THE STORY OF
PAINTING

THE STORY OF
PAINTING

SISTER WENDY BECKETT
Contributing Consultant PATRICIA WRIGHT

DORLING KINDERSLEY
LONDON • NEW YORK • SYDNEY • MOSCOW
IN ASSOCIATION WITH THE NATIONAL GALLERY OF ART, WASHINGTON, D.C.
www.dk.com

A DORLING KINDERSLEY BOOK
www.dk.com

Project editors *Janice Lacock,*
Edward Bunting, Susannah Steel
Art editors *Claire Legemah, Tassy King*
Editor *Joanna Warwick*
Assistant editor *Neil Lockley*
Senior editor *Gwen Edmonds*
Managing editor *Sean Moore*
Managing art editor *Toni Kay*
Production manager *Meryl Silbert*

All views and interpretations expressed in this
book are the authors'

Rembrandt, *Self-portrait* (etching)

Author's Acknowledgments
I dedicate this book to Toby Eady. With him I would like to associate
all at Dorling Kindersley who worked so hard on it, especially Sean Moore,
who commissioned the book, and Patricia Wright, my gifted co-writer;
Gwen Edmonds, Janice Lacock, Susannah Steel, and Edward Bunting who
laboured with such patience to get it right.

Note on painting titles
In *The Story of Painting* we have used authentic titles for paintings where they are known or,
in their absence, one that will serve as well, e.g. *Still Life with Peaches*. Where paintings have
a popular title that was obviously not formulated by the artist, the title appears in quotation
marks, e.g. *"The Arnolfini Marriage"*. For ancient works we use a simple description,
not set in italics, e.g. Fresco with dolphins.

First published in Great Britain in 1994 by
Dorling Kindersley Limited
9 Henrietta Street, London WC2E 8PS

6 8 10 9 7 5

A CIP catalogue record for this book is available
from the British Library
ISBN 0 7513 0133 7

Colour reproduction by GRB Editrice s.r.l.
Printed in Italy by A. Mondadori Editore, Verona

FOREWORD

Donatello, Florentine
heraldic lion, 1418–20

Pisanello, *Duke of Rimini*
(portrait medal), 1445

Art has long been a passionate concern to me, and I have often been puzzled by media questions as to why this is so, and when my interest began. It seems to me that we are all born with the potential to respond to art. Unfortunately, not all of us have the good fortune to have this potential activated, as it were. This book is my faltering attempt to offer the security of a knowledgeable background, which will help to make whatever art we see more accessible. Some people are certainly held back from a fearless gaze at painting, because they fear their own ignorance. Truly to look remains one's personal responsibility, and nobody else's response (and certainly not my own) can be a substitute. But knowledge must come to us from outside, from reading, listening, and viewing. If we know that we know, we can perhaps dare to look. Love and knowledge go hand in hand. When we love, we always want to know, and this book will succeed if it starts the reader on the track that leads to more reading, greater knowledge, greater love and, of course, greater happiness.

Van Eyck, *Musicians* from
the *Ghent Altarpiece*, 1432

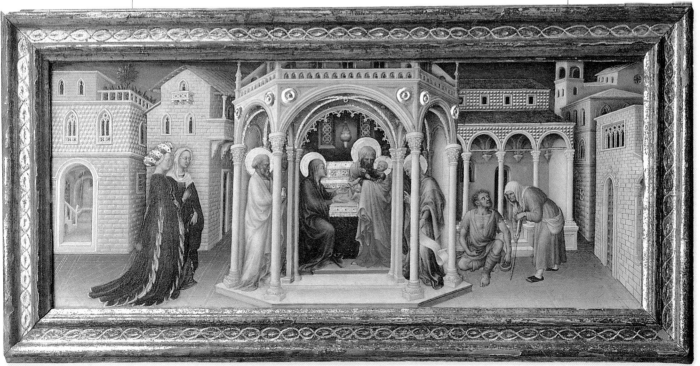

Gentile da Fabriano, *The Presentation of the Child in the Temple, 1423*

Mantegna, ceiling fresco in
the Gonzaga Palace, c. 1470

CONTENTS

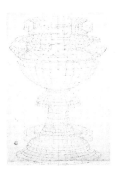

Giotto,
Madonna and Child

Paolo Uccello,
Study of a Chalice

Nicholas Hilliard, *The
Artist's Father* (miniature)

Antonello da Messina,
Portrait of a Young Man

Piero della Francesca,
The Baptism of Christ

Francisco Goya,
Doña Teresa Sureda

Sir Henry Raeburn, *The
Rev Robert Walker skating*

Vincent van Gogh,
Dr Gachet

Camille Corot,
Ville d'Avray

Anton Mengs,
Portrait of Winkelmann

Sir John Everett Millais, *Death of Ophelia*

Edgar Degas,
Girl Drying Herself

Georges Seurat,
Les Poseuses

Ernst Ludwig Kirchner,
Berlin Street Scene

INTRODUCTION
PAINTING
BEFORE GIOTTO

Our word "history" comes, by way of Latin, from the Greek word *historien*, which means "to narrate", and that word comes from another Greek word, *histor*, "a judge". History not only tells a story, but it passes judgment on it, puts it in order, and gives it meaning. The story of painting is one that is immensely rich in meaning, yet its value is all too often hidden from us by the complexities of its historians. If we forget the densities of history and simply surrender to the wonder of its story, we are reclaiming our birthright.

The preface to our story opens with the earliest examples of Western painting, created by our first artistic ancestors: Paleolithic man. From here through to Giotto – with whom the story really begins – we pass through the ancient worlds of Egypt and Greece, the great Roman Empire, early Christian and Byzantine worlds, and close with the magnificent illuminated manuscripts created by European monks during the Middle Ages.

Revellers, from the Tomb of the Leopards, Tarquinia, Italy, c. 470 BC

THE FIRST PAINTINGS

That art is truly our birthright can be seen from its ancient beginnings. It does not begin in history, but actually in prehistory, thousands of years ago. Our Palaeolithic ancestors, living between 30,000 and 8,000 BC, were small, hairy, and unlettered, and even archaeology can say little about them with certainty. But one thing is radiantly clear, and that is that these

Stone Age cave dwellers were artists, and not only artists in that they could describe in visual terms the animals with which they came into daily contact – such art may be no more than illustration. Cave painting is much more than this: it is art in the grand manner, great art, manifested in works of subtlety and power that have never been surpassed.

The paintings on the walls of the Altamira caves were the first to be discovered in modern times, in 1879. The caves are near Santander in northern Spain. The discovery had such fundamental implications for archaeology that it was at first dismissed as a forgery. This great bison *(1)* is painted on the ceiling of a long, narrow corridor leading from a subterranean cave in Altamira. It does not stand alone. A whole herd surges majestically across the roof, one animal overlapping another – horses, boars, mammoths, and other creatures, all the desired quarry of the Stone Age huntsman. They assert a powerful animal presence, despite the confusion.

CAVE PAINTING TECHNIQUE

The caves are fully underground, and therefore permanently in darkness. Archaeologists have discovered that the artists painted with the aid of small stone lamps, filled with animal fat or marrow. The initial designs were engraved into the soft rock, or thin lines of paint were blown onto the wall through a hollow reed. To make coloured paint, the artists used ochre, a natural mineral that could be crushed to a powder that would yield red, brown, and yellow pigments, while black may have been made from powdered charcoal. Powdered pigments were either rubbed onto the wall with the hands, producing

1 Bison from Altamira cave, c. 15,000–12,000 BC, 195 cm (77 in) (bison length only)

2 Wounded bison attacking a man, detail from cave painting at Lascaux, France, c. 15,000 10,000 BC, 110 cm (43 in) (bison length only)

very delicate gradations of tone akin to soft pastel painting, or mixed with some form of binding fluid, such as animal fat, and applied with crude reed or bristle brushes. The means were simple, yet the effect, especially in the strange silence of the cave, is overwhelming.

SIGNIFICANCE OF THE CAVE PAINTINGS

It is thought that these paintings had some deep importance to prehistoric society. The bison seems to be almost quivering with power as it displays its massive chest, dense hindquarters, and short, thin legs. It brandishes an aggressive pair of horns. Was this animal sacred to some ritual? We may never know the true significance of the cave paintings, but they almost certainly served a ritualistic, even magical function. How much the art was produced for its own sake – and this cannot be entirely ruled out – will remain a mystery.

The extraordinary naturalism and anatomical accuracy in the portrayal of animals in these paintings is believed to be connected with the purpose they served. The artists were also hunters, and their lives depended on the animals whose images they painted in the caves. Is it possible that these hunter-artists believed that by accurately depicting the animals' power, strength, and speed, they would acquire magical power? With this they might be able to take control of the animal's spirit and remove its strength before the hunt. Many of the paintings show the animals wounded or pierced with arrows, and some examples even show evidence of actual physical attacks on the painted image.

The naturalism with which animals are painted and drawn does not extend to the portrayal of humans – perhaps for this very reason. People are rarely represented, but when they are, it is by the crudest recognizably human shape, or more often by symbolic forms, as can be seen in the image of the prostrate man in this startling painting *(2)*, which dates from between 15,000 and 10,000 BC. It is in the most celebrated of all the sites of ancient cave paintings: the Lascaux caves in the Dordogne, France. The stick-like man is lying in front of a bristling, disembowelled bison. Below him is a figure that looks as if it could be a bird, or possibly a totem or banner displaying an image of a bird. The painting has an awesome power: we have to confess our ignorance of its meaning, yet this lack of knowledge does not affect our response – unless, indeed, it deepens it. In this alone, prehistoric art is representative of all art to follow.

THE ANCIENT WORLD

Strangely enough, it is a long time before painting rises again to the quality of the cave art of Stone Age society. The Egyptians were interested mainly in architecture and sculpture, and in many of their paintings, particularly those that decorated their tombs, they gave drawing precedence over colour.

Some paintings, or fragments, have been preserved from a variety of other cultures of ancient Europe: Minoan, Mycenaean, and Etruscan. Then came the civilizations of Greece and Rome. From a modern point of view, a feature common to almost all ancient painting traditions is a shortage of examples surviving today.

The Egyptians loved the terrestrial world too much to believe that its pleasures necessarily ended with death. Egyptians believed that the rich and the powerful, at least, could enjoy the pleasures of life in perpetuity, as long as the image of the deceased was reproduced on their tomb walls. Much Egyptian painting, therefore, was done for the sake of the dead. It is possible, however, that the Egyptians did not feel that great expense was required to ensure a good afterlife, and that they chose painting as a labour-saving and cost-cutting device. Instead of the expensive art of the sculptor or the stone carver, a cheaper art form – painting – was employed. It is certain, at any rate, that the ceremonial, formal painting style used for tomb walls was not the only one available. We now know that living (and wealthy) Egyptians had murals in their homes, and that these were done in richly textured, painterly styles. Unfortunately, only small fragments of these murals survive.

ANCIENT EGYPTIAN TOMB PAINTING

Perhaps one of the most impressive images from Egyptian tombs is that of the "*Geese of Medum*" (3), three majestic birds from the tomb of Nefermaat (a son of Sneferu, the first pharaoh of the 4th dynasty) and his wife Itet, dating from over 2,000 years before Christ. The geese form only a detail in a pictorial frieze in a tomb at the ancient town of Medum, but already they hint at the vitality and power of the sculptural triumphs to come in the years ahead. Another Egyptian tomb painting, from the tomb of Ramose, shows a funeral procession of *Lamenting Women (4)*. Ramose was a minister under two pharaohs of the 18th dynasty, Amenhotep III and Amenhotep IV (Akhenaten). The women in the painting are flat and schematic (look at their feet), but their anguished gestures vibrate with grief.

4 Lamenting Women, *wall painting from the tomb of Ramose, Thebes (Egypt), c. 1370 BC*

To the ancient Egyptians it was the "eternal essence" that mattered: what constituted their view of constant, unchanging reality. Thus their art was not concerned with the changeable variation of externals for visual appeal, and even their keen observations of nature (evidently painted from memory) were subject to rigid standardization of forms, often becoming symbols. It is not from any kind of "primitivism" that their scenes appear decidedly unreal – their technical skill and evident understanding of natural forms makes this clear enough. It is, rather, the direct consequence of the essentially

3 "Geese of Medum",
*c. 2530 BC, approximately
46 x 175 cm (18 x 69 in)*

intellectual function of their art. Each subject was shown from whatever angle would make it most clearly identifiable, and according to a rank-based scale, large or small dependent on social hierarchy. This resulted in a highly patterned, schematic, and almost diagrammatic appearance. This over-riding concern with clarity and "thorough" representation applied to all subject matter: hence, the human head is always shown in profile, yet the eyes are always drawn from the front. For this reason, there is no perspective in Egyptian paintings – everything appears two-dimensional.

STYLE AND COMPOSITION

Most Egyptian wall paintings, as in this example, a *Fowling Scene (5)* from a nobleman's tomb in Thebes, were created with the *fresco secco* technique. In this method, tempera (see glossary, p.390) is applied to plaster that has been allowed to dry first, unlike the true *buon fresco* technique in which the

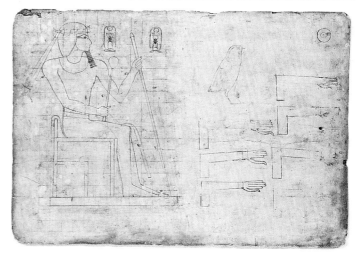

6 Pharaoh Tuthmosis III, *Egyptian painting on a drawing board, c. 1450 BC, 37 cm (14½ in) high*

EGYPTIAN RULES OF REPRESENTATION

In Egyptian art, representation of the full-length human figure was organized within the so-called "rule of proportion", a strict, geometric grid system that ensured the accurate repetition of the Egyptian ideal form on any scale and in any position. It was a foolproof system, regulating the exact distances between parts of the body, which was divided into 18 equal-sized units and placed in relation to fixed points on the grid. It even specified the exact width of the stride in walking figures, and the distance between the feet (which were both shown from the inside view) in standing figures. Before beginning a figure, artists would first draw a grid of the required size onto the surface, and then fit the figure within it. A surviving 18th-dynasty wooden drawing board shows the Pharaoh Tuthmosis III drawn within such a grid (6).

It was not only tombs that the Egyptians decorated: they also painted sculpture. This beautiful painted limestone sculpture, of the *Head of Nefertiti (7)*, who was wife of the Pharaoh Akhenaten, is thought to have been a workshop model, because it was found in the ruins of a sculptor's studio. It is as poignant as a Botticelli head (see p.94), with the same touching and exquisite wistfulness. It also demonstrates a loosening of the rigid conven-tions that governed earlier (and later) Egyptian art, because Akhenaten broke with the traditional style. During his reign, the paintings, carvings, and sculptures that were produced were refreshingly graceful and original.

5 Fowling Scene *from the tomb of Nebamun, Thebes, Egypt, c. 1400 BC, 81 cm (31 in) high*

painting is made on wet plaster (see p.46). The wildlife of the papyrus marshes and Nebamun's retriever cat are shown in great detail, yet the scene is idealized. The nobleman stands in his boat, holding three birds he has just caught in his right hand, and his throwing-stick in his left. He is accompanied by his wife, who appears in an elaborate costume with a perfumed cone on her head, holding a bouquet. Between Nebamun's legs squats the small figure of his daughter, picking a lotus flower from the water (this is an example of how, as mentioned above, it was conventional for figures to be shown large or small according to their status). Originally this painting was only one part of a larger work, which also included a fishing scene.

7 Head of Nefertiti, *c. 1360 BC*

AEGEAN CULTURES OF THE BRONZE AGE

The Bronze Age Minoan civilization (3000–1100 BC), named after the mythical King Minos, was the earliest to develop in Europe. Its home was the small island of Crete, in the Aegean Sea between Greece and Turkey, and its society developed roughly in parallel to that of its African neighbour, Egypt. Despite their proximity and certain shared influences, Egyptian and Minoan cultures remained very separate, though the latter was to have enormous influence on the art of ancient Greece. Crete formed the centre, both culturally and geographically, of the Aegean world. Also in parallel with Minoan civilization was that of the Cyclades, an Aegean island group. Idols have been recovered from this society (8), objects whose ancient, quasi-neolithic forms are reduced to the barest abstraction, but still retain the magical power of the fetish. Here we have a weird forerunner of the abstract art of our own century in which the human body is seen in geometrical terms with an immense raw power, contained and controlled by linear force. Originally the idols had painted eyes, mouths, and other features.

8 Female idol from Amorgos, an island in the Cyclades Archipelago (now part of Greece), c. 2000 BC

MINOAN AND MYCENAEAN ART

Minoan art is largely represented by its carvings and painted pottery, and it is not until 1500 BC, during the great "Palace period", that we see paintings at all; and generally these have only survived in fragments. Although a certain degree of Egyptian stylization is apparent in the schematic repetition of human figures, for instance, Minoan representation reveals a naturalism and suppleness largely absent in Egyptian art. The Minoans took inspiration from nature and their art exhibits an astonishing degree of realism. They were a seafaring civilization and their paintings reflected their knowledge of the oceans and of sea creatures, such as dolphins.

9 Fresco with dolphins, from the Palace of Knossos, Crete, c. 1500–1450 BC

10 "Toreador Fresco" from the royal palace at Knossos, Crete (restored detail), c. 1500 BC, 80 cm (31½ in) high including borders

This lively example (9) is from the Palace of Knossos, which was excavated in the first two decades of the 20th century. Another recurrent Minoan theme is bull jumping, a ritual thought to be connected with Minoan religion. A second work from the royal palace of Knossos, the *"Toreador Fresco"* (10), is one of the best-preserved Minoan paintings, although fragmentary. The fragments have been pieced together to reveal three acrobats, two girls (they are fair-skinned), and a darker-skinned man somersaulting over a magnificent bull. The usual interpretation of this picture is as a "time-lapse" sequence. The girl on the left is taking hold of the bull's horns in preparation to leap; the man is in mid-vault; the girl on the right has landed and steadies herself with arms outstretched, like a modern gymnast.

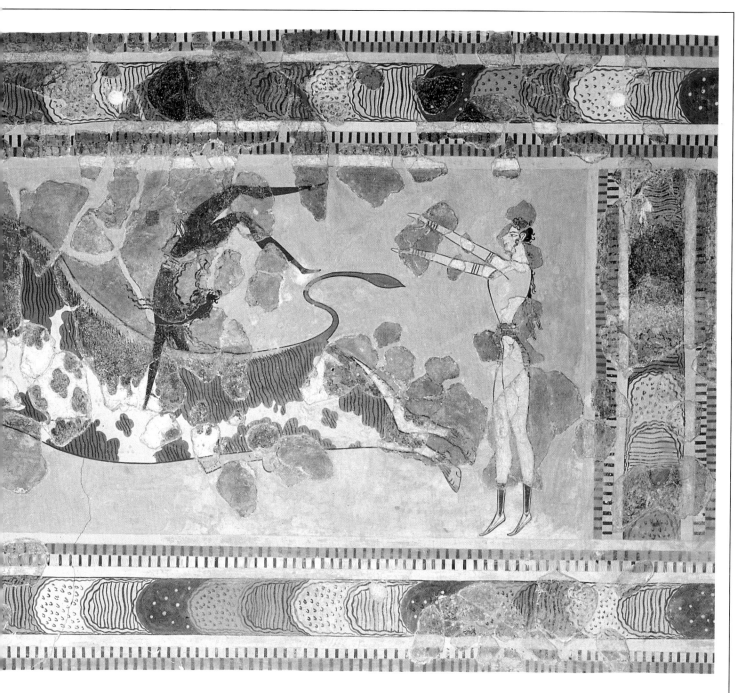

The Mycenaean civilization was a Bronze Age culture of mainland Greece. It came to succeed the ancient Minoan culture in Crete, emerging around 1400 BC to became the dominant culture on the island. Its history and legends form the background to the writings of the Greek poet Homer (c. 750 BC), whose epic poems, the *Odyssey* and the *Iliad*, reflect the "heroic age": the end of the Mycenaean period. One of the most

enduring images from Mycenaean art is this funeral mask *(11)*, thought for a time to be of the Mycenaean King Agamemnon, who, in Homeric legend, was the leader of the Greeks in the Trojan Wars. All that is certain is that it is a death mask, and that it was taken from one of the royal tombs of the Mycenaean period, in the 16th century BC. Besides a certain love of gold, it reveals the immense dignity of the Mycenaean image of humankind. This highly expressive mask is a great iconic depiction of what it means to be a human being.

Fragments of Mycenaean paintings found at two sites (Tiryns and Pylos) in Greece represent what must have been impressive mural cycles. Many of the Mycenaean and Minoan murals were not frescoes in the usual sense of the word, but, like the Egyptian murals, were produced by applying tempera paint (see glossary, p.390) to plaster that had already dried. Subjects of Mycenaean murals included scenes from everyday

11 Funeral mask from the royal tombs at Mycenae, c. 1500 BC

life, as well as depictions of the natural world. Mycenean art was rather solemn in nature in comparison with Minoan art. These two traditions formed the background from which the art of the Greeks later emerged.

The Mycenaean civilization collapsed around 1100 BC. Its ending marks the end of the Bronze Age in Greece. There followed a period of around 100–150 years, known as the "Dark Age", about which less is known in Aegean culture. After that, prehistory ended, and the period of written history began. Around 650 BC, archaic Greece emerged as Europe's most advanced civilization.

GREECE'S NEW VISION

Like their Cretan predecessors, the Greeks were far less conscious of the tomb than the Egyptians. They have left us a number of bronze statuettes, which are highly esteemed. But their painting – an art on which their writers assure us they lavished great skill – is almost totally lost. One reason for this is that, unlike the Egyptians, the Minoans, and the Mycenaeans, who painted only murals, the Greeks painted mainly on wooden panels that have perished over time.

The Roman scholar Pliny the Elder (AD 23/4–79), whose detailed descriptions of Greek painting and the ancient world greatly influenced successive generations, is the major source of information on Greek painting. In every other school of art, the truth of such descriptions can be judged by the painting that survives. This is not true of Greek painting, and so the value of what Pliny said can never be assessed.

Almost our only hint of the beauty of Greek painting is in the relatively minor, especially utilitarian art of vase painting. The word *vase*, first used as a broad term for ancient Greek pottery in the 18th century, can be misleading. The Greeks never made vases purely for decorative purposes, as can happen today, but always had a specific purpose in mind. Greek potters made a range of products, in a variety of shapes, such as storage jars, drinking vessels, bottles for perfume and ointment, and containers for liquids used in ceremonies.

In the Greek vase paintings we can see a concern with anatomy, and a preoccupation with the human figure, which became the central motif of Greek art and philosophy. We see a departure from what the Egyptian tomb paintings showed, with their preconceived formulae for representing the world, and a whole new way of viewing art opens up with respect to what the eye can see, and what the mind dictates.

STYLES IN GREEK VASE PAINTING

If vase painting is a minor art, then it has some major practitioners. The Athenian artist Exekias, who lived about 535 BC, signed at least two of his black-figure pots as their "painter", and his style, with its poetry and perfection of balance, is instantly recognizable. It is worth noting that he made the pottery as well as its decoration. Exekias' work is important because it reveals the direction representational art would take, signifying the leap from a "hieroglyphic" symbolic representation of objects in the world to one that attempted to show the world as it really appears. This is particularly evident in his treatment of the boat's sail in this superb kylix (a shallow, two-handled drinking cup), *Dionysos in His Boat (12)*. Dionysos, the god of wine, vegetation, and fruitfulness, lies stretched out in repose as he carries the secret of wine to humankind. His symbolic vines twirl around the mast and soar fruitfully into the sky, a wonderful adaption to the difficult circular composition of the kylix. The ship, with its gleaming sail, glides majestically over the pink and orange world of Heaven and Earth, where dolphins play around the sacred presence, and the scene is alive with an amazing sense of wholeness.

12 Exekias, Dionysos in His Boat, on a kylix (a shallow, two-handled drinking cup), c. 540 BC

13 Berlin Painter, Pallas Athena, on an amphora (a two-handled storage pot), c. 480 BC

the "figures" were not painted; instead, the black background was painted around them, leaving the red clay colour to stand for the figures, which were then painted with anatomical details. Greater naturalistic effects were possible, and the vivid scenes depicted on the vases became more and more complex and ambitious. A good example of this new development is the painting from the interior of a drinking bowl *(14)* made by the potter Brygos (the artist is known simply as the Brygos Painter). Although the subject matter – a woman holding the head of a drunken youth while he is sick – is not appealing, the figures are presented with subtlety and dignity. The woman's clothing in particular gives her a tender grace.

PORTRAYING THE HUMAN FORM

The way the Greeks represented the human body had a direct influence on the development of Roman art, and all later Western art. Since we can no longer see many Greek paintings themselves, we have to rely on Greek sculpture to trace the progress of the human nude. Early Greek statues, such as the 6th-century BC *Kouros* shown here *(15)*, were based on the grid system of the ancient Egyptians. (*Kouros* means a young man, and in the sculpture of the time it means a statue of a standing youth.) Gradually the lines softened, as shown in the 5th-century BC *"Kritios Boy" (16)*, named after the sculptor Kritios, in whose style it was made. Eventually we see the realistic musculature of classical 5th-century BC statues, such as the *Discus Thrower (17)*. This is a Roman copy of the original by the Greek sculptor Myron.

14 Brygos Painter, "The End of the Party" *on a drinking bowl, c. 490 BC*

Greek vase painting is typically concerned with story-telling, and many vases carry images of incidents recounted in Homer's *Iliad* and *Odyssey*, written in the 8th century BC. Vases decorated with narratives date from times preceding Homer to the Classical Greek period, which succeeded the Archaic period around 480 BC, and indeed long beyond.

We cannot fully appreciate Greek vase painting unless we see both the image and the vase as a whole. A key figure in the *Odyssey*, Pallas Athena, the guardian deity of Athens, appears on a lidded shoulder amphora (a storage pot with two handles) by an anonymous artist whom scholars have named the Berlin Painter, around 480 BC *(13)*. The darkly gleaming, black glazed curve of the jar makes the goddess seem to retreat from our gaze, while allowing us to glimpse her in her stately sweetness. She is shown holding out a jug of wine to Hercules, who is on the other side on the jar, both keeping their privacy inviolate, yet communicating. It is a wonderfully controlled and reverent work, both simple and complex.

The amphora is an example of the red-figure technique, invented around 530 BC, which succeeded black-figure pottery. In the red-figure technique

15 Kouros (statue of a standing youth), late 6th century BC

16 "Kritios Boy", c. 480 BC

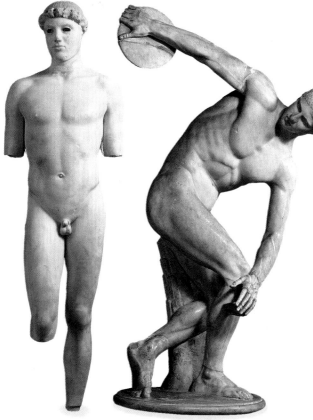

17 Discus Thrower (Roman copy), original c. 450 BC

18 Revellers, from the Tomb of the Leopards, Tarquinia, Italy, c. 470 BC

ETRUSCAN PAINTING

The mysterious Etruscan civilization existed in the Italian peninsula at the time Greek civilization spread to southern Italy in the 8th century BC. Once thought to have come from Asia Minor, it is now more commonly believed to have originated in Italy. Its art was influenced by Greek art, but maintained a style of its own, which the Greeks valued highly. Some early Etruscan art, as typified by a wall painting from the Tomb of the Leopards at Tarquinia (18), displays a joyful quality. The men, who may be dancing, carry a cup of wine, a double flute, and a lyre.

However, much of the surviving art has a slightly sinister edge to it, an awareness of the uncontrollable nature of life and all its implications. Among some impressive Etruscan tomb paintings, contemporary with the classical period in Greece, is this fresco from a tomb in the Rivo di Puglia, where a brightly coloured procession of *Mourning Women (19)* advances with implacable force. They form a fascinating contrast to the mourning women in Ramose's tomb (see p.12). The Egyptian women grieve over the human loss that death brings with it, while the Etruscans mourn the remorseless and inescapable advance of fate.

PAINTING IN CLASSICAL GREECE

The most significant Greek painter of the early classical period (c. 475–450 BC) is Polygnotos, who has been credited with being the first to give life and character to the art of painting. None of his pictures survive, but Pliny left a description of his *"Discus Thrower"*. The most important Greek painting surviving from the 4th century BC is *The Rape of Persephone (20)*, on the wall of a tomb in the same burial complex as that of Philip II of Macedon, who died in 356 BC. Full of the vitality and naturalism of art at that time, this haunting image shows how the Greeks explained the seasons. Persephone is the daughter of Demeter, goddess of fertility. Persephone is carried off by Hades to the underworld, from which she will emerge as the new growth of spring. The great cycle of the seasons is tapped by this painting, and the myth lives on through it.

19 Mourning Women, from a tomb at Rivo di Puglia, Italy (detail), late 5th century BC, height 55 cm (22 in)

20 The Rape of Persephone, *from a tomb at Vergina, Greece, c. 340* BC

HELLENISTIC ART

By the time of his death in 323 BC, Alexander the Great (356–323 BC) had extended his Empire as far as the Middle East, conquering Greece's old enemy Persia, and also Egypt. However, the empire was then divided up among Alexander's generals, who established a series of independent states, throughout which there spread a new cosmopolitan culture, blending that of both East and West. This is known today as Hellenistic culture, and it prevailed in the Mediterranean region until well after the Roman Empire became the dominant power. Its heart was Athens but its other important centres (ruled by Greek kings and speaking Greek) were in Syria, Egypt, and Asia Minor. A Roman mosaic known as the *"Alexander Mosaic" (21),* found at the House of the Faun at Pompeii, is known to have been based on a Hellenistic painting. It depicts the Battle of Issus, fought between Alexander and the Persian King Darius III in 333 BC. The scene is violent and lively, and the artist displays sophisticated technical skills (he knows about foreshortening – see glossary, p.390) that gives the work a great immediacy of impact.

Hellenistic culture soon developed a love of "art for its own sake". The Eastern influence led to a more decorative, sumptuous art, and religious elements retired to the background. In their place were paintings of gardens (including, arguably, the first landscapes), still lifes, portraits, and everyday scenes of contemporary life. The popularity of this tendency, curiously dubbed "baroque" by historians (see p.172), is recorded by Pliny, who wrote that art could be found in barbers' and cobblers' shops, as well as palaces.

An overwhelming concern of Hellenistic artists was "truth" to reality, and they tended to depict dramatic, often violent action. They developed a style that paralleled the vivid literary tradition of the Roman poet Virgil (70–19 BC). A definitive example of the artistic philosophy of Hellenistic

21 "Alexander Mosaic" *(Roman copy of a late Hellenistic painting), c. 80* BC

22 Hagesandrus, Polydorus, and Athenodorus, Laocoön and His Two Sons, 1st century AD

unprecedented naturalism and a relaxed, lyrical quality. These features are especially evident in this beautiful and modern-looking wall painting from the Roman town of Stabiae, *Young Girl Gathering Flowers (23)*. (Stabiae was a small resort, less well known than Pompeii or Herculaneum, that was destroyed together with these towns in the same eruption of the volcano Vesuvius in AD 79.) The young woman glides gently away from us with a poignant charm. We do not see her face, as if she were deliberately withholding from us the unearthly beauty that seems appropriately associated with the ethereal flowers she plucks. She vanishes into the mists and eludes us, leaving behind her only a suggestion of what Roman painting may have been like.

The happy accident that left us the young girl makes it even more painful to realize how much we must have lost. We can easily forget the vulnerability of painting, and how easily master works can be destroyed.

ILLUSIONISTIC WALL PAINTINGS
We also have a substantial number of examples of Roman paintings from Pompeii, but many of these are clearly works of provincial artists. Massively influenced by Greek painting (which the Romans admired as much as Greek sculpture and copied for wealthy houses), these do not necessarily reflect

art, dating from the 1st century AD, is *Laocoön and His Two Sons (22)*. This sculpture depicts a horrifying scene from Virgil's *Aeneid*, in which a Trojan priest named Laocoön and his two sons were strangled by two sea snakes. This was a punishment from the gods because Laocoön had tried to warn the Trojans about the Greeks' wooden horse. Without the warning, the Trojans were tricked, pulling the horse into their city and bringing about their own downfall. This is a sculpture, not a painting, but it does give us some hint of what Hellenistic painting must have been like. The sculpture was rediscovered in 1506 and had a strong influence on many Renaissance artists, including Michelangelo (p.116), who referred to it as "a singular miracle of art". Among those who were inspired by it was the Mannerist El Greco (see p.146), who is known to have produced three paintings featuring the Laocoön story.

PAINTINGS OF THE ROMAN EMPIRE
Hellenistic styles continued to exert strong influences on artists long past the official end of the Hellenistic period, set by historians at the Battle of Actium in 27 BC. Soon after this battle the Roman Republic, under Caesar Augustus, was transformed into an Empire and became the dominant power in the Western world for three centuries and more. All Hellenistic paintings that survive today are from the Roman period, many being by Roman artists who copied Hellenistic paintings. These 1st-century Roman paintings reveal an

23 **Young Girl Gathering Flowers,** *c. 15 BC–AD 60, height 30 cm (12 in)*

the achievements of more talented painters. Still, these works have great charm. It is to their credit that the Romans, even in the small remaining sample of their homes that we can look at today, commissioned so many paintings.

The Romans' interest in landscape, as such, is likely to be Hellenistic in origin. Roman artists were also probably continuing a Hellenistic tradition when they embellished the interior walls of houses with illusions of expensive decorative facings and slabs of coloured marble. Such skills were applied in the palaces of the Caesars on the Palatine Hill.

What sets Roman art apart from Hellenistic influences is an interest in facts – in places, faces, and historical events. Roman artists were specially interested in space (which may shed an interesting light on the collective Roman psyche). They also knew how to open up space on a wall by means of mock images of porticoes, architraves, and parapets, which themselves framed illusions of landscapes and figures.

This wall painting *(24),* from the hall of the Villa of Livia in Prima Porta, just outside Rome, is a charming example of an artist's attempt to create an illusion of a garden, as though the wall did not exist. Painted in the fresco technique, it shows birds, fruit, and trees in realistic detail. A low trellis separates us from a narrow patch of grass. Beyond that is another low wall, before the fruit trees begin.

24 *Wall painting from Villa of Livia, near Rome (detail), late 1st century AD, approximately 275 cm (9 ft 2 in) wide*

25 Still Life with Peaches, c. AD 50, approximately 35 x 34 cm (14 x 13½ in)

This illusionism is seen not only in large-scale wall paintings, but also in small works, such as this remarkably fresh and modern-looking still life of peaches and a jug of water, painted in about AD 50, in Herculaneum *(25)*. It reveals an understanding of natural light, where the artist has attempted to show the various effects of light falling onto and through objects, and displays consistent use of chiaroscuro (the depiction of light and dark) as a means of giving volume to form and enhancing the illusion of reality. Once again, this skill is first seen in Hellenistic work, revealing the extent to which ideas were imported into Rome.

ROMAN PORTRAITURE

The wall painting known as "*The Baker and His Wife*" *(26)*, a 1st-century work from Pompeii, is now thought not to portray a baker, but a lawyer and his wife. (Archaeologists are still trying to establish who owned the house in which this mural was found.) But, whoever this young couple was, the portrait remains essentially Roman, with all the interest concentrated on their personalities. The husband, a slightly uncouth, gawky, earnest young man, looks at the viewer with anxious appeal, while the wife looks away into the distance, musing and holding her writing stylus to her delicately pointed chin. Both seem lonely, as if their differently directed gaze reveals something of their marriage. They live together, but they do not share their lives, and there is an added

poignancy; the house of Neo (whatever his profession may prove to be, we do know that this was the name of the building in which the painting was situated) was still unfinished at the time of the eruption, so it is possible that this lonely marriage was of tragically short duration.

THE FAIYUM MUMMIES

Perhaps the most compelling Roman painting has an equal claim to be called Egyptian: the two cultures blended together with an eerie aptness when European realism met African lyricism during the Roman control of North Africa. Excavations have unearthed mummies from the cemetery in Faiyum, a town (today, a district rather than a town) near Cairo. These mummies are protected in a variety of wrappings ranging from *papier-mâché* to wooden boxes. With each mummy is a panel on which a portrait of the deceased is painted in encaustic (a medium consisting of pigments suspended in hot wax). This mummy case *(27)* is known to have been made for the body of a man named Artemidorus, for this name is inscribed on it. The silhouettes below his portrait show Egyptian deities.

The Faiyum portraits show all ages, from young to old, but those of young adults are the most touching. It may be that they were intended to give a sense of the individual's nature, his or her spirit, rather than the outer appearance, and for this purpose, some may have been idealized. Yet this *Bearded Youth (28)*, whose large eyes look so solemnly into ours, seems hauntingly real. Whether he looked like this or not, it is easy to believe that this was what he was like within.

26 "The Baker and His Wife" ("Neo and His Wife"), 1st century AD, 58 x 52 cm (23 x 20½ in)

22

27 Mummy case and portrait, from Faiyum, Egypt, 2nd century AD

28 Bearded Youth, 2nd century AD, 43 x 22 cm (17 x 8½ in)

is carved into the likeness of a scroll that twists in a spiral up the column. The "scroll" is more than 180 m (600 ft) in length and contains over 2,500 human figures. It shows a series of scenes from Trajan's triumphant campaigns in Dacia (the present-day Romania). The examples shown on this page depict soldiers and builders at work constructing the walls of a fortification *(29)*. The reliefs are shallow and have a painterly feel to them. They make up a continuous and clearly intelligible narrative, leading the "reader" through 150 episodes in succession.

During the 16th century the carvings on this column were an important inspiration and influence for the artists of the Renaissance (see p.80), who regarded the column's dense carvings as an idealized, three-dimensional demonstration of what two-dimensional art was really about.

ROMAN SCULPTURE

Long after the ancient Roman civilization had disappeared, examples of its sculpture have continued to be visible in all parts of the empire. In Rome itself, the great narrative reliefs on Trajan's Column and the Arch of Titus in the Forum were on display to visitors and inhabitants of the city. Trajan's Column is as tall as a ten-storey building and stands on a pedestal two stories high. It was built in AD 113 to honour the Emperor Trajan, a gilded statue of whom (replaced in the 16th century by a statue of St Peter) was placed at the top. The marble outer surface of the column

29 Detail from Trajan's Column, AD 113

EARLY CHRISTIAN AND MEDIEVAL ART

The great Roman empire was in decline by the early 2nd century AD, and by the 3rd century its political life had degenerated into chaos. When the Emperor Diocletian divided the empire in half, splitting East from West, the final collapse of the Western section *was set in motion. In the 5th century, the Western empire succumbed to the Germanic barbarians. In the East, at Byzantium, a new, Christian-based empire slowly emerged, destined to endure for a thousand years, and with it a new art form, born out of Christianity.*

In Rome, in the network of ancient burial chambers known as the catacombs, there is a series of wall paintings dating from the time when the Christians were persecuted in the 3rd and 4th centuries AD. In style, these paintings bear the marks of the continuing Greco-Roman tradition. Unimpressive as art, this figure *(30)* is nonetheless deeply moving as an image of faith. It carries a secret charge of conviction that compensates for any technical incompetence.

THE FIRST GOLDEN AGE OF BYZANTINE ART

In 313, after 300 years of Christian persecution, the Emperor Constantine recognized the Christian church as the official religion of the Roman Empire. Early Christian art differed from the Greco-Roman tradition in subject matter more than style. Later, in the east, it evolved into Byzantine art, as artists turned away from Greco-Roman style to develop an entirely new style. The importance of Byzantine art is seen

30 Wall painting from catacombs of Rome, 3rd century, 40 x 27 cm (16 x 10½ in)

in its profound influence on Gothic art (see pp.36–77). It was the first part of a tradition that was to remain predominantly Christian, and was to run right through the Middle Ages to the time of the Renaissance.

The emotional yet straight-faced intensity of the "Faiyum" paintings of 2nd-century Egypt (see p.22) lingers on into the early Christian mosaics created between 526 and 547 in the church of San Vitale, Ravenna, capital of the area liberated from the Goths by Byzantium). These mosaics achieved a maturity of stylistic convention – restrained elegance,

emotional austerity, and a "frozen", authoritative solemnity – that would form the basis for all Byzantine art. The artist who created the image of *Justinian and His Attendants (31)* gave us a great and lordly image of a mid 6th-century Byzantine emperor. Slender, imperious, remote, and exalted, Justinian is shown with his bishop, clergy, and a representative section of his army: an image of the united forces of church and state, and an echo of the deification of kings practised during the Roman Empire. All Justinian's princely qualities are also seen, in due proportion, in his

31 Justinian and His Attendants, *from the* Great Cycle *of mosaics at the church of San Vitale, Ravenna, c. 526–547*

attendant lords. They gleam far above us, both materially and spiritually, aloft on the Basilica walls. There is an equally glittering companion mosaic on the other side of the altar, depicting Justinian's wife, the Empress Theodora.

That same century, we can find both the emotional intensity of Faiyum and the priestly remoteness of Ravenna, in an icon from the Monastery of St Catherine on Mount Sinai. Icons, a great tradition within the life of the Eastern church, were religious images, usually of Christ, the Madonna, or the saints. They were painted on small and often portable panels for devotional purposes, and each detail of the image could be charged with a special religious significance. The *Virgin and Child Enthroned Between St Theodore and St George (32)* has

32 Virgin and Child Enthroned Between St Theodore and St George, icon from Mount Sinai, c. 6th century AD, 68 x 48 cm (27 x 19 in)

all the sacred beauty that gives icons their unique power. Mary has wide eyes, which are intended to suggest her purity of heart: she is a woman of vision, one who sees God. She does not look at the small King on her lap: as her Lord, the Child can, as it were, fend for Himself, and it is on us that the Virgin bends her sternly maternal look. The two accompanying saints are dear to the Eastern church tradition – George, the holy warrior and dragon killer (though here his sword is sheathed), and Theodore, less well known to us today, another

33 Christ as Ruler of the Universe, the Virgin and Child, and Saints, c. 1190

26

warrior. Both saints wear the uniforms of the Imperial Guard, but as weapons each now holds a Cross. The angels behind the throne look upwards, alerting us to the hand of God that beckons and announces the Child. The Child holds in His hand a symbolic scroll. God is silent, only the angels see Him, though the eyes of the saintly figures seem to suggest that they sense the divine presence. The four halos of the Madonna, Child, and saints form a Cross and alert us to the message that the closed scroll must contain. It is a strange, mystical work, and this kind of painting continues to this day in Eastern churches.

THE SECOND GOLDEN AGE OF BYZANTINE ART

In the 8th and 9th centuries, the Byzantine world was torn with bitter controversy over the use of pictures or carvings in religious life. Any human image that was at all realistic could be seen as a violation of the commandment not to worship any "graven image". In 730, Emperor Leo III decreed any image of Christ, the Virgin, or any saint or angel, in human form, to be illegal. The decree gave power to religious militants known as iconoclasts (image breakers) who saw to it that, for over a century, religious art was restricted to non-human imagery such as leaves or abstract patterns. There was a steady migration of Byzantine artists to the West.

When the law was abolished in 843, and human images were tolerated again, resumption of contact with the artists of the West led to a renewed influence of classical form and illusionistic qualities.

This mosaic, from the apse (a domed recess behind the altar) of the Cathedral of Monreale, Sicily (33), is a large-scale, quintessentially Byzantine work in which the figure of Christ is huge and authoritative. He looms out at us from the sanctuary, a great, luminous image of power; not the gentle Jesus, but the "Judge". Beneath Him the enthroned Madonna with Child, and the standing figures of archangels and saints, are all seen, rightfully, as small. They are beautiful, but relatively unimportant. The golden background of the mosaic is one of the most distinctive features of Byzantine art and continued into the Gothic era (see p.40).

INTIMATE ICON

Not all Byzantine art was on such a grand scale. One of the most beautiful small icons from the period is the so-called "Vladimir Madonna" (34). This was probably painted in Constantinople in the 12th century and later taken to Russia. The position of the Virgin and Child, their faces touching tenderly, introduces a new note in sacred art. Previously the two figures had appeared as symbols of the Christian faith – Christ and His Mother not sharing any emotional closeness. Here they appear in their intimate, human relationship.

34 "Vladimir Madonna", c. 1125, 75 x 53 cm (30 x 21 in)

RUSSIAN ART

Russia was converted to Christianity in the 10th century, and eventually took over the Byzantine tradition, making it very much its own. The most exquisite example of this meeting of two very dissimilar cultures, at the highest point in the development of Russian Byzantine art, is surely this vivid *Trinity (35)*, painted by Andrei Rublev (c. 1360–1430). Rublev is the most famous of Russian icon painters. The figures represent the three angels that appeared to Abraham in the Old Testament. This is grace made visible, and it is this Byzantine heritage that gives special poignancy to the mysterious works of El Greco (see p.146) 300 years later.

36 David and Goliath, fresco at Tahull, Spain, c. 1123

35 Andrei Rublev, Trinity, c. 1422–27, 140 x 112 cm (55 x 44 in)

THE "DARK AGES" IN WESTERN EUROPE

The phrase "Dark Ages" is sometimes used to refer to the early Middle Ages in European civilization, up to the beginning of the High Middle Ages around 1100. The thousand-year period from 400 to 1400 was a time of gradual mingling of influences from the Greco-Roman tradition, Christianity, and Byzantine art, as well as the growing Celtic and Germanic cultures of the North. Despite its pejorative implication, this was far from being an artistically barren or regressive period filling the empty space between the Roman empire and the Renaissance, as was believed for centuries, it was a period of development and metamorphosis within the stronghold of Christianity. The "Dark Ages" held the seeds of future scientific and technical innovation and prepared the way for such things as the coming invention of printing.

The art of the Western church was less mystical and more human than that of the Byzantine empire, and throughout the Middle Ages, painting was the preferred manner of popular religious instruction, at a time when a large majority of people were illiterate. Even the poorest church buildings covered their walls with brightly coloured biblical stories, often to spectacular effect. In the tiny Catalan church of Santa Maria, at Tahull, Spain, the 12th-century frescoes have only four main colours: white, black, ochre, and vermilion, with touches of blue and orange. This passionate simplicity is repeated in the forms as David sways forward to decapitate an inert Goliath *(36)*. David, in adolescent garb, is slight, dreamy, and defenceless, while Goliath, immense in his huge armour, is the consummate worldling whom the children of God, even poor shepherds such as the young David, defeat.

ILLUMINATED MANUSCRIPTS

The art of the nomadic barbarian peoples who had conquered the West was mostly object-based, small scale, and portable. After conversion to Christianity it was logical that this highly decorative art form should be translated into a religious art that is also small scale and portable: the illuminated manuscript. This most accessible and perhaps even most lovely of early medieval artefacts has been discussed by some critics as being the work of craftsmen, but where do we draw the line? The original meaning of the Latin word *ars* was "craftsmanship", the exact equivalent of the Old High German word *kunst,* which originally meant knowledge or wisdom, and by extension came to mean a craft or skill. The discipline of a trained eye and a trained hand was essential to create an object either for delight or for function or – the continual desire of the creator – for both. The distinction between aristocratic art and plebeian craft is only a modern one. It dwindles away into insignificance when we look at the work of the great "craftsmen" of the Middle Ages.

THE CAROLINGIAN EMPIRE

The single most powerful political figure in Europe in the early middle ages was Charlemagne. His contemporary name translates as "Charles the Great", and Charlemagne is a version of the Latin for this. The adjective relating to his time is *Carolingian.*

Charlemagne's armies took control of extensive territories in northern Europe from 768 to 814. With his military might, he was responsible for the enforcement of Christianity in the North, and for a revival of the art of antiquity that had flourished before the collapse of the Roman Empire in the West 300 years earlier.

When Charlemagne was crowned emperor of what is now France and Germany in 800, he became a great patron of the arts. He was fluent in Latin and could understand Greek, though he could hardly write at all. He wanted his artists to reflect both the Christian message and the magnificence and importance of his own empire. For his court at Aachen, he recruited the greatest scholar known in Europe at that time, Alcuin of York, an Englishman from Northumbria.

Charlemagne commissioned several glorious sets of illuminated Latin Gospels. Some of the work that these contain has an almost classical majesty, a magnificent serenity. The emperor sent artists to Ravenna (see p.25), where they could study the early Christian and Byzantine murals and mosaics, whose style offered itself as more appropriate to the religious development of the new empire than did the pagan art of Greece and Rome. He may have employed Greek artists to work on some of the illuminated Gospels. The Byzantine influence, together with elements from early Christian,

37 St Matthew *from the* Harley Golden Gospels, *c. 800, 37 x 25 cm (14½ x 10 in)*

Anglo-Saxon, and Germanic art, are seen in these illuminated manuscripts. These traditions combined to produce the Carolingian style, embodied in this painting *(37)* from the *Harley Golden Gospels.* This book was produced under Charlemagne and takes its present name from a collector, Lord Harley, who once owned it. St Matthew writes his Gospel in a setting that displays a rather lopsided perspective, but is eminently balanced emotionally. He leans forward to listen to the Holy Spirit, calmly collected, half smiling. His emblem, an angel, hovers above him with equal poise, and expressing the same quiet happiness.

38 *Symbols of the Evangelists, from the* Book of Kells, *c. 800,*
33 x 24 cm (13 x 9½ in)

CELTIC ILLUMINATION

The missionary zeal of the Christian church, which spread its influence across Europe, is seen at its most intense in the relatively tiny Christian stronghold of Celtic Ireland, which had converted to Christianity in the 5th century. Advanced Celtic monastic communities were also established in Britain and northern Europe. The intricate art that was created in all these communities reveals a blend of Celtic and Germanic styles. In their convoluted manner, the Celtic manuscripts appeal to us across the centuries with a remarkable intensity.

There can be few works of art more exquisite in every sense than the *Book of Durrow*, the *Lindisfarne Gospels*, or the *Book of Kells*. This last, created by Irish monks on the island of Iona in the 8th and early 9th centuries, and later taken to the monastery of Kells in Ireland, is possibly the greatest work of manuscript illumination ever created. The figurative images have an iconic strength, as we see in the page that shows the symbols of the four evangelists: Matthew's angel, Mark's lion, Luke's ox, and John's eagle *(38)*.

ILLUMINATED INITIALS

But the true glory of the *Book of Kells* is in the illuminated initials. Here intricacy becomes so integrated, so wild yet so controlled – a marvellous paradox – that it is impossible even to imagine how such lace-like perfection could have been drawn by the unaided human hand. One of the most

wonderful initial pages presents the words *Christi autem generatio* ("the birth of Christ") from St Matthew's Gospel. The word *Christi*, shortened to "*XPI*", fills most of the page; *autem* is abbreviated as *h*, while *generatio* is spelt out *(40)*.

The shortened form of the name of Christ is made out of the two characters XP, the Greek letters *chi* and *rho*. This is the symbolic abbreviation known as the *Chi-Rho*. The entire ornate pattern is based upon the material form and spiritual meaning of these two characters.

The whole page is densely covered with a network of lines, faces, shapes, and animals (human figures are not often the main focus of Irish illuminations). There are three figures of men (or angels), three being the mystic trinitarian number; there are butterflies, cats playing with mice (or are they kittens?), and a fine otter, upside down and clutching a fish in its mouth. But we have to search these creatures out, disguised as they are by a glorious swirl of geometric patterning. The floating human faces, glimpsed here and there amid the tracery, make clear to us that the central and all-encompassing reality in life is Christ. His very name, even in its abbreviated form, simply subsumes all else.

The ambitious approach of this page is more easily appreciated if we compare it with its equivalent in the *Lindisfarne Gospels (39)*. This manuscript was produced in Northumberland, in northern England, shortly before 698, by the monk Eadfrith. Here too the illumination is magnificent, but it is much less complicated in its layout and scope.

39 Chi-Rho *page from the* Lindisfarne Gospels, *c. 690,*
34 x 25 cm (13½ x 10 in)

40 Chi-Rho page from the Book of Kells, *c. 800, 33 x 24 cm (13 x 9½ in)*

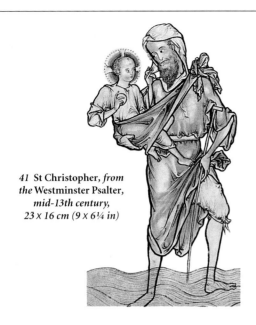

41 St Christopher, from the Westminster Psalter, mid-13th century, 23 x 16 cm (9 x 6¼ in)

43 Christ and the 24 Elders, from the Apocalypse of Beatus, c. 1028–72, 37 x 55 cm (14½ x 22 in)

42 St Peter, from the Oscott Psalter, c. 1270, 30 x 19 cm (12 x 7½ in)

SPANISH ILLUMINATION

The very smallness of manuscript art gives it an intimacy that can prove tremendous. The most dramatic of medieval illuminations tend to be Spanish. The book of Revelation, the final and apocalyptic book of the Bible, provided a never-failing source of blazingly powerful images. The monk Beatus, who lived in the 8th century at Liebana in Spain, wrote a commentary on the Apocalypse (as Revelation is also known) that entranced the visual imaginations of a whole series of painters for centuries to come. Here is how another monk (probably Spanish or Spanish-trained), who worked at the monastery of Saint-Sever in Gascony, envisioned *Christ and the 24 Elders* in an 11th-century copy of Beatus *(43)*. Around the outer edge of a great circle containing Christ and His blessed are the souls of the saints, pure and free as birds. There is a wonderful exhilaration in the image of the elders, including the four evangelists, waving their goblets to toast the triumphant Lord, while the winged saints stretch out longing hands towards the celestial glory.

ENGLISH ILLUMINATION

Like the Irish monks, the British also produced manuscripts of great beauty, this being one of the very few periods in which the least visual of national groups, the English speakers, attained international fame as artists. Matthew Paris, who died in 1259, was a monk at the flourishing Abbey of St Albans, just outside London, and his 42 years in the cloister were mainly distinguished by a series of books that he not only wrote, but illustrated, giving them the benefit of his remarkable draughtsmanship. In this example from the *Westminster Psalter*, the patron saint of travellers, *St Christopher (41)*, is shown carrying the Christ Child across the river.

Another outstanding work from St Albans, known as the *Oscott Psalter (42)*, illustrated by an artist who is not named, shows the same nervous delicacy of line, with an elegance and psychological subtlety that enchant the viewer. St Peter, identifiable by the keys he holds and the fact that he stands on a rock, is one of ten saints depicted in the psalter.

44 The Death of Harold's Brothers, *from the* Bayeux Tapestry, *c. 1066–77 (detail)*

45 *Page from the* St Denis Missal, *c. 1350, 23 × 16 cm (9 × 6¼ in)*

ENGLISH EMBROIDERY

The so-called *Bayeux Tapestry* is not really a tapestry, but a woollen embroidery supported by cloth. For a long time it was thought to have been made in Normandy for Queen Matilda, wife of William the Conqueror, by her "court ladies". However, it has recently been proved to have been commissioned by Bishop Odo, William's half-brother, and made in England. It displays the same jerky animation that we find in English manuscripts. A sort of Anglo-Saxon glorified comic strip, it tells its exciting story of the Norman Conquest of England with economy and charm. It takes the form of a long cloth frieze, with upper and lower borders that provide a commentary on the action in the main panel. In this particular scene *(44)*, the brothers of the English King Harold are slain by Norman soldiers. The top border is given over to decorative, almost emblematic animals, while the bottom one is filled with images of dead soldiers and an assortment of their abandoned weapons and armour.

FRENCH ILLUMINATION

A lovely missal (a book of texts for church services through the year) survives from the 14th century at the abbey of St Denis in Paris. It is by a follower of Jean Pucelle, an illuminator with a workshop in Paris. One page shows liturgical text for the feast day of St Denis *(45)*, with a magnificent pictorial "O" and two other miniatures telling of the saint's relationships with the royal family. Even if we do not know the legends about the stag that hid in a church when pursued by Prince Dagobert, and how the prince and his father King Clotaire are eventually reconciled through a dream appearance of St Denis, we can still enjoy the pale and meticulous figurines, living out their holy adventures in the missal.

ROMANESQUE PAINTING

In an illustration in a mid 13th-century French *Bible moralisée* (biblical text with moralizing commentary), God the Father is seen as an architect *(46)*. This work shows the increasing return to the natural-looking style of Roman art (see p.20) – especially visible in the relaxed drapery and the suggestion of volume beneath – a style that would reach unprecedented heights of realism in Gothic painting. Although, as was typical of medieval paintings, the artist did not leave us his name, the picture has an almost Giottoesque power (see p.46). Almost 600 years later, William Blake would also show God bending over a compass in an illustration in his book *The Ancient of Days (47)*. But Blake's God is narrowed by geometry, and this artist is rebelling against the rule of cold law, and glorying in the majesty of a strong, free deity. God strides through space, barely contained by the brilliant blue and scarlet borders of the human imagination. The great swirls of His royal robes recall the sculptural pleats on the figures in Reims Cathedral. God is utterly intent upon his creative work, putting forth every effort of his mighty will to control and discipline the wild waters, stars, planets, and earths of His world. He will soon, we feel, send it spinning into space, but first, He orders it. He labours with barefoot concentration, the perfect integrator of art and skill.

When the Florentine artist Giotto (see p.46) started producing frescoes in the early 14th century, his genius was so massive that he changed the course of European painting. However, the illuminators' art did not come to an immediate end. Contemporary with Giotto and past his time, influenced but yet distinct, the manuscript artists continued with their intricate craft, reaching greater heights precisely because Giotto had set them free from any imaginative limitation.

47 William Blake, illustration from The Ancient of Days, *1794*

CLASSICAL INFLUENCES

Other works that can be seen to prefigure Giotto's naturalism include the paintings and mosaics of the Italian artist Pietro Cavallini (active 1273–1308). He worked mainly in Rome, and Giotto would have seen examples of his art there early in his career. Cavallini's style was strongly influenced by classical Roman art. Unfortunately, his work has been preserved for us, for the most part, only in fragments.

This example is a detail from his best surviving fresco, in the church of Santa Cecilia in Trastevere, Rome *(48)*. The three seated Apostles shown here form part of a larger group surrounding the figure of Christ in the Last Judgment. In the unidentified but youthful Apostle in the centre, we see a sweetness and a gravity that has great human appeal as well as a supernatural power. He is an accessible saint, yet still incontrovertibly a "saint".

46 **God the Father as Architect,** *illustration in a French* Bible moralisée *from the mid-13th century, 34 x 25 cm (13½ x 10 in)*

48 Pietro Cavallini,
The Last Judgment,
c. 1295 (detail)

GOTHIC PAINTING

The Gothic style began with the architecture of the 12th century, at the height of the Middle Ages, when Europe was putting the memory of the "Dark Ages" behind it and moving into a radiant new era of prosperity and confidence. At the same time, Christianity was entering a new and triumphant phase of its history, and so the age of chivalry was also the time of the building of the magnificent Gothic cathedrals, such as those in the northern French towns of Chartres, Reims, and Amiens. In the realm of painting, the change to the new style became visible around a century after the first of these cathedrals rose. In contrast to the Romanesque and Byzantine styles, the most noticeable feature of the art of the Gothic period is its increased naturalism. This quality, which first appeared in the work of Italian artists in the late 13th century, became the dominant painting style throughout Europe until the end of the 15th century.

Ambrogio Lorenzetti, Allegory of Good Government: Effects of Good Government in the City and in the Country, *1338–39 (detail)*

GOTHIC TIMELINE

The Gothic era in painting spanned more than 200 years, starting in Italy and spreading to the rest of Europe. Towards the end of this period there were some artists in parts of the North who resisted Renaissance influences and kept to the Gothic tradition. As a result, the end of the Gothic timeline overlaps with both the Italian and the Northern Renaissance timelines (see pp.80–81, 150–51).

CIMABUE, MAESTA, 1280–85
Although this painting shows strong Byzantine influences, Cimabue's work marked a departure from that tradition in the more three-dimensional rendering of space and the apparent humanity of his Madonna. In addition, the drapery is much softer than that in Byzantine art (p.42).

GIOTTO, DEPOSITION OF CHRIST, C. 1304–13
Giotto's art heralded an entirely new tradition of painting, and his art even belongs in some ways to the Renaissance. This fresco from the Arena Chapel, Padua, is a good example of his characteristic psychological intensity, spatial clarity, and solidity of form (p.47).

WILTON DIPTYCH, C. 1395
Although little is known about the origin of this work, it is a perfect example of the courtly International Gothic style that swept Europe at the end of the 14th century. The rich blue and the crowded composition of the panel showing the Virgin surrounded by angels contrasts with the simplicity of the left-hand panel, with its gold background (p.54).

1290	1310	1330	1350	1370	1390

DUCCIO, THE HOLY WOMEN AT THE SEPULCHRE, 1308–11
Duccio's most celebrated work is his wonderful Maestà altarpiece. It still impresses, even though now dismembered and partially dispersed, with its huge Virgin in Majesty. It was free-standing, and the back showed scenes from the life of Christ (p.45).

SIMONE MARTINI, THE ANGEL AND THE ANNUNCIATION, 1333
The Sienese artist Simone Martini painted several versions of the Annunciation. In this glittering example, the fluid lines of the draperies of the Virgin and the angel clearly reveal the solid forms beneath them – a characteristic feature of Gothic painting (p.50). The similarly-named Angel of the Annunciation, a diptych panel showing the angel without Mary, is another display of Martini's consummate skill in the portrayal of drapery (p.51).

ROGIER VAN DER WEYDEN, DEPOSITION, C. 1435
In the hands of this great Flemish artist, the removal of Christ's body from the Cross is a moment of intense emotional drama. Everyone in the scene is overwhelmed by grief, though each expresses it differently (p.67).

ROBERT CAMPIN, PORTRAIT OF A WOMAN, C. 1420–30
Northern artists began to show individual personalities in their head-and-shoulders portraits of wealthy townsfolk (p.61).

MASTER OF AVIGNON PIETA, PIETA, C. 1470
Depictions of the Pietà, the Virgin Mary viewing or holding the dead body of her Son, abound in Gothic art. This poignant 15th-century version was created by an anonymous artist in France (p.66).

HIERONYMUS BOSCH, TEMPTATION OF ST ANTHONY, 1505
Bosch stands out among his peers for the bizarre and fantastic images that appear in many of his paintings (p.72).

1410	1430	1450	1470	1490	1510

JAN VAN EYCK, THE ARNOLFINI MARRIAGE, 1434
Van Eyck was one of the first artists to exploit the new medium of oil paint. In this double portrait, one of his most famous paintings, he uses it to great effect in the realistic rendering of light and shadows. The unifying result of this treatment was extremely original in its time. The interior domestic setting is found in many of the paintings of contemporary Netherlandish artists (p.65).

MATTHIAS GRÜNEWALD, CRUCIFIXION, C. 1510–15
The German artist Grünewald typifies the emphasis on horrific suffering of some late Gothic art. His Crucifixion scene has a harrowing intensity (p.76).

EARLY GOTHIC ART

In the early Gothic period, art was produced chiefly for religious purposes. Many paintings were teaching aids, to make Christianity "visible" to an illiterate population; others were displayed, like icons (see p.27), to enhance contemplation and prayer. The early Gothic masters created images of great spiritual purity and intensity, and, in doing so, preserved the memory of the Byzantine tradition. But there was much that was new as well: strikingly persuasive figures, perspective, and a wonderful elegance of line.

AMIENS CATHEDRAL
This cathedral, with its pointed arches and ornate stonework, is typical of the High Gothic architecture of 13th-century France. Building work commenced in 1220.

THE MIDDLE AGES
Gothic art belongs chiefly to the last three centuries of the Middle Ages. The Middle Ages extended from the fall of Rome in 410 until the start of the Renaissance in the 15th century.

STAINED GLASS
The Gothic cathedral at Chartres attracted the most accomplished makers of stained glass. It has three rose windows, a popular Gothic feature. In the windows under the north rose (above), completed c. 1230, are the figures of St Anne holding the Virgin Mary as a child, and four Old Testament figures, including David and Solomon.

The term "Gothic" denotes a period of time rather than describing a set of identifiable features. Although there are certain recognizable characteristics of Gothic style, Gothic art's numerous manifestations are easier to make sense of if we bear in mind that the period spanned over 200 years, and that its influence spread throughout Europe. The Italians were the first to use the term "Gothic", and they used it as a derogatory word for art that was produced during the late Renaissance (see p.139), but that was of a medieval appearance. The word was a reference to the "barbaric past" – in particular to the Goths, a Northern, Germanic people of ancient times whose armies had invaded Italy and sacked Rome in the year 410. Eventually the word Gothic lost its derogatory overtones and was adopted as a broad term describing the new style of architecture and art that emerged after the Romanesque period (see p.34) and before the Renaissance.

THE INFLUENCE OF GOTHIC ARCHITECTURE

The innovation that separates the churches of the Gothic period from the Romanesque architecture was a new type of ceiling construction, the ribbed vault. With this strengthening structure, the supporting walls no longer needed to be so massive. In addition, flying buttresses were employed as load-bearing devices on the outside of the building, so that not all the weight of the roof needed to be supported by the columns and walls. Thus the walls could be thinner and large parts could be given over to glass, allowing in more light.

A common misconception about Gothic architecture is that the pointed arch was one of its innovations. In fact, such arches were not new, but enjoyed much greater popularity in Gothic designs than at any earlier time. More variable in shape than semicircular arches, they offered architects greater freedom of choice.

The first churches to be built in the Gothic style were in France, notably at Notre Dame in Paris, St Denis in Paris, and at Chartres. A less elaborate, but similar, style appeared in England, for instance at Salisbury; and Gothic churches were also built in Germany, Italy, Spain, and the Netherlands. In all of them there was a startling

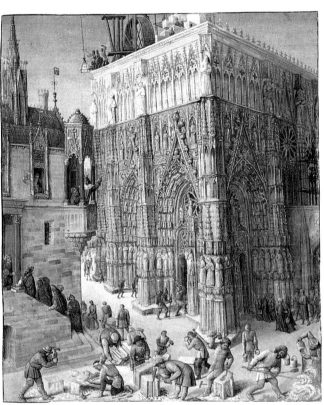

*49 Jean Fouquet, **The Building of a Cathedral**, from a 15th-century manuscript copy of the writings of the 1st-century Jewish historian Josephus*

and revolutionary use of stained glass. Coloured light now flooded the interior, creating a new and unearthly atmosphere. Whereas before each coloured panel had to be held in place by stonework, Gothic craftsmen learned to make a mesh of lead tracery to hold the glass in place. The art of making stained glass windows reached its greatest height in the church of Sainte Chapelle in Paris (50), where windows make up three-quarters of the wall area.

EMERGENCE OF GOTHIC PAINTING

Gothic painting has its beginnings in Italy. Painting in 13th-century Italy was still dominated by Byzantine art, which was known in Italy as "the Greek manner". Painting was much slower to assimilate the Gothic influence than architecture and sculpture. It was not until the end of the 13th century that the Gothic style appeared in painting, in the brilliant panel paintings of Florence and Siena. Early Gothic painting displayed a greater realism than had been found in Romanesque and Byzantine art. There is an obvious fascination with the effects of perspective and in creating an illusion of real-looking space.

RIBBED VAULTS

The ribbed vaulting and delicate, pointed arches of the Lady Chapel in Wells Cathedral, England are typical of the Gothic style. So too is the light that streams into the chapel through the large windows. This part of the cathedral was completed in 1326.

SCULPTURE

This figure of Simeon holding Christ is from the exterior of the north transept of Chartres Cathedral. It illustrates the shift from the rigid Romanesque style of sculpture towards more personalized and elegant figures, typified by the folds in the drapery. This was echoed in Gothic painting.

50 Interior of the church of Sainte Chapelle, Paris, 1243–48

OTHER WORKS BY CIMABUE

Crucifix
(Church of San Domenico, Arezzo)

Virgin and Child Enthroned
(Church of Santa Maria dei Servi, Bologna)

St Luke
(Upper Church, Basilica of San Francesco, Assisi)

St John
(Pisa Cathedral, Pisa)

Virgin and Child With Six Angels
(Louvre, Paris)

The Gualino Madonna
(Galleria Sabauda, Turin)

51 *Cimabue*, Maestà, *1280–85, 386 x 225 cm (12 ft 8 in x 7 ft 5 in)*

Many of the pictures show a sinuous elegance and delicacy. Other characteristics of the Early Gothic style are an interest in pictorial story-telling, and a heightened, often passionate, expression of spirituality.

TURNING AWAY FROM BYZANTINE ART

The most prominent artist working in Florence at the end of the 13th century was Cimabue (Cenni di Peppi, c.1240–c.1302), who is traditionally held to be Giotto's teacher. So many works have been attributed to him that his name has almost come to represent a group of like-minded artists rather than an individual, though we know he existed.

Although Cimabue remained a painter in the Byzantine style, he went a long way towards liberating himself from the flatness of traditional icon-painting, and in doing this he took the first steps in the quest for realism that has played such a fundamental role in Western painting.

We know that in 1272 Cimabue travelled to Rome, which was then the main centre in Italy for muralists. The mural painters and mosaic makers of that time were particularly interested in creating a greater naturalism in their work,

52 *Duccio*, Maestà, *main front panel, 1308–11, 213 x 396 cm (7 x 13 ft)*

and Cimabue may well have shared their concern. Cimabue is best known for his *Maestà (51)*, originally on the altar of the church of Santa Trinità in Florence. The word *maestà* means "majesty", and was used to refer to a painting of the Madonna and Child in which the figure of Mary sits on a throne and is surrounded by angels. Cimabue's *Maestà* has a great sweetness and dignity, surpassing in emotional content the rigid, stylized figures of the Byzantine icon. The handling of the soft texture of the drapery, together with the "open", three-dimensional space created by the inlaid throne on which the Madonna and Child sit; all this is new and exciting.

DUCCIO AND THE SIENESE SCHOOL

Regardless of all the developments he initiated, Cimabue's work still has a certain flatness if we compare it with the works of the great, and almost contemporary, Sienese painter Duccio (Duccio di Buoninsegna, active 1278–1318/19).

During the 13th and 14th centuries the city of Siena vied with Florence in the splendour of its arts. If Giotto (see p.46) revolutionized Florentine art, then Duccio and his followers were responsible for their own smaller, but very significant, revolution to the south. Duccio is a painter of tremendous power. His greatest work was his *Maestà*, commissioned for Siena Cathedral in 1308 and installed there in 1311 with great ceremony. A chronicler recorded the

53 *Duccio,* **The Holy Women at the Sepulchre**
(from the Maestà*), 1308–11, 102 x 53 cm (40 x 21 in)*

festivities: "The Sienese took [the *Maestà*] to the cathedral on the 9th June, with great devotions and processions ... ringing all the bells for joy, and this day the shops stayed closed for devotions". It is extraordinary that this great work was in later times cut up and sold, at least in part because it was no longer appreciated. The beneficial result of this cultural folly is that museums all around the world now have panels from the *Maestà*.

Duccio's *Maestà* was painted on both sides; the front was in three parts. The main panel *(52)* showed the Mother and Child enthroned, surrounded by angels and saints. At the base of the main panel ran a predella (a pictorial strip along the bottom), decorated with scenes from Christ's childhood. A corresponding strip at the top displayed scenes from the last years of the life of the Virgin. Both these strips are now lost. The reverse was painted with scenes from the life of Christ (26 are known).

Among the scenes from the back of the *Maestà* that remain in Siena is *The Holy Women at the Sepulchre (53)*. It is the moment in the Passion when the three Marys discover Christ's empty tomb, and are told by the Angel Gabriel that He has risen. This painting is a work of such powerful austerity and grace that we become conscious of the urgency of its Christian message.

It is not the psychology of the women that interests Duccio (as it would Giotto), but the wonder of the sacred interaction between them, at this all-important point in the story of the Passion. The figures in the painting sway towards one another, yet there is never actual contact. We are being shown a world of inwardness that none of us can understand, not even the artist himself. The wonderful self-containedness and detachment of Duccio's work is one of his most distinctive qualities.

KINGDOM OF ITALY

Pisa • • Florence
• Siena

• Rome

PAPAL STATES

KINGDOM OF THE TWO SICILIES

ITALY

During the Gothic period the independent states of the Italian peninsula were generous and competitive patrons of the arts. The political map of Italy changed many times – this one dates from 1450. In earlier times, the Papal States had occupied a larger area in the north, and the southern mainland was part of the Kingdom of Naples, which was taken over by Sicily in 1443. The Papal States and the north of Italy were both parts of the Holy Roman Empire.

CONTEMPORARY ARTS

1264
Italian philosopher and theologian Thomas Aquinas begins writing his *Summa Theologica*

1290s
Cavallini (see p.34) creates a series of mosaics in Santa Maria in Trastevere, Rome, and some frescoes in Santa Cecilia in Trastevere, Rome

1296
Building work commences on Florence Cathedral

1307
Dante (see p.47) begins writing his epic poem *The Divine Comedy*

MARCO POLO

In 1271 Marco Polo, a Venetian merchant, travelled to China with his father and uncle. This French miniature shows the Polos receiving their safe-conduct documents from Kublai Khan, the emperor of the Mongol empire in China. Whilst acting as an ambassador for Kublai Khan, Marco Polo saw lapis-lazuli stone being extracted from quarries in Afghanistan. This was to become an important pigment in Italian painting. When Polo returned to Italy in 1295, accounts of his travels provoked a fashion for all things oriental.

He seems to paint from a distance, whereas Giotto (see p.46) wholly identifies with his stories, creating real dramas, and involving us as he tells them. Although the stiffly formal composition of the front of the *Maestà* reveals strong ties with the Byzantine tradition, the influence of Northern Europe (which Duccio received second-hand through the sculpture of Nicola and Giovanni Pisano, see p.46) can be seen in the graceful, undulating forms of the figures – an early example of the refined charm that characterizes the whole period of Gothic art.

With Duccio, we see a real change of style, and his influence was greater than Cimabue's. His figures seem to have volume, and their robes relax into fluid, sinuous lines, which also describe the forms beneath. Though the panels on the reverse of the *Maestà* are small, they are painted with an epic sense of scale, and a bold simplicity new to Italian painting. The *Maestà* is the only extant work we know to be by Duccio, although not all of it is by his hand. As far as we know, he always worked on a small scale.

JESUS CALLING THE APOSTLES

Another small panel from the predella on the reverse of Duccio's masterpiece, *The Calling of the Apostles Peter and Andrew (54)* is a luminous and bare image of tremendous power.

Duccio divides the world into three: a great golden heaven, a greeny-gold sea, and a rocky shore, where Jesus stands at the picture's edge. At the centre are the two brothers Andrew and Peter, stunned by the incursion of the miraculous into their workaday existence. They have fished all night in vain; Jesus shouts to them to cast their net to one side, and they humour the stranger by obeying Him. The net comes up laden with fish, but they hardly seem to look at it. Peter turns questioningly to Jesus while Andrew stands motionless, looking out at us.

The clothes of the two disciples are pale in hue, whereas Jesus, in token of His spiritual profundity, wears blood-crimson to symbolize His Passion, and purple to indicate His royal status; and the gold edging of His robe outlines His figure, dividing it from the golden background.

54 Duccio, The Calling of the Apostles Peter and Andrew *(from the* Maestà *), 1308/11, 43 x 46 cm (17 x 18 in)*

THE CALLING OF THE APOSTLES PETER AND ANDREW

In this panel from his *Maestà*, Duccio portrays the scene from Christ's life when He summons the two Galilean fishermen, Peter and his brother Andrew, to be His disciples. He is calling them to become "fishers of men" and bring new followers to Christ.

THE APOSTLE ANDREW

Andrew is shown in the moment of the revelation of his faith. Whereas his brother Peter (who, according to the Scriptures, was always the active one) confronts Jesus, Andrew appears to be listening to another, unseen calling. As he pauses in his task of hauling in the nets laden with fish, he stands transfixed, with an expression of slow comprehension dawning on his face.

JESUS' CARVED HALO

The halo as a symbol of divinity was originally attributed to the sun gods Apollo, Mithras and Helios, and signified the sun's radiance and power. It first appeared in Christian art in the 4th century. Here, Christ's halo is carved into a wooden panel – a feature of Gothic panel painting, which would also often incorporate precious stones. The patterned surface of the halo attracts and reflects light, thereby intensifying its radiance, and distinguishing it from the background.

CHRIST CALLING

Duccio portrays Jesus as a regal, authoritative figure. With His hand outstretched towards the two fishermen Peter and Andrew, He does not exactly invite, but gently commands. He stands barefoot on the rock, a symbol for the Church, and communes with Peter, whose name, meaning "the rock", was chosen by Jesus.

THE FISHING NET

The net comes up full, and this suggests that the apostolic mission will be richly rewarding. Although clearly suspended in the water, the net is superimposed over the transparent green sea (enlivened by the layer of warm gold beneath). Duccio shows little concern with three-dimensional space – the boat is a kind of wooden "envelope" slicing into the water with just enough depth to accommodate the two fishermen.

55 Giotto, Madonna and Child, probably c. 1320/30, 85 x 62 cm (34 x 24½ in)

GIOTTO, FATHER OF WESTERN PAINTING

Whereas Duccio was a reinterpreter of Byzantine art, his great Florentine contemporary, Giotto (Giotto di Bondone, c. 1267–1337) transformed it. His revolutionary approach to form, and his way of depicting realistic "architectural" space (so that his figures are in scale in relation to his buildings and the surrounding landscape), mark a great leap forward in the story of painting. Gothic painting is widely regarded as reaching its height in Giotto, who so splendidly subsumed and reinvigorated all that had gone before. For the first time, we have in European painting what the historian Michael Levey calls "a great creative personality". The true age of the "personalities", however, was the Renaissance, and it is not without cause that writers on the Renaissance always begin it with Giotto. Giant-like, he straddles the two periods, being of his

time, and before his time. His dates, however, place him firmly in the time we call Gothic, with its climate of spiritual grace, and a spring-time delight in the freshness of colour and the beauty of the visible world. What the Gothic artists had achieved was to depict a solidity of form, where earlier painters had shown an essentially linear world, lacking in bulk, thin in substance despite its spiritual forcefulness.

INFLUENCES ON GIOTTO

We know that Giotto went to Rome in 1300 and painted a fresco in the Lateran Palace. He under-stood the innovations of Pietro Cavallini (see p.34), the Roman artist whose strong, beautiful frescoes and mosaics show an amazing grasp of naturalism. Giotto's frescoes did not assimilate the Roman influence from within the Byzantine style, as Cimabue's panel paintings did; they went further, and transcended it. The real world was primary for Giotto. He had a true feeling for natural form, a wonderful sculptural solidity, and an unaffected humanity, that changed the course of art.

Equal with Giotto in stature and innovation, and massively important to the way Giotto visualized his world, were Italy's greatest sculptors of the period, Nicola Pisano (d. 1278) and his son Giovanni (c. 1250 until after 1314).

Nicola Pisano came to live in Tuscany, Giotto's native province, in 1250. He was devoted to studying the sculptures of classical Rome, but more importantly he brought with him a new and vital influence; his special inspiration was the Gothic art of Northern Europe. The French court of Anjou, which had established itself in Naples in c. 1260, had brought a new influence to Italian sculpture (see column, p.41). Pisano's art showed a convincing solidity of form and human individuality (see column, right), far removed from the rather wooden, stylized nature of all other sculpture in Tuscany in his time (see column, left).

If we look at Giotto's paintings in direct relation to Pisano's sculpture, Giotto's pictorial "leap" is partly explained: sculptural form and space have entered the flat space of painting, and the paintings breathe, released once and for all from the rigid and stylized Byzantine tradition.

Giotto's panel paintings are necessarily physically smaller than his frescoes, but in them he seems to transcend size. Even a small *Madonna and Child (55)* has a weight of human significance that makes it seem large. Mary looks out on us with tender dignity, and the Child, kingly in person, sits on her arm as on a throne. Yet we are not kept at a distance: we approach with reverence, but we do not stay shyly away.

EARLY SCULPTURE

Guido da Como (active 1240–60) was a contemporary of the sculptors, Nicola and Giovanni Pisano. However, his work belongs to the earlier, rigidly stylistic tradition. His figures, such as these riders and their horses, lack physical vitality.

GIOTTO'S FRESCOES

The Arena Chapel in Padua is decorated with Giotto's greatest surviving work, a cycle of frescoes painted about 1305–06 showing scenes from the life of the Virgin and from the Passion. The frescoes run all the way round the chapel.

Giotto's *Deposition of Christ (56)*, which is one of the frescoes on the north wall of the Arena Chapel, is the end of the same adventure we see starting in Duccio's *Calling of the Apostles* (see p.44). Giotto has called all his forces into play in this visualization of one of the great episodes in the story of Christ. In contrast to the towering, remote heights of Duccio's and Cimabue's enthroned Madonnas, Giotto brings the action down to our human eye-level, creating a startling truthfulness, and transforming the familiar event into a humanly real, intensely moving drama. The great square is vibrant with activity, with saintly mourners, each clearly distinct and intent on a specific action. His Mother, a woman of almost masculine determination (Giotto always

depicts her as tall and stately), clasps the dead body to herself, controlled and tragic. Mary Magdalene humbly holds His feet, contemplating through her tears the marks of the nails. St John makes a wild gesture of despairing grief, flinging back his arms, offering his breast to the terrible reality. The older men, Nicodemus and Joseph of Arimathea, stand to the side, reticent, mournful, while Mary's companions, who supported her at the foot of the cross, wail and lament and shed the tears that she does not. Such a bloodstained earth is no place for the angels, but they swoop and somersault with the roarings of their sorrow.

One lone and leafless tree on the arid hillside behind hints at the horror of the death, yet the darkened blue of the sky has a secret luminosity. Giotto and his contemporaries knew, even if the wildly passionate angels do not, that Christ would rise again. The strange self-possession of the Virgin may spring from this prophetic inner certainty, and it is a measure of Giotto's

DANTE
Dante Alighieri (1265–1321) is one of Italy's greatest poets. His most famous work, the *Divine Comedy*, was considered innovatory because it was written in Tuscan (the language of the common people) rather than Latin. The allegorical poem was divided into three parts and told the story of the poet's journey through Hell, Purgatory, and Paradise. It is filled with detailed descriptions of real people as well as legendary ones. Giotto, for example, appears in the *Purgatorio* section. Here, Dante is shown reading from the *Divine Comedy*.

56 Giotto, Deposition of Christ, c. 1304–13, 230 × 200 cm (7 ft 7 in × 6 ft 7 in)

PISANO'S SCULPTURES
Nicola Pisano's *Allegory of Strength* is one of the supporting column figures from the Baptistery pulpit at Pisa, Italy. Completed in 1260, the pulpit is acknowledged as Pisano's masterpiece. Many of Pisano's sculptures had a strong influence on Giotto.

GIOTTO'S CAMPANILE
Although we now think of Giotto primarily as a painter, he was also a skilled architect and sculptor. In 1334 he was appointed architect of Florence's city walls and fortifications. He also designed a *campanile* (bell tower) for the cathedral, although when it was built (above) only the lower sections were completed to Giotto's original specifications.

57 Giotto, The Kiss of Judas, c. 1305–06, 200 x 185 cm (6 ft 7 in x 6 ft 1 in)

ARENA CHAPEL
The Arena Chapel in Padua was founded by Enrico Scrovegni in 1303 to atone for the sins of his father, a notorious usurer. The chapel contains many of Giotto's finest frescoes, including *The Kiss of Judas*.

narrative conviction that we should ponder these possibilities. The very colour and forms, so clear, solid, and whole, so forthright, reassert this mystic certainty, without any concession to the apparent hopelessness. Six centuries afterwards, the great French artist Henri Matisse (see p.336) was to say that we need not know the Gospel story to catch the meaning of a Giotto painting: it carries its own truth within.

MOMENT OF BETRAYAL
Giotto has a startling power to organize the excitement of a scene around a central image. *The Kiss of Judas (57)*, another fresco from the Arena Chapel, sways and surges, every actor alive and functioning, either for or against Christ. Torches blaze and weapons whirl.

But at the heart there is only a tragic stillness, as Jesus looks into the mock-friendly eyes of His disciple Judas, and truth confronts falsehood with sorrowful love. The betrayer and the betrayed form the solid centre, with the jaundiced yellow of Judas' cloak billowing over the figure of Christ as if to swallow Him up. As in all Giotto's work, the heads are of the utmost importance, the natural focal point of the human dramas.

Time and again in the cycle, it is the facial expression, the direction of the eyes, sheer body language, that expresses the emotion. Artists working in the Byzantine style had a formula for the head: they painted a three-quarter view, and so the characters looked sideways. The effect of this was to exclude any personal involvement with the viewer or among themselves. But, for Giotto, art was all about involvement.

THE KISS OF JUDAS

Judas Iscariot was the Apostle who betrayed Jesus to the authorities, and then, unable to live with the consequences of his action, hanged himself. Giotto's painting depicts the moment when Judas identifies Jesus to the high priests and soldiers, with a kiss.

A FROZEN MOMENT
Christ and Judas provide the only still part in this impassioned scene. Christ is an image of constancy, His calm brow and steady eye contrasting with Judas' already troubled, frowning face. Giotto has suspended time, and Jesus' searching gaze silently communicates both foreknowledge that He is being betrayed, and understanding of Judas' heart.

PETER DEFENDS JESUS
All action draws our attention to the main figures of Christ and Judas. The swords and torches fan out from them, almost as an extended halo, or sway towards them. The gesticulating priest on the right is counterbalanced by the Apostle Peter on the left, who, in his anger, has cut off a soldier's ear.

THE ARREST
In the dense, organic mass of soldiers, Giotto creates an unstoppable, tidal force. They advance in one movement towards Christ, who is already engulfed in Judas' cloak. Many are indistinguishable, non-persons, their ranks merely punctuated by the repeated diagonals of their weapons.

COMBINING GOTHIC ELEMENTS

The most quintessential Gothic artist is Simone Martini (c. 1285–1344). Of the Sienese painters, he is the only one who can be said to have rivalled his teacher, the great Duccio. As Simone was, artistically, a direct descendant of Duccio, his art still held links with the Byzantine tradition of remote spirituality. It also acknowledged Giotto's spatial innovations and the elegant Gothic style of Northern Europe (represented by France), which was by then popular in Siena. As early as 1260, the French monarch, Robert of Anjou, brought his court to Naples, and before 1317, Simone was called to the court to paint a commission for the king. Simone was greatly influenced by the art of the Angevin court, with its characteristic elegance and courtly refinement that distinguished the French Gothic tradition from the early Italian developments. The influence of Northern Gothic style (see p.60) on Italian art is strongest in Simone's work: his concern with graceful form, and with uninterrupted, free-flowing line and pattern; the mannerisms and delicate gestures of his figures; and the "precious" quality and craftsmanship of his paintings reveal him as the definitive artist of the "Gothic-Italian" genre, and an early exponent of the International Gothic style (see p.54).

GOTHIC GRACE

Simone's figures have an extraordinary physical fluidity: whether angelic or human, they sway and sweep across the scene, dazzlingly beautiful, like some magical inhabitants both of our

58 Simone Martini, The Angel and the Annunciation, *1333, 265 x 305 cm (8 ft 8 in x 10 ft)*

event, is considered to have been a diptych, the right panel of which is now lost. It contained the Virgin, to whom the angel extends an arm, holding an olive branch. The absence of the Virgin is almost a *felix culpa* (happy mischance) since we are each forced to take her place, entering into the silent drama.

FAMILY CONFLICT

Simone's graciousness and love of beautiful clothes is not superficial and he can combine it with an electric sense of conflict. *Christ Discovered in the Temple (60)* is an extraordinary evocation of the generation gap, as the Child Jesus and His Mother oppose each other with dismaying incomprehension, and St Joseph tries ineffectually to bridge the gap between them. This is the chilling moment when Jesus reaches that crucial stage in growing up, when we come to realize that even those we love and trust do not understand and cannot be expected to. We are each alone and each singular, and this applies even to the best of families.

59 *Simone Martini,* **The Angel of the Annunciation,** *c. 1333, 30.5 x 22 cm (12 x 8½ in)*

world and of Heaven; feet are firmly on the earth, yet the whole being breathes the enchantments of another reality. There is no artist quite like Simone, both in the great daring of his colour combinations and in the persuasive force with which he invites us to enter the world of his singular imagination. This applies equally to his later, more intensely passionate works. His sense of drama is poignantly clear in *The Angel and the Annunciation (58)* in the Uffizi Gallery, Florence. In it we see Mary shrinking, almost aghast at the solemnity of being asked to bear God's Son.

But even at this moment of profound spiritual bewilderment, Mary sways with the Gothic grace that is so characteristic of Simone's art. She is all in blue, usually understood to symbolize the heavens. The angel is a dazzle of golden colour. The observer is aware of a sacred encounter in which heaven and earth become one. Mary and the angel lock eyes, each affecting the other. *The Angel of the Annunciation (59)*, another version of the same

60 *Simone Martini,* **Christ Discovered in the Temple,** *1342, 50 x 35 cm (20 x 14 in)*

61 **Pietro Lorenzetti,** St Sabinus before the Governor, *c. 1342,*
37.5 X 33 cm (14¾ X 13 in)

THE LORENZETTI BROTHERS

If Simone is a worthy disciple of Duccio, then his contemporaries, the two Lorenzetti brothers, Pietro (active 1320–48) and Ambrogio (active 1319–48), are stamped with the mark of Giotto, though both are Sienese. They represent Giotto "Duccioed", painting great columnar forms that yet have a tender grace. Their paintings reveal a stronger affinity with Giotto's unique psychological vitality than with the conscious elegance and refined craftsmanship of their own most illustrious contemporary, Simone Martini. Both brothers died suddenly in 1348, probably victims of that great European epidemic, the Black Death (see p.58).

There is near monumentality as well as a great gentleness in Pietro Lorenzetti's panel painting of *St Sabinus before the Governor (61)*. Sabinus, one of the four patron saints of Siena, refuses to offer sacrifice to the strange little idol as directed by the Roman Governor of Tuscany. The white-clad figure of the saint, who exudes an air of calm stillness and resolution, commands our attention, whilst the seated figure of the governor is depicted with his back to the observer. We are aware of spaciousness, both literally and of the mind.

Ambrogio, the younger brother, combines the weighty and the perceptive in his small painting *The Charity of St Nicholas of Bari (63)*. It depicts the moment in the legend when the saint throws the three golden balls into the bedroom of the daughters of an impoverished aristocrat.

62 *Ambrogio Lorenzetti,* **Allegory of Good Government: Effects of Good Government in the City and the Country** *, 1338–39, 2.4 X 14m (8 X 46 ft)*

PANORAMIC LANDSCAPE

The masterpiece of early landscape painting that is Ambrogio's particular claim to fame is his fresco depicting the *Effects of Good Government in the City and the Country (62)*, commissioned for the interior of the Palazzo Pubblico in Siena. Never did any state have its ideal so superbly set before it. The Lorenzetti vision is of a world blissfully ordered, painted with remarkable naturalism and sharp observation, based on the city of Siena itself. A companion painting, representing the consequences of bad government in the city, is also in the Palazzo Pubblico, but is, unfortunately, badly damaged.

This sort of bird's-eye, panoramic view is so familiar to us today, though more commonly in the form of a photograph, that we may not realize the extraordinarily avant-garde nature of this painting. It is the first attempt to show a real place in a real setting with its real inhabitants, and to make this wholly secular theme appear as jewel-like and precious as anything religious. This is not Bethlehem or Nazareth, but the actual worldly city of Siena, with its streets and shops and its patchwork of fields. Parts of the present-day town can even be recognized.

The panorama is painted from a variety of viewpoints and the buildings are not in scale with the figures. It depicts a time of peace, in which commerce, industry, and agriculture are all shown to be flourishing, and the inhabitants, who are depicted in a variety of pursuits, are clearly contented.

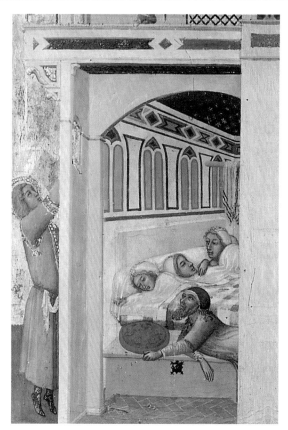

63 *Ambrogio Lorenzetti,* **The Charity of St Nicholas of Bari,** *c. 1332, 30 × 20 cm (11¾ × 8 in)*

The balls (from which we derive the pawnbroker's sign) will serve as dowries for the girls. Their father looks up, stunned, and the eldest daughter raises an astonished head as well.

PALAZZO PUBBLICO
Building work on the Palazzo Pubblico (town hall) in Siena began in 1298. Ambrogio Lorenzetti's panoramas of the city were painted on its interior walls.

CONTEMPORARY ARTS
1322
Consecration of Cologne Cathedral, one of Germany's great Gothic buildings
1330
Andrea Pisano begins work on the bronze doors of the Florence Baptistery
1348
Italian poet Boccaccio starts writing *The Decameron*, a collection of 100 short stories told by evacuees from a plague-bound city

INTERNATIONAL GOTHIC STYLE

By the end of the 14th century, the fusion of Italian and Northern European art had led to the development of an International Gothic style. For the next quarter of a century, leading artists travelled from Italy to France, and vice versa, and all over Europe. As a consequence, ideas spread and merged, until eventually painters in this International Gothic style could be found in France, Italy, England, Germany, Austria, and Bohemia.

FROISSART'S CHRONICLES

In the mid-14th century the French cleric Jean Froissart wrote a history of contemporary wars. The chronicle was richly decorated throughout; this illustration shows the Battle of Crécy, which took place in 1346. The battle was one of a series that were fought by France and England between 1337 and 1453, a period referred to as the Hundred Years' War. By 1360, the English, under Edward III, had captured much of northern France and profited financially while the French suffered. However, gradually the French regained territory and had reconquered most of France by 1453.

DIPTYCH

Diptychs are paintings in two, normally equal, parts, often linked together with hinges. Most Gothic diptychs depict the praying figure of the owner or donor of the painting in one panel, and the Madonna and Child in the other.

The influence of Simone Martini (see p.50) had spread far. He had left Italy in either 1340 or 1341 to work at the papal court, which was then in Avignon, France (see column, right). His extreme pictorial refinement was very much to the court's taste. The International Gothic style had a particularly courtly and aristocratic flavour, infused with a specially Flemish concern for naturalistic detail and, unlike the diverse strands of early Gothic art, it had a distinct and unified character. One classic example of the truly International style is the *Wilton Diptych (64)* now kept in the National Gallery, London. This exquisitely delicate, self-consciously monarchial work has proven impossible to attribute, and difficult to date. In fact, it could have been painted at any time during the reign of Richard II (1377–99) and, more significantly – attesting to its truly international style – scholars have been unable to agree on the nationality of the artist, only that he could have been English, French, Flemish, or Bohemian. The title of the painting is not original: it was once housed at Wilton House in Wiltshire, England.

The *Wilton Diptych* depicts Richard II of England kneeling before the Madonna and Child. He is accompanied by two English saints, Edmund (carrying an arrow) and Edward the Confessor (holding a ring); the third figure is John the Baptist. All the angels wear jewels in the form of a white hart, the personal emblem of King Richard. The painting may be intended to emphasize Richard's "divine right" (royal authority) as confirmed by the blessing he receives from the Christ Child. It also contains a clear reference to the Epiphany, with three kings worshipping the infant Jesus.

64 Anonymous, The Wilton Diptych, c. 1395, 46 x 29 cm (18 x 11½ in) each panel

Les Très Riches Heures is one of a genre of 15th-century illustrated prayer books known as "books of hours". The "hours" were prayers to be said at one of seven hours of the day. A book of hours would naturally contain a calendar, and this became the opportunity for a display of the illuminator's talent. Sadly, this particular example was unfinished at the time of the Limbourgs' and the Duc de Berry's deaths.

Each month is marked by an enchanting scene, usually showing appropriate seasonal activities. In August *(65)* we see courtly lovers riding to hunt with their falcons, while the great white ducal castle gleams in the distance and the peasants swim happily in the winding stream. The blue upper part of the painting shows an astrological hemisphere. With its mixture of courtly refinement and everyday reality, this miniature is representative of many in the book.

The Garden of Eden (66) was painted separately from the rest of *Les Très Riches Heures* and inserted into it later. It is a great enclosed circle showing the world as it was intended to remain before Adam and Eve's fall from grace. The whole story of the loss of Eden and human self-will is set graphically before us. Adam and Eve are finally ejected from the lush greenery of Eden onto a dangerous rocky shore. The Limbourgs' consciousness of tragedy is no less acute for being so chivalric in its manner. For all their elegance, they are as aware as all great artists that pain is our human lot.

65 *The Limbourg Brothers,* August, *from* Les Très Riches Heures du Duc de Berry, *1413–16, 29 x 20 cm (11½ x 8 in)*

MASTERS OF ILLUMINATION

The ancient art of book illumination (see pp.28–33) was still the prevailing form of painting in France at the beginning of the 15th century. It reached new heights, however, in the work of the Limbourg brothers, Pol, Herman, and Jehanequin, exponents of the International Gothic style. They came from Gelderland, a province of the Netherlands, but worked in France. They were the only other Gothic painters to take such orderly joy as that shown by Ambrogio Lorenzetti (see p.52) in the city and its environment, its people, and its rulers. The Limbourg brothers all died suddenly in 1416, probably of the plague.

The Limbourgs' joint masterpiece, *Les Très Riches Heures,* was commissioned by the wealthy and extravagant manuscript collector, the Duc de Berry (see column, right).

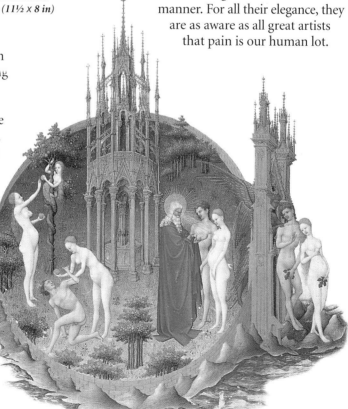

66 *The Limbourg Brothers,* The Garden of Eden *from* Les Très Riches Heures du Duc de Berry, *1413–16, 20 x 20 cm (8 x 8 in)*

MANUSCRIPT ILLUMINATION
This 15th-century illumination shows a lady painting the Virgin and Child. Women of the upper classes were not expected to work, but activities such as illuminating and weaving were acceptable occupations.

DUC DE BERRY
Jean, Duc de Berry, was a younger brother of Charles V of France. He ordered the building of a number of castles and filled each with specially commissioned works of art, including tapestries, paintings, and jewels. He is reputed to have owned 1,500 dogs.

POPE MARTIN V
The election of Pope Martin V in 1417 ended a period of crisis in the Western church known as the Great Schism (1378–1417), during which rival French and Italian popes held office. There were disagreements even before the Schism, and for 67 years (1309–76) the papal court was relocated from Rome to Avignon in France. During this period, Avignon became an important centre for artists.

GENTILE DA FABRIANO

International Gothic art is also exemplified by the well-travelled and influential Italian artist Gentile da Fabriano (c. 1370–1427), who helped to spread the International Gothic style across extensive areas of Italy. He crams every sector of his great panels with romantic activity, delighting, with his affectionate detail, in the sheer variety of a world he does not present too realistically, but just realistically enough to be convincing. It is a novelist's world, rich in human interest and engagingly plotted.

Most of Gentile's works, on which his reputation was made in his own lifetime, have not survived. Of those that are still known today, the most extraordinary is *The Adoration of the Magi (67)*. In this scene a cast of thousands, or so it seems, throngs the stage, providing constant interest and animation, but without any confusion of the story line. The Magi – the three kings from the East (see also column, p.98) – have come to adore the Christ Child with all their exotic, oriental retinue: camels, horses, dogs, dwarfs, and courtiers. But all attention is focused on the tiny figure of Christ, leaning forward from His Mother's clasp to lay a loving hand on the great hulking mass of the old king kneeling before Him.

As in the case of Simone Martini's *Angel of the Annunciation (58)*, the elaborate and sumptuously decorated, vaulted Gothic frame is an integral part of the work, and has direct bearing on the compositional structure. The *Adoration* was commissioned by Palla Strozzi, the richest man in Florence, for the church of Santa Trinità.

67 Gentile da Fabriano, **The Adoration of the Magi,** *finished 1423, 300 x 282 cm (9 ft 10 in x 9 ft 4 in)*

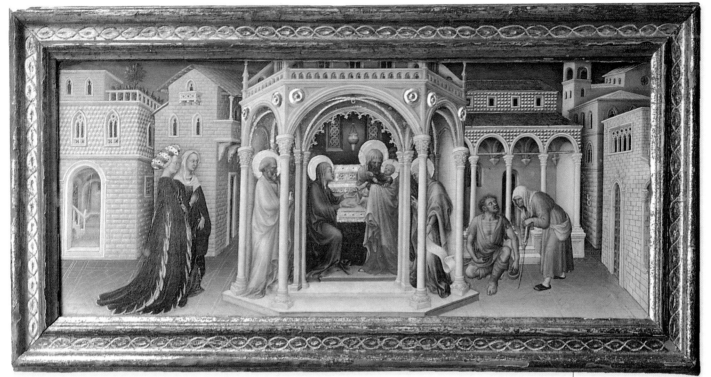

68 Gentile da Fabriano, **The Presentation of the Child in the Temple,** *1423, 25 x 65 cm (10 x 26 in)*

The strong anecdotal feeling in Gentile da Fabriano's work is also clear in *The Presentation of the Child in the Temple (68)*. The sacred event is the central feature of the painting, but on either side life goes on, with two stately women gossiping, and beggars seeking alms.

PAINTER AND MEDALLIST

This same lucidity of Gentile's is also seen in his fellow Italian artist Antonio Pisanello (c. 1395–1455/6). For decades it was thought that almost all of his frescoes had perished. Happily, a number have recently been uncovered in Mantua.

His panel painting *The Virgin and Child with St George and St Anthony Abbot (69)* shows an extraordinary confrontation. The almost savage rusticity of St Anthony the Hermit, in his rust-coloured cloak, is contrasted with the urban sophistication of St George, attired with the utmost modishness from large, white hat to elaborately spurred bootlets. (St George has no halo, but this is more than compensated for by his hat.)

Yet, despite the bizarre fascination of these two saintly figures, never for a single moment does Pisanello let us forget the importance of the Virgin and Child. They hang in the air, enclosed in what seems to be the circle of the sun, and it is they who integrate and give meaning to the scene.

69 Antonio Pisanello, **The Virgin and Child with St George and St Anthony Abbot,** *mid-15th century, 47 x 29 cm (18½ x 11½ in)*

> **"** *Michelangelo …in speaking of Gentile [da Fabriano], used to say that his hand in painting corresponded to his name.* **"**
>
> **Giorgio Vasari,**
> **Lives of the Painters,**
> **1568**

PISANELLO MEDAL
Pisanello was as famous for his portrait medals as he was for his paintings. The medals carried a likeness of the patron on one side and an allegory or landscape on the reverse. This example, produced c. 1445, shows the Duke of Rimini.

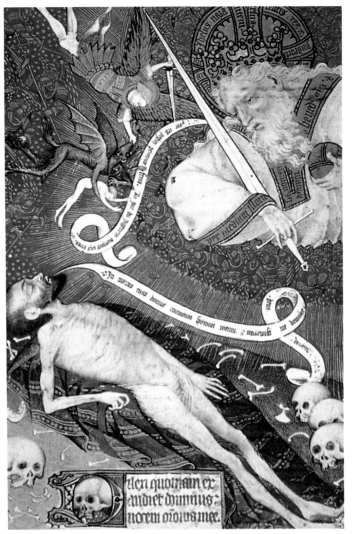

*70 The Master of the Rohan Hours, **The Dead Man before His Judge**, c. 1418–25, 27 x 19 cm (10½ x 7½ in)*

THE BLACK DEATH AND THE ARTS

Some Gothic art clearly shows the impact of the great medieval disaster, the Black Death. This epidemic, now probably of bubonic and pneumonic plague, devastated Europe from 1347 to 1351, claiming almost a third of the population. Many contemporaries viewed the Black Death as a judgment from God on the corruption of His people. This provoked a wave of popular enthusiasm, not, unfortunately, for religion itself, but for the "comfort religion" that excessive penances, like flagellation, provide. Artists, such as the Master of the Rohan Hours, reflected their interest in death and judgment in their work. The terrible realism of the miniature illumination *The Dead Man before His Judge (70)*, for example, presents a striking contrast with the Limbourgs' miniatures (see p.55). Here, the unknown artist shows his unflinching consciousness of the meaning and inevitability of death. The painting, with its archaic perspective and spatial ambiguities,

seems to be all the more impressive for these qualities. The horror of such death is intensified by the way the pock-marked and rotting corpse fills the page, seeming near to us, and striking even the casual viewer with holy dread.

The dead man's last prayer is written in Latin on a white scroll: "Into Thy hands I commend my spirit; thou hast redeemed me, O Lord, the God of truth."

God holds a globe and a sword as symbols of His power and as the Supreme Judge. In response to the dead man's prayers, He replies in French: "For your sins you shall do penance. On judgment day you shall be with Me."

The small figures at the top left of the miniature depict St Michael, aided by his army of inconspicuous angels, attacking a devil who is attempting to take possession of the dead man's soul, represented by an adolescent nude.

SIENESE ASSURANCE

Other examples of contemporary art in the International Gothic style seem to be unaffected by the terror of the Black Death. Indeed, in our confused and divided times, there seems to be a happy inner security in many of the Gothic painters that is infinitely poignant. It may have a touch of the fairy tale about it, as it does in the delightful Sienese master, Sassetta (Stefano di Giovanni, 1392–1450), whose panel painting *The Meeting of St Anthony and St Paul (71)* shows the enduring influence of French illuminated manuscripts. The two hermits meet in a "Red Riding Hood" sort of woods, and embrace as simply as children, affirming love in the desert.

The panel is one of a series telling the story of St Anthony Abbot, said to be the founder of monasticism. At the top we see St Anthony, who at the age of 90 abandoned his hermit life after having a vision, setting out to visit St Paul the Hermit, who was by then 113. On his journey he encounters a centaur (half man and half horse), a symbol of paganism. St Anthony blesses him and converts him to Christianity.

The foreground shows the story's conclusion as the two saints greet each other fondly, their staffs lying on the ground beside them (St Anthony's staff is always shown as a T-shaped crutch) as they lean in to one another.

For almost all of Sassetta's life, the Sienese people lived peacefully (apart from a short period in the 1430s) under a republican government. This meant that they could enjoy a fertile relationship with their rival, the bigger and more powerful neighbouring city of Florence.

Sassetta was the most important Sienese artist of the 15th century. His art was steeped in the Sienese Gothic tradition, but he happily absorbed influences from the great, innovative Florentine artists of the day, such as Masaccio (see p.82) and the sculptor Donatello (see p.83).

CHAUCER

By 1500, the language of the English court had changed from French to English. The change to the use of English is seen much earlier in the writings of Geoffrey Chaucer. Born in 1343 to a wealthy London family, he became one of King Edward III's attendants, a position that enabled him to travel and earn enough money to write. His most famous work, *The Canterbury Tales*, describes a wonderful cross-section of 14th-century society, while for the first time using a poetic language that could be understood by everybody in the country.

71 Sassetta, The Meeting of St Anthony and St Paul, *c. 1440, 48 x 35 cm (19 x 14 in)*

OTHER WORKS BY SASSETTA

St Thomas Aquinas before a Crucifix (Vatican Museum, Rome)

St Francis Renounces his Earthly Father (National Gallery, London)

The Mystic Marriage of St Francis (Musée Condé, Chantilly)

The Journey of the Magi (Metropolitan Museum of Art, New York)

The Burning of Jan Geus (National Gallery of Victoria, Melbourne)

The Betrayal of Christ (Detroit Institute of Arts)

INNOVATION IN THE NORTH

In the 15th century the International Gothic style developed in two directions: both could be called revolutions. One was in the South, in Florence, and was the birth of the Italian Renaissance (see p.82). The other took place in the North, in the Low Countries, where painting went through an independent but equally radical transformation: this was the beginning of the Northern Renaissance movement (see p.148).

THE NETHERLANDS

In the 15th century the area shown above (with modern boundaries) was known either as the Low Countries or as the Netherlands. Flanders (shaded) was the centre of artistic activity. Netherlandish and Flemish were used interchangeably, although the latter refers to the smaller area of Flanders.

The new form of painting that appeared in the Netherlands at the beginning of the 15th century was distinguished by a depth of pictorial reality that had not been seen before. It rejected the seductive elegance and overtly decorative elements of the International Gothic style, and whereas before, in the sacred painting of the 14th century, there was a sense of the viewer being offered glimpses of Heaven – of putting an insignificant foot in the door, so to speak – the Flemish painters brought the sacred down to our real world. Instead of depicting a form of high drama for which the world served as a kind of grand stage, artists chose to portray real-life domestic interiors – living rooms and bedrooms that revealed the commonplace belongings of everyday human existence. We find a growing peace with the world and one's place in it in the work of the Northern painters. Robert Campin (active 1406–44), one of the earliest great Northern innovators and the teacher of van der Weyden (see p.67), is now believed to be the artist known as the Master of Flémalle. (This name is derived from a group of panel paintings that were thought to have originated in an abbey at Flémalle-lez-Liège.) In fact, Campin lived and worked in Tournai (both these places were in Flanders).

THE SACRED IN THE EVERYDAY

In his *Nativity (72)*, Campin presents an intense abundance, a world crowded with individuals and the unromantic realities of being alive. He portrays a puny newborn Christ, a sullen midwife, coarse shepherds, and a cow in its rickety stable, yet everything is solid, lovely, true, and despite its realism, all is pervaded by a deep, though unself-conscious faith.

Even more striking is Campin's *Virgin and Child Before a Firescreen (73)*, where simple domesticity is emphasized by the wickerwork firescreen that provides the Virgin's halo. By tradition, International Gothic style indicated holiness with a golden circle.

The painting's upper left-hand corner contains a view of a town seen through the open window. Little landscapes like this were

72 Robert Campin, Nativity, c. 1425, 85 x 71 cm (34 x 28 in)

73 *Robert Campin,* **The Virgin and Child Before a Firescreen,** *c. 1430, 63 x 49 cm (25 x 19½ in)*

GLIMPSE OF A TOWNSCAPE
This detail from Virgin and Child Before a Firescreen *shows a miniature landscape glimpsed through the open window. Campin depicts a busy town dominated by a Gothic-style church. The gabled buildings are typical of contemporary Netherlandish architecture.*

CHIVALRY
Many medieval paintings illustrated chivalry, which was part of the contemporary concept of knighthood. Gradually the basic forms of chivalry, with an emphasis on valour, honour, courtesy, loyalty, and chastity, gave way to the courtly love inspired by Arthurian romances. This was a movement towards the idea of unfulfilled desire – love as a religion in itself. On this painted Flemish shield, a lady stands before a kneeling knight who vows to honour her or die.

often seen in Netherlandish painting, and the idea of encapsulating the world through a window was later attractive to Italian artists.

Spirituality and reality are now brought together, and the setting is Campin's own world: the bourgeois interior. Once we have an alliance of the sacred and the commonplace, it becomes possible for representational painting in all its specificity to express the sacred. The close attention given to ordinary objects – each awarded absolute clarity – invested them with a quality of silent, mystical significance. There is an aura of mystery here, and the seemingly ordinary can be startling and powerfully present, and this is fully applicable to portraiture.

Up to this time, portraiture as we understand it today had not existed since antiquity. Paintings that resembled "portraits" had served specific functions, such as recording an event. Robert Campin was the first to look at people with a new artistic eye, bringing out the psychological individuality of the subject. His *Portrait of a Woman (74),* with its animated face peering out from a plain white headdress, shows his mastery of light effects. His focus is sharp, forcing us to look at what he paints. The

74 *Robert Campin,* **Portrait of a Woman,** *c. 1420–30, 40 x 28 cm (16 x 11 in)*

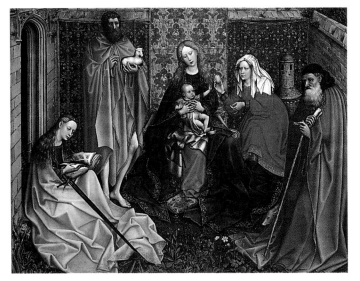

75 Follower of Robert Campin, Madonna and Child with Saints in an Enclosed Garden, *c. 1440/60,* *120 x 148cm (47 x 58½ in)*

portrait is a good example of the new style of painting in the Netherlands. Portraits began to reveal less of a family look and more of the individuality of the sitter. Campin introduced a new facial type that continued in van der Weyden (see p.67).

In *Madonna and Child with Saints in an Enclosed Garden (75)*, a follower of Campin attains the same comforting assurance that Campin showed in his *Nativity* (see p.60). The enclosed garden in which Mother and Child are shown with a group of saints is the Garden of Paradise – a "managed" Paradise. A walled or fenced garden is a traditional symbol of the virginity of Mary.

A NEW REALISM

This inner certainty reaches its peak in Jan van Eyck (1385–1441), a contemporary of Campin and one of the enduring influences on his century. He had an eye almost miraculously responsive to every detail of his world, not just in that he saw it, but that he understood its value. Van Eyck's natural habitat was one of luminous clarity; he saw the most ordinary things with a wonderful sharpness and a great sense of their awesome beauty. We know little about him personally, but he is the most overwhelming of painters in the convictions he enables us to share.

Like the 17th-century Dutch painter Vermeer (see p.208), van Eyck takes us into the light, and makes us feel that we, too, belong there. Van Eyck's meticulously detailed *Adoration of the Lamb (76)* is part of a huge altarpiece; painted

76 Jan van Eyck, Adoration of the Lamb (*detail*)*, completed 1432, 135 x 235 cm (53 x 93 in)*

77 Jan van Eyck, **Annunciation,** *c. 1434/36, 92 x 37 cm (36½ x 14½ in)*

Jan, about whom we have the most information, was mostly responsible, or whether it was Hubert, about whom we know almost nothing. For what it is worth, Hubert is given precedence in the inscription. It reads: "The painter Hubrecht Eyck, than whom none was greater, began this work, which his brother Jan, who was second to him in art, completed at the behest of Jodoc Vijdt…"

This panel shows the sacrificial Lamb on the high altar, its sacred blood pouring into a chalice. Angels surround the altar, carrying reminders of the Crucifixion and in the foreground gushes the Fountain of Life. Coming from the four corners of the earth are the worshippers, a diverse collection that includes prophets, martyrs, popes, virgins, pilgrims, knights, and hermits. It is likely, as with many great religious works of the time, that van Eyck would have been advised by a theologian, and these figures seem to represent the hierarchy of the Church. Set in a beautiful, lush landscape, the holy city gleams on the horizon, its outline very much that of a Dutch city; the church on the right is probably Utrecht Cathedral. This is a detail from the vast altarpiece, but its very perfection and accuracy, its convincingness, explain why this mystic vision has laid such a hold on the affections of those who see it. The *Ghent Altarpiece* envelops the viewer in a mood of contemplation, but any more rigorous analysis becomes a massive intellectual effort. We can move more easily into a smaller painting, such as his long, slender *Annunciation (77)*.

SYMBOLIC LIGHT IN VAN EYCK
As we look at the *Annunciation*, we become warmly conscious of the gentle radiance of the light, illuminating everything it embraces, from the dim upper roofing to the glancing gleam of the angel's jewels. The clarity would be too intense were it not also soft, an integrating, enveloping presence. This diffused presence, impartial in its luminescence, is also a spiritual light, surrogate of God Himself, who loves all that He has made.

The symbolism goes even deeper: the upper church is dark, and the solitary window depicts God the Father. Below though, wholly translucent, are three bright windows that remind us of the Trinity, and of how Christ is the light of the world. This holy light comes in all directions, most obviously streaming down towards the Virgin as the Holy Spirit comes to overshadow her: from this sacred shadow will arise divine brightness. Her robes swell out as if in anticipation, and she answers the angelic salutation "*Ave Gratia Plena*" ("Hail, full of

on both sides, it is the largest and most complex altarpiece produced in the Netherlands in the 15th century. This monumental work still hangs in its original setting, the Cathedral of St Bavo in Ghent, drawing the worshipper deeper and deeper into the sacred world it makes visible. There has been much debate over the parts the two van Eyck brothers, Jan and Hubert, played in the creation of the *Ghent Altarpiece*: whether

COPIED ELEMENTS
In this book illustration (attributed to a later Flemish painter), elements derived from *"The Arnolfini Marriage"* include the inscription, mirror, beads, and brush.

grace") with a humble *"Ecce Ancilla Domini"* ("Behold the handmaid of the Lord"). But with charming literalness, van Eyck writes her words reversed and inverted, so that the Holy Spirit can read them. The angel is all joy, all smiles, all brightness: the Virgin is pensive, amazed, unbejewelled. She knows, as the angel apparently does not, what will be the cost of her surrender to God. Her heart will be pierced with grief when her Child is crucified, and we notice that she holds up her hands in the symbolic gesture of devotion, but also as if in unconscious anticipation of a piercing.

The angel advances over the tiles of a church, where we can make out David slaying Goliath. (Goliath represents the power – ultimately fruitless – of the Devil.) The message the angel gives Mary sets her forth on her own road to the giant-slaying that is her motherhood and holiness.

OIL: A NEW PAINTING MEDIUM

The van Eycks started their careers as manuscript illuminators. The often miniature detail and exquisite rendering found in van Eyck paintings, such as The *Annunciation*, reveal a strong affinity with this art form. However, the single factor that most distinguishes the van Eycks from the art of manuscript illumination was the medium they used.

For many years Jan van Eyck was wrongly credited with the "discovery of painting in oil". In fact, oil painting was already in existence, used to paint sculptures and to glaze over tempera paintings. The van Eycks' real achievement was the development – after much experimentation – of a stable varnish that would dry at a consistent rate. This was created with linseed and nut oils, and mixed with resins.

The breakthrough came when Jan or Hubert mixed the oil into the actual paints they were using, instead of the egg medium that constituted tempera paint. The result was brilliance, translucence, and intensity of colour as the pigment was suspended in a layer of oil that also trapped light. The flat, dull surface of tempera was transformed into a jewel-like medium, at once perfectly suited to the representation of precious metals and gems and, more significantly, to the vivid, convincing depiction of natural light.

Van Eyck's inspired observations of light and its effects, executed with technical virtuosity through this new, transparent medium, enabled him to create a brilliant and lucid kind of reality. The invention of this technique transformed the appearance of painting.

A MARRIAGE PORTRAIT

"The Arnolfini Marriage" (78) is a name that has been given to this untitled double portrait by Jan van Eyck, now in the National Gallery, London. It is one of the greatest celebrations of human mutuality. Like Rembrandt's *"Jewish Bride"* (see p.204, another picture that had no known title of its maker's giving), this painting reveals to us the inner meaning of a true marriage.

The bed, the single burning candle, the solemn moment of joining as the young groom is about to place his raised hand in his betrothed's, the fruit, the faithful little dog, the rosary, the unshod feet (since this is the ground of a holy union), and even the respectful space between Giovanni Arnolfini and his wife, Giovanna Cenami, are all united in the mirror's reflection. All these details exalt us and at the same time make us aware of the human potential for goodness and fulfilment.

78 Jan van Eyck, "The Arnolfini Marriage", 1434, 82 x 60 cm (32¼ x 23½ in)

"The Arnolfini Marriage"

This title has traditionally been given to this painting because it was thought to be a form of "wedding certificate" for Giovanni Arnolfini and Giovanna Cenami, who married in Bruges in 1434. He was an Italian merchant, she the daughter of an Italian merchant. Their grave, youthful faces both have a lovely responsibility that is typical of van Eyck.

Convex mirror

The mirror is painted with almost miraculous skill. Its carved frame is inset with ten miniature medallions depicting scenes from the life of Christ. Yet more remarkable is the mirror's reflection, which includes van Eyck's own tiny self-portrait, accompanied by another man who may have been the official witness to the ceremony.

Symbolic candle

The solitary flame burning in bright daylight can be interpreted as the bridal candle, or God's all-seeing eye, or simply as a devotional candle. Another symbol is St Margaret (the patron saint of women in childbirth), whose image is carved on the high chairback.

An elaborate signature

As today, marriages in 15th-century Flanders could take place privately rather than in church. Van Eyck's Latin signature, in the Gothic calligraphy used for legal documents, reads: "Jan van Eyck was present", and has been interpreted by some as an indication that the artist himself served as a witness.

Symbol of faithfulness

Almost every detail can be interpreted as a symbol. The companion dog is seen as a symbol of faithfulness and love. The fruits on the window ledge probably stand for fertility and our fall from Paradise. Even the discarded shoes are not thought to be incidental, but to signify the sanctity of marriage.

79 Master of the Avignon Pietà, Pietà, *c. 1470, 160 x 215 cm (5 ft 3 in x 7 ft 1 in)*

THE SPREAD OF NATURALISM

The new realism of the Netherlands had begun
to spread in the first quarter of the 15th century,
and by the 1450s its influence was widespread
throughout northern Europe and as far as Spain
and the Baltic. The *Pietà (79)*, painted by an
unknown artist in Avignon, France, retains
the flat golden background of early Gothic
and Byzantine painting, but we hardly notice.
Our attention is completely absorbed by this
passionate meditation on the death of Christ.
It takes place in no earthly location, only in the
heart of the praying and kneeling donor on the
left. For sheer impact, this wonderful and terrible
painting is unsurpassed until we meet the Passion
scenes of Bosch (see p.72). We can see that the
Gothic era was a freely emotional period, one
that accepted tears as a natural expression of
our frail vulnerability.

The strangely named Petrus Christus (1410–72/3)
is another Fleming with a mysterious sense of
emotional truth. He was a follower of van Eyck
(who was possibly his teacher) and many of his
works reveal his debt to the older Fleming. To

80 Petrus Christus, The Man of Sorrows, *c. 1444–72/3,
11.5 x 8.5 cm (4½ x 3⅜ in)*

van Eyck's influence was added that of Antonello da Messina (see p.111), whose art Petrus Christus certainly knew. This led Christus to somewhat "Italianize" van Eyck's style. The tiny picture *Man of Sorrows (80)* in Birmingham, England, shows the crucified Jesus wearing His crown of thorns and displaying three of His wounds. He is flanked by two angels, one of whom holds a lily and the other a sword, symbolizing innocence and guilt. This is the Last Judgment, at which every man must face his judge: it captures the attention of the viewer, making it impossible to avoid the reality of the Passion and ultimately its significance for us.

THE INFLUENTIAL VAN DER WEYDEN

Rogier van der Weyden (1399/1400–64) is another giant of the Northern tradition. He was a pupil of van Eyck and Campin, and became the most influential Northern artist of the first half of the 15th century. Though he began his career relatively late (in his late twenties), he was very successful and had a large workshop with many assistants. The success of his art at the court of Philip the Good, Duke of Burgundy (see right), ensured and prolonged the popularity of his style. His paintings were exported to other parts of Europe, reaching Castille, Spain, in 1445 and Ferrara, Italy, in 1449, and his fame became widespread.

Van der Weyden was a master of expressing human emotion; he moves us in a way that van Eyck cannot. Perhaps the best example of this is his *Deposition (81)*. It is of its nature an emotional subject; the handling of any dead body is a disturbing experience, let alone that of a young man executed in the full flower of his beauty, and this young man is, of course, Christ. But no artist has ever imbued this scene with more majestic pathos than van der Weyden. Like a great sculptured frieze, the holy mourners spread across the surface of the painting. Christ and His Mother echo the same position: He falls from the Cross physically dead; she falls to the ground emotionally dead.

Van der Weyden explores all the degrees and kinds of grief, from the controlled and grave anguish of St John on the left, prominent in pink, to the anguished abandon of Mary Magdalene on the right, a striking colour composition of red, palest yellow, and purple.

The extravagance of the emotion never escapes the artist's control. All remains firmly believable and we are swept into an experience that is at once beautiful and terrible.

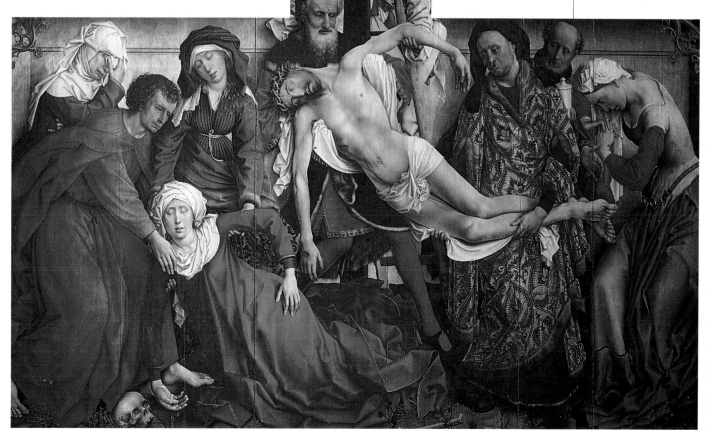

81 Rogier van der Weyden, Deposition (The Descent from the Cross), *c. 1435, 220 x 260 cm (7 ft 3 in x 8 ft 6 in)*

OTHER WORKS BY VAN DER WEYDEN

The Sforza Triptych
(Musée des Beaux Arts, Brussels)

Lamentation for Christ at His Entombment
(Uffizi, Florence)

Francesco d'Este
(Metropolitan Museum of Art, New York)

Portrait of Jean de Gros
(Art Institute of Chicago)

GUILDS

In medieval Europe most tradespeople and artisans, including painters, belonged to a guild. These men (above) would have been members of the glassblowers' guild. Guilds served to keep a particular craft profitable, protect standards, and provide social benefits. They were a vital part of city life and members were often represented on town councils. Some of the large guilds representing several crafts were split into confraternities, each with a patron saint.

OTHER WORKS BY VAN DER GOES

The Adoration of the Kings
(Staatliche Museen, Berlin)

The Fall of Man
(Kunsthistorisches Museum, Vienna)

Death of the Virgin
(State Museum, Bruges)

Donor with Saint John the Baptist
(Walters Art Gallery, Baltimore)

POWERFUL PORTRAITURE

The compositional structure of the *Deposition*, with its shallow space and cropped shape, deliberately excludes any distracting background, thereby concentrating all attention on the dramatic scene. A similar effect is achieved in another van der Weyden painting, his *Portrait of a Lady (82)*. Here, the stark background focuses all our attention on the sitter. The subject has a haunting quality, a sense of almost painful reserve, as if she was willing to give the artist only her exterior. Yet he has circumvented her resistance and brought us into contact with the lady in her actuality. Her unadorned

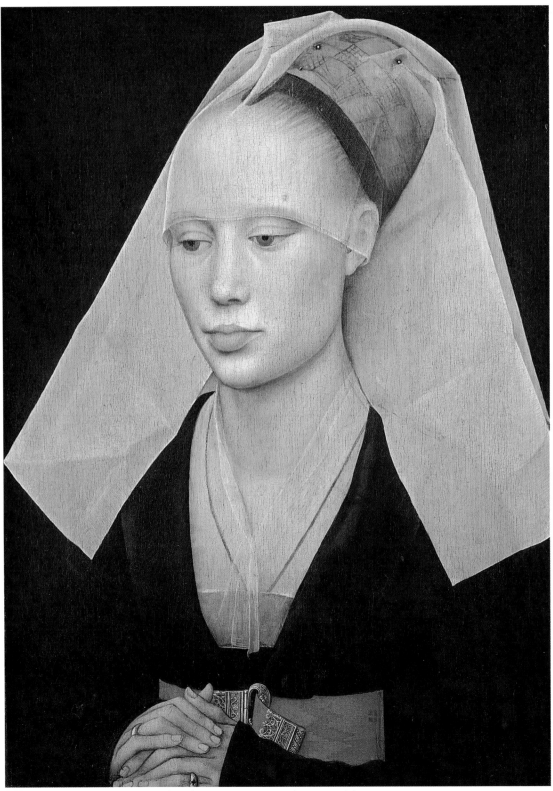

82 Rogier van der Weyden, Portrait of a Lady, c. 1460, 37 x 27.5 cm (14½ x 10¾ in)

83 Hugo van der Goes, The Portinari Altarpiece, c. 1476, 254 x 140 cm (100 x 55 in) each wing, 254 x 305 cm (8 ft 4 in x 10 ft) central panel

clothing and downcast gaze suggest modesty. To the modern observer she has an exceptionally high forehead; in fact, this was the fashion, achieved by plucking the hairline.

It has been suggested that the woman is Marie de Valengin, the daughter of Philip the Good, Duke of Burgundy (see p.67), but this identification is somewhat doubtful.

A GRAND SCALE

Hugo van der Goes (c. 1436–82) is an extraordinary painter, and produced paintings on a surprisingly large scale, both literally and in the unprecedented monumentality of the figures. His most famous work, *The Portinari Altarpiece (83)*, now in the Uffizi, Florence, was to prove very influential in Italy, where it decorated the church of the Hospital of Santa Maria Nuova in Florence. It was commissioned by a Florentine banker, Tommaso Portinari, who lived in Bruges and acted as the Flanders agent for the powerful Italian de' Medici family (see pp.93, 97). The dimensions of the painting, which when open measures over 2.5 m (8 ft) long, were dictated by a Florentine precedent.

Van der Goes is said to have died of religious melancholia, and knowing this, we may persuade ourselves that we see a barely controlled passion in his work. But without this biographic information, it may simply strike us as immensely dignified. Like the wings, the central panel, *The Adoration of the Shepherds*, shows two different scales in use, with the angels strangely small in comparison to the rest of the scene. This was a common device in medieval painting; it makes it easy to spot the important characters.

SAINTS AND THE DONOR'S FAMILY

The two large figures of St Margaret and St Mary Magdalene, who appear in the right panel of The Portinari Altarpiece, *are presenting Portinari's wife, Maria, and their daughter. St Margaret (patron saint of childbirth) can be identified by the fact that she is standing on a dragon. According to legend, she was swallowed by a monster, but burst out of it. Mary Magdalene carries the jar of ointment with which she anointed Christ's feet.*

SHRINE BY MEMLING

One of Memlings' most famous works is the Shrine of St Ursula. The carved wooden casket is in the shape of a Gothic chapel with six painted panels. Each panel tells the myth of St Ursula's pilgrimage to Rome with 11,000 virgins from England. On their return they were massacred by pagans from Cologne. The shrine is now the centrepiece of the Memling Museum in Bruges, Belgium.

MEMLING'S PLACIDITY

Van der Goes' vision is immensely powerful, and his paintings combine the gravity of van Eyck and the emotional intensity of van der Weyden. Certainly the power in his work is absent in that of the other Flemings, such as Gerard David (see p.71) and Hans Memling. Memling (also known as Memlinc; c. 1430/35–94) was possibly trained in the workshop of van der Weyden (see p.67), but also contains influences from Dieric Bouts (see below), a follower of van Eyck. Although a German by birth, Memling settled in Bruges, Flanders, and it was there that he lived and worked. In fact, he worked so successfully that he became one of Bruges' wealthiest citizens.

Memling is a gentle artist, unobtrusively regarding the world about him and sharing his response with us. His *Portrait of a Man with an Arrow (84)* is immediately likeable. Various possibilities have been suggested as to the meaning of the arrow: something about his kindly and mild countenance seems to rule out

84 Hans Memling, Portrait of a Man with an Arrow, c. 1470/5, 32.5 x 26 cm (12¾ x 10¼ in)

the possibility that he is a soldier. We are shown a very human gentleman, but one with firm and sensual lips. This small masterpiece grows on us the longer we contemplate it.

There could not be a greater contrast than between this and the work of Memling's contemporary, Bosch (see p.72), in whose work we often find a face that appears mean with suppressed hatreds.

A VAN DER WEYDEN FOLLOWER

Of all the Northern painters, the greatest influence on the Dutch-born painter Dieric Bouts (c. 1415–75) was van der Weyden (see p.67), who was possibly his teacher. Bouts did most of his work in Louvain, Flanders, where he was appointed the official city painter in 1468. His paintings are recognizable for their solemn dignity and deeply religious feeling. The spare composition and simple rendering of the drapery folds in Bouts' sensitively painted and elegant *Portrait of a Man (85)* are typical. He was an accomplished landscape painter, and here we get a glimpse of a landscape through the open window.

85 Dieric Bouts, Portrait of a Man, 1462, 32 x 20 cm (12½ x 8 in)

LATE GOTHIC PAINTING

Gerard David, Hieronymus Bosch, and Matthias Grünewald were all early 16th-century artists and contemporaries of the other Northern artists Albrecht Dürer, Lucas Cranach, and Hans Holbein (see pp.148–162). However, the paintings of the former artists maintain connections with the Gothic tradition, while the latter were strongly influenced by the Italian Renaissance (see p.79). Thus the two strands of Gothic and Renaissance art coexisted in Northern Europe in the first half of the 16th century.

Gerard David (c. 1460–1523) was Memling's natural successor in Bruges at the end of the 15th century, and was a highly successful artist with a busy workshop. He is a wholly delightful painter, whose childlike Madonna makes an immediate and unforced emotional appeal. In *The Rest on the Flight into Egypt (86)*, she holds grapes for her baby, a symbol of the wine of His adult Passion, yet her quiet and abstracted expression is not one of foreboding. She seems enwrapped with her baby Jesus in a timeless reverie, while all the burden is borne by the active St Joseph in the background, and the watchful ass.

The distinct early 15th-century style of the Low Countries, which we see in the paintings of Campin and van Eyck (see pp.60–65), comes to its peak in David's paintings. We find in him the

THE HANSA

The Hanseatic League was formed in the 14th century as an association of German towns to protect its merchants in foreign parts and to extend trade. It grew to encompass 200 cities in Germany, the Low Countries, and England. Hansa merchants exported wool, cloth, metals, and furs to the East, and imported pigments, raw materials, silk, spices, and a variety of other oriental goods into Europe.

BRUGES

Until the late 15th century Bruges was the hub of international commerce in northern Europe. Bruges was a self-governing commune and the city was also the headquarters of the Hanseatic League. Although self-governing, the city was, like the rest of Flanders, under the overlordship of the Dukes of Burgundy until 1477. Bruges lost its trading dominance after the River Zwijn became unnavigable and Antwerp assumed its position of influence.

86 *Gerard David,* **The Rest on the Flight into Egypt,** *c. 1510, 44 x 45 cm (17½ x 17¾ in)*

87 Hieronymus Bosch, **The Temptation of St Anthony** *(central panel), c. 1505, 132 x 120 cm (52 x 47 in)*

monumental qualities of the Northern tradition, vitalized by a new pictorial vision, that would influence Quentin Massys and Jan Gossaert (see p.163). In these two, the divergent traditions of North and South come together again, though this happened later, when Italian Renaissance art was exerting an enormous and compelling influence. Northern art kept its sharp veracity, but with Italian modulations.

THE UNIQUE VISION OF BOSCH

The extraordinary painter Hieronymus Bosch (c. 1450–1516) stands apart from the prevailing Flemish traditions in painting. His style was unique, strikingly free, and his symbolism, unforgettably vivid, remains unparalleled to this day. Marvellous and terrifying, he expresses an intense pessimism and reflects the anxieties of his time, one of social and political upheaval.

Very little is known about Bosch, which somehow seems fitting since his work is so enigmatic. We know that he adopted the name of the Dutch town of s'Hertogenbosch (near Antwerp) as his own, that he belonged to an ultra-orthodox religious community called the Brotherhood of Mary, and that in his own day he was famous. Many of his paintings are devotional, and there are several on the theme of the Passion. He is specially famous for his fantastic, demon-filled works, one of which is *The Temptation of St Anthony (87)*.

The central panel of this triptych illustrates the kneeling figure of St Anthony being tormented by devils. These include a man with a thistle for a head, and a fish that is half gondola. Bizarre and singular as such images seem to us, many would have been familiar to Bosch's contemporaries because they relate to Flemish proverbs and religious terminology. What is so extraordinary is that these imaginary creatures are painted with utter conviction, as though

88 Hieronymus Bosch, The Path of Life, *c. 1500–02, 135 × 90 cm (53 × 35½ in)*

they truly existed. He has invested each bizarre or outlandish creation with the same obvious realism as the naturalistic animal and human elements. His nightmarish images seem to possess an inexplicable surrealistic power.

Even a more naturalistic painting like *The Path of Life (88)* contains sinister elements. Apart from the dog snarling at the poverty-stricken old man, and the animal bones and skull in the foreground, robbers attack a traveller in the back-ground, and a gallows is visible on the skyline above the old man's head. *The Path of Life* is on the outer face of the wings of a triptych. The three inside panels display Bosch's tragic view of human existence, dwelling upon the triumph of sin. Man's exile from Paradise is shown on the left, the infinite variation of human vice in the centre, and its consequence – exile to Hell – on the right.

ILLUSTRATED ALLEGORIES

In *The Ship of Fools (89)* Bosch is imagining that the whole of mankind is voyaging through the seas of time on a ship, a small ship, that is representative of humanity. Sadly, every one of the representatives is a fool. This is how we live, says Bosch – we eat, drink, flirt, cheat, play silly games, pursue unattainable objectives. Meanwhile our ship drifts aimlessly and we never reach the harbour. The fools are not the

89 Hieronymus Bosch, The Ship of Fools, *c. 1490–1500, 58 × 33 cm (23 × 13 in)*

> *"The master of the monstrous… the discoverer of the unconscious."*
>
> **Carl Gustav Jung,** on Hieronymus Bosch

DRAMA

Mummers like these, who appear in a 14th-century French illumination, were a common sight in the Middle Ages in the towns of northern Europe. They were masked players who travelled around in groups and put on entertainments and mystery plays in the streets and private houses. The religious community that Bosch belonged to is also known to have performed mystery plays.

DEATH AND THE MISER

This moralistic panel from Bosch's middle phase is an example of the 15th-century Flemish insistence on exposing the folly and vices of humanity. Religious sects proliferated in the Low Countries at that time, and Bosch belonged to one with strongly orthodox beliefs.

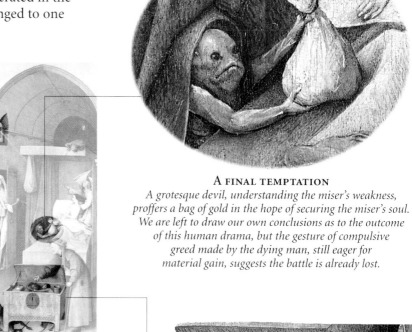

A FINAL TEMPTATION

A grotesque devil, understanding the miser's weakness, proffers a bag of gold in the hope of securing the miser's soul. We are left to draw our own conclusions as to the outcome of this human drama, but the gesture of compulsive greed made by the dying man, still eager for material gain, suggests the battle is already lost.

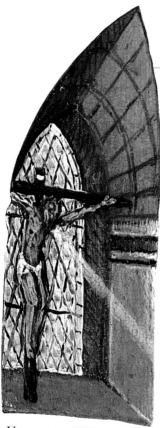

UNSEEN CRUCIFIX

At the heart of this painting is the battle for the miser's soul. His guardian angel pleads – perhaps in vain – for his salvation, and attempts to guide the dying man's attention to the small crucifix away off to the upper left, unseen by the miser and ignored.

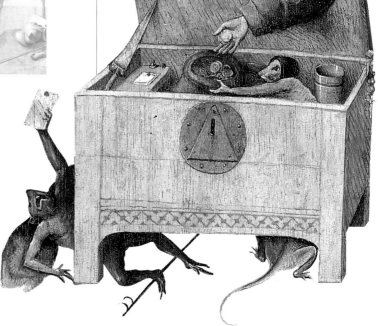

MONEY – THE FOCAL POINT

Lust, gluttony, and material greed were ranked among the worst of vices and were popular subjects of 15th-century religious sermons. The strongbox is given a prominent position, as the cause of the miser's possible damnation. He does not seem to see, as Bosch ensures we do, that the strongbox is alive with malicious, verminous creatures from the underworld, and that he carrries his key next to his rosary in vain.

SELF-PORTRAIT?

In the foreground, a small demon looks sideways at us amidst the miser's discarded silks, a face often seen in Bosch paintings, lean, pinched, and unhopeful. It has been suggested that this is a sardonic portrait of Bosch himself.

irreligious, since prominent among them are a monk and a nun, but they are all those who live "in stupidity". Bosch laughs, and it is a sad laugh. Which one of us does not sail in the wretched discomfort of the ship of human folly? Eccentric

90 Hieronymus Bosch, Death and the Miser, c. 1485/90, 93 x 30.5 cm (36½ x 12 in)

and secret genius that he was, Bosch not only moved the heart but scandalized it into full awareness. The sinister and monstrous things that he brought forth are the hidden creatures of our inward self-love: he externalizes the ugliness within, and so his misshapen demons have an effect beyond curiosity. We feel a hateful kinship with them. *The Ship of Fools* is not about other people, it is about us.

A MORAL TALE

Another of Bosch's panel paintings, *Death and the Miser (90)*, serves as a warning to anyone who has grabbed at life's pleasures, without being sufficiently detached, and who is unprepared to die. Who can feel indifferent to this fable? In a long and concentrated format Bosch sets out the whole painful scenario.

The naked and dying man has been a man of power: at the bed's foot, but sundered now by a low wall, lies his armour. His riches have come through combat; the sick man has fought for his wealth and stored it close to him. He appears twice, the second time in full health, soberly dressed because he hoards his gold, dense with satisfaction as he adds another coin. Demons lurk all around, death puts a leering head around the door (notice the sick man's surprise: death is never expected), and the final battle begins. It is one he must wage without his armour. Behind him stands a pleading angel. Before him, even now proffering gold, lurks a demon. Above the bed, expectant and interested, peers yet another demon. The outcome of the story is left undecided. We hope desperately that the miser will relinquish empty possessiveness and accept the truth of death.

GRÜNEWALD'S DARK VISION

The final flowering of the Gothic came relatively late, in the work of the German artist, Matthias Grünewald (his real name was Mathis Neithart, otherwise Gothart, 1470/80–1528). He was possibly an exact contemporary of Dürer (see p.152), but while Dürer was deeply influenced by the Renaissance, Grünewald ignored it in his choice of subject matter and style. Much of his work has not survived to this day, but even from the small amount that has come down to us, it is possible to see Grünewald as one of the most powerful of all painters. No other painter has ever so terribly and truthfully exposed the horror of suffering, and yet kept before us, as Bosch does not, the conviction of salvation. His *Crucifixion (91)*, part of the many-panelled

PHILIP II
The Spanish King Philip II (1527–98) was an admirer of the work of Bosch and amassed a substantial collection of his paintings. The son of the Emperor Charles V, Philip brought Spain out of the Middle Ages and into the Renaissance era. He commissioned many works by Titian (see p.131).

PANEL PAINTINGS
While painting on wooden panels was widespread across Europe, the timber used varied. In Italy poplar was the most common. North of the Alps there was a greater choice of wood, and oak, pine, silver fir, lime, beech, and chestnut were all used. Italian panels were left rough at the back while Northern European panels were beautifully finished. Those from Bruges were often stamped with a seal.

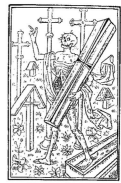

WORLD'S END
As at the end of most centuries, a number of people feared that the world would end in 1500. As a result apocalyptic images of death were widespread.

> *A kind of typhoon of unrestrained art, which carries you as it passes… you leave it in a state of lasting hallucination.*

J. K. Huysman on Grünewald's *Crucifixion*

MEDIEVAL MEDICINE
Up until the Renaissance, medical knowledge was rudimentary. Diseases and ailments were usually treated with herbal cures, blood-letting by leeches, or by supernatural "cures". Superstition dictated, for example, that sickness could be avoided by carrying holy relics, or texts taken from the Bible. This illustration, dating from the 14th century, shows a very docile patient undergoing a primitive lobotomy operation.

91 Matthias Grünewald, Crucifixion, *c. 1510–15, 270 x 305 cm (8 ft 10 in x 10 ft)*

Isenheim Altarpiece, is now kept in Colmar. It was commissioned for the Antonite monastery at Isenheim and was intended to give support to patients in the monastic hospital. Christ appears hideous, his skin swollen and torn as a result of the flagellation and torture that He endured. This was understandably a powerful image in a hospital that specialized in caring for those suffering from skin complaints.

The more accessible *Small Crucifixion (92)* engages us very directly with the actual death of the Saviour. The crucified Lord leans down into our space, crushing us, leaving us no escape, filling the painting with his agony. We are hemmed in by the immensities of darkness and mountain, alone with pain, forced to face the truth. The Old Testament often talks of a "suffering servant", describing him in Psalm 22 as "a worm and no man": it is of Grünewald's Christ that we think. In this noble veracity, Gothic art reached an electrifying greatness.

92 Matthias Grünewald, The Small Crucifixion, *c. 1511/20, 61 x 46 cm (24 x 18 in)*

CRUCIFIXION

This is the central panel of Grünewald's large, multi-panelled *Isenheim Altarpiece*. It is an extraordinary record of intense and disfiguring human suffering. Because he worked in a hospital, Grünewald based his image of suffering on the patients whose torments he witnessed. These were mostly sufferers from skin diseases, which were common at the time.

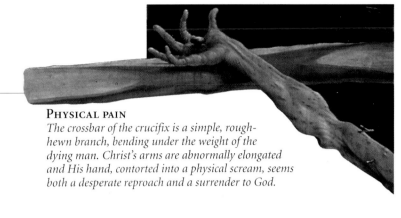

PHYSICAL PAIN
The crossbar of the crucifix is a simple, rough-hewn branch, bending under the weight of the dying man. Christ's arms are abnormally elongated and His hand, contorted into a physical scream, seems both a desperate reproach and a surrender to God.

FAMILY GRIEF
Divided from the stoic figure of John the Baptist by the monstrous dying Christ are the traumatized relatives and friends. Mary collapses into herself, either swooning from exhaustion or from a need to shut out the vision of her crucified Son. Grünewald originally painted her as an upright figure, but later arched her body into this pitiful state. She is supported by the despairing St John the Evangelist.

ST JOHN'S PROPHECY
St John the Baptist stands barefoot, wearing the animal skins that symbolize his time in the wilderness, and carrying a book. He seems unbowed by the horror of the moment and is unshakable in his prophetic conviction – inscribed against the night sky – "He will increase while I decrease". John delivers the Christian message of hope and redemption, balancing the desolation of the scene.

AGONY VISUALIZED
Grünewald takes the Gothic concern with suffering, sin, and mortality to its furthest extreme. Here in graphic detail is Christ the victim, physically repulsive in His brutalized condition and far removed from the heroic, athletically beautiful Christs of the Renaissance. Grünewald's vision is one of horror, a metaphor for the supreme cruelty and degradation of which humanity is capable, and by the same token, of the supreme mercy of Christ's benediction.

LAMB OF GOD
The lamb, used as a sacrificial animal by the Jews, was adopted by the early Christians as a symbol of Christ's sacrifice. It is associated with St John, who on seeing Jesus declared, "Behold the Lamb of God". The lamb normally holds a Cross and its sacrificial blood flows into a chalice.

THE ITALIAN RENAISSANCE

In the arts and sciences as well as society and government, Italy was the major catalyst for progress during the Renaissance: the rich period of development that occurred in Europe at the end of the Middle Ages. Because of the number of different fields in which it applied, "Renaissance" is a word with many layers of meaning. Accordingly, Renaissance painting cannot signify any one common or clearly definable style. As Gothic painting had been shaped by the feudal societies of the Middle Ages, with its roots in the Romanesque and Byzantine traditions, Renaissance art was born out of a new, rapidly evolving civilization. It marked the point of departure from the medieval to the modern world and, as such, laid the foundations for modern Western values and society.

Giovanni Bellini, **The Feast of the Gods,** *1514 (detail)*

Italian Renaissance Timeline

The Renaissance in Italy started gradually, its beginnings being apparent even in Giotto's work, a century before Masaccio was active (see p.46). The quest for scientific precision and greater realism culminated in the superb balance and harmony of Leonardo, Raphael, and Michelangelo. The influence of Humanism (see p.82) is reflected in the increase of secular subjects. In the final phase of the Renaissance, Mannerism became the dominant style.

Masaccio, Adam and Eve, 1427
Leonardo wrote that Masaccio "showed by his perfect works, how those who take for their inspiration anything but Nature – mistress of all masters – weary themselves in vain"; and in 1830, Eugène Delacroix wrote of him: "Born in poverty, almost unknown during the best part of his short life, he carried out singlehanded the greatest revolution ever known in painting." This revolution was his vision of the world: of mortal beings portrayed with honesty and tenderness, living and breathing in a terrestrial world of air, light, and space (p.83).

Piero della Francesca, Resurrection of Christ, c. 1450
Clarity and dignity characterize Piero's art. Influenced by Roman Classicism and Florentine innovation, his paintings combine complex mathematical structures with brilliant colour and crystalline light (p.102).

Leonardo da Vinci, Virgin of the Rocks, c. 1508
A true "Renaissance man", Leonardo was a great painter as well as a sculptor, architect, inventor, engineer, and an expert in such fields as botany, anatomy, and geology. His distinctively lyrical art reveals his compelling belief in nature as a source of inspiration (p.120).

1420	1440	1460	1480	1500

Fra Angelico, Beheading of St Cosmas and St Damian, 1438–40
This is part of the predella (a strip along the lower edge) of the altarpiece in the priory of San Marco, Florence. Fra Angelico's paintings have a delicate grace that belies their dynamism. There are elements of Gothic style, but the figures move in real, observed landscapes, and are defined by natural light (p.90).

Sandro Botticelli, Primavera, c. 1482
Botticelli is known best for his secular paintings – elaborate pagan allegories and mythological scenes. But his paintings are recognizable for their sheer beauty of line, free of discord. His art is notable for its peculiarly gentle, wistful melancholy. As he aged, this deepened to an anxious sadness; his figures became emaciated, sometimes with tortured expressions. This was possibly a reaction to contemporary political and religious tensions (p.94).

MICHELANGELO, IGNUDO (NUDE) FROM THE SISTINE CHAPEL, C. 1508–12

Michelangelo is another "giant" of the High Renaissance. However, in contrast with the lyricism of Leonardo's paintings, Michelangelo's art is characterized by gravity. Created on an epic scale, it is peopled with superhuman forms, of severe athletic beauty (p.122).

TITIAN, VENUS AND ADONIS, C. 1560

Titian was the greatest of the Venetian artists, and one of the world's supreme artists, with a profound influence on the development of Western painting. His late works are unsurpassed in their haunting and fragile beauty, strikingly suggestive of some 20th-century art (p.134).

EL GRECO, MADONNA AND CHILD WITH ST MARTINA AND ST AGNES, C. 1597–99

El Greco is the great religious Mannerist. His passionate vision surpasses the stylish manipulations of later Mannerists. After travels in Venice and Rome, he settled in Toledo in Spain. His work displays a mystic fervour that accurately represents the religious intensity of Counter-Reformation Spain (p.115).

CORREGGIO, VENUS, SATYR, AND CUPID, C. 1514–30

Correggio's imagery can seem too sweet for modern tastes. But beneath the outward charm is a tough appreciation of sensual truth (p.142).

1520	1540	1560	1580	1600

TINTORETTO, THE CONVERSION OF ST PAUL, C. 1545

The Venetian artist Tintoretto was a leading late Renaissance painter. After studying briefly under Titian, he evolved a distinctive, dynamic style with startling contrasts of colour and tone, sweeping vistas, and dramatic movement. His paintings exhibit a religious intensity and a passionate "expressionism" that move him into the realm of Mannerism, away from the Classicism of the High and Early Renaissance (p.134).

RAPHAEL, BINDO ALTOVITI, C. 1515

Raphael was a successor to Leonardo, whose early influence on him was profound. Raphael was also attracted to classical art, so that his paintings possess heroic grandeur, and his portraits a new, graceful spontaneity (p.128).

THE EARLY RENAISSANCE

The name "Renaissance" – meaning "rebirth" – is given to a period of broad cultural achievement spanning three centuries. The idea of rebirth lies at the heart of all Renaissance achievement: artists, scholars, scientists, philosophers, architects, and rulers believed that the way to greatness and enlightenment was through the study of the Golden Ages of the ancient Greeks and Romans. They rejected the more recent, medieval past, which constituted the Gothic era. Instead of this, inspired by Humanism, they looked to the literary and philosophical traditions, and the artistic and engineering achievements, of Greco-Roman antiquity.

BRUNELLESCHI AND FLORENTINE ARCHITECTURE
The cupola of Florence's Cathedral is considered to be the greatest triumph of the architect Filippo Brunelleschi. It has a diameter of 45 m (150 ft), and the marble ribs on the exterior exert a powerful centripetal force which supports the whole structure. Its eight faces are held in place by the continuously self-supporting masonry system, which is in itself a remarkable feat of structural engineering. The dome was completed in 1418, becoming the focal point of the city and proclaiming Florence to be the cultural capital of the Renaissance.

HUMANISM
Humanism was an important cultural movement of the Renaissance, in which prime importance was given to human reason rather than to God's revelation. Erasmus (see p.154) was its great theorist. Classical Latin and Greek texts were the main sources, but Humanist education also included the liberal arts, such as grammar, rhetoric, poetry, and ethics. Humanistic thinking was brought to the world of diplomacy by Machiavelli, and to architecture by Alberti (see p.88).

Renaissance painting began in Italy in the middle of the 13th century, and its influence rapidly spread throughout Europe, reaching its peak at the end of the 15th century. Renaissance artists believed their art was a continuation of the great antique tradition of Greece and Rome, an insight that came originally from Giotto (see p.46). With his joyful spiritual vision, Giotto is like the Gothic artists. But his ability to present stories from the Bible as very naturalistic, human dramas and his way of depicting his figures as solid, weighty characters were Renaissance qualities. Giotto showed what could be done, how an artistic vision could encompass the exciting new understanding of Humanism and Classicism, which were to be so important to Renaissance artists. With antiquity as a model and Giotto as a guide, painters of the early Italian Renaissance entered a new phase of pictorial representation, based on the reality of human existence.

MASACCIO AND FLORENCE
Of course the transition from Gothic to Renaissance did not happen overnight, but it can come as a surprise to see that the next great Italian painter after Giotto (who died in 1337) was not born until 1401, and therefore not active until nearly a century after Giotto's death. This gap is largely explained by the Black Death (see p.58), the first spread of which devastated Europe in the 14th century, reaching Italy first in 1347 and sweeping across Europe over the next four years. The consequences were far-reaching, and in addition to the massive physical loss, medieval society underwent great changes. Artistic revolution in the North, in the Low

93 Masaccio, The Virgin and Child, 1426, 135 × 75 cm (53 × 29½ in)

Countries (see pp.60–70), was leading painting in new directions through its increasing naturalism, secularism, and technical mastery. In the South, it seemed as if Giotto had never been. Miraculously, there was a second spring with the birth of the Florentine painter,

Masaccio (Tomasso de Giovanni di Simone Guidi, 1401–28). It is Masaccio who is the revolutionary founder of Renaissance painting. Of the Italian painters, he was the one who really saw what Giotto had initiated, and made it accessible to all who followed.

Masaccio is forever young because he died when he was 27, yet his art seems to be outstandingly mature. His name is a nickname, meaning something like "Tom the Hulk", and his art is hulking too. But it is the hulk of genius, monumental, strong and convincing, true heir to the humanity and spatial depth of Giotto. One of his early works, painted for a church in Pisa, has an almost architectonic concentration. In *The Virgin and Child* (*93*), the central panel of a now scattered polyptych (multiple painting), the Madonna is sculptural in her blocky dignity, seated on a throne of classic weight, shadowed and austere, with her Child completely stripped of Byzantine kingliness. This Jesus is a real baby, sucking his fingers and staring into space. It represents the antithesis of the courtly refinement of the International Gothic style of Gentile da Fabriano, for instance (see p.56). Yet the pathos is heightened, not diminished: there is strength and vulnerability, beautifully combined, and even the angel musicians have a chubby earnestness.

LINKS WITH SCULPTURE

As Giotto was influenced by the sculpture of the Pisanos (see p.46), so was Masaccio by their Florentine sculptural descendants as it were, the two senior artists: Donatello (Donato di Niccolo, 1386–1466, see right), and Lorenzo Ghiberti (1378–1455, see p.102, column). The influence of sculpture on early Renaissance painting, and inherently on the development of the Western tradition in painting, cannot be overstressed. Masaccio's understanding of three-dimensional form, architectural space, and of perspective owed a great debt to the technical and scientific achievements pioneered by Donatello, Ghiberti, and the Florentine architect Brunelleschi (Filippo di Ser Brunelleschi, 1377–1446, see column, left). Sculptural realism lies at the heart of Renaissance painting, to culminate in the epic monumentality of Michelangelo's art during the High Renaissance (see p.120).

As Giotto translated Pisano's carvings into pictorial form, Masaccio drew inspiration from Donatello's freestanding sculptures and reliefs, and applied sculptural considerations to his paintings: creating images of convincingly solid objects, in a feasible space, with optical perspective. More significantly, he applied the sculptor's understanding of the effects of real light falling onto objects, and filtering through spaces, surpassing Giotto's already monumental leap towards understanding and reinventing the world through painting.

From now on the lovely play that can characterize the finest Gothic art (though less often that of Giotto or Duccio) has disappeared. Masaccio lives in a wholly serious world. His *Adam and Eve Expelled from Paradise* (*94*), in Florence's Brancacci Chapel, wail with unselfconscious horror, blinded with grief,

94 Masaccio, Adam and Eve Expelled from Paradise, *c. 1427, 205 x 90 cm (81 x 35½ in)*

DONATELLO'S DAVID

Donatello was one of a group of brilliant sculptors who led the way for painters in the early Renaissance (see also p.105). He visited Rome, where he was inspired by the freedom of movement achieved in the nude figures of classical sculpture, and afterwards (c. 1434) created this bronze figure of the young King David. This overtly sensual work was one of the first nude statues of the Renaissance.

RESTORATION OF FRESCOES

Time and the elements, in particular modern pollution, have caused serious deterioration in the surface of many of the frescoes produced during the Renaissance. As a result, to repair the damage and to prevent more from occurring, many famous works, including Masaccio's Brancacci Chapel frescoes and Michelangelo's Sistine Chapel ceiling (see p.122), have been substantially restored. This has resulted in some controversy as not all art critics and historians are in agreement that all the work has been sensitively carried out. Some argue that the tonal values of the work have been ignored.

THE TRINITY

The doctrine of the Trinity – of God as three separate beings, yet remaining one entity – lies at the heart of the Christian "mystery". It is first mentioned in Matthew's Gospel (28: 19), as comprising Father, Son, and Holy Spirit. Masaccio's *Trinity* was commissioned for the church of Santa Maria Novella in 1425. It was covered over in 1570 with a panel painting by Vasari (see p.98), and only rediscovered in 1861.

MOTHER OF CHRIST
Mary the Virgin is the only one of the non-divine beings who looks directly out at us. She stands upright and dry-eyed, and points with a gesture both implacable and supplicating, towards her crucified Child and gives the viewer a concentrated glance of terrible reproach.

THE DONORS
The figures of the Trinity, and of Mary and St John, appear as solidly real as the two donors. Yet the donors are both included in and excluded from this timeless scene. Spatially they belong: they share the same scale (traditionally donors were shown on a specially reduced scale) and are bathed in the same light that illuminates the interior of the vault. But symbolically the donors remain "outside" the scene, because they have been positioned on a lower step, as though on the predella (a painted border strip) of an altarpiece, which locates them firmly in the world of the viewer.

THE TRINITY
Masaccio's Trinity *is part of a Renaissance pictorial tradition in which the Father is generally depicted as an aged and bearded patriarch, standing behind and above the crucified Son. He is often shown supporting both ends of the the crossbar of the crucifix, thus echoing His Son's sacrifice. Between them flits the white geometry of the Holy Spirit, traditionally depicted as a dove (see also p.101). The Spirit is the third person of the Trinity, but is here perhaps the most eye-catching in the sheer brilliance of the white smudge that bisects the fresco.*

PERSPECTIVE
Vasari recorded his admiration for Masaccio's Trinity *when he described its sophisticated spatial structure as: "a barrel vault drawn in perspective, and divided into squares with rosettes which diminish and are foreshortened so well, that there seems to be a hole in the wall". Masaccio had interpreted Brunelleschi's (p.82) theories of perspective with such clarity, that in the past it was believed that Brunelleschi was actually directly involved in the production of the painting.*

95 Masaccio, The Trinity, 1425, 670 x 315 cm (22 ft x 10 ft 4 in)

unaware of anything but their loss of happiness. Eve is so sheerly ugly as she screams aloud from misery that we are startled into attention and into pity.

MASACCIO'S TRINITY

What distinguishes Masaccio is his majesty; there never was a more massive, more dignified, more noble and yet more human painter. The wonder of this painting of *The Trinity (95)* is that it shows us six *human* images. Central are Father and Son. Although they are in the most moving way human (a real, suffering Jesus showing compassion for His fellow men and women as He dies, and a real Father upright in His splendid dignity as He holds up the Crucifix and shows us His surrendered Son) in Their

majesty we can well accept that these two figures are divine. Divinity is by definition a mystery, something we cannot comprehend, but Masaccio makes the mystery of the Trinity humanly accessible. Below the great central vertical pole of the Trinity, symmetrically fanning out on either side, are the four non-divine actors in the drama. Only one – Mary – is looking directly out of the picture. Balancing the figure of Christ's mother, Mary, on the other side of the Cross is St John, equally-massive, equally solid, though he is looking not towards us, but towards Christ.

Beyond them, sealing in the picture, are the donors – large, profiled, solidly present as our representatives. At the very bottom of the painting there is a seventh character: the skeleton, representing Adam and Everyman. This is the human truth which underlies all religious dogma. Above the skeleton, on the stone wall of the narrow tomb in which it lies, is written the inscription "I was once what you are and what I am you will become". The universal nature of Masaccio's *Trinity*, encompassing the wide realm of mortal decay and spiritual salvation, belongs to a medieval tradition.

There is an immense authority about this young artist. *St Peter Healing with His Shadow (96)* is one of a pair of scenes from the Brancacci Chapel cycle, situated at either side of the altar. (The other is *The Distribution of the Goods of the Church*, and the pair share a common perspective.) St Peter strides towards the viewer down a narrow street of houses built in the Florentine style. One man in his entourage, wearing the short smock of a stonecutter, might be intended as a portrait of Donatello; another, younger man, his beard not yet grown, might be Masaccio's self-portrait (he is positioned facing directly out of the picture in the manner of self-portraits of the time). Peter's shadow is rendered with remarkable confidence in view of the fact that, prior to this, no technique for painting shadows had been developed. The cripples are depicted with a vividness and individuality astonishingly advanced for the early 15th century.

Masaccio's concerns with the true appearance of things earned him this singular appraisal from the art historian Vasari (see p.98):

THE BRANCACCI CHAPEL
Several of Masaccio's frescoes cover the upper walls of the Brancacci family chapel in the church of Santa Maria del Carmine in Florence. This cycle of frescoes became a model for Florentine artists in the late Renaissance, including Michelangelo (see p.120).

OTHER WORKS BY MASACCIO
Crucifixion of St Peter (Staatliche Museen, Berlin-Dahlem)

Virgin with St Anne (Uffizi, Florence)

Tribute Money (Brancacci Chapel, Florence)

96 Masaccio, St Peter Healing with His Shadow, 1425 (detail of fresco)

"With regard to painting we are indebted first of all to Masaccio, who first painted people's feet actually standing on the ground, and by doing so eliminated that awkwardness, common to all artists before him, of having the figures standing on tiptoe. We must also be grateful to him for having given his figures such liveliness and relief that he deserves the same credit as if he had invented Art itself".

THE "SMALLER" ART OF MASOLINO

Masaccio's greatness can best be seen if we compare him with Masolino (Tommaso di Cristoforo Fini da Panicale, 1383– c. 1447), nearly 20 years his senior, with whom he often worked. (It has been suggested that "Masolino", also a nickname, was coined to mark the difference between "Big Tom", Masaccio, and "Small Tom", Masolino.) He is unfairly seen as small, but only in comparison. On his own, he is still temperamentally in the Gothic era, as we

98 Masaccio, St Jerome and St John the Baptist, c. 1428, 115 x 55 cm (45 x 21½ in)

99 Masolino, St Liberius and St Matthias, c. 1428, 115 x 55 cm (45 x 21½ in)

see in his graceful *Annunciation (97)*, in which he shows us his love of the decorative and elegant, flowing line that is truly Gothic. But when paired with the bigger Tom, Masolino too stretched out into the true Renaissance.

The best proof of Masolino's ability to grow can be seen in a comparison between two panels, *St Jerome and St John the Baptist (98)* and *St Liberius and St Matthias (99)*, which hang to either side of an altarpiece. All four saints have a hulking presence typical of Masaccio – they certainly stand with their feet flat on the ground – yet it is now fairly certain that the former panel is largely by Masaccio, while the latter is mainly the work of Masolino. (Previously, both were attributed to Masaccio.)

DOMENICO THE INNOVATOR

The Venetian artist Domenico Veneziano (Domenico di Bartolomeo di Venezia, active c.1438–61) was one of the most important painters of the early Renaissance, working in Florence. His importance lies not so much in his personal achievement, as in the breadth and significance of his influence – for he was the teacher of Piero della Francesca (see p.100).

What we find so beautifully in Domenico is a splendour of light that emanates from a single source, breathing air into the space and unifying forms within it. He gives us the first radiant indication of that water-born silveriness that is one of the Venetian gifts to the visual world. Domenico had also a dazzlingly original mind. We admire – rightly – the great Masaccio; we love the limpid Domenico. His *St John in the Desert (100)* is a magical work. Light pours in blinding clarity over a glittering barrenness,

97 Masolino, Annunciation, probably c. 1425/30, 148 x 115 cm (58¼ x 45 in)

100 *Domenico Veneziano,* St John in the Desert, *c. 1445,*
28.5 × 32.5 cm (11¼ × 12¾ in)

with the tender, naked saint the only softness to
be seen. He is stripping off his worldly clothes,
like a young athlete getting ready for the race.
That the race is very present to him, and that
it is a contest of the spirit is sublimely clear. But
if it is an all-demanding vocation to which this
slender youth is called, it is one lived in the
exhilaration of a high plateau.

There is a strange relationship between this
classical-looking nude, with his medieval golden
halo, and his setting in a landscape reminiscent
of Netherlandish (even Byzantine) art; and this
juxtaposition illustrates the meeting of the spiritual, pagan, and physical worlds. This is a deeply
Renaissance way of visualizing the story, as we
can see if we compare it with the painting of the
same subject by Giovanni di Paolo (c.1403–83).
This is Giovanni's *St John the Baptist Retiring to
the Desert (101),* an archaic and bewitching Gothic
fantasy that sends the youthful saint out like a
young adventurer to seek his heavenly fortune.

101 *Giovanni di Paolo,* St John the Baptist Retiring to the Desert, *c. 1454,*
30 × 39 cm (11¾ × 15½ in)

PERSPECTIVE: SCIENCE INTO ART

The Renaissance concept that most gripped the Florentine artist Paolo Uccello (Paolo di Dono, 1397–1475), whose name is also a nickname (*uccello* means "bird" – given to him for his love of birds), was not so much that of light as perspective. Significantly, he was apprenticed with the architect Ghiberti (see p.102, column) at the beginning of his career.

In a story recounted by Vasari, Uccello once worked all night on this science, whereby the confusion of the world could be ordered into submission. His wife reported him crying out in ecstasy, "Oh, how great is this perspective!" and, on being called to bed, saying that he would not leave his "sweet mistress perspective". He seized upon it with an intellectual passion that might have produced a rather rigid art.

Put very simply, the art of perspective is the representation of solid objects and three-dimensional space in accordance with our

optical perception of these things (and in direct opposition to a purely symbolic or decorative form of representation). We see the world "in perspective": objects appear smaller as they recede into the distance; the walls of a corridor or an avenue of trees, for instance, appear to converge as they stretch into the distance. The laws of perspective are based upon these converging lines meeting eventually at a single, fixed "vanishing point", which may be visible – such as when an avenue of trees stretches as far as the eye can see – or is an imagined "vanishing point" as when the converging lines of a room continue, in our imagination only, beyond the far wall.

One of Uccello's greatest works, which demonstrates his fascination with perspective, is *The Hunt in the Forest (102)*. Everything in it is organized upon a distant and almost unseen stag, a vanishing stag: the vanishing point. The bright little hunters, with their horses, hounds,

ALBERTI

The Florentine artist, architect, and antiquarian Leon Battista Alberti (1404–72) was one of the first to construct a formula of perspective that could be applied to two-dimensional paintings.

*102 Paolo Uccello, **The Hunt in the Forest**, 1460s, 75 x 178 cm (29½ x 70 in)*

and beaters, run from all sides among the slim, bare trunks of a darkly wooded landscape. While all this activity is frenzied, it is exquisitely purposeful and sane. Throughout this painting, we feel Uccello's comfort and his poetry.

Uccello was not the first Florentine to explore perspective. Brunelleschi, the architect who built Florence Cathedral's revolutionary dome (see p.82), demonstrated linear perspective as an element in architectural design in about 1413. However, it was Leon Battista Alberti (see left) who pioneered its application to painting. His 1435 treatise *On Painting* had a widespread influence on contemporary artists. How widespread it was is something that we can never really prove. The fact remains that after Uccello, Brunelleschi, and above all Alberti, every artist had become alerted to the potential of this astonishing new insight.

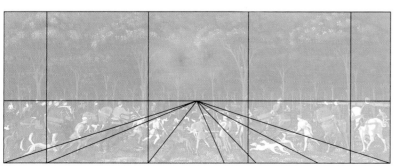

THE VANISHING POINT

That Uccello's Hunt in the Forest *demonstrates an effective rendering of perspective is shown in this miniature version. Lines have been added artificially to draw attention to features of the general composition that lead the eye to the vanishing point. At this point, the leading stag is disappearing into the forest.*

UCCELLO'S STUDIES

The complex perspective framework of Uccello's paintings was the result of meticulous study. In this drawing of a chalice he tackles the perspective problems of drawing a rounded object in three-dimensional space.

103 Fra Angelico, The Beheading of St Cosmas and
St Damian, *c. 1438–40, 37 x 46 cm (14½ x 18 in)*

THE DEVOUT ART OF FRA ANGELICO

The Dominican monk Fra Angelico (Fra
Giovanni da Fiesole, c. 1400–55) was active at
about the same time as Masaccio. He painted
with great religious gravity and in remarkably
luminous tones, but he is insufficiently seen as
the bold experimenter that he truly was – not
in theme, but in manner.

Despite the implications of his name, there
is a satisfying humanity about Fra Angelico that
takes pleasure in the substance of the material
world. No questions are left unanswered in his
Beheading of St Cosmas and St Damian (103).
It is a scene of intense chromatic brightness,
every form and hue bathed in the relentless light
of a summer morning. The landscape is wholly
realized, from the clarity of the white towers to
the tall, dark cypresses and the receding swoops
and rises of a hilly countryside. The two saints
wait, blindfolded against the brightness and
horror, and the three already decapitated sprawl
in the messy scarlet of their blood, each head
rolling on the grass in its hoop of halo. It is real
death, painted without recourse to melodrama,
but seen with the half-smile of a total believer.

It is tempting to look at the *Virgin and Child
Enthroned with Angels and Saints (104)* and
regard it as charming but conventional, since the
graceful, sinewy lines and strong local colour are
derived from the Gothic tradition. But a closer
look reveals that Fra Angelico was fully aware
of the progressive tendencies in painting – of
perspective and use of light especially – and the

SAN MARCO AND THE DOMINICANS

The Dominican order, of which Fra Angelico was a member, moved to the convent of San Marco in Florence in 1436. It was funded by Cosimo de' Medici, who also donated more than 400 classical texts to the library. It was at San Marco that Fra Angelico painted many of his best-known frescoes, including *The Annunciation*.

LUCA DELLA ROBBIA

Much admired in his time, Luca della Robbia (1400–82) was a Florentine sculptor. He carved the beautiful marble *cantoria* (choir gallery) for Florence Cathedral in 1431–38. The carvings illustrate the 150th Psalm and depict angels, boys, and girls playing musical instruments, singing, and dancing.

OTHER WORKS BY FRA ANGELICO

The Madonna of Humility (National Gallery of Art, Washington)

The Annunciation (Convent of San Marco, Florence)

St James Freeing Hermogenes (Kimbell Art Museum, Fort Worth, Texas)

Virgin and Child with St Dominic and St Peter Martyr (Church of San Domencino, Cortona)

Virgin and Child (Cincinnati Art Museum)

104 Fra Angelico, The Virgin and Child Enthroned with Angels and Saints, c. 1438–40, 220 x 229 cm (7 ft 3 in x 7 ft 6 in)

We peer past the agonized figure on the Cross to attempt – in vain – to decipher the carpet. Equally, past the reverential angels beside the throne, in a naturalistic landscape, we see light catching the tips of trees, glancing off leaves, escaping past the trunks to reveal a distant land. The total effect is anything but conventional.

SACRED AND PROFANE

All the same, Fra Angelico was the model of a good monk, just as Fra Filippo Lippi (c.1406–69) was not. Giovanni da Fiesole chose in his young maturity to become a monk, and his admiring brethren called him the "Reverend Angel" (*Fra Angelico*). In the 19th century he was thought to be a saint. But young Filippo (Lippo) was left an orphan and brought up by the Carmine monks in Florence: no other calling was suggested to him, though it became scandalously clear that he had no capacity for a life of frugal chastity. It is a story with a happy ending, in that he eventually met a woman to cherish (incidentally, a nun who had been "conventized" in much the same unthinking fashion as he was encouraged in his choice) and both were dispensed from their vows, and their marriage blessed.

Lippi's version of the *Virgin and Child (105)* surrounded by angels and saints may be compared with that of his truly devout brother in religion (see p.91). Lippi painted his version some years after Masaccio produced his frescoes in the Brancacci Chapel in Florence (see p.85), and these were a crucial influence on Lippi's work.

105 Fra Filippo Lippi, Virgin and Child, *c. 1440–45, 215 x 244 cm (7 ft 1 in x 8 ft)*

sculptural influence on his representation of physical space is pronounced. There is a strong formal patterning, real bodies stand in true relation to one another, and there is an unconventional delight in the near-primitivism of the animals in the carpet and in the tiny but significant Crucifixion that looms sternly up in the centre.

106 Fra Filippo Lippi, Annunciation, *c. 1448–50, 68 x 152 cm (27 x 60 in)*

However, the monumentality of form Lippi learned from Masaccio was to be tempered with a delicacy and sweetness, similar to that found in Fra Angelico's paintings, and the serene mystical quality of his later paintings reveal growing Netherlandish influences in Italy.

Lippi's Virgin has a rounded physical presence, statuesque and forbidding despite its fullness, and the chubby Child looks rather disparagingly down on the kneeling St Frediano. The angels too are heavily present, crowded in upon one another in a confusion of light-filled space. There is too much going on. The marbled walls behind push down on us, and the jewelled brightness of material and form takes on an almost claustrophobic weight. But when he simplifies his scene, it is rare to find a painter more moving than Fra Lippi.

His *Annunciation (106)* is a heavenly little work, with diaphanous veilings exquisitely rendered, and a lovely tenderness in the pure and gentle girl and her angelic messenger. This panel is thought to have been part of the bedroom furniture of some great noble, possibly Piero de' Medici (who patronized Lippi). The Medici family emblem – three feathers in a diamond ring – appears carved in stone beneath the vase of lilies, and in the companion piece, *Seven Saints (108)*, all the saints are "connected" with the Medici: name saints of the family males. The seven sit dreamily on a marble garden seat, only St Peter Martyr, with his emblematic hatchet in his head, looking glum.

That saints in general are happy seems a congenial belief to Filippo. His own son, the model for many of the Infant Jesus images, was himself to become a painter and likewise express a fundamental well-being. But Lippi junior, Filippino

(1457–1504), was orphaned at ten and brought up by Botticelli (see p.94), who had been taught by Lippi senior. Filippino's work shows that Lippi tendency to happiness, shadowed by the Botticelli sense of human frailty. There is a quivering gentleness in Filippino that is uniquely his own. *Tobias and the Angel (107)* is a moving work, but it floats ethereally before us, scarcely seeming to acknowledge the earth.

107 Filippino Lippi, Tobias and the Angel, probably c. 1480, 32.5 x 23.5 cm (12¾ x 9 in)

COSIMO DE' MEDICI

The Medici family dominated Florentine political life for much of the 15th and 16th centuries. The glorious epoch of the family began with Cosimo (1389–1464) who commissioned work from Ghiberti, Donatello, and Fra Angelico. His descendant, Cosimo I (1519–1574), depicted above, became Duke of Florence in 1537. He was a skilled but ruthless soldier who managed to annex the republic of Siena to Tuscany in 1555. He too was a great patron of the arts and had his own collection of Etruscan antiquities. This portrait, painted in 1537, is by Jacopo Pontormo (see pp.139–141).

108 Fra Filippo Lippi, Seven Saints, c. 1448–50, 68 x 152 cm (27 x 60 in)

ANATOMICAL EXACTITUDE

The work of the Florentine artist Antonio Pollaiuolo (c. 1432–98) and his brother Piero (c. 1441–94/96) influenced that of Botticelli. According to Vasari (see column, p.98), Antonio was one of the first artists to carry out dissections of the human body in order to study the underlying systems and structures. *The Martyrdom of St Sebastian*, completed in 1475 and from which this detail is taken, clearly shows the results of this research.

BOTTICELLI: LYRICAL PRECISION

After Masaccio, Sandro Botticelli (Alessandro di Moriano Filipepi, 1444/5–1510) comes as the next great painter of the Florentine tradition. The new, sharply contoured, slender form and rippling sinuous line that is synonymous with Botticelli was influenced by the brilliant, precise draftsmanship of the Pollaiuolo brothers (see below, left), who trained not only as painters, but as goldsmiths, engravers, sculptors, and embroidery designers. However, the rather stiff, scientifically formulaic appearance of the Pollaiuolos' painting of *The Martyrdom of St Sebastian* (see left), for instance, which clearly

109 Sandro Botticelli, Primavera, c. 1482, 315 x 205 cm (10 ft 4 in x 6 ft 9 in)

follows anatomical dictates, finds no place in the paintings of Botticelli. His sophisticated understanding of perspective, anatomy, and the Humanist debate of the Medici court (see p.82) never overshadows the sheer poetry of his vision. Nothing is more gracious, in lyrical beauty, than Botticelli's mythological paintings *Primavera* and *The Birth of Venus* (see p.96), where the pagan story is taken with reverent seriousness and Venus is the Virgin Mary in another form. But it is also significant that no-one has ever agreed on the actual subject of *Primavera (109)*, and a whole shelf in a library can be taken up with different theories;

> **"** *… [Botticelli] appears almost as if haunted by the idea of communicating the unembodied values of touch and movement.* **"**
>
> **B. Berenson,**
> *The Italian Painters of the Renaissance,* 1896

MYTHICAL FIGURES

Botticelli's *Primavera* is an allegory on the harmony of nature and humankind and contains many mythical figures including Venus (the link between nature and civilization) and Mercury. At the extreme right of the painting, the figure of Zephyr (the west wind of spring) is seen chasing Chloris, who is then transformed into Flora, the goddess of flowers. A blindfolded Cupid shoots his arrows at the Three Graces (the handmaidens of Venus) who were believed to represent the three phases of love: beauty, desire, and fulfillment. This illustration shows a woodcut of Cupid, who was one of the most popular figures in Renaissance art.

THE BIRTH OF VENUS

This secular work was painted onto canvas, which was a less expensive painting surface than the wooden panels used in church and court pictures. A wooden surface would certainly be impractical for a work on such a scale. Canvas is known to have been the preferred material for the paintings of non-religious and pagan subjects that were sometimes commissioned to decorate country villas in 15th-century Italy.

WOODED SHORE

The trees form part of a flowering orange grove – corresponding to the sacred garden of the Hesperides in Greek myth – and each small white blossom is tipped with gold. Gold is used throughout the painting, accentuating its role as a precious object and echoing the divine status of Venus. Each dark green leaf has a gold spine and outline, and the tree trunks are highlighted with short diagonal lines of gold.

THE WEST WIND

Zephyr and Chloris fly with limbs entwined as a twofold entity: the ruddy Zephyr (his name is Greek for "the west wind") is puffing vigorously, while the fair Chloris gently sighs the warm breath that wafts Venus ashore. All around them fall roses – each with a golden heart – which, according to legend, came into being at Venus' birth.

THE SHELL

Botticelli portrays Venus in the very first suggestion of action, with a complex and beautiful series of twists and turns, as she is about to step off her giant gilded scallop shell onto the shore. Venus was conceived when the Titan Cronus castrated his father, the god Uranus – the severed genitals falling into the sea and fertilizing it. Here what we see is actually not Venus' birth out of the waves, but the moment when, having been conveyed by the shell, she lands at Paphos in Cyprus.

NYMPH

The nymph may well be one of the three Horae, or "The Hours", Greek goddesses of the seasons, who were attendants to Venus. Both her lavishly decorated dress and the gorgeous robe she holds out to Venus are embroidered with red and white daisies, yellow primroses, and blue cornflowers – all spring flowers appropriate to the theme of birth. She wears a garland of myrtle – the tree of Venus – and a sash of pink roses, as worn by the goddess Flora in Botticelli's Primavera *(p.94–95).*

110 Sandro Botticelli, **The Birth of Venus,** *c. 1485–86, 175 x 280 cm (5 ft 9 in x 9 ft 2 in)*

but though scholars may argue, we need no theories to make *Primavera (109)* dear to us. In this allegory of life, beauty, and knowledge united by love, Botticelli catches the freshness of an early spring morning, with the pale light shining through the tall, straight trees, already laden with their golden fruit: oranges, or the mythical Golden Apples of the Hesperides?

At the right Zephyr, the warm wind of Spring, embraces the Roman goddess Flora, or perhaps the earth nymph Chloris, diaphanously clad and running from his amorous clasp. She is shown at the moment of her metamorphosis into Flora, as her breath turns to flowers which take root over the countryside. Across from her, we see Flora as a goddess, in all her glory (or perhaps her daughter Persephone, who spends half her time beneath the earth, as befits the patron saint of flowers) as she steps forward clad in blossoms. In the centre is a gentle Venus, all dignity and promise of spiritual joy, and above her, the infant Cupid aims his loving arrows. To the left, the Three Graces dance in a silent reverie of grace, removed from the others in time also, as indicated by the breeze that wafts their hair and clothes in the opposite direction from Zephyr's gusts. Mercury, the messenger of

the gods, provides another male counterpart to the Zephyr. Zephyr initiates, breathing love into the warmth he brings to a wintry world, and Mercury sublimates, taking the hopes of humanity and opening the way to the gods.

Everything in this miraculous work is profoundly life-enhancing. Yet it offers no safeguards against pain or accident: Cupid is blindfolded as he flies, and the Graces seem enclosed in their own private bliss. So the poetry has an underlying wistfulness, a sort of musing nostalgia for something that we cannot possess, yet something with which we feel so deeply in tune. Even the gentle yet strong colours speak of this ambivalence: the figures have an unmistakable presence and weight as they stand before us, moving in the slowest of rhythms. Yet they also seem insubstantial, a dream of what might be rather than a sight of what is.

This longing, this hauntingly intangible sadness is even more visible in the lovely face of Venus as she is wafted to our dark shores by the winds, and the garment, rich though it is, waits ready to cover up her sweet and naked body. We cannot look upon love unclothed, says *The Birth of Venus (110)*; we are too weak, maybe too polluted, to bear the beauty.

LORENZO DE' MEDICI
Succeeding in 1469 as head of the Medici family, Lorenzo "*Il Magnifico*" (the Magnificent) was a courageous, if autocratic, leader. He was a patron of the arts and assisted many artists, including Michelangelo and Leonardo da Vinci. Botticelli had some patronage from Lorenzo, but his chief patron was a cousin of *Il Magnifico* called Lorenzo di Pierfrancesco de' Medici, or "Lorenzino".

111 Sandro Botticelli, The Adoration of the Magi, *c. 1485–86, 175 x 280 cm (5 ft 9 in x 9 ft 2 in)*

Botticelli accepted that paganism, too, was a religion and could bear profoundly philosophical significance. His religious paintings manifest this belief by converging all truths into one.

He seems to have had a personal devotion to the biblical account of *The Adoration of The Magi (111)*, setting it in a ruined classical world. This was not an uncommon Renaissance device, suggesting that the birth of Christ brought fulfilment to the hopes of everyone, completing the achievements of the past.

But no painter felt this with the intensity of Botticelli. We feel that he desperately needed this psychic reassurance, and that the wild graphic power of his *Adoration*'s great circles of activity, coming to rest on the still centre of the Virgin and her Child, made visible his own interior circlings. Even the far green hills sway in sympathy with the clustered humans as if by magnetic attraction around the incarnate Lord.

Botticelli was not the only Florentine to be blessed or afflicted by an intensely anxious temperament. In the 1490s, the city of Florence was overtaken by a political crisis. The Medici government fell, and there followed a four-year period of extremist religious rule under the zealot Savonarola (see column, facing page). Either in response to this, or possibly out of some desire of his own for stylistic experimentation, Botticelli produced a series of rather clumsy-looking religious works – the *San Bernabo Altarpiece* is an example.

THE STRANGE WORLD OF PIERO DI COSIMO

Piero di Cosimo (1462–1521) did not live, like Botticelli, in the enlightened ambience of the Medici court. He was a man who actively required some sort of seclusion so as to conserve his energies and explore his preoccupations. (He even went so far as to live on boiled eggs, we are told, cooking them 50 at a time, so as to be free of the mundane concerns of the mere body.) Yet in *The Visitation with St Nicholas and St Anthony Abbot (112)*, he displays a wonderful sense of the body, its weight and presence. When he shows the Virgin Mary, still bewildered by the angelic annunciation of her sacred pregnancy, coming to greet her elderly cousin Elizabeth, also blessed with a miraculous pregnancy, the two women approach each other with a touching reverence.

Each is primarily conscious of the child in her womb, and Elizabeth is about to cry out to tell Mary that the unborn John the Baptist within her has leapt for joy at the nearness of the unborn Jesus. Piero merely shows us the two touching each other with a wondering reverence, yet the profundities are all the more present for being unexpressed.

But, as in all Piero's pictures, there are strange elements here. The women are flanked by two elderly saints: St Nicholas, identifiable by the three golden balls at his feet (the dowry he anonymously threw into the house of an impoverished father of three marriageable daughters, see p.53); and St Anthony Abbot, whose unromantic emblem of a pig rootles happily in the background. To the right, behind Elizabeth, a furious scene, swarming with violence, depicts the massacre of the innocents, and in the shadows behind Mary, we find a quiet and almost insignificant nativity. Do the saints, engrossed in their reading and writing, "see" these things in their minds? What is actually happening and what is imagined?

Piero leaves us with engrossing problems to ponder. "The strangeness of Piero's brain," as Vasari (see column, left) described it, is seen even more in his non-religious paintings like this mysterious *Allegory (113)*, with its mermaid, comical white stallion, and winged maiden, standing on a tiny island and holding the beast by a thread. We look with delight, but never find an answer. Piero's interest in animals and the exotic is revealed in many of his paintings. He included a snake in his *Portrait of Simonetta Vespucci*, a satyr and a dog in *Mythological Scene*, and various animals in his *Hunting Scene*.

113 Piero di Cosimo, Allegory, c. 1500, 56 x 44 cm (22 x 17⅓ in)

112 Piero di Cosimo, The Visitation with St Nicholas and St Anthony Abbot, c. 1490, 184 x 189 cm (6 ft ½ in x 6 ft 2 in)

THE DUKE OF URBINO

One of Piero della Francesca's patrons was the first Duke of Urbino, Federigo da Montefeltro, whose portrait he painted (above). The Duke led several armies during the territorial battles of the 15th century, but was also a renowned scholar. His palace at Urbino was one of the important small courts of Italy and contained his extensive library.

THE MISERICORDIA

The Compagnia della Misericordia was founded in Florence in the 13th century to carry out missions of mercy, such as transporting the sick to hospital, and the dead to burial. In 1445, the organization commissioned Piero della Francesca to paint an altarpiece for Borgo Sansepolcro. The central figure in the work is the Madonna of Mercy, who was patroness of the Misericordia. The organization is still in operation today.

PIERO DELLA FRANCESCA'S SOLEMN GENIUS

The "other" Piero is far better known, and with justice. It can come as a shock to learn that the present admiration for Piero della Francesca (c. 1410/20–92) is of comparatively recent origin. His intensely still and silent art went out of fashion not long after his death, and its sublime restraint of expression was seen as inadequacy. Yet Piero della Francesca is one of the truly great masters of all time. He was born in the small town of Borgo Sansepolcro in Umbria, central Italy. In Piero's wide vision we can see the lovely defining light and sculptural form of Masaccio (see p.82) and Donatello (see p.83), brilliant clarity of colour, together with a new interest in "real" landscape, that was influenced by his master Domenico Veneziano (see p.86) and by Flemish artists. When his eyes dimmed in later life, Piero turned increasingly to his other abiding interest, mathematics, and as a branch of mathematics, perspective (see p.88). He was also a theorist, and, like Alberti (see p.88), wrote two treatises on the mathematics of art.

RELIGIOUS LANDSCAPES

The Baptism of Christ (114) takes place in an eternal dimension, even though those little streams and terraced hills are purely Umbrian. Piero's admiration of ancient art, which he studied in Rome around 1450, is manifested in the dignity and classical form of Christ, and of St John and the angels. The tall and slender column of manhood that is Jesus, Son of the Most High, is paired with the tall and slender column of the tree. The tree in turn is aligned with the majestic figures of the waiting angels. John the Baptist is another vertical, a slightly inclining one, solemnly performing his sacramental baptism with water from the river that, as told in legend, has stopped flowing at Christ's feet. A disrobing penitent, leaning forwards, both continues and varies the vertical theme. A group of theologians debates, clothes brightly reflected in the stilled water.

The invisible element, the Holy Spirit, is all-pervading, as a pure, crystalline early morning light, and in material form as a dove hovering horizontally with outspread wings, sanctifying the baptism with golden rays (only barely visible now), that shine down over Christ's head. The dove is the only presence in the baptismal group that could be reflected in the limpidity of the waters, but is not; it is unseen by all eyes but our own. There is such poetry in the sunlight and the high sky, the flowers, and the simple brightness of the garments, that it is impossible not to believe, as Piero does, that we who contemplate the scene are literally blessed.

114 *Piero della Francesca,* **The Baptism of Christ,** *1450s, 168 × 117 cm (66 × 46 in)*

Even a detail like the great over arching mass of foliage in the trees overhead seems to be weighted with holy significance. But Piero never presses home any symbolism, he never intrudes to put forward an interpretation. It has been remarked that everything in this picture is mathematically calculated to give the maximum impact, and one can even draw diagrams to show the underlying intelligence behind the structure. But our response comes immediately, affected unconsciously by this intelligence. Piero has that rare gift: he is effective – his pictures work; and he affects – we are moved by them.

THE BAPTISM OF CHRIST

This was originally the central panel of a large triptych. The rest of this triptych was painted by Matteo di Giovanni in about 1464. Piero's natural, almost casual depiction of this solemn ritual belies the work's sophisticated composition, and though its structure can be reduced to strict mathematical proportions, it is one of Piero's least mathematically controlled paintings.

ANGELS
The compact trio of angels is divided from the mortal world by the tree. They stand together with a charming degagé air, holding hands, their large and lovely flat feet planted solidly on the grassy meadow. The angels are witnessing Christ's baptism and affirm its importance with serene certainty. Piero shows us only a glimpse of the wing of the far angel, in which a few flecks of gold are still visible, and the landscape visible beneath.

CHRIST
The ritual anointing is performed in the deep, silent absorption of prayer, signified by the quiet concentration of John and Jesus. Christ's body has the whiteness of a bleached shell, His outer cleanliness echoing His symbolic purification through baptism – presided over by the Holy Spirit in the form of a white dove. A kind of spiritual force field separates John from Christ. He moves towards Christ, yet his free hand does not enter the unbroken divide between them.

DISTANT TOWN
Piero shows us the small town of Borgo Sansepolcro, with its fortified towers appearing piteously small and insignificant in the distance. Piero's treatment of the distinctly Umbrian landscape immediately distinguishes him from his contemporaries and displays an unprecedented naturalism. It reveals the extent to which Piero was influenced by Netherlandish art.

BENDING FIGURE
The half-naked figure standing at the river's edge in the middle distance is stripping off his clothes in readiness for his own baptism. His nakedness is symbolic of his humility before the Almighty, and contrasts sharply with the extravagant and even kingly headgear and costume of the high priests, who stand farthest away and are given the smallest stature in Piero's hierarchy. The identity of the penitent is hidden – a temporary concealment hinting at the new life he will enter into after baptism. His body – like Christ's – is bathed in a brilliant white light.

PIERO'S MASTERPIECES

Although Piero has a claim to being the perfect painter, every one of whose paintings are wonderfully good, his greatest work is the fresco that makes magnificent the church of St Francis in the town of Arezzo, near Piero's birthplace. *The Story of the True Cross (115)* runs around the walls, telling all aspects of the legend, from the supposed beginning of the Cross as a tree growing in Paradise, up to the miraculous Finding of the Cross by St Helena, the mother of Constantine the Great. The story is legend from start to finish, yet Piero treats it with such reverent solidity that archetypal truths are revealed. When the Queen of Sheba, proceeding in stately fashion toward her encounter with Solomon, "adores the wood of the Cross", the quiet passion of that bending neck tells us of the meaning of adoration, and its loveliness.

Although she and her maidens are cut from the same cloth pictorially (tall, willowy, swan-necked beauties) it is only the queen who understands the challenge of the holy and prostrates her regal self. Behind her the pages gossip, beside her the maids of honour look interestedly on. She alone has understood the full dimensions of the finding. As ever in Piero, there is an air of silence so profound as to halt all movement in its tracks, and immortalize the scene that is depicted.

Another work, the *Resurrection of Christ (116)*, has actually been described as the greatest picture ever painted (its only rival for this honour being Velázquez's *Las Meninas*, see p.194). The two masterpieces are utterly different, Piero's having a unique sublimity. Its gravely heroic Christ, impassive and heraldic, enters life as a sombrely compassionate Conqueror, lifting the sleeping world up onto a new plane of being. It was painted for the town hall of Borgo Sansepolcro – Italian for "the Holy Sepulchre."

116 **Piero della Francesca,** Resurrection of Christ, *early 1450s,* 225 x 205 cm (7 ft 5 in x 6 ft 9 in)

115 *Piero della Francesca,* **The Story of the True Cross,** *c. 1452–57, 335 × 747 cm (11 ft × 24 ft 6 in)*

SOLIDITY IN MANTEGNA'S ART

There is something of Piero's silent massiveness in Andrea Mantegna (1431–1506), the first great artist from northern Italy. He belongs to the Florentine tradition in that his art showed the expressly Florentine concerns with scientific debate and classical aspiration, but as the leading artist of northern Italy he belonged also to that of nearby Venice. He is first heard of as a young man in Padua, struggling, by means of a lawsuit, to free himself from his teacher and adoptive father, Francesco Squarcione.

A sort of lonely freedom is basic to Mantegna's temperament, as we understand it, and there is something rather appropriate in his dual attempt to gain his legal independence and to plot with fierce intellectual clarity the frescoes on the walls of the Eremitani chapel. Although nearly all this work was destroyed or damaged during World War II, enough remains to indicate the almost awesome originality of his painterly approach.

The irony is that Mantegna would have claimed not originality, but a rigorous conservatism, and his art is a rejection of the more relaxed, painterly styles that were emerging in Venetian art. He may have benefitted from the teaching of Squarcione, who did at least possess an unrivaled set of antique drawings, but the sculptural quality of Mantegna's art makes it far more likely that he was influenced by local

examples of work by Donatello (see pp.83, 105). Many of Mantegna's paintings take on the appearance of a pictorial bas-relief akin to Donatello's and Ghiberti's sculpted panels (see p.102), and these works subsequently influenced High Renaissance painting, notably that of Raphael (see p.125).

For some, this sculptural bias has made Mantegna's art seem bloodless. It is severe, monumental, thought out from within. But it can strike us as all the more impressively emotional for that very need, experienced so intensely, to protect himself from the vulnerability of self-exposure. The task is impossible, since every major artist can only create from his own heart, and the attempt to conceal is as revealing as the desire to expose. Mantegna had left Padua to be court artist at Mantua when he painted *The Death of the Virgin (117)*, a great tableau where emotion is frozen into a sort of icy

117 *Andrea Mantegna,* **The Death of the Virgin,** *c.1460, 54 × 42 cm (21¼ × 16½ in)*

passion. The Apostles gathered around the bier are heavy with minutely observed grief. The Virgin is revealed with direct, personal simplicity in the humiliation of death. The drama is framed and given its context by the vast Mantuan landscape, which gleams in remote perfection behind the window. The waters lie still, the ramparts offer the pretence of human inviolability, and the serene sun bathes lakes, palaces, priests, and the dead Virgin in the same quiet light.

PERSPECTIVE SKILLS

This fresco was painted on a ceiling of the Gonzaga Palace in Mantua by Mantegna in 1465–74. In creating the illusion of an opening to the sky, the artist makes humorous use of Albertian perspective (see p.89), especially in the foreshortening of the winged figures.

OTHER WORKS BY PIERO DELLA FRANCESCA

Madonna of Mercy
(Borgo Sansepolcro)

Federigo da Montefeltro
(Uffizi, Florence)

The Nativity
(National Gallery, London)

St Jerome in the Desert
(Staatliche Museen, Berlin-Dahlem)

SINOPIA

This was a technique of using red ochre to draw initial guides for fresco painting. Each day, a section of the sinopia was plastered over and painted. The 1966 flood in Florence damaged a number of Renaissance frescoes. As part of the restoration work, some were removed from the walls on which they were created, thereby exposing the sinopia. This provided insight into the artists' working practices and showed that they often introduced changes between the drawing of the original guides and the final representations.

118 *Andrea Mantegna*, Portrait of a Man, *probably c. 1460, 24 x 19 cm (9½ x 7½ in)*

people's oppressor. Her expression is remote and impassive, and we perceive her extreme detachment of will in the way she averts her head, refusing to confront emotionally the reality of what she has done, as she passes the head to her shrinking attendant. She has resolutely turned her back on the pathos of Holofernes's dead foot, which rises up behind her like an accusing ghost. On one level, the painting is all calmness and immobility; on another, there is a revulsion of spirit so violent that there has to be a total psychological distancing.

This wonderful paradox, Mantegna's special gift, is fortuitously duplicated for us, for he painted another version *(119)*, in sombre richness of colour. The stony non-colour of the tent and the figures contained within its shade changes to a harmony of radiant pinks, oranges, ochres, and blue-greens. One work, in Washington *(120)*, emphasizes the distancing; the other, in Dublin *(119)*, the intensity. Both have a still and stately beauty that is unforgettable.

PORTRAITS OF THE GONZAGAS

Mantegna was commissioned to paint portraits of members of the influential Gonzaga family in Mantua. Even in these intimate pictures, which are unique for their historical immediacy, he always contrives to show us both the actual, which we can recognize, and the hidden ideal, which we can revere. This is apparent even in this small-scale work, the *Portrait of a Man (118)*, where the unknown sitter is strongly individual and yet recalls to us the moral imperatives of duty and courage.

MANTEGNA'S GRISAILLE

In his love for the solid reality of sculpture, Mantegna went so far as to perfect a form of grisaille (monochrome painting that imitates the effect and colour of stone relief). The texture resembles stone, yet in his hands it was fully alive. He might have chiselled out the dramatic panel of *Judith and Holofernes (119)*, where the Junoesque heroine stands impassively before the rigid folds of the tent in which she has murdered her

119 *Andrea Mantegna*, Judith and Holofernes, *1495–1500, 48 x 37 cm (19 x 14½ in)*

120 Andrea Mantegna, Judith and Holofernes, c. 1495, 30 × 18 cm (12 × 7 in)

DONATELLO'S JUDITH

As a close personal friend of Cosimo de' Medici, Donatello was given the artistic freedom to produce this highly controversial sculpture of Judith slaying Holofernes in 1456. The Jewish heroine who murdered the Philistine (Assyrian) general Holofernes to protect her people was meant to symbolize humility overcoming pride, but the bronze was considered too disturbing by many Florentines, who petitioned successfully for its removal from the Piazza della Signoria.

OTHER WORKS BY MANTEGNA

Crucifixion
(Louvre, Paris)

St Sebastian
(Kunsthistorisches Museum, Vienna)

Dead Christ
(Brera Gallery, Milan)

Virgin and Child with the Magdalen and St John the Baptist
(National Gallery, London)

Dido
(Montreal Museum of Fine Arts)

The Dead Christ with Two Angels
(Statens Museum for Kunst, Copenhagen)

RENAISSANCE VENICE

Painting that was produced in Renaissance Venice belonged to the northern Italian tradition and had an identity and genealogy all its own. While Venetian artists also explored problems of perspective and mathematics, and were unavoidably influenced by the fertile art of Medician Florence – the heartland of the Renaissance – there emerged in Venice a new, essentially "painterly" tradition. Venetian painting showed less concern with sculptural form and hard-edged delineation, placing more emphasis on colour and nuances of light. From the beginning, it contained a peculiarly gentle lyricism, quite distinct from the Florentine tradition.

VENETIAN TRADE

In the 16th century Venice was an independent and imperial city with a state-owned arsenal of ships employing 10,000 workers. The city was the Italian gateway to the Mediterranean for trading in silks, pigments, and spices. Venice was renowned as the centre of the pigment trade, and it is known that Raphael, for example, sent an assistant there from Rome to purchase particular colours.

The artist great enough to lead painting into its next phase, and in doing so, greatly influence the course of Western painting since, was Giovanni Bellini (c. 1427–1516). He belonged to a family of artists, composed of his father Jacopo (c. 1400–70/71) and his brother Gentile (c. 1429–1507). The two brothers were taught by their father (who had been a pupil of Gentile da Fabriano, see p.56) in accordance with the artistic tradition in Venice, in which skills were passed down through generations. The two generations of Bellinis became the most influential group of artists in northern Italy; and just as the early Renaissance is bound up with 15th-century Florentine culture, the Bellinis were responsible for the distinctly Venetian heritage of the High Renaissance of the late 15th to early 16th centuries.

INFLUENCE OF MANTEGNA

Although Mantegna (see p.103) stands alone, he had, in fact, a close and fruitful relationship with the Bellini family of Venice. (He was even a literal relation, in that he married Nicolosia, sister to Giovanni and Gentile. She does not seem to have softened him much – he remained litigious and over-sensitive to the end.) But the hard beauty of

AGONY IN THE GARDEN

This theme was popularized in the Renaissance by artists such as Bellini, Mantegna, and El Greco (see p.146). After the Last Supper and before His arrest Christ retired to the Mount of Olives to pray. The "agony" is the contest between Christ's human weakness and His divine confidence and belief in His resurrection. In Renaissance paintings of this scene Christ traditionally kneels on a rocky outcrop as the three disciples sleep.

121 Andrea Mantegna, **The Agony in the Garden,** *c. 1460, 63 x 81 cm (25 x 32 in)*

Mantegna's own work certainly affected that of his brothers-in-law. Giovanni Bellini is one of the supreme painters of all the ages, able to accept the spare majesty of Mantegna and yet transform it into his own subtle sweetness. Sometimes we can actually watch influences being absorbed.

Both painters, coincidentally, have a version of *The Agony in the Garden* in the National Gallery, London. Mantegna's *(121)* is thought to have been painted about five years before Bellini's, and the younger artist, Bellini, always regarded his own work as lesser in quality. Yet the contest is very close; both paintings have a gaunt and rocky landscape setting, appropriate for the austerity of the drama. Both excel in figural perspective, showing the sleeping Apostles in abrupt foreshortening. Both have the praying Christ half turned away, isolated on His jut of stone, bare feet vulnerable in His absorption upon His Father and His fate. In both paintings we see in the distance the approaching figures of the soldiers coming to arrest Jesus, led by the betraying disciple Judas.

But the two works are subtly different. It is not just that Mantegna is far more interested in the actual geophysical structure of the rocks, but that Bellini's world *(122)* is less aggressive, less confrontational. It may only be a question of degree, yet it modifies the feeling of the picture, makes it more tender, more visually ambiguous. It is here that Bellini's greatest gift is displayed, his sense of light in all its specificity.

It is sacred "time" in Mantegna, the "hour" of which Jesus spoke, removed from the mundane time of the normal day. Mantegna's sky, like his frozen and brooding city, is eternal. But Bellini shows us a real city faintly glimmering into visibility beneath the gentle skies of early morning. Light is beginning to flood with its warmth the cold night where Jesus has laboured in painful prayer, and the Angel of Consolation, solid in Mantegna, floats solitary and ethereal in Bellini, a dawn apparition that will dissolve into cloud.

The mature Bellini understood light with mystical fervour. It had a sacred significance for him, one that he could share with us without ever lapsing into the explicit. Bellini is an extraordinary artist, a man sensitive to beauty, aware of the significance of form, and inspired by a passionate love, both of the visible and the invisible, that makes his work moving on every level. There is no Bellini painting that we cannot respond to with joy and a deeper understanding of what our existence is all about.

BELLINI FAMILY

The Bellinis formed one of the most prominent and successful families of Renaissance painters. Father Jacopo's silverpoint sketchbook was the inspiration for many of Giovanni's paintings, which in turn inspired the young Giorgione and Titian. It featured mythological characters (such as Perseus with the head of the Gorgon, shown here), as well as classical, biblical, and imaginative subjects.

122 *Giovanni Bellini*, The Agony in the Garden, *c. 1460, 81 x 127 cm (32 x 50 in)*

123 Giovanni Bellini, **The Madonna of the Meadow,** *c. 1500–05, 67 × 86 cm (26½ × 34 in)*

ST JEROME

This detail from *St Jerome* by Ghirlandaio (see p.121) shows equipment used to copy ancient texts. Jerome was a popular figure in Renaissance art as he symbolized the ideal of the Humanist scholar. His great achievement was to translate the Bible into Latin.

The Madonna of the Meadow (123) may appear to be a typical Madonna, albeit a very enchanting one. But it is, in its understated manner, almost a revolutionary painting. Scholars have always pitted Florence against Venice, ever since Vasari, the great early art historian (see p.98), quoted his hero, Michelangelo, as lauding form above colour, and deploring the Venetian concentration on the latter. In this sense, Giovanni Bellini is the "first" Venetian painter.

He initiates in us the awareness of a magical, enveloping brightness, a palpable light in which all colours shine at their loveliest. In this colour-world, there is no longer man and woman in the midst of nature, but humanity as part of nature, another expression of its truth. The very texture of the harsh soil, the low lattices, the defended well, all have an undemonstrative integrity that has some mysterious, inexplicable connection with the strong pyramid of Mother and Child at the centre of the picture.

Madonnas are a common idiom in Renaissance painting. There was hardly an artist who did not attempt this great theme. We can understand why. The wonderful thing about the Madonna and Child theme is that it appeals both to the specifics of Christianity (where the humanity of Christ is a central mystery) and to the human values on which all religion is based, throughout the world.

Every painter had a mother. Every psyche has been affected by this fact. To explore this fundamental of human existence had an irresistible fascination for the artist. No-one has ever been more sensitive to this fundamental subject than Bellini. Every one of his Madonnas has an aesthetic and a spiritual force that makes them all memorable. He understands, at an elemental level, the meaning of motherhood and childhood, and this is the basis of the conviction that we see behind his Madonnas. This is only a sample, but an excellent one.

MADONNA OF THE MEADOW

Bellini was famed for his paintings of the Madonna and Child. From his 65-year-long career, no fewer than 14 of the major works that survive are on this, his favourite theme. It is one of the most ancient of all religious subjects, yet Bellini was able to invigorate what had become a formula, an icon, with a fully convincing depiction of both the sacred and the human.

HARBINGER
OF DEATH

A large raven broods heavily over the meadows: a reminder of the ever-present figure of death. Death, however, assumes a small scale in comparison to the monumental serenity of the Madonna and Child, who affirm life after death. The bird perches high up in the small, thin, leafless trees that sway imperceptibly against the luminous pallor of the sky. Though its role is symbolic, the bird is integrated into the natural order of life.

VENETIAN LANDSCAPE

On the right, divided from death by the towering figure of Mary, are the sober activities of life. Despite the gloomy presence of death, the daily life of the natural world goes calmly on. A farmer tends to the livestock in the field. Above them, an insubstantial line of cloud drifts slowly over the softly gleaming ramparts of the little city, whose concerns of government and commerce are rightly distanced from the great theme of life and death that Bellini dwells upon. And this is no walled garden, with cherubim and angels floating amid exotic flowers and cultivated hedgerows, but the real, solid world – Bellini's world – in the province of Venice.

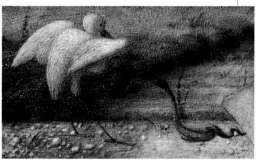

MORTAL STRUGGLE

Easy to miss in the middle distance, and on the side of death, is a little egret fighting with a snake. Wings raised in a threatening gesture, the egret circles the snake. This combat symbolizes the fight between good and evil. It may also refer to Christ's struggle before His sacrifice, and the reason for His sacrifice – the serpent's entry into the Garden of Eden. (It is interesting to note that there is a pair of egrets in the foreground of Mantegna's Agony in the Garden, see p.106.)

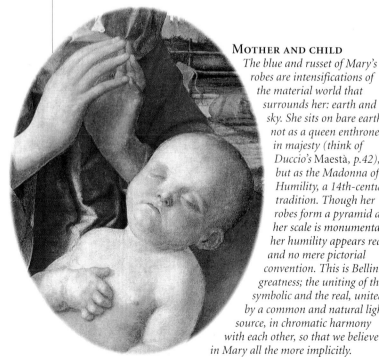

MOTHER AND CHILD

The blue and russet of Mary's robes are intensifications of the material world that surrounds her: earth and sky. She sits on bare earth, not as a queen enthroned in majesty (think of Duccio's Maestà, p.42), but as the Madonna of Humility, a 14th-century tradition. Though her robes form a pyramid and her scale is monumental, her humility appears real, and no mere pictorial convention. This is Bellini's greatness; the uniting of the symbolic and the real, united by a common and natural light source, in chromatic harmony with each other, so that we believe in Mary all the more implicitly.

THE CITY STATES OF ITALY

During the Renaissance northern Italy was one of the wealthiest regions in Europe. Genoa and Venice both had populations of around 100,000 by 1400 and were the main centres of trade. Florence, with a population of 55,000, was the centre for manufacture and distribution. A sense of civic pride known as *campanilismo* ("love for the bell tower") was characteristic of the Italian city dweller.

MUSIC IN THE RENAISSANCE

This painting by Lorenzo Costa, dating from c. 1500, shows a lute player and singers performing a *frottola*; a simple song for one or a group of voices with an instrumental accompaniment. During the 16th century it became the prevailing form of refined music. The *frottola* later developed into the madrigal.

OTHER WORKS BY BELLINI

Pietà
(Brera Gallery, Milan)

St Francis in Ecstasy
(The Frick Collection, New York)

Virgin and Child Between St John the Baptist and St Catherine
(Accademia, Venice)

The Doge Leonardo Loredan
(National Gallery, London)

Virgin and Child
(Museum of Art, New Orleans)

124 *Giovanni Bellini*, St Jerome Reading, *c. 1480/90, 49 x 39 cm (19½ x 15½ in)*

There is this same magical involvement in his *St Jerome Reading (124)* where the centre of attention is not the noble saint, still less his attendant lion comfortably snuggled at his back, but the wonderful white hare, nibbling at the leaves with the same disinterested attitude as the saint brings to his mental fodder, his book. St Jerome, that renowned scholar, is oblivious, but the little animal is bright in the wintry sunlight, and makes us aware of the beauty of the created world, with its rocks, leaves, lagoons, and stones.

A splendid Bellini, *The Feast of the Gods (125)*, was modified into even greater splendour by no less an artist than Titian (see p.131). It is still quintessentially Bellini: all the gods are characterized and something of their legends and relationships given pictorial form, all in a golden light of high classical dignity. Another sign of his greatness as an artist is that having led the way for Giorgione and Titian (who heralded an entirely new phase of painting), the aging Bellini allowed himself to be led by the younger artists and, adapting his own style, produced masterpieces even in his eighties.

125 *Giovanni Bellini*, The Feast of the Gods, *1514, 170 x 188 cm (5 ft 7 in x 6 ft 2 in)*

OIL PAINT AND THE FLEMISH INFLUENCE IN VENICE

If Bellini eventually outgrew Mantegna's influence, there were other, perhaps lesser artists, who were guided by it on their way to achieving their own summits, and to remaining there.

The Sicilian artist Antonello da Messina (c. 1430–79) is a rather perplexing figure, mainly because Vasari falsely credited him with the sole popularization in Italy of van Eyck's use of oil (see p.64). Antonello is the first important artist from southern Italy, but he did not belong to any Southern school; instead he found his influences abroad, in Flemish art.

Because the influence of Flemish art is strikingly visible in his paintings, Antonello provides an important bridge between Italy and the Netherlands. His visit to Venice in 1475, where he came into close contact with Giovanni Bellini, was to play a major role in the history of Venetian painting.

Some people, then, consider that Antonello introduced oil painting techniques, after they had already been mastered by the Flemish artists, to Venice. Others take the view that he had a sophisticated knowledge of the medium, having learned it in Naples, where he probably studied under a Flemish-influenced artist, and that this made the crucial impact on artists who were already experimenting with oil paints. The argument is not a terribly important one. Whatever the case, the result of this meeting of

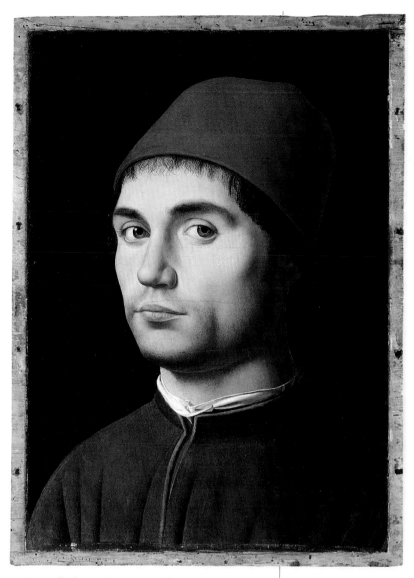

126 *Antonello da Messina*, Portrait of a Young Man, *c. 1465, 35 x 25 cm (14 x 10 in)*

127 *Antonello da Messina*, Virgin Annunciate, *c. 1465, 45 x 34 cm (17¾ x 13½ in)*

the traditions was that, in Italy, oil painting techniques were pioneered exclusively by Venetian artists before they spread to other artistic centres. Antonello himself needs no spurious claims to attention. From the example of Piero della Francesca (see p.100), and especially Mantegna, he learned the importance of solid truth-telling. His forms are almost too clear and sharp; in them we see a "Flemish" intense scrutiny of detail contrasted with an Italian broad generosity of form. He bathes his forms in the most romantic of lights.

His *Portrait of a Young Man (126)* is lit from within, despite the unexceptional and pudgy face, and in a great work like the *Virgin Annunciate (127)*, there is a concentrated simplicity that makes the Virgin affect us with immense impact. Interestingly, the artist presents the Virgin as a devotional portrait, rather than showing the Annunciation itself.

MODERN ANATOMY

In 1543 the Flemish professor Andrea Vesalio (1514–64) wrote his *De Humani Corporis Fabrica* which became the first standard work of modern anatomy. It has been suggested that the drawings in the book were produced in Titian's studio in Venice.

FASCINATION WITH EXTERNALS

Carlo Crivelli (1430/5–c. 1495) also belongs to a Venetian artistic family. Like Antonello da Messina, he, too, has a clear cut manner that is unmistakable, influenced by Mantegna but applying the fine wire of his outline in an almost mannered style. "Fashion" is the word that springs to mind.

Crivelli's art reveals an ardent interest in externals and their lucid perfections – perhaps also partly owing to the Flemish influence of Antonello – but never in the actual spiritual substances involved (surprisingly, since he painted only religious subjects).

It is rather in material substance that Crivelli excels, enthralling us with the rotundity of a pear or the angular swirl of a damask skirt, winning us over to share his delight in gorgeous things. When he attempts an emotional theme we may feel embarassed, but on his own level, he is superb. His *Madonna and Child Enthroned, with Donor (128)* soars aloft with such elegance

128 Carlo Crivelli, Madonna and Child Enthroned, with Donor, c. 1470, 130 x 55 cm (51 x 21½ in)

and wit (note the dragon-like arms of the throne: brutality subdued to the service of religion) that we may miss the tiny, kneeling donor. He is tacked onto the real interest of the artist, which is not holiness and people praying, but shapes and their self-assured interplay.

Cima da Conegliano (Giovanni Battista Cima, c. 1459/60–1517/18) lived all his life in the environs of Venice, in the small provincial town of Conegliano (from which his name is derived). The strongest influence on him was that of Mantegna, though from early in his career he was also influenced by Giovanni Bellini. Cima is not a great painter, and his work developed very little throughout his artistic life, but he has a spontaneous innocence, a sense of the fitting,

129 Cima da Conegliano, St Helena, c. 1495, 40 x 32.5 cm (16 x 12¾ in)

and a technical amplitude as well, that make his work very appealing. *St Helena (129)* is a fine example of his work. She is tall and stately, with her slender Cross on one side and a slender living tree on the other, and dominates the green hills before which she appears. The hills are crowned by little cities where, we sense, her discovery of the True Cross (see column, p.102), however apocryphal, has changed the lives of the citizens. It is not by accident that she looms so large. Her stature is built into the picture's meaning as much as are her queenly bearing and her severe self-possession.

130 *Cosimo Tura*, Madonna and Child in a Garden, *c. 1455, 53 x 37 cm (21 x 14½ in)*

THE FERRARESE SCHOOL

Tura and Cossa, artists in the independent city state of Ferrara (see column, p.115), were also admiring contemporaries of Mantegna. Cosimo Tura (c. 1430–95) is perhaps the greater of the two, with his highly original and easily recognizable blending of the suave and the exciting. Like Crivelli, he rarely goes deep, but he gives us a superbly integrated surface, with a similar metallic wiriness and hard-edged control. There is wit and a tenderness in *Madonna and Child in a Garden (130)*, exquisite in its form and its daring chromatic contrasts. The Virgin steeples her long, thin fingers over the sleeping child, as if to make a refuge for him, and the rosy blooms that cluster behind her, like a cushioned throne, make us conscious that both these tender creatures of God are in need of cushioning: there are dark gleams from the night background, caused only by light catching on fruit and leaf, but the effect is subtly sinister.

Francesco del Cossa (c. 1435–c. 1477) has humanized this insouciant austerity. Though Cossa was Ferrarese, his *St Lucy (131)* belongs to the Florentine tradition, infused with the hard-edged contours of Mantegna and tinged with the peculiar metallic quality of his contemporary, Tura – though the effect is a softer one, largely due to its being painted in the more gently luminous medium of oil paint.

Cossa's St Lucy is so monumental, so luminously afloat in her golden air, it takes us time to realize her spray is not composed of flowers, but two stalked eyes. The original Lucy was wrongly credited with being martyred by having her eyes torn out (see column, right), and this grisly emblem always accompanies her depiction.

131 *Francesco del Cossa*, St Lucy, after 1470, 79 x 56 cm (31 x 22 in)

STORY OF HASDRUBAL'S WIFE

Hasdrubal was a Carthaginian general who fought against the Romans in the second century BC. He surrendered to Scipio in 146 BC. His wife is reputed to have been so ashamed of his cowardice that she threw herself and her children into the fire at the temple where they were sheltering.

CASSONI

The workshops of Renaissance painters were busy for much of the time in the production of objects other than paintings and altarpieces, such as plates, chests (*cassoni*), beds, and coats of arms. *Cassoni* were carved, inlaid, painted chests for storing linen, clothes, and household items. Brides often used them to keep their trousseaux and many *cassoni* were decorated with narrative paintings and family coats of arms.

THE FLIGHT INTO EGYPT

After being warned in a dream that Herod was seeking to kill the infant Jesus, Joseph took Mary and the Child away to Egypt until after Herod's death. The story of their journey to Egypt was a popular theme in Renaissance art and often contained guardian angels and a dramatic evening landscape.

The last of the great Ferrarese artists, Ercole de' Roberti, maintained the Mantegna–Tura–Cossa sobriety and classic formality. *The Wife of Hasdrubal and Her Children (132)* may be an unusual subject (see column, left), but we respond immediately to the solidity of these three human creatures, anguished, in frantic motion, yet still with a semi-sculptural stillness.

CARPACCIO: THE STORY-TELLER

Vittore Carpaccio (1455/65–1525/26), though essentially Venetian, was clearly influenced by the great artists of the Ferrarese school, and also by Giovanni Bellini's brother, Gentile. Carpaccio had probably been taught by the Bellini patriarch, Jacopo, and was an assistant to Giovanni. The element that is peculiarly his own is that of story-telling, of which he had an instinctive mastery. The delicacy of detail in his work may suggest a medieval naïveté, yet he is a highly sophisticated painter who can use narrative simplicities as a pleasurable means to his ends.

Carpaccio can rise above the picturesque. *The Flight into Egypt (133)* may not present us with wholly serious actors: Mary is most sumptuously clad and has obviously used some of her rose-red silks to fashion a tunic for St Joseph. But all lighthearted ness is forgotten in the glory of the setting. In a sunset sky of striking verisimilitude we see why Carpaccio gives us the impression of being, despite all, a major artist. The light bathes an

132 *Ercole de' Roberti*, The Wife of Hasdrubal and Her Children, *c. 1480/90, 47 x 30.5 cm (18½ x 12 in)*

ordinary lakeside town and its surroundings – unimpressive, undramatic, and yet completely satisfying and convincing. There can be a delib-

133 *Vittore Carpaccio*, The Flight into Egypt, *c. 1500, 72 x 112 cm (28¼ x 44 in)*

134 Vittore Carpaccio, **The Dream of St Ursula,** *1494, 275 x 265 cm (9 ft x 8 ft 8 in)*

erately Gothic charm in Carpaccio's legend cycles, as in the wholly delightful *Dream of St Ursula (134)*. This is one of a series of paintings Carpaccio produced for the confraternity of St Ursula. She was a legendary Breton princess who led a pilgrimage to Rome with 11,000 virgins who had converted to Christianity. The story ends with the massacre of the entire company by villainous Huns (see column, p.70). The neat little bed, and the sleeping saint have

an enamelled charm that will happily survive her coming martyrdom, signified by the entering angel bearing the symbolic palm. Carpaccio's meticulous recording of the material world has provided historians with insight into the material reality of 15th-century Venice. This faithful representation of the visible world, composed of many tiny parts, reappears in the work of another Venetian artist in the 18th century, Canaletto (see p.234).

(see column, p.70)

FERRARA

During the Renaissance Ferrara became a lively centre for the arts and the court of the Este family encouraged individual artists from throughout Italy. Many impressive secular buildings were built in the city during the 15th century including the Palazzo dei Diamanti.

THE HIGH RENAISSANCE

Since Renaissance means "new birth", it is obvious that it cannot stand still. Once something is born, it begins to grow. But never has there been growth as lovely as that of painting as it matured into the High Renaissance. Here we find some of the greatest artists ever known: the mighty Florentines, Leonardo da Vinci and Michelangelo; the Umbrian, Raphael; and, equal in might, the Venetians – Titian, Tintoretto, and Veronese.

By a happy chance, a common theme links the lives of four of the famous masters of the High Renaissance – Leonardo, Michelangelo, Raphael, and Titian. Each began his artistic career with an apprenticeship to a painter who was already of good standing, and each took the same path of first accepting, then transcending, the influence of his first master. The first of these, Leonardo

SFUMATO

This term, derived from the Italian *fumo*, meaning smoke, is particularly applied to the work of Leonardo. It defines the gradual and imperceptible transition between areas of different colour, without the use of sharp outlines. The capacity to blur over harsh outlines, especially in portrait paintings, was considered the sign of a highly skilled and distinguished painter.

EQUESTRIAN MONUMENTS

This monument to Bartolommeo Colleoni was begun by Verrocchio c. 1481 and completed after his death. During this period, riders on horseback were a popular subject for monuments. Their popularity is attributed to the influence of the classical statue of Emperor Marcus Aurelius that stood in the Campidoglio in Rome. Donatello also made works commemorating Renaissance soldiers.

135 Andrea del Verrocchio, The Baptism of Christ, c. 1470, 180 x 152 cm (5 ft 11 in x 5 ft)

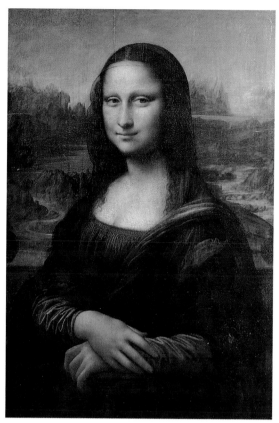

136 Leonardo da Vinci, Mona Lisa, 1503, 77 x 53 cm (30½ x 21 in)

mathematical excellence, scientific daring … the list is endless. This overabundance of talents caused him to treat his artistry lightly, seldom finishing a picture, and sometimes making rash technical experiments. *The Last Supper*, in the church of Santa Maria delle Grazie in Milan, for example, has almost vanished, so inadequate were his innovations in fresco preparation.

Yet the works that we have salvaged remain the most dazzlingly poetic pictures ever created. The *Mona Lisa (136)* has the innocent disavantage of being too famous. It can only be seen behind thick glass in a heaving crowd of awe-struck sightseers. It has been reproduced in every conceivable medium: it remains intact in its magic, for ever defying the human insistence on comprehending. It is a work that we can only gaze at in silence.

Leonardo's three great portraits of women all have a secret wistfulness. This quality is at its most appealing in *Cecilia Gallarani (137)*, at its most enigmatic in the *Mona Lisa*, and at its most

> *"The first object of the painter is to make a flat plane appear as a body in relief and projecting from that plane."*
>
> Leonardo da Vinci

da Vinci (1452–1519), was the elder of the two Florentine masters. He was taught by Andrea del Verrocchio 1435–88), an engaging painter whose great achievement was his sculpture (see p.116, column). Verrocchio also had considerable influence on the early work of Michelangelo (see p.120). Verrocchio's best-known painting is the famous *Baptism of Christ (135)*, famous because the youthful Leonardo is said to have painted the dreamy and romantic angel on the far left, who compares more than favourably with the stubby lack of distinction in the master's own angel immediately beside him.

LEONARDO: RENAISSANCE POLYMATH
There has never been an artist who was more fittingly, and without qualification, described as a genius. Like Shakespeare, Leonardo came from an insignificant background and rose to universal acclaim. Leonardo was the illegitimate son of a local lawyer in the small town of Vinci in the Tuscan region. His father acknowledged him and paid for his training, but we may wonder whether the strangely self-sufficient tone of Leonardo's mind was not perhaps affected by his early ambiguity of status. The definitive polymath, he had almost too many gifts, including superlative male beauty, a splendid singing voice, magnificent physique,

137 Leonardo da Vinci, Cecilia Gallarani, c. 1485, 54 x 39 cm (21¼ x 15½ in)

LEONARDO'S THEORIES

Between 1473 and 1518 Leonardo wrote a series of papers which were then collected together as his *Treatise on Painting*. One section, written in 1492, is devoted to linear perspective. The page shown here demonstrates his technique for transferring a figure onto the sides of a curved vault. This technique prefigured the later style known as *trompe l'oeil* (paintings that "deceive the eye").

INVENTIVE SKETCHES

Leonardo's sketches reveal a man with endless imagination and scientific interest. As well as anatomical studies and caricature, he also produced many mechanical drawings, inventing objects as diverse as war engines, water-mills, spinning machines, tanks, and even helicopters (shown above).

confrontational in *Ginevra de' Benci (138)*. It is hard to gaze at the *Mona Lisa*, because we have so many expectations of it. Perhaps we can look more truly at a less famous portrait, *Ginevra de' Benci*. It has that haunting, almost unearthly beauty peculiar to Leonardo.

A WITHHELD IDENTITY

The subject of *Ginevra de' Benci* has nothing of the Mona Lisa's inward amusement, and also nothing of Cecilia's gentle submissiveness. The young woman looks past us with a wonderful luminous sulkiness. Her mouth is set in an unforgiving line of sensitive disgruntlement, her proud and perfect head is taut above the unyielding column of her neck, and her eyes seem to narrow as she endures the painter and his art. Her ringlets, infinitely subtle, cascade down from the breadth of her gleaming forehead (the forehead, incidentally, of one of the most gifted intellectuals of her time). These delicate ripples are repeated in the spikes of the juniper bush.

The desolate waters, the mists, the dark trees, the reflected gleams of still waters, all these surround and illuminate the sitter. She is totally fleshly and totally impermeable to the artist. He observes, rapt by her perfection of form, and shows us the thin veil of her upper bodice and the delicate flushing of her throat. What she is truly like she conceals; what Leonardo reveals to us is precisely this concealment, a self-absorption that spares no outward glance.

138 Leonardo da Vinci, Ginevra de' Benci, c. 1474, 39 x 37 cm (15½ x 14½ in)

GINEVRA DE' BENCI

Leonardo's exquisite portrait of Ginevra de' Benci was described by Vasari (see p.98) as a "beautiful thing". It was originally larger, but was cut down (because of damage) to this powerfully compact format by later owners. The back of the panel depicts a wreath of laurel and palm encircling a juniper sprig (see right). The three are connected by a scroll bearing the inscription "She adorns her beauty with virtue".

JUNIPER LEAVES

The young woman's name, Ginevra, is related to the Italian word ginepro, *meaning juniper. Appropriately, Leonardo has set her pale, marble-like beauty against the dark, spiky leaves of a juniper bush. She is well described by spikiness, we may imagine, and the bitter appeal of the gin that comes from the juniper berry is also adumbrated by this setting.*

RESERVED CHARACTER

Ginevra's rose-pink cheek and lips are painted with supreme delicacy and restraint. This effect is so subtle, so cool, that it admirably conveys her inner restraint, her firm control over her emotions. Her heavy, half-closed lids cast a shadow over the irises of her eyes, and the almost total absence of reflected light serves to reduce the communication between us and her. A slight cast in her left eye accentuates the lack of focus in her expression and her gaze is directed over our shoulder.

INSUBSTANTIAL LANDSCAPE

In contrast to the woman, with her firm, sculptural presence, the middle-distance landscape quivers with uncertainty, rendered with thin, fluid paint. Each brushmark is visible over the next, and the trees are merely thin stalks, their trunks painted with delicate, tremulous brush strokes. This part of the picture is a prime example of Leonardo's sfumato *(see p.116).*

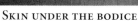

SKIN UNDER THE BODICE

Ginevra's skin is rendered with absolutely smooth, "invisible" brush strokes. This is achieved by working wet-in-wet, and by the use of glazes and loose, "oily" paint, so that the colour and contours of each brush stroke blend imperceptibly to form a continuous, uninterrupted surface. It is seen through her diaphanous bodice, which is given only the slightest definition. If it were not for the gilt pin holding it together, we would perhaps not notice it at all.

> **" . . . I cannot live under pressures from patrons, let alone paint."**
>
> Michelangelo, quoted in Vasari's *Lives of the Artists*

MACHIAVELLI

The Florentine statesman Niccolo Machiavelli (1469–1527) is remembered as the author of *Il Principe* (The Prince, 1532), a rational analysis of political power. His main argument was that a ruler must be prepared to do evil if he judges that good will come of it. After his death he developed a reputation as an amoral cynic and this was reinforced by criticism from his enemies in Church and State. In the present century a more balanced view prevails.

139 Leonardo da Vinci, Virgin of the Rocks, c. 1508, 190 x 120 cm (75 x 47 in)

INTERIOR DEPTH

We can always tell a Leonardo work by his treatment of hair, angelic in its fineness, and by the lack of any rigidity of contour. One form glides imperceptibly into another (the Italian term is *sfumato*; see column, p.116), a wonder of glazes creating the most subtle of transitions between tones and shapes. The angel's face in the painting known as the *Virgin of the Rocks (139)* in the National Gallery, London, or the Virgin's face in the Paris version of the same picture, have an interior wisdom, an artistic wisdom that has no pictorial rival.

This unrivalled quality meant that few artists actually show Leonardo's influence: it is as if he seemed to be in a world apart from them. Indeed he did move apart, accepting the French King Francis I's summons to live in France. Those who did imitate him, like Bernardino Luini of Milan (c. 1485–1532), caught only the outer manner, the half-smile, the mistiness *(140)*.

The shadow of a great genius is a peculiar thing. Under Rembrandt's shadow, painters flourished to the extent that we can no longer distinguish their work from his own. But Leonardo's was a chilling shadow, too deep, too dark, too overpowering.

MICHELANGELO: A DOMINANT FORCE IN FLORENCE AND ROME

Michelangelo Buonarroti (1475–1564), on the contrary, exerted enormous influence. He, too, was universally acknowledged as a supreme artist in his own lifetime, but again, his followers all too often present us with only the master's outward manner, his muscularity and gigantic grandeur; they miss the inspiration. Sebastiano del Piombo (c. 1485–1547), for example, actually used a drawing (at least a sketch) made for him by Michelangelo for his masterwork, *The Raising of Lazarus*. Masterwork it is: yet how melodramatic it appears if compared with Michelangelo's own painting,

Michelangelo resisted the paintbrush, vowing with his characteristic vehemence that his sole tool was the chisel. As a well-born Florentine, a member of the minor aristocracy, he was temperamentally resistant to coercion at any time. Only the power of the pope, tyrannical by position and by nature, forced him to the Sistine and the reluctant achievement of the world's greatest single fresco. His contemporaries spoke about his *terribilità*, which means, of course, not so much being terrible as being awesome. There has never been a more literally awesome artist than Michelangelo: awesome in the scope of his imagination, awesome in his awareness of the significance – the spiritual significance – of beauty. Beauty was to him divine, one of the ways God communicated Himself to humanity.

140 Bernardino Luini, Portrait of a Lady, c. 1520/25, 77 x 57 cm (30½ x 22½ in)

141 Domenico Ghirlandaio, The Birth of John the Baptist, *c. 1485-90 (detail of fresco panel)*

Like Leonardo, Michelangelo too had a good Florentine teacher, the delightful Domenico Ghirlandaio (c. 1448–94). Later, he was to claim that he never had a teacher, and figuratively, this is a meaningful enough statement. However, his handling of the claw chisel does reveal his debt to Ghirlandaio's early influence, and this is evident in the cross-hatching of Michelangelo's drawings – a technique he undoubtedly learned from his master. The gentle accomplishments of a work like *The Birth of John the Baptist (141)* bear not the slightest resemblance to the huge intelligence of an early work of Michelangelo's like *The Holy Family (142*; also known as the *Doni Tondo).* This is somehow not an attractive picture with its chilly, remote beauty, but its stark power stays in the mind when more accessible paintings have been forgotten.

142 Michelangelo, The Holy Family, *c. 1503, 120 cm (47 in) diameter*

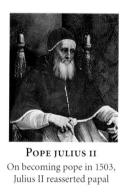

POPE JULIUS II
On becoming pope in 1503, Julius II reasserted papal authority over the Roman barons and successfully backed the restoration of the Medici in Florence. He was a liberal patron of the arts, commissioning Bramante to build St Peter's Church, Michelangelo to paint the Sistine Chapel, and Raphael to decorate the Vatican apartments.

SIBYLS

These were female seers of ancient Greece and Rome. They were also known as oracles. Like the Jewish prophets of the Old Testament, many sibyls had their sayings recorded in books. Jewish prophets spoke unbidden, whereas sibyls tended to speak only if consulted on specific questions. They sometimes answered in riddles or rhetorical questions.

THE SISTINE CHAPEL

All the same, it is the Sistine ceiling that displays Michelangelo at the full stretch of his majesty. Recent cleaning and restoration have exposed this astonishing work in the original vigour of its colour. The sublime forms, surging with desperate energy, tremendous with vitality, have always been recognized as uniquely grand. Now these splendid shapes are seen to be intensely alive in their colour, indeed shockingly so for those who liked them in their previous dim grandeur.

The story of the Creation that the ceiling spells out is far from simple, partly because Michelangelo was an exceedingly complicated man, partly because he dwells here on profundities of theology that most people need to have spelt out for them, and partly because he has balanced his biblical themes and events with giant *ignudi*, naked youths of superhuman grace *(143)*. They express a truth with surpassing strength, yet we do not clearly see what this truth actually is. The meaning of the *ignudi* is a personal one: it cannot be verbalized or indeed theologized, but it is experienced with the utmost force.

SEERS AND PROPHETS

There is the same power, though in more comprehensible form, in the great prophets and seers that sit in solemn niches below the naked athletes. Sibyls were the oracles of Greece and Rome (see column, left). One of the most famous was the Sibyl of Cumae, who, in the *Aeneid*, gives guidance to Aeneas on his journey to the underworld. Michelangelo was a heavyweight intellectual and poet, a profoundly educated man and a man of utmost faith;

144 Michelangelo, The Erythraean Sibyl *from the Sistine Chapel ceiling, 1508–12*

his vision of God was of a deity all "fire and ice", terrible, august in His severe purity. The prophets and the seers who are called by divine vocation to look upon the hidden countenance of God have an appropriate largeness of spirit. They are all persons without chitchat in them.

The *Erythraean Sibyl (144)* leans forward, lost in her book. The artist makes no attempt to show any of the sibyls in appropriate historical garb, or to recall the legends told of them by the classical authors. His interest lies in their symbolic value for humanity, proof that there have always been the spiritual enlightened ones, removed from the sad confusions of blind time.

The fact that the sibyls originated in a myth, and one dead to his heart (which longed for Christian orthodoxy) only heightens the drama. At some level we all resent the vulnerability of our condition, and if only in image, not reality, we take deep comfort in these godlike human figures. Some of the sibylline seers are shown as aged, bent, alarmed by their prophetic insight.

143 Michelangelo, Ignudo *from the Sistine Chapel ceiling, 1508–12*

THE ERYTHRAEAN SIBYL

In the Sistine Chapel, sibyls from the ancient Greek and Roman culture are "twinned" with Old Testament prophets. The God of the Jews spoke to the prophets. The sibyls, too, were wise women with superior spiritual inspiration, capable of explaining God's message to all humanity. The prophets proclaimed to the Jews alone, whereas the sibyls prophesied to the Greeks. The Erythraean Sibyl lived in the town of Erythrae in Ionia (in what is now southwest Turkey). There were many others, such as, for instance, the Egyptian Sibyl.

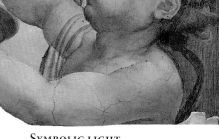

SYMBOLIC LIGHT
The cherub holds a lit torch, and the flame that issues from it looks almost like a fiery bird, the Holy Spirit come before His Pentecostal time. Significantly, the sibyl has not needed to wait for the lamp to be lighted: her light is from within, and her sureness of vision is contrasted with a dim little cherub, who rubs his eyes with baby fists.

FLOWING ROBE
Michelangelo's original colours are believed to have had a startling, luminous quality. The Sistine Chapel frescoes gradually darkened with the passage of time and in the present century three attempts have been made – the latest from 1980 to 1990 – to restore their original appearance.

PENSIVE HEAD
The sibyl leans forward, lost in her book. She turns the page with the calm deliberation of one who "sees", one in command, touched by divine clairvoyance. She is inspired and infallible, and her stately head is undaunted by what she reads. Her role as illuminator and interpreter "to spread good tidings to all the nations" (Mark 16: 15) is evidenced by the opened book, turned outwards for all to see.

TURNING THE PAGES OF TIME
The great stature of the pacific sibyl reassures us at a subliminal level, and maybe all the more effectively for that. She needs only one muscular arm to turn the pages of the future; the other hangs in relaxation. She is poised to rise and act, yet remains still, concentrating on her reading. The book rests on a lectern covered with a blue cloth, symbolizing its divine content. The colours sing in splendour, pinks glazed to whiteness by the intensity of the light.

145 Michelangelo, **The Last Judgment,** *west wall of Sistine Chapel, 1536–41, 1463 x 1341 cm (48 x 44 ft)*

The implicit sense of God's majesty (rather than His fatherhood) is made explicit in the most alarming *Last Judgment (145)* known to us. It is Michelangelo's final condemnation of a world

he saw as irredeemably corrupt, a verdict essentially heretical, though at that time it was thought profoundly orthodox. His judging Christ is a great, vengeful Apollo, and the power in this terrible painting comes from the artist's tragic despairs. He paints himself into the judgment, not as an integral person, but as a flayed skin, an empty envelope of dead surface, drained of his personhood by artistic pressure. The only consolation, when even the Virgin shrinks from this thunderous colossus, is that the skin belongs to St Bartholomew, and through this martyr's promise of salvation we understand that perhaps, though flayed alive, the artist is miraculously saved.

As grandly impassive as the Erythraean Sibyl is the heroic Adam in *The Creation of Adam (146)*, lifting his languid hand to his Creator, indifferent to the coming agonies of being alive.

INFLUENCES ON RAPHAEL

After the complexities of Leonardo and Michelangelo, it is a relief to find Raphael (Raffaello Sanzio, 1483–1520), a genius no less than they, but one whose daily ways were those of other men. He was born in the small town of Urbino, an artistic centre (see p.100), and received his earliest training from his father. Later, his father sent him to Pietro Perugino (active 1478–1523) who, like Verrocchio and Ghirlandaio, was an artist of considerable gifts. But while Leonardo and Michelangelo quickly outgrew their teachers and show no later trace of influence, Raphael

MICHELANGELO'S DAVID
Michelangelo began work on the colossal figure of David in 1501, and by 1504 the sculpture (standing at 4.34 m/14 ft 3 in tall) was in place outside the Palazzo Vecchio. The choice of David was supposed to reflect the power and determination of Republican Florence and was under constant attack from supporters of the usurped Medicis. In the 19th century the statue was moved to the Accademia.

146 Michelangelo, **The Creation of Man** *from Sistine Chapel ceiling, 1511–12*

147 Pietro Perugino, **Crucifixion with the Virgin, St John, St Jerome, and St Mary Magdalene,** *c. 1485, centre 101 x 57 cm (39½ x 22½ in)*

EXPLORER'S GLOBE
The 15th century saw an unprecedented enlargement of the known world as explorers opened up the New World of the Americas as well as the Far East. The explorers' maps made possible the production of the first terrestrial globe in 1492 (above). Painters were able to take advantage of the exotic pigments that were shipped into Italian ports.

had a precocious talent right from the beginning and was an innate absorber of influences. Whatever he saw, he took possession of, always growing by what was taught to him. An early Raphael can look very like a Perugino. In fact, Perugino's *Crucifixion with the Virgin, St John, St Jerome, and St Mary Magdalene (147)* was thought to be by Raphael until evidence proved it was given to the church of San Gimigniano in 1497, when Raphael was only 14. It is undoubtedly a Perugino, calmly emotional, and pious rather than passionate. A fascinating context for this scene of quiet faith is the notorious unbelief on the part of the artist, who was described by Vasari as an atheist. He painted what would be acceptable, not what he felt to be true, and this may account for the lack of real emotive impact.

EARLY RAPHAEL
There are still echoes of the gentle Perugino in an early Raphael like the diminutive *St George and the Dragon (148)*, painted when he was in his early twenties; the little praying princess is very Peruginesque. But there is a fire in the knight and his intelligent horse, and a nasty vigour in the convincing dragon that would always be beyond Perugino's skill. Even the horse's tail is electric, and the saint's mantle flies wide as he speeds to the kill.

148 Raphael, **St George and the Dragon,** *1504–06, 28 x 22 cm (11 x 8½ in)*

ST GEORGE
The portrayal of St George and the dragon in art symbolizes the conversion of a heathen country to Christianity. Often the place of conversion would be represented by a young woman. St George is patron saint of several European cities including Venice, and was made patron of England in 1222.

150 Raphael, The Alba
Madonna, *c. 1510,
95 cm (37½ in)
diameter*

POPE LEO X

As the second son of the
Medicean ruler Lorenzo
the Magnificent (see p.97),
Pope Leo X (1475–1521)
had an easy passage to high
office. He is best remem-
bered as a patron of the
arts and he established a
Greek college in Rome.
He encouraged the work
of artists such as Raphael
(who painted this portrait).
Despite his undoubted
inadequacies as the
spiritual head of
Christendom, his under-
standing of the human
need for great art and
architecture made him of
central importance. Such
worldliness undoubtedly
helped provoke the
Reformation (see p.169).

Raphael spent
his first sojourn in
Florence (1504–08) to
sublime purpose. At that time
Leonardo and Michelangelo were both working
there, and as a result Raphael adopted new
working methods and techniques –
particularly influenced by Leonardo
– and his paintings took on a more
vigorous graphic energy. We may
think we see a hint of what he took
from Leonardo in a work like the
Small Cowper Madonna (149), with
its softness of contour and perfection
of balance. Both faces, the Virgin's
almost smiling, almost praying,
wholly wrapped up in her Child,
and that of the Child, wholly at
ease with His Mother, dreamily
looking out at us with abstracted
sweetness, have that inwardness
we see in Leonardo, but made
firm and unproblematic. Behind
the seated figures we see a tranquil
rural landscape with a church
perched on a hill.

149 Raphael, Small Cowper Madonna
(detail), 1505, 60 x 45 cm (24 x 17 ½ in)

RAPHAEL'S LATER WORK

Raphael returned to the subject of the Madonna
and Child several times, each time in an intimate,
gentle composition. *The Alba Madonna (150),*
on the other hand, has a Michelangelic heroism
about it; tender as always in Raphael, but also
heavy; masses wonderfully composed in tondo
form; a crescendo of emotion that finds its
fulfilment in the watchful face of Mary. The
world stretches away on either side, centred on
this trinity of figures, and the movement sweeps
graciously onwards until it reaches the furthest
fold of Mary's cloaked elbow. Then it floods
back, with her bodily inclination towards the
left, and the meaning is perfectly contained:
love is never stationary, it is given and returned.
Raphael's life was short, but while he lived he
was one of those geniuses who continually
evolve and develop. He had an extraordinary
capacity (like, though greater than, Picasso's)
to respond to every movement in the art world,
and to subsume it within his own work.

THE ALBA MADONNA

Like Bellini, Raphael became a *Madonniere* – a painter of
Madonnas. Depicted like Bellini's *Madonna of the Meadow*
(see p.109) in an open landscape, *The Alba Madonna* is an example
of the Renaissance "Madonna of Humility" tradition. However,
all comparison with Bellini ends here, and it is the influence of
Michelangelo that is more evident in *The Alba Madonna*, not least
in its tondo format – derived from Michelangelo's *Holy Family*
(c. 1503), which Raphael saw in Rome (see p.121).

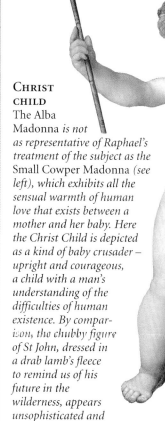

CHRIST CHILD

The Alba
Madonna *is not
as representative of Raphael's
treatment of the subject as the
Small Cowper Madonna (see
left), which exhibits all the
sensual warmth of human
love that exists between a
mother and her baby. Here
the Christ Child is depicted
as a kind of baby crusader –
upright and courageous,
a child with a man's
understanding of the
difficulties of human
existence. By compar-
ison, the chubby figure
of St John, dressed in
a drab lamb's fleece
to remind us of his
future in the
wilderness, appears
unsophisticated and
truly childlike.*

HEROISM

*The relatively
close tonal range
and restrained palette
of* The Alba Madonna *is
perfectly suited to her self-contained, gentle heroism. It is wholly
unlike the rosy glow and brilliant hues of the* Small Cowper Madonna.
The Alba Madonna's *whole demeanour, as well as her quietly mournful
gaze, expresses dignity, spiritual strength, and solidity. She meditates
on a small wooden cross that symbolizes Christ's Crucifixion.*

MADONNA'S FOOT

*The military style of the sandal
worn by the Madonna emphasizes
her warrior-like demeanour. Like
her Son, she assumes an heroic stance.
The ground on which she sits is
sprinkled with small flowers, some
in bloom. The petals are painted
delicately over the primary layer of
green earth. The flowers that St John
has gathered are anemones that
grow behind him. Round the picture
from where he kneels are a white
dandelion, what could be another
anemone, a plantain, a violet, and
three lilies, not yet in flower.*

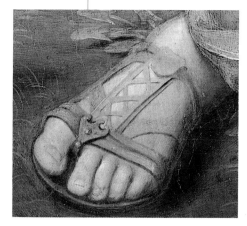

UMBRIAN COUNTRYSIDE

*Beyond the statuesque figure of
the Madonna, in the open Umbrian
landscape, is a small wood filled with
odd, tightly-foliaged trees. Beyond the
wood, still further into the distance,
are tiny horsemen. The activities of
the horsemen, too minute to make
out, are reduced almost to nothingness
by the giant-like form of the Madonna,
her remote gaze echoing their physical
distance and their essential irrelevance.*

151 Raphael, Bindo Altoviti, *c. 1515,*
60 x 44 cm (23½ x 17⅓ in)

Since Vasari (see p.98) described the picture
commissioned by *Bindo Altoviti (151)* as "his
portrait when young", historians have liked
to think that this radiant youth was Raphael
himself. He was indeed said to be unusually
handsome, pensive, and fair, which is exactly
what this portrait shows us. But it is now agreed
that it is Bindo when young, and since he was at
this time a mere 22 (and Raphael 33, with only
five years left to him), this is not an "imagined"
youth but the real boy who takes up so self-
conscious a stance before the painter.

Raphael is one of the most acute of all
portraitists, effortlessly cleaving through the
external defences of his sitter, yet courteously
colluding with whatever image the ego would
seek to have portrayed. This duality, looking
beneath the surface and yet remaining wholly
respectful of the surface, gives an additional
layer of meaning to all his portraits. We see,
and we know things that we do not see; we are
helped to encounter rather than to evaluate.

Bindo Altoviti was beautiful, successful (as
a banker), and rich: rather like Raphael himself.
There may have been some feeling of fellowship
in the work, as the noble countenance is
sensitively fleshed out for us. Half the face is
in shadow, as if to allow the sitter his
mystery, his maturing, his private
destiny. The lips are full and
sensual, balanced by the

152 Raphael, The
School of Athens,
*1510–11, 772 cm
(25 ft 4 in) wide
at base*

deep-set eyes with their confront-ational stare, almost defiant. The ruffled shirt is half-covered by the young man's locks, calculatedly casual, at odds in their dandyish profusion with the plain beret and the rich but simple doublet. He holds a darkened hand dramatically to his breast, maybe to show off the ring, maybe to indicate psychic ease.

But Raphael has not given him the real world for his setting. Bindo Aldoviti stands in a nowhere place of luminous green, outside the scope of time in his eternal youth, fearless because he is protected by art from human uncertainties.

There is an aptness in the areas of darkness in which the great doublet sleeve loses itself. For all his debonaire poise, this is a young man threatened. For the viewer who knows how short Raphael's own life was to be, the thought that this might be a self-portrait is seductively plausible. There is a sense in which every portrait is one of the self, since we never escape our own life enough to see with divine vision what is objectively there: this shows us both men, painter and banker, "when young".

Raphael is out of favour today; his work seems too perfect, too faultless for our slipshod age. Yet these great icons of human beauty can never fail to stir us: his Vatican murals can stand fearlessly beside the Sistine ceiling. *The School of Athens (152)*, for example, monumentally immortaliz-ing the great philosophers, is unrivalled in its classic grace. Raphael's huge influence on succes-sive artists is all the more impressive considering his short life.

THE HIGH RENAISSANCE IN VENICE

There is always a happy sureness, a sense of belonging, of knowing how things work, in Raphael, and it is this confidence that seems most to distinguish him from that other genius who died young, the Venetian Giorgione (Giorgio da Castelfranco, 1477–1510).

Giorgione achieved far less than Raphael (and his life was still shorter). Even the few works said to be by him are often contested, yet he has a hauntingly nostalgic grace found nowhere else in art. He trained in the workshop of the great Venetian painter Giovanni Bellini (see p.107), whose softness of contour and warm, glowing colour continue in Giorgione's work. He does

153 Giorgione, The Tempest, *1505–10, 83 x 73 cm (32½ x 28¾ in)*

not belong, as Raphael does, to this world, not even in the rarefied way that we find in his great successors, Titian (see p.131) and Tintoretto (see p.134). His alliance is to another spirit, yet one to which we instinctively respond, even if we do not always understand the logic of his works.

The Tempest (153) is one of the most argued-over works in existence. Its importance in relation to the development of Venetian painting lies in the predominance of landscape for its own sake. Fortunately, everyone accepts that this painting is by Giorgione, but who is this motionless soldier, brooding quietly in the storm, and who the naked gypsy, feeding her child and apparently unaware of any company? Attempts to read the scene as a novel version of the Flight into Egypt are usually foiled by the inexplicable fact of the woman's nakedness. Despite this, countless scenarios have been provided, all ingenious and all of them making some sense.

Elucidation has not been helped by scientific analysis, which reveals that the first draft of the work included a second naked woman, bathing in the stream. The "real meaning" may elude us, but perhaps that elusiveness is the meaning. We are shown the world lit up with the startling clarity of a sudden flash of lightning, and in that revelation we are able to behold mysteries that were hitherto concealed within the darkness.

❝ *While we may term other works paintings, those of Raphael are living things; the flesh palpitates, the breath comes and goes, every organ lives, life pulsates everywhere.* **❞**

Vasari, *Lives of the Artists*

BALDASSARE CASTIGLIONE

This portrait by Raphael is of the Renaissance diplomatist and writer Baldassare Castiglione. He was employed in the service of a number of Italian dukes in the early 16th century. His treatise *Il Cortegiano*, published in 1528, described the court at Urbino and defined the correct etiquette for courtiers to learn. Another feature of the book was its popularization of Humanist philosophy (see p.82, column).

154 Giorgione (finished by Sebastiano del Piombo),
The Three Philosophers, *c. 1509, 121 x 141 cm (47½ x 55½ in)*

The intensely poetic nature of the few undoubted Giorgiones brought a quality into Venetian High Renaissance art that it was never completely to lose. Even though finished by Michelangelo's friend, Sebastiano del Piombo,

The Three Philosophers (154) shows the potency of this lyrical richness. The actual subject-matter seems not to have mattered to the artist. He apparently began by intending a picture of the Magi (see p.98), the three eastern kings who saw the star at Christmastide and journeyed to the manger. The Magi were also believed to be astronomers, star-gazers, and from this Giorgione travelled mentally to the concept of philosophical search, plotting the stars with a sextant and pondering on their meaning.

Here too are the three ages of man, with the work being embarked upon by the serious youth, held mentally and debated by the man of maturity, and stored in material form by the elderly sage, glorious in his silken raiment.

Every detail of the three has a psychological significance: the boy is dressed in springtime simplicity, and he is solitary, as is often a youthful circumstance. Who can share his dreams and hopes? The two adult men turn inwards to themselves, seeming to converse, yet both as lonely as the passionate boy. They are elders, no longer fervent, but they bring to their problem a weighty earnestness.

The philosopher at the centre has the look of a man of affairs as he holds his hands free for work. Beside him, the older man grasps the visible signs of his thinking, a sky chart. The three human figures occupy only a half of the

BIRTH TRAYS

Like *cassoni* (see p.114), birth trays were another unusual form of Renaissance art. These colourfully painted wooden trays were used to carry gifts to new mothers and were then preserved as family heirlooms. This example from the first half of the 15th century depicts the Triumph of Love. Its 12-sided shape is typical of the period.

155 Giorgione, **The Adoration of the Shepherds,** *c. 1505/10, 91 x 111 cm (36 x 43½ in)*

picture, though. The rest – the part that gives them their significance – is tree and rock. In the rock is a dark cave, and beyond it, a rich landscape burnished by the late sun.

Two possibilities are open: to venture into the unknown, the dark cave, or to move out into the familiar beauty of the countryside; to go within, into the spirit, or to go without, into the world and its rewards. Each man, alone, faces the invitation, seriously debating the wiser course, not consulting, but responsibly considering.

It is the landscape, with its autumnal ambience, that gives the work its poignancy. Scholars tells us that the old man's beard suggests to them the philosophies of Aristotle, that the middle figure wears the oriental dress reminiscent of Islamic thought, and that the sextant in the boy's motionless hand indicates the new natural philosophy that we now call "science", but the information, true or not, seems irrelevant. The point is the poetry, the touch of interior gravity, the choice.

FORERUNNER OF TITIAN
A perfect example of Giorgione melting into Titian, who certainly finished some of Giorgione's paintings after his early death, is *The Adoration of the Shepherds (155)*, also called *The Allendale Nativity*. The balance of opinion now gives this solely to Giorgione, but it could equally be by Titian. In a way, the subject of the painting, or at least the focus of the artist's greatest interest, is the evening light, and this emphasis on light and landscape, first influenced by Giorgione, remained one of Titian's most enduring concerns. It unifies all it touches, and although there are certain activities taking place in the background, the overriding impression is of stillness and silence.

The business of the normal world has come to a stop. Parents, Child, and shepherds seem lost in an eternal reverie, a prolonged sunsetting that will never move to clocktime. Even the animals are rapt in prayer, and the sense of being shown not an actual event, but a spiritual one, is very persuasive. Giorgione transports us beyond our material confines, without denying them.

TITIAN: THE "MODERN" PAINTER
Titian (Tiziano Vecellio, c. 1488–1567), who was Giorgione's successor, was destined to have one of the longest life spans in artistic history – in contrast to Giorgione and Raphael – and was one of those few very fortunate artists (Rembrandt and Matisse were two others) who changed and grew at every stage, reaching a climactic old age. The early Titian is wonderful enough; the later Titian is incomparable.

Before working with Giorgione, Titian spent time in the workshop of Giovanni Bellini (see p.107). Bellini's mastery of oil painting techniques, which had transformed Venetian painting, was of huge importance to Titian's art – and by the same token, to the direction of subsequent Western painting. It is in Titian's paintings that we find a freedom prophetic of the art of today: the actual material of the paint is valued for its inherent expressive qualities – in harmony with, but distinct from, the narrative of the paintings. Titian is perhaps the most important of all the great painters of the Renaissance. Unlike his predecessors, who were trained as engravers, designers for goldsmiths, and other crafts, he devoted all his energies to painting, and as such was a forerunner of the modern painter.

156 *Titian,* Christ appearing to the Magdalen (Noli me Tangere), *c. 1512, 109 x 91 cm (42¾ x 36 in)*

Christ Appearing to the Magdalen (Noli me Tangere) (156) shows the youthful Titian delighting in the human interplay between the ardent Magdalen, all rich and spreading drapery, and the austere Christ, who withdraws from her with infinite courtesy.

Christ almost dances in resurrection freedom; she is recumbent with the heaviness of earthly involvements. A little tree tells us that newness of life has only just begun, and a great world stretches away towards the blue hills, remote, witnessing, leaving Mary Magdalene to her own choices. There is a touch of loneliness in the picture, a hint, too, of Giorgionesque nostalgia for a lost poetry. But fundamentally the mood has an earthly vigour.

OTHER WORKS BY TITIAN
Sacred and Profane Love
(Borghese Gallery, Rome)

Bacchanal of the Andrians
(Prado, Madrid)

Venus of Urbino
(Metropolitan Museum of Art, New York)

The Rape of Europa
(Isabella Stewart Gardner Museum, Boston)

Franciscan Friar with a Book
(National Gallery of Victoria, Melbourne)

A Young Man
(Staatliche Museen, Berlin-Dahlem)

TITIAN SELF-PORTRAIT
This painting was completed by Titian towards the end of his life when he was revered as an artist of great magnitude. He had revolutionized oil painting techniques, and was to be a great influence on artists such as Tintoretto and Rubens. He was ceremonially buried in Santa Maria dei Frari in Venice.

NOLI ME TANGERE
Titian's painting (see left) depicts the biblical story of Christ appearing before Mary Magdalene after His Resurrection. He forbids her to touch Him (*Noli me tangere*) but asks her to tell the disciples that He is risen. Mary mistook Him for a gardener, so He is shown holding a hoe.

RANUCCIO FARNESE

Ranuccio Farnese (1530–65) was the grandson of Pope Paul IV, and belonged to one of the most influential families in Italy. This portrait was painted in 1542. By then he already held the privileged position of Prior of the Order of the Hospital of St John of Jerusalem (the "Knights of Malta"), whose emblem, the Maltese Cross, is emblazoned on his cloak. Titian painted another portrait of a young aristocrat in 1542, the infant Clarissa Strozzi. Both pictures evince a warm sympathy for youth. They are full of the poignant realization of the tension between the playful world of childhood and the adult responsibilities awaiting the sitter in later life.

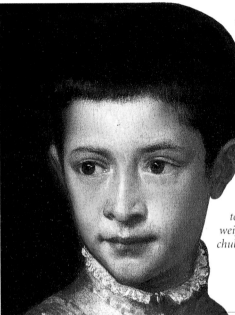

VISION OF YOUTH

At the top of the painting, above the curving swell of the satin, Titian admits the true reality of the unadorned boy, who belongs still to the realm of childhood. He has a child's fresh, unmarked skin, and his eyes are bright with reflected light. Bashfully, he does not meet our gaze, and his still-unformed mouth expresses an habitual amusement. In sharp contrast to the military paraphernalia weighing him down, we see the tender chubbiness of an untried adolescent.

MILITARY SYMBOL

The heraldic cross on Ranuccio's coat is given a metallic sheen. Thick white paint has been dragged over the graduated greys of the cross and has been applied unmixed, to create the sharpest highlights. This is the Maltese Cross, the emblem of the Knights of Malta, an order of chivalry founded in the 13th century. The order's original purpose was to administer a hospital in Jerusalem for soldiers wounded in the Holy Land while on service in the Crusades.

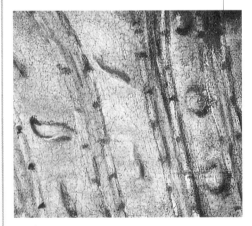

BOY'S TUNIC

The immediate focal point of this marvellous painting is the boy's brilliant red and gold satin tunic, contrasting with the warm, peachy flush of his cheeks. The rich cloth dazzles and shimmers in the light falling on the boy's chest, the red almost bleached out so that bright gold and silver remains, like the plumage of a bird. We are reminded of the tender vulnerability of the boy by the many small crimson slits that, in conjunction with the weapons, create an undercurrent of violence and pain.

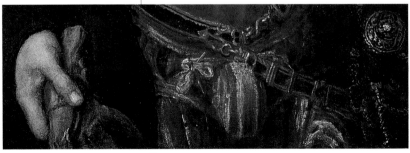

BELT AND CODPIECE

At the bottom of the painting we see the attributes of manhood – the prominent, highlighted codpiece, closed but potent for the future: many family hopes hang upon this and his putative heirs – and the clutter of belts and sword, whose steely glint is picked out in small, dot-like strokes. Titian's portrait is built upon the contrast between the innocence of youth (Ranuccio is about 12) and the outward trappings of someone belonging to one of Italy's most powerful aristocratic families.

157 Titian, Ranuccio Farnese, 1542, 90 x 74 cm (35 x 29 in)

VENUS AND OTHER MYTHS

Mythological subjects featured strongly in Titian's later work, especially in the *poesie*, a series of paintings he made for Philip II of Spain. Venus is a particularly popular figure in Renaissance art appearing in the works of Botticelli, Giorgione, Bronzino, and Correggio as well as Titian. The Roman goddess of love and fertility, Venus is the mother of Cupid, the little god of love.

ITALIAN BANKING

The first modern bank had opened in Venice in the 12th century. However, during the Renaissance, Florentine banks became the most important in Europe, many having branches around the continent. The influential Medici family owed much of its wealth and power to its banking activities. These gold florins (above) were minted and circulated in Renaissance Florence.

TITIAN'S PORTRAITURE

This portrait *(157)* from Titian's middle years shows an artist of far greater depth of spiritual insight. Now he is not revelling in the sheer technique that turns thought into image; now he is painting from his own depths, and we feel the image arises almost spontaneously.

Ranuccio Farnese (157) portrays a very young man, splendid in his courtly attire. A silver cross gleams on one breast and light sparkles on the poignard below it. But the heraldic and warlike aspects are in shadows: what is real to the boy is the glove in his other hand, a hand visibly bare,

prepared to take on the burden of living, both unafraid and unprotected. He has not yet grown into his years, and the look of expectancy on the young face is full of an unformed innocence.

We admire the dignity that Titian has seen as appropriate, but we are also touched by the all-enveloping blackness in which Ranuccio is like a small, lighted candle.

Titian's insight is almost frightening in its realism. What he does do, with superb technical skill, is show us the truth of an individual with all the attendant weakness, and yet produce a picture that is supremely beautiful.

158 Titian, Venus and Adonis, c. 1560, 107 x 136 cm (42 x 53½ in)

THE LATE TITIAN

At the very end of his life, Titian painted many mythological scenes, as deeply poetic as those of the long-dead Giorgione, but with a deeper and sadder tone. Sometimes he would repeat a composition, as if seeking the total expression of some unrealized vision. One such repeated theme is that of *Venus and Adonis (158)*, in which the goddess of love pleads with the young and beautiful Adonis to stay with her, knowing in prophetic insight that he will be killed while

hunting. Adonis will not listen, will not – typical of inexperience – believe that he can die. He is every young man going off to war or to adventure, and Venus is every woman striving to hold him back. There is a painful irony in that she is the one being who is most desired of all men, most lovely of the gods and most loved; but the excitement of the hunt has greater charm for Adonis even than sexual bliss, and he impatiently rebuffs her. There is even a sense of older woman/ younger man, another irony, since Venus is immortal and Adonis merely thinks himself so, with tragic results.

It is the quivering colour tones that make late Titian so marvellous, the soft and shimmering beauty of the flesh. Venus shows us her superb back and buttocks, beguilingly rounded, full of promise. Adonis is a hard and virile counterpart to her softness. Her coiled hair suggests her deliberateness – this is no dishevelled lady of the bedchamber, and indeed they are sleeping out- doors, under a brooding sky. The great hounds, wiser than their master, sense something amiss, and even Cupid weeps with pity.

EMOTIONAL INTENSITY

So supreme an artist is Titian that it is surprising to read that Ruskin, that most insightful of Victorian critics, thought he was surpassed by Tintoretto (1518–1594). Tintoretto's original name was Jacopo Robusti, but he came to be known as *Il Tintoretto*, meaning "little dyer" after his father's profession. In a city as small as Venice, all artists knew one another, and it is no

PUTTI
Nude children, often winged, known as *putti* (plural of the Italian *putto*, meaning a little boy) appeared in many early Renaissance paintings and sculptures. Often meant to depict angels and cupids, they originally graced the art of the ancient Greeks and Romans. This bronze statue of a *putto* with a dolphin was fashioned by Verrocchio c. 1470. (see p.116).

159 Tintoretto, The Conversion of St Paul, c. 1545, 152 x 236 cm (5 ft x 7 ft 9 in)

160 Tintoretto, **The Last Supper,** *1592–94, 366 x 569 cm (12 ft x 18 ft 8 in)*

surprise to learn that Tintoretto, about 30 years Titian's junior, declared his ambition was to combine Titian's colour with Michelangelo's drawing. "Drawing", as Michelangelo would haughtily agree, is hardly the word to use for Venetian chromatic unities: form coalesces out of light, very softly. Tintoretto, though, was an almost "hard" Venetian, in that he painted in a fury of inspiration, dashing down his first ideas and scumbling them into a whole.

The passion of his attack makes its tempestuous presence seen: there is constant excitement and a sense of the tremendous. Only a gigantic talent could hold this trembling emotion and keep it both genuine and humble, and all the major Tintorettos do indeed affect us with their total honesty and their overwhelming emotional force. A very early work, painted when he was in his twenties, *The Conversion of St Paul (159),* shows this extravagance of imaginative power.

Most painters show the conversion of St Paul as dramatic, since the not-yet saint was thrown bodily from his horse and received the divine message lying terrified on his back. But none of the other works has the wild turbulence of Tintoretto's scene. The whole visible world breaks into chaotic disfunction, as the divine

erupts into our normality. On the right, a horse stampedes away with rider and streaming banners, on the left another horse screams and rears, while its stricken rider is dazzled by the heavenly brightness above. Mountains surge, trees toss, men stagger and fall, the skies darken with ominous clouds. Paul lies in the centre, overshadowed by his fallen horse. But he does not panic; he stretches out his desperate hands, passionate for salvation.

Many of his most potent images are still in their Venetian settings. *The Last Supper (160)* is still in the chancel of San Giorgio Maggiore (see right). It is an idiosyncratic version of the Last Supper, the meal commemorated every time the Eucharist (Holy Communion) is celebrated. Little is shown of the interaction between the Apostles (we have to look hard to find Judas, usually a focal point). Tintoretto's one interest is in the gift of the Eucharist, and although many things are happening around this miracle, with cats, dogs, and servants included in the scene, all is insubstantial except for Christ and the Food of Heaven. There is a feeling that only Christ is truly real. Angels flicker and fade in the flashes of His glory, and human presence takes on some sort of nebulous coherence only when

PALLADIAN ARCHITECTURE

The influential architect Andrea Palladio (1508–80) produced a number of buildings in Vicenza, but perhaps his most famous work is San Giorgio Maggiore in Venice. Begun in 1565, the church has the facade of a classical temple.

CHRIST AT THE SEA OF GALILEE

The contrast between Duccio's picture (see p.44) of the scene in which Christ first summons Peter and Andrew, and Tintoretto's extraordinary painting could not be greater. Once again we see Christ at the Sea of Galilee, here in the middle of a violent storm. He stands on the water and calls to His amazed Apostles. But as Duccio's panel painting was all certainty and calm – the moment of revelation, frozen in time and silent – Tintoretto's canvas reveals an uncertain world, filled with danger, doubt, and confusion.

THE BOAT AND FISHERMEN

The painting is largely composed of sharp, jagged shapes and wild zigzagging movement. Not least among these is the boat, whose mast is exaggeratedly curved into a thorn shape, bending almost to breaking point in the wind. The fishermen are picked out in rough, dry daubs of paint. Only two have halos: Peter (with the brighter halo), who, with all sense of personal danger lost, leaps into the water towards Christ, and another Apostle, who steers the boat towards the shore.

STILL POINT

Amidst the violence of the storm, only the figure of Christ and the upright tree are still. All else is in turmoil. The little branch growing out of the side of the tree is flowering – a symbol of hope – and seems untroubled by the violent storm. Its grey-green leaves and tiny white petals are painted with single, thick daubs of paint.

STORMY SEA

The thrashing waves echo the drama of the storm-filled sky, with its glancing, flashing light and rolling clouds. Earth colours have been added to the greens and greys of the turbulent waves, and the warm red ground shows through linking the water to the solid earth, thereby increasing its sense of destructive might. The sharp zigzag of waves, razor-edged with thick white paint, leads our eye back and forth between Christ and the boat, and gives the impression of the earth opening up.

VISIONARY FIGURE

Christ's robes are rapidly painted, with great bravura (His halo is a quick white swirl). The thick, creamy paint forming his lower robes gives them solidity, and their strange metallic pink is made by crimson glazes over the top. Tintoretto's Christ belongs to an essentially visionary world: His body lacks substance. His feet are merely outlines in white paint, with the green of the sea showing through, and His finger melts into the distant shore.

161 Tintoretto, **Christ at the Sea of Galilee,** *c. 1575/80, 117 x 169 cm (46 in x 66½ in)*

haloed with holy brightness. There is not a moment's pretence of realism, only of underlying and sacred meaning. We either take this to heart or find it too intense.

A late Tintoretto shows *Christ at the Sea of Galilee (161)*. It is a work of immense emotional intensity. Far from presenting a frozen moment in time, it shows more than could be conveyed in a flickering instant. It is as if life could never stay still long enough to reveal what is sacred. Instead, Tintoretto paints a timeless scene of confrontation. Christ stands on the surface of a wildly tossing sea and calls His disciples. He is taut with summons, a solitary figure of majestic instancy, beckoning His divine invitation.

The Apostles are a dim mass of anxious humanity, battered by the wild sea, helpless under the storm clouds. The voice of Jesus releases them from their fearful anonymity. Peter leaps joyfully into the waters, eyes fixed only on Jesus. The ugly trenches of the waves lie between servant and Master, but Tintoretto has no doubt at all that the two will meet. Violence is powerless in the presence of God, and in consequence has no authority over a seeker after God. Tintoretto shows nature as a thing almost

of torn paper, threatening and yet defanged. In an interesting touch, we are not shown the face of Christ, only His averted profile. Peter, who looks upon Him fully, can dare the leap of faith.

Even in a lovely secular work like *Summer (162)*, there is an ecstatic, spring-like vitality in Tintoretto's paintings that makes the very corn "immortal wheat" in the words of the 17th-century English cleric and mystic poet Thomas Traherne. This earthly image is reminiscent of the third great Venetian artist, Veronese.

OTHER WORKS BY TINTORETTO

Crucifixion
(Scuola di San Rocco, Venice)

Bearded Man
(National Gallery of Canada, Ottawa)

Resurrection
(Queensland Art Gallery, Brisbane)

162 Tintoretto, **Summer,** *c. 1555, 106 x 194 cm (42 x 76 in)*

VERONESE'S MATERIAL WORLD

Veronese (Paolo Caliari, 1528–88) has been called the first "pure" painter, in that he is practically indifferent to the actuality of what he paints, and totally taken up with an almost abstract sensitivity to tone and hue. His works glow from within, decorative art at its noblest.

Veronese may not be as profound an artist as Titian or Tintoretto, but it is easy to underestimate him. His fascination for the way things look, their capacity for ideal beauty, raises his art to a high level. He shows not what is but what, ideally, could or should be, celebrating materiality with a magnanimous seriousness.

To take the superficial so earnestly is to raise it to another order of being. His *St Lucy and a Donor (163)* does not really show us a martyr; he expects us to know the story of this saint and provide the context ourselves. What he does show is the glory of young womanhood, all satins and silks and sunlit beauty. Her lovely face is enraptured, slightly timid, and a closer

163 Paolo Veronese, **St Lucy and a Donor**, *probably c. 1580, 180 x 115 cm (71 x 45 in)*

inspection of the martyr's palm, held away from her, as if reluctantly received, shows her usual emblem, an eye. But the allusion could not be more reticent, more present for form's sake. We see the elderly donor more as an admirer in the worldly way than as a devotee of her cult. The work is one of great amplitude, of confidence, and bodily delight.

The Finding of Moses (164) shows the same healthy and hopeful nature: there is an obvious and unaffected pleasure in the sheer opulence of the dress of Pharaoh's daughter and of her maidens. Everybody, including the infant Moses, is good-looking, elegant, and happy. The characters in the scene all look refreshingly uncomplicated. Trees balance the landscape to left and right. The lady looks affectionately at the attractive child. The biblical scene as such has solemn overtones, but not for Veronese. What delights him is its beautiful humanity.

It is easy to underestimate Veronese, to see him as a superb decorator producing colourful tableaux. But he carries decoration to the point where it reveals the intensity of experienced beauty and becomes powerful art in its own right. Veronese's work glows out at us with an awareness of the potential of a material world that is supremely beautiful.

164 Paolo Veronese, **The Finding of Moses**, *probably 1570/75, 58 x 44.5 cm (23 x 17½ in)*

THE ITALIAN MANNERIST PERIOD

Like "Renaissance", the term "Mannerism" applies to a broad and diverse movement, and to a certain artistic standpoint, rather than any one style. It developed out of the High Renaissance, which was in decline by the early part of the 16th century, and lasted roughly 60 years, between 1520 and 1580. Mannerist art was influenced by the work of such High Renaissance artists as Michelangelo and Raphael (who died in 1520).

The word "Mannerism" is derived from the Italian word maniera, which in the 16th century meant "style" in the sense of elegance. Because of this implication of elegance, Mannerism has long been a somewhat misleading term that has caused much confusion and disagreement among art historians. Nevertheless "style", in this sense of the word, does constitute a crucial element of Mannerism, while Mannerist painting is also often highly "mannered" in the modern sense of the word. Mannerist painting is characterized by its self-consciously sophisticated, often contrived or exaggerated elegance, its heightened or sharp colour combinations, its complex and highly inventive composition, and the technical bravado and the free-flowing line favoured by its painters.

EARLY MANNERIST PAINTING IN FLORENCE

The High Renaissance was exceptionally rich in minor painters, artists whose work often slid imperceptibly into Mannerism as they exaggerated their styles, intent upon creating excitement in the viewer. Even if this sounds contrived and self-conscious, there is nevertheless an emotional charge in the great Mannerists that can be highly effective.

Rosso (Giovanni Battista di Jacopo, 1494–1540) was known in France, where he emigrated, as Rosso Fiorentino, "the Florentine". He was a deeply neurotic man, and his art was almost wantonly a flouting of normal expectations. He employed bold, dissonant colour contrasts, and his figures often filled the entire picture frame. *Moses and the Daughters of Jethro (165)*, for example, is a fantastic jumble of nude bodies – huge, agitated, Michelangelo-like wrestlers, with a pale, terrified, half-stripped girl standing aghast amidst the carnage. Rosso is painting an idea of violence, rather than specifics, and he does so succinctly and expertly.

Pontormo (Jacopo Carucci, 1494–1556) was also an over-sensitive and neurotic man. He was sometimes known to withdraw completely from the world in order to live in seclusion. Like Rosso, his art is excitable and strange, striking us with a sort of enjoyable agitation.

Pontormo and Rosso were taught by the gifted Florentine Andrea del Sarto (1486–1531), whose soft forms, gentle colours, and emotional gestures provided a counterbalance to the rigorous athleticism of Michelangelo in Rome. His smudgy sweetness was influential, moving the Classicism of the High Renaissance towards a new Mannerist expression.

THE LAURENTIAN LIBRARY
In 1523 the Medici family commissioned Michelangelo to design a library that would hold 10,000 books and manuscripts. This, the Laurentian Library, became a forerunner of Mannerist architecture. It was 1559 before Michelangelo designed the staircase, which is recognized as a masterpiece of decorative architecture inspired by classical forms.

165 Rosso, **Moses and the Daughters of Jethro** *c. 1523, 160 x 117 cm (63 x 46 in)*

SANTA FELICITA

The Church of Santa Felicita in Florence contains the Capponi Chapel which houses Pontormo's *Deposition* as its altarpiece. The facade of the church was remodelled in 1564 with a porch added by Vasari to support the corridor connecting the Palazzo Vecchio with the Pitti Palace.

The essentially monochrome *Portrait of a Young Man (167)* is a good example of the subtle use of colour in Andrea del Sarto's work – and some contemporaries rated him as one of the four best painters of his time.

Pontormo's masterpiece is his *Deposition (166)*, painted for the altarpiece of a private chapel in Florence. Its strangely luminescent quality and lucid, unearthly light were created partly to compensate for the darkness of the chapel, but also reflect the work's emotional intensity. There is an overriding sense of vulnerability and loss; and this makes the contrast between the beautifully

167 *Andrea del Sarto*, **Portrait of a Young Man**, *c. 1517, 72.5 x 57 cm (28½ x 22½ in)*

athletic, long-limbed, classical bodies and the facial expressions of anxiety and confusion all the more pitiful. Pontormo's portrait of *Monsignor della Casa (168)* is brilliantly observed, with the prelate's long, aristocratic face giraffe-like above his auburn beard. He is hemmed in by the walls of his room, rigid and defensive, challenging the onlooker with his arrogance, and yet so pleasingly decorative to view.

166 *Pontormo*, **Deposition**, *c. 1525/28, 312 x 190 cm (10 ft 3 in x 6 ft 3 in)*

168 *Pontormo*, **Monsignor della Casa**, *c. 1541/44, 102 x 79 cm (40 x 31 in)*

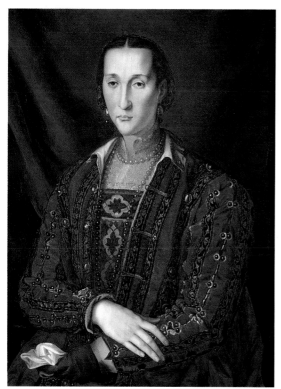

169 *Agnolo Bronzino,* Eleanora di Toledo, *c. 1560,*
85 x 65 cm (34 x 26 in)

BRONZINO'S CHILL VISION

Pontormo was the teacher and almost foster-
father of the strangely brilliant Agnolo Bronzino
(1503–72). In Pontormo's reclusive moods
Bronzino, too, was barred entrance. This may
have been because Pontormo, who was deeply
religious in a fanatic manner, picked up disturbing
undercurrents in his protégé's work. There is
a cold brilliance in Bronzino that can be very
unappetizing, even when we admire his skill.

The court did not find him unattractive,
however: his icy and rather bitter portraits
were much admired in his day, and he became
the leading Mannerist painter in Florence. His
portrait of *Eleanora di Toledo (169)* shows her
opulently dressed, dripping with costly pearls
and grimly displeased.

Bronzino's *Allegory with Venus and Cupid
(170)* used to be known as *Venus, Cupid, Folly,
and Time.* It was commissioned by Cosimo I of
Florence as a present for Francis I. The painting
was described by Vasari as a many-sided allegory about sensual pleasure and a variety of
unspecified dangers that lurk beneath the
surface. Some have seen it as referring to incest,
inherently perverse. But in 1986 a doctor suggested an extremely plausible explanation of the
allegory, arguing that it was a reference to
syphilis. The tortured figure on the left is an
intricately worked illustration crammed with
the clinical symptoms of the disease and one or

two of the side effects of treatments that were
used in the 16th century. The allegory, by this
reading, is that illicit love is attended by Fraud,
who offers a honeycomb. A child representing
the deceived will rushes to enjoy pleasure. The
result of the ignorant embrace is syphilis. Time
exposes the sickness by pulling away the blue
backcloth, to reveal the truth that is hidden
from Venus and Cupid.

SPIRITUALITY OF CORREGGIO

A Renaissance painter with a Mannerist mind
was Correggio (Antonio Allegri, c. 1489–1534),
who lived in Parma. He was one of the very
great artists, intensely physical and yet steadily
aware of light and its spiritual significance.
Correggio was a follower of Mantegna (see
p.103), and that inner solidity keeps his
excesses reasonable and, still more, lovable.

A turning point in the development of
Correggio's artistic identity came after a stay in
Rome as a young man, where he saw at first hand
the work of Michelangelo (see p.120) and Raphael

CONTEMPORARY ARTS
1542 University of Pisa founded by Cosimo de' Medici
1548 Hotel de Bourgogne, the first roofed theatre, opens in Paris
1553 The violin begins to develop into its modern form
1561 The English philosopher Francis Bacon is born
1578 The catacombs of Rome are discovered

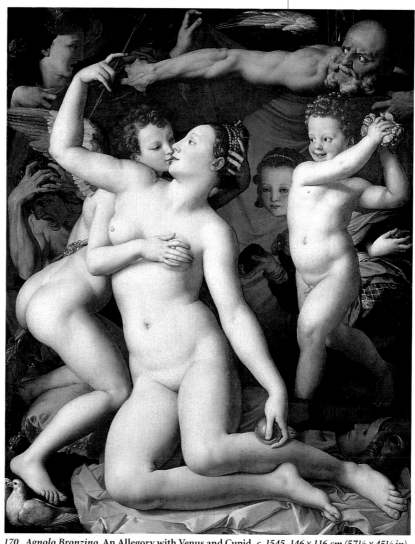

170 *Agnolo Bronzino,* An Allegory with Venus and Cupid, *c. 1545, 146 x 116 cm (57½ x 45½ in)*

**171 Correggio, The Mystic Marriage of St Catherine,
c. 1510/15, 28 x 21 cm (11 x 8¼ in)**

(see p.124). He soon became the leading artist
in Parma. His *Venus, Satyr, and Cupid (172)*
has a complete sensual abandon, yet there is
an innocence in its fleshliness, a feeling of
living in the age before the Expulsion from
Eden. Each body reflects the moonlight
individually and differently, the proportions
subtly wrong, but thereby all the more
morally reassuring.

There is precisely the same sort of fleshly
sweetness in his religious pictures, such as
The Mystic Marriage of St Catherine (171).
The legend, that Catherine had a vision in
which the Child Jesus betrothed her with a
ring, is no longer thought of as literally true,
yet it has a deeper meaning, one of consecration,
and above all, of the vow of chastity. St Catherine
kneels, oblivious to her saintly partner, who
leans forward with an expression of deep
reverence. Indeed the whole painting, small but
emotionally expansive, is infused with a profound
awareness of the sacred.

Correggio was important as a precursor to
the Mannerism movement, rather than a
Mannerist artist himself. In fact, his greatest
contribution to Mannerism and the Baroque
(see p.176) are his wonderful illusionistic
ceiling frescoes, painted inside the domes of
great churches in Parma.

Unfortunately, these frescoes defy reproduction.
We have to stand inside Parma Cathedral,
looking up into the light-filled *Assumption of
the Virgin*; we have to be there in the church
of San Giovanni Evangilista, tilting our heads
in awe at *The Vision of St John the Evangelist*.
Only experience enables us to appreciate the
skill of foreshortening and the over-whelming
impression of actuality, which were to culminate
in the technical wizardry of the Mannerists.

THE ELEGANCE OF PARMIGIANINO

Parmigianino (Girolamo Francesco Maria
Mazzola, 1503–40) was an artist of the utmost
elegance, subsuming all reality in sheer grace.
The Madonna with the Long Neck (173) is his
best-known and most typical picture. Mary is
a swanlike lady, set amid a wholly improbable
scene of ruins and curtains, elongated not only

172 Correggio, **Venus, Satyr, and Cupid,** *1524/25,
190 x 124 cm (6 ft 3 in x 48½ in)*

173 Parmigianino, **The Madonna with the Long Neck,** *1534–40, 215 x 132 cm (85 x 52 in)*

GRINDING PIGMENTS

This red ochre drawing by Parmigianino shows a workshop assistant grinding pigments. During their apprenticeships the artists learned to identify, grind, and blend the pigments. In oil painting the pigments would be suspended in vegetable oils derived from linseed, walnuts, sunflower seeds, poppy seeds, or other plant sources. Using a build-up of different-coloured pigments on the canvas imparted a light and liquidity that would be impossible using egg tempera.

ISABELLA D'ESTE

Recognized during the Renaissance for her exceptional talent and intellectual ability, Isabella d'Este (1474–1539) was a great patron of literature and art. She gathered a coterie of intellectuals, one of whom was Baldassare Castiglione (see p.129), to educate her, and employed the great artists of the time, including Correggio. There are portraits of her by a number of artists, notably Leonardo and Titian (shown above).

of neck but of person, with a long, elegant Child on her lap, insecurely posed but unworryingly so, since this is a world where the vulgarities of gravity do not apply. A long-legged angel, ravishingly beautiful, is only the first of a throng of similar exquisites. Everything sweeps upwards, like the background pillar, as if floating heavenwards and bearing us all along in its sweep.

DOSSI IN FERRARA

Dosso Dossi (c. 1490–1542), from Ferrara, is touched with the same light of fantasy as Parmigianino (see p.142). He was Court Painter to Lucrezia Borgia (see column, left), and there has been speculation that it is she who was the inspiration behind the magical *Circe and Her Lovers in a Landscape (174)*. It is an enchanting picture in a double sense, not least because of the possible initial misreading of Circe's body. Her left leg is modestly cloaked, but at first it can seem strangely absent, as if she strides across from another world into ours. The men magicked into animals have both pathos and humour, with a touch of cruelty congenial to the Borgia ménage. Yet Circe has a yearning face, and perhaps the strongest note in the picture is one of sadness and desire.

LOTTO IN VENICE

There is this same strain of sadness in Lorenzo Lotto (c. 1480–1556), a highly idiosyncratic painter who mingles his sadness with a disinterested human curiosity. He always gives us a slanting view, provocative and thoughtful, coloured by

175 Lorenzo Lotto, St Catherine, c. 1522, 57 x 50 cm (22½ x 20 in)

Giovanni Bellini's continuing influence in Venice. Lotto is famous especially for his portraits, where his weird and original insights found splendid scope, but even in an apparent religious image, there is the same enigmatic and offbeat inventiveness. *St Catherine (175)* tilts her charming head to one side and regards us thoughtfully. She has generously hidden from us her spiked wheel, covering it with the rich folds of her green mantle, and she rests her hands comfortably on its rotundity. The artist clearly suspects that her neck cross is essentially as much adornment as is her pearled crown, yet we believe totally in her. We may not believe in this Catherine as a saint, but that she is a real woman whom Lotto painted comes across with great clarity.

BECCAFUMI IN SIENA

Domenico Beccafumi (1485–1551) was the last great Sienese artist of the High Renaissance, just as Dossi was the last great Ferrarese. He is not an easy painter, with his sudden transitions from dark to light, his oddly proportioned figures, and his unusual acidic colours reminiscent of the Florentine Mannerist Rosso Fiorentino (see p.139). Beccafumi's figures can seem to loom up at us, disconcertingly, and his use of perspective, though sophisticated,

174 Dosso Dossi, Circe and Her Lovers in a Landscape, c. 1525, 101 x 136 cm (39½ x 53½ in)

176 Domenico Beccafumi, **The Fall of the Rebel Angels,**
c. 1524, 345 × 225 cm (11 ft 4 in × 7 ft 5 in)

is personal to himself. *The Fall of the Rebel Angels
(176)* is a tangle of dimly lit forms, hallucinatory
in its horror, yet shot though with the memories
of Sienese graciousness (see p.43).

EL GRECO: PASSIONATE VISIONARY

The greatest Mannerist of them all is the Spanish
painter El Greco (Domenicos Theotokopoulos,
1541–1614, called "El Greco" because he was
born in Crete). His artistic roots are diverse:
he travelled between Venice, Rome, and Spain
(settling in Toledo). The Christian doctrines
of Spain made a crucial impact on his approach
to painting, and his art represents a blend of
passion and restraint, religious fervour and
Neo-Platonism, influenced by the mysticism
of the Counter-Reformation (see p.176, 187).

El Greco's elongated figures, ever straining
upwards, his intense and unusual colours, his
passionate involvement in his subject, his ardour
and his energy, all combine to create a style that
is wholly distinct and individual. He is the great
fuser, and also the transfuser, setting the stamp
of his angular intensity upon all that he creates.
To the legacies of Venice, Florence, and Siena, he
added that of the Byzantine tradition, not necessarily in form but in spirit (although he did in
fact train as an icon painter in his early years in

177 El Greco, **Madonna and Child with St Martina and
St Agnes,** *1597–99, 194 × 103 cm (76 × 40½ in)*

Crete). El Greco always produces icons, and it is
this interior gravity of spirit that gives his odd
distortions a sacred rightness.

The *Madonna and Child with St Martina
and St Agnes (177)* sweeps us up from our
natural animal level, there at the bottom with

GALILEO GALILEI
The foremost philosopher, physicist, and astronomer of the Renaissance was Galileo (1564–1642). He held an heliocentric view of the world (believing that the world revolved around the sun) and was considered a heretic by the Church. He developed a telescope (shown above) that was powerful enough to show the mountains and valleys of the moon.

In 1633 he was put under house arrest for his astronomical teachings; later he was forced to disown them publicly.

St Martina's pensive lion and St Agnes' lamb, balancing with unnatural poise on the branch of her arm. Martina's palm of martyrdom acts like a signal, as do the long, impossibly slender fingers of Agnes.

We are drawn irresistibly up, past the flutter of cherubic wing and the rich swirl of virginal robe, kept to the pictorial centre by those strangely papery or sheet-like clouds peculiar to El Greco. Up, up, rising through the curve of Mary's cloak until we are drawn to the heart of the work, the Child and, above Him, the oval serenity of the Madonna's countenance. We are continually on the move, but never left to our own devices. We are guided and directed by El Greco, with praying figures at the corners to hold us in the right position.

UNRESOLVED QUESTIONS

Such a dramatic and insistent art can seem too obtrusive: we may long to be left to ourselves. But this psychic control is essential to El Greco, the great – in the nicest sense – manipulator. Even when we cannot really understand the picture, as in the *Laocoön (178)*, we have no doubt that something portentous is taking place and that we are diminished to the extent we cannot participate. The literal reference to the Trojan priest and his sons is clear enough (see p.20). But who are the naked women, one of whom seems to be double-headed? Even if the extra head is indicative of the work being unfinished, it is still uncannily apposite. *The Laocoön* was overpainted after El Greco's death, and the "second head" that looks into the painting was obliterated, while the two standing frontal nudes were given loincloths. Later, these features were restored to the form that we see now.

The serpents seem oddly ineffectual, thin and meagre; we wonder why these muscular males have such trouble overcoming them. And we feel that this is an allegory more than a straightforward story, that we are watching evil and temptation at work on the unprotected bodies of mankind. Even the rocks are materially unconvincing, made of the same non-substance as the high and clouded sky.

The less we understand, the more we are held enthralled by this work. It is the implicit meaning that always matters most in El Greco, that which he conveys by manner rather than by substance, gleaming with an unearthly light that we still, despite the unresolved mysteries, do not feel to be alien to us. No other of the great Mannerists carried manner to such height or with such consistency as El Greco.

OTHER WORKS BY EL GRECO

Lady in a Fur Wrap (Pollock House, Glasgow)

The Burial of Count Orgaz (Church of Santo Tome, Toledo)

The Resurrection (Prado, Madrid)

St Bonaventura (National Gallery of Victoria, Melbourne)

St Francis in Ecstasy (Museum of Fine Arts, Montreal)

St Peter in Tears (Nasjonalgalleriet, Oslo)

178 El Greco, Laocoön, c. 1610, *137 x 173 cm (54 x 68 in)*

LAOCOÖN

El Greco's painting depicts events best known to us from Virgil's *Aeneid*, but El Greco probably knew them from the Greek writer Arctinus of Miletus. Laocoön tried to dissuade the Trojans from letting in the treacherous wooden horse (which led to the sacking of Troy). In the Arctinus version Laocoön, a priest, was killed by serpents sent by Apollo for breaking his priestly rule of celibacy (in Virgil the gods intervened openly on the Greek side).

MYSTERY WITNESSES

The figures who appear to watch the scene with indifference are a mystery. One, a woman, seems to be two-headed, with one head looking out of the painting. The figures could be Apollo and Athena, come down to witness the judgment on Laocoön.

COILED SERPENT

El Greco's wonderful circular invention of the boy wrestling with the serpent creates a powerful physical tension. We are kept in suspense as to whether the boy will end the same way as his brother lying dead on the ground. El Greco's unique and unorthodox style admits an unprecedented freedom. Around the boy's outstretched arm there is a broad band of black, which has no spatial "meaning" as such, and which emphasizes the rigidity of the arm and the desperate efforts of the boy. The line flows around the strange, stone-coloured figures.

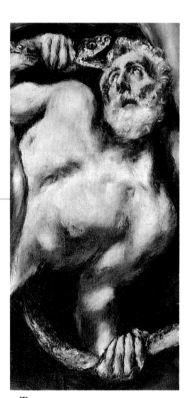

THE EPONYMOUS SUFFERER

The anguished head of Laocoön is an example of the artist's characteristic light, rapid, feathery brushwork. Where skin meets skin – in between toes, lips, nostrils – he has applied crimson or vermilion, breathing life and a suggestion of life-blood into the death-like steely greys of the flesh.

A SPANISH TROY

The allegorical horse in the middle distance trots towards the city, which is spread out under a glowering, doom-laden sky. It is a beautiful landscape, in which the vibrant, red-earth ground is covered with a lattice of silvers, blues, and greens. However, this is not the ancient city of Troy, but El Greco's home town of Toledo in Spain. El Greco painted Laocoön *during the time of the Spanish Catholic Counter-Reformation, and his allegorical drama, of transgressing mortals and vengeful gods, set unequivocally in his own modern Spain, is an indication of the orthodoxy of the artist's religious beliefs.*

THE NORTHERN RENAISSANCE

Having closed the Gothic chapter with the anguished realism of Matthias Grünewald, in order to concentrate on that most momentous of movements, the Italian Renaissance, we now return to the North, picking up the thread where we left off.

The 16th century heralded a new era for painting in the Netherlands and Germany. Northern artists were influenced by the great innovations in the South; many artists travelled to Italy to study; and the Renaissance concern for bringing modern science and philosophy into art was also evident in the North. There was, however, a difference of outlook between the two cultures. In Italy, change was inspired by Humanism, with its emphasis on the revival of the values of classical antiquity. In the North, change was driven by another set of preoccupations: religious reform, the return to ancient Christian values, and the revolt against the authority of the Church.

Pieter Brueghel, The Wedding Feast, *c. 1567–68 (detail)*

NORTHERN RENAISSANCE TIMELINE

The Renaissance in the North crystallized around the intense vision and realism of Dürer's work. Other painters in both Germany and the Netherlands followed the Northern impulse for precise observation and naturalism in the fields of landscape painting (Patinir and Brueghel) and portraiture (Holbein). As in Italy, the Northern Renaissance ended with a Mannerist phase. Mannerism was to last about a generation longer in the North than it did in Italy, where it was outmoded by 1600.

ALBRECHT DÜRER, MADONNA AND CHILD, C. 1505
Dürer's work is characterized by an intense scrutiny that enabled him to depict the innermost depths of his subjects. He sees through to the heart of his subject, whether his theme is portraiture or religious (p.153).

LUCAS CRANACH, CRUCIFIXION WITH THE CONVERTED CENTURION, 1536
In the course of his long career, Cranach developed two styles. Popular paintings such as nudes were sold privately to wealthy patrons, and court paintings were produced on official commission. These were either portraits or religious works. This Crucifixion, which alludes to the Gospel story of the centurion, shows Cranach tackling the task of devotional work. His sincerity is compromised by his own personal commitment to Humanism and his support for the Reformation, which questioned the value of religious imagery (p.158).

1500	1515	1530	1545

JOACHIM PATINIR, CHARON CROSSING THE STYX, 1515–24
Elements of Gothic style are visible in Patinir's work from the early Northern Renaissance. Charon, the mythical ferryman, is taking his passenger to Hades, the Greek equivalent of Hell, which is depicted as a war-torn landscape with burning buildings and tortured, despairing people in the manner of Hieronymus Bosch (see p.72). This work is, at the same time, an early foreshadowing of the Northern landscape tradition (p.166).

HANS HOLBEIN THE YOUNGER, CHRISTINA OF DENMARK, 1538
In the work of Holbein, we find the other face of portrait painting, in contrast to that of Dürer. Holbein was able to show the surface, without close inquiry into the inner life of the sitter. This distanced approach suited his work as a court and diplomatic portraitist to Henry VIII of England. Christina was not a queen but the Duchess of Milan and a member of the Danish aristocracy. She granted Holbein an audience of only three hours in which to sketch for this powerful picture (p.160).

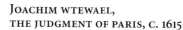

JOACHIM WTEWAEL,
THE JUDGMENT OF PARIS, C. 1615
Wtewael was one of the leading Mannerist painters in the
Northern Netherlands. His work shows a preoccupation with
elegant figure painting, in which the subjects are invariably
seen in distorted poses and a characteristically acidic range of
colours. This scene has the typically artificial Mannerist setting,
a fantasy woodland populated with elegant creatures (p.165).

SCHOOL OF FONTAINEBLEAU,
DIANA THE HUNTRESS, C. 1550
The Gothic castle at Fontainebleau
outside Paris was developed by King
Francis I (1514–47) as a cultural and
artistic centre. The king employed artists
and sculptors from Italy, and Fontaine-
bleau became an entry point through
which Southern influence made its way
into Northern Europe. The poets of the
school of Fontainebleau treated Diana
as the most important of the gods, more
so even than Venus. The way Diana is
painted shows well the sinuous line and
decorative pose that appeared in so much
Mannerist art (p.164).

PIETER BRUEGHEL, THE
WEDDING FEAST, 1567–68
This is one of a number of works in
which Brueghel took as his theme the
life of the contemporary peasant. For
a sophisticated intellectual, it was an
extraordinary achievement to enter
so profoundly into the crude vitality
of these scenes. Despite their rough
humour, Brueghel's peasant scenes
exude an almost guilty compassion
for the degradation in which the
peasants lived (p.168).

| 1560 | 1575 | 1590 | 1610 |

PIETER BRUEGHEL, HUNTERS IN THE SNOW, 1565
It was part of Brueghel's universality that he excelled in
landscapes as well as focusing closely on human nature. In 1565
he painted a series of landscapes linked to months of the year,
thus continuing the tradition of calendar illustrations seen in
the "books of hours" (see p.55). In the books of hours, peasant
activities were shown in alternate panels with scenes from court
life. In Brueghel's series, only the peasant scenes are known,
at least today. Another of this series is Gloomy Day (see p.171).

BARTHOLOMEUS SPRANGER,
VULCAN AND MAIA, C. 1590
Frankly sensuous poses, attenuated figures,
and a strong element of fantasy make this
a quintessential work of Mannerism (p.165).

DÜRER AND GERMAN PORTRAITURE

Dürer was so great an artist, so searching and all-encompassing a thinker, that he was almost a Renaissance in his own right – and his work was admired by contemporaries in North and South alike. The 16th century saw the emergence of a new type of patron, not the grand aristocrat but the bourgeois, eager to purchase pictures in the newly developed medium of woodcut printing. The new century also brought an interest in Humanism and science, and a market for books, many of which were illustrated with woodcuts. The accuracy and inner perception of Dürer's art represent one aspect of German portraiture; another is seen in the work of that master of the court portrait, Holbein.

OTHER WORKS BY DÜRER

Young Girl Wearing a Beret
(Staatliche Museen, Berlin-Dahlem)

A Young Man
(Palazzo Rosso, Genoa)

Virgin and Child
(Alte Pinakothek, Munich)

Salvator Mundi
(Metropolitan Museum of Art, New York)

Adam
(Prado, Madrid)

Adoration of the Trinity
(Kunsthistorisches Museum, Vienna)

Impressive though others may be, the great German artist of the Northern Renaissance is Albrecht Dürer (1471–1528). We know his life better than the lives of other artists of his time: we have, for instance, his letters and those of his friends. Dürer travelled, and found, he says, more appreciation abroad than at home. The Italian influence on his art was of a particularly Venetian strain, through the great Bellini (see p.106), who, by the time Dürer met him, was an old man. Dürer was exceptionally learned, and the only Northern artist who fully absorbed the sophisticated Italian dialogue between scientific theory and art, producing his own treatise on proportion in 1528. But although we know so much about his doings, it is not easy to fathom his thinking.

Dürer seems to have united a large measure of self-esteem with a deep sense of human unfulfilment. There is an undercurrent of exigency in all he does, as if work was a surrogate for happiness. He had an arranged marriage, and friends considered his wife, Agnes, to be mean and bad-tempered, though what their real marital relations were, nobody can tell. For all his apparent openness, Dürer is a reserved man, and perhaps it is this rather sad reserve that makes his work so moving.

The Germans still tended to consider the artist as a craftsman, as had been the conventional view during the Middle Ages. This was bitterly unacceptable to Dürer, whose *Self-portrait (179)* (the second of three) shows him as slender and aristocratic, a haughty and foppish youth, ringletted and impassive. His stylish and expensive costume indicates, like the dramatic mountain view through the window (implying wider horizons), that he considers himself no mere limited provincial. What Dürer insists on above all else is his dignity, and this was a quality that he allowed to others too.

Even a small and early Dürer has this momentousness about it. His *Madonna and Child (180)*, which manifestly follows the Venetian precedent of the close-up, half-figure portrait, was once thought to be by Bellini. To Dürer, Bellini was an example of a painter who could make the ideal become actual. But Dürer can never quite believe in the ideal, passionately though he longs for it. His Madonna has a portly, Nordic handsomeness, and the Child a snub nose and massive jowls. All the same, He holds His apple

179 Albrecht Dürer, Self-portrait, 1498, 52 x 40 cm (20½ x 16 in)

180 *Albrecht Dürer,* **Madonna and Child,** *c. 1505, 50 x 40 cm (20 x 16 in)*

❝*I hold that the perfection of form and beauty is contained in the sum of all men.***❞**

Dürer, Four Books on Human Proportions, 1528

DÜRER WOODCUTS
In 1498 Dürer produced his first great series of woodcuts: a set of illustrations for the Apocalypse (the Book of Revelations). He would complete more than 200 woodcuts during his lifetime. The illustration above is a detail of one of these, *The Four Horsemen of the Apocalypse.* This is an allegorical representation of War, Hunger, Plague, and Death.

ART IN GERMANY AND THE LOW COUNTRIES
During the High Renaissance a number of Italian artists visited Northern Europe, but were generally critical of Northern art. Despite this, the North had a strong tradition of learning and the arts. There were many lively centres of artistic and intellectual achievement such as Vienna, Nuremberg, and Wittenberg. Certainly by Dürer's time a Renaissance in the North was overdue.

in exactly the same position as in Dürer's great engraving of Adam and Eve, and this attitude is pregnant with significance. The Child seems to sigh, hiding behind His back the stolen fruit that brought humanity to disaster and that He is born to redeem. On one side is the richly marbled wall of the family home; on the other, the wooded and castellated world. The sad little Christ faces a choice, ease or the laborious ascent, and His remote mother seems to give Him little help. Beautiful though the work is in

colour, and fascinating in form, it is this personal emotion that always makes Dürer an artist who touches our heart, somehow putting out feelers of moral sensibility.

There is an almost obsessive quality about a great Dürer. One feels the weight of a sensibility searching into the inner truth of his subject. It is this inwardness that interests Dürer, an inner awareness that is always well contained within the outer form (he is a great portrait painter) but which lights it from within.

Having rejected the Gothic art and philosophy of Germany's past, Dürer is the first great Protestant painter, calling Martin Luther (see column, p.156) "that Christian man who has helped me out of great anxieties". These were secret anxieties, that hidden tremulousness that keeps his pride from ever becoming complacent. Although there is no reason why any Catholic artist should not have painted *The Four Apostles (181)*, nor why such an artist should not equally have chosen first John and Peter (indisputably biblical Apostles), then Paul and Mark (mere disciples, not ordained by Christ in the Gospel story, though they were great preachers of the Word), it strikes a definitely Protestant note.

These four embody the four temperaments: sanguine, phlegmatic, choleric, and melancholic. Dürer had a consistent interest in medicine and its psychological concomitants, since in some way he found humankind mysterious.

*181 Albrecht Dürer, **The Four Apostles**, 1523–26, 215 x 75 cm (85 x 29½ in) (each panel)*

THE FOUR APOSTLES

Together the four Apostles make a whole, just as the four temperaments meet within an individual. Dürer is depicting many things at once: the wholeness of humanity, the unity that makes a church, the need to live united without a hierarchy, the interests of various kinds of men. The painting is infinitely satisfying, full, strong, almost sculptural in its awareness of space. The four stand against a black background, heroic in their individualism and their comradeship.

PAUL AND MARK
Mark is the choleric man, with angry eyes aglare. He is looking away to the right, almost as if to ward off danger. Masking him is the melancholic Paul, a tall brooder, who holds his Gospel closed and is watching us suspiciously out of the corner of his eye. Paul is visually redeemed by the amplitude of his flowing white garments, so creamy and so heavy that they fall in deep, shadowed folds. Shadows are part of melancholy, yet they have great dignity.

JOHN AND PETER
John is the sanguine man, hopeful and at peace, his ruddy cheeks matched by the full, flowing red of his cloak and by the auburn curls on his handsome head. As the writer of one of the Gospels, he holds a book. Peter, the phlegmatic, holds his papal keys impassively. He stands with bald head shining, face inexpressive, his body hidden behind John's impressive bulkiness. (There is surely a touch of acid wit in so diminishing the impulsive Peter, the appointed Keeper of the Keys.)

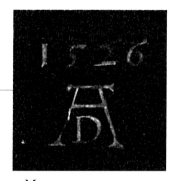

MONOGRAM AND YEAR
Dürer's distinctive "AD" monogram appears on virtually all his work. As if to emphasize his non-Italian, Germanic identity, he usually ignored the common practice of adding a Latin phrase to the signature. On the rare occasions when he did, he described himself as "Albertus Durer Noricus" – Albrecht Dürer of Nuremberg.

JOHN'S GOSPEL
St John's normal attribute is a chalice, the cup used at the Last Supper and, in symbolic form, at communion. Dürer departs from tradition by using St John's Gospel as an attribute. The open page shows the first words of a chapter, which on close inspection prove to be the German text of Luther's Bible translation, another indication of Dürer's Protestant sympathies.

182 Albrecht Dürer, The Painter's Father, 1497, 50 x 40 cm (20 x 16 in)

MARTIN LUTHER
This portrait of the religious reformer Martin Luther (1483–1546) is by Cranach. In 1517 Luther drafted 95 theses opposing the contemporary emphasis on ritual and denouncing the decadence of the Church. In 1521 Luther (then under house arrest) translated the New Testament into German. By 1546 much of Germany had been converted to Protestantism.

Dürer came from a Hungarian family of goldsmiths, his father having settled in Nuremberg in 1455. In *The Painter's Father (182)* Dürer shows the face with respectful sensitivity. The technique is pencil-like, precise, and enquiring; the description achieved has a hard brilliance. However, the rest of the picture may be incomplete, or not all Dürer's work. The rudimentary background is a far cry from the detailed one in Dürer's own *Self-portrait* (see p.152), and the sitter's clothing is hardly more than sketched in.

THE SEDUCTIVE NUDES OF CRANACH
Lucas Cranach, the Elder (1472–1553), born one year after Dürer, is as self-determined as Dürer but without his spiritual concentration. From an early stage in his career, Cranach was able to obtain copies of Dürer's woodcut prints, and his familiarity with these was to have lasting influence on his painting, with its sharp definition and brilliant colour.

Cranach was almost two painters in one – artistically schizophrenic, as it were. His most popular works are the decidedly seductive nudes with which he delighted his aristocratic patrons. These coy creatures have the rare distinction of fitting in with modern tastes, being slender, free-spirited, and even kinky. They have a sort of refined sexuality, but it is also cold and teasing: we are tempted to think that Cranach did not really care for women and may even have feared them. His *Nymph of the Spring (183)* has hung

up her hunting arrows, but the presence of a pair of partridges (birds of Venus) suggests that it is the human heart that she hunts. A distinctly diaphanous wisp of silk draws attention to her loins by "covering" them, she wears her jewellery provocatively, and she is clearly only pretending to be asleep, propped up on the thick, sensual velvet of her dress. She sprawls before us, part of the landscape and in a sense its essence. A Latin inscription on the upper left reminds us that this is a nymph of a sacred fountain. She is not a secular image, despite her alluring nakedness. We are warned not to break, not to shatter her holy slumbers. Love, Cranach is telling us, is something we have to approach with delicate reverence. A meaningful landscape surrounds her. Close by is the mysterious, symbolic cave in the rock – again, an image of sacred sexual symbolism, the female hollow. Beyond that there is the world of commerce and battle, church and family, in which the sacred realities of sex are played out in actual life.

THE HOLY ROMAN EMPIRE

This was a confederation of kingdoms and princi-palities across Europe, though the German lands were always the chief component. The emperor was elected by the German princes together with a number of archbishops.

183 Lucas Cranach, the Elder, **The Nymph of the Spring,** *after 1537, 48 x 73 cm (19 x 29 in)*

CRANACH'S COURT PAINTINGS

The other Cranach was also in great demand at the German courts, these being the excessively (and superficially) religious mini-courts of the Germanic states. He had a large workshop, which was busied with the production of copies of his more successful or popular pictures. His religious scenes are not always very convincing, even if the orthodoxy is impeccable: the soldier in his *Crucifixion with the Converted Centurion (185)*, a Teuton down to his monstrous feathered hat and studded armour, seems out of place beneath the Cross.

His portraits of these same Teutons, though, when the religious trappings are left aside, can be hypnotically powerful. He painted a great many court portraits, always ornately extravagant and materially decadent in mood. The fanatic precision of the dress, the elaboration of necklaces and rippling hair, and, above the grandeur, the wistful child face, make his *Princess of Saxony (184)* one of the most appealing images of the

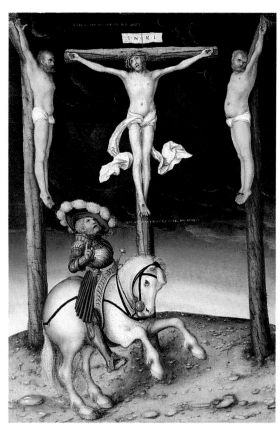

185 **Lucas Cranach the Elder,** The Crucifixion with the Converted Centurion, *1536, 50 x 35 cm (20 x 14 in)*

child in art. She is both regal and vulnerable, a princess in her splendid attire of golden chains and her scarlet-and-white dress, and a child in her open-eyed and wondering innocence. Cranach perplexes the eye with the intermingling of her soft, waving hair with her golden chains, an apt symbol for a princess.

HANS HOLBEIN THE YOUNGER

Cranach's little girl, over-dressed and over-decorated, makes an interesting contrast with Holbein's little boy *(186)*, who carries the splendour of his attire without question. The boy is, of course, not some anonymous Saxon, however noble, but the only son of the mighty King Henry VIII of England.

Hans Holbein (1497/8–1543) was educated in his father's studio in Augsburg, but early in his career he left his native Germany for Basle in Switzerland. It was in Basle that Holbein met the reformist scholar Desiderius Erasmus (see column, p.154). Erasmus provided an entry to English court circles, where Holbein eventually received royal patronage from King Henry VIII.

The English penchant for the portrait found its complete satisfaction in Holbein's shrewd, subtle, and respectful eye, his infinitely accurate and yet ennobling hand. The small Edward was the apple of his fearsome father's eye.

184 **Lucas Cranach the Elder,** A Princess of Saxony, *c. 1517, 43 x 34 cm (17 x 13½ in)*

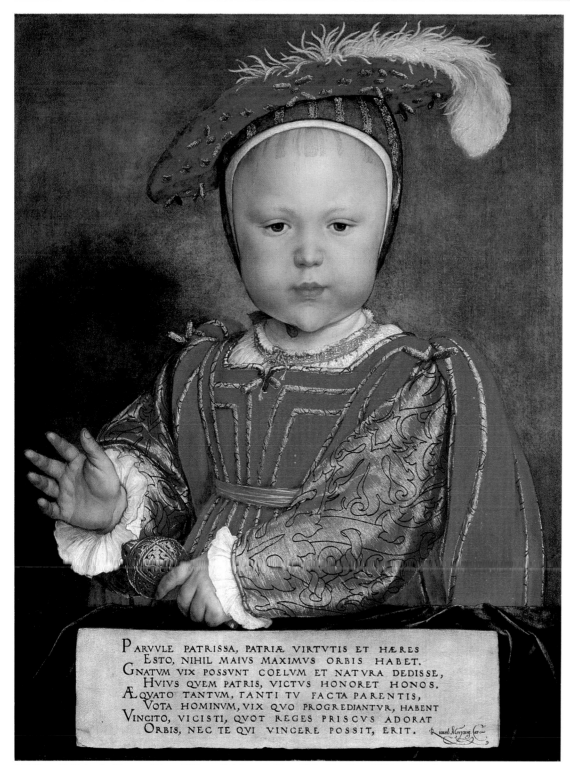

186 Hans Holbein, the Younger, **Edward VI as a Child,** *probably c. 1538, 57 x 44 cm (22½ x 17⅓ in)*

CONTEMPORARY ARTS

1512
First use of the word "masque" to denote a poetic drama

1515
The first nationalized factories for the production of tapestries are opened in France

1520
The Royal Library of France founded by King Francis at Fontainebleau

1549
Court jesters appear in Europe

FREDERICK THE WISE
Lucas Cranach spent most of his career as the Court Painter to Frederick the Wise, Elector of Saxony. The Electorate of Saxony was an independent state with a hereditary title (although part of the Holy Roman Empire, see p.157) which Frederick inherited in 1486. He was an intelligent, forward-thinking man who founded the University of Wittenberg and invited Luther to lecture on religious reform. He was also a great patron of artists and poets.

Holbein shows him as an apple: round, sweet, wholesome, red. It is hard to believe that Edward, who died at 15, was genuinely so bouncing a baby, but Holbein makes us credit both his health and his natural dignity. This is a princely baby, the all-important son whom Henry had sought with such savage desire in a marital history that left its mark on Europe. Holbein's intense interest in human personality, the facial characteristics that distinguish one individual from another, might seem to have little scope in dealing with a child. A child, after all, is not yet a fully achieved personality: he or she is essentially potential. Yet it is precisely this potential that Holbein shows. This face has all the soft indeterminacy of a baby, united into the hard reality of a ruler. It is the child as future king, royal child, Edward VI.

HOLBEIN AS COURT PAINTER

Holbein left the city of Basle in 1526 to go to England, where he became Court Painter to Henry VIII. His first visit lasted seven years and he painted many portraits of the English aristocracy. As Court Painter he was employed to paint the prospective wives of the king, but only managed to complete pictures of Anne of Cleves and Christina of Denmark, whom Henry did not marry (shown above). He also painted a mural of Henry VIII with Jane Seymour. This hung in the Whitehall Palace, but was destroyed when the palace burned down in 1698.

OTHER WORKS BY HOLBEIN

An Englishman
(Kunstsammlung, Basle)

A Woman
(Institute of Art, Detroit)

Sir Thomas Godsalve and his son John
(Gemäldegalerie, Dresden)

Henry VIII
(Fundaçion Thyssen-Bornemisza, Madrid)

A Merchant of the German Steelyard
(Royal Collection, Windsor)

Lady Margaret Butts
(Isabella Stewart Gardner Museum, Boston)

187 Hans Holbein, the Younger, The Ambassadors, *1533, 207 x 210 cm (6 ft 9½ in x 6 ft 11 in)*

An elaborate vanitas

In his portraits of the adult rich and powerful, we see the full extent of Holbein's scope. *The Ambassadors* (187, originally named *Jean de Dinteville and Georges de Selve*) is a memorial to two extremely wealthy, educated, and powerful young men. Jean de Dinteville (on the left) was the French ambassador to England in 1533, when the portrait was painted, and was aged 29.

On the right is Georges de Selve, an eminent scholar who had recently become a bishop; he was just 25. He was not a diplomat at the time of the painting, but later became French ambassador to Venice, at that time ruled by Spain.

This picture fits into a tradition of works that show learned men with their books and instruments. Between the two Frenchmen stands a table that has an upper and a lower shelf.

Objects on the upper shelf represent the study of the heavens, while those on the lower shelf stand for the educated pursuits on earth. At the left end of the upper shelf is a celestial globe – a map of the sky – in a frame that can be used to calculate astronomical measures. Next to it is an elegant portable brass sundial. Next is a quadrant – a navigational instrument for calculating the position of a ship as it travels, by measuring the change in the apparent position of fixed stars. To the right of this is a polyhedral (multi-sided) sundial, and then another astronomical instrument, a torquetum, which, along with the quadrant, was used for measuring the position of heavenly bodies.

Almost unnoticed, in the top left corner of the painting, a silver crucifix is seen, representing the goal of salvation, not forgotten amid the splendour and advanced scientific knowledge.

On the lower shelf at the left is a book, which proves to have been a recent guide to arithmetic for merchants (published in 1527). Behind it is the globe, representing geographical knowledge. The set square emerging from the book probably represents the skill of map-making. The lute was the chief courtly instrument of the time and stands for the earthly love of music. At the end of the bent-back tip, one string can be seen to be broken, representing the sudden breakage of death. Beneath the lute, next to a pair of compasses, is a copy of a Lutheran hymn book. The flutes beside them were popular instruments for all levels of society.

To this grand image of youth in its prime, Holbein has slashed across the foreground his reminder of human mortality. We realize that this strange shape, when viewed from a certain angle, is actually a human skull that has been cunningly distorted by stretching it sideways in so-called anomorphic projection.

Renaissance miniatures

In the 16th century Henry VIII relaunched the 15th-century fashion for miniature paintings. Nicholas Hilliard (1547–1619) became the most successful miniature portraitist, using his skills as an artist and as a jeweller to create exquisite masterpieces. Generally, miniaturists concentrated on the head and shoulders only, and used bright colours for details. This simple miniature is of Richard Hilliard, the artist's father.

Nicolaus Kratzer

Holbein and Nicolaus Kratzer struck up a friendship in 1527 when working together on a ceiling in Greenwich Palace. Kratzer was an astronomer and an astrologer, and is said to have lent Holbein the instruments we see in *The Ambassadors*. In 1519 he was appointed "Astronomer and Deviser of the King's Horologes" and in this post he encouraged Henry VIII to popularize science and mathematics. This portrait is by Holbein and shows Kratzer working on a polyhedral sundial.

Most of Holbein's portraits are of lords and ladies, but there are a few that reveal more of his private life. One such is the haunting *Portrait of the Artist's Wife with Katherine and Philipp (188)*. Artists have always painted their families, but this is the saddest version on record. He lived very little with his wife and children in Basle (the reasons for this may have been political, religious, or financial), but this tragic little trio have all the withering marks of the unloved.

The dim-eyed wife presses down on the children, plain, pale little beings, all unhappy and all ailing. Holbein, that superb manipulator of the human face, cannot have meant to reveal their wretchedness and expose his neglect with such drastic effect. It is as if his art is stronger than his will and for once Holbein is without defences.

We might describe him as an un-Germanic German, since he left for Switzerland when he was still a teenager and then worked in England for Henry VIII. While Dürer and those influenced by Dürer (which includes practically all

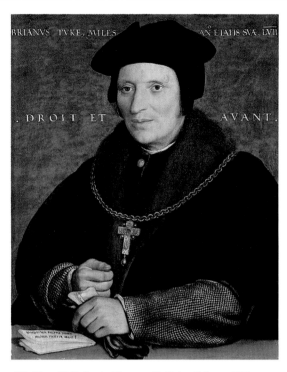

189 Hans Holbein, the Younger, Sir Brian Tuke, c. 1527, 49 x 39 cm (19½ x 15½ in)

German Renaissance artists except Holbein) had an intense interest in the personal self of the sitter, Holbein was essentially discreet. A court painter *par excellence*, he always maintains a dignified distance. We see the sitter's exterior, what he or she looked like, but we never pass into the inner sanctuary. The sole exception, which is what makes it so extraordinarily interesting, is this painting of his wife and children. Here his courtly shield is down, perhaps because of the artist's personal sense of guilt. He was not a good husband or father, and while he can carry off any other portrait with superb technical aplomb, he catches his breath and opens the inner door when he paints the family that he abandoned and neglected.

A much more characteristic Holbein is *Sir Brian Tuke (189)*, with his clever, sensitive face, his air of unflinching probity, the tenseness of his half-smile and his clenched hand. A folded piece of paper on the table quotes a biblical passage in which Job appeals to God for rest from anxiety. We would know, without having sufficient knowledge to recall that Tuke served Henry VIII, that here was a man who was noble but imperilled – though in fact, he flourished.

Holbein's work is never cold nor lacking in involvement, as we can see in *The Ambassadors*, *Christina of Denmark*, and *Sir Brian Tuke*; but he protects his sitters from psychological exposure and, indirectly, protects himself. What a contrast with Dürer, who always leaves both the sitter and himself open to the most personal scrutiny.

188 Hans Holbein, the Younger, The Artist's Wife with Katherine and Philipp, c. 1528, 77 x 65 cm (30½ x 26 in)

NORTHERN MANNERISM

The Italianate influence on the Northern painters, who had been nurtured in the Gothic tradition, initially produced a sometimes uneasy admixture of styles. On the one hand, it resulted in a convincing monumentalism, seen, for example, in the art of Jan Gossaert (see below) and Lucas Cranach the Elder (see p.156). On the other hand, it encouraged the Northern Mannerist trend. This can be characterized by a rather superficial, even contrived, Italianate gloss.

OTHER WORK BY GOSSAERT

A Man with a Rosary
(National Gallery, London)

Virgin and Child
(Musée Marmottan, Paris)

A Gentleman
(Statens Museum for Kunst, Copenhagen)

Portrait of Anna de Bergh
(Mcnay Art Institute, San Antonio, Texas)

A Woman as the Magdalen
(Museum Mayer van der Bergh, Antwerp)

Adam and Eve
(Fundaçion Thyssen Bornemiza, Madrid)

190 Jan Gossaert (Mabuse), **Portrait of a Merchant,** *c. 1530, 63.5 x 48 cm (25 x 19 in)*

clash between the spirit of Northern realism and this intense, masculine, Italianate face. The portrait stands apart from much of Northern portraiture of the time, which formed a strong and distinct tradition of its own, with a direct and realistic attitude to nature, and a resistance to the classical influences coming from Italy.

There is the same feeling of jarring, but wonderfully so, in Gossaert's *Danaë (191)*, in which a Flemish housewife, demure and expectant, sits in an Italianate classical arcade, the divine gold (for Jove came to her in this disguise) filtering down to her like thickened light.

Two Netherlandish painters straddle the divide between the Gothic and Renaissance worlds: Gossaert and Patinir. The first of these, Jan Gossaert (c. 1478–1532), even bridges the North/South divide, in that he worked in Italy, where he was influenced by Michelangelo and Raphael (both working there at that time), and invented an Italian-sounding name, "Mabuse", from his native town of Maubeuge in the province of Hainaut.

So here we see an artist from the Netherlands, with a heritage of van Eyckian observation (see p.64) and van-der-Weydenish sincerity (see p.67), but with a desire to be flamboyantly classical, as it were. He can be extremely moving, when he finds a theme that suits his strange blend of talents and intentions. The mixture works well enough in his *Portrait of a Merchant (190)*, painted about 20 years after Grünewald's *Crucifixion* (see p.76), despite the perceptible

191 Jan Gossaert, **Danaë,** *1527, 115 x 95 cm (45 x 37½ in)*

THE COURT OF FONTAINEBLEAU

One of the most distinguished artists at the court of Fontainebleau was Francesco Primaticcio who, between 1530 and 1560, created elegant sculptures as well as paintings such as the one shown above, *The Rape of Helen*. The style of the painting is self-consciously sensuous and elegant, placing emphasis on the female nude, which was to symbolize the secularization of art in the 16th century.

SCHOOL OF FONTAINEBLEAU

If France can be considered to be part of the "North", as it is at least in the sense of being non-Italianate, then Jean Clouet (1485/90–1540/1) and the School of Fontainebleau are notable examples of a painterly Renaissance in the North. The patronage of the French King Francis I attracted Italian artists to the royal court at Fontainebleau. Francis sought for himself the haughty, kingly image that Italian Mannerist artists created for their sitters. The Florentine artist Rosso Fiorentino (see p.139) and later Francesco Primaticcio (1504–70; see column, left), who was born in Bologna and trained at Mantua, brought their cultivated influence to the Fontainebleau Court.

Clouet, a native Frenchman and Court Painter to King Francis I (or it may have been François Clouet, his son) has given us the quintessential king in his *Francis I (192)*. The portrait is all majestic bulk, with any human frailties not so much hidden as frozen out of countenance. It is an icon, a diplomatic effigy, alarming in its careless assumption of superhuman stature. The School of Fontainebleau based its practice on the elegancies of Italian visitors like Rosso, and all its practitioners (many of whom are by now anonymous) may be from the South, yet there is a languid realism that is different from Italian Mannerist chic. There is, too, a touch of the clumsy, not very Gallic but extremely Northern.

Diana the Huntress (193), with her leaping mastiff and the enveloping forest, is a true wood nymph, innocent of the coyness of a Cranach hunting nude (see p.157) and striding out with lovely animal vigour.

193 School of Fontainebleau, Diana the Huntress, c. 1550, 190 x 132 cm (75 x 52 in)

SPREAD OF MANNERISM IN THE NORTH

This elongated, elegant, and slightly unreal form of art was not confined to Fontainebleau. Its elegance appealed to the aristocratic North in general, and there are some supreme examples outside the confines of Paris.

Joachim Wtewael (or Uytewael, 1566–1638) was one such example from the Northern Netherlands (what is known today simply as the Netherlands). He was born in Utrecht, and in his early career he travelled in Italy and France before settling down in Utrecht. He became an important exponent of the Mannerist style in his country, though he tended to ignore the advances in naturalism being achieved by his contemporaries, such as Dürer and Cranach.

192 Jean Clouet, Francis I, c. 1525, 97 x 73 cm (38 x 28¾ in)

194 Joachim Wtewael, **The Judgment of Paris,** *c. 1615, 55 x 74 cm (21½ x 29 in)*

Wtewael's *The Judgment of Paris (194),* in which the Trojan shepherd prince Paris awards the golden apple to the goddess he considers the most beautiful, is a highly Mannerist concoction. The self-conscious poses of the three divine ladies, the suave gestures of Paris as he makes his all-important choice, even the attendant animals with their delicate horns and slender legs, recall that world of mythical romance in which Mannerism flourishes.

Another eminent painter in the Mannerist style was the Flemish artist Bartholomeus Spranger (1546–1611). Born in Antwerp, he too travelled in Italy and France when young. He worked in Vienna, then settled permanently in Prague. In 1581 Spranger became Court Painter to the Emperor Rudolf II, and he had much influence on the Academy of Haarlem.

Spranger's *Vulcan and Maia (195)* has an almost disturbingly erotic force. Maia is looped across the knee of the massive and saturnine Vulcan, like a living bow to which he will fit his arrow. One long, intrusive finger stabs her in the heart, and she writhes suggestively under its impact. In some ways a rather unpleasant picture, it is nevertheless strong and, in a weird way, beautiful. There is a lightness, an aristocratic innocence, about the art of Fontainebleau, which vanishes once Mannerism moves from the sunlit groves of courtly Paris to the dark,

Teutonic forests of the true North. An almost sinister quality pervades the art of Spranger and his followers, never overpowering but flavoursome, almost gamy.

195 Bartholomeus Spranger, **Vulcan and Maia,** *c. 1590, 23 x 18 cm (9 x 7 in)*

NORTHERN LANDSCAPE TRADITION

Landscape painting became one of the most enduring and characteristic features of Northern painting throughout the 16th century. Before this, there had been the small cameo landscapes, spied through windows and doorways of the earlier interior scenes (see p.61). These delightful features now began to attain their rightful scale, and as they did so they became a sort of large stage for all the small activities of humankind. Yet it is not until Brueghel appears that we see the truly Flemish, lyrical understanding of nature, unlocked from its servitude to human concerns and shown in all its glory.

ALCHEMY
During the 16th and 17th centuries the science of alchemy underwent a revival in northern Europe. Alchemists believed it was possible to turn base metal into gold and argued that through this process they would discover a way to make human society perfect. They also believed that a magician (the Magus) controlled the Universe and would use charms, symbols, and charts to contact the hidden forces of the world.

The Flemish artist Joachim Patinir (c. 1480– c. 1525) is one who provided links between the Gothic world and the Renaissance. While Jan Gossaert (see p.163) had been a link between North and South, Patinir mediated between past and future. He has a Gothic imagination, a profoundly medieval sense of the world – that small ball held in the divine hand – but he has also a prophetic sense of distance and the spaciousness of true landscape. We can see Dürer (see p.152) in him, Dürer's prints being available to him at that time (see p.153). We also catch a glimpse of the medieval illuminated manuscripts (see p.28). *Charon Crossing the Styx (196),* with its vision of Hell as war, shows his style well.

THE GERMAN LANDSCAPE
Albrecht Altdorfer (c.1480-1526), like his fellow German, Lucas Cranach the Elder (p.156), was a stay-at-home. He may well have seen some of the topographical watercolours that Dürer brought home with him after his roamings across the Alps. After Altdorfer's own trips along the river Danube, landscape was to become his passion. Altdorfer's landscapes are of a peculiarly Germanic character, bristling with wild forests and lonely, wolf-infested glades. They are fearsome, though magnificent, and they even contain the hint of irrationality overcoming sobriety. Altdorfer does maintain control, but we feel the threat.

196 *Joachim Patinir,* **Charon Crossing the Styx,** *1515–24, 63 x 102 cm (25 x 40 in)*

landscape-based but uses the landscape to make some mysterious moral point. We can never quite comprehend the meaning of an Altdorfer work – there is always an elusive element – which is perhaps one of the reasons why he remains so consistently a source of delight and interest.

PIETER BRUEGHEL THE ELDER

The only rival to Dürer as greatest of the Northerners is a so-called peasant painter, Pieter Brueghel (1525–69). Born in Breda in the Flemish province of Brabant, he was the forefather of a whole tribe of painterly Brueghels, Jans and Pieters; but none ever take our breath away with wonder as does Pieter the First. The "peasant" nickname is particularly unbecoming in that he was a travelled and highly cultivated man, friend of Humanists and patronized by the learned Cardinal

197 Albrecht Altdorfer, Christ Taking Leave of His Mother, *perhaps 1520, 140 x 110 cm (55 x 43 in)*

OTHER WORKS BY ALTDORFER

Nativity
(Staatliche Museen, Berlin-Dahlem)

Farewell of St Florian
(Uffizi, Florence)

The Beautiful Virgin of Regensburg
(The Church of St Johannes, Regensburg)

Lot and His Daughters
(Kunsthistorisches Museum, Vienna)

Landscape with a Footbridge
(National Gallery, London)

Danube Landscape (198) is one of the first examples of a painting that is content to have no human beings in it at all. It stands or falls by the sheer quality of the sky, the trees, the distant river, the blue mountains. We are offered a romantic substitute for mankind, one purer and more open to the ethereal heavens. Altdorfer believes in the sacramental value of what he paints, and it is his conviction that convinces.

But he can also people his landscapes, and with remarkable effect. *Christ Taking Leave of His Mother (197)* has an extraordinary, gawky power. The vague gestures towards graciousness fall completely flat, and we see that almost comic awkwardness of the enormous feet of the supportive mourner. We also see a that there is a sad dichotomy between the ruined castellations on the left, on the side of the women, and the wild encroachments of the forested world of the men on the right. There seems to be a painful absence of communication, an accepted harshness, and we come to a painful realization that this is of the essence of any saying of goodbyes. This striking scene makes a rough, embarrassing, ardent picture that is quite unforgettable.

Altdorfer is an unexpected painter and with many more personae in his repertoire than we might expect. Surprisingly, he has a feel for allegory, which has produced some of the most enchanting small paintings in all Northern art (there is a wonderful example in the Gemäldegalerie in Berlin). This art is

198 Albrecht Altdorfer, Danube Landscape, *c.1520–25, 30 x 22 cm (11¾ x 8½ in)*

Granvella. Despite his travels to France and Italy around 1553, the strongest influences on his work were from Bosch (see p.72) and Patinir (see p.166). In Breughel's paintings we see a continuation of the Netherlandish tradition: from Bosch's fantastic inventions (which later, in Breughel's hands, resided in a more gently comic nature); and from Patinir's reverent and passionate landscapes. Breughel's paintings are supremely un-Italianate, and the classical quest for the ideal form finds no place in his art.

The only relevant application of Breughel's nickname is that he not infrequently painted peasants, works that some think satirical but that others regard as carrying a heavy weight of compassion and affectionate concern.

The famous *Wedding Feast (199)* certainly shows us the round and stupid faces of the guests, the fat and silly bride drunk with complacency beneath her paper canopy-crown, the table agog with intent eaters. But our smile, like Breughel's, is a painful one. She is so pathetic, the poor, plain young woman in her little hour of triumph, and if the guests are gobbling down their food, we see the food, humble plates of porridge or custard, served on a rough board in a decorated but realistic barn.

These are the poor, these their wretched celebrations. The child licks with lingering gusto at her empty bowl, and the piper, who yet must play until he receives his food, stares at the porridge with the longing of the truly hungry. Only the insensitive would find *The Wedding Feast* comic. There is a very real sense in which our reactions to *The Wedding Feast* put us morally to the test. This is a wholly serious subject, the degradation of the working class, treated with

OTHER WORKS BY BREUGHEL

The Beggars
(Louvre, Paris)

The Triumph of Death
(Prado, Madrid)

Massacre of the Innocents
(Royal Collection, Hampton Court Palace)

The Land of Cockaigne
(Alte Pinakothek, Munich)

The Three Soldiers
(Frick Collection, New York)

Children's Games
(Kunsthistorisches Museum, Vienna)

Wedding Dance
(Detroit Institute of Arts)

The Parable of the Blind
(Nazionale di Capodimonte, Naples)

Harbour of Naples
(Galleria Doria Pamphili, Rome)

199 Pieter Breughel, **The Wedding Feast,** *c. 1567–68, 114 × 164 cm (44½ × 64½ in)*

disinterested humour, which we are meant to see through. Not to understand Breughel's concern and compassion condemns us.

The Tower of Babel (200) has a horrifying complexity, dwarfing the human figures in their authoritarian pride, reducing the most gigantic of labours to the pointless scurrying of ants. This is Babel, and it is our own local experience: the humans are both pathetic and doomed in their conceits. Breughel was a highly educated and sophisticated painter, with a scholar's insight into myth and legend. His version of the ancient story of the Tower of Babel is far removed from

200 Pieter Brueghel, The Tower of Babel, 1563, 114 x 155 cm (44½ x 61 in)

THE REFORMATION

The term Reformation describes the period of ecclesiastical dispute between the papacy and the various national churches of Europe throughout the 16th century. The nailing of Luther's 95 theses to the door of the Schlosskirke in Wittenberg is considered the catalyst that resulted in the reform of the Roman Catholic church and the establishment of the Protestant churches. The final agreement was that a nation should follow the religion of its sovereign. This woodcut shows rival Protestant and Catholic preachers competing for followers.

THE TOWER OF BABEL

A version of the ancient story of the Tower of Babel is told in chapter 11 of the book of Genesis. The people ambitiously set out to build a tower to reach the heavens. As a punishment for their pride, God confused the people's language so they could not understand one another, and He scattered them over the face of the Earth. In art, the idea of linguistic confusion is shown in the different races of people, and the tower is seen in a chaotic and unfinished state.

a mere illustration of a biblical passage. Brueghel, in fact, never works on the surface but always at depth. Whether it is the Fall of Icarus in Greek myth or the building of Babel in biblical story, it is meaning that concerns him, visual meaning.

But the great glory of Brueghel, his real claim to be ranked among the world's greatest, lies in his landscapes, in particular the set of months, *à la* Limbourg brothers (see p.55), that he painted for a wealthy citizen of Antwerp. One of these is *Gloomy Day* (see p.170). Only five remain, but they have never been surpassed for their truth,

their dignity, and their mysterious spiritual power. Brueghel never forces a moral. The most reticent of painters, he merely exposes the vastness of nature that surrounds our everyday life, so that we will respond to the challenge of reality. But it is a most delicate challenge, one that makes demands on our imagination.

This is the world, Brueghel tells us, in all its diversity, majesty, mystery, and beauty. How do we respond to it? The intense pleasure that these pictures provide should not mask from us their deep moral seriousness.

GLOOMY DAY

Brueghel's innovative portrait of a landscape in the grip of winter is one of a series of paintings based on the Northern seasonal calendar. It represents the dark, cold winter months of February and March, and follows the Northern pictorial tradition (derived from illuminated manuscripts) of the labours of the months (see p.55).

MOUNTAINOUS LANDSCAPE

The wild, violent face of nature is given concrete form in the jagged mountain-tops and glowering black storm-clouds on the far horizon. Shown at a distance, it remains a threatening and ever-present force that dictates daily existence. The sombre blacks and chilling whites provide a cool background to the red-browns and warm umbers of the peasants' habitat, and assert the contrast between the wild and the domesticated. Comforting wisps of smoke trailing from chimneys are matched by the icy puffs of frozen cloud above the mountain range.

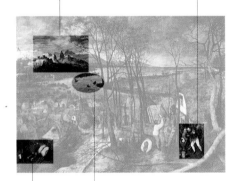

CARNIVAL TIME

Near a group of men absorbed in the February task of pollarding willows is another intimate group that provides more clues to the time of year. A man is greedily eating the Carnival fare of waffles, and the child's paper crown – common fancy dress for Epiphany and Shrovetide processions – and lantern also denote Carnival. Our attention is first caught by the bright red and light tan of the clothing of the three figures, then led downward and along the shore, then up again, to rest finally at the horizon and thundering sky.

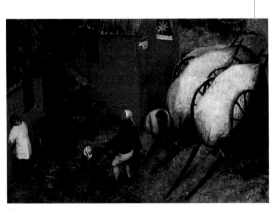

THE VILLAGE

From our vantage point we see the peasants' vulnerable position and their insect-like activities within this great celebration of raw nature. If we look closely we can find touches of bawdy humour typical of Brueghel: to the left a man urinates against the wall of an inn (following his own, smaller, dictates of nature, perhaps).

FOUNDERING SHIPS

Like the village scene, this detail is not immediately apparent at first sight. The terrible catastrophe of ships crashing on the rocks is depicted as merely another incidental detail within the greater drama of the landscape. We see the irony (even if the villagers cannot) of their innocent attempts to "harness" nature by pollarding their willows, while the the destructive might of nature passes unheeded beyond them.

201 Pieter Brueghel, **Gloomy Day,** *1565, 117 x 163 cm (46 x 64 in)*

THE LEGEND
OF FAUST

Between 1507 and 1540
numerous references were
made in German society to
a dealer in the black market
by the name of Faust, who
was said to have made a
pact with the devil. Faust
became a renowned
magician and charlatan
and was driven on from
town to town until he
disappeared. The first
printed Faust story
appeared in 1587 and its
anti-Catholic sympathies
fuelled the troubles of the
Reformation. The legend
was truly popularized in
the 17th century by the
playwright Christopher
Marlowe, whose version
was performed throughout
Europe. In the 19th century
it was made into a classic of
German literature by the
poet Goethe.

Gloomy Day (201) is about the dark days of February and March, lightened only by the Carnival festivities. Yet we sense instinctively that this painting is about far more than the end of winter. Brueghel shows us a vast, elemental universe, through which a wild river rages. Overhead, the sky is in tumult, a great, wild mass of cloud, threatening and descending. The villagers may labour, or they may play: their activities seem so small within the vast context of human reality. Lightning glints on tree trunks and village roofs. The foreground is relatively bright, which is, of course, the illusion that human activity is intended to create. Immersed in our work or play, we easily forget the threat of nature's violence and of the dark.

Hunters in the Snow (202) is both sensuously overwhelming, the very feel of the cold made visual, and emotionally expanding. The mysterious space of the valley and its mountain, its lakes, and its bare trees, its tiny inhabitants and its far-ranging birds, all lies before our view. Like the gods themselves, we look upon "the world". Every detail informs us of the season as the bonfire blazes and the hounds slink wearily home. The dazzle of white conceals the details but reveals the wholeness, with only humanity at leisure to play, and only the young at that. The grandeur of Brueghel's vision is one that he is able to share with the viewer completely.

He takes us into an awareness of what it means to live in the physical world, its mountains, valley, and rivers, its snows, its birds, its animals, its trees. No other painter has such a breadth of vision, so unencumbered by the persona. We feel this is not what Brueghel saw (and what we now see) but what actually and objectively is. This is his great and unique contribution to art.

202 Pieter Brueghel, **Hunters in the Snow,** *1565, 117 x 162 cm (46 x 63¾ in)*

BAROQUE AND ROCOCO

Originally a Portuguese word meaning rough or irregularly shaped, "Baroque" came into use as an art term – not a complimentary one – from the world of pearl collecting. The Baroque style was a new direction in the arts that emerged in Rome at the turn of the 17th century, partly as a reaction to the artificiality of the Mannerist style of the 16th century. The new art was committed both to genuine emotion and to the imaginatively ornamental. Human drama became a vital element in Baroque paintings, typically acted out with highly expressive, theatrical gestures, lit with striking chiaroscuro and featuring rich colour combinations.

The Rococo style developed as a successor to the Baroque in a wide range of arts, including architecture, music, and literature as well as painting. Its emphasis was on lightness, decoration, and stylistic elegance. The Rococo style emerged in Paris in the early 18th century, and soon spread to the rest of Europe.

Caravaggio, Bacchus, 1590s (detail)

BAROQUE AND ROCOCO TIMELINE

The Baroque period in painting corresponds roughly to the 17th century. In Italy and Spain, the Catholic church, in its campaigning, Counter-Reformation mood, put pressure on artists to seek the most convincing realism possible. In the North too, Rembrandt and Vermeer, each in their separate ways, pushed forward the limits of realism. Rococo art began with Watteau and became the ruling European style for most of the 18th century.

CARAVAGGIO, THE DEATH OF THE VIRGIN, 1605/06

Caravaggio's religious works were executed in true Counter-Reformation spirit. Nevertheless, the unprecedented realism in this work caused its rejection by the priests who commissioned it (p.177).

POUSSIN, THE HOLY FAMILY ON THE STEPS, 1648

Poussin's deeply classical sense of balance is revealed in every corner of this composition, particularly in the pyramidal shape of the Holy Family and the plinth-like step supporting them. Despite the classical feel, the work's emotional force and spiritual intensity place it well within the mainstream of Baroque art (as opposed to the Neoclassicism of the 18th century, p.216).

REMBRANT, SELF-PORTRAIT, 1659

Realism was crucial to Baroque painting, and Rembrandt provides a prime example of Dutch portraiture of the Baroque period. This self-portrait shows us a face stripped of all pretensions – the artist is looking earnestly at himself and painting what he sees, producing great art from personal failure (p.202).

| 1600 | 1620 | 1640 | 1660 | 1680 |

RUBENS, DESCENT FROM THE CROSS, 1612–14

Rubens, a Flemish Catholic, was one of the greatest painters of all time. His work is supremely balanced and yet passionate (p.186).

VELAZQUEZ, FRANCISCO LEZCANO, 1636–38

Velázquez was Court Painter at the Royal Court of Spain, immortalizing its royalty and senior court personalities, including the dwarves (jesters), whom he portrayed with his characteristic dignity (p.196).

VERMEER, KITCHEN MAID, 1656–61

Vermeer's use of light gave his paintings a silent clarity, the sensation of a moment preserved, of the recording of that precious quality of simply existing. His choice of subjects was undramatic – typically a scene of complete ordinariness (p.210).

TIEPOLO, WEDDING ALLEGORY, C. 1758

The Venetian artist Tiepolo was the most celebrated and sought-after painter of his time, admired for his soaring imagination and mastery of composition. His most famous work is perhaps the fresco cycle in the Residenz at Würzburg. This magnificent ceiling fresco is in the Rezzonico Palace (now a museum) in Venice (p.232).

WATTEAU, "EMBARKATION FOR CYTHEREA", 1717

Rococo art began in Paris, where Watteau settled as a young man. He inititated the Rococo era and invented a new genre, known as fêtes galantes. This painting shows some of its key features: an open-air scene crowded with wistfully depicted lovers. They have just taken their vows at the shrine of Venus and are ready to leave the island. Although the fêtes galantes approach might suggest an admiration for frivolity, there is an underlying sadness in all of Watteau's works (p.224).

HOGARTH, A SCENE FROM THE BEGGAR'S OPERA, 1728/29

While Rococo fashions ruled in London, one British artist was independently building a new genre – satirical painting. Hogarth's narratives, though humorous, were profoundly moral. (p.235).

FRAGONARD, BLINDMAN'S BUFF, PROBABLY C. 1765

Fragonard, too, following Watteau and Boucher, was a Rococo painter. In this open-air scene, an innocent game takes place in a carefree atmosphere, but the players are overshadowed by the landscape (p.228).

1700	1720	1740	1760	1780

CANALETTO, VENICE: THE BASIN OF SAN MARCO ON ASCENSION DAY, C. 1740

Canaletto is famous for his accurate and elaborately detailed records of city views. He painted within the Rococo tradition, and Venice is a supremely Rococo city, both fantastical and imaginative. Yet Canaletto is more interested in straightforward architecture and elegance of proportion than in fantasy. His work foreshadows the Neoclassical art that belongs to the late 18th century (p.234).

CHARDIN, STILL LIFE, C. 1760/65

Chardin was an artist of the Rococo period who would not allow the frivolous tone of the art of his time to influence him. His sober and restrained pictures often contain a moral or spiritual meaning. Sometimes it is an explicit one, contained in the action of the painting, but otherwise, as here, the message is conveyed simply in the solemn, sacramental atmosphere (p.231).

ITALY: A CATHOLIC VISION

During the Renaissance, Florence and Venice had dominated the art world, but during the Baroque period Rome became the great artistic centre, visited by artists from all over Europe. Having survived the Protestant Reformation, the Catholic church emerged more vigorous than ever as a result of its own parallel process of revitalization, the Counter-Reformation. As Catholics, artists in Italy were required to endorse the authority of the Church and to make the scriptures a palpable reality to its people. The heightened emotional content and the persuasive realism of Baroque painting provided such means.

THE SCULPTURE OF BERNINI

The Italian sculptor and architect Gianlorenzo Bernini (1598–1680) was influential in the formation of Baroque style. Bernini designed the sweeping twin colonnades that surround the piazza in front of St Peter's Church in Rome. He described these as "like the mother church embracing the world". Between 1645 and 1652 he completed this sculpture (above) of St Teresa of Avila, a religious reformer, for the Cornaro family chapel. The elegance of St Teresa's draperies and the drama of her facial expression embody the essential "realist" characteristics of Baroque sculpture.

ITALIAN ARCHITECTURE

The rebuilding of Rome in the 16th century under the pontificate of Sixtus V transformed the architectural vista of the city. The most successful architect of the time was Carlo Maderno (1566–1623) who designed the quintessentially early Baroque facade of St Peter's in 1603. Francesco Borromini (1599–1667) was a contemporary of Bernini and Maderno, but his best work is seen in the smaller churches, such as San Carlo alle Quattro Fontane.

As the Church had done, painting now underwent its own kind of reformation. The new style was not given the name Baroque until the 19th century, and for 200 years it was simply thought of as a form of post-Renaissance Classicism, associated especially with Raphael (see p.126). Italian artists in the 17th century moved away from the complexities of Mannerism to a new style of painting that had more in common with the grandeur of form of the High Renaissance. Pioneering this change were two artists of far-reaching importance: Caravaggio, the great proto-realist, working in Rome, and Annibale Carracci, the founder of the classical landscape tradition, in Bologna (see p.182).

CARAVAGGIO: BEAUTY IN TRUTH

The art establishment of the 19th century scorned Baroque painting, and perhaps the first and the greatest painter to be affected by this scorn was Caravaggio (Michelangelo Merisi da, 1573–1610), who moved to Rome from Milan in around 1592.

Caravaggio's early works consisted largely of genre paintings (see glossary, p.390), such as *The Lute Player (203)*: a youth so full, rich, and rosy that he has been mistaken for a girl. It is without doubt a girlish beauty, curls seductive on the low forehead, gracefully curving hands fondling the gracefully curved lute, soft lips parting in song or invitation. Perhaps some viewers found this charm frightening, with

203 Caravaggio, The Lute Player, c. 1596, 94 x 120 cm (37 x 47 in)

204 Caravaggio, Bacchus, 1590s, 94 x 85 cm (37 x 33½ in)

the Apostles. This woman was all they had left of their Master. Mary Magdalene is huddled in sorrow, and the men mourn in their different but equally painful manner. Mary is not shown in the customary way, ascending to Heaven in glory; we are confronted with both a human corpse and human loss. Above the body swirls a great scarlet cloth, mutely hinting at the mystery of being Mother of a divine Son: blood red for passionate love, for virtual martyrdom, for the upward movement of her soul. There is a copper bowl at the Magdalen's feet: she has been washing the body. Every realistic detail makes the work more and not less religious, one of the great sacred icons of our culture, with immense impact.

its air of decadence, of pleasure up for sale: but Caravaggio does not approve or, for that matter, disapprove of this young man: he presents him with an underlying sadness, a creature whose favours will fade, like the fruit and the flowers, and whose music will end in the darkened room.

Bacchus (204) may well be the same model but here in classical guise, the young wine god holding out the cup of pleasure. But corruption and decay are never far away: the worm-hole in the apple, and the overripe pomegranate, remind us of the transience of all things. Light and darkness, good and evil, life and death: the chiaroscuro of his style plays masterfully with these fundamental realities.

OFFENDING RELIGIOUS SENSIBILITIES

Viewers may have been alarmed by the sensuality of *The Lute Player,* but what really drew down condemnation was the uncompromising realism of Caravaggio's religious works. The Carmelite priests who commissioned *The Death of the Virgin (205)* rejected it, finding it indecent. There was a rumour that the model for the Virgin had been a drowned prostitute. It is certainly a shocking picture, light striking with brutal finality upon the plain and elderly face of the corpse, sprawled across the bed with two bare feet stuck out unromantically into space, and the feet are dirty. What shocks us is the sense of real death, real grief, with nothing tidied up or deodorized. If Mary was human, then she really died; and the lack of faith was that of the horrified priests who rejected this masterpiece, not that of the artist. A poor, aged, worn Virgin makes perfect sense theologically, and so does the intense grief of

205 Caravaggio, The Death of the Virgin, 1605/06, 370 x 244 cm (12 ft 2 in x 8 ft)

Caravaggio lived the life of an "avant-gardist" – liberated from convention, both in his art and in his life. Earlier artists had not been models of virtue, but he was astonishing in his freedom from constraint, his quarrels and rages, and even his one killing, bringing him much merited disfavour. Yet, however wild his life, down to the miserable and early death on a lonely seashore, there is nothing wild or undisciplined about his painting. It has an overwhelming truthfulness that, merely in itself, is beautiful.

It is almost impossible to overestimate the influence of Caravaggio. For the first time, as it were, an artist looked at the full reality of human existence, its highs and its lows, its glories and its sordid materiality. He accepted this and loved it into great art. If we respond to Rembrandt in his human truthfulness, it is to some extent because Caravaggio first responded as an artist to the full spectrum of real life. This is to deal only with the simple truthfulness of his eye: equally influential was his awareness of the importance of light and dark, the chiaroscuro, which he introduced to European painting, and which was dominant for centuries to come.

PALPABLE ASTONISHMENT

The Supper at Emmaus (206) still has its power to shock, with the strangely "unspiritual" Christ, a youth with plump, pointed face and loose locks, unbearded and undramatic. Why should Christ not look like this? The unpretentious face allows the drama to be inherent in the event.

The basket of fruit, balanced on the edge of the table, spells out the significance of Christ's apparition – nothing is left of our earthly securities if death has lost its absoluteness.

Caravaggio's way of homing in on the essentials – or perhaps of bringing them up to, and through, the invisible barrier of the picture plane, into the space occupied by the viewer – made a profound impression upon his contemporaries. He told his story through every element in the work, not least light and shadow. From Jesus, light spreads outwards; Caravaggio can tell his story by means of simple effects that nature itself provides. After Caravaggio, a new emphasis on reality, on natural drama, and on the infinite fluctuations of light can be seen in nearly every artist. Like Giotto, like Masaccio, Caravaggio was an art-historical hinge.

206 Caravaggio, **The Supper at Emmaus,** *1600–01, 140 x 195 cm (55 x 77 in)*

THE SUPPER AT EMMAUS

After His Resurrection Jesus meets two of His disciples walking on the road from Jerusalem to Emmaus. Caravaggio shows the moment when, at supper that evening, Jesus reveals Himself to the disciples in the breaking of the bread. It is the manner in which He blesses the supper that suddenly unveils to them that this is their "dead" master, come back to them. Their astonishment is breathtakingly portrayed, while the innkeeper looks on, baffled and uncomprehending.

SUDDEN REACTION

The disciple on the right (the shell he wears is the badge of a pilgrim) makes the more dramatic gesture as he recognizes Jesus. His outstretched arms echo the Crucifixion, and one dramatically foreshortened arm appears to stretch right out of the picture towards the viewer. This contrasts with the equally sudden but more contained reaction of the other disciple, on the left, whose tattered elbow seems to protrude from the picture but in a more restrained way.

A YOUTHFUL CHRIST

The image of Christ is that of a young man, almost a youth. Caravaggio may have been influenced by paintings by Leonardo in his unusual depiction of Christ without a beard. He is serene and remote, having transcended the agonies leading up to and during His Crucifixion, and the difficulties of mortal life. He appears, as stated in Mark's Gospel, "in another likeness". Amid the rich, dark tones and the enveloping shadows, His face is flooded in a clear light, which falls from the left (Caravaggio's customary light source). Although the innkeeper stands in the path of the light, his shadow misses Christ, falling instead onto the back wall.

STILL LIFE

The basket of fruit – subtly past its best and teetering on the edge of the table – projects into "our" space, insisting on our attention and rightful admiration. The mostly autumnal fruits are chosen for their symbolic meaning, though the Resurrection was in spring. The pomegranate symbolizes the crown of thorns, and the apples and figs man's original sin. The grapes signify the Eucharistic wine, symbolic of the blood of Christ.

207 Orazio Gentileschi, **The Lute Player,** *probably c. 1610, 144 x 129 cm (56½ x 50½ in)*

FATHER AND DAUGHTER

We can see Caravaggio's profound influence even on a relatively unadventurous painter like Orazio Gentileschi (properly Orazio Lomi, 1563–1639). Although Gentileschi's *The Lute Player (207)* is emphatically feminine and very different from Caravaggio's lascivious boy, she too is caught by the light, held in its beams amidst the slanting darkness, lovely and fresh in her innocent music making.

The innocent and rightful desire of feminist art critics to reinstate women artists in the canon has perhaps rather unbalanced our appreciation of Orazio's work. He is a splendid artist, sensitive and strong. The lute player gleams seductively out of the shadows and is totally convincing. It is only because his daughter has been wrongfully slighted (many of her works were incorrectly attributed to her father) that we pass over him to dwell on the work of his daughter, Artemisia (1593–1652/3).

She was a precociously talented painter, and almost as passionate and powerful as her father. In fact she is closer in nature to Caravaggio. Yet she is not incapable of producing a gentler image, as when she portrays herself as the allegory

WOMEN ARTISTS

Artemisia Gentileschi was one of the first important women artists whose work it is possible to attribute with certainty. As women were excluded from life classes with nude models (which formed the basis of traditional academic training) they were at a disadvantage. Other female artists such as Rachel Ruysch (1664–1750) and Judith Leyster (1609–60) were painting during this period and the work by Rachel Ruysch shown above is typical of the detailed flower paintings of the Baroque era.

of painting *(208)*. Perhaps the fact that the legendary originator of the art of painting was a woman enabled her to make this exception. This is an unglamorized self-portrait but a delightful one, the round face of the woman intent upon her work and her gown green in the Caravaggioesque light.

Despite the unpretentious approach, the passion and intensity of her paintings make Artemisia almost unique among female artists before the 20th century. It may be – as modern historians like to speculate – because she was raped by one of her father's friends, and this left her with a special insight into violence and betrayal. Like any woman artist, she had to battle against the unexpressed absolutes of her culture, which included the belief in a "natural" inferiority of women, and this too may have fuelled the fire with which she depicts *Judith Slaying Holofernes (209)*. The head of the oppressor (see p.105, column) is being visibly sawed off and palpable blood is oozing sickeningly down the mattress.

It is hard to avoid sexist generalities; to avoid saying that it is because she is a woman that she immerses us in the material practicalities of a slaughter. It is a human characteristic to be able to imagine an event in all its dimensions, which is what Artemisia does. She makes us aware of both the courageous heroism of Judith, saviour of her people, slayer of the tyrant, and of what it means to slay another human being.

208 Artemisia Gentileschi, **Self-portrait as the Allegory of Painting,** *1630s, 97 x 74 cm (38 x 29 in)*

209 *Artemisia Gentileschi,* Judith Slaying Holofernes, *c. 1612–21,*
200 x 163 cm (6 ft 7 in x 5 ft 4 in)

THE CARRACCI FAMILY

The Carracci family of Bologna was also influenced by Caravaggio – as who was not – but here the influence is a subtle one. This talented family of artists comprised two brothers, Agostino (1557–1602) and Annibale (1560– 1609), and their cousin Ludovico (1556–1619). They were interested less in the clash of light and shade than in that of temperaments. It was the drama they had in common with Caravaggio, but with differing emphases.

The greatest of the three was Annibale, who combined classical strength with realistic observation. Annibale united High Renaissance monumentalism with Venetian warmth and strong colour, and in his paintings he achieved a form of dignified naturalism that could express the idealism, and delicacy of sentiment, that Caravaggio's revolutionary realism could not. There is unforced nobility in his painting of *Domine Quo Vadis? (210)* (Where are you going, Lord?), the question legend had St Peter put when he fled Rome for fear of persecution and met with a vision of Christ going the other way. No dirty feet here, and yet we are conscious of the confrontation, and that it is taking place in a real setting; idealized figures, though strong and convincing, but bare earth and unromantic trees. The touch of the ideal kept it more acceptable than the stark vision of Caravaggio, and this accessibility had an aptness in the time of the Counter-Reformation (see p.187).

THE BIRTH OF OPERA

In keeping with the aesthetic beliefs of the High Baroque period, opera aimed to be a fusion of all possible artistic forms (instrumental music, singing characters, and drama). The first documented example of an opera is *La Dafne* by Jacopo Peri (1561–1633). The art of opera reached its maturity with Claudio Monteverdi (1567–1643) who wrote *Orfeo* in Mantua in 1607. The first public opera house was opened in 1637 in Venice. In the same year, Monteverdi resumed writing for the stage after a 30-year break. This portrait of Monteverdi (above) is by his contemporary, Domenico Feti.

210 Annibale Carracci, **Domine Quo Vadis?,** *1601–02, 77 x 56 cm (30½ x 22 in)*

THE CLASSICAL LANDSCAPE

The peaceful landscape, T*he Flight into Egypt (211)*, is an example of the Carraccis' far-reaching legacy. The classical landscape tradition begins here, where harmony, classical balance, and idealism – where all is well with the world – are combined with strong mood and real personal drama. Annibale exploited the innate

211 Annibale Carraci, **The Flight into Egypt,** *c. 1603, 121 x 225 cm (47½ x 88½ in)*

expressive potential of the landscape, through nuances of light and atmosphere, so that it played as important a role as the narrative about which the painting ostensibly revolves.

Domenichino (Domenico Zampieri, 1581–1641) was a pupil of the teaching academy founded by the Carraccis in 1582. His interests lay increasingly in Classicism and landscapes as he developed, but he knew how to put these techniques to religious effect. *Landscape with Tobias Laying Hold of the Fish (212)* takes the story of the magical fish (see column, right) and sets it in a world so large, so full of potential, that the narrative is swallowed whole.

ELSHEIMER: FROM GERMANY TO ITALY

By the 17th century Northern Europe possessed a strong realist tradition of landscape and genre painting (though in the long run, Italian landscape was more influential). One of the many Northerners working in Italy at the beginning of the 17th century was the German landscape painter Adam Elsheimer (1578–1610). His paintings combine Northern clarity and eye for the "truth" with the Southern quest for the idyllic. Another scene from the story of Tobias appears in *Tobias and the Archangel Raphael Returning with the Fish (213)*. This painting was for many years attributed to Elsheimer but is now thought to be by a later artist imitating Elsheimer's style. Tobias is depicted gingerly

212 **Domenichino,** Landscape with Tobias Laying Hold of the Fish, *perhaps c. 1617-18, 45 x 34 cm (17¾ x 13⅜ in)*

making his way homeward with his huge fish. The artist is attracted to the mysterious romance of nature, and this is a work of wonderful silence, as boy and protective spirit move through the lonely evening.

TOBIAS AND THE MIRACULOUS FISH
The book of Tobit is in the Apocrypha, included in the Bible by the Orthodox and Catholic churches. Tobit, the father of Tobias, loses his sight after sparrow droppings fall in his eyes while he is asleep. Believing his death to be imminent, he sends Tobias to collect a debt owed to him. The Archangel Raphael accompanies Tobias, without revealing his identity. Whilst bathing in the River Tigris, Tobias is attacked by a great fish, which he catches and guts, under Raphael's instructions. He burns the heart and liver, later using these to exorcize demons from his wife Sarah. On reaching home, he uses the burnt gall of the fish to restore his father's sight.

CONTEMPORARY ARTS

1606
First open-air opera, in Rome

1615
Inigo Jones becomes England's chief architect

1616
Death of Shakespeare

1632
Building work begins on the Taj Mahal in India

1642
All theatres in England are closed by order of the Puritans

1661
The Royal Academy of Dance is founded in France by Louis XIV

1665
Bernini completes the high altar canopy (baldachin) for St Peter's, Rome

1667
John Milton begins to write *Paradise Lost*

213 *After Adam Elsheimer,* Tobias and the Archangel Raphael Returning with the Fish, *mid-17th century, 19 x 28 cm (7½ x 11 in)*

214 *Guido Reni*, Susannah and the Elders, *c. 1600-42,*
117 x 150 cm (46 x 59 in)

THE NEGLECTED MASTER

One former pupil of the Carracci Academy came to eclipse the Carracci family in fame, both in the city of Bologna and throughout Europe. This was Guido Reni (1575–1642), a man of reclusive temperament, whom the German poet Goethe considered a "divine" genius. Reni has had the misfortune to lose his fame over the years, as our civilization has become increasingly secular-minded and his works seem too emphatic in their piety.

The truly "Baroque" nature of his paintings brought Reni much of the contempt later expressed for Baroque art. It is an unfair judgment and it is slowly being rectified as the wonderful pictorial emotion and the genuine seriousness of this great painter are progressively being re-understood.

215 *Guido Reni*, Deianeira Abducted by the Centaur Nessus,
1621, 295 x 194 cm (9 ft 8 in x 6 ft 4 in)

To take one example of Reni's religious work, *Susannah and the Elders (214)* is a painting that confounds the ignorance of prejudice. The story is about a Jewish heroine who is surprised when bathing by two religious elders, who try to blackmail her into immorality. Susannah displays the opposite of surface piety: she faces her tormentors with the indignation of the innocent. She sees no reason for fear, trusting in God and her own blamelessness.

Reni is equally powerful in mythological works. *Deianeira Abducted by the Centaur Nessus (215)* is a work of thrilling majesty. Hercules is on a journey with his wife, Deianeira, when they come to a river, where the ferryman is the centaur Nessus. He takes Hercules across first, then tries to ravish Deianeira. The picture shows him ready to gallop off with her on his back. Bodies gleam in the sunlight: the man-beast hard and straining, the abducted woman vulnerable in her fleshly softness. Garments fly, clouds gather, a great equine leg is paralleled by the slender human form, the nearness underscoring the cruel unlikeness. Deianeira casts an anguished glance upward to the gods, one arm reaching out for help. On every level, visual and emotional, this is a painting that learns from Raphael and Caravaggio alike.

HUMAN DRAMA IN GUERCINO

Like Reni, Guercino (Giovanni Francesco Barbieri, 1591–1666) also fell into disrepute. Perhaps this is even less reasonable, for he is one of the great narrative painters, a draughtsman of infinite ability and a superb colourist as well, especially in his earlier years. The name by which we know him was a sort of nickname and is best translated as "Squinty". It indicates a disability, but no man ever used a squint to better effect. He was influenced by the Carracci, and like the Carracci also, by Venetian painting.

Character, interaction, passions in conflict: these are things that Guercino portrays with total confidence. *Christ and the Woman Taken in Adultery (216)* makes its point mainly through the gestures of the hands, as Jesus and the accusers signal their difference of principle (see column, below right). The noble head of Christ, imperturbably calm amid the hubbub, is just sufficiently unidealized to make the incident seem credible. Guercino shows us divine love as a great force of compassion, infinitely demanding and infinitely forgiving.

Guercino is an intensely dramatic artist, playing with light and shade with dazzling skill. We are moved by meaning in his work, but also by its sheer visual beauty.

> **"***A great draughtsman and a most felicitous colourist; he is a prodigy of nature, a miracle.***"**
>
> **Carracci on Guercino in a letter of 1617**

THE WOMAN TAKEN IN ADULTERY

This story is told in St John's Gospel. Temple officials and members of the Pharisee sect try to trick Jesus into giving judgment (so that they can accuse Him of usurping authority). They bring before Him a woman who has been caught in the act of adultery, punishable in Roman law by stoning. Jesus pauses, writing with one finger in the dust, then replies, "He that is without sin among you, let him cast the first stone." At this the accusers leave the scene. Jesus finally says to the woman, "Go, and sin no more."

216 Guercino, Christ and the Woman Taken in Adultery, *c. 1621, 98 x 122 cm (38½ x 48 in)*

FLEMISH BAROQUE

In the 17th century, Flanders was the main stronghold of Catholicism in an otherwise Protestant northern Europe. It remained under Spanish rule when the Northern Netherlands won independence, and the greatest outside influences on Flemish art were Spain and the Counter-Reformation. This is clearly seen in both Rubens and van Dyck.

For a century, Spain had been the major military force in Europe. It had used its power to back up the might of the Catholic Church in Northern Europe – precisely where Catholicism was under the strongest attack from the Protestant Reformation. In the Netherlands, when the North won its independence, Flanders remained within the Catholic fold, in an ever closer relationship with Spain. The two Catholic countries had in common the religious idealism of the Counter-Reformation, and, linked as they were by their history, they shared similarities in their art. At the start of the 17th century, as a result of this consolidation with Spain, industry in Flanders flourished, and the arts, which were centred in Antwerp, benefited from the increasingly prosperous culture.

The greatest of the Northern Baroque painters was the Antwerp-based Peter Paul Rubens (1577–1640). He has something of Domenichino's largeness of spirit (see p.183), but greatly magnified. The wonderful mixture of Italian grandeur and Flemish lucidity, and feeling for light, climaxes in the paintings of Rubens. His work is infused with a kind of Catholic Humanism that admits sensuous delight along with religious sentiment, and it has an energetic, optimistic spirituality.

In 1600 Rubens went to Italy to study. He travelled widely over the next decade, notably to Spain, where he became friends with a Spanish artist who was 22 years his junior and who was of perhaps even greater stature: the incomparable Velázquez (see p.194).

Rubens wrote, "I consider the whole world to be my native land," and this confident generosity of spirit, this cosmopolitan view of the world, is manifested in his works. So expansive was his genius that he easily took the elements that he admired of the High Renaissance masters and assimilated them into his own strongly independent vision. His paintings reveal a supremely confident use of colour – always rich and generous – that he learned from studying the works of the great Venetian, Titian. His figures have a massiveness of form that runs in a clear line back to Michelangelo.

RUBENS' RELIGIOUS WORKS

Rubens spent some time in Rome and the influence of his Italian contemporary, Caravaggio (see p.176), proved to be an enduring one. This revealed itself most emphatically in Rubens' religious paintings, to which, in true Baroque form, Rubens gave popular appeal and an utterly physical presence. We cannot always tell from an artist's religious painting how personal is his faith: probably we can never tell, faith being so

217 Peter Paul Rubens, Descent from the Cross, *1612–14, 420 x 310 cm (13 ft 9 in x 10 ft 2 in)*

218 Peter Paul Rubens, Deborah Kip, Wife of Sir Balthasar Gerbier, and her Children, *probably 1629/40, 165 × 178 cm (5 ft 5¼ in × 5 ft 10 in)*

integral a part of our nature. But we know that Rubens cherished his religion and tried to live by it. We can imagine that we see this earnestness in his wonderfully energetic *Descent from the Cross (217).* Here we can see Caravaggio's influence, in the dramatic lighting and humane realism, but also that of Michelangelo, in the muscular, classical form of the dead Christ.

The painting still hangs in Antwerp Cathedral, for which it was painted, a great descent indeed, as the limp body (the only non-active element in the picture) drops down the whole length of the frame. All the activity is kept central, a thick and vital column of emotion and movement, passion expressing itself physically, all the light kept steady on the deadness of the Christ. His weight presses down almost unbearably, His death making it impossible for love to reach out. The mourners feel with despair that they have had something of their own life taken away in the Crucifixion of their Lord.

RUBENS AS A PORTRAITIST

But Rubens is no escapist. He never flatters the truth into acceptability: he reveals what defects he sees, though sitters may not have recognized them when displayed for all to see in a portrait.

One of his great group portraits, *Deborah Kip, Wife of Sir Balthasar Gerbier, and Her Children (218),* shows a family that is not happy. The three older children are grim and questioning, the little girls looking out at us with hesitant reserve. They are beautiful children, but they are tense – as is the elder brother, leaning tautly forwards. The baby is unaware of tension, but the mother seems lost in her sadness.

The father of the family was a cruel and unprincipled man, and Rubens does not gloss this over. Deborah Kip is gloriously dressed in damasks and silks, but the family stands in a setting of ominous clouds. The glow and the beauty are observed, but with foreboding. There is deep sentiment, but no sentimentality.

THE COUNTER-REFORMATION

This was a movement that took place within the Catholic Church at the time of the Protestant Reformation (see p.169). The Roman church found itself in need of reform, particularly so if it was to win back regions that had turned Protestant. Pope Paul III (1468–1549, shown above) summoned the Council of Trent (1545–63), which redefined Catholic doctrines and introduced disciplinary reforms. New religious orders, including the Jesuits, were founded to lead the counter-offensive against the Protestants. Later the more rational types of church reform were replaced by the paranoia of the Inquisition (see p.197), which used extreme measures against Protestant "heretics".

AN AMBASSADOR'S SKILL

Rubens' vitality and tenderness – an unusual combination – could make him seem unlikely to be a success as a political artist. But his genius was immense and he was a highly successful ambassador for his country, the Spanish Netherlands, so he was used to moving in the highest political circles.

Almost all the crowned heads of Europe knew personally, and valued aesthetically, the great Rubens. He was the obvious choice for Marie de' Medici, the widowed Queen Mother of France, who needed artistic help in her state of rivalry with her own son, Louis XIII.

Louis came of age in 1614 and duly became king but, like many a parent, unfortunately, Marie was unable to accept her son as a functioning adult, and she clung tenaciously to her status. The French court came to be beset with the political problems arising from this sordid rivalry. Louis was forced to have his mother exiled to the provinces, and she was not allowed to return until 1620. She moved into the Luxembourg Palace, a splendid Baroque building on the left bank of the Seine, whose refurbishment and decoration became her main occupation for the next five years.

Her plan was to commission two cycles entailing some 48 vast canvases altogether. One was to illustrate the romance and triumph of her career, the other the events of her late husband's. Marie de' Medici had never been beautiful and was always overweight. King Henry IV had indeed been a hero, but the only cycle to come near completion was the one focusing on Marie. No other artist but Rubens could have carried this off without becoming ludicrous. The series is far from ludicrous: it is magnificent. Without eliding the truth, merely gently shading it, Rubens provides one splendid canvas after another, making a mountain of art out of a molehill of fact.

His method is splendidly exemplified in *The Apotheosis of Henri IV and the Proclamation of the Regency (219)*, which is set in terms of classical myth. Rubens' lips may have twitched as he painted this, but his artist's hand is rock steady. It is a beautiful, vibrant picture, completely integrated, one of the great narratives of art.

Facing *The Apotheosis of Henri IV* at the opposite end of the long gallery in which the cycle was originally housed was *The Queen Triumphant*, a brilliant piece of court portraiture. Other memorable successes were *The Education of the Princess*, *The Disembarkation at Marseilles*, and *The Birth of the Dauphin*.

If weaknesses in the cycle are looked for, they are to be found in a small minority of the paintings. *Louis XIII Comes of Age*, for instance, appears to lack conviction, and this is thought to be indicative of the lingering hostility between the officially reconciled royal figures.

219 Peter Paul Rubens, **The Apotheosis of Henri IV and the Proclamation of the Regency,** *c. 1621/25, 391 × 727 cm (12 ft 11 in × 23 ft 10 in)*

THE APOTHEOSIS OF HENRI IV

Rubens conceived the *Apotheosis of Henri IV* as the climactic work in a great cycle depicting events in the career of Marie de' Medici. It is a huge canvas, 4 m high and over 7 m in length (13 by 24 ft), commissioned for Marie de' Medici's palace where it stretched across the entire end wall of the gallery in which it was hung. Its full title, *The Apotheosis of Henri IV and the Proclamation of the Regency,* explains the double nature of the composition. With great success, Rubens has depicted two separate events (both proclaimed on the same day) within one canvas: the death of the king (who was assassinated in 1610) and the regency of his widow.

REGENCY OF MARIE DE' MEDICI
On the right-hand side, the embattled Spirit of France kneels and offers the orb to the unwilling widow (depicted in deep mourning). Above her, a figure representing the regency offers her a rudder. The French aristocracy, and the heavenly graces, plead with her to overcome her humble reluctance.

APOTHEOSIS OF HENRI IV
On the left, Henri IV is taken up to Heaven where he will be deified (the meaning of apotheosis). He is carried by Saturn (sickle in hand), the god of time and death, who delivers him to Jupiter, the supreme god of power, leaning down from Olympia to receive him. Jupiter's eagle, bearing a thunderbolt in its claws, symbolizes the ascending soul. The serpent, shot through with arrows, is an allusion to the king's assassin.

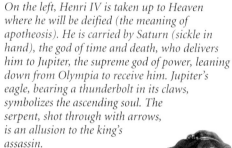

MINERVA'S SHIELD
The gruesome shield, bearing the severed head of the hideous gorgon Medusa, is an attribute of Minerva, the goddess of war and wisdom. In thanks for her help, Perseus made Minerva a gift of Medusa's head (which still retained its power to turn living things to stone). Unlike Mars, Minerva is a warrior of just causes, hence her presence here beside the widow. This same shield can be found in Rubens' Judgment of Paris, *behind the naked figure of Minerva (see p.190).*

220 *Peter Paul Rubens,* **The Judgment of Paris**, *1635–38, 145 x 194 cm (57 x 76 in)*

THE RUBENS LOOK

Rubens is unfortunate in that today's attitude towards the fat is in direct opposition to that of the 17th-century Flemings. They loved a full-bodied woman, and most of Rubens' superb nudes are too large for our taste. But he is very much more than the painter of the fair and fat.

Rubens was the most fortunate artist in history: handsome, healthy (until gout in later life), well-educated, sensible, good-humoured, wealthy, an innate diplomat and recognized as such by the crowned heads of Europe, twice married, both times with blissful success – so much so that he openly celebrated it in his paintings – and one of the greatest and most influential artists ever born. He used all his gifts with unselfish industry, climaxing his good fortune by being a thoroughly good man. It is typical of his happy career that at a young age he became Court Portraitist at Mantua in Italy (see column, p.104) and that in 1609, at 32, he became Court Painter to the Infanta Isabella and Archduke Albert in Brussels (see column, left).

The glory of Rubens' work is its vigour, its happy and profound consciousness of the significance of being alive and alert, of never wasting what a context offers. But as well as that, there is what one can only call a sweetness in him, shown most remarkably by the Rubens

"look". People in his paintings tend to give one another a look of whole-hearted trust, an acceptance of difference and a confidence in its worth. An example is *The Judgment of Paris (220)*. Paris looks at the naked goddesses with a lovely reverence – the Rubens "look". It is returned by

221 *Jacob Jordaens,* **The Four Evangelists**, *c. 1625, 134 x 118 cm (52½ x 46¼ in)*

222 Peter Paul Rubens, **Marchesa Brigida Spinola Doria**
1606, 152 × 99 cm (60 × 38¾ in)

VAN DYCK'S GRAND ELEGANCE

The closest to Rubens in gift, and at times in style, in the North, was Anthony van Dyck (1599–1641). In his youth, Rubens had a very aristocratic elegance that reminds us of van Dyck. An example from his early twenties is his regal-looking portrait of *Marchesa Brigida Spinola Doria (222)*, in which the face, gentle in its self-assurance, proclaims the work of Rubens.

Van Dyck can manage just as much grandeur, skilfully deploying all his arts to make his own *Marchesa (223)*, of the great Grimaldi family, appear almost immortal in her lofty state. In his portraits, van Dyck suppresses the "earthiness" and animal vitality so forceful in Rubens' paintings, and in its place we find an elegance and psychological presence that his aristocratic subjects doubtless found pleasing. The slave who holds the parasol is humankind: the lady is on another plane – yet not quite. Somehow van Dyck manages to make us believe in his lady, with a subtlety not evident in Rubens' portrait.

Venus, innocently amazed at her victory. It has been remarked that her surprise is justified; that Juno, with her back arched above her furs, is the true winner. (The third goddess, Minerva, seems to look on with amused curiosity.) The legend takes on a special significance, quite apart from preceding the Trojan war. What interests this supremely balanced painter is the encounter between what could have been a vulgar youth and an unclad queen. Rubens lends the scene dignity and graciousness.

JORDAENS – RUBENS' SUCCESSOR

Rubens ran a workshop in Antwerp, with a large stable of assistants. One artist who is known to have worked with him in Antwerp is Jacob Jordaens (1593–1678), who gained a great deal from his association with Rubens and flourished over the years, producing coarse-grained but vital works. Jordaens' *The Four Evangelists (221)* is painted with vigour: the thick brushwork is very different from Rubens' technique.

Jordaens worked best as a painter of genre works and typically chose modest subjects; but after Rubens' death in 1640 it was he who filled the post of Antwerp's leading artist, perpetuating Rubens' influence and producing a great many public works over his long career.

223 Anthony van Dyck, **Marchesa Elena Grimaldi**, *1623, 241 × 133 cm (95 × 52 in)*

224 *Anthony van Dyck,* Charles I of England out Hunting, *c. 1635–38, 266 × 207 cm (8 ft 8½ in × 6 ft 9½ in)*

Portrait painting was a lucrative business, and van Dyck really excelled at it. Like Rubens (in whose Antwerp workshop he briefly worked) he travelled extensively, enjoying an illustrious career before settling in 1632 in England. It was at the court of Charles I, that doomed monarch, that his gifts flourished, influencing generations of portrait painters in England and throughout the rest of Europe. The diminutive king featured in many of van Dyck's paintings, in a variety of symbolic roles, sometimes in armour, and sometimes on horseback. One portrait in the Louvre, *Charles I of England out Hunting (224),* is the greatest piece of public relations ever created. By sheer force of genius, van Dyck presents us with an icon of the heroic, of the grave scholar king who yet loves the chase. Noble tree, noble seat, noble monarch: van Dyck integrates the three into a most memorable image. Charles knighted him, and we feel he deserved it.

SPANISH BAROQUE

Painting in 17th-century Spain was profoundly influenced by the Church, at least partly because of the religious zeal of the Spanish Hapsburg dynasty. King Philip II and his two successors, Philip III and IV, maintained religious orthodoxy by means of the dreaded Spanish Inquisition, a council for the persecution of all forms of "heresy", including Protestantism. Spanish Baroque art was largely devotional in nature, though the period can boast a little court painting and some mythological, genre, and still-life work.

Despite the tense atmosphere of religious conformity presided over by the Hapsburg régime, Caravaggio's liberating influence (see p.176) is fairly widespread in Spanish painting in the early part of the 17th century. Caravaggio's rich contrasts and dark palette were well suited to the Spanish tradition, in which a tendency towards grim and graphic realism was already well established, especially in religious sculpture (see column, p.198).

"Caravaggism" found an early exponent in Jusepe de Ribera (1591–1652), who painted with dark colours and, often, disturbingly sinister undercurrents. Ribera went to Italy – first to Rome, where he absorbed Caravaggio's influence, then to Spanish-ruled Naples. He remained in Italy for the rest of his life and enjoyed great success. There is more piety, and sensual pleasure, in Ribera's religious paintings than in those of Caravaggio and, equally, a deeper level of pain and suffering. There is a terrifying degree of pain in this mythological work *(225)*, in which Apollo punishes Marsyas by skinning him alive. Marysas, who was a skilled flautist, had challenged Apollo to a music contest, but had lost. As victor, Apollo was allowed to choose the punishment.

Ribera found his models among urchins and beggars, and portrayed them as they really were. His beggar-boys, even his philosophers, confront us with all their physical imperfections: rotting teeth, deformed limbs, dirty skin, and aged flesh, breathing a harsh and unprecedented social realism into 17th-century painting.

SPAIN IN THE 17TH CENTURY

From the reign of Philip II (1556–98) onwards, the Hapsburg monarchy had to struggle to keep control over Spain's vast empire. At the beginning of the 17th century, the country was in economic decline due to the number of wars it had to fund. It was also weakened by the loss of land to France under the Treaty of the Pyrenees in 1659, and by several serious outbreaks of the plague. At the same time, Spain experienced a renaissance in its artistic and intellectual life.

DON QUIXOTE

Miguel de Cervantes (1547–1616) was the most successful Spanish novelist of the 17th century. His most famous work, *Don Quixote*, was written while he was in prison in Seville. The novel is a satire on the current fashion for chivalry but also portrays the theory of the human ideal and the frailty of man. The two characters represent the many fluctuating features of insanity, and the detailed descriptions of the Spanish countryside give the book a powerful resonance. By 1605 the book was in print in Madrid; this illustration (above) shows the popular 1608 edition.

225 Jusepe de Ribera, **The Flaying of Marsyas,** *183 x 234 cm (6 ft x 7 ft 8 in)*

**OTHER WORKS BY
VELAZQUEZ**

*Cardinal Don
Ferdinand of Austria*
(Prado, Madrid)

The Rokeby Venus
(National Gallery,
London)

*The Infanta
Maria Teresa*
(Kunsthistorisches
Museum, Vienna)

*The Moorish
Kitchen Maid*
(National Gallery,
Edinburgh)

Count Olivares
(The Hermitage,
St Petersburg)

*The Infante
Balthasar Carlos*
(The Wallace
Collection, London)

*The Painter
Juan de Pareja*
(Metropolitan Museum
of Art, New York)

VELAZQUEZ: SPANISH GENIUS

When Diego Velázquez (1599–1660) first made
his bid for painterly glory (barely out of his teens)
he was influenced by Caravaggio (see p.176).
There is the same surety of form and control of
light, but beyond this, all real comparison ends.
Velázquez was unique, one of the very greatest
of painters, and he developed a vision of human
reality that owed little to outside influence.

The only image of royalty comparable to the
van Dyck portraits of the Stuart King Charles I
(see p.192) is that given by Velázquez of the
Hapsburgs, whom he served as Court Painter;
but, again, the comparison is a superficial one.
Velázquez did not merely glorify his king and
court, though he did that as a matter of course;
he was also oddly intent on rising in social status.
In time he did win his way to a mild friendship
with Philip IV. The king was a poor politician
(see left), but his saving grace was that he did
appreciate the genius fate had sent him as
Court Painter and rewarded him accordingly.

The sheer beauty of Velázquez' court
paintings, official statements in an age without photography of what the monarch and
entourage looked like, undoes all attempts at
labelling. *Las Meninas (226)* ("the maids of
honour") is now hung in pride of place, behind
bulletproof glass, visibly the greatest treasure of
its great museum, the Prado, Madrid.

226 Diego Velázquez, Las Meninas, 1656, 318 x 276 cm (10 ft 5 in x 9 ft ½ in)

LAS MENINAS

At one level, this picture is easy to read: at the centre is the little princess, the Infanta Margarita Teresa, with her maids clustered round her, her tutors, page, and dwarf in attendance, and her gigantic dog. From the dog we work our way up by stages to the distant reflection of the king and queen. Here is the whole world of the inner court, presented obliquely, in reverse order of importance. Painted for the king's private summer quarters, this work is both a portrait of his young daughter and a sophisticated, innovative tribute to the king himself. It portrays a single moment, each figure responding to the entrance of the king.

MINIATURE PORTRAITS
In the rear mirror, our attention drawn to it by the silhouetted courtier, we see a reflection of the king and queen. Whether it actually reflects them, or the painting Velázquez is working on, nobody knows for certain. Secure in their position, the royal pair can easily afford to become a mere reflection behind their child. Even as pale shadows, they can dominate, surely the subtlest of compliments.

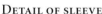

SELF-PORTRAIT
The painter, Velázquez himself, stands at the far left, intent upon a canvas looming impressively upwards, while the large copies of Rubens' paintings behind him are diminished (there is irony here) by the shadows. The red cross on Velázquez' chest signifies his subsequent knighthood and was added to the painting two or three years later.

DETAIL OF SLEEVE
Viewed at close quarters, the fluid, seemingly hasty brushmarks, have an abstract, almost arbitrary quality. But as the viewer steps back to take in the whole scene, these patches miraculously assume the solid structure of the child's arm enclosed within the gauzy fabric of her sleeve.

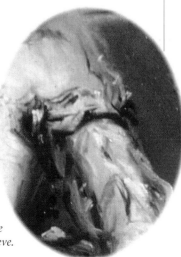

COURT LIFE
There is a sense of life as actively lived, life held still for a passing moment – not a moment of special significance, however; merely one of the thousands passing every hour: and this one lives on. The figures of the Infanta's entourage appear and recede in a vast cave of shadows. All have been identified as historical personages except for the man standing quietly on the right.

Earlier in his career, Velázquez had contributed to the grand projects inaugurated by Philip IV. These included a splendid new palace, the Buen Retiro, built in 1631–35, in whose many rooms some 800 paintings were hung. Its principal ceremonial room, known as the Hall of Realms, contained 27 paintings by Spanish artists, including Velázquez' *Surrender of Breda*, alongside a number of works by Zurbarán (see p.197). The king's next project was the Torre de la Parada, a hunting lodge in the grounds of the Pardo Palace. Velázquez, despite the king's increasing interest in foreign artists, contributed portraits of the young crown prince Balthasar Carlos, and two of the court dwarves, one of whom, *Francisco Lezcano (228)*, is shown here.

228 Diego Velázquez, Francisco Lezcano, 1636–38, 107 x 83 cm (42 x 32½ in)

Velázquez' use of paint intrigued his royal friends. They pointed out to one another, quite intelligently, that his pictures had to be viewed at a distance, when the rough and apparently glancing dabs of colour would suddenly, miraculously, integrate themselves into the image. Lace, gold, the glitter of light jewels, the rosy flush of a young cheek, the weary droop of an aged head: Velázquez could catch them all and hold them for us to see. He could do this with a religious image: no *Christ on the Cross (227)* has a more mournful human dignity than his.

He could teach us that the court dwarf *(228)*, who often used to serve as a jester (see left) and a figure of fun, had the same tragic dignity and unalienable humanity as the dying Jesus.

He could take a theme from mythology and show us that paganism, too, is a religion and so draws its force from the movements of the human spirit. *The Forge of Vulcan (229)* is a masterpiece of contrasts between two kinds of being. On the one hand, there is the luminous, epicene, and effeminate youth, visitant from another world, blandly confident of his ability to make himself understood. On the other, there is the team of blacksmiths, male to their core, wiry, and astonished – and yet at the same time clearly unimpressed. The two worlds meet with mutual incomprehension and with mutual disesteem, yet Velázquez laughs so low in his chest that the joke may go unheard.

*227 Diego Velázquez, **Christ on the Cross**, 1631–32, 248 x 169 cm (8 ft 1 in x 5 ft 6½ in)*

229 *Diego Velázquez*, **The Forge of Vulcan**, *1630, 223 x 290 cm (7 ft 4 in x 9 ft 6 in)*

ZURBARAN: A SACRAMENTAL CALM

Francisco Zurbarán (1598–1664) was a contemporary of Velázquez and worked in Velázquez' native town of Seville. The two were largely unlike in style, except that Zurbarán's paintings display that pleasing solidity of form and plasticity of paint found in Velázquez' early work (see p.196). It is in still life that we find Zurbarán at his finest. *Still Life with Oranges (230)* has a sacramental monumentality, a modest certainty of the value of things, the fruit laid out on an altar, the flower silent beside the humble mug, three images bathed in sunlight and conveying an indescribable sense of the sacred.

230 *Francisco Zurbarán*, **Still Life with Oranges**, *1633, 60 x 107 cm (23½ x 42 in)*

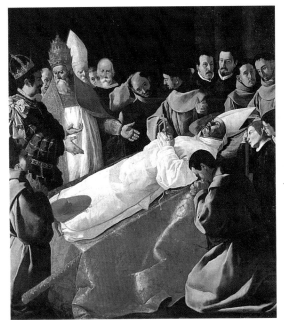

231 **Francisco Zurbarán**, The Lying-in-state of St Bonaventura, *c. 1629, 250 x 225 cm (8 ft 2 in x 7 ft 5 in)*

The Lying-in-state of St Bonaventura (231) has the same weight of lucid significance, of "event" that is uneventful. The work hovers between time and eternity, intent upon the unseen that gives the seen its meaning. The human actors in the drama (and we might say that the dead saint is the most vital of these) are spotlit against profound darkness. The mystery of our journey from birth to death becomes almost tangible.

MURILLO: A FORGOTTEN MASTER

The next great 17th-century Spanish master after Velázquez and Zurbarán is another artist who lived in Seville, Bartolomé Esteban Murillo (1617–82). Sadly, Murillo is easy to misjudge; at his weakest, which is not all that infrequent, he has a softness that can only be called sentimental. The mistake is to take the weak Murillo as the only Murillo. It is true that he is never as strong or as deep as Velázquez or Zurbarán, but he has his own gentle strengths and depths. Murillo can make us catch our breath with his unworldly but convincing images.

Murillo is often accused of being too soft, too anodyne, perhaps because of our modern desire to face life whole, with all its cruelty. It is a wish that runs contrary to Murillo's personal world of family love and understanding.

Some of our surprise may come from the realization, unexpected, that sweetness can be made to work. *The Holy Family (232)*, with its tenderly involved St Joseph and the absence of anything resembling heavy symbolism, has a charm that increases the longer the picture is looked at. The small mongrel and the cosseted child are both painted with the insight of love.

But we can perhaps best appreciate the genuine if not monumental gifts of this artist in one of his rare secular works. *Two Women at a Window (233)* is a splendid image, reticent, creamily beautiful, certain of its own understanding of the two figures. One of them is almost certainly a duenna – an older woman employed by the family to be both a governess and a chaperon. She is laughing, but we are not shown her laughter: only her creased-up cheeks, flushed with mirth. Her twinkling eyes assure us that what makes the young woman smile to herself, unaffected, makes the older woman crinkle up with sardonic glee. She sees more, and understands with sharper wit, than the pretty child, and Murillo shows us this with the most delicate understatement.

In this wonderful picture, the great strong vertical of the shutter, and the equally strong horizontal of the window ledge, frame the two women. The girl, who is the emotional centre of the picture, looks out at life with ironic detachment, but Murillo, and the older woman, know that her practical options are severely circumscribed.

232 **Bartolomé Esteban Murillo**, The Holy Family, *1650, 144 x 188 cm (56½ x 74 in)*

233 Bartolomé Esteban Murillo, Two Women at a Window, c. 1670, 127 × 106 cm (50 × 41¾ in)

A DUTCH PROTESTANT VISION

The United Provinces of the Northern Netherlands claimed their independence in 1579, but it took 30 years of armed conflict to drive the Spanish from their soil. A treaty was signed in 1648, and this Protestant region, with its Reformation affinities and Northern realist heritage, now evolved its own tradition. Life was lived out in a dramatic atmosphere, first of revolution and later of the fight to defend the hard-won freedom. A new order began, based on social justice and spiritual austerity. Churches were stripped bare for Calvinist worship, and in painting, there was renewed emphasis on realism and simple, everyday things.

It can be difficult to realize that Rubens (1577–1642, see p.186) and Rembrandt (van Rijn, 1606–1669) were contemporaries, their lives overlapping for the first half of the 17th century. Both lived in the Low Countries, though Rubens was based at Antwerp in Flanders, and Rembrandt at Amsterdam in the North, in the country that was known then as the United Provinces, and today is called "the Netherlands" or, more conversationally, "Holland".

Rubens seems to belong to an older age, more classical and international. Rembrandt is emphatically a Dutchman, and his vision comes primarily from himself and not from antiquity. Both are magnificent, but it is Rembrandt to whom we feel closest, perhaps because of his fascination for the self-portrait, which makes us able to "read" him at every stage of his emotional life. The human face fascinated him from the beginning, a fortunate circumstance that brought him many lucrative commissions. However, it is never the externals that intrigue Rembrandt, whether in his own face or that of others. It is the inner workings of the mind, an obsession that eventually lost him his successful position and the respect of his peers. Yet in Rembrandt's paintings, the two worlds of inner and outer are not in opposition. It is precisely through the body, so wonderfully conjured up in the medium of paint, that Rembrandt unveils to us the nature of the sitter, even the passing moods, as well as the deep-seated attitudes.

Rembrandt was a miller's son; in other words, he came from a middle-class background. This was significant of his times, for alongside the independence struggle, Dutch society was changing and the middle class was growing. As it grew it created a strong new demand for realistic paintings, such as serious institutional portraits and images of working life. Rembrandt was one of those born painters who started young and was recognized almost at once. His earliest work, with its love for melodrama and keen interest in the humanity of his models, is essentially merely a hint at what is to come. His painting of a biblical story, *The Blinding of Samson (234)*, is superbly done; we flinch involuntarily from the sinister, silhouetted shape of the sword about to jab into a defenceless eye, and we tremble to see the tumultous violence that is raging within the dark and claustrophobic spaces of the cave. Samson writhes in anguish, Delilah flits away, half-gloating, half horrified, and the pressure builds up so high that it threatens to topple over into farce. We can see the same "overweight" of story in the early self-portraits, too.

234 Rembrandt, The Blinding of Samson, 1636, 236 x 300 cm (7 ft 9 in x 9 ft 10 in)

The *Self-portrait at the Age of About 21 Years (235)*, dark and secretive, shows Rembrandt in early adulthood, perhaps deliberately acting the part of the "artist". In his mid-life self-portraits he is more reflective, obviously successful, and quietly confident, gazing dispassionately out at us. A late work *(236)*, ten years before his death in relative poverty, shows a face stripped of all pretensions, looking earnestly, not at us, but at himself, judging himself not unkindly but with disinterested truthfulness. It is one of the most moving confessions of personal inadequacy ever made, great art won from personal failure.

PORTRAIT INTERPRETATION

Rembrandt is essentially a master story-teller. Sometimes, even in the portraits, he simply puts into our grasp the materials of the "story" and trusts us to enter into it by ourselves. *Portrait of a Lady with an Ostrich-feather Fan (237)* haunts us with its tranquil sadness, its bravery and

235 *Rembrandt*, Self-portrait at the Age of About 21 Years, *c. 1627, 20 x 16 cm (8 x 6¼ in)*

wisdom. Where do we see all this? Why should we be certain that the unknown lady has a history of sorrow and of exceptional joy? Rembrandt merely puts her before us, with light lingering as if with love on the once-beautiful face, the acceptant hands, the great, free sweep of the feather. Sometimes, though, he plays out

236 *Rembrandt*, Self-portrait, *1659, 84 x 66 cm (33 x 26¼ in)*

237 *Rembrandt*, Portrait of a Lady with an Ostrich-feather Fan, *c. 1660, 100 x 83 cm (39 x 32½ in)*

238 *Rembrandt,* Joseph Accused by Potiphar's Wife, *1655, 106 x 98 cm (41¾ x 38½ in)*

REMBRANDT'S ETCHINGS

Etching is a method of engraving in which the image is scratched onto a waxy coating on a metal plate, using a needle. The plate is then immersed in acid, which eats ("etches") into the metal where the image has been scratched. The technique is more versatile than the earlier metal-engraving process, as it enables the artist to alter the tone during the procedure. Etching reached its greatest heights as an art form with Rembrandt, who made his first etching in 1628. He enjoyed experimenting with different-textured papers and inks, and often reworked his etchings several times. His etchings cover a variety of subjects, including portraits, biblical stories, and scenes of daily life.

THE QUESTION OF ATTRIBUTION

In recent years many paintings that were thought to be by Rembrandt have been reattributed to other artists who worked in his workshop. Since the beginning of the 20th century over a third of the 988 "Rembrandts" have been reattributed. Experts check the colour, brushwork, and subject matter to confirm the correct artist. Today many of Rembrandt's old work-shop assistants are gaining new respect for having produced renowned paintings.

the story for us, counting upon our educated knowledge of the context. *Joseph Accused by Potiphar's Wife (238)* is an incident from the book of Genesis that has intrigued many artists. Old Potiphar, his young wife, and a handsome young Jewish slave: the outcome is as might be expected, except that Joseph is one of the heroes, and he repulses his master's wife and her advances. Woman scorned that she is, the wife accuses Joseph of attempted rape.

Rembrandt makes no distinction here between virtuous and vicious: all merit his compassion. Central is the wife, shifty of eye, false of gesture, clearly not really expecting to be believed. Sad in the shadows, Potiphar listens, and as clearly, does not believe. He knows his wife, and knows his servant. Chivalry ties his hands. The miracle

is that Rembrandt makes us see all this marital interplay, and the sorrow of it, neither party able to be truthful with each other, yet hating the falseness. Ignored amid the passionate privacies of husband and wife, Joseph waits for his public disgrace. He is wholly unassertive, unaggressive, and – most movingly – unself-pitying. He too understands that Potiphar cannot afford to ignore his wife's histrionics, and in a sense, it is only Joseph, the victim, who is capable of accepting the situation. Without a single overt sign, Rembrandt makes us aware that Joseph commits his cause to God, and rests in peace. The wife is isolated in her finery, concerned only with herself. Even the hand meant to gesticulate towards her rapist is not directed at him, but at his red cape hanging over her bed. Her other hand presses painfully to her breast. She is suffering, not only from her sexual rejection by a younger man, but from her own awareness of her life. Rembrandt involves us in her personality, just as he does in the unbelieving husband, who reaches out, not to her, but to her chair, the material realm where these two have their only contact. Joseph is lost in the gloomy vastness of the chamber, yet a faint nimbus (an emanation of light) enhaloes him.

Rembrandt has allowed light and colour to tell us the meaning of the event and make it move us with its inextricable human complexity and its profound sadness, redeemed only by blind faith in an unseen Providence.

A TENDER UNION

Perhaps the greatest and most profound of all Rembrandt's works is the mysteriously entitled "*Jewish Bride*" (239). This is the 19th century title, since Rembrandt left the work unnamed, and it is a suitable title because no viewer can help but be stirred by the picture's sense of the sacred, and the biblical garb suggests that the couple are Jewish. Who these two people are we shall probably never know, but they are clearly married. Both are past their first youth; they are plain in looks and rather careworn, though splendidly attired.

The husband enfolds his wife with an embrace of heartbreaking tenderness. One hand is on her shoulder and the other on the gift of his love, the golden chain that hangs on her breast. This chain is gold, it is his gift; it is still a chain. It is this aspect of love, that it binds, that its wonder is inseparable from its weight, that seems to preoccupy the woman. She is weighing up the responsibilities of loving and being loved, of receiving and of giving. It is not by chance that her other hand rests upon her womb, since children are the ultimate responsibility of married love.

Love binds, love weighs, love is the most serious experience that we can ever know in our life. It is Rembrandt's awareness of this profound truth, and the glorious visual beauty with which he makes it accessible to us, that makes the "*Jewish Bride*" so unforgettable.

239 Rembrandt, "The Jewish Bride", 1665–67, 122 × 168 cm (48 × 66 in)

"THE JEWISH BRIDE"

"The Jewish Bride" is one of Rembrandt's late works, and one of his most beautiful. Its superb harmony, of red and gold and warm browns, is built around the most profound and compassionate insight into human relationships. It received its current title only in the 19th century, a title that implies that this could be an imaginary portrayal of one of the celebrated biblical marriages: Tobias and Sarah, for instance, or Isaac and Rebekah. But the couple's dress and jewellery, together with the powerful sense of two distinct, living personalities, suggests rather that it is a portrait of an unknown couple.

CARING EMBRACE
This is surely one of the most tender of all paintings. Few depictions of mortal love reveal such depth with such subtlety. His hand lies flat across her bosom, symbolically as well as physically tender. Her hand rests on his, with the gentlest pressure, both acknowledging and returning his caress but again delicately, as though the full significance of their union lies deeper within.

AUTHENTIC EXPRESSION
Despite the opulence and beauty of the wedding costumes, the overwhelming impact of this great painting lies in its simple emotional authenticity. The groom is a little care-worn, his hair is thinning, and there are lines around his mouth and eyes. He makes no grand displays of devotion, and there is no sense of male victory but rather a quiet certainty as he inclines his head towards her, lost in thought almost as though listening to her thoughts. They do not formally address us as witnesses to their betrothal, and the intimacy is such that we feel we are intruding upon a very private moment.

SHIMMERING SLEEVE
The great billowing sleeve swells out like soft golden armour. The paint is heavily built up, and Rembrandt has used short, staccato brush strokes to recreate the many little pleats and folds that shimmer in the light. Touches of thick, white paint provide the brightest points. Thick, encrusted paint glints and shimmers across the surface of the canvas, and one senses that their costumes are stiff and heavy, expensively brocaded. The bride's jewellery is picked out in dots and blobs of paint, again highlighted with white.

240 William Heda, Still Life, 1637, 45 x 55 cm (17¾ x 21½ in)

THE DUTCH STILL-LIFE TRADITION
Humankind, fashioned from earth and spirit, and forever struggling towards the goal of integration, fascinated Rembrandt; still life did not greatly attract him, yet in his own milieu we find some wonderful examples of this genre.

A still life may be said to make a statement, while Rembrandt asks a question. And yet there is infinite curiosity in a work like Heda's (Willem Claesz, 1597–1680). His *Still Life (240)* of a tablecloth, silvery in the light, gleaming with goblets and glasses and wide plates and littered with the remnants of a meal, is painted with the utmost dignity and respect.

De Heem (Jan Davidsz, 1606–1683/84) paints a *Vase of Flowers (241)* as time defied, nature held eternally in a radiant present for our delectation; it is the other pole of the genre. Heda is silent, and de Heem sings aloud with pleasure: both enhance for us the meaning of the ordinary, achieving the same effect, in their own smaller fashion, as does Rembrandt. One might suspect that something in the Dutch temperament responds to the quietness of a still life. It demands from the artist the ability to discard the heights and lows of drama; which suggests, does it not, the flatness of the Dutch landscape?

RADIANT TRANSPARENCY
One of the glories of a great still life is that it is as great in the parts as it is in the whole. This is the aftermath of a meal, but the uneaten nut is a whole world in itself, the fallen glass has a radiant transparency, and we can pick out every detail of the scene with increasing pleasure. Notice how the light gleams on the edge of the knife blade, how the tankard changes in tone when we see it through the bell-shaped end of the glass. Heda shows refraction changing the outline of the tankard and the play of light.

241 Jan de Heem, Vase of Flowers, *c. 1645, 69 x 57 cm (27 x 22½ in)*

**OTHER WORKS BY
VERMEER**

The Little Street
(Rijksmuseum,
Amsterdam)

A Lady with Her Maid
(The Frick Collection,
New York)

*Interior with an
Astronomer*
(Louvre, Paris)

*Interior with a
Music Lesson*
(The Royal Collection,
Windsor Castle)

*Head of a Girl with a
Pearl Earring*
(Mauritshuis, The Hague)

*Interior with a
Girl at a Window*
(Gemäldegalerie,
Dresden)

THE SILENCE OF VERMEER

There is something about the reverent awareness
of the still life painter that reminds one of the
great solitary of 17th-century Holland, Jan Vermeer
(1632–75). He was not literally solitary, having
11 children and a powerful family of in-laws,
but none of the hubbub that must have filled
his small house is ever evident in his miraculous
paintings, far less any suggestion of family.

Vermeer does not need brightness in his
paintings. *Woman Holding a Balance (242)*, for
example, has the shutters almost closed, with
light stealing obliquely round the edges. It
catches the downy fur on the lady's jacket, the
decorated linen that falls gracefully round her
tilted head, the pearls gleaming on the shadowed table. It glances off a finger here and a
necklace there, but it insists only on its silence.
Silence "expresses" the purity of what exists:
pure because it exists. This picture has some
symbolism in that the lady is testing her empty
balance, and the picture behind her shows the
Last Judgment (see right).

But the meaning is equally in the "balance"
that we experience in the actual painting: darkness
and light are held in dynamic equilibrium, and
in fact the picture as a whole displays a variety
of balances – warm human flesh against the
silky and furry garment, the unstable human
hand against the frozen certainties of metal.

242 Vermeer, Woman Holding a Balance, *c. 1664, 42.5 x 38 cm (16¾ x 15 in)*

WOMAN HOLDING A BALANCE

This painting is also known as *Woman Weighing Gold*. It is a solemn, allegorical work, in which a young woman stands before the symbols of her material wealth, weighing them for their value, whilst behind her, in the painting on the wall, the figure of Christ can be seen "weighing" souls. The young woman is clearly pregnant, and it is significant that the two strongest accents of warm orange/gold do not emanate from her jewels or her gold but from the small window, high up in the wall, from which the light falls directly onto her stomach. It is tempting to read deeper meaning into this, as comparisons with annunciation paintings (see for example pp.50, 63, 86, and 92) unavoidably spring to mind.

MOOD OF CONTEMPLATION
Her knowing expression, with gently tilted head and almost closed eyes, shows her to be more than just idly enjoying her treasures. Rather, she is at a moment when she contemplates the meaning of value itself. She is dressed richly but simply, her head covered by a plain white hood that is "beaded" with drops of light. On the wall opposite her is a mirror, suggestive of her quiet self-contemplation.

JUDGMENT DAY
The painting on the wall is a version of the Last Judgment *possibly by the 16th-century Flemish altarpiece painter Jean Bellagambe (c. 1480–c. 1535). The air of serenity and contentment in the quiet room contrasts with the pitiful chaos of the damned, who are painted as flat, dim silhouettes behind the intensely vital, living form of the woman.*

A SIMPLE BALANCE
The woman will weigh her gold and pearls on a delicate brass balance with a gesture of infinite grace. The balance is rendered so finely that in parts it is barely visible, and touches of glimmering light shine on the empty pans. This is appropriate since we are again reminded of the other, final weighing depicted behind her.

FAMILY VALUABLES
A rich blue tablecloth has been pushed back, and scattered over the table-top, spilling out of jewellery boxes, is her collection of pearls and gold. Each little orb consists of a single droplet of light, made from individual touches of paint that are jewel-like in themselves. The flat coins, or gold weights, are given a sense of roundness by just the slightest highlight.

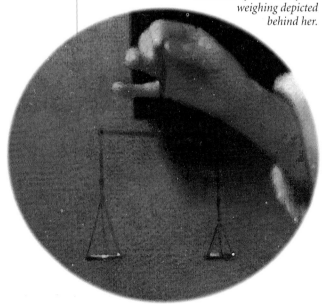

243 Vermeer, View of Delft, 1658, 100 x 117 cm (39 x 46 in)

We come to believe that Vermeer's pictures have a reality – not like everyday reality, but greater, less fragile. It is his unique triumph to concentrate with absolute – or so it seems – optical fidelity on the minutiae of material things. Every texture has its complete integrity in painterly form. He elides, of course, but we are unaware of it, and this sense of total truth, offered to us through a reverence for what is bodily present, effortlessly acquires a sense of the spiritual.

TRANSCENDING THE CITY
The French writer Marcel Proust, who centred his whole literary work upon the recovery, alive and powerful, of memory, thought *View of Delft* (243) the greatest work ever painted. On one level, it appears so unassuming: a topographical setting-out of the appearance of this Dutch city. Vermeer is not inventing, only describing. But he takes the bare facts of the city and its approaches and, without manipulation, renders them transcendent.

That city shining out at us across the water is both Delft and the heavenly Jerusalem, the city of peace. It offers profound variety, not in extravagance but in its simple mixture of roofs and towers, of churches and houses, of sunlit areas and swathes of lovely shadow. Overhead, the sky arches, the rain clouds lift and disperse, the lofty area of blue almost visibly grows.

The tiny figures on the near quayside are vital: they are us, not in the holy city yet, still sundered and yearning, but with great hope.

Boats are moored and no obstacle presents itself. It is the utter ordinariness of the scene that is so piercingly evocative of the Paradise world. Even when Vermeer paints a *Kitchen Maid (244)* he bathes the kitchen in a quiet radiance. She is merely pouring out milk, but there is a sense of luminous stillness, of time gently slowed, of body translucent with soul, of secular holiness. The simplicities of her yellow bodice and her blue working apron gleam out at us, not beautiful in themselves, but beautiful because light makes all it shines on share its own brightness. Her plain, broad, peasant face is lost in absorption with her task, rather as we think Vermeer must have been as he painted her. He is one of the artists who is immediately accessible, which makes his years of neglect all the more astonishing.

HALS' BRAVADO
Frans Hals (c.1582/83–1666) also knew neglect, but his case is not the same as Vermeer's. We can sympathize with the bewilderment, for example, of the wealthy Coymans family at seeing the finery of young *Willem Coymans (245)* depicted by a rash dribble of paint, with rough slashes pleating his linen sleeve and a rather brutal sensuality lightly informing his face. Willem himself, however, may well have liked his portrait very much indeed (Hals' patrons tended to be delighted with his versions of them).

Willem has a daredevil gallantry, a look of dissipated splendour that any young man might find highly appealing to his self-esteem. Hals does not delve deep into personality like Rembrandt (see p.200) or contemplate all sitters under the noble light of Vermeer (see p.208).

244 Vermeer, Kitchen Maid, 1656–61, 45 x 40 cm (17¾ x 16 in)

245 *Frans Hals,* **Portrait of Willem Coymans,** *1645, 77 x 63 cm (30½ x 25 in)*

ALLA PRIMA TECHNIQUE

Until the 17th century most artists who used oils underpainted their surfaces first, to achieve a consistent surface. Frans Hals was one of the pioneers of the *alla prima* (Italian for "at first") technique in which the paint is applied directly to the ground without underpainting. The effect of this technique is clearly visible in the broad brush strokes and spontaneous textural qualities of much of Frans Hals' work. With the development of better pigments in the 19th century the technique became more popular.

He first made his reputation with a series of portraits, ranging from the celebrated *Laughing Cavalier* to a variety of low-life sketches of gypsies and drunkards, which were all painted in the years 1620–25 and were all delightful renderings of the nuances of expression in the sitters' smiling or leering faces. Hals' family came from Antwerp in Flanders and moved to Haarlem, in the Protestant North, when he was just a child. One is tempted to imagine what he would have produced had he stayed in the Catholic South, where his inclination towards extravagant display would certainly have found a wider field of expression than that of portraiture. Hals paints what he sees, with a sort of daredevil carelessness. He leaps upon the tightrope of pictorial art, rarely stumbling, but astonishing us with his emphatic facility. He achieves "the mostest with the leastest", to adapt the words of an American general.

Much of the work of Hals appeals to us because of its light, virtuoso quality, but in his impoverished old age he rose to a gravity that puts the stamp of greatness on his work.

246 *Frans Hals,* The Women Regents of the Haarlem Almshouse, *1664, 170 x 250 cm (5 ft 7 in x 8 ft 2 in)*

247 *Pieter de Hooch,* A Dutch Courtyard, *c. 1660, 68 x 58 cm (27 x 23 in)*

His *Women Regents of the Haarlem Almhouse (246)*, painted shortly before the artist's own almshouse death, is a totally serious picture. He has forgotten the ego that spurred him on to witty bravura. Here he shows us not merely the outward look of these tired and elderly women, but something of their individual personalities, and something of their corporate attitude to the responsibilities of their office.

DUTCH GENRE PAINTING

Pieter de Hooch (1629–84) has the uneasy distinction of making us aware of how great is Vermeer. De Hooch is a semi-Vermeer – all the ingredients but lacking the magic. It is as if some of Frans Hals' worldly confidence had seeped into the work, making it parochial.

Yet of course, it is the celebration of the parochial that gives de Hooch his charm, a very real charm, inadequate only in comparison with the very greatest of his contemporaries. *A Dutch Courtyard (247)* has an enchanting immediacy, with its occupants "snapped" as if by a camera. The sense of reality is seductive; at any moment the girl, we feel, will go inside through the open door, and we will go with her. The illusion is of a merely temporary pause in activity, of daylight and weather, of work and play.

This feeling of time held still and on the point of moving forward is also the beauty of *The Skittle Players Outside an Inn (248)* by Jan Steen (1626–79). Much of his work has a coarse vitality,

248 *Jan Steen*, **The Skittle Players Outside an Inn**, *c. 1652, 33 x 27 cm (13 x 10½ in)*

249 *Albert Cuyp*, Herdsman with Cows by a River, *c. 1650, 45 × 74 cm (17¾ × 29 in)*

with peasants junketing and a general air of happy vulgarity. But this painting is marvellous, evocative of an evening in early summer, with the viewer made privy to a moment of calm enjoyment. Calm enjoyment is also the constant theme of Albert Cuyp (1620–91), the enjoyment being mostly on the part of cows, which are washed in a heavenly golden radiance, inhabiting a natural paradise on our behalf *(249)*. The herd stands peacefully in the peaceful waters, the ships move past them slowly into the light. It is essentially a communication of serenity. Sunlight and its bovine enjoyers do not seem the stuff of great art, and this is one of the enchantments of the Baroque. It makes its beauty out of the ordinary with great gusto. Often the focus is on the land or sea, flat fields becoming as spaciously beautiful as the romantic mountains of earlier or later art.

Jacob van Ruisdael (1628/9–82), can take a *Forest Scene (250)*, a tangle of trees and glimpsed water, a great dead horizontal of stricken branch and root, dark skies forming and humankind departing, and without tidying it up or making a moral, give us a moving depiction of the tangle of our complex and vulnerable lives. He has a greater weight than any other Dutch landscape artist. There is almost a sense of a tragic dimension, but never one without hope. His uncle, Salomon van Ruisdael (c.1600–70), works the same magic with river scenes.

Pieter Saenredam (1597–1665), focusing on another aspect of the workaday, takes us into the great spaces of church interiors, like

250 *Jacob van Ruisdael*, Forest Scene, *c. 1660/65, 105 × 131 cm (41 × 51½ in)*

251 Pieter Saenredam, The Grote Kerk, Haarlem, *1636–37, 60 × 82 cm (23½ × 32¼ in)*

**WILLIAM III
OF ORANGE**
As Stadholder (ruler) of the
United Provinces, William
III of Orange (1650–1702)
rescued his country from
the hands of Louis XIV in
the Franco-Dutch wars of
1672–79. He was a sincere
Calvinist and a respected
patron of the arts. He had
grown up in the uncertain
climate of the rule of the
anti-Orange party led by
Johann de Witt. In the
revolution of 1672 he
overthrew his enemies
and became Stadholder.
He became King of
Britain and Ireland in the
"Glorious Revolution" of
1688, when the Whigs and
Tories invited him to invade
the country and claim the
throne for himself and his
wife Mary (daughter of
the British King James II).

The Grote Kerk, Haarlem (251). The play of
light on these silent architectural masses has an
almost Vermeerish profundity, a strange immediacy. It would be easy to get carried away into
speculation about the meaning of "interiors",
which these pictures seem to be about, and so
it is useful to remember that Saenredam, who
specializes in church interiors, somehow also
manages to get the same "inner" quality when
he paints church exteriors.

The Dutch seemed to have an insatiable love
for the actualities of their surroundings: their
Calvinism, however tolerantly held, makes the
idea of explicitly religious painting unappealing,
and we can feel a great weight of quasi-religious
significance being quietly removed, to rest upon
landscape, still life, and portraiture. There was
still room for the so-called "history" painting
genre, but the most popular narrative painting
was that of Gerard Dou (1613–75).

Dou's works were small, exquisitely finished,
and technically perfect. Although this praise
sounds rather mechanical, there is no doubt
that, at his best, Dou well deserved his reputation.
These small, jewel-like pictures still delight
and allure: it may be for the sheer contrast
between their tiny size and their intensity of
focus. Dou had been Rembrandt's pupil, but he
seems to have taken little of the master's spirit.
The cluttered but brilliant cave interior of *The*

Hermit (252) has Dou's own technical intricacy
but nothing of Rembrandt's spiritual intensity,
and they remain essentially genre works.

252 Gerard Dou, The Hermit, *1670,
46 × 34 cm (18 × 13½ in)*

THE GRAND TOUR
A favourite pastime of the
young rich in the 17th
and 18th centuries was
to go on the Grand Tour.
Accompanied by a servant,
a young aristocrat would
tour Europe, culminating
in a stay in Italy to
appreciate the arts of
classical antiquity. This
18th-century caricature
shows a horrified father
meeting his fashionable
returning son.

FRANCE: A RETURN TO CLASSICISM

Dutch painters loved landscape, and they acquired great skill in its depiction, but the great names in landscape painting in the 17th century were French. Foremost among these were Nicolas Poussin and Claude Lorrain, who both lived for years in Italy and were strongly influenced by Italy's natural Classicism, however dissimilar they were in other ways.

PIERRE PUGET

Recognized as the greatest French Baroque sculptor, Pierre Puget (1620–94) originally trained as a ship's sculptor in Marseilles. His earliest work is on the portals of the town hall in Toulon, completed in 1656. He created his most famous work, the *Milo of Crotona*, for Louis XIV's palace at Versailles. The sculpture shown above, *The Assumption of the Virgin*, is now kept in Marseilles.

The lure of Rome, the heartland of the Baroque style, was strong in the first half of the 17th century, so much so that the French painting tradition, which was classical at heart, was considerably weakened by the exodus of artists. Among these was Nicolas Poussin (1594– 1665), who enjoyed considerable fame in Rome and painted many important works there. It took the persuasive powers of Louis XIII and his Chief Minister, Cardinal Richelieu (see p.223), to entice Poussin back from Rome in 1640.

The King had made previous attempts to rejuvenate the French tradition in painting, but he had met with little real success. A tradition still existed, and was even growing, in France,

and it was both delicate in palette and dignified in approach. But the French School did not develop until Poussin's arrival from Rome. His art drew on Carracci's legacy of Venetian harmony and ideal beauty (see p.182). In Italy, he had studied the High Renaissance masters, together with antique sculpture, and he was also influenced by the arch-classicist Domenichino (see p.183), who was 13 years his senior and who ran a successful workshop in Rome.

Poussin's art represents a rejection of the emotional aspects of Italian Baroque, but at the same time sacrifices none of the Baroque's spiritual intensity and richness – which distinguishes him from Neoclassical art (see p.256).

253 Nicolas Poussin, The Holy Family on the Steps, 1648, 68 x 98 cm (27 x 38½ in)

In a sense, his aims in painting have more in common with those of the Renaissance artists (see pp.79–138). Poussin brought to the Baroque an austere, restrained Classicism, combined with a clear, glowing light.

He is an artist of the utmost intelligence, achieving total integration of every element within his pictures. But it is a visual intelligence, a massive understanding of beauty, so that what could be daunting in its orderliness is radiant with supreme grace. This great painterly intellect moves us rather than convinces us. In the words that John Donne, the 17th-century English poet, used to describe his beloved, it could be said of Poussin that his "body thought". It is this wonderful incarnation of vision in actuality that makes Poussin supreme.

AUSTERE BEAUTY

The Holy Family on the Steps (253) might seem, at first viewing, not a landscape work at all. This is, broadly, quite correct: the concentration is upon the five human figures in the centre. But they form a great equilateral triangle, based upon the long, low step that acts as a plinth and a barrier. Mary is a sacred plinth herself, a holy barrier that holds Jesus up for us to see but is His earthly safeguard. So protected, the naked Child leans down to His nude cousin, little John the Baptist, who is untended by his own mother, St Elizabeth, all of whose longing attention is fixed upon Mary's Child.

Balancing her, humbly seated in shadow, sits St Joseph, whose elegant feet emerge into astonishingly clear light. Three objects line the lower margin: a basket of fruit, symbolic of the world's fertility that will spring from this Family: a fertility of grace. Near Joseph, as if under his care, are two containers – a classical vase, reminiscent of the Greeks, and a box, which recalls the eastern kings and their costly gifts.

Material riches lie at the base, then, and from here the painting soars up, the eye being led by balustrade and pillar, to the porticos that open on infinity and the endless sky. The Holy Family is clearly not sitting on the steps of a real building: this is more an idealized version of an entrance, though it lacks symmetry. The glories of this world are asymmetrical; only the perfect balance of the Holy Family has the beauty of pure rationality. The centre is an apple offered to the Holy Child by our representative, John.

The fruit of the fall is here redeemed, and the discreet orange trees indicate that redemption has now happened. There is fruit galore, fruit for us all. Mary holds Jesus almost as if He is living fruit, and at once we pick up eucharistic resonances. In Poussin there is always subtlety

254 Nicolas Poussin, Self-portrait, 1650,
97 x 73 cm (38 x 29 in)

upon subtlety, but at no time is it either forced subtlety or mere conceptual cleverness. He takes his concepts into his own depths, and there he finds their proper form. This painting is of an ascent, powered by the insistent verticals and made credible by the exquisite placement of continual stepping-stones of horizontals.

The austere *Self-portrait* in the Louvre *(254)* makes no concessions to vanity. Poussin looks out gravely, with his fleshy nose and secretive eyes, and his lips shut with that firmness so obvious in all his work. He encompasses himself with canvases that are also geometrical intensifiers. His background, he implies, is one of severe order. Yet the only actual picture we see – a young woman being embraced – has a romantic charm. The other rectangles of canvas, as well as the door, are blank, and all the frames are blank. While seeming to expose himself, Poussin is actually preserving his secrecy.

NICOLAS POUSSIN
Poussin aimed to achieve a unity of mood in each picture by developing his theory of modes. According to this theory, the subject and the emotional situation of the painting dictate the appropriate treatment. Poussin also used a miniature stage set to practice composition and lighting for his paintings.

SHEPHERDS AND ARCADIA

To educated people in the 17th century the name Arcadia readily evoked the pastoral tradition, that easy-going genre of poetry that had developed in parallel with epic writing since the time of the classical Greeks. The tradition stems from the carefree, open-air life that was supposedly enjoyed by shepherds and shepherdesses, who spent all summer guarding their flocks. Consequently they had plenty of time in which to play their flutes and compose love poems, which they might sing to one another, perhaps in a contest.

Best remembered of the pastoral poets were Theocritus in Sicily and Virgil in Italy, whose *Eclogues* are the best remembered of all. Arcadia is mentioned in the *Eclogues*, and occasionally in literature since the Renaissance.

The phrase "*et in Arcadia ego*" cannot be traced to any known source in the classics. It means either "I, the one who is dead, was once in Arcadia too," or "I, Death, am in Arcadia too." The Italian painter Guercino (see p.185) made a painting with this same theme in 1620.

Poussin himself produced two paintings on the "Death in Arcadia" theme. The first (the Chatsworth version) was painted between 1630 and 1632. In it, a group of shepherds discovers with shock that a tomb, with its disturbing message, exists in their idyllic countryside.

They are shown leaning forwards in a tense attitude, confronting the fearsome discovery. In the version shown here (the Louvre version, *255*), originally entitled *Happiness Subdued by Death* and painted in 1638–40, the shepherds form a more relaxed group around the tomb. Instead of reacting dramatically they seem to be pondering the meaning of the inscription. Each of the four shepherds is expressing his or her own personal emotional response. Without overemphasis, Poussin makes us clearly aware of those vulnerable humans in all their individuality.

Poussin's Arcadia is a silent place; even the shepherds seem to be communicating by gesture rather than by word. They seem to have found, to their bewilderment, their first evidence of death. It is evidence, too, that their beautiful country has a history, has been lived in and died in, and yet this history has been completely forgotten. They puzzle out the inscription on the tomb with wonder and fear.

What gives this picture its force, of course, is its relevance to our own personal histories. We pass a milestone in human maturity when we come to an emotional understanding of death and of our own relative insignificance in the context of human history. Countless generations lived before us and will live after us. In all the magnificence of their youthful beauty, the shepherds must accept this.

255 Nicolas Poussin, Et in Arcadia Ego, *c. 1638–40, 85 × 121 cm (33½ × 47½ in)*

ET IN ARCADIA EGO

Historically, Arcadia was the central plateau of the mountainous region of southern Greece and was inhabited by shepherds and hunters. But Arcadia was also an earthly paradise, a pastoral idyll celebrated by poets and artists as early as the 3rd century BC. It was the home of romantic love, ruled over by Pan, the rustic god of "all things": flocks and herds, woods and fields. Its native shepherds and shepherdesses shared their simple paradise with nymphs, satyrs, centaurs, and the bacchantes.

SILENT COMMUNICATION
The shepherds and shepherdess respond in different ways to the discovery of death. Some are content to ponder its significance, while others question and decipher. All, however, are silent, revealing their sadness or curiosity through individual gestures and expressions. One young shepherd looks up at the young woman beside him with an especially urgent communication, as though struck with sudden realization of his own immortality.

LANDSCAPE
Although this is one of Poussin's mature works, his treatment of the landscape is not as stylistically developed as is his treatment of form and colour throughout the rest of the painting. The line of trees and foliage serves primarily to enclose the scene and act as a backdrop to the main focus of attention, which centres on the discovery of a tomb.

"I TOO WAS ONCE IN ARCADIA"
The inscription is the central focal point of the whole work. All our attention is directed to it, reinforced by the puzzled gestures of the shepherds as they run their fingers over the tomb as though hoping to discover its mysterious identity. The painting takes on the nature of an elegy as they quietly and solemnly contemplate the significance of the words (see left).

CLASSICAL FORM
Poussin has not portrayed the simple and carefree shepherds and shepherdesses supposed to inhabit Arcadia, but instead classically formed, sober and dignified figures from antiquity. The young woman manifests the classical ideal, with her smooth brow and fine nose, the proportions of her head to her body, and above all, her noble, statuesque bearing. In her figure, we can see Poussin's distinctive late handling of colour. It is sharp, strong, and clear, and the artist's growing passion for order and clarity is paramount. The four figures form a tight cluster around the tomb, the balance equally distributed among them.

The Funeral of Phocion (256) shows Poussin's landscape art at its most profound. There is a story in this painting, one of those classic tales of great moral meaning that were so dear to him. Phocion was an Athenian general who argued for peace at a time when the majority were for war with Macedon. His enemies used Athens' democratic system to have him condemned.

Poussin shows this victim of judicial murder being carried to his burial by a mere two faithful slaves. They carry him through a world teeming with antique activity. Behind them the great city can be seen, with its temple, its domed capitol proclaiming Athenian order, its inhabitants peacefully busy at their rightful occupations.

Yet all this outward stability is made into a lie by the sad pair in the foreground, moving disconsolately through the wholly civilized terrain on their uncivilized task. Justice has been flouted, cruelty and envy have triumphed: the great pacific state apparatus grinds on with massive and unreal dignity. The eye is entranced by the sheer intelligibility and interest of the scene, by the nobility of the concept and the beauty of its execution. It is as intense as any poetry, yet the poetry is always epic. Poussin can daunt, but he is worth all our effort.

CLAUDE'S PASTORAL IDYLLS

Claude (Claude Gellée, 1600–82), whose Frenchness was marked by adding "Lorrain" to his name, was a fellow inhabitant of Rome with Poussin. Claude too is a very great artist, but not an intellectual. Where Poussin thought out a work, Claude used his intuition. One understood the classic world, the other entered it by imagination: both visions are wonderful.

Claude is forever making us free of the classical paradise-that-never-was (or at least, not literally) so that it is subliminally the essence of his work. He sees the landscape of the Roman Campagna (a low-lying plain surrounding Rome) as bathed in a golden light, a place in harmony with the nymphs or else with the heroes of the Bible. We feel it is much the same for Claude whether we gaze across the wooded hills with Paris and the three goddesses he must assess for the most beautiful in *The Judgment of Paris (257)*, or with the biblical Isaac and Rebekah, who have come to celebrate their marriage in *Landscape with the Marriage of Isaac and Rebekah (258)*. The "subject" is not what the title indicates. Paris and Isaac and Rebekah are excuses, pretexts for his venture into the lovely lost world of pastoral poetry.

256 Nicolas Poussin, The Funeral of Phocion, *1648, 47 × 71 cm (18½ × 28 in)*

257 *Claude Lorrain,* **The Judgment of Paris,** *1645/46, 112 x 150 cm (44 x 59 in)*

THE JUDGMENT OF PARIS

At the wedding of the Greek hero Peleus to his bride Thetis, all the gods are invited except Eris, goddess of Strife. In revenge she throws down a golden apple inscribed "to the fairest", insisting that Paris, son of the King of Troy, must award the apple to one of three goddesses: Minerva, Venus, and Juno. Venus promises Paris the love of any woman he chooses and describes Helen, wife of the King of Sparta. Paris accordingly awards the apple to Venus, then abducts Helen and carries her back to Troy. This act provokes the Trojan war – in which Paris is fatally wounded.

Both landscapes are made glorious by their trees, by the amazing sense they provide of immense spaciousness. The eye roams untrammelled to the distant hills and follows the curves of the shining waters. It is not a real landscape, but its power to arouse emotion is real.

To the modern eye, *The Marriage of Isaac and Rebekah* might seem to work better than the *Judgment of Paris* if only because Claude's great weakness is thought to be his painting of the human figure. In *The Marriage* the tiny human forms dancing and feasting in the glade are as removed from us in space as they are in time. We stand at a height looking down, and although in the Bible this marriage was an important event for the continuance of the "seed of Abraham", it is the landscape that matters here, that dwarfs the human celebrants into relative insignificance. Claude clearly recognized this by his very title. Yet the landscape, so shadowed, so immemorial, does not fight the theme of marriage; it reinforces it.

In *The Judgment of Paris* we are much closer to the drama. The four actors (five if we include the infant Cupid, who clings to his mother) are fairly large and also fairly individualized. The painting captures a moment at the start of the judgment. Juno, as queen, is the first of the three goddesses to speak, putting her case as the most beautiful to Paris. He is perching rather insecurely on his rock, almost dislodged by the vigour of her approaches. Minerva, as befits a wise woman, abstracts herself from the scene and in so doing becomes its appropriate but unwitting centre. It is on her white body, as she leans forward to tie her sandal, that Claude's golden light so lovingly lingers.

258 *Claude Lorrain,* **Landscape with the Marriage of Isaac and Rebekah,** *1648, 149 x 197 cm (58¾ x 77½ in)*

THE CLAUDE GLASS
Named after Claude
Lorrain, the Claude Glass
was used in the 17th and
18th centuries by landscape
painters. A small, convex
glass mirror backed in
black or silver would
be used to reflect the
landscape in miniature
and in terms of light and
shade. This restraining
of the colours enabled the
artist to assess the relative
tonality between different
parts of the landscape.
The 18th-century Claude
Glass shown above is
in a lined carrying case.

259 Claude Lorrain, Landscape with Ascanius Shooting the Stag of Silvia, *1682, 120 x 150 cm (47 x 59 in)*

Very occasionally theme matters in Claude, as
in his last painting, *Landscape with Ascanius
Shooting the Stag of Silvia (259)*. Here again is
the whole lovely expanse of nature, but this time
it is all affected by the dreadful certainty that
murder is to be done and the balance of the
Italian pre-Roman peace destroyed. Claude
homes in on the tension of the one moment
when Ascanius would still be able, if he chose,
to hold back the arrow. The world waits in fear,
and stag and man are locked in puzzled
questioning. We need not know the legend to
guess what will happen. We have indeed destroyed
our sacred stag and brought down upon ourselves
the end of peace. All the tragedy of the daily
newspaper is implicit in this great painting.

THE ART OF THE EVERYDAY
Poussin, sublime by nature, said that those who
painted "mean subjects" did so because of "the
weakness of their talents". This obviously has
no reference to Claude, but it might indicate
why the le Nain brothers and Georges de la Tour
were relatively unappreciated. The le Nains took
for their subject the humble lives of the peasants.
Landscape with Peasants (260), by Louis le Nain
(1593–1648) has, in fact, a lovely sweep of
dullish scenery that seduces by its resolute lack
of excitement. Peasants stand or sit, quiet amid
the quietness, unaffected as is the painter by any
need to become "interesting".

260 Louis le Nain, Landscape with Peasants, *c. 1640, 47 x 57 cm (18½ x 22½ in)*

LIGHT AND DARKNESS

Georges de la Tour (1593–1652) did not exactly choose "mean subjects", but he painted with a light-and-shade duality that relates to the Caravaggesque tradition (see p.177), and he did so in a manner that verges on the simplistic. His forms are sparse, his design bare. He was a provincial painter, and his unusual freedom from accustomed conventions might well have seemed inadequate or "mean" to a classicist. *The Repentant Magdalen (261)* concentrates with semi-brutal fierceness on the legendary period that the Magdalen, who had been a sinner, spent in lamenting her past. But it seems rather to be the picture of abstract thought. The Magdalen is shown as lost in profound musing, her hand caressing the skull, a "vanitas" motif, which is repeated in its mirrored reflection. The candle – the only source of light – is masked by the dome of bare bone, and the Magdalen does not so much repent as muse. With great daring, the major part of the picture is more darkness, with the young woman looming up out of the shadow like a second Lazarus. It is a work hard to forget, yet its power is difficult to explain. Vulgar? Or spiritually intense?

261 *Georges de la Tour*, **The Repentant Magdalen**, *c. 1635, 113 x 93 cm (44 x 36½ in)*

THE PHILOSOPHY OF DESCARTES

Regarded as the founder of modern philosophy, Descartes (1596–1650) was a French philosopher and mathematician. His *Discourse on Method*, published in 1637, explains the basis of his theory of dualism –"I think therefore I am". He argued that reason reigns supreme and that it is vital to systemize knowledge. The idea of God is so complex that no man could have invented it and so God must have planted the idea into man's mind.

CARDINAL RICHELIEU

Under Louis XIII, France was a weak country, with the Protestant population forming a state within a state. Richelieu (1585–1642) became Minister of State in 1624 and his first task was to reduce the power of the Huguenots. He was to remain a vital pioneering force in France until the ascendency of Louis XIV, and he survived many plots against his life. He died leaving Louis XIV in a position of absolute power over a stronger and more unified country.

ROCOCO

With Antoine Watteau we move into the Rococo era. This style evolved in France and became a dominant influence in 18th-century art through most of Europe. The word was not a flattering term (few art labels ever have been); it was coined in the early 19th century, deriving from the French word rocaille. *This was the name of a style of interior decoration that made use of shell patterns and other ornamental stonework. Rococo art was thought of as thin, airy-fairy, not the serious art of the past.*

The Rococo style emerged in the early 18th century as an exaggeratedly decorative variation of the Baroque. Perhaps, at first, only the French took it seriously; its first great champion was Jean Antoine Watteau (1684–1721). There is an underlying sadness in his pictures that gives a painful note to all his airs and graces, a wistfulness that belongs more to the 17th than the 18th century. Watteau was born in Flanders and lived most of his short life in exile in France. His work evinces a poignant sense of never belonging, of having no lasting stake in the world, that is

CONTEMPORARY ARTS

1710
Sir Christopher Wren completes St Paul's Cathedral, London

1711
The first European porcelain is made at Meissen, near Dresden in Saxony

1719
The English novelist Daniel Defoe publishes *Robinson Crusoe*

1729
Johann Sebastian Bach composes the *St Matthew Passion*

1742
Handel composes *The Messiah*

1759
The French writer Voltaire writes *Candide*

FETES GALANTES
Watteau arrived in Paris in 1702 and soon made a reputation as the inventor of a new artistic genre known as *fêtes galantes*. The name means "a feast of courtship" and was coined by members of the French Academy in 1717. It applies to any open-air scene with a mixed company, such as musicians, actors, and flirtatious lovers, all enjoying themselves out of doors.
Many of Watteau's contemporaries favoured the genre, using it to portray the manners and fashions of the aristocracy.

262 Jean Antoine Watteau, "Embarkation for Cytherea", 1717, 129 x 194 cm (50½ x 76 in)

specific to Watteau's own circumstances but has a moving relevance to us all. His training and early artistic development took place outside the confines of Paris, which is lucky for us, since the Parisian art world was becoming increasingly academic. He studied in Luxembourg under Claude Audran. Here he was fully able to absorb Rubens' great *Life of Maria de' Médici* cycle (see p.188), and we can see something of the sensual dynamism of Rubens – only in miniature form – in Watteau's delicate paintings.

LOVE AND PATHOS

Watteau was the inventor of a new art genre (though few ever could make his poetic use of it): *fêtes galantes*, in which lovers sang and danced and flirted, always on the edge of loss.

263 Jean Antoine Watteau, Italian Comedians, *probably 1720, 63 x 76 cm (25 x 30 in)*

This example, "*Embarkation for Cytherea*" *(262)*, is in fact misnamed, but has been so immemorially. It shows lovers leaving, not embarking for, the fabled isle of lovers, on which they have made their vows to the shadowy Venus who is hidden in the undergrowth. The act of taking vows has made them into inseparable pairs, but they leave with reluctance. Never again will love be so accessible and so certain: in leaving the seclusion of Venus and her bower they set all at risk and jeopardize their happiness. Watteau has no need to make this explicit. His pairs of lovers are satiated with fulfilment, yet move sadly and slowly. Love does not bring joy.

Watteau's other famous theme differs only at the literal level: his many scenes featuring the troupes of actors, Italian or French, who entertained the court. These two nationalities had different approaches to drama, but both traditions were based on the theme of love and its disappointments. *Italian Comedians (263)* has its jester and its gaily posturing actors, its pretty ladies, and its flirtations. But at the centre is the strange, tragic figure of Pierrot, taller than anyone else, starkly visible in his silken whites, motionless and heraldic.

There is even a blasphemous echo of Pilate presenting Christ to the mockery of the people, and it is impossible to say that Watteau did not explicitly intend this echo. No crown of thorns, but a crown of flowers lies neglected and rejected on the steps. All gleams, and there is laughter, but we are strangely chilled.

COMMEDIA DELL'ARTE

The Italian *commedia dell'arte* began as an anti-literary form of theatre based on improvisation, with juggling and acrobatics. It had a set of stock characters, the foremost of which were a rich, foolish old man and his clever servant Harlequin. Two others were Columbine and Pierrot, the latter being the embodiment of out-spoken simplicity. With its anti-establishment character it was banned by the French nobility in 1687. In 1716 the Italian actors were recalled by the Duc d'Orléans, Louis XV's Regent from 1713 to 1723. Scripts were eventually written for the *commedia dell'arte*; these had a delicate verbal style, and often an erotic undercurrent.

DIANA BATHING

Diana (known as Artemis to the Greeks) has several identities: as chastity, and more commonly, as the huntress, in which guise she appears in this painting. To the Romans, she had three personifications: Diana for the earth, Hecate for the underworld, and Luna for the moon – which explains the crescent moon she wears in her hair.

PEARLS
This detail reveals how the surface of the painting is covered in a network of fine cracks. The smooth, uninterrupted finish of Diana's perfect skin seems all the more delicate. Pearls suggest the moon, both in their gentle gleam and their lovely rotundity, and these are Diana's only ornaments. She needs nothing else, suggests Boucher, her godhead is apparent.

ATTENDANT NYMPH
Boucher has chosen to depict Diana after the hunt; to have shown her in active pursuit of game would not have suited his temperament at all. Instead, we are presented with what is essentially a boudoir scene, a fine young lady seated on her expensive silks and pampered by her handmaiden – except that this happens to be the goddess Diana, attended by a reverent nymph who dries her feet, and seated in a secluded woodland glade.

DIANA'S HOUNDS
Diana as the Huntress is shown with hunting dogs, arrows, and quiver. One of the dogs, alerted by a noise in the undergrowth, lifts its head and sniffs the air. This is an allusion, perhaps, to the doomed mortal, Actaeon, who, according to legend, accidentally stumbles upon the scene and, as punishment for beholding the naked goddess, is turned into a stag and devoured by his own dogs.

SPOILS OF THE HUNT
A rabbit and two doves have been strung onto Diana's dainty bow. Diana was often depicted in opposition to Venus, the goddess of love. Here, Venus' attribute of a pair of doves – symbols of love and lust – has been vanquished by chastity. The birds' earthy, vital nature contrasts sharply with Diana's unearthly, pure skin.

264 *François Boucher,* Diana Bathing, *1742, 57 x 73 cm (22½ x 28¾ in)*

BOUCHER'S SOLID STYLE

After Watteau came François Boucher (1703–70), a fuller and more solid painter, less magical but more robust. This contrast may be the outward reflection of the fact that he was in relatively better health than Watteau, whose constitution was frail. Boucher demonstrates the Rococo fear of the solemn, and his art – more than that of Watteau – reveals the truly Rococo spirit of decoration.

Yet, despite this ornamental spirit, Boucher's entrancing ladies, who are usually shown sweetly displaying to us their naked charms, are not trivial. At his best, Boucher succeeds in making us share in his worship of the female body, its vulnerable roundness, and its essential innocence. There is far more to Boucher than appears at first viewing. He is a great celebrator,

and a work like his masterpiece, *Diana Bathing (264)*, celebrates not only the firmly rounded goddess and her eager companion, but the civilized terrain of parkland as well. This is a cultured landscape, in which the savagery of nature has been tamed.

At the start of the 20th century Boucher was held in very low esteem, seen merely as a decorator and an artist of charm but little substance. His work in fact is very out of key with contemporary attitudes, especially feminism. Strangely, however, he has been creeping up in critical esteem as the spirit of his work – which is genuinely reverential – becomes more apparent to the discerning eye. Creative beauty in all its forms moved him emotionally and his eye dwells as lovingly on the dogs and the riverbank as it does on the nymphs.

MADAME DE POMPADOUR

As official mistress of the French King Louis XV, Madame de Pompadour was a powerful figure in French artistic life. She was a great patron of the arts, commissioning a number of painters and poets, and had a huge influence on the king's policies. She also founded the Military school and the porcelain factory at Sèvres.

Boucher never ogles, but – and in this respect he is akin to Rubens – lifts his hat and sweeps low the plumes. *Venus Consoling Love (265)* floats deliciously onto the canvas, one naked goddess and three naked children. They have an eerie similarity, all four, to the fatly feathered pair of nesting birds among the reeds. Nothing here is real or meant to be. But the sense of pleasure in ideal beauty is very real, and makes the work into much more than a triviality.

BEFORE THE REVOLUTION

Fragonard (Jean-Honoré, 1732–1806) followed Boucher. He came from the town of Grasse in southeastern France, which was and is the centre of the French perfume industry. Fragonard was a rapid and spontaneous painter. He was as skilled as his teacher Boucher in sharing his pleasure in young women and their bodies, but more alert to their emotions.

Fragonard had a keen and endearing sense of human folly, especially when set in the expanses of the natural world. In his *Blindman's Buff (266)* a children's game is merrily being played out by adults. Despite the light, bright and airy atmosphere there is a sense of foreboding in the painting. The gathering clouds that dominate

265 *François Boucher,* Venus Consoling Love, *1751, 107 x 84 cm (42 x 33 in)*

half the canvas suggest to us, yet surely not explicitly to the painter, that the French Revolution was to come before his death. The Revolution had very unfortunate consequences for Fragonard, as it ruined his patrons and deprived him of commissions. After 1793, despite previous success, he lived in obscurity for the rest of his life.

A Young Girl Reading (267) is aglow with the softest of umbers, the rich colour darkening and paling as it follows the girl's young contours. Her back is supported by a sort of maternal abundance of rosy pillow, but there is an almost horizontal element in the board under her arm except when her charming sleeve has overlapped its rigid outline. She is intent upon her book, as unprotected as any Boucher nymph.

The sweetness of *A Young Girl Reading*, its almost Renoirish charm (see p.298), should not blind us to its strength and solidity. There is a geometrical framework to the softness of the adolescent reader: a strong, vertical swathe of yellow-brown wall, and the gleaming horizontal bar of the armrest. It is this ability to transcend decoration that distinguishes Fragonard. Look at the girl's neck and bosom: delicious frills and ribbons, and the crinkling descent of the silks, yet there is the firm basis of a real, plump, human body. As in *Blindman's Buff*, the literal theme of this picture is held in an unstated context of solemnity. Like Boucher, Fragonard is more profound than he seems, and his genuine sensitivity is becoming increasingly apparent.

266 *Jean-Honoré Fragonard,* Blindman's Buff, *probably c. 1765, 216 x 198 cm (7 ft 1 in x 6 ft 6 in)*

267 *Jean-Honoré Fragonard, A Young Girl Reading, c. 1776, 81 x 65 cm (32 x 26 in)*

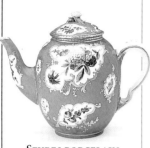

CHARDIN: WEIGHT AND SOBRIETY IN A ROCOCO ERA

Jean-Baptiste-Siméon Chardin (1699–1779), who is so unlike the pleasure-loving Fragonard, taught the young Fragonard before he found a more congenial mentor in Boucher.

Chardin is categorized as "Rococo" only by date, as it were. Despite his charming choice of subjects, frequently painting small children and young servants, he did not have it in him to create other than from his depth. *The Attentive Nurse (268)* simply shows a young nursemaid preparing the supper egg. She stands in the kitchen engrossed in her task, a coloured column of lovely rectitude. The table is laid as for a sacrament: the bread and the goblet take on a sacred significance, and the great white water jug has baptismal import.

None of the mysterious significance contained in *The Attentive Nurse* is overt. It is simply that the scene has overtones. The whites here – the cloth, eggs, jug, and towel – are so pure; and the pinky oranges in the petticoat and the bread, picked up and intensified in the floor and bowl,

268 Jean-Baptiste-Siméon Chardin, **The Attentive Nurse,** *probably 1738, 46 x 37 cm (18 x 14½ in)*

269 *Jean-Baptiste-Siméon Chardin,* **Still Life with Game,**
c. 1760/65, 50 x 60 cm (20 x 23½ in)

are so ruddy with the goodness of health, that
we feel unable to accept the work at face value.
Often in Chardin there are underlying moral
messages or implications, as we see in *The
House of Cards (270)* (life's instability and the
child's ignorance of it) or *Soap Bubbles* (not
illustrated – the uselessness, the vanity in the
biblical sense, of most human activities). But,
paradoxically, the more explicit the moral, the
less its effect.

It is the implicit moralities, like the sacramental
overtones of the nurse with her egg, or the
similar message contained in one of the great
still lifes *(269)* (from one of the greatest of all
the still-life painters) that most move us. The
slaughtered bird and hares, all small and harmless
creatures, lie in solemn state on their altar of the
kitchen ledge. A dusky shadow glimmers on the
wall, and the slab seems lit from within. Chardin
is paying homage to a ritual sacrifice, offered
on our behalf. And not only the animals: the
vegetable world, too, is one of sacrifice, and
Chardin duly bows his head before it.

Chardin never ventured upon what his age
would have considered a major theme: his work
is essentially domestic, quiet, undramatic. It is
his treatment that makes his themes major.

270 *Jean-Baptiste-Siméon Chardin,* **The House of Cards,**
c. 1735, 82 x 66 cm (32¼ x 26¼ in)

TIEPOLO AND ITALIAN ROCOCO

The Italians also had their great Rococo artists, especially in Venice, where the sway and sparkle of the omnipresent waters make a fitting setting. Giambattista Tiepolo (1696–1770) is the quintessential master of this style; all the decorative vitality and glowing colour of the Venetian tradition finds its culmination in him. His exuberance is held under masterly control; he has a natural gaiety that is supremely imaginative and capable of flights of visual wit that have never been excelled.

Tiepolo's greatest work was done mostly in fresco. In these vast, soaring compositions the sheer extent of space to be covered draws from his stupendous best. There is, therefore, a pleasing congruity in his often being commissioned to paint ceilings. This he did with enormous panache and skill, something we may miss if we see his work in a museum, where it has been removed from above our heads and pallidly hung upon a wall.

But the great ceiling at the Museo ca Rezzonico in Venice *(271)* still remains in place, arching superbly over our heads and worth any amount of neck craning. It was painted to celebrate the marriage of two Venetian princely houses, the families of Ludovico Rezzonico and Faustina Savorgnan, which Tiepolo does in a delightful allegory. Ludovico, the bridegroom, leans expectantly forward, the lion of St Mark at his side, holding aloft the banner that shows the two coats of arms united into one. Apollo, the sun god, surges forward in his chariot, bringing the modest bride. Fame blows her trumpet, goddesses, *putti*, and birds rejoice, and in the distance the goddess of fertility, half concealed, contemplates the face of the child that will be conceived. The mirror of the future is still blank, but the glory Tiepolo has created makes it impossible to believe that there can be anything ahead but glory.

Tiepolo borrowed the motif of Apollo's chariot and horses from the ceiling of the Kaisersaal at the bishop's palace in Würzburg (see p.231), his masterpiece of 1750–53. Tiepolo brings the same radiant conviction to mythological subjects too. The theme of the painting that is currently entitled *Queen Zenobia Addressing Her Soldiers (272)* has been the subject of much speculation. It is now known to have been commissioned by the Zenobio family of Venice

271 Giambattista Tiepolo, **Allegory of the Marriage of Rezzonico to Savorgnan,** *1758*

272 Giambattista Tiepolo, **Queen Zenobia Addressing Her Soldiers,** *c. 1730, 262 x 366 cm (8 ft 7 in x 12 ft)*

TIEPOLO DRAWINGS
While it is for his paintings that Tiepolo is most famous, the many sketches he left behind have a considerable reputation of their own. Tiepolo would tirelessly sketch out the characters, and then they would be transferred to his ceiling masterpieces. This sketch (shown above) illustrates Tiepolo's ability to use chiaroscuro (depiction of light and shade) and his grasp of perspective. The woman is believed to be Truth, a mythical personification who appears in several of Tiepolo's paintings.

and that the helmeted female figure is Queen Zenobia. She was an extremely powerful, 3rd-century ruler of Palmyra, but we do not need to know the story behind the painting to appreciate its power. What Tiepolo shows us with brilliant force is the confrontation of male and female, but, in 18th-century terms, reversed. It is the woman who dominates, the men who listen submissively. The woman is all-powerful, and dynamic, while the men, despite their masculine bulk, await her commands passively. It is a sparkling and witty work, yet wholly serious.

LATE ROCOCO IN VENICE

The Rococo, dying out in the rest of Europe as it became increasingly regarded as frivolous, still found great painters in Venice. The best of their art shows the real strength of Rococo, its wonderful energy. Francesco Guardi (1712– 93), with his lyrical capriccios (imaginary landscape arrangements, half real and half surreal) is one of the last of this school. The most famous of a family of painters, his art is loose and impressionistic, airy and delightful. We may not totally believe in his architecture, but we accept its fantasy on its own terms. If he shows us *A*

Seaport and Classical Ruins in Italy (273), we take uncomplicated pleasure in its cloudy grandeur, a fitting site for the imagination to play in. What charms us in Guardi is his ability both to convince intellectually (we believe we are seeing a real place) and to enchant us romantically (we also feel that this is a poetic creation). Poetry that convinces us is the most enduring.

273 Francesco Guardi, **A Seaport and Classical Ruins in Italy,** *1730s, 122 x 178 cm (48 x 70 in)*

BELLOTTO

Canaletto's nephew
Bernardo Bellotto
(1721–80) caused much
confusion in the 18th
century by calling
himself Canaletto. He
trained with his uncle
in Venice but left in
1747 for the courts of
northern Europe,
particularly Dresden
and Warsaw. His work
was considered so
reliable that architects
rebuilding Warsaw
after World War II
copied buildings
and details from
his pictures.

PORTRAITS OF CITIES

An early exponent of a new stylistic current
leading to a renewed Classicism – but an artist
who was still very much a part of the Rococo
world – was the Venetian landscape painter
Canaletto (Antonio Canale, 1697–1768). He was
born only one year after Tiepolo (see p.232) and
several years before Guardi (see p.233) – both
quintessential Rococo artists – yet his art can
be seen as rigorously Neoclassical.

Canaletto adopted the city portrait as his
chosen subject early in his career and stuck to it,
becoming famous in his lifetime for his accurate
and elaborately detailed records of city views.
Since many of Canaletto's paintings are of his
birthplace, Venice itself, a fantastical and imaginative city, they may indeed have a Rococo exterior,
but the spirit is pure sobriety.

A splendid example of Canaletto's feeling
for texture, for slate and stone and wood, with
distant water and high sky, is seen in this behind-
the-scenes view of Venice, sloppy and untidy,
yet all held in the context of the loveliest of
cities. *The Stonemason's Yard (274)* even sounds
unromantic, yet Canaletto has seen the yard as a
wonderful setting for the interplay of light and
shadow, declivity and height.

*Venice: The Basin of San Marco on Ascension
Day (275)* is bathed in the hard light of a classical
sun. Its verticals are severe and perfectly balanced,
and its architectural masses are unmistakably
solid; yet Canaletto paints with such love and
appreciation of his city that the result is beguiling.
There is no atmospheric poetry here, except for
the lyrical quality of the sky.

275 *Canaletto,* Venice: the Basin of San Marco on Ascension
Day, *probably c. 1740, 122 x 183 cm (48 x 72 in)*

Canaletto was specially admired by English
visitors to Venice, who responded immediately
to his rationality. He went to England in 1745
and lived there for ten years, producing many
views of London, though these were unappreciated.

His nephew, Bernardo Bellotto (1721–80, see
column, left), sometimes also known, confusingly,
as Canaletto, imitated his more famous uncle.
They are hard to distinguish, and one could argue
(to my view, falsely) that to see a Canaletto is to
see a Bellotto. Yet Bellotto is a more detailed
painter, a great master of extent, in which the
air seems crystal clear and we possess the view
like a god. This divine amplitude characterizes
both uncle and nephew, so characteristic of them
both that the confusion of their identities is
almost inevitable.

HOGARTH: FOUNDER OF AN ENGLISH TRADITION

The British taste for art was less visual than
factual. British patrons liked portraits of themselves, as well as landscape views of their homes
and estates and of foreign cities they visited.
Ironically, William Hogarth (1697–1764), Britain's
first major artist, though a truthful and vigorous
portrait painter, made his name in the unusual
genre of pictorial satire, another art form

274 *Canaletto,* The Stonemason's Yard, *c. late 1720s, 125 x 163 cm (49 x 64 in)*

276 **William Hogarth,** The Graham Children, *1742, 163 × 183 cm (5 ft 4 in × 6 ft)*

**HOGARTH
ENGRAVINGS**
William Hogarth
(1697–1764) trained as an
engraver and popularized
the use of a sequence of
anecdotal pictures to
portray social and moral
issues. He saw himself
as the defender of the
common man and the
upholder of sensible British
values in the face of French
fashions and mannerisms.
The engraving shown
above is of *Gin Lane*,
a fictitious street in which
the dire consequences of
gin-drinking are clearly
demonstrated. The work
was completed by Hogarth
in 1751 and is one of a pair,
the other illustrating the
noble qualities of British
beer. Engravings such as
these sold for one shilling
and were popular across
the social spectrum.

The Graham Children (276) can bear comparison
with the works of the great Velázquez (see p.194)
in its sense of immediacy, of sharing with us a
particular moment in time. The painting shows
four children who, with their cat and their caged
bird, sparkle happily out at us. Only after a time
do we glimpse the deeper implications of this
scene: the cat, electric with desire, is after the
bird, and its lively chirping, which the children
take to be a response to their own music, is in
reality a frantic cry for their protection. Only
the baby sees what the cat is up to, and as a baby,
does not understand. Hogarth is showing us
innocence threatened, and the shadow falls
on the laughing children too.

congenial to his countrymen, and which Hogarth
took to new heights, creating an entirely new art
form. Hogarth was a lively and dogmatic man,
and greatly opposed to the "Italianate" Rococo
styles that were popular in London at this time.
He was a decided nationalist, and, finding the
English art scene to be hopelessly provincial,
contributed to the development of Britain's
earliest art institutions. He was all for building
a truly British tradition, one that did not take
its lead from the continent but instead reflected
the British way of life.

In his portraiture, Hogarth broke new ground
in depicting the rising English middle class in
ways that had previously been reserved for
nobility, and his keen sense of human absurdity
drew him irresistibly to satire as a suitable and
lucrative means for social and judicial commentary. He tends to see his subject as if it were a
piece of theatre.

A Scene from the Beggar's Opera (277) is taken
from the great satirical play by John Gay, written
in 1728. Captain Macheath, the highwayman,
stands grandly in the centre, while his two lady-
loves plead with their villainous, hypocritical
fathers. Hogarth gets the utmost enjoyment out
of the twofold satire, of good and bad not being
what they seem, and of a man in love with two
women who gets himself in a tangle. This is the
witty Hogarth, but he has a deeper side too.

277 **William Hogarth,** A Scene from the Beggar's Opera, *1728/29, 51 × 61 cm (20¼ × 24 in)*

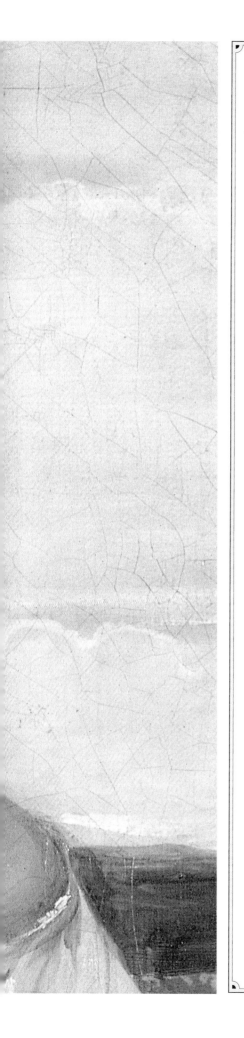

NEOCLASSICISM AND ROMANTICISM

Neoclassicism was born out of a rejection of the Rococo and late Baroque styles, around the middle of the 18th century. Neoclassical artists wanted a style that could convey serious moral ideas such as justice, honour, and patriotism. They yearned to re-create the simple, dignified style of the art of classical Greece and Rome. Some succeeded, but the movement suffered from a certain bloodlessness, a spirit of academic narrowness.

Romanticism began in the same era, but it was an approach that had to do with the modern rather than the antique, and it was about wildness and expression rather than control. Romantic artists had no fixed laws relating to beauty or the proprieties of subject matter. Instead, Romanticism was a creative outlook, a way of life.

A vast gulf existed between these two outlooks, and the debate between them was long and at times bitter; but in the end, Romanticism emerged as the dominant artistic movement of the first half of the 19th century.

Eugène Delacroix, An Orphan Girl in the Graveyard, 1824 (detail)

NEOCLASSICISM AND ROMANTICISM TIMELINE

Neoclassicism began in the middle of the 18th century (well before the Rococo style finally went out of use) and was in decline by the early 19th century. Likewise, early traces of Romanticism in painting are found in the 1740s; for instance, in Gainsborough. Romantic painting became a recognized movement by the 1780s, continuing into the mid-19th century.

JOHN SINGLETON COPLEY, THE COPLEY FAMILY, 1776–77
Copley's portrait of his own family is an example of the effects of European Neoclassical influence (chiefly that of Reynolds) on an artist arriving from the New World. When living in America, Copley had been known for his unvarnished but convincing realism. In England, in response to the prevailing fashion, he idealized and made his figures elegant, but in the event all too often diminishing his original insight (p.246).

GEORGE STUBBS, MARES AND FOALS, 1762
By specializing, George Stubbs attained a degree of distinction that guaranteed him lasting fame. He dedicated himself to the horse, and this is one of his many horse pictures that leave humans out altogether. It gives a glimpse of these wild creatures as superior beings to whom the landscape truly belongs (p.247).

SIR JOSHUA REYNOLDS, LADY CAROLINE HOWARD, 1778
Reynolds was England's leading academic painter and possibly the best portraitist. He is an eclectic painter, leaning heavily to the classic, which gives dignity to his pictures of contemporary aristocrats. Here he gives an atmosphere of grandeur, almost heroism, to a simple portrait of a child (p.244).

1740   1750   1760   1770   1780   1790

THOMAS GAINSBOROUGH, MR AND MRS ANDREWS, 1749
This unforgettable portrait haunts us with its startlingly original treatment. The poses and facial expressions are individual and convincing, and yet paradoxically the two figures are made to look like dolls or porcelain figures. They are positioned in the corner of the composition, allowing two-thirds of the painting to be devoted to landscape. Nature is an important element in all of Gainsborough's portraits, and he had a profound influence on the English landscape painters in the 19th century, notably Constable (p.240).

JACQUES-LOUIS DAVID, THE OATH OF THE HORATII, 1784–85
This was the first really famous image from the Neoclassical school. David was on the side of the Revolution when it came in 1789, and this subject evoked revolutionary patriotism. The composition is carefully orchestrated: for instance, the exaggerated weakness and softness of the women on the right contrast with the rigid, heroic pose of the three young men on the left (p.253).

JOHN CONSTABLE, THE WHITE HORSE, 1819

This is one of the Suffolk scenes that have become part of the canon of great paintings in the English landscape tradition. Constable's work has a unique freshness. There is a brilliant use of broken colour, with an immediacy and convincing truth. With his robust, work-a-day scenes from the country-side near his home, Constable breached classical rules on what constituted the "correct" sort of landscape to paint (p.270).

FRANCISCO GOYA, COLOSSUS, 1810–12

Goya was influenced, when first at the Spanish royal court, by the Neoclassicist, Anton Raphael Mengs, but over the years of his career he moved more and more in the direction of Romanticism. He is an artist of the very greatest stature and exercised considerable influence on the development of Romanticism throughout Europe. The Colossus is an example of Goya's ability to realize an image that seems to come from our inner consciousness, powerful but with no single, unambiguous message (p.252).

EUGENE DELACROIX, DEATH OF SARDANAPALUS, 1827

Delacroix' Romanticism has a solid underpinning of the classic. Rubens and Géricault encouraged him to see the emotional effect of strong colour. This painting shows the energy and exoticism of his work, but he always retained a certain detachment and inner control (p.261).

1800	1810	1820	1830	1840	1850

JEAN-AUGUSTE INGRES, THE BATHER, 1808

Ingres became the "high priest" of Neoclassicism in France. He had a special preference for the backs and necks of his nudes, often making them into prominent features of his paintings and frequently distorting them or elongating them in order to suit the needs of his highly sophisticated compositions. This was typical of the Neoclassical painters, for whom control over subject matter was central to their whole approach to art. Ingres' distortions went even further than in this example, but they were nearly always achieved in such a way as to make anatomical "falsehoods" seem as plausible as reality itself (p.256).

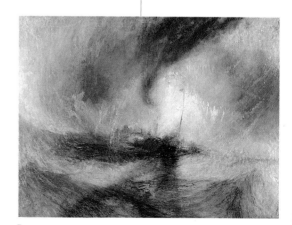

J.M.W. TURNER, STEAMBOAT IN A SNOWSTORM, 1842

In Turner's seascapes we see to the full the emotive power of Romantic art. Yet, like all truly great artists, Turner retains control over what is happening in this painting. Here he shows a ship in mortal danger in a storm at sea. No matter how imaginative or extreme the subject, he is still aware of perspective and its imperatives (p.265).

THE BRITISH SCHOOL

In British painting of the 18th century there was a mixture of both the Romantic and the Neoclassical tendencies. On the one hand there was the marvellous lyricism of Thomas Gainsborough, always including the natural environment in his portraits, many of which were more in the way of being landscapes. On the other hand there was the educated, classical approach of Sir Joshua Reynolds, appealing to the ideals of polite society of his time – which was known, then as well as today, as the Age of Reason.

One of the artists who led English painting into its great period was Thomas Gainsborough (1727–88). He called himself "a wild goose at best", and it was this ravishing originality, within the bounds of gentlemanly appeal, that made him so popular. A supreme portrait painter, his great love was the landscape, and his finest works give us both. His achievements in landscape painting paved the way for Constable's radically naturalistic approach to landscape, and for the English Romantic tradition (see p.264). Gainsborough's

landscapes are reminiscent of Watteau's *fêtes galantes* (see p.224): whimsical, idyllic scenes, peopled with delicate creatures. In Gainsborough, however, these are transformed into large-scale lyrical landscapes, refreshing in their truth to nature. The most famous of Gainsborough's early portraits is the unconventional *Mr and Mrs Andrews (278)*. The young newlyweds pose in their ancestral fields, she in the height of fashion, scowling over her silks, he casual and somehow adolescent.

278 *Thomas Gainsborough*, Mr and Mrs Andrews, *c. 1749, 71 x 120 cm (28 x 47 in)*

A NEW STYLE OF PORTRAIT

The Andrews portrait takes its verve from its paradoxically real and unreal portrayal of the sitters, who appear doll-like, and yet are nonetheless totally convincing; and from its strikingly original composition. Its originality lies in the positioning of its subjects off-centre, flanked by an unidealized, genuinely 18th-century English landscape of farmland with its cornfield, sturdy oak tree, and changeable sky.

Their position emphasizes their status as landowners. They appear to be surveying the landscape around them, a landscape that plays an important part in its own right, no longer merely as a decorative, fanciful backdrop (as had been the custom for such outdoor portraits). The portrait is not finished. Mrs Andrews is believed to have made the rather odd request that she be painted holding a pheasant, which probably accounts for the blank patch in her lap. Gainsborough clearly finds the couple comic, yet he paints with an admirably straight face.

279 Thomas Gainsborough, The Painter's Daughters Chasing a Butterfly, *late 1750s, 115 x 105 cm (45 x 41 in)*

PATHOS AND CELEBRATION

As Gainsborough matured, his sensibility became more delicate, more "finely tuned", as did his confidence in his ability to catch a likeness. His lyrical landscape backgrounds, lightly sketched, became more idealized (though never unbelievable) and were executed with increasing freedom. Gainsborough is very sensitive to the pathos of beauty or heroism, graces that time will transform, and there can be a heartbreaking pensiveness in some of his portraits.

There is pathos, for example, in his repeated portraits of his two daughters, Molly (Mary) and Margaret, plain girls whom he dearly loved and whose future was to be unhappy – both were psychically fragile. Our foreknowledge of this unhappiness to come seems sublimely shared in his enchanting picture of them in their childhood: *The Painter's Daughters Chasing a Butterfly (279).* Only the young chase the butterfly: the adult knows sadly that it is hard to catch, and may die as a result. For children, the chase itself is sheer pleasure without misgivings, and Gainsborough subtly expresses, at one and the same time, the happiness of innocence and the sadness of maturity.

OTHER WORKS BY GAINSBOROUGH

Captain Thomas Matthew
(Museum of Fine Arts, Boston)

John Smith, Clerk to the Drapers' Company
(Queensland Art Gallery, Brisbane)

Crossing the Ford
(Christchurch Mansion, Ipswich)

Mrs Susannah Gardiner
(Tate Gallery, London)

Mrs George Drummond
(Montreal Museum of Fine Arts)

Lady in a Blue Dress
(Philadelphia Museum of Art)

A Lady
(Bridgestone Museum of Art, Tokyo)

George III
(Royal Collection, Windsor Castle)

*280 Thomas Gainsborough, **Mrs Richard Brinsley Sheridan,** 1785/86, 220 x 154 cm (7 ft 3 in x 5 ft ½ in)*

Gainsborough was one of the great "independents" and his influence on portraiture was only limited. However, his landscapes were important as models for the young John Constable (see p.268), who wrote, "I fancy I see Gainsborough in every hedge and hollow tree."

RAMSAY THE CATALYST

Perhaps the greatest portrait painter in 18th-century Britain is the unfairly forgotten Scot, Allan Ramsay (1713–84). The English writer Horace Walpole, one of the shrewdest men of his age, remarked that "Reynolds seldom succeeds in women," whereas "Ramsay is formed to paint them." A great Ramsay is usually treasured by the family that originally commissioned it, and he has fallen from critical view for far too long.

This portrait, *Mrs Allan Ramsay (281)*, is of Ramsay's second wife, Margaret Lindsay (1726–82). The first Mrs Ramsay, Anne Bayne, had died in childbirth, thereby forever destroying Ramsay's confidence in the invulnerability of love. His second wife is very lovely, sweet and fresh, but he paints her with a touching anxiety, a haunting fear that her beloved life may fade away as inevitably as the flowers at her side.

Ramsay's delicate style introduced a blend of Baroque Italian Classicism, with French Rococo charm, into English painting. His personality – contrasting so noticeably with that of Hogarth, the pragmatic social commentator – gave impetus for change, and the active ingredients for this great period in British painting.

MRS RICHARD

MRS RICHARD BRINSLEY SHERIDAN
Elizabeth Linley (1754–92), a singer of great beauty and charm, had been known to Gainsborough since childhood. She eloped to France with the dramatist Richard Brinsley Sheridan (1751–1816) in 1772 and they married a year later. They settled in London, living much beyond their means until Sheridan became a successful playwright, as well as a Member of Parliament.

THE PLAYWRIGHT'S WIFE
Pathos, again, is inherent in this portrait of *Mrs Richard Brinsley Sheridan (280)*. She had a tempestuous marriage with the great playwright Sheridan, as well as being renowned for her singing voice and her unearthly beauty. Her loneliness, and her elusive charm, are all conveyed to us in her portrait. Only the grave and lovely face is solid: all else is thin, diaphanous, unstable. Her mood is echoed by the wistful melancholy of the setting sun.

Full-length portraits, particularly of ladies placed in a natural setting, were a special tradition in 18th-century English and French painting; they were noticed on the continent, and copied, by Goya among others (see p.248).

*281 Allan Ramsay, **Margaret Lindsay, Mrs Allan Ramsay,** early 1760s, 68 x 55 cm (27 x 22 in)*

MRS RICHARD BRINSLEY SHERIDAN

The rather incompatible natures of the subject of this portrait and her husband (see column, p.242) meant that the former spent much of her time in the country, where she was happiest, while her wayward spouse stayed in London. She was an appropriate subject for Gainsborough's new, Romantic approach to portraiture, where all elements combine to express the gently melancholic mood of the sitter.

FACE

She is depicted as truly belonging in this environment, and her hair, caught by the wind, is treated in the same way as the leaves on the tree. Her plaintive expression (the focal point of the painting) and whole demeanour seem to express the wish she made to her husband to "Take me out of the whirl of the world, place me in the quiet and simple scenes of life that I was born for." Her wistful mood is echoed by the setting sun.

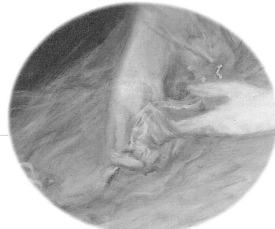

DISTANT TREE

A solitary tree in the distance has been superimposed over the sky. Its trunk is a few simple arabesques, and the fluffy clumps of foliage are all painted in the same direction. Pink underpainting is visible in the sky, which echoes the pinks and blues of her costume.

HANDS

In comparison to her face, her pale arms are relatively flatly painted, with virtually no modelling or shading. Her hands seem to lose themselves in the folds of her dress and scarf. The transparent scarf is composed of a network of fluid squiggles weaving in and out of her fingers. It unifies the figure into one single romantic gesture as it twists and tumbles down from around her shoulders and across her chest, falling through her arms and onto her knees and feet.

RHYTHM OF COLOUR AND FORM

The lightly suggested feet are subordinate to the major rhythms of the composition. Gainsborough has worked largely wet-in-wet, with loosely-woven layers of washes, a technique that produces softness of definition. At the speed of a glance, he has zig-zagged his brush down the expanse of her dress to her feet. Our eye moves automatically to the distant tree and then up and down through the foliage behind her, where her diagonal pose begins the circular rhythm anew.

RAEBURN: BRILLIANT PORTRAITIST

Raeburn, a fellow Scot, was clearly influenced by Ramsay, and at his peak is practically his equal. One would love to know whether it was the Rev. Walker himself or Raeburn who hit upon the wonderful pose of the skater *(282)*. This extraordinary image, with the dark outline of a minister in his sombre black, intent upon balancing his movement across the ice, has the superb background of mist and mountains. The man is so solid, the world so nebulous. He fixes his gaze adamantly upon the unseen and skates his way forward. We can see the muscles in play as his skates score the ice, and yet where he is going, and why this image is appropriate, baffles us still.

REYNOLDS' GRAND MANNER

Joshua Reynolds (1723–92), who was knighted for his great success as a portrait painter, is less sensitive than Gainsborough but more balanced. Unlike the latter, who had little formal education, and preferred the company of actors and musicians to scholars, Reynolds was decidedly

283 *Sir Joshua Reynolds*, Lady Caroline Howard, *1778, 143 x 113 cm (56 x 44½ in)*

an intellectual. From early on in his training, Reynolds had immersed himself in the art of the Renaissance, and he shared an interest in antiquity with the Italian and French Neoclassical artists. These influences led to his revival of the "Grand Manner", set in a modern context (see column, left). He was, without question, considered the leading portrait artist in Britain in his day, although, like Gainsborough, his passion lay outside the field of portraiture.

History painting was for Reynolds the highest form of art, and he contrived to instil Classicism and heroism into his portraits of the English ruling class. The threat to Reynolds' standing in England – especially from Gainsborough's popularity – did not arise until fairly late in the day, and Reynolds' influence on English art endured for many years. He became the first president of the Royal Academy on its foundation in 1768, and his enormous influence formed the basis for academic painting (see column, left).

Reynolds was an influential theorist whose lectures at the Royal Academy still make useful reading, and he encapsulates the aristocratic dignity of his age. He can hover alarmingly on the edge of the sentimental, especially in his idealization of childhood, but when he catches youthful freshness, he is very appealing. Here is one of the best examples of his portraiture: *Lady Caroline Howard (283)*, with her rosebush and her general air of simplicity, has a pensiveness that does not make extravagant claims, but lets us enjoy this quiet and rosy child.

282 *Sir Henry Raeburn*, The Rev. Robert Walker Skating, *mid-1790s, 73 x 60 cm (29 x 24 in)*

AMERICA AND ENGLAND:
A SHARED LANGUAGE

If the forgotten Ramsay (see p.242) is arguably the greatest portrait painter of the time, then the equally overlooked American artist Gilbert Stuart (1755–1828), 42 years his junior, may be the most original. Stuart, as his name suggests, was originally of Scottish ancestry. He arrived in London at the age of 20 and trained under a fellow American, the hugely successful history painter Benjamin West (see right).

Stuart was also a great success in London. His work was so acclaimed that at a later stage it was even confused with that of Gainsborough. This is a double-edged compliment: he has his own style, which is almost recklessly truthful. His time may be too early to speak of a specifically American style, but there is a homespun brilliance in his work that we do not find in European artists.

There is superb observation in his *Mrs Richard Yates (284)*: what other artist would have dared show her vestigial moustache? The gradations of facial colour, too, and the alertness to the light glancing and dulling on her dress and cap, are all prophetic of the Impressionists (see p.294). After running into serious financial problems, Stuart returned to live permanently in America in 1793. He is probably known mainly because he painted George Washington, but despite his popularity he is not at his best as a public artist. It is the sheer domesticity of Mrs Richard Yates, a merchant's wife, that calls out his reserves of sensitive observation

285 Benjamin West, Self-portrait, c 1770, 77 x 61 cm (30¼ x 25⅛ in)

284 Gilbert Stuart, Mrs Richard Yates, 1793/94, 77 x 63 cm (30¼ x 25 in)

HISTORY PAINTING: A POPULAR GENRE

A more famous, though less interesting artist than Gilbert Stuart is Benjamin West (1738–1820), whose enormous reputation as a history painter was gained in England rather than his native America.

West's style relied very much on accuracy of detail and historical fact, and he was influenced by Neoclassical artists such as Anton Mengs (see p.248) when he was in Rome in 1760. West's great historical dramas, which so impressed his contemporaries, leave us rather unmoved. They seem to be generated from the mind rather than the heart.

But the heart is always involved in painting a self-portrait, and here we see him at his best *(285)*. There is wishful thinking, perhaps, in this self-portrait – that of a quiet, elegant gentleman, dressed in the fashionable severity of urban style, contemplating us with aristocratic serenity. West's sketch seems an adjunct to his portrait and is in fact placed on the perimeter. Half his face and his body are deeply shadowed, with all this suggests of a divided and secretive persona.

ANGELICA KAUFFMAN

Angelica Kauffman was a friend of Joshua Reynolds and fellow member of the Royal Academy. She began as a fashionable portraitist, then became more interested in historical subjects. In the 1770s she painted a series of decorative murals for the architect Robert Adam. In 1781 she remarried and moved to Rome. This piece of Neoclassical Meissen ware (fine porcelain) is decorated with a portrait of Angelica Kauffman.

AMERICAN INDEPENDENCE

A disagreement between the government in London and the American colonists over increases in tax is seen as the initial catalyst of the American Revolution. George Washington (1732–99, shown above) was appointed Commander-in-Chief of the army and on July 4th, 1776 the Declaration of Independence was signed. George Washington proved to be an excellent leader and was inaugurated as the first president in 1789.

286 John Singleton Copley, **The Copley Family,** *1776-77, 185 x 292 cm (6 ft 1 in x 9 ft 7in)*

COPLEY: AN UNFULFILLED TALENT

If Britain gave West the opportunity he needed, it both rewarded and damaged John Singleton Copley (1738–1815). His American works show a realism and a truthfulness that is marvellously alive. Moving to England involved him in the elegance of Neoclassicism and the influence of Reynolds' Grand Manner; but, for Copley, this was not a fruitful involvement.

The change is evident in *The Copley Family (286)*. In this painting, which was carefully worked up from preliminary studies, his father-in-law's face and hands and the glorious doll in the left-hand corner are examples of his early style. Here it is thrillingly convincing. For the remainder of the picture, Copley idealizes and abstracts, and the whole, though impressive, is somehow derivative: we have seen this kind of "Grand Manner" portraiture before in the work of Reynolds, Gainsborough, and West, for example. It remains a fascinating work, as much for its weakness as its strength. One of the weaknesses

287 George Stubbs, **Mares and Foals,** *1762,
100 x 190 cm (39 x 75 in)*

he himself were an honorary member of the species. Stubbs did not totally disdain to paint humans, who after all were the source of his equestrian commissions. But *Mares and Foals (287)* is one of his many pictures that has no human component. There is certainly no sentimentality either, yet these stately mothers and children, trustfully grouped together with artless poetry, evince a tender vision of nature at its most inspiring.

The horses group themselves with classic elegance against an archetypal English landscape. Stubbs is profoundly moved by their beauty and he communicates to us his own secret conviction that it is they to whom the landscape truly belongs. Thick-limbed humanity, with its clumsy trapping of clothes and its intrusive apparatus for living, is so inferior to these bare, gleaming creatures of the wild that yet honour us with their comradeship.

that is paradoxically a strength comes from our uncertainty as to where this family group is located. Are they inside – as is suggested by the brocaded sofa and the gilt-edged curtain, not to mention the expensive carpet? Or are they assembled outside – as seems to be indicated by the backdrop, with its distant hills and intrusive foliage? The two settings are cleverly linked. The carpet is patterned with leaves and there is a flower motif on the sofa.

GREAT EQUESTRIAN PAINTING

The one great Anglo-Saxon master of the century, George Stubbs (1724–1806), was, like Gainsborough, a lover of the portrait and the countryside, but all his passion is concentrated on the horse. Stubbs does not merely look at horses: in his time he dissected them (literally), meditated upon them, and entered into every aspect of this noble but non-human being, as if

288 George Stubbs, **A Horse Frightened by a Lion,** *1770,
94 x 125 cm (37 x 49 in)*

Idyllic though it is, Stubbs does not cheat. The sky is darkening with storm clouds, and shadows already fall around the mares and foals. Only the very centre of the meadow, where they actually stand, is still sunlit.

Stubbs was equally sensitive to the vulnerability of animal life. *A Horse Frightened by a Lion (288)* comes straight from a Freudian nightmare. Blown by the wind, under some heavenly spotlight that gleams with eerie fierceness on its terrified body, a white horse halts in abrupt horror as a leonine head looks out at it from the darkness. It is a frozen tableau of fear. He leaves its outcome to our imagination.

HORSE PAINTINGS

George Stubbs' (1724–1806) horse paintings are a testimony to the 18th-century gentleman's passionate interest in improved stock breeding techniques. The formal discipline of Stubbs' composition is Neoclassical in spirit but the artist's romantic perception of the horse is demonstrated by his move towards Romanticism in his later years. The implied and described violence in paintings, such as *A Horse Frightened by a Lion*, appeal strongly to our emotions.

OTHER WORKS BY STUBBS

Otho with Larkin Up (Tate Gallery, London)

Repose After Shooting (Yale Center for British Art, New Haven, Connecticut)

Portrait of Lady Laetitia Lade (Royal Collection, Windsor)

Returning from the Hunt (Museum of Art, San Antonio, Texas)

GOYA

The greatest artist of the 18th century, without any qualification, was a Spaniard – Francisco Goya. He was a man of irrepressible originality and determination. After initially being influenced by the German-born Neoclassical artist Anton Mengs, he developed in his own way and painted, above all, with a truly Spanish vision.

Anton Raphael Mengs (1728–79) was a founder of Neoclassicism, in association with Johann Winckelmann (see column, left). He is more significant to us today, however, for his extremely influential style of Neoclassical portraiture. Perhaps even more importantly, he was also the Court Painter to King Charles III of Spain. The king was a committed antiquarian and social reformer, and he had a natural preference for Mengs' serious, dignified, and pragmatic approach, which is admirably demonstrated in Mengs' *Self-portrait (289)*. It was Mengs who invited Goya to Madrid – in 1771.

GOYA: A SPANISH GENIUS

The influence of Mengs can be seen in the early work of Francisco Goya (1746–1828), particularly in his first portraits. Beyond that Goya fits into no category: his career spanned some 60 years, undergoing several metamorphoses, changing, and maturing in new ways right up to the mid-1820s. Goya seems to have worked solely from the centre of his own genius. With the hindsight of history we can see that his essentially personal

290 Francisco Goya, **Marquesa de Pontejos**, *c. 1786, 210 x 127 cm (83 x 50 in)*

289 Anton Mengs, **Self-portrait**, *1744, 73 x 55 cm (29 x 22 in)*

vision of the modern world places him as an early Romantic (see p.259). His art was more in tune with the Baroque mixture of classical form and emotive personal expression – he cited Velázquez, Rembrandt, and Nature as his masters – than with the disciplined idealism of the Neoclassicists.

Goya possessed two outstanding gifts. He could pierce through the external façade of any sitter, to unmask the interior truth, a gift dangerous for any but the prudent. But he coupled with it a marvellous decorative sense, as is clear from his disarming portrait of the *Marquesa de Pontejos (290)*. His work has such sheer beauty that even those almost pilloried in his portraits seem not to have grasped what had happened, being overwhelmed by wonder of the paint.

291 Francisco Goya, **The Family of King Charles IV**, *1800, 280 x 336cm (9ft 2 in x 11 ft ½ in)*

AN AMBITIOUS FAMILY PORTRAIT

The Family of King Charles IV (291), a portrait of the ruling Borbón family, who were haughtily remote from their countryfolk, shows the sitters for what they are: vain and pompous. Yet they continued to patronize Goya throughout his career. The portrait is breathtaking in its cruel insight and its beauty. The royals are spread out like a frieze, heavy, dull-faced, and self-satisfied, squashed together with little elegance and no style. We wince for them, we pity the poor, stupid king and his vixenish queen, and sigh over the impenetrable crassness of their stumpy heir. Then we look again, at the dazzle of attire, the silks and laces, the infinite delicacy with which decoration, ribbons, jewels, and sashes are found to be glittering, gleaming, blazing out at us with undiminished glamour.

In every portrait, Goya puts his finger on the living pulse of the sitter. He does so with such intensity of power that we positively need the decorative qualities to offset the impact. When we look at his *Thérèse Louise de Sureda (292)*, our eyes dwell with continual fascination on the chair with its wonderfully inconsistent canary shade, and on the dress, which is a gleaming

292 Francisco Goya, **Thérèse Louise de Sureda**, *c. 1803/04, 120 x 81 cm (47 x 31 in)*

THE ROYAL FAMILY

In 1779 Goya was appointed to the position of First Court Painter under King Charles IV of Spain, who came to the throne in 1778. Court life under Charles IV was extravagant and self-indulgent, and full of personal intrigues. This miniature of the royal family in profile (above) was painted on silk by an unknown artist. It is of interest because of the way it shows the close resemblance between family members.

TAPESTRY CARTOONS

Goya worked at various times between 1774 and 1794 at the Royal Tapestry Factory, painting cartoons – the paintings from which the weavers copied their tapestries. Many of the cartoons have been lost, but 63 of Goya's are known today, either in their original form as cartoons or as the finished tapestries. This photograph shows a tapestry of Goya's cartoon *The Vintage* on the loom. Weavers worked the tapestry from the back, studying the cartoon through the threads.

THE CAPRICES

Between 1797 and 1799
Goya produced a series of
80 satirical prints, known
as the Caprices. Goya's
friend Leandro Fernández
de Moratín told Goya of
some caricatures he had
seen in England, and of
how effectively they had
ridiculed the establishment.
This is an example of
Goya's Caprices (above),
entitled *The Sleep of
Reason*. It was first sketched
in 1797 and printed in
1798. In Spain such overt
political criticism was not
tolerated and the Caprices
were threatened with a
ban by the Inquisition.

**NAPOLEON'S
INVASION OF SPAIN**

In December 1807
Napoleon Bonaparte
(1769–1821) marched
130,000 French troops into
northern Spain. By the
spring of 1808 he had
effectively taken control of
Madrid, and by June he had
deposed King Ferdinand
VII, appointing his
(Napoleon's) own brother
Joseph as King of Spain.
As a result a guerilla war
began between the people
of Spain and the French
occupying forces. This
culminated in the resistance
uprising of May 2nd, 1808,
and the execution of
Spanish insurgents by
French soldiers at various
sites across Madrid on
the following day.

blue-black shot through with red and green – because the colour makes it possible, through its seductions, for us to accept the force of the sitter's implacable gaze. Doña Teresa was a friend of Goya's in that her husband (also a painter) was one of Goya's drinking companions. But she was a "friend" mainly in the sense that Goya knew her and, we suspect, disliked her. She is well rounded, a compact bundle of womanhood, but she is tense and angry. She will not submit to the painter, challenging him with her glare and her uprightness, carefully coiffured but not for the warmth of love's embraces. There can be no comparable portrayal of a woman at once so attractive and so hostile.

Goya made his living by working for royalty and the establishment, and his political views appear confused: they may necessarily have been ambiguous. But it is impossible not to believe that he had an inborn hatred of tyranny. His art suggests a vehement independence, and perhaps his greatest painting may be his version of a French war crime, the shooting of hostages after the Spanish people rose against Napoleon Bonaparte's rule in 1808. *The Third of May 1808 (293)* was painted six years after the event it portrays. This is only partly a patriotic picture, if it is that at all. It is not the French that Goya condemns but our communal cruelty. It is humankind that holds the rifles, but humankind at its most utterly conscienceless. The victims, too, are Everyman, the huddled mass of the poor who have no defender.

Goya manages to make us feel that we are both executioners and executed, as if the dual potential for good or evil that we all possess were animated before us. Intensity of fear, pain, and loss on one side, and the extremity of brutality on the other: which fate is the worse? Who is really destroyed in this terrible painting, the depersonalized French or the individualized Spanish? Behind the dying rises a hillock, bright with light; the soldiers stand in a shadowy and sinister no-man's-land. Meanwhile, in the central background, the city endures.

This is a very dark painting, psychologically, but the really dark works were to be painted later, in Goya's sick old age, when he was deaf and lonely, a prey to the irrational fears that are subliminally present in all his work, giving it a secret bite. He used these fears to create images of our darkest imaginings – not just his own, or they would fail to produce their terrible effect. Goya's last works have a ghastly sanity in their insanity, as if all demarcations had gone, and we had all fallen through into the abyss.

293 Francisco Goya, The Third of May 1808, *1814, 260 x 345 cm (8 ft 6 in x 11 ft 4 in)*

THE THIRD OF MAY 1808

The Third of May 1808 is one of a pair of paintings focusing on the brutal suppression and subsequent mass executions of Spanish civilians who had risen against French troops on May 2nd, 1808. Only when King Ferdinand VII was finally restored to power in 1813 did Goya quickly send him a petition asking to commemorate the "most notable and heroic actions or scenes of our glorious insurrection against the tyrant of Europe".

FIRING SQUAD
The soldiers are depicted as faceless automatons. Their bodies are locked together, like some form of destructive insect. They stand unfeasibly close to their victims, emphasizing the brutal and tragically ludicrous nature of the scene, and crudely mirror David's great Neoclassical painting, The Oath of the Horatii *(see p.253). But whereas David's soldiers represent unity of will, Goya's represent only the mindless anonymity of the war machine.*

CHRIST FIGURE
Our attention is immediately drawn to the man kneeling with outstretched arms, evoking the Crucifixion, about to be shot almost at point-blank range. However, his heroic gesture cannot detract from the overwhelming despair and mortal terror that is depicted all around him, and his white shirt, brightly lit by the soldiers' lamp, we know will shortly be splattered with red.

"GLORIOUS INSURRECTION"
Despite his declared intention to immortalize the "heroic actions" of his countrymen, Goya has instead produced an image of a slaughterhouse. A dead man, lying face down in a pool of blood, thrusts disturbingly into the foreground. He has been crudely foreshortened and appears twisted and mangled. His outflung arms suggest a supplication, mutely (and perhaps more eloquently) echoing the courageous, dramatic gesture of the next victim, who will shortly join the pile of corpses in the foreground.

GOYA'S DEATH
By 1825 Goya's health had deteriorated. He spent his remaining years in exile at Bordeaux in France. In 1826 he made the long, hard journey to revisit Madrid, after which his eyesight became so weak that he had to paint with the aid of a magnifying glass. Goya died on the night of April 15th, 1828 in Bordeaux, and remained buried there until 1901, when his body was moved to Madrid. Later, in 1929, it was exhumed again and moved to a tomb in the Hermitage of San Antonia de la Florida. This painting of the original Bordeaux tomb is by Goya's old friend Antonio Brugada.

OTHER WORKS BY GOYA

Don Manuela Silvela
(Prado, Madrid)

The Marqués de Castro Fuerte
(Museum of Fine Arts, Montreal)

The Duke of Osuna
(Frick Collection, New York)

The Duke of Wellington
(National Gallery of New Zealand, Wellington)

Isabel de Porcel
(National Gallery, London)

Young Woman with a Letter
(Musée Lille)

294 Francisco Goya, The Colossus, *1810–12, 115 x 105 cm (45 x 41 in)*

The Colossus (294) has a subtitle, *Panic.* It shows all humanity in flight, streaming away like ants from unimaginable horror – an analogy for the monstrous destruction of war, one of the bloodiest in Spain's history (see column, p.250). Goya has visualized this dread for us, given it concrete form: a huge, hostile presence fills the sky, not yet looking down at the terrified masses below, merely flexing his muscles. Existence is not what we had thought: here are different rules and we do not know what they are. What we are contemplating is our common nightmare.

Goya gives this fear an awesomely convincing form. He is painting his own dreads, but his genius reveals them to be our own. They may in fact be more our own than we realize.

The Colossus is in fact looking away from the fleeing people: are we perhaps seeing more of a threat in this mysterious form than is literally there? He can even be seen as a protective Colossus, the native genius of Spain, arising in might to challenge Napoleon. Yet somehow this benign interpretation does not spring readily to mind.

There is a darkness in Goya, an anger, a wildness, that represents something within our hearts, repress it though we may. It is precisely this irrational fury of the imagination, prefiguring the Romantics – poets such as Shelley, Keats, and Byron, or composers such as Schumann or Berlioz – that gives Goya the edge over his contemporary, the great French Neoclassical artist Jacques-Louis David.

THE NEOCLASSICAL SCHOOL

Neoclassicism clearly proved to be a popular philosophy among artists in the middle of the 18th century. It manifested itself in a variety of national schools, in varying degrees of intensity. In England, it was found in a modified form, in the work of Reynolds and his followers. In Italy it was important, for Rome was the world centre for Neoclassical thought, attracting such personalities as the first "true" Neoclassicist, Anton Mengs. But Neoclassicism did not really become established as a coherent movement in the arts until it emerged in quintessential form in the late 18th century, in France.

In the middle of the 18th century, as in the middle of the 17th (see p.216), artists turned to Classicism in reaction against the frivolity of art of the previous generation. The 18th-century Neoclassicist philosophy was reformist in character, calling for a revival of ancient standards of seriousness, morality, and idealism. It was taken up readily by artists and writers who found themselves in the midst of social and political upheaval.

With the French Revolution (see column, p.255) breaking out in 1789, its potential for use in propaganda was not wasted. Jacques-Louis David's (1748–1826) style is nobly classical, the whole image so integrated that each section supports the other and there is a fine concentration of significance. The first great Neoclassical painting, painted in 1784–85, *The Oath of the Horatii (295)* is theatrical, but it is honestly so.

THE OATH OF THE HORATII

An argument between the peoples of Rome and Alba threatened to lead to war and so it was decided that each side (the Horatii and the Curatii) would send three men to fight for their city. After the battle only one man remained alive, Horatius. He discovered that his sister had been betrothed to one of the enemy Curatii. In revenge he slew his sister and was found guilty of murder but managed to get a reprieve from the death sentence. In art, the three brothers are usually shown swearing a sacrificial oath in front of their father.

295 *Jacques-Louis David,* The Oath of the Horatii, *1784–85, 335 × 427 cm (11 ft × 14 ft)*

296 Jacques-Louis David, Madame Récamier, *1800, 175 x 244 cm (5 ft 9 in x 8 ft)*

**NEOCLASSICAL
SCULPTURE**

The first fully Neoclassical
sculptor was Antonio
Canova (1757–1822), who
began his career in Venice.
He established a
reputation as a unique
modifier of the classical
Greco-Roman style, his
most famous piece being
The Three Graces. He ran
a large studio producing
a wide range of pieces,
including commissions for
Napoleon and Wellington
and the beautiful *Psyche
Revived by the Kiss of
Love* illustrated above.

All elements in the painting are geared towards
facilitating our understanding of the drama:
three brave Romans are vowing their lives away
for their country. The uprightness of their intent
is shown in the straightness of their outstretched
arms as they receive swords from their father.
Great symmetrical arches stabilize their act of
taking the vow, setting it in a noble context. The
austerity and clarity of the colours emphasize the
selflessness and totality of their fervour.

The men are hard, concentrated, active; across
the room huddle the women, soft, distracted,
passive. The contrast between them is absolute,
and it is in this uncompromising climate of
absolutes that David feels most at home.
When David painted *The Oath of the Horatii,*
the Revolution was not far away, and the picture
contains a clear reference to this.

Probably the works of David that are most
compatible to present-day sensibilities are his
portraits. Here we have no need to set him in
his historical setting before we can respond fully:
he is wonderful in the sheer conciseness of his
vision. There are no superfluities, yet the bareness
has a confident rightness about it.

Madame Récamier (296) is the epitome of
Neoclassical charm. We see that she knows she
has charm, and that she is almost consciously
watching its effect upon the painter. Everything
on and about her is sophisticatedly simple: she
scorns, we feel, the vulgarity of devices, but she
is all one living device, forcing us to accept her
at her own valuation. David sees that she is
lovely, and makes us see it as well: she reclines
because she is sure of the power of her charm,
secure behind the ivory chill of her pose. But he
seeks to know her at a level below the conscious,
and in that lies the forcefulness of the image.

A MARTYR OF THE REVOLUTION

The absoluteness of *The Oath of the Horatii* (see
p.253), intrinsically overstated but subjectively
real, is what makes *The Death of Marat (297),*
a revolutionary icon. David was very involved
in the Revolution, debating in the assembly with
a furious excitement, and was intellectually swept
away, along with many others. Marat, whom he
here idealizes as a modern saint, was assassinated
by the royalist Charlotte Corday, who prepared
for her act with fasting and prayer.

The real Marat was a politician of particularly hideous appearance who was obliged to take frequent baths because of a severe skin infection. David shows him fair and martyred, struck down amid his labours for the common good. But the literal truth is unimportant here. David painted the truth he wanted to believe, a deliberate act of propaganda, and the sheer wanting, the passionate faith in the revolution and its sanctifying power, gives the work a gigantic force. If we forget Marat himself and generalize, here is an image of death in its purity. Everything conspires to recall the Christian martyrs – the dark background lightens to the right, as if heavenly glory awaited the dying saint. Yet this is brilliant legerdemain because at no point does David cheat by using Christian imagery: it is all done by subtle reminiscence.

THE FRENCH REVOLUTION

In 18th-century France, the poorest people were forced to assume the burden of the highest taxes whilst the aristocracy and clergy were exempted from payment. On July 14th, 1789, the masses (known as *sans-culottes*, illustrated above) attacked the Bastille (the royal prison) hoping to find a stock of weapons.

It was against this background that on August 4th, 1789, the Constituent Assembly voted to abolish the *ancien régime* (feudal society). In 1791 the royal family tried to flee Paris but were captured and the trial and execution of Louis XVI took place in January 1793.

297 Jacques-Louis David, The Death of Marat, *1793, 160 x 125 cm (63 x 49 in)*

MAXIMILLIAN DE ROBESPIERRE

A leading radical in the National Assembly and an early member of the Jacobin Club, Robespierre (1758–94) derived his ideas from the doctrines of Rousseau. On June 8th, 1794, Robespierre held "The Fête of the Supreme Being" which was stage-managed by Jacques-Louis David. This new religious group was based on the disestablishment of the church and the worship of nature as a deity.

298 Jean-Auguste Ingres, The Bather, 1808,
146 x 97 cm (57½ x 38 in)

NEOCLASSICISM'S GREATEST HEIGHTS

Ingres (Jean-Auguste Dominique, 1780–1867)
studied under Jacques-Louis David, who was
32 years his senior, but eventually he emerged as
the leading exponent of Neoclassicism in France.
Ingres was greatly influenced by David, especially
in his earlier works. Like David, Ingres was a
strange man, almost fanatic in his meticulousness,
so dedicated to the ideal that he could not accept
the real if it fell below his aspirations.

Ingres was a passionate admirer of Raphael,
the supreme classicist, and it almost seems that
his whole art is a yearning for that earlier certainty
represented by Raphael. He is renowned for
painting the female back, not as it is, but as he
felt it ought to be, with additional vertebrae
to provide the perfect elongation. *La Grande
Odalisque (299)* is a superb example of this.
A great curve of naked back sweeps from the line
of her neck, outlining her backbone and ending
in the voluptuous fullness of her buttock. She is
like a glassy stream, breaking into a waterfall at
the barrier of the jewelled fly-whisk, with the
tumult of hands, legs, and feet flowing to the
edge of the canvas.

Parmigianino, the Italian Mannerist painter,
did much the same, lengthening the beautiful
neck of his Madonnas (see p.142). But the
Mannerists intended to excite by their use of
forms; Ingres does not. His intention is to get
us to accept his forms as actual, as classically
perfect, and in their weird beauty they come
close to it. *The Bather* (also known as *The
Valpinçon Bather, 298)* is an example of this.
It is a heavily sensual picture, the naked back
exposed amidst the contrived setting of a great
sway of olive-green drapery and the wonderful
pillowy whites of a bed's edge.

She has been given the name *The Bather* in an attempt to make sense of her position and her cap, but Ingres hardly needs the trappings. It is that heavy, dimpled back he needs, over-long in its luscious curvature, obsessing the artist and affecting the viewer through the force of his emotion. The same impossible curve distinguishes his Thetis. *Thetis Entreating Jupiter (300)*, in which the male is as impossibly broad as the female is supple, is a comic picture, quite unintentionally, because of this bodily fixation.

Ingres believed that "drawing is the probity of art", and his linear grace carries him magnificently through most hazards. But Thetis is stretching out an arm with elastic bones, a dislocated limb that halts us in our gaze and alerts us to the comely deformations the artist is trying to persuade us to accept. Ingres obviously feels that Jupiter has an iconic majesty, which has an odd truth to it, but the clam-like beauty at his knees undoes whatever faith we have managed for Jupiter. The picture fails, but so gloriously, so alarmingly, that it fascinates still.

300 Jean-Auguste Ingres, *Thetis Entreating Jupiter, 1811, 350 x 257 cm (11 ft 6 in x 8 ft 5 in)*

THETIS AND JUPITER
The legend of Thetis entreating Jupiter is told in the *Iliad*. Thetis, the mother of Achilles, is sent by her son to Jupiter with a petition concerning his quarrel with Agamemnon. In paintings the scene usually depicts Jupiter, sceptre in hand, enthroned on Mount Olympus. Thetis kneels before him and is seen imploring with the god to intervene in her son's fate.

299 Jean-Auguste Ingres, *La Grande Odalisque, 1814, 91 x 163 cm (36 x 64 in)*

CONTEMPOARAY ARTS
1764
Mozart composes his first symphony at the age of 8 years
1792
Mary Wollstonecraft writes *A Vindication of the Rights of Women*
1804
The English Watercolour Society is founded
1813
Jane Austen writes *Pride and Prejudice*
1818
The Prado Museum is founded in Madrid
1826
The US Academy of Design is founded
1837
Dickens' *The Pickwick Papers* is serialized
1862
Victor Hugo writes *Les Misérables*

MARIE ANTOINETTE

After marrying the Dauphin in 1770, Marie Antoinette (1755–93) became Queen of France on the coronation of her husband Louis XVI in 1774. Unfortunately the miseries of France became identified with her extravagances. As a feminist Marie Antoinette supported female artists, including Vigée-Lebrun, and was involved in the march on Versailles in 1789. After the execution of her husband in 1793 she was placed under arrest and was guillotined in 1793.

THE FRENCH SALON

The Salon of 1667 was the first official art exhibition held in France and was limited to members of the Royal Academy. The term *Salon* derived from the Salon d'Apollon, in the Louvre, where the annual exhibitions were first held. Until the 19th century the limited number of artists who were allowed to show at these salon exhibitions had a monopoly on publicity and sales of art. This painting, *L'Innocence*, is by Adolph-William Bouguereau (1825–1905), who was one of the key supporters of the 19th-century salon.

301 Elisabeth Vigée-Lebrun, Countess Golovine, c. 1797–1800, 83 x 67 cm (33 x 26½ in)

ROYALIST IN REVOLUTIONARY TIMES

(Marie) Elisabeth (Louise) Vigée-Lebrun (1755–1842) was a clear-minded supporter of the monarchy. She fits uncomfortably within the revolutionary climate that so excited David. She understood Neoclassicism but transcended its formalities, delighting in the freedoms of the Baroque, with its strong, contrasting colours. A charming woman, she made friends with Marie Antoinette and had an instinct for the socially acceptable. At times, her insight can take her beyond this, as in her fine portrait of the

Countess Golovine (301). It is impossible not to warm to the completely feminine frankness of this Russian aristocrat, her ingenuous gesture with her scarlet cape and the seductive simplicity with which her rosy face smiles out at us beneath the carefully dishevelled black curls. This is a strong woman, for all her charm, and Vigée-Lebrun must have recognized an equal. At the outbreak of the Revolution, Vigée-Lebrun went into exile in Italy. She went to London in 1802, where she painted several important portraits, returning to Paris in 1805.

THE GREAT FRENCH ROMANTICS

If applied to the arts today, the word Romantic suggests a certain theatricality and sentimental idealism. Its original meaning, however, had quite different associations. While Neoclassicism was associated with the culture of antiquity, the Romantic was associated with the modern world. Romanticism admitted the "irregular": the wild and uncontrolled aspects of nature (both animal and human, both beautiful and ugly). The necessary strategy for such expression was inevitably incompatible with the dogma of Neoclassicism and its fixed notions about beauty and subject matter.

JEAN-JACQUES ROUSSEAU

Jean-Jacques Rousseau, (1712–78) the political philosopher and author, had a great influence on the Neoclassical period. It was not until 1750 that he made his name as a writer with his *Discourse on the Sciences and the Arts* which argued that there was a schism between the demands of contemporary society and the true nature of human beings. His argument for "Liberty, Equality, and Fraternity" became the battle cry of the French Revolution.

The pastoral idyll suggested by some of the country scenes of Gainsborough (see p.240) was fast disappearing under the Industrial Revolution, while in France, revolution of a more violent kind brought irrevocable change to the social order. The grandeur and idealism of Neoclassicism were at odds with the realities and hardships of an increasingly industrial society. Prefigured by Goya (see p.252), Romanticism stands for an outlook, an approach, a sensibility towards modern life. France was its true home, and that of its earliest innovators, Théodore Géricault (1791–1824) and Eugène Delacroix (1798–1863).

If Ingres (see p.256) was the great Neoclassicist, these were the great Romantics. Their art was diametrically opposed to his, and in the bitter debate between the two schools, theirs proved the stronger. Ingres was concerned mainly with the control of form and with outward perfection as a metaphor for inner worth. The Romantics were far more interested in the expression of emotion – through dramatic colour, freedom of gesture, and by their choice of exotic and emotive subject matter. *The Raft of the Medusa (302)* was enormously important as a symbol of Romanticism in art.

302 **Théodore Géricault, The Raft of the Medusa**, *1819, 491 x 717 cm (16 ft 1 in x 23 ft 6 in)*

303 Théodore Géricault, Woman with the Gambling Mania, *c. 1822, 77 x 65 cm (30½ x 26 in)*

GÉRICAULT'S RAFT

The raft carried survivors from a French naval ship, *La Méduse*, which sank en route to West Africa in 1816. The captain and senior officers took to the lifeboats and left a makeshift raft for the 150 passengers and crew. During 13 days adrift on the Atlantic, all but 15 died. Géricault's choice of this grim subject for a gigantic canvas went against traditional artistic rules. It also implied criticism of the government, for the appointment of this unseamanlike captain had been an act of political favouritism.

This radical work was accepted, but grudgingly, by the artistic establishment: the gold medal it won at the Paris Salon of 1819 was merely a way of denying Géricault the controversy he sought. Géricault forces us, almost physically, to accept the reality of human suffering and death. It is death in the most terrible conditions, anguished, tortured, long-drawn-out, without nobility or privacy. The drama is all in the physical details. It is as if Géricault eschews the use of colour as

too trivial, too joyous, for such a scene. There is no space for the viewer in which to escape the terrible impact of that rough triangle of raft. It juts out at us, a blow in the solar plexus.

Disappointed with its tepid reception in France, Géricault took the painting to England, where he stayed for a few years, deeply impressed by Constable (see p.268).

Géricault's life was short but intense. He sought after the real with a hungry passion, but it was to make the real transcendent that he sought. There is a hypnotic power in his portraits of the insane, such as *Woman with the Gambling Mania (303).* These tragic and haunted faces had some personal resonance for him. He is not regarding their sufferings objectively; there is a moving intensity of reaction. He makes us feel that the potential for these various imbalances are endemic to us all. It is our own possible future that we contemplate.

DELACROIX: THE GREAT ROMANTIC

Géricault had a preoccupation with death and the morbid that is absent in his contemporary, Delacroix, whose characteristic is a sense of the romantic fullness of being alive. After Géricault's death in 1824, Delacroix was regarded as the sole leader of the Romantic movement, but his art was very much his own, and soon transcended Géricault's early influence. Like Géricault, Delacroix received a classical training (in fact they first met as students of the Neoclassicist Pierre-Narcisse Guérin) but, despite much

304 Eugène Delacroix, An Orphan Girl in the Graveyard, *1824, 65 x 54 cm (26 x 21½ in)*

305 Eugène Delacroix, **The Death of Sardanapalus,** *1827, 391 x 496 cm (12 ft 10 in x 16 ft 3 in)*

criticism from the salons, he went on to develop a uniquely animated and expressive style, greatly influenced by Rubens (see p.186), employing a characteristically vivid palette that places him as one of the great colourists. He has an almost Rubensian energy, a wild and sometimes reckless vitality that is the exact visual equivalent of Byronism. Like Byron (see column, p.262) he can be histrionic at times, but generally he exults with the vigour of the truly great and carries the viewer uncritically away.

Delacroix is an extremely active artist. When he paints *An Orphan Girl in the Graveyard (304),* she is not a tearful or passive orphan, but a vibrant young beauty, avid for life, alarmed and alerted by the nearness of death, but slack-mouthed and bare-shouldered as she looks away from the graves towards rescue. Her eyeballs have the gleam of a frightened horse, but the tenseness of her neck muscles is completely healthy. She is not a victim, despite her label.

The Death of Sardanapalus (305) shows Delacroix at his most brilliantly unpleasant – appropriately, for Sardanapalus was an Assyrian dictator. The gorge rises to see female slaves treated as chattels just like the horses and jewels. If sado-masochism is to be glorified, this is its glorification. Only Delacroix, with his almost innocent delight in movement and colour, could even attempt to carry it off.

Like Géricault, Delacroix exulted in horses, especially those from the exotic wastes of Arabia or Africa. But he did not share the younger Romantics' interest in contemporary, local reality. When he deals with modern events he distances himself by setting them in a far-away, exotic location. Such detachment sets him apart from the Romantic movement as such, though not from the Romantic attraction to the exotic. It also reveals his concern that art should still strive to attain the timelessness and seeming universality of the great art of the past.

OTHER WORKS BY
DELACROIX

*The Assassination of
the Bishop of Liège*
(Louvre, Paris)

Education of the Virgin
(National Museum of
Western Art, Tokyo)

Hercules and Alcestis
(Phillips Collection,
Washington, DC)

Odalisque
(Musée des Beaux
Arts, Dijon)

Death of Valentino
(Kunsthalle, Bremen)

The Lion Hunt
(Chicago Art Institute)

Death of Ophelia
(Neue Pinakothek,
Munich)

LORD BYRON

One of Delacroix's great heroes was the poet George Byron (1788–1824). Byron had supported the Greeks in their struggle against the Turks since he visited Greece in 1809–10 and witnessed the terrible conditions in which they were living. With the outbreak of the War of Independence in 1821 Byron sailed to Argostoli to lead a private army of soldiers. Soon he became disillusioned with the internal fighting within his ranks and his efforts were overshadowed by mutinies and illness. He died of a fever on April 19th, 1824. This illustration shows Byron dressed in the national Greek costume.

TRAVEL JOURNALS

In the mid-19th century it became popular for artists to go on tours of distant countries. In 1832 Delacroix travelled to North Africa and filled seven notebooks with drawings and watercolour sketches like these studies (shown above) of the walls around Meknès. The experiences of his six-month tour of Morocco and Algeria fuelled his imagination for the next 30 years.

Delacroix spent time in Tangiers and Morocco, and he remained in tune with this romantic world all his life. He felt a temptation to the violent, the extreme, and exorcized it in his paintings of the Near East, rather than of his own periodically turbulent country. Here, in a wild swoop of motion and a rolling swirl of colour, he can show *Arabs Skirmishing in the Mountains (306)*. He claimed to have seen these attacks and even taken part, but their truest origin is in his imaginative bonding with the warriors. He is himself in all parts of the picture, in the frenzy of the horses, the manoeuvres of the fighters, their pain and anger, their courage and despair. He is at one with the landscape, wild and high, desolate, infertile, yet fiercely loved.

The citadel on the cliffs, though, remains, above the smoke and the fury, and that, too, is to be understood personally. Delacroix never loses himself in his greatest works but, with instinctive tact, leaves always a place for detachment. There is an inner stability that keeps the work from bluster, however near the edge it may go.

306 Eugène Delacroix, Arabs Skirmishing in the Mountains, 1863, 92 x 75 cm (36½ x 30 in)

ARABS SKIRMISHING IN THE MOUNTAINS

Delacroix produced this painting a few months before his death in 1863. It has been suggested that it depicts a battle between the Moroccan Sultan's tax collectors and local rebels, and Delacroix may have come into contact with such incidents when he travelled to Meknès with the Moroccan foreign minister in 1832. (An entry in his diary of 1832 suggests this.) Historical details are, however, irrelevant to the real subject of the painting, which is a Romantic celebration of drama, colour, light, and of the exotic. It is primarily a story-teller's painting, reinvented 31 years after Delacroix's Moroccan journey, and whatever its connection with real events, it exists as a purely fictitious scene.

DISTANT ACTION
The gunmen fighting in the distance are picked out largely by their headdresses and guns, within the brilliant cloud of dust, or possibly heat haze. The livid, broken surface of the horse's flank (below), which provides a sharp focal point for the foreground, gradually gives way to a broader, more relaxed application of paint as the action recedes, culminating in the ghostly fortress on the mountain.

DISTINCTIVE BRUSHWORK
Delacroix's distinctive broken brushwork recalls the flame-like motion of El Greco's (see p.145) and contrasts utterly with his Neoclassical contemporary, Ingres (see p.256). The action of the narrative is imitated in the actual paint surface, through a kind of visual onomatopoeia. It is alive with writhing, swirling brushmarks, and there are no straight lines or flat, uninterrupted surfaces; the vegetation waves, and even the men's rifles seem animated.

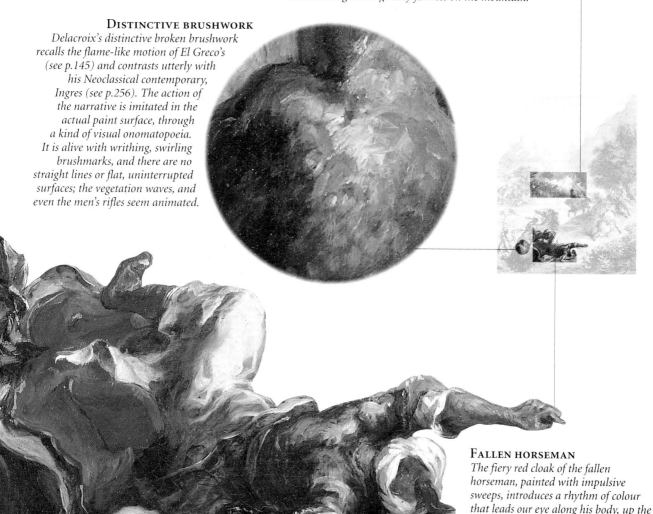

FALLEN HORSEMAN
The fiery red cloak of the fallen horseman, painted with impulsive sweeps, introduces a rhythm of colour that leads our eye along his body, up the path described by vegetation to the line of kneeling riflemen, where the direction is reinforced by the emphatic diagonals of their rifles. The sweeping movement then continues on, led by the galloping horseman, into the more distant action.

ROMANTIC LANDSCAPES

In their landscape paintings the Romantics gave free rein to their daring and their imagination. Art lovers in the 19th century may have lamented the lost rational serenity of the 17th-century master Claude Lorrain (see p.220), but many of them also saw that Turner was his equal. Turner's revelations of atmosphere and light answered the need for a new artistic language. Constable surprised the world with a new awareness of, and a new openness to, nature as it actually is, and not in any idealized or stylized form.

JOHANN WOLFGANG
VON GOETHE

Germany's greatest poet, Goethe (1749–1832) pioneered Romanticism in German literature in the 1770s. He believed that great art must simulate the creative force of nature. In his later life he also studied various sciences including optics. Goethe's writings on art included a book on the theory of colour which opposed Newton's discovery that there were seven colours in the spectrum and argued that there were only six in natural daylight conditions.

The French were by no means the only Romantics: Germany was the original "land of the Goths". A touch of that heavy symbolism that so often characterizes German art is seen in Caspar David Friedrich (1774–1840). It is primarily the countryside that Friedrich sees as a symbol, a mute praise of its unseen and unseeable Creator. Germanic mysticism has never been very exportable, and Friedrich is only today being seen as a powerful, significant artist. Religious art without an explicit religion is not easy to paint, but Friedrich succeeds.

Monk by the Shore (307) has a daring simplicity. Three great bands stretch across it: sky, sea, land, with the one vertical note of the human being, who gathers the muteness of nature into himself and gives it a voice. "Monk" comes from the Greek for "alone", and it is this loneliness that Friedrich shares with us. In the sense of this picture, we are all monks and we all stand on the shore of the unknown.

THE ENGLISH ROMANTIC TRADITION

True Romanticism – in the sense of the broad movement that was bound up with the demise of Neoclassicism – necessarily belongs to France. On the other hand, speaking strictly chronologically, a Romantic tradition had emerged earlier in England than it did in France; in a way it had been there all along, in the form of a particularly English sensibility towards the landscape – exemplified in the paintings of Gainsborough (see p.240). This early sensibility reached its full Romantic expression in the works of England's two great landscape painters: Turner and Constable.

TURNER'S LANDSCAPES

Turner (Joseph Mallord William, 1775–1851) disturbed those who met him by conforming so little to the accepted idea of a great artist. He remained an unrepentant Cockney, not over scrupulous about cleanliness or correct pronunciation, but passionately intent on the things that mattered to him. He was recognized as great from the beginning, and his career was a source of baffled but resoundingly affirmative reactions throughout his life. If his pourings and soakings of paint were beyond comprehension, they bore the certain stamp of genius.

We associate Turner with colour, but his early work is dark, the actuality of the scene being an over-riding concern, and beyond this, its inherent drama. In mid-career, it is light itself that has begun to fascinate him. Place never loses its necessity, but it is as a focus for the light, as a precious receptacle, that it matters.

He was friendly with a group of English watercolourists who were at that time developing an art that was very much based on the atmosphere of a place, as well as its topographical fact. This new art form was called the "picturesque". Turner's early training was as a watercolourist, and he would eventually come to realize watercolour's special potential for freedom of expression in his oil paintings, creating a completely unprecedented new language.

Mortlake Terrace (308) is without obvious drama. There is an early summer evening, the Thames flowing gently by, pleasure boats venturing out, tall trees lining the terrace and swaying lightly in the breeze. Shadows fall across the short grass, a few bystanders watch, a small dog leaps onto the parapet. Nothing really happens, yet the drama is as vibrant as ever. It is light that

307 *Caspar David Friedrich,* Monk by the Shore, *1810, 110 x 170 cm (43 x 67 in)*

308 J.M.W. Turner, Mortlake Terrace, *c. 1826, 92 x 122 cm (36½ x 48 in)*

is the artist's preoccupation; all is a pretext for his enamoured rendering of this delicacy of sunlight. Light quivers in the air, it bleaches the far hills, it makes the trees translucent, it throws a dark, diagonal patterning on the dull turf that takes on an entranced quality; light hides the world, and reveals it.

The Napoleonic wars ended in 1815, and the Continent became accessible once more. Turner began his long series of travels in European countries. Particularly important were his trips to Italy: in 1819 he spent three months in Rome and then visited Naples, Florence, and Venice. He revisited Italy in 1829, 1833, 1840, and 1844. His understanding of the mechanics of light was greatly enhanced by the times he spent in Italy, especially Venice, and this is what marked the beginning of his last and greatest phase.

Steamboat in a Snowstorm (309) shows Turner at his most impassioned. We are presented with a whirlwind of frenetic energy, almost tactile communication of what it means to be in a storm at sea, and a snowstorm at that. The opacity of the driven snow, the dense clouds

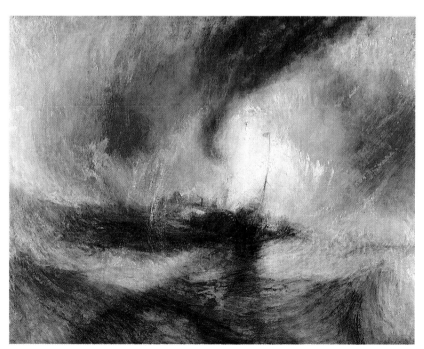

309 J.M.W. Turner, Steamboat in a Snowstorm, *1842, 91 x 122 cm (36 x 48 in)*

swirling from the smokestacks, the furious commotion of the water, all combine with almost frightening realism. And yet, take away the title, change the century, and we would think we were looking at an abstract.

This is the greatness of Turner, an almost reckless appreciation of natural wildness, controlled solely by the power of the artist's understanding. In controlling the scene, Turner seems to control nature itself, a godlike quality, and he communicates this orderliness to us. The viewer experiences the wildness, and yet is able to hold it in perspective. There can be few things more exhilarating than to encounter the full force of a great Turner.

EXHILARATION OF LIGHT

In Turner's work from this time until his old age, light has conquered so completely that all dissolves in its radiance. In these pictures, the Romantic glorification and love of nature's drama are shown to the fullest. It is here that the deeply poetic nature of Romantic painting first finds supreme visual form. As his rival John Constable (see p.268) put it, late Turners are as though "painted with tinted steam".

Approach to Venice (310) needs its title, since we are presented with a haze of coloured nothingness, through which there looms the bright accents of what we make out to be boats and a far-off steeple. The water is golden with light, but so is the sky: where does one end and the other start? There is no perspectival depth, just space, height, clouds, dazzle, glory.

The impression given is of immense exhilaration, almost ecstatic in its power; the natural is allied with the spiritual. Turner has torn the world into paper shreds and thrown them up to the sun: there they catch fire and he paints them for us, crying "Alleluia!"

Not until the 20th century, with Pollock, Rothko, and de Kooning (see pp.368–372) was there such a daring disregard for realism. Yet Turner knew precisely what he was aiming at. The clouds of glory, the lakes of light, the stone and mortar transformed into citadels of Heaven: these are not inventions. Few people have not seen the extravagances of glory that the sun produces with casual ease morning after morning. It was Turner's special gift to know that these extremes of light and colour demand from the artist an extremity of technique.

TURNER'S TECHNIQUE
This caricature by Richard Doyle entitled *Turner Painting One of His Pictures* was painted for the *Almanack of the Month* in 1846. It makes the point that Turner's love of chrome yellow, which he had used consistently since the 1820s, was still considered shocking by the public. Turner's use of luminous yellows, blues and pinks was his most characteristic feature.

310 J.M.W. Turner, **Approach to Venice,** *c. 1843, 62 x 94 cm (24½ x 37 in)*

APPROACH TO VENICE

Turner visited Venice several times. He painted *Approach to Venice* on what was probably his last visit there. As a late work it exceeds, stylistically, his earlier paintings of Venice, pushing further his daring with Romantic atmospherics and departing from the topographic reality of the Venetian sea- and townscape even more than before.

DISTANT CITY

The mysterious and unnamed procession of barges moves silently through water that, more than anything, resembles liquid gold, towards the shimmering, floating city of Venice. The distant city seems to be dissolving, no more on firm ground than the barges themselves, and takes on the quality of a mirage. Indeed, when this painting was exhibited in London, a critic for the weekly magazine The Spectator wrote: "beautiful as it is in colour it is but a vision of enchantment".

DARKENING SKY

Turner has created a canopy of orange and blue over the setting sun. These are the strongest touches of colour in the painting and suggest that the colours of the sunset have not yet reached their peak of intensity before they finally disappear. Over a smooth (and now heavily cracked) surface, these "abbreviated" clouds have been quickly and lightly rendered, and Turner has created a wonderful sense of transition as the sky moves rapidly from day to night.

MOONLIGHT
ON THE WATER

Beyond the ostensible subject matter of Approach to Venice, with its important-looking barges sailing towards Venice, is the real subject of the painting: the duel between sunset and moonrise. To the right of the canvas, the sun is setting in a spread of diffused, pale lemon light. To the left, casting its cooler reflection down the length of the picture, is the ascending full moon. When Turner first exhibited this painting, he accompanied it with these lines from a poem by Byron:

> "The moon is up, and yet
>   it is not night,
> The sun as yet disputes
>   the day with her."

LAYERED SURFACE

Turner habitually prepared his canvases with a thick layer of white oil ground, which would largely obliterate the "tooth" of the canvas. Over this smooth surface he would apply thin, pale washes of those colours that were to be used full strength later. This resulted in a fresh, glowing surface over which he built up subsequent layers. To the barge on the left he has added thick, crusted paint, which, having a jewelled effect, catches natural light falling onto the picture and provides areas of focus. Conversely, the shadows of the dark barge on the right have been applied with thin washes of black so that they appear to sink within the surface.

NEOCLASSICAL ARCHITECTURE

The distinction between Greek and Roman architecture came to be better understood in the 18th century due to the rediscovery of early Doric temples in southern Italy and Sicily and also due to the publication in 1762 of Stuart and Revett's *Antiquities of Athens.* Neoclassical architecture rejected the plasticity of the Baroque with its incorrect use of form and instead concentrated on perfecting the classical form. This photograph shows the Pantheon (temple dedicated to all the Roman gods) in the gardens at Stourhead in southwest England.

LANDSCAPE GARDENS

During the course of the 18th century, the landscape gardens of England progressed from the Arcadian landscape (seen at Stourhead and Stowe), through the Ideal landscape, to the Romantic idyll. The greatest landscape artist of the period was Capability Brown (1716–83), who led the movement away from the formal towards the natural. Brown used smooth lawns, lakes, dells, and ha-has (sunken fences that do not interrupt the view) to create a poetic whole with spatial variety and contrasting moods.

CONSTABLE – POETRY IN REALITY

Turner's Romanticism, though full of drama, is not melodramatic, and indeed "Romantic" does not preclude the humble and ordinary as we have already seen in Turner's treatment of a quiet sunset at Mortlake (see p.265).

Constable (1776–1837) is as intense as Turner and, in his less obvious manner, fully as daring, but he always reverences the factuality of what he paints. Since he sees those facts as purely poetic, there is no loss of intensity. Turner loved the grandiose and the magnificent. Venice was his natural habitat. Constable loved the ordinary, and his love and natural dwelling place was the flat land of his beloved Suffolk. He is the natural heir to Gainsborough's lyricism (see p.240), but

whereas Gainsborough was still largely concerned with extracting the beautiful and harmonious in the natural landscape, Constable saw the long meadows and winding canals, the old bridges, and the slimy posts by the rivers, as being inherently as lovely as anything the heart of man could desire. All his youth and all his hope of Heaven were intimately connected with these rural simplicities, already under threat from industry as he began his arduous and none too successful career as an artist.

Turner lived unmarried; Constable needed the solace of a wife to share his loneliness. Even shared, this loneliness is always discernible. The sun may shine and the trees wave in the breeze, but a Constable landscape carries a deep sense

JOHN RUSKIN

The art critic John Ruskin (1819–1900) took it upon himself to rescue Turner from obscurity. In 1843 he wrote his treatise *Modern Painters* in defence of Turner, which he then developed into a series of volumes concerning artistic tastes and ethics. Ruskin belonged to the Romantic school in his conception of the artist as inspired prophet and teacher. His personal life, however, was deeply unhappy and he died a lonely Christian socialist fighting against the onslaught of the Industrial Revolution.

311 John Constable, Wivenhoe Park, Essex, 1816, 56 x 102 cm (22 x 40 in)

of loss and yearning. After the early death of his beloved wife, this yearning becomes even more apparent. Yet it is a resigned yearning and an acceptance of life as it is, and of the consolation given by the beauty of the material world, our nearest image of lost Eden.

The intensity of Constable's poetry was not obvious to himself: he believed that he was the most throughgoing of realists. Even an early work, though, like *Wivenhoe Park, Essex (311)*, despite its conscientious fulfilment of the owner of the park's desire to illustrate every aspect of his property (which Constable found "a great difficulty") is still a work of imaginative ardour. The reality of all he portrays is evident: there fish the Wivenhoe tenants, on the fish-stocked lake; there wander the dairy cows, belonging to the farm; there, tiny in the distance, is the family in the trap; there in the background is the stately home. Yet all this is bathed in a silvery sunlight, so that the waters shimmer and the shadows beneath the great, spreading trees entice the viewer towards their shade.

Over the earth and water towers a pale and clouded sky, hinting at rain to come, the blissful rain that every estate needs. Peace and silence, contentment and prosperity are all imagined and realized in the actual details, so that Wivenhoe Park is both real and ideal, both in our world and removed from it.

OTHER WORKS BY CONSTABLE

Hampstead Heath
(Fitzwilliam Museum, Cambridge)

View at Epsom
(Tate Gallery, London)

Naworth Castle
(National Gallery of Victoria, Melbourne)

Coast at Brighton, Stormy Weather
(Yale Center for British Art, New Haven, Connecticut)

View of Salisbury
(Louvre, Paris)

The Watermill
(National Museum, Stockholm)

Wooded Landscape
(Art Gallery of Ontario, Toronto)

SONGS OF INNOCENCE

As a child, the English poet William Blake (1757–1827) saw visions from which he drew lifelong inspiration. One of William Blake's most significant inventions was the printed book in which the illustrations were completely intergrated with the text, both being printed from a single metal plate.

The two mediums of poetry and engraving came together triumphantly in 1789 when he published his *Songs of Innocence*. This illustration shows the original title page. The fictional world of *Songs of Innocence* is Christian and pastoral with the innocence of childhood celebrated as a spiritual force. Five years later Blake wrote the antithesis of this idyll entitled the *Songs of Experience*. In his last years Blake produced some of his finest engravings, illustrating, among others, the book of Job.

312 John Constable, The White Horse, *probably 1819, 130 x 188 cm (51 x 74 in)*

THE UNTRADITIONAL CONSTABLE

"Constable's England" has become so familiar to us that it is difficult to understand the impression his paintings made on his contemporaries. His work has come to shape our conceptions of the beautiful in the English landscape, but his contemporaries were accustomed to a very different kind of representation of the natural landscape. There were set formulas, strictly adhered to, concerning the correct way to create distance, harmony, and mood. Constable's naturalistic, vivid greens, for instance, totally upturned these formulas, which were based on the use of warm browns in the foreground and pale blues in the far distance – and his depiction of the random or "unbeautiful" aspects of the landscape was counter to accepted standards of composition and to the conventions of appropriate subject matter.

When Delacroix (see p.260) visited England in 1825 he was enormously impressed with Constable's animated brushwork, and the optical freshness that resulted from his use of broken colour to create tone. On his return, Delacroix is believed to have reworked his large *Massacre at Chios*, enlivening the surface of the painting to make it echo its emotive subject.

It was his great "six-foot" canvases that Constable valued most, but modern taste finds even greater beauty in the studies and sketches with which he prepared for them. The wild passion of a Constable study has a marvellous vigour that the sedate control of the finished works may lack. *White Horse (312)* is such a magnificent picture, with the white streak of the horse uniting both sides of the river, the greenery almost palpable, the sense of actuality so piercing, that it is almost a shock to find that his oil sketches, such as *Dedham from Langham (313)*, can be even more immediate and evocative, even more vital.

313 John Constable, Dedham from Langham, *c. 1813, 13.5 x 19 cm (5¼ x 7½ in)*

PREPARATORY SKETCHES

Constable adopted a systematic approach to painting from nature, making oil sketches on the spot then later working them up into larger works. *Dedham from Langham* was one of a number of preliminary sketches of the same scene. Constable said of it, "Nature is never seen, in this climate at least, to greater perfection than at about 9 o'clock in the morning of July and August when the sun has gained sufficient strength to give splendour to the landscape 'still gemmed with the morning dew'".

ENGLISH MYSTICISM

Romanticism provided an outlet for the spiritual expression and individuality that Neoclassicism, with its emphasis on the ideal and on stoic heroism, largely denied.

Both William Blake and Samuel Palmer worked primarily as watercolourists rather than as oil painters, yet both have the peculiarly English quality of nostalgic realism that is so pronounced in Constable. Both were poets, Blake (1757–1827) literally so (see column, p.270) and Palmer temperamentally, and there is a haunting awareness of time and its passing in their works.

Blake's *Job and His Daughters (314)* is a clumsy, archaic vision that is nevertheless extremely powerful. Blake later went on to illustrate the book of Job. His strange, visionary art found a more sympathetic response after his death, and he achieved cult status among the Pre-Raphaelites of the 19th century (see p.276). Blake's wood engravings contained the crucial element of mystery and innocence that his followers also admired in the paintings of the German primitives, and of the 18th-century Romantic group, the Nazarenes.

Samuel Palmer (1805–81) was an avid follower of Blake, nearly 50 years younger than him and influenced particularly by his few landscape works, which had been commissioned as illustrations

315 Samuel Palmer, Coming from Evening Church, *1830, 30 x 20 cm (12 x 8 in)*

314 William Blake, Job and His Daughters, *1799–1800, 27 x 38 cm (10½ x 15 in)*

for a school edition of Virgil's *Eclogues* (see p.218). Palmer's *Coming from Evening Church (315)* is just as naïvely independent of styles and schools as Blake's art, and has much the same spiritual innocence. Palmer developed a way of working with mixed media – such as Indian ink, watercolour, and gouache – that resulted in an intense luminosity, reminiscent of the medieval illuminated manuscripts (see pp.28-34).

Constable was an artist in the largest sense, as Blake and Palmer were not, but his influence continued in their work – in their particularly English strain of deeply personal love of the land, and in their awareness of its mystical importance to our spiritual well-being.

THE ANCIENTS

In 1826 Samuel Palmer (1805–81) moved to Shoreham in England and founded a group of artists known as The Ancients. The name of the group was derived from their passion for the medieval world and their concentration on pastoral subjects with a mystical outlook. Palmer's work was largely forgotten until the Neo-Romantics rediscovered him during World War II.

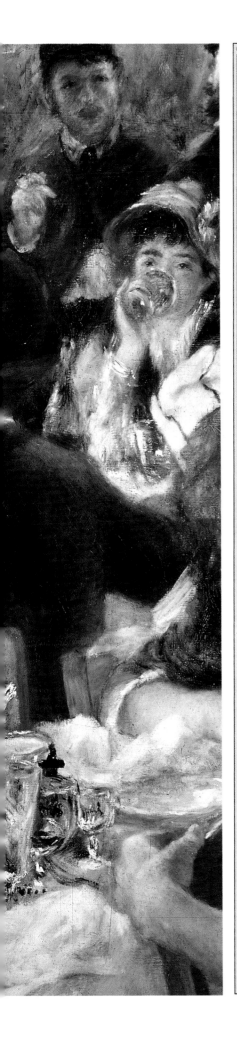

THE AGE OF IMPRESSIONISM

In the middle of the 19th century, painters began to look at reality with a new alertness. Academic conventions had become so solidified and entrenched that artists such as Gustave Courbet could see no point in them. He painted peasant life as it truly was, thereby shocking and alienating the art world establishment.

The label for this reaction was "Realism", but the next generation of artists ultimately found it too material a vision. They too rejected idealized and emotional themes, but they sought to go much further. Studio painting seemed in itself unnatural to them when the real world was "out there": it was there that they painted, outside, seeking to capture the fleeting effects of light and give the real impression of a passing moment. Rather contemptuously, they were known as Impressionists and their most characteristic figures were Claude Monet and Auguste Renoir, who captured the poetry of the here and now.

Auguste Renoir, **The Boating Party Lunch,** *1881 (detail)*

AGE OF IMPRESSIONISM TIMELINE

Realism as a style was based upon a new attitude to social truth; it accepted the sordid conditions of real life. Impressionism was not social but personal, less "life" than "experience". If we want historical dates, it lasted from the first Impressionist exhibition of 1874 to the last in 1886, but artists escape these neat time boxes, and Impressionists reach back to the Realists and forward to the Post-Impressionists.

JEAN-FRANCOIS MILLET, THE GLEANERS, 1857
The village of Barbizon was the home of a group of artists who shared a common desire for a greater naturalism in landscape painting than that provided by Romanticism or academic painting. Millet shared this desire, painting peasants with a strong sense of their dignity, imbued with compassion for their laborious lifestyle (p.281).

SIR JOHN EVERETT MILLAIS, OPHELIA, 1851–52
The Pre-Raphaelites were a group of English artists who rejected the studio conventions of their day and harked back to medieval simplicities. Ophelia is a fine example of their weird amalgam of specific detail and Romantic theme (p.276).

CAMILLE COROT, VILLE D'AVRAY, C. 1867–70
Corot's long career began in the 1820s, during the Romantic era, and this painting is an example of his late work. It shows his deeply poetic response to the timeless qualities of classical landscapes, that nostalgic world of the lost paradise from which we are all inevitably barred. He taught the Barbizon painters how to see this world and make it real, and the Impressionists learnt from him too (p.280).

1850	1860	1870

GUSTAVE COURBET, BONJOUR MONSIEUR COURBET, 1854
Courbet, like the Pre-Raphaelites, believed in the importance of the specific, but far more flamboyantly. He himself was the centre of his art, and we see him here splendidly confident. It is not theories that make his paintings work, but sheer artistic power (p.283).

EDOUARD MANET, LE DEJEUNER SUR L'HERBE, 1863
Manet painted with a naked truth that stripped away the social pretences of his time. It was not the subject of his work that was startling (a picnic in the woods was a well-established theme), but its alarming realism, its refusal to pretend, to hide in an antique guise. He was not specifically an Impressionist, but his artistic discoveries were an enormous influence on Impressionism (p.284).

AUGUSTE RENOIR, THE BOATING PARTY LUNCH, 1881
While other Impressionists were fascinated with the ever-changing patterns of nature, Renoir was more interested in people. He took simple pleasure in whatever met his good-humoured attention and aimed to give the impression, the sensation, of his subject matter. This painting shows Renoir's skill in capturing delightful scenes of modern life and recording how the Parisians spent their leisure time. He also shows relationships between people – such as that of the pair on the right (p.298).

ALFRED SISLEY, MEADOW, 1875
Sisley came from an English family living in France, and can be considered the one true Impressionist. He never developed beyond it. His landscapes are not as robust as Monet's, but are subtle, lyrical, and peaceful. The place shown here is unimportant, but Sisley catches the quality of light and the changing shadows perfectly (p.301).

EDGAR DEGAS, FOUR DANCERS, C. 1899
Degas often exhibited with the Impressionists, although he studied the Old Masters throughout his life and was a superb draughtsman. This late work is a good example of how he could seize upon the unbalance of an actual scene in the real world, and make art from what he had found. He learnt this from photography and the strange magic of the Japanese printmakers (p.292).

1880   **1890**   **1900**

JAMES WHISTLER, NOCTURNE IN BLUE AND GOLD: OLD BATTERSEA BRIDGE, 1872–75
American by birth, Whistler moved to Europe and lived first in Paris, then London. Nocturne in Blue and Gold reveals his debt to the Impressionists. He had looked at them, but also, and more significantly, at the Japanese, with their use of a non-realistic, seemingly two-dimensional composition, and the skilful choice of a few highly significant details. Whistler was interested in the Realist and Impressionist movements, but took from them what he needed to create a decorative style that was his alone (p.302).

CLAUDE MONET, THE WATERLILY POND, 1899
A quintessential work of Impressionism, this is one of Monet's numerous waterlily studies, some of which border on the abstract with their floating shapes and surface reflections (p.296).

THE PRE-RAPHAELITES

Towards the middle of the 19th century, a small group of young artists in England reacted vigorously against what they felt was "the frivolous art of the day": this reaction became known as the Pre-Raphaelite movement. Their ambition was to bring English art (such as it was) back to a greater "truth to nature". They deeply admired the simplicities of the early 15th century, and they felt this admiration made them a "Brotherhood".

While contemporary critics and art historians worshipped Raphael (see p.125) as the great master of the Renaissance, these young students rebelled against what they saw as Raphael's theatricality and the Victorian hypocrisy and pomp of the academic art tradition. The friends decided to form a secret society, the Pre-Raphaelite Brotherhood, in deference to the sincerities of the early Renaissance before Raphael developed his grand manner. The Pre-Raphaelites adopted a high moral stance that embraced a sometimes unwieldy combination

316 Sir John Everett Millais, Ophelia, *1851–52, 75 x 112 cm (30 x 44 in)*

of symbolism and realism. They painted only serious – usually religious or romantic – subjects, and their style was clear and sharply focused. It entailed a unique insistence on painting everything from direct observation.

The group initially caused outrage when the existence of their secret brotherhood became known after their first works were exhibited in 1849. They also offended with their heavily religious and realist themes that were so unlike the popular historical paintings. However, the Royal Academy continued to exhibit Pre-Raphaelite paintings, and after 1852 their popularity burgeoned. Their work, though certainly detailed and for the most part laboriously truthful, became progressively old-worldish, and this

317 William Holman Hunt, On English Coasts, *1852, 43 x 58 cm (17 x 23 in)*

decision to live in the past, while deploying the judgments of the present, makes the work of an artist such as John Everett Millais (1829–96) appear disturbingly unintegrated. His *Ophelia (316)*, Hamlet's drowned lover, was modelled with painstaking attention on a real body in water, surrounded by a ravishing array of genuine wild flowers (see column, p.276).

Millais spent four months painting the background vegetation on the same spot in Surrey, England. He then returned to London to paint his model, Elizabeth Siddal, posing in a bath full of water, so determined was he to capture the image authentically. The result is oddly dislocated, as if the setting, girl, and flowers did not belong together, each keeping its own truth and ignoring that of the others.

LUMINOUS COLOUR

William Holman Hunt (1827–1910), a fellow art student and friend of Millais, was more alerted to the theatricalities of his age, and *On English Coasts (317)* is a political allegory on the theme of strayed and unprotected sheep. Yet the weirdly acidic colours, even though honestly come by, strike unpleasantly on the eye. We are constrained into belief, but against our will: the bright yellow is so garishly bright and so are the aggressive greens of the sea.

The Pre-Raphaelites achieved such intense luminosity in their work by painting pure colours onto a canvas that had been prepared with white paint, sometimes reapplied fresh before each day's work, so as to give the hues added brilliance.

CHARLES DICKENS
The English author Charles Dickens (1812–70) is considered one of the greatest novelists of the 19th century. His early life was one of poverty and hard work, but he managed to educate himself and find a job as a journalist for the *Morning Herald.* His first printed work, *Sketches By Boz,* was published in 1836 and from this date onwards he became a prolific writer, completing many serialized novels including *Hard Times,* published in 1865 (illustrated above). As an important literary figure, Dickens found ready listeners for his criticism of Millais' *Christ in the House of His Parents.* He objected to the imagery, and style, calling it "mean, odious, repulsive and revolting".

WILLIAM MORRIS

William Morris (1834–96) became a lifelong friend of Edward Burne-Jones whilst they were studying at Oxford University. Along with several other craftsmen, Morris founded a manufacturing and decorating firm in 1861. The firm produced works based on the ideal of a medieval guild, in which the artists both designed and executed the work. Products included furniture, stained glass, tapestries, carpets, and wallpaper (illustrated above).

DANTE GABRIEL ROSSETTI

Rossetti (1828–82) was born into an intellectual and creative Italian family but spent most of his life in London. Throughout the 1840s his poetry and painting prospered and he completed many symbolic historical paintings. He met Elizabeth Siddal in 1850 whom he then married in 1860 after a troubled courtship. His wife, however, was weak and died only two years later, leaving Rossetti a broken man. For her burial Rossetti insisted on placing his complete poetry manuscripts in her coffin, which he then retrieved in 1869 by exhuming her body. He fell into depression and in 1872 attempted suicide but did not die. He lingered on in a alcoholic and drug-induced haze until his death in 1882.

LITERARY INFLUENCES

Dante Gabriel Rossetti (1828–82), the third founding member of the Pre-Raphaelites, became the recognized leader and even formed a second grouping of the brotherhood in 1857, after Millais and Hunt had gone their separate ways. Rossetti came from an artistic and versatile Italian family, and it was perhaps the confidence engendered by this background, and his dynamic personality, rather than his artistic talent, that earned him his prominent position.

Rossetti was a poet as well as a painter, and in common with the other Pre-Raphaelites, his art was a fusion of artistic invention and authentic renderings of literary sources. The brotherhood drew heavily from Shakespeare, Dante, and contemporary poets such as Robert Browning and Alfred Lord Tennyson – Rossetti in particular was greatly attracted to Tennyson's reworkings of the Arthurian legends. He specialized in soulful maidens of extraordinary looks for his romantic themes, using his beautiful but neurotic wife Elizabeth Siddal as his model. Her striking face, with its long-nosed, languid expression, appears in many pictures. After Elizabeth's

318 Rossetti, The Day Dream, 1880, 160 x 92 cm (63 x 36½ in)

319 Edward Burne-Jones, The Golden Stairs, 1876–80, 270 x 117 cm (106 x 46 in)

death, Rossetti's model was William Morris' wife Janey (a Siddal look-alike). She is the one we see in *The Day Dream (318)*.

Edward Burne-Jones (1833–98), who was a great influence on the French Symbolists (see p.321), was a friend of Rossetti and Morris. He places his introspective, medievalized heroines in *The Golden Stairs (319)* in a dreamlike never-neverland that comes close to his own unworldly convictions. This romanticized world may cloy, but there are many who feel at home in the serious play of the Pre-Raphaelites, and have no difficulty in responding to their themes.

REALISM IN FRANCE

Neither a Romantic nor a Realist, it was Camille Corot, who early in the 19th century, showed that these two approaches were not necessarily in opposition. He united great truth with great lyricism, but it was his astonishing truthfulness that ultimately made the greater impact. Honoré Daumier began to look at the social realities of his day with a boldness he had learnt from Corot, and so did the Barbizon School of painters. This Realism, now fully deserving its capital "R", came to its full maturity in the astonishing work of Gustave Courbet.

After the emotional extremes of the Romantics (see p.259), it comes almost as a relief to enter the gentler world of Corot's imagination (Jean-Baptiste-Camille, 1796–1875). Corot's style was far removed from the heroics of the Romantics. He saw the world, both natural and man-made, with an innocent truthfulness that greatly influenced the Barbizon School of artists, as well as practically every painter of landscape in the latter half of the 19th century.

In 1825 Corot went to Italy, a journey that influenced his approach to painting for the rest of his life; subsequently, it affected the whole development of modern landscape painting. It was in Italy that Corot first experienced the benefits of painting *en plein air* (see column, right), and his authentic depiction of light and nuance set a new precedent in French landscape painting. He came to place great importance on the Italian practice of making sketches *in situ*, valuing these for their spontaneity, truthfulness, and atmosphere. He was deeply responsive to the timeless serenity of the classical landscape; its quietness found a response within, and his Italian landscapes express this profound and lovely silence.

A View near Volterra (320) was not painted on the spot: Corot saw this view as he travelled in this strange region of Italy and some years later, referring to his original sketch, he painted it both as what he remembered and for what it meant to him. The truth then is emotional rather than factual, but it is truth nonetheless: the quiet rocks and sunlit foliage bear within them a sense of the antique. Many generations have lived on the sites of the ancient Etruscans

PAINTING EN PLEIN AIR
The French landscape painter Charles Daubigny (1808–79) was one of the earliest exponents of *plein air* (open air) painting and was to have a significant influence on the later Impressionist painters. The invention of metal paint tubes allowed long-term storage of oil paints, making trips into the countryside feasible using the new portable easels. Many of the Impressionists settled and painted in the riverside communities along the banks of the River Seine. This illustration shows Camille Corot (1796–1875) painting *en plein air* under an umbrella.

OTHER WORKS BY COROT

Morning near Beauvais
(Museum of Fine Arts, Boston)

La Rochelle
(Cincinnati Art Museum)

In the Dunes
(Rijksmuseum, The Hague)

Souvenir of Palluel
(National Gallery, London)

The Ferryman
(Louvre, Paris)

Landscape at Orleans
(Bridgestone Museum of Art, Tokyo)

Canal in Holland
(Philadelphia Museum of Art)

The Happy Island
(Museum of Fine Arts, Montreal)

320 Camille Corot, A View near Volterra, 1838, 70 x 95 cm (27½ x 37½ in)

321 *Camille Corot,* Ville d'Avray, *c. 1867–70,
40 x 60 cm (19½ x 26 in)*

(see p.18), and their presence still lives on subliminally. Corot paints the place and its feel, evoking our own memories to unite with his. The place is dreamlike, yet fundamental in its solidity. No artist ever made mere substance so spiritual as did Corot.

Corot can be so unassuming that his true greatness is missed. He never dramatizes or exaggerates, never strikes any kind of attitude. Few painters have ever had such a mastery of tone, of the imperceptible gradations by which one colour melts into another. His landscapes are often small but perfect, with a simplicity so profound as to be totally satisfying. He may not have beautified his undramatic countrysides but the excitement is in the veracity of his vision.

Corot's early and less critically successful landscapes paved the way for Impressionism. In his later years, he would modify his art, painting again and again an entrancing forest glade, dappled and peaceful. This is the fashionable Corot, and this too is lovely, but it is a declension from the unique magic of his disregarded early work. A typical and lovely example of late Corot is *Ville d'Avray (321)*: feathery trees, pale sky, pure white of the distant houses, silvery water, and young people bright amidst all the flowers and grasses. The one abiding component is a contemplative stillness that Corot never lost.

DAUMIER THE SATIRIST

We do not know what Corot thought of the French painters Daumier and Millet, but he gave financial help to Daumier in his blind old age, and to Millet's widow. Honoré Daumier

(1808–79) was greatly influenced by Corot's work – though the caustic wit and the overtly socio-political content of Daumier's caricatures and lithographs (see column, left) would appear to have little in common with the serenity of Corot's art. Though he was acknowledged as one of the most important cartoonists of the 19th century during his lifetime, it is only since his death that Daumier's qualities as a serious painter have been recognized. His directness of vision and lack of sentimentality in the way he painted actual experiences make his works some of the most powerful examples of Realism.

While Corot was comfortably well off and never had to earn his living, Daumier struggled throughout his career as a satirist to support himself, suffering censorship and imprisonment because of the subversive nature of his art. He was a committed Republican with an intense political passion for the poor, drawing such strong caricatures that his own contemporaries found it hard to take him seriously as a fine artist. He gave Corot his painting *Advice to a Young Artist (322)* in gratitude for an act of generosity by Corot that released Daumier from financial worry in his final years. Two men are alone in the studio, the unmade bed the only sharp colour. The young man is tense, the older man intent, perhaps marking time while he finds the encouraging yet sincere words to offer as advice. The stress is wholly on personal interaction, with the entire context conjured up out of just a few props.

322 *Honoré Daumier,* Advice to a Young Artist, *probably after 1860, 41 x 33 cm (16 x 12 in)*

MILLET AND THE BARBIZON SCHOOL

In the 1830s a group of landscape artists moved out of Paris to the small village of Barbizon on the outskirts of the Forest of Fontainebleau, where they were often joined by Corot. He was a great influence on the group, but they were also affected by Constable's landscapes (see p.268) in their desire for a greater naturalism and a truthful depiction of the countryside.

Jean-François Millet (1814–75) settled in Barbizon in 1849 and was soon associated with the School. Although in later life he turned to painting pure landscape, he is more famous for his peasant pictures, the truth of which arises from his own personal experience as the son of a farm labourer. Some now think these paintings sentimental, but they were considered radical in their day for their social realism. Millet was a sad and laborious painter, apt to see life as very dark – the temperamental opposite of Corot, with his luminous world of serenity and light – but people clearly responded to his art, although

they were still baffled by Daumier's. Millet's style was simplified, diluted, yet powerful, imbuing the ordinary with a strong sense of dignity and a monumental weight.

Millet's most famous work is probably *The Gleaners (323)*. We see three peasant women at work in a golden field: two of them are bowed in measured toil, assiduously gathering the scraps left behind by the harvesters, while the third binds together her pathetic sheath. Millet makes inescapable the realization that it is hard, back-breaking work. The women's faces are not only darkened by the sun, but seen as almost brutish, with thick, heavy features. Yet, beasts of burden though they are, he regards them with reverence. We feel awed at their massive power and the sheer beauty of the classical frieze they create silhouetted against the meadow. This is a setting of great natural loveliness: golden corn, peaceful sky, the rhythmic movement of distant labourers. The background is a pastoral idyll; the foreground a pastoral reality.

MILLET'S SKETCHES

Jean-François Millet (1814–75) was the most famous painter of rural life in 19th-century France. Although renowned as a painter, some of Millet's best works are his drawings, which invest the ordinary with depth and dignity. Millet is known to have said that he aimed "to make the trivial serve to express the sublime". Millet was admired by many artists including van Gogh (see p.316).

323 Jean-François Millet, **The Gleaners,** *1857, 83 x 111 cm (33 x 44 in)*

THE PARIS COMMUNE
In July 1870 the French declared war on Prussia. After only two months the French leader Napoleon III was forced to surrender and an angry, humiliated mob declared the Third French Republic. Patriotic radicals in Paris sought to republicanize the country and elect a municipal council: the Commune. Barricades were established by the Communards and the State French troops had to retake the city by force. By the end of the conflict 20,000 Parisians had been killed and the Communards had shot many high-ranking hostages. This illustration shows a female petrol-bomber defending the barricades.

THE PAINTER'S STUDIO
Dissatisfied with the space allotted to him at the Universal Exhibition of 1855, Gustave Courbet decided to establish his own pavillion called *Le Realismé* to show his works. One of the paintings exhibited was *The Painter's Studio* which proved that secular art could now convey the deep seriousness previously only expected from religious paintings.
There were many interpretations of the painting, including a theory that it was a covert denouncement of Napoleon III. Courbet, however, stated that it shows "all the people who serve my cause, sustain me in my ideal, and support my activity".

COURBET, THE GREAT REALIST

The Pre-Raphaelites' (see p.276) concept of Realism was a fundamentally different one, their work often displaying a superficial, outward impression of nature and expressing sentiments quite removed from reality. The greatest Realist, in a much truer sense, was the brash, anti-intellectual, and largely self-taught artist, Gustave Courbet (1819–98). He was by nature prone to rhetorical flourishes and was not as down-to-earth as he himself thought, but he had no tincture of the dreamy hankering after the past that characterizes the Pre-Raphaelites. Courbet's defiantly non-conformist stance and his commitment to concrete reality was an important influence on a subsequent generation of artists.

Courbet lived by his belief that artists should paint only "real and existing things", striding resolutely into the future and taking, he generally felt, possession of it. He was impressed by Caravaggio's robust expression (see p.176) and by the Dutch masters Hals (p.210) and Rembrandt (p.200). Their influences can also be traced in Courbet's own admirers. His landscapes are always vital with a savage sort of power and he prided himself on this uninhibited zest. The son of a rural bourgeois landowner, he was by nature a rough, coarse, and passionate man and he sublimated these qualities in his art. He called himself "a socialist, a democrat and a Republican and above all a Realist, that is to say a sincere lover of genuine truth".

Courbet's work has a heavy realism that is unflinching in its restless scrutiny. All his qualities, including an indefinable something that eludes the viewer, are present in his masterpiece, *The Painter's Studio (324)*. This is an intensely personal work, yet it keeps its secrets: nobody has ever quite discovered what is meant by its full title – *A Real Allegory Summing Up Seven Years of My Artistic and Moral Life*. Courbet claimed to have assembled, imaginatively, in this one canvas, all the significant influences of his life, some generalized and some apparently

324 Courbet, The Painter's Studio, 1855, 361 x 597 cm (11 ft 10 in x 19 ft 17 in)

personified. The people are of all kinds and conditions, all totally authentic, all centred on the artist himself, who paints a ravishing landscape while a nude model presses herself affectionately against his chair. These visitors are all guests, whom he seems to have invited for a purpose. Courbet actually described this strange allegory in a letter to his friend, the novelist Jules Champfleury, writing that the figures on the left were those who "live on death", while the figures on the right "live on life".

Although the portraits on the right are identifiable – Champfleury himself is depicted among the onlookers, along with other elegant Parisian friends of Courbet, such as the journalist and socialist Pierre Proudhon and the poet Charles Baudelaire (see p.286) – the characters on the left, veiled in semi-darkness, could represent people from Courbet's past or previous influences in his life: there may even be a disguised portrait of the Emperor Napoleon III. We may smile at this naïve self-importance, yet we are also

325 *Gustave Courbet*, Bonjour Monsieur Courbet, *1854, 130 x 150 cm (51 x 59 in)*

impressed. Courbet had every right to see himself as a major painter who understood materiality so profoundly as to make it appear to become more than it really was.

THE OMNISCIENT ARTIST
Courbet's vanity is not rare in those with creative talent, but few have put their weakness to such effective use. *Bonjour Monsieur Courbet (325)* shows the painter as he sees himself, very handsome and virile, detached from the softness of civilized living, striding forth along a country lane. Courbet's devoted patron, Alfred Bruyas, and his servant, bow reverentially to the artist as if he is their superior, and it is clear that Courbet heartily agrees. There is an innocent conceit in the tilt of the artist's noble head, in the condescension of his affable smile. The dusty path, the bordering weeds and grasses, the dog – every detail of this wholly ordinary part of France is grasped completely in its truth and left undramatized. We are drawn into what Courbet saw and smelt and heard, not through any dramatic overemphasis but from his enormous painterly conviction.

This self-image of the artist existing above and beyond the mediocrities of "bourgeois" civilization was to find full expression in the works and lives of the next generation of painters, particularly Manet and Degas, who benefited from Courbet's artistic advances and laid the foundations of "modern" expression.

OTHER WORKS BY COURBET

Hunters in the Snow (Musée des Beaux Arts, Besançon)

Reflection of a Gypsy (National Museum of Western Art, Tokyo)

Landscape (National Museum, Stockholm)

Girls on the Banks of the Seine (Petit Palais, Paris)

The Waterfall (National Gallery of Canada, Ottawa)

Woman with a Parrot (Metropolitan Museum of Art, New York)

The Grotto of the Loue (Kunsthalle, Hamburg)

THE INFLUENCE OF MANET & DEGAS

Courbet's richness of colour and insistence on his own personal vision were immensely influential on other artists, teaching them to believe only what they could see with their own eyes. Manet abandoned the conventional practice of subtle blending and polished "finish", using instead bold colours to explore the harsh, realistic contrasts created by sunlight. Degas, influenced by photography and the simplicities of Japanese prints, adapted his skills as a draughtsman to create startlingly new compositions with his figures.

THE NEW PARIS

When Napoleon III became Emperor in 1851 he set about making Paris the new centre of Europe. Napoleon employed the architect Baron Haussmann (shown above) to redesign and rebuild central Paris, using a new network of interconnecting tree-lined boulevards. During the rebuilding he also created new parks, squares, and municipal buildings. Haussmann's ruthless plans displaced over 350,000 people and led to more social problems, including increased visibility of prostitution on the wide-open boulevards.

SALON DES REFUSES

The "Salon of the Rejected" was formed after the official 1863 Salon turned down over 4,000 paintings. The alternative salon was ordered by the Emperor Napoleon III, and many artists, including Manet, Cézanne, and Whistler were happy to find a place to show their rejected works. When the Salon des Refusés opened in May 1863, over 7,000 people visited on the first day, but the exhibition received very little critical acclaim. The Salon des Refusés inspired other artists to develop their own salons and increased the influence of art dealers. This illustration shows a contemporary cartoon parodying the jury system of the Salon.

326 Edouard Manet, Le Déjeuner sur l'Herbe, 1863, 206 x 265 cm (6 ft 10 in x 8 ft 8 in)

Edouard Manet (1832–83) took Courbet's realism one step further, so blurring the boundary between objectivity and subjectivity that painting has never recovered from his quiet revolution. After Impressionism, art can never return to a dependence upon a world that exists "out there" apart from the individual artist. Yet it was a quiet revolution only in that Manet was a reticent, gentlemanly artist who desired nothing better than conventional success at the Paris Salons

(see column, p.284). Temperamentally Courbet's opposite, with his very fashion-conscious, witty, and urbane attitude, Manet was the archetypal *flâneur* (see column, right) and was well liked. To the end he could not understand why his work was so reviled by the Parisian art world and seen as an offence. Fortunately a private income enabled him to pursue his course without undue financial distress, but one cannot imagine even a starving Manet ever compromising.

"THE FATHER OF MODERN ART"

In the past Manet has been included in the all-embracing term of Impressionism, but his art is Realist rather than Impressionist. It was Manet's attitude that influenced the group of younger painters who subsequently became known as the Impressionists. They were also affected by his radical use of strong flat colour, broken brushwork, harsh natural lighting, and the generally "raw", fresh appearance of his paintings.

Manet was an extremely cultured and sophisticated man from a well-to-do bourgeois background, yet he painted with a simplicity that is startling. His painting *Le Déjeuner sur l'Herbe (326)* is the work of an educated artist. The central group is based upon a print that is itself based upon a work by Raphael – nothing Pre-Raphaelite about Manet – and a picnic in the woods was a well-established artistic subject.

What shocked the critics and the public was the startling modernity of it all: the naked woman had a timeless body, but her face and attitude were unmistakably contemporary. One wonders whether the scandal would have been less if the men too had been unclothed. Manet made his subject seem so horribly likely, a scene that might greet the eye of anyone taking a stroll in the woods.

Ironically, it was the very power of this painting that made it a popular failure, coupled with Manet's highly idiosyncratic use of perspective. The girl bathing in the brook is neither in the picture, nor out of it. Her proportions are "wrong" in relation to the others, so that the three picnickers are enclosed within what seem like two distinct styles of painting: the stooping bather seems flattened and too remote, while the superb still life of carelessly spilled clothes and fruit looks overpoweringly real.

In the centre, Victorine Meurent, Manet's favourite model, looks out unabashed and shamelessly at the very intruder each viewer fears might be himself or herself. That classical nymphs should feel at ease with their bodies had long been accepted, but in portraying a modern, fleshly woman realistically, Manet stripped away the social pretences of his time.

THE FLANEURS

During the heyday of the Impressionist movement the streets and cafes of Paris became the setting for fashionable posing by artists and writers. A *flâneur* was the particularly Parisian phenomenon: an elegant gentleman idler who paid meticulous attention to his appearence but still maintained serious artistic or literary concerns. Manet was renowned in Parisian circles for his fashion-conscious appearance and held a life-long love for fashion in all its variety and detail.

CONTEMPORARY ARTS

1851
The Great Exhibition is held in Hyde Park, London

1865
Lewis Carroll publishes *Alice in Wonderland*

1867
Karl Marx publishes *Das Kapital*

1877
The Rijksmuseum is built in Amsterdam

1887
Sir Arthur Conan Doyle writes the first Sherlock Holmes story, *A Study in Scarlet*

1892
Tchaikovsky composes the *Nutcracker Suite*

THE FRANCO-PRUSSIAN WAR

At the onset of the Franco-Prussian war Manet and Degas joined the French National Guard whilst other Impressionist artists, such as Monet, Sisley, and, Pissarro fled to England. After only a couple of months the French army was forced to surrender and the Germans, under Bismarck, took the French province of Alsace and most of Lorraine. The French were forced to pay an indemnity of five billion francs. This illustration shows a contemporary cartoon parodying the abilities of all the leaders involved.

EMILE ZOLA

Emile Zola (1840–1902) was a supporter of Manet's work and in return the artist painted a portrait of Zola in 1867–68. The pair would regularly meet up at the Café Guerbois to discuss topical subjects. Zola produced a pamphlet defending Manet's work and remained friends with several Impressionist artists until 1886 when he published his novel *L'Oeuvre*. The novel centred around an artist-hero (based on a mixture of Manet and Cézanne) who dreams of success but finds only failure.

While Courbet sought to shock, Manet considered such a deliberate intention ill-bred and was suprised at the reaction to this work. Yet we can also sympathize with any incomprehension on the viewer's part: Manet is still not an easy artist. What we find so amazing is the blindness shown by his contemporaries to the great beauty of his art. The strong yet soft image of a young body set against the bosky magic of the woods – this is so entrancing that it remains a mystery why so few could actually "see" what was portrayed.

PARISIAN AVANT-GARDE

Manet was a close friend of the innovative French poet Charles Baudelaire (1821–67), whose essay *The Painter of Modern Life* – challenging artists to capture the great spectacle of life in the modern city – was an enduring influence on Manet's work. In each of Manet's paintings we can perceive a constant challenge to his contemporaries to see, as he did, the grandeur, beauty, and tragedy of modern life; urging artists to look at the world around them, instead of to the past, for their inspiration. He painted philosophers in the guise of modern beggars, street entertainers, prostitutes, courtesans, and people on the edges of society, as well as those situated comfortably within it. He was particularly sensitive to urban alienation and the constantly changing and evolving nature of cities. As such, Manet's contribution to modern "expression", and to the history of modern art, is profound. For all this, his art still maintained firm links with the past – particularly Velázquez (see p.194), Goya (p.248), and the Dutch masters (p.200) – learning from them in a modern context. These links were finally broken by the Impressionists in their entirely new approach to visualizing the physical world around them.

It could seem that Manet's main interest was the figure, but in fact it was the material world as actually seen, as experienced at one fleeting moment, in sunlight or shadows, and created anew. His still lifes are particularly moving. In *Still Life With Melon and Peaches (327)*, the light gleams upon the incandescent white of the tablecloth. Its texture is firmly distinguished from the soft white of the rose that lies on it. The picture not only plays with white but runs through an exhilarating gamut of luminous greens and yellows. The strong black of the bottle and the table, mixed from many colours, creates a dramatic contrast with the bright hues, while Manet's dexterous brush strokes give life and vitality to these blocks of strong colour. He shows us a world at its most vulnerable and yet its most lovely.

327 Edouard Manet, **Still Life with Melon and Peaches,** *c. 1866, 69 x 92 cm (27 x 36½ in)*

328 *Edouard Manet, Gare Saint-Lazare, 1873, 94 x 115 cm (37 x 45 in)*

OTHER WORKS BY MANET

The Suicide
(Bührle Foundation, Zürich)

Portrait of Armand Brun
(Bridgestone Museum of Art, Tokyo)

Olympia
(Musée d'Orsay, Paris)

The Spanish Singer
(Metropolitan Museum of Art, New York)

The Waitress
(National Gallery, London)

House at Rueil
(National Gallery of Victoria, Melbourne)

Philosopher with a Hat
(Art Institute of Chicago)

The Artist's Wife
(Nasjonalgalleriet, Oslo)

CONTEMPORARY THEMES

Yet the human figure remains central to Manet's work. Victorine Meurent, that insouciant young beauty, continued to be his favourite model. Ten years after *Le Déjeuner sur l'Herbe*, Meurent is still undaunted, still self-contained and at ease with her body in *Gare Saint-Lazare (328)*. This work takes the theme of a railway station (which might seem mundane, perhaps, to the modern mind) and treats it with a compelling sense of adventure, yet also with an offbeat humour.

Always responsive to avant-garde developments, Manet was in turn influenced by the younger group of Impressionists and in particular by Monet (see p.294), with whom he became good friends. Although he never became an Impressionist, *Gare Saint-Lazare* reflects Manet's growing interest in their art and marks an important progression in his own artistic methods: Manet made his initial studies for the painting inside his studio using posed models and then worked *en plein air* on site to finish the picture.

Meurent is at the far left in *Gare Saint-Lazare*, unsymmetrical, as is usual in real life. Under a gorgeous confection of a hat, her mass of red hair streams down unrepentantly and she is dressed with a flourish of Parisian chic. Little crinkles of lace froth around her sensual throat,

a velvet band draws our attention to the neat triangle above her trim body, and she holds on her lap a book, emphatically unread, and a winsome puppy, dozing above her frilly cuffs. She enchants us with her unconcerned air. Equally unconventionally, the other character in the picture shows us only her spacious back, large swathes of starched white and a huge blue sash on which light and shade flicker and fade; the little girl is as expensively dressed as her companion, but posed to appear unaware of our presence; her whole attention is on the station, always an intriguing place for children. Manet keeps the focus of our attention on this little girl by obscuring from us what she sees, beyond a blur of smoke and the dimly-lit atmosphere of the station.

It is the young girl's rapt, childish excitement, her sense of wonder at the modern world before her, that is the theme of this painting, and her attitude is made all the more evident in the boredom of the adult beside her who waits casually, passing the time away, concerned mainly with herself. Manet keeps our attention wholly where he wants it to be: on the dull, swirly background, the intense and particularized personalities, and

HOMAGE TO DELACROIX

This painting by Fantin-Latour (see p.289), completed in 1864, shows a gathering of the artistic and literary avant-garde entitled *Homage to Delacroix*. The painting shows Fantin-Latour, Baudelaire, Manet, and Whistler, among others, grouped around a portrait of their artistic hero, Delacroix. In spite of his association with progressive artists, Fantin-Latour was a traditionalist and produced meticulous portraits and lithographs in his later years.

THE BAR AT THE FOLIES-BERGERE

In his review of Manet's last great work, *The Bar at the Folies-Bergère*, the French art critic Paul Alexis described the barmaid as: "standing at her counter, a beautiful girl, truly alive, truly modern". A dedicated urbanite to the very end, Manet re-created the fashionable world he knew and loved best, in all its splendour, and its failures.

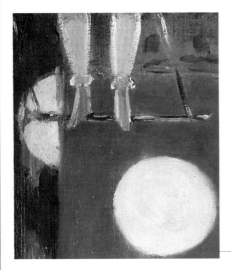

TRAPEZE ACT

It can come as a surprise to discover, tucked away in an upper corner, above the white glare of the electric lights, the bizarre presence of a pair of legs in little green boots. This is in fact the reflection of a trapeze act. The Folies-Bergère was a Parisian music hall that pioneered "variety" entertainment; its promenades were frequented by prostitutes.

THE "CUSTOMER"

Manet was accused of ignorance of the laws of perspective, for we see the reflection of a customer who seems to be conversing with the barmaid, but his bodily presence is missing – which we would expect to see, considering his position in reflection. Manet's critics failed to see the subtlety of his invention: we, the viewers, are in the position that the "customer" would rightly occupy, and so we take his place.

SUZON

The Bar at the Folies-Bergère was painted in the year before Manet's death, when he was already seriously ill. There is an unmistakable sadness beneath the bored expression of the barmaid, Suzon, who, though surrounded by gay electric lights (a new, very modern feature of the Folies-Bergère), is remote and distracted. As with much of Manet's work, the superficial gaiety of the busy Paris night-life is offset by a sense of private alienation.

MANET'S FRIENDS

Apart from the utterly solid figure of Suzon and her bar laden with refreshments, the rest of the painting is a mere reflection. Wisps of blue-grey paint, trailed over the surface of the canvas, evoke the smoky atmosphere and indicate the flatness of the mirror's surface. Cameo portraits of Manet's friends (Méry Laurent and Jeanne Demarsy) can be picked out in the blur of the teeming audience.

329 Edouard Manet, **The Bar at the Folies-Bergère,** *1882, 97 x 130 cm (38 x 51 in)*

ANTONIN PROUST
Manet and Proust were schoolboys and students together and were to remain life-long friends. In 1850 Manet and Proust joined Thomas Couture's art academy in Paris and there developed their animosity towards the art establishment. Proust's *Souvenirs de Manet,* published in 1897, is the source usually quoted for some of Manet's earliest sayings. It celebrates their unfailing friendship and expounds the glories of Manet's genius. Manet died in April 1883 after six months of constant pain. Proust was a main speaker at his funeral which was also attended by many famous artists including Monet, Renoir, Pissarro, and Sisley.

the vague impressions of a foreground. It is this new sensitivity to the fleeting, mobile reality of time that Manet gave to other artists, and which was so important to the progress of the Impressionist movement.

THE FINAL MASTERPIECE

This sense of the small, fleeting moment held perpetually still is supremely conveyed in *The Bar at the Folies-Bergère (329)*. Manet also plays with the deceptiveness of space: there are reflections that reflect falsely, and it is hard to locate ourselves in the work. The barmaid looks out with the sad dignity of the exploited, as much a comestible as the wine in the bottles or the fruit in the bowl. Like the exquisite vase of flowers on the bar, she seems to have been plucked and set before the viewer. Manet died relatively young, and knowing this, we find his late flower studies to be among his most poignant works. There we find fragile flowers, so lovely yet so mortal, contrasted with their vases, also lovely but capable of indefinite existence. There are deep emotions in Manet, but never on the surface.

It is impossible to overestimate the haunting beauty with which Manet embraces every detail of this last great canvas, his valediction to the world of high art, and it is fitting that this final work is a scene from modern Parisian life.

FANTIN-LATOUR –
A PAINTER OF STILL LIFES

Manet had a particularly wide circle of friends and artists including Monet, Renoir, Cézanne, and Bazille, an early Impressionist painter who died in 1870 in the Franco-Prussian war (see column, p.286). There were other artists who were friends with the Impressionists, but who never quite crossed over into the fleetingness of their world. Henri Fantin-Latour (1836–1904), for example, who was especially famous for the exuberant beauty of his flower arrangements, always remained a Realist, painting his flowers with the objectivity achieved from prolonged contemplation. *Flowers and Fruit (330),* with its meticulous detail, shows little awareness of the way Manet, Monet, or Renoir would dissolve the blooms into iridescence. His group portrait *Homage to Delacroix* (see column, p.287) reveals Fantin-Latour's friendship with some of the most advanced artists of the day, yet the dark, brooding colours and the substantial feel of each figure confirms his preference for consistent, realistic images.

330 Henri Fantin-Latour, **Flowers and Fruit,** *1865, 64 x 57 cm (25½ x 22½ in)*

331 Berthe Morisot, **The Harbour at Lorient,** *1869, 44 x 73 cm (17½ x 29 in)*

BERTHE MORISOT

The Morisot family was part of Manet's social circle, and his brother (Eugène Manet) eventually married the beautiful Berthe (1841–95). Morisot learned from Manet how to catch the passing hour and make it stay still for her, how to render the exquisite delicacy of light without hardening it into what it is not. During her early years she was taught by Corot and was also in contact with Charles-François Daubigny, an artist of the Barbizon School (see p.281). She was influenced by their honesty in capturing the true, changeable atmosphere of the landscape as it truly appeared before their own eyes.

Morisot enjoyed an intense, mutually respectful relationship with Manet. This influence was offset by her affiliation with the Impressionist group, with whom she exhibited regularly (while Manet remained aloof). Her eventual adoption of a lighter Impressionist palette was itself of considerable influence on Manet's late works. Morisot is not a strong painter in the Manet sense, but only a strong woman could have forced this work through: women's art was universally derided at that time. *The Harbour at Lorient (331)* is one of her finest paintings, a truly Impressionist work, in which the landscape is not subordinate to the figure and all is painted with the same care and the same ease. Great areas of contrasting blue shimmer as still water reflects unstill sky, powerfully geometric diagonals anchoring the picture, and the wonderful freshness of the morning as a girl sits on the embankment, a blithely blurred image under her pink parasol. The world hovers at the corner of the eye, delightful and unobtrusive.

MARY CASSATT

The other important woman Impressionist, Mary Cassatt (1845–1926), was as upper-class as Morisot, but her family lived in Pittsburgh, America, not in Paris. It was after she came to France in 1868 to paint and exhibit with the Impressionist group that she became modestly well known. Her art has an amplitude, a solidity very different from Morisot's, and gender is one of the few things they have in common. Cassatt's grave dignity is never over-emphatic. Her *Girl Sewing (332)* is made beautiful by the sheer variousness of the soft light. It pinkens the path behind the young woman, glows red in the flowers, and plays with a cascading grace over her simple frock. We are held by her attitude of childlike endeavour, lips set in concentration, and by the sheer brilliance with which her physical presence is captured. Cassatt was also an accomplished and brilliant printmaker, and the widespread influence of Japanese prints is especially evident in her prints and drawings.

THE INFLUENCE OF MANET AND DEGAS

332 Mary Cassatt, Girl Sewing,
1880–82, 92 x 63 cm (36½ x 25 in)

Cassatt's art shows her interest in physicality. This is very understandable since it was Degas, not Manet, who was Cassatt's mentor. Degas (Hilaire-Germain-Edgar, 1834–1917), a cynic in later life and a misogynist at every age, was condescendingly surprised at Cassatt. He admitted her power, quite against his will. Yet this power of draughtsmanship, and the ability to make a body palpably real, is very much his own.

DEGAS AS DRAUGHTSMAN

Degas is a far greater painter than Cassatt, and his graphic powers have never been excelled: his genius for line combined with a rich colour sense to produce work that will always ravish the viewer. Like Manet, he was separate from the Impressionist group (though unlike Manet, he did exhibit with them). He was sceptical of studying nature for its own sake and was instead drawn to Classicism.

Degas remained remote from life as much through his wealthy upbringing as his temperament. That his temperament was that of a voyeur seems certain: he looked on, not only from a distance, but from a height. This was so instinctive to him that it rarely offends us. Such a curiosity is shown in *Madame René de Gas (333)*, painted when he visited a branch of the family in New

PARIS OPERA HOUSE
The new Paris Opera House, designed by Jean Garnier, opened in January 1875 and Degas was a frequent visitor. He had held a season ticket to the old opera house where he studied ballet classes. With the opening of the new opera house his interest in ballet grew and became a major subject of his work in the late 1870s.

EDGAR DEGAS
In 1861 Degas met Manet whilst copying a Velázquez in the Louvre, and was introduced by him to the circle of young Impressionists. Degas' main protégée was Mary Cassatt, whom he met in Paris in 1874 and whom he asked to exhibit at the fourth Impressionist exhibition of 1879. Degas often worked in pastel, especially in the 1880s, when his sight began to fail and he chose to work using stronger colours and more simplified compositions. For the last 20 years of his life he lived alone, almost blind, as a recluse and devoted much of his time to modelling sculptures (which would be cast after his death).

333 Edgar Degas, Madame René de Gas, 1872/73, 73 x 92 cm (29 x 36½ in)

DEGAS' DANCERS

Over half of Degas' paintings depict the young ballerinas who performed between the main acts at the Paris opera (see p.291). Although Degas painted the dancers in intimate behind-the-scenes situations, he viewed them with a cool detachment. Only one of Degas' ballet sculptures was exhibited (in 1881), and at the time it was considered unusually realistic because Degas dressed the sculpture in real clothes. This illustration shows a bronze sculpture of a young dancer based on a number of pencil sketches.

DEGAS AND HORSE RACING

In the mid-19th century horse racing became extremely popular in Parisian society. Both Manet and Degas were part of the well-bred racing fraternity and attended many of the races at Longchamp in the Bois de Boulogne. Degas preferred to depict the moments before the race began, such as those in the painting illustrated above. He produced over 300 works of art on the race course theme.

334 Edgar Degas, Four Dancers, *c.1899, 151 x 180 cm (59½ x 71 in)*

Orleans. His brother René had married a woman who went blind; Edgar Degas at least did not need to fear that the intensity of his stare would disturb her. He shows her gazing blankly, plump and well-dressed, and we sense what her darkened world is like. The picture is strangely indistinct except for the face, where she is truly "herself". For the rest, she exists in cloudy spaciousness, her skirts spreading widely around her, the couch a sketchy background, nothing on the wall except light. The tight constraint of her hairstyle, unbecomingly scraped back, gives a certain pathos. Degas is sensitive to her situation, yet full of admiration: "My poor Estelle... is blind. She endures this in an amazing way; she is seldom helped around the house".

There is a tragic irony in the fact that Degas himself was to suffer from poor eyesight and eventually became unable to paint at all. His later work, mostly painted in the more direct medium of pastel, has a wild, instinctive rightness, as if his hand "knew" what his eye could barely see. *Four Dancers (334)* is not in pastel, but the oil is used with a pastel-like freedom. He makes no attempt at obvious design. The dancers move out of the painting backwards so that we just glimpse them as they move away. This unbalanced

composition, learned from photography (see column, p.293) and Japanese prints, shows Degas' understanding of this effect. The viewer is intrigued, forced to accept the painter's logic rather than that of convention. The colours, too, are vivid, insistent, glaringly bright, and this is part of Degas' theme: the stage is at all times artificially lit and our distance from it makes the colours become both loud and blurred, creating an impression of distance and glamorous dazzle.

UNIDEALIZED NUDES

For one who so openly professed contempt for women, Degas was strangely fascinated by the female nude. But he also brutally demystifies it: the women he depicts are wholly unideal and lacking in individuality. Instead, his interest is in form, the figure being reduced to an animating agent. He loved, he said, to paint as if "through the keyhole", catching his subjects when they thought themselves unobserved. The pastel painting *Girl Drying Herself (335)* is typical. We see only the back of this young woman as she stands with gawky tension upon her clothes. It is the rosy gleam of the light that provides romance and the hollow and swell of her muscles as she dries herself with animal vigour.

335 *Edgar Degas, Girl Drying Herself, 1885, 82 x 50 cm (31½ x 20 in)*

DEGAS AND PHOTOGRAPHY

By the time of the Impressionists, technical advances had led to the development of the "snap-shot" camera. The availability of instant unposed photography, with blurrings and accidental cropping off of figures created a sense of spontaneity which the Impressionists also sought to achieve. Edgar Degas was inspired by the pioneer photographer, Eadweard Muybridge, whose freeze-framed photographs of humans and animals in motion revolutionized the depiction of movement in art. This illustration shows the type of camera used by Degas.

THE GREAT IMPRESSIONISTS

Impressionism was officially "born" in 1874, when the term was applied to a relatively diverse collection of artists who exhibited at the Salon des Refusés that year. Many of the works had a comparatively coarse, unfinished appearance, which gave a strong sense of immediacy that incensed the critics. Although these artists were all individualistic, with disparate ideas and attitudes, they were united in their desire to achieve a greater naturalism in art, and their work revealed a startling new freshness and luminosity.

(see column, left)

THE BIRTH OF IMPRESSIONISM

The term "Impressionism" appeared after the first group exhibition of 1874 when a journalist, Louis Leroy, made a sarcastic attack on Monet's painting entitled *Impression: Sunrise.* Mr Leroy's satirical review argued "wallpaper in its embryonic state is more finished" and, although derisory, the term was quickly adopted by others. The first show was held in Paris in the vacated studios of the photographer Nadar, and this was followed by seven more exhibitions until 1886.

Critics found the independent exhibitors an easy target, especially the younger artists, Monet, Renoir, Morisot, and Sisley. These artists established a pictorial style that continued to the end of the decade and, after their first shows, consciously adopted the "Impressionist" label (see column, left). Cézanne, Pissarro, Degas, Gauguin – even some mainstream Salon artists – also exhibited at the Impressionist shows. Degas, though he had little stylistic affiliation with the Impressionists, wanted to support an alternative salon that would undermine the monopoly of the official Salons and provide a public arena for an innovative kind of painting based on real life.

Degas' concentration on formal line rather than on the effects of colour make him quite different from his contemporaries, Monet and Renoir. Claude Monet (1840–1926), in particular, is the quintessential Impressionist, and as such his world is exhilaratingly beautiful. Monet's style, like that of the other Impressionists, was characterized by a light, colourful palette, and he often applied unmixed paints directly onto a canvas prepared with a pure white coating. This bright surface enhanced the luminosity of each colour and increased the broken, disharmonious appearance of the picture.

What fascinates Monet in *Woman with a Parasol (336)* (also called *Madame Monet and Her Son*) is not the identities of the models, but the way the light and breeze are held upon the canvas for our perpetual delectation. One summer's day a young woman stood on a small rise in the ground, grass and flowers hiding all sight of her feet. She seems to have floated here, borne along by her dappled sunshade, radiant in the sheer brightness of the hour. Her dress is alive with reflected hues, gleaming gold or blue or palest pink. The colours never settle down, any more than do her pleats and folds, which swirl against the glitter of the clouds and the intense blue sky. Monet saw this, held it still, and made it pictorially accessible to our eyes. We look up over the variegated grass with its luminous shadows, and we are dazzled.

THE SERIES PAINTINGS

Monet's contemporaries were used to controlling the motionless images they painted in their studios, so that their work corresponded not with what was actually seen in real life – which was never still – but with what was thought to be seen. Monet took away these comforting labels of certainty. He did this most alarmingly in his great series paintings, where he surveyed the same subject in different weather conditions at different times of day or seasons. As the

336 Claude Monet, Woman with a Parasol, 1875, 100 x 81 cm (39 x 31 in)

337 Claude Monet, **Rouen Cathedral, West Façade, Sunlight,** *1894,*
100 x 66 cm (39¼ x 26 in)

Rouen Cathedral,
The Portal Seen from the
Front (Harmony in Brown)

Rouen Cathedral,
The Portal, Grey Weather
(Harmony in Grey)

Rouen Cathedral,
Morning Sun
(Harmony in Blue)

Rouen Cathedral,
The Portal and the Saint-
Romain Tower, Morning
Effect (Harmony in White)

enveloping light changes, so do the forms that had hitherto been thought constant and permanent. Monet used his brilliant palette to capture the optical effects created by natural light across a landscape or a townscape, paying little attention to the incidental details and using highly visible, sketchy, "undiscriminating" brushwork to capture the scene quickly.

Rouen Cathedral had seemed an unchangeable reality, but as Monet painted that identical west front with its spires and entrance arches – always from the same viewpoint – he saw how it was constantly transformed by the light: now richly ruddy, the thick, crusty paint echoing the rough stonework, the welcoming gates very visible, the great picture window a mystery of dark appeal; then pale, shimmery, fluid, and shifting, almost without detail in the richness of the glare. He usually worked on several canvases at once, softening the stonework in dull weather with a harmonious palette of grey and heightening

it with white and cobalt blue when the sun was at its most brilliant. *Rouen Cathedral, West Façade, Sunlight (337)* makes its statement solely through this light. It was this sensitivity to the changing, transforming light – in the strictest sense, creative light – that was Monet's greatest gift as a painter. This, of course, was for him the great fascination of the series paintings, and he explored this fascination to the utmost.

Monet extended his pleasure to the mechanics of water gardens during the final years of his life, working directly with nature: at last he had the time and the money to create his own garden and paint it. Some of his final waterlily murals, painted on enormous canvases, are almost abstract with their floating shapes and surface reflections, but *The Waterlily Pond (338)* is held firmly in the world of actuality by the Japanese bridge that curves across the centre. Even here, without that unifying curve, we might read this riot of greens, blues, and golds as an abstraction.

338 **Claude Monet**, The Waterlily Pond, *1899, 90 x 92 cm (35 x 36½ in)*

THE WATERLILY POND

Monet moved to a house at Giverny in northwest France in 1883, and lived there for the rest of his life. His garden was his main source of inspiration during his remaining years, and in 1893 he increased its area by purchasing an adjoining site that contained a pond. Here he created his celebrated water garden. This is one of 18 paintings belonging to Monet's late series, in which the arched, Japanese-style bridge, that he had constructed over his waterlily pond, forms the central motif.

VERTICAL BRUSHWORK

This version of the waterlily pond reveals the garden in full summer, with dense, bright green foliage. Beyond the tense, arching curve of the bridge, the foliage is a soft mass of confusion: greens, blues, pinks, and purples merge in and out of one another, and definition is almost non-existent. However, the vertical rhythm of the brushwork prevents the foliage from melting into incoherence, and it helps maintain the strong formal structure, repeating the verticals of the bridge and the sides of the canvas.

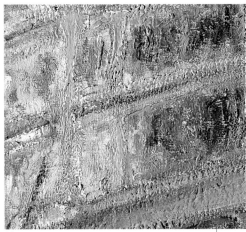

THE JAPANESE BRIDGE

In this detail we can see Monet's characteristic "dry" paint surface. A heavily loaded brush was dragged over the canvas where previous applications were allowed to dry first. The result is a richly-textured, encrusted surface, built up over time, which attracts light falling onto the canvas. The thick crust of paint imitates the solid structure of the bridge, standing out in sharp definition against the amorphous vegetation and transient light.

MONET'S SIGNATURE

The effect of The Waterlily Pond is an overwhelming sense of life, blocking out the sky and pushing in from all directions, almost vulgar in its lushness. Within the gloom of a deep shadow, not immediately visible amid such vibrancy, Monet's signature and the date of the painting can be found. The signature has been added in red, which has also been used to pick out individual flowers.

HORIZONTAL BRUSHWORK

The vertical rhythms of the foliage are continued into the deep shadows and bright reflections in the water. However, the unified downward movements of this brushwork are counterbalanced by bold horizontal brushstrokes, running from side to side across the canvas, which describe the receding bands of waterlilies stretched across the pond. These bands of colour are applied with thick sculptural paint over the top of the reflections and shadows in the water, "anchoring" them by asserting the flatness of the water's surface. This continuous criss-cross interplay of brushwork maintains a lively tension between the painting's two-dimensional abstract properties and its illusion of three-dimensional space.

339 Auguste Renoir, The Boating Party Lunch, *1881, 130 × 175 cm (51 × 69 in)*

CONTEMPORARY LIFE

Auguste Renoir (1841–1919) and Monet worked closely together during the late 1860s, painting the same scenes of popular river resorts and views of a bustling Paris. Renoir was by nature more solid than Monet, and while Monet fixed his attentions on the ever-changing patterns of nature, Renoir was particularly entranced by people and often painted friends and lovers. His early work has a quivering brightness that is gloriously satisfying and fully responsive to what he is painting, as well as to the effects of the light.

Renoir seems to have had the enviable ability to see anything as potentially of interest. More than any of the Impressionists, he found beauty and charm in the modern sights of Paris. He does not go deep into the substance of what he sees but seizes upon its appearance, grasping its generalities, which then enables the spectator to respond with immediate pleasure. "Pleasure" may be decried by the puritanical instinct within us all, but it is surely the necessary enhancer that

life needs. It also signifies a change from Realism: the Impressionists' paintings have none of the laboured toil of Millet's peasants, for example: instead they depict delightful, intimate scenes of the French middle class at leisure in the country or at cafés and concerts in Paris. Renoir always took a simple pleasure in whatever met his good-humoured attention, but he refused to let what he saw dominate what he wanted to paint. Again he deliberately sets out to give the impression, the sensation of something, its generalities, its glancing life. Maybe, ideally, everything is worthy of attentive scrutiny, but in practice there is no time. We remember only what takes our immediate notice as we move along.

In *The Boating Party Lunch (339)*, a group of Renoir's friends are enjoying that supreme delight of the working man and woman, a day out. Renoir shows us interrelationships: notice the young man intent upon the girl at the right chatting, while the girl at the left is occupied with her puppy. But notice too the loneliness, however relaxed, that can be part of anyone's experience at a lunch party. The man behind the girl and her dog is lost in a world of his own, yet we cannot but believe that his reverie is a happy one. The delightful debris of the meal, the charm of the young people, the hazy brightness of the world outside the awning: all communicates an earthly vision of paradise.

RENOIR'S PORTRAITS

One of Renoir's early portraits, *A Girl with a Watering Can (340),* has all the tender charm of its subject, delicately unemphasized, not sentimentalized, but clearly relished. Renoir stoops down to the child's height, so that we look at her world from her own altitude. This, he hints, is the world that the little one sees – not the actual garden that adults see today, but the nostalgic garden that they remember from their childhood. The child is sweetly aware of her central importance. Solid little girl though she is, she presents herself with the fragile charm of the flowers. Her sturdy little feet in their sensible boots are somehow planted in the garden, and the lace of her dress has a floral rightness; she also is decorative. With the greatest skill, Renoir shows the child, not amid the actual flowers and lawns, but on the path. It leads away, out of the picture, into the unknown future when she will no longer be part of the garden but an onlooker, an adult, who will enjoy only her memories of the present now depicted.

340 *Auguste Renoir,* A Girl with a Watering Can, *1876, 100 x 73 cm (39 x 29 in)*

341 *Auguste Renoir,* Bather Arranging Her Hair, *1893, 92 x 74 cm (36½ x 29 in)*

RENOIR'S LATE STYLE

Although he may seem a happy hedonist, Renoir was in fact a serious artist. At one stage he changed his whole style, feeling that he had gone as far as he could with Impressionism and was in danger of becoming superficial. His late style is firmer, with a cleaner edge to his figures, and the last works have a classical solidity. In *Bather Arranging Her Hair (341),* he has preserved the solid feel of the bodily form and irradiated it with luminous colour. The girl's lovely body is set out amid the disarray of her many-coloured garments: her corset, her hat, the white material draped around that round and rosy flesh. Renoir persuades us that the girl herself does the stripping and the presenting, and we feel she loves her body, as she should. He gazes worshipfully, not at her, the person, but at her body, the outer her, and he delights in painting her soft, glowing skin. Her bright but concentrated expression hints that the distinction would not mean much to her; she is an innocent country beauty.

DURAND-RUEL

Paul Durand-Ruel (1831–1922) was the first art dealer to give consistent support to the Impressionists. He was introduced to Monet by the artist Daubigny whilst in England during the Franco-Prussian war and became the sole financial backer of a number of the Impressionist artists. In 1886 he achieved a breakthrough with an exhibition of Impressionist works in New York and in 1905 his exhibition of hundreds of paintings brought the artists' work to London. Monet's international acclaim was due wholly to the support and investment of Durand-Ruel during the 1870s.

342 *Camille Pissaro,* Orchard in Bloom, Louveciennes, *1872, 45 x 55 cm (17½ x 22 in)*

CAMILLE PISSARRO

Camille Pissarro is seen as the patriarchal figurehead of the Impressionist movement and is the only artist to have had work shown at all eight of the Impressionist exhibitions. During the Franco-Prussian war (see p.286) Pissarro joined Monet in England and was influenced by the English landscape tradition of Turner and Constable. In 1872 he returned and settled in Pontoise where he became a friend and mentor of Cézanne. Pissarro's art centres on the people who work the soil and he is renowned for his paintings of peasant girls going about their daily chores.

CAMILLE PISSARRO

Camille Pissarro (1830–1903) was the patriarch of the Impressionists, not only because he was slightly older, but because of his benign and generous character. After meeting Corot in 1857, Pissarro was encouraged to abandon his formal training to paint in the open air and, despite his age, he became one of the most receptive of the Impressionists to new ideas. He was a passionate champion of progress, sometimes to the detriment of his own individual expression. He was the only artist to have shown work at all eight Impressionist exhibitions.

Pissarro was a dedicated painter and enormously prolific. He tended to stray in and out of pure Impressionism as the spirit took him, unconcerned with the rigours of style. He was the outsider of the group, perhaps, a man of mixed blood (Portuguese, Jewish, and Creole), and he was instinctively reponsive to the underlying architecture of nature. His paintings, with their almost naïve simplicity and unpolished surface, influenced Gauguin (see p.322), van Gogh (p.316), and Cézanne (p.310), who called himself the "pupil of Pissarro".

Orchard in Bloom, Louveciennes (342) is a work with bones under the painterly flesh: the path that we notice in the foreground leads us with a real sense of distance through the flowering brightness of impressionistic trees. There is a

343 *Camille Pissarro,* Peasant Girl with
a Straw Hat, *1881, 73 x 60 cm (29 x 24 in)*

sunlit gentleness peculiar to this balanced, wise artist with his sense of freedom and restrained exhilaration. *Peasant Girl with a Straw Hat (343)* has a beautiful simplicity, a fullness of form not contradicted but given significance by the haze of the background. Pissarro himself was a very good human being, and even without knowing this we do seem to find a lovely wholesomeness in his people and places. The girl is supremely unpretentious, unconcerned with herself, her whole being – sun-reddened nose and all – illuminated by the strong, bright light of day.

In his fifties, Pissarro became fascinated by the Neo-Impressionists and their great interest in the science of optics. He experimented with the Divisionist techniques of Seurat (see p.314) with (for Pissarro) relative unsuccess. The work was not appreciated by the public either, and he converted back to the spontaneity of true Impressionism. He was a major Impressionist – Cézanne considered him their leader – though he has been somewhat overshadowed by Monet and his other great "pupils".

ALFRED SISLEY

Alfred Sisley (1839–99) was rather an outsider in that his family, though permanently resident in France, was actually English. Sisley, however, has been called the most consistent of the Impressionists. All the others, even Monct in his late, great semi-abstractions, moved on from, or at least through, Impressionism. Sisley, once he saw the meaning of the movement, stayed with it. While other Impressionists sought their inspiration in Paris, he preferred, like Pissarro, to live in the countryside and paint rural scenes.

Sisley's art was not as robust as Monet's, but his paintings are some of the most subtly beautiful of the Impressionists, and they are heavenly in their peaceful celebration of nature. *Meadow (344)* lies quietly under the sun, vibrant with variety and chromatic glory. It is a scene that is easy to look at, a strip of field and a humble fence, yet Sisley has seen that it is alive all over with the intensity of being. The miracle is that the intensity is so wholly without tension; Sisley seems to dream in paint.

ALFRED SISLEY
As an artist Alfred Sisley is known to have felt like an outsider from the main group of Impressionist painters. However, many of his landscapes are considered among the most lyrical and harmonious works of Impressionism. Born of English parents, he moved to France and joined the studio of Charles Gleyre in 1862, where he met Renoir and became close friends with Monet.

344 Alfred Sisley, Meadow, *1875, 55 x 73 cm (22 x 29 in)*

AMERICAN VISION

Impressionism became a worldwide movement, as international as the Gothic style of ages past, and artists as far away as Japan and Australia began to paint modern-day subjects in the open air. American artists such as James Whistler, Thomas Eakins, and Winslow Homer travelled to Europe to study painting. Skilfully, they took from Realism and Impressionism what each of them personally needed.

> **"** *Art should stand alone, and appeal to the artistic sense of eye or ear, without confounding this with emotions entirely foreign to it.* **"**
>
> James Whistler

James Abbott McNeill Whistler (1834–1903), though he lived in London by choice, was an American. A flamboyant character, he was one of the most well-known and colourful figures of the European art world in the 19th century.

In 1855 Whistler left America and travelled to Paris to train as an artist. He entered the studio of Charles Gleyre, an advocate of Realism, and became, for a time, an enthusiastic follower of Gustave Courbet (see p.282). He was a dandy and a wit, very much at home as a Parisian *flâneur* like his two contemporaries, Manet and Degas. When his early work received more success in England, he left Paris in 1859 and moved to London, where he began to paint a favourite and enduring subject, the Thames.

AN AMERICAN ENGLISHMAN

Whistler hovered on the brink of Impressionism during the 1860s and at one stage came close to painting mere "sensation". But it was Japanese prints that influenced his style, and he was one of the first artists to understand and absorb the lessons of Japanese art, rather than imitate it. He translated the two-dimensional qualities, cool tones, and significant details of *Japonisme* into a highly individual treatment of colour harmony and tone on a flat, decorative surface.

Nocturne in Blue and Gold: Old Battersea Bridge (345) shows Whistler's interest in harmonious arrangements of colour and pattern. Its musical title gives emphasis to the sparse notes of colour that blaze on a dimly seen background, suggesting that we are given only an impression of what is seen, not its actuality; his elongated bridge is far more reminiscent of the stylistic imagery of *Japonisme* than of the real Old Battersea Bridge. Yet despite its apparent vagueness, the painting has genuine power. This is how London would have looked in the days of smoking chimneys. We catch a sense of mystery, even glamour, the last perhaps an index of Whistler's American nature: the transatlantic traveller, as we know from the novels of Henry James (see column, p.305), finds London far more romantic than the average Londoner.

Whistler is at his best when he plays with shapes and colours and it is their intrinsic interaction that delights him, rather than the play of light itself. *The White Girl (346)* is a great piece of decorative art. Jo Heffernan, his mistress, pleasingly occupies the centre of the picture. There is a marvellous subtlety in the different whites: the thick hanging of the patterned curtain; the soft whiteness of her dress; the rose she holds in her hand, while her dark, beautiful face in its rough cascade of auburn hair is sadly enigmatic.

345 James Whistler, Nocturne in Blue and Gold, *1872–75, 68 x 50 cm (27 x 20 in)*

OSCAR WILDE
The playwright, novelist, poet, and wit, Oscar Wilde (1854–1900) was one of Whistler's closer friends. Whilst travelling to the USA on a lecture tour in 1882 Wilde is believed to have said, when asked if he had anything to declare, "Only my genius". He married in 1884, and in 1891 wrote the novel *The Picture of Dorian Gray*, in which the main character is believed to have been based on his male lover, the poet John Gray. His most famous work, however, was *The Importance of Being Earnest*, written for the theatre in 1895. Wilde's brief but brilliant career ended in ruin when he was sentenced to two years in prison for homosexual practices.

OTHER WORKS BY WHISTLER
Old Westminster
(Museum of Fine Arts, Boston)

Grey and Green: the Silver Sea
(Art Institute of Chicago)

Nocturne: River Scene
(Glasgow University)

Three Figures: Pink and Grey
(Tate Gallery, London)

A Woman
(National Museum of Western Art, Tokyo)

Self-portrait
(Detroit Institute of Art)

Man with a Pipe
(Museé d'Orsay, Paris)

346 James Whistler,
The White Girl,
*1862, 213 x 108 cm
(84 x 42½ in)*

347 Winslow Homer, Breezing Up, 1876, 62 x 97 cm (24½ x 38 in)

WINSLOW HOMER

Winslow Homer (1836–1910), was only lightly touched by Impressionism. He visited Paris in 1867, and was also impressed by Manet's broad tonal contrasts, but he explored light and colour within a firm construction of clear outlines. Whistler's art seems a rejection of all that Homer represents, with his emphasis on clarity and objective, convincing solidity. Homer's watercolours have an incandescent brightness, his oils are beautifully solid, and he is better described by Realism than Impressionism.

Breezing Up (347) has a spectacular vividness. The sea (Homer's favourite subject) frisks and sways almost palpably under the keel of the small boat, the three boys and the fisherman brought before us by the slightest of touches.

AMERICA AND HER LEADERS

In the late 19th century the USA was undergoing economic and social changes which would have repercussions across the whole world. Between 1880 and 1900 the population of the country doubled with the arrival of nine million immigrants. The country was also re-emerging from a period of economic depression and was stimulated by industrialization, the growth of the railways, and the discovery of more silver and gold in the west of the country.
  The election in 1880 produced a compromise president, James Garfield (1831–81)(shown above), but interparty strife led to his assassination by a disappointed and deranged office-seeker on July 2nd 1881.

348 Thomas Eakins, The Biglin Brothers Racing, c. 1873, 60 x 91 cm (24 x 36 in)

This is one particular day when the wind begins to rise at sea with all the emotions freshly to hand for the painter. The sun shines and the air of excitement runs all along the horizon, ending with the filling – and balancing – sails that punctuate the far right of the picture.

THOMAS EAKINS

If Homer is a supreme watercolourist, then Thomas Eakins (1844–1916) is a supreme oil painter of the American Realist tradition. *Breezing Up* is wonderful, but it seems just that slight shade less convincing than *The Biglin Brothers Racing (348)*, one of Eakins' greatest works. Eakins persuades us that we too would have seen this, had we stood in Philadelphia one summer's morning to watch the racers exercise.

349 *John Singer Sargent,* Mrs Adrian Iselin, *1888, 154 x 93 cm (61 x 37 in)*

We would not have seen this scene, of course: the Biglin brothers would have vanished from sight before we had time to notice how the sunlight catches doublet and oar, or how the distant riverbank is as dim and dense as foliage. Eakins has held the image and created a work of such atmosphere that when we look at the painting the moment seems full and long – not at all like a snap shot. In the light of this comparison, Homer's glimpsed sailors begin to seem far more impressionistic than at first sight.

SARGENT THE SOCIETY PAINTER

John Singer Sargent (1856–1925) is essentially known as a society painter and, except for his marvellous watercolours of nature, he painted almost only high society. Often there was a great swagger of fashionable dress, but *Mrs Adrian Iselin (349)* is too élite for such embellishments. She glitters before us in austere black with the domineering haughtiness of a *grande dame*. For those who think Sargent pandered to his sitters, he has faithfully depicted her large and ugly ear. At his best, Sargent could be as ruthless as Goya, and with something of his technical brilliance.

POST-IMPRESSIONISM

Art history loves labels, and Post-Impressionism is the label for the diverse art that immediately followed Impressionism (this label roughly covers the period between 1886 and 1910). The Impressionists had destroyed forever an artistic belief in the objective truth of nature. Painters now understood that what we see depends on how we see, and even more when we see: the "objective view" was in fact subject to both perception and time. We live in an essentially fleeting and uncontrollable world and it is the glory of art to wrestle with this concept.

The greatest of all wrestlers was Paul Cézanne, who understood, as no artist before him ever had, the personal need of the artist to respond to what he saw and make a visual and enduring image of its wayward and multi-dimensional beauty. Another Post-Impressionist giant, Georges Seurat, sought a more scientific analysis of colour in his painting, though his art transcended his theories. Other artists chose to portray the world, not just by its physical, outward appearance, but by its inner, less tangible realities, exploring new symbolic associations with colour and line.

Paul Gauguin, Riders on the Beach, *1902 (detail)*

POST-IMPRESSIONISM TIMELINE

Post-Impressionism is the name given to a group of painters in the last two decades of the 19th century. They have very little in common except their starting point – the Impressionists. Paul Cézanne, Paul Gauguin, and Vincent van Gogh are all geniuses of a high order, but the movement we call Post-Impressionism also embraces, in its capacious sweep, small groups such as the Nabis.

VINCENT VAN GOGH, THE ARTIST'S BEDROOM, 1889

Van Gogh used colour to convey emotion more than to represent objects: this painting carries a poignant message of loneliness, hinted at by the extra chair, waiting for an eagerly expected companion (Gauguin). This room is in the house at Arles that van Gogh shared with Gauguin from October 1888 to May 1889. He painted this scene in 1888 and made two copies of it in 1889 (this is one of them) when he was in the asylum at St Rémy (p.316).

EDOUARD VUILLARD, THE READER, 1896

To the Nabi artists it was important to show beauty in simple scenes, such as this superbly decorative painting with its assemblage of patterned fabrics (p.328).

1885 **1890** **1895**

GEORGES SEURAT, THE LIGHTHOUSE AT HONFLEUR, 1886

Seurat was that rare thing, both scientist and artist. He was enthralled by the newly emerging science of optics and developed a style of painting called Pointillism, which used innumerable dots of colour. The eye combines these as we do in real life, but his vision was of a world supremely pure and controlled, painfully different from actuality (p.315).

HENRI DE TOULOUSE-LAUTREC, RUE DES MOULINS, 1894

The witty, searching art of Lautrec often depicted nightclub and drinking scenes, or portrayed the denizens of Parisian low life. Here, two prostitutes are shown queuing up for a medical examination, and the sadness and shame of their position in society are held up to our gaze. Lautrec was influenced by the Japanese and their complete freedom from conventional notions of composition; the centre of attention was often off-centre. His style was perfectly suited to poster art, to which he brought great new zest and life. In all his work there is a fluidity and passion that captures the vitality of city life (p.320).

EDVARD MUNCH, FOUR GIRLS ON A BRIDGE, 1889-1900

A strange man, Munch experienced overwhelmingly gloomy emotions. It was to express the intensity of these emotions that his art was directed. Personally he found the pain of life too much to bear, but artistically he struggled to express this pain and make beauty out of it. Symbolism struck a deep chord within him: with its high colour and formal simplicity, it offered him a refuge from his fears. This Nordic gloom lived on to influence Expressionism, which dominated Germanic art after World War I (p.325).

PIERRE BONNARD, THE LETTER, C. 1906

Bonnard was a leading member of the Nabis, who in some ways were a transitional movement between Post-Impressionism and the art of the 20th century. Bonnard was interested in oriental philosophy and mysticism. He was influenced by Japanese art, imitating the graphic simplicity of Japanese woodcuts. The Letter is a typical example of his many paintings of everyday life. The model is one who frequently appears in Bonnard's pictures, his partner and later wife, Marthe. She is portrayed with a wonderful concision, and Bonnard takes an uncomplicated pleasure in the patterns into which the image falls (p.326).

PAUL CEZANNE, LE CHATEAU NOIR, 1900/04

At all stages of his career Cézanne was a supreme master. This picture is a fine example of the Post-Impressionist tension between actuality and illusion, description and abstraction, reality and invention. We are forced to read it not only as a wooded landscape with a château, but equally as a flat plane, upon which colours of different chromatic and tonal values have been arranged (p.312).

1900   1905   1910

PAUL GAUGUIN, NEVERMORE, 1897

The English title Nevermore, *appearing in the corner of this painting, is the keynote of a poem,* The Raven *by Edgar Allan Poe, which was a favourite of the French Symbolists. However, the painting is not exactly an illustration of the poem. Poe writes about a devilish raven that prevents him from adoring his beloved, who is absent. For Gauguin the girl is the main feature in the painting, and the bird is reduced to a toy-like caricature. Gauguin is concerned to show the capacity of art to escape from rationality and naturalism, in order to describe more accurately the inner workings of the heart and mind (p.324).*

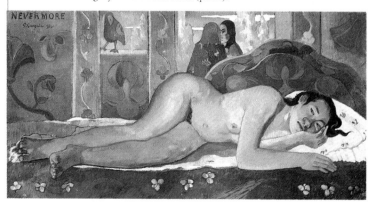

GUSTAV KLIMT, THE KISS, 1907/08

Gustav Klimt came from a family of artists and craftsmen, his father being a gold engraver. As one of Austria's most prominent artists he helped found two radical groups, the Vienna Secession and the Vienna Workshop. The Kiss is a gloriously decorative work, a fusion of two figures into one, with a suggestion of anxiety in the tense grip of the hands and the averted face of the girl (p.325).

POST-IMPRESSIONIST ARTISTS

Like the Renaissance, Impressionism made an irreversible difference, so that one naturally senses that all art since that time has been "after Impressionism". The artists who rejected Impressionism towards the end of the 19th century painted not only what they observed, but what they felt, finally setting painting free to deal with emotions as well as material reality. They experimented with new subjects and techniques, moving art closer to abstraction and winning tremendous freedom for the next generation of artists.

350 Paul Cézanne, The Artist's Father, 1866, 199 x 119 cm (78 x 47 in)

Post-Impressionism was never a movement – the term was unknown to the artists involved during their own lifetimes (see column, p.311). It encompasses a group of artists with diverse styles and ideals who became dissatisfied with the limitations of Impressionism and departed from it in various directions. Never again could it be so taken for granted that painting has a direct relation to the exterior world.

CEZANNE'S EARLY WORK

Paul Cézanne (1839–1906) is certainly as great an artist as any that ever lived, up there with Titian, Michelangelo, and Rembrandt. Like Manet and Degas, and also Morisot and Cassatt, he came from a wealthy family – his was in Aix-en-Provence, France. His banker father seems to have been an uncultivated man, of whom his highly nervous and inhibited son was afraid. Despite parental displeasure, Cézanne persevered with his passionate desire to become an artist. His early paintings display little of the majesty of his late work, though today they are rightfully awarded the respect that he certainly never received for them.

His early years were difficult and his career was, from the beginning, dogged with repeated failure and rejection. In 1862 he was introduced to the famed circle of artists who met at the Café Guerbois in Paris, which included Manet, Degas, and Pissarro, but his awkward manners and defensive shyness prevented him from becoming an intimate of the group. However, Pissarro was to play an important part in Cézanne's later development (see p.300).

One of the most important works of his early years is the portrait of his formidable father. *The Artist's Father (350)* is one of Cézanne's "palette-knife pictures", painted in short sessions between 1865 and 1866. Their realistic content and solid style reveal Cézanne's admiration for Gustave Courbet (see p.282). Here we see a craggy, unyielding man of business, a solid mass of manhood, bodily succinct from the top of his black beret to the tips of his heavy shoes. The uncompromising verticals of the massive chair are echoed by the door, and the edges of

351 Paul Cézanne, Abduction, c. 1867, 90 x 117 cm (35 x 46 in)

ROGER FRY
The term
Post-Impressionism was
coined by the English
art critic Roger Fry
(1866–1934) to describe
the group of artists who
came immediately after
the Impressionists. These
artists were centred in
Paris and chose to reject
the Impressionists'
concentration on the
external, fleeting
appearances of their
world. Fry was curator
of the Metropolitan
Museum of Art in New
York between 1906 and
1910 and introduced the
Post-Impressionists to
Great Britain by exhibitions
which he arranged at the
Grafton Galleries in 1910
and 1912. Artists he
displayed included
Gauguin, Cézanne,
and van Gogh.

the small still life by Cézanne on the wall just behind: everything corresponds to the absolute verticals of the edges of the canvas itself, further accentuating the air of certainty about the portrait. Thick hands hold a newspaper – though Cézanne has replaced his father's conservative newspaper with the liberal *L'Evénement*, which published articles by his childhood friend, Emile Zola (see p.286). His father devours the paper, sitting tensely upright in the elongated armchair. Yet it is a curiously tender portrait too. Cézanne seems to see his father as somehow unfulfilled: for all his size he does not fully occupy the chair, and neither does he see the still life on the wall behind him, which we recognize as being one of his son's. We do not see his eyes – only the ironical mouth and his great frame, partly hidden behind the paper.

MYSTERY OF NATURE

Cézanne was in his twenties when he painted *The Artist's Father*. Wonderful though it is, with its blacks and greys and umbers, it does not fully indicate the profundity of his developing genius. Yet even in this early work, Cézanne's grasp of form and solid pictorial structures which came to dominate his mature style are already essential components. His overriding concern with

form and structure set him apart from the Impressionists from the start, and he was to maintain this solitary position, carving out his unique pictorial language.

Abduction, rape, and murder: these are themes that tormented Cézanne. *Abduction (351)*, an early work full of dark miseries, is impressive largely for its turgid force, held barely under his control. These figure paintings are the most difficult to enter into: they are sinister, with passion in turmoil just beneath the surface.

Cézanne's late studies of the human body are most rewarding, his figures often depicted as bathers merging with the landscape in a sunlit lightness. This became a favourite theme for Cézanne and he made a whole series of pictures on the subject. This mature work is dictated by an objectivity that is profoundly moving for all its seeming emotional detachment.

It was before nature that Cézanne was seized by a sense of the mystery of the world to a depth never expressed by another artist. He saw that nothing exists in isolation: an obvious insight, yet one that only he could make us see. Things have colour and they have weight, and the colour and mass of each affects the weight of the other. It was to understand these rules that Cézanne dedicated his life.

**OTHER WORKS BY
CÉZANNE**
Basket of Apples
(Art Institute of
Chicago)

Mont Sainte Victoire
(Courtauld Institute,
London)

Still Life of Fruit
(Barnes Foundation,
Marion, Penn.)

The Card Players
(Metropolitan Museum
of Art, New York)

Poplars
(Musée d'Orsay, Paris)

Self-portrait
(Bridgestone Museum
of Art, Tokyo)

L'Estaque
(Bührle Foundation,
Zürich)

MONT SAINTE-VICTOIRE

The Sainte-Victoire mountain near Cézanne's home in Aix-en-Provence was one of his favourite subjects and he is known to have painted it over 60 times. Cézanne was fascinated by the rugged architectural forms in the mountains of Provence and painted the same scene from many different angles.

He would use bold blocks of colour to achieve a new spatial effect known as "flat-depth" to accommodate the unusual geological forms of the mountains. Cézanne travelled widely in the Provence region and also enjoyed painting the coast at L'Estaque.

352 Paul Cézanne, Le Château Noir, 1900/04, 74 x 97 cm (29 x 38 in)

STRUCTURE AND SOLIDITY

From 1872, under Pissarro's influence, Cézanne painted the rich Impressionist effects of light on different surfaces and even exhibited at the first Impressionist show. But he maintained his concern for solidity and structure throughout, and abandoned Impressionism in 1877. In *Le Château Noir (352)*, Cézanne does not respond to the flickering light as an Impressionist might; he draws that flicker from deep within the substance of every structure in the painting. Each form has a true solidity, an absolute of internal power that is never diminished for the sake of another part of the composition.

It is the tension between actuality and illusion, description and abstraction, reality and invention, that makes Cézanne's most unassuming subjects so profoundly satisfying and exciting, and which provided a legacy for a revolution of form that led the way for modern art.

The special attraction of still life to Cézanne was the ability, to some extent, to control the structure. He brooded over his apples, jugs, tables, and curtains, arranging them with infinite variety. *Still Life with Apples and Peaches (353)* glows with a romantic energy, as hugely present as Mont Sainte-Victoire (see column, left). Here too is a mountain, and here too sanctity and victory: the fruits lie on the table with an active power that is not just seen but experienced. The jug bulges, not with any contents, but with its own weight of being. The curtain swags gloriously, while the great waterfall of the napkin absorbs and radiates light onto the table on which all this life is earthed.

353 Paul Cézanne, Still Life with Apples and Peaches, c. 1905, 81 x 100 cm (32 x 40 in)

LE CHATEAU NOIR

The château in this painting derives its name from rumours about its owner, rather than from its appearance. It was built in the 18th century by an industrialist from Marseilles, who manufactured lampblack paint (derived from soot). He also used it to decorate the interior walls and furniture of the château. As a result, he was associated with black magic among the local people, who believed that the château was also home to the devil.

BROKEN LINE
Again, Cézanne emphasizes the physical, plastic reality of the painting. The jagged lines describing the overhanging branches are fragmented, beginning and ending in mid-air. They are valued as much for their formal role in maintaining the strong vertical, horizontal, and diagonal balance of the composition as for their descriptive function: Cubism's debt to Cézanne is paramount (see p.346). The impossibly rich, deep blues and greens of the sky, applied right up to and overlapping the branches, fight for dominance, creating a continuous tension between decorative flatness and spatial depth.

PATCH OF SKY
The deep blue of this patch of sky, visible through the trees, is painted with no concessions to illusory depth. The strong blue of the sky "jumps" forward over the quieter colours of the surrounding foliage, insisting that we read the picture not only as a wooded landscape with a château, but equally as a flat plane upon which colours of differing chromatic and tonal values have been arranged.

BRUSHWORK
This detail shows us Cézanne's characteristic diagonal brushwork, and the way in which he counterbalances the disjunctures created by his abstract treatment of space (see above) with a unifying application of paint. Cézanne thus realizes his belief that a painting should be both structurally convincing and formally independent. The slanting, generally equal-sized brushmarks range across the surface of the canvas and, as such, must do the job of describing form through relative values of colour alone, in a process that Cézanne called modulation.

THE CHATEAU
The slender, Gothic-arched windows of the château reveal nothing but the intense blue of the sky. The complementary relationship of the yellow building and the blue windows emphatically affirms the colour harmony of the work, and its ambiguity between "solid" sky and "ephemeral" stone. The building seems in turn both impressively permanent, and also a shallow façade through which the blue hills and sky are visible. It is an intensely blue painting, made even bluer by the intervals of yellow ochre, and united by the more neutral greens.

LES POSEUSES

Seurat painted
Les Poseuses using
preparatory sketches to
demonstrate his belief
in premeditated art,
in contrast to the
spontaneity of
Impressionism. The
nude model is shown in
three different positions
within a room in which
one wall is filled by
Seurat's painting
La Grand Jatte.
The same models are
believed to have been
used in both paintings,
allowing the viewer
to experience a fluid
connection between
the formality of fashion
in *La Grand Jatte*
and the classical
naked form in
Les Poseuses.

SEURAT AND DIVISIONISM

It is possible, though perhaps improbable, that Georges-Pierre Seurat (1859–91), had he lived longer, might have been in the league of Cézanne. Like the great Masaccio at the beginning of the Renaissance (see p.82), like Giorgione (p.129) and Watteau (p.224), he died tragically young – yet after just a few years of painting he left us some marvellous work. He believed that art should be based on a system and developed Impressionism towards a rigorous formula. He invented a method he called optical painting – also known as Divisionism, Neo-Impressionism, or Pointillism – in which dots of colour laid beside one another blend together in the viewer's eye. He believed that these dots of intense colour, placed schematically in precise patterns, could imitate the resonant effects of light falling onto various colours more accurately than the more random, intuitive practice of the Impressionists. Seurat's systematic approach was based on his study of the new theory of colour science. As a theory it sounds daunting, and in the hands of imitators it does daunt, being a theory that is more poetic than literal in its truth. A silent and secretive young man, Seurat perhaps needed this theory psychologically, and he made wonderful use of it in his paintings.

Seurat differed from the Impressionists in more than just his scientific approach. He was influenced by Ingres (see p.256) and the great Renaissance artists, and his work has a gravity that relates more to the classical tradition than to the casual intimacy and transience of Impressionism. And though, like the Impressionists, Seurat worked on small studies in the open air so that he could faithfully record the effects of light on the landscape, his large compositions were produced entirely in the studio according to his own strict laws of painting. To the themes already well mapped out by the Impressionists, such as city life, seascapes, and

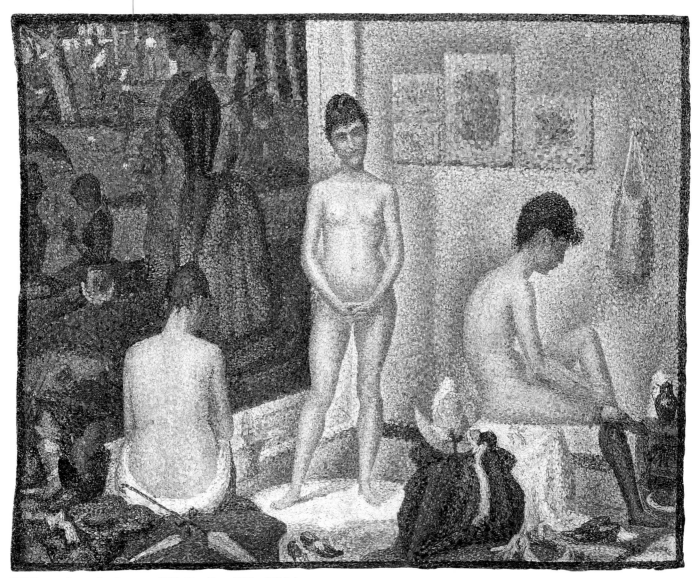

354 Georges Seurat, Les Poseuses, *1888, 39 x 49 cm (15½ x 19½ in)*

355 *Georges Seurat,* **The Lighthouse at Honfleur,** *1886, 68 x 82 cm (26½ x 32 in)*

entertainment, Seurat added a sense of mystery and even monumentality, as well as a controlled geometry. In *Les Poseuses (354)* there is a sense of exquisite rightness, of flesh in all its individuality still beautifully conforming to a pattern. These images of a classical female nude are nymph-like in their delicacy, but with an austerity that is unique to Seurat.

ART REPLACING NATURE

Les Poseuses was painted in Seurat's studio in artificial light, and the large landscape serving as a backdrop to it is *Sunday Afternoon on the Island of the Grande Jatte*, a summer scene he painted between 1884 and 1886 of strollers by the River Seine, on the outskirts of Paris.

La Grande Jatte is important, both within Seurat's limited oeuvre, and historically. This was the painting that he hung at the last Impressionist show in 1886, despite the reluctance of the other, older exhibitors. Seurat represented a new generation of painters who heralded the disintegration of the Impressionist ideal, and whether the older painters liked it or not, a new order was rapidly being established. Pissarro alone fought for Seurat's right to exhibit with them and saw his colour theory as the progressive

step Impressionism needed. Pissarro briefly adopted Divisionism himself, but found it too inhibiting and soon abandoned it.

Seurat's landscapes also heroically subdue nature to the "dot" of his colour theory, and they have an interior quiet that prevails magnificently over natural confusion. Seurat organized what he saw, but he did so with the tact of genius. We realize that no landscape ever really looked so clean, so uncluttered, and so integrated, but he makes us suspend our disbelief.

Everything in the landscape painting *The Lighthouse at Honfleur (355)* is arranged with such formal perfection that removing any one element would destroy the balance. Pale, magical, severe, it absolutely needs the wooden structure in the foreground. This geometric form of sharp angles allows Seurat to move spaciously back into the far glimmer of the sea, rhyming all the other horizontals and verticals delicately with it: one upright like the lighthouse tower, redeployed by the boathouse; one flat like the boat, re-echoed by the top bar of the sawing frame. The sun bleaches the whole scene, so that colour, too, rhymes and is compatible. This is how life ought to be, he tells us, and nature is replaced by art.

VAN GOGH

Seurat was one kind of genius, contained and silent. The other kind we find in a Dutch-born painter, Vincent van Gogh (1853–90), whose turbulent, seeking life everyone knows. The sad tale of van Gogh cutting off his ear is now part of common genius mythology. The unhappiness documented in a flood of letters to his brother, Theo, is transformed in his art into a passionate search for stability, truth, life itself. He has the rare power, something like that of Rembrandt (see p.200), to take the ugly, even the terrible, and make it beautiful by sheer passion.

Van Gogh's formative years as a painter reveal his confusion and restlessness as he worked in various jobs in search of a meaningful existence. At 20 he left Holland for England, then lived for a short time in Belgium as a missionary, and in 1886, aged 33, he left for Paris. Through Theo's work as an art dealer (see column, p.317), he met other artists – Degas (p.291), Pissarro (p.300), Seurat (p.314), Lautrec (p.320) – and learnt about Impressionist techniques. He arrived at his artistic vocation by a slow and tortuous route, but it wasn't until he had fully absorbed the influences of Impressionism and *Japonisme* (see column, p.290) and made his own experiments with colour (see column, p.317) that he discovered his true genius.

VAN GOGH AT ARLES

In 1888, leaving Theo in Paris, he went to Arles, in Provence, where, in the last two years of his life, he produced his most remarkable works. *The Artist's Bedroom (356)* has the utmost power and poignancy (this is a copy he painted to comfort himself while in the asylum at St. Rémy; see column, p.318). Two pillows and chairs hint at his eager anticipation of Gauguin's arrival (see p.322). It was his dream that Arles would become a centre for painters, but Gauguin's reluctant visit ended in disaster.

356 Vincent van Gogh, The Artist's Bedroom, *1889, 71 x 90 cm (28 x 35 in)*

357 *Vincent van Gogh,* Farmhouse in Provence, *1888, 46 x 61 cm (18 x 24 in)*

Farmhouse in Provence and *La Mousmé* were painted in the year van Gogh moved to Arles. If Seurat subdued nature to reflect his intellect, van Gogh heightened it to echo his emotions. *Farmhouse in Provence (357)* has a terrible, life-threatening fertility about it. Wheat surges about the farm on all sides; the flaming ears of grain almost overwhelm the small figure who wades through them. The wall suddenly comes to an end, devoured by the encroaching army of ripening wheat, red flowers, and vegetation.

The farm has a beleaguered air, taking some trees into its protection; elsewhere, out in the field, trees are stunted and sparse. Farm buildings huddle together, while the sky maintains an utter neutrality. Nature always comes to van Gogh in this threatening manner, yet he never gives in: he wrestles with it, capturing its wildness on his canvas. The sheer attention he has given to every blade of wheat gives him a moral ascendancy over such power.

La Mousmé (358) is of "a Japanese girl – provincial in this case – 12 to 14 years old," as van Gogh explained to Theo. He laboured on this work, lured by the simplicity and tautness he so admired in Japanese art, and he presents this dull-faced adolescent solely in terms of decorative masses. Her dress is built up of curving stripes above and solid red dots on blue below.

The chair sweeps round her in schematic arches; hands and face are an opaque pinky-brown, seemingly boneless hands dangle from her sleeves, and her face is doll-like. Her body curves flatly against a background of mottled green. So much

358 *Van Gogh,* La Mousmé, *1888, 73 x 60 cm (29 x 24 in)*

THE DECLINE

The first clear signs of van Gogh's mental instability appeared whilst he and Gauguin were sharing the Yellow House in Arles in 1888. One evening he threatened Gauguin, lost control, cut off his own right ear lobe, and presented it to a local prostitute. He was then taken to the hospital suffering from loss of blood and hallucinations. By May 1889 van Gogh had left Arles and had committed himself voluntarily to the asylum in St Rémy. During two years in the asylum van Gogh produced over 200 paintings and in 1890 Pissarro persuaded him to move to Auvers where he was placed in the hands of Dr Gachet (shown above). However, within a couple of months van Gogh fell ill, and in July 1890 he committed suicide.

OTHER WORKS BY VAN GOGH

The Farmhouse
(Rijksmuseum, Amsterdam)

Sunflowers
(National Gallery, London)

Portrait of Dr Paul Gachet
(Musée d'Orsay, Paris)

Windmills at Montmartre
(Bridgestone Museum of Art, Tokyo)

Two Peasants
(Bührle Foundation, Zürich)

Bed of Irises
(National Gallery of Canada, Ottawa)

Hospital at St Rémy
(Hammer Collection, Los Angeles)

about *La Mousmé* is pathetic. She looks out at us so warily that we too feel slightly uncomfortable. Her eyes are alive, brown, and hurt, as if she knows that life will not treat her well. Van Gogh directs on the child such a force of passionate attention, such a totality of respect, such confidence in the power of vision to raise him up from the hell of existence, that the picture is an awesome success. Qualities like beauty or grace become irrelevant. To make us see through his eyes is the triumph of the painter, and van Gogh triumphs often.

VAN GOGH'S SELF-PORTRAITS

Few artists have been as interested in the self-portrait as van Gogh. *Self-portrait (359)* is overpowering in its purity and realism: this is the real face of the artist, with a rough, red beard, unhappy mouth, and hooded eyes. His is an identity barely held in existence under the pressure of the whirling blue chaos. His face may be solid enough, but his clothes lose their identity as the lines swirl and jostle and deconstruct, showing us just how he felt as a mentally tormented and suffering individual.

359 Vincent van Gogh, Self-portrait, 1889, 65 x 54 cm (26 x 21½ in)

SELF-PORTRAIT

In May 1889, after his violent breakdown in Arles, van Gogh entered the asylum at St Rémy. With his brother Theo's financial assistance, van Gogh was able to have his own bedroom, and also a studio where – whenever his condition and the asylum authorities allowed – he could continue to paint. It was at the asylum, just six weeks after another severe breakdown, that van Gogh painted this very beautiful self-portrait in September 1889. It is one of two self-portraits van Gogh painted that same month, both of which are notable for their calm and dignified portrayal, and their sense of fortitude, despite the misery of his situation. The skilful use of contrasting colours, the sensitive draughtsmanship, and the sense of mature control all point to a superior mind, however disturbed the artist's feelings.

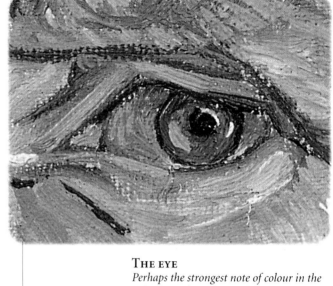

THE EYE

Perhaps the strongest note of colour in the painting is the surprisingly vivid patch of green under the eye. It acts as a focal point, drawing our attention to van Gogh's steady and penetrating gaze. The structure of the eye is emphatically "level"; a straight, dark, horizontal line defines his heavy brow, and every detail of the eye is clearly delineated; but whilst the set features show resoluteness, at the same time the acid greens in the face, clashing against the reds of the hair and beard, suggest passion held under restraint.

SWIRLING BACKGROUND

Within the overall cool harmonies of silver-grey, silver-green, and blues, van Gogh's head glows like a flame. Here is a painting of great contrasts. Everything outside the vivid head is subdued. The disturbed background hints at the precariousness of his own stability, symbolized by his neat waistcoat, and his shirt buttoned to the neck, and by his pose, suggestive of stillness and calm. The background can be distinguished from the figure only by the texture of the swirling brush strokes, which are otherwise virtually identical in colour to the body.

A NEW PORTRAIT

Each brush stroke is laid on side by side, without blending or modelling. Around this time van Gogh conceived of a new kind of portraiture, based on the innate expressive qualities of colour. In the same month that he painted this picture, he wrote to Theo, expressing his wish to paint portraits that contain the vibrancy of life that he found in Delacroix's paintings: "by a wedding of two complementary colours, their mingling and their opposition, the mysterious vibrations of kindred tones".

TOULOUSE-LAUTREC

Toulouse-Lautrec came from an aristocratic family but was physically deformed as a result of inbreeding and a childhood accident. This self-parodying photograph shows Lautrec dressed as a samurai warrior.

TOULOUSE-LAUTREC'S PARIS

If van Gogh escaped from his overwhelming burdens by committing suicide, Henri de Toulouse-Lautrec (1864–1901) escaped into the sordid nightlife of Paris. Only there, submerged within a raucous and raunchy crowd, could he forget that he was a scion of one of the noble families in France with an unfortunate disability. A model once said he had "a genius for distortion", but his genius, though acid, was not embittered or dark. His deformity set him free, paradoxically, from a need to accept any normal responsibilities, and though he killed himself with his excesses, he also created a witty, wiry art that still attracts. His paintings and prints reveal the strong attraction to Japanese art that he shared with van Gogh: he employed typically oblique Japanese perspectives with an off-centre focus, and his art is characterized by a self-assured

361 Henri de Toulouse-Lautrec, Rue des Moulins, *1894, 83 x 60 cm (33 x 24 in)*

simplicity of line, dramatic colour, and flat shape. Lautrec's art was well-suited to poster design and, aided by newly perfected techniques for printing posters, he revolutionized the discipline, breathing a new vibrancy and immediacy into it. In all his work there is a fluidity and passion that captures the vitality of city life.

Quadrille at the Moulin Rouge (360) has a rough energy that contrasts with the controlled vigour of the artist's line. There is life here, but no joy. However, there is also no self-pity, and though the life he shows us is horrible, it is at least lived with determination. Gabrielle, a dancer at the Moulin Rouge nightclub and one of Lautrec's favourite models, faces us with an almost comic expression of tipsy intentness as she stands aggressively in the centre of the hall.

Lautrec does not often go deep, but when he does, he can appal. The two prostitutes in *Rue des Moulins (361)* are not seeking custom (this he paints with a very wry laugh). They are lining up for the obligatory medical examination for licensed prostitutes, and their raddled faces are painfully pathetic. The first is aged of body, with loose, wrinkled thighs and fallen bosom. The other appears slightly younger, and although her body is less ravaged, her face is cruelly worn. Even the background of this picture is a lurid red. Vice is killing them both, despite the state medical intrusions. Lautrec does not glorify his whores; his world is one of harsh reality.

360 Henri de Toulouse-Lautrec, Quadrille at the Moulin Rouge, *1892, 81 x 60 cm (31 x 24 in)*

THE INFLUENCE OF SYMBOLISM

Symbolism began as a literary movement that championed the imagination as the most important source of creativity. It soon filtered into the visual arts as another reaction to the limited, representational world of Realism and Impressionism. Inspired by the symbolist poetry of the French poets Stéphane Mallarmé, Paul Verlaine, and Arthur Rimbaud, the Symbolist painters used emotive colours and stylized images to float into our consciousness their dreams and moods, sometimes painting exotic, dream-like scenes.

Though it was towards the end of his career that Symbolism became artistically significant, it is still true to regard Gustave Moreau (1826–98) as a precursor of Symbolist ideals and a patriarchal figure. In age he was much closer to Realism (his dates are almost contemporary with those of Manet, see p.285, or Courbet, p.282), but he ignored both Realism and Impressionism to pursue his own, distinctively individual style.

There could sometimes be a lurid and rather sickly strain in Symbolist work: the story of Salome, for example, with all its Freudian implications of woman destroying man, crops up continually. Moreau's *Salome (362)* is one of the more playful versions of this deadly myth, and we can enjoy its intense light and colour without thinking too much of its sinister

363 *Odilon Redon,* Anemones and Lilacs in a Blue Vase, *after 1912, 74 x 60 cm (29 x 23½ in)*

implications. Many of Moreau's other pictures are populated with strange beasts and mystic figures, and this escape from the world of reality, coupled with his idiosyncratic temperament, made him a significant figure among the other Symbolists.

REDON'S FLOWER PAINTINGS

Odilon Redon (1840–1916) is another escaper into a land of dreams. He did not have a major gift, but the pleasure of his art is pure and deep. He used colour in a completely personal and uninhibited way, but it was his subject matter, so elusive and fantastical, that made him a quintessential Symbolist. Like Moreau, he had a haunting imagination, but his exquisite bunches of flowers are his greatest achievement. *Anemones and Lilacs in a Blue Vase (363)* is typical of the soft, delicate imagery he could produce using iridescent pastels. These are radiant flowers, picked and preserved and glowing eternally for the viewer.

362 *Gustave Moreau,* Salome, *1876, 143 x 103 cm (56 x 40½ in)*

STÉPHANE MALLARMÉ
Stéphane Mallarmé (1842–98) was a leading Symbolist poet and friend of many of the symbolist artists. The basic principles of this artistic movement were to express ideas through colour and line and to concentrate on mystical or fantastical images. This illustration shows an etching of Mallarmé, completed by Gauguin, with a raven in the background. The raven is believed to be a direct reference to Edgar Allan Poe's influential symbolist poem *The Raven*, which was published in 1875. In 1886 the French poet Jean Moréas published the *Symbolist's Manifesto* which was inspired by Mallarmé's poetry.

PAUL SÉRUSIER
The painter and art theorist Paul Sérusier (1863–1927) had a great influence on the Symbolist and Nabis movements (see p.326). The painting shown above is of the *Bois d'Amour* at Pont-Aven, where Sérusier painted whilst being advised on colour by his friend Gauguin. The painting is also known as *The Talisman* because the younger painting generation saw it as the symbol of new artistic freedom and possibilities. Sérusier published his treatise on art in 1921.

364 *Paul Gauguin,* The Vision After the Sermon, *1888, 73 x 92 cm (29 x 36½ in)*

CLOISONNISM

Emil Bernard's *Buckwheat Harvest* (shown above) is a good example of the technique known as Cloisonnism (*cloison* is French for partition). This style of painting is associated with the Pont-Aven school and is characterized by dark outlines enclosing areas of bright, flat colour, similar to the effect achieved by stained glass. Gauguin and Bernard (1868–1941) worked together at Pont-Aven between 1888 and 1891, and Bernard is believed to have had a stimulating effect on Gauguin's work.

A SINGULAR VISION

Paul Gauguin (1848–1903) is best known for the art he painted after he fled to the South Seas to escape Europe and his family, but essentially he drew the inspiration for his work from within himself. Though he took to painting as a professional quite late, his early development as an amateur was influenced by the Impressionists, especially Pissarro (see p.300), whose systematic, broken brushwork Gauguin adopted. Gauguin was introduced to the Impressionists as a rich Parisian stockbroker and began to buy their art: he even exhibited his own work at some of their shows from 1879. Yet when he finally became a full-time artist in 1883, he was already feeling the constraints of the Parisian art scene.

Gauguin sought to be untrammelled by any conventions in his art. The Impressionists were influenced by nature; Gauguin was influenced by his own version of nature. He found freedom and quiet at Pont-Aven, Brittany, where he soon became the chief figure of the Pont-Aven artists (see column, left). It was in this isolated region that he developed the distinctive symbolic and primitive elements of his art. Inspired by medieval stained glass and folk art, he began to paint simplified shapes heavily outlined in black. The Breton peasants, with their simple faith and archaic lifestyles, also appealed to him and became a recurrent theme.

The Vision After the Sermon (364) was painted two years before he left for Tahiti, but it is as primitive as anything Tahitian. Gauguin blended reality with the inner experience of a vision and heightened it with symbolic colour. He offered the painting to the local Breton church, but the priest was suspicious and thought he was being mocked. Only today does the spiritual power of the painting become vitally clear.

LAST YEARS IN FRANCE

Gauguin had long abandoned his Dutch wife and children, and in 1888 he agreed to visit van Gogh in Arles. It seems fitting that the two were friends, though perhaps "friend" is not the right word: both were solitary men, desperately seeking for healing companionship. It was the breakdown of their shaky relationship that drove van Gogh, the more fragile, to the hysterical mutilation of his own ear. Gauguin spent his remaining two years in France moving around restlessly, and left in April 1891 for Tahiti, where he spent much of the rest of his life.

VISION AFTER THE SERMON

Gauguin depicts a sermon that has just been preached on the subject of Jacob wrestling with the Angel, an Old Testament story. Probably religion had an exotic fascination for Gauguin, though he could only see its mysteries from without. He imagines Jacob at dawn, struggling to overcome his superhuman opponent and make him reveal his name. Gauguin felt he was up against the superhuman and he too wrestled with his demon/angel to find his real identity.

JACOB AND THE ANGEL

Gauguin's compact image was inspired by a study of wrestlers by the Japanese master Katsushika Hokusai, whose illustrations influenced many of Gauguin's contemporaries (see also column, p.290). The struggle takes place in an airless, shadowless space of saturated red in which the combatants seem to float, out of proportion to the world around them. Gauguin truly realized his desire to tackle a devotional work in a new way.

PRAYING PRIEST

There is no literal contest here, as we can guess from the downcast eyes of the women and the priest: it is in their imaginations that life and death meet in battle. Their tightly-grouped heads are magnified so that we feel like part of the crowd; we have to peer over the tops of their heads to see the vision. Much of the painting is conceived as completely flat planes of colour; only the curving forms of the women's headdresses are painted in a three-dimensional style – the white folds have a heavy, sculptural feel.

THE TWO HALVES OF THE CANVAS

Gauguin makes his composition all absolutes and opposites: brilliant reds screaming against blazing whites; hordes of women and one sole male (the priest, in the lower right-hand corner), violence and meditation, enveloping garments and bare faces. A great tree trunk slices the picture diagonally into two separate halves: the real world on the left, containing the simple Breton women and a straying cow that paws the red earth; and the visionary world on the right, where the angel and the man wrestle. The man won, however, as Gauguin expected his viewers to remember.

366 Paul Gauguin, Nevermore, 1897, 60 x 115 cm (24 x 45 in)

Gauguin escaped to the South Seas in search of a primitive lifestyle where his art could flourish. Despite his disgust at the entrenched colonial society he found there (see column, left), he painted the Polynesians as images of a heavenly state of total freedom. Gauguin impresses his own version of nature upon us, creating stylized, flattened shapes and using intense, exotic colours with what may seem like reckless abandon, but which are carefully calculated for the greatest effect. In *Riders on the Beach (365)* he paints the sands pink not, we feel, because he actually

"saw" any pinkness there, but because only pink sands could express his feelings. Yellow would have been too intrusively real: it is not a logical scene but a magical one, and the peace and joy are symbolic, not literal. It is a painting of an idyllic state of life, gentle and radiant people effortlessly in control of their horses, freedom on every side, intoxicating seascape, wide, clouded skies, man and woman in perfect amity.

SINISTER UNDERCURRENTS

Although Gauguin transformed the Polynesian women into goddess figures – obeying no rules but those of his imagination – he also knew well the sad depravations of their real lives, and produced some dark and disturbing images in response to what he saw.

The young girl depicted in *Nevermore (366)*, painted after he had lived in the South Seas for several years, shows how he had come to terms with the haunted otherness of the interior life the women led. The girl is spread out before us, her golden body a sinister green as she ponders the mystery of her existence. A sightless raven, painted as a decorative detail, perches outside her window as a symbolic "bird of death" (inspired by the poem *The Raven* by Edgar Allan Poe, a favourite of the Symbolists).

Two women speak urgently together while the girl lies isolated and afraid on her splendid yellow pillow. The semi-abstract patternings we can see in paintings such as this are expressions of internal, psychological rhythms rather than outward events. Gauguin's skill lies in refusing to explain this complex mystery, even though he suggests there may be an answer. However long we contemplate *Nevermore*, it retains and in fact deepens its mystery before us.

365 Paul Gauguin, Riders on the Beach, 1902, 73 x 92 cm (29 x 36½ in)

MUNCH'S INTENSE EMOTIONALISM

Symbolist painting was not restricted to France alone. The Norwegian artist Edvard Munch (1863–1944) was a gloomy man, perpetually haunted by illness, madness and death, who used all his psychic weakness to create electrifying art.

Munch began painting in Oslo, where the predominant style was Social Realism, and it was only when he went to Paris in 1888 that he began to experiment. Van Gogh's swirling, emotive brushwork is detectable in Munch's more disturbing paintings, but he was also attracted to the work of Gauguin and the Symbolist painters, and he became close friends with the Symbolist poet Stéphane Mallarmé (see column, p.321).

He began to use the Symbolists' stylized forms, decorative patterning, and highly charged colours to express his own anxieties and pessimism. A precursor of Northern Expressionism (see p.340), he was one of those great artists whose main intention was to make an emotional statement, and who subdued all the elements of a picture to that end.

Munch can paint what seems an innocuous image. There are many versions of *Four Girls on a Bridge (367)*, a theme which clearly stirred something deep within him, and each work has a sinister undertone. The girls are all young and slender, passively leaning towards or away from the water. We feel uneasily that the water must represent something: time? their coming sexual power? They are on the "bridge", the dark, heavy shapes of the future at the far side of the bridge looming ahead. Yet to spell out the full meaning is to diminish it. Munch is a Symbolist whose ideas work at a subliminal level.

367 Edvard Munch, Four Girls on a Bridge, 1899–1900, 136 x 126 cm (53½ x 49½ in)

The greater his unhappiness, the more overtly autobiographical his art became. In the 1890s he produced a series of paintings called the *Frieze of Life* which he described as "a poem of life, love, and death". In 1908 he suffered from a severe mental illness and though he never left Norway again, his undisputed originality made a great impact on the next generation of artists.

GUSTAV KLIMT

Just as Munch can be associated with both Symbolism and Expressionism, so the art of the Austrian painter, Gustav Klimt (1862–1918), is a curious and elegant synthesis of Symbolism and Art Nouveau (see column, p.327). The Austrians responded enthusiastically to the decorative artifice of Art Nouveau, and Klimt is almost artifice incarnate. He painted large ornamental friezes of allegorical scenes, and produced fashionable portraits, uniting the stylized shapes and unnatural colours of Symbolism with his own essentially harmonious concept of beauty. *The Kiss (368)* is a fascinating icon of the loss of self that lovers experience. Only the faces and hands of this couple are visible; all the rest is a great swirl of gold, studded with coloured rectangles as if to express visually the emotional and physical explosion of erotic love.

368 Gustav Klimt, The Kiss, 1907/08, 180 x 180 cm (71 x 71 in)

CONTEMPORARY ARTS

1880
Rodin produces *The Thinker*

1886
The Statue of Liberty is dedicated to the American people

1889
The French begin the construction of the Eiffel Tower

1890
Oscar Wilde publishes *The Picture of Dorian Gray*

1895
Tchaikovsky's *Swan Lake* is performed in St Petersburg

1900
Puccini's opera *Tosca* is performed in Rome

1901
The first Nobel prizes are awarded

THE NABIS

Two French artists straddle the gap between Post-Impressionism and the moderns: Pierre Bonnard and Edouard Vuillard. Difficult to place artistically, they are thought of as Intimists, and leaders of a group known as the Nabis. Both painters lived well into the 20th century, yet, with their love of the gentle domesticities of life that was such a feature of the work of the Nabis, neither seems to belong truly to the world of modern art.

Inspired by Sérusier's painting *The Talisman* (see column, p.321), Pierre Bonnard (1867–1947) and Edouard Vuillard (1868–1940) formed a group known as the Nabis (Hebrew for seers or prophets) in 1892. The decorative was the keynote to their art: as their associate Maurice Denis (see column, p.329) wrote, "A picture, before being a warhorse, a nude, or some anecdote, is essentially a surface covered with colours arranged in a certain order." Disillusioned with Paris and Impressionism, the Nabis admired Gauguin and Japanese art and embraced many aspects of oriental mysticism, endeavouring to express the spiritual in their work.

THE JAPANESE NABI

Bonnard fell the deepest under the oriental influence, being known to his friends as "the Japanese Nabi". It was the graphic concision of Japanese woodcuts that appealed so strongly to him, with their lovely purity of line and colour. As Bonnard's art matured, the colours he used became much richer and deeper, so that the whole meaning is revealed in the colour.

The Letter (369) has a Japanese-like simplicity, the young woman so intent upon her writing and the tilt of her head suggesting the depth of her concentration. But that bent head is wonderfully feminine, with its glowing clumps of chestnut brown, the elegance of the little comb, the neat little nose, snub and flirtatious, and the expressive curves of her mouth. Bonnard is concerned with this woman less as a personality than as an enchantment – a very Japanese trait. He has walled her in deliciously for his own delight, with a gorgeous rim of crimson seatback, an interestingly variegated wall, and on the open, free side, a box and an envelope of entrancing hues. The green box is the palest colour in the painting, directing our eyes upwards towards the deep, rich blues of her modest dress and her downturned head. Bonnard makes no great statement about life or about this particular living creature. He looks at her instead with the most delicate and uncomplicated pleasure.

Bonnard, like Japanese artists, was interested in painting everyday life, in freezing the intimacies of a personal scene. Many of his paintings show images of the same model. This was Marthe, a sadly neurotic woman whom he eventually married, and who separated him from all his friends, yet who seems to have provided him with endless visual interest.

Fortunately, Marthe always loved to be painted, especially while in the bath, and many of his major paintings show her fully submerged in the water. There is an almost ecstatic brightness in the sensuous shades of her body and the water in *The Bath (370)*, and it has too often been thought that Bonnard's art is just a last dying effulgence of Impressionism. But he goes further, daringly and powerfully. Bonnard is not

369 Pierre Bonnard, The Letter, c. 1906, 55 x 48 cm (22 x 19 in)

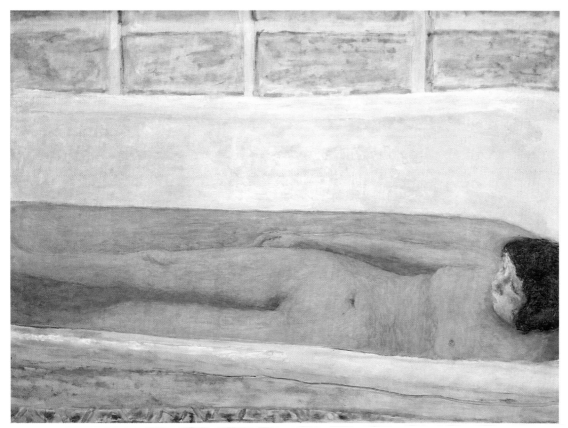

370 Pierre Bonnard, **The Bath,** *1925, 85 x 120 cm (34 x 47 in)*

ART NOUVEAU
In the 1890s a new decorative art movement known as Art Nouveau developed, inspired by naturalistic, organic forms. The movement was developed by sculptors, jewellery makers, potters, and, most importantly, poster artists. The roots of the movement were in England, but French artists, such as Bonnard and Vuillard, were also influenced by the swirling shapes and bright colours of the new style. This illustration shows a brooch designed in 1904 by Paco Durrio, a Spaniard who worked in France. It perfectly encapsulates the spirit of Art Nouveau – a sensuous subject and a fluid form.

interested in the atmospheric nuances of light, as the Impressionists were, but rather in rhythm, shape, texture, colour, and the endless decorative possibilities of the visual world.

CEZANNE'S INFLUENCE

The Nabis all shared an admiration for Cezanne (p.310), certainly the dominant influence on all early 20th-century artists. Maurice Denis' work *Homage to Cézanne* (see column, p.329) shows Bonnard and Vuillard clearly visible among several artists as they gather around one of Cézanne's paintings. When Bonnard paints a landscape he shows us not only what we can see but what the landscape feels like, as it were: he makes a leap into otherness, into sensation.

Stairs in the Artist's Garden (371) was painted near the end of his life and it is an extraordinary picture, like all his great variations on the theme of the garden. The stairs lead up the centre and then vanish as the grandeur of the blossoms overwhelms us. Exuberant colours mass to the left; huge fountains of springtime green erupt to the right. Ahead is a sunburst of bright bushes, piercingly golden and incandescently red, and there are more flowers overhead, allowing the intense blues of the skies to act as a backdrop. It is theatrical, a stage set, and the stage is set not for a play but for life. Bonnard wants to stir us into accepting the wonder of being alive. We are

liberated from our factual limitations into this radiant freedom. Taking Cézanne's chromatic majesty a step further, he etherealizes the weightiness that Cézanne felt essential, and is a great enough artist to succeed at it.

371 Pierre Bonnard, **Stairs in the Artist's Garden,** *1942/44, 63 x 73 cm (25 x 29 in)*

VUILLARD'S INTIMATE ART

By comparison, Bonnard's friend Vuillard may seem modest. His art is certainly more delicate, and he is interested less in colouristic fireworks than in the gentle, muted subtleties of textures and patterned cloth. His mother, with whom he gladly lived for much of his life, was a dressmaker, and he spent much of his time among women as they worked away in small rooms, absorbed and talkative. The happy, unforced charm of his art never cloys, never becomes obvious, and always remains tender and alive. His works are for the most part very small, as humbly befits their theme.

JAPANESE INFLUENCES

Vuillard's early paintings, as a member of the Nabis group, were highly influenced by the Japanese sketches that he had seen at the Ecole des Beaux Arts in 1890. The role of drawing, and particularly of silhouette, in achieving simplification of form was crucial to much of Vuillard's work. The sketch illustrated above was produced by Vuillard in 1890 using Indian ink and a Japanese brush. The artist was also closely involved with the theatre and was employed by the the theatre mogul of Paris, Coquelin cadet, to capture backstage scenes in the traditional Japanese style.

OTHER WORKS BY VUILLARD

In Bed
(Musée d'Orsay, Paris)

Girl in an Interior
(Tate Gallery, London)

Woman Before a Mirror
(Bridgestone Museum of Art, Tokyo)

Portrait of Madame Bonnard
(National Gallery of Victoria, Melbourne)

Woman Seated on a Sofa
(Art Institute of Chicago)

The Dining Room
(Neue Pinakothek, Munich)

The Lady in Green
(Glasgow Art Gallery)

*372 Edouard Vuillard, **The Reader**, 1896, 213 x 155 cm (7 ft x 5 ft 1 in)*

373 Edouard Vuillard, Vase of Flowers on a Mantelpiece, c.1900, 36 x 30 cm (14½ x 12 in)

Vuillard's lifelong exposure to dress materials through his mother's work, as well as the textile designs of his uncle, was clearly a formative influence on his art. *The Reader (372)* is one of a series of panels that he painted for a friend's library, and for this reason it was atypically large. Here we see how the furnishings of a room, its wallpapers, carpets, and upholstery, can nearly submerge the human presence there. We almost tremble for the reader, so bravely intent upon her book amid the jungle of the interior, and perhaps the women watching her from the doorway tremble too. Yet Vuillard cannot but paint from love, and the threat of so many clamouring designs is diffused, held at bay by the warm charm of his colour.

SMALL-SCALE INTERIORS

Vase of Flowers on a Mantelpiece (373) is exquisitely modest by comparison. We cannot see the whole mantelpiece, merely a section of it; nor can we see the entirety of the armchair beneath, merely part of the curve of its back, with the pattern of its upholstery. Vuillard stops short of painting the fire too, though the pink roses in a vase suggest that this is not the season for fires. But neither is it the season for emptiness: the mirror reflects a small, dimly-lit, furnished room, and the genius of Vuillard is to keep us engrossed as we try to read what we half see. The one unmistakable area of clarity is the vase of flowers itself, one large rose surrounded by its clustering companions. It is a picture in which

nothing seems to happen, yet which is a perpetually fascinating scene. We are drawn, irresistibly, into the encompassing warmth of Vuillard's own love of the ordinary.

WALTER SICKERT

The English painter Walter Sickert (1860–1942) was not one of the Nabis, but was influenced by this group, particularly Bonnard and Vuillard, and he was important as a link between English and French art at the end of the 19th century. Although he was a pupil and studio assistant of Whistler (see p.302) in the 1880s and worked with Degas (p.291) in Paris in 1883, Sickert's paintings also show an intimism (see glossary, p.390) comparable to the Nabis' work, and a shared interest in unusual compositions.

Some of Sickert's paintings are Victorian England's equivalent of the Nabis' quiet images of bourgeois French culture. But Sickert also painted dark, and sometimes sinister, images of the underworld. *La Hollandaise (374)* demands no knowledge of art history to announce this woman's profession. Poor, unidealized creature that she is, she nevertheless has the whore's appeal. Sickert paints her with an economy that is almost cruel, obliterating the features of her face to expose her naked body and scraping the paint thinly across her flesh: Sickert is clearly as interested in what she is as with how she looks, and he conveys both brilliantly.

HOMAGE TO CEZANNE
This painting was completed by Maurice Denis (1870–1943) in 1900 to commemorate Cézanne's first one-man exhibition held in 1895. The painting shows a group of artists, including Redon (to the left of the composition), Vollard (behind the easel), and many of the Nabis gathered around a Cézanne still life which was once owned by Gauguin. Cézanne and the Nabis were linked by Vollard, who had begun to deal in the Nabis' paintings and was also having great success in selling much of Cézanne's work.

CAMDEN TOWN MURDER SERIES
In September 1907 Emily Dimmock, a well-known north London prostitute, was found dead with her throat cut in her lodgings in Camden Town. The body was found by her lover when he returned from his night shift. A commercial artist, Robert Wood, was accused of her murder but was acquitted after a long and exciting trial. Sickert, who is known to have followed the trial reports, adopted the name *Camden Town Murder* as a general designation for several series of etchings, paintings, and drawings. Each painting in the series features a naked woman and a clothed man who personify the tragedy of poverty and deprivation.

374 W. Sickert, La Hollandaise, 1906, 50 x 40 cm (20 x 16 in)

THE 20TH CENTURY

It has been calculated that there are more artists practising today than were alive in the whole Renaissance, all three centuries of it. But we are no longer following one story-line: we are in a new situation, where there is now no mainstream. The stream has flowed into the sea and all we can do now is to trace some of the main currents.

20th-century art is almost indefinable, and ironically we can consider that as its definition. This makes sense, as we live in a world that is in a constant state of flux. Not only is science changing the outward forms of life, but we are beginning to discover the strange centrality of our subconscious desires and fears. All this is completely new and unsettling, and art naturally reflects it.

The story of painting now loses its way temporarily: it enters upon an encounter with the unknown and the uncertain. Only the passage of time can reveal which artists in our contemporary world will last, and which will not.

Wassily Kandinsky, Improvisation 31 (Sea Battle), *1913 (detail)*

20TH-CENTURY TIMELINE

We have dates in the 20th century, and pictures to attach to them, but there is no longer a coherent time sequence. This can be irritating to the tidy-minded, but it is in fact exciting in its adventurous freedom. With so many interesting artists, some of whom time may vindicate as of great importance, there is only space to touch briefly on those who seem to many observers to be part of the story, and not just footnotes.

PABLO PICASSO, LES DEMOISELLES D'AVIGNON, 1907
This picture is the one work that could be considered essential to the art of the 20th century. From its bizarre malformations and hideous energy have flowed a torrent of creative and innovative power. It startled Georges Braque, and it startles us still: it is a supreme and repulsive masterpiece (p.347).

WASSILY KANDINSKY, IMPROVISATION 31 (SEA BATTLE), 1913
It seems to be agreed that Kandinsky was the first totally abstract artist of the modern period. His art matured to an almost formal geometry, but initially, as here, it had a wild and wonderful connection with the real world, with shapes that are symbols of an imaginary sea battle (p.354).

PAUL KLEE, DEATH AND FIRE, 1940
Klee is a great colourist and an endlessly creative painter, both enchanting and profound. Only he can depict death and fire with a smile and a sacred tremor. This is characteristic of his unique approach, both to the matter and the manner of painting (p.358).

1900	1910	1920	1930	1940

HENRI MATISSE, THE CONVERSATION, 1909
Equal with Picasso (if not indeed greater), Matisse is the great master of our century. He is a skilful simplifier of form and a marvellous manipulator of colour, though he never uses these talents for their own sake, but always to create a design that at every point has a meaning (p.337).

PIET MONDRIAN, DIAMOND PAINTING IN RED, YELLOW, AND BLUE, C. 1921/25
Mondrian is the great purist of art. He limited himself to a few basic colours, arranged in solemn squares. His art is profound, expressing in this bare form a noble conception of life (p.360).

SALVADOR DALI, THE PERSISTENCE OF MEMORY, 1931
Some artists are greatly gifted, but have little to express. This is not entirely true of Dali, but it can be said that what he wanted to express was his own self-importance. Sometimes his experience coincides with our own, which is why this picture of melting watches – time going into a flux – is so unforgettable (p.364).

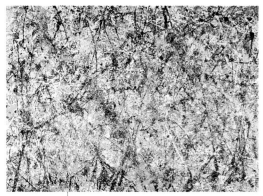

JACKSON POLLOCK, NUMBER 1, 1950 (LAVENDER MIST), 1950

Picasso and Matisse dominated the first half of our century. In the second half, the major figure is probably Jackson Pollock. Whether for good or ill, he "liberated" artists from the palette and the brush, from design and intention. He splattered his paint, swirling it out from its tins, as he danced on the horizontal canvas. It was an innovation of genius and surprisingly personal to Pollock himself (p.369).

MARK ROTHKO, UNTITLED (BLACK AND GREY), 1969

For some decades, Rothko has held his position as one of the great spiritual artists of our time. His mature work is always of the same format: there is a large canvas in which two rectangles of colour hover before us. We sense a deep emotion, but though the critics have spoken about "the veil of the temple" and other mystical metaphors, no explanation wholly convinces (p.370).

LUCIAN FREUD, STANDING BY THE RAGS, 1988–89

Although it is stretching the point to speak of a school of London, it is still true that a group of figurative artists is at work there. Lucian Freud is perhaps the most significant, a ruthless and clinical observer of humanity who dissects his subject on the canvas with memorable power. Such vulnerability would be unbearable to contemplate, were there the slightest touch of criticism or even of distancing. It is himself Freud dissects, and us with him. Here he shows us a nude standing against a background of paint rags from his studio. He makes everything that could be made of both these subjects, and of the many contrasts between them (p.386).

1950	1960	1970	1980	1990

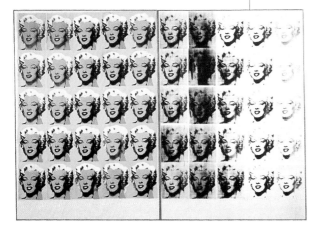

ANDY WARHOL, MARILYN DIPTYCH, 1962

There are still two vociferous attitudes towards Warhol. Is he a genius or a mountebank? Perhaps looking at the Marilyn Diptych we may feel that he is both: an artist who capitalized on his natural vulgarity and laziness, and used them to create icons for our times. One weakness, obsessive interest in the media stars, is here set to work. He makes a subtle comment on the reality of this interest, while conveying its fascination (p.380).

JASPER JOHNS, DANCERS ON A PLANE; MERCE CUNNINGHAM, 1980

Jasper Johns is a difficult artist, and none of his works is simple or easily comprehensible. There is always a concept controlling what he creates. Yet these creations are so supremely beautiful that they can be enjoyed even without full understanding. There is a reason behind every mark in Dancers on a Plane, *and if we learn to love it we may want to investigate these secret complexities. But it is the love that matters (p.381).*

AFRICAN INFLUENCES

Many of the Fauvists were inspired by African art and had their own collections of masks and statues. The fashion for tribal art had been started by Gauguin and the African influence can be seen in several of the paintings Matisse completed around 1906. This Kwele mask, shown above, closely resembles a famous piece once owned by André Derain. The whitened face suggests that it may have been part of the ancestors cult in central Africa.

FAUVISM

Between 1901 and 1906, several comprehensive exhibitions were held in Paris, making the work of Vincent van Gogh, Paul Gauguin, and Paul Cézanne widely accessible for the first time. For the painters who saw the achievements of these great artists, the effect was one of liberation and they began to experiment with radical new styles. Fauvism was the first movement of this modern period, in which colour ruled supreme.

375 *Maurice de Vlaminck,* **The River,** *c. 1910, 60 x 73 cm (23½ x 28¾ in)*

Fauvism was a short-lived movement, lasting only as long as its originator, Henri Matisse (1869–1954), fought to find the artistic freedom he needed. Matisse had to make colour serve his art, rather as Gauguin needed to paint the sand pink to express an emotion (see p.324). The Fauvists believed absolutely in colour as an emotional force. With Matisse and his friends, Maurice de Vlaminck (1876–1958) and André

376 *André Derain,* Charing Cross Bridge, *1906, 80 x 100 cm (32 x 39 in)*

Derain (1880–1954), colour lost its descriptive qualities and became luminous, creating light rather than imitating it. They astonished viewers at the 1905 Salon d'Automne: the art critic Louis Vauxcelles saw their bold paintings surrounding a conventional sculpture of a young boy, and remarked that it was like a Donatello *"parmi les fauves"* (among the wild beasts). The painterly freedom of the Fauves and their expressive use of colour gave splendid proof of their intelligent study of van Gogh's art (see pp. 316-18). But their art seemed brasher than anything seen before.

VLAMINCK AND DERAIN

During its brief flourishing, Fauvism had some notable adherents, including Rouault (p.341), Dufy (p.339), and Braque (p.350). Vlaminck had a touch of wild-beastishness, at least in the dark vigour of his internal moods: even if *The River (375)* looks at peace, we feel a storm is coming. A self-professed "primitive", he ignored the wealth of art in the Louvre, preferring to collect the African masks that became so important to early 20th-century art (see column, p.334).

Derain also showed a primitive wildness in his Fauve period – *Charing Cross Bridge (376)* bestrides a strangely tropical London – though as he aged he quenched his fire to a classic calm. He shared a studio with Vlaminck for a while and *The River* and *Charing Cross Bridge* seem to share a vibrant power: both reveal an unself-conscious use of colour and shape, a delight in the sheer patterning of things. This may not be profound art but it does give visual pleasure.

CONTEMPORARY
ARTS
1902
Chekov writes
The Three Sisters
1907
Stravinsky composes
his first symphony
1908
Constantin Brancusi
completes his
sculpture *The Kiss*
1916
Frank Lloyd Wright
designs the Imperial
Hotel in Tokyo
1922
James Joyce writes
Ulysses
1927
The first "talkie" film,
The Jazz Singer,
is produced
1928
Eugene O'Neill wins
the Nobel Prize
for literature
1931
The Empire State
Building is completed
in New York City

MATISSE, MASTER OF COLOUR

The art of our century has been dominated by two men: Henri Matisse and Pablo Picasso. They are artists of classical greatness, and their visionary forays into new art have changed our understanding of the world. Matisse was the elder of the two, but he was a slower and more methodical man by temperament and it was Picasso who initially made the greater splash. Matisse, like Raphael (see p.124), was a born leader and taught and encouraged other painters, while Picasso, like Michelangelo (see p.120), inhibited them with his power: he was a natural czar. Each demands his own separate space, and we start with Matisse.

> ❝*Instinct must be thwarted just as one prunes the branches of a tree so that it will grow better.*❞
>
> Henri Matisse

THE GREEN STRIPE
Matisse painted this unusual portrait of his wife in 1905. The green stripe down the centre of Amélie Matisse's face acts as an artificial shadow line and divides the face into two distinct sides. Instead of dividing the face in the conventional portraiture style, with a light and a dark side, Matisse divides the face chromatically, with a cool and warm side. The natural light is translated directly into colours and the highly visible brush strokes add to the sense of artistic drama.

377 Henri Matisse, Madame Matisse, Portrait with a Green Stripe, 1905, 40.5 × 32.5 cm (16 × 12¾ in)

378 Henri Matisse, The Conversation, *1909, 177 x 217 cm (5 ft 9¾ in x 7 ft 1½ in)*

AFRICAN TRAVELS
In January 1912 Matisse
set off on the first of two
trips to Morocco. His
appetite for African
primitive art had been
whetted by a visit to
Tangiers in 1906 and he
was eager to go back to
capture the wonderful light
and vitality of Africa. When
Matisse arrived in Morocco
it had been raining for
two weeks and the rain
was to continue for some
time. These unusual
climatic conditions left
the landscape green
and verdant which in
turn affected Matisse's
paintings. This
photograph shows a
piece of traditional
Moroccan textile
owned by Matisse.

Matisse's art has an astonishing force and lives by innate right in a paradise world into which Matisse draws all his viewers. He gravitated to the beautiful and produced some of the most powerful beauty ever painted. He was a man of anxious temperament, just as Picasso (see p.346), who saw him as his only rival, was a man of peasant fears, well concealed. Both artists, in their own fashion, dealt with these disturbances through the sublimation of painting: Picasso destroyed his fear of women in his art, while Matisse coaxed his nervous tension into serenity. He spoke of his art as being like "a good armchair" – a ludicrously inept comparison for such a brilliant man – but his art was a respite, a reprieve, a comfort to him.

Matisse initially became famous as the "King of the Fauves" (see p.334), an inappropriate name for this gentlemanly intellectual: there was no wildness in him, though there was much passion. He is an awesomely controlled artist, and his spirit, his mind, always had the upper hand over the "beast" of Fauvism.

In his green stripe portrait of his wife *(377)* he has used colour alone to describe the image. Her oval face is bisected with a slash of green and her coiffure, purpled and top-knotted, juts against a frame of three jostling colours. Her right side repeats the vividness of the intrusive green, on her left, the mauve and orange echo the colours of her dress. This is Matisse's version of the dress, his creative essay in harmony.

THE EXPERIMENTAL YEARS

Matisse's Fauvist years were superseded by an experimental period, as he abandoned three-dimensional effects in favour of dramatically simplified areas of pure colour, flat shape, and strong pattern. The intellectual splendour of this dazzlingly beautiful art appealed to the Russian mentality, and many great Matisses are now in Russia. One is *The Conversation (378)*, in which husband and wife converse. But the conversation is voiceless. They are implacably opposed: the man – a self-portrait – is dominating and upright, while the woman leans back sulkily in her chair. She is imprisoned in it, shut in on all sides. The chair's arms hem her in, and yet the chair itself is almost indistinguishable from the background: she is stuck in the prison of her whole context. The open window offers escape; she is held back by an iron railing. He towers above, as dynamic as she is passive, every line of his striped pyjamas undeviatingly upright, a wholly directed man.

HENRI MATISSE
Matisse's artistic career
was long and varied,
covering many different
styles of painting from
Impressionism to near
Abstraction. Early on
in his career Matisse
was viewed as a Fauvist
(see p.334), and his
celebration of bright
colours reached its peak
in 1917 when he began
to spend time on the
French Riviera at Nice
and Vence. Here he
concentrated on reflecting
the sensual colour of
his surroundings and
completed some of his
most exciting paintings.
In 1941 Matisse was
diagnosed as having
duodenal cancer and
was permanently
confined to a wheelchair.
It was in this condition
that he completed the
magnificent Chapel
of the Rosary
in Vence.

OTHER WORKS BY MATISSE

Woman with a Red Chair
(Baltimore Museum of Art)

The Pink Studio
(Pushkin Museum, Moscow)

Odalisque
(Bridgestone Museum of Art, Tokyo)

Two Models Resting
(Philadelphia Museum of Art)

Woman with a Violin
(The Orangerie, Paris)

The Snail
(Tate Gallery, London)

Oceania, the Sea
(Musées Royaux des Beaux Arts, Brussels)

*379 Henri Matisse, **Odalisque with Raised Arms**, 1923, 65 x 50 cm (25½ x 19¾ in)*

His neck thickens to keep his outline straight and firm, an arrow of concentrated energy. The picture cannot contain him and his head continues beyond it and into the outside world. He is greater than it all, and the sole "word" of this inimical conversation is written in the scroll of the rail: *Non.* Does he say no to her selfish passivity? Does she say no to his intensity of life? They deny each other forever.

SUPREME DECORATION

But denial is essentially antipathetic to Matisse. He was a great celebrator, and to many his most characteristic pictures are the wonderful odalisques he painted in Nice (he loved Nice for the sheer quality of its warm, southern light). Though such a theme was not appreciated at the time, it is impossible for us to look at *Odalisque with Raised Arms (379)* and feel that Matisse is exploiting her. The woman herself is unaware of him, lost in private reverie as she surrenders to the sunlight, and she, together with the splendid opulence of her chair, her diaphanous skirt, and the intricately decorated panels on either side, all unite in a majestic whole that celebrates the glory of creation. It is not her abstract beauty that attracts Matisse, but her concrete reality. He reveals a world of supreme decoration: for example, the small black patches of underarm hair on the odalisque are almost a witty inverted comma mark round the globes of her breasts and the rose pink centre of each nipple.

SCULPTING IN PAPER

Picasso and Matisse were active to the end of their lives, but while Picasso was preoccupied with his ageing sexuality, Matisse moved into a period of selfless invention. In this last phase, too weak to stand at an easel, he created his papercuts, carving in coloured paper, scissoring

381 Raoul Dufy, Regatta at Cowes, *1934, 82 x 100 cm (32¼ x 39 in)*

out shapes, and collaging them into sometimes vast pictures. These works, daringly brilliant, are the nearest he ever came to abstraction. *Beasts of the Sea (380)* gives a wonderful underwater feeling of fish, sea cucumbers, sea horses, and water-weeds, the liquid liberty of the submarine world where most of us can never go. Its geometric rightness and chromatic radiance sum up the two great gifts of this artist and it is easy to see why he is the greatest colourist of the 20th century. He understood how elements worked together, how colours and shapes could come to life most startlingly when set in context: everything of Matisse's works together superbly.

DUFY'S JOYOUS ART

One painter who truly found his artistic self through Matisse and the Fauves was another Frenchman, Raoul Dufy (1877–1953). He is still hard to categorize, one of the important painters about whom the critics have not yet entirely made up their minds. His art seems too light of heart and airy, unconcerned with any conventions that persuade the doubter of his seriousness. He is in fact utterly serious, but serious about joy, about the need to be free and disinterested, with no personal stake in life. His painting *Regatta at Cowes (381)* leaps with glorious unconcern across the canvas, so superbly organized that it almost seems artless. If some later artists have tried to imitate Dufy's apparent incoherence, none has had his profound purity that makes everything cohere. This kind of art either comes naturally, or fails.

les bêtes de la mer... H. matisse 50

380 Henri Matisse, Beasts of the Sea, *1950, 295.5 x 154 cm (9 ft 8 in x 5 ft ½ in)*

> ### BEASTS OF THE SEA
> Matisse chose to challenge the traditional beliefs of the artistic establishment by turning to the use of bright, colourful collage. His first use of scissors and paper was in 1931 but it was purely as a design approach for his larger paintings. However, following his ill-health, he turned to collage as an art in itself. In 1950, when he was over 80 years old, he cut one of his most beautiful collages in memory of the South Seas, which he had visited 20 years earlier. *Beasts of the Sea* includes symbols of aquatic life on the ocean bed, on the surface of the water, of the island itself, and of the sky above. By playing the bright colours against each other, Matisse achieved tonal resonances which would have a great influence on the colour painters of the 1960s.

EXPRESSIONISM

In the north of Europe the Fauves' celebration of colour was pushed to new emotional and psychological depths. Expressionism, as it was generally known, developed almost simultaneously in different countries from about 1905. Characterized by heightened, symbolic colours and exaggerated imagery, it was German Expressionism in particular that tended to dwell on the darker, sinister aspects of the human psyche.

EXPRESSIONISM

The term "Expressionism" can be used to describe various art forms but, in its broadest sense, it is used to describe any art that raises subjective feelings above objective observations. The paintings aim to reflect the artist's state of mind rather than the reality of the external world. The German Expressionist movement began in 1905 with artists such as Kirchner and Nolde, who favoured the Fauvist style of bright colours but also added stronger linear effects and harsher outlines.

DIE BRÜCKE

In 1905 a group of German Expressionist artists came together in Dresden and took the name Die Brücke (The Bridge). The name was chosen by Schmidt-Rottluff to indicate their faith in the art of the future, towards which their work would serve as a bridge. In practice they were not a cohesive group, and their art became an angst-ridden type of Expressionism. The achievement that had the most lasting value was their revival of graphic arts, in particular, the woodcut using bold and simplified forms.

382 Georges Rouault, Prostitute at Her Mirror, 1906, 70 x 60 cm (27½ x 23½ in)

Although Expressionism developed a distinctly German character, the Frenchman, Georges Rouault (1871–1958), links the decorative effects of Fauvism in France with the symbolic colour of German Expressionism. Rouault trained with Matisse at Moreau's academy and exhibited with the Fauves (see p.335), but his palette of colours and profound subject matter place him as an early, if isolated Expressionist. His work has been described as "Fauvism with dark glasses".

Rouault was a deeply religious man and some consider him the greatest religious artist of the 20th century. He began his career apprenticed to a stained-glass worker, and his love of harsh, binding outlines containing a radiance of colour gives poignancy to his paintings of whores and fools. He himself does not judge them, though the terrible compassion with which he shows his wretched figures makes a powerful impression: *Prostitute at Her Mirror (382)* is a savage indictment of human cruelty. She is a travesty of femininity, although poverty drives her still to prink miserably before her mirror in the hope of work. Yet the picture does not depress, but holds out hope of redemption. Strangely enough, this work is for Rouault – if not exactly a religious picture – at least a profoundly moral one. She is a sad female version of his tortured Christs, a figure mocked and scorned, held in disrepute.

THE BRIDGE TO THE FUTURE

Die Brücke (The Bridge) was the first of two Expressionist movements that emerged in Germany in the early decades of the 20th century. It was formed in Dresden in 1905.

The artists of Die Brücke drew inspiration from van Gogh (see p.316), Gauguin (p.322), and primitive art. Munch was also a strong influence, having exhibited his art in Berlin from 1892 (p.325). Ernst Ludwig Kirchner (1880–1938), the leading spirit of Die Brücke, wanted German art to be a bridge to the future. He insisted that the group, which included Erich Heckel (1883–1970) and Karl Schmidt-Rottluff (1884–1976), "express inner convictions… with sincerity and spontaneity".

Even at their wildest, the Fauves had retained a sense of harmony and design, but Die Brücke abandoned such restraint. They used images of the modern city to convey a hostile, alienating world, with distorted figures and colours. Kirchner does just this in *Berlin Street Scene (383)*, where the shrill colours and jagged hysteria of his own vision flash forth uneasily. There is a powerful sense of violence, contained with difficulty, in much of their art. Emil Nolde (1867–1956), briefly associated with Die Brücke, was a more profound Expressionist who worked

383 Ernst Ludwig Kirchner, Berlin Street Scene, *1913, 121 × 95 cm (47½ × 37½ in)*

in isolation for much of his career. His interest in primitive art and sensual colour led him to paint some remarkable pictures with dynamic energy, simple rhythms, and visual tension. He could even illuminate the marshes of his native Germany with dramatic clashes of stunning colour. Yet *Early Evening (384)* is not mere drama: light glimmers over the distance with an exhilarating sense of space.

DEGENERATE ART
With the rise of Hitler and the Nazi party in the 1930s, many contemporary artists were discredited and forced to flee Germany or go into camps. The term "degenerate art" was coined by the authorities to describe any art which did not support the Nazi Aryan ideology. The first degenerate art exhibition opened in Munich in 1937, with paintings by van Gogh, Picasso, and Matisse torn from their frames and hung randomly amongst the work of asylum inmates. The exhibition was so successful that it went on a propaganda tour throughout Germany and drew millions of visitors. Many artists were deeply affected by being labelled "Degenerate" and Ernst Kirchner actually committed suicide as a result in 1938.

384 Emil Nolde, Early Evening, *1916, 74 × 101 cm (29 × 39½ in)*

WORLD WAR I

World War I broke out in 1914 following the assassination of Archduke Ferdinand (heir to the throne of Austria-Hungary) in Sarejevo by nationalists. This single event ignited localized problems which spread into an international conflict. Within months the whole of Europe and parts of North Africa were in conflict. Austria-Hungary declared war on Serbia (believing the Serbians had devised the Sarejevo plot) and Austria's ally Germany declared war on Russia and France and then immediately invaded Belgium. In response, Britain declared war on Germany, and the stage was set for five years of incessant fighting and for the death of 10 million people. By April 1917 the allies included Britain, France, Russia, Japan, Italy, and the USA. Many artists were affected by the war, particularly Max Beckmann who was deeply affected by his work as a medical orderly on the front lines.

OTHER WORKS BY BECKMANN

Souvenir of Chicago
(Fogg Art Museum, Cambridge, Mass.)

Two Women
(Museum Ludwig, Cologne)

The Dream
(Staatsgalerie Moderner Kunst, Munich)

Masquerade
(Art Museum, St Louis)

Carnival
(Tate Gallery, London)

Sea Lions in the Circus
(Kunsthalle, Hamburg)

385 Max Beckmann, Self-portrait, 1944, 95 x 60 cm (37½ x 23½ in)

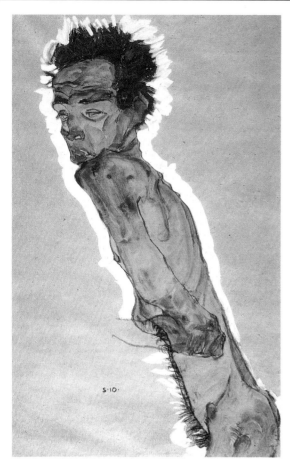

386 Egon Schiele, **Nude Self-portrait,**
1910, 110 x 35.5 cm (43 x 14¼ in)

Die Brücke collapsed as the inner convictions of each artist began to differ, but arguably the greatest German artist of the time was Max Beckmann (1884–1950). Working independently, he constructed his own bridge, to link the objective truthfulness of great artists of the past with his own subjective emotions. Like some other Expressionists, he served in World War I and suffered unbearable depression and hallucinations as a result. His work reflects his stress through its sheer intensity: cruel, brutal images are held still by solid colours and flat, heavy shapes to give an almost timeless quality. Such an unshakeable certainty of vision meant that he was hated by the Nazis, and he ended his days in the United States, a lonely force for good. He is perhaps just discernible as a descendant of Dürer in his love of self-portraits and blend of the clumsy and suave with which he imagines himself: in *Self-portrait (385)*, he looks out, not at himself, but at us, with a prophetic urgency.

AUSTRIAN EXPRESSIONISM

The Austrian Expressionist painter Egon Schiele (1890–1918) died when he was only 28 and we do not really know whether he would have developed from the self-pitying adolescent

angst that was the main theme of his work. *Self-portrait (386)*, however, is a most moving theme in itself: a pathetic and yet powerful exposure of Schiele's vulnerability. He is mere skin and bone, not yet fully there as a person. He has outlined his body with a glowing line of white to indicate to us both his sense of imprisonment and his limitations: notice how his arm disappears almost at the elbow – yet paradoxically it also suggests growth and potential. He is an unhappy, scrawny youth, the wild and exaggerated expanse of pubic hair perhaps indicating the centre of his unhappiness. His may seem too individualistic a view, yet in his hysterical way he is expressing the fears and doubts of many young people. He is wonderful, unsettling, and strangely innocent.

Oskar Kokoschka (1886–1980) was another Austrian artist of enormous Expressionist power. He said of his art, "It was the Baroque inheritance I took over unconsciously". He rejected harmony, but insisted on vision, and his art stakes its all on this visionary intensity, which plays havoc with more staid conventions.

In 1914 he fell passionately in love with Alma Mahler, the widow of the Austrian composer, Gustav Mahler. In its wild, dreamy way *Bride of the Wind (387)* commemorates the emotional storms and insecurities of that relationship with a sophisticated psychological insight: Alma, the "bride", sleeps complacently, while Kokoschka, flayed and disintegrating within the twisting brush strokes and sinuous ribbons of colour, agonizes alone in silence.

OSKAR KOKOSCHKA

Oskar Kokoschka first made a name for himself in 1909–10 with his psychological portraits in which the sitter's soul was believed to be exposed to the world. His paintings altered radically after his traumatic experiences in World War I and he began to paint Expressionist landscapes. In 1914 Kokoschka began an affair with Alma Mahler, Gustav Mahler's widow, which inspired one of his most powerful paintings *Bride of the Wind.* This relationship ended in 1915, but Kokoschka could not accept the break. He is known to have made a life-size doll of his lover which he carried around with him at all times. His obsession with Alma was brought to an abrupt end in 1922, and he smashed the doll's skull after a night of heavy drinking.

387 Oskar Kokoschka, **Bride of the Wind,** *1914, 181 x 221 cm (5 ft 11¼ x 7 ft 3 in)*

ARTISTIC EMIGRES

As the centre of artistic interest, Paris attracted many foreign painters in the early 20th century, and within a few years of each other three Jewish émigrés, Chaim Soutine, Marc Chagall, and Amedeo Modigliani, had all arrived in the city. Though they became friends and gained inspiration from the recent innovations in art, they were each highly original artists and their paintings stand alone, defying categorization and imitation.

The three painters that we look at here were all born outside France, and they remained outsiders to the Parisian art scene for more than merely cultural reasons (Soutine and Chagall were both Russian and Modigliani was Italian). These painters shared the isolation of being "other", never truly belonging to any group or adhering to a single manifesto.

A PASSIONATE EXPRESSIONIST

Chaim Soutine (1894–1943) came to Paris in 1913. He was the only painter in the city who was in the least like Georges Rouault (see p.341) and as a Parisian Expressionist, he belonged to the "School of Paris". Soutine's style of applying thickly encrusted paint was quite different from Rouault's, but his wild, chaotic spirit, sorrowful and vehement, is like that of the Frenchman. Just as Rouault, despite his Fauvist connections, is seen as inherently Expressionist, so Soutine was a natural, though singular, Expressionist.

Soutine's religion was the earth. He painted the sacredness of the country with a passion that makes his art hard to read. *Landscape at Ceret (388)* is so dense that it could be abstract, and it does take enormous liberties with the earthly facets, but when we do "read" it, hill and tree and road take on a new significance for us.

388 Chaim Soutine, Landscape at Ceret, c.1920–21, 56 x 84 cm (22 x 33 in)

DREAMS OF THE HEART

Marc Chagall (1887–1985) arrived in Paris in 1914 penniless, like Soutine. He combined his fantasies with sensuous colour and modern art techniques he learnt in France. He played with reality in a completely original and even primitive way. At heart he was a religious painter, using the word in its widest sense: he painted the dreams of the heart, not the mind, and his fantasy is never fantastic. It speaks beyond logic to the common human desire for happiness.

His early work in particular seems lit up from within by a psychic force that flows from his Jewish upbringing in Russia. *The Fiddler (389)* is a mythic figure, the celebrant of Jewish births, marriages, and deaths, but he bears this weight of the community alone, almost alienated from the common lot – notice the luminous green of the fiddler's face and how he hovers magically, unsupported in the air.

MODIGLIANI'S MANNERED ART

The third great "outsider" among the *émigrés* in Paris died all too soon. The Italian Amedeo Modigliani (1884–1920) destroyed himself through drink and drugs, driven desperate by his poverty and bitterly ashamed of it. Modigliani was a young man of fey beauty,

389 Marc Chagall, The Fiddler, *1912/13, 188 × 158 cm (6 ft 2 in × 5 ft 2 in)*

390 Amedeo Modigliani, Chaim Soutine, *1917, 91 × 60 cm (36 × 23½ in)*

and his work has a wonderful slow elegance that is unusual, but compelling. Through the influence of the Rumanian sculptor Constantin Brancusi, he fell under the spell of primitive sculpture, especially from Africa. He went on to develop a sophisticated, mannered style built upon graceful, decorative arabesques and simplified forms. It is hard for us to imagine why it did not attract patrons. He is famous now for his elegant, elongated nudes, but it is his portraits that are the most extraordinary.

Chaim Soutine (390) whose own art was so off-beat, appeals to Modigliani for what he is bodily and for what he could become spiritually. Soutine rears up out of the frame like a gawky pillar. His nose is brutish in its spread, his eyes asymmetrical, his hair a shaggy mess. All this uncouthness is contrasted by his slender wrists and hands, by an impression we have of a man yearning for a homeland, set upon forming one out of his own substance if no place is provided. There is sadness here, but also determination: the thick red mouth is resolutely closed.

OTHER WORKS BY CHAGALL

The Cattle-Dealer (Öffentliche Kunstsammlung, Basle)

The Juggler (Art Institute of Chicago)

The Eiffel Tower (National Gallery of Canada, Ottawa)

War (Pompidou Centre, Paris)

The Martyr (Kunsthaus, Zürich)

The Blue Circus (Tate Gallery, London)

Peasant Life (Guggenheim Museum, New York)

PICASSO AND CUBISM

After Cubism, the world never looked the same again: it was one of the most influential and revolutionary movements in art. The Spaniard Pablo Picasso and the Frenchman Georges Braque splintered the visual world not wantonly, but sensuously and beautifully with their new art. They provided what we could almost call a God's-eye view of reality: every aspect of the whole subject, seen simultaneously in a single dimension.

> *"...The art of painting original arrangements composed of elements taken from conceived rather than perceived reality."*
>
> Guillaume Apollinaire, *The Beginnings of Cubism*, 1912

It is understandable that Pablo Picasso (1881–1973) found Spain at the turn of the century too provincial for him. Picasso's genius was fashioned on the largest lines, and for sheer invention no artist has ever bettered him: he was one of the most original and versatile of artists, with an equally powerful personality. Throughout the 20th century people have been intrigued and scandalized by Picasso's work, uncertain of its ultimate value.

391 Pablo Picasso, Family of Saltimbanques, 1905, 213 x 230 cm (7 ft x 7 ft 7 in)

392 Pablo Picasso, Les Demoiselles d'Avignon, *1907, 244 x 234 cm (8 ft x 7 ft 8 in)*

THE EARLY YEARS

Picasso's Blue Period, from 1901 to 1904, sprang from his initial years of poverty after moving to Paris and modulated into a Rose Period as he slowly began to emerge into prominence. Although still only in his youth when he started painting, Picasso had overwhelming ambition, and his *Family of Saltimbanques (391)* was, from the start, meant to be a major statement. It is a very large, enigmatic work from the Rose Period, revealing his superb graphic skill and the subtle sense of poverty and sadness that mark those early years. The five itinerant acrobats are strained and solitary in the barren, featureless landscape; the lonely girl seems not to belong to their world, though she too is melancholy and belongs by right of mood. There is something portentous about the picture, some unstated

mystery. We feel that Picasso, too, does not know the answer – only the question. Already art is an emotional medium for Picasso, reflecting his moods and melancholia as he seeks to find fame as an artist.

THE FIRST CUBIST PAINTING

While still in his twenties, but finally over his self-pitying Blue and Rose periods, Picasso fundamentally changed cognitive reality with a work his friends called *Les Demoiselles d'Avignon (392)* after a notorious place of prostitution. These demoiselles are indeed prostitutes, but their initial viewers recoiled from their advances with horror. This is the one inevitable image with which a discussion of 20th-century art must be concerned. It was the first of what would be called the Cubist works, though the boiled pink

PICASSO'S PHASES

Pablo Picasso (1881–1973) had several distinct phases during his long career, including his Blue Period, and his later Rose Period. He began his blue paintings in 1901 reflecting his sadness at a friend's death. Picasso felt that blue was the colour of solitude, and melancholy, which certainly reflected his own bleak circumstances at the time. Directly after his Blue Period Picasso moved on to his Rose Period in 1905. Some believe that the warm tones of this period of work were influenced by Picasso's habit of smoking opium. One of Picasso's most creative phases took place between 1908 and 1912 and is known as Analytical Cubism (see p.348). In this style, which he developed with Georges Braque, Picasso used disintegrated and reassembled forms in shades of black and brown.

CUBISM

This movement in painting was developed by Picasso and Braque around 1907 and became a major influence on Western art. The artists chose to break down the subjects they were painting into a number of facets, showing several different aspects of one object simultaneously. The work up to 1912 concentrated on geometrical forms using subdued colours. The second phase, known as Synthetic Cubism, used more decorative shapes, stencilling, collage, and brighter colours. It was then that artists such as Picasso and Braque started to use pieces of cut-up newspaper in their paintings.

colour of the hideous young women is far removed from later Cubism, with its infinite subtleties of grey and brown. It is almost impossible to overestimate the importance of this picture and the profound effect it had on art subsequently. The savage, inhuman heads of the figures are the direct result of Picasso's recent exposure to tribal art, but it is what he does with their heads – the wild, almost reckless freedom with which he incorporates them into his own personal vision and frees them to serve his psychic needs – that gives the picture its awesome force.

Whether he did this consciously or not we do not know, since he was a supremely macho man: *Les Demoiselles* makes visible his intense fear of women, his need to dominate and distort them. Even today when we are confronted with these ferocious and threatening viragoes, it is hard to restrain a frisson of compassionate fear.

394 Pablo Picasso, Nude Woman in a Red Armchair, 1932, 130 x 97 cm (51 x 38 in)

At first Picasso did not dare to show it even to his admirers, of whom there were always many. But Georges Braque (see p.350) was haunted and affronted by its savage power, and eventually he and Picasso began to work out together the implications of this new kind of art. Cubism involved seeing reality simultaneously from all angles, of meshing the object in the network of its actual context: as Cézanne had indicated, there were to be no bounding lines to truth, but a form emerging from all different aspects intuited together (see column, p.347). The results are hard to read, even though the Cubists confined themselves mostly to unpretentious and familiar objects such as bottles and glasses of wine, or musical instruments (see p.350).

BEYOND CUBISM

Picasso would have scorned any thought of limiting himself to a single style. He experimented continually, his versatility and creativity always amazing his contemporaries. Whenever he seemed to have settled in a particular mode of seeing, he changed again almost overnight.

Picasso soon became a wealthy man and when the scandal of his early artistic methods had died down, he revived it with his subject matter. He is even more autobiographical an artist than Rembrandt or van Gogh and it was the women in his life who provided the changing drama: each new relationship precipitated a new

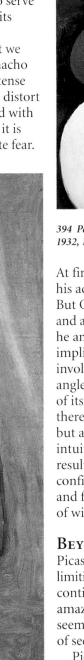

393 Pablo Picasso, The Lovers, 1923, 130 x 97 cm (51 x 38 in)

wave of creativity, with a new model and a new vision. *The Lovers (393)* shows him in a classical vein, soberly and simply giving substantial form to an almost theatrical drama. This was the period of his infatuation with Olga Kokhlova, the well-bred Russian ballerina whom he rashly married and whose elegant influence on him was soon to be angrily denied as their relationship faltered. There is a balletic grace in *The Lovers* and, pictorially thrifty though he was, Picasso never completely discarded the styles as he did the women.

THE ARTIST'S PLEASURE

The mistress who inspired the most enchanting art in him was Marie-Thérèse, a large, pacific girl with whose rounded body shapes he loved to play on canvas. Picasso was so various an artist, so astonishing in his inventions that every viewer may well have a favourite period, yet (though this may be too subjective a reaction) the work inspired by Marie-Thérèse seems to come from a depth that is perhaps unequalled in his other work. *Nude Woman in a Red Armchair (394)* is the last time we see Picasso relatively benign. There is something in Marie-Thérèse's willing vunerability, in her material fecundity of shape, that Picasso finds positively reassuring.

All the Marie-Thérèse paintings – at least until the affair began to disintegrate – are remarkably satisfying: rich, gracious, almost sweet, and yet deeply challenging. Picasso plays with both the rotundity of her body and with the powerful paradox of her extreme youth (she was only 17 when they met), yet the physical satisfaction that she brought him, succouring and nurturing him, was as though this simple child was in a sense a mother figure to him. *Nude Woman in a Red Armchair*, with its luminous physicalities – which even the armchair seems to share as it curls and glows around her body – still expresses the dichotomy of Marie-Thérèse's double role in Picasso's treatment of her face: she is both full moon and crescent moon, full face and in profile. It is impossible not to feel the thrilling communication of the artist's pleasure. This sense of fulfilment, rare in Picasso at any stage, never reappeared after he lost interest in Marie-Thérèse and her warm charms.

PICASSO'S LATER MISTRESSES

Subsequent mistresses such as Dora Maar, an intellectual, or François Gillot, another artist – both fiercely determined women – brought out Picasso's cruelty, his determination not to be impressed. Even in his old age, when he was cared for by his second wife, Jacqueline Roque, Picasso still used her as ammunition in his battle

against fate. He raged against his loss of sexual power in these final years and sought to compensate for it through the phenomenal weight of his artistic powers.

Picasso's portrait of Dora Maar, *Weeping Woman (395)*, painted the same year as his great picture *Guernica*, has a terrible power. It is a deeply unattractive picture, the shrill acids of its yellows and greens fighting bitterly and unrelentingly with the weary reds, sickly whites, and sinister purples. But it is also unattractive in the sense that it conveys Picasso's venomous desire to mutilate his sitter. Dora Maar's tears were almost certainly tears caused by Picasso himself. They reveal her anguished need for respect; Picasso repays her with a vicious savagery.

Power was Picasso's special gift. He had the ability to turn even the most incidental of themes into powerful works with an often overbearing force. If we accept that all beauty has power, we can range artists along a line, at one end or the other. Vermeer, Claude, and Matisse would be at the beauty end, and Rembrandt and Poussin at the power end, together with Picasso.

395 Pablo Picasso, Weeping Woman, *1937, 55 x 46 cm (21½ x 18 in)*

396 *Georges Braque*, Still Life: Le Jour, *1929, 115 x 147 cm (45 x 58 in)*

GEORGES BRAQUE

Georges Braque (1882–1963) was the only artist ever to collaborate with Picasso as an equal. He admitted that they were like climbers roped together, each pulling the other up. From 1907 they worked so closely together, exploring the planes and facets of the same subject matter, that some of their work appears almost identical. Although they developed their own natural autonomy as artists, they carried Cubism to another level that was brighter and more legible.

Their joint discovery was remarkably brief for the effect it has had. Braque never excelled in these early works, though he never fell below Picasso's standards either. His Synthetic Cubist painting (see column, p.347) of *Still Life: Le Jour (396)* is restrained in colour, is hardly playful at all, and is somehow less exuberant than Picasso's Cubist work – though Braque delights in the originality of the shapes and textures. But by this time the two artists had long parted, and their innate differences are clear.

JUAN GRIS

There was a third great Cubist, the Spaniard Juan Gris (1887–1927). He died young and never moved on from the style, though he progressively brightened and clarified it. With this single-mindedness, Gris can be thought of as the one absolute Cubist. *Fantômas (397)* has a harlequinish gaiety with its shifting planes and witty celebration of newspapers, magazines, and entertainment. With its stylish sophistication, we would never think it was a Braque or Picasso.

397 *Juan Gris*, Fantômas, *1915, 60 x 73 cm (23½ x 29 in)*

THE AGE OF MACHINERY

Interest in and appreciation of machinery was clearly in the air in the early decades of the 20th century. For a group of young Italian "Futurist" artists, the progress offered by machinery epitomized their increasing fascination with dynamic speed and motion. Though they translated this idea of progress into a frenetic exultation of the glory of war and the destruction of museums, their visual understanding of motion remained exciting.

The Italian Futurists, like the members of Die Brücke in Germany, aimed to free art from all its historical restraints and celebrate the new beauty of the modern age (see column, right). Umberto Boccioni (1882–1916), Gino Severini (1883–1966), and Giacomo Balla (1871–1958), who all joined Futurism in 1910, wanted to express the onrush of events in the world with pictures of motion, dynamism, and power.

In *Street Noises Invade the House (398)*, Boccioni attempts to give this sensation and succeeds remarkably well. Noise becomes something seen, something literally invasive of privacy. Boccioni said of the picture: "all life and the noises of the street rush in at the same time as the movement and the reality of the objects outside." The surging incoherence of the forms is both chaotic and ordered.

398 **Umberto Boccioni**, **Street Noises Invade the House**, *1911, 100 x 107 cm (39¼ x 42 in)*

ORPHISM

The term "Orphism" was coined by Apollinaire with reference to the singer and poet of Greek myth, Orpheus, who reflected the desire of artists to bring a new lyricism into their work. This type of art has been attributed to Delaunay, who concentrated on the power of colour over form. He managed to achieve a fusion of Cubism, Fauvism, and Futurism, to produce the first real forerunner to abstract art. Apollinaire viewed such esoteric paintings as the only "pure" art as they are created entirely by the artist without recourse to any outside influences.

399 Fernand Léger, Two Women Holding Flowers, 1954, 97 x 132 cm (38 x 52 in)

400 Robert Delaunay, Homage to Blériot, 1914, 250 x 251 cm (8 ft 2½ in x 8 ft 3 in)

FRANCE AND THE MACHINE AGE

Fernand Léger (1881–1955) was initially influenced by Cubism, but after his experience of trench warfare in World War I, he converted to Socialism. Like the Futurists, he admired the harmonious union of man with modern machinery. He developed an unusual blend of abstraction and representational imagery that conveyed something of the smooth, ordered quality of machines. *Two Women Holding Flowers (399)* shows the simplicity and power of this later style, though it is still only partially realistic. The full, schematic forms of the women were meant to be easily assimilable to ordinary people, for whom Léger felt immense respect, though it is the great bright blocks of colour that give his women their true interest. All the same, there is a sort of epic splendour in this art to which most people find themselves responding instinctively.

The machine age inspired not only Léger and the Futurists, but Robert Delaunay (1885–1941). *Homage to Blériot (400)* shows Delaunay's intoxication with the aeroplane and Blériot, the first pilot to fly the English Channel. Initially, it may seem to be an abstract picture, but it is full of visual clues. Blériot's plane whirls high above the Eiffel Tower, while figures and planes dazzle in and out of swirling multi-coloured circles, reminiscent of a propellor (see column, left).

TOWARDS ABSTRACTION

In 1911, a new group of German artists began exhibiting their work to the public. Der Blaue Reiter was to become the high point of German Expressionism, but it also opened the way towards abstraction with its stand for free experimentation and originality. It is Wassily Kandinsky, the most influential member of the group, who is most often credited with the distinction of painting the first "abstract" picture, in 1910.

Der Blaue Reiter (The Blue Rider) was formed in 1911 and succeeded the first Expressionist movement, Die Brücke (see p.340), which dissolved in 1913. The group included Franz Marc (1880–1916), Wassily Kandinsky (1866–1944), and August Macke (1887–1914), and celebrated the art of children and primitives, but had no

precise artistic programme. The most active proponent of this essentially romantic and rather spiritual view of art (see column, right) was Franz Marc, a young artist who was killed in World War I. Marc saw animals as the betrayed but uncontaminated guardians of what was left of innocence and unspoilt nature.

THE BLUE RIDER
This was the name given, in 1911, to a group of Munich Expressionist artists by the two most important members, Franz Marc and Wassily Kandinsky. Two touring exhibitions of paintings were transported around Germany, with other artists such as Macke, Klee, and Braque also represented. This illustration shows the front cover of *Der Blaue Reiter* published in 1912 by Marc and illustrated with a woodcut by Kandinsky.

401 Franz Marc, Deer in the Forest II, *1913/14, 110.5 × 100.5 cm (43½ × 39⅔ in)*

THEOSOPHISTS
The term "theosophy" is derived from the Greek words *theos*, "God" and *sophia*, "wisdom". As a religious philosophy, theosophy can be traced back to ancient roots, but it re-emerged in the late 19th century and influenced artists such as Kandinsky and Mondrian. The classic formulation of theosophical teachings is *The Secret Doctrine* written by Mme Blavatsky, an American theosophist. She argues that the "essence" of an object is more important than the attributes of the object. The new artists, like Kandinsky, believed their abstract art would lead the people to spiritual enlightenment.

RUSSIAN REVOLUTION

The Russian Revolution of 1917 had its origins partly in the inability of the existing order to manage the Russian role in World War I. There were two main groups of revolutionaries: the liberals, who believed that Russia could still win the war and create a democracy; and the Bolsheviks, who thought the war was lost and wanted to transform the whole economy. The avant-garde movement was adopted by the state (though not for long) and became a major vehicle for "agitprop" (a mixture of agitation and propaganda). Artists were encouraged to design for posters and political rallies.

Like August Macke, Marc chose to express these feelings with emphatic, symbolic colours. He painted animals with a profoundly moving love: a love for what they represented and could still experience, unlike humanity. *Deer in the Forest II (401)* is made up of a dense network of shapes and lines that border on the abstract. Together they create a forest of experience through which we can see, as if emerging from the undergrowth, the small forms of the deer. The animals are utterly at peace, at home in the forest of the world. It is a stylized and luminous vision of a species that can live without the angers of the ego.

August Macke, who was also to be killed in the coming war, was another artist with a gentle, poetic temperament. He took a simple delight in the joys common to us all, which makes his senseless destruction especially painful. *Woman in a Green Jacket (402)* floats onto the canvas, blissfully detached and pacific. Of the group, he was the most sensitive to form and colour, and the hues in this picture irradiate gently within strong shapes to create sensuous areas of light.

402 August Macke, Woman in a Green Jacket, *1913, 44 x 43.5 cm (17⅓ x 17 in)*

KANDINSKY AND ABSTRACTION

However, neither Marc nor Macke were abstract painters. It was Kandinsky who found that the "interior necessity", which alone could inspire true art, was forcing him to leave behind the representational image. He was a Russian who had first trained as a lawyer. He was a brilliant and persuasive man. Then, when already in his thirties, he decided to go to Munich in 1897 to study art. By the time Der Blaue Reiter was established, he was already "abstracting" from the image, using it as a creative springboard for his pioneering art. Seeing a painting of his own, lying on its side on the easel one evening, he had been struck by its beauty, a beauty beyond what he saw when he set it upright. It was the liberated colour, the formal independence, that so entranced him.

Kandinsky, a determined and sensitive man, was a good prophet to receive this vision. He preached it by word and by example, and even those who were suspicious of this new freedom were frequently convinced by his paintings. *Improvisation 31 (403)* has a less generalized title, *Sea Battle*, and by taking this hint we can indeed see how he has used the image of two tall ships shooting cannonballs at each other, and abstracted these specifics down into the glorious commotion of the picture. Though it does not show a sea battle, it makes us experience one, with its confusion, courage, excitement, and furious motion.

Kandinsky says all this mainly with the colour, which bounces and balloons over the centre of the picture, roughly curtailed at the upper corners, and ominously smudged at the

403 Wassily Kandinsky, Improvisation 31 (Sea Battle), *1913, 140 x 120 cm (55 x 47 in)*

bottom right. There are also smears, whether of paint or of blood. The action is held tightly within two strong ascending diagonals, creating a central triangle that rises ever higher. This rising accent gives a heroic feel to the violence.

These free, wild raptures are not the only form abstraction can take, and in his later, sadder years, Kandinsky became much more severely constrained, all trace of his original inspiration lost in magnificent patterings.

Accent in Pink (404) exists solely as an object in its own right: the "pink" and the "accent" are purely visual. The only meaning to be found lies in what the experience of the picture provides, and that demands prolonged contemplation. What some find hard about abstract art is the very demanding, time-consuming labour that is implicitly required. Yet if we do not look long and with an open heart, we shall see nothing but superior wallpaper.

404 Wassily Kandinsky, Accent in Pink, 1926, 101 x 81 cm (39½ x 31¾ in)

PAUL KLEE

Paul Klee was an introverted Swiss painter who spent most of his adult life in Germany until he was expelled by the Nazis in 1933. His work is impossible to clarify, except to say that it is hardly ever wholly abstract, but equally, never truly realistic. He had a natural sensitivity to music, the least material of the arts, and it runs through all his work, clarifying his spellbinding colour and dematerializing his images.

66 *Colour and I are one. I am a painter.* 99
Paul Klee

Paul Klee (1879–1940) was one of the greatest colourists in the story of painting, and a skilled deployer of line. His gravest pictures may have an undercurrent of humour, and his powers of formal invention seem infinite. After making an early choice whether to pursue painting or music as a career, he became one of the most poetic and inventive of modern artists. He taught at the Bauhaus in Weimar and Dessau (see column, left) and then at the Düsseldorf

BAUHAUS ARCHITECTURE

The Bauhaus school of art and architecture was developed by Walter Gropius (1883–1969) around the old Weimar Academy in 1919. The early teachers at the school included artists such as Klee and Kandinsky, and a close relationship was established between the artists and local industry. Many products, including furniture and textiles, were chosen for large-scale production. In 1925 the Bauhaus moved to Dessau and established a group of large cooperative buildings (illustrated above). The Bauhaus style was impersonal, severe, and geometrical, using a strict economy of line and pure materials. Gropius left the Bauhaus group and after moving to Berlin in 1932 the Bauhaus was closed down by the Nazis. This dissolution of the group actually encouraged individuals to travel and helped disseminate Bauhaus ideas throughout the Western world.

405 *Paul Klee*, The Golden Fish, *1925/26, 50 x 69 cm (19¾ x 27¼ in)*

Academy. Until his explusion from Düsseldorf by the Nazis, Klee painted and drew on a very small scale, yet the small size of his pictures does not effect their internal greatness.

The Golden Fish (405) glides through the kingdom of its underwater freedom, all lesser fish leaving a clear space for its gleaming body. This is a magical fish with runic signs upon his body, scarlet fins, and a great pink flower of an eye. He hangs majestically in the deep, dark blue magic of the sea, which is luminous with secret images of fertility. The great fish draws the mysteriousness of his secret world into significance. We may not understand the significance, but it is there. The sea and its creatures are arranged in

406 **Paul Klee,** Diana in the Autumn Wind, *1934, 63 x 48 cm (24¾ x 19 in)*

glorious homage, belittled but also magnified by this bright presence. This quiet nobility, the brightness, the solitude, the general respect: all are true of Klee himself. Whether the art world knew it or not, he was their "golden fish".

IMAGES OF DEATH AND FEAR

Klee painted with intense rapidity and sureness and it is impossible to indicate the full breadth of his range, his unfailing magic, and his poetry. *Diana in the Autumn Wind (406)* gives a hint of his sense of movement. Leaves flying in a moist breeze are, at the same time, the Virgin goddess on the hunt, and yet also a fashionably dressed woman from Klee's social circle. The eeriness of the dying year takes shape before our eyes and beyond all this are lovely balancing forms that exist in their own right. This work is strangely pale for Klee, yet the gentle pallor is demanded by the theme: he hints that Diana is disintegrating under the force of autumnal fruitfulness.

BOOK BURNING

At the peak of Klee's career in the early 1930s he came under surveillance from the Chamber of Culture. Joseph Goebbels, the Nazi minister of propaganda, organized hundreds of book burnings in German university towns. Thousands of books were destroyed for being "non-conformist to the spirit of a new Germany", including those by Marx and Freud. Hundreds of intellectuals and artists were forced to flee the country, including Kandinsky (who fled to France), and Klee (who went to Switzerland). Other left-wing intellectuals were not so fortunate and died in concentration camps.

OTHER WORKS BY KLEE

Old Sound
(Öffentliche Kunstsammlung, Basel)

Garden Gate
(Kunstmuseum, Berne)

The Dancer
(Art Institute of Chicago)

Flower Terrace
(National Museum of Modern Art, Tokyo)

Fire at Evening
(Museum of Modern Art, New York)

Watchtower of Night Plants
(Staatsgalerie Moderner Kunst, Munich)

Land of Lemons
(Phillips Collection, Washington, DC)

407 Paul Klee, Death and Fire, *1940, 46 x 44 cm (18 x 17⅓ in)*

Klee died relatively young of a slow and wasting disease, his death horribly mimicked by the death of peace that signified World War II. His last paintings are unlike any of his others. They are larger, with the forms often enclosed by a thick black line, as if Klee were protecting them against a violent outrage. The wit is gone and there is a huge sorrow, not personal, but for foolish and wilful humanity.

Death and Fire (407) is one of Klee's last paintings. A white, gleaming skull occupies the centre, with the German word for death, *Tod*, forming the features of its face. A minimal man walks towards death, his breast stripped of his heart, his face featureless, his body without substance. Death is his only reality, his facial features waiting there in the grave for him. But there is fire in this picture too: the sun, not yet set, rests on the earth's rim, which is also the hand of death. The upper air is luminous with fire, presenting not an alternative to death, but a deeper understanding of it. The man walks forward bravely, into the radiance, into the light. The cool, grey-green domain of death accepts the fire and offers wry comfort.

Three mysterious black stakes jag down vertically from above, and the man strikes the skull with another. If fate forces him down into the earth, he does not go passively or reluctantly: he cooperates. Death's head is only a half-circle, but the sun that it balances in its hand is a perfect globe. The sun is what endures the longest, what rises highest, what matters most, even to death itself. Klee understood his death as a movement into the deepest reality, because, as he said, "the objective world surrounding us is not the only one possible; there are others, latent". He reveals a little of that latent otherness here.

PURE ABSTRACTION

Shapes and colours have always had their own emotional force: the designs on ancient bowls, textiles, and furnishings are abstract, as are whole pages of medieval manuscripts. But never before in Western painting had this delight in shape as such, in colour made independent of nature, been taken seriously as a fit subject for the painter. Abstraction became the perfect vehicle for artists to explore and universalize ideas and sensations.

Several artists claimed to be the first to paint an abstract picture, rather as early photographers had wrangled over who had invented the camera. For abstract art, the distinction is most often given to Wassily Kandinsky (see p.354), but certainly another Russian artist, Kasimir Malevich, was also among the first.

RUSSIAN SUPREMATISM

Although Chagall and Soutine (see p.344) both left Russia to seek inspiration in France, the early 20th century saw an amazing renewal in Russian art. Since the far-off days of the icon painters (see pp.27–28), there had been nothing in this great country but the monotony of academic art. Now, as if unconsciously anticipating the coming revolution of 1917, one great painter after another appeared. They were not universally welcomed in their homeland, and more than one artist sought a response elsewhere, but some of the most significant painters dedicated their lives and their art to their country.

They are difficult artists. Kasimir Malevich (1878–1935), who founded what he called Suprematism (see column, right), believed in an extreme of reduction: "The object in itself is meaningless…the ideas of the conscious mind are worthless". What he wanted was a non-objective representation, "the supremacy of pure feeling." This can sound convincing until one asks what it actually means. Malevich, however, had no doubts as to what he meant, producing objects of iconic power such as his series of *White on White* paintings or *Dynamic Suprematism (408),* in which the geometric patterns are totally abstract.

Malevich had initially been influenced by Cubism (see p.347) and primitive art (p.334), which were both based on nature, but his own movement of Suprematism enabled him to construct images that had no reference at all to reality. Great solid diagonals of colour in *Dynamic Suprematism* are floating free, their severe sides denying them any connection with the real world, where there are no straight lines. This is a pure abstract painting, the artist's main theme being the internal movements of the personality. The theme has no precise form,

and Malevich had to search it out from within the visible expression of what he felt. They are wonderful works, and in their wake came other powerful Suprematist painters such as Natalia Goncharova and Liubov Popova.

408 Kasimir Malevich, Dynamic Suprematism, *1916, 102 x 67 cm (40 x 26½ in)*

409 Piet Mondrian, The Grey Tree, 1912, 79 x 108 cm (31 x 42½ in)

MONDRIAN'S ABSTRACT PURITY

Kandinsky's late style had a geometrical tendency and Suprematist abstraction revolved largely around the square, but the real artist of geometry was the Dutchman Piet Mondrian (1872–1944). He seems to be the absolute abstract artist, yet his early landscapes and still lifes were relatively realist.

> **"** *The important task of all art is to destroy the static equilibrium by establishing a dynamic one.* **"**
>
> **Piet Mondrian in *Circle*, 1937**

NEO-PLASTICISM

Although a founding member of De Stijl ("the style") group of artists, Piet Mondrian preferred his art to be viewed as Neo-Plasticism. The first De Stijl journal, published in 1917, emphasized the importance of austere abstract clarity and Mondrian's work certainly followed this agenda. In 1920 he published a Neo-Plasticism pamphlet asking artists to denaturalize art and to express the ideal of universal harmony. Mondrian restricted his paintings to primary colours, black, white, and grey, using lines to divide his canvases.

The Grey Tree (409) adumbrates the abstractions that were a half-way house to his geometrical work, yet it also has a foothold in the real world of life and death. *The Grey Tree* is realist art on the point of taking off into abstraction: take away the title and we have an abstraction; add the title and we have a grey tree. He claimed to have painted these pictures from the need to make a living, yet they have a fragile delicacy that is precious and rare. Mondrian sought an art of the utmost probity: his greatest desire was to attain personal purity, to disregard all that pleases the narrow self and enter into divine simplicities. That may sound dull, but he composed with a lyrical sureness of balance that makes his art as pure and purifying as he hoped.

Mondrian imposed rigorous constraints on himself, using only primary colours, black and white, and straight-sided forms. His theories and his art are a triumphant vindication of austerity. *Diamond Painting in Red, Yellow, and Blue (410)* appears to be devoid of three-dimensional space, but it is in fact an immensely dynamic picture. The great shapes are dense with their chromatic tension. The varying thicknesses of the black borders contain them in perfect balance. They integrate themselves continually as we watch, keeping us constantly interested. We sense that this is a vision of the way things are intended to be, but never are.

410 Piet Mondrian, Diamond Painting in Red, Yellow, and Blue, c. 1921/25, 143 x 142 cm (56¼ x 56 in)

ART OF THE FANTASTIC

Between the two World Wars, painting lost some of the raw, modern energy it began the century with and became dominated by two rather philosophical movements, Dada and Surrealism, which arose partly as a reaction to the senseless atrocities of World War I. But artists were also becoming introspective, concerned with their own subconscious dreams: Sigmund Freud's psychoanalytical theories were well known by this time, and painters explored their own irrationalities and fantasies in search of a new artistic freedom.

One artist who prefigured the Surrealists' idea of fantasy with his fresh, naïve outlook on the world was the Frenchman, Henri Rousseau (1844–1910). Like Paul Klee (see p.356), he defies all labels, and although he has been numbered among the Naïves or Primitives (two terms for untrained artists), he transcends this grouping. Known as *Le Douanier,* after a lifelong job in the Parisian customs office, Rousseau is a perfect example of the kind of artist in whom the Surrealists believed: the untaught genius whose eye could see much further than that of the trained artist.

Rousseau was an artist from an earlier era: he died in 1910, long before the Surrealist painters championed his art. Pablo Picasso (p.346), half-ironically, brought Rousseau to the attention of the art world with a dinner in his honour in 1908: an attention to which Rousseau thought himself fully entitled. Although Rousseau's greatest wish was to paint in an academic style, and he believed that the pictures he painted were absolutely real and convincing, the art world loved his intense stylization, direct vision, and fantastical images.

Such total confidence in himself as an artist enabled Rousseau to take ordinary book and catalogue illustrations and turn each one into a piece of genuine art: his jungle paintings, for instance, were not the product of any first-hand experience and his major source for the exotic plant life that filled these strange canvases was actually the tropical plant house in Paris.

Despite some glaring disproportions, exaggerations, and banalities, Rousseau's paintings have a mysterious poetry. *Boy on the Rocks (411)* is both funny and alarming. The rocks seem to be like a series of mountain peaks and the child effortlessly dwarfs them. His wonderful stripy garments, his peculiar mask of a face, the uncertainty as to whether he is seated on the peaks or standing above them, all comes across with a sort of dreamlike force. Only a child can so bestride the world with such ease, and only a childlike artist with a simple, naïve vision can understand this elevation and make us see it as dauntingly true.

METAPHYSICAL PAINTING

Giorgio de Chirico (1888–1974) was an Italian artist who originated what we now call Metaphysical painting (known as *Pittura Metafisica*), which also influenced the Surrealists' art. It was World War I and its brutalities that shocked de Chirico and his fellow Italian, Carlo Carrà (see column, p.362), into a new way of looking at reality in 1917. De Chirico painted real locations and objects within strange contexts and from unusual perspectives. The result is an uneasy assemblage of images in a peculiarly silent world.

> **"** *Surrealism is destructive, but it destroys only what it considers to be shackles limiting our vision.* **"**
> **Salvador Dali in** *Declaration,* 1929

411 Henri Rousseau, **Boy on the Rocks,** *1895/97, 55 x 46 cm (21¾ x 18 in)*

412 *Giorgio de Chirico,* **The Uncertainty of the Poet,** *1913, 106 x 94 cm (41¾ x 37 in)*

The Surrealists saw in de Chirico's paintings the importance of the mysterious world of dreams and the unconscious. They were influenced by the quality of enigma in his work, and especially by the unexpected juxtapositioning of objects, which became a distinguishing factor of much

Surrealist art. De Chirico hoped to rise above the bare facts in his art, transmitting the magical experience beyond reality: he wanted his vision to be shown through reality, but not limited by it in any way.

De Chirico's theories do not really explain the power of his work, and in fact he found this art hard to sustain, so that it dwindled surprisingly soon into a brilliant but imitative classicism of a kind. While at his brief best, however, de Chirico is as magical as he hopes, and *The Uncertainty of the Poet (412),* with its melancholy, deserted piazza, the suggestively scattered bananas, and the great bulk of the twisted, headless female bust is a genuinely unsettling picture.

FROM DADA TO SURREALISM

The German, Max Ernst (1891–1976), is hard to categorize: he invented one new method after another during his career, including frottage (laying paper over textured surfaces, making a rubbing with graphite, and using the marks as chance starting points for an image). Untrained as an artist, Ernst originally studied philosophy. In 1919 he founded the Cologne branch of the Dada group (see column, left). Dada appeared in Paris the same year and though it lasted only until 1922, it became a precursor of Surrealism.

413 *Max Ernst,* **The Entire City,** *1934, 50 x 61 cm (19¾ x 24 in)*

414 Joan Miró, Woman and Bird in the Moonlight, *1949, 81 x 66 cm (32 x 26 in)*

Dada reflected the mood of the time: it was a literary and artistic movement of young artists who, like de Chirico, were appalled and disillusioned by the atrocities of World War I. They expressed their sense of outrage by challenging established art forms with irrational and imaginative concepts in their work so that it frequently appeared nonsensical.

In 1922, Ernst settled in Paris and he became instrumental in the evolution of Surrealism from Dada by using childhood memories to influence his subject matter. His mind was extraordinarily fertile, which attracted a group of Surrealist writers, and after Dada ended, he became an intimate with this group.

Ernst took from de Chirico the idea of unconnected objects in strange, atmospheric settings, and turned them into pictures in a more modern context, full of fear and apprehension. He is an uneven artist, but his best works have a personal sense of mythology to them. *The Entire City (413),* with its uncanny streaks of frottage, and the great clear moon above with its vacant centre, strikes an unhappy chord of recognition. Although we recognize the familiar floorboard pattern, Ernst makes us feel the sad likelihood that we are also receiving a prevision of our future.

Surrealism began officially in 1924 with a manifesto drawn up by the Surrealist writer André Breton (1896–1966). Called "Surrealists" to stress the idea of being above or beyond reality, the group combined the irrationality of

Dada with the idea of pure, unreasoned thought through subconscious dreams and free association – a concept heavily inspired by Sigmund Freud's theories on dreams. The group took a sentence from the poet Lautréamont to explain their search for the fantastical: "Beautiful as the chance encounter of a sewing machine and an umbrella on an operating table."

MIRO AND MAGRITTE

Surrealist artists placed great value on children's drawings, the art of the insane, and untrained amateur painters whose art sprang from pure creative impulses, unrestrained by convention or aesthetic laws. Surrealism generally took the form of fantastic, absurd, or poetically loaded images. It was a potent, if inexplicable, force in the work of many artists, of whom Joan Miró (1893–1983) is perhaps the most uncanny. An introspective Spanish artist, he was one of the truly major Surrealists. His art appears far more spontaneous than that of Ernst or Dali (see p.364) in rejecting traditional images and devices in painting. *Woman and Bird in the Moonlight (414)* is a personal celebration of some deep joy. The figures tumble together with instinctive sureness, magical shapes that move in and out of recognition as if the woman and the bird could at any time exchange identities.

The Belgian René Magritte (1898–1967) was a practitioner of realist Surrealism, pressed into imaginative servitude. He began by imitating the avant-garde, but he genuinely needed a more poetic language which was influenced

ANTONI GAUDÍ

Before Surrealism had been created at the beginning of the 20th century the Spanish architect Antoni Gaudí (1852–1926) had already demonstrated the power of abstract forms and Surrealist fantasy in architecture. His most famous creations all encompass fluidity of form, with organic and abstract shapes, often using mosaic tiling to create arabesque decoration. The detail illustrated above is taken from the Parque Güell in Barcelona, designed by Gaudí in 1900–14 for his patron Don Basilio Güell. Several of the Surrealist artists, including Joan Miró, acknowledged drawing inspiration from Gaudí and other Catalan art.

415 René Magritte, The Fall, *1953, 80 x 100 cm (31½ x 39⅓ in)*

416 *Salvador Dali,* The Persistence of Memory, *1931, 24 x 33 cm (9½ x 13 in)*

by de Chirico's Metaphysical paintings. He had a mischievous mind, and his weirdly bowler-hatted men in *The Fall (415)* drop through the sky with complete composure, expressing something of the oddity of life as we know it. His art, painted with such clarity that it appears highly realistic, typifies the Surrealist love of paradoxical visual statements and though things may seem normal, there are anomalies everywhere. *The Fall* has a weird rightness about it, and it is in tapping our own secret understanding of sublunar peculiarity that Surrealism appeals.

DALI'S DREAM PHOTOGRAPHS

Salvador Dali (1904–89), whose graphic gifts were never affected by his mental imbalance, painted profoundly unpleasant and yet striking images of the unreality in which he felt at home. But he painted the unreality with meticulous realism, which is why they are so disturbing. He described these works as "hand-painted dream photographs" and their power lies precisely in their paradoxical condition as snapshots of things that, materially, do not exist.

It is easy, in theory, to disregard Dali, but difficult in practice. *The Persistence of Memory (416),* with its melting watches and the distorted face (like a self-portrait) in the centre, has an intensity and an applicability that we cannot shrug off. Dislike it though we may, this sense of time gone berserk, of a personal world collapsed under the pressure of the contemporary, has an inescapable power. And distasteful though it is, *The Persistence of Memory* is one of the great archetypal images of our century.

DUBUFFET AND ART BRUT

Though not a Surrealist as such, Jean Dubuffet (1901–85) shared some of the Surrealists' influences, in particular children's drawings, art of the insane, and the absurd and irrational. He had a large collection of work by psychotics which he called *Art Brut* – Raw Art.

Although he was still a young man when he trained as an artist in Paris, Dubuffet was in his forties before he began painting in earnest. On the surface, his art bears very little obvious relation to that of the Surrealists, though he painted with a Surrealist philosophy. His pictures are crude and rough, totally devoid of the illusionist trickery or persuasiveness employed by Dali and Magritte. Nor do they possess the Surrealist tendency towards enigma and mystery. Instead, his art was, as he would say, *Art Brut –* aggressively unsophisticated "outsider art".

We can be taken aback by a work such as *Nude with a Hat (417).* It seems to have been gouged out of a primitive material context. The nude glares out at us, her big eyes, confrontational mouth, and great, flat, egotistical hat making her a powerful and dynamic icon. Only the two small circles in the centre remind us that this is a nude and these are her breasts. Dubuffet is concerned with a whole different scenario: woman as demon, as a psychic force. It is the great flat hat that matters, not her nakedness. It is this reversal of the accepted and the conventional on which Dubuffet builds his art. It is wonderful stuff, but deeply challenging.

417 *Jean Dubuffet,* Nude with a Hat, *1946, 80 x 64 cm (31½ x 25 in)*

418 Giorgio Morandi, Still Life, 1946, 37.5 x 46 cm (14¾ x 18 in)

ISOLATION AND OBSESSION

In this period between the two world wars, Giorgio Morandi and Alberto Giacometti stood apart from their artistic contemporaries. Both painters absorbed the broad influence of Surrealism early on in their careers, but soon abandoned these affiliations to pursue their own singular and intensely individual languages. Morandi was Italian, Giacometti Swiss, and like their cultural disparities, their art has little common ground. However, they share the trait of being obsessive artists, returning to the same subject again and again.

Giorgio Morandi (1890–1964) was one of the real geniuses of Italian 20th-century painting. He was an unusual man who lived a very quiet life in Bologna, and his own quiet personality is the predominant trait in his art. His early paintings are influenced by de Chirico's Metaphysical paintings, but he soon evolved his own unique vision – one that he did not deviate from for the rest of his life. He painted still lifes – often the same group of bottles, jugs, and other humble domestic ware – and they quiver on the canvas with an almost breathless reverence. *Still Life (418)* has the inner peace of visual prayer. For him, these are objects of the deepest mystery and he has that rare artistic power of making us understand just what he experiences as he contemplates them.

THE HUMAN FORM IN SPACE

Alberto Giacometti (1901–66) spent a large proportion of his career as a sculptor and returned to painting at a relatively late stage. Like Morandi, his early paintings – especially those made in Paris where he settled in 1922 – were essentially Surrealist with their disturbing, aggressively ambiguous vein. He later abandoned this form of expression to work directly from life, thus severing all points of contact with the Surrealists. Giacometti spent the rest of his life engaged in one long, ongoing struggle to convey the solid presence of the human form in space. He tended to work obsessively on a series of paintings, working continuously on one particular image at a time. His tendency to wipe out every night what he had created during the day gives a poignancy to what has survived. *Jean Genet (419)*, for example, the Parisian thief-turned-writer, intrigued Giacometti in both aspects of his unique personality.

Giacometti was fascinated both by the creative Genet, the writer, and by the obsessive Genet, the thief. Something of Giacometti's double fascination is apparent in this portrait. Genet looks up almost blindly into the world of mysterious materiality. This is the world from which he was excluded, and which he yet longs to possess. All of these subtleties are present in Genet's portrait: a small, tense figure, blindly intent upon a world that eludes him. There is mastery here and menace, as well as a sense of the magical.

OTHER WORKS BY MORANDI

Still life
(Australian National Gallery, Canberra)

Flowers
(Collezione d'Arte Religiosa Moderna, Vatican Rome)

Still life with a Green Dish
(Gemeentemuseum, The Hague)

Still life with Bottles
(Scottish National Gallery of Modern Art, Edinburgh)

Landscape of Grizzana
(Fondazione Magnani Rocca, Parma)

Metaphysical Picture
(Hermitage, St Petersburg)

419 Alberto Giacometti, Jean Genet, 1955, 65 x 54 cm (25½ x 21¼ in)

PRE-WAR AMERICAN PAINTING

There have always been interesting American artists, and at least two 19th-century painters, Thomas Eakins and Winslow Homer, influenced the course of future art in the United States. During the 1920s and '30s, Edward Hopper and Georgia O'Keeffe emerged as the inspirational new painters of distinctive American traditions. Hopper's work was strongly realist, his still, precise images of desolation and isolated individuals reflecting the social mood of the times. O'Keeffe's art was more abstract, often based on enlarged plants and flowers, and infused with a kind of Surrealism she referred to as "magical realism". She may not have been a great painter, but her art was highly influential.

AMERICAN SCENE PAINTING

Edward Hopper (1882–1967) painted American landscapes and cityscapes with a disturbing truth, expressing the world around him as a chilling, alienating, and often vacuous place. Everybody in a Hopper picture appears terribly alone. Hopper soon gained a widespread reputation as the artist who gave visual form to the loneliness and boredom of life in the big city. This was something new in art, perhaps an expression of the sense of human hopelessness that characterized the Great Depression of the 1930s.

THE FEDERAL ART PROJECT

Instigated by President Franklin D. Roosevelt as part of his "New Deal" in 1935, the Federal Art Project aimed to alleviate the worst effects of the American Depression. At its peak, the FAP employed over 5,000 people across the country to decorate public buildings and to create new art centres and galleries. Lasting until 1943, the project employed virtually all the major American artists of the period, either as teachers or practitioners.

420 Edward Hopper, Cape Cod Evening, 1939, 77 x 102 cm (30¼ x 40 in)

Edward Hopper (1882–1967) has something of the lonely gravity peculiar to Thomas Eakins (see p.305), a courageous fidelity to life as he feels it to be. He also shares Winslow Homer's (p.304) power to recall the feel of things. For Hopper, this feel is insistently low-key and ruminative. He shows the modern world unflinchingly; even its gaieties are gently mournful, echoing the disillusionment that swept across the country after the start of the Great Depression in 1929 (see column, right). *Cape Cod Evening (420)* should be idyllic, and in a way it is. The couple enjoy the evening sunshine

421 Georgia O'Keeffe, **Jack-in-the-Pulpit No. IV,** *1930, 102 x 76 cm (40 x 30 in)*

outside their home, yet they are a couple only technically and the enjoyment is wholly passive as both are isolated and introspective in their reveries. Their house is closed to intimacy, the door firmly shut and the windows covered. The dog is the only alert creature, but even it turns away from the house. The thick, sinister trees tap on the window panes, but there will be no answer.

Georgia O'Keeffe (1887–1986), like Mary Cassatt (see p.291), and Berthe Morisot (p.290), is a female artist who no story of painting can neglect: like them, she added something. She married the photographer Alfred Stieglitz in 1924 and his close-ups of vegetation and New York skyscrapers inspired her own art.

Her *Jack-in-the-Pulpit* series starts with a highly realistic image which is abstracted and magnified until the last work shows just the "jack", the stamen. Perhaps the fourth in the *Jack-in-the-Pulpit (421)* series has the greatest impact. We are confronted by a great blaze of intense blue, haloed by a jagged outline of luminous green and centred by a radiant candle of stamen. An ardour of white flame soars upwards, seemingly imprisoned and yet intimately connected with the light at the leaf's edges. The inner flame burns somehow out of sight, triumphing. O'Keefe's ability to make the totally real become mystically unreal had few immediate imitators, but she has steadily influenced art for much of this century.

GEORGIA O'KEEFFE

The artist Georgia O'Keeffe (1887–1986) was one of the pioneers of Modernism in America. She was a member of the circle surrounding the photographer and art dealer Alfred Stieglitz (1864–1946), whom she married in 1924. O'Keeffe is best known for her close-up, quasi-photographic images of flowers, which have generally been judged as sensuous and sexually suggestive. From the 1930s she spent every winter in New Mexico, where she was inspired by the desolate beauty of the desert landscape. After her husband's death in 1946, she moved to New Mexico permanently.

THE GREAT DEPRESSION

This term describes the economic slump which affected the USA and Europe between 1929 and 1939. In the USA the economic boom of the 1920s ended with the Wall Street Crash of October 1929. By 1932 one out of every four American workers was unemployed. By 1933 the total value of world trade had fallen by more than half as countries abandoned the gold standard and stopped importing foreign goods. In the USA President Roosevelt offered the people a New Deal, which included a huge relief programme financed by public funds. But it was not until World War II, and the growth of the arms industry that any real recovery was established.

ABSTRACT EXPRESSIONISM

However great a disaster World War II was, it did at least mean that artists such as Piet Mondrian and Max Ernst, in leaving Europe for the safety of the USA, greatly extended their artistic influence. It is impossible to estimate how much they affected American art, but the fact remains that in the 1940s and '50s, for the first time, American artists became internationally important with their new vision and new artistic vocabulary, known as Abstract Expressionism.

The first public exhibitions of work by the "New York School" of artists – who were to become known as Abstract Expressionists – were held in the mid '40s. Like many other modern movements, Abstract Expressionism does not describe any one particular style, but rather a general attitude; not all the work was abstract, nor was it all expressive. What these artists did have in common were morally loaded themes, often heavyweight and tragic, on a grand scale. In contrast to the themes of social realism and regional life that characterized American art of

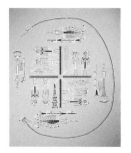

*422 Jackson Pollock, **The Moon-Woman Cuts the Circle**, 1943, 109.5 x 104 cm (43 x 41 in)*

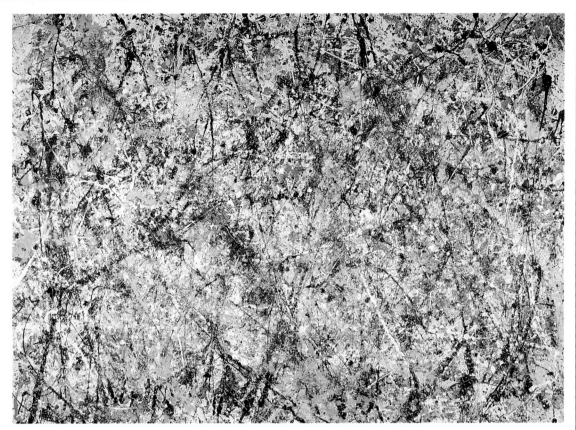

423 Jackson Pollock, **Number 1, 1950 (Lavender Mist),** *1950, 221 x 300 cm (7 ft 3 in x 9 ft 10 in)*

previous decades, these artists valued, above all, individuality and spontaneous improvisation. They felt ill at ease with conventional subjects and styles, neither of which could adequately convey their new vision. In fact, style as such almost ceased to exist with the Abstract Expressionists, and they drew their inspiration from all directions.

BREAKING THE ICE
It was Jackson Pollock (1912–56) who blazed an astonishing trail for other Abstract Expressionist painters to follow. De Kooning (see p.371) said, "He broke the ice", an enigmatic phrase suggesting that Pollock showed what art could become with his 1947 drip paintings (see column, p.368).

The Moon-Woman Cuts the Circle (422) is an early Pollock, but it shows the passionate intensity with which he pursued his personal vision. This painting is based on a North American Indian myth. It connects the moon with the feminine and shows the creative, slashing power of the female psyche. It is not easy to say what we are actually looking at: a face rises before us, vibrant with power, though perhaps the image does not benefit from laboured explanations. If we can respond to this art at a fairly primitive level, then we can also respond to a great abstract work such as *Lavender Mist (423).* If we cannot, at least we can appreciate the fusion of colours and

the Expressionist feeling of urgency that is communicated. *Moon-Woman* may be a feathered harridan or a great abstract pattern; the point is that it works on both levels.

ACTION PAINTING
Pollock was the first "all-over" painter, pouring paint rather than using brushes and a palette, and abandoning all conventions of a central motif. He danced in semi-ecstasy over canvases spread across the floor, lost in his patternings, dripping and dribbling with total control. He said: "The painting has a life of its own. I try to let it come through." He painted no image, just "action", though "action painting" seems an inadequate term for the finished result of this creative process. *Lavender Mist* is 3 m long (nearly 10 ft), a vast expanse on a heroic scale. It is alive with coloured scribble, spattered lines moving this way and that, now thickening, now trailing off to a slender skein. The eye is kept continually eager, not allowed to rest on any particular area. Pollock has put his hands into paint and placed them at the top right – an instinctive gesture eerily reminiscent of cave painters (see p.11) who did the same. The overall tone is a pale lavender, made airy and active. At the time Pollock was hailed as the greatest American painter, but there are already those who feel his work is not holding up in every respect.

OTHER WORKS BY POLLOCK
White Light
(Museum of Modern Art, New York)

The Deep
(Pompidou Centre, Paris)

Blue Poles
(Australian National Gallery, Canberra)

No. 23
(Tate Gallery, London)

Watery Paths
(Galleria d'Arte Moderne, Rome)

Eyes In the Heat
(Guggenheim Foundation, Venice)

Untitled Composition
(Scottish National Gallery of Art, Edinburgh)

424 *Lee Krasner,* Cobalt Night, *1962, 237 x 401 cm (7 ft 9⅓ in x 13 ft 2 in)*

Lee Krasner (1908–84), who married Pollock in 1944, was not celebrated at all during his lifetime (cut short in 1956 by a fatal car crash), but it was actually she who first started covering the canvas with a passionate flurry of marks. The originality of her vision, its stiff integrity and its great sense of internal cohesion, is now beginning to be recognized. *Cobalt Night (424)* at 4 m (over 13 ft) is even larger than *Lavender Mist* and has the same kind of heroic ambition.

MARK ROTHKO

The other giant of Abstract Expressionism is the Russian-born Mark Rothko (1903–70). Just as there are some who feel a little uneasy about the status of Pollock, and others who would fiercely defend it, so too with Rothko. Like Pollock, he was initially influenced by Surrealism and its capacity for freedom of expression, but his greatest works are his mature abstracts. These paintings are often not hung as he originally intended. He wanted dim lighting and an atmosphere of contemplation; he rarely gets it. He rejected the extreme religious connotations given to his great walls of colour, saying that his work had an essentially emotional rather than mystical meaning. He insisted that the theme, the subject, was different and could only be communicated by personal involvement in an atmosphere of solitude. Yet to many it appears that all Rothkos have identical formats: oblongs of delicate colour held floating in a coloured setting, the edges ravelled like heavenly clouds. Those who love Rothko consider him one of the most important painters of the 20th century.

Rothko's art represented an alternative Abstract Expressionism to Pollock's: he placed greater emphasis on colour and gravity than on the excitement of gesture and action. Such

425 *Mark Rothko,* Untitled (Black and Grey), *1969, 207 x 194 cm (6 ft 9⅓ in x 6 ft 4 in)*

demarcations, however, can be dangerous, since the Abstract Expressionists rarely aligned themselves into such rigid camps. *Untitled (Black and Grey) (425)* was painted the year before Rothko killed himself. The chromatic luminosities of the earlier years had long been quenched by a deepening sadness: the emotion conveyed here is of deep sorrow. We must take what comfort we can in recognizing that the grey area is greater than the black and that though the black has a heavy, deadening solidity the grey is still shot through with undershades, with potential.

Arshile gorky

It may have been his soul-shattering early experiences as an Armenian refugee, and the resulting insecurities, that made Arshile Gorky (1905–48) begin his artistic career so heavily under the influence of Picasso (see p.346) that it seemed an individual style would never emerge. Born Vosdanig Manoog Adoian, Gorky emigrated to the USA in 1920, moving to New York in 1925 to study and then teach art. Before he too killed himself (see column, right), Gorky did indeed find his own voice, released partly through his contact with Surrealism in America. *Waterfall (426)* shows a lovely tumble of free images, the sweetly floating flat patches of colour and shapes of his maturity. Strangely, the images do truly resemble a waterfall: something in the

427 *Willem de Kooning,* Woman and Bicycle, *1952–53, 194 × 124 cm (76 × 49 in)*

surge down the canvas suggests a great sweep of water, the sunlight dazzling on hidden rocks behind. There is a springtime freshness about Gorky's work that gives his suicide an added poignancy. It is as if only in his art did he find happiness, freedom, and acceptance.

De kooning

Gorky was an important influence on the development of Abstract Expressionism and also on one of its most vital figures, his friend Willem de Kooning (1904–). De Kooning was born in Holland, but has lived mainly in the USA.

426 *Arshile Gorky,* Waterfall, *1943, 154 × 113 cm (60½ × 44½ in)*

TRAGIC LIFE

Arshile Gorky was a potent force in American art, forging a link between Surrealism and Abstraction. At the peak of his powers he suffered from a series of tragedies. In 1946 a fire destroyed many of his paintings and he was diagnosed as having cancer. In 1948 he broke his neck in a car accident and his wife left him. Soon afterwards he hanged himself.

Though there were many Abstract Expressionists, the most vital seems to be de Kooning: even in Pollock's lifetime, de Kooning was hailed as his major rival. His ability to take a theme, whether landscape or portrait, and treat it with wild and wonderful freedom still impresses. His northern European background and the impulsive passion of his style, however, still bear some resemblance to Chaim Soutine (see p.344).

We are shaken with a visceral shock when we encounter de Kooning's women. *Woman and Bicycle (427)* is all teeth, eyes, and enormous bosom. She sits like a mantis, with a gleeful expectancy lighting her wedge of a face. This is a woman totally devoid of glamour, let alone charm, yet the poor giantess is dolled up in her tasteless finery, waiting for her prey. We shrink, we smile (such hideousness), we feel a little afraid. She is, above all, impressive and wickedly so. It is as much a tribute as a taunt.

At his lyrical best, de Kooning can overwhelm us with his beauty. *Door to the River (428)* balances most delicately on the cusp of abstraction. Great thick bars of colour that slash and sprawl across the canvas create an unmistakable door; through

429 *Clyfford Still*, 1953,
236 × 174 cm (7 ft 9 in × 5 ft 8½ in)

the vertical bars gleams the intense blue of the distant river. This is not de Kooning delighting us with his wit, but rather drawing us right into the heart of great art. A work of art is great to the extent that to encounter it is to be changed. *Door to the River* passes this test triumphantly.

CLYFFORD STILL

With Clyfford Still (1904–80), landscape moved majestically over the cusp and into pure abstraction. Still is set apart from other artists of the New York School by the fact that for most of his career he lived and worked at a remove from the art world of New York – although he lived and taught in the great city during the height of Abstract Expressionism in the mid 1950s.

Still rejected references to the real world in his art and attempted to sever colour from any links and associations. Most of his paintings are variations on a theme. He made grandiose claims for his work as being transcendent and numinous, and a painting such as *1953 (429)* does suggest why he felt able to make such claims. An objective viewer might feel he overstates his case, and yet this is a wonderful painting. The expanse of blue is dotted with black, two passionate streaks of red at the base, and great jagged slashes of colour at the top. It is as if the mountains have opened to show us both the brightness and the darkness within, and it is this power to suggest a psychic significance that distinguishes Still's art.

428 **Willem de Kooning**, Door to the River, *1960, 205 × 178 cm (6 ft 8 in × 5 ft 10 in)*

430 Franz Kline, Ballantine, 1948–60, 183 × 183 cm (6 ft × 6 ft)

FRANZ KLINE

If Franz Kline (1910–62) suggests urban land-scapes in his art, it is only in the sense of girders set against the sky. It is as if the struts of a bridge or some unsupported scaffolding had inspired him to see the sheer majesty of pure, isolated shape. His work resembles nothing more than oriental calligraphy writ large. Much of it is black and white, with all the subtle shadings and blurring that distinguish great Chinese calligraphy. There is a sort of passionate rightness about a work such as *Ballantine (430)* that is immediately convincing. This personal building of a shape like a bridge, with an oriental freedom of handling, may not be especially profound but it remains immensely satisfying.

BARNETT NEWMAN

Barnett Newman (1905–70) was one of the most prestigious of the New York School painters. Originally an art critic, he was an ardent supporter of the Abstract Expressionists, explaining and popularizing their work across America. Everyone was surprised when he suddenly blossomed forth as a painter himself, producing enormous "colour field" canvases: often a solid block of a single colour punctuated by what Newman called "zips". *Yellow Painting (431)* is a perfect example: two straight white lines that differ slightly in width (though their length is identical) zip vertically through the painting at either edge. Their pristine whiteness makes us aware of the rich canary yellow which, we discover on inspection, is bisected by another zip, this time yellow, faintly outlined in places with a shadowy white. The sheer size of the painting and its baffling simplicity keep us looking. The longer we look, the more aware we are of the strength and purity of the

yellow, and indeed of the white. This is a strangely uplifting experience, as though colour draws us into itself whilst enlarging our horizons. With these works, Newman prefigures both the decorative panels of the Colourists (see p.375) and the spartan canvases of the Minimalists (see p.377).

ROBERT MOTHERWELL

Although his work has a monolithic simplicity, Newman was a noted intellectual. So indeed was Robert Motherwell (1915–91), the youngest of the Abstract Expressionists and a philosopher whose work exerts an enormous, though fundamentally mysterious moral power.

Motherwell has said that "without ethical consciousness a painter is only a decorator". This remark makes sense in the context of the series that he painted as an emotional response to the Spanish Civil War of 1936–39. These works are elegies mourning the self-inflicted death of

THE IRASCIBLES

Discontented with the Metropolitan Museum of Art's stance on avant-garde painting, a group of American artists, including, Newman, Pollock, Still, and Rothko, wrote a letter to the museum announcing that they would not exhibit in the gallery. After an article in the *New York Herald* criticized their tactics, the group became known as "The Irascible 18". The most vocal of the group was Jackson Pollock, who argued that each era must choose a different artistic style to express the thoughts of contemporary culture.

431 Barnett Newman, Yellow Painting, 1949, 171 × 133 cm (5 ft 7½ in × 52⅜ in)

432 Robert Motherwell, Elegy to the Spanish Republic No. 70, *1961, 175 × 290 cm (5 ft 9 in × 9 ft 6 in)*

a great civilization. Heavy swags of black, like a bull's testicles, hang down the picture space, reminding us that this is the land of bullfights which end with a noble beast slaughtered. There is a sombre dignity and emotional grandeur to *Elegy to the Spanish Republic No. 70 (432)* and at first sight we may only be aware of a massive area of black against the luminous pallor of the background: yet the background shades are subtle greys and a pale blue. The solid black swings up and falls down heavily, fissured by thin and ominous dark lines. Even without the title we would know this is an elegy. Motherwell is mourning, but his grief – a very Spanish touch – has a great nobility of restraint.

PHILIP GUSTON

Philip Guston (1913–80) began painting as an Abstract Expressionist and there are probably still some people who regard the delicate grace of those works as his best. But he underwent a conversion, suffering a revulsion against what he had come to feel was too pretty, and started what we could call a second career as the most plebeian of figurative painters.

The Painter's Table (433), painted towards the end of his life, could be described as uniquely autobiographical: there is the ashtray and still-smoking cigarette; there are the books to keep a painter's mind alert, and there is a paint box with solid squiggles of paint on the lid – a witty reminder of an earlier career as an abstract artist. But the box is closed, pressed down by one of the solid boots which became almost his trademark: life is a heavy business and we are not borne miraculously through it. Dead centre is a wonderful eye, the essential requisite of the painter. Notice, though, that the eye looks through the table into infinity, the painter's task, and that the nail he has driven into the table casts a bleeding red shadow. There are mysterious shapes, too, in the picture, that tease our imaginations; why should a painter's life be fully explicable?

433 Philip Guston, The Painter's Table, *1973, 196 × 229 cm (6 ft 5 in × 7 ft 6 in)*

AMERICAN COLOURISTS

Abstract Expressionism, although it developed increasingly serious implications with its interior subject matter and artistic gaze, also liberated a wonderful flood of abstract art in the next generation of American painters. But to call these artists "the second generation" of Abstract Expressionists is perhaps unhelpful. They reacted against the "self-importance" and theoretical "spirituality" of painters such as Barnett Newman, seeking to free the artistic image from the obsessively metaphysical and make it a purely optical experience.

The painters that followed the Abstract Expressionist movement were less intense in their concentration, but wider and more diverse in the effects they sought. The Abstract Expressionists were profoundly serious – tragedy was essentially their theme – while the Colourists, or "Stainers", used colour to express joy rather than sorrow. They stained canvases with paint or created large areas of colour to communicate visually the wonder of human existence. Colour has an effect on us all: it communicates meaning in its very being, irrespective of image or theme. It was this elementary power that the Colourists relied upon, bypassing the intellect to appeal to a deeper self.

HELEN FRANKENTHALER

American art has several great Colourists. One is Helen Frankenthaler (1928–), whose method of staining the canvas with paint had such a wide influence on painting. She was influenced by Pollock's "all over" painting (see p.369), and her innovative approach is in some ways an extension of Pollock's pouring and dripping process, though the effect is very different. She mixed thin washes and transparent stains and impregnated the bare, untreated canvas with them so that the colour no longer sat on the surface of the canvas, but became the picture surface itself. *Wales (434)* shows her technique in its lovely simplicity, yet the more we look, the more subtle it is.

Frankenthaler demands a place in art history as a pioneer of the staining technique, but this seems relatively unimportant compared with the end to which she put this means. Her style has been well-imitated, but never with such inspired power. The eye moves over *Wales* with continual pleasure: it is a superb example of a work which has no "meaning" and yet provides profound intellectual satisfaction.

MORRIS LOUIS

When Morris Louis (1912–62) visited Frankenthaler's studio in 1954, he learnt from her the technique of using stains as a means of creating, not on the canvas, but in it, making the work seem to

434 Helen Frankenthaler, Wales, 1966, 287 x 114 cm (113 x 45 in)

> *"A bridge between Pollock and all possibilities."*
>
> Morris Louis on Helen Frankenthaler in 1953

STAIN PAINTING
From 1952 a new genre of painting known as "stain painting" was developed by Helen Frankenthaler, who had evolved her own style of Abstract Expressionism (see pp.368-74) under the influences of Jackson Pollock and Arshile Gorky. The technique she developed involved using thinned paint to cover a whole unprimed canvas. The colours, having lost their glossy coating, float into and away from the surface creating nebulous but controllable space, while at the same time the spectator's awareness of the texture of the canvas denies the sense of extended illusion. In 1963 Frankenthaler started to use acrylic paints, which produced the same density of colour saturation but were more controllable.

435 Morris Louis, Beta Kappa, 1961, 262 x 439 cm (8 ft 7 in x 14 ft 5 in)

emerge from its own necessities. *Beta Kappa (435)* (the works are distinguished by Greek letters so that no shade of interpretation may creep into our experience of the paintings) is a late work, one of Louis' series of *Unfurleds*, where diagonal stripes across the canvas create a purely decorative effect. The painting is over 4 m (14 ft) long, yet the area in the centre of the picture has been left daringly bare. We cannot take in, with just one look, the pourings down either side, so we must move between the edges, seeking an integration. Finally, we are forced to submit to the challenging nothingness of the picture, which its coloured borders only make more evident.

RICHARD DIEBENKORN

Not all the great American painters live in New York. Richard Diebenkorn (1922–1994) has lived for many years in San Francisco, and his famous *Ocean Park* series is named after a local suburb there. The wonderful rectangles he paints are both similar to one another and yet completely different. He has found, as Mark Rothko did (see p.370), a format that sets him free to explore the nuances of colour, and it is serious play.

Stripes and diagonals divide *Ocean Park No. 64 (436)* into three sections, differently hued and sized. The absolute verticals highlight the swimming softness of the blue background and the subtle shifts and variations of paint application, so that in this work we really do recall the varying depths of the great Pacific Ocean. But this is also a park, fenced in and bounded both at every edge and from within. Diebenkorn uses colour so creatively that we begin to understand the world a little better.

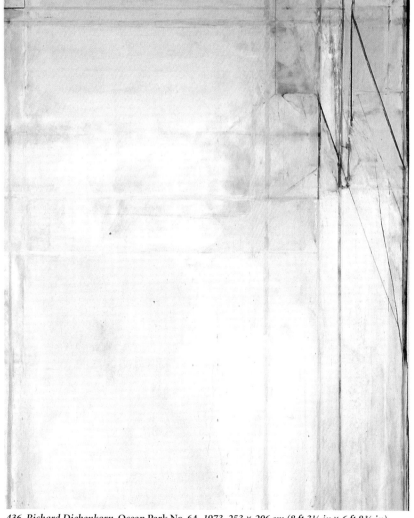

436 Richard Diebenkorn, Ocean Park No. 64, 1973, 253 x 206 cm (8 ft 3½ in x 6 ft 8¾ in)

MINIMALISM

If Abstract Expressionism dominated the 1940s and '50s, Minimalism belonged to the '60s. It grew out of the restrained, spartan art of Abstract Expressionists such as Mark Rothko and Barnett Newman. A broad concept, Minimalism refers either to the paring down of visual variation within an image, or to the degree of artistic effort required to produce it. The result is an art form that is purer and more absolute than any other, stripped of incidental references and uncorrupted by subjectivity.

Ad Reinhardt (1913–67) could be said to be the quintessential Minimalist. He began as an "all-over" painter (see p.379) in the 1940s, but he matured into what he called his "ultimate" paintings in the 1950s: hard-edged, severely minimal abstract works. He darkened his palette and suppressed the contrast between adjacent colours to such an extent that after 1955 his art was restricted to the slow tonalities of deep black and almost-black colours. An inspirational teacher and outspoken theoretician, he believed passionately in reducing art to its purest form and, by extension, to its most spiritually pure state. Within the great luminous expanse of *Abstract Painting No. 5 (437)*, and its smooth, deep, blue-black surface, the artist's hand has

437 Ad Reinhardt, Abstract Painting No. 5, 1962, 152 x 152 cm (5 ft x 5 ft)

AD REINHARDT

In the 1940s Reinhardt passed through his stage of "all-over" painting into a style close to certain of the Abstract Expressionists, particularly Robert Motherwell (see p.374), with whom he jointly edited *Modern Artists in America* in 1950. During the 1950s he turned to monochromatic (usually all-black) paintings and this reduction of his work to pure aesthetic essences reflects his fundamental belief that "Art is art. Everything else is everything else." Reinhardt's radical reduction of art to a simple chromatic abstraction was not initially accepted by the critics, but fellow artists understood his need to liberate art from the confines of contextual judgment.

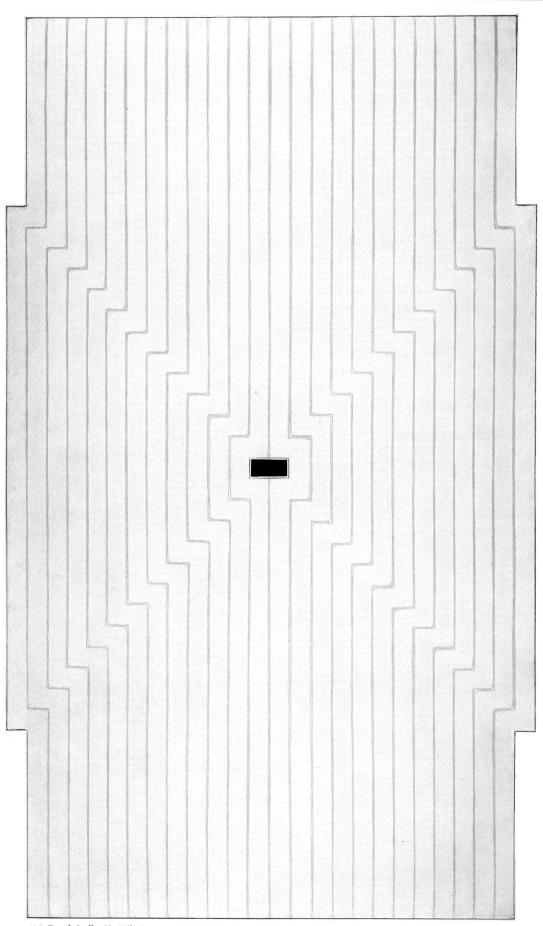

" *...Non-objective, non-representational, non-figurative, non-imagist, non-expressionist, non-subjective.* **"**

Ad Reinhardt, describing Minimalist painting in 1962

STELLA AND MINIMALISM

The trend in minimal art developed in the 1950s in the USA. Only the most simple geometric forms were used. The impersonal nature of the genre is seen as a reaction to the high emotiveness of Abstract Expressionism. In his early work from 1958 to 1960, Frank Stella produced a kind of painting that was more abstract than any before. He confined himself to single colours, at first using black, and then aluminium paint, as in *Six Mile Bottom*, shown here. The artist chose the metallic paint because it has a quality that repels the eye, creating a more abstract appearance. Another striking aspect of Stella's work is that the structures appear to follow the shape of the canvas.

438 Frank Stella, Six Mile Bottom, 1960, 300 x 182 cm (9 ft 8 in x 5 ft 11½ in)

deliberately made itself invisible. We can see, just emerging, the faint outlines of a cross – almost as though Reinhardt himself has not painted it. This is not a Christian cross; if it is a religious icon it is in the broadest sense, with an infinite vertical and an infinite horizontal – the unfathomable dimensions of the human spirit.

FRANK STELLA

Frank Stella (1936–) became a pivotal figure of 1960s' American art. In 1959, he produced a series of controversial pictures for the exhibition "16 Americans" at the Museum of Modern Art in New York. The works he presented were "all-over" unmodulated pictures dissected by strips of untouched canvas, creating severe geometric patterns. He consciously eliminated colour, using black and then silver-coloured aluminium paint to reduce the idea of illusion; even his painting process became systematic and Minimalist. His art ignores the rectangular limits of traditional canvases, reminding us that whatever connotations his paintings may evoke, they remain essentially coloured objects. Often considered merely a shaped pattern, *Six Mile Bottom (438)* is a highly successful work and one could claim that it implies a central order in worldly affairs. The geometric bareness of Stella's early work has been influential, but he developed into such a colourful, exuberant, multi-dimensional artist, continually experimenting and challenging, that one wonders at the stately purity of his early work. Was Stella's explosive buoyancy as yet undiscovered in 1959, or does it lurk within those strange rigidities of *Six Mile Bottom*?

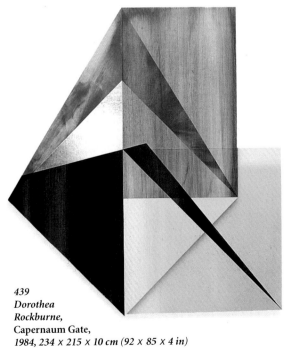

439
Dorothea
Rockburne,
Capernaum Gate,
1984, 234 x 215 x 10 cm (92 x 85 x 4 in)

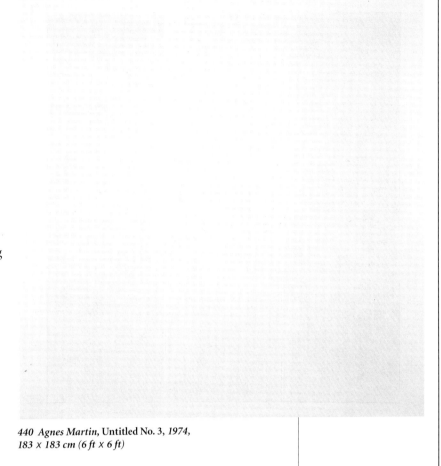

440 Agnes Martin, Untitled No. 3, 1974, *183 x 183 cm (6 ft x 6 ft)*

MARTIN AND ROCKBURNE

There is never going to be universal agreement over contemporary painters but there are some that, to this writer, are of unmistakable greatness: the Canadian, Agnes Martin (1912–), is one. *Untitled No. 3 (440)* is simply a 183-cm (6-ft) square in which a fragile, almost non-colour, border encloses three great strips. The palest of pinks lies in the middle, bordered by two rectangles of watery purple or blue. The gentleness and delicate serenity of this work is exposed to our gaze without anything, as it were, seeming to happen. One has to stay with a Martin, looking as if into the waters of a lake, until the work begins to open up and flower.

With Dorothea Rockburne (1922–) there is much more to grasp and keep hold of. She is a profoundly intellectual artist, often taking her inspiration from Old Masters, and she combines powerful austerity with a great lyrical insight. Some of her most wonderful work has been with oil and gold leaf (like the medieval illuminators) on linen prepared in a traditional way with gesso. She folds and creates geometric majesty from these simple means in *Capernaum Gate (439)*, using the utmost splendour of saturated hues and making us see her work as iconic, as something sacred.

> ### ALL OVER PAINTING
> The term "all-over" painting was first used to describe the "drip" paintings of Jackson Pollock (see p.368). However, since then the term has been applied to any art where the overall treatment of the canvas is relatively uniform in colour or pattern. Often the traditional perception of the canvas having a top, bottom, or centre is no longer viable and the painting becomes purely an experience.

POP ART

It is a moot point as to whether the most extraordinary innovation of 20th-century art was Cubism or Pop Art. Both arose from a rebellion against an accepted style: the Cubists thought Post-Impressionist artists were too tame and limited, while Pop Artists thought the Abstract Expressionists pretentious and over-intense. Pop Art brought art back to the material realities of everyday life, to popular culture (hence "pop"), in which ordinary people derived most of their visual pleasure from television, magazines, or comics.

POP ART

The term "Pop Art" was first used by the English critic Lawrence Alloway in a 1958 issue of *Architectural Digest* to describe those paintings that celebrate post-war consumerism, defy the psychology of Abstract Expressionism, and worship the god of materialism. The most famous of the Pop artists, the cult figure Andy Warhol (shown above), recreated quasi-photographic paintings of people or everyday objects.

Pop Art emerged in the mid 1950s in England, but realized its fullest potential in New York in the '60s where it shared, with Minimalism (see p.377), the attentions of the art world. In Pop Art, the epic was replaced with the everyday and the mass-produced awarded the same significance as the unique; the gulf between "high art" and "low art" was eroding away. The media and advertising were favourite subjects for Pop Art's often witty celebrations of consumer society. Perhaps the greatest Pop artist, whose innovations have affected so much subsequent art, was the American artist, Andy Warhol (1928–87).

WARHOL'S PRINTS

Opinions, in the past, have differed wildly as to whether Warhol was a genius or a con-artist extraordinaire. Having begun his career as a commercial artist, he incorporated commercial photographs into his own work, at first screen printing them himself and then handing the process over to his studio (known as "The Factory"): he devised the work, they executed it. In the *Marilyn Diptych (441)*, the image has deliberately been screen-printed without any special skill or accuracy, and the colour printing on the right is, at best, approximate. Yet the

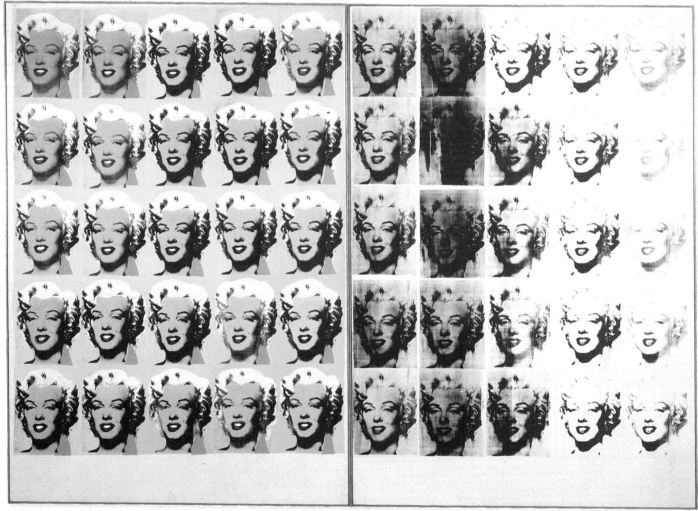

441 Andy Warhol, Marilyn Diptych, 1962, 205 x 145 cm (80¾ x 57 in) each panel

442 Roy Lichtenstein, Whaam, 1963, 173 x 406 cm (5 ft 8 in x 13 ft 4 in)

Marilyn Diptych is an interesting and impressive work, rising from something deep within Warhol's psyche. He was an avid fan of the famous and understood the ephemeral nature of this fame, but he was even more interested in the idea of the American public's devotion to fame as a cultural symbol of his times. In giving herself up to the publicity machine, Monroe was destroyed as a person and Warhol's utterly detached documentary style of portraiture echoes the impersonality and the isolation of this fame. In *Marilyn Diptych* a sea of Monroe faces, alike and yet subtly different, confront us with an iconic mask. It is an unforgettable work.

Roy lichtenstein

Ironically, Warhol's first venture into Pop Art was based on images taken from comic books, but the dealer to whom he showed his work was not interested: he had already been won over by the art of fellow American Roy Lichtenstein (1923–), another of Pop Art's major figures.

There is of course an element of nostalgia in work such as Lichtenstein's – the comic book world is that of childhood and early adolescence with all its innocence and hopes. Lichtenstein saw the iconic dimensions of these images and re-created them on the grand scale favoured by the Abstract Expressionists. His *Whaam (442)* is not an actual transcription from a comic book but an image he has taken and reduced to its essentials, to its streamlined power. *Whaam* is about violence and about how we can remove ourselves from it. The image is a narrative diptych: on one side are the powers of good, the avenging angel of the aeroplane; on the other the powers of evil, the enemy destroyed

in a stylized blaze of punitive power. Lichtenstein uses simple shapes and colours and copies the dot process used in printing to restore us to the simplified world of moral black and white, and to our nostalgic childhood simplicities.

Jasper johns

Dancers on a Plane; Merce Cunningham (443), is Jasper Johns' (1930–) tribute to the work of Merce Cunningham, the avant-garde American choreographer. Visually, *Dancers on a Plane* is extremely beautiful; conceptually, it is extremely

443 Jasper Johns, Dancers on a Plane; Merce Cunningham, 1980, 200 x 162 cm (6 ft 7 in x 5 ft 3½ in)

complex. Johns' supreme gift is to create a demanding concept visually – he so delights the eye that he leads us into mental exploration of this concept. *Dancers on a Plane* shows the complexities of religious fulfilment (how the earthly side of life, the left side, will be divinely transformed after death, the right side) and sexual relationships, the four-dimensional nature of dance movement shown on "one plane", the flat canvas, with the steps matching one another in a partnership. It is a thoroughly rewarding picture which repays the time devoted to its contemplation. Equally, it gives pleasure on the merest glance; Johns satisfies on all levels.

ROBERT RAUSCHENBERG

The influence of Dada and Surrealism on Robert Rauschenberg (1925–) led him to a wholly new art form, using commonplace objects in unusual juxtapositions. Called "combine" paintings, they are Rauschenberg's speciality. *Canyon (445)* is one such work. He has assembled a bewildering *mélange* of images and techniques: oil painting combined with screen-printed photographs, newspaper text, and sheer painterly scrawl. But below this hubbub of intense life hovers the gaunt, outstretched wings of a dead bird. There is a vertiginous sense of soaring, of taking off into the canyon of the unknown. We feel that

445 Robert Rauschenberg, Canyon, 1959, 220 x 179 x 57.5 cm (7 ft 2½ in x 5 ft 10½ in x 22¾ in)

the canyon is not so much in the picture as below it: it is not out there, safely framed, but in here in our own personal space. The ledge on which the bird perches juts out into the viewers' world at a diagonal, and hanging limply from it is a cushion, tightly composed into two sac-like bags that seem weirdly erotic and pathetic. All the elements of the work, two-dimensional as well as three-dimensional, combine into a sense of closure, as though we were truly trapped within the high blank walls of a stone canyon. There can be an inspired lunacy in Rauschenberg which does not always come off, but when it does his images are unforgettable.

DAVID HOCKNEY

Technically, it is true to say that the Pop movement started with Richard Hamilton and David Hockney (1937–) in England. Hockney's early work made superb use of the popular magazine-style images on which much of Pop Art is based. However, when Hockney moved to California in the 1960s, he responded with such artistic depth to the sea, sun, sky, young men, and luxury that his art took on a wholly new, increasingly naturalistic dimension. Though one might consider *A Bigger Splash (444)* a simplistic rather than a simplified view of the world, it nevertheless creates a delightful interplay between the stolid pink verticals of a Los Angeles setting and the exuberance of spray as the unseen diver enters the pool. There is no visible human presence here, just that lonely, empty chair and a bare, almost frozen world. Yet that wild white splash can only come from another human, and a great deal of Hockney's psyche is involved in the mix of lucidity and confusion of this picture.

444 David Hockney, A Bigger Splash, 1967, 243 x 244 cm (7 ft 11⅔ in x 8 ft)

EUROPEAN FIGURATIVE PAINTING

While Abstraction obsessed American artists for decades, the human figure never lost its significance in European painting. England eventually challenged American pride in the 1970s with a school of painters that included Lucian Freud and Frank Auerbach. British artists on the whole do not form "schools", and seem to work alone, which is perhaps indicative of a national tendency towards eccentricity.

The strangely disturbing figurative art of Balthus (1908–), a Frenchman of Polish descent, has never been linked to a European school or movement. Balthus, the nickname used by Count Balthasar Klossowski de Rola since the age of 13, works in isolation with a classic majesty that can seem quite incongruous in our hectically unaristocratic age. His art is effective because this quiet sense of hierarchy comes naturally to him. Haunted by the griefs of our modern times, he chooses to deal with them obliquely, rather as Matisse did. His art is enigmatic, infused with a dignified stillness and monumentality.

BALTHUS

In the most sensitive and subtle of ways *The Game of Cards (446)* is concerned with awakening sexuality. Both young people have childlike bodies, but their facial expressions indicate that they are on the verge of entering a new world of sexual interplay. Their innocence, soon to be lost in bodily consciousness, moves Balthus, and he shares with us his emotional sympathy and his pleasure in their "game".

The Game of Cards is obviously about far more than the title suggests: the young people cannot look at one another directly without flirtatious timidity. Both reach out with one

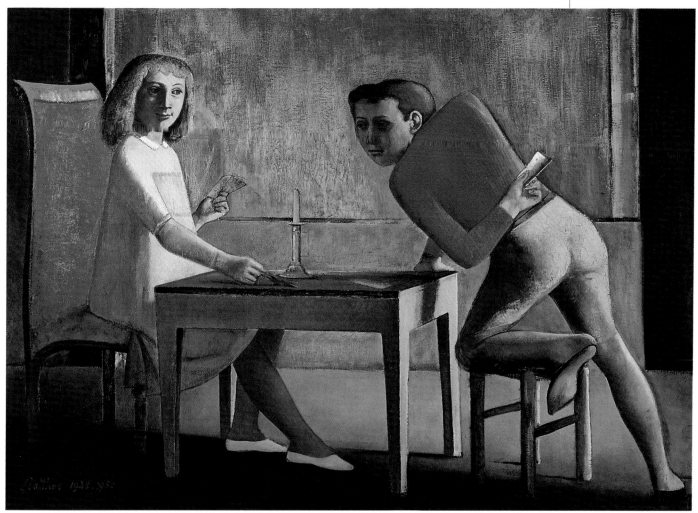

446 Balthus, The Game of Cards, *1948–50, 140 x 194 cm (55 x 76 in)*

FRANCIS BACON

In 1945 British art was reawakened by the arrival of Francis Bacon. Many of Bacon's paintings were unreservedly violent, showing isolation and despair, using smudged paint and distorted human figures. Bacon proclaimed that the violence was inherent in the act of painting itself – in the struggle to remake reality on the canvas.

hand while drawing back with the other. The girl offers not only her hand but her delicate feet in her white plimsolls, edged towards the boy. The boy is barricaded behind a table, determined to keep his secrets to himself (his unshod feet point away from her) and yet, as the angle of his body suggests, he is deeply attracted to her.

Everything in this picture is symbolic: the great protective chair against which the girl does not lean, the low, unprotected stool which is all the young male has for support, even the mysterious brightness of the upper background and the shadows in which the activity is taking place. Is the candle at the centre of the table a sacred image, a votive candle, or is it a phallic image, indicative of what is to come? It is certainly not a source of light because it is unlit. There are clear ambiguities present here, but no answer is given. Balthus does not prophesy.

FRANCIS BACON

By the 1970s a London School had emerged, though it did not share the same qualities as the pre-war Paris or post-war New York Schools, where the artists frequently met and shared their ideas. It included several major artists, of whom the best known is the Irishman Francis Bacon (1909–92), who moved to London in 1925.

Bacon is under reassessment: is his work a terrible indictment of the human condition, or did he wantonly create chaos for the wicked fun of it? Bacon, however, is very far from fun. His early works most certainly convey a great weight of grief and doubt, while his later paintings are overwhelmingly oppressive. Balthus' art reveals a secretive world full of obsession; Bacon's work exposes a world riddled with horror and anxiety.

Portrait of Isabel Rawsthorne Standing in a Street in Soho (447) has a deliberately long-winded title. The picture is tightly framed, with Bacon's friend entrapped like a bull in a ring, an arena. The curved wheel of a passing motor car suggests the horn of a bull at the same time. The woman presents an image of wary tension as she looks around quickly, her skirt aswirl with motion. The dullness of the long title adds force to her plight: a street in London's Soho – and such anxiety? Her face is hideous with brooding concentration, yet we can see that she is beautiful. She is ready to break loose from her cage.

Bacon developed a unique and inimitable technique which included rubbing the canvas with various cloths, chosen for their different textures, to smudge and blur the paint. He also used dramatic contrasts of thin and thick paint, which he applied to the canvas with a violence akin to defacement. In this picture, Bacon has splattered wet paint in several places to indicate the role of chance, of uncertainty and risk. Not even the great coiled spring of a female can be certain of her freedom. By involving us emotionally, he shows the mark of a great painter.

LEON KOSSOFF

Two other British artists are of European-Jewish origin. Frank Auerbach (1931–) and Leon Kossoff (1926–) were both taught by the painter David Bomberg, whose art went neglected by the world until after his death (see column, p.385). Both are awesomely dedicated, working full-time in their studios, Auerbach encrusting his early work with more and more paint until it came alive and Kossoff incessantly repainting the same familiar places and people. Both work from life; Bacon painted from memory, believing that the elusive qualities of the human presence were more honestly recreated by an equivalent painterly ambiguity.

447 Francis Bacon, **Portrait of Isabel Rawsthorne Standing in a Street in Soho,** *1967, 198 x 147 cm (78 x 58 in)*

Kossoff is like the great Swiss sculptor and painter, Alberto Giacometti (see p.365), who each night scratched out the day's work, never satisfied. For Kossoff too, painting becomes a repeated exercise, and he gains new insights through his experimentation. Then, suddenly, he understands visually and the picture is begun and finished very quickly. The sweep of his hurried paint is clearly visible as he drives himself to catch the truth before it vanishes once more. In a sense it is his own truth that he forever pursues, since the things he paints are the intimate companions of his own life.

Kossoff's aged parents are portrayed in *Two Seated Figures No. 2 (448)*, a subject that he has brooded over productively for years. Every part of their body language is intelligible to him, but he must make visual sense of it and portray this couple with fitting dignity. Unembarrassed, Kossoff paints with a keen observation: his father, a hard-working man, is now too old to be a true consort to his wife. He crouches awkwardly in his chair, seemingly unsure of himself.

Kossoff has said that his parents "obsessed" him as a subject. Here he is coming to grips with the changes in parental dominance as he has previously known it, and with the changes in the marital relationship itself. But he looks on with the steady love of the observer, admitting no grief, playing with no explicit memories. It is a marvellously reticent painting, and all the more moving for that restraint.

*449 Frank Auerbach, **The Sitting Room**, 1964, 128 x 128 cm (50⅓ x 50⅓ in)*

FRANK AUERBACH

Auerbach, like Kossoff, paints only deeply loved, personal things. He tries with a passion to capture their essence and always fails. But he fails gloriously. He spent nearly a year on *The Sitting Room (449)*, in the home of E.O.W., one of his few constant models, and he painted her there three times a week. Here is where they are most intimate, the model in one chair and her daughter in another, where every object has meaning for both of them. What he wants to show is not the bare sight of the room, but the sense of it seen anew each time.

Auerbach's images are built up of flat shapes of solid colour, so that the depth in each picture has to be sought for. The surfaces of his early paintings are built up to the degree of a sculpted relief, the great gouges and mounds of paint taking on an almost independent reality. The earthy colours in *The Sitting Room* have an emotional rightness, for this is his soul's soil, from which his art grows. He has painted and repainted endlessly, refusing to dramatize or play the illusory games of an illustrator. Suddenly the image coheres and moves forward from its obscurity. The human memory is never reliably sharp: the certainty is vital but the forms often cannot be strictly delineated.

*448 Leon Kossoff, **Two Seated Figures No. 2**, 1980, 244 x 183 cm (8 ft x 6 ft)*

LUCIAN FREUD

Lucian Freud, like Francis
Bacon, has a serious claim
to be considered as part of
the story of painting. He
has painted landscapes,
still lifes, and portraits,
but his most powerful
art deals with the naked
human body. He sees it in
all its chromatic wonder
and its astonishing
vulnerability. He almost
seems to paint what is
underneath the skin,
exposing the secret truth
of his models, all of whom
are people he knows well.
His desire is not to create
paintings that are like the
subjects, but that are the
subjects, so that there are
two realities, one on the
canvas, one walking free.

LUCIAN FREUD

Lucian Freud (1922–), grandson of the German
psychoanalyst Sigmund Freud, is a resolutely
realist artist, and frighteningly so. He began by
painting tightly-controlled, Surrealist-influenced
portraits and still lifes and rarely painted nudes
before 1965–66; yet he subsequently painted
some of the most powerful and original nude
pictures in Western painting. Freud developed
an increasingly "fleshy" style, seeking ways of
conveying the physical reality of humans in a
concrete world with ever greater intensity, and
with an increasing interest in the wonder of
skin tones. He directs a clinical eye on his
subject that is chilling in its objectivity.

Standing by the Rags (450) is a recent work
and a superb example of Freud at his greatest.
He shows us a woman in all her raw fleshiness
standing in the full exposure of the sunlight.
It is almost as if Freud paints beneath the skin
with his dazzling sensitivity to the variations
in her skin tone. These pinks, blues, and yellows

450 Lucian Freud, Standing by the Rags, *1988–89, 169 x 138 cm (66½ x 54⅓ in)*

451 Anselm Kiefer, Parsifal 1, 1973,
325 x 220 cm (10 ft 8 in x 7 ft 2½ in)

importance of his theme obscures our judgment here: only time will tell. *Parsifal 1 (451)* is from a series based on the Wagner opera. The theme is a weighty one, and critics have seen these works as an expression of the roughly hewn nature of the true Germanic spirit, as well as a meditation on the nature and growth of an individual artist. Kiefer uses unusual techniques, so that the overlapping strips of wallpaper, laid horizontally across one another and painted black at the edges, physically look like floorboards of rough wood. This wood echoes the great forests of his native land and every swirl and textural mark seems to bear some great significance for him.

GEORG BASELITZ

Those unacquainted with contemporary art may well feel an ironic gratitude to Georg Baselitz (1938–) because his work is immediately recognizable. His almost invariable inversion of his images has been criticized as a gimmick: why, after all, are the two figures in *Adieu (452)* upside down? The intention is in fact a serious and aesthetic one: he wants to use the human figure with an almost abstract freedom so that his work is not easily understood and, as too often happens, forgotten. As we puzzle over the upturned figures and the strange "starter flag" of the background, we absorb something of the artist's power and his fascination and delight in evading familiar constructions. It is too early to know how important an artist he is, but he is a good example of an interesting contemporary about whom we can make up our own minds.

are visually extraordinary – have we ever seen skin like this before? The woman plunges down towards us; the floorboards beneath her feet provide the only perspective and are so vertiginous that we instinctively move back, as if she were to fall out on top of us. Despite their wild disarray, the rags are safely tucked away behind her, barricaded by her bent arm and the weighty flesh of her body. These rags are among some of the most beautiful things Freud has ever painted. They gleam with a soft luminosity, their whiteness extending from deep shadows of grey through all possible intermediate tones up to a sharp pallor. The firm human flesh is played off against the loose compression of the rag pile. The woman is limited by the definition of her shape; the rag pile extends indefinitely in three directions. Every aspect of this disjuncture delights Freud's painterly heart.

ANSELM KIEFER

Among today's German artists, many critics would back Anselm Kiefer (1945–) for his staying power: he is a romantic painter, an expressionist in the German Expressionist tradition with a deep need to give visual form to the idea of repentance. His subject matter largely revolves around the terrible injustices suffered by the Jews in Germany, and it may be that the

452 Georg Baselitz, Adieu, 1982, 205 x 300 cm (6 ft 8¾ in x 9 ft 10 in)

EPILOGUE

This is both an afterword and a foreword: hundreds and thousands of artists come after the disappearance of the "story line" into the maze of contemporary artistic experience and these same artists may of course be the forerunners of a new story. In the present context of the end of the century it is impossible to know which threads will lead us through the maze and which are in fact dead-ends. I can only then give a very personal, subjective sample of contemporary art and single out just three artists who I hope will endure.

One – Robert Natkin – is a senior artist and a supreme colourist who has up until recently resisted being called an abstract painter. Clearly, to Natkin every part of his canvas is vital with what he calls narrative interest. A communication is being made, visually – an experience is being enacted; but this event, so searching and enriching to the spirit, is carried out by means of shapes and colours, integrating into a wholeness. Natkin floats his colours on, denies them, deepens them, teases them into new complexities, always with a masterly elegance that is overwhelmingly beautiful. *Farm Street (453)* is one of a series inspired by worship at Farm Street, a Jesuit Church in central London. The picture offers the viewer an entry into worship, not just the painter's but our own. It is a humbling and uplifting work, with its wonderful luminosities. Yet Natkin offends many critics by being too beautiful, purity being suspect in these days of dilemma.

453 **Robert Natkin**, Farm Street, *1991, 152 x 183 cm (60 x 72 in)*

454 Joan Mitchell, Sunflowers, 1990–91, 280 x 400 cm (110¼ x 157½ in)

The great Joan Mitchell also offends with her beauty, but she saves herself in overcritical circles by drawing the beauty, not just from her own vision, like Natkin, but from the seen world. Her home for many years was in Giverny where Claude Monet had made his home and miraculous garden (see p.297), but she asserted that she never looked at the view. The "view" is in her own house, the flowers on the table or in the garden, and she paints them with enormous grace and compassion. *Sunflowers (454)* has almost the sad glory of Van Gogh's version. It is a theme that Mitchell has painted many times. She has said "If I see a sunflower drooping I can droop with it, and draw it and feel it until its death."

MODERN RELIGIOUS ART

The Renaissance marks the high point of religious art but since then it has almost died out. It is therefore all the more astonishing then that contemporary Britain should produce an artist like Albert Herbert. A profoundly educated painter, who paints from his own inner experience, his own need, he creates biblical images of astonishing conviction. Here is Jonah, happily journeying within the security of his whale, and real life, represented by its goose girl and her geese, threaten and alarm him. In *Jonah and the Whale (455)* Herbert is using biblical imagery to express powerfully and magnificently a truth about the human heart.

455 Albert Herbert, Jonah and the Whale, c. 1988, 28 x 35 cm (11 x 14 in)

The story of painting continues, even if the chapter we are in is not ready to be read. It will in the end be read and appreciated, just as we appreciate the art of the past. We have the adventure of looking at contemporary art without guidelines or labels, and that is a precious part of the story.

GLOSSARY

Abstract art Art that does not represent objects or people from the observable world.

Acrylic paint A type of paint made with a synthetic acrylic resin as the medium. It dries more quickly than oil paints (see column, p.376).

Altarpiece A religious work of art placed above and behind the altar.

Annunciation A popular subject in Gothic, Renaissance and Counter-Reformation art: the moment of the announcement to the Virgin Mary by the Angel Gabriel that she shall concieve and bear a son and that he shall be called Jesus (see column, p.63).

Byzantine Esssentially Christian art produced in the Eastern Roman Empire between the 5th century AD and 1453, when Constantinople fell to the Turks.

Chiaroscuro (Italian: "light dark") The technique of suggesting three-dimensional form by varying tones of light and dark paint.

Complementary colour The true contrast of any colour. The complementary of each primary colour – red, blue, and yellow – is the combination of the other two. Red and green; blue and orange; and yellow and violet are the basic pairs. In painting, placing complementary colours next to each other makes both appear brighter.

Diptych A picture made up of two panels, usually hinged (see column, p.54).

Donor The commissioner of a painting, who in medieval and Renaissance art, is often portrayed within the painting.

En plein air (French: "in the open air") Painting out of doors.

Fetish An object, often sculpted, that was believed to be the embodiment of a spirit.

Foreshortening A technique for depicting an object at an angle to the plane of the picture by making use of perspective so that the object appears shorter and narrower as it recedes.

Fresco The wall-painting technique in which pigment, mixed with water, is applied to a layer of wet plaster. When dry, the wall and the colours are inseparable. This is known as *buon fresco* or true fresco. *Fresco secco* refers to the technique of applying paint to dry plaster.

Genre painting Paintings depicting scenes from daily life.

Grisaille A monochrome painting in shades of grey. Renaissance artists used it to imitate the look of sculptural relief.

Ground A preparatory surface of primer or paint applied to the canvas before painting.

Icon A painting on a panel depicting Christ, the Virgin Mary, or a saint in a traditional Byzantine style.

Immaculate Conception In Christian theology, the doctrine that the Virgin Mary was conceived without the stain of original sin.

Impasto A thick layer of paint.

Intimism A style adopted by a sub-group of the Nabis, in which bourgeois domestic interiors are depicted in an informal and intimate way.

Japonisme The influence of Japan on European art, in particular Impressionist and Post-Impressionist painting.

Maestà (Italian: "majesty") An altarpiece showing the Madonna and Child enthroned and surrounded by saints and angels.

Medium In paint, the vehicle (substance) that binds the pigment – for instance, in oil paint the medium

is an oil (poppy oil, etc.); in tempera the medium is egg.

Odalisque A female slave or concubine.

Oil painting Painting in which oils such as linseed, walnut, or poppy are used as the medium binding the pigment.

Painterly The rendering of form by means of colour rather than outline.

Palette-knife pictures Paintings in which the paint is applied and manipulated with a palette knife.

Panel A painting on wood (see column, p.75).

Passion The sufferings of Christ between the Last Supper and His Crucifixion.

Perspective A system of depicting a three-dimensional form on a two-dimensional surface. In linear perspective, objects are depicted in diminishing size and parallel lines converge with increasing distance.

Primary colours The three colours from which all others are derived – red, yellow, and blue.

Scumbling A technique in which a thin layer of paint is unevenly applied over another layer to create a broken effect as areas of the under colour show through.

Sfumato A soft, smoky effect, created by colours and tones overlapping and blending, changing imperceptibly from light to dark (see column, p.116).

Still life A painting or drawing of inanimate objects.

Tempera Paint in which pigment is dissolved in water and mixed with gum or egg yolk.

Tondo A circular painting.

Tooth The irregular texture of a canvas, which enables paint to adhere.

INDEX

PICTURE CREDITS

Every effort has been made to trace the copyright holders and we apologize in advance for any unintentional omissions. We would be pleased to insert the appropriate acknowledgement in any subsequent edition of this publication.

INTRODUCTION

1. Altamira cave/Ancient Art and Architecture Collection **2.** Lascaux cave/Ancient Art and Architecture Collection **3.** Hirmar Fotoarchiv **4.** Tomb of Ramose, Thebes/Mary Jellife/Ancient Art Architecture Collection **5.** The Trustees of The British Museum, London **6.** The Trustees of The British Museum, London **7.** Tomb of Nefermaat, Medum/Ancient Art and Architecture Collection **8.** National Archaeological Museum, Athens/ Bridgeman Art Library, London **9.** Palace of Knossos, Crete/Sonia Halliday Photographs **10.** Museo Heraklion, Crete/Scala **11.** National Archaeological Museum, Athens **12.** Staatliche Antikensammlung Munich/Bridgeman Art Library, London **13.** Antiken Museum, Basel und Sammlung Ludwig /Foto Clare Niggli **14.** Colorphoto Hans Hinz **15.** Museo Nazionale, Athens/Scala **16.** Acropolis Museum, Athens **17.** Museo delle Terme, Rome/Scala **18.** Archiv für Kunst und Geschichte, Berlin **19.** Museo Nazionale, Naples **20.** Fratelli Fabbri, Milan/Bridgeman Art Library, London **21.** Museo Nazionale, Napoli/Scala **22.** The Vatican Museum, Vatican/ Ancient Art and Architecture Collection **23.** Archaeological Museum, Naples/ Bridgeman Art Library, London **24.** Metropolitan Museum of Art, New York/ Bridgeman Art Library, London **25.** Museo Nazionale, Naples/Scala **26.** Museo Nazionale, Naples **27.** The Trustees of the British Museum, London **28.** Ancient Art and Architecture Collection **29.** Courtauld Institute Galleries, London **30.** Catacombe di Priscilla, Rome/Scala **31.** San Vitale, Ravenna/Scala **32.** Monastery of Saint Catherine, Mount Sinai/ Ancient Art and Architecture Collection **33.** Duomo, Monreale/ Scala **34.** Gallerie Statale Trat'Jakov, Moscow/Scala **35.** Gallerie Statale Trat'Jakov, Moscow/ Bridgeman Art Library, London **36.** Museu Nacional d'Art de Catalunya/ Calveras/Sagrista **37.** By permission of The British Library, London **38.** The Board of Trinity College, Dublin **39.** The British Library, London/Bridgeman Art Library, London **40.** The Board of Trinity College, Dublin **41.** By permission of The British Library, London **42.** By permission of The British Library, London **43.** Bibliothéque Nationale, Paris **44.** City of Bayeux/Bridgeman Art Library, London **45.** By Courtesy of the Board of Trustees of the V&A, Victoria and Albert Museum, London **46.** Österreichische Nationalbibliothek, Vienna **47.** The Trustees of The British Museum, London **48.** S. Cecilia Trastevere, Rome/Scala

GOTHIC

49. Bibliotheque Nationale, Paris/ Bridgeman Art Library, London **50.** Sainte Chapelle, Paris/Sonia Halliday Photographs **51.** Uffizi, Florence/Scala **52.** Museo dell'Opera Metropolitana, Siena/Scala **53.** Museo dell'Opera Metropolitana, Siena/Scala **54.** Samuel H Kress Collection, National Gallery of Art, Washington DC **55.** Samuel H Kress Collection, National Gallery of Art, Washington DC **56.** Scrovegni Chapel, Padua/Scala **57.** Scrovegni Chapel, Padua/Scala **58.** Uffizi, Florence/Scala **59.** Samuel H Kress Collection, National Gallery of Art, Washington DC **60.** Walker Art Gallery, Liverpool/Board of Trustees of the National Museums and Galleries on Merseyside **61.** Courtesy of Board of Trustees The National Gallery, London **62.** Palazzo Publico, Siena/Scala **63.** Louvre, Paris/Bridgeman Art Library, London **64.** Courtesy of Board of Trustees The National Gallery, London **65.** Musée Conde, Chantilly/Giraudon/ Bridgeman Art Library, London **66.** Musée Conde, Chantilly/ Giraudon/Bridgeman Art Library, London **67.** Uffizi, Florence/Scala **68.** Louvre, Paris/©Photo Ph.Sebert **69.** Courtesy of Board of Trustees The National Gallery, London **70.** Bibliotheque Nationale, Paris/ Courtauld Institute Galleries, London **71.** National Gallery of Art, Washington DC **72.** Musée des Beaux Arts, Dijon **73.** Courtesy of Board of Trustees The National Gallery, London **74.** Courtesy of Board of Trustees The National Gallery, London **75.** Samuel H Kress Collection, National Gallery of Art, Washington DC **76.** Cathedral of St Bavo, Ghent/Giraudon/ Bridgeman Art Library, London **77.** Andrew W Mellon Collection, National Gallery of Art, Washington DC **78.** Courtesy of Board of Trustees The National Gallery, London **79.** Louvre, Paris/Giraudon **80.** By Permission of Birmingham Museum and Art Gallery **81.** Museo del Prado, Madrid **82.** Andrew W Mellon Collection, National Gallery of Art, Washington DC **83.** Uffizi, Florence/Scala **84.** Andrew W Mellon Collection, National Gallery of Art, Washington DC **85.** Courtesy of Board of Trustees The National Gallery, London **86.** Andrew W Mellon Collection, National Gallery of Art, Washington DC **87.** Museu Nacional de Arte Antiga, Lisbon/Bridgeman Art Library, London **88.** Louvre, Paris/© Photo Ph.Sebert **89.** Louvre, Paris/© Photo Ph.Sebert **90.** Samuel H Kress Collection, National Gallery of Art, Washington, DC **91.** Colmar/ Bridgeman Art Library, London **92.** Samuel H Kress Collection, National Gallery of Art, Washington DC

ITALIAN RENAISSANCE

93. Courtesy of Board of Trustees The National Gallery, London **94.** Branacci Chapel, Florence/Scala **95.** Santa Maria Novella, Florence/ Scala **96.** Chiesa del Carmine, Florence/Scala **97.** Andrew W Mellon Collection, National Gallery of Art, Washington DC **98.** Courtesy of Board of Trustees The National Gallery, London **99.** The National Gallery, London **100.** Samuel H Kress Collection, National Gallery of Art, Washington DC **101.** Courtesy of Board of Trustees The National Gallery, London **102.** Ashmolean Museum, Oxford **103.** Louvre, Paris/© Photo Ph. Sebert **104.** Museo di Marco, Florence/Scala **105.** Louvre, Paris/© Photo Ph.Sebert **106.** Courtesy of Board of Trustees, The National Gallery, London **107.** Samuel H Kress Collection, National Gallery of Art, Washington, DC **108.** Courtesy of Board of Trustees The National Gallery, London **109.** Uffizi, Florence/Scala **110.** Uffizi, Florence/Scala **111.** Andrew W Mellon Collection, National Gallery of Art, Washington DC **112.** Samuel H Kress Collection, National Gallery of Art, Washington DC **113.** Samuel H Kress Collection, National Gallery of Art Washington, DC **114.** Courtesy of Board of Trustees The National Gallery, London **115.** San Francesco, Arezzo/Scala **116.** Pinacoteca Communale Sansepolcro/Scala **117.** Museo del Prado, Madrid **118.** Samuel H Kress Collection, National Gallery of Art, Washington DC **119.** The National Gallery of Ireland, Dublin **120.** Photo Richard Carafetti, Widener Collection, National Gallery of Art, Washington DC **121.** Courtesy of Board of Trustees The National Gallery, London **122.** Courtesy of Board of Trustees The National Gallery, London **123.** Courtesy of Board of Trustees The National Gallery, London **124.** Samuel H Kress Collection, National Gallery of Art, Washington DC **125.** Widener Collection, National Gallery of Art, Washington DC **126.** Courtesy of Board of Trustees The National Gallery, London **127.** Galleria Nazionale della Sicilia, Parma/ Scala **128.** Samuel H Kress Collection, National Gallery of Art, Washington DC **129.** Samuel H Kress Collection, National Gallery of Art, Washington DC **130.** Samuel H Kress Collection, National Gallery of Art, Washington DC **131.** Samuel H Kress Collection, National Gallery of Art, Washington DC **132.** Ailsa Mellon Bruce Fund, National Gallery of Art, Washington DC **133.** Andrew W Mellon Collection, National Gallery of Art, Washington DC **134.** Accademia, Venice/Scala **135.** Uffizi, Florence/ Scala **136.** Louvre, Paris/© Photo Ph.Sebert **137.** Czartorisky Museum, Krakow/Scala **138.** Ailsa Mellon Bruce Fund, National Gallery of Art, Washington DC **139.** Courtesy of Board of Trustees The National Gallery, London **140.** Andrew W Mellon Collection, National Gallery of Art, Washington DC **141.** Santa Maria Novella, Florence/Scala **142.** Uffizi, Florence/ Scala **143.** Sistine Chapel, Vatican/© Nippon Television Network Corporation 1994 **144.** Sistine Chapel, Vatican © Nippon Television Network Corporation 1994 **145.** Sistine Chapel, Vatican/Scala **146.** Sistine Chapel, Vatican/© Nippon Television Network Corporation 1994 **147.** Andrew W Mellon Collection, National Gallery of Art Washington DC **148.** Andrew W Mellon Collection, National Gallery of Art, Washington DC **149.** Photo José Naranjo, Widener Collection, National Gallery of Art, Washington DC **150.** Andrew W Mellon Collection, National Gallery of Art, Washington DC **151.** Samuel H Kress Collection, National Gallery of Art, Washington DC **152.** Stanze di Raffaello, Vatican/Scala **153.** Accademia, Venice/Scala **154.** Kunsthistorisches Museum, Vienna **155.** Samuel H Kress Collection, National Gallery of Art, Washington DC **156.** Courtesy of Board of Trustees The National Gallery, London **157.** Samuel H Kress Collection, National Gallery of Art, Washington DC **158.** Widener Collection, National Gallery of Art, Washington DC **159.** Samuel H Kress Collection, National Gallery of Art, Washington DC **160.** San Giorgio Maggiore, Venice/Scala **161.** Samuel H Kress Collection, National Gallery of Art, Washington DC **162.** Samuel H Kress Collection, National Gallery of Art, Washington DC **163.** Samuel H Kress Collection, National Gallery of Art, Washington DC **164.** Andrew W Mellon Collection, National Gallery of Art, Washington DC **165.** Uffizi, Florence/ Scala **166.** Santa Felicità, Florence/Scala **167.** Courtesy of Board of Trustees The National Gallery, London **168.** Samuel H Kress Collection, National Gallery of Art, Washington DC **169.** Samuel H Kress Collection, National Gallery of Art, Washington DC **170.** Courtesy of Board of Trustees The National Gallery, London **171.** Samuel H Kress Collection, National Gallery of Art, Washington DC **172.** Louvre, Paris/© Photo Ph.Sebert **173.** Uffizi, Florence/ Scala **174.** Samuel H Kress Collection, National Gallery of Art, Washington DC **175.** Samuel H Kress Collection, National Gallery of Art, Washington DC **176.** Pinacoteca Nazionale, Siena/ Scala **177.** Widener Collection, National Gallery of Art, Washington DC **178.** Samuel H Kress Collection, National Gallery of Art, Washington DC

NORTHERN RENAISSANCE

179. Museo del Prado, Madrid **180.** Samuel H Kress Collection, National Gallery of Art, Washington DC **181.** Blauel/ Gnamm Artothek, München Alte Pinakothek **182.** Courtesy of Board of Trustees The National Gallery, London **183.** Gift of Clarence Y Palitz, National Gallery of Art, Washington DC **184.** Ralph and Mary Booth Collection, National Gallery of Art, Washington DC **185.** Samuel H Kress Collection, National Gallery of Art, Washington DC **186.** National Gallery of Art, Washington DC **187.** Courtesy of Board of Trustees The National Gallery, London **188.** Kustmuseum, Basel/ Colorphoto Hans Hinz, Basel **189.** Andrew W Mellon Collection, National Gallery of Art, Washington DC **190.** Ailsa Mellon Bruce Fund, National Gallery of Art, Washington DC **191.** Joachim Blauel, Artothek, München Alte Pinakothek **192.** Louvre, Paris/© Photo Ph.Sebert **193.** Louvre, Paris/© Photo Ph.Sebert **194.** Courtesy of Board of Trustees, The National Gallery, London **195.** Kunsthistoriches Museum, Vienna **196.** Museo del Prado, Madrid **197.** Courtesy of Board of Trustees The National Gallery, London **198.** Blauel/Gnamm Artothek/ München Alte Pinakothek **199.** Kunsthistorisches Museum, Vienna **200.** Kunsthistorisches Museum, Vienna **201.** Kunsthistorisches Museum, Vienna **202.** Kunsthistorisches Museum, Vienna

BAROQUE AND ROCOCO

203. Hermitage, St Petersburg/Scala **204.** Uffizi, Florence/ Scala **205.** Louvre, Paris/RMN, Paris **206.** Courtesy of Board of Trustees The National Gallery, London **207.** Ailsa Mellon Bruce Fund, National Gallery of Art, Washington DC **208.** The Royal Collection, Kensington Palace, London/© Her Majesty The Queen **209.** Uffizi, Florence/ Scala **210.** Courtesy of Board of Trustees The National Gallery, London **211.** Doria Pamphili Gallery, Rome/Scala **212.** Courtesy of Board of Trustees, The National Gallery, London **213.** Courtesy of Board of Trustees, The National Gallery, London **214.** Courtesy of Board of Trustees, The National Gallery, London **215.** Louvre, Paris/RMN, Paris **216.** By Permission of Governors of Dulwich Picture Gallery **217.** Antwerp Cathedral/ Visual Arts Library **218.** Andrew W Mellon Fund, National Gallery of Art, Washington DC **219.** Louvre, Paris/RMN, Paris **220.** Courtesy of Board of Trustees The National Gallery, London **221.** Louvre, Paris/© Photo Ph.Sebert **222.** Samuel H Kress Foundation, National Gallery of Art, Washington DC **223.** Widener Collection, National Gallery of Art, Washington DC **224.** Louvre, Paris/© Photo Ph.Sebert **225.** Musées Royaux des Beaux Arts du Belgique, Brussels **226.** Museo del Prado, Madrid **227.** Museo del Prado, Madrid **228.** Museo del Prado, Madrid **229.** Museo del Prado, Madrid **230.** Collection Contini Bonacossi **231.** Louvre, Paris/RMN, Paris **232.** Museo del Prado, Madrid

233. Widener Collection, National Gallery of Art, Washington DC
234. Staatliches Kunstinstitut Frankfurt/Arthothek
235. Staatliche Museen Kassel, Gemaldegalerie Alte Meister
236. Andrew W Mellon Collection, National Gallery of Art, Washington DC **237.** Widener Collection, National Gallery of Art, Washington DC **238.** Andrew W Mellon Collection, National Gallery of Art, Washington DC
239. Rijksmuseum Foundation, Amsterdam **240.** Louvre, Paris/RMN, Paris **241.** Andrew W Mellon Fund, National Gallery of Art, Washington DC **242.** Widener Collection, National Gallery of Art, Washington DC **243.** Mauritshuis, The Hague **244.** Rijksmuseum Foundation, Amsterdam
245. Andrew W Mellon Collection, National Gallery of Art, Washington DC **246.** Frans Hals Museum, Haarlem **247.** Andrew W Mellon Collection, National Gallery of Art, Washington DC
248. Courtesy of Board of Trustees The National Gallery, London
249. Courtesy of Board of Trustees The National Gallery, London
250. Widener Collection, National Gallery of Art, Washington DC
251. Courtesy of Board of Trustees The National Gallery, London
252. Timken Collection, National Gallery of Art, Washington DC
253. Samuel H Kress Foundation, National Gallery of Art, Washington DC **254.** Louvre, Paris/RMN, Paris **255.** Louvre, Paris/Giraudon **256.** Earl of Plymouth: On loan to the National Museum of Wales **257.** Ailsa Mellon Bruce Fund, National Gallery of Art, Washington DC
258. Courtesy of Board of Trustees, The National Gallery, London
259. Ashmolean Museum, Oxford
260. Samuel H Kress Collection, National Gallery of Art, Washington DC **261.** Ailsa Mellon Bruce Fund, National Gallery of Art, Washington DC **262.** Louvre, Paris/© Photo Ph.Sebert
263. Samuel H Kress Collection, National Gallery of Art, Washington DC **264.** Louvre, Paris/© Photo Ph.Sebert
265. Chester Dale Collection, National Gallery of Art, Washington DC **266.** Samuel H Kress Collection, National Gallery of Art, Washington DC **267.** Gift of Mrs Mellon Bruce in Memory of her Father, Andrew W Mellon, National Gallery of Art, Washington DC **268.** Samuel H Kress Collection, National Gallery of Art, Washington DC
269. Samuel H Kress Collection, National Gallery of Art, Washington DC **270.** Andrew W Mellon Collection, National Gallery of Art, Washington DC
271. Museo Ca Rezzonico, Venice/Bridgeman Art Library, London
272. Samuel H Kress Collection, National Gallery of Art, Washington DC **273.** Samuel H Kress Collection, National Gallery of Art, Washington DC
274. Courtesy of Board of Trustees The National Gallery, London
275. Courtesy of Board of Trustees The National Gallery, London
276. Courtesy of Board of Trustees The National Gallery, London
277. Paul Mellon Collection, National Gallery of Art, Washington DC

Neoclassicism and Romanticism

278. Courtesy of Board of Trustees The National Gallery, London
279. Courtesy of Board of Trustees The National Gallery, London
280. Andrew W Mellon Collection, National Gallery of Art, Washington DC **281.** National Gallery of Scotland, Edinburgh
282. National Gallery of Scotland, Edinburgh **283.** Andrew W Mellon Collection, National Gallery of Art, Washington DC
284. Andrew W Mellon Collection, National Gallery of Art, Washington DC **285.** The Baltimore Museum of Art: Gift of Dr Morton K Blaustein, Barbara Hirschhorn and Elisabeth B Roswell, in memory of Jacob and Hilda K Blaustein **286.** Andrew W Mellon Fund, National Gallery of Art, Washington DC **287.** Tate Gallery, London **288.** Walker Art Gallery, Liverpool/Tate Gallery, London **289.** Uffizi, Florence/Bridgeman Art Library, London
290. Andrew W Mellon Collection, National Gallery of Art, Washington DC **291.** Museo del Prado, Madrid **292.** Gift of Mr and Mrs P H B Frelinghuysen in memory of her father and mother Mr and Mrs H O Havemeyer/National Gallery of Art, Washington DC **293.** Museo del Prado, Madrid **294.** Museo del Prado, Madrid **295.** Louvre, Paris/© Photo Ph.Sebert
296. Louvre, Paris/© Photo Ph.Sebert **297.** Musées Royaux des Beaux Arts de Belgique, Brussels
298. Louvre, Paris/© Photo Ph.Sebert **299.** Louvre, Paris/RMN, Paris **300.** Bernard Terlay/Musée Granet, Aix en Provence
301. University of Birmingham
302. Musée des Beaux Arts, Rouen/Giraudon **303.** Louvre, Paris/© Photo Ph.Sebert
304. Louvre, Paris/© Photo Ph.Sebert **305.** Louvre, Paris/Giraudon **306.** Chester Dale Fund, National Gallery of Art, Washington DC **307.** Staatliche Museen zu Berlin Preussischer Kulturbesitz Nationalgalerie
308. Andrew W Mellon Collection, National Gallery of Art, Washington DC **309.** Tate Gallery, London **310.** Andrew W Mellon Collection, National Gallery of Art, Washington DC **311.** Widener Collection, National Gallery of Art, Washington DC **312.** Widener Collection, National Gallery of Art, Washington DC **313.** Tate Gallery, London **314.** Rosenwald Collection, National Gallery of Art, Washington DC **315.** Tate Gallery, London

The Age of Impressionism

316. Tate Gallery, London
317. Tate Gallery, London
318. "By Courtesy of the Board of Trustees of the V&A", Victoria and Albert Museum, London **319.** Tate Gallery, London **320.** Chester Dale Collection, National Gallery of Art, Washington DC **321.** Gift of Count Cecil Pecci-Blunt, National Gallery of Art, Washington DC
322. Gift of Duncan Phillips, National Gallery of Art, Washington DC **323.** Louvre, Paris/Giraudon **324.** Louvre, Paris/Giraudon **325.** Musée Fabre, Montpellier **326.** Louvre, Paris/Giraudon **327.** Gift of Eugene and Agnes E Meyer, National Gallery of Art, Washington DC **328.** Gift of Horace Havemeyer in memory of his mother Louisine W Havemeyer, National Gallery of Art, Washington DC **329.** The Courtauld Institute Galleries, London **330.** Musée d'Orsay/Sp A Harris **331.** Ailsa Mellon Bruce Collection, National Gallery of Art, Washington DC **332.** Louvre, Paris/© Photo Ph.Sebert
333. Chester Dale Collection, National Gallery of Art, Washington DC **334.** Chester Dale Collection, National Gallery of Art, Washington DC **335.** Gift of the W Averall Harriman Foundation in Memory of Marie N Harriman, National Gallery of Art, Washington DC **336.** Collection of Mr and Mrs Paul Mellon, National Gallery of Art, Washington DC
337. Chester Dale Collection, National Gallery of Art, Washington DC **338.** Courtesy of Board of Trustees The National Gallery, London **339.** Bridgeman Art Library, London/Phillips Collection, Washington DC
340. Chester Dale Collection, National Gallery of Art, Washington DC **341.** Chester Dale Collection, National Gallery of Art, Washington DC **342.** Ailsa Mellon Bruce Collection, National Gallery of Art, Washington DC **343.** Ailsa Mellon Bruce Collection, National Gallery of Art, Washington DC
344. Ailsa Mellon Bruce Collection, National Gallery of Art, Washington DC **345.** Tate Gallery, London **346.** Tate Gallery, London
347. Gift of the W L and May T Mellon Foundation, National Gallery of Art, Washington DC
348. Gift of Mr and Mrs Cornelius Vanderbilt Whitney, National Gallery of Art, Washington DC
349. Gift of Ernest Iselin, National Gallery of Art, Washington DC

Post-Impressionism

350. Collection of Mr and Mrs Paul Mellon, National Gallery of Art, Washington DC
351. Fitzwilliam Museum, University of Cambridge, England
352. Gift of Eugene and Agnes E Meyer, National Gallery of Art, Washington DC **353.** Gift of Agnes and Eugene E Meyer, National Gallery of Art, Washington DC
354. Courtesy of Board of Trustees The National Gallery, London
355. Collection of Mr and Mrs Paul Mellon, National Gallery of Art, Washington DC **356.** Musée d'Orsay/© Photo Ph.Sebert
357. Ailsa Mellon Bruce Collection, National Gallery of Art, Washington DC **358.** Chester Dale Collection, National Gallery of Art, Washington DC **359.** Musée d'Orsay/Giraudon, Paris
360. Chester Dale Collection, National Gallery of Art, Washington DC **361.** Chester Dale Collection, National Gallery of Art, Washington DC **362.** Musée Gustav Moreau, Paris/Giraudon
363. Musée du Petit Palais, Paris/Lauros/Giraudon **364.** National Gallery of Scotland, Edinburgh
365. Museum Folkwang, Essen
366. Courtauld Institute Galleries, London **367.** Christies Colour Library **368.** Fotostudio Otto
369. Chester Dale Collection, National Gallery of Art, Washington DC **370.** Tate Gallery, London **371.** Ailsa Mellon Bruce Collection, National Gallery of Art, Washington DC **372.** Musée du Petit Palais, Paris/© Phototheque des Musées de la Ville de Paris
373. Ailsa Mellon Bruce Collection, National Gallery of Art, Washington DC **374.** Tate Gallery, London

The 20th Century

375. Chester Dale Collection, National Gallery of Art, Washington DC/© ADAGP, Paris and DACS, London 1994
376. John Hay Whitney Collection, National Gallery of Art, Washington DC/© ADAGP, Paris and DACS, London 1994
377. Statens Museum für Kunst Copenhagen/© Sucession H Matisse/DACS 1994 **378.** Museo dell'Ermitage, Leningrad/Scala/© Sucession H Matisse/DACS 1994
379. Chester Dale Collection, National Gallery of Art, Washington DC/© Sucession H Matisse/DACS 1994 **380.** Ailsa Mellon Bruce Collection, National Gallery of Art, Washington DC/© Sucession H Matisse/DACS 1994
381. Ailsa Mellon Bruce Collection, National Gallery of Art, Washington DC/© DACS 1994
382. Musée National D'Arte Moderne, Paris/© ADAGP, Paris and DACS 1994 **383.** Brücke Museum/"Copyright Dr Wolfgang and Ingeborg Henze-Ketterer, Wichtrach/Bern" **384.** Offentliche Kunstsammlung, Kunstmuseum, Basel/© Nolde Stiftung Seebüll
385. Artothek/Staatsgalerie moderner Kunst, Munich/© DACS 1994 **386.** Albertina Graphics Collection, Vienna/Bridgeman Art Library
387. Offentliche Kunstsammlung Kunstmuseum, Basel, Ph Martin Bühler/© DACS 1994 **388.** Tate Gallery, London **389.** Chester Dale Collection, National Gallery of Art, Washington DC **390.** Artothek Stedelijk Museum/© ADAGP, Paris and DACS, London 1994
391. Picasso/Chester Dale Collection, National Gallery of Art, Washington DC/© DACS 1994
392. Museum of Modern Art, New York/Giraudon, Paris, © DACS 1994 **393.** Chester Dale Collection, National Gallery of Art, Washington DC/© DACS 1994
394. Tate Gallery, London/© DACS 1994 **395.** Tate Gallery/© DACS 1994 **396.** Chester Dale Collection, National Gallery of Art, Washington DC/ADAGP, Paris and DACS, London 1994
397. Chester Dale Fund, National Gallery of Art, Washington DC
398. Sprengel Museum, Hannover
399. Tate Gallery, London/© DACS 1994 **400.** Offentliche Kunstsammlung Kunstmuseum, Basel, Ph Martin Bühler/ADAGP, Paris and DACS, London 1994
401. Staatliche Kunsthalle Karlsruhe EV **402.** © Rheinisches Bildarchiv/ Museum Ludwig, Cologne **403.** Ailsa Mellon Bruce Fund, National Gallery of Art, Washington DC/© ADAGP, Paris and DACS, London 1994
404. Musée National D'Arte Moderne, Paris/© ADAGP, Paris and DACS, London 1994
405. Kunsthalle, Hamburg/DACS 1994 **406.** Paul Klee Stiftung, Kunstmuseum, Bern/© DACS 1994
407. Paul Klee Stiftung, Kunstmuseum, Bern/© DACS 1994
408. Artothek, Museum Ludwig, Cologne **409.** Collection Haagsgemente Museum, The Hague/International Licensing Partners, Amsterdam **410.** Gift of Herbert and Nanette Rothschild, National Gallery of Art, Washington DC/International Licensing Partners, Amsterdam
411. Chester Dale Collection, National Gallery of Art, Washington DC **412.** Tate Gallery, London/© DACS 1994 **413.** Tate Gallery, London/© SPADEM/ADAGP, Paris and DACS, London 1994 **414.** Tate Gallery, London/© ADAGP, Paris and DACS, London 1994 **415.** Private Collection, Houston/Bridgeman Art Library/© ADAGP, Paris and DACS, London 1994 **416.** Metropolitan Museum of Art, New York/© DEMART PRO ARTE BV/DACS, London 1994 **417.** Moderner Museet, Stockholm/© ADAGP, Paris and DACS, London 1994
418. Tate Gallery, London/© DACS 1994 **419.** Tate Gallery, London/© ADAGP, Paris and DACS, London, 1994 **420.** John Hay Whitney Collection, National Gallery of Art, Washington DC
421. Alfred Stieglitz Collection, Bequest of Georgia O'Keeffe, National Gallery of Art, Washington DC/© 1994 The Georgia O'Keeffe Foundation/Artists Rights Society (ARS), New York **422.** Musée National d'Art Moderne, Paris/Lauros-Giraudon/©1994 Pollock-Krasner Foundation/Artists' Rights Society (ARS), New York **423.** Ailsa Mellon Bruce Fund, National Gallery of Art, Washington DC/© 1994 Pollock-Krasner Foundation/Artists' Rights Society (ARS), New York **424.** Gift of Lila Acheson Wallace, National Gallery of Art, Washington DC **425.** Gift of the Mark Rothko Foundation, National Gallery of Art, Washington DC/© 1994 Kate Rothko-Prizel and Christopher Rothko/ Artists' Rights Society (ARS), New York **426.** Tate Gallery, London/© ADAGP, Paris and DACS, London 1994
427. Whitney Museum of American Art, New York/© 1994 Willem de Kooning/Artists' Rights Society (ARS), New York
428. Whitney Museum of American Art, New York, Purchased with Funds from the friends of the Whitney Museum of American Art/© 1994 Willem de

COLUMN PICTURE CREDITS

ACKNOWLEDGEMENTS

Dorling Kindersley would like to thank:

Colin Wiggins for reading the manuscript; Frances Smythe at the National Gallery of Art, Washington DC; Miranda Dewar at Bridgeman Art Library; Sister Anne Marie; David Stirling-Wylie and Gillian M. Walkley; Julia Harris-Voss and Jo Walton; Simon Hinchliffe, Tracy Hambleton-Miles, Tina Vaughan, Kevin Williams, Sucharda Smith, Zirrinia Austin, Samantha Fitzgerald, Simon Murrell, and Kirstie Hills.

Textbook of Tinnitus

Aage R. Møller • Berthold Langguth •
Dirk De Ridder • Tobias Kleinjung •

Editors

Textbook of Tinnitus

Editors
Aage R. Møller
The University of Texas at Dallas
School of Behavioral and Brain
Sciences, Richardson, Texas, USA
amoller@utdallas.edu

Berthold Langguth
University of Regensburg
Department of Psychiatry
Psychotherapy and Psychosomatics
Regensburg, Germany
Berthold.Langguth@medbo.de

Dirk De Ridder
BRAI²N/TRI Tinnitus Clinic and
Department of Neurosurgery
University Hospital Antwerp
Wilrijkstraat 10
2650 Edegem
Belgium
dirk.de.ridder@uza.be

Tobias Kleinjung
University of Regensburg
Department of Otorhinolaryngology
Regensburg, Germany
tobias.kleinjung@klinik.uni-regensburg.de

ISBN 978-1-60761-144-8   e-ISBN 978-1-60761-145-5
DOI 10.1007/978-1-60761-145-5
Springer New York Dordrecht Heidelberg London

Library of Congress Control Number: 2010934377

Printed on acid-free paper

Springer is part of Springer Science+Business Media (www.springer.com)

Foreword

REFLECTIONS ON A 1,000-DAY ADVENTURES IN A RESEARCH PROJECT.

October is a very nice month in the Egyptian desert. It is also when the "Rally of the Pharaons" takes place; an intensive ride in the sand where the main objective is not to get stuck or lost and to arrive at the right place before most of the others.

In 2004, like other times, I was participating and enjoying the concentration, the scenery, and the short nights in a camp, preparing the mind and the equipment for the next day. The next day, half an hour before the end of the stage, I passed the wheel to an impatient navigator who wanted his moment of piloting glory.

A few minutes later, the car went to the wrong side of a mountain, "rolled over" several times, and landed upside down at the bottom of the hill.

Whiplash, stressful emotion, and lack of oxygen to the ear (dissection of the carotid artery); I had just landed at the perfect scenario for developing something that was totally unknown to me until then: TINNITUS!!

After 6 months of panic and useless wondering to find a cure, I was left with two choices: live with it or try to do something about it. Although accepting to live with it was probably the best cure at that moment, I chose to try to do something about it. Not out of generosity or because I thought I was called upon the task by higher duties, because:

1. Unlike other pathologies, *time* was on my side: I was not going to die or get worse over time
2. I had *experience* in organizing research
3. I had the *motivation* to walk in other people's lives and invite them into a project I believed in
4. I had the *time,* having sold my main business believing I could not lead as well anymore
5. I had the *money, and*
6. I did not want to regret that I had not tried

The "program" turned out to be a venture in frustration and hope, a balancing act between logic and instinct, and maybe a little, but important milestone for successful therapies in the future. Also, and not surprisingly, it was a human adventure about people and their beliefs, their weaknesses, and their strengths. Here is how I remember it and what I would consider if it started again.

As an independent entrepreneur, I wanted to give some structure to my program, but without losing flexibility and making sure I would not "play doctor." The main immediate points were:

1. How to finance it and through what entity
2. How to choose the people
3. How to choose and coordinate the research program, and my role in it, and
4. How and when to end it, the businessman's "exit strategy"

How to Finance It and Through What Entity

(a) An existing pharmaceutical company would seem the most immediate choice. However, their managers are guided by long-term survival of their companies and, consequently by considerations such as short-term cash flow, risk, time to market a product, and reimbursement by health care, and are often not open to innovation if it overlaps existing businesses (like in the case of new hearing aids).

(b) Co-investing with government funding was not really an option. Tinnitus, not being a life-threatening disease, would not get a lot of attention. Moreover, government projects have a long bureaucratic approval process and once funded, they lack the flexibility to change directions during the research if the interim results so suggest.

(c) An existing association was another obvious choice. Scott Mitchell, member of the board of ATA, has written many interesting articles and believes that public non-profit organizations appear to be the best vehicle for funding tinnitus research. Although I agree with him to some extent, it is normal that every time you are managing other people's money, you are somewhat restricted by present logic and paradigms, and have to allocate a lot of time and resources for explanations and accounting to "shareholders," in addition to public awareness, prevention, support to patients, etc.

(d) *Direct funding to individuals by an individual*

As more individuals live longer and achieve financial success, they reach a point where they feel they can use their money and their experience to make a difference in a field other than their own – and make it their "legacy."

Teaming up with one of these individuals would be risky because they are, in all likelihood strong personalities who bring into a program their style, their objectives, and their people, and since it is their "legacy" after all, often want a lot of exposure.

In addition, I wanted to try to bring together cross-border and interdisciplinary knowledge into a field where not enough was yet known to make it interesting to future participants (industry, governments, and associations) and had my own ideas on what was important – and what was going to make this possible.

Chances of improving were higher because we started from zero.

My program would be based on the idea that tinnitus research was still in a phase where to get to the next step it was better to stay away from too many "models," and that some of it had to be done by somebody who was willing to fail, make mistakes, change his mind, not understand, and ultimately not base his decisions on risk/reward, but on people who were willing to work on a project for the right reasons and with the right attitude.

"Life is like a game of chess; the first moves are very important, but until the game is over you still have some good moves to play."

Anne Frank

How to Choose the People

I have always been involved in science – and yet know very little. My father was a brilliant scientist, with many researchers around him. I never tried to compete directly, but learned a lot from "back stage" and over the years. He had a sign in his office that said: "if you want to lose money spend it on boats, women and research." Even if we had not spent a lot of time together, I must have taken that part from him!

The process of choosing the scientists whom I would have liked to meet each other and work together was very intuitive, but I can try to list a few characteristics that I think are common to successful scientists – they:

- Are optimistic, but realistic
- Do not promise more than what they can deliver
- Are capable of giving bad news
- Take pleasure and attention in the growth of people around them
- Simplify and explain complicated things in a simple way
- See a problem and turn it into an opportunity
- Do not have what is called the "not invented here syndrome": they listen with an open mind to other people's ideas
- Recognize today's assumptions and question them
- Look beyond the obvious
- Find a way to look at something new without rejecting the current concept
- Don't look at an idea only to see what is wrong with it and how they can reject it
- Think and work a lot – genius ideas are a result of it
- Have a high sense of responsibility
- Always want to do things better and
- *Try to do the best they can.*

Some of these characteristics usually surface even in a short interview and I always saw some of them in the people who have at some stage participated in the TRI research program. I am naturally honored that they have accepted to work with TRI as I never took it for granted.

"The scientific mind does not so much provide the right answers as ask the right questions."

Claude Levi Strauss

How to Choose and Coordinate the Research Program, and My Role in it

A traditional program would have three main components.

Leadership, to clearly identify the objectives so as to produce the results.

Organization, to identify the different functions and to allocate them to the best people.

Administration, to allocate the resources where and when necessary.

One difference in this case was that none of the participants was directly employed and that the relationship was based more on attitude and trust than otherwise. Each had their own existing activity.

The main objective was not to organize an effective research program, but to encourage multidisciplinary, interdisciplinary exchange in the belief that the right people would seize the opportunity.

Personal interaction coupled with the exposure to different therapeutic areas would combine the knowledge without setting boundaries of research, and ultimately, individuals would choose their partners in the program.

Their partners would possibly be from different areas, different levels, and different countries and cultures, and that combination would increase understanding, innovation, and the feeling that the "mission" was doable.

Over time strategic groups and their performance obligations would form. Diversification would increase the effort of coordinating their work, but would naturally identify specific areas of research.

Workgroups in pharmacology, neurostimulation, auditory stimulation, somatosensory modulation, and eventually tinnitus clinics (when the need for integrating research and clinical medicine became more evident) were formed, but these were based more on the individuals who chose to work together than on an imposed structure or organization.

Somehow the dynamics were quite different than those of a company.

Later, I would have worked more closely to improve the connection between innovation and actual therapy. I knew that existing commercial compounds generated less problems. I also had learned that successful players design the most incisive clinical trials and were not necessarily hung up on publishing a lot.

The dynamics were a strange mix of what I had lived in the past, and my role was going to shape accordingly.

Rod Davis, coach of the Team New Zealand sailing team, wrote an interesting article to explain coaching and support: The Invisible Hand. He says coaching is a weird combination of teaching, mentoring, being the hatchet man (at times), and being a "nanny," throw it all in a blender and make something good out of it. Coaching, Rod writes, is not rocket science. In fact, it is not a science at all, it is art. Coaches provide the environment for driven talent to become champions. The ones with talent who take full advantage of the opportunities presented became champions.

Environment means unloading distractions. It means create a belief in the ability to perform in tasks that are the most important to them. He adds that a big part of self-confidence is self-responsibility: if someone knows that it is up to him to be in control of his own destiny and knows he has done all that is needed to be ready, how can he not be self-confident?

This improves the chances of success, but there are no guarantees. There are thousands of pieces to the puzzle, but if the environment is right, the end result is certainly more likely to be positive.

Interestingly enough, two successive research coordinators failed in their mission, probably because they did not see the program the same way.

I was going to try and follow Rod's "art," keeping in mind that it was also my role – at least at the beginning, to add strong leadership and sense of the mission, just like Grant Dalton does with the very successful Team New Zealand.

"I came in understanding that the magnitude of the issues facing the country required that I put together a team that I could delegate a whole range of different tasks to and who would be able to work well together. Over the last 6 months I have relearned that lesson – that my most important job is to get the right people in the right place, give them the freedom to innovate and to think creatively about problems,

hold them accountable for results, and make sure they are cooperating with each other and communicating on an ongoing basis."

President Barack Obama, August 2009

How and When to End it

Basic research delivers the technology platform, the ideas, and concepts, but they are often not at first accepted by industry or peers. This is the innovation gap and it needs to be bridged by the public hand. At a certain point, there needs to be an investment of the government to share the risk: political will is not only the weakest link in the chain, but also the hardest to fix.[1]

Governments, whose biggest expense is becoming health care, have a difficult task in choosing priorities. As an example, a very small percentage of cancer research spending would make a huge difference in other areas, including tinnitus.

Maybe a better way to look at it would be to present the issue in a more global way. Now that the majority of researchers agree that tinnitus is a malfunction or reorganization that takes place with the neurons in the brain, its research implications go together with the understanding of other pathologies such as Alzheimer's or Parkinson's that are more easily understood as terribly detrimental.

Public nonprofit organizations should help bridge the gap to government involvement in addition to encouraging awareness and prevention.

Contrary to many, I believe that it is important that at a certain point the individual sponsor disappears. A more structured and long-term mechanism has to take place. People and programs should not depend solely on the sponsor.

In this specific case, the objective was to install new energy toward an "undervalued" problem and contribute to make it a stand-alone research area for medicine. Only time will tell how much has been achieved toward that end.

"You can have a dialogue about solving future problems all you like, but if you do not behave any differently when you go out of here, it won't make any difference."

Dennis Meadows
"Limits to growth"

Conclusions

Strategy is about the future and then making decisions based on that. The worst thing you can do is not to have an opinion, and not make decisions.[2]

More than ever, success depends on our ability to learn and to create value from what we learn.

In these times of uncertainty, scientists and physicians have to be agents of change in the right direction, accelerate science, advance medicine, and also direct it in a more integrated and patient-driven experience that is comprehensive to all.

---

[1]Peter Gruss, President Max-Planck-Society
[2]Alan Mulally, President Ford Motor Company

Individuals still play an important role in sponsoring and discovery. It is everybody's task to create the environment and attitude for positive change.

Whether we made a change, and if the change was meaningful we will not know for years and maybe never. But I believe it would be a mistake to loose the momentum and coordination that TRI has created.

On a personal note, I have met some extraordinary people and scientists, although my tinnitus is still there, I believe that we have cured people who otherwise would still be suffering. I believe I will be cured in the next 3–5 years and that I will have that cure available before it enters the global market.

Is that enough?

It is one of the best things I ever did!

Matteo de Nora

Preface

Tinnitus (ringing in the ears) has many forms, and the severity of tinnitus ranges widely from being a slight nuisance to affecting a person's daily life. How loud the tinnitus is perceived does not directly relate to how much it distresses the patient. Thus, even tinnitus very close to the hearing threshold can be a disabling symptom that amounts to a major burden, it can reduce the quality of life by generating anxiety and concentration problems impairing the ability to do intellectual work, making it difficult to sleep; causing depression and tinnitus can ultimately lead to suicide. Tinnitus can occur at young age, but its prevalence steadily increases with the degree of age-related hearing loss and can reach 12–15% for people aged 65 and over. Moreover, tinnitus incidence is increasing dramatically with increased leisure noise, more work-related noise trauma, and longer lifespan.

The different forms of tinnitus have similarities with different kinds of pain; many forms of pain and tinnitus are phantom sensations. Another important commonality is that pain and tinnitus lack detectable signs; imaging tests (structural MRI, CT, etc.) and common electrophysiological test results are the same whether or not a person has tinnitus.

For a long time, it was believed that the anatomical location of the physiological abnormalities that caused the tinnitus was the ear. However, it was later understood that most forms of tinnitus are caused by abnormalities in the central nervous system and that these abnormalities are often caused by expression of neural plasticity.

Many structures of the body, such as the ear, the auditory nervous system, the somatosensory system, other parts of the brain, and muscles of the head and the neck are directly or indirectly involved in different forms of tinnitus. To treat and understand the pathology of tinnitus, therefore, requires the involvement of many specialties of medicine, surgery, psychology, and neuroscience.

Tinnitus may occur after noise exposure and administration of pharmacological agents, but the cause of subjective tinnitus is often unknown. Severe tinnitus is often accompanied by symptoms, such as hyperacusis (lowered tolerance to sound) and distortion of sounds. Affective disorders, such as phonophobia (fear of sound) and depression, often occur in individuals with severe tinnitus. With such differences in attributes, it is not reasonable to expect that a single cause can be responsible for severe tinnitus, again a factor that makes managing the tinnitus patient a challenge for health care professionals.

Realizing the complexity of tinnitus has highlighted the importance of interdisciplinary research, and the fact that most forms of tinnitus are disorders of the nervous system has put emphasis on neuroscience, both in studies and in the treatment of tinnitus.

However, few clinicians are specifically trained in tinnitus treatment, and there is a lack of suitable books that describe how to diagnose and treat each of these many forms of tinnitus most effectively.

Each of the authors contributing to the "Textbook of Tinnitus" were, therefore chosen from many specialties of medicine, surgery, psychology, and neuroscience, and came from diverse areas of expertise, such as Neurology, Neurosurgery, Audiology, Otolaryngology, Psychiatry, Clinical- and Experimental Psychology, Pharmacology, Dentistry, and Neuroscience.

Unlike pain, which has considerable literature, including a book with the title "Textbook of Pain" now in its fifth edition, there is no comprehensive book that covers the many aspects of tinnitus. This book, therefore, fills a void by providing relevant information about tinnitus as a disease and how to treat it effectively. The "Textbook of Tinnitus" is directed toward the clinician and gives detailed information about the diagnosis of many different forms of tinnitus and their treatment. The book also provides an overview of what is known about the pathophysiology of different kinds of tinnitus.

It has become more and more evident that neural plasticity plays an important role, not only in adapting the nervous system to changes in demand and after injuries, but also as a cause of symptoms and signs of disease. Such diseases have been called "plasticity disorders." The role of neural plasticity in creating symptoms of disease, such as many forms of tinnitus, has only been described in a few books directed to neurologists and researchers in neuroscience. This means the medical community in general is often unaware that functional changes in the nervous system can be the cause of a patient's complaints, and that hampers the diagnosis of disorders, such as tinnitus. Therefore, the effective treatment of tinnitus also requires knowledge about neural plasticity as a cause of diseases. This is one of the aspects of tinnitus that is covered in the "Textbook of Tinnitus."

The fact that tinnitus is not a single disease, but a group of diseases means tinnitus cannot be effectively treated by a single approach, and several disciplines of health care must be involved in managing the patient with tinnitus. Treatment of the patient with severe tinnitus requires collaborations between clinicians in many different fields of medicine, audiology, and psychology. Accordingly, tinnitus research and treatment have been performed by a variety of disciplines, viewing the problem from various perspectives, focusing on different targets, and using diverse approaches. New developments regarding the treatment have prompted the involvement of neurosurgeons, neurologists, psychiatrists, and dentists. Therefore, an important challenge for the future consists in improving cooperation between different disciplines involved in tinnitus research and treatment.

It is a challenge to translate the results from basic research into clinical practice. The "Textbook of Tinnitus" provides the basis for multidisciplinary management of the tinnitus patient using the most modern methods of treatment. The book represents a new and broad interdisciplinary approach to tinnitus by bringing together in a single book, contributions from many different areas of basic science and clinical research and health care to guide the management of the tinnitus patient. This is the first time that such broad efforts have been made regarding the treatment of tinnitus.

The 95 chapters in this book express the independent views of the authors, some of which may diverge and some may complement one and another. The editors have made no attempts to modify individual authors' views, only attempts have been made to achieve a similar style of writing in the different chapters.

The book describes both the theoretical background of the different forms of tinnitus and detailed knowledge of state-of-the-art treatment of tinnitus written for clinicians by clinicians and researchers in tinnitus. It provides up-to-date information in forms that are suitable for those who diagnose and treat patients with tinnitus in their clinical praxis as otolaryngologists, neurologists, psychiatrists, neurosurgeons, clinical audiologists, dentists, and psychologists. The book can also serve as a reference for clinicians who do not treat tinnitus patients routinely because of its organization and extensive subject index.

The book has five sections, I Basics about tinnitus, II Causes of tinnitus, III Differential diagnosis of tinnitus, IV Clinical characteristics of different forms of tinnitus, and V Management of tinnitus.

The first section describes the basic aspects of tinnitus and the symptoms that often accompany the disorder, such as hyperacusis and misophonia. This section includes chapters on the epidemiology of tinnitus in children as well as adults and discusses the role of genetics in tinnitus. The anatomy and physiology of the normal auditory system and the pathologic system are the topics of other chapters; chapters on pain and similarities between tinnitus and pain are also included, as are chapters that discuss the use of special forms of neuroimaging for studies of tinnitus. Modeling of the pathologies of tinnitus is the topic of two chapters, and one chapter discusses how clinical trials are performed. The last part of the section concerns how tinnitus is perceived and approached by members of different specialties in the research and treatment of tinnitus, including a chapter about how tinnitus is viewed by the patients themselves.

Section II has chapters about different causes of tinnitus, such as the role of disorders of the ear, age, and exposure to noise and ototoxic substances. Diseases associated with tinnitus, such as vestibular schwannoma and Ménière's disease, are the topics of other chapters in this section. Yet another chapter covers the cause of somatosensory tinnitus. Other chapters concern the role of different disorders of the central nervous system. The role of disorders of the masticatory system, including that of the temporomandibular joint, is the topic of the last chapter in the section.

Section III discusses the diagnosis of tinnitus and a chapter presents a diagnostic algorithm for tinnitus, followed by chapters on how the different diagnostic methods are performed. Chapters covering otologic, audiologic, and neuro-otologic assessment and examination follow a chapter about history and questionnaires. A chapter describes the diagnosis of somatosensory tinnitus, and another the assessment of temporomandibular disorders. The last chapter in the section covers psychological and psychiatric assessments.

The chapters of Section IV cover the clinical characteristics of the different forms of tinnitus. In order to better meet the need of clinicians, the section is organized according to symptoms and syndromes as presented by the patients. The chapters describe the management of tinnitus with sudden hearing loss, hyperacusis and phonophobia, intermittent tinnitus, and pulsatile tinnitus. Tinnitus that occurs together with other symptoms, such as, Ménière's disease, headache, and psychiatric disorders (depression, anxiety, and insomnia), are also covered in separate chapters. Finally, posttraumatic tinnitus and tinnitus caused by blast injuries that occur in wars are described.

The chapters of Section V concern management of the various forms of tinnitus. The chapters provide an extensive coverage of the available treatments. The chapters review treatments, such as counseling, cognitive behavioral treatment, and auditory training, which include various forms of sound stimulation. Specific treatment programs, such as the Tinnitus Retraining Therapy (TRT) and the Neuromonics program are described. The chapters also discuss different kinds of pharmacologic treatment. Treatment using botulinum toxin and different forms of surgical treatment are covered in separate chapters. Other chapters describe different forms of neuromodulation, and one chapter discusses complementary treatments. The two final chapters include the treatment of tinnitus and pain and strategies for TMJ disorders as their topics.

Many of the contributors to "Textbook of Tinnitus" are involved in research sponsored by the international research organization, "The Tinnitus Research Initiative" (TRI). The goal of the TRI is to improve the treatment for tinnitus through advances in the understanding of the pathophysiology of tinnitus. This organization has promoted collaborative interdisciplinary research on tinnitus during the past 5 years. It has now been converted into an international research foundation, the TRI Foundation.

TRI's goal is to provide a basis for collaborations between researchers and clinicians from different fields to achieve an integrated approach to studies of the pathophysiology of tinnitus and develop and test treatments of different forms of tinnitus.

The Editors thank Mr. Matteo de Nora for his support to research on tinnitus through the TRI Foundation and for his support in the preparation of this book. We also acknowledge valuable support from The University of Texas at Dallas School of Behavioral and Brain Sciences. Amanda Miller provided editorial help and Paige Wahl provided general assistance in the preparation of this book.

Dallas, February 2010   Aage R. Møller
                                                                         Berthold Langguth
                                                                         Dirk De Ridder
                                                                         Tobias Kleinjung

Contents

Contributors

Umberto Ambrosetti, MD
Department of Specialist Surgical Sciences, University of Milan, Fondazione
IRRCCS Ca Granda Ospedale Maggiore Policlinico, Via Pace 9, 20122, Milano,
Italy
umberto.ambrosetti@unimi.it

George E. Anthou Esq
132 Greens Ave, Cannonsburg PA, 15317, USA
ganthou@hotmail.com

Moisés A. Arriaga, MD, MBA, FACS
Department of Otolaryngology, Louisiana State University Health Sciences Center,
New OrleansLA, USA
Our Lady of the Lake Hearing and Balance Center, 7777 Hennessy Blvd,
Suite 709 Baton Rouge LA, 70808, USA
maa@neurotologic.com

David M. Baguley, BSc MSc MBA PhD
Cambridge University Hospitals, Hills Road, Cambridge, CB2 2QQ, UK
dmb29@cam.ac.uk

Carey Balaban, PhD
Department of Otolarynology, Eye and Ear Insitute, University of Pittsburgh,
203 Lothrop St, Pittsburgh PA, 15213, USA
cbalaban@pitt.edu

Giovanna Baracca
Fondazione Ascolta e Vivi, via Foppa 15, 20144, Milano, Italy
baracca.giovanna@libero.it

Michael Behr, Dr. med. dent
Department of Prosthodontics, Regensburg University Medical Center,
Franz-Josef-Strauss-Allee 11, 93053, Regensburg, Germany
michael.behr@klinik.uni-regensburg.de

Eric C. Bielefeld, PhD, CCC-A
The Ohio State University, 110 Pressey Hall, 1070 Carmack Road, Columbus,
OH, 43210, USA
bielefeld.6@osu.edu

Eberhard Biesinger, Dr.med. (PhD)
Department of Klinikum Traunstein, Maxplatz 5, 83278, Traunstein, Germany
Dr.Eberhard.Biesinger@t-online.de

LucaDel Bo
Fondazione Ascolta e Vivi, via Foppa 15, 20144 Milano, Italy
delbo@sordita.it

Daniel J. Bosnyak
Department of Psychology, Neuroscience, and Behavior, McMaster University,
Hamilton ON, Canada, L8S4K1
bosnyak@mcmaster.ca

Ralf Bürgers, PhD, DMD
Department of Prosthodontics, University Medical Center Regensburg,
Franz-Josef-Strauss-Allee 11, 93053, Regensburg, Germany
ralf.buergers@klinik.uni-regensburg.de

Anthony T. Cacace, PhD
Department of Communication Sciences & Disorders, Wayne State University,
207 Rackham, 60 Farnsworth Detroit MI, 48202, USA
cacacea@wayne.edu

Claudia Barros Coelho, MD, PhD
Rua Mostardeiro, 32/32 Porto Alegre- RS -Brazil, 90430-000
claudiabarroscoelho@gmail.com

Tatjana Crönlein, Dr. phil
Dept of Psychiatry and Psychotherapy, University Hospital of Regensburg,
Universtitaetsstr. 84, 93053, Regensburg, Germany
tatjana.croenlein@medbo.de

Paul B. Davis, PhD MAudSA (CC)
Audiology, Health Professions Division, Nova Southeastern University,
3600 South University Drive, Fort Lauderdale, FL, 33328, USA
pauldavi@nova.edu

Dirk De Ridder, MD, PhD
BRAI²N TRI Tinnitus Clinic & Dept of Neurosurgery,
University Hospital Antwerp, Wilrijkstraat 10, 2650, Edegem, Belgium
dirk.de.ridder@uza.be

Isabel Diges, PhD
Department of Otorhinolaryngology, Tinnitus and Hiperacusis Clinic,
Hospital Universitario Fundacion Alcorcon, c/ Budapest, 1, 28922
Alcorcon Madrid, Spain
idiges8@gmail.com

Ana Belén Elgoyhen, PhD
University of Buenos Aires, School of Medicine,
National Research Council (CONICET), Institute for Research in Genetic
Engineering and Molecular Biology, Vuelta de Obligado 24, 901428,
Buenos Aires, Argentina
elgoyhen@dna.uba.ar

Paolo Enrico, PhD
Department of Biomedical Sciences, University of Sassari,
V.le S. Pietro 43/B07100, Sassari, Italy
enrico@uniss.it

Stella Forti
Audiology Unit, Fondazione IRRCCS Ca' Granda Ospedale Maggiore Policlinico,
Via Pace 920122, Milan, Italy
aut_est@yahoo.it

Peter Geisler, MD
Dept of Psychiatry, Psychosomatics and Psychotherapy, University Hospital of
Regensburg, Universitaetsstr. 8493053, Regensburg, Germany
peter.geisler@medbo.de

Vénéra Ghulyan-Bédikian, PhD
106, Bd de Hambourg, 13008, Marseille, France
V_Ghulyan@hotmail.com

Ron Goodey, MD Otolaryngologist
3 Wootton RoadRemuera, Auckland1050, New Zealand
rongoodey@xtra.co.nz

Martin Gosau, MD, DMD
Department of Cranio-Maxillo-Facial Surgery,
University Medical Center Regensburg, Franz-Josef-Strauss-Allee 11, 93053,
Regensburg, Germany
martin.gosau@klinik.uni-regensburg.de

Karoline V. Greimel, PhD
Salzburg University Hospital, Muellner Hauptstasse 48, 5020, Salzburg, Austria
k.greimel@salk.at

Sebastian Hahnel, DMD
University Medical Center Regensburg, Department of Prosthodontics,
Franz-Josef-Strauss-Allee 11, 93053, Regensburg, Germany
sebastian.hahnel@klinik.uni-regensburg.de

Göran Hajak, Dr. med.
Dept of Psychiatry and Psychotherapy, University Hospital of Regensburg,
Universtitaetsstr. 84, 93053, Regensburg, Germany
goeran.hajak@medbo.de

Thomas Hartmann, Dipl.-Psych
Department of Psychology, University of Konstanz, P.O. Box 25, 78457,
Konstanz, Germany
thomas.hartmann@uni-konstanz.de

Carlos Herraiz, MD, PhD
Tinnitus and Hiperacusis Clinic, Department of Otorhinolaryngology, Hospital
Universitario Fundacion Alcorcon, c/ Budapest, 128922, Alcorcon, Madrid, Spain
cherraizp@seorl.net

Michael E. Hoffer, MD
Department of Otolaryngology, Naval Medical Center San Diego, 34800 Bob
Wilson Drive San Diego CA, 92134, USA
Michael.hoffer@med.navy.mil

Pawel Jastreboff, PhD, DSc
Department of Otolaryngology, Tinnitus and Hyperacusis Center, Emory University
School of Medicine, Atlanta GA, USA
pjastre@emory.edu

James A. Kaltenbach, PhD
Department of Neurosciences, NE-63, Lerner Research Institute,
Cleveland Clinic, 9500 Euclid Avenue, Cleveland, OH, 44195, USA
kaltenj@ccf.org

Eman Khedr, MD
Department of Neurology, Assiut University Hospital, Assiut 71511, Egypt
emankhedr99@yahoo.com

Andrea Kleine-Punte, MSci
University Department of Otorhinolaryngology, Head and Neck Surgery, Antwerp
University Hospital, University of Antwerp, Wilrijkstr 10, 2650, Edegem-Antwerp,
Belgium
Andrea.kleine.punte@uza.be

Tobias Kleinjung, MD
Department of Otorhinolaryngology, University Hospital of Regensburg,
Regensburg, Germany
tobias.kleinjung@klinik.uni-regensburg.de

Michael Koller, PhD
Center of Clinical Studies, University Hospital of Regensburg, Regensburg,
Germany
michael.koller@klinik.uni-regensburg.de

Orianna Kong MAud (Hons)
The University of Auckland, 92019, Auckland, New Zealand
audiology@auckland.ac.nz

Birgit Kröner-Herwig, PhD
Department of Clinical Psychology & Psychotherapy
Georg-Elias-Müller-Institute of Psychology, University of Goettingen,
Gosslerstr. 14, 37073, Göttingen, Germany
bkroene@uni-goettingen.de

Benoit Lafont, MD
Hôpitaux Hopital Nord, 13915, Marseille Cedex 20, France
Beloit.Lafont@ap-hm.fr

Michael Landgrebe, MD
Department of Psychiatry and Psychotherapy, University Hospital of
Regensburg, Regensburg, Germany
michael.landgrebe@medbo.de

Berthold Langguth, MD
Department of Psychiatry and Psychotherapy, University of Regensburg,
Universitätsstraße 84, 93053, Regensburg, Germany
Berthold.Langguth@medbo.de

Miguel J A Láinez, MD, PhD
Department of Neurology, University Clinic Hospital, University of Valencia,
Avda Blasco Ibáñez 17, 46010, Valencia, Spain
jlaineza@meditex.es

Edward Lobarinas, PhD, CCC-A
Department of Communicative Disorders and Sciences, Center for Hearing and
Deafness, State University of New York at Buffalo, 137 Cary Hall,
3435 Main StreetBuffalo NY, 14214, USA
el24@buffalo.edu

Isabel Lorenz, Dipl.-Psych
Department of Psychology, University of Konstanz, D2578457, Konstanz, Germany
isabel.lorenz@uni-konstanz.de

Jacques Magnan, MD
University Aix-Marseille II, Hopital Nord, 13915 Marseille Cedex 20, France
jmagnan@ap-hm.fr

Jane E Magnusson
Department of Sport and Exercise Science, The University of Auckland,
92019, Auckland, New Zealand
j.magnusson@auckland.ac.nz

William Hal Martin, PhD
Department of Otolaryngology, Oregon Health and Science University,
Portland, OR, USA
martinw@ohsu.edu

Jason G. May, MD
Department of Otolaryngology – Head and Neck Surgery, School of Medicine,
Wayne State University, 4201St Antoine #5E, Detroit, MI, 48201, USA
jmay@med.wayne.edu

Manuela Mazzoli, MD
ORL-Otochirurgia, Az. Ospedaliera-Università di Padova,
via Giustiniani 2, Padova 35128, Italy
manuela.mazzoli@gmail.com

Don J. McFerran, MA, FRCS
Department of Otolaryngology, Colchester Hospital University,
NHS Foundation Trust, Lexden Rd., Colchester CO33NB, UK
donmcferran@aol.com

Olivier Meeus, MD
Department of Otorhinolaryngology, Head and Neck Surgery, Antwerp University
Hospital, University of Antwerp, Wilrijkstr 10, 2650, Edegem-Antwerp, Belgium
Olivier.meeus@uza.be

Nadia Müller, Dipl. Psych
University of Konstanz, P.O. Box 25, 78457, Konstanz, Germany
nadia.mueller@uni-konstanz.de

Aage R. Møller, PhD (DMedSci)
The University of Texas at Dallas School of Behavioral and Brain Sciences, GR 41,
800 W Campbell Rd, Richardson, TX, 75080, USA
amoller@utdallas.edu

Matteo De Nora
Tinnitus Research Initative Foundation, Bezirksklinikum Regensburg,
Universitätsstr. 84, 93053, Regensburg, Germany
Foundation@tinnitusresearch.org

Arnaud Norena, PhD
Université de Provence, Centre St Charles, Pôle 3C - Case B,
3, Place Victor Hugo F 13331, Marseille Cedex 03, France
arnaud.norena@univ-provence.fr

Michel Paolino, MD
Centre Médical Clairval, 317,Bd du Redon13009, Marseille, France
michel.paolino@wanadoo.fr

Anna Piera, MD
Department of Neurology, University Clinic Hospital, University of Valencia,
Avda Blasco Ibáñez 17, 46010, Valencia, Spain
jlaineza@meditex.es

Alejandro Ponz, MD, PhD
Department of Neurology, University Clinic Hospital, University of Valencia,
Avda Blasco Ibáñez 17, 46010, Valencia, Spain
jlaineza@meditex.es

Benjamin Questier
1 Place de l'Eglise, 69270, Saint Romain au Mont d'Or, France
bquestier@gmail.com

Virginia Ramachandran, AuD
Division of Audiology, Department of Otolaryngology - Head and Neck Surgery,
Henry Ford Hospital, 2799W. Grand Blvd, Detroit MI, 48202, USA
vramach1@hfhs.org

Charbel Rameh, MD, PhD
Hopital Nord, 13915, Marseille Cedex 20, France
charbelramed@hotmail.com

Larry E. Roberts, PhD
Department of Psychology, Neuroscience, and Behavior, McMaster University,
1280 Main Street West Hamilton ON, Canada, L8S4K1
roberts@mcmaster.ca

Carina Andrea Bezerra Rocha,
Rua São Vincente de Paulo, 650/82, São Paulo-SP-Brazil,
01229-010
carinabr.fisio@gmail.com

Carla Vanina Rothlin, PhD
School of Medicine, Yale University,
300 Cedar St TAC S625A, New Haven, CT, 06520, USA
carla.rothlin@yale.edu

Richard Salvi, PhD
Center for Hearing & Deafness, 137 Cary Hall, University of Buffalo,
3435 Main Street Buffalo NY, 14214, USA
salvi@buffalo.edu

Philipp G. Sand, MD
Department of Psychiatry, University of Regensburg, Franz-Josef-Strauss-Allee 11,
Regensburg, Germany
philipp.sand@klinik.uni-regensburg.de

Tanit Ganz Sanchez, MD, PhD
Discipline of Otolaryngology, University of São Paulo School of Medicine, Instituto
Ganz Sanchez, Av Padre Pereira de Andrade, 545/174F, São Paulo-SP-Brazil,
05469-000
tanitsanchez@gmail.com

Winfried Schlee, PhD
University of Konstanz, P.O. Box 25, 78457, Konstanz, Germany
winfried.schlee@uni-konstanz.de

Hannah Schulz, Dipl. Psych
University of Konstanz, P.O. Box 25, 78457, Konstanz, Germany
Hannah.schulz@uni-konstanz.de

Grant D Searchfield, BSc MAud (Hons) PhD (Audiology) MNZAS
Section of Audiology School of Population Health,
The University of Auckland, Auckland, New Zealand
g.searchfield@auckland.ac.nz

Georgina Shakes, BSc (Hons), DClinPsychol, CPsychol
Mt Eden Road, Symonds Street, P.O. Box 8050, Auckland1150, New Zealand
prac92@ihug.co.nz

Susan E Shore, PhD
Departments of Otolaryngology and Molecular and Integrative Physiology,
Kresge Hearing Research Inst, University of Michigan, 1150 West Medical
Center Drive, Room 5434A Ann Arbor MI, 48109-5616, USA
sushore@umich.edu

Paul F. Smith, PhD
Dept. of Pharmacology and Toxicology, School of Medical Sciences, University of
Otago Medical School, Dunedin, New Zealand
paul.smith@stonebow.otago.ac.nz

Wei Sun, PhD
Center for Hearing and Deafness, 137 Cary Hall,
University of Buffalo, Buffalo NY, 14214, USA
weisun@buffalo.edu

Chiemi Tanaka, MA, CCC-A PhD
Department of Communicative Disorders and Sciences, Center for Hearing and
Deafness, State University of New York at Buffalo, 137 Cary Hall, 3435 Main
StreetBuffaloNY, 14214, USA
ctanaka@buffalo.edu

Dayse Távora-Vieira, BSc (Sp Path & Aud) MAudSA (CC)
University of Western Australia, Perth, Medical Audiologist Services, 51, Colin St,
West Perth, WA6005 Australia
dayse.tavora@gmail.com

Ambrosetti Umberto
Audiology Unit, Department of Specialist Surgical Sciences, University of
Milan, Fondazione IRRCCS Ca' Granda Ospedale Maggiore Policlinico,
Via Pace 9, 20122, Milan, Italy
umberto.ambrosetti@unimi.it

Paul Van de Heyning, MD, PhD
Department of Otorhinolaryngology Head and Neck
Surgery, Antwerp University Hospital, University of Antwerp,
Wilrijkstr 10, 2650, Edegem-Antwerp, Belgium
paul.van.de.heyning@uza.be

Sven Vanneste, MA, MSc
BRAI²N TRI Tinnitus Clinic and Department of Neurosurgery,
University Hospital Antwerp, Wilrijkstraat 10, 2650, Edegem, Belgium
sven.vanneste@ua.ac.be

Nathan Weisz, Dr. rer. nat
Department of Psychology, University of Konstanz, P.O. Box 25, 78457,
Konstanz, Germany
nathan.weisz@uni-konstanz.de

Yu-Lan Mary Ying, MD
Department of Otolaryngology, Baylor College of Medicine, One Baylor Plaza ,
NA-102 Houston TX, 77030, USA
ylmying@yahoo.com

Florian Zeman, MA
Center of Clinical Studies, University Hospital of Regensburg, Regensburg,
Germany
florian.zeman@klinik.uni-regensburg.de

Chapter 1
Introduction

Aage R. Møller

Keywords Tinnitus • Objective tinnitus • Subjective tinnitus • Impact of tinnitus • Treatment • Neural plasticity • Hyperacusis • Phonophobia

Abbreviations

CNS   Central nervous system
EEG   Electroencephalography
PAG   Periaquaductal gray

Introduction

Tinnitus can affect the entire life of an individual, can prevent intellectual work, and impair the quality of life in general; in some instances, tinnitus can cause suicide. Severe tinnitus is often accompanied by hyperacusis and affective disorders such as phonophobia and depression.

Tinnitus and auditory hallucinations are perceptions of sounds in the absence of external noise. Subjective tinnitus and hallucinations are phantom sounds. Tinnitus is different from hallucinations and objective tinnitus that is caused by sounds generated in the body and conducted to the ear. Tinnitus is hearing of meaningless sounds. Hallucinations consist of meaningful sounds such as music or speech and occur in schizophrenia, after intake of certain drugs, and it may occur (rarely) in temporal lobe disorders. This book will not cover hallucinations.

There are two main kinds of tinnitus, namely, objective and subjective tinnitus. Objective tinnitus is caused by sounds generated in the body and conducted to the ear. It may be caused by turbulence of blood flow or muscle contractions. Individuals with subjective tinnitus have no visible signs of disease, and the disease has few detectable physical correlates. Objective tinnitus may be detected by an observer using auscultation, whereas subjective tinnitus can only be observed by the person who has the tinnitus.

Subjective tinnitus can have many forms: it can be high frequency sounds similar to the sounds of crickets, like a high- or low-frequency tone, and constant or pulsatile. Tinnitus can be present at all times or can appear only sometimes. However, it is usually not possible to relate a specific event to the appearance of tinnitus.

Patients' description of their symptoms is the only cue, and this may be misleading because they point to the ear, which is rarely the site of the pathology. It is abnormal neural activity in the brain that causes subjective tinnitus. This abnormal neural activity may originate in the ear but it is more likely generated somewhere in the brain.

There are two ways in which abnormal neural activity that may be interpreted as a sound can occur in the brain. One is through neural activity in the periphery of the auditory system that emulates the activity elicited by sound, which reaches the ear. The other way is through abnormal neural activity generated somewhere in the ascending auditory pathways. The way the neural activity that causes tinnitus is generated is not known in detail, but recent studies indicate that the activity is different from that elicited by sound stimulation, which means that the different forms of tinnitus may be generated in different ways.

There is evidence that tinnitus, after some time (chronic tinnitus), becomes fundamentally different

A.R. Møller (✉)
The University of Texas at Dallas, School of Behavioral
and Brain Sciences, GR 41, 800 W Campbell Rd,
Richardson, TX 75080, USA
e-mail: amoller@utdallas.edu

A.R. Møller et al. (eds.), *Textbook of Tinnitus*,
DOI 10.1007/978-1-60761-145-5_1, © Springer Science+Business Media, LLC 2011

from acute tinnitus. This change over time is important for treatment of tinnitus, and there is evidence that treatments are less effective after tinnitus has persisted for more than 5 years [1].

Tinnitus is not perceived in the same way as normal physical sounds, and there are indications that the way tinnitus is perceived has to do with perception of "self" (see Chap. 73) [2].

It is not known where in the nervous system sensory activation reaches conscious awareness, and neural activity in other parts of the CNS than that of normal sounds may give rise to the tinnitus sensation. It is not known what features of neural activity are important for eliciting awareness of a sensory signal, and even less is known about which kind of neural activity causes awareness of tinnitus (see Chap. 10) [3].

Contemporary understanding of which qualities of neural activity gives awareness of sensory stimulation includes neural synchrony, coherence of activity in many neurons in cortical or other structures, and neural connectivity. There is considerable evidence that activation of neural plasticity plays an important role in many forms of tinnitus (see Chap. 12). These characteristics of tinnitus have similarities with equally variant forms of pain. In particular, central neuropathic pain has many similarities with severe tinnitus, as will be discussed in this book (Chap. 14). Tinnitus and neuropathic pain are typical examples of "plasticity disorders" [4], where the symptoms are caused by plastic changes that are not beneficial to an individual person.

Sensory awareness and affective reactions (distress) are probably caused by different kinds of neural activity and probably occur in different parts of the CNS.

Such separation of perception is known for pain, where the lateral tract of the spinothalamic system produces awareness while the medial system produces the affective and emotional reaction to pain and activates distress networks.

More recently, some abnormal physiological signs have been found to be abnormal in individuals with some forms of tinnitus. One abnormality is with regard to the high-frequency component of electroencephalographic (EEG) recordings, known as gamma activity (see Chap. 21). The amplitude of the gamma activity is increased while the amplitude of another common component of the EEG, the alpha activity, is decreased (see Chap. 17). Animal experiments have shown that some forms of evoked potentials are altered (often increased) after exposure to sounds of an intensity that

in humans causes tinnitus, and which has shown signs of hyperactivity in recordings from specific nuclei [5, 6].

The signs of tinnitus at a local anatomical level are often different from those of a global brain level, and there are indications that non-auditory regions of the brain are activated abnormally in some forms of subjective tinnitus (see Chap. 17) [7]. Many different parts of the CNS are involved with tinnitus and there is evidence that parts that normally are not activated by sounds may also be involved in generating the sensation of tinnitus (see Chap. 73).

Also, animal experiments have shown evidence of non-auditory structures, for example, the hippocampus, being involved [8, 9]. Studies in humans have shown evidence of involvement of limbic structures [10]. Other studies have indicated that nonclassical pathways are abnormally involved in some forms of tinnitus [11, 12].

The degree and the impact of tinnitus on an individual person vary widely for the different kinds of tinnitus and also from person to person. It often fluctuates over time and with differing circumstances. Tinnitus is common, but only in a relatively few individuals does it cause distress or other problems. Many people who do not have tinnitus under normal environmental circumstances will experience tinnitus when placed in a room that is silent, such as the test rooms used for audiological testing.

Tinnitus is a phantom sensation of different kinds of sounds, but rarely are these sounds comparable with natural sounds or even with sounds that can be synthesized electronically.

Different methods have been used to estimate the intensity (loudness) of tinnitus. Visual analog scales have been used to estimate the strength of tinnitus, but methods such as loudness balance often give results that are unrealistically low [13]. The results of loudness matching show that most forms of tinnitus have loudness in the range of 20 dB even in situations where the tinnitus is regarded to be unbearable.

The effect of tinnitus on an individual person varies, and the degree of annoyance is not directly related to the perception of tinnitus. Like the impact of severe pain depends on whether it is regarded to be escapable or inescapable, also the impact of tinnitus on a person's quality of life largely varies. Studies have indicated that inescapable and escapable pain involved different lamina of the PAG [14] and the hypothalamic–midbrain neural circuits [15].

While tinnitus is described as a sound, similar sensations cannot be evoked by sound stimulation and it is assumed that the neural activity that causes tinnitus is different from that evoked by sound stimulation. The abnormal neural activity that causes tinnitus cannot be detected by imaging methods that are available. Some physiological methods can provide some insight in abnormal neural activity, but most of these methods are restricted to use in animals.

Tinnitus, especially severe tinnitus, is often accompanied by abnormal perception of (physical) sounds such as hyperacusis (lowered tolerance for all kinds of sounds) (see Chap. 3) and phonophobia (fear of sound). Hyperacusis also occurs in connection with other diseases such as autism.

In some individuals, tinnitus is associated with distress of affective (emotional) symptoms. These two qualities, perception and distress, are caused by activation of different parts of the nervous system. This is similar to pain where the lateral spinothalamic system is engaged in the perception of pain, whereas the medial spinothalamic system mediates the distress or affective component of pain. Animal experiments have indicated that pain that is perceived as escapable involves anatomically different parts of the periaquaductal gray (PAG) than pain that is perceived as inescapable. It is not known if there are similarities regarding tinnitus.

It is particularly true that when limbic structures (the emotional brain) become activated, tinnitus becomes a problem [2] (see Chaps. 10 and 73).

Treatment of Tinnitus

Subjective tinnitus is the most challenging of common disorders of hearing. So far, the available forms of treatment have had little to moderate success. Many different treatments are in use and even more have been tried and discarded. Often the goal of treatment of severe tinnitus has been to eliminate the symptoms, but this is rarely achieved. However, it is often possible to reduce some of the effects of the tinnitus, so that a patient gains quality of life and would perhaps be able to work in spite of the remaining effects of the disorder. This means that it is often possible to gain quality of life for the patient by such management of the tinnitus. Setting the goal to eliminate tinnitus will often make the patient disappointed when this goal is not met, and the

patient may try to find another treatment option, which most likely will be equally disappointing.

There are no known objective tests that can determine the severity of tinnitus and even detect whether tinnitus is present or not. Treatment must therefore rely on the patient's own assessment of his/her tinnitus. Some functional abnormalities have been detected in some individuals with tinnitus using functional imaging methods that can relate the abnormalities to specific brain regions. However, these methods are still in development and are not yet available for general clinical diagnosis of tinnitus.

Research on tinnitus has lagged behind similar disorders such as pain. There are two kinds of sound perception that are not caused by sounds reaching the ear from outside the body: tinnitus and auditory hallucinations.

Tinnitus Can Occur Together with Other Diseases

Tinnitus may occur together as one of the symptoms of a specific disease, such as Ménière's disease (see Chaps. 38 and 60), where tinnitus is one of the three (or four) symptoms that define the disease (the others are paroxysmal vertigo and fluctuating low-frequency hearing loss). Vestibular schwannoma are almost always accompanied by tinnitus (see Chap. 39). Individuals with Wilson's disease often have tinnitus. Tinnitus is often one of the symptoms of intracranial hypotension [16]. Traumatic injuries to the auditory nerve often result in tinnitus. Down's syndrome may also be associated with a higher incidence of tinnitus than non-Down's syndrome individuals. It has been reported that autistic individuals have an abnormal perception of loudness [17], but little is known about tinnitus.

Many conditions have tinnitus as part of their symptoms; most noticeable are Ménière's disease and vestibular schwannoma.

Tinnitus is often associated with hearing loss of various kinds, but hearing loss also occurs without tinnitus. Individuals with tinnitus often have hearing loss, but tinnitus may also occur, although rarely, in individuals with normal or near-normal hearing. In a study by Friedland and co-authors [18], a correlation was found between low-frequency hearing loss and risk of cardiovascular diseases. These investigators found that the shape of a person's audiogram correlated strongly with cardiovascular changes and peripheral arterial disease. Hypertension has been found to be associated with a lower incidence of tinnitus, as compared to normotension and hypotension [19].

Tinnitus often occurs after head injuries. Injury to the auditory nerve, which may occur from surgical manipulation or head trauma, often results in tinnitus. Blast injuries, such as those occurring in recent wars, result in a high incidence of tinnitus in connection with closed head injuries.

Tinnitus is more prevalent at old age, but results of epidemiologic studies vary widely, mainly because the criteria for tinnitus chosen in the different studies have been different. Most studies have concerned people who have sought professional help for their tinnitus.

Tinnitus may occur after exposure to loud noise and as complication in treatment with certain drugs such as some antibiotics (ototoxic antibiotics), aspirin, idometacin, and diuretic (furosemide) quinine (see Chap. 42).

Tinnitus often occurs together with depression [20], and it is often said that depression is a co-morbidity to tinnitus. However, it could also be possible that the physiological abnormalities that cause tinnitus are similar or that tinnitus and depression have the same risk factors. Misophonia (dislike of specific sound) may occur together with tinnitus or alone. The "exploding head syndrome" may also occur with tinnitus or alone (see Chap. 4).

Plastic Changes in the Brain Can Cause Tinnitus

Tinnitus is regarded to be a complex hyperactive disease, or rather tinnitus is a symptom with complex causes that indicate hyperactive neural activity. There is evidence that the neural activity that causes at least some forms of tinnitus is different from that evoked by sound. Earlier it was assumed that tinnitus was caused by increased firing rate of neurons occurring without sensory input. Recent studies indicate that other forms of abnormal activity somewhere in the nervous system, in particular how neural activity in populations of nerve cells are inter-related, may be the cause of some forms of tinnitus. Evidence has been presented that abnormal synchrony and temporal coherence of the activity in populations of neurons may be the important factors for causing tinnitus [21, 22]. Activation

of the nervous systems with temporal (periodic or non-periodic) signals, such as those occurring from sensory stimulation with sounds, creates coherence in the neural activity in a population of neurons because many neurons are activated by the same source. There are reasons to believe abnormal communications between nerve fibers or nerve cells (ephaptic transmission) may be involved in creating an abnormally high degree of temporal coherence of neural activity without any physical sensory input (see Chaps. 10 and 13).

There is considerable evidence that activation of neural plasticity plays an important role in many forms of tinnitus (see Chap. 12). Activation of neural plasticity can alter the connectivity in the brain by unmasking dormant synapses. This is another factor that may be involved in some forms of tinnitus. There is also some evidence that the anatomically located regions activated in tinnitus are different from those that are activated by sound. There are indications that the neural activity that causes the awareness (conscious perception) of tinnitus is different from that which causes the affective (distress) reactions. Such separation in processing of sounds that represent different kinds of information may be similar to the separation of different kinds of sensory signals described as stream segregation. The separation processing that leads to conscious perception and the processing that causes distress may indicate that these occur in different parts of the thalamus: the ventral part for processing of awareness and the medial and dorsal parts for the activity that causes affective symptoms. The dorsal and medial thalamus has subcortical connections to the amygdala. All these forms of changes in the function of the nervous system have few or no detectable morphological correlates.

Many aspects of tinnitus that have lasted a long time (e.g., more than 5 years) are different from tinnitus that has only lasted a short time (less than 5 years). Perhaps most important, tinnitus that has lasted a long time is more difficult to treat than tinnitus that has only lasted a short time [1].

Impact of Tinnitus on an Individual Person

The degree and the impact on an individual person from tinnitus vary widely from person to person and often vary over time. Only rarely has it been possible to relate the character and the severity to events or specific diseases.

There are no objective tests that can determine the existence of tinnitus nor is it possible to evaluate the severity of tinnitus by any known test. The lack of objective tests may sometimes set the patients' description into question. The cause (meaning what caused the tinnitus to start) is often elusive. Only rarely has it been possible to relate the character and the severity to events or specific diseases.

The lack of objective signs to classify tinnitus according to severity has affected attempts to study the epidemiology of tinnitus. This is probably the most important reason why different studies typically show different incidence and prevalence values.

References

1. Møller MB and AR Møller, (1990) Vascular compression syndrome of the eighth nerve: Clinical correlations and surgical findings., in Neurologic clinics: Diagnostic neurotology and otoneurology, IK Arenberg and DB Smith, Editors. 1990, WB Saunders Publishing Co: Philadelphia. 421–39.
2. Jastreboff PJ (1990) Phantom auditory perception (tinnitus): Mechanisms of generation and perception. Neurosci Res 8:221–54.
3. Eggermont JJ, (2007) Pathophysiology of tinnitus, in Tinnitus: Pathophysiology and treatment, progress in brain research, B Langguth et al. Editors. 2007, Elsevier: Amsterdam. 19–35.
4. Møller AR (2008) Neural Plasticity: For Good and Bad. Progress of Theoretical Physics Supplement No 173:48–65.
5. Syka J (2002) Plastic changes in the central auditory system after hearing loss, restoration of function, and during learning. Physiol Rev 82:601–36.
6. Szczepaniak WS and AR Møller (1996) Evidence of neuronal plasticity within the inferior colliculus after noise exposure: A study of evoked potentials in the rat. Electroenceph Clin Neurophysiol 100:158–64.
7. Schaette R and R Kempter (2008) Development of hyperactivity after hearing loss in a computational model of the dorsal cochlear nucleus depends on neuron response type. Hear Res 240:57–72.
8. Goble TJ, AR Møller and LT Thompson (2009) Acute corticosteroid administration alters place-field stability in a fixed environment: comparison to physical restraint and noise exposure. Hear Res 253:52–9.
9. Lanting CP, E de Kleine and P van Dijk (2009) Neural activity underlying tinnitus generation: Results from PET and fMRI. Hear Res 255:1–13.
10. Lockwood AH, DS Wack, RF Burkard et al (2001) The functional anatomy of gaze-evoked tinnitus and sustained lateral gaze. Neurology 56:472–80.
11. Møller AR, MB Møller and M Yokota (1992) Some forms of tinnitus may involve the extralemniscal auditory pathway. Laryngoscope 102: 1165–71.
12. Cacace AT, JP Cousins, SM Parnes et al (1999) Cutaneous-evoked tinnitus. II: Review of neuroanatomical, physiological and functional imaging studies. Audiol Neurotol 4:258–68.
13. Vernon J (1976) The loudness of tinnitus. Hear Speech Action 44:17–9.
14. Keay KA, CI Clement, A Depaulis et al (2001) Different representations of inescapable noxious stimuli in the periaqueductal gray and upper cervical spinal cord of freely moving rats. Neurosci Lett 313:17–20.
15. Lumb BM (2002) Inescapable and escapable pain is represented in distinct hypothalamic-midbrain circuits: specific roles of Ad- and C-nociceptors. Exp Physiol 87:281–86.
16. Couch JR (2008) Spontaneous intracranial hypotension: the syndrome and its complications. Curr Treat Options Neurol. 10:3–11.
17. Khalfa S, N Bruneau, B Rogé et al (2004) Increased perception of loudness in autism. Hear Res 198:87–92.
18. Friedland DR, Cederberg C, Tarima S (2009) Audiometric pattern as a predictor of cardiovascular status: development of a model for assessment of risk. Laryngoscope 19:473–86.
19. Podoshin L, J Ben-David and CB Teszler (1997) Pediatric and Geriatric Tinnitus. Int Tinnitus J 3:101–3.
20. Langguth B, T Kleinjung, B Fischer et al. (2007) Tinnitus severity, depression and the Big Five personality traits, in Tinnitus: Pathophysiology and treatment, progress in brain research, B Langguth et al. Editors. 2007, Elsevier: Amsterdam. 221–33.
21. Eggermont JJ and LE Roberts (2004) The neuroscience of tinnitus. Trends Neurosci 27:676–82.
22. Eggermont JJ (2007) Correlated neural activity as the driving force for functional changes in auditory cortex. Hear Res 229:69–80.

Chapter 2
Different Forms of Tinnitus

Aage R. Møller

Keypoints

1. Subjective tinnitus has many forms and may be regarded as a group of disorders rather than a single disorder.
2. There are a few objective ways to distinguish between the different forms of tinnitus.
3. Tinnitus has been classified subjectively according to:
   (a) Intensity: Often using a visual analog scale or loudness matching.
   (b) Character: High frequency (like crickets), low frequency (rumbling), tonal, pulsatile, constant, or intermittent.
   (c) Other features such as the ability to modulate the tinnitus by manipulating their jaw, moving their eyes, or applying pressure on neck regions.
   (d) Whether referred to one ear, both ears, or perceived as being inside the head.
4. Some diseases, such as Ménière's disease, are accompanied with tinnitus; such tinnitus may be different from other forms of tinnitus.
5. Some forms of tinnitus are associated with affective disorders such as depression or phonophobia.
6. Subjective tinnitus is often accompanied by abnormal perception of sounds, known as hyperacusis (lowered tolerance for sounds) or hypersensitivity to sounds.

A.R. Møller (✉)
The University of Texas at Dallas, School of Behavioral and Brain Sciences, GR 41, 800 W Campbell Rd, Richardson, TX 75080, USA
e-mail: amoller@utdallas.edu

Keywords Objective tinnitus • Subjective tinnitus • Somatosensory tinnitus • Modulation of tinnitus • Abnormal perception of sounds

Abbreviations

AVM	Arterio-venous malformations
EEG	Electroencephalography
MEG	Magnetoencephalography
TMJ	Temporomandibular joint

Introduction

Subjective tinnitus is a broad group of sensations that are caused by abnormal neural activity in the nervous system that is not elicited by sound activation of sensory cells in the cochlea. Subjective tinnitus is by far the most common kind of tinnitus. Subjective tinnitus is phantom sounds that have similarities with the phantom limb symptoms and central neuropathic pain (see Chap. 14) [1, 2].

It is a general problem that the same name (tinnitus) is used for so many different forms of subjective tinnitus with different characteristics, different severities, and different causes. Having the same name used for fundamentally different disorders, such as the different forms of tinnitus, is an obstacle in treatment as well as research. The fact that tinnitus is not a single disorder but many makes epidemiological studies difficult to interpret. Different epidemiological studies have come up with very different numbers for the prevalence of tinnitus to some extent, because different definitions of tinnitus and its severity were employed in different studies.

It is agreed that the incidence of tinnitus increases with age and is more common in people who have had exposure to loud noise. Studies of the prevalence of tinnitus in individuals above the age of 50 years have shown values from 7.6% to 20.1% (see Chap. 5).

In general, subjective tinnitus has no physical signs, and there are no objective clinical diagnostic tests that can distinguish between the different forms of subjective tinnitus. Only the patient's own description can serve as a basis for a clinical evaluation. Only recently have laboratory research methods been developed that might provide some insight into the different anatomical locations of the abnormalities associated with different forms of tinnitus. Neuroimaging methods are now beginning to provide some information on the functional changes in the brain of individuals with tinnitus (see Chap. 18). Electrophysiologic tests (electroencephalography, EEG, and magnetoencephalography, also known as MEG) can provide some information about plastic changes in the brain associated with tinnitus (see Chap. 20). These methods may become the basis for future clinical tests that can make a differential diagnosis of the different kinds of tinnitus possible and then relate it to pathology.

Subjective for Objective Measures of Tinnitus

Loudness matching and the use of a visual analog scale have been used for estimations of the loudness of an individual's tinnitus. However, loudness matching results in unrealistically low values [3–5]. The use of a visual analog scale seems to give more realistic values.

In the absence of objective tests, tinnitus has been classified according to its perceived severity. Reed classifies tinnitus into three broad groups: mild tinnitus, moderate tinnitus, and severe chronic tinnitus [3]. Mild tinnitus is defined as tinnitus that does not interfere noticeably with everyday life, moderate tinnitus may cause some annoyance and may be perceived as unpleasant, and severe chronic tinnitus affects a person's entire life. These classifications rely on the individual person's own description of their tinnitus. Similar classifications have been used for pain (see [6]).

The Anatomical Location of the Physiological Abnormality

Like other phantom sensations, such as phantom limb syndrome, tinnitus is often referred to a different anatomical location than that of the pathology. Since tinnitus has the character of sound, it is often referred to one or both ears. Naturally, tinnitus has been regarded as a pathology located in the ear. Therefore, individuals with tinnitus often seek medical assistance from an ear specialist. However, examination of the ear in most cases finds nothing to be wrong. Also much of the research conducted early had been directed to the ear for studies of the pathology of tinnitus.

The anatomical location of the physiological anomaly of subjective tinnitus is often unknown and is likely to be different from where the tinnitus is referred (one ear, both ears, or in the middle of the head). Instead, the anatomical location of the abnormality that causes tinnitus is the brain. However, it is not obvious which region of the brain the pathology is located, and the abnormal function is not necessarily restricted to regions that are normally activated by sound stimulation.

Many forms of tinnitus are caused by activation of neural plasticity, which makes it difficult to identify the cause and the location of the primary pathology.

Activation of neural plasticity may change many neural processes, re-route information, alter the relation between inhibition and excitation, and change temporal coherence of activity in the population of neurons that may be involved in different forms of tinnitus.

It is possible that different characteristics of tinnitus distinguish the different kinds of tinnitus. There is recent evidence that the pathology of tinnitus that is pulsating is different from tinnitus that is not pulsating (see Chap. 59).

The pathology of tinnitus that is caused by external factors may be different from tinnitus that occurs without external factors being involved.

Deprivation of sensory input may constitute such external factors. It is known to be powerful in turning on neural plasticity, and there are many examples of how restoring input to the auditory nervous system can alleviate tinnitus [7] (see Chaps. 74 and 77). The fact that these methods provide relief from tinnitus supports the hypothesis that neural plasticity has been activated by the absence of signals to the nervous system.

Tinnitus occurs together with age-related hearing loss (see Chap. 36) and noise-induced hearing loss (see Chap. 37), as well as after administration of ototoxic antibiotics, some diuretics (furosemide), and quinine [8].

Tinnitus caused by noise exposure may normally abate after ending the exposure, but the tinnitus may sometimes remain present after ending exposure and may last indefinitely, which indicates that generation of tinnitus is caused by a stable pathologic state of neural circuits. These neural networks, which generate that kind of tinnitus, have bistable properties: one normal and another pathologic.

Exposure to loud sounds can cause tinnitus (see Chap. 37), and so can administration of ototoxic drugs. It is not known if the cause is the reduction in input to the auditory nervous system that turns neural plasticity on, or if it is overstimulation or possibly the morphological damage from overstimulation that activates neural plasticity.

There is evidence that the pathology of subjective tinnitus that occurs in Ménière's disease (see Chaps. 38 and 60) is different from other forms of tinnitus because it can be reduced or eliminated by sympathectomy [9], which has not been shown effective in other kinds of tinnitus. Tinnitus in Ménière's disease may therefore be a specific form of tinnitus that is different from other forms.

Tinnitus almost always occurs together with vestibular schwannoma (earlier known as acoustic tumors) (see Chap. 39). There are reasons to believe that the pathology of these forms of tinnitus is also different, although studies have not been published that could support this hypothesis. It has also been shown that there are other specific differences between the tinnitus that accompanies vestibular schwannoma and other forms of tinnitus. Thus, Cacace (1994) found some specific signs that occurred regarding tinnitus after operations for vestibular schwannoma [10], consisting of gaze-evoked or gaze-modulated tinnitus (see Chap. 39). He ascribed it to a phenomenon of deafferentation-induced plasticity. Acoustic schwannoma is one of the few risk factors for tinnitus that is almost 100%. The tinnitus does not normally disappear after removal of the tumor [11]. Injury of the auditory nerve from trauma, surgical operation, or viral infection (neuritis) is also associated with a high risk of tinnitus.

Traumatic head injuries are often associated with tinnitus.

Tinnitus often occurs with migraine headaches. It seems likely that the pathology of these forms of tinnitus differs from each other, although studies have not confirmed this hypothesis.

Tinnitus also accompanies disorders such as temporomandibular joint (TMJ) [12, 13]. Tinnitus, in connection with TMJ disorders, often disappears when the TMJ disorder is treated successfully (see Chap. 95). The pathology of these forms of tinnitus may be related to the anatomical connections between the trigeminal caudal nucleus and cochlear nuclei [14] (see Chap. 9).

Tinnitus often accompanies neck disorders (see Chap. 80) [15]. However, there is often no known cause to the tinnitus (idiopathic tinnitus). These forms of tinnitus are known as "somatosensory tinnitus," and the reason for this abnormal cross-modular interaction may be the involvement of the nonclassical pathways. The pathology of these forms of tinnitus is likely to be different and therefore require different kinds of treatment. The pathology may be related to the anatomical connections between the upper spinal cord (C_{2-4}) and cochlear nuclei (see Chap. 9).

Subjective tinnitus is often accompanied by an abnormal perception of sounds, such as hyperacusis (decreased tolerance for sounds in general, see Chap. 3), phonophobia (fear of sound), and misophonia (dislike of specific sounds) (see Chap. 4). Some individuals with tinnitus hear sounds as being distorted, spoiling the enjoyment of music. This distortion may also make it difficult to understand speech.

Many individuals who have tinnitus (about two-thirds) can modulate their tinnitus by signals from the somatosensory system, such as from eye movements [16], manipulations of their jaw, and applying various pressure on specific neck regions [17–19]. These forms of tinnitus can be managed by somatosensory-oriented treatment [20], and such individuals may be a subgroup with a different pathology.

Affective symptoms accompany some forms of tinnitus [21]. It seems likely that such forms of tinnitus are different from other forms and that their pathology may differ as well (see Chap. 62).

Conclusion

Tinnitus is not a single disorder and the symptoms vary substantially. The causes of different individual's tinnitus also have wide variants. The fact that a disorder with such differences has the same name is an obstacle in studies of tinnitus and patient management.

References

1. Møller AR, (2007) Tinnitus and pain, in Tinnitus: Pathophysiology and treatment, progress in brain research, B Langguth et al, Editors. 2007, Elsevier: Amsterdam. 47–53.

2. Møller AR (1997) Similarities between chronic pain and tinnitus. Am. J. Otol. 18:577–85.

3. Reed GF (1960) An audiometric study of 200 cases of subjective tinnitus. Arch. Otolaryngol. 71:94–104.

4. Fowler EP (1942) The illusion of loudness of tinnitus-its etiology and treatment. Ann. Otol. Laryngol. 52:275–85.

5. Vernon J (1976) The loudness of tinnitus. Hear Speech Action 44:17–9.

6. Møller AR (2006) Neural plasticity and disorders of the nervous system. Cambridge: Cambridge University Press.

7. Van de Heyning P, K Vermeire, M Diebl et al (2008) Incapacitating unilateral tinnitus in single-sided deafness treated by cochlear implantation. Ann. Otol. Rhinol. Laryngol. 117:645–52.

8. Rizzi MD and K Hirose (2007) Aminoglycoside ototoxicity. Curr. Opin. Otolaryngol. Head Neck. Surg. 15:352–7.

9. Passe EG (1951) Sympathectomy in relation to Ménière's disease, nerve deafness and tinnitus. A report of 110 cases. Proc. Roy. Soc. Med. 44:760–72.

10. Cacace AT, TJ Lovely, DJ McFarland et al (1994) Anomalous cross-modal plasticity following posterior fossa surgery: Some speculations on gaze-evoked tinnitus. Hear. Res. 81:22–32.

11. Berliner KI, C Shelton, W Hitselberger et al (1992) Acoustic tumors: Effect of surgical removal on tinnitus. Am. J. Otol. 13:13–7.

12. Morgan DH (1992) Tinnitus of TMJ origin. J. Craniomandibular practice 10:124–9.

13. Wright DD and DK Ryugo (1996) Mossy fiber projections from the cuneate nucleus to the cochlear nucleus in the rat. J. Comp. Neurol. 365:159–72.

14. Zhou J and S Shore (2004) Projections from the trigeminal nuclear complex to the cochlear nuclei: A retrograde and anterograde tracing study in the guinea pig. J. Neurosci. Res. 78:901–7.

15. Montazem A (2000) Secondary tinnitus as a symptom of instability of the upper cervical spine: Operative management. Int. Tinnitus. J. 6:130–3.

16. Coad ML, AH Lockwood, RJ Salvi et al (2001) Characteristics of patients with gaze-evoked tinnitus. Otol. Neurotol. 22:650–4.

17. Rubinstein B (2003) Tinnitus and craniomandibular disorders – is there a link? Swed. Dental J. Suppl. 95:1–46.

18. Pinchoff RJ, RF Burkard, RJ Salvi et al (1998) Modulation of tinnitus by voluntary jaw movements. Am. J. Otol. 19:785–9.

19. Abel MD and RA Levine (2004) Muscle contractions and auditory perception in tinnitus patients and nonclinical subjects. Cranio. 22:181–91.

20. Levine RA, EC Nam, Y Oron et al, (2007) Evidence for a tinnitus subgroup responsive to somatosensory based treatment modalities, in Tinnitus: Pathophysiology and treatment, progress in brain research, B Langguth et al, Editors. 2007, Elsevier: Amsterdam. 195–207.

21. Langguth B, T Kleinjung, B Fischer et al, (2007) Tinnitus severity, depression and the big five personality traits, in Tinnitus: Pathophysiology and treatment, progress in brain research, B Langguth et al, Editors. 2007, Elsevier: Amsterdam. 221–33.

Chapter 3
Hyperacusis and Disorders of Loudness Perception

David M. Baguley and Don J. McFerran

Keypoints

1. There are several forms of loudness perception disorder.
2. The terminology of such disorders is often confused.
3. The most commonly used terms in an audiological context are hyperacusis, denoting a generalized reduced tolerance for sound, as well as phonophobia, denoting a fear of sounds.
4. The majority of people with a loudness perception disorder also have tinnitus. Just under one half of individuals with tinnitus also describe some degree of loudness perception disorder.
5. There are few rigorous studies regarding the epidemiology of loudness perception disorders; the true prevalence of hyperacuis and phonophobia remains a matter of conjecture.
6. Some loudness perception disorders are associated with disorders of facial nerve function with consequent loss of the acoustic reflex. Most cases have no such association and the underlying pathological mechanism is unclear.
7. Various management strategies have been suggested, including the use of tinnitus therapies, with or without the use of sound therapy, and psychological therapies.

Keywords Tinnitus • Hyperacusis • Hypersensitivity • Loudness discomfort • Migraine

D.M. Baguley (✉)
Cambridge University Hospitals, Hills Road, Cambridge, CB2 2QQ, UK
e-mail: dmb29@camacuk

Introduction

Most people dislike certain sounds, irrespective of their intensity; chalk screeching on a blackboard or the sound of skin catching on a child's balloon are common examples of this. Many people recognize that their sound tolerance varies with their mood, so that someone who is tired, stressed, or anxious may find sounds within their normal tolerance zone unpleasantly loud. Similarly, one person's unbearably loud concert may be another's ideal outing. Because of this interpersonal and temporal variation, clinical disorders of sound tolerance were not recognized until relatively recently, and even when recognized, were thought to be exceptional. In 1987, Vernon [1] stated "In our Tinnitus Clinic, where more than 4,000 patients have been seen, hyperacusis has been seen only four times." As knowledge of tinnitus has improved, recognition of disorders of loudness tolerance has also improved. However, this is still a confused and under researched area.

The fact that clinical recognition of disorders of sound tolerance is relatively recent is not to say that these issues have arisen in modern times. For example, Wilkie Collins uses hyperacusis as an essential element of the plot in his gripping novel "the Woman in White" (1860). Mr Fairlie is the uncle and guardian of Laura, and is derelict in his duty (leading to his niece's downfall) as he is unable to tolerate spoken conversation and thus advise her. For example, Mr Fairlie states:

"Pray excuse me, but could you contrive to speak in a lower key? In the wretched state of my nerves, loud sound of any kind is indescribable torture to me You will pardon an invalid?" (see also Chap. 57).

A.R. Møller et al. (eds.), *Textbook of Tinnitus*,
DOI 10.1007/978-1-60761-145-5_3, © Springer Science+Business Media, LLC 2011

Definitions

There is still no unified standard of nomenclature for disorders of sound tolerance. Some of the commonly used words are shown in Table 3.1.

Part of the reason for this wide range of terminology is that disorders of sound tolerance are treated by several disciplines. As well as Audiology and Otolaryngology, Neurologists and Psychiatrists encounter patients with symptoms of altered sound tolerance and, hence, have developed their own terminology. Sound tolerance is also an important consideration for those involved in the public health issues of environmental and occupational noise.

Hyperacusis

The word "hyperacusis" first appeared in the medical literature in 1938 [2]. A later modification to "hyperacusis dolorosa" [3] captured the emotional impact but was not widely adopted. The dictionary definition given in Table 3.1 implies the ability to detect sound at abnormally low intensities, or, in other words, better than average hearing; this is not how the term is used in the clinical literature. Subsequent attempts to define hyperacusis have included "unusual tolerance to ordinary environmental sounds" [1], "consistently exaggerated or inappropriate responses that are neither threatening nor uncomfortably loud to a normal person" [4], and "abnormal lowered tolerance to sound" [5]. A more recent definition [6] describes hyperacusis as "abnormal increased sound-induced activity within the auditory pathways". As a result, sounds that are nonintrusive, or unnoticed by the general population, are uncomfortable to people with hyperacusis. The common thread to all these definitions is that sounds in general, rather than specific sounds, are unpleasant to individuals with hyperacusis.

Some workers have applied a different meaning to hyperacusis. Gordon [7] defined it as increased sensitivity to quiet sounds or, in other words, unusually acute hearing and coined the term "audiosensitivity" for what audiologists would regard as hyperacusis. The word "audiosensitivity" is not commonly used. To further complicate matters, a new term has recently appeared, namely, "conductive hyperacusis" [8, 9].

Table 3.1 Some of the words and phrases used to describe disorders of loudness tolerance

	Synonyms	Derivation	Definition
Recruitment	Loudness recruitment	*Fr* recruter	"An abnormally large increase in the perceived loudness of a sound caused by a slight increase in its intensity" (Dorland)
Hyperacusis	Hyperacousia Hyperacusia Hyperakusis Acoustic hyperaesthesia Auditory hyperaesthesia	*Gk* hyper (above) akousis (hearing)	"Exceptionally acute hearing, the hearing threshold being unusually low" (Dorland) "An abnormal, lowered tolerance to sound" (Baguley, 2003) [50]
Phonophobia		*Gk* phone (voice or sound) phobia (fear)	"Irrational fear of sounds or of speaking aloud" (Dorland)
Misophonia		*Gk* misos (hatred) phone (voice or sound)	"A negative reaction to sound results from an enhanced limbic and autonomic response, without abnormal enhancement of the auditory system" Jastreboff and Hazell [6]
Dysacousis	Auditory dysesthesia dysacousia dysacusis	*Gk* dys (bad) akousis (hearing)	"A condition in which certain sounds produce discomfort" (Dorland)
Odynacusis		*Gk* odyne (pain) akousis (hearing)	"lowered uncomfortable loudness levels" (Levitin et al. 2005) [51]
Auditory allodynia		*L* auditorius (pertaining to hearing) *Gk* allos (other) odyne (pain)	"substantial aversion to certain sounds" (Levitin et al. 2005) [51]
Collapsed sound tolerance			Term coined by the Hyperacusis Network (www.hyperacusis.net) and synonymous with hyperacusis

This is a phenomenon associated with dehiscence of the superior semicircular canal in which the person may have normal air conduction thresholds on pure tone audiometry but better-than-normal bone conduction. This results in an air-bone gap, and the person often complains of hyper-awareness of somatosounds.

Phonophobia

Phonophobia, literally meaning fear of sound, is a widely used term in neurology, particularly in association with migraine. Woodhouse and Drummond [10] reported that at least 50% of migraine attacks are accompanied by increased sensitivity to sound, and uncomfortable loudness levels are reduced during attacks. From an audiological point of view, however, phonophobia implies reaction to certain sounds that have specific emotional associations for that person. Thus, the reduced sound tolerance seen in migraine might be better described as hyperacusis. True phonophobia in isolation is unusual; Hazell et al. [11] reported that only 56% of individuals with reduced loudness tolerance had pure phonophobia.

Misophonia

The condition misophonia (see also Chap. 4) was proposed in 2003 [12] to convey many of the same sentiments as phonophobia but removing the phobic connotation as an automatic accompaniment. This is potentially useful as in some health economies it is not lawful to treat a phobic condition unless one is a licensed psychologist or psychiatrist. In 2004, Jastreboff and Hazell [6] describe misophonia as "a negative reaction to sound results from an enhanced limbic and autonomic response, without abnormal enhancement of the auditory system." They suggest that phonophobia is a subsection of misophonia where fear is the chief component. The word "misophonia" has yet to enter widespread usage and is not a recognized term in many healthcare databases such as Medline. It does, however, add a useful definition to the terminology of reduced loudness tolerance, and its usage should probably be encouraged.

Recruitment

Recruitment or, to use the full title, loudness recruitment [13, 14], is a common finding in individuals with cochlear hearing loss associated with outer hair cell dysfunction. It is characterized by an abnormally large increase in the perceived loudness of a sound caused by a slight increase in its intensity. This is not modulated by mood or levels of anxiety.

The boundaries between these definitions can occasionally seem blurred, and it is also quite possible for a person to have more than one form of reduced sound tolerance. For example, a person with a cochlear hearing loss may display recruitment but also have phonophobia. In the Audiology/Otology literature, hyperacusis is quite frequently used as an all-embracing term for all forms of reduced sound tolerance, adding to the confusion. Additionally, present terminology does not describe some clinical presentations, such as the hyper-vigilance to novel auditory events seen in individuals with autism spectrum disorder [15, 16] or the marked auditory startle seen in some with cerebral palsy [17].

Acoustic Shock

Recently, considerable interest has been developed about auditory symptoms arising in response to sudden, unexpected sounds [5, 18] (see also Chap. 4). The causative signal does not have to be particularly loud and does not reach a level that causes noise-induced hearing loss. The phenomenon has developed particular relevance among people wearing headsets or using telephone handsets in working environments such as call centres. Acoustic shock undoubtedly predates call centers, and wearing a headset is probably not essential to the diagnosis. Almost all affected individuals describe pain in or around their ears. Other symptoms include tinnitus, vestibular disturbance, hyperacusis, hyper-vigilance, anxiety, headache, numbness, burning, tingling, blockage, pressure, fullness, echoing, or hollow feelings in the ear. Much remains to be discovered about the character of the sounds that trigger this condition, the characteristics of the individuals who develop the symptoms, and the correct methods of managing the disorder. The pathogenesis of the condition has included theories of overactivity of the tensor tympani muscle, cochlear damage, central auditory mechanisms, or a post-traumatic stress disorder. A UK working group has been set up, "The Acoustic Shock Programme" and has proposed the following definitions for those indviduals who develop acoustic shock in the workplace while using communications equipment:

- An acoustic incident is a sudden, unexpected, noise event which is perceived as loud, transmitted through a telephone or headset.
- Acoustic shock is an adverse response to an acoustic incident resulting in alteration of auditory function.

Epidemiology of Reduced Loudness Tolerance

There is still a dearth of published work on the demographics of reduced sound tolerance, but it certainly seems more common than Vernon's original observation [1]. A Polish study into the prevalence of tinnitus [19] included a question on hyperacusis; 10,349 people responded, of whom 15.2% reported hyperacusis. The symptom was more common in men, more common in those of higher socio-economic class, and more common in urban dwellers. Among individuals who had tinnitus, the prevalence of hyperacusis was 40%. A well-designed study by Andersson et al. [20] examined responses to a questionnaire administered partly over the internet and partly via the conventional postal system. This showed a point prevalence of hyperacusis of 9% in the web respondents and 8% in the postal group. The prevalence of requiring ear protection for everyday sounds was notably lower at 2 and 3% for the web and postal respondents, respectively. Interestingly, a proportion of respondents also reported sensitivity to other sensory modalities, particularly light and odours, and this increased sensitivity was higher in the respondents who also reported sound sensitivity. In addition, those who reported hyperacusis were also more likely to report dizziness, hearing loss, and headaches. These estimates of the prevalence of hyperacusis do not make a distinction between people who have a mild dislike of extremely loud sounds and those whose sound tolerance has a significant impact on their ability to live a normal life. Consequently, they almost certainly over-estimate the number of people who have clinically important hyperacusis (see also Chaps. 5 and 6).

One way to obtain an approximate prevalence figure for significant hyperacusis is to use a process of extrapolation from other data sources. The prevalence of hyperacusis in individuals who have tinnitus and vice versa has been well documented. Patients attending a tinnitus clinic have a hyperacusis prevalence of approximately 40% [21, 22]. Among those whose chief complaint is hyperacusis, the prevalence of tinnitus has been reported as 86% [23]. If 5% of the adult population have troublesome tinnitus [24], and 40% of those have troublesome hyperacusis, then a prevalence of significant hyperacusis of 2% can be derived [5].

Altered loudness tolerance is seen in conjunction with several other common conditions, most notably migraine [25] and post-traumatic stress disorder [26]. It is also thought to be more common in conditions such as depression, though there is little robust scientific support for this assertion.

Pathophysiology of Reduced Loudness Tolerance

A review by Katzenell and Segal [27] separated disorders of loudness tolerance into those associated with conditions of the peripheral auditory system, diseases of the central nervous system, hormonal diseases, and infectious diseases. However, they also concluded that in many cases, there was no identifiable cause, and that in these cases, the central auditory system was the likely culprit. The peripheral causes discussed by Katzenell and Segal [27] included Bell's palsy, Ramsay Hunt syndrome, and individuals who have undergone a stapedectomy. However, in all these cases, the stapedial reflex might have been affected, either due to direct damage to the stapedius muscle (stapedectomy) or due to damage to the facial nerve that innervates stapedius (Bell's palsy, Ramsay Hunt syndrome). Without a functioning stapedius, part of the ear's protective reflex is lost and more sound energy can reach the cochlea. As the auditory system is then responding correctly to the amount of energy reaching the cochlea, it is a moot point as to whether this constitutes a true abnormality of loudness tolerance.

Peripheral causes of hyperacusis, however, are relatively uncommon. The majority have no obvious cause, but a number of cases of hyperacusis are associated with specific conditions; these examples of so-called

Table 3.2 Conditions associated with reduced loudness tolerance

Migraine
Depression
Posttraumatic stress disorder
Head injury
Lyme disease
Williams syndrome
Multiple sclerosis
Addison's disease
Fibromyalgia/pain
Multiple sclerosis (case report)
Middle cerebral artery aneurysm (case report)

Table 3.3 Hyperacusis in Williams syndrome

References	N	Percentage with hyperacusis	Notes
Klein et al. (1990) [4]	65	95	
Van Borsel et al. (1997) [52]	82	95	Complaint of sensitivity to "noise": example given of a power-saw
Levitin et al. (2005) [51]	118	91	
Blomberg et al. [31]	38	13	Used Khalfa et al. [41] questionnaire

"syndromic hyperacusis" are shown in Table 3.2. Because the underlying pathology for some of these conditions is at least partially understood, it is useful to examine their pathological mechanisms to try and obtain clues about hyperacusis in general.

Some cases of familial migraine have been shown to be associated with mutations in a central nervous system calcium gene. It has been speculated that if this faulty gene is present, calcium channels within the cochlea or central auditory pathways could be involved, resulting in the episodic hypersensitivity to sound [28].

Lyme disease is a tick borne infection caused by a bacterium, *Borrelia burgdorferi*. The infection affects many organs including the nervous system, and hypersensitivity to sound is a well-recognized symptom [29]. In some cases, the facial nerve is affected. Hence, the stapedial reflex may be deficient, resulting in the same mechanism described above for Bell's palsy. However, there are also cases where the facial nerve function and stapedial reflex are normal and, in these cases at least, the problem is likely to be in the central auditory system.

Several of the other conditions associated with central hyperacusis, such as depression, migraine, posttraumatic stress disorder, and posthead injury syndrome, are thought to be related to disturbances of 5 hydroxytryptamine (5 HT, serotonin) function [18, 27]. 5 HT is known to be involved in central auditory pathways. It has been suggested that the hyperacusis is a manifestation of this disturbed 5 HT function [30].

Williams syndrome is a rare chromosomal abnormality caused by deletion of part of chromosome 7, which includes the Elastin Gene. Affected individuals have characteristic elfin features, developmental delay, cardiac problems, and hypercalcaemia. Diagnosis is accomplished by detecting the abnormal gene sequence using fluorescence in situ hybridization (FISH test). Traditionally, it has been thought that at least 90% of individuals with William's syndrome experience hyperacusis; and for all intents and purposes, that symptom has been regarded as a defining characteristic of the condition (Table 3.3). It is interesting, however, to note that when a validated questionnaire is used, as in the Blomberg et al. study [31], the prevalence of hyperacusis falls, and it may be that what is experienced in Williams syndrome is an aversion to all sound rather than an abnormality of loudness tolerance. Marriage and Barnes [30] suggested that the hyperacusis of Williams syndrome is another example of hyperacusis, secondary to problems of 5 HT function. This theory is yet to be proved.

There are several theories as to the cause of nonsyndromic hyperacusis. The medial efferent part of the central auditory system sends neurons to the outer hair cells; it is thought that these modulate the cochlea's response to sound [32]. Thus, a defect of the medial efferent system might lead to reduced damping of the cochlea. Sahley and Nodar [33] suggested that stress causes the release of endogenous opiates or dynorphins under the inner hair cells. This could potentiate the cochlear neurotransmitter glutamate, which might lead to enhanced auditory nerve activity.

The neurophysiological model supplies possible mechanisms for both hyperacusis and misophonia (including phonophobia) [6]. In hyperacusis, the incoming auditory signal undergoes a process of abnormal enhancement or amplification in subconscious auditory pathways. This then causes secondary activation of the limbic system and autonomic nervous system. The mechanism by which the incoming signal is enhanced is obscure. In misophonia, the auditory pathways behave normally but the limbic and auto-nomic nervous systems are in a heightened state of excitation and therefore react abnormally to normal auditory input.

An elegant piece of work by Formby et al. [34] examined auditory plasticity by allocating normal hearing volunteers to wear either sound attenuating earplugs or sound generators for a 2-week period. Wearing ear plugs resulted in the participants reporting increased loudness perception, whereas wearing sound generators resulted in increased sound tolerance. This experiment supports the hypothesis that loudness perception is directly related to central auditory gain and not only demonstrates the plasticity of the auditory system but also provides support for the use of sound therapy in the management of loudness perception disorders (see also Chap. 13).

Baguley and Andersson [5] attempted to incorporate beliefs and thoughts about the effects of noise and listening situations, in which discomfort is experienced with a model explored in the literature on pain, called the "fear avoidance model" [35, 36], originally developed by Lethem et al. [37]. The central concept of the model is fear of pain, with varying degrees of severity from just plain pain to exacerbation of pain following exposure. The two end-points in the process are either "confrontation" or "avoidance," with the latter leading to maintained avoidance and possibly even a phobic state. The observation from the pain literature that fear of pain can serve a causal role in leading to disability (fear of injury leads to inactivity, and that inactivity in itself leads to even more pain and disability) is relevant for hyperacusis as well. In light of the experimental evidence recently provided by Formby et al. [34] that ear protection leads to increased noise sensitivity, it was postulated that avoidance of auditory stimulation is likely to sensitize the auditory system, which in turn can exacerbate the hyperacusis. In a recent book on tinnitus [24], a three-component understanding of hyperacusis was proposed that involved consideration of sensitivity, annoyance, and fear of injury (Fig. 3.1). While the first two of these factors have been extensively researched in the literature on noise sensitivity [38], *fear* of the pain experience in itself, the risk of becoming hearing impaired, getting worse tinnitus, and so on, might be a further factor that plays a significant role in explaining the avoidance of sounds in hyperacusis. It is too narrow to just focus on fear of injury, however; and in a slightly revised version of the three-component model, "fear" is considered a factor which is a more broad construct

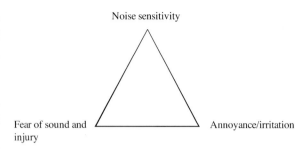

Fig. 3.1 Three-component model of hyperacusis [24]

including fear of the actual pain experience when noise is confronted. The noise sensitivity refers to the actual sensation of pain that is an aversive reaction not necessarily involving cognitive appraisal. The annoyance/irritation dimension is similar to the construct proposed more recently by Jastreboff and Hazell [6] – misophonia – and is more closely linked to cognitive appraisal. What is left out in the figure and in the discussions on hyperacusis overall is the possible effect of noise sensitivity on cognitive capacity, such as attention and memory performance. Moreover, the link between noise exposure and stress responses, including cardiovascular responses, sleep, etc., has largely been ignored in the literature on hyperacusis.

Engel [39] proposed that disease should be considered within a biopsychosocial framework, and this idea has come to underpin much of health psychology. The biological element is the pathophysiology of the condition, the psychological element, the emotional and behavioural impact, and the social element – initially society's view of a symptom/condition – but more literally taken to mean the social consequences (e.g., work or respect) of that state. Baguley and Andersson [5] considered hyperacusis within a biopsychosocial framework, arguing that an exclusive focus upon only one of these elements (such as the pathophysiology of hyperacusis) is not helpful.

A novel perspective of hyperacusis has been provided by Dubal and Viaud-Delmon [40], who sought to determine if an association exists between hyperacusis and magical ideation (the latter concept describing "nonrational" beliefs about the world), it may be a model of the distorted cognitions in psychosis. Using the Khalfa et al. [41] questionnaire (see below) to assess hyperacusis, Dubal and Viaud-Delaman demonstrated an association, proposing that magical ideation might give a predisposition for heightened auditory sensitivity. More work in this area is awaited with interest.

Assessment

Clinical History

The diagnosis of hyperacusis is essentially made by taking a detailed clinical history, which will often take considerable time to elucidate. A structured framework for a hyperacusis history has been proposed by Baguley and Andersson [5] (Table 3.4).

Examination

Clinical examination of patients with hyperacusis is frequently normal and does not contribute to the diagnosis or direct subsequent treatment. Nevertheless, there are occasions when the examination may supply useful information and it is important that all patients have the reassurance that a thorough assessment provides. In addition to examination of the ears, particular attention should be given to cranial nerve function as a small but significant number of hyperacusis patients have disorders of cranial nerve function, in particular, disorders of the facial nerve.

Audiometry

All audiometric testing in hyperacusis patients must be undertaken with the utmost care. Exposing people to the sensory stimulus that distresses them runs the risk of increasing that distress and exacerbating the situation rather than helping. Many patients require nothing more than a pure tone audiogram. Even this can prove upsetting for some patients, and the initial presentation of the test tone may need to be at a much lower level than normally used. The use of loudness discomfort levels (LDLs) has been advocated for this patient population [6], both as an aid to diagnosis and as an outcome measure. This is not without issue, as there is marked inter- and intra-participant variability in results [42, 43], evident in both tonal and speech-based protocols [5]. Further, subjecting the patient to sound, either at or above their threshold of discomfort, may undermine clinical rapport and therapeutic trust. Arguments for undertaking the test are the need to determine the extent of the problem for individuals, perhaps most pertinently in a medico-legal context, and to determine the efficacy of therapy. There is

Table 3.4 Structured diagnostic hyperacusis interview [5]

Background questions
1. Family situation
2. Work situation
   – Current or previous work history?
3. Sick leave
   – On extended sick-leave? (for the last six months for example)
   – Part-time or full time?

Noise sensitivity questions
4. Onset of noise sensitivity?
5. Gradual or sudden?
6. Development over time (worse–better)?
7. Laterality?
8. Type of sounds? (e.g., clatter, talk, paper noises etc)
9. Perception of sounds being unclear/distorted? If so, what kind of sounds?
10. Reactions to sounds? Fear? Pain? Annoyance? Uncomfortable? Other?
11. Hearing impairment and related compensations (e.g., hearing aids)?
12. Tinnitus and related distress?
13. What is most bothersome? Hearing loss, tinnitus, or the hyperacusis?
14. Does exposure to loud sounds increase the sensitivity?

Other diagnoses and medical history of relevance
15. Episodes of depression? If yes, how many episodes in life?
16. Any contact with psychiatry?
17. Migraine?
18. Tension headace?
19. Other sensitivities and medical problems?
    (a) Light
    (b) Touch
    (c) Pain
    (d) Smell
    (e) Allergy
    (f) Balance disturbance
20. Whiplash?
21. Temporomandibular joint dysfunction or problems with teeth?
22. Hypertension or other cardiovascular issues?
23. Medications?
24. Avoidance of places and activities because of hyperacusis?
    (a) Things not done/stopped because of hyperacusis?
    (b) Thing not done yet in life and now very unlikely/impossible because of hyperacusis?
    (c) Use of ear protection? What kind, when and where?

no consensus on this issue at present. Other tests that use sound stimuli that are likely to exceed the threshold for discomfort should be avoided. These include stapedial reflex estimation and evoked response audiometry.

Imaging

Patients with hyperacusis may require imaging, with similar indications as for tinnitus. These indications include asymmetric symptoms, asymmetric audiometric findings, or associated neurological symptoms or signs. Care should be taken when choosing the imaging modality. Magnetic resonance imaging (MRI) is the usual modality of choice for investigating the cerebellopontine angles, but it produces considerable sound levels. Although ear defenders are routinely employed when performing MRI scans, these may not attenuate the sound sufficiently to make it a comfortable experience for a hyperacusis patient. Consideration may need to be given to using a quieter, less-sensitive modality such as computed tomography (CT).

Self-Report

Until recently, there was no method of recording the impact that reduced sound tolerance had on individuals. However, this has been addressed and there are now two self-report questionnaires. Khalfa et al. [41] devised a questionnaire based on 14 items and normalized on 201 volunteers from the general population. A three-factor solution of attentional, emotional, and social factors was derived. In a clinical setting, this questionnaire has low negative impact on patients, but the fact that of the sample population only 4 or 5 might have been expected (from the data above) to have clinically significant hyperacusis. Nelting et al. [44] developed a similar tool using 27 items on 226 individuals with a complaint of hyperacusis. A three-factor solution was derived, with cognitive reactions, actional or somatic behaviour, and emotional factors identified. This latter questionnaire is currently only available in German, but hopefully the arrival of these questionnaires marks a step forward in the study of reduced sound tolerance.

An alternative approach to the scaling of the severity of hyperacusis was proposed by Dauman and Bouscau-Faure [45], who formulated a multiple activity scale for hyperacusis (MASH) which measures the impact of the symptom upon everyday activities. Whilst this undoubtedly captures an aspect of the disability associated with hyperacusis, in that patients may describe a major impact upon family activities such as supermarket shopping or cinema attandance, it should be noted that what is a commonplace activity for an individual in one culture may be exceptional in another context.

Management

The first response of many patients and clinicians is to try and escape from sound, whether by moving to a naturally quiet environment or by using sound attenuating devices such as ear plugs or earmuffs. Unfortunately, observation would suggest that this generally makes the situation worse. It is thought that by reducing the expected sound input, the central auditory gain is increased which exacerbates the loudness hypersensitivity. It is important to explain this carefully to patients, as to many it seems counterintuitive to expose someone who is distressed by noise to the very thing that is causing the distress. If their job or recreation involves noise exposure, they may need appropriate sound protection devices such as general earmuffs and plugs or musician's, shooter's, or motorcyclist's plugs. It must be carefully stressed that these are only to be worn when the noise levels are genuinely high and must not be worn at other times.

Any associated condition such as Lyme disease, depression, or post-traumatic stress disorder should be treated by the appropriate clinical teams at the same time as the loudness perception is addressed.

Sound therapy is widely used in the treatment of hyperacusis, either as a stand-alone treatment modality or as part of Tinnitus Retraining Therapy (TRT). Using therapy on its own can be undertaken using techniques of either densensitization or recalibration. With decalibration, sound generators are set to levels just below the patient's threshold of discomfort and slowly increased as tolerance improves. There is some support for this method [46], though in practice relatively few clinicians use this approach. For recalibration, the devices are set to a comfortable, consistent level with the intention of resetting the central auditory gain in much the same fashion that Formby et al. [34] demonstrated with normal volunteers. Norena and Chery-Croze [47] used what they described as an "enriched auditory environment" in patients with hyperacusis. The stimuli were used for several hours a day (for 15 weeks) and consisted of pure tone stimuli (100-ms duration and 100-ms intervals) within the audiometric area affected by hearing ;oss. This meant that the sound stimulation was given at the same frequency range as the hearing loss: i.e., if the hearing loss was in the region 3–6 kHz, sound stimulation of 3–6 kHz was administered.

The sound stimulation was achieved by listening to a CD, and significant improvements in measures of loudness scaling were reported. Due to the small number of patients and some of their characteristics (the presence of hearing loss being an example), this work should be regarded as preliminary but of major interest. For sound therapy for hyperacusis in general, there is a paucity of robust evidence of efficacy to date.

TRT was introduced by Jastreboff and Hazell (1993) [6, 53] as a novel method of dealing with tinnitus. It was recognized that this could be adapted slightly and applied to patients with reduced sound tolerance. In TRT, the first therapeutic step is to allocate each new patient to a category. Category 0 patients have mild or recent onset symptoms. Category 1 and 2 patients have significant tinnitus with normal hearing or hearing loss, respectively. Category 3 patients have hyperacusis without prolonged enhancement from sound exposure. Category 4 patients have tinnitus and/or hyperacusis with prolonged worsening of the symptoms following sound exposure. Those patients with significant hyperacusis, namely category 3 and 4 patients, receive counselling and treatment with wearable binaural sound generators. The protocol for wearing the sound generators varies according to the category. In category 3, patients are advised to slowly increase the sound to the highest level that does not cause annoyance or discomfort or interfere with the hearing. The generators should be worn continuously and may need frequent adjustment. In category 4 patients, the generator output should be set close to threshold or even put in the ear but not initially switched on. The output is then slowly increased, changing the level every 6–8 weeks. If the patients have tinnitus as well as decreased loudness tolerance, the loudness tolerance should be addressed first even if this runs the risk of temporarily worsening the tinnitus. There are a limited number of trials showing the outcome of TRT in the treatment of hyperacusis and all have methodological flaws. However, the studies that are available by Gold et al. [48], McKinney et al. [49], and Hazell et al. [11] have all shown positive outcomes. In the latest of these trials [11], 60.4% of treated patients had normal LDLs by 25 months [11].

Psychological treatments, particularly cognitive behavioural therapy (CBT) (Andersson et al. 1999 [54]), probably have a role to play, in particular for those patients who have significant associated anxiety and distress. There is a paucity of evidence for this promising approach to date, but what evidence does exist is reviewed by Baguley and Andersson [5].

There is no evidence about how to treat patients with acoustic shock. Many clinicians treat it as a form of acute phonophobia, but this is based on intuition rather than science. Much effort is being spent investigating the nature of sounds that triggers acoustic shock in the hope that telecommunications equipment can be fitted with suitable filtering circuitry.

As with tinnitus, there is considerable value in a self-help approach to hyperacusis. The Hyperacusis Network (www.hyperacusis.net) is an important resource in this regard, with well-informed and well-moderated forums and much positive advice.

Summary

Disorders of loudness tolerance have received much less attention than tinnitus and still remain in the shadows. Far from being a rare and obscure condition, research has shown hyperacusis to be a common symptom, especially among patients with tinnitus. Various mechanisms have been suggested, and it seems likely that different mechanisms can apply to different patients. Although there is meagre published information on the management of sound hypersensitivity, the research that is available suggests that a programme of careful and gradual desensitization is effective for the majority.

Acknowledgment David Baguley's research is supported by an East of England NHS Senior Academic Clinical Fellowship.

References

1. Vernon, JA. Pathophysiology of tinnitus: a special case – hyperacusis and a proposed treatment. Am J Otol 1987; 8: 201–202
2. Perlman, HB. Hyperacusis. Ann Otol Rhinol Laryngol 1938; 47: 947–953
3. Mathisen, H. Phonophobia after stapedectomy. Acta Otolaryngol 1969; 68: 73–77

4. Klein, AJ, Armstrong, BL, Greer, MK, and Brown, III FR. Hyperacusis and otitis media in individuals with Williams syndrome. Journal of Speech Hear Disord 1990; 55: 339–344

5. Baguley, DM and Andersson, G. Hyperacusis: Mechanisms, Diagnosis and Therapies. San Diego, Plural, 2007

6. Jastreboff, PJ and Hazell, JWP. Tinnitus Retraining Therapy. Cambridge, Cambridge University Press, 2004

7. Gordon, AG. Abnormal middle ear muscle reflexes and audiosensitivity. Br J Audiol 1986; 20: 95–99

8. Minor, LB, Cremer, PD, Carey, JP, Della Santina, CC, Streubel, SO, and Weg, N. Symptoms and signs in superior canal dehiscence syndrome. Ann N Y Acad Sci 2001; 942: 259–273

9. Banerjee, A, Whyte, A, and Atlas, MD. Superior canal dehiscence: review of a new condition. Clin Otolaryngol 2005; 30: 9–15

10. Woodhouse, A and Drummond, PD. Mechanisms of increased sensitivity to noise and light in migraine headache. Cephalgia 1993; 13: 417–421

11. Hazell, JWP, Sheldrake, JB, and Graham, RL. Decreased sound tolerance: predisposing factors, triggers and outcomes after TRT. In: Patuzzi R (ed) Proceedings of the Seventh International Tinnitus Seminar 2002. Perth, University of Western Australia, 2002: 255–261

12. Jastreboff, PJ. Tinnitus retraining treatment for patients with tinnitus and decreased sound tolerance. Otolaryngol Clin N Am 2003; 36: 321–336

13. Fowler, EP. A method for the early detection of otosclerosis. Arch Otolaryngol 1936; 24: 731–741

14. Moore, BCJ. Cochlear Hearing Loss. London, Whurr, 1998

15. Gomes, E, Pedroso, FS, and Wagner, MB. Auditory hypersensitivity in the autistic spectrum disorder. Pro Fono 2008; 20: 279–284

16. Gomot, M, Belmonte, MK, Bullmore, ET, Bernard, FA, and Baron-Cohen, S. Brain hyper-reactivity to auditory novel targets in children with high-functioning autism. Brain 2008; 131: 2479–2488

17. Goldberg, J, Anderson, DE, and Wilder, S. Startle reflex habituation in children with cerebral palsy. Percept Mot Skills 1979; 48(3 Pt 2): 1135–1139

18. Westcott M. Case study: management of hyperacusis associated with post-traumatic stress disorder. In: Patuzzi R (ed) Proceedings of the Seventh International Tinnitus Seminar 2002. Perth, University of Western Australia; 2002: 280-285

19. Fabijanska, A, Rogowski, M, Bartnik, G, and Skarzynski, H. Epidemiology of tinnitus and hyperacusis in Poland. In: Hazell JWP (ed) Proceedings of the Sixth International Tinnitus Seminar. London, The Tinnitus and Hyperacusis Centre; 1999: 569–571

20. Andersson, G, Lindvall, N, Hursti, T, and Carlbring, P. Hypersensitivity to sound (hyperacusis): a prevalence study conducted via the Internet and post. Int J Audiol 2002; 41: 545–554

21. Bartnik, G, Fabijanska, A, and Rogowski, M. Our experience in treatment of patients with tinnitus and/or hyperacusis using the habituation method. In: Hazell JWP (ed) Proceedings of the Sixth International Tinnitus Seminar. London, The Tinnitus and Hyperacusis Centre; 1999: 416–417

22. Jastreboff, PJ and Jastreboff, MM. Tinnitus retraining therapy (TRT) as a method for treatment of tinnitus and hyperacusis patients. J Am Acad Audiol 2000; 11: 162–177

23. Anari, M, Axelsson A, Eliasson, A, and Magnusson, L. Hypersensitivity to sound Questionnaire data, audiometry and classification. Scand Audiol 1999; 28: 219–230

24. Andersson, G, Baguley, DM, McKenna, L, and McFerran, DJ. Tinnitus: A Multidisciplinary Approach. London, Whurr, 2005

25. Silberstein, SD. Migraine symptoms: results of a survey of self-reported migraineurs. Headache 1995; 35: 387–396

26. Fagelson, MA. The association between tinnitus and post-traumatic stress disorder. Am J Audiol 2007; 16: 107–117

27. Katzenell, U, and Segal, S. Hyperacusis: review and clinical guidelines. Otol Neurotol 2001; 22: 321–326

28. Baloh, RW. Neurotology of migraine. Headache 1997; 37: 615–621

29. Nields, JA, Fallon, BA, and Jastreboff, PJ. Carbamazepine in the treatment of Lyme disease-induced hyperacusis. J Neuropsychiatry Clin Neurosci 1999; 11: 97–98

30. Marriage, J and Barnes, NM. Is central hyperacusis a symptom of 5 hydroxytryptamine (5-HT) dysfunction? J Laryngol Otol 1995; 109: 915–921

31. Blomberg, S, Rosander, M, and Andersson, G. Fears, hyperacusis and musicality in Williams syndrome. Res Dev Disabil 2006; 27: 668–680

32. Sahley, TL, Nodar, RH, and Musiek, FE. Efferent Auditory System: Structure and Function. San Diego, Singular, 1997

33. Sahley, TL and Nodar, RH. A biochemical model of peripheral tinnitus. Hear Res 2001; 182: 43–54

34. Formby, C, Sherlock, LP, and Gold, SL. Adaptive plasticity of loudness induced by chronic attenuation and enhancement of the acoustic background. J Acoust Soc Am 2003; 114: 55–58

35. Asmundson, GJ, Norton, PJ, and Norton, GR. Beyond pain: the role of fear and avoidance in chronicity. Clin Psychol Rev 1999; 19: 97–119

36. Vlaeyen, JW and Linton, SJ. Fear-avoidance and its consequences in chronic musculoskeletal pain: a state of the art. Pain 2000; 85: 317–332

37. Lethem, J, Slade, PD, Troup, JDG, and Bentley, G. Outline of a fear-avoidance model of exaggerated pain perception-I. Behav Res Ther 1983; 21: 401–408

38. Stansfeld, SA. Noise, noise sensitivity and psychiatric disorder: epidemiological and psychophysiological studies. Psychol Med Suppl 1992; 22: 1–44

39. Engel, GL. The need for a new medical model: a challenge for biomedicine. Science 1997; 196: 129–136

40. Dubal, S and Viaud-Delmon, I. Magical ideation and hyperacusis. Cortex 2008; 44: 1379–1386

41. Khalfa, S, Dubal, S, Veuillet, E, Perez-Seliaz, F, Jouvent, R, and Collet, L. Psychometric normalisation of a hyperacusis questionnaire. ORL J Otorhinolaryngol Relat Spec 2002; 64: 436–442

42. Stephens, SD, Blegvad, B, and Krogh, HJ. The value of some suprathreshold auditory measures. Scand Audiol 1977; 6: 213–221

43. Valente, M, Potts, LG, and Valente, M. Differences and intersubject variability of loudness discomfort levels measured in sound pressure level and hearing level for TDH-50P and ER-3A earphones. J Am Acad Audiol 1997; 8: 59–67

44. Nelting, M, Rienhoff, NK, Hesse, G, and Lamparter, U. The assessment of subjective distress related to hyperacusis with

a self-rating questionnaire on hypersensitivity to sound. Laryngorhinootologie 2002; 81: 32–34

45. Dauman, R and Bouscau-Faure, F. Assessment and amelioration of hyperacusis in tinnitus patients. Acta Otolaryngol 2005; 125: 503–509

46. Vernon, JA and Meikle, MB. Tinnitus masking. In: Tyler RS (ed) Tinnitus Handbook. San Diego: Singular Thomson Learning 2000: 313–356

47. Noreña, AJ and Chery-Croze, S. Enriched acoustic environment rescales auditory sensitivity. Neuroreport 2007; 18: 1251–1255

48. Gold, S, Formby, C, Frederick, EA, and Suter, C. Shifts in loudness discomfort level in tinnitus patients with and without hyperacusis. In: Patuzzi R (ed) Proceedings of the Seventh International Tinnitus Seminar 2002. Perth, University of Western Australia, 2002: 170–172

49. McKinney, CJ, Hazell, JWP, and Graham, RL. Changes in loudness discomfort level and sensitivity to environmental sound with habituation based therapy. In: Hazell J (ed) Proceedings of the Sixth International Tinnitus Seminar. Cambridge, The Tinnitus and Hyperacusis Centre; 1999: 499–501

50. Baguley, DM. Current perspectives on hyperacusis J Royal Society of Medicine, 2003, 96, 1–4

51. Levitin, DJ, Cole, K, Lincoln, A and Bellugi, U. Aversion, awareness and attraction: investigating claims of hyperacusis in the Williams syndrome phenotype, Journal of Child Psychology and Psychiatry, 2005, 46, 514–523

52. Van Borsel, J, Curfs, LMG and Fryns, JP. Hyperacusis in Willams syndrome: a sample survey study. Genetic Conselling, 1997, 8, 121–126

53. Jastreboff, PJ and Hazell, JWP. A neurophysiological approach to tinnitus: clinical implications. British Journal of Audiology, 1993, 27, 7–17

54. Andersson, G, Lyttkens, L and Larsen, HC. Tinnitus and anxiety sensitivity. Scandinavian J of Behaviour Therapy 1999, 27, 57–64

Chapter 4
Misophonia, Phonophobia, and "Exploding Head" Syndrome

Aage R. Møller

Keypoints

1. Misophonia, phonophobia, and "exploding head" syndrome have symptoms that may occur together with some forms of tinnitus or they can occur alone.
2. These sensations are different from hyperacusis which is a lowered tolerance to most kinds of sounds.
3. Misophonia is a dislike of specific kinds of sounds.
4. Attempts have been made to treat misophonia using the same methods as used for treating tinnitus.
5. Phonophobia is a fear of specific sounds related to the implication of the sounds.
6. The non-classical auditory pathways providing a subcortical route to the amygdala may be involved in phonophobia.
7. The "exploding head" syndrome is the experience of a very loud and sudden noise that seems to originate from within the head. It often occurs during sleep and wakes up the individual.
8. The "exploding head" syndrome may have similarities with REM sleep behavior disorder (RBD).

Keywords Tinnitus • Misophonia • Phonophobia • Exploding head syndrome

Abbreviations

CNS   Central nervous system
DST   Decreased sound tolerance
RDB   REM sleep behavior disorder
REM   Rapid eye movement (sleep)
TRT   Tinnitus retraining therapy

A.R. Møller (✉)
The University of Texas at Dallas, School of Behavioral and Brain Sciences, GR 41, 800 W Campbell Rd, Richardson, TX 75080, USA
e-mail: amoller@utdallas.edu

Introduction

There are several forms of decreased sound tolerance (DST); probably, the most common one is hyperacusis, which is a decreased tolerance level of (nonspecific) sounds, independent on their significance or importance (see Chap. 3). Misophonia is a decreased tolerance to specific sounds and phonophobia is fear of sounds: both disorders are based on the perceived implications or meanings of those sounds, whereas hyperacusis is not related to the comfort of the sound. The "exploding head" syndrome is hearing loud unexpected sounds, mostly during sleep or drowsiness. The prevalence of misophonia and phonophobia is unknown, and there are no known effective treatments. These abnormal reactions to sound are different from hyperacusis because the reactions are related to the significance of the sounds and are different from the common reaction to loud sounds that occur unexpectedly and which can cause a general body reaction known as a startle response. The "exploding head" syndrome is not a reaction to sound but occurs spontaneously. Even less is known about these symptoms than misophonia and phonophobia, and the available treatments are unsatisfactory.

The fact that these three different syndromes are not generally known opens the possibility of many kinds of maltreatment and misinformation from health care professionals, who often administer large batteries of tests, which are ineffective. Patients often go to one physician after another searching in vain for help.

Misophonia

Misophonia is defined as "dislike of certain specific sounds," thus comparable with the term "phonophobia."

Misophonia has been regarded a phantom sensation similar to tinnitus [1]. It has been discussed in connection with tinnitus and tolerance to sounds [2, 3]. Misophonia is different from hyperacusis in that it is only experienced in response to specific sounds, unlike hyperacusis, which is a lowered tolerance to all sounds (above a certain intensity) (see Chap. 3). A better word than misophonia may be "unpleasant" or "annoying." These sounds that are unpleasant may also elicit autonomic reactions of various kinds.

Misophonia can occur together with tinnitus and hyperacusis, but may also occur alone. Treatment of misophonia has been discussed by Jastreboff, who suggested similar treatment to that used for tinnitus, namely the tinnitus retraining therapy (TRT) [4]. Beneficial effects of treatment of misophonia using TRT have been reported [2, 5, 6].

One can only guess about the anatomical location of the physiological abnormalities that cause misophonia. Since misophonia is related to specific sounds (its difference from hyperacusis), the anatomical location of the physiological abnormality that causes misophonia must be structures that are activated by highly processed sounds, thus located after auditory information has been subjected to considerable processing and selection. It seems likely that the location would be that of object (and frequency) processing sounds. It was mentioned in Chap. 8 that different kinds of sound are processed in different parts of the brain (stream segregation). This means the anatomical location of the abnormality that causes misophonia is located more central than that of hyperacusis because more neural processing of the sounds has occurred to cause misophonia compared with hyperacusis.

The anatomical location of the physiological abnormality may be in the inferior part of the temporal lobe where processing of object ("what") information in humans occurs (see Chap. 8).

Phonophobia

Phonophobia means fear of sound and it is related to the content (or significance) of the sound. Some kinds of sounds can invoke fear in most people. Sounds that are understood not to be signaling an eminent danger usually do not invoke fear. This can be explained by considering the normal route of sensory signals to the amygdala through the "high route" [7, 8] (see Fig 9. in Chap. 8). The input to the high route comes through the classical auditory pathways where sounds use the ventral part of the thalamus from where connections lead to the primary auditory cortex, secondary cortex, association cortices, and from there to the lateral nucleus of the amygdala. This allows control by higher CNS regions of the flow of information in the high route and can therefore control the information that reaches the amygdala.

The situation is different if the non-classical pathways are active because there is a subcortical route to the amygdala from the dorsal and medial thalamus that is not controlled by higher CNS centers. Some individuals with severe tinnitus have signs that they use the non-classical auditory pathways [9], (see Chaps 8 and 10).

Functional imaging studies have supported the results of the reports that indicate an increased activity of structures of the limbic system [10].

"Exploding Head" Syndrome

"Exploding head" syndrome is a condition that causes the sufferer to occasionally experience a tremendously loud noise as if originating from within his or her own head. The "exploding head" symptoms usually occur during sleep or drowsiness [11]. Individuals with these symptoms explain it as explosions in the head. This syndrome can also cause the sufferer to feel an extreme rush of adrenaline kick going through his or her head, sometimes multiple times.

The "exploding head" syndrome and the abnormal perceptions that some people with tinnitus may experience is unpleasant and even described as a terrifying sensation of flashing lights, the sound of an explosion, gunshot, door slamming, roar, waves crashing against rocks, loud voices, a ringing noise, or the sound of an electrical short circuit. In some cases, an instant flash of what is perceived as video "static" is reported [12]. The "exploding head" syndrome may have similarities with audiogenic seizures, which has been studied in animals where it was found that the inferior colliculus was involved [13].

The exploding head phenomenon may be a failure to prepare the nervous system for sleep. It may be an exaggeration of the events that normally occur in the transition between being awake and being at sleep.

The normal transition between wakefulness and sleep requires that the reticular system changes the excitability of not only the motor system but also other CNS systems. Many people experience sounds that are perceived to be louder moments before falling asleep. This may have to do with the different steps needed in the process of changing the excitability (or gain) in sensory systems to preparation for sleep that are not fully synchronized.

The "exploding head" syndrome may be a result of failure of the automatic gain control that normally compresses the range of amplitudes of sounds. The auditory nervous system would not be able to process sounds in the enormous range of intensities of normal sounds without extensive gain control. Different stages of the auditory system have automatic gain control. The first structure that performs gain control is the cochlea, where amplification in the cochlea by the action of the outer hair cells decreases with the intensity of sounds. The amplification of this "cochlear amplifier" is to some extent controlled by the central nervous system through the olivocochlear bundle that is a part of the descending auditory pathway (see [14] and Chap. 8).

The "exploding head" phenomenon may have similarities with what is known as REM sleep behavior disorder (RBD) [15]. In some individuals, the system that normally keeps skeletal muscles paralyzed during REM sleep malfunctions causing violent behavior during REM sleep [16]. RBD is assumed to be caused by failure of the reticular system to maintain paralysis of skeletal muscles. Many people experience hyperacusis just before falling asleep, thus a sign that the reticular formation has affected the processing of auditory information.

Other forms of little known malfunctions of the reticular formation may be responsible for similar phenomena that may occur immediately after waking up. Some individuals can occasionally experience total paralysis for a few moments. This seems to be caused by a failure of the reticular formation to release the paralysis that occurs normally during REM sleep.

The symptoms of the "exploding head" can be reduced by reassurance of the harmlessness of the condition and the symptoms often ameliorate spontaneously with time. In a study, clomipramine, a tricyclic agent with both antidepressant and antiobsessional properties, has been reported to provide immediate relief of the symptoms [11]. None of the participants in these studies had any neurological disorders [11].

References

1. Jastreboff PJ (1990) Phantom auditory perception (tinnitus): Mechanisms of generation and perception. Neurosci Res 8:221–54.
2. Jastreboff MM and P Jastreboff (2002) Decreased sound tolerance and tinnitus retraining therapy (TRT). Aust NZJ Audiol 21:74–81.
3. Jastreboff PJ and MM Jastreboff (2003) Tinnitus retraining therapy for patients with tinnitus and decreased sound tolerance. Otolaryngol Clin North Am 36:321–36.
4. Jastreboff PJ, (2007) Tinnitus retraining therapy, in Tinnitus: Pathophysiology and treatment, progress in brain research, B Langguth et al, Editors. 2007, Elsevier: Amsterdam. 415–23.
5. Jastreboff PJ and MM Jastreboff (2006) Tinnitus retraining therapy: a different view on tinnitus. ORL J Otorhinolaryngol Relat Spec 68:23–9.
6. Dobie RA, (2004) Overview: Suffering from Tinnitus, in Tinnitus: Theory and management, JB Snow, Editor. 2004, BC Decker Inc.: Hamilton. 1–7.
7. LeDoux JE (1992) Brain mechanisms of emotion and emotional learning. Curr Opin Neurobiol 2:191–7.
8. Møller AR (2003) Sensory systems: Anatomy and physiology. 2003, Amsterdam: Academic Press.
9. Møller AR, MB Møller and M Yokota (1992) Some forms of tinnitus may involve the extralemniscal auditory pathway. Laryngoscope 102: 1165–71.
10. Lockwood A, R Salvi, M Coad et al (1998) The functional neuroanatomy of tinnitus. Evidence for limbic system links and neural plasticity. Neurology 50:114–20.
11. Sachs C and E Svanborg (1991) The exploding head syndrome: polysomnographic recordings and therapeutic suggestions. Sleep 14:263–6.
12. Teixido M and K Connolly (1998) Explosive tinnitus: An underrecognized disorder. Otolaryngology – Head and Neck Surgery 118:108–9.
13. Pierson MG and J Swann (1991) Ontogenetic features of audiogenic seizure susceptibility induced in immature rats by noise. Epilepsia 32:1–9.
14. Møller AR (2006) Hearing: Anatomy, physiology, and disorders of the auditory system, 2nd Ed. 2006, Amsterdam: Academic Press.
15. Olson EJ, BF Boeve and MH Silber (2000) Rapid eye movement sleep behaviour disorder: demographic, clinical and laboratory findings in 93 cases. Brain 123:231–9.
16. Schenck CH, JL Boyd and MW Mahowald (1997) A parasomnia overlap disorder involving sleepwalking, sleep terrors, and REM sleep behavior disorder in 33 polysomnographically confirmed cases. Sleep 20:972–81.

Chapter 5
Epidemiology of Tinnitus in Adults

Aage R. Møller

Keypoints

1. Many studies have addressed the prevalence of tinnitus, but the definition of tinnitus has varied.
2. Some studies have reported that as many as 80% of the adult population experience tinnitus at some point.
3. Six large population studies in different countries reported prevalence of prolonged tinnitus, varying between 4.4 and 15.1% for adults and between 7.6 and 20.1% for individuals below the age of 50 years. One of the studies reported that 2.4% of the population responded "yes" to the description of tinnitus as "tinnitus plagues me all day."
4. A study in four cities in England found that tinnitus, on average, occurred in 17.5% of the participants in the age group of 40–60 years and 22.2% in participants above the age of 60 years.
5. Since tinnitus has many forms and its prevalence varies with age and, to some extent, gender, the prevalence of tinnitus cannot be described by a single number.
6. The prevalence of tinnitus increases monotonically up to the age of approximately 70 years, above which the prevalence either becomes constant or decreases slightly with age.
7. The prevalence of tinnitus is lower in women up to 75 years, above which the gender difference becomes small.
8. There is some evidence that noise exposure increases the risk of tinnitus.
9. The odds of having tinnitus increases with the degree of hearing loss when measured at 4 kHz.
10. While reported "trouble hearing" increases monotonically with age, "bothersome tinnitus" increases with age only up to the age group of 65–74, after which it becomes independent of age or decreases slightly with age.

Keywords Tinnitus • Epidemiology • Prevalence • Adults • Hearing loss • Noise exposure

Introduction

Understanding the incidence and prevalence of a disease in a defined population is important for improvement of health and prevention of diseases. Accurate determination of the prevalence of a condition, such as tinnitus, which does not have objective signs, depends on the ability to define the disease to the members of the population that is studied.

Tinnitus affects different groups of people differently, such as different age groups, and the prevalence of tinnitus in women and men is also different. This means that a single number cannot describe the prevalence of tinnitus. It is therefore important to define the part of the population that is studied.

Tinnitus is often accompanied by hyperacusis (lowered tolerance for sound, see Chaps. 3 and 57), misophonia (dislike of certain sounds), and phonophobia (fear of certain sounds); see Chaps. 4 and 57. While the prevalence of tinnitus, in general, is poorly known, the prevalence of these symptoms is even less known. The effect of tinnitus on a person's quality of life depends more on the distress it causes and less on how a person perceives his or her tinnitus. However, the prevalence of distress from tinnitus is poorly known.

A.R. Møller (✉)
The University of Texas at Dallas, School of Behavioral and Brain Sciences, GR 41, 800 W Campbell Rd, Richardson, TX 75080, USA
e-mail: amoller@utdallas.edu

A.R. Møller et al. (eds.), *Textbook of Tinnitus*,
DOI 10.1007/978-1-60761-145-5_5, © Springer Science+Business Media, LLC 2011

When discussing the prevalence of tinnitus, it is the troubled tinnitus that is of the greatest interest because that is the form of tinnitus that affects the quality of life and which may have severe consequences for the person who has tinnitus. Troubled tinnitus may result in the inability to work and may have such a severe effect on a person that it causes suicide.

This chapter discusses population studies of the prevalence of tinnitus. Few studies have addressed the incidence of tinnitus which will not be discussed, and the natural history of tinnitus is not understood (see Chaps. 63 and 64) [1].

For studies of the prevalence of tinnitus, the greatest challenge lies in defining the tinnitus. As has been discussed in many of the chapters in this book, tinnitus has many forms (see especially Chaps. 2–4 and 17). Tinnitus varies widely among individuals not only in strength but also in character, and many investigators have proposed different classification schemes for tinnitus (for a review see Heller 2003) [2]. An individual's tinnitus can vary widely from time to time. Many forms of tinnitus change from day to day and even change over the course of one day.

In that way, tinnitus has many similarities with pain. When the task is to obtain accurate information regarding its prevalence of tinnitus and pain, there are many aspects of these two symptoms that must be taken into account as has been discussed in Chaps. 14 and 94.

Tinnitus can noticeably decrease the quality of life or it can just be a small annoyance. In fact, most people who have tinnitus do not regard it as anything important. One study reported that 0.5–1% of individuals with tinnitus indicated that the condition severely affected their ability to live a normal life [3]. Other studies have reported different estimates of prevalence of such forms of tinnitus.

The degree of distress tinnitus can cause is not related to the character or the perceived strength of the disorder as it is described by the persons who have tinnitus. The perceived severity of tinnitus depends on many different factors; one being a person's personality (see Chaps. 27, 63 and 64). The perception of tinnitus is also influenced by external circumstances. These factors all make it difficult to obtain an accurate estimate of the prevalence of tinnitus that affects a person's life. Different definitions of such forms of tinnitus have been used by individual investigators. This is one of the reasons that the results reported by different epidemiologic studies differ considerably, and

different studies report prevalence of tinnitus that varies from study to study. The lack of objective signs of tinnitus is another source of uncertainty in studies of this disorder, and only self-reported evaluation of a person's tinnitus is available. Most epidemiologic studies have not attempted to distinguish between the different origins of the tinnitus, not even distinguishing between objective and subjective tinnitus.

Another source of variation in the results of different epidemiologic studies of tinnitus is shared with other voluntary studies, namely, that not all persons selected for a study respond. Normally, epidemiologic studies will spend a considerable effort finding out if the group of non-responders is different from the group that responds.

Another reason for varying results in different studies is that questions are formulated differently. Some studies have used written questions distributed to groups of people more or less representative of the general population. Some studies have enrolled individuals seeking professional help for their tinnitus. The participants in some studies must therefore be regarded as being a selected group of individuals that may not be representative of the general population.

Tinnitus depends on many factors, which makes it important to obtain a multi-dimensional description of its epidemiology. Thus, it is not meaningful to just describe the prevalence with a single number.

Estimates of the Prevalence of Tinnitus

Data from the National Center for Health Statistics, US Department of Health, Education, and Welfare (1968), indicate that 30% of the general population are affected by tinnitus, and that 6% of them (1.8% of the general population) have incapacitating symptoms [2]. Other studies have presented values of prevalence that vary between 7.6 and 20.1% (see Table 5.1).

Prevalence of Tinnitus as a Function of Age

One of the main variables in the prevalence of tinnitus is age, and studies have therefore expressed the prevalence of tinnitus as a function of age. Table 5.1 compares the

Table 5.1 Prevalence of self-reported tinnitus in adults by decade of life from several population-based, epidemiologic studies

Age (year)	I (%)	II (%)	III (%)	IV (%)	V (%)	VI (%)
20–29	5.7	7.5	5.1	1.4		9.8
30–39	7.4	5.8	6.0	2.0		9.6
40–49	9.9	8.9	7.2	3.7		11.8
50–59	12.5	18.6	10.1	5.7	7.3	16.9
60–69	16.3	20.3	13.0	7.9	10.1	20.2
70–79	14.4	21.3	12.6	9.4	8.7	24.0
>80	13.6		14.1	8.3	5.5	22.9
<50	14.2	20.1	12.1	7.6	8.2	20.1
Adult	10.2	14.2	8.4	4.4		15.1
Participants	34,050	2,556	59,343	99,435	3,737	47,410

I: United Kingdom National Study of Hearing (1980–1986); II: Gothenburg, Sweden (1989); III: US NHIS Hearing Supplement (1990); IV: Disability Supplement (1994–1995); V: Beaver Dam, WI Hearing Loss Study (1993–1995); VI: Nord Trondelag, Norway Hearing Loss Study (1996–1998)

Data from Hoffmann and Reed [4]

reported prevalence in several studies from the United Kingdom, Sweden, Norway, and the US.

All published studies show values of prevalence of tinnitus that are not the same for different age groups. All published studies seem to agree that the risk of getting tinnitus increases with age up to about 65 years, after which age prevalence is either independent of or decreases slightly with increasing age.

The design of the studies, the results of which are shown in Table 5.1, all had differences, which make it difficult to compare the results. The first study (United Kingdom National Study of Hearing) used a postal questionnaire sent to people in Cardiff, Glasgow, Nottingham, and Southampton in age groups between 17 and more than 80 years. In the questionnaire, tinnitus was defined as "prolonged spontaneous tinnitus" that lasts for more than 5 min and occurs not exclusively after loud sounds [5].

In the study from Gothenburg, Sweden, questionnaires were mailed and had blinded response (no follow-up of non-responders). Tinnitus was defined as an ear noise that occurs "often or always" and sounds like a peep, chirping, roaring, wind blowing in the trees, etc., [6]. In the same study, 2.4% of the population suffered from the worst severity degree defined as "tinnitus plaques me all day."

The United States National Health Interview Survey (US NHIS) is a household survey with personal interviews of non-institutionalized civilians from randomly chosen areas constituting a nationally representative sample. The participants in this study had tinnitus that was defined as "having been bothered by ringing in the ears or other funny noises in the head in the past

12 months" [7]. The 1994–1995 US NHIS Disability Supplement study, Phase I, used an impairment and disability-screening questionnaire. Chronic tinnitus was defined in the interview as "now having a ringing, roaring, or buzzing in the ears that has lasted for at least 3 months" [8, 9].

The participants in the Beaver Dam, WI Hearing Loss study had significant tinnitus that was defined as "buzzing, ringing, or noise in the ears in the past year of at least moderate severity and/or tinnitus that caused difficulty in falling asleep" (Nondahl 2002) [10].

The Nord Trondelag, Norway Hearing Loss study used a self-administered questionnaire filled out in study clinics prior to the hearing examination [11]. Tinnitus was defined as "bothered by ringing in the ears." The participants in this study were thus individuals who had sought professional help for their tinnitus. The results may therefore not be representative of the general population.

While there are large differences between the values of prevalence arrived at by different studies, there is agreement that the prevalence of tinnitus increases with age. Less clear is the relationship to gender, but studies show a tendency for tinnitus to occur more frequently in men than in women. Epidemiological studies of prevalence show a slightly larger prevalence of tinnitus in men, but the results are not consistent.

Most studies show an increase in the prevalence of tinnitus with age in the age groups up to 65–74 and considerably lower prevalence in individuals above 75 years than in the age group of 65–74 years. Since tinnitus of an individual rarely decreases the prevalence arrived at in epidemiologic studies, at least up to

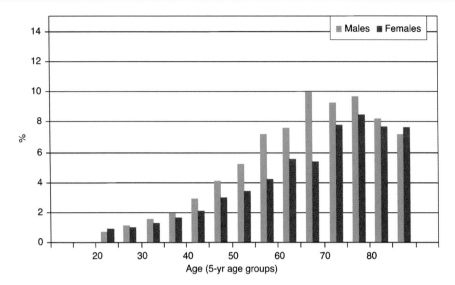

Fig. 5.1 Age- and sex-specific prevalence (in percentage of total study population) of chronic tinnitus ("ringing, roaring or buzzing in the ears or head now that has lasted at least 3 months"), based on 1994–1995 US National Health Interview Survey Disability Supplement. The study had 99,435 participants. Reproduced from Hoffman and Reed [4] with permission by BC Decker Inc.

the age of 70 can be regarded as being cumulative, above which it does not seem to increase very much.

This pattern of age relations of prevalence of tinnitus is clearly seen in the graphic representation of the results of another study (Fig. 5.1).

This graph shows that the prevalence of tinnitus for both men and women increases with age and that it levels out and even decreases above a certain age. The prevalence of tinnitus is higher for men than for women up to the age of 75, and the prevalence of tinnitus reaches its highest value earlier in life for men than for women. At the age of 75, the prevalence in women catches up with that of men, and above the age of 75 the prevalence of tinnitus is about the same for men and women. This pattern is thus similar to that of the prevalence of cardiovascular disease.

That the prevalence is less in the group of 80 years of age may have to do with tinnitus being associated with diseases, which may have caused early death. Therefore, those who die before the age of 80 may have had a higher prevalence of tinnitus than those who live beyond the age of 80 years. Again, it may suggest that tinnitus has similar risk factors as diseases that can cause early death, such as cardiovascular disorders.

Animal studies have shown that rats genetically predisposed for high blood pressure also acquire more hearing loss from noise exposure than animals not genetically predisposed for hypertension (normotensive

Table 5.2 Tinnitus prevalence by age and gender (%), standardized to the Australian population, using 1996 Australian census data

Age (years)	Women	Men	Participants
< 60	23.6	32.3	28.0
60–69	30.5	35.1	32.7
70–79	28.7	32.7	30.5
80+	27.7	21.5	25.4
All ages	28.6	32.2	30.3

Data from Sindhusake et al. [14]

rats) [12, 13]. There may also be (unknown) relations between cardiovascular factors and tinnitus in humans.

Those individuals who survive the age of 80 may, thus, have fewer risk factors that shorten lifespan and which are the same risk factors for tinnitus. It may therefore be more representative to compare the values for the higher age groups, such as the 60–69 years, where the prevalence arrived at in different studies varies between 20.3 and 8.7%.

Other studies found similar trends of prevalence of tinnitus increasing with age between 50 and 75 years, above which the prevalence decreased in two different studies: one from the US and one from Australia (Table 5.2).

It has been pointed out that the influence on daily life from tinnitus is different and that the ways in which questions asked of participants in epidemiologic studies

Table 5.3 Percentages of adult population reporting tinnitus and its effects

	Cardiff	Glasgow	Nottingham	Southampton
Starting number (N)	1035	2,787	1,028	1,954
Usable replies (N)	730 (71%)	2,033 (75%)	726 (71%)	1,511 (77%)
Tinnitus (%)	17.9	18.6	18.1	15.5
Annoyance: moderate (%)	4.1	4.1	4.4	3.8
Severe (%)	0.7	2.8	0.4	0.7
Combined (%)	4.8	6.9	4.8	4.5
Sleep disturbance (%)	3.8	7.3	5.4	4.4
Severe effect on life (%)	0.4	0.5	0.4	0.5

Data from Coles [15]

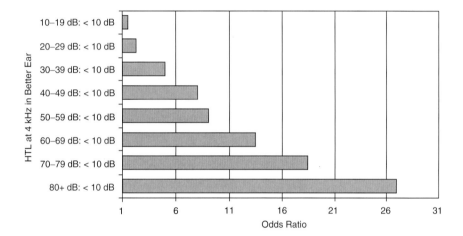

Fig. 5.2 Bar graph showing how the odds of having tinnitus increase as hearing threshold level (HTL) at 4 kHz increases in the United Kingdom National Study of Hearing. Because the prevalence of tinnitus in people with 4 kHz thresholds less than 10 dB (the reference group) was about 1%, the odds ratios in this case are very close to the actual prevalence rates in percentage. After Coles [16]. Reproduced from Dobie [1] with permission from BC Decker Inc

are formulated influence the results. This is one of the reasons for the difference in results of epidemiologic studies.

A study from four cities in the UK (Table 5.3) [15], which reported that tinnitus occurred in an average of 17.5% of individuals, showed that annoyance was classified to be moderate or severe in 5.3% on average for the cities studied. This study also showed a similar pattern of age relationship (14.5% in persons younger than 40 years, 17.5% in the group of 40–60 years, and 22.2% in individuals older than 60 years).

Although the reported prevalence of tinnitus varies between different studies, twenty percent of people who say they have tinnitus reported their condition as "severe tinnitus." This means that about 80% of

patients with tinnitus suffer little and are not seeking treatment.

Hearing Loss and Tinnitus

A study shows that the risk of having tinnitus (expressed as odds ratio[1]) increases with the degree of hearing loss at 4 kHz [16] (Fig. 5.2)

---

[1]Odds ratio: A measure of the size of an effect describing the strength of association between two binary data values. It is different from the relative risk because it treats the two variables to be compared symmetrically.

Fig. 5.3 Prevalence of self-reported hearing loss ("lot of trouble hearing" or "any trouble hearing") and bothersome tinnitus. Reproduced from Hoffmann and Reed [4] with permission by BC Decker Inc.; based on US National Health Interview Survey, Hearing Supplement 1990

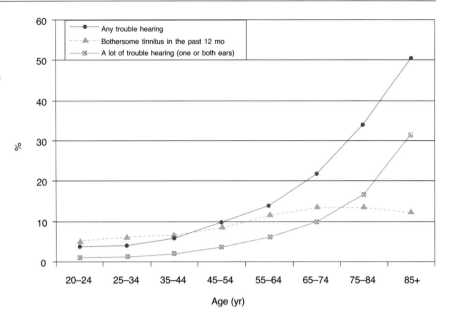

"Trouble Tinnitus" Compared with "Trouble Hearing"

There is considerable difference between having tinnitus and being troubled by tinnitus (having "trouble tinnitus"). The same is the case for hearing; having "trouble hearing" is a distinction from just having hearing loss. In a study based on the US National Health Interview Survey, participants were asked to report whether they had a "lot of trouble hearing" or "any trouble hearing," and for tinnitus the participants were asked if they had "bothersome tinnitus." In this study, the reported hearing trouble only increased slightly after age of 65, when self-reported problems were concerned (Fig. 5.3).

It is evident that while hearing loss increases monotonically with age, the prevalence of bothersome tinnitus levels off and even decreases after the age of 70 years, thus, in agreement with other studies reported above. That bothersome tinnitus reaches a level of about 14% in the 65- to 74-year age group should be noted.

Can Hearing Loss Cause Tinnitus?

The prevalence of tinnitus increases with age, and it has been discussed whether hearing loss can be a

contributing cause of this increase in the prevalence of tinnitus with age. Audiometric data show that hearing loss increases with age [17, 18] (see Chap. 36) The results of studies discussed in this chapter show that the prevalence of tinnitus increases with age, but it is not known if it is age-related changes in the ear and the nervous system that cause the tinnitus to increase with age or if it is the age-related hearing loss that causes the increase in prevalence of tinnitus. Population studies have shown that individuals with tinnitus, on average, have hearing loss affecting mostly high frequencies [19] (Fig. 5.4).

Other studies (Table 5.4) have confirmed the difference in prevalence of tinnitus between men and women.

There is considerable evidence that deprivation of input to the auditory nervous system can cause tinnitus (see Chaps. 11–13 and 21). There is also evidence that noise exposure can cause hearing loss (see Chap. 37), but it is not known if it is the noise exposure, as such, or the associated hearing loss that causes the tinnitus.

The hearing loss shown in Fig. 5.4 is slightly greater in males than in females, resembling what is found in population studies of hearing and showing signs of a 4-kHz dip, indicating that some of the hearing loss is likely to have been caused by noise exposure.

As an example of the diversity of tinnitus, it has been shown that the type of hearing (shape of the audiogram) is related to the character of the tinnitus

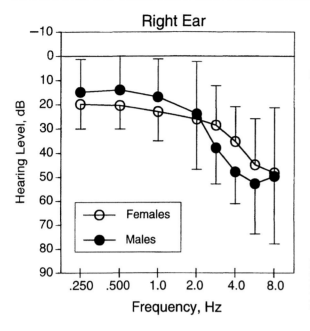

Fig. 5.4 Mean hearing thresholds in the right ear for female and male patients with tinnitus. Data are from patients who attended a tinnitus clinic. From Henry et al. [19]

Table 5.4 Prevalence in percentages for males and females

Age	Male (%)	Female (%)
18–24	4.3	5.2
25–24	5.8	6.2
45–64	10.6	9.5
65+	12.3	13.9

Prevalence based on a self report of "bothersome tinnitus" as a function of age, sex, and percentage of each characteristic in the population; based on the 1990 Hearing Supplement to the National Health Interview Survey. Data from Hoffmann and Reed [4]

(Fig. 5.5). Patients with low-pitched tinnitus (<1,500 Hz) tend to have much more severe hearing losses, especially in the low frequencies, than do patients with higher pitched tinnitus.

Again, it must be emphasized that these data are also from tinnitus clinics, thus, only including people who have sought professional help. While tinnitus does occur in individuals with normal hearing, people with tinnitus usually have hearing loss, and deprivation of sound activation of the nervous system can cause tinnitus by activating neural plasticity, as discussed in Chap. 12. However, the prevalence of troubled tinnitus does not increase above the age of 65, while audiometric hearing loss does continue to increase with age above 65.

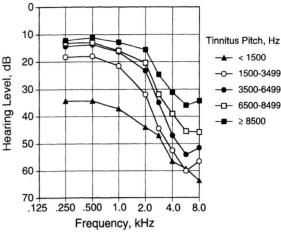

Fig. 5.5 Mean hearing threshold of the right ear for individuals in each group of patients according to the pitch of their tinnitus. Data are from patients who attended a tinnitus clinic. From Henry et al. [19]

The fact that tinnitus cannot be measured objectively as can hearing loss means that comparing tinnitus with audiometrical hearing loss may be regarded to be an invalid comparison. However, as seen in Fig. 5.3, the subjective trouble with hearing also increases with age while the prevalence of tinnitus is not changing above the age of 65. This could be because the debut of tinnitus above that age is rare or that some individuals who had tinnitus before the age of 65 improve and that counteracts an increase in the new cases of tinnitus. This question cannot be answered because the natural history of tinnitus is poorly known. Studies that have concerned the natural history of tinnitus have only reported on the presence of the disorder, not its severity [20, 21, 22] or how the individuals perceive their tinnitus. There are two reasons why the prevalence of tinnitus may be higher in a population of individuals with hearing loss. One reason is that hearing loss implies a certain degree of deprivation of input to the auditory system (see Chap. 11), which is known to be able to activate neural plasticity, and known to be involved in many forms of tinnitus (see Chaps. 12 and 13). Another reason that there may be a relationship between the prevalence of tinnitus and hearing loss is that the same factors that cause hearing loss may cause tinnitus. Such common factors may be age, cardiovascular disorders, and noise exposure.

When the kind of tinnitus individuals with hearing loss have is correlated with the shape of their audiograms, it follows that there are distinct correlations between the pitch of an individual's tinnitus and the individual's audiogram (Fig. 5.5). This is yet another complexity of tinnitus that makes it difficult to establish clear data on its prevalence.

It was shown in a study of patients with tinnitus of different pitch that patients with low-pitched tinnitus (less than 1,500 Hz) tend to have much more severe hearing losses, especially at the low frequencies, than do patients with higher pitched tinnitus.

The studies reported in the two preceding graphs concerned patients who had sought help for their tinnitus. This means that the participants do not represent a random selection of people. There are many reasons why people seek professional help and equally many reasons why people do not seek professional help.

Other Risk Factors for Tinnitus

Noise exposure and noise that induced hearing loss is another factor anecdotally reported to cause tinnitus in individuals.

Risk factors for tinnitus other than age are hearing loss, diseases such as middle-ear disorders, Ménière's disease, cerebrovascular diseases, and, in particular, hearing loss of various causes and environmental factors such as exposure to noise and administration of certain medications such as ototoxic antibiotics and acetylsalicylate.

Noise exposure increases the risk of tinnitus, and, at the same time, it causes hearing loss. The question is, therefore, if the tinnitus from noise exposure is caused by the hearing loss associated with noise exposure. The increased prevalence of tinnitus in males may have to do with the increased noise exposure in males and subsequent higher frequency of hearing loss in men [17].

Tinnitus and Suffering

Tinnitus is a sensation, and suffering may be related to and possibly a consequence of having tinnitus. The prevalence of tinnitus, counting all forms, is of little interest from a health care perspective because most individuals with tinnitus are not bothered to an extent that it affects their daily life, and few will seek medical attention except for those who want to be sure that their tinnitus is not a sign of a serious disease. In that way, tinnitus has similarities with pain. Most people have experienced pain in one form or another, but only a few have severe pain that causes suffering.

References

1. Dobie RA, (2004) Overview: Suffering from Tinnitus, in Tinnitus: Theory and management, JB Snow, Editor. 2004, BC Decker Inc.: Hamilton. 1–7.
2. Heller A (2003) Classification and epidemiology of tinnitus. Otolaryngol Clin N Am 36:239–48.
3. Erlandsson SI and LR-M Hallberg (2000) Prediction of quality of life in patients with tinnitus. PBr J Audiol 34:11–20.
4. Hoffmann HJ and GW Reed, (2004) Epidemiology of Tinnitus, in Tinnitus: Theory and management, JB Snow, Editor. 2004, BC Decker: Hamilton. 16–41.
5. Davis A, (1995) Hearing in adults. The prevalence and distribution of hearing impairment and reported hearing disability, in MRC Institute of Hearing Research's National Study of Hearing. 1995, Whurr Publishers Ltd.: London.
6. Axelsson A and A Ringdahl (1989) Tinnitus–a study of its prevalence and characteristics. Br J Audiol 23:53–62.
7. Ries P, (1994) Prevalence and characteristics of persons with hearing trouble: United States, 1990–91, in Vital and health statistics. 1994, National Center for Health Statistics: Hyattsville (MD).
8. Adams P and M Marano, (1995) Current estimates from the National Health Interview Survey, 1994., in Vital and health statistics. 1995, National Center for Health Statistics: Hyattsville (MD).
9. Benson V and M Marano, (1998) Current estimates from the National Health Interview Survey 1995., in Vital and health statistics. 1998, National Center for Health Statistics: Hyattsville (MD).
10. Nondahl D, K Cruickshanks, T Wiley et al (2002) Prevalence and 5-year incidence of tinnitus among older adults: the epidemiology of hearing loss study. J Am Acad Audiol 13:323–31.
11. Tambs K, H Hoffman, H Borchgrevink et al (2003) Hearing loss induced by noise, ear infections, and head injuries: results from the Nord-Trøndelag Hearing Loss Study. Int J Audiol 42:89–105.
12. Borg E (1981) Noise, hearing, and hypertension. Scand Audiol 10:125–6.
13. Borg E and AR Møller (1978) Noise and blood pressure: Effects on lifelong exposure in the rat. Acta Physiol Scand 103:340–42.
14. Sindhusake D, P Mitchell, P Newall et al (2003) Prevalence and characteristics of tinnitus in older adults: the Blue Mountains Hearing Study. Int J Audiolog 42:289–94.
15. Coles RRA, (1981) Epidemiology of tinnitus, in Ciba Foundation Symposium 85. 1981, Pitman Books Ltd. 16–34.

16. Coles R, (2000) Medicolegal issues, in Tinnitus handbook, R Tyler, Editor. 2000, Singular Publishing: San Diego. 399–417.

17. Møller MB (1981) Hearing in 70 and 75 year-old people. results from a cross-sectional and longitudinal population study. Am J Otolaryngol 2:22–9.

18. Spoor A (1967) Presbycusis values in relation to noise induced hearing loss. Int Audiol 6:48–57.

19. Henry JA, M Meikle and A Gilbert, (1999) Audiometric correlates of tinnitus pitch, in Proceedings of the Sixth International Tinnitus Seminar, J Hazell, Editor. 1999, The Tinnitus and Hyperacusis Centre: London. 51–7.

20. Rubinstein B, T Österberg and U Rosenhall (1992) Longitudinal fluctuations in tinnitus reported by an elderly population. J. Audiol Med 1:149–55.

21. Rosenhall U and AK Karlsson (1991) Tinnitus in old age. Scand Audiol 20:165–71.

22. Rosenhall U (2003) The influence of ageing on noise-induced hearing loss. Noise Health 5:47–53.

Chapter 6
Epidemiology of Tinnitus in Children

Claudia Barros Coelho

Keypoints

1. Children experience tinnitus and might present similar suffering as observed in adults but they rarely mention the symptom unless directly asked about it.
2. Difficulty on concentration, sleeping, hearing, leisure activities, sports practice, and hyperacusis are the most frequent complaints associated to tinnitus in children.
3. Only a few population studies have been performed and have disclosed prevalence rates from 6% to 59%. Many factors might be implicated in the large inter-study variability of tinnitus prevalence in children.
4. Age, gender, hearing loss, motion sickness, hyperacusis, and noise exposure have been suggested as risk factors to development of tinnitus in children.
5. A proper model to investigate children should be developed for the purpose of obtaining accurate information about the prevalence of tinnitus in children.
6. Preventive measures should aim at hearing education about the risk of hearing loss and tinnitus. Prevention of noise exposure should be promoted as early as possible.

Keywords Tinnitus • Epidemiology • Children • Hyperacusis • Preventive measures • Sleep

C.B. Coelho (✉)
Department of Otolaryngology and Head and Neck Surgery, University of Iowa, Iowa City, IA, USA
and
Grupo de Pesquisa em Otologia, Hospital de Clínicas de Porto Alegre, Posto Alegre, RS, Brazil
e-mail: claudiabarroscoelho@gmail.com

Abbreviations

OR	OR
TTS	Temporary threshold shift
HL	Hearing Level

Introduction

Children rarely mention tinnitus unless they are asked specifically about it. The frequency with which they mention the symptom spontaneously ranges from 1.6% to 6.5% [1–4]. Therefore, the observed proportion of children who seek professional help does not represent all children with tinnitus. Also, investigating tinnitus is seldom a part of routine pediatric otolaryngological practice. For these reasons, the prevalence of the symptom is generally underestimated in childhood [5].

Children who experience tinnitus may suffer in a similar way as adults with tinnitus. Difficulty in concentration, sleeping, hearing, and hyperacusis are the most frequent complaints associated with tinnitus in children [1, 6–8]. The symptoms might affect many kinds of leisure activities such as sports [1] as well as cause a decrease in school performance [9, 10]. The symptoms may significantly interfere with children's life in general, which will inevitably affect their entire families as well [11].

Terms such as "ringing" [2, 12], "beeping" or "buzzing," and a "high-pitched noise" or "whistling" [6] have been used by children to describe tinnitus sounds.

Some hypotheses have been presented regarding why children rarely report tinnitus spontaneously. (1) Children rarely refer to symptoms that are not associated with pain [13]; (2) children have a less-developed body image [14]; (3) there are specific differences in the ascending

A.R. Møller et al. (eds.), *Textbook of Tinnitus*,
DOI 10.1007/978-1-60761-145-5_6, © Springer Science+Business Media, LLC 2011

auditory pathways in children [15]; (4) children may perceive tinnitus as a familiar experience [16]; (5) children may be more easily distracted by events of the external environments [17]; (6) do not perceive the medical significance of the symptom [18]; and (7) children's attention process is different from that in adults, and this might also have an effect on how they perceive tinnitus.

In order to diagnose tinnitus in children, it is therefore important to ask children specifically if they have tinnitus.

Studying Tinnitus in Children

When studying tinnitus in childhood, it must be kept in mind that a child is not a miniature version of the adult. Children obviously do not possess adult brains. The organs of perception linking the child to the external world are still under maturation. The organization of sensory systems in the brain [15] (see also Chap. 8) and perception and attention in a child are different from adult, promoting a different perception and attitude to the world.

Other obstacles in studies of tinnitus in children are related to the fact that children tend to give positive answers to please the interviewer [19] and it is important to minimize and parents preoccupations that children's their might have after being aware of tinnitus.

In managing tinnitus in children, it is important to distinguish between the perception of the tinnitus and the impact that the tinnitus has on a person (tinnitus suffering) [5]. Lack of information about the prevalence of tinnitus suffering in children makes it difficult to judge the impact of tinnitus on children.

Epidemiological Studies

Although the existence of tinnitus in childhood has been reported since the 1970s there is still great uncertainty regarding the prevalence of tinnitus in children.

Population Studies

The few population studies that have been published were done in only a few countries and have shown widely different values of prevalence (from 6% to 59%) (Table 6.1).

Many different factors may have contributed to the discrepancies between the results of the different studies that have been published: (1) the criteria used for defining tinnitus may have been different; (2) hearing criteria may have been different; (3) age range may have been different; (4) methodological factors – interview or questionnaires most likely were different; (5) studies have used different statistical procedures, with different sample sizes; (6) the effect of confounding variables may also have contributed to the variations, for example, social and economic classes, ethnic, and cultural background may have varied; (7) different behavioral factors may have influenced the results such as emotional problems; (8) the effect of environmental factors such as exposure to noise may have been different.

Two studies of the prevalence of tinnitus in children had many participants recruited from otolaryngological clinics. Aust [20] screened children who sought help for otological complaints and Savastano [4] evaluated a general population of children using a specific protocol to investigate tinnitus (Table 6.2). They found tinnitus in 7% and 34%, respectively.

Factors that may Promote Tinnitus (Risk Factors)

Risk factors refer to an increase in the chance that an event is going to occur; in the present situation, this means the likelihood that a child will get tinnitus. Identification of risk factors plays an important role toward understand the etiology of tinnitus. Identification of risk factors might help understanding the symptoms and develop strategies for prevention of tinnitus (see Chap. 69). They can be identified by logistic regression models where the risk odds is determined while controlling for irrelevant factors. The OR (OR) is the likelihood that an event will occur; in our case, the likelihood of occurrence of tinnitus versus the chance of absence of tinnitus. The OR for a predictor tells the relative amount by which the odds of the outcome increases (OR > 1.0) or decreases (OR < 1.0). Decrease in OR is a sign that a protective factor against the occurrence of an event is present.

Table 6.1 Epidemiological studies of tinnitus in children

Author	Place	N	Age	Study design	Diagnosis based on	Prevalence	Prevalence	Prevalence
Nodar [12]	USA	2000	10–18	Longitudinal	Questionnaire "Do you hear a noise in your ears like ringing, buzzing, or a click?"		13.3% normal hearing	58.6% hearing impaired
Stouffer et al. [19]	Canada	161	7–12	Cross-sectional	Interview "Do you hear a noise in your head for more than 5 min?"		13% in normal hearing 6% after an answer (consistency criteria)	29% in hearing impaired 24% after an answer (consistency criteria)
Holgers and Svedlund [21]	Sweden	964	7	Cross-sectional	Questionnaire "After listening to loud music or other loud sounds/noise, have you afterwards heard aringing, buzzing or other sort of noise in your ears, even if the loud music or noise has been turned off?" "Have you heard a ringing,in the ears, without first having listened to loud music or other loud sounds?"		13% in normal hearing	8.8% in hearing impaired
Holgers and Pettersson [29]	Sweden	671	13–16	Cross-sectional	Questionnaire "How often do you experience tinnitus?" "How often is tinnitus annoying?" "Thoughts about tinnitus"		53% tinnitus perception	27% tinnitus annoyance
Coelho et al. [1]	Brazil	506	5–12	Randomized cross-sectional	Tinnitus sensation "Do you hear a noise inside your ears/head?" "Describe the sounds perceived" and "locate".		Tinnitus perception 37.7% normal hearing 50% Hearing impaired 50%	Tinnitus annoyance 19% normal hearing 17.8% hearing impaired

(continued)

Table 6.1 (continued)

Author	Place	N	Age	Study design	Diagnosis based on	Prevalence	Prevalence	Prevalence
Aksoy et al. [8]	Turkey	1020	6–16	Cross-sectional	Questionnaire "Have you ever had noises in your head or ears?" "Nowadays do you hear noises in your head or ears?"	9.2% tinnitus perception	5.8% tinnitus annoyance	
Bulbul et al. (2009) [34]	Turkey	428	11–18	Cross-sectional	Questionnaire "Do you have tinnitus (ringing in the ears)?" "Do have tinnitus after listening high volume music?"	33.4% tinnitus	35.2% tinnitus after listening high volume	
Savastano [4]	Italy	1100	6–16	Observational	Interview	34% tinnitus perception 22% tinnitus annoyance	76.4% normal hearing	24.6% hearing impaired
Aust [20]	Germany	1420	7–12	Observational	Interview	7.2% tinnitus	26.4% normal hearing	75.3% hearing impaired

To our knowledge, only two studies on tinnitus prevalence in children have so far used such statistical analysis.

The following risk factors have been identified on tinnitus in children.

Age

The risk for tinnitus sensation and tinnitus annoyance increases with age by 1.1 times, for every year among children in the Brazilian study [1] and by a factor of 1.2 according to Nodar [12]. Aksoy et al. [8] reported a progressive increase on tinnitus incidence around the age of 13–14 years from 10 to 18 years and 6 to 16 years have observed.

Gender

Holgers and Svedlund [21] found a higher prevalence of tinnitus among girls, as well as a higher prevalence of depressive and anxiety symptoms. Coelho et al. [1] found that boys had an OR of 0.

To present, tinnitus suffering when compared to girls means that the male gender was a protective factor for the development of tinnitus among children. These findings could be related to: (1) girls present a higher tendency to express symptoms than boys, including those related to affective disorders [22]; (2) spontaneous otoacoustic emissions are more frequent among females [23] and have been described as a possible tinnitus etiology[24]; (3) genetic differences among genders associated with neurotransmitter expressions pursuing an action on auditory pathway, including serotonin [25] and female reproductive hormones affect GABA receptors in the brain [26] (see Chap. 10).

Hearing Loss

Tinnitus is more frequent in children with normal hearing [12, 19] than in hearing impaired children, but children with profound hearing loss have lower prevalence of tinnitus than children with moderate loss [27]. Comparison of children with middle ear disease to those with sensorineural hearing loss showed that 43.9% of children with middle ear disease had

tinnitus while 29.5% with sensorineural hearing loss had tinnitus [16].

Children with hearing loss had an OR of 3.3 regarding tinnitus that could not be related to sound exposure according to a Swedish study from Holgers and Svedlund [21].

Similar findings were made by Coelho et al. [1] using a regression model where tinnitus was less prevalent in children with moderate to profound sensorineural hearing loss, than in those children with minimum to mild hearing loss. Minimum to mild hearing loss was a risk factor for tinnitus with an OR of 1.8 for tinnitus sensation and 2.4 for tinnitus suffering. Moderate to profound hearing loss (including deafness) was also considered risk factors with ORs of 0.5 for tinnitus sensation and 1.1 for tinnitus suffering.

The fact that a mild loss on hearing is a risk factor for tinnitus in children may be explained by the finding that even a mild hearing loss (thresholds at 30 dB HL) could promote tonotopic reorganization of the auditory cortex [28].

Temporary Threshold Shifts

Holgers and Petterson [29] have reported that individuals with temporary threshold shift (TTS) from noise exposure had an OR of 1.4 to present spontaneous tinnitus and 2.0 to noise-induced tinnitus. When comparing participants who sometimes experienced TTS to participants who did not have TTS, the OR was 2.8 to present spontaneous tinnitus and 8.4 to noise-induced tinnitus.

Noise Exposure

Holgers and Petterson [29] found that adolescents who attended concerts and discos/clubs had an OR of 1.4 regarding noise-induced tinnitus. Individuals who visited concerts 6–12 times per year had an OR of 4.4, compared to those who never went to concerts. Children who visited discos/clubs had an OR of 3.8.

Coelho et al. [1] reported that history of noise exposure was a risk factor for both tinnitus sensation and tinnitus suffering with ORs of 1.8 and 2.8, respectively. They found that firecrackers were the most frequent kind of noise exposure. Such noise may have peak levels of 145–165 dB HL at a distance of 2 m or less from the explosion site [30]. Risk of exposure to excessive noise from toys has also been mentioned on the literature [31, 32]. Exposure to high levels of noise from toys and firecrackers were reported by 25% of children who sought medical care because of noise trauma [33].

Tinnitus is also often associated with the use of music players such as the walkman and iPOD devices both in the right ear ($p = 0.004$) and in the left ear ($p = 0.000$) [34].

Activation of neural plasticity by overexposure or reduced impact to the auditory nervous system caused by hearing loss may cause tinnitus (see Chaps. 12 and 13). The reorganization on the tonotopic map of the primary auditory cortex following noise trauma is one sign of activation of neural plasticity that has been documented in several studies [35, 36] and it has been suggested that tinnitus may be related to such reorganization [37–39].

Motion Sickness

Motion sickness was found to be a risk factor for tinnitus sensation with an OR of 1.8 [1]. Motion sickness has been highly associated to migraine and vestibular symptoms in children [40].

Hyperacusis

Hyperacusis and tinnitus are related symptoms [41] (see Chap. 3). Coelho et al. [1] showed that hyperacusis was the highest risk factor for tinnitus in children, with an OR of 4.2, but tinnitus was not a risk factor for hyperacusis [1, 42].

Conclusions

The remedy from some of the shortcomings of present studies is as follows.

The available data regarding the epidemiology of tinnitus have a high degree of variations among different studies. There is therefore a need of more studies to bring down the variability. This chapter has pointed to some factors that have contributed to the variations in the results among different studies. Cross over or cohort studies with randomized samples representative of the whole population should be considered. Participants for such studies could be recruited from schools where stratification and randomization of the participants can be achieved. Participants from a school environment have fewer dropouts; consents from parents can easily be obtained. Multivariate regression models should be used to describe risk factors.

Some of the problems with present studies are related to the definition of tinnitus. Standardized interviews such as: "Do you hear a noise (sound) in your ears or in your head that last more than 5 min?" should be used in evaluation of the tinnitus, and evaluation of the impact on everyday life is important. Questions such as "Does this noise (sound) bother you?" should be included in the questionnaires.

Audiological testing is important for evaluating tinnitus etiology and standardized methodology, and classification of results should be used.

An epidemiological surveillance system would be the basic action to prevent tinnitus. Efficient preventive measures should aim at hearing education and prevention of noise exposure as early as possible (see Chap. 69).

References

1. Coelho, CB, TG Sanchez, and RS Tyler, Tinnitus in children and assciated risk factors. Prog Brain Res, 2007 **166**:179–91
2. Mills, RP, DM Albert, and CE Brain, Tinnitus in childhood. Clin Otolaryngol Allied Sci, 1986 **11**(6):431–4
3. Nodar, R and M Lezak, Paediatric tinnitus: a thesis revisited. J Laryng Otol, 1984 **9**:234–5
4. Savastano, M, Characteristics of tinnitus in childhood. Eur J Pediatr, 2006 **166**(8):797–801
5. Coelho, CB and RS Tyler, Management of tinnitus in children, in Paediatric Audiological Medicine, V Newton, Editor 2009, Wiley & Sons: West Sussex, 418–27
6. Martin, K and S Snashall, Children presenting with tinnitus: a retrospective study. Br J Audiol, 1994 **28**(2):111–5
7. Gabriels, Children with tinnitus in 5th International Tinnitus Seminar. 1996 Portland: USA American Tinnitus Association
8. Aksoy, S, et al, The extent and levels of tinnitus in children of central Ankara. Int J Pediatr Otorhinolaryngol, 2007 **71**(2):263–8
9. Drukier, GS, The prevalence and characteristics of tinnitus with profound sensori-neural hearing impairment. Am Ann Deaf, 1989 **134**(4):260–4
10. Kentish, RC, SR Crocker, and L McKenna, Children's experience of tinnitus: a preliminary survey of children presenting to a psychology department. Br J Audiol, 2000 **34**(6):335–40

11. Kentish, RC and SR Crocker, Scary monsters and waterfalls: tinnitus narrative therapy for children, in Tinnitus Treatment Clinacal Protocols, R Tyler, Editor 2006, Thieme: New York

12. Nodar, RH, Tinnitus aurium in scholl age children: a survey. J Aud Res, 1972 **12**:133

13. Graham, J, Tinnitus aurium. Acta Otolaryng, 1965 **Suppl**(202):24–6

14. Leonard, G, F Black, and J Schramm, Tinnitus in Children, in Pediatric Otolaryngology, CD Bluestone, S Stool, and S Arjona, Editors 1983, W Saunders: Philadelphia, 271–277

15. Møller AR and P Rollins, The non-classical auditory system is active in children but not in adults. Neurosci Lett, 2002 **319**:41–4.

16. Mills, RP and JR Cherry, Subjective tinnitus in children with otological disorders. Int J Pediatr Otorhinolaryngol, 1984 **7**(1):21–7

17. Viani, LG, Tinnitus in children with hearing loss. J Laryngol Otol, 1989 **103**(12):1142–5

18. Savastano, M, A protocol of study for tinnitus in childhood. Int J Pediatr Otorhinolaryngol, 2002 **64**(1):23–7

19. Stouffer, J, et al, Tinnitus in normal-hearing and hearing-impaired children. In IV International Tinnitus Seminar 1991 Kugler Publications: Bordeaux

20. Aust, G, Tinnitus in childhood. Int Tinnitus J, 2002 **8**(1): 20–6

21. Holgers, K and Svedlund C, Tinnitus in childhood. J Psychosomat Res, 2003 **55**(2):135

22. Eley, TC, P Lichtenstein, and J Stevenson, Sex differences in the etiology of aggressive and nonaggressive antisocial behavior: results from two twin studies. Child Dev, 1999 **70**(1):155–68

23. Penner, MJ, Linking spontaneous otoacoustic emissions and tinnitus. Br J Audiol, 1992 **26**(2):115–23

24. Burns, EM, KH Arehart, and SL Campbell, Prevalence of spontaneous otoacoustic emissions in neonates. J Acoust Soc Am, 1992 **91**(3):1571–5

25. Weiss, LA, et al, Sex-specific genetic architecture of whole blood serotonin levels. Am J Hum Genet, 2005 **76**(1):33–41

26. Tremere, LA, JK Jeong and R Pinaud, Estradiol shapes auditory processing in the adult brain by regulating inhibitory transmission and plasticity-associated gene expression. J Neurosci, 2009 **29**(18):5949–63

27. Graham, JM, Tinnitus in children with hearing loss. Ciba Found Symp, 1981 **85**:172–92

28. Norena, AJ and JJ Eggermont, Enriched acoustic environment after noise trauma reduces hearing loss and prevents cortical map reorganization. J Neurosci, 2005 **25**(3): 699–705

29. Holgers, KM and B Pettersson, Noise exposure and subjective hearing symptoms among school children in Sweden. Noise Health, 2005 **7**(27):27–37

30. Smoorenburg, GF, Risk of noise-induced hearing loss following exposure to Chinese firecrackers. Audiology, 1993 **32**(6):333–43

31. Axelsson, A, et al, Noisy toys – a risk of hearing injuries? Lakartidningen, 1984 **81**(45):4162–6

32. Rytzner, B and C Rytzner. Schoolchildren and noise. The 4 kHz dip-tone screening in 14391 schoolchildren. Scand Audiol, 1981 **10**(4):213–6

33. Segal, S, et al, Inner ear damage in children due to noise exposure from toy cap pistols and firecrackers: a retrospective review of 53 cases. Noise Health, 2003 **5**(18):13–8.

34. Bulbul, SF, et al, Subjective tinnitus and hearing problems in adolescents. Int J Pediatr Otorhinolaryngol, 2009 **73**(8): 1124–31

35. Robertson, D and DR Irvine, Plasticity of frequency organization in auditory cortex of guinea pigs with partial unilateral deafness. J Comp Neurol, 1989 **282**(3):456–71

36. Komiya, H and JJ Eggermont, Spontaneous firing activity of cortical neurons in adult cats with reorganized tonotopic map following pure-tone trauma. Acta Otolaryngol, 2000 **120**(6):750–6

37. Rauschecker, JP, Auditory cortical plasticity: a comparison with other sensory systems. Trends Neurosci, 1999 **22**(2):74–80

38. Norena, A, et al, Psychoacoustic characterization of the tinnitus spectrum: implications for the underlying mechanisms of tinnitus. Audiol Neurootol, 2002 **7**(6):358–69

39. Norena, AJ and JJ Eggermont, Changes in spontaneous neural activity immediately after an acoustic trauma: implications for neural correlates of tinnitus. Hear Res, 2003 **183**(1–2):137–53

40. Uneri, A and D Turkdogan, Evaluation of vestibular functions in children with vertigo attacks. Arch Dis Child, 2003 **88**(6):510–1

41. Tyler, RS and LJ Baker, Difficulties experienced by tinnitus sufferers. J Speech Hear Disord, 1983 **48**(2):150–4

42. Coelho, CB, TG Sanchez, and RS Tyler, Hyperacusis, sound annoyance and loudness hypersensitivity in children. Prog Brain Res, 2007 **166**:169–78

Chapter 7
Genetic Risk Factors in Chronic Tinnitus

Philipp G. Sand

Keypoints

1. Individual susceptibility to chronic tinnitus is shaped by the interplay of genetic and environmental factors.
2. Whereas many environmental risks including noise trauma and medication side effects are already well understood, heritable risks remain to be specified.
3. Pilot biometric studies in twins have produced heritability estimates of up to 0.39 in subgroups of affected patients but are still burdened with confounders.
4. The current review addresses the quest for molecular genetic biomarkers of tinnitus and the candidate genes examined so far.
5. Of these, genes encoding neurotrophic factors BDNF and GDNF give promising results that warrant further study.
6. Public attitude toward advances in genetic testing for tinnitus is as yet unexplored and deserves consideration in future research.

Keywords Tinnitus • Association study • Familial clustering • Genetic risk • Heritability • Mutation screening • Tinnitus susceptibility

Abbreviations

BDNF	brain-derived neurotrophic factor
CNTF	ciliary neurotrophic factor
GDNF	glial cell-derived neurotrophic factor
HTTLPR	serotonin transporter gene length polymorphic region
HTR1A	serotonin receptor 1A
HTR3A	serotonin receptor 3A
HUNT-II	North-Trøndelag Health Study II (1995–1997)
PRNP	Prion protein
SLC6A4 (5-HTT)	solute carrier 6A4 (serotonin transporter)

Introduction

Tinnitus is a common clinical syndrome with an estimated 30 million sufferers in the United States [1]. Of those who develop a chronic form of tinnitus, the majority also experience varying degrees of hearing loss. However, the relationship between both conditions is complicated by dissimilar age-specific prevalence rates and interfering risk factors. For tinnitus, these comprise male sex, cigarette smoking, occupational noise exposure, lower income, higher body mass index, and reduced general health status, among others [2]. It is also evident from anecdotal reports that environmental risks interact with heritable susceptibility to chronic tinnitus that is as yet poorly defined [3]. Together, these elements have become a focus of public awareness [4] that is accelerating scientific research into the biological underpinnings of tinnitus. The present review summarizes the latest advancements on innate factors that may help account for interindividual differences in severity and course of symptoms.

P.G. Sand (✉)
Department of Psychiatry, University of Regensburg,
Universitaetsstr. 84, 93053 Regensburg, Germany
e-mail: philipp.sand@klinik.uni-regensburg.de

A.R. Møller et al. (eds.), *Textbook of Tinnitus*,
DOI 10.1007/978-1-60761-145-5_7, © Springer Science+Business Media, LLC 2011

Familial Aggregation of Chronic Tinnitus

Limited evidence is currently available on the familial clustering of chronic tinnitus. In siblings of affected individuals, a twofold risk has been noted relative to the general population [2]. A multicentre investigation involving 198 families from six European countries confirmed familial aggregation of tinnitus, albeit to a lesser extent than clustering observed for age-related hearing impairment [5]. A Danish study of 956 monozygotic and dizygotic twins found no evidence of heritability for chronic tinnitus in male individuals, but estimated heritability at .039 in female individuals [6]. Owing to the elderly age of the participants ($\geq$70 years), the impact of other determinants of physical health on prevalence rates is a concern.

Few attempts have been made so far to identify specific features of tinnitus that are highly heritable and that may serve to define subgroups at risk. In 1,147 Belgian individuals with tinnitus, effects of familial loading on the curvature of the audiogram were investigated in an effort to distinguish highly heritable from sporadic conditions [7]. The authors claimed an association of familial forms of tinnitus with flat audiograms, but replication is lacking. Others have proposed that tinnitus in conjunction with hearing loss may predict familial tinnitus [8].

A pilot investigation in Norway has addressed the respective contributions of genetic and environmental factors to chronic tinnitus as part of the Nord-Trøndelag Hearing Loss Study [9]. In this study, epidemiological findings were merged with public registry data on the relatedness between individuals and gave a heritability estimate of 0.106 for a broadly defined tinnitus phenotype. Results were based on data from 51,975 individuals in 17 of 23 municipalities of a rural county (age range: 20–101 years; mean age: 50 years). Participants underwent pure-tone audiometry and completed self-report questionnaires between 1996 and 1998, providing information on occupational and leisure noise exposure, medical history, and symptoms of hearing impairment. Valid audiometry and questionnaire data refer to a core sample of 50,132 individuals [10]. While the authors argue that selection toward individuals with poor hearing is unlikely to have occurred in ~90% of participants who had been recruited as part of an earlier general health survey (HUNT-II), a weakness

of the study is the specification of tinnitus-related complaints. Participants were asked whether or not they were "bothered by ringing in their ears," i.e., tinnitus annoyance was used as a surrogate of tinnitus perception. As has been noted before, reference to the term "bothersome tinnitus" is liable to produce conservative estimates of the syndrome's actual prevalence [1]. Pending the detailed publication of findings from this Norwegian population, the likelihood of type II errors in future studies may be reduced by a standardized evaluation of severity with attention to wording, the exclusion of known confounders, and further narrowing of the syndrome.

Candidate Gene Studies

A number of candidate genes have been investigated in individuals diagnosed with chronic tinnitus using either a case–control design (e.g., [11]) or a systematic mutation screening approach [12] (Table 7.1). From these investigations, there is little support for the notion of a serotonin-related etiology of tinnitus [13]. Specifically, negative associations of tinnitus with serotonin receptor genes 1A and 3A [12, 14], plus the serotonin transporter gene have been documented [15]. In contrast, positive findings have emerged for two genes that encode neurotrophic factors [11, 16]. Thus, the risk for developing tinnitus in conjunction with hearing impairment was significantly reduced in carriers of a missense variant in the gene encoding brain-derived neurotrophic factor (BDNF) [11]. When information from BDNF variants was combined with data on variants in the gene encoding glial cell-derived neurotrophic factor (GDNF), 16% of the variance in tinnitus severity could be explained [16]. Neurotrophins play key roles in tonotopic organization of the central auditory pathway [17, 18] and have been implicated in defective neuroregeneration in the cortex and hippocampus [19]. Both BDNF and GDNF protect the inner ear against trauma [20] and BDNF expression patterns dynamically respond to traumatic acoustic stimuli [21]. While BDNF expression is decreased in the primary auditory cortex, upregulation occurs within days in the inferior colliculus in what has been considered a putative correlate of ongoing neuronal repair. Together, these experimental data

Table 7.1 A synopsis of published investigations of candidate genes in chronic tinnitus

Candidate gene	Chromosomal locus	Study	Outcome
HTR1A	5q11	Kleinjung et al. [12]	Systematic screening for mutations produces no novel variants in individuals with chronic tinnitus
BDNF	11p13	Sand et al. [11]	Carriers of the BDNF Val66Met variant differ from other individuals with regard to comorbid hearing impairment ($p=0.01$)
SLC6A4 (5-HTT)	17q11	Sand et al. [15]	No significant effect of 5-HTTLPR carrier status on tinnitus severity
CNTF	11q12	Kleinjung et al. [25]	No significant effect of CNTF null mutation carrier status on self-ratings of tinnitus severity
PRNP	20p12	Kleinjung et al. [26]	No significant effect of carrier status for a coding variant on tinnitus scores as measured by TQ
HTR3A	11q23	Kleinjung et al. [14]	No significant effect of a silent HTR3A variant on tinnitus severity
GDNF	5p13	Kleinjung et al. [16]	Five GDNF and BDNF variants account for 16% of variance in subjective tinnitus severity ($p=0.03$)

warrant further exploration of neurotrophin-related signaling in animal models of tinnitus and can serve as a starting point for a targeted search of tinnitus biomarkers in humans.

Outlook

It is currently too early to speculate on the possible benefits that can be expected from future genetic tests for tinnitus, or even to predict when such tests may become available. However, genetic testing for other communication disorders (e.g., for deafness) has underscored the importance of providing potential consumers of these services with full information on all aspects of genetic evaluation [22]. Public education will need to address cost effectiveness and the appropriate use of resources. Many related issues, e.g., prenatal testing and gene therapy, are not without controversy and have given rise to individual and societal concerns over recommending tests for heritable syndromes. Adequate understanding of the needs and desires of parents and family members is therefore essential to guide the application of new genetic technologies to clinical practice [23]. In the largest survey of parents of children with hearing loss conducted in the USA to date, positive feelings about advances in

the genetics of hearing loss prevailed [24], but no surveys exist to gauge interest in a DNA-based test for tinnitus. Unlike rare monogenic disorders of hearing, tinnitus is presumed to feature a much more complex mode of inheritance [8], which will call for a judicious interpretation of test results that rely on only one or few emerging risk factors.

References

1. Snow, JB, Tinnitus, in The Senses: A Comprehensive Reference, Volume 3, Audition, P Dallos, D Oertel, Editors 2008:301–308
2. Hoffman, HJ, Reed, GW, Epidemiology of Tinnitus, in Tinnitus: Theory and management, JB Snow, Editor 2004: 16–41
3. Sand, PG, Langguth, B, Kleinjung, T, Eichhammer, P, Genetics of chronic tinnitus Prog Brain Res, 2007 166: 159–168
4. Groopman, J, That buzzing sound: The mystery of tinnitus The New Yorker, 09 Feb 2009
5. Hendrickx, JJ, Huyghe, JR, Demeester, K, Topsakal, V, Van Eyken, E, Fransen, E, Mäki-Torkko, E, Hannula, S, Jensen, M, Tropitzsch, A, Bonaconsa, A, Mazzoli, M, Espeso, A, Verbruggen, K, Huyghe, J, Huygen, PL, Kremer, H, Kunst, SJ, Manninen, M, Diaz-Lacava, AN, Steffens, M, Parving, A, Pyykkö, I, Dhooge, I, Stephens, D, Orzan, E, Pfister, MH, Bille, M, Sorri, M, Cremers, CW, Van Laer, L, Van Camp, G, Wienker, TF, Van de Heyning, P, Familial aggregation of tinnitus: a European multicentre study B-ENT, 2007 Suppl 7:51–60

6. Petersen, HC, Andersen, T, Frederiksen, H, et al The heritability of tinnitus – a twin study Arhus (Denmark): Nordic Epidemiology Congress: June 2002
7. Demeester, K, van Wieringen, A, Hendrickx, JJ, Topsakal, V, Fransen, E, Van Laer, L, De Ridder, D, Van Camp, G, Van de Heyning, P, Prevalence of tinnitus and audiometric shape B-ENT, 2007 Suppl 7:37–49
8. Ryan, AF, Mullen, LM, Molecular Biology of Hearing and Tinnitus, in Tinnitus: Theory and management, JB Snow, Editor 2004:43–51
9. Kvestad, E, Hearing loss and tinnitus: Genetic and Environmental Effects. Abstract, Programme for Environment, Genetics and Health, The Research Council of Norway Research Seminar, 30–31 Oct 2008
10. Borchgrevink, HM, Tambs, K, Hoffman, HJ, The Nord-Trøndelag Norway Audiometric Survey 1996–98: unscreened thresholds and prevalence of hearing impairment for adults >20 years Noise Health, 2005 7:1–15
11. Sand, P, Kleinjung, T, Langguth, B, Eichhammer, P, Fischer, B, Pratt, C, Pfluegl, S, Niebling, H, Hajak, G, Investigation of a BDNF missense variant in chronic tinnitus Int J Neuropsychopharmacol, 2006a 9: S1
12. Kleinjung, T, Langguth, B, Fischer, B, Hajak, G, Eichhammer, P, Sand, PG, Systematic screening of the Serotonin Receptor 1A (5-HT1A) gene in chronic tinnitus J Otology, 2006 2:83–85
13. Simpson, JJ, Davies, WE, A review of evidence in support of a role for 5-HT in the perception of tinnitus Hear Res, 2000 145:1–7
14. Kleinjung, T, Fischer, B, Vielsmeier, V, Langguth, B, Sand, P, Serotonin-Rezeptor 3A-Genvarianten bei Patienten mit chronischem Tinnitus 79th Annual Meeting of the German Society of Oto-Rhino-Laryngology, Bonn, 2008b
15. Sand, P, Langguth, B, Kleinjung, T, Fischer, B, Stoertebecker, P, Pfluegl, S, Niebling, H, Hajak, G, Eichhammer, P, Investigation of the 5-HTTLPR in chronic tinnitus Am J Med Genet (Neuropsychiatr Genet), 2006b 141B:763
16. Kleinjung, T, Frank, E, Vielsmeier, V, Landgrebe, M, Langguth, B, Sand, P, BDNF and GDNF variants predict tinnitus severity Otolaryngol Head Neck Surg, 2009 141 Suppl 1:180–181
17. Staecker, H, Galinovic-Schwartz, V, Liu, W, Lefebvre, P, Kopke, R, Malgrange, B, Moonen, G, Van De Water, TR, The role of the neurotrophins in maturation and maintenance of postnatal auditory innervation Am J Otol, 1996 17:486–492
18. Reser, DH, Van de Water, TR, Implications of neurotrophin supported auditory neuron survival for maintenance of the tonotopic organization of the central auditory pathway Acta Otolaryngol, 1997 117:239–243
19. Morris, JK, Maklad, A, Hansen, LA, Feng, F, Sorensen, C, Lee, KF, Macklin, WB, Fritzsch, B, A disorganized innervation of the inner ear persists in the absence of ErbB2 Brain Res, 2006 1091:186–199
20. Martin, DM, Raphael, Y, Gene-based diagnostic and treatment methods for tinnitus Int Tinnitus J, 2003 9:3–10
21. Tan, J, Rüttiger, L, Panford-Walsh, R, Singer, W, Schulze, H, Kilian, SB, Hadjab, S, Zimmermann, U, Köpschall, I, Rohbock, K, Knipper, M, Tinnitus behavior and hearing function correlate with the reciprocal expression patterns of BDNF and Arg31/arc in auditory neurons following acoustic trauma Neuroscience, 2007 145:715–726
22. Burton, SK, Withrow, K, Arnos, KS, Kalfoglou, AL, Pandya, A, A focus group study of consumer attitudes toward genetic testing and newborn screening for deafness Genet Med, 2006 8:779–783
23. Arnos, KS, Ethical and social implications of genetic testing for communication disorders J Commun Disord, 2008 41: 444–457
24. Withrow, KA, Tracy, KA, Burton, SK, Norris, VW, Maes, HH, Arnos, KS, Pandya, A, Impact of genetic advances and testing for hearing loss: results from a national consumer survey Am J Med Genet A, 2009 149A:1159–1168
25. Kleinjung, T, Fischer, B, Langguth, B, Eichhammer, P, Hajak, G, Sand, P, Prevalence of a CNTF null mutation in individuals with chronic tinnitus Otolaryngol Head Neck Surg, 2007 137 Suppl 1:247
26. Kleinjung, T, Langguth, B, Vielsmeier, V, Landgrebe, M, Sand, P, Investigation of the Prion protein in individuals with chronic tinnitus Otolaryngol Head Neck Surg, 2008a 139 Suppl 1:151

Chapter 8
Anatomy and Physiology of the Auditory System

Aage R. Møller

Keypoints

1. The auditory system consists of four anatomically separate structures:

    (a) those that conduct the stimulus to the receptors
    (b) the receptors
    (c) the auditory nerve
    (d) the central auditory nervous system

2. The most important part regarding tinnitus is the auditory nervous system.
3. The auditory nervous system consists of two parallel ascending pathways that project to auditory cortices and two (reciprocal) descending pathways that project to nuclei of the auditory pathways.
4. The nuclei in the ascending auditory pathways process information in a serial hierarchical fashion, and processing occurs in modules with specific functions.
5. Two separate ascending sensory pathways have been identified in the auditory pathways: classical pathways and the non-classical pathways. Also, the somatosensory and visual pathways have two different ascending tracts.
6. The classical pathways are also known as the lemniscal system, or the specific system, and the non-classical pathways are also known as the extralemniscal system, or the unspecific system. The non-classical pathways have been divided into the defuse system and the polysensory pathways.

7. The classical and non-classical pathways process information differently and have different central targets, especially regarding connections to the thalamus and the cerebral cortex.
8. The non-classical ascending auditory pathways branch off the classical pathways at several levels, the most prominent being the central nucleus of the inferior colliculus.
9. The auditory pathways receive input from the somatosensory system at the external nucleus of the inferior colliculus and from the dorsal cochlear nucleus as well.
10. The auditory pathways are mainly crossed, but there are extensive connections between nuclei at the two sides at two levels: the pontine nuclei (superior olivary complex) and the midbrain level (inferior colliculus). There are also extensive connections between the two sides at the cerebral cortical level.
11. The auditory nerve sends collaterals to cells in all these divisions of the cochlear nucleus. That is the earliest sign of the anatomical basis for parallel processing of information. Parallel processing occurs throughout the ascending pathways by axons branching to connect to more than one group of nerve cells.
12. Descending auditory pathways are abundant, in particular, the cortico-thalamic pathways, but little is known about their function. The descending pathways are largely reciprocal to the ascending pathways. The descending pathways reach as far caudal as the receptors in the cochlea.
13. The classical sensory pathways are interrupted by synaptic contacts with neurons in the ventral parts of the thalamus, which project to the primary sensory cortices.
14. The non-classical sensory pathways use the dorsal and medial thalamus as relay, the neurons of which

A.R. Møller (✉)
The University of Texas at Dallas, School of Behavioral and Brain Sciences, GR 41, 800 W Campbell Rd, Richardson, TX 75080, USA
e-mail: amoller@utdallas.edu

A.R. Møller et al. (eds.), *Textbook of Tinnitus*,
DOI 10.1007/978-1-60761-145-5_8, © Springer Science+Business Media, LLC 2011

project to secondary and association cortices thus bypassing the primary sensory cortices.

15. Neurons in the dorsal and medial thalamus make direct (subcortical) connections with other parts of the CNS, such as structures of the limbic system, while the classical sensory systems connect to other parts of the CNS, mainly via association cortices.

16. There are anatomical connections between the upper spinal cord and the dorsal cochlear nucleus and between the caudal trigeminal nucleus and the dorsal cochlear nucleus. There are anatomical connections between the somatosensory system and midbrain nuclei of the non-classical auditory system.

17. Neurons in the nuclei of the classical pathways respond distinctly to specific sensory stimuli and have distinct frequency selectivity.

18. Sound stimulation may increase the firing rate of auditory nerve fibers, but saturation occurs for most fibers at low sound intensities.

19. Periodic sounds cause many nerve fibers to become locked to the waveform of the sound, and consequently, the firing of such fibers becomes time locked to each other. It subsequently causes the discharge of many neurons in the ascending auditory pathways, which then become time locked to each other.

20. Stream segregation implies that different types of information (for example, spatial and object information) are processed in anatomically different parts of the sensory nervous system.

21. Parallel processing allows the same information to be processed in anatomically different parts of the nervous system, while stream segregation implies that different kinds of information are processed in anatomically different structures.

22. Much less is known about the functional role of the non-classical pathways compared to the classical pathways, but neurons of the nuclei of the non-classical pathways respond less distinctly and are broader tuned than cells in the classical pathways and respond to a broad range of stimuli. They also integrate information on wider spatial scales than the classical pathways.

23. Neurons in the nuclei of the classical auditory pathways, up to and including the primary auditory cortex, respond only to one sensory modality

(sound) while neurons of higher order cortices (secondary and association cortices) integrate information from several sensory systems and respond to different sensory modalities. This response can be modulated by input from non-sensory brain areas such as the amygdala.

24. Some neurons in the ascending non-classical pathways respond to more than one sensory modality. Their response to sound can be modulated by other sensory input.

25. The non-classical pathways make direct (subcortical) connections from the thalamus to other parts of the CNS, such as structures of the limbic system, while the classical sensory systems connect to other such parts of the CNS mainly via association cortices.

26. Stimulation of the somatosensory system affects perception of sounds in children, indicating involvement of the non-classical auditory system in children.

27. There are no signs of cross-modal interaction in adults, except with some forms of tinnitus and in autistic individuals, indicating that the non-classical auditory pathways are not normally active in adults.

28. Sensory systems connect to motor systems, the limbic system, reticular activating system, and the autonomic nervous system through subcortical and cortical routes.

29. There is considerable interaction between different systems in the brain, such as between different sensory systems and between sensory systems and non-sensory systems.

Keywords Ear • Auditory pathways • Anatomy • Non-classical pathways • Physiology • Cross-modal interaction

Abbreviations

AAF	Anterior auditory (cortical) field
AES	Anterior ectosylvian sulcus area
AI	Primary auditory cortex
AII	Secondary auditory cortex
AN	Auditory nerve
AVCN	Anterior ventral cochlear nuclei
C_2	Upper segment of the cervical spine
CN	Cochlear nucleus

COCB	Crossed olivocochlear bundle
DC	Dorsal cortex (of IC)
DNLL	Dorsal nucleus of the lateral lemniscus
DPOAE	Distortion product otoacoustic emission
DRG	Dorsal root ganglion
DZ	Dorsal auditory zone
ED	Posterior ectosylvian gyrus dorsal part
EI	Posterior ectosylvian
EV	Posterior ectosylvian gyrus
IC	Inferior colliculus
ICC	Central nucleus of the IC
ICX	External nucleus of the IC
IHC	Inner hair cells
In	Insular
LL	Lateral lemniscus
LSO	Lateral superior olive
MG	Medial geniculate body
MSO	Medial superior olive
NLL	Nucleus of the lateral lemniscus
NTB	Nucleus of the trapezoidal body
OCB	Olivocochlear bundle
OHC	Outer hair cells
PAF	Posterior auditory (cortical) field
PVCN	Posterior ventral cochlear nuclei
SH	Stria of Held (intermediate stria)
SM	Stria of Monakow (dorsal stria)
SOC	Superior olivary complex
SOE	Spontaneous otoacoustic emission
Sp5	Trigeminal nucleus
Te	Temporal cortex
TEOAE	Transient evoked otoacoustic emissions
UCOCB	Uncrossed olivocochlear bundle
Ve	Auditory cortex ventral area
VNLL	Ventral nucleus of the lateral lemniscus
VP	Auditory cortex ventral posterior area

Introduction

This chapter reviews anatomy and physiology of the auditory system, emphasizing structures and function that are likely to be involved with tinnitus. For general coverage of auditory anatomy and physiology of the auditory system, see [1]. The following chapter (Chap. 10) discusses pathologies of the auditory system.

Main Components of the Auditory System

The mammalian auditory system consists of four main parts: the apparatus that conducts sounds to the cochlea; the cochlea, where sounds are separated according to their frequency the sensory transduction occurs; the auditory nerve and the ascending auditory pathways, consisting of classical and non-classical including the primary and secondary auditory cortices; and association cortices with two streams (object or "what" and spatial or "where") and extra-cortical structures that receive projections from the primary and secondary auditory cortices [1].

Anatomy

The most important parts of the auditory system, regarding most forms of tinnitus, are the function of the cochlea, the auditory nerve, and the central auditory nervous system.

The outer and middle ear that conducts sounds to the inner ear becomes important for tinnitus when impairments reduce the sound that reaches the cochlea where the sensory cells are located.

The cochlea is a very complex structure with essentially two fluid systems with different ionic composition (Fig. 8.1). The most important structures for transduction of sound into a neural code in auditory nerve fibers are the sensory cells (hair cells) that are located along the basilar membrane (Fig. 8.2). There are two kinds of sensory cells (inner and outer hair cells) (Fig. 8.1) that are morphologically similar but have complete different functions.

The auditory nervous system involves structures in the pons, midbrain, thalamus and cerebral cortex (Fig. 8.3).

Classical Pathways

The fibers of the auditory nerve terminate in the cochlear nuclei, which has three main divisions, the anterior and posterior ventral cochlear nuclei (AVCN

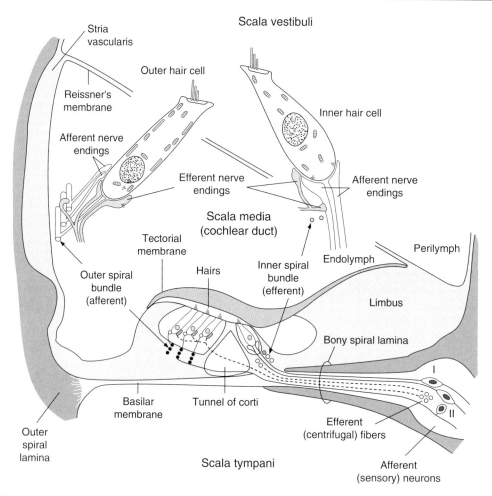

Fig. 8.1 Schematic drawing of a cross-section of the cochlea showing the organ of Corti. Outer and inner hair cells are shown as inserts (from A.R. Møller Sensory Systems, Academic Press 2003). (Redrawn from Shepherd GM. *Neurobiology*. New York: Oxford University Press, 1994. [2])

and PVCN), and the dorsal cochlear nuclei (DCN) (Figs. 8.4 and 8.5). Each fiber of the auditory nerve bifurcates and one of the branches divides again making it possible for each nerve fiber to connect to neurons in each of the three divisions of the cochlear nucleus (Fig. 8.5). This represents the first example of parallel processing allowing the same information to be processed in (three) different populations of nerve cells.

The sensory cells in the cochlea are innervated by the auditory nerve that conducts signals to the cochlear nucleus complex, which is the first nucleus of the ascending auditory pathways.

The cochlear nucleus has three main divisions: the dorsal cochlear nucleus (DCN), the anterior ventral cochlear nucleus (AVCN), and the posterior ventral cochlear nucleus (PVCN).

Cells in the three divisions of the cochlear nucleus project to the central nucleus of the inferior colliculus (ICC) through three fiber tracts, the dorsal (stria of Monaco), medial (stria of Held), and ventral striae (trapezoidal body) that joins into the lateral lemniscus (LL) (Fig. 8.6). Fibers in these three striae give off collaterals to the nuclei of the superior olivary complex and some fibers are interrupted in some of these nuclei.

There are two different ascending pathways from the cochlear nucleus to the cerebral auditory cortices, known as the classical and the non-classical pathways. The classical pathways also known as the lemniscal, or

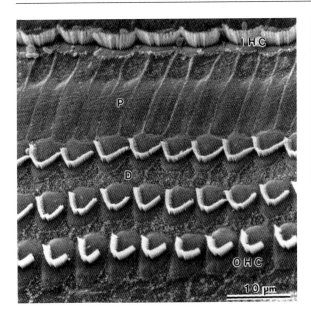

Fig. 8.2 Scanning electron micrographs of inner hair cells (IHC) and outer hair cells (OHC) in a monkey after that the tectorial membrane has been removed. From: Harrison RV and Hunter-Duvar IM. An Anatomical Tour of the Cochlea. In: *Physiology of the Ear*, edited by Jahn AF and Santos-Sacchi J. New York: Raven Press, 1988, p. 159–171 [3]

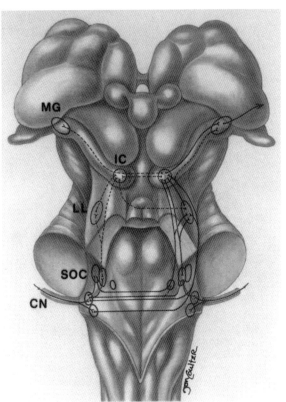

Fig. 8.3 Schematic drawing of the anatomical locations of the ascending auditory pathway. *AN* auditory nerve, *CN* cochlear nucleus, *SOC* superior olivary complex, *LL* lateral lemniscus, *NLL* nucleus of the lateral lemniscus, *IC* inferior colliculus, *MG* medial geniculate body (From Møller, A.R. 1988. Evoked potentials in intraoperative monitoring Williams and Wilkins, Baltimore [4])

the distinct pathways, are the best known. The non-classical pathways are also known as the extralemniscal, or diffuse, pathways. The main differences between these two pathways are in the thalamus.

The classical auditory pathways are mainly crossed, but there are extensive connections between the inferior colliculi at the midbrain level (Fig. 8.6) with the result that each one of the two side's cerebral cortices receives approximately equal amounts of input from both ears. Sounds are thus represented bilaterally at the cortex, despite that the pathways are mainly crossed below the inferior colliculus. This has a clinical importance because lesions (tumors, strokes, traumatic injuries, etc.) on one side's auditory cortex have only subtle clinical manifestations (normal audiograms, and only impaired speech discrimination for low-redundancy speech [6]). There are no known connections between the two sides' thalamic nuclei.

The cells of the ICC project to the ventral part of the thalamic auditory nucleus, the medial geniculate body (MGB) that projects to the primary auditory cortex, and several other divisions of the auditory cortex, including the secondary cortex (AII) and the anterior and posterior auditory fields (AAF and PAF) (Fig. 8.7).

Cells in the inferior colliculus project to the auditory thalamic nucleus, the medial geniculate body (MGB). The thalamus plays a fundamental role in auditory processing. It consists of two different cell groups; one is the ventral part, belonging to the classical ascending pathways, which project to the primary auditory cortex. The other parts, the medial and dorsal parts, belong to the non-classical pathways and have fundamentally different functions. The cells project not to primary auditory cortex but bypass the primary cortex and connect directly to the secondary auditory cortex. In addition, these neurons connect to several parts of the brain, such as the amygdala, thus providing as subcortical route to the emotional brain.

Cells in the thalamic nuclei of the classical pathways project to the primary and secondary auditory

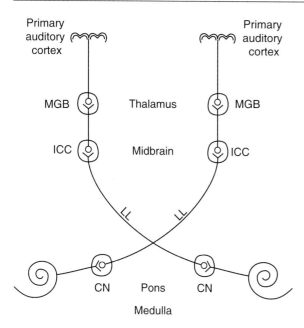

Fig. 8.4 Schematic drawing of the anatomical locations of the ascending auditory pathway. *AN* auditory nerve, *CN* cochlear nucleus, *SOC* superior olivary complex, *LL* lateral lemniscus, *NLL* nucleus of the lateral lemniscus, *IC* inferior colliculus, *MG* medial geniculate body (From Møller, A.R. 2006. Hearing intraoperative monitoring Williams and Wilkins, Baltimore [4])

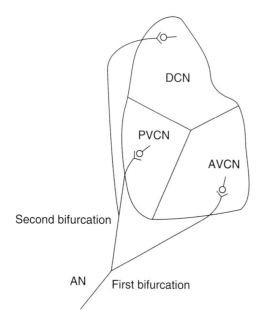

Fig. 8.5 Schematic drawing of the cochlear nucleus to show the auditory nerve's connections with the three main divisions and the cochlear nucleus. *DCN* dorsal cochlear nucleus, *PVCN* posterior ventral cochlear nucleus, *AVCN* anterior ventral cochlear nucleus. (Reprinted from Møller, A.R., Sensory Systems: Anatomy and Physiology. 2003, Amsterdam: Academic Press, with permission from Elsevier. [5])

cortices, whereas the thalamic nuclei of the non-classical pathways project to the secondary auditory cortex and association cortices, skipping the primary cortex. The dorsal and medial thalamus also provide a subcortical route to several structures such as the amygdale.

The Non-classical Pathways

While all neurons in the classical pathways up to and including the primary auditory cortex only respond to one sensory modality, some neurons in the non-classical pathways also respond to other sensory modalities. Likewise, other modalities of sensory input can change the response to auditory stimulation. This means that the non-classical auditory pathways receive input from other sensory systems, such as the somatosensory system and the visual system.

Anatomical Basis for Cross-modal Interaction

The fact that the non-classical ascending auditory system receives input from more than one system is the basis for sensory cross-modal interaction.

What was originally known as the extralemniscal system begins at the midbrain through connections from the ICC to two other parts of the inferior colliculus (IC), the external nucleus (ICX) and the dorsal cortex of the IC (DC) [7] (Fig. 8.8). The ICX also receives projections from the dorsal part of the spinal cord [8], thus providing input from the somatosensory system to the auditory pathways [9].

The results shown in Fig. 8.8 were based on animal studies with the cat. More recent anatomical studies in the guinea pig have shown that the external nucleus of the inferior colliculus (ICX) receives anatomically verified connections from the trigeminal ganglion[1]

---

[1]Some authors use the term "ganglion" for the trigeminal nucleus, but it seems more appropriate to use the term "nucleus" for clusters of nerve cells where synaptic communication occurs. The word "ganglion" should be reserved for clusters of cell bodies, such as the dorsal root ganglia. This is in accordance with the definitions by Stedman's Electronic Medical Dictionary: A ganglion is: originally, any group of nerve cell bodies in the central or peripheral nervous system; currently, an aggregation of nerve cell bodies located in the peripheral nervous system.

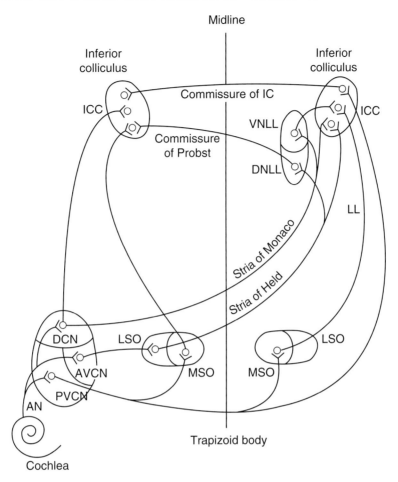

Fig. 8.6 More detailed drawing of the ascending auditory pathways from the ear to the central nucleus of inferior colliculus (ICC). *AVCN* anterior ventral cochlear nucleus, *PVCN* posterior ventral cochlear nucleus, *DCN* dorsal cochlear nucleus, *LSO* lateral superior olive, *NTB* nucleus of the trapezoidal body, *MSO* medial superior olive, *SH* stria of Held (intermediate stria), *SM* stria of Monakow (dorsal stria), *LL* nucleus of the lateral lemniscus, *DNLL* dorsal nucleus of the lateral lemniscus, *VNLL* ventral nucleus of the lateral lemniscus, *ICC* central nucleus of the inferior colliculus. (Modified from Møller, A.R., Sensory Systems: Anatomy and Physiology. 2003, Academic Press, Amsterdam. Reproduced with permission from Elsevier [5])

[10], mostly from the spinal (caudal) part of the fifth nerve nucleus [11].

The ICX, which is a part of the non-classical auditory pathways, receives anatomically verified connections from the trigeminal ganglion, as shown in studies in guinea pigs [10], mostly from the spinal (caudal) fifth nerve nucleus[2] (Sp5) [11]. For a review of the influence on auditory processing in the brainstem from somatosensory activation, see Dehmel et al. [12].

Cells in the ICX and the DC project to dorsal and medial parts of the thalamic auditory nucleus. These cells do not project to the primary auditory cortex as do the cells from the ventral part of the thalamus, but project to the AII division of the auditory cerebral cortex and to association cortices (Fig. 8.9). This means that the non-classical pathways skip a step in cortical activation compared with the classical pathways.

There is one more important difference between the connections from the dorsal and medial thalamatic nuclei and the ventral nuclei. The dorsal and the medial nuclei, in addition to projecting to the cerebral cortex, also make connections to several non-auditory parts of the brain, such as structures of the amygdala, which

---

[2]In neuroanatomy, a nucleus is a group of nerve cell bodies in the brain or spinal cord that can be demarcated from neighboring groups on the basis of either differences in cell type or the presence of a surrounding zone of nerve fibers or cell-poor neuropil.

Classical auditory
pathways

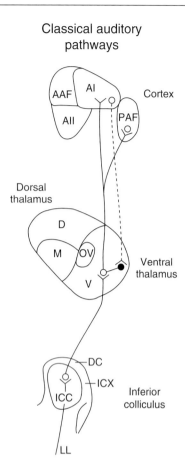

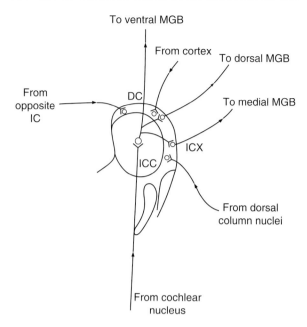

Fig. 8.8 Schematic drawing of the connections from the ICC to the ICX and DC and connections from these nuclei to other structures. Efferent input from the cerebral cortex and connections to the DC and ICX from the somatosensory system (dorsal column nuclei) and from the opposite IC are also shown (From: Møller, A. R. (2003) *Sensory Systems: Anatomy and Physiology*. Academic Press: Amsterdam. [5], reproduced with permission from Elsevier)

Fig. 8.7 Schematic drawing of the ascending pathways from the central nucleus of the inferior colliculus (ICC) to the ventral portion of the thalamic nucleus, the medical geniculate body (MGB), and their connections to auditory cortical radiations. Most of the connections have reciprocal descending connections; only one of which is shown in this graph (between AI and the MGB). *M* medial (or magnocellular) division of MGB, *D* dorsal division, *V* ventral division, *OV* ovoid part of the MGB (From Møller, A.R. (2003) *Sensory Systems: Anatomy and Physiology*. Academic Press: Amsterdam. [5], reproduced with permission from Elsevier)

connect to many other structures such as the hypothalamus (Fig. 8.9).

The connections to limbic structures such as the amygdala are especially important in relation to tinnitus (see Chaps. 21 and 73). The classical and the non-classical pathways make important connections to the lateral nucleus of the amygdala through two different routes, known as the "high route" and the "low route" [13], respectively (Fig. 8.10). The low route uses a subcortical connection from the lateral and medial thalamus while the high route uses a long chain of neurons in the primary–secondary auditory cortices

followed by neurons in several parts of the association cortices. Studies have indicated that the low route is not normally active in adults who do not have tinnitus, but there are indications that the non-classical auditory pathways are active in children [14] and in some individuals with tinnitus [15]. This means also that the subcortical connections to the amygdala are active in children and some individuals with tinnitus and also in other possible disorders [16] such as some forms of autism [17, 18].

Other Anatomical Bases for Interaction between Senses

These connections to nuclei of the IC from the spinal cord and the trigeminal nucleus were, for a long time, believed to be the only connections between the somatosensory system and the auditory system. Recent studies have shown that connections also exist from the somatosensory system to more peripheral levels of

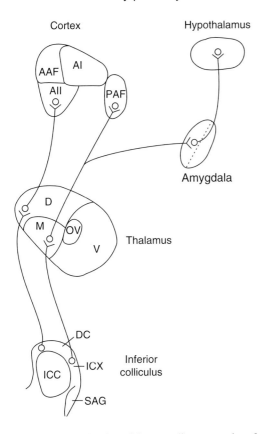

Nonclassical
auditory pathways

Fig. 8.9 Schematic drawing of the ascending connections from the ICX and DC to the thalamic nuclei (MGB) and some of their cortical radiations. *M* medial (or magnocellular) division of MGB, *D* dorsal division, *V* ventral division, *OV* ovoid part of the MGB. Connections from the MGB to auditory cortical areas and the basolateral nuclei of the amygdala are also shown (From: Møller, A. R. (2003) *Sensory Systems: Anatomy and Physiology*. Academic Press: Amsterdam, reproduced with permission from Elsevier [5])

the ascending auditory pathways. Thus, somatic sensory neurons project to several central auditory structures, including DCN, perhaps the VCN, and parts of inferior colliculus (IC) (the external nucleus). Both first- and second-order somatosensory neurons have been found to project to auditory structures [12, 20, 21]. The projections from primary structures originate from spinal dorsal roots, mainly C_2 but also more caudal roots, and the trigeminal nerve [22]. The projections from secondary somatosensory structures mainly originate from the spinal dorsal column nuclei, the

caudal trigeminal nucleus (Sp5), and DRG [11]. Some neurons in the Sp5 and the dorsal column nuclei project to both the CN and the external cortex of IC by way of axon collaterals [23].

Histological studies in guinea pigs have shown that there are connections between the trigeminal nucleus, as well as the marginal cell areas of the cochlear nucleus and the magnocellular portion of the ventral cochlear nucleus. It is mostly the ophthalmic and mandibular divisions of the trigeminal nerve that give rise to these connections [24] and the DCN [21] (for more details see Chap. 9). (For a review of the influence on auditory processing in the brainstem from somatosensory activation see Dehmel et al. [12]).

Early studies involving cats showed direct projections from dorsal column nuclei and the spinal trigeminal nuclei to the cochlear nuclei [25]. Later studies using decerebrated paralyzed cats have shown that electrical stimulation of the dorsal column in the spinal cord and spinal trigeminal nucleus could inhibit the response from cells in the DCN [26]. Direct connections from the C_2 area of the dorsal horn of the spinal cord to the cochlear nuclei have been shown in anatomical studies [27].

The skin around the ears and of the scalp is innervated both by fibers of the C_2 dorsal root and by the trigeminal nerve. This may explain the beneficial effect of electrical stimulation on tinnitus when performed on these areas of skin [28].

There are also anatomically verified connections between the caudal trigeminal nucleus and the dorsal cochlear nucleus [24] (see Chap. 9), and there is also anatomical evidence that the trigeminal nucleus innervates the cochlea [29].

These more recent studies extend the anatomical basis for interaction between the auditory and somatosensory functions, which are the anatomical basis for the cross-modal interaction discussed below.

This also means that the non-classical pathways indeed use the lemniscal system, making the earlier used name "extralemniscal system" irrelevant. The name used in this book (non-classical) seems to be more appropriate.

Projection fibers from these somatic sensory neurons form a laminar pattern of "en passant terminal endings" from ventromedial to dorsolateral within the ventrolateral regions of ICX, including the ventral border of IC and the ventromedial edge of IC (or pericentral regions).

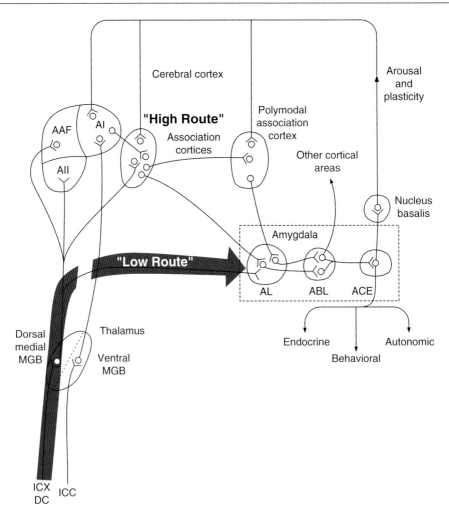

Fig. 8.10 Schematic drawing of the connections between the classical and the non-classical routes and the lateral nucleus of the amygdala (AL), showing the "high route" and the "low route." Connections between the basolateral (ABL) and the central nuclei (ACE) of the amygdala and other CNS structures are also shown. (From: Møller AR. *Neural plasticity and disorders of the nervous system.* Cambridge: University of Cambridge Press, 2006 [19], with permission from Cambridge University Press based on LeDoux, J.E. 1992. Brain mechanisms of emotion and emotional learning. Curr. Opin.Neurobiol. 2, 191–197)

A study has shown a novel projection from the basolateral nucleus of the amygdala to the inferior colliculus in bats [30].

Descending Systems

Descending auditory systems have been described as having three different parts. It may be more suitable to describe the descending systems as reciprocal to the ascending systems (see Fig. 8.11) [31].

The axons of the most peripheral parts of the descending pathways (olivocochlear bundle, OCB, Fig. 8.12a, b) terminate on hair cells in the cochlea, mostly outer hair cells. Since these hair cells control mechanical properties of the basilar membrane, the descending pathways can influence the mechanical properties of the basilar membrane and thereby affect auditory sensitivity and frequency selectivity.

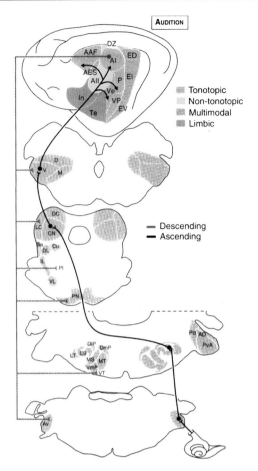

Fig. 8.11 The ascending (*black*) and descending (*blue*) pathways of the classical auditory system connecting to the different regions of the auditory cortex, *AI* primary auditory cortex, *AII* Secondary auditory cortex, *AAF* anterior auditory field, *AES* anterior ectosylvian sulcus area, *DZ* dorsal auditory zone, *ED* posterior ectosylvian gyrus, dorsal part, *EI* posterior ectosylvian, *Ve* auditory cortex, ventral area, *VP* auditory cortex, ventral posterior area, *In* insular, *Te* temporal cortex, *EV* posterior ectosylvian gyrus, reproduced from Winer JA and CC Lee (2007) The distributed auditory cortex. Hear. Res. 229:3–13, with permission from Elsevier [22]

Physiology

The Ear

The basilar membrane of the cochlea separates sounds according to their frequency in such a way that the population of sensory cells that are activated is a direct function of the frequency (or spectrum) of the sounds that reaches the ear. One kind of hair cells, the inner hair cells, is activated by the motion of the basilar membrane and controls the discharges in the auditory nerve fibers. The outer hair cells are also activated by sound, but they have a mechanical role in that they elongate and shorten in response to sound, thereby acting as "motors" that amplify the motion of the basilar membrane. This action is most pronounced for low sound intensities where the action of the outer hair cells adds approximately 50 dB of sensitivity to the ear. The fact that their action is dependent on the intensity of the sounds that reach the ear makes the function of the cochlea become highly non-linear and the outer hair cells act to compress sounds. The active role of the outer hair cells also causes the cochlea to generate sound under certain circumstances (otoacoustic emissions) (for a review see Kim et al. [34]).

The non-linearity of the outer hair cells manifests by several measures used in clinical diagnosis. The active role of the outer hair cells can be detected by recording the otoacoustic emission of the ear by placing a microphone in the ear canal. There are several kinds of such otoacoustic emission. Spontaneous otoacoustic emission (SOE), the ear producing sound without receiving sound (in silence), is relatively rare. The most commonly studied kinds of otoacoustic emission that arc also used clinically are transient elicited otoacoustic emission (TEOAE) and distortion product otoacoustic emission (DPOAE) (Fig. 8.13)., reproduced with permission from Elsevier

The Nervous System

The physiology of the classical pathways has been studied extensively, mainly by recordings from single auditory nerve fibers of the auditory nerve and from cells in the nucleus and the cerebral cortex. Little is known about the response from cells in the nuclei of the non-classical pathways. Only a few studies have concerned the physiology of the descending pathways and little is known about the function of these anatomically extensive systems.

When studied using pure-tone stimuli, all auditory nerve fibers and cells in the nuclei of the ascending auditory pathways display frequency selectivity. The sharpness of the auditory nerve's fiber tuning varies systematically with the frequency to which they are tuned (their best frequency; see Fig. 8.14). The sharpness of the tuning also varies with the sound intensity as shown in Fig. 8.15a

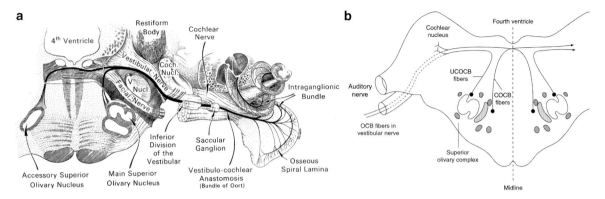

Fig. 8.12 (**a**) Origin of efferent supply to the cochlea. (Reprinted from Schucknecht HF: *Pathology of the ear.* Cambridge, MA, Harvard University Press, 1974 with permission from Harvard University Press. [32]). (**b**) Olivocochlear system in the cat. The uncrossed olivocochlear bundle (UCOCB) and the crossed olivocochlear bundle (COCB) are shown.

(Redrawn from Pickles, J.O. 1988. An Introduction to the Physiology of Hearing, (2nd ed) Academic Press, London, with permission from Elsevier [33]). Reproduced from A.R. Møller, Hearing: Anatomy, Physiology, and Disorders of the Auditory System, 2nd Ed. Academic Press, 2006 [1] with permission from Eleseuier

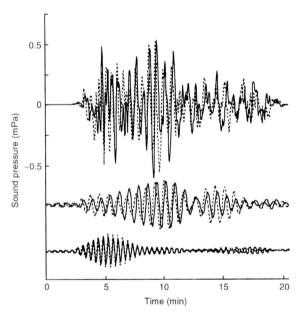

Fig. 8.13 Click evoked otoacoustic emission (TEOAE). The *solid* and the *dashed lines* are the response in two different body positions. From: Büki B, Avan P and Ribari O. The Effect of Body Position on Transient Otoacoustic Emission. In: *Intracranial and Intralabyrinthine Fluids*, edited by Ernst A, Marchbanks R and Samii M. Berlin: Springer Verlag, 1996, p. 175–181. [35] Reproduced from A.R. Møller, Sensory Systems, Academic Press, 2003 reproduced with the permission from Elsevier

that shows tuning of an auditory nerve fiber in response to broad-band noise stimuli, and Fig. 8.15b shows the sharpness of the tuning of an auditory nerve fiber is an

almost linear function of the sound intensity. The frequency to which the fiber is tuned decreases with increasing sound intensity. The sharpness of the tuning of the basilar membrane is greater for low-intensity sounds compared with sounds of higher intensity (Fig. 8.15c), thus following a similar pattern as the tuning of auditory nerve fibers, indicating that the cause of the non-linearity seen in the tuning of auditory nerve fibers is some property of the cochlear mechanics.

The shape and sharpness (frequency selectivity) of the frequency tuning of cells in the nucleus and the cerebral cortex vary among cells. Some have a higher degree of selectivity than auditory nerve fibers, other cells are more broadly tuned, and the tuning curves of some cells have more than one peak (Fig. 8.16).

When more complex sounds are used, the response pattern becomes different from that obtained to steady test sounds, as has been shown for cells in the cochlear nuclei. These cells show more complex response pattern to sounds, the frequency of which is varied at different rates. The response becomes dependent on rate of tonal change (Fig. 8.17). This means that the response to complex sounds cannot be deduced from knowledge about the response to simple sounds such as pure tones with steady frequency. This non-linear behavior is apparent in the responses from cells in the cochlear nucleus and it becomes more pronounced in the responses from cells of higher order nuclei of the auditory system, including the cerebral cortices.

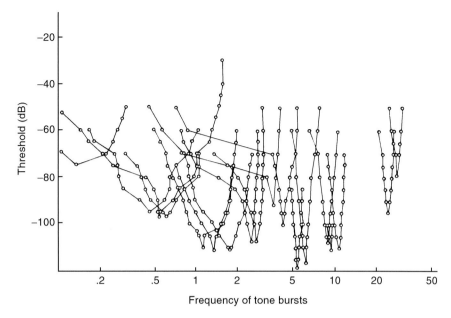

Fig. 8.14 Typical frequency threshold curves of single auditory nerve fibers in a cat. The different curves show the thresholds of individual nerve fibers as a function of the frequency of the stimulus tones. The left-hand scale gives the thresholds in arbitrary decibel values. From Kiang, N.Y.S., Watanabe, T., Thomas, E.C., Clark, L. 1965. Discharge patterns of single fibers in the cat's auditory nerve MIT Press, Cambridge, MA [36], reproduced with permission from MIT Press

Moreover, because cells in auditory nuclei and the cerebral cortex receive input from many fibers, the width and the center frequency of their tuning become dependent on the efficacy of the synapses that connect the fibers to the cells. Since synaptic efficacy can be altered by activation of neural plasticity, the tuning of cells is not static but subject to change.

Non-classical System

Much less is known about the physiology of the non-classical pathways. Few studies have been published on the response from cells in the nuclei that belong to the non-classical pathways as opposed to those belonging to the classical pathways. It is known, however, that the responses of cells in the non-classical pathways are generally less distinct, and tuning is broader in neurons of the non-classical pathways compared with the classical pathways. Perhaps the most important aspect of the auditory non-classical pathways for understanding the pathologies of tinnitus is the interactions between signals from other sensory systems that

occur causing cross-modal interactions; the effect of the use of the medial and dorsal thalamic nuclei with their subcortical connections; and the absence of connections to the primary cortices.

Cross-modal Interaction

It has become more and more evident that there is considerable interaction between systems that earlier were regarded as being separate. The old concept that certain functions of the brain are contained in certain areas of the brain has gradually been eroded. It was earlier regarded as an axiom that the information from the different sense organs was processed in specific and separate parts of the brain. That somatosensory signals can interfere with hearing is discussed in several parts of this book. The anatomy of sensory systems as described above involves both the non-classical pathways and connections between the dorsal column nuclei and the cochlear nucleus, which also receives connections from the trigeminal ganglion. Physiological

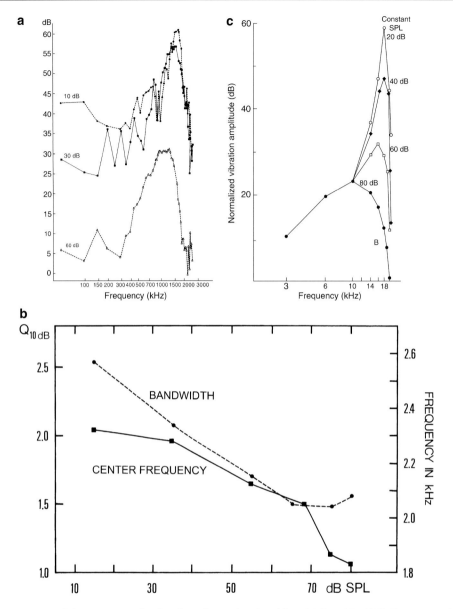

Fig. 8.15 (**a**) Estimates of frequency transfer function of a single auditory nerve fiber in a rat at different stimulus intensities (given in dB SPL), obtained by Fourier transforming cross-correlograms of the responses to low-pass–filtered pseudorandom noise (3,400 Hz cutoff). The amplitude is normalized to show the ratio (in dB) between the Fourier-transformed cross-correlograms and the sound pressure and the individual curves would have coincided if the cochlear filtering and neural conduction had been linear. Modified from Møller, A.R. 1983. Frequency selectivity of phase-locking of complex sounds in the auditory nerve of the rat. Hear. Res. 11, 267–284. [37]. Reproduced with permission from Elsevier. (**b**) Shift in the center frequency (*solid lines*) and the width of the tuning of a single auditory nerve fiber (*dashed line*) in the auditory nerve of a rat as a function of the stimulus intensity. The width is given a "Q10dB" which is the center frequency divided by the width at 10 dB above the peak

(Reprinted from Møller, A.R. 1977. Frequency selectivity of single auditory nerve fibers in response to broadband noise stimuli. Reproduced from J. Acoust. Soc. Am. 62, 135–142, with permission from the American Institute of Physics [38]) (**c**) Vibration amplitude at a single point of the basilar membrane of a guinea pig obtained using pure tones as test sounds at four different intensities. The amplitude scale is normalized, and the individual curves would have coincided if the basilar membrane motion had been linear. From Johnstone, B.M., Patuzzi, R., Yates, G.K. 1986. Basilar membrane measurements and the traveling wave. Hear. Res. 22, 147–153 [Johnstone, 1986 #1116] based on results from Sellick, P.M., Patuzzi, R., Johnstone, B.M. 1982. Measurement of basilar membrane motion in the guinea pig using the Mossbauer technique. J. Acoust. Soc. Am. 72, 131–141. [39]. Reproduced with permission from the American Institute of Physics

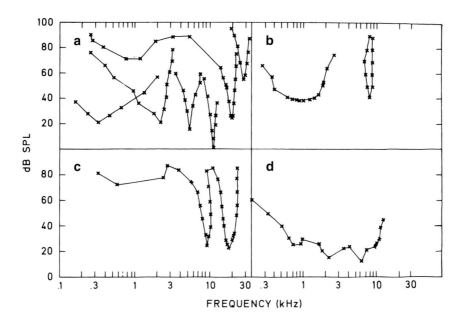

Fig. 8.16 Examples of frequency tuning curves with different shapes obtained from neurons of the superior olivary complex of the cat. From Guinan Jr., J.J., Norris, B.E., Guinan, S.S. 1972. Single auditory units in the superior olivary complex. II. Location of unit categories and tonotopic organization. Int. J. Neurosci. 4, 147–166. [40]. Reproduced with permission from Elsevier

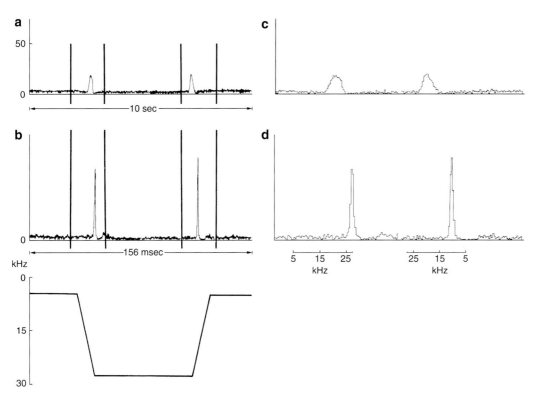

Fig. 8.17 Period histograms of a cell in the cochlear nucleus of a rat in response to tones the frequency of which was varied between 5 and 25 kHz at different rates. (**a**) and (**c**): Slow rate, (**b**) and (**d**): Fast rate. The *top histograms* (**a** and **c**, slow rate) show the responses obtained when the duration of a full cycle was 10 s and the *lower histograms* (**b** and **d**, fast rates) show the responses obtained when the duration of a complete cycle was 156 ms. The change in the frequency of the stimulus tone was accomplished by having a trapezoidal waveform control of the frequency of the sound generator (**e**). The two *left-hand graphs* (**a** and **b**) are histograms of a full cycle of the modulation and the *right-hand graphs* (**c** and **d**) show the details between the *vertical lines* in the *left-hand graphs*. From Møller, A.R. 1974. Coding of sounds with rapidly varying spectrum in the cochlear nucleus. J. Acoust. Soc. Am. 55, 631–640. [41]. Reproduced with the permission from the American Institute of Physics

studies have shown that the non-classical auditory path-ways are active in children [14] and in some individuals with tinnitus [15].

As mentioned above, it has been shown in several studies that there are anatomically verified connections between the trigeminal nucleus and the dorsal cochlear nucleus, as well as between the upper part of the spinal cord and the dorsal cochlear nucleus.

Physiological studies in animals (guinea pigs) have shown that multisensory integration occurs in the DCN, thus confirming that the anatomical con-nections discussed above are also physiologically active. This means that the synapses that connect the axons to the cells in the DCN are effective. Electrical stimulation of the trigeminal ganglion elicited unit responds in the VCN with latencies from 5 to 17 ms, indicating that the anatomically verified pathway from the trigeminal ganglion to the VCN is function-ally active [42, 43].

These connections between the somatosensory system and the cochlear nucleus are most likely the basis for findings that electrical stimulation of the skin around ears suppresses tinnitus in some individ-uals [44] (see Chap. 43). Such stimulation would therefore activate both the dorsal gray of the upper spinal cord and the spinal nucleus. The observed effect on tinnitus may therefore come from either spi-nal connection to cochlear (DCN) nuclei or the trigeminal nucleus.

The effect of electrical stimulation of the skin around the ears has been verified in animal experiments.

After exposure to loud tones, recordings from cells in the DCN of hamsters showed that such exposure caused hyperactivity. When the skin at the base of the ears was stimulated electrically, the response would be either suppressed in both control animals and exposed animals; excited in controls and suppressed in tone-exposed animals; suppressed and excited; or excited in both controls and tone exposed [45]. The suppression was sig-nificantly higher during and after stimulation than in controls, with the effect slightly greater after the stimulation than during stimulation.

The pathways for this cross-modal interaction have been studied in animals and it has been shown that there is both physiological and anatomical evidence for cross-modal interaction in the dorsal cochlear nucleus [43].

In one study in hamsters using tracing experiments, it was found that the DCN received input from the spinal trigeminal nucleus (that is commonly regarded to be involved in face pain), but also the dorsal raphe nucleus seems to be involved along with the locus coeruleus [46].

These studies indicate that the cross-modal interaction in the dorsal cochlear nucleus may involve a direct and an indirect pathway. Therefore, relieving tinnitus through somatosensory electrical stimulation may involve manip-ulations of both auditory and non-auditory neural circuits.

It is mainly somatic receptors in the upper body that can modulate activity elicited by sound stimulation in the neurons of the non-classical auditory pathways [7]. In order for this to occur, the non-classical auditory pathways must be active. The non-classical auditory system has the ability of cross-modal interactions because neurons in that system receive signals from more than one sensory modality. There are no signs of the non-classical auditory system being active in adults who do not have tinnitus. Adults who do not have tin-nitus do not have signs that the non-classical pathways are active. This means that some forms of cross-modal interactions require re-routing of information, so that the non-classical auditory system becomes active. As mentioned above, there are signs of such cross-modal interaction between the somatosensory system and the auditory system in young children [14], in some indi-viduals with tinnitus [15], and in some autistic indi-viduals [17, 18].

This means that there is physiologic evidence that multisensory integrations occur in the DCN in guinea pigs [43, 47], in the ICX in cats [7], and the ICX in rats [48]. There may be differences between the animals that have been studied and humans; it is not known how these results from animals can be applied to humans. Studies in humans of the ability of somatosensory stim-ulation to affect sound perception, in terms of loudness, seem to show that such interaction occurs normally in children but not in adults [15]. Stimulation of the soma-tosensory system can affect the loudness and character of tinnitus in some individuals [15], and there are other studies that show evidence that somatosensory activa-tion can affect the loudness and the character of tinnitus [49–51]. Studies have also shown evidence of interac-tion between the somatic and visual systems [52].

Conclusions

The description of the anatomy and physiology of the auditory system in this chapter covers what was regarded to be relevant regarding tinnitus. There are many aspects of the anatomy and physiology that are not included, and which were judged to be less related to the topic of this book. A more detailed description of the anatomy and physiology of the auditory system can be found in Møller, A. R. (2006) *Hearing: Anatomy, Physiology, and Disorders of the Auditory System, 2nd Ed.* Academic Press: Amsterdam [1].

References

1. Møller AR (2006) Hearing: anatomy, physiology, and disorders of the auditory system, 2nd ed. Amsterdam: Academic Press.
2. Shepherd GM (1994) Neurobiology. New York: Oxford University Press. 760.
3. Harrison RV and IM Hunter-Duvar, (1988) An anatomical tour of the cochlea, in Physiology of the ear, AF Jahn and J Santos-Sacchi, Editors. Raven Press: New York. 159–71
4. Møller AR (1988) Evoked potentials in intraoperative monitoring. Baltimore: Williams and Wilkins.
5. Møller AR (2003) Sensory systems: anatomy and physiology. Amsterdam: Academic Press.
6. Korsan-Bengtsen MM (1973) Distorted speech audiometry. Acta Otolaryng. Suppl. 310.
7. Aitkin LM (1986) The auditory midbrain, structure and function in the central auditory pathway. Clifton, NJ: Humana Press.
8. Aitkin LM, H Dickhaus, W Schult et al (1978) External nucleus of inferior colliculus: auditory and spinal somatosensory afferents and their interactions. J. Neurophysiol. 41:837–47.
9. Aitkin LM, CE Kenyon and P Philpott (1981) The representation of auditory and somatosensory systems in the external nucleus of the cat inferior colliculus. J. Comp. Neurol. 196:25–40.
10. Jain R and S Shore (2006) External inferior colliculus integrates trigeminal and acoustic information: unit responses to trigeminal nucleus and acoustic stimulation in the guinea pig. Neurosci. Lett. 395:71–5.
11. Zhou J and S Shore (2006) Convergence of spinal trigeminal and cochlear nucleus projections in the inferior colliculus of the guinea pig. J. Comp. Neurol. 495:100–12.
12. Dehmel S, YL Cui and SE Shore (2008) Cross-modal interactions of auditory and somatic inputs in the brainstem and midbrain and their imbalance in tinnitus and deafness. Am. J. Audiol. 17:S193–209.
13. LeDoux JE (1992) Brain mechanisms of emotion and emotional learning. Curr. Opin. Neurobiol. 2:191–7.
14. Møller AR and P Rollins (2002) The non-classical auditory system is active in children but not in adults. Neurosci. Lett. 319:41–4.
15. Møller AR, MB Møller and M Yokota (1992) Some forms of tinnitus may involve the extralemniscal auditory pathway. Laryngoscope 102:1165–71.
16. Møller AR (2008) Neural plasticity: for good and bad. Progress of Theoretical Physics Supplement No 173:48–65.
17. Møller AR (2007) Neurophysiologic abnormalities in autism, in New autism research developments, BS Mesmere, Editor. Nova Science Publishers: New York.
18. Møller AR, JK Kern and B Grannemann (2005) Are the non-classical auditory pathways involved in autism and PDD? Neurol. Res. 27:625–9.
19. Møller AR (2006) Neural plasticity and disorders of the nervous system. Cambridge: Cambridge University Press.
20. Pfaller K and J Arvidsson (1988) Central distribution of trigeminal and upper cervical primary afferents in the rat studied by anterograde transport of horseradish peroxidase conjugated to wheat germ agglutinin. J. Comp. Neurol. 268:91–108.
21. Zhou J and S Shore (2004) Projections from the trigeminal nuclear complex to the cochlear nuclei: a retrograde and anterograde tracing study in the guinea pig. J. Neurosci. Res. 78:901–7.
22. Kanold PO and ED Young (2001) Proprioceptive information from the pinna provides somatosensory input to cat dorsal cochlear nucleus. J. Neurosci. 21:7848–58.
23. Li H and N Mizuno (1997) Single neurons in the spinal trigeminal and dorsal column nuclei project to both the cochlear nucleus and the inferior colliculus by way of axon collaterals: a fluorescent retrograde double-labeling study in the rat. Neurosci. Res. 29:135–42.
24. Shore SE, Z Vass, NL Wys et al (2000) Trigeminal ganglion innervates the auditory brainstem. J. Comp. Neurol. 419: 271–85.
25. Itoh K, H Kamiya, A Mitani et al (1987) Direct projections from dorsal column nuclei and the spinal trigeminal nuclei to the cochlear nuclei in the cat. Brain Res. 400: 145–50.
26. Young ED, I Nelken and RA Conley (1995) Somatosensory effects on neurons in dorsal cochlear nucleus. J. Neurophysiol. 73:743–65.
27. Zhan X, T Pongstaporn and DK Ryugo (2006) Projections of the second cervical dorsal root ganglion to the cochlear nucleus in rats. J. Comp. Neurol. 496:335–48.
28. Shulman A (1987) External electrical tinnitus suppression: a review. Am. J. Otol. 8:479–84.
29. Vass Z, SE Shore, AL Nuttall et al (1997) Trigeminal ganglion innervation of the cochlea – a retrograde transport study. Neuroscience 79:605–15.
30. Marsh RA, CD Grose, JJ Wenstrup et al (1999) A novel projection from the basolateral nucleus of the amygdala to the inferior colliculus in bats. Soc. Neurosci. Abstr. 25:1417.
31. Winer JA and CC Lee (2007) The distributed auditory cortex. Hear. Res. 229:3–13.
32. Schucknecht HF (1974) Pathology of the ear. Cambridge, MA: Harvard University Press.
33. Pickles JO (1988) An Introduction to the physiology of hearing, 2nd ed. London: Academic Press.
34. Kim S, DR Frisina and RD Frisina (2002) Effects of age on contralateral suppression of distortion product otoacoustic emissions in human listeners with normal hearing. Audiol. Neurootol. 7:348–57.
35. Büki B, P Avan and O Ribari (1996) The effect of body position on transient otoacoustic emission, in Intracranial and intralabyrinthine fluids, A Ernst, R Marchbanks and M Samii, Editors. Springer Verlag: Berlin. 175–81.

36. Kiang NYS, T Watanabe, EC Thomas et al (1965) Discharge patterns of single fibers in the cat's auditory nerve. Cambridge, MA: MIT Press.

37. Møller AR (1983) Frequency selectivity of phase-locking of complex sounds in the auditory nerve of the rat. Hear. Res. 11:267–84.

38. Møller AR (1977) Frequency selectivity of single auditory nerve fibers in response to broadband noise stimuli. J. Acoust. Soc. Am. 62:135–42.

39. Sellick PM, R Patuzzi and BM Johnstone (1982) Measurement of basilar membrane motion in the guinea pig using the Mossbauer technique. J. Acoust. Soc. Am. 72: 131–41.

40. Guinan Jr. JJ, BE Norris and SS Guinan (1972) Single auditory units in the superior olivary complex. II. Location of unit categories and tonotopic organization. Int. J. Neurosci. 4:147–66.

41. Møller AR (1974) Coding of sounds with rapidly varying spectrum in the cochlear nucleus. J. Acoust. Soc. Am. 55:631–40.

42. Shore SE, H El Kashlan and J Lu (2003) Effects of trigeminal ganglion stimulation on unit activity of ventral cochlear nucleus neurons. Neuroscience 119:1085–101.

43. Shore SE (2005) Multisensory integration in the dorsal cochlear nucleus: unit responses to acoustic and trigeminal ganglion stimulation. Eur. J. Neurosci. 21:3334–48.

44. Shulman A, J Tonndorf and B Goldstein (1985) Electrical tinnitus control. Acta Otolaryngol. 99:318–25.

45. Zhang J and Z Guan (2008) Modulatory effects of somatosensory electrical stimulation on neural activity of the dorsal cochlear nucleus of hamsters. J. Neurosci. Res. 86:1178–87.

46. Zhang J and Z Guan (2007) Pathways involved in somatosensory electrical modulation of dorsal cochlear nucleus activity. Brain Res. 1184:121–31.

47. Shore SE, S Koehler, M Oldakowski et al (2008) Dorsal cochlear nucleus responses to somatosensory stimulation are enhanced after noise-induced hearing loss. Eur. J. Neurosci. 27:155–68.

48. Szczepaniak WS and AR Møller (1993) Interaction between auditory and somatosensory systems: a study of evoked potentials in the inferior colliculus. Electroencephalogr. Clin. Neurophysiol. 88:508–15.

49. Cacace AT, JP Cousins, SM Parnes et al (1999) Cutaneous-evoked tinnitus. II: review of neuroanatomical, physiological and functional imaging studies. Audiol. Neurotol. 4:258–68.

50. Cacace AT, JP Cousins, SM Parnes et al (1999) Cutaneous-evoked tinnitus. I: phenomenology, psychophysics and functional imaging. Audiol. Neurotol. 4:247–57.

51. Cacace AT, TJ Lovely, DJ McFarland et al (1994) Anomalous cross-modal plasticity following posterior fossa surgery: some speculations on gaze-evoked tinnitus. Hear. Res. 81:22–32.

52. Hotta T and K Kameda (1963) Interactions between somatic and visual or auditory responses in the thalamus of the cat. Exp. Neurol. 8:1–13.

Chapter 9
Interaction Between Somatosensory and Auditory Systems

Aage R. Møller and Susan Shore

Keypoints

1. Studies in animals (guinea pigs) have shown projections from the dorsal column nuclei and the caudal trigeminal nucleus to cells in the cochlear nucleus (CN).
2. Recordings from single cells in the DCN and evoked potentials indicate that the pathways from the trigeminal nucleus are functional.
3. Electrical stimulation of the dorsal column and the cervical dorsal root ganglia elicits short and long latency inhibition separated by a transient excitatory peak in DCN single units.
4. Electrical stimulation of the trigeminal nucleus elicits excitation in some DCN units and inhibition in others.
5. Dorsal cochlear nucleus neurons show greater sensitivity to somatosensory stimulation, and the interaction between somatic stimulation and sound stimulation is greater after exposure to loud sounds that cause hearing loss and probably tinnitus. These findings may be explained by increased innervation of the cochlear nucleus by somatosensory fibers after noise exposure.

Keywords Tinnitus • Cross-modal interaction • Cochlear nucleus • Trigeminal system • Dorsal column system

Abbreviations

ANF	Auditory nerve fibers
CN	Cochlear nucleus
DCN	Dorsal cochlear nucleus
GCD	Granule cell domain
DRG	Dorsal root ganglion
PSTH	Post stimulus time histogram
Sp5	Spinal trigeminal nucleus
Sp5C	Caudal spinal trigeminal nucleus
TG	Trigeminal ganglion
TN	Trigeminal nucleus
VCN	Ventral cochlear nucleus

Introduction

It has been known for many years that information from different senses are coordinated in many parts of the cerebral cortex, but it is only recently that it has become evident that different senses interact with each other at subcortical levels. One of the routes of sensory interaction is the connection between the dorsal root ganglion or dorsal column nuclei [1] and the cochlear nucleus (CN); another is the connection between the trigeminal ganglion or caudal trigeminal nucleus (Sp5C) and cochlear nuclei (CN) [1–3]. These connections are the anatomical basis for some of the cross-modal interactions observed in animal experiments, in humans, and in some individuals with tinnitus (see Chap. 10).

It is of particular interest that the interaction between stimulation of the somatosensory system and sound stimulation is enhanced by previous intense sound overstimulation of the kind that normally results in tinnitus [4]. In this chapter, we will discuss the anatomical and physiological bases for cross-modal

A.R. Møller (✉)
The University of Texas at Dallas, School of Behavioral and Brain Sciences, GR 41, 800 W Campbell Rd, Richardson, TX 75080, USA
e-mail: amoller@utdallas.edu

A.R. Møller et al. (eds.), *Textbook of Tinnitus*,
DOI 10.1007/978-1-60761-145-5_9, © Springer Science+Business Media, LLC 2011

interaction and the possible relationship to tinnitus by the subcortical connections between the somatosensory system and the auditory system. Histological and physiological studies in animals will be reviewed. Interactions between the auditory system and other systems in general were discussed in the preceding chapter (Chap. 8).

Anatomical Basis for Interaction Between the Somatic System and the CN

Histological studies in guinea pigs have shown that there are connections between the trigeminal system (trigeminal ganglion and trigeminal nucleus) and the marginal cell areas of the CN, and the magnocellular portion of the ventral cochlear nucleus (VCN), and the dorsal cochlear nucleus (DCN) [5]. Studies of the functional role of these connections using electrical stimulation of the trigeminal ganglion (TG) showed responses from cells in the CN, indicating that these anatomically verified pathways from the trigeminal ganglion to the VCN can be activated [6, 7]. The latencies varied considerably, from 5 to 17 ms, indicating that different pathways may be involved.

Several studies have found connections between the dorsal column of the spinal cord and cells along the medial edge of the VCN, the dorsal ridge of the anterior ventral cochlear nucleus (AVCN) (i.e., subpeduncular corner between the AVCN and the inferior cerebellar peduncle), and lamina of the granule cell domain (GCD) [1, 3]. These axons of the dorsal column originate from the C_2 dorsal roots of the spinal cord. Likewise, it has been found that electrical stimulation of the dorsal root ganglion elicits responses from cells in the DCN [8]. The projection from somatosensory nuclei to the CN is particularly abundant in granule cell regions in layer 2 of the DCN. The small cell cap region of CN and also larger cells in deep DCN receive projections from cells in the Sp5 [5, 9] and the dorsal column nuclei [5, 10–14].

The dorsal column nuclei receive innocuous somatosensory input and proprioceptive sensory input [15, 16]; caudal trigeminal nucleus (Sp5C) receives pain and temperature information from regions of the face and mouth. This nucleus also receives proprioceptive signals from the vocal tract, including the temporomandibular joint and tongue muscles [17]. The substantia gelatinosa layer of the Sp5C that is analogous to the lamina II in the dorsal horn of the spinal cord primarily receives nociceptive afferents.

Effects of Trigeminal Nerve Activation on CN Activity

Studies in the guinea pig have shown that electrical stimulation of the ophthalmic/mandibular divisions of the trigeminal ganglion where neurons project to the CN [18] elicit responses from neurons in the VCN [6] and excite (Fig. 9.1) or inhibit neurons in the DCN (Fig. 9.2) [7, 19].

In the post-stimulus histograms of the response from cells in the DCN shown in Figs. 9.1 and 9.2, the stimulus artifact is seen at 25 ms, indicating the time at which the electrical stimulus was applied to the TG. The four channels of recordings were obtained simultaneously and, in the example illustrated in Fig. 9.2, the electrical stimulation of three of these had an inhibitory effect on spontaneous activity. In this recording, the latency of the inhibition was approximately 12 ms; in other similar recordings, the latency varied between 5 and 20 ms, indicating multisynaptic pathways would be the underlying neural circuits producing these responses [7].

The results of these studies show that the trigeminal pathways can alter the spontaneous activity in both the VCN and the DCN. This change in spontaneous activity of CN neurons might explain tinnitus' loudness modulation from trigeminal system stimulation observed in some individuals with what is known as somatic tinnitus.

Other studies [8] using recordings of evoked potentials have shown that electrical stimulation of spinal nerves in the neck can elicit a response from cells in the DCN. The C_2 root mediates mechanoreception and proprioception of the pinna and the surrounding skin. The evoked potentials were largest in response to stimulation of the cervical nerves corresponding to mechanoreception and proprioception in the pinna (C_2), neck (C_7), and forelimbs (C_8) [8]. These results show a similarity with the effect of TG stimulation [6]. Other studies have shown that stimulation of the femoral nerve can activate cells in the DCN as evidenced by fos expression [21].

Combining electrical stimulation of the trigeminal systems with sound stimulation shows that these two kinds of activation of CN neurons interact in a nonlinear

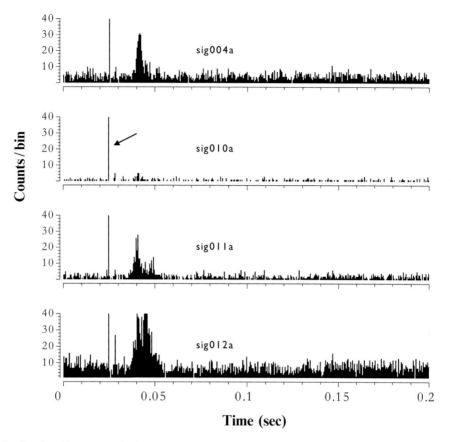

Fig. 9.1 Poststimulus time histograms of DCN unit responses to trigeminal ganglion - stimulation show excitation. Responses of four different unit clusters from four channels (4, 10, 11, 12) of a 16-channel electrode in the same animal, but with different penetration. Stimulation was at 80 μA, 100 ms/phase bipolar pulses, 100 presentations. Bin width, 0.5 ms. *Arrow* – electrical stimulus artifact indicates onset of TN stimulation. *Inset at right* shows location of the stimulating electrode in the ophthalmic region of the TG. (Reproduced from Shore, S., Zhou, J. and Koehler, S. (2007) Neural mechanisms underlying somatic tinnitus. In: *Tinnitus: Pathophysiology and Treatment, Progress in Brain Research.* pp. 107–123. Eds. B. Langguth, G. Hajak, T. Kleinjung, A. Cacace, A. R. Møller. Elsevier: Amsterdam. [20] Reproduced with permission of Elsevier

way; one modality can inhibit or enhance the response to another modality, depending on the time interval between the sound and the electrical stimulations (Fig. 9.3).

It is seen from Fig. 9.3 that the interaction between these two stimuli depends on the interval between the stimuli. When the acoustic stimulus precedes the TG stimulation, the response to the acoustic stimulus is suppressed, the effect being the greatest when the two stimuli are presented within a small interval. Somatosensory stimulation can alter the firing rate to acoustic stimulation, even when it precedes the acoustic stimulation by as much as 90 ms and stimulation and the effect still persist for the duration of the sound stimulation [7].

The interaction between these two kinds of stimulation is different in different cells as illustrated in Fig. 9.4b, which shows the discharge rate as a function of the interval between sound stimulation and the stimulation of the TG for three different cells in the DCN. The firing rate of one of the cells increases when the interval between the stimuli is increased from 20 to 95 ms. Another cell shows a depression that is the largest when the interval is 60 ms; the third cell depicted in Fig. 9.4 has very little effect of the combination of the two stimuli.

Other studies of the interaction between stimulation of the somatic sensory system and sound [8, 22, 23] have shown that sound-evoked responses are influenced by electrical stimulation of the dorsal column of the spinal cord in a similar way as stimulation of the trigeminal system. The responses from cells in the DCN to electrical activation of dorsal

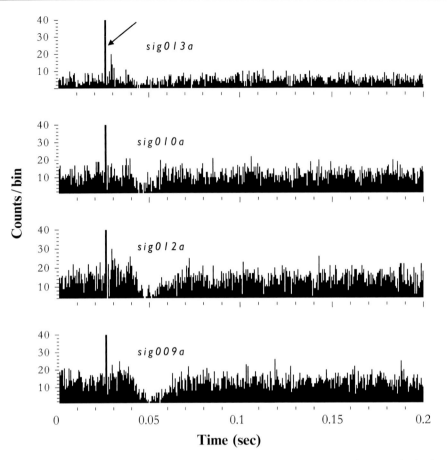

Fig. 9.2 Poststimulus time histograms of DCN unit responses to trigeminal ganglion stimulation show inhibition in a similar recording as shown in Fig. 9.1. *Arrow* – electrical stimulus artifact indicates onset of TN stimulation. Inset at right shows location of the stimulating electrode in the ophthalmic region of the TG. (Reproduced from Shore, S., Zhou, J. and Koehler, S. (2007) Neural mechanisms underlying somatic tinnitus. In: *Tinnitus: Pathophysiology and Treatment, Progress in Brain Research.* pp. 107–123. Eds. B. Langguth, G. Hajak, T. Kleinjung, A. Cacace, A. R. Møller. Elsevier: Amsterdam. [20] Reproduced with permission of Elsevier

root ganglia (DRG) are similar to those obtained by stimulation of dorsal column nuclei, but they have longer latencies [8].

Interaction Between the Somatosensory System and the DCN After Sound Over Stimulation

It is of particular interest regarding tinnitus that the interaction between the somatosensory system and the auditory system is larger after sound overstimulation that causes hearing loss and probably tinnitus [4].

Studies in the guinea pig have shown that the bimodal interaction was enhanced after noise exposure. The interaction between somatic and auditory stimulation in animals that have not been exposed to loud sounds varies among different cells, some showing enhancement and some showing suppression as shown above (Figs. 9.1 and 9.2). This is also the case in noise-exposed animals. However, two weeks after noise exposure, more cells showed suppression than in animals that were not exposed to noise, 75% compared with 49%. This difference developed over time after noise exposure, and it was very small, one week after noise exposure.

Noise exposure also decreased the threshold to trigeminal stimulation, and the spontaneous discharge

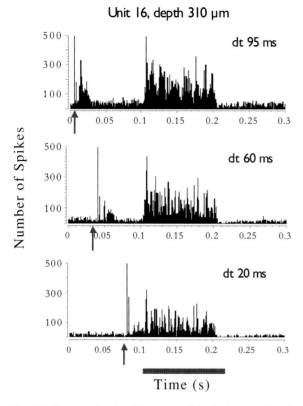

Unit 16, depth 310 μm

Fig. 9.3 Poststimulus time histograms of the discharges of a cell in the DCN in response to electrical stimulation of the TG, and sound stimulation (broadband noise at 30 dB SPL). The electrical stimulation (80 μA, 100 ms/phase bipolar pulses) precedes the sound stimulus by 95 ms in the top histogram, 60 ms in the histogram in the middle, and 20 ms in the bottom histogram. The acoustic stimulus is indicated by the *bar* below the histograms and the *arrow* indicates the time when the stimulation of the TG was applied. Each histogram represents the responses to 100 presentations of these stimuli. (Reproduced from Shore, S., Zhou, J. and Koehler, S. (2007) Neural mechanisms underlying somatic tinnitus. In: *Tinnitus: Pathophysiology and Treatment, Progress in Brain Research*. pp. 107–123. Eds. B. Langguth, G. Hajak, T. Kleinjung, A. Cacace, A. R. Møller. Elsevier: Amsterdam. [20] Reproduced with permission of Elsevier)

rates of cells in the DCN increased [4]. The increase in the responses from cells in the DCN to somatosensory stimulation may be a compensation for lost auditory input because of the hearing loss caused by the sound exposure. The duration of the inhibitory response to trigeminal stimulation decreased and its amplitude increased after noise exposure (Fig. 9.4).

The observed changes in the response properties of DCN cells after noise exposure might be caused by activation of neural plasticity that has strengthened

the synaptic coupling to the somatic source of input to some cells in the DCN. There are other examples that show that loss of one kind of sensory input has enhanced input from other senses. The most profound example might be invasion of visual fibers into the auditory cortex after interruption of auditory input [24].

We believe that the observed suppression of the responses to broad band noise is a result of the summation of weak responses from cartwheel cells to the noise and stronger and long-lasting activation of these cells by the input from the trigeminal nucleus, which in turn leads to inhibition of fusiform cells. Facilitation of the response to noise stimuli, on the other hand, may occur because of long-term potentiation of direct activation of fusiform cells by granule cells. Cartwheel cells excite each other and inhibit fusiform cells (see Fig. 9.6). Stimulation of the TG may excite cells in the ventral cochlear nucleus (multipolar onset cells), which can inhibit vertical cells and fusiform cells [6].

The circuits of the DCN relevant to interactions from somatosensory nuclei are shown in Fig. 9.6, which illustrates the situation before (a) and after (b) noise exposure.

Based on their findings that the vesicular glutamate transporters (VGLUT1 and VGLUT2) are differentially associated with auditory nerve and somatosensory inputs to the CN, respectively [25], Zeng et al. [26] examined the relative distributions of VGLUT1 and 2 after unilateral deafening. After unilateral intracochlear injections of kanamycin (1 and 2 weeks), VGLUT1 immunoreactivity in the magnocellular CN ipsilateral to the cochlear damage was significantly decreased, reflecting decreased auditory nerve input as expected. On the other hand, VGLUT2, which is associated with the non-auditory inputs, including somatosensory inputs, *increased* in regions that received non-auditory input 2 weeks after deafening, suggesting the possibility of axonal sprouting of these somatosensory inputs to the CN. These morphologic changes may be the cause of the observed increase in the response to trigeminal stimulation (Fig. 9.5).

These results should be viewed in the light of earlier studies that have shown that noise exposure causes morphologic changes in the cochlear nucleus [27]. Other studies [5] have shown enhanced cartwheel cell activity after noise damage, which could be responsible for the increase in suppressive bimodal integration demonstrated above [4].

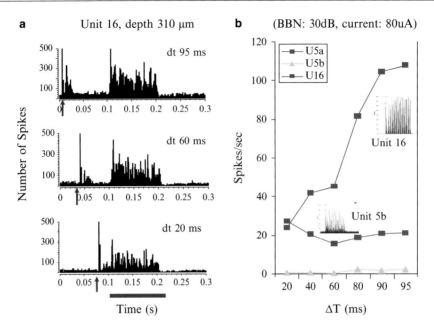

Fig. 9.4 Quantification of the spike rates achieved in (**a**) for unit 16. Spike rates for two other units, 5a and 5b, are also shown. *Insets*: Poststimulus time histograms for responses to BF tone bursts indicate unit types: Unit 16 is a P-Buildup, Unit 5b may be a cartwheel cell (Reproduced from Shore, S., Zhou, J. and Koehler, S. (2007). Neural mechanisms underlying somatic tinnitus. In: *Tinnitus: Pathophysiology and Treatment, Progress in Brain Research*. pp. 107–123. Eds. B. Langguth, G. Hajak, T. Kleinjung, A. Cacace, A. R. Møller. Elsevier: Amsterdam. [20])

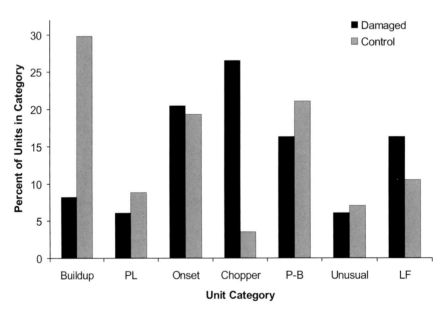

Fig. 9.5 Responses to trigeminal stimulation are redistributed at 1 and 2 weeks after noise overexposure. The percentage of single units with excitatory, inhibitory, or excitatory/inhibitory responses after trigeminal nucleus stimulation at 80 µA is shown. Following noise exposure, inhibitory responses predominate, whereas the normal animals show more excitatory than inhibitory responses. The increased incidence of inhibition by trigeminal stimulation in noise-damaged animals may signify a change in the distribution of trigeminal inputs to the cochlear nucleus granule cells following cochlear damage. (Reproduced from: Shore, S. E., Koehler, S., Oldakowski, M., Hughes, L. F. and Syed, S. (2008) Dorsal cochlear nucleus responses to somatosensory stimulation are enhanced after noise-induced hearing loss. *Eur J Neurosci*. 27, 155–168). [4] Reproduced with permission of Wiley

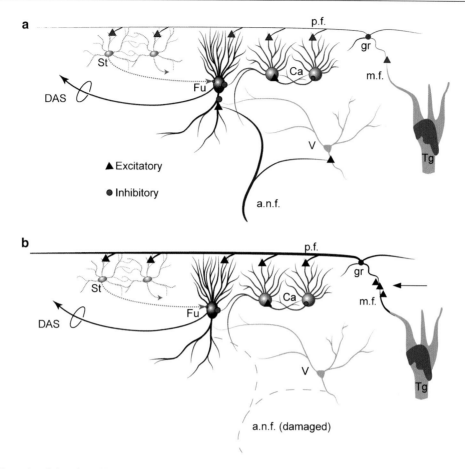

Fig. 9.6 Schematic of dorsal cochlear nucleus circuitry putatively involved in bimodal integration in normal and noise-damaged animals (**a**) Normal system. Trigeminal ucleus (Tg) stimulation excites cochlear nucleus granule cells (gr), which, in turn, excite stellate (St), cartwheel (Ca), and fusiform (Fu) or giant (not shown) cells. *DAS* dorsal acoustic stria, *p.f.* parallel fibers. (**b**) Noise-damaged system. ANF input to basal dendrites of Fu cells is weakened. (Reproduced after Shore, S. E. (2005) Multisensory integration in the dorsal cochlear nucleus: unit responses to acoustic and trigeminal ganglion stimulation. *Eur J Neurosci* 21, 3334–3348. [7] and from: Shore, S. E., Koehler, S., Oldakowski, M., Hughes, L. F. and Syed, S. (2008) Dorsal cochlear nucleus responses to somatosensory stimulation are enhanced after noise-induced hearing loss. *Eur J Neurosci.* 27, 155–168). [4]

Conclusion

Studies in the guinea pig have shown that stimulation of the dorsal column of the upper spinal cord or the trigeminal ganglion or nucleus can elicit excitation or inhibition of neurons in the cochlear nuclei. These studies also indicate that such stimulation can modulate the sound-driven activity in the cochlear nuclei. The effect of somatosensory stimulation on the neural activity in the cochlear nuclei is greater in animals that have noise-induced hearing loss and probably tinnitus when studied 2 weeks after the noise exposure, but not immediately after noise exposure (Fig. 9.5).

References

1. Zhan X, T Pongstaporn and DK Ryugo (2006) Projections of the second cervical dorsal root ganglion to the cochlear nucleus in rats. J Comp Neurol 496:335–48.
2. Dehmel S, YL Cui and SE Shore (2008) Cross-modal interactions of auditory and somatic inputs in the brainstem and midbrain and their imbalance in tinnitus and deafness. Am J Audiol 17:S193–209.
3. Pfaller K and J Arvidsson (1988) Central distribution of trigeminal and upper cervical primary afferents in the rat studied by anterograde transport of horseradish peroxidase conjugated to wheat germ agglutinin. J Comp Neurol 268:91–108.
4. Shore SE, S Koehler, M Oldakowski et al (2008) Dorsal cochlear nucleus responses to somatosensory stimulation are

enhanced after noise-induced hearing loss. Eur J Neurosci 27:155–68.

5. Zhou J and S Shore (2004) Projections from the trigeminal nuclear complex to the cochlear nuclei: a retrograde and anterograde tracing study in the guinea pig. J Neurosci Res 78:901–7.

6. Shore SE, H El Kashlan and J Lu (2003) Effects of trigeminal ganglion stimulation on unit activity of ventral cochlear nucleus neurons. Neuroscience 119:1085–101.

7. Shore SE (2005) Multisensory integration in the dorsal cochlear nucleus: unit responses to acoustic and trigeminal ganglion stimulation. Eur J Neurosci 21:3334–48.

8. Kanold PO and ED Young (2001) Proprioceptive information from the pinna provides somatosensory input to cat dorsal cochlear nucleus. J Neurosci 21:7848–58.

9. Haenggeli CA, T Pongstaporn, JR Doucet et al (2005) Projections from the spinal trigeminal nucleus to the cochlear nucleus in the rat. J Comp Neurol 484:191–205.

10. Zhou J and S Shore (2006) Convergence of spinal trigeminal and cochlear nucleus projections in the inferior colliculus of the guinea pig. J Comp Neurol 495:100–12.

11. Wolff A and H Kunzle (1997) Cortical and medullary somatosensory projections to the cochlear nuclear complex in the hedgehog tenrec. Neurosci Lett 221:125–8.

12. Wright DD and DK Ryugo (1996) Mossy fiber projections from the cuneate nucleus to the cochlear nucleus in the rat. J Comp Neurol 365:159–72.

13. Weinberg RJ and A Rustioni (1987) A cuneocochlear pathway in the rat. Neuroscience 20:209–19.

14. Itoh K, H Kamiya, A Mitani et al (1987) Direct projections from dorsal column nuclei and the spinal trigeminal nuclei to the cochlear nuclei in the cat. Brain Res 400:145–50.

15. Brodal A (2004) The central nervous system. Third Edition. New York: Oxford University Press.

16. Møller AR (2006) Neural plasticity and disorders of the nervous system. Cambridge: Cambridge University Press.

17. Jacquin MF, M Barcia and RW Rhoades (1989) Structure-function relationships in rat brainstem subnucleus interpolaris: IV. Projection neurons. J Comp Neurol 282:45–62.

18. Shore SE, Z Vass, NL Wys et al (2000) Trigeminal ganglion innervates the auditory brainstem. J Comp Neurol 419:271–85.

19. Jain R and S Shore (2006) External inferior colliculus integrates trigeminal and acoustic information: unit responses to trigeminal nucleus and acoustic stimulation in the guinea pig. Neurosci Lett 395:71–5.

20. Shore S, J Zhou and S Koehler, (2007) Neural mechanisms underlying somatic tinnitus, in Tinnitus: Pathophysiology and Treatment, Progress in Brain Research, B Langguth et al, Editors. Elsevier: Amsterdam. 107–23.

21. McKitrick DJ and FR Calaresu (1993) Expression of Fos in rat central nervous system elicited by afferent stimulation of the femoral nerve. Brain Res 632:127–35.

22. Saadé NE, YR Bassim, SF Atweh et al (1989) Auditory influences via cochlear nucleus on cuneate neurons in decerebrate-decerebellate cats. Brain Res 486:403–6.

23. Saadé NE, AS Frangieh, SF Atweh et al (1989) Dorsal column input to cochlear neurons in decerebrate-decerebellate cats. Brain Res 486:399–402.

24. Horng SH and M Sur (2006) Visual activity and cortical rewiring: activity-dependent plasticity of cortical networks, in Reprogramming the Brain, Progress in Brain Research, AR Møller, Editor. Elsevier: Amsterdam. 3–11.

25. Zhou J, N Nannapaneni and S Shore (2007) Vessicular glutamate transporters 1 and 2 are differentially associated with auditory nerve and spinal trigeminal inputs to the cochlear nucleus. J Comp Neurol 500:777–87.

26. Zeng C, N Nannapaneni, J Zhou et al (2009) Cochlear damage changes the distribution of vesicular glutamate transporters associated with auditory and nonauditory inputs to the cochlear nucleus. J Neurosci 29:4210–7.

27. Morest DK, MD Ard and D Yurgelun-Todd (1979) Degeneration in the central auditory pathways after acoustic deprivation or over-stimulation in the cat. Anat Rec 193:750.

Chapter 10
Pathology of the Auditory System that Can Cause Tinnitus

Aage R. Møller

Keypoints

1. Symptoms such as tinnitus can be caused by damage and diseases that affect the conductive apparatus of the ear, its receptor organs, the auditory nerve, and nerve cells in the nuclei of the auditory system, including the cerebral auditory cortex.
2. Tinnitus can also be caused by activation of neural plasticity (causing *plasticity diseases*), which can cause altered function at the cellular level in the brain and re-routing of information.
3. The brain is not a fixed system but it is continuously shaped and re-shaped by signals it receives from the outside world.
4. Neural plasticity is a property of the nervous system that becomes apparent only when turned on. Activation of neural plasticity can be beneficial or harmful.
5. Activation of beneficial neural plasticity facilitates recovery from damage to the nervous system (such as from strokes). In sensory systems, it may serve to compensate for loss of function or to adapt the nervous system to change in demand. Expression of neural plasticity can make the nervous system adapt to changing demands (prostheses such as cochlear and cochlear nucleus implants).
6. Activation of harmful neural plasticity is involved in creation of symptoms of disease (*plasticity disorders*) such as some forms of tinnitus, central neuropathic pain, and some forms of muscle spasm.

7. Activation of neural plasticity can change processing of information and cause:
   (a) Reorganization and re-routing of information in the central nervous system.
   (b) Change in the balance between inhibition and excitation.
   (c) Increased synchrony of activity of single nerve cells.
   (d) Increased temporal coherence of activity in populations of nerve cells.
8. Deprivation of input, overstimulation, injuries, and unknown intrinsic factors can promote expression of neural plasticity.
9. Many forms of tinnitus are phantom sensations caused by activation of neural plasticity and similar to phantom sensations in other sensory systems causing central neuropathic pain, paresthesia, and spasm in motor systems.
10. Many forms of tinnitus are associated with changes in processing of information that may involve hyperacusis and distortion of sounds.
11. Abnormal (pathologic) changes in connectivity may occur because of activation of neural plasticity that opens (unmask) dormant synapses or close (mask) synapses that are conducting normally.
12. Activation of non-classical pathways is an example of change in connectivity.
13. Tinnitus is often accompanied by cross-modal interaction, which may be explained by an abnormal activation of non-classical sensory pathways through re-routing of information.
14. Involvement of the non-classical pathways may explain symptoms of mood disorders, phantom sensations, improved perceptual capabilities, or atypical sensory experiences that often accompany severe tinnitus.

A.R. Møller (✉)
The University of Texas at Dallas, School of Behavioral
and Brain Sciences, GR 41, 800 W Campbell Road,
Richardson, TX 75080, USA
e-mail: amoller@utdallas.edu

A.R. Møller et al. (eds.), *Textbook of Tinnitus*,
DOI 10.1007/978-1-60761-145-5_10, © Springer Science+Business Media, LLC 2011

Keywords Tinnitus • Neural plasticity • Deprivation of input • Coherence of neural activity • Hyperacusis • Cross-modal interaction

Abbreviations

EEG   Electroencephalography
EPSP   Excitatory post synaptic potentials
HFS   Hemifacial spasm
MEG   Magnetoencephalography
SPL   Sound pressure level
TMS   Transcranial magnetic stimulation

Introduction

Since tinnitus appears as a sound, it is often referred to the ear. For many years, the ear was therefore assumed to be the anatomical location of the pathology that caused subjective tinnitus. Jürgen Tonndorf was one of the first investigators who proposed a neurophysiologic cause for some forms of tinnitus and suggested a model for generation of tinnitus involving the central nervous system [1]. It was a major progress in understanding the pathology of many forms of tinnitus when it became more generally accepted that most forms of tinnitus are phantom sounds caused by abnormal function of neural circuits in the brain [2]. It is now evident that while the pathology that causes tinnitus may start with an event involving the ear, the pathology that causes most forms of persistent subjective tinnitus is in the central nervous system where some abnormal neural activity is generated and interpreted in a similar way as activity generated when sound reaches the ear.

Many different factors have been suspected to be involved in causing tinnitus, such as pathologies of the ear, the auditory nerve, and various parts of the central auditory nervous system. Damage to the auditory nerve from trauma, including surgical trauma and ionized radiation, are common causes of tinnitus, as are viral infections. It is not known exactly how trauma to the auditory nerve can cause tinnitus. One hypothesis has been that ephaptic transmission[1] between denuded auditory nerve fibers (see Chap. 84) occur after trauma and, more recently, it has been suggested that such transmission may occur between nerve cells in the auditory nervous system.

Factors such as overstimulation and deprivation of signals to the auditory nervous system have also been suggested as causing tinnitus through activation of neural plasticity.

Subjective tinnitus has many similarities with phantom sensations from other senses, such as paresthesia of the somatosensory system, and in particular, with central neuropathic pain, which we will discuss in another chapter (see Chap. 14).

Similar "phantom sensations" as tinnitus rarely occur in vision (phosphene), olfaction (phantosmia), olfactory hallucinations, or abnormal taste (metallic taste). In the vestibular system, some forms of vertigo may be phantom sensations.

There is considerable evidence that activation of neural plasticity is involved in many forms of tinnitus [3–6] (see Chap. 12). We are, however, far from fully understanding the nature of the abnormalities that cause many forms of tinnitus, and how it is brought about is still being investigated; hypotheses regarding the pathology of tinnitus are constantly created and abandoned [7].

It has been pointed out in several places in this book that tinnitus is not a single disorder but many different ones. This is a major obstacle in attempts to understand its pathology, as it is for developing effective treatments. This means that the pathologies that can cause tinnitus are likely numerous and the anatomical location of the pathologies of these different kinds of tinnitus varies between the ear, the auditory nerve, and many different parts of the brain.

The pathological processes involved are poorly understood, but they may be different for varying kinds of tinnitus. Imbalance between inhibition and excitation has been suggested. Ephaptic transmission between axons in the auditory nerve has been suggested [7, 8], but some forms of ephaptic transmission between nerve cells in the central nervous system may also be involved. It is known that such ephaptic transmission plays a role in some forms of epilepsy [9]. Increased temporal coherence may be promoted by abnormal (ephaptic) transmission between auditory nerve fibers mimicking sound activation or between cells in the central nervous system.

---

[1] Ephaptic transmission is transmission between axons and nerve cells without synaptic transmission. It may occur when bare axons or nerve cells are in close contact with each other so that one can activate the other electrically.

Anatomical Location of the Physiologic Abnormalities

The symptoms and signs of most diseases occur not because of a single event or because of damage to a single structure; the symptoms and signs of most disorders are caused by a cascade of events that occur at the same time, although there may not have been any signs or symptoms if they had occurred alone or one at a time. Most disorders of the nervous system involve a cascade of structures in the brain. While only one structure is pathologic, many structures may behave abnormally because they receive abnormal signals from the pathologic structures. It is an obstacle to research and treatment of many sensory disorders such as tinnitus and pain that several brain structures may behave abnormally even when only one of the structures is pathologic [10, 11]. The reason is that a faulty structure of a sensory system sends abnormal signals to other structures, which then behave abnormally, either because they relay abnormal activity or because the abnormal activity has affected the function of the structure in question.

Many mistakes in the diagnosis and the treatment are done because the treatment has been directed to the wrong structure.

There are other reasons why focus can be directed to the wrong structure. Phantom sensations are by definition not referred to the structure where the abnormal neural activity causing the sensations is generated. This is most obvious from the phantom limb, where a person feels pain in a leg that has been amputated. In a similar way, the pain in central neuropathic pain may be referred to a specific body part, but the abnormal neural activity is generated in the brain without any input from sensors in the body. Naturally, tinnitus is often referred to the ear and that can be the case even when the individual is deaf or has had the auditory nerve severed.

It was a major progress in understanding the pathophysiology of tinnitus when it became accepted that most forms of subjective tinnitus are caused by abnormal neural activity in the nervous system occurring without input from the ear. The fact is that tinnitus can occur in deaf individuals and after severance of the auditory nerve lends strong evidence to the hypothesis that the anatomical location of the physiologic abnormality is the central nervous system in many individuals with tinnitus, and input from the ear is not involved, at least not in later stages of the disorder.

In the hypothetical example in Fig. 10.1, the abnormal activity was caused by neural plasticity that was activated by deprivation of input and which activated a chain of structures. The abnormal activity in this chain of structures will subsequently reach neurons in the parts of the brain that generate the symptoms of tinnitus. It is important to identify the structure in the beginning of the chain that is pathologic. Aiming treatment at neural structures that are functioning normally but produce abnormal input because they receive abnormal input is not effective in treating the disease in question.

Aiming treatment at structures that behave abnormally because they receive signals from structures that are pathologic may affect the perception of tinnitus because it may interrupt the flow of the abnormal signals that cause the tinnitus but will not yield permanent relief because the pathology is still unaffected. Such treatment may, however, ameliorate the symptoms as long as the treatment is applied. Similar situations exist regarding other common diseases, such as central neuropathic pain (see Chap. 14) and diabetes type 2 (Fig. 10.2).

Often two factors (or more) must be present at the same time to cause symptoms and signs of disease (Fig. 10.3). One example is diabetes type 2, where a cascade of events in a chain of structures result in changes that produce symptoms of diabetes neuropathy characterizing the disease.

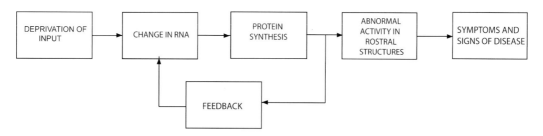

Fig. 10.1 Hypothetical flow chart of events in a series of structures as a result of deprivation of input. From Møller AR. *Neural plasticity and disorders of the nervous system.* Cambridge: University of Cambridge Press, 2006. Reproduced with permission from Cambridge University Press. Neurological Research with permission from W.S. Maney and Son Ltd [10]

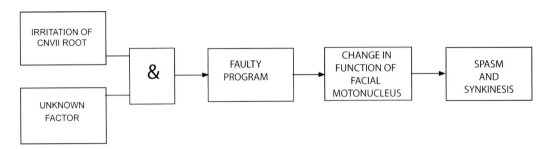

Fig. 10.2 Hypothetical flowchart of disorders where two factors must be present together in order to cause symptoms of disease. From Møller AR. *Neural plasticity and disorders of the nervous system.* Cambridge: University of Cambridge Press, 2006. Reproduced with permission from Cambridge University Press. Neurological Research with permission from W.S. Maney and Son Ltd [10]

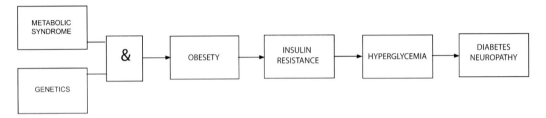

Fig. 10.3 Hypothetical flowcharts of events that occur in development of type 2 diabetes neuropathy. From Møller AR. *Neural plasticity and disorders of the nervous system.* Cambridge: University of Cambridge Press, 2006. Reproduced with permission from Cambridge University Press. Neurological Research with permission from W.S. Maney and Son Ltd [10]

The Ear

There are two ways the ear can be involved in causing tinnitus; one is by producing the kind of neural activity in the auditory nerve that is interpreted by the nervous system as a sound. The other way the ear can cause tinnitus is by depriving input to the nervous system that will turn on neural plasticity. Injury to the ear (see Chap. 34) may cause tinnitus because of the deprivation of input to the auditory nervous system it causes and which is known to be able to cause hyperactivity in specific structures through activation of neural plasticity [6, 12, 13]. Cochlear damage such as from noise exposure (see Chap. 37) or age-related changes (see Chap. 36) can also cause deprivation of input to the auditory system. Deprivation of input is a strong promoter of neural plasticity, which in turn causes changes in the nervous system that involves the generation of neural activity that may be interpreted as sound-evoked neural activity.

Studies have shown that passing electrical current through the cochlea in some patients with tinnitus can ameliorate their tinnitus [14, 15]. This is a strong sign that the ear is involved in causing and maintaining some forms of tinnitus.

Another sign that the ear is involved in causing some forms of tinnitus is the success of severing the auditory nerve in treatment of the disorder [16, 17]. This is, however, a controversial matter and other investigators have found that severing or damaging the auditory nerve does not affect tinnitus and may, in fact, make tinnitus worse [18].

If tinnitus is caused by deprivation of input to the nervous system, passing electrical current through the cochlea [15, 19] that may activate either hair cells or auditory nerve fibers and may thus compensate for deprivation.

Such electrical stimulation applied to the cochlea may, however, also activate the trigeminal nerve fibers, of which innervate the mucosa that lines the middle ear cavity including the cochlea capsule. Other studies have shown that electrical stimulation of the cochlear capsule can alleviate some forms of tinnitus [20]. Again, that may not have been caused by stimulating auditory receptors but instead by stimulating receptors in the mucosa of the middle ear cavity. These receptors are innervated by the trigeminal nerve fibers that terminate in the trigeminal nucleus. The cells these fibers terminate on project to cochlear nuclei known to be involved in tinnitus [21–23] (see Chaps. 8 and 9).

The ear is probably the cause of the tinnitus in only a few of those individuals who have severe chronic tinnitus, and severance of the auditory nerve is rarely done now. Pulec has emphasized [16, 17] that the auditory nerve must be sectioned centrally to the spiral ganglion in order to relieve tinnitus. This may mean that disconnecting the ear may not be the (entire) reason for the success of auditory nerve sectioning in tinnitus, and it indicates that the cause of the tinnitus may be the auditory nerve rather than the ear in some of the individuals who benefitted from this procedure.

The Auditory Nerve

Traumatic injury to the auditory nerve almost always causes tinnitus. This may occur in surgical operation and head trauma. Surgical trauma and ionized radiation used to treat vestibular schwannoma may cause loss of hearing and tinnitus, but moderate injury to the auditory nerve may cause only little change in the hearing threshold with a large decrease in speech discrimination and tinnitus. Viral infections, such as the herpes zoster virus, can affect the auditory nerve and cause hearing loss and tinnitus. The Ramsay Hunt syndrome is caused by the herpes zoster virus, and although it primarily affects the facial nerve, it can also affect the auditory-vestibular nerve and cause tinnitus [24]. Other viral infections, such as the Coxsackie B virus, have also been reported to cause tinnitus [25].

The neural activity in slightly injured nerves is altered in different ways and the results on its ability to activate its target cells can vary widely and have different consequences (Fig. 10.4). Injuries to the auditory nerve may make some nerve fibers unresponsive and may cause changes (slowing) in the propagated conduction in the nerve fibers; the change is normally not the same for all nerve fibers. Such temporal dispersion (decreased coherence) in the nerve impulses that arrive at the target neuron can have widely different effects in the excitation of the target neuron: it can fail to activate the target neuron (Fig. 10.4), it can activate it in a similar way as before the injury occurred, or the injury can actually cause an increase in the excitation of the target neuron because it causes a prolonged excitatory post-synaptic potential (EPSP). This means that the effect of slight injury to the auditory nerve could have widely

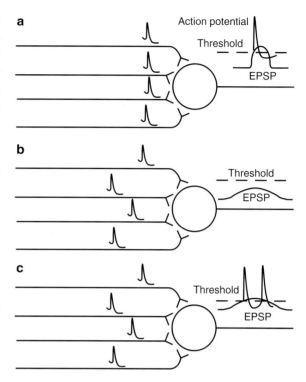

Fig. 10.4 Hypothetical illustration of the effect of spatial integration by a cell on which many axons converge. (**a**) Little spatial dispersion. (**b**) Increased spatial dispersion but the high threshold of the neuron prevent it from firing. (**c**) Large degree of spatial dispersion and low threshold of the neuron. The prolonged EPSP makes the neuron fire twice. (From: Møller AR. *Neural plasticity and disorders of the nervous system.* Cambridge: University of Cambridge Press, 2006. Reproduced with permission from Cambridge University Press [26])

different effects on the neurons in the cochlear nucleus, including increased excitation that could be associated with tinnitus.

Altered time pattern of discharges in the auditory nerve from continuous type pattern may occur as a result of damage to the ear or, more likely, from damage to the auditory nerve may induce tinnitus.

Bursting neural activity that often results from injuries can activate target cells that were not activated by steady firing, even if the mean discharge rate is not altered after changing to burst mode of firing (Fig. 10.5). Such bursting activity can open synapses not normally conducted when the incoming neural activity is a continuous stream of impulses. Bursting activity has been linked to tinnitus but not to hearing loss.

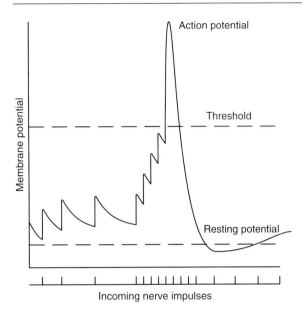

Fig. 10.5 Hypothetical description of the effect of burst activity on excitation of a cell. (From: Møller AR. *Neural plasticity and disorders of the nervous system*. Cambridge: University of Cambridge Press, 2006, Reproduced with permission from Cambridge University Press [26])

The Central Nervous System

There are many ways that pathways of the central nervous system can be involved in tinnitus, hyperacusis, and other symptoms that occur together or independently.

Sound causes both excitation and inhibition in the nervous system and if this balance is upset toward less inhibition, the "amplification" in neural networks may be so high that self-oscillations occur, and thus, may explain some forms of tinnitus. Reduced inhibition in the auditory nervous system is assumed to promote the development of some kinds of tinnitus. The role of altered balance between inhibition and excitation has been studied in the dorsal cochlear nucleus (DCN) in animal models of tinnitus [5, 13].

The changes in the nervous system that cause the abnormal activity perceived as tinnitus may be initiated by abnormal activity from the ear or an injured auditory nerve. However, it often progresses over time when structures of the central nervous system become involved. That the pathologic processes that cause the tinnitus develop further over time is supported by the observation that tinnitus becomes more resistant to treatment, the longer a person has had the tinnitus [27]. This means

that the role of the ear in the pathology of tinnitus may diminish over time.

The changes in the function of the central nervous system through activation of neural plasticity may start by abnormal or absent input from the ear, but after some time the abnormal functioning may have reached a stable pathologic state. This may occur in accordance with Hebb's principle ("neurons that fire together wire together"). This means that the function of the sensory system may have two stable states: one that is the normal state and the other that is the pathologic state. If this hypothesis is correct, it means that there is a similarity with the bilateral state of the spinal cord in some forms of central neuropathic pain [28] (see Chap. 14).

Various forms of injuries to the central nervous system, and in particular changes in function, caused by activation of neural plasticity can be involved in causing tinnitus. This means that tinnitus can be a regarded as being caused by harmful neural plasticity, thus a plasticity disease [29]. Change in synaptic efficacy through activation of neural plasticity, changes in the relation between inhibition and excitation, and re-routing of information to another part of the brain than normally activated by sound are the most important causes of many forms of subjective tinnitus. Establishment of ephaptic transmission is another change in function that has been suggested to be involved in some forms of tinnitus.

Activation of neural plasticity is the most common cause of tinnitus (see Chap. 12). The central nervous system consists of many subsystems that are connected in a complex way. When these connections change, which may occur when neural plasticity is activated, a manifold of symptoms from different parts of the brain may result. The most important is perhaps that activation of neural plasticity may switch on the non-classical pathways, which has several implications: one of which is a form of cross-modal interaction and another is establishment of a subcortical route to the amygdala (see Chap. 8). Other possible effects are redirection of signals to other parts of the brain than those that are normally activated by sound. Misophonia and phonophobia (see Chap. 4) are examples of signs of pathologies that may result from such redirection of information.

Changes in the function of the central nervous system through activation of neural plasticity can also cause diseases that have similarities with some forms of tinnitus, such as central neuropathic pain (see Chap. 14).

Neural Plasticity

Neural plasticity is the ability of the nervous system to change its function on the basis of experience [26]. Neural plasticity is a normal property of the nervous system that only becomes apparent when turned on.

Activation of neural plasticity can be purposeful and beneficial, or it can be purposeful but not beneficial. Activation of neural plasticity can make it possible to adapt to changing demand, after damage to a region of the brain or spinal cord; activation of neural plasticity can re-route information to regions that are undamaged; or it can be harmful, creating symptoms and signs of disease. We have called the diseases that are caused by activation of such harmful plasticity, *plasticity diseases* [29].

Neural plasticity has similarities with learning as well as differences. The neural mechanisms are similar, involving change in synaptic efficacy causing long-term depression (LTD) and long-term potentiation (LTP) [30], but learning is different from neural plasticity in many ways. What is learned must be recalled, while the result of plastic changes is always available. The difference can be illustrated by learning to pronounce uncommon word and names, which is a matter of neural plasticity, while learning what to say must be actively recalled, thus a matter of memorizing and learning. Activation of neural plasticity is involved in the normal childhood development and aging processes.

Changes in the function of the nervous system that occur because of activation of neural plasticity are mainly changes in synaptic efficacy [31], it can also include other changes in the function of nerve cells such as change in protein synthesis [12]. These changes occur with little delay and cannot be detected using common clinical tests. Changes in synaptic efficacy may start a sequence of events that include formation of new synapses and elimination of other synapses. Later, change in function may cause morphological changes such as creation of new connections according to the Hebb's principle [32]. The plastic changes may include sprouting of axons, programmed cell death, etc. There are few physiological tests that can reveal such morphological changes and cannot be detected by available clinical diagnostic methods.

The immediate effect that is caused by change in synaptic efficacy is reversible, and the function may recover when the factors that initiated the plasticity are no longer present. The effects that follow, and which involves morphological changes, are more difficult to reverse (see Chaps. 10 and 15). This has an immediate clinical effect in that it causes plasticity diseases such as tinnitus and central neuropathic pain to become more difficult to successfully treat after being present a long time.

There are two fundamentally different effects of activation of neural plasticity: one is beneficial and one is harmful. The beneficial effect is the best known; it makes it possible to adapt to changing demands, and change functions to function areas of the brain after injuries such as from strokes. The other effect of activation of neural plasticity is harmful, causing symptoms and signs of diseases such as some forms of tinnitus and neuropathic pain. We have called such diseases "plasticity diseases." Some forms of tinnitus belong to a group of diseases where activation of neural plasticity plays an important role for creating symptoms. Many forms of tinnitus are thus plasticity diseases.

The pathology of plasticity diseases is complex, and several factors are often involved in causing a plasticity disorder [26]. The effect of several factors may add up, and in some disorders two or more factors must be present at the same time in order to cause the symptoms of the disease in question. Hemifacial spasm (HFS) is such an example of more than one factor being necessary for causing the symptoms of the disorder [33, 34]. Irritation of the facial nerve root seems to be the cause because moving the blood vessel off the facial nerve root is a very effective treatment. The fact that blood vessels in close contact with the nerve root is common while HFS is a very rare disorder shows that another (unknown) factor must also be present to cause the symptoms of HFS.

In such a situation, it may be sufficient to treat both the factors if both are necessary to cause symptoms. An example of that is HFS that is caused by hyperactivity in the facial motonucleus, but a blood vessel in close contact with the facial nerve root is one of the two (or more) factors that are necessary for causing the spasm that is the characteristic symptom of HFS. It is therefore sufficient to treat one of the causes, and naturally the selection in moving the blood vessel off the nerve root is typically chosen. Some forms of tinnitus may also have several factors that all need to be present in order for symptoms to manifest but where it would be sufficient to treat just one of these factors.

Other studies have shown evidence that the symptoms (spasm in one side of the face) are not caused by pathologies of the facial nerve but instead hyperactivity of the facial motonucleus, probably caused by activation of neural plasticity [34]. This means that HFS is also a plasticity disorder with similarities such as tinnitus and central pain.

There is now considerable evidence that activation of harmful neural plasticity is the cause of many forms of tinnitus, and perhaps also other symptoms that often occur together with tinnitus, such as hyperacusis and perhaps phonophobia and misophonia. Tinnitus is therefore one of several forms of "plasticity disorders." It may be appropriate to speculate how a common property of the nervous system, such as neural plasticity, can be harmful to an individual person.

The Role of Ephaptic Transmission in Tinnitus

One of the first hypotheses regarding hyperactive disorders such as face pain (trigeminal neuralgia) and HFS [35] was ephaptic transmission between the axons of the trigeminal nerve, the myelin of which had been damaged. The theory about ephaptic transmission between injured (denuded) nerve fibers has been further developed and applied to peripheral nerves and dorsal spinal roots [36, 37]. A similar hypothesis was proposed for the auditory nerve to explain the cause of tinnitus [8].

Such direct communication between denuded axons (ephaptic transmission) was hypothesized to promote temporal coherent firing of many nerve fibers. Ephaptic transmission [8, 36, 37] may occur after injuries, such as in connections with surgical trauma and perhaps in conjunction with vestibular schwannoma [38] – conditions that are known to often be associated with tinnitus. However, the question about ephaptic transmission between nerve fibers in cranial nerve roots is controversial, and the hypothesis has never been proven. For another disorder that can be cured by moving a blood vessel off a cranial nerve root, HFS, it was shown to be unlikely to occur for any long period [39].

From having been the established theory in disorders such as trigeminal neuralgia, HFS, and some vestibular disorders (disabling positional vertigo), it was shown in studies of patients undergoing microvascular decompression operations for HFS that the signs of this disorder are related to hyperactivity of the facial motonucleus rather than ephaptic transmission in the nerve root [39]. However, the fact that the HFS can be effectively treated by moving a blood vessel off the facial nerve root implicates the nerve root with the disease. Likely, the explanation is that development

and maintaining the symptoms of these diseases involve several steps where the vascular irritation of a nerve root is just one.

Another form of ephaptic transmission, direct and synchronous activation of many nerve cells, has been hypothesized to be involved in causing epileptic seizures by synchronizing the firing of many neurons in a neuron pool, without being caused by transmission by chemical synapses [9].

Not only that, such "non-synaptic" mechanisms may occur not only from electrotonic coupling through gap junctions but also that the effect of the electrical field outside cell bodies can activate neighboring cells, thus causing ephaptic transmission and thereby causing many nerve cells to fire in synchrony. Ionic interactions (e.g., increases in the extracellular concentration of K^+) may have similar effects. This form of ephaptic transmission is believed to be involved in causing some forms of epileptic seizures [9]. It has been shown that some forms of tinnitus are caused by localized epileptic-like activity [4].

Higher packing density favors that kind of abnormal transmission between nerve cells and may be a contributing cause of symptoms in, for example, autistic individuals where it is known that the packing density of cells in the brain is greater than normal [40]. Similar phenomena may be involved in forms of tinnitus that often occur in conjunction with traumatic brain damage, such as closed head injuries (see Chap. 67).

The Role of the Non-Classical Auditory Pathways

There are many ways the central nervous system can be involved in causing and maintaining tinnitus. The most common cause is the change in function that occurs through activation of neural plasticity, which can change the excitability of synapses (synaptic efficacy), activate dormant synapses, and make synapses dormant which can re-route information (see Chap. 12).

One example is re-routing information to the non-classical auditory pathways. The non-classical auditory pathways are normally active in children, as indicated by the presence of a cross-modal interaction, where perception of sound is affected by electrical stimulation of the somatosensory system (the median nerve at the wrist) [41]. Such cross-modal interaction does not normally occur in adults but has been shown to occur in some individuals with tinnitus [42–44], indicating that the non-classical auditory pathway is involved in causing tinnitus in some individuals with tinnitus [42, 43]. The non-classical pathways (see Chap. 8) [45] have input from other sensory systems and provide a direct subcortical route to the amygdala, which may explain why some individuals with tinnitus also have affective symptoms such as depression and phonophobia.

It has been shown that female reproductive hormones influence neural transmission and enhance among other things GABA receptors [46].The difference in the incidence of tinnitus in males and females may be related to this effect of female reproductive hormones on GABAergic inhibition.

Involvement of Non-Auditory Parts of the Central Nervous System

There is evidence from animal experiments that parts of the brain other than auditory pathways may be functioning abnormally when tinnitus is induced through activation of neural plasticity by, for example, stimulation with loud sounds [13, 47]. For instance, it has been shown that place cells in the hippocampus function abnormally in animals exposed to intense noise, which would have caused tinnitus in humans [48].

Since many systems are connected to each other, pathology in one part may result in pathologic activity in many systems of the brain with wide and unexpected consequences.

Causes of Hearing Loss and Tinnitus

There are many ways the nervous system can be involved in causing hearing loss and tinnitus from factors such as noise exposure and administration of ototoxic substances. The cause of the tinnitus could be deprivation of signals that the ear sends to the auditory nervous system. The fact that tinnitus only occurs in some individuals with hair cell injuries indicates that factors other than injuries to hair cells are necessary for the development of tinnitus, emphasizing the complexity of tinnitus. More than one factor must often be present for tinnitus to manifest.

Effect of Exposure to Loud Noise and Ototoxic Substances

Noise exposure and administration of ototoxic drugs are common causes of hearing loss. It has been assumed that this is caused by damage to hair cells. However, it has become evident that matters are more complex and the auditory nervous system is also involved (see Chap. 37). Tinnitus often accompanies hearing loss caused by noise exposure or administration of ototoxic antibiotics and other ototoxic drugs (see Chap. 42) [49]. These agents have mostly been assumed to cause damage to hair cells in the cochlea. However, these assumptions may also have to be revised as more information about the involvement of the nervous system is gained.

Noise exposure or administration of ototoxic drugs causes hearing loss. Noise exposure and administration of ototoxic dugs have been assumed to primarily have these adverse effects by damaging hair cells (especially outer hair cells) in the cochlea, thus impairing the cochlear amplifier (see Chap. 37) [45]. However, animal studies have provided evidence that the effect is more complex [50, 51].

Animal experiments have shown that exposure to high-intensity sounds causes changes to occur in the response from structures of the ascending auditory pathways such as the cochlear nucleus [52], as well as in non-auditory structures such as the hippocampus [48]. Exposure to loud sounds may cause tinnitus because of the resulting hearing loss and deprivation of input to the auditory system, activating neural plasticity.

Deprivation of Input to the Auditory Nervous System

There is evidence that severance of the auditory nerve can in fact cause tinnitus or make existing tinnitus worse [18]. Lack of input to the auditory nervous system as a cause of tinnitus is supported by the finding that tinnitus can be ameliorated by cochlear implants [53, 54] (see Chap. 77) or by applying high-frequency (4,800 Hz) impulses to the round window of the cochlea [55].

Hearing loss causes deprivation of input to the auditory nervous system and can activate neural plasticity.

Another reason that deprivation of input from certain parts of the cochlea, such as the high-frequency (basal) part, causes tinnitus may be that such input normally provides inhibitory influence on neurons in the auditory nervous system.

There is some evidence that the effect of overexposure to sound is not only on the cochlea but also affecting the auditory nervous system, especially the cochlear nucleus where noise exposure has been reported to cause morphological changes [56]. Other investigators have reported physiological changes after exposure to loud noise [48, 52, 57, 58].

Neural plasticity may also be activated by abnormal input, including overexposure to noise (see Chap. 12).

The central nervous system may act on the hair cells through the descending pathways olivocochlear bundle. We discussed earlier age-related hearing loss (presbycusis) and showed that it can have influence from the central nervous system [59] in addition to the well-known degeneration of cochlear hair cells (Chap. 36).

There is evidence from other studies that deprivation of input to a structure such as the sensory cerebral cortex may result in the unused part being taken over by other systems. For example, an unused auditory cortex can be taken over by the visual system [60]. It is now well accepted that children who are born with hearing deficits or acquire hearing deficits early in life must have input to their auditory system re-established in order to ensure a normal development of the auditory system. Little is known about the possibility of early deficits in hearing causing tinnitus.

Signs of Tinnitus

There are few external signs of tinnitus except the individual's testimony. Cross-modal interaction occurs in some individuals with tinnitus (discussed in Chap. 9). Some can modulate their tinnitus by muscle contractions or change of gaze and some individuals cause tinnitus by stimulation of the skin [43, 44, 61]. There are possibly some signs of electroencephalography (EEG) or magnetoencephalography (MEG) changes that are specific to tinnitus [62].

Interaction between the Auditory and Somatosensory System

Animal experiments have shown that axons from one sense can grow into the brain territory of another sense if activation of that sense is suppressed or not existing such as in congenitally deaf individuals [60].

There is evidence from several studies that an abnormal cross-modal interaction occurs together with tinnitus in some individuals [42–44, 61, 63]. Several different explanations for such cross-modal interaction have been presented. One explanation involves the non-classical auditory pathways. It was mentioned in Chap. 8 that the non-classical auditory pathways receive input from other sensory systems. This means that activation of the non-classical pathways can make interaction from other sensory systems possible, but signs of function of the non-classical pathways (cross-modal interaction) have been shown only in children [41] and under some pathologic conditions such as tinnitus and autism [64]. While the non-classical pathways seem to be active in some animals used in auditory experimentation, such interaction does not seem to be normal in adult humans, but it is a normal phenomenon in children [41], which may be one of the reasons that children seem to react differently to tinnitus (see Chap. 6). When cross-modal interaction occurs in adults, it may be regarded as pathologic and can be involved in symptoms such as tinnitus or can occur together with tinnitus [42].

Other possibilities for cross-modal interaction involve the anatomical connections between the caudal trigeminal nucleus and the DCN dorsal column nuclei.

The connections between the DCN and the dorsal column nuclei and the trigeminal nucleus (as described in Chaps. 8 and 9) provide the anatomical substrate for one form of cross-modal interaction. These connections, shown to be active in animals, may not be active in humans under normal circumstances. The synapses on neurons in the DCN through which they receive somatosensory input may normally be dormant, but reduced auditory input to these neurons may activate the synapses that mediate somatosensory input to these cells [63, 65]. This assumption is supported by the finding that the response of DCN neurons to somatosensory input is increased in animals that have noise-induced hearing loss [66]. It is known from other studies that decreased use of synapses cause some of the synapses to become dormant, and some may become eliminated and their place on a cell membrane becomes taken over by other synapses (see [26]).

There are other mechanisms that could contribute to these effects. One example is the activation of $GABA_B$ receptors in the DCN that regulate dendritic excitability and excitatory inputs [67, 68]. $GABA_B$

receptors in CN could modulate glutamatergic neurotransmission. The GABAergic inputs could come from several cell types, some of which also contain glycine receptors [69, 70]. Similar processes could occur in the ICX that receive direct input from DCN neurons. Effects that are present at the level of the DCN may become enhanced within the IC.

Some studies [71, 72] found that tinnitus often occurs together with TMJ problems and often resolves when the TMJ problems have been successfully treated [73, 74]. A population study involving 989 consecutive patients [75], however, did not find a higher prevalence of tinnitus in patients with TMJ problems (7.28%) than what occurs in the general population (10–14%). These anomalies may be explained by interaction between the auditory system and the somatosensory system.

A different and perhaps an even stronger indication of an abnormal interaction between sensory systems is the observation made by some individuals with tinnitus that stimulation of the skin results in perceiving a sound. A person with tinnitus mentioned that when he dried his back with a towel, he would hear a swishing sound.

Some individuals can turn their tinnitus on and off or make it change its pitch or loudness by performing certain motor or sensory manipulations [76]. Also, a change in eye gaze, from a neutral head-referenced position, is one such behavior that can evoke or modulate tinnitus [61]. These phenomena are signs of interactions between the auditory system and the somatosensory system.

Tinnitus that Occurs as a Part of the Symptoms of Other Diseases

Tinnitus, and especially hyperacusis, may occur with other symptoms of some diseases such as Ménière's disease, Wilson's disease, and some forms of autism.

Ménière's Disease

Tinnitus is one of the three (or four) symptoms of Ménière's disease (see Chaps. 38 and 60). Since the two other symptoms of this disorder (fluctuating hearing loss and vertigo) are closely related to the function of the ear, it has been assumed that tinnitus that occurs as a part of the symptoms of Ménière's disease is also caused

by a malfunction of the structures in the ear. There are indications that the tinnitus in Ménière's disease is different from other kinds of tinnitus. For example, it can be shown to be affected by sympathectomy [77], not known to be effective in other kinds of tinnitus.

The symptoms – fluctuating hearing loss, tinnitus, and vertigo – of Ménière's disease (see Chaps. 42 and 60) have been regarded to be caused by local changes in the fluid system of the inner ear. The finding that stimulating vestibular receptors with air puffs applied to the middle ear cavity can ameliorate at least some of the symptoms of Ménière's disease [78] is an indication that the nervous system is involved in causing the pathology of Ménière's disease.

Applying air puffs to the inner ear, thus stimulating the receptors in the inner ear, may have an effect by activating neural plasticity. These observations indicate that the pathology of the disease is not limited to the inner ear, but the nervous system may also be involved in creating the symptoms of Ménière's disease.

This observation was developed into a clinical method using a device named the "Meniett." The results of clinical tests have shown beneficial effects of such treatment [79, 80].

Migraine

It has been hypothesized that symptoms such as phonophobia, tinnitus, fluctuation in hearing perception, and increased noise sensitivity [81] that often occur during migraine attacks are caused by an effect on cochlear blood vessels as a component of basilar artery migraine. Evidence has been presented that trigeminal neurogenic inflammation is involved in the development of vascular migraine with its components such as tinnitus and phonophobia [81].

Disorders that Affect the Auditory Nerve

Different kinds of injury can cause tinnitus. Thus, vestibular schwannoma, although these tumors often originate from the superior vestibular nerve, cause some destruction of the auditory nerve, and tinnitus almost always occurs in individuals with vestibular schwannoma (see Chap. 39) [43, 80]. Physical trauma to the auditory nerve, which may occur in head injuries caused by accidents, explosions (see Chap. 67), or surgery, may cause injuries to the auditory nerve by manipulations and heat from electro-coagulations. Temporomandibular joint disorders are often accompanied by tinnitus [74, 75] (see Chap. 96). Cerebrovascular diseases may also be accompanied by tinnitus (see Chap. 41). The common headache is often accompanied by tinnitus (see Chap. 61). Also, viral infections can result in tinnitus. Very little is known about how several different kinds of these injuries to the auditory nerve may cause tinnitus.

Head Injuries

It is known that head injury is often associated with tinnitus (see Chap. 67). Head injuries of various forms, such as from blast injuries, also result in many other symptoms such as epileptic seizures [9]. Close contact between many nerve cells, such as from abnormally dense packing of nerve cells, promotes ephaptic transmission. There are reasons to believe that ephaptic transmission between nerve cells may contribute to tinnitus in head injuries, which means nerve cells can be activated by field potentials in adjacent cells.

Some case reports have shown that disorders of the cerebral cortex (temporal lobe) may be associated with tinnitus [82], supporting the hypothesis that tinnitus can originate from the cortex.

Rare diseases such as Williams syndrome [83] and some forms of autism [64] are associated with hyperacusis.

Tinnitus and Stress

Stress seems to influence the tinnitus of people who already have the disorder, and stress may cause tinnitus [82, 84]. This could occur in many ways, one is direct effect on the hair cells through secretion of norepinephrine. Another cause of stress could be through an effect on the nervous system. It has been reported that tinnitus sometimes occurs just before a person faints [85]. This has been related to an effect on the

inner ear fluid systems from a hemodynamic imbalance [85]. It could also naturally be caused by change in sympathetic activity that accompanies syncope or it could be caused by the effect of low blood pressure on the brain. Syncope may be regarded as a situation where systemic blood pressure has become lower than the range where the auto-regulation can keep blood flow in the brain constant, independent of systemic blood pressure.

The abundant innervation of both cochlear and vestibular sensory cells by the efferent fibers of the olivocochlear bundles (see Chap. 8) could affect the function of the hair cells and possibly the balance of the fluid volumes in the inner ear.

Many sympathetic nerve fibers terminate close to hair cells in both the cochlea and the vestibular apparatus [86]. These fibers secrete norepinephrine in response to activation of the sympathetic nervous system. Epinephrine secreted from these fibers can alter the function of the hair cells and increase their sensitivity; that may explain why sympathectomy has a beneficial effect on tinnitus in Ménière's disease [77]. Sympathetic blockage (stellate ganglion block) has also been shown to reduce sudden hearing loss [87], thus, a further sign of an effect of the sympathetic innervation of the cochlea.

What is the Neural Code of Tinnitus?

It is not known which properties of the discharge in single auditory nerve fibers are interpreted as a sound. It was earlier thought that increased firing rates would signal the presence of sound, but the discharge rate of auditory nerve fibers in animals that have been treated in ways that would cause tinnitus in humans (such as by using administration of ototoxic antibiotics) is not elevated but rather reduced [88–91]. The same is the case for acute injury to the cochlea [92]. Other animal experiments have shown that administration of salicylate, in dosages that are known from humans to give tinnitus, can cause an increase in the spontaneous discharge rates of single auditory nerve fibers [93, 94].

Eggermont and coworkers have found that longtime (4 months) stimulation with frequency bands (two octave wide and 80 dB sound pressure level [SPL]) of sounds of moderate intensity decreases the responsiveness of cells in the primary auditory cerebral cortex that are tuned to the frequencies of the stimulation and increases the responsiveness of cells that are tuned to frequencies of the edge of the spectrum of the stimulus sounds [95]. More recently, it was found that similar effects could be obtained using lower stimulus intensity (68 dB SPL) and shorter time of exposure (6 weeks) [96].

Recent research has shown evidence that synchrony of the firing (temporal coherence) in large groups of nerve cells is more likely to be the neural code that causes the sensation of the presence of sounds, and most likely many forms of tinnitus [49, 97, 98], than discharge rate.

It has been hypothesized that phase-locking discharge in many auditory nerve axons is the neural code that signals the presence of sound [8] and thus, also probably the code that falsely communicates a sound is present when not causing tinnitus. Animal studies have indicated that the coherence of temporal patterns of activity in individual neurons in a pool of neurons is important for providing the normal awareness of the presence of a sound, including tinnitus. This means that correlation of neural activity in populations of nerve cells in the auditory nervous system is most likely what causes tinnitus [49, 98] (see Chap. 16).

Thus, there is considerable evidence that tinnitus is not directly related to the discharge rate of auditory nerve cells, which seems surprising because tinnitus is regarded as a hyperactive disorder. These observations, however, are in agreement with other studies that indicate that the discharge rate of auditory nerve fibers does not communicate information about the strength (intensity) of sounds [99].

Such phase locking occurs normally in response to sounds because the same source drives the nerve activity. It can also occur pathologically through an abnormal coupling between nerve fibers or nerve cells, known as ephaptic transmission.

Which Structures Function Abnormally in Individuals with Tinnitus?

Which parts of the auditory pathways have abnormal function in individuals with tinnitus is not known. Many studies have focused on the primary auditory cortex but there is also evidence that subcortical connections from the dorsal and medial thalamus to the lateral nucleus of the amygdala may convey sensation of tinnitus. The sensory cerebral cortices are just another processing station. The anatomical location where perception occurs is much higher, but it is unknown exactly in which structures neural activity causes sensory perception.

The amygdala nuclei have connections to most parts of the brain, which means that this route could be important in some forms of tinnitus. The medial and dorsal parts of the auditory thalamic nuclei are parts of the non-classical auditory pathways. Signs of activation of these pathways have been shown as a constant phenomenon in children below the age of 12 years [41]. Adults thus do not normally have such signs, but some individuals with tinnitus have similar signs of involvement of the non-classical auditory pathways as young children [42]. Other studies have shown an increased activation of the amygdala in some individuals with tinnitus [100].

Detectable Changes in Function of the Auditory Nervous System in Tinnitus

There are a few objective signs that can provide information about the magnitude of tinnitus and its character, and indeed there are no available objective tests that can determine if a person has tinnitus at all. The character and the magnitude of the annoyance and distress caused by tinnitus can only be assessed by interviewing the person. While there are no clinically recognized methods for objectively assessing the severity of tinnitus or helping distinguish between different forms of tinnitus, some laboratory methods have shown promise for being of clinical value. It has, however, recently been shown that some forms of tinnitus are associated with specific abnormalities in EEG and MEG recordings. The future will tell whether these techniques will be applied in clinics for diagnosing tinnitus.

Another promising method is to use transcranial magnetic stimulation (TMS) as a test of the ability for electrical stimulation of specific parts of the cerebral cortex to beneficially affect an individual's tinnitus [101–103].

Change in Tonotopic Maps

Studies have shown indications of abnormalities in the tonotopic organization of the cerebral auditory cortex in patients with tinnitus using magnetoencephalograpic (MEG) recordings [104]. The functional importance of the tonotopic organization is, however, unknown; it is not known if the observed changes are primary to the pathology of tinnitus or caused by the effect of abnormal neural input to the auditory cerebral cortex.

Much attention has been paid to these observed changes in the tonotopic organization in individuals with tinnitus [104, 105]. The functional importance of normal tonotopic organization is unknown. Therefore, it is not known what the implications of altering the tonotopic organization might be.

Tonotopic map changes and change in tuning acuity of neurons in the auditory system can be explained by change in synaptic efficacy that may occur because neural plasticity has been turned on. Many of the synapses that connect these inputs to a cell are normally dormant. By unmasking synapses and masking other synapses, it is possible to change the tuning of cells, shift their center frequency, and change the width of the tuning. The width of the tuning is determined by how many inputs are active, which thus determines the shape of the tuning curve of the cell in question. This means that masking and unmasking of synapses can change the tonotopic organization of auditory nuclei and in the auditory parts of the cerebral cortex.

Pathology of a specific structure can make many other structures behave abnormally without having a pathologic function simply because they receive abnormal input [29]. For example, the observed change in tonotopic organization in the cerebral cortex may not be caused by pathologies of the cerebral cortex, but the reorganization and abnormal response of cortical structures can equally be caused by pathologic neural activity generated by more peripheral structures and delivered to a normally functioning cerebral cortex.

Conclusion

Of the different pathologies that affect the auditory system, tinnitus is the most complex disorder and it affects many people. It is also the one least known about and has the least effective treatments of common disorders of the ear. It has been falsely regarded as an ear disease for many years, and not until relatively recently has it become generally accepted that the anatomical location of most forms of tinnitus is the central nervous system. Most forms of tinnitus are phantom sensations caused by activation of harmful neural plasticity; it is thus a plasticity disorder that has many similarities to central neuropathic pain. Its management requires a multidisciplinary approach.

References

1. Tonndorf J (1987) The analogy between tinnitus and pain: a suggestion for a physiological basis of chronic tinnitus. Hear. Res. 28:271–5.
2. Jastreboff PJ (1990) Phantom auditory perception (tinnitus): mechanisms of generation and perception. Neurosci. Res. 8:221–54.
3. Møller AR (2003) Tinnitus, in Neurotology, RK Jackler and D Brackmann, Editors. St. Louis: Mosby.
4. Møller AR (2003) Pathophysiology of tinnitus. In: Otolaryngologic Clinics of North America, A Sismanis, Editor. Amsterdam: W.B. Saunders, 249–66.
5. Kaltenbach JA and CE Afman (2000) Hyperactivity in the dorsal cochlear nucleus after intense sound exposure and its resemblance to tone-evoked activity: a physiological model for tinnitus. Hear. Res. 140:165–72.
6. Salvi RJ, J Wang and D Ding (2000) Auditory plasticity and hyperactivity following cochlear damage. Hear. Res. 147: 261–74.
7. Bauer CA, JG Turner, DM Caspary et al (2008) Tinnitus and inferior colliculus activity in chinchillas related to three distinct patterns of cochlear trauma. J. Neurosci. Res. 86: 2564–78.
8. Møller AR (1984) Pathophysiology of tinnitus. Ann. Otol. Rhinol. Laryngol. 93:39–44.
9. Dudek FE, T Yasumura and JE Rash (1998) Non-synaptic' mechanisms in seizures and epileptogenesis. Cell Biol. Int. 22:793–805.
10. Møller AR (2009) Plasticity diseases. Neurol. Res. 31: 1023–30.
11. Møller AR (2006) Neural Plasticity in Tinnitus, in Reprogramming the Brain, Progress in Brain Research, AR Møller, Editor. 2006, Elsevier: Amsterdam, 367–74.
12. Sie KCY and EW Rubel (1992) Rapid changes in protein synthesis and cell size in the cochlear nucleus following eighth nerve activity blockade and cochlea ablation. J. Comp. Neurol. 320:501–8.
13. Kaltenbach JA (2007) The dorsal cochlear nucleus as a contributor to tinnitus: mechanisms underlying the induction of hyperactivity, in Tinnitus: Pathophysiology and Treatment, Progress in Brain Research, B Langguth et al, Editors. Amsterdam: Elsevier, 89–106.

14. Aran JM and I Cazals (1981) Electrical suppression of tinnitus, in Ciba Foundation Symposium 85. London: Pitman Books Ltd., 217–25.

15. Cazals Y, M Negrevergne and JM Aran (1978) Electrical stimulation of the cochlea in man: hearing induction and tinnitus suppression. J. Am. Audiol. Soc. 3:209–13.

16. Pulec JL (1995) Cochlear nerve section for intractable tinnitus. ENT J. 74:469–76.

17. Pulec JL (1984) Tinnitus: surgical therapy. Am. J. Otol. 5: 479–80.

18. House JW and DE Brackmann (1981) Tinnitus: surgical treatment, in Tinnitus (Ciba Foundation Symposium 85). London: Pitman Books Ltd.

19. Portmann M, Y Cazals, M Negrevergne et al (1979) Temporary tinnitus suppression in many through electrcial stimulation of the cochlea. Acta Otolaryngol. (Stockh.) 87:249–99.

20. Uddman R, T Grunditz, A Larsson et al (1988) Sensory innervation of the ear drum and middle-ear mucosa: retrograde tracing and immunocytochemistry. Cell Tissue Res. 252:141–6.

21. Young ED, I Nelken and RA Conley (1995) Somatosensory effects on neurons in dorsal cochlear nucleus. J. Neurophysiol. 73:743–65.

22. Zhou J and S Shore (2004) Projections from the trigeminal nuclear complex to the cochlear nuclei: a retrograde and anterograde tracing study in the guinea pig. J. Neurosci. Res. 78:901–7.

23. Shore SE, Z Vass, NL Wys et al (2000) Trigeminal ganglion innervates the auditory brainstem. J. Comp. Neurol. 419: 271–85.

24. Yanagida M, K Ushiro, T Yamashita et al (1993) Enhanced MRI in patients with Ramsay-Hunt's syndrome. Acta Otolaryngol. Suppl. 500:58–61.

25. Langguth B, H Stadtlaender, M Landgrebe et al (2007) Tinnitus and Coxsackie B infections: a case series. Neuro Endocrinol. Lett. 28:554–5.

26. Møller AR (2006) Neural plasticity and disorders of the nervous system. Cambridge: Cambridge University Press

27. Møller MB, AR Møller, PJ Jannetta et al (1993) Vascular decompression surgery for severe tinnitus: selection criteria and results. Laryngoscope 103:421–7.

28. Dubner R and AI Basbaum, (1994) Spinal dorsal horn plasticity following tissue or nerve injury, in Textbook of Pain, PD Wall and R Melzack, Editors. Edinburgh: Churchill Livingstone, 225–41.

29. Møller AR (2008) Neural plasticity: for good and bad. Prog. Theoret. Phys. 173:48–65.

30. Abraham WC (2003) How long will long-term potentiation last?. Philos. Trans. R. Soc. Lond. B, Biol. Sci. 358:735–44.

31. Wall PD (1977) The presence of ineffective synapses and circumstances which unmask them. Philos. Trans. R. Soc. (Lond.) 278:361–72.

32. Hebb DO (1949) The organization of behavior. New York: Wiley.

33. Møller AR and PJ Jannetta (1984) On the origin of synkinesis in hemifacial spasm: results of intracranial recordings. J. Neurosurg. 61:569–76.

34. Møller AR (1993) Cranial nerve dysfunction syndromes: pathophysiology of microvascular compression, in Neurosurgical Topics Book 13, "Surgery of Cranial Nerves of the Posterior Fossa," Chapter 2, DL Barrow, Editor. Park Ridge, IL: American Association of Neurological Surgeons, 105–29.

35. Gardner WJ (1962) Concerning the mechanism of trigeminal neuralgia and hemifacial spasm. J. Neurosurg. 19:947–58.

36. Seltzer Z and M Devor (1979) Ephaptic transmission in chronically damaged peripheral nerves. Neurology 29:1061–4.

37. Rasminsky M (1980) Ephaptic transmission between single nerve fibers in the spinal nerve roots of dystrophic mice. J. Physiol. (Lond.) 305:151–69.

38. Cacace AT (2003) Expanding the biological basis of tinnitus: crossmodal origins and the role of neuroplasticity. Hear. Res. 175:112–32.

39. Møller AR (1987) Hemifacial spasm: ephaptic transmission or hyperexcitability of the facial motor nucleus? Exp. Neurol. 98:110–9.

40. Møller AR (2007) Neurophysiologic abnormalities in autism, in New Autism Research Developments, BS Mesmere, Editor. New York: Nova Science Publishers.

41. Møller AR and P Rollins (2002) The non-classical auditory system is active in children but not in adults. Neurosci. Lett. 319:41–4.

42. Møller AR, MB Møller and M Yokota (1992) Some forms of tinnitus may involve the extralemniscal auditory pathway. Laryngoscope 102:1165–71.

43. Cacace AT, TJ Lovely, DJ McFarland et al (1994) Anomalous cross-modal plasticity following posterior fossa surgery: some speculations on gaze-evoked tinnitus. Hear. Res. 81: 22–32.

44. Cacace AT, JP Cousins, SM Parnes et al (1999) Cutaneous-evoked tinnitus. II: Review of neuroanatomical, physiological and functional imaging studies. Audiol. Neurotol. 4: 258–68.

45. Møller AR (2006) Hearing: anatomy, physiology, and disorders of the auditory system, 2nd Ed. Amsterdam: Academic Press.

46. Tremere LA, JK Jeong and Pinaud R (2009) Estradiol shapes auditory processing in the adult brain by regulating inhibitory transmission and plasticity-associated gene expression. J. Neurosci. 29:5949–63

47. Szczepaniak WS and AR Møller (1995) Evidence of decreased GABAergic influence on temporal integration in the inferior colliculus following acute noise exposure: a study of evoked potentials in the rat. Neurosci. Lett. 196:77–80.

48. Goble TJ, AR Møller and LT Thompson (2009) Acute corticosteroid administration alters place-field stability in a fixed environment: comparison to physical restraint and noise exposure. Hear. Res. 253:52–9.

49. Eggermont JJ (2007) Pathophysiology of tinnitus, in Tinnitus: Pathophysiology and Treatment, Progress in Brain Research, B Langguth et al, Editors. Amsterdam: Elsevier, 19–35.

50. Canlon B, E Borg and A Flock (1988) Protection against noise trauma by pre-exposure to a low level acoustic stimulus. Hear. Res. 34:197–200.

51. Miller JM, CS Watson and WP Covell (1963) Deafening effects of noise on the cat. Acta Otolaryngol. Suppl. 176:1–91.

52. Szczepaniak WS and AR Møller (1996) Evidence of neuronal plasticity within the inferior colliculus after noise exposure: a study of evoked potentials in the rat. Electroenceph. Clin. Neurophysiol. 100:158–64.

53. Sininger YS, JP Mobley, W House et al (1987) Intra-cochlear electrical stimulation for tinnitus suppression in a patient with near-normal hearing, in Proceedings of the III International Tinnitus Seminar, Karlsruhe, West Germany, H Feldmann, Editor. Harsch Verlag.

54. Van de Heyning P, K Vermeire, M Diebl et al (2008) Incapacitating unilateral tinnitus in single-sided deafness treated by cochlear implantation. Ann. Otol. Rhinol. Laryngol. 117:645–52.

55. Rubinstein JT, RS Tyler, A Johnson et al (2003) Electrical suppression of tinnitus with high-rate pulse trains. Otol. Neurotol. 24:478–85.

56. Morest DK, MD Ard and D Yurgelun-Todd (1979) Degeneration in the central auditory pathways after acoustic deprivation or over-stimulation in the cat. Anat. Rec. 193:750.

57. Syka J, N Rybalko and J Popelar (1994) Enhancement of the auditory cortex evoked responses in awake guinea pigs after noise exposure. Hear. Res. 78:158–68.

58. Syka J and N Rybalko (2000) Threshold shifts and enhancement of cortical evoked responses after noise exposure in rats. Hear. Res. 139:59–68.

59. Willott JF, JG Turner and VS Sundin (2000) Effects of exposure to an augmented acoustic environment on auditory function in mice: roles of hearing loss and age during treatment. Hear. Res. 142:79–88.

60. Horng SH and M Sur (2006) Visual activity and cortical rewiring: activity-dependent plasticity of cortical networks, in Reprogramming the Brain, Progress in Brain Research, AR Møller, Editor. Amsterdam: Elsevier, 3–11.

61. Cacace AT, JP Cousins, SM Parnes et al (1999) Cutaneous-evoked tinnitus. I: Phenomenology, psychophysics and functional imaging. Audiol. Neurotol. 4:247–57.

62. Gerken GM (1996) Central tinnitus and lateral inhibition: an auditory brainstem model. Hear. Res. 97:75–83.

63. Dehmel S, YL Cui and SE Shore (2008) Cross-modal interactions of auditory and somatic inputs in the brainstem and midbrain and their imbalance in tinnitus and deafness. Am. J. Audiol. 17:S193–209.

64. Khalfa S, N Bruneau, B Rogé et al (2004) Increased perception of loudness in autism. Hear. Res. 198:87–92.

65. Shore S, J Zhou and S Koehler (2007) Neural mechanisms underlying somatic tinnitus, in Tinnitus: Pathophysiology and Treatment, Progress in Brain Research, B Langguth et al, Editors. Amsterdam: Elsevier, 107–23.

66. Shore SE, S Koehler, M Oldakowski et al (2008) Dorsal cochlear nucleus responses to somatosensory stimulation are enhanced after noise-induced hearing loss. Eur. J. Neurosci. 27:155–68.

67. Caspary DM, A Raza, Lawhorn B et al (1990) Immunocytochemical and neurochemical evidence for age-related loss of GABA in the inferior colliculus: implications for neural presbycusis. J. Neurosci. 10:2363–72

68. Caspary DM, TM Holder, LF Hughes et al (1999) Age-related changes in GABA$_A$ Receptor subunit composition and function in rat auditory system. Neuroscience 93:307–12.

69. Shore SE, RH Helfert, SC Bledsoe et al (1991) Descending projections to the dorsal and ventral divisions of the cochlear nucleus in guinea pig. Hear. Res. 52:255–68.

70. Mugnaini E (1985) GABA neurons in the superficiallayers of the rat dorsal cochlear nucleus:light and electron microscopic immunocytochemestry. J. Comp. Neurol. 235:6181.

71. Tuz HH, EM Onder and RS Kisnisci (2003) Prevalence of otologic complaints in patients with temporomandibular disorder. Am. J. Orthod. Dentofacial. Orthop. 123:620–3.

72. de Felício CM, MO Melchior, CL Ferreira et al (2008) Otologic symptoms of temporomandibular disorder and effect of orofacial myofunctional therapy. Cranio 26:118–25.

73. Wright EF (2007) Otologic symptom improvement through TMD therapy. Quintessence Int. 38:564–71.

74. Morgan DH (1992) Tinnitus of TMJ origin. J. Craniomandibular Pract. 10:124–9.

75. Upton LG and SJ Wijeyesakere (2004) The incidence of tinnitus in people with disorders of the temporomandibular joint. Int. Tinnitus J. 10:174–6.

76. Levine RA, M Abel and H Cheng (2003) CNS somatosensory-auditory interactions elicit or modulate tinnitus. Exp. Brain Res. 153:643–8.

77. Passe EG (1951) Sympathectomy in relation to Ménière's disease, nerve deafness and tinnitus. A report of 110 cases. Proc. R. Soc. Med. 44:760–72.

78. Densert B and K Sass (2001) Control of symptoms in patients with Ménière's disease using middle ear pressure applications: two years follow-up. Acta Otolaryngol. (Stockh.) 121:616–21.

79. Odkvist LM, S Arlinger, E Billermark et al (2000) Effects of middle ear pressure changes on clinical symptoms in patients with Ménière's disease – a clinical multicentre placebo-controlled study. Acta Otolaryngol. Suppl. 543:99–101.

80. Mattox DE and M Reichert (2008) Meniett device for Meniere's disease: use an compliance at 3 and 5 years. Otol. Neurotol. 29:29–32.

81. Vass Z, PS Steyger, AJ Hordichok et al (2001) Capsaicin stimulation of the cochlea and electric stimulation of the trigeminal ganglion mediate vascular permeability in cochlear and vertebro-basilar arteries: a potential cause of inner ear dysfunction in headache. Neuroscience 103:189–201.

82. Hurst RW and SI Lee (1986) Ictal tinnitus. Epilepsia 27:769–72.

83. Borsel van J, LMG Curfs and JP Fryns (1997) Hyperacusis in Williams syndrome: a sample survey study. Genet. Couns. 8:121–6.

84. Horner KC (2003) The emotional ear in stress. Neurosci. Biobehav. Rev. 27:437–46.

85. Pirodda A, C Brandolin, MC Raimond et al (2009) Tinnitus as a warning for preventing vasovagal syncope. Med. Hypotheses 73:370–1.

86. Densert O (1974) Adrenergic innervation in the rabbit cochlea. Acta Otolaryngol. (Stockh.) 78:345–56.

87. Haug O, WL Draper and SA Haug (1976) Stellate ganglion blocks for idiopathic sensorineural hearing loss. Arch Otolaryngol. 102:5–8.

88. Liberman MC (1978) Auditory-nerve response from cats raised in low-noise chamber. J. Acoust. Soc. Am. 63:442–55.

89. Liberman MC and NYS Kiang (1978) Acoustic trauma in cats. Acta Otolaryngol. (Stockh.) 358:1–63.

90. Salvi RJ (1976) Central components of the temporary threshold shift, in Effect of Noise on Hearing, D Henderson et al, Editors. New York: Raven Press, 247–60.

91. Salvi RJ and WA Ahroon (1983) Tinnitus and neural activity. J. Speech Hear. Res. 26:629–32.

92. Evans EF (1976) Temporary sensorineural hearing losses and eighth nerve changes, in Effect of Noise on Hearing, D Henderson, et al, Editors, New York: Raven Press, 199–221.

93. Evans EF, JP Wilson and TA Borerwe (1981) Animal models of tinnitus, in Ciba Foundation Symposium 85. London: Pitman Books Ltd.

94. Evans EF and TA Borerwe (1982) Ototoxic effects of salicylate on the responses of single cochlear nerve fibers and on cochlear potentials. Br. J. Audiol. 16:101–8.

95. Noreña AJ, B Gourévitch, N Aizawa et al (2006) Spectrally enhanced acoustic environment disrupts frequency representation in cat auditory cortex. Nat. Neurosci. 9:932–9.

96. Pienkowski M and JJ Eggermont (2009) Long-term, partially-reversible reorganization of frequency tuning in mature cat primary auditory cortex can be induced by passive exposure to moderate-level sounds. Hear. Res. 257: 24–40.

97. Eggermont JJ and LE Roberts (2004) The neuroscience of tinnitus. Trends Neurosci. 27:676–82.

98. Eggermont JJ (2007) Correlated neural activity as the driving force for functional changes in auditory cortex. Hear. Res. 229:69–80.

99. Müller M, D Robertson and GK Yates (1991) Rate-versus-level functions of primary auditory nerve fibres: evidence of square law behavior of all fibre categories in the guinea pig. Hear. Res. 55:50–6.

100. Lockwood A, R Salvi, M Coad et al (1998) The functional neuroanatomy of tinnitus. Evidence for limbic system links and neural plasticity. Neurology 50:114–20.

101. Kleinjung T, V Vielsmeier, M Landgrebe et al (2008) Transcranial magnetic stimulation: a new diagnostic and therapeutic tool for tinnitus patients. Int. Tinnitus J. 14:112–8.

102. De Ridder D, G De Mulder, V Walsh et al (2004) Magnetic and electrical stimulation of the auditory cortex for intractable tinnitus. J. Neurosurg. 100:560–4.

103. De Ridder D, G De Mulder, V Walsh et al (2005) Transcranial magnetic stimulation for tinnitus : a clinical and pathophysiological approach: influence of tinnitus duration on stimulation parameter choice and maximal tinnitus suppression. Otol. Neurotol. 147:495–501.

104. Mühlnickel W, T Elbert, E Taub et al (1998) Reorganization of auditory cortex in tinnitus. Proc. Natl. Acad. Sci. U.S.A. 95:10340–3.

105. Bartels H, MJ Staal and FW Albers (2007) Tinnitus and neural plasticity of the brain. Otol. Neurotol. 28:178–84.

Chapter 11
The Role of Auditory Deprivation

Aage R. Møller

Keypoints

1. Deprivation of input to the auditory system can cause two kinds of change in function: It can alter the balance between inhibition and excitation and can activate neural plasticity.
2. Hearing loss of any kind, such as conductive hearing loss or cochlear hearing loss, causes decreased input to the auditory nervous system.
3. Noise-induced hearing loss is an example of deprivation of auditory stimulation and overexposure, which in itself may activate neural plasticity.
4. Altered balance between inhibition and excitation can change the gain in the auditory system. If the gain is increased, it may cause hyperactivity in the form of tinnitus.
5. The effect on the balance between inhibition and excitation is likely to abate when normal input to the auditory system is established.
6. Activation of neural plasticity, which may occur because of sensory stimulation, may last after restoring normal sensory stimulation.
7. Plastic changes may become permanent, and reversal of neural plasticity may require special actions.

Keywords Tinnitus • Sound deprivation • Neural plasticity • Inhibition • Temporal coherence

A.R. Møller (✉)
The University of Texas at Dallas, School of Behavioral and Brain Sciences, GR 41, 800 W Campbell Road, Richardson, TX 75080, USA
e-mail: amoller@utdallas.edu

Introduction

The effect on the nervous system of sensory deprivation can be profound, and is different when it occurs at birth or shortly thereafter, compared with occurring during adult life. The anatomical and functional development of the nervous system depends on sensory stimulation. Therefore, sound deprivation can have a stronger effect on young individuals than on adults. The fact that there are indications that the nonclassical pathways are normally active in children [1, 2] while not normally active in adults, may influence the way children react to deprivation of sound compared with adults.

Deprivation of input to the auditory system can mainly cause two different kinds of change in the function of the auditory nervous system, both of which can cause tinnitus: (1) It can decrease or shift the balance between excitation and inhibition and thereby increase the gain in the auditory nervous system and (2) deprivation of sensory stimulation can activate neural plasticity involving change in synaptic efficacy and sprouting of axons [3]. The effect of sound deprivation may not be easily observed because children do not complain of tinnitus in the same way as adults (see Chap. 6).

There are many ways that the auditory nervous system can be deprived of normal stimulation. Any form of hearing loss can cause some degree of sensory deprivation, whether it occurs through obstruction of the ear canal, disorders of the middle ear (see Chap. 34), or from disorders of the cochlea (see Chap. 35), it may have the same effect on the nervous system.

Tinnitus is common after noise-induced hearing loss (see Chap. 37). The reduced hearing may activate

A.R. Møller et al. (eds.), *Textbook of Tinnitus*,
DOI 10.1007/978-1-60761-145-5_11, © Springer Science+Business Media, LLC 2011

neural plasticity, causing the form of tinnitus that occurs after exposure to loud sounds; however, overexposure in itself may also activate neural plasticity and thereby cause tinnitus. The tinnitus that occurs after exposure to noise, which causes hearing loss, or after a brief period of deprivation of sound often disappears after some time. In some instances, however, exposure to loud noise, especially impulsive or high-frequency sounds such as fire alarms, can cause permanent tinnitus.

It was earlier believed that increased neural firing was the cause of tinnitus, but more recent studies seem to indicate that temporal and spatial coherence of activity is more important for eliciting a sensation of the presences of sound including tinnitus [4, 5]. Noreña and Eggermont [6] showed a slight increase in spontaneous firing in cells in the auditory cortex after acoustic trauma.

Many different parts of the nervous system have been implicated in tinnitus. Some investigators have found evidence of altered spontaneous activity that is different at different levels of the auditory system [7]. There is evidence that tinnitus may be associated with less neural excitation in the periphery of the ascending auditory pathway but greater activity in more central structures. Some have hypothesized that increased synchrony of neural firing can cause tinnitus. Other investigators have hypothesized that temporal coherence of firing in large groups of nerve cells is the cause of some forms of tinnitus [4, 8].

The frequency tuning in the cochlea is the basis for the tuning of nerve cells throughout the auditory nervous system. The acuity of tuning to sounds depends on the intensity of the sound; the higher the intensity, the broader the tuning [9, 10]. Increased temporal coherence of firing in many nerve cells may be caused by the broadening of the cochlea's tuning that occurs at higher sound intensities, thus causing a greater degree of overlap of different cells' response areas in the cortex. Unmasking of dormant synapses of interneurons, which often occur as a result of activation of neural plasticity, may also cause increased coherence of neural firing [3]. Changes in the relation between excitation and inhibition may likewise cause increased coherence and increased spontaneous firing. Both such changes may therefore be caused by reduced sensory stimulation.

Change in Balance Between Inhibition and Excitation

Single auditory nerve fibers have both excitatory and inhibitory response areas that mainly surround the excitatory areas [11]. The inhibition that is present in the response of single auditory nerve fibers is not caused by synaptic inhibition, but it is instead a form of suppression that is a result of cochlear nonlinearities [8]. Similar arrangement of suppression and excitation is present throughout the auditory nervous system, where the suppression is caused by synaptic inhibition. This means that a sound such as a tone will activate both inhibition and excitation (see Chap. 15). This suppression or inhibition is similar to what is in the visual system known as lateral inhibition. If pathologies of the cochlea result in a greater reduction of inhibition than excitation in a population of neurons, they may become sufficiently active to produce awareness of sound without sound reaching the ear, thus tinnitus. Tinnitus can be suppressed by proper arrangement of sound stimulation. Thus, sound in certain frequency regions can suppress some forms of tinnitus, and that may occur because such sounds contribute more to inhibition than excitation of specific populations of nerve cells. There are some indications that high-frequency sounds elicit stronger inhibitory influence on neurons in the cochlear nucleus more than low frequencies. This means that high-frequency hearing loss, which is common, may cause tinnitus because it reduces normally occurring inhibition. This can also explain why high-frequency stimulation can be effective in reducing some forms of tinnitus.

The interaction between inhibition and excitation is present along the ascending pathways including the cerebral cortices. Lateral inhibition is especially prevalent in the inferior colliculus where interaction between excitation and inhibition is especially prevalent. It has been shown that selective damage to sensory cells (acoustic trauma) in the cochlea that reduces the evoked potentials recorded from the auditory nerve, in fact, increases the discharge rate of many neurons in the inferior colliculus [12], indicating that the deprivation stimulation caused by cochlear trauma has decreased inhibition in these third-order neurons of the ascending auditory pathways. The observed changes suggest that these cells receive inhibitory input from high-frequency regions of their response areas and this inhibition has been reduced by deprivation of stimulation caused by cochlear trauma.

Josef Syka and his collaborators have shown that acoustic trauma causes increased activity in central auditory structures [13, 14]. This means many investigators agree that neural activity in the auditory periphery is decreased by acoustic trauma while it is increased at central levels such as the inferior colliculus and the cerebral cortex. Reduced inhibitory activity could explain these changes that go in opposite directions in the periphery and the central auditory structures. Also, the edge effect [15] may be a consequence of lateral inhibition. The fact that tinnitus is more prevalent in elderly individuals may be explained by the reduction in inhibition that normally occurs with age [16], thereby shifting the balance between excitation and inhibition toward excitation.

The hypothesis that deprivation of high-frequency sounds is involved in many forms of tinnitus is supported by animal (chinchilla) studies that show that auditory nerve fibers tuned to high frequencies tend to have elevated spontaneous activity [17]. This indicates that normal suppression was reduced after the noise exposure assumed to have caused tinnitus. Mathematical modeling predicts that the response of cells in the dorsal cochlear nucleus after noise trauma depends on the cell type, one type of cells become hyperactive, whereas another type is not affected by acoustic trauma [18].

Studies of temporal integration in the inferior colliculus of rats have shown decreased signs of GABAergic inhibitory activity in the cochlear nucleus after acoustic trauma [19]; administration of $GABA_A$ receptor agonists (benzodiazepines) reversed these changes [20].

Experience from treatment of people with tinnitus has also supported the hypothesis that deprivation of auditory stimulation decreases inhibition in the auditory nervous system.

Watanabe et al. [21] in a study of 600 individuals with tinnitus found that therapy with narrow band noise could suppress tinnitus in 66% of individuals, more so in individuals with presbycusis than sudden deafness. Souliere et al. [22] studied the effect of cochlear implants on loudness, annoyance, daily duration, location, and residual inhibition of tinnitus in 33 postlingual deafened individuals. Eighty-five percent of these individuals had tinnitus. The study showed a significant reduction in

both loudness and annoyance. Fifty-four percent of the individuals who had tinnitus before implantation had a loudness decrease of 30% or more; 43% had a decrease in annoyance of 30% or more. The duration of the tinnitus decreased 30% or more in 48% of the individuals who had tinnitus before implantation. The fact that many of the participants in these studies experienced contralateral residual inhibition and tinnitus suppression suggests that a central mechanism contributed to their tinnitus.

Using a computational model of a lateral inhibition neural network, Kral and Majernik [23] showed evidence that lateral inhibition might be involved in some forms of tinnitus. These investigators suggested that the spontaneous activity in the auditory nerve, when subjected to lateral inhibition, can cause phantom perceptions in the absence of auditory stimulation that many individuals experience when placed in silence, such as in an acoustically shielded chamber used for audiologic testing. Kral and Majernik [23] suggested that neural noise normally generated in neural networks is generally masked by a sound stimuli or ambient broadband acoustic noise. Inhibition may balance excitation in response to broadband noise, but the spectrum of other kinds of noise determines to what extent the response will be suppressed by inhibition or whether excitation dominates.

Rubinstein et al. [24] have shown that stimulation with electrical impulses at a high rate applied to the cochlea can reduce tinnitus in some individuals. The fact that especially high-frequency electrical stimulation of the cochlea has a beneficial effect on tinnitus in both deaf individuals [22] as well as individuals who do not have much hearing loss (see Chap. 77) [22] supports these hypotheses. Other investigators [25, 26, 27] found that electrical stimulation of the cochlea can reduce some forms of tinnitus by counteracting the effect of reduced activation of the auditory nervous system.

Activation of Neural Plasticity

Considerable evidence has been presented that activation of neural plasticity is involved in many forms of tinnitus (see Chaps. 12, 13, and 14) [28]. Many forms of tinnitus are therefore "plasticity disorders" [29].

The strongest promoter of neural plasticity is deprivation of sensory stimulation [3].

The effect of activation of neural plasticity can be changes in the function of the nervous system that occur with a short delay and last for just a short period for a long time.

It is assumed that acoustic trauma causes deprivation of input to the auditory nervous system because of the hearing loss it causes. There is, however, also the possibility that overstimulation may activate neural plasticity, which in turn can cause changes in the function of the nervous system that may result in tinnitus.

Studies in animals have shown evidence that auditory deprivation can cause cortical map modifications, and such cortical plasticity is associated with decreased inhibition [30].

There are several ways that deprivation of sensory stimulation can immediately affect functions of the auditory nervous system. These matters are discussed in Chap. 12.

References

1. Møller AR and P Rollins (2002) The non-classical auditory system is active in children but not in adults. Neurosci Lett. 319:41–4.
2. Møller AR (2006) Hearing: Anatomy, Physiology, and Disorders of the Auditory System, 2nd Ed. Amsterdam: Academic.
3. Møller AR (2006) Neural plasticity and disorders of the nervous system. Cambridge: Cambridge University Press.
4. Eggermont JJ and LE Roberts (2004) The neuroscience of tinnitus. Trends Neurosci. 27:676–82.
5. Møller AR (1984) Pathophysiology of tinnitus. Ann Otol Rhinol Laryngol. 93:39–44.
6. Noreña AJ and JJ Eggermont (2003) Changes in spontaneous neural activity immediately after an acoustic trauma: Implications for neural correlates of tinnitus. Hear Res. 183:137–53.
7. Syka J (2002) Plastic changes in the central auditory system after hearing loss, restoration of function, and during learning. Physiol Rev. 82:601–36.
8. Ruggero MA (1992) Responses to sound of the basilar membrane of the mammalian cochlea. Curr Opin Neurobiol. 2:449–56.
9. Johnstone BM, R Patuzzi and GK Yates (1986) Basilar membrane measurements and the traveling wave. Hear Res. 22:147–53.
10. Møller AR (1977) Frequency selectivity of single auditory nerve fibers in response to broadband noise stimuli. J Acoust Soc Am. 62:135–42.
11. Sachs MB and NYS Kiang (1968) Two tone inhibition in auditory nerve fibers. J Acoust Soc Am. 43:1120–8.
12. Wang J, D Ding and RJ Salvi (2002) Functional reorganization in chinchilla inferior colliculus associated with chronic and acute cochlear damage. Hear Res. 168:238–49.
13. Syka J, N Rybalko and J Popelar (1994) Enhancement of the auditory cortex evoked responses in awake guinea pigs after noise exposure. Hear Res. 78:158–68.
14. Syka J and J Popelar (1982) Noise impairment in the guinea pig. I. Changes in electrical evoked activity along the auditory pathway. Hear Res. 8:263–72.
15. Gerken GM (1996) Central tinnitus and lateral inhibition: an auditory brainstem model. Hear Res. 97:75–83.
16. Caspary DM, A Raza, BA Lawhorn Armour et al (1990) Immunocytochemical and neurochemical evidence for age-related loss of GABA in the inferior colliculus: Implications for neural presbycusis. J Neurosci. 10:2363–72.
17. Salvi RJ and WA Ahroon (1983) Tinnitus and neural activity. J Speech Hear Res. 26:629–32.
18. Schaette R and R Kempter (2008) Development of hyperactivity after hearing loss in a computational model of the dorsal cochlear nucleus depends on neuron response type. Hear Res. 240:57–72.
19. Szczepaniak WS and AR Møller (1995) Evidence of decreased GABAergic influence on temporal integration in the inferior colliculus following acute noise exposure: A study of evoked potentials in the rat. Neurosci Lett. 196:77–80.
20. Szczepaniak WS and AR Møller (1996) Effects of (-)-baclofen, clonazepam, and diazepam on tone exposure-induced hyperexcitability of the inferior colliculus in the rat: possible therapeutic implications for pharmacological management of tinnitus and hyperacusis. Hear Res. 97:46–53.
21. Watanabe K, T Kamio, D Ohkawara et al (1977) Suppression of tinnitus by band noise masker–a study of 600 cases. Nippon Jibiinkoka Gakkai Kaiho. 100:900–6.
22. Souliere CJ, P Kileny, TA Zwolan et al (1992) Tinnitus suppression following cochlear implantation. A multifactorial investigation. Arch Otolaryngol Head Neck Surg. 118:1291–7.
23. Kral A and V Majernik (1996) On lateral inhibition in the auditory system. Gen Physiol Biophys. 15:109–27.
24. Rubinstein JT, RS Tyler, A Johnson et al (2003) Electrical suppression of tinnitus with high-rate pulse trains. Otol Neurotol 24:478–85.
25. Portmann M, Y Cazals, M Negrevergne et al (1979) Temporary. tinnitus suppression in many through electrcial stimulation of the cochlea. Acta Otolaryngol (Stockh). 87:249–99.
26. Cazals Y, M Negrevergne and JM Aran (1978) Electrical stimulation of the cochlea in man: Hearing induction and tinnitus suppression. J Am Audiol Soc. 3:209–13.
27. Aran JM and I Cazals (1981) Electrical suppression of tinnitus, in Ciba Foundation Symposium 85. 1981, Pitman Books Ltd: London. 217–25.
28. Bartels H, MJ Staal and FW Albers (2007) Tinnitus and neural plasticity of the brain. Otol Neurotol. 28:178–84.
29. Møller AR (2008) Neural Plasticity: For Good and Bad. Progress of Theoretical Physics Supplement No 173:48–65.
30. Rajan R (2001) Plasticity of excitation and inhibition in the receptive field of primary auditory cortical neurons after limited receptor organ damage. Cereb Cortex. 11:171–82.

Chapter 12
The Role of Neural Plasticity in Tinnitus

Aage R. Møller

Keypoints

1. There is evidence from many studies that plastic changes in the central nervous system are involved in causing many forms of tinnitus.
2. Expression of neural plasticity may cause symptoms of sensory system disorders by changing neural processing and rerouting of information.
3. Rerouting of information through activation of neural plasticity may explain the occurrence of affective symptoms (mood disorders), phantom sensations, improved perceptual capabilities, or atypical sensory experiences such as phantom sensations, tinnitus, and neuropathic pain.
4. Changes in the processing of information may cause hyperacusis and distortion of sounds in connection with some forms of tinnitus.
5. There is evidence that the nonclassical auditory pathways in adults may be activated through expression of neural plasticity, causing cross-modal interaction in some individuals with tinnitus.

Keywords Tinnitus • Neural plasticity • Hyperacusis • Plasticity disorders • Nonclassical pathways • Extralemniscal pathways

Abbreviations

CNS   Central nervous system
MVD   Microvascular decompression

A.R. Møller (✉)
The University of Texas at Dallas, School of Behavioral and Brain Sciences, GR 41, 800 W Campbell Road, Richardson, TX 75080, USA
e-mail: amoller@utdallas.edu

Introduction

Plastic changes in the brain are involved in many forms of tinnitus and also in abnormal perception of sounds such as hyperacusis, as discussed in Chap. 10. Neural plasticity may also be involved in the affective disorders that often accompany tinnitus, such as phonophobia and depression.

Many forms of tinnitus are phantom sensations; the sensation is caused entirely by activity in the central nervous system that is maintained without any signals from the body, including the ear. Therefore, tinnitus has similarities with the phantom limb syndrome and central neuropathic pain. These symptoms belong to a group of adverse and harmful effects that can occur when neural plasticity is turned on and they have been termed "plasticity disorders" [1]. Deprivation of input to the nervous system is the strongest factor that can activate neural plasticity. Activation of neural plasticity is involved in many forms of tinnitus, and the topic has been reviewed recently by many authors in journal articles [2–5] and books [6, 7]. Since deprivation of sensory signals in general is a strong promoter of plastic changes, deprivation of sound is also an important factor in tinnitus as it can worsen existing tinnitus and cause the disorder in individuals who do not experience it in normal-sound environments.

Effects of Activation of Neural Plasticity

There are thus two fundamentally different effects of activation of neural plasticity; one being beneficial and the other being harmful, causing symptoms and signs of disease. The harmful effects are thus called "plasticity disorders" [1].

A.R. Møller et al. (eds.), *Textbook of Tinnitus*,
DOI 10.1007/978-1-60761-145-5_12, © Springer Science+Business Media, LLC 2011

Plastic changes can alter the processing of sounds, cause hyperactivity that may cause tinnitus, and re-route signals in the CNS, which may cause hyperacusis and affective symptoms and promote coherent firings of many neurons in a pool of neurons. It has been hypothesized that such increased coherence may be the cause of tinnitus.

Neural plasticity is a property of the nervous system that can change its function in various ways. The changes in function occur only when neural plasticity is activated. Neural plasticity may be activated, or turned on, by sensory experience such as reduced sensory signals (deprivation of input), by overstimulation, and by injuries of various kinds [7]. Intrinsic factors may turn on neural plasticity without any known cause.

The immediate effect of activation of neural plasticity would explain why a person who is placed in a silent room experiences tinnitus immediately. The effect that occurs later would explain why a certain treatment is more successful early in a disease.

Rerouting of Information

Activation of neural plasticity can open routes that are normally blocked because of ineffective synapses [8] by unmasking such dormant synapses [7, 9] (see Chap. 10). This property may be especially important for tinnitus. There are indications that the nonclassical pathways are becoming activated in that way in some individuals with tinnitus [10]. Activation of the nonclassical pathways may result in a different processing of sounds and can explain cross-modal interaction because the nonclassical auditory pathways receive input not only from ear but also from sensory receptors of other sensory systems, such as the somatosensory system. The nonclassical pathways also involve subcortical routes to the amygdala and other limbic structures by activating what has been called the "low route" [11] from the dorsal and medial thalamus [12]. Limbic structures have been shown to be abnormally activated in some individuals with tinnitus [13] using imaging techniques.

Several studies have shown evidence that tinnitus may be associated with affective syndromes such as depression and fear (phonophobia) which may be explained by an abnormal establishment of a subcortical route from the dorsal and medial thalamus to the lateral nucleus of the amygdala.

What Can Activate Neural Plasticity?

Many factors can activate neural plasticity including sensory experience. In connection with tinnitus, reduced sensory input from the ear to the auditory nervous system is an important factor for developing tinnitus. However, overstimulation can also activate neural plasticity causing tinnitus. Other factors that can activate neural plasticity are intrinsic factors such as inflammation; unknown factors may also be involved in turning on neural plasticity and causing or contributing to tinnitus.

Deprivation of Signals to the Nervous System

Most individuals who have tinnitus suffer from hearing loss, but a few have very little hearing loss or actually possess normal hearing.

There is considerable evidence that tinnitus may occur after damage to the ear or the auditory nerve that may cause reduced input to the central nervous system. This can have two different effects: It can change the balance between inhibition and excitation and it can promote activation of neural plasticity. Damage to the ear can reduce input to the central auditory system and shift the balance between inhibition and excitation. Deprivation, as such, is unlikely to be the cause of tinnitus but can start a sequence of events of central modifications of the function of the auditory system and likely other parts of the central nervous system. Decreased input to the nervous system can activate neural plasticity.

Sounds that reach the ear cause both inhibition and excitation; decreased input to the nervous system may also change the relation between inhibition and excitation. Sound deprivation can occur because of pathologies of the ear or the auditory nerve, as well as a lack of environmental sounds.

The effect of deprivation of sound increases with age. In a study of 120 normal hearing young adults, it was found that 64 experienced tinnitus when seated in a silent room used for audiologic tests after a short time period (4 min). None of the participants experienced tinnitus in ordinary environments [14]. Placed in a room of silence is also likely to increase the tinnitus of individuals who have tinnitus in ordinary environments.

Interruption of input from the ear to the auditory system (deafferentation of the auditory periphery) can induce neural plasticity, causing changes in the function of the central nervous system from deprivation of input that may cause some forms of tinnitus. Age-related hearing loss (see Chap. 36) is the most common situation where deprivation of sound causes tinnitus and also hearing loss. Cochlear hearing loss from noise exposure (see Chap. 37) is another example of decreased signals from the ear that may cause tinnitus because it activates neural plasticity.

Middle-ear diseases can lead to tinnitus through activating neural plasticity by reducing the sound that reaches the cochlea (see Chap. 34). When appropriately treated or compensated by amplification, the tinnitus is likely to improve or disappear completely.

Age-related hearing that often occurs in elderly individuals mainly affects high-frequency hearing loss. Hearing loss is more likely to cause tinnitus in older individuals than when occurring in younger individuals. This may be because inhibition in the nervous system decreases with age [15], which just adds to the effect of reduced sound that normally causes inhibition.

Altered time pattern of discharges in the auditory nerve from continuous type of pattern to burst pattern that may occur as a result of damage to the ear or more likely from damage to the auditory nerve may induce tinnitus. Another factor that seems more plausible as a cause of tinnitus is synchrony of the discharges in many nerve fibers [16, 17].

The fact that there are many individuals who have considerable hearing loss but no tinnitus means deprivation or reduced input to the auditory system does not always turn on harmful plasticity. This means neural plasticity turned on by deprivation of input to the auditory system is not the only cause of tinnitus.

Overexposure

Exposure to loud sounds, especially impulsive noise, can cause immediate tinnitus [18, 19] in addition to hearing loss (see Chap. 37). In most people, the tinnitus decreases with time after the end of the exposure. In some individuals, a single exposure can cause a lifetime of tinnitus, thus creating a best-able situation where the nervous system has two stable conditions; one normal and one that is pathological. A one-time exposure may cause tinnitus because permanent damage has occurred to the ear. Changes in function of the nervous system induced by activation of neural plasticity may have two

permanent states: one normal and one pathologic, which can explain why permanent tinnitus may occur after a single exposure. The cause of the tinnitus from noise exposure may be changes in the ear or the nervous system through activation of neural plasticity, or by the deprivation of input to the auditory nervous system that occurs because of the damage caused by the overexposure. There are indicators that overexposure in itself can turn neural plasticity on.

In order to correct this bi-stable property, it is not only necessary to reverse the cause of the pathologic changes but the state of the neural circuitry must also be flipped back to restore normalcy (see Chap. 14). Conditions caused by plastic changes can be permanent because of Hebb's principle: neurons that fire together will eventually also connect morphologically together ("wire together") [7].

Treatment of Plasticity Disorders

Similarly to what is experienced from neuropathic pain, tinnitus becomes difficult to treat the longer it persists. This was shown in a study of the efficacy of MVD of the auditory nerve for treatment of tinnitus in patients who had had their tinnitus for different lengths of time [20]. There was a marked difference when the participants were divided according to the time they had had their tinnitus. Of the 72 patients – 40 men and 32 women – who underwent MVD for tinnitus, 18.2% had total relief, 22.2% showed marked improvement, 11.1% had slight improvement, and 2.8% (two patients) became worse. Those who experienced total relief or marked improvement had had their tinnitus for a shorter period than those who had had their tinnitus for a longer period, 2.9 and 2.7 years, respectively; those who only achieved slight improvement or no improvement at all had had their tinnitus much longer, 5.2 and 7.9 years, respectively.

The finding that there was a marked difference between the outcome in men and women is more difficult to explain. Of the women, 54.8% had relief or some improvement of their tinnitus, but only 29.3% of the men had such improvements. The participants in this study all had severe tinnitus (it can serve as a reminder of the seriousness of severe tinnitus that two of the participants who did not have any improvement committed suicide within a year after the MVD operation).

Development of Beneficial and Harmful Plasticity

It seems reasonable to assume that beneficial neural plasticity has developed as a result of natural selection (Darwinian), but development of harmful plasticity causing plasticity disorders seems contradictory to natural selection that is normally assumed to favor the development of favorable functions such as beneficial plasticity. Activation of beneficial neural plasticity that causes adaptation to changing demands and redirection of signals from injured parts of the brain to functional parts seems in accordance with common hypotheses about Darwinian development. These functions are likely to have developed according to the principle of natural selection of the fittest [21] and are purposive and beneficial to an individual person. It is less obvious how harmful plasticity has developed, but it could be argued that plasticity disorders are caused by maladaptive plasticity.

If this hypothesis is accepted, one can ask if nature tries to correct its mistakes and if harmful plasticity (plasticity disorders) can be expected to vanish as development goes forth. Mistakes in evolution may disappear, if they cause disadvantages to survival or the accomplishment of reproduction. It is questionable whether tinnitus is a disadvantage in reproduction. It may be assumed that the goals of natural selection are to improve reproduction. It is questionable if plasticity disorders such as tinnitus can affect the ability to reproduce, in particular, since they mainly occur late in life after the end of the reproductive period, which for women is around the age of 40, but much higher for men. Plasticity disorders that occur late in life do not affect the ability to reproduce and thus there is little evolutionary pressure to eliminate such disorders by natural selection.

References

1. Møller AR (2008) Neural Plasticity: For Good and Bad. Progress of Theoretical Physics Supplement No 173:48–65.
2. Henry JA, KC Dennis and MA Schechter (2005) General review of tinnitus: prevalence, mechanics, effects, and management. J Speech Lang Hear Res 48:1204–35.
3. Saunders JC (2007) The role of central nervous system plasticity in tinnitus. J Commun Disord 40:313–34.
4. Plewnia C, M Bartels and C Gerlof (2003) Transient suppression of tinnitus by transcranial magnetic stimulation. Ann Neurol 53:263–6.
5. Bartels H, MJ Staal and FW Albers (2007) Tinnitus and neural plasticity of the brain. Otol Neurotol 28:178–84.
6. Møller AR (2007) The role of neural plasticity, in Tinnitus: Pathophysiology and Treatment, Progress in Brain Research, B Langguth et al, Editors. Elsevier: Amsterdam. 37–45.
7. Møller AR (2006) Neural plasticity and disorders of the nervous system. Cambridge: Cambridge University Press.
8. Wall PD (1977) The presence of ineffective synapses and circumstances which unmask them. Phil Trans Royal Soc (Lond) 278:361–72.
9. Møller AR (2001) Symptoms and signs caused by neural plasticity. Neurol Res 23:565–72.
10. Møller AR, MB Møller and M Yokota (1992) Some forms of tinnitus may involve the extralemniscal auditory pathway. Laryngoscope 102:1165–71.
11. LeDoux JE (1992) Brain mechanisms of emotion and emotional learning. Curr Opin Neurobiol 2:191–7.
12. Møller AR (2003) Sensory Systems: Anatomy and Physiology. Amsterdam: Academic.
13. Lockwood A, R Salvi, M Coad et al (1998) The functional neuroanatomy of tinnitus. Evidence for limbic system links and neural plasticity. Neurology 50:114–20.
14. Tucker DA, SL Phillips, RA Ruth et al (2005) The effect of silence on tinnitus perception. Otolaryngol Head Neck Surg 132:20–4.
15. Caspary DM, TA Schatteman and LF Hughes (2005) Age-related changes in the inhibitory response properties of dorsal cochlear nucleus output neurons: role of inhibitory inputs. J Neurosci 25:10952–9.
16. Eggermont JJ (2005) Tinnitus: neurobiological substrates. Drug Discov Today 10:1283–90.
17. Baguley DM (2002) Mechanisms of tinnitus. Br Med Bull 63:195–212.
18. Smoorenburg GF (1993) Risk of noise-induced hearing loss following exposure to Chinese firecrackers. Audiology 32:333–43.
19. Humes LE, LM Joellenbeck and JS Durch (2005) Noise and Military Service: Implications for Hearing Loss and Tinnitus. 2005: Institute of Medicine of the National Academies.
20. Møller MB, AR Møller, PJ Jannetta et al (1993) Vascular decompression surgery for severe tinnitus: Selection criteria and results. Laryngoscope 103:421–7.
21. De Ridder D and P Van de Heyning (2007) The Darwinian plasticity hypothesis for tinnitus and pain, in Tinnitus: Pathophysiology and Treatment, Progress in Brain Research, B Langguth et al, Editors. Elsevier: Amsterdam. 55–60.

Chapter 13
Neural Synchrony and Neural Plasticity in Tinnitus

Larry E. Roberts

Keypoints

1. Most individuals with chronic tinnitus have high-frequency hearing loss, induced by noise exposure, otological disease, or the aging process. Physiological evidence suggests that in such individuals, tinnitus is likely caused not by irritative processes that persist in the ear after cochlear injury, but by changes that occur in central auditory pathways when the ear is partly disconnected from the brain.

2. In animals, hearing loss induced by experimental noise trauma leads to a reorganization of tonotopic maps in the primary auditory cortex, such that frequencies near the edge of normal hearing come to be overrepresented at the expense of frequencies in the hearing loss region. Neurons show increased spontaneous firing rates in cortical and subcortical auditory structures, and in the auditory cortex, increased synchronous activity in the region of hearing impairment.

3. Evidence from physiological, psychoacoustic, and human brain imaging studies suggests that increased neural synchrony (temporally coupled neural activity) in the hearing loss region may be an important mechanism contributing to tinnitus. Tinnitus spectra and residual inhibition functions overlap the region of auditory threshold shift, consistent with this hypothesis.

4. Several forms of neural plasticity may contribute to changes in spontaneous firing rates and neural synchrony that develop after hearing loss. Because the tuning of auditory neurons can be modified by acoustic training procedures throughout the lifespan, it may be possible to reverse some of the neural changes underlying tinnitus.

5. For this goal to be achieved, it must be possible to modify auditory representations by acoustic training in individuals with tinnitus, and the neural modifications induced by training must intersect with the underlying tinnitus mechanisms. Auditory plasticity in normal hearing individuals and people with tinnitus requires further study.

Keywords Mechanism of tinnitus • Neural synchrony • Cortical reorganization • Neural plasticity • Tinnitus spectrum • Residual inhibition

Abbreviations

HL	Hearing level
CF	Center frequency
RI	Residual inhibition
ASSR	Auditory steady-state response
AM	Amplitude modulation
EEG	Electroencephalogram
MEG	Magnetoencephalography

Introduction

Although our understanding of the mechanisms of tinnitus comes from many sources, two recent lines of research, in particular, have provided insight into the question of how the sensation of tinnitus is generated. The first line of research has shown that hearing loss induced by noise exposure in animal models leads to a reorganization of tonotopic maps in the primary auditory cortex, such that frequencies near the edge of nor-

L.E. Roberts (✉)
Department of Psychology, Neuroscience, and Behavior,
McMaster University, 1280 Main Street West, Hamilton,
Ontario, Canada L8S 4K1
e-mail: roberts@mcmaster.ca

A.R. Møller et al. (eds.), *Textbook of Tinnitus*,
DOI 10.1007/978-1-60761-145-5_13, © Springer Science+Business Media, LLC 2011

mal hearing come to be overrepresented at the expense of frequencies in the hearing loss region [1–3]. Because hearing loss is a putative cause of tinnitus, it was suggested that this overrepresentation, or changes in neuron response properties associated with it, may underlie tinnitus percepts [4, 5]. The second line of research demonstrated that neural representations for sound in the primary auditory cortex are not fixed after early development but can be modified over the lifespan by procedures such as deafferentation or auditory training that alter the organism's experience with sound [6, 7]. This phenomenon is called "neural plasticity" (see Chap. 12). These two lines of research have converged to ask whether neural plasticity may be involved in the generation of tinnitus, and if so, whether acoustic training procedures might be designed to reduce tinnitus or prevent its development when hearing loss occurs.

This chapter reviews evidence from animal models of hearing loss, human psychoacoustic studies, and brain imaging experiments that suggests that tinnitus is generated by abnormal synchronous (temporally coupled) neural activity that develops in the auditory cortex when central auditory structures are deafferented by cochlear pathology. It is useful to formulate a perspective on the neural basis of tinnitus, because treatment procedures designed to reduce tinnitus must interact with this mechanism if tinnitus is to be altered. I also briefly review evidence for neural plasticity in the auditory system and ask whether the rules that describe auditory plasticity in normal hearing individuals apply as well to individuals with tinnitus. This cannot be assumed, because people with tinnitus experience not only some degree of hearing loss but also an auditory sensation that may interfere with the remodeling process. In a later chapter (Chap. 72), we discuss current approaches to sensory training from the perspective of research on these two questions.

The Neural Synchrony Model of Tinnitus

It is widely recognized that most individuals who have tinnitus also have sensorineural hearing loss caused by injury, otological disease, noise exposure, or the aging process. Even when auditory thresholds are in the normal range (≤25 dB HL), tinnitus sufferers often have evidence for restricted cochlear dead regions [8] or show threshold elevations in the audiogram on the order of 10 dB in the tinnitus frequency range compared

to age-matched controls [9] suggesting that some degree of hearing impairment is present. In most cases, however, it is doubtful that chronic tinnitus is generated by irritative processes that persist in the cochlea damaged by hearing loss. Damage to the cochlea caused by lesioning or noise exposure typically leads not to an increase in spontaneous activity in auditory nerve fibers, which might be expected from such processes, but rather to a decrease in auditory nerve activity, pointing to a reduction of input to central auditory structures [5]. These observations suggest that the sensation of tinnitus in the majority of individuals is generated not in the ear but by changes that have occurred in central auditory pathways when the brain has been partly disconnected from the ear by hearing loss (deprivation of input, see Chap. 11). Consistent with this understanding, most individuals who had tinnitus before removal of a vestibular schwannoma with sectioning of the auditory nerve also had tinnitus after the operation. Tinnitus is also a predictable outcome after sectioning of the auditory nerve in individuals who did not have tinnitus before their operations for vestibular schwannomas or other conditions [10] (see Chap. 39).

Animal models of hearing loss have begun to give a picture of the changes that occur in central auditory pathways following auditory deafferentation. The understanding supported by these studies is summarized in Fig. 13.1a (from [5]), which depicts the primary auditory cortex of a cat that has sustained a high-frequency hearing loss induced by noise trauma. The left side of the figure shows the undamaged region, including thalamocortical afferents synapsing on input neurons followed by feed-forward (i) and lateral (ii) inhibition after one synaptic delay. Feed-forward inhibition is functionally dissociable from lateral inhibition [11] and quenches target neurons after their depolarization, which may protect thalamocortical synapses from down-regulation (and preserve their cochleotopic tuning) when the neurons are driven by uncorrelated input from horizontal fibers in the tonotopic map. Animal studies have shown that when a region of the tonotopic map is disconnected from the ear by cochlear damage (right side of Fig. 13.1a), auditory neurons in the affected region begin to respond preferentially to input conveyed by horizontal fibers as their thalamocortical input is impaired or lost. As a consequence, the cortical tonotopic map "reorganizes" when the affected neurons begin to express the tuning preference of their neighbors, leading to an overrepresentation of edge frequencies in the tonotopic gradient

Fig. 13.1 Central effects of hearing loss in the cat. (**a**) Tonotopic map of primary auditory cortex depicting intact thalamocortical input to neurons in a low-frequency region (*left*) and diminished thalamocortical input to a high-frequency region affected by hearing loss (*right*). Neurons in the damaged region begin to express the tuning of their unaffected neighbors via horizontal fibers when their thalamocortical input is lost. Feed-forward (i) and lateral (ii) inhibition is depicted in the intact low-frequency region. Graphic from Eggermont and Roberts [5] (with permission). (**b**) Tonotopic representation in a normal cat (*solid line*) and in a cat with high-frequency hearing loss induced by noise trauma (*open circles*). The abscissa is transcortical distance from a reference point near the apex of the basilar membrane. An overrepresentation of edge frequencies is seen in the hearing impaired cat. Data from Rajan and Irvine [2] (with permission)

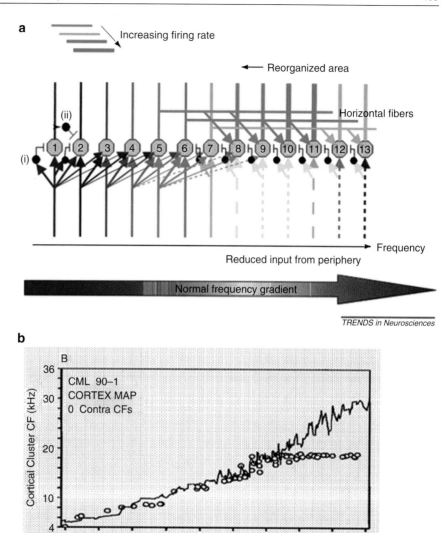

(an example is shown in Fig. 13.1b, from [2]). It has been proposed that this overrepresentation of edge frequencies may correspond to the tinnitus percept, which was thought to be confined to the edge of normal hearing. However, this is doubtful not only because of evidence to be presented below but also because it is not obvious how the activity of the affected neurons would be heard in terms other than their original cochleotopic tuning.

Other changes in the response properties of auditory neurons documented by animal studies of hearing loss are more likely to contribute to the tinnitus percept. One such change is that neurons in cortical and subcortical auditory structures (but not auditory nerve fibers) increase their spontaneous firing rates as input from the ear is diminished. This effect could reflect an

adaptive rescaling of neuron input/output functions by homeostatic plasticity [12] when afferent input to central auditory structures is impaired, or inhibitory deficits consequent on deafferentation, or most probably both factors. At the level of the cortex, increased spontaneous firing has been observed to occur across the tonotopic map, including tonotopic regions that are affected by hearing loss (typically high-frequency regions) as well as regions that are less affected (typically low-frequency regions). Increased spontaneous neural activity is likely to be an important factor in the development of tinnitus, although it has been suggested by several investigators that uncorrelated neural activity may not be sufficient to generate a coherent sound percept. A second change that may occur is an increase in the *temporally synchronous activity* of a population of neurons, which is expressed as an increase in cross-correlated neural firing when compared to control animals [13]. This change is more closely confined to the hearing loss region and appears to reflect synchronous network activity that is forged over lateral connections by neuroplastic mechanisms operating in this region [14], possibly because the quenching effect of feed-forward inhibition is lost. It should be noted that although thalamocortical input to the affected tonotopic region is affected by cochlear injury, the output of the synchronously active neurons remains intact. The neural synchrony model of tinnitus suggests that this output (which is conveyed to the thalamus by nerve fibers more numerous than the forward path) is processed by other brain regions and generates the tinnitus percept (see Chap. 12).

This picture of the neural mechanism of tinnitus has implications for the psychoacoustic properties of tinnitus. One implication is that when participants in a study are asked to rate sounds of different frequencies for similarly to their tinnitus, ratings should not be restricted to the region of the audiometric edge (although contrast enhancement at the edge may contribute [15]), but should instead span the region of hearing loss, increasing in proportion to the depth of hearing impairment. This result should be obtained for individuals with tonal tinnitus as well as tinnitus with wider bandwidths because audiometric function is similar among these tinnitus types [16]. Independent studies by laboratories in France [17], Canada [9], and New Zealand [18] have confirmed this prediction (see Fig. 13.2). A further implication is that post-masking suppression of tinnitus by band-limited noise maskers (called "residual inhibition," or RI, in the tinnitus literature) should increase proportionately as the center frequency (CF) of the masking sound enters the tinnitus frequency region. This is because these masking sounds (which are presented at intensity levels exceeding the hearing threshold and the tinnitus sound) should reinject feed-forward inhibition into the affected regions of the cortical tonotopic map, temporarily disrupting the synchronous activity underlying tinnitus and weakening the tinnitus percept. This prediction has also been confirmed (Fig. 13.2; from [9]). It should be noted that RI does not appear to be caused by habituation of the affected neurons to frequencies contained in the masker. On the contrary, these neurons are actually more easily driven by amplitude-modulated sounds presented to the tinnitus frequency region during RI than during tinnitus (see Fig. 13.3, from [19, 20]),

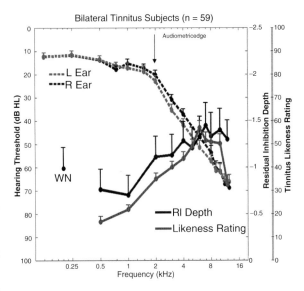

Fig. 13.2 Relation of the tinnitus spectrum (likeness rating) and the residual inhibition function (RI depth) to hearing loss in bilateral tinnitus ($n=59$ cases). To obtain the tinnitus spectrum, the participants rated the pitch of each of 11 sounds for its likeness to their tinnitus. A rating exceeding 40 corresponded to a sound that was beginning to resemble the tinnitus. Likeness ratings diminished at 12 kHz, probably because these sounds were not well matched for loudness owing to the depth of hearing loss at this frequency. RI was measured following presentation of band-limited noise maskers differing in center frequency (CF) (band pass ±15% of CF). A rating of −5 corresponded to "tinnitus gone." From Roberts et al. [9]

possibly because their capture by synchronous network activity underlying tinnitus has been disrupted. Rapid rescaling of subcortical auditory input to the frequencies contained in the masker could also contribute to this effect [21]. Other brain imaging results that support the neural synchrony model include evidence for (1) a degraded frequency (tonotopic) representation above ~2 kHz in the region of primary auditory cortex in individuals with tinnitus compared to controls [22] (this reorganization resembling that seen in animal models of hearing loss) and (2) increased spontaneous oscillatory brain activity in individuals with tinnitus [23]. The latter effect tracks the laterality of the tinnitus percept and may reflect augmented network underlying this condition.

As described here, the neural synchrony model accords an important role to the primary auditory cortex in the generation of tinnitus percepts. However, neuron response properties, including increased spontaneous activity and map reorganization, are also altered by hearing loss in subcortical auditory structures [24, 25], although neural synchrony in these regions has not yet

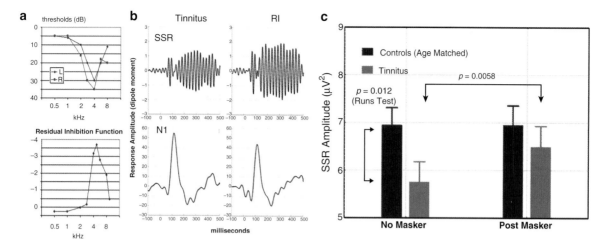

Fig. 13.3 Electromagnetic correlates of residual inhibition (RI). (**a**) Audiogram and corresponding RI function for a single individual with hearing loss around 4 kHz. A band-limited masker (±15% of CF) centered at 4 kHz in the notch region corresponded to the tinnitus sensation and gave good RI. This masker was used to induce RI in this individual in (**b**). (**b**) The brain response evoked by 4 kHz 40-Hz AM probe tones (duration 0.5 s) delivered after 30 s of masking when the person was experiencing RI (*top right* panel) or tinnitus (*top left* panel, no preceding masker). This brain response (called the 40-Hz auditory steady-state response or ASSR, measured here by magnetoencephaology [MEG]) localizes tonotopically to the region of the primary auditory cortex (see Fig. 13.4a) and gives a picture of neural activity occurring in this region (the 4-kHz region in this recording). The ASSR is larger in RI

compared to tinnitus (Roberts, Weisz, Wienbruch and Bosnyak, 2001, unpublished data). Unlike the ASSR, the N1-evoked response (localizing to secondary auditory cortex) adapted after masking (*lower* panel). (**c**) Subsequent research using electroencephalographic (EEG) recordings [19] found that enhancement of the ASSR after masking is specific to individuals with tinnitus ($n=14$, $p=0.0058$) and is not seen in age-matched controls ($n=14$, $p=0.99$). Without masking ASSR amplitude is reduced in tinnitus ($p=0.012$) returning toward normal levels after masking. Unlike the ASSR, the N1 adapted after masking ($p=0.007$, results not shown; cf. (**b**) *lower*). It should be noted that in (**c**), the probe stimulus (5 kHz) was matched for intensity to a 1-kHz 65-dB SL tone in the region of normal hearing (a procedure that controls for loudness recruitment in individuals with tinnitus)

been studied. Changes occurring in subcortical structures could be projected to the primary cortex and determine some of the effects seen there, as well as some distinct properties of tinnitus including its modulation by somatosensory inputs in many patients [26, 27]. Alternatively, the changes seen in subcortical nuclei could be sculpted by returning output from the auditory cortex, which may recruit a brain network supporting tinnitus percepts. Functional brain imaging studies have implicated several brain areas in tinnitus [28–31], including frontal and limbic areas that may subserve, respectively, the attentional and emotional aspects of tinnitus described by Jastreboff [32] in a comprehensive model of tinnitus published more than a decade ago.

These lines of evidence pointing to a role for neural synchrony in tinnitus have implications for how sensory training might best be conducted (see Chap. 72). The neural synchrony hypothesis implies that the goal of training should be to disrupt the synchronous neural activity believed to underlie tinnitus percepts.

When significant residual hearing is present (delivered by surviving on-target thalamocortical projections or thalamocortical radiations), this goal could be attempted by training suprathreshold sounds in the tinnitus frequency region. These sounds may reinject feed-forward inhibition into the tonotopic map and/or rescale neuron transfer functions in subcortical structures to represent the trained frequencies, thereby disrupting neural synchrony and strengthening thalamocortical synapses previously down-regulated by abnormal synchronous network behavior. Maskers that induce RI may operate in a similar fashion, although repeated induction of RI does not appear to convey a lasting benefit [33], at least in the absence of active auditory training. Alternatively, acoustic training in the region of normal hearing could convey uncorrelated inputs into the affected map region via lateral connections, disrupting neural synchrony or suppressing it by lateral inhibition. Before considering research on various approaches (see Chap. 72), it is useful to briefly consider what is known about how auditory remodeling works in individuals with normal hearing, and how it may contribute to the development of tinnitus.

Neuroplastic Remodeling in Tinnitus

A feature common to the neural synchrony model and the wider framework of Jastreboff [32] is a role for neural plasticity in the generation of tinnitus percepts. Although direct evidence is lacking and not easily procured, there are compelling reasons to propose a role for such mechanisms in tinnitus. Spike-timing-dependent plasticity [34] appears to be general property of cortical neurons, and this mechanism, acting in concert with increased spontaneous firing rates consequent on inhibitory deficits and homeostatic plasticity [12], would be expected to facilitate the formation of synchronous networks in regions of the primary auditory cortex affected by hearing loss. Synchronous activity appears to be expressed over cortical distances that exceed those expected from thalamocortical radiations, which implicates temporal coincidence mediated by horizontal fibers as a driving mechanism [14]. From the limited data available, it appears that cross-correlated activity develops within hours of hearing loss and grows over time [13], although the limit of this growth is not known. Neural plasticity has the potential to explain the variability that is seen in tinnitus percepts among affected individuals, with the addition of no new principles.

In the last 15 years, much has been learned about how neural plasticity remodels auditory representations in normal hearing animals. Experience with sound has a profound effect on tonotopic organization and the tuning properties of auditory neurons in the developing brain [35, 36] and after maturity as well [37, 38]. Neural modeling during development appears to be driven largely by the spectrotemporal statistics of the acoustic input, such that neural representations become tuned to the sounds present in the animal's environment. After maturity, top–down mechanisms begin to play an additional role, preferentially gating neural plasticity in the auditory cortex for sounds that are important for behavioral goals [6, 39]. Several response properties are affected by acoustic training in mature organisms, including shifts in the tuning preference of

auditory neurons toward the trained stimuli [6, 7], spike rates induced by these stimuli [40, 41], tuning bandwidth [42, 43], response latency in post-stimulus time histograms [41, 42], and tonotopic map expansions for the trained sounds [44]. However, passive immersion in a distinctive acoustic environment can still have profound effects on neuron response properties and neural organization in the adult brain [38], which may reflect, at least in part, changes in subcortical auditory nuclei that are driven unselectively by stimulus input. These broad principles derived from animal studies appear to be applicable to humans as well [45–48], although much remains to be discovered about the specific rules that guide remodeling in both domains and the mechanisms that underlie them.

Whether these principles apply as well to individuals with tinnitus is less well established. A brain response that is relevant to this question is the stimulus-driven "auditory steady-state response" (ASSR, shown earlier in Fig. 13.3b). This response is evoked in the electroencephalogram by sounds that are amplitude modulated (AM) near 40 Hz, localizes tonotopically to cortical sources in the region of primary auditory cortex, and gives a picture of changes occurring in or projecting to this region during auditory training (see Fig. 13.4a). In individuals with normal hearing, acoustic training to detect single pulses of enhanced amplitude in a 40-Hz AM 2 kHz sound of 1-s duration has been found to modify temporal population activity expressed in the primary auditory cortex. This effect is expressed as an advance in the phase of the ASSR, which reflects a reduction in the time delay between the 40-Hz response and stimulus waveforms (see Fig. 13.4b). The phase advance is a robust phenomenon that consolidates after 24–72 h, increases with continued training, relates perceptual performance, and does not require explicit behavioral training for its appearance [48]. ASSR amplitude is also increased by auditory training, implying more neurons depolarizing synchronously to represent the trained sound [48]. However, the training effect on ASSR amplitude lags that on phase, does not correlate well with perception, and is not observed when multiple sound frequencies are presented during training [49].

These results are from individuals with normal hearing who were studied in order to discover rules that guide remodeling in the human brain. What happens when individuals with tinnitus are trained? The answer to this question is presently not well established.

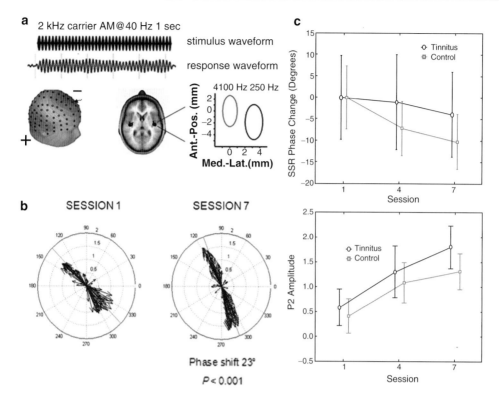

Fig. 13.4 Effects of auditory training on auditory-evoked potentials. (**a**) Response evoked by a 2-kHz tone amplitude modulated at 40 Hz (ASSR). The stimulus waveform and the response waveform recorded at electrode Cz are shown, together with the bipolar scalp topography (128 sensors). In inverse modeling, the cortical generators for an ASSR evoked by a carrier frequency of 4,100 Hz localized medial to those for an ASSR evoked by a carrier frequency of 250 Hz, in the region of primary auditory cortex. (**b**) Compass plots showing the amplitude (vector length) and phase (vector angle) of the ASSR at each of 128 sensors, before (*left* panel) and after (*right* panel) seven sessions of acoustic training. Individuals with normal hearing who did not have tinnitus ($n = 9$) were trained to detect a single 40-Hz AM pulse of enhanced amplitude in a stimulus of 1-s duration (carrier frequency 2 kHz). A phase shift of 23° was observed ($p < 0.001$, advance of the response waveform toward the stimulus waveform), but the amplitude enhancement did not reach significance. (**c**) *Upper* panel: The phase shift (over seven sessions of training) did not reach significance in the participants who had tinnitus ($p = 0.44$) but was present in their age-matched controls ($p = 0.006$). In both groups, the carrier frequency was 5 kHz (in the tinnitus frequency region of the individuals with tinnitus). Negative values indicate a shift of ASSR phase toward the stimulus waveform. *Lower* panel: The P2 transient-evoked response (latency ~180 ms) increased with training in both groups, suggesting that secondary auditory areas are remodeled normally in individuals who have tinnitus (cf. [49])

In a preliminary study [20], we found that while a group of control participants age matched to a tinnitus group showed the expected phase advance when trained on a 5-kHz 40-Hz AM sound ($n = 11, p = 0.006$), only two of eight participants with tinnitus did so, resulting in a nonsignificant group effect overall ($p = 0.44$, see Fig. 13.4c, upper panel). It is possible that synchronous neural activity underlying tinnitus may have obstructed or reset training effects in the primary auditory cortex of the participants who had tinnitus (5 kHz was chosen for study because it is in the tinnitus frequency range). However, remodeling of secondary auditory cortical areas appeared to be normal in those

who had tinnitus. The P2 (latency ~180 ms) auditory-evoked potential, which localizes to cortical sources in this region and is known to be highly plastic [49], showed a normal enhancement in both groups after auditory training (Fig. 13.4c, lower panel). Several other long latency (>100 ms) auditory evoked potentials localizing to secondary cortex or beyond are known to increase with acoustic training in the laboratory in normal hearing individuals (in order of increasing latency: N1 [50], N1c [49], Ta [51], P2 [47–49, 52], N2 [53], MMN [54]), or to be enhanced for musical sounds in trained musicians (N1c [55], P2 [55–57], anterior frontotemporal sources [58]), induced frontotemporal gamma oscillations [59]). These evoked potentials reveal a distributed neural system for auditory (and perhaps other) learning in the human brain that may overlap with neural structures involved in tinnitus. However, the behavior of the responses during acoustic training in tinnitus is unknown.

Most studies of human auditory learning have employed active training procedures in which adults attended to and processed the sound stimuli while making discriminative decisions. However, there is growing evidence that remodeling of equal magnitude occurs when the sounds are presented as background cues, even when individuals are engaged in watching a subtitled film and have no knowledge of auditory task structure [47, 48, 60]. The ASSR and P2 effects described above were remodeled equally by active training, compared to when the auditory stimuli were presented passively as background sounds to individuals with normal hearing [48]. Animals housed in distinctive sound environments with no processing demands also display significant auditory remodeling, even in adulthood [37, 38]. A working hypothesis based on animal data is that these effects are produced by a rescaling of neuron input/output transfer functions in subcortical auditory structures by fundamental mechanisms that are stimulus driven and expressed in the auditory cortex throughout the lifespan. Explicit auditory training may produce additional changes mediated by attention, but this more mature mechanism is not a prerequisite for remodeling. The fact that auditory representations are modified by passive as well as active exposure could be good news for tinnitus, to the extent that arduous training regimens may be avoided.

Overview and Conclusion

Animal research in the last two decades has established that neural plasticity is a fundamental property of neurons in the auditory system. Evidence has also accumulated that hearing loss leads to changes in central auditory pathways, including tonotopic map reorganization and increased neuron firing rates in primary auditory cortex that may be forged by neuroplastic mechanisms into abnormal synchronous network behavior that generates tinnitus. In this Chapter, I have summarized physiological, psychoacoustic, and brain imaging evidence pointing to a role for neural synchrony in tinnitus.

Also reviewed were results from animal research indicating that cortical representations for sound in the primary auditory cortex are not fixed after early development as was once believed, but can be modified by auditory training well into adulthood. The findings have spawned renewed research into the question of whether tinnitus can be reduced or eliminated by acoustic training designed to normalize aberrant auditory neural representations. For this goal to be achieved, it must be possible to modify auditory representations by acoustic training in individuals with tinnitus, and the neural modifications induced by training must intersect with tinnitus mechanisms. Preliminary research suggests that areas of secondary auditory cortex remodel normally in individuals with tinnitus compared to normal controls, although whether this is true of the primary auditory cortex requires further study.

Acknowledgments The research of the author reported herein was supported by grants from the Canadian Institutes for Health Research, the Natural Sciences and Engineering Research Council of Canada, the American Tinnitus Association, and the Tinnitus Research Initiative. I thank my colleague Daniel Bosnyak for his role and Phillip Gander, Victoria Mosher, Graeme Moffat, and David Thompson for their contributions.

References

1. Robertson D, DRF Irvine (1989) Plasticity of frequency organization in auditory cortex of guinea pigs with partial unilateral deafness. J. Comp. Neurol. 282:456–461.
2. Rajan R, DRF Irvine (1998) Neuronal responses across cortical field A1 in plasticity induced by peripheral auditory organ damage. Audiol. Neuro Otol. 3:123–144.
3. Noreña AJ, M Tomita, JJ Eggermont (2003) Neural changes in cat auditory cortex after a transient pure-tone trauma. J. Neurophysiol. 90:2387–2401.
4. Rauschecker JP (1999) Auditory cortical plasticity: a comparison with other sensory systems. Trends Neurosci. 22:74–80.
5. Eggermont JJ, LE Roberts (2004) The neuroscience of tinnitus. Trends Neurosci. 27:676–682.
6. Fritz J, M Elhilali, S Shamma (2005) Active listening: task-dependent plasticity of spectrotemporal receptive fields in primary auditory cortex. Hear. Res. 206:159–176.
7. Weinberger NM (2007) Auditory associative memory and representational plasticity in the primary auditory cortex. Hear. Res. 229:54–68.
8. Weisz N, T Hartmann, K Dohrmann et al (2006) High-frequency tinnitus without hearing loss does not mean absence of deafferentation. Hear. Res. 222:108–114.

9. Roberts LE, G Moffat, M Baumann et al (2008) Residual inhibition functions overlap tinnitus spectra and the region of auditory threshold shift. J. Assoc. Res. Otolaryngol. 9:417–435.

10. House JW, DE Brackman (1981) Tinnitus: surgical treatment. Ciba Found. Symp. 85:204–216.

11. Rajan R (2001) Plasticity of excitation and inhibition in the receptive field of primary auditory cortical neurons after limited receptor organ damage. Cereb. Cortex. 11:171–182.

12. Turrigiano GG, SB Nelson (2004) Homeostatic plasticity in the developing nervous system. Nat. Rev. Neurosci. 5:97–107.

13. Noreña AJ, JJ Eggermont (2003) Changes in spontaneous neural activity immediately after an acoustic trauma: implications for neural correlates of tinnitus. Hear. Res. 183:137–153.

14. Eggermont JJ (2007) Correlated neural activity as the driving force for functional changes in auditory cortex. Hear. Res. 229:69–80.

15. Llinás R, FJ Urbano, E Leznik et al (2005) Rhythmic and dysrhythmic thalamocortical dynamics: GABA systems and the edge effect. Trends Neurosci. 28:325–333.

16. Roberts LE, G Moffat, DJ Bosnyak (2006) Residual inhibition functions in relation to tinnitus spectra and auditory threshold shift. Acta Otolaryngol. Suppl. 556:27–33.

17. Noreña A, C Micheyl, S Chéry-Croze, L Collet (2002) Psychoacoustic characterization of the tinnitus spectrum: implications for the underlying mechanisms of tinnitus. Audiol. Neurootol. 7:358–369.

18. Kay F (2008) Towards improving the assessment of tinnitus pitch. Section of Audiology, Faculty of Medical and Health Sciences, University of Auckland.

19. Bosnyak DJ, PE Gander, LE Roberts (2008) The 40-Hz auditory steady-state response in tinnitus tracks age-related deficits in intracortical inhibition but does not follow the tinnitus percept. Annual Meeting of the Society for Neuroscience 2008. Washington: Society of Neuroscience 2008 Planner 850.13.

20. Roberts LE, DJ Bosnyak (2010) Neural synchrony and neural plasticity in tinnitus. In: Searchfield GD, Goodey R Editors. Proceedings of Tinnitus Discovery: Asia-Pacific Tinnitus Symposium. N Z Med J. 123:39–50.

21. Dean I, NS Harper, D McAlpine (2005) Neural population coding of sound level adapts to stimulus statistics. Nat. Neurosci. 8:1684–1689.

22. Wienbruch C, I Paul, N Weisz et al (2006) Frequency organization of the 40-Hz auditory steady-state response in normal hearing and in tinnitus. Neuroimage. 33:180–194.

23. Weisz N, S Muller, W Schlee et al (2007) The neural code of auditory phantom perception. J. Neurosci. 27:1479–1484.

24. Finlayson PG, JA Kaltenbach (2009) Alterations in the spontaneous discharge patterns of single units in the dorsal cochlear nucleus following intense sound exposure. Hear. Res. doi:10.1016.

25. Zeng C, N Nannapaneni, J Zhou et al (2009) Cochlear damage causes changes in the distribution of vesicular glutamate transporters associated with auditory and nonauditory inputs to the cochlear nucleus. J. Neurosci. 29:4210–4217.

26. Cacace AT (2003) Expanding the biological basis of tinnitus: crossmodal origins and the role of neuroplasticity. Hear. Res. 175:112–132.

27. Shore SE, S Koehler, M Oldakowski, LF Hughes, S Syed (2008) Dorsal cochlear nucleus responses to somatosensory stimulation are enhanced after noise-induced hearing loss. Eur. J. Neurosci. 27:155–168.

28. Lockwood AH, MA Wack, RF Burkard et al (2001) The functional anatomy of gaze-evoked tinnitus and sustained lateral gaze. Neurology. 56:472–480.

29. Mühlau M, JP Rauschecker, E Oestreicher et al (2006) Structural brain changes in tinnitus. Cereb. Cortex. 16:1283–1288.

30. Lanting CP, E de Kleine, P van Dijk (2009) Neural activity underlying tinnitus generation: Results from PET and fMRI. Hear. Res. 255:1–13.

31. Schlee W, T Hartmann, B Langguth et al (2009) Abnormal resting-state cortical coupling in chronic tinnitus. BMC Neurosci. doi:10.1186/1471-2202-10-11.

32. Jastreboff PJ (1995) Tinnitus as a phantom perception: Theories and clinical applications. In: Vernon J, Moeller AR, editors. Mechanisms of Tinnitus Boston, MA: Allyn and Bacon, pp 73–94.

33. Terry AMP, DM Jones, BR Davis, R Slater (1983) Parametric studies of tinnitus masking and residual inhibition. Br. J. Audiol. 17:245–256.

34. Markram H, J Lübke, M Frotscher et al (1997) Regulation of synaptic efficacy by coincidence of postsynaptic APs and EPSPs. Science. 275:213–215.

35. Zhang LI, S Bao, MM Merzenich (2001) Persistent and specific influences of early acoustic environments on primary auditory cortex. Nat. Neurosci. 4:1123–1130.

36. de Villers-Sidani E, KL Simpson, YF Lu et al (2008) Manipulating critical period closure across different sectors of the primary auditory cortex. Nat. Neurosci. 11:957–965.

37. Stanton SG, RV Harrison (1996) Abnormal cochleotopic organization in the auditory cortex of cats reared in a frequency augmented environment. Aud. Neurosci. 2:97–107.

38. Pienkowski M, JJ Eggermont (2009) Long-term, partially-reversible reorganization of frequency tuning in mature cat primary auditory cortex can be induced by passive exposure to moderate-level sounds. Hear. Res. doi:10.1026/j.hearres 2009.07.011.

39. Weinberger NM (2007) Associative representational plasticity in the auditory cortex: a synthesis of two disciplines. Learn. Mem. 14:1–16.

40. Blake DT, F Strata, AK Churchland, MM Merzenich (2002) Neural correlates of instrumental learning in primary auditory cortex. Proc. Natl. Acad. Sci. USA. 99:10114–10119.

41. Kilgard MP, MM Merzenich (2002) Order-sensitive plasticity in adult primary auditory cortex. Proc. Natl. Acad. Sci. USA. 99:3205–3209.

42. Brown M, DR Irvine, VN Park (2004) Perceptual learning on an auditory frequency discrimination task by cats: association with changes in primary auditory cortex. Cereb. Cortex. 14:952–965.

43. Kilgard MP, PK Pandya, J Vazquez, A Gehi, CE Schreiner, MM Merzenich (2001) Sensory input directs spatial and temporal plasticity in primary auditory cortex. J. Neurophysiol. 86:326–338.

44. Recanzone GH, CE Schreiner, MM Merzenich (1993) Plasticity in the frequency representation of primary auditory cortex following discrimination training in adult owl monkeys. J. Neurosci. 13:87–103.

45. Kuhl PK (2004) Early language acquisition: cracking the speech code. Nat. Rev. 5:831–843.

46. Alain C, JS Snyder, Y He et al (2007) Changes in auditory cortex parallel rapid perceptual learning. Cereb. Cortex. 17:1074–1084.

47. Sheehan KA, GM McArthur, DV Bishop (2005) Is discrimination training necessary to cause changes in the P2 auditory

event-related brain potential to speech sounds? Brain Res. Cogn. Brain Res. 25:547–553.

48. Gander PE, DJ Bosnyak, LE Roberts (2010) Acoustic experience but not attention modifies neural population phase expressed in human primary auditory cortex. Hear. Res. do1:10.1016 (on-line ahead of print).

49. Bosnyak DJ, RA Eaton, LE Roberts (2004) Distributed auditory cortical representations are modified by training at pitch discrimination with 40-Hz amplitude modulated tones. Cereb. Cortex. 14:1088–l099.

50. Okamoto H, H Stracke, O Thiede, C Pantev (2009) Listening to tailor-made notched music reduces tinnitus loudness and tinnitus-related auditory cortex activity. Proc. Natl. Acad. Sci. USA doi:10.1073/pnas.0911268107.

51. Alain C, JS Snyder, Y He, KS Reinke (2007) Changes in auditory cortex parallel rapid perceptual learning. Cereb. Cortex. 17:1074–1084.

52. Tremblay K, N Kraus, T McGee, C Ponton, B Otis (2001) Central auditory plasticity: changes in the N1-P2 complex after speech-sound training. Ear. Hear. 22:79–90.

53. Fujioka T, B Ross, R Kakigi, C Pantev, LJ Trainor (2006) One year of musical training affects development of auditory cortical-evoked fields in young children. Brain. 129:2593–608.

54. Menning H, LE Roberts, C Pantev (2000) Plastic changes in the auditory cortex induced by intensive frequency discrimination training. Neuroreport. 11:817–822.

55. Shahin A, DJ Bosnyak, LJ Trainor, LE Roberts (2003) Enhancement of neuroplastic P2 and N1c auditory evoked potentials in musicians. J. Neurosci. 23:5545–5552.

56. Shahin A, LE Roberts, LJ Trainor (2004) Enhancement of auditory cortical development by musical experience in children. Neuroreport. 15:1917–1921.

57. Kuriki S, S Kanda, Y Hirata (2006) Effects of musical experience on different components of MEG responses elicited by sequential piano-tones and chords. J. Neurosci. 26:4046–4053.

58. Shahin AJ, LE Roberts, C Pantev, M Aziz, TW Picton (2007) Enhanced anterior-temporal processing for complex tones in musicians. Clin. Neurophysiol. 118:209–220.

59. Shahin AJ, LE Roberts, W Chau, LJ Trainor, LM Miller (2008) Music training leads to the development of timbre-specific gamma band activity. Neuroimage. 41:113–122.

60. Ross B, K Tremblay (2009) Stimulus experience modifies auditory neuromagnetic responses in young and older listeners. Hear. Res. 248:48–59.

Chapter 14
Similarities Between Tinnitus and Pain

Aage R. Møller

Keypoints

1. Both pain and tinnitus have many different forms.
2. Tinnitus and central neuropathic pain are phantom sensations similar to the phantom limb symptoms that occur without any physical stimulation of sensory receptors.
3. Tinnitus and neuropathic pain are typical examples of "plasticity disorders" where the symptoms are caused by plastic changes that are not beneficial to an individual person.
4. Central neuropathic pain and tinnitus have no physical signs.
5. The severity of pain and tinnitus are difficult to assess quantitatively even under laboratory circumstances. Only the patients' own perception is a true measure of the severity of central pain and subjective tinnitus.
6. The perception of pain and tinnitus is affected by many factors such as actual circumstances, expectation, stress, and a person's emotional state.
7. Many forms of pain are best described as suffering; the same is the case for severe subjective tinnitus.
8. Pain and tinnitus can have strong emotional components, it often prevents or disturbs sleep, and it can interfere with or prevent intellectual work.
9. It is difficult to get reliable data on epidemiology of tinnitus and central neuropathic pain because of their subjective nature and large variability.
10. Activation of neural plasticity is involved in causing and maintaining central neuropathic pain and many forms of subjective tinnitus.
11. The nervous system is the site of the anomalies that cause central neuropathic pain and many forms of tinnitus. Both tinnitus and pain involve a cascade of neural structures.
12. The pathology of the nervous system in some forms of central neuropathic pain is stable in the pathologic state. It may be similar for some forms of tinnitus.
13. Pain that is perceived as escapable uses a different part of the periaquadctal gray than pain that is perceived as inescapable. It is not known if tinnitus also has such distinctions.
14. Severe tinnitus is often accompanied by hyperacusis (lowered tolerance to sounds); pain may be accompanied by allodynia (pain from normally innocuous touch of the skin) hyperpathia (exaggerated reaction to acute pain), and hypersensitivity (lowered threshold for painful stimulation).
15. Some forms of tinnitus and pain can be modulated by electrical stimulation of the skin.
16. Electrical stimulation of several cortical structures can modulate both pain and tinnitus.
17. The sympathetic nervous system can modulate pain and some forms of tinnitus.

Keywords Tinnitus • Pain • Central neuropathic pain • Hyperacusis • Allodynia

Abbreviations

DCN	Dorsal cochlear nucleus
NST	Nucleus of the tractus solitaries
PAG	Periaquadctal gray
TENS	Transderm electrical nerve stimulation
VCN	Ventral cochlear nucleus
WDR	Wide dynamic range neurons

A.R. Møller (✉)
The University of Texas at Dallas, School of Behavioral
and Brain Sciences, GR 41, 800 W Campbell Rd,
Richardson, TX 75080, USA
e-mail: amoller@utdallas.edu

A.R. Møller et al. (eds.), *Textbook of Tinnitus*,
DOI 10.1007/978-1-60761-145-5_14, © Springer Science+Business Media, LLC 2011

Introduction

It was Jürgen Tonndorf [1] who first drew attention to the similarities between tinnitus and pain. Other investigators have later elaborated on the many similarities between tinnitus and severe chronic pain (central neuropathic pain) [2–5]. Activation of neural plasticity is involved and both are examples of "plasticity diseases" [6]. Pain gets far more attention than tinnitus. The fifth edition of the Wall and Melzack's Textbook of Pain has over 1,200 pages; Weiner's Pain Management has over 1,500 pages. Textbooks devoted to tinnitus are essentially non-existent (this book is the first textbook on tinnitus). The research literature on pain is far greater than that on tinnitus; a search in PubMed came up with approximately 400,000 articles about pain vs. approximately 6,000 for tinnitus. Literature about hyperacusis and phonophobia is sparse.

Many forms of tinnitus have similarities with central neuropathic pain, in that activation of neural plasticity is involved in creating the symptoms. Central neuropathic pain is a particular condition where the symptoms are caused by abnormal activity in populations of neurons in the spinal cord and brain that occurs without signals from receptors in the body.

Subjective tinnitus and central neuropathic pain are phantom sensations where the sensations are not elicited by activation of receptors. Central neuropathic pain and some forms of tinnitus are symptoms with very few, if any, objective signs. Despite that, both central neuropathic pain [7] and severe tinnitus [8] can affect a person's entire life, the entire family, as well as social and working relationships. Both these disorders may prevent or disturb sleep and interfere with intellectual work. There are examples of people who like their work but retire because of tinnitus.

Other similarities include the lack of effective treatment, diverse etiology, and sparse knowledge about the anatomical and physiologic bases for these disorders. The treatments a patient with either one of these disorders may receive depend on the specialty of the physician they choose to consult, and the specific interest of the physician or surgeon. In only a few forms of central neuropathic pain and tinnitus can any underlying disease be found.

There are many forms of tinnitus and many forms of pain. Some common forms of pain such as headache and back pain can be managed by simple analgesics. No such general treatment is known for tinnitus. Peripheral neuropathic pain, migraine, and fibromyalgia are complex pain conditions that have less satisfactory treatments. Central neuropathic pain can often be managed by medication. Brain and spinal cord injuries can cause both pain and tinnitus that are difficult to treat.

A separate chapter (Chap. 15) describes the basic anatomy and physiology of pain. Here, we will discuss the similarities between some forms of subjective tinnitus and central neuropathic pain, both being phantom sensations, with activation of neural plasticity playing a central role in their cause. The similarities between treatment of pain and tinnitus are discussed in chapter 94.

Common Features of Subjective Tinnitus and Central Pain

Both central neuropathic pain [9, 10] and subjective tinnitus [11] have many different forms (see Chap. 2). Different forms of disorders with the same name cause difficulties in studying their pathologies and treatments. It would be more appropriate to consider both central and subjective tinnitus as groups of different disorders rather than a single disorder.

Most forms of subjective tinnitus and central neuropathic pain are phantom sensations, which mean that the symptoms are not caused by physical stimulation, but are similar to symptoms that occur after amputations. This is known as phantom limb syndrome, where pain and other sensations are felt as if coming from the limb that no longer exists [12]. The symptoms of many forms of tinnitus and central neuropathic pain are felt as coming from a different anatomical location than the actual pathology and physiological anomaly that cause the symptoms. The anatomical locations of the pathologies of most forms of central pain and most forms of tinnitus are in the brain, although the pain is often referred to a specific part of the body. This is well known from studies of central pain and it is also evident from some observations regarding tinnitus. Tinnitus is often referred to the ear, although tinnitus may occur in deaf people and after severance of the auditory nerve, thus similar to the pain that is felt as coming from an amputated leg. Neural plasticity activated by the absence of input from receptors in an amputated limb is the main cause of the phantom limb syndrome.

Some forms of tinnitus are caused by deprivation of auditory inputs as evidenced from the fact that tinnitus can be caused by middle ear disorders (see Chap. 34) and disappears when sound conduction to the ear is restored, either by treating the conductive pathology such as otosclerosis or by a hearing aid (see Chaps. 56 and 76) or cochlear implants (see Chap. 77). Many people get tinnitus when placed in a silent environment [13].

Neural plasticity plays an important role in creating central tinnitus and central pain, and activation of neural plasticity also plays a role in tinnitus that is caused by pathology in the ear and in acute pain caused by stimulation of nociceptors.

Both tinnitus and central neuropathic pain are examples of harmful effects of plastic changes, thus forms of "plasticity disorders" [6] caused by neural plasticity going awry. Activation of such maladaptive neural plasticity causes abnormal neural activity and re-routing of information. Activation of neural plasticity is involved in many forms of subjective tinnitus and central neuropathic pain as has been discussed in other parts of this book (see Chaps 10 and 15). The way plasticity is turned on is often unknown and probably more complex than what it is for creating phantom limb symptoms.

Both pain and tinnitus can cause suffering; that may be a different condition than tinnitus and pain that does not cause suffering. Tinnitus that causes suffering, or is "bothersome" [14], may activate other neural circuits than tinnitus that does not have these qualities. It has been shown that pain that is "escapable" and pain that is perceived as being "inescapable" activate different parts of a neural structure, the periaquaductal gray (PAG) [15], and different parts of the hypothalamus and midbrain [16].

Peripheral processes can contribute to the initiation of chronic neuropathic pain as well as many forms of tinnitus. Peripheral and central sensitization have been shown to play an important role in the creation of hyperactivity that is the cause of central neuropathic pain [9, 10]. The same is probably the case for tinnitus, although it has not been studied to the same extent as pain [17]. The fact that different mechanisms can initiate processes that result in changes in the central nervous system that cause many forms of tinnitus may explain some of the differences in the symptoms that patients experience [9, 18]. The same is the case for central pain.

Another similarity between tinnitus and pain is that the severity of these disorders cannot be substantiated by objective tests. Even health care professionals may sometimes misjudge the severity of these diseases. Individuals with tinnitus as well as individuals with pain have no attributes of illness and therefore do not attract much attention and sympathy. Relatives and friends may doubt the seriousness of their diseases. In the absence of objective test results, health professionals may even sometimes think that their patients may be malingering. This makes both tinnitus and central pain disorders some of the most challenging disorders for clinicians.

Prevalence of Central Pain and Tinnitus

One of the problems in getting reliable epidemiologic data is similar for pain and tinnitus, namely that the definition of the severity varies among individuals with these conditions. These problems are greater for central neuropathic pain than other neuropathic pain conditions, and it is greater for tinnitus than for other hearing disorders, such as hearing loss from exposure to noise (see Chap. 37), which have been studied extensively as has age-related hearing loss (presbycusis) (see Chap. 36). No reliable information about the epidemiology of central neuropathic pain is available, nor is the prevalence of other chronic pain conditions such as peripheral neuropathic pain that commonly occurs in individuals with diabetes neuropathy completely known [18, 19].

The prevalence of chronic neuropathic pain may be greater than commonly assumed and its prevalence is likely to increase in the future. This is very similar to tinnitus, where the prevalence seems to increase. The prevalence of both central pain and tinnitus increases after middle age, which means that age-related changes add to the factors that cause tinnitus and pain (see Chap. 36).

Tinnitus is estimated to effect 13–20% of the overall population of the United States [20]. These complaints, often associated with hearing loss, increase with age to 27–34% of the population older than 70 years reporting significant tinnitus [21]. Twenty percent to 45% of tinnitus sufferers also have hyperacusis; a few individuals only have hyperacusis [22] (see also Chap. 5).

One reason for the increased incidence of tinnitus is the increased occurrence of head injuries (see Chap. 67), which also is associated with pain conditions. From 10 to 30% of people with spinal cord injuries have central pain. Individuals with head injuries often have central pain and tinnitus [23, 24] (see Chap. 67). After strokes, 1–8% have central pain [19, 25].

The prevalence of post-surgical neuropathic pain has been estimated to be 2–3% of the population in the developed world [18]. This problem is poorly recognized. Equally poorly recognized is postoperative tinnitus. It occurs often after surgical removal of vestibular schwannoma where the concerns are about preserving facial function and hearing, which has improved after introduction of intraoperative neurophysiologic monitoring [26]. However, little is known about how to reduce the risk of tinnitus.

Neuroanatomical Similarities Between Tinnitus and Pain

The neuroanatomy of hearing and pain has many similarities. The neural pathways for acute pain have similarities with the classical and non-classical ascending auditory pathways. The medial tract of the spinothalamic system may be regarded as the non-classical pathways of the somatosensory system (see Chap. 15). The fibers of the lateral spinothalamic tract terminate in neurons in the ventral thalamus corresponding to the classical pathway, whereas the medial spinothalamic tract terminates in the dorsal and medial thalamus and thus resembles the non-classical pathways of other sensory systems. The lateral spinothalamic tract provides information about the location of the pain and the medial tract provides information about the nature of the pain (see Chap. 15).

The medial and dorsal thalamus have subcortical connections to several regions of the brain, such as the limbic system, and the neurons in the cortical projections of the dorsal thalamus bypass the primary somatosensory cortex. These neurons terminate directly on neurons in the secondary and association cortices while the classical pathways project to primary cortices.

Functional Similarities Between Pain and Tinnitus

Tinnitus has similarities with several characteristics of central neuropathic pain. Repeating painful stimulations

causes increasing intensity of pain, known as the "wind up" phenomenon [27]. When a noxious stimulation is repeated at a short interval, the pain from the second presentation feels stronger. This is thus a form of abnormal temporal integration of painful stimulation. In other studies, it has been shown that temporal integration of pain signals is different in individuals with signs of neuropathic pain and individuals without central neuropathic pain [28].

A few similar studies have been done regarding temporal integration of sound in individuals with tinnitus [29], but animal experiments indicate that strong sound stimulation changes the temporal integration in the inferior colliculus as assessed using evoked potential techniques [30].

Sensitization and Modulation of Pain and Tinnitus

It is well known that peripheral and central sensitization can play important roles in creation of pain. Together with re-organization of neural circuits, this is regarded as the cause of central neuropathic pain. Evidence is accumulating that similar processes affecting the auditory system may play important roles in some forms of tinnitus.

Peripheral Sensitization

There are several ways in which peripheral sensitization of receptors in the body and the ear can contribute to pain and tinnitus. One way is through activation of the sympathetic nervous system, which can cause sympathetic nerve fibers that terminate near receptors to secrete norepinephrine, which increases the sensitivity of the receptors. Epinephrine secreting nerve fibers have been identified near receptors in the skin and close to the receptors (hair cells) in the cochlea [31]. Thus, the fact that sympathectomy is an effective treatment for tinnitus when it is a symptom of Ménière's disease [32] indicates that the sympathetic nervous system is involved in at least the kind of tinnitus that occurs in Ménière's disease.

The sympathetic nervous system may even activate the receptors without external stimulation, so they send information to the nervous system similar to when normal stimulation of the receptors occurs with physical stimuli. The most extreme of such sympathetically induced pain is reflex sympathetic dystrophy (RSD), now known as complex regional pain syndrome type I [33].

Central Sensitization

Certain kinds of neurons in the dorsal horn of the spinal cord (and the trigeminal nucleus), known as the wide dynamic range (WDR) neurons, are believed to have important roles in central sensitization of pain circuits ([9, 34, 35], see also [36]). Activation of neural plasticity that can change synaptic efficacy also plays an important factor in creating the abnormal states of the neural circuits in the dorsal horn associated with central pain [37] (see Chap. 15).

Activation of neural plasticity in the neural circuits of the dorsal horn is important because it can change the excitability of neurons (central sensitization) and re-route information by making dormant synapses become active [38]. Also, it can make synapses that are normally active become dormant.

It has been hypothesized that reorganization of the neural circuits in the spinal cord plays an important role for creation and maintaining central neuropathic pain. Doubell has proposed that the pain circuits in the dorsal horn of the spinal cord (and the trigeminal nucleus) can operate in four main different states [34] (see Chap. 15).

Similar hypotheses may apply to some forms of tinnitus, but hypotheses about the pathology of tinnitus are less uniform and less detailed. Studies in animals in which tinnitus conditions were induced by deprivation of input to the auditory system [39] or by overstimulation [40] have shown evidence that some neurons in the inferior colliculus have the ability to change their function in a similar way as the WDR neurons.

Interaction Between Sensory Systems

The old concept that certain functions of the brain are done in specific parts of the brain has gradually been eroded. It has become more and more evident that considerable interaction between many systems in the brain and the spinal cord occurs normally, as well as in diseases where certain interactions have adverse and harmful effects. It was earlier regarded as an axiom that the information from the different sense organs was processed in specific and separate parts of the brain.

Anatomical Aspects

We have discussed in Chap. 10 how somatosensory signals can interfere with hearing when the non-classical auditory pathways are active such as it is in children [41] and in some individuals with tinnitus [42]. This can occur in two different ways. One way is through connections that neurons in the dorsal column nuclei and the trigeminal nucleus make with neurons in the dorsal cochlear nucleus (DCN) [43–45] (see Chap. 9). The other way is through activation of the non-classical ascending auditory pathways, which receive input from other senses through connections to the inferior colliculus [46] (see Chap. 8).

Physiologic Signs of Cross-Modal Interaction

Certain anomalies of sensory systems in individuals with central pain have similarities with anomalies that occur in connection with some forms of tinnitus. One such anomaly is cross-modal sensory interaction, which means that the perception of one sensory modality can be affected by stimulation of another sense.

It has been known for a long time that acute pain sensations elicited by stimulation of pain receptors can be modulated by stimulation of nerve fibers, which innervate receptors that mediate innocuous sensory stimuli (touch, etc.). This is a normal phenomenon involving Aβ fibers in the spinal cord, which have inhibitory influence on cells that receive nocuous input from pain receptors (Fig. 14.1). This fact is used in treatment of pain, using electrical stimulation of the skin. This method is in routine use under the name of transderm electrical nerve stimulation (TENS) [47], and it has shown effectiveness for acute pain [48] as well as central pain [49]. It relies of stimulation of large sensory fibers, which can have an inhibitory influence on pain cells in the spinal cord and activate neural plasticity and thereby is effective in reducing pain not caused by activation of pain receptors (central neuropathic pain).

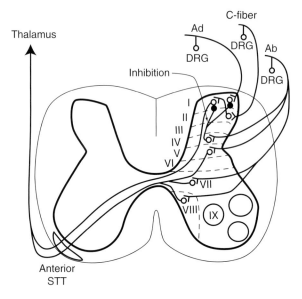

Fig. 14.1 Schematic illustration of the connections through which innocuous sensory input mediated by large myelinated (Aβ) fibers can inhibit pain neurons in lamina I that receive noxious input from Aδ fiber and C fibers via interneurons and which give rise to axons of the STT. Reproduced from: Møller AR (2006) Neural plasticity and disorders of the nervous system. Cambridge: Cambridge University Press, with permission by Cambridge University Press [9]

Modulation of tinnitus by activation of the somatosensory system [50, 51] has been demonstrated by electrical stimulation of the median nerve at the wrist [42], manipulation of neck muscles [52, 53], from temporomandibular problems [54, 55], and from changing one's gaze [50, 56, 57]. Functional imaging studies indicate that gaze-evoked tinnitus is caused by neural activity associated with eye movements that enters the auditory system [58]. These effects seem to be mediated through cross-modal interaction between the auditory system and the somatosensory system.

The anatomical and physiologic bases for these interactions are not as well known as the modulation of pain by somatosensory stimulation. Electrical stimulation of the skin around the ears can modulate tinnitus in some individuals [59] (see Chap. 91), and there are two different theories to explain this. One hypothesis states that sensory cells in these areas of the skin activate axons that become parts of dorsal spinal root C_2, which terminate on cells in the brainstem [60] (DCN and VCN) (See Chap. 9). Some of the axons from these cells terminate on cells in the dorsal cochlear nucleus (DCN) [43, 61]. Other studies have implicated the DCN in some forms of tinnitus [62, 63] (see Chap. 8).

The other way that somatic stimulation can affect the auditory system is through the non-classical ascending auditory pathways [64]. The non-classical auditory pathways receive input not only from the ear but also from other sensory systems such as the somatosensory system [45, 46] (see Chap. 8).

A different kind of interaction on pain [65] and possibly tinnitus is that from the vagus nerve. Earlier, little attention was paid to the vagus nerve; the focus has been on the motor functions of the vagus nerve. However, approximately 80% of the nerve fibers are afferent fibers. The discovery that electrical stimulation of the vagus nerve could treat epilepsy renewed the attention to the vagus nerve. Electrical stimulation of the vagus nerve is an approved treatment for epilepsy in the US [66] and is in clinical use for controlling epileptic seizures. Electrical stimulation has also been used for treatment of depression.

Electrical stimulation of the left vagus nerve has been shown to suppress some forms of pain [65] (see Chap. 94), and research is now aimed at other applications such as treatment of depression and control of severe tinnitus.

Afferent vagus nerve fibers terminate in the nucleus of the tractus solitaries (NST), which connect to many parts of the brain. The vagus nerve supplies cholinergic input to many structures in ways that have similarities to that of the basal nucleus of Meynert, which provides arousal and promote cortical plasticity [67, 68].

Central neuropathic pain is often associated with allodynia (pain from light touch stimulation). This may be similar to the rarely reported perception of sound by rubbing the skin, such as by a towel.

References

1. Tonndorf J (1987) The analogy between tinnitus and pain: a suggestion for a physiological basis of chronic tinnitus. Hear Res 28:271–5.
2. Møller AR (1997) Similarities between chronic pain and Tinnitus. Am J Otol 18:577–85.
3. Møller AR (2000) Similarities between severe tinnitus and chronic pain. J Amer Acad Audiol 11:115–24.
4. Folmer RL, SE Griest and WH Martin (2001) Chronic tinnitus as phantom auditory pain. Otolaryngol Head Neck Surg 124:394–400.
5. Bartels H, MJ Staal and FW Albers (2007) Tinnitus and neural plasticity of the brain. Otol Neurotol 28:178–84.
6. Møller AR (2008) Neural Plasticity: for Good and Bad. Progress of Theoretical Physics Supplement No 173:48–65.

7. Closs SJ, V Staples, I Reid et al (2009) The impact of neuropathic pain on relationships. J Adv Nurs 65:402–11.

8. Shipton E (2008) Post-surgical neuropathic pain. ANZ J Surg 78:548–55.

9. Møller AR (2006) Neural plasticity and disorders of the nervous system. Cambridge: Cambridge University Press, with permission by Cambridge University Press.

10. McMahon SB and M Koltzenburg, eds. Wall and Melzak's Textbook of Pain. 5th ed. 2006, Elsevier, Churchill, Livingstone: Amsterdam.

11. Langguth B, G Hajak, T Kleinjung et al (2007) Tinnitus: pathophysiology and treatment, progress in brain research. Prog Brain Res 166:1–542.

12. Jastreboff PJ (1990) Phantom auditory perception (tinnitus): mechanisms of generation and perception. Neurosci Res 8:221–54.

13. Tucker DA, SL Phillips, RA Ruth et al (2005) The effect of silence on tinnitus perception. Otolaryngol Head Neck Surg 132:20–4.

14. Gerken GM, PS Hesse and JJ Wiorkowski (2001) Auditory evoked responses in control subjects and in patients with problem tinnitus. Hear Res 157:52–64.

15. Keay KA, CI Clement, A Depaulis et al (2001) Different representations of inescapable noxious stimuli in the periaqueductal gray and upper cervical spinal cord of freely moving rats. Neurosci Lett 313:17–20.

16. Lumb BM (2002) Inescapable and escapable pain is represented in distinct hypothalamic-midbrain circuits: specific roles of Ad- and C-nociceptors. Exp Physiol 87:281–86.

17. Zenner HP, M Pfister and N Birbaumer (2006) Tinnitus sensitization: sensory and psychophysiological aspects of a new pathway of acquired centralization of chronic tinnitus. Otol Neurotol 27:1054–63.

18. Dworkin RH (2002) An overview of neuropathic pain: syndromes, symptoms, signs, and several mechanisms. Clin J Pain 18:343–9.

19. Schwartzman RJ, J Grothusen, TR Kiefer et al (2001) Neuropathic central pain: epidemiology, etiology, and treatment options. Arch Neurol. 58:1547–50.

20. Coles RAA and SA Sook (1998) Hyperacusis and phonophobia in hyperacusic and nonhyperacusic subjects. Br J Audiol 22:228.

21. Ruth R and JI Hall, (1999) Patterns of audiologic findings for tinnitus patients, in Proceedings Sixth International Tinnitus Seminar, J Hazell, Editor. The Tinnitus and Hyperacusis Center: London. 442–5.

22. Hamill-Ruth RJ, RA Ruth, DC Castain et al (2000) Mangement of Tinnitus and Hyperacusis using a Multidiciplinary Pain Model. Am Pain Soc Bull.

23. Dimberg E and T Burns (2005) Management of common neurologic conditions in sports. Clin Sports Med 24:637–62.

24. Nölle C, I Todt, R Seidl et al (2004) Pathophysiological changes of the central auditory pathway after blunt trauma of the head. J Neurotrauma 21:251–8.

25. Häusler R and R Levine (2000) Auditory dysfunction in stroke. Acta Otolaryngol 120:689–703.

26. Møller AR (2006) Intraoperative Neurophysiologic Monitoring, 2nd Edition. Totowa, New Jersey: Humana Press Inc.

27. Herrero JF, JM Laird and JA Lopez-Garcia (2000) Wind-up of spinal cord neurones and pain sensation: much ado about something? Prog Neurobiol 61:169–203.

28. Møller AR and T Pinkerton (1997) Temporal integration of pain from electrical stimulation of the skin. Neurol Res 19:481–8.

29. Quaranta A, V Sallustio and A Scaringi, (1999) Cochlear function in ears with vestibular schwannomas., in Third International Conference on Acoustic Neurinoma and other CPA Tumors, M Sanna et al, Editors. Monduzzi Editore: Rome, Italy. 43–50.

30. Szczepaniak WS and AR Møller (1996) Effects of (−)-baclofen, clonazepam, and diazepam on tone exposure-induced hyperexcitability of the inferior colliculus in the rat: possible therapeutic implications for pharmacological management of tinnitus and hyperacusis. Hear Res 97:46–53.

31. Densert O (1974) Adrenergic innervation in the rabbit cochlea. Acta Otolaryngol. (Stockh.) 78:345–56.

32. Passe EG (1951) Sympathectomy in relation to Ménière's disease, nerve deafness and tinnitus. A report of 110 cases. Proc Roy Soc Med 44:760–72.

33. Baron R, (2006) Complex regional pain syndromes, in Wall and Melzack's Textbook of Pain, SB McMahon and M Koltzenburg, Editors. Elsevier: Amsterdam. 1011–27.

34. Doubell TP, RJ Mannion and CJ Woolf, (1999) The dorsal horn: state-dependent sensory processing, plasticity and the generation of pain, in Handbook of Pain, PD Wall and R Melzack, Editors. Churchill Livingstone: Edinburgh. 165–81.

35. Price DD, S Long and C Huitt (1992) Sensory testing of pathophysiological mechanisms of pain in patients with reflex sympathetic dystrophy. Pain 49:163–73.

36. Brodal A (2004) The central nervous system third edition. New York: Oxford University Press.

37. Dubner R and AI Basbaum, (1994) Spinal dorsal horn plasticity following tissue or nerve injury, in Textbook of Pain, PD Wall and R Melzack, Editors. Edinburgh: Churchill Livinstone. 225–41.

38. Wall PD (1977) The presence of ineffective synapses and circumstances which unmask them. Phil. Trans. Royal Soc. (Lond.) 278:361–72.

39. Gerken GM, SS Saunders and RE Paul (1984) Hypersensitivity to electrical stimulation of auditory nuclei follows hearing loss in cats. Hear Res 13:249–60.

40. Szczepaniak WS and AR Møller (1996) Evidence of neuronal plasticity within the inferior colliculus after noise exposure: a study of evoked potentials in the rat. Electroenceph Clin Neurophysiol 100:158–64.

41. Møller AR and P Rollins (2002) The non-classical auditory system is active in children but not in adults. Neurosci Lett 319:41–4.

42. Møller AR, MB Møller and M Yokota (1992) Some forms of tinnitus may involve the extralemniscal auditory pathway. Laryngoscope 102: 1165–71.

43. Kanold PO and ED Young (2001) Proprioceptive information from the pinna provides somatosensory input to cat dorsal cochlear nucleus. J Neurosci 21:7848–58.

44. Zhou J and S Shore (2004) Projections from the trigeminal nuclear complex to the cochlear nuclei: a retrograde and anterograde tracing study in the guinea pig. J Neurosci Res 78:901–7.

45. Dehmel S, YL Cui and SE Shore (2008) Cross-modal interactions of auditory and somatic inputs in the brainstem and midbrain and their imbalance in tinnitus and deafness. Am J Audiol 17:S193–209.

46. Aitkin LM (1986) The auditory midbrain, structure and function in the central auditory pathway. Clifton, NJ: Humana Press.

47. Willer JC (1988) Relieving effect of TENS on painful muscle contraction produced by an impairment of reciprocal innervation: an electrophysiological analysis. Pain 32:271–4.

48. Rakel B and R Frantz (2003) Effectiveness of transcutaneous electrical nerve stimulation on postoperative pain with movement. J Pain Symptom Manage 4:455–64.

49. Cooney WP (1997) Electrical stimulation and the treatment of complex regional pain syndromes of the upper extremity. Hand Clin. 13.

50. Cacace AT, JP Cousins, SM Parnes et al (1999) Cutaneous-evoked tinnitus. II: review of neuroanatomical, physiological and functional imaging studies. Audiol Neurotol 4:258–68.

51. Cacace AT, JP Cousins, SM Parnes et al (1999) Cutaneous-evoked tinnitus. I: phenomenology, psychophysics and functional imaging. Audiol. Neurotol 4:247–57.

52. Levine RA, EC Nam, Y Oron et al, (2007) Evidence for a tinnitus subgroup responsive to somatosensory based treatment modalities, in Tinnitus: Pathophysiology and Treatment, Progress in Brain Research, B Langguth et al, Editors. Elsevier: Amsterdam. 195–207.

53. Levine RA, M Abel and H Cheng (2003) CNS somatosensory-auditory interactions elicit or modulate tinnitus. Exp Brain Res 153:643–8.

54. Upton LG and SJ Wijeyesakere (2004) The incidence of tinnitus in people with disorders of the temporomandibular joint. Int Tinnitus J 10:174–6.

55. Morgan DH (1973) Temporomandbular joint surgery. Correction of pain, tinnitus, and vertigo. Den Radiogr Photogr 46:27–46.

56. Coad ML, AH Lockwood, RJ Salvi et al (2001) Characteristics of patients with gaze-evoked tinnitus. Otol Neurotol 22:650–4.

57. Cacace AT, TJ Lovely, DJ McFarland et al (1994) Anomalous cross-modal plasticity following posterior fossa surgery: some speculations on gaze-evoked tinnitus. Hear Res 81:22–32.

58. Lockwood AH, DS Wack, RF Burkard et al (2001) The functional anatomy of gaze-evoked tinnitus and sustained lateral gaze. Neurology 56:472–80.

59. Shulman A, J Tonndorf and B Goldstein (1985) Electrical tinnitus control. Acta Otolaryngol 99:318–25.

60. Zhan X, T Pongstaporn and DK Ryugo (2006) Projections of the second cervical dorsal root ganglion to the cochlear nucleus in rats. J Comp Neurol 496:335–48.

61. Young ED, I Nelken and RA Conley (1995) Somatosensory effects on neurons in dorsal cochlear nucleus. J Neurophysiol 73:743–65.

62. Kaltenbach JA (2000) Neurophysiologic mechanisms of tinnitus. J Am Acad Audiol 11:125–37.

63. Kaltenbach JA (2007) The dorsal cochlear nucleus as a contributor to tinnitus: mechanisms underlying the induction of hyperactivity, in Tinnitus: Pathophysiology and Treatment, Progress in Brain Research, B Langguth et al, Editors. Elevier: Amsterdam. 89–106.

64. Møller AR (2006) Hearing: Anatomy, physiology, and disorders of the auditory system, 2nd Ed. Amsterdam: Academic Press.

65. Kirchner A, F Birklein, H Stefan et al (2000) Left vagus nerve stimulation suppresses experimentally induced pain. Neurology 55:1167–71.

66. Groves DA and VJ Brown (2005) Vagal nerve stimulation: a review of its applications and potential mechanisms that mediate its clinical effects. Neurosci Biobehav Rev 29:493–500.

67. Weinberger NM, R Javid and B Lepan (1993) Long-term retention of learning-induced receptive-field plasticity. Proc Nat Acad Sci 90:2394–8.

68. Kilgard MP and MM Merzenich (1998) Plasticity of temporal information processing in the primary auditory cortex. Nature Neurosci 1:727–31.

Chapter 15
Anatomy and Physiology of Pain

Aage R. Møller

Keypoints

1. Pain is a subjective sensation that has no objective correlates.
2. Pain has many forms, and the perception of pain is affected by many factors including actual circumstances expectation, stress, and the emotional state of the person.
3. Many forms of pain are best described as suffering.
4. Pain may be divided into two large groups: pain that is caused by direct stimulation (physical or chemical) of specific receptors (nociceptors) and pain that is not caused by stimulation of nociceptors. There is also a third kind of pain in which activation of neural plasticity plays an important role.
5. Stimulation of nociceptors that are located in the skin, the cornea, tooth pulp, muscles, joints, peripheral nerves, the respiratory system, and viscera causes acute pain that has both a fast and a slow component.
6. Pain can also be caused by trauma or inflammatory processes generated in nerves or in the nervous system and not from activation of specific pain receptors.
7. Expression of neural plasticity can create pain (central neuropathic pain) that is caused by neural activity in the brain without peripheral input.
8. Transmission of pain in the dorsal horn of the spinal cord (and the trigeminal nucleus) can be modulated by input from skin receptors (Aβ fibers) and descending activity from supraspinal sources.
9. The sympathetic nervous system can modulate the sensitivity of nociceptors and the transmission of pain signals in the spinal cord and the trigeminal nucleus.
10. Activation of neural plasticity can also cause change in processing of nociceptor-elicited pain signals causing hyperpathia (exaggerated and prolonged response to painful stimuli) and allodynia (painful sensation from light touch of the skin).
11. The vagus nerve is involved in some forms of pain, and electrical stimulation may reduce pain.

Keywords Somatic pain • Visceral pain • Neuropathic pain • Central neuropathic pain • Neural plasticity

Abbreviations

CNS	Central nervous system
DLPT	Dorsolateral pontomesencephalic tegmentum
IASP	International Association for the Study of Pain
NA	Norepinephrine
NST	Nucleus of the solitary tract
PAG	Periaquaductal grey
RVM	Rostral ventromedial medulla
SI	Primary somatosensory cortex
STT	Spinothalamic tract
VPI	Ventral posterior inferior (thalamus)
VPL	Ventral posterior lateral (thalamus)
VPM	Ventral posterior medial (thalamus)

Introduction

Some forms of pain have similarities with tinnitus, as discussed in another chapter (Chap. 14). There are further anatomical and physiologic aspects of pain that

A.R. Møller (✉)
The University of Texas at Dallas, School of Behavioral and Brain Sciences, GR 41, 800 W Campbell Rd, Richardson, TX 75080, USA
e-mail: amoller@utdallas.edu

A.R. Møller et al. (eds.), *Textbook of Tinnitus*,
DOI 10.1007/978-1-60761-145-5_15, © Springer Science+Business Media, LLC 2011

make it appropriate to include a chapter on the anatomy and physiology of pain in a book on tinnitus. Pain can have many forms; it can be constant or intermittent. It can cause little or moderate discomfort or it can be disabling, preventing sleep and intellectual work. Pain can cause fear of a serious disease, and its perception can change just from assurance that it is not a sign of a serious disease. Pain that is not a sign of a serious disease, thus, mainly affects quality of life.[1] Pain that is not a sign of a serious disease usually receives little attention from health care personnel.

Pain is related more to suffering than to any other quality; but again, there is large individual variation. Helplessness and expectations are important.

Pain is the most common reason for visits to the emergency room and plays an important role in diagnosis of many forms of diseases. However, training of physicians in this particular area is often inadequate in the US and falls short of providing the basis for effective treatment and care for patients with various degrees of pain.

Pain is a subjective sensation that lacks objective signs; it cannot be measured with any clinical methods, only the patient's own description can provide information about its strength, character, and the location on the body to which it is referred. Estimates of the intensity of pain can be obtained using a visual analog scale, but it still depends on the individual's judgment about the pain.

The basic research that is devoted to pain is much less than what seems justified by the degree of suffering from idiopathic pain. Many forms of pain are in many ways an enigma. Many forms of pain are not caused by diseases. Available treatments are often ineffective, and some treatments cause severe side effects. Different kinds of narcotics are effective pain treatments but are restricted by legal measures because of fear for addiction or because physicians hesitate to prescribe them because of fear of legal actions.

Pain is often regarded as a somatosensory sense and is often discussed in textbooks together with sensory systems. However, the sensation of pain is more complex than somatosensory sensations; it is a much more variable sensation than somatosensory perceptions such as touch, vibrations, and warmth and cool.

It has been said that the only pain that is tolerable is someone else's pain.[2]

This chapter provides a brief description of the anatomy and physiology of pain. More detailed descriptions can be found in Wall and Melzack "Textbook of pain" and in Møller "Neural plasticity and disorders of the nervous system".

Different Kinds of Pain

Pain can be divided into two broad classes of acute and chronic pain according to how long the pain has lasted. The term "chronic pain" is usually used for pain that lasts more than 3 months. However, chronic pain is not related to the pathology of the pain or to its etiology [1–3] and thus is an arbitrary distinction. The International Association for the Study of Pain (IASP) regards pain that lasts more than 6 months to be chronic pain. Chronic pain may be caused by diseases such as rheumatoid arthritis but is often caused by re-organization of the central nervous system (CNS) (central neuropathic pain) or a combination of these two causes.

Another way of categorizing pain is as somatic and visceral pain. Somatic pain is caused by activation of pain receptors in the skin, muscles, joints, etc. Visceral pain originates in viscera from mechanical or chemical stimulation, including inflammation. Another way of dividing pain is in somatic pain, visceral pain, and neuropathic pain. Devor and Boive [4, 5] have defined three main types of pain (see Fig. 15.1). There is considerable overlap between these kinds of pain [4]. The term "neuropathic pain" describes pain that originates in the nervous system. It can be divided into peripheral and central neuropathic pain. The term "neuropathic pain" theoretically covers all pain caused by nerves, the spinal cord, and the brain, but the term is used by neurologists to describe pain caused by peripheral nerves and cranial nerves. The term "central neuropathic pain" is used for pain caused by abnormal neural activity in the central nervous system (spinal cord and brain). This kind of pain occurs without input from pain receptors. Central neuropathic pain[3] is a phantom sensation that

---

[1]International Association for the Study of Pain (IASP) definition of pain: An unpleasant sensory and emotional experience associated with tissue damage or potential damage or described in such terms.

[2]René Leriche, French surgeon, 1879–1955

[3]Neuropathic pain: Neurologists use the term "neuropathic pain" only in reference to pain from peripheral and cranial nerves, although the term relates to pain from the nervous system in general.

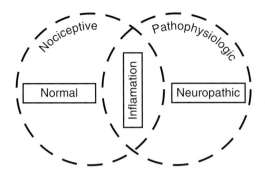

Fig. 15.1 A classification of pain that defines two main overlapping groups of pain namely, nociceptive pain that can occur as a normal condition and as a result of inflammatory processes; and pathophysiological pain that includes neuropathic pain and pain caused by inflammatory processes [4]. From Møller AR (2006) Neural plasticity and disorders of the nervous system [6]. Reproduced with permission from Cambridge University Press

has similarities to some forms of tinnitus. All other forms of pain are caused by activation of pain receptors. Pain receptors are localized in the skin, muscle tendons, fascia, and viscera. Heat, chemicals, and inflammatory processes can activate pain receptors.

Central pain is caused by a lesion or dysfunction in the CNS [3], according to the IASP.

Central neuropathic[4] pain is caused by abnormal neural activity in the CNS that may be caused by functional re-organization of the nervous system, most likely elicited through activation of neural plasticity and thus not caused by activation of pain receptors. Central neuropathic pain is a "phantom" sensation similar to that experienced from amputated limbs and tinnitus. Phantom sensations are caused by the expression of neural plasticity [7, 8] and are therefore "plasticity diseases" similar to tinnitus [9]. The term "central neuropathic pain" is used to distinguish pain that is not caused by morphologically verifiable lesions of nerves in the CNS [10] from causes that have morphological or chemical correlates.

These different categories of pain may overlap and interact with each other, and, in particular, central neuropathic pain may begin with somatic pain of some kind.

Pain causes many different reactions and is often associated with activation of other parts of the nervous system than those that are traditionally regarded as

pain pathways. The autonomic nervous system is often activated in connection with pain. Pain can also cause activation of limbic structures, such as the amygdala and the cingulate gyrus [11, 12], causing emotional (affective) reactions such as anger, fear, anxiety, and depression, which can be related to activation of the amygdala. This activation may occur through cortical routes from the dorsal thalamus [13, 14], through activation of the medial spinothalamic tract (see below). Severe pain that has lasted a long time is often accompanied by allodynia (pain from normally innocuous stimulation) or hyperpathia and hyperalgesia (exaggerated and prolonged response to stimulation of nociceptors). The periaquaductal gray (PAG) [15, 16] is often activated. It has been shown that pain that is considered "escapable" activates different anatomical parts of the PAG than pain that is "inescapable" [15].

Somatic Pain

Somatic pain is caused by activation of pain receptors in the body. It can occur from tissue damage, traumatic injuries, and surgical operations. It is a common cause of acute pain. Ischemia also causes pain by stimulation of certain pain receptors. These kinds of pain occur rapidly and are normally short lasting. Inflammation of the skin, joints, and muscles are other common causes of somatic pain, but pain can last a long duration of time if the inflammation is chronic. Unmyelinated axons can grow into scar tissue, such as from operations of the spinal cord and cause central pain [17]. Muscle and joint pain, such as in rheumatoid arthritis, are common causes of chronic pain.

Visceral Pain

Visceral pain is not perceived in the same way as somatic pain. The pain is not felt at the anatomical location of the cause of the pain. Pain that originates in the viscera and the heart is often referred to locations on the surface of the body [1, 18–20]. Such pain is known as referred pain. The location of the pain is less specific than somatic pain and varies among individuals [1]. Visceral pain often has an emotional component such as being perceived as inescapable [21].

---

[4] Central neuropathic pain is a subgroup of central pain that is caused by abnormal activity in the CNS that is a result of functional changes in the CNS.

The reason why pain from viscera is poorly local-ized is most likely related to the fact that none of the secondary neurons in the spinal cord receive only visceral input; there are much fewer visceral afferent fibers than somatic afferent fibers [22]. Another reason may be that the vagus nerve can mediate pain from viscera [23].

Pathways

Peripheral nerves that carry signals from pain receptors are layer I and II of the dorsal horn. In the head, pain fibers travel in the fifth, ninth, and tenth cranial nerves to terminate in the caudal (spinal) part of the trigeminal nucleus. Central pain pathways include both ascending and descending pathways. Ascending pain pathways are often regarded as part of the somatosensory system, known as the anterior lateral system.

The different parts of the anterior lateral tracts carry pain information from the spinal cord and the trigeminal nucleus to the reticular formation, the periaquaductal gray (PAG), and to the dorsal and ventral thalamus. From here, pain information can reach several parts of the brain. Some forms of visceral pain are carried in the vagus nerve that terminates in the nucleus of the solitary tract, and from there travel to several parts of the brain [23].

The trigeminal nucleus has similarities with the dorsal horn of the spinal cord. It is an elongated struc-ture in the brainstem that reaches from the midbrain into the upper part of the spinal cord (Fig. 15.2). Its rostral parts are concerned with innocuous stimulation of the skin in the face and mucosa in the nose and

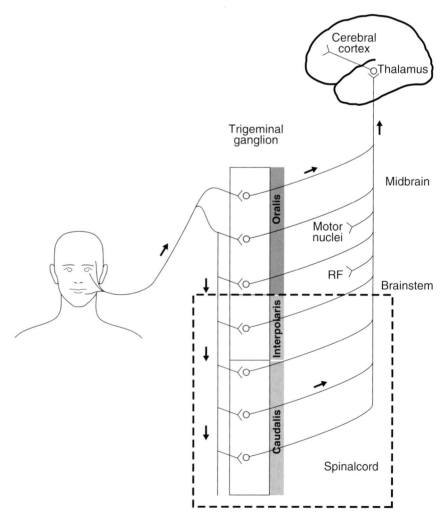

Fig. 15.2 Pain pathways from the head of the trigeminal nucleus (indicated by *dashed rectangle*). RF: Reticular formation. Adapted from Sessle [25]. From Møller AR (2006) Neural plasticity and disorders of the nervous system [6]. Reproduced with permission from Cambridge University Press

mouth. The caudal part is mostly involved with noxious stimulation and thus pain. The connections to the dorsal cochlear nucleus make this a structure of importance for tinnitus (see Chap. 9). The trigeminal nucleus is the site of pathologies that cause a particular kind of pain, trigeminal neuralgia, that consists of attacks of excruciating pain in one of the three radiations of the trigeminal nerve [24].

Neural Circuitry in the Spinal Cord

Dorsal root fibers from pain receptors make synaptic contact with cells in layer I and II of the dorsal horn (Fig. 15.3); most of the axons of these cells cross the midline at the segmental level and ascend in the anteriorlateral tracts [26]. C fibers terminate mainly on cells in lamina II of the dorsal horn (Fig. 15.3) (Rexed's classification [27]). The axons of these cells make synaptic contact with cells in lamina I. (Lamina I is also known as the substantia gelatinosa.) Aδ fibers terminate on cells in layer I, and collateral fibers of these Aδ fibers terminate in lamina IV and V of the dorsal horn [26].

Some of the interneurons in lamina I send collaterals to segments above and below their own segment. These fibers travel in the tract of Lissauer (dorsolateral fasciculus), forming part of the anteriorlateral tract, mainly the spinothalamic tract (STT) [26] (Fig. 15.4). These cells receive input from nociceptors that respond to different modalities of noxious stimuli [28].

The anterior lateral tract consists of the spinoreticular, the spinotectal, and spinothalamic tracts, the latter being the best known and probably the most important.

Cells in lamina VI, VII, and VIII in the so-called "intermediate zone" receive input from large diameter fibers that innervate receptors for innocuous and nocuous (painful) stimulations from large areas of skin. Some cells receive input from viscera.

The neurons in lamina I send axons crossing the midline to form the lateral tract of the STT that ascends toward the thalamus. The lateral STT is crudely organized somatotopically and mediates the magnitude and quality of pain ("What" in Fig. 15.3). The anterior portion of the STT communicates awareness and spatial information about pain (Fig. 15.5 "Where"). The fibers of this tract originate in cells in deeper layers of the dorsal horn, layers V and VII and fibers from cells in the intermediate and also from layer VI, VII, and VIII of the intermediate zone of the dorsal horn.

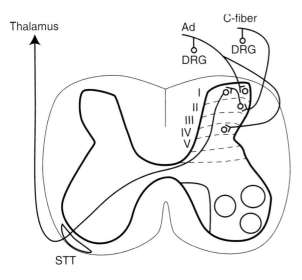

Fig 15.3 Illustration of the termination of Aδ fibers and C fibers in the dorsal horn. DRG: Dorsal root ganglia. Lamina I and II are also known as substantia gelatinosa. From Møller AR (2006) Neural plasticity and disorders of the nervous system [6]. Reproduced with permission from Cambridge University Press

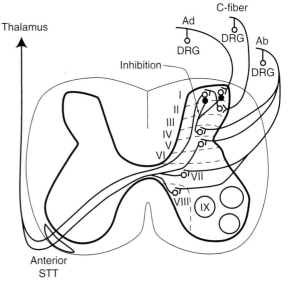

Fig 15.4 Schematic illustration of the connections through which innocuous sensory input mediated by large myelinated (Aβ) fibers can inhibit pain neurons in lamina I that receive noxious input from Aδ fiber and C fibers via interneurons and which give rise to axons of the STT. From Møller AR (2006) Neural plasticity and disorders of the nervous system [6]. Reproduced with permission from Cambridge University Press

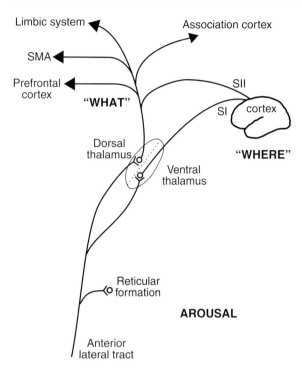

Limbic system

Association cortex

SMA

Prefrontal
cortex

"WHAT"

SII

SI   cortex

Dorsal
thalamus

Ventral
thalamus

"WHERE"

Reticular
formation

AROUSAL

Anterior
lateral tract

Fig 15.5 Simplified diagram of pathways involved in mediating the sensation of nociceptor pain. Central pain pathways project to primary cortices conveying spatial ("where") information. Objective ("what") information can reach many different parts of the CNS such as the prefrontal cortex, supplementary motor area (SMA), and the amygdala. Information that travels in the anterior lateral pathways can also reach the reticular formation and thereby contribute to arousal [14]. From Møller AR (2006) Neural plasticity and disorders of the nervous system [6]. Reproduced with permission from Cambridge University Press

Large diameter (Aβ) fibers from sensory receptors in the skin respond to innocuous stimuli and project to cells in lamina III, IV, and V [28] (Figs 15.3 and 15.4). The axons of these fibers form the anterior STT tract. Large Aβ fibers that terminate on cells in the dorsal horn can inhibit cells that respond to noxious stimulation, and innocuous sensory input can thereby modulate (inhibit) conduction of pain impulses in the dorsal horn.

The fibers of the STT terminate in several parts of the thalamus; as many as six areas have been identified [28].

The anterior STT targets the ventral thalamus (ventral posterior lateral (VPL), the ventral posterior medial (VPM), ventral posterior inferior (VPI) nuclei, and several nuclei in the medio-dorsal thalamus) [28]. The neurons of the VPL and VPI project to the primary somatosensory cortex (SI). This pathway probably gives rise to the sensation of the fast phase of pain,

which is clearly localized. The fibers of the lateral portion of the STT (Fig. 15.3) originate mainly in cells in lamina I of the dorsal horn that receive input from C fibers via neurons in lamina II. This part of the lateral portion of STT mediates the burning sensation of pain.

The lateral tract projects to the dorsal and medial portion of the thalamus from where axons travel to the insula and limbic structures. The cells of these structures project to secondary somatosensory cortices on both sides and to other non-sensory structures, and to some extent to area 3a (SI) [28] (Fig. 15.3) [29] as well.

The lateral tract communicates object information ("What" in Fig. 15.5) about pain and it is responsible for affective qualities of painful stimulation, thus similar to the non-classical pathways of the auditory system (see Chap. 8) that may evoke fear and other emotional reactions to sound in individuals with tinnitus.

The fact that pure C-fiber activation reaches the SI cortex means that C fibers may produce a sensation of pressure or touch, in addition to a sensation of burning pain.

There is considerable individual variation in the pain pathways [30], however, and many of the studies of the neuroanatomy of pain have been done in animals; the results may not be directly applicable to humans.

The spinoreticular tract is mainly bilateral, and its main target is the reticular formation of the brainstem. The spinomesencephalic tract has as its main target the periaquaductal gray (PAG). This means that only the STT has connections to the ventral thalamus, and from there connects to the SI. The spinoreticular and spinomesencephalic tracts are important for control of pain processing. These structures, through descending systems, can modulate traffic in ascending pain pathways and thereby cause suppression and enhancement of pain sensations (see p. xx).

The fibers of many parts of the anterior lateral tracts send collateral fibers to many locations along their ascending paths. Many of these collaterals terminate in the reticular formation of the brainstem, thus affecting wakefulness.

Neural Plasticity in the Spinal Cord

Neural plasticity, regarding processing of pain signals in the dorsal horn of the spinal cord (and the trigeminal nucleus), is extensive and has been studied in detail. Evidence has been presented that the dorsal pain circuits in the dorsal horn can operate in four different states. Doubell [31] has described these states in the following way:

State 1 is the normal state, where low-threshold mechanoreceptors mediate sensations such as that of touch, vibration, pressure, warmth, or cool. When the spinal cord is in this state, stimulation of high threshold receptors causes localized sensations that are clearly recognized as painful without emotional engagement.

State 2 represents a change in function that is characterized by suppression of transmission of both normal innocuous somatosensory information and the neural activity that normally elicit painful sensations. In this state, descending signals from the brain cause reactions such as "flight or fight", mediated by the NA–serotonin descending pathways, Fig. 20.

The changes in state 2 represent the way hypnosis, placebo, suggestions, distraction, and cognition can affect (suppress) the perception of painful stimuli. Switching from state 1 (normal function) to stage 2 can be affected by administration of opioids, alpha-adrenergic agents, and $GABA_A$ antagonists (bicuculine). The known freedom of pain that often is present during a short period after an accident is probably an example of the changes that represent state 2.

In state 3 function of the neural circuits in the dorsal horn, the excitability of cells is higher than normal, thus almost opposite to that of state 2. In stage 3, the nociceptive receptive fields of neurons in the dorsal horn neurons becomes larger through activation of ineffective (dormant) synapses [32]. This is presumably caused by an increased synaptic efficacy facilitating neural transmission together with reduced inhibition. Stimulation of sensory receptors thereby elicits larger than normal neural activity and sensory activation that normally does not elicit a sensation of pain causes painful sensitivity. This is believed to be one way that light touch can cause a painful sensation known as allodynia. Similar mechanisms may be responsible for the exaggerated prolonged pain experience from moderately strong painful stimuli known as hyperpathia.

Pathologies of nerves may promote a switch of the function of neural circuits in the dorsal horn to stage 3 [33].

State 4 has many similarities with stage 3; one major difference being that the abnormal conditions are caused by an anatomical re-organization, while the changes in function in stage 3 are caused by functional changes (altered synaptic efficacy, etc.). The changes in morphology that is a characteristic of stage 4 include programmed deaths of cells (apoptosis), degeneration or atrophy of synapses, creation of new synapses, and modification of the contacts between cells and synapses. In state 3, Aβ fibers may make synaptic contact with cells that are innervated by C fibers [31]. Instead of normally terminating on cells in layers III–V of the spinal horns of the spinal cord, they may invade the territories of C fibers (lamina II), which can explain why normally innocuous stimulation is perceived as painful (allodynia).

In summary, state 1 is the normal state of the spinal cord's dorsal horn (and the trigeminal nucleus); state 2 represents decreased response to painful stimulation. State 3 represents the opposite with abnormally high excitability. Finally, state 4 is a (anatomically) permanent state of such increased excitability that causes permanent pain and redirection of information.

Change from stage 1, the normal function occurs when neural plasticity is tuned on first, causing a change in synaptic efficacy and as a further step when state 4 is reached as a result of structural changes. State 4 is a stable stage that is more difficult to reverse than that of 2 and 3. The change in function that occurs in state 2 probably reverses automatically to the normal stage or to state 3.

Modulation of Pain

The best known way to modulate pain is by administrating common pain relieving medications such as aspirin, ibuprofen, naprosyn, and by opioids that act on several different opioid receptors (mu, kappa, and delta receptors), that are found in many structures, best known are those found in the brainstem in the RVM and PAG. The COX1 and COX2 enzyme systems are involved in pain and analgesics of various kinds are aimed at modulating this enzyme system, either acting on both COX1 and COX2 or specifically on COX2. Selective COX2 inhibitors were introduced some years ago but were in general found to have unacceptable side effects or/and did not offer the benefits that were expected in the form of less risk for stomach bleedings.

Pain can be naturally modulated by peripheral mechanisms and by central mechanisms. Peripheral mechanisms involve modulation of the sensitivity of pain receptors, and central mechanisms involve complex descending neural pathways that can control the impulse traffic in the ascending pain pathways. The modulation has often been described as sensitization that increases the sensitivity of pain sensations and as de-sensitization that decreases pain sensations. The anatomical bases for different systems that can modulate acute pain are described below.

Peripheral Modulation of Pain

Peripheral modulation of pain consists mainly of sensitization of pain receptors and can occur through secretion of norepinephrine from sympatric nerve fibers that terminate close to the receptors. This kind of modulation is caused by the sympathetic nervous system.

Descending Pathways

As in sensory systems, pain pathways have extensive descending pathways (Figs. 15.6–15.8) that exert control over impulse traffic in the ascending pathways. Together with the sympathetic nervous system, these descending pathways can sensitize pain receptors (peripheral sensitization) or block pain impulses from reaching the brain in the spinal cord, such as often occurs after trauma and which is a part of "flight or fight" reactions. The results are often freedom of pain in the first short period after a serious trauma.

Three or four separate descending systems, which can modulate the transmission of pain signals in the ascending pathways, have been identified [34]. These are the rostral ventromedial medulla (RVM) (Fig. 15.6), the dorsolateral pontomesencephalic tegmentum (DLTP) (Fig. 15.7) [35], and the NA–Serotonin pathway. In addition, ascending activity from stimulation of nociceptors can be modulated by the norepinephrine (NA)–serotonin pathway that originates in the brainstem reticular formation (Fig. 15.8). In addition, the vagus nerve may also be regarded as a descending pathway that can modulate pain [36, 37].

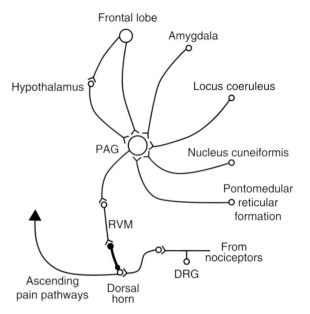

Fig 15.6 Input to the PAG and pathways through which modulation of transmission of pain signals by the PAG can occur through the RVM pathway. From Møller AR (2006) Neural plasticity and disorders of the nervous system [6]. Reproduced with permission from Cambridge University Press

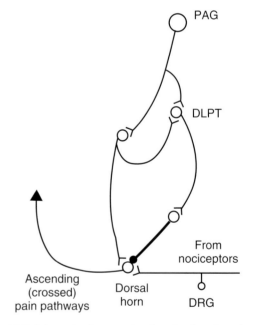

Fig 15.7 Schematic diagram showing the dorsolateral pontomesencephalic tegmentum pathway (DLTP). From Møller AR (2006) Neural plasticity and disorders of the nervous system [6]. Reproduced with permission from Cambridge University Press

The RVM and DLTP pathways originate in supraspinal structures. The modulation occurs mainly by influencing neurons in lamina I and II of the dorsal horn.

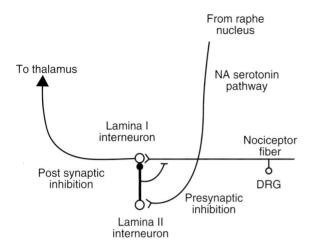

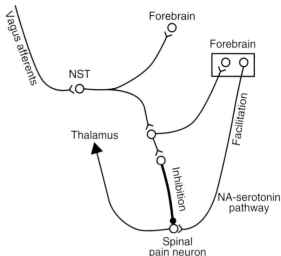

Fig 15.8 Schematic diagram showing the descending pathways from raphe nucleus (NA–serotonin pathway) that terminate on pain neurons in the dorsal horn [18]. From Møller AR (2006) Neural plasticity and disorders of the nervous system [6]. Reproduced with permission from Cambridge University Press

Fig 15.9 Schematic illustration of the innervation by the vagus nerve of organs in the lower abdomen involving the NST showing how these connections can have inhibitory influence on spinal pain neurons and how they connect with neurons in the forebrain. From Møller AR (2006) Neural plasticity and disorders of the nervous system [6]. Reproduced with permission from Cambridge University Press

The PAG is involved in two of these pathways through at least one interneuron in the RVM. The RVM's target is neurons in lamina I and II of the dorsal horn [38]. The DLPT also targets neurons in the dorsal horn, but it is mainly excitatory (facilitating). There are three types of RVM neurons, on-cells, off-cell and neutral cells. The on-cells that excite dorsal horn pain cells are inhibited by opioids. The off-cells, that are excited by opioids inhibit pain cells in the dorsal horn. The RVM is the main source of serotonin.

It is worth noting that these descending systems have two parts, an inhibitory and an excitatory part, which means that at least the RVM and DLTP can both enhance and suppress impulse traffic in pain circuits in the dorsal horn and the trigeminal nucleus. There are thus parallel inhibitory and excitatory descending pathways. The net effect of activation of these descending systems depends on the balance between the activity in the inhibitory and excitatory paths. This is one of the anatomical substrates for the complex modulation of pain sensations.

The Role of the Vagus Nerve

Much less is known about the neural circuits through which the vagus nerve can modulate pain impulses. Approximately 80% of the fibers in the vagus nerve are afferent (ascending) fibers, but so far most studies have

concerned the efferent (descending) fibers of the vagus nerve. The afferent fibers terminate in the nucleus of the solitary tract (NST). Recent studies have found that the nucleus can influence many structures of the brain and the spinal cord, including pain circuits (Fig. 15.9). It is not completely understood how vagus stimulation can control central pain, but the effect seems to be related to the fact that the vagus nerve can influence some of the neurons in the dorsal horn neurons that mediate pain [37, 39]. Studies have shown indications that the vagus nerve may be involved in the opioid induced analgesia. Studies in rats have shown that after severing of the vagus nerve, the analgesic effect of morphine decreases [37]. This means that intact function of the vagus nerve is necessary for the analgesic effect of morphine.

Electrical stimulation of the vagus nerve can reduce the pain from controlled stimulation of nociceptors. It also reduces the temporal integration of pain elicited by consecutive impulses ("wind-up") as well as pain from tonic pressure [36]. Pain sensation such as from electrical stimulation normally show temporal integration and the threshold at high stimulus rates is much higher than the threshold of sensation, which does not show any noticeable temporal integration for stimulus rates between 1 and 100 pps. In an individual with signs of central neuropathic pain, the temporal integration for pain is abolished and the difference between pain threshold and that of sensation is much smaller than normal [40].

Studies in cats and monkeys have shown that electrical stimulation of the vagus nerve can attenuate the response from neurons in the dorsal horn to many different types of noxious and innocuous stimuli [41].

The results of many studies indicate that the vagus nerve can affect the central processing of pain (central inhibition). The effect of vagal activity on pain may be mediated through the NA–serotonin descending system (Fig. 15.8) [42] as well as endocrine from the adrenal medullae [39].

The complexity of both the descending pathways and modulation of central pain impulses may explain some paradoxical effects. For example, benzodiazepines that are effective in treating pain caused by muscle contractions may enhance other forms of pain see Møller [6].

Animal (rat) experiments have shown that activity in vagal afferents under the diaphragm can modulate somatic pain impulses such as mechanical hyperalgesia [39]. The effect was induced by endocrine signals released from the adrenal medulla. It was concluded that the brain could control the sensitivity of nociptors all over the body, even when the effect is elicited for an anatomical far distance. This means that nociptors are under the control of circulating catecholamines in a way that is different from other modulation of the sensitivity of nociceptors, such as that by the sympathetic nervous system.

Placebo Effect

The common way of testing treatments is to compare the results of the active treatment verses the inactive (sham) treatment when administered in similar ways.

The expectation of pain relief from what was presumed to be an effective treatment often causes a beneficial effect of the inactive treatment. This is known as the placebo effect.

Placebo effect is the beneficial effect that is obtained from administration of inactive medication or other forms of sham treatment while the participants are told

that they are treated for their symptoms. It is now recognized that the placebo effect is real, at least regarding pain [43]. The placebo effect may be regarded as another way of modulating the flow of pain impulses. Many treatments have placebo effects, and it is well known that placebo treatment can reduce pain and has been recognized as a form of treatment for pain [44, 45]. The placebo effect on pain could be caused by endogenous opioids that were liberated because of the expectation of a beneficial effect from the treatment that, unknowingly to the participant in the study, was a sham treatment.

A study of postoperative patients supported that hypothesis and showed that the participants who responded positively to placebo experienced increased pain after administration of naloxone.[5] Those who did not respond to placebo did not respond to naloxone either [45]. Perception of pain is very complex. It is not surprising that emotional factors are involved in many forms of pain, making it understandable that the observed effect of placebo treatment for pain is also complex [39, 44]. Involvement of limbic structures and descending pathways from the prefrontal cortex most likely plays important roles, both in some forms of pain perception and in the beneficial effect of treatment with placebos [9].

Conclusion

Pain has many different forms from minor pain that may be regarded as a nuisance to pain that has a wide range of symptoms regarding perception, degree of suffering, and how it can affect the entire life of a person. While the anatomy of acute pain is not more complicated than that of sensory systems, the anatomy of pain that causes serious suffering is complex, and it may involve large parts of the brain. The physiology of acute pain involves similar circuits as the somatosensory systems but severe pain may involve activation of circuits that can modulate pain, and it may re-route information to many different parts of the brain through activation of neural plasticity.

[5]Naloxone: An antidote to opiates that counteracts the pain relieving effect of opioids.

References

1. Cousins M and I Power, (1999) Acute and postoperative pain, in Textbook of Pain, PD Wall and R Melzack, Editors. Churchill Livingstone: Edinburgh. 447–91.

2. Long DM, (1999) Chronic back pain, in Handbook of Pain, PD Wall and R Melzack, Editors. Churchill Livingstone: Edinburgh. 539–8.

3. Merskey H and N Bogduk, (1994) Classification of chronic pain. IASP Press: Seattle. 1–222.

4. Devor M and Z Seltzer, (1999) Pathophysiology of damaged nerves in relation to chronic pain, in Textbook of Pain, PD Wall and R Melzack, Editors. Churchill Livingstone: Edinburgh. 129–64.

5. Boivie J, (1999) Central pain, in Textbook of Pain, PD Wall and R Melzack, Editors. Churchill Livingstone: Edinburgh. 879–914.

6. Møller AR (2006) Neural plasticity and disorders of the nervous system. Cambridge: Cambridge University Press

7. Jastreboff PJ (1990) Phantom auditory perception (tinnitus): Mechanisms of generation and perception. Neurosci Res 8:221–54.

8. Melzack R (1992) Phantom limbs. Sci Am 266:120–6.

9. Møller AR (2008) Neural Plasticity: For Good and Bad. Progress of Theoretical Physics Supplement No 173: 48–65.

10. Woolf CJ and RJ Mannion (1999) Neuropathic pain: Aetiology, symptoms, mechanisms, and managements. The Lancet 353:1959–64.

11. Hassenbusch SJ, PK Pillay and GH Barnett (1990) Radiofrequency cingulotomy for intractable cancer pain using stereotaxis guided by magnetic resonance imaging. Neurosurg 27:220–3.

12. Lenz FA, M Rios, A Zirh et al (1998) Painful stimuli evoke potentials recorded over the human anterior cingulate gyrus. J Neurophys 79:2231–4.

13. LeDoux JE (1992) Brain mechanisms of emotion and emotional learning. Curr Opin Neurobiol 2:191–7.

14. Møller AR (2003) Sensory systems: Anatomy and physiology. Amsterdam: Academic Press.

15. Keay KA, CI Clement, A Depaulis et al (2001) Different representations of inescapable noxious stimuli in the periaqueductal gray and upper cervical spinal cord of freely moving rats. Neurosci Lett 313:17–20.

16. Morgan MM and P Carrive (2001) Activation of periaqueductal gray reduces locomotion but not mean arterial blood pressure in awake, freely moving rats. Neuroscience 102:905–10.

17. Brisby H (2006) Pathology and possible mechanisms of nervous system response to disc degeneration. J Bone and Joint Surg 88A Suppl. 2:68–71.

18. Cousins MJ and PO Bridenbbaugh (1998) Neural blockade in clinical anesthesia and management of pain. Philadelphia: Lippingcott-Raven.

19. Ruch TC, (1979) Pathophysiology of pain, in The brain and neural function, TC Ruch and HD Patton, Editors. W.B.Saunders: Philadelphia. 272–324.

20. Procacci P, M Zoppi and M Maresca, (1999) Heart, vascular and haemopathic pain, in Textbook of Pain, PD Wall and R Melzack, Editors. Churchill Livingstone: Edinburgh. 621–39.

21. Blackburn-Munro G and RE Blackburn-Munro (2001) Chronic pain, chronic stress and depression: Coincidence or consequence? J Neuroendocrinol 13:1009–23.

22. Cervero F (1994) Sensory innervation of the viscera: Peripheral basis of visceral pain. Physiol Rev 74:95–138.

23. Berthoud HR and WL Neuhuber (2000) Functional and chemical anatomy of the afferent vagal system. Autonomic Neurosci 85:1–17.

24. Sweet WH (1986) The treatment of trigeminal neuralgia (tic douloureux). N Engl J Med 315:174–7.

25. Sessle BJ (1986) Recent development in pain research: Central mechanism of orofacial pain and its control. J. Endodon. 12:435–44.

26. Brodal P (1998) The central nervous system. New York: Oxford Press.

27. Rexed BA (1954) Cytoarchitectonic atlas of the spinal cord. J Comp Neurol 100:297–379.

28. Dostrovsky JO and AD Craig, (2006) Ascending projection systems, in Wall and Melzak's Textbook of Pain, SB McMahon and M Koltzenburg, Editors. Elsevier: Amsterdam. 187–203.

29. Kakigi R, T Diep, Y Qiu et al (2003) Cerebral responses following stimulation of unmyelinated C-fibers in humans: Eletro- and magneto-encephalographic study. Neurosci. Res.

30. Inui K, DT Tran, M Qiu et al (2002) Pain-related magnetic fields evoked by intra-epidermal electrical stimulation in humans. Clin Neurophysiol 113:298–304.

31. Doubell TP, RJ Mannion and CJ Woolf, (1999) The dorsal horn: State-dependent sensory processing, plasticity and the generation of pain, in Handbook of Pain, PD Wall and R Melzack, Editors. Churchill Livingstone: Edinburgh. 165–81.

32. Hong CZ and DG Simons (1998) Pathophysiologic and electrophysiologic mechanisms of myofascial trigger points. Arch Phys Med Rehab 79:863–72.

33. Yakhnitsa V, B Linderoth and BA Meyerson (1999) Spinal cord stimulation attenuates dorsal horn hyperexcitability in a rat model of mononeuropathy. Pain 79:223–33.

34. Fields HL, AI Basbaum and MM Heinricher, (2006) Central nervous system mechanisms of pain modulation, in Wall and Melzak's Textbook of Pain, SB McMahon and M Koltzenburg, Editors. Elsevier: Amsterdam. 125–42.

35. Fields HL and AI Basbaum, (1999) Central nervous system mechanism of pain modulation, in Textbook of Pain, PD Wall and R Melzack, Editors. Churchill Livingstone: Edinburgh. 309–29.

36. Kirchner A, F Birklein, H Stefan et al (2000) Left vagus nerve stimulation suppresses experimentally induced pain. Neurology 55:1167–71.

37. Gebhart GF and A Randich (1992) Vagal modulation of nociception. Am Pain Soc J 1:26–32.

38. Basbaum AI, CH Clanton and HL Fields (1978) Three bulbospinal pathways from the rostral medulla of the cat: And autoradiographic study of pain modulating systems. J Comp Neurol 178:209–24.

39. Jänig W, SG Khasar, JD Levine et al (2000) The role of vagal visceral afferents in the control of nociception. The

biological basis for mind body interaction. Prog Brain Res 122:271–85.

40. Møller AR and T Pinkerton (1997) Temporal integration of pain from electrical stimulation of the skin. Neurol Res 19:481–8.

41. Chandler MJ, SF Hobbs, DC Bolser et al (1991) Effects of vagal afferent stimulation on cervical spinothalamic tract neurons in monkeys. Pain 44:81–7.

42. Tanimoto T, M Takeda and SS Matsumoto (2002) Suppressive effect of vagal afferents on cervical dorsal horn neurons

responding to tooth pulp electrical stimulation in the rat. Exp Brain Res 145:468–79.

43. Hróbjartsson A and PC Gøtzsche (2001) Is the placebo powerless? An analysis of clinical trials comparing placebo with no treatment. N Engl J Med 344:1594–602.

44. Grevert P, LH Albert and A Goldstein (1983) Partial antagonism of placebo analgesia by naloxone. Pain 16: 129–43.

45. Levine JD, NC Gordon and HL Fields (1978) The mechanism of placebo analgesia. Lancet 654–7.

Chapter 16
Behavioral Animal Models of Tinnitus, Pharmacology, and Treatment

Richard Salvi, Edward Lobarinas, and Wei Sun

Keypoints

1. Tinnitus research on humans is difficult, primarily because the pathophysiology of tinnitus is still not well understood.
2. A number of animal models have been developed in order to study conditions that may lead to tinnitus and evaluate treatments for efficacy and safety before being used in human trials.
3. Current tinnitus animal models fall into five general subtypes:

   a. Lick suppression
   b. Operant conditioning
   c. False-positive models
   d. Avoidance conditioning
   e. Startle reflex models

4. Animal models have evaluated tinnitus induced primarily by:

   a. High doses of sodium salicylate
   b. High doses of quinine
   c. High-level noise exposure

5. A number of tinnitus treatments that target specific mechanisms have been proposed and tested in animal models. These include:

   a. Calcium channel antagonists
   b. GABA agonists
   c. NMDA antagonists
   d. Benzodiazepines
   e. Potassium channel modulators
   f. Transcranial magnetic stimulation

6. Tinnitus animal models provide important guidance in the development of new drug therapies.

Keywords Animal models • Drug therapy • Startle reflex • Tinnitus

Abbreviations

BW	Bandwidth
GABA	γ-Aminobutyric acid
GPIAS	Gap prepulse inhibition of the acoustic startle
NBN	Narrow band noise
NBPIAS	Noise burst prepulse inhibition of the acoustic startle
NMDA	N-methyl-D-aspartic acid
rTMS	Repeated transcranial magnetic stimulation
SC	Scopolamine
SIPAC	Schedule induced polydipsia avoidance conditioning
SS	Sodium Salicylate

Introduction

Behavioral Models of Tinnitus

Over the last 15–20 years, a number of animal models have been developed to facilitate basic research into the biological basis of tinnitus. While the models vary from measuring reflexes to advanced conditioning paradigms, they share a basic feature: animals must discriminate between quiet and the presence of a real sound. When tinnitus is present, the ability to detect quiet becomes compromised and animals behave as if a real sound was present. The following chapter will

R. Salvi (✉)
Center for Hearing and Deafness, University at Buffalo, 137 Cary Hall, Buffalo, NY 14214, USA
e-mail: salvi@buffalo.edu

A.R. Møller et al. (eds.), *Textbook of Tinnitus*,
DOI 10.1007/978-1-60761-145-5_16, © Springer Science+Business Media, LLC 2011

introduce a number of animal models and review some of the treatments that have been evaluated using these models. These advances provide the framework to accelerate preclinical and basic research toward the biological mechanisms of tinnitus and the effects of potential treatments. The reader will appreciate the ingenious and creative ways in which researchers have shown that, indeed, animals appear to experience tinnitus.

Animal Models to Assess Tinnitus

Conditioned Lick Suppression: Jastreboff developed the first behavioral model of tinnitus [1] using a conditioned, lick-suppression paradigm. Water-deprived animals were allowed to lick for water when sound was present; however, during randomly presented quiet intervals an unavoidable foot shock was administered at the end of the interval. Delivery of foot shock suppressed licking during quiet intervals, but not during sound intervals. In this conditioned-suppression paradigm, animals learned to lick when sound was present and to suppress licking during quiet. After being conditioned, animals in the experimental group were given a tinnitus-inducing agent (e.g., a high dose of sodium salicylate) while animals in the control group were given a placebo (e.g., saline). During the tinnitus testing phase, the foot shock was turned off and the lick-suppression behavior began to extinguish as foot shock was no longer presented at the end of quiet intervals. The animals in the experimental group that experienced tinnitus during the quiet intervals quickly began to lick during the silent intervals, and the conditioned lick suppression extinguished rapidly. In contrast, the control group did not experience tinnitus during the testing phase and the rate of extinction was much slower as quiet intervals continued to suppress licking, because these intervals were still associated with shock. Tinnitus was assumed to be present if lick suppression extinguished more rapidly in the experimental group (tinnitus) than in the control group. The lick-suppression paradigm was then used to assess the presence, pitch, and loudness of tinnitus induced by high doses of salicylate or quinine [2–5]. While the conditioned lick-suppression model provided useful data, it had some important limitations. First, the onset and offset of tinnitus could not be assessed repeatedly in the same animal. Instead, the technique required two groups, an experimental tinnitus group and a control group. The analysis was based on comparison of group data rather than data from individual animals. Second, the behavior extinguished after 4–5 days. Therefore, tinnitus could only be assessed over a short time interval. With this model, it was not possible to determine if tinnitus was permanent or temporary, or to measure the time course of tinnitus onset and cessation.

Heffner modified the Jastreboff-conditioned lick-suppression paradigm, so that water-deprived hamsters could avoid foot shock if they ceased licking for water during quiet intervals [6]. Hamsters were then exposed to high-intensity noise from 1 to 4 h. Following noise exposure, the foot shock was turned off and rate of extinction of lick suppression in the noise-exposed group was compared to the control group. Tinnitus assessment began 5 days postexposure, as physiological data suggested that tinnitus would begin at this time. Most of the animals exposed for 4 h at the highest intensity (127 dB SPL) extinguished more rapidly than the control animals; this was interpreted as evidence of noise-induced tinnitus. However, only a few animals exposed at lower levels for shorter durations exhibited signs of tinnitus. The results of this study were important for two reasons. First, the results indicated only high-level and long-duration exposures reliably induced tinnitus 5–9 days postexposure, while low-level and short-duration exposures seldom induced tinnitus. Second, only a subset of hamsters developed tinnitus as expected from human reports of noise-induced tinnitus. Heffner's method, however, has some of the same limitations as the Jastreboff paradigm: (a) a separate control group is needed to infer if tinnitus is present; (b) the behavior extinguishes in 4–5 days making it difficult to determine if tinnitus is permanent or temporary; (c) it is not possible to determine the time course of tinnitus and whether the tinnitus is temporary or permanent.

Operant Conditioning: Bauer and colleagues developed a tinnitus animal model by training food-deprived rats to press a bar for food in the presence of white noise and to stop responding during quiet intervals paired with foot shock [7]. At random intervals, a test tone was substituted for white noise without shock. When the stimuli were test tones, the group of salicylate-treated rats continued to press for food more often than the control group. The explanation for this behavioral difference was that salicylate-treated rats perceived the tones as "noisy" due to the presence of tinnitus and, therefore, suppressed bar pressing behavior less than controls. This approach allowed for long-term assessment of tinnitus; however, a limitation of this technique was that differences in behavior attributed to tinnitus occurred only at elevated sound levels, often at low frequencies, contrary to tinnitus reported in humans. Thus, results could be more reflective of changes to suprathreshold hearing induced by salicylate, such as changes in sound tolerance, rather than tinnitus. This technique continues to be refined and the authors report that rats with tinnitus have a constant noise floor and require a larger signal-to-noise ratio than normal control in order to hear tones above their tinnitus.

False-Positive Response Models: Guitton used an increase in "false-positive" responses in quiet to infer the presence of tinnitus [8]. Rats were trained to jump onto a pole when sounds were presented in order to avoid foot shock. During quiet intervals, the shock was turned off and animals could safely remain on the cage floor. In the training phase, rats reliably climbed the pole during sound intervals (hits) and seldom jumped on the pole during quiet intervals (false positive). Rats were then treated for 4 days with 300 mg/kg/d of sodium salicylate. Salicylate-treated rats showed a progressive increase in false-positive responses during quiet intervals over the 4 days of salicylate treatment, indicative of tinnitus. After salicylate treatment ended, the false-positive rate began to decline and reached control levels 2 days postsalicylate, indicating cessation of tinnitus. This behavioral paradigm has several appealing features. It does not extinguish, it does not require a separate control group, and it can be used to assess the onset and recovery of tinnitus. There are, however, some potential limitations with this technique. First, once an animal develops tinnitus, there would no longer be any safe periods in the test chamber. In other words, the animal would need to jump on the pole and remain there 100% of the time, i.e., when the noise was present and when tinnitus was present. Consequently, only a few trials could be run per test session. Second, if an animal developed permanent tinnitus, then it would always jump on the pole, making it difficult to distinguish between tinnitus-induced false positives and false positives due to lack of stimulus-controlled behavior. Finally, over time, an animal with permanent tinnitus might learn to distinguish a phantom sound from a real sound and no longer climb on the pole during quiet periods. Data from other animal models,

including the authors of this chapter, suggest that over time some animals learn to discriminate their tinnitus from real sound, or that a low-level tinnitus becomes the animals' "quiet" state.

Ruttiger combined food-reinforced operant conditioning with a false-positive model. His group trained rats to activate a liquid feeder when white noise was presented, and to withhold their response during quiet periods when no food was delivered [9]. After rats were treated with 350 mg/kg of salicylate, they increased their "false-positive" response rate during the quiet intervals, suggesting that they were perceiving tinnitus. The intensity of the phantom sound was estimated to be around 30 dB SPL since the false-positive rate to the 350 mg/kg dose of salicylate was similar to the number of response evoked by a real noise of 30 dB SPL. Lowering the dose of salicylate reduced the false-positive rate in periods of quiet. The main limitation of this technique is the large amount of time needed to train the animals. Other limitations include the ability to detect the frequency of the tinnitus, whether animals can learn to discriminate tinnitus from real sound over time, and extinction of the ability of quiet to reduce responding. Despite these limitations, this method can reliably detect the presence, intensity, and persistence of tinnitus.

Schedule Induced Polydipsia Avoidance Conditioning (SIPAC): The authors of this chapter developed SIPAC to evaluate the onset, offset, and pitch of transient or persistent tinnitus. Under SIPAC, food-restricted animals (85% free feeding weight) are placed under a fixed, 1-min time interval (FT = 1) food reinforcement schedule while water is available in the experimental chamber (animals receive one pellet per minute). Each daily session is 150 min, under which animals receive 150, 45-mg food pellets. Over a few days, animals become polydipsic; they begin to exhibit large bursts of drinking following food pellet delivery. Typically, total session licks for each session range from 2,000 to as high as 10,000 licks. Initially, a 4-kHz narrow band noise (NBN) is played in the background on half of the trials while the other half has no sound (quiet). Once the animals become polydipsic, a brief foot shock is delivered if animals lick in the presence of the 4-kHz NBN. Within 2–3 days animals restrict their licking in the presence of sound and lick predominantly during quiet intervals (<10% licks in the presence of sound). In the final training stage, the sound trials are generalized to 4, 8, 12, 16, and 20 kHz NBN or 16 kHz tone. Licking in the presence of these sounds also results in brief foot shock. However, no shock is delivered if the animals lick during the quiet intervals. The presence of tinnitus is inferred by a decrease in the licks that occurs during the quiet intervals, while sound intervals are expected to remain unchanged. Recent advancements in the SIPAC technique have allowed the estimation of the pitch of salicylate, quinine, and unilateral noise-induced tinnitus (only one ear is exposed to the noise, the other ear is left unexposed to hear the real sound). The pitch was estimated to be in the 12–16 kHz range for salicylate and quinine-induced tinnitus and 12–20 kHz for noise-induced tinnitus, depending on the frequency of the noise trauma. These ranges are consistent with previously published results using other animal models.

Gap Prepulse Inhibition Acoustic Startle (GPIAS): Turner [10] developed an efficient technique to assess tinnitus, which we refer to as GPIAS. The dependent measure in GPIAS is the amplitude of a sound-evoked reflex in response to an acoustic startle stimulus (115 dB noise burst, 20 ms). The acoustic startle reflex is a rapid extension and reflection of a series of muscles resulting in pressure exerted on a platform. The changes in pressure are detected by a piezo transducer attached to the bottom of the platform. Presentation of the startle stimulus reliably induces a robust startle response. However, the amplitude of the response to the startle can be suppressed when a low-level stimulus, or prepulse, precedes the startle stimulus. Similarly, a detectable silent gap embedded in an otherwise continuous low-level background noise presented before the startle stimulus can also suppress the startle reflex. Suppression of the startle reflex by a prepulse or gap is referred to as prepulse, or gap prepulse, inhibition as shown on Fig. 16.1. In the Turner study, the gap prepulse stimulus was a 50-ms silent interval embedded in otherwise continuous noise (60 dB SPL, broad band noise, or narrow band noise centered at 10 or 16 kHz); the gap preceded the startle stimulus by 100 ms. In untreated rats, the gap prepulse suppressed the startle response by 50–65%, relative to trials with no gaps. However, in unilaterally noise-exposed rats believed to have tinnitus, prepulse inhibition was normal except for gaps embedded in noise centered at 10 kHz. The authors concluded that the rats had 10 kHz tinnitus that partially filled in the silent gap embedded in the narrow band noise and reduced the ability of the rats to detect

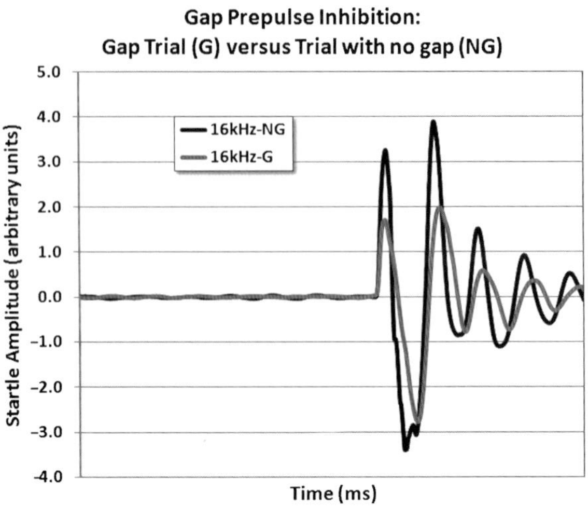

Gap Prepulse Inhibition: Gap Trial (G) versus Trial with no gap (NG)

Fig. 16.1 Startle reflex amplitude as a function of condition. When no gap (*NG*) is presented during a trial with a steady-state background noise, there is a large startle reflex in response to a brief 115 dB SPL (20 ms) startle stimulus. On a subsequent trial, a gap is presented before the startle stimulus (*G*). Detection of the gap significantly reduces the startle response

gaps in 10 kHz noise. In contrast, gap prepulse inhibition was normal for gaps embedded in broadband noise or narrowband noise centered at 16 kHz, presumably because rats could differentiate the 10 kHz tinnitus from the broadband noise or 16 kHz narrow band noise. More importantly, the same animals that showed impaired GPIAS at 10 kHz also showed evidence of 10 kHz tinnitus measured with an operant bar press discrimination task [11].

Methods of Inducing Tinnitus

Salicylate-Induced Tinnitus: In our first experiments, we used SIPAC to determine which dose of salicylate would reliably induce tinnitus [12] and to find out if these results were consistent with previous reports. Figure 16.2 shows the typical behavior of a rat with salicylate-induced tinnitus. During baseline testing, the rat made 2,000–4,000 licks in quiet (>90% correct) and almost no licks in sound (40 dB SPL). Following baseline measures, the rat was injected with saline for 2 days. Licks in quiet remained high (correct) while licks in sound remained low, indicating that the injections had no adverse effects on performance. Next, the animal was injected with 150 mg/kg of salicylate for

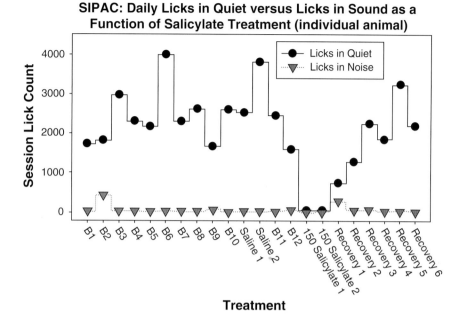

Fig. 16.2 Individual data for the SIPAC tinnitus animal model. During baseline (*B1–B10*), animals avoid shock by drinking during quiet intervals and restricting drinking during noise intervals that are paired with shock. Saline treatment has no effect on licks in quiet. When treated with 150 mg/kg of salicylate, animals cannot discriminate the quiet intervals and behave as if they hear sound consistent with tinnitus. By day 3 post-treatment, the animal returns to baseline levels. Note that licks in noise remain unchanged

two consecutive days. On these days, licks in quiet were far below a 99.9% confidence interval established during baseline/saline conditions, providing a statistical method for detecting the presence of tinnitus in an individual animal. The licks in quiet remained low during the first 2 days of recovery, indicating residual tinnitus. However, the ratio then returned to baseline levels, indicating the absence of tinnitus. A dose of 50 mg/kg of salicylate was also administered to the rat (not shown). This dose failed to suppress licks in quiet, indicating that the treatment was too low to induce tinnitus-like behavior. Finally, the animal was treated with 100 mg/kg of salicylate (not shown), which partially suppressed licks in quiet on the first day, but the effect disappeared by the second day. This result suggested that the 100 mg/kg does not reliably induce tinnitus.

Salicylate Dose–Response: The mean (*n* = 5) salicylate dose–response data are shown in Fig. 16.3. Licks in sound remained low during the entire experiment, indicating that the response was under stimulus control and real sound remained audible. Licks in quiet during saline treatment and the 50 mg/kg dose of salicylate were high, similar to baseline, indicating an absence

of tinnitus. In contrast, licks in quiet were significantly reduced during the 150 mg/kg and 350 mg/kg doses of salicylate, indicating the presence of tinnitus. Licks in quiet were slightly reduced with the 100 mg/kg dose, but the reduction was not statistically significant, indicating an absence of tinnitus. To study the recovery from salicylate-induced tinnitus, we measured licks in quiet after salicylate treatment ended. Licks in quiet were greatly depressed during treatment with 150 mg/kg, remained low 1–2 days posttreatment, and fully recovered to baseline values by the third day.

Quinine-Induced Tinnitus: Jastreboff was the first to report evidence of tinnitus in animals treated with high doses of quinine [4]. Quinine, an antimalarial agent, and its derivatives are still used in sub-Saharan Africa and in military populations serving overseas. High doses of quinine can be quite toxic and have been known to cause birth defects in humans [13]. In addition, high doses of quinine have been reported to induce tinnitus [14, 15]. The mechanism of action by which quinine induces tinnitus is not well understood, but may be related to effects on calcium channel signaling and hyperactivity. We evaluated the effects of quinine using SIPAC and GPIAS to determine the dose, duration, and pitch characteristics

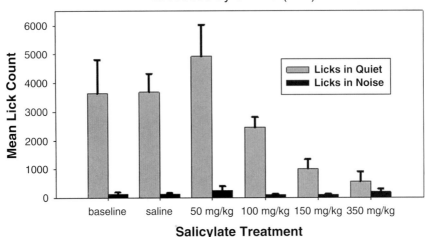

Fig. 16.3 Salicylate dose–response function. Animals drink during quiet intervals with no shock and refrain from drinking during noise intervals that are paired with shock. When treated with saline or a low dose of salicylate (50 mg/kg), animals can still discriminate quiet from sound intervals. When the dose of salicylate exceeds 100 mg/kg, animals behave during quiet intervals as if a sound was there, indicated by a decrease in licks in quiet. These results are consistent with the presence of tinnitus. Note that behavior to the real sound intervals remains unchanged

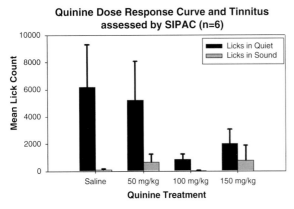

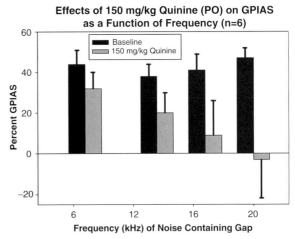

Fig. 16.4 Quinine dose–response function. Animals drink during quiet intervals with no shock and refrain from drinking during noise intervals that are paired with shock. When treated with saline or a low dose of quinine (50 mg/kg), animals can still discriminate quiet from sound intervals. When the dose of quinine is increased to 100–150 mg/kg, animals behave during quiet intervals as if a sound was there, indicated by a decrease in licks in quiet. These results are consistent with the presence of tinnitus. Note that behavior to the real sound intervals remains unchanged

Fig. 16.5 Effects of 150 mg/kg quinine on GPIAS. Compared to baseline measures, there is a progressive decrease in GPIAS at 12–20 kHz. These results indicate that animals cannot reliably detect silent gaps embedded in NBN 12–20 kHz, suggesting the presence of tinnitus. Note that behavior gaps in lower frequency NBN (6 kHz) remains unchanged

of quinine-induced tinnitus. Figure 16.4 shows the effects of quinine on SIPAC. At 100–150 mg/kg, quinine significantly reduced licks in quiet, indicating the presence of tinnitus. We repeated the experiment using GPIAS, and

again found a dose–dependent reduction in the ability to detect silent gaps. The effects on GPIAS are shown on Fig. 16.5. Note that the pitch of quinine-induced tinnitus was 16–20 kHz.

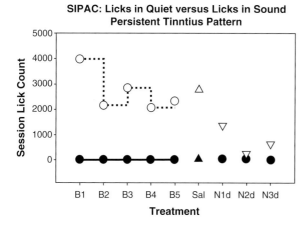

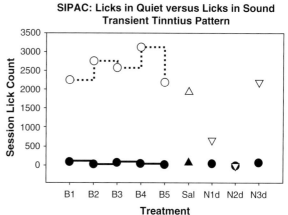

Fig. 16.6 Animals were evaluated for the presence of tinnitus using SIPAC after a 120-dB SPL unilateral noise exposure. Some animals, as indicated by *downward open triangles*, develop evidence of tinnitus (decreased licks in quiet) that was still present 3 days postnoise trauma

Fig. 16.7 Animals were evaluated for the presence of tinnitus using SIPAC after a 120-dB SPL unilateral noise exposure. Some animals, as indicated by *downward open triangles*, develop evidence of tinnitus (decreased licks in quiet). However, the tinnitus is only transient and licks in quiet recover to baseline levels by day 3 postnoise trauma

Noise-Induced Tinnitus: We first used SIPAC to determine if individual rats developed tinnitus after unilateral exposure to narrow band noise centered at 11 kHz (120 dB, 2 h). The exposure resulted in a 35–50 dB high-frequency hearing loss (confirmed by auditory brainstem response) immediately after the exposure, but hearing remained nearly normal in the contralateral, unexposed ear. As shown in Fig. 16.6, some rats developed persistent tinnitus (open downward triangles). Note a large decrease in the number of licks in quiet from baseline (B1–5) after noise exposure (N1d–N3d), indicating the presence of tinnitus. Other rats developed transient tinnitus for a day or two (Fig. 16.7, licks in quiet, open downward triangles), and then recovered to baseline by postnoise day 3. Some rats, however, failed to develop noise-induced tinnitus (not shown), consistent with other studies [6]. These results are in agreement with human studies showing that some individuals develop noise-induced tinnitus while others do not (see Chap. 37). These data illustrate the importance of assessing tinnitus in individual rats rather than solely assessing group data.

In addition to SIPAC, we recently evaluated the effect of unilateral noise-induced hearing loss on the development of tinnitus under GPIAS. Like previous studies, animals show a range of variability in their susceptibility to noise-induced hearing loss and noise-induced tinnitus. However, we have found that the maximum hearing loss and tinnitus pitch resulting from the unilateral noise trauma is often ½–1 octave

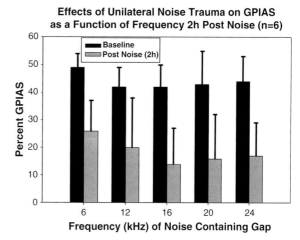

Fig. 16.8 Effects of 12 kHz unilateral noise trauma on GPIAS. Compared to baseline measures, there is a decrease in GPIAS across all frequencies tested 2 h post-exposure. These results indicate that animals cannot reliably detect silent gaps embedded in NBN 6–24 kHz, suggesting the presence of an early onset broadband or loud tinnitus

above the noise exposure. For instance, when one group of animals was exposed to 12 kHz bandpass noise (123 dB SPL) unilateral noise trauma, GPIAS was reduced initially across multiple frequencies as shown in Fig. 16.8 (2 h postnoise). However, recovery typically occurred at frequencies both below the noise trauma and greater than one octave above the noise trauma and by day 4 postnoise, there was complete recovery (Fig. 16.9). Increasing the frequency of the noise trauma to 16 kHz narrow band noise (120 dB SPL, 1 h) shifted evidence of tinnitus to 20 kHz (Fig. 16.10); results are consistent with the maximum hearing loss in the exposed ear.

In order to ensure that the tinnitus effects observed were not the result of hearing loss, we ran noise burst

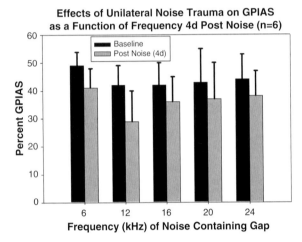

Fig. 16.9 Effects of 12 kHz unilateral noise trauma on GPIAS 4 days postnoise exposure. There is nearly complete recovery of GPIAS across all frequencies relative to 2 h posttrauma (Fig. 16.8), indicating that the transient tinnitus is no longer present

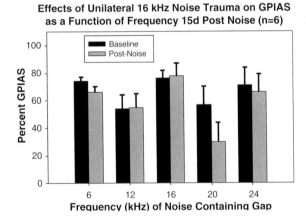

Fig. 16.10 Effects of 16 kHz unilateral noise trauma on GPIAS. Compared to baseline measures, there is a decrease in GPIAS at 20 kHz that persists at 15 days post-exposure. These results indicate that animals cannot reliably detect silent gaps embedded in NBN at 20 kHz, suggesting the presence of persistent high-frequency tinnitus. Note that animals can reliably detect gaps when the carrier noise frequency is lower or higher than 20 kHz

prepulse inhibition (NBPIAS). Under NBPIAS, a brief 60 dB SPL narrow band prepulse (50–100 ms, 6, 12, 16, 20, and 24 kHz) was presented in a quiet background 100 ms before the startle stimulus. Similar to GPIAS, if the animal detects the prepulse preceding the startle stimulus, the acoustic startle reflex will be greatly reduced compared to conditions in which no prepulse is present, resulting in a high percentage of NBPIAS. We found that unilaterally exposed animals could easily perform this task and had robust NBPIAS, indicating that the animals were able to detect the 60 dB prepulse tone. In contrast, GPIAS was reduced when gaps were inserted into continuous NBN of the same frequencies and intensities as tested by NBPIAS. To further confirm the status of the unexposed ear and exposed ears, distortion product otoacoustic emissions (DPOAE) were obtained from both the traumatized and nontraumatized ears. We found that the nonexposed ear did not differ from baseline measures, while the traumatized ear showed large reductions or absent DPOAE, consistent with the effects of noise on outer hair cell function in the noise-exposed ear. The results from GPIAS, NBPIAS, and DPOAE were consistent with the presence of tinnitus in the 12–20 kHz frequency region, and not the result of hearing loss.

Tinnitus Treatments

A number of potential tinnitus suppressing drugs have been evaluated in animal models. The following section presents an overview of drugs from different classes that have been suggested or hypothesized as potential treatments for tinnitus (see also Chaps. 78 and 79).

Nimodipine: This calcium channel antagonist was reported to block quinine-induced tinnitus in a dose-dependent manner [4] in rats. A subsequent human trial found evidence that a small subset of patients showed a reduction of tinnitus severity with nimodipine treatment; however, this study lacked an appropriate placebo control [16], and more research is needed on Nimopidine to determine whether it is a viable treatment for some forms of chronic tinnitus.

Tiagabine and Gabapentin: The efficacy of tiagabine (GABA agonist that inhibits GABA reuptake) and gabapentin (anticonvulsant, antihyperalgesic, antinociceptive, mechanism of action unknown) was evaluated in rats with persistent noise-induced tinnitus [11]. Tiagabine was found to have no effect on the behavioral manifestations of tinnitus, whereas gabapentin, at clinically relevant doses (1 and 2.5 mg/kg), significantly reduced tinnitus. However, a recent human clinical trial failed to show that gabapentin was effective in treating tinnitus [17]; while another found that gabapentin reduced the annoyance of tinnitus in a subgroup of patients [18].

The Excitatory Neurotransmitter Glutamate: It has been hypothesized that salicylate-induced tinnitus arises because salicylate increases neural excitation by enhancing glutamate-sensitive NMDA (*N*-methyl-d-aspartic acid) receptor currents in the cochlea [8, 19, 20]. To test this hypothesis, rats were given intraperitoneal injections of salicylate to induce tinnitus. Salicylate-induced tinnitus was suppressed when NMDA receptor antagonists (MK801, 7-chlorokynurenate) were applied to the round window of both cochleas [8, 21]. However, a recent human clinical trial found that the NMDA antagonist flupirtine was ineffective in treating tinnitus.

Vigabatrin: Previous studies have suggested that loss of tonic GABA-mediated inhibition could lead to increased neural excitability and tinnitus [22, 23]. To test this hypothesis, unilateral acoustic overstimulation was used to induce tinnitus in rats tested with an operant-conditioned suppression method [22]. The psychophysical discrimination function (suppression ratio vs. intensity) of noise-exposed rats showed evidence of tinnitus-like behavior at suprathreshold levels of the 20 kHz discrimination function compared to the control group. Treatment with low and high doses of vigabatrin (30 or 81 mg/kg) abolished the tinnitus-like behavior. However, tinnitus-like behavior re-emerged during the drug washout period. These results suggested that upregulating GABA-mediated inhibition may suppress noise-induced tinnitus. However, since only group data were presented, it is not clear if vigabatrin can suppress tinnitus in all animals or just some. In addition, since tinnitus assessment was based on discrimination performance obtained at suprathreshold levels, it was not clear whether vigabatrin could abolish tinnitus-like behavior measured in quiet as is done with other techniques (e.g., SIPAC). One concern with using vigabatrin clinically is its serious side effects (e.g., ataxia, psychotic episodes) [24]. These risk factors, unfortunately, reduce vigabatrin's therapeutic utility for tinnitus treatment.

Memantine: Memantine, a spasmolytic drug and NMDA antagonist with antiglutamatergic properties, has been suggested as a possible drug to treat tinnitus [25, 26]. We evaluated the ability of memantine to suppress salicylate-induced tinnitus using SIPAC. In control experiments, we first identified the dose of memantine alone (≤3 mg/kg/d) that did not disrupt behavior. We then induced tinnitus with 200 mg/kg of sodium salicylate (SS), and then administered memantine (M) at 3 mg/kg to see if it would suppress salicylate-induced tinnitus. Treatment with memantine failed to abolish salicylate-induced tinnitus (Fig. 16.11).

Scopolamine: Recently, the anti-cholinergic drug scopolamine (SC) has been suggested as a possible drug to treat tinnitus [26]. We first determined the dose of scopolamine *alone* (≤1 mg/kg/d) that did not disrupt the behavioral response. Then, we induced tinnitus with 150 mg/kg of sodium salicylate (SS). SS alone caused a significant decrease of licks in quiet, indicative of tinnitus. SC alone had no effect on licks in quiet. Afterwards, rats were treated with SS plus SC. SC caused a slight increase in the number of licks, but did not suppress salicylate-induced tinnitus [27].

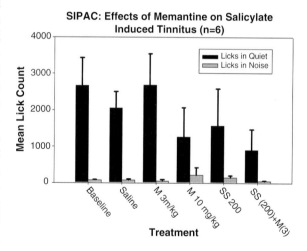

Fig. 16.11 Memantine dose–response function. Animals drink during quiet intervals with no shock and refrain from drinking during noise intervals that are paired with shock. When treated with saline or a low dose of memantine (*M*), animals can still discriminate quiet from sound intervals. When the dose of M is increased to 10 mg/kg, SIPAC is disrupted suggesting that this dose may have some nonspecific side effects. Animals were then treated with 200 mg/kg salicylate and behave during quiet intervals as if a sound was there, indicated by a decrease in licks in quiet. Concurrent treatment with 3 mg/kg M fails to reverse salicylate-induced tinnitus. Note that behavior to the real sound intervals remains unchanged

Alprazolam and L838417: If tinnitus is the result of loss of central inhibition in response to peripheral hearing loss, it is possible that increasing endogenous inhibition might suppress the aberrant signals of tinnitus. To test this hypothesis, we evaluated the benzodiazepine, alprazolam, and the GABA-A agonist L838417 on salicylate or noise-induced tinnitus using GPIAS. Alprazolam, 0.5 mg/kg, failed to reduce evidence of 16–20 kHz tinnitus in animals treated with 250 mg/kg salicylate. Furthermore, higher doses of alprazolam (>1 mg/kg) exhibited strong sedation effects and attenuated overall startle response amplitudes.

A separate group of animals was exposed to 120 dB SPL unilateral noise trauma with a 16-kHz narrow band noise (BW = 100 Hz). Following noise trauma, animals were tracked for 15 days. Animals showing evidence of 16–20 kHz tinnitus were treated with 10 mg/kg of L838417 at 2 and 15 days posttrauma. L838417 has similar anxiolytic effects as the benzodiazepine, or Chlordiazepoxide, but does not exhibit sedative effects, making it an ideal candidate for the GPIAS paradigm. Initial results showed a partial reversal of noise-induced tinnitus at 48 h and no effect on noise-induced tinnitus at 15 days. These results suggested that early administration of L838417 treatment following noise trauma may reduce the presence of tinnitus temporarily or inhibit the development of permanent tinnitus. However, after 15 days of administration, the drug has little effect on tinnitus. Interestingly, new hypotheses are emerging regarding potential differences between the acute phase and the chronic phase of tinnitus, in regard to their neural locus. Early tinnitus is believed to have a more peripheral component and reside subcortically, while chronic tinnitus may result from more central plasticity changes. These differences could explain some of the results obtained among studies.

Potassium Channels and Tinnitus: Potassium channel dysfunction has been implicated in brain hyperactive disorders such as epilepsy [28, 29]. One of the functions of potassium channels is to regulate the resting state of neurons and the depolarization threshold. The emergence of highly selective potassium channel modulators has brought forth new potential therapies for central hyperactivity. We have begun to evaluate potassium channel modulators and their effect on salicylate or noise-induced tinnitus. Preliminary data show that BK potassium channel agonists reverse the effect of salicylate-induced tinnitus, and may slightly reduce evidence of noise-induced tinnitus. However, further validation is needed to determine if these effects can be replicated and if the effects on salicylate are a drug-on-drug interaction or a reduction of the tinnitus percept.

Repeated Transcranial Magnetic Stimulation (rTMS): Transcranial magnetic stimulation is an approved therapeutic technique for the treatment of depression [30, 31]. It has also been evaluated in humans for the treatment of tinnitus [32–35]. One hypothesis of rTMS for the treatment of tinnitus is that magnetic pulse stimulation may "break up" synchronous activity in the brain associated with the perception of tinnitus.

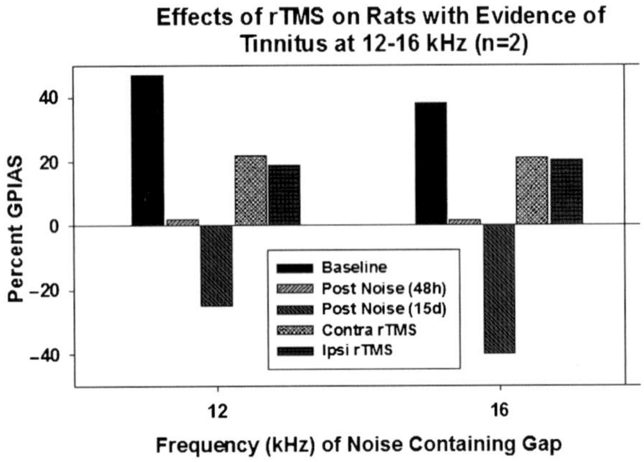

Fig. 16.12 Animals with evidence of tinnitus at 12–16 kHz were treated to two sessions (one ipsi, one contra) of repeated Transcranial Magnetic Stimulation (*rTMS*). The animals were awake and restrained and treated with 100 pulses per session. Results suggest a partial reversal of tinnitus, indicated by an increase in GPIAS

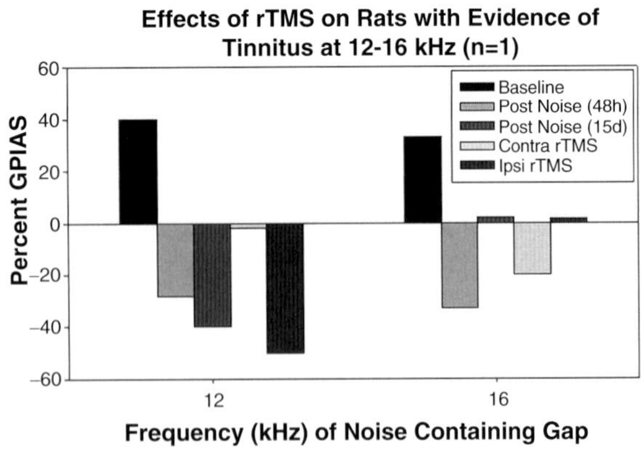

Fig. 16.13 A single animal with evidence of tinnitus at 12–16 kHz was treated to two sessions (one ipsi, one contra) of repeated Transcranial Magnetic Stimulation (*rTMS*). The animal was awake and restrained and treated with 100 pulses per session. Results suggest no benefit from rTMS in either the ipsilateral or the contralateral condition

Although the use of rTMS for tinnitus is still in its early stages, there have been some positive results in a select number of tinnitus patients (see Chap. 88). When we evaluated rTMS on rats ($n=4$) with noise-induced tinnitus, we found transient suppression after a single rTMS session (100 pulses) in two of the rats (Fig. 16.12), no change in one rat, and increased tinnitus in one rat (Fig. 16.13). The results suggested that there might be a biological basis for the efficacy of rTMS for at least some tinnitus patients.

Current Studies

Advances in our understanding of neural disorders and the development of novel pharmacological agents to manage central disorders provide newfound opportunities for potential tinnitus treatments. Engineered compounds and nanoparticles allow more efficient and effective targeting of specific receptors and channels. A combined preclinical approach among physiological, microbiological, and behavioral studies of tinnitus is likely to accelerate the finding of new potential treatments to manage or eradicate tinnitus. New human clinical trials with drugs that modulate NMDA activity are ongoing and show promising results on noise-induced tinnitus.

Summary

While no treatments are available that are effective in all tinnitus patients, a number of significant advancements have been made in tinnitus research. Physiological and functional brain imaging studies have suggested that increased activity along the central auditory pathway is present during tinnitus. Theories of tinnitus have moved away from the inner ear to a central generator for chronic tinnitus. Clinical work is ongoing for better classification of tinnitus subtypes, better patient selection is being implemented for human drug studies, and a number of animal models have been developed. This last point is of critical importance as tinnitus can currently only be assessed from a person's or an animal's subjective experience. However, the animal models allow researchers to find biological correlates of behavioral evidence of tinnitus and explore how tinnitus develops from trauma to the inner ear. Additionally, while the locus may remain unclear, preclinical drug trials can be performed to determine if potential treatments reduce behavioral evidence of tinnitus in animals. These advancements have come a long way in establishing tools necessary to reveal the biological markers of tinnitus and to develop effective treatment strategies.

Acknowledgments The authors would like to thank Daniel Stolzberg for his important contributions in developing the GPIAS animal model of tinnitus.

References

1. Jastreboff PJ, JF Brennan and CT Sasaki (1988) An animal model for tinnitus. Laryngoscope 98:280–6.
2. Jastreboff PJ (1994) Instrumentation and tinnitus: A neurophysiological approach. Hear Instrum 45:7–11.
3. Hazell J and JB Sheldrake. The Tinnitus and Hyperacusis Centre [website]. [cited 2006 15 April]; Available from: http://www.tinnitus.org.
4. Jastreboff PJ, JF Brennan and CT Sasaki (1991) Quinine-induced tinnitus in rats. Arch Otolaryngol Head Neck Surg 117:1162–6.
5. Londero A, JP Lefaucheur, D Malinvaud et al (2006) Magnetic stimulation of the auditory cortex for disabling tinnitus: Preliminary results. Presse Med 35:200–6.
6. Heffner HE and IA Harrington (2002) Tinnitus in hamsters following exposure to intense sound. Hear Res 170:83–95.
7. Bauer CA, TJ Brozoski, R Rojas et al (1999) Behavioral model of chronic tinnitus in rats. Otolaryngol Head Neck Surg 121:457–62.
8. Guitton MJ, J Caston, J Ruel et al (2003) Salicylate induces tinnitus through activation of cochlear NMDA receptors. J Neurosci 23:3944–52.
9. Ruttiger L, J Ciuffani, HP Zenner et al (2003) A behavioral paradigm to judge acute sodium salicylate-induced sound experience in rats: A new approach for an animal model on tinnitus. Hear Res 180:39–50.
10. Turner JG, (2006) Gap detection as a high throughput, objective behavioral screen for tinnitus, in The future treatment of tinnitus: First Tinnitus Research Initiative meeting 27–29 July 2006. 2006: Regensburg, Salzstadel, Germany.
11. Bauer CA and TJ Brozoski (2001) Assessing tinnitus and prospective tinnitus therapeutics using a psychophysical animal model. J Assoc Res Otolaryngol 2:54–64.
12. Lobarinas E, W Sun, R Cushing et al (2004) A novel behavioral paradigm for assessing tinnitus using schedule-induced polydipsia avoidance conditioning (SIP–AC). Hear Res 190:109–14.
13. Phillips-Howard PA and D Wood (1996) The safety of antimalarial drugs in pregnancy. Drug Saf 14:131–45.
14. Roche RJ, K Silamut, S Pukrittayakamee et al (1990) Quinine induces reversible high-tone hearing loss. Br J Clin Pharmacol 29:780–2.

15. Smilkstein MJ, KW Kulig and BH Rumack (1987) Acute toxic blindness: Unrecognized quinine poisoning. Ann Emerg Med 16:98–101.

16. Davies E, E Knox and I Donaldson (1994) The usefulness of nimodipine, an L-calcium channel antagonist, in the treatment of tinnitus. Br J Audiol 28:125–9.

17. Witsell DL, MT Hannley, S Stinnet et al (2007) Treatment of tinnitus with gabapentin: A pilot study. Otol Neurotol 28:11–5.

18. Bauer CA and TJ Brozoski (2006) Effect of gabapentin on the sensation and impact of tinnitus. Laryngoscope 116:675–81.

19. Miller B, M Sarantis, SF Traynelis et al (1992) Potentiation of NMDA receptor currents by arachidonic acid. Nature 355:722–5.

20. Peng BG, S Chen and X Lin (2003) Aspirin selectively augmented N-methyl-d-aspartate types of glutamate responses in cultured spiral ganglion neurons of mice. Neurosci Lett 343:21–4.

21. Guitton MJ, R Pujol and JL Puel (2005) m-Chlorophenylpiperazine exacerbates perception of salicylate-induced tinnitus in rats. Eur J Neurosci 22:2675–8.

22. Brozoski TJ, TJ Spires and CA Bauer (2007) Vigabatrin, a GABA transaminase inhibitor, reversibly eliminates tinnitus in an animal model. J Assoc Res Otolaryngol 8:105–18.

23. Szczepaniak WS and AR Møller (1995) Evidence of decreased GABAergic influence on temporal integration in the inferior colliculus following acute noise exposure: A study of evoked potentials in the rat. Neurosci Lett 196:77–80.

24. Tartara A, R Manni, CA Galimberti et al (1992) Six-year follow-up study on the efficacy and safety of vigabatrin in patients with epilepsy. Acta Neurol Scand 86:247–51.

25. Oestreicher E, W Arnold, K Ehrenberger et al (1998) Memantine suppresses the glutamatergic neurotransmission of mammalian inner hair cells. ORL J Otorhinolaryngol Relat Spec 60:18–21.

26. Wallhausser-Franke E, B Cuautle-Heck, G Wenz et al (2006) Scopolamine attenuates tinnitus-related plasticity in the auditory cortex. Neuroreport 17:1487–91.

27. Lobarinas E, G Yang, W Sun et al (2006) Salicylate- and quinine-induced tinnitus and effects of memantine. Acta Otolaryngol Suppl 556:13–9.

28. Wang B, BS Rothberg and R Brenner (2009) Mechanism of increased BK channel activation from a channel mutation that causes epilepsy. J Gen Physiol 133:283–94.

29. Lee US and J Cui (2009) {beta} subunit-specific modulations of BK channel function by a mutation associated with epilepsy and dyskinesia. J Physiol 587:1481–98.

30. Padberg F, P Zwanzger, ME Keck et al (2002) Repetitive transcranial magnetic stimulation (rTMS) in major depression: Relation between efficacy and stimulation intensity. Neuropsychopharmacology 27:638–45.

31. George MS, EM Wassermann, WA Williams et al (1995) Daily repetitive transcranial magnetic stimulation (rTMS) improves mood in depression. Neuroreport 6:1853–6.

32. Langguth B, T Kleinjung, E Frank et al (2008) High-frequency priming stimulation does not enhance the effect of low-frequency rTMS in the treatment of tinnitus. Exp Brain Res 184:587–91.

33. Londero A, B Langguth, D De Ridder et al (2006) Repetitive transcranial magnetic stimulation (rTMS): A new therapeutic approach in subjective tinnitus? Neurophysiol Clin 36:145–55.

34. Kleinjung T, P Eichhammer, B Langguth et al (2005) Long-term effects of repetitive transcranial magnetic stimulation (rTMS) in patients with chronic tinnitus. Otolaryngol Head Neck Surg 132:566–9.

35. Langguth B, P Eichhammer, M Zowe et al (2004) Low frequency repetitive transcranial magnetic stimulation (rTMS) for the treatment of chronic tinnitus – are there long-term effects? Psychiatr Prax 31 Suppl 1:S52–4.

Chapter 17
Objective Signs of Tinnitus in Humans

Bertold Langguth and Dirk De Ridder

Keypoints

1. Different methods have successfully been used for detecting tinnitus-related changes in the brain; chief among them are neuroimaging, electroencephalography and magnetoencephalography.
2. These methods make it possible to detect noninvasively neuronal activity in the human brain and determine the anatomical location of the activity.
3. Findings from neuroimaging have already contributed to a better understanding of the pathophysiological changes underlying the different forms of tinnitus
4. The different neuroimaging methods hold the potential to be further developed as methods for diagnosis, outcome assessment, and outcome prediction.
5. Replication of studies with larger sample sizes and clinically well-characterized individuals with tinnitus is needed.

Keywords Tinnitus • Neuroimaging • Electroencephalography • Magnetoencephalography • Functional magnetic resonance tomography • Positron emission tomography • Diagnosis • Pathophysiology

Abbreviations

EEG   Electroencephalography
fMRI   Functional magnetic resonance imaging
MEG   Magnetoencephalography
MRI   Magnetic resonance imaging

B. Langguth (✉)
Department of Psychiatry and Psychotherapy, University of Regensburg, Universitätsstraße 84, 93053 Regensburg, Germany
e-mail: Berthold.Langguth@medbo.de

PET   Positron emission tomography
SPECT Single positron emission computed tomography

Introduction

Many forms of tinnitus are phantom perceptions of sound and therefore related to functional changes in the brain. Identification of the "neuronal correlate" of such forms of tinnitus is of utmost importance for a deeper understanding of the pathophysiology and the development of new effective treatments for these kinds of tinnitus. It should be stressed that tinnitus is most likely a network property and that the "neural correlate" should be understood as such, and should not be viewed as one phrenological "tinnitus hotspot" somewhere in the brain. Several different methods have been increasingly used during the last two decades for the detection of tinnitus-related changes in the brain and in attempts to find where in the brain the physiologically abnormal neural activity is generated and to which extent the pathophysiological changes in humans correspond to those in animal models of tinnitus. In detail, these methods are structural and functional neuroimaging methods and source-localized electroencephalography (EEG) and magnetoencephalography (MEG). These methods make it possible to detect neuronal activity noninvasively in the human brain and determine the anatomical location of the activity. Even the most cautious interpretation of the available data, most of them come from small samples, indicates the potential of neuroimaging, EEG, and MEG as valuable tools in tinnitus research. These methods provide windows to the brain that allow detecting the localization of

A.R. Møller et al. (eds.), *Textbook of Tinnitus*,
DOI 10.1007/978-1-60761-145-5_17, © Springer Science+Business Media, LLC 2011

tinnitus-related changes in the brain. This knowledge is indispensable for a better understanding of the pathophysiology of tinnitus (see Chap. 21). Very importantly, imaging techniques can be applied both in animals and in humans and can so contribute to bridge the gap between the knowledge coming from clinical data and animal models of tinnitus [1].

Neuroimaging may not only serve as a tool for improved understanding of the pathophysiology but also have an impact on future diagnosis and treatment of tinnitus patients. This can be best illustrated by the recent development of brain stimulation techniques for the treatment of tinnitus (see Chaps. 88 and 90). Neuroimaging findings of increased neural activity in the auditory cortex of tinnitus patients prompted the suggestion to treat tinnitus by focal modulation of this activity with electric or magnetic stimulation. Neuroimaging has the potential to be further developed as an objective diagnostic tool for tinnitus. Most findings from studies of tinnitus-related brain changes come from comparison of groups of individuals with tinnitus with matched groups of individuals who do not have tinnitus. The results of such studies do not automatically mean that each individual with tinnitus has an identical abnormality as the ones detected when groups of individuals are compared. Further studies with larger sample sizes will be needed to estimate sensitivity and specify of different techniques for the diagnosis of tinnitus, since there is not yet enough evidence that any of the presented methods can be recommended for use in routine diagnostic management of tinnitus patients.

A further potential application of neuroimaging is for distinguishing between different forms of tinnitus. It may be assumed that differences in the perceptual characteristics of tinnitus, in the emotions surrounding tinnitus and in the response to specific treatments, would be reflected by specific patterns of neural activity, which could be detected by the use of imaging techniques. By contributing to this differential diagnosis, imaging may in the future also serve as predictor of the efficacy of specific treatments and for the assessment of treatment outcome. This will help to exactly identify the neuronal mechanisms by which specific treatment interventions exert their effects. This knowledge in turn can be useful for improving efficacy of those treatment interventions.

Whereas EEG and MEG measure directly the electrical and magnetic field, which is induced by neuronal activity, "functional imaging" methods such as functional Magnetic Resonance Imaging (fMRI) or Positron Emission Tomography (PET) measure changes in cerebral blood flow, blood oxygenation, and glucose uptake based on the assumption that alterations of neuronal activity are reflected by changes in the hemodynamic or metabolic responses. Results of the use of these methods in the investigation of tinnitus and the results from such studies are summarized in the following chapters.

Tinnitus-related functional changes of neural activity have been investigated with fMRI, PET, and Single Positron Emission Computed Tomography (SPECT). The different methods differ in the correlates of neuronal activity they detect (e.g., cerebral blood flow or glucose uptake) and in their ability to measure resting neuronal activity or stimulus-evoked changes of neuronal activity. Results from the use of these methods for the study of tinnitus will be presented in detail in Chap. 18. High-resolution Magnetic Resonance Imaging (MRI) data have demonstrated changes in the volume of specific brain structures in tinnitus patients. However, it remains to be elucidated, whether these alterations are a consequence of longer lasting changes in functional activity or whether they rather represent a marker for increased vulnerability to develop tinnitus. This will be discussed further in Chap. 19.

Chapter 20 concerns electrophysiologic methods for studies of neural activity. While the EEG records the electrical field, which is produced by neural activity, MEG records the magnetic field changes. The use of MEG and EEG is based on the assumption that electrical activity either from electrodes placed on the scalp (EEG) or from measurement of the small changes in the magnetic field that can be measured outside head (MEG) correlates with neural activity in populations of nerve cells. Typically, EEG is recorded by many electrodes placed over the surface of the scalp. Signals recorded by these electrodes can be used to construct a map of the brain's electrical activity. Both EEG and MEG are characterized by high temporal but low spatial resolution. MEG is more sensitive for currents that are directed tangential to the surface of the skull, whereas EEG detects radial sources best. Both methods have the advantage that they do not produce noise that can interfere with auditory recordings as the imaging methods do. EEG and MEG can be used both for measuring resting brain activity and for recording neural activity elicited by sound.

Reference

1. Paul, A K, Lobarinas, E, Simmons, R, Wack, D, Luisi, J C, Spernyak, J, Mazurchuk, R, bdel-Nabi, H, and Salvi, R (2008) Metabolic imaging of rat brain during pharmacologically-induced tinnitus. Neuroimage 15;44(2):312–8

Chapter 18
Functional Neuroimaging

Berthold Langguth and Dirk De Ridder

Keypoints

1. Different functional imaging methods, such as SPECT, PET, and fMRI, have been used for investigating tinnitus.
2. Neuroimaging methods have provided windows to the brain that allow detection of the localization of tinnitus-related changes in the brain.
3. Such studies have shown signs of abnormalities in many parts of the brain, including auditory brain regions but also nonauditory brain areas involved in sensory integration, in attention, or in emotional evaluation.
4. New treatment strategies have evolved from fMRI and PET findings of abnormal neuronal activity in the auditory cortex.

Keywords Tinnitus • Neuroimaging • Electroencephalography • Magnetoencephalography • Functional magnetic resonance tomography • Positron emission tomography • Diagnosis • Pathophysiology

Abbreviations

FDG-PET	Fluor-deoxy-glucose PET
fMRI	Functional Magnetic Resonance Imaging
PET	Positron emission tomography
rCBF	Regional cerebral blood flow
SPECT	Single positron emission computed tomography
[¹⁵O]-H₂O PET	Positron emission tomography with radioactively labeled water

B. Langguth (✉)
Department of Psychiatry and Psychotherapy,
University of Regensburg, Universitätsstraße 84,
93053 Regensburg, Germany
e-mail: Berthold.Langguth@medbo.de

Introduction

Tinnitus-related functional changes of neural activity have been investigated with functional imaging techniques such as single photon emission computed tomography (SPECT), positron emission tomography (PET), and functional magnetic resonance imaging (fMRI). The different methods and the results of their use in the investigation of subjects with tinnitus will be presented in detail in the following sections. Finally, we will discuss how the different techniques have contributed to identify the anatomical location of the functional abnormalities that cause some forms of tinnitus.

Single Photon Emission Computed Tomography (SPECT)

SPECT (single photon emission computed tomography) scanning makes use of a radioactive tracer emitting gamma rays to measure blood flow in regions of the brain (regional cerebral blood flow, rCBF). The emission of photons is recorded by a camera that provides a 3D image of the anatomical location of indicators of neural activity. To obtain a SPECT scan, the individual person receives an injection of a small amount of a radio-labeled compound, e.g., Technetium-HMPAO. The distribution of this compound is related to blood flow and is used as a measure for local neural activity.

A study of rCBF using SPECT [1] in 45 depressed individuals, of whom 27 had severe tinnitus, found decreased CBF in the right frontal lobe Brodmann area 45 (Broca, pars triangularis), the left parietal lobe area 39 (angular gyrus, part of Wernicka's area), and the left visual association cortex area 18 (secondary visual cortex, V2) in tinnitus patients compared with nontinnitus patients. In patients with tinnitus, the CBF was increased in the primary, secondary, and auditory association areas of the temporal lobe (Brodmann's area 41, primary auditory cortex; area 21, middle temporal gyrus; area 22, superior temporal gyrus) as compared to gender-matched controls and depressed patients who did not have tinnitus. The study also showed signs that the superior temporal gyrus bilaterally (primary and secondary auditory cortex) and three further brain areas were more active in depressed patients who had tinnitus than in depressed patients without tinnitus: Brodmann areas 18 (V2), 39 (inferior parietal, angular gyrus), and 45 (Broca's homologue, VLPFC) [1]. Another study in two individuals who had tinnitus found differences in the temporal, frontal, parietal, hippocampal, and amygdala regions when compared with normative Tc-HMPAO SPECT data [2].

Positron Emission Tomography

PET has a similarity to SPECT and makes use of a radioactive tracer (a short-lived radioactive isotope) to identify the anatomical location of indicators of neural activity such as blood flow or glucose metabolism.

As the radioactive atoms in the compound decay, they release positively charged positrons. When a positron collides with a negatively charged electron, they are both annihilated and two photons are emitted. The photons move in opposite directions and are detected by the sensor ring of the PET scanner. Reconstruction of the three-dimensional paths of the articles provides information about the maximum accumulation or metabolism of the short-lasting radio-labeled isotope at a higher resolution than obtained with a SPECT scan (1 cm for SPECT).

PET retains unique advantages in studies of auditory processing over fMRI because it is not associated with any noticeable noise, as are fMRI machines, which produce up to 130 dB noise at the location where the person who is scanned is placed. Unlike fMRI, PET can be used to study individuals with cochlear implants or other kinds of implanted

electrodes, which do not allow use of fMRI [3]. PET is also much less sensitive to body movements, such as those from arterial pulsations in the brainstem. On the other hand, PET is not widely available, is relatively expensive, and is always associated with exposure to ionized radiation, which precludes repetitive imaging sessions.

The two PET methods have been used in the investigation of tinnitus: one uses a radioactively labeled glucose (FDG PET), which reflects metabolic activity, and the other type uses radioactively labeled water ($[^{15}O]$-H_2O PET), which provides a measure for cerebral blood flow.

Studies Using $[^{15}O]$-H_2O PET

Estimates of changes in rCBF using PET with radioactively labeled water ($[^{15}O]$-H_2O PET) have been used as an indicator of changes in neural activity during transient reduction of tinnitus loudness, e.g., by the administration of lidocaine [4, 5].

Several PET studies of rCRB took advantage of the fact that few individuals can modulate their tinnitus by orofacial movements [6, 7] or eye movements, a condition which may occur after surgical operations in the cerebellopontine angle [8]. Thus, Giraud et al. [9] found that such forms of tinnitus are associated with an increase in CBF bilaterally, especially in auditory temporoparietal association areas.

Individuals with unilateral tinnitus who could alter the loudness of their tinnitus by orofacial movements showed indications that neural activity in areas adjacent to the *contralateral* auditory cortex increased and decreased in parallel to the reported change in loudness of tinnitus [10]. In contrast, auditory stimulation in the same individuals resulted in *bilateral* activation of the auditory cortex, suggesting that the abnormal neural activity that caused the sensation of tinnitus originated in the central auditory system rather than the cochlea [10]. When investigating subjects with gaze-evoked tinnitus, Lockwood et al. [11] found signs of CBF alterations in a large part of the frontal, parietal, and temporal cortex, as well as the lateral pontine tegmentum and the primary auditory cortex. Whereas lateral gaze reduced rCBF in the temporal lobe in control subjects, this was not the case in individuals with tinnitus whose condition worsened during lateral gaze. This finding suggests that gaze-evoked tinnitus may be caused by reduced gaze-evoked inhibition of the auditory cortex [11].

Tinnitus was also associated with more widespread activation of neural structures in the brain not activated by sound stimulation, including activation of limbic structures, which indicated that plastic changes of the auditory nervous system had occurred (see Chap. 12).

Several investigators using PET scans have shown indications that intravenous administration of lidocaine can modulate tinnitus [4, 5, 12, 13]. Most studies of the effect of lidocaine on tinnitus have been done in individuals where lidocaine decreased the loudness of the tinnitus. In such a study, Reyes et al. [5] found that the decrease in the loudness of the tinnitus was associated with changes in the neural activity in the right auditory association cortex. These findings were confirmed and extended by Plewnia et al. [4], who found changes in CBF in a broad region of the auditory cortex (middle temporal gyrus), including areas involved in the integration of sensory stimuli (gyrus angularis) and cognitive processing (posterior cingulated cortex) of sensory stimuli.

In a recent study, Andersson et al. [14] showed evidence that reduction of tinnitus loudness during a cognitive task (silent backward counting) is accompanied by reduced CBF in auditory cortex.

Taken together, measurements of rCBF with [^{15}O]-H$_2$O PET have consistently provided evidence for tinnitus-related increases of neural activity in auditory pathways as well as in some nonauditory neural systems. However, the use of this technique depends on the ability to influence the loudness of the tinnitus by specific interventions, which means that it can only be used in individuals who can modulate their tinnitus.

Studies Using FDG-PET

Another, and perhaps more direct method for getting estimates of neural activity uses measurements of regional glucose uptake (FDG-PET) that is related to metabolic activity and, in turn, is a marker for steady-state neuronal activity. This technique has been applied to measure steady-state brain activity in individuals with tinnitus [15–17].

This method does not depend on the ability to change the tinnitus as does the [^{15}O]-H$_2$O PET and can therefore be used for diagnostic purposes in almost every tinnitus patient. The results of using this form of imaging in individuals with tinnitus was first described by Arnold et al. in 1996 [15]. These investigators found asymmetric activation of the auditory cortex, predominantly on the left side and independent of tinnitus perceived laterality in tinnitus patients as compared to controls. Nine out of ten patients with tinnitus (two right sided, six left sided, and two with tinnitus centered in the head) had signs of significantly increased metabolic activity in the left primary auditory cortex (Brodmann area 41, primary auditory cortex), and one had increased activity in the right cortex. In one patient, in whom the severity of the tinnitus fluctuated up and down, repeated PET scans showed that the metabolic activity of the left primary auditory cortex changed in a similar way as the loudness of the tinnitus changed. These results were confirmed by a case series [18] and two studies involving larger sample sizes [16, 17] all of which demonstrated asymmetry in the auditory cortices of tinnitus patients with higher levels of spontaneous neuronal activity predominantly on the left side, irrespective of tinnitus laterality. An example for a FDG PET scan of a tinnitus patient is given in Fig. 18.1

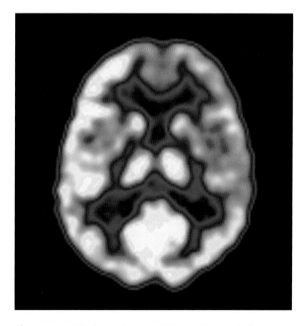

Fig. 18.1 [18F] deoxyglucose (FDG) positron emission tomography (PET) of a patient with right-sided tinnitus. The transversal slice through the temporal brain region shows unilaterally increased metabolic activity in projection to the left auditory cortex

The unilateral activation pattern resembles findings from Lookwood and colleagues, who observed unilateral auditory cortex activation in individuals with tinnitus using a different method [10]. A major limitation of all published FDG PET studies of tinnitus patients is that data analysis has been restricted to the auditory cortex by using a region of interest approach [19].

Functional Magnetic Resonance Imaging (fMRI)

fMRI is a specialized form of MRI that is used for identifying regions of the brain, where neural activity increases in response to neural stimulation, such as sensory stimulation. The use of fMRI is based on the finding that magnetic properties of hemoglobin depend on its oxygenation level and the observation that blood flow and blood oxygenation is closely related to neural activity. Regional changes in hemoglobin oxygenation occur because of local neuronal activation e.g., in response to a stimulus or during a specific task. Blood oxygenation level-dependent (BOLD) contrast is the basis of brain mapping using fMRI. BOLD contrast provides in vivo real-time maps of blood deoxygenation in the brain under normal physiological conditions. Brain regions of increased oxygen consumption are depicted by comparison of two MRI images: one at rest and one with increased oxygen consumption due to a specific task.

The use of fMRI offers several advantages over PET. First, participants are not exposed to ionized radiation; second fMRI is easier to perform, less expensive, and more widely available. Furthermore, fMRI provides high spatial resolution ($1 \times 1 \times 1$ mm) [20].

The fMRI obtained in individuals with bilateral tinnitus show symmetrical activation in all investigated areas of the auditory pathways (auditory cortex, thalamus, and inferior colliculus) while all published studies show that in individuals with unilateral tinnitus altered activation patterns only of structures contralateral to where the tinnitus is perceived were observed [21–24]. Lanting et al. found an increased sensitivity of the contralateral inferior colliculus to the loudness of the presented acoustic stimuli, whereas Melcher and Smits observed reduced neuronal activation in the contralateral inferior colliculus in individuals with tinnitus.

For the correct interpretation of these data, it is important to remember that functional MRI activation always represents a comparison between two activation states. Energy usage by the brain depends largely on firing rate [25], and it has been shown that high-frequency activity in the gamma range correlates with the BOLD signal in the auditory cortex [26, 27]. Thus, increased spontaneous neural activity, such as postulated in tinnitus patients, may imply only a limited increase in activity during stimulation with sound due to a ceiling effect. According to this saturation model, hypoactivation in fMRI has been interpreted as a possible indicator of pathologically increased neuronal spontaneous activity.

Functional MRI can also provide information about the tonotopic organization of the auditory cortex (Fig. 18.2). In individuals with pure-tone tinnitus, fMRI during presentation of a tone with the frequency of the tinnitus has made it possible to determine the anatomical localization of the representation of the tinnitus frequency in the primary and secondary auditory cortices. The fMRI technique has been used for finding the best placement of the stimulating electrode for epidural cortical stimulation [28]. However, there

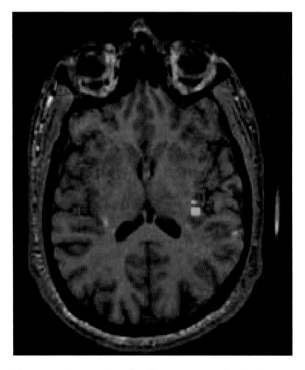

Fig.18.2 Visualization of auditory cortex activation induced by sounds of different frequencies: activation induced by 4 kHz is displayed in green, activation caused by 0,5 kHz in red

are no fMRI studies available that investigated systematically potential alterations of the tonotopic map in tinnitus patients.

In a recent study, fMRI studies were combined with an emotional paradigm in order to identify tinnitus-related changes in emotional processing (Rosengarth et al., personal communication). The study showed signs of abnormal neural activity in the hippocampus, the parahippocampal gyrus, and the amygdala that were independent from depressive comorbidity. These results provide further experimental evidence for the involvement of limbic brain structures in tinnitus [29, 30].

Summary of the Use of Imaging Methods for Studies of Tinnitus

A summary of the findings of functional imaging studies in tinnitus is given in table 1 and in Fig. 18.3 PET

studies have shown which areas of the brain are involved in the tinnitus network: primary [10, 15, 17, 31] and secondary auditory cortex, extending into the temporoparietal junction (=auditory association area) [1, 2, 9, 31]; (para)hippocampus [10]; medial geniculate body [10]; anterior [32] and posterior cingulate cortex [4, 33]; and precuneus and inferior lateral parietal cortex [12]. Voxel-based morphometry adds the subgenual anterior cingulate cortex extending into the nucleus accumbens area [34], and both VBM and fMRI add inferior colliculus [21, 24, 35]. Most of the neural networks activated by tinnitus overlap with brain regions that are involved in attention to and processing of normal sounds include the primary and secondary auditory cortex, parahippocampus, amygdala, as well as the right superior, middle, and inferior dorsolateral prefrontal cortex [33, 36] have the important difference that tinnitus-related activity seems to be predominantly unilateral. More recent studies have shown that other brain areas are activated by aversive sound stimulation

Table 18.1 Synopsis of the results of imaging studies in individuals with tinnitus

Area	Individuals with tinnitu s compared to controls		Individuals with tinnitus: changes in tinnitus, induced by:		
	Steady-state metabolism	Effects of sound stimulation	Somatosensory modulation	Gaze	Lidocaine
Primary auditory cortex	⇧[1,2,3]	⬆[4,6] A[12,13]	↕[4]		
Secondary auditory cortex		A[12,13]			
Auditory assoc. cortex			↕[4]	↕[5]	↕[6,7,9,10]
Thalamus		A[13]	↕[4]		
Inferior Colliculus		⬆[14] ⬇[11] A[13]			
Auditory brainstem				↕[8]	
Limbic system		⬆[4]			↕[7,10]
Frontal lobe					↕[6,7]

Legend:

⇧: increased asymmetry of FDG uptake

⬆: increased response to sound; ⬇: reduced response to sound

↕: increased and reduced rCBF corresponding to increased and reduced tinnitus

A : Abnormal assymetry

Studies:

FDG-PET: **1**: Arnold et al. 2006; **2**: Wang et al. 2001; **3**: Langguth et al. 2006

H$_2$O-PET: **4**: Lockwood et al. 1998; **5**: Giraud et al. 1999; **6**: Mirz et al. 1999; **7**: Mirz et al. 2000; **8**: Lockwood et al. 2001; **9**: Reyes et al. 2002; **10**: Plewnia et al. 2007

fMRI: **11**: Melcher et al. 2000; **12**: Kovacs et al. 2006; **13**: Smits et al. 2007; **14**: Lanting et al. 2008

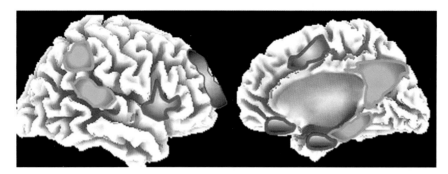

Fig.18.3 Schematic tinnitus network, as composed by integrating data from SPECT PET, fMRI and MEG studies. Areas of neuronal activity predominantly related to the acoustic tinni- tus percept are displayed in blue, areas involved in the to emotional system are marked in orange

and are related to the reward and emotional system, such as nucleus accumbens and insula [37].

New treatment strategies have evolved from fMRI and PET findings of abnormal neuronal activity in the auditory cortex [38, 39]. The results of several pilot studies using low-frequency transcranial magnetic stimulation (see Chap. 88) and direct electrical stimulation of the auditory cortex (see Chap. 90), which have been based on findings in imaging studies, have shown promising results for treatment of some forms of tinnitus. The application of brain stimulation for treatment of tinnitus patients most likely requires guidance by neuroimaging studies. Areas of the auditory cortex that have shown signs of increased metabolic activity have been identified as targets for stimulation. PET scan is now used for guidance of treatment. Preliminary findings suggest that the results of PET scanning may also serve as a predictor of the outcome of treatment [17, 32, 40].

Even data that come from relatively small sample sizes emphasize the value of fMRI, SPECT, and PET for developing new therapeutic strategies, but also show the potential of these procedures to become clinical tools for the diagnostic differentiation between different forms of tinnitus and for the assessment of treatment outcome.

References

1. Gardner, A, Pagani, M, Jacobsson, H, Lindberg, G, Larsson, SA, Wagner, A, et al. Differences in resting state regional cerebral blood flow assessed with 99mTc-HMPAO SPECT and brain atlas matching between depressed patients with and without tinnitus. Nucl Med Commun. 2002;23(5):429–39
2. Shulman, A. A final common pathway for tinnitus – the medial temporal lobe system. Int Tinnitus J. 1995;1(2):115–26
3. Johnsrude, IS, Giraud, AL, Frackowiak, RS. Functional imaging of the auditory system: the use of positron emission tomography. Audiol Neurootol. 2002;7(5):251–76
4. Plewnia, C, Reimold, M, Najib, A, Brehm, B, Reischl, G, Plontke, SK, et al. Dose-dependent attenuation of auditory phantom perception (tinnitus) by PET-guided repetitive transcranial magnetic stimulation. Hum Brain Mapp. 2007; 28(3):238–46
5. Reyes, SA, Salvi, RJ, Burkard, RF, Coad, ML, Wack, DS, Galantowicz, PJ, et al. Brain imaging of the effects of lidocaine on tinnitus. Hear Res. 2002;171:43–50
6. Levine, RA, Abel, M, Cheng, H. CNS somatosensory-auditory interactions elicit or modulate tinnitus. Exp Brain Res. 2003;153(4):643–8
7. Sanchez, TG, Guerra, GC, Lorenzi, MC, Brandao, AL, Bento, RF. The influence of voluntary muscle contractions upon the onset and modulation of tinnitus. Audiol Neurootol. 2002;7(6):370–5
8. Cacace, AT, Lovely, TJ, McFarland, DJ, Parnes, SM, Winter, DF. Anomalous cross-modal plasticity following posterior fossa surgery: some speculations on gaze-evoked tinnitus. Hear Res. 1994;81:22–32
9. Giraud, AL, Chery-Croze, S, Fischer, G, Fischer, C, Vighetto, A, Gregoire, MC, et al. A selective imaging of tinnitus. Neuroreport. 1999;10:1–5
10. Lockwood, AH, Salvi, RJ, Coad, ML, Towsley, ML, Wack, DS, Murphy, BW. The functional neuroanatomy of tinnitus: evidence for limbic system links and neural plasticity. Neurology. 1998;50:114–20
11. Lockwood, AH, Wack, DS, Burkard, RF, Coad, ML, Reyes, SA, Arnold, SA, et al. The functional anatomy of gaze-evoked tinnitus and sustained lateral gaze. Neurology. 2001;56:472–80
12. Mirz, F, Pedersen, B, Ishizu, K, Johannsen, P, Ovesen, T, Stodkilde-Jorgensen, H, et al. Positron emission tomography of cortical centers of tinnitus. Hear Res. 1999;134:133–44
13. Andersson, G, Lyttkens, L, Hirvela, C, Furmark, T, Tillfors, M, Fredrikson, M. Regional cerebral blood flow

during tinnitus: a PET case study with lidocaine and auditory stimulation. Acta Otolaryngol. 2000;120:967–72

14. Andersson, G, Juris, L, Classon, E, Fredrikson, M, Furmark, T. Consequences of suppressing thoughts about tinnitus and the effects of cognitive distraction on brain activity in tinnitus patients. Audiol Neurootol. 2006;11(5):301–9

15. Arnold, W, Bartenstein, P, Oestreicher, E, Romer, W, Schwaiger, M. Focal metabolic activation in the predominant left auditory cortex in patients suffering from tinnitus: a PET study with [18F]deoxyglucose. ORL J Otorhinolaryngol Relat Spec. 1996;58:195–9

16. Wang, H, Tian, J, Yin, D. Positron emission tomography of tinnitus-related brain areas. Zhonghua Er Bi Yan Hou Ke Za Zhi. 2000;35(6):420–4

17. Langguth, B, Eichhammer, P, Kreutzer, A, Maenner, P, Marienhagen, J, Kleinjung, T, et al. The impact of auditory cortex activity on characterizing and treating patients with chronic tinnitus–first results from a PET study. Acta Otolaryngol Suppl. 2006;(556):84–8

18. Smith, JA, Mennemeier, M, Bartel, T, Chelette, KC, Kimbrell, T, Triggs, W, et al. Repetitive transcranial magnetic stimulation for tinnitus: a pilot study. Laryngoscope. 2007;117(3):529–34

19. Eichhammer, P, Hajak, G, Kleinjung, T, Landgrebe, M, Langguth, B. Functional imaging of chronic tinnitus: the use of positron emission tomography. Prog Brain Res. 2007; 166:83–8

20. Yacoub, E, Duong, TQ, Van De Moortele, PF, Lindquist, M, Adriany, G, Kim, SG, et al. Spin-echo fMRI in humans using high spatial resolutions and high magnetic fields. Magn Reson Med. 2003;49(4):655–64

21. Melcher, JR, Sigalovsky, IS, Guinan, JJ, Jr, Levine, RA. Lateralized tinnitus studied with functional magnetic resonance imaging: abnormal inferior colliculus activation. J Neurophysiol. 2000;83:1058–72

22. Lanting, CP, De, KE, Bartels, H, Van, DP. Functional imaging of unilateral tinnitus using fMRI. Acta Otolaryngol. 2008;128(4):415–21

23. Londero, A, Lefaucheur, JP, Malinvaud, D, Brugieres, P, Peignard, P, Nguyen, JP, et al. Magnetic stimulation of the auditory cortex for disabling tinnitus: preliminary results. Presse Med. 2006;35(2 Pt 1):200–6

24. Smits, M, Kovacs, S, De, RD, Peeters, RR, Van, HP, Sunaert, S. Lateralization of functional magnetic resonance imaging (fMRI) activation in the auditory pathway of patients with lateralized tinnitus. Neuroradiology. 2007;49(8):669–79

25. Attwell, D, Laughlin, SB. An energy budget for signaling in the grey matter of the brain. J Cereb Blood Flow Metab. 2001;21(10):1133–45

26. Mukamel, R, Gelbard, H, Arieli, A, Hasson, U, Fried, I, Malach, R. Coupling between neuronal firing, field potentials, and FMRI in human auditory cortex. Science. 2005; 309(5736):951–4

27. Nir, Y, Fisch, L, Mukamel, R, Gelbard-Sagiv, H, Arieli, A, Fried, I, et al. Coupling between neuronal firing rate, gamma LFP, and BOLD fMRI is related to interneuronal correlations. Curr Biol. 2007;17(15):1275–85

28. De Ridder, D, De Mulder, G, Menovsky, T, Sunaert, S, Kovacs, S. Electrical stimulation of auditory and somatosensory cortices for treatment of tinnitus and pain. Prog Brain Res. 2007;166:377–88

29. Jastreboff, PJ. Phantom auditory perception (tinnitus): mechanisms of generation and perception. Neurosci Res. 1990;8:221–54

30. Møller, AR. Pathophysiology of tinnitus. Otolaryngol Clin North Am. 2003;36:249–66

31. Lockwood, AH, Salvi, RJ, Burkard, RF, Galantowicz, PJ, Coad, ML, Wack, DS. Neuroanatomy of tinnitus. Scand Audiol Suppl. 1999;51:47–52

32. Plewnia, C, Reimold, M, Najib, A, Reischl, G, Plontke, SK, Gerloff, C. Moderate therapeutic efficacy of positron emission tomography-navigated repetitive transcranial magnetic stimulation for chronic tinnitus: a randomised, controlled pilot study. J Neurol Neurosurg Psychiatry. 2007;78(2): 152–6

33. Mirz, F, Gjedde, A, Ishizu, K, Pedersen, CB. Cortical networks subserving the perception of tinnitus–a PET study. Acta Otolaryngol Suppl. 2000;543:241–3

34. Muhlau, M, Rauschecker, JP, Oestreicher, E, Gaser, C, Rottinger, M, Wohlschlager, AM, et al. Structural brain changes in tinnitus. Cereb Cortex. 2006;16(9):1283–8

35. Landgrebe M, Langguth B, Rosengarth K, Braun S, Koch A, Kleinjung T, et al. Structural brain changes in tinnitus: Grey matter decrease in auditory and nonauditory brain areas. Neuroimage. 2009;46(1):213–8

36. Voisin, J, Bidet-Caulet, A, Bertrand, O, Fonlupt, P. Listening in silence activates auditory areas: a functional magnetic resonance imaging study. J Neurosci. 2006; 26(1):273–8

37. Zald, DH, Pardo, JV. The neural correlates of aversive auditory stimulation. Neuroimage. 2002;16:746–53

38. De Ridder, D, De Mulder, G, Walsh, V, Muggleton, N, Sunaert, S, Møller, A. Magnetic and electrical stimulation of the auditory cortex for intractable tinnitus Case report. J Neurosurg. 2004;100(3):560–4

39. Langguth, B, Eichhammer, P, Wiegand, R, Marienhegen, J, Maenner, P, Jacob, P, et al. Neuronavigated rTMS in a patient with chronic tinnitus effects of 4 weeks treatment. Neuroreport. 2003;14:977–80

40. Richter, GT, Mennemeier, M, Bartel, T, Chelette, KC, Kimbrell, T, Triggs, W, et al. Repetitive transcranial magnetic stimulation for tinnitus: a case study. Laryngoscope. 2006;116(10):1867–72

Chapter 19
Findings from Structural Neuroimaging

Berthold Langguth and Michael Landgrebe

Keypoints

1. Structural differences in brain morphology have been detected in individuals with tinnitus compared to control groups.
2. These structural alterations involve auditory and limbic brain structures, suggesting that tinnitus may arise when alterations in both auditory and limbic brain structures occur.
3. It has yet to be clarified whether the observed structural changes represent causes or consequences of tinnitus.

Keywords Tinnitus • Neuroimaging • Magnetic resonance imaging • Voxel based morphometry • Morphological segmentation

Abbreviations

MRI   Magnetic resonance imaging
TMS   Transcranial magnetic stimulation
VBM   Voxel based Morphometry

Introduction

Recent studies, in the search for neural correlates of tinnitus functional neuroimaging, have been complemented by structural imaging research. The search for structural differences between individuals with tinnitus and control groups can in some instances identify brain areas, which are involved in the pathophysiology of tinnitus. Similar to functional imaging, the exact clinical characterization of the pathology of an individual patient is of the utmost importance as is the control for confounding factors such as hearing loss or psychiatric comorbidity. In the interpretation of imaging results, it must be considered that differences in brain structure between individuals with and without tinnitus may be signs of (1) changes that have occurred before the tinnitus became manifest, thus signs of risk factors, (2) the consequences of tinnitus that reflect plastic changes involved in tinnitus pathogenesis, or (3) a combination of both.

Structural imaging studies for research purposes are usually based on high-resolution magnetic resonance imaging (MRI). Different analyses can reveal either changes in gray matter volume of specific brain regions in an individual person (individual morphologic segmentation; [1]) or alterations in the concentration or ratio of volume of gray and white matter at the group level without any restriction to a specific brain region (voxel-based morphometry, VBM; [2]). The major advantage of VBM is that it is a semi-automatic, investigator-independent method, which allows researchers to detect structural alterations in the brain without an a priori hypothesis. This method is therefore ideally suited to give accurate insights into physiological [3] and pathophysiological (e.g., [4]) neuroplastic processes.

Studies Using Voxel-Based Morphometry

Two VBM studies have been published to date [5, 6]. In both studies, individuals with tinnitus and similar clinical characteristics (normal audiogram, no psychiatric

B. Langguth (✉)
Department of Psychiatry and Psychotherapy,
University of Regensburg, Universitätsstraße 84,
93053 Regensburg, Germany
e-mail: Berthold.Langguth@medbo.de

A.R. Møller et al. (eds.), *Textbook of Tinnitus*,
DOI 10.1007/978-1-60761-145-5_19, © Springer Science+Business Media, LLC 2011

comorbidity) have been investigated. Both studies revealed structural changes in the auditory and non-auditory system. Muhlau et al. found an increase of gray matter in the medial geniculate nucleus of the thalamus and a decrease of gray matter in the subcallosal region, including the nucleus accumbens. In the study of Landgrebe et al., areas of decreased gray matter were found to be located in the inferior colliculus and the hippocampus. Interestingly, tinnitus has been described after lesions occuring in the inferior colliculus [7] and the hippocampus [8]. The decrease of gray matter in the inferior colliculus suggests that hyperactivity in that area, as demonstrated in animal studies (see Chap. 16) and in functional imaging studies in humans (see Chap. 18), may be a compensatory mechanism. An increase in thalamic gray matter concentration may be the consequence of deprivation of input to the auditory nervous system due to a dysfunction in the auditory periphery. Change in the function of the inferior colliculus may also influence corticothalamic loops.

The Role of Limbic Structures in Tinnitus

In some individuals with tinnitus, the observed change that occurs in non-auditory brain regions, such as the hippocampal [6] and subcallosal regions of the orbito-frontal cortex [5], provides further evidence of the limbic system's involvement in the generation and maintenance of tinnitus and associated symptoms, as postulated by several models of tinnitus pathophysiology [9, 10]. These findings support the assumption that tinnitus arises if there is (1) increased neuronal activity in specific parts of the central auditory pathways as a consequence of hearing loss (deprivation of input to the auditory nervous system) and (2) a central deficit in cancelation of meaningless signals in the auditory pathways.

Thus, several types of studies seem to agree that tinnitus-related activity in the central auditory pathways is relayed in parallel to limbic structures, which might act to evaluate the importance of the auditory signal. Habituation to meaningless sensory signals, which are mediated by the subcallosal region, the nucleus accumbens, and the hippocampus, is normally assumed to cancel out the tinnitus signal at the thalamic level and prevents the signal from being consciously perceived [5]. However, if this filter fails, increased

activity in the central auditory system (e.g., due to altered sensory input) might be consciously perceived as tinnitus and the limbic structures may become involved in forming negative emotional associations with the tinnitus sound.

The Auditory Cortex

Surprisingly, both of the VBM studies mentioned above did not show any changes in the auditory cortex, despite the fact that functional imaging (see Chap. 18) as well as TMS studies (see Chap. 88) indicate that the auditory cortex is involved in the pathophysiology of tinnitus. This could be due to the high inter-individual variability in the morphology of the auditory cortex, which makes it difficult to detect changes of gray matter density with VBM. A study that used a different technique for assessing potential structural changes in the auditory cortex, namely individual morphological segmentation of the medial partition of Heschl's gyrus [1], found that individuals with tinnitus had significantly smaller auditory cortex volumes than controls. In individuals with unilateral tinnitus, this effect was almost only seen in the hemisphere ipsilateral to the affected ear. In bilateral tinnitus, the volume of the medial Heschl's gyrus was substantially reduced in both hemispheres. This tinnitus-related volume reduction occurred across the full extent of medial Heschl's gyrus and was not limited only to the high-frequency part usually most affected by hearing loss-induced deprivation of input to the auditory nervous system.

Conclusion

High-resolution magnet resonance imaging has revealed alterations of the brain structure both in the central auditory pathways and in the limbic system of individuals with tinnitus. Whether the observed structural changes may represent the cause or the effect of tinnitus is yet to be explained. Longitudinal studies may indicate whether the observed structural changes result from tinnitus-related functional changes or whether they constitute a vulnerability factor in the generation of the abnormal neural activity that causes tinnitus.

References

1. Schneider, P, Andermann, M, Wengenroth, M, Goebel, R, Flor, H, Rupp, A, et al. Reduced volume of Heschl's gyrus in tinnitus. Neuroimage. 2009;45(3):927–39

2. Ashburner, J, Friston, KJ. Voxel-based morphometry–the methods. Neuroimage. 2000;11:805–21

3. Draganski, B, Gaser, C, Busch, V, Schuierer, G, Bogdahn, U, May, A. Neuroplasticity: changes in grey matter induced by training. Nature. 2004;427:311–2

4. May, A, Ashburner, J, Buchel, C, McGonigle, DJ, Friston, KJ, Frackowiak, RS, et al. Correlation between structural and functional changes in brain in an idiopathic headache syndrome. Nat Med. 1999;5(7):836–8

5. Muhlau, M, Rauschecker, JP, Oestreicher, E, Gaser, C, Rottinger, M, Wohlschlager, AM, et al. Structural brain changes in tinnitus. Cereb Cortex. 2006;16(9):1283–8

6. Landgrebe M, Langguth B, Rosengarth K, Braun S, Koch A, Kleinjung T, et al. Structural brain changes in tinnitus: Grey matter decrease in auditory and nonauditory brain areas. Neuroimage. 2009;46(1):213–8

7. Stimmer, H, Borrmann, A, Loer, C, Arnold, W, Rummeny, EJ. Monaural tinnitus from a contralateral inferior colliculus hemorrhage. Audiol Neurootol. 2009;14(1):35–8

8. Corkin, S, Amaral, DG, Gonzalez, RG, Johnson, KA, Hyman, BT. H M's medial temporal lobe lesion: findings from magnetic resonance imaging. J Neurosci. 1997;17(10): 3964–79

9. Jastreboff, PJ. Phantom auditory perception (tinnitus): mechanisms of generation and perception. Neurosci Res. 1990;8:221–54

10. Møller, AR. Pathophysiology of tinnitus. Otolaryngol Clin North Am. 2003;36:249–66

Chapter 20
A Global Brain Model of Tinnitus

Winfried Schlee, Isabel Lorenz, Thomas Hartmann, Nadia Müller, Hannah Schulz, and Nathan Weisz.

Keypoints

1. Subjective tinnitus is characterized by the perception of a phantom sound in the absence of any physical source.
2. While transient tinnitus usually lasts only a couple of seconds to a few hours, chronic tinnitus is an ongoing conscious perception of sound for more than 6 months with low incidence of spontaneous remissions.
3. Empirical studies in animals and humans often show enhancement of cortical excitability in the auditory areas associated with the tinnitus.
4. Theoretical and experimental studies suggest an additional involvement of extra-auditory cortical regions, especially the frontal cortex, the parietal cortex, and the cingulum.
5. Using magnetoencephalograpic recordings, we found that these areas are functionally connected with each other and form a global fronto–parietal–cingulate network.
6. The top–down influence of this global network on auditory areas is associated with the distress that is perceived by many individuals with tinnitus.
7. We suggest that both entities – the enhanced excitability of the central auditory system and the integration with a global cortical network – are important to generate and maintain a conscious percept of tinnitus.
8. This chapter will concentrate on how a conscious perception of tinnitus is formed and maintained throughout a lifetime.

Keywords Chronic tinnitus • Conscious perception • Global network • Cortical connectivity • Top–down • Long-range connectivity

Abbreviations

ACC	Anterior cingulate cortex
AM	Amplitude modulation
dB	Decibel
DPFC	Dorsolateral prefrontal cortex
EEG	Electroencephalography
ERS	Event-related synchronization
Hz	Hertz
MEG	Magnetoencephalography
OF	Orbitofrontal cortex
PCC	Posterior cingulate cortex
PDC	Partial directed coherence
PET	Positron emission tomography
rCBF	Regional cerebral blood flow
SLIM	Synchronization by loss of inhibition model
SPL	Sound pressure level
SSR	Steady state response

Introduction

Subjective tinnitus is characterized by a conscious perception of a sound in the absence of any physical source. This sound is typically described as a tone, a hissing or roaring noise, and in some cases as a combination of several sounds. Transient tinnitus, a phenomenon perceived by a large percentage of the population at least once in a lifetime, typically lasts a few seconds to a few hours. A far smaller percentage (5–15%) of people in western societies reports hearing their tinnitus constantly for more than 6 months [1]. Such an

W. Schlee (✉)
Department of Psychology, University of Konstanz,
P.O. Box 25, 78457, Konstanz, Germany
e-mail: winfried.schlee@uni-konstanz.de

A.R. Møller et al. (eds.), *Textbook of Tinnitus*,
DOI 10.1007/978-1-60761-145-5_20, © Springer Science+Business Media, LLC 2011

ongoing perception of tinnitus has the potential to impair the ability to concentrate, to disturb sleep, to affect social interactions, and it may even cause psychiatric problems. Indeed, about 1–3% of the general population reports that their tinnitus adversely affects their quality of life [2].

In this chapter, we will concentrate on how a conscious perception of tinnitus is formed and maintained in the brain. In general, our sensory systems constantly receive an overwhelming amount of sensory input, which – although being processed within the nervous system e.g., primary sensory regions – does not enter our consciousness completely. In fact, most of the stimuli remain unconscious and our conscious perception is limited to only a few sensory events. In recent years, several studies have investigated the neural mechanisms for the conscious perception of sensory stimuli [3–6] and with the Global Neural Workspace Hypothesis, Dehaene et al. proposed a model for conscious visual perception that explains several empirical findings and observations [3, 4]. In short, this model points out two requirements for conscious perception: (1) activation of the respective sensory area and (2) the entry of this activity into a global network of long-range cortical couplings. In light of this view, we want to review the current knowledge about chronic tinnitus and suggest a model for the perception of tinnitus.

In the following chapter, we will summarize the findings of altered activity in the central auditory and nonauditory regions as well as the cross-talk between auditory and nonauditory areas in tinnitus. We will give a short overview of the studies on conscious perception of external stimuli. Finally, we suggest a model for tinnitus perception that has the potential to explain several tinnitus phenomena and propose new methods of tinnitus therapy.

Increased Excitability of the Central Auditory System

Many individuals with tinnitus are able to localize their tinnitus to one or both ears. In most cases, the tinnitus sensation is accompanied by an audiometrically measurable damage to the cochlea. Thus, one may think that the tinnitus is generated within the ears; however, this is most likely not the case. If the phantom sound was generated within the ears, a transection of the auditory nerve would reliably eliminate the ongoing

perception of the tinnitus sound. To date, there is much evidence refuting this view. There are only a small percentage of patients in whom the auditory nerve section leads to relief from tinnitus. The majority of patients still experience tinnitus after surgical sectioning of the auditory nerve [7, 8]. Furthermore, if tinnitus was generated in the periphery, a systematic enhancement of spontaneous activity in auditory nerve fibers would be present. As summarized by Eggermont and Roberts [9], changes in the spontaneous firing rate of the auditory nerve are rather unsystematic. When tinnitus is induced experimentally in animals, spontaneous auditory nerve activity may be enhanced, reduced, or even remain the same. Thus, the tinnitus perception is elicited irrespective of the utilized technique and the accordant changes in auditory nerve activity. These results suggest that for the majority of individuals, the sensation of tinnitus originates from central rather than peripheral parts of the auditory system. There is a large body of studies demonstrating the importance of central structures in tinnitus. Tinnitus-related changes of spontaneous activity can be found throughout the central auditory system. The spontaneous firing rate is enhanced in the dorsal cochlear nucleus [10], the inferior colliculus, and the primary and the secondary auditory cortex [9].

Neuroimaging studies in humans also suggest a hyperactive auditory cortex in tinnitus. In some individuals, tinnitus can temporarily be suppressed by masking or lidocaine application. Mirz et al. [11] used this effect to investigate changes in regional cerebral blood flow (rCBF) during tinnitus suppression in the positron emission tomograph (PET). They reported a significant reduction of rCBF in the right temporal lobe during tinnitus suppression. However, changes in nonauditory structures were also observed, which will be discussed in the next section. In another PET study, individuals with tinnitus were distracted from their symptoms with the serials seven test (counting silently backwards in steps of seven), which led to a reduction of rCBF in the left and the right auditory cortices [12]. Neuroimaging recordings of tinnitus patients during resting state differ from recordings of individuals who do not have tinnitus inasmuch as the individuals with tinnitus experience an ongoing phantom sound. Using magnetoencephalography (MEG) in resting state recordings, Weisz et al. [13] reported a significant enhancement of delta (1–4 Hz) activity and a concomitant reduction of alpha (8–12 Hz) activity in individuals with tinnitus. These changes were most prominent in the temporal regions and correlated with the subjective rating of tinnitus distress. A later analysis on an extended dataset also showed a significant increase of gamma frequencies (40–90 Hz) in the left and right temporal lobe of the tinnitus group [14]. These results fit well into a recently proposed framework that explains enhanced synchronization of auditory activity by a reduction of cortical inhibition ("Synchronization by Loss of Inhibition Model," SLIM, [15]). Synchronized alpha activity is often assumed to be an indicator for active cortical inhibition mechanisms: A decrease in alpha power is associated with an increase in cortical excitability [16–18], while an increase in alpha power (also called Event-Related Synchronization, ERS) reflects inhibition [16]. The alpha desynchronization, as observed in chronic tinnitus, reflects a release of inhibition and thus favors the synchronization of neuronal activity. Altogether, the elevated rCBF (in PET), the enhancement of gamma band synchronization (in MEG), and the augmented spontaneous firing rate (single-unit recordings in animals) all act as an indicator for increased excitability of the auditory cortex in tinnitus.

Integration of Auditory and Nonauditory Brain Activity

Changes in brain activity accompanying tinnitus are not restricted to the auditory cortices. In the study by Mirz et al. referred to above, tinnitus suppression was accompanied by a reduction of rCBF in the temporal lobe, but also in the frontal lobe and posterior brain regions [11]. The MEG study by Weisz et al. [13] demonstrates alpha power decrease and delta power increase mainly located in the temporal lobe, but also extending into frontal and parietal sites.

Furthermore, there are also reports of structural changes in gray and white matter regarding chronic tinnitus. In a voxel-based morphometry study, Mühlau displayed a decrease of gray matter density in subcollosal regions and a gray matter increase in the posterior thalamus, and the medial geniculate body for tinnitus patients compared with healthy controls [19].

These results suggest an involvement of extra-auditory brain regions in the generation and/or perception of the phantom tinnitus sound. As hypothesized earlier by Jastreboff, the neural activity that causes tinnitus is generated within the auditory system, while nonauditory

regions are involved in encoding the conscious percept as well as the emotional evaluation of it [20]. This hypothesis is supported by a study conducted in the 1960s, which revealed that a disconnection of the prefrontal cortex resulted in a reduction of tinnitus annoyance in most of the surviving patients [21]. Also, almost all clinicians are aware of anecdotal evidence that chronic tinnitus patients are often not aware or disturbed by their tinnitus (e.g., when distracted), but it can become the focus of attention or brought back into conscious awareness at any time. Based on these results and theoretical considerations, we postulate the existence of a widespread tinnitus network functionally connecting auditory and nonauditory brain regions. If such a network existed, there should be a considerable difference in the long-range cortical networks between participants with tinnitus and control participants who do not report an ongoing perception of tinnitus. Furthermore, if the connectivity between auditory and nonauditory regions encodes tinnitus distress, a correlation between the functional inter-regional connectivities and tinnitus distress should be revealed. We challenged these suppositions in three studies with MEG recordings in tinnitus and nontinnitus control participants.

In the first study, we employed auditory steady-state responses (SSR) to entrain the tinnitus network and investigated long-range functional connectivity across various nonauditory brain regions [22]. We presented amplitude-modulated (AM) tones of three different carrier frequencies to 22 participants (12 individuals with tinnitus and 10 controls). One of these stimuli was designed to match the individual tinnitus sound and the two other were control tones that were 1.1 and 2.2 octaves below the frequency of the tinnitus. Cortical connectivity was analyzed by means of phase synchronization in the participants with tinnitus and in healthy controls. We found a deviating pattern of long-range functional connectivity in tinnitus that was strongly correlated with individual ratings of tinnitus intrusiveness. Phase couplings between the anterior cingulum and the right frontal lobe as well as phase couplings between the anterior cingulum and the right parietal lobe demonstrated significant *condition* times *group* interactions. They were correlated with individual tinnitus distress ratings in the tinnitus condition. This study provided the first evidence for tinnitus-related alterations in the long-range synchronization between distant brain regions outside auditory areas.

The second study aimed to investigate the cortical networks in the resting state [23]. The analysis was based on a sample of 41 participants: 21 individuals with chronic tinnitus and 20 healthy control participants who did not have tinnitus. Cortical coupling was again analyzed by means of phase-locking analysis between distant brain regions. We found a significant decrease of inter-areal coupling in the alpha (9–12 Hz) band and a significant increase of inter-areal coupling in the 48–54 Hz gamma frequency range for the tinnitus group. Furthermore, an inverse relationship ($r = -0.71$) of the alpha and gamma network coupling was observed for all participants. Discrimination analysis revealed a separation of 83% between the tinnitus and the control group based on the alpha and gamma couplings. Post hoc analysis showed an influence of tinnitus manifestation on gamma coupling. In the participants who had a short tinnitus history, the left temporal cortex was predominant in the gamma network, whereas in the participants who had a longer tinnitus duration, the gamma network was more widely distributed across the cortex.

This study demonstrated disturbances in the long-range cortical coupling in individuals with tinnitus under resting conditions. The resting state is of particular interest for tinnitus research since individuals with this condition typically report an enhanced perception of the tinnitus when they are in a quiet surrounding. The results of the second study are in line with several other findings demonstrating the emergence of functional connectivity across widely distributed brain areas, in association with a conscious perception of the stimulus [3, 4, 6, 24, 25]. This connectivity may be an important mechanism of the brain in binding different features of the stimulus to form a comprehensive perception. Additionally, this connectivity might serve as an amplifier that enhances the neuronal activity in sensory areas (e.g., [3]).

In a recently published framework on chronic tinnitus, Weisz et al. proposed a top–down influence of higher order brain areas on the cortical activity in the auditory cortex [15]. With the third study [26] we specifically aimed to assess this top–down influence using partial directed coherence (PDC) – a measure that is based on the concept of Granger causality and allows for investigating the directionality of information flow between distant brain regions in the frequency domain.

Using MEG, we investigated the long-range cortical networks of individuals with chronic tinnitus ($n = 23$)

and healthy controls ($n = 24$) in the resting state. A beam-forming technique was applied to reconstruct the brain activity at source level, and the directed functional coupling between all voxels was analyzed by means of Partial Directed Coherence. Within a cortical network hubs are brain structures that either influence a great number of other brain regions or are influenced by a great number of other brain regions. A strong outflow in this context indicates that this brain area considerably influences the activity of other brain structures. In the tinnitus group, two brain regions were identified with stronger outflow and one site with a weaker outflow. Stronger outflows were located in the prefrontal cortex and in the posterior part (parieto-occipital/occipital) of the brain. The weaker outflow was found in the orbitofrontal cortex (OFC). All these changes in the outflow behavior were found for the gamma frequency band above 30 Hz. A strong inflow means that this brain area is strongly driven by other brain regions.

With respect to the inflow characteristics, we found two sites with significant group differences. The OFC received more inflow in the high-frequency gamma range in the tinnitus group compared to the control group. Posterior parts of the cortex received less inflow from other brain areas in a broad frequency range, including slow waves, alpha, low beta, and gamma frequencies. Furthermore, we found the inflow to the temporal cortices correlated positively with subjective ratings of tinnitus distress: the more the activity in the temporal cortices was driven by other brain regions, the stronger the subjective distress reported by the participants. Additionally, we demonstrated that the inflow to the temporal cortex mainly originates from the prefrontal cortex and the posterior part of the brain; both are structures that we have characterized with a strong outflow within this network.

A Short Notion on Long-Range Cortical Networks

Long-range synchronization of distant brain regions has been first reported by Gray et al. [27]. They revealed synchronized oscillatory responses between neighboring columns in the visual cortex of the cat. Based on this finding, they proposed that synchronization combines different features of the visual pattern, which is processed in different specialized columns of the visual cortex to form a common percept of the visual scene. While Gray et al. reported synchronization between cortical columns within the visual cortex, further studies demonstrated synchronization also over longer distances in the brain using noninvasive recording techniques: Miltner et al. [28] revealed long-range synchronization between the visual cortex and somatosensory areas during an associative learning task. Hummel and Gerloff [29] showed that successful performance in a visuotactile discrimination task significantly correlates with long-range coherence between the visual and the sensorimotor cortex. Melloni et al. [6] used different masks to manipulate whether a test stimulus was visible or invisible to the participants. They found significantly different gamma phase locking across widely separated regions of the brain for the "visible" and the "invisible" condition. Supp et al. [30] visually presented familiar and unfamiliar objects and revealed different patterns of long-range coupling between frontal, temporal, and parietal areas. This leads to the assumption that successful communication between widely distributed brain areas depends on long-range synchronization (also called "long-range coherence" or "long-range coupling"). Furthermore, in the "Communication Through Coherence" model, Pascal Fries also suggested that the absence of synchronization between distant brain regions prevents communication between them. Hence, irritations in the synchronization pattern can lead to major disturbances of brain functions.

Indeed, abnormal patterns of long-range functional coupling were reported in several pathologies. For instance, Uhlhaas and Singer [31] investigated schizophrenic patients during a Gestalt perception task and discovered a reduction of beta-band phase synchrony that might be related to their impairment in grouping stimulus elements to form a coherent percept. A reduction of long-range synchronization has also been detected in Alzheimer's disease [32] and autism [33, 34]. Le van Quyen et al. [35] reported a decrease of long-range synchrony for the preictal phase in epilepsy with the epileptic focus. This isolation was accompanied by an increase of local synchrony within the epileptic focus. Silberstein et al. [36] discovered an increase of cortico-cortical coupling in Parkinson's disease that correlated with the strength of Parkinsonism. Therapeutic interventions like the application of L-dopa or electrical stimulation of the subthalamic nucleus resulted in a reduction of the cortico-cortical coupling and Parkinson symptoms.

The theoretical framework on conscious perception suggested by Dehaene et al. asserts the existence of a global neuronal workspace that is distributed over the whole cortex. It is mainly located in the parietal lobe, the frontal lobe, the cingulate cortex, and the sensory systems [3, 4]. In order to form a conscious percept of a stimulus, two conditions are required: first, neuronal activity of the sensory cortex of the respective modality and second, an entry into the global neuronal workspace and thus long-range coupling between the widely distributed workspace neurons. According to this model, bidirectional coupling between this fronto–parietal–cingulate network and the sensory areas is needed for conscious perception (i.e., awareness of the stimulus). Activity of sensory areas without this coupling would remain preconscious. Furthermore, Dehaene and colleagues proposed that top–down influence from the global workspace on sensory areas enhances the neuronal activity therein.

Altogether, long-range connectivity might serve two important roles in brain function: First, the long-range connectivity might be a way to bind various stimulus features and integrate information from different brain regions to form a conscious perception of the (usually) external stimulus. Second, it is suggested that higher order brain regions might influence the excitability in sensory regions via long-range connections (so-called top–down modulation, [15]).

A Global Brain Model of Tinnitus

In this chapter, we propose a model for the conscious perception of the tinnitus sound, which is based on the above-mentioned studies on long-distance cortical coupling and extends earlier tinnitus models by Jastreboff [20], Eggermont and Roberts [9], and Weisz et al. [15]. Two levels of tinnitus-related neuronal processing are distinguished in this framework: the *local* (or *sensory*) level refers to the activity in the auditory areas. The *global* level refers to long-range cortical network of functionally connected brain areas.

The Sensory Level

Tinnitus is frequently associated with hyperactivity and enhanced synchronization of neuronal activity in the auditory cortex. Animal studies have shown a systematic enhancement of spontaneous neuronal activity of the dorsal cochlear nucleus, the inferior colliculus, the primary auditory cortex, and the secondary auditory cortex (see [9] for a review). Moreover, studies in humans with chronic tinnitus revealed tinnitus-related changes in oscillatory activity of the temporal cortex [13, 14, 37, 38]. In a very recent study, we investigated rock musicians who perceived a transient tinnitus after a loud (~120 dB SPL for ~2 h) band practice. Resting-state activity in the MEG was recorded at two time points: immediately after the practice and at a second day without exposure to loud music. We found a strong enhancement of gamma frequency power (55–85 Hz) in the right temporal cortex during the perception of transient tinnitus, which was also observed on the single participant level in 13 of 14 participants and, importantly, was not correlated with the degree of hearing loss (Ortmann et al., submitted).

The hyperactivity in auditory areas (i.e., enhanced spontaneous firing rate as observed in animal studies) and the stronger synchronization of neuronal activity (as observed through an increase of oscillatory power in the gamma frequency range) both argue for an enhanced excitability of the auditory cortex in tinnitus [9]. The absence of an alpha effect in our transient tinnitus study could imply that a down-regulation of inhibition sets in after synchronization of excitatory neurons and could play a crucial role in the transition to chronic tinnitus. A down-regulation of inhibition would require less excitatory activity to ignite a tinnitus-related cell assembly, putatively evolving into "spontaneous synchronization" (i.e., where spontaneous activity (firing) of neurons suffices for synchronization of excitatory neurons [15]). We suggest that the enhanced spontaneous synchronization of circumscribed tonotopically organized regions of the central auditory system is one necessary prerequisite for the perception of tinnitus.

The Global Level

A second requirement for the conscious perception of tinnitus is the activation of a global network characterized by long-range coupling between distant cortical regions. The brain contains a highly organized pattern of functional connectivity for which we report multiple evidence of disturbance in cases of tinnitus. Based on our studies, we suppose the tinnitus-related global network

to spread over the entire cortex. However, four core regions are emphasized particularly: (a) the dorsolateral prefrontal cortex (DPFC), (b) the orbitofrontal cortex (OFC), (c) the anterior cingulate cortex (ACC), and (d) the precuneus/posterior cingulate cortex (PCC). Furthermore, top–down influence of these higher order regions on the auditory cortices modulates the neuronal activity therein. The prefrontal cortex and the precuneus/PCC regions are the main areas for this top–down modulation. This idea of a tinnitus-related global network is an application of the global workspace hypothesis as suggested by Dehaene et al. onto chronic tinnitus [3, 4]. They postulated the existence of global workspace neurons that are distributed over distant areas of the cortex, characterized by a disproportionally large amount of long-range excitatory connections. Information that is processed within this network can easily be accessed by various brain systems; hence, it is hypothesized that this workspace is the basis for conscious perception. People with chronic tinnitus report an ongoing perception of the tinnitus sound. Thus, we propose that the tinnitus sound is constantly kept in the global workspace.

Furthermore, we suppose a top–down influence from the fronto-parietal-cingulate network on the temporal cortices that enhances the neuronal excitability therein. The magnitude of this influence is mediated by the subjectively perceived tinnitus distress. Support for this assumption comes from the above-described study in which we demonstrated significant correlations between the strength of the inflow hubs and the tinnitus distress. As outlined above, we presume that desynchronized alpha activity reflects a state of reduced intracortical inhibition and enhanced neuronal excitability. In a previous MEG-study [13], we demonstrated that the decrease of alpha power in temporal regions correlated strongly with the tinnitus distress as reported by the participants in our study. Two mechanisms are likely to influence alpha power decreases in the resting state:(1) a profound hearing loss that is frequently associated with the occurrence of tinnitus might lead to loss of lateral inhibition in the tonotopically ordered auditory cortex and thus increase the excitability of the auditory cortex and (2) a top–down influence from higher order brain regions on the temporal cortex might further affect the cortical excitability. Here, we assert that the later mechanism plays the more prominent role in tinnitus of the chronic state. This is largely supported by the fact that temporal alpha desynchronization

Fig. 20.1 Global Brain
Model of Tinnitus. Abnormal
activity sensory level and at
the global level is required
for a perception of tinnitus.
The global network amplifies
the neuronal activity by
top–down influence. Higher
tinnitus distress is associated
with stronger top–down
amplification

Low Distress:
Weak Top-Down Amplification

High Distress:
Strong Top-Down Amplification

Global Level:
Global Network with
Top-Down Amplification
on the Auditory Cortex

Sensory Level:
Hyperactivity of the central
auditory system

correlates well with the tinnitus distress ratings, but not
with hearing loss (Fig. 20.1).

In summary, the models state that there are two processes that modulate excitability in the auditory cortices:
at the sensory and the global level. The explanation at the
sensory level takes into account that chronic tinnitus is
usually associated with a profound damage to the hearing system (ear or auditory nerve). The reduced sensory
input leads to a decrease of inhibitory mechanisms in the
central auditory system and ultimately to an enhancement of cortical excitability therein (and favors the
synchronization of spontaneous neuronal activity).
We assume that this is the central mechanism in the generation of the phantom sound at tinnitus onset. The second explanation emphasizes a top–down influence of the
global tinnitus network on the auditory cortices. We suggest that tinnitus-related information is processed in the
globally extended fronto–parieto–cingulate network
with influence on the auditory cortex. The magnitude of
this influence is positively associated with the strength of
the perceived tinnitus distress. Stronger tinnitus distress
is characterized by stronger top–down influence leading
to a marked alpha desynchronization, which is a neuronal
signature of reduced cortical inhibition. We suppose that
this mechanism is especially involved in the maintenance of the tinnitus-related enhancement of neuronal
excitability in later periods of the tinnitus history. This
is supported by the fact that we found significant correlations between tinnitus distress and top–down connectivity,
but no results for the bottom–up connectivity.

Implications of the Model
for the Treatment of Tinnitus

The proposed model explains the partial success of
current therapies for tinnitus like Neurofeedback (see
Chap. 87), transcranial magnetic stimulation (TMS),
and cognitive therapies (see Chap. 73). Repetitive transcranial magnetic stimulation (rTMS) (see Chap. 88)
aims to reduce the enhanced excitability in the auditory
cortex, which leads to a reduction of tinnitus loudness
[39–43]; however, a complete relief of tinnitus is rare.
Regarding the global brain model of tinnitus, this is
not surprising. Even if rTMS successfully reduces the
enhanced excitability in the auditory cortices, the
amplification by the global network would constantly
fight against it. On the other hand, it has been shown
that cognitive therapies also reduce tinnitus symptoms
to some extent [20, 44]. In our proposed framework,
we speculate that cognitive therapies are able to alter
the tinnitus-related global network by changing the
conscious elaboration of the tinnitus percept. This can
potentially reduce the top–down amplification of the
global network on the temporal lobe and thus lower
the enhanced excitability therein, though there is still an
untreated abnormal pattern of spontaneous activity in
the temporal cortex that results from damage to the
peripheral hearing system. If this abnormal spontaneous activity reaches a certain threshold, it can enter the
global network again by means of the "bottom–up
mode" as explained above.

Therefore, we stress the importance of a combination of both branches in tinnitus therapy: reducing the enhanced excitability in the auditory cortex on the one hand (e.g., via rTMS), and changing the global network on the other hand (e.g., via cognitive therapies). We strongly suggest combining both treatment approaches and expect synergy effects that improve the benefit from current tinnitus therapies.

Acknowledgments This work was supported be the Deutsche Forschungsgemeinschaft (DFG), the Tinnitus Research Initiative (TRI), and the Zukunftskolleg of the University of Konstanz.

References

1. Heller, AJ, Classification and epidemiology of tinnitus Otolaryngol Clin North Am, 2003 36:239–248
2. Dobie, RA, Depression and tinnitus Otolaryngol Clin North Am, 2003 36:383–388
3. Dehaene, S, Changeux, J-P, Neural Mechanisms for access to consciousness, in The Cognitive Neurosciences III, Gazzaniga, M, Editor 2004
4. Dehaene, S, Changeux, J-P, Naccache, L, Sackur, J, Sergent, C, Conscious, preconscious, and subliminal processing: a testable taxonomy Trends Cogn Sci, 2006 10:204–211
5. Gaillard, R, Dehaene, S, Adam, C, Clemenceau, S, Hasboun, D, Baulac, M, Cohen, L, Naccache, L, Converging intracranial markers of conscious access PLoS Biol, 2009 7:e61
6. Melloni, L, Molina, C, Pena, M, Torres, D, Singer, W, Rodriguez, E, Synchronization of neural activity across cortical areas correlates with conscious perception J Neurosci, 2007 27:2858-2865
7. Dandy, WE, The surgical treatment of intracranial aneurysms of the internal carotid artery Ann Surg, 1941 114:336–340
8. Silverstein, H, Transmeatal labyrinthectomy with and without cochleovestibular neurectomy Laryngoscope, 1976 86:1777–1791
9. Eggermont, JJ, Roberts, LE, The neuroscience of tinnitus Trends Neurosci, 2004 27:676–682
10. Kaltenbach, JA, The dorsal cochlear nucleus as a participant in the auditory, attentional and emotional components of tinnitus Hear Res, 2006 216–217:224–234
11. Mirz, F, Pedersen, B, Ishizu, K, Johannsen, P, Ovesen, T, Stodkilde-Jorgensen, H, Gjedde, A, Positron emission tomography of cortical centers of tinnitus Hear Res, 1999 134:133–144
12. Andersson, G, Juris, L, Classon, E, Fredrikson, M, Furmark, T, Consequences of suppressing thoughts about tinnitus and the effects of cognitive distraction on brain activity in tinnitus patients Audiol Neurootol, 2006 11:301–309
13. Weisz, N, Moratti, S, Meinzer, M, Dohrmann, K, Elbert, T, Tinnitus perception and distress is related to abnormal spontaneous brain activity as measured by magnetoencephalography PLoS Med, 2005 2:e153
14. Müller, S, Analyse des neuromagnetischen Spektrums bei Tinnitus Department of Psychology, 2007 Diploma Thesis
15. Weisz, N, Dohrmann, K, Elbert, T, The relevance of spontaneous activity for the coding of the tinnitus sensation Prog Brain Res, 2007 166:61–70
16. Klimesch, W, Sauseng, P, Hanslmayr, S, EEG alpha oscillations: the inhibition-timing hypothesis Brain Res Brain Res Rev, 2007 53:63–88
17. Romei, V, Rihs, T, Brodbeck, V, Thut, G, Resting electroencephalogram alpha-power over posterior sites indexes baseline visual cortex excitability Neuroreport, 2008 19:203–208
18. Sauseng, P, Klimesch, W, Stadler, W, Schabus, M, Doppelmayr, M, Hanslmayr, S, Gruber, WR, Birbaumer, N, A shift of visual spatial attention is selectively associated with human EEG alpha activity Eur J Neurosci, 2005 22:2917–2926
19. Muhlau, M, Rauschecker, JP, Oestreicher, E, Gaser, C, Rottinger, M, Wohlschlager, AM, Simon, F, Etgen, T, Conrad, B, Sander, D, Structural brain changes in tinnitus Cereb Cortex, 2006 16:1283–1288
20. Jastreboff, PJ, Phantom auditory perception (tinnitus): mechanisms of generation and perception Neuroscience Res, 1990 8:221–254
21. Beard, AW, Results of leucotomy operations for tinnitus J Psychosom Res, 1965 9:29–32
22. Schlee, W, Dohrmann, K, Hartmann, T, Lorenz, I, Müller, N, Elbert, T, Weisz, N, Assessment and modification of the tinnitus-related cortical network Semin Hear, 2008 29:270–287
23. Schlee, W, Hartmann, T, Langguth, B, Weisz, N, Abnormal resting-state cortical coupling in chronic tinnitus BMC Neurosci, 2009 10:11
24. Super, H, Spekreijse, H, Lamme, VA, Two distinct modes of sensory processing observed in monkey primary visual cortex (V1) Nat Neurosci, 2001 4:304–310
25. Tononi, G, Koch, C, The neural correlates of consciousness: an update Ann N Y Acad Sci, 2008 1124:239–261
26. Schlee, W, Müller, N, Hartmann, T, Lorenz, I, Weisz, N, Mapping Cortical Hubs in Tinnitus BMC Biology, 2009 7:80
27. Gray, CM, Konig, P, Engel, AK, Singer, W, Oscillatory responses in cat visual cortex exhibit inter-columnar synchronization which reflects global stimulus properties Nature, 1989 338:334–337
28. Miltner, WH, Braun, C, Arnold, M, Witte, H, Taub, E, Coherence of gamma-band EEG activity as a basis for associative learning Nature, 1999 397:434-436
29. Hummel, F, Gerloff, C, Larger interregional synchrony is associated with greater behavioral success in a complex sensory integration task in humans Cereb Cortex, 2005 15:670-678
30. Supp, GG, Schlogl, A, Trujillo-Barreto, N, Muller, MM, Gruber, T, Directed cortical information flow during human object recognition: analyzing induced EEG gamma-band responses in brain's source space PLoS ONE, 2007 2:e684
31. Uhlhaas, PJ, Singer, W, Neural synchrony in brain disorders: relevance for cognitive dysfunctions and pathophysiology Neuron, 2006 52:155–168
32. Stam, CJ, Functional connectivity patterns of human magnetoencephalographic recordings: a 'small-world' network? Neurosci Lett, 2004 355:25–28
33. Just, MA, Cherkassky, VL, Keller, TA, Kana, RK, Minshew, NJ, Functional and anatomical cortical underconnectivity in autism: evidence from an FMRI study of an executive func-

tion task and corpus callosum morphometry Cereb Cortex, 2007 17:951–961

34. Just, MA, Cherkassky, VL, Keller, TA, Minshew, NJ, Cortical activation and synchronization during sentence comprehension in high-functioning autism: evidence of underconnectivity Brain, 2004 127:1811–1821

35. Le Van Quyen, M, Navarro, V, Martinerie, J, Baulac, M, Varela, FJ, Toward a neurodynamical understanding of ictogenesis Epilepsia, 2003 44 Suppl 12:30–43

36. Silberstein, P, Pogosyan, A, Kuhn, AA, Hotton, G, Tisch, S, Kupsch, A, Dowsey-Limousin, P, Hariz, MI, Brown, P, Cortico-cortical coupling in Parkinson's disease and its modulation by therapy Brain, 2005 128:1277–1291

37. Kahlbrock, N, Weisz, N, Transient reduction of tinnitus intensity is marked by concomitant reductions of delta band power BMC Biol, 2008 6:4

38. Lorenz, I, Muller, N, Schlee, W, Hartmann, T, Weisz, N, Loss of alpha power is related to increased gamma synchronization-A marker of reduced inhibition in tinnitus? Neurosci Lett, 2009 453:225–228

39. De Ridder, D, De Mulder, G, Walsh, V, Muggleton, N, Sunaert, S, Møller, A, Magnetic and electrical stimulation of the auditory cortex for intractable tinnitus. Case report J Neurosurg, 2004 100:560–564

40. De Ridder, D, Verstraeten, E, Van der Kelen, K, De Mulder, G, Sunaert, S, Verlooy, J, Van de Heyning, P, Møller, A, Transcranial magnetic stimulation for tinnitus: influence of tinnitus duration on stimulation parameter choice and maximal tinnitus suppression Otol Neurotol, 2005 26:616–619

41. Khedr, EM, Rothwell, JC, Ahmed, MA, El-Atar, A, Effect of daily repetitive transcranial magnetic stimulation for treatment of tinnitus: comparison of different stimulus frequencies J Neurol Neurosurg Psychiatry, 2008 79: 212–215

42. Kleinjung, T, Steffens, T, Sand, P, Murthum, T, Which tinnitus patients benefit from transcranial magnetic stimulation? Otolaryngol Head Neck Surg, 2007 137:589–595

43. Plewnia, C, Reimold, M, Najib, A, Reischl, G, Plontke, SK, Gerloff, C, Moderate therapeutic efficacy of positron emission tomography-navigated repetitive transcranial magnetic stimulation for chronic tinnitus: a randomised, controlled pilot study J Neurol Neurosurg Psychiatry, 2007 78:152–156

43. Kaldo, V, Levin, S, Widarsson, J, Buhrman, M, Larsen, HC, Andersson, G, Internet versus group cognitive-behavioral treatment of distress associated with tinnitus: a randomized controlled trial Behav Ther, 2008 39:348–359

Chapter 21
A Heuristic Pathophysiological Model of Tinnitus

Dirk De Ridder*

Keypoints

1. Tinnitus pathophysiology should explain both tinnitus distress and tinnitus intensity.
2. Distress in tinnitus is most likely generated by an aspecific distress network consisting of the amygdala–anterior cingulate and anterior insula.
3. Tinnitus intensity might be encoded by gamma band activity in the contralateral auditory cortex.
4. This gamma band activity might result from thalamocortical dysrhythmia.
5. Tinnitus distress can be seen as phase-synchronized co-activation of the auditory cortex activity and the aspecific distress network.
6. For tinnitus to be perceived consciously, it requires the auditory cortex activity be embedded in a larger network.
7. This larger network could be the global workspace, the self-perception network.
8. The tinnitus network changes in time, hypothetically via an allostatic mechanism.
9. In chronic tinnitus, the parahippocampus, insula, and dorsolateral prefrontal cortex networks are critical.
10. The parahippocampus is involved via its auditory sensory gating mechanism, suppressing redundant auditory information.

Keywords Tinnitus • Gamma • Theta • Thalamocortical dysrhythmia • Distress • Deafferentation • Plasticity • Reorganization • Networks

Abbreviations

AC	Auditory cortex
ACC	Anterior cingulate cortex
BA	Brodman area
BOLD	Blood oxygen level dependent
BPS	Band pass small
BPW	Band pass wide
BRAI²N	Brain research center antwerp for innovative & interdisciplinary neuromodulation
CAS	Complex adaptive systems
DACC	Dorsal part of ACC
DLPFC	Dorsolateral prefrontal cortex
EEG	Electroencephalography
ERP	Event related potential
FMRI	Functional magnetic resonance imaging
Hz	Hertz
IC	Inferior colliculus
ICA	Independent component analysis
IPS	Intraparietal sulcus
IEEG	Intracranial EEG
LORETA	Low resolution electro tomography
LTP	Long term potentiation
MCS	Minimally conscious state
MD	Mediodorsal
MEG	Magnetoencephalography
MGB	Medial geniculate body
NB	Nucleus basalis
OF	Other frequency
PET	Positron emission tomography
PCC	Posterior cingulate cortex

D. De Ridder (✉)
TRI Tinnitus Clinic Antwerp, BRAI²N & Department of Neurosurgery, University Hospital Antwerp, Wilrijkstraat 10, 2650 Edegem, Belgium
e-mail: dirk.de.ridder@uza.be

*With a critical review by the members of the TRI neurostimulation workgroup: Nathan Weisz, Berthold Langguth, Marco Congedo, Winnie Schlee, Arnaud Norena. Other reviewers include Ana Belen Elgoyhen, Elsa van der Loo, Sven Vanneste, Mark Plazier, Thomas Elbert, Paul van de Heyning, and Aage Møller. Not every idea presented in this heuristic model has full support of all the reviewers.

PVS	Persistent vegetative state
RTMS	Repetitive transcranial magnetic stimulation
SMA	Supplementary motor area
SPL	Superior parietal lobule
STG	Superior temporal gyrus
STS	Superior temporal sulcus
TF	Tinnitus frequency
TQ	Tinnitus questionnaire
TPJ	Temporoparietal junction
TRI	Tinnitus research initiative
VMPFC	Ventromedial prefrontal cortex
VTA	Ventral tegmental area

Introduction

If rational treatments for tinnitus are to be developed, its pathophysiology needs to be understood. However, current knowledge of auditory system physiology is largely insufficient for this purpose. Available data on auditory physiology and the neural correlate of tinnitus can be supplemented by translating physiological data from other systems studied more extensively, such as the visual and somatosensory systems, and by extrapolating from pathophysiological mechanisms known in potentially analogous symptoms such as pain. Being aware of the limitations and the potential risks of such an approach, the proposed model has to be considered as a heuristic approach that results in the generation of testable hypotheses and needs to be corrected and improved accordingly.

Pathophysiology of Tinnitus

The pathophysiological working model of tinnitus has to include the mechanisms involved in the generation of the auditory percept and the intensity of a phantom sound as well as the mechanisms causing the tinnitus-related distress.

Tinnitus Intensity

The auditory system consists of two main parallel pathways supplying auditory information to the cerebral cortex; the same two ascending systems also have a descending counterpart, the tonotopically organized parvalbumin staining lemniscal system and the non-tonotopic calbindin staining extralemniscal system [1–4]. The lemniscal pathways use the ventral part of the medial geniculate body, the neurons of which project to the primary auditory cortex, whereas the extralemniscal pathways use the dorsal part of the medial geniculate body that projects to the secondary auditory cortex and association cortices, thus bypassing the primary cortex [5], Table 21.1. While neurons in the lemniscal pathways only respond to auditory stimulation, many neurons in the extralemniscal pathway are multimodal. Neurons in the ventral thalamus fire in a tonic or semi-tonic mode while neurons in the dorsal thalamus fire in bursts [6, 7]. Burst firing consists of dense packets of action potentials followed by periods of quiescence [8]. Information theory suggests that, in general, both tonic and burst firing efficiently transmit information about the stimulus. Burst and tonic firing might therefore be parallel computations in the auditory and other sensory systems [8, 9] (Table 21.1).

Based on the differences between the two parallel auditory pathways – the lemniscal being tonotopic and the extralemniscal being less tonotopic – it has been hypothesized that white-noise tinnitus may be caused by synchronous hyperactivity of burst firing in the non-tonotopic extralemniscal system, whereas pure-tone tinnitus may be the result of increased synchronous tonic firing in the tonotopic (lemniscal) system [43]. Narrow band tinnitus could be the result of a co-activation of the lemniscal and extralemniscal pathways.

Tinnitus Distress Matrix

The same subjectively reported tinnitus intensity can be related with severe distress in some people but may well be tolerated in others. The emotional component involved in tinnitus is most likely generated in the emotional circuit imbedded in our brain. Components of the emotional system are the amygdala, the subgenual and dorsal anterior cingulate cortex (ACC), the anterior insula, the ventromedial prefrontal cortex (VMPFC), and the orbitofrontal cortex [44–47]. Some of these areas such as the amygdala [48], the ACC [49], and the orbitofrontal cortex [50] are also involved in the reward system, together with the ventral tegmental area, nucleus accumbens, and mediodorsal nucleus of the thalamus [51].

Table 21.1 Differences between the lemniscal and extralemniscal systems [10]

The extralemniscal system – aka the non-specific system, the non-tonotopic system, or the non-classical system – has the following characteristics
- Phylogenetically old [11, 12]
- Unconscious reflexes [13, 14]
- To secondary cortex [1, 2, 15, 16]
- Less tonotopic [1, 7, 17, 18]
- Slow spontaneous firing rate [19] [20]
- Variable latency response [18, 21, 22]
- Rapid habituation to repetitive stimuli [17, 18, 22]
- Fires predominantly in burst mode [6, 7]
- Stimulus detector [23, 24]
- Non-linear [24–26]
- Overrides tonic mode [24–26]
- Processes changes in auditory environment [24, 27]
- Calbindin positive [1, 16, 28]
- CB increases after deafferentation [29–32]
- Multimodal [17, 33–36]

The lemniscal system – aka the specific system, the tonotopic system, or classical system – has the following characteristics
- Phylogenetically recent [11, 12]
- Conscious perception [13, 14]
- To primary sensory area [1, 2, 15, 16]
- Tonotopic [1, 7, 17, 18]
- Higher spontaneous firing rate [37, 38] [39–41]
- Short latency response [18, 21, 22]
- Slower habituation to repetitive stimuli [17, 18, 22]
- Fires in tonic mode [6, 7]
- Feature detector [23, 24]
- Linear [24–26]
- Weaker than burst mode [24–26]
- Processes the content of change in the auditory environment [24, 27]
- Parvalbumin positive [1, 16, 28]
- PV decreases after deafferentation [42]
- Unimodal [34]

The brain resolves perceptual ambiguity by anticipating the forthcoming sensory environment, generating a template against which to match observed sensory evidence. The ventromedial prefrontal cortex has been implicated as the source of this template [52]. Positive feedback results when sensory evidence is indeed as predicted and raises hemodynamic activity in the ventral striatum (nucleus accumbens) and the posterior cingulated cortex, related to a reward and storing the received information, respectively; negative feedback activates the dACC and the anterior insula, mediated via the habenula [53]. Thus, when the brain has not obtained the information, it needs to guide subsequent behavior,

it activates the dACC–insula network to get more information.

Whenever new information is presented, the brain cannot compare this to a template, and therefore activity levels of the dorsal ACC (dACC) might also reflect the salience of the new information for predicting future outcomes [54, 55], guiding optimal decision making in an uncertain world [56].

Functional connectivity studies reveal that the dACC is functionally connected to the anterior insula [57] as well as the thalamus and brainstem [58]. The combined dACC–anterior insula activity possibly subserves intrinsic alertness [58], as the dACC and anterior insula are co-activated during states of arousal [55, 59, 60] and anticipatory arousal [61]. It has been shown that the amount of baseline activity in the dACC and insula predicts how intense a subsequent pain stimulus is being perceived [62]. The combined anterior insula and dACC activation has been suggested to act as a switch from the interoceptive default state to an exteroceptive executive brain state [63].

The human dACC has developed a parallel specialization for motivational drive via a thalamocortical pathway relaying in the mediodorsal thalamus [49]. The direct activation of both the interoceptive cortex and the dACC by the distinct homeostatic modalities corresponds with the simultaneous generation of both a sensation and a motivation [49, 64]. Thus, the function of the dACC might be to integrate motivationally important information with appropriate autonomic and motor responses [61] related to the survival needs of the body [64]. This might be based on the reward learning system, which uses dopamine as one of its major neurotransmitters. Dopamine neurons emit an alerting message about the surprising presence or absence of rewards [65, 66]. Dopamine neurons in the ventral tegmental area (VTA) are activated by rewarding events that are better than predicted, remain uninfluenced by events that are as good as predicted, and are depressed by events that are worse than predicted.

The right anterior insula has been implicated in interoceptive awareness [64, 67] related to the autonomic nervous system, the amygdala could be a relevance detector [68], and the ventromedial prefrontal cortex could be a major link between the autonomic nervous system, regulation of emotion, and stress reactivity [69]. Imaging studies on distress in posttraumatic stress disorder (PTSD) demonstrate activation of the amygdala, insula, medial prefrontal cortex, and anterior cingulate cortex [70], which overlaps with the distress network noted in pain and tinnitus. In anxiety disorders (such as social phobia, specific phobia, or PTSD) during emotional processing, the amygdalae and insulae are hyperactive; in PTSD specifically, the dACC and medial prefrontal cortex are hypoactive [71]. This could hypothetically reflect the brain's suppression of the salience (dACC [54]) of the traumatic template (VMPFC [52]). Thus, even though the same network is active, its composing structures might be differentially activated depending on the task and pathology involved.

In tinnitus, using whole head magnetoencephalography (MEG) phase synchronization analysis has shown that functional connectivity between ACC and the right frontal lobe and ACC and right parietal lobe is correlated to tinnitus intrusiveness, a measure of tinnitus distress. The phase synchronization between ACC and right frontal lobe was inversely correlated with tinnitus intrusiveness, whereas the phase synchronization between ACC and right parietal lobe was positively correlated with tinnitus intrusiveness [72]. Even though no specific studies have looked at the tinnitus distress, Positron Emission Tomography (PET) studies have demonstrated activation of this distress network as well. Tinnitus distress, as measured by the Tinnitus Questionnaire (TQ) [73], is correlated with anterior cingulate activity [74], and the anterior insula is activated in tinnitus [75].

It has been suggested that there is a lateralization of the two components of the autonomic system, with the right insula controlling the sympathetic system and the left insula the parasympathetic system [59, 76, 77]. The same lateralization has been found in the ventromedial prefrontal cortex [78, 79], consistent with earlier data on hemispheric lateralization of parasympathetic and sympathetic control [80]. This could explain why the difference between severe but compensating and severe but decompensating tinnitus distress is related to activation of the right anterior insula (Vanneste submitted), confirmed by heart rate variability data correlated to anterior insula spontaneous activity (van der Loo, unpublished data). Both studies are based on Low Resolution brain Electric Tomography (LORETA) EEGs [81] (Fig. 21.1).

Based on the clinical analogies between tinnitus distress and pain distress and based on neuroimaging data, it is tempting to speculate that the tinnitus distress network and the pain matrix are identical [82]: unpleasantness of pain activates the anterior cingulate [83] and orbitofrontal cortices, amygdala, hypothalamus, posterior insula, primary motor cortex, and frontal pole [84]. One may further speculate that the perception of tinnitus and pain intensity could be related to auditory and somatosensory cortex activation, respectively, but that the distress associated with its perception might be related to activation of a common general non-specific "distress network." This notion is supported by a recent study that demonstrates activation of this distress network during unpleasant symptoms in a somatoform disorder, even in the absence of a real physical stimulus [85].

Furthermore, the emotional network involved in pain and dyspnea [86] is similar, suggesting that the distress network might be a non-specific system that can be activated by many different kinds of external and internal stimuli.

The conscious perception of tinnitus distress and pain distress could be due to a co-activation of the thalamocortical auditory and somatosensory activity and distress network activity, possibly through synchronization of neuronal activity [72]. This heuristic model can also explain the clinical observation that tinnitus distress is frequently related to the development of tinnitus in stressful periods. Thus, a person in which the distress network is already sensitized, for whatever reason (divorce, work-related problems, etc.), would be more vulnerable to develop distressing tinnitus by increased activation of the auditory system. Once established, the co-activation between the auditory pathways and the distress network might stabilize and become self-sustaining.

Developmental and Adult Plasticity

Plasticity refers to the capacity of the nervous system to modify its organization [87]. The response of the nervous system to environmental changes can involve functional and structural changes. These changes can be induced not only by normal sensory input but also by abnormal sensory input, adaptation to damage of the nervous system, or sensory deprivation [87]. There seems to be a greater potential for plastic changes during development than during adulthood, even though similar mechanisms seem to govern both developmental and adulthood plasticity.

Fig. 21.1 2D: 2 LORETA images of tinnitus distress. From left to right are the horizontal (*left*), sagittal (*middle*), and coronal (*right*) sections through the voxel with maximal significant statistical difference. 3D reconstruction of the "distress network"

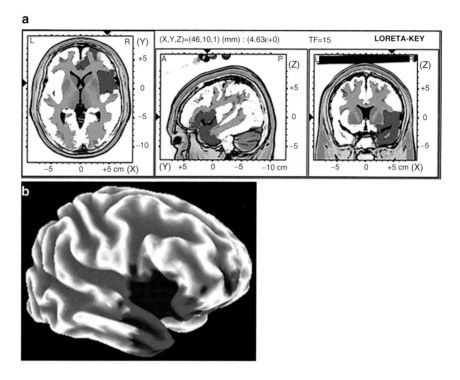

Any alteration of auditory input during the development of the tonotopy will result in reorganization of the tonotopic map according to the altered pattern of incoming neural activity. Thus, the Lamarckian and Darwinian (pangenesis) principle of "use it or lose it" guides both development and subsequent changes in the tonotopy. The auditory system develops in two stages [88, 89]. A first stage of synapse formation or auditory tract formation is genetically determined [90] and requires the release of a chemotropic factor [89, 91]. This is followed by fine-tuning of the synapses, leading to the formation of a tonotopic structure [92]. The development of tonotopy requires electrical activity resulting from auditory input during a critical period [93, 94]. It is the result of self-organization [95] via apoptotic resorption of surplus synapses and neurons [91, 96].

The mature auditory system still demonstrates an important capacity for reorganization, adjusting itself to any change in the auditory environment [97, 98]. The tonotopic maps are not rigid and may alter or reorganize under influence of normal physiological stimuli, as in learning, adjusting the tonotopic map to relevant environmental stimuli [97, 99, 100]. However, the plastic changes also occur in pathological situations

such as sound overexposure [101], partial unilateral hearing loss [93, 102], or tinnitus [103].

In addition, the tonotopic map can also reorganize via direct cortical stimulation, as demonstrated in the big brown bat. Electrical auditory cortex stimulation can change the tonotopic map at a cortical [104], thalamic [105], or inferior colliculus level [97, 105], suggesting that the corticofugal pathway is involved in this tonotopical reorganization [98]. This corticofugal system acts as a positive feedback system, which in combination with lateral inhibition sharpens and adjusts tuning of neurons in the thalamus and inferior colliculus [98, 106]. In other words, the corticofugal system acts as a mechanism for reorganization of the thalamus and the inferior colliculus [105], adjusting the tonotopy to auditory experience [97].

Focal electrical stimulation of the cortex activates this corticofugal system resulting in reorganization of the thalamus and inferior colliculus [107], all the way to the cochlea [108], as well as the auditory cortex itself [104]. It induces tonotopic changes by decreasing best frequencies slightly higher than those electrically stimulated, and increasing best frequencies slightly lower than those electrically stimulated [104].

Auditory cortex plasticity is under the influence of the major neuromodulatory systems, such as the cholinergic nucleus basalis [99, 109], the dopaminergic ventral tegmental area [110], the serotoninergic dorsal raphe [111], and the noradrenergic locus coeruleus. The effects on the auditory cortex are understandably not identical for all these neuromodulatory systems. For example, the effect of the nucleus basalis [109] and the VTA [110] can be summarized as follows:

Stimulation of	NB	VTA
Size of functional auditory cortex	Increased	Increased
Size of functional AI	No change	Increased
Stimulus frequency representation	Increased	Increased
Adjacent frequency representation	Decreased	Increased
Spectral selectivity	Increased	No change
Non-monotonic responses	Increased	No change
Frequency specificity of the effects	Sharper	Broader
Tuning of secondary auditory cortex	Yes	No
Temporal asymmetry of the effects	Yes	No
Modulation of stimulus-following rate	Undetermined	Yes
Cross-area synchronization	Yes	Does not apply

The differential effects of these neuromodulatory systems on auditory cortex plasticity might benefit future tinnitus treatments.

Plasticity and Reorganization in Tinnitus

After noise trauma, tonotopic organization in the cortex is changed such that cortical neurons with characteristic frequencies in the frequency region of the hearing loss no longer respond according to their place in the tonotopic map but reflect instead the frequency tuning of their less affected neighbors [112, 113]. Providing an acoustically enriched environment, spectrally matching the hearing loss prevents this reorganization [114]. Neurons in the reorganized region also demonstrate spontaneous hyperactivity

and increased neural synchrony [115–117], which can also be abolished by providing a spectrally matched and enriched acoustic environment. Magnetic source imaging studies [103] confirm this reorganization in humans: the auditory cortex is reorganized such that the frequency area corresponding to the tinnitus pitch is represented adjacent to where magnetic activity is expected on the tonotopic axis. Furthermore, in this study, the amount of reorganization was correlated with the perceived strength of the tinnitus, similarly to what is found in phantom pain [118]. In tinnitus patients, this reorganization is not correlated with the amount of hearing loss [103], which is the primary activator of changes in tonotopic maps [119]. This suggests that reorganization of the cortical tonotopic map, changes in neuron response properties, and tinnitus are correlated.

Deafferentation, Tinnitus, and Synchronized Auditory Hyperactivity

In tinnitus, firing rate and synchrony of firing are increased both in the extralemniscal and in the lemniscal systems. In the extralemniscal system, increased firing is observed [120–122] in the dorsal and external inferior colliculus [120], the thalamus [123], and the secondary auditory cortex [121, 122]. Furthermore, quinine, known to generate tinnitus, induces an increased regularity in burst firing, at the level of the auditory cortex, inferior colliculus, and frontal cortex [124]. This fits with the fact that in tinnitus an increased synchrony is found in the cochlear nerve [125–127] and auditory cortex [128, 129]. In tinnitus, an increased tonic firing rate is present in the lemniscal system as demonstrated in the lemniscal dorsal cochlear nucleus [130–135], inferior colliculus [136–139], and primary auditory cortex [140]. Interestingly, in the primary auditory cortex, not only tonic firing is increased, generating the phantom sound, but also the burst firing [129] at a regular basis.

Repetitive stimulus presentation results in decreased neuronal response to that stimulus, known as auditory habituation at the single cell level [141], also known as auditory-mismatch negativity at multiple cell level [141, 142]. Tinnitus is usually constantly present, i.e., there is no auditory habituation to this specific activation at this specific frequency.

This corresponds, to some extent, to habituation deficits described in chronic pain.

The Neural Correlate of Tinnitus: Gamma Band Thalamocortical Firing

The EEG power spectrum (of the oscillation rate) and the level of consciousness are correlated [143]. Slow delta frequencies (0.5–4 Hz) are recorded in patients under deep sleep, anaesthesia, and coma. Somewhat higher frequencies, called theta waves (4–7 Hz), are noted in light sleep, and alpha waves (8–13 Hz) are recorded from all sensory areas in a resting state. Frontal beta waves (13–30 Hz) are recorded predominantly when people pay attention to external or internal stimuli. Synchronization of separate gamma band activities (30–80 Hz), present in different thalamocortical columns [144], is proposed to bind [145, 146] distributed neural gamma activity into one coherent auditory percept [147–152]. In general, coherent gamma band activity is present only in locally restricted areas of the cortex for short periods of time [152–156]. Thus, persisting gamma activity localized in one brain area can be considered pathological.

Recent data from the visual system suggest stimuli that reach consciousness and those that do not reach consciousness are characterized by a similar increase of local gamma oscillations in the EEG [157, 158]. Thus, gamma band activity, per se, is not related to conscious perception. Data from the olfactory bulb, as homologue for the thalamus, indicate that percept of odor could be related to amplitude modulation of the gamma band, suggesting that the gamma band is no more than a carrier wave [159, 160]. This idea is based on the fact that a signal (information) must sometimes be attached or superimposed on other voltages at frequencies that move easier in the transmission medium. Attaching signals to other carrier signals is called modulation. Carrier waves are known frequencies that can be readily detected (using a narrow bandwidth receiver tuned to transmitted signal). Retrieving the tinnitus-related information from the gamma carrier wave might therefore be attempted by different methods: by amplitude modulation analysis, frequency modulation analysis, pulse modulation analysis, or by completely different methods such as principal or independent component analysis (ICA) of the spectrally filtered gamma band or raw EEG.

In clinical practice, source analysis of the gamma band activity in tinnitus patients can be performed with LORETA EEGs [81]. If gamma band activity is localized in the auditory cortex, an ICA of the raw EEG filtered for gamma band activity can be performed, and the independent component that co-localizes with the gamma band activity could be considered to contain the tinnitus-related information. Intracranial recordings (iEEG) give a unique way to measure brain activity directly at the site of the electrode, bypassing skin and skull resistance. Comparing these intracranial recordings to simultaneously recorded scalp EEG activity, validation of the independent components measured at scalp level has been given at the site of the intracranial electrode [161]. According to our data, the ICA of scalp EEG could indeed serve as a tool to detect the neural correlate of tinnitus, similarly to what has been suggested for contralateral auditory cortex gamma band activity [162, 163]. Incorporating this concept into the thalamocortical dysrythmia model of Llinas (see below for further information), 40 Hz is a carrier wave, carrying the tinnitus-related information, which could potentially be represented by a co-localized gamma band filtered independent component (Fig. 21.2).

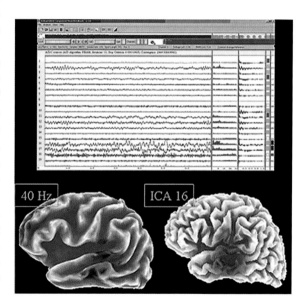

Fig. 21.2 Independent component analysis performed on a 19-channel EEG recording in a patient with right-sided pure-tone tinnitus. The 16th independent component co-localizes with 40 Hz activity. Note that this component is not based on gamma band filtered EEG, which would be essential for if looking for the tinnitus information carried on the gamma wave

Thalamocortical Dysrhythmia

Tinnitus correlates with gamma band activity, and Llinas has developed this hypothesis further in this thalamocortical dysrhythmia model [163]. This model can be summarized as follows: the thalamus and cortex are interconnected and act in a coherent way. In the sleeping state, the thalamus fires at 4–7 Hz (1–3 Hz during slow wave sleep); in the resting awake state the thalamus fires around 10 Hz, driving the cortex to fire at the same rate [164]. When auditory stimuli are presented, the thalamocortical rhythm becomes activated and increases its firing rate to gamma band activity (>30 Hz). However, in a deafferented state, the thalamocortical columns fire in a burst mode with a frequency of 4–7 Hz. This leads to a decrease of lateral inhibition in the adjacent areas and results in a halo of gamma band activity, called the edge effect. It is hypothesized that this spontaneous and constant gamma band hyperactivity causes tinnitus [156].

Tinnitus is usually constantly present, which suggests that tinnitus-related gamma activity is continuously present, in contrast to normal physiological gamma activity, which waxes and wanes [152–156]. Therefore, it should be possible to retrieve this gamma band activity from the auditory cortex by analyzing short-term recordings of spontaneous electrical activity from the brain. Magnetoencephalography studies demonstrate that indeed gamma band activity is increased in the auditory cortex contralaterally to the side of tinnitus perception [162]. Whether the gamma band activity in the auditory cortex is related to the percept per se or is just an intensity coding mechanism is not clear. The first LORETA EEG data suggest that the spontaneous gamma band activity might be encoding tinnitus intensity [165].

Using data from implanted electrodes overlying the secondary auditory cortex, power versus frequency plots can be made of spontaneous electrical activity. The normal power versus frequency plots demonstrate the typical individual alpha peak of the sensory cortices. In thalamocortical dysrhythmia tinnitus, a theta peak can sometimes be found on iEEG recordings (De Ridder, submitted) similarly to what has been described for MEG. When recording during a period of residual inhibition, after electrical stimulation at the area of the theta peak when no more tinnitus is present, the theta peak disappears, suggesting that the theta peak is causally related to the tinnitus, either the theta

itself or, hypothetically, via the decrease of nested gamma [166]. This seems to confirm Llinas' model, at least at a cortical level.

When analyzing four implanted patients, in whom stimulation results in a decrease of tinnitus intensity, iEEG recordings can be performed with tinnitus at two different tinnitus intensities: one performed while the tinnitus is at rest and another performed during a period of residual inhibition. Theta band activity is higher on all poles of the electrodes when tinnitus intensity is high in comparison with low ($Z = -1.826$, $p = 0.068$), a nearly significant result with only four patients.

Using co-registration of the preoperative functional Magnetic Resonance Imaging (fMRI) and the postoperative CT, it can be shown that gamma band activity is highest at the area of Blood Oxygen-Dependent Level (BOLD) activation in all patients. These data give some support at a group level for the idea of thalamocortical dysrhythmia.

Tinnitus is usually constantly present, indicating that no habituation occurs for the tinnitus-related neuronal activity. Using EEG-mismatch negativity, abnormalities have been demonstrated in tinnitus sufferers who are specific to frequencies located at the audiometrically normal lesion edge as compared to normal hearing controls [167], which is compatible with Llinas' thalamocortical dysrhythmia model [163].

Thalamocortical Dysrhythmia and Reorganization Go Hand in Hand

Increased "synchrony" in theta and gamma band firing in thalamocortical dysrhythmic tinnitus may induce cortical reorganization by simple Hebbian plasticity mechanisms [168]: cells that fire together, wire together. This model would predict that over time the tinnitus-related neuronal changes become more and more stabilized and the tinnitus more difficult to treat. Hebbian learning in the adult requires that the event is behaviorally relevant, i.e., input from nucleus basalis (NB) and VTA in addition to the firing of cortical cells or thalamocortical circuits in parallel. Therefore, the model would emphasize appraisal of the tinnitus, only predicting long-term changes when the tinnitus is given significant attention. The central nucleus of the amygdala and midbrain–striatal dopamine systems are critically involved in the alteration of attentional and emotional processing of initially neutral stimuli by associative learning [169–171], via its influence on the VTA [169]and nucleus basalis [170]. The insula and anterior cingulate receive the most pronounced innervations from the VTA [172]. It has been demonstrated that 10–50 Hz stimulation at the VTA (in contrast to the MD nucleus of the thalamus) activates the anterior cingulate via a dopaminergic pathway in a frequency-dependent manner [173].

Thus, co-activation of the dorsal ACC with the anterior insulae could result in attaching salience [54, 174, 175] to the tinnitus sound, resulting in reward-based Hebbian long-term plasticity as a (clinically negative) consequence. The dACC exerts a top–down influence on secondary auditory cortex (BA22) gamma band responses [176]. Cortical gamma band activity with associated attentive behavior is under control of the dopaminergic VTA [177]. Stimulating the VTA together with an auditory stimulus of a particular tone increases the cortical area and selectivity of the neural responses to that sound stimulus in AI and via coherent activity in A2 as well [110].

The anterior insula is not only involved in sound detection and in the entry of the sound into awareness but also in allocating auditory attention and in processing of novel versus familiar auditory stimuli [178]. Lesions in the anterior insula lead to contralateral auditory agnosia [179–181].

Under physiological situations, the hippocampus detects new information, which is not already stored in its long-term memory as it arrives. The resulting novelty signal is conveyed through the subiculum, accumbens, and ventral pallidum to the VTA where it contributes (along with salience and goal information) to the novelty-dependent firing of these cells. This results in dopamine release within the hippocampus producing an enhancement of Long-Term Potentiation (LTP) and learning [182]. In the auditory system, the auditory input enters the hippocampus via the parahippocampus [183, 184]. Complex novel sounds in humans activate the left and right superior temporal gyrus and the left inferior and middle frontal gyrus as well as the left parahippocampal gyrus [185]. In a similar fashion, the left superior temporal and left parahippocampal gyrus, along with left inferior frontal regions, are associated with listening to meaningful sounds [186]. The parahippocampal area is involved in sensory gating of irrelevant or redundant auditory information after both 100 ms and 400 ms [183]. This

area is activated with the dACC, which peaks at 120 ms and after 240 ms [187]. It is of interest that onset of auditory hallucinations is related to activation of the left anterior insula and right middle temporal gyrus [188, 189], associated with deactivation of the parahippocampal area and anterior cingulate [188].

Thus, in summary, the amygdala might perceive a sound as salient or not [190], which activates the VTA [169] to mobilize the dACC and insulae [173], switching the default state to an executive brain state [63]. The dACC exerts a top–down influence on A2 [191], from where the left parahippocampal area is also activated if the sound is novel [185] or meaningful [186]. The VTA and the (tinnitus) sound result in plastic changes in the primary auditory cortex and from there in the secondary auditory cortex [110]. The posterior parahippocampus is the main node of entry for auditory information from A2 to the medial temporal lobe memory system, where salient information is encoded into long-term memory [184]. The parahippocampus also has an auditory gating function, suppressing irrelevant or redundant auditory information [183], as the dACC does somewhat earlier [187, 192]. Thus, when the dACC and parahippocampus are deactivated, as in the onset of complex auditory phantom percepts (hallucinations), the irrelevant and redundant information is not suppressed anymore, and the activation of the anterior insula and temporal cortex permits the internally generated auditory information to be perceived consciously and attended to [178]. Thus, it can be hypothesized that tinnitus onset could be characterized by deactivation of the dACC and parahippocampus, with activation of the insula and superior temporal gyrus.

Extending Thalamocortical Dysrhythmia to Darwinian Plasticity: Reverse Thalamocortical Dysrhythmia

Thalamocortical dysrhythmia predicts that the hyperactive symptoms related to gamma band activity are expressed at the lesion edge, thus adjacent to the missing sensory input. However, both in the auditory system [193] and in the somatosensory system [194], phantom perceptions are those coming from the missing input and not from the edge. This could be explained by including Darwinian plasticity to the thalamocortical dysrhythmia model. Sensory deafferentation results in expansion of the adjacent non-deafferented region into the vacated area, both in the somatosensory and in the auditory cortex. It has been suggested that a reverse form of plasticity could also exist: deafferented sensory cortex neurons seek information elsewhere in an attempt to survive (hence the name Darwinian plasticity). Neurophysiological and neuroanatomical data, functional imaging, clinical and human electrical brain stimulation data suggest a Darwinian model of brain plasticity. This model is capable of explaining deafferentation-induced symptomatology, which was not well explained by classical plasticity [195]. Whereas the lemniscal thalamocortical dysrhythmia model predicts a reduction of the oscillation frequency in deafferentiated thalamocortical columns, the proposed reverse thalamocortical dysrhythmia model can explain that the deafferented thalamocortical units also oscillate at gamma frequencies and thus can generate phantom percepts that fit the clinical data. Due to increased lateral inhibition related to gamma activity, a halo of low-frequency activity will develop at the lesion edge. This could be called reverse thalamocortical dysrhythmia, which explains that the perceived tinnitus pitch matches the deafferented frequencies (Fig. 21.3).

Cortical reorganization in tinnitus can be visualized using MSI (Magnetic Source Imaging, a fusion of MEG and MRI; Muhlnickel, Elbert et al. [103]). However, MEG is an expensive technique, restricted to a very limited amount of research centers. Therefore, using fMRI as a means of visualizing tinnitus would be advantageous in routine clinical practice, as this technique is available at many clinics and can provide images at high resolution.

fMRI measures a relative difference in oxygen consumption between a resting state and activated state. BOLD contrast takes advantage of the fact that the magnetic properties of haemoglobin depend on its oxygenation. The blood oxygenation in turn reflects changes in neuronal activity. As such, BOLD contrast can be used to provide in vivo real-time maps of blood oxygenation in the brain under normal physiological conditions [196]. Thus, a focal area of increased oxygen consumption can be depicted by subtraction of two MRI images, one at rest and one with increased oxygen consumption due to a specific task. As increased oxygen consumption is correlated to increasing metabolic demands, the BOLD effect is related to event-related synchronization of gamma band activity [197], and BOLD is highly coupled to gamma local field potentials (EEG) in the auditory cortex [198, 199]. This strongly suggests that fMRI can visualize the gamma band-synchronized activity associated with tinnitus.

A scanning paradigm, using music as a stimulus, adequately visualizes the auditory pathways in tinnitus

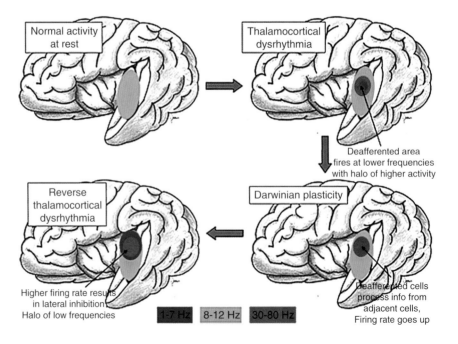

Fig. 21.3 Heuristic pathophysiological model of tinnitus intensity generation (Figure by Jan Ost, RN)

Normal activity at rest

Thalamocortical dysrhythmia

Deafferented area fires at lower frequencies with halo of higher activity

Darwinian plasticity

Deafferented cells process info from adjacent cells, Firing rate goes up

Reverse thalamocortical dysrhythmia

Higher firing rate results in lateral inhibition Halo of low frequencies

1-7 Hz   8-12 Hz   30-80 Hz

patients [200]. fMRI activation is symmetrical in patients with bilateral tinnitus at all investigated areas of the auditory pathways (auditory cortex, thalamus, and inferior colliculus). fMRI activation is significantly decreased in patients with right-sided tinnitus in the left primary auditory cortex (AC) and in the left inferior colliculi (IC). In patients with left-sided tinnitus, fMRI activation is significantly decreased in the right medial geniculate body (MGB). In summary, the contralateral auditory pathways seem to be involved in patients with unilateral tinnitus. fMRI activation always represents a difference in neural activity instead of absolute neural activity. An increase of spontaneous neural activity, such as postulated in tinnitus patients, would mean that the affected brain area during the rest condition is more active than the unaffected side, and that the active condition (sound presentation) will only give rise to a limited increase in activity due to a ceiling effect (known as the saturation model) in comparison to the non-affected side. This can explain the fact that constant pathological neuronal hyperactivity can be correlated to hypoactivation in fMRI [200].

A similar study for tinnitus using tinnitus pitch and character-specific stimuli is currently being conducted. In this study, we compare BOLD activation for tinnitus-specific sound presentation to non-tinnitus sounds presented in the scanner. Only tinnitus-specific sounds induce a significant BOLD change, as demonstrated by a lateralization effect, in contrast to non-tinnitus sounds, which generate a bilateral symmetrical BOLD activation.

Even for tinnitus-specific frequencies, the exact representation might be important. For patients suffering from pure-tone tinnitus, auditory presentation of a pure tone generates a marked asymmetrical BOLD activation, whereas presentation of a narrow band noise creates less BOLD activation, and a white noise generates almost no asymmetry (Kovacs, unpublished data) (Fig. 21.4). However, as mentioned before, auditory tract activation is insufficient to objectively diagnose tinnitus solely based on functional imaging.

A disadvantage of fMRI studies is that a contrast is needed, e.g. by presenting a sound and comparing this to a resting state or other conditions (e.g. other sound). The active condition may include different unspecific components, e.g., different arousal and differences in a patient's understanding of verbal instruction. Therefore, fMRI studies might suffer from various confounds. The fact that the fMRI-related activation changes are

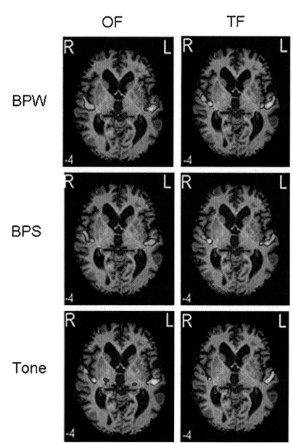

Fig. 21.4 Tinnitus frequency-specific BOLD changes on fMRI in a patient with left-sided pure-tone tinnitus. Auditory presentation of non-tinnitus sound (*OF* other frequency) generates a bilateral BOLD activity on white noise (*BPW* band pass wide), narrow band noise (*BPS* band pass small), and pure tones. In contrast, for the tinnitus frequency (TF), a pure tone generates a marked asymmetrical BOLD activation, a narrow band noise less so, and a white noise creates almost no asymmetry

specific for the perceived phantom sound (Fig. 21.4) does, however, suggest that fMRI can indeed be used to study tinnitus.

Isolated Thalamocortical Dysrhythmia and the Global Workspace Model (Electrophysiologically Explored)

As tinnitus is a persistent conscious auditory percept, it is important to understand the neural correlates of auditory consciousness, defined as the minimal neuronal mechanisms jointly sufficient for any auditory conscious percept [201]. This understanding is an essential requirement for defining neurostimulation targets to suppress this auditory phenomenon. It has been suggested by Crick and Koch that in the visual system V1 activation is necessary but insufficient for visual awareness [202, 203]. Thus, isolated thalamocortical dysrhythmia in the primary auditory cortex is most likely not enough to generate the conscious percept of tinnitus. Studies in patients in persistent vegetative state (PVS), who are awake but without awareness – without conscious percepts [204] – demonstrate that these patients have a decreased metabolism in a network of areas consisting of midline areas, such as the anterior cingulate (ACC), which extends into the ventromedial prefrontal cortex (VMPFC), and the posterior cingulate (PCC), which extends into the precuneus. However, the lateral cortical regions also have less metabolic activity, more specifically the parietal and dorsolateral prefrontal cortex areas [205]. Not only is metabolism decreased in these patients, but functional connectivity is also decreased between the intralaminar nuclei of the thalamus and ACC/VMPFC and PCC/precuneus regions, and between ACC/VMPFC and PCC/precuneus [204, 205]. Recovery from PVS is associated with normalization of metabolism and connectivity, suggesting this decreased metabolism and loss of connectivity is critically involved and causally related to the neural correlate of consciousness [206, 207]. Extending these studies to auditory processing of patients in PVS, it was shown that the activation associated with auditory stimuli was restricted to the primary auditory cortex bilaterally in patients in a PVS without functional connectivity between the secondary auditory cortex and temporal and prefrontal association cortices [208], similarly to what has been shown for pain processing [209]. Based on these data, it can be proposed that activity restricted to the primary auditory cortex does not lead to auditory conscious perception, similarly to the somatosensory and visual system, but that this auditory activity becomes conscious when functionally connected to the ACC/VMPFC and prefrontal cortex (BA10) [206].

Baars has proposed the global workspace theory [210], which was extended and electrophysiologically refined for the visual system by Dehaene [211, 212]. The global workspace model, as perfected by Dehaene, can be translated to the auditory system as follows [213]: in (unconscious) preconscious processing, auditory stimulus processing is blocked at the level of the global neuronal workspace, i.e., it remains limited to the primary auditory cortex, while the global workspace is temporarily occupied by another task or is non-active, such as in PVS. A preconscious auditory stimulus may be temporarily buffered within the primary auditory cortex (discussed below) and later accessed by the frontoparietal system, once it is released by its present distracting task. In this case, information switches from unconscious to conscious. Conscious processing occurs when the accumulated stimulus-evoked activation exceeds a threshold and evokes a dynamic state of global reverberation [214] ("ignition") across multiple high-level cortical areas forming a "global neuronal workspace," particularly involving prefrontal, cingulate, and parietal cortices, the same areas that are decreased in metabolism and functional connectivity in PVS. These areas can maintain the information online and broadcast it to a variety of other processors, thus serving as a central hub for global access to information – a key property of conscious states.

Subliminal processing corresponds to a data-limited situation where the auditory stimulus reaches only specialized cerebral sensory networks (i.e., secondary and auditory association areas), without reaching a threshold for global ignition and, thus, without global reportability. The orientation and depth of subliminal processing may nevertheless depend on the top–down state of attention.

So, when an auditory stimulus is presented, it will activate the primary auditory cortex after about 17 to 30 ms [215, 216] and the primary auditory cortex (A1) remains activated up to 300 ms generating a Pa (P50), Nb, Na, P1 en N100 ERP [217]. This persistent A1 activation is characterized by an early (85 ms) posterior and a late (115 ms) anterior N1 component [218, 219]. In other words, the primary auditory cortex neurons synchronize multiple times to generate positive and negative ERP peaks. At 50 ms, the information is not only processed in the primary, secondary, and association auditory cortex [220] but also in the frontal cortex [183, 221], more specifically, in Brodmann's areas 6 and 24 [192, 221, 222]. There might be a parallel signal transmission to the ACC and auditory cortex analogous to what has been shown for the somatosensory system. Somatosensory stimuli arrive at the ACC and somatosensory cortex simultaneously, as evidenced by intracranial recordings of evoked potentials [223]. This might reflect simultaneous processing of sensory and affective components of the stimulus. Auditory information processing is dependent on sensory gating, a mechanism of suppression of irrelevant auditory input or auditory habituation. Sensory gating seems to depend both on frontal and on auditory cortex activity [192, 221, 222, 224], and predominantly on gamma band activity [225]. At 100 ms, the auditory information also arrives in the posterior parahippocampus [183] and is still present frontally at the dorsal anterior cingulate extending into the insula, electrophysiologically recorded as N100 [226–228]. At the same time, information is processed in the PCC [227]. After 200 ms, the information will still be processed in the auditory cortices, ACC in VMPFC, extending to frontopolar cortex (BA10), and posteriorly in the precuneus (coming from PCC), altogether generating a N200 ERP [220, 229]. The anterior circuit, which is activated earlier, is most likely related to attentive processes, whereas the posterior activity is more related to sensory memory updating. After 300 ms, the information also extends into the temporoparietal junction and inferior and superior parietal area [230, 231], which is required for conscious perception (in the visual system). It has to be mentioned that a P300 is different from a P600 in its neural generators (P600 has generator in basal ganglia) [232], suggesting that any positive peak between 250 and 900 ms should not be called a P300 as is commonly done [233]. After 400 ms, the signal (if semantic) reaches the parahippocampus again [183], mediating sensory gating (presenting repetitious stimuli and measuring the degree of neural inhibition that occurs) [234] of irrelevant or redundant auditory input [183].

The Functional Networks of the Brain

The brain is organized into multiple systems that have distinct and potentially competing functional roles [235]; at least four functional systems have been described by functional connectivity analysis:

1. The dorsal attention system, which is associated with externally directed cognition, includes regions in the frontal eye fields, ventral premotor cortex, superior parietal lobule, intraparietal sulcus, and motion-sensitive middle temporal area [236–238].

2. The hippocampal-cortical memory system, a network of regions that are active during passive mental states linked to internally directed cognition (the default network) [239, 240], includes regions in ventral medial prefrontal cortex, posterior inferior parietal lobule, retrosplenial cortex, posterior cingulate, and the lateral temporal lobe [235, 236, 239, 241, 242].

3. The frontoparietal control system is an executive control system guiding decision making by integrating information from the external environment with stored internal representations [243]. It includes many regions identified as supporting cognitive control and decision-making processes including lateral prefrontal cortex, anterior cingulate cortex, and inferior parietal lobule [235].

4. The emotional system is a network based on functional connectivity with the amygdala and includes subgenual and dorsal anterior cingulate, orbitofrontal, insular, and dorsolateral prefrontal cortex, as well as strong interactions between amygdala and parahippocampal gyrus [244].

The global workspace has not been delineated anatomically. It can be hypothesized that the areas involved in the global workspace overlap with regions of these four networks.

However, that is still more than the minimal requirement for conscious perception [201].

Sleep studies have shown that the inferior and midfrontal gyrus, inferior parietal area, and medial parietal area are less active in Rapid Eye Movement (REM) sleep in comparison to wakefulness [245], suggesting that these areas are important for wakefulness and processing of external input but less important for awareness. The superior frontal and superior parietal areas with the intraparietal sulcus are equally active during wakefulness and REM sleep, as well as the VMPFC [245], suggesting that these areas are important for awareness/consciousness and could potentially be the minimal network required for awareness. It is striking that the dorsal attentional network, which selects and links stimuli and responses and hereby influences subsequent processing of stimuli in sensory cortex, is located in exactly the same areas: intraparietal sulcus (IPS) and superior parietal lobule (SPL), and dorsal frontal cortex along the precentral sulcus [237, 246], except for the VMPFC. The ventral attentional network, which interrupts and resets ongoing activity, consists of the temporoparietal junction (including the STS and gyrus), the inferior parietal lobule, and the mid and inferior frontal gyrus as well as the frontal operculum, and anterior insula [237, 246]. Thus, the inferior parietal and mid- and inferior frontal area, which are less active in REM compared to wakefulness [245] and are part of a resetting network [246], might be critically involved in updating current conscious information processing with novel external input.

Thus, based on both PVS and sleep studies, it can be proposed that the network consisting of the superior frontal–superior parietal–VMPFC–intralaminar nuclei has to be functionally connected for internally or externally generated auditory stimuli to be consciously perceived. These areas are activated after 200–300 ms and are involved in the generation of the P300, which is one of the requirements for stimuli to be perceived consciously (in the visual system).

Subliminal stimuli can be deeply processed and activate similar brain areas as consciously perceived stimuli [158]. Both perceived and non-perceived visual stimuli cause a similar increase of local (gamma) oscillations in the EEG, but only perceived words induce a transient long-distance synchronization of gamma oscillations across widely separated regions of the brain [157, 158], compatible with the global workspace model. Furthermore, only visual stimuli that are consciously perceived induce enhanced theta oscillations over frontal regions and demonstrate an increase of the P300 component of the event-related potential and an increase in power and phase synchrony of gamma oscillations [158].

As previously mentioned, the neural generators of the auditory P300 are the inferior parietal lobe/temporoparietal junction (TPJ), the supplementary motor cortex (SMA), the dorsal anterior cingulate cortex (dACC), the superior temporal gyrus (STG), the insula, and the dorsolateral prefrontal cortex [231] (in other words, the ventral attentional network plus dorsolateral prefrontal cortex). Thus, the P300 seems to interrupt and reset ongoing activity to what is being processed in the DLPFC, or in working memory [247]. This is very similar to the frontoparietal control system [235].

It has been suggested that the P300 is the electrophysiological correlate of global workspace activation, implying that the global workspace consists of the dorsolateral prefrontal cortex, dACC, SMA, and inferior parietal area extending into the STS [248].

If auditory cortex activation is essential but not sufficient for auditory conscious perception, where is the percept being transformed into a conscious percept? Data from monkey studies in the somatosensory system suggest it could be the prefrontal cortex [249]. Activity of primary somatosensory cortex neurons covaries with the stimulus strength but not with the animal's perceptual reports. This is similar in tinnitus: tinnitus intensity correlates with gamma band activity in the contralateral auditory cortex [165]. In contrast, the activity of the medial premotor cortex (MPC) neurons does not co-vary with the stimulus strength but does so with the animal's perceptual reports [249]. In further agreement with the global workspace model, it has been demonstrated in the somatosensory system that the neural correlate of subjective sensory experience gradually builds up across cortical areas starting at the somatosensory cortex and ending in the premotor areas of the frontal lobe [250], which might have a hidden sensory function [251]. This idea of premotor cortex activity related to conscious sensory perception fits with the sensorimotor contingency philosophy of consciousness [252] described in the book *Action in Perception* [253], which suggests that seeing is a way of acting, a way of exploring the environment. This intentionality driven sensation dates back to Aristotle and Thomas Aquinas [254] and has been proposed to be a working mechanism in olfaction as well [255]. Thus, neural activity alone is not sufficient to produce vision, but neural activity contributes to experience only as enabling mastery and exercise of laws of sensorimotor contingency [252].

It is of interest that it was shown that N1, P2, and P3 are attenuated in chronic tinnitus patients [256, 257]. However, no source analysis was performed, and N1 attenuation is not found all the time [258]. One explanation can be that N1 is only attenuated in patients with low distress [259]. Another study found a difference in N1-P2 in unilateral tinnitus sufferers on the basis of N1-P2 intensity dependence and N1-P2 amplitude. A bilateral tinnitus group differed from controls by greater intensity dependence of the N1-P2 component and shorter N1 latency [260]. Using MEG, it was also shown that amplitude ratio M200/M100 represents a clear-cut criterion to distinguish between tinnitus patients and individuals without tinnitus [261], and the abnormal M200/M100 normalized when the tinnitus disappeared [262].

However, this M200/M100 abnormality in tinnitus patients could not be confirmed by another study [263].

Based on the above-mentioned heuristic model, it can be hypothesized that the ERPs should be performed with tinnitus-matched sound and non-tinnitus–matched sound. Obtaining a LORETA ICA of N100 should correlate to two aspects of tinnitus: one component relating to tinnitus distress (the ACC component) and one component to tinnitus intensity (auditory cortex component). In a similar way, the P/N 200 should be analyzed by ICA to make the distinction between distress and intensity. Similarly, the P300 should be analyzed for the presence of tinnitus, with P3a gamma band activity examined for the presence of distress and P3b for the presence of the sound.

It can be further hypothesized that the P50 (and N400) might be abnormal in tinnitus, as there is no sensory gating involved for the tinnitus-matched sound, whereas the P50 and N400 could be normal for non-tinnitus–matched sound.

PET studies have shown which areas of the brain are involved in the tinnitus global workspace network (Fig. 21.5): primary [75, 264–267] and secondary auditory cortex, extending into the temporoparietal junction (the auditory association area) [265, 268], (para)hippocampus [75], medial geniculate body, [75], anterior [74] and posterior cingulate cortex [269, 270], and precuneus and inferior lateral parietal cortex [271]. Voxel-based morphometry adds the subgenual ACC extending into the nucleus accumbens area [272], the hippocampus, and the inferior colliculus [273], which is confirmed by fMRI [274, 275]. Magnetoencephalography also finds abnormal spontaneous activity as well in the prefrontal cortex (BA10) [276]. Most of the tinnitus network overlaps with an aversive sound-processing network consisting of the primary and secondary auditory cortex, parahippocampus, amygdala, and right superior, middle,

and inferior dorsolateral prefrontal cortex [277]. Later studies extended the aversive sound network to the auditory association, nucleus accumbens, and insula area [278].

The Tinnitus Network Changes in Time

Clinical data suggest that the longer tinnitus lasts the more difficult it becomes to treat. This has been shown for microvascular decompressions [279–285] and transcranial magnetic stimulations [269, 286–288]. Even though it is most likely a gradual continuous change, tinnitus duration of 4 years might be a practical point for clinicians to differentiate acute from chronic tinnitus (De Ridder, in press, Neurosurgery). This was first noted in microvascular decompressions by Møller, later by others performing the same surgery [279–285], and most recently was extended to rTMS investigations [286, 287]. A MEG study looking at phase-locked connectivity in the tinnitus network found that in patients with a tinnitus history of less than 4 years, the left temporal cortex was predominant in the gamma network, whereas in patients with tinnitus duration of more than 4 years, the gamma network was more widely distributed including more frontal and parietal regions [289]. Thus, even though the areas involved might still be the same, the functional connectivity and weight of the hubs between the involved areas might change.

In a recent EEG study, these network changes were also analyzed spectrally. Results indicate that the generators involved in tinnitus of recent onset (<4 years) seem to change in time with increased synchronized activity contralaterally in the auditory cortex, DLPFC/premotor cortex, dACC, and inusla. This is associated with an increase in gamma band connectivity between

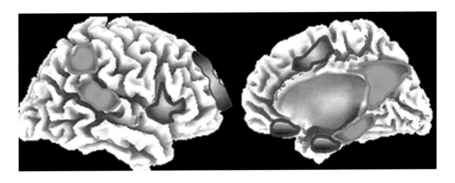

Fig. 21.5 The tinnitus global workspace network, as summarized from functional neuroimaging studies. *Red*: anterior distress network. *Blue*: posterior tinnitus intensity network

the parahippocampal cortex, auditory cortex, and the insula ipsilaterally to the tinnitus side and DLPFC contralaterally to the tinnitus side. All other connections seem to decrease in time (vanneste, submitted).

It is interesting to note that in chronic tinnitus, the degree of response to auditory cortex rTMS on TQ distress was correlated with tinnitus-associated activation of the anterior cingulate cortex [74].

Recently, the idea of allostasis, defined as the adaptive process for actively maintaining stability (homeostasis) through change [290], has been introduced in medicine [290]. It has been shown that allostasis is controlled by the brain [291, 292]. Homeostasis relates to the mechanisms that maintain stability within the physiological systems and hold all the parameters of the organisms internal milieu within limits that allow an organism to survive [290, 293, 294]. Allostasis, on the other hand, relates to the maintenance of stability outside of the normal homeostatic range, where an organism must vary all the parameters of its physiological systems to match them appropriately to chronic demands, for example, by resetting the system parameters at a new set point [290, 295, 296]. An allostatic state has been defined as a state of chronic deviation of the regulatory systems from their normal state of operation with establishment of a new set point [296]. It has been especially investigated with regard to the Darwinian [297] adaptive nature of stress and its possible maladaptive consequences, called allostatic load. The allostatic load then leads to pathology [291, 292, 298]. Drug addiction is hypothesized to involve a change in drug reward set point and reflects an allostatic, rather than a homeostatic, adaptation (i.e., outside the normal set point) [295, 296].

The brain areas controlling allostasis in stress are suggested to be the amygdala and the prefrontal cortex [291, 292, 297], as well as the ACC and insula [175]. Based on parallels between addiction and pain, it has been suggested that in chronic pain the concomitant tolerance (adaptive decreases of the drug's efficacy) and hyperalgesia might be the result of the development of a new allostatic equilibrium [299]. Conceptually, in chronic tinnitus, a new allostatic equilibrium could develop, resulting in hyperacusis and persistence of the phantom sound. The dorsal ACC is involved in adaptive decision making and value evaluation [300] by adapting its activity when a new piece of information is witnessed, reflecting its salience for predicting future outcomes [54] by utilizing dopamine

reward prediction error signals, but only when something can be learned [301]. Thus, the dorsal ACC might be involved in resetting this equilibrium. Metaphorically speaking, the dorsal ACC attributes salience to the phantom sound and resets its equilibrium allostaticly, so that the sound remains consciously perceived via resetting the parahippocampal auditory gating.

The allostatic equilibrium resetting can be located in the dACC and parahippocampus, as both regions are involved in auditory sensory gating [183, 192], i.e. suppression of irrelevant or redundant auditory information. Thus, if there is an allostatic reset of what auditory information is important or not, the dACC will be important as well as the parahippocampal area.

The parahippocampus is functionally connected to the inferior lateral parietal cortex regions along the midline including posterior cingulate and retrosplenial cortex extending into the precuneus, and subgenual ACC extending into the ventral medial prefrontal cortex [241].

The posterior parahippocampus is the main node of entry for auditory information to the medial temporal lobe memory system, where salient information is encoded into long-term memory [184]. The left parahippocampal gyrus along with left inferior frontal and left superior temporal regions are specifically associated with listening to meaningful sounds [186]. The parahippocampal area has also been linked to the unpleasantness of the auditory information [302], in contrast to the left amygdale, which is related to the salience of the aversive auditory (verbal) information [190].

Based on visual system data, it has been suggested that the parahippocampal cortex may play a broad role in contextual association [303, 304]. If complex auditory phantom phenomena (such as auditory hallucinations) and simple auditory phantom phenomena (such as tinnitus) share common pathophysiological mechanisms, it is of interest to note that at onset of auditory hallucinations, the parahippocampus becomes deactivated as well as the anterior cingulate [188]. Furthermore, when analyzing the difference between responders and non-responders to auditory cortex stimulation by means of LORETA EEG, non-responders demonstrate increased theta activity in the left parahippocampus, whereas responders have increased gamma band (30–40 Hz) activity in the (left) parahippocampal area $t(9) = 1.98$; $p < 0.05$ (van der Loo, unpublished data). Perception involves the processing of sensory stimuli and their translation into conscious experience. A novel percept can, once synthesized, be maintained or discarded from awareness. Visual perception is associated with distributed bilateral activation in the posterior thalamus and regions in the occipito-temporal, parietal, and frontal cortices. In contrast, sustained perception is associated with activation of the left prefrontal cortex and left (para) hippocampus [305]. Thus, if tinnitus is considered a sustained auditory perception, it could explain why amytal tests of the amygdalohippocampal area are capable of suppressing tinnitus in chronic unilateral tinnitus [306].

The Tinnitus Network: A Summary

A stimulus only makes sense if it is related to and incorporated the person's self-percept. Therefore, the self-perception network, consisting of the ACC-vmPFC, PCC–precuneus, superior frontal-parietal, and STS, has to be activated for the tinnitus to be consciously perceived (Fig. 21.6). This is supported by the data from PVS patients.

The tinnitus intensity is related to auditory cortex activity, which might be controlled by dACC–insula baseline activity, expressing that the tinnitus is salient.

The tinnitus percept, per se, might not be encoded in the auditory cortex but be represented by DLPFC–premotor activity, connected to the self-perception network via the PCC–precuneus activity. This could be analogous to the somatosensory processing, where

stimulus intensity is encoded by somatosensory cortex activity and the conscious percept in the frontal cortex. The parahippocampus might serve as an entry to auditory memory, pulling the missing information due to deafferentation from memory (Fig. 21.6).

The Tinnitus Network: Future Perspectives

Since the recent development of network science [307–311] to study complex adaptive systems (CAS), these analyses have been introduced in brain science [312–318] as well. The underlying idea is that CAS, whether it is the internet, ant societies, social interactions, the weather, or economy, are structured by similar universal rules [319].

Network topology describes how different nodes in a network are connected or linked. It was initially assumed that networks predominantly form randomly, in which each node is connected to another node randomly, characterized by a Poisson distribution of its connectivity [307]. All nodes are equal in this network. More recently, scale-free networks have been described [311], in which some nodes are more connected and more clustered (i.e., have a shorter path length, turning them into hubs). This suggests that some nodes are clearly more critical with regard to the robustness of the network. Both random and scale-free

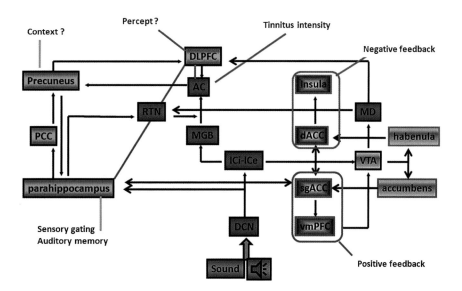

Fig. 21.6 Heuristic tinnitus
network interactions

networks are very robust to random errors, but scale-free networks are more sensitive to attacks on hubs. Eighty percent of nodes can be removed in scale-free networks without failure, but if some critically important hubs are removed, the network system fails. Most likely, these scale-free networks become incorporated into hierarchical networks [320], permitting incorporation of modularity and scale-free behavior of the network.

The approach to studying complex adaptive systems has recently been extended to the human brain, as the brain clearly fulfils the criteria of a complex adaptive system [312, 313, 315]. The topological network approach can be applied to brain anatomy [318, 321], electrical [317, 322] and magnetic brain activity [314], and blood oxygenation changes (fMRI) [312, 313].

The entire brain is not ruled by one network, but most likely different topologies exist depending on the brain area and functional state of the brain. The brainstem is organized like a small world, but is not scale free [323]. The cerebellum seems to be structured like a regular or strictly local network [324], the hippocampus more like a random [324] and small world network, and the cortex has both small world [312, 325] and scale-free [326, 327] properties. These different network systems might be integrated in a hierarchical system of functional modules [320].

This network approach to studying the brain of patients with tinnitus could benefit the future neuromodulation management for individuals with this condition. Based on this short introduction to network analysis, it becomes clear that if tinnitus is related to scale-free hub disability, neuromodulation makes sense, as with limited targeting the persistent tinnitus network might be normalized again. This will, however, be impossible in random networks and will not be useful in regular networks. A recent study demonstrates that the hubs in tinnitus might consist of the PCC, dACC, and sgACC, extending into the OFC and parahippocampal area [328]. More similar studies with higher resolution will permit future pathophysiologically-based hub targeting in tinnitus.

Conclusion

There is insufficient literature to develop an evidence-based neuropathophysiological model of tinnitus, but a heuristic model can be conceived when available

tinnitus data are supplemented by knowledge from other sensory systems, as well as the limbic, autonomic, and motor systems. Since it has been suggested that plasticity uses similar mechanisms in all sensory areas, extrapolating information from other sensory systems seems acceptable.

Tinnitus intensity is correlated with increased gamma activity in the contralateral auditory cortex, possibly as a reaction on reduced auditory input via thalamocortical or reverse thalamocortical dysrhythmia, resulting in lack of inhibition and increased synchrony, which in turn may lead to topographic map reorganization in the auditory cortex.

The tinnitus percept, per se, is almost certainly not related to isolated synchronous gamma band activity in the auditory cortex, but requires co-activation of the ill-defined global workspace or a self-perception network.

The distress some tinnitus patients perceive seems to be correlated to increased activity in the amygdala, anterior cingulate, and right anterior insula. Tinnitus distress might also be the result of synchronization of auditory thalamocortical dysrhythmia and distress network activation.

In time, the neural generators of tinnitus might change, possibly only by spectral modifications within the tinnitus global space network, hypothetically based on an allostatic mechanism.

Future studies, applying techniques from network science might demonstrate which hubs are critical for maintaining the tinnitus percept and therefore could be good targets for tinnitus neuromodulation treatments.

References

1. Jones EG (2001) The thalamic matrix and thalamocortical synchrony. Trends Neurosci 24:595–601.
2. Jones EG (1998) Viewpoint: the core and matrix of thalamic organization. Neuroscience 85:331–45.
3. Molinari M, ME Dell'Anna, E Rausell et al (1995) Auditory thalamocortical pathways defined in monkeys by calcium-binding protein immunoreactivity. J Comp Neurol 362: 171–94.
4. Munkle MC, HJ Waldvogel and RL Faull (2000) The distribution of calbindin, calretinin and parvalbumin immunoreactivity in the human thalamus. J Chem Neuroanat 19:155–73.
5. Møller AR (2003) Sensory systems: anatomy and physiology. Amsterdam: Academic Press.
6. He J and B Hu (2002) Differential distribution of burst and single-spike responses in auditory thalamus. J Neurophysiol 88:2152–6.

7. Hu B, V Senatorov and D Mooney (1994) Lemniscal and non-lemniscal synaptic transmission in rat auditory thalamus. J Physiol 479 (Pt 2):217–31.

8. Chacron MJ, A Longtin and L Maler (2004) To burst or not to burst? J Comput Neurosci 17:127–36.

9. Oswald AM, MJ Chacron, B Doiron et al (2004) Parallel processing of sensory input by bursts and isolated spikes. J Neurosci 24:4351–62.

10. De Ridder D, T Menovsky and P Van de Heyning, eds. Tinnitus as a central auditory processing disorder. Current controversies in central auditory processing disorder, ed. AT Cacace and DJ McFarland. 2008, Plural Publishing: San Diego. 291–305.

11. Strominger NL, LR Nelson and WJ Dougherty (1977) Second order auditory pathways in the chimpanzee. J Comp Neurol 172:349–65.

12. Parvizi J and AR Damasio (2003) Differential distribution of calbindin D28k and parvalbumin among functionally distinctive sets of structures in the macaque brainstem. J Comp Neurol 462:153–67.

13. Tennigkeit F, DW Schwarz and E Puil (1996) Mechanisms for signal transformation in lemniscal auditory thalamus. J Neurophysiol 76:3597–608.

14. McCormick DA and HR Feeser (1990) Functional implications of burst firing and single spike activity in lateral geniculate relay neurons. Neuroscience 39:103–13.

15. Jones EG (2003) Chemically defined parallel pathways in the monkey auditory system. Ann N Y Acad Sci 999:218–33.

16. Chiry O, E Tardif, PJ Magistretti et al (2003) Patterns of calcium-binding proteins support parallel and hierarchical organization of human auditory areas. Eur J Neurosci 17:397–410.

17. Bordi F and JE LeDoux (1994) Response properties of single units in areas of rat auditory thalamus that project to the amygdala. I. Acoustic discharge patterns and frequency receptive fields. Exp Brain Res 98:261–74.

18. Calford MB (1983) The parcellation of the medial geniculate body of the cat defined by the auditory response properties of single units. J Neurosci 3:2350–64.

19. Sherman SM and C Koch (1998) The synaptic organization of the brain. ed. G Shepherd. Oxford: Oxford University Press.

20. Disterhoft JF and J Olds (1972) Differential development of conditioned unit changes in thalamus and cortex of rat. J Neurophysiol 35:665–79.

21. Bordi F, J LeDoux, MC Clugnet et al (1993) Single-unit activity in the lateral nucleus of the amygdala and overlying areas of the striatum in freely behaving rats: rates, discharge patterns, and responses to acoustic stimuli. Behav Neurosci 107:757–69.

22. Bartlett EL and PH Smith (1999) Anatomic, intrinsic, and synaptic properties of dorsal and ventral division neurons in rat medial geniculate body. J Neurophysiol 81:1999–2016.

23. Mooney DM, L Zhang, C Basile et al (2004) Distinct forms of cholinergic modulation in parallel thalamic sensory pathways. Proc Natl Acad Sci USA 101:320–4.

24. Sherman SM (2001) A wake-up call from the thalamus. Nat Neurosci 4:344–6.

25. Sherman SM (2001) Tonic and burst firing: dual modes of thalamocortical relay. Trends Neurosci 24:122–6.

26. Swadlow HA and AG Gusev (2001) The impact of 'bursting' thalamic impulses at a neocortical synapse. Nat Neurosci 4:402–8.

27. Ramcharan EJ, CL Cox, XJ Zhan et al (2000) Cellular mechanisms underlying activity patterns in the monkey thalamus during visual behavior. J Neurophysiol 84:1982–7.

28. Tardif E, O Chiry, A Probst et al (2003) Patterns of calcium-binding proteins in human inferior colliculus: identification of subdivisions and evidence for putative parallel systems. Neuroscience 116:1111–21.

29. Syka J (2002) Plastic changes in the central auditory system after hearing loss, restoration of function, and during learning. Physiol Rev 82:601–36.

30. Forster CR and RB Illing (2000) Plasticity of the auditory brainstem: cochleotomy-induced changes of calbindin-D28k expression in the rat. J Comp Neurol 416:173–87.

31. Caicedo A, C d'Aldin, M Eybalin et al (1997) Temporary sensory deprivation changes calcium-binding proteins levels in the auditory brainstem. J Comp Neurol 378:1–15.

32. Garcia MM, R Edward, GB Brennan et al (2000) Deafferentation-induced changes in protein kinase C expression in the rat cochlear nucleus. Hear Res 147:113–24.

33. Itoh K, H Kamiya, A Mitani et al (1987) Direct projections from the dorsal column nuclei and the spinal trigeminal nuclei to the cochlear nuclei in the cat. Brain Res 400:145–50.

34. Møller AR (2000) Hearing: its physiology and pathophysiology. San Diego: Academic Press.

35. Szczepaniak WS and AR Møller (1993) Interaction between auditory and somatosensory systems: a study of evoked potentials in the inferior colliculus. Electroencephalogr Clin Neurophysiol 88:508–15.

36. Leinonen L, J Hyvarinen and AR Sovijarvi (1980) Functional properties of neurons in the temporo-parietal association cortex of awake monkey. Exp Brain Res 39:203–15.

37. Kawaguchi Y and Y Kubota (1993) Correlation of physiological subgroupings of nonpyramidal cells with parvalbumin- and calbindin D28k-immunoreactive neurons in layer V of rat frontal cortex. J Neurophysiol 70:387–96.

38. Kawaguchi Y (2001) Distinct firing patterns of neuronal subtypes in cortical synchronized activities. J Neurosci 21:7261–72.

39. Solbach S and MR Celio (1991) Ontogeny of the calcium binding protein parvalbumin in the rat nervous system. Anat Embryol 184:103–24.

40. Baimbridge KG, MR Celio and JH Rogers (1992) Calcium-binding proteins in the nervous system. Trends Neurosci 15:303–8.

41. Caillard O, H Moreno, B Schwaller et al (2000) Role of the calcium-binding protein parvalbumin in short-term synaptic plasticity. Proc Natl Acad Sci USA 97:13372–7.

42. Rausell E, CG Cusick, E Taub et al (1992) Chronic deafferentation in monkeys differentially affects nociceptive and nonnociceptive pathways distinguished by specific calcium-binding proteins and down-regulates gamma-aminobutyric acid type A receptors at thalamic levels. Proc Natl Acad Sci USA 89:2571–5.

43. De Ridder D, E van der Loo, K Van der Kelen et al (2007) Do tonic and burst TMS modulate the lemniscal and extralemniscal system differentially? Int J Med Sci 4:242–6.

44. Phillips ML, WC Drevets, SL Rauch et al (2003) Neurobiology of emotion perception I: The neural basis of normal emotion perception. Biol Psychiatry 54:504–14.

45. Phan KL, T Wager, SF Taylor et al (2002) Functional neuroanatomy of emotion: a meta-analysis of emotion activation studies in PET and fMRI. Neuroimage 16:331–48.

46. Dalgleish T (2004) The emotional brain. Nat Rev Neurosci 5:583–9.

47. Ghashghaei HT, CC Hilgetag and H Barbas (2007) Sequence of information processing for emotions based on the anatomic dialogue between prefrontal cortex and amygdala. Neuroimage 34:905–23.

48. Baxter MG and EA Murray (2002) The amygdala and reward. Nat Rev Neurosci 3:563–73.

49. Craig AD (2002) How do you feel? Interoception: the sense of the physiological condition of the body. Nat Rev Neurosci 3:655–66.

50. Kringelbach ML (2005) The human orbitofrontal cortex: linking reward to hedonic experience. Nat Rev Neurosci 6:691–702.

51. Ikemoto S (2007) Dopamine reward circuitry: two projection systems from the ventral midbrain to the nucleus accumbens-olfactory tubercle complex. Brain Res Rev 56:27–78.

52. Summerfield C, T Egner, M Greene et al (2006) Predictive codes for forthcoming perception in the frontal cortex. Science 314:1311–4.

53. Ullsperger M and DY von Cramon (2003) Error monitoring using external feedback: specific roles of the habenular complex, the reward system, and the cingulate motor area revealed by functional magnetic resonance imaging. J Neurosci 23:4308–14.

54. Behrens TE, MW Woolrich, ME Walton et al (2007) Learning the value of information in an uncertain world. Nat Neurosci 10:1214–21.

55. Critchley HD (2005) Neural mechanisms of autonomic, affective, and cognitive integration. J Comp Neurol 493:154–66.

56. Kennerley SW, ME Walton, TE Behrens et al (2006) Optimal decision making and the anterior cingulate cortex. Nat Neurosci 9:940–7.

57. Margulies DS, AM Kelly, LQ Uddin et al (2007) Mapping the functional connectivity of anterior cingulate cortex. Neuroimage 37:579–88.

58. Mottaghy FM, K Willmes, B Horwitz et al (2006) Systems level modeling of a neuronal network subserving intrinsic alertness. Neuroimage 29:225–33.

59. Critchley HD, DR Corfield, MP Chandler et al (2000) Cerebral correlates of autonomic cardiovascular arousal: a functional neuroimaging investigation in humans. J Physiol 523 (Pt 1):259–70.

60. Critchley HD, RN Melmed, E Featherstone et al (2002) Volitional control of autonomic arousal: a functional magnetic resonance study. Neuroimage 16:909–19.

61. Critchley HD, CJ Mathias and RJ Dolan (2001) Neural activity in the human brain relating to uncertainty and arousal during anticipation. Neuron 29:537–45.

62. Boly M, E Balteau, C Schnakers et al (2007) Baseline brain activity fluctuations predict somatosensory perception in humans. Proc Natl Acad Sci USA 104:12187–92.

63. Sridharan D, DJ Levitin and V Menon (2008) A critical role for the right fronto-insular cortex in switching between central-executive and default-mode networks. Proc Natl Acad Sci USA 105:12569–74.

64. Craig AD (2003) Interoception: the sense of the physiological condition of the body. Curr Opin Neurobiol 13:500–5.

65. Schultz W (1998) Predictive reward signal of dopamine neurons. J Neurophysiol 80:1–27.

66. Schultz W, P Dayan and PR Montague (1997) A neural substrate of prediction and reward. Science 275:1593–9.

67. Critchley HD, S Wiens, P Rotshtein et al (2004) Neural systems supporting interoceptive awareness. Nat Neurosci 7:189–95.

68. Sander D, J Grafman and T Zalla (2003) The human amygdala: an evolved system for relevance detection. Rev Neurosci 14:303–16.

69. Hansel A and R von Kanel (2008) The ventro-medial prefrontal cortex: a major link between the autonomic nervous system, regulation of emotion, and stress reactivity? Biopsychosoc Med 2:21.

70. Vermetten E, C Schmahl, SM Southwick et al (2007) Positron tomographic emission study of olfactory induced emotional recall in veterans with and without combat-related posttraumatic stress disorder. Psychopharmacol Bull 40:8–30.

71. Etkin A and TD Wager (2007) Functional neuroimaging of anxiety: a meta-analysis of emotional processing in PTSD, social anxiety disorder, and specific phobia. Am J Psychiatry 164:1476–88.

72. Schlee W, N Weisz, O Bertrand et al (2008) Using auditory steady state responses to outline the functional connectivity in the tinnitus brain. PLoS One 3:e3720.

73. Goebel G and W Hiller (1994) [The tinnitus questionnaire. A standard instrument for grading the degree of tinnitus. Results of a multicenter study with the tinnitus questionnaire]. HNO 42:166–72.

74. Plewnia C, M Reimold, A Najib et al (2007) Moderate therapeutic efficacy of positron emission tomography-navigated repetitive transcranial magnetic stimulation for chronic tinnitus: a randomised, controlled pilot study. J Neurol Neurosurg Psychiatr 78:152–6.

75. Lockwood AH, RJ Salvi, ML Coad et al (1998) The functional neuroanatomy of tinnitus: evidence for limbic system links and neural plasticity. Neurology 50:114–20.

76. Oppenheimer S (1993) The anatomy and physiology of cortical mechanisms of cardiac control. Stroke 24:I3–5.

77. Critchley HD, R Elliott, CJ Mathias et al (2000) Neural activity relating to generation and representation of galvanic skin conductance responses: a functional magnetic resonance imaging study. J Neurosci 20:3033–40.

78. Cerqueira JJ, OF Almeida and N Sousa (2008) The stressed prefrontal cortex. Left? Right! Brain Behav Immun 22:630–8.

79. Hilz MJ, O Devinsky, H Szczepanska et al (2006) Right ventromedial prefrontal lesions result in paradoxical cardiovascular activation with emotional stimuli. Brain 129:3343–55.

80. Hilz MJ, M Dutsch, K Perrine et al (2001) Hemispheric influence on autonomic modulation and baroreflex sensitivity. Ann Neurol 49:575–84.

81. Pascual-Marqui RD, CM Michel and D Lehmann (1994) Low resolution electromagnetic tomography: a new method for localizing electrical activity in the brain. Int J Psychophysiol 18:49–65.

82. Moisset X and D Bouhassira (2007) Brain imaging of neuropathic pain. Neuroimage 37 Suppl 1:S80–8.

83. Price DD (2000) Psychological and neural mechanisms of the affective dimension of pain. Science 288:1769–72.

84. Kulkarni B, DE Bentley, R Elliott et al (2005) Attention to pain localization and unpleasantness discriminates the functions of the medial and lateral pain systems. Eur J Neurosci 21:3133–42.

85. Landgrebe M, W Barta, K Rosengarth et al (2008) Neuronal correlates of symptom formation in functional somatic syndromes: a fMRI study. Neuroimage 41:1336–44.

86. von Leupoldt A, T Sommer, S Kegat et al (2009) Dyspnea and pain share emotion-related brain network. Neuroimage 48:200–6.

87. Bavelier D and H Neville (2002) Developmental neuroplasticity. in Encyclopedia of the human brain, V Ramachandran, Editor. Academic Press: Amsterdam. 561–78.

88. Whitehead MC and DK Morest (1985) The development of innervation patterns in the avian cochlea. Neuroscience 14:255–76.

89. Kandel ER (1991) Cellular mechanisms of hearing and the biological basis of individiuality. in Principles of neural science, E Kandel, J Schwartz and T Jessell, Editors. Appleton & Lange: Norwalk, CT. 1009–31.

90. Snyder RL and PA Leake (1997) Topography of spiral ganglion projections to cochlear nucleus during postnatal development in cats. J Comp Neurol 384:293–311.

91. Staecker H, V Galinovic-Schwartz, W Liu et al (1996) The role of the neurotrophins in maturation and maintenance of postnatal auditory innervation. Am J Otol 17:486–92.

92. Rubsamen R (1992) Postnatal development of central auditory frequency maps. J Comp Physiol A 170:129–43.

93. Harrison RV, D Ibrahim and RJ Mount (1998) Plasticity of tonotopic maps in auditory midbrain following partial cochlear damage in the developing chinchilla. Exp Brain Res 123:449–60.

94. Sininger YS, KJ Doyle and JK Moore (1999) The case for early identification of hearing loss in children. Auditory system development, experimental auditory deprivation, and development of speech perception and hearing. Pediatr Clin North Am 46:1–14.

95. Deacon T, (1997) Evolution and intelligence: beyond the argument from design. in The origin and evolution of intelligence, A Scheibel and J Schopf, Editors. 1997, Jones and Bartlett: Boston. 103–36.

96. Sanes DH, J Song and J Tyson (1992) Refinement of dendritic arbors along the tonotopic axis of the gerbil lateral superior olive. Brain Res Dev Brain Res 67:47–55.

97. Gao E and N Suga (1998) Experience-dependent corticofugal adjustment of midbrain frequency map in bat auditory system. Proc Natl Acad Sci USA 95:12663–70.

98. Suga N, E Gao, Y Zhang et al (2000) The corticofugal system for hearing: recent progress. Proc Natl Acad Sci USA 97:11807–14.

99. Weinberger NM and JS Bakin (1998) Learning-induced physiological memory in adult primary auditory cortex: receptive fields plasticity, model, and mechanisms. Audiol Neurootol 3:145–67.

100. Recanzone GH, CE Schreiner and MM Merzenich (1993) Plasticity in the frequency representation of primary auditory cortex following discrimination training in adult owl monkeys. J Neurosci 13:87–103.

101. Cohen YE and JC Saunders (1994) The effect of acoustic overexposure on the tonotopic organization of the nucleus magnocellularis. Hear Res 81:11–21.

102. Dietrich V, M Nieschalk, W Stoll et al (2001) Cortical reorganization in patients with high frequency cochlear hearing loss. Hear Res 158:95–101.

103. Muhlnickel W, T Elbert, E Taub et al (1998) Reorganization of auditory cortex in tinnitus. Proc Natl Acad Sci USA 95:10340–3.

104. Chowdhury SA and N Suga (2000) Reorganization of the frequency map of the auditory cortex evoked by cortical electrical stimulation in the big brown bat. J Neurophysiol 83:1856–63.

105. Zhang Y and N Suga (2000) Modulation of responses and frequency tuning of thalamic and collicular neurons by cortical activation in mustached bats. J Neurophysiol 84:325–33.

106. Zhang Y, N Suga and J Yan (1997) Corticofugal modulation of frequency processing in bat auditory system. Nature 387:900–3.

107. Ma CL, JB Kelly and SH Wu (2002) AMPA and NMDA receptors mediate synaptic excitation in the rat's inferior colliculus. Hear Res 168:25–34.

108. Xiao Z and N Suga (2002) Modulation of cochlear hair cells by the auditory cortex in the mustached bat. Nat Neurosci 5:57–63.

109. Kilgard MP and MM Merzenich (1998) Cortical map reorganization enabled by nucleus basalis activity. Science 279:1714–8.

110. Bao S, VT Chan and MM Merzenich (2001) Cortical remodelling induced by activity of ventral tegmental dopamine neurons. Nature 412:79–83.

111. Ji W and N Suga (2007) Serotonergic modulation of plasticity of the auditory cortex elicited by fear conditioning. J Neurosci 27:4910–8.

112. Eggermont JJ and H Komiya (2000) Moderate noise trauma in juvenile cats results in profound cortical topographic map changes in adulthood. Hear Res 142:89–101.

113. Norena AJ, M Tomita and JJ Eggermont (2003) Neural changes in cat auditory cortex after a transient pure-tone trauma. J Neurophysiol 90:2387–401.

114. Norena AJ and JJ Eggermont (2005) Enriched acoustic environment after noise trauma reduces hearing loss and prevents cortical map reorganization. J Neurosci 25:699–705.

115. Seki S and JJ Eggermont (2003) Changes in spontaneous firing rate and neural synchrony in cat primary auditory cortex after localized tone-induced hearing loss. Hear Res 180:28–38.

116. Norena AJ and JJ Eggermont (2003) Changes in spontaneous neural activity immediately after an acoustic trauma: implications for neural correlates of tinnitus. Hear Res 183:137–53.

117. Norena AJ and JJ Eggermont (2006) Enriched acoustic environment after noise trauma abolishes neural signs of tinnitus. Neuroreport 17:559–63.

118. Flor H, T Elbert, S Knecht et al (1995) Phantom-limb pain as a perceptual correlate of cortical reorganization following arm amputation. Nature 375:482–4.

119. Rajan R (1998) Receptor organ damage causes loss of cortical surround inhibition without topographic map plasticity. Nat Neurosci 1:138–43.

120. Chen GD and PJ Jastreboff (1995) Salicylate-induced abnormal activity in the inferior colliculus of rats. Hear Res 82:158–78.

121. Eggermont JJ and M Kenmochi (1998) Salicylate and qui-nine selectively increase spontaneous firing rates in sec-ondary auditory cortex. Hear Res 117:149–60.

122. Eggermont JJ (2003) Central tinnitus. Auris Nasus Larynx 30 Suppl:S7–12.

123. Jeanmonod D, M Magnin and A Morel (1996) Low-threshold calcium spike bursts in the human thalamus. Common physiopathology for sensory, motor and limbic positive symptoms. Brain 119 (Pt 2):363–75.

124. Gopal KV and GW Gross (2004) Unique responses of auditory cortex networks in vitro to low concentrations of quinine. Hear Res 192:10–22.

125. Møller AR (1984) Pathophysiology of tinnitus. Ann Otol Rhinol Laryngol 93:39–44.

126. Cazals Y, KC Horner and ZW Huang (1998) Alterations in average spectrum of cochleoneural activity by long-term salicylate treatment in the guinea pig: a plausible index of tinnitus. J Neurophysiol 80:2113–20.

127. Martin WH, JW Schwegler, J Scheibelhoffer et al (1993) Salicylate-induced changes in cat auditory nerve activity. Laryngoscope 103:600–4.

128. Ochi K and JJ Eggermont (1996) Effects of salicylate on neural activity in cat primary auditory cortex. Hear Res 95:63–76.

129. Ochi K and JJ Eggermont (1997) Effects of quinine on neu-ral activity in cat primary auditory cortex. Hear Res 105:105–18.

130. Brozoski TJ, CA Bauer and DM Caspary (2002) Elevated fusiform cell activity in the dorsal cochlear nucleus of chin-chillas with psychophysical evidence of tinnitus. J Neurosci 22:2383–90.

131. Zhang JS and JA Kaltenbach (1998) Increases in spontaneous activity in the dorsal cochlear nucleus of the rat following expo-sure to high-intensity sound. Neurosci Lett 250:197–200.

132. Zacharek MA, JA Kaltenbach, TA Mathog et al (2002) Effects of cochlear ablation on noise induced hyperactivity in the hamster dorsal cochlear nucleus: implications for the origin of noise induced tinnitus. Hear Res 172:137–43.

133. Kaltenbach JA and CE Afman (2000) Hyperactivity in the dorsal cochlear nucleus after intense sound exposure and its resemblance to tone-evoked activity: a physiological model for tinnitus. Hear Res 140:165–72.

134. Kaltenbach JA, DA Godfrey, JB Neumann et al (1998) Changes in spontaneous neural activity in the dorsal cochlear nucleus following exposure to intense sound: rela-tion to threshold shift. Hear Res 124:78–84.

135. Kaltenbach JA, MA Zacharek, J Zhang et al (2004) Activity in the dorsal cochlear nucleus of hamsters previously tested for tinnitus following intense tone exposure. Neurosci Lett 355:121–5.

136. Jastreboff PJ (1990) Phantom auditory perception (tinni-tus): mechanisms of generation and perception. Neurosci Res 8:221–54.

137. Jastreboff PJ, JF Brennan and CT Sasaki (1988) An animal model for tinnitus. Laryngoscope 98:280–6.

138. Jastreboff PJ and CT Sasaki (1986) Salicylate-induced changes in spontaneous activity of single units in the infe-rior colliculus of the guinea pig. J Acoust Soc Am 80:1384–91.

139. Gerken GM (1996) Central tinnitus and lateral inhibition: an auditory brainstem model. Hear Res 97:75–83.

140. Komiya H and JJ Eggermont (2000) Spontaneous firing activity of cortical neurons in adult cats with reorganized tonotopic map following pure-tone trauma. Acta Otolaryngol 120:750–6.

141. Ulanovsky N, L Las and I Nelken (2003) Processing of low-probability sounds by cortical neurons. Nat Neurosci 6:391–8.

142. Naatanen R, P Paavilainen, H Tiitinen et al (1993) Attention and mismatch negativity. Psychophysiology 30:436–50.

143. Zeman A (2002) Consciousness, a user's guide. 2002, New Haven: Yale University Press. 77–110.

144. Steriade M (2000) Corticothalamic resonance, states of vigilance and mentation. Neuroscience 101:243–76.

145. Gray CM, P Konig, AK Engel et al (1989) Oscillatory responses in cat visual cortex exhibit inter-columnar syn-chronization which reflects global stimulus properties. Nature 338:334–7.

146. Gray CM and W Singer (1989) Stimulus-specific neuronal oscillations in orientation columns of cat visual cortex. Proc Natl Acad Sci USA 86:1698–702.

147. Tiitinen H, J Sinkkonen, K Reinikainen et al (1993) Selective attention enhances the auditory 40-Hz transient response in humans. Nature 364:59–60.

148. Joliot M, U Ribary and R Llinas (1994) Human oscillatory brain activity near 40 Hz coexists with cognitive temporal binding. Proc Natl Acad Sci USA 91:11748–51.

149. Llinas R, U Ribary, D Contreras et al (1998) The neuronal basis for consciousness. Philos Trans R Soc Lond B Biol Sci 353:1841–9.

150. Llinas R, U Ribary, M Joliot et al (1994) Content and context in temporal thalamocortical binding. in Temporal coding in the brain, G Buzsaki, R Llinas and W singer, Editors. Springer-Verlag: Berlin. 251–72.

151. Ribary U, AA Ioannides, KD Singh et al (1991) Magnetic field tomography of coherent thalamocortical 40-Hz oscilla-tions in humans. Proc Natl Acad Sci USA 88:11037–41.

152. Crone NE, D Boatman, B Gordon et al (2001) Induced electrocorticographic gamma activity during auditory per-ception. Brazier Award-winning article, 2001. Clin Neurophysiol 112:565–82.

153. Steriade M, F Amzica and D Contreras (1996) Synchronization of fast (30–40 Hz) spontaneous cortical rhythms during brain activation. J Neurosci 16:392–417.

154. MacDonald KD and DS Barth (1995) High frequency (gamma-band) oscillating potentials in rat somatosensory and auditory cortex. Brain Res 694:1–12.

155. Menon V, WJ Freeman, BA Cutillo et al (1996) Spatio-temporal correlations in human gamma band electrocortico-grams. Electroencephalogr Clin Neurophysiol 98:89–102.

156. Llinas R, FJ Urbano, E Leznik et al (2005) Rhythmic and dysrhythmic thalamocortical dynamics: GABA systems and the edge effect. Trends Neurosci 28:325–33.

157. Gaillard R, S Dehaene, C Adam et al (2009) Converging intracranial markers of conscious access. PLoS Biol 7:e61.

158. Melloni L, C Molina, M Pena et al (2007) Synchronization of neural activity across cortical areas correlates with conscious perception. J Neurosci 27:2858–65.

159. Freeman WJ (2003) The wave packet: an action potential for the 21st century. J Integr Neurosci 2:3–30.

160. Freeman WJ and LJ Rogers (2002) Fine temporal resolution of analytic phase reveals episodic synchronization by state transitions in gamma EEGs. J Neurophysiol 87:937–45.

161. Van der Loo E, M Congedo, M Plazier et al (2007) Correlation between independent components of scalp EEG and intracranial EEG (iEEG) time series. International Journal of Bioelectromagnetism 9:270–5.

162. Weisz N, S Muller, W Schlee et al (2007) The neural code of auditory phantom perception. J Neurosci 27:1479–84.

163. Llinas RR, U Ribary, D Jeanmonod et al (1999) Thalamocortical dysrhythmia: a neurological and neuropsychiatric syndrome characterized by magnetoencephalography. Proc Natl Acad Sci USA 96:15222–7.

164. Hughes SW and V Crunelli (2005) Thalamic mechanisms of EEG alpha rhythms and their pathological implications. Neuroscientist 11:357–72.

165. van der Loo E, S Gais, M Congedo et al (2009) Tinnitus intensity dependent gamma oscillations of the contralateral auditory cortex. PLoS One 4:e7396.

166. Lisman J and G Buzsaki (2008) A neural coding scheme formed by the combined function of gamma and theta oscillations. Schizophr Bull 34:974–80.

167. Weisz N, S Voss, P Berg et al (2004) Abnormal auditory mismatch response in tinnitus sufferers with high-frequency hearing loss is associated with subjective distress level. BMC Neurosci 5:8.

168. Eggermont JJ and LE Roberts (2004) The neuroscience of tinnitus. Trends Neurosci 27:676–82.

169. El-Amamy H and PC Holland (2007) Dissociable effects of disconnecting amygdala central nucleus from the ventral tegmental area or substantia nigra on learned orienting and incentive motivation. Eur J Neurosci 25:1557–67.

170. Holland PC (2007) Disconnection of the amygdala central nucleus and the substantia innominata/nucleus basalis magnocellularis disrupts performance in a sustained attention task. Behav Neurosci 121:80–9.

171. Maddux JM, EC Kerfoot, S Chatterjee et al (2007) Dissociation of attention in learning and action: effects of lesions of the amygdala central nucleus, medial prefrontal cortex, and posterior parietal cortex. Behav Neurosci 121:63–79.

172. Oades RD and GM Halliday (1987) Ventral tegmental (A10) system: neurobiology. 1. Anatomy and connectivity. Brain Res 434:117–65.

173. Onn SP and XB Wang (2005) Differential modulation of anterior cingulate cortical activity by afferents from ventral tegmental area and mediodorsal thalamus. Eur J Neurosci 21:2975–92.

174. Seeley WW, V Menon, AF Schatzberg et al (2007) Dissociable intrinsic connectivity networks for salience processing and executive control. J Neurosci 27:2349–56.

175. Taylor KS, DA Seminowicz and KD Davis (2009) Two systems of resting state connectivity between the insula and cingulate cortex. Hum Brain Mapp. 30:2731–45.

176. Mulert C, G Leicht, O Pogarell et al (2007) Auditory cortex and anterior cingulate cortex sources of the early evoked gamma-band response: relationship to task difficulty and mental effort. Neuropsychologia 45:2294–306.

177. Montaron MF, JJ Bouyer, A Rougeul et al (1982) Ventral mesencephalic tegmentum (VMT) controls electrocortical beta rhythms and associated attentive behaviour in the cat. Behav Brain Res 6:129–45.

178. Bamiou DE, FE Musiek and LM Luxon (2003) The insula (Island of Reil) and its role in auditory processing. Literature review. Brain Res Brain Res Rev 42:143–54.

179. Engelien A, D Silbersweig, E Stern et al (1995) The functional anatomy of recovery from auditory agnosia. A PET study of sound categorization in a neurological patient and normal controls. Brain 118 (Pt 6):1395–409.

180. Habib M, G Daquin, L Milandre et al (1995) Mutism and auditory agnosia due to bilateral insular damage – role of the insula in human communication. Neuropsychologia 33:327–39.

181. Fifer RC (1993) Insular stroke causing unilateral auditory processing disorder: case report. J Am Acad Audiol 4:364–9.

182. Lisman JE and AA Grace (2005) The hippocampal-VTA loop: controlling the entry of information into long-term memory. Neuron 46:703–13.

183. Boutros NN, R Mears, ME Pflieger et al (2008) Sensory gating in the human hippocampal and rhinal regions: regional differences. Hippocampus 18:310–6.

184. Engelien A, E Stern, N Isenberg et al (2000) The parahippocampal region and auditory-mnemonic processing. Ann N Y Acad Sci 911:477–85.

185. Muller BW, M Juptner, W Jentzen et al (2002) Cortical activation to auditory mismatch elicited by frequency deviant and complex novel sounds: a PET study. Neuroimage 17:231–9.

186. Engelien A, O Tuscher, W Hermans et al (2006) Functional neuroanatomy of non-verbal semantic sound processing in humans. J Neural Transm 113:599–608.

187. Tanaka E, K Inui, T Kida et al (2008) A transition from unimodal to multimodal activations in four sensory modalities in humans: an electrophysiological study. BMC Neurosci 9:116.

188. Hoffman RE, AW Anderson, M Varanko et al (2008) Time course of regional brain activation associated with onset of auditory/verbal hallucinations. Br J Psychiatry 193:424–5.

189. Shergill SS, MJ Brammer, E Amaro et al (2004) Temporal course of auditory hallucinations. Br J Psychiatry 185:516–7.

190. Anderson AK and EA Phelps (2001) Lesions of the human amygdala impair enhanced perception of emotionally salient events. Nature 411:305–9.

191. Mulert C, G Juckel, M Brunnmeier et al (2007) Rostral anterior cingulate cortex activity in the theta band predicts response to antidepressive medication. Clin EEG Neurosci 38:78–81.

192. Kurthen M, P Trautner, T Rosburg et al (2007) Towards a functional topography of sensory gating areas: invasive P50 recording and electrical stimulation mapping in epilepsy surgery candidates. Psychiatry Res 155:121–33.

193. Norena A, C Micheyl, S Chery-Croze et al (2002) Psychoacoustic characterization of the tinnitus spectrum: implications for the underlying mechanisms of tinnitus. Audiol Neurootol 7:358–69.

194. Ramachandran VS and W Hirstein (1998) The perception of phantom limbs. The D. O. Hebb lecture. Brain 121 (Pt 9): 1603–30.

195. De Ridder D and P Van de Heyning (2007) The Darwinian plasticity hypothesis for tinnitus and pain. Prog Brain Res 166:55–60.

196. Ogawa S, TM Lee, AR Kay et al (1990) Brain magnetic resonance imaging with contrast dependent on blood oxygenation. Proc Natl Acad Sci USA 87:9868–72.

197. Brookes MJ, AM Gibson, SD Hall et al (2005) GLM-beamformer method demonstrates stationary field, alpha ERD and gamma ERS co-localisation with fMRI BOLD response in visual cortex. Neuroimage 26:302–8.

198. Nir Y, L Fisch, R Mukamel et al (2007) Coupling between neuronal firing rate, gamma LFP, and BOLD fMRI is related to interneuronal correlations. Curr Biol 17:1275–85.

199. Mukamel R, H Gelbard, A Arieli et al (2005) Coupling between neuronal firing, field potentials, and FMRI in human auditory cortex. Science 309:951–4.

200. Smits M, S Kovacs, D De Ridder et al (2004) Lateralization of signal change in the auditory pathway in patients with lateralized tinnitus studied with functional Magnetic Resonance Imaging (fMRI). Radiology 233, supplement:abstract 12-06.

201. Crick F and C Koch (2003) A framework for consciousness. Nat Neurosci 6:119–26.

202. Crick F and C Koch (1990) Toward a neurobiological theory of consciousness. Semin Neurosci 2:263–75.

203. Crick F and C Koch (1995) Are we aware of neural activity in primary visual cortex? Nature 375:121–3.

204. Laureys S (2007) Eyes open, brain shut. Sci Am 296:84–9.

205. Laureys S, S Goldman, C Phillips et al (1999) Impaired effective cortical connectivity in vegetative state: preliminary investigation using PET. Neuroimage 9:377–82.

206. Laureys S, ME Faymonville, A Luxen et al (2000) Restoration of thalamocortical connectivity after recovery from persistent vegetative state. Lancet 355:1790–1.

207. Laureys S, M Boly and P Maquet (2006) Tracking the recovery of consciousness from coma. J Clin Invest 116:1823–5.

208. Boly M, ME Faymonville, P Peigneux et al (2004) Auditory processing in severely brain injured patients: differences between the minimally conscious state and the persistent vegetative state. Arch Neurol 61:233–8.

209. Boly M, ME Faymonville, P Peigneux et al (2005) Cerebral processing of auditory and noxious stimuli in severely brain injured patients: differences between VS and MCS. Neuropsychol Rehabil 15:283–9.

210. Baars BJ (1993) How does a serial, integrated and very limited stream of consciousness emerge from a nervous system that is mostly unconscious, distributed, parallel and of enormous capacity? Ciba Found Symp 174:282–90; discussion 91–303.

211. Dehaene S, M Kerszberg and JP Changeux (1998) A neuronal model of a global workspace in effortful cognitive tasks. Proc Natl Acad Sci USA 95:14529–34.

212. Dehaene S and L Naccache (2001) Towards a cognitive neuroscience of consciousness: basic evidence and a workspace framework. Cognition 79:1–37.

213. Dehaene S, JP Changeux, L Naccache et al (2006) Conscious, preconscious, and subliminal processing: a testable taxonomy. Trends Cogn Sci 10:204–11.

214. Edelman GM (1993) Neural Darwinism: selection and reentrant signaling in higher brain function. Neuron 10:115–25.

215. Liegeois-Chauvel C, A Musolino, JM Badier et al (1994) Evoked potentials recorded from the auditory cortex in man: evaluation and topography of the middle latency components. Electroencephalogr Clin Neurophysiol 92:204–14.

216. Yvert B, A Crouzeix, O Bertrand et al (2001) Multiple supratemporal sources of magnetic and electric auditory evoked middle latency components in humans. Cereb Cortex 11:411–23.

217. Zouridakis G, PG Simos and AC Papanicolaou (1998) Multiple bilaterally asymmetric cortical sources account for the auditory N1m component. Brain Topogr 10:183–9.

218. Loveless N, S Levanen, V Jousmaki et al (1996) Temporal integration in auditory sensory memory: neuromagnetic evidence. Electroencephalogr Clin Neurophysiol 100:220–8.

219. Jaaskelainen IP, J Ahveninen, G Bonmassar et al (2004) Human posterior auditory cortex gates novel sounds to consciousness. Proc Natl Acad Sci USA 101:6809–14.

220. Saletu M, P Anderer, GM Saletu-Zyhlarz et al (2008) Event-related-potential low-resolution brain electromagnetic tomography (ERP-LORETA) suggests decreased energetic resources for cognitive processing in narcolepsy. Clin Neurophysiol 119:1782–94.

221. Korzyukov O, ME Pflieger, M Wagner et al (2007) Generators of the intracranial P50 response in auditory sensory gating. Neuroimage 35:814–26.

222. Grunwald T, NN Boutros, N Pezer et al (2003) Neuronal substrates of sensory gating within the human brain. Biol Psychiatry 53:511–9.

223. Frot M, F Mauguiere, M Magnin et al (2008) Parallel processing of nociceptive A-delta inputs in SII and midcingulate cortex in humans. J Neurosci 28:944–52.

224. Rosburg T, P Trautner, OA Korzyukov et al (2004) Short-term habituation of the intracranially recorded auditory evoked potentials P50 and N100. Neurosci Lett 372:245–9.

225. Clementz BA, LD Blumenfeld and S Cobb (1997) The gamma band response may account for poor P50 suppression in schizophrenia. Neuroreport 8:3889–93.

226. Grau C, L Fuentemilla and J Marco-Pallares (2007) Functional neural dynamics underlying auditory event-related N1 and N1 suppression response. Neuroimage 36:522–31.

227. Meyer M, S Baumann and L Jancke (2006) Electrical brain imaging reveals spatio-temporal dynamics of timbre perception in humans. Neuroimage 32:1510–23.

228. Atcherson SR, HJ Gould, MA Pousson et al (2006) Long-term stability of N1 sources using low-resolution electromagnetic tomography. Brain Topogr 19:11–20.

229. Potts GF, J Dien, AL Hartry-Speiser et al (1998) Dense sensor array topography of the event-related potential to task-relevant auditory stimuli. Electroencephalogr Clin Neurophysiol 106:444–56.

230. Volpe U, A Mucci, P Bucci et al (2007) The cortical generators of P3a and P3b: a LORETA study. Brain Res Bull 73:220–30.

231. Mulert C, O Pogarell, G Juckel et al (2004) The neural basis of the P300 potential. Focus on the time-course of the underlying cortical generators. Eur Arch Psychiatry Clin Neurosci 254:190–8.

232. Frisch S, SA Kotz, DY von Cramon et al (2003) Why the P600 is not just a P300: the role of the basal ganglia. Clin Neurophysiol 114:336–40.

233. Andreassi J (2000) Psychophysiology, human behavior and physiological response. Mahwah, NJ: Lawrence Erlbaum Associates.

234. Cromwell HC, RP Mears, L Wan et al (2008) Sensory gating: a translational effort from basic to clinical science. Clin EEG Neurosci 39:69–72.

235. Vincent JL, I Kahn, AZ Snyder et al (2008) Evidence for a frontoparietal control system revealed by intrinsic functional connectivity. J Neurophysiol 100:3328–42.

236. Vincent JL, AZ Snyder, MD Fox et al (2006) Coherent spontaneous activity identifies a hippocampal-parietal memory network. J Neurophysiol 96:3517–31.

237. Fox MD, M Corbetta, AZ Snyder et al (2006) Spontaneous neuronal activity distinguishes human dorsal and ventral attention systems. Proc Natl Acad Sci USA 103: 10046–51.

238. Fox MD, AZ Snyder, JL Vincent et al (2005) The human brain is intrinsically organized into dynamic, anticorrelated functional networks. Proc Natl Acad Sci USA 102: 9673–8.

239. Buckner RL, JR Andrews-Hanna and DL Schacter (2008) The brain's default network: anatomy, function, and relevance to disease. Ann N Y Acad Sci 1124:1–38.

240. Raichle ME, AM MacLeod, AZ Snyder et al (2001) A default mode of brain function. Proc Natl Acad Sci USA 98:676–82.

241. Kahn I, JR Andrews-Hanna, JL Vincent et al (2008) Distinct cortical anatomy linked to subregions of the medial temporal lobe revealed by intrinsic functional connectivity. J Neurophysiol 100:129–39.

242. Greicius MD and V Menon (2004) Default-mode activity during a passive sensory task: uncoupled from deactivation but impacting activation. J Cogn Neurosci 16:1484–92.

243. Miller EK (2000) The prefrontal cortex and cognitive control. Nat Rev Neurosci 1:59–65.

244. Stein JL, LM Wiedholz, DS Bassett et al (2007) A validated network of effective amygdala connectivity. Neuroimage 36:736–45.

245. Maquet P, P Ruby, A Maudoux et al (2005) Human cognition during REM sleep and the activity profile within frontal and parietal cortices: a reappraisal of functional neuroimaging data. Prog Brain Res 150:219–27.

246. Corbetta M, G Patel and GL Shulman (2008) The reorienting system of the human brain: from environment to theory of mind. Neuron 58:306–24.

247. Manes F, B Sahakian, L Clark et al (2002) Decision-making processes following damage to the prefrontal cortex. Brain 125:624–39.

248. Dehaene S, C Sergent and JP Changeux (2003) A neuronal network model linking subjective reports and objective physiological data during conscious perception. Proc Natl Acad Sci USA 100:8520–5.

249. de Lafuente V and R Romo (2005) Neuronal correlates of subjective sensory experience. Nat Neurosci 8:1698–703.

250. de Lafuente V and R Romo (2006) Neural correlate of subjective sensory experience gradually builds up across cortical areas. Proc Natl Acad Sci USA 103:14266–71.

251. de Lafuente V and R Romo (2002) A hidden sensory function for motor cortex. Neuron 36:785–6.

252. O'Regan K and A Noë (2001) A sensorimotor account of vision and visual consciousness. Behav Brain Sci 24:883–917.

253. Noë A (2004) Action in Perception. Cambridge, MA: MIT Press.

254. Aquinas ST (1268) Commentaries on Aristotle's on sense and what is sensed and on memory and recollection. Washington, DC: The Catholic University of America Press.

255. Freeman WJ (1999) How brains make up their minds. London: Phoenix.

256. Attias J, D Urbach, S Gold et al (1993) Auditory event related potentials in chronic tinnitus patients with noise induced hearing loss. Hear Res 71:106–13.

257. Attias J, V Furman, Z Shemesh et al (1996) Impaired brain processing in noise-induced tinnitus patients as measured by auditory and visual event-related potentials. Ear Hear 17:327–33.

258. Shiraishi T, K Sugimoto, T Kubo et al (1991) Contingent negative variation enhancement in tinnitus patients. Am J Otolaryngol 12:267–71.

259. Delb W, DJ Strauss, YF Low et al (2008) Alterations in Event Related Potentials (ERP) associated with tinnitus distress and attention. Appl Psychophysiol Biofeedback 33:211–21.

260. Norena A, H Cransac and S Chery-Croze (1999) Towards an objectification by classification of tinnitus. Clin Neurophysiol 110:666–75.

261. Hoke M, H Feldmann, C Pantev et al (1989) Objective evidence of tinnitus in auditory evoked magnetic fields. Hear Res 37:281–6.

262. Pantev C, M Hoke, B Lutkenhoner et al (1989) Tinnitus remission objectified by neuromagnetic measurements. Hear Res 40:261–4.

263. Jacobson GP, BK Ahmad, J Moran et al (1991) Auditory evoked cortical magnetic field (M100–M200) measurements in tinnitus and normal groups. Hear Res 56:44–52.

264. Arnold W, P Bartenstein, E Oestreicher et al (1996) Focal metabolic activation in the predominant left auditory cortex in patients suffering from tinnitus: a PET study with [18F]deoxyglucose. ORL J Otorhinolaryngol Relat Spec 58:195–9.

265. Lockwood AH, RJ Salvi, RF Burkard et al (1999) Neuroanatomy of tinnitus. Scand Audiol Suppl 51:47–52.

266. Eichhammer P, G Hajak, T Kleinjung et al (2007) Functional imaging of chronic tinnitus: the use of positron emission tomography. Prog Brain Res 166:83–8.

267. Langguth B, P Eichhammer, A Kreutzer et al (2006) The impact of auditory cortex activity on characterizing and treating patients with chronic tinnitus – first results from a PET study. Acta Otolaryngol Suppl 84–8.

268. Giraud AL, S Chery-Croze, G Fischer et al (1999) A selective imaging of tinnitus. Neuroreport 10:1–5.

269. Plewnia C, M Reimold, A Najib et al (2007) Dose-dependent attenuation of auditory phantom perception (tinnitus) by PET-guided repetitive transcranial magnetic stimulation. Hum Brain Mapp 28:238–46.

270. Mirz F, A Gjedde, K Ishizu et al (2000) Cortical networks subserving the perception of tinnitus – a PET study. Acta Otolaryngol Suppl 543:241–3.

271. Mirz F, T Ovesen, K Ishizu et al (1999) Stimulus-dependent central processing of auditory stimuli: a PET study. Scand Audiol 28:161–9.

272. Muhlau M, JP Rauschecker, E Oestreicher et al (2006) Structural brain changes in tinnitus. Cereb Cortex 16:1283–8.

273. Landgrebe M, B Langguth, K Rosengarth et al (2009) Structural brain changes in tinnitus: grey matter decrease in auditory and non-auditory brain areas. Neuroimage 46:213–8.

274. Melcher JR, IS Sigalovsky, JJ Guinan, Jr. et al (2000) Lateralized tinnitus studied with functional magnetic resonance imaging: abnormal inferior colliculus activation. J Neurophysiol 83:1058–72.

275. Smits M, S Kovacs, D De Ridder et al (2007) Lateralization of functional magnetic resonance imaging (fMRI) activation in the auditory pathway of patients with lateralized tinnitus. Neuroradiology 49:669–79.

276. Weisz N, S Moratti, M Meinzer et al (2005) Tinnitus perception and distress is related to abnormal spontaneous brain activity as measured by magnetoencephalography. PLoS Med 2:e153.

277. Mirz F, A Gjedde, H Sodkilde-Jrgensen et al (2000) Functional brain imaging of tinnitus-like perception induced by aversive auditory stimuli. Neuroreport 11:633–7.

278. Zald DH and JV Pardo (2002) The neural correlates of aversive auditory stimulation. Neuroimage 16:746–53.

279. De Ridder D, H Ryu, G De Mulder et al (2005) Frequency specific hearing improvement in microvascular decompression of the cochlear nerve. Acta Neurochir (Wien) 147:495–501; discussion 501.

280. De Ridder D, K Heijneman, B Haarman et al (2007) Tinnitus in vascular conflict of the eighth cranial nerve: a surgical pathophysiological approach to ABR changes. Prog Brain Res 166:401–11.

281. Møller MB, AR Møller, PJ Jannetta et al (1993) Vascular decompression surgery for severe tinnitus: selection criteria and results. Laryngoscope 103:421–7.

282. De Ridder D, H Ryu, AR Møller et al (2004) Functional anatomy of the human cochlear nerve and its role in microvascular decompressions for tinnitus. Neurosurgery 54:381–8; discussion 8–90.

283. Jannetta P, (1997) Outcome after microvascular decompression for typical trigeminal neuralgia, hemifacial spasm, tinnitus, disabling positional vertigo, and glossopharyngeal neuralgia. in Clinical neurosurgery, S Grady, Editor. 1997, Williams and Wilkins: Baltimore. 331–84.

284. Ryu H, S Yamamoto, K Sugiyama et al (1998) Neurovascular compression syndrome of the eighth cranial nerve. What are the most reliable diagnostic signs? Acta Neurochir (Wien) 140:1279–86.

285. Brookes GB (1996) Vascular-decompression surgery for severe tinnitus. Am J Otol 17:569–76.

286. De Ridder D, E Verstraeten, K Van der Kelen et al (2005) Transcranial magnetic stimulation for tinnitus: influence of tinnitus duration on stimulation parameter choice and maximal tinnitus suppression. Otol Neurotol 26:616–9.

287. Kleinjung T, T Steffens, P Sand et al (2007) Which tinnitus patients benefit from transcranial magnetic stimulation? Otolaryngol Head Neck Surg 137:589–95.

288. Khedr EM, JC Rothwell, MA Ahmed et al (2008) Effect of daily repetitive transcranial magnetic stimulation for treatment of tinnitus: comparison of different stimulus frequencies. J Neurol Neurosurg Psychiatr 79:212–5.

289. Schlee W, T Hartmann, B Langguth et al (2009) Abnormal resting-state cortical coupling in chronic tinnitus. BMC Neurosci 10:11.

290. Sterling P and J Eyer (1988) Allostasis: a new paradigm to explain arousal pathology. in Handbook of life stress, cognition and health, S Fisher and J Reason, Editors. 1988, Wiley: New York. 629–49

291. McEwen BS (2007) Physiology and neurobiology of stress and adaptation: central role of the brain. Physiol Rev 87:873–904.

292. McEwen BS (2008) Central effects of stress hormones in health and disease: understanding the protective and damaging effects of stress and stress mediators. Eur J Pharmacol 583:174–85.

293. Cannon W (1929) Organization for physiological homeostasis. Physiol Rev 9:399–431.

294. Bernard C (1865) Introduction a l'Etude de la Médicine Expérimentale. Paris: JB Baillière.

295. Koob GF and M Le Moal (2008) Addiction and the brain antireward system. Annu Rev Psychol 59:29–53.

296. Koob GF and M Le Moal (2001) Drug addiction, dysregulation of reward, and allostasis. Neuropsychopharmacology 24:97–129.

297. Korte SM, JM Koolhaas, JC Wingfield et al (2005) The Darwinian concept of stress: benefits of allostasis and costs of allostatic load and the trade-offs in health and disease. Neurosci Biobehav Rev 29:3–38.

298. McEwen BS (2002) Protective and damaging effects of stress mediators: the good and bad sides of the response to stress. Metabolism 51:2–4.

299. Celerier E, JP Laulin, JB Corcuff et al (2001) Progressive enhancement of delayed hyperalgesia induced by repeated heroin administration: a sensitization process. J Neurosci 21:4074–80.

300. Walton ME, PL Croxson, TE Behrens et al (2007) Adaptive decision making and value in the anterior cingulate cortex. Neuroimage 36 Suppl 2:T142–54.

301. Holroyd CB, OE Krigolson, R Baker et al (2009) When is an error not a prediction error? An electrophysiological investigation. Cogn Affect Behav Neurosci 9: 59–70.

302. Gosselin N, S Samson, R Adolphs et al (2006) Emotional responses to unpleasant music correlates with damage to the parahippocampal cortex. Brain 129:2585–92.

303. Eichenbaum H and PA Lipton (2008) Towards a functional organization of the medial temporal lobe memory system: role of the parahippocampal and medial entorhinal cortical areas. Hippocampus 18:1314–24.

304. Aminoff E, N Gronau and M Bar (2007) The parahippocampal cortex mediates spatial and nonspatial associations. Cereb Cortex 17:1493–503.

305. Portas CM, BA Strange, KJ Friston et al (2000) How does the brain sustain a visual percept? Proc Biol Sci 267:845–50.

306. De Ridder D, H Fransen, O Francois et al (2006) Amygdalohippocampal involvement in tinnitus and auditory memory.Acta Otolaryngol Suppl 50–3.

307. Strogatz SH (2001) Exploring complex networks. Nature 410:268–76.

308. Watts DJ and SH Strogatz (1998) Collective dynamics of 'small-world' networks. Nature 393:440–2.

309. Albert R and AL Barabasi (2000) Topology of evolving networks: local events and universality. Phys Rev Lett 85:5234–7.

310. Albert R and AL Barabasi (2000) Dynamics of complex systems: scaling laws for the period of boolean networks. Phys Rev Lett 84:5660–3.

311. Barabasi AL and R Albert (1999) Emergence of scaling in random networks. Science 286:509–12.

312. Achard S, R Salvador, B Whitcher et al (2006) A resilient, low-frequency, small-world human brain functional network with highly connected association cortical hubs. J Neurosci 26:63–72.

313. Bassett DS, E Bullmore, BA Verchinski et al (2008) Hierarchical organization of human cortical networks in health and schizophrenia. J Neurosci 28:9239–48.

314. Bassett DS, A Meyer-Lindenberg, S Achard et al (2006) Adaptive reconfiguration of fractal small-world human brain functional networks. Proc Natl Acad Sci USA 103:19518–23.

315. Bullmore E and O Sporns (2009) Complex brain networks: graph theoretical analysis of structural and functional systems. Nat Rev Neurosci 10:186–98.

316. Salvador R, J Suckling, C Schwarzbauer et al (2005) Undirected graphs of frequency-dependent functional connectivity in whole brain networks. Philos Trans R Soc Lond B Biol Sci 360:937–46.

317. Stam CJ and JC Reijneveld (2007) Graph theoretical analysis of complex networks in the brain. Nonlinear Biomed Phys 1:3.

318. van den Heuvel MP, CJ Stam, M Boersma et al (2008) Small-world and scale-free organization of voxel-based resting-state functional connectivity in the human brain. Neuroimage 43:528–39.

319. Barabasi AL (2009) Scale-free networks: a decade and beyond. Science 325:412–3.

320. Oltvai ZN and AL Barabasi (2002) Systems biology. Life's complexity pyramid. Science 298:763–4.

321. Hagmann P, L Cammoun, X Gigandet et al (2008) Mapping the structural core of human cerebral cortex. PLoS Biol 6:e159.

322. Ponten SC, L Douw, F Bartolomei et al (2009) Indications for network regularization during absence seizures: weighted and unweighted graph theoretical analyses. Exp Neurol 217:197–204.

323. Humphries MD, K Gurney and TJ Prescott (2006) The brainstem reticular formation is a small-world, not scale-free, network. Proc Biol Sci 273:503–11.

324. Buzsaki G (2006) Rhythms of the brain. Oxford: Oxford University Press.

325. Yu S, D Huang, W Singer et al (2008) A small world of neuronal synchrony. Cereb Cortex 18:2891–901.

326. Eguiluz VM, DR Chialvo, GA Cecchi et al (2005) Scale-free brain functional networks. Phys Rev Lett 94:018102.

327. Miller KJ, LB Sorensen, JG Ojemann et al (2009) Power-law scaling in the brain surface electric potential. PLoS Comput Biol 5:e1000609.

328. Schlee W, N Mueller, T Hartmann et al (2009) Mapping cortical hubs in tinnitus. BMC Biol 7:80.

Chapter 22
Methodology of Clinical Trials for Tinnitus

Michael Landgrebe, Berthold Langguth, Florian Zeman, and Michael Koller

Keypoints

1. There is no established methodology for clinical trials of tinnitus treatment.
2. Inter-study comparability is difficult due to insufficient characterization of investigated samples and variation of the used assessment and outcome measures.
3. Clinical trials in tinnitus should follow standards set by the guidelines of Good Clinical Practice, by the Consort statements, and should be registered in a clinical trial registry.
4. The design of the clinical trial depends on the clinical question, which should be answered by the study.
5. Placebo-controlled randomized trials represent the gold standard for testing efficacy of treatment approaches. However, in order to save resources, a stepwise approach seems reasonable, which involves pilot open trials as a first step to screen for potentially promising treatments and which is followed in case of positive outcome by randomized controlled trials.
6. Due to the heterogeneity of tinnitus, the best possible characterization of the investigated study sample, with respect to clinical or neurobiological characteristics, is highly desirable.
7. Outcome criteria for therapeutic trials have to be reliable, valid, specific, and relevant.
8. Trial design should be based on statistical estimation of sample sizes and power in order to minimize the risk of type I and type II errors.
9. To enhance inter-study comparability, international accepted standards for patient assessment and outcome measurement should be followed.
10. Standardization of clinical trial methodology will enhance clinical research in tinnitus by facilitating data comparison across trials and allowing pooled data analyses of multicenter study results in international databases.

Keywords Tinnitus • Clinical trials • Placebo • Inter-study comparability

Introduction

Clinical trials are conducted in order to answer questions regarding the safety and efficacy of new treatment options. Ideally, clinical trials will answer these questions as accurately as possible. However, there are several constraints for the design and conduct of a clinical trial, such as recruitment of patients (especially when large sample sizes are required or selective inclusion and exclusion criteria are being imposed), adherence of patients, or financial resources. Thus, the optimal trial design has to find a balance between adequacy to address the clinical question and feasibility as defined by the research infrastructure.

M. Landgrebe (✉)
Department of Psychiatry, Psychosomatics, and Psychotherapy, University of Regensburg, Universitätsstraße 84, 93053 Regensburg, Germany
and
Interdisciplinary Tinnitus Clinic, University of Regensburg, Regensburg, Germany
e-mail: michael.landgrebe@medbo.de

Randomized Controlled Trials: Bias Reduction and Ethical Issues

The gold standard for evaluating treatment efficacy is the randomized controlled clinical trial (RCT) [1].

A.R. Møller et al. (eds.), *Textbook of Tinnitus*,
DOI 10.1007/978-1-60761-145-5_22, © Springer Science+Business Media, LLC 2011

Randomization is the key element and refers to the fact that patients are assigned to a treatment or a control group *by chance*. That is, a patient who has been found eligible to participate in the trial and has also provided informed consent to do so, has an equal chance to be assigned to either the treatment or the control condition. Neither the patient nor the physician is involved in this decision. In practice, treatment assignment is laid down in a randomization code that is compiled before the start of the trial by using tables of random numbers or generating a list of random numbers by computerized tools. The important conceptual and methodological consequence of randomization is – given that the sample size is sufficiently high – that any known and unknown factors related to the patient (patient history, co-morbidity, gender, age, expectations) are balanced out across treatment and control condition. Thus, the process of randomization establishes structural equivalence and eliminates biases (i.e., systematic errors that jeopardize the interpretation of study results) that are due to confounding factors.

A second major technique to reduce bias is blinding. The idea is to keep the treatment assignment of patients confidential throughout the course of the trial and ensure that all patients are treated in a consistent way. Ideally, neither patients nor doctors know which treatment or control group a patient is assigned to; this is called a double-blind study. An even more strict design is a triple-blind study, in which neither the patient and the doctor nor the researcher assessing treatment outcome or being involved in data analysis have information regarding treatment assignment. There are cases, however, in which only the patient can be blinded; this is a single-blind study. A study in which treatment assignment is known to all participants is called an open study.

The fact that randomized trials impose the element of chance regarding treatment assignment and require blinding as an additional methodological feature gives rise to substantial ethical concerns. The two most popular, and conflictive, points of criticisms read as follows: (1) patients in the treatment arm may be exposed to a dangerous regimen whose safety is not yet proven; (2) patients in the control arm may be withheld from a potential beneficial new treatment option. There is broad and undisputed social and scientific consensus that randomized controlled trials have to comply with the highest ethical standards. The two most important ethical requirements are sufficient evidence regarding the safety of the new treatment option, and, at the same time, uncertainty regarding the reliability and magnitude of its potential benefit. This state of uncertainty is called equipoise: only then a randomized trial may be conducted as a decision experiment to clarify whether there is a reliable and clinical meaningful difference between treatment and control condition.

Further Considerations When Planning a RCT

Clinical trials can be performed as monocentre or multicentre trials. Performance of RCT as multicentre trials makes it possible to include a larger sample in shorter time and also allows controlling for specific center effects, but the organization also becomes more demanding. It should also be mentioned that not in all situations are RCTs the best solution. First of all, RCTs are methodologically demanding, expensive, and time consuming. Therefore, there should be pilot data available that identify the treatment approach under the study as promising and allow estimation of the effect size of the intervention. Knowledge of the sample size, in turn, is a necessary prerequisite for sample size and power calculations. However, identifying an intervention as "promising" is a difficult task. One practical approach may be a stepwise process starting with a smaller, open pilot trial. If the results of the pilot trial have been promising, the next step can be to test this intervention in a RCT. Furthermore, data from the pilot trial may help to identify inclusion or stratification criteria. Alternatively, RCTs may be started based on promising results of preclinical experiments (e.g., animal studies). However, the lack of in vitro bioassays or validated animal models is a major problem in the development of new drugs for tinnitus therapy.

Recent promising advances in this field, however, may facilitate drug development in the near future (see Chap. 16), but it remains to be determined to what extent data from drug trials in the available animal models can be extrapolated to efficacy in humans. Another problem of RCTs is that the efficacy of a treatment is, in general, evaluated by assessing the mean change of the outcome measure for each group. Using this approach, individual patients with a very good treatment response may be missed. Hence, in addition to the evaluation of group averages, study results should be analyzed for predictors of positive treatment response or subgroups of responders. The search for predictors of treatment response may be further facilitated by pooling the information from different trials in meta-analyses or databases, assuming that the studies have been performed according to specific standards [2]. It is important to note that such post hoc data-driven analyses have to be interpreted carefully and require further prospective confirmatory studies because they are never corrected for multiple comparisons.

Given the complexity of tinnitus and the many treatment options and possible combinations available, tinnitus may be a target for complex interventions. The UK's Medical Research Council (MRC) has developed a conceptual and methodological framework for complex interventions [3]. The continuum of increasing evidence comprises five consecutive phases [4, 5]:

1. Theory: the theoretical basis is laid down suggesting a specific intervention will have the expected effect (preclinical phase).
2. Modeling: all components of the interventions are described and their interrelations and expected outcomes are specified.
3. Exploratory trial: preliminary evidence is obtained that this treatment has the intended effect. This phase helps to improve the final study design, intervention, and control groups, as well as assessment strategies.
4. Confirmatory randomized controlled clinical trial (RCT): this crucial phase is designed to answer whether the complex intervention really works.
5. Long-term implementation: this final step includes a subsequent study that evaluates the validity of the complex intervention under real-life circumstances.

Promising examples applying this model have been published [4, 5], which may also serve as a general model for clinical tinnitus research.

Control Groups

Placebo-controlled trials can be performed in cross-over designs or parallel group designs. In cross-over designs, each patient represents his own control, which minimizes the influence of confounding factors. Furthermore, a much smaller sample size is sufficient

to reach the same statistical power. However, the main shortcomings are that a cross-over design limits follow-up periods and requires a wash-out period before switching to the other kind of intervention (placebo or active treatment) in order to avoid the effects of the first intervention influencing the second intervention. The estimation of a sufficient duration of the wash-out time is sometimes difficult, since both known factors (e.g., long half-life times of pharmaceutical agents) and unknown factors (e.g., induced neuroplastic changes in the central nervous system, which may occur with a delay after treatment) may play a role. Thus, the design of a cross-over trial always involves a trade-off between study duration and the risk of potential carry-over effects, which may confound study results. Moreover, cross-over designs cannot be used when the timing of the intervention is critical, e.g., for the investigation of acute treatment intervention in tinnitus with recent onset.

Parallel group designs, in contrast, allow long observation periods and do not have to deal with potential carry-over effects. However, in addition to the already mentioned requirement of larger sample sizes, differences between groups, with respect to potential confounding variables, may become relevant. Such factors include, but are not limited to, age, gender, tinnitus cause and duration, tinnitus severity at baseline, level of hearing loss, co-morbid psychiatric symptoms (depression or anxiety), etc. Despite randomization, these factors may be unequally distributed in different treatment groups, especially when relatively small sample sizes are investigated. In such cases, these confounding factors have to be considered in the interpretation of the results.

As described earlier, blinding of the study is an important issue [1] to keep treatment regimens consistent and to control for effects of associated anticipation and expectation. Whenever possible, clinical trials should therefore use double blinding, which means both patient and therapist are blinded. In pharmacological trials, the use of placebo medication allows effective double blinding. However, in nonpharmacological treatments, blinding represents a substantial problem (e.g., repetitive transcranial magnetic stimulation [6, 7]) or may almost not be possible (e.g., cognitive behavioral therapy). For such interventions, waiting list controls or "treatment as usual" controls are sometimes used. However, these controls are vulnerable to expectations and unspecific effects of the interaction between patient and therapist and tend to overestimate the effects of the active intervention. Quite generally, the choice of the optimal control condition becomes more difficult when nonpharmacologic interventions such as psychotherapy, physiotherapy, or brain stimulation are tested [8].

Trial Duration and Follow-Up

One limitation of current clinical trials in tinnitus is their short duration typically ending after 3 months. Since tinnitus represents in many cases a chronic condition often characterized by significant spontaneous changes in intensity, assessment of treatment effects beyond 3 months would be desirable. This is even more important in treatments, which exert their effect with delay (e.g., behavioral focused treatments like cognitive behavioral therapy or tinnitus retraining therapy). Furthermore, longer follow-up periods enable researchers to determine adherence rates to treatments, which have been reported to be quite low for some kind of interventions (e.g., the use of white-noise generators [9]).

Sample Size and Statistical Testing

Clinical trials may have different goals. They can be performed in order to find the optimal dose of a treatment or to demonstrate noninferiority of a specific intervention in comparison to a standard one. In most cases, the aim of a clinical trial is to determine whether or not a treatment is effective for a given indication. To achieve this, it is important that the trial has been designed in a way that false-positive and false-negative errors are minimized. False-positive means that the trial suggests a treatment is more effective than placebo, when this is not actually true; the results of the trial are due to other influences. This kind of error can be minimized by using good blinding conditions, matching for potential confounding variables, and use of randomization procedures. False-negative results mean that the trial suggests a treatment is not more effective than placebo; the reason for this result can also be that the sample size of the trial was too small in order to detect the difference between both study arms. To avoid this problem of insufficient power, definition of

clinically meaningful changes (e.g., a reduction of a given number of points in a tinnitus questionnaire), power analysis, and determination of sample size is essential. Whenever possible, power calculations should be based on the results of existing studies or the preliminary findings of pilot studies [10]. After completion of the trial, statistical testing should also address the issue of potential false-negative errors. Treatment efficacy will be determined by analysis of the treatment effect on the primary outcome variable. To avoid the statistical problem of multiple testing, the primary outcome measure should be restricted to one variable. Other variables may be included as secondary outcome measures. Finally, drop-outs from the study may represent a substantial problem in the statistical analyses of the trial. Data from patients who dropped out of the trial should not be disregarded; one option is the so-called "last observation carried forward" (LOCF) approach. This kind of analysis is also called "intention-to-treat" analysis, which is the most widely used approach in analyses of clinical trials. However, if the drop-out rate gets too high, analyses and interpretation of results become difficult. Drop-out rates may increase in study populations with high spontaneous remission rates (i.e., the patients have no need to further stay in the trial), long study durations, or mild forms of tinnitus. These problems have to be kept in mind during the design of the trial. In general, it is advisable to seek statistical consultation by an expert in clinical trials in advance of planning the trial, in order to avoid such problems.

Statistical Significance and Clinical Relevance

There is a crucial distinction between statistical significance and clinical relevance. Statistical significance refers to the fact that a finding is statistically reliable. It is important to note that empirical research, in general, can never prove a finding is 100% correct. All solid research can do is minimize the error that false conclusions are drawn from data. In the behavioral and medical sciences, there is consensus that an error rate of less than 5% is tolerable, often expressed as $p < 0.05$ (sometimes stricter levels of significance are applied, such as $p < 0.01$ or $p < 0.001$). Obtaining a difference between the treatment and the control group accepting $p < 0.05$ means that if the experiment is repeated 100 times, in roughly 95% of the cases the difference will show up again and 5% of the experiments will fail to observe the effect.

Whether a result reaches statistical significance generally depends the mean difference between the two groups, the variability of the results (standard deviation), and on the sample size. As the number of participants increases, the difference between groups required to reach statistical significance becomes smaller. As an example, with a sample size of several hundred patients, mean improvements of one or two points on a tinnitus scale may reach statistical significance. Such results are frequently criticized with the argument that such a difference may not be clinically relevant.

Clinical relevance relates to the magnitude of an effect. Thus, clinical relevance is not a statistical or methodological issue; it refers to the fact that clinicians and/or patients regard a difference between a new treatment and a control treatment as "large enough" or "important." For instance, a difference in success rates between treatment and control of 10% may be considered clinically relevant. The definition of clinically important differences is particularly challenging with regard to questionnaire data. Questionnaires are used for detecting meaningful changes of clinical symptoms. Since the currently available questionnaires have not been developed and validated for detecting treatment-induced changes, empirical data about the minimal

change required for clinical relevance is limited. For the tinnitus questionnaire, a reduction of five points has been proposed as a minimum change for an individual patient in order to be of clinical relevance [11].

Reporting Clinical Trials: Consolidated Standards of Reporting Trials

Consolidated standards of reporting trials (CONSORT) encompass various initiatives developed by the CONSORT group to alleviate the problems arising from inadequate reporting of randomized controlled trials. The main product of the CONSORT group is the CONSORT Statement [12, 13], which represents an evidence-based minimum set of recommendations for reporting randomized trials. It offers a standard way for authors to prepare reports of trial findings, facilitating their complete and transparent reporting, reducing the influence of bias on their results, and aiding their critical appraisal and interpretation. The CONSORT Statement comprises a 22-item checklist (Table 22.1) and a flow diagram (Fig. 22.1), along with some brief descriptive text. The checklist items focus on reporting how the trial was designed, analyzed, and interpreted. The flow diagram displays the progress of all participants throughout the trial.

Table 22.1 The CONSORT Statement 2001 checklist (items to include when reporting a randomized trial) is intended to be accompanied with the explanatory document that facilitates its use

Paper section and topic	Item	Descriptor
Title and *abstract*	1	How participants were allocated to interventions (e.g., "random allocation", "randomized", or "randomly assigned").
Introduction		
Background	2	Scientific background and explanation of rationale.
Methods		
Participants	3	Eligibility criteria for participants and the settings and locations where the data were collected.
Interventions	4	Precise details of the interventions intended for each group and how and when they were actually administered.
Objectives	5	Specific objectives and hypotheses.
Outcomes	6	Clearly defined primary and secondary outcome measures and, when applicable, any methods used to enhance the quality of measurements (e.g., multiple observations, training of assessors).
Sample size	7	How sample size was determined and, when applicable, explanation of any interim analyses and stopping rules.

(continued)

Table 22.1 (continued)

Paper section and topic	Item	Descriptor
Randomization – sequence generation	8	Method used to generate the random allocation sequence, including details of any restrictions (e.g., blocking, stratification)
Randomization – allocation concealment	9	Method used to implement the random allocation sequence (e.g., numbered containers or central telephone), clarifying whether the sequence was concealed until interventions were assigned.
Randomization – implementation	10	Who generated the allocation sequence, who enrolled participants, and who assigned participants to their groups.
Blinding (masking)	11	Whether or not participants, those administering the interventions, and those assessing the outcomes were blinded to group assignment. If done, how the success of blinding was evaluated.
Statistical methods	12	Statistical methods used to compare groups for primary outcome(s); Methods for additional analyses, such as subgroup analyses and adjusted analyses.
Results		
Participant flow	13	Flow of participants through each stage (a diagram is strongly recommended). Specifically, for each group report the numbers of participants randomly assigned, receiving intended treatment, completing the study protocol, and analyzed for the primary outcome. Describe protocol deviations from study as planned, together with reasons.
Recruitment	14	Dates defining the periods of recruitment and follow-up.
Baseline data	15	Baseline demographic and clinical characteristics of each group.
Numbers analyzed	16	Number of participants (denominator) in each group included in each analysis and whether the analysis was by "intention-to-treat". State the results in absolute numbers when feasible (e.g., 10/20, not 50%).
Outcomes and estimation	17	For each primary and secondary outcome, a summary of results for each group, and the estimated effect size and its precision (e.g., 95% confidence interval).
Ancillary analyses	18	Address multiplicity by reporting any other analyses performed, including subgroup analyses and adjusted analyses, indicating those prespecified and those exploratory.
Adverse events	19	All important adverse events or side effects in each intervention group.
Discussion		
Interpretation	20	Interpretation of the results, taking into account study hypotheses, sources of potential bias or imprecision and the dangers associated with multiplicity of analyses and outcomes.
Generalizability	21	Generalizability (external validity) of the trial findings.
Overall evidence	22	General interpretation of the results in the context of current evidence.

From ref. [13]. For more information, visit www.consort-statement.org

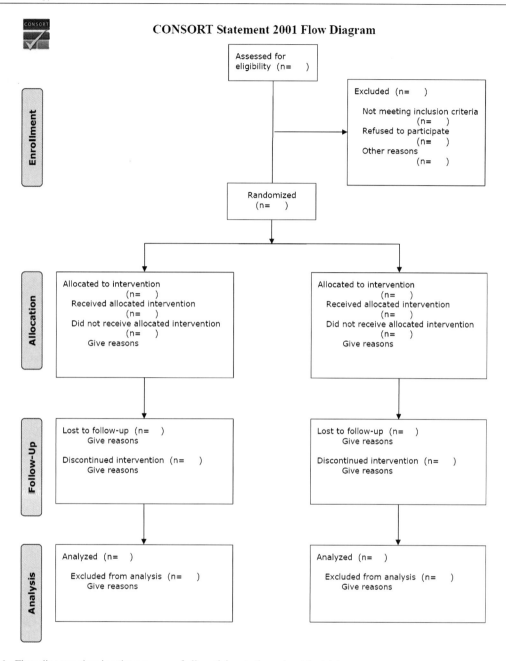

Fig. 22.1 Flow diagram showing the progress of all participants throughout the trial

Regulatory Requirements of Clinical Trials

Good Clinical Practice

Good clinical practice (GCP) is an international quality standard for clinical trials involving human subjects that is provided by the International Conference on Harmonization [14]. GCP guidelines include protection of human rights for subjects in clinical trials, but they also include standards on how clinical trials should be conducted and define the roles and responsibilities of clinical trial sponsors, clinical research investigators, and monitors.

Ethical Issues

There is international consensus that all studies that involve a medical or therapeutic intervention on patients must be approved by a supervising ethics committee. In some countries, this body is called institutional review board (IRB). Most ethics committees or IRBs are located at the local investigator's hospital or institution, but there also exists a central IRB for investigators who work at smaller institutions. The main function of ethics committees or IRBs is to ensure that clinical trials are performed according to ethical standards. Major issues include full and informed consent of participating human subjects, qualification of staff, performance of clinical trials according to GCP, as well as the design of the trial. Informed consent is clearly a necessary condition for, but does not ensure, ethical conduct. The final objective is to serve the community of patients, or future patients, in a best possible and most responsible way.

Ethical difficulties can arise when treatments have been established over time, even if their evidence has never been clearly documented in a well-conducted trial. This is, for example, the situation in steroid treatment for acute hearing loss with tinnitus [15]. Placebo-controlled randomized clinical trials are required in order to investigate whether steroids have a beneficial effect or not in this group of patients. However, this would imply that patients, who are randomized to placebo treatment in such trials, would be deprived of an established and potentially effective treatment. On the other hand, as long as no placebo-controlled RCTs are available, a large number of patients all over the world receive a treatment with unknown efficacy.

Trial Registration and Publication of Study Protocols

Public registration of clinical trials has been introduced with the primary purpose of improving public access to clinical trials where individuals with serious diseases and conditions might find experimental treatments. Moreover, registration of clinical trials became an important methodological requirement since it ensures sample sizes, primary outcome measures, and statistical analysis methods are performed according to a properly planned study design. Registration of clinical trials further allows controlling for publication bias (negative studies have a higher risk to be never published) and facilitates coordination between efforts of different research groups. Several public clinical trial registries exist; the largest of them is www.ClinicalTrials.gov that is run by the United States National Library of Medicine (NLM) at the National Institutes of Health, currently holding registrations from over 60,000 trials from more than 150 countries in the world. In addition, it has become good research practice to publish short versions of study protocols before starting a clinical trial [16, 17].

Specifics of Tinnitus Trials

In the design of clinical trials for tinnitus, several aspects are of specific importance and are therefore discussed in detail. These include heterogeneity of diagnoses, duration of illness, and outcome assessment.

Study Population – Tinnitus Subtypes

An important aspect in the design of clinical trials is the establishment of criteria to stratify or classify tinnitus patients. Tinnitus can occur as a result of insults to the ear, such as from noise exposure or administration of specific pharmacologic agents. It can also be caused by ear or head injuries, some diseases of the ear, and ear infections. In some cases, the causative agent remains unknown. Moreover, the manifestation of tinnitus can vary, ranging from intermittent tinnitus perception with little impact on daily life to a devastating roar that occurs 24 h a day preventing sleep and the ability to do intellectual work, leading to social isolation. Tinnitus is also often associated with other symptoms, such as hyperacusis and distortion of sounds. Affective disorders such as anxiety, phonophobia, and depression often accompany severe tinnitus and that can lead to suicide. With such differences in etiology and symptoms, heterogeneity within tinnitus patients is expected. If a treatment would exist that suppresses all forms of tinnitus irrespective of its etiology or its clinical characteristics, defining subgroups would not be necessary. However, analysis of available clinical trials reveals a high variability in treatment outcomes, which is most probably due to the fact that patients included in a clinical trial suffer from different forms of tinnitus [18]. The fact that a subgroup of patients who have intermittent tinnitus that sounds like a typewriter, popcorn, or ear clicking receive significant benefit from carbamazepine [19, 20] indicates that "subtyping" tinnitus is highly recommended.

Two different strategies can be used to account for the inhomogeneity of tinnitus. Either a more homogeneous group is created by selective inclusion criteria or different groups within a large sample are stratified according to specific criteria. Criteria for selection or stratification have to be identified in both strategies. Among the criteria that have been suggested for delineating different forms of tinnitus are objective versus subjective tinnitus, perceptual characteristics such as pulsatile versus nonpulsatile tinnitus, the perceived localization, the duration, the frequency composition, the response to specific interventions (lidocaine, sound stimulation, somatic maneuvers), or co-morbidities such as hearing loss or concurrent psychiatric symptoms. However, there is no generally established classification system for the different forms of tinnitus to date, and there is an urgent need for further research in order to identify classification criteria. In addition to clinical and audiologic aspects, new neuroimaging methods may provide further information (see Chap. 17). Also, the identification of subgroups by cluster analysis of different clinical variables has been proposed [21].

However, all efforts of stratifying tinnitus patients into subgroups is self-limited by the amount of available patients and the time needed to recruit them. The use of very selective inclusion criteria has the consequence that results cannot be generalized to other forms of tinnitus. Therefore, defining subgroups is always a compromise between homogeneity on one side and sample size and generalizability on the other side. However, the chances for significant results in clinical treatment trials increase with homogeneous samples, e.g., when known predictor variables for a specific treatment are considered in the design of a clinical trial. Frequently, at the time of the design of a clinical trial, it is not yet known which subgroup of tinnitus patients may benefit best from treatment. A practical approach

in this situation is a standardized assessment of potentially relevant clinical characteristics and a post hoc analysis of responder groups. As is later described, such analyses have to be interpreted carefully. They always have to be considered as exploratory and require confirmation in further studies.

Patients who undergo any additional tinnitus-specific treatment should be excluded from a clinical trial in order to minimize potential confounding factors that may influence treatment outcome. This may be difficult for long-term treatments such as hearing aids or white-noise generators. At least the use of these devices should be documented. An additional strategy to address this issue is the documentation of baseline stability by repeated tinnitus assessments before initiation of the intervention under study.

Also, relevant comorbid disorders like depression or anxiety may be excluded from study participation, except when the treatment to be tested is specifically focusing on this given comorbidity in tinnitus (e.g., antidepressants in tinnitus patients with comorbid depressive symptoms). As an example for the significance of defining subgroups for clinical trials, we will discuss the relevance of tinnitus duration in more detail.

Duration of Tinnitus

Acute and chronic forms of tinnitus differ in many respects. First of all, pathological mechanisms are likely to be different. Acute tinnitus is frequently accompanied by acute hearing loss. It is expected that an intervention that can improve hearing function will also have a beneficial effect on tinnitus. Examples of such interventions are steroid administration or treatment with hyperbaric oxygen. However, it is expected that an intervention that improves tinnitus by restoring hearing after acute hearing loss only has a beneficial effect in acute tinnitus with acute hearing loss and not in chronic tinnitus. For such an intervention, it is important to establish the therapeutic window for successful administration.

In general, tinnitus that persists more than 6 months is considered chronic [16]. However, this distinction is arbitrary and is based on national definitions, not on pathophysiologic knowledge. For example, in a current study, subacute tinnitus is defined as having between 3 and 12 months duration (see clinical trials identifier: NCT00772980). Recent neuroimaging data indicate that there may be different stages of chronification over the course of several years, which differ in their pathophysiology [22], further underlining the relevance of tinnitus duration in addition to the distinction between acute and chronic.

Whereas initiation of tinnitus may be triggered by pathologies in the inner ear, the relevant pathological changes of tinnitus chronification take place within the central nervous system. Alone, this makes it obvious that the success of specific treatment interventions will depend on tinnitus duration. Therefore, acute and chronic forms of tinnitus should not be included in the same treatment trial. Otherwise, the chance of a nonresponding subgroup is artificially increased. Another problem in the acute phase of tinnitus is the high spontaneous recovery rate. Until now, there were no reliable predictors of spontaneous remission. Therefore, large sample sizes were needed for detecting significant differences between an intervention and placebo. Furthermore, if tinnitus is only of transient and mild character, the drop-out rate may be increased leading to statistical difficulties. On the other hand, for some interventions, there may be a short therapeutic window and treatment in general may become more difficult with increasing tinnitus duration [11]. Hence, there is a need for clinical trials that investigate treatment interventions both at early stages of tinnitus and in chronic tinnitus. However, in the design of a clinical trial, the duration of tinnitus should be considered as an important criterion. How this is reflected in the design of the clinical trial, e.g., by selection or stratification of the study population, depends on the intervention and its assumed mechanism.

Outcome Measures

Since tinnitus is a purely subjective phenomenon, assessment of treatment effects is not trivial. At the same time, the use of an adequate outcome is probably the single most important factor in the design of clinical trials. One possibility for tinnitus measurement is the assessment of tinnitus loudness, either by a visual analogue scales (VAS) or by matching or masking methods. However, psychoacoustic methods like loudness matching or minimal masking level are subjective methods and can give only indirect approximations of tinnitus intensity. Furthermore, assessments of tinnitus loudness have shown only limited reliability, and there is only a poor correlation between the intensity of the tinnitus as qualified by matching techniques and the degree of annoyance the tinnitus creates [23]. Hence, evaluating treatment effects on tinnitus should rather focus on tinnitus associated with suffering than on tinnitus loudness alone. For the assessment of tinnitus severity, there are several validated questionnaires available (see Chap. 47). However, most of the questionnaires for assessment of tinnitus severity have been designed and validated for diagnostic purposes in order to discriminate subgroups (e.g., to separate mild from severely affected tinnitus patients [24]) but not for evaluating treatment-induced changes. Thus, the available questionnaires are not specifically sensitive for the assessment of treatment-related changes in tinnitus severity. Furthermore, it is not clear which change in these questionnaires is of clinical relevance [25]. It should also be noted that most of the questionnaires have been validated by using the Beck Depression Inventory (BDI), and therefore their scores correlate highly with the BDI scores [26]. Hence, in a sample of tinnitus patients with comorbid depression, an intervention that has an antidepressant effect, but no effect on tinnitus, would probably result in reduced tinnitus scores, just by reducing depressive symptoms.

Efforts are underway in order to design specific questionnaires to evaluate treatment-induced changes in tinnitus [24]. Currently, there is consensus that until such an evaluative questionnaire is validated in different languages and internationally established, the use of one of the available validated questionnaires for the assessment of tinnitus severity is the most appropriate outcome measurement. There is widespread recognition that consistency between research centres, in how intervention outcomes are measured, would allow better comparability of different trials. At the first Tinnitus Research Initiative meeting held in Regensburg in July 2006, which gathered worldwide tinnitus experts, an attempt was made to establish a consensus both for patient assessments and for outcome measurements [2]. There was an agreement that the questionnaire most widely used and validated in most languages is the tinnitus handicap inventory [27], which should for the sake of comparability be included in every trial. It should also be noted that the first Phase III trials currently performed for a tinnitus drug use the TBF-12 as main outcome criterion, which is essentially a short version of the THI with selection of 12 sensitive items out of the 25 items of the THI [28]. If the trials are successful and the drug is approved by the U.S. Food and Drug Association (FDA) and the European Medicines Agency (EMEA), the TBF-12 might become a reference for further pharmacologic trials.

In this context, it should also be emphasized that each clinical trial should have only one primary outcome measure – a validated questionnaire. The primary outcome measure has to be defined a priori (i.e., before the trial starts) and is the main criterion for statistical determination of the efficacy of the treatment under trial. Additional measures may be included as secondary outcome measures (e.g., assessing change in depressive symptoms using the Beck Depression Inventory [29]).

Outlook and New Challenges

Taken together, although efforts in finding effective treatment strategies for tinnitus are increasing, the situation in the therapeutic daily routine is disappointing. Hence, there is a big need to facilitate clinical research in order to find new effective treatment options. Major tasks will be defining and better characterization of tinnitus subgroups based on clinical symptomatology and treatment response as well as detecting predictors for therapy response. To achieve these goals, a large number of tinnitus patients have to be investigated and systematically included in clinical trials. If these investigations were performed in a standardized way, data could be pooled for analysis, which would significantly increase statistical power and enable detection of potential predictors. Unfortunately, studies currently conducted are very heterogeneous, with respect to quality of the design and outcome measures used, thereby jeopardizing the comparability of the results. Hence, future research may be very much facilitated, if there is an overall consensus about key diagnostic and outcome measures and the will to share these results for analyses via an international tinnitus database. Promising attempts have been made to find such agreements [2], which would be the basis for internationally acting research networks.

References

1. Friedman, LM, Furberg, CD, DeMets, DL Blindness. 3rd ed. New York: Springer; 1998
2. Langguth, B, Goodey, R, Azevedo, A, Bjorne, A, Cacace, A, Crocetti, A, et al Consensus for tinnitus patient assessment and treatment outcome measurement: Tinnitus Research Initiative meeting, Regensburg, y 2006. Prog Brain Res, 2007; 166:525–36
3. MRC Health Services and Public Health research Board. A framework for development and evaluation of RCTs for complex interventions to improve health. London: MRC; 2006
4. Klinkhammer-Schalke, M, Koller, M, Ehret, C, Steinger, B, Ernst, B, Wyatt, JC, et al Implementing a system of quality-of-life diagnosis and therapy for breast cancer patients: results of an exploratory trial as a prerequisite for a subsequent RCT. Br J Cancer, 2008; 99(3):415–22
5. Klinkhammer-Schalke, M, Koller, M, Wyatt, JC, Steinger, B, Ehret, C, Ernst, B, et al Quality of life diagnosis and therapy as complex intervention for improvement of health in breast cancer patients: delineating the conceptual, methodological, and logistic requirements (modeling). Langenbecks Arch Surg, 2008; 393(1):1–12
6. Lisanby, SH, Gutman, D, Luber, B, Schroeder, C, Sackeim, HA Sham TMS: intracerebral measurement of the induced electrical field and the induction of motor-evoked potentials. Biol Psychiatry, 2001; 49(5):460–3
7. Loo, CK, Taylor, JL, Gandevia, SC, McDarmont, BN, Mitchell, PB, Sachdev, PS Transcranial magnetic stimulation (TMS) in controlled treatment studies: are some "sham" forms active? Biol Psychiatry, 2000; 47(4):325–31
8. Tyler, RS, Noble, W, Coelho, C Considerations for the design of clinical trials for tinnitus Acta Otolaryngol Suppl, 2006; 556:44–9
9. Dobie RA Clinical Trials and Drug Therapy In: Snow JB, editor Tinnitus: Theory and Management Hamilton, USA: BC Decker; 2004; 266–77
10. Cohen J Statistical Power Analysis for the Behavioral Sciences, 2nd ed. Hillsdale, NJ: Lawrence Erlbaum; 1988
11. Kleing, T, Steffens, T, Sand, P, Murthum, T, Hajak, G, Strutz, J, et al Which tinnitus patients benefit from transcranial magnetic stimulation? Otolaryngol Head Neck Surg, 2007; 137(4):589–95
12. Altman, DG, Schulz, KF, Moher, D, Egger, M, Davidoff, F, Elbourne, D, et al The revised CONSORT statement for reporting randomized trials: explanation and elaboration. Ann Intern Med, 2001; 134(8):663–94
13. Moher, D, Schulz, KF, Altman, DG The CONSORT statement: revised recommendations for improving the quality of reports of parallel-group randomised trials. Lancet, 2001; 357(9263):1191–4
14. International conference on harmonisation of technical requirements for registration of pharmaceuticals for human use (ICH) adopts consolidated guideline on good clinical practice in the conduct of clinical trials on medicinal products for human use. Int Dig Health Legis, 1997; 48(2):231–4
15. Wei, PBC, Mubiru, S, O'Leary, S Steroids for idiopathic sudden sensorineural hearing loss. Cochrane Database Syst Rev, 2006; 25(1):CD003998
16. Landgrebe, M, Binder, H, Koller, M, Eberl, Y, Kleing, T, Eichhammer, P, et al Design of a placebo-controlled,

randomized study of the efficacy of repetitive transcranial magnetic stimulation for the treatment of chronic tinntius. BMC Psychiatry, 2008; 8(1):23

17. Chalmers, I, Altman, DG How can medical journals help prevent poor medical research? Some opportunities presented by electronic publishing. Lancet, 1999; 353(9151):490–3

18. Møller, AR A double-blind placebo-controlled trial of baclofen in the treatment of tinnitus Am J Otol, 1997; 18(2):268–9

19. Mardini, MK Ear-clicking "tinnitus" responding to carbamazepine. N Engl J Med, 1987; 317(24):1542

20. Levine, RA Typewriter tinnitus: a carbamazepine-responsive syndrome related to auditory nerve vascular compression. ORL J Otorhinolaryngol Relat Spec, 2006; 68(1):43–6

21. Tyler, R, Coelho, C, Tao, P, Ji, H, Noble, W, Gehringer, A, et al Identifying tinnitus subgroups with cluster analysis. Am J Audiol, 2008; 17(2):S176–84

22. Schlee, W, Hartmann, T, Langguth B, Weisz, N Abnormal resting-state cortical coupling in chronic tinnitus. BMC Neurosci, 2009; 10:11

23. Hiller, W, Goebel, G Factors influencing tinnitus loudness and annoyance. Arch Otolaryngol Head Neck Surg, 2006; 132(12):1323–30

24. Meikle, MB, Stewart, BJ, Griest, SE, Tin, WH, Henry, JA, Abrams, HB, et al Assessment of tinnitus: measurement of treatment outcomes. Prog Brain Res, 2007; 166: 511–21

25. Tyler, RS, Oleson, J, Noble, W, Coelho, C, Ji, H Clinical trials for tinnitus: study populations, designs, measurement variables, and data analysis. Prog Brain Res, 2007; 166: 499–509

26. Langguth, B, Kleing, T, Fischer, B, Hajak, G, Eichhammer, P, Sand, PG Tinnitus severity, depression, and the big five personality traits. Prog Brain Res, 2007; 166:221–5

27. Newman, CW, Jacobson, GP, Spitzer, JB Development of the tinnitus handicap inventory. Arch Otolaryngol Head Neck Surg, 1996; 122(2):143–8

28. Greimel, KV, Leibetseder, M, Unterrainer, J, Albegger, K Can tinnitus be measured? Methods for assessment of tinnitus-specific disability and presentation of the Tinnitus Disability Questionnaire. HNO, 1999; 47(3): 196–201

29. Beck, AT, Steer, RA Internal consistencies of the original and revised beck depression inventory. J Clin Psychol, 1984; 40(6):1365–7

Part II
Tinnitus Seen by Different Specialties

Chapter 23
The Otolaryngologist

Tobias Kleinjung

Keypoints

1. This chapter describes the role of the otolaryngologist (ENT specialist) in the diagnosis and treatment of tinnitus.
2. Apart from the general practitioner, the otolaryngologist is the first point of contact for many tinnitus patients.
3. Otological diagnosis must be performed in patients with acute tinnitus and basic audiological screening must be arranged.
4. The acute treatment of new-onset tinnitus is also the domain of the otolaryngologist.
5. In patients with chronic tinnitus, the role of the otolaryngologist – ideally as part of a multidisciplinary team – is to coordinate further diagnostic and therapeutic measures.

Keywords Otolaryngology • Tinnitus • Hearing loss • Counseling

Introduction and History

Advances in science in recent decades have completely redefined the role of the otolaryngologist in terms of the diagnosis and treatment of tinnitus. In the past, the otolaryngologist was often working alone in managing patients with tinnitus. The spectrum of therapeutic options available to the otolaryngologist was soon exhausted, particularly when treating patients with chronic tinnitus with no underlying otological cause. The great suffering experienced by these patients prompted committed otolaryngologists to repeatedly undertake heroic, but usually frustrated curative efforts, even extending as far as sectioning the eighth cranial nerve [1]. A wide variety of therapeutic approaches, all of which had the labyrinth as their focus, also failed to yield successful outcomes [2]. The justifiable demands of patients for further help led in many cases to a profound disturbance of the doctor–patient relationship. "You must learn to live with your tinnitus" – a comment frequently heard from the lips of doctors – was tantamount to admitting further treatment attempts would be futile. The frustrated patient often looked for a new doctor or sought refuge in paramedical treatments. The recognition that mechanisms unfolding outside the ear are key factors in the etiology and perception of tinnitus brought with it a change in the management of tinnitus patients. It became clear that to concentrate solely on the labyrinth cannot do justice to the problem of tinnitus. The development of the neurophysiological model of tinnitus [3] showed how successful treatment strategies can be designed that are outside the core competency area of the otolaryngologist. In patients with chronic tinnitus, the brain has now become the focus of treatment attempts. Aside from diagnostic and exploratory measures, the role of the otolaryngologist – as part of a team – is to coordinate the treatment of patients with tinnitus in conjunction with specialists from other disciplines.

T. Kleinjung (✉)
Department of Otorhinolaryngology, University of Regensburg, Franz-Josef-Strauss-Allee 11, 93053 Regensburg, Germany
e-mail: tobias.kleinjung@klinik.uni-regensburg.de

A.R. Møller et al. (eds.), *Textbook of Tinnitus*,
DOI 10.1007/978-1-60761-145-5_23, © Springer Science+Business Media, LLC 2011

The Role of the Otolaryngologist in a Modern Tinnitus Clinic

Patients with new-onset tinnitus generally seek an appointment first with an otolaryngologist. Thus, it is an important part of the otolaryngologist's role to be the primary point of contact for the tinnitus patient. In Germany, tinnitus patients make up a large proportion (20–25%) of people seeking medical help from an otolaryngology clinic [4]. For this reason, every otolaryngologist in clinical practice should acquire competence in the management of tinnitus patients; as a rule, such competence should extend beyond the knowledge gained in the course of specialist training, which tends to focus on surgical treatments. The otolaryngologist should acquire the understanding of the pathophysiology of tinnitus and the capacity to empathize with the patient. During the initial consultation, it is important to collect information about circumstances relating to the onset of tinnitus, the nature of the tinnitus, any possible concomitant hearing loss, as well as the patient's psychosocial background (see Chap. 47). The importance of this first contact with the patient is immeasurable. The needs of an otherwise healthy patient with the symptom "tinnitus" must be taken seriously, but every effort must be made to keep the patient from being overly focused on this symptom. Catastrophic statements such as "Your tinnitus might be a sign of a brain tumor" may have devastating consequences for the patient's further clinical course.

Otological diagnosis is a core competency area for the otolaryngologist (see Chap. 48). The purpose of otological diagnosis is to identify potential diseases of the external ear, middle ear, or inner ear that might be a possible cause of tinnitus. In many patients, this may result in a straightforward therapy, such as the removal of wax from the ear canal. For other diseases, such as otosclerosis, surgery (see Chap. 83) may lead to the abolition of tinnitus. In most tinnitus patients, however, an otological examination will reveal no abnormal findings.

Otological diagnosis should always be followed by audiological testing, which can discriminate between different forms of hearing loss. Such information should enable the otolaryngologist to explain to the patient how the tinnitus might have developed. This can help many tinnitus patients cope with their tinnitus and perhaps require no further therapy.

For patients who need further therapy, the otolaryngologist should direct the patient to an appropriate specialist in areas, such as the temporomandibular joint, cervical spine, etc., for further diagnostic work up.

Once the results of all investigations have been completed by all the specialists involved, a team conference should be held to draw up a treatment strategy for the individual patient. The interdisciplinary approach permits personalized treatment strategies that can be tailored to the requirements of the individual patient. Even though many forms of tinnitus remain "incurable" in the classic sense, this modus operandi brings a higher degree of satisfaction both for patients and for the physicians treating them.

Tinnitus that occurs as a part of sudden hearing loss should be treated with appropriate medications, such as intravenous steroid therapy (see Chap. 56) and rheologically active medication [5]. The usefulness of such vasoactive infusion therapies is still under debate in the English-speaking world [2].

The otolaryngologist can also make important contributions on a scientific level. As the first point of contact, the otolaryngologist will be familiar with many different patients and can therefore be useful in the recruitment, follow-up, and the assessment of patients in clinical studies.

References

1. House, JW and DE Brackmann. Tinnitus: surgical treatment. In Tinnitus (Ciba Foundation Symposium 85) 1981, Pitman: London
2. Conlin, AE and LS Parnes. Treatment of sudden sensorineural hearing loss: I A systematic review. Arch Otolaryngol Head Neck Surg, 2007, **133**(6):573–81
3. Jastreboff, PJ, JW Hazell, and RL Graham. Neurophysiological model of tinnitus: dependence of the minimal masking level on treatment outcome. Hear Res, 1994, **80**(2):216–32
4. Goebel, G. Verhaltensmedizinische Aspekte und Therapie des chronischen Tinnitus. Psychoneuro, 2004, **30**(6):330–6
5. Michel, O, T Jahns, M Joost-Enneking, P Neugebauer, M Streppel, E Stennert. [The Stennert antiphlogistic-rheologic infusion schema in treatment of cochleovestibular disorders]. HNO, 2000, **48**(3):182

Chapter 24
The Role of the Audiologist in Tinnitus Practice

Grant D. Searchfield and David M. Baguley

Keypoints

1. Audiologists play a significant role in most models of tinnitus health care provision, including both the assessment and management of tinnitus as reported by Henry et al. (Am J Audiol 14:49–70, 2005; Am J Audiol 14:21–48, 2005).
2. Audiologists have expertise assessing auditory function; training in auditory physiology and psychology prepares them to provide tinnitus counseling; and they are able to fit hearing aids and other instruments for tinnitus therapies.
3. In some situations, the Audiologist will be part of a multidisciplinary team (e.g., in a large metropolitan hospital) that may potentially include Otologists, Neurologists, Hearing Therapists, and Psychologists.
4. In other circumstances, the Audiologist may work in comparative isolation and be responsible for the majority of tinnitus care.
5. In this chapter, the authors consider the Audiologists' perspectives of tinnitus.
6. We describe Audiologists' skills and attributes in their role in tinnitus management; present models for tinnitus practice; and introduce a Matrix framework from within which clinicians can choose strategies for patients with varying needs.

Keywords Tinnitus • Audiology • Assessment • Rehabilitation

G.D. Searchfield (✉)
Audiology Section, School of Population Health, The University of Auckland, Private Bag 92019, Auckland, New Zealand
e-mail: g.searchfield@auckland.ac.nz

What is an Audiologist?

Audiologists are professionals trained in the clinical application of hearing science. Audiology exists as a health care profession in English speaking countries, the Americas, and the Pacific Rim; elsewhere similar roles are undertaken by medically qualified professions or technicians [1]. Henceforth, in this chapter, we use the name "Audiologist" to identify professionals with nonmedical University qualifications in audiology. However, much of what we discuss could equally apply to Audiological Physicians, Hearing aid Acousticians, and others who provide nonmedical assessment and management of tinnitus.

Audiologists have a broad scope of practice encompassing most aspects of hearing assessment and management. This practice includes behavioral and electrophysiological evaluations of hearing, rehabilitation of hearing loss through technology (hearing aids, cochlear implants), hearing loss prevention, and assessment and management of balance and tinnitus. Due to the strong association between hearing loss and tinnitus (see Chaps. 34 and 35), it is not surprising that most Audiological associations or registration bodies recognize that tinnitus is at the core of audiology practice.

"Audiologists are qualified to evaluate, diagnose, develop management strategies, and provide treatment and rehabilitation for tinnitus patients" [2].

Audiology began to develop as a distinct profession after World War II [3]. Shortly after this, audiological methodology (such as hearing aids) began to be applied for treating tinnitus [4, 5]. The use of sound as a treatment medium became more common with the development of ear-level maskers in the 1970s and the use of this technology in newly developed tinnitus clinics [4, 6]. The profile of audiology in tinnitus management rose again in the 1990s with the widespread adoption of Tinnitus Retraining Therapy (TRT, [7]). The current decade has seen the continued development and diversification of tinnitus management methods available to audiologists. Some notable additions to the audiologists' armory being Tinnitus Activities Treatment [8], Audiologic Tinnitus Management [9, 10], Neuromonics [11], and modified versions of TRT [12]. As the scale of tinnitus worldwide has become apparent, Hearing aid manufacturers and technology companies have also become more involved in improving management tools. A comprehensive survey of hearing health care practice internationally identified that audiologists are responsible for tinnitus management in most countries [1] .

Audiology Skills Applied to Tinnitus

The skills that audiologists acquire during their training and practice of "general" audiology are directly applicable to the more specialized area of tinnitus (Table 24.1). For example, audiologists need to counsel anxious hearing aid candidates and provide support to emotional parents on diagnosis of hearing loss in children. This counseling is not too dissimilar to counseling the distressed tinnitus sufferer.

Most educational programs in audiology offer limited training specific to tinnitus [10], but there are many regular opportunities for audiologists to gain further tinnitus knowledge. Scientific meetings, such as the International Tinnitus Seminars and Tinnitus Research Initiative meetings, are excellent opportunities to learn of the latest scientific developments in the field. Annual training workshops, such as one hosted annually by Iowa University as well as the European Tinnitus Course in Cambridge, build on existing knowledge to provide additional skills toward tinnitus practice. Audiologists should also have sufficient training to implement practice models described in this book and in other publications [13, 14]. Many established tinnitus clinics (including those at Addenbrooke's Hospital and The University of Auckland) are willing to share experiences and clinical protocols with clinicians new to the field.

Diagnosis and Assessment

Given that patients with hearing and balance issues are internationally being referred directly to an audiologist, care should be taken to ensure effective and efficient diagnosis. This will usually involve four themes:

Table 24.1 Consideration of audiological skills in general use and as applied to tinnitus. American Speech and Hearing Association audiology scope of practice guidelines [56] were used to formulate the categories of audiology practice

General audiology	Tinnitus audiology
Hearing loss prevention and promotion	Tinnitus prevention and promotion
Identification of auditory and balance disorders	Identification of tinnitus and tinnitus related pathology
Behavioral and electrophysiological assessment of auditory function	Behavioral and electrophysiological assessment of tinnitus
Intraoperative monitoring of audiology function	Intraoperative monitoring of audiology function during tinnitus-related neurosurgery
Assessment and management of Auditory Processing Disorders	Evaluation and intervention of tinnitus (and Hyperacusis) in recovery from head and neck trauma
Otoscopy and middle ear function tests examining for the obstruction of external auditory meatus and middle ear pathology	Evaluation of potential contribution of external and middle ears to tinnitus symptoms.
Assessing the "Hearing needs" of patients	Tinnitus needs assessment
Referral and consultation with other professionals	Referral and consultation with other professionals
Development of intervention and rehabilitation plans	Tinnitus management plan
Select and fit hearing aids and/or assistive devices to improve hearing	Select and fit hearing aids and/or sound generating devices for tinnitus management
Assessment and management of severe-profound hearing loss with Cochlear Implants	Assessment and management of tinnitus accompanying severe-profound hearing loss with Cochlear Implants
Use counseling to address psychosocial aspects of hearing loss and provide communication skills	Tinnitus counseling
Assessment of hearing intervention outcomes	Tinnitus outcomes measurement

- Identification of treatable otological pathology
- Assessment of hearing and tinnitus testing
- Assessment of tinnitus handicap
- Identification of treatable psychological symptoms, such as anxiety and depression

Each of these themes are now discussed in turn. Given appropriate teaching and support, there is no reason why an audiologist should not diagnose otological pathology. A protocol approach is advocated, wherein investigations and onward referral are indicated by the presence of certain symptoms or test findings. An example is in centers located in the UK (Cambridge and Liverpool for example) where patients with unilateral tinnitus and/or asymmetric hearing thresholds are referred for Magnetic Resonance Scanning by the audiologist leading the Tinnitus Clinic. Similarly, when an autoimmune hearing loss is suspected, appropriate serological tests can be requested. When abnormalities are found an otological opinion is then necessary. This extension to the traditional audiologist scope of practice allows a direct-access model of service provision that is both efficient and cost effective.

Audiometric testing is clearly an essential element of the assessment of the tinnitus patient, and in many patients tympanometry will also be routinely undertaken. The issue of testing for loudness tolerance in the tinnitus population, many of whom may have hyperacusis, is somewhat controversial and discussed in Chap. 3. There are well-established audiometric methods of tinnitus pitch and intensity matching (see Chap. 24). The clinical utility of such measures is not high, however. Electrophysiological measures of tinnitus are being developed and opportunities may exist for audiologists to implement these in clinical practice.

The assessment of tinnitus handicap is another essential element in patient management. Many questionnaire instruments are available to determine the impact of tinnitus. These questionnaires typically inquire as to the effects of tinnitus on work or leisure activities, sleep emotion, and in some cases hearing [15, 16]. The clinician must choose one or two questionnaires that are reliable, sensitive to change with treatment, and are of low impact to the patient. The need for a universal outcome measure for tinnitus treatments has been recognized [17]. Whether clinicians are willing to move from existing questionnaires to a standard index will be tested in the next few years.

The assessment of anxiety and depression is also strongly indicated in tinnitus patient management. *The Beck Depression Inventory* [18] and *State-Trait Anxiety Inventory* [19] are the gold standard in this regard, but the questionnaires may alarm some individuals, promoting greater distress. The Hospital Anxiety and Depression Scale [20] is in widespread use in tinnitus clinics in the UK, and is a low impact screen for these symptoms. As psychologists developed the scale, it is credible to that community which helps onward referral.

Management

Audiology-based methods of tinnitus intervention demonstrate their benefits across psychological and audiological/neurophysiological domains, including but not limited to attention, habituation, and learning [21]. Most strategies used by audiologists incorporate the use of sound making devices along with counseling [22] (see Chap. 74). Although it has been argued that the used of sound stimulation has limited benefit over counseling [23] and even that it is counterproductive [24], there is increasing evidence that placed in an appropriate counseling framework sound does provide additional assistance [11, 25]. How sound should be used and with what counseling approach is most appropriate has been a source of considerable debate [26, 27]. Although treatment strategies used by audiologists differ, fundamentally they are actually very similar – sound therapy and counseling. The most appropriate intervention used by audiologists should be governed by the needs of the individual seeking help. At a bare minimum, an audiologist should be able to offer positive advice and refer to other clinicians involved in tinnitus management. The major elements of tinnitus management from an audiology perspective are described below.

Tinnitus Needs Assessment

A key stage in preparing an audiological management plan is determining the needs of the individual. This tinnitus needs assessment attempts to identify how the tinnitus affects an individual. Using tinnitus questionnaires can help identify general emotional and lifestyle needs of patients. The Client-Orientated Scale of Improvement (COSI, [28]) is a widely used needs assessment tool in hearing aid selection. The COSI-Tinnitus [29] can be used to identify an individual's specific needs and goals for tinnitus management. Through dialog and acknowledgment of the tinnitus sufferer's complaints the groundwork for counseling can be laid. The patient's needs can be addressed through variations of counseling and sound therapy.

Audiological Interventions

Specific counseling (see Chap. 70), masking (see Chap. 74), and habituation (see Chap. 75) based treatments are mentioned elsewhere in the book. We describe them briefly here considering the role of Audiologists.

Counseling

To help patients understand tinnitus and facilitate their coping with the condition, clinical approaches to the management of tinnitus include the use of counseling (see Chap. 70). In this context, audiology counseling interventions can range from simply providing advice, to bibliotherapy [30], directive counseling [31], and psychoeducation [32]. In some cases, referral for formal psychological assessment and treatment will be indicated, e.g., CBT [33] (see Chap. 54), though some patients may be resistant to that [34]. Audiologists should be able to address patient concerns and misplaced beliefs due to broad knowledge of auditory physiology, psychology, and aural rehabilitation. Counseling accompanying the fitting of sound devices would be very similar to the counseling of an audiologist should provide individuals with hearing aids in a comprehensive aural rehabilitation program. Some audiologists use CBT-based techniques, which address a patient's reaction to tinnitus, and provide relaxation training and cognitive restructuring as part of their scope of practice (e.g., [36]).

Masking

Tinnitus masking uses sound to cover tinnitus to some degree and should be used with counseling [6]. Masking could be considered the core audiological-based treatment for tinnitus [37]. During the 1990s, masking became somewhat maligned as a treatment method, but the principles and clinical application still remains a useful tool for audiologists. Masking is commonly associated with the use of ear-level devices produced by hearing aid manufacturers with whom audiologists should have strong working relationships. Audiologists familiar with tonal masking in audiometry should understand that tinnitus masking does not obey normal peripheral masking rules [38, 39]. Tinnitus masking is likely due to central processing mechanisms, similar perhaps to informational masking [40]. Complex sounds may be more useful in this treatment than constant broadband noise commonly in use [41].

Habituation

Habituation is the decline in responses to a signal that is not important [42]. The most well-known clinical models of tinnitus habituation are the model of Hallam et al. [43] and Tinnitus Retraining Therapy [7]. Audiologists have tended to gravitate toward the TRT model due to familiarity with; the auditory system as expressed in the underlying model [44]; directive counseling and the use of instruments for sound therapy [45]. TRT has been simplified to suit different clinical settings [12] and other published management protocols exploit the aspects of habituation [8].

Sound Therapy Technology

Audiology has a strong technology focus; this is also the case in its tinnitus role.

Although tinnitus patients often crave silence, this silence can "feed" the tinnitus by increasing the tinnitus signal relative to background noise. With little competition the auditory system will naturally divert attention resources to the remaining signal – tinnitus [48]. While avoiding silence is simple advice, it does help patients who fail to make the connection between tinnitus perception and background noise levels. Desktop sound generating devices produce a variety of different sounds (for example, ocean waves, rain, and running water), and these have been found useful to reduce tinnitus effects at night [49]. Nighttime is often when tinnitus sufferers experience heightened tinnitus awareness due to low sound levels and absence of other competing sensory input. Desktop devices are available through hearing aid distributors or electronics retailers.

The value of digital music players (e.g., MP3 players) as tinnitus aids have been recognized by both patients and audiologists [9]. Sounds can be produced by computer programs in the clinic or downloaded from the Internet. Use of prerecorded sounds is an easy way of obtaining treatment sounds that patients find comfortable and easy to listen too. Music can be used in an informal way to promote positive emotional effects to reduce tinnitus [50]. The Neuromonics treatment [11] uses music in a customized form as part of its audiology-focused treatment protocol. Although each year the size of digital players decreases and their battery capacity increases, they are still less convenient to wear on a regular basis than hearing aid style sound generators [52]. Personal music players also do not address any accompanying hearing handicap the way hearing aids or combination devices do.

Hearing aid style in-the-ear and behind-the-ear sound generators produce noise stimuli of variable intensity and frequency. The selection and manufacture of these devices is much the same as for hearing aids, but without the sophistication of signal processing necessary for amplification. Hearing aids themselves are often an underrated tinnitus management technology. Detailed protocols for the fitting of hearing aids in tinnitus treatment are available [29] (Chap. 74). The development of more advanced signal processing appears to have increased success rates [29, 53]. Audiologists are intimately familiar with hearing aids, including their selection, electroacoustic, and subjective evaluation of performance. Hearing aids have the benefit of addressing hearing as well as tinnitus needs. Combination instruments combine a hearing aid with a built-in tinnitus masker. They are available from a limited number of hearing aid manufacturers, but they attempt to combine the benefits of amplification with generated sound [54]. The technology, in these devices, has in the past lagged behind that of the best hearing

aids. However, this technology gap appears to being addressed by some manufacturers. A potential advantage of combination devices is their independence from environmental sound levels for effect. In persons with severe to profound hearing loss, cochlear implants become a management option [55].

Matrix Approach to Therapy Selection

Several authors have suggested a progressive management approach based on tinnitus severity and how it manifests itself [14, 56]. One approach to therapy selection is to use a Matrix model in which the audiologist selects intervention depending on the needs of the individual. Selecting the most appropriate elements from both psychological and technological axes can target individual needs assessed during an interview. The key to successfully implementing such an approach is to understand the problems the patient reports and their reaction to each treatment element. Individuals with high emotional needs are provided with more in depth counseling. Those with greater complexity of auditory injury may require more complex technological solutions. The potential strengths of audiologists in this management role are their ability to work across both technology and counseling strategies (Fig. 24.1).

Referring on

Within the context of an audiologist led Tinnitus Service, there will be patients who need to access professionals of other disciplines when issues arise that are beyond the scope of the audiologist's practice. The majority of these will be referrals to Otology and Psychology services, but there may also be occasions when referral to disciplines, such as Hearing Therapy (for addition counseling), Neurology (e.g., Head injury), Maxillofacial surgery (e.g., temporomandibular joint assessment), or Physiotherapy (for one-to-one instruction in relaxation techniques) may be indicated. Building relationships with professionals of such disciplines is an essential part of developing a Tinnitus Clinic. The ease with which these relationships are formed will vary with context and may be most straightforward in a University Acute Hospital

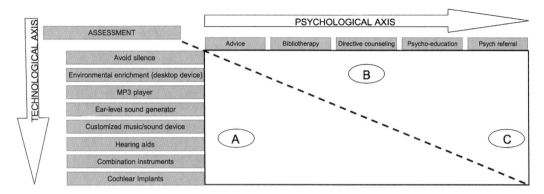

Fig. 24.1 Matrix of audiological management combining the psychological and technical aspects of audiology practice: (**a**) an individual with low psychological impact of tinnitus, but a hearing loss may simply require good advice and a hearing aid fitting. (**b**) A person with normal hearing though fear of tinnitus may not require a technological solution, but the individual may need to understand the cause and neurophysiological basis of tinnitus – directive counseling is one way of providing this. (**c**) Patients with significant anxiety, depression, and hearing loss are likely to be best served by hearing aids (or combination instruments) along with referral to psychology or psychiatry services

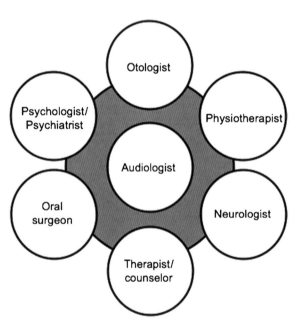

Fig. 24.2 Hub and spoke model of key relationships from an audiologist led service

Table 24.2 Audiology counseling scope of practice and referral guidelines, based on Flasher and Fogle

Within scope of practice	Referral
Interviewing the patient/family	Chemical dependence
Presenting the diagnosis	Child or elder abuse
Providing information about the diagnosis	Chronic depression
Discussing interventions for the diagnosis	Legal conflicts
Dealing with the patient's reaction to the diagnosis	Marital problems
Supporting the strengths of the person and their efforts to regain function	Personality disorders
Supporting the strengths of the family to help them interact optimally with the patient	Sexual abuse and sexual problems
Creating supportive empowerment for the patient and family to develop the ability to manage their own problems and be independent of the clinician	Suicidal ideation

setting. Outside the hospital setting, audiologists need to seek out professionals to network within a useful way (Fig. 24.2).

A clear framework for which issues lie within, and without, the boundaries of clinical practice for an audiologist has been developed by Flasher and Fogle 54. The areas that are considered to lie within and outside boundaries are detailed in Table 24.2. This framework deserves some reflection. The issues said to be within boundaries are wide ranging and may be challenging for those who see audiology as primarily a technical profession. The issues beyond boundaries are specific and some of those listed may well arise in a tinnitus context – legal conflicts and marital problems potentially being the most common. Stating that these issues are beyond boundaries does not mean that the audiologist should ignore them. Rather, it indicates that the issue should be acknowledged, as should the fact that it is outside the scope of an audiologist, and additional help and support sought from appropriate practitioners.

Summary and conclusions

Audiologists should feel that they have the skills to implement many of the tinnitus treatments in this book. Useful protocols for managing tinnitus have also been published elsewhere [32]. Increasingly, audiologists are adopting evidence-based practice models [55]. Tinnitus practice models should also reflect current evidence and audiologists should adapt their methods based on the evidence available. Audiologists should have the training and flexibility to incorporate changes in the understanding of physiology, psychology, assessment, and management technologies as they occur. In many respects, audiology practice is one of human-technology interaction. Rapid advancement in sound technology applications and hearing instruments should see audiologists among those at the forefront of tinnitus treatment innovation for the foreseeable future.

References

1. Goulios H and RB Patuzzi (2008) Audiology education and practice from an international perspective. Int J Audiol 47:647–64.
2. AAA. Audiologic Guidelines for the Diagnosis & Management of Tinnitus Patients. 2000 [cited; Available from: http://www.audiology.org/resources/documentlibrary/Pages/TinnitusGuidelines.aspx.
3. Ansberry M (1948) The Veterans Administration program in the fields of audiology and speech correction. J Speech Discord 3:115–8.
4. Vernon J (1977) Attempts to relieve tinnitus. J Am Audiol Soc 2:124–31.
5. Saltzman M and M Ersner (1947) A hearing aid for the relief of tinnitus aurium. Laryngoscope 57:358–66.
6. Hazell JW, GR Williams and JB Sheldrake (1981) Tinnitus maskers – successes and failures: A report on the state of the art. J Laryngol Otol Suppl 4: 80–7.
7. Jastreboff PJ and JWP Hazell (1993) A neurophysiological approach to tinnitus management. Br J Audiol 27:7–17.
8. Tyler RS, AK Gehringer, W Noble et al (2006) Tinnitus activities treatment, in Tinnitus treatment: Clinical protocols, RS Tyler, Editor. Thieme: New York 2006. 116–31.
9. Henry JA, TL Zaugg and MA Schechter (2005) Clinical guide for audiologic tinnitus management II: Treatment. Am J Audiol 14:49–70.
10. Henry JA, TL Zaugg and MA Schechter (2005) Clinical guide for audiologic tinnitus management I: Assessment. Am J Audiol 14:21–48.
11. Davis PB, B Paki and PJ Hanley (2007) Neuromonics tinnitus treatment: Third clinical trial. Ear Hear 28:242–59.
12. Aazh H, B Moore and B Glasberg (2008) Simplified form of tinnitus retraining therapy in adults: a retrospective

study. BMC Ear Nose Throat Disord. 8:7. 1472-6815/8/7: 1472-6815/8/7
13. Henry JA, MA Schechter, CL Loovis et al (2005) Clinical management of tinnitus using a "progressive intervention" approach. J Rehabil Res Dev 42:95–116.
14. Noble W (2001) Tinnitus self-assessment scales: Domains of coverage and psychometric properties. Hear J 54:20.
15. Robinson SK, JR McQuaid, ES Viirre et al (2003) Relationship of tinnitus questionnaires to depressive symptoms, quality of well-being, and internal focus. Int Tinnitus J 9:97–103.
16. Meikle MB (2002) A conceptual framework to aid the diagnosis and treatment of severe tinnitus. Aus N Z J Audiol 24:59–67.
17. Beck A, C Ward, M Mendelson et al (1961) An inventory for measuring depression. Arch Gen Psychiatry 4:561–71.
18. Spielberger CD (1983) Manual for the State-Trait Anxiety Inventory (STAI). Consulting Psychologists Press: PaloAlto, CA.
19. Zigmond A and R Snaith (1983) The hospital anxiety and depression scale. Acta Psychiatr Scand 67:361–70.
20. Tyler RS (2005) Neurophysiological models, psychological models, and treatments for tinnitus, in Tinnitus Treatment: Clinical Protocols, R Tyler, Editor. Thieme Medical Publishers, Inc.: New York. 1–22.
21. Folmer RL, WH Martin, Y Shi et al (2005) Tinnitus sound therapies, in Tinnitus Treatment: Clinical Protocols, R Tyler, Editor. Thieme Medical Publishers, Inc.: New York. 176–86.
22. Hiller W and C Haerkotter (2005) Does sound stimulation have additive effects on cognitive-behavioral treatment of chronic tinnitus? Behav Res Ther 43:595–612.
23. McKenna L and R Irwin (2008) Sound therapy for tinnitus – sacred cow or idol worship?: An investigation of the evidence. Audiol Med 6:16–24.
24. Folmer RL and JR Carroll (2006) Long-term effectiveness of ear-level devices for tinnitus. Otolaryngol Head Neck Surg 134:132–7.
25. Jastreboff MM (1999) Controversies between cognitive therapies and TRT counseling, in Proceedings of the Sixth International Tinnitus Seminar, Cambridge UK. September 5th–9th 1999, JW Hazell, Editor. The Tinnitus and Hyperacusis Centre: London. 288–91.
26. Kroener-Herwig B, E Biesinger, F Gerhards et al (2000) Retraining therapy for chronic tinnitus. A critical analysis of its status. Scand Audiol 29:67–78.
27. Dillon H, A James and J Ginis (1987) Client oriented scale of improvement (COSI) and its relationship to several other measures of benefit and satisfaction provided by hearing aids. J Am Acad Audiol 8:27–43.
28. Searchfield G (2006) Hearing aids and tinnitus, in Tinnitus Treatment: Clinical Protocols, R Tyler, Editor. 2006, Thieme Medical Publishers, Inc.: New York. 161–75.
29. Davis P (1995) Living with tinnitus. 1995, Rushcutters Bay, N.S.W.: Gore & Osment.
30. Hazell JWP (1999) The TRT method in practice, in Proceedings of the Sixth International Tinnitus Seminar, September 5th–9th 1999, JWP Hazel, Editor. Tinnitus and Hyperacusis Centre: London.
31. Tyler R (2006) Tinnitus Treatment: Clinical Protocols. New York: Thieme.
32. Andersson G, D Baguley, L McKenna et al (2005) Tinnitus: A Multidisciplinary Approach. Whurr: London.

33. McFerran DJ and DM Baguley (2009) Is psychology really the best treatment for tinnitus? Clin Otolaryngol 34:99–101.

34. Sweetow RW (1986) Cognitive aspects of tinnitus patient management. Ear Hear 7:390–6.

35. Vernon J and A Schleuning (1978) Tinnitus: A new management. Laryngoscope 88:413–9.

36. Feldmann H (1981) Homolateral and contralateral masking of tinnitus. J Laryngol Otol Suppl 4:60–70.

37. Penner MJ (1987) Masking of tinnitus and central masking. J Speech Hear Res 30:147–52.

38. Oh EL and RA Lutfi (1999) Informational masking by everyday sounds. J Acoust Soc Am 106:3521–8.

39. Henry JA, B Rheinsburg and T Zaugg (2004) Comparison of custom sounds for achieving tinnitus relief. J Am Acad Audiol 15:585–98.

40. Worden FG (1973) Auditory habituation, in Habituation: Physiological Substrates, HVS Peeke and MJ Herz, Editors. Academic Press: New York. 109–33.

41. Hallam RS, S Rachman and R Hinchcliffe (1984) Psychological aspects of tinnitus, in Contributions to Medical Psychology, S Rachman, Editor. Pergamon: Oxford. 31–53.

42. Jastreboff PJ (1990) Phantom auditory perception (tinnitus): Mechanisms of generation and perception. Neurosci Res 8:221–54.

43. Jastreboff PJ (1994) Instrumentation and tinnitus: A neurophysiological approach. Hear Instrum 45:7–11.

44. Tyler RS and CJ Bergan (2001) Tinnitus retraining therapy: A modified approach. Hear J 54:36.

45. Davis PB, RA Wilde and LG Steed (2003) A habituation-based rehabilitation technique using the acoustic desensitisation protocol, in Proceedings of the Seventh International Tinnitus Seminar, Perth, Australia: March 5th–9th, 2002, RB Patuzzi, Editor. 2003, Physiology Dept., University of Western Australia: Perth, Australia. 188–91.

46. Heller MF and M Bergman (1953) Tinnitus aurium in normally hearing persons. Ann Otol Rhinol Laryngol 62:73–83.

47. Handscomb L (2006) Use of bedside sound generators by patients with tinnitus-related sleeping difficulty: Which sounds are preferred and why? Acta Otolaryngol Suppl 556:59–63.

48. Hann D, GD Searchfield, M Sanders et al (2008) Strategies for the selection of music in the short-term management of mild tinnitus. Aus N Z J Audiol 30:129–40.

49. Folmer RL, WH Martin, Y Shi et al (2006) Tinnitus sound therapies, in Tinnitus Treatment: Clinical Protocols, R Tyler, Editor. Thieme Medical Publishers, Inc.: New York. 176–86.

50. Trotter MI and I Donaldson (2008) Hearing aids and tinnitus therapy: A 25-year experience. J Laryngol Otol 122:1052–6.

51. Sandlin RE and R Olsson (1999) Evaluation and selection of maskers and other devices used in the treatment of tinnitus and hyperacusis. Trends Amplif 4:6–26.

52. Tyler RS (1995) Tinnitus in the profoundly hearing-impaired and the effects of cochlear implants. Ann Otol Rhinol Laryngol Suppl 165:25–30.

53. Tyler RS, GB Haskell, SA Gogel et al (2008) Establishing a tinnitus clinic in your practice. Am J Audiol 17:25–37.

54. Flasher LV and PT Fogle (2003) Counseling skills for speech-language pathologists and audiologists. 2003: Cengage Learning.

55. Cox RM (2005) Evidence-based practice in audiology. J Am Acad Audiol 16:408–9.

56. Association AS-L-H (2003) Scope of Practice in Audiology. Ad Hoc Committee on Scope of Practice in Audiology http://www.asha.org/policy.

Chapter 25
Tinnitus from the Perspective of the Psychologist

Karoline V. Greimel and Birgit Kröner-Herwig

Keypoints

1. Tinnitus is always both a medical and a psychological phenomenon.
2. A medical condition might be responsible for the emergence of tinnitus, but psychological factors play an important role in individual processing of inner noises.
3. Characteristics of tinnitus-like loudness do not determine the tinnitus-related distress.
4. The primary goal of psychological interventions is to promote habituation and to improve the patient's ability to reduce the impact of tinnitus on the quality of life.
5. Psychological approaches offer:

    (a) Diagnostic assessment
    (b) Management of tinnitus

6. Psychological interventions should be an integral part of tinnitus management and not be made dependent on existence of a mental disorder.
7. Early referrals to a psychologist are desirable to conduct a thorough assessment of tinnitus-related complaints and to undertake a comprehensive functional analysis of the problem.

Keywords Tinnitus • Psychological assessment • Psychoeducation • Psychological treatment • Multiprofessional team

K.V. Greimel (✉)
Salzburg University Hospital, Muellner Hauptstrasse 48,
5020 Salzburg, Austria
e-mail: k.greimel@salk.at

Abbreviations

CBT   Cognitive behavioral treatment
CNS   Central nervous system

The Psychological Perspective on Tinnitus

Tinnitus always has to be regarded as being both a medical and a psychological phenomenon. Even if there is a medical reason for the emergence of tinnitus (e.g., hair cell damage), it is the brain that generates the inner noise when interpreting an altered pattern of nerve signals. This "abnormal" perception is further processed by the brain, and then psychological factors come in to play an important role regarding how the tinnitus is evaluated and coped with. Nevertheless, when proposing a "psychological dimension" of tinnitus, it does not mean that tinnitus is a mental disorder. To classify patients with tinnitus on the basis of hypothesized underlying medical conditions as "organic" or "nonorganic" (respectively "psychogenic") is not reasonable either. Likewise, it is not at all advisable to attempt to modify the patient's personality. Instead, the consequences of tinnitus (i.e., behavior and cognition regarding tinnitus) must be made the central issue in psychological assessment and intervention.

Due to the fact that tinnitus is not verifiable by any objective measurement, patients easily get the feeling that their sensations are not taken seriously. They are afraid that their symptoms are considered to be imagined, not real or feigned. For that reason, it is important to emphasize the validity of tinnitus as a sensory experience to the patients.

A.R. Møller et al. (eds.), *Textbook of Tinnitus*,
DOI 10.1007/978-1-60761-145-5_25, © Springer Science+Business Media, LLC 2011

Psychological Approaches: Assessment, Psychoeducation/Counseling, Psychological Treatment

The primary goal of psychological interventions is to improve the patient's ability to reduce the impact of tinnitus on the quality of life, i.e., to teach and improve coping strategies. Psychological approaches can offer assessment and management of tinnitus.

Psychological Assessment

A comprehensive assessment is essential before the implementation of therapy. Apart from medical and audiological parameters, perceptual, attentional, emotional, and behavioral aspects have to be equally considered. Topics of psychological assessment include characteristics of tinnitus (loudness, localization, pitch of sound) and the progression of tinnitus (onset, duration, intensity, increasing and decreasing factors). Beyond that, cognitive-emotional evaluation and coping (e.g., catastrophic thinking, helplessness, anger, sadness, etc.), psychological impairments related to tinnitus (depression, irritability, sleeping problems, and so on), effects of tinnitus on life (e.g., work, social interactions), sources of stress apart from tinnitus (e.g., live events, daily hassles), operant factors (e.g., avoidance behavior), comorbidity (e.g., mental disorders, hearing loss), treatment history, and treatment expectations have to be evaluated (see Table 25.1).

In addition, sometimes it might be important to disentangle connections between tinnitus and other afflictions, preventing tinnitus from becoming a scapegoat for all other problems. Assessment of tinnitus also

Table 25.1 Main topics of psychological assessment

Characteristics of tinnitus
Progression of tinnitus
Cognitive emotional evaluation and coping responses to tinnitus
Psychological impairments related to tinnitus and effects of tinnitus on daily life
Sources of stress apart from tinnitus
Operant factors
Further medical and psychological problems(comorbidity)
Treatment history and treatment expectations

includes the patient's view of his/her problem: Although from a psychological perspective, the etiology of tinnitus can be neglected most of the time, the way in which patients interpret the cause for tinnitus can be essential for coping efforts. Patients may indicate that the *intensity* or *loudness* of their tinnitus causes difficulties in the areas of sleep, concentration, hearing, social relationships, or work and is therefore made responsible for their increasing anxiety and depression. However, as research shows, there appears to be little correlation between the subjective loudness of the tinnitus and the degree to which a person is impaired by it [1, 2]. Tinnitus distress cannot be regarded as dependent on the severity of the tinnitus sensation or as a function of "loudness." A variety of features of tinnitus, together with characteristics of the individual, have to be considered in assessing tinnitus-related distress. It is the patient's reaction to tinnitus rather than the symptom itself that separates the individual who simply "experiences" tinnitus from the individual who seeks medical or psychological help because of tinnitus [3].

Psychological assessment is accomplished through interviews, questionnaires, severity rating, and so on. Sometimes, diaries are used for documenting frequency, duration, intensity, and other parameters of tinnitus impairment. The introduction of diaries arouses fear in some patients that it might cause exacerbation of tinnitus because attention is focused on it. However, this is not harmful. On the contrary, it might rather be an opportunity to make patients aware of the alliance between attention direction and perception.

Psychoeducation/Psychological Counseling

An understanding of the assumed neurobiological basis of tinnitus, and its cognitive, emotional, and behavioral factors is essential for successful coping. Knowledge about tinnitus ought to be enhanced, and patients are asked to take psychological aspects of tinnitus into account. Educational programs cover topics like assumptions about the causes of tinnitus, give information about exacerbating factors and the prognosis, and give an overview of treatment possibilities, etc.

Many patients are afraid that tinnitus might become worse over time, that they will go deaf, and they consider the disorder to be a severe illness. Such beliefs and concerns shift attention to tinnitus and increase its awareness. Patients need to be taught about the relationship between selective attention on tinnitus and its cognitive-emotional and behavioral consequences.

It is also important to inform patients that a large number of individuals are not impaired at all and are able to cope effectively with tinnitus. Poor coping has been found to be associated with the lack of control over sound and failure to habituate [4]. Besides the perception of noises, various other problems may contribute to a negative emotional status and patients may incorrectly attribute it entirely to tinnitus. In addition, patients often are worried that tinnitus becomes worse over time. However, research has shown quite the opposite: the number of complaints tends to decline the longer the tinnitus has been present [5, 6].

Instead of focusing on the unrealistic goal of tinnitus elimination, modifying the ways of coping is a more realistic goal. However, this can be challenging and involves assisting patients in the identification of aggravating factors and dealing with negative emotions (e.g., anxiety, anger, depression, etc.), sleeping problems, interference with social and recreational activities, concentration dysfunctions, and deterioration of performance.

Sometimes, patients also need help avoiding countless ineffective treatments and considerable costs.

Psychological Treatment

Treatment has to be tailored to the specific needs of patients, and patients should become active participants in all assessment and treatment procedures. Psychological approaches depend on the working alliance between therapist and patient rather than on so-called compliance. Psychological treatment is a collaborative effort rather than directive approach [7].

Before beginning any psychological treatment, a therapeutic rationale has to be developed and offered to the patient. A general hypothetical model of tinnitus tolerance was first developed by Hallam [8] and enhanced by Kröner-Herwig [9].

This model of tinnitus tolerance described by Hallam [10] suggests that tinnitus can be equated with any other auditory stimulus to which a person may or may not attend and that habituation to tinnitus noises

and development of tolerance is the normal response, even though this process may take time. Habituation takes place when an originally new stimulus becomes "well known" and has no relevance for taking any action. Habituation fails if the stimulus is endowed with a negative evaluation (threat, impairment, anxiety). Attention to the inner noise is correlated with distress since it is associated with negative thoughts yes, but it might be German-English; and may also interfere with other activities (e.g., falling asleep or reading a book).

In this model, suffering from tinnitus is explained as a failure of habituation or adaptation. At least three classes of variables are considered influential to the process. These variables can be divided into:

- *Sensory factors*: The characteristics of the stimulus (i.e., intensity and quality).
  It is assumed that noises which are more salient and show a more variable and irregular pattern require a longer period of habituation.
- *Perceptual factors*: Environmental conditions (e.g., intensity of other stimuli and the competing demands on attention).
  For some patients, masking by natural sounds will frequently occur. Different activities and competing sensory perceptions ought to divert attention from tinnitus.
- *Psychological factors*: It is assumed that the more meaningful, especially the more threatening, a stimulus is the more attention it will receive, which creates a positive feedback loop: the more tinnitus is attended to the more the person is involved in negative cognitive emotional processing. High levels of cortical arousal are supposed to delay habituation. A patient's style of information processing and general distractibility may influence habituation as well. Furthermore, CNS pathology affecting the neural pathways involved in attention, habituation, and appraisal has to be considered as well (see Fig 25.1).

Psychological therapies aim to assist patients in controlling attention by learning to direct attention away from tinnitus (attention-control techniques) and in bringing negative cognitive processes under self-control (cognitive restructuring techniques). Behavior modification techniques aim at reducing avoidance behavior motivated by tinnitus and increasing adaptive problem solving. In addition, different forms of relaxation

Fig.25.1 Hypothetical model of tinnitus tolerance (from Hallam [10], p. 160)

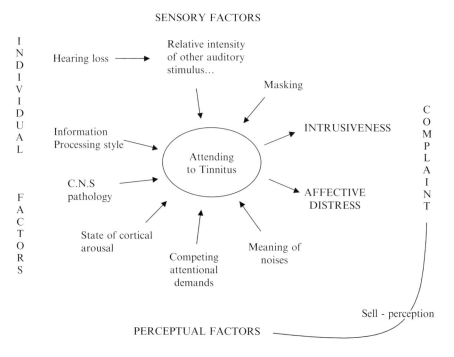

SENSORY FACTORS

training, including biofeedback, are offered to find a way of coping with tension related to tinnitus, sleeping difficulties or other sources of stress (see Chap. 71).

General Recommendations Regarding Treatment Protocols

Psychological interventions should be an integral part of tinnitus management and not be based on the existence of a mental disorder, despite the fact that in some cases anxiety or depressive disorders can accompany tinnitus attributed distress. Early referrals to a psychologist are desirable to undertake an assessment of tinnitus-related complaints, identification of psychiatric comorbidity, and to undertake a comprehensive functional analysis of the problem.

Figures 25.2 and 25.3 show two different models of cooperation between medicine and psychology. Referrals to psychologists after various medical and audiological treatments have failed in removing or diminishing tinnitus are counterproductive. And simply telling the patient to accept and ignore the ringing in their ear is not enough – if it were they would have already done so. Giving the information that "nothing

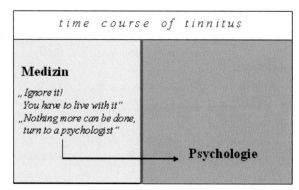

Fig. 25.2 Dichotomous model

more can be done" and that the tinnitus might be "psychogenic" is often interpreted by patients as uncaring and insensitive. Such sentiments hamper the search for and acceptance of psychotherapeutic help (see Fig. 25.2).

McFadden [11] stated that "treatment of psychological factors without adequate preparation of the patient often results in confusion and alienation." It is vital to inform the patient that while the tinnitus is "real," the maladaptive response is creating the distress, and this is where patients themselves can intervene. Moreover, cognitive-behavioral therapy (CBT), albeit a primarily psychological approach, may have

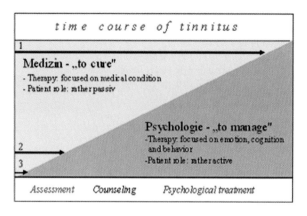

Fig. 25.3   Cooperative model

significant neurophysiological consequences, as suggested by the principles of neuroplasticity and cortical reorganization [12–14]. Resistance is often minimized when the patient recognizes that this approach works on the biological level as well.

When tinnitus is experienced, a patient will very likely consult his or her doctor first. From the very beginning physicians, audiologists, and psychologists should work together as partners (see Fig. 25.3). Medical assessments and interventions prevail at that the beginning (see yellow triangle in Fig. 25.3). Psychological assessment, counseling, and treatment should become more significant over the course of time (see blue triangle in Fig. 25.3).

While medical interventions attempt to remove ("to cure") tinnitus, psychological intervention rather supports patients in learning to tolerate the noises and handle tinnitus-related impairments ("to manage"). The patient role is very different in medical and psychological settings as well. While doctors "treat" a disease and patients are more or less passive recipients of treatment, patients have to actively participate in psychological approaches. The collaborative style maximizes patient involvement, encourages the patient to take responsibility, and minimizes the feeling that the therapist is imposing his or her own view.

The time of referral to a psychologist and psychotherapist has to be planned carefully as well. The arrows in Fig. 25.3 show different time points. The treatment management symbolized by arrow 1 shows an example where tinnitus exclusively is seen as a medical condition. Psychological factors are neglected. Patients expect that tinnitus is being removed by medical

interventions. When this goal fails (which is the case in chronic tinnitus most of the time), patients increasingly get disappointed and frustrated. In response, they might visit other doctors ("doctor-shopping") or become desperate and hopeless. The medical expert should be helpful in deciding when is the right moment for seeking the cooperation of a psychologist by assessing the cognitive-emotional and behavioral impact of tinnitus on the patient early and repeatedly. Arrow 3 characterizes quite the opposite: The patient is referred to a psychologist, without (or insufficiently) performing medical and audiological assessments. In this case, tinnitus is considered exclusively "psychogenic." Medical and audiological factors are ignored. Both ways have their shortcomings in the long run. In any medical condition which is predisposed to become chronic, medical as well as behavioral variables have to be considered equally. It is mainly the cognitive, emotional, and behavioral response to tinnitus that separates patients experiencing the symptoms from patients who are suffering from tinnitus, and behavior can be changed at any time. Due to that, psychologists play an important role in tinnitus management regardless of the existence of psychiatric disorders.

References

1. Coles, RRA and Baskill, JL (1995) Absolute loudness of tinnitus. Tinnitus clinic data In: Proceedings of the Fifth International Tinnitus Seminar 135–141. American Tinnitus Association: Portland, Oregon
2. Traserra, J, Doménech, J, Fusté, J, Carulla, M and Traserra-Coderch, J (1995) Subjective and objective intensity of tinnitus In: Proceedings of the Fifth International Tinnitus Seminar 193–194. American Tinnitus Association: Portland, Oregon
3. Sweetow, RW (1986) Cognitive aspects of tinnitus-patient management. Ear Hear **7**, 390–396
4. Hallam, RS, Jakes, SC and Hinchcliffe, R (1988) Cognitive variables in tinnitus annoyance. Brit J Cin Psychol **27**, 213–222
5. Tyler, RS and Baker, LJ (1983) Difficulties experienced by tinnitus sufferers. JSHD **48**, 150–154
6. Andersson, G, Vretblad, P, Larsen, H and Lyttkens, L (2001) Longitudinal follow-up of tinnitus complaints. Arch Otolaryngol Head Neck Surg **127**, 175–179
7. Wilson, PH and Henry, JL (2000) Psychological management of Tinnitus. In: Tinnitus Handbook 263–279 Ed RS Tyler, Singular: San Diego
8. Hallam, RS (1984) Psychological aspects of tinnitus. In: Contributions to Medical Psychology 31–53 Ed S Rachmann. Pergamon: Oxford

9. Kroener-Herwig, B (1997) Die Psychologische Behandlung des chronischen Tinnitus. Beltz: Weinheim

10. Hallam, RS (1987) Psychological Aroaches to the evaluation and management oftinnitus distress. In: Tinnitus 156–175 Ed J Hazell. Churchill Livingstone: Edinburgh

11. McFadden, D (1982) Tinnitus: Facts, Theories and Treatments. National Academy: Washington, DC

12. Kilgard, MP and Merzenich, MM (1998) Plasticity of temporal information processing in the primary auditory cortex. Nat Neurosci **1**, 727–731

13. Rauschecker, JP (1999) Auditory cortical plasticity: a comparison with other sensory systems. Trends Neurosci **22**, 74–80

14. Møller, AR (2003) Pathophysiology of tinnitus Otolaryngol. Clin North Am **36**, 249–266

Chapter 26
The Neurologist

Miguel J. A. Láinez, Alejandro Ponz, and Anna Piera

Keypoints

1. Subjective tinnitus is not a disease, but a symptom and the many forms of tinnitus probably have different pathophysiology.
2. For a long time, it was believed that tinnitus arose from the ear and that the anatomical location of the physiological abnormalities which cause tinnitus was the ear. However, it was later understood that most forms of tinnitus were caused by the expression of neural plasticity.
3. The fact that most forms of tinnitus are disorders of the nervous system puts emphasis on neuroscience for treatment of tinnitus.
4. This chapter is focused on the treatment of tinnitus and how neurologists can be involved in the evaluation and diagnosis of patients with tinnitus.

Keywords Tinnitus • Phantom perception • Neural plasticity • Auditory pathway • Neurotology

Abbreviation

TRI   Tinnitus research initiative
GABA   Gamma amino butyric acid
TMS   Transcranial magnetic stimulation

M.J.A. Láinez (✉)
Department of Neurology, Hospital Clínico Universitario, University of Valencia (Spain), Avenida Blasco Ibáñez, 17, 46010 Valencia, Spain
e-mail: jlaineza@meditex.es

Introduction

There are two main types of tinnitus – objective and subjective tinnitus (see Chap. 2). Objective tinnitus is caused by sounds generated in the body and then transmitted to the ear, whereas subjective tinnitus is caused by an abnormal neural activity. Objective tinnitus is rare, but subjective tinnitus is a frequent disorder that occurs with different severity; it can be just noticeable, an annoyance, or it can cause suffering that severely reduces the quality of life. There are no objective tests that can measure subjective tinnitus, and the only person who can evaluate a person's tinnitus is the person who has the tinnitus. This is one of the aspects of subjective tinnitus that is similar to central neuropathic pain [1] (see Chap. 14).

It is generally agreed that subjective tinnitus is not a disease, but a symptom, and the many forms of tinnitus probably have different pathophysiology. For a long time, it was believed that tinnitus arose from the ear and that the anatomical location of the physiological abnormalities that cause tinnitus was the ear. However, it was later understood that most forms of tinnitus were phantom sounds [2] caused by the expression of neural plasticity [1] (Chap. 12). Realizing the complexity of tinnitus has highlighted the importance of interdisciplinary research. The fact that most forms of tinnitus are disorders of the nervous system has placed emphasis on neuroscience in the studies of tinnitus (see Chap. 10).

Objective tinnitus is caused by sound generated in the body, reaching the ear through conduction in body tissues [1] (see Chap. 10). The source can be turbulent flow of blood in an artery, where there is a constriction, or it can be caused by muscle contractions. Unlike subjective tinnitus, an observer can often hear objective tinnitus using a stethoscope.

A.R. Møller et al. (eds.), *Textbook of Tinnitus*,
DOI 10.1007/978-1-60761-145-5_26, © Springer Science+Business Media, LLC 2011

Subjective tinnitus consists of meaningless sounds that are not associated with a physical sound, and only the person who has the tinnitus can hear it. This chapter discusses subjective tinnitus and focuses on neurologic evaluation of patients with tinnitus, describing the methodology for obtaining a clinical history to classify the tinnitus and make suggestions to the patient regarding the treatment to relieve tinnitus.

Tinnitus is a Neurological Entity

Tinnitus is considered a phantom perception similar to neuropathic pain, sharing a similar pathophysiology and clinical symptoms. Both neuropathic pain and tinnitus are perceptions that occur without the physical stimulation of receptors, which are considered to be the result of maladaptative neural plasticity (see Chaps. 12 and 34).

The expression of neural plasticity can change the balance between excitation and inhibition, promote hyperactivity, and the activation of specific parts of the nervous system not normally involved in processing sounds, such as the nonclassical auditory pathways (extralemniscal pathways) (see Chap. 8). The strongest promoter of expression of neural plasticity is the deprivation of input, which explains why tinnitus often occurs together with hearing loss [1] (see Chap. 11).

Different treatments, such as training and sound exposure to magnetic stimulation, including the use of neuromodulation, are based on the assumption that hyperactivity and reorganization of the nervous system are the causes of many of the different forms of tinnitus.

How the Clinical Neurologist is Involved in Tinnitus Diagnosis?

Individuals with mild tinnitus often do not need any treatment, but some need an assurance that their tinnitus is not a sign, therefore, of a severe disease. A detailed clinical history is essential in all patients with severe tinnitus with an aim to find an etiology if possible. A consensus at a first Tinnitus Research Initiative (TRI) meeting (www.tinnitusresearch.org) agreed upon items that should be assessed, and it has created a tinnitus questionnaire designed for assessing the severity of tinnitus and comorbidity [3].

In parallel to the otologists examination necessary in all patients with tinnitus, the neurologist should focus on patients who are suspected of having neurological disorders that may be involved in causing tinnitus or which occur as comorbidity to tinnitus. Examples are vascular malformations and brain tumors. Intermittent types of tinnitus may occur in individuals with migraine and epilepsy (see Chap. 61). Participation of neurologists is also important in the management of patients with somatic tinnitus that occurs without an apparent cause. A multidisciplinary approach should be employed for treating patients with severe tinnitus, selecting the most suitable therapies for each patient [3].

Treatment of Tinnitus with a Neurological View

While the pathophysiology of the different forms of tinnitus remains poorly understood, electrophysiologic and functional neuroimaging studies have recently shown the evidence of an association between severe chronic tinnitus and abnormal functioning of the central nervous system (CNS) [1, 2] (see Chap. 10). Abnormal neuronal firing within the auditory pathway may account for the perception of sound when there is no physical sound present (tinnitus). In detail, neuroimaging studies demonstrated that tinnitus is associated with increased activity of the inferior colliculus [4, 5], the thalamus [6, 7], the auditory cortex [8, 9], and the limbic structure (amygdala) [10, 11]. Evidence has been presented that the activation of neural plasticity is involved in chronic tinnitus as well as failing homeostatic mechanisms, thus resembling the pathologies of chronic pain syndromes [12–14]. Animal models of tinnitus suggest that Ca^{2++} signaling pathways as well as imbalance between the GABAergic and glutamatergic system are among known involved mechanisms [15].

Effective therapies of tinnitus have been based on known pathophysiology of tinnitus. Modulation of somatic inputs by transcranial magnetic stimulation (TMS) (see Chap. 88) and retraining therapy, alone or in combination, have been used (see Chap. 73).

TMS is a noninvasive method that can relieve tinnitus by modulating the excitability of neurons in the auditory cortex to decrease the hyperexcitability believed to cause some forms of tinnitus (see Chap. 88) by direct electrical stimulation of the cerebral cortex (see Chap. 90). All these treatments are aimed at reversing hyperexcitability of the auditory pathways in the central and peripheral nervous system.

Medications used for reducing the increased neuronal excitability, anticonvulsants, have been repeatedly used for the treatment of tinnitus as well as antidepressants, benzodiazepines, acamprosate, and melatonin [15] (see Chaps. 78 and 79). Other methods that are in use for the treatment of tinnitus act to modulate or stimulate the somatic sensory system similar to what is used to treat central neuropathic pain (see Chaps. 91 and 94).

References

1. Møller AR (2003) Pathophysiology of tinnitus In: Sismanis A (Ed) Otolaryngologic Clinics of North America. WB Saunders, Amsterdam, pp 249–66.
2. Jastreboff PJ (1990) Phantom auditory perception (tinnitus): Mechanisms of generation and perception. Neurosci Res. 8:221–54.
3. Langguth B, Goodey R, Azevedo A, Bjorne A, Cacace A, Crocetti A, Del Bo L, De Ridder D, Diges I, Elbert T, Flor H, Herraiz C, Ganz Sanchez T, Eichhammer P, Figueiredo R, Hajak G, Kleinjung T, Landgrebe M, Londero A, Lainez MJ, Mazzoli M, Melkle MD, Melchor J, Rauschecker JP, Sand PG, Struve M, Van de Heyning P, Van Dijk P, Vergara R (2007) Consensus for tinnitus patient assessment and treatment outcome measurement: Tinnitus Research Initiative meeting, Regensburg, July 2006. Prog Brain Res. 166: 525–36
4. Melcher JR et al (2000) Lateralized tinnitus studied with functional magnetic resonance imaging: Abnormal inferior colliculus activation. J Neurophysiol. 83(2):1058–72
5. Melcher JR, RA Levine, C Bergevin et al (2009) The auditory midbrain of people with tinnitus: Abnormal sound-evoked activity revisited. Hear Res. 257:63–74.
6. De Ridder D, van der Loo E, Van der Kelen K, Menovsky T, van de Heyning P, Møller A (2007) Theta, alpha and beta burst transcranial magnetic stimulation: Brain modulation in tinnitus. Int J Med Sci. 4(5):237–41
7. Llinas R, Urbano FJ, Leznik E, Ramirez RR and van Marle HJ (2005) Rhytimic and dysrhytmic thalamocortical dynamics: GABA Systems and the Edge effect. Trends Neurosci. 28:325–33
8. Arnold W, Bartenstein P, Oestreicher E, Romer W and Schwaiger M (1996) Focal metabolic activation in the predominant left auditory cortex in patients suffering from tinnitus: A PET study with [18F] deoxyglucose. ORL J Otorhinolaryngol Relat Spec. 58:195–9
9. Mirz F, Pedersen B, Ishizu K, Johannsen P, Ovesen T, Stodkilde-Jorgensen H and Gjedde A (1999) Positron emission tomography of cortical centers of tinnitus. Hear Res. 134:133–44
10. De Ridder D, Fransen H, Francois O, Sunaert S, Kovacs S, Van De Heyning P (2006) Amygdalohippocampal involvement in tinnitus and auditory memory. Acta Otolaryngol Suppl. (556):50–3
11. Lockwood AH, Salvi RJ, Burkard RF, Galantowicz PJ, Coad ML and Wack DS (1999) Neuroanatomy of tinnitus. Scand Audiol Suppl. 51:47–52
12. De Ridder D, Van de Heyning P (2007) The Darwinian plasticity hypothesis for tinnitus and pain. Prog Brain Res. 166:55–60
13. Flor H, Elbert T, Knecht S, Wienbuch C, Pantev C, Birbaumer N, Larbig W, and Taub E (1995) Phantom limb pain as a perceptual correlate of cortical reorganization following arm amputation. Nature. 375:482–4
14. Møller AR (2006) Neural Plasticity and Disorders of the Nervous System. Cambridge University Press, Cambridge
15. Eggermont JJ (2005) Tinnitus: neurobiological substrates. Drug Discov Today. 10:1283–90

Chapter 27
The Psychiatrist

Berthold Langguth

Keypoints

1. Tinnitus is not a psychiatric disorder, but shares some relevant aspects with psychiatric disorders.
2. Tinnitus is frequently accompanied by psychiatric comorbidities.
3. Tinnitus research can benefit from recent advances in psychiatric research, e.g., in neuroimaging, genetics or clinical trials methodology.
4. Diagnosis of psychiatric comorbidity and psychopharmacologic treatment should be performed by psychiatrists, and psychotherapy by psychotherapists.
5. A multidisciplinary collaborative approach seems to be the most promising strategy both for the management of the tinnitus patients and for tinnitus research.

Keywords Tinnitus • Brain disorder • Psychiatry • Psychosomatics • Psychotherapy • Multidisciplinarity

Introduction

Traditionally, tinnitus is treated by otologists and audiologists. This can reasonably be explained by the fact that tinnitus is a sound and thus subjectively located to in the ears. It is common to seek help for hearing problems from otologists and hearing specialists (audiologists). Recent advances in neuroimaging and

neuroscientific neuroscience, however, have initiated a paradigmatic shift by demonstrating that tinnitus is generated by an alteration of neural activity in the brain.

Tinnitus as a Brain Disorder

The central auditory system is involved in most forms of tinnitus, but also nonauditory brain areas, such as the frontal cortex or the limbic system. The changes in the central auditory system that cause tinnitus not only arise from auditory deprivation, but can also be caused or modulated by somatosensory input. Whether changes that occur in neural activity in the central auditory pathways are perceived as tinnitus depend on the degree of coherence of neural activity in populations of neurons and synchronous coactivation of a global neural network. The extent to which limbic brain structures are involved may determine the emotional burden (see Chaps. 9, 10, 13, 17, and 21 for more details).

Thus, many studies have demonstrated that the location of the pathology underlying tinnitus and tinnitus distress is in the brain. Hence, there is no doubt that the specific experience of neuroscientists, neurologists, and psychiatrists in the investigation of brain disorders can provide important contributions to tinnitus research.

Should Tinnitus be Considered to be a Psychiatric Disorder?

That the anatomical localization of tinnitus pathology is the brain does not automatically mean that tinnitus should be classified as a neurological or psychiatric

B. Langguth (✉)
Department of Psychiatry and Psychotherapy, University of Regensburg, Universitätsstraße 84, 93053 Regensburg, Germany
and
Interdisciplinary Tinnitus Clinic, University of Regensburg, Universitätsstraße 84, 93053 Regensburg, Germany
e-mail: Berthold.Langguth@medbo.de

A.R. Møller et al. (eds.), *Textbook of Tinnitus*,
DOI 10.1007/978-1-60761-145-5_27, © Springer Science+Business Media, LLC 2011

233

disorder and treated by these disciplines. Other factors have to be considered, such as which discipline is best equipped to provide diagnostic and therapeutic management of patients with tinnitus. Also, historical aspects, the organization of the different national health care systems or the currently used diagnostic classification systems, may play a role in the choice of specialist best able to care for patients with tinnitus.

Taking into account all these aspects, one may find several arguments for classifying tinnitus as a psychiatric disorder in addition to the fact that the pathology of tinnitus is localized in the brain: (1) Tinnitus as a perceptual disorder shares phenomenological similarities with auditory hallucinations; (2) Emotional and cognitive impairment are core symptoms of tinnitus, and there are high rates of psychiatric comorbidity (see Chap. 62); (3) Psychoeducation (counseling) is probably the most widely used treatment for tinnitus, and psychotherapy is the only intervention for which efficacy has been shown in a Cochrane meta analysis [1]; (4) Also, most promising results of pharmacologic treatment have been shown for drugs used to treat psychiatric disorders, such as antidepressants or anticonvulsants [2] (see Chap. 78).

On the other hand, the importance of hearing disorders as the most important risk factor for tinnitus has been recognized, highlighting the relevance of detailed otologic and audiologic assessment. Treatments, which compensate for hearing loss, such as hearing aids or cochlear implants, have been clearly shown to improve tinnitus (see Chaps. 74 and 77) [3]. These arguments alone already justify that tinnitus patients are treated primarily by otologists and audiologists. There is probably general agreement that otologists and audiologists are most competent to provide information about hearing, but also to give recommendations on how to deal with hearing disorders and tinnitus. This is similar to other diseases, where one would expect, for example, the diabetologist to give recommendations for physical activity and eating behavior and not the behavioral therapist. Nevertheless, many ear specialists may benefit from some psychological training about how to best convey information or behavioral recommendations in their management of patients with tinnitus.

The Role of the Psychiatrist

Similar like audiological diagnosis and treatment require competent professionals, specific training is needed for psychiatric diagnosis and psychotherapeutic treatment. In this context, a clear distinction is also necessary between counseling, which comprises general information delivery and behavioral recommendation for tinnitus patients and psychotherapy. While counseling may be primarily the task of otologists or audiologists, cognitive behavioral therapy can best be performed by a specifically trained psychotherapist. Involvement of a specialist is also needed for the diagnosis and treatment of the frequently occurring psychiatric comorbidities.

But who is this specialist? Even among medical doctors there is confusion about the different "psycho-disciplines." Which discipline can provide the best benefit to patients with tinnitus: psychology or psychiatry, psychotherapy or psychosomatics, psychoanalysis or behavioral therapy? There is no general answer to this question because competences of the different disciplines vary across countries and health systems but an orientation can be given. Diagnosis of psychiatric disorders can be made by psychiatrists and specifically trained psychologists. The different forms of psychotherapy all require specific training. Both psychologists and psychiatrists can be trained to become psychotherapists. Legally, pharmacologic treatment can only be prescribed by psychiatrists or other medical doctors.

Tinnitus: A Psychosomatic Disorder?

The term psychosomatics highlights the interaction between psychological and somatic aspects of health and diseases. Psychosomatics can be considered as a reaction to the body–soul dualism, which influenced our thinking since Descartes. However, recent advances in neuroscience clearly demonstrate that psychological factors, such as motivation, emotions, beliefs, or expectations, are related to neural activity in specific brain circuits and that successful psychotherapeutic treatment induces changes in these brain networks. Thus, neither the distinction between "somatic" and "psychological" etiology for a symptom or a disease, nor the distinction between somatic and psychological treatment can be justified anymore. This also has important consequences for the still widespread assumption that symptoms without a detectable somatic correlate have a nonsomatic, ergo psychological, etiology. There is no reason to believe that there should be more unresolved psychological conflicts in individuals with tinnitus than in individuals who do not have tinnitus. There is also no evidence for any etiological relationship between psychological conflicts and the emergence of tinnitus. On the contrary, we know that tinnitus has always a neuronal correlate. If it is not possible to detect such changes in every patient, then this only reflects the present lack of methods and perhaps lack of knowledge. Any form of successful intervention, whether sensorial (hearing aids), physical (physiotherapy), pharmacologic, or psychological, exert their effect through the modulation of neural activity.

Conclusion

It is not helpful to distinguish between somatic and psychological causes for tinnitus. Instead, research should be directed toward identifying the neuronal correlates of the different forms of tinnitus and their comorbidities. It would be a mistake to ignore knowledge and methodological experience from biological psychiatric research. For example, neuroimaging is a valuable tool for targeting neuromodulation, and genetic research can contribute to the identification of molecular structures that can be manipulated by pharmacologic treatment.

Psychiatrists have an important role in clinical management of the patient with tinnitus. When there is suspicion of psychiatric comorbidity, a referral to a psychiatrist is critical and necessary when the patient has suicidal tendencies. (Criteria on how to identify these situations are given in Chap. 54 Tinnitus with psychiatric comorbidity). Prescription of psychopharmacologic drugs is best done by psychiatrists and whenever psychotherapy is indicated for the treatment of tinnitus, it should be performed by a trained psychotherapist.

It becomes clear that no single clinical specialty will be able to cover all relevant aspects of diagnosis and therapy for the different forms of tinnitus. Instead, close collaboration between different disciplines seems to be the most promising strategy, both for the clinical management of tinnitus patients and for tinnitus research. Our own experience from close interdisciplinary collaboration at tinnitus centers has taught us that such a concept that can be realized successfully to the benefit of patients with tinnitus.

References

1. Martinez, DP, Waddell, A, Perera, R, Theodoulou, M. Cognitive behavioural therapy for tinnitus. Cochrane Database Syst Rev, 2007; (1):CD005233
2. Langguth, B, Salvi, R Elgoyhen, AB. Emerging pharmacotherapy of tinnitus. Expert Opin Emerg Drugs, 2009; 14(4):687–702
3. Van de Heyning, P, Vermeire, K, Diebl, M, Nopp, P, Anderson, I, De Ridder, D. Incapacitating unilateral tinnitus in single-sided deafness treated by cochlear implantation. Ann Otol Rhinol Laryngol, 2008; 117(9):645–52

Chapter 28
The Neurosurgeon

Dirk De Ridder

Keypoints

1. Neurosurgeons can contribute in a similar fashion to treatments of tinnitus as they currently do in pain treatment.
2. Neurosurgeons should collaborate with other clinicians and basic neuroscientists to help elucidate the pathophysiology of tinnitus.
3. Invasive neuromodulation can be helpful in selected forms of intractable tinnitus.
4. Different intracranial pathologies exist that can cause tinnitus amenable to surgical treatment, both of the non-pulsatile and of the pulsatile type.
5. Non-pulsatile tinnitus can be considered analogous to pain and results from changes in neural networks of the brain.
6. Pulsatile tinnitus is mostly related to anomalies of blood vessels in and around the brain.

Keywords Tinnitus • Neurosurgeon • Tinnitus • Pulsatile • Non-pulsatile • Neurosurgery • Neuromodulation

Abbreviations

CPA   Cerebellopontine angle
CSF   Cerebrospinal fluid
ENT   Ear nose and throat
Gy   Gray (unit of absorbed radiation)
MRI   Magnetic resonance imaging
TMS   Transcranial magnetic stimulation

Introduction

Tinnitus has traditionally been a field belonging to ear nose and throat (ENT) surgeons, audiologists, and psychiatrists, except for some forms of pulsatile tinnitus, such as anomalies of the cerebral blood vessels, which have usually been treated by neurosurgeons.

Recently, both basic research [1] and clinical research [2, 3] have focused on the brain's involvement in the generation of tinnitus, opening the tinnitus field up to neurologists and neurosurgeons specialized in the field of tinnitus (see also Chap. 26).

Neurosurgeons treat patients with pain in an invasive way, and based on the analogy between some forms of pain and tinnitus [4–7], both of which can be considered deafferentation or phantom phenomena [8], the step to treating tinnitus for neurosurgeons is not as big as it looks at first sight (see Chap. 94).

A patient's referral to a neurosurgeon for pain relief was once considered bad news, because the choice of procedures was limited to the creation of lesions, offering significant risk and only modest success [9]. Neurosurgery used to be considered the "pursuit of the impossible by the irrepressible" [10]. In a similar way, the tinnitus field still considers the neurosurgeon a last resort, when everything else fails and the patient is suicidal or distressed by the tinnitus. Neurosurgical approaches to tinnitus are still too often described as "the half mad being operated upon by the mad" [10].

Advances in technology and an improved understanding of pain have helped to develop more effective procedures to such an extent that a recent textbook [11]

D. De Ridder (✉)
BRAI²N and Department of Neurosurgery,
TRI Tinnitus Clinic Antwerp, University of Antwerp,
Wilrijkstraat 10, 2650 Edegem, Belgium
e-mail: dirk.de.ridder@uza.be

A.R. Møller et al. (eds.), *Textbook of Tinnitus*,
DOI 10.1007/978-1-60761-145-5_28, © Springer Science+Business Media, LLC 2011

discusses more than 30 types of procedures used in more than 18 major categories of pain [9]. However, as stated in the textbook, this does not mean that the neurosurgical procedures should always be the first line of treatment, as chances for pain relief are greatest when neurosurgery is but one piece of a comprehensive plan incorporating all possible treatment modalities [9].

Neurosurgeons treat the cause of pain (for example, disk surgery and microvascular decompressions) or use invasive neuromodulation when the cause of the pain is unknown or cannot be treated. In a similar way, the neurosurgeon should be involved in tinnitus treatment, dealing with the cause of the tinnitus, and by using neuromodulation to treat the symptoms.

There are indeed a series of pathologies that can cause tinnitus, either as their principal symptom or as one in a constellation of symptoms. Knowing the clinical course of the tinnitus in these pathologies is needed in order to be able to prognostically address these pathologies surgically. Some examples of specific diseases that often have tinnitus among their symptoms and that can be treated surgically are vestibular schwannoma, Arnold-Chiari malformations, arachnoid cysts, and others. Treatment of such diseases belongs to the classical repertoire of neurosurgery. However, neuromodulation through electrical (or magnetic) stimulation or lesioning, which are effective methods in treating disorders such as tinnitus and some forms of pain, also belong to the armamentarium of modern neurosurgery. Although neurosurgical procedures are traditionally the last resort in the battle against tinnitus, it is of interest for the tinnitus field to learn from neurosurgical pain management, which has brought relief to many patients with pain where other treatments have been ineffective. There are reasons to believe that neurosurgical treatment of tinnitus may evolve to become as widely used for treatment of tinnitus as it is now for treatment of pain.

However, brain surgeons should not limit themselves to developing new treatments for tinnitus based on analogy with pain. As a brain surgeon, one has a unique and unparalleled access to the brain, permitting recordings directly from the brain. It is important that they team up with basic neuroscientists to collaborate in order to gain as much valuable information as possible during the short window of direct brain access [12]. The power of intraoperative studies of brain function has a long history beginning with Penfield in the 1930s [13], extending to modern times where large parts of our understanding of the function of many systems of the human brain is based on intraoperative studies in patients undergoing neurosurgical operations [14, 15].

The neurosurgeon treating tinnitus should ideally work in a multidisciplinary team consisting of not only clinicians but also basic neuroscientists. Therefore, as long as no standardized neurosurgical treatments become available for tinnitus suppression, the neurosurgeon should not limit himself/herself to be a "sophisticated manual laborer" but should also be a "researcher" attempting to better understand the pathophysiology of tinnitus in order to develop new treatments for this elusive symptom (see Chaps. 21, 90, and 94).

Neurosurgical Approaches to Tinnitus

Tinnitus can be divided into two entirely different entities: pulsatile and non-pulsatile tinnitus [16–18]. Pulsatile tinnitus is usually related to vascular anomalies or intracranial hyper- or hypotension and is not related to an abnormal function of the auditory system. Non-pulsatile tinnitus, on the other hand, is critically related to an abnormal function of the auditory system.

Non-Pulsatile Tinnitus

Non-pulsatile tinnitus can be considered an auditory phantom phenomenon [8], resulting from auditory deprivation or deafferentation [1]. Any lesion along the auditory tract altering its normal function can cause non-pulsatile tinnitus. Ménière's disease, vestibular schwannoma, cerebellopontine angle (CPA) lesions, arachnoid cysts, microvascular compressions, Chiari malformation, and brain tumors are causes of non-pulsatile tinnitus that can be treated surgically.

If no cause for a patient's tinnitus can be found and thus no causal treatment can be offered, attempts to provide permanent relief from treatments such as electrical stimulation should be tried. First, non-invasive stimulations at different targets of the auditory system (promontory stimulation, transcranial magnetic stimulation

[TMS], transcranial direct current stimulation, transcutaneous electrical nerve stimulation) to test if a permanent implant could be beneficial should be performed. However, no prognostic relation has yet been shown between the effect of TMS aimed at the auditory cortex or cortical electrical stimulation at the level of the auditory cortex.

In *Vestibular schwannoma*, a high-pitch tinnitus (described as ringing or steam from a kettle) is present in 60–85% of the participants in a recent study [19]. Since the advent of stereotactic irradiation, vestibular schwannomas are often treated by radiosurgery, especially gamma knife radiosurgery. This seems to have a similar effect on tinnitus as microsurgery, although it seems to induce less tinnitus in the short term after treatment. Studies have shown that the tinnitus in 12–46% of such patients improves after the treatment [20] and tinnitus develops in only 4% of the patients after radiosurgery [20, 21]. The tinnitus experienced by patients who underwent microscopic surgery for removal of vestibular schwannoma disappeared in 16–50% of the participants in a study [22, 23]. Other studies have shown that after surgery to remove vestibular schwannoma, the tinnitus is reduced in 16% of patients, in 55% it does not change, and in 29% it becomes worse [22, 24, 25], especially when hearing is saved in surgery [24]. While the prevalence of tinnitus before and after operations, where hearing preservation is not attempted, is not significantly different, there are significant differences in tinnitus before and after operations where hearing is saved. When tinnitus is absent preoperatively, 85% of the hearing preservation group develops tinnitus after the operation while only 31% of patients in whom hearing preservation was not attempted developed tinnitus [24]. The results of other studies are, however, more optimistic, showing that only 8% of patients developed tinnitus after hearing preservation operations for vestibular schwannoma [26].

Gamma knife treatment has advantages over surgery as well as disadvantages. Gamma knife radiosurgery is less invasive and requires shorter hospitalization and convalescence periods [27]. The development of facial palsy or paresis is extremely rare (1% if irradiation dose is <14 Gy), and hearing can be saved in almost 80% of patients if 13 Gy as the maximum dose is respected [28]. The technique is, however, limited to lesions less than 3 cm in size and carries a greater risk

for the development of post-treatment hydrocephalus and a certain, though small, risk of dedifferentiation into a neoplasia (malignancy). In small lesions (<1.5 cm) without serviceable hearing microsurgery and gamma knife treatment have comparable rates of tinnitus, tumor control, facial nerve function, and trigeminal function. However, stereotactic radiosurgery has a greater risk of long-term balance problems compared to microsurgery [29]. In general, gamma knife surgery might be better for vestibular schwannoma treatment in the short term [30], with similar effects on improvement and worsening of tinnitus as surgery. Surgery after failed gamma knife treatment has an increased risk for facial palsy due to strong adhesions [31] (see Chap. 85).

Other CPA *lesions* [32] such as meningioma, epidermoid tumors, lipoma, choroid plexus papilloma, epithelial cysts, teratoma, cavernoma, and hemangioma are sometimes associated with non-pulsatile tinnitus, usually together with other symptoms depending on the location of the lesion and the degree of brainstem, cerebellar, or cranial nerve compression.

Arachnoid cysts are a rare cause of non-pulsatile tinnitus. It is a congenital or posttraumatic/post-inflammatory disorder [33, 34], leading to vague symptoms [35]. However, infratentorial [36] arachnoid cysts can sometimes mimic Ménière's disease as well. Arachnoid cysts producing tinnitus can occur in the CPA [35, 37, 38], but also retroclival, retrocerebellar, and lateral of the cerebellum [39], with postoperative improvement of the tinnitus [39]. Usually, symptoms of intracranial hypertension are associated with non-pulsatile tinnitus [35, 40]. Surgical treatment consists of marsupialization[1] or excision of the cyst [40]. Also supratentorial Sylvian fissure arachnoid cysts can generate isolated tinnitus, and tinnitus suppression can be the result of marsupialization of the cysts if they act as a mass lesion [41]. Supratentorial cysts can also mimic Ménière's disease [42]. Imaging studies using intrathecal contrast to verify if an arachnoid cyst-like lesion communicates with normal cerebrospinal fluid (CSF) flow can help to ascertain whether an arachnoid cyst could act as a mass lesion and thus be symptomatic or not. Magnetic resonance imaging (MRI) sequences looking for a flow void within the cyst can be helpful as well [43].

---

[1] Marsupialization: Surgical alteration of a cyst or similar enclosed cavity by making an incision and suturing the flaps to the adjacent tissue, creating a pouch. (From: The American Heritage® Stedman's Medical Dictionary.)

Ménière's syndrome is a clinical entity consisting of episodic vertigo, fluctuating sensory hearing loss, tinnitus, and aural fullness (see Chap. 38). This syndrome is caused histopathologically by endolymphatic hydrops that can be caused by many pathologies – traumatic (acoustic, iatrogenic, or temporal bone trauma and labyrinthine concussion), infectious/inflammatory (autoimmune inner ear, see Chap. 60), Cogan's syndrome, chronic otitis media, viral or serous labyrinthitis, syphilis, tumoral (leukemia), congenital (deafness, Mondini dysplasia), or in the setting of connective tissue or bone disease (Letterer-Siwe disease, Paget's disease, otosclerosis), and others [44]. Tinnitus worsens both in intensity and as a function of duration and bilateral disease [45]. It is perceived as worse than in a comparable group of tinnitus sufferers due to acoustic trauma or otosclerosis [45].

In Ménière's disease, any kind of surgery, whether vestibular nerve section, cochlear nerve section, endolymphatic sac surgery [46], or gentamicin injections [47], never seems to produce greater than 50% tinnitus control – a small improvement upon the 30% spontaneous disappearance in its natural history [48]. Endolymphatic sac surgery, independent on whether decompression, exclusion, or shunting is done, improves or cures tinnitus in 40% of patients with Ménière's disease [49]. This is similar to intratympanic gentamycin application, a less invasive technique with 27–69% tinnitus improvement [50–52].

In a recent review paper on vestibular nerve section performed for tinnitus [53], the proportion of patients in whom tinnitus was exacerbated postoperatively ranged from 0 to 60%, with a mean of 16.4%. The proportion of patients in whom tinnitus was unchanged was 17–72% (mean 38.5%), and in whom tinnitus was improved was 6–61% (mean 37.2%). These results are similar to gentamycin and endolymphatic sac surgery. In the majority of patients undergoing vestibular nerve section, ablation of auditory efferent input (and thus total efferent dysfunction) to the cochlea was not associated with an exacerbation of tinnitus [53].

In *otosclerosis*, tinnitus is very common; up to 91% of individuals with otosclerosis have tinnitus and 38% is severely affected by it [54]. Successful stapedectomy causes disappearance of non-pulsatile tinnitus in up to 40–73% tinnitus [55–60] with another 32–37%

improving. In individuals who did not have tinnitus before stapedectomy, the risk of developing it after the surgery is almost non-existent. Only in 10%, the operation does not improve the tinnitus [60] and in another 8% it worsens [57]. Rarely, otosclerosis also produces arterial pulsatile tinnitus, due to a neovascularization at the site of stapes fusion. Stapedectomy can sometimes cure this rare form of pulsatile tinnitus [17].

A *tumor* in the auditory cortex, compressing the auditory cortex, can cause ipsilateral fluctuating non-pulsatile tinnitus as the sole symptom, probably due to a direct influence on normal cortical sound processing. Removal of the lesion resulted in abolishing the tinnitus in 4 out of 5 patients who had the operation [41]. Tumors elsewhere along the auditory tract (for example, the brainstem) rarely present with tinnitus only but usually give rise to additional symptoms related to the tumor's closeness of other neural structures in the brainstem.

For *intractable non-pulsatile tinnitus*, auditory brainstem implants [61] (see Chap. 77) and auditory cortex stimulations can give relief in intractable non-pulsatile tinnitus [62–64]. These treatments are based on a recently developed pathophysiological model for non-pulsatile tinnitus, based on auditory deprivation or deafferentation as the initial trigger for tinnitus generation. Studies have shown that a decrease of auditory input induces a slowing of auditory information processed in the thalamocortical loop generating slow wave activity (delta en theta oscillations) [7, 65], with a decrease in lateral inhibition [66] and a halo or edge of increased activity [7, 67]. This is also called thalamocortical dysrhythmia [7] associated with cortical reorganization [68, 69]. The most likely mechanism that links hyperactivity and reorganization is synchrony [1]. Synchronization of the gamma band activity could possibly induce topographical reorganization via simple Hebbian mechanisms (cells that fire together wire together) [1]. Therefore, it seems logical to try and modify this tinnitus-related auditory cortex reorganization/hyperactivity in an attempt to suppress the tinnitus. This can be achieved using neuronavigation-guided TMS, a technique that is capable of modulating cortical activity. If TMS is capable of suppressing tinnitus, the effect could be maintained by implantation of electrodes at the area of signal abnormality on the auditory cortex. The first results in patients with unilateral pure-tone tinnitus have shown statistically significant tinnitus suppression, without suppressing white or narrow band noise in individuals who responded to TMS with decreased tinnitus [63]. More recent trials also suggested that narrow band tinnitus is suppressible with novel stimulation designs consisting of closely spaced spikes of very high frequencies [70].

Reafferentation of the auditory thalamocortical system after it has been deprived of input can also be achieved by cochlear implants (see Chap. 77). Almost, immediately after the introduction of cochlear implants for hearing improvement, it was noted that the electrical intracochlear stimulation ameliorated tinnitus in a large proportion of individuals [71, 72]. Multiple studies since then have replicated these results indicating that cochlear implants inserted for hearing improvement can also modulate tinnitus [73–77], not only unilaterally but also bilaterally in a majority of individuals [78]. A recent study using cochlear implant insertion in patients with incapacitating tinnitus and ipsilateral complete hearing loss and contralateral preserved hearing demonstrates similarly promising results [79]. Using promontory stimulation as a preoperative non-invasive test in this selected group of patients might predict good outcomes in tinnitus suppression.

A limit to this technique is that it can only be used in patients with unilateral complete hearing loss. This could potentially be extended to people with high-frequency hearing loss but preserved low-frequency hearing, as a recent paper has shown that short hybrid cochlear implants can preserve low-frequency hearing [80]. Another option is to use extracochlear stimulation for tinnitus suppression. The first attempts for developing extracochlear electrical stimulation have been made [76, 81] as well.

Pulsatile and Pseudopulsatile Tinnitus

Many causes of pulsatile tinnitus are amenable to interventional neuroradiological procedures or neurosurgical interventions, whereas most problems involving pseudopulsatile tinnitus are the domain of the ENT surgeon (see Table 28.1). For an overview of these pathologies, the reader is referred to Chap. 59.

Table 28.1 Surgically treatable causes of tinnitus

Pulsatile tinnitus	Non-pulsatile tinnitus
Venous	Vestibular schwannoma (acoustic neuroma)
Benign intracranial hypertension	Other cerebellopontine angle lesions
Chiari malformation	Arachnoid cyst
High jugular bulb	Menière's disease
Sigmoid sinus diverticulum	Otosclerosis
Sigmoid-transverse aneurysm	Microvascular compression
Aberrant veins aneursm	Chiari malformation
Arterial	Brain tumor
Carotid stenosis	*Symptomatic*
Aberrant carotid artery	Cochlear implant
Glomus tumor	Brainstem implant
Vascular lesions of petrous bone/skull base	Auditory cortex implant
Arteriovenous malformation	*Pseudopulsatile tinnitus*
Aneurysm	Palatal myoclonus
Canal dehiscence	Middle ear myoclonus
Benign intracranial hypertension	Patulous eustachian tube
Carotid-cavernous fistula	
Intrameatal vascular loop	
Somatosensory pulsatile tinnitus syndrome	
Idiopathic	

Conclusion

Stimulated by recent developments in our understanding of the pathophysiology of tinnitus, treatment has shifted from purely otological approaches to brain-based approaches. Therefore, neurosurgeons should become more involved in treating this elusive symptom.

Tinnitus actually consists of two entirely different entities with a different pathophysiology, different clinical symptoms, and different treatment. Before tinnitus patients are told "to learn to live with their tinnitus" it can be suggested to look for possible causes for both non-pulsatile and pulsatile tinnitus as this can result in an otoneurosurgical treatment. In patients with non-pulsatile tinnitus, non-invasive trials with promontory or TMS can potentially help select candidates for a permanent implant as a treatment for tinnitus. Neurosurgeons should be involved not only in the surgical treatment of operable causes but also in the exploration of possible pathophysiological mechanisms, making use of their unique ability to record activity directly from the brain when performing intracranial surgery.

References

1. Eggermont JJ and LE Roberts (2004) The neuroscience of tinnitus. Trends Neurosci 27:676–82.
2. Lockwood AH, RJ Salvi and RF Burkard (2002) Tinnitus. N Engl J Med 347:904–10.
3. Lockwood AH, RJ Salvi, RF Burkard et al (1999) Neuroanatomy of tinnitus. Scand Audiol Suppl 51:47–52.
4. Møller AR (2000) Similarities between severe tinnitus and chronic pain. J Am Acad Audiol 11:115–24.
5. Møller AR (1997) Similarities between chronic pain and tinnitus. Am J Otol 18:577–85.
6. Tonndorf J (1987) The analogy between tinnitus and pain: a suggestion for a physiological basis of chronic tinnitus. Hear Res 28:271–5.
7. Llinas RR, U Ribary, D Jeanmonod et al (1999) Thalamocortical dysrhythmia: a neurological and neuropsychiatric syndrome characterized by magnetoencephalography. Proc Natl Acad Sci USA 96:15222–7.
8. Jastreboff PJ (1990) Phantom auditory perception (tinnitus): mechanisms of generation and perception. Neurosci Res 8: 221–54.
9. Giller CA (2003) The neurosurgical treatment of pain. Arch Neurol 60:1537–40.
10. Dan NG (1995) The personality of the neurosurgeon. Acta Neurochir (Wien) 132:217–21.
11. Burchiel KJ (ed) (2002) Surgical management of pain. Thieme: New York.
12. Abbott A (2009) Neuroscience: Opening up brain surgery. Nature 461:866–8.
13. Penfield W and E Boldrey (1937) Somatic motor and sensory representation in the cerebral cortex of man as studied by electrical stimulation. Brain 60:389–443.
14. Anderson WS, SO O'Hara, HC Lawson et al (2006) Plasticity of pain-related neuronal activity in the human thalamus. In Reprogamming the brain, AR Møller (Ed). Elsevier: Amsterdam, 353–64.
15. Ojemann GA (2003) The neurobiology of language and verbal memory: observations from awake neurosurgery. Int J Psychophysiol 48:141–6.
16. Sismanis A (1997) Pulsatile tinnitus. Int Tinnitus J 3: 39–40.
17. Sismanis A (1998) Pulsatile tinnitus. A 15-year experience. Am J Otol 19:472–7.
18. Sismanis A (2003) Pulsatile tinnitus. Otolaryngol Clin North Am 36:389–402, viii.
19. Kentala E and I Pyykko (2001) Clinical picture of vestibular schwannoma. Auris Nasus Larynx 28:15–22.
20. Selch MT, A Pedroso, SP Lee et al (2004) Stereotactic radiotherapy for the treatment of acoustic neuromas. J Neurosurg 101 Suppl 3:362–72.
21. Hempel JM, E Hempel, B Wowra et al (2006) Functional outcome after gamma knife treatment in vestibular schwannoma. Eur Arch Otorhinolaryngol 263:714–8.
22. Fahy C, TP Nikolopoulos and GM O'Donoghue (2002) Acoustic neuroma surgery and tinnitus. Eur Arch Otorhinolaryngol 259:299–301.
23. Dandy W (1941) Surgical treatment of Ménière's disease. Surg Gynaecol Obstet 72:421–5.
24. Kanzaki J, A Satoh and T Kunihiro (1999) Does hearing preservation surgery for acoustic neuromas affect tinnitus? Skull Base Surg 9:169–76.
25. Berliner KI, C Shelton, WE Hitselberger et al (1992) Acoustic tumors: effect of surgical removal on tinnitus. Am J Otol 13:13–7.
26. Catalano PJ and KD Post (1996) Elimination of tinnitus following hearing preservation surgery for acoustic neuromas. Am J Otol 17:443–5.
27. Karpinos M, BS Teh, O Zeck et al (2002) Treatment of acoustic neuroma: stereotactic radiosurgery vs. microsurgery. Int J Radiat Oncol Biol Phys 54:1410–21.
28. Regis J, M Tamura, C Delsanti et al (2008) Hearing preservation in patients with unilateral vestibular schwannoma after gamma knife surgery. Prog Neurol Surg 21:142–51.
29. Coelho DH, JT Roland, Jr., SA Rush et al (2008) Small vestibular schwannomas with no hearing: comparison of functional outcomes in stereotactic radiosurgery and microsurgery. Laryngoscope 118:1909–16.
30. Pollock BE (2008) Vestibular schwannoma management: an evidence-based comparison of stereotactic radiosurgery and microsurgical resection. Prog Neurol Surg 21:222–7.
31. Shuto T, S Inomori, S Matsunaga et al (2008) Microsurgery for vestibular schwannoma after gamma knife radiosurgery. Acta Neurochir (Wien) 150:229–34; discussion 34.
32. Lalwani AK (1992) Meningiomas, epidermoids, and other nonacoustic tumors of the cerebellopontine angle. Otolaryngol Clin North Am 25:707–28.
33. Yanaka K, T Enomoto, T Nose et al (1988) Post-inflammatory arachnoid cyst of the quadrigeminal cistern. Observation of development of the cyst. Childs Nerv Syst 4:302–5.
34. Lesoin F, P Dhellemmes, M Rousseaux et al (1983) Arachnoid cysts and head injury. Acta Neurochir (Wien) 69:43–51.
35. Hadley MN, TW Grahm, CP Daspit et al (1985) Otolaryngologic manifestations of posterior fossa arachnoid cysts. Laryngoscope 95:678–81.
36. O'Reilly RC and EK Hallinan (2003) Posterior fossa arachnoid cysts can mimic Meniere's disease. Am J Otolaryngol 24:420–5.
37. Takano S, T Maruno, S Shirai et al (1998) Facial spasm and paroxysmal tinnitus associated with an arachnoid cyst of the cerebellopontine angle – case report. Neurol Med Chir (Tokyo) 38:100–3.
38. Zennaro O, F San-Gali, V Darrouzet et al (1992) Arachnoid cysts of the cerebellopontine angle. Rev Laryngol Otol Rhinol (Bord) 113:47–50.
39. Ottaviani F, CB Neglia, A Scotti et al (2002) Arachnoid cyst of the cranial posterior fossa causing sensorineural hearing loss and tinnitus: a case report. Eur Arch Otorhinolaryngol 259:306–8.
40. Haberkamp TJ, EM Monsell, WF House et al (1990) Diagnosis and treatment of arachnoid cysts of the posterior fossa. Otolaryngol Head Neck Surg 103:610–4.
41. Kovacs S, R Peeters, M Smits et al (2006) Activation of cortical and subcortical auditory structures at 3 T by means of a

functional magnetic resonance imaging paradigm suitable for clinical use. Invest Radiol 41:87–96.

42. Buongiorno G and G Ricca (2003) Supratentorial arachnoid cyst mimicking a Meniere's disease attack. J Laryngol Otol 117:728–30.

43. De Ridder D, G Alessi, M Lemmerling et al (2002) Hemilingual spasm: a new neurosurgical entity? Case report. J Neurosurg 97:205–7.

44. Borjab DI, SA Bhansali and RA Battista (1994) Peripheral vestibular disorders. In Neurotology, R Jackler, D Brackmann (eds). Mosby: St. Louis.

45. Herraiz C, MC Tapia and G Plaza (2006) Tinnitus and Meniere's disease: characteristics and prognosis in a tinnitus clinic sample. Eur Arch Otorhinolaryngol 263:504–9.

46. Meyershoff W (1992) Tinnitus. In Otolaryngology head and neck surgery, W Meyershoff, D Ria (Eds). Saunders Company: Philadelphia, 435–46.

47. Kaasinen S, I Pyykko, H Ishizaki et al (1995) Effect of intratympanically administered gentamicin on hearing and tinnitus in Meniere's disease. Acta Otolaryngol Suppl 520 Pt 1:184–5.

48. Vernon J, R Johnson and A Schleuning (1980) The characteristics and natural history of tinnitus in Meniere's disease. Otolaryngol Clin North Am 13:611–9.

49. Quaranta N, G De Thomasis, A Gandolfi et al (2001) Long-term audition results in patients with chronic endolymphatic hydrops after selective vestibular neurotomy and endolymphatic sac surgery. Acta Otorhinolaryngol Ital 21:131–7.

50. Quaranta A, A Scaringi, A Aloidi et al (2001) Intratympanic therapy for Meniere's disease: effect of administration of low concentration of gentamicin. Acta Otolaryngol 121:387–92.

51. Seidman M (2002) Continuous gentamicin therapy using an IntraEAR microcatheter for Meniere's disease: a retrospective study. Otolaryngol Head Neck Surg 126:244–56.

52. De Valck CF, V Van Rompaey, EL Wuyts et al (2009) Tenotomy of the tensor tympani and stapedius tendons in Meniere's disease. B-Ent 5:1–6.

53. Baguley DM, P Axon, IM Winter et al (2002) The effect of vestibular nerve section upon tinnitus. Clin Otolaryngol Allied Sci 27:219–26.

54. Sobrinho PG, CA Oliveira and AR Venosa (2004) Long-term follow-up of tinnitus in patients with otosclerosis after stapes surgery. Int Tinnitus J 10:197–201.

55. Glasgold A and F Altmann (1966) The effect of stapes surgery on tinnitus in otosclerosis. Laryngoscope 76:1524–32.

56. Gersdorff M, J Nouwen, C Gilain et al (2000) Tinnitus and otosclerosis. Eur Arch Otorhinolaryngol 257:314–6.

57. Ayache D, F Earally and P Elbaz (2003) Characteristics and postoperative course of tinnitus in otosclerosis. Otol Neurotol 24:48–51.

58. Oliveira CA (2007) How does stapes surgery influence severe disabling tinnitus in otosclerosis patients? Adv Otorhinolaryngol 65:343–7.

59. Sparano A, JP Leonetti, S Marzo et al (2004) Effects of stapedectomy on tinnitus in patients with otosclerosis. Int Tinnitus J 10:73–7.

60. Szymanski M, W Golabek and R Mills (2003) Effect of stapedectomy on subjective tinnitus. J Laryngol Otol 117:261–4.

61. Soussi T and SR Otto (1994) Effects of electrical brainstem stimulation on tinnitus. Acta Otolaryngol 114:135–40.

62. De Ridder D, G De Mulder, V Walsh et al (2004) Magnetic and electrical stimulation of the auditory cortex for intractable tinnitus. Case report. J Neurosurg 100:560–4.

63. De Ridder D, G De Mulder, E Verstraeten et al (2006) Primary and secondary auditory cortex stimulation for intractable tinnitus. ORL J Otorhinolaryngol Relat Spec 68:48–54; discussion 55.

64. De Ridder D, G De Mulder, E Verstraeten et al (2007) Auditory cortex stimulation for tinnitus. Acta Neurochir Suppl 97:451–62.

65. Weisz N, S Moratti, M Meinzer et al (2005) Tinnitus perception and distress is related to abnormal spontaneous brain activity as measured by magnetoencephalography. PLoS Med 2:e153.

66. Llinas R, FJ Urbano, E Leznik et al (2005) Rhythmic and dysrhythmic thalamocortical dynamics: GABA systems and the edge effect. Trends Neurosci 28:325–33.

67. Weisz N, S Muller, W Schlee et al (2007) The neural code of auditory phantom perception. J Neurosci 27:1479–84.

68. Muhlnickel W, T Elbert, E Taub et al (1998) Reorganization of auditory cortex in tinnitus. Proc Natl Acad Sci USA 95:10340–3.

69. Norena AJ and JJ Eggermont (2006) Enriched acoustic environment after noise trauma abolishes neural signs of tinnitus. Neuroreport 17:559–63.

70. De Ridder D, S Vanneste, E van der Loo et al (2010) Burst stimulation of the auditory cortex: a new form of neurostimulation for noise-like tinnitus suppression. J Neurosurg 112:1289–94.

71. Brackmann DE (1981) Reduction of tinnitus in cochlear-implant patients. J Laryngol Otol Suppl 4:163–5.

72. House JW and DE Brackmann (1981) Tinnitus: surgical treatment. Ciba Found Symp 85:204–16.

73. Miyamoto RT, MK Wynne, C McKnight et al (1997) Electrical suppression of tinnitus via cochlear implants. Int Tinnitus J 3:35–8.

74. Aschendorff A, G Pabst, T Klenzner et al (1998) Tinnitus in cochlear implant users: the Freiburg experience. Int Tinnitus J 4:162–4.

75. Di Nardo W, I Cantore, F Cianfrone et al (2007) Tinnitus modifications after cochlear implantation. Eur Arch Otorhinolaryngol 264:1145–9.

76. Hazell JW, LJ Meerton and MJ Conway (1989) Electrical tinnitus suppression (ETS) with a single channel cochlear implant. J Laryngol Otol Suppl 18:39–44.

77. Ito J and J Sakakihara (1994) Tinnitus suppression by electrical stimulation of the cochlear wall and by cochlear implantation. Laryngoscope 104:752–4.

78. Yonehara E, R Mezzalira, PR Porto et al (2006) Can cochlear implants decrease tinnitus? Int Tinnitus J 12:172–4.

79. Van de Heyning P, K Vermeire, M Diebl et al (2008) Incapacitating unilateral tinnitus in single-sided deafness treated by cochlear implantation. Ann Otol Rhinol Laryngol 117:645–52.

80. Gantz BJ, C Turner, KE Gfeller et al (2005) Preservation of hearing in cochlear implant surgery: advantages of combined electrical and acoustical speech processing. Laryngoscope 115:796–802.

81. Matsushima J, N Sakai, M Sakajiri et al (1996) An experience of the usage of electrical tinnitus suppressor. Artif Organs 20:955–8.

Chapter 29
The Dentist

Ralf Bürgers and Michael Behr

Keypoints

1. Patients with tinnitus are *prima facie* beyond the responsibility of dentists.
2. Studies of the prevalence of tinnitus in people with temporomandibular disorders (TMD) (give values from 2 to 59%) and the prevalence of TMD in patients with tinnitus ranging from 7 to 95%. Evidence about the relationship between TMD and tinnitus is conflicting and it is not known if it is causal or coincidental.
3. Patients with TMD-related tinnitus can benefit from TMD therapy but TMD therapy in patients with tinnitus without any signs of TMD is not recommended.

Keywords TMD • Tinnitus • Dentist

Abbreviations

CMD Craniomandibular disorder(s)
MPD Myofascial pain dysfunction
TMD Temporomandibular disorder(s)
TMJ Temporomandibular joint

Introduction

Tinnitus is generally regarded as a symptom of the ear or an auditory disorder. Therefore, patients with tinnitus are *prima facie* beyond the responsibility of

R. Bürgers (✉)
Department of Prosthetic Dentistry, University Medical Center Regensburg, 93042 Regensburg, Germany
e-mail: ralf.buergers@klinik.uni-regensburg.de

dentists or maxillofacial surgeons. Additionally, patients suffering from tinnitus do not primarily consult a dentist, and most patients will not relate their "ear symptoms" to possible stomatognathic or temporomandibular disorders. The understanding of tinnitus symptoms and knowledge on the pathophysiology of different forms of tinnitus has, however, changed in recent years. Tinnitus researchers have benefited from learning from other fields of medicine, from cooperating with other disciplines, and from "thinking outside the box" [1]. Today, tinnitus is seen as a symptom presenting in many forms, and the contribution of dental science to a better understanding of tinnitus is appreciated by "traditional tinnitus therapists", such as otolaryngologists, audiologists, psychologists, and psychiatrists.

Temporomandibular Disorders

Dentists and maxillofacial surgeons have long known that tinnitus symptoms are not uncommon in patients with temporomandibular joint (TMJ) and masticatory muscle disorders – also referred to as Costen's syndrome – [2], craniomandibular disorders (CMD), myofascial pain dysfunction (MPD), temporomandibular dysfunction, or temporomandibular joint syndrome [3]. Nowadays, these terms are summarized under the heading "temporomandibular disorders" (TMD) [4, 5]. TMD are considered as a cluster of various joint and muscle disorders and a subgroup of general musculoskeletal and rheumatologic disorders, but should be regarded as a distinct group of diseases and symptoms [6]. The complex signs and symptoms of TMD are generally described as pain or tenderness in the region of the TMJ or the masticatory muscles (myofascial pain), limitation or disturbance of mandibular movements, joint sound (clicking and crepitation), locking, oral parafunction, masticatory muscle hyperactivities (bruxism, clenching, and rocking of teeth), and fatigue in the jaws [3, 6]. Unfortunately, since the classification of the different forms of TMD is still not agreed upon, numerous ways of categorizing TMD have been proposed [7]. In general, TMD can be classified as a joint disorder (including structural deviations, mechanical derangements, and inflammatory disorder or arthritis), muscle disorder, and a combination of both [4, 6]. Clinicians who treated patients with TMD as a main complaint have noted that these patients often present with ear symptoms as a secondary complaint. Therefore, related conditions such as tinnitus were improved and often eliminated after treatment of their TMJ problems [8–11]. Tinnitus and TMD symptoms show many parallels in their clinical appearance. Knowledge of the etiology of both symptoms and disorders is limited. Thus, valid and reproducible diagnostic criteria are lacking. As a result, conflicting opinions exist on therapeutic proceedings for patients with tinnitus and TMD. Success rates of specific therapies remain unpredictable, which in turn transforms patients of both groups into an "unpopular" group of patients.

Prevalence of Temporomandibular Joint Disorders

The literature contains conflicting evidence about the prevalence of tinnitus in individuals with TMD as a main complaint (ranging from 2 to 59%), but most studies report a much higher prevalence of tinnitus in patients with TMD than in the general population. Unfortunately, most of the presented studies are mainly descriptive and have not been designed to compare between patients with symptoms and a reference group (Table 29.1). Studies of the general population showed prevalence of tinnitus from 14.2 to 20.1% (please see Chap. 5). Vice versa, information on the prevalence of TMD in patients with tinnitus is also incongruent (ranging from 7 to 95%) (Table 29.2). However, incidence of TMD was found to be higher in patients with tinnitus than in the general population, where tinnitus occurred in 16–59% for reported symptoms and in 33–86% for clinical signs [12].

Relation Between TMD and Ear Problems

Many different manifestations lead to the diagnosis of TMD, and a discrepancy exists between reported

Table 29.1 Studies reporting tinnitus in patients with TMD as the main complaint

Source	Prevalence of tinnitus, no (%)	
	Patients with TMD	General population
Bernstein et al. [35]	36/86 (42%)	–
Bush [8]	35/105 (33%)	–
Bürgers (unpublished)	30/82 (37%)	68/951 (7%)
Camparis et al. [36]	54/100 (54%)	–
Cooper et al. [37]	301/837 (36%)	–
Dolowitz et al. [38]	200/338 (59%)	46/326 (14%) and 121/368 (33%)
Gelb et al. [39]	311/742 (42%)	–
Gelb et al. [40]	71/200 (36%)	–
Goodfriend [31]	24/168 (14%)	–
Hankey [41]	6/68 (9%)	–
Koskinen et al. [42]	9/47 (19%)	–
Myrhaug [32]	436/1,391 (31%)	–
Parker et al. [9] and Chole et al. [28]	199/338 (59%)	45/326 (14%) and 118/365 (33%)
Rubinstein et al. [43]	93/376 (25%)	–
Tuz et al. [10]	91/200 (46%)	13/50 (26%)
Upton et al. [44]	72/989 (7%)	–
Wedel et al. [45]	8/350 (2%)	–
Wright et al. [46]	101/267 (38%)	–

Table 29.2 Studies reporting TMD in patients with tinnitus as the main complaint

| Source | Prevalence of TMD, no (%) | |
	Patients with tinnitus	General population
Bernhardt et al. [47]	18/30 (60%) >2 TMD symptoms	697/1,907(37%)
Bosel et al. [17]	129/340 (38%)	–
Kempf et al. [48]	110/138[a] (80%)	–
Linsen et al. [49]	17/22 (77%)	–
Morgan [23]	19/20 (95%)	–
Peroz [13]	TMJ sounds 9/40 (23%)	1/35 (3%)
	Muscle tenderness 27/40 (93%)	8/35 (23%)
	Bruxism 25/40 (63%)	13/35 (37%)
Rubinstein et al. [43]	47/102 (46%)	–
Tullberg et al. [50]	101/120 (84%)	–
Upton et al. [44]	72/989 (7%)	–
Vernon et al. [18]	69/1,002 (7%)	–

[a]Patients with inner ear dysfunction

symptoms and clinical findings. Therefore, epidemiological studies on TMD (as well as on tinnitus) should not be compared without restrictions. Nevertheless, the simultaneous occurrence of tinnitus and TMD has led to the assumption that there may be a relationship between the two conditions. The initial claim relating tinnitus symptoms, temporomandibular joint, and masticatory muscle disorders was made by Costen in 1934, who described a syndrome of ear and sinus symptoms relating to disturbed TMJ function [2]. Although Costen's structural and mechanical theories on the correlation of TMD and tinnitus have now been discarded, his considerations started numerous scientific efforts to reveal the linkage between both symptoms [13–16]. At this point, many questions on this topic remain unexplained. We still do not know whether ear symptoms (such as tinnitus and TMD) are coexistent, independent, or unrelated [8, 17–22] or whether both diseases have a causal connection [23–30]. Since TMD and tinnitus occur frequently in humans, their coincidence may not mean these two diseases have common causes or common risk factors. Authors reporting causal associations between tinnitus and TMD have based their conclusions mainly on clinical, epidemiological, anatomical, and histological investigations [23–27].

For example, the simultaneous occurrence of bruxism (grinding of teeth) as a symptom of TMD and tinnitus may be explained by two different ways: patients with bruxism (TMD as a main complaint, shifting therapeutic responsibilities toward dentists) generate tinnitus symptoms through overloading their masticatory muscles and the temporomandibular joint or patients with tinnitus (tinnitus as a main complaint, shifting

therapeutic responsibilities toward otorhinolaryngologists, audiologists, psychiatrists, etc.) process ear symptoms through grinding their teeth nightly. In addition to these causal explanations, these symptoms may occur without any causal relationship, or the presence of a third "disease" such as mental pressure, physic stress, or specific medication can act as a shared reason or a collective trigger causing TMD and tinnitus as secondary complaints [9, 19, 20]. Parker and Chole assumed that the relationship between TMD and tinnitus may be that both are responses to emotional stress [9]. However, attempts to find such a specific collective trigger for tinnitus and TMD symptoms remain speculative [21]. TMD-related tinnitus has been classified as objective tinnitus in most studies [26, 31, 32]. In contrast, Shulman and co-workers considered TMD-related tinnitus as subjective idiopathic tinnitus that was thought to directly or indirectly extend from a temporomandibular joint dysfunction on the auditory system [33, 34].

Besides epidemiological studies on TMD-related tinnitus and the steric adjacency of the *Porus acusticus* and the TMJ, a causal relationship between both symptoms has been observed. Ren and Isberg, for example, stated that in 53 patients with unilateral tinnitus and anterior disk displacement, disk displacement was found to be present in the ipsilateral joints in all patients, whereas the contralateral joint was asymptomatic in 50 patients (94%) [27]. In some patients, the intensity and quality of tinnitus can be altered (in most cases an enhancement) by mandibular movements, by pressure applied to the TMJ, or by biting [3, 13, 18, 24]. These alterations may indicate that increased activity of the masticatory muscles or pressure on the TMJ increases or even causes the perception of tinnitus, which in turn corroborates the theory that TMD is the causal trigger of tinnitus [3]. Nevertheless, up to now, no conclusive explanation exists for this phenomenon. It should be mentioned that some authors could not find any epidemiological correlation between TMD and tinnitus symptoms [8, 18, 22]. It should also be mentioned that the innervations of the TMJ and adjacent tissue project to cells in the upper part of the spinal cord and the trigeminal nucleus, which in turn project to cochlear nucleus (see Chaps. 8 and 9). This may explain why some individuals with TMD also have tinnitus.

From a dental perspective, tinnitus is possibly a secondary complaint of TMD or vice versa. Therefore, evaluation of possible involvement of the TMJ and masticatory muscle disorders seems feasible in all patients with tinnitus, as well as using TMD therapy in patients with TMD symptoms (TMD-related tinnitus). In contrast, TMD therapy in patients with tinnitus but without any signs of TMD is not based on scientific evidence.

References

1. Møller, AR, Tinnitus: presence and future. Prog Brain Res, 2007;166:3–16
2. Costen, JB, A syndrome of ear and sinus symptoms dependent upon disturbed function of the temporomandibular joint. 1934. Ann Otol Rhinol Laryngol, 1997;106:805–819
3. Rubinstein, B, Tinnitus and craniomandibular disorders – is there a link? Swed Dent J Suppl, 1993;95:1–46
4. Bell, WE (1990) Temporomandibular disorders: classification, diagnosis and managment. Yearbook Medical Publishers: Chicago
5. McNeill, C, Mohl, ND, Rugh, JD, Tanaka, TT, Temporomandibular disorders: diagnosis, management, education, and research. J Am Dent Assoc, 1990;120:253–257
6. Zarb, GA, Carlsson, GE, Sessle, BJ, Mohl, ND (1994) Temporomandibular joint and masticatory muscle disorders. Munksgaard: Copenhagen
7. Nielsen, IL, Ogro, J, McNeill, C, Danzig, WN, Goldman, SM, Miller, AJ, Alteration in proprioceptive reflex control in subjects with craniomandibular disorders. J Craniomandib Disord, 1987;1:170–178
8. Bush, FM, Tinnitus and otalgia in temporomandibular disorders. J Prosthet Dent, 1987;58:495–498
9. Parker, WZ, Chole, RA, Tinnitus, vertigo, and temporomandibular disorders. Am J Orthod Dentofacial Orthop, 1995;107:153–158
10. Tuz, HH, Onder, EM, Kisnisci, RS, Prevalence of otologic complaints in patients with temporomandibular disorder. Am J Orthod Dentofacial Orthop, 2003;123:620–623
11. Luz, JG, Maragno, IC, Martin, MC, Characteristics of chief complaints of patients with temporomandibular disorders in a Brazilian population. J Oral Rehabil, 1997;24:240–243
12. Helkimo, M (1979) Epidemiological surveys of dysfunction of the masticatory system, in Temporomandibular joint function and dysfunction, GA Zarb, GE Carlsson, Editors, Munksgaard: Copenhagen, 175–192
13. Peroz, I, Dysfunctions of the stomatognathic system in tinnitus patients compared to controls. HNO, 2003;51:544–549
14. Sicher, H, Temporomandibular articulation in mandibular overclosure. J Am Dent Assoc, 1948;36:131–139
15. Sicher, H, Structural and functional basis for disorders of the temporomandibular articulation. J Oral Surg (Chic), 1955;13:275–279
16. Shapiro, HH, Truex, RC, The temporomandibular joint and the auditory function. J Am Dent Assoc, 1943;30: 1147–1168
17. Bosel, C, Mazurek, B, Haupt, H, Peroz, I, [Chronic tinnitus and craniomandibular disorders Effectiveness of functional therapy on perceived tinnitus distress]. HNO, 2008;56:707–713
18. Vernon, J, Griest, S, Press, L, Attributes of tinnitus that may predict temporomandibular joint dysfunction. Cranio, 1992;10:282–287
19. Brookes, GB, Maw, AR, Coleman, MJ, 'Costen's syndrome' – correlation or coincidence: a review of 45 patients with temporomandibular joint dysfunction, otalgia and other aural symptoms. Clin Otolaryngol Allied Sci, 1980;5:23–36
20. Laskin, DM, Block, S, Diagnosis and treatment of myofacial pain-dysfunction (MPD) syndrome. J Prosthet Dent, 1986; 56:75–84
21. Turp, JC, Correlation between myoarthropathies of the masticatory system and ear symptoms (otalgia, tinnitus). HNO, 1998;46:303–310
22. Moss, RA, Sult, SC, Garrett, JC, Questionnaire evaluation of craniomandibular pain factors among college students. J Craniomandibular Pract, 1984;2:364–368
23. Morgan, DH, Tinnitus of TMJ origin: a preliminary report. Cranio, 1992;10:124–129
24. Rubinstein, B, Axelsson, A, Carlsson, GE, Prevalence of signs and symptoms of craniomandibular disorders in tinnitus patients. J Craniomandib Disord, 1990;4:186–192
25. Pinto, OF, A new structure related to the temporomandibular joint and middle ear. J Prosthet Dent, 1962;12:95–105
26. Arlen, H, The otomandibular syndrome: a new concept. Ear Nose Throat J, 1977;56:60–62
27. Ren, YF, Isberg A, Tinnitus in patients with temporomandibular joint internal derangement. Cranio, 1995;13:75–80
28. Chole, RA, Parker, WS, Tinnitus and vertigo in patients with temporomandibular disorder. Arch Otolaryngol Head Neck Surg, 1992;118:817–821
29. Lam, DK, Lawrence, HP, Tenenbaum, HC, Aural symptoms in temporomandibular disorder patients attending a craniofacial pain unit. J Orofac Pain, 2001;15:146–157
30. Ciancaglini, R, Loreti, P, Radaelli, G, Ear, nose, and throat symptoms in patients with TMD: the association of symptoms according to severity of arthropathy. J Orofac Pain, 1994;8:293–297
31. Goodfriend, DJ, Deafness, tinnitus, vertigo and neuralgia. Arch Otolaryngol, 1947;46:1–35
32. Myrhaug, H, The incidence of ear symptoms in cases of malocclusion and temporo-mandibular joint disturbances. Br J Oral Surg, 1964;2:28–32

33. Shulman, A, Clinical classification of subjective idiopathic tinnitus. J Laryngol Otol Suppl, 1981;(4):102–106

34. Shulman, A, Subjective idiopathic tinnitus: a review. J Laryngol Otol Suppl, 1981;(4):1–9

35. Bernstein, JM, Mohl, ND, Spiller, H, Temporomandibular joint dysfunction masquerading as disease of ear, nose, and throat. Trans Am Acad Ophthalmol Otolaryngol, 1969;73:208–217

36. Camparis, CM, Formigoni, G, Teixeira, MJ, de Siqueira, JT, Clinical evaluation of tinnitus in patients with sleep bruxism: prevalence and characteristics. J Oral Rehabil, 2005;32:808–814

37. Cooper, BC, Alleva, M, Cooper, DL, Lucente, FE, Myofacial pain dysfunction: analysis of 476 patients. Laryngoscope, 1986;96:1099–1106

38. Dolowitz DA, Ward JW, Fingerle CO, Smith CC, The role of muscular incoordination in the pathogenesis of the temporomandibular joint syndrome. Trans Am Laryngol Rhinol Otol Soc, 1964;44:253–255

39. Gelb, H, Calderone, JP, Gross, SM, Kantor, ME, The role of the dentist and the otolaryngologist in evaluating temporomandibular joint syndromes. J Prosthet Dent, 1967;18:497–503

40. Gelb, H, Bernstein, I, Clinical evaluation of two hundred patients with temporomandibular joint syndrome. J Prosthet Dent, 1983;49:234–243

41. Hankey, GT, Painful disorders of the temporomandibular joint. Proc R Soc Med, 1962;55:787–792

42. Koskinen, J, Paavolainen, M, Raivio, M, Roschier, J, Otological manifestations in temporomandibular joint dysfunction. J Oral Rehabil, 1980;7:249–254

43. Rubinstein, B, Carlsson, GE, Effects of stomatognathic treatment on tinnitus: a retrospective study. Cranio, 1987; 5:254–259

44. Upton, LG, Wijeyesakere, SJ, The incidence of tinnitus in people with disorders of the temporomandibular joint. Int Tinnitus J, 2004;10:174–176

45. Wedel, A, Carlsson, GE, Factors influencing the outcome of treatment in patients referred to a temporomandibular joint clinic. J Prosthet Dent, 1985;54:420–426

46. Wright, EF, Bifano, SL, The relationship between Tinnitus and Temporomandibular Disorder (TMD) therapy. Int Tinnitus J, 1997;3:55–61

47. Bernhardt, O, Gesch, D, Schwahn, C, Bitter, K, Mundt, T, Mack, F, Kocher, T, Meyer, G, Hensel, E, John, U, Signs of temporomandibular disorders in tinnitus patients and in a population-based group of volunteers: results of the Study of Health in Pomerania. J Oral Rehabil, 2004;31: 311–348

48. Kempf, HG, Roller, R, Muhlbradt, L, Correlation between inner ear disorders and temporomandibular joint diseases. HNO, 1993;41:7–10

49. Linsen, S, Schmidt-Beer, U, Koeck, B, Tinnitus-Verbesserung durch Kiefergelenk-Distraktions-Therapie. Dtsch Zahnarztl Z, 2006;61:27–31

50. Tullberg, M, Ernberg, M, Long-term effect on tinnitus by treatment of temporomandibular disorders: a two-year follow-up by questionnaire. Acta Odontol Scand, 2006;64: 89–96

Chapter 30
The Pharmacologist

Ana Belén Elgoyhen and Carla Vanina Rothlin

Keypoints

1. One in 10 adults has subjective tinnitus, and for 1 in 100 adults, tinnitus severely affects their quality of life.
2. Despite the significant unmet clinical need for a safe and effective drug targeting tinnitus relief, there is currently not a single FDA-approved drug on the market.
3. Since in some individuals, tinnitus causes irritability, agitation, stress, depression, insomnia, and interferes with normal life, even a drug that produces a small but significant effect would have a huge therapeutic impact.
4. A glimpse of hope is appearing in the near future, as some pharmaceutical industries now have compounds targeting tinnitus in their pipeline.
5. If these compounds finally reach the market, they will set a new era that will revolutionize the treatment of tinnitus.

Keywords Tinnitus • Phantom sound • Animal models • Lead compounds • Drug discovery

Tinnitus: A Clinical Unmet Need

Despite the significant unmet clinical need for a safe and effective drug targeting tinnitus relief, there is currently not a single FDA-approved drug on the market. For the majority of tinnitus sufferers who seek medical advice, the treatment goals are aimed at symptomatic relief (i.e. reduce or eliminate the tinnitus that is referred to as inside the head and/or ears). Symptomatic treatment is usually justified, because serious underlying pathologies are rare (see Sect. 30.2). Over four million prescriptions are written each year for tinnitus relief in Europe and the US, but these are all off-label prescriptions from a wide variety of therapeutic drugs, many of which are associated with considerable side effects or are ineffective in relieving tinnitus. There is, therefore, a large need for an effective drug therapy targeted at tinnitus, with minimal side effects compared to current medications prescribed off-label. Since in some individuals, tinnitus causes irritability, agitation, stress, depression, insomnia, and interferes with normal life, even a drug that produces a small but significant effect would have a huge therapeutic impact. However, disappearance of tinnitus should be the ultimate goal.

Tinnitus can be Pharmacologically Targeted

While the initial lesion might affect the peripheral organ of the auditory system, the neural correlate of the perceived sound is most likely in the central auditory circuitry [1] and there is growing evidence that changes in neuronal activity in different parts of the auditory pathway, including the dorsal cochlear nucleus, inferior colliculus, thalamus, and/or auditory cortex may be involved in tinnitus pathology [2–9]. Neuronal excitability can be modulated by different neurotransmitters, neuromodulators, and voltage-gated channel acting compounds [10–14], so there is no reason to believe that activity-driven changes underlying

A.B. Elgoyhen (✉)
Instituto de Investigaciones en Ingeniería Genética y Biología Molecular, Consejo Nacional de Investigaciones Científicas y Técnicas, Buenos Aires 1428, Argentina
and
Departamento de Farmacología, Facultad de Medicina, Universidad de Buenos Aires, Buenos Aires 1121, Argentina
e-mail: elgoyhen@dna.uba.ar

A.R. Møller et al. (eds.), *Textbook of Tinnitus*,
DOI 10.1007/978-1-60761-145-5_30, © Springer Science+Business Media, LLC 2011

tinnitus cannot be pharmacologically targeted. The fact that a local anesthetic, the voltage-gated sodium channel blocker lidocaine [15], given intravenously, leads to the temporary disappearance of tinnitus or a major change in the nature of the tinnitus in 70% of patients [16–22], indicates that Pharmacologic agents can have beneficial effects on many forms of tinnitus.

Challenges Toward Developing a Tinnitus Drug

The quest for effective tinnitus therapies faces significant challenges. First, tinnitus is only a symptom that might be the manifest of different underlying pathologies. Differential diagnosis of triggering events and temporal onset should allow for a more rational and effective pharmacological approach. Therefore, the careful classification of tinnitus patients together with the search for drugs that can successfully target each underlying pathology becomes a priority. Moreover, the current limited understanding of the neural substrates of tinnitus, together with the lack of adequate animal models that can faithfully recapitulate its pathology, hampers the screen for new molecules in preclinical studies. Finally, because the first tinnitus drugs are yet to be approved, regulatory agencies such as the Food and Drug Administration (FDA) or the European Medicines Agency (EMEA) lack standardized protocols for their approval process. The often considerable placebo effect is another obstacle in selecting new substances for tinnitus treatment.

Many pharmacological agents have been used off-label to treat individuals with tinnitus. These include anticonvulsants, anxiolytic, antidepressants, NMDA antagonists, cholinergic antagonists, antihistamines, vasodilators, and antipsychotics, to name a few (see Chap. 78) [23, 24]. Some drugs have been reported to provide moderate relief of symptoms in a subset of patients. Careful clinical observations along with data from clinical trials have provided useful clues for deciding on a rational course of drug therapy for selected patients. However, most drugs have not proven sufficient effectiveness in randomized controlled clinical trials in order to be marketed specifically for tinnitus, highlighting the importance of selectively targeting the underlying pathological cause of tinnitus.

The first step toward designing a successful strategy in the search for tinnitus drugs would most likely include finding criteria by which to stratify tinnitus patients included in trials. As previously discussed, tinnitus often occurs as a result of insults to the ear, such as from noise exposure or administration of specific pharmacologic agents. It can also be caused by ear or head injuries, some diseases of the ear, and ear infections [1, 25]. In some cases, the causative agent remains unknown. Therefore, the identification of the triggering cause should aid in selecting the most adequate pharmacological approaches. In addition, tinnitus sounds can take a variety of forms, such as buzzing, ringing, whistling, hissing, or a range of other sounds. It can be a benign sound that is heard only occasionally or it can be devastating roars that occur 24 h a day, which prevent its sufferers from sleep or the ability to do intellectual work. All degrees of subjective tinnitus occur in between these extremes. Tinnitus is also often associated with other symptoms, such as hyperacusis and distortion of sounds [25]. Affective disorders, such as anxiety, phonophobia, and depression, often accompany severe tinnitus, and that form of tinnitus can lead to suicide. With such differences in etiology and symptoms, heterogeneity within tinnitus patients is expected. Thus, the tinnitus drug discovery endeavor faces the "one drug won´t fit all" situation. The fact that a subgroup of patients who have intermittent tinnitus that sounds like a typewriter, popcorn, or ear clicking receives significant benefit from carbamazepine [26, 27] indicates that "subtyping" tinnitus is highly needed for successful treatment. Efforts toward establishing subgroups of tinnitus are under way [28] and will most likely aid the selection of patients in future clinical trials.

An additional challenge in the design of drugs for the treatment of tinnitus derives from the fact that the neural substrates underlying tinnitus are far from being fully understood. An increase in spontaneous firing rates or neuronal synchrony in different parts of the auditory pathway as well as changes in cortical tonotopy have been proposed as potential correlates of tinnitus [1, 29]. Modern drug discovery is mostly centered on the identification of new lead molecules that interact with discrete molecular targets. This is a reductionistic approach that mainly focuses on sites of drug action. Although it has been useful in developing molecules such as statins (inhibitors of HMG CoA reductase) and HIV protease inhibitors [30], central nervous system acting drugs owe their clinical effectiveness to actions at multiple molecular targets [31]. Thus, this reductionistic approach is most likely inadequate for a central nervous system disorder such as tinnitus.

Although a well-defined neuronal target would ease the path toward drug discovery, the empirical approach that has been used for most central nervous system disorders should not be precluded in the case of tinnitus. The importance of this approach in central nervous system drug discovery can be appreciated in the case of morphine and barbiturates, whose mechanisms of action were unknown when these drugs were introduced for human use [30]. In fact, most central nervous system acting drugs were discovered serendipitously. Thus, for example, valproic acid was used as an organic solvent in research laboratories for eight decades, until the observation of action against pentylenetetrazol-induced convulsions in rodents was made [32]; chlorpromazine was used to enhance recovery from surgical anesthesia before it was found to alleviate some symptoms of schizophrenia [33]; gabapentin was first developed as an anticonvulsant and is now used for treating neuropathic pain [34]. Thus, following these past experiences with central nervous system acting drugs, the search for drugs to alleviate tinnitus should not wait until the neural correlates are identified.

Before a compound is judged suitable for testing in humans, it must first demonstrate safety and efficacy in animal models. A drawback in the development of a tinnitus drug is the lack of validated animal models in which to test or screen for compounds. The basic dilemma faced by the animal researcher who wants to study tinnitus is whether or not the animals have the disorder. The experimenter has to find a way by which a rodent tells him about the ringing in its head. Several animal models are being developed, which are based either on noise exposure or on the administration of salicylate (see Chap. 16 and [35–37]). An additional challenge is imposed by the fact that, in humans, tinnitus is accompanied by the activation of a distress network that involves the limbic system [38–40]. This is probably not recapitulated in the animal models. However, animal models that have been developed for complex central nervous diseases such as depression or schizophrenia do not completely recapitulate the disease itself. Moreover, they are only of limited value for predicting treatment efficacy in humans [41]. However, in spite of all these drawbacks, these animal models have proven useful. In addition, in psychiatric

diseases, empiric pharmacology has driven science. Thus, the serendipitous observation that central nervous system acting drugs like chlorpromazine calmed inmates of a psychiatric asylum has given way to the dopamine theory of schizophrenia and to the serotonin theory of depression and anxiety [41, 42]. These theories remain the pillars of the animal models used for preclinical validation, in spite of the fact that there is more to the major psychoses than alterations in these two neurotransmitter systems. Thus, the search for drugs to treat tinnitus should not wait for the refinement of the animal models. Moreover, the identification of compounds that alleviate tinnitus would not only lead to a better treatment but would also serve as a possible starting point for the understanding of the neural correlates of this condition, and thereof for the generation of better animal models, which target these neural substrates.

Finally, since no drug having tinnitus as its primary indication has been approved so far, there are no standardized protocols for the approval of a tinnitus drug by regulatory agencies like the FDA and EMEA. Therefore, the first pharmaceutical industry to develop a tinnitus drug will have to pave the way. In addition, tinnitus being a subjective phenomenon, assessment of outcome is probably the single most important factor in conducting a clinical trial. Widespread recognition that consistency between research centers in the ways that patients with tinnitus are assessed and how outcomes following interventions are measured would facilitate more effective co-operation and more meaningful evaluations. At the first Tinnitus Research Initiative meeting held in Regensburg in July 2006, which gathered worldwide tinnitus experts, an attempt was made to establish a consensus both for patient assessments and for outcome measurements [43].

Tinnitus and the Pharmaceutical Industry

Pharmaceutical companies are aware of the fact that there is a large market for a drug indicated for tinnitus relief. Evidence for this exists in the scores of patents that have been filed worldwide on potential drugs that may offer relief. Furthermore, tinnitus can be found attached to long lists of indications in many more patents filed on molecules aimed at a range of diverse therapeutic classes. As indicated above, in spite of the fact that there is a significant unmet clinical need for a safe and effective drug targeting tinnitus relief, there is no FDA-approved drug currently on the market. The Royal National Institute for Deaf People, in the UK, estimates that a novel tinnitus drug could have a product value of US $689 million in its first year of launch [44]. However, there are very few pharmaceutical and/ or biotechnology companies with tinnitus compounds in their R&D pipeline. A search carried out in the investigational drug databases Pharmaprojects (http:// www.pharmaprojects.com), AdisInsight (http://www. adisinsight.com), Prous DDR (http://www.prous.com), and IDdb3 (http://science.thomsonreuters.com) shows that the following companies are developing a compound for tinnitus: Epicept, a lidocaine patch at phase II; Sound Pharmaceuticals, ebselen, a glutathione peroxidase mimetic and inducer at phase II; Auris Medical, AM101, an NMDA receptor antagonist, at phase II; Ipsen, a ginkgo biloba extract, at phase I; Merz, neramexane, an NMDA antagonist and an $\alpha9$ $\alpha10$ nicotinic cholinergic receptor blocker [45], at phase III; and GSK, vestipitant, a neurokinin 1 receptor antagonist [46], at phase II.

From the above, it can be concluded that there are a few companies with tinnitus compounds in their pipelines in spite of the existence of such a huge market for this clinically unmet need. This most likely derives from the existing challenges described in the previous section. The lack of serendipitous discoveries of effective treatments for tinnitus has severely limited insight into disease pathology, which is often gained by such fortuitous pharmacological findings. It is the absence of a fully determined mechanism for tinnitus that makes research into this area potentially very high risk. However, if any of the above compounds reaches the market, they will set a turning point both in the treatment of tinnitus as well as in the development of future compounds.

Potential Pharmacological Targets

The search for drugs that target tinnitus is hampered by the lack of a deep knowledge of the underlying neural substrates of this pathology. Initially considered an inner ear pathology, it is now clear that at least chronic tinnitus is a central nervous system disorder. As indicated above, changes in cortical tonotopy, as well as

increase in spontaneous firing rates and neuronal synchrony in different parts of the auditory pathway, have been proposed as potential correlates of tinnitus [1, 29].

After noise trauma induced hearing loss, one of the main causes leading to tinnitus, changes in tonotopic organization in the cortex are observed. Cortical neurons with characteristic frequencies in the frequency region of the hearing loss no longer respond according to their place in the tonotopic map, but reflect instead the frequency tuning of their less affected neighbors [47–49]. Magnetic source imaging studies confirm this reorganization in human patients [50]. This suggests that reorganization of the cortical tonotopic map and tinnitus are correlated. Interestingly, providing an acoustically enriched environment spectrally matching the hearing loss prevents this reorganization [51, 52]. Thus, preventing neuronal reorganization by an acoustically rich environment might become a treatment strategy to prevent the establishment of the long-term plastic changes that follow exposure to noise trauma. However, most clinicians are faced with the problem of treating tinnitus patients when tinnitus is most likely a chronic condition in which tonotopic rearrangements along the auditory pathway are already established. Can established tonotopic rearrangements in the auditory cortex be reversed? Experiments in laboratory animals that combine sound exposure with electric stimulation of certain neuronal pathways/circuits show promising results. In the primary auditory cortex, dopamine release has been observed during auditory learning that remodels the sound frequency representations [53]. The stimulation of dopaminergic neurons in the ventral tegmental area of rats, together with an auditory stimulus of a particular tone, increases the cortical area and selectivity of the neural responses to that sound stimulus in the primary auditory cortex while it decreases the representations of nearby sound frequencies [54]. In addition, episodic electrical stimulation of the nucleus basalis of rats, paired with an auditory stimulus, results in a massive progressive reorganization of the primary auditory cortex in the adult rat. Receptive field sizes can be narrowed, broadened, or left unaltered depending on specific parameters of the acoustic stimulus paired with nucleus basalis activation [55]. The nucleus basalis contains both cholinergic and gabaergic neurons [56, 57]. Thus, taken together, these results indicate that sound therapy coupled with drugs that can modulate the neurotransmission of the pathways/circuits involved in the described plastic events would be an interesting avenue to investigate.

Additional neural correlates of tinnitus include neuronal spontaneous hyperactivity in the reorganized region and increased neural synchrony [48, 52, 58]. Neuronal hyperactivity can be modulated by many multiple drugs that target either voltage-gated ion channels or neurotransmitter receptors. However, examples of such drugs like benzodiazepines, anticonvulsants, NMDA antagonists, and calcium antagonists, although effective in some patients, have not proven effective in double-blind placebo-controlled clinical trials [23]. Recently, in a preliminary report using a rat behavioral model, the potassium channel modulator Maxipost (BMS-204352) reduced behavioral evidence of salicylate-induced tinnitus in a dose-dependent manner [59]. This compound is a KCa1.1 (BK) and a Kv7 positive modulator [60, 61]. Since potassium ion channels play an important role in regulating the resting potential and spontaneous and evoked neural activity, potassium channel modulators represent potential important compounds for tinnitus therapy.

The above are only some few challenging ideas concerning ways to revert altered neuronal activity, synchrony, and tonotopy observed in the auditory pathway in tinnitus. However, it is a reductionistic approach, since it only takes into account changes observed in the auditory pathway. As has been shown in the somatosensory system, auditory cortex activation is essential, but probably not sufficient for auditory conscious perception [62, 63]. Moreover, for most patients, tinnitus is more than mere changes in the auditory pathway and implicates the activation of a distress network [38–40]. This brings us back to the notion that central nervous system acting drugs, in particular, owe their clinical utility to actions at multiple molecular targets [31]. This is most likely the scenario we are facing in the search of a drug to alleviate tinnitus.

The Time is Right

For many years, the standard of care for dealing with tinnitus patients has been, "You need to learn to live with it." Although we are far away from fully understanding tinnitus, the chances for a solution are much brighter than they were a decade ago. The development of behavioral measures of tinnitus in animals combined with physiological, biochemical, molecular, and imaging techniques are likely to provide important insights into the underlying causes of tinnitus. Tinnitus animal models will provide a way to screen for drugs that can suppress the disorder. The potential market for an FDA-approved drug to treat tinnitus is huge. Several existing drugs have been reported to provide significant relief from tinnitus in subsets of patients. Looking toward an exciting future, patients and clinicians may finally receive encouraging news if the compounds under development by several pharmaceutical industries finally reach the market. If they do, they will set a new era that will revolutionize the treatment of tinnitus.

Acknlowledgments Ana Belén Elgoyhen is supported by an International Research Scholar Grant from the Howard Hughes Medical Institute, a Research Grant from ANPCyT (Argentina), the University of Buenos Aires (Argentina), and the Tinnitus Research Initiative.

References

1. Eggermont JJ (2007) Pathophysiology of tinnitus. Prog Brain Res 166:19–35.
2. Eggermont JJ (2008) Role of auditory cortex in noise- and drug-induced tinnitus. Am J Audiol 17:S162–9.
3. Kaltenbach JA and DA Godfrey (2008) Dorsal cochlear nucleus hyperactivity and tinnitus: are they related? Am J Audiol 17:S148–61.
4. Bauer CA, JG Turner, DM Caspary et al (2008) Tinnitus and inferior colliculus activity in chinchillas related to three distinct patterns of cochlear trauma. J Neurosci Res 86:2564–78.
5. Lanting CP, E De Kleine, H Bartels et al (2008) Functional imaging of unilateral tinnitus using fMRI. Acta Otolaryngol 128:415–21.
6. Reyes SA, RJ Salvi, RF Burkard et al (2002) Brain imaging of the effects of lidocaine on tinnitus. Hear Res 171:43–50.
7. Melcher JR, IS Sigalovsky, JJ Guinan, Jr. et al (2000) Lateralized tinnitus studied with functional magnetic resonance imaging: abnormal inferior colliculus activation. J Neurophysiol 83:1058–72.
8. Schlee W, T Hartmann, B Langguth et al (2009) Abnormal resting-state cortical coupling in chronic tinnitus. BMC Neurosci 10:11.
9. Smits M, S Kovacs, D de Ridder et al (2007) Lateralization of functional magnetic resonance imaging (fMRI) activation in the auditory pathway of patients with lateralized tinnitus. Neuroradiology 49:669–79.
10. Lambert RC, T Bessaih and N Leresche (2006) Modulation of neuronal T-type calcium channels. CNS Neurol Disord Drug Targets 5:611–27.
11. Surmeier DJ, J Ding, M Day et al (2007) D1 and D2 dopamine-receptor modulation of striatal glutamatergic signaling in striatal medium spiny neurons. Trends Neurosci 30:228–35.

12. Wonnacott S, J Barik, J Dickinson et al (2006) Nicotinic receptors modulate transmitter cross talk in the CNS: nicotinic modulation of transmitters. J Mol Neurosci 30:137–40.

13. Slassi A, M Isaac, L Edwards et al (2005) Recent advances in non-competitive mGlu5 receptor antagonists and their potential therapeutic applications. Curr Top Med Chem 5:897–911.

14. Blank T, I Nijholt, MJ Kye et al (2004) Small conductance Ca2+-activated K+channels as targets of CNS drug development. Curr Drug Targets CNS Neurol Disord 3:161–7.

15. Muroi Y and B Chanda (2009) Local anesthetics disrupt energetic coupling between the voltage-sensing segments of a sodium channel. J Gen Physiol 133:1–15.

16. Duckert LG and TS Rees (1983) Treatment of tinnitus with intravenous lidocaine: a double-blind randomized trial. Otolaryngol Head Neck Surg 91:550–5.

17. Israel JM, JS Connelly, ST McTigue et al (1982) Lidocaine in the treatment of tinnitus aurium. A double-blind study. Arch Otolaryngol 108:471–3.

18. Kalcioglu MT, T Bayindir, T Erdem et al (2005) Objective evaluation of the effects of intravenous lidocaine on tinnitus. Hear Res 199:81–8.

19. Lenarz T (1986) Treatment of tinnitus with lidocaine and tocainide. Scand Audiol Suppl 26:49–51.

20. Melding PS, RJ Goodey and PR Thorne (1978) The use of intravenous lignocaine in the diagnosis and treatment of tinnitus. J Laryngol Otol 92:115–21.

21. Merchant SN and N Merchant (1985) Intravenous lignocaine in tinnitus. J Postgrad Med 31:80–2.

22. Trellakis S, J Lautermann and G Lehnerdt (2007) Lidocaine: neurobiological targets and effects on the auditory system. Prog Brain Res 166:303–22.

23. Darlington CL and PF Smith (2007) Drug treatments for tinnitus. Prog Brain Res 166:249–62.

24. Patterson MB and BJ Balough (2006) Review of pharmacological therapy for tinnitus. Int Tinnitus J 12:149–59.

25. Møller AR (2007) Tinnitus: presence and future. Prog Brain Res 166:3–16.

26. Levine RA (2006) Typewriter tinnitus: a carbamazepine-responsive syndrome related to auditory nerve vascular compression. ORL J Otorhinolaryngol Relat Spec 68:43–6; discussion 6–7.

27. Mardini MK (1987) Ear-clicking "tinnitus" responding to carbamazepine. N Engl J Med 317:1542.

28. Tyler R, C Coelho, P Tao et al (2008) Identifying tinnitus subgroups with cluster analysis. Am J Audiol 17:S176–84.

29. Eggermont JJ (2005) Tinnitus: neurobiological substrates. Drug Discov Today 10:1283–90.

30. Enna SJ and M Williams (2009) Challenges in the search for drugs to treat central nervous system disorders. J Pharmacol Exp Ther. 329: 404–11.

31. Spedding M, T Jay, J Costa e Silva et al (2005) A pathophysiological paradigm for the therapy of psychiatric disease. Nat Rev Drug Discov 4:467–76.

32. Henry TR (2003) The history of valproate in clinical neuroscience. Psychopharmacol Bull 37 Suppl 2:5–16.

33. Carpenter WT and JI Koenig (2008) The evolution of drug development in schizophrenia: past issues and future opportunities. Neuropsychopharmacology 33:2061–79.

34. Johannessen Landmark C (2008) Antiepileptic drugs in non-epilepsy disorders: relations between mechanisms of action and clinical efficacy. CNS Drugs 22:27–47.

35. Bauer CA (2003) Animal models of tinnitus. Otolaryngol Clin North Am 36:267–85.

36. Jastreboff PJ and JF Brennan (1994) Evaluating the loudness of phantom auditory perception (tinnitus) in rats. Audiology 33:202–17.

37. Turner JG (2007) Behavioral measures of tinnitus in laboratory animals. Prog Brain Res 166:147–56.

38. De Ridder D, H Fransen, O Francois et al (2006) Amygdalohippocampal involvement in tinnitus and auditory memory. Acta Otolaryngol Suppl 556:50–3.

39. Jastreboff PJ and MM Jastreboff (2006) Tinnitus retraining therapy: a different view on tinnitus. ORL J Otorhinolaryngol Relat Spec 68:23–9; discussion 9–30.

40. Bauer CA (2004) Mechanisms of tinnitus generation. Curr Opin Otolaryngol Head Neck Surg 12:413–7.

41. Hurko O and JL Ryan (2005) Translational research in central nervous system drug discovery. NeuroRx 2:671–82.

42. Frankenburg FR and RJ Baldessarini (2008) Neurosyphilis, malaria, and the discovery of antipsychotic agents. Harv Rev Psychiatry 16:299–307.

43. Langguth B, R Goodey, A Azevedo et al (2007) Consensus for tinnitus patient assessment and treatment outcome measurement: Tinnitus Research Initiative meeting, Regensburg, July 2006. Prog Brain Res 166:525–36.

44. Vio MM and RH Holme (2005) Hearing loss and tinnitus: 250 million people and a US$10 billion potential market. Drug Discov Today 10:1263–5.

45. Plazas PV, J Savino, S Kracun et al (2007) Inhibition of the alpha9alpha10 nicotinic cholinergic receptor by neramexane, an open channel blocker of N-methyl-D-aspartate receptors. Eur J Pharmacol 566:11–9.

46. Brocco M, A Dekeyne, C Mannoury la Cour et al (2008) Cellular and behavioural profile of the novel, selective neurokinin1 receptor antagonist, vestipitant: a comparison to other agents. Eur Neuropsychopharmacol 18:729–50.

47. Eggermont JJ and H Komiya (2000) Moderate noise trauma in juvenile cats results in profound cortical topographic map changes in adulthood. Hear Res 142:89-101.

48. Norena AJ and JJ Eggermont (2003) Changes in spontaneous neural activity immediately after an acoustic trauma: implications for neural correlates of tinnitus. Hear Res 183: 137–53.

49. Norena AJ, M Tomita and JJ Eggermont (2003) Neural changes in cat auditory cortex after a transient pure-tone trauma. J Neurophysiol 90:2387–401.

50. Muhlnickel W, T Elbert, E Taub et al (1998) Reorganization of auditory cortex in tinnitus. Proc Natl Acad Sci USA 95:10340–3.

51. Norena AJ and JJ Eggermont (2005) Enriched acoustic environment after noise trauma reduces hearing loss and prevents cortical map reorganization. J Neurosci 25:699–705.

52. Norena AJ and JJ Eggermont (2006) Enriched acoustic environment after noise trauma abolishes neural signs of tinnitus. Neuroreport 17:559–63.

53. Stark H and H Scheich (1997) Dopaminergic and serotonergic neurotransmission systems are differentially involved in auditory cortex learning: a long-term microdialysis study of metabolites. J Neurochem 68:691–7.

54. Bao S, VT Chan and MM Merzenich (2001) Cortical remodelling induced by activity of ventral tegmental dopamine neurons. Nature 412:79–83.

55. Kilgard MP and MM Merzenich (1998) Cortical map reorganization enabled by nucleus basalis activity. Science 279:1714–8.

56. Gritti I, L Mainville and BE Jones (1993) Codistribution of GABA- with acetylcholine-synthesizing neurons in the basal forebrain of the rat. J Comp Neurol 329:438–57.

57. Gritti I, L Mainville, M Mancia et al (1997) GABAergic and other noncholinergic basal forebrain neurons, together with cholinergic neurons, project to the mesocortex and isocortex in the rat. J Comp Neurol 383:163–77.

58. Seki S and JJ Eggermont (2003) Changes in spontaneous firing rate and neural synchrony in cat primary auditory cortex after localized tone-induced hearing loss. Hear Res 180:28–38.

59. Lobarinas E, W Dalby-Brown, D Stolzberg et al (2009) Effects of the BK Agonists BMS-204352 and the Enantiomeric Compound ("R-Enantiomer") on Transient, Salicylate Induced Tinnitus in Rats. Association for Research in Otolarygol Baltimore, MD.

60. Nardi A and SP Olesen (2008) BK channel modulators: a comprehensive overview. Curr Med Chem 15:1126–46.

61. Korsgaard MP, BP Hartz, WD Brown et al (2005) Anxiolytic effects of Maxipost (BMS-204352) and retigabine via activation of neuronal Kv7 channels. J Pharmacol Exp Ther 314:282–92.

62. de Lafuente V and R Romo (2005) Neuronal correlates of subjective sensory experience. Nat Neurosci 8:1698–703.

63. de Lafuente V and R Romo (2006) Neural correlate of subjective sensory experience gradually builds up across cortical areas. Proc Natl Acad Sci U S A 103:14266–71.

Chapter 31
The Neuroscientist

James A. Kaltenbach

Keypoints

1. This chapter reviews the current state of knowledge of tinnitus from the neuroscientist's perspective.
2. Tinnitus is viewed as a disorder involving changes in the rate and timing of spontaneous discharges at multiple levels of the auditory system.
3. Its mechanisms vary, depending on etiology, but most commonly the disorder stems from increases in the excitability of neurons in the central auditory system.
4. Most of the available data suggest that this increase is synaptic in origin, caused by shifts in the balance of excitatory and inhibitory inputs to neurons.
5. However, other mechanisms, such as shifts in the expression of ion channels that determine the resting membrane potential of neurons, may also play a contributing role.
6. Since these changes occur at multiple levels of the auditory system, it is likely that new therapies that will prove most effective will be those that take a system-wide approach rather than those that target specific generator sites.

Keywords Tinnitus • Dorsal cochlear nucleus • Plasticity • Excitotoxicity • Neurodegeneration • Inferior colliculus • Auditory cortex

Abbreviations

DCN   Dorsal cochlear nucleus
GABA   Gamma amino butyric acid
IC   Inferior colliculus
LTD   Long-term depression
LTP   Long-term potentiation
NMDA N-Methyl-D-aspartate
rTMS   Repetitive TMS
TMS   Transcranial magnetic stimulation

Introduction

Over the past 20 years, a great deal has been learned about tinnitus mechanisms from neuroimaging studies in humans and neurophysiological studies in animals. We now have substantial literature examining where and how activity in the auditory system is altered by tinnitus-inducing agents. Coupled with the growing number of behavioral studies demonstrating that animals develop tinnitus after exposure to various tinnitus-inducing agents, the available evidence provides us with compelling reasons to suspect that some of the reported changes in activity underlie the percepts of tinnitus. This chapter reviews the current state of knowledge of tinnitus from a neuroscientist's perspective.

Is Tinnitus Primarily a Peripheral or Central Problem?

The term "ringing of the ears" implies that tinnitus is largely a problem of the ear. However, we now have a considerable body of evidence that the major changes underlying tinnitus can occur peripherally or centrally. House and Brackman [1] found that tinnitus persisted in 62% of patients in whom input to the brain from the auditory nerve was surgically abolished. In many of

J.A. Kaltenbach (✉)
Department of Neurosciences, NE-63, Head and Neck Institute/
Lerner Research Institute, The Cleveland Clinic, 9500 Euclid
Avenue, Cleveland, OH 44195, USA
e-mail: kaltenj@ccf.org

A.R. Møller et al. (eds.), *Textbook of Tinnitus*,
DOI 10.1007/978-1-60761-145-5_31, © Springer Science+Business Media, LLC 2011

these patients, the post-surgical tinnitus was worse than the pre-surgery tinnitus. Other studies have reported that tinnitus develops secondarily following surgical removal of eighth-nerve tumors (vestibular Schwannoma) [1–3], a procedure that can lead to major impairment of the auditory nerve. These findings point to the central auditory system as an important source of tinnitus, although there is little doubt that tinnitus in most cases begins with trauma in the auditory periphery. Thus, although agents such as noise or aminoglycoside, which cause hearing loss, often also cause tinnitus (see Chaps. 37, 42), they either have a weak long-term effect on spontaneous activity in the auditory nerve or cause this peripheral activity to decrease [4–6].

At the same time, it is important to acknowledge that in 38% of House and Brackman's patients, tinnitus was abolished by eighth-nerve section. Although spontaneous activity is reduced following noise or amino-glycoside treatment, other alterations have been found in the auditory nerve, such as increase spontaneous bursting activity (see next section), which could potentially be tinnitus producing. Moreover, some studies suggest that sodium salicylate can cause increases in spontaneous activity and changes in the timing of spontaneous spikes in the auditory nerve that could generate tinnitus percepts [7–11]. Thus, it seems likely that some forms of tinnitus may originate peripherally, although, as discussed in the following section, most contemporary studies of tinnitus have focused on the central auditory system for the reasons given above.

Neurophysiological Correlates of Tinnitus

The most commonly reported effects of tinnitus-inducing agents on neurons in the auditory system are increases in spontaneous activity, bursting activity, and synchronous discharges. Chronic increases in spontaneous activity can be induced in the dorsal cochlear nucleus (DCN) [12–18], inferior colliculus (IC) [15, 19–26], and auditory cortex [27–31] using exposure or treatment conditions that have been shown in a variety of other studies to induce tinnitus in animals [17, 21, 32–39]. Increased spontaneous activity occurs in the IC and auditory cortex after salicylate treatment [40–45]. There is evidence for increased spontaneous activity in the DCN following treatment with cisplatin [44]

(see Chap. 16) and in the auditory cortex following treatment with quinine [46]. Both salicylate and quinine have also been shown to cause tinnitus in animals at doses known from other studies to cause increased spontaneous activity in the auditory system [47–49]. That the increase in activity is likely to be perceptually sound evoking is supported by the following:

1. The hyperactivity displays similar spatial and temporal distribution patterns as increases in activity evoked by tonal stimulation.
2. It is well established from electrophysiological studies that increases in activity are observed throughout the central auditory system during sound stimulation, so there can be little doubt that sound percepts are linked to increases in discharge rates.
3. Cochlear and central auditory prosthetics are based on the notion that auditory percepts can be evoked by stimuli designed to increase discharge rates of auditory neurons.
4. Increased activation has been observed in the IC and auditory cortex of individuals with tinnitus [50–59].
5. Stimulation of the somatosensory system via the trigeminal nucleus or cervical nerves modulates both spontaneous activity in central auditory centers [60–63] and tinnitus [64–67]. Taken together, these findings give strong support to the view that tinnitus is linked to changes in discharge rates in the central auditory system.

However, just increased discharge rates, per se, may not be the whole story. Noise exposure, and salicylate cause increases in a specific type of activity called bursting discharges in the auditory system. Chronic increases in bursting activity have been observed in the auditory nerve following noise exposure [6], in the DCN following noise exposure [14], and in the IC following salicylate and noise exposure [23, 41]. No increased bursting has been found in the auditory cortex following noise exposure, salicylate, or quinine [23, 46, 68, 69]. Increases in bursting activity, even if limited to the auditory brainstem, may be an important correlate of tinnitus. Bursts of spikes carry an important feature that is likely to signal the presence of sound, namely, periodicities, and brief clusters of spikes with nearly identical interspike intervals. Of these, periodicities in firing are critical to the ability of neurons to encode the frequency of sounds [70, 71]. If bursting is increased, then periodicities in a restricted frequency range would probably also be increased, and this could lead to perception of a tinnitus-like sound in a correspondingly restricted pitch range.

In addition to increased discharge rates and increased bursting activity, there is evidence for an increase in synchrony of discharges among neurons in the IC following noise exposure [23] and in the auditory cortex following noise or quinine administration [27, 30, 69]. Increased synchrony of auditory nerve fibers following salicylate treatment is suggested by increases in the amplitude of 200 and 900 Hz peaks in the frequency spectrum of ongoing ensemble activity [9–11]. This means that instead of impulses being more or less randomly related across the neural population, the impulses become increasingly coincident. This is sometimes referred to as temporal coherence (see Chaps. 12 and 13). Neurons showing increased synchrony occur in frequency bands of the hearing loss that are also the areas in which tonotopic map reorganization occurs. Increased synchrony has been hypothesized to be a neural correlate of tinnitus [72, 73] (see Chaps. 12 and 13). Pitch percepts corresponding to frequency regions with increased synchrony might be enhanced, leading to the often pitch-like percepts of tinnitus.

In summary, central auditory nuclei and cortical areas develop some of the types of changes following cochlear trauma that are also evoked by acoustic stimulation. Issues that will be addressed next are what the underlying triggers of changes in spontaneous activity might be as well as what mechanisms underlie their induction.

The Triggers of Tinnitus-Related Activity

The Role of Deafferentation

Tinnitus is often viewed as a deafferentation disorder triggered by loss of normal input from the auditory periphery. Evidence for a deafferentation mechanism of tinnitus comes from a wide range of clinical and experimental observations. Tinnitus is most commonly associated with hearing loss. Between 80 and 90% of tinnitus patients have an associated hearing loss [74] (see Chap. 5). Tinnitus can be induced by surgical damage to [75, 76] as well as compression or tumors of the eighth nerve [2, 3, 77, 78] (see Chap. 39). Tinnitus is also sometimes seen in association with

conductive hearing loss [79–81] (see Chap. 83). All these conditions involve impairment of peripheral auditory functions, so there is good reason from human observations alone to suspect that loss of peripheral function and peripheral input are key triggers of tinnitus. Animal models have also yielded evidence consistent with a deafferentation-induced mechanism of tinnitus. Tinnitus percepts in animals and tinnitus-related changes in activity in the IC have been found to be associated with loss of spiral ganglion cells [23]. The induction of tinnitus-related hyperactivity in the dorsal cochlear nucleus has been found to be correlated with loss of outer hair cells [45]. This is consistent with reports that tinnitus is often found to be associated with defects in outer hair cell function, as reflected by alterations of transient-evoked or distortion product otoacoustic emissions (see review of [82]). It has been hypothesized that loss of outer hair cells may induce hyperactivity in the dorsal cochlear nucleus by causing loss of peripheral input to the granule cell system [45]. This hypothesis builds on the facts that the granule cell domain in the cochlear nucleus receives input from type II spiral ganglion neurons, which originate from outer hair cells [83–85], and there is some evidence that granule cells are among the recipients of type II input [86]. Moreover, activation of granule cells influences the level of activity of the principal cells of the DCN, the likely generators of tinnitus signals [13, 41, 60, 87].

Deafferentation can also involve loss of input to auditory structures from non-auditory areas. This possibility is raised by the fact that many subjects with tinnitus possess disorders of other systems. For example, many cases of somatic tinnitus (such as that experienced by people who can change the loudness or pitch of their tinnitus by manipulations of head and neck musculature) occur in people with somatic pathologies of the head and neck, including craniofacial anomalies, temporomandibular joint disorders, or inflammatory conditions of the neck muscles [64, 65, 88]. Furthermore, Levine [65] found that in his patients with somatic tinnitus, when the tinnitus was monaural, it was usually on the same side as the somatic disorder. Lastly, an increasing number of articles suggest that tinnitus can be induced or exacerbated by emotional conditions such as stress and anxiety [89–91]. There are several levels of the auditory pathway where auditory centers receive input from non-auditory areas. The best described example, in terms of circuitry, is the dorsal cochlear nucleus, whose output is modulated by the cochlear granule cell system. This system receives input not only from auditory sources but also from cuneate and trigeminal nuclei and ganglion of the somatosensory system [61, 92–94] (see Chap. 9) and a variety of other pathways [87]. Since activation of the granule cell system is known to affect the level of spontaneous activity [13, 60, 95], conditions in which inputs from these areas are impaired or damaged could affect output of the dorsal cochlear nucleus via their effects on the granule cell system.

The Role of Plasticity

There are two general mechanisms by which deafferentation might induce tinnitus-related activity in the central auditory system by activating neural plasticity (see also Chaps. 12 and 13). The most frequently hypothesized mechanism is a shift in the balance of excitatory and inhibitory synaptic inputs to central target neurons toward the side of excitation. Such a shift could involve direct loss of inhibitory inputs (disinhibition) and/or an increase in excitatory inputs.

Several lines of evidence indicate that both a loss of inhibition and an increase in excitation occur centrally after loss of auditory nerve input and that such changes involve plasticity. First, loss of primary afferent input leads to loss of inhibitory influence in brainstem auditory nuclei, as signaled by reductions in glycinergic and GABAergic neurotransmission [96–104]; these reductions change over time, suggestive of a temporal or possibly homeostatic plasticity mechanism [105]. Second, there are suggestions of up-regulations of excitatory synapses – for example, cochlear ablation, noise exposure, and conductive hearing loss trigger up-regulations of cholinergic and glutamatergic systems in the central auditory systems [106–113]. Some of these adjustments vary over time. Third, degeneration of second-order neurons in the brain following noise exposure [114] is followed by regrowth of excitatory and inhibitory terminals, but a more complete return of excitatory than inhibitory synapses, indicating a reorganization of synaptic connections that favors excitation [115].

A second mechanism that could lead to tinnitus-related activity is an increase in excitability of neurons caused by alterations in their intrinsic membrane properties. Such alterations might involve up- or down-regulations of specific ion-conductance channels. Studies pointing to changes in the intrinsic membrane properties of cochlear nucleus neurons following cochlear deafferentation have been published. Cochlear ablation was found to cause increases in membrane resistances of neurons in the ventral cochlear nucleus (Francis and Manis, 2000). Hearing impairment has also been found to be associated with decreases in the expression of the two-pore domain potassium channels and reductions of Kv3.1 channels in central auditory neurons [116, 117]. Changes in spike waveform have been observed in the dorsal cochlear nucleus after noise exposure [14]. The relationship between these changes and alterations in spontaneous activity has not yet been determined.

Non-deafferentation Triggers of Tinnitus Induction

Deafferentation is not the only triggering mechanism by which tinnitus-related activity could be induced. Some inducers of tinnitus may act through non-deafferentation mechanisms, such as excitotoxicity or activity-dependent plasticity.

Excitotoxicity

Excess release of excitotoxic neurotransmitters in the brain caused by acoustic overstimulation could lead to degeneration of second-order neurons, many of which may be inhibitory. Glutamate is the most common excitatory and most powerfully excitotoxic neurotransmitter in the nervous system. It is also the excitatory transmitter of hair cells, auditory nerve fibers, granule cells of the cochlear nucleus, and the main projection neurons that make up the ascending auditory pathway. Normally, toxicity of this transmitter is prevented by its reuptake following its release by the presynaptic membranes. However, under certain conditions, such as when there is excessive sound stimulation, glutamate is released in excess, and this excess can sometimes overwhelm the reuptake mechanism. This leads to its accumulation in the synaptic cleft. Excess glutamate binds to N-methyl-D-aspartate (NMDA) receptors, which stimulates excess calcium influx into postsynaptic neurons via the calcium channels of NMDA receptors; the excess calcium stimulates intracellular enzymes that are damaging to cells and can culminate in apoptosis.

A case for excitotoxicity acting through excess glutamate release in the auditory system is suggested by the following: Overstimulation would be expected to cause excess release of glutamate from excitatory terminals in and beyond the cochlear nucleus. An increase in glutamate release and a decrease in glutamate uptake have been found to occur in the cochlear nucleus and persist for at least 5 days following acoustic overstimulation [110]. This would be expected to result in an accumulation of glutamate in the synaptic cleft and thereby trigger excitotoxic injury. Evidence consistent with this hypothesis is the finding that degeneration occurs in broad areas of the cochlear nucleus well beyond zones of peripheral deafferentation [114, 118]. These findings have been interpreted as possibly resulting from excitotoxic injury in the central auditory system [110, 118]. The loss of second-order neurons by this mechanism would be expected to shift the balance of excitation and inhibition in the central auditory system in ways that could be tinnitus inducing.

Activity-Dependent Plasticity

One of the most commonly described mechanisms by which synaptic excitability of neurons is chronically shifted is long-term potentiation (LTP). This is a long-lasting enhancement in synaptic transmission between two neurons that results from stimulating them synchronously. LTP results in a sensitization of neurons to their inputs, which is manifest as an augmentation in the response of the postsynaptic neuron to its excitatory inputs. Another manifestation of LTP is an increase in spontaneous activity [119]. If LTP occurs in the auditory system, it seems likely that the affected neurons would become hypersensitive and spontaneously hyperactive. A related, but opposing process is long-term depression (LTD), which is manifest as a reduction in the response of neurons to their inputs. These activity-dependent phenomena were originally discovered in the hippocampus and have been implicated as neural mechanisms of long-term memory. They are now known to be ubiquitous throughout the brain.

The question at hand is whether inducers of tinnitus can cause LTP in auditory neurons. There is evidence that LTP can be induced in various auditory centers by synchronous stimulation of pre- and postsynaptic neurons. LTP has been demonstrated by this method in the dorsal cochlear nucleus [120–122], inferior colliculus

[123, 124], and auditory cortex [125, 126]. Thus far, it is not known whether tinnitus inducers can cause LTP in these same brain areas. However, it has been hypothesized that noise might increase the probability of synchronous firing of pre- and postsynaptic firing and thereby cause induction of LTP [127]. This possibility seems plausible since acoustic stimuli increase the frequency of firing and the occurrence of coincident spikes in the auditory system [29]. Induction of tinnitus by LTP and excitotoxicity offers an explanation of why tinnitus often occurs without any accompanying hearing loss.

Why Tinnitus Does Not Always Accompany Hearing Loss

If tinnitus is the result of increases in neuronal activity (increased discharge rate and bursting) and/or increased synchrony triggered by loss or overstimulation of afferent input to the auditory centers of the brain from the ear, and also possibly involving non-auditory inputs to these centers, then why do many people with hearing loss have no tinnitus? [128, 129] The simplest explanation is that the direction of the shift in the balance of excitation and inhibition following cochlear injury may depend on the pattern of cochlear injury. Tinnitus induction would be expected to occur when there is more degeneration centrally of inhibitory than excitatory neurons, causing disinhibition and an increase in excitation. However, it is conceivable that certain patterns of peripheral injury may not be sufficient to shift the balance of excitation and inhibition or could even favor a shift toward the side of greater inhibition. Support for this concept is demonstrated by the finding that tinnitus-related hyperactivity is initially absent following induction of noise-induced threshold shift but emerges slowly over several days following the noise exposure, only after a transient decline of activity [16]. Moreover, it has been shown that when cochlear injury induced by cisplatin is restricted to outer hair cells, there is a strong relationship between the degree of centrally recorded hyperactivity and the amount of outer hair cell loss, but when the outer hair cell loss is accompanied by mild damage to the inner hair cells, particularly disarray of their stereocilia, activity is not elevated centrally. However, when the inner hair cell injury becomes more severe or outer hair cell loss is accompanied by inner hair cell loss, hyperactivity is clearly apparent [45]. This suggests that the effect of peripheral injury on central auditory activity depends on the balance and type of injury to the two hair cell populations and their connecting primary afferents.

Implications for Tinnitus Treatment

The state of knowledge on tinnitus mechanisms has provided a much-needed theoretical framework for conceiving and testing new therapeutic treatments for tinnitus over the past decade. Among the various modalities that have received the most attention are drug therapy, electrical stimulation, and transcranial magnetic stimulation. Efforts also continue to improve treatment through sound therapy and psychological counseling.

Drugs that are attracting interest as potential tinnitolytic agents are those that decrease neural activity. Initial studies with gabapentin were suggestive of a tinnitolytic effect in animals and some human subjects [130]. However, more recent clinical trials showed that when the effects are compared with placebo across a sample of patients, no significant difference was observed [131, 132]. Thus, if gabapentin has a tinnitolytic effect, it may be that only a small proportion of patients who have been treated with gabapentin experience benefit. Agents that activate the inhibitory receptors for $GABA_A$ and $GABA_B$ receptors (e.g., benzodiazepine and baclofen, respectively) have been found to have a suppressive effect on tinnitus-related activity in animals [133, 134]; studies with these agents in clinical trials have yielded mixed results. While baclofen was not found to have a significant effect on tinnitus [135], there are indications that administration of benzodiazepines, benefits many patients suffering from tinnitus [136] (see review of Gananca et al. [137]) (see also Chap. 30). In some patients, the benefit may be achieved primarily by reducing the severity of the emotional reaction to tinnitus, but there is usually a subgroup that also experiences a decrease in the loudness of tinnitus.

There has been growing interest in targeting NMDA receptors, which are implicated in plasticity for tinnitus treatment. The data thus far are preliminary, but there are indications that NMDA receptor antagonists (acam-

prosate, caroverine, ifenprodil) have tinnitolytic effects in animals [36, 138–140]. Preliminary results suggest that the NMDA receptor antagonist, neramexane, may reduce tinnitus-related activity in the DCN of animals [141]. A recent clinical trial with neramexane yielded results suggestive of a significant tinnitolytic effect in human subjects [142]. The drug is now being tested in a phase III clinical trial: http://clinicaltrials.gov/ct2/show/ (NCT00405886) (see also Chaps. 22 and 30).

Electrical stimulation studies have been conducted in areas of the brain that have been implicated as sites of tinnitus generation. The benefits have been most remarkable for patients stimulated at the cochlear level, either transtympanically or intracochlear using a cochlear implant [143, 144] (see also Chap. 77). Stimulation of the dorsal cochlear nucleus using the auditory brainstem implant has been found to be effective in suppressing tinnitus [145], and there are some recent indications that stimulation of the auditory cortex can suppress tinnitus [146–148].

Another approach that has generated considerable interest is repetitive transcranial magnetic stimulation (rTMS). This procedure is used primarily to stimulate the auditory cortex or nearby areas (see Chap. 88). A recent review of the literature [149] concluded that rTMS is a promising approach for the treatment of patients with certain forms of tinnitus. At present, the results of both stimulation modalities vary significantly across studies and within studies across individuals. This variability may stem from differences in stimulus parameters, differences in what parameters are optimal for each patient, and differences in the precise location of the stimulating electrode(s) or magnetic field relative to the primary generator sites giving rise to the tinnitus-producing signals. The fact that tinnitus has many forms (see Chap. 2) also contributes to the variability in the results of treatments. However, the findings provide a proof of concept that stimulation of auditory areas can, under optimal conditions, bring considerable relief to a significant number of tinnitus patients.

Summary and Conclusions

The foregoing review of tinnitus summarizes the areas of the nervous system that display activity changes believed to underlie the percepts of tinnitus. The available evidence indicates that tinnitus is associated with more than one type of change in the auditory system. At the brainstem level, increases in bursting and non-bursting spontaneous activity are clearly demonstrable after noise exposure and salicylate treatment, while at the cortical level, increases in non-bursting spontaneous activity and neural synchrony are more apparent. The literature review also indicates that tinnitus of different etiologies likely involves different structures and possibly different mechanisms. This is best demonstrated by clinical studies showing that sectioning the eighth nerve sometimes alleviates tinnitus, but more commonly tinnitus persists and is often worsened following this procedure. This suggests that there may not be a single final common path for tinnitus and supports that there are many forms of tinnitus (see Chap. 2). Another important concept is that tinnitus of central origin emerges as a consequence of activation of neural plasticity, which alters the excitability of neurons, primarily by shifting the balance of their excitatory and inhibitory inputs, but also possibly by shifting the balance of ion channels that control the resting membrane potential.

Our current state of knowledge provides a useful framework for developing new therapeutic approaches to tinnitus treatment. The multi-tiered distribution of tinnitus-related changes suggests that the most effective treatments for tinnitus will be those that take a system-wide approach rather than those that target specific structures. Therapies that quiet resting activity throughout the auditory system without lowering the activity of other brain pathways and without compromising sensitivity to sound will bring the type of benefits desired by most patients with tinnitus. A demonstration that such effects can be achieved on a short timescale is already indicated by the brief periods of tinnitus suppression provided by residual inhibition, somatic modulation of tinnitus, and, in some cases, by lidocaine. The goal now is to exploit these mechanisms further to increase the duration of the suppression to bring a longer lasting period and possibly chronic state of relief from tinnitus. With the foundation presently in place, we have good reason to expect that this knowledge will lead to major improvements in the treatment of tinnitus.

Acknowledgments The experiments conducted by the author, which contributed in part to this review, were supported by NIH grant R01 DC009097.

References

1. House, JW, Brackman, DE, Tinnitus: surgical treatment. In: Evered, D, Lawrenson, G (Eds), Tinnitus Ciba Found Symp 85. London: Pitman, 1982, pp 204–216
2. Berliner, KI, Shelton, C, Hitselberger, WE, Luxford, WM, Acoustic tumors: effect of surgical removal on tinnitus. Am J Otol, 1992;13:13–17
3. Fahy, C, Nikolopoulos, TP, O'Donoghue, GM, Acoustic neuroma surgery and tinnitus. Eur Arch Otorhinolaryngol, 2002;259:299–301
4. Dallos, P, Harris, D, Properties of auditory nerve responses in absence of outer hair cells. J Neurophysiol, 1978;41: 365–383
5. Liberman, MC, Dodds, LW, Single-neuron labeling and chronic cochlear pathology. II. Stereocilia damage and alterations of spontaneous discharge rates. Hear Res, 1984;16: 43–53
6. Liberman, MC, Kiang, NY, Acoustic trauma in cats Cochlear pathology and auditory-nerve activity. Acta Otolaryngol Suppl, 1978;358:1–63
7. Evans, EF, Borerwe, TA, Ototoxic effects of salicylates on the responses of single cochlear nerve fibers and on cochlear potentials. Br J Audiol, 1982;16:101–108
8. Mulheran, M, Evans, EF, A comparison of two experimental tinnitogenic agents: the effect of salicylate and quinine on activity of cochlear nerve fibers in the guinea pig. In: Hazell, J (Ed), Proceedings of the Sixth International Tinnitus Seminar. London: The Tinnitus and Hyperacusis Center, 1999, pp 189–192
9. Martin, WH, Schwegler, JW, Scheibelhoffer, J, Ronis ML, Salicylate induced changes in cat auditory nerve activity. Laryngoscope, 1993;103:600–604
10. Cazals, Y, Horner, KC, Huang, ZW, Alterations in average spectrum of cochleoneural activity by long-term salicylate treatment in the guinea pig: a plausible index of tinnitus. J Neurophysiol, 1998;80:2113–2120
11. Lenarz, T, Schreiner, C, Snyder, RL, Ernst, A, Neural mechanisms of tinnitus. Eur Arch Otorhinolaryngol, 1993;249:441–446
12. Kaltenbach, JA, Godfrey DA, Neumann, JB, McCaslin, DL, Afman, CE, Zhang, J, Changes in spontaneous neural activity in the dorsal cochlear nucleus following exposure to intense sound: relation to threshold shift. Hearing Res, 1998;124:78–84
13. Shore, SE, Koehler, S, Oldakowski, M, Hughes, LF, Syed, S, Dorsal cochlear nucleus responses to somatosensory stimulation are enhanced after noise-induced hearing loss. Eur J Neurosci, 2008;27:155–168
14. Finlayson, PG, Kaltenbach, JA, Alterations in the spontaneous discharge patterns of single units in the dorsal cochlear nucleus following intense sound exposure. Hear Res, 2009;256:104–117
15. Imig, TJ, Durham, D, Effect of unilateral noise exposure on the tonotopic distribution of spontaneous activity in the cochlear nucleus and inferior colliculus in the cortically intact and decorticate rat. J Comp Neurol, 2005;490: 391–413
16. Kaltenbach, JA, Afman, CE, Hyperactivity in the dorsal cochlear nucleus after intense sound exposure and its

resemblance to tone-evoked activity: a physiological model for tinnitus. Hear Res, 2000;140:165–172

17. Brozoski, TJ, Bauer, CA, Caspary, DM, Elevated fusiform cell activity in the dorsal cochlear nucleus of chinchillas with psychophysical evidence of tinnitus. J Neurosci, 2002;22:2383–2390

18. Zhang, JS, Kaltenbach, JA, Increases in spontaneous activity in the dorsal cochlear nucleus of the rat following exposure to high intensity sound. Neurosci Lett, 1998;250:197–200

19. Gerken, GM, Saunders, SS, Paul, RE, Hypersensitivity to electrical stimulation of auditory nuclei follows hearing loss in cats. Hear Res, 1984;13:249–259

20. Ma, WL, Hidaka, H, May, BJ, Spontaneous activity in the inferior colliculus of CBA/J mice after manipulations that induce tinnitus. Hear Res, 2006;212:9–21

21. Kwon, O, Jastreboff, MM, Hu, S, Shi, J, Jastreboff, PJ, Modification of single unit activity related to noise-induced tinnitus in rats. In: Proc of the 6th Internat Tinn Sem,1999, pp 459–462

22. Brozoski, TJ, Ciobanu, L, Bauer, CA, Central neural activity in rats with tinnitus evaluated with manganese-enhanced magnetic resonance imaging (MEMRI). Hear Res, 2007;228:168–179

23. Bauer, CA, Turner, JG, Caspary, DM, Myers, KS, Brozoski, TJ, Tinnitus and inferior colliculus activity in chinchillas related to three distinct patterns of cochlear trauma. J Neurosci Res, 2008;86:2564–2578

24. Salvi, RJ, Wang, J, Ding, D, Auditory plasticity and hyperactivity following cochlear damage. Hear Res, 2000;147 (1–2):261–274

25. Mulders, WH, Robertson, D, Hyperactivity in the auditory midbrain after acoustic trauma: dependence on cochlear activity. Neuroscience, 2009;164:733–746

26. Dong, S, Mulders, WH, Rodger, J, Robertson, D, Changes in neuronal activity and gene expression in guinea-pig auditory brainstem after unilateral partial hearing loss. Neuroscience, 2009;159:1164–1174

27. Seki, S, Eggermont, JJ, Changes in spontaneous firing rate and neural synchrony in cat primary auditory cortex after localized tone-induced hearing loss. Hear Res, 2003;180:28–38

28. Komiya, H, Eggermont, JJ, Spontaneous firing activity of cortical neurons in adult cats with reorganized tonotopic map following pure-tone trauma. Acta Otolaryngol, 2000;120:750–756

29. Eggermont, JJ, Komiya, H, Moderate noise trauma in juvenile cats results in profound cortical topographic map changes in adulthood. Hear Res, 2000;142:89–101

30. Noreña, AJ, Eggermont, JJ, Enriched acoustic environment after noise trauma abolishes neural signs of tinnitus. Neuroreport, 2006;17:559–563

31. Mahlke, C, Wallhäusser-Franke, E, Evidence for tinnitus-related plasticity in the auditory and limbic system, demonstrated by arg31 and c-fos immunocytochemistry. Hear Res, 2004;195:17–34

32. Heffner, HE, Harrington, IA, Tinnitus in hamsters following exposure to intense sound. Hear Res, 2002;170:83–95

33. Zheng, Y, Baek. JH, Smith, PF, Darlington CL Cannabinoid receptor down regulation in the ventral cochlear nucleus in a salicylate model of tinnitus. Hear Res, 2007;228:105–111

34. Jastreboff, PJ, Brennan, JF, Coleman, JK, Sasaki, CT, Phantom auditory sensation in rats: an animal model for tinnitus. Behav Neurosci, 1988;102:811–822

35. Kaltenbach, JA, Zacharek, MA, Zhang, JS, Frederick, S, Activity in the dorsal cochlear nucleus of hamsters previously tested for tinnitus following intense tone exposure. Neurosci Lett, 2004;355:121–125

36. Guitton, MJ, Dudai, Y, Blockade of cochlear NMDA receptors prevents long-term tinnitus during a brief consolidation window after acoustic trauma. Neural Plast, 2007;2007:80904

37. Turner, JG, Brozoski, TJ, Bauer, CA, Parrish, JL, Myers, K, Hughes, LF, Caspary, DM, Gap detection deficits in rats with tinnitus: a potential novel screening tool. Behav Neurosci, 2006;120:188–195

38. Rüttiger, L, Ciuffani, J, Zenner, HP, Knipper, M, A behavioral paradigm to judge acute sodium salicylate-induced sound experience in rats: a new approach for an animal model on tinnitus. Hear Res, 2003;180:39–50

39. Tan, J, Rüttiger, L, Panford-Walsh, R, Singer, W, Schulze, H, Kilian, SB, Hadjab, S, Zimmermann, U, Köpschall, I, Rohbock, K, Knipper, M, Tinnitus behavior and hearing function correlate with the reciprocal expression patterns of BDNF and Arg31/arc in auditory neurons following acoustic trauma. Neuroscience, 2007;145:715–726

40. Jastreboff, PJ, Sasaki, CT, Salicylate-induced changes in spontaneous activity of single units in the inferior colliculus of the guinea pig. J Acoust Soc Am, 1986;80:1384–1391

41. Chen, G-D, Jastreboff, PJ, Salicylate-induced abnormal activity in the inferior colliculus of rats. Hear Res, 1995;82:158–178

42. Manabe, Y, Saito, T, Saito, H, Effects of lidocaine on salicylate-induced discharges of neurons in the inferior colliculus of the guinea pig. Hear Res, 1997;103:192–198

43. Wallhäusser-Franke, E, Mahlke, C, Oliva, R, Braun, S, Wenz, G, Langner, G, Expression of c-fos in auditory and non-auditory brain regions of the gerbil after manipulations that induce tinnitus. Exp Brain Res, 2003;153:649–654

44. Melamed, SB, Kaltenbach, JA, Church, MW, Burgio, DL, Afman, CE, Cisplatin-induced increases in spontaneous neural activity in the dorsal cochlear nucleus and associated outer hair cell loss. Audiology, 2000;39:24–29

45. Kaltenbach, JA, Rachel, JD, Mathog, TA, Zhang, JS, Falzarano, PR, Lewandowski, M, Cisplatin induced hyperactivity in the dorsal cochlear nucleus and its relation to outer hair cell loss: relevance to tinnitus. J Neurophys, 2002;88:699–714

46. Eggermont, JJ, Kenmochi, M, Salicylate and quinine selectively increase spontaneous firing rates in secondary auditory cortex. Hear Res, 1998;117:149–160

47. Jastreboff, PJ, Brennan, JF, Sasaki, CT, Quinine-induced tinnitus in rats. Arch Otolaryngol Head Neck Surg, 1991;117:1162–1166

48. Bauer, CA, Brozoski, TJ, Rojas, R, Boley, J, Wyder, M, Behavioral model of chronic tinnitus in rats. Otolaryngol Head Neck Surg,1999;121:457–462

49. Lobarinas, E, Sun, W, Cushing, R, Salvi, R, A novel behavioral paradigm for assessing tinnitus using schedule-induced polydipsia avoidance conditioning (SIP-AC). Hear Res, 2004;190:109–114

50. Melcher, JR, Sigalovsky, IS, Guinan, JJ Jr, Levine, RA, Lateralized tinnitus studied with functional magnetic resonance imaging: abnormal inferior colliculus activation. J Neurophysiol, 2000;83:1058–1072

51. Lanting, CP, De Kleine, E, Bartels, H, Van Dijk, P, Functional imaging of unilateral tinnitus using fMRI. Acta Otolaryngol, 2008;128:415–421

52. Lockwood, AH, Salvi, RJ, Coad, ML, Towsley, ML, Wack, DS, Murphy, BW, The functional neuroanatomy of tinnitus: evidence for limbic system links and neural plasticity. Neurology, 1998;50:114–120

53. Arnold, W, Bartenstein, P, Oestreicher, E, Romer, W, Schwaiger, M, Focal metabolic activation in the predominant left auditory cortex in patients suffering from tinnitus: a PET study with [18F]deoxyglucose. ORL J Otorhinolaryngol Relat Spec, 1996;58:195–199

54. Andersson, G, Lyttkens, L, Hirvela, C, Furmark, T, Tillfors, M, Fredrikson, M, Regional cerebral blood flow during tinnitus: a PET case study with lidocaine and auditory stimulation. Acta Otolaryngol, 2000;120:967–972

55. Giraud, AL, Chery-Croze, S, Fischer, G, Fischer, C, Vighetto, A, Gregoire, MC, Lavenne, F, Collet, L, A selective imaging of tinnitus. Neuroreport, 1999;10:1–5

56. Lockwood, AH, Wack, DS, Burkard, RF, Goad, ML, Reyes, SA, Arnold, SA, Salvi, RJ, The functional anatomy of gaze-evoked tinnitus and sustained lateral gaze. Neurology, 2001;56:472–480

57. Wang, H, Tian, J, Yin, D, Positron emission tomography of tinnitus-related brain areas. Zhonghua Er BiVan Hou Ke Za Zhi, 2000;35:420–424

58. Mirz, F, Gjedde, A, Ishizu, K, Pedersen, CB, Cortical networks subserving the perception of tinnitus-a PET study. Acta Otolaryngol Suppl, 2000;543:241–243

59. Reyes, SA, Salvi, RJ, Burkard, RF, Coad, ML, Wack, DS, Galantowicz, PJ, Lockwood, AH, Brain imaging of the effects of lidocaine on tinnitus. Hear Res, 2002;171: 43–50

60. Kanold, PO, Young, ED, Proprioceptive information from the pinna provides somatosensory input to cat dorsal cochlear nucleus. J Neurosci, 2001;21:7848–7858

61. Shore, SE, Zhou, J, Somatosensory influence on the cochlear nucleus and beyond. Hear Res, 2006;216–217:90–99

62. Shore, SE, Vass, Z, Wys, NL, Altschuler, RA, Trigeminal ganglion innervates the auditory brainstem. J Comp Neurol, 2004;19:271–285

63. Shore, SE, Multisensory integration in the dorsal cochlear nucleus: unit responses to acoustic and trigeminal ganglion stimulation. Eur J Neurosci, 2005;21:3334–3348

64. Levine, RA, Somatic (craniocervical) tinnitus and the dorsal cochlear nucleus hypothesis. Am J Otolaryngol, 1999;20: 351–362

65. Levine, RA, Somatic tinnitus. In: Snow, JB Jr (Ed), Tinnitus: Theory and management. Hamilton, Ontario, Canada: Decker, 2004, pp 108–124

66. Levine, RA, Abel, M, Cheng, H, CNS somatosensory–auditory interactions elicit or modulate tinnitus. Exp Brain Res, 2003;153:643–648

67. Abel, MD, Levine, RA, Muscle contractions and auditory perception in tinnitus patients and nonclinical subjects. Cranio, 2004;22:181–191

68. Ochi, K, Eggermont, JJ, Effects of salicylate on neural activity in cat primary auditory cortex. Hear Res, 1996;95: 63–76

69. Ochi, K, Eggermont, JJ, Effects of quinine on neural activity in cat primary auditory cortex. Hear Res, 1997;105:105–118

70. Evans, EF, Place and time coding of frequency in the peripheral auditory system: some physiological pros and cons. Audiology, 1978;17:369–420

71. Joris, PX, Smith, PH, The volley theory and the spherical cell puzzle. Neuroscience, 2008;154:65–76

72. Eggermont, JJ, Pathophysiology of tinnitus. Prog Brain Res, 2007;166:19–35

73. Eggermont, JJ, Roberts, LE, The neuroscience of tinnitus. Trends Neurosci, 2004;27:676–682

74. Vernon, JA (Ed), Tinnitus: Treatment and Relief. Boston, MA: Allyn & Bacon, 1997

75. Cacace, AT, Lovely, TJ, McFarland, DJ, Parnes, SM, Winter, DF, Anomalous cross-modal plasticity following posterior fossa surgery: some speculations on gaze-evoked tinnitus. Hear Res, 1994;81:22–32

76. Cacace, AT, Expanding the biological basis of tinnitus: crossmodal origins and the role of neuroplasticity. Hear Res, 2003;175:112–132

77. Møller, MB, Møller, AR, Jannetta, PJ, Jho, HD, Vascular decompression surgery for severe tinnitus: selection criteria and results. Laryngoscope, 1993;103:421–427

78. Møller, AR, Møller, MB, Microvascular decompression operations. Prog Brain Res, 2007;166:397–400

79. Nodar, RH, Graham, JT, An investigation of frequency characteristics of tinnituis associated with Meniere's disease. Arch Otolaryngol Head Neck Surg, 1965;82:28–31

80. Hazell, JW, Tinnitus II: surgical management of conditions associated with tinnitus and somatosounds. J Otolaryngol, 1990;19:6–10

81. Mills, RP, Cherry, JR, Subjective tinnitus in children with otological disorders. Int J Pediatr Otorhinolaryngol, 1984;7:21–27

82. Lonsbury-Martin, BL, Martin, GK, Otoacoustic emissions and tinnitus. In: Snow, JB Jr (Ed), Tinnitus: Theory and Management. Hamilton, Ontario, Canada: Decker, 2004, pp 69–78

83. Brown, MC, Ledwith, JV III, Projections of thin (type-II) and thick (type-I) auditory nerve fibers into the cochlear nucleus of the mouse. Hear Res, 1990;49:105–118

84. Benson, TE, Brown, MC, Postsynaptic targets of type II auditory nerve fibers in the cochlear nucleus. J Assoc Res Otolaryngol, 2004;5:111–125

85. Shore SE, Moore JK, Sources of input to the cochlear granule cell region in the guinea pig. Hear Res, 1998;116(1–2):33–42

86. Berglund AM, Brown MC, Central trajectories of type II spiral ganglion cells from various cochlear regions in mice. Hear Res, 1994;75(1–2):121–130.

87. Godfrey, DA, Godfrey, TG, Mikesell, NL, Waller, HJ, Yao, W, Chen, K, Kaltenbach, JA, Chemistry of granular and closely related regions of the cochlear nucleus In: Syka, J (Ed), Acoustical Signal Processing in the Central Auditory System. New York: Plenum, 1997, pp 139–153

88. Rubinstein, B, Tinnitus and craniomandibular disorders – is there a link? Swed Dent J Suppl, 1993;95:1–46

89. Seydel, C, Reisshauer, A, Haupt, H, Klapp, BF, Mazurek, B, The role of stress in the pathogenesis of tinnitus and in the ability to cope with it. HNO, 2006;54:709–714

90. Schmitt, C, Patak, M, Kröner-Herwig, B, Stress and the onset of sudden hearing loss and tinnitus. Int Tinnitus J, 2000;6:41–49

91. Mazurek, B, Stöver, T, Haupt, H, Klapp, BF, Adli, M, Gross, J, Szczepek, AJ, The significance of stress: its role in the auditory system and the pathogenesis of tinnitus. HNO, 2010;58:162–172

92. Wright, DD, Ryugo, DK, Mossy fiber projections from the cuneate nucleus to the cochlear nucleus in the rat. J Comp Neurol, 1996;365:159–172

93. Weinberg, RJ, Rustioni, AA, Cuneocochlear pathway in the rat. Neuroscience, 1987;20:209–219

94. Itoh, K, Kamiya, H, Mitani, A, Yasui, Y, Takada, M, Mizuno, N, Direct projections from the dorsal column nuclei and the spinal trigeminal nuclei to the cochlear nuclei in the cat. Brain Res, 1987;400:145–150

95. Manis, PB, Responses to parallel fiber stimulation in the guinea pig dorsal cochlear nucleus in vitro. J Neurophysiol, 1989;61:149–161

96. Suneja, SK, Potashner, SJ, Benson, CG, Plastic changes in glycine and GABA release and uptake in adult brain stem auditory nuclei after unilateral middle ear ossicle removal and cochlear ablation. Exp Neurol, 1998;151:273–288

97. Suneja, SK, Potashner, SJ, Benson, CG, Glycine receptors in adult guinea pig brain stem auditory nuclei: regulation after unilateral cochlear ablation. Exp Neurol, 1998;154: 473–488

98. Potashner, SJ, Suneja, SK, Benson, CG, Altered glycinergic synaptic activities in guinea pig brain stem auditory nuclei after unilateral cochlear ablation. Hear Res, 2000;147:125–136

99. Asako, M, Holt, AG, Griffith, RD, Buras, ED, Altschuler, RA, Deafness-related decreases in glycine-immunoreactive labeling in the rat cochlear nucleus. J Neurosci Res, 2005;81:102–109

100. Wang, H, Brozoski, TJ, Turner, JG, Ling, L, Parrish, JL, Hughes, LF, Caspary, DM, Plasticity at glycinergic synapses in dorsal cochlear nucleus of rats with behavioral evidence of tinnitus. Neuroscience, 2009;164:747–759

101. Abbott, SD, Hughes, L, Bauer, CA, Salvi, R, Caspary, DM, Detection of glutamate decarboxylase isoforms in rat inferior colliculus following acoustic exposure. Neuroscience, 1999;93:1375–1381

102. Milbrandt, JC, Holder, TM, Wilson, MC, Salvi, RJ, Caspary, DM, GAD levels and muscimol binding in rat inferior colliculus following acoustic trauma. Hear Res, 2000;147:251–260

103. Bledsoe, SCJ, Nagase, S, Miller, JM, Altschuler, RA, Deafness induced plasticity in the mature central auditory system. Neuroreport, 1995;7:225–229

104. Caspary DM, Raza A, Lawhorn Armour BA, et al. Immunocytochemical and neurochemical evidence for age-related loss of GABA in the inferior colliculus: implications for neural presbycusis. J Neurosci, 1990;10:2363–2372

105. Schaette, R, Kempter, R, Development of tinnitus-related neuronal hyperactivity through homeostatic plasticity after hearing loss: a computational model. Eur J Neurosci, 2006;23:3124–3138

106. Chang, H, Chen, K, Kaltenbach, JA, Zhang, J, Godfrey, DA, Effects of acoustic trauma on dorsal cochlear nucleus neuron activity in slices. Hear Res, 2002;164:59–68

107. Kaltenbach, JA, Zhang, J, Intense sound-induced plasticity in the dorsal cochlear nucleus of rats: evidence for cholinergic receptor upregulation. Hear Res, 2007;226:232–243

108. Jin, YM, Godfrey, DA, Wang, J, Kaltenbach, JA, Effects of intense tone exposure on choline acetyltransferase activity in the hamster cochlear nucleus. Hear Res, 2006;216–217: 168–175

109. Illing, RB, Kraus, KS, Meidinger, MA, Reconnecting neuronal networks in the auditory brainstem following unilateral deafening. Hear Res, 2005;206:185–199

110. Muly, SM, Gross, JS, Potashner, SJ, Noise trauma alters D-[3H]aspartate release and AMPA binding in chinchilla cochlear nucleus. J Neurosci Res, 2004;75:585–596

111. Suneja, SK, Potashner, SJ, Benson, CG, AMPA receptor binding in adult guinea pig brain stem auditory nuclei after unilateral cochlear ablation. Exp Neurol, 2000;165:355–369

112. Rubio, ME, Redistribution of synaptic AMPA receptors at glutamatergic synapses in the dorsal cochlear nucleus as an early response to cochlear ablation in rats. Hear Res, 2006;216–217:154–167

113. Whiting, B, Moiseff, A, Rubio, ME, Cochlear nucleus neurons redistribute synaptic AMPA and glycine receptors in response to monaural conductive hearing loss. Neuroscience, 2009;163:1264–1276

114. Kim, J, Morest, DK, Bohne, BA, Degeneration of axons in the brainstem of the chinchilla after auditory overstimulation. Hear Res, 1997;103:169–191

115. Kim, JJ, Gross, J, Potashner, SJ, Morest, DK, Fine structure of long-term changes in the cochlear nucleus after acoustic overstimulation: chronic degeneration and new growth of synaptic endings. J Neurosci Res, 2004;77:817–828

116. Holt, AG, Asako, M, Duncan, RK, Lomax, CA, Juiz, JM, Altschuler, RA, Deafness associated changes in expression of two-pore domain potassium channels in the rat cochlear nucleus. Hear Res, 2006;216–217:146–153

117. von Hehn, CA, Bhattacharjee, A, Kaczmarek, LK, Loss of Kv31 tonotopicity and alterations in cAMP response element-binding protein signaling in central auditory neurons of hearing impaired mice. J Neurosci, 2004;24:1936–1940

118. Morest, DK, Kim, J, Potashner, SJ, Bohne, BA, Long-term degeneration in the cochlear nerve and cochlear nucleus of the adult chinchilla following acoustic overstimulation. Microsc Res Tech, 1998;41:205–216

119. Kimura, A, Pavlides, C, Long-term potentiation/depotentiation are accompanied by complex changes in spontaneous unit activity in the hippocampus. J Neurophysiol, 2000;84:1894–1906

120. Fujino, K, Oertel, D, Bidirectional synaptic plasticity in the cerebellum-like mammalian dorsal cochlear nucleus. Proc Natl Acad Sci U S A, 2003;100:265–270

121. Oertel, D, Young, ED, What's a cerebellar circuit doing in the auditory system? Trends Neurosci, 2004;27:104–110

122. Tzounopoulos, T, Kim, Y, Oertel, D, Trussell, LO, Cell-specific, spike timing-dependent plasticities in the dorsal cochlear nucleus. Nat Neurosci, 2004;7:719–725

123. Wu, SH, Ma, CL, Sivaramakrishnan S, Oliver DL, Synaptic modification in neurons of the central nucleus of the inferior colliculus. Hear Res, 2002;168:43–54

124. Zhang, Y, Wu, SH, Long-term potentiation in the inferior colliculus studied in rat brain slice. Hear Res, 2000;147: 92–103

125. Seki, K, Kudoh, M, Shibuki, K, Long-term potentiation of Ca²⁺ signal in the rat auditory cortex. Neurosci Res, 1999; 34:187–197

126. Kudoh, M, Shibuki, K, Long-term potentiation in the auditory cortex of adult rats. Neurosci Lett, 1994;171:21–23

127. Tzounopoulos, T, Mechanisms of synaptic plasticity in the dorsal cochlear nucleus: plasticity-induced changes that could underlie tinnitus. Am J Audiol, 2008;17:S170–S175

128. König, O, Schaette, R, Kempter, R, Gross, M, Course of hearing loss and occurrence of tinnitus. Hear Res, 2006;221:59–64

129. Schaette, R, Kempter, R, Predicting tinnitus pitch from patients' audiograms with a computational model for the development of neuronal hyperactivity. J Neurophysiol, 2009;101:3042–3052

130. Bauer, CA, Brozoski, TJ, Effect of gabapentin on the sensation and impact of tinnitus. Laryngoscope, 2006;116:675–681

131. Piccirillo, JF, Finnell, J, Vlahiotis, A, Chole, RA, Spitznagel, E Jr, Relief of idiopathic subjective tinnitus: is gabapentin effective? Arch Otolaryngol Head Neck Surg, 2007;133:390–397

132. Witsell, DL, Hannley, MT, Stinnet, S, Tucci, DL, Treatment of tinnitus with gabapentin: a pilot study. Otol Neurotol, 2007;28:11–15

133. Szczepaniak, WS, Møller, AR, Evidence of decreased GABAergic influence on temporal integration in the inferior colliculus following acute noise exposure: a study of evoked potentials in the rat. Neurosci Lett, 1995;196:77–80

134. Zhang, JS, Kaltenbach, JA, Effects of GABAB receptor activation on sound-induced hyperactivity in the DCN of hamsters in vivo. In: ARO Abs, 2000 #5020

135. Westerberg, BD, Roberson, JB Jr, Stach, BA, A double-blind placebo-controlled trial of baclofen in the treatment of tinnitus. Am J Otol, 1996;17:896–903

136. Bahmad, FM Jr, Venosa, AR, Oliveira, CA, Benzodiazepines and GABAergics in treating severe disabling tinnitus of predominantly cochlear origin. Int Tinnitus J, 2006;12:140–144

137. Gananca, MM, Caovilla, HH, Gananca, FF, Gananca, CF, Munhoz, MS, da Silva, ML, Serafini, F, Clonazepam in the pharmacological treatment of vertigo and tinnitus. Int Tinnitus J, 2002;8:50–53

138. Azevedo, AA, Figueiredo, RR, Tinnitus treatment with acamprosate: double-blind study. Braz J Otorhinolaryngol, 2005;71:618–623

139. Azevedo, AA, Figueiredo, RR, Treatment of tinnitus with acamprosate. Prog Brain Res, 2007;166:273–277

140. Ehrenberger, K, Topical administration of Caroverine in somatic tinnitus treatment: proof-of-concept study. Int Tinnitus J, 2005;11:34–37

141. Budzyn, B, Kaltenbach, JA, Effects of neramexane on tinnitus-related hyperactivity in the dorsal cochlear nucleus. In: Abstract for the 3rd meeting of the Tinnitus Research Initiative, Stresa, Italy, 2009

142. Althaus, M, Clinical development of new drugs for the treatment of tinnitus using the example of Neramexane. In: Abstract for the 3rd meeting of the Tinnitus Research Initiative, Stresa, Italy, 2009

143. Pan, T, Tyler, RS, Ji, H, Coelho, C, Gehringer, AK, Gogel, SA, Changes in the tinnitus handicap questionnaire after cochlear implantation. Am J Audiol, 2009;18:144–151

144. Rubinstein, JT, Tyler, RS, Johnson, A, Brown, CJ, Electrical suppression of tinnitus with high-rate pulse trains. Otol Neurotol, 2003;24:478–485

145. Soussi, T, Otto, SR, Effects of electrical brainstem stimulation on tinnitus. Acta Otolaryngol, 1994;114:135–140

146. De Ridder, D, Vanneste, S, van der Loo, E, Plazier, M, Menovsky, T, van de Heyning, P, Burst stimulation of the auditory cortex: a new form of neurostimulation for noise-like tinnitus suppression. J Neurosurg, 2010;112:1289–1294

147. De Ridder, D, De Mulder, G, Verstraeten, E, Van der Kelen, K, Sunaert, S, Smits, M, Kovacs, S, Verlooy, J, Van de Heyning, P, Møller, AR, Primary and secondary auditory cortex stimulation for intractable tinnitus. ORL J Otorhinolaryngol Relat Spec, 2006;68:48–54

148. Seidman, MD, Ridder, DD, Elisevich, K, Bowyer, SM, Darrat, I, Dria, J, Stach, B, Jiang, Q, Tepley, N, Ewing, J, Seidman, M, Zhang, J, Direct electrical stimulation of Heschl's gyrus for tinnitus treatment. Laryngoscope, 2008;118:491–500

149. Kleinjung, T, Steffens, T, Londero, A, Langguth, B, Transcranial magnetic stimulation (TMS) for treatment of chronic tinnitus: clinical effects. Prog Brain Res, 2007;166:359–367

Chapter 32
Tinnitus from the Perspective of a Patient

George E. Anthou

Keyword ROTC Reserve Officer Training Corps

In my wish to perhaps help others suffering from tinnitus and the constant ringing and hissing in both ears since March 16, 1996, I thought it would be appropriate to provide a historical background on how this intractable problem came about in my life. As those who are suffering from tinnitus, I am aware it is a symptom and not a disease and that it can be brought about from a number of variable causes that include: (1) use of excess alcohol, (2) caffeine, (3) aspirin in heavy doses, (4) certain mediations, (5) hardening of the arteries, (6) high blood pressure, (7) infection of the ear canal or eardrum, (8) Ménière's disease (inner ear disorder), and (9) exposure to loud noise(s). In my particular case, the latter is the cause of my tinnitus.

Let me first describe my upbringing. Upon graduation from Washington and Jefferson College in June of 1955, I was commissioned as Second Lieutenant in the United States Army in connection with having enrolled in ROTC (a 4-year Reserve Office Training Corp). In that same month and year, I was posted at the United States Transportation School at Ft. Eustis, Virginia a short distance from Williamsburg, Virginia. In February of 1956, I was assigned to serve as a part of the post-war occupation of then West Germany and stationed at the United States seventh Army Headquarters near the city of Stuttgart. Although I was attached to a Transportation Unit, we were required to take part in maneuvers every 3 months. On those occasions, as an officer, I carried a 45-caliber pistol and was required to fire it on the firing range. On other occasions, I was designated the "firing

line officer" on the firing range to supervise the firing of 50-caliber machine guns by enlisted men in our unit. Occasionally, I also fired the 50-caliber machine gun. Knowledge of fire power and the use of weapons was necessary because, as I recall, we were informed of the possible menace by the Russian Army, which had divided the country into East and West Germany. In any event, ZI must say that the noise from firing the 45-caliber pistol and alternately firing the 50-caliber machine gun was deafening. It must also be remembered that at that time, we had no ear protectors or any other device(s) to shield us from the horrendous noise. After completing a few rotations as "firing line officer" I noticed some "ringing" in my right ear; although it was slight, I reported it to my Company Commander.

He suggested that I make an appointment with the resident Army physician, who, after a quick examination and test, stated that I had a 10/11% hearing loss but, did not issue any Order excusing me from being on the firing range. I mentioned this encounter with the military physician because the examination was so casual and did not address my problem with the onset of tinnitus. However, I was so troubled that a continuation of exposure to extremely loud noise on the firing line would aggravate the tinnitus that I again approached my Company Commander who shared my concerns. Accordingly, he issued an Executive Order excusing me from the firing range altogether.

After that, I was assigned to the Motor Pool for the remainder of my tour until June 1957 when I received an Honorable Discharge as a First Lieutenant. Thereafter, although the mild tinnitus continued in my right ear, it was more of an irritating problem but, more importantly, did not interfere with my studies at the University of Washington and Lee Law School (Lexington, Virginia), where I was admitted shortly after my discharge from the Army.

G.E. Anthou (✉)
132 Greenside Ave, Canonsburg, PA 15317, USA
e-mail: ganthou@hotmail.com

A.R. Møller et al. (eds.), *Textbook of Tinnitus*,
DOI 10.1007/978-1-60761-145-5_32, © Springer Science+Business Media, LLC 2011

I should note, in particular, that I was not taking any medication for the mild tinnitus in my right ear. In other words, I led a normal life and had no health problems since my discharge in June of 1957. However, to my great misfortune, all that changed on the night of March 16, 1996. On that night, as a solicitor for a local municipality, I attended a meeting of the Planning Commission to review a plan for a real estate developer who was seeking a special exception of the building code for the construction of apartments in the municipality. After a lengthy review of the plans, the meeting was adjourned.

As I was about to enter my car, the fire sirens on the tower next to the municipal building sounded off and since my car doors were locked, my only option was to place my fingers in each ear in hopes of diminishing the extremely loud sirens. All I could do was wait until the sirens turned off and then enter my car because I had no other choice. In other words, had I attempted to open my car door I would have exposed my ears to even louder noise. I knew immediately that my tinnitus was greatly increased by the exposure to the sirens because as I drove home, the ringing was louder and was now not only the right ear but also in the left ear, which previous to this incident was absent of any tinnitus. When I arrived home, my wife asked me why my face was so ashen and I related the above incident. I also told her that in the few seconds that I was exposed to the screeching of these sirens, loud hissing in both ears was immediately noticeable. I was not only devastated but fell into deep depression right away because, in my opinion, the mild tinnitus prior to this incident was forever aggravated.

As a result of the increased tinnitus, now in both ears, I could not sleep. At the suggestion of my wife, I took a couple of aspirins, but this did not reduce the loud tinnitus at all nor did it help me to fall asleep. In the morning, after a completely restless night, I was frantic and wanted to see a doctor as soon as possible. My wife called a family friend who recommended an eminent and highly respected otologist. When my wife called the otologist's office, she was informed that the doctor was attending a conference in Europe. However, after explaining the urgency of the matter, the office secretary scheduled an appointment to be seen immediately after her return in 2 weeks time. In the interim, I called another otologist whose office made an appointment for me. At that visit, I related the circumstances of exposure to the sirens to the doctor and he proceeded to conduct an examination. At the end of the exam, he gave me a prescription for Zoloft to help me cope with the tinnitus. That particular doctor advised me to return to my law office and "work on a brief and forget the tinnitus." I responded that with constant loud hissing in both ears, I could not return to my law practice since I could not concentrate on my work, and furthermore, I was extremely depressed and disheartened about my condition. Incidentally, the Zoloft I was taking at the time caused me to feel dazed and weak. Upon the return of the otologist recommended by my family friend, an appointment was confirmed. Upon my arrival, I underwent a battery of tests to determine if there was any loss of hearing arising out of exposure for the loud sirens. The tests revealed that there was some loss of hearing, especially at high-pitched sounds. However, my hearing was not greatly diminished. Also during that visit, it was decided that I should cease taking Zoloft, and Xanax was prescribed instead.

I was also advised that it might be helpful and therapeutic to see a psychologist. I was agreeable to this approach and an appointment was made with a psychologist at a nearby geriatric center. This course of action was followed for approximately 4 months. However, since the otologist concluded that this regimen was not as helpful as she had anticipated, she recommended a consultation with one of the most eminent psychiatrists at a psychiatric hospital. I must say that this particular psychiatrist was very helpful because I found him to be sincerely interested in my plight. His candid and positive assessment of my depression occasioned by my tinnitus was helpful as well. Despite those efforts, my otologist determined, through many discussions, that my depression was so deep and pervasive that I might harm myself. Accordingly, in early December of 1996, she informed me that the department of neurology at a university hospital was performing experimental surgery (referred to as microvascular decompression of the eighth cranial nerve) for those who were suffering from loud tinnitus. Although the outcome of that particular surgery was uncertain and indeed questionable, the otologist suggested that it might be a matter that I might consider in view of my intractable tinnitus. Moreover, she concluded that emotionally, I was a suitable candidate for this procedure. As I recall, I met with the surgical team to thoroughly discuss the surgery. I also remember the admonition of the chief surgeon, specifically, that the surgery (1) may reduce the tinnitus, (2) may make the tinnitus louder, (3) may cause a loss of hearing altogether, or (4) may not accomplish anything at all. Naturally, after hearing these, fear and anxiety swept over me but, taking into consideration the debilitating and constant hissing in both ears, it was necessary for me to consider the above scenario and to make a decision about the proposed surgery. My wife and I deliberated about this and ultimately I harkened back to my days in law school to what I remembered in my class on the subject of negligence to convince me to go forward with the surgery. The rationale in one of the cases under study had to do with how one should approach a serious problem, which was enunciated as follows: "when embarking on a course of conduct, one must weigh the magnitude of the risk(s) against the utility of the conduct." If the risk(s) outweighs the particular conduct contemplated, then the utility of the conduct must be abandoned.

"On the other hand, if the utility of the conduct outweighs the risk(s), then one must proceed with the conduct." In my decision, which was supported by my wife, we concluded that the hope we placed in the surgical procedure outweighed the risk(s) of potential harm because of the intractable and debilitating condition arising out of the loud and unceasing ringing in both my ears. In this context, we believed we were making the correct decision in going through with the microvascular decompression surgery of the eighth cranial nerve. Thus, in late December 1996, the surgical team scheduled me to undergo a microvascular decompression operation for my left eighth nerve. The decision to operate on the left side was made by the neurological team on the premise that since it was the side which was damaged most recently, the chance of any success would be more likely than the right side, where the tinnitus first surfaced while I was on military duty in May 1956.

The surgery began with an incision just below the hairline behind the left ear as muscle and fascia were dissected. Then a burr hole was placed and extended with the craniectomy extending to the skull floor. The dura was then opened to view the eighth nerve. Finally, a piece of Teflon felt was interposed between the nerve and vessel.

I was then taken to the recovery room and when I gained consciousness, it felt like "a ton of bricks" (emphasis supplied) had struck my head. Fortunately, nurses stayed with me (in 12-h shifts), and in 4 days I was discharged.

After the surgical procedure, I had follow-up visits with various members of the surgical team as well as the otologist. At first, it appeared to me that the tinnitus had diminished slightly but after a few months, the tinnitus had returned to the level prior to the surgery. Of course, I was quite disappointed. However, I had been advised by the surgical team that this was one of the likely results of the surgery.

I consulted with my otologist about the current state of my condition and reported that I still had difficulty sleeping due to the constant hissing in both ears.

She then recommended that I purchase a "Sound Soother" with a timer. I mention this because this machine or device replicates different sounds such as water fall and the rush of ocean waves. This helped me to begin sleep, although to a small degree, but in a few hours I could hear the hissing again, which thus disturbed my sleep to such an extent that I abandoned the "Sound Soother." When I returned to my law practice a few months after the surgery, on the advice of my otologist, I purchased a set of head phones under the name of "Viennatoners" (operated by batteries) to wear during the daytime hours and at work.

Although these "head phones" somewhat "masked" the tinnitus, I found them not only impracticable (it was difficult to make or accept office phone calls), but also of little benefit in attempting to manage the tinnitus, so I abandoned this approach after a few months.

In the meantime, even though I had not experienced any reduction of tinnitus incident to the microvascular decompression operation, I met with the surgical team and my otologist to seek their opinion about undergoing a second surgical procedure on the right side because the tinnitus was unbearable. After taking another series of tests, it was determined once again that I was physically and mentally able to tolerate such a surgical procedure. Thus, in early June of 1997, I underwent another microvascular decompression operation – this time of the eighth cranial nerve on the right side. One might question why I would subject myself to another operation when the first one was not successful. The answer, to me at least, was quite ordinary and simple, that is to say that due to suffering tinnitus 24/7, I was rather desperate and willing to accept the risk inherent in such a surgical procedure. Despite all the pain and suffering from this operation, I came out of it without any side effects and anxiously waited for some positive result even though I had tinnitus on that side since my military days. However, after a number of months, I was again disappointed that there was no degree of reduction of the tinnitus.

I continued to visit my otologist to take hearing tests, which indicated that although I was extremely sensitive to high-pitched sounds (termed Hyperacusis), my hearing was not diminished as a result of the tinnitus. It was of some comfort to know that my hearing was quite good under the circumstances. It should be noted that I continued visiting my psychiatrist, only instead of visits every 3 months, my appointments has been reduced to twice a year. I find, even at this present time, that the sessions were of immeasurable benefit to me. During the visits to the psychiatrist for the past 14 years, newer medications have helped me manage my tinnitus.

I currently take Effexor to calm my nerves during the day and Clonazepam has been the drug of choice before I go to bed because it begins my sleep cycle and I am able to get at least 6 h of sleep without hearing the hissing sound of tinnitus. During the early days of my tinnitus, a group of us suffering from the same nagging disability would call each other to offer comfort and support. Indeed, I found that some in our group who were experiencing very loud tinnitus were taking Clonazepam during the day and night because it was so debilitating. One unfortunate lady, who was in our group, was suffering so much from loud constant ringing and hissing (bi-laterally) that she could not sleep at all and after a number of months, in ultimate desperation, took her own life.

Of course, I must also say that suffering from the intractable effects of tinnitus has changed my lifestyle dramatically. Thus, I must be careful to avoid noisy venues and places. As a consequence, since the onset of aggravation of my tinnitus in 1996, I have not attended the symphony, movies, concerts, weddings, sports events, and crowded restaurants. Even a set of keys accidentally dropped in our kitchen, the banging of a door, or the whirling of a mixer all cause heightened noise, which, in turn, increases the hissing ring in each ear. On some such occasions, it seems to be especially loud and there is no relief until I go to bed with the aid of Clonazepam. Nor have I been able to utilize my lawn mower or my snowplow. Not surprisingly, because of the tinnitus, I have found myself speaking to friends, colleagues, and others in a low tone and invariably, they ask me to speak louder. On occasions when I cannot avoid noise (loud church choir for example), I find it necessary to place foam earplugs (which I always carry with me) in my ears for some protection. As one can see, my quality of life has been substantially changed due to my tinnitus. On the other hand, I am fortunate to have a patient and supportive wife, an otologist whose specialty in the study of tinnitus has given me encouragement to be positive and a psychiatrist who has provided me with years of counseling and drug therapy, all of whom have given me hope to continue my fractured life as best I can under stressful circumstances.

If I may offer some gratuitous advice to anyone who suffers from tinnitus, I would first urge him or her to never surrender to this nagging problem. I would also encourage them to be their own advocate by reading the vast information available in books, periodicals, and medical journals on the subject of tinnitus. The reservoir of information on the Internet is also a tremendous source of knowledge on the subject.

Lastly, I would counsel that if one is struggling with tinnitus, a specialist in otology be sought and not, with due respect, merely a family practice physician.

I am hopeful that the recitation of events that have occupied my life since June of 1996 may be of comfort and benefit to others who are suffering from this persistent and unyielding malady.

Chapter 33
Introduction

Tobias Kleinjung and Dirk De Ridder

There are many causes of tinnitus, and the origin of many incidences of tinnitus is unknown. A common cause of severe tinnitus is deprivation of signals to the central auditory system (see Chap. 11). This may occur through conductive hearing loss, cochlear hearing loss, and pathologies of the auditory nerve. The relation between tinnitus and hearing loss is discussed in Chap. 35 (see also Chaps. 8 and 10).

Only a few incidences of tinnitus are direct consequences of pathologies of the ear. Tinnitus is more frequently caused by deprivation of input to the central auditory pathway because of hearing loss. Many authors agree that the initial cause of tinnitus, when accompanied with hearing loss, has a peripheral origin that may trigger a series of reactions in the central nervous system, resulting in tinnitus. The anatomical location of the pathology may be the cochlea, but it is often the auditory nervous system (see Chap. 10). The finding that both deaf people and individuals with normal hearing can have severe tinnitus clearly indicates that tinnitus is not always linked to hearing loss.

Restoration of hearing can often also reduce the tinnitus, provided the restoration occurs before the tinnitus has been allowed to continue over a long period of time.

This section describes the possible causes of conductive hearing loss located in the external ear and middle ear (Chap. 34). Most incidences of tinnitus occur together with sensorineural hearing loss such as age-related hearing loss (presbycusis (Chap. 36) and noise-induced hearing loss (Chap. 37). Complications in medical treatment can cause tinnitus, such as through ototoxic antibiotics and cytostatica (Chap. 42). One of these symptoms that define Ménière's disease is tinnitus (Chap. 38). Surgical manipulations of the auditory nerve can cause tinnitus (Chap. 40). Pathologies that affect the auditory nerve, such as vestibular schwannoma (Chap. 39), are often accompanied by tinnitus, as are surgical trauma to the auditory nerve. Pathologies that affect other parts of the auditory nervous system, such as cerebrovasular diseases (Chap. 41), can cause tinnitus but such cases are rare. The somatosensory system is involved in some forms of tinnitus (Chap. 43), and disorders such as those affecting the temporomandibular system are often accompanied by tinnitus (Chap. 44).

T. Kleinjung (✉)
Department of Otorhinolaryngology, University Hospital of Regensburg, Regensburg, Germany
e-mail: tobias.kleinjung@klinik.uni-regensburg.de

A.R. Møller et al. (eds.), *Textbook of Tinnitus*,
DOI 10.1007/978-1-60761-145-5_33, © Springer Science+Business Media, LLC 2011

Chapter 34
Conductive and Cochlear Hearing Loss

Tobias Kleinjung

Keypoints

1. Any kind of hearing loss may be accompanied by tinnitus.
2. This chapter describes possible causes of conductive hearing loss located in the external ear and middle ear.
3. Pathologies of this area include neoplastic changes (e.g., tumors), inflammatory disease (e.g., otitis media), or disorders of unknown origin (e.g., otosclerosis).
4. Cochlear hearing loss of genetic origin can be classified in to syndromic and non-syndromic forms.
5. Labyrinthitis can occur due to bacterial or viral infection or in the context of immunological disease.

Keywords Hearing loss • Inner ear • Middle ear • Otitis media • Otosclerosis • Tinnitus

Abbreviations

AIED Autoimmune inner ear disease
NSHL Non-syndromic hearing loss
SHL   Syndromic hearing loss

Introduction

Virtually any pathology involving the ear appears to have the capacity to cause hearing loss and tinnitus may accompany the hearing loss at any time. Pathology

T. Kleinjung (✉)
Department of Otorhinolaryngology, University of Regensburg, Franz-Josef-Strauss-Allee 11, 93053 Regensburg, Germany
e-mail: tobias.kleinjung@klinik.uni-regensburg.de

involving the external ear and middle ear leads to conductive hearing loss, whereas a pathological change in the cochlea causes cochlear hearing loss. In most cases, tinnitus cannot be regarded as a direct consequence of the pathological changes, but rather hearing loss causes deprivation of input to the central auditory pathway activating neural plasticity (see Chap. 10). The tinnitus that occurs together with hearing loss is, in most cases, subjective tinnitus. Only very rarely can conductive hearing loss cause objective tinnitus, generally because of vascular turbulence. The effect of conductive hearing loss is the same as that of an earplug, and tinnitus might be interpreted as intensified perception of body sounds that occurs because sounds from the outside are reduced.

If the hearing loss is reduced or eliminated, tinnitus may also disappear after a certain period. Many forms of conductive hearing loss, in particular, can be treated successfully by surgical interventions (Chap. 83), leading to improvement of hearing and disappearance of tinnitus. If hearing loss persists, the accompanying tinnitus also usually persists. Often, the frequency of maximum hearing loss coincides with the frequency of the tinnitus.

Causes of Conductive Hearing Loss

Changes in the Territory of the External Auditory Canal

Pathologies leading to conductive hearing loss with subsequent tinnitus can be of a mechanical, inflammatory, or neoplastic nature. It may affect the ear canal or the middle ear. Genetic factors as well as exogenous noxious agents (thalidomide embryopathy [1]) may be involved in the development of auditory canal anomalies.

A.R. Møller et al. (eds.), *Textbook of Tinnitus*,
DOI 10.1007/978-1-60761-145-5_34, © Springer Science+Business Media, LLC 2011

Obstruction of the external auditory canal by wax is a mundane reason for sudden onset of hearing loss and tinnitus. Inflammation of the external auditory canal (swimmer's otitis) may cause very painful swelling, redness, and discharge from the external auditory canal due to bacterial (*Pseudomonas aeruginosa*, *Staphylococcus aureus*) or, more rarely, fungal infection. When the external auditory canal becomes blocked, tinnitus may develop together with the hearing loss [2]. Neoplastic disorders leading to increasing stenosis and finally occlusion of the external auditory canal may be benign or malignant. Exostoses[1] of the external auditory canal are benign new bone formations that occur with an incidence of 3–6% [3]. They may cause recurrent inflammation of the external ear canal with conductive hearing loss and transient tinnitus [4]. Apart from the constitutional factors, repeated thermal irritation of the external auditory canal by frequent contact with cold water (swimmer's ear, surfer's ear) has long been regarded as a predisposing factor [5].

Malignant neoplasms of the external auditory canal are far less common. These may arise from skin cells (basal cell carcinoma, squamous cell carcinoma, malignant melanoma) or in the ceruminous glands (adenocarcinoma, adenoid cystic carcinoma) [6]. Congenital changes resulting in partial occlusion or atresia of the external auditory canal can cause hearing loss and possibly tinnitus. Severe forms may also be accompanied by an auricular anomaly in addition to complete atresia of the external auditory canal. As syndromic components, external ear anomalies may also occur in association with further dysmorphologies, for example, mid-facial dysplasia (mandibulofacial dysostosis, Treacher-Collins syndrome [7]), or craniofacial dysostoses (Crouzon syndrome [8]). These anomalies may be accompanied by additional anomaly of the middle ear, which can be detected by high-resolution computed tomography [9].

Pathological Conditions of the Middle Ear

Eustachian tube dysfunction leads to impairment of the function of the middle ear. Disturbances affecting opening and closure of the Eustachian tube are an important factor in the pathogenesis of many middle ear conditions because the ventilation and drainage of the middle ear no longer function properly. The sequelae may include chronic mucoid otitis media (glue ear), recurrent acute otitis media, or chronic otitis media. Disturbances affecting opening and closure of the Eustachian tube may be caused by mechanical blockage of the tubal orifice (adenoids, tumor), by inflammatory swelling of the tubal mucosa, or by muscular insufficiency such as may occur in individuals with cleft palate [10, 11]. Conductive hearing loss, sometimes accompanied by tinnitus, may develop subsequent to Eustachian tube dysfunction.

A patulous Eustachian tube is a special condition in which there is a permanently open connection between the tube and the nasopharynx. This condition may entail a variety of symptoms, such as autophony, aural fullness, and the unpleasant sensation of hearing one's own respiratory sounds. Reduced muscle tone and weight loss are the main factors predisposing to the development of patulous Eustachian tube.

Acute otitis media often occurs secondary to rhinitis or pharyngitis. The common organisms that cause otitis media are streptococci, *Haemophilus influenzae*, and staphylococci. The main symptoms are earache and hearing loss. In many cases tinnitus may occur as an additional symptom. The tinnitus may be objective, having a vascular origin. It may be perceived as pulsatile pounding and buzzing sounds that occur in acute inflammatory stage by dilatation of vessels and high pulse amplitude of blood flow. Chronic otitis media is an umbrella term that covers several different middle ear pathologies. If it lasts for several years, there may be different extents of irreversible tissue destruction in the middle ear. In addition to perforation of the eardrum and defects in the ossicular chain, enzymatic degradation processes associated with cholesteatoma[2] may occur and may, in particular, lead to destructive erosion of the bony walls of the middle ear toward the cranial base. The common consequence of these

---

[1] Exostosis: A cartilage-capped bony projection arising from any bone that develops from cartilage. Stedman's Electronic Medical Dictionary.

[2] Cholesteatoma: Squamous metaplasia or extension of squamous cell epithelium inward to line an expanding cystic cavity that may involve the middle ear or mastoid, erode surrounding bone, and become filled with a mass of keratinized squamous cell epithelial debris, usually resulting from chronic otitis media. The lesion often contains cholesterol clefts surrounded by inflammatory and foreign body giant cells, hence the name *cholesteatoma*. Stedman's Electronic Medical Dictionary.

pathologies is increasing conductive hearing loss with recurrent mucous or purulent discharge. Individuals in whom cholesteatoma is associated with erosion of the bony walls of the structures of the labyrinth, may also have sensorineural hearing loss and even deafness because the pathologies have spread to the cochlea.

There are three different causes of traumatic eardrum perforation: direct mechanical or thermal injury, a pressure wave in the external auditory canal, or an otobasis fracture. Depending on the extent of hearing loss, the possibility of a concomitant injury to the ossicular chain or the cochlea must also be considered.

Otosclerosis causes stapedial ankylosis, which in turn causes conductive hearing loss. Otosclerosis can also affect the bony labyrinth characterized by bone resorption and remodeling processes (otospongiosis). Otosclerosis is responsible for 5–9% of all hearing losses and 18–22% of all conductive hearing losses [12]. The condition is encountered almost exclusively in Caucasians, very rarely occurring in Asians and almost never in Blacks [13]. The female-to-male ratio is approximately 2:1. The precise etiology remains unclear [14]. Alongside genetic factors [15], the role of inflammatory processes (localized measles virus infection of the otic capsule [16]), endocrine factors [17], and immunological disease [18] have been considered in the etiopathogenesis.

Independently of sex and age, tinnitus is a concomitant symptom in 65–91% of individuals with otosclerosis [19, 20]. Tinnitus already develops in many individuals with otosclerosis years before the onset of noticeable hearing loss. Tinnitus sometimes persists despite an optimal hearing outcome from surgical management (see Chap. 83).

Otosclerotic processes may spread to the cochlea and that may be responsible for persisting tinnitus. This condition, known as "cochlear otosclerosis" by many authors, causes signs of sensorineural hearing loss [21–23]. It is also associated with changes in the stria vascularis, the organ of Corti and the spiral ligaments, as demonstrated in histopathological and radiological studies [24–26].

Tumors affecting the middle ear are rare. The glomus tumor (synonyms: paraganglioma, chemodectoma) is one kind of benign tumor of the middle ear, displaying destructive growth. Two locations of glomus tumors occur: glomus tympanicum tumors (which are limited to the middle ear) and glomus jugulare tumors (lesions that affect both the middle ear and the bulb of the jugular vein) [27]. In histological terms, the tumors consist of non-chromaffin paraganglionic cells along the course of cranial nerves IX and X.

The majority of glomus tumors occur in adulthood, with a female-to-male predominance of 6:1 [28]. Glomus tumors can generally be diagnosed clinically on the basis of the symptom triad of conductive hearing loss, pulsatile tinnitus, and a red middle-ear tumor that can be seen through the eardrum using otoscopy [29]. In some patients, pulsatile objective tinnitus can be detected objectively by inserting a stethoscope or microphone into the external auditory canal. The sound is probably produced by the formation of microvascular shunts within the tumor mass [30]. With increasing tumor infiltration into the jugular foramen, additional deficits related to caudal cranial nerves IX–XI may become evident.

Facial nerve schwannoma is another – very rare – benign tumor affecting the middle ear, characterized by slowly progressive facial paralysis as well as conductive hearing loss. Wegener's granulomatosis,[3] Langerhans cell histiocytosis,[4] and sarcoidosis[5] are among the tumor-like lesions that potentially involve the middle ear and are also accompanied by tinnitus, in addition to conductive hearing loss [31].

Malignant tumors that may involve the middle ear are squamous cell carcinoma and adenoid cystic carcinoma.

---

[3] Wegener's granulomatosis: a disease, occurring mainly in the fourth and fifth decades, characterized by necrotizing granulomas and ulceration of the upper respiratory tract, with purulent rhinorrhea, nasal obstruction, and sometimes with otorrhea, hemoptysis, pulmonary infiltration and cavitation, and fever; exophthalmos, involvement of the larynx and pharynx, and glomerulonephritis may occur; the underlying condition is a vasculitis affecting small vessels, and is possibly due to an immune disorder. Stedman's Online Medical Dictionary.

[4] Langerhans cell histiocytosis: a set of closely related disorders unified by a common proliferating element, the Langerhans cell. Three overlapping clinical syndromes are recognized: a single site disease (eosinophilic granuloma), a multifocal unisystem process (Hand-Schuller-Christian syndrome), and a multifocal, multisystem histiocytosis (Letter-Siwe syndrome.) Formerly this process was known as histiocytosis X. Stedman's Online Medical Dictionary.

[5] Sarcoidosis: a systemic granulomatous disease of unknown cause, especially involving the lungs with resulting interstitial fibrosis, but also involving lymph nodes, skin, liver, spleen, eyes, phalangeal bones, and parotid glands; granulomas are composed of epithelioid and multinucleated giant cells with little or no necrosis. Stedman's Online Medical Dictionary.

Causes of Sensorineural Hearing Loss

The causal factors responsible for the development of sensorineural hearing loss can be many and varied. Apart from congenital factors, the etiology may include infectious diseases, autoimmune diseases, toxic lesions (see Chap. 42), noise-related injury (see Chap. 37), traumatic damage (see Chap. 67), or age-induced changes (presbycusis, see Chap. 36). Furthermore, fluctuating sensorineural hearing loss is one of the three signs of Ménière's disease (see Chaps. 38 and 60) and sudden hearing loss (Chap. 56). Depending on the cause, the form of sensorineural hearing loss can be different and have varying severity. All forms of hearing loss may be accompanied by tinnitus of varying severity. The following discussion will deal with those forms of sensorineural hearing loss that are not covered in separate chapters of their own.

Sensorineural Hearing Loss of Genetic Origin

Impairment of hearing is the most common sensorineural pathology affecting humans. Approximately, one-half of all the cases of prelingual hearing impairment have a genetic cause [32–34]. A distinction is made between genetic hearing loss occurring as a component of a specific (genetic) syndrome (30%) and non-syndromic hearing loss that occurs in the absence of any other genetic diseases or developmental anomalies [35]. Syndromic hearing loss (SHL) can be inherited in an autosomal dominant, autosomal-recessive, or X-linked manner [34], and can be associated with developmental anomalies of the inner ear or petrous portion of the temporal bone like Mondini[6] or Scheibe[7] dysplasia; frequently there is also a link with other organic disorders, such as thyroid disease (Pendred syndrome), renal dysfunction (Alport syndrome), or

eye disease (Usher syndrome) [34]. Children with Down's syndrome are more likely to have congenital permanent inner ear hearing loss than the general population (which has an incidence of 1:1,000). From teenage years onward, they are likely to develop degenerative cochlear changes, and most will have significant hearing loss by the age of 40 years [34, 36]. Of non-syndromic hearing loss (NSHL), 80% have autosomal recessive, 18% an autosomal dominant, and 2% an X-linked or mitochondrial inheritance pattern [32]. In the majority, a single gene defect leads to the phenotypical development of hearing loss, which may not have its onset until later in life. In recent years, many gene loci and mutations have been described that are responsible for various forms of hearing loss. For example, known mutations affect the GJB2 gene – which codes for connexin-26 – and the GJB6 gene (connexin-30) [37] (see also Chap. 7).

Infections

Inflammation of the cochlea may develop together with acute or chronic otitis media when bacteria enters the cochlea through the round or oval window, or may develop together with meningitis where bacteria enters the cochlea and the vestibular apparatus via the internal auditory canal, the cochlear aqueduct, or the vestibular aqueduct. The resulting sensorineural hearing loss is often accompanied with tinnitus. Because of the involvement of the vestibular apparatus, the symptoms are often dominated by pronounced rotatory vertigo accompanied by nausea and vomiting. Meningitis is often followed by the cochlea being filled with bone (labyrinthitis ossificans or "white cochlea"), with complete obliteration of the membranous labyrinth [38]. The bacteria in borreliosis or syphilis can spread via blood to the inner ear. Many kinds of infections can cause damage to the cochlea or the inner ear as a whole. Especially serious ones are congenital rubella or cytomegalovirus infections, which may lead to severe sensorineural hearing loss or to deafness. Of the postnatal viral infections of the inner ear, epidemic parotitis (mumps) typically causes unilateral deafness without vestibular involvement [39]. Herpes zoster oticus that is caused by reinfection with the varicella zoster virus can cause blisters in the external auditory canal and the pinna in addition to sensorineural hearing loss and

[6] Mondini dysplasia: Congenital anomaly of osseus and membranous otic labyrinth characterized by aplastic cochlea and deformity of the vestibule and semicircular canals with partial or complete loss of auditory and vestibular function; may be associated with dilated vestibular aqueduct and spontaneous cerebrospinal fluid otorrhea resulting in meningitis.

[7] Scheibe dysplasia: Hearing impairment due to cochleosaccular dysplasia; usually autosomal recessive inheritance. Stedman's Online Medical Dictionary.

tinnitus, vestibular symptoms, and facial nerve palsy. When the facial nerve is involved it is known as the Ramsey Hunt syndrome [40]. In addition to infection of the nerve sheaths, the symptoms may also be caused by secretion of toxins into the perilymph spaces of the inner ear [41].

Immunogenic Labyrinthitis

Sensorineural hearing loss may occur together with immunological diseases as a heterogeneous group of sensorineural hearing loss types under the heading "autoimmune inner ear disease" (AIED) [42]. Possible target structures for antibodies are the stria vascularis in the organ of Corti and the blood vessels supplying the inner ear [43]. AIED is characterized by progressive, often fluctuating and usually bilateral, sensorineural hearing loss with tinnitus and vertigo, more often in women. Progression over time is too rapid to suggest presbycusis and too slow for a diagnosis of sudden deafness. AIED patients respond well to immunosuppressant corticosteroid therapy. Some patients with AIED present with a systemic autoimmune disease, such as Wegener's granulomatosis (see footnote 3), Cogan syndrome,[8] or relapsing polychondritis[9] [44]. No specific test battery that will unequivocally show the presence of an autoimmune reaction to structures of the inner ear has yet been described. The recommendation is to use general laboratory tests (antinuclear antibodies, antineutrophil cytoplasmatic antibodies, etc.) to screen patients who are suspected of having an autoimmune disease for the presence of systemic signs [45].

---

[8] Cogan syndrome: Typical Cogan syndrome is characterized by interstitial keratitis and vestibuloauditory dysfunction. There is generally a brief episode of inflammatory eye disease (interstitial keratitis) followed by bilateral audiovestibular symptoms. The interstitial keratitis usually occurs with sudden onset and is characterized by photophobia, lacrimation, and eye pain. The vestibuloauditory dysfunction is usually bilateral, presenting with tinnitus, sensorineural hearing loss, and acute episodes of vertigo.

[9] Relapsing polychondritis: a degenerative disease of cartilage producing a bizarre form of arthritis, with collapse of the ears, the cartilaginous portion of the nose, and the tracheobronchial tree; death may occur from chronic infection or suffocation because of loss of stability in the tracheobronchial tree; of autosomal origin. Stedman's Online Medical Dictionary.

Age-Related Hearing Loss

Age-related hearing loss is the commonest of all forms of hearing loss (see Chap. 36). It affects more than 40% of people over the age of 65 [46]. Apart from physiological age-related processes, endogenous and exogenous factors such as hypoxia, exposure to loud noise, hypertension, hypercholesterolemia, or diabetes mellitus may cause or contribute to hearing loss in old age [47]. Consequently, excessive noise exposure and atherosclerosis contribute to the development of presbycusis in industrialized countries. The reported presence of tinnitus together with presbycusis varies between 8 and 72% [48–50]. The risk for the development of tinnitus rises with increasing age and with increasing exposure to noise [51].

References

1. Takemori S, Tanaka Y, Suzuki JI. Thalidomide anomalies of the ear. Arch Otolaryngol, 1976;102(7):425–7
2. Ostrowski VB, Wiet RJ. Pathologic conditions of the external ear and auditory canal. Postgrad Med, 1996;100(3):223–8, 233–7
3. Adams WS. The aetiology of swimmer's exostoses of the external auditory canals and of associated changes in hearing. J Laryngol Otol, 1951;65(4):232–50; concl.
4. Mlynski R, Radeloff A, Brunner K, Hagen R. [Exostoses of the external auditory canal Is the cold water hypothesis valid for patients in continental areas?] HNO, 2008; 56(4):410–6. German
5. Van Gilse, PHG. Des observations ultérieures sur la genèse des exostoses du conduit externe par l'irritation d'eau froide. Acta Otolaryngol, 1938;2:343–352
6. Breau RL, Gardner EK, Dornhoffer JL. Cancer of the external auditory canal and temporal bone. Curr Oncol Rep, 2002;4(1):76–80
7. Horbelt CV. A review of physical, behavioral, and oral characteristics associated with Treacher Collins syndrome, Goldenhar syndrome, and Angelman syndrome. Gen Dent, 2008;56(5):416–9
8. Rice DP. Clinical features of syndromic craniosynostosis. Front Oral Biol, 2008;12:91–106
9. Jahrsdoerfer RA, Yeakley JW, Aguilar EA, Cole RR, Gray LC. Grading system for the selection of patients with congenital aural atresia. Am J Otol, 1992;13(1):6–12
10. Timmermans K, Vander Poorten V, Desloovere C, Debruyne F. The middle ear of cleft palate patients in their early teens: a literature study and preliminary file study. B-ENT, 2006;2(Suppl 4):95–101
11. Phua YS, Salkeld LJ, de Chalain TM. Middle ear disease in children with cleft palate: protocols for management. Int J Pediatr Otorhinolaryngol, 2009;73(2):307–13

12. Chole RA, McKenna M. Pathophysiology of otosclerosis. Otol Neurotol, 2001;22(2):249–57

13. Altmann F, Glasgold A, Macduff JP. The incidence of otosclerosis as related to race and sex. Ann Otol Rhinol Laryngol, 1967;76(2):377–92

14. Markou K, Goudakos J. An overview of the etiology of otosclerosis. Eur Arch Otorhinolaryngol, 2009;266(1):25–35

15. Ali IBH, Thys M, Beltaief N, Schrauwen I, Hilgert N, Vanderstraeten K, Dieltjens N, Mnif E, Hachicha S, Besbes G, Arab SB, Van Camp G. A new locus for otosclerosis, OTSC8, maps to the pericentromeric region of chromosome 9. Hum Genet, 2008;123(3):267–72

16. Niedermeyer HP, et al., Measles virus and otosclerosis. Adv Otorhinolaryngol, 2007;65:86–92

17. Lippy WH, Berenholz LP, Schuring AG, Burkey JM. Does pregnancy affect otosclerosis? Laryngoscope, 2005;115(10):1833–6

18. Dahlqvist A, Diamant H, Dahlqvist SR, Cedergren B. HLA antigens in patients with otosclerosis. Acta Otolaryngol, 1985;100(1–2):33–5

19. Gristwood RE, Venables WN. Otosclerosis and chronic tinnitus. Ann Otol Rhinol Laryngol, 2003;112(5):398–403

20. Sobrinho PG, Oliveira CA, Venosa AR. Long-term follow-up of tinnitus in patients with otosclerosis after stapes surgery. Int Tinnitus J, 2004;10(2):197–201

21. Sellari-Franceschini S, Ravecca F, De Vito A, Berrettini S. [Progressive sensorineural hearing loss in cochlear otosclerosis]. Acta Otorhinolaryngol Ital, 1998;18(4 Suppl 59):59–65

22. Shinkawa A, Sakai M, Ishida K. Cochlear otosclerosis 30 years after stapedectomy confirmed by CT, MRI. Auris Nasus Larynx, 1998;25(1):95–9

23. Linthicum F, Jr. Post-stapedectomy cochlear otosclerosis. Ear Nose Throat J, 2009;88(4):872

24. Hinojosa R, Marion M. Otosclerosis and sensorineural hearing loss: a histopathologic study. Am J Otolaryngol, 1987;8(5):296–307

25. Ramsden R, Rotteveel L, Proops D, Saeed S, van Olphen A, Mylanus E. Cochlear implantation in otosclerotic deafness. Adv Otorhinolaryngol, 2007;65:328–34

26. Mafee MF. Use of CT in the evaluation of cochlear otosclerosis use of CT in the evaluation of cochlear otosclerosis. Radiology, 1985;156(3):703–8

27. Alford BR, Guilford FR. A comprehensive study of tumors of the glomus jugulare. Laryngoscope, 1962;72:765–805

28. Gulya AJ. The glomus tumor and its biology. Laryngoscope, 1993;103(11 Pt 2 Suppl 60):7–15

29. Horn KL, Hankinson H. (1994) Tumors of the jugular foramen, in Neurotology, RK Jackler, DE Brackmann, Editors, Mosby: New York, 1059–64

30. Sismanis A. (1997) Pulsatile tinnitus, in Clinical otology, GB Hughes, ML Pensak, Editors, Thieme: New York, 445–60

31. Wackym PA, Friedman I. (2000) Unusal tumors of the middle ear and mastoid, in Tumors of the ear and temporal bone, RK Jackler, CLW Driscoll, Editors, Lippincott Williams & Wilkins: Philadelphia, 128–45

32. Birkenhager R, Aschendorff A, Schipper J, Laszig R. [Non-syndromic hereditary hearing impairment]. Laryngorhinootologie, 2007;86(4):299–309; quiz 310–3

33. Kitamura K, Takahashi K, Tamagawa Y, Noguchi Y, Kuroishikawa Y, Ishikawa K, Hagiwara H. Deafness genes. J Med Dent Sci, 2000;47(1):1–11

34. Bayazit YA, Yilmaz M. An overview of hereditary hearing loss. ORL J Otorhinolaryngol Relat Spec, 2006;68(2):57–63

35. Smith RJ, Bale JF, Jr, White KR. Sensorineural hearing loss in children. Lancet, 2005;365(9462):879–90

36. Hess C, Rosanowski F, Eysholdt U, Schuster M. [Hearing impairment in children and adolescents with Down's syndrome]. HNO, 2006;54(3):227–32

37. Batissoco AC, Abreu-Silva RS, Braga MC, Lezirovitz K, Della-Rosa V, Alfredo T, Jr, Otto PA, Mingroni-Netto RC. Prevalence of GJB2 (connexin-26) and GJB6 (connexin-30) mutations in a cohort of 300 Brazilian hearing-impaired individuals: implications for diagnosis and genetic counseling. Ear Hear, 2009;30(1):1–7

38. Douglas SA, Sanli H, Gibson WP. Meningitis resulting in hearing loss and labyrinthitis ossificans – does the causative organism matter? Cochlear Implants Int, 2008;9(2):90–6

39. Hviid A, Rubin S, Muhlemann K. Mumps. Lancet, 2008;371(9616):932–44

40. Sweeney CJ, Gilden DH. Ramsay Hunt syndrome. J Neurol Neurosurg Psychiatry, 2001;71(2):149–54

41. Sugiura M, Naganawa S, Nakata S, Kojima S, Nakashima T. 3D-FLAIR MRI findings in a patient with Ramsay Hunt syndrome. Acta Otolaryngol, 2007;127(5):547–9

42. McCabe BF. Autoimmune sensorineural hearing loss. Ann Otol Rhinol Laryngol, 1979;88(5 Pt 1):585–9

43. Ruckenstein MJ. Autoimmune inner ear disease. Curr Opin Otolaryngol Head Neck Surg, 2004;12(5):426–30

44. Broughton SS, Meyerhoff WE, Cohen SB. Immune-mediated inner ear disease: 10-year experience. Semin Arthritis Rheum, 2004;34(2):544–8

45. Bovo R, Ciorba A, Martini A. The diagnosis of autoimmune inner ear disease: evidence and critical pitfalls. Eur Arch Otorhinolaryngol, 2009;266(1):37–40

46. Cruickshanks KJ, Wiley TL, Tweed TS, Klein BE, Klein R, Mares-Perlman JA, Nondahl DM. Prevalence of hearing loss in older adults in Beaver Dam, Wisconsin The Epidemiology of Hearing Loss Study. Am J Epidemiol, 1998;148(9):879–86

47. Mazurek B, Stöver T, Haupt H, Gross J, Szczepek A. [Pathogenesis and treatment of presbyacusis current status and future perspectives]. HNO, 2008;56(4):429–32; 434–5

48. Rosenhall U, Karlsson AK. Tinnitus in old age. Scand Audiol, 1991;20(3):165–71

49. Nondahl DM, Cruickshanks KJ, Wiley TL, Klein R, Klein BE, Tweed TS. Prevalence and 5-year incidence of tinnitus among older adults: the epidemiology of hearing loss study. J Am Acad Audiol, 2002;13(6):323–31

50. do Carmo LC, Médicis da Silveira JA, Marone SA, D'Ottaviano FG, Zagati LL, Dias von Söhsten Lins EM. Audiological study of an elderly Brazilian population. Braz J Otorhinolaryngol, 2008;74(3):342–9

51. Ahmad N, Seidman M. Tinnitus in the older adult: epidemiology, pathophysiology and treatment options. Drugs Aging, 2004;21(5):297–305

Chapter 35
Tinnitus and Hearing Loss

Giovanna Baracca, Luca Del Bo, and Umberto Ambrosetti

Keypoints

1. Damage in the external, middle, or internal ear can contribute to the emergence of tinnitus because of the hearing loss it causes.
2. The two components of the external ear are the auricle and the outer auditory canal.
   (a) The occlusion of the ear canal produces an alteration in sound transmission that may cause tinnitus to develop.
   (b) Ear canal inflammation may cause tinnitus.
3. The middle ear is an impedance transformer and the site of several pathologies that all may cause tinnitus.
   (a) Acute otitis is accompanied by fever, strong pain in the ear, conductive hearing loss and discharge from the ear.
   (b) Otitis media with effusion is a chronic presence of seromucous secretions in the middle ear cavity without signs of acute inflammation.
   (c) Otitis media is an inflammation of the middle ear causing conductive hearing loss.
   (d) Cholesteatoma is a mass of keratinizing squamous cells or epithelial debris that may occur in the middle ear cavity; it can erode body structures.
   (e) Otosclerosis involves a bony formation around the stapes, impeding its motion.
4. The first symptom of otosclerosis is often tinnitus.

5. Tinnitus often occurs in association with hearing loss of cochlear origin.
   (a) Acoustic trauma is one of the most common risk factors for the development of tinnitus and one of the major causes of permanent sensorineural hearing loss.
   (b) Administration of ototoxic drugs can cause hearing loss, tinnitus, and vertigo or dizziness.
   (c) Age-related changes can cause tinnitus and hearing loss.
   (d) Tinnitus is one of the three symptoms that define Ménière's disease.
   (e) Changes (decrease) in cochlear blood perfusion can lead to cochlear damage with hearing loss and tinnitus
   (f) Abrupt change in barometric pressure (barotraumas) can cause damage to the cochlea and may lead to tinnitus.
6. Hearing loss due to ear diseases may trigger a series of reactions in the central nervous system, which leads to the tinnitus.
7. Head trauma can lead to tinnitus, and balance disorders are very common after mild to severe head traumas.

Keywords Tinnitus • Hearing loss • External ear • Middle ear • Internal ear • Cochlea

Abbreviations

CF	Characteristic frequency
CNS	Central nervous system
dB	Decibel
Hz	Hertz
IHC	Inner hair cell
kHz	Kilohertz
OHC	Outer hair cell
SGN	Spiral ganglion neuron

G. Baracca (✉)
Department of Surgical Specialist Sciences,
University of Milan, Milano, Italy
and
Fondazione Ascolta e Vivi, via Foppa 15, 20144 Milano,
Italy
e-mail: baracca.giovanna@libero.it

A.R. Møller et al. (eds.), *Textbook of Tinnitus*,
DOI 10.1007/978-1-60761-145-5_35, © Springer Science+Business Media, LLC 2011

Introduction

The peripheral auditory system includes the external, the middle, and the internal ear, as well as the acoustic nerve. Damage in one of these structures can contribute to the emergence of tinnitus, associated with hearing loss (Table 35.1). Different mechanisms of the pathophysiology of tinnitus have been hypothesized from the study of the relation between tinnitus and hearing loss, as summarized in the present chapter (see also Chaps. 8 and 10).

Hearing Loss and Tinnitus Caused by External Ear Damage

The two components of the external ear are the auricle and the outer auditory canal, which conveys acoustical waves to the eardrum. The function of the auricle is to direct sounds into the entrance of the ear canal and it acts as an acoustic filter. The auricle is important for directional hearing in the vertical plane and about the direction to the sound source, either frontal or back. Comparison of the input from both ears helps to localize sounds in space.

The external ear canal is 24–27-mm long from the entrance to the ear drum. The external auditory canal amplifies frequencies between 2,000 and 4,000 Hz when the sound source is located in front of an observer [1].

Table 35.1 Main pathologies in the ear which may cause tinnitus

Subjective tinnitus	Causes
Pathologies: external ear	Occlusion of the ear canal
	External otitis
Pathologies: middle ear	Acute otitis media
	Otitis media with effusion
	Chronic otitis media
	Suppurative otitis media
	Cholesteatoma
	Otosclerosis
Pathologies: internal ear	Ototoxic drugs induced hearing loss
	Noise induced hearing loss
	Presbycusis
	Ménière's disease
	Alteration in blood flow
	Barotrauma
	Head trauma

Occlusion of the Ear Canal

Occlusion of the ear canal causes hearing loss on the affected ear. If an obstruction occurs in only one ear, it causes perception of annoying echoes and distortion that may develop into tinnitus. The most common cause of occlusion in the ear canal is the presence of ear wax (cerumen). Ear wax is produced by particular sweat glands located in the ear canal wall. Its function is to protect the ear skin from infections and the ear canal from the entry of foreign bodies. Normally, it moves out of the ear canal automatically. Accumulation of wax in the ear may lead to a wax plug, which is caused by an increased secretion of ear wax, change in the composition of the wax, or anatomical changes in the ear canal (e.g., stenosis, osteoma, esostosi) that prevent the normal movement of wax thus causing buildup. Common symptoms due to the presence of a wax plug are hearing loss, aural fullness, and tinnitus, which typically worsen when water penetrates into the ear. (Ear wax is not completely solvable in water and has a hygroscopic compound.) The presence of a foreign body in the ear canal is another cause of occlusion. These include cotton, gauzes, or even living organisms such as insects, which can be very annoying. The appropriate therapy is the removal of the foreign bodies.

Cancers of the ear canal skin are rare; occlusion-induced symptoms include tinnitus. After a proper assessment, therapy may either be surgical or pharmacological.

External Otitis

Ear canal inflammation is called external otitis. It is always accompanied by itching or pain due to the rich innervation of the skin in the ear canal, and sometimes by fever. Additional symptoms may be discharge, hearing loss, and tinnitus. Signs may include redness and edema with the possible presence of secretions [2].

Ear canal infections can be caused by bacteria or fungi. Anatomical changes in the ear canal can increase the likelihood of infections; frequent and aggressive bathing and bath detergents are such factors. Others include changes of pH in the ear canal. Pharmacological treatment is very important to prevent the spread of infections to neighboring areas. Tinnitus usually disappears with the recovery from inflammation.

Compromised sound transmission to the internal ear by an obstruction of the ear canal causes sound deprivation, which enhances the existing tinnitus and may cause tinnitus in individuals who did not previously have the disorder. This is because deprivation of sound activates neural plasticity (see Chap. 12). Most individuals who are placed in a silent environment will experience tinnitus [3–5].

Hearing Loss and Tinnitus Caused by Damage to the Middle Ear

The middle ear consists of the eardrum and the ossicular chain (malleus, incus, and stapes), which transmits the sounds that reach the eardrum to the cochlear fluids through movements of the stapes footplate located in the oval window. The main function of the middle ear is to optimize energy transfer from the air to the cochlear fluids. It does so by acting as an impedance transformer [6]. Direct transfer of sound energy to internal ear fluids is inefficient because of large differences in the impedance of air and the fluid of the cochlea [7].

The ossicular chain is kept in place by four ligaments and two muscles, the tensor tympani and stapedius muscle. The tensor tympani muscle, with more tonic fibers, is innervated by a branch of the mandibular nerve (a branch of the trigeminal nerve). The stapedius muscle, with more phasic fibers, is innervated by the facial nerve. In humans, contraction of the stapedius muscle can be elicited by a strong sound, whereas the tensor tympani muscle contracts when swallowing and yawning. The acoustic stapedius reflex extends the dynamic range of human hearing, improving word intelligibility of loud sounds [8] and improves discrimination in noise by alternating low frequency sounds that can mask high frequency sounds.

Myoclonus (repetitive abnormal contractions) of the muscles may cause objective tinnitus [9], which may either be perceived as a rhythmic clicking or buzzing [10]. A single instance of continuous and high-frequency tinnitus has been described [11].

The middle ear is connected to the rhinopharynx through the Eustachian Tube. The tube is normally closed, except during swallowing and intense efforts when opened by the peristafilini muscles to allow air to enter the tympanic cavity, thus permitting replacement of air and normalization of pressure to ambient pressure.

Acute Otitis Media

Inflammatory diseases of the middle ear can cause tinnitus; damages to the epithelium in the tympanum and Eustachian tube dysfunction prevent the physiological absorption of air and promote stagnation of secretions, causing alterations in the function of the middle ear. Acute otitis is mainly caused by bacterial infections originating in the nasal cavities. It is accompanied by fever, strong pain in the ear, and conductive hearing loss [12]. It may progress into perforation of the ear drum and discharge from the middle ear.

Otitis Media with Effusion

Otitis media with effusion is characterized by a chronic presence of seromucous secretions in the middle ear cavity without signs of acute infection but with the presence of conductive hearing loss, aural fullness, and sometimes tinnitus. The associated dysfunction of the Eustachian tube prevents normal ventilation of the middle ear cavity causing negative pressure in the middle ear with secretion of fluids from the mucosa [13]. Treatment is either pharmacological or surgical.

Chronic Otitis Media

Chronic otitis is the consequence of protracted inflammation of the middle ear with alterations of the eardrums, usually perforation. The ossicular chain may be affected, calcified, or destroyed. Conductive hearing loss and tinnitus are generally also present [14].

In all these disorders, the normal functions of the middle ear has deteriorated and sound transmission to the cochlea is compromised causing conductive hearing loss often accompanied by aural fullness and tinnitus, which is described by patients as a broadband noise in most cases.

Cholesteatoma

Cholesteatoma is a mass of squamous cells or epithelial debris, a keratinizing lesion that occurs in the middle ear. It may be either congenital or acquired [15].

Cholesteatoma may grow in a way that involves the entire middle ear cavity by eroding the mastoid bone. Clinical presentation is similar to that of chronic otitis, and the common treatment is surgical and involves removal of the pathologic tissue.

Otosclerosis

Otosclerosis is a disease of the cochlear capsule characterized by the formation of soft, vascular bone around the stapes. This causes fixation of the stapes footplate in the oval window [16], resulting in conductive hearing loss and often tinnitus. A genetic factor plays a role in the occurrence of otosclerosis [17, 18], as evident from the fact that it is more common in some families and occurs more often in women. Hearing loss is initially conductive and is greatest for low frequencies, but it increases with progression of the disease. After some time, the disease progresses to the cochlea where it causes ossification causing sensorineural hearing loss and involving high frequencies. Often the first symptom of otosclerosis is tinnitus, which is typically described as ringing, whistling, or roaring. The common treatment of otosclerosis consists of replacement of the stapes by a prosthesis inserted in the footplate, which can restore hearing to near normal and often results in resolution of the tinnitus [19]. A hearing aid is an alternative option, which also can reduce the tinnitus because it restores the ability to hear environmental sounds (see Chap. 74).

Hearing Loss and Tinnitus Caused by Cochlear Damage

The cochlea is a coiled tube containing the sensory cells of audition. The cochlea separates sounds according to frequency before they are transduced by the sensory cells into a neural code in auditory nerve (see Chaps. 8 and 10).

Tinnitus often occurs in association with hearing loss and a common pathophysiology has been hypothesized. Both tinnitus and hearing loss are often associated with other conditions, such as noise trauma, ototoxic drugs, head trauma, Ménière's disease, cochlear hydrops, presbycusis, and genetics alterations and syndromes. Several studies have clearly described how these conditions are associated with hearing impairment, but the exact mechanisms generating tinnitus are still under investigation. Several proposed potential mechanisms are complex and controversial.

In the past years, hearing impairments have been regarded as the effect of injuries to hair cells, mainly OHC. However, it has become evident that disorders of the cochlea can indirectly influence the function of the CNS. Symptoms such as tinnitus and hearing loss are likely to have components that originate in the CNS, causing deprivation and changed balance between inhibition and excitation [1, 20]. Some symptoms may also promote an expression of neural plasticity, which in turn can cause symptoms such as tinnitus, hyperacusis, changed dynamic range, or redirection of information (see Chap. 12).

This new approach to understand the pathophysiology of hearing impairment has blurred the distinction between cochlear and nervous system disorders. Sensorineural hearing loss related to cochlear damage is often characterized by alterations in speech perception and recruitment of loudness; in the past, they were regarded to be related only to damage of hair cells, whereas recent studies have shown that they may also be caused by a change in the function of the central nervous auditory system. In conclusion, hearing impairments may both be the result of a combination of deficits in the auditory periphery and the effect of changes in the CNS. In recent years, evidence has accumulated that plastic changes in the central auditory nervous system can cause tinnitus.

Any factor able to alter the level of the spontaneous activity in the auditory nerve may theoretically result in tinnitus [21]. Bauer [22] proposed that tinnitus is the result of reversible OHC dysfunction and decoupling stereocilia from the tectorial membrane. Schwaber [23] theorized that the basic pathophysiology of tinnitus involves an alteration in stereocilia stiffness that results in an increase in the discharge rate of hair cells. Møller [24] analyzed the link between tinnitus and hearing loss and concluded that tinnitus is not directly related to the degree of the hearing loss. Tinnitus may be the result of a combination of causes.

Factors involved in damage of the cochlea, most commonly related to tinnitus and hearing loss, are discussed in separate chapters (Chaps. 36, 37 and 42).

Ménière's Disease

Ménière's disease [25] is a progressive disorder defined by periodic attacks of vertigo, fluctuating sensorineural hearing loss, tinnitus, and aural fullness [26] (see Chaps. 38 and 60). Several authors have agreed that Ménière's disease is not a single disorder, but rather a family of different disorders. It has been customary to include patients who do not show all symptoms in the term Ménière's disease. For instance, patients who only have tinnitus with aural fullness and a mild temporary hearing loss limited to low frequencies may also be classified as having Ménière's disease.

In the early stages of the diseases, hearing loss only affects low frequencies and is almost completely reversible, but as the disease progresses residual hearing worsens definitively and spreads to higher frequencies. Symptoms are first unilateral, but in many patients they will, in the course of the disease, involve the contralateral ear after 10 or 15 years. Tinnitus may persist between acute attacks, but typically increases in 1 or 2 days before vertigo (Regarding contemporary hypothesis about Ménière's Disease, see Chaps. 38 and 60.).

Alterations in Blood Flow in the Cochlea

The cochlea needs a correct blood supply to preserve its function [27]. The labyrinthine artery is an end-artery, and the inner ear has no collateral blood supply. Even minimal alterations in blood perfusion can lead to cochlear damage. Additionally, vulnerability of the cochlea causes high-energy consumption from the blood supply required to keep the cochlear fluids in perfect balance.

It has been hypothesized that the entity and the frequencies involved in hearing loss may depend on the location of the vascular accident; the district of the cochlea permeates the thrombosis downstream or the bleedings will be affected by damage.

Many systemic diseases that cause hearing loss are also accompanied by tinnitus such as those that are caused by circulatory and microcirculatory alterations [28, 29]. Many hypotheses have been proposed to explain the pathology of sudden hearing loss that occurs without any additional symptoms. One hypothesis regards vascular impairment [30]. It has been suggested that viral infections can also cause sudden hearing loss [31] through a viral attack of endothelial cells, even though no conclusive evidence has been yet found. Hearing loss may be profound at its onset and often accompanied by tinnitus. Hearing may deteriorate within a few hours; fortunately, it is almost always limited to one ear and the chance of spontaneous recovery is good.

Hearing function is generally recovered spontaneously in one-third of patients; it is improved in one-third and is maintained with no change in the remainder of patients. In some cases hearing will improve, while tinnitus will remain the same. Different therapeutic approaches have been used such as administration of steroids, antiviral agents, or hyperbaric oxygen treatment [32, 33].

Barotrauma

Tinnitus can present after diving in water or during a flight, especially in conjunction with cold or allergy symptoms. In these cases, a barotrauma may have caused the symptoms because abrupt change in barometric pressure has affected the cochlear fluids. Tinnitus may either be temporary or persistent. If the trauma has been so severe that it caused a rupture of the eardrum or the round windows (fistula), resulting in hearing loss and/or vertigo, tinnitus often occurs. Adequate medical or surgical treatment is necessary to restore hearing and relieve the tinnitus.

Head Trauma

Tinnitus and balance symptoms are common after both mild and severe head trauma. A temporal bone fracture that may occur after head injury can lead to cochlear damage with severe hearing loss, vertigo, and tinnitus [34]. Acute vertigo typically lasts for several days and then resolves, but dizziness may persist. Hearing loss is often permanent. Tinnitus may decrease or persist together with hearing loss.

Head trauma without a temporal bone fracture can cause cochlear damage [35] with symptoms such as dizziness, tinnitus, and sometimes hearing loss. These symptoms may be temporary or occur sometime after the injury. The symptoms may last for several months and then gradually abate, while tinnitus often remains. The mechanisms that lead to hearing disorders by concussion are not fully known; it has been suggested that the higher nervous structures are involved.

Head trauma can also cause blood effusion into the tympanic cavity, as well as rupture of the eardrum and dislocation of the ossicular chains, resulting in conductive hearing loss and tinnitus. These injuries often require adequate surgical treatment.

Conclusion

Many studies have focused on the relationship between tinnitus and other symptoms, such as hearing loss. However, no clear explanation has been published regarding the cause of tinnitus. Many authors agree that the initial cause of tinnitus, when occurring together with hearing loss, has a peripheral origin that may trigger a series of reactions in the CNS, resulting in tinnitus. The anatomical location of the pathology may be the cochlea, but it is often the auditory nervous system (see Chap. 10). The finding that both people with hearing loss and individuals with normal hearing can have severe tinnitus clearly indicates that tinnitus is not always linked to hearing loss.

References

1. Møller, A.R. (2006) Hearing. Anatomy, Physiology, and Disorders of the Auditory System. 2nd Edition. Academic: San Diego, CA.
2. Osguthorpe, J.D. and Nielsen, D.R. (2006) Otitis externa: review and clinical update. Am. Fam. Physician 74, 1510–1516.
3. Heller, M.F. and Bergman, M. (1953) Tinnitus aurium in normally hearing persons. Ann. Otol. Rhinol. Laryngol. 62, 73–83.
4. Sanchez, T.G., Medeiros, B.R., Levy, C.P., et al. (2005) Tinnitus in normally hearing patients: clinical aspects and repercussions. Rev. Bras. Otorrinolaringol. (English Edition) 71, 427–431.
5. Del Bo, L., Forti, S., Ambrosetti, U., et al. (2008) Tinnitus aurium in persons with normal hearing: 55 years later. Otol. Neurotol. 139, 391–394.
6. Møller, A.R. (1965) An experimental study of the acoustic impedance of the middle ear and its transmission properties. Acta Otolaryngol. 60, 129–149.
7. Rosowski, J.J. (1991) The effects of external- and middle-ear filtering on auditory threshold and noise-induced hearing loss. J. Acoust. Soc. Am. 90, 124–135.
8. Borg, E. and Zakrisson, J.E. (1975) The activity of the stapedius muscle in man during vocalization. Acta Otolaryngol. 79, 325–333.
9. Golz, A., Fradis, M., Netzer, A., Ridder, G.J., Westerman, S.T. and Joachims, H.Z. (2003) Bilateral tinnitus due to middle-ear myoclonus. Int. Tinnitus J. 9, 52–55.
10. Badia, L., Parikh, A. and Brookes, G.B. (1994) Management of middle ear myoclonus. J. Laryngol. Otol. 108, 380–382.
11. Bento, R.F., Sanchez, T.G., Miniti, A. and Tedesco-Marchesi, A.J. (1998) Continuous, high-frequency objective tinnitus caused by middle ear myoclonus. Ear Nose Throat J. 77, 814–818.
12. Ramakrishnan, K., Sparks, R.A. and Berryhill, W.E. (2007) Diagnosis and treatment of otitis media. Am. Fam. Physician 76, 1650–1658.
13. Grimmer, J.F. and Poe, D.S. (2005) Update on eustachian tube dysfunction and the patulous eustachian tube. Curr. Opin. Otolaryngol. Head Neck Surg. 13, 277–282.
14. Verhoeff, M., van der Veen, E.L., Rovers, M.M., Sanders, E.A. and Schilder, A.G. (2006) Chronic suppurative otitis media: a review. Int. J. Pediatr. Otorhinolaryngol. 70, 1–12.
15. Persaud, R., Hajioff, D., Trinidade, A., et al. (2007) Evidence-based review of aetiopathogenic theories of congenital and acquired cholesteatoma. J. Laryngol. Otol. 121, 1013–1019.
16. Stankovic, K.M. and McKenna, M.J. (2006) Current research in otosclerosis. Curr. Opin. Otolaryngol. Head Neck Surg. 14, 347–351
17. Gordon, M.A. (1989) The genetics of otosclerosis: a review. Am. J. Otol. 10, 426–438.
18. Aggarwal, R. and Saeed, S.R. (2005) The genetics of hearing loss. Hosp. Med. 66, 32–36.
19. Glasgold, A. and Altman, F. (1966) The effect of stapes surgery on tinnitus in otosclerosis. Laryngoscope 76, 1524–1532.
20. Møller, A.R. (2006) Neural Plasticity and Disorders of the Nervous System. Cambridge University Press: Cambridge.
21. Simpson, J.J. and Davies, W.E. (1999) Recent advances in the pharmacological treatment of tinnitus. Trends Pharmacol. Sci. 20, 12–18.
22. Bauer, C.A. (2003) Animal models of tinnitus. Otolaryngol. Clin. North Am. 36, 267–285.
23. Schwaber, M.K. (2003) Medical evaluation of tinnitus. Otolaryngol. Clin. North Am. 36, 287–292.
24. Møller, A.R. (2003) Pathophysiology of tinnitus. Otolaryngol. Clin. North Am. 36, 249–266.
25. Ménière, P. (1861) Maladies de l'oreille interne offrant des symptomesde la congestion cerebral apoplectiforme. Gaz. Med. Paris 16, 88.
26. Paparella, M.M. (1984) Pathogenesis of Ménière's disease and Ménière's syndrome. Acta Otolaryngol. Suppl. 406, 10–25.
27. Nakashima, T., Naganawa, S., Sone, M., Tominaga, M., Hayashi, H., Yamamoto, H., Liu, X. and Nuttall, A.L. (2003) Disorders of cochlear blood flow. Brain Res. Rev. 43, 17–28.

28. Burch-Sims, G.P. and Matlock, V.R. (2005) Hearing loss and auditory function in sickle cell disease. J. Commun. Disord. **38**, 321–329.

29. Duck, S.W., Prazma, J., Bennett, P.S. and Pillsbury, H.C. (1997) Interaction between hypertension and diabetes mellitus in the pathogenesis of sensorineural hearing loss. Laryngoscope **107**, 1596–1605.

30. Hughes, G.B., Freedman, M.A., Haberkamp, T.J. and Guay, M.E. (1996) Sudden sensorineural hearing loss. Otolaryngol. Clin North. Am. **29**, 393–405.

31. Merchant, S.N., Durand, M.L. and Adams, J.C. (2008) Sudden deafness: is it viral? ORL J. Otorhinolaryngol. Relat. Spec. **70**, 52–60; discussion 60–62.

32. Rauch, S.D., Chen, C.Y. and Halpin, C.F. (2005) Our experience in diagnostics and treatment of sudden sensorineural hearing loss. Otol. Neurotol. **26**, 317.

33. Zadeh, M.H., Storper, I.S. and Spitzer, J.B. (2003) Diagnosis and treatment of sudden-onset sensorineural hearing loss: a study of 51 patients. Otolaryngol. Head Neck Surg. **128**, 92–98.

34. Johnson, F., Semaan, M.T. and Megerian, C.A. (2008) Temporal bone fracture: evaluation and management in the modern era. Otolaryngol. Clin. North Am. **41**, 597–618.

35. Katsarkas, A. and Baxter, J.D. (1976) Cochlear and vestibular dysfunction resulting from physical exertion or environmental pressure changes. J. Otolaryngol. **5**, 24–32.

Chapter 36
Cochlear and Non-cochlear Age-Related Hearing Loss and Tinnitus

Aage R. Møller

Keypoints

1. Age-related changes are some of the most common causes of disorders of sensory systems.
2. The most common age-related change in hearing is elevation of the hearing threshold beginning at the highest audible frequencies, progressing toward lower frequencies while deepening.
3. Age-related changes in hearing are often, but not always, accompanied by tinnitus.
4. Age-related changes in hearing function may be caused by:

   (a) Degeneration of sensory receptor cells, in the cochlea
   (b) Change in the conduction velocity of sensory nerve fibers
   (c) Change in the access to neural transmitters, such as gamma amino butyric acid (GABA), and subsequent increases in GABA receptor sites

5. Change in processing of information may also occur, causing deterioration of speech comprehension.
6. Animal studies have shown that the progression of age-related changes in hearing might be affected (slowed down) by exposure to sound ("enhanced sound environment") indicating expression of neural plasticity plays a role in some age-related changes of sensory functions.
7. The large individual variability in age-related changes in hearing has many causes, such as exposure to loud sounds, environmental factors, genetics, different expression of genes (epigenetics), and unknown factors.

Keywords Presbycusis • Age-related hearing loss • Tinnitus • Neural plasticity

Abbreviations

ARHI   Age-related hearing impairment
EPSP   Excitatory postsynaptic potentials
GABA   Gamma amino butyric acid

Introduction

Age-related impairment of hearing (presbycusis[1]) is the most common disorder of the auditory system. The most obvious changes in hearing that occur with increasing age are an elevated hearing threshold for high frequencies. Presbycusis normally refers to the elevation of hearing threshold. In addition, the elevation of hearing threshold and impaired processing of sound, known as phonemic regression[2] may occur. Many individuals acquire tinnitus in old age, and it often accompanies presbycusis. However, it may also occur together with minimal hearing loss. Most elderly people have tinnitus when placed in a silent room, such as a room used for audiologic tests.

---

[1]Presbycusis: Loss of hearing associated with aging; manifest as reduced ability to perceive or discriminate sounds; the pattern and age of onset vary (Stedman's Electronic Medical Dictionary).

[2]Phonemic regression: a decrease in intelligibility of speech out of proportion to the pure tone hearing loss associated with aging (Stedman's Electronic Medical Dictionary).

A.R. Møller (✉)
The University of Texas at Dallas, School of Behavioral and Brain Sciences, GR 41, 800 W Campbell Rd, Richardson, TX 75080, USA
e-mail: amoller@utdallas.edu

A.R. Møller et al. (eds.), *Textbook of Tinnitus*,
DOI 10.1007/978-1-60761-145-5_36, © Springer Science+Business Media, LLC 2011

Epidemiology of Presbycusis

Normally, hearing loss increases gradually with age, as shown in many studies. Spoor et al. [1] have reviewed the literature and presented average audiograms for different age groups from eight different population studies based on a total of 7,617 ears – including both men and women (Fig. 36.1). This classical study of age-related hearing loss included the effect of environmental factors, such as noise exposure, and did not show the individual variations.

There is a distinct difference between hearing loss in men and women (Fig. 36.1), but that may be at least partly a result of different degrees of noise-induced hearing loss. It has been preferentially men who were working in industries with heavy noise exposure. This effect of noise exposure is particularly prominent with participants in the older studies, such as those summarized by Spoor with the hearing loss depicted in Fig. 36.1. Some of the individual variations in presbycusis may thus be attributed to environmental factors, mainly the varying degree of exposure to sounds.

Large individual variations were mentioned in several studies. One study [2] quantified these variations (Fig. 36.2). This study showed the individual variations in hearing loss and in speech discrimination. Also, this study included individuals who have had exposure to noise that caused hearing loss, affecting mostly men.

It seems likely that genetic factors also play a role. In fact, a gene that affects age-related hearing loss has been identified in a mice strain [3]. There are many genetic disorders that affect hearing in general [4], but not specifically regarding the deterioration of hearing with age. A study that specifically addressed genetic predisposition for age-related hearing loss [5] found that approximately half of the variance of Age-Related Hearing Impairment (ARHI) is attributable to environmental risk factors. The other half is linked to genetic factors.

Gates and co-authors [6] described the results of a large population study (Farmingham). Hearing sensitivity and word recognition tests in 1662 men and women between the age of 60 and 90 showed that the pure-tone thresholds increased with age at a rate that did not differ by gender. However, men had poorer hearing threshold in general. This means the result of noise exposure had its full effect on hearing thresholds before a person reaches the age of 60 , which is the age at which this population study began. Maximum word recognition ability declined with age more rapidly in men than in women and was also poorer in men than women at younger ages.

One more recent study [7] found that the hearing threshold increased approximately 1 dB per year in individuals of 60 years and above. Females of 70 years and above had a faster rate of change in hearing threshold at 0.25 to 3, 10, and 11 kHz than females in the age group of 60–69 years.

Other authors [8] found a true gender difference in hearing threshold, including a difference in older individuals where women have less age-related hearing loss. Jerger et al. also referred to the hypothesis about

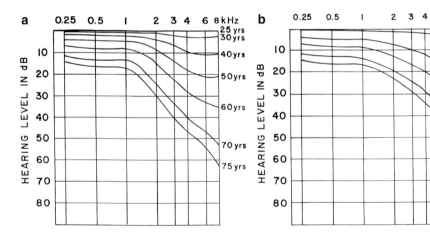

Fig. 36.1 (**a**) Average hearing loss in different age groups of men. Combined results from eight different published studies based on a total of 7,617 ears. (**b**) Average hearing loss in different age groups of women. Results from eight different published studies based on 5,990 ears. Reprinted from Møller AR (2006) Neural plasticity and disorders of the nervous system [1] with permission

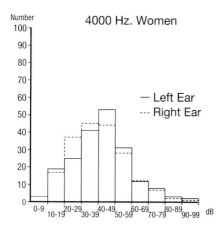
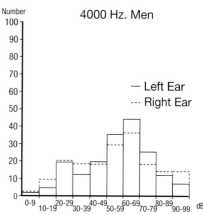

Fig. 36.2 Distribution of hearing loss at different frequencies from a cross-sectional population study of hearing in people of age 70; for women (*left* column) and men (*right* column). Solid lines represent left ear and dashed lines represent right ear. Data from Møller [2]

cardiovascular diseases promoting hearing loss [8], or perhaps, the same genetic factors that promote development of cardiovascular disorders also promote hearing loss. For example, animals studies of rats with predisposition for hypertension also acquire more age related hearing loss and more hearing loss from noise exposure [9, 10]. Other animal experiments have shown the progression of the age-related elevation of the hearing threshold can be arrested by appropriate sound stimulation [11].

Epidemiology of Age-Related Tinnitus

Tinnitus almost always occurs together with hearing loss (see Chaps. 35 and 37). Tinnitus is one of the three symptoms that define Ménière's disease (see Chaps. 38 and 60). Tinnitus is also often associated with presbycusis, but different studies of the prevalence of tinnitus have arrived at different results. The reported concomitant presence of tinnitus varies between 8 and 72% [12–14]. The risk for the development of tinnitus rises with increasing age and with increasing noise exposure [15]. In the age group of 55–65 years, one study found that tinnitus occurred in 19.3% or 11.8%, depending on the questions asked in such studies [16]. Other studies have found very varying incidences of tinnitus together with age-related hearing loss [13, 14], but it is generally agreed that the incidence of tinnitus increases with age [15].

Tinnitus is related not only to the size of the hearing loss but also to the shape of the audiogram, being more common in individuals with a high-frequency, steeply sloping audiogram than in individuals with a flat audiogram [16].

Tinnitus cannot be measured in a similar way as in the case of hearing loss. The evaluation depends on the individual's own assessments of the severity of his or her tinnitus. This adds uncertainties to epidemiologic studies of the prevalence of tinnitus and is the main cause of the differences reported by different authors.

Most people above the age of 60 have experienced some form of tinnitus, but these epidemiologic studies have only included individuals with tinnitus of a certain severity. Some of the causes of variations between the studies of individual investigators are diverse definitions of the different degrees of tinnitus, such as "bothersome tinnitus." Most epidemiologic studies are performed using written questionnaires. The outcome of such epidemiological studies is affected not only by the definitions used for the level of severity, but also in the way the questions are phrased about the participant's perception of his or her tinnitus.

The use of common medications that are associated with tinnitus such as certain diuretics increases with age [17] and this may count for some of the observed age-related increase in the incidence of tinnitus.

As is the case for presbycusis, environmental factors such as noise exposure, exposure to chemicals, and other environmental factors, thus similar reasons for causing more hearing loss in men than women, influence the occurrence of tinnitus. This was confirmed by the findings that tinnitus is more common in males than in females [16].

Pathology of Presbycusis

Many studies have shown that hair cells, especially outer hair cells, are injured in individuals with presbycusis [18] and that these injuries correspond to the hearing loss, as it is reflected in a person's audiogram.

The hearing loss, as it is described by the pure tone audiogram, has been attributed to impairment or loss of cochlear hair cells – mostly affecting outer hair cells. Outer hair cells function to amplify the basilar membrane vibration (act as motors), but the outer hair cells probably do not participate in the signal transduction; that is done by inner hair cells [19] (see Chap. 8). The fact that the morphological changes in the cochlea are so apparent has made investigators and clinicians focus on this aspect of aging in hearing. More recent studies have shown evidence that hair cell damage is not the only cause of presbycusis.

Although morphologic changes in the cochlea of individuals with presbycusis are convincing, it is not the only reason for presbycusis. Other changes in the auditory system that occur normally with age also contribute to the loss of hearing. The abundant efferent innervation of especially outer hair cells makes it possible for the function of outer hair cells to be modulated by signals from the central nervous system (see Chap. 8). Plastic changes that affect the auditory nervous system may thereby affect the transduction process in the cochlea by changing the amplification in the cochlear amplifier. This means that the pathology causing hearing to deteriorate with age is located not only in the cochlea but also in the CNS.

The nervous system is involved in noise-induced hearing loss, as confirmed by the finding that noise-induced hearing loss can be reduced by pre-exposure to moderately strong sounds [20, 21].

It is difficult to distinguish between the deterioration of the hearing from noise exposure from that caused by age-related factors, although the shape of the audiogram of age-related hearing is different from the common noise-induced hearing loss (Chap. 37). The age-related hearing loss is greatest at high frequencies, whereas noise-induced hearing loss is, as a rule, greatest around 4 kHz [19].

The complexity of presbycusis is supported by the results of animal studies where different kinds of rats' hearing loss during their lifetime were studied while the rats were housed under different conditions; with and without noise exposure.

In this study, three groups of rats were exposed to 85 dB, 105 dB, and no noise for 8 h every day during their lifetime [9]. Each group of rats consisted of normotensive and spontaneous hypertensive[3] rats. The hearing loss from noise exposure in the 85 dB group was minimal when compared with those that, were not exposed to noise. The animals in the group that were exposed to 105 dB noise acquired considerable hearing loss. However, it was different for normotensive rats compared with spontaneous hypertensive rats, acquiring an average hearing loss of 30 dB and 60 dB, respectively [22]. The larger hearing loss from exposure to noise in the spontaneous hypertensive rats did not seem to be caused by the elevated blood pressure as such because hypertension induced by ligation of a kidney artery in normotensive rats did not cause larger noise-induced hearing loss [23]. Ligation of one kidney artery caused similar elevation of blood pressure as observed with age in the spontaneous hypertensive rats.

The results of these studies points to a genetic cause of the larger age-related hearing loss in spontaneous hypertensive rats when compared with that of normotensive rates. The genetic cause of hypertension also resulted in greater noise-induced hearing loss in spontaneously hypertensive rats rather than the effect of the high blood pressure as such. These animal studies have thus supported the hypothesis that genetic predisposition for hypertension also promotes hearing loss. The genetic abnormality of spontaneous hypertensive rats also predisposed the rats for acquiring larger than normal elevation of hearing threshold with age. That one genetic abnormality or risk factor can predispose, for more than one pathologic sign is not uncommon.

It has been hypothesized that female reproductive hormones may be involved in causing hearing loss [24]. Estrogen affects auditory neural function, as evidenced from its effect on auditory brainstem responses (ABR) [25]. It is known that female reproductive hormones can modulate the function of GABA receptors [26]. That may be the basis for the effect of female reproductive hormones on hearing loss.

The increased release of the afferent transmitter glutamate can exert a direct as well as an indirect neurotoxic effect at higher concentrations [27]. The age-related reduction in dopamine receptors may also be involved in the effect of age on the incidence of tinnitus [28].

---

[3] Spontaneous hypertensive rats: Rats with genetic predisposition for greater increase in blood pressure with age than normal.

Loss of the inhibitory neural transmitter, GABA, that occurs with age may promote presbycusis [29] and perhaps, in particular, tinnitus. The change in female reproductive hormones with age may therefore affect the development of presbycusis, and this effect may cause some of the differences between the development of presbycusis in men and women. The pathology of presbycusis is far more complex than just damaged hair cells.

It was mentioned above that the central nervous system could influence the function of the hair cells in the cochlea. Injuries to cochlear hair cells can also influence the function of the auditory nervous system. The auditory nervous system can influence how normal hair cells (especially outer hair cells) are damaged or get an abnormal injured function.

While injuries to cochlear hair cells can themselves cause symptoms, pathologies of hair cells can also promote expressions of neural plasticity, which can cause symptoms of hyperactivity, redirection of information, etc. (see Chap. 12). This may explain why injuries to cochlear hair cells are not the sole reason for the symptoms of age-related changes. Hearing loss that occurs when hair cells are injured is therefore not only caused by these injuries as such, but the function of the central auditory nervous system pathways may also be altered. This contributes to hearing loss caused by cochlear pathologies.

In a similar way, the fact that tinnitus is often associated with injuries to hair cells does not mean that it is the hair cells that generate the abnormal neural activity that causes tinnitus. The anatomical location of the abnormal function that causes these symptoms is thus not only the cochlear hair cells, but changes in the function of specific structures of the auditory nervous system may also contribute to some forms of tinnitus.

Presbycusis and age-related tinnitus are caused by a complex combination of deficits in the cochlea and changes in the central auditory nervous system [30, 31]. Advances in our knowledge about the disorders of the auditory system have now blurred the distinction between cochlear and nervous system disorders.

Problems to understand speech, even after that the loss in hearing sensitivity has been compensated for by amplification is common in elderly individuals. Age-related changes in the auditory nerve, where the variation in diameter of auditory nerve fibers increases with age [32] (Fig. 36.3), might contribute to hearing problems. Greater variation in the diameter of auditory nerve fibers in turn causes the conduction velocity to

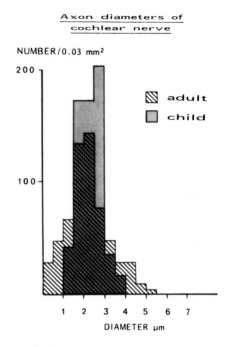

Fig. 36.3 Distribution of diameters of myelinated auditory nerve fibers in humans. Results obtained in an adult are compared with that found in a child. Reprinted from Spoendlin H and A Schrott (1989) Analysis of the human auditory nerve. Hear. Res. 43: 25–38. [32] Reproduced with permission of Elsevier

vary. Subsequently, the arrival time of neural activity at the cochlear nucleus will vary with the degree and kind of injury. This result in a temporal dispersion can have different effects on activation of cochlear nucleus cells [33] (Fig. 36.4). It is evident from Fig. 36.4 that increased temporal dispersion can cause both decreased excitation of target neurons or increased excitation. The latter may be a cause of some forms of tinnitus. Processing in the other nuclei and the cerebral cortex of the auditory system may also change as a result of age-related changes, contributing to difficulties in understanding speech.

Epidemiology of Age-Related Tinnitus

As has been pointed out in other parts of this book, data on epidemiology of tinnitus in general are sparse, and epidemiologic data on age-related are few. A study of the prevalence of tinnitus in children and the elderly [34] found the incidence of tinnitus in presbycusis to be 11%. A study in Sweden of 153 individuals from age 70 to 79

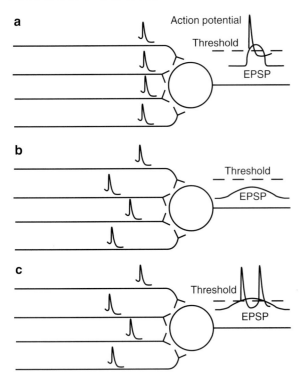

Fig. 36.4 Hypothetical illustration of the effect of spatial integration by a cell on which many axons converge. (**a**) Little spatial dispersion (**b**) Increased spatial dispersion, but the high threshold of the neuron prevents it from firing. (**c**) Large degree of spatial dispersion and low threshold of the neuron. The prolonged EPSP makes the neuron fire twice. From Møller AR (2006) Neural plasticity and disorders of the nervous system. 2006, Cambridge: Cambridge University Press [33]. Reproduced with permission of Cambridge University Press

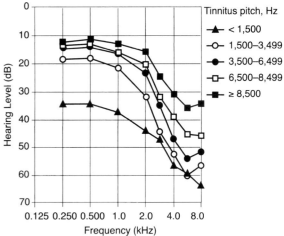

Fig. 36.5 Graph showing the odds of having tinnitus as a function of hearing loss at 4 kHz. Data from a study in the United Kingdom, National Study of Hearing [37]

showed that the incidence of tinnitus increased from 31% at age 70, to 44% at age 79. A few participants (11) in this study had less tinnitus at age 79 compared with what they had at age 70, thus some form of remission [35, 36].

Relationship Between Hearing Loss and Tinnitus

While there are individuals with tinnitus who have normal or near normal hearing, most forms of tinnitus are associated with hearing loss. A study has shown a clear relationship between hearing loss at 4 kHz and the odds of having tinnitus [37] (Fig. 36.5).

It should be noted that 4 kHz is the frequency of greatest hearing loss from noise exposure, and it can be assumed that a noticeable portion of the hearing loss of many of the participants in this study comes from noise exposure (see Chap. 37).

There are also individuals with considerable hearing loss who do not have tinnitus. Hearing loss may therefore not be regarded to always cause tinnitus, although hearing loss – including conductive hearing loss – may be associated with tinnitus, because deprivation of sound activates neural plasticity (see Chaps. 11 and 12).

Individuals with low-frequency tinnitus tend to have more severe hearing loss than people with high-frequency tinnitus [38] (see Fig. 36.6). Tinnitus in connection with age-related hearing loss can have several causes. It can be caused by activation of neural plasticity because of reduced input to the nervous system from the ear (deprivation of sensory input is a strong promoter of plastic changes) (see Chap. 12). It can be caused by aging factors other than those that cause hearing loss. The reduced GABA activity that occurs with age [39] reduces inhibition in general in the nervous system and that may promote hyperactivity, which can cause tinnitus.

It has become evident that risk factors for age-related deterioration of CNS functions causing disorders, such as different forms of dementia, overlap with risk factors for cardiovascular diseases [40]. Little is known about the relation between dementia and hearing loss or about the risk factors for presbycusis and various forms of dementia. However, it has been found that many of the changes that occur with age can be slowed down or prevented by appropriate exposure to sound [11].

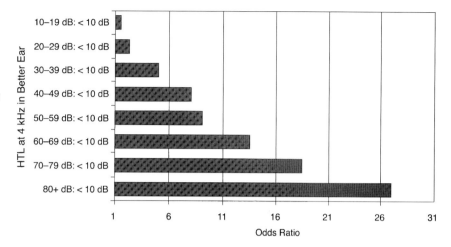

Fig. 36.6 Audiograms of individuals with tinnitus in different frequency ranges. Reproduced from Henry JA, M Meikle and A Gilbert, (1999) Audiometric correlates of tinnitus pitch, in *Proceedings of the Sixth International Tinnitus Semminar*, J Hazell, Editor. The Tinnitus and Hyperacusis Centre: London. 51–7. [38]

Conclusion

The cause of tinnitus is complex, as discussed in several chapters in this book. Although the likelihood of having tinnitus increases with age, as does hearing loss, the casual relationship between hearing loss and tinnitus is complex and many other factors than hearing loss are involved in causing age-related tinnitus.

References

1. Spoor A (1967) Presbycusis values in relation to noise induced hearing loss. Int Audiol 6:48–57.
2. Møller MB (1981) Hearing in 70 and 75 year-old people. results from a cross-sectional and longitudinal population study. Am J Otolaryngol 2:22–9.
3. Johnson KR, LC Erway, SA Cook et al. (1997) A major gene affecting age-related hearing loss in C57BL/6J mice. Hear Res 114:83–92.
4. Topsakal V, G Van Camp and P Van de Heyning (2005) Genetic testing for hearing impairment. B-ENT 1:125–35.
5. Fransen E, L Van Laer, N Lemkens et al. (2004) A novel Z-score-based method to analyze candidate genes for age-related hearing impairment. Ear Hear 25:133–41.
6. Gates G, A, JCJ Cooper, WB Kannel et al. (1990) Hearing in the elderly: the Framingham cohort, 1983–1985. Part I. Basic audiometric test results. Ear Hear 11:247–56.
7. Lee FS, LJ Matthews, JR Dubno et al. (2005) Longitudinal study of pure-tone thresholds in older person. Ear Hear 26:1–11.
8. Jerger J, R Chmiel, B Stach et al. (1993) Gender affects audiometric shape in presbyacusis. J Am Acad Audiol 4(1):42–9
9. Borg E and AR Møller (1978) Noise and blood pressure: Effects on lifelong exposure in the rat. Acta Physiol Scand 103:340–42.
10. Borg E (1982) Noise induced hearing loss in normotensive and spontaneously hypertensive rats. Hear Res 8:117–30.
11. Willott JF, TH Chisolm and JJ Lister (2001) Modulation of presbycusis: current status and future directions. Audiol Neurotol 6:231–49.
12. Do Carmo LC, JA Médicis da Silveira, SA Marone et al. (2008) Audiological study of an elderly Brazilian population. Braz J Otorhinolaryngol 74:342–9.
13. Nondahl DM, KJ Criuckshanks, TL Wiley et al. (2002) Prevalence and 5-year incidence of tinnitus among older adults: the epidemiology of hearing loss study. J Am Acad Audiol 13:323–31.
14. Rosenhall U and AK Karlsson (1991) Tinnitus in old age. Scand. Audiol 20:165–71.
15. Ahmad N and M Seidman (2004) Tinnitus in the older adult: epidemiology pathophysiology and treatment options. Drugs Aging 21:297–305.
16. Demeester K, A van Wieringen, JJ Hendrickx et al. (2007) Prevalence of tinnitus and audiometric shape. B-ENT Suppl 7:37–49.
17. Borghi C, C Brandolini, MG Prandin et al. (2005) Prevalence of tinnitus in patients withhypertension and the impact of different anti hypertensive drugs on the incidence of tinnitus: A prospective, single-blind, observational study. Current Therapeutic Research 66:420–32.
18. Johnsson LG and HL Hawkins (1972) Sensory and neural degeneration with aging, as seen in microdissections of the human inner ear. Ann Otol Rhinol Laryngol 81:179–93.
19. Møller AR (2006) Hearing: Anatomy, Physiology, and Disorders of the Auditory System, 2nd Ed. 2006, Amsterdam: Academic Press.
20. Miller JM, CS Watson and WP Covell (1963) Deafening effects of noise on the cat. Acta Oto Laryng Suppl. 176 1–91.
21. Canlon B, E Borg and A Flock (1988) Protection against noise trauma by pre-exposure to a low level acoustic stimulus. Hear Res 34:197–200.
22. Borg E (1981) Noise, hearing, and hypertension. Scand Audiol 10:125–6.
23. Borg E (1982) Noise induced hearing loss in rats with renal hypertension. Hear Res 8:93–9.
24. Hultcrantz M, R Simonoska and AE Stenberg (2006) Estrogen and hearing: a summary of recent investigations. Acta Otolaryngol 126:10–4.

25. Elkind-Hirsch KE, WR Stoner, BA Stach et al. (1992) Estrogen influences auditory brainstem responses during the normal menstrual cycle. Hear Res 60:143–8.

26. Malyala A, MJ Kelly and OK Rønnekleiv (2005) Estrogen modulation of hypothalamic neurons: activation of multiple signaling pathways and gene expression changes. Steroids 70:397–406.

27. Pujol R, G Rebillard, PJ L. et al. (1990) Glutamate neurotoxicity in the cochlea: a possible consequence of ischaemic or anoxic conditions occurring in ageing. Acta Otolaryngol Suppl. 476:32–6.

28. Mukherjee J, BT Christian, KA Dunigan et al. (2002) Brain imaging of 18F-fallypride in normal volunteers: blood analysis, distribution, test-retest studies, and preliminary assessment of sensitivity to aging effects on dopamine D-2/D-3 receptors. Synapse 46:170–88.

29. Caspary DM, A Raza, Lawhorn et al. (1990) Immunocytochemical and neurochemical evidence for age-related loss of GABA in the inferior colliculus: Implications for neural presbycusis. J Neurosci 10:2363–72.

30. Syka J (2002) Plastic changes in the central auditory system after hearing loss, restoration of function, and during learning. Physiol Rev 82:601–36.

31. Mazelova J, J Popelar and J Syka (2003) Auditory function in presbycusis: peripheral vs. central changes. Exp Gerontol 38:87–94.

32. Spoendlin H and A Schrott (1989) Analysis of the human auditory nerve. Hear Res 43:25–38.

33. Møller AR (2006) Neural plasticity and disorders of the nervous system. 2006, Cambridge: Cambridge University Press

34. Podoshin L, J Ben-David and CB Teszler (1997) Pediatric and Geriatric Tinnitus. Int Tinnitus J 3:101–3.

35. Rubinstein B, T Österberg and U Rosenhall (1992) Longitudinal fluctuations in tinnitus reported by an elderly population. J Audiol Med 1:149–55.

36. Khaw KT (1997) Epidemiological aspects of ageing. Philos Trans R Soc Lond B Biol Sci 352:1829–35.

37. Coles R, (2000) Medicolegal issues, in Tinnitus Handbook, R Tyler, Editor. 2000, Singular Publishing: San Diego. 399–417.

38. Henry JA, M Meikle and A Gilbert, (1999) Audiometric correlates of tinnitus pitch, in Proceedings of the Sixth International Tinnitus Semminar, J Hazell, Editor. The Tinnitus and Hyperacusis Centre: London. 51–7.

39. Caspary DM, JC Milbrandt and RH Helfert (1995) Central auditory aging: GABA changes in the inferior colliculus. Exp. Gerontol 30:349–60.

40. Fillit H, DT Nash, T Rundek et al. (2008) Cardiovascular risk factors and dementia. Am J Geriatr Pharmacother 6:100–18.

Chapter 37
Noise-Induced Hearing Loss: Implication for Tinnitus

Donald Henderson, Eric C. Bielefeld, Edward Lobarinas, and Chiemi Tanaka

Keypoints

1. Noise-induced hearing loss (NIHL) is often associated with tinnitus.
2. The shape and depth of the audiogram in patients with NIHL varies considerably.
3. Characteristics of tinnitus (sensation level, pulsatile versus continuous, perceived pitch) also vary widely across individuals.
4. The relationship between the pattern of hearing loss and the characteristics of the tinnitus is complex and a relevant topic of research.
5. This chapter focuses on three topics relevant to NIHL and tinnitus:

   (a) The relationship between the parameters of a noise exposure and the resulting hearing loss.
   (b) The cochlear pathologies underlying permanent hearing loss and temporary hearing loss and how they differ.
   (c) Noise-induced tinnitus and the animal modeling of tinnitus used to study the relationship between noise and tinnitus.

Keywords Temporary threshold shift • Permanent threshold shift • Kurtosis • Noise interactions • Tinnitus

Abbreviations

ATS   Asymptotic threshold shift
CNS   Central nervous system

EAM External auditory meatus
GPIAS Gap-prepulse inhibition of the acoustic startle
IHC Inner hair cell
NBN Narrow band noise
NIHL Noise-induced hearing loss
NIOSH National Institute for Occupational Safety and Health
OHC Outer hair cell
OSHA Occupational Safety and Health Administration
PTS Permanent threshold shift
TTS Temporary threshold shift

Introduction

Hearing loss from exposure to noise can either be temporary or permanent, depending on the level or duration of the exposure. The audiological symptoms associated with both noise-induced temporary threshold shift (TTS) and permanent threshold shift (PTS) include an elevation in hearing thresholds with particular vulnerability in the 3–6 kHz region; decreased frequency resolution and increased vulnerability to masking; abnormal growth of loudness; compromised temporal processing (i.e. decreased temporal summation of acoustic power and increased forward masking); and, of course, tinnitus (see review by Henderson et al. [1]).

There have been scores of studies on the relationship between noise exposure, the resultant hearing loss, changes in cochlear tuning, and the pathological basis for the corresponding audiometric symptoms (see Review articles by Saunders et al., Lieberman, Henderson and Hamernik [2–4]). However, our understanding of the biological basis of tinnitus is not as well understood (see review by McFadden and Wightman [5]).

D. Henderson (✉)
Center for Hearing and Deafness,
Department of Communicative Disorders and Sciences,
State University of New York at Buffalo,
Buffalo, NY 14214, USA
e-mail: donaldhe@buffalo.edu

A.R. Møller et al. (eds.), *Textbook of Tinnitus*,
DOI 10.1007/978-1-60761-145-5_37, © Springer Science+Business Media, LLC 2011

Tinnitus is a particularly interesting problem because noise exposures primarily damage the auditory periphery (cochlea) while evidence of tinnitus is often clearly central in origin. A fundamental question is what the changes in the operation of the cochlea that leads to a phantom perception generated in the central nervous system (CNS).

Acoustic parameters of Noise-Induced Hearing Loss (NIHL)

A review of the relationship between the parameters of noise exposure and temporary or permanent hearing loss is a reasonable place to begin an examination of the relation between noise exposure and tinnitus.

Temporary Threshold Shift (TTS)

Exposure to loud sound can lead to acute TTS, or if the noise is loud enough or long enough the hearing loss

can be PTS. The most comprehensive study of TTS was done in the 1940s and 1950s by Hallowell Davis [6] and his distinguished colleagues. They systematically studied the relationship between the acoustic variables of *frequency*, *intensity*, and *duration* and the perceptual correlates of loudness changes, pitch coding, and tinnitus.

A summary of their findings is schematically illustrated in Fig. 37.1 and includes the following results: (1) Exposure to pure tones or noise above 90 dB SPL can shift an individual's hearing threshold; (2) The magnitude of the hearing loss caused by a specific tone depends on the frequency of the tone, i.e. high frequencies such as 2,000 and 4,000 Hz caused a larger threshold shift than low frequencies (500 Hz). Note that the 500 Hz tone caused a broad hearing loss that was roughly equal in magnitude to the 2,000 and 4,000 Hz tones, but that the 500 Hz tone required a 32-min exposure while the 2,000 and 4,000 Hz tones required only 4-min exposures to elicit the same threshold shifts (Fig. 37.1a); (3) The peak of threshold shift in the audiogram was typically 1/2 to 1 octave above the frequency of the exposure (Fig. 37.1a–c); (4) The magnitude of TTS grew

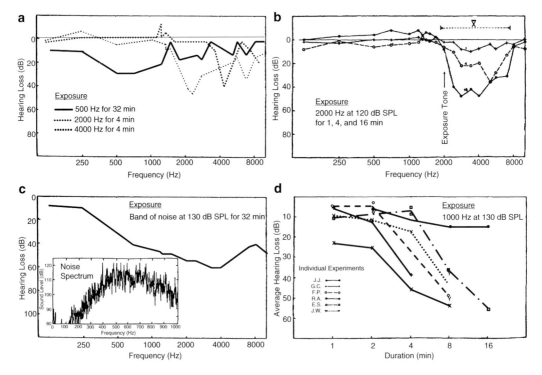

Fig. 37.1 Pattern of TTS from exposure to tones and noise. (**a**) Average TTS following exposure to either 500, 2,000, or 4,000 Hz; (**b**) growth of hearing loss for 2000 Hz tone at 120 dB SPL for 1, 4,

or 16 min; (**c**) average hearing loss from exposure to band of noise (*insert*) at 130 dB SPL for 32 min; (**d**) individual subject's exposure to 1000 Hz at 130 dB SPL. Adapted from Davis et al. [6]

with duration of exposure; (5) There was substantial inter- and intra-subject variability (Fig. 37.1b). One subject develops less than 15 dB of TTS after 16 min while another subject develops 50 dB after only an 8-min exposure to the 1,000 Hz tone. The variability across subjects is especially puzzling given that they all had the same pre-exposure audiogram and received exactly the same noise exposure; (6) Wide band noise caused a pattern of hearing loss with a "notch" or peak ranging between 3 and 6 kHz. Since the external auditory meatus (EAM) acts like a ¼ wave resonator, the actual location of the notch (3, 4, or 6 kHz) partially depends on the length of the subject's EAM. Larger subjects with longer EAMs tend to have notches at lower frequencies, while smaller subjects with shorter EAMs tend to have notches at higher frequencies.

The authors used binaural loudness balancing techniques to compare the loudness between an exposed and non-exposed ear. They reported a change in loudness with TTS (i.e. the degree of loudness shift is greater at low sensation levels, but the difference is reduced or disappears at high levels of stimulation). This phenomenon has been termed 'recruitment' [7]. With regard to frequency coding, they reported a diplacusis (i.e. for the same stimulus, the normal and ear with TTS develop different pitches). Finally, without analyzing the observation, they reported that a number of the subjects developed a buzzing or ringing in their ears which has become known as tinnitus. The tinnitus following a pure tone exposure was reported to have a much more consistent and defined pitch than the tinnitus following a noise exposure. Most of the subjects completely recovered. However, several were left with a permanent hearing loss. The results of Davis et al. [6] on the development of TTS have been expanded and confirmed by a number of investigators (series summary by Ward [8]). The early collection of research raises several questions. What is the relation between TTS and PTS in cases of more extreme exposures? What are the underlying changes in cochlear anatomy and physiology that lead to the constellation of symptoms associated with TTS and tinnitus?

Given that the audiological symptoms are essentially the same for both the TTS and PTS, it is reasonable to assume that the underlying changes in the cochlea are similar between the two conditions. However, this assumption ultimately proves to be too difficult to confirm or deny. An interesting perspective on TTS and PTS is provided in the literature on asymptotic threshold

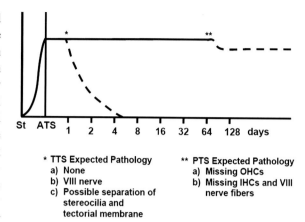

Fig. 37.2 Model of transition from temporary and permanent threshold shift using ATS paradigm

shift (ATS) [9–11]. ATS refers to the phenomenon where hearing loss grows over the first 8–24 h of a noise exposure. Hearing then stabilizes at an asymptotic level and remains at the same level for weeks or months of a constant noise exposure. If subjects are studied at different time points (i.e. 24-h exposure to 60 days), an interesting trend emerges (see Fig. 37.2). Both the 24 h subjects and the 60 day subjects have the same magnitude of threshold shift. When the 24-h subjects are removed from the noise, they begin to recover to normal sensitivity and suffer no PTS or cochlear damage. However, for subjects exposed to 60 days of noise, even though they have the same magnitude of threshold shift, when they are removed from noise they recover slowly and only partially [12]. The transition from TTS to PTS illustrates how the conditions produce the same apparent threshold shift on the audiogram but with significant differences in the underlying pathology.

Pathology of TTS

The term "TTS" suggests the pathological changes might be insignificant. However, in cases of TTS the cochlea can suffer a fairly wide spectrum of possible anatomical changes, from substantial temporary pathological damage to subtle, non-symptomatic pathological changes.

Nordmann et al. [13] have shown that TTS exposure can be associated with a disconnection between the tallest outer hair cell (OHC), stereocilia, and the tectorial membrane due to changes in the structure of the organ of Corti. The assumption is partial recovery

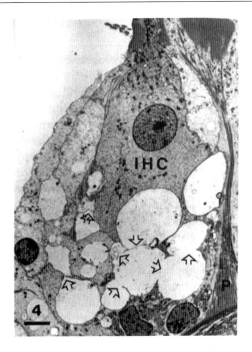

Fig. 37.3 Inner hair cell after noise exposure. Note *arrows* identify swollen VIII nerve dendrites

results from structural recovery of the supporting cells and eventual reattachment of the stereocilia to the tectorial membrane. Also, the VIII nerve dendrites under the inner hair cells (IHCs) suffer excitotoxicity [14, 15], leading to de-afferentation of the IHC (Fig. 37.3). However, studies of IHC/VIII nerve fiber excitotoxicity with kainic acid (which mimics the effects of noise) show that the swollen VIII nerve dendrites recover and become functional again [16]. Consequently, part of TTS is likely due to the repairable excitotoxicity. Finally, the cochlea can sustain permanent losses of OHCs that are not sufficient in number to impair threshold detection. Collectively, the pathology associated with TTS may be repairable, or the permanent changes are too minor to be detected with typical audiological measures, so PTS would not be observed audiometrically.

Permanent Threshold Shift (PTS)

The relationship between the parameter of a noise and PTS are similar to TTS, but the levels required to cause PTS are higher or the durations are longer.

For humans the threshold for causing PTS with years of daily repeated noise exposures is approximately 85 dBA [17]. The assumption is that repeated daily exposure for 5–10 years will lead to PTS. The predictive course of NIHL prepared by ISO1999 is associated with large degrees of variability, consequently making the prediction for an individual questionable. The underlying assumption of the ISO1999 procedure is that the degree of HL is related to the total energy of the exposure. The U.S. Occupational Health and Safety Administration (OHSA) considers 85 dB(A) to be the "action" level where workers are monitored and 90 dB(A) is permissible for 8 h. For each 5 dB increase in level, there is a halving of the duration (for example 95 dB(A) for 4 h is equivalent to 100 dB(A) for 2 h). In 1995, the National Institute for Occupational Safety and Health (NIOSH) prepared a recommendation for a noise standard that has a maximum tolerable exposure of 85 dB for 8 h and a 3 dB trading ratio (88 dB(A) for 2 h equals 91 dB(A) for 1 h), but the NIOSH amendment has not been enacted into law.

The effects of continuous and impulse/impact noise are different. For example, in the relationship between the noise level and ATS or PTS, for either laboratory studies or in large demographic studies, hearing loss grows at the rate of 1.7 dB for each dB of noise above the threshold for damage [18]. The relationship between the noise level and hearing loss changes dramatically with exposure to impulse, impact, and high level bursts of continuous noise. To illustrate, chinchillas were exposed to impact noises of equal energy, i.e. the impacts' peak levels × the number of repetitions were counterbalanced so that each group had equal amounts of acoustic energy (102–135 dB SPL) (Fig. 37.4) [19]. As seen in Fig. 37.4, the hearing loss was approximately the same for exposure to impacts of 102–119. However, above 119 dB, the hearing loss increased dramatically in spite of the equal energy that each exposure had. The interpretation of these results is that for the lower levels 99–119 dBA, the impact noises caused the same cochlear damage and HL because the ear was responding to the total energy of the exposure. However, at higher levels the hearing loss is more related to the peak level of the impact. This can suggest direct mechanical damage. This and a number of experiments with high level exposure [11, 20] lead/led to the formulation of the "critical level" hypothesis [21]

Fig. 37.4 Average PTS at 4,000 Hz for chinchilla exposed to impact noise ranging from 107 to 143 dB peak SPL at either rate of 1/s (**a**) or 4/s (**b**). From Henderson and Hamernik [19]

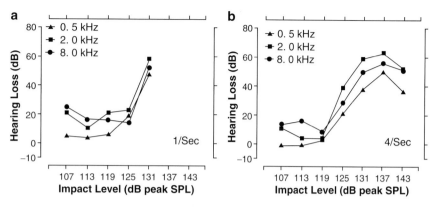

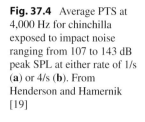

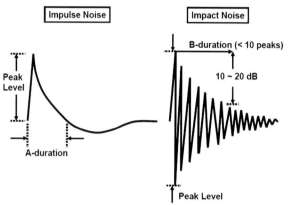

Fig. 37.5 Schematic of impulse and impact noise. Impulses are created by explosive phenomenon while impacts are consequence of hard object colliding. From Henderson and Hamernik [22]

which assumes that high level exposures damage the ear causing direct mechanical failure.

The threshold of direct mechanical failure or "critical level" depends on the duration of the exposure. For example, for gunfire with peak levels of approximately 140–165 dB pSPL and impulse durations of approximately 1 ms, the "critical level" is between 150 and 155 dB pSPL peak level. For impact noise with duration of 200 ms, the "critical level" for mechanical failure is approximately 120 dBA. Short duration impulse and impact noises are shown in Fig. 37.5 [22].

When a noise exceeds the "critical level", damage to the cochlea is immediate and direct, as seen Fig. 37.6. This figure illustrates a number of pathologies associated with exposure to "gunfire" and the resultant mechanical failures. These failures range from dramatic damage as seen in Fig. 37.6a [23], where the organ of Corti is ripped from the basilar membrane

(Note the split of the cuticular plate between first and second row of OHC; this type of damage allows endolymph to bathe the OHCs and cause their death), to a more subtle damage where OHCs are separated from their Deiters' cups (Fig. 37.6b).

When a continuous noise exposure is terminated, recovery of function proceeds almost immediately in the affected cochlear region and hearing sensitivity recovers to baseline or to a stable level of PTS. However, with exposure to high level impact/impulse noise, the time course of recovery may be complicated and tri-phasic. For example, there is a rapid recovery for 15 min–1 h, a rebound where hearing loss increases over a 2–6 h period, and then finally a slower recovery to a stable level of hearing or hearing loss.

NIHL and Tinnitus

There is no question about the strong correlation between NIHL and tinnitus. In the review of the clinical and experimental literature on noise and tinnitus for the military, it is stated, "... noise doses associated with hearing loss are likely to be associated with tinnitus". However, they were not specific about the exact relationship between HL and tinnitus, i.e. the percentage of people with hearing loss that suffer tinnitus or the magnitude of the hearing loss and tinnitus. They did report that exposure to impulse noise is more likely to produce tinnitus than exposure to continuous noise. More recently, a study evaluating soldiers exposed to blast trauma in Iraq and Afghanistan found that 49% of combat personnel exposed to blasts developed tinnitus. Moreover, tinnitus ranked as the chief audiologic complaint. These new findings provide direct evidence

Fig. 37.6 Chinchilla exposed
to impulse noise of 155 dB
peak SPL. (**a**) Mechanical
damage when organ of Corti
(**d**) is ripped from basilar
membrane (**c**) From Hamernik
et al. [23]; (**b**) OHC separated
from Dieter's cells

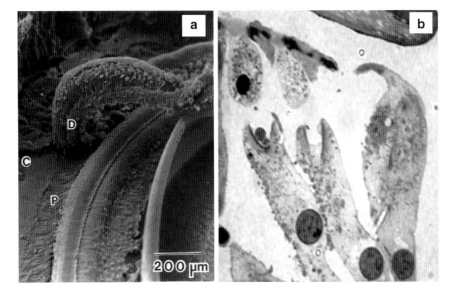

of noise overexposure and subsequent tinnitus. However, more studies are needed to characterize the persistence and features of this tinnitus.

The correlation between NIHL and tinnitus remains far from perfect. There is still a large gap in our knowledge on how peripheral damage (by noise) in the cochlea leads to abnormal neural activity in the brain and the false perception of tinnitus. Two possible causes of tinnitus may be secondary neural degeneration (i.e. VIII nerve to cochlear nucleus, etc.) in the CNS or changes in the balance of excitation and inhibition in auditory pathways. Morest and colleagues [24] have reported neural degeneration in the auditory system secondary to cochlear degeneration caused by noise. The implication of the noise-induced CNS degeneration for perception is not clear. TTS, which presumably does not cause CNS degeneration, can also cause tinnitus. The alternative hypothesis for tinnitus and NIHL is a change in balance of excitation-inhibition. Salvi and colleagues [25] have experimental data showing rapid changes in the inferior colliculus and auditory cortex after NIHL. After traumatic noise exposure, the spontaneous activity of the VIII nerve remains normal, but the spontaneous activity of the cochlear nucleus can increase with "bursts" of neural responses [26]. In addition, studies of evoked potentials (inferior colliculus, auditory cortex) after acute noise exposure show an elevation of threshold as well as enhancement of the amplitude of the evoked potential [25, 27]. These findings suggest that the hearing loss caused a release of inhibition. With the development of animal models of tinnitus, we can expect more information for the relationship between cochlear pathology, changes in neural firing patterns, and tinnitus.

Animal Models of Tinnitus

Jastreboff was the first to develop an animal model of tinnitus over 20 years ago. The initial studies looked at the effects of high doses of sodium salicylate and the development of transient tinnitus in rats. The model used a creative and straightforward lick-suppression paradigm that required discrimination between real sound and quiet. When the animals are exposed to high-dose salicylate, they fail to discriminate between quiet conditions and audible sound conditions. Since the animals failed to perceive the quiet intervals they continued to drink in the presence of a quiet/calm state. The inability to perceive the quiet state is interpreted to mean that the animals are experiencing tinnitus induced by the salicylate.

A similar technique was developed by Heffner. However, there were a number of notable differences. Heffner used an operant food-reinforced behavioral technique whereby gerbils could avoid shock if they refrained from responding during quiet intervals. Responding was allowed during sound. More importantly, Heffner used varying levels of unilateral tone trauma (10 kHz, 124 or 127 dB SPL, for 0.5, 1, 2, or 4 h) to induce tinnitus. The key findings were threefold. First, regardless of sound intensity or duration not all animals developed tinnitus, highlighting individual differences in susceptibility of tinnitus. Second, the probability of tinnitus increased as a function of sound intensity. Finally, only long duration, high intensity tone trauma resulted in tinnitus. Tinnitus was seldom reported for low intensity or short duration trauma. Thus, there is a direct relationship between the trauma duration or level and the probability of developing tinnitus.

The most recent animal model of tinnitus relies on the acoustic startle response to a brief startling broadband or band-pass noise. Presentation of this stimulus reliably induces a large motor startle in rats that can be measured on a pressure sensitive plate. However, when a brief low intensity signal is presented before the startling sound, a significant reduction in startle amplitude is observed. This is known as pre-pulse inhibition. The acoustic signal preceding a startling sound that is audible serves to reduce the startle response. Another way of inhibiting the startle is by presenting a silent gap in a low-level continuous background noise before a startling stimulus. In this paradigm, there is always a background band-pass noise running throughout the session. At random intervals, startling sounds are presented and elicit large startle responses. On some trials, silent gaps are embedded in the continuous noise 100 ms before the startle sound. If these are detected, the amplitude of the startle response is decreased. This is known as gap-prepulse inhibition.

We have performed a number of preliminary studies to evaluate the suitability of the gap-prepulse inhibition of the acoustic startle (GPIAS) model on detecting the presence of noise induced tinnitus. When we pooled the results across a number of preliminary studies we found a direct correlation with the level of noise trauma and the probability of chronic tinnitus. When animals were exposed to a 123 dB SPL (12 kHz, NBN, BW = 100 Hz, 2 h) noise exposure (Fig. 37.7), approximately 33% showed evidence of tinnitus. Raising the noise exposure level to 126 dB SPL increased the percentage of animals with evidence of tinnitus to 75%. In contrast, when salicylate was used to induce transient tinnitus the incident level was 100%. As not all animals were tracked long term, the data from noise exposure is related to evidence of tinnitus of 2–15 days post noise. Further studies are

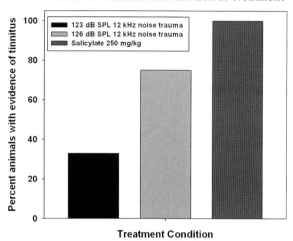

Percent of Tinnitus as a function of Treatment

Fig. 37.7 The percentage of animals with evidence of tinnitus after unilateral noise trauma increased from 33% at 123 dB SPL (NBN centered at 12 kHz, BW = 100 Hz, duration of 1 h) to 75% at 126 dB SPL (NBN centered at 12 kHz, BW = 100 Hz, duration 1 h). Pharmacologically-induced transient tinnitus with a high dose of sodium salicylate (250 mg/kg, 1 h pre-session, i.p.) yielded evidence of tinnitus in all the animals tested. Group sizes were 12, 12, and 24 rats (Harlan SASCO Sprague Dawley, adult males, mean body weight 375 g)

needed to determine the percentage of animals that develop long-term chronic tinnitus.

In addition to the duration of tinnitus, we were also interested in the pitch of noise-induced tinnitus. Evidence from human studies suggests that there is a relationship between the frequency of the maximal hearing loss and the pitch of the tinnitus. When animals were unilaterally exposed to 12 kHz noise at 123 dB SPL, tinnitus was observed between 12 and 16 kHz (Fig. 37.8). Immediately after the noise exposure, however, animals failed to detect gaps at multiple frequencies. This effect disappeared within 24 h, but evidence of tinnitus remained in the 12–16 kHz region. Increasing the level of the unilateral 12 kHz NB noise to 126 dB SPL led to a nearly complete loss of gap-induced prepulse inhibition at 16 kHz (Fig. 37.9). Changing the center frequency of the noise from 12 to 16 kHz resulted in the maximum loss of gap-induced prepulse inhibition occurring at 20 kHz instead of 16 kHz (Fig. 37.10). Audiometrically, these changes in the "pitch" of the tinnitus would seem to be related to a shift in the location of maximal OHC trauma in the cochlea, but that relationship has yet to be confirmed anatomically.

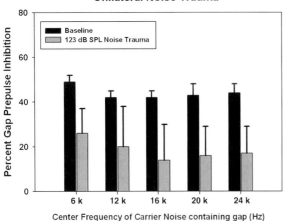

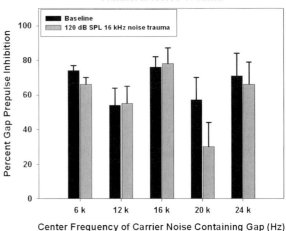

Fig. 37.8 The percentage gap prepulse inhibition before and after 123 dB SPL unilateral noise trauma (NBN centered at 12 kHz, BW = 100 Hz, duration of 1 h). Baseline shows robust inhibition (40–50%) of the startle response when a gap is presented before the startling stimulus (100 ms gap, 100 ms before a 115 dB SPL, 20 ms Band-pass noise 5–10 kHz). In contrast, post exposure gap prepulse inhibition decreases by more than 50% with gaps in 16 kHz carrier NBN showing the largest drop. The decrease in the ability to detect the gap was interpreted as evidence of tinnitus

Fig. 37.10 The percentage gap prepulse inhibition before and after 120 dB SPL unilateral noise trauma (NBN centered at 16 kHz, BW = 100 Hz, duration of 1 h). Post exposure gap prepulse inhibition decreases by more than 50% at 20 kHz. The decrease in the ability to detect the gap was interpreted as evidence of tinnitus centered primarily around 20 kHz

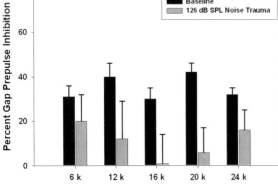

Fig. 37.9 The percentage gap prepulse inhibition before and after 126 dB SPL unilateral noise trauma (NBN centered at 12 kHz, BW = 100 Hz, duration of 1 h). Baseline shows significant inhibition (30–40%) of the startle response when a gap is presented before the startling stimulus (100 ms gap, 100 ms before a 115 dB SPL, 20 ms Bandpass noise 5–10 kHz). In contrast, post exposure gap prepulse inhibition decreases by more than 50%, with gaps in the 16 kHz carrier NBN showing the largest drop resulting in them being virtually indistinguishable from trials with no gaps. The decrease in the ability to detect the gap was interpreted as evidence of tinnitus centered primarily around 16 kHz

One limitation of the GPIAS model is that the startle response is dependent on binaural hearing. If the unilateral acoustic trauma is excessive, the startle stimulus is less effective at producing a strong startle response. Because of this, it is advantageous to limit the hearing loss to the high frequencies. There is also clinical value of limiting the NIHL as tinnitus induced by noise tends to be perceived at higher frequencies. The startle stimulus can also be moved so that it is a band-pass noise within the audible range of even the exposed ear. This can increase the effectiveness of the startle stimulus following the exposure.

Despite the gaps of knowledge that still exist regarding the biological basis for tinnitus and the basis for tinnitus susceptibility, a number of research groups have been steadily narrowing the gaps. Progress is likely to accelerate as animal models continue to be developed and act as a platform for basic science and pre-clinical drug therapy models. However, challenges still remain for understanding tinnitus. However, NIHL is known to be one of the key catalysts for the development of chronic tinnitus. A concerted effort using animal models, human and animal imaging studies, physiological, behavioral, and pharmacological studies will likely enhance our knowledge base and move us closer to providing strategies to reduce the impact of tinnitus.

Conclusions

The hearing loss caused by exposure to noise can be either temporary or permanent. In addition to a loss of hearing sensitivity, traumatic noise exposure degrades signal detection in background noise, reduces the dynamic range of loudness, and can induce tinnitus. The deleterious effects of noise are related to each of the primary dimensions of sound: frequency, intensity, and duration of exposure. Our current noise standards are over 40 years old (from 1968), and do not reflect modern scientific research or our understanding of the effects of noise. For example, research has shown that certain types of noise exposure (combinations of continuous noise with impulse/impact noise) or noise combined with ototoxic solvents pose an increased risk to hearing compared with simple continuous noise exposures. Since the initial noise legislation of 1968, much has been learned about the mechanisms through which noise causes hearing loss, and in the last 10 years, much progress has been made in unraveling the mystery of noise-induced tinnitus.

References

1. Henderson D, M Subramaniam, MA Gratton et al (1991) Impact noise: the importance of level, duration, and repetition rate. J Acoust Soc Am 89:1350–7.
2. Henderson D and RP Hamernik (1995) Biologic bases of noise-induced hearing loss. Occup Med 10:513–34.
3. Liberman MC (1990) Quantitative assessment of inner ear pathology following ototoxic drugs or acoustic trauma. Toxicol Pathol 18:138–48.
4. Saunders JC, SP Dear and ME Schneider (1985) The anatomical consequences of acoustic injury: A review and tutorial. J Acoust Soc Am 78:833–60.
5. McFadden D and FL Wightman (1983) Audition: some relations between normal and pathological hearing. Annu Rev Psychol 34:95–128.
6. Davis H, CT Morgan, JE Hawkins et al (1943) Temporary deafness following exposure to loud tones and noise. Acta Otolaryngol Suppl LXXXVIII.
7. Jerger JF (1952) A difference limen recruitment test and its diagnostic significance. Laryngoscope 62:1316–32.
8. Ward WD (1968) Susceptibility to auditory fatigue. Contrib Sens Physiol 3:191–226.
9. Carder HM and JD Miller (1971) Temporary threshold shifts produced by noise-exposure of long duration. Trans Am Acad Ophthalmol Otolaryngol 75:1346–54.
10. Carder HM and JD Miller (1972) Temporary threshold shifts from prolonged exposure to noise. J Speech Hear Res 15:603–23.
11. Mills JH (1973) Temporary and permanent threshold shifts produced by nine-day exposures to noise. J Speech Hear Res 16:426–38.
12. Bohne BA (1977) Growth of cochlear damage with increasing severity of exposure. Trans Sect Otolaryngol Am Acad Ophthalmol Otolaryngol 84:420–1.
13. Nordmann AS, BA Bohne and GW Harding (2000) Histopathological differences between temporary and permanent threshold shift. Hear Res 139:13–30.
14. Puel JL, C d'Aldin, J Ruel et al (1997) Synaptic repair mechanisms responsible for functional recovery in various cochlear pathologies. Acta Otolaryngol 117:214–8.
15. Pujol R and JL Puel (1999) Excitotoxicity, synaptic repair, and functional recovery in the mammalian cochlea: a review of recent findings. Ann N Y Acad Sci 884:249–54.
16. Zheng XY, J Wang, RJ Salvi et al (1996) Effects of kainic acid on the cochlear potentials and distortion product otoacoustic emissions in chinchilla. Hear Res 95:161–7.
17. ISO1999 (1990) Acoustics – determination of occupational noise exposure and estimation of noise-induced hearing impairment. International Organization for Standardization.
18. Mills JH, WY Adkins and RM Gilbert (1981) Temporary threshold shifts produced by wideband noise. J Acoust Soc Am 70:390–6.
19. Henderson D and R Hamernik (1986) A parametric evaluation of the equal energy hypothesis, in Basic & Applied Aspects of Noise Induced Hearing Loss, R Salvi et al, Editors, pp 369–78.
20. Bohne BA (1976) Safe level for noise exposure? Ann Otol Rhinol Laryngol 85:711–24.
21. Ward WD, PA Santi, AJ Duvall, 3 rd et al (1981) Total energy and critical intensity concepts in noise damage. Ann Otol Rhinol Laryngol 90:584–90.
22. Henderson D and RP Hamernik (1986a) Impulse noise: critical review. J Acoust Soc Am 80:569–84.
23. Hamernik RP, G Turrentine, M Roberto et al (1984) Anatomical correlates of impulse noise-induced mechanical damage in the cochlea. Hear Res 13:229–47.
24. Morest DK, J Kim, SJ Potashner et al (1998) Long-term degeneration in the cochlear nerve and cochlear nucleus of the adult chinchilla following acoustic overstimulation. Microsc Res Tech 41:205–16.
25. Salvi RJ, J Wang and D Ding (2000) Auditory plasticity and hyperactivity following cochlear damage. Hear Res 147:261–74.
26. Kaltenbach JA and CE Afman (2000) Hyperactivity in the dorsal cochlear nucleus after intense sound exposure and its resemblance to tone-evoked activity: a physiological model for tinnitus. Hear Res 140:165–72.
27. Sun W, L Zhang, J Lu et al (2008) Noise exposure-induced enhancement of auditory cortex response and changes in gene expression. Neuroscience 156:374–80.

Chapter 38
Tinnitus and Ménière's Disease

Yu-Lan Mary Ying and Moises A. Arriaga

Keypoints

1. Ménière's disease is characterized by a triad of symptoms: fluctuating hearing loss, attacks of vertigo, and tinnitus. Some authors have included aural fullness.
2. Patients often seek treatment for the severe vertigo attacks, but may have had other otologic symptoms for some time prior to the onset of vertigo.
3. Tinnitus that occurs in Ménière's disease is best characterized as a low pitched, narrow band of noise, resembling a "roaring sound."
4. The tinnitus may change with the fluctuations in hearing loss, and tinnitus increases as hearing loss worsens with the progression of the disease.
5. During the active phase of Ménière's disease, the vertigo can be debilitating and dominating the symptoms.
6. As the disease stabilizes, the tinnitus can become a serious and a severe problem.
7. It is believed that endolymphatic hydrops (imbalance in volume of the fluid systems of the inner ear) is the cause of the symptoms of Ménière's disease, but there is still uncertainty regarding many aspects of the pathology of the disease.

Keywords Tinnitus • Cochlear implants • Promontory stimulation • Treatment

Y.-L.M. Ying (✉)
Department of Otolaryngology – Head and Neck Surgery,
Baylor College of Medicine, Neurosensory Center,
6501 Fannin Street, Suite NA 102
Houston, Texas 77030
e-mail: ylmying@yahoo.com

Abbreviations

AAO-HNS	American Academy of Otolaryngology – Head and Neck Surgery
DHI	Dizziness Handicap Inventory
HHIA	Hearing Handicap Inventory for Adults
PA	Pure tone average
THI	Tinnitus Handicap Inventory

Introduction

Ménière's disease is defined by the presence of three symptoms (or four); intermittent vertigo, fluctuating hearing loss, and tinnitus with aural fullness occurring on one side. Some authors have added aural fullness as a fourth symptom. It was first described by Prosper Ménière in his original publication in 1861. Its diagnosis is largely based on the clinical history and hearing tests. Individuals with Ménière's disease experience incapacitating attacks of vertigo, associated with nausea and vomiting lasting for hours [1]. The sudden attacks of vertigo last anywhere from 30 min to several hours, with unilateral hearing loss occurring together with tinnitus; often aural fullness is present as well. Audiological findings include fluctuating low frequency and progressive sensorineural hearing loss with tinnitus. The course of Ménière's disease is unpredictable and highly variable among individuals and can be accompanied with periods of remission. Disequilibrium may persist for 24–72 h after the attack before resolving completely.

Tinnitus may be the first symptom of Ménière's disease and may precede the remaining symptoms by months or years. Fluctuating cochlear signs, such as tinnitus, hearing impairment, and/or fullness in the ear

A.R. Møller et al. (eds.), *Textbook of Tinnitus*,
DOI 10.1007/978-1-60761-145-5_38, © Springer Science+Business Media, LLC 2011

Table 38.1 Diagnosis of Ménière's disease

Certain Ménière's disease

Definite Ménière's disease, plus histopathologic confirmation

Definite Ménière's disease

Two or more definitive spontaneous episodes of vertigo 20 min or longer

Audiometrically documented hearing loss on at least one occasion

Tinnitus or aural fullness in the treated ear

Other causes excluded

Probable Ménière's disease

One definitive episode of vertigo

Audiometrically documented hearing loss on at least one occasion

Tinnitus or aural fullness in the treated ear

Other causes excluded

Possible Ménière's disease

Episodic vertigo of the Ménière type without documented hearing loss or

Sensorineural hearing loss, fluctuating or fixed, with disequilibrium but

without definitive episodes

Other causes excluded

Adapted from Committee on Hearing and Equilibrium guidelines for the diagnosis and evaluation of therapy in Ménière's disease. American Academy of Otolaryngology – Head and Neck Foundation, Inc. Otolaryngol Head Neck Surg. 1995; 113(3):181

were present prior to onset of the first vertigo attack in more than 50% of patients in a study by [2].

Criteria for the diagnosis of Ménière's disease can be divided into four categories as possible, probable, definite, and certain (Table 38.1). Furthermore, scales of dizziness [i.e., Dizziness Handicap Inventory (DHI)], hearing loss [i.e., Hearing Handicap Inventory for Adults (HHIA)], and tinnitus [i.e., Tinnitus Handicap Inventory (THI)] have been developed to quantify the symptoms associated with Ménière's disease.

The Committee on Hearing and Equilibrium of the American Academy of Otolaryngology – Head and Neck Surgery (AAO-HNS) published its most updated guidelines for defining, reporting, and interpreting results of the treatment of Ménière's disease in 1995 [3]. (For detailed discussion see Chap. 60)

Epidemiology

Reports on incidence and prevalence vary among investigators [4]. The results of studies of the prevalence of Ménière's disease in the US vary from 218 per 100,000 people [5], thus approximately 0.2% of the population. The latter study was performed by the Mayo Clinic [6]. The reported prevalence of Ménière's disease throughout the world varies, in average it is about 1% CHECK). One study finds it to be more common in industrialized countries and in adult white populations [7]. Studies have reported the prevalence of Ménière's disease in England as 56/100,000 [8] and 157/100,000 [9]. In Japan, the reported prevalence of Ménière's disease is low, one study by Shojaku and Watanabe (1997) [10] found a prevalence of between 21.4 and 36.6/100,000. In Finland, the prevalence has been reported to be 43/100,000 and the incidence 4.3/100,000 [11]. In Sweden, Stahle reported an incidence of 45/100, using more stringent criteria than some other studies [12]. In Italy, the reported prevalence is low, 45/100,000, with an incidence of only 8/100,000 [13].

The prevalence increases linearly with age up to 60 years. There is a slight female preponderance, and the typical age of onset is 30–60 years. Bilateral Ménière's disease incidence ranges from 10 to 70%, increasing the frequency with time [14]. Genetic predisposition has been reported in families with Ménière's disease [15, 16]. Factors such as diet, weather changes, as well as emotional and physical stress can also precipitate vertigo attacks and make any symptom complex and worse. Some of the variance in the incidence reported by different investigators may have been caused by differences in the definition of Ménière's disease.

The symptoms of Ménière's disease are signs of an imbalance in the volumes of the fluids in the inner ear, known as endolymphatic hydrops [17]. Cochlear hydrops causing fluctuating low-frequency hearing loss, tinnitus, and aural fullness without associated vertigo may precede Ménière's disease with eventual development of the full syndrome occurring in 37–42% of patients [18]. Lermoyez's syndrome is a variant of Ménière's disease, where hearing loss and tinnitus precede an attack of vertigo by days or months, with improvement of hearing after vertigo episodes. Patients with severe and long-term Ménière's disease are at risk of developing Tumarkin otolithic crisis or drop attacks of falling because of loss of lower-extremity muscle tone without loss of consciousness. The incidence is reported as 7% of patients with Ménière's disease to as high as 72% in one report [19]. The cause is thought to be a sudden stimulation of the vestibular end organs by shift of the utricular macula or rupture of inner ear membranes, but the exact cause is unknown [20].

The frequency of vertigo attacks varies widely with a mean of 6–11 episodes per year [21]. Spells tend to change in severity over a period of time, becoming milder but still unpredictable. The decrease in hearing and tinnitus can occur before or during the vertigo attack. Typically, the disease eventually "burns out" with the decline and cessation of vertigo, but there is progressive deterioration of hearing. Hearing fluctuates in the early course of disease but eventually becomes progressively worse, stabilizing at about 50 dB pure tone average (PA) and 50% word discrimination score [18]. The hearing loss in Ménière's disease begins at low frequencies, thus, different from many other causes of hearing loss such as noise induced hearing loss, hearing loss caused by ototoxic substances, and presbycusis that mainly affect hearing at high frequencies. Eventually, hearing loss in individuals with Ménière's disease involves all frequencies. Tinnitus that occurs in Ménière's disease is often described as a harsh roaring machine-like sound that is more pronounced during vertigo attacks. Hyperacusis (decrease tolerance to sounds, see Chap. 3) and distortion of sound in the affected ear can also be present. Tinnitus and aural fullness prevail during life in the majority of individuals with Ménière's disease [22].

Pathophysiology

Despite the long history of Ménière's disease, the etiology and pathophysiology of this condition are still unknown. Most hypotheses of the pathogenesis of Ménière's disease include anatomical abnormalities of the endolymphatic fluid system, but other hypotheses involve viral infection, autoimmune disease, allergy, and activation of neural plasticity. That endolymphatic hydrops is the cause of the symptoms of Ménière's disease has been supported by histopathological findings, although not all patients with the histopathology have the typical symptoms [23, 24]. The hydrops are believed to be caused by mechanical obstruction to endolymphatic flow or by intrinsic malfunction of the endolymphatic system, resulting in an overabundance of endolymphatic volume and/or pressure [25].

Dysfunction of the spiral ligament fibrocytes, which interferes with the recycling of K^+ ions and results in osmotic imbalance, can cause expansion of the endolymphatic compartment [26].

Schuknecht developed a theory of gradual distention of the endolymphatic system that leads to a rupture of membranous labyrinth and sudden release of a large volume of endolymph into perilymphatic space [20]. It is suggested that sensory and neural structures are injured from exposure to the potassium-rich endolymph, resulting in vertigo and hearing loss. As the rupture heals and hemostasis is restored in the inner ear compartments, the symptoms subside. Dohlman (1980) [27] suggested that increase of potassium occurs in the perilymph during a Ménière's attack and that potassium-rich fluid surrounding the vestibular nerve is the cause of the experienced vertigo. Zenner (1987) [28] found that perilymphatic potassium intoxication leads to a longitudinal contraction of the outer hair cells. This results in their decoupling from the tectorial membrane. Dulon et al. (1987) [29] demonstrated that small changes in the osmolarity of the surrounding in vitro medium induce fast contractions (hypo-osmotic solution) or elongations (hyperosmotic solution) in isolated outer hair cells. However, the hypotheses that assume that Reissner's membrane ruptures before an attack occurs have been questioned.

Another theory proposed by Gibson and Arenberg (1997) [30] is a disturbance in longitudinal flow of endolymph from the cochlear duct to the endolymphatic sac due to a narrow vestibular aqueduct, resulting in hydrops.

It has been suggested that longitudinal flow was involved in maintaining endolymph homeostasis. However, measurements of the dispersal of markers in the endolymph [17] have failed to support these hypotheses. These measurements were interpreted to suggest that the normal state of the endolymph is maintained without a significant involvement of volume flow at all [17]. The situation is different in abnormal states, such as is assumed to be present in Ménière's disease where the volume of inner ear fluid is abnormal. In such situations, the longitudinal volume flow of the endolymph may contribute to homeostasis.

The role of the endolymphatic sac is complex and poorly understood. It seems to act as a "bidirectional overflow" system that responds to the endolymph volume disturbance [17].

In other hypotheses, the sac is postulated to actively regulate the flow by maintaining an osmotic gradient and secreting glycoproteins that attract movement of the endolymph toward the sac. The sac produces saccin, a hormone thought to increase the volume of endolymph, which may promote faster flow [30].

It has been suggested that the endolymphatic sac is primarily responsible for the immuno-defense of the inner ear [31]. It is hypothesized that a viral infection leads to an inflammatory immune and microvascular-mediated injury. Circulating immune complexes and serum auto-antibodies to inner ear antigens are greater in Ménière's disease patients than in controls [32–34]. This suggests that circulating immune complexes may be involved in the pathogenesis of Ménière's disease, either as a direct cause of damage or as a by-product of an underlying autoimmune abnormality [33]. This hypothesis is supported by the clinical experience of beneficial effect of treatment with corticosteroids [35].

As early as in 1923, Duke (1923) [36] proposed an allergic theory for Ménière's disease. However, it was not until 1970s that studies showed an improvement in the symptoms of this disease after desensitization to inhalant allergens and an elimination diet for allergies to food.

> Pulec (1973) [37], in discussing Ménière's disease, reported allergies were related to the sensorineural hearing loss and symptoms of Ménière's disease among 36% patients. Fourteen percent of his Ménière's disease patients responded to allergy treatment. In a case-control study, Derebery and Valenzuela (1992) [38] found an inhalant allergy in 41.6% and a food allergy in 40.3% of patients with Ménière's disease answering a self-reported questionnaire, in comparison with rates of 27.6 and 17.4% in their control population.

Furthermore, a significant percentage of patients with Ménière's disease and allergy showed improvement in both allergy and Ménière's symptoms when treated with desensitization and diet control [39]. Hence, symptoms of food allergy should be questioned for patients with endolymphatic hydrops and fluctuant hearing loss, as suggested by Shambaugh and Wiet (1980) [40].

Inspired by the benefits from treatment with air-pressure (pressure chamber) [41–43] by applying air-puffs to the inner ear (using the Meniett device), it has been suggested that activation of neural plasticity may be involved in creating the symptoms of Ménière's disease [44].

Tinnitus Associated with Ménière's Disease

Tinnitus in Ménière's disease is best characterized as a low pitched, narrow band of noise, usually described as a "roaring sound", corresponding to the low-frequency sensorineural hearing loss [45–47]. In the early stages of the disease, tinnitus may be intermittent. As the disease progresses, tinnitus becomes permanent, but its intensity fluctuates. Hearing loss and tinnitus normally increase over time. After a long time, the end state of Ménière's disease "burnt-out" where the effects of vertigo attacks have ceased, tinnitus may become the most disturbing complaint.

As Stahle (1988) [48] described in his results of an epidemiologic study in Sweden, the tinnitus quality fluctuated in its intensity and paralleled the control of vertigo symptom and ear blockage. In a separate group of patients with control of their chief vertigo complaint, the ear blockage persisted, as did the tinnitus. Herraiz et al. (2006) [49] found a statistical association between tinnitus intensity and worse hearing loss or hyperacusis in 102 patients with Ménière's disease, uninfluenced by the number of vertigo spells. In the initial phases of Ménière's disease, tonal-tinnitus is usually not present, as opposed to in the later stages of the disease where tonal-tinnitus is described by a number of patients [50].

Pathophysiology of Tinnitus in Ménière's Disease

Tinnitus in Ménière's disease may be caused by similar mechanisms as other forms of tinnitus that are related to injuries of the cochlea (see Chap. 10). Hearing loss may cause tinnitus through the effect of deprivation of input to the auditory system that activates neural plasticity (see Chap. 12).

Management and Treatments

There is no known cure for Ménière's disease, and treatments are aimed at reduction of its symptoms. Vertigo is often the most debilitating symptom of

Ménière's disease, and most treatments focus on relieving this symptom. The tinnitus of Ménière's disease may well remit with improvement in low-frequency hearing as a result of medical or surgical treatment. For a detailed discussion of treatment of Ménière's disease, see Chap. 60.

Treatments specifically directed toward tinnitus in Ménière's disease are similar to treatments of other forms of tinnitus described in the chapters in Part VI of this book.

Neural Plasticity

The reason that overpressure can relieve symptoms of Ménière's disease is not known, but it has been hypothesized that neural plasticity is involved in at least one or more of the symptoms of Ménière's disease [51]. These symptoms are assumed to be caused by an imbalance of the volumes of the fluid in the inner ear [17], the causes of which are unknown. The finding that applying air-puffs to the inner ear can ameliorate the symptoms, thus stimulating the vestibular sensory cells, indicates that functional abnormalities may be involved in causing the symptoms of Ménière's disease and an activation of neural plasticity may be involved.

References

1. Minor LB, DA Schessel, JP Carey (2004) Ménière's Disease. Curr Opin Neurol. 17:9–16.
2. Tokumasu K, A Fujino, H Naganuma et al (1996) Initial Symptoms and Retrospective Evaluation of Prognosis in Ménière's Disease. Acta Otolaryngol Suppl (Stockh). 524:43–49.
3. Anonymous (1995) Committee on Hearing and Equilibrium Guidelines for the Diagnosis and Evaluation of Therapy in Ménière's Disease. American Academy of Otolaryngology – Head and Neck Foundation, Inc. Otolaryngol Head Neck Surg. 113:181.
4. Arenberg IK, TJ Balkany, G Goldman et al (1980) The Incidence and Prevalence of Meniere's Disease – A Statistical Analysis of Limits. Otolaryngol Clin NA. 13:597–601.
5. Ervin SE (2004) Meniere's Disease: Identifying Classic Symptoms and Current Treatments. AAOHN J. 52:156–158.
6. Wladislavosky-Waserman P, G Facer et al (1984) Meniere's Disease: A 30-Year Epidemiologic and Clinical Study in Rochester, MN, 1951–1980. Laryngoscope. 94:1098–1102.
7. Friberg U, J Stahle, A Svedberg (1984) The Natural Course of Menieres' Disease. Acta Otolaryngol. Suppl. 406:72–77.
8. Minor LB, DA Schessel, JP Carey (2004) Ménière's Disease. Curr Opin Neurol. 17:9–16.
9. Cawthorne T, AB Hewlett (1954) Ménière's Disease. Proc. R. Soc. Med. 47:663–670.
10. Shojaku H, Y Watanabe (1997) The Prevalence of Definite Cases of Ménière's Disease in the Hida and Nishikubiki Districts of Central Japan: A Survey of Relatively Isolated Areas of Medical Care. Acta Otolaryngol. Suppl. 528:94–96.
11. Kotimaki J, M Sorri, E Aantaa et al (1999) Prevalence of Ménière's Disease in Finland. Laryngoscope. 109:748–753.
12. Stahle J, C Stahle, IK Arenberg (1978) Incidence of Ménière's Disease. Arch Otol. 104.2:99–102.
13. Celistino D, G Ralli (1991) Incidence of Ménière's Disease in Italy. Am J Otol. 12.2:135–138.
14. Haye, R, S Quist-Hanssen (1976) The Natural Course of Ménière's Disease. Acta Otolaryngol. 82–4:289.
15. Frykholm C, HC Larsen, N Dahl et al (2006) Familial Ménière's Disease in Five Generations. Otol Neurotol. 27:681–686.
16. Klar J, C Frykholm, U Friberg et al (2006) A Ménière's Disease Gene Linked to Chromosome 12p123. Am J Med Genet B Neuropsychiatr Genet. 141B:463–467.
17. Salt AN (2001) Regulation of Endolymphatic Fluid Volume. Ann N Y Acad Sci. 942:306–312.
18. Grant IL, DB Welling (1997) The Treatment of Hearing Loss in Ménière's Disease. Otolaryngol Clin North Am. 30:1123.
19. Kentala E, M Havia, I Pyykko (2001) Short-Lasting Drop Attacks in Ménière's Disease. Otolaryngol Head Neck Surg. 124:526.
20. Schuknecht HF (1993) Endolymphatic Hydrops. Pathology of the Ear. 2nd ed. Philadelphia, Lea & Febiger. 506.
21. Stahle, J, Friberg, U, Svedberg A. Long term progression of Meniere's disease. Am J Otol. 1989; 10:170
22. Green JD Jr, DJ Blum, SG Harner (1991) Longitudinal Followup of Patients with Ménière's Disease. Otolaryngol Head Neck Surg. 104:783.
23. Schuknecht HF, AJ Gulya (1983) Endolymphatic Hydrops: An Overview and Classification. An Otol Rhinol Laryngol. Suppl. 106:1–20.
24. Rauch SD, SN Merchant, BA Thedinger (1989) Ménière's Syndrome and Endolymphatic Hydrops Double-Blind Temporal Bone Study. Ann Otol Rhinol Laryngol. 98: 873–883.
25. Vasama JP, FH Linthicum Jr (1999) Ménière's Disease and Endolymphatic Hydrops Without Ménière's Symptoms: Temporal Bone Histopathology. Acta Otolaryngol. 119:297.
26. Nin F, H Hibino, K Doi, T Suzuki, Y Hisa, Y Kurachi (2008) The endocochlear potential depends on two K+ diffusion potentials and an electrical barrier in the stria vascularis of the inner ear. Proc Natl Acad Sci USA. 105:1751–6.
27. Dohlman GF (1980) Mechanism of the Meniere Attack. ORL J Otorhinolaryngol Relat Spec. 42:10–19.
28. Zenner HP (1987) Modern Aspects of Hair Cell Biochemistry, Motility and Tinnitus. In Proceedings, Third International Tinnitus Seminar, Munster Edited by H Feldmann Karlsruhe, Germany, Harsch Verlag.
29. Dulon D, JM Aran, J Schacht (1987) Osmotically Induced Motility of Outer Hair Cells: Implications for Ménière's Disease. Arch Otorhinolaryngol. 244:104–107.

30. Gibson WP, IK Arenberg (1997) Pathophysiologic Theories in the Etiology of Ménière's Disease. Otolaryngol Clin North Am. 30.6:961.
31. Arenberg IK, C Lemke, GE Shambaugh Jr (1997) Viral Theory for Ménière's Disease and Endolymphatic Hydrops: Overview and New Therapeutic Options for Viral Labyrinthitis. Ann NY Acad Sci. 830:306.
32. Brookes GB (1986) Circulating Immune Complexes in Ménière's Disease. Arch Otolaryngol Head Neck Surg. 112.5:536.
33. Derebery MJ, VS Rao, TJ Siglock et al (1991) Ménière's Disease: An Immune Complex-Mediated Illness? Laryngoscope. 101.3:225–229.
34. Gottschlich S, PB Billings, EM Keithley et al (1995) Assessment of Serum Antibodies in Patients with Rapidly Progressive Sensorineural Hearing Loss and Ménière's Disease. Laryngoscope. 105.12 Pt 1:1347.
35. Wackym PA, I Sando (1997) Molecular and Cellular Pathology of Ménière's Disease. Otolaryngol Clin North Am. 30.6:947.
36. Duke, WW (1923) Ménière's Syndrome Caused by Allergy. JAMA. 81:2179.
37. Pulec JL (1973) Ménière's Disease – Etiology, Natural History, and Results of Treatment. Otolaryngol Clin North Am. 6.1:25–39.
38. Derebery MJ, S Valenzuela (1992) Ménière's Syndrome and Allergy. Otolaryngol Clin N Am. 25:213.
39. Derebery MJ (2000) Allergic Management of Ménière's Disease: An Outcome Study. Otolaryngol Head Neck Surg. 122.2:174.
40. Shambaugh GW, RJ Wiet (1980) The Diagnosis and Evaluation of Allergic Disorders With Food Intolerance in Ménière's Disease. Otolaryngol Clin North Am. 13.4: 671–679.
41. Ingelstedt S, A Ivarsson,O Tjernström (1976) Immediate Relief of Symptoms During Acute Attacks of Meniere's Disease, Using a Pressure Chamber. Acta Otolaryngol. 85:368–378.
42. Densert B, O Densert (1982) Overpressure in Treatment of Meniere's Disease. Laryngoscope. 92:1285–1292.
43. Densert B, K Sass (2001) Control of Symptoms in Patients with Ménière's Disease Using Middle Ear Pressure Applications: Two Years Follow-Up. Acta Otolaryngol. 121:616–621.
44. Møller AR (2008) Neural Plasticity: For Good and Bad. Progr Theor Phys Suppl. 173:48–65
45. Grahm JT, HA Newby (1962) Acoustical Characteristics of Tinnitus, Particularly Treatment. Arch Otolaryngol 75:162–168.
46. Nodal RH, JT Graham (1965) An Investigation of the Frequency of Characteristics of Tinnitus Associated with Ménière's Diseases. Arch Otolaryngol. 82:28–31.
47. Reed GF (1960) An Audiometric Study of Two Hundred Cases of Subjective Tinnitus. Arch Otolaryngol. 71:94–104.
48. Stahle J (1988) My Experience with Ménière's Disease. Audio Digest-39. Pulec JL (1973) Ménière's Disease – Etiology, Natural History, and Results of Treatment. Otolaryngol Clin North Am. 6.1:25–39.
49. Herraiz C, F Plaza, G De Ios Santos (2006) Tinnitus Retraining Therapy in Meniere Disease. Acta Otorrinolaringol Esp. 57:96–100.
50. Vernon JA (1978) Information from UOHSC Tinnitus clinic. ATA Newsl. 3:1–4.
51. Møller AR (2008) Neural Plasticity: For Good and Bad. Progr Theor Phys Suppl. 173:48–65.

Chapter 39
Tinnitus and Vestibular Schwannoma: Overview and Clinical Correlations

Jason May, Virginia Ramachandran, and Anthony T. Cacace

Keypoints

1. Historical overview considering aspects of medical and audiological evaluation of patients with vestibular schwannoma and tinnitus.
2. Treatment modalities and outcomes are discussed together with a review of relevant postsurgical issues.
3. The value of asymmetrical hearing loss, vestibular complaints, and facial nerve problems in establishing the index-of-suspicion for medical and allied-health professionals regarding the presence of vestibular schwannoma.
4. It is indicated that it is difficult to predict the likelihood of tinnitus following microsurgery for tumor resection
5. Stereotactic radiosurgery does not appear to have a substantial influence on tinnitus.
6. Atypical forms of tinnitus may occur as postsurgical complications, particularly when hearing is lost completely and abruptly during surgery.
7. Tinnitus after severing the auditory nerve causing unilateral deafferention of the auditory periphery causes a cascade of reactive changes in the peripheral and central nervous systems that can result in anomalous forms of cross-modal plasticity.
8. Gaze-evoked, gaze-modulated, and other forms of somatic (cutaneous-evoked) tinnitus can result.

Keywords Vestibular schwannoma • Acoustic neuroma • Tinnitus • Gaze-evoked tinnitus • Cutaneous-evoked tinnitus • Audiology • Neuro-otology • Microsurgery • Neurosurgery • Gamma knife radiosurgery

Abbreviations

CPA	Cerebellar pontine angle
ABR	Auditory brainstem response
IAC	Internal auditory canal
CT	Computerized tomography
MRI	Magnetic resonance imaging
fMRI	Functional magnetic resonance imaging
LINAC	Linear accelerator
PET	Positron emission tomography
GET	Gaze-evoked tinnitus
Cm	Centimeter
Mm	Millimeter
TCR	Trigemino-cardiac reflex
NF2	Neurofibromatosis type 2, NF2

Introduction

Background

Vestibular schwannoma, earlier known as acoustic neuroma or vestibular neuroinoma, is a benign tumor of the VIIIth cranial (cochlear–vestibular) nerve that constitutes between 6 and 10% of all intracranial tumors and 80–90% of all tumors of the cerebellopontine angle (CPA [1]).[1]

A.T. Cacace (✉)
Department of Communication Sciences & Disorders, Wayne State University, 207 Rackham, 60 Farnsworth, Detroit, MI 48202, USA
and
Department of Otolaryngology, Wayne State University, Detroit, MI, USA
e-mail: cacacea@wayne.edu

---

[1]While vestibular schwannoma has been recommended as the official nomenclature of this disease [2], the terms acoustic tumor, acoustic neuroma, and vestibular neurinoma remain interchangeable among clinicians.

A.R. Møller et al. (eds.), *Textbook of Tinnitus*,
DOI 10.1007/978-1-60761-145-5_39, © Springer Science+Business Media, LLC 2011

The incidence of vestibular schwannoma is estimated at 17.4 cases per million [3]. These tumors originate from the nerve sheath and consist of Schwann cells in a collagenous matrix; typically arising from within the bony portion of the internal auditory canal (IAC) at the myelin–glial junction (Obersteiner-Redich zone) and growing outward from the porus acousticus to the CPA [1]. They are generally well-circumscribed and produce symptoms by displacing adjacent anatomical and neural structures without invasion.

Vestibular schwannoma are typically slow growing [average rate-of-growth: 0.2 cm per year)], but can grow as rapidly as 2 cm per year. Initially, symptoms arise due to VIIth and VIIIth nerve compression, but as the tumor size increases (2–3 cm), the fourth ventricle can become compressed and hydrocephalus can result from total obstruction; trigeminal symptoms can also occur once the tumor exceeds 3 cm. If growth continues, brainstem compression, cerebellar-tonsil herniation, and death can result.

In this class of tumors, 95% are unilateral, nonhereditary, and manifest in individuals between the ages of 40–60 years [1]. The exception is Neurofibromatosis type 2 (NF2), a disease characterized by bilateral vestibular schwannoma, usually presenting before 21 years-of-age. Neurofibromatosis type 2 can be inherited through an autosomal dominant transmission or as a result of de novo mutations. The genetic mutation responsible for NF2 is caused by a defect located on chromosome 22, band q11-13.1. Additionally, these patients also have higher occurrence rates of meningiomas, ependymomas, and Schwannoma of other cranial nerves.

Presenting Symptomatology

The most common presenting symptom of vestibular Schwannoma is asymmetrical sensorineural hearing loss. Loss of pure tone hearing sensitivity typically progresses slowly over many years and is often, but not always, accompanied by reduced performance on tests of monosyllabic word recognition, absence and/or decay of the acoustic-stapedius reflex, and abnormalities of the auditory brainstem response (ABR). A harbinger of this disease is the occurrence of word recognition scores that are much worse than would be expected based upon the pure-tone average (0.5, 1, 2 kHz, respectively) or the roll-over effect for monosyllabic

words, if a complete psychometric function (percent correct word recognition vs. stimulus level) is generated (e.g., [4]). Decreased pure tone hearing sensitivity and other audiometric abnormalities are thought to occur as a consequence of direct injury to the cochlear-vestibular nerve, interruption of the cochlear blood supply, brainstem involvement, or a combination of factors [5]. Indeed, unilateral tinnitus can be the *initial* and *only* presenting symptom signaling tumor presence [6]. Recent estimates indicate that approximately 10% of individuals with vestibular schwannoma will present themselves in this manner [7]. The presentation of unilateral tinnitus, in and of itself, is an indication for further work-up.

Although vertigo is *not* a commonly presenting symptom, disequilibrium or unsteadiness can be seen in 40–50% of patients. Presumably, if destruction of vestibular nerve fibers is sufficiently slow, most patients will compensate over a period of time. Headaches are found in 50–60% of patients, but are rarely observed as a presenting symptom. Similarly, facial-nerve weakness is also rare, occurring less than 1% of the time as a presenting symptom [7].

Management Options and Their Relationship to Tinnitus

The treatment options for vestibular schwannoma include planned observation, surgical extirpation, and radiation. With respect to the first option, because these tumors are typically benign and slow growing, they can be carefully observed over a period of time and re-evaluated to determine if more aggressive treatments are necessary. This strategy is often applied in older adults that are poor candidates for surgery, in individuals with small tumors, in instances when the involved side is the only hearing ear, and/or if tumor growth is less than 2–3 mm per year.

Since the late 1800s, surgical procedures have undergone vast improvements. The current goals of surgery are: (1) complete tumor extirpation to cure the underlying disease, (2) preservation of facial nerve function, and when possible, (3) preservation of hearing. However, depending on size and growth patterns, these ambitious goals cannot always be attained and consequently, surgical co-morbidities remain as a distinct reality.

To appreciate the evolution of this field, we provide here some historical background and relevant vignettes based on the more detailed review of Machinis and colleagues [8]. Briefly, the first documented surgery performed by von Bergmann (1890) was unsuccessful as the patient died prior to localization of the tumor. Sternberg (1900) is credited with the first accurate pathological description of the tumor. In a two-stage operation circa 1894, Sir Charles Ballance described the finger dissection of vestibular schwannoma, which he called an "encapsulated fibro-sarcoma" (Ballance 1907) [9]. While the first decade of the twentieth century saw continued, albeit limited attempts at tumor resection, the failure rate of surgery was alarmingly high. Apparently, the high failure rate was due to small craniotomies leading to cortical herniation and eventual death.

With respect to the suboccipital approach, several key individuals (e.g., Woolsey, Fraenkel, and Krause) made definitive advancements [10]. Subsequently, Panse (1904) [11] proposed, but never performed, a surgical technique through the petrous bone, which would later be described as the translabrynthine approach (see [12] for additional historical insights). However, at this early juncture, the translabrynthine approach did not gain popularity because it did not provide adequate access to the CPA and because there was a high rate of meningitis postoperatively. Consequently, it was not until Cushing described the bilateral suboccipital approach that complications and mortality rates approached what might be considered acceptable levels [13].

The surgical approach advocated by Cushing aimed at subtotal intracapsular resection. Initially, morbidity and mortality rates were high (approximately 75% and 40, respectively); however, after 30 operations, Cushing reduced the mortality rate to 20% and with more experience, the mortality rate dropped to 7.7% (based on a series of 176 cases). Cushing advanced the field by avoiding herniation and medullary compression during surgery and by making a large curvilinear incision between both mastoid processes [13]. Nevertheless, a disappointing 5-year survival rate of 50% could not be overcome, due in large part to tumor recurrence.

Subsequently, Cairns (1931) reported the first complete removal of a vestibular schwannoma with preservation of facial-nerve function. Progress in this area continued as Olivecrona reported an impressive 40% facial nerve preservation rate, with recovery of facial-nerve function in another 20% [8]. Improvements in

diagnosis, surgical care, and advances in the suboccipital approach further improved mortality rate to approximately 2.4% [14].

Introduction of the operating microscope was a key element to advancing surgical outcome, preservation of hearing and facial-nerve function and reduction of other morbidities [8]. This instrumental innovation also allowed for the perfection of the translabrynthine approach and for the introduction of the middle cranial fossa approach. Other advancements came with the advent of the polytome Pantopaque imaging technique [14], which led to the identification of small tumors in the IAC. With the available imaging techniques and use of the operating microscope, House and colleagues lowered the mortality rate to the range of 0.8–5% [15]. Use of the auditory brainstem response (ABR), use of the ABR, computerized tomography (CT), and magnetic resonance imaging (MRI) further revolutionized diagnosis. Thus, based on these historical trends and innovations, three surgical approaches have withstood the test-of-time and are considered the mainstay of the surgeon's arsenal. These include the translabrynthine, retrosigmoid/suboccipital, and middle cranial fossa approaches, each having specific advantages and disadvantages.

In the contemporary surgical literature, William House is credited with perfecting the translabrynthine approach [7]. Because no brain retraction is used, this technique is considered by some to be the safest approach. In the absence of a high riding jugular bulb and/or an anteriorly placed sigmoid sinus, the translabrynthine approach provides excellent access to the lateral CPA. Thus, with the fundus and lateral portion of the IAC completely exposed, the facial nerve can be dissected easily. The disadvantage of this approach is that hearing is always sacrificed during surgery.

The retrosigmoid/suboccipital and middle cranial fossa approaches are considered the procedures-of-choice in cases where hearing preservation is attempted. While the retrosigmoid/suboccipital approach can be applied to all vestibular schwannoma, of the available procedures, it has the advantage of providing the widest exposure and best operative field visualization of the posterior fossa. However, limited access to the lateral CPA near the IAC, poor visualization of the VIIth and VIIIth cranial nerves, and the potential for cerebrospinal fluid leaks, both peri and -postoperatively, are clear disadvantages.

The middle cranial fossa approach, also introduced and perfected by William House, is considered the procedure-of-choice for small intracanalicular tumors. Advantages of this approach include access to the lateral third of the IAC and the fact that it is an *extra-dural* procedure. The disadvantages include risk to the facial nerve, limited access to the posterior fossa, potential for dural laceration (particularly in patients over 65), and the need for temporal lobe retraction. As the facial nerve lies on the anterior surface of the canal, tumor removal can be hindered by this approach.

Stereotactic Radiosurgery

In addition to the surgical procedures noted above, stereotactic radiosurgery has become a viable management tool. This treatment modality can be used either alone or in combination with microsurgery, particularly in those instances where tumors are incompletely excised. While different types of radiosurgery are available [linear accelerator (LINAC) and gamma knife], gamma knife is the approach used most frequently. Gamma knife treatment involves a single-session application of collimated beams of cobalt radiation to a localized intracranial location. This approach allows for high doses of radiation to the location of the lesion while registering smaller doses to surrounding structures, thus minimizing morbidity [16]. The effectiveness of this method occurs through interference with the cellular life-cycle, thereby inhibiting growth of the tumor. Individuals, who have tumors less than 2.5–3.0 cm including the absence of or limited tumor-related symptoms, are considered candidates [17, 18]. Age, hearing status, facial movement, facial sensation, balance, vertigo, and tinnitus are other factors that are given consideration in patient selection [19]. As gamma knife radiosurgery requires only a local anesthetic and has a relatively fast recovery time, it is an appealing and often a superior option for individuals who may not be medically able to undergo surgery.

Outcomes of gamma knife radiosurgery are considered good when viewed in terms of tumor control and cranial nerve morbidity, particularly with the advent of improved dosing strategies. However, hearing and balance function may be adversely affected [20]. Direct comparison of the effectiveness of gamma knife radiosurgery to microsurgery is difficult because tumor size and patient characteristics are confounding variables and randomization of patient selection has been difficult.

Because gamma knife radiosurgery is typically limited to smaller tumors, better facial-nerve function and hearing outcomes have been observed with this modality. However, severity of tinnitus and vertigo are generally unchanged following this type of treatment [21].

As with any treatment modality, complications are inevitable. With gamma knife radiosurgery, complications can include facial twitching, weakness, numbness, pain, trigeminal-nerve dysfunction, watery or dry eyes, hydrocephalus, hearing loss, tinnitus, balance disturbances, and vertigo [18, 22]. Some post-treatment effects, such as hearing loss, may have a delayed onset [16], although lower doses of radiation have been shown to reduce complication rates [23]. Gamma knife radiosurgery may also be associated with a small risk for developing radiation-induced malignancies [20], and in cases where enlargement of the tumor occurs, surgery may be necessary [24]. Unfortunately, in those instances when tumors fail to respond to radiation, management through salvage surgery may be more difficult, thus resulting in poorer outcomes [25].

Tinnitus and Vestibular Schwannoma

While it has been estimated that tinnitus is the sole symptom in 10% of patients presenting with vestibular schwannoma, it is present in 60% along with asymmetrical hearing loss. In their series of individuals undergoing hearing preservation surgery, Levo et al. (2000) [26] observed that tinnitus worsened postoperatively in 6–20%, remained unchanged in 25–60%, and improved or resolved in 30–50% of individuals. Based on logistic regression analysis to determine which of eight independent variables were prognostic for the presence or absence of postoperative hearing, Rastogi and colleagues (1995) [27] found that porus acousticus widening was the best prognostic indicator. In this series, the presence or absence of tinnitus did *not* play a significant role in their outcome data. In studying tumor size and age, Fahy et al. (2002) [28] were unable to predict tinnitus outcome postoperatively. They also failed to show a statistically significant association between changes in tinnitus and quality-of-life. Nevertheless, they found that tinnitus improved in 16%, was unchanged in 55%, and actually worsened in 29% of patients. Based on these data, it remains unpredictable which patients will have worsening tinnitus postoperatively.

There are several surgical factors that have been examined in regard to tinnitus symptom outcomes. For example, Schaller et al. (2008) [29] showed that the intraoperative occurrence of the trigemino-cardiac reflex (TCR) during surgery was a negative prognostic factor not only for hearing preservation but also for the presence of ipsilateral postoperative tinnitus. The TCR occurred in 17% of patients undergoing tumor resection; 60% of those patients had postoperative tinnitus vs. 17% of those who did not have TCR. Kanzaki et al. (1999) [30] addressed the question of surgical technique on postoperative tinnitus. Based on questionnaires obtained from 202 patients, they found an increase in tinnitus in those individuals undergoing hearing preservation surgery vs. those patients undergoing translabrynthine surgery. In cases where hearing preservation was attempted, tinnitus was present in 78.6% preoperatively and increased to 89.3% postoperatively. Individuals who underwent a translabrynthine approach decreased from 72.7% preoperatively to 67.3% postoperatively. The outcome of surgery to preserve hearing showed no predictive value with respect to tinnitus occurrence or estimated tinnitus loudness. This study indicates that while hearing preservation is a distinct surgical outcome, individuals remain at risk of developing tinnitus. In a series of vestibular schwannoma surgeries using the middle cranial fossa approach ($n=311$) where the facial nerve was preserved 99% of the time and where hearing was preserved 49% of the time (in smaller tumors), Haid (1998) [31] found that 45% of individuals also had a reduction in tinnitus severity.

Tinnitus and Gamma Knife Radiosurgery

Tinnitus outcomes from gamma knife radiosurgery treatments tend to be reported by the presence/absence of tinnitus or use of a visual-analog scale as a method to gauge tinnitus severity. As noted previously, while available data suggest that tinnitus tends to remain unchanged following this treatment modality, the type of outcome measures used to track these changes lack the necessary precision to demonstrate clinically significant changes. To our knowledge, no attempts have been made to measure relevant psychoacoustic parameters of tinnitus perception, such as pitch and loudness, prior to and following gamma knife radiosurgery.

Based on a nonrandomized prospective study of 63 patients who underwent gamma knife radiosurgery and 28 patients who underwent microsurgery using a suboccipital approach, Myrseth and colleagues (2009) [21] found no change in tinnitus severity using a visual-analog scale for either group, despite the fact that decreases in hearing sensitivity were observed in both groups. In a retrospective questionnaire-based study and chart review comparing gamma knife radiosurgery with translabrynthine microsurgery in individuals with non-serviceable hearing and small tumors, Coelho and colleagues (2008) [19] noted that tinnitus was present post-treatment in 7/21 (33%). This occurred in 2/12 (17%) in the gamma knife radiosurgery group; and 5/9, 56% in the translabrynthine microsurgery group). Of those in the gamma knife group without tinnitus, 9/10 showed no post-treatment changes, while one had new onset of tinnitus. Of those with tinnitus prior to treatment, both noted post-treatment changes. Of four individuals in the translabrynthine group without tinnitus preoperatively, one noted new onset tinnitus. Of the five that had preoperative tinnitus, one noted improvement and two had no change and got worse. While this information is of interest, the small sample size limits the generalizing power of these data. In a retrospective analysis of 123 patients with vestibular schwannoma treated with gamma knife radiosurgery, Hempel et al. (2006) [32] found that the presence or absence of tinnitus remained stable in 90% of patients. In this sample, approximately 4% reported tinnitus onset, while 6% reported tinnitus cessation following treatment. Interestingly, seven patients also reported improvement in hearing sensitivity, but there is no report of how hearing loss may or may not have correlated with changes in tinnitus. Bertalanffy and colleagues (2001) [33] found that in a group of individuals undergoing gamma knife radiosurgery with preoperative tinnitus ($n=32$), tinnitus improved in six cases (46%), was unchanged in five cases (38%), and worsened in two cases (15%). Tinnitus appeared as a new symptom in one patient. Régis and colleagues (2002) [34] reported a decrease in tinnitus for approximately 16% of patients following gamma knife radiosurgery. Niranjan and colleagues (1999) [35] found that of 29 patients with intracanalicular tumors who underwent gamma knife radiosurgery, 7/13 who had preoperative tinnitus continued to experience tinnitus at a long-term post-surgical follow-up.

The post-treatment stability of tinnitus is interesting in light of hearing preservation outcomes with gamma knife radiosurgery. Based on the Gardner–Robertson classification scheme [36], hearing outcomes tend to fluctuate compared to changes in tinnitus. Given the typical high correlation of tinnitus to hearing loss, additional audiometric information may be helpful in future studies better understand these effects. Régis and colleagues (2008) [37] provided some information regarding the relationship between hearing loss and tinnitus by noting that in a sample of 184 patients followed for 3 years or longer, the presence of tinnitus preoperatively was viewed a protective factor for hearing preservation, although it was not speculated why this might be the case.

The mechanism(s) of pathology for complications of gamma knife radiosurgery may include effects of tumor swelling prior to shrinkage, cochlear-nerve toxicity, and/ or damage to cochlear structures due to radiation exposure. Direct radiation-induced cochlear-nerve toxicity has been speculated to be a causative factor for hearing loss [38, 39], which suggests that the basal turn of the cochlea near the modiolus and the inferior-most extension are most susceptible to high radiation doses. Using the ABR as a physiologic measure to distinguish cochlear from retro-cochlear effects, Bertalanffy and colleagues (2001) [33] showed that that cochlear function was generally unaffected by this type of treatment.

Atypical Forms of Postsurgical Tinnitus

Even with the best of efforts and skills of the neurosurgeon and neuro-otologist, hearing can be lost completely and abruptly during microsurgery. While the consequence of profound unilateral hearing loss occurs as a direct result of the translabrynthine procedure, if the tumor size exceeds 2 cm, a high probability of profound unilateral hearing loss is also expected [27], regardless of the surgical approach used. Consequently, complete loss of hearing in the course of tumor resection results in a unilateral deafferentation of the auditory periphery. This acute injury sets the stage for a cascade of reactive changes in afferent/efferent pathways that can result in gaze-evoked, gaze-modulated, and/or other forms of somatic tinnitus.

In its purest form, gaze-evoked tinnitus (GET) is a phenomenon whereby horizontal or vertical deviation of eye position, from a neutral head-referenced position, results in an auditory sensation. While exact

mechanisms are unknown, it has been postulated that these cross-modal effects may occur from reactive sprouting of neurons to unoccupied (denervated) synaptic sites, unmasking of silent synapses, and/or ephaptic interactions [40, 41]. It has also been suggested that time from deafferentation to the onset of symptoms may provide insight about potential mechanisms underlying these effects. Rapid onset of GET suggests unmasking of silent synapses, whereas longer delays may be consistent with sprouting, changes in strength of existing neural connections, ephaptic interactions, or a combination of processes [41–43].

Initial descriptions documenting the phenomenology of GET were brief case reports [44–46]. In-depth series of cases were subsequently reported [40], and these observations were followed by detailed methods for quantifying the visual-spatial coordinates and psychoacoustic properties of this phenomenon with contemporary psychophysical methods [47, 48]. Gaze-evoked tinnitus is distinguished from *gaze-modulated tinnitus* in which there is typically an area of visual space where the tinnitus is absent; tinnitus only becomes manifest after change in eye position exceeds certain spatial coordinates of gaze. In contrast, gaze-modulated tinnitus occurs when existing constant tinnitus is altered in some way (change in loudness or pitch) by change in eye position. However, there are terminological disparities in the literature that tend to obfuscate our understanding. For example, in their sample of individuals with gaze-modulated tinnitus, Coad and colleagues (2001) [49] suggest that "eye movement" is the relevant parameter. This description is in contrast to a report from the same laboratory whereby activations were maintained by sustained lateral gaze [42]. Giraud et al. (1999) [48] also use the term "eye movement" to describe their effects. We suspect that the term "eye movement" is a misnomer, but this specific use of terminology will require clarification.

With greater recognition of this phenomenon, several groups have tried to estimate the prevalence of gaze-modulated tinnitus based on either retrospective or prospective convenience samples [43, 49, 50]. Prevalence estimates range from 1.8 to 32% [43, 49, 50]. However, the incidence of GET is unknown, but in all likelihood, it is not as commonly observed as the gaze-modulated form.

While there is no agreed upon treatment for gaze-evoked or gaze-modulated tinnitus, Sanchez and Pio (2007) [51] describe a case whereby daily eye movement exercises had the effect of suppressing the underlying tinnitus perception. The mechanism(s)-of-action is/are unknown and theoretical accounts remain to be adequately explained. Nevertheless, this interesting observation is worthy of further investigation and replication.

Cutaneous-Evoked Tinnitus

Also observed following skull-base surgery for gross total excision of mass lesions (glomus jugulare tumor, vestibular schwannoma) were documented reports of cutaneous-evoked tinnitus [52, 53]. In one individual, the trigger zone for cutaneous-evoked tinnitus was a circumscribed area in the upper aspect of the hand by the wrist area. Activation of this area by stroking the skin produced a tonal tinnitus approximating 800 Hz. In another presentation, simultaneously touching the right index finger and thumb triggered an auditory noise-like sensation.

Imaging Gaze-Evoked, Gaze-Modulated, and Cutaneous-Evoked Tinnitus with Functional (fMRI) and Positron Emission Tomography (PET)

As individuals can either turn their tinnitus on and off and/or modulate the percept with change in eye gaze, the potential exists for localizing the source of the tinnitus-related activity through various forms of neuroimaging methodologies (e.g., fMRI or PET). In these investigations, individuals with GET serve as their own endogenous generators and act as their own controls. The first account of imaging GET was reported by Cacace and colleagues (1996) [54] using fMRI. This innovation was possible because it allowed for the on-off paradigm commonly used in fMRI studies to be applied [55]. By comparing the differences in activation between *tinnitus on* and *tinnitus off* conditions, tinnitus generator sites could in theory be localized. In one example where fMRI was successful in this regard, activations were observed in the upper brainstem and frontal cortex (superior colliculus and frontal-eye fields) [54, 56, 57]. This approach set the stage for other types of imaging studies on tinnitus and allowed other investigators to replicate and expand upon these

original results (e.g., Giraud et al., 1999 and Lockwood et al., 2001) [42, 48].

With respect to cutaneous-evoked tinnitus, using fMRI and a finger tapping opposition task, Cacace and colleagues (1999) [53] were able to validate that finger tapping in one hand activated specific auditory pathways. When the finger tapping opposition task was performed with the right hand, which served to trigger the tinnitus, activation of the left temporal cortex (i.e., the superior portion of the Sylvian fissure and inferior aspect of the parietal operculum) was observed contralateral to the motor activation task. This cortical activation was in addition to the expected motor area activation sites in or near the Rolandic sulcus. Importantly, the finger tapping opposition task with the opposite hand only activated sites associated with the motor system, thus documenting the specificity of this phenomenon by using an objective test.

The occurrence of GET and cutaneous-evoked tinnitus expand our perspective on the biological basis of tinnitus by considering these phenomena in the context of lesion-induced cross-modal plasticity. Obviously, these conditions are sufficiently different from other forms of tinnitus, and these manifestations require an expansion of the existing models and frameworks to account for these phenomena.

Conclusions

The detection, management, and treatment of vestibular schwannoma has evolved over a period of time, whereby current treatment options have reduced mortality to near zero and minimized substantially the surgical morbidity. This current state-of-affairs is due to technical innovations in imaging and electrophysiology allowing for early diagnosis, improvements in surgical technique, use of the operating microscope, and availability of alternative treatment options. Tinnitus and vestibular schwannoma are intimately related. Unilateral tinnitus can serve as a red flag to signal the presence of this disease, prompting further evaluation and ultimately resulting in early diagnosis and better surgical outcomes. Tinnitus outcomes vary with treatment type. Following microsurgery, it is unpredictable if tinnitus will get better or worse. However, with stereotactic radiosurgery, tinnitus is generally unchanged following treatment. Lastly, in cases where hearing is lost completely and abruptly during surgery, gaze-evoked, gaze-modulated, or other forms of somatic (cutaneous-evoked) tinnitus can result. These later types of tinnitus, which may be a consequence of cross-modal plasticity, are not accounted for by available models of tinnitus generation and require special consideration in future theories. Nevertheless, they serve to expand the biologic basis of tinnitus and provide additional insight to the complexity of this phenomenon under various conditions and circumstances [58].

References

1. Cummings, C W, Arriaga, M, Brackmann, D, Flint, P, Lee, H, Haughey, B, Richardson, M, Robbins, K, Schuller, D, and Thomas, J (2005) Otolaryngology – Head and Neck Surgery, 5th ed. Mosby: Elsevier, pp 3803–3840
2. National Institutes of Health Consensus Development Conference, Statement on Acoustic Neuroma, December 11-13, 1991. The Consensus Development Panel. Arch Neurol, 51: 201–207
3. Stangerup, S E, Caye-Thomasen, P, Tos, M, and Thomsen, J (2006) The natural history of vestibular schwannoma. Otol Neurotol, 27: 547–552
4. Cacace, A T (1981) Acoustic neuroma: An audiological evaluation. New York State J Med, 81: 744–749
5. Glasscock, M (1968) History of the diagnosis and treatment of vestibular schwannoma. Arch Otolaryngol, 88: 578–585
6. House, W F, and Graham, M D (1973) Surgery of acoustic tumors. Otolaryngol Clin North Am, 3: 245–266
7. Kutz, J W, Roland, P S, and Isaacson, B (2009) Skull base, vestibular schwannoma (Vestibular schwannoma). eMedicine, http://emedicinemedscapecom/article/882876-overview: 693–697
8. Machinis, T G, Fountas, K N, Dimopoulos, V, and Robinson, J S (2005) History of acoustic neurinoma surgery. eMedicine http://wwwmedscapecom/viewarticle/503952
9. Ballance, C A (1907) Some Points in the Surgery of the Brain and Its Membranes. London, Macmillan
10. Creed, L, and Seeger, J F (1984) Radiologic evaluation of the vestibular schwannoma. Ariz Med J, 41:739–743
11. Panse, R (1904) Ein Gliom des Akustikus. Arch Ohrenheilkd, 61: 251–255
12. Nguyen-Huynh, A T, Jackler, R K, Pfister, M, and Tseng, J (2007) The aborted early history of the translabyrinthine approach: a victim of suppression or technical prematurity? Otol Neurotol, 28: 269–279
13. Cushing, H (1917) Tumors of the Nervus Acusticus and the Syndrome of the Cerebellopontine Angle. Philadelphia: Saunders
14. Dandy, W (1941) Results of removal of acoustic tumors by the unilateral approach. Arch Surg, 42: 1026–1033
15. Weit, R J, Teixido, M, and Liang, J G (1992) Complications in vestibular schwannoma surgery. Otolaryngol Clin North Am, 25: 389–412
16. Flickinger, J C (2003) Radiation treatment for vestibular schwannoma. In: Glasscock, M E, Gulya, A J (Eds), Glasscock-Shambaugh Surgery of the Ear, 5th ed. Hamilton: Decker Inc, pp 693–697
17. Abram, S, Rosenblatt, P, and Holcomb, S (2007) Stereotactic radiation techniques in the treatment of acoustic schwannoma. Otolaryngol Clin North Am, 40: 571–588
18. Myrseth, E, Pedersen, P H, Møller, P, and Lund-Johansen, M (2007) Treatment for vestibular schwannoma Why, when, and how? Acta Neurochir (Wien), 149: 647–660
19. Coelho, D H, Roland, J T, Rush, S A, Narayana, A, St Clair, E, Chung, W, and Golfinos, J G (2008) Small vestibular schwannoma with no hearing: Comparison of functional outcomes in stereotactic radiosurgery and microsurgery. Laryngoscope, 118: 1909–1916
20. Wackym, P A (2005) Stereotactic radiosurgery, microsurgery, and expectant management of vestibular schwannoma: Basis for informed consent. Otolaryngol Clin North Am, 38: 653–670
21. Myrseth, E, Møller, P, Pedersen, P H, and Lund-Johansen, M (2009) Vestibular schwannoma: Surgery or gamma knife radiosurgery? A prospective, nonrandomized study. Neurosurgery, 64: 654–661
22. Kondziolka, D, Lunsford, L D, McLaughlin, M, and Flickinger, J C (1998) Long-term outcomes after radiosurgery for vestibular schwannoma. N Engl J Med, 339: 1426–1433
23. Chung, W Y, Liu, K D, Shiau, C Y, Wu, H M, Wang, L W, Guo, W Y, Ho, D M, and Pan, D H (2005) Gamma knife surgery for vestibular schwannoma: 10-year experience of 195 cases. J Neurosurg, 102: Suppl 87–96
24. de Ipolyi, A R, Yang, I, Buckley, A, Barbaro, N M, Cheung, S W, and Parsa, A T (2008) Fluctuating response of a cystic vestibular schwannoma to radiosurgery: Case report. Neurosurg, 62: E1164–E1165
25. Pollack, B E (2006) Management of vestibular schwannoma that enlarge after stereotactic radiosurgery: Treatment recommendations based on a 15 year experience. Neurosurg, 58: 241–248
26. Levo, H, Blomstedt, G, and Pyykkö, I (2000) Tinnitus and vestibular schwannoma surgery. Acta Otolaryngol 543: Suppl 28–29
27. Rastogi, P, Cacace, A T, and Lovely, T J (1995) Factors influencing hearing preservation in acoustic tumor surgery. Skull Base Surg, 5: 137–142
28. Fahy, C, Nikolopoulos, T P, and O'Donoghue, G M (2002) Vestibular schwannoma surgery and tinnitus. Eur Arch Otorhinolaryngol, 259: 299–301
29. Schaller, B J, Rasper, J, Filis, A, and Buchfelder, M (2008) Difference in functional outcome of ipsilateral tinnitus after intraoperative occurrence of the trigemino-cardiac reflex in surgery for vestibular schwannoma. Acta Neurochir (Wien), 150: 157–160
30. Kanzaki, J, Sato, A, and Kunihiro, T (1999) Does hearing preservation surgery for acoustic neuroma affect tinnitus? Skull Base Surg, 9: 169–176
31. Haid, C (1998) Acoustic tumor surgery on tinnitus. Int Tinn J 4: 155–158
32. Hempel, J M, Hempel, E, Wowra, B, Schichor, C, Muacevic, A, and Riederer, A (2006) Functional outcome after gamma knife treatment in vestibular schwannoma. Eur Arch Otorhinolaryngol, 263: 714–718

33. Bertalanffy, A, Dietrich, W, Aichholzer, M, Brix, R, Ertl, A, Heimberger, K, and Kitz, K (2001) Gamma knife radiosurgery of acoustic neurinomas. Acta Neurochir (Wien), 143: 689–695

34. Régis, J, Pellet, W, Delsanti, C, Dufour, H, Roche, P H, Thomassin, J M, Zanaret, M, and Peragut, J C (2002) Functional outcome after gamma knife surgery or microsurgery for vestibular schwannoma. J Neurosurg, 97: 1091–1100

35. Niranjan, A, Lunsford, L D, Flickinger, J C, Maitz, A, and Kondziolka, D (1999) Dose reduction improves hearing preservation rates after intracanalicular acoustic tumor radiosurgery. Neurosurg, 45: 753–762

36. Gardner, G, and Robertson, J H (1988) Hearing preservation in unilateral vestibular schwannoma surgery. Ann Otol Rhinol Laryngol, 97: 55–66

37. Régis, J, Tamura, M, Delsanti, C, Roche, P H, Pellet, W, and Thomassin, J M (2008) Hearing preservation in patients with unilateral vestibular schwannoma after gamma knife surgery. Prog Neurol Surg, 21: 142–151

38. Pollack, A G, Marymont, M H, Kalapurakal, J A, Kepka, A, Sathiaseelan, V, and Chandler, J P (2005) Acute neurological complications following gamma knife surgery for vestibular schwannoma. J Neurosurg, 103: 546–551

39. Linskey, M E, Johnstone, P A, O'Leary, M, and Goetsch, S (2003) Radiation exposure of normal temporal bone structures during stereotactically guided gamma knife surgery for vestibular schwannoma. J Neurosurg, 98: 800–806

40. Wall, M, Rosenburg, M, and Richardson, D (1987) Gaze-evoked tinnitus. Neurology, 37, 1034–1046

41. Cacace, A T, Lovely, T J, McFarland, D J, Parnes, S M, and Winter, D F (1994) Anomalous cross-modal plasticity following posterior fossa surgery: Some speculations on gaze-evoked tinnitus. Hear Res, 81. 22–32

42. Lockwood, A H, Wack, D S, Burkard, R F, Coad, M L, Reyes, S A, Arnold, S A, and Salvi, R J (2001) The functional anatomy of gaze-evoked tinnitus and sustained lateral gaze. Neurology, 56: 472–480

43. Baguley, D M, Phillips, J, Humphriss, R L, Jones, S, Axon, P R, and Moffat, D A (2006) The prevalence and onset of gaze modulation of tinnitus and increased sensitivity to noise after translabyrinthine vestibular schwannoma excision. Otol Neuro-Otol, 27: 220–224

44. Whittaker, C K (1982) Tinnitus and eye movement. Am J Otol, 4: 188

45. Whittaker, C K (1983) Intriguing change in tinnitus with eye movement. Am J Otol, 4: 273

46. House, W F (1982) Letter to the editor. Am J Otol, 4: 188

47. Cacace, A T, Lovely, T J, Winter, D F, Parnes, S M, and McFarland, D J (1994) Auditory perceptual and visual-spatial characteristics of gaze-evoked tinnitus. Audiology, 33: 291–303

48. Giraud, A L, Chery-Croze, S, Fischer, G, Fisher, C, Vighetto, A, Grégoire, M C, Lavenne, F, and Collet, L (1999) A selective imaging of tinnitus. Neuroreport, 10: 1–5

49. Coad, M L, Lockwood, A, Salvi, R, and Burkard, R (2001) Characteristics of patients with gaze-evoked tinnitus. Otol Neuro-Otol, 22: 650–654

50. Biggs, N D, and Ramsden, R T (2002) Gaze-evoked tinnitus following vestibular schwannoma resection: A de-afferentation plasticity phenomenon? Clin Otolaryngol Allied Sci, 27: 338–343

51. Sanchez, T G, and Pio, M R B (2007) The cure of a gaze-evoked tinnitus by repetition of gaze movements. Int Arch Otorhinolaryngol, 3: 345–349

52. Cacace, A T, Cousins, J P, Parnes, S M, McFarland, D J, Semenoff, D, Holmes, T, Davenport, C, Stegbauer, K, and Lovely, T J (1999) Cutaneous evoked tinnitus: II Review of neuroanatomical, physiological and functional imaging studies. Audiol Neurootol, 4, 258–268

53. Cacace, A T, Cousins, J P, Parnes, S M, Semenoff, D, Holmes, T, McFarland, D J, Davenport, C, Stegbauer, K, and Lovely, T J (1999) Cutaneous evoked tinnitus: I Phenomenology, psychophysics and functional imaging. Audiol Neurootol, 4: 247–257

54. Cacace, A T, Cousins, J P, Moonen, C T W, van Gelderen, P, Miller, D, Parnes, S M, and Lovely, T J (1996) In-vivo localization of phantom auditory perceptions during functional magnetic resonance imaging of the human brain. In: Reich, GE, and Vernon, J A (Eds), Proceeding of the Fifth International Tinnitus Seminar, American Tinnitus Association, Portland, OR, pp 397–401

55. Cacace, A T, Tascicyan, T, and Cousins, J C (2000) Principles of functional magnetic resonance imaging: Application to auditory neuroscience. J Am Acad Audiol, 11: 234–272

56. Cacace, A T, Lovely, T J, Parnes, S M, Winter, D F, and McFarland, D J (1996) Gaze-evoked tinnitus following unilateral peripheral auditory deafferentation: A case for anomalous cross-modal plasticity. In: Salvi, R J, Hendersen, D, Fiorino, F, and Colletti, V (Eds) Auditory System Plasticity and Regeneration. New York: Thieme Medical Publishers, pp 354–358

57. Cacace, A T (1999) Delineating tinnitus-related activity in the nervous system: Application of functional imaging at the fin de siècle. In: Hazell J W P (Ed), Proceedings of the Sixth International Tinnitus Seminar, 1999, Cambridge, UK THC London, pp 39–44

58. Cacace, A T (2003) Expanding the biological basis of tinnitus: Cross-modal origins and the role of neuroplasticity. Hear Res, 175: 112–132

Chapter 40
Microvascular Compression of the Vestibulocochlear Nerve

Dirk De Ridder and Aage R. Møller

Keypoints

1. Microvascular contacts or compressions of the vestibulocochlear nerve can result in tinnitus.
2. For nonpulsatile tinnitus, the contact is most often at the central nervous system segment.
3. For pulsatile tinnitus and typewriter tinnitus, the contact is at the peripheral nervous system segment. The tinnitus is unilateral and characterized by intermittent paroxysms of tinnitus.

   (a) A typical development consists of progressively more frequent bouts of tinnitus, which last longer and longer.
   (b) If bilateral vascular compressions exist, the tinnitus alternates between the left and right side, and does not occur on each side simultaneously.

4. Associated symptoms are correlated with related contacts/compressions of nearby nerves and include overt or cryptogenic hemifacial spasms, geniculate neuralgia, optokinetically induced short bouts of disabling positional vertigo, and tinnitus frequency-specific hearing loss.
5. Auditory brainstem responses (ABRs) correlate with disease progress and clinical symptoms and can be used diagnostically.

   (a) Tinnitus is causally related to a decrease in amplitude of peak II in the ipsilaterally elicited ABR.
   (b) Tinnitus frequency-specific hearing loss is causally related to prolongation of the ipsilateral interpeak latency (IPL) I–III.
   (c) Prolongation of contralateral IPL III–V occurs and is a sign of slowed signal transmission in the brainstem.

6. Magnetic resonance imaging sequences with constructive interference in steady state can visualize most vascular contacts/compressions of the auditory nerve.
7. Microvascular decompression should be performed before irreversible nerve damage is induced; clinically, the procedure should be performed before 4–5 years.

Keywords Pulsatile • Tinnitus • Vascular conflict • Microvascular compression • MVC • MVD

Abbreviations

AAO	American Academy of Otolaryngology
AAOO	American Academy of Ophthalmology and Otolaryngology
ABR	Auditory brainstem response
CISS	Constructive interference in steady state
CVCS	Cochleovestibular compression syndrome
ENT	Ear nose and throat
HFS	Hemifacial spasm
IPL	Interpeak latency
MRI	Magnetic resonance imaging
MVC	Microvascular compression
MVD	Microvascular decompression
PNS	Peripheral nervous system
TGN	Trigeminal neuralgia

D. De Ridder (✉)
BRAI²N and Department of Neurosurgery, TRI Tinnitus
Clinic Antwerp, University of Antwerp, Wilrijkstraat 10,
2650 Edegem, Belgium
e-mail: dirk.de.ridder@uza.be

A.R. Møller et al. (eds.), *Textbook of Tinnitus*,
DOI 10.1007/978-1-60761-145-5_40, © Springer Science+Business Media, LLC 2011

Introduction

Definition of Microvascular Compression

A blood vessel compressing a cranial nerve induces a nerve stimulation leading to a hyperactive cranial nerve syndrome [1, 2] with or without a loss of function. It is diagnosed almost solely based on the history taken, and a magnetic resonance imaging (MRI) is used for exclusion of other pathology and as a possible confirmation.

Primary and Secondary Microvascular Compressions

Microvascular compression (MVC) can occur as such or can be induced based on a general lack of space in the posterior fossa, such as seen in the Arnold–Chiari malformation [3–5] or associated with space-occupying lesions. This can result in a direct compression [6, 7] or indirect compression [8], but can also occur contralaterally, possibly due to a decrease in intracranial space [9–13]. In Sindou's series [4] of 39 patients with Arnold–Chiari malformation,[1] nine suffered from trigeminal neuralgia. After decompressing the foramen magnum, five of these nine individuals got rid of their pain, whereas the remaining four persons required a second microvascular decompression (MVD) operation. In this series of trigeminal neuralgias treated by MVD, the nerve was compressed between the pons and petrous bone in 3.9% of persons studied, due to the small size of the posterior fossa [14]. Removal of a tentorial meningioma can improve sudden hearing loss related to an MVC of the vestibulocochlear nerve based on the same premises [8].

Signs and Symptoms of Microvascular Compression

Examples of MVC syndromes are trigeminal neuralgia, glossopharyngeal neuralgia, hemifacial spasm [HFS], disabling positional vertigo, tinnitus, and otalgia.[2]

Other clinical syndromes such as spasmodic torticollis [15], cyclic oculomotor spasm with paresis [16], superior oblique myokymia [17, 18], and abducens spasm [19] may also be initiated by vascular compressions of the respective cranial nerves (nerves intermedius, spinal accessory nerve, and oculomotor and trochlear nerves). The incidence of the different MVC syndromes seems to be related to the length of the central nervous system (CNS) segment [20].

MVC of cranial nerves usually occurs unilaterally and, thus, induces unilateral symptoms [21–25] characterized by paroxysmal and intermittent spells of hyperactivity. The paroxysms typically become more frequent over time, the intermittent symptom-free periods become shorter and terminate in a constant dysfunction [26–28]. The symptoms of MVC can often be evoked by specific triggers [21, 26–28]. MVC syndromes are most common in late middle age (mean age 50 years) [21–25].

MVC of the vestibulocochlear nerve can cause any of the following paroxysmal symptoms depending on the place of compression: vertigo disabling positional vertigo [29], tinnitus [30, 31], hearing loss [32], or ear pressure (Dirk De Ridder unpublished observation).

MVC rarely presents bilaterally (1–12%) [23, 25, 33, 34]; if it does, the pain or spasm alternates sides and never occurs on both at the same time. There usually is a delay between the onset of symptoms from one side and the development of symptoms of the other side [24, 35, 36], with only 2–3% of the bilateral cases starting simultaneously. Bilateral MVC has a higher incidence in familial cases [33, 35].

MVC syndromes that affect more than one cranial nerve occur rarely (incidence 2.8%) [24]. The combination may occur unilaterally (1.5%) or bilaterally (1.3%). The mean age is higher than for unilateral symptoms, 63.2 vs. 55.3 years, which is similar to bilateral MVCs (61.4 years) [24]. If one blood vessel contacts two or more cranial nerves, symptoms do not develop at the same moment in time [37]. The best-known double compression syndrome is called the tic convulsif, consisting of a combination of HFS and trigeminal neuralgia [38], which can occur even bilaterally [37, 39].

These data suggest that if bilateral tinnitus is due to MVC it is expected that the left- and the right-sided component should start at different moments in time and with a different pitch. Theoretically, true bilateral tinnitus (i.e., with same pitch) could occur if the compression is at the level of the cochlear nucleus.

---

[1] Arnold-Chiari malformation: displacement of the medulla and cerebellar tonsils and vermis through the foramen magnum into the upper spinal canal; often associated with other cerebral anomalies.

[2] Otalgia: Earache.

Cochleovestibular Compression Syndrome

A recent meta-analysis has confirmed that blood vessels in contact with the vestibulocochlear nerve can result in otological symptoms, including hearing loss and tinnitus [40, 41].

Whereas initially it was proposed that only vascular compression of the root entry zone of a cranial nerve could cause symptoms [42], it was later suggested that any vascular contact along the CNS segment (between the internal acoustic meatus and the brainstem) could result in tinnitus [20]. Vascular loops inside the internal acoustic meatus along the morphologically more resistant peripheral nervous system (PNS) segment, however, were described to produce either typewriter tinnitus [43] or pulsatile tinnitus [41, 44]. Typewriter tinnitus consists of paroxysms of tinnitus perceived as Morse code, machine gun-like staccato, or typewriter sound and has been shown to be responsive to treatment with carbamazepine [43], thus analogous to trigeminal neuralgia.

Diagnostic Criteria of Cochleovestibular Compression Syndrome

Based on the analogy with other vascular compression syndromes, tinnitus caused by MVC would be expected to be unilateral and have short-lasting paroxysms with the tinnitus-free intervals becoming progressively shorter – ending in constant tinnitus. This kind of tinnitus would be expected to occur in middle-aged individuals and would not be anticipated to be associated with a flat hearing loss, as the typical MVC disorders (HFS and TGN) are not associated with complete weakness or complete loss of sensation in the entire distribution of the cranial nerve. Persistent compression can result in changes in the characteristics of pain and sensory impairment [26]. In a similar fashion, long-standing HFS could result in facial palsy or Bells's palsy [45]. Similarly, chronic vestibular nerve compression can lead to hypofunctioning of the labyrinth, clinically expressed as gait instability [25].

Both parts of the vestibulocochlear nerve might be compressed at the same time, and symptoms from the vestibular nerve would be expected in individuals with tinnitus from MVC. A similar evolution is noted, with progressively more vertiginous spells and shorter symptom-free periods [25, 28]. In contrast to Ménière's disease, the spells are shorter lasting and have no aura and no postictal period. In a chronic stage, persistent instability is noted [25, 46].

It is of interest, however, that in Ryu's study, 73% of the patients with a MVC were diagnosed as having Ménière's disease [28]. The main electrophysiological difference between Ménière's disease and cochleovestibular compression syndrome (CVCS) is that in Ménière's disease there are no abnormalities in peak II and interpeak latency (IPL) I–III of the auditory brainstem response (ABR) [47]. Two more nerves are in close relationship with the cochleovestibular nerve: the intermediate and the facial nerve. Vascular contact with the nervous intermedius is associated with geniculate neuralgia [22]. At the acute stage, intermittent paroxysmal bouts of otalgia occur; at a later stage, a deep, dull hemifacial pain develops [22].

Vascular contact with the root exit zone of the facial nerve can result in HFS [48, 49] and concomitant contact with the cochleovestibular nerve. The same vessel can cause auditory signs including low frequency tinnitus and hearing loss [31, 50].

Characteristic Features of Tinnitus as a MVC Syndrome

Selection Criteria

1. Intermittent paroxysmal spells of tinnitus lasting only seconds
   (a) Hearing loss at the tinnitus frequency
2. Associated ipsilateral symptoms from adjacent cranial nerves
   (a) Cryptogenic or overt HFSs
   (b) Bouts of otalgia or feeling pressure in the ear
   (c) Vertiginous spells: short lasting, optokinetically induced
3. Positive MRI for vascular compression
4. Positive brainstem auditory evoked potential using Møller's criteria

Classification of Cochleovestibular Compression Syndrome

The characteristics of CVCS can be classified into four different groups based on the American Academy of

Ophthalmology and Otolaryngology's (AAOO) (later renamed the American Academy of Otolaryngology [AAO]) criteria of Ménière's disease [51, 52], relating to the certainty of the diagnosis of CVCS as the cause of tinnitus [53]:

• Possible CVCS: initially intermittent unilateral tinnitus spells without associated symptoms.
• Probable CVCS: possible CVCS with associated symptoms (vertigo spells; ipsilateral cryptogenic or overt HFS; ipsilateral pressure feeling in the ear, ipsilateral ear pain, or deep, dull hemifacial pain; ipsilateral frequency-specific hearing loss).
• Definite CVCS: probable CVCS with abnormal ABR and/or abnormal MRI.
• Certain CVCS: definite CVCS is surgically proven.

Pathophysiology of the CVCS

A cranial nerve has two parts, a CNS segment and a PNS segment separated by a transition zone, known as the root entry or root exit zone (for sensory and motor nerves, respectively) or Obersteiner–Redlich zone. The length of the CNS segment is different in every cranial nerve, with sensory fibers, in general, having a longer CNS segment than motor fibers [54]. For the VIIIth cranial nerve, the CNS segment encompasses the entire cisternal trajectory of the cochleovestibular nerve with the root entry zone located at the entrance of the internal auditory canal, thus the root entry zone is located at the internal auditory meatus.

Functional Anatomy

The cochlear nerve contains approximately 30,000 axons [55], 90% of which are myelinated (type I) and 10% of which are unmyelinated (type II) [56]. (For details, see Chaps. 8 and 36.) Myelinated nerve fibers represent the afferent neurons from the inner hair cells and the efferent neurons to the outer hair cells. Unmyelinated nerve fibers, on the contrary, represent the efferent neurons to the inner hair cells and the afferent neurons from the outer hair cells [56].

The average axon diameter of the PNS segment is fairly constant at ±3 μm [56] or 4.2–5.5 μm [57], suggesting conduction velocities of approximately 12 m/s [58] (11.6 ± 1.6 m/s). Whether differences exist in fiber spectrum, especially with regards to fiber diameter between apical and basal fibers in humans, is still debated, so it is not known whether a direct correlation exists between axonal diameters and tonotopy in humans; however, it has been suggested [57].

The auditory system is tonotopically organized. This means neurons sensitive to specific acoustic frequencies are topographically arranged in an orderly manner [59–62]. As the cochlea is tonotopically organized (Von Bekesy's place theory of pitch perception) – as well as the cochlear nuclei, the inferior colliculus, and the auditory cortex – the cochlear nerve has to be tonotopically organized too [31], as shown in animal studies [63]. The cochlear nerve (as other cranial nerves) rotates as it travels through the auditory canal and cisternal segment of the subarachnoidal space toward the cochlear nucleus [64]. The tonotopy follows this rotation as well. This tonotopy has been demonstrated in humans as well as in studies of MVDs of the vestibulocochlear nerve [31]. It has also been demonstrated by means of an MRI technique using 3D reconstructions of high-resolution (0.6 mm slice thickness), heavily T2-weighted images (constructive interference in steady state, CISS) [65] also known as virtual endoscopy [66].

Pathophysiological Model of CVCS

Several hypotheses have addressed the pathology of MVC in general. Some of them concern the cranial nerve and some concern the respective nucleus. HFS has been studied extensively, and evidence for hyperactivity in the facial motonucleus has been presented [48]. There is no evidence supporting the old hypothesis that blood vessels elongate and their brain "sags" with age [2, 67–70]. It is not known whether the formation of vascular loops in the posterior fossa that can come close to cranial nerve increases with age [69]. MVC has been claimed to cause focal demyelination (see Chap. 84), but little evidence of demyelination or other morphological changes in cranial nerves in individuals with symptoms of cranial nerve vascular compression has been published.

Focal demyelination, if it exists because of MVC, could cause ectopic excitation [68, 71–73] (see Chap. 84). Such ectopic excitation might cause dysfunction of the cochlear nerve, most likely leading to a reorganization of the auditory nuclei in the auditory brainstem through activation of neural plasticity. Subsequently, the entire auditory tract, including the auditory cortex, can become hyperactive, resulting in gamma band activity, which may cause tinnitus [74, 75].

Microvascular Compressions Can Result in Tinnitus due to Abnormal Signal Transmission

Animal (cat) studies have described the tonotopic organization of the auditory nerve. The tonotopic organization of the human auditory nerve [31] has been related to the site of vascular contact and the frequency-specific dysfunction of the cochlear nerve revealed as the frequency-specific hearing loss and a frequency-specific tinnitus [31, 41].

Nonfrequency-specific click evoked auditory brainstem potentials are used routinely in an attempt to discover early demyelination. If the close contact with a blood vessel causes demyelination, frequency-specific ABR would be expected to be able to detect such focal demyelination. (For details about the anatomy of the auditory nerve, see Chap. 36 and [76].)

The neural generators of the auditory evoked responses (ABRs) in humans have been determined [59, 76]. The generators of the ABR in humans are not the same as the generators of the ABR in animals, including those in monkeys [76].

Peak I in humans is generated in the distal part of the cochlear nerve; peak II is generated in its CNS segment; peak III in the cochlear nuclei; peak IV in the superior olivary complex; peak V in the lateral lemniscus; and peak VI in the inferior colliculus (see Table 40.1) [76].

The IPL I–III would therefore be expected to be increased. If the vascular compression occurs at the CNS segment [20], peak II would be expected to be affected. Evoked potentials, in general, are the result of synchronized firing pattern as a reaction to a sensory stimulus [76]. The more synchronized the nerves fire, the higher the summated amplitude will be. If MVC of the cochlear nerve creates functional impairment of

some fibers, the temporal coherence of firing will decrease, resulting in a decrease of the amplitude of peak II. This hypothesis is supported by clinical findings that show a peak II decrease in individuals with tinnitus ipsilateral to MVCs with recurrence of peak II when surgical decompression is successful [53]. This suggests that the tinnitus is causally related to dysfunctional signal transmission at the site of compression in the initial stage of compression.

1. Chronic MVC results in frequency-specific hearing loss at tinnitus frequency.

In the first 2 years, no significant changes in ABR are noted in patients presenting with tinnitus and MVC [53]. Once peak II decreases are noted, IPL I–III prolongs [53].The fact that the IPL I–III prolongation is related to the duration of the tinnitus furthermore suggests that this is a dynamically progressive pathology [53] and that the effect of vascular contact with blood vessels creates changes over time, both electrophysiologically [53] and clinically [53].

The IPL I–III prolongation seems to be significantly related statistically to the degree of tinnitus after normalization for age [53]. Postoperatively, a shortening of the IPL I–III is not related to a clinical improvement in tinnitus but to an improvement in tinnitus frequency-specific hearing loss [53].

Schwaber and Hall [46] analyzed auditory brainstem evoked potentials in cochleovestibular compressions: IPL I–III interval difference ≥0.2 ms occurs in 66% of patients with a diagnosis of an MVC syndrome. Wave II amplitude <33% (in comparison with the contralateral) occurs in 57%. Contralateral IPL III–V interval difference ≥0.2 ms occurs in 30%; the ipsilateral IPL I–III absolute interval ≥2.3 ms occurs in 24%. Contralateral IPL III–V absolute interval ≥2.2 ms occurs in 2% of patients diagnosed with an MVC syndrome. This is associated with hearing loss for high frequencies in 65% of patients, a mid-frequency hearing loss in 27% of patients, and a low frequency loss in 8% of patients. A flat hearing loss was not seen in patients diagnosed with a MVC in Schwaber's series [46].

While the ABR changes (increased IPL I–III) indicate that the conduction velocity in the auditory nerve has decreased, intracranial recordings from patients undergoing MVD operations for severe tinnitus [77] did not find any significantly increased latencies when compared with individuals with some hearing loss who did not have tinnitus, confirming that IPL I–III is related

Table 40.1 Summary of relative time duration and possible mechanism related to electrophysiological changes and clinical symptoms for microvascular compression of the VIIIth cranial nerve for tinnitus

Time (years)	Mechanism	ABR	Clinical
0–2	Vascular compression	No ABR changes	Intermittent tinnitus?
	↓	↓	↓
>2	Disrupted signal transmission	Peak II decrease ipsilateral	Tinnitus
	↓	↓	↓
>4	Demyelination?	IPL I–III prolongation ipsilateral	Hearing loss at tinnitus frequency
	↓	↓	↓
>4	Compensation in brainstem	IPL III–V contralateral	?

to hearing loss and not tinnitus, per se. When compensated for hearing loss, individuals with tinnitus do not have significant changes in auditory evoked potentials from the peripheral part (IPL I–III) of the ascending pathways but a slight change in the potentials recorded from the inferior colliculus.

Signals transmitted via the compressed nerve fibers arrive at the cochlear nuclei in delay (IPL I–III prolongs) in comparison with the contralateral input. Because auditory input arrives bilaterally, this slowing down of nerve conduction in the auditory nerve of the affected ear (ipsilateral IPL I–III) will be counterbalanced by slowing down the auditory signals coming from the contralateral ear (De Ridder, submitted). As this slowing down can only occur in the brainstem, this will result in an increase in IPL III–V in the contralateral side. As such, a pathophysiological explanation can be proposed for Møller's criteria of MVC syndromes of the cochleovestibular nerve.

Criteria of microvascular compression of the VIIIth nerve [29]:

- Ipsilateral IPL I–III ≥2.3 ms
- Contralateral IPL III–V ≥2.2 ms
- IPL I–III difference ≥0.2 ms
- IPL III–V difference ≥0.2 ms
- IPL I–III difference ≥0.16 ms if low or absent peak II
- IPL III–V difference ≥0.16 ms if low or absent peak II
- Peak II amplitude <33%

2. Chronic tinnitus might be due to tinnitus frequency-specific hearing loss.

Whereas initially tinnitus is causally related to abnormal signal transmission in the peripheral part of the cochlear nerve at the site of the compression, electrophysiologically demonstrated by peak II decrease ipsilateral to the tinnitus side, chronic tinnitus might be the result of deafferentation due to hearing loss caused by slowing down of signal transmission in the peripheral part of the cochlear nerve, electrophysiologically related to IPL I–III prolongation. It is known that the most common cause for tinnitus is auditory deprivation, inducing the development of an auditory phantom percept [78]. Therefore, it is likely that when the compression has resulted in a hearing loss this will result in tinnitus, specifically at the frequency of hearing loss [31, 53, 79–81]. It has also been shown that the neural network in the brain that generates tinnitus changes with time [82], with a marked change before and after 4 years of tinnitus duration. This could explain why tinnitus that has lasted a long time is more difficult to treat by surgical decompression than acute tinnitus [28, 30, 31, 83, 84]. MVD is less successful in treatment of tinnitus that has lasted for longer than 3–5 years than tinnitus that has lasted a shorter period [31], coinciding temporally with the tinnitus-related brain network changes.

Conclusion

It is evident from several studies that MVD operations are more successful in treating tinnitus that has not lasted too long (less than 3–5 years). Studies have shown cure rates of 30% of patients and 30% improved. Worsening of tinnitus caused by MVD operations and other complications are rare but can be severe and life threatening.

After a MVD operation, the hearing threshold of the frequency of the tinnitus may improve if IPL I–III normalizes and peak II reoccurs.

The following pathophysiological mechanism can be suggested for tinnitus: when a blood vessel comes into contact with the auditory part of the VIIIth nerve and starts interfering with normal signal transmission, initially no electrophysiological changes can be retrieved. After 2 years, when enough fibers are involved a decrease in peak II on the ABR develops. When the close contact with a blood vessel continues, IPL I–III may increase, associated with hearing loss at the tinnitus frequency. This signal transmission slowing at the side of the compression is compensated by a contralateral slowing in the brainstem (contralateral IPL III–V prolongs). When hearing loss develops, tinnitus might relate more to the deafferentation, which induces network changes in the brain based on neural plasticity, and tinnitus at that stage has become a phantom percept. These tinnitus network changes alter in time, which might explain why surgical decompression has to be performed before 4 years in order to be successful.

References

1. Møller AR (1991) The cranial nerve vascular compression syndrome: II. A review of pathophysiology. Acta Neurochir (Wien) 113:24–30.
2. Jannetta PJ (1975) Neurovascular cross-compression in patients with hyperactive dysfunction symptoms of the eighth cranial nerve. Surg Forum 26:467–9.
3. Rosetti P, NO Ben Taib, J Brotchi et al (1999) Arnold Chiari Type I malformation presenting as a trigeminal neuralgia: case report. Neurosurgery 44:1122–3; discussion 3–4.
4. Sindou M (1999) discussion on Arnold Chiari Type I malformation presenting as a trigeminal neuralgia: case report. Neurosurgery 44:1123–4.
5. Kanpolat Y, A Unlu, A Savas et al (2001) Chiari Type I malformation presenting as glossopharyngeal neuralgia: case report. Neurosurgery 48:226–8.
6. Glocker FX, JK Krauss, G Deuschl et al (1998) Hemifacial spasm due to posterior fossa tumors: the impact of tumor location on electrophysiological findings. Clin Neurol Neurosurg 100:104–11.
7. Barker FG II, PJ Jannetta, RP Babu et al (1996) Long-term outcome after operation for trigeminal neuralgia in patients with posterior fossa tumors. J Neurosurg 84:818–25.
8. De Ridder D, T Menovsky, C Van Laer et al (2008) Remote tentorium meningioma causing sudden sensorineural deafness. Surg Neurol 70:312–7; discussion 318.
9. Matsuura N and A Kondo (1996) Trigeminal neuralgia and hemifacial spasm as false localizing signs in patients with a contralateral mass of the posterior cranial fossa. Report of three cases. J Neurosurg 84:1067–71.
10. Cappabianca P, G Mariniello, A Alfieri et al (1997) Trigeminal neuralgia and contralateral mass. J Neurosurg 86:171–2.
11. Haddad FS and JM Taha (1990) An unusual cause for trigeminal neuralgia: contralateral meningioma of the posterior fossa. Neurosurgery 26:1033–8.
12. Koenig M, K Kalyan-Raman and ON Sureka (1984) Contralateral trigeminal nerve dysfunction as a false localizing sign in acoustic neuroma: a clinical and electrophysiological study. Neurosurgery 14:335–7.
13. Mase G, M Zorzon, L Capus et al (1994) Trigeminal neuralgia due to contralateral meningioma of the posterior cranial fossa. J Neurol Neurosurg Psychiatry 57:1010.
14. Sindou M, T Howeidy and G Acevedo (2002) Anatomical observations during microvascular decompression for idiopathic trigeminal neuralgia (with correlations between topography of pain and site of the neurovascular conflict). Prospective study in a series of 579 patients. Acta Neurochir (Wien) 144:1–12; discussion 143.
15. Jho HD and PJ Jannetta (1995) Microvascular decompression for spasmodic torticollis. Acta Neurochir (Wien) 134:21–6.
16. Kommerell G, E Mehdorn and UP Ketelsen (1985) Oculomotor paralysis with cyclic spasms; electromyographic and electron microscopic indications of chronic peripheral nerve irritation. Fortschr Ophthalmol 82:203–4.
17. Samii M, SK Rosahl, GA Carvalho et al (1998) Microvascular decompression for superior oblique myokymia: first experience. Case report. J Neurosurg 89:1020–4.
18. Scharwey K, T Krzizok, M Samii et al (2000) Remission of superior oblique myokymia after microvascular decompression. Ophthalmologica 214:426–8.
19. De Ridder D and T Menovsky (2007) Neurovascular compression of the abducent nerve causing abducent palsy treated by microvascular decompression. Case report. J Neurosurg 107:1231–4.
20. De Ridder D, A Møller, J Verlooy et al (2002) Is the root entry/exit zone important in microvascular compression syndromes? Neurosurgery 51:427–33; discussion 33–4.
21. Resnick DK, PJ Jannetta, D Bissonnette et al (1995) Microvascular decompression for glossopharyngeal neuralgia. Neurosurgery 36:64–8; discussion 8–9.
22. Lovely TJ and PJ Jannetta (1997) Surgical management of geniculate neuralgia. Am J Otol 18:512–7.
23. Fukushima T (1995) Microvascular decompression for hemifacial spasm: result in 2890 cases. In Neurovascular surgery, L Carter, R Spetzler and M Hamilton, Editors. McGraw-Hill, Inc: New York, 1133–45
24. Kobata H, A Kondo, K Iwasaki et al (1998) Combined hyperactive dysfunction syndrome of the cranial nerves: trigeminal neuralgia, hemifacial spasm, and glossopharyngeal neuralgia: 11-year experience and review. Neurosurgery 43:1351–61; discussion 61–2.
25. Møller MB, AR Møller, PJ Jannetta et al (1993) Microvascular decompression of the eighth nerve in patients with disabling positional vertigo: selection criteria and operative results in 207 patients. Acta Neurochir (Wien) 125:75–82.
26. Burchiel KJ and KV Slavin (2000) On the natural history of trigeminal neuralgia. Neurosurgery 46:152–4; discussion 4–5.
27. Ehni G and H Woltman (1945) Hemifacial spasm. Arch Neurol Psychiatry 53:205–11.
28. Ryu H, S Yamamoto, K Sugiyama et al (1998) Neurovascular compression syndrome of the eighth cranial nerve. What are

the most reliable diagnostic signs? Acta Neurochir (Wien) 140:1279–86.

29. Møller MB (1990) Results of microvascular decompression of the eighth nerve as treatment for disabling positional vertigo. Ann Otol Rhinol Laryngol 99:724–9.

30. Møller MB, AR Møller, PJ Jannetta et al (1993) Vascular decompression surgery for severe tinnitus: selection criteria and results. Laryngoscope 103:421–7.

31. De Ridder D, H Ryu, AR Møller et al (2004) Functional anatomy of the human cochlear nerve and its role in microvascular decompressions for tinnitus. Neurosurgery 54:381–8; discussion 8–90.

32. Okamura T, Y Kurokawa, N Ikeda et al (2000) Microvascular decompression for cochlear symptoms. J Neurosurg 93:421–6.

33. Pollack IF, PJ Jannetta and DJ Bissonette (1988) Bilateral trigeminal neuralgia: a 14-year experience with microvascular decompression. J Neurosurg 68:559–65.

34. Rushton JG, JC Stevens and RH Miller (1981) Glossopharyngeal (vagoglossopharyngeal) neuralgia: a study of 217 cases. Arch Neurol 38:201–5.

35. Tacconi L and JB Miles (2000) Bilateral trigeminal neuralgia: a therapeutic dilemma. Br J Neurosurg 14:33–9.

36. Brisman R (1987) Bilateral trigeminal neuralgia. J Neurosurg 67:44–8.

37. Fonoff ET, VP Araujo, YS de Oliveira et al (2009) Neurovascular compression in painful tic convulsif. Acta Neurochir (Wien) 151:989–93.

38. Cook BR and PJ Jannetta (1984) Tic convulsif: results in 11 cases treated with microvascular decompression of the fifth and seventh cranial nerves. J Neurosurg 61:949–51.

39. Felicio AC, O Godeiro Cde, Jr., V Borges et al (2007) Bilateral hemifacial spasm and trigeminal neuralgia: a unique form of painful tic convulsif. Mov Disord 22:285–6.

40. Chadha NK and GM Weiner (2008) Vascular loops causing otological symptoms: a systematic review and meta-analysis. Clin Otolaryngol 33:5–11.

41. Nowe V, D De Ridder, PH Van de Heyning et al (2004) Does the location of a vascular loop in the cerebellopontine angle explain pulsatile and non-pulsatile tinnitus? Eur Radiol 14:2282–9.

42. Jannetta PJ (1977) Observations on the etiology of trigeminal neuralgia, hemifacial spasm, acoustic nerve dysfunction and glossopharyngeal neuralgia. Definitive microsurgical treatment and results in 117 patients. Neurochirurgia (Stuttg) 20:145–54.

43. Levine RA (2006) Typewriter tinnitus: a carbamazepine-responsive syndrome related to auditory nerve vascular compression. ORL J Otorhinolaryngol Relat Spec 68:43–6; discussion 6–7.

44. De Ridder D, L De Ridder, V Nowe et al (2005) Pulsatile tinnitus and the intrameatal vascular loop: why do we not hear our carotids? Neurosurgery 57:1213–7; discussion 1217.

45. Jannetta PJ and DJ Bissonette (1978) Bell's palsy: a theory as to etiology. Observations in six patients. Laryngoscope 88:849–54.

46. Schwaber MK and JW Hall (1992) Cochleovestibular nerve compression syndrome. I. Clinical features and audiovestibular findings. Laryngoscope 102:1020–9.

47. Møller MB (1988) Controversy in ménière's disease: results of microvascular decompression of the eighth nerve. Am J Otol 9:60–3.

48. Møller AR (1993) Cranial nerve dysfunction syndromes: Pathophysiology of microvascular compression. In: Neurosurgical Topics Book 13, 'Surgery of Cranial Nerves of the Posterior Fossa,' Chapter 2. D.L. Barrow, ed. American Association of Neurological Surgeons, Park Ridge, Illinois, pp. 105–129.

49. Møller AR and PJ Jannetta (1985) Hemifacial spasm: results of electrophysiologic recording during microvascular decompression operations. Neurology 35:969–74.

50. Møller MB and AR Møller (1985) Audiometric abnormalities in hemifacial spasm. Audiology 24:396–405.

51. CHE A-H (1995) Committee on hearing and equilibrium guidelines for the diagnosis and evaluation of therapy in Meniere's disease. American Academy of Otolaryngology-Head and Neck Foundation, Inc. Otolaryngol Head Neck Surg 113:181–5.

52. Beasley NJ and NS Jones (1996) Meniere's disease: evolution of a definition. J Laryngol Otol 110:1107–13.

53. De Ridder D, K Heijneman, B Haarman et al (2007) Tinnitus in vascular conflict of the eighth cranial nerve: a surgical pathophysiological approach to ABR changes. Prog Brain Res 166:401–11.

54. Hamlyn PJ (1999) Neurovascular compression of the cranial nerves in neurological and systemic disease. Elsevier: Amsterdam.

55. Spoendlin H and A Schrott (1988) The spiral ganglion and the innervation of the human organ of Corti. Acta Otolaryngol 105:403–10.

56. Spoendlin H and A Schrott (1990) Quantitative evaluation of the human cochlear nerve. Acta Otolaryngol Suppl 470:61–9; discussion 69–70.

57. Felix H, LG Johnsson, MJ Gleeson et al (1992) Morphometric analysis of the cochlear nerve in man. Acta Otolaryngol 112:284–7.

58. Nguyen BH, E Javel and SC Levine (1999) Physiologic identification of eighth nerve subdivisions: direct recordings with bipolar and monopolar electrodes. Am J Otol 20:522–34.

59. Møller AR (2000) Hearing: its physiology and pathophysiology. Academic Press: San Diego.

60. Bear M, BW Connors and M Paradiso (2001) Neuroscience: exploring the brain. Lippincott Williams and Wilkins: Baltimore, 349–95.

61. Purves D, G Augustine, D Fitzpatrick et al (1997) Neuroscience. Sinauer Associates: Sunderland, 223–44.

62. Shepherd G (1994) Neurobiology. Oxford University Press: New York.

63. Sando I (1965) The anatomical interrelationships of the cochlear nerve fibers. Acta Otolaryng (Stockh) 59:417–36.

64. Silverstein H, H Norrell, T Haberkamp et al (1986) The unrecognized rotation of the vestibular and cochlear nerves from the labyrinth to the brain stem: its implications to surgery of the eighth cranial nerve. Otolaryngol Head Neck Surg 95:543–9.

65. Casselman JW, R Kuhweide, M Deimling et al (1993) Constructive interference in steady state-3DFT MR imaging of the inner ear and cerebellopontine angle. AJNR Am J Neuroradiol 14:47–57.

66. Nowe V, JL Michiels, R Salgado et al (2004) High-resolution virtual MR endoscopy of the cerebellopontine angle. AJR Am J Roentgenol 182:379–84.

67. Jannetta PJ (1983) Hemifacial spasm: treatment by posterior fossa surgery. J Neurol Neurosurg Psychiatry 46:465–6.

68. Møller AR (1999) Vascular compression of cranial nerves: II: pathophysiology. Neurol Res 21:439–43.

69. Wilkins RH (1985) Neurovascular compression syndromes. Neurol Clin 3:359–72.

70. Dandy W (1934) Concerning the cause of trigeminal neuralgia. Am J Surg 24:447–55.

71. Love S and HB Coakham (2001) Trigeminal neuralgia: pathology and pathogenesis. Brain 124:2347–60.

72. Eidelman BH, VK Nielsen, M Møller et al (1985) Vascular compression, hemifacial spasm, and multiple cranial neuropathy. Neurology 35:712–6.

73. Schwaber M (1994) Vascular compression syndromes. In Neurotology, R Jackler and D Brackmann, Editors. Mosby: St Louis, 881–903.

74. van der Loo E, S Gais, M Congedo et al (2009) Tinnitus intensity dependent gamma oscillations of the contralateral auditory cortex. PLoS One 4:e7396.

75. Weisz N, S Muller, W Schlee et al (2007) The neural code of auditory phantom perception. J Neurosci 27:1479–84.

76. Møller AR (2006) Hearing: anatomy, physiology, and disorders of the auditory system, 2nd Ed. Academic Press: Amsterdam.

77. Møller AR, MB Møller, PJ Jannetta et al (1992) Compound action potentials recorded from the exposed eighth nerve in patients with intractable tinnitus. Laryngoscope 102: 187–97.

78. Jastreboff PJ (1990) Phantom auditory perception (tinnitus): mechanisms of generation and perception. Neurosci Res 8:221–54.

79. De Ridder D (2004) Modulation of brain functions in tinnitus. Neuromodulation 7:146.

80. De Ridder D, H Ryu, G De Mulder et al (2005) Frequency specific hearing improvement in microvascular decompression of the cochlear nerve Acta Neurochir (Wien) 147:495–501.

81. Norena A, C Micheyl, S Chery-Croze et al (2002) Psychoacoustic characterization of the tinnitus spectrum: implications for the underlying mechanisms of tinnitus. Audiol Neurootol 7:358–69.

82. Schlee W, T Hartmann, B Langguth et al (2009) Abnormal resting-state cortical coupling in chronic tinnitus. BMC Neurosci 10:11.

83. Jannetta P (1997) Outcome after microvascular decompression for typical trigeminal neuralgia, hemifacial spasm, tinnitus, disabling positional vertigo, and glossopharyngeal neuralgia. In Clinical neurosurgery, S Grady, Editor. Williams and Wilkins: Baltimore, 331–84.

84. Brookes GB (1996) Vascular-decompression surgery for severe tinnitus. Am J Otol 17:569–76.

Chapter 41
Causes of Tinnitus: Cerebrovascular Diseases

Miguel J.A. Láinez, Alejandro Ponz, and Anna Piera

Keypoints

1. Tinnitus can be divided into two broad groups: objective and subjective tinnitus.
2. Several layers of complexity are involved in the pathophysiology and the cause of tinnitus, and it is rarely known what causes an individual's tinnitus.
3. Disorders that affect the brain are often accompanied by tinnitus.
4. Cerebrovascular diseases can be the cause of both objective and subjective tinnitus.
5. This chapter discusses cerebrovascular diseases as a cause of tinnitus and how it is produced.

Keywords Tinnitus • Cerebrovascular diseases • Arterial pulsatile tinnitus • Venous pulsatile tinnitus

Abbreviations

CTA	Angiotomography
CVD	Cerebrovascular diseases
DAVF	Dural arteriovenous fistula
GJT	Glomus jugular tumor
HJB	High jugular bulb
MRA	Magnetic resonance angiography
PT	Pulsatile tinnitus
RI	Resistive index

M.J.A. Láinez (✉)
Department of Neurology, Hospital Clínico Universitario.
University of Valencia, Avenida Blasco Ibáñez, 17,
46010 Valencia, Spain
e-mail: jlaineza@meditex.es

Introduction

Tinnitus can be divided into two broad groups: objective and subjective tinnitus. Objective tinnitus is caused by sound generated in the body reaching the ear through conduction in body tissues [1]. The source can be turbulent flow of blood in an artery where there is a constriction, or it can be caused by muscle contractions. Unlike subjective tinnitus, an observer using a stethoscope or a person listening to the individual at a close distance may hear the sound. Subjective tinnitus is meaningless sounds that are not associated with a physical sound and only the person who has the tinnitus can hear it.

Several layers of complexity are involved in the pathophysiology and the cause of tinnitus, and it is rarely known what causes an individual's tinnitus (idiopathic tinnitus). Disorders of the central nervous system (CNS) or disorders that affect the function of the CNS are often accompanied by tinnitus. In the large group of cerebrovascular diseases, some cause tinnitus as an isolated symptom, but tinnitus is often associated with other symptoms. Such diseases can cause both objective tinnitus (e.g., pulsatile tinnitus in carotid-cavernous fistula) and subjective tinnitus such as those from ischemia of the inferior colliculus that can activate subcortical auditory pathways, and thereby cause tinnitus. This chapter discusses cerebrovascular diseases as a cause of tinnitus as well as the mechanisms, which cause the tinnitus. We will distinguish between pulsatile tinnitus and non-pulsatile tinnitus.

Pulsatile Tinnitus

Pulsatile tinnitus is perceived by an individual as pulsations in the tinnitus that are synchronous with the heart, and it is similar to pulsating sounds or a rushing

A.R. Møller et al. (eds.), *Textbook of Tinnitus*,
DOI 10.1007/978-1-60761-145-5_41, © Springer Science+Business Media, LLC 2011

sound (see chapter 59). Pulsatile tinnitus can be subjective or objective. Objective tinnitus can result from blood flow through a constriction causing the flow to become turbulent. Objective tinnitus that is strongly associated with the timing of the heart beat is most likely caused by turbulent flow in arteries or veins of the head or neck area located adjacent to the ear, on the surface of the head, or just inside the head. Patients with such problems require special imaging studies and often require surgery to resolve the issues.

This type of tinnitus can be heard as several characteristic sounds including a lower pitched thumping or booming. Objective tinnitus can also be caused by respiration and heard as a blowing sound, which is coincidental with respiration. Tinnitus that sounds like clicking, rhythmic sounds can be caused by muscle contractions in the head, such as those from muscles in the palate or the middle ear muscles.

Patients with pulsatile tinnitus may need a thorough medical evaluation to locate the cause of their tinnitus. Many published studies describe methods for treating objective tinnitus [2, 3]. Vascular imaging techniques have been employed to help determine the site of lesion, but there are many forms of pulsatile tinnitus that have no known cause (idiopathic category). This can be caused by failure to properly interpret imaging studies or miss the trouble spots that may be tangled in other structures or hidden by bone or other tissue. A clinical interview is crucial to identify this type of tinnitus [4–7].

Arterial Pulsatile Tinnitus: Differential Diagnosis

Many different pathologies of the cerebrovascular system have been reported as cause of pulsatile tinnitus. Some are listed below.

Cervical Arterial Stenosis

Stenosis of the carotid or the subclavian arteries are typical causes of pulsatile tinnitus, ipsilateral, or contralateral to the side of tinnitus. Often, the intensity or the appearance of tinnitus is not related to the degree of stenosis. Doppler ultrasonography is a useful test for use in tinnitus clinics to distinguish between these causes of pulsatile tinnitus [8, 9]. When stenosis of the

carotid artery is symptomatic, endarterectomy also relieves tinnitus [10–12].

Aberrant Internal Carotid Artery and Other Morphologic Abnormalities

Internal carotid artery morphologic abnormalities that can present with pulsatile tinnitus are mainly tortuousities (having many turns and twists) and coiling of the artery. Head bruit causing objective tinnitus can be evaluated by angiotomography or magnetic resonance angiography (MRA) of the head and neck, which can differentiate these abnormalities from other more serious vascular disorders [13, 14].

Cervicocephalic Arterial Dissection

Pulsatile tinnitus rarely occurs together with cervicocephalic arterial dissection. Tinnitus may occur together with ischemia caused by arterial dissection in carotid stenosis, causing Horner's syndrome. Dissection of the vertebral artery may cause vertigo and dysgeusia. Angiography is essential if there is a high degree of suspicion of such pathologies, and delay in the diagnosis should be avoided [15].

Fibromuscular Dysplasia of Cervical Arteries

Pulsatile tinnitus often occurs together with stenosis of the carotid artery. Fibromuscular dysplasia of the vertebral artery can also cause tinnitus [16]. Symptoms such as tinnitus, vertigo, headache, and cervicofacial hypoesthesia might lead a person to seek medical help from a neuro-otologist. Fibromuscular dysplasia may cause pulsatile tinnitus directly because of its stenosing angiopathy and indirectly by activation of sympathetic nervous system through its effect on a sympathetic plexus.

Dural Arteriovenous Fistulas (DAVF)

Pulsatile tinnitus is a common symptom in individuals with intracranial dural arteriovenous fistulas [17]. The occurrence of pulsatile tinnitus is related to the location of the fistula and the location of the arteries feeding the fistula. Yeh et al. have published an interesting study in which they compared the characteristics of

DAVF and carotid duplex sonography [18]. They showed that the occurrence of pulsatile tinnitus is highly correlated with the location of the DAVF and its feeding arteries. They also showed that the resistive index[1] and the end diastolic velocity in the external carotid artery are related to the presence of DAVF in pulsatile tinnitus patients by sonography [18]. Although this technique is not considered to provide a definitive diagnosis, sonography may assess pulsatile tinnitus in patients who are candidates for angiography [19].

Carotid-Cavernous Fistula

Carotid-cavernous fistula is a rare vascular abnormality that may develop following traumatic injury to the skull base; it may also be spontaneous. Objective tinnitus caused by this pathology is of acute or subacute onset, and an early intervention, endovascular of surgical, is needed to prevent permanent disability. Pulsatile tinnitus occurs together with carotid-cavernous fistula – other symptoms being papillary abnormalities, proptosis, headaches, and papilledema [20–24].

Aneurysms

Petrous carotid aneurysms and other located aneurysms are serious causes of tinnitus. Pulsatile tinnitus may be a symptom of the compression by the aneurysm when located near auditory structures. Hemorrhage, secondary to an aneurysm, can produce tinnitus as an acute symptom in addition to other symptoms derived from the subarachnoid hemorrhage [25, 26].

Vertebrobasilar and Carotid Dolichoectasia

Dolichoectasia[2] is an angiopathy characterized by dilatation, elongation, and tortuosity of brain arteries. It most frequently involves the vertebral and basilar arteries, but involvement of both the vertebrobasilar and carotid systems is rare. A magnetic resonance angiography (MRA) imaging or a computed tomographic angiography (CTA) can show an enlarged tortuosity of these arteries, often producing compression of the cranial portion of vestibulocochlear nerve [27].

Persistent Trigeminal Artery

Persistent trigeminal arteries are rare and represent a remnant of the fetal carotid-basilar circulation. They typically extend from the internal carotid artery to the basilar artery. In rare instances, a persistent trigeminal artery is associated with a carotid-cavernous fistula; patients with this condition may have pulsatile tinnitus in addition to other symptoms such as ptoptosis, eye pain, conjunctival injection, diplopia, and decreased visual acuity [28].

Subclavian Steal Syndrome

This syndrome is characterized by a subclavian artery stenosis located proximal to the origin of the vertebral artery. In this case, the subclavian artery steals reverse flow of blood from the vertebrobasilar artery circulation to supply the arm during exertion, resulting in vertebrobasilar insufficiency. As the vertebrobasilar arterial system feeds both the peripheral and central auditory and vestibular systems, symptoms such as dizziness, recurrent vertigo, hearing loss, and tinnitus [29] may occur in the subclavian steal syndrome.

Internal Auditory Canal Vascular Loops

A vascular loop entering the internal auditory meatus can be another cause of pulsatile tinnitus. Normally, the wall of the internal auditory meatus prevents vibrations of an artery from reaching the cochlea, but structural differences between the internal acoustic meatus and pericarotid area can originate tinnitus. De Ridder et al. insulated the carotid artery preventing arterial pulsations be transmitted to the bone. Abnormalities in the surgical interpositioning of Teflon felt between the arterial loop and the cochlea can eliminate this form of tinnitus [30].

Ischemic and Hemorrhagic Infarctions of the Posterior Circulation

These kinds of infarcts may cause tinnitus, but it is unknown what exactly causes the tinnitus [31–34].

---

[1] Doppler resistive index (RI) is the peak systolic velocity – the end diastolic velocity divided by the peak systolic velocity.

[2] Dolichoectasia: The term "dolichoectasia" means elongation and distension. It is used to characterize arteries throughout the human body that have shown significant deterioration of their tunica intima (and occasionally the tunica media), weakening the vessel walls and causing the artery to elongate and distend.

Brainstem Telangiectasias

Capillary telangiectasia (dilation of small or terminal vessels) is often found incidentally on magnetic resonance imaging because it is normally associated with only minor neurologic symptoms. There has been little evidence about whether such lesions are responsible for symptoms at all. In some individuals, telangiectasia is associated with tinnitus and sensorineural hearing loss. The auditory brain stem responses (ABR) in such individuals have abnormalities regarding waves III and IV. Another sign is asymmetry in optokinetic nystagmus that is present in some individuals [35].

Proatlantal Intersegmental Artery

Primitive carotid-vertebral and carotid-basilar anastomoses are formed early during human embryogenesis at approximately 24 days. From cephalic to caudal direction, these anastomoses are cranial extensions of the primitive internal carotid, trigeminal, otic, hypoglossal, and proatlantal intersegmental arteries. The proatlantal intersegmental artery maintains the posterior circulation until the vertebral arteries are fully developed, between the 7th and 8 gestational weeks. Normal and abnormal morphofunctional aspects of prenatal and postnatal forms of the proatlantal intersegmental artery have been described. When the proatlantal intersegmental artery fails to obliterate, it can produce symptoms affecting the function of vertebrobasilar structures such as hearing, tinnitus, and dizziness. In some individuals, these arteries do not give noticeable symptoms and are only found incidentally [36].

Venous Pulsatile Tinnitus: Differential Diagnosis

Glomus Jugular Tumor

Glomus jugular tumors are benign and slow-growing lesions that can be locally aggressive because of their proximity to lower cranial nerves and major vascular structures [37]. These lesions are known causes of pulsatile tinnitus and other symptoms by their compression of the nerves of the skull base [38]. Surgical resection is often complicated; the possibilities of

using radiosurgery are limited and combinations of both localized surgery in the middle ear and gamma knife surgery have shown good results.

High Jugular Bulb

The jugular bulb is normally surrounded by a bony layer in the jugular fossa. It is named a high jugular bulb (HJB) if it is anatomically above the inferior surface of the bonny annulus, extending into the middle ear or located above the basal turn of the cochlea. HJB is a frequent cause of objective pulsatile tinnitus. It may be dehiscent or aberrant. Techniques using endovascular management and surgery using ligation and embolization have been described to relieve this abnormality [39].

Sigmoid or Jugular Diverticulum

Jugular bulb diverticulum is a rare condition. It has been reported that unilateral auditory symptoms may accompany this disorder, although some individuals are asymptomatic. Some individuals with this condition are referred to clinics of neurotology centers with symptoms of unilateral sensorineural hearing loss and tinnitus. Tomographic venography is a useful tool to diagnose the condition [40, 41].

Condylar Vein Abnormalities

One of the most important venous foramina of the human skull is the condylar canal. This structure is described as the most stable and permanent venous emissary, with a prevalence of nearly 100%. It has been reported that patients with dural arteriovenous fistula of the anterior condylar vein have symptoms related to an unusual venous drainage. Pulsatile tinnitus may be the symptom of alarm for abnormalities of the jugular venous system [42].

Venous Angioma of Posterior Fossa

Venous angioma can cause tinnitus by affecting the auditory pathway [43–45] and the structures of the inner ear, thus similar to brainstem telangiectasias and other vascular malformations of the brainstem and other posterior fossa locations.

Sinus Thrombosis

Dural and profound sinus thrombosis commonly presents with headaches and some neurological symptoms depending on the location of the thrombosis and the surrounding edema and infarct. Dural sinus thrombosis may cause tinnitus with headaches in some individuals, more common if the course of the symptoms is subacute. The complaint from sigmoid sinus thrombosis may be unilateral head pain and unilateral pulsatile tinnitus [46–49].

Cerebrovascular Diseases with Subjective Tinnitus

Some cerebrovascular disorders can cause pulsatile tinnitus by affecting the auditory system at different levels. For example, a brain ischemic infarct located in the inferior colliculus can produce an acute or subacute tinnitus, and even chronic tinnitus as a sequela, by its effect on the auditory pathway.

References

1. Møller, AR (2003) Pathophysiology of tinnitus. In: Sismanis A (Ed) Otolaryngologic Clinics of North America. WB Saunders: Amsterdam, 249–266
2. Hafeez F, Levine RL, Dulli DA. Pulsatile tinnitus in cerebrovascular arterial diseases. J Stroke Cerebrovasc Dis 1999;8(4):217–223
3. Sismanis A. Pulsatile tinnitus. Otolaryngol Clin North Am 2003;36(2):389–402, viii
4. Sanchez TG, Murao M, de Medeiros IR, Kii M, Bento RF, Caldas JG, Alvarez CA, Raggiotto CH. A new therapeutic procedure for treatment of objective venous pulsatile tinnitus. Int Tinnitus J 2002;8(1):54–7
5. Shulman A, Goldstein B, Strashun AM. Central nervous system neurodegeneration and tinnitus: a clinical experience Part I: Diagnosis. Int Tinnitus J 2007;13(2):118–31
6. Shulman A, Goldstein B, Strashun AM. Central nervous system neurodegeneration and tinnitus: a clinical experience Part II: translational neurovascular theory of neurodegenerative CNS disease and tinnitus. Int Tinnitus J 2008;14(1):43–51
7. Liess BD, Lollar KW, Christiansen SG, Vaslow D. Pulsatile tinnitus: a harbinger of a greater ill? Head Neck 2009; 31(2):269–73
8. Gutmann R, Wollenberg B, Krampert B, Mees K. Incidence of Doppler ultrasound detectable stenoses of cervical arteries in patients with cochlear-vestibular symptoms. Laryngorhinootologie 1993;72(10):502–5 German
9. Hartung O, Alimi YS, Juhan C. Tinnitus resulting from tandem lesions of the internal carotid artery: combined extracranial endarterectomy and intrapetrous primary stenting. J Vasc Surg 2004;39(3):679–81
10. Bertora GO, Bergman JM. Doppler ultrasonography in tinnitus patients. Int Tinnitus J 2002;8(2):124–6
11. Kirkby-Bott J, Gibbs HH. Carotid endarterectomy relieves pulsatile tinnitus associated with severe ipsilateral carotid stenosis. Eur J Vasc Endovasc Surg 2004;27(6):651–3
12. Daneshi A, Hadizadeh H, Mahmoudian S, Sahebjam S, Jalesi A. Pulsatile tinnitus and carotid artery atherosclerosis. Int Tinnitus J 2004;10(2):161–4
13. Sonmez G, Basekim CC, Ozturk E, Gungor A, Kizilkaya E. Imaging of pulsatile tinnitus: a of 74 patients. Clin Imaging 2007;31(2):102–8
14. Sismanis A, Girevendoulis A Pulsatile tinnitus associated with internal carotid artery morphologic abnormalities Otol Neurotol 2008;29(7):1032–6
15. Pelkonen O, Tikkakoski T, Luotonen J, Sotaniemi K. Pulsatile tinnitus as a symptom of cervicocephalic arterial dissection. J Laryngol Otol 2004;118(3):193–8
16. Foyt D, Carfrae MJ, Rapoport R. Fibromuscular dysplasia of the internal carotid artery causing pulsatile tinnitus. Otolaryngol Head Neck Surg 2006;134(4):701–2
17. Brocks C, Bela C, Gaebel C, Wollenberg B, Sommer K. A dural fistula as a rare cause for a pulse-synchronized tinnitus aurium. Laryngorhinootologie 2008;87(8):573–8
18. Yeh SJ, Tsai LK, Jeng JS. Clinical and carotid ultrasonographic features of intracranial dural arteriovenous fistulas in patients with and without pulsatile tinnitus. J Neuroimaging 2009 May 18
19. Tan TY, Lin YY, Schminke U, Chen TY. Pulsatile tinnitus in a case of traumatic temporal extradural arteriovenous fistula: carotid duplex sonography findings before and after embolization. J Clin Ultrasound 2008;36(7):432–6
20. Hurst RW, Howard RS, Zager E. Carotid cavernous fistula associated with persistent trigeminal artery: endovascular treatment using coil embolization. Skull Base Surg 1998;8(4):225–8
21. Robertson A, Nicolaides AR, Taylor RH. Spontaneous carotido-cavernous fistula presenting as pulsatile tinnitus. J Laryngol Otol 1999;113(8):744–6
22. Mohyuddin A Indirect carotid cavernous fistula presenting as pulsatile tinnitus J Laryngol Otol 2000;114(10):788–9
23. Rivarés Esteban JJ, Gil Paraíso PJ, Marín García J, Campos del Alamo MA, Martín Martín JM, Navarro Díaz F. Post-traumatic carotid cavernous fistula as a cause of objective tinnitus. An Otorrinolaringol Ibero Am 2002;29(2):117–24 Spanish
24. Lerut B, De Vuyst C, Ghekiere J, Vanopdenbosch L, Kuhweide R Post-traumatic pulsatile tinnitus: the hallmark of a direct carotico-cavernous fistula J Laryngol Otol 2007;121(11):1103–7 Epub 2007 Feb 13
25. Depauw P, Caekebeke J, Vanhoenacker P. Objective pulsatile tinnitus caused by intrapetrous dissecting aneurysms. Clin Neurol Neurosurg 2001;103(3):197–9
26. Moonis G, Hwang CJ, Ahmed T, Weigele JB, Hurst RW. Otologic manifestations of petrous carotid aneurysms AJNR. Am J Neuroradiol 2005;26(6):1324–7

27. Titlic M, Tonkic A, Jukic I, Buca A, Kolic K, Batinic T. Tinnitus caused by vertebrobasilar dolichoectasia. Bratisl Lek Listy 2007;108(10–11):455–7

28. Ali S, Radaideh MM, Shaibani A, Russell EJ, Walker MT. Persistent trigeminal artery terminating in the posterior inferior cerebellar artery: case report. Neurosurgery 2008; 62(3):E746–8; discussion E746–8

29. Psillas G, Kekes G, Constantinidis J, Triaridis S, Vital V. Subclavian steal syndrome: neurotological manifestations. Acta Otorhinolaryngol Ital 2007;27(1):33–7

30. De Ridder D, De Ridder L, Nowé V, Thierens H, Van de Heyning P, Møller A. Pulsatile tinnitus and the intrameatal vascular loop: why do we not hear our carotids?. Neurosurgery 2005;57(6):1213–7; discussion 1213–7

31. Häusler R, Levine RA Auditory dysfunction in stroke Acta Otolaryngol 2000;120(6):689–703

32. Szirmai A Cochleovestibular dysfunction caused by cerebrovascular diseases Int Tinnitus J 2005;11(1):63–5

33. Lee H, Whitman GT, Lim JG, Yi SD, Cho YW, Ying S, Baloh RW. Hearing symptoms in migrainous infarction. Arch Neurol 2003;60(1):113–6

34. Lee H. Sudden deafness related to posterior circulation infarction in the territory of the nonanterior inferior cerebellar artery: frequency, origin, and vascular topographical pattern. Eur Neurol 2008;59(6):302–6; Epub 2008 Apr 11

35. Espinosa PS, Pettigrew LC, Berger JR Clin Neurol Neurosurg 2008 May;110(5):484–91 Hereditary hemorrhagic telangectasia and spinal cord infarct: case report with a of the neurological complications of HHT Epub 2008 Mar 4

36. Li TH, Lan MY, Liu JS, Tseng YL, Wu HS, Chang YY. Type II proatlantal intersegmental artery associated with objective pulsatile tinnitus. Neurology 2008;71(4):295–6

37. Ramina R, Maniglia JJ, Fernandes YB, Paschoal JR, Pfeilsticker LN, Neto MC, Borges G. Jugular foramen tumors: diagnosis and treatment. Neurosurg Focus 2004;17(2):E5

38. Liu JK, Mahaney K, Barnwell SL, McMenomey SO, Delashaw JB Jr. Dural arteriovenous fistula of the anterior condylar confluence and hypoglossal canal mimicking a jugular foramen tumor. J Neurosurg 2008;109(2):335–40

39. Yoon BN, Lee TH, Kong SK, Chon KM, Goh EK. Management of high jugular bulb with tinnitus: transvenous stent-assisted coil embolization. Otolaryngol Head Neck Surg 2008;139(5):740–1

40. Bilgen C, Kirazli T, Ogut F, Totan S. Jugular bulb diverticula: clinical and radiologic aspects. Otolaryngol Head Neck Surg 2003;128(3):382–6

41. Bush ML, Jones RO, Given C. The value of CT venography in the diagnosis of jugular bulb diverticulum: a series of 3 cases. Ear Nose Throat J 2009;88(4):E4–7

42. Raghuram K, Curé JK, Harnsberger HR. Condylar jugular diverticulum. J Comput Assist Tomogr 2009;33(2):309–11

43. Forte V, Turner A, Liu P. Objective tinnitus associated with abnormal mastoid emissary vein. J Otolaryngol 1989;18(5):232–5

44. Papanagiotou P, Grunwald IQ, Politi M, Struffert T, Ahlhelm F, Reith W. Vascular anomalies of the cerebellopontine angle. Radiologe 2006;46(3):216–22 German

45. Chen CC, Cheng PW, Tseng HM, Young YH. Posterior cranial fossa tumors in young adults. Laryngoscope 2006; 116(9):1678–81

46. Houdart E, Chapot R, Merland JJ. Aneurysm of a dural sigmoid sinus: a novel vascular cause of pulsatile tinnitus. Ann Neurol 2000;48(4):669–71

47. Sigari F, Blair E, Redleaf M. Headache with unilateral pulsatile tinnitus in women can signal dural sinus trombosis. Ann Otol Rhinol Laryngol 2006;115(9):686–9

48. Krishnan A, Mattox DE, Fountain AJ, Hudgins PA. CT arteriography and venography in pulsatile tinnitus: preliminary results. AJNR Am J Neuroradiol 2006;27(8):1635–8

49. White JB, Kaufmann TJ, Kallmes DF. Venous sinus thrombosis: a misdiagnosis using MR angiography. Neurocrit Care 2008;8(2):290–2

Chapter 42
Complications to Medical Treatment

Paolo Enrico and Ron Goodey

Keypoints

1. When medical treatment is blamed, tinnitus may be harder to treat.
2. Adverse consequences are better accepted and more easily managed if the patient had been well informed before treatment started and had acknowledged and accepted the risk.
3. Ear syringing, suctioning, instrumentation, local anaesthetic injection, grommet insertion, dental treatment, hyperbaric oxygen therapy, and ototoxic ear drops are all relatively minor procedures that may be blamed for tinnitus.
4. Major ear operations may cause hearing loss and tinnitus.
5. Ototoxic drugs can cause hearing loss and tinnitus after administration systemically, intrathecally, or topically to extensive wounds or burns as well as from use as eardrops.
6. Onset of tinnitus is occasionally blamed on radiation therapy, noisy organ imaging, medical equipment accidents, neck manipulation, and general anesthetic.
7. Tinnitus can be triggered by procedures on any region of the body when there have been excessive pain and associated anxiety, fear, and anger.
8. The medical treatments most commonly accused of causing tinnitus are treatments with drugs. Usually, the tinnitus improves when the drug is withdrawn, provided there is no permanent damage to the cochlea or powerful associated factors.

9. Drugs with proven ototoxicity and that also cause tinnitus include aminoglycoside antibiotics, antineoplastic drugs, anti-inflammatory drugs, loop diuretics, antimalarials, and others. The ototoxicity may be synergistic with other agents that damage the inner ear.
10. Drugs that are not usually considered ototoxic but are sometimes blamed for causing tinnitus include lidocaine, anticonvulsants, antidepressants, cannabinoids, antihypertensives, beta-adrenergic blocking agents, opioids (buprenorphine), caffeine, and antihistamines. At times, drugs from within most of these groups are also credited with ameliorating tinnitus.

Keywords Tinnitus • Complication of treatment • Medical misadventure • Ototoxicity • Pathogenesis • Drug-induced tinnitus • Therapy-induced tinnitus

Introduction

Many differing medical treatments are thought by patients to have triggered the onset of their tinnitus [1]. Indeed, there are a variety of mechanisms and pathways by which this may occur. Medical treatment can result in reduced or abnormal stimulation through the auditory, somatosensory, vestibular, and other sensory pathways. Activity in central pathways can be affected directly. Unwanted effects of medical treatment may be temporary, but are associated with tinnitus that may persist once triggered. Medical treatment of almost any type throughout the entire body may be blamed as the trigger for the onset of tinnitus when that treatment has had powerful emotional associations and was accompanied by severe pain.

Tinnitus tends to be worse, and its management more difficult when the onset has been associated with fear or anger. Unfortunately, for the patient and therapist, when

R. Goodey (✉)
Section of Otolaryngology, Department of Surgery, University of Auckland, 3 Wootton Road, Remuera, Auckland 1050, New Zealand
e-mail: rongoodey@xtra.co.nz

A.R. Møller et al. (eds.), *Textbook of Tinnitus*,
DOI 10.1007/978-1-60761-145-5_42, © Springer Science+Business Media, LLC 2011

the onset of tinnitus is perceived as being a complication of medical treatment, it is usually associated with anger and often with fear and anxiety as well. This can make management difficult. The main exception is when the possibility of tinnitus developing had been anticipated, clearly explained, and then accepted by the patient as an acceptable trade-off for life-saving treatment.

As clinicians, we may sometimes support a patient's claim for compensation for tinnitus, which the patient attributes to medical treatment they had received. More often, however, many of us encourage our patients to disassociate their tinnitus from such emotionally charged triggers. We justify doing so on the basis that the association is unproven and that dwelling on it makes the tinnitus more intrusive and harder to manage. A review of the tinnitus literature shows that we seldom investigate a suspected relationship between the onset of tinnitus and a medical treatment, let alone report it.

This chapter is an opportunity to review not only the situations in which tinnitus is acknowledged as a complication of medical treatment but also situations that have been largely ignored in scientific literature as causes of tinnitus but which, in one author's experience, occasionally are. The editors are to be congratulated for making it possible to consider all situations in which tinnitus may be a complication of medical treatment. Some of the sections in Part 1 of this chapter express unsubstantiated opinions acquired from Dr. Goodey's otological practice and his discussions with colleagues. They are presented as a challenge to other colleagues for wider consideration. Part 2 of this chapter focuses entirely on drug therapy as a trigger for tinnitus. It discusses drugs with proven ototoxicity, and some of those that are sometimes accused of causing tinnitus but not considered ototoxic. Part 2 draws heavily on Dr Enrico's extensive knowledge and experience as a neuropharmacologist.

Part 1: Procedural Treatments that May Cause Tinnitus

Minor Procedures in and Around the Ear

Often, procedures that clean the ear of wax and/or debris also reduce or eliminate any associated tinnitus. However, such procedures may occasionally trigger or aggravate tinnitus. Other procedures in the region may also trigger or aggravate tinnitus. Quite often (but not always), temporomandibular joint dysfunction may be aggravated by the same procedures and consequently aggravate the associated tinnitus.

Ear Syringing

Ear syringing is only occasionally mentioned in journal articles as a trigger for the onset of tinnitus [1–3]. However, it is frequently acknowledged as a trigger by patient support groups [4]. Even some of the more professional support groups find it necessary to produce brochures on the association [5, 6]. Mostly, they provide balanced and generally reassuring information. In such brochures, the triggering of tinnitus is sometimes attributed to ear syringing, but only when it is "poorly performed." Many otologists who deal with patients troubled by tinnitus accept that some of these patients appropriately attribute the onset of their tinnitus to ear syringing.

Occasionally, syringing-induced tinnitus has been associated with rupture of the tympanic membrane (especially if it was already weakened). Rarely, there has been major trauma to the middle ear, and inner ear as well, especially if a carelessly attached nozzle came off with the pressure used. However, more commonly, any trauma attributable to syringing has been relatively minor and confined to the ear canal. The symptoms associated with the onset of tinnitus induced by syringing are pain and vertigo. Tinnitus is especially likely to have occurred and persisted if the doctor or nurse continued to syringe an ear after the patient had wanted them to stop.

Syringing should be avoided in those with a weakened or perforated eardrum (or a grommet) or with an infected ear canal. The water used must be at body temperature. The nozzle must be firmly attached; it should have a smooth and rounded tip; and it must be directed at the posterior canal wall. If pain or vertigo is induced, the procedure must be stopped immediately.

Ear Suctioning

Ear suctioning is often recommended as a safe alternative to syringing, and it usually is. It is the treatment of choice when there is a perforation or a grommet (tympanostomy tube) or if the ear canal is infected. However, noise levels at the suction tip are sometimes loud enough to be distressing to the patient and to trigger tinnitus [7–11], even when there is no measurable change in the audiogram.

Tinnitus is more likely to be triggered if the suction noise is excessively loud because of the material being aspirated. In this context, noise levels of 96 dB have been measured at the suction tip [12]. Tinnitus is more likely to be triggered if the commencement of the suction noise is abrupt and unexpected. If inner ear damage occurs, it may be a direct consequence of noise energy. Alternatively, inner ear damage could result from violent contraction of the stapedius muscle, as can be caused by a sound blast. However, Dr. Goodey is not aware of any patients in whom the annular ligament has been damaged and a perilymphatic fistula caused as a result of suctioning.

During suctioning, tinnitus and hyperacusis may occur and persist without any persisting change in hearing. In some of these, the situation may be identical with "acoustic shock disorder" described in comparable situations [13, 14]. Associated symptoms may include acute ear pain, muffled hearing, a feeling of fullness and numbness, and occasionally vertigo. Tinnitus and hyperacusis may persist when all the other symptoms have settled. In such situations, the inner ear may have been protected by the intermittent pattern and relatively short duration. A possible mechanism for the symptoms could be contraction of tensor tympani.

Suctioning of a mastoidectomy cavity or through a perforation often triggers vertigo. Occasionally, this is followed by persistent tinnitus, especially if suctioning was continued after the patient had become distressed.

A wise microscopist will always ask in advance whether the patient is intolerant to loud noise and always instruct their patient to tell the microscopist to stop if the suction noise is hurtful, causes vertigo, or is otherwise distressing.

Cleaning the Ear Canal Skin with Instruments

Cleaning of the ear canal with instruments often causes superficial ulceration and sometimes lacerations. Occasionally, a patient reports that it triggered their tinnitus. Ear canal injury or infection may also lead to

chronic changes in the ear canal skin, which may then have a continuing effect on tinnitus.

Trauma Affecting the Middle Ear and/or Inner Ear

Clumsy instrumentation or failure to adjust to sudden head movement (such as during removal of a foreign body) can cause damage not only to the ear canal skin but also to the tympanic membrane, ossicular chain, and – through inadvertent manipulation of the chain – the inner ear. Tinnitus may result even without measurable hearing loss.

Injection of Local Anaesthetic

Injection of local anaesthetic into the ear canal in preparation for a minor surgical procedure occasionally triggers severe vertigo, which may last several hours and be extremely distressing for the patient. Accompanying tinnitus is insignificant because the vertigo is so distressing. Occasionally, tinnitus persists after nausea and vertigo have subsided. The development of effective topical anaesthetics has largely eliminated the need for injections of local anaesthetic into the ear canal for minor procedures [15].

Insertion of a Grommet

Quite commonly, insertion of a grommet to relieve Eustachian tube dysfunction or a middle ear effusion also reduces any associated tinnitus. Occasionally, however, insertion of a grommet may trigger or aggravate tinnitus, even when there has been no reaction to the local anaesthetic used and when the procedure has been gentle. In this situation, the tinnitus usually subsides or reverts to its previous level if the grommet is removed promptly, and the resulting hole was covered with a rice paper patch.

Dental Treatment

Case history questionnaires may include dental treatment as an item associated with the onset of tinnitus [16]. In Dr. Goodey's experience, dental treatment can be a potent trigger or aggravator of tinnitus. The tinnitus tends to be more severely affected on the side of the dental treatment and occurs more often if the procedure has been prolonged and painful and associated with anxiety. There is usually associated temporomandibular joint dysfunction and sometimes aggravation of chronic neck problems as well. However, dental treatment as a trigger for tinnitus receives little or no attention in the literature, whereas dental disorders as triggers for tinnitus do receive some attention [17–19].

Without associated factors, noise from dental drilling is seldom, if ever, loud enough and prolonged enough to cause hearing loss and tinnitus in patients. However, dentists and their assistants may occasionally suffer occupational noise-induced hearing loss and tinnitus after many years of exposure [20]. Malfunction of an air drill can cause a sudden and unexpected loud blast of noise and result in tinnitus and associated symptoms described as the acoustic shock disorder in the section "Ear suctioning" of this chapter.

Barotrauma

In the context of medical treatment, barotrauma is only likely to be blamed as the trigger for tinnitus when there has been difficulty in equalizing while hyperbaric oxygen was being used as an adjunct to therapy [21]. The incidence of barotrauma as a consequence of hyperbaric oxygen therapy has been assessed and correlated with conditions being treated [22, 23]. An associated incidence of tinnitus gets little mention. Occasional patients are adamant that their tinnitus occurred or became worse during hyperbaric oxygen treatment. If equalizing problems have occurred during a previous treatment session, or are anticipated, then a mini grommet will give complete protection during subsequent treatments. When treatment in a hyperbaric chamber is required following a diving accident, then any inner ear damage can usually be attributed to the original accident and not to the treatment.

Ototoxic Ear Drops

When the eardrum is perforated or has a grommet, there is potential for ototoxic components in ear drops to cause sensorineural hearing loss and trigger tinnitus. The incidence of this occurring has been very low

considering the widespread use over a large number of years [24]. However, hearing loss and tinnitus from the use of such drops do occur. The risk is probably minimized if such drops are only used when the middle ear mucosa is inflamed. A modern clinician is unwise to allow such drugs to be used in high-risk ears or once the middle ear mucosa is healthy [25]. Fluoroquinalone antibiotic drops are now available, which are proven clinically and experimentally to be nonototoxic [26–28]. Unfortunately, they tend to be much more expensive and also less well tolerated, especially by children. Nevertheless, with expert panels in the US, Canada, United Kingdom, and Australia all advocating the use of fluoroquinalones, a clinician who continues to prescribe potentially ototoxic drops has to be prepared to justify the need for these types of medications.

Major Procedures in and Around the Ear

Stapedectomy, labyrinthectomy, tympanoplasty, simple myringoplasty (especially with an overlay graft, which involves more manipulation of the malleus), mastoid surgery, vestibular nerve section, and vestibular schwannoma surgery can all trigger tinnitus. However, these have all been dealt with in the section "Complications of surgical treatment". Any resulting tinnitus is usually associated with additional sensorineural hearing loss.

As with the minor ear procedures, these more major operations only occasionally cause damage and tinnitus. More often, they reduce or relieve pre-existing hearing impairment and associated tinnitus or they have no effect on tinnitus.

Occasional Causes of Unexpected Tinnitus and Sometimes of Cochlear Hearing Loss

Radiation Therapy

Prior irradiation increases the incidence of ototoxicity, including tinnitus, during subsequent treatment with cytotoxic drugs [29]. Usually, the possibility of such life-saving treatment causing hearing loss and tinnitus will have been understood and accepted as a risk by patient. Occasionally, this is not the case, and the unexpected symptoms greatly increase the patient's distress. In the past, irradiation to reduce vascularity of a glomus tumor has caused unexpected cochlear damage and tinnitus. Irradiation is no longer used in this context. However, the inner ear is occasionally damaged during irradiation of intracranial tumors, even when cytotoxic drugs are not used. Resultant hearing loss may be accompanied by tinnitus. In Dr. Goodey's experience, tinnitus is more likely to occur if postirradiation necrosis of the external ear canal also occurs. Presumably, this is because of the added effect of somatosensory stimulation. Subsequent care of the ear canal helps reduce the impact of the tinnitus.

Noise from Organ Imaging Equipment Especially MRI

Patients sometimes attribute their tinnitus or its increased intrusiveness to the noise associated with having an MRI [30]. Noise levels have been measured in excess of 93 dB [30] and continue throughout the relatively lengthy procedure. There is no associated increased hearing loss. Probably, anxiety, fear, and the claustrophobic environment have contributed, even though the patient has blamed the noise alone for the onset or aggravation of their tinnitus. Any patient with troublesome tinnitus should use hearing protection during an MRI.

Medical Equipment Accidents

During otologic surgery, noise levels generated by otologic drills have been measured as 82–106 dB and by suctions measured as 71–84 dB. These are considered acceptable levels. No change in postoperative bone conduction was found [31]. Others have recorded noise levels from air turbine drills of 116 dB and at suction tips of 96 dB [12]. It is widely accepted that there is a high risk of inner ear damage if a drill burr comes in contact with an intact ossicular chain or suction is applied to perilymph in the oval or round window or lateral canal fistula. A hose becoming detached from a compressed air cylinder has triggered severe hearing loss and tinnitus. Other incidents have been reported anecdotally and include a gas explosion.

Neck Manipulation

Patients regularly claim that manipulation of their neck was the trigger for their tinnitus. The resultant tinnitus can usually be modulated by neck movement suggesting proprioceptor disturbance–triggered somatosensory tinnitus. However, in some patients, neck manipulation triggered severe temporary vertigo as well as persistent tinnitus. It may be that on some occasions, neck manipulation triggers tinnitus (and sometimes vertigo) through temporary effects on the vertebral arteries. In others, radiological evidence of facet joint damage caused by manipulation has been demonstrated [32]. If a patient's neck is to be manipulated vigorously, there should be preceding organ imaging expertly read, the therapist should be experienced, and the therapist should stop immediately if untoward symptoms start to develop.

General Anaesthetic

Tinnitus may be triggered after almost any type of surgical procedure, but mostly if the procedure was under general anaesthetic and a relaxant has been used. There may be postoperative suboccipital headache as well. In these circumstances, the tinnitus can usually be modulated by the neck. Some anesthetists maintain gentle traction on the head and neck while relaxants are wearing off and claim that this reduces the incidence of postoperative headache. In Dr. Goodey's experience, this maneuver can reduce postoperative tinnitus as well. It is a wise precaution in a patient who already has troublesome tinnitus, especially if they blame it on a previous operation under general anesthesia.

Sometimes, postoperative tinnitus is associated with temporomandibular joint pain and can be modulated by the jaw. In these circumstances, difficulty with intubation may have been the mechanism.

General Reaction to Painful Procedures

In Dr. Goodey's experience, distressing and painful surgery anywhere in the body can act as the trigger for the onset of tinnitus. The resulting tinnitus may be extremely distressing and difficult to manage. This occurs most often if the pain experienced has been excessive because of complications or inadequate anesthesia, and especially when there are powerful emotional associations because of the nature of the surgery and the consequences of it.

Occasionally, there may be associated sudden hearing loss suggesting microembolism, especially after breast, orthopedic, and cardiac surgery.

Most often there is no measurable change in hearing. There may be some pre-existing hearing impairment, which may have predisposed the patient to the onset of tinnitus in response to the powerful triggering effects of pain, anxiety, fear, and anger.

Part 2: Drug Therapies, Which May Cause Tinnitus

Ototoxicity from Medical Therapy

Over 150 medications and chemicals have been reported to be potentially able to induce hearing loss and/or tinnitus, possibly by acting on both peripheral and central acoustic structures [33–35]. Drug-induced ototoxicity may be reversible or irreversible and associated with both acute and long-term administration of drugs. Among the major classes of ototoxic drugs are the aminoglycosides and other antimicrobial agents, antineoplastic drugs, anti-inflammatory drugs, loop diuretics, antimalarial drugs, and others (Table 42.1). Due to their importance in clinical practice, some ototoxic drugs are discussed in more detail below.

The pharmacological and chemical heterogeneity of drugs, which share the ability to induce hearing loss and/or tinnitus, is noteworthy. Unfortunately, research in this field is often limited by several problems, among which is the lack of a good animal model. As a consequence, the neurobiological basis of drug-induced ototoxicity is still largely unknown and may involve biochemical and physiological changes in discrete parts of the acoustic system [35]. So far, there is no evidence of a common pathway leading to drug-induced damage of acoustic structures.

Chemotherapy of Microbial Diseases

Aminoglycosides

Aminoglycosides are an important group of antibacterial drugs used primarily against Gram-negative aerobic and facultative anaerobic bacteria. Streptomycin is also effective against several tubercular and nontubercular mycobacteria, including *Mycobacterium tuberculosis*, the etiological agent of tuberculosis. Aminoglycosides are bactericidal and act by binding to the 30 S subunit of bacterial ribosomes, disrupting the elongation of the peptide chain; they may also impair translational accuracy resulting in misreading of the mRNA sequence. Aminoglycosides are poorly absorbed from the gastrointestinal tract and, therefore, are usually administered parenterally by injection or infusion. Aminoglycosides are well distributed into bodily fluids, except for the eye and the central nervous system. As their metabolism within the body is negligible, aminoglycosides are excreted unaltered by glomerular filtration (serum half-life of 2–3 h). They are also found in breast milk but, as they are not well absorbed orally, these drugs are considered compatible with use during breastfeeding [36]. Aminoglycosides are classified as an FDA pregnancy category D (positive evidence of human fetal risk, but the benefits from use in pregnant women may be acceptable despite the risk). Therefore, they should be used during pregnancy only when the alternatives are worse.

All aminoglycosides are able to induce both reversible and irreversible damage at cochlear, vestibular, and renal level. Nevertheless, aminoglycosides are still among the most commonly used antibiotics worldwide, mainly because of their cost effectiveness [33], but also to face the emergence of bacterial strains with advanced patterns of antimicrobial resistance [37, 38]. Aminoglycoside toxicity correlates with the total amount of drug administered and occurs in almost all patients exposed to a toxic dose. The risk of toxicity is increased if impaired renal function is allowed to cause the serum level to rise [39]. Abnormally high sensitivity to the ototoxic effects of aminoglycosides (idiosyncrasy) may also be an inherited trait, and several mutations at the mitochondrial genome level have been identified [40, 41]. Cochlear and vestibular structures appear to differ in sensitivity to aminoglycosides-induced damage. Indeed, streptomycin and gentamicin are mainly toxic at the vestibular level, while amikacin, neomycin, dihydrostreptomycin, and kanamycin act primarily at the cochlear level [34, 41]. Netilmicin appears to be as effective as gentamicin, but is less ototoxic [38, 41].

Both animal and human studies show that aminoglycosides affect outer hair cells first and later the inner hair cells. Degeneration of hair cells usually starts at the basal turn and progresses toward the apex. The mechanisms of aminoglycoside-induced ototoxicity

Table 42.1 Drugs which are claimed to cause ototoxicity and/or tinnitus

	Ototoxic	Tinnitus
Drugs acting at synaptic and neuroeffector junctional sites		
β2-selective adrenergic receptor agonists		
Procaterol		+
Nonselective β adrenergic receptor antagonists		
Timolol		+
Serotonin receptor agonists		
Almotriptan		+
Eletriptan		+
Ergonovine		+
Methyl ergonovine		+
Drugs acting on the central nervous system		
Anticonvulsants		
Valproic acid	+	
Flecainide		+
Antidepressants – Tricyclic		
Desipramine		+
Amitriptyline		+
Antidepressants – SSRI		
Fluoxetine		+
Citalopram		+
Autacoids: drug therapy of inflammation		
NSAIDs		
Acetyl salicylic acid	+	+
Meclofenamic acid		+
Diclofenac		+
Ketoprofene		+
Indomethacin		+
Diflunisal		+
Acemetacine		+
Oxaprozin		
Corticosteroids		
Methylprednisolone		+
Antihistamine agents		
Chlorphenamine		+
Hydroxyzine		+
Doxylamine		+
Prometazine		+
Drugs affecting renal and cardiovascular function		
Loop diuretics		
Furosemide	+	+
Ethacrinic acid	+	+
Torasemide	+	+
Bumetanide	+	+
Inhibitors of carbonic anhydrase		
Diclofenamide		+
Antiarrhythmics		
Flecainide		+
Dihydrochinidine	+	
ACE inhibitors		
Enalapril		+
Imidapril		+
Benazepril		+

(continued)

Table 42.1 (continued)

	Ototoxic	Tinnitus
Moexipril		+
Calcium channel blockers		
Nicardipine		+
Angiotensin II receptor antagonis		
Irbesartan		+
Drugs affecting gastrointestinal function		
Sulphasalazine		+
Chemotherapy of parasitic infections		
Chloroquine	+	
Hydroxychloroquine	+	+
Mefloquine		+
Quinine		+
Sulfadoxine – pyrimethamine		+
Chemotherapy of microbial diseases		
Aminoglycosides	+	+
Macrolides		
Eritromycin	+	
Azithromycin		+
Clarithromycin		+
Quinolones		
Lomefloxacin	+	+
Moxifloxacin	+	+
Rufloxacin		+
Cinoxacin		+
Cephalosporins		
Ceftibuten		+
Cefepime		+
Lincosamides		
Lincomycin		+
Tetracyclines		
Minocycline		+
Sulfonamides		
Cotrimoxazole		+
Sulfadiazine		+
Glycopeptides		
Teicoplanin	+	+
Vancomycin	+	+
Antivirals		
Ganciclovir	+	
Lopinavir		+
Ritonavir		+
Antifungal		
Amphotericin B	+	
Griseofulvine	+	
Chemotherapy of neoplastic diseases		
Platinum compounds		
Cisplatin	+	+
Carboplatin	+	+
Oxaliplatin	+	
Immunomodulators		
Muromonab CD3	+	+
Hormones and hormone antagonists		
Bisphosphonates		
Risedronate		+

have not been fully characterized; however, several mechanisms have been proposed, including disruption of mitochondrial protein synthesis, generation of reactive oxygen species (ROS), and excitotoxicity from enhancement of the glutamatergic N-methyl-D-aspartate (NMDA) receptor function [39, 41].

Approaches to Protection

Due to the widespread use of these drugs, prevention of aminoglycosides-induced ototoxicity is very important. Patients should also be questioned for symptoms of tinnitus, decreased hearing, dizziness, disequilibrium, and problems of ocular fixation. Careful monitoring of serum levels together with audiological or vestibular function tests are essential components of the standard of care required to reduce the incidence of aminoglycoside ototoxicity.

Scientific research is now focused on the biological mechanisms underlying aminoglycosides-induced damage in order to develop coherent attempts at protection such as administration of antioxidants or iron chelators, interference with cell death signaling pathways, and blockade of glutamate NMDA receptor [41–44]. At present, experimental evidence shows a decrease in ototoxicity when antioxidants or iron chelators are co administered with aminoglycosides. However, successful translation of experimental evidence to the clinic is a slow process requiring consideration of many points. Therefore, the currently more "orthodox" approach of monitoring serum drug levels and ototoxicity symptoms remains the standard of care [39, 45].

It may be impractical to monitor serum drug levels and perform audiological or vestibular function tests on all patients receiving treatment with aminoglycosides. It is essential to do so in those patients with high risk for developing ototoxicity, including those receiving prolonged treatment courses, those who have had previous aminoglycoside therapy, those with sensorineural hearing loss, or patients in whom inner ear damage would create a disproportionately major handicap. Because the incidence of ototoxicity is related to the serum aminoglycoside concentrations, it is critical to reduce the maintenance dosage of these drugs in patients with impaired renal function or who are concomitantly taking loop diuretics [46] or nephrotoxic drugs. The elderly are especially at risk from aminoglycosides, as their

renal function may be significantly impaired without increase in serum creatinine.

Idiosyncratic hearing loss induced by aminoglycosides is, in theory, preventable by genetic screening to identify those at risk (e.g., individuals with the m.1555 A>G mutation). The use of such genetic screening is questioned because of the high cost of the tests. However, when the expenses of genetic screening are compared to the lifelong management of a profoundly deaf child, the cost effectiveness of genetic screening may prove very favorable [40].

Chemotherapy of Neoplastic Diseases

Platinum Compounds–Cisplatin

In theory, any drug with the capacity to destroy malignant cells should be regarded as having the potential to damage the cells of the cochlea and cause hearing loss and tinnitus. Cisplatin (*cis*-diamminedichloroplatinum) is an inorganic platinum coordination complex used alone or in combination with other anti-cancer agents. Its main application is in the medical therapy of malignancies including sarcoma, small-cell lung cancer, germ cell tumors, lymphoma, and ovarian cancer [36, 47]. Cisplatin disrupts DNA function in several ways. It inhibits DNA synthesis by the formation of DNA crosslinks; it denatures the double helix and covalently binds to DNA bases interfering with replication and transcription [48, 49]. Cisplatin is administered parenterally either by the intravenous or by the intraperitoneal route. It is not metabolized but is excreted mainly by the kidney (>90%). A few studies have examined the excretion of cisplatin into human milk with contradictory results, and therefore, breastfeeding during cisplatin therapy should be considered contraindicated. Cisplatin is nephrotoxic, neurotoxic, mutagenic in bacteria, produces chromosomal aberrations in animal cells in tissue culture, and is teratogenic and embryotoxic in mice [50]. There are no adequate well-controlled studies in pregnant women [51], and Cisplatin is therefore classified as FDA pregnancy category D.

Cisplatin ototoxicity seems to be mediated by the generation of ROS in the cochlear tissue and has been shown to act on at least three major targets: the organ of Corti, the spiral ganglion cells, and the lateral wall [52]. Increased ROS and organic peroxide following the administration of ototoxic doses of cisplatin would overwhelm the antioxidant potential of the cochlear cells, leading to calcium influx, which would activate the apoptotic pathway causing cell death [39, 52]. Several genetic variants have been associated with increased sensitivity to cisplatin-induced ototoxicity [52–54]. Research in this field is still in an early phase. However, it is conceivable that a better understanding of the genetic variants associated with cisplatin-induced ototoxicity may be an important step toward case selection and safer cisplatin treatment [53, 55, 56].

The clinical presentation of cisplatin-induced damage to the inner ear includes tinnitus and high-frequency sensorineural hearing loss. The hearing loss is usually modest but can be permanent and can progress to involve the lower frequencies. The tinnitus is often more irksome than the modest loss of hearing. The risk of inner ear damage is increased by prior irradiation and concomitant use of aminoglycosides.

Approaches to Protection

In general, patients who embark on antineoplastic chemotherapy are not only well monitored but also well informed. They are aware and have accepted the possibility of adverse consequences of drugs, including the development of tinnitus and some loss of hearing. Nevertheless, research on new methods of protection against ototoxicity (such as chemoprotection) is definitely needed. At present, the only strategy for reducing cisplatin-induced ototoxicity is based on limiting the total dose per cycle, the cumulative dose, and the dose intensity, which inevitably limits the antineoplastic effectiveness [57, 58]. Various strategies have been proposed to reduce cisplatin ototoxicity by chemoprotectants; in particular, an "upstream approach" to prevent the generation of ROS with antioxidants and a "downstream approach" using inhibitors of molecules involved in the apoptotic cell death pathway (such as caspases and p53). Indeed, the administration of several antioxidants does seem to be able to limit cisplatin ototoxicity [44, 59, 60]. Unfortunately, this approach has limited clinical usefulness because of the potential for negative interaction between antioxidants and antineoplastic drugs, resulting in reduced therapeutic effectiveness.

A particularly important issue in protection from cisplatin ototoxicity is the extensive use of this drug in pediatric patients, mainly because of its effectiveness in increasing the survival rate for children with cancer [47, 61, 62]. While new anti-cancer treatment protocols are very successful in improving pediatric patient survivals, they also subject the children to toxicities, which may profoundly affect a child's life and development [63, 64]. The reported incidence of cisplatin-induced ototoxicity in children varies from 10 to 85% of cases. Nevertheless, the implications of hearing loss to speech and language development are very important in very young children, whereas educational and psychosocial problems are more important for older children [63].

A child's age at treatment and the cumulative dose of cisplatin are the two most important risk factors in predicting moderate to severe hearing loss in children [62, 65]. During cisplatin therapy and a subsequent follow-up, pediatric patients should be audiometrically tested for the development of drug-induced sensorineural hearing loss [63, 66].

Several recent reports have shown a protective effect of amifostine, a thiolic cytoprotectant, in pediatric cancer patients treated with cisplatin [67–69]. However, evidence is contradictory, and more research is needed [70–72].

Chemotherapy of Parasitic Infections

Malaria is one of the most severe public health problems worldwide and a leading cause of death and disease in many third-world countries [73]. In Western world countries in which malaria has never existed or has been eliminated, the greater majority of cases occur either in travelers returning home or in migrants arriving from areas where malaria is endemic – "imported malaria" [74].

Each year, millions of people from malaria-free countries travel to areas where malaria is common and are therefore subjected to antimalarial chemoprophylactic treatment, which includes administration of several ototoxic drugs [75–78].

Quinolines and Related Compounds

Intravenous quinine dihydrochloride is currently the first-line antimalarial drug for the treatment of severe malaria in the UK [79]. Quinine is also sometimes used for night cramps and chloroquinine for arthritis; chloroquine and hydroxychloroquine are also used in the treatment of rheumatoid arthritis and lupus associated arthritis. Quinoline derivatives are thought to exert their antimalarial effect by reaching high concentrations in the *Plasmodium* digestive vacuole and preventing the biocrystallization of toxic heme released during proteolysis of hemoglobin into hemozoin. Failure to inactivate toxic heme would poison the parasite, possibly via oxidative damage to plasma membranes [36, 80]. Quinolines are well absorbed from the gastrointestinal tract and may also be administered parenterally either by injection or by infusion. Although rare in western countries, quinine and quinidine overdose may lead to severe toxicity and death related to cardiovascular and neurological effects, particularly in children [81, 82]. Although several skeletal and muscular malformations have occurred in laboratory animals, quinoline derivatives appear safe in human pregnancy and during lactation [83–85].

Quinine is known to cause reversible hearing loss and tinnitus in both humans and animal studies [86–88]. Ototoxicity also has been reported in association with the use of other quinoline-type antimalarial drugs including chloroquine, hydroxychloroquine, and mefloquine [89–91]. The biological bases of quinolines-induced ototoxicity have not been fully resolved. However, some experimental evidence suggests that quinine may affect the function of calcium-dependent potassium channels and reversibly alter the mechanical properties of outer hair cells [92–95].

Approaches to Protection

Quinoline derivatives cause hearing impairment and tinnitus without vestibular disturbance. Both the hearing loss and the tinnitus are usually reversible, but the changes can progress to cochlear degeneration, permanent hearing impairment, and increased likelihood that the tinnitus will persist [96, 97]. Young and unborn children are probably more susceptible to quinoline-induced hearing loss [98, 99]. The ototoxic effects of quinine may be potentiated by doxycycline, an antibiotic, which is sometimes used with quinine in the prophylaxis or treatment of malaria [100]. On its own, doxycycline is not thought to be ototoxic. It has been reported that chloroquine-induced damage to the cochleovestibular system can recover if the medication is

stopped and appropriate therapy is instituted with steroids and plasma expanders [89].

Mefloquine is also ototoxic, but in addition to hearing impairment and tinnitus, it may also cause vestibular disturbance [99, 101]. The tinnitus and hearing impairment are more likely to be permanent than with the other antimalarial drugs.

Salicylates

Acetylsalicylic acid (aspirin) was one of the first drugs to have come into common usage. Despite the introduction of new agents, it is still the analgesic, antipyretic, and anti-inflammatory drug most widely used in the world [102, 103]. Approximately 35,000 metric tones are produced and consumed annually, which is enough to make over 100 billion standard aspirin tablets every year [102, 104]. Besides its use as analgesic, antipyretic, and anti-inflammatory agent, aspirin is also extensively used in the prevention and treatment of various aspects of cardiovascular disease [105, 106], and it is under investigation in a number of other medical conditions including cancer [103, 107, 108].

Most pharmacological effects of salicylates are due to inhibition of prostaglandin formation via blockade of cyclooxygenase. Although there is no agreement about their molecular mechanisms of action, salicylates probably act because of their content in salicylic (orthohydroxybenzoic) acid [36, 102]. Aspirin also possesses distinct protein-acetylating capabilities, which may account for its unique pharmacological profile [109]. Salicylates are rapidly adsorbed from the gastrointestinal tract and well distributed in the body tissues and fluids. About 50% of orally administered aspirin is de-acetylated to salicylate in the liver immediately after absorption. Common metabolites are salicyluric acid, salicyl phenolic or acyl glucuronides, and gentisic acid. Salicylates are excreted in the urine. Plasma half-life of aspirin is about 15 min while the half-life of salicylate is between 2 and 12 h. Aspirin taken in low dose during pregnancy is generally considered safe. However, full-dose aspirin taken in the third trimester is considered to be in FDA pregnancy category D. Aspirin is excreted into human milk in small amounts and should be given to nursing mothers with caution [110].

Salicylates have been recognized as ototoxic longer than almost any other drug [111]. The main ototoxic effects of salicylates are sensorineural hearing loss and tinnitus. Salicylate-induced hearing loss is typically mild to moderate, symmetrical, and flat or high frequency [112, 113]. The tinnitus is often described as a continuous high pitch sound of mild loudness. The neurobiological mechanism of salicylate-induced hearing loss and tinnitus remains obscure. However, several papers have shown that multiple actions of salicylates throughout the acoustic system may contribute. Salicylates administration profoundly affects cochlear function, possibly through downregulation of outer hair cells electromotile response with resultant decrease in cochlear neural output [114, 115]. Several other neurotransmitter systems are involved in salicylates ototoxicity at central level, including the glutamatergic and GABAergic system [112, 116–118]. Interestingly, sodium salicylate has been shown to partially protect against cisplatin ototoxicity and aspirin to partially protect against aminoglycoside ototoxicity, possibly because of their antioxidant properties [42, 119, 120].

Approaches to Protection

Salicylate-induced hearing loss is almost always reversible. Associated tinnitus usually subsides as hearing recovers, although this is not always the case. Quite large doses (6–8 g daily) are required to cause hearing loss and tinnitus [117]. The onset of tinnitus can be helpful as an early indicator of salicylate intoxication or salicylism [121, 122]. Salicylism is a potentially fatal poisoning that, partly because of the enormous amount of aspirin produced and consumed annually, remains a common cause for treatment in emergency departments, especially of children [123]. It is also noteworthy that salicylate intoxication is being reported increasingly often as a consequence of the use of herbal medicines [124–126].

Miscellaneous Drugs that are not Considered Ototoxic

Several different drugs may cause or aggravate tinnitus often without an effect on hearing. Some of these drugs may ease tinnitus in some patients, yet aggravate or cause it in others. Among these drugs are lidocaine,

anticonvulsants, antidepressants, cannabinoids antihypertensives, β-adrenergic blocking agents, opioids (buprenorphine), caffeine, antihistamines, and several others. Unfortunately, the available evidence on the vast majority of these drugs is scarce and much of it anecdotal.

Lidocaine

Lidocaine is the prototypical amide-type local anesthetic, as well as one of the drugs most consistently reported as being efficacious in relieving subjective tinnitus. Available data consistently report that intravenous lidocaine is able to dose dependently inhibit tinnitus in approximately 60% of patients [127–130], although some authors report lower figures [131]. In some patients, tinnitus inhibition is complete, while in a small number of patients an exacerbation is perceived. Lidocaine is a voltage-gated sodium channel blocker able to reduce nerve cell responsiveness to stimuli in a time- and voltage-dependent fashion [132–134]. Lidocaine can also reversibly block voltage-gated potassium channels at concentrations compatible with plasma levels linked to tinnitus inhibition [135]. Since voltage-gated potassium channels are reported to play a key role in the encoding of auditory information, this effect of lidocaine may be relevant [136–139]. The site of action of lidocaine still remains unclear; earlier studies found a cochlear involvement [128, 140]; however, much evidence is now accumulating, which indicates a central site of action. In particular, auditory brainstem responses [141] and brain imaging techniques showed a central action of lidocaine and suggested that this drug may affect the functional linkage of several brain areas including auditory thalamus, auditory cortex, dorsolateral prefrontal cortex, and limbic system [142–144].

Anticonvulsants

Anticonvulsant drugs are increasingly used in the treatment of several nonepileptic conditions, including various psychiatric disorders, pain syndromes, and tinnitus [145]. Evidence of benefit from antiepileptic drugs in nonepileptic conditions varies among different drugs, but there is, in general, a lack of randomized double-blind trials in the literature [145, 146]. Diverse pharmacological mechanisms of action are responsible for the therapeutic effects of antiepileptic drugs including effects on voltage-gated sodium and calcium channels, and neuronal inhibition mediated by γ-aminobutyric acid receptors. However, it may be hypothesized that the common final action is to reduce the tendency of neurons in sensory pathways to fire spontaneously or at inappropriately high frequencies. Carbamazepine, sodium valproate, and phenytoin are all incriminated as triggers and aggravators of tinnitus in some patients while they may help reduce it in others. Unfortunately, clear scientific evidence is unavailable at the moment.

Antidepressants

Antidepressants are widely used in many therapeutic protocols, including those for the management of tinnitus [147, 148]. This may be mainly because of the well-described comorbidity between major depressive disorders and tinnitus [147, 149, 150].

Among all antidepressants used for tinnitus, a particular interest has been paid to tricyclic drugs mainly because of the analgesic effect of this class of drugs [151, 152], in view of the proposed etiological correspondence between tinnitus and neuropathic pain [153, 154]. However, tricyclics may trigger or aggravate tinnitus in some patients. Amitriptyline has been reported as causing tinnitus in one case [155] and subsequently reported as being helpful in treating major depressive symptoms in tinnitus [156]. Recent evidence confirms the tinnitus-inducing effect of amitriptyline in some patients [157].

Selective Serotonin Reuptake Inhibitors (SSRIs) are the most widely prescribed antidepressants in many countries, mainly because of their clinical effectiveness and the reduced toxicity when compared to tricyclics. SSRIs are supposed to act by inhibiting the reuptake of serotonin into the presynaptic cell, thus causing a temporary increase in levels of 5-HT within the synaptic cleft. Despite their antidepressant effectiveness, SSRIs are frequently reported as inducing tinnitus either as a side effect of therapy or as a consequence of drug discontinuation syndrome [158–160]. Fluoxetine occasionally has a dramatic triggering effect, which may persist after the drug is stopped. The specific effectiveness of SSRIs in tinnitus has been recently questioned by several high-quality studies [148, 161, 162].

Among atypical antidepressants, the aminoketone bupropion acts as a norepinephrine and dopamine reuptake inhibitor and also as a nicotinic antagonist.

Bupropion was originally marketed as an antidepressant but is now a fundamental drug in smoking cessation therapies along with nicotine replacement products [163, 164]. Bupropion is among the most frequently prescribed psychotropic drugs in the United States. It is not considered an ototoxic drug, but its association with tinnitus has been consistently reported in case reports as well as literature [165, 166]. Bupropion-induced tinnitus appears to be a temporary effect that disappears after the drug is discontinued. More research is needed to clarify the relationship between bupropion use and the development of tinnitus.

Cannabinoids

Cannabinoids (mainly tetrahydrocannabinol, cannabidiol, β-caryophyllene, and cannabigerol) are now being increasingly used in the treatment of several conditions including spasticity, multiple sclerosis, painful conditions (including neuropathic pain), asthma, and closed-angle glaucoma [167–169]. Natural and synthetic cannabinoids interact with the bodily endocannabinoid system by binding to specific G-protein–coupled cannabinoid receptors (CB1 and CB2). Agonists to CB receptors activate multiple intracellular signal transduction pathways, leading to a very complex picture involving inhibition of adenylate cyclase, activation of inwardly rectifying K channels, alteration of intracellular Ca levels, and influences on other ion channels and kinases [170–172]. Cannabinoid receptors are differentially expressed in the body tissues. CB1 is present in the brain and in the periphery it is present in adipose tissue, the gastrointestinal tract, skeletal muscles, heart, and in the reproductive system. CB2 is mainly expressed in the immune system [173].

As well as the chemically pure drug (such as Dronabinol and nabilone), cannabinoids are also available in some jurisdictions in the form of dried *Cannabis indica* leafs (marijuana). They are then generally self-administered by inhalation of marijuana smoke or through the gastrointestinal system. Despite consistent evidence of clinical efficacy and relative safety [174, 175], medical cannabis remains a controversial issue, mainly because marijuana is one of the most widely used recreational drugs in the world and remains illegal in many countries.

Cannabis smoke has been anecdotally reported to temporarily cause tinnitus in some patients, but dramatically relieves it in some others. However, despite the reported occurrence of CB1 in the cochlear nucleus [176], there is no scientific evidence available of a direct role of cannabinoids in neurobiological basis of tinnitus [177]. However, more research on cannabinoids and tinnitus may be advisable, since a potential for clinical use may be obscured by other considerations. [175]

Drug-Induced Ototoxicity: Final Considerations

Ototoxicity is an adverse effect of several classes of drugs, such as the aminoglycosides, antineoplastic drugs, anti-inflammatory drugs, loop diuretics, antimalarial drugs, and others. Further, occasional cases of ototoxicity have been reported for a wide variety of other therapeutic compounds and chemicals.

Ototoxic agents can impair the sensory processing of sound at many cellular or subcellular sites. Much research has been performed to investigate the causes and the pathophysiology of ototoxicity to try to prevent this complication. However, the neurobiological mechanisms underlying ototoxicity have not been established for most of these drugs, and structure–toxicity relationships have not been determined. It is therefore quite difficult to predict the ototoxic potential of new drugs, and rational approaches to the prevention of ototoxicity are still lacking. In addition, the simultaneous administration of multiple agents, which are potentially ototoxic, can lead to synergistic loss of hearing. Exposure to loud noise may also potentiate hearing loss due to ototoxic drugs.

Drug-induced ototoxicity, although not life threatening, may induce considerable damage and cause severe disability. When increasing ototoxicity occurs, the ototoxic medication has to be discontinued if permanent hearing loss and/or tinnitus are to be minimized.

Although ototoxic injury is sometimes unavoidable, certain measures may reduce the risk. Prevention of drug-induced ototoxicity is generally based upon consideration and avoidance of relevant risk factors, as well as on monitoring renal function, serum drug concentrations, and cochlear and auditory functions before and during drug therapy.

Conclusions

- The treating physician should consider choosing a therapeutically equivalent nonototoxic drug whenever one is available, especially in patients with a heightened risk such as pre-existing cochlear hearing loss and renal insufficiency.
- During therapy with potentially ototoxic medications, the lowest dose compatible with therapeutic efficacy should be used.
- When indicated, periodically monitor serum peak and trough levels.
- Simultaneous use of multiple ototoxic medications (e.g., aminoglycosides and loop diuretics) should be avoided whenever clinical circumstances permit, as their concomitant use may increase the risk of permanent deficit.
- When early detection is important, audiological monitoring should include the very high frequencies as, generally, ototoxic drugs first destroy hearing in the very high frequencies, which are not normally tested (those above 8,000 Hz).
- Should a patient develop auditory (hearing loss and/or tinnitus) or vestibular (vertigo and/or disequilibrium) symptoms during therapy with a potentially ototoxic medication, audiometric testing and otological assessment should be arranged urgently especially if there is reluctance to stop the ototoxic medication.

References

1. Coles RA (1996) Compensable tinnitus from causes other than noise, in Proceedings of the Fifth International Tinnitus Seminar: July 12–15, 1995. Portland, Oregon, USA, GE Reich and JA Vernon, Editors. 1996, American Tinnitus Association: Portland, OR. 367–72.
2. Jayarajan V (2003) Tinnitus following ear syringing, in Proceedings of the Seventh International Tinnitus Seminar, Perth, Australia : March 5th–9th, 2002, RB Patuzzi, Editor. 2003, Physiology Dept., University of Western Australia: Perth, Australia. 340–5.
3. Jayarajan V (2003) The effect of significant life events in tinnitus generation, in Proceedings of the Seventh International Tinnitus Seminar, Perth, Australia : March 5th–9th, 2002, RB Patuzzi, Editor. 2003, Physiology Dept., University of Western Australia: Perth, Australia. 238–42.
4. Saunders J (1992) Tinnitus: What is that noise in my head? 1992, Auckland, NZ: Sandalwood Enterprises. 104.

5. Robinson P and A Wright. "Are there links between ear syringing, ear problems and tinnitus?". Ear Syringing (fact-sheet) cited; Available from: rnid.org.uk.

6. Tungland OP. Ear Syringing and Tinnitus. Information for Everyone 2005 cited; Available from: www.tinnitus.org.uk.

7. Jang CH, CH Song, SH Kim et al (2004) Influence of suction tube noise on hearing in pediatric patients who received ventilation tube insertion. Chang Gung Med J 27:734–40.

8. Katzke D and G Sesterhenn (1982) Suction-generated noise in the external meatus and sensorineural hearing loss. J Laryngol Otol 96:857–63.

9. Pante HJ and P Reuter (1977) Reduction of noise in suction devices. Dtsch Zahnarztl Z 32:490–2.

10. Parkin JL, GS Wood, RD Wood et al (1980) Drill- and suction-generated noise in mastoid surgery. Arch Otolaryngol 106:92–6.

11. Spencer MG (1980) Suction tube noise and myringotomy. J Laryngol Otol 94:383–6.

12. Ray CD and R Levinson (1992) Noise pollution in the operating room: a hazard to surgeons, personnel, and patients. J Spinal Disord 5:485–8.

13. Westcott M (2008) Tonic Tensor Tympani Syndrome – An explanation for everyday sounds causing pain in tinnitus and hyperacusis clients [poster], in IXth International Tinnitus Seminars: Together with the Audiological Seminars: 15–18 June 2008. Göteborg, Sweden. 2008: Göteborg, Sweden. 69.

14. Westcott M (2009) Somatosensory tinnitus and Tonic Tensor Tympani Syndrome (TTTS) [poster abstract], in From clinical practice to basic neuroscience and back: An international conference on tinnitus: Third Tinnitus Research Initiative Meeting, Stresa, Italy. June 24–26, 2009. 2009, TRI: Stresa, Italy. 73.

15. Bingham B, M Hawke and J Halik (1991) The safety and efficacy of Emla cream topical anesthesia for myringotomy and ventilation tube insertion. J Otolaryngol 20:193–5.

16. Langguth B, R Goodey, A Azevedo et al (2007) Consensus for tinnitus patient assessment and treatment outcome measurement: Tinnitus Research Initiative meeting, Regensburg, July 2006. Prog Brain Res 166:525–36.

17. Kempf HG, R Roller and L Muhlbradt (1993) Correlation between inner ear disorders and temporomandibular joint diseases. HNO 41:7–10.

18. Brookler KH and MA Hamid (2008) An approach to tinnitus management. Ear Nose Throat J 87:616–21.

19. Bernhardt O, D Gesch, C Schwahn et al (2004) Signs of temporomandibular disorders in tinnitus patients and in a population-based group of volunteers: Results of the Study of Health in Pomerania. J Oral Rehabil 31:311–9.

20. Altinoz HC, R Gokbudak, A Bayraktar et al (2001) A pilot study of measurement of the frequency of sounds emitted by high-speed dental air turbines. J Oral Sci 43:189–92.

21. Farri A, GC Pecorari, A Enrico et al (2002) Hyperbaric oxygen therapy application in otorhinolaryngology and head and neck surgery: state of the art and review of literature. Acta Otorhinolaryngol Ital 22:227–34.

22. Blanshard J, A Toma, P Bryson et al (1996) Middle ear barotrauma in patients undergoing hyperbaric oxygen therapy. Clin Otolaryngol Allied Sci 21:400–3.

23. Fiesseler FW, ME Silverman, RL Riggs et al (2006) Indication for hyperbaric oxygen treatment as a predictor of tympanostomy tube placement. Undersea Hyperb Med 33:231–5.

24. Abello P, JB Vinas and J Vega (1998) Topical ototoxicity: review over a 6-year period. Acta Otorrinolaringol Esp 49:353–6.

25. Mahadevan M, DA Wabnitz, DL McIntosh et al (2008) Survey on the use of ototopical medications by New Zealand otolaryngologist/head and neck surgeons. N Z Med J 121:U2898.

26. Daniel SJ and R Munguia (2008) Ototoxicity of topical ciprofloxacin/dexamethasone otic suspension in a chinchilla animal model. Otolaryngol Head Neck Surg 139:840–5.

27. Ikiz AO, B Serbetcioglu, EA Guneri et al (1998) Investigation of topical ciprofloxacin ototoxicity in guinea pigs. Acta Otolaryngol 118:808–12.

28. Wai TK and MC Tong (2003) A benefit-risk assessment of ofloxacin otic solution in ear infection. Drug Saf 26:405–20.

29. Marshall NE, KV Ballman, JC Michalak et al (2006) Ototoxicity of cisplatin plus standard radiation therapy vs. accelerated radiation therapy in glioblastoma patients. J Neurooncol 77:315–20.

30. Vernon J, L Press and T McLaughlin (1996) Magnetic resonance imaging and tinnitus. Otolaryngol Head Neck Surg 115:587–8.

31. Chen B, Y Wang, D Wang et al (2004) Evaluation of safety on the noise of drills in the tympanoplasty. Lin Chuang Er Bi Yan Hou Ke Za Zhi 18:4–5.

32. Kraft CN, R Conrad, M Vahlensieck et al (2001) Non-cerebrovascular complication in chirotherapy manipulation of the cervical vertebrae. Z Orthop Ihre Grenzgeb 139:8–11.

33. Arslan E, E Orzan and R Santarelli (1999) Global problem of drug-induced hearing loss. Ann N Y Acad Sci 884:1–14.

34. Cianfrone G, M Pace, R Turchetta et al (2005) Guida ed aggiornamento sui farmaci ototossici, tinnitogeni e vertigogeni. Acta Otorhinolaryngol Ital 25:28.

35. Yorgason JG, JN Fayad and F Kalinec (2006) Understanding drug ototoxicity: molecular insights for prevention and clinical management. Expert Opin Drug Saf 5:383–99.

36. Brunton LL, JS Lazo and KL Parker (2005) Goodman and Gilman's The Pharmacological Basis of Therapeutics Laurence Brunton, Editors. McGraw-Hill, New York.

37. Durante-Mangoni E, A Grammatikos, R Utili et al (2009) Do we still need the aminoglycosides? Int J Antimicrob Agents 33:201–5.

38. East JE, JE Foweraker and FD Murgatroyd (2005) Gentamicin induced ototoxicity during treatment of enterococcal endocarditis: resolution with substitution by netilmicin. Heart 91:e32.

39. Rybak LP and V Ramkumar (2007) Ototoxicity. Kidney Int 72:931–5.

40. Bitner-Glindzicz M and S Rahman (2007) Ototoxicity caused by aminoglycosides. BMJ 335:784–5.

41. Selimoglu E (2007) Aminoglycoside-induced ototoxicity. Curr Pharm Des 13:119–26.

42. Chen Y, WG Huang, DJ Zha et al (2007) Aspirin attenuates gentamicin ototoxicity: from the laboratory to the clinic. Hear Res 226:178–82.

43. Perletti G, A Vral, MC Patrosso et al (2008) Prevention and modulation of aminoglycoside ototoxicity (Review). Mol Med Rep 1:10.

44. Sergi B, AR Fetoni, A Ferraresi et al (2004) The role of antioxidants in protection from ototoxic drugs. Acta Otolaryngol Suppl 552:42–5.

45. Rizzi MD and K Hirose (2007) Aminoglycoside ototoxicity. Curr Opin Otolaryngol Head Neck Surg 15:352–7.

46. Bates DE, SJ Beaumont and BW Baylis (2002) Ototoxicity induced by gentamicin and furosemide. Ann Pharmacother 36:446–51.

47. Mir O, S Ropert and F Goldwasser (2009) Cisplatin as a cornerstone of modern chemotherapy. Lancet Oncol 10:304.

48. Kyrtopoulos SA, LM Anderson, SK Chhabra et al (1997) DNA adducts and the mechanism of carcinogenesis and cytotoxicity of methylating agents of environmental and clinical significance. Cancer Detect Prev 21:391–405.

49. Shamkhani H, LM Anderson, CE Henderson et al (1994) DNA adducts in human and patas monkey maternal and fetal tissues induced by platinum drug chemotherapy. Reprod Toxicol 8:207–16.

50. Hartmann JT and HP Lipp (2003) Toxicity of platinum compounds. Expert Opin Pharmacother 4:889–901.

51. Mir O, P Berveiller, S Ropert et al (2008) Use of platinum derivatives during pregnancy. Cancer 113:3069–74.

52. Rybak LP, CA Whitworth, D Mukherjea et al (2007) Mechanisms of cisplatin-induced ototoxicity and prevention. Hear Res 226:157–67.

53. Oldenburg J, SD Fossa and T Ikdahl (2008) Genetic variants associated with cisplatin-induced ototoxicity. Pharmacogenomics 9:1521–30.

54. Riedemann L, C Lanvers, D Deuster et al (2008) Megalin genetic polymorphisms and individual sensitivity to the ototoxic effect of cisplatin. Pharmacogenomics J 8:23–8.

55. Huang RS, S Duan, SJ Shukla et al (2007) Identification of genetic variants contributing to cisplatin-induced cytotoxicity by use of a genomewide approach. Am J Hum Genet 81:427–37.

56. Knoll C, RJ Smith, C Shores et al (2006) Hearing genes and cisplatin deafness: a pilot study. Laryngoscope 116:72–4.

57. Rademaker-Lakhai JM, M Crul, L Zuur et al (2006) Relationship between cisplatin administration and the development of ototoxicity. J Clin Oncol 24:918–24.

58. Zuur CL, YJ Simis, RS Verkaik et al (2008) Hearing loss due to concurrent daily low-dose cisplatin chemoradiation for locally advanced head and neck cancer. Radiother Oncol 89:38–43.

59. Fetoni AR, B Sergi, A Ferraresi et al (2004) Protective effects of alpha-tocopherol and tiopronin against cisplatin-induced ototoxicity. Acta Otolaryngol 124:421–6.

60. Thomas Dickey D, LL Muldoon, DF Kraemer et al (2004) Protection against cisplatin-induced ototoxicity by N-acetylcysteine in a rat model. Hear Res 193:25–30.

61. Bertolini P, M Lassalle, G Mercier et al (2004) Platinum compound-related ototoxicity in children: long-term follow-up reveals continuous worsening of hearing loss. J Pediatr Hematol Oncol 26:649–55.

62. Coradini PP, L Cigana, SG Selistre et al (2007) Ototoxicity from cisplatin therapy in childhood cancer. J Pediatr Hematol Oncol 29:355–60.

63. Helt-Cameron J and PJ Allen (2009) Cisplatin ototoxicity in children: implications for primary care providers. Pediatr Nurs 35:121–7.

64. Knight KR, DF Kraemer and EA Neuwelt (2005) Ototoxicity in children receiving platinum chemotherapy: underestimating a commonly occurring toxicity that may influence academic and social development. J Clin Oncol 23:8588–96.

65. Li Y, RB Womer and JH Silber (2004) Predicting cisplatin ototoxicity in children: the influence of age and the cumulative dose. Eur J Cancer 40:2445–51.

66. Dhooge I, C Dhooge, S Geukens et al (2006) Distortion product otoacoustic emissions: an objective technique for the screening of hearing loss in children treated with platin derivatives. Int J Audiol 45:337–43.

67. Fisher MJ, BJ Lange, MN Needle et al (2004) Amifostine for children with medulloblastoma treated with cisplatin-based chemotherapy. Pediatr Blood Cancer 43:780–4.

68. Fouladi M, M Chintagumpala, D Ashley et al (2008) Amifostine protects against cisplatin-induced ototoxicity in children with average-risk medulloblastoma. J Clin Oncol 26:3749–55.

69. Freyer DR, L Sung and GH Reaman (2009) Prevention of hearing loss in children receiving cisplatin chemotherapy. J Clin Oncol 27:317–8; author reply 8–9.

70. Katzenstein HM, KW Chang, M Krailo et al (2009) Amifostine does not prevent platinum-induced hearing loss associated with the treatment of children with hepatoblastoma: a report of the Intergroup Hepatoblastoma Study P9645 as a part of the Children's Oncology Group. Cancer 115:5828–35.

71. Marina N, KW Chang, M Malogolowkin et al (2005) Amifostine does not protect against the ototoxicity of high-dose cisplatin combined with etoposide and bleomycin in pediatric germ-cell tumors: a Children's Oncology Group study. Cancer 104:841–7.

72. Sastry J and SJ Kellie (2005) Severe neurotoxicity, ototoxicity and nephrotoxicity following high-dose cisplatin and amifostine. Pediatr Hematol Oncol 22:441–5.

73. World Health Organization (2008) World Malaria Report 2008.

74. Centers for Disease Control and Prevention (2008) Malaria Surveillance – United States, 2007. MMWR 58:16.

75. Ashley E, R McGready, S Proux et al (2006) Malaria. Travel Med Infect Dis 4:159–73.

76. Berman J (2004) Toxicity of commonly-used antimalarial drugs. Travel Med Infect Dis 2:171–84.

77. Centers for Disease Control and Prevention (2009) The Pre-Travel Consultation – Malaria, in Health Information for International Travel 2010. 2009.

78. Gkrania-Klotsas E and AM Lever (2007) An update on malaria prevention, diagnosis and treatment for the returning traveller. Blood Rev 21:73–87.

79. Lalloo DG, D Shingadia, G Pasvol et al (2007) UK malaria treatment guidelines. J Infect 54:111–21.

80. Sullivan DJ, Jr., IY Gluzman, DG Russell et al (1996) On the molecular mechanism of chloroquine's antimalarial action. Proc Natl Acad Sci U S A 93:11865–70.

81. Huston M and M Levinson (2006) Are one or two dangerous? Quinine and quinidine exposure in toddlers. J Emerg Med 31:395–401.

82. Taylor S (2004) Quinine intoxications: a continuing problem. Br J Clin Pharmacol 57:817; author reply.

83. Nosten F, R McGready, U d'Alessandro et al (2006) Antimalarial drugs in pregnancy: a review. Curr Drug Saf 1:1–15.

84. Ostensen M and M Motta (2007) Therapy insight: the use of antirheumatic drugs during nursing. Nat Clin Pract Rheumatol 3:400–6.

85. Ward SA, EJ Sevene, IM Hastings et al (2007) Antimalarial drugs and pregnancy: safety, pharmacokinetics, and pharmacovigilance. Lancet Infect Dis 7:136–44.

86. Alvan G, KK Karlsson, U Hellgren et al (1991) Hearing impairment related to plasma quinine concentration in healthy volunteers. Br J Clin Pharmacol 31:409–12.

87. Jastreboff PJ, JF Brennan and CT Sasaki (1991) Quinine-induced tinnitus in rats. Arch Otolaryngol Head Neck Surg 117:1162–6.

88. Paintaud G, G Alvan, E Berninger et al (1994) The concentration-effect relationship of quinine-induced hearing impairment. Clin Pharmacol Ther 55:317–23.

89. Bortoli R and M Santiago (2007) Chloroquine ototoxicity. Clin Rheumatol 26:1809–10.

90. Gurkov R, T Eshetu, IB Miranda et al (2008) Ototoxicity of artemether/lumefantrine in the treatment of falciparum malaria: a randomized trial. Malar J 7:179.

91. Hadi U, N Nuwayhid and AS Hasbini (1996) Chloroquine ototoxicity: an idiosyncratic phenomenon. Otolaryngol Head Neck Surg 114:491–3.

92. Jarboe JK and R Hallworth (1999) The effect of quinine on outer hair cell shape, compliance and force. Hear Res 132:43–50.

93. Karlsson KK and A Flock (1990) Quinine causes isolated outer hair cells to change length. Neurosci Lett 116:101–5.

94. Karlsson KK, M Ulfendahl, SM Khanna et al (1991) The effects of quinine on the cochlear mechanics in the isolated temporal bone preparation. Hear Res 53:95–100.

95. Zheng J, T Ren, A Parthasarathi et al (2001) Quinine-induced alterations of electrically evoked otoacoustic emissions and cochlear potentials in guinea pigs. Hear Res 154:124–34.

96. Jung TT, CK Rhee, CS Lee et al (1993) Ototoxicity of salicylate, nonsteroidal antiinflammatory drugs, and quinine. Otolaryngol Clin North Am 26:791–810.

97. Shine NP and H Coates (2005) Systemic ototoxicity: a review. East Afr Med J 82:536–9.

98. Coutinho MB and I Duarte (2002) Hydroxychloroquine ototoxicity in a child with idiopathic pulmonary haemosiderosis. Int J Pediatr Otorhinolaryngol 62:53–7.

99. Taylor WR and NJ White (2004) Antimalarial drug toxicity: a review. Drug Saf 27:25–61.

100. Karbwang J, KN Bangchang, A Thanavibul et al (1994) Quinine toxicity when given with doxycycline and mefloquine. Southeast Asian J Trop Med Public Health 25:397–400.

101. AlKadi HO (2007) Antimalarial drug toxicity: a review. Chemotherapy 53:385–91.

102. Amann R and BA Peskar (2002) Anti-inflammatory effects of aspirin and sodium salicylate. Eur J Pharmacol 447:1–9.

103. Yasuda O, Y Takemura, H Kawamoto et al (2008) Aspirin: recent developments. Cell Mol Life Sci 65:354–8.

104. www.aspirin-foundation.com. 2009 cited.

105. Bjorklund L, MA Wallander, S Johansson et al (2009) Aspirin in cardiology – benefits and risks. Int J Clin Pract 63:468–77.

106. Wolff T, T Miller and S Ko (2009) Aspirin for the primary prevention of cardiovascular events: an update of the evidence for the U.S. Preventive Services Task Force. Ann Intern Med 150:405–10.

107. Cuzick J, F Otto, JA Baron et al (2009) Aspirin and non-steroidal anti-inflammatory drugs for cancer prevention: an international consensus statement. Lancet Oncol 10:501–7.

108. Elwood PC, AM Gallagher, GG Duthie et al (2009) Aspirin, salicylates, and cancer. Lancet 373:1301–9.

109. O'Kane P, L Xie, Z Liu et al (2009) Aspirin acetylates nitric oxide synthase type 3 in platelets thereby increasing its activity. Cardiovasc Res 83:123–30.

110. Ressel G (2002) AAP updates statement for transfer of drugs and other chemicals into breast milk. American Academy of Pediatrics. Am Fam Physician 65:979–80.

111. Marchese-Ragona R, G Marioni, P Marson et al (2008) The discovery of salicylate ototoxicity. Audiol Neurootol 13:34–6.

112. Cazals Y (2000) Auditory sensori-neural alterations induced by salicylate. Prog Neurobiol 62:583–631.

113. Koren G (2009) Hearing loss in a woman on aspirin: the silent pharmacokinetic parameter. Ther Drug Monit 31:1–2.

114. Ermilov SA, DR Murdock, D El-Daye et al (2005) Effects of salicylate on plasma membrane mechanics. J Neurophysiol 94:2105–10.

115. Frolenkov GI (2006) Regulation of electromotility in the cochlear outer hair cell. J Physiol 576:43–8.

116. Puel JL (2007) Cochlear NMDA receptor blockade prevents salicylate-induced tinnitus. B-ENT 3 Suppl 7:19–22.

117. Puel JL and MJ Guitton (2007) Salicylate-induced tinnitus: molecular mechanisms and modulation by anxiety. Prog Brain Res 166:141–6.

118. Sun W, J Lu, D Stolzberg et al (2009) Salicylate increases the gain of the central auditory system. Neuroscience 159:325–34.

119. Hyppolito MA, JA de Oliveira and M Rossato (2006) Cisplatin ototoxicity and otoprotection with sodium salicylate. Eur Arch Otorhinolaryngol 263:798–803.

120. Minami SB, SH Sha and J Schacht (2004) Antioxidant protection in a new animal model of cisplatin-induced ototoxicity. Hear Res 198:137–43.

121. Dargan PI, CI Wallace and AL Jones (2002) An evidence based flowchart to guide the management of acute salicylate (aspirin) overdose. Emerg Med J 19:206–9.

122. Samlan SR, MT Jordan, SB Chan et al (2008) Tinnitus as a measure of salicylate toxicity in the overdose setting. West J Emerg Med 9:146–9.

123. Michael JB and MD Sztajnkrycer (2004) Deadly pediatric poisons: nine common agents that kill at low doses. Emerg Med Clin North Am 22:1019–50.

124. Baxter AJ, R Mrvos and EP Krenzelok (2003) Salicylism and herbal medicine. Am J Emerg Med 21:448–9.

125. Bell AJ and G Duggin (2002) Acute methyl salicylate toxicity complicating herbal skin treatment for psoriasis. Emerg Med (Fremantle) 14:188–90.

126. Hofman M, JE Diaz and C Martella (1998) Oil of wintergreen overdose. Ann Emerg Med 31:793–4.

127. Baguley DM, S Jones, I Wilkins et al (2005) The inhibitory effect of intravenous lidocaine infusion on tinnitus after translabyrinthine removal of vestibular schwannoma: a double-blind, placebo-controlled, crossover study. Otol Neurotol 26:169–76.

128. Haginomori S, K Makimoto, M Araki et al (1995) Effect of lidocaine injection of EOAE in patients with tinnitus. Acta Otolaryngol 115:488–92.

129. Otsuka K, JL Pulec and M Suzuki (2003) Assessment of intravenous lidocaine for the treatment of subjective tinnitus. Ear Nose Throat J 82:781–4.
130. Sanchez TG, AP Balbani, RS Bittar et al (1999) Lidocaine test in patients with tinnitus: rationale of accomplishment and relation to the treatment with carbamazepine. Auris Nasus Larynx 26:411–7.
131. Kalcioglu MT, T Bayindir, T Erdem et al (2005) Objective evaluation of the effects of intravenous lidocaine on tinnitus. Hear Res 199:81–8.
132. Butterworth JFt and GR Strichartz (1990) Molecular mechanisms of local anesthesia: a review. Anesthesiology 72:711–34.
133. Chevrier P, K Vijayaragavan and M Chahine (2004) Differential modulation of Nav1.7 and Nav1.8 peripheral nerve sodium channels by the local anesthetic lidocaine. Br J Pharmacol 142:576–84.
134. Scholz A (2002) Mechanisms of (local) anaesthetics on voltage-gated sodium and other ion channels. Br J Anaesth 89:52–61.
135. Trellakis S, D Benzenberg, BW Urban et al (2006) Differential lidocaine sensitivity of human voltage-gated potassium channels relevant to the auditory system. Otol Neurotol 27:117–23.
136. Bortone DS, K Mitchell and PB Manis (2006) Developmental time course of potassium channel expression in the rat cochlear nucleus. Hear Res 211:114–25.
137. Grigg JJ, HM Brew and BL Tempel (2000) Differential expression of voltage-gated potassium channel genes in auditory nuclei of the mouse brainstem. Hear Res 140:77–90.
138. Holt AG, M Asako, RK Duncan et al (2006) Deafness associated changes in expression of two-pore domain potassium channels in the rat cochlear nucleus. Hear Res 216-217:146–53.
139. Kaczmarek LK, A Bhattacharjee, R Desai et al (2005) Regulation of the timing of MNTB neurons by short-term and long-term modulation of potassium channels. Hear Res 206:133–45.
140. Shiomi Y, K Funabiki, Y Naito et al (1997) The effect of intravenous lidocaine injection on hearing thresholds. Auris Nasus Larynx 24:351–6.
141. Ruth RA, TJ Gal, CA DiFazio et al (1985) Brain-stem auditory-evoked potentials during lidocaine infusion in humans. Arch Otolaryngol 111:799–802.
142. Giraud AL, S Chery-Croze, G Fischer et al (1999) A selective imaging of tinnitus. Neuroreport 10:1–5.
143. Staffen W, E Biesinger, E Trinka et al (1999) The effect of lidocaine on chronic tinnitus: a quantitative cerebral perfusion study. Audiology 38:53–7.
144. Reyes SA, RJ Salvi, RF Burkard et al (2002) Brain imaging of the effects of lidocaine on tinnitus. Hear Res 171:43–50.
145. Ettinger AB and CE Argoff (2007) Use of antiepileptic drugs for nonepileptic conditions: psychiatric disorders and chronic pain. Neurotherapeutics 4:75–83.
146. Rogawski MA and W Loscher (2004) The neurobiology of antiepileptic drugs for the treatment of nonepileptic conditions. Nat Med 10:685–92.
147. Dobie RA (1999) A review of randomized clinical trials in tinnitus. Laryngoscope 109:1202–11.
148. Robinson SK, ES Viirre and MB Stein (2007) Antidepressant therapy in tinnitus. Hear Res 226:221–31.
149. McKenna L, RS Hallam and R Hinchcliffe (1991) The prevalence of psychological disturbance in neurotology outpatients. Clin Otolaryngol Allied Sci 16:452–6.
150. Zoger S, J Svedlund and KM Holgers (2006) Relationship between tinnitus severity and psychiatric disorders. Psychosomatics 47:282–8.
151. Mico JA, D Ardid, E Berrocoso et al (2006) Antidepressants and pain. Trends Pharmacol Sci 27:348–54.
152. Reisner L (2003) Antidepressants for chronic neuropathic pain. Curr Pain Headache Rep 7:24–33.
153. Møller AR (1997) Similarities between chronic pain and tinnitus. Am J Otol 18:577–85.
154. Møller AR (2000) Similarities between severe tinnitus and chronic pain. J Am Acad Audiol 11:115–24.
155. Feder R (1990) Tinnitus associated with amitriptyline. J Clin Psychiatry 51:85–6.
156. Koshes RJ (1992) Use of amitriptyline in a patient with tinnitus. Psychosomatics 33:341–3.
157. Mendis D and M Johnston (2008) An unusual case of prolonged tinnitus following low-dose amitriptyline. J Psychopharmacol 22:574–5.
158. Ahmad S (1995) Venlafaxine and severe tinnitus. Am Fam Physician 51:1830.
159. Farah A and TE Lauer (1996) Possible venlafaxine withdrawal syndrome. Am J Psychiatry 153:576.
160. Leiter FL, AA Nierenberg, KM Sanders et al (1995) Discontinuation reactions following sertraline. Biol Psychiatry 38:694–5.
161. Baldo P, C Doree, R Lazzarini et al (2006) Antidepressants for patients with tinnitus. Cochrane Database Syst Rev 4:CD003853.
162. Robinson SK, ES Viirre, KA Bailey et al (2005) Randomized placebo-controlled trial of a selective serotonin reuptake inhibitor in the treatment of nondepressed tinnitus subjects. Psychosom Med 67:981–8.
163. Kisely S and LA Campbell (2008) Use of smoking cessation therapies in individuals with psychiatric illness : an update for prescribers. CNS Drugs 22:263–73.
164. Siu EC and RF Tyndale (2007) Non-nicotinic therapies for smoking cessation. Annu Rev Pharmacol Toxicol 47:541–64.
165. Humma LM and MP Swims (1999) Bupropion mimics a transient ischemic attack. Ann Pharmacother 33:305–7.
166. Settle EC, Jr. (1991) Tinnitus related to bupropion treatment. J Clin Psychiatry 52:352.
167. Ashton JC and ED Milligan (2008) Cannabinoids for the treatment of neuropathic pain: clinical evidence. Curr Opin Investig Drugs 9:65–75.
168. Ben Amar M (2006) Cannabinoids in medicine: a review of their therapeutic potential. J Ethnopharmacol 105:1–25.
169. Di Marzo V and LD Petrocellis (2006) Plant, synthetic, and endogenous cannabinoids in medicine. Annu Rev Med 57:553–74.
170. Dalton GD, CE Bass, C Van Horn et al (2009) Signal transduction via cannabinoid receptors. CNS Neurol Disord Drug Targets 8:422–31.
171. Demuth DG and A Molleman (2006) Cannabinoid signalling. Life Sci 78:549–63.
172. Howlett AC (2002) The cannabinoid receptors. Prostaglandins Other Lipid Mediat 68–69:619–31.
173. Mouslech Z and V Valla (2009) Endocannabinoid system: an overview of its potential in current medical practice. Neuro Endocrinol Lett 30:153–79.

174. Aggarwal SK, GT Carter, MD Sullivan et al (2009) Medicinal use of cannabis in the United States: historical perspectives, current trends, and future directions. J Opioid Manag 5:153–68.

175. Cohen PJ (2009) Medical marijuana: the conflict between scientific evidence and political ideology. Part two of two. J Pain Palliat Care Pharmacother 23:120–40.

176. Zheng Y, JH Baek, PF Smith et al (2007) Cannabinoid receptor down-regulation in the ventral cochlear nucleus in a salicylate model of tinnitus. Hear Res 228:105–11.

177. Raby WN, PA Modica, RJ Wolintz et al (2006) Dronabinol reduces signs and symptoms of idiopathic intracranial hypertension: a case report. J Ocul Pharmacol Ther 22: 68–75.

Chapter 43
Tinnitus Caused and Influenced by the Somatosensory System

Tanit Ganz Sanchez and Carina Bezerra Rocha

Keypoints

1. It is now recognized that many forms of tinnitus-related neural activity are much more complex and multimodal than ever thought.
2. It has become evident that contribution of non-auditory pathways is involved in eliciting or modulating many forms of tinnitus.
3. Many forms of tinnitus can be modulated by different actions such as forceful muscle contractions of the head and neck as well as eye movements.
4. Somatosensory stimulation such as that from pressure of myofascial trigger points, cutaneous stimulation at specific locations, electrical stimulation of the median nerve and hand, finger movements, and orofacial movements can also modulate or cause tinnitus, as can pressure applied to the temporomandibular joint or lateral pterygoid muscle.
5. This chapter discusses the causes of somatosensory tinnitus and in particular the influence from both head and neck regions on the auditory pathways in individuals with tinnitus.

Keywords Tinnitus • Somatic • Somatosensory • Central nervous system • Muscle • Cervical spine • Temporomandibular joint.

Abbreviations

MTP   Myofascial trigger point
AMTP   Active myofascial trigger point
LMTP   Latent myofascial trigger point

T.G. Sanchez (✉)
Otolaryngology Department, University of São Paulo Medical School, Av. Padre Pereira de Andrade, 545/174-F, São Paulo, SP, Brazil 05469-000
e-mail: tanitsanchez@gmail.com

Introduction

For many years, tinnitus was thought to arise almost exclusively from abnormal neuronal activity within the auditory pathway. However, accumulated evidence suggested that tinnitus-related neural activity is much more complex and multimodal than previously anticipated.

More often than ever thought, tinnitus can be evoked or modulated by inputs from somatosensory, somato-motor, and visual-motor systems in some individuals. This means that the psychoacoustic attributes of tinnitus might be changed temporarily by different stimuli, such as:

– Forceful muscle contractions of head, neck, and limbs [1–3];
– Eye movements in horizontal or vertical axis [4–7];
– Pressure of myofascial trigger points [8];
– Cutaneous stimulation of the hand/fingertip region [4] and the face [9];
– Electrical stimulation of the median nerve and hand [10];
– Finger movements [11];
– Orofacial movements [12];
– Pressure applied to the temporomandibular joint or lateral pterygoid muscle [13, 14].

Such temporary changes are known as modulation of tinnitus. So, the contribution of non-auditory pathways has become more and more evident in eliciting or modulating existent tinnitus.

Although this phenomenon is yet to be fully understood, it seems to be clinical evidence of the existing neural connections between the somatosensory and auditory systems, whose "activation" may play a role in tinnitus. Anatomic and physiological findings in animal studies have shown that the trigeminal and dorsal root ganglia relay some afferent somatosensory information from the periphery to secondary sensory neurons in the brainstem, specifically, the spinal trigeminal nucleus and dorsal column nuclei, respectively [15]. Each of these structures sends excitatory projections to the cochlear nucleus. Mossy fibers from the spinal trigeminal and dorsal column nuclei terminate in the granule cell domain while en passant boutons from the ganglia terminate in the granule cell domain and core region of the cochlear nucleus. Single unit and evoked potential recordings in the dorsal cochlear nucleus indicate that these pathways are physiologically active.

So, these clinical findings strongly suggest that those who are able to modulate their tinnitus should be considered as a specific subgroup of patients. Among all types of modulating factors that have been described, we are particularly interested in the influence of both head and neck regions on the auditory pathways.

Now, there is yet no consensus on the definition of "somatosensory tinnitus," and this term has been used with different meanings. A group of researchers in the Tinnitus Research Initiative is presently working to define and differentiate "somatosensory tinnitus" (primary origin in head and neck trauma, dental or cervical manipulation, or even in unknown chronic pain) from "somatosensory modulation" (auditory origin with temporary somatosensory influence in loudness, pitch, or localization). Although many aspects still need clarification, we have already progressed in establishing some specific causes, methods of diagnosis, and treatment options to this subgroup, which will be described in this chapter.

Theories About Tinnitus Modulation

It is widely known that reorganization or re-mapping of specific central nervous areas occurs as a normal response of brain tissue to injury [16, 17]. However, as any double-edged sword, it is not possible to predict whether injury-induced plasticity will end up in limited or cross-modal effects, which in turn may result in compensatory or pathologic effects. Neuroplasticity is often implicated in tinnitus, and aberrant cross-modal plasticity seems to play a role in recently described cases of tinnitus evoked by somatosensory activation. This suggests that abnormal interaction between

different sensory modalities, sensorimotor systems, neurocognitive, and neuroemotional networks may contribute to certain aspects of tinnitus [17].

Tinnitus modulation indicates that the psychoacoustic attributes of tinnitus change temporarily during some sort of stimuli [18]. Some of these modulation patterns (gaze-evoked, finger-evoked, and cutaneous-evoked tinnitus) were first described after acute unilateral total deafferentation of the auditory afferents, usually caused by the removal of skull base and posterior cranial fossa tumors. Some authors have hypothesized that in this form of modulation, important plastic changes occurred in the central nervous system after such deafferentation.

However, our own clinical experience showed that other types of modulation occur regardless of any surgical manipulation or degree of hearing loss [2, 3, 19]. An altered afferent input to the auditory pathway may be the initiator of a complex sequence of events finally resulting in the generation of tinnitus at the central level of the auditory nervous system. The effects of neural plasticity can generally be divided into early and later modifications, depending on the time of onset. Unmasking of dormant synapses, diminishing of (surround) inhibition, and generation of new connections through axonal sprouting are early manifestations of neural plasticity, resulting in lateral spread of neural activity and development of hyperexcitability regions in the central nervous system. The remodeling of tonotopic receptive fields within auditory structures (dorsal cochlear nucleus, inferior colliculus, and auditory cortex) seems to be a late manifestation of neural plasticity. The modulation of tinnitus by stimulating the somatosensory system might be explained by activating auditory regions through the non-classical pathway.

Tinnitus Modulation by Muscle Contractions

Sometimes tinnitus patients spontaneously report that contractions of head and neck muscle may change the loudness or pitch of their tinnitus. However, recent studies showed that a surprisingly large number of patients modulate tinnitus when they are specifically tested for it. Levine initially found that 68% of patients with tinnitus experienced some kind of modulation when performing muscular contractions [1, 20]. Regardless of etiology or audiometric pattern, 71% could modify their tinnitus with a variety of cephalo-cervical isometric maneuvers or extremity contractions [21]. The head/neck isometric maneuvers were much more effective in modulating tinnitus than contractions of the limbs. Using a control group, Sanchez et al. pointed out that 65.3% of patients modulated loudness or pitch of their tinnitus during muscle contractions, while 14% of asymptomatic subjects could evoke tinnitus perception during the same maneuvers [2]. Later, other studies confirmed that the majority of tinnitus patients can modulate the phantom sound by stimulation of the somatosensory system [3, 19, 21, 22].

Considering the structure of the auditory pathway, it consists of several well-defined centers, although precise information about their interaction is still lacking. The cochlear nucleus is the first central nucleus of the auditory pathway, receiving information from the cochlear hair cells. In higher portions of the auditory pathway, the lemniscal system sends the received information to the primary cortical auditory areas, whereas the extralemniscal portion of the ascending pathways transmits auditory information to associated areas [10]. Many neurons of the extralemniscal system receive information from other sensorial tracts, such as the somatosensory system [23, 24]

The cuneate and gracile nuclei collectively form the dorsal medullary nucleus, whose position in the somatosensory system is analogous to that of the cochlear nucleus in the auditory system. It receives information directly from the dorsal roots, which in turn get information from the proprioceptive, tactile, and vibratory receptors of the body surface. The lateral cuneate nucleus is the end point of afferent fibers from the neck, ear, and suboccipital muscles, and carries information on head and ear position needed to process the acoustic information [25]. Because of reciprocal connections between the auditory and somatosensory systems, these authors postulated that projections from the cuneate to the cochlear nucleus may lead to excitation of the cochlear nucleus. Nevertheless, some electrophysiological studies in cats showed that the final effect of cuneate nucleus activation is the inhibition of the dorsal cochlear nucleus [26]. The exact mechanisms responsible for somatic modulation of tinnitus are currently unclear. If one considers that tinnitus results from aberrant neuronal activity within the auditory pathway, this could mean that somatosensory stimuli coming from

head and neck muscle contractions might, through a multisynaptic pathway, disinhibit the ipsilateral cochlear nucleus, producing an excitatory neuronal activity within the auditory pathway that results in tinnitus.

As muscular contraction represents an activation of the somatosensory system, these anatomical connections between both systems might explain the influence of voluntary muscle contractions upon some types of tinnitus, thereby stimulating or inhibiting this symptom and presenting clinically as a modulation factor. In fact, we have seen patients with a typical history of acoustic trauma that could also clearly evoke tinnitus by several different stimuli, including during abdominal contraction.

Tinnitus Modulation Through Myofascial Trigger Points

Myofascial trigger points (MTP) are small hypersensitive spots located within the palpable taut bands of skeletal muscle fibers. Either spontaneously or under mechanical stimulation, they may cause local and referred pain [27].

MTP may be active (AMTP) when their stimulation causes a pattern of referred pain that is similar to the patient's pre-existent pain complaint or may aggravate such pain [28]. They are frequently found on the neck, shoulders, pelvic girdle, and masticatory muscles [29], where they provoke spontaneous pain or movement-related pain.

MTP can also be latent (LMTP), which are located in symptom-free areas and provoke local and referred pain only when stimulated [28].

Although MTP may be detected in pain-free subjects, they are typical of patients with myofascial pain syndrome, who often complaint of an associated tinnitus [30].

Travell and Simons first reported that MTP palpation of the sternal division of the sternocleidomastoid evoked a sound perception in a tinnitus-free patient [27]. Later, Eriksson et al. described a patient who noticed differences in tinnitus when palpating a MTP in the sternocleidomastoid. Such association has also been verified in studies where tinnitus patients had their conditions improved through anesthesia-based MTP deactivation [31].

Recently, Rocha et al. (2007) [8] investigated whether myofascial trigger points could modulate tinnitus and examined the association between tinnitus and MTP. They evaluated 94 subjects with tinnitus and 94 without the disorder, who underwent bilateral digital pressure of nine muscles of the head, neck, and shoulder girdle usually tested in myofascial pain syndromes (infraspinatus, levator scapulae, superior trapezius, splenius capitis, scalenus medius, sternal portion of sternocleidomastoid, posterior digastric, superficial masseter, and anterior temporalis). Temporary tinnitus modulation was observed in 56% of the subjects during digital pressure, mainly in the masseter, splenius capitis, sternocleidomastoid, and temporalis muscles. The rate of tinnitus modulation was significantly higher on the same side of MTP tinnitus subjects to examination in six out of the nine muscles. A strong association between tinnitus and the presence of MTP was observed, as well as a laterality association between the ear with tinnitus and the side of the body with MTP [19].

We initially assumed that only AMTP (related to pain) would be able to modulate tinnitus. However, the compression of LMTP may also end up with modulation of tinnitus. One possible explanation is that both active and latent MTP evoke referred pain when stimulated. Another interesting discovery of this study was the fact that MTP located in head and neck muscles produced more tinnitus modulation than those located in the shoulder girdle, which supports previous study [2, 20] findings, in which head and neck muscular contraction maneuvers produced more modulation than those of the members. These results can be possibly explained by neuroanatomy, since connections between somatic and auditory pathways at the cephalic level would be richer.

One of the mechanisms that explains referred pain is transmission by autonomic pathways [32]. The autonomic phenomena referred to other areas besides the MTP region can be explained by increased sensitivity of sensory nerve endings (thin terminal axons) at the MTP region and consequent neural mechanisms to spread referred pain [25]. Whenever those LMTP remain in a given subject for lengthy periods, they give rise to sensitization of nervous fibers associated to vasoconstriction due to increased sympathetic neurovegetative activity [33]. According to Hubbard and Berkoff, sympathetic activity explains the autonomic symptoms associated with MTP and provides a mech-

anism through which local injury and nociception cause local tension. It is now accepted that there is direct sympathetic innervation to the intrafusal fibers of muscle spindles. In some tinnitus patients, the sympathetic nervous system apparently plays an important role. Studies have found that blocking the sympathetic input to the ear or a sympathectomy can alleviate tinnitus in some patients. Thus, the autonomic nervous system (sympathetic) may explain some of the findings regarding the effects of MTP stimulation on tinnitus.

Thus, the possible explanation for the relationship between tinnitus and MTP would be not only somatosensory–auditory system interactions but also the influence of the sympathetic system.

Tinnitus Modulation During Tender Point Compression

Tender points are discrete areas of pain in response to palpation on body surfaces and can be identified in many people, but those suffering from chronic pain disorders tend to be more affected. The difference between MTP and tender points is the location of pain and the point of maximum tenderness that causes the symptoms. MTP refers pain to a distant spot upon pressure; tender points do not [34]. Researchers have been debating whether trigger points are a subset of tender points.

Even with such similarities, there has been no report of tender points being able to modulate tinnitus. However, during the examination of 11 patients with tinnitus and frequent regional pain for at least 3 months in the head, neck, and shoulder girdle (ten with myofascial pain syndrome and one with only tender points), we surprisingly found that 5 of them modulated tinnitus upon digital pressure on some tender points, besides the modulation by trigger points. Moreover, two other patients only modulated tinnitus by tender points, including the subject who did not have myofascial pain syndrome.

As this finding appeared by chance during the development of a study focused to trigger points, new clinical studies with bigger samples are necessary in order to demonstrate a possible relationship between tender points and tinnitus, with or without an associated myofascial trigger point.

Tinnitus Associated with Cervical Whiplash

As a consequence of cervical whiplash, extensive injuries to the cervical joints, ligaments, and discs may occur [35]. These bony and soft tissue injuries may lead to a variety of clinical manifestations [36]. Neck pain is the most common symptom, reported in 88–100% of cases [37]. Surprisingly, tinnitus and other otological symptoms are found in approximately 10–15% of the patients [38–40]. However, among 109 patients evaluated, none reported otological symptoms in the acute phase following the whiplash injury [41]. In our opinion, a possible explanation might involve the secondary vicious muscular postures that patients adopt in order to avoid neck pain. Considering the relation previously described between tinnitus modulation and muscular tension, myofascial trigger and tender points [8, 19, 31, 42], it is possible that secondary findings in patients with whiplash injury may justify the later onset of tinnitus. As the relationship between whiplash itself and tinnitus is yet controversial, caution is recommended whenever attributing these symptoms to such an injury.

On the other hand, some studies have suggested a possible link between whiplash and temporomandibular joint dysfunction [43–45]. Whiplash might induce joint lesions and posttraumatic malocclusions, which would lead to dysfunction of the masticatory muscle, resulting in tinnitus [46]. However, other researchers claim that temporomandibular joint dysfunction is not associated with whiplash injuries [47–49].

In short, although whiplash is considered a cervical spinal disorder, its relation with tinnitus is controversial. Furthermore, evidence of somatosensory modulation of tinnitus in such patients is not yet supported by the literature.

Acknowledgments The authors wish to thank Tinnitus Research Initiative for the creation and incentive of the workgroup of Somatosensory Tinnitus and Modulating Factors.

References

1. Levine, RA. Somatic modulation appears to be a fundamental attribute of tinntus. In: Hazell, JPW, ed. Proceedings of the Sixth International Tinnitus Seminar. London: The Tinnitus and Hyperacusis Center; 1999:193–7.

2. Sanchez, TG; Guerra, GCY; Lorenzi, MC; Brandão, AL; Bento RF. The influence of voluntary muscle contractions upon the onset and modulation of tinnitus. Audiol. Neurootol. 2002; 7:370–5.

3. Sanchez, TG; Lima, AS; Brandao, AL; Lorenzi, MC; Bento RF. Somatic modulation of tinnitus:test reliability and results after repetitive muscle contraction training. Ann. Otol. Rhinol. Laryngol. 2007; 116:30–5

4. Cacace, AT; Cousins, JP; Parnes, SM; McFarland, DJ; Semenoff, D; Holmes, T; Davenport, C; Stegbauer, K; Lovely, TJ. Cutaneous-evoked tinnitus. II. Review of neuroanatomical, physiological and functional imaging studies. Audiol. Neurootol. 1999; 4:247–57.

5. Coad, ML; Lockwood, A; Salvi, R; Burkard, R. Characteristics of patients with gaze-evoked tinnitus. Otol. Neurotol. 2001; 22(5):650–4.

6. Baguley, DM; Phillips, J; Humphriss, RL; Jones, S; Axon, PR; Moffat, DA. The prevalence and onset of gaze modulation of tinnitus and increased sensitivity to noise after translabyrinthine vestibular schwannoma excision. Otol. Neurotol. 2006; 27:220–4.

7. Sanchez, TG; Pio, MRB. Abolição de zumbido evocado pela movimentação ocular por meio de repetição do deslocamento do olhar:um método inovador. Arq. Otorhinolaryngol. 2007; 11:451–3.

8. Rocha, CA; Sanchez TG. Myofascial trigger points: another way of modulating tinnitus. Prog. Brain Res. 2007; 166:209–14.

9. Sanchez, TG; Marcondes, RA; Kii, MA; Lima, AS; Rocha, CAB; Ono, CR; Bushpiegel, C. A different case of tinnitus modulation by tactile stimuli in a patient with pulsatile tinnitus. Presented at II Meeting of Tinnitus Research Initiative, Mônaco, 2007:21–3.

10. Møller, AR; Rollins, PR. The non-classical auditory pathways are involved in hearing in children but not in adults. Neurosci. Lett. 2002; 319:41–4.

11. Cullington, H. Tinnitus evoked by finger movement: Brain plasticity after peripheral deafferentation. Neurology. 2001; 56:978.

12. Pinchoff, RJ; Burkard, RF; Salvi, RJ; Coad, ML; Lockwood, AH. Modulation of tinnitus by voluntary jaw movements. Am. J. Otol. 1998; 19:785–9.

13. Björne, A. Tinnitus aurum as an effect of increased tension in the lateral pterygoid muscle. Otolaryngol. Head Neck Surg. 1993; 109:969.

14. Rubinstein, B. Tinnitus and craniomandibular disorders – is there a link? Swed. Dental J. Suppl. 1993; 95:1–46.

15. Shore, S; Zhou, J; Koehler, S. Neural mechanisms underlying somatic tinnitus. Prog. Brain Res. 2007; 166:107–23.

16. Chen, R; Cohen, LG; Hallett, M. Nervous system reorganization following injury. Neuroscience. 2002; 111:761–73.

17. Cacace, AT. Expanding the biological basis of tinnitus: crossmodal origins and the role of neuroplasticity. Hear. Res. 2003; 175:112–32.

18. Sanchez, TG; Kii, MA. Modulating tinnitus with visual, muscular and tactile stimulation. Semin Hear, Tinnitus: Part II. 2008; 29:350–60.

19. Rocha, CACB; Sanchez, TG; Siqueira, JTT. Myofascial trigger points:a possible way of modulating tinnitus? Audiol. Neurootol. 2008; 13:153–60.

20. Levine, RA. Somatic (craniocervical) tinnitus and the dorsal cochlear nucleus hypothesis. Am. J. Otolaryngol. 1999; 20:351–62.

21. Levine, RA; Abel, M; Cheng, H. CNS somatosensory–auditory interactions elicit or modulate tinnitus. Exp. Brain Res. 2003; 153(4):643–8.

22. Møller, AR; Møller, MB; Yokota, M. Some forms of tinnitus may involve the extralemniscal auditory pathway. Laryngoscope 1992; 102:1165–71.

23. Hotta, T; Kameda, K. Interactions between somatic and visual or auditory responses in the thalamus of the cat. Exp. Neurol. 1963; 8:1–13.

24. Thompson, RF; Smith, HE; Bliss, D. Auditory, somatic, sensory, and visual response interactions and interrelations in association and primary cortical fields of the cat. J. Neurophysiol. 1963; 26:365–78.

25. Wright, DD; Ryugo, DK. Mossy fiber projections from the cuneate nucleus to the cochlear nucleus in the rat. J. Comp. Neurol. 1996; 365:159–72.

26. Young, ED; Nelken, I; Conley, RA. Somatosensory effects on neurons in dorsal cochlear nucleus. J. Neurophysiol. 1995; 73:743–65.

27. Travell, J; Simons, DG. Myofascial pain and dysfunction: The trigger point manual, upper half of body. Baltimore: Williams & Wilkins; 1999.

28. Aronoff, GM. Myofascial pain syndrome and fibromyalgia: a critical assessment and alternate view. Clin. J. Pain. 1998; 14:74–8.

29. Davidoff, RA. Trigger points and myofascial pain: towards understanding how they affect headaches. Cephalalgia. 1998; 18:436–48.

30. Hong, CZ; Hsueh, TC. Difference in pain relief after trigger point injections in myofascial pain patients with and without fibromyalgia. Arch. Phys. Med. Rehabil. 1996; 77:1161–6.

31. Estola-Partanen, M. Muscular tension and tinnitus:an experimental trial of trigger point injections on tinnitus [dissertation]. Tampere: Faculty of Medicine, University of Tampere; 2000.

32. Wang, F; Audette, J. Electrophysiologic characteristics of the local twitch response in subjects with active myofascial pain of the neck compared with a control group with latent trigger points. Am. J. Phys. Med. Rehabil. 2000; 79:203.

33. Wyant, GM. Chronic pain syndrome and their treatment II. Trigger points. Canad. Anaesth. Soc. J. 1979; 26:216–9.

34. Simons DG. Myofascial pain syndromes: Where are we? Where are we going? Arch. Phys. Med. Rehabil. 1988; 69:207–12.

35. Yoganandan, N; Pintar, FA; Cusick, JF. Biomechanical analyses of whiplash injuries using an experimental model. Accid. Anal. Prev. 2002; 34:663–71.

36. Scholten-Peeters, GG; Bekkering, GE, Verhagen, AP et al. Clinical practice guideline for the physiotherapy of patients with whiplash-associated disorders. Spine 2002; 15:412–22.

37. Vibert, D; Häusler, R. Acute peripheral vestibular deficits after whiplash injuries. Ann. Otol. Rhinol. Laryngol. 2003; 112:246–51.

38. Oosterveld, WJ; Kortschot, HW; Kingma, GG; de Jong, HA; Saatci MR. Electronystagmographic findings following cervical whiplash injuries. Acta. Otolaryngol. 1991; 111:201–5.

39. Claussen, CF; Claussen, E. Neurootological contributions to the diagnostic follow-up after whiplash injuries. Acta. Otolaryngol. 1995 (suppl 520):53–4.

40. Tranter, RM; Graham, JR. A review of the otological aspects of whiplash injury. J. Forensic Leg. Med. 2009; 16:53–5.

41. Rowlands, RG; Campbell, IK; Kenyon, GS. Otological and vestibular symptoms in patients with low grade (Quebec grades one and two) whiplash injury. J. Laryngol. Otol. 2009; 123:182–5.

42. Eriksson, M; Gustafsson, S; Axelsson, A. Tinnitus and trigger points: a randomized cross-over study. In: Reich, GE; Vernon, JA, eds. Proceedings of the Fifth International Tinnitus Seminar, Portland, OR, 1995:81–3.

43. Friedman, MH; Weisberg, J. The craniocervical connection: a retrospective analysis of 300 whiplash patients with cervical and temporomandibular disorders. Cranio 2000; 18:163–7.

44. Garcia, R; Arrington, JA. The relationship between cervical whiplash and temporomandibular joint injuries: an MRI study. Cranio 1996; 14:233–9.

45. Krogstad, BS; Jokstad, A; Dahl, BL; Soboleva, U. Somatic complaints, psychologic distress, and treatment outcome in two groups of TMD patients, one previously subjected to whiplash injury. J. Orofac. Pain. 1998; 12:136–44.

46. Boniver, R. Temporomandibular joint dysfunction in whiplash injuries:association with tinnitus and vertigo. Int. Tinnitus J. 2002; 8:129–31.

47. Bergman, H; Andersson, F; Isberg, A. Incidence of temporomandibular joint changes after whiplash trauma:a prospective study using MR imaging. Am. J. Roentgenol. 1998; 171: 1237–43.

48. McKay, DC; Christensen, LV. Whiplash injuries of the temporomandibular joint in motor vehicle accidents: speculations and facts. J. Oral Rehabil. 1998; 25:731–46.

49. Ferrari, R; Schrader, H; Obelieniene, D. Prevalence of temporomandibular disorders associated with whiplash injury in Lithuania. Oral Surg. Oral Med. Oral Pathol. Oral Radiol. Endod. 1999; 87:653–7.

Chapter 44
Tinnitus and the Masticatory System

Michael Behr

Keypoints

1. Epidemiologic data indicate a frequent association between temporomandibular joint disorders and tinnitus.
2. It is extremely unlikely that tinnitus is Directly caused by a mechanical relationship between the masticatory system and the middle ear.
3. Increased muscle tension of masticatory muscles may cause clonus of the palatine muscle via reflex muscle hypertension.
4. Increased muscle tension of masticatory muscles can influence tinnitus via somatosensory afferents.
5. In certain patients, occlusional appliances have been shown to normalize increased muscle tension and improve tinnitus, even if evidence for their efficacy is limited.

Keywords Tinnitus • Temporomandibular joint • Temporomandibular diseases • Masticatory muscles • Bruxism

Abbreviations

CNS   Central nerve system
DCN   Dorsal cochlear nucleus
TMD   Temporomandibular disorder
TMJ   Temporomandibular joint

M. Behr (✉)
Department of Prosthetic Dentistry, University Medical Center Regensburg, 93042 Regensburg, Germany
e-mail: michael.behr@klinik.uni-regensburg.de

Introduction

Patients with tinnitus frequently complain about temporomandibular disorders (TMD). Otological symptoms in connection with TMD have been widely described in the literature [1–4]. Some studies even reported that TMD treatment can successfully alleviate or cure tinnitus symptoms [5, 6], suggesting a potential causal relationship between TMD and tinnitus.

Disorders of the masticatory system may exert an influence on tinnitus via mechanical connections between the temporomandibular system and the ear or via neuronal influences. This chapter discusses the possible relationship between tinnitus and the masticatory system.

Temporomandibular Joint Disorders and Middle Ear Function

The structures of the middle ear and the temporomandibular joint derive from the first brachial arch. All muscle of the masticatory system and the tensor tympani muscle and the tensor veli palatine muscle are innervated by branches of the trigeminal nerve. In contrast, the M. stapedius, the stapes, the mimic muscles, and the sternocleidomastoid muscle derive from the second branchial arch. These muscles are innervated by the facial nerve.

The ontogenetic development of the masticatory system and the middle ear associates a close anatomical relationship (Fig. 44.1). There is a fibrous connection between the discal apparatus of the temporomandibular joint (TMJ) and the malleus of the middle ear [7, 8]. By this connection, pathologies of the TMJ may theoretically

A.R. Møller et al. (eds.), *Textbook of Tinnitus*,
DOI 10.1007/978-1-60761-145-5_44, © Springer Science+Business Media, LLC 2011

Fig. 44.1 Discomalleolar and sphenomandibular ligament. Cranial and lateral view

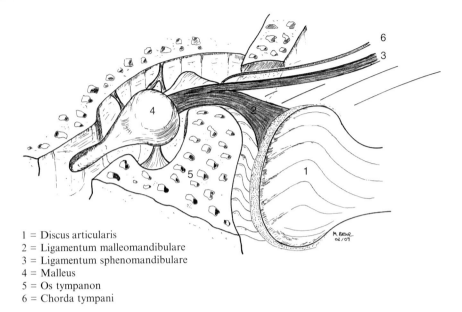

1 = Discus articularis
2 = Ligamentum malleomandibulare
3 = Ligamentum sphenomandibulare
4 = Malleus
5 = Os tympanon
6 = Chorda tympani

cause dysfunction of the middle ear, which in turn could cause tinnitus. However, recent anatomical studies have found no evidence for the hypothesis that traction of the discomalleolar ligament may trigger movement in the middle ear ossicles [7–9]. Also, a possible influence on middle ear ossicles via the sphenomandibular ligament has been discussed, but this may only be relevant in some rare cases of surgical manipulation [8] or traumatic mandibular dislocation [9, 10].

In summary, little evidence exists that an anterior dislocation of the articular disc (internal derangement) causes tinnitus via a mechanical influence on middle ear function, since such symptoms may only be provoked by an extensive protruded dislocation of the mandible.

Masticatory Muscle and Muscles of the Middle Ear

Muscles of the masticatory and the middle ear system (M. tensor veli palatini, M. tensor tympani) are both innervated by the trigeminus nerve. Neuromuscular dysfunction of the masticatory muscles may induce a "reflex hypertonia" of the tensor muscles of the middle ear [11]. The irregular tonus of the tensor veli palatini may result in a dysfunction of the Eustachian tube, which can result in aural congestion and tinnitus [12, 13]

(Fig. 44.2). Even if there are conflicting views about the exact role of the tensor veli palatini, the levator veli palatini, and the tensor tympani muscle in Eustachian tube dysfunction, in the rare cases of tinnitus due to palatinal myoclonus, a potential influence of masticatory muscles should be considered.

Removable occlusal appliances made of resin have been recommended to relax masticatory muscles to eliminate or alleviate hearing symptoms triggered by TMJ disorders. However, up to now, occlusal appliances have not been proven to reduce or eliminate masticatory muscle dysfunction such as bruxism (grinding of the teeth). Nevertheless, some authors believe that a "perfect" reconstruction of the occlusal contacts of mandibular teeth, in association with maxillary teeth, may cure or at least alleviate masticatory muscle spasms [14–16]. Other authors argue that changing the occlusal relationship between the upper and lower jaw is not effective for reducing muscle hyperactivity [17–19]. A review of the *Cochrane Collaboration* concluded "the evidence is insufficient for affirming that the occlusal splint is effective for treating sleep bruxism" [20]. So, it is questionable whether occlusal appliances may have a beneficial influence on dysfunction of the tensor veli palatini or the tensor tympani muscles if there is no evidence for an effect on masticatory muscle function.

However, even if only a little evidence exists that the treatment of masticatory muscle hyperactivity has an

Fig. 44.2 Eustachian tube, middle ear, and temporomandibular joint. View from cranial to medial and from anterior to posterior

1 = Discus articularis
2 = Discomalleolar ligament
3 = Sphenomandibular ligament
4 = Cartiledge Eustachian tube
5 = A. carotis interna
6 = Malleus
7 = Eardrum
8 = M. tensor tympani
9 = M. pterygoideus med.
10 = M. tensor veli palatini
11 = M. dilatator tubae
12 = M. salpinopharyngeus
13 = Palate muscles

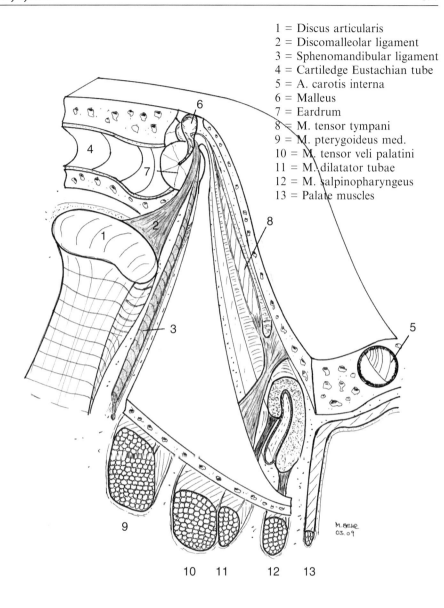

impact on the tensor veli palatini, the use of occlusional appliances should be considered as a potential treatment approach in patients who suffer from tinnitus due to palatinal myoclonus.

Somatosensory Influences on the Central Auditory System

Many individuals can modulate their tinnitus by movements of the head and neck. The contraction of facial mimic muscles [21], as well as also clenching the jaw or moving the head or neck, can cause change in tinnitus. The most common change is an increase or decrease in loudness [22, 23].

Afferent nerves from head and neck muscles, particularly the second cervical nerve and the trigeminal nerve or ganglion, are known to interact with central auditory pathways in the dorsal cochlear nucleus (DCN) (see Chap. 9) [24–31]. Recent studies have attributed the DCN as a key role in the development of tinnitus [30, 31]. The trigeminal input to the DCN may suppress neural activity generated by sounds produced by chewing, self-vocalization, or respiration. Input to the DCN from the pinna area may serve localization of sounds in animals that can move their pinna. It has been hypothesized that the DCN is also involved in movement programs, which orient the head and body toward the source of the perceived sound [27]. In studies on cats, pressure or stretching the head and neck structures evokes inhibitory and excitatory responses in neurons of the DCN with a predominance of inhibitory responses [27]. In this way, somatosensory input to the DCN may modulate excitability in central auditory pathways and it may cause aberrant neuronal activity in central auditory pathways, which may be perceived as tinnitus (see Chap. 10).

If tinnitus can be modulated by manipulation of somatosensory afferents from head and neck structures, dentists may contribute to the treatment of tinnitus. It has been emphasized that the position of the mandible and the hyoid may influence the posture of the head and the cervical spine, or vice versa [32]. Occlusal changes during dental treatment may alter the resting position of the hyoid and the mandible. If the occlusion contacts in the resting position shift the mandible into a protruded, retruded, or laterally displaced

position, a muscular imbalance may occur, not only in the chewing muscles but, also in the muscles of the cervical spine (Fig. 44.3). Thus, imbalance of the occlusal system may result in abnormal somatosensory input to the DCN from the second cervical nerve and the trigeminal, which in turn modulates neuronal activity in other parts of the central auditory pathways. This mechanism has been studied in detail in animal experiments [25] and is assumed to account for the association between head and neck pathologies and tinnitus. However, it is controversial to which extent can occlusal equilibration or the use of occlusal appliances contribute to normalization of masticatory and neck muscle tension [18, 33].

Regarding indications for interventions such as those of occlusal appliances, it should also be considered that temporomandibular dysfunction may have existed for a long time before the start of tinnitus, and the condition may even be congenital. The association between craniofacial anomalies, malocclusion, and TMJ disorders has been widely investigated [34–38]. Despite the conflicting evidence in the literature, at

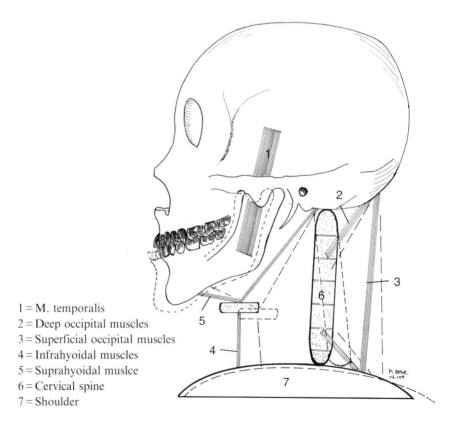

1 = M. temporalis
2 = Deep occipital muscles
3 = Superficial occipital muscles
4 = Infrahyoidal muscles
5 = Suprahyoidal muslce
6 = Cervical spine
7 = Shoulder

Fig. 44.3 Association between the posture of the mandible and the surrounding structures of the hyoid and cervical spine area

least one tendency has been recognized, namely that tenderness of the masticatory muscles may be associated with shorter posterior facial height and a shorter mandible. Increased tenderness of shoulder muscles was found in individuals with larger cranial base angles, reduced mandibular prognathism, and larger inclination and vertical jaw relationship [36]. The tenderness of these muscles may stimulate somatosensory input through the second cervical spinal root and may thus cause or affect tinnitus.

Despite the limited evidence about the exact nature of the association between TMJ disorders and tinnitus, patients who perceive their tinnitus differently by moving their mandible, head, or neck should be examined by a dentist [39]. If a change in the mandibular resting position by dental treatment has a beneficial effect on a patient's tinnitus, occlusal appliances or orthodontic treatment should be considered for alleviating the tinnitus.

References

1. Koskinen J, Paavolainen M, Raivio M, Roschier J (1980) Otological manifestations in temporomandibular joint dysfunction. J Oral Rehabil 7.249 54
2. Ogutcen-Toller M, Juniper RP (1993) The embryologic development of the human lateral pterygoid muscle and its relationships with the temporomandibular joint disc and Meckel's cartilage. J Oral Maxillofac 51:772–8
3. Kuttila S, Kuttila M, Le BY, Alanen P, Suonpaa J (2005) Recurrent tinnitus and associated ear symptoms in adults. Int J Audiol 44:164–70
4. Ramirez LM, Ballesteros LE, Sandoval GP (2008) Topical review: temporomandibular disorders in an integral otic symptom model. Int J Audiol 47:215–27
5. Gelb H, Calderone JP, Gross SM, Kantor ME (1967) The role of the dentist and the otolaryngologist in evaluating temporomandibular joint syndromes. J Prosthet Dent 18:497–503
6. Vernon J, Griest S, Press L (1992) Attributes of tinnitus associated with the temporomandibular joint syndrome. Eur Arch Otorhinolaryngol 249:93–4
7. Komori E, Sugisaki M, Tanabe H, Katoh S (1986) Discomalleolar ligament in the adult human. Cranio 4:299–305
8. Loughner BA, Larkin LH, Mahan PE (1989) Discomalleolar and anterior malleolar ligaments: possible causes of middle ear damage during temporomandibular joint surgery. Oral Surg Oral Med Oral Pathol 68:14–22
9. Sencimen M, Yalcin B, Dogan N, Varol A, Okcu KM, Ozan H, et al (2008) Anatomical and functional aspects of ligaments between the malleus and the temporomandibular joint. Int J Oral Maxillofac Surg 37:943–7
10. Cheynet F, Guyot L, Richard O, Layoun W, Gola R (2003) Discomallear and malleomandibular ligaments: anatomical study and clinical applications. Surg Radiol Anat 25:152–7
11. Arlen H (2009) The otomandibular system. Clinical Management of Head, Neck and TMJ Pain Dysfunction. Philadelphia: WB Saunders and Co, 171–80
12. Malkin DP (1987) The role of TMJ dysfunction in the etiology of middle ear disease. Int J Orthod 25:20–1
13. Zipfel TE, Kaza SR, Greene JS (2000) Middle-ear myoclonus. J Laryngol Otol 114:207–9
14. Ramfjord SP (1961) Bruxism, a clinical and electromyographic study. J Am Dent Assoc 62:21–44
15. Dawson PE (1973) Temporomandibular joint pain-dysfunction problems can be solved. J Prosthet Dent 29:100–12
16. Kerstein RB, Farrell S (1990) Treatment of myofscial pain-dysfunction syndrome with occlusal equilibration. J Prosthet Dent 63:695–700
17. Kardachi BJ, Bailey JO, Ash MM (1978) A comparison of biofeedback and occlusal adjustment on bruxism. J Periodontol 49:367–72
18. Clark GT, Adler RC (1985) A critical evaluation of occlusal therapy: occlusal adjustment procedures. J Am Dent Assoc 110:743–50
19. Turp JC, Komine F, Hugger A (2004) Efficacy of stabilization splints for the management of patients with masticatory muscle pain: a qualitative systematic review. Clin Oral Investig 8:179–95
20. Macedo CR, Silva AB, Machado MA, Saconato H, Prado GF (2007) Occlusal splints for treating sleep bruxism (tooth grinding). Cochrane Database Syst Rev 4:CD005514
21. Yamamoto E, Nishimura H, Iwanaga M (1985) Tinnitus and/or hearing loss elicited by facial mimetic movement. Laryngoscope 95:966–70
22. Levine RA (1999) Somatic (craniocervical) tinnitus and the dorsal cochlear nucleus hypothesis. Am J Otolaryngol 20:351–62
23. Lockwood AH, Salvi RJ, Burkard RF (2002) Tinnitus. N Engl J Med 347:904–10
24. Shore SE, Vass Z, Wys NL, Altschuler RA (2000) Trigeminal ganglion innervates the auditory brainstem. J Comp Neurol 419:271–85
25. Shore S, Zhou J, Koehler S (2007) Neural mechanisms underlying somatic tinnitus. Prog Brain Res 166:107–23
26. Shore SE (2005) Multisensory integration in the dorsal cochlear nucleus: unit responses to acoustic and trigeminal ganglion stimulation. Eur J Neurosci 21:3334–48
27. Kanold PO, Young ED (2001) Proprioceptive information from the pinna provides somatosensory input to cat dorsal cochlear nucleus. J Neurosci 21:7848–58
28. Møller AR (2006) Neural plasticity in tinnitus. Prog Brain Res 157:365–72
29. Kaltenbach JA (2000) Neurophysiologic mechanisms of tinnitus. J Am Acad Audiol 11:125–37
30. Kaltenbach JA (2007) The dorsal cochlear nucleus as a contributor to tinnitus: mechanisms underlying the induction of hyperactivity. Prog Brain Res 166:89–106
31. Kaltenbach JA (2006) The dorsal cochlear nucleus as a participant in the auditory, attentional and emotional components of tinnitus. Hear Res 216–217:224–34
32. Rocabado M (1983) Biomechanical relationship of the cranial, cervical, and hyoid regions. J Craniomandibular Pract 1:61–6

33. Behr M, Stebner K, Kolbeck C, Faltermeier A, Driemel O, Handel G (2007) Outcomes of temporomandibular joint disorder therapy: observations over 13 years. Acta Odontol Scand 65:249–53

34. Winnberg A, Pancherz H, Westesson PL (1988) Head posture and hyo-mandibular function in man. A synchronized electromyographic and videofluorographic study of the open-close-clench cycle. Am J Orthod Dentofacial Orthop 94:393–404

35. Bergamini M, Pierleoni F, Gizdulich A, Bergamini C (2008) Dental occlusion and body posture: a surface EMG study. Cranio 26:25–32

36. Sonnesen L, Bakke M, Solow B (2001) Temporomandibular disorders in relation to craniofacial dimensions, head posture and bite force in children selected for orthodontic treatment. Eur J Orthod 23:179–92

37. Sonnesen L, Kjaer I (2007) Cervical vertebral body fusions in patients with skeletal deep bite. Eur J Orthod 29:464–70

38. Sonnesen L, Kjaer I (2008) Anomalies of the cervical vertebrae in patients with skeletal Class II malocclusion and horizontal maxillary overjet. Am J Orthod Dentofacial Orthop 188:15–20

39. Goodey R (2007) Tinnitus treatment: state of the art. Prog Brain Res 166:237–46

Chapter 45
Introduction

Berthold Langguth

Keypoints

1. Tinnitus is not a single clinical or pathophysiologic entity. There are many forms of tinnitus that differ in their pathophysiology.
2. Exact diagnosis is required in each patient in order to provide the best management of tinnitus.
3. It is especially important to identify those patients who can be treated by specific interventions and those in which tinnitus is a symptom of a severe underlying disease and those patients who require immediate therapeutic action.
4. Exact diagnosis is also of great importance in clinical trials.
5. In the future, new methods such as functional neuroimaging may be found to have additional diagnostic value.

Keywords Tinnitus • Diagnosis • Heterogeneity • Pathophysiology • Diagnostic algorithm

Tinnitus can be experienced as a ringing, roaring, clicking, hissing, or buzzing. Tinnitus can start together with hearing loss but can also occur after neck trauma or during stressful live events. In some individuals, tinnitus is accompanied by insomnia, others have difficulty in concentrating, and some complaint about hyperacusis. Some individuals report that their tinnitus worsens by environmental sound; in others, the same sound may relieve their tinnitus. These clinical observations clearly show that tinnitus is not a single disease entity, but that there are many different forms of tinnitus that are likely to vary in their pathophysiology and in their response to treatment interventions. This, in turn, implies that an exact differential diagnosis is of utmost importance in the management of tinnitus.

This insightful view on tinnitus is not new. Already, more than 200 years ago (coupled with the systematic application of specific therapeutic interventions), diagnostic criteria for tinnitus were developed. The goal at that time was to identify patients who responded to galvanism, which was the then available therapy (Fig. 45.1, [1]).

It is assumed that the exact pathophysiological changes in an individual determine the efficacy of specific causally oriented therapies. In contrast, the mechanisms involved in generating the sensation of a sound when no sound reaches the ear may be less relevant for therapeutic methods that aim at habituation to the sound, such as tinnitus retraining therapy or cognitive behavior therapy. Hence, the increasing popularity of these methods in the last several decades has shifted the diagnostic focus. Clinical characteristics of the sound a person perceives with a potential reflection of its generating mechanism, such as sound characteristics, laterality, or duration, have been considered as less important. Instead, the interest has focused on detailed information about how the tinnitus impairs an individual's life and its psychosocial consequences. Fully acknowledging the relevance of the latter information for the management of an individual with tinnitus, ignoring the pathophysiologic hetereogenity would be a mistake and can even be dangerous. First, those subforms of tinnitus, which can be treated causally [2] or highly efficiently [3] with specific interventions, may not be identified. Second, tinnitus can be

B. Langguth (✉)
Department of Psychiatry and Psychotherapy, University of Regensburg, Universitätsstraße 84, 93053 Regensburg, Germany
and
Interdisciplinary Tinnitus Clinic, University of Regensburg, Universitätsstraße 84, 93053 Regensburg, Germany
e-mail: Berthold.Langguth@medbo.de

A.R. Møller et al. (eds.), *Textbook of Tinnitus*,
DOI 10.1007/978-1-60761-145-5_45, © Springer Science+Business Media, LLC 2011

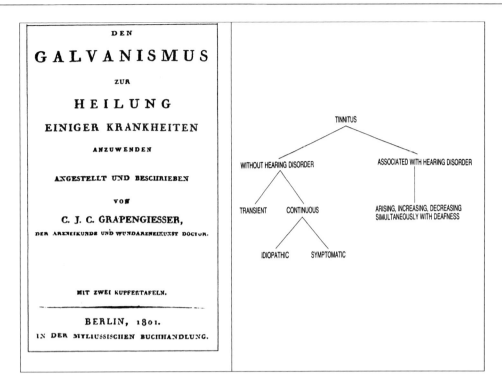

Fig. 45.1 Diagnostic algorithm from 1801 for identifying those tinnitus patients, who responded better to galvanism [1]

the first symptom of potentially dangerous diseases, some of which may even become life threatening if left undiagnosed and untreated (e.g., carotid dissection and vestibular schwannoma). Therefore, each patient with tinnitus requires a careful and systematic diagnostic approach.

In this section (Part. III), a diagnostic algorithm (Chap. 46) will first be presented, which provides guidance for systematic diagnosis of clinically relevant and specific forms of tinnitus. The diagnostic steps, which are recommended in all patients, include a detailed case history (Chap. 47) and otological (Chap. 48) and audiological examinations (Chap. 49). Depending on the findings in these primary diagnostic procedures, further diagnostic steps for exactly diagnosing specific subforms of tinnitus may or may not be required. Indications for further diagnostic steps are, for example, acute tinnitus, pulsatile tinnitus, or severe general impairment of the individual.

Chapter 46, "Diagnostic Algorithm," will give a synoptic overview about the diagnostic process and provide orientation of which diagnostic procedures are indicated in which case. These procedures are then described in detail in Chaps. (49) Neurotologic

Assessment, (50) Neurologic Examination, (52) Diagnosis of Somatosensory Tinnitus, (53) TMJ Assessment, and (54) Psychological/Psychiatric Assessment. Parts II (causes of tinnitus) and IV (clinical characteristics of the different forms of tinnitus) concern these specific forms of tinnitus and their management. It should be noted that the proposed diagnostic approach refers mainly to the identification of currently known subforms of tinnitus with a well-understood pathophysiologic mechanism that also holds therapeutic relevance, such as tinnitus together with sudden hearing loss, or pulsatile tinnitus associated with a neurovascular conflict.

However, the frequently observed high variability in treatment outcome in clinical trials [4, 5] suggests the existence of further subforms of tinnitus, the specific clinical characteristics of which we do not yet know and for which our knowledge of the exact pathophysiologic underpinnings is still incomplete. This, in turn, may result in a vicious cycle: it is difficult to identify new promising treatments if we do not know according to which criteria tinnitus patients should be stratified. However, as long as no effective treatments are available, it is difficult to identify clinically relevant criteria for stratification. Different strategies may help overcome this problem. First, standardized assessment of clinical characteristics in clinical trials will provide the opportunity to identify clinical characteristics that predict responses to specific interventions. For this purpose, an effort has been made at the TRI meeting in Regensburg 2007 to arrive at a consensus about such a standard (http://www.tinnitusresearch.org; [6]). Also, the advent of new techniques such as functional neuroimaging or transcranial magnetic stimulation has shown some promise for better diagnosis of the different forms of tinnitus. Recent findings using these techniques suggest that clinical criteria such as tinnitus duration [7] or sound characteristics (pure tone vs. narrow band noise [8]) may have specific pathophysiologic reverberations and therefore seem to be relevant criteria for stratifying patients with tinnitus.

References

1. Grapengiesser CJC Versuche, den Galvanismus zur Heilung einiger Krankheiten anzuwenden Berlin: Myliussische Buchhandlung; 1801.
2. Van de Heyning P, K Vermeire, M Diebl et al (2008) Incapacitating unilateral tinnitus in single-sided deafness treated by cochlear implantation. Ann Otol Rhinol Laryngol. 1179:645–52.
3. Mardini MK (1987) Ear-clicking "tinnitus" responding to carbamazepine. N Engl J Med. 317.24:1542.
4. Møller AR (1997) A double-blind placebo-controlled trial of baclofen in the treatment of tinnitus. Am J Otol. 18.2: 268–9.
5. Langguth B, M Landgrebe, G Hajak et al (2008) Tinnitus and transcranial magnetic stimulation. Semin Hear. 29.3:288–99.
6. Langguth B, R Goodey, A Azevedo et al (2006) Consensus for tinnitus patient assessment and treatment outcome measurement: Tinnitus Research Initiative Meeting, Regensburg. Prog Brain Res. 166:525–36.
7. Schlee W, T Hartmann, B Langguth et al (2009) Abnormal resting-state cortical coupling in chronic tinnitus. BMC Neurosci. 10.11.
8. De Ridder D, E van der Loo, K Van der Kelen et al (2007) Do tonic and burst TMS modulate the lemniscal and extralemniscal system differentially? Int J Med Sci. 4.5:242–6.

Chapter 46
Algorithm for the Diagnostic and Therapeutic Management of Tinnitus

Berthold Langguth, Ebergard Biesinger, Luca Del Bo, Dirk De Ridder, Ron Goodey, Carlos Herraiz, Tobias Kleinjung, Miguel J.A. Lainez, Michael Landgrebe, Michel Paolino, Benjamin Questier, Tanit G. Sanchez, and Grant D. Searchfield

Keypoints

1. Tinnitus can be a symptom of a wide range of different underlying pathologies and accompanied by many different comorbidities, indicating the need for comprehensive multidisciplinary diagnostic assessment.
2. Basic diagnostics should include a detailed case history, assessment of tinnitus severity, clinical ear examination, and audiological measurement of hearing function. For a considerable number of patients, these first diagnostic steps in combination with counseling will be sufficient.
3. Further diagnostic steps are indicated if the findings of basic diagnostics point to acute tinnitus onset, a potentially dangerous underlying condition (e.g., carotid dissection), a possible causal treatment option, or relevant subjective impairment.
4. Further diagnostic management should be guided by clinical features. There is increasing evidence that phenomenologic and etiologic aspects determine the pathophysiology and the clinical course of tinnitus. In a hierarchical diagnostic algorithm, the first differentiation should be between pulsatile vs. non-pulsatile tinnitus. In case of non-pulsatile tinnitus, differentiation between acute tinnitus with hearing loss, paroxysmal tinnitus, and chronic tinnitus is recommended. Further diagnostic procedures of constant non-pulsatile tinnitus will depend on concomitant symptoms and etiological conditions.
5. All diagnostic and therapeutic steps should be accompanied by empathic and insightful counseling.
6. The ultimate treatment goal is the complete relief from tinnitus. If causally oriented treatment options are available, these should be preferred. However, in many cases, only symptomatic therapies can be offered, and then the treatment goal in clinical practice will be defined as the best possible reduction of unpleasant hearing sensations and accompanying symptoms, that is, to improve quality of life.

Keywords Tinnitus • Pathology • Etiology • Comorbidity • Symptom • Diagnosis • Therapy

Abbreviations

AVM	Arterio-venous malformation
ABR	Auditory brainstem responses
BIH	Benign intracranial hypertension
CBT	Cognitive behavioral therapy
CHQ	Case history questionnaire
CSF	Cerebrospinal fluid
CT	Computer tomography
ECoG	Electrocochleography
EEG	Electroencephalography
FDA	US Food and Drug Administration
LP	Lumbar puncture
MRI	Magnetic resonance imaging
MVC	Microvascular compression
OAE	Otoacoustic emissions
PTSD	Posttraumatic stress disorder
SOL	Space occupying lesion
THI	Tinnitus handicap inventory
TMJ	Temporomandibular joint

B. Langguth (✉)
Department of Psychiatry and Psychotherapy, University of Regensburg, Universitätsstraße 84, 93053 Regensburg, Germany
and
Interdisciplinary Tinnitus Clinic, University of Regensburg, Regensburg, Germany
e-mail: Berthold.Langguth@medbo.de

A.R. Møller et al. (eds.), *Textbook of Tinnitus*,
DOI 10.1007/978-1-60761-145-5_46, © Springer Science+Business Media, LLC 2011

TMS	Transcranial magnetic stimulation
tDCS	Transcranial direct current stimulation
TRT	Tinnitus retraining therapy
TQ	Tinnitus questionnaire
VEMP	Vestibular evoked myogenic potentials

Introduction

Diagnostic and therapeutic management of tinnitus is challenging for a variety of reasons. Multiple etiologies can result in the same phantom sound percept. Even though hearing disorders are the most important risk factors for the development of tinnitus, other diseases such as brain tumors, neck injuries, temporomandibular dysfunction, or emotional disorders generally covered by other disciplines (e.g., neurology, psychiatry, orthopaedics, dentistry, or neurosurgery) can be critically involved in the etiology or continuation of tinnitus. Therefore, the requirements of comprehensive tinnitus diagnosis and treatment can only be met by an integrated multidisciplinary approach.

Although tinnitus itself is not dangerous, it can be the first sign of potentially dangerous diseases that can even become life threatening if left undiagnosed and untreated. Furthermore, tinnitus by itself may become life threatening if accompanied by suicidal tendencies.

The authors[1] of this chapter developed an algorithm in order to provide guidance for diagnosis and treatment of tinnitus based on currently available evidence (see Fig. 46.1).[2] In particular, this algorithm is intended to assist clinicians who occasionally see tinnitus patients and may not be fully aware of the complexity of

the condition. Subgroups of tinnitus require specific management or can benefit from specific treatment. Even if some of these conditions are relatively rare, considering the possibility of their occurrence is warranted because of the availability of specific treatment options.

A stepwise decision-tree approach for tinnitus management is proposed, starting with basic diagnostic steps, which are recommended in all patients [1] (Fig. 46.1, white boxes), and includes history taking for associated symptoms (Fig. 46.1, red boxes). Depending on the findings of the first step, further diagnostic or therapeutic measures may or may not be necessary (see also Table 46.1). The second step consists of tailored technical tests (Fig. 46.1, yellow boxes) for the diagnosis of specific tinnitus-related disorders (blue boxes), leading to a causal and therapeutic management. For cases in which a causally oriented treatment is not available, not possible, or not sufficiently successful, symptomatic treatment options can be offered (Fig. 46.1, grey boxes). It is emphasized that the entire diagnostic workup should be accompanied by empathic and insightful counseling (Chap. 70).

More detailed descriptions of the different diagnostic and therapeutic steps can be found in the specific book chapters in Part II (Causes of Tinnitus), Part III (Differential Diagnosis of Tinnitus), and Part IV (Clinical Characteristics of Different Forms of Tinnitus).

Basic Diagnostic Assessment

This first step, to be performed in every patient and not requiring any sophisticated instrumentation, will reveal enough clinical information about tinnitus, hearing, and comorbidities to decide whether further diagnostic steps are needed – if yes, the diagnostic assessment indicates which of them would be most appropriate. These basic diagnostics should include an in-depth case history including assessment of tinnitus severity (using screening tools or questionnaires) (for details see Chap. 47); clinical ear examination (for details, see Chap. 48); and audiological measurement [1] (for details, see Chap. 49.

As previously discussed, for a considerable number of patients, these first diagnostic steps in combination with counseling will be sufficient (see Table 46.1). For example, further diagnostic steps are not necessary if there is no hint of a dangerous underlying disease and

---

[1]The authors are clinicians from different specialties who all have extensive experience in the management of tinnitus patients. The algorithm for the diagnostic and therapeutic management of tinnitus patients has been developed in the framework of the Tinnitus Research Initiative (http://www.tinnitusresearch.org). In order to avoid bias due to specific disciplines or specific health care systems, the group was multidisciplinary (consisting of otolaryngologists, audiologists, neurologists, psychiatrists, psychotherapists, and a neurosurgeon) and multinational (Belgium, Brazil, France, Germany, Italy, New Zealand, and Spain).

[2]In the original powerpoint version of the flowchart (available at http://www.tinnitusresearch.org), a mouse click on any item opens a separate slide, which provides more detailed additional information. In order to avoid redundancy, only the synopsis is presented in this chapter.

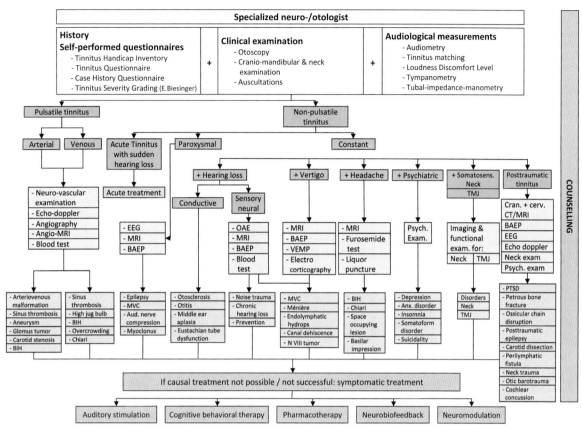

Fig. 46.1 Diagnostic and therapeutic algorithm. In the original powerpoint version of the flowchart (available at http://www.tinnitus-research.org), a mouse click on any item of the flowchart opens a separate slide, which provides more detailed additional information

Table 46.1 Further diagnostic or therapeutic measures that may or may not be necessary

Indications for further detailed diagnostic steps	Indications for immediate therapeutic management
Subjective impairment by tinnitus	Tinnitus with suicidality or with severe impairment
Heart synchronous pulsatile tinnitus	Acute tinnitus with sudden hearing loss
Tinnitus with hearing loss of unknown etiology	
Posttraumatic tinnitus	

Following basic assessment further diagnostic and therapeutic procedures may or may not be necessary. Here important indications for further diagnostic steps and immediate treatment are summarized

if the patient is not impaired by the tinnitus. However, the basic assessment will also identify those cases where further diagnostic and/or therapeutic steps are required and those where further steps should be performed immediately.

An example for a life-threatening emergency is concomitant suicidal tendencies, which require immediate therapeutic action (see Chap. 54). Other conditions, such as acute tinnitus in combination with sudden hearing loss of recent onset, should also be treated as soon as possible (see Chap. 56). In conditions where a severe underlying disease cannot be excluded or when a patient is bothered by his tinnitus, further diagnostic steps are clearly indicated.

Further diagnostic procedures should be guided by clinical features (Fig. 46.1, red boxes). In a hierarchical diagnostic algorithm, the first differentiation should be between pulsatile vs. non-pulsatile tinnitus. This differentiation acknowledges the fundamental pathophysiological difference between these two forms of tinnitus.

Pulsatile Tinnitus

It is important to note that pulsatile refers to heart synchronous or respiration synchronous (venous hum) pulsatile tinnitus. Pulsatile tinnitus with a rhythm different from the heart rate or respiration rate should be classified here as pseudopulsatile or non-pulsatile tinnitus (see Chap. 59). Further diagnostic assessment of heart synchronous pulsatile tinnitus requires a neurovascular examination (yellow box). Diseases such as arteriovenous malformation, sinus venous thrombosis, benign intracranial hypertension, or high jugular bulb may be identified as potential causes of pulsatile tinnitus. A detailed description of the diagnostic management of pulsatile tinnitus is found in the chapter on pulsatile tinnitus.

Non-pulsatile Tinnitus

Non-pulsatile tinnitus is much more common than pulsatile tinnitus and requires further differentiation according to chronicity, concomitant symptoms, and etiologic factors. As a first step, a differentiation between acute tinnitus with sudden hearing loss, paroxysmal tinnitus, and chronic tinnitus can be useful. In case of acute tinnitus accompanied by sudden hearing loss, diagnostic and therapeutic procedures should not be postponed in order to identify possible causes for the hearing loss and start appropriate treatment. This is described in detail in the chapter on sudden hearing loss and tinnitus.

Paroxysmal or intermitent tinnitus can be a symptom of auditory nerve compression, superior canal dehiscence syndrome, Ménière's disease, palatal myoclonus, or even epilepsy (blue boxes). For a differential diagnosis, magnetic resonance imaging (MRI), auditory-evoked potentials, and electroencephalography (EEG) are indicated (yellow boxes) (for more details, see Chap. 58).

Further diagnostic procedures of constant non-pulsatile tinnitus will depend on concomitant symptoms and etiological conditions (Fig. 46.1, red boxes). Constant non-pulsatile tinnitus can be accompanied by conductive or sensorineural hearing loss. Conductive hearing loss can be caused by otosclerosis, different forms of otitis, or Eustachian tube dysfunction. More information about tinnitus with conductive hearing loss is given in Chap. 34.

In case of sensorineural hearing loss, further diagnostic procedures are indicated for identifying the exact etiology. These can include magnetic resonance imaging (MRI) and auditory brainstem responses (ABR) (e.g., for excluding vestibular schwannoma) and also otoacoustic emissions for assessment of outer hair cell function (detailed description in Chaps. 35 and 36).

Diagnostic assessment and therapeutic management of tinnitus occurring together with vertigo is indicative of specific pathologies such as Ménière's disease, superior canal dehiscence, or damage to the vestibulocochlear system. More details are found in Chaps. 36, 38–40, 60, and 84.

If tinnitus presents with associated headache, increased intracranial pressure has to be excluded. Potential underlying pathologies such as space occupying lesions (SOL), benign intracranial hypertension (BIH), disorders of cerebrospinal fluid (CSF) circulation, or craniocervical anomalies can be diagnosed by MRI. In specific cases, lumbar puncture and furosemide tests may help determine whether reduced CSF pressure also alleviates tinnitus (more details are found in Chap. 61).

The co-occurrence of depression, anxiety, and insomnia with severe tinnitus has been frequently described. Immediate action is required when a patient reports acute suicidal thoughts. A detailed explanation of diagnostic procedures in case of psychiatric comorbidity is provided in Chap. 58, 63–65.

When tinnitus is associated with neck or temporomandibular dysfunction or pain, a more detailed examination of these systems should be considered. Radiologic tests are indicated if structural alterations are suspected, whereas functional impairments can be best detected by physical examination performed by experienced dentists and physiotherapists. More details are presented in Chap. 43, 44, 52, 53, and 95.

Specific diagnostic tests are indicated if tinnitus begins or worsens within 3 months after a traumatic event. It is important to note that a delay of several weeks between trauma and tinnitus onset does not exclude a potential etiologic relationship. Traumatic events may cause tinnitus in different ways. The indication for further diagnostic procedures depends on the trauma mechanism. In particular, noise, ear, head, neck, and even emotional trauma should be considered. In case of posttraumatic pulsatile tinnitus, immediate diagnostic workup for vascular pathologies (especially carotid dissection) is mandatory. A detailed description of pathologies, which can occur as a consequence of trauma and which may be involved in the generation of tinnitus, is given in Chap. 66. A separate chapter is devoted to blast injuries (Chap. 67) since tinnitus has become one of the most relevant warfare-related health problems in the last years. Blast injuries are a particular diagnostic challenge since the tinnitus-inducing mechanisms may include noise, ear, head, neck, and emotional trauma.

Hyperacusis and phonophobia occur frequently together with tinnitus and require specific management, which is described in detail in Chaps. 3 and 4.

Symptomatic Treatment

Symptomatic treatment should be considered in every patient who feels impaired by his tinnitus if specific causally oriented treatments are not available, not sufficiently effective, or not indicated for any other reason. Cognitive behavioral therapy (CBT) (see Chap. 71) and auditory stimulation with counseling are the most established treatment options. Auditory stimulation can be essentially differentiated in the use of sound for masking or partially masking tinnitus (see Chaps. 74 and 75) and in attempts to compensate for hearing deficits, for example, by hearing aids (see Chaps. 74, 76, and 77). Also, specific forms of sound stimulation with a frequency composition according to the individual audiogram have been proposed (see Chap. 75). Tinnitus retraining therapy (TRT), a specific combination of auditory stimulation and counseling, is widely used and described in Chap. 73.

Pharmacotherapeutic options for the treatment of tinnitus are limited. However, even if there is currently no drug, which is approved by the US Food and Drug Administration (FDA) for the treatment of tinnitus, there are some promising results from clinical studies indicating beneficial effects of specific drugs for subgroups of patients (Chap. 78). Neuromodulatory approaches have been proposed very recently. Most evidence is available for transcranial magnetic stimulation (TMS); neurobiofeedback, transcranial direct current stimulation (tDCS), cutaneous stimulation, and cortical electrical stimulation have also demonstrated promising results. A description of how these techniques are performed and which results have been obtained is given in the respective Chaps. 86, 88–90.

In summary, a wide range of different pathologies can underlie tinnitus. The diagnostic challenge can best be met by a stepwise approach consisting of basic assessment procedures followed by more detailed diagnostic tests in selected patients. Here, important indications for further diagnostic steps and immediate treatment are summarized. If these diagnostic procedures do not reveal causally oriented treatment options or if results from such therapies are not satisfying, the available symptomatic treatment possibilities should be considered. It should also be mentioned that this algorithm is based on currently available knowledge and is expected to evolve and be refined with time and criticism.

Reference

1. Langguth, B., Goodey, R., Azevedo, A., Bjorne, A., Cacace, A., Crocetti, A., et al. (2007) Consensus for tinnitus patient assessment and treatment outcome measurement: Tinnitus Research Initiative Meeting, Regensburg, July 2006. Prog. Brain Res., 166: p. 525–36.

Chapter 47
History and Questionnaires

Berthold Langguth, Grant D. Searchfield, Eberhard Biesinger, and Karoline V. Greimel

Keypoints

1. A detailed case history is required in all tinnitus patients in order to obtain the necessary information for deciding about the therapeutic management.
2. Qualitative data can be best obtained by case history questionnaires or a structured interview.
3. A case history should contain information about the history and descriptive characteristics of the tinnitus, about specific behavioral, social, interpersonal, and emotional consequences of tinnitus, about factors that may either exacerbate or reduce tinnitus severity, about previous tinnitus treatments, and about relevant comorbidities.
4. Quantitative assessment of tinnitus severity is relevant for both clinical management and research applications.
5. Various validated questionnaires are available for quantifying tinnitus distress, disability, or handicap.
6. The selection of the questionnaire should be based not only on purpose (What should be assessed?) but also on psychometric data of the questionnaire and the availability of the questionnaire in a specific language.
7. Numeric rating scales and visual analogue scales are easy applicable tools for quantifying different aspects of tinnitus (such as loudness or annoyance).

B. Langguth (✉)
Department of Psychiatry and Psychotherapy, University of Regensburg, Universitätsstraße 84, 93053, Regensburg, Germany
and
Interdisciplinary Tinnitus Clinic, University of Regensburg, Regensburg, Germany
e-mail: Berthold.Langguth@medbo.de

Keywords Tinnitus • Case history • Questionnaire • Structured interview • Quantitative assessment • Clinical management • research applications • Visual analogue scales

Introduction

Tinnitus has many forms and many characteristics. However, tinnitus is not readily apparent to others, and currently no objective procedures are yet established for diagnosis of tinnitus. The assessment of the perceptual aspects of tinnitus is difficult. Only by listening to the patient can one find out whether a patient has tinnitus and what form of tinnitus he/she has. The case history is of high importance for correct diagnosis in all areas of medicine; this is especially true for tinnitus, since it is fundamentally a self-report phenomenon. Moreover, the subjective nature of tinnitus is a challenge not only in the clinical management of the individual with tinnitus but also for research applications.

Therefore, in addition to an otologic (see Chap. 48) and audiologic assessment (see Chap. 49), a detailed case history is required in all tinnitus patients in order to obtain the necessary information for deciding about the therapeutic management (see Chap. 46). In many patients, a comprehensive diagnostic assessment including a detailed case history can be sufficient for tinnitus management. If a severe disorder (e.g., tumor or carotid dissection) can be excluded and the tinnitus is not perceived as a problem, no treatment is necessary. In all other cases, the detailed case history represents the first therapeutic step, since the patients can make their experience known, they see that their complaints are taken seriously and that the clinician is competent, caring, and understands the effects of tinnitus.

A.R. Møller et al. (eds.), *Textbook of Tinnitus*,
DOI 10.1007/978-1-60761-145-5_47, © Springer Science+Business Media, LLC 2011

For the clinical management of the individual patient information about the perceptual characteristics of tinnitus (e.g., pulsatile or non pulsatile), its time course (e.g., recent onset or chronic), influencing factors (e.g., reduction by environmental sound), and associated symptoms (e.g., reduced sound tolerance) are important. These qualitative data can be best obtained by case history questionnaires or a structured interview.

Loudness of tinnitus can be evaluated quantitatively either by rating or by matching methods (see Chap. 49). In addition to details about the tinnitus percept, information about the perceived severity and the impact on an individual's life also have to be assessed. Personality, comorbidities, or environmental circumstances contribute more to tinnitus-related distress, impairment, disability, and handicap than the perceptual characteristics of tinnitus [1, 2]. Therefore, the evaluation of tinnitus consequences on a person's life needs to be multidimensional, taking into account psychological and social factors.

Screening tools allow an estimation of tinnitus severity based on a few questions, whereas for quantitative assessment of tinnitus severity, many psychometrically validated questionnaires are available. These questionnaires are helpful tools for quantifying disabling and handicapping effects of tinnitus, providing insight into how the tinnitus sensation generates a disability at a personal level and a handicap on the societal level. Responses on these questionnaires can be summed resulting in a total score or subscale scores. Based on the score, the tinnitus severity of an individual patient can be determined (e.g., in low, medium, moderate, or severe).

If a patient is moderately or severely impaired, additional assessment by a psychologist or a psychiatrist is frequently necessary. Psychological and psychiatric assessment involves the integration of information from multiple sources and tools, including the clinical interview, rating scales, questionnaires, and the observation of the patient's behavior during the interview. It is not only *what* the patients say but also *how* they say it that is of relevance. Sometimes, interviews with significant others or reports from previous therapists or physicians provide further important information.

The clinician also needs to be aware that when people complain about tinnitus, other problems may be contributing to any negative emotional state. For example, a coexistent hearing impairment or hyperacusis, balance problems, pain, anxiety, or depression may contribute to the person's difficulties. Daily stressors or major life events may also have an impact on the person's ability to cope with the tinnitus, and patients may attribute their feelings of depression and anxiety incorrectly to the tinnitus. An aim of the initial assessment may also be to disentangle causal connections between tinnitus distress, other stressors, and negative emotional states.

Another important area of investigation concerns the risk of suicide. Rather than avoiding asking questions about suicide, the clinician should address this issue directly. Patients may consider suicide as a means to escape from tinnitus or it may be concurrent to a depressive disorder (for more detailed information see Chap. 54). If results indicate the potential for self-harm, the clinician should manage for this or refer the patient to another specialist.

In addition to clinical applications, quantitative assessment by tinnitus questionnaires is an important tool for all kinds of different research applications.

This chapter reviews methods for obtaining qualitative and quantitative information about a condition, which is purely subjective in its nature, namely a patient's tinnitus and its disabling and handicapping effects. It is our intent to provide a useful and practical reference for both clinicians and researchers seeking information about the availability of different methods. Also, the limitations of the different methods will be discussed in order to allow the readers to select the most appropriate method for their specific clinical or research application (see Table 47.1).

Case History

A detailed history and primary source of descriptive data of the patient's tinnitus or tinnitus-related conditions can be obtained through the initial intake, either

Table 47.1 Questions to consider when performing an assessment

(1) *What do I want to know?* > Kind of information.
   (e.g., tinnitus characteristics, tinnitus related impairments, comorbidity)
(2) *Why do I want it to know?* > Reason for evaluation.
   (e.g., for screening, treatment planning, measuring treatment outcome)
(3) *How can I get the information?* > Choice of appropriate assessment tools.
   (e.g., interview, rating scales, questionnaires, protocols)

by a questionnaire or by structured interviews. The goal of the intake interview is to arrive at a thorough understanding of the nature of the tinnitus by exploring a broad range of inquiry, including causal, descriptive, and diagnostic variables. This information, together with otologic and audiological assessment, is the basis for further diagnostic and therapeutic management. In detail, the following areas should be explored comprehensively:

(1) The history and descriptive characteristics of the tinnitus;
(2) Specific behavioral, social, interpersonal, and emotional consequences of tinnitus;
(3) Factors that may either exacerbate or reduce tinnitus severity;
(4) Previous tinnitus treatments;
(5) Relevant comorbidities.

Many practitioners prefer questionnaires. Case history questionnaires offer advantages of standardized questions to provide reliable and complete information; furthermore, they require less clinician time than interviews. Detailed patient information can be especially important in medicolegal cases.

Several case history questionnaires have been published [3–5], but many clinicians and researchers have developed their own questionnaires in which they include those questions that they consider important and relevant. In the context of a consensus workshop on tinnitus assessment in Regensburg in July 2006, an "items list" for tinnitus case history questionnaires (see Table 47.2) has been compiled including items that are common to most questionnaires in current use and are considered important by experts in the field. This list consists of 14 essential (level A) items and 21 highly desirable (level B) items. Also, a case history questionnaire has been developed, which can be used as an example of how these items might be expressed (Tinnitus Sample Case History Questionnaire (TSCHQ), available in English, French, Spanish, Italian, German, Portuguese, Flemish, and Czech languages at http://www.tinnitusresearch.org [4]).

Depending on their individual background, some clinicians will consider additional items as relevant (e.g., a clinician with physiotherapeutic experience will be interested in more detailed information about postural complaints). The item list should therefore only be considered as a core list to which individual specializations should be added. In the following description, we want to give some examples about the relevance of the proposed items for further diagnostic or

Table 47.2 "Items list" for tinnitus case history questionnaires [4]

Items are ordered according to their level of significance: **Category "A" (= essential) in bold type.**

Background
1. **Age.**
2. **Gender.**
3. Handedness.
4. **Family history of tinnitus (parent, sibling, children).**

Tinnitus history
5. **Initial onset. Time?**
6. **Initial onset. Mode? Gradual or abrupt?**
7. Initial onset. Associated events? Hearing change, Acoustic trauma, Otitis media,
   Head trauma, Whiplash, Dental Treatment, Stress, Other.
8. **Pattern. Steady? Pulsatile? Other?**
9. **Site. Right ear? Left ear? Both ears? (symmetrical?) Inside head?**
10. Intermittent or constant?
11. Fluctuant or non-fluctuant?
12. **Loudness. Scale 1-100. At worst & at best?**
13. Quality. Own words/Give a list of choices.
14. Pure tone or Noise? Uncertain/polyphonic?
15. Pitch. Very high? High? Medium? Low?
16. **Percentage of awake time aware of tinnitus?**
17. Percentage of awake time annoyed by tinnitus?
18. Previous tinnitus treatments (no, some, many)?

Modifying influences
19. **Natural masking? Music, everyday sounds, other sounds?**
20. Aggravated by loud noise?
21. **Altered by head and neck movement or touching of head or upper limbs (specification of the respective movements)?**
22. Daytime nap. Worse? Better? No effect?
23. Effect of nocturnal sleep on daytime tinnitus?
24. Effect of stress?
25. Effect of medications? Which?

Related conditions
26. **Hearing impairment?**
27. **Hearing aids (No, left ear, right ear, both ears; effect on tinnitus)?**
28. **Noise annoyance or intolerance?**
29. Noise induced pain?
30. Headaches?
31. Vertigo/dizziness?
32. Temporomandibular disorder?
33. Neck pain?
34. Other pain syndromes?
35. Under treatment for psychiatric problems?

therapeutic procedures. A comprehensive description of the clinical characteristics of the different forms of tinnitus is found in Part V.

Demographic data, such as age, are of relevance since the causes of tinnitus are different in younger and older people. In elderly people, tinnitus is frequently associated with presbycusis [6]; other causal factors such as noise exposure may be more prominent in younger patients [7]. A positive family history of tinnitus complaints can point to a genetic form of hearing loss as an underlying disorder. There is also some suggestion that genetic factors may play a role for individual susceptibility to tinnitus [8] (see Chap. 7).

The duration of tinnitus is of high relevance for further diagnostic and therapeutic management. Whereas acute tinnitus, especially with abrupt onset, may be a sign of an acute dangerous disease, this is only very rarely the case in chronic tinnitus. Also, acute tinnitus requires an entirely different therapeutic management than chronic tinnitus. The circumstances under which tinnitus started are also important (e.g., onset of tinnitus related to neck trauma needs a different diagnostic work-up than tinnitus that started during a stressful live event).

Concerning the sound characteristics that patients report, the differentiation between pulsatile and non-pulsatile tinnitus is of greatest importance. In patients who describe pulsatile sounds, particularly if synchronous with the heartbeat, vascular origin should be suspected. Pulsatile tinnitus requires specific diagnostic procedures (see Chap. 46). Low-pitched tinnitus with intermittent occurrence may be a cue for the diagnosis of Ménière's disease. Neurophysiologic differences have been suggested for tinnitus resembling "a pure tone" and "noise," and response to specific therapeutic procedures may depend on this distinction [9, 10].

Tinnitus loudness can be assessed with numeric rating scales or visual analogue scales and gives an estimate of the subjectively perceived loudness of the patient's tinnitus. The percentage of time patients are aware of their tinnitus varies enormously between "sometimes in quiet environments" and "always." Also, there is a difference between the time patients are aware and the time patients are annoyed by their tinnitus. These factors are important for determining how intrusive the tinnitus may be in a specific patient.

Factors that improve or worsen tinnitus can be important predictors for treatment success (e.g., use of a sound generator if environmental sounds reduce tinnitus). Determination of therapies that have been trialed, successfully or not, can also provide useful information as to a future treatment choice. When therapies in the past have failed, it should be asked exactly how the therapy had been performed. Possible reasons for failing could be an inadequate performance or insufficient duration of a given treatment.

There are several health disorders, which are frequently associated with tinnitus, such as hearing loss, hyperacusis, neck or temporomandibular joint disorders, vertigo, insomnia, headache, anxiety, or depression. These comorbidities may be a cause or a consequence of tinnitus. In all cases, the co-occurrence of these disorders is of relevance for the therapeutic management. Irrespective of whether there is a causal relationship or not, successful treatment of tinnitus comorbidities can improve the patient's quality of life enormously. This, in turn, may also improve the patient's ability to cope with tinnitus, even if perceptual characteristics remain largely unchanged (see chapters in Part V for more details).

Although case history questionnaires are useful tools for obtaining information, they should not replace a thorough clinical intake interview. However, the use of a case history questionnaire can make the intake interview more efficient by providing an opportunity to discuss relevant items in detail. Patients should be encouraged to clarify questions when they are uncertain how to answer. The discussion allows patients to also describe in their own words aspects of special importance to them. The discussion of the different items helps establish rapport between the clinician and the patient. In this context, it is always helpful to ask patients what bothers them the most about their tinnitus. This varies from patient to patient and has implications for the therapeutic management. If, for example, a patient suffers mainly from the lack of control, this can be addressed by cognitive–behavioral therapy; if the main complaint is difficulty in sleeping, the treatment of the sleeping problem should also be the main focus. Furthermore, the impact of tinnitus on the person's work, sleep (falling asleep and staying asleep), participation in enjoyable activities, social interaction (with friends, family, and partner), and the general lifestyle has to be examined. Reactions to tinnitus can be very different, and it is the patient's reaction to tinnitus that causes problems rather than the sound by itself. If this message reaches the patient during the intake interview, a very important first step toward treatment has been achieved.

Quantitative Assessment of Tinnitus

Many people with tinnitus are neither bothered nor concerned about their tinnitus. There is also a group of patients who see a physician only because they are concerned that their tinnitus may be a sign of a serious ear or brain disease. Apart from those, all other people with tinnitus who seek medical attention are to some extent bothered by their tinnitus. However, there is a large variability in distress, ranging from those who have learned to cope but would welcome some relief from the sound, to those who have severe problems with tinnitus in their daily lives. It has been repeatedly shown that the loudness or the pitch of the tinnitus sensation does not predict suffering [1, 2, 11]. Methods that directly quantify tinnitus distress, disability, and handicap are more appropriate for assessing the amount of suffering. Screening tools allow an estimation of tinnitus severity based on a few questions, whereas for quantitative assessment of tinnitus severity several questionnaires are available.

Psychometric and Methodological Aspects

Different methodological aspects have to be considered in the use of quantitative measurement techniques.

Validity

Is there a specific questionnaire assessing disability, handicap, or coping styles? In general, the validity of an instrument is reflected by its ability to yield "truthful," "correct," or "real" information (see also Fig. 47.1). Validation strategies include content validity, criterion-related validity, and construct validity. Content validity demonstrates to which extent the items of the scale reflect the characteristics to be measured;

criterion-related validity measures how well the instrument correlates with a "gold standard"; and construct validity reflects the degree to which an instrument purports to measure a theoretic construct of the characteristics to be assessed [12, 13].

Standardization and Norming

Can data assessed at place X at time X be compared to those at place Y and time Y?

Is there a specific score high or low as compared to most other patients?

Standardization means that data are always assessed and performed in the same standardized way. Relevant issues can be whether a questionnaire is completed as an electronic version or as a paper version, or whether it is completed before or after the first consultation. Only a standardized way of assessment allows comparison across individuals, time, and clinical settings. Norming means obtaining information about the distribution of measures in a target population in the form of means, standard deviations, or percentiles. Normative data allow placement of the score of an individual in context of a target population.

Reliability

Does the tinnitus questionnaire have high test–retest reliability and stability?

Reliability describes the precision of the instrument and includes internal consistency but also reproducibility. Internal consistency reflects the inter-item consistency of a scale or subscales. It is expected that several items

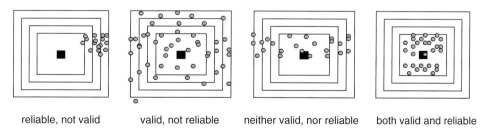

reliable, not valid   valid, not reliable   neither valid, nor reliable   both valid and reliable

Fig. 47.1 Validity and reliability

that assess the same construct (e.g., tinnitus handicap) correlate with each other. The statistical measure of this internal consistency is Cronbach's α.

Reproducibility can be differentiated in short- and long-term reproducibility. Short-term reproducibility may reflect effects of day-to-day fluctuations; long-term reproducibility describes stability over longer time intervals. This is of relevance when a questionnaire is used for evaluating effects of a specific intervention. If there is a lack of knowledge about the changes in a questionnaire score over time occurring without any treatment intervention, one cannot rely on uncontrolled observations of treatment effects. Documented changes in tinnitus scores may not be due to the treatment, per se, but rather due to measurement error of the questionnaire used for assessing treatment outcome.

Responsiveness

Is the questionnaire sensitive for treatment-induced changes?

Responsiveness reflects the ability of a questionnaire to register changes following an individual's response to a treatment intervention. This is especially required when an instrument is used as treatment outcome measure. This aspect of measurement instruments has also been characterized as evaluative [14, 15]. Variables that are stable over time and reflect, for example, the individual's personality are called *trait* parameters, whereas variables that reflect mainly the actual condition are called *state* variables.

From an evaluative questionnaire, one would expect that it samples mainly *state* variables that are likely to change under treatment. A large amount of change-insensitive *trait* variables are useless for detecting treatment effects and may even obscure them. In contrast, the inclusion of *trait* parameters can be useful for an instrument designed for diagnostic use (e.g., for discriminating between individuals with severe vs. mild tinnitus, see Table 47.5).

Another factor related to the responsiveness of a questionnaire is the number of response options for each item. A questionnaire, which consists of items that can only be answered with two or three levels (e.g., yes and no), is, in general, less sensitive to changes than a questionnaire with five or more answer options per item.

It should be noted that the currently available tinnitus questionnaires have not been specifically designed for evaluating treatment-related changes, but most of them have been used as outcome measurers in clinical trials. New questionnaires specifically designed to evaluate treatment-related changes will emerge in the near future [15].

Feasability

Is the questionnaire easily applicable?

Feasibility reflects the property of an instrument to be practically applicable in a real-world context. As an example, in order to be applicable in a busy clinical practice, tinnitus questionnaires should be brief and easy to administer, understand, score, and interpret.

Cultural and Language Bias

Questionnaires designed and tested in one population and language are not necessarily equally applicable in another. Questionnaires developed in one culture do not necessarily measure the same factors in another, even if the language is the same [16]. Likewise, translation from one language to another can introduce changes in meaning. One way of addressing these variations is to validate the questionnaire in each language and setting. This may lead to some items from the original questionnaire being moved into a different factor or rejected as invalid. While this approach has merit in optimizing the questionnaire for a particular population, there are at least two significant downsides: (1) considerable time is required to validate the questionnaire in each setting and (2) cross-population comparisons become difficult. The latter of these two issues is most troublesome for researchers who might want to compare outcomes from two populations using the "same" questionnaire. For example, a questionnaire developed in the US but optimized for New Zealand might omit questions [16]. If two treatments are compared between these countries and found to have the same questionnaire scores, it cannot be assumed that the treatments are equally effective because they actually do not ask the same questions. On the other hand, if the original questionnaire is used in its original form in both countries, cultural idiosyncrasies mean that they still measure different factors.

This paradox is a limitation of questionnaires. Any "worldwide" standard should retain as many of its original items and factor structure when validated in different populations. Researchers should recognize the potential for population differences when using questionnaires.

Screening of Tinnitus Severity

In the daily routine of an audiological or otolaryngologic clinic, there is a high need for fast and reliable classification of tinnitus patients according to their severity. Those who suffer from tinnitus require an entirely different management than those who simply experience tinnitus,

but are only slightly impaired by it. Here, a screening tool is presented that consists of three questions and allows screening for tinnitus severity in an objective and economic way (B-Scale; [17]; Table 47.3).

Another possibility of a single, global measure of the impact of tinnitus on individuals is the following global item [15]:

How much of a problem is your tinnitus?

Not a problem	0
A small problem	1
A moderate problem	2
A big problem	3
A very big problem	4

Table 47.3 B-scale for screening of tinnitus severity [17]
Grading of tinnitus impairment by asking the following three questions

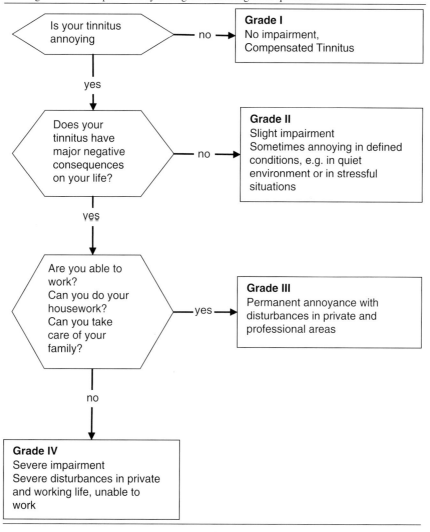

Fig. 47.2 Correlation between the screening question "How much of a problem is your tinnitus?" and the score in the Tinnitus Questionnaire [30] (*N*: 281; *r*=0.70)

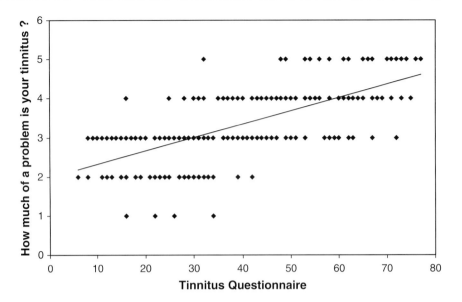

Tinnitus Questionnaires

Preliminary data from the tinnitus clinic in Regensburg show that this five-level response scale correlates highly with the score of the tinnitus questionnaire (see Fig. 47.2), indicating that it is a reliable, well-functioning global item for screening patients.

Tinnitus Questionnaires

Different questionnaires are available to assess specific aspects of patients with tinnitus (see Table 47.4). These questionnaires are score driven, which means that the responses to single items are scored and then summed or averaged. Thus, total scores or subscale scores can be calculated.

There are specific questionnaires for assessing tinnitus-related cognitions (TCQ) or coping styles (TCSQ). The other questionnaires mainly aim to quantify tinnitus distress, disability, or handicap. Items of the different scales largely overlap. Accordingly, there is a relatively high correlation between the total scores of the different tinnitus severity and handicap questionnaires.

In addition to clinical applications, quantitative assessment by tinnitus questionnaires allows research applications. For example, tinnitus questionnaires have been successfully used for investigating the relationship between personality and psychopathology and their impact on tinnitus severity [18]. Furthermore, tinnitus questionnaires provide a method for researchers to quantify tinnitus severity as a criterion for subject selection. That is, self-report measures allow investigators to select only those patients indicating a certain degree of tinnitus severity to be included in a particular study. Minimum and maximum values of the individual's tinnitus score are defined in the research protocol as inclusion criterion, if it is expected that the treatment under study shows best effects in patients with specific tinnitus severity (see Chap. 22). Furthermore, self-report measures can be used to evaluate the effectiveness of a particular experimental treatment. Even if none of the currently available questionnaires has been specifically designed to be sensitive to treatment-related changes, there is general consensus that questionnaire scores are the best available measures of tinnitus consequence and should be used as primary outcome variables in randomized clinical trials for tinnitus treatment [4, 19].

Table 47.4 gives an overview about the most widely used quantitative tinnitus questionnaires in the English language. In the following discussion, each of these questionnaires is presented in detail. A description of the questionnaire is followed by a short explanation of how the questionnaire is scored and interpreted. Psychometric characteristics of the questionnaire are presented, strengths and weaknesses of the instrument are discussed, and finally it is indicated whether validated translations for the questionnaire are available.

Even if self-report questionnaires have been proven to be useful tools both in the clinical management of

Table 47.4 Quantitative Tinnitus Questionnaires

Questionnaire	Number of items	Response options for each item	Factors
Tinnitus Severity Scale [20]	15	Four levels: wording of response options varies between item	One-dimensional
Subjective Tinnitus Severity Scale [21]	16	Two levels: yes and no	One-dimensional
Tinnitus Questionnaire [24, 25]	52	Three levels: true, partly true, not true	Five factors (1 – emotional distress, 2 – auditory perceptual difficulties, 3 – intrusiveness, 4 – sleep disturbances, 5 – somatic complaints)
Tinnitus Handicap/Support Scale [36]	28	Five levels: 1=strongly disagree; 5=strongly agree	Three factors (1 – perceived attitudes, 2 – social support, 3 – disability/handicap)
Tinnitus Handicap Questionnaire [27]	27	100 levels: 0=strongly disagree; 100=strongly agree	Three factors (1 – physical, emotional, social consequences of tinnitus, 2 – interfering effects of tinnitus on the hearing ability of the patient, 3 – the patient's view of tinnitus)
Tinnitus Handicap Inventory [42]	25	Three levels: 4=yes, 2=sometimes, 0=no	Three factors (1 – functional, 2 – emotional, 3 – catastrophic)
Tinnitus Reaction Questionnaire [29]	26	Five levels: 0=not at all; 4=almost all of the time	Four factors (1 – general distress, 2 – interference, 3 – severity, 4 – avoidance)
Tinnitus Cognitions Questionnaire [61]	26	Five levels; negative items: never=0, frequently=4, positive items: never=4, frequently=0	Three factors (1 – positive evaluation of tinnitus, 2 – hoplesness/despair. 3 – helplessness/victimization)
Tinnitus Coping Style Questionnaire [62]	33	Seven levels: never=1; always=7	Two factors (1 – effective coping, 2 – maladaptive coping)
Tinnitus Severity Index [54]	12	Version 1: three and four levels; Version 2: three to five levels	One-dimensional
Tinnitus Beeinträchtigungs Fragebogen (TBF-12) [60]	12	Three levels: 4=yes, 2=sometimes, 0=no	Two factors (1 – emotional-cognitive impairment, 2 – functional-communicative impairment)

tinnitus and in research applications, some caution is advised in their use and interpretation. First, completing a questionnaire might not only measure specific aspects of a patient's tinnitus but also influence the patient's tinnitus. Especially, catastrophizing statements may induce or reinforce maladaptive coping strategies (e.g., statements about suicide). Also, statements such as, "I cannot sleep because of my tinnitus," may induce incorrect attributions. A patient, who repeatedly reads such a statement, may become convinced that his insomnia may be a caused by his tinnitus, which is not necessarily true and might result in incorrect beliefs such as, "as long as I have my tinnitus I will never be able to sleep well."

Second, it should be considered that self-report questionnaires can be subject to dissimulation or aggravation. Thus, just as a low score cannot exclude a significant impact of the tinnitus on a patient's life, a high score is not proof of severe suffering. Therefore,

questionnaire results always have to be evaluated in the context of the clinical impression and the patient's tinnitus-related behavior.

Tinnitus Severity Scale (TSS) [20]

The tinnitus severity scale (TSS) aims at quantifying individuals' cognitive and behavioral responses to tinnitus. The 15 items are categorized under the factors intrusiveness (four items), distress (six items), hearing loss (three items), sleep disturbance (one item), and medication (one item). Responses refer to the past week and range in score from 1 (no impact) to 4 (most impact). Each item is weighted from 1 to 3 points (total weight score=39 points). The total score is calculated by multiplying each item's score by its weight and summing these products, resulting in a range between

Table 47.5 Important aspects of questionnaire construction[a]

Purpose	Discriminative questionnaires Quantitative diagnosis	Evaluative questionnaires Assessment of treatment outcome
1. Item selection	Responses of different patients or subjects should be heterogeneous (spread widely across the response continuum)	Lack of response heterogeneity is not a problem, may even improve an item's ability to show clear changes resulting from treatment
2. Item reduction	Items that most subjects answer the same are unable to reveal diagnostic differences and should be deleted	Delete any items that testing reveals are insensitive to change (regardless of whether they are sensitive to diagnostic differences)
3. Item response scaling	The chosen scaling should facilitate uniform interpretation by subjects (wording should not be ambiguous or confusing) Too much resolution may decrease subjects' response reliability	An items sensitivity to change is generally proportional to the number of response options it provides. Response scales should have high resolution (sufficient gradations) to register changes even if small
4. Test–retest reliability	Within-subject variance should be small, between-subject variance should be large and stable (reliability indicating stable individual differences)	Within-subject variance should be small when functional status remains constant, but show large changes in scores when functional status improves
5. Content validity	All or most of the important dimensions of the health problem should be addressed	Address only those dimensions capable of showing treatment-related change
6. Construct validity	Questionnaire scores should be highly correlated with well-established, comparable measures administered at that same time	Questionnaire scores after treatment should bear the predicted relationship to the same measures administered before treatment

[a]Modified from [15]

39 points (39 weighting points×1-point item score) and 156 points (39 weighting points×4-point item score). The TSS has acceptable test–retest reliability ($r=0.86$). No other psychometric data are available, limiting clinical and research applications. Validated translations of the English scale into other languages are not published.

Subjective Tinnitus Severity Scale (STSS) [21]

The 16-item subjective tinnitus severity scale (STSS) was developed to provide a simple questionnaire to assess tinnitus severity. Each question is answered with either a "yes" or a "no" response. Ten of the 16 items earn a point if the response is "yes" (e.g., "Are you almost always aware of your tinnitus?"), whereas the other six items earn a point if the response is "no" (e.g., "When you are busy, do you quite often forget about your tinnitus?"), summing up to scores between 0 and 16 with higher scores reflecting greater overall severity. A Cronbach's α of 0.84 indicates high consistency reliability. The validity was established in a sample of 30 patients, where mean STSS scores were found to correlate highly with two independent clinical ratings of severity.

The STSS is extremely simple to administer and score. The lack of a classification scheme for the total score limits its diagnostic use. Furthermore, no data about test–retest reliability are available, limiting its applicability for measuring treatment outcome.

The original questionnaire is in the English language, validated translations in Dutch [22] and French [23] have been published.

Tinnitus Questionnaire (TQ) [24]

The 52-item Tinnitus Questionnaire (TQ) developed by Hallam and colleagues has been designed to measure several dimensions of patients' tinnitus complaints, namely emotional distress, auditory perceptual difficulties, and sleep disturbance. Questions either relate to the "noises" in the ear as the major cause of distress or reflect lack of coping skills.

Individuals indicate their level of agreement to each statement using one of the three response alternatives: true (2 points), partly true (1 point), or not true (0 points).

Affirmative responses to an item (indicated by true) are identified as complaints about tinnitus, with the exception of the items 1, 7, 32, 40, 44, and 49, which are reverse scored because they are considered positive statements. Possible scores range from 0 to 104 points, with higher scores reflecting greater tinnitus complaints.

The TQ instrument has been found to have high internal consistency reliability (Cronbach's α=.91–.95) and high test–retest reliability (r=.91–.94) [25, 26]. The high test–retest reliability suggests good stability over time.

High correlations were also found between the TQ and measures of tinnitus handicap (Tinnitus Handicap Questionnaire (THQ) [27], tinnitus handicap inventory (THI) [28], and tinnitus distress (TRQ) [29]. Factor analyses conducted in separate populations were consistent with the factors originally identified by Hallam and colleagues in the United Kingdom supporting the instrument's validity.

The TQ has been found to measure a number of different dimensions of tinnitus complaints and is a stable measure over time. In this connection, the TQ would be useful as an outcome measure in determining the effectiveness of treatment. However, the responsiveness of the TQ to changes has not been evaluated, and no data are available to assist the clinician in determining what is considered a statistically significant or clinically relevant change in scores following intervention for a given patient.

The TQ has been translated into the German language and extensively validated [30–32]. Factor analysis of the German translation of the TQ revealed that the dimensions of emotional and cognitive distress, intrusiveness, auditory perceptual difficulties, sleep disturbances, and somatic complaints can be differentiated [32]. This validation also resulted in a different scoring system, where some items were not used at all and others loaded in two factors, resulting in a maximum score of 84 points. Further translations in Dutch and French are based on the German version [33]. Recently, a Chinese version of the TQ has been validated [34]. Also, a short version of the TQ has been presented in the German language (Mini TQ, [31]), which has also been validated in Portuguese [35]. Furthermore, official translations of the Mini TQ in most European languages are available at http://www.eutinnitus.com/country-selection.php.

Tinnitus Handicap/Support Scale (TH/SS) [36]

The 28-item tinnitus handicap/support scale (TH/SS) assesses the attitudes of significant others toward the person with tinnitus. Three factors were identified, including perceived attitudes or reactions of others (factor 1; 9 items), social support (factor 2; 10 items), and personal and social handicaps (factor 3; 9 items). Each statement on the scale is scored from 1 (strongly disagree) to 5 (strongly agree). The reliability of the TH/SS has not been examined. Construct validity of the TH/SS was assessed using a 10-item Tinnitus Severity Questionnaire (TSQ). This is the only questionnaire that has been designed to assess the influence of significant others in the overall management process, which can be helpful for counseling. The lack of retest reliability data limits both its clinical and its scientific use.

The questionnaire is in the English language and has not been validated in any other language.

Tinnitus Handicap Questionnaire (THQ) [27]

The Tinnitus Handicap Questionnaire (THQ) description has been developed to be broad in scope but sensitive to patients' perceived degree of tinnitus handicap. By factor analysis, three factors have been differentiated. Factor 1 (15 items) reflects the physical, emotional, and social consequences of tinnitus; factor 2 (8 items) assesses the effects of tinnitus and hearing; and factor 3 (4 items) explores the patient's view on tinnitus.

For each item, the individual responds with a number between 0 and 100 indicating how much he or she disagrees (0=strongly disagree) or agrees (100=strongly agrees) with the statement. After inverting scores obtained on items 25 and 26 by subtracting them from 100, mean scores can be calculated for the total or for each of the three factors. Higher scores indicate greater handicap.

The THQ demonstrated high internal consistency and reliability for the total scale (Cronbach's α=0.95), factor 1 (0.95), and factor 2 (0.88). Factor 3 yielded a low alpha (0.47), which may be due to the small number of items comprising this factor. A similar factor structure has been obtained in Australian [26] and New Zealand [37] samples.

Adequate construct validity of the THQ was documented by relative high correlations ($r > 0.50$) with perceived tinnitus loudness, life satisfaction, hearing threshold, depression, and general health status. High test–retest correlations have been obtained assessed over a 6-week period for the total score ($r = 0.89$), factor 1 ($r = 0.89$), and factor 2 ($r = 0.90$), whereas factor 3 yielded inadequate retest reliability ($r = .50$) [38]. Normative data for the THQ are available [27]. The percentile ranking allows determining severity for an individual patient relative to other patients with tinnitus. Comparison of the scores for Factor 1 (emotional and social effects) and Factor 2 (hearing) has been used to guide clinicians in treatment selection (high Factor 1, greater psychological management; high Factor 2, hearing aids [39]).

The 100-point response scale may be relatively sensitive for changes [40], but it may be somewhat problematic, especially for items, dealing with subjective strength of belief.

According to their authors, the THQ is among the most widely used questionnaires [40]. A French translation of the THQ has been validated [41]; official (unvalidated) translations in various languages are available at http://www.uihealthcare.com/depts/med/otolaryngology/clinics/tinnitus/questionnaires/index.html.

Tinnitus Handicap Inventory (THI) [42]

The 25-item Tinnitus Handicap Inventory consists of three subscales. The functional subscale (11 items) evaluates role limitations, the emotional subscale (nine items) reflects affective responses to tinnitus, and the catastrophic subscale (five items) probes the most severe reactions to tinnitus. However, the distinctness of the subscales has been questioned, and the use of only the total score was recommended [43].

For each item of the inventory, the patient responds with "yes" (4 points), "sometimes" (2 points), or "no" (0 points). The responses are summed, with a total score ranging from 0 to 100 points. Higher scores represent greater perceived handicap. Handicap severity

categories (0–16: no; 18–36: mild; 38–56: moderate; 58–100: severe) have been developed based on quartiles calculated for the total THI score [44].

The THI has very good internal consistency reliability (Cronbach's $\alpha = 0.93$) and high test–retest reliability for the total score ($r = 0.92$), as well as the subscales (ranging from 0.84 to 0.94). Test–retest reliability assessed on average 20 days after the initial administration was also high for the total score and the three subscales. A 95% confidence interval of 20 points for the total scale suggests that in an individual, a difference of 20 points or more between pre- and post-treatment administration can be considered statistically significant. Convergent validity was assessed using the THQ, whereas construct validity was assessed using the Beck Depression Inventory, Modified Somatic Perception Questionnaire, symptom rating scales (e.g., sleep disturbance, annoyance), and perceived tinnitus pitch and loudness. High convergent validity with the TQ has been demonstrated recently [28].

The THI is briefly and easily administered and scored. It assesses the domains of function that are addressed by many available treatment interventions.

The test–retest data allow clinicians to judge effects of treatment interventions. Further data about retest stability over longer time intervals are desirable in order to evaluate changes in perceived handicap over the medium and long term.

The THI is the most widely used tinnitus questionnaire, as evidenced by the number of citations. Validated translations are published in Danish [45], Spanish [46], Korean [47], Portuguese [48, 49], German [50], Italian [51], and Chinese [52].

In a consensus meeting, the (additional) use of the THI has been recommended for clinical studies in order to facilitate comparability between studies [4].

Tinnitus Reaction Questionnaire (TRQ) [29]

The Tinnitus Reaction Questionnaire has been developed for quantifying the psychological distress associated with tinnitus [29]. The 26 items of the TRQ relate to distress consequences such as anger, confusion, annoyance, helplessness, activity avoidance, and panic.

Each item on the TRQ is scored on a 5-point scale, ranging from 0 to 4 points. The scores are summed with the total score ranging from 0 to 104 points, with higher scores reflecting greater distress.

The TRQ has high internal consistency reliability (Cronbach's $\alpha=.96$), as well as test–retest reliability ($r=.88$). Concerning construct validity, there are moderate to high correlations between the TRQ and clinician ratings and self-reported measures of anxiety and depression. A factor analysis revealed the factor's general distress, interference, severity, and avoidance.

The TRQ represents an easy clinical tool for assessing tinnitus distress. However, no cut-off values for severity categories are available. High test–retest reliability over a period ranging from 3 days to 3 weeks indicates short-term stability of the TRQ and its usefulness in quantifying treatment outcome, at least for short interventions. However, no data are available about what is considered a statistically significant or a clinically relevant change of the score. A French translation of the TRQ has been validated [23] and compared with the English version, demonstrating only minor effects of language [53].

The Tinnitus Severity Index

The Tinnitus Severity Index is a 12-item questionnaire that measures the effect of tinnitus on work and social activities and overall quality of life [54]. The 12 items of the TSI are totaled for a single severity index. This is one of the shorter tinnitus questionnaires that has been published. There have been two versions of the TSI, the original [54] using 3- and 4-point scales and a modified version using primarily a 5-point scale, with two 4-point questions and one 3-point question [55]. The TSI has had limited use outside of the US, but the original version has been normed in New Zealand as well [37]. The TSI has good internal consistency in both US and NZ (Cronbach's $\alpha>0.87$) populations. The TSI has been found to correlate to the subjective rating of tinnitus loudness but not hearing loss [37]. The TSI and THQ are correlated ($r=0.77$, $p<0.05$), suggesting that each questionnaire is measuring similar, but not exactly the same, elements of tinnitus [37]. The TSI scores have been shown to improve following comprehensive audiology-based tinnitus management

programs [56, 57], and use of SSRIs has improved scores [58]. Persons with tinnitus following head injuries have greater TSI scores than those whose tinnitus develops from other injuries [59].

The Tinnitus Handicap Questionnaire (Tinnitus Beeinträchtigungs Fragebogen; TBF-12)

Based on the Tinnitus Handicap Inventory (THI) [42], a short version in German language has been developed [60]. The number of items was reduced based on rigorous psychometrical testings. The final German version encompasses 12 items and distinguishes between the factors emotional cognitive (items 3, 4, 6, 8, 10, 11, and 12) and functional communicative impairments (items 1, 2, 5, 7, 9).

The internal consistency reliability of the TBF is high (Cronbach's $\alpha=0.90$). The TBF-12 is easy to understand and administer, psychometrically robust, and well suitable as a screening instrument in primary care. The TBF-12 is currently used as the primary outcome measure for evaluation of the efficacy of a pharmacologic compound in phase III trials. In case the trials will be positive and the compound will be approved by the Food and Drug Administration (FDA) or the European Agency for the Evaluation of Medical Products (EMEA), it will set a standard for further drugs to be approved. In the context of the phase III trial, the questionnaire has been translated and linguistically evaluated in Spanish, Dutch, French, Portuguese, Czech, Spanish, Polish, and English, as well as in African languages.

Tinnitus Cognitions Questionnaire (TCQ) [61]

In contrast to the scales assessing distress, disability, or handicap, the Tinnitus Cognitions Questionnaire (TCQ) focuses on the patient's reaction to tinnitus from a cognitive perspective. The 26 items assess positive and negative thoughts associated with tinnitus [61], especially important in the context of the psychological management of tinnitus. The TCQ consists of 13 negative items and 13 positive items, which are clearly separated. Each of the items is rated on a five-point scale (0–4). The negative items (1–13) are scored 0–4, whereas the positive items (14–26) are reverse scored, 4–0. The addition of the item scores reveals the total TCQ score, which can range from 0 to 104, with higher scores reflecting a tendency toward more negative and less positive thoughts in response to tinnitus.

The TCQ yielded both good test–retest reliability ($r=.88$) and internal consistency reliability (Cronbach's $\alpha=.91$). A factor analysis revealed that the negative and positive cognitions represent independent factors. Construct and convergent validity was assessed between the TCQ-total, TCQ-positive, and TCQ-negative scores, as well as other measures of tinnitus-specific symptomatology (e.g., distress, handicap, complaint behavior), depression, automatic thoughts, and loss of control. The TCQ showed moderate correlations with other tinnitus-related measures (i.e., TRQ, THQ, and TQ), with the TCQ-negative subscale demonstrating higher correlations with each of the tinnitus- and non-tinnitus measures.

The TCQ is different from other questionnaires by focusing on cognitive responses in individuals with tinnitus. The information gleaned from the TCQ responses is especially useful in the context of cognitive–behavioral therapy for screening or stratifying patients, but also for outcome measurement. However, the latter requires data about test–retest reliability. It has to be considered that reporting about cognitions or thoughts may not be identical to engaging in these thoughts. No validated translations of the instrument have been published.

Tinnitus Coping Style Questionnaire (TCSQ) [62]

The Tinnitus Coping Style Questionnaire (TCSQ) is a 33-item scale developed to assess adaptive and coping strategies and consists of two factors [62]. Eighteen items comprise the maladaptive coping factor; the other fifteen items comprise the effective coping subscale.

For each item, the patient indicates how frequently he/she employs each of the coping strategies on a 1 ("never") to 7 ("always") scale. Higher scores on the

maladaptive coping subscale reflect poorer coping skills, whereas higher scores on the effective coping dimension are characterized by better acceptance of the tinnitus and use of a broad range of adaptive coping skills.

The internal consistency reliability values for the maladaptive coping and effectiveness coping subscales were 0.90 and 0.89, respectively. The two subscales were not significantly correlated ($r=0.13$). Maladaptive coping strategies were significantly associated with measures of tinnitus severity, depression, and anxiety. In contrast, effective coping was not correlated with any of the tinnitus adjustment measures [62].

The TCSQ is specifically focused on coping strategies used by tinnitus sufferers. Information obtained with the TCSQ is fundamental in developing a cognitive–behavioral therapy program. After probing test–retest reliability of the instrument, the TSCQ might also be suitable for monitoring changes during cognitive–behavioral therapy.

Other Questionnaires

Beside tinnitus-related questionnaires, several other instruments referring to different comorbid conditions may be useful as part of a broad assessment of the patient and their problems. A large variety of self-report questionnaires are available for assessing depression, anxiety, sleep disorders, or health-related quality of life. A detailed description of these questionnaires is beyond the scope of this chapter. In general, these instruments are not necessary for basis assessment in every patient but may be helpful in specific cases.

VAS Scales

Rating scales (visual analogue scales or Likert-type scales/numerical rating scales) can be used for assessing different characteristics of tinnitus, such as loudness or annoyance. Examples for such scales are given in Fig. 47.3. Rating scales are easy to understand, but sometimes patients report difficulties, because generally the maximum end of the scale is only very vaguely defined.

Fig. 47.3 Numeric rating scale (NRS) and visual analogue scale (VAS) of loudness of tinnitus.

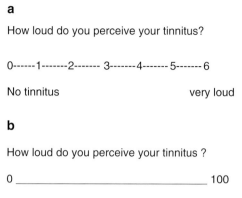

a

How loud do you perceive your tinnitus?

0------1-------2------- 3-------4------- 5------- 6

No tinnitus   very loud

b

How loud do you perceive your tinnitus ?

0 _____ 100

Example for a numeric rating scale / Likert like scale (a) and a visual analogue scale (b) for assessment of subjectively perceived tinnitus loudness.

Apart from loudness and annoyance, other qualitative features of tinnitus can also be easily assessed with rating scales (e.g., intrusiveness or ability to ignore tinnitus). This can provide an opportunity to understand what the most important problem is for a given patient and may lead to the use of more individually tailored assessment and monitoring tool, such as tinnitus diaries or tinnitus protocols.

A big advantage of rating scales is that they are fast to perform and can be repeated easily, e.g., in the form of tinnitus protocols. Unfortunately, there is limited psychometric data for visual analogue and numeric rating scales. One recent study shows that in individuals with tinnitus who do not seek medical attention, loudness rating scores are much lower than in those who seek help for their tinnitus [63]. It has also been shown that results of visual analogue loudness scale correlate with the THI scores ($r = 0.56$) [64].

Tinnitus Protocols

Tinnitus protocols are self-report instruments for assessing different aspects of tinnitus over time. As an example, tinnitus loudness, annoyance, mood, and stress can be assessed daily, and results can be displayed in a diagram (see Fig. 47.4).

A tinnitus protocol can be an appropriate tool to examine changes of different tinnitus aspects over time,

and correlations between intensity of tinnitus (e.g., loudness, annoyance) and different psychobehavioral factors such as mood or stress. This allows, for example, the detection of triggers or rhythmic changes over time. As shown in the example in Fig. 47.3, such a protocol can reveal that mood and stress are correlated closer to tinnitus annoyance than loudness. By monitoring different parameters over a certain period of time, the patient can learn that it is not just the noise that borders them but other emotional, cognitive, and behavioral factors that influence tinnitus perception and reaction. This can be helpful to motivate patients for cognitive–behavioral therapy.

Conclusion

There are different forms of tinnitus that require specific management. The intake interview is of highest importance for obtaining comprehensive information about the patient's tinnitus in order to be able to make an exact diagnosis. Collected information from the interview, observation of the patient, and the various self-report scales should enable the clinician to formulate a view about the nature of the tinnitus, its time course, its perceptual characteristics, its comorbidities, the difficulties experienced by the patient, the person's coping strategies, loudness the consequences

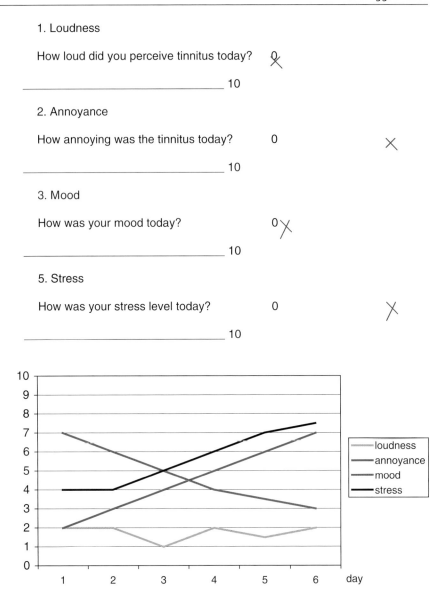

Fig. 47.4 Example of a
tinnitus protocol

1. Loudness

How loud did you perceive tinnitus today?

_____ 10

2. Annoyance

How annoying was the tinnitus today?   0

_____ 10

3. Mood

How was your mood today?

_____ 10

5. Stress

How was your stress level today?   0

_____ 10

of the tinnitus for the person's life. Based on all these information, a specific treatment program may be developed, which is likely to be effective for an individual patient.

References

1. Meikle, MB, Vernon, J, Johnson, RM. The perceived severity of tinnitus Some observations concerning a large population of tinnitus clinic patients. Otolaryngol Head Neck Surg, 1984;92(6):689–96

2. Jakes, SC, Hallam, RS, Chambers, C, Hinchcliffe, R. A factor analytical study of tinnitus complaint behaviour. Audiology, 1985;24(3):195–206

3. Stouffer, JL, Tyler, RS. Characterization of tinnitus by tinnitus patients. J Speech Hear Disord, 1990;55(3): 439–53

4. Langguth, B, Goodey, R, Azevedo, A, Bjorne, A, Cacace, A, Crocetti, A, et al. Consensus for tinnitus patient assessment and treatment outcome measurement: Tinnitus Research Initiative Meeting, Regensburg, 2006. Prog Brain Res, 2007;166:525–36

5. Henry, JA, Jastreboff, MM, Jastreboff, PJ, Schechter, MA, Fausti, SA. Assessment of patients for treatment with tinnitus retraining therapy. J Am Acad Audiol, 2002;13(10): 523–44

6. Hoffman HJ, Reed GW. Epidemiology of tinnitus. In: Snow JB, editor. Tinnitus: Theory and Management. London: BC Ker, 2004;16–41

7. Coelho, CB, Sanchez, TG, Tyler, RS. Tinnitus in children and associated risk factors. Prog Brain Res, 2007;166:179–91

8. Sand, PG, Langguth, B, Kleing, T, Eichhammer. Genetics of chronic tinnitus. Prog Brain Res, 2007;166:159–68

9. De Ridder, D, van der Loo, E, Van der Kelen, K, Mesky, T, Van de Heyning, P, Møller, A. Do tonic and burst TMS modulate the lemniscal and extralemniscal system differentially? Int J Med Sci, 2007;4(5):242–6

10. De Ridder, D, van der Loo, E, Van der Kelen, K, Mesky, T, Van de Heyning, P, Møller, A. Theta, alpha and beta burst transcranial magnetic stimulation: brain modulation in tinnitus. Int J Med Sci, 2007;4(5):237–41

11. Hiller, W, Goebel, G. Factors influencing tinnitus loudness and annoyance. Arch Otolaryngol Head Neck Surg, 2006;132(12):1323–30

12. Hyde, ML. Reasonable psychometric standards for self-report outcome measures in audiological rehabilitation. Ear Hear, 2000;21(4 Suppl):24 S–36 S

13. Ventry IM, Schiavetti N. Evaluating Research in Speech Pathology and Audiology. Reading, MA: Addison Wesley, 1980

14. Kirshner, B, Guyatt, G. A methodological framework for assessing health indices. J Chronic Dis, 1985;38(1):27–36

15. Meikle, MB, Stewart, BJ, Griest, SE, Tin, WH, Henry, JA, Abrams, HB, et al. Assessment of tinnitus: measurement of treatment outcomes. Prog Brain Res, 2007;166:511–21

16. Searchfield GD, Jerram C. Tinnitus assessment. In: Searchfield GD, Goodey R, editors. Tinnitus Discovery: Asia Pacific Tinnitus Symposium, 2010

17. Biesinger, E, Heiden, C, Greimel, V, Lendle, T, Hoing, R, Albegger, K. Strategies in ambulatory treatment of tinnitus. HNO, 1998;46(2):157–69

18. Langguth, B, Kleing, T, Fischer, B, Hajak, G, Eichhammer, P, Sand, PG. Tinnitus severity, depression, and the big five personality traits. Prog Brain Res, 2007;166:221-5

19. Dobie, RA. A review of randomized clinical trials in tinnitus. Laryngoscope, 1999;109:1202–11

20. Sweetow, RW, Levy, MC. Tinnitus severity scaling for diagnostic/therapeutic use. Hear Instrum, 2009;41:20–46

21. Halford, JB, Anderson, SD. Tinnitus severity measured by a subjective scale, audiometry and clinical judgement. J Laryngol Otol, 1991;105(2):89–93

22. van Veen, ED, Jacobs, JB, Bensing, JM. Assessment of distress associated with tinnitus. J Laryngol Otol, 1998;112(3):258–63

23. Meric, C, Pham, E, Chery-Croze, S. Validation of French translation of the "Tinnitus Reaction Questionnaire", Wilson et al 1991. Encephale, 1997;23(6):442–6

24. Hallam, RS, Jakes, SC, Hinchcliffe, R. Cognitive variables in tinnitus annoyance. Br J Clin Psychol, 1988;27(Pt 3):213–22

25. Hallam RS. Manual of the Tinnitus Questionnaire. London: The Psychological Corporation/Harcourt Brace, 1996

26. Henry, JL, Wilson, PH. The psychometric properties of two measures of tinnitus complaint and handicap. Int Tinnitus J, 1998;4(2):114–21

27. Kuk, FK, Tyler, RS, Russell, D, Jordan, H. The psychometric properties of a tinnitus handicap questionnaire. Ear Hear, 1990;11(6):434–45

28. Baguley, DM, Humphriss, RL, Hodgson, CA. Convergent validity of the tinnitus handicap inventory and the tinnitus questionnaire. J Laryngol Otol, 2000;114(11):840–3

29. Wilson, PH, Henry, J, Bowen, M, Haralambous, G. Tinnitus reaction questionnaire: psychometric properties of a measure of distress associated with tinnitus. J Speech Hear Res, 1991;34(1):197–201

30. Goebel, G, Hiller, W. The tinnitus questionnaire A standard instrument for grading the degree of tinnitus. Results of a multicenter study with the tinnitus questionnaire. HNO, 1994;42:166–72

31. Hiller, W, Goebel, G, Rief, W. Reliability of self-rated tinnitus distress and association with psychological symptom patterns. Br J Clin Psychol 1994;33(Pt 2):231–9

32. Hiller, W, Goebel, G. A psychometric study of complaints in chronic tinnitus. J Psychosom Res, 1992;36(4):337–48

33. Meeus, O, Blaivie, C, Van de, HP. Validation of the Dutch and the French version of the Tinnitus Questionnaire. B-ENT, 2007;3(Suppl 7):11–7

34. Kam, AC, Cheung, AP, Chan, PY, Leung, EK, Wong, TK, Tong, MC, et al. Psychometric properties of a Chinese (Cantonese) version of the Tinnitus Questionnaire. Int J Audiol, 2009;48(8):568–75

35. Cerejeira, R, Cerejeira, J, Paiva, S, Goncalves, P, Firmino, H, Quartilho, M, et al. The Portuguese version of Mini-Tinnitus Questionnaire: brief screening test for assessment of tinnitus-induced stress. Otol Neurotol, 2009;30(1):112–5

36. Erlandsson, SI, Hallberg, LR, Axelsson, A. Psychological and audiological correlates of perceived tinnitus severity. Audiology, 1992;31(3):168–79

37. Searchfield, GD, Jerram, C, Wise, K, Raymond, S. The impact of hearing loss on tinnitus severity Australian and New Zealand. J Audiol 2007;29:67–76

38. Newman, CW, Wharton, JA, Jacobson, GP. Retest stability of the tinnitus handicap questionnaire. Ann Otol Rhinol Laryngol, 1995;104(9 Pt 1):718–23

39. Searchfield GD. Hearing aids and tinnitus. In: Tyler R, editor. Tinnitus: Treatment. New York: Thieme, 2007;161–75

40. Tyler, RS, Oleson, J, Noble, W, Coelho, C, Ji, H. Clinical trials for tinnitus: study populations, designs, measurement variables, and data analysis. Prog Brain Res, 2007;166:499–509

41. Meric, C, Pham, E, Chery-Croze, S. Translation and validation of the questionnaire Tinnitus Handicap Questionnaire, 1990. J Otolaryngol, 1997;26(3):167–70

42. Newman, CW, Jacobson, GP, Spitzer, JB. Development of the Tinnitus Handicap Inventory. Arch Otolaryngol Head Neck Surg, 1996;122(2):143–8

43. Baguley, DM, Andersson, G. Factor analysis of the Tinnitus Handicap Inventory. Am J Audiol, 2003;12(1):31–4

44. Newman, CW, Sandridge, SA, Jacobson, GP. Psychometric adequacy of the Tinnitus Handicap Inventory (THI) for evaluating treatment outcome. J Am Acad Audiol, 1998;9(2):153–60

45. Zachariae, R, Mirz, F, Johansen, LV, Andersen, SE, Bjerring, P, Pedersen, CB, Reliability and validity of a Danish adaptation of the Tinnitus Handicap Inventory, Scand Audiol, 2000;29(1):37–43

46. Herraiz, C, Hernandez, CJ, Plaza, G, Tapia, MC, de los, SG. Disability evaluation in patients with tinnitus. Acta Otorrinolaringol Esp, 2001;52(6):534–8

47. Kim, JH, Lee, SY, Kim, CH, Lim, SL, Shin, JN, Chung, WH, et al. Reliability and validity of a Korean adaptation of the Tinnitus Handicap Inventory. Korean J Otholaryngol, 2002;45:328–34

48. Paula Erika, AF, Cunha, F, Onishi, ET, Branco-Barreiro, FC, Gananca, FF. Tinnitus Handicap Inventory: cross-cultural adaptation to Brazilian Portuguese. Pro Fono, 2005;17(3): 303–10

49. Dias, A, Cordeiro, R, Corrente, JE. Tinnitus annoyance assessed by the tinnitus handicap inventory. Rev Saude Publica, 2006;40(4):706–11

50. Kleing, T, Fischer, B, Langguth, B, Sand, PG, Hajak, G, Dvorakova, J, et al. Validation of the German-Version Tinnitus Handicap Inventory (THI). Psychiatr Prax, 2007;34(S1):140–2

51. Monzani, D, Geese, E, rara, A, Gherpelli, C, Pingani, L, Forghieri, M, et al. Validity of the Italian adaptation of the Tinnitus Handicap Inventory; focus on quality of life and psychological distress in tinnitus-sufferers. Acta Otorhinolaryngol Ital, 2008;28(3):126–34

52. Kam, AC, Cheung, AP, Chan, PY, Leung, EK, Wong, TK, van Hasselt, CA, et al. Psychometric properties of the Chinese (Cantonese) Tinnitus Handicap Inventory. Clin Otolaryngol, 2009;34(4):309–15

53. Meric, C, Pham, E, Chery-Croze, S. Validation assessment of a French version of the tinnitus reaction questionnaire: a comparison between data from English and French versions. J Speech Lang Hear Res, 2000;43(1):184–90

54. Meikle, MB, Griest, S, Stewart, BJ, Press, LS. Measuring the negative impact of tinnitus: A brief severity index. Abstr Midwinter Res Meet Assoc Res Otolaryngol, 1995; 18:167

55. Folmer, RL, Carroll, JR. Long-term effectiveness of ear-level devices for tinnitus. Otolaryngol Head Neck Surg, 2006;134(1):132–7

56. Folmer, RL. Long-term reductions in tinnitus severity. BMC Ear Nose Throat Disord, 2002;2(1):3

57. Henry, JA, Schechter, MA, Zg, TL, Griest, S, Jastreboff, PJ, Vernon, JA, et al. Outcomes of clinical trial: tinnitus masking versus tinnitus retraining therapy. J Am Acad Audiol, 2006;17(2):104–32

58. Folmer, RL, Shi, YB. SSRI use by tinnitus patients: interactions between depression and tinnitus severity. Ear Nose Throat J, 2004;83(2):107–8, 110, 112

59. Folmer, RL, Griest, SE. Chronic tinnitus resulting from head or neck injuries. Laryngoscope, 2003;113(5):821–7

60. Greimel, KV, Leibetseder, M, Unterrainer, J, Albegger, K. Can tinnitus be measured? Methods for assessment of tinnitus-specific disability and presentation of the Tinnitus Disability Questionnaire. HNO, 1999;47(3):196–201

61. Wilson, PH, Henry, JL. Tinnitus cognitions questionnaire: development and psychometric properties of a measure of dysfunctional cognitions associated with tinnitus. Int Tinnitus J, 1998;4(1):23–30

62. Budd, RJ, Pugh, R. Tinnitus coping style and its relationship to tinnitus severity and emotional distress. J Psychosom Res, 1996;41(4):327–35

63. Demeester, K, Van, WA, Hendrickx, JJ, Topsakal, V, Fransen, E, Van, LL, et al. Prevalence of tinnitus and audiometric shape. B-ENT, 2007;3(Suppl 7):37–49

64. Figueiredo, RR, Azevedo, AA, Oliveira, PM. Correlation analysis of the visual-analogue scale and the Tinnitus Handicap Inventory in tinnitus patients. Braz J Otorhinolaryngol, 2009; 75(1):76–9

Chapter 48
Clinical Otologic Assessment

Tobias Kleinjung

Keypoints

1. This chapter describes the diagnostic procedures of the otorhinolaryngologist, which can be performed in an office setting.
2. The otologic assessment is important for the identification of underlying causes that might be accessible to medical or surgical intervention.
3. Special attention should be paid to all kinds of objective tinnitus, which is often caused by an organic pathology of the ear or the neck.
4. The combination of otological, radiological, and audiological findings will help to make the correct diagnosis.

Keywords Tinnitus • Otoscopy • Endoscopy • Auscultation • Doppler ultrasound

Introduction

Some disorders of the conductive apparatus of the ear can cause both objective and subjective tinnitus. As already described in Chap. 23, the otorhinolaryngologist is often the first port of call for patients with new-onset tinnitus. Otologic diagnosis in patients with tinnitus should therefore concentrate on conditions that might cause tinnitus. When taking the history of a patient with tinnitus, it is essential to enquire about ear pain, sensation of aural fullness, otorrhea, sinunasal problems, hearing loss, and a history of previous infection or surgery involving the ear. Methods used in otological examination of a patient with tinnitus include tympanic microscopy, endoscopy of the nasopharynx, auscultation and Doppler ultrasound examination of the neck vessels, and auscultation of the aural region.

Inspection of the external ear can reveal developmental anomalies that may be important for diagnosis of tinnitus. Surgical scars detected during examination of the retro-auricular region may be an indication of previous middle ear surgery, another possible cause of tinnitus.

Otoscopy

Examination of the external auditory canal and tympanic membrane is performed ideally using a microscope with up to 10× magnification. Normally, the external auditory canal is wide and the tympanic membrane is transparent. Attention should be paid to bony exostoses[1] and tumors on the skin lining the ear canal. The long process of the incus is often visible through the tympanic membrane in many cases, as well as the manubrium of the malleus with the umbo. Reddening of the tympanic membrane or increased vascular markings is indicative of acute otitis media. Otoscopy can detect fluid build-up in the tympanic cavity. Negative air pressure in the tympanic cavity causes retraction of the tympanic membrane and suggests Eustachian tube dysfunction. Perforations of the tympanic membrane indicate chronic otitis media.

T. Kleinjung (✉)
Department of Otorhinolaryngology, University of Regensburg, Franz-Josef-Strauss-Allee 11, 93053 Regensburg, Germany
e-mail: tobias.kleinjung@klinik.uni-regensburg.de

[1]Exostosis: A cartilage-capped bony projection arising from any bone that develops from cartilage. From: Stedman's Electronic Medical Dictionary.

A.R. Møller et al. (eds.), *Textbook of Tinnitus*,
DOI 10.1007/978-1-60761-145-5_48, © Springer Science+Business Media, LLC 2011

The presence of cholesteatoma[2] may cause the epitympanic perforation to be filled with keratin debris or granulation tissue. Stinking otorrhea is also characteristic of the presence of a cholesteatoma. In many cases, large tympanic membrane perforations permit inspection of the auditory ossicular chain and assessment of the tympanic mucosa. Otoscopy findings are usually normal in otosclerosis. Schwartze's sign[3] is a rare finding, consisting of a pink blush of the mucosa near the promontory that can be seen through a translucent tympanic membrane. It is a sign of proliferation and dilatation of blood vessels at the promontory and should be regarded as indication of cochlear otosclerosis [1].

Movement of the tympanic membrane in time with the patient's respiration on forced nasal breathing is indicative of a patulous Eustachian tube. Pulsatile movement of the tympanic membrane may indicate the presence of a glomus tumor. This bluish-red tumor growing in a grape-like cluster may cause the tympanic membrane to bulge outward. In advanced cases, the tumor may also impinge into the external auditory canal. Rhythmic movements of the tympanic membrane are also noted in patients with myoclonus[4] of the tensor tympani muscle.

Valsalva's maneuver and Toynbee's maneuver are clinical tests of Eustachian tube function. In Valsalva's maneuver, patients pinch their nose tightly between thumb and forefinger and then attempt to breathe out forcibly while also keeping their mouth closed. An outward bulging tympanic membrane during a Valsalva's maneuver is an indication that the Eustachian tube functions normally and that air can reach the middle ear via the Eustachian tube. In Toynbee's maneuver, the patient is instructed to swallow, again with nose pinched closed. This normally results in a negative air pressure in the tympanic cavity that can be detected by otoscopy as an inward retraction of the tympanic membrane. Objective measure of Eustachian tube function can be obtained by tympanometry (see Chap. 49).

Endoscopy

Further examination of possible causes of dysfunction of the Eustachian tube can be done by examination of the nasal and pharyngeal structures using rigid or flexible endoscopes. Polypoid mucosal changes in the nasal cavity are indicative of chronic rhinosinusitis that may affect the function of the Eustachian tube. Attention should also be paid to the possible presence of space-occupying lesions in the nasopharynx that may obstruct the tubal orifice (hypertrophied lymphatic tissue, nasopharyngeal carcinomas). Many patients with a patulous Eustachian tube have a widening of the opening of the Eustachian tube in the nasopharynx [2]. Biopsy of suspected space-occupying lesions should be done for histopathological examination. Objective tinnitus may be caused by myoclonus of the palatine muscles (the tensor and levator veli palatini). Twitching of these muscles can be observed by endoscopy.

Auscultation

Auscultation of the ear and neck vessels can be important in the diagnosis of objective tinnitus [3]. A stethoscope can be used to detect signs of carotid artery stenosis, such as what may occur from atherosclerosis, vascular compression, and arteriovenous malformations. Dural AV fistulas can be detected by auscultation of the upper neck and in the post-auricular region. According to [4], the use of an electronic stethoscope is more sensitive than classic auscultation techniques. If a patient's tinnitus is affected by compression of the neck or from turning the head, it is a sign that the cause is of venous origin. Such maneuvers would have no effect on pulsatile tinnitus of arterial origin [5]. Abnormal auscultatory findings require further clarification using Doppler ultrasound or angiography. Direct auscultation of the middle ear performed with a Toynbee tube inserted into the external auditory canal makes it possible to hear the tinnitus that is caused by contractions of the stapedius or tensor tympani muscles of the middle ear [6].

---

[2]Cholesteatoma: Squamous metaplasia or extension of squamous cell epithelium inward to line an expanding cystic cavity that may involve the middle ear or mastoid, erode surrounding bone, and become filled with a mass of keratinized squamous cell epithelial debris, usually resulting from chronic otitis media. The lesion often contains cholesterol clefts surrounded by inflammatory and foreign body giant cells, hence the name cholesteatoma. From: Stedman's Electronic Medical Dictionary.

[3]Schwartze's sign: A pink blush behind the tympanic membrane, sometimes seen in otosclerosis because of hyperemia of the mucous membrane around the promontory. First described by Schwartze in 1873. From: Dorland's Medical Dictionary.

[4]Myoclonus: One or a series of shock-like contractions of a group of muscles of variable regularity, synchrony, and symmetry, generally due to a central nervous system lesion.

Supplementary Radiological Diagnosis

Radiological examinations may be justified when otologic examinations are inconclusive regarding pathologies that may be involved in causing tinnitus [7]. High-resolution computed tomography (CT) of the petrous portion of the temporal bones can be used to detect and examine structural bony changes of the external ear and its surroundings, the middle ear, and inner ear.

MRI can be used to visualize a fluid-filled cochlea. Finally, this technique is used to diagnose intra- or extrameatal acoustic neurinomas. Detailed information regarding these techniques is provided in Chap. 19.

Doppler studies of vessels on the neck are helpful in the diagnosis of pulsatile tinnitus (see Chap. 59). In some countries (e.g., Germany), ultrasound techniques are part of an otologic examination. Doppler ultrasound allows visualization of carotid stenoses, arterial dissections, and arteriovenous malformations. Sismanis and Smoker [8] also recommend extending the use of this modality to include the subclavian arteries. Digital subtraction angiography is employed for the preoperative assessment of a glomus tumor, permitting identification of the main supplying vessel on the basis of the tumor blush. Interventional embolization of the supplying vessels during the same session prepares for efficient control of bleeding during subsequent surgical resection.

References

1. Nakashima, T., Sone, M., Fujii, H., Teranishi, M., Yamamoto, H., Otake, H., Sugiura, M., Naganawa, S. (2006) Blood flow to the promontory in cochlear otosclerosis. Clin. Otolaryngol. **31**, 110–115.
2. Grimmer, J. F., Poe, D. S. (2005) Update on Eustachian tube dysfunction and the patulous Eustachian tube. Curr. Opin. Otolaryngol. Head Neck Surg. **13**, 277–282.
3. Tewfik, S. (1974) Phonocephalography: An objective diagnosis of tinnitus. J. Laryngol. **88**, 869–875.
4. Sismanis, A., Williams, G. H., King, M. D. (1989) A new electronic device for evaluation of objective tinnitus. Otolaryngol. Head Neck Surg. **100**, 644–645.
5. Sismanis, A. (2003) Pulsatile tinnitus. Otolaryngol. Clin. North. Am. **36**, 389–402.
6. Badia, L. B., Parikh, A., Brookes, G. B. (1994) Management of middle ear myoclonus. J. Laryngol. Otol. **108**, 380–382.
7. Branstetter, B. F. 4th, Weissman, J. L. (2006) The radiologic evaluation of tinnitus. Eur. Radiol. **16**, 2792–2802.
8. Sismanis, A., Smoker, W. R. K. (1994) Pulsatile tinnitus: recent advantages in diagnosis. Laryngoscope. **104**, 681–688.

Chapter 49
Audiologic Clinical Assessment

Umberto Ambrosetti and Luca Del Bo

Keypoints

1. Tinnitus may be the symptom of many different disorders.

   An accurate assessment of a patient's history, symptoms, and signs is important to establish a correct diagnosis.

   The tinnitus handicap inventory (THI) and the visual analog scale (VAS) are very useful tests to evaluate the handicap caused by tinnitus and the entity of tinnitus, respectively.

2. An objective assessment of ear, head, neck, and temporomandibular articulation should be performed.

3. Pure-tone audiometry (the frequency range from 125 to 16 KHz), tympanometry, acoustic middle-ear reflex testing, speech recognition threshold testing, and speech discrimination tests help determine the type of hearing loss and the status of the middle ear.

4. Otoacoustic emission (OAEs) testing allows for precise evaluation of the outer hair cell function.

5. Acufenometry is performed to determine pitch and loudness of tinnitus by defining minimum masking levels (MMLs), loudness discomfort levels (LDLs), and the residual inhibition.

6. Auditory brainstem responses (ABR) are used in selected patients for further evaluation and exclusion of disorders such as vestibular schwannoma.

Electrocochleography (ECochG) is used in order to evaluate the electric phenomena of the inner ear.

Keywords Tinnitus • Assessment • Pure-tone audiometry • Speech audiometry • Impedance • Otoacoustic emissions • Acufenometry • Brainstem-evoked potentials.

Abbreviations

ABR	Auditory brainstem response
AEP	Auditory evoked potential
dB	Decibel
DPOAE	Distortion product otoacoustic emissions
ECochG	Electrocochleography
fMRI	Functional Magnetic Resonance Imaging
HL	Hearing level
Hz	Hertz
IHCs	Inner hair cells
LDL	Loudness discomfort level
MEG	Magneto Encephalographic
MLR	Middle latency response
MML	Minimum masking level
MRI	Magnetic resonance imaging
OAE	Otoacoustic emissions
OHCs	Other hair cells
PET	Positron emission tomography
RI	Residual inhibition
NMR	Nuclear magnetic resonance
CT	Computed tomography
TEOAE	Transiently evoked otoacoustic emissions
THI	Tinnitus handicap inventory
VAS	Visual analog scale
WN	White noise

L. Del Bo (✉)
Fondazione Ascolta e Vivi, via Foppa 15, 20144 Milan, Italy
e-mail: delbo@sordita.it

A.R. Møller et al. (eds.), *Textbook of Tinnitus*,
DOI 10.1007/978-1-60761-145-5_49, © Springer Science+Business Media, LLC 2011

Introduction

An audiologic diagnosis is crucial to identify auditory system pathologies. In particular, an accurate assessment must precede any further treatment. A detailed assessment may even be therapeutic for patients with tinnitus, as it often reduces many of the patient's concerns and reactions to their disease. Audiologic assessments can rule out severe diseases, which may have been of great concern to the patient, and the real cause of tinnitus is identified.

Tinnitus may be the symptom of many different disorders of the human auditory system that must be accurately investigated in order to reach a diagnosis that allows the best treatment. These treatments allow for the cure or management of the patient's tinnitus by means of medical or surgical therapies, as well as specific dietary regimens or other available treatments.

Audiological History

The medical history of patients with subjective tinnitus should include information about infectious diseases during childhood, previous surgical interventions, endocrine and metabolic disorders, and hypertension. Middle-ear diseases (stenosis and insufficiency of the Eustachian tube, secretive otitis media, acute and chronic otitis media, tympanosclerosis with a close or open tympanum, or otosclerosis) and inner ear diseases (toxic drug–induced damage, exposure to acoustic traumas, Ménière's disease, or presbyacusis) should also be included in the history.

Also, alterations in the skeleton, either congenital or induced by injuries and traumas, should be investigated, as well as posture variations due to pathologies of lumbosacral and cervical vertebral column, pelvic girdle, and, in particular, the stomatognatic apparatus [1, 2].

The characteristic of tinnitus should be determined, including duration, intensity, loudness, continuity, intermittence, pulsatility, variations produced by physical effort, and psychological effects [3, 4].

The tinnitus handicap inventory (THI) questionnaire [5] is a very useful instrument to evaluate the handicap caused by tinnitus; it is simple, short, and immediate. McCombe and colleagues [6] reduced the THI questionnaire scorings into a grading scale to estimate the development of tinnitus: Grade 1 (0–16), slight tinnitus; Grade 2 (18–36), mild tinnitus; Grade 3 (38–56), moderate tinnitus; Grade 4 (58–76), severe tinnitus; and Grade 5 (78–100), catastrophic tinnitus.

The visual analog scale (VAS) is a scale ranging from 0 to 10, which is used to quantify the entity of the disease as tinnitus, hyperacusis, or deafness by directly evaluating the symptoms reported by the patient [7, 8].

Objective Examination

Once all the significant anamnestic data have been collected, the objective examination of the outer and middle ear along with all the ear, nose, and throat area is to be performed.

The areas relating to the auricle, mastoid, and temporomandibular articulation must be investigated in order to identify possible malformations, stenosis, atresia in the external auditory canal, or any asymmetry between the two auricles, which is indicative of malformations or associated syndrome. Palpation of the whole auricular area must then be performed and, in particular, it must be investigated whether the patient experiences pain on both sides of the temporomandibular joint (TMJ) either with a closed mouth or during mastication.

The cartilagineous and bone portions of the auditory canal and the tympanic membrane are then examined: an operating microscope should be used, which allows a stereoscopic visualization. The examination of the external auditory canal may reveal build-up of wax or epidermal residues that must be removed in order to allow the examination of the tympanic membrane. Earwax must be totally removed, even when it is "spread" on the tympanic membrane or located in the anterior tympano-meatal corner. In fact, in these cases, earwax can often be difficult to remove with a simple remove wash without causing a sense of ear occlusion, hearing loss, or tinnitus. Hairs or hair fragments in the ear canal may also be accurately removed, as they may cause tinnitus, which resolves spontaneously after removal. Dermatologic diseases in the skin of the ear canal or anatomic stenosis, caused by single or multiple osteomas, may also be looked for.

The color of the tympanic membrane, which normally appears pearly, must be carefully examined for its brightness and the possible presence of air blisters, scars, dermo-epidermal blisters, single retraction pockets, or partial and total perforations.

In case of tympanic perforation, its extension and localization must be carefully assessed, as well as the possible presence of otorrhea, which should be removed by means of an aspirator if it is abundant. Small granulations, if present, must also be removed in order to proceed with a proper assessment of the tympanic membrane.

Once the external auditory canal has been duly cleaned, secretion-induced crusts must be removed from the tympanic membrane; after removing any residue that can mask tympanic perforations or retraction pockets, the presence of whitish tissue must be investigated, in particular, in the epitympanum, pathognomonic of cholesteatomatous chronic otitis.

Besides the otologic clinical assessment, an objective examination of both nose and throat must be performed, possibly with the aid of a fiber-optic endoscopy.

In case of pulsating tinnitus, the large vessels of the ear and neck must be ausculted in order to identify objective tinnitus [9, 10].

Diagnostic imaging is required if the clinical assessment reveals a suspicion of expansive growth pathologies in the middle ear or pontocerebellar corner. Computed tomography (CT) and gadolinium magnetic resonance imaging (MRI) of the cerebellopontine angle is warranted to exclude a vestibular schwannoma in case of audiologic suspicion (asymmetric hearing loss, no middle-ear reflexes). Further diagnostic work-up may include echo-doppler of supra-aortic trunks or the cochlear labyrinth, as warranted. Angio-MRI may be done if vascular diseases are suspected. Additional diagnostic imaging techniques, such as positron emission

tomography (PET), functional magnetic resonance imaging (fMRI), magneto encephalographic (MEG) – all used in clinical research – have not yet been included in clinical diagnostic protocols.

Hematochemical analyses provide information on possible metabolic disorders (dyslipidemia, altered blood viscosity), flogistic diseases (immunocomplexes, antibodies), endocrine diseases (dysthyroidism, diabetes), and others.

In case of isolated tinnitus, causing or favoring factors should be investigated within the vascular system (hypertension, vertebrobasilar insufficiency) or within the neurologic system (epilepsy).

Psychiatric etiology should also always be considered (hysteria, psychosis, schizophrenia), as well as any manifestation of anxiety or depression [4].

Audiometric Evaluation

Several audiometric tests are required to complete a clinical examination of patients with tinnitus. This includes both subjective and objective tests (Table 49.1), which should be carried out in a succession to allow a comprehensive evaluation of the auditory system, from the periphery to the central auditory nervous system.

Audiometric evaluation should include the following tests:

– Pure-tone thresholds
– Speech recognition thresholds
– Acoustic middle-ear reflex testing (reflex tone decay only if comfortably tolerated by patient) and tympanometry

Table 49.1 List of subjective and objective audiologic examinations and relating aims in tinnitus diagnosis

Subjective examination	Objective examination	Aim
Pure-tone thresholds		Auditory threshold assessment and damage site localization
	Tympanmetry and acoustic reflex testing	Middle ear and Eustachian tube function, cochlear and retrocochlear dysfunctions
Speech recognition thresholds and discrimination		Damage site definition and confirmation, communication capabilities assessment
	Otoacustic emissions	Outer hair cell function
Acufenometry		Tinnitus pitch and loudness, MML and RI definition
Loudness disconfort level (LDL)		Doscomfort threshold definition
	Acoustic evoked potentials: ECochG, ABR, MLR	Acoustic nerve function assessment and threshold confirmation

- Tinnitus loudness and pitch matching
- Minimum masking levels (MMLs)
- Loudness discomfort levels (LDLs) to speech and pure tone
- Residual inhibition (RI)
- Distortion-product otoacoustic emissions (DPOAEs)
- Evoked potentials (ABR)

Pure-Tone Thresholds

The first test to be performed is a plain pure-tone audiogram [11] with the patient sitting in a soundproof booth; pure tones of known intensity and frequency are delivered through insert earphones, or through supra-aural headphones, and an audiometer, which is controlled by the examiner.

Clinical audiometers usually have a frequency range from 125 to 8,000 Hz, at an intensity range between 10 and 120 dB hearing level (HL). However, for use in patients with tinnitus, the range must be extended up to 16,000 Hz [12, 13].

Audiometer calibration must be performed at least once a year, since it is important to be able to detect even minor threshold variations from normal conditions [14]. This test, despite being a relatively simple one, actually requires an experienced examiner with excellent clinician–patient communication skills, so that the most precise threshold can be obtained.

In case of large degree of asymmetry in hearing threshold between the two sides, "masking" noise should be delivered to the healthier ear, so that this latter does not perceive the acoustic stimulus via bone conduction [15]. The "cross-talk" effect is different for different earphone types, being much greater for supra-aural head transmission than for insert earphones (see [16], page 299).

Bone conduction audiometry that allows direct stimulation of the inner ear (hair cells), "bypassing" the ear canal and middle-ear transmission system, makes it possible to separately evaluate the hearing threshold without the influence of the conductive apparatus.

For that, a small vibrator is placed on the patient's mastoid bone. The vibrator allows delivery of stimuli frequency ranging from 250 to 4,000 Hz, and the highest deliverable intensity varies according to the tested frequency [17].

When the air conduction threshold is worse than the bone conduction one, it is an indication of conductive hearing loss. When both thresholds are equal and elevated, it is a sign of sensorineural hearing loss.

Elevation of the hearing threshold, even a mild one, within the frequency range 8,000–16,000 Hz may be the cause of acute tinnitus.

Elevation of the hearing threshold in the frequency range between 3,000 and 6,000 Hz (determined in steps of half octaves) must also be investigated; such hearing loss may be an indication of isolated selective damages to the auditory system that could lead to frequency-specific tinnitus in this frequency range. Some individuals with tinnitus have several dips in their audiograms, which may be indications of contact between a blood vessel and the auditory nerve root (see Chap. 40).

Tympanometry and Acoustic Middle-Ear Reflex Testing

Tympanometry measures the change in the ear's acoustic impedance when the air pressure in the ear canal is varied. The results appear as a curve of the acoustic impedance (or more often its inverse, known as the acoustic admittance). The term "immittance" is often used to describe the acoustic compliance of the ear. Tympanometry cannot be carried out when the external auditory duct is occluded or the tympanic membrane is perforated.

This method gives objective clinical information; it is a non-invasive exam and a quick one.

The examination is performed by introducing into the external auditory canal a probe equipped with a soft end cap, ensuring pneumatic capacity, besides the following three additional functions: (1) it generates a sound called "probe tone" (220 Hz–65 dB HL); (2) by means of a pump, it varies the pressure from positive values (+200 mm/H_2O) to negative values (−400 mm/H_2O); and (3) a microphone records the sound pressure in the ear canal. The sound pressure in the ear canal is a measure of the ear's acoustic impedance (or admittance).

One single exam allows, in a very short time, three different tests to be performed: tympanometry, assessment of acoustic stapedial reflexes, and assessment of the Eustachian tube function.

The test has two parts: one is tympanometry, which evaluates the compliance (mobility) of the middle ear. The second test uses similar techniques to record

Table 49.2 Recordable tympanograms and associated physiopathologic conditions

Tympanogram	Morphology	Clinical significance
A	Bell-shaped with a peak zero pressure or close	Normal
B	Flat line or ruler-like	Fixation of the tympano-ossicular chain
C	A bell shaped with a peak shifted to the negative pressure values	Negative pressure in the middle ear (otitis with effusion or Eustachian tube stenosis)

contractions of the middle-ear muscles (mainly the stapedius muscle) elicited by a loud tone presented to the same or the opposite ear. A normally functioning middle ear has a tympanogram that is bell shaped with a peak center on zero pressure (Type A); a tympanogram showing a flat line is, instead, consistent with an increase in rigidity of the tympanic ossicular system (Type B); a bell-shaped tympanogram with a peak shifted to the negative pressure values on the graph (Type C) is indicative of pressure in the middle-ear cavity that can be caused by secretive otitis media or Eustachian tube stenosis [18] (Table 49.2).

Tympanometry allows the evaluation of the function of the Eustachian tube, such as its ability to open during deglutition. Once the tympanogram has been obtained, external auditory canal pressure is increased to +200 mm H_2O, and the patient is asked to swallow; under normal conditions, the tympanogram changes as a sign of air coming out of the middle ear and returns to normal after deglutition. This test is crucial for tinnitus evaluation, since altered tubal function is associated to tinnitus appearance.

The acoustic middle-ear reflex (stapedial reflex) is elicited with tones in the frequency range 500–1,000 and in the range of 2,000–4,000, applied to the contralateral or the ipsilateral stimulus one at a time. Contraction of the middle-ear muscles (stapedius and tensor tympani) causes the ear's acoustic impedance to change, and that makes a non-invasive way of recording the response of the acoustic middle-ear reflex. If the middle-ear pressure is different from the ambient pressure, as indicated by the tympanogram, it has to be equalized before testing the acoustic middle-ear reflex. Under normal conditions, the threshold for the acoustic middle-ear reflexes for tones is 90 dB HL in a normally hearing individual. It is slightly (2–10 dB) lower when elicited from the ipsilateral ear.

Cochlear hearing loss is associated with a distortion phenomenon called "recruitment of loudness", so that a sound is perceived louder than normal. This should be distinguished from hyperacusis, which is a lowered tolerance for sounds (see Chap. 3). The stapedial reflex threshold, as recorded for different frequencies, allows the physician to objectively determine recruitment of loudness.

Assessment of the decay of the response of the acoustic middle-ear reflex at prolonged stimulation may be an indication of auditory nerve diseases (Anderson's test) [19]. However, the reliability of this test has been disputed.

It has been estimated that 40% of individuals with tinnitus also have hyperacusis. Such patients may experience discomfort from acoustic overstimulation, such as in testing the acoustic middle-ear reflex.

Speech Recognition Thresholds and Speech Discrimination

In order to properly assess an individual's hearing capacity and quantify its impact on speech recognition, threshold, and speech discrimination scores, speech audiometry is used, by means of words and sentences as test sounds. Recorded speech material is preferred to live voice presentation. Standardized lists of words and sentences are delivered at different intensities, to one ear at a time, recording the number of correct answers given by the patient. The healthier ear must be masked in patients with a marked tone threshold asymmetry when the ear with hearing loss is tested.

Under normal conditions, the articulation curve is S shaped; in cases of conductive hearing loss, the curve is shifted to the right. In patients with cochlear or retrocochlear hearing loss, the shape of the curves, in addition to being shifted to the right, are changed, and 100% intelligibility will not be achieved.

Otoacoustic Emissions

The damage to other hair cells (OHCs) is believed to be involved in the development of peripheral tinnitus in individuals with a normal hearing sensibility [20, 21]. Recording of otoacoustic emissions (OAEs) is important because it allows to identify changes in the function of the OHC.

OAEs are weak sounds generated by the electromotility of the OHC, which pass through the middle-ear ossicles and tympanic membrane and can be measured in the external ear canal [22].

Recordings of OAEs are objective tests of cochlear (OHC) function and their presence, in general, is indicative of normal hearing. This test is very sensitive to cochlear damage that involves OHCs and can often be detected before clinical evidence of hearing loss is present. Successful recording of OAEs depends on normal function of the middle ear.

In the clinical practice, particularly in the study of tinnitus, the subclasses of OAEs, which are most useful and utilized, are transiently evoked otoacoustic emissions (TEOAEs) and distortion-product otoacoustic emissions (DPOAEs).

TEOAEs are less affective by contralateral white-noise suppression in individuals with tinnitus than in individuals with similar hearing impairments and without tinnitus [23]. One explanation of this observation may be a hyperactivity of the OHCs resulting from pathological cochlear activity [24].

Recording of distortion-product otoacoustic emissions (DPOAEs) can provide a detailed and tonotopic OHC test that can identify small areas of cochlear damage; DPOAEs are recorded at frequencies as high as 8–10 kHz with up to 10 points/octave.

The value of recording DPOAEs in patients with tinnitus has been controversial [25–29].

Tinnitus Loudness and Pitch Matching

Acufenometry is the technique used to determine the frequency range (pitch) of tinnitus, its subjective intensity (loudness), the ability of sounds to mask the tinnitus of an individual person, and the residual inhibition of tinnitus. The test becomes difficult to perform when the tinnitus has the character of complex noise.

It is well known that one tone may be masked by another pure tone with enough intensity. Narrowband noises also have masking characteristics similar to those of pure tones while tinnitus that sounds like wideband noises do not have similar masking features. A tone may easily be masked by a wideband noise, while a wideband noise is hardly ever masked by a pure tone.

Tinnitus that is referred to one ear may be masked by sounds applied to the ipsilateral as well as the contralateral ear. Contralateral masking requires higher sound levels than ipsilateral masking [30].

Masking or suppressing tests make it possible to determine the tone intensity or noise that completely suppresses the perception of tinnitus. Once the type of sound that effectively masks the tinnitus has been found, the stimulus intensity is then increased 2 dB steps, up to a level where the tinnitus can no longer be heard.

The intensity difference, measured in dB, between the hearing threshold for the masking tone and the level of minimum masking intensity is the "minimum masking level" (MML).

In most patients, the MML plotted as a function of frequency intersects with the hearing threshold, indicating the specific frequency of tinnitus [31].

Hyperacusis is studied by determining the level of acoustic stimulation threshold that produces discomfort (loudness discomfort level – LDL) to the patient.

Hyperacusis is defined as a lower than normal discomfort level (see Chap. 3). Hyperacusis is different from recruitment of loudness, which is a perception that sounds arc abnormally loud, and the threshold of the acoustic middle-ear reflex is lower than it would be for the same hearing loss that occurs without recruitment. Masking noise may often induce temporary tinnitus suppression or a temporary relief from tinnitus, known as "residual inhibition" (RI) or "residual suppression" [31–34].

To perform the test, the noise level established for MML is raised by 10 dB and presented for exactly 1 min.

The examiner waits for a few seconds and then asks, "Does your tinnitus sound the same as before, or is there any difference?" The residual inhibition is present if the patient reports a lower level of tinnitus. The total duration of residual inhibition is recorded and measured in seconds [35]. As a masker intensity is increased to +20 dB, the depth and duration of RI increase.

RI is one of the few procedures that may reduce or eliminate tinnitus for a brief period.

The presence of RI, in individuals with hearing loss, allows efficient control of tinnitus by means of hearing aid, which provides sufficient amplification at the frequencies of the tinnitus [36].

Auditory-Evoked Potentials

Essentially, four kinds of auditory-evoked potentials are in clinical use (Table 49.3). These tests cannot be done in patients with hearing loss exceeding 80–90 dB HL.

When elicited by a transient sound, click, or short tone burst, electrocochleography (ECochG) records the sound-evoked potentials generated in the cochlea (cochlear microphonics and summating potentials) and in the distal portion of the auditory nerve (compound action potential). ECochG is performed by placing a recording electrode either deep in the ear canal or using a needle that is inserted through the tympanic membrane to come in contact with the cochlea capsule. It allows a detailed evaluation of the electric phenomena occurring in the cochlea and in the distal portion of the auditory nerve [37].

Recording of the auditory brainstem response (ABR) allows evaluation of the auditory threshold when elicited by high-intensity clicks or tone bursts (approximately 65 dB HL). ABR recordings provide information about the integrity of the ascending auditory pathways up to the midbrain level (inferior colliculus).

ABR recordings provide diagnostic information about auditory nerve injuries, presence of vestibular schwannoma, and other pathologies of the lower auditory pathways. ABR test requires the application of three surface electrodes placed on the patient's skin after degreasing the skin and spreading a conductive paste [to forehead center (or better on the top of the head of Cz), ear lobes]. The response to 2,000 click sounds delivered through a headset is normally averaged to get an interpretable record.

By increasing the frequency of the acoustic stimulation (high rate potential), further information may be obtained concerning the latencies of the components of the ABR recordings; Selters and Brackman [38]

reported that the ABR had a high sensitivity for deflecting the presence of vestibular schwannoma when the recorders are compensated for age-related changes in hearing threshold.

Godey and colleagues [39] reported that the ABR alone detected vestibular schwannoma in 92% of patients, while together with recordings of acoustic middle-ear reflex and caloric vestibular responses, the sensitivity was 98%.

References

1. Bjorne A (2007) Assessment of temporomandibular and cervical spine disorders in tinnitus patients. Prog Brain Res 166:215–9.
2. Rocha CA and TG Sanchez (2007) Myofascial trigger points: another way of modulating tinnitus. Prog Brain Res 166:209–14.
3. Langguth B, T Kleinjung, B Fischer et al (2007) Tinnitus severity, depression, and the big five personality traits. Prog Brain Res 166:221–5.
4. Prosser S and A Martini (2007) Argomenti di audiologia. Omega Edizioni. 418–20.
5. Newman CW, GP Jacobson and JB Spitzer (1996) Development of the tinnitus handicap inventory. Arch Otolaryngol Head Neck Surg 122:143–8.
6. McCombe A, D Baguley, R Coles et al (2001) Guidelines for the grading of tinnitus severity: the results of a working group commissioned by the British Association of Otolaryngologists, Head and Neck Surgeons, 1999. Clin Otolaryngol Allied Sci 26:388–93.
7. Henry JA, MM Jastreboff, PJ Jastreboff et al (2003) Guide to conducting tinnitus retraining therapy initial and follow-up interviews. J Rehabil Res Dev 40:157–77.
8. Meikle MB, BJ Stewart, SE Griest et al (2008) Tinnitus outcomes assessment. Trends Amplif 12:223–35.
9. Bjorne A (1993) Tinnitus aereum as an effect of increased tension in the lateral pterygoid muscle. Otolaryngol Head Neck Surg 109:969.
10. Møller AR (2003) Pathophysiology of tinnitus. Otolaryngol Clin North Am 36:249–66, v–vi.
11. Haller RW (2002) Puretone evaluation, in Handbook of clinical audiology, J Katz, Editor. Lippincott Williams & Wilkins: Baltimore. 71–8.
12. Berlin C (1982) Ultra-audiometric hearing in the hearing impaired and the use of upward-shifting translating hearing aids. Volta Rev 84:352–63.
13. Fausti SA and JM Rappaport (1985) High-frequency audiometry. Semin Hear 6:369–86, 97–404.
14. Wilberg LA (1985) Calibration: puretone, speech and noise signal, in Handbook of clinical audiology, J Katz, Editor. Williams & Wilkins: Baltimore. 116–50.
15. Konig E (1963) The use of making noise and its limitations in clinical audiometry. Acta Otolaryngol (Suppl) 180:1–64.
16. Møller AR (2006) Hearing: anatomy, physiology, and disorders of the auditory system, 2nd Ed. Academic Press, Amsterdam.

Table 49.3 Different types of auditory evoked potential and investigated site

Auditory evoked potential	Investigated site
ECochG	• Cochlea
	• Auditory nerve
ABR	• Auditory nerve
	• Nuclei of the ascending auditory pathway
MLR	• Thalamus
	• Primary auditory areas

17. Dirks D (1985) Bone conduction testing, in Handbook of clinical audiology, J Katz, Editor. Williams & Wilkins: Baltimore. 202–23.

18. Jerger J (1970) Clinical experience with impedance audiometry. Arch Otolaryngol 92:311–24.

19. Dirks D and SE Morgon (2000) Tynpanometry and acoustic reflex testing, in The ear comprensive otology, RF Canalis and PR Lambert, Editors. Lippincott Williams & Wilkins: Philadelphia. 223–9.

20. Jastreboff PJ (1990) Phantom auditory perception (tinnitus): mechanisms of generation and perception. Neurosci Res 8:221–54.

21. Lenarz T, C Schreiner, RL Snyder et al (1993) Neural mechanisms of tinnitus. Eur Arch Otorhinolaryngol 249:441–6.

22. Kemp DT (1978) Stimulated acoustic emissions from within the human auditory system. J Acoust Soc Am 64: 1386–91.

23. Attias J, I Bresloff and V Furman (1996) The influence of the efferent auditory system on otoacoustic emissions in noise induced tinnitus: clinical relevance. Acta Otolaryngol 116:534–9.

24. Zweig G and CA Shera (1995) The origin of periodicity in the spectrum of evoked otoacoustic emissions. J Acoust Soc Am 98:2018–47.

25. Norton SJ, AR Schmidt and LJ Stover (1990) Tinnitus and otoacoustic emissions: is there a link? Ear Hear 11:159–66.

26. Mitchell CR, DJ Lilly and JA Henry (1995). Otoacoustic emissions in subjects with tinnitus and normal hearing, in 5th International Tinnitus Seminars. Am Tinnitus Association: Portland.

27. Shiomi Y, J Tsuji, Y Naito et al (1997) Characteristics of DPOAE audiogram in tinnitus patients. Hear Res 108:83–8.

28. Gouveris H, J Maurer and W Mann (2005) DPOAE-grams in patients with acute tonal tinnitus. Otolaryngol Head Neck Surg 132:550–3.

29. Ozimek E, A Wicher, W Szyfter et al (2006) Distortion product otoacoustic emission (DPOAE) in tinnitus patients. J Acoust Soc Am 119:527–38.

30. Cusimano F and E Martines (1995) Acufeni, in Manuale di audiologia, M Del Bo, Editor. Masson: Milano. 413.

31. Feldmann H (1971) Homolateral and contralateral masking of tinnitus by noise-bands and by pure tones. Audiology 10:138–44.

32. Josephson EM (1931) A method of measurement of tinnitus aurium. Arch Otolaryngol 14:282.

33. Vernon J, S Griest and L Press (1990) Attributes of tinnitus and the acceptance of masking. Am J Otolaryngol 11:44–50.

34. Terry AM, DM Jones, BR Davis et al (1983) Parametric studies of tinnitus masking and residual inhibition. Br J Audiol 17:245–56.

35. Henry JA (2004) Audiologic assessment, in Tinnitus: theory and management, JB Snow, Jr., Editor. BC Decker: Hamilton [Ont.]. 220–36.

36. Vernon J, A Schleuning, L Odell et al (1977) A tinnitus clinic. Ear Nose Throat J 56:181–9.

37. Ferraro JA and R Ferguson (1989) Tympanic ECochG and conventional ABR: a combined approach for the identification of wave I and the I–V interwave interval. Ear Hear 10:161–6.

38. Selters WA and DE Brackmann (1977) Acoustic tumor detection with brain stem electric response audiometry. Arch Otolaryngol 103:181–7.

39. Godey B, X Morandi, L Beust et al (1988) Sensitivity of auditory brainstem response in acoustic neuroma screening. Acta Otolaryngol (Stockh) 118:501–4.

Chapter 50
Clinical Otoneurological Examination

Carlos Herráiz

Keypoints

1. The relevance of the anterior labyrinth (cochlea) in tinnitus generation opens the possibility that some patients will show damage in the posterior labyrinth as a whole inner ear disease.
2. The connections between the central vestibular pathways and the auditory, visual, and somatosensory systems could be also implicated in the mechanisms of tinnitus.
3. An exhaustive otoneurological examination is recommended in those patients we suspect a vestibular affection. The medical history will give us the most important information for the etiology and the severity of the symptoms.
4. The examination is driven toward three main systems: cranial pairs and cerebellum, the vestibulo-ocular reflex, and the vestibulo-spinal reflex.
5. A basic office exam can give us much information about the affected side and the compensation stage.
6. The instrumental examination, mostly performed in the chronic stages, will objectify and measure some aspects of the vestibular impairment. The oculomotor system examination and vestibulo-ocular reflex (rotatory and caloric stimulation) will be tested with the videonystagmograph.
7. The vestibulo-spinal reflex will be checked using the dynamic posturography. This instrument will test

the balance and lateropulsion from a dizzy patient, as well as the strategies for keeping the equilibrium right over specific sensorineural afferent disruption (visual, somatosensory, and vestibular).
8. Understanding the mechanisms and pathophysiology of the vestibular system will help us to connect the multiple sensory pathways involved in some forms of tinnitus.

Keywords Tinnitus • Dizziness • Vertigo • Videonystagmography • Dynamic posturography

Introduction

The cochlea is the location of the pathology that causes some forms of tinnitus, but there is now evidence that the central nervous system (CNS) is the anatomical location of the abnormal neural activity that causes many forms of tinnitus. There is also evidence that these changes are caused by activation of neural plasticity and that acoustic deprivation is the most important cause and chronic maintenance of these changes [1]. The abnormal neural activity that causes tinnitus may be generated along the peripheral and central auditory pathways (CAP), or in other systems connected to these pathways such as the somatosensory or the limbic–amygdala complex. While there is evidence that connections between the central vestibular pathways and the auditory, visual, and somatosensory systems might be implicated in causing some forms of tinnitus, there is no evidence of similar interaction with the vestibular system. It is therefore only when vestibular disorders accompany tinnitus that it is important to perform a complete otoneurological examination.

C. Herráiz (✉)
Department of Otorhinolaryngology, Hospital Universitario
Fundación Alcorcón, C/Budapest, 1, 28922,
Alcorcón Madrid, Spain
and
Tinnitus and Hyperacusis Clinic, Otorhinolaryngology,
Hospital Quirón, Madrid, Spain
e-mail: cherraizp@seorl.net

A.R. Møller et al. (eds.), *Textbook of Tinnitus*,
DOI 10.1007/978-1-60761-145-5_50, © Springer Science+Business Media, LLC 2011

417

Medical History

Dizziness can represent a group of highly heterogeneous symptoms and sensations. Vertigo is the sensation of motion or spinning from oneself or from the environment and is often accompanied by vegetative symptoms. It is secondary to vestibular disorders in the majority of cases (central or peripheral). Imbalance or unsteadiness describes a loss of equilibrium on movement, or in situations in which there are conflicting sensory cues. It can represent the normal pattern of compensation after an acute vestibular lesion or a poor compensation if the symptoms are persistent after a few months. Multisensory disorders (visual, somatosensory, motor, or cerebellar) can manifest imbalance. Dizziness is any vague sensation of discomfort in the head: light-headedness, disorientation, floating, etc. Poor vestibular compensation or psychiatric disorders such as depression, anxiety, or hyperventilation can cause it. The syncope is secondary to cardiovascular disorders with reduced cerebral blood flow. Severe bilateral peripheral vestibular disorders or central diseases can produce a lack of stabilization of the visual field with passive whole-body movement called oscillopsia [2, 3]. Duration of vertigo, trigger factors, characteristics and frequency of spells, and presence of vegetative symptoms will help us in the diagnosis of the disease (Tables 50.1 and 50.2).

Otoneurologic Examination

The otoneurological examination is driven toward three main systems: cranial nerves and the cerebellum, the vestibulo-ocular reflex, and the vestibulo-spinal reflex.

Table 50.2 Differences between peripheral and central vertigo

	Peripheral vertigo	Central vertigo
Clinical symptoms	Harmonic[a]	Dys-harmonic
Optocinetic/pursuit test	Normal	Altered
Nystagmus	Direction-fixed	Direction-changing, dissociated
Compensation process	Usual	Unusual
Hearing	Altered	Normal

[a]Harmonic: nystagmus towards the healthy side + lateropulsion towards the affected side + spinnin sensation towards the healthy side

Nystagmus

Nystagmus is an involuntary rhythmic oscillation of the eyes, usually occurring simultaneously in both eyes. Ocular nystagmus is a pendular eye movement with similar speed toward both sides. It is related to abnormal visual fixation associated to loss of central vision. The vestibular nystagmus has a slow phase followed by a fast phase (saccadic movement) toward the opposite side. Nystagmus may be caused by any peripheral or central vestibular disorders of brainstem origin affecting control of the eye muscles. Nystagmus classification is given in Table 50.3. When the fast phase of nystagmus beats toward the healthy ear, it is a sign of peripheral vestibular problems. The intensity of the nystagmus increases when the patient looks toward the side to which the fast phase beats. Nystagmus can be spontaneous, gaze evoked, or voluntarily induced. Vestibular nystagmus is reduced when the patient fixes the gaze. A few individuals have nystagmus without

Table 50.1 Causes of vertigo and imbalance according to duration of the symptom

Seconds	Minutes/hours	Days	Months
BPPV	Ménière's disease	Vestibular neuritis	Vestibular neuroma
Perilymphatic Fistula	Endolymphatic hydrops	Sudden deafness	Ototoxicity
DSSC Sdr.	Vestibular migraine	Labyrinthitis	Bilateral vestibular disorders: genetic, bilateral MD, idiopathic
Cerebellar disorders	Perilymphatic fistula	Ramsay–Hunt syndrome	
Falls	Vertebrobasilar stroke	Cerebrovascular stroke	Psychiatric disorders
	Seizures	Multiple sclerosis	
	VIII nerve vascular compresion syndrome	Viral infections of the brain stem	
	Central paroxysmal vertigo of the cerebral stem	Vertebrobasilar insufficiency	
	Panic attack		
	Postural phobic vertigo		

BPPV: benign paroxysmal positional vertigo; DSSC Sdr: dehiscent superior semicircular canal syndrome; MD: Ménière's disease

any known disease. These kinds of nystagmus involve eye movements in the horizontal plane.

The examination of nystagmus involves having the patient follow the examiner's finger in both directions of gaze, but no more than 30 grades. The use of Frenzel glasses abolishes the gaze fixation making nystagmus appear more intense [2, 3]. Vertical nystagmus is rare and a sign of central nervous system diseases.

There are computerized tests of the vestibular ocular reflex (VOR) that measure gain and phase of the VOR. The gain is a measure of how accurately the eyes move in the direction opposite of head movement and the phase angle is a measure of the timing of the movement of the eyes. The videonistagmography tests the oculomotor movements (saccadic, pursuit, optokinetic) and the VOR through a double stimulation: rotatory and caloric (Figs. 50.1 and 50.2). The examination of postural vertigo through Dix-Hallpike maneuvers will diagnose benign positional paroxystic vertigo. A fistula test is performed with the patient sitting with their head 60° backward, so the horizontal canal of the vestibular apparatus is in the vertical position. With a snugly fitting pneumatic otoscope, alternate positive and negative pressure is rapidly applied to the external ear canal. If the patient becomes dizzy and gets nystagmus, it is a sign of the presence of a perilymphatic fistula.

Table 50.3 Characteristics of nystagmus

Direction	Direction-changing
	Direction-fixed
	Disconjugated
Plane	Horizontal, horizonto-rotatory, rotatory, vertical, oblique
Intensity	Three degrees (Alexander's law)
Mode of occurrence	Spontaneous, gaze-evoked, induced (optokinetic, head shaking, fistula test, drugs)
Specific forms	Endpoint N, congenital N, periodic alternate N

Tullio Phenomenon

Vertigo that is induced by high intensity sound is known as the Tullio phenomenon. It is positive in dehiscent superior semicircular canal syndrome and in the perilymphatic fistula. Making the Valsalva maneuver will typically induce vertigo in a patient who has a perilymphatic fistula or patients with an Arnold–Chiari malformation [4].

Unsteadiness and lateropulsion can be a consequence of vestibulo-spinal reflex (VSR) disorders.

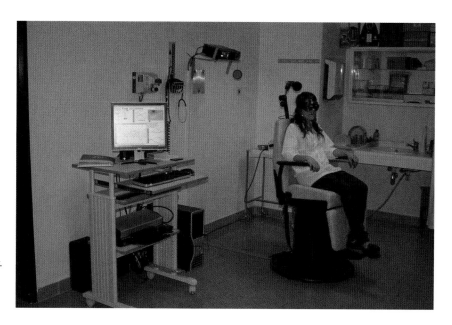

Fig. 50.1 Videonystagmography. It includes the eye camera, the rotatory chair, and the hardware/ software for data analysis

Fig. 50.2 Report of the VNG data for caloric responses. Graphic representation of the nystagmus according to the four stimulation processes, diagram of Freyss showing the represented values and objective data of preponderance and reflectivity of the labyrinths

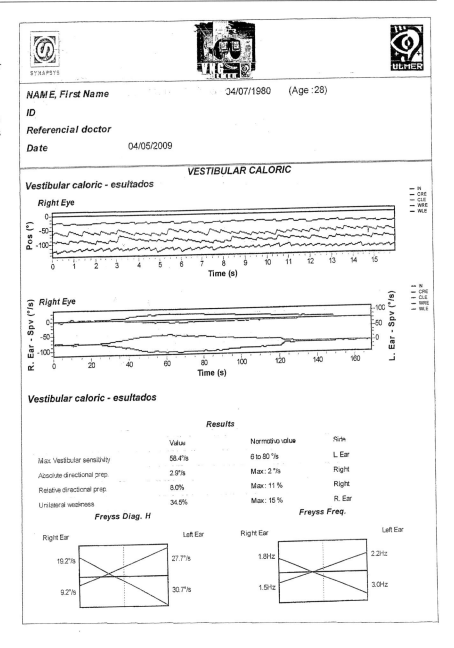

Romberg, Unterberger, and the test of the gait with the Babinksy–Weil test should be performed in all tinnitus patients with vestibular symptoms. Dynamic posturography is a computerized method to evaluate the VSR and the equilibrium strategies: visual, vestibular, and propioceptive (Fig. 50.3). Recording of the vestibular-evoked myogenic potentials (VEMP) is a novel technique to test the saccula function.

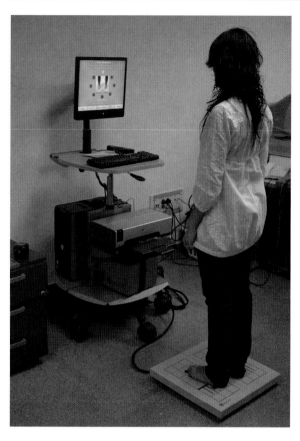

Fig. 50.3 Dynamic posturography for vestibular rehabilitation

Conclusions

Otoneurological examination in patients with tinnitus can be useful in the diagnosis of only some forms of tinnitus where the vestibular system is suspected to be involved, such as in connection with vestibular schwannoma. If vertigo or any kind of dizziness occurs together with tinnitus, an otoneurologic examination may be justified. Such examination must be done by a person who understands the mechanisms and pathophysiology of the vestibular system. Tests of the vestibulo-ocular and vestibulo-spinal reflexes are important in the examination of the vestibular disorders.

References

1. Møller A (2007) The role of neural plasticity in tinnitus. Prog Brain Res 166:37–45.
2. Busis S and Busis N (1994) The neurotologic examination. In Neurotology. Jackler R, Brackmann D Eds. Mosby: St Louis, MS, p. 186–187.
3. Bartual and Perez N (1998) El sistema vestibular y sus alteraciones. Masson Ed. Barcelona, Spain, p. 125–129.
4. Carmona S, Marelli E (2009) Neuro-Otologia. Akadia Ed. Buenos Aires, Argentina, p. 79–82.

Chapter 51
Diagnosis of Tinnitus: Neurological Examination

Miguel J.A. Láinez, Anna Piera, and Alejandro Ponz

Keypoints

1. There is an urgent need for a set of assessment methods to be agreed upon and utilized by the international tinnitus research community.
2. Neurological examination of tinnitus patients is essential to achieve a good diagnostic approach to the different forms of objective and subjective tinnitus.
3. This chapter summarizes the neurological examination in tinnitus, including the protocol used in the authors' tinnitus clinic, which is based on the consensus of the Tinnitus Research Initiative (TRI).

Keywords Tinnitus • Questionnaire (TSCHQ) • Tinnitus handicap inventory (THI) • Neurological examination • Doppler sonography

Abbreviations

MR	Magnetic resonance
MRA	Magnetic resonance angiography
SCM	Sternocleidomastoid
TCCS	Transcranial color coded sonography doppler
HAM-D	Hamilton rating scale for depression
TCD	Transcranial doppler
TMJ	Temporo-mandibular joint
TRI	Tinnitus Research Initiative
TSCHQ	Tinnitus sample case history questionnaire

M.J.A. Láinez (✉)
Department of Neurology, Hospital Clínico Universitario,
University of Valencia, Avenida Blasco Ibáñez, 17,
46010 Valencia, Spain
e-mail: jlaineza@meditex.es

Introduction

Chronic tinnitus, the phantom perception of sound, can be a debilitating and life-altering experience. It affects millions of people in western countries. Despite the enormous social and economic burden tinnitus causes, no well-established treatment for this specific disorder is available. Among the reasons for this unsatisfactory situation are the difficulties in assessing tinnitus, as it is a purely self-reported phenomenon.

There is an urgent need for a set of assessment methods to be agreed upon and utilized by the international tinnitus research community. This includes assessment of patients with tinnitus and subsequent measurement of outcomes following intervention [1].

There is a need for standardization of the ways patients with tinnitus are assessed and the way outcomes of interventions are measured to facilitate more effective cooperation and more meaningful evaluations and comparisons of the outcomes of treatment. So far, three meetings organized by the TRI were held in 2006, 2008, and 2009 to develop a consensus for patient assessments and outcome measurements. This has already contributed to better cooperation between research centers in finding and evaluating treatments for tinnitus by making it possible to better compare the results of studies and treatments [2].

During these workshops, the participants reviewed provisional consensus summaries, and after receiving feedback from all authors, a final consensus was created, giving consideration to the possibility of further modifications [2].

This chapter summarizes the neurological examination in tinnitus, making a brief introduction of protocol used in the authors' tinnitus clinic, based on the consensus arrived at by workshops arranged by the TRI.

A.R. Møller et al. (eds.), *Textbook of Tinnitus*,
DOI 10.1007/978-1-60761-145-5_51, © Springer Science+Business Media, LLC 2011

Evaluation of Patients with Tinnitus

Case History

Information about the history and descriptive characteristics of the patient's tinnitus or tinnitus-related conditions could be obtained by questionnaires and related interviews. The best example is a tinnitus sample case history questionnaire (TSCHQ), in which demographic data and other clinical data are compiled:

- Name, date of birth
- Age, gender, handedness, family tinnitus history
- Time of onset of symptoms
- Was the beginning perception gradual or abrupt
- Was the onset of tinnitus related to loud blast of sound, whiplash, change in hearing, stress, or others
- Is the tinnitus pulsatile or not pulsatile
- Is the tinnitus specific to the right or left ear, the head, or is it similar in both ears
- Constant or intermittent
- Loudness (scale 0–100)
- Sounds like noise, tone(s), sounds of crickets, other
- High pitch, medium, or low frequency (hum)
- Percent of total awake time with tinnitus (1–100%)
- Treatments received
- Can the tinnitus be masked by sound
- Is the tinnitus worse in a noisy environment
- Somatic modulation: can head and neck maneuvers, TMJ movement change the tinnitus
- Stress influence
- Hearing problem and hearing aids
- Hyperacusis
- Physical discomfort
- Neck pain
- TMJ disorder
- Psychiatric problems [1]

Psychophysical measures of perceived tinnitus intensity and severity are important for proper diagnosis. Even though these instruments are not specifically designed to be sensitive to treatment-related changes, they have been used as outcome measures in clinical trials. Tinnitus handicap inventory (THI) and Hamilton rating scale for depression (HAM-D) are used if there is psychiatric comorbidity like anxiety and depression [3–6]. Psychopathological aspects of patients with tinnitus and psychiatric comorbidity are discussed extensively in Chaps. 54, 62–64.

Neurological Examination

Neurological examination is essential in tinnitus patients to achieve a good diagnostic approach to the etiology in secondary tinnitus or in objective and subjective tinnitus. Below are the algorithms used by our clinic according to tinnitus workshops and publications. The patient's case history should always be taken into account when using these suggested assessments (see also Chap. 50).

Vital Signs

1. Blood pressure, pulse rate and character
2. Inspection:
   a. General appearance: anxiety, sadness, attention
   b. Head: irregularities or other deformities in cranial scars and signs of previous trauma; anomalies in temporal arteries
   c. Eyes: Ophthalmologic abnormalities can provide many clues to the etiology of tinnitus – bilateral exophthalmos in thyroid disease, unilateral proptosis in carotid-cavernous fistula, recent skew at basal inspection.

Higher Cortical Functions

A basic neurological examination of higher cortical functions like language and speech are needed to determine if a patient has neurologic, as opposed to psychiatric, disease.

Cranial Nerves

- Optic nerve CN II. Visual acuity and visual fields should be obtained in addition to ophthalmoscopic examination. These tests are indicated if intracranial hypertension or changes in vision caused by any vascular disorders or brain lesion along the optic pathway are suspected.
- The extraocular motor nerves CN III, IV, and VI control the eyelids, pupils, pupillary reflexes, eye movements, and nystagmus. Examination of the eyes begins with inspection – looking for any obvious ocular malalignment or skew, abnormal lid position, or abnormalities of the position of the globe within

the orbit. In routine cases where there are no eye complaints and the likelihood of abnormality is low, the ocular motility examination may be limited to assessing versional pursuit movements in the six cardinal positions of gaze, including full lateral gaze to each side, as well as upgaze and downgaze when looking to either side. If an abnormality of one or more extraocular motor nerves is found in a patient with tinnitus, a few causes should be considered:

1. Carotid-cavernous fistula
2. Ischemic or hemorrhagic ictus in the brainstem area
3. Carcinomatous meningitis – the term carcinomatous meningitis, also called leptomeningeal metastasis, leptomeningeal carcinomatosis, or leptomeningeal dissemination is correct in that case (see footnote)[1]
4. Inflammatory/autoimmunity diseases
5. Horner syndrome in carotid dissection and head trauma
6. Space-occupying lesions

Evaluating nystagmus and other ocular oscillations is essential. Nystagmus is a complex topic. When faced with a patient with nystagmus or similar abnormal eye movements, the usual clinical action includes two steps: deciding if the nystagmus is an indication of neurologic pathology and if so, whether the pathology is central or peripheral. Depending on the etiology [7], nystagmus in patients with tinnitus may be a sign of a neurological disorder or may be the sign of a vestibular disorder as described below.

– Trigeminal nerve CN V. Only a basic examination evaluating the sensitivity in the face of the three nerve branches needs to be checked in the tinnitus neurologist clinic.
– Facial nerve CN VII. Examination of the motor aspect of the facial nerve is essential in patients with tinnitus when the cause may be a vestibular schwannoma. Tinnitus rarely occurs together with Bell's palsy.

– Vestibular auditory nerve CN VIII. This nerve is mainly examined by the otologist and the audiologist (see Chap. 48 and 49).
– Glossopharyngeal and vagus nerves CN IX and X. The voice, ability to swallow, and dysphasia are functions affected. Nuclear and infranuclear processes that may affect CN IX and X include intramedullary and extramedullary neoplasm, all of which may cause tinnitus. Tinnitus may occur together with glomus jugulare tumors, skull base fracture, surgical trauma, demyelinating disease, or brainstem ischemia. Some of the examinations needed are done by otologists. Palatal myoclonus hyperactivity of muscles innervated by CN IX, in a few cases neuropathic, cause objective tinnitus and are almost always associated with reduced voluntary contraction.
– Spinal accessory nerve CN XI. The examination is limited to evaluation of the functions of the spinal portions. One sternocleidomastoid (SCM) muscle acts to turn the head to the opposite side or to tilt it to the same side. Acting together, the SCMs thrust the head forward and flex the neck. Hyperactivity of the SCM and trapezius may cause spasmodic torticollis in cervical dystonia and in a few patients, it can modulate or cause tinnitus.
– Hypoglossal nerve CN XII. A purely motor nerve, associated with the tongue. Hypoglossal palsy in patients with tinnitus may indicate the presence of infections or neoplastic meningitis, trauma of the skull base, or cervical surgical trauma.

Motor and Sensory Systems

A basic neurological motor and sensitive examination is needed in order to rule out focal neurologic disorders, which are never specific in patients with tinnitus, but necessary to rule out. Some ischemic lesions, brain tumors, and infiltrative disorders may cause tinnitus as a symptom [8, 9].

Cerebellar Function, Gait, and Posture

The cerebellum refines motor commands and is necessary for normal control and regulation of muscle contraction, but it is not involved in the generation of motor commands. It is important to assess cerebellar functions in patients with tinnitus when a secondary cause of the

[1]Leptomeningeal dissemination is a condition in which a solid tumor diffusely spreads to the leptomeninges. Lung tumors, breast tumors, and malignant melanoma comprise the majority of solid tumors spreading to the leptomeninges. Alternative definition: an infiltration of carcinoma cells in the arachnoid and subarachnoid space may be primary or secondary.
Synonyms: leptomeningeal carcinoma, leptomeningeal carcinomatosis, meningeal carcinomatosis, leptomeningeal metastasis.

tinnitus is suspected to be in the posterior fossa, near to the cerebellopontine angle. Examples of such causes are vestibular schwannoma, arteriovenous malformations of the posterior fossa, cholesteatoma, and ischemic lesions of vertebrobasilar territory. Depending on the parts of the cerebellum and its annexes involved, patients may suffer from various combinations of tremor, incoordination, difficulty walking, dysarthria, and nystagmus. Thus, examination of coordination in multi-joint movements, the finger–nose maneuver to examine appendicular coordination, tremor, muscle resistance to passive movement, eye movements, equilibratory coordination, gait, and articulation of speech are indicated.

Neurovascular Examination

A neurovascular examination is essential to a clinical neurovascular examination in patients with tinnitus because pulsatile and intermittent tinnitus can be secondary to many aspects of diseases such as atherosclerotic disease [10], dural arteriovenous fistulas, aneurysms, and other vascular disorders [11] [benign intracranial hypertension (pseudotumor cerebri), etc.].

Inspection

Hardening and tenderness of temporal arteries may reflect giant cell arthritis or may be an indirect sign of an arteriovenous fistula.

Auscultation

Auscultation of the head is sometimes useful. Bruits may be heard best over the temporal regions of the skull, the eyeballs, and the mastoids. Cephalic bruits may occur with angiomas, aneurysms, arteriovenous malformations, neoplasms that compress large arteries, and in the presence of atherosclerotic plaques that partially occlude cerebral or carotid arteries. Ocular bruits usually signify occlusive intracranial cerebrovascular disease. A carotid bruit may be transmitted to the mastoid, resulting in objective tinnitus. An ocular bruit in a patient with an arteriovenous aneurysm may disappear when carotid compression is applied.

Neurovascular Examination with Supra-Aortic and Transcranial Doppler Test

Transcranial Doppler (TCD) is an imaging test that measures blood flow velocity using ultrasound. It is also known as Transcranial Doppler sonography. Used more recently, transcranial color coded sonography Doppler (TCCS), eco-duplex, and power imaging are tests that can measure the velocity of blood flow through the brain's blood vessels [12, 13]. The tests are relatively quick and inexpensive ways to aid in the diagnosis of emboli, stenosis, and vasospasm from a subarachnoid hemorrhage, as well as other vascular problems. TCD is often used in conjunction with other tests, such as magnetic resonance (MR), magnetic resonance angiography (MRA), carotid duplex ultrasound, and CT scans.

Two methods of recording may be used in TCD studies. The first uses "B-mode" imaging, which displays a two-dimensional image as seen by the ultrasound probe. Once the desired blood vessel is found, blood flow velocities may be measured with a pulsed Doppler probe, which provides graphical information about blood flow velocities over time. Together, these make a duplex test. The second method uses only the second probe function, relying instead on the training and experience of the clinician in finding the correct vessels.

The equipment used for these tests is becoming increasingly portable, making it possible to use them at hospital bedsides, a doctor's office, or a nursing home for both inpatient and outpatient studies, and TCD can be used routinely in daily neurovascular examinations by the office of a neurologist.

Applications of Carotid and Transcranial Doppler Sonography in Patients with Tinnitus

Arterial Stenosis

Doppler sonography is very sensitive to detect carotid and vertebrobasilar stenosis and allows an accurate measure of the size of the stenosis (degree of occlusion).

Arteriovenous Malformations

Doppler sonography can detect indirect signs of arteriovenous malformations and dural fistula, revealing coincidental blood supply from other intracranial or extracranial vessels. TCD with echo enhancement is very sensitive to detect these malformations directly, although it is slightly less sensitive than MRA [14].

Benign Intracranial Hypertension

TCD provides useful information on cerebral circulation even under raised intracranial pressure. The systolic spike in blood flow as measured by TCD and the size of the arterial pulse (pulsatility index) are useful diagnostic parameters for both acute intracranial hypertension and benign intracranial hypertension. In benign intracranial hypertension, which is a known cause of tinnitus, the pulsatility index measured by TCD is highly correlated with the values of intracranial pressure and cerebral blood flow, thus making it possible to assess and monitor the therapeutic response in patients with such pathologies.

Lumbar Puncture

Lumbar puncture is a diagnostic and, at times, therapeutic procedure that is performed in order to collect a sample of cerebrospinal fluid for biochemical, microbiological, and cytological analysis. Very rarely, this procedure is used as a treatment to relieve increased intracranial pressure. Lumbar puncture is performed in patients with tinnitus if an infiltrative or inflammatory cause is suspected, for example, carcinomatous meningitis, subacute encephalitis, cerebral sarcoidosis, or subacute/chronic infections of the central nervous system in general. These conditions rarely cause tinnitus. It is important to recognize that they may be important exceptions.

The value of neuroimaging as a complementary tool in the diagnosis of tinnitus patients is discussed in Chap. 18.

References

1. Langguth B, G Hajak, T Kleinjung et al (2007) Tinnitus: Pathophysiology and Treatment, Progress in Brain Research. Prog Brain Res 166:1–542.
2. Langguth B, R Goodey, A Azevedo et al (2007) Consensus for Tinnitus Patient Assessment and Treatment Outcome Measurement: Tinnitus Research Initiative Meeting, Regensburg, 2006. Prog Brain Res. 166:525–36.
3. Monzani D, E Genovese, A Marrara et al (2008) Validity of the Italian Adaptation of the Tinnitus Handicap Inventory Focus on Quality of Life and Psychological Distress in Tinnitus-Sufferers. Acta Otorhinolaryngol Ital. 3:126–34.
4. Nondahl DM, KJ Cruickshanks, DS Dalton et al (2007) The Impact of Tinnitus on Quality of Life in Older Adults. J Am Acad Audiol. 3:257–66.
5. Belli S, H Belli, T Bahcebasi et al (2008) Assessment of Psychopathological Aspects and Psychiatric Comorbidities in Patients Affected By Tinnitus. Eur Arch Otorhinolaryngol. 5.3:279–85.
6. Ito M, K Soma, R Ando (2009) Association Between Tinnitus Retraining Therapy and A Tinnitus Control Instrument. Auris Nasus Larynx. 36(5):536–40.
7. Rzeski M, A Stepień, Z Kaczorowski (2008) Evaluation of the Function of the Vestibular System in Patients with Nigraine. Neurol Neurochir Pol. 2.6:518–24.
8. DeJong's (2009) Neurologic Examination. Lippincott Williams and Wilkins.
9. Brazis WP, C Masdeu, J Biller (2007) Localization in Clinical Neurology. Lippincott Williams and Wilkins. 5th Ed.
10. Troost BT (1979) Dizziness and Vertigo in Vertebrobasilar Disease. Part II. Central Causes and Vertebrobasilar Disease. Curr Conc Cerebrovasc Dis Stroke. 14:21–24.
11. Mattox DE, P Hudgins (2008) Algorithm for Evaluation of Pulsatile Tinnitus. Acta Otolaryngol. 8.4:427–31.
12. Bertora GO, JM Bergman (2002) Doppler Ultrasonography in Tinnitus Patients. Int Tinnitus J. 8.2:124–6.
13. Nakagawa M, N Miyachi, K Fujiwara (2008) A Convenient Sonographic Technique for Diagnosis of Pulsatile Tinnitus Induced by a High Jugular Bulb. J Ultrasound Med. 1:139–40.
14. Offergeld C, S Schellong, A Schmidt et al (2008) Diagnostic Value of Color-Coded Doppler Sonography in Neuro-otologic Disorders. Ultraschall. 6:627–32.

Chapter 52
Diagnosis of Somatosensory Tinnitus

Tanit Ganz Sanchez and Carina Bezerra Rocha

Keypoints

1. The contribution of non-auditory pathways to the pathology of tinnitus has become more and more evident.
2. Because many different stimuli can modulate tinnitus (forceful muscle contractions of the head and neck, eye movements, pressure of myofascial trigger points, cutaneous stimulation of the face, orofacial movements, etc.), it is important to diagnose somatosensory tinnitus and somatosensory modulation of tinnitus.
3. This chapter discusses how somatosensory tinnitus and somatosensory modulation of tinnitus can be diagnosed, mostly by means of anamnesis and physical evaluation. The chapter provides practical information to the health care professionals regarding such diagnosis.

Keywords Tinnitus • Somatosensory • Central nervous system • Muscle • Cervical spine • Temporomandibular joint

Abbreviations

MTP Myofascial trigger points
PA   Pressure algometry
TMJ Temporomandibular joint

T.G. Sanchez (✉)
Department of Otolaryngology, University of São Paulo
Medical School, Av. Padre Pereira de Andrade, 545/174-F,
São Paulo, SP, Brazil 05469-000
e-mail: tanitsanchez@gmail.com

Introduction

It is now generally accepted that many incidences of tinnitus can be evoked or modulated by inputs from the somatosensory system, the somatomotor, and the visual-motor systems. Some individual's tinnitus can be modulated by stimulation of parts of the somatosensory system. Such tinnitus is known as somatosensory tinnitus (other names have been used and the name somatosensory tinnitus has been used for other forms of tinnitus). Somatosensory tinnitus is different from tinnitus that is not affected by activations of non-auditory systems. We will call such tinnitus auditory tinnitus. The effect of somatosensory stimulation on tinnitus can be demonstrated by inducing forceful muscle contractions of the head, neck, and limbs [1–3]; by orofacial movements [4–8]; by applying pressure to myofascial trigger points (MTP) [9]; or by stimulating the skin of the face and hands [4, 10]. Eye movements can often induce tinnitus or modulate existing tinnitus [5]. Among these and other types of modulating factors that have been described (see Chap. 43), the influence of stimulating head and neck regions on the auditory pathways are particularly interesting.

Definition of Somatosensory Tinnitus

The terms "somatosensory tinnitus" and "somatic tinnitus" have been used with different meanings. Efforts are now made to differentiate between somatosensory tinnitus (primary origin in head and neck disorders) and somatosensory modulation of tinnitus.

A.R. Møller et al. (eds.), *Textbook of Tinnitus*,
DOI 10.1007/978-1-60761-145-5_52, © Springer Science+Business Media, LLC 2011

Somatosensory Tinnitus

Somatosensory tinnitus is suspected when a patient's history shows at least one of the following events has occurred before the onset of tinnitus:

– Head or neck trauma
– Manipulation of teeth or jaw or cervical spine
– Recurrent pain episodes in head, neck, or shoulder girdle
– Increase of both pain and tinnitus at the same time
– Inadequate postures during rest, walking, working, or sleeping
– Intense periods of bruxism (grinding of the teeth) during day or night

Other forms of stimulation of structures of the head and neck may or may not cause the loudness, pitch, or localization of somatosensory tinnitus to change.

The most important characteristic of somatosensory tinnitus is that it is related to problems of the head and neck, rather than to problems of the ear.

The complexity of somatosensory tinnitus requires that patients with this disorder be evaluated by an integrated team including an experienced dentist and physiotherapist (or similar professions, depending on the organization of local health care structures) to evaluate possible bone and muscular disorders of the face and neck as well as dental problems. Prompt diagnosis is important because treatment must be started as early as possible to obtain the best results (see Chap. 80).

Somatosensory Modulation of Tinnitus

Somatosensory modulation of tinnitus may be perceived as transient changes in loudness, pitch, or localization of the tinnitus. Such modulation of tinnitus can be induced in individuals with either auditory or somatosensory tinnitus. Since the tinnitus of many individuals can be elicited or modulated by somatosensory stimulation (65–80%) [1, 2], all patients who seek help for their tinnitus should be tested for somatosensory modulation. If a patient spontaneously reports that his/her tinnitus changes temporarily during common daily movements of the jaw or neck (opening mouth, clenching teeth, or turning head) or by applying pressure on the temples, mandible, cheek, mastoid, or neck with a fingertip, it is a strong sign

that the patient has somatosensory modulation of tinnitus. Other signs of somatosensory modulation may become evident when a professional examines the patient and actively searches for modulation of the tinnitus by applying different kinds of stimuli to different locations on the patient's body. The patient may mention an immediate change in the loudness of the tinnitus (increase or decrease assessed by a visual analogue scale) or changes in the pitch or the localization of the tinnitus. If this occurs during at least one maneuver involving the somatosensory, somatomotor, or visual-motor systems, it is a strong sign that the patient has somatosensory tinnitus. The effect of many kinds of modulation is short lasting and it is difficult to use a questionnaire to evaluate tinnitus before and after such maneuvers. However, a simple instrument such as a visual analogue scale can be used to quickly evaluate the magnitude of the induced changes in tinnitus.

Different stimuli can be used to detect somatosensory modulation of a patient's tinnitus, such as active jaw movements (with and without resistance by the examiner), opening and closing the mouth, moving chin forward and backward, or lateralizing chin right and left. Passive muscular palpation can be used to find MTPs or tender points in the masseter, temporalis, and lateral pterygoid muscles. The fatigue test (teeth closed with spatula between them in anterior, right, and left positions for a duration of 1 min) is another useful test that can reveal somatosensory tinnitus.

Such movements increase the signals elicited by the tense muscles in the area innervated by the sensory part of the trigeminal nerve, which is anatomically and physiologically connected to the acoustic pathways [11].

Active neck movements (with and without resistance by the examiner) such as moving neck forward and backward, rotation right and left, and lateralization right and left can be used to test if signals from the neck can modulate the patient's tinnitus. Passive muscular palpation searching for MTPs or tender points in the trapezius (upper fibers), sternocleidomastoid (sternal division), splenius capitis (near the mastoid process), and splenius cervicis are other important tests.

The jaw and upper cervical spine are considered to be a part of an integrated motor system; therefore, observing the posture of the patient is also important for diagnosis and treatment of tinnitus that can be modulated with somatosensory stimulation. For example, if a patient has the mandible and/or neck protruded forward, this might suggest an attempt to compensate for wrong dental occlusion.

Gaze-Evoked Tinnitus or Gaze-Modulated Tinnitus

Eye movements can both cause tinnitus and modulate tinnitus (gaze-evoked tinnitus or gaze-modulated tinnitus) [5]. Influence of gaze on tinnitus can be tested by having the patient start looking straight forward (a neutral position) and then gaze first to the maximal right and then left; after that, looking upwards and downwards. Each position should be maintained for 5–10 s. With the patient placed in a silent environment, changes in tinnitus may occur during each eye movement.

Methods for measuring modulation of tinnitus are not yet standardized. Some centers only describe it as "present" or "absent," and some use a visual analogue scale (from 0 to 10 or from 0 to 100). Toward standardization, we propose a scale for modulation of tinnitus that is centered at 0 (rest state of tinnitus) and ranging from minus 5 (disappearance) to plus 5 (biggest increase ever thought).

Other Indications of Somatosensory Tinnitus

Bone problems of the temporomandibular joint (TMJ) and the neck (osteophits, arthrosis, spondylosis, etc.) may justify the presence of pain and management of accompanying muscular problems (which also can occur in isolation). Such bone problems can seldom be reversed completely, but an approach directed to treat the muscular tension may also lead to control of somatosensory tinnitus and the associated pain (Chap. 80). It may therefore be recommended that the TMJ and neck disorders may be diagnosed and treated to allow better tinnitus control.

Although modulation of tinnitus can occur regardless of the presence of pain, some extra clues to diagnosing somatosensory tinnitus may be added if pain is also included in the following rationale:

- Does the patient have frequent regional pain?
- If so, is it in the head, neck, and shoulder girdle?
- If so, has it a similar duration as the patient's tinnitus?
- If so, does the patient's tinnitus become worse when the pain increases?

In general, a patient's history, together with a clinical examination by a physician might be sufficient for diagnosing temporomandibular and neck disorders in most patients, but complimentary exams (X-ray, computed tomography, or magnetic resonance imaging) may be helpful in reaching a firm diagnosis.

Myofascial Trigger Points

MTP are hyperirritable spots in skeletal muscles, which are associated with hypersensitive palpable nodules in taut bands. Basically, there are two kinds of MTPs: active or latent. Active MTP cause clinical pain complaint and refer patient-recognized pain during palpation. A latent MTP may have all the other clinical characteristics of an active MTP and always has a taut band that increases muscle tension and restricts range of motion. It does not provoke spontaneous pain and it is painful only when palpated (upon palpation, the latent MTP can provoke pain and altered sensation in its distribution expected from a MTP in that muscle) [12].

The diagnosis of active MTP is very important for the treatment of myofascial pain syndrome, for pain release, and possibly even for tinnitus relief.

The relationship between MTP, myofascial pain syndrome, and tinnitus has been studied during the preceding years (see Chaps. 9, 43, and 80). Tender points should also be identified and their possible modulation of the patient's tinnitus must likewise be determined.

Palpation should be performed with sustained deep single-finger pressure during up to 10 s with a spade-like pad at the end of the distal phalanx of the index finger or through pincer palpation (thumb and finger) moving across the muscle band at the hypersensitive area (Figs. 52.1 and 52.2).

When a palpable taut band and spot tenderness is detected, the patient should be asked (Fig. 52.3) if he/she feels any sensation in other area besides the one being pressed upon; if the sensation is like the one that

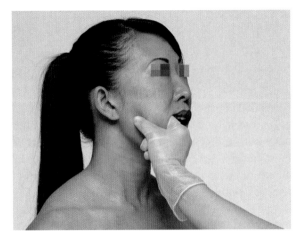

Fig. 52.1 Examination of the trigger point in the masseter muscle

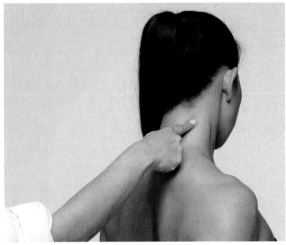

Fig. 52.2 Examination of the trigger point in the splenius cervicis muscle

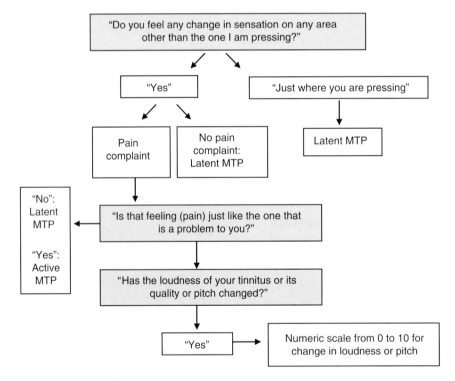

Fig. 52.3 Questions asked during MTP evaluation

is a problem to the patient; and finally, if the loudness or pitch of the tinnitus changed.

The ten muscles in the head, neck, and shoulder girdle (infraspinatus, levator scapulae, trapezius, splenius capitis, splenius cervicis, scalenus medius, sternocleidomastoid, digastric, masseter, and temporalis)

should all be examined for the presence of MTPs [12]. The examination is expected to reveal whether MTPs were present or not, and if so, in which muscles, in which side of the body relative to the tinnitus, and if palpation of one or more MTPs modulated the patient's tinnitus. If tender points were present, the patient

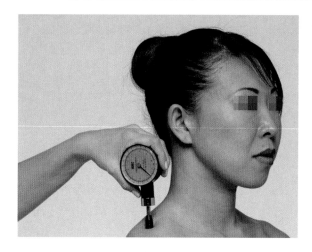

Fig. 52.4 Pressure algometry

should be asked if palpation of the tender points affected their tinnitus.

Manual palpation of the muscles is the easiest way of examining patients for somatosensory tinnitus. However, a more objective measurement may be obtained using a hand-held force gauge with a rubber tip to measure the pressure required for eliciting MTP activity [pressure algometry (PA)]. PA has been used to document the tenderness of MTP and is also applied to measure the referred pain threshold and pain tolerance. The reliability and validity of measurements using PA have been established [13, 14]. Pre- and posttherapeutic effectiveness of various procedures on MTP have been assessed by measurement of pressure threshold with PA (Fig. 52.4).

Conclusions

The ability to correctly diagnose somatosensory tinnitus and somatosensory modulation of tinnitus relies mainly on the patient's history and a thorough physical examination. However, these forms of tinnitus have only recently been studied in detail. Knowledge about the signs of these forms of tinnitus is therefore not generally known. Health care professionals may need to be informed about how to diagnose these forms of tinnitus in their daily routine of treating patients with tinnitus.

Acknowledgments The authors thank the Tinnitus Research Initiative for the creation and support of the workgroup of Somatosensory Tinnitus and Modulating Factors.

References

1. Levine, RA. Somatic modulation appears to be a fundamental attribute of tinnitus. In: Hazell, JPW, ed. Proceedings of the Sixth International Tinnitus Seminar. London: The Tinnitus and Hyperacusis Center; 1999: 193–7.
2. Sanchez, TG; Guerra, GCY; Lorenzi, MC; Brandão, AL; Bento, RF. The influence of voluntary muscle contractions upon the onset and modulation of tinnitus. Audiol. Neurootol. 2002; 7: 370–5.
3. Sanchez, TG; Lima, AS; Brandao, AL; Lorenzi, MC; Bento, RF. Somatic modulation of tinnitus: test reliability and results after repetitive muscle contraction training. Ann. Otol. 2007; 116: 30–5.
4. Cacace, AT; Cousins, JP; Parnes, SM; McFarland, DJ; Semenoff, D; Holmes, T; Davenport, C; Stegbauer, K; Lovely, TJ. Cutaneous-evoked tinnitus. II. Review of neuroanatomical, physiological and functional imaging studies. Audiol. Neurootol. 1999; 4: 247–57.
5. Coad, ML; Lockwood, A; Salvi, R; Burkard, R. Characteristics of patients with gaze-evoked tinnitus. Otol. Neurotol. 2001; 22(5): 650–4.
6. Baguley, DM; Phillips, J; Humphriss, RL; Jones, S; Axon, PR; Moffat, DA. The prevalence and onset of gaze modulation of tinnitus and increased sensitivity to noise after translabyrinthine vestibular schwannoma excision. Otol. Neurotol. 2006; 27: 220–4.
7. Sanchez, TG; Pio, MRB. Abolição de zumbido evocado pela movimentação ocular por meio de repetição do deslocamento do olhar: um método inovador. Arq. Otorhinolaryngol. 2007; 11: 451–3.
8. Pinchoff, RJ; Burkard, RF; Salvi, RJ; Coad, ML; Lockwood, AH. Modulation of tinnitus by voluntary jaw movements. Am. J. Otol. 1998; 19: 785–9.
9. Rocha, CACB; Sanchez, TG; Siqueira, JTT. Myofascial trigger points: a possible way of modulating tinnitus? Audiol. Neurootol. 2008; 13: 153–60.
10. Sanchez, TG; Marcondes, RA; Kii, MA; Lima, AS; Rocha, CAB; Ono, CR; Bushpiegel, C. A different case of tinnitus modulation by tactile stimuli in a patient with pulsatile tinnitus. Presented at II Meeting of Tinnitus Research Initiative, Mônaco, 2007; 21–3.
11. Shore, S; Zhou, J; Koehler, S. Neural mechanisms underlying somatic tinnitus. Prog. Brain Res. 2007; 166: 107–23.
12. Travell, J; Simons, DG. Myofascial Pain and Dysfunction: The Trigger Point Manual, Upper Half of Body. Baltimore: Williams & Wilkins; 1999.
13. Fischer, AA. Pressure threshold meter: its use for quantification of tender spots. Arch. Phys. Med. Rehabil. 1986; 67: 836–8.
14. Kraus, H; Fischer, AA. Diagnosis and treatment of myofascial pain. Mt. Sinai J. Med. 1991; 58: 235–9.

Chapter 53
Differential Diagnosis of Temporomandibular Joint and Masticatory Muscle Disorders in Patients with Tinnitus

Ralf Bürgers, Martin Gosau, Sebastian Hahnel, and Michael Behr

Keypoints

1. This chapter aims at providing non-dental healthcare specialists engaged in tinnitus treatment with a description of a short screening of individuals with tinnitus to clarify the involvement of temporomandibular disorders (TMD) in such patients. A screening test for TMD seems to be reasonable for all tinnitus patients. Patients with a positive TMD screening should be referred to an experienced TMD specialist.
2. TMD short screening consists of an anamnesis, an examination of the temporomandibular joint (TMJ) (jaw motion and TMJ sounds), and an examination of the masticatory muscles (palpation, isometric contraction, and parafunction).
3. Individuals with TMD-related tinnitus suffer more frequently from masticatory muscle pain than from joint syndromes, whereby the majority of individuals with TMD-related tinnitus – in contrast to patients with tinnitus only – describe their tinnitus as fluctuating.

Keywords TMD • Tinnitus • Short screening

Abbreviations

N   Newton
TMD   Temporomandibular disorder(s)
TMJ   Temporomandibular joint

R. Bürgers (✉)
Department of Prosthetic Dentistry,
University Medical Center Regensburg,
93042 Regensburg, Germany
e-mail: ralf.buergers@klinik.uni-regensburg.de

Introduction

Diagnosis of temporomandibular disorders (TMD) should be made on the basis of the medical history and clinical examination of a patient. It is the opinion of this author that diagnosis of TMD requires a detailed evaluation by a dentist or physician with advanced experience in treating temporomandibular joint (TMJ) and masticatory muscle disorders. This chapter, however, cannot provide a detailed and comprehensive tutorial, neither for diagnosing TMJ and masticatory muscle disorders nor for differentiating between the various forms of TMD; such information can only be obtained from textbooks such as "Temporomandibular Joint and Masticatory Muscle Disorders" by Zarb et al. [1]. The present chapter aims at providing health care specialists of different fields who are engaged in tinnitus treatment a brief guide regarding how to best clarify possible TMD involvement in patients. Patients who have tested positive for TMD and tinnitus should be referred to an experienced TMD specialist for further diagnosis and therapy. The differential diagnosis should rule out pain resulting from other causes but with similar symptoms, such as trigeminal neuralgia and atypical facial pain [2].

It is well documented that individuals with both tinnitus and TMD have more pain and higher dysfunction index scores than individuals with only TMD [3–7]. Therefore, screenings of patients with tinnitus for related TMD can be brief. Patients with a suspicion of having TMD and those without a clear diagnosis may be referred to a TMD specialist for further diagnosis. A short screening can be conducted in approximately 5 min, because it is known that TMD is often accompanied by tinnitus; it may therefore be reasonable to screen all patients with tinnitus for TMD complaints.

TMJ Short Screening Procedure

Often, patients with tinnitus will not relate their "ear symptoms" to possible stomatognathic[1] or TMD. Furthermore, many patients with chronic TMD, such as joint clicking or grinding of their teeth, hesitate to consult a dentist or report their symptoms to an otorhinolaryngologist because they regard them (mostly free of pain) as "normal" and not pathogenic. Therefore, screening for TMD should be generally included in examinations of patients with tinnitus [1, 5]. Short screenings to evaluate the incidence of TMD in patients with tinnitus have been described in the literature [8, 9]. The screening described below is adapted to the specific conditions in TMD-related tinnitus. When TMJ involvement is found (positive screening), the patient should be referred to an experienced dentist or TMD specialist for a more detailed diagnosis and TMD therapy [10].

Anamnesis

Ask the patients about pain in the face, jaw, temple, in front of the ear, in the neck, or in the shoulders in the past month and let them point to the area the pain is felt. All patients with tinnitus should be asked if they have had treatments for TMD in the past (such as splint therapy, physiotherapy, medications, etc.), if they have had pain in their temple and tinnitus from mental pressure or medication [2, 11–13].

Patients who have pain in the TMJ or the masticatory muscles (myofascial pain) should have detailed diagnostic tests for TMD.

Jaw Motion

The vertical range and opening pattern of the mandible [10, 14] should be tested (Fig. 53.1). Ask the patient to close their mouth with teeth lightly touching and then slowly open their mouth as wide as possible, even if it is painful.

1. Note if the patient has an initial deviation to one side but corrects to the midline before reaching the maximum mandibular opening or an uncorrected deviation of the jaw to one side.
2. Measure the maximum unassisted opening from the incisal edge of the maxillary central incisor to the opposing mandibular incisor.
3. Ask the patient to do largest possible movements of the mandible: left lateral excursion and right lateral excursion, protrusion, and retrusion.

Patients who have reproducible opening deviations or limited vertical range (<40 mm) or with painful mandible movements should have detailed diagnostic tests for TMD.

TMJ Sounds

Ask the patient if they hear any sounds when opening and closing their mouth. Place left index finger over the patient's right TMJ and the right index finger over the left TMJ; ask the patient to slowly open the mouth as wide as possible, even if it is painful (Fig. 53.2). Palpation has to be done bilaterally.

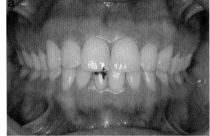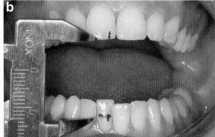

Fig. 53.1 Estimation of the maximum mandibular opening and deviations. (**a**) Orientation lines on mandibular and maxillary central incisor. (**b**) Measurement of maximum mandibular opening with sliding caliper

---

[1] Stomatognatic system: mouth and jaws and closely associated structures.

Fig. 53.2 Palpation of the temporomandibular joint (TMJ) for the evaluation of joint sounds. (**a**) Lateral, preauricular palpation with index finger. (**b**) Dorsal, intraauricular palpation with little finger

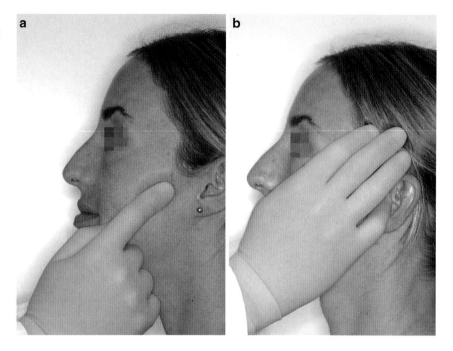

Record clicking (short) or continuous sounds, like a stone grinding against another stone (crepitus). Ask the patient if the palpation was painful.

More detailed diagnostic tests for TMD are needed in patients who have reproducible TMJ sounds or joint pain during palpation.

In addition to the lateral palpation (preauricular), the TMJ palpation may also be performed from dorsal (intraauricular) direction, with the examiner's fingers in the right and left acoustic meatus, finger pads orientated forward.

Masticatory Muscle Tenderness

Palpation and isometric contraction of the muscles of mastication (Fig. 53.3) may be useful for detecting muscle tenderness. Ask the patient to open their mouth and take the cheek between index finger and thumb. Have the patient lightly clench to identify the *masseter muscle* and then palpate the whole muscle in a passive state (approximately 2 lb/10 N of pressure). Ask the patient to lightly clench and move the mandible forward and backward to identify the *Temporalis muscle*

and palpate the entire muscle in a passive state (approximately 2 lb/10 N of pressure).

The examiner holds up the mandible with both hands below the chin while asking the patient to open their mouth and hold the position for 1 min (*abduction isometric contraction*).

Deposit two cotton rolls or swabs between the upper and lower jaw in the region of the premolars and ask the patient to clench and hold with constant pressure for 1 min (*adduction isometric contraction*).

More detailed diagnostic tests for TMD are needed in patients with masticatory muscle palpation pain or muscle pain during isometric contraction.

Palpation of the remaining masticatory muscles (medial pterygoid, lateral pterygoid, stylohoid, suprahyoid, and digastricus) may also be done, but localizing these muscles may be difficult even for experienced TMD specialists. Myogelosis and hypertrophies should also be noticed. Movements of the head or cervical spine can cause changes in tinnitus perception [15] (see Chap. 9). Disorders of the neck or cervical spine may influence TMD-related tinnitus and should therefore –if existent – be further examined by a specialist.

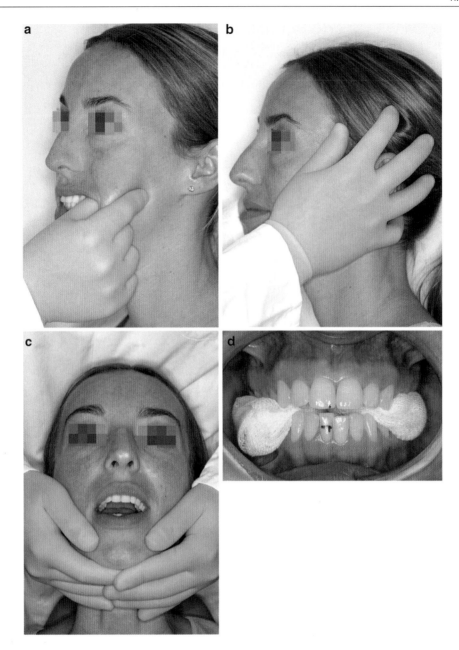

Fig. 53.3 Masticatory muscle palpation. (**a**) Digital palpation of masseter muscle between index finger and thumb. (**b**) Palpation of temporalis muscle in toto. (**c**) Abduction isometric contraction during mouth opening. (**d**) Adduction isometric contraction through clenching two swabs between the upper and lower jaw in the premolar region

Parafunction[2]

Ask the patient for grinding of their teeth (bruxism), clenching and rocking of teeth. Examine the oral cavity for hard tissue attritions (not age-based) or soft tissue impressions (of the tongue or inside of the cheek).

Hypertrophies of the masticatory muscles (masseter) and asymmetries of the face should be recorded associated with occlusal trauma. Also called *parafunctional habits* or *oral habits*. (From Mosby's Dental Dictionary, 2nd edition. © 2008 Elsevier, Inc. All rights reserved.)

---

[2]Parafunction: the habitual movements (e.g., bruxism, clenching, and rocking of teeth using teeth for tools) that are normal motions associated with mastication, speech, or respiratory movements and that result in worn facets and other problems

because they are indicators for parafunctions. More detailed diagnostic tests for TMD are needed in patients with signs of parafunction. Patients should be asked if their tinnitus changes during mandible movements or palpation of joint and masticatory muscles.

Special Considerations in Patients with Tinnitus

One of the difficulties in diagnosing patients with both TMD and tinnitus is to distinguish patients who have tinnitus because of TMD from patients who hear tinnitus independently of their TMD. In patients with TMD-related tinnitus, therapy should primarily focus on TMD. Often the tinnitus will abate after successful TMD treatment. In patients whose TMD and tinnitus are independent of each other, TMD therapy is unlikely to affect the tinnitus. Such patients should therefore be referred to a tinnitus specialist. Patients with both symptoms are often classified as having tinnitus or TMD.

Individuals with tinnitus have been described to suffer more frequently from masticatory muscle pain (and especially from myofascial pain) than from joint symptoms [3, 6, 16]. However, Henderson et al. reported that tinnitus does not occur more frequently in patients with TMD involving disc displacement than in patients with physiological disc position [17]. Therefore, TMD diagnosis and related short screenings in patients with tinnitus should particularly focus on examining the masticatory muscle system and muscular disorders. Most individuals with TMD-related tinnitus describe their tinnitus as fluctuating, and TMD occlusal splint therapy has been found significantly more effective in patients with fluctuating tinnitus than in patients with continuous and severe tinnitus [16, 18]. Patients with TMD might be diagnostically separated from patients with tinnitus-related TMD because of the character of their disorder (joint disorder vs. muscle pain) (Fig. 53.4). So far, such unequivocal signs that should allow distinction between the pathology in these two groups have not been described. The quality of the tinnitus might be a predictable indicator for the involvement of the TMJ and masticatory muscle system, which should therefore be examined even more thoroughly in patients with tinnitus of a specific quality (fluctuating tinnitus).

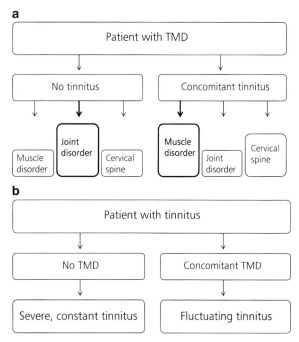

Fig. 53.4 Special considerations in patients with tinnitus, TMD, and TMD-related tinnitus. (**a**) TMD symptoms in patients with or without tinnitus. (**b**) Tinnitus symptoms in patients with or without TMD

Conclusions

There are several reasons why testing for TMD would be beneficial to patients with tinnitus, especially for patients with TMD who do not have a known cause of tinnitus. It is known that patients with tinnitus benefit from efficient treatment of their TMD and, therefore, patients with tinnitus should be screened for TMJ problems, as every patient with TMD should be asked if they have tinnitus [1, 19].

References

1. Zarb, GA., Carlsson, GE., Sessle, BJ. and Mohl, ND. (1994) Temporomandibular joint and masticatory muscle disorders. Copenhagen, Munksgaard.
2. Turp, JC. (1998) Correlation between myoarthropathies of the masticatory system and ear symptoms (otalgia, tinnitus). HNO **46**: 303–310.
3. Camparis, CM., Formigoni, G., Teixeira, MJ. and de Siqueira, JT. (2005) Clinical evaluation of tinnitus in patients with sleep bruxism: prevalence and characteristics. J. Oral Rehabil. **32**: 808–814.
4. Bernhardt, O., Gesch, D., Schwahn, C., Bitter, K., Mundt, T., Mack, F., Kocher, T., Meyer, G., Hensel, E. and John, U. (2004) Signs of temporomandibular disorders in tinnitus patients and

in a population-based group of volunteers: results of the Study of Health in Pomerania. J. Oral Rehabil. **31**: 311–319.

5. Keersmaekers, K., De Boever, JA. and Van Den, BL. (1996) Otalgia in patients with temporomandibular joint disorders. J. Prosthet. Dent. **75**: 72–76.

6. Tuz, HH., Onder, EM. and Kisnisci, RS. (2003) Prevalence of otologic complaints in patients with temporomandibular disorder. Am. J. Orthod. Dentofacial. Orthop. **123**: 620–623.

7. Rubinstein, B., Axelsson, A. and Carlsson, GE. (1990) Prevalence of signs and symptoms of craniomandibular disorders in tinnitus patients. J. Craniomandib. Disord. **4**: 186–192.

8. Bosel, C., Mazurek, B., Haupt, H. and Peroz, I. (2008) Chronic tinnitus and craniomandibular disorders. Effectiveness of functional therapy on perceived tinnitus distress. HNO **56**: 707–713.

9. Hankey, GT. (1962) Painful disorders of the temporomandibular joint. Proc. R. Soc. Med. **55**: 787–792.

10. Dworkin, SF. and LeResche, L. (1992) Research diagnostic criteria for temporomandibular disorders: review, criteria, examinations and specifications, critique. J. Craniomandib. Disord. **6**: 301–355.

11. Chan, SW. and Reade, PC. (1994) Tinnitus and temporomandibular pain-dysfunction disorder. Clin. Otolaryngol. Allied Sci. **19**: 37–80.

12. Seligman, DA. and Pullinger, AG. (1989) Association of occlusal variables among refined TM patient diagnostic groups. J. Craniomandib. Disord. **3**: 227–236.

13. Parker, WS. and Chole, RA. (1995) Tinnitus, vertigo, and temporomandibular disorders. Am. J. Orthod. Dentofacial. Orthop. **107**: 153–158.

14. Koskinen, J., Paavolainen, M., Raivio, M. and Roschier, J. (1980) Otological manifestations in temporomandibular joint dysfunction. J. Oral Rehabil. **7**: 249–254.

15. Levine, RA. (1999) Somatic (craniocervical) tinnitus and the dorsal cochlear nucleus hypothesis. Am. J. Otolaryngol. **20**: 351–362.

16. Tullberg, M. and Ernberg, M. (2006) Long-term effect on tinnitus by treatment of temporomandibular disorders: a two-year follow-up by questionnaire. Acta Odontol. Scand. **64**: 89–96.

17. Henderson, DH., Cooper, JC., Bryan, GW. and Van Sickels, JE. (1992) Otologic complaints in temporomandibular joint syndrome. Arch. Otolaryngol. Head Neck Surg. **118**: 1208–1213.

18. Bush, FM. (1987) Tinnitus and otalgia in temporomandibular disorders. J. Prosthet. Dent. **58**: 495–498.

19. Morgan, DH. (1992) Tinnitus of TMJ origin: a preliminary report. Cranio **10**: 24–129.

Chapter 54
Psychologic/Psychiatric Assessment

Michael Landgrebe and Berthold Langguth

Keypoints

1. Psychiatric comorbidity occurs frequently in patients with tinnitus, especially in moderate to severe forms.
2. Depression and anxiety are the most frequently found comorbid conditions.
3. Tinnitus severity and impairment in quality of life can be linked to psychiatric symptoms.
4. For every professional who treats tinnitus patients, it is important to recognize signs of potential psychiatric comorbidity.
5. Potential warning signs are high scores in tinnitus questionnaires. Screening instruments that are easy to use may help to identify comorbid psychiatric disorders such as depression or anxiety.
6. Further diagnosis and treatment should be done by specialists such as psychiatrists or psychologists.
7. Patients who appear suicidal should be promptly referred to a psychiatrist.

Keywords Psychiatric comorbidity • Quality of life • Suicidality • Diagnostic screening • Depression • Anxiety disorder

Introduction

Chronic tinnitus represents a frequent condition experienced by about 10–20% of the general population (see Chaps. 5 and 6). One to two percent of individuals with tinnitus have reduced quality of life [1]. Psychiatric comorbidity occurs especially in individuals with severe tinnitus [2]. Major depression, anxiety, and somatoform disorders are frequently reported as comorbid conditions to tinnitus [3–7]. However, psychosis and personality disorders may also be associated with tinnitus [8]. Major depressive disorder and anxiety disorder occur most frequently in individuals with chronic disabling tinnitus; a prevalence rate of 60% or more has been reported [5, 9, 10]. From a clinical point of view, it is important to note that chronic disability and suffering in tinnitus patients is frequently linked to concomitant depressive symptoms [11] and improvement of depression is paralleled by an improvement of functional disability [12]. Several studies have shown that tinnitus severity and tinnitus-related distress is correlated with depression [4, 6, 7]. Psychiatric comorbidity, especially depression and anxiety disorders, is a common phenomenon in tinnitus patients and adds considerably to the suffering and impairment in quality of life. It is, therefore, important that clinicians who treat tinnitus patients are observant to any comorbid psychiatric symptoms, especially depression and anxiety, and provide treatment of tinnitus that takes any affective symptoms into account. Effective treatment regimes for tinnitus aimed at the cause of the patient's symptoms are still missing, and treatment of comorbid psychiatric disorders can substantially reduce the burden of the disease and improve the quality of life of individuals with tinnitus. The difference between a severely suffering tinnitus patient and a well-compensated individual is sometimes adequate treatment of a psychiatric comorbidity. Thus, it is important that comorbid psychiatric disorders are diagnosed and efficiently treated.

M. Landgrebe (✉)
Department of Psychiatry, Psychosomatics, and Psychotherapy, University of Regensburg, Universitaetsstrasse 84, 93053 Regensburg, Germany
e-mail: michael.landgrebe@medbo.de

A.R. Møller et al. (eds.), *Textbook of Tinnitus*,
DOI 10.1007/978-1-60761-145-5_54, © Springer Science+Business Media, LLC 2011

Management of Psychiatric Comorbidity

In this chapter, we will focus on the detection of comorbid psychiatric disorders; for the exact clinical description and the clinical management, we refer to Chaps. 62–64.

Detection of Psychiatric Comorbidity in a Nonpsychiatric Setting

The majority of tinnitus patients do not show any signs of psychiatric comorbidity, especially those who have mild forms of tinnitus, which are well managed. However, if tinnitus patients suffer from depression or anxiety, it is important to recognize and treat these disorders.

In clinical practice, patients primarily seek medical help for their tinnitus, not of their depression or anxiety. Depending on the health care system, patients with tinnitus seek help from a general practitioner, an otorhinolaryngologist, or an audiologist, but rarely from a psychiatrist. Patients seek help because of their tinnitus; additional symptoms, which may be present are only mentioned in passing. Most patients are reluctant to talk about affective symptoms such as mood disturbances or anxiety in a nonpsychiatric setting and that increases the likelihood that these symptoms are overlooked, as has been shown in large survey studies. In practitioner offices, correct diagnosis of a major depression represents a substantial problem; patients with mild to moderate depression are particularly at risk of being overlooked [13]. Clinicians who are not specialized in psychiatry yet caring for tinnitus patients should ask the questions: (a) What are the signs that a psychiatric comorbidity is likely when treating a patient with tinnitus? (b) What are reasonable screening instruments for psychiatric disorders? (c) What should be done if comorbid psychiatric disorders are suspected? (d) How patients with risk of suicide should be managed?

Warning Signs of Potential Psychiatric Comorbidity

Most individuals with tinnitus do not suffer substantially and have little or no impairment of their quality of life. They are also typically able to work and are not restricted by their tinnitus in their everyday life. Some patients with tinnitus seek medical help because they are concerned their tinnitus may be a sign of a dangerous disease such as a brain tumor. Information about the pathophysiology of tinnitus, counseling (see Chap. 70), and a suitable test to rule out a vestibular schwannoma is sufficient, and any psychiatric comorbidity appears to be unlikely in these cases. Severe and disabling tinnitus, however, is often accompanied by symptoms such as depressed mood and anxiety. Tinnitus severity can be assessed either by scales, which are easy to perform [14], or by a validated questionnaire (see Chap. 42). Patients with grade III and IV of Biesinger (Table 54.1) or high scores in tinnitus questionnaires (i.e., a total score of more than 47 in the tinnitus questionnaire of Goebel and Hiller [15] or more than 37 in the Tinnitus Handicap Inventory) should be examined with focus on signs of depression or anxiety [16].

What are Reasonable Screening Instruments for Psychiatric Symptoms?

The most frequent symptoms of depression are depressed mood, loss of interest, and sleep disorders. However, in a nonpsychiatric setting, circumstances such as time limitations often do not allow an extensive interview to specifically explore all potential symptoms of depression or anxiety. Also, specific training and experience is required for assessing affective signs and should be done by a psychiatrist or psychologist. However, everybody who treats tinnitus patients should be familiar with screening instruments for frequent psychiatric disorders, which are based on a few key questions and are easy to perform.

Table 54.1 Tinnitus grading according to Biesinger et al. [14]

Grade I	Tinnitus is well compensated. No psychological strain
Grade II	Tinnitus appears only in silence and is disturbing during periods of stress and pressure
Grade III	Tinnitus interferes continuously in the private and professional area. Emotional, cognitive and physical disturbances occur
Grade IV	Tinnitus leads to the complete decompensation in the private area; disability

Table 54.2 Screening questions for different forms of anxiety disorders according to the MINI International Neuropsychiatric Interview (M.I.N.I.; Sheehan et al. [18])

Disorder	Screening question
Panic disorder	Have you, on more than one occasion, had spells or attacks when you suddenly felt anxious, frightened, uncomfortable or uneasy, even in situations where most people would not feel that way? Did the spells surge to a peak, within 10 min of starting?
Agoraphobia	Do you feel anxious or uneasy in places or situations where you might have a panic attack or panic-like symptoms, or where help might not be available or escape might be difficult: like being in a crowd, standing in a line (queue), when you are away from home or alone at home, or when crossing a bridge, traveling in a bus, train or car?
Social phobia	In the past month were you fearful or embarrassed being watched, being the focus of attention, or fearful of being humiliated? This includes things like speaking in public, eating in public or with others, writing while someone watches, or being in social situations
Specific phobia	In the past month have you been bothered by recurrent thoughts, impulses, or images that were unwanted, distasteful, inappropriate, intrusive, or distressing? (e.g., the idea that you were dirty, contaminated or had germs, or fear of contaminating others, or fear of harming someone even though you didn't want to, or fearing you would act on some impulse, or fear or superstitions that you would be responsible for things going wrong, or obsessions with sexual thoughts, images or impulses, or hoarding, collecting, or religious obsessions

For depression, the following two questions have been proposed:

1. During the past month have you often been bothered by feeling down, depressed, or hopeless?
2. During the past month have you often been bothered by little interest or pleasure in doing things [17]?

If the patient answers with "yes" to one of the both questions, depression is likely and referral to a psychiatrist or psychologist should be made. Similar screening questions for anxiety disorders are used in standardized, semi-structured diagnostic interviews like the MINI International Neuropsychiatric Interview (M.I.N.I.; [18]; see Table 54.2) and can be used for screening for anxiety disorders.

What to Do if a Patient with Tinnitus is Suspected to also Have Depression and Anxiety

A patient who is suspected of suffering from depressive symptoms, anxiety, or any other psychiatric disorder should be referred to a psychiatrist for further diagnostic and therapeutic management. In clinical practice, this may sometimes be difficult, since patients may interpret the referral to a psychiatrist as a sign they are not taken seriously or are considered to be "crazy." This can be easily avoided by careful explanation that tinnitus can cause a high amount of distress and that the treatment concept will include approaches for reducing tinnitus (e.g., hearing aids, noise generators). However, the patient should understand that the amount of suffering induced by tinnitus should be treated by specialists (e.g., by some form of cognitive behavioral therapy or by pharmacologic treatment). Also, a close collaboration with psychiatrists and psychologists, which are interested in tinnitus and have experience with diagnosis and management of tinnitus patients, will make it easier for otologists or audiologists to refer their patients for psychiatric diagnosis and therapy.

How to Manage a Suicidal Patient?

The suicidal patient is a rare but clinically important issue in the management of tinnitus patients. Signs of suicidal thoughts must always be taken serious. Individuals with chronic, severe tinnitus have an increased risk of suicide, especially when comorbid depressive disorders are present [19–21]. The important questions in this context are first, how to find out if a patient is at risk of suicide and second, how to find out whether asking about the patient's suicidal thoughts may prompt the patient to commit suicide. The most prominent risk factor for suicide and suicidal ideas is a depressive disorder [22, 23]. Hence, a severe depressed mood, which cannot be modulated and is accompanied by social withdrawal, is an important warning sign of high risk of suicide. If one suspects that a patient is at

Table 54.3 Screening questions and assessment of suicidality according to the MINI International Neuropsychiatric Interview (M.I.N.I.; Sheehan et al. [18])

Question	Score if "Yes"
Think you would be better off dead or wish you were dead?	1
Want to harm yourself?	2
Think about suicide?	6
Have a suicide plan?	10
Attempt suicide	10
In your lifetime: Did you ever make a suicide attempt	4

Suicide risk current: 1–5 points = low; 6–9 points = moderate; 10 or more points = high

risk of suicide, the seriousness of the patient's suicidal thoughts should be evaluated by directly asking the patient about suicidal ideations or even asking if the patient has concrete plans of how to commit suicide. Discussing the issue of suicide with a patient should not increase the risk of them actually committing suicide. On the contrary, most patients feel relieved to have the opportunity to talk about their thoughts. Although there is no general rule of how to manage patients who are suicidal, one possible approach to this sensitive area is to first talk about passive suicidal ideas. This may be introduced by asking, for example, "In the past month did you think that you would be better off dead or wish you were dead?" Further screening questions to estimate the risk that the patient will actually commit suicide are given in Table 54.3. If it becomes clear from the clinical interview that the patient is suffering from suicidal ideas, the patient should be immediately referred to a psychiatrist. A patient with serious suicidal and concrete plans of how to commit suicide is an emergency, in which many physicians would recommend hospitalization for treatment.

References

1. Axelsson, A, Ringdahl, A Tinnitus – a study of its prevalence and characteristics Br J Audiol, 1989;23(1):53–62
2. Hiller, W, Goebel, G A psychometric study of complaints in chronic tinnitus J Psychosom Res, 1992;36(4):337–48
3. Belli, S, Belli, H, Bahcebasi, T, Ozcetin, A, Alpay, E, Ertem, U Assessment of psychopathological aspects and psychiatric comorbidities in patients affected by tinnitus Eur Arch Otorhinolaryngol, 2008;265(3):279–85
4. Unterrainer, J, Greimel, KV, Leibetseder, M, Koller, T Experiencing tinnitus: which factors are important for perceived severity of the symptom? Int Tinnitus J, 2003;9(2):130–3
5. Zoger, S, Svedlund, J, Holgers, KM Psychiatric disorders in tinnitus patients without severe hearing impairment: 24 month follow-up of patients at an audiological clinic Audiology, 2001;40(3):133–40
6. Zoger, S, Svedlund, J, Holgers, KM Relationship between tinnitus severity and psychiatric disorders Psychosomatics, 2006;47(4):282–8
7. Konzag, TA, Rubler, D, Bandemer-Greulich, U, Frommer, J, Fikentscher, E [Psychological comorbidity in subacute and chronic tinnitus outpatients] Z Psychosom Med Psychother, 2005;51(3):247–60
8. Marciano, E, Carrabba, L, Giannini, P, Sementina, C, Verde, P, Bruno, C, et al. Psychiatric comorbidity in a population of outpatients affected by tinnitus Int J Audiol, 2003;42(1):4–9
9. Harrop-Griffiths, J, Katon, W, Dobie, R, Sakai, C, Russo, J Chronic tinnitus: association with psychiatric diagnoses J Psychosom Res, 1987;31(5):613–21
10. Sullivan, MD, Katon, W, Dobie, R, Sakai, C, Russo, J, Harrop-Griffiths, J Disabling tinnitus Association with affective disorder Gen Hosp Psychiatry, 1988;10(4):285–91
11. Dobie, RA Depression and tinnitus Otolaryngol Clin North Am, 2003;36(2):383–8
12. Katon, W, Sullivan, M, Russo, J, Dobie, R, Sakai, C Depressive symptoms and measures of disability: a prospective study J Affect Disord, 1993;27(4):245–54
13. Wittchen, HU, Pittrow, D Prevalence, recognition and management of depression in primary care in Germany: the Depression 2000 study Hum Psychopharmacol, 2002;17 Suppl 1:S1–11
14. Biesinger, E, Heiden, C, Greimel, V, Lendle, T, Hoing, R, Albegger, K [Strategies in ambulatory treatment of tinnitus] HNO, 1998;46(2):157–69
15. Goebel, G, Hiller, W [The tinnitus questionnaire A standard instrument for grading the degree of tinnitus Results of a multicenter study with the tinnitus questionnaire] HNO, 1994;42(3):166–72
16. Crocetti, A, Forti, S, Ambrosetti, U, Bo, LD Questionnaires to evaluate anxiety and depressive levels in tinnitus patients Otolaryngol Head Neck Surg, 2009;140(3):403–5
17. Whooley, MA, Simon, GE Managing depression in medical outpatients N Engl J Med, 2000;343(26):1942–50
18. Sheehan, DV, Lecrubier, Y, Sheehan, KH, Amorim, P, Janavs, J, Weiller, E, et al. The Mini-International Neuropsychiatric Interview (MINI): the development and validation of a structured diagnostic psychiatric interview for DSM-IV and ICD-10 J Clin Psychiatry, 1998;59 Suppl 20:22–33
19. Jacobson, GP, McCaslin, DL A search for evidence of a direct relationship between tinnitus and suicide J Am Acad Audiol, 2001;12(10):493–6
20. Lewis, JE, Stephens, SD, McKenna, L Tinnitus and suicide Clin Otolaryngol Allied Sci, 1994;19(1):50–4
21. Turner, O, Windfuhr, K, Kapur, N Suicide in deaf populations: a literature review Ann Gen Psychiatry, 2007;6:26
22. Hawton, K, van Heeringen, K Suicide Lancet, 2009;373(9672):1372–81
23. Lejoyeux, M, Leon, E, Rouillon, F [Prevalence and risk factors of suicide and attempted suicide] Encephale, 1994;20(5):495–503

Part V
Clinical Characteristics of Different Forms of Tinnitus

Chapter 55
Introduction

Berthold Langguth, Dirk De Ridder, and Tobias Kleinjung

Keypoints

1. Tinnitus has many forms and many concomitant symptoms.
2. Specific subforms of tinnitus, which are characterized by phenomenological properties of the tinnitus sound, acuity, a specific time course, specific etiologies, or specific accompanying symptoms, require specific diagnostic and therapeutic management.

Keywords Subforms • Etiology • Chronicity • Comorbidity • Concomittant symptoms • Types • Tinnitus

Introduction

There is increasing consensus among clinicians that tinnitus is not a disease entity. Rather, there are many different forms of tinnitus that vary in their pathophysiology and probably also in their response to treatment interventions [1]. This, in turn, implies that differentiation of the different forms of tinnitus is essential for successful therapeutic management. Differentiation according to clinical characteristics seems to be the best feasible strategy.

B. Langguth (✉)
Department of Psychiatry and Psychotherapy, University of Regensburg, Universitätsstraße 84, 93053, Regensburg, Germany
and
Interdisciplinary Tinnitus Clinic, University of Regensburg, Universitätsstraße 84, 93053, Regensburg, Germany
e-mail: Berthold.Langguth@medbo.de

This means that diagnostic and therapeutic management should be individualized according to phenomenological characteristics of the tinnitus sound (e.g., pulsatile or non-pulsatile), comorbidities (e.g., vertigo, headache, and psychiatric symptoms), time course (e.g., acute tinnitus with hearing loss), or etiologic aspects (e.g., posttraumatic tinnitus). The chapters of this section deal with the most clinically relevant specific forms of tinnitus and their diagnostic and therapeutic management.

Acute sudden hearing loss with tinnitus (see Chap. 56) represents a specific subform, which requires immediate attention. In such a situation, therapeutic activities are primarily directed toward restoration of hearing. Based on data from animal models, it is assumed that after acute onset, there is a short therapeutic window for specific therapies [2, 3].

Hyperacusis and phonophobia occur frequently together with tinnitus [4]. An exact description is given in Chaps. 3 and 4. The focus of Chap. 57 is the management of tinnitus patients where hyperacusis and phonophobia are main complaints.

Both pulsatile and paroxysmal tinnitus have to be considered as specific entities and point at characteristic underlying pathologies. These subforms of tinnitus require specific diagnostic and therapeutic management which is described in the chapters on pulsatile tinnitus (Chap. 59) and intermittent tinnitus (Chap. 58).

Low-pitch tinnitus co-occurring with fluctuating vertigo and low-frequency hearing loss is characteristic for Ménière's syndrome with endolymphatic hydrops as an underlying pathology (see Chap. 60).

When tinnitus is accompanied by headache, pathologies should be considered, which result in increased or reduced intracranial pressure. These include space-occupying lesions and pseudotumor cerebri as well as low intracranial pressure syndrome. The diagnostic and therapeutic management of these and other syndromes are outlined in the chapter on tinnitus with headache (Chap. 61).

Severely impaired tinnitus patients frequently suffer from psychiatric comorbidities with depression, anxiety, and insomnia being the most frequent [5]. Even if a patient presents primarily because of his tinnitus, sometimes the management of the psychiatric comorbidities is in the foreground. This is definitively the case when a patient reports acute suicidal ideation. The different psychiatric comorbidities and their therapeutic management are covered in Chap. 62 with the subchapters Tinnitus and Depression (Chap. 63), Tinnitus and Anxiety (Chap. 64), and the chapter Tinnitus and Insomnia (Chap. 65).

The last two chapters of this section are devoted to tinnitus with a specific etiology. Whenever tinnitus occurs in conjunction with a traumatic event, specific diagnostic management is indicated (see Chap. 66) [6]. This is not only necessary for the best possible treatment of tinnitus itself but also to avoid further complications since tinnitus after trauma can be a symptom of a severe underlying condition that may become life threatening if left untreated (e.g., carotid dissection) [7]. A separate chapter is devoted to blast injuries (Chap. 67) as a specific form of posttraumatic tinnitus. This form of tinnitus is of high clinical relevance, since tinnitus has become one of the most relevant warfare-related health problems in the last few years [8]. Furthermore, blast injuries are a particular diagnostic challenge, since the tinnitus-inducing mechanisms may include noise, ear, head, neck, and emotional trauma [9, 10].

References

1. Møller, AR. Tinnitus: presence and future. Prog Brain Res, 2007;166: 3–16
2. Puel, JL, Ruel, J, Guitton, M, Wang, J, Pujol, R. The inner hair cell synaptic complex: physiology, pharmacology and new therapeutic strategies. Audiol Neurootol, 2002 Jan;7(1): 49–54
3. Norena, AJ, Eggermont, JJ. Enriched acoustic environment after noise trauma abolishes neural signs of tinnitus. Neuroreport, 2006 Apr 24;17(6): 559–63
4. Andersson, G, Juris, L, Kaldo, V, Baguley, DM, Larsen, HC, Ekselius, L. Hyperacusis – an unexplored field Cognitive behavior therapy can relieve problems in auditory intolerance, a condition with many questions. Lakartidningen, 2005 Oct 31;102(44): 3210–2
5. Crocetti, A, Forti, S, Ambrosetti, U, Bo, LD. Questionnaires to evaluate anxiety and depressive levels in tinnitus patients. Otolaryngol Head Neck Surg, 2009 Mar;140(3): 403–5
6. Folmer, RL, Griest, SE. Chronic tinnitus resulting from head or neck injuries. Laryngoscope, 2003 May;113(5): 821–7
7. Liess, BD, Lollar, KW, Christiansen, SG, Vaslow, D. Pulsatile tinnitus: a harbinger of a greater ill? Head Neck, 2009 Feb;31(2): 269–73
8. http://www.vba.va.gov/bln/21/ 2010 Ref Type: Internet Communication
9. Garth, RJ. Blast injury of the auditory system: a review of the mechanisms and pathology. J Laryngol Otol, 1994 Nov;108(11): 925–9
10. Ritenour, AE, Wickley, A, Ritenour, JS, Kriete, BR, Blackbourne, LH, Holcomb, JB, et al. Tympanic membrane perforation and hearing loss from blast overpressure in Operation Enduring Freedom and Operation Iraqi Freedom wounded. J Trauma, 2008 Feb;64(2 Suppl): S174–8

Chapter 56
Sudden Hearing Loss and Tinnitus

Carlos Herráiz

Keywords Tinnitus • Sensorineural hearing loss • Hyperacusis • Sudden deafness • Transtympanic • Steroids

Abbreviations

ABR   Auditory brainstem response
AIEDA   Autoimmune inner ear disease
FTA   Fluorescent treponemal antibody absorbed (FTA-ABS) test for syphilis
MRI   Magnetic resonance imaging
RCT   Randomized clinical trials
SNHL   Sensory neural hearing loss
SSNHL   Sudden sensory neural hearing loss
TTS   Transtympanic steroids

Introduction

Hearing loss can occur suddenly when the ear canal becomes occluded or the middle ear becomes damaged from trauma. However, the term sudden hearing loss is mainly used for suddenly occurring sensory neural hearing loss. Sudden sensory neural hearing loss (SSNHL) was first described by De Klein in 1944 [1]. SSNHL is a dramatic condition for the patient that twenty-first century medicine still has no explanation of; there is no known cure. The mechanisms, the etiology, and the treatment remain hypothetical. The SSNHL definition is also controversial among authors. The most detailed criteria have been proposed by Stokroos [2], who described SSNHL as an acute deafness with abrupt onset, generally within 3 days, of more than 30-dB hearing loss at three consecutive frequencies. Different authors have used different definitions of SSNHL [3].

Incidence of SSNHL

SSNHL occurs suddenly, over less than 3 days; it normally affects only one ear. The incidence of SSNHL has been reported to be 5–20 per 100,000 inhabitants per year in the United States [4] and 8–14.6 in Holland [5]. A recent epidemiological study conducted during 2004 in Saxony, Germany, with a population of almost half a million, showed an incidence of 160 per 100,000 inhabitants [6].

Some incidences of SSNHL have been reported in childhood. The prevalence is higher in young and healthy individuals. Many individuals with SSNHL recover spontaneously. There are many causes of hearing loss similar to etiologies that could be regarded as other forms of sensorineural hearing loss (SNHL) [4], and they have to be ruled out before the diagnosis of SSNHL is made. Endolymphatic hydrops, according to the Fetterman series, is the second most common cause of acute hearing loss (5.5%) after idiopathic sudden hearing loss. Ménière's disease was the next most frequent diagnosis (1.9%), followed by vestibular schwannoma (1.7%), perilymphatic fistula (0.7%), and autoimmune inner ear disease (0.6%). Other authors find that vestibular schwannoma accounts for 4% of acute unilateral hearing loss [7].

C. Herráiz (✉)
Department of Otorhinolaryngology, Hospital Universitario Fundación Alcorcón, C/Budapest, 1. Alcorcón, 28922 Madrid, Spain
and
Tinnitus and Hyperacusis Clinic. Otorhinolaryngology, Hospital Quirón, Madrid, Spain
e-mail: cherraizp@seorl.net

A.R. Møller et al. (eds.), *Textbook of Tinnitus*,
DOI 10.1007/978-1-60761-145-5_56, © Springer Science+Business Media, LLC 2011

Causes of SSNHL

Up until now, the etiological of most SSNHL is unknown. In only 10% of the SSNHL is it possible to find a plausible cause [4]. Many causes have been suggested, such as disturbances in the cochlear blood flow, inflammatory processes secondary to viral infections, and autoimmune reactions.

Decrease of the Inner Ear Blood Flow

Blood flow in the inner ear may be reduced because of hemorrhage or arterial occlusion, which may occur from thrombosis or vascular spasm. Pathological studies describe processes of fibrosis and cochlear ossification in individuals who have had sudden deafness [8]. The vascular causes may be suspected in individuals with a history of previous thrombi-embolisms, artherosclerosis, heart surgery, or thrombocytopenia due to aplastic anemia or leukemia.

Spontaneous recovery makes impairment of the cochlea's blood supply for longer than 1 h an unlikely cause [9].

Rupture of the Cochlear Membranes

The rupture of the cochlear membranes causes contact between the perilympha and the endolympha, altering the electrolytic balance and resulting in damage to hair cells.

A perilymphatic fistula to the middle ear is known to cause sudden hearing loss. Intense physical exercise, Valsalva maneuvers, or barotrauma can cause rupture of the oval or round window membrane. It has been estimated that perilymph fistulae may explain almost thirty percent of the SSNHL [10].

Autoimmune Inner Ear Disease

Autoimmune inner ear disease (AIED) is characterized by rapidly progressive bilateral hearing loss, usually symmetrical and fluctuant, although some individuals experience sudden hearing loss in only one ear.

Viral Theory

The viral theory is the most referred in the literature. Viral infections like mumps, rubella, herpes, or spurma retrovirus have been related to sudden hearing loss, although there is no clear evidence to confirm this theory [11–13].

Clinical Course

Sudden hearing loss starts with a rapidly progressive hearing impairment, either suddenly or within a few hours, often when the person wakes up. Sixty-three percent of people with SSNHL have ear pain initially and 41% experience aural pressure during a few days [11]. Tinnitus appears in 91% of individuals with SSNHL [4]. Tinnitus has been reported to develop days before the SSNHL occurred or it can occur simultaneously or days after to the SSNHL. Some individuals describe facial paresthesia.

Vertigo has been reported to occur in 43% of individuals with SSNHL [11]. Some patients refer a rotatory motion with vegetative manifestations during a few days. Often unsteadiness and involuntary movement of the body toward the affected side occur for weeks. The presence of spontaneous nystagmus in SSNHL has been reported to occur in half of individuals with SSNHL. The recurrence rate of hearing loss in long-term follow-up has been reported to be significantly higher (51.2%) in the group who had spontaneous nystagmus than in the individuals without nystagmus (27.9%) [14].

Diagnosis

A diagnosis of individuals with rapidly occurring hearing loss requires complete auditory examination: tone and speech audiometry, tympanometry, and stapedial reflex test. Auditory brainstem responses or MRI to rule out retrocochlear diseases and laboratory tests such as the antinuclear antibodies, erythrocyte sedimentation rate, and tests for rheumatoid factor have been proposed for diagnosis of SSNHL and to detect treatment responders [15]. However, none of the laboratory parameters have been proven to have a high sensitivity or specificity. A test to rule out syphilis (FTA) is also recommended [16].

The assessment of the vestibular system may be useful to detect possible vestibular complications for prognosis. Vestibular-evoked myogenic potentials (VEMP) have demonstrated saccular damage in patients with SSNHL without vertigo, suggesting a saccular deterioration in those patients with profound high-frequency hearing loss [17].

Prognosis

A spontaneous recovery has been described in 45–65% of the cases [11]. Some individuals with SSNHL have a complete recovery while most have partial improvement of hearing. Specific factors that affect the prognosis of SSNHL are the severity of the hearing loss; a greater impairment on high frequencies or the presence of vestibular symptoms significantly reduces the prognosis [11, 18]. However, Fetterman [4] did not find that the audiometric profile made any differences regarding prognosis, but "U"-shaped audiograms predict higher fluctuations and recurrences of the episodes of SSNHL. Age or speech recognition threshold did not influence the course of the disease.

Treatment

The high rate of spontaneous recovery and the difference in definition of SSNHL makes it difficult to compare the results presented in published studies [19].

Blood Flow Increase

Vasodilatation: *histamine, verapamil, papaverine, novocaine, nicotinic acid, naftidrofuryl, Egb 761.*

Studies that have followed a valid design do not show significant differences between treated individuals and control groups [20–22].

Reduction in the blood viscosity: Dextran, papaverine, pentoxifiline.

A recent multicenter and randomized study evaluated the benefits of rheopheresis, a method to reduce the plasma viscosity and improve microcirculation for treatment of SSNHL [23]. The rheopheresis group (two sessions within 3 days) was compared to a group that received steroid treatment (methyl-prednisolone 250 mg per day, 3 days and tapered oral dosing) and to intravenous hemodilution (500 ml 6% hydroxyethil starch plus 600 mg pentoxifyline per day during 10 days). There was not a placebo control group in this study. None of the tested treatments were superior regarding providing overall good recovery of hearing.

Defibrinogenase Therapy: Baxtrobin

Administration of baxtrobin, a trombine-like enzyme that reduces the levels of fibrinogen and the blood viscosity [24] did not present better results than expected with placebo.

Anti-inflammatory Treatment: Corticosteroids

Systemic Steroids

Corticosteroids are the most effective treatment for SSNHL. A placebo-controlled study demonstrated the efficacy of dexamethasone or methyl-prednisolone. Seventy-eight percent of the patients with moderate and severe hearing loss who received such treatment had partial or total recovery of hearing compared with placebo [25].

In a descriptive study by Moon [26], SSNHL participants who showed any improvement after early steroid therapy were analyzed to evaluate the beginning time and the plateau time of hearing improvement. It was shown that 93.1% had an onset of improvement within 14 days of beginning the treatment. Complete recovery or completed improvement was achieved in 80.4% of the participants within 1 month and in 92.2% within 2 months after treatment [26].

After 1 month, the possibility of improvement decreases [2], but Stokroos did not find differences in starting a treatment within the first 24 h and during the first 10 days [2]. Better recovery was found in participants who had the most hearing loss around 4 kHz [4].

Transtympanic Steroid Therapy

Many publications regarding randomized clinical trials (RCT) have demonstrated the benefit of transtympanic steroids (TTS) as a rescue treatment after systemic steroids for SSNHL. Methyl-prednisolone showed the most promising profile, when considering drug concentration in the endolymph [27]. Battaglia obtained better results in those patients who received a combined therapy, oral steroids (60 mg per day, 7 days) plus TTS (dexamethasone 12 mg/ml once per week, 3 weeks), compared to the group that received TTS plus oral placebo. This last combination was more effective than oral steroids and transtympanic placebo [28].

Antiviral Therapy

There was no difference in the benefit from treatment with antiviral drugs (acyclovir) or administration of steroids [5], nor have other studies with valacyclovir [29, 30] shown any benefit of the antiviral drug for SSNHL.

Hyperbaric Oxygen Therapy

Administration of hyperbaric oxygen treatment has been described but is controversial [2].

Surgery

If a perilymphatic fistula is the cause of SSNHL, surgical treatment of the fistula can improve hearing [31].

Other Treatments

Ozone therapy (autohaemotherapy) has been tried in a RCT for sudden hearing loss [32]. A 100 ml of the patient's own blood with a gaseous mixture of oxygen and ozone was re-injected twice a week for 10 sessions. Seventy-seven percent of the treated patients showed a significant hearing recovery compared to 40% in the placebo group. Pure-tone averages and speech reception thresholds were also significantly better.

Tinnitus and SSNHL

Tinnitus is a common symptom in SSNHL. Approximately 91% of individuals with SSNHL report that they have tinnitus in the affected ear or in both ears [4]. Tinnitus occurs at the same time as hearing loss in some individuals with SSNHL and may be the first symptom before hearing loss. Tinnitus begins some days after the hearing impairment in some individuals. The tinnitus may be caused by sound deprivation caused by the hearing loss, which is known to be able to start central nervous system reorganization processes that can lead to tinnitus (see Chaps. 10, 12 and 21) and hyperacusis (see Chaps. 3 and 4).

Tinnitus Characteristics

We have previously shown [32] that 6.6% of the first 213 patients referred to our tinnitus clinic had SSNHL. Tinnitus onset was sudden in approximately 92% of the patients. The intensity of the tinnitus fluctuated in 46% of patients. Tinnitus psychoacoustical characteristics are shown in Table 56.5.

The tinnitus in SSNHL can imply a greater handicap than the hearing loss [2]. When the hearing resolves, either through treatment or spontaneously, the tinnitus may improve or disappear. Tinnitus may be a prognostic sign for the hearing loss [33].

Tinnitus Management

Tinnitus that accompanies SSNHL can be treated in a similar way as other forms of tinnitus (see chapters in Section V). All treatments for sudden hearing loss can be effective in treating the tinnitus. The use of steroids, vasodilatation drugs, and procedures or the hyperbaric oxygen therapy is often used when tinnitus accompanies SSNHL. At early stages of SSNHL, sound stimulation is beneficial because it can prevent reorganization processes secondary to sound deprivation in the auditory nervous system. As remapping could be the physiological substrate for tinnitus development, customized sound enrichment would help to decrease the possibility of tinnitus and hyperacusis [34, 35] (see Chaps. 74, 75 and 76).

Conclusion

Most forms of SSNHL have no known cause. In management of patients with SSNHL, it is important to rule out other causes. Retrocochlear diseases, such as vestibular schwannoma and other central nervous system tumors, have been described to occur in 4% of SSNHL. They can be ruled out through tests such as ABR or MRI. Published results regarding the prognosis of SSNHL vary among studies. Some studies show 45–65% spontaneous recovery. The severity of the hearing loss, the audiometric profile, and the presence of vestibular symptoms affect the prognosis. Delay on starting treatment is associated with a worse prognosis. Steroid treatment is proven to be the most effective treatment, although it is not largely effective. Recent studies show promising results regarding the efficacy of steroids delivered through the eardrum. More than 50% of the patients showed a significant improvement of such treatment when administered after the failure of conservative therapy. Tinnitus accompanies most incidences of SSNHL. Tinnitus usually improves when hearing is partial or totally recovered, and individuals can also benefit from other forms of tinnitus treatment when there is no improvement of hearing.

References

1. De Klein A. Sudden complete o partial loss of function of the octavus-system in apparently normal persons. Acta Otolaryngol (Stockh) 1944; 32: 409–429
2. Stokroos RJ, Albers FWJ. Therapy of idiopathic sudden sensorineural hearing loss. A review of the literature. Acta Oto-rhino-laryngol Belg., 1996; 50: 77–84
3. Shikowitz MJ Sudden sensorineural hearing loss. Med Clin North Am. 1991; 75(6): 1239–50
4. Fetterman BL, Sanders JE, Luxford WM. Prognosis and Treatment of Sudden Sensorineural Hearing loss. Am J Otol 1996; 17: 529–536
5. Stokroos RJ, Albers FW, Tenvergert EM. Antiviral treatment of idiopathic sudden sensorineural hearing loss: a prospective, randomized, double-blind clinical trial. Acta Otolaryngol 1998; 118: 488–95
6. Klemm E, Deutscher A, Mösges R. A present investigation of the epidemiology in idiopathic sudden sensorineural hearing loss. Laryngorhinootologie 2009; 88: 524–527
7. Hughes GB, Freedman MA, Haberkamp TJ, Guay ME. Sudden neurosensorial hearing loss. Otolaryngol Clin North Am 1996; 29: 393–405
8. Belal A. The effect of vascular occlusion on the Human Inner Ear. J Laryngol Otol, 1979; 93: 955–68
9. Perlman HB, Kimura RS, Fernandez C. Experiments on temporary occlusion of the internal auditory artery. Laryngoscope 1959; 69: 591–613
10. Duckert LG, Meyerhoff W. Sudden hearing loss. In Meyerhoff WL, ed. Diagnosis and management of hearing loss. Philadelphia WB Saunders, 1980; 12–22
11. Van Dishoeck HAE, Bierman TA. Sudden perceptive deafness and viral infection. Ann. Otol Rhinol laryngol, 1957; 66: 963–80
12. Mattox DE, Simons FB. Nautral history of sudden sensorineural hearing loss. Ann Otol Rhinol Laryngol 1977; 86: 463–480
13. Kobayashi H, Suzuki A, Nomura Y. Unilateral hearing loss following rubella infection in an adult. Acta Otolaryngol (Stockh), 1994; 514: 49–51
14. Junicho M, Fushiki H, Aso S et al. Prognostic value of initial electronystagmography findings in idiopathic sudden sensorineural hearing loss without vértigo. Otol Neurotol 2008a; 29: 905–909
15. Süslü N, Yilmaz T, Gürsel B. Utility of anti-HSP 70, TNF-alfa, ESR, antinuclear antibody and antiphospholipid antibodies in the diagnosis and treatment of sudden s12ensorineural hearing loss. Laryngoscope 2009; 119: 341–6
16. Garcia-Berrocal JR, Ramirez-Camacho R, Trinidad A. Autoimmune hearing loss: improving diagnostic performance. Acta Otorrinolaryngol Esp 2007; 58: 138–42
17. Hong SM, Byun JY, Park CH et al. Saccular damage in patients with idiopathic sudden sensorineural hearing loss without vertigo. Otolaryngol Head Neck Surg 2008; 139: 541–5
18. Byl FMJ. Sudden hearing loss: eight years of experience and suggested pronostic table. Laryngoscope, 1984; 94 (5 Pt 1): 647–51
19. Plontke SK, Bauer M, Meisner C. Comparison of pure-tone audiometry analysis in sudden hearing loss studies: lack of agreement for different outcome measures. Otol Neurotol 2007; 28: 753–63
20. Kronenberg J, Almagor M, Bendet E, Kushnir D. Vasoactive therapy versus placebo in the treatment of Sudden Hearing loss: a double blind clinical study. Laryngoscope 1992; 102: 65–8
21. Kohen W, Nickol HJ. Horsturz-zur altersabhangigkeit der therapieergebnisse unter berucksichtiguntg vom naftodrofuryl (Dusodril). HNO, 1985; 33: 36–9
22. Hoffmann F, Beck C, Schutz A, Offerman P. Ginkgoextrakt EGB 171 (Tebonin)/HAES versus Naftidrofuryl (Dusodril)/HAES. Eine randomisierte studie zur horsturztherapie. Laryngol, Rhinol Otol, 1994; 73: 149–52

23. Mösges R, Köberlein J, Heibges A et al. Rheopheresis for idiopathic sudden hearing loss: results from a large prospective, multicenter, randomized, controlled clinical trial. Eur Arch Otorhinolaryngol 2008; 266: 943–53

24. Kubo T Matsunaga T. Efficacy of defibrinogenation and steroid therapies on sudden deafness. Arch Otolaryngol Head Neck Surg 1988; 114: 649–652

25. Wilson WR, Byl FM, Laird N. The efficacy of steroides in the threatment of idiopathic sudden hearing loss. Arch Otolaryngol 1980; 106: 772–6

26. Moon IS, Kim J, Lee SY et al. How long should the sudden hearing loss patients be followed after early steroid combination therapy?. Eur Arch Otorhinolaryngol 2009; 266: 1391–5

27. Parnes LS, Sun AH, Freeman DJ. Corticosteroid pharmacokinetics in the inner ear fluids: an amimal study followed by clinical application. Laryngoscope, 1999; 109: 1–17

28. Battaglia A, Burchette R, Cuevas R. Combination therapy (intratympanic dexamethasone + high-dose prednisone taper) for the treatment of idiopathic sudden sensorineural hearing loss. Otol Neurotol. 2009; 30: 254–5

29. Tucci DL, Farner JC Jr, Kithc RD et al. Treatment of sudden sensorineural hearing loss with systemic steroids and valacyclovir. Otol Neurotol 2002; 23: 301–8

30. Westerlaken BO, Stokroos RJ, Wit HP et al. Treatment of sudden sensorineural hearing loss with antiviral therapy: a prospective, randomized, double-blind clinical trial. Ann Otol Rhinol Laryngol 2003; 112: 993–1000

31. Ragab A, Shreef E, Behiry E et al. Randomised, double-blinded, placebo-controlled, clinical trial of ozone therapy as treatment of sudden sensorineural hearing loss. J Laryngol Otol 2009; 123: 54–60

32. Ruben RJ, Yankelowitz SM. Spontaneous perilymphatic fistula in children. Am J Otol. 1989; 10(3): 198–207

33. Herraiz C. Tinnitus management with retraining therapies. Doctoral Thesis. Universidad Autonoma Madrid, June 2002.

34. Hikita-Watanabe N, Kitahara T, Horii A, Kawashima T, Doi K, Okumura SI. Tinnitus as a prognostic factor of sudden deafness. Acta Otolaryngol. 2009 May 12: 1–5. [Epub ahead of print]

35. Norena AJ, Eggermont JJ. Enriched acoustic environment after noise trauma abolishes neural signs of tinnitus. Neuroreport 2006; 17: 559–563

Chapter 57
Tinnitus and Hyperacusis/Phonophobia

Carlos Herráiz and Isabel Diges

Keypoints

1. Hyperacusis is a decreased sound tolerance.
2. Prevalence of the disease is described in 9–15% of the population, but increases among tinnitus patients.
3. Pathophysiological mechanisms involve some disruptions in the amplification and regulation processes of the external hair cells, disorders of the efferent system (medial and lateral olivocochlear pathways), or effects to the central sound processing at the subcortical level.
4. The role of some neurotransmitters (serotonin, GABA), which are also involved in other hyperacusis-related diseases (migraine, depression), can be relevant in this disorder.
5. Other theories confirm the effect of the endorphins that activates the excitatory function of the glutamate, the main auditory neurotransmitter, increasing its toxicity.
6. The activation of the limbic and autonomic nervous systems produces the emotional reaction of the hyperacusis (anxiety, fear, and depression).
7. Proposed treatments are based on acoustic stimulation: progressive introduction of white sound (tinnitus retraining therapy TRT) and customized sounds based on the damaged hearing frequencies.
8. Noise generators and hearing aids can be fitted in severe cases.
9. The role of some drugs involved in the metabolism of serotonin and GABA opens new approaches for the management of hyperacusis.

C. Herráiz (✉)
Department of Otorhinolaryngology, Hospital Universitario
Fundación Alcorcón, c/Budapest 1. Alcorcon,
28922 Madrid, Spain
e-mail: cherraizp@seorl.net

Keywords Tinnitus • Decreased sound tolerance • Hyperacusis • Recruitment • Phonophobia • Efferent system • Tinnitus retraining therapy • Hearing aid

Abbreviations

LDL	Loudness discomfort level
DST	Decreased sound tolerance
OHC	Outer hair cells
IHC	Inner hair cells
MOCB	Medial olivocochlear bundle
LOCB	Lateral olivocochlear bundle
5HT	Serotonin
ABR	Auditory brain responses
THS	Test of Hypersensitivity to Sound
BBNG	Broad band noise generators

Introduction

Hyperacusis is defined as a decreased tolerance to environmental sounds or the abnormal avoidance response to sounds that they are not annoying to the general population (see Chap. 3). It is a disorder of the normal amplification process of the auditory pathways. A decrease in the loudness discomfort levels (LDL) to environmental noise is observed in individuals with hyperacusis scores below 90 dBHL for some authors [1] or below 100 dBHL according to others [2]. Auditory hypersensitivity affects all sounds, although some specific noises can be more annoying according to their frequency spectrum or intensity.

The hyperacusis has to be distinguished from other symptoms that could co-exist simultaneously or develop as isolated forms. Misophonia (from the

Greek "miso: hate") is a "dislike of certain specific sounds," and is different from phonophobia – a fear of certain sounds [2] (see Chap. 4). The anatomical and physiological basis is generally unknown, and these clinical entities have been regarded as belonging to the field of psychology. Phonophobia and misophonia are related to the type or the source of the sound and not specifically to its loudness. Hyperacusis is an abnormally low tolerance of sounds and may have to do with faulty gain control in the auditory pathways causing an abnormal activation of emotional reactions from the limbic and autonomous systems. Conversely, phonophobia is an abnormal reaction from the limbic and autonomous systems with normal auditory neural activity.

Recruitment of loudness is a pure cochlear physical phenomenon that depends on the outer hair cells. It is caused by the stimulation of the neighboring neural fibers to the damaged cochlear areas after exposure to intense sounds. There is a breakdown in the relation between the stimulus loudness and the intensity of the patient's acoustic sensation. The result is a distortion of, and an annoyance to, the sound.

There are a few epidemiological studies related to hyperacusis and decreased sound tolerance (DST). Fabijanska performed a wide study, sending a specific questionnaire to the general population by postal mail. Of 10,349 returned questionnaires, the study showed that 15.2% of the population referred hypersensitivity to sound [3].

The study published by Andersson in 2002 was conducted in Sweden through the Internet. Nine percent of the 595 responders reported a DST. These data were confirmed through postal mail to 589 individuals, where 8% of the sample showed the same results [4].

Some studies have described the prevalence of DST among tinnitus patients. Between 40% [2] and 59% [5] in a tinnitus clinic sample reported symptoms of hyperacusis. The prevalence of tinnitus in DST patients rises up to 86% [6].

Mechanisms of Hyperacusis

The mechanisms of hyperacusis generation and persistence could involve a peripheral origin, principally the cochlea, or could be a disorder of the central auditory pathways.

The amplification of the acoustic pressure wave from the active movements of the outer hair cells (OHC) facilitates the stimulation of the inner hair cells (IHC). This mechanism can be damaged due to an increased amplification of sound from the OHC [2]. Hyperexcitability of these cells would overstimulate the action of the IHC. The OHC's active movements would excessively amplify a sound of moderate intensity and, therefore, it will be annoying. Distortion product measurements in these patients would show increased values [2, 7].

Contralateral otoacoustic emission suppression through white noise stimulation is a useful tool to test the efferent system function. We found some abnormalities in the medial olivocochlear bundle (MOCB) pathways as the cause of DST [8]. Other authors, such as Baguley, have not found any change in LDL scores after section of olivocochlear fibers (efferent fibers) when performing a vestibular neurectomy for disabling vertigo (the MOCB travels with the vestibular nerve at the point where it is sectioned) [9].

The lateral olivocochlear bundle (LOCB) originates in the lateral superior olivary complex and innervates through unmyelinated axons, the primary afferent dendrites of the cochlear nerve near their synapses with inner hair cells. LOCB terminals are more complex, with evidence for cholinergic, GABAergic, dopaminergic, and peptidergic transmission [10]. Activation of the LOCB can evoke either slow enhancement (cholinergic) or suppression (dopaminergic) of auditory nerve response. LOCB feedback maintains the binaural balance in neural excitability required for accurate localization of sounds in space [11]. Its function has been associated with the control to glutamate excitotoxicity in afferent nerve terminals in acute acoustic injury [12], and it has a protective effect over neural damage from intense sound exposition, mainly based on the dopaminergic regulation.

DST could be caused by LOCB impairment. Clinical diagnosis of LOCB function is based on auditory brainstem responses (ABR) [13], which would increase by ipsilateral stimulation and decrease in response to contralateral stimulation. Otoacoustic emissions will not be affected because the LOCB does not affect the function of the outer hair cells. It can be hypothesized that the dopaminergic LOCB synapses would be a suitable target for treatments. It has been shown that after acute acoustic injury, perfusion with dopaminergic agonists reduces cochlear damage [12].

Table 57.1 Cause of hyperacusis from ear disorders range

Cochlear diseases	Ménière's disease/endolymphatic hydrops
	Perylimphatic fistula
	Sudden deafness
	Acoustic trauma/noise induced hearing loss
	Otoesclerosis
After surgical procedures	Post stapedectomy
	After transtympanic tube placement
	After wax removal
Stapedial reflex disorders	Sdr. Ramsay hunt
	Bell's facial palsy
Muscular disorders	Mystenia gravis

Table 57.2 Causes of hyperacusis related to central nervous system disorders

Migraine
Depression
Sd. Postraumatic stress
Craneoencephalic trauma
Lyme's disease (*Borrelia burgdorferi*)
Williams Sdr.
BZD dependence Sdr.
Chronic postviral fatigue Sdr.
Serotonine disfunction
Tay-Sachs Sdr. (*gangliosidosis 2*)
Multiple sclerosis
Benign intracranial hypertension Sdr.

BZD benzodiazepines

Other possible mechanisms of peripheral disorders that could cause DST would be the recruitment phenomenon; although recruitment of loudness is regarded to be different from hyperacusis, it is included in DST. Cochlear hearing loss (which occurs in Ménière's disease), sudden sensorineural hearing loss, or immunological inner ear disease shows a reduction in LDL and the presence of acoustic distortion. Other possible causes of hyperacusis would be damage of the acoustic middle-ear reflex mediated by the facial nerve. Bell's palsy, other facial palsies, neuro-muscle disorders such as myasthenia gravis, or stapes surgery may present DST in many patients. This kind of DST, however, usually abates spontaneously over time. Table 57.1 shows the most relevant etiologies.

Serotonin (5HT) has been involved in some diseases such as migraine, depression, or posttraumatic stress syndrome – disorders associated with DST that may modulate auditory signals [14]. (5HT) has an important role for central auditory processing (CAP) and can be decreased in older people. A study performed in elderly patients showed that treatment with a selective serotonin release inhibitor (citalopram) improved the results of auditory processing and speech discrimination tests [15].

A second mechanism described in hyperacusis is based on the role of the endogen endorphins [16]. Anxiety and stress increase the liberation of endorphins in the IHC–auditory nerve synapses. These substances potentiate the excitatory effect of the glutamate and therefore may increase excitation in the auditory periphery. Table 57.2 gives a list of central disorders associated with hyperacusis.

The inhibitory neurotransmitter GABA acts at several levels on the acoustic pathways. Even the function of the cochlea depends on GABA transmission at IHC synapses. A decrease in the action of GABA will increase neural activity and could be a correlate for hyperacusis. $GABA_A$ receptor agonists, such as benzodiazepines, could be used for some forms of hyperacusis. The author has used pregabalin for DST management with good results in some patients. Pregabalin affects many receptors and produces a dose-dependent increase in glutamic acid decarboxylase activity, increasing neuronal GABA levels.

Diagnosis of Hyperacusis

There is no objective measurement of hyperacusis because it is a subjective symptom (Table 57.3). A complete audiological examination, however, can be useful in the diagnosis of hyperacusis. Tonal and speech audiograms, tympanometry, and the study of the acoustic middle-ear reflex should be performed in all patients. ABR can rule out vestibular schwannoma and other retrocochlear diseases (multiple sclerosis) and is also useful for the diagnosis of auditory nerve neuropathy. An increase in the amplitude of the ipsilateral ABR responses and a decrease in the contralateral ABR in normal hearing subjects would rule out a LOCB disorder [13].

The study of OHC function and the MOCB efferent system can be performed through otoacoustic emissions (OEA). Study of the MOCB efferent system can be useful for diagnosis of some causes of DST. The discomfort threshold, which is the sound intensity that is annoying and not tolerable, can be determined. Its

Table 57.3 Classification of hyperacusis according to the loudness discomfort level and dynamic range

Degree	Dynamic range	Loudness discomfort level
No hyperac.	≥60 dB	≥95 dB in all the frequencies
Mild	50–55 dB in any frequency	80–90 dB in 2 or more frequencies
Moderate	40–45 dB in any frequency	65–75 dB in 2 or more frequencies
Severe	≤35 dB in any frequency	≤60 dB in 2 or more frequencies

Table 57.5 Grades of hyperacusis considering the GUF

Degree	Score
Mild	≤10
Moderate	From 11 to 17
Severe	From 18 to 25
Very severe	26–45

Studies of Hyperacusis in a Tinnitus Clinic

Table 57.4 List of affected or avoided activities due to DST

Concerts	Social life	Sport spectacles
Going to the restaurants	Going to church	House keeping
Going to the cinema	Working	Taking care of the children
Shopping	Driving	Others

normal values are more than 90 dBHL, which are lower than the pain thresholds. It has to be tested several times because patients may have an initial fear of sounds, which would initially give lower thresholds than the real tolerance level.

Many individuals with DST will avoid different activities, affecting quality of life. The use of visual analogue scales for evaluation of hyperacusis handicap is useful (described in Table 57.4). Another system that has been proposed, named MASH, classifies the hyperacusis in four grades according to a broad list of activities: mild (≤3), moderate (from 3.1 to 5), severe (from 5.1 to 7), and very severe (≥7) [17].

In recent years, some specific questionnaires for DST have been developed and are useful tools in clinical diagnosis. The "self-rating Questionnaire on Hypersensitivity to Sound" published by Nelting and Rienhoff [18], evaluated DST according to three factors: cognitive reactions to hyperacusis, behavioral changes, and emotional responses to external sound. It was based on 15 questions; the scores went from 0 to 45. Every question had four possible answers: never (0 points), sometimes (1 point), often (2 points), and always (3 points). The score obtained can be divided into four grades, as we can see in Table 57.5. This questionnaire was originally written in German and it has been translated into Spanish [19]. Another published questionnaire was written by Khalfa [20]. It is based on 14 items and evaluates three dimensions: attention, social interaction, and emotion.

In a study on 250 consecutive patients [5], we described the clinical characteristics of hyperacusis and tinnitus in DST patients. Direct questions and specific questionnaires were used to evaluate the interference of DST and tinnitus on quality of life. Auditory and psychoacoustic measurements were done on all participants. The answer to a question "do you feel more uncomfortable with environmental sounds than a majority of people?" was affirmative for 54% of the participants. Fifty-two participants had to stop one or more activities from a list of eleven (shopping, driving, taking care of children, going to church, etc.) because of DST. Sixty-three percent of the tinnitus clinic population showed LDL ≤90 dBHL, which was our definition of hyperacusis. Sixty-one percent were women, whose average age was 51 years (±14). Anxiety or stress was reported by 65% of the group, and 15% described the presence of different phobias: height, closed spaces, or insects. Sleeping problems were also very common (51%), and in two-thirds of the cases, tinnitus was the main problem for lack of sleep. A hearing impairment over 25 dBHL in any frequency was present in 83% of the participants.

The tinnitus of the DST group was predominantly in the left ear (52%), 27% in the right ear, and bilateral or cephalic in 21%. The average time the participants had experienced their symptoms was 6.6 years. The symptoms were present all day in 81% and had fluctuant intensity in 42% of the participants. The tinnitus increased by anxiety in 63% of the participants by loud external sound (27%) and postural changes (10%). The Tinnitus Handicap Inventory (THI) was used for evaluation of the severity and degree of annoyance. An average of 47 points was obtained. The visual analogue scale on tinnitus loudness scored 6.5 ± 2 (range 1–10).

Psychoacoustic measurement of tinnitus pitch showed that 46% had high- frequency tinnitus (>2 kHz) 34% from 0.5 to 2 kHz, and 14% of the participants matched their tinnitus to low frequencies. Average loudness was 9.8 dB ± 8.5 and minimum masking level was 19.3 dB ± 18.5. Two percent reported a temporally complete elimination of the tinnitus with residual inhibition, whereas 56% obtained a partial reduction. Forty-two percent had no changes after sound exposure.

The Spanish version of the Sound Hypersensitivity Questionnaire (THS) was evaluated in another study with 40 participants with DST who were referred to our Tinnitus and Hyperacusis Clinic.

Seventy percent of the participants were female; average age was 48 ± 11 years. Hearing loss was present in 77% of the participants. THS average was 20.1 ± 10.0 points (range 1–45). The questions "I cannot listen or pay attention when intense or annoying sounds from my surroundings are present," "I have to leave when there are intense surrounding sounds," and "I am worried of hearing loss because of exposure to intense sounds" were answered with "yes" by most of the participants. There was a significant correlation ($p < 0.05$) between higher scores of the THS and a higher score in the visual analogue scale and the number of affected activities. The group of DST patients with hearing loss had higher scores in THS, but there was no correlation between the degree of hearing loss (pure-tone average) and the THS scores. Ninety percent of the participants presented tinnitus. The presence of tinnitus and its handicap, according to a visual analogue scale and the THI evaluation, were also correlated with higher THS scores. There was no significant relation between THS values and sex, age, possible etiology, duration of the disease, and loudness discomfort levels [19].

Therapeutical Approaches

There is one basic pillar for hyperacusis treatment: acoustic stimulation. Reaching this objective requires two steps. The first one is counseling. A professional can be able to change the patient's negative feelings about causes of hyperacusis, possibilities for its control, treatment options, and prognosis. Counseling should be focused on positive and evidence-based medicinal information, reducing the patient's emotional reaction and behaviors.

The second step is acoustic stimulation. Controlled and progressive exposure to sound has been demonstrated to be a useful tool in hyperacusis management, as we will see later in this chapter. Patients should avoid regular use of hearing plugs, except for the activities they are not able to perform without ear protection. The continuous use of the earplugs will increase the loudness discomfort levels and will decrease sound tolerance. The combination of counseling and white noise stimulation was developed by Jastreboff on the basis of a neurophysiologic model of tinnitus and named *Tinnitus Retraining Therapy (TRT)* (see Chap. 73). TRT has demonstrated its efficacy for hyperacusis management [2] and is now in routine use in many clinics. According to TRT, sound therapy can be delivered using three systems.

– *Environmental sound enrichment.* Different devices are useful for sound enrichment. A progressive increase in the volume of different kinds of sounds

is used to increase sound tolerance in a slow but constant way. This method is effective for mild or moderate hyperacusis.

– *Broad band noise generators (BBNG).* According to Jastreboff's criteria, broad band noise generators should be used when LDL were 80–85 dB or less. Jastreboff reported that 30 percent of the tinnitus patients required hyperacusis management before treatment of their tinnitus [21]. The BBNG is designed to produce two sounds with different spectrums: one covers low and middle frequencies and the other one covers some high frequencies. The digital noise generators can be customized to each patient's preferences. The patient starts the therapy at the maximum volume tolerated without feeling annoyance. In some patients, the volume and time of exposure to the generator has to be increased on a weekly or monthly basis and extended to up to 8 h a day.

– *Hearing Aids.* Patients with hearing loss and moderate or severe hyperacusis will require DST management before being fitted with a hearing aid. This symptom could lead the patient to reject the device. There is also a possibility that the hyperacusis and tinnitus could increase. In a recent study, 41 percent of DST patients in our clinic experienced increased loudness of their tinnitus after exposure to loud sounds [5] (see also Chap. 74). The fitting process has to be slow, progressive, and made in accordance to the patient's tolerance. We recommend that patients first use their hearing aid in quiet places. The use of the device and environmental sound exposure should be increased after this initial period of adjustment. The hearing aid compression systems and the maximum output of the device should be adjusted to avoid annoyance. The use of auditory training and broad band noise generators before the hearing aid fitting helps improve the LDL, dynamic range, and the speech comprehension. This method has been used by other authors, such as Knáster [22, 23], who obtained a reduction of the LDL (recruitment coefficient) in 59% of participants who had unilateral DST and 94% in bilateral DST.

The results of TRT in the management of DST are convincing. Gold reduced the LDL for 2, 3, and 4 kHz in more than 12 dBHL [24] at the end of treatment. Hazell reported that 45 percent of the patients he treated returned to regular LDL after 6 months, and 61% of the patients had regular LDL in 2 years. The number of activities the patient had to give up because of his DST was reduced from 3.5 to 1.1 after 15 months of TRT [25].

Noreña and Chery-Croze [26] have hypothesized that hyperacusis is caused by enhancement of neural activity in the auditory pathways caused by deprivation of input to the auditory nervous system at the hearing impaired frequencies (see also Chap. 11). The introduction of external sound limited to the impaired frequencies (inverse to the one showed at the audiogram) could progressively reduce the amplification in the auditory nervous system and thereby decrease hyperacusis. The intensity of the sound stimulus should be customized according to the hearing loss as it appears in the audiogram. The differences between TRT's recommended noise stimulation and that suggested in Noreña's study is that in Norena's study, it is limited to the impaired frequencies; there is not a progression of the stimulus intensity. The intensity of the sound used should be kept the same during all training. Our method is based on stimulation with sound (or CDs) of different frequency ranges (2–8 kHz, 4–12 kHz, etc.), but there is no customized intensity for each frequency. The sound intensity is increased gradually according to patient's improvement.

Although TRT is the most used method to treat hyperacusis worldwide, treatment with drugs can be used alone or in combination with sound treatment. Those patients we suspect of having a cochlear hyperexcitability may improve with administration of salicylates because of their ototoxicity [27]. Typical recruitment from non-compensated cochlear diseases (Ménière's disease, sudden deafness, fluctuant sensorineural hearing loss, etc.) can be managed through steroid therapy (systemically or transtympanic delivery). The use of diuretics, betahistine, and sulpiride are common on these clinical entities and can give some relief during acute crisis.

One of the mechanisms described for central hyperacusis has been associated with a decrease in serotonin. Drugs that are selective serotonin reuptake inhibitors (paroxetine, fluoxetine, sertraline) can therefore be helpful to some patients with DST [14, 28]. Drug or cognitive management of anxiety and depression can successfully treat the emotional component of hyperacusis. DST mechanisms based on GABA disorders can be alleviated using $GABA_A$ agonists such as benzodiazepines. Other drugs, such as pregabalin and gabapentin, facilitate the GABA transport over the blood–brain barrier, among other effects. The authors' personal experiences have shown pregabalin to be a useful drug for acute and severe DST in patients with normal hearing.

Conclusions

Hyperacusis is a decreased tolerance to sounds and is estimated to affect 9% of the general population. Pathophysiological mechanisms can be cochlear diseases or disorders in the central auditory pathways, with an abnormal activation of the limbic system that increases the psychological and emotional reaction to the symptom. The combination of professional counseling and acoustic stimulation using controlled sounds (TRT) has been proven to provide relief of decreased sound tolerance in many patients with DST.

References

1. Goldstein B, Shulman A. Tinnitus-hyperacusis and the loudness discomfort level test-A preliminary report. Int Tinnitus J 1996;2:83-89
2. Jastreboff PJ, Jastreboff MM. Tinnitus retraining therapy (TRT) as a method for treatment of tinnitus and hyperacusis patients. J Am Acad Audiol 2000;11:162-177
3. Fabijanska A, Rogowski M, Bartnik G et al. Epidemiology of tinnitus and hyperacusis in Poland. In: Hazell J, ed. Proceedings of the Sixth International Tinnitus Seminar. London: Tinnitus and Hyperacusis Center; 1999 569-71
4. Andersson G, Lindvall N, Hursti T, Carlbring hypersensitivity to sound (hyperacusis): a prevalence study conducted via the internet and post. Int J Audiol 2002;41:545-54
5. Herraiz C, Hernández Calvín J, Plaza G, et al. Estudio de la hiperacusia en una unidad de acúfenos. Acta Otorrinolaringol Esp 2003;54:617-622
6. Anari M, Axelsson A, Eliasson A et al. Hypersensitivity to sound. Scand Audiol 1999;28:219-30
7. Hesse G, Masri S, Nelting M et al. Hypermotility of outer hair cells: DPOAE findings with hyperacusis patients. In Hazell J, ed. Proceedings of the Sixth International Tinnitus Seminar. London: Tinnitus and Hyperacusis Center; 1999 342-4
8. Sahley TI, Nodar RH, Musick FE. Efferent Auditory System: Structure and Function. San Diego; Singular, 1997
9. Baguley DM, Axon PR, Winter IM, Moffat DA. The effect of vestibular nerve section upon tinnitus. Clin Otolaryngol 2002;27:219-26
10. Eybalin M. Neurotransmitters and neuromodulators of the mammalian cochlea. Physiol Rev 1993;73:309-373
11. Darrow KN, Maison SF, Liberman MC. Cochlear efferent feedback balances interaural sensitivity. Nat Neurosci. 2006;9(12):1474-6

12. D'Aldin C, Puel JL, Leducq R et al. Effects of a dopaminergic agonist in the guinea pig cochlea. Hear Res 1995;90: 202-11

13. Darrow KN, Maison SF, Liberman MC. Selective removal of lateral olivocochlear efferents increases vulnerability to acute acoustic injury. J Neurophysiol 2007;97:1778-85

14. Marriage J, Barnes NM. Is central hyperacusis a symptom of 5-hydroxytryptamine (5-HT) dysfunction?. J Laryngol Otol 1995;109:915-921

15. Cruz OL, Kasse CA, Sanchez M, Barbosa F, Barros FA. Serotonin reuptake inhibitors in auditory processing disorders in elderly patients: preliminary results. Laryngoscope. 2004;114(9):1656-9

16. Sahley TI, Nodar RH. A biochemical model of peripheral tinnitus. Hear Res. 2001;152(1-2):43-54

17. Daumann R, Bouscau-Faure F. Assessment and amelioration of hyperacusis in tinnitus patients. Acta Oto-Laryngol 2005;125:503-9

18. Nelting M, Rienhoff NK, Hesse G et al. Die Erfassung des subjektiven Leidens uner Hyperakusis mit einem Selbstbeurteilungsbogen zur Geräuschüberempfindlichkeit (GÜF). Laryngo-Rhino-Otol 2002;81:327-334

19. Herraiz C, De los Santos, Diges I et al. Assessment of hyperacusis: the self-rating questionnaire on hypersensitivity to sound. Acta Otorrinolaringol Esp 2006;57:303-306

20. Khalfa S, Dubal S, Veuillet E et al. Psychometric normalization of a hyperacusis questionnaire. ORL J Otorhinolaryngol Relat Spec 2002;64:436-42

21. Jastreboff PJ, Jastreboff MM. Decreased sound tolerance. In Snow JB ed. Tinnitus: Theory and Management. Hamilton EEUU, BC Decker Inc; 2004 8-15

22. Knaster J. Reentrenamiento auditivo en la hipoacusia neurosensorial. Acta Otorrinolaringol Es 1988;39(5):327-9

23. Domínguez LJ, Rodríguez C, Vallés H, Iparraguirre V, Knaster J. Entrenamiento auditivo con ruido blanco de banda ancha. Acta Otorrinolaringol Esp 2001;52:111-119

24. Gold SL, Frederick EA, Formby C. Shifts in dynamic range for hyperacusis patients receiving tinnitus retraining therapy (TRT). In: Hazell J, ed. Proceedings of the Sixth International Tinnitus Seminar. London: Tinnitus and Hyperacusis Center; 1999 297-301

25. Hazell JWP, Sheldrake JB, Graham RL. Decreased sound tolerance: predisposing factors, triggers and outcomes after TRT. In: Patuzzi R. ed. Proceedings of the Seventh International Tinnitus Seminar 2002. Perth: University of Western Australia, 2002:255-61

26. Noreña AJ, Chery-Croze S. Enriched acoustic environment rescales auditory sensitivity. Neuroreport. 2007;18: 1251-5

27. Jastreboff PJ, Mattox DE. Treatment of hyperacusis by aspirin. In: Popelka GR ed. Abstracts of the Twenty-First Annual Midwinter Research Meeting of the Association for Research in Otolaryngology. Mt. Royal (NJ): Association for Research in Otolaryngology;1998 52

28. Simpson J, Davies WE. A review of evidence in support of a role for 5-HT in the perception of tinnitus. Hear Res 2000;145:1-7

Chapter 58
Clinical Description of a Different Form of Tinnitus: Intermittent Tinnitus

Miguel J.A. Láinez, Anna Piera, and Alejandro Ponz

Keypoints

1. Intermittent (paroxysmal) tinnitus is a form of non-pulsatile tinnitus.
2. An intermittent nature can be the only sign that intermittent tinnitus is different from other forms of tinnitus.
3. Intermittent tinnitus may be accompanied by irregular symptoms of other neurotologic disorders.
4. Both objective and subjective tinnitus may be intermittent.
5. A wide range of pathologies may cause intermittent tinnitus, but the cause of most forms is unknown.

Keywords Paroxysmal (intermittent) tinnitus • Myoclonus • Temporomandibular joint changes • Cerebellopontine angle changes • Migraine • Auditory hallucinations • Audiogenic seizures

Abbreviations

ABR	Auditory brainstem response
AGS	Audiogenic seizures
CPA	Cerebellopontine angle
CSF	Cerebrospinal fluid
EEG	Electroencephalography
GABA	Gamma amino butyric acid
IC	Inferior colliculus
TMJ	Temporomandibular joint

M.J.A. Láinez (✉)
Department of Neurology, Hospital Clínico Universitario,
University of Valencia (Spain), Avenida Blasco Ibáñez, 17,
46010 Valencia, Spain
e-mail: jlaineza@meditex.es

Introduction

Suddenly occurring non-pulsatile tinnitus (intermittent tinnitus) can be the only symptom or it can be accompanied by neurotologic symptoms like vertigo, headaches, visual changes, and disturbances of consciousness.

Like constant tinnitus, intermittent tinnitus can be objective or subjective, depending on the pathology; objective tinnitus is caused by physical sounds generated in the body, which can also be heard by an observer. Subjective tinnitus is caused by abnormal neural activity, and only the patient can hear the tinnitus.

Objective Intermittent Tinnitus

Some important pathology should be ruled out in patients who present with intermittent objective tinnitus. The most important disorders that may occur together with objective tinnitus are palatal and middle-ear muscle myoclonus and temporomandibular joint (TMJ) disorders.

Palatal and Middle-Ear Muscle Myoclonus

Tinnitus produced by middle-ear myoclonus is objective intermittent tinnitus, and is rare; only a few cases are reported in the literature. In middle-ear myoclonus, otoscopic examination shows visible rhythmic movements of the eardrum, and weak clicking sounds are heard in the ear by auscultation. Tympanometry confirms rhythmic changes in middle-ear compliance. Middle-ear myoclonus can be accompanied by palatal myoclonus or can be the only manifestation. Palatal myoclonus is an uncommon rhythmic "shock-like" involuntary movement of the muscles of the soft palate, throat, and other structures derived from the branchial arcs. Objective intermittent tinnitus associated with palatal myoclonus can be related to hearing impairment; however, this relation is not always present. Examination of muscles of the soft palate and throat shows rhythmic involuntary movements and, in some cases, spontaneous clicking sounds by auscultation near the ear [1–3].

Temporomandibular Joint Changes (Synchrony with Joint Movements)

The TMJ is a complex, sensitive, and highly mobile joint. Millions of people suffer from temporomandibular disorders. Tinnitus associated to TMJ changes is synchronic with joint movement and is easy to provoke during the examinations. Several disorders of TMJ cause tinnitus: luxation, condyle malposition, bruxism, degenerative arthropathy, capsulitis, and many others. These disorders are also very common in inflammatory arthropathies. Regardless of the cause of a TMJ disorder, all of them can be common causes of intermittent tinnitus, and a routine examination for these disorders is needed in all tinnitus clinics [4–6].

Subjective Intermittent Tinnitus

Subjective intermittent tinnitus, which is much more common than objective tinnitus, can occur together with pathologies such as cerebellopontine angle (CPA) disorders.

Cerebellopontine Angle Disorders

CPA disorders may be suspected in patients with unilateral hearing loss and unilateral intermittent tinnitus with or without dizziness. Audiological and imaging studies of the posterior fossa are used to rule out disorders of the CPA. Lesions of the CPA are frequent and represent 6–10% of all intracranial tumors. Vestibular schwannoma (acoustic neuroma)

and meningioma are the two most frequent lesions and account for approximately 85–90% of all CPA tumors. The other 10–15% encompasses a large variety of lesions including aneurysms, epidermoid cysts, arachnoidal cysts, Arnold–Chiari malformations, lipoma, and melanomas. Such lesions are now detected more frequently because of the sensitivity and accuracy of magnetic resonance imaging (MRI) [7–10].

Recently, Levine has described a subtype of intermittent tinnitus, called typewriter tinnitus, with an excellent response to treatment with carbamazepine, in which vascular compression of the auditory nerve was suspected to be the cause in five of six patients that were studied. This suggests that surgical decompression may also be effective in such patients [11].

Audiogenic Seizures and Epilepsy

The inferior colliculus (IC) plays an important role in many pathophysiological conditions that involve hearing (including tinnitus, age-related hearing loss, and audiogenic seizures (AGS)). AGS occur frequently in rodents and can be genetically mediated. AGS can also be readily induced in experimental animals [12]. AGS can be induced in normal animals by administration of drugs that are GABA receptor antagonists. Glutamate-mediated excitation is a critical element of neurotransmission in IC neurons, and excessive activation of glutamate receptors in the IC is implicated in AGS. Such neurotransmitter abnormalities cause excessive firing of IC neurons that act as the critical initiation mechanism for triggering seizures in response to intense acoustic stimuli, thus AGS. The IC plays a role in the integration of acoustic-motor and acoustic-limbic integration, as well as in acute and chronic AGS. García-Caraisco et al. [13] have demonstrated in animal experiments that chronic kindled AGS change behavioral expressions in a similar way as those that occur in temporal lobe epileptic seizures mixed with audiogenic seizure activity, which is known to be dependent on brainstem networks. This form of AGS involves subcortical intermittent pattern of tinnitus manifestation [14, 15].

Tinnitus, as an intermittent pathologic cortical manifestation, has been described in only a few patients while electroencephalography (EEG) was monitored, and was determined that the tinnitus originated from the contralateral mid-temporal area [16].

Auditory Hallucinations

Auditory hallucinations can be simple or complex. Therefore, tinnitus could be considered an auditory hallucination. Several studies with transcranial magnetic stimulation have reported a benefit in improving both auditory hallucinations and tinnitus by modulating cerebral cortex activity. New results of studies and new questions about the neurobiological basis of mental and neural disorders have concerned whether there is a common substrate in tinnitus and auditory hallucinations [17, 18].

Migraine with Basilar Aura

Vertigo, dysarthria, and tinnitus may occur together with basilar aura in individuals with migraine. It has been reported to occur in 50% of individuals with basilar aura. Other symptoms are diplopia, bilateral visual symptoms, bilateral paresthesia, hearing loss, decreased level of consciousness, and ataxia. For management of patients with tinnitus and headache, it is important to obtain information about how the tinnitus may be regarded as a symptom that precedes headache [19–21].

Cerebrospinal Fluid Pressure Changes

Both intracranial hypotension and hypertension (pseudotumor cerebri) have been suggested as possible causes of intermittent tinnitus. A lumbar puncture is needed to measure pressure changes in cerebrospinal fluid (CSF), and in most cases, a neuroimaging technique (MRI or CT) is necessary to rule out other brain lesions [22–24].

Phantom Sensations Without Evidence of Cortical or Auditory System Dysfunctions

In spite of the many different pathologies that may cause intermittent tinnitus, in some patients no pathology can be found and the tinnitus remains a phantom intermittent sensation – an expression of an abnormally high correlation of activity in many nerve cells in cortical and subcortical parts of the auditory system [25, 26].

Techniques used in Diagnosis of Intermittent Tinnitus

Several different techniques are useful in the diagnostic workup of patients with intermittent tinnitus; the most important are MRI, auditory brainstem responses (ABR), and in some patients, EEG.

Magnetic Resonance Imaging

MRI is performed in almost all patients with intermittent tinnitus in order to rule out CPA disorders, cortical ectopias, and indirect signs of benign intracranial hypertension of licuoral hypotension.

Electroencephalography

EEG is only indicated if there are further signs of seizure and when tinnitus is accompanied by symptoms of consciousness disturbance.

Basal EEG recordings performed with provocation maneuvers like flashing light and hyperventilation in some cases may be useful. EEG can help determine if temporal lobe discharges are present.

Role of Auditory Brainstem Responses

ABR are indicated only in intermittent tinnitus for screening auditory nerve compression and can provide prognosis for microvascular compression [27].

References

1. Abdul-Baqi KJ. Objective high-frequency tinnitus of middle-ear myoclonus. J Laryngol Otol. 2004 118(3):231–3.
2. Howsam GD, Sharma A, Lambden SP, Fitzgerald J, Prinsley PR. Bilateral objective tinnitus secondary to congenital middle-ear myoclonus. J Laryngol Otol. 2005 119(6):489–91.
3. Elziere M, Roman S, Nicollas R, Triglia JM. Objective tinnitus associated with essential palatal myoclonus: report in a child. Int Tinnitus J. 2007 13(2):157–8.

4. De Felício CM, Melchior Mde O, Ferreira CL, Da Silva MA. Otologic symptoms of temporomandibular disorder and effect of orofacial myofunctional therapy. Cranio. 2008 26(2):118–25.

5. Ramirez LM, Ballesteros LE, Sandoval GP. Topical review: temporomandibular disorders in an integral otic symptom model. Int J Audiol. 2008 47(4):215–27.

6. Ramírez LM, Ballesteros LE, Sandoval GP. Otological symptoms among patients with temporomandibular joint disorders. Rev Med Chil. 2007 135(12):1582–90. Epub 2008 Feb 13, Spanish.

7. Espir M, Illingworth R, Ceranic B, Luxon L. Intermittent tinnitus due to a meningioma in the cerebellopontine angle. J Neurol Neurosurg Psychiatry. 1997 62(4):401–3.

8. Takano S, Maruno T, Shirai S, Nose T. Facial spasm and intermittent tinnitus associated with an arachnoid cyst of the cerebellopontine angle – case report. Neurol Med Chir (Tokyo). 1998 38(2):100–3.

9. Chatrath P, Frosh A, Gore A, Nouraei R, Harcourt J. Identification of predictors and development of a screening protocol for cerebello-pontine lesions in patients presenting with audio-vestibular dysfunction. Clin Otolaryngol. 2008 33(2):102–7.

10. Gultekin S, Celik H, Akpek S, Oner Y, Gumus T, Tokgoz N. Vascular loops at the cerebellopontine angle: is there a correlation with tinnitus. AJNR Am J Neuroradiol. 2008 29(9):1746–9. Epub 2008 Jul 24.

11. Levine RA. Typewriter tinnitus: a carbamazepine-responsive syndrome related to auditory nerve vascular compression. ORL J Otorhinolaryngol Relat Spec. 2006 68(1):43–6; discussion 46–7. Epub 2006 Mar.

12. Pierson MG, Swann J. Ontogenetic features of audiogenic seizure susceptibility induced in immature rats by noise. Epilepsia. 1991 32:1–9.

13. García-Caraisco N. A critical review on the participation of inferior colliculus in acoustic-motor and acoustic-limbic networks involved in the expression of acute and kindled audiogenic seizures. Hear Res. 2002 168(1–2):208–22.

14. Gordon AG. Temporal lobe epilepsy and auditory symptoms. JAMA. 2003 290(18):2407.

15. Doretto MC, Cortes-de-Oliveira JA, Rossetti F, Garcia-Cairasco N. Role of the superior colliculus in the expression of acute and kindled audiogenic seizures in Wistar audiogenic rats. Epilepsia. 2009 50(12):2563–74.

16. Cendes F, Kobayashi E, Lopes-Cendes I. Familial temporal lobe epilepsy with auditory features. Epilepsia. 2005 46 Suppl 10:59–60.

17. Boksa P. On the neurobiology of hallucinations. J Psychiatry Neurosci. 2009 34(4):260–2.

18. Horiguchi J, Miyaoka T, Shinno H. Pathogenesis and symptomatology of hallucinations (delusions) of organic brain disorder and schizophrenia. Psychogeriatrics. 2009 9(2):73–6.

19. Dash AK, Panda N, Khandelwal G, Lal V, Mann SS. Migraine and audiovestibular dysfunction: is there a correlation? Am J Otolaryngol. 2008 29(5):295–9. Epub 2008.

20. Rzeski M, Stepie A, Kaczorowski Z. Evaluation of the function of the vestibular system in patients with migraine. Neurol Neurochir Pol. 2008 42(6):518–24.

21. Evans RW, Ishiyama G. Migraine with transient unilateral hearing loss and tinnitus. Headache. 2009 49(5):756–8.

22. Mackenzie RA, Lethlean AK, Shnier R, Blum PW. Chronic intracranial hypotension. J Clin Neurosci. 1998 5(4):457–60.

23. Wall M. Idiopathic intracranial hypertension (pseudotumor cerebri). Insight. 2008 33(2):18–25.

24. Wall M. Idiopathic intracranial hypertension (pseudotumor cerebri). Curr Neurol Neurosci Rep. 2008 8(2):87–93.

25. Eggermont JJ. Correlated neural activity as the driving force for functional changes in auditory cortex. Hear Res. 2007 229(1–2):69–80. Epub 2007 Jan 16.

26. Dohrmann K, Elbert T, Schlee W, Weisz N. Tuning the tinnitus percept by modification of synchronous brain activity. Restor Neurol Neurosci. 2007 25(3–4):371–8.

27. Kehrle HM, Granjeiro RC, Sampaio AL, Bezerra R, Almeida VF, Oliveira CA. Comparison of auditory brainstem response results in normal-hearing patients with and without tinnitus. Arch Otolaryngol Head Neck Surg. 2008 134(6):647–51.

Chapter 59
Pulsatile Tinnitus

Dirk De Ridder

Keypoints

1. Pulsatile tinnitus, in general, is not related to pathology of the auditory system.
2. Two main types of pulsatile tinnitus exist: arterial heart beat synchronous pulsatile tinnitus and venous respiratory synchronous pulsatile tinnitus.
3. The main causes of pulsatile tinnitus are related to aberrant/ectopic, stenosis, or other pathologies of blood vessels, either arterial or venous.
   (a) MRI, CT, or classical angiography are diagnostic tools for pulsatile tinnitus.
4. Benign intracranial hypertension is another common cause of pulsatile tinnitus.
   (a) Funduscopy and lumbar puncture with measurement of cerebrospinal pressure are diagnostic tests for benign intracranial hypertension.
5. In 15–30% of patients, no cause can be found for the pulsations.
6. Pseudopulsatile tinnitus groups a number of muscle-related tinnitus types mimicking pulsatile tinnitus.

Keywords Pulsatile • Tinnitus • Venous • Hum • Arterial • Intracranial hypertension

Abbreviations

ABR   Auditory brainstem response
AV   Anterior-venous
AVM   Arterial venous malformation
BIH   Benign intracranial hypertension
CT   Computerized (axial) tomography
EEG   Electroencephalography
ICA   Internal carotid artery
IPL   Interpeak latencies
MRA   Magnetic resonance angiography
MRI   Magnetic resonance imaging
MVC   Microvascular compression
MVD   Microvascular decompression
TMJ   Temporomandibular joint

Introduction

Tinnitus can be subdivided into two entirely different entities: pulsatile and non-pulsatile tinnitus [1–3]. Most forms of pulsatile are heart beat synchronous, where arterial pulsations modulate the tinnitus. The arterial pulsations are most likely transmitted to the cochlea via the cerebrospinal fluid, a mechanism similar to what has been proposed as an explanation for bone conduction [4–6]. Respiration synchronous tinnitus is rare, but an individual may perceive hearing their own breathing sounds because of an open Eustachian tube as tinnitus.

Pulsatile tinnitus synchronous with the heart beat seems to be related to arterial causes; pulsatile tinnitus synchronous with respiration is most likely due to venous causes. Venous pulsatile tinnitus might be equally or even more prevalent than arterial heart beat synchronous tinnitus [2, 7], even though it is not as well known as arterial pulsatile tinnitus. Thus, pulsatile tinnitus, in general, is not associated with pathology of the auditory pathways per se, which is in contrast to the more common non-pulsatile tinnitus.

D. De Ridder (✉)
TRI Tinnitus Clinic Antwerp, BRAI²N Department
of Neurosurgery, University Hospital Antwerp,
Wilrijkstraat 10, 2650 Edegem, Belgium
e-mail: dirk.de.ridder@uza.be

A.R. Møller et al. (eds.), *Textbook of Tinnitus*,
DOI 10.1007/978-1-60761-145-5_59, © Springer Science+Business Media, LLC 2011

Arterial pulsations may modulate existing tinnitus or cause tinnitus. The tinnitus caused by arterial pulsations being transmitted to the cochlea are forms of objective tinnitus.

Since heart beat synchronous tinnitus is predominantly vascular in origin, almost all causes of pulsatile tinnitus can be diagnosed by magnetic resonance imaging and magnetic resonance angiography, except for benign intracranial hypertension [1–3].

Causes of Pulsatile Tinnitus

Heart Beat Synchronous Pulsatile Tinnitus

Arteriovenous malformations (AVM) of the dura are the best known causes of arterial pulse synchronous pulsatile tinnitus [8, 9]. Such abnormal communications between the arterial and venous systems may be congenital or acquired [10]. Often AVMs result from chronic mastoiditis or other causes occluding the sigmoid-transverse sinus, such as trauma. As a natural repair mechanism, vascular bypasses tend to develop around the occlusion, resulting in a dural AVM. If the dural AVM is symptomatic or if it is asymptomatic with leptomeningeal drainage, these lesions are often treated with embolization, usually in multiple sessions. If intractable with endovascular, treatment involving surgical excision of the AVM and dura is often done [11] (Table 59.1).

Posttraumatic pulsatile tinnitus can be the result of a carotid dissection, AV fistula, or caroticocavernous fistula. In 16–27% of carotid dissections, pulsatile tinnitus is experienced at the side of the dissection but is usually associated with other focal or global symptoms [12]. In contrast, in (non-traumatic) vertebral artery dissection, only 5% of patients present with pulsatile tinnitus [13].

Carotid dissection in the neck is a relatively common condition. Most dissections are spontaneous, likely related to activities that cause a sudden stretch of the pharyngeal portion of the carotid artery. Traumatic carotid dissections occur in approximately 1% of all patients with blunt injury mechanisms [14]. Carotid dissections are characterized by a triad of neck and head pain, Horner's syndrome, and pulsatile tinnitus. Others present with transient or persistent brain ischemia. Strokes are due to the embolization of thrombus

Table 59.1 Causes of pulsatile tinnitus

Pulsatile tinnitus
Venous
Benign intracranial hypertension
Chiari malformation
High jugular bulb
Sigmoid sinus diverticulum
Sigmoid-tranverse sinus aneurysm
Arterial
Carotid stenosis
Glomus tumor
Vascular lesions of petrous bone/skull base
Arteriovenous malformation/fistula (dural, carotidocavernous, etc.)
Intrapetrous aneurysm
Hyperdynamic state (anemia, thyreotoxicosis, pregnancy, etc.)
Paget's disease
Carotid or vertebral artery dissection
Somatosensory pulsatile tinnitus syndrome
Congenital vascular anomalies
Microvascular compression
Intrameatal vascular loop
Benign intracranial hypertension

material from the lumen of the dissected artery to the intracranial arteries, most often the middle cerebral artery [15]. Carotid dissection is asymptomatic in less than 10% of the patients, whereas in more than 90% of patients, carotid territory ischemia and/or local signs and symptoms on the side of dissection develop. Local signs and symptoms on the side of dissection include head (65–68%), facial (34–53%), or neck pain (9–26%), as well as Horner syndrome (28–41%) and cranial nerve palsy (8–16%), in particular the hypoglossal nerve. The facial nerve may also be involved; dysgeusia results mainly from involvement of the chorda tympani (0.5–7.0%) or the glossopharyngeal nerve. Transient pareses of the ocular motor (III, IV, and VI) and trigeminal nerves have been observed. In three-fourths of carotid dissections, an ischemic event occurs, which includes ischemic stroke in 80–84%, transient ischemic attack in 15–16%, amaurosis fugax in 3%, ischemic optic neuropathy in 4%, and retinal infarct in 1% [12].

Treatment consists of anticoagulants or antiplatelet agents, and healing occurs within 3–6 months with a resolution of stenosis in 90% of patients, and recanalization of occlusions in as many as 50% [14]. In cerebral hemodynamicly, compromised patients without an irreversible infarct emergency stenting can be considered [14].

Posttraumatic AV fistulas often result in pulsatile tinnitus. The sinus fistulas are often the result of a venous thrombosis, similarly to the non-traumatic variant of AV fistulas. The most common posttraumatic fistula is the carotid-cavernous fistula. These are characterized by pulsatile tinnitus, pulsating exophthalmia, chemosis, and visual deficit of the afflicted side.

Carotid-cavernous fistulas are the most common arteriovenous fistula. They are divided in the more common (70%) [16] direct high- and rare indirect low-flow fistulas. Low-flow fistulas are usually associated with atherosclerosis, hypertension, and collagen vascular disease, or may develop in females during the peripartum period [16]. They can be spontaneous (low-flow) [17] or high-flow posttraumatic [18]. Spontaneous high-flow fistulas are very rare [19]. Carotid-cavernous fistulas are characterized by pulsatile tinnitus (50% in low flow [20] and more frequently in high flow), pulsating exophthalmia, chemosis, and visual deficit of the fistula side [21]. Treatment consists predominantly of endovascular treatment [22], although high obliteration rates have been described 1-3 months after gamma knife surgery [23].

Dural arteriovenous malformations are the best known causes of arterial pulse synchronous pulsatile tinnitus. Often AVMs result from chronic mastoiditis or other causes occluding the sigmoid-transverse sinus, such as posttraumatic thrombosis. As a natural repair mechanism, vascular bypasses tend to develop around the occlusion, resulting into a dural AVM [24]. If the dural AVM is symptomatic, or if it is asymptomatic with leptomeningeal drainage, these lesions should be embolized, usually in multiple sessions [25, 26]. In benign lesions with only tinnitus or embolization failures, gamma knife surgery is an alternative option if no cortical venous drainage is present [27]. If intractable with endovascular or radiosurgical treatment, surgical excision of the AVM and dura can be proposed [11, 28, 29]. Not only transverse or sigmoid sinus AV fistulas can generate pulsatile tinnitus: sagittal sinus AV fistulas [30] and carotid-cavernous fistulas can generate pulsatile tinnitus as well, which disappears after embolization or gamma knife surgery.

For posttraumatic AV fistulas, the reader is referred to Chap. 66 [21].

It is not only dural fistulas or carotid-cavernous AVMs or fistulas that can present with arterial pulsations but also AVMs of the external ear [31], hypoglossal canal [32], and even the parotid gland [33] can cause pulsatile tinnitus.

Carotid stenosis is a common cause [1–3] of arterial pulsatile tinnitus. The most common cause is artherosclerotic disease [34, 35], but fibromuscular dysplasia [8, 36] can also cause pulsatile tinnitus. This kind of pulsatile tinnitus typically disappears when compressing the ipsilateral, internal, or common carotid artery. The diagnosis can be confirmed by sonography, MRI, CT, or classical angiography. Treatment of the extracranial carotid artery stenosis can consist of dilation and stenting or carotid endarterectomy. Ipsilateral carotid endarterectomy for tinnitus is effective in reducing or abolishing tinnitus in more than 90% of patients with demonstrated ICA stenosis related to pulsatile tinnitus. Proximal lesions lend themselves to carotid endarterectomy, whereas distal lesions have been treated by stenting [37]. For the rarer intracranial carotid artery stenosis, two approaches have been used; an initial balloon occlusion test under transcranial doppler and EEG monitoring can verify whether the ipsilateral carotid artery can be sacrificed. If so, one option is to ligate the symptomatic carotid artery. The other option is to dilate and stent the intracranial portion of carotid artery, resulting in a disappearance of the arterial pulsatile tinnitus. A major problem still faced today is that stents might occlude. Thus, this elegant technique still remains experimental until the coagulation problems can be better controlled [38]. Overall, almost 70% of patients with carotid stenosis are cured by intervention, and most of these patients experience (close to 90%) immediate relief of tinnitus [37].

It is not only a stenosed internal or external carotid artery that can lead to pulsatile tinnitus; a stenotic subclavian [39] or external carotid artery [40] can also generate a treatable form of arterial pulsatile tinnitus. Reversal of blood flow in an aberrant occipital artery can also cause pulsatile tinnitus, and this condition can also be treated by stenting [41].

Hyperdynamic flow in the internal carotid artery can generate pulsatile tinnitus, as seen in basilar artery atresia with predominant flow in both carotids [42]. The hyperdynamic flow can also be due to anemia [43], thyrotoxicosis, or pregnancy.

It has been suggested that a mechanism by which one does not normally hear the pulsations of the carotids is due to a dampening effect of a pericarotid venous plexus [42]. Extensive pneumatization around the carotid artery could, however, reduce this dampening effect and result in the perception of arterial pulsations [44].

Aneurysms of the petrous carotid artery can lead to pulsatile tinnitus [8, 9, 45–47]. This may be caused by the aneurysm obliterating this venous plexus, allowing the arterial pulsations to be transmitted directly to the cochlea and resulting in the perception of the arterial pulsations. However, this is not the only mechanism involved, as aneurysms of the anterior communicating artery have also been related to pulsatile tinnitus [48].

Congenital Vascular Anomalies

The persistent stapedial artery, a normal fetal artery that ordinarily disappears before birth, can cause pulsatile tinnitus. The persistent stapedial artery runs through the obturator foramen between the crura of the stapes and across the promontory in the middle ear, leaving the middle ear to run along the tympanic portion of the facial nerve canal near the geniculate fossa, finally exiting the facial nerve canal to supply the territory of the middle meningeal artery, which never develops in the case of a persistent stapedial artery. Consequently, the foramen spinosum, the entry of the middle meningeal artery in the skull does not develop either [49].

Aberrant and ectopic internal carotid arteries have also been implicated in arterial pulsatile tinnitus [7]. An aberrant carotid artery is a congenital anomaly in which the cervical internal carotid artery never develops. Instead, the inferior tympanic artery (a branch of the ascending pharyngeal artery) enlarges, anastomoses with the caroticotympanic artery in the middle ear, and resumes the usual course of the internal carotid artery in the horizontal portion of the petrous carotid canal. The aberrant carotid artery may be dehiscent and visible through the tympanic membrane as it courses through the middle ear [49].

Glomus tumors, or paraganglioma, are associated with unilateral hearing loss in 80% of cases and with pulsatile tinnitus in 60% [50]. These tumors occur predominantly in women (6:1), and should thus be differentiated from benign intracranial hypertension (BIH). Diagnosis is confirmed by MRI and/or angiography. Some glomus tumors (1–3%) are endocrinologically active and secrete catecholamines [50]. As glomus tumors are mostly benign lesions (less than 3% metastasize) growing less than 2 cm in 5 years, treatment options are either a "wait and scan" policy or embolization and surgery [51]. If the tinnitus is incapacitating, the embolization with surgery option

can be helpful. The glomus tumor cell is radiation insensitive, but irradiation can reduce the vascularity responsible for the pulsatile tinnitus.

Other vascular lesions of the petrous bone or skull base – such as hemangiopericytoma [52], plasmacytoma [52], giant cell tumors [53], and neuroendocrine carcinoma [54], amongst others – are also known to cause tinnitus that can be treated by otoneurosurgical methods.

Pulsatile tinnitus that occurs in individuals with Paget's disease can be explained in a similar way, especially when the temporal bone is involved [10, 34]. It has indeed been suggested that increased vascularization with intraosseous arteriovenous shunts may be responsible for the pulsatile tinnitus [10].

Microvascular compressions of the cochlear nerve can cause incapacitating pulsatile or non-pulsatile tinnitus [55, 56]. A meta-analysis has shown that individuals with pulsatile tinnitus are 80 times more likely to have a vascular loop in close contact with the root of the auditory nerve than individuals with non-pulsatile tinnitus [57]. Most vascular compressions, however, cause non-pulsatile tinnitus. This is similar to other disorders of microvascular compressions (MVC) of cranial nerve roots, such as trigeminal neuralgia and hemifacial spasm, which also do not have pulse synchronous bouts of pain in the distribution of the trigeminal nerve or pulse synchronous hemifacial spasms. The diagnosis of microvascular compression in individuals with tinnitus is based on the clinical picture and confirmed by auditory brainstem-evoked potentials and magnetic resonance imaging [58] [59–61] (see Chap. 40).

However, if the vascular loop extends into the internal auditory meatus, it can cause arterial pulse synchronous tinnitus via CSF/bone conduction [42, 62]. Studies of MRIs of individuals with pulsatile tinnitus, after exclusion of other causes, have shown a statistically significant high number of vascular loops in the internal auditory canal in comparison with individuals with non-pulsatile tinnitus [62]. Placement of shredded Teflon between the vascular loop and the nerve (microvascular decompression, MVD) has abolished pulse synchronous tinnitus [42]. Pathophysiologically, the sharp turn of the vascular loop in the triangular internal auditory canal creates a turbulence, which creates sound waves that are concentrically irradiating. The internal auditory canal has a cave or funnel effect guiding the sound waves towards its end – the top of the triangle where the cochlea is located. The sounds waves in the CSF–bone interface are transferred to the cochlea via bone conduction. High-frequency waves carry less energy than low-frequency waves and are therefore reflected more easily than the longer low-frequency waves. This could explain why pulsatile tinnitus is matched to low frequencies.

A new form of pulsatile tinnitus has been described and called the somatosensory pulsatile tinnitus syndrome [63]. It is characterized by a high-pitched, pulse synchronous tinnitus, where the pulsations can be suppressed by strong contractions or normal compressions of the neck and jaw muscles (somatic testing) [63]. This form of tinnitus is hypothesized to be related to heart synchronous somatosensory activation of the central auditory pathway or to failure of the somatosensory–auditory central nervous system interactions, which normally suppresses heart somatosounds [63].

A *semicircular canal dehiscence* can be the cause of pulsatile tinnitus (7%) [64, 65], especially when gaze evoked. Twenty-five percent of patients with dehiscence have this kind of tinnitus.

Dehiscence of a semicircular canal is described most often for the superior canal [66], but posterior [67–70, 71, 72] and lateral semicircular canal dehiscences have also been described[73]. Hyperacusis to bone-conducted sounds is also commonly found in 39% of patients. The most typical signs of canal dehiscence are, however, autophony and "blocked ear" (94%) [74], sound-induced vertigo (97%) (Tulio's sign), and oscillopsia. The autophony does not present with audible breathing such as that in a patulous Eustachian tube [7]. Most patients also complain of chronic dysequilibrium. In addition, most patients will have sound or Valsalva-evoked eye movements in the plane of the dehiscent canal. Tragal pressure evokes the nystagmus in 54% (Hennebert's sign) and one-fifth of patients show sound-evoked head movements.

Patients may describe very unusual findings – hearing their joints moving, hearing their eye movements, hearing their heart beat, hearing their heels strike during walking, or the ability to hear a tuning fork placed at a distal extremity – due to increased bone conduction. Treatment of symptomatic patients consists of surgical plugging (the better method) or resurfacing of the canal [75].

Venous Hum

A venous hum was originally attributed to an impingement of the transverse process of the second vertebra in the jugular vein [76]. However, venous pulsatile tinnitus can have many different causes. BIH, also known as pseudotumor cerebri or idiopathic intracranial hypertension [77], is another possible cause of pulsatile tinnitus. Sismanis [2] showed that 40% of individuals he studied with pulsatile tinnitus were diagnosed with BIH. Other studies find that only 2% of the individuals with BIH had pulsatile tinnitus [7]. BIH almost exclusively afflicts young overweight women [77, 78]. Clinical symptoms include arterial pulsatile tinnitus, venous hum, headache, and blurry vision. Patients with BIH can also complain of aural fullness, low-frequency hearing loss, and vertigo [1, 2, 77]. Oddly enough, the venous hum presents most often unilaterally (80%) and can be the only symptom of BIH [2]. High intracranial pressure can cause more prominent symptoms that may occur after lying down (such as in the morning when waking up) or bending over or when coughing or performing other maneuvers that raise intracranial pressure. A suspicion of BIH can be confirmed by compressing the ipsilateral jugular vein, stopping the flow in the ipsilateral sigmoid sinus, which causes the venous hum to disappear. When the tinnitus disappears, the pressure-like headaches tend to increase because the intracranial pressure increases due to the reduced drainage of CSF.

About half of all individuals with BIH have low-frequency sensorineural hearing loss; this disappears on ipsilateral jugular vein compression as well. Papilledema is often present [77, 78], and magnetic resonance angiography (MRA) and MRI are usually negative. An empty sella, present in 25% of such individuals [2], should, however, raise suspicion of BIH as it can be related to prolonged intracranial pressure. Spontaneous cerebrospinal fluid leak should also be considered a sign of possible intracranial hypertension [79]. Diagnosis is usually confirmed by lumbar puncture (opening pressure > 20 cm water). Treatment consists of weight loss, diuretics, or ventriculoperitoneal or lumboperitoneal shunting. BIH is usually idiopathic, but venous sinus outflow obstruction can be the cause [78] and also occurs after posterior fossa surgery (unpublished results).

The Arnold–Chiari malformation is a clinical entity in which there is a tonsillar herniation in the foramen magnum. Four different types exist, but only Chiari type I occurs frequently in the Western world. Seven to ten percent [80] of individuals with Arnold–Chiari malformations complain of tinnitus, which can be both non-pulsatile and pulsatile [81]. Pulsatile tinnitus most commonly consists of a venous hum, likely caused by raised intracranial pressure since it worsens on bending over and on Valsalva maneuvers. The pulsations normally disappear on ipsilateral jugular vein compression, which also causes improvement of the low sensorineural hearing loss, as the tinnitus may be masking normal hearing. No ABR changes have been noted in individuals with this kind of tinnitus. After surgical treatment of individuals with Arnold–Chiari malformations (decompression), this form of tinnitus often disappears [81]. The non-pulsatile tinnitus that occurs in such individuals is usually intermittent, and the cause is unknown; it may be caused by stretching of the cochlear nerve, such as by microvascular compression or brainstem traction [82]. ABR changes have been noted in 75% of patients and consist of prolongation of the IPL III–V in 100% of the patients and prolongation of IPL I–III in 30% [82]. Prolongation of IPL III–V may be due to brainstem traction and/or contralateral microvascular compression of the auditory nerve [83]; the IPL I–III may be caused by ipsilateral microvascular compression of the auditory nerve [84, 85]. Posterior fossa decompression, which consists of opening the foramen magnum and widening the dura mater, can therefore result in improving the non-pulsatile tinnitus in three out of four patients with Chiari malformation (De Ridder, unpublished results), similarly to what is seen in trigeminal neuralgia in patients with Arnold–Chiari malformation [86]. The improvement of such patients may be due to a secondary auto decompression of the vestibulocochlear nerve, analogous to what is suggested in surgical removal of posterior fossa tumors [87].

Sigmoid Sinus Diverticulum

A common cause for venous pulsatile tinnitus is a sigmoid sinus diverticulum [7], in which a diverticulum enters into the mastoid bone. The perceived pulsations most likely result from turbulent flow in the diverticulum, which is transmitted to the cochlea via bone conduction. Transmastoid reconstruction of the sigmoid sinus, as described for venous aneurysms, can result in a permanent cure for the pulsations [88].

High Jugular Bulb

A high jugular bulb can also cause venous hum, as a result of its close and direct contact with the cochlea. When the high bulb is dehiscent, it can be seen as a bluish mass in the hypotympanum on otoscopy [89], in contrast to the reddish mass in the anterior middle ear, which suggests a dehiscent/aberrant carotid artery [89]. In the same way as described for benign intracranial hypertension, the venous hum disappears on compression of the ipsilateral jugular vein. A high jugular bulb can be diagnosed by CT imaging. Surgically, ligating or lowering the jugular bulb and interposing Teflon or bonewax can abolish or diminish this form of tinnitus [90, 91]. Transvenous stent-assisted coil embolization has been used as well for treating this condition [92].

Abnormal veins, such as an abnormal posterior condylar emissary vein [93] and abnormal mastoid emissary veins [94], have been described as surgically treatable causes of venous pulsatile tinnitus as well.

Like arterial aneurysms, a sigmoid-transverse venous aneurysm can be causally related to venous pulsatile tinnitus [95–97]. After coagulation of the aneurysm and reconstruction of the sinus wall [96], or after endovascular treatment [97], the pulsations can disappear.

Pseudopulsatile Tinnitus

There exist pathologies that mimic pulsatile tinnitus. Causes for this non-vascular tinnitus are palatal myoclonus [98], tensor tympani spasms [99, 100], stapedial muscle myoclonus [101], and a patulous Eustachian tube [102]. These pathologies generate neither arterial pulse synchronous nor respiratory rate synchronous tinnitus, but tend to fluctuate in intensity (as in a stormy wind) or are perceived as clicks. The clicking palatal myoclonus is often bilateral and is caused by contractions of the peritubal muscles, especially the levator veli palatine muscles which snap the Eustachian tube open, breaking surface tension. It can be effectively treated by botulinum toxin [103] or radiofrequency lesioning [104] of the peritubal muscles. Tensor tympani spasms and stapedial muscle contractions together are called middle-ear myoclonus. It generates rhythmic contractions (40–200 Hz) of the tympanic membrane coinciding with the tinnitus. It can be perceived as a "rushing wind" noise by the patient and can be treated by sectioning of the tendons of both these muscles resulting in an immediate improvement [100, 101, 105]. In some patients, stapedial muscle contractions can be treated by selective sectioning of stapedial tendons [101]. The stapedius contractions create a buzzing sound, whereas the tensor typani has a clicking sound. The objective tubal tinnitus in a patulous Eustachian tube is often associated with autophonia and audible breathing. The somatosounds arise as a result of the walls of the Eustachian tube snapping together [102], with respiration associated with tympanic contractions. Botulinum toxin [106] and/or transsection of the tensor veli palatini muscle tendon may be a useful method of treatment if the patient experiences objective tinnitus, which is very distressing [102].

Conclusion

Pulsatile tinnitus can be divided into arterial heart beat synchronous pulsatile tinnitus and respiratory synchronous venous hum. It is important to look for a cause of the pulsations by neuroimaging tools, as many causes can be treated successfully. Idiopathic intracranial hypertension should be excluded as a non-vascular possible cause for the pulsations.

Pseudopulsatile tinnitus mimics pulsatile tinnitus but is not synchronous with the heart beat and therefore not of vascular origin. Instead, it is mostly of muscular origin.

References

1. Sismanis A (1997) Pulsatile tinnitus. Int Tinnitus J 3:39–40.
2. Sismanis A (1998) Pulsatile tinnitus. A 15-year experience. Am J Otol 19:472–7.
3. Sismanis A (2003) Pulsatile tinnitus. Otolaryngol Clin North Am 36:389–402, viii.
4. Freeman S, JY Sichel and H Sohmer (2000) Bone conduction experiments in animals – evidence for a non-osseous mechanism. Hear Res 146:72–80.
5. Sohmer H and S Freeman (2004) Further evidence for a fluid pathway during bone conduction auditory stimulation. Hear Res 193:105–10.
6. Sohmer H, S Freeman, M Geal-Dor et al (2000) Bone conduction experiments in humans – a fluid pathway from bone to ear. Hear Res 146:81–8.
7. Mattox DE and P Hudgins (2008) Algorithm for evaluation of pulsatile tinnitus. Acta Otolaryngol 128:427–31.
8. Waldvogel D, HP Mattle, M Sturzenegger et al (1998) Pulsatile tinnitus – a review of 84 patients. J Neurol 245:137–42.
9. Dietz RR, WL Davis, HR Harnsberger et al (1994) MR imaging and MR angiography in the evaluation of pulsatile tinnitus. AJNR Am J Neuroradiol 15:879–89.
10. Levine SB and JB Snow, Jr. (1987) Pulsatile tinnitus. Laryngoscope 97:401–6.
11. Awad I and D Barrow (1993) Dural arteriovenous malformations. Park Ridge, IL: American Association Neurological Surgeons.
12. Baumgartner RW and J Bogousslavsky (2005) Clinical manifestations of carotid dissection. Front Neurol Neurosci 20:70–6.
13. Arnold M, MG Bousser, G Fahrni et al (2006) Vertebral artery dissection: presenting findings and predictors of outcome. Stroke 37:2499–503.
14. Redekop GJ (2008) Extracranial carotid and vertebral artery dissection: a review. Can J Neurol Sci 35:146–52.
15. Selim M and LR Caplan (2004) Carotid artery dissection. Curr Treat Options Cardiovasc Med 6:249–53.
16. Das JK, J Medhi, P Bhattacharya et al (2007) Clinical spectrum of spontaneous carotid-cavernous fistula. Indian J Ophthalmol 55:310–2.
17. Robertson A, AR Nicolaides and RH Taylor (1999) Spontaneous carotico-cavernous fistula presenting as pulsatile tinnitus. J Laryngol Otol 113:744–6.
18. Liang W, Y Xiaofeng, L Weiguo et al (2007) Traumatic carotid cavernous fistula accompanying basilar skull fracture: a study on the incidence of traumatic carotid cavernous fistula in the patients with basilar skull fracture and the prognostic analysis about traumatic carotid cavernous fistula. J Trauma 63:1014–20; discussion 20.
19. Yu JS, T Lei, JC Chen et al (2008) Diagnosis and endovascular treatment of spontaneous direct carotid-cavernous fistula. Chin Med J (Engl) 121:1558–62.
20. Halbach VV, RT Higashida, GB Hieshima et al (1987) Dural fistulas involving the cavernous sinus: results of treatment in 30 patients. Radiology 163:437–42.
21. D'Alise M, C Caetano and H Batjer (1997) Vascular complications of head injury, in Cerebrovascular disease, H Batjer, Editor. Philadelphia: Lippincott-Raven.
22. Miller NR (2007) Diagnosis and management of dural carotid-cavernous sinus fistulas. Neurosurg Focus 23:E13.
23. Onizuka M, K Mori, N Takahashi et al (2003) Gamma knife surgery for the treatment of spontaneous dural carotid-cavernous fistulas. Neurol Med Chir (Tokyo) 43:477–82; discussion 82–3.
24. Chaudhary MY, VP Sachdev, SH Cho et al (1982) Dural arteriovenous malformation of the major venous sinuses: an acquired lesion. AJNR Am J Neuroradiol 3:13–9.
25. Raupp S, WJ van Rooij, M Sluzewski et al (2004) Type I cerebral dural arteriovenous fistulas of the lateral sinus: clinical features in 24 patients. Eur J Neurol 11:489–91.
26. van Rooij WJ, M Sluzewski and GN Beute (2007) Dural arteriovenous fistulas with cortical venous drainage: incidence, clinical presentation, and treatment. AJNR Am J Neuroradiol 28:651–5.
27. Soderman M, G Edner, K Ericson et al (2006) Gamma knife surgery for dural arteriovenous shunts: 25 years of experience. J Neurosurg 104:867–75.
28. Bavinzski G, B Richling, M Killer et al (1996) Evolution of different therapeutic strategies in the treatment of cranial dural arteriovenous fistulas – report of 30 cases. Acta Neurochir (Wien) 138:132–8.

29. Steinberg GK, SD Chang, RP Levy et al (1996) Surgical resection of large incompletely treated intracranial arteriovenous malformations following stereotactic radiosurgery. J Neurosurg 84:920–8.

30. Arat A and S Inci (2006) Treatment of a superior sagittal sinus dural arteriovenous fistula with Onyx: technical case report. Neurosurgery 59:ONSE169–70; discussion ONSE-70.

31. Woo HJ, SY Song, YD Kim et al (2008) Arteriovenous malformation of the external ear: a case report. Auris Nasus Larynx 35:556–8.

32. Manabe S, K Satoh, S Matsubara et al (2008) Characteristics, diagnosis and treatment of hypoglossal canal dural arteriovenous fistula: report of nine cases. Neuroradiology 50: 715–21.

33. Chen MC, WY Chung, CB Luo et al (2010) Arteriovenous malformation in the parotid region presenting as pulsatile tinnitus: A case report. Head Neck 32:262–7.

34. Sismanis A and WR Smoker (1994) Pulsatile tinnitus: recent advances in diagnosis. Laryngoscope 104:681–8.

35. Sismanis A, MA Stamm and M Sobel (1994) Objective tinnitus in patients with atherosclerotic carotid artery disease. Am J Otol 15:404–7.

36. Malek AM, RT Higashida, VV Halbach et al (2000) Patient presentation, angiographic features, and treatment of strangulation-induced bilateral dissection of the cervical internal carotid artery. Report of three cases. J Neurosurg 92:481–7.

37. Singh DP, AJ Forte, MB Brewer et al (2009) Bilateral carotid endarterectomy as treatment of vascular pulsatile tinnitus. J Vasc Surg 50:183–5.

38. De Ridder D, H Fransen, L De Waele et al (2002) Intracranial stenting for pulsatile tinnitus. Proceedings of VIIth International Tinnitus Seminar P4.

39. Lehmann MF, C Mounayer, G Benndorf et al (2005) Pulsatile tinnitus: a symptom of chronic subclavian artery occlusion. AJNR Am J Neuroradiol 26:1960–3.

40. Fernandez AO (1983) Objective tinnitus: a case report. Am J Otol 4:312–4.

41. Cowley PO, R Jones, P Tuch et al (2009) Pulsatile tinnitus from reversal of flow in an aberrant occipital artery: resolved after carotid artery stenting. AJNR Am J Neuroradiol 30:995–7.

42. De Ridder D, L De Ridder, V Nowe et al (2005) Pulsatile tinnitus and the intrameatal vascular loop: why do we not hear our carotids? Neurosurgery 57:1213–7; discussion 1213–7.

43. Cochran JH, Jr. and PW Kosmicki (1979) Tinnitus as a presenting symptom in pernicious anemia. Ann Otol Rhinol Laryngol 88:297.

44. Topal O, SS Erbek, S Erbek et al (2008) Subjective pulsatile tinnitus associated with extensive pneumatization of temporal bone. Eur Arch Otorhinolaryngol 265:123–5.

45. Moonis G, CJ Hwang, T Ahmed et al (2005) Otologic manifestations of petrous carotid aneurysms. AJNR Am J Neuroradiol 26:1324–7.

46. Liu JK, ON Gottfried, A Amini et al (2004) Aneurysms of the petrous internal carotid artery: anatomy, origins, and treatment. Neurosurg Focus 17:E13.

47. Depauw P, J Caekebeke and P Vanhoenacker (2001) Objective pulsatile tinnitus caused by intrapetrous dissecting aneurysm. Clin Neurol Neurosurg 103:197–9.

48. Austin JR and DR Maceri (1993) Anterior communicating artery aneurysm presenting as pulsatile tinnitus. ORL J Otorhinolaryngol Relat Spec 55:54–7.

49. Weissman JL and BE Hirsch (2000) Imaging of tinnitus: a review. Radiology 216:342–9.

50. Horn K and H Hankinson (1994) Tumors of the Jugular Foramen, in Neurotology, R Jackler and D Brackmann, Editors. St Louis: Mosby. 1059–68.

51. Jackson CG, PF Harris, ME Glasscock, 3 rd et al (1990) Diagnosis and management of paragangliomas of the skull base. Am J Surg 159:389–93.

52. Megerian CA, MJ McKenna and JB Nadol, Jr. (1995) Non-paraganglioma jugular foramen lesions masquerading as glomus jugulare tumors. Am J Otol 16:94–8.

53. Rosenbloom JS, IS Storper, JE Aviv et al (1999) Giant cell tumors of the jugular foramen. Am J Otolaryngol 20:176–9.

54. Leonetti JP, MA Shirazi, S Marzo et al (2008) Neuroendocrine carcinoma of the jugular foramen. Ear Nose Throat J 87:86, 8–91.

55. Ryu H, S Yamamoto, K Sugiyama et al (1998) Neurovascular compression syndrome of the eighth cranial nerve. What are the most reliable diagnostic signs? Acta Neurochir (Wien) 140:1279–86.

56. Ryu H, S Yamamoto, K Sugiyama et al (1998) Neurovascular decompression of the eighth cranial nerve in patients with hemifacial spasm and incidental tinnitus: an alternative way to study tinnitus. J Neurosurg 88:232–6.

57. Chadha NK and GM Weiner (2008) Vascular loops causing otological symptoms: a systematic review and meta-analysis. Clin Otolaryngol 33:5–11.

58. Møller MB, AR Møller, PJ Jannetta et al (1993) Vascular decompression surgery for severe tinnitus: selection criteria and results. Laryngoscope 103:421–7.

59. Brookes GB (1996) Vascular-decompression surgery for severe tinnitus. Am J Otol 17:569–76.

60. Ko Y and CW Park (1997) Microvascular decompression for tinnitus. Stereotact Funct Neurosurg 68:266–9.

61. De Ridder D, H Ryu, AR Møller et al (2004) Functional anatomy of the human cochlear nerve and its role in microvascular decompressions for tinnitus. Neurosurgery 54:381–8; discussion 8–90.

62. Nowe V, D De Ridder, PH Van de Heyning et al (2004) Does the location of a vascular loop in the cerebellopontine angle explain pulsatile and non-pulsatile tinnitus? Eur Radiol 14:2282–9

63. Levine RA, EC Nam and J Melcher (2008) Somatosensory pulsatile tinnitus syndrome: somatic testing identifies a pulsatile tinnitus subtype that implicates the somatosensory system. Trends Amplif 12:242–53.

64. Hillman TA, TR Kertesz, K Hadley et al (2006) Reversible peripheral vestibulopathy: the treatment of superior canal dehiscence. Otolaryngol Head Neck Surg 134:431–6.

65. Brantberg K, J Bergenius, L Mendel et al (2001) Symptoms, findings and treatment in patients with dehiscence of the superior semicircular canal. Acta Otolaryngol 121:68–75.

66. Minor LB, PD Cremer, JP Carey et al (2001) Symptoms and signs in superior canal dehiscence syndrome. Ann N Y Acad Sci 942:259–73.

67. Brantberg K, D Bagger-Sjoback, T Mathiesen et al (2006) Posterior canal dehiscence syndrome caused by an apex cholesteatoma. Otol Neurotol 27:531–4.

68. Krombach GA, E Di Martino, S Martiny et al (2006) Dehiscence of the superior and/or posterior semicircular canal: delineation on T2-weighted axial three-dimensional turbo spin-echo images,

maximum intensity projections and volume-rendered images. Eur Arch Otorhinolaryngol 263:111–7.

69. Krombach GA, E DiMartino, T Schmitz-Rode et al (2003) Posterior semicircular canal dehiscence: a morphologic cause of vertigo similar to superior semicircular canal dehiscence. Eur Radiol 13:1444–50.
70. Mikulec AA and DS Poe (2006) Operative management of a posterior semicircular canal dehiscence. Laryngoscope 116:375–8.
71. Bassim MK, KG Patel and CA Buchman (2007) Lateral semicircular canal dehiscence. Otol Neurotol 28:1155–6.
72. Bance M (2004) When is a conductive hearing loss not a conductive hearing loss? Causes of a mismatch in air-bone threshold measurements or a "pseudoconductive" hearing loss. J Otolaryngol 33:135–8.
73. Merchant SN and JJ Rosowski (2008) Conductive hearing loss caused by third-window lesions of the inner ear. Otol Neurotol 29:282–9.
74. Zhou G, Q Gopen and DS Poe (2007) Clinical and diagnostic characterization of canal dehiscence syndrome: a great otologic mimicker. Otol Neurotol 28:920–6.
75. Minor LB (2005) Clinical manifestations of superior semicircular canal dehiscence. Laryngoscope 115:1717–27.
76. Cutforth R, J Wiseman and RD Sutherland (1970) The genesis of the cervical venous hum. Am Heart J 80:488–92.
77. Jindal M, L Hiam, A Raman et al (2009) Idiopathic intracranial hypertension in otolaryngology. Eur Arch Otorhinolaryngol 266:803–6.
78. Donaldson JO (1981) Pathogenesis of pseudotumor cerebri syndromes. Neurology 31:877–80.
79. Schlosser RJ, BA Woodworth, EM Wilensky et al (2006) Spontaneous cerebrospinal fluid leaks: a variant of benign intracranial hypertension. Ann Otol Rhinol Laryngol 115:495–500.
80. Paul KS, RH Lye, FA Strang et al (1983) Arnold–Chiari malformation. Review of 71 cases. J Neurosurg 58:183–7.
81. Wiggs WJ, Jr., A Sismanis and FJ Laine (1996) Pulsatile tinnitus associated with congenital central nervous system malformations. Am J Otol 17:241–4.
82. Ahmmed AU, I Mackenzie, VK Das et al (1996) Audiovestibular manifestations of Chiari malformation and outcome of surgical decompression: a case report. J Laryngol Otol 110:1060–4.
83. Møller AR (1997) A double-blind placebo-controlled trial of baclofen in the treatment of tinnitus. Am J Otol 18:268–9.
84. Møller AR, PJ Jannetta and MB Møller (1981) Neural generators of brainstem evoked potentials. Results from human intracranial recordings. Ann Otol Rhinol Laryngol 90:591–6.
85. Møller AR, PJ Jannetta and LN Sekhar (1988) Contributions from the auditory nerve to the brain-stem auditory evoked potentials (BAEPs): results of intracranial recording in man. Electroencephalogr Clin Neurophysiol 71:198–211.
86. Sindou M (2004) Discussion on trigeminal neuralgia and venous compression. Neurosurgery 55:338.
87. De Ridder D, T Menovsky, C Van Laer et al (2008) Remote tentorium meningioma causing sudden sensorineural deafness. Surg Neurol 70:312–7; discussion 8.

88. Otto KJ, PA Hudgins, W Abdelkafy et al (2007) Sigmoid sinus diverticulum: a new surgical approach to the correction of pulsatile tinnitus. Otol Neurotol 28:48–53.
89. Jastreboff PJ, CG Gray and DE Mattox (1998) Tinnitus and hyperacusis, in Otolaryngology, head & neck surgery, CW Cummings et al, Editors. St Louis: Mosby. 3198–222.
90. Couloigner V, AB Grayeli, D Bouccara et al (1999) Surgical treatment of the high jugular bulb in patients with Meniere's disease and pulsatile tinnitus. Eur Arch Otorhinolaryngol 256:224–9.
91. Golueke PJ, T Panetta, S Sclafani et al (1987) Tinnitus originating from an abnormal jugular bulb: treatment by jugular vein ligation. J Vasc Surg 6:248–51.
92. Yoon BN, TH Lee, SK Kong et al (2008) Management of high jugular bulb with tinnitus: transvenous stent-assisted coil embolization. Otolaryngol Head Neck Surg 139:740–1.
93. Lambert PR and RW Cantrell (1986) Objective tinnitus in association with an abnormal posterior condylar emissary vein. Am J Otol 7:204–7.
94. Forte V, A Turner and P Liu (1989) Objective tinnitus associated with abnormal mastoid emissary vein. J Otolaryngol 18:232–5.
95. Houdart E, R Chapot and JJ Merland (2000) Aneurysm of a dural sigmoid sinus: a novel vascular cause of pulsatile tinnitus. Ann Neurol 48:669–71.
96. Gologorsky Y, SA Meyer, AF Post et al (2009) Novel surgical treatment of a transverse-sigmoid sinus aneurysm presenting as pulsatile tinnitus: technical case report. Neurosurgery 64:E393–4; discussion E4.
97. Zenteno M, L Murillo-Bonilla, S Martinez et al (2004) Endovascular treatment of a transverse-sigmoid sinus aneurysm presenting as pulsatile tinnitus. Case report. J Neurosurg 100:120–2.
98. MacKinnon DM (1968) Objective tinnitus due to palatal myoclonus. J Laryngol Otol 82:369–74.
99. Badia L, A Parikh and GB Brookes (1994) Management of middle ear myoclonus. J Laryngol Otol 108:380–2.
100. Zipfel TE, SR Kaza and JS Greene (2000) Middle-ear myoclonus. J Laryngol Otol 114:207–9.
101. Golz A, M Fradis, D Martzu et al (2003) Stapedius muscle myoclonus. Ann Otol Rhinol Laryngol 112:522–4.
102. Virtanen H (1983) Objective tubal tinnitus: a report of two cases. J Laryngol Otol 97:857–62.
103. Penney SE, IA Bruce and SR Saeed (2006) Botulinum toxin is effective and safe for palatal tremor: a report of five cases and a review of the literature. J Neurol 253:857–60.
104. Aydin O, M Iseri and M Ozturk (2006) Radiofrequency ablation in the treatment of idiopathic bilateral palatal myoclonus: a new indication. Ann Otol Rhinol Laryngol 115:824–6.
105. Bento RF, TG Sanchez, A Miniti et al (1998) Continuous, high-frequency objective tinnitus caused by middle ear myoclonus. Ear Nose Throat J 77:814–8.
106. Olthoff A, R Laskawi and E Kruse (2007) Successful treatment of autophonia with botulinum toxin: case report. Ann Otol Rhinol Laryngol 116:594–8.

Chapter 60
Ménière's Disease and Tinnitus

Michel Paolino and Vénéra Ghulyan-Bedikian

Keypoints

1. Ménière's disease is a clinical syndrome that comprises vertigo, sensorineural hearing loss, subjective tinnitus, and aural fullness.
2. The tinnitus is classically low pitched and evolves with the progression of the disease.
3. The diagnosis of Ménière's disease is based on patient history, a clinical examination, a complete oto-neurological assessment, and a MRI.
4. The differential diagnosis distinguishes Ménière's disease from vestibular schwannoma, microvascular conflict of the VIII cranial nerve, and migraines.
5. Antivertiginous, antihistamines, loop diuretics, antiemetics, and benzodiazepines are effective in managing the acute attacks.
6. The following therapies are recommended for inter-crises periods:

   (a) Dietetic recommendations including low-salt diet
   (b) Medication (antihistaminics, diuretics, osmo-regulators, vasodilators, antiemetics, corticoids, benzodiazepines)
   (c) Relaxation therapy, tinnitus retraining therapy, sound therapy, etc.
   (d) Coordinated treatment of temporomandibulaires and cervical disorders
   (e) Intratympanic therapy with gentamycin or steroids
   (f) Surgical approach by endolymphatic mastoid shunt or endolymphatic sac decompression, vestibular neurotomia, and labyrinthectomia.

7. Some medications as well as transtympanic therapy seem particularly interesting, because they provide improvements of both vertigo and tinnitus while preserving the hearing in the majority of patients who have this treatment.
8. Conservative treatments should be exhausted and surgery reserved for patients with disabling and refractory vertigo, but surgery cannot prevent the progression of the tinnitus.

Keywords Ménière's disease • Tinnitus • Vertigo • Hearing loss • Endolymphatic hydrops • Psychosomatic incidence

Abbreviations

AAO-HNS	American Academy of Otolaryngology – Head and Neck Surgery
ABR	Auditory brainstem response
BPPV	Benign paroxysmal positional vertigo
CBT	Cognitive-behavioral therapy
DPOAEs	Distortion product otoacoustic emissions
ECoG	Electrocochleography
MRI	Magnetic resonance imaging
SP	Summating potential

Ménière's Disease: Pathogenesis, Symptoms, and Clinical Manifestations

Ménière's disease represents one of the many causes of tinnitus. Since its first description in 1861, several etiological theories have been proposed to explain the pathogenesis of this disease: endolymphatic hydrops, autoimmune disorders, viral infections, allergic processes,

M. Paolino (✉)
Department of Oto-Neurology, IMERTA,
C.H.P. Clairval, Marseille, France
e-mail: michel.paolino@wanadoo.fr

A.R. Møller et al. (eds.), *Textbook of Tinnitus*,
DOI 10.1007/978-1-60761-145-5_60, © Springer Science+Business Media, LLC 2011

and activation of neural plasticity. Ménière's disease is a syndrome that comprises of three (or four) symptoms:

– Recurrent episodes of spontaneous vertigo lasting from several minutes to a few hours, which can be followed by residual unsteadiness.
– Fluctuating and slowly progressive sensorineural hearing loss, usually unilateral and initially prevailing at low frequencies.
– Subjective tinnitus and sensation of aural fullness, pressure, or discomfort. The tinnitus is referred to the affected ear and described as a low-frequency "buzz" or "roar," but as the disease progresses, it sometimes includes a high-pitched component.

Ménière's disease usually starts in only one ear but can evolve into a bilateral form. It is characterized by periods of exacerbation and remission. The crises are frequently severe, incapacitating, unpredictable, and usually accompanied by anxiety, headaches, and autonomic manifestations (nausea, vomiting, diaphoresis, pallor, tachycardia, diarrhea, etc.).

At the beginning, the tinnitus complaint is secondary. Classically, it becomes worse during vertigo attacks but may significantly improve or even disappear afterward. However, with the progression of the disease, the tinnitus can become permanent, persisting between attacks. Its evolution is then unfavorable due to a significant increase in anxiety.

Besides the above-described classic form, some physicians have also included patients with incomplete clinical features as forms of Ménière's disease. In fact, the frequency and the intensity of the crises, the association of symptoms, and their impact on the patient's quality of life can vary from one patient to another. These various clinical forms can be classified into three groups:

– Predominantly cochlear forms where hearing loss and tinnitus are "in the foreground" and the vertigo is either absent or atypical
– Predominantly vestibular forms with typical vertigo crises, which are not necessarily preceded by tinnitus or aural fullness, and the hearing loss does not always affect the low frequencies
– Separate forms with initially typical vertigo crises without cochlear signs.

These symptoms that have similarities with the vertiginous crises of migraine should be distinguished from those of Ménière's disease. Later, the cochlear symptoms usually occur together with a pattern of vestibular signs. Signs of endolymphatic hydrops sometimes are later added by vestibular symptoms, and the disease evolves into a typical Ménière's disease.

Diagnostic Criteria

The diagnosis is established with patient history, a clinical examination, a complete oto-neurological assessment, and possibly a MRI of the brain.

Patient History

Patient history is very important for correct diagnosis of Ménière's disease because it can provide information about symptoms during acute attacks. Clinical testing is usually only done between acute attacks. On completing the initial history, the onset, duration, frequency and intensity of crises, the association of symptoms, and their impact on the patient's quality of life should be determined. A typical vertigo attack with no associated hearing loss suggests that the disease is possibly Ménière's disease. A single definitive episode of vertigo that occurs together with the other symptoms of Ménière's disease makes the diagnosis probable but an exact diagnosis of Ménière's disease requires two or more definitive episodes of vertigo and hearing loss associated with tinnitus and/or aural fullness [1].

Clinical Examination

Clinical testing is usually only done between acute attacks and can be normal at the earlier stages of the disease. As the disease progresses, it reveals audio-vestibular abnormalities.

The Romberg test[1] shows axial deviation while the Babinski–Weil test[2] and the Fukuda stepping

---

[1] Romberg test: The patient stands with feet together, eyes open, and hands by the sides. The patient closes their eyes while the examiner observes for a full minute to note occurrence of a fall or axial deviation toward the affected side.

[2] Babinski–Weil test: the patient walks with eyes closed, ten steps forward and ten steps backward several times; the examiner looks for a deviation from the straight path, bending to the affected side when walking forward and to the other when walking backward.

test[3] show drift toward the affected side. However, these tests are not always reliable when the patient has myo-articular and/or orthopedic problems.

Audiometric and Oto-Neurologic Examination

Pure-tone audiometry should be obtained and should show low-frequency sensorineural hearing loss that gets better or disappears after crises. However, as the disease progresses, the hearing loss often reaches high frequencies and can even change to a flat hearing loss.

Speech audiometry should show normal speech intelligibility and can confirm that the hearing loss is indeed of cochlear origin. Tympanometry can rule out middle-ear problems. The Weber-test[4] should be lateralized toward the healthy or better ear. The Rinne test[5] should be positive. In patients with Ménière's disease, it usually does not indicate any difference between the auditory thresholds for air and bone conductance.

Metz-test[6] shows objective recruitment that is more marked in Ménière's disease compared to the other cochlear pathologies.

The Reflex Decay Test shows that the stapedius reflex is well maintained and can confirm the cochlear origin of the disease.

If the patient accepts, a Glycerol test[7] may be helpful if the patient's history and tests are inconclusive. Hearing thresholds, particularly at low frequencies, often improves after administration of glycerol to patients with Ménière's disease.

Recording of distortion product otoacoustic emissions (DPOAEs) provides information about the function of the outer hair cells which may be impaired by abnormal pressure (or rather volume [2]) of the endolymphatic fluid. The combination of vestibular-evoked myogenic potentials and DPOAEs with the glycerol test is suggested for early diagnosis of Ménière's disease and for the differential diagnosis in patients presenting a first attack of vertigo with or without hearing loss [3].

Studies have disagreed regarding the value of recording DPOAEs and cochlear microphonics for differential diagnosis in patients with and without hydrops [4]. The auditory brainstem response (ABR) typically does not show abnormalities in agreement with the assumption that the disease is not affecting retrocochlear functions. The diagnostic value of recordings of the summating potential (SP) that is a component of the electrocochleogram (ECoG) has been advocated by some investigators [5, 6] while others, Eggermont 1979, [7] have been critical regarding the value of ECoG in diagnosis of Ménière's disease, in particular for hearing loss less than 50 dB. The large individual variation in the SP is an obstacle in its use as a diagnostic criterion.

---

[3] Fukuda stepping test: The patient stands with eyes closed, arms outstretched and wearing ear muffs. The patient marches in place 50 steps at the pace of a brisk walk while keeping the eyes closed. The observer looks for any rotation. Rotation of 30° or more is considered a positive test.

[4] Weber test: A test in which the stem of a vibrating tuning fork is placed on the midline of the head to ascertain which ear the sound is heard by bone conduction. The sound will be perceived in the affected ear when a unilateral conductive hearing loss is present or in the unaffected ear when there is a unilateral sensorineural hearing loss. The result of this test is combined with the result of the Rinne test to interpretation of the type of hearing loss. (From Stedman' Electronic Medical Dictionary).

[5] Rinne test: Tests the ability to hear by air conduction with the ability to hear by bone conduction. By placing the tines of a vibrating tuning fork near the pinna, the acoustic stimulus is presented by air conduction; by placing the stem of a vibrating tuning fork on the mastoid process, the acoustic stimulus is presented by bone conduction. In conductive hearing losses, the stimulus is heard louder and longer by bone conduction. In sensorineural hearing losses, the stimulus is heard louder and longer by air conduction. The result of the test is reported for each ear as air conduction and is found to be greater than bone conduction, or vice versa. This information is combined with the result of the Weber tuning fork test in interpreting the type of hearing loss.

---

[6] Metz test: The test compares the threshold of the acoustic middle-ear reflex and loudness perception.

[7] Glycerol test: Glycerol is administered orally 1.5 ml/kg of body weight dissolved in the equal amount of the physiological saline. A positive result is defined as a threshold improvement of the audiogram of 10 dB or more in at least three frequencies (500, 1,000, or 2,000 Hz). The speech audiometry must show an improvement of 10% of the discrimination. However, the oral glycerol test prohibits food intake before the testing, requires a long examination time, and is associated with side effects such as headache, nausea, and vomiting. The intravenous glycerol test (intravenous injection of 100 ml glycerol (10%) over 30 min) is known to have no such disadvantages.

Vestibular Examination

Nystagmography[8] can quantify the vestibular abnormalities. Spontaneous horizontal or horizontal-rotatory nystagmus is common in individuals with Ménière's disease. As soon as the crisis starts, nystagmus beating toward the affected side occurs. But the direction of the eye movements is quickly reversed, confirming a unilateral vestibular deficit. The nystagmus is then very intense and occurs even when the eyes are directed toward the affected side (grade III[9]) nystagmus). Typically it diminishes with time. After the crisis, the nystagmus which is sensitized by the suppression of ocular fixation, disappear from direct observation, but can always be reactivated by the Head shaking test[10] or by vibratory stimulation of the mastoid. If high-frequency vibratory stimulation of the mastoid reveals a latent nystagmus, it is an indication of a unilateral vestibular deficit. In patients with Ménière's disease who have a normal caloric test, the direction of the nystagmus triggered by the head shaking and vibratory tests is usually discordant and informs us on the evolution of the disease.

The Dix Hallpike test[11] is typically negative in Ménière's disease. However, detailed attention should be paid to the realization of this test because the spontaneous or latent nystagmus due to the Ménière's disease can be sensitized or revealed in the decubitus position. In addition, the possibility of benign paroxysmal positional vertigo (BPPV) should not be overlooked. BPPV can be either idiopathic or, due to the mechanical disruption and distortion of the utricle and saccule, related to the progression of Ménière's disease.

Magnetic Resonance Imaging

A MRI of the brain with Gadolinium contrast can determine whether the internal auditory canals are open and that the morphology of structures in the posterior fossa is normal.

Differential Diagnosis

An expert clinical judgment is required to distinguish between true Ménière's disease and several other conditions characterized by vertigo, hearing loss, and tinnitus, such as cochlear otosclerosis; bacterial or viral labyrinthitis; temporal bone trauma; V, VII, and VIII neuroma; meningioma; cholesteatoma; and migraine. The complete oto-neurological assessment including an ABR, ECoG, and MRI of the posterior fossa makes it possible to differentiate Ménière's disease from these etiologies.

Distinguishing Ménière's disease from vestibular schwannoma and vascular conflict of the VIII cranial nerve are the most important factors. Kentala and Pyykkö (2000) [8] compared test results from 128 individuals with vestibular schwanomma and 243 with Ménière's disease and found that 38% of patients with small and medium-sized vestibular schwannoma had an association of all the symptoms of a typical Ménière's disease. In 69% of the patients, the attacks lasted from 5 min to 4 h and occurred only once or twice a year. In addition, half of the patients had spontaneous nystagmus and 61% of the patients had caloric asymmetry. Tinnitus in these patients was either mild or intense (in 49 and 12% of cases, respectively).

Vascular conflict of the VIII nerve is characterized by intermittent paroxysms of dizziness and unilateral tinnitus, which can become more frequent over time (see also Chap. 40). In a chronic stage, this condition

---

[8] Nystagmography: The technique of recording nystagmus. Frenzel glasses or videonystagmography mask should be used to eliminate the visual fixation that may suppress the nystagmus.

[9] Grade III nystagmus: Spontaneous nystagmus that occurs when the eyes are directed to the center, right, and left. The intensity of this nystagmus increases when the gaze direction is the same at the quick phase of the nystagmus.

[10] Head shaking test: The patient is positioned upright and instrumented with a videonystagmography mask that suppresses the visual fixation and records the eye movements. The examiner grasps the patient's head and moves it briskly approximately 30° to either side in the horizontal plane around the vertical axis. The head shaking for a frequency of about 2 Hz is continued for 20 cycles and then abruptly stopped. A head shaking nystagmus indicates a dynamic imbalance between the ears. It is usually beating toward the "better" ear during about 30 s and can be followed by a second phase of nystagmus that is weaker, decays more slowly, and is directed toward the "bad" ear. The main value of seeing a secondary phase is that one can clearly identify the primary phase, which is sometimes very short.

[11] Dix Hallpike test: test for eliciting paroxysmal vertigo and nystagmus in which the patient is brought from the sitting to the supine position with the head hanging over the examining table and turned to the right or left (45°); vertigo and nystagmus are elicited when the head is rotated toward the affected ear. Frenzel glasses or videonystagmography mask are used to eliminate the visual fixation that may suppress the nystagmus.

induces persistent unsteadiness [9, 10] often associated with constant tinnitus. Unfortunately, this condition, which has a similar course as Ménière's disease, is often not recognized. In a study by Ryu and coworkers, it was even shown that up to 73% of the patients diagnosed preoperatively as having Ménière's disease were successfully treated for vascular conflict of the vestibular nerve [11].

Patients with Ménière's disease have normal ABR with normal interpeak latency I–III [12].

Ménière's disease also has similarities with migraine (see a recent review by Minor, 2004 [13] and Chap. 38). However, the glycerol test is negative for migraine, the crises of dizziness always start in the early morning, and there is often a family or personal history of migraines. In addition, individuals with migraine-associated dizziness usually have normal hearing, and when a sensorineural hearing loss is present, it rarely progresses, thus, different from individuals with Ménière's disease [14] (see also Chap. 38).

Treatment

There are several different treatments available for Ménière's disease, and the choice of treatment requires careful consideration. Both medical and surgical treatments are in general use, but there is not a consensus regarding the specific treatment and a divergence of different protocols currently in use.

Management of Acute Attacks

During an attack, the treatment is aimed at alleviating the acute symptoms.

Vertigo is often the most disabling symptom of Ménière's disease, and the medical treatment seeks, above all, to control these symptoms. The intravenous injections of *Acetylleucine* used in some countries are effective in alleviating vertigo attacks. The action of *Acetylleucine* is not understood, but studies in animal models suggest that it acts mainly on abnormally hyperpolarized and/or depolarized vestibular neurons by restoring their membrane potential [15]. Administration of *Acetylleucine* does not have any proven effect on tinnitus.

A randomized double-blind clinical study showed that *betahistine dimesylate* 12 mg as well as a fixed combination of *cinnarizine* 20 mg and *dimenhydrinate* 40 mg are highly effective and safe treatment options for Ménière's disease and may be used in both the management of acute episodes and long-term treatment. These drugs, commonly used to treat vestibular disorders, reduce tinnitus in approximately 60% of patients with Ménière's disease [16].

Some physicians prescribe loop diuretics to normalize the balance of fluid volumes in the inner ear. For example, intravenous injections of 40 mg *furosemide* in the morning during 3–5 days are effective treatments but require checking the blood electrolytes. Tinnitus should be watched since furosemide can give tinnitus.

During crises, intravenous injections of 40 ml of 30% *Glucosé-hyper* in the morning and evening for 3 days are also effective treatments. Corticosteroids (such as *Methylprednisolon* 20 mg in intravenous perfusion) are used by some physicians for the management of acute vertigo attacks. Treatment for preventing nausea and vomiting, which can be very intense during a crisis, should also be available. The following antiemetics are often prescribed:

Compazine (per os or suppository) – 5 mg every 12 h as needed.

Meclizine (per os) – dose ranges from 12.5 mg twice a day to 50 mg three times a day.

Métopimazin (per os) – 1 or 2 (15 mg) tablets three times a day.

Métoclopramid – intramuscular or intravenous injections of a 10 mg/2 ml vial three times a day.

Benzodiazepines (for example: *Lorazepam* sublingual tablets, 0.5 mg twice a day) are used to relieve the anxiety accompanying Ménière's attacks.

Therapies for Inter-crises Periods

The purpose of treatment is to reduce the number of attacks while trying to prevent further hearing loss and damage to the vestibular system. This form of treatment depends on the inter-crises symptoms, their intensity, and their impact on the patients' quality of life.

Non-invasive Therapies

If the symptoms disappear after the crisis, the patient only needs dietetic recommendations such as to avoid caffeine, alcohol, tobacco, and aspartame, which worsen tinnitus and other Ménière's disease symptoms. A low-salt diet is also important.

To reduce the frequency of vertigo attacks and alleviate the inter-crises symptoms, *Betahistine* (16 mg three times a day or 24 mg twice a day) is often beneficial [17]. Diuretics (such as *furosemide* 20 mg a day, two times a week with a control of electrolytes), osmoregulators (such as *glycerol* or *mannitol*), or vasodilators (for example, Buflomedil 150 mg twice a day) can also be effective in selected patients. However, there is insufficient evidence that this medication has any significant effect on Ménière's disease-related tinnitus [18, 19].

A randomized and controlled clinical study showed the effectiveness of the combination of *diphenidol* (25 mg/d), *acetazolamide* (250 mg/48 h), and *prednisone* (0.35 mg/kg) on the tinnitus, as well as the frequency and duration of vertigo [20].

Corticosteroids are especially helpful in bilateral forms, in particular, if an autoimmune cause is suspected. Desensitizing therapies for allergies have been shown to be effective to relieve the Ménière's disease symptoms, including tinnitus in some patients [21, 22].

Depending on the presence of psychosomatic components, the social–professional impact of tinnitus, and other Ménière's disease symptoms, a patient's regular follow-up by a multidisciplinary team may be beneficial. Relaxation therapy may be beneficial in some patients because of its beneficial effects on unsteadiness, as well as on tinnitus. It should be associated with standard methods of tinnitus management (see Part V – Management of Tinnitus). Balance rehabilitation can improve a patient's balance.

Intratympanic Therapy

When vertigo persists despite optimal medical management, an intratympanic therapy with gentamycin or steroids may be proposed to control the vertigo. The intratympanic administration of low-dose gentamycin provides long-term vertigo control, whilst preserving hearing and vestibular function in the majority of patients [23]. In addition, it is effective to treat the tinnitus in Ménière's disease [24, 25]. New protocols have been developed to reduce the risk of permanent gentamycin ototoxicity. The one-shot injection protocols present a minimal risk to hearing, whereas repeated or continuous application protocols result in higher gentamycin doses in the cochlea and can cause damage to hearing [2, 26]. In a review of literature, Dodson and Sismanis (2004) [27] suggest that this therapy should mainly be proposed to patients with Ménière's disease who do not have useful hearing. The authors recommend intratympanic therapies with steroids for Ménière's patients with normal hearing, which have some success in controlling vertigo.

Treatments that can control vertigo may not always improve tinnitus in Ménière's patients. A prospective double-blind placebo-controlled trial by Garduno-Anayaet et al. (2005) [28] showed relief of tinnitus in 48% of the patients who were treated with intratympanic dexamethasone. It was also shown that the inner-ear perfusion via transtympanic delivery of dexamethasone 4 mg/ml improves hearing, tinnitus, and aural pressure in patients with a cochlear form of Ménière's disease [29]. Nonetheless, Araujo et al. (2005) [30] reported that a prospective randomized placebo-controlled but single-blind trial showed that intratympanic dexamethasone had no significant effect on severe tinnitus compared to placebo.

Surgical Approach

Surgical treatment should be a last resort and is reserved for Ménière's patients who are refractory to medical therapy. Conservative and destructive surgical procedures are used according to the severity of the crises, the degree of serviceable hearing, and the condition of the contralateral ear.

Endolymphatic Sac Surgery

Conservative surgery by endolymphatic mastoid shunt or endolymphatic sac decompression without sac incision is the operation most often practiced. It can lead to a temporary decrease in vertigo occurrence and intensity, while generally preserving hearing [31]. However, the literature reveals disagreement regarding the effectiveness of this approach in reducing vertigo.

Sectioning of the Vestibular Nerve

Sectioning of the vestibular nerve is effective in controlling vertigo while preserving hearing in most patients. Thus, it is available for patients with serviceable hearing who have failed all other treatments and are especially incapacitated by Ménière's disease. Dandy (1941) [32], described how he treated patients with Ménière's disease by sectioning the eighth cranial nerve. Later, this technique has been refined and now, most typically, only the vestibular nerve is sectioned. Different techniques are in use for sectioning the vestibular nerve, such a retromastoid (retrolabyrinthine) approach to the cerebello pontine angle, and a middle fossa approach has been used as well. Endoscope-assisted, minimally invasive retrosigmoid approach that is now recommended rather than the middle fossa or retrolabyrinthine approaches is simpler, more reliable, and has lower risk of complications [33–35]. Analysis of 18 publications mentioning tinnitus status after vestibular neurotomy in a total of 1,318 patients shows that the tinnitus had worsened after the operation from 0 to 60%, but most of the patients had no change in their tinnitus (17–72%) and others even reported improvements of 6–61% [36]. Thus, vestibular neurotomy does not consistently worsen tinnitus, but the risk is present.

For patients with unilateral Ménière's disease and total deafness, labyrinthectomy can be undertaken as a last resort.

The procedures that control the episodic vertigo by destroying the vestibular function in the affected ear should be reserved for patients who have handicapping vertigo, which persists in spite of conservative treatments. Typically, the balance improves significantly after these procedures, thanks to compensatory and substitutive mechanisms. The ability to compensate for loss of vestibular input decreases with age, and for people over the age of 50 years, the compensation takes a long time and is rarely complete. These operations, however, cannot prevent the progression of hyperacusis or tinnitus.

Microvascular Decompression

Cranial nerve roots in contact with a blood vessel have been associated with specific diseases such as hemifacial spasm, trigeminal neuralgia, glossopharyngeal neuralgia, and geniculate neuralgia. Also, blood vessels in close contact with the root of the vestibular nerve have been associated with a specific disorder such as a specific vestibular disorder [disabling positional vertigo (DPV)] [37, 38], and blood vessels in contact with the auditory nerve have been associated with some special forms of tinnitus [10]. Microvascular decompression operations (MVD) for DPV have shown beneficial effect in about 85% of patients [39] (see Chap. 40). MVD operations for tinnitus are effective in giving relief of tinnitus in some patients with this condition [10] (see Chap. 84).

The fact that vascular loops have been reported to be in contact with the vestibular nerve in patients with Ménière's disease does not mean that contact with a blood vessel is associated with symptoms. Studies have shown that vascular loops in contact with cranial nerve roots occur frequently without giving specific symptoms from the respective cranial nerve [40] (see Chap. 40).

Other Forms of Treatment

Applying Air Puffs to the Inner Ear

It has been shown that applying air pressure to the inner ear can relieve some of the symptoms of Ménière's disease [41, 42]. This was first realized by placing individuals with Ménière's disease in a pressure chamber. These findings have later been explored, and a practical device that a person can wear was developed (the Meniett, now marketed by Medtronic, Inc.). This device provides a series of air puffs to the sealed ear canal. Using this device requires that ventilation tubes (PE tubes) are inserted in the eardrum to make it possible for the air puffs to reach the middle-ear cavity. The Meniett device is now in use for management Ménière's disease.

The efficacy of such treatment was studied by Odkvist et al. (2000) [43] in a prospective randomized placebo-controlled, multicenter clinical trial. The study had

56 participants with active Ménière's disease, age 20–65 years, with a hearing loss of 20–65 dB PTA. Thirty-one participants completed 2 weeks using the Meniett device and 25 patients completed the 2 weeks with the placebo device. A grommet (PE tube) was inserted in the eardrum on the affected side 2 weeks before the study began. The active group experienced significant improvement concerning the frequency and intensity of vertigo, dizziness, aural pressure, and tinnitus, assessed using a visual analogue scale (VAS). The placebo group experienced no difference from the normal course of their disease. Pure-tone threshold improved at the frequencies 500 and 1,000 Hz after active treatment, but there were no improvement of hearing after placebo treatment. Boudewyns et al. reported a significant decrease in the median number of vertigo spells without any improvement in hearing status, tinnitus and functional level, or self-perceived dizziness handicap [44].

In another study, Densert and Sass (2001) [45] found beneficial effect on the symptoms in 37 individuals with Ménière's disease, 31 of whom had failed to respond to medical treatment in a 2-year follow-up; 19 were free from vertigo spells; 15 had a significantly fewer vertigo spells; and 3 did not respond to pressure treatment. These three individuals later had treatment with gentamicin injections, one of these three became deaf in the affected ear. None of the patients' conditions when treated with air puffs became worse [45]. All participants in the study reported improvement in functionality of at least two levels, according to the AAO-HNS functionality scale.

References

1. Beasley NJ, NS Jones (1996) Ménière's disease: evolution of a definition. J Laryngol Otol. 110.12: 1107–1113.
2. Salt AN, RM Gill, SK Plontke (2008) Dependence of hearing changes on the dose of intratympanically applied gentamicin: a meta-analysis using mathematical simulations of clinical drug delivery protocols. Laryngoscope. 118.10: 1793–1800.
3. Magliulo G, G Cianfrone, M Gagliardi et al (2004) Vestibular evoked myogenic potentials and distortion-product otoacoustic emissions combined with glycerol testing in endolymphatic hydrops: their value in early diagnosis. Ann Otol Rhinol Laryngol. 113.12: 1000–1005.
4. Fetterman BL (2001) Distortion-product otoacoustic emissions and cochlear microphonics: relationships in patients with and without endolymphatic hydrops. Laryngoscope. 111.6: 946–954.
5. Rotter A, S Weikert, J Hensel et al (2008) Low-frequency distortion product otoacoustic emission test compared to ECoG in diagnosing endolymphatic hydrops. Eur Arch Otorhinolaryngol. 265.6: 643–649.
6. Ferraro JA, JD Durrant (2006) Electrocochleography in the evaluation of patients with Ménière's disease/endolymphatic hydrops. J Am Acad Audiol. 17.1: 45–68.
7. Eggermont JJ (1979) Summating potentials in Ménière's disease. Arch Otorhinolaryngol 222: 63–75.
8. Kentala E, M Havia, I Pyykko (2001) Short-lasting drop attacks in Ménière's disease. Otolaryngol Head Neck Surg. 124.5: 526.
9. Schwaber MK, JW Hall (1992) Cochleovestibular nerve compression syndrome. I. Clinical features and audiovestibular findings. Laryngoscope. 102.9: 1020–1029.
10. Møller MB, AR Møller, PJ Jannetta et al (1993) Microvascular decompression of the eighth nerve in patients with disabling positional vertigo: selection criteria and operative results in 207 patients. Acta Neurochir (Wien). 125.1–4: 75–82.
11. Ryu H, S Yamamoto, K Sugiyama et al (1998) Neurovascular compression syndrome of the eighth cranial nerve. What are the most reliable diagnostic signs. Acta Neurochir (Wien). 140.12: 1279–1286.
12. Møller MB (1988) Controversy in Ménière's disease: results of microvascular decompression of the eighth nerve. Am J Otol. 9.1: 60–63.
13. Minor LB, DA Schessel, JP Carey (2004) Ménière's disease. Curr Opin Neurol 17: 9–16.
14. Battista RA (2004) Audiometric findings of patients with migraine-associated dizziness. Otol Neurotol. 25.6: 987–992.
15. Vibert N, PP Vidal (2001) In vitro effects of acetyl-dl-leucine (tanganil) on central vestibular neurons and vestibulo-ocular networks of the guinea-pig. Eur J Neurosci. 13.4: 735–748.
16. Novotný M, R Kostrica (2002) Fixed combination of cinnarizine and dimenhydrinate versus betahistine dimesylate in the treatment of Ménière's disease: a randomized, double-blind, parallel group clinical study. Int Tinnitus J. 8.2: 115–123.
17. Ganança MM, HH Caovilla, FF Ganança (2009) Comparable efficacy and tolerability between twice daily and three times daily betahistine for Ménière's disease. Acta Otolaryngol. 129.5: 487–492.
18. Simpson JJ, WE Davies (1999) Recent advances in the pharmacological treatment of tinnitus. Trends Pharmacol Sci. 20.1: 12–18.
19. Thirlwall AS, S Kundu (2006) Diuretics for Ménière's disease or syndrome. Cochrane Database Syst Rev. 19.3: CD003599.
20. Morales-Luckie E, A Cornejo-Suarez, MA Zaragoza-Contreras et al (2005) Oral administration of prednisone to control refractory vertigo in Ménière's disease: a pilot study. Otol Neurotol. 26.5: 1022–1026.
21. Derebery MJ (2000) Allergic management of Ménière's disease: an outcome study. Otolaryngol Head Neck Surg. 122.2: 174–182.
22. Thai-Van H, MJ Bounaix, B Fraysse (2001) Ménière's disease: pathophysiology and treatment. Drugs. 61.8: 1089–1102.
23. Suryanarayanan R, JA Cook (2004) Long-term results of gentamicin inner ear perfusion in Ménière's disease. J Laryngol Otol. 118.7: 489–495.

24. Eklund S, I Pyykkö, H Aalto et al (1999) Effect of intratympanic gentamicin on hearing and tinnitus in Ménière's disease. Am J Otol. 20.3: 350–356.

25. Diamond C, O'Connell DA, Hornig JD et al (2003) Systematic review of intratimpanic gentamicin in Menière's disease. J Otolaryngol. 32.6: 351.361.

26. De Beer L, R Stokroos, H Kingma (2007) Intratympanic gentamicin therapy for intractable Ménière's disease. Acta Otolaryngol. 127.6: 605–612.

27. Dodson KM, A Sismanis (2004) Intratympanic perfusion for the treatment of tinnitus. Otolaryngol Clin North Am. 37.5: 991–1000.

28. Garduño-Anaya MA, H Couthino De Toledo, R Hinojosa-González et al (2005) Dexamethasone inner ear perfusion by intratympanic injection in unilateral Ménière's disease: a two-year prospective, placebo-controlled, double-blind, randomized trial. Otolaryngol Head Neck Surg. 133.2: 285–294.

29. Light JP, H Silverstein (2004) Transtympanic perfusion: indications and limitations. Curr Opin Otolaryngol Head Neck Surg. 12.5: 378–383.

30. Araújo MF, CA Oliveira, FM Bahmad (2005) Intratympanic dexamethasone injections as a treatment for severe, disabling tinnitus: does it work? Arch Otolaryngol Head Neck Surg. 131.2: 113–117.

31. Brinson GM, DA Chen, MA Arriaga (2007) Endolymphatic mastoid shunt versus endolymphatic sac decompression for Ménière's disease. Otolaryngol Head Neck Surg. 136.3: 415–421.

32. Dandy WE (1941) Surgical treatment of Ménière's disease. Surg. Gynecol. Obstet. 72: 421–425.

33. Magnan J, G Bremond, A Chays et al (1991) Vestibular neurotomy by retrosigmoid approach: technique, indications, and results. Am J Otol. 12.2: 101–104.

34. Miyazaki H, A Deveze, J Magnan (2005) Neuro-otologic surgery through minimally invasive retrosigmoid approach: endoscopc assisted microvascular decompression, vestibular neurotomy, and tumor removal. Laryngoscope. 115.9: 1612–1617.

35. Li CS, JT Lai (2008) Evaluation of retrosigmoid vestibular neurectomy for intractable vertigo in Ménière's disease: an interdisciplinary review. Acta Neurochir. (Wien). 150.7: 655–661.

36. Baguley DM, P Axon, IM Winter et al (2002) The effect of vestibular nerve section upon tinnitus. Clin Otolaryngol Allied Sci. 27.4: 219–226.

37. Møller MB, AR Møller, PJ Jannetta et al (1986) Diagnosis and surgical treatment of disabling positional vertigo. J. Neurosurg. 64: 21–28.

38. Jannetta PJ, MB Møller and AR Møller (1984) Disabling positional vertigo. New Engl. J. Med. 310.26: 1700–1705.

39. Møller MB, AR Møller, PJ Jannetta et al (1993) Microvascular decompression of the eighth nerve in patients with disabling positional vertigo: Selection criteria and operative results in 207 patients. Acta Neurochir (Wien). 125: 75–82.

40. Sunderland S (1948) Microvascular relations and anomalies at the base of the brain. J. Neurol. Neurosurg Psychiatry. 11: 243–257.

41. Ingelstedt S, A Ivarsson and O Tjernström (1976) Immediate relief of symptoms during acute attacks of Ménière's disease, using a pressure chamber. Acta Otolaryngol. 85: 368–378.

42. Densert B, O Densert (1982) Overpressure in treatment of Ménière's disease. Laryngoscope 92: 1285–1292.

43. Odkvist LM, S Arlinger, E Billermark et al (2000) Effects of middle ear pressure changes on clinical symptoms in patients with Ménière's disease – a clinical multicentre placebo-controlled study. Acta Otolaryngol Suppl. 543: 99–101.

44. Boudewyns AN, FL Wuyts, M Hoppenbrouwers et al (2005) Meniett therapy: rescue treatment in severe drug-resistant Ménière's disease? Acta Otolaryngol. 125.12: 1283–1289.

45. Densert B and K Sass (2001) Control of symptoms in patients with Ménière's disease using middle ear pressure applications: Two years follow-up. Acta Otolaryng (Stockh.). 121: 616–621.

Chapter 61
Tinnitus with Headaches

Miguel J.A. Láinez, Anna Piera, and Alejandro Ponz

Keypoints

1. Patients with tinnitus frequently have headaches, but the relation between these two disorders is not always casual.
2. Headaches and tinnitus could be symptoms of the same disease.
3. Idiopathic intracranial hypertension is a syndrome in which headaches and tinnitus often occur together.
4. Headaches and tinnitus often occur together with other focal symptoms in symptomatic intracranial hypertension.
5. Intracranial vascular abnormalities such as arteriovenous malformations (AVMs) can occur together with any kind of headache with paroxysmal tinnitus.
6. Tinnitus may be one of the signs of a basilar migraine.
7. Headaches are a very frequent symptom after head trauma, and tinnitus is also common in the posttraumatic syndrome.
8. When a patient with tinnitus presents with headaches, a careful neurological examination that may include neuroimaging should be completed.

Keywords Tinnitus • Headache • Idiopathic intracranial hypertension • Arteriovenous malformations • Symptomatic intracranial hypertension • Brain tumor • Basilar migraine

Abbreviations

AVM   Arteriovenous malformation
CPA   Cerebellopontine angle
CSF   Cerebrospinal fluid
DCN   Dorsal cochlear nucleus
IIH   Idiopathic intracranial hypertension
MR   Magnetic resonance
MRI   Magnetic resonance imaging
TNC   Trigeminal nucleus caudalis

M.J.A. Láinez (✉)
Department of Neurology, Hospital Clínico Universitario,
University of Valencia, Avenida Blasco Ibáñez, 17, 46010
Valencia, Spain
e-mail: jlaineza@meditex.es

Introduction

Headaches are the most frequent reason for neurological consultation [1]. The lifetime prevalence of headaches has been estimated in 66% of the general population with a current prevalence of 47% [2]; with these high prevalence rates, it is not surprising that patients with tinnitus also have headaches. However, the relation between these two disorders is not always casual.

Headaches and tinnitus are both symptoms of the same disease; patients with increased or decreased cerebrospinal fluid (CSF) pressure, basilar migraine, or carotid dissection experience both symptoms. Headaches are also common in patients with chronic tinnitus; the relationship between these symptoms is unclear.

Headaches and Tinnitus as Symptoms of the Same Disease

Idiopathic Intracranial Hypertension (Pseudotumor Cerebri)

In an alert and orientated patient without localized neurological signs, idiopathic intracranial hypertension (IIH) is characterized by the symptoms and signs of elevated CSF pressure. It occurs most frequently in obese women of childbearing age, but women can

A.R. Møller et al. (eds.), *Textbook of Tinnitus*,
DOI 10.1007/978-1-60761-145-5_61, © Springer Science+Business Media, LLC 2011

develop IIH at any age. A headaches is the more prominent symptom; it is usually severe, daily, and referred
to the entire head; it can be throbbing or pressing and
often worsens with Valsalva maneuvers or postural
changes. Nausea is a common symptom and, less frequently, so is vomiting [3, 4].

Tinnitus referred to inside of the head occurs in
approximately two-thirds of individuals with IIH. This
type of tinnitus is more often perceived as a pulsatile
bruit-like sound that is synchronous with the heartbeat
and not a high-frequency ringing sound. The tinnitus is
often unilateral and disappears after jugular compression
on the side to which the tinnitus is referred. The tinnitus
has been attributed to the intensified vascular pulsations
that are transmitted to the wall of the venous sinuses by
the CSF. The pulsatile compressions were thought to
convert laminar blood flow to turbulent flow [3].

Episodes of transient blurred vision of brief duration
are frequent, and papilledema is the hallmark sign in a
neurological examination. However, it is important to
remember that IIH may occur occasionally without
papilledema. Horizontal diplopia is also common.

An increase of CSF pressure (>200 mm H_2O in the
non-obese, >250 mm H_2O in the obese) measured by
lumbar puncture confirms the diagnosis. After the
lumbar puncture, headaches and tinnitus improve. The
diagnosis of IIH requires neuroimaging to rule out
other causes of intracranial hypertension [5, 6].

MRI and MR angiography are recommended; if
MRI cannot be obtained, a computed tomography scan
with contrast is the second best choice.

If a patient is overweight, losing weight is recommended. In order to reduce the increase of CSF pressure, diuretics are recommended; acetazolamide is the
most commonly used drug, but furosemide is an alternative. A furosemide test (40–80 mg each morning for
3–10 days) has been proposed to rule out the IIH.

Topiramate is also an alternative in combination
with diuretics. If the medical treatment fails, surgery
should be considered: optic nerve sheath fenestration
and shunting procedures could be performed [3, 6].

Symptomatic Intracranial Hypertension and Intracranial Hypotension

All space-occupying lesions in the brain produce, or
can produce, increased CSF pressure and, because of
this, headaches are a usual manifestation. The most

common type of "brain tumor headache" is a tension-type
headache; usually, it is moderate or severe, worsens in
the morning, and, in few cases, is accompanied by
nausea and vomiting. The more typical and classically
mild, early morning frontal headache that resolves
after wakeup is uncommon in brain tumor patients. In
other space-occupying lesions, such as subdural hema-
tomas or brain abscesses, headaches are an earlier
and more frequent symptom [7].

Tinnitus has been described as a symptom of intracranial hypertension, but the prevalence is unknown.
Usually the tinnitus is described as constant and ringing high-frequency sound. Tinnitus is more common
in individuals with tumors of the posterior fossa, especially in space-occupying lesions of the cerebellopontine angle (tumors, aracnoid cysts). Some individuals
with such lesions complain of intermittent tinnitus
[8, 9]. Headache and tinnitus usually improve or disappear after resolution of the intracranial hypertension.

Tinnitus has also been described in patients with
such hindbrain abnormalities as Arnold–Chiari malformation. In these cases, headache and tinnitus should
appear with manoeuvres that transiently increase
intracranial and intra-abdominal pressure. Coughing,
sneezing, and physical exercise typically trigger attacks
of tinnitus [7].

In low CSF pressure syndrome, headache is also the
main clinical feature. It is typically an orthostatic headache that is present when the patient is upright and is
relieved when lying down. It may be throbbing, and
the location is predominantly posterior. Changes in
hearing (echoed, distant, or muffled) and tinnitus have
been described as associated symptoms; these symptoms can also appear in an upright position and improve
or disappear by lying down [10, 11]. These symptoms
may be related with stretching the VIII nerve or
changes in the pressure of the perilymphatic fluid in
the inner ear [12].

Vascular Abnormalities

All kinds of vascular malformations can produce headache and tinnitus. Both are more prominent in arteriovenous malformations (AVM) and arteriovenous fistula
[13]. The headaches in individuals with AVMs often
fulfill criteria for migraine with aura, but all types of
headaches have been described. The tinnitus often
occurs episodically. Both tinnitus and headaches are

more common in individuals with vascular abnormalities located to the posterior fossa, and the tinnitus may be a relevant symptom in lesions near the VIII nerve [14, 15].

Carotid and vertebral dissections are other causes of acute headaches and tinnitus. Headaches are usually severe and persistent, neck pain is also common and tinnitus is frequently paroxysmal [13].

Acute headaches, papilledema, and seizures are the most typical signs of sinus thrombosis, but tinnitus can also be a prominent symptom [16].

If a vascular abnormality is suspected, imaging such as MRI and MR angiography is indicated. In some cases, a Seldinger[1] angiography could be indicated.

Posttraumatic Syndrome

Headaches are a cardinal symptom of the posttraumatic syndrome [17–19] caused by either head trauma and/or whiplash injury. In the acute phase, there are autonomic symptoms like dizziness, nausea and vomiting, orthostatic reactions, and problems with regulation of body temperature. These signs are accompanied by different degrees of cognitive problems or other often poorly defined neuropsychologic deficits, such as irritability and increased low tolerance and sensitivity to light and noise [20, 21]. Other forms of pain that resemble primary headache disorders may develop after head injury. The most frequently occurring pattern resembles a tension-type headache and occurs in more than 80% of individuals who have had head trauma. Some such individuals have typical migraine with or without aura triggered by the head impact. Even a cluster-like syndrome has been described in some individuals who have had head trauma [22].

Tinnitus is also a frequent symptom in individuals who have had head and neck trauma and is part of the post-concussion syndrome. The frequency of tinnitus is also high in individuals after blast injury (see Chap. 67). Usually, the tinnitus is continuous, and after

neck injury, it has the characteristics of somatic tinnitus [23, 24] (see Chaps. 9 and 43).

Migraine with Basilar Aura

Vertigo, dysarthria[2], and tinnitus may occur together with basilar aura in individuals with migraine. Tinnitus has been reported to occur alone or in combination with other symptoms in 50% of individuals with basilar aura. Other symptoms are diplopia, bilateral visual symptoms, bilateral paresthesia, hearing loss, decreased level of consciousness, and ataxia. For the management of patients with tinnitus and migraine, it is important to obtain information about how their tinnitus may be regarded as a symptom that precedes headaches [25, 26].

Headaches in Individuals with Tinnitus

The prevalence of headaches in individuals with tinnitus, and vice versa, is unknown. Both tinnitus and headaches have common signs, which suggest that each one of these symptoms could amplify each other and one of these symptoms might cause the other. Both disorders are frequent, under recognized, and under treated; they cause a high degree of disability, and both are often accompanied by psychiatric disorders [27, 28]. The most remarkable finding is that these two symptoms share some common mechanism in their tendency to become chronic. Studies in animals have shown that DCN neurons receive input from the trigeminal system [29].

Lack of normal inhibition of the caudal trigeminal nucleus (TNC) may be an important mechanism in the cause of headache [30]. In both headaches and tinnitus, an increase of the somatosensory influence might play an important role in making these symptoms chronic [29, 31]. In a series of 149 patients with chronic tinnitus (mean duration: 1.5 years), we found a prevalence of headaches in 47%; in the patients with unilateral tinnitus who could modulate their tinnitus by

---

[1] Seldinger angiography: A method of percutaneous insertion of a catheter into a blood vessel or space. A needle is used to puncture the structure and a guide wire is threaded through the needle; when the needle is withdrawn, a catheter is threaded over the wire; the wire is then withdrawn, leaving the catheter in place. Stedman's Electronic Medical Dictionary.

[2] Dysarthria: A disturbance of speech due to emotional stress, brain injury, or paralysis, in co-ordination, or spasticity of the muscles used for speaking. Stedman's Electronic Medical Dictionary.

somatic stimulation, the prevalence of headaches was 89%. These patients had tension-type headaches, predominantly unilateral and related with the tinnitus side. More results are necessary to establish the exact relation between the evolution of both these symptoms and the response to treatment.

References

1. Casado Menéndez I (2009) Analysis of the reasons for visits to a neurology office in Asturias. Neurologia. 24(5):309–14. Spanish

2. Stovner LJ, C Andrée (2008) Eurolight Steering Committee impact of headache in Europe: a review for the Erolight project. J Headache Pain. 9(3):139–46.

3. Friedman DI, JJ Corbett (2006) High cerebrospinal fluid pressure. In: The Headaches. 3rd edition. Olesen J, Goadsby PJ, Ramadan NM, Tfelt-Hansen P, Welch KMA, eds. Lippincot Willians and Wilkins, Philadelphia. 925–33.

4. Wall M, D George (1991) Idiopathic intracranial hypertension: A prospective study of 50 patients. Brain. 114:155–180.

5. Headache Classification Subcommittee of the International Headache Society (2004) The International Classification of Headache Disorders: 2nd edition. Cephalalgia. 24(Suppl 1):9–160.

6. Wall M (2008) Idiopathic intracranial hypertension (pseudo-tumor cerebri). Curr Neurol Neurosci Rep. 8(2):87–93.

7. Friedman DI, M Wall, SD Silberstein (2008) Headache associated with abnormalities in intracranial structure and function: High cerebrospinal fluid pressure headache and brain tumor. In: Wolff's Headache. Silberstein SD, Lipton RB, Dodick DW, eds. Oxford University Press, New York. 489–511.

8. Chatrath P, A Frosh, A Gore et al (2008) Identification of predictors and development of a screening protocol for cerebello-pontine lesions in patients presenting with audio-vestibular dysfunction. Clin Otolaryngol. 33(2):102–7.

9. Gultekin S, H Celik, S Akpek et al (2008) Vascular loops at the cerebellopontine angle: is there a correlation with tinnitus. AJNR Am J Neuroradiol. 29(9):1746–9.

10. Mackenzie RA, AK Lethlean, R Shnier (1998) Chronic intracranial hypotension. J Clin Neurosci. 5(4):457–60.

11. Mokri B, WI Schievink (2008) Headache associated with abnormalities in intracranial structure and function: Low cerebrospinal fluid pressure headache. In: Wolff's Headache. Silberstein SD, Lipton RB, Dodick DW, eds. Oxford University Press, New York. 513–31.

12. Portier F, C Monteguiaga, E Rey et al (2002) Spontaneous intracranial Hypotension. A rare cause of labyrinthine hydrops Ann Otol Rhinol Laryngol. 112: 817–820.

13. Diener HC, DW Dodick (2008) Headache associated with vascular disorders. In: Wolff's Headache. Silberstein SD, Lipton RB, Dodick DW, eds. Oxford University Press, New York. 473–88.

14. Levine RA (2006) Typewriter tinnitus: a carbamazepine-responsive syndrome related to auditory nerve vascular compression. ORL J Otorhinolaryngol Relat Spec. 68(1):43–6; discussion 46–7.

15. Komatsu F, S Sakamoto, Y Takemura et al (2009) Ruptured tectal arteriovenous malformation demonstrated angiographically after removal of an unruptured occipital lobe arteriovenous malformation. Neurol Med Chir (Tokyo). 49(1): 30–2.

16. Sigari F, E Blair, M Readleaf (2006) Headache with unilateral pulsatile tinnitus in women can signal dural sinus thrombosis. Ann Otol Rhinol Layngol. 115(9):686–9.

17. Láinez JM (2005) Cefalea atribuída a traumatismo craneal y cervical. In: Diagnóstico y tratamiento de la cefalea. Gómez F, Jiménez MD, eds. Ergon, Madrid. 233–48.

18. Young WB, RC Packard, N Ramadan (2001) Headaches associated with head trauma. In: Wolffs Headache and Other Head Pain. 7th edition. Silberstein SD, Lipton RB, Dalessio DJ, eds. Oxford University Press, New York.

19. Evans RW (2004) Postraumatic headaches. Neurol Clin. 22: 237–49.

20. Ramadan NM, MJA Láinez (2006) Chronic postraumatic headaches. In: The Headaches. 3rd edition. Olesen J, Goadsby PJ, Ramadan NM, Tfelt-Hansen P, Welch KMA, eds. Lippincort Willian and Wilkin, Philadelphia. 873–77.

21. Keidel M (2000) Posttraumatic headache. In: Drug Treatment of Migraine and Other Frequent Headaches, Diener HC, ed. Karger, Basel. Monogr Clin Neurosci. 17:329–36.

22. Láinez JM, A Piera (2006) Cefalea postraumática. In: Manejo de las cefaleas refractarias. Pascual J, Láinez JM, eds. Ergon, Madrid. 99–113.

23. Rowlands RG, IK Campbell, GS Kenyon (2009) Otological and vestibular symptoms in patients with low grade (Quebec grades one and two) whiplash injury. J Laryngol Otol. 123(2):182–5.

24. Nageris BI, J Attias, R Shemesh (2008) Otologic and audiologic lesions due to blast injury. J Basic Clin Physiol Pharmacol. 19(3–4):185–91.

25. Rzeski M, A Stepie , Z Kaczorowski (2008) Evaluation of the function of the vestibular system in patients with migraine. Neurol Neurochir Pol. 42(6):518–24.

26. Evans RW, G Ishiyama (2009) Migraine with transient unilateral hearing loss and tinnitus. Headache. 49(5):756–8.

27. Kalaydjian A, K Merikangas (2008) Physical and mental comorbidity of headache in a nationally representative sample of US adults. Psychosom Med. 70(7):773–80. Epub 2008 Aug 25.

28. Andersson G, P Carlbring, V Kaldo et al (2004) Screening of psychiatric disorders via the Internet. A pilot study with tinnitus patients. Nord J Psychiatry 58(4):287–91.

29. Dehmel S, YL Cui, SE Shore (2008) Cross-modal interactions of auditory and somatic inputs in the brainstem and midbrain and their imbalance in tinnitus and deafness. Am J Audiol. 17(2):S193–209.

30. Goadsby PJ (2005) Headache 45(Suppl 1):S14–9.

31. Bartsch T, PJ Goadsby (2003) The trigeminocervical complex and migraine: current concepts and synthesis. Curr Pain Headache Rep 7:371–6.

Chapter 62
Tinnitus and Psychiatric Co-morbidity

Michael Landgrebe and Berthold Langguth

Keypoints

1. Tinnitus is often accompanied by psychiatric co-morbidity, especially in severe forms of tinnitus.
2. Many different co-morbid psychiatric disorders have been reported in individuals with severe tinnitus; among them are depression, anxiety, somatoform disorders, psychosis, personality disorders, and body-concept disorders.
3. The exact relationship between tinnitus and psychiatric disorders may vary from patient to patient. Psychiatric disorders may evolve as a consequence of tinnitus, may represent vulnerability factors, may be consequences of another causal event (e.g., trauma), or may just co-occur with tinnitus without any known cause.
4. All forms of co-morbid psychiatric disorders should be treated specifically.

Keywords Tinnitus • Psychiatric co-morbidity • Affective disorders • Tinnitus severity • Psychotherapy • Psychopharmacotherapy

Introduction

Tinnitus, the perception of a phantom sound, is reported by up to 20% of the general population (see Chap. 5) but most of those who have tinnitus are not severely affected by their tinnitus. Nevertheless, there is a group of individuals with tinnitus, who are severely suffering and sometimes become even suicidal because of their tinnitus [1]. For management of the patient with tinnitus, it is important what causes tinnitus-related distress and disability. It has been shown that individuals with tinnitus with low and high distress do not differ regarding the character of their tinnitus such as pitch, loudness, or tinnitus variability [2, 3]. What, however, differs between these two groups is the presence of psychiatric co-morbidity. Patients with high scores in tinnitus questionnaires such as the tinnitus handicap inventory suffer much more frequently from psychiatric disorders than those with low scores in the tinnitus questionnaires [2, 4–7]. The most frequently reported psychiatric symptoms in this patient group are symptoms of depression and anxiety [4, 7–9]. The incidence of psychiatric disorders such as posttraumatic stress disorder [10, 11], somatoform disorder [12], psychosis [13], obsessive-compulsive disorder [14], or body-image disorder [15] is high among individuals with tinnitus. Published studies agree that there is a high degree of correlation between severe tinnitus and symptoms of depression and anxiety, but the results from different studies vary. This is probably due to differences in kinds of studies (e.g., population survey vs. primary care vs. highly specialized tinnitus centers; [16]). Differences in the used diagnostic criteria [17] also contribute to the variation in results. The exact relationship between tinnitus and psychiatric disorders vary from patient to patient; it may depend on the order of onset of the two symptoms. Psychiatric disorders may develop as a consequence of the individual's tinnitus or because of the individual's vulnerability factors. The interplay between tinnitus and psychiatric symptoms is often complex, and that makes it difficult to determine if tinnitus has caused a reactive psychiatric co-morbidity in an individual patient or if a pre-existing

M. Landgrebe (✉)
Department of Psychiatry, Psychotherapy and Psychosomatics, University of Regensburg, Universitaetsstrasse 84, 93053, Regensburg, Germany
and
Interdisciplinary Tinnitus Clinic, University of Regensburg, Regensburg, Germany
e-mail: michael.landgrebe@medbo.de

but compensated psychiatric disorder flares up due to the tinnitus, or whether a well-managed tinnitus reappears due to the onset of a psychiatric disease.

Recent studies indicate that assessment of psychiatric co-morbidity should not be restricted to chronic tinnitus, but that affective disorders may also occur in acute stages of tinnitus [18]. Also therapeutic interventions should be considered in acute tinnitus, since the amount of distress in the acute stage (<1 week duration) seems to predict the amount of suffering in the chronic situation [19].

Finally, psychiatric disorders that occur together with tinnitus should always be treated specifically, independent on how they are related to the patient's tinnitus. Efficient treatment of the concurrent psychiatric disorder reduces the burden of disease and improves the quality of life of the tinnitus patient. Special emphasis must be directed to emergency of treatment in tinnitus patients who are suicidal (see Chap. 54).

The topic of the following chapters concerns the most frequent co-morbid psychiatric conditions, i.e., emotional trauma, depression, and anxiety including etiological and pathophysiological considerations and the therapeutic management.

References

1. Lewis, JE, Stephens, SD, McKenna, L. Tinnitus and suicide. Clin Otolaryngol Allied Sci, 1994 Feb;19(1):50–4
2. Henry, JL, Wilson, PH. Coping with tinnitus: two studies of psychological and audiological characteristics of patients with high and low tinnitus-related distress. Int Tinnitus J, 1995;1(2):85–92
3. Meikle, MB, Vernon, J, Johnson, RM. The perceived severity of tinnitus. Some observations concerning a large population of tinnitus clinic patients. Otolaryngol Head Neck Surg, 1984 Dec;92(6):689–96
4. Crocetti, A, Forti, S, Ambrosetti, U, Bo, LD. Questionnaires to evaluate anxiety and depressive levels in tinnitus patients. Otolaryngol Head Neck Surg, 2009 Mar;140(3):403–5
5. Marciano, E, Carrabba, L, Giannini, P, Sementina, C, Verde, P, Bruno, C, et al. Psychiatric comorbidity in a population of outpatients affected by tinnitus. Int J Audiol, 2003 Jan;42(1):4–9
6. Sullivan, MD, Katon, W, Dobie, R, Sakai, C, Russo, J, Harrop-Griffiths, J. Disabling tinnitus association with affective disorder. Gen Hosp Psychiatry, 1988 Jul;10(4):285–91
7. Zoger, S, Svedlund, J, Holgers, KM. Relationship between tinnitus severity and psychiatric disorders. Psychosomatics, 2006 Jul;47(4):282–8
8. Belli, S, Belli, H, Bahcebasi, T, Ozcetin, A, Alpay, E, Ertem, U. Assessment of psychopathological aspects and psychiatric comorbidities in patients affected by tinnitus. Eur Arch Otorhinolaryngol, 2008 Mar;265(3):279–85
9. Halford, JB, Anderson, SD. Anxiety and depression in tinnitus sufferers. J Psychosom Res, 1991;35(4–5):383–90
10. Fagelson, MA. The association between tinnitus and posttraumatic stress disorder. Am J Audiol, 2007 Dec;16(2):107–17
11. Hinton, DE, Chhean, D, Pich, V, Hofmann, SG, Barlow, DH. Tinnitus among Cambodian refugees: relationship to PTSD severity. J Trauma Stress, 2006 Aug;19(4):541–6
12. Hiller, W, Janca, A, Burke, KC. Association between tinnitus and somatoform disorders. J Psychosom Res, 1997 Dec; 43(6):613–24
13. D'Amelio, R, Delb, W. Comorbidity of schizophrenic psychosis and tinnitus. A hitherto neglected theme in research and therapy. HNO, 2008 Jul;56(7):670–2
14. Folmer, RL, Griest, SE, Martin, WH. Obsessive-compulsiveness in a population of tinnitus patients. Int Tinnitus J, 2008; 14(2):127–30
15. Stuerz, K, Lafenthaler, M, Pfaffenberger, N, Kopp, M, Gutweniger, S, Guenther, V. Body image and body concept in patients with chronic tinnitus. Eur Arch Otorhinolaryngol, 2009 Jul;266(7):961–5
16. Andersson, G, Kaldo-Sandstrom, V, Strom, L, Stromgren, T. Internet administration of the Hospital Anxiety and Depression Scale in a sample of tinnitus patients. J Psychosom Res, 2003 Sep;55(3):259–62
17. Andersson, G, Carlbring, P, Kaldo, V, Strom, L. Screening of psychiatric disorders via the Internet. A pilot study with tinnitus patients. Nord J Psychiatry, 2004;58(4):287–91
18. Konzag, TA, Rubler, D, Bandemer-Greulich, U, Frommer, J, Fikentscher, E. Psychological comorbidity in subacute and chronic tinnitus outpatients. Z Psychosom Med Psychother, 2005;51(3):247–60
19. D'Amelio, R, Archonti, C, Scholz, S, Falkai, P, Plinkert, PK, Delb, W. Psychological distress associated with acute tinnitus. HNO, 2004 Jul;52(7):599–603

Chapter 63
Tinnitus and Depression

Berthold Langguth and Michael Landgrebe

Keypoints

1. There is an increased prevalence of depressive symptoms in individuals with tinnitus.
2. Affective disorders, together with personality factors, play an important role in creating the distress experienced by many individuals with tinnitus.
3. The co-occurrence of tinnitus and depression may be explained by the involvement of limbic brain structures in the pathophysiology of tinnitus.
4. Tinnitus is associated with neuroendocrine alterations, which are characteristic for depressive disorders.
5. Patients with tinnitus and depression should be efficiently treated.
6. Efficient treatment of co-morbid depressive symptoms has to consider a large variety of possible underlying disorders.

Keywords Tinnitus-related distress • Depression • Psychiatric co-morbidity • Limbic brain areas • Quality of life • Suicide

Abbreviations

DCN   Dorsal cochlear nucleus
PTSD   Post traumatic stress disorder
ICD   International classification of diseases
DSM   Diagnositic and statistical manual of mental disorders

Introduction

There is abundant evidence of increased prevalence of depressive symptoms in individuals with tinnitus [1–10]. This is especially the case in individuals with disabling tinnitus [2, 3]. Also, high correlations between scores in tinnitus severity measures and depression scales have been reported [6, 9]. Thus, the occurrence of co-morbid depression may explain to some extent why some individuals suffer severely from tinnitus, whereas other individuals are not bothered by their tinnitus. Further studies have shown an additional role for specific personality traits such as anxiety, obsessiveness, neuroticism, or agreeableness [9, 11, 12]. However, it is important to note that all these findings are mainly derived from studies that used self-report questionnaires for the assessment of depressive symptoms, not from structured interviews. This difference is important, since the presence of depressive symptoms does not automatically mean that a patient fulfills diagnostic criteria for a depressive disorder. Depressive symptoms may be indicative of a depressive disorder, but they can also occur in the context of a large variety of other psychiatric disorders, such as bipolar disorders, personality disorders, anxiety disorders, dementia, or addiction, just to name a few. Therefore, further studies using structured interviews will be needed to determine exactly the prevalence of co-morbid psychiatric disorders in tinnitus.

B. Langguth (✉)
Department of Psychiatry and Psychotherapy, University of Regensburg, Universitätsstraße 84, 93053 Regensburg, Germany
and
Interdisciplinary Tinnitus Clinic, University of Regensburg, Regensburg, Germany
e-mail: Berthold.Langguth@medbo.de

Depression

Diagnosis of Depression

For non-psychiatrists, detection of depressive symptomatology is obviously difficult. However, the use of simple screening questions may help to identify potential depression. The following two questions have been proposed as a screening method for depression: "During the past month have you often been bothered by feeling down, depressed, or hopeless?"; "During the past month have you often been bothered by little interest or pleasure in doing things?" [13]. If the patient answers with "yes" to one of the questions, depression is likely and further diagnosis by a psychiatrist or psychologist should be initiated. A more detailed screening instrument is the Mini-International Neuropsychiatric Interview [M.I.N.I., [14]]. As mentioned above, depressive symptoms may occur in a variety of psychiatric diseases. The exact differential diagnosis is of importance, since it has important consequences for the therapeutical management. For example, depressive symptoms can occur in the context of a bipolar affective disorder or a posttraumatic stress disorder, which requires completely different therapeutic management than major depression. Thus, when screening questions suggest potential co-morbid depression, a psychiatrist should be involved in further diagnostic assessment and therapeutic management.

The exact diagnostic classification may further depend on the classification system. The most widely used classification systems are the "*Diagnostic and Statistical Manual of Mental Disorders*" of the American Psychiatric Association (DSM-IV) [15] and the "*International Classification of Diseases*" of the WHO (ICD-10) [16]. Classification criteria for major depression (DSM IV) and depressive disorders (ICD 10) are displayed in Tables 63.1 and 63.2.

Interplay Between Tinnitus and Depression

Given the association between tinnitus and depressive symptoms, the question about the nature of the relationship arises. Clinical experience suggests that all kinds of relationships may occur: Depressive symptoms may develop as a reaction to tinnitus. Specific vulnerability factors such as anxious or obsessive personality traits may contribute to the development of such depressive reactions. In other cases, where tinnitus exists for a long time without causing any substantial distress, a depressive episode may lead to decompensation of the tinnitus with subsequent impairment in quality of life. There is also the possibility that tinnitus and depressive symptoms are consequences of a third condition (e.g. traumatic event). Finally, tinnitus and depressive disorders may also co-occur incidentally since both are relative frequent conditions. In clinical practice, differential diagnosis of all relevant factors contributing to tinnitus distress is of importance, since all these factors may represent potential targets for treatment. As an example, let us consider a patient who complains about chronic tinnitus with variations of perceived distress, ranging between severe disturbances to none at all. Psychiatric exploration may reveal a co-morbid seasonal affective disorder or a co-morbid bipolar disorder, which explains the variations in tinnitus distress. In this case, the co-morbid psychiatric condition should be specifically treated with the primary aim of mood stabilization, which in turn will lead to decreased variations of distress and impairment.

Similarities Between the Pathophysiology of Tinnitus and Depression

Pathophysiologic models of tinnitus have claimed the involvement of frontal and limbic brain regions. In his neurophysiological model of tinnitus, Jastreboff hypothesized in detail that the prefrontal cortex may be the brain structure that integrates sensory and emotional aspects of tinnitus and may be involved in the emotional and autonomic reaction to tinnitus [17]. The activation of the non-classical (extralemniscal) ascending auditory pathways in some forms of tinnitus [18] (see Chap. 10) may explain the coactivation of cortical association areas, limbic areas, and the autonomic nervous system [19]. Recent neuroimaging studies (in non-depressed individuals with tinnitus) have confirmed the involvement of the prefrontal cortex, the subgenual frontal cortex, and the amygdalo-hippocampal area in the pathophysiology of tinnitus (for review see [20, 21] or Chap. 17, 18, 19).

Table 63.1 DSM IV criteria of major depression [15]

A. Five (or more) of the following symptoms have been present during the same 2-week period and represent a change from previous functioning; at least one of the symptoms is either depressed mood or loss of interest or pleasure: Note: Does not include symptoms that are clearly due to a general medical condition, or mood-incongruent delusions or hallucinations.

1. Depressed mood most of the day, nearly every day, as indicated by either subjective report (e.g. feels sad or empty) or observation made by others (e.g. appears tearful). Note: In children and adolescents, this can be an irritable mood;
2. Markedly diminished interest or pleasure in all (or almost all) activities most of the day, nearly every day (as indicated by either a subjective account or observations made by others);
3. Significant weight loss when not dieting or weight gain (e.g. a change of more than 5% of body weight in a month), or change in appetite nearly every day. Note: In children, consider failure to make expected weight gains;
4. Insomnia or hypersomnia nearly every day;
5. Psychomotor agitation or retardation nearly every day (observable by others, not merely subjective feelings of restlessness or being slowed down);
6. Fatigue or loss of energy nearly every day;
7. Feelings of worthlessness or excessive or inappropriate guilt (which may be delusional) nearly every day (not merely self-reproach or guilt about being sick);
8. Diminished ability to think or concentrate, or indecisiveness, nearly every day (either by subjective account or as observed by others);
9. Recurrent thoughts of death (not just fear of dying), recurrent suicidal ideation without a specific plan, or a suicide attempt or a specific plan for committing suicide.

B. The symptoms do not meet criteria for a Mixed Episode.
C. The symptoms cause clinically significant distress or impairment in social, occupational, or other important areas of functioning.
D. The symptoms are not due to the direct physiological effects of a substance (e.g. a drug of abuse, a medication) or a general medical condition (e.g. hypothyroidism).
E. The symptoms are not better accounted for by bereavement (i.e. after the loss of a loved one), the symptoms persist for longer than 2 months, or are characterized by marked functional impairment, morbid preoccupation with worthlessness, suicidal ideation, psychotic symptoms, or psychomotor retardation.

Table 63.2 ICD 10 criteria for depressive episode [16]

A. General criteria for depressive episode:
1. The depressive episode should last for at least 2 weeks.
2. The episode is not attributable to psychoactive substance use or any organic mental disorder.
B. Presence of at least two of the following symptoms:
1. Depressed mood to a degree that is definitively abnormal for the individual, present for most of the day and almost every day, largely uninfluenced by environmental circumstances, and sustained for at least 2 weeks.
2. Marked loss of interest or ability to enjoy activities that were previously pleasurable.
3. Decreased energy or increased fatigability.
C. An additional symptom or symptoms from the following should be present, to give a total of at least four:
1. Loss of confidence and self-esteem and feelings of inferiority;
2. Unreasonable feelings of self-reproaches or excessive and inappropriate guilt;
3. Recurrent thoughts of death or suicide or any suicidal behavior;
4. Complaints or evidence of diminished ability to concentrate or think, accompanied by indecisiveness or vacillation;
5. Change in psychomotor activity, with agitation or inhibition;
6. Sleep disturbances of any type;
7. Changes in appetite (decrease or increase) with corresponding weight change;
D. There may or may not be the somatic syndrome.

These brain areas are well known as critical parts of brain networks, functionally altered in individuals with depressive disorders [22, 23]. Thus, imaging data suggest that the neuronal correlates of tinnitus and depression overlap in limbic networks, which provides a possible explanation for the co-occurrence of tinnitus and depressive symptoms.

In this context, an important role for the dorsal cochlear nucleus (DCN) has also been proposed [24]. There is increasing evidence from animal studies that the DCN is an important contributor to tinnitus. There are direct projections from the DCN to brain stem structures such as the locus coeruleus, reticular formation, and raphe nuclei which are the principle sites for synthesis of serotonine and noradrenaline and are implicated in the control of attention and emotional responses. Thus, attentional and emotional disorders, such as anxiety and depression, commonly associated with tinnitus may result from an interplay between these non-auditory brainstem structures and the DCN [24].

Also, serotonergic dysfunction, which is assumed to play an important role in the pathophysiology of depression [25], has been suggested to be involved in tinnitus [26, 27]. However, evidence for this hypothesis is scarce.

Finally, neuroendocrine alterations such as a hypothalamic–pituitary–adrenal axis dysfunction, which are pathognomonic for stress-related disorders such as depression or posttraumatic stress disorder (PTSD) [28, 29] have been described in tinnitus patients [30, 31], indicating another pathophysiological overlap between tinnitus and affective disorders. Interestingly, a recent study has shown that tinnitus patients differ only slightly from controls in physiological reactivity during stress tests, indicating relatively normal psychophysiological reactivity [32].

Depression

Treatment Options for Depression

There are several reasons why patients with tinnitus and depression should be promptly and efficiently treated. Efficient treatment depends on the exact etiology of co-morbid depressive symptoms to tinnitus. If diagnostic assessment reveals a major depression (see Table 63.1), standard treatment options include antidepressants and psychotherapy. There is a large variety of antidepressants available, which differ in their mechanisms of action and side effects. Also, there are some antidepressants that specifically address specific symptoms of depression. For example, amitriptylin and mirtazapin have sedative effects and are preferentially used in patients with insomnia, whereas venlafaxine, duloxetine, and bupropion exert an activating effect and are preferred in patients who suffer from loss of energy. Thus, the choice of the best antidepressant is complex and depends on previous patient's experience with specific drugs, the predominant symptoms of depression and co-morbidities. Also, cognitive behavioral therapy has been shown to be efficient in the treatment of depression. Further non-pharmacologic treatment options include light therapy, sleep deprivation, aerobic exercise, transcranial magnetic stimulation or electroconvulsive therapy.

Several antidepressants have been investigated for their use in tinnitus [33, 34] (see Chap. 78). Two randomized double-blind placebo-controlled studies investigated the effects of antidepressants in patients with tinnitus and co-morbid depression [35, 36]. The tricyclic nortriptyline significantly reduced depression scores, tinnitus disability scores, and tinnitus loudness relative to placebo [1]. Also the serotonin reuptake inhibitor sertraline was significantly more effective than placebo in reducing tinnitus severity [2]. In both studies, reduction in tinnitus disability scores correlated high with reduction of depression scores, suggesting that antidepressants have beneficial results in depressed tinnitus patients, but that this is mainly due to the antidepressant effect of the drug.

However, induction or worsening of tinnitus has also been reported in the context of treatment with antidepressants, both as a side effect of drugs such as phenelzine, amitriptyline, protriptyline, doxepin, imipramine, fluoxetine, trazadone, bupropion, and venlafaxine. Worsening of tinnitus has also been associated with withdrawal of antidepressants (venlafaxine and sertraline) [37]. Interestingly, transcranial magnetic stimulation of the dorsolateral prefrontal cortex, performed for the treatment of depression, has also been described to induce and worsen tinnitus in rare cases [38]. This suggests that tinnitus can be generated or worsened by modulation of neural activity in the frontal cortex. Thus, the complex interactions between antidepressant treatment and tinnitus may be explained by antidepressant-induced modulation of frontal cortex networks [39], which in turn may result in altered top–down control of activity in the central auditory pathways.

Suicidal Tendency

Depression can become life-threatening by leading to suicidal ideation. The most important risk factor for suicide is depressive disorder, both in tinnitus patients [40–42] and in non-tinnitus patients [43, 44]. Further risk factors include male gender, elder age, and social isolation [3]. In tinnitus patients with depression, suicidal tendencies have to be assessed because a high risk of suicide requires immediate action. This sensitive area can be approached by asking the patient about passive suicidal ideations (for more details, see Chap. 54). It is important to know that asking about suicidal thoughts does not increase the risk of committing suicide.

References

1. Sullivan, MD, Katon, W, Dobie, R, Sakai, C, Russo, J, Harrop-Griffiths, J Disabling tinnitus Association with affective disorder Gen Hosp Psychiatry, 1988 Jul;10(4): 285–91

2. Halford, JB, Anderson, SD Anxiety and depression in tinnitus sufferers J Psychosom Res, 1991;35(4–5):383–90

3. Henry, JL, Wilson, PH Coping with tinnitus: two studies of psychological and audiological characteristics of patients with high and low tinnitus-related distress. Int Tinnitus J, 1995;1(2):85–92

4. Folmer, RL, Griest, SE, Meikle, MB, Martin, WH Tinnitus severity, loudness, and depression Otolaryngol Head Neck Surg, 1999 Jul;121(1):48–51

5. Marciano, E, Carrabba, L, Giannini, P, Sementina, C, Verde, P, Bruno, C, et al Psychiatric comorbidity in a population of outpatients affected by tinnitus Int J Audiol, 2003 Jan; 42(1):4–9

6. Robinson, SK, McQuaid, JR, Viirre, ES, Betzig, LL, Miller, DL, Bailey, KA, et al Relationship of tinnitus questionnaires to depressive symptoms, quality of well-being, and internal focus Int Tinnitus J, 2003;9(2):97–103

7. Unterrainer, J, Greimel, KV, Leibetseder, M, Koller, T Experiencing tinnitus: which factors are important for perceived severity of the symptom? Int Tinnitus J, 2003; 9(2):130–3

8. Zoger, S, Svedlund, J, Holgers, KM Relationship between tinnitus severity and psychiatric disorders Psychosomatics, 2006;47(4):282–8

9. Langguth, B, Kleinjung, T, Fischer, B, Hajak, G, Eichhammer, P, Sand, PG Tinnitus severity, depression, and the big five personality traits Prog Brain Res, 2007;166:221–5

10. Crocetti, A, Forti, S, Ambrosetti, U, Bo, LD Questionnaires to evaluate anxiety and depressive levels in tinnitus patients Otolaryngol Head Neck Surg, 2009 Mar;140(3): 403–5

11. Weber, JH, Jagsch, R, Hallas, B The relationship between tinnitus, personality, and depression Z Psychosom Med Psychother, 2008;54(3):227–40

12. Folmer, RL, Griest, SE, Martin, WH Obsessive-compulsiveness in a population of tinnitus patients Int Tinnitus J, 2008;14(2):127–30

13. Whooley, MA, Simon, GE Managing depression in medical outpatients N Engl J Med, 2000 Dec 28;343(26):1942–50

14. Sheehan, DV, Lecrubier, Y, Sheehan, KH, Amorim, P, Janavs, J, Weiller, E, et al The Mini-International Neuropsychiatric Interview (MINI): the development and validation of a structured diagnostic psychiatric interview for DSM-IV and ICD-10 J Clin Psychiatry, 1998;59 Suppl 20:22–33; quiz 34–57:22–33

15. American Psychiatric Association Diagnostic and Statistical Manual of Mental Disorders – DSM-IV-TR (4th edition, Text Revision) 4th ed Washington, DC: 2000

16. International Statistical Classification of Diseases and Related Health Problems 10th Revision 2007

17. Jastreboff, PJ Phantom auditory perception (tinnitus): mechanisms of generation and perception Neurosci Res, 1990; 8:221–54

18. Møller, AR, Møller, MB, Yokota, M Some forms of tinnitus may involve the extralemniscal auditory pathway Laryngoscope, 1992 Oct;102(10):1165–71

19. Møller, AR Pathophysiology of tinnitus Otolaryngol Clin North Am, 2003;36:249–66

20. Lanting, CP, De, KE, Van, DP Neural activity underlying tinnitus generation: results from PET and fMRI Hear Res, 2009 Sep;255(1–2):1–13

21. Adjamian, P, Sereda, M, Hall, DA The mechanisms of tinnitus: Perspectives from human functional neuroimaging Hear Res, 2009 Apr 11

22. Drevets, WC, Price, JL, Furey, ML Brain structural and functional abnormalities in mood disorders: implications for neurocircuitry models of depression Brain Struct Funct, 2008 Sep;213(1–2):93–118

23. Mayberg, HS Positron emission tomography imaging in depression: a neural systems perspective Neuroimaging Clin N Am, 2003 Nov;13(4):805–15

24. Kaltenbach, JA The dorsal cochlear nucleus as a participant in the auditory, attentional and emotional components of tinnitus Hear Res, 2006 Jun;216–217:224–34

25. Neumeister, A Tryptophan depletion, serotonin, and depression: where do we stand? Psychopharmacol Bull, 2003; 37(4):99–115

26. Tyler, RS, Coelho, C, Noble, W Tinnitus: standard of care, personality differences, genetic factors ORL J Otorhinolaryngol Relat Spec, 2006;68(1):14–9

27. Simpson, JJ, Davies, WE (2000) A review of evidence in support of a role for 5-HT in the perception of tinnitus. Hear Res, 145:1–7

28. Holsboer F, Ising M (2008) Central CRH system in depression and anxiety – evidence from clinical studies with CRH1 receptor antagonists. Eur J Pharmacol, 583(2–3):350–7

29. Nemeroff, CB The corticotropin-releasing factor (CRF) hypothesis of depression: new findings and new directions Mol Psychiatry, 1996 Sep;1(4):336–42

30 Hebert, S, Lupien, SJ Salivary cortisol levels, subjective stress, and tinnitus intensity in tinnitus sufferers during noise exposure in the laboratory Int J Hyg Environ Health, 2009 Jan;212(1):37–44

31. Hebert, S, Lupien, SJ The sound of stress: blunted cortisol reactivity to psychosocial stress in tinnitus sufferers Neurosci Lett, 2007 Jan 10;411(2):138–42

32. Heinecke, K, Weise, C, Schwarz, K, Rief, W Physiological and psychological stress reactivity in chronic tinnitus J Behav Med, 2008 Jun;31(3):179–88

33. Robinson, S Antidepressants for treatment of tinnitus Prog Brain Res, 2007;166:263–71

34. Baldo, P, Doree, C, Lazzarini, R, Molin, P, McFerran, DJ Antidepressants for patients with tinnitus Cochrane Database Syst Rev, 2006;(4):CD003853

35. Sullivan, M, Katon, W, Russo, J, Dobie, R, Sakai, C A randomized trial of nortriptyline for severe chronic tinnitus Effects on depression, disability, and tinnitus symptoms Arch Intern Med, 1993 Oct 11;153(19):2251–9

36. Zoger, S, Svedlund, J, Holgers, KM The effects of sertraline on severe tinnitus suffering – a randomized, double-blind, placebo-controlled study J Clin Psychopharmacol, 2006 Feb;26(1):32–9

37. Robinson, SK, Viirre, ES, Stein, MB Antidepressant therapy in tinnitus Hear Res, 2007 Apr;226(1–2):221–31

38. Marcondes, R, Fregni, F, Pascual-Leone, A Tinnitus and brain activation: insights from transcranial magnetic stimulation Ear Nose Throat J, 2006 Apr;85(4):233–8

39. Ishizaki, J, Yamamoto, H, Takahashi, T, Takeda, M, Yano, M, Mimura, M Changes in regional cerebral blood flow following antidepressant treatment in late-life depression Int J Geriatr Psychiatry, 2008 Aug;23(8):805–11

40. Lewis, JE, Stephens, SD, McKenna, L Tinnitus and suicide Clin Otolaryngol Allied Sci, 1994 Feb;19(1):50–4

41. Turner, O, Windfuhr, K, Kapur, N Suicide in deaf populations: a literature review Ann Gen Psychiatry, 2007 Oct 8;6:26:26

42. Jacobson, GP, McCaslin, DL A search for evidence of a direct relationship between tinnitus and suicide J Am Acad Audiol, 2001 Nov;12(10):493–6

43. Lejoyeux, M, Leon, E, Rouillon, F Prevalence and risk factors of suicide and attempted suicide Encephale, 1994 Sep;20(5):495–503

44. Hawton, K, van, HK Suicide Lancet, 2009 Apr 18;373(9672):1372–81

Chapter 64
Tinnitus and Anxiety

Michael Landgrebe and Berthold Langguth

Keypoints

1. Individuals with tinnitus often suffer from anxiety.
2. Such co-morbid anxiety is associated with increased severity of tinnitus and distress as well as general impairment of quality of life.
3. Similar brain areas are involved in the pathogenesis of tinnitus and anxiety disorders indicating a close interrelationship between these two disorders.
4. Hyperacusis and phonophobia represent specific problems in a subset of tinnitus patients who require special attention.
5. Treatment of concurrent anxiety symptoms in tinnitus patients is essential.
6. Treatment options include pharmacological (e.g. antidepressants) and psychotherapeutic (e.g. cognitive behavioral therapy, tinnitus-retraining therapy) approaches.

Keywords Anxiety • Chronic tinnitus • Pharmacotherapy • Psychotherapy

Abbreviations

CIDI-SF   Composite diagnostic interview
ICD   International classification of diseases
SNRI   Selective serotonin and noradrenalin reuptake inhibitor

M. Landgrebe (✉)
Department of Psychiatry, Psychosomatics, and Psychotherapy, University of Regensburg, Universitaetsstrasse 84, 93053 Regensburg, Germany
and
Interdisciplinary Tinnitus Clinic, University of Regensburg, Regensburg, Germany
e-mail: michael.landgrebe@medbo.de

SSRI   Selective serotonin reuptake inhibitor
WHO   World Health Organization

Introduction

Anxiety belongs to the most basic physiological emotions of human beings. It represents a biosocial signal contributing to the development of normal interpersonal relations and a risk-sensitive interaction with the environment. Anxiety is an indicator of thread and points to potential dangers. The subjective perception of anxiety and its related threads, however, is very much influenced by learning processes, which gradually leads to modified perceptions and cognitive evaluations of internal and external dangers. This, in turn, determines the individual level of tolerated anxiety and forms the behavioral styles to recover safety. Hence, anxiety subserves important physiological functions, which are essential for survival. In this respect, anxiety does not represent a pathological symptom. However, it gains clinical relevance in cases of too much or too little anxiety.

Symptomatology, Epidemiology, and Etiopathogenesis of Anxiety Disorders

Anxiety as a symptom may be part of almost every psychiatric disease. If anxiety reaches an extraordinary level, is subjectively perceived as unrealistic, causes a high burden, and impairs social functioning, it may be regarded as a disease and the diagnosis of an anxiety disorder may be fulfilled. In general, anxiety appears

A.R. Møller et al. (eds.), *Textbook of Tinnitus*,
DOI 10.1007/978-1-60761-145-5_64, © Springer Science+Business Media, LLC 2011

always on different levels; i.e. an emotional, cognitive (e.g. subjective beliefs regarding danger), a motor (e.g. behavioral attitudes such as fight, fright, or flight), and an autonomic level (e.g. somatic reactions such as tachycardia, stress hormone secretion, etc.). In the International Classification of diseases of the WHO (ICD-10), diagnostic criteria for several anxiety disorders have been defined. These are phobic disorders (ICD-10: F40; e.g. agoraphobia, social, and specific phobias) and other anxiety disorders (ICD-10: F41; e.g. panic disorder, generalized anxiety disorder, anxiety and depression mixed). Phobic disorders are characterized in that way, the anxiety mainly occurs in specific situations or in response to specific things which are normally not dangerous to the individual (e.g. fear of public places, busses, etc. or fear of specific things, e.g., spiders). In contrast, in the other anxiety disorders, symptoms occur independently of specific triggers. Both forms of anxiety disorders have in common that individuals try to avoid situations associated with anxiety. This, in turn, stabilizes the symptoms, because avoidance behavior prevents them from realizing that the anticipated danger is not real and hampers them from learning adaptive strategies.

Similar avoidance behavior is also found in tinnitus patients. Especially, in people suffering from hyperacusis, phonophobia develops frequently and noise is avoided. However, the avoidance of sound is counterproductive, since there is clear evidence that reduced environmental sound increases phantom auditory perceptions such as tinnitus [1]. Hence, this avoidance behavior represents one core target of cognitive behavioral therapeutic interventions, both in anxiety disorders and in tinnitus.

Anxiety disorders are prevalent. Lifetime prevalence rates range from about 1.2% for panic disorder up to 5% for specific phobias. Due to diverging diagnostic criteria, prevalence rates vary substantially between studies. The most frequent anxiety disorder seems to be social phobia, where lifetime prevalence rates of 13.3% have been reported [2]. The lifetime prevalence for anxiety disorders overall is about 10% [3]. Anxiety is even more frequent in individuals with tinnitus. Various studies reported anxiety in 19% up to 45% [4–6]. A recent study using an Internet-adapted version of the WHO short form of the Composite Diagnostic Interview (CIDI-SF [7]) found 12-month prevalence rates of 60% for generalized anxiety disorder, 83% for specific phobia, 67% for social phobia, 58% for agoraphobia, and

21% for panic disorder in a self-selected population of tinnitus patients [7]. Although these data have to be interpreted with caution, because they have been collected by internet survey and verification of the diagnoses by a psychiatrist was not performed, this study, together with the others, indicates that anxiety is a common phenomenon among individuals with tinnitus. Its clinical relevance is further underlined by the fact that tinnitus severity and distress are linked to co-morbid anxiety and depression [8], which is very often also a co-morbid condition in anxiety disorders. Hence, detection and diagnosis of anxiety symptoms in tinnitus patients represents an important task for every health care professional dealing with tinnitus patients. Especially, in severe forms with substantial impairment in quality of life, the probability of a co-morbid psychiatric disorder such as anxiety or depression is increased. In those cases, detailed exploration for anxiety symptoms should be performed. Screening questions, which are used in structured clinical interviews, may be helpful (see Chap. 54). However, in case of suspicion of an anxiety disorder, further diagnosis and treatment should be done by a psychiatrist or psychologist. Potential treatment options will be discussed later in this chapter.

The etiopathogenesis of anxiety symptoms is multifactorial. Anxiety patients are often characterized by some accentuated personality traits (e.g. introversion and neuroticism). Other important factors are dysfunctional cognitive processes, anxiety sensitivity, and attentional bias. A behavioral consequence of these dysfunctional cognitions is biased perceptions of potential dangers, misinterpretation of physiological signs (such as heart beat) as signals of danger, and the feeling of being unable to control these symptoms. Many aspects of such dysfunctional cognitions are also frequently found in tinnitus patients, even if they do not suffer from anxiety symptoms. For example, being unable to control their tinnitus and the fear that the tinnitus will get worse are very often mentioned by tinnitus patients as one major reason to seek medical help. It is important to note that these fearful beliefs depend to a large extent on the interaction and communication between patient and health care providers. By exaggerating the risk of dangerous diseases, which may underlie tinnitus (e.g. brain tumors), medical doctors may cause anxiety, and can also do so by informing the patient that there is no help for their tinnitus and that they have to live with it. Hence, the way information about tinnitus – its pathophysiological basis and potential treatment options – is provided may be critical for the way a patient learns to deal with tinnitus. Informing the patient in an empathic way and providing hope are important factors for preventing the development of anxiety (see Chap. 70). This is even more important since there is evidence that anticipatory processes and dysfunctional activation of a cortical distress network seems to play a role in the pathophysiology of tinnitus [9]. Cognitive behavioral treatment strategies in tinnitus patients focus on these dysfunctional cognitive and anticipatory processes and have been shown to be able to improve quality of life in tinnitus patients [10].

On a neurobiological level, many different brain regions have been identified to be involved in the generation of arousal and anxiety. The arousal level is under the control of brain stem nuclei, mainly the locus coeruleus [11]. But arousal alone is not equal to anxiety. Anxiety depends also on connoted emotions, which are generated within the limbic system and involves structures such as the amygdale, hippocampus, septal nuclei, and the hypothalamus. Recent studies point to a critical role of the amygdale in generation of anxiety, especially in the formation of emotional, anxiety-related memories [12]. There is emerging evidence that the limbic system is also involved in the pathogenesis of tinnitus. A variety of studies have shown functional activations [13–15], as well as structural alterations [16, 17], in limbic areas in individuals with tinnitus, pointing to a role of these structures in the pathogenesis of tinnitus. This is further underlined by the fact that the severity of tinnitus is closely related to concurrent symptoms of anxiety and depression [18]. Just by treating these symptoms, the functional impairment of tinnitus patients may be improved [19].

In summary, anxiety is a frequent symptom, which may occur as a normal physiological phenomenon but also in the context of almost every somatic or psychiatric disorder. Anxiety is a common phenomenon in individuals with tinnitus, and prevalence rates of anxiety disorders are very high. Furthermore, anxiety is often associated with depression. Neurobiology shows that tinnitus and both depression and anxiety share similar neural circuits underlining the close interrelationship of these syndromes. Finally, tinnitus severity is associated with co-morbid anxiety and depression, indicating the necessity to detect and treat these symptoms when treating patients with tinnitus.

Hyperacusis and Phonophobia

Hyperacusis and phonophobia, which often occur together with tinnitus, may complicate treatment of tinnitus in some patients. Hyperacusis has been defined as lowered tolerance to ordinary environmental sounds, or as a consistently exaggerated [20] or inappropriate response to sounds that are neither threatening nor uncomfortably loud to a typical person [21]. In phonophobia, specific sounds evoke negative emotions such as anxiety and fear. Phonophobia represents a form of a specific phobia. Hyperacusis may occur in context of some underlying somatic conditions such as disorders of the facial nerve (e.g. Bell's palsy) or neuropsychiatric disorders such as migraine, depression, or posttraumatic stress disorder (see Chap. 3, see (22)). Prevalence rates of hyperacusis in the general population vary between 9% [23] and 15% [24]. Among tinnitus patients attending a tinnitus clinic, prevalence rates of up to 40% have been reported [22].

The pathophysiological mechanisms of hyperacusis are not yet identified, and several potential mechanisms have been discussed [22]. Among these, alterations of serotonergic neurotransmission have been postulated [25]. Evidence for this hypothesis derives from findings that hyperacusis tends to occur in diseases where serotonergic neurotransmission is altered (e.g. migraine, depression, or posttraumatic stress disorder), indicating again a close pathophysiological relationship of tinnitus and hyperacusis to depression and anxiety. But also via direct connections from the central auditory system to the amygdale, specific or more general sounds can induce emotions of fear and anxiety. These unconscious conditioning processes, linking sounds to emotions, have been postulated to be one major mechanism by which hyperacusis may occur [26]. Treatment strategies such as tinnitus-retraining therapy aim to disconnect these dysfunctional connections [27].

Treatment Strategies

The importance of efficient treatment of co-morbid anxiety symptoms in tinnitus patients has already been extensively discussed in this chapter. However, before treatment can be initiated, a clear diagnosis of the anxiety disorder should be made, which requires in most cases the consultation of a psychiatrist. In cases of a diagnosed anxiety disorder, principal treatment options are pharmacotherapy and psychotherapy. First-line pharmacological treatment options for anxiety disorders such as panic disorder, social phobia, and generalized anxiety disorder are antidepressants, predominantly serotonin reuptake inhibitors (SSRI) and combined serotonin and noradrenalin reuptake inhibitors (SNRI; e.g. venlafaxine or duloxetine). But also mirtazapine or tricyclic antidepressants may have beneficial effect. For patients with tinnitus and anxiety, improvement of tinnitus has been reported under treatment with antidepressants (see Chap. 63). The selection of an antidepressant for the individual patient may depend on other symptoms such as agitation and/or sleep problems or concurrent other medical conditions or the necessity of other medication, which may increase the risk of unfavorable drug–drug interactions. Therefore, it is advisable that pharmacological treatment is managed by a psychiatrist. Besides classical antidepressants, some other substances may sometimes have beneficial effects in treatment of tinnitus patients with anxiety. For example, the antiepileptic drug pregabalin has been shown to be effective in the treatment of generalized anxiety disorder and has recently also been approved for this indication. Thus, pregabalin represents an additional option for the treatment of anxiety disorders in tinnitus patients.

In contrast to antidepressants and pregabalin, which exert their anxiolytic effects after continuous treatment over weeks to months, benzodiazepines have acute anxiolytic properties. Several pilot studies also suggest beneficial effects of benzodiazepines on tinnitus (see Chap. 78). However, benzodiazepines are regarded to be addictive, and therefore regular use over longer periods of time should be avoided. Also, protracted tinnitus has been reported after discontinuation of benzodiazepines [28]. Thus, the administration of benzodiazepines in treatment of anxiety in tinnitus patients should be restricted to use as rescue medication. For this purpose, short-acting substances such as alprazolam should be preferred. Sometimes, already, the availability of this efficient rescue medication gives the patient some form of control over his/her symptoms and reduces the fear of developing severe anxiety or panic attacks.

Psychotherapy is the other important treatment option, especially in patients with tinnitus who are severely affected and have psychological distress symptoms [29]. Cognitive behavioral therapy aims at modifying dysfunctional cognitions and avoidance behavior in the context of tinnitus. A recent meta-analysis of 285 tinnitus patients showed that tinnitus-specific cognitive behavioral therapy contributes to a positive management of tinnitus and leads to improvement in quality of life [10]. However, this meta-analysis did not reveal improvement in the subjective loudness of tinnitus or on associated depression. The latter suggests that patients with tinnitus and co-morbid anxiety or depression may require specific forms of psychotherapy, which focus primarily on their co-morbid psychiatry disorders.

Avoidance of unpleasant sounds represents a substantial problem in individuals who have hyperacusis and phonophobia in addition to their tinnitus. Both hyperacusis and phonophobia can be efficiently treated by cognitive behavioral therapy [30]. Another treatment option represents tinnitus-retraining therapy, which is based on the neurophysiological model of tinnitus [26] (see also Chap. 73). This model postulates involvement of the limbic and autonomic nervous systems in all cases of clinically significant tinnitus and points out the importance of both conscious and subconscious connections between limbic and auditory pathway structures. Tinnitus-retraining therapy aims at extinction of these dysfunctional unconscious connections in order to allow habituation to tinnitus. Similarly, tinnitus-retraining therapy is also assumed to be efficient for the treatment of hyperacusis [27].

In summary, in patients with tinnitus and concurrent anxiety symptoms or anxiety disorder, a broad variety of pharmacological and available psychotherapeutic treatment options can have beneficial effect on both tinnitus and anxiety. Decisions for the best individual treatment require psychiatric experience and depend on individual symptoms that may be concomitant with other medical conditions and depending on the individual patient's acceptance.

References

1. Heller MF, Bergman M. Tinnitus aurium in normally hearing persons. Ann Otol Rhinol Laryngol 1953;62(1):73–83
2. Kessler RC, Crum RM, Warner LA, Nelson CB, Schulenberg J, Anthony JC. Lifetime co-occurrence of DSM-III-R alcohol abuse and dependence with other psychiatric disorders in the

National Comorbidity Survey. Arch Gen Psychiatry 1997; 54(4):313–21

3. Somers JM, Goldner EM, Waraich P, Hsu L. Prevalence and incidence studies of anxiety disorders: a systematic review of the literature. Can J Psychiatry 2006;51(2):100–13

4. Belli S, Belli H, Bahcebasi T, Ozcetin A, Alpay E, Ertem U. Assessment of psychopathological aspects and psychiatric comorbidities in patients affected by tinnitus. Eur Arch Otorhinolaryngol 2008;265(3):279–85

5. Marciano E, Carrabba L, Giannini P, Sementina C, Verde P, Bruno C, et al. Psychiatric comorbidity in a population of outpatients affected by tinnitus. Int J Audiol 2003;42(1):4–9

6. Zoger S, Svedlund J, Holgers KM. Psychiatric disorders in tinnitus patients without severe hearing impairment: 24 month follow-up of patients at an audiological clinic. Audiology 2001;40(3):133–40

7. Andersson G, Carlbring P, Kaldo V, Strom L. Screening of psychiatric disorders via the Internet. A pilot study with tinnitus patients. Nord J Psychiatry 2004;58(4):287–91

8. Zoger S, Svedlund J, Holgers KM. Relationship between tinnitus severity and psychiatric disorders. Psychosomatics 2006;47(4):282–8

9. Landgrebe M, Frick U, Hauser S, Hajak G, Langguth B. Association of tinnitus and electromagnetic hypersensitivity: hints for a shared pathophysiology? PLoS ONE 2009;4(3): e5026.

10. Martinez DP, Waddell A, Perera R, Theodoulou M. Cognitive behavioural therapy for tinnitus. Cochrane Database Syst Rev 2007 24;(1):CD005233.

11. Hoehn-Saric R, Merchant AF, Keyser ML, Smith VK. Effects of clonidine on anxiety disorders. Arch Gen Psychiatry 1981; 38(11):1278–82

12. LaBar KS, Cabeza R. Cognitive neuroscience of emotional memory. Nat Rev Neurosci 2006;7(1):54–64

13. Giraud AL, Chery-Croze S, Fischer G, Fischer C, Vighetto A, Gregoire MC, et al. A selective imaging of tinnitus. Neuroreport 1999;10:1–5

14. Lockwood AH, Salvi RJ, Coad ML, Towsley ML, Wack DS, Murphy BW. The functional neuroanatomy of tinnitus: evidence for limbic system links and neural plasticity. Neurology 1998;50:114–20

15. Mirz F, Gjedde A, Ishizu K, Pedersen CB. Cortical networks subserving the perception of tinnitus – a PET study. Acta Otolaryngol Suppl 2000;543:241–3

16. Landgrebe M, Langguth B, Rosengarth K, Braun S, Koch A, Kleinjung T, et al. Structural brain changes in tinnitus: grey matter decrease in auditory and non-auditory brain areas. Neuroimage 2009;46(1):213–8

17. Muhlau M, Rauschecker JP, Oestreicher E, Gaser C, Rottinger M, Wohlschlager AM, et al. Structural brain changes in tinnitus. Cereb Cortex 2006;16(9):1283–8

18. Holgers KM, Erlandsson SI, Barrenas ML. Predictive factors for the severity of tinnitus. Audiology 2000;39(5):284–91

19. Katon W, Sullivan M, Russo J, Dobie R, Sakai C. Depressive symptoms and measures of disability: a prospective study. J Affect Disord 1993;27(4):245–54

20. Vernon JA. Pathophysiology of tinnitus: a special case – hyperacusis and a proposed treatment. Am J Otol 1987; 8(3):201–2

21. Klein AJ, Armstrong BL, Greer MK, Brown FR, III. Hyperacusis and otitis media in individuals with Williams syndrome. J Speech Hear Disord 1990;55(2):339–44

22. Baguley DM. Hyperacusis. J R Soc Med 2003;96(12): 582–5

23. Andersson G, Lindvall N, Hursti T, Carlbring P. Hypersensitivity to sound (hyperacusis): a prevalence study conducted via the Internet and post. Int J Audiol 2002; 41(8):545–54

24. Fabijanska A, Rogowski M, Bartnik G, Skarzynski H. Epidemiology of tinnitus and hyperacusis in Poland. 569–571. 1999. London, The Tinnitus and Hyperacusis Centre. Proceedings of the Sixth International Tinnitus Seminar. Hazell, J. W. P.Ref Type: Serial (Book, Monograph)

25. Marriage J, Barnes NM. Is central hyperacusis a symptom of 5-hydroxytryptamine (5-HT) dysfunction? J Laryngol Otol 1995;109(10):915–21

26. Jastreboff PJ, Hazell JW. A neurophysiological approach to tinnitus: clinical implications. Br J Audiol 1993;27(1):7–17

27. Jastreboff PJ, Jastreboff MM. Tinnitus Retraining Therapy (TRT) as a method for treatment of tinnitus and hyperacusis patients. J Am Acad Audiol 2000;11(3):162–77

28. Busto U, Fornazzari L, Naranjo CA. Protracted tinnitus after discontinuation of long-term therapeutic use of benzodiazepines. J Clin Psychopharmacol 1988;8(5):359–62

29. Andersson G, Lyttkens L. A meta-analytic review of psychological treatments for tinnitus. Br J Audiol 1999; 33(4):201–10

30. Andersson G, Juris L, Kaldo V, Baguley DM, Larsen HC, Ekselius L. Hyperacusis – an unexplored field. Cognitive behavior therapy can relieve problems in auditory intolerance, a condition with many questions. Läkartidningen 2005;102(44):3210–2

Chapter 65
Tinnitus and Sleep

Tatjana Crönlein, Peter Geisler, and Göran Hajak

Keypoints

1. Disturbed sleep is a frequent problem in persons suffering from tinnitus.
2. Insomnia may persist over years even after successful treatment of tinnitus and specific therapy of sleep.
3. Sleep-disturbed tinnitus patients are more impaired the more severe their tinnitus is.
4. Since disturbed sleep is a risk factor for mental and somatic health, sleep-disturbed tinnitus patients need special therapeutic and diagnostic care.
5. The results of sleep tests in sleep-disturbed tinnitus patients show similarities with insomnia patients, and their psychological symptoms are similar.
6. The prevalence of organic sleep disorders is high in older persons, and therefore differential diagnostic measures are important in this population.
7. Insomnia in sleep-disturbed tinnitus patients can be treated with hypnotics or with insomnia-specific psychotherapy.
8. Insomnia-specific cognitive behavior therapy may improve both sleep and tinnitus.

Keywords Tinnitus • Sleep • Insomnia • Behavior therapy

Abbreviations

BDI   Beck Depression Inventory
CBT   Cognitive behavior therapy
CPAP   Continuous positive air pressure
ESS   Epworth sleepiness scale
PI   Psychophysiological insomnia
PLMS   Periodic limb movements in sleep
PSQI   Pittsburgher sleep quality index
RLS   Restless legs syndrome
SAS   Sleep apnea syndrome
SDTP   Sleep disturbed tinnitus patients
TP   Tinnitus patients

Introduction

"I know how my night sleep is going to be just from the way my tinnitus is during the day." This sentence uttered by a patient in our sleep disorder center describes the special combination of tinnitus and insomnia. The definition of sleep includes decreased responsiveness to external stimuli. The first studies on sleep depth had been performed on the basis of acoustic threshold. E. Kohlschütter described in his dissertation "Zur Festigkeit des Schlafes" (Henle Zeitschrift) in 1862 that the acoustic arousal threshold increases at the beginning of sleep and declines at the end, a result that has been later confirmed [1]. Noise level beyond this threshold prevents or interrupts sleep. Tinnitus, as an internal stimulus, is a special phenomenon in sleep research. However, only a few studies about insomnia and tinnitus have been published. Is disturbed sleep that is experienced by tinnitus sufferers a logical consequence of the tinnitus? Then why do only some tinnitus sufferers develop insomnia? And how can it be treated if tinnitus is a permanent sleep-preventing stimulus?

T. Crönlein (✉)
Sleep Disorders Center, Department of Psychiatry, Psychosomatic and Psychotherapy, University Clinic of Regensburg, Universitätsstr. 84, 93053, Regensburg, Germany
e-mail: tatjana.croenlein@medbo.de

A.R. Møller et al. (eds.), *Textbook of Tinnitus*,
DOI 10.1007/978-1-60761-145-5_65, © Springer Science+Business Media, LLC 2011

Prevalence

Disturbed sleep is a major problem associated with tinnitus. Hallam reported that disturbed sleep is one of the three most important components of tinnitus complaints, next to difficulties in hearing and emotional stress [2]. The prevalence of disturbed sleep in persons with tinnitus varies from 25 to 77% [3–8]. Tyler and Baker found that 57% of 72 tinnitus patients (TP) experienced difficulties getting to sleep [4]. In a larger sample of 436 TP, 15% reported disturbed sleep [5]. Epidemiologic data are dependent on whether samples are tinnitus sufferers [6] or individuals with tinnitus [7, 8], and whether the sample is representative for the population in general [6] or whether it regards a defined subpopulation, for example military personnel [3]. Another reason that different investigators arrive at different values of prevalence may be that the quality of sleep had varied over the time of an investigation.

Insomnia occurs more frequently in individuals with recent onset tinnitus [8]. While 45% of individuals experiencing tinnitus onset less than 1 year reported disturbed sleep, only 26% of individuals who had tinnitus for more than 11 years reported similar sleep issues. Thus, there seems to be an acute and a chronic type of insomnia in individuals with tinnitus. However, there are no published data that support whether these are two distinct forms of insomnia or merely a variation of one form. Nevertheless, the chronic form seems to be more severe since tinnitus and insomnia become more pronounced the longer a patient suffers from these conditions. In a follow-up study in Oregon, 43 of 175 participants still reported having sleep problems after being treated. In this group, loudness and severity were significantly greater [8]. In a follow-up study, after 5 years of treatment in a university clinic in Sweden, 62% TP still reported having sleep problems [9].

The fact that insomnia becomes a persistent problem only in some individuals with tinnitus indicates a special relationship between tinnitus and disturbed sleep. This is considered to be a diagnostic and therapeutic challenge.

Clinical Data of Sleep-Disturbed Tinnitus Patients

Subjective sleep studies of sleep-disturbed tinnitus patients (SDTP) show that there is a higher incidence of problems falling asleep than being awakened by tinnitus. Furthermore, less than half of tinnitus sufferers who had problems falling asleep also reported being awakened by their tinnitus [6]. Results from studies of the relationship between the loudness of tinnitus and sleep are contradictory. Some studies report an influence of loudness on disturbed sleep [7, 10] while others do not [11]. Surprisingly, only a minority of tinnitus sufferers with disturbed sleep reported that their tinnitus interferes with their sleep [6]. Studies indicate that SDTP predominantly suffer from delayed sleep onset and that individuals with tinnitus have a tendency to perceive disturbed sleep independent of their tinnitus.

Subjective sleep studies provide only limited information about the effect of tinnitus on sleep because they are based on memory. Individuals with insomnia often underestimate their sleep [12, 13]. Only three published studies used polysomnographic techniques to assess the participants' sleep.

One study shows that individuals with insomnia but no tinnitus have a shorter sleep duration compared to that in healthy controls [14], thus similar to SDTP. Another study [15] compared objective and subjective sleep data as well as clinical data to investigate the hypothesis that SDTP resemble individuals with primary insomnia, daytime vigilance, depression, and daytime tiredness of individuals with primary insomnia and SDTP. No differences in objective sleep measurements were found, but both groups had low sleep efficiencies and long sleep onset latencies. In addition, no differences were found in subjective ratings of daytime sleepiness (ESS) or depression (BDI), both scores being within the normal range. Similar results were obtained in tests of sustained attention performance (QM), which is sensitive to effects of sleep deprivation. These results and those of other studies [7] support the hypothesis that insomnia in TP is not a consequence of depression. Furthermore, polysomnographic[1] of tinnitus patients [14–16] measurements reflect subjective disturbed sleep in SDTP. The polysomnographic results in SDTP and individuals with insomnia are similar.

---

[1] Polysomnography: physiologic measures of sleep which are electroencephalography (EEG), electroencephalography (EOG), and electromyography (EMG).

Model

Since not all tinnitus sufferers develop insomnia, disturbed sleep and tinnitus probably do not have a common somatic mechanism, and it is not clear whether insomnia is a consequence or a comorbid condition to TP. Patients, however, regard the relationship between tinnitus and sleep disturbance to be clear, and many patients believe that their tinnitus is the cause of their disturbed sleep. This mechanism is probably valid in acute tinnitus and is in line with a commonly expected relationship between a disturbing noise and sleep. A higher prevalence of insomnia in persons who suffer from acute tinnitus can be explained with the so-called adjustment insomnia.

The essential characteristic of "adjustment insomnia" is the existence of an identifiable stressor. The insomnia is expected to resolve as soon as the stressor is eliminated. The fact that sleep disturbance becomes less frequent with the duration of tinnitus [8] can be explained by habituation to the tinnitus in some SDTP.

Nevertheless, there is a chronic form of insomnia which cannot be explained with "adjustment insomnia" criteria, where insomnia exists as a comorbid condition. Tinnitus is erroneously held responsible for disturbed sleep by the patient as well as the physician, and insomnia persists without a precipitating factor. Similarities between SDTP and patients with psychophysiological insomnia found in clinical studies support this assumption [15]. Psychophysiological insomnia essentially is a conditioned sleep disorder with a heightened somatic and mental level of arousal that results from a cycle of symptoms such as the urge for sleep, focus on the inability to sleep, and focus on sleep-related cues [17].

There seems to be an overlap between several psychological aspects of tinnitus and features of psychophysiological insomnia. Andersson and Westin proposed classical conditioning, selective attention, and appraisal of tinnitus as mediating factors for the distress experienced by tinnitus sufferers [18]. Similar factors exist in psychophysiological insomnia [19, 20]. Insomnia and tinnitus distress in its chronic form reinforce each other [15]. SDTP perceive tinnitus in the acute phase as a sleep-preventing stimulus. The perspective that it is permanent and inescapable triggers a vicious cycle of insomnia with an obsession on sleep, selective attention to tinnitus, and the inability to sleep in addition to mental and somatic hyperarousal [15]. While the actual sound becomes less prominent after some time, it is rather the attitude that tinnitus prevents sleep that reinforces insomnia. It is therefore understandable that such patients feel their tinnitus is severe [11]. In a study of tinnitus sufferers attending our tinnitus center, we found a clear correlation between tinnitus severity and degree of sleep disturbance (Fig. 65.1).

Consequences of Disturbed Sleep

Restorative sleep is a basic condition of health, and impaired daytime functioning is one of the diagnostic criteria of insomnia (ICSD-2, 2005). An increasing number of studies have indicated that insomnia is a risk factor for physical and mental health disorders [21–23]. Insomnia is associated with impairment of vitality, general health, and a physical ability to function that is not insignificant, even when compared to disorders such as depression or congestive heart failure [22]. Furthermore, studies have shown that insomnia is associated with an increased risk for arterial hypertension [24], coronary heart diseases, psychiatric disorders such as depression [23, 25], accidents, and impaired productiveness on the job [26, 27]. Insomnia itself, therefore, is a major health problem, and disturbed sleep in tinnitus sufferers is a serious medical problem.

Therapy

Several different treatments, such as pharmacologic agents [28] and cognitive behavior therapy, are available to treat insomnia [29].

Two kinds of pharmacologic agents are in common use: benzodiazepines and sedative antidepressants. Both have problems, especially for long-term use. Benzodiazepine, a $GABA_A$ receptor agonist, such as zolpidem, zopiclone, and zaleplon [30] has limited duration of beneficial effect [31]. While intermittent intake of hypnotics has shown to be effective [32], adaptation (or tolerance) is a problem when used for long periods. Despite that recent studies suggest that an intake of up to 6 months of Z-substances is not harmful [33]; chronically, sleep-disturbed patients

Fig. 65.1 Correlation between tinnitus severity and severity of psychophysiological insomnia in 31 sleep-disturbed tinnitus patients

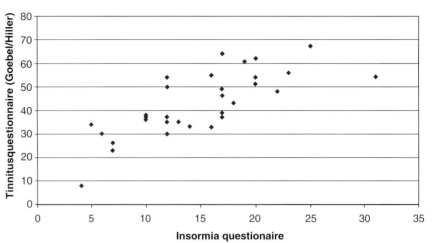

such as SDTP normally need a medication for an even longer period of time.

Especially in the case of chronic insomnia in SDTP, cognitive behavior therapy (CBT) should be applied since it targets the symptoms that modulate distress. Components are bed time restriction [34], stimulus control, relaxation therapy, and sleep education [35]. Several studies have shown that CBT has a positive and long-lasting effect on primary insomnia [29, 36]. In a follow-up three months after participating in a CBT program specially designed for insomnia and tinnitus, an improvement in sleep as well as tinnitus could be seen.

Alternation of dysfunctional attitudes and behavior patterns leads to patients' regaining control of pre-sleep ease and as a consequence results in a better likelihood for falling asleep.

Assessment of Results of Treatment

The Pittsburgher sleep quality index (PSQI) [37] is the most preferred sleep questionnaire in sleep research so far. It is designed to measure sleep quality, and it also assesses symptoms of sleep-related breathing disorders. The insomnia severity index is a commonly used instrument for measuring severity of insomnia

syndrome [38]. Sleep protocols are a useful tool for quantifying therapy effects as well as diagnostic purposes.

Other Syndromes That Occur Together with Sleep Disturbances

Sleep Apnea

One study [16] showed that sleep apnea syndrome (SAS) occurred in 10 out of 26 SDTP and PLMS in three of these patients. Detecting organic sleep disorders in SDTP is very important since even a mild severity of SAS or PLMS may have an impairing effect on insomnia in SDTP because of its sleep fragmentation effect. Once sleep is disturbed and leads to nocturnal awakening, SDTP have problems falling back asleep. People may attribute nightly awakening to tinnitus and present it to the therapist that way. Studies of the prevalence of sleep-related breathing disorders in individuals with tinnitus have not been published, and there are no data available about the effect of CPAP therapy on the severity of SDTP with SAS. Sleep apnea is not always associated with a high body mass index, excessive snoring, and/or regular alcohol consumption.

Especially in older persons, sleep apnea may occur without these symptoms. Sleep medication such as Benzodiazepines and other sedative agents may worsen sleep-related breathing disorders.

Restless Leg Syndrome

Restless legs syndrome (RLS), especially if associated with PLMS, may also have an impairing effect on sleep in SDTP. Periodic limb movement disorder (PLMS) is characterized by episodes of repetitive, stereotyped leg movements during sleep. It may but need not lead to sleep fragmentation. A study found PLMS without RLS to occur in 15% of individuals with insomnia, and its occurrence increases with age (34% of people over 60 years) [39] (reference needed). Certain sedative drugs, such as benzodiazepines, may worsen insomnia when an SAS or PLMS is present.

Conclusion

Insomnia in tinnitus sufferers is a condition that decreases the quality of life and may be regarded as a serious health problem. It is important to rule out organic sleep disorders such as sleep apnea and RLS as a cause for insomnia. Disturbed sleep in persons with tinnitus should be treated specifically. An early treatment of disturbed sleep is useful to prevent insomnia becoming chronic. Cognitive behavior therapy is a promising tool to this end.

References

1. Rosenthal, L, Bishop, C, Helmus, T, Krstevska, S, Roehrs, T, Roth, T. Auditory awakening thresholds in sleepy and alert individuals. Sleep, 1996;19(4):290–5
2. Hallam, RS, Jakes, SC, Hinchcliffe, R. Cognitive variables in tinnitus annoyance. Br J Clin Psychol, 1988;27(Pt 3):213–22
3. Alster, J, Shemesh, Z, Ornan, M, Attias, J. Sleep disturbance associated with chronic tinnitus. Biol Psychiatry, 1993; 34(1–2):84–90
4. Tyler, RS, Baker, LJ. Difficulties experienced by tinnitus sufferers. J Speech Hear Disord, 1983;48(2):150–4
5. Sanchez, L, Stephens, D. A tinnitus problem questionnaire in a clinic population. Ear Hear, 1997;18(3):210–7
6. Axelsson, A, Ringdahl, A. Tinnitus – a study of its prevalence and characteristics. Br J Audiol, 1989;23(1):53–62

7. Hallam, RS. Correlates of sleep disturbance in chronic distressing tinnitus. Scand Audiol, 1996;25(4):263–6
8. Folmer, RL, Griest, SE. Tinnitus and insomnia. Am J Otolaryngol, 2000;21(5):287–93
9. Andersson, G, Vretblad, P, Larsen, HC, Lyttkens, L. Longitudinal follow-up of tinnitus complaints. Arch Otolaryngol Head Neck Surg, 2001;127(2):175–9
10. Slater R, Jones D, Davis B, Terry M. Project into psychological aspects of adjustment to subjective tinnitus and the effectiveness of tailored masking, London 1983
11. Meikle, MB, Vernon, J, Johnson, RM. The perceived severity of tinnitus Some observations concerning a large population of tinnitus clinic patients. Otolaryngol Head Neck Surg, 1984;92(6):689–96
12. Hauri, P, Olmstead, E. What is the moment of sleep onset for insomniacs? Sleep, 1983;6(1):10–5
13. Knab, B, Engel, RR. Perception of waking and sleeping: possible implications for the evaluation of insomnia. Sleep, 1988;11(3):265–72
14. Burgos, I, Feige, B, Hornyak, M, Haerter, M, Weske-Heck, G, Voderholzer, U, et al. Chronic tinnitus and associated sleep disturbance. Somnologie, 2005;9:133–8
15. Cronlein, T, Langguth, B, Geisler, P, Hajak, G. Tinnitus and insomnia. Prog Brain Res, 2007;166:227–33
16. Eysel-Gosepath, K, Selivanova, O. Characterization of sleep disturbance in patients with tinnitus. Laryngorhinootologie, 2005;84(5):323–7
17. Harvey, AG. A cognitive model of insomnia. Behav Res Ther, 2002;40(8):869–93
18. Andersson, G, Westin, V. Understanding tinnitus distress: introducing the concepts of moderators and mediators. Int J Audiol, 2008;47(Suppl 2):S106–11
19. Espie, CA, Broomfield, NM, MacMahon, KM, Macphee, LM, Taylor, LM. The attention-intention-effort pathway in the development of psychophysiologic insomnia: a theoretical review. Sleep Med Rev, 2006;10(4):215–45
20. Perlis, ML, Giles, DE, Mendelson, WB, Bootzin, RR, Wyatt, JK. Psychophysiological insomnia: the behavioural model and a neurocognitive perspective. J Sleep Res, 1997; 6(3):179–88
21. Katz, DA, McHorney, CA. Clinical correlates of insomnia in patients with chronic illness. Arch Intern Med, 1998; 158(10):1099–107
22. Katz, DA, McHorney, CA. The relationship between insomnia and health-related quality of life in patients with chronic illness. J Fam Pract, 2002;51(3):229–35
23. Riemann, D, Voderholzer, U. Primary insomnia: a risk factor to develop depression? J Affect Disord, 2003;76(1–3): 255–9
24. Suka, M, Yoshida, K, Sugimori, H. Persistent insomnia is a predictor of hypertension in Japanese male workers. J Occup Health, 2003;45(6):344–50
25. Breslau, N, Roth, T, Rosenthal, L, Andreski. Sleep disturbance and psychiatric disorders: a longitudinal epidemiological study of young adults. Biol Psychiatry, 1996;39(6):411–8
26. Godet-Cayre, V, Pelletier-Fleury, N, Le, VM, Dinet, J, Massuel, MA, Leger, D. Insomnia and absenteeism at work. Who pays the cost? Sleep, 2006;29(2):179–84
27. Leger, D, Massuel, MA, Metlaine, A. Professional correlates of insomnia. Sleep, 2006;29(2):171–8

28. Dundar, Y, Dodd, S, Strobl, J, Boland, A, Dickson, R, Walley, T. Comparative efficacy of newer hypnotic drugs for the short-term management of insomnia: a systematic review and meta-analysis. Hum Psychopharmacol, 2004; 19(5):305–22

29. Morin, CM, Bootzin, RR, Buysse, DJ, Edinger, JD, Espie, CA, Lichstein, KL. Psychological and behavioral treatment of insomnia:update of the recent evidence (1998–2004). Sleep, 2006;29(11):1398–414

30. Dundar, Y, Boland, A, Strobl, J, Dodd, S, Haycox, A, Bagust, A, et al. Newer hypnotic drugs for the short-term management of insomnia: a systematic review and economic evaluation. Health Technol Assess, 2004;8(24):iii–x, 1–125

31. Perlis, M, Gehrman, P, Riemann, D. Intermittent and long-term use of sedative hypnotics. Curr Pharm Des, 2008;14(32):3456–65

32. Hajak, G, Cluydts, R, Allain, H, Estivill, E, Parrino, L, Terzano, MG, et al. The challenge of chronic insomnia: is non-nightly hypnotic treatment a feasible alternative? Eur Psychiatry, 2003;18(5):201–8

33. Krystal, AD, Walsh, JK, Laska, E, Caron, J, Amato, DA, Wessel, TC, et al. Sustained efficacy of eszopiclone over 6 months of nightly treatment: results of a randomized, double-blind, placebo-controlled study in adults with chronic insomnia. Sleep, 2003;26(7):793–9

34. Spielman, AJ, Saskin, P, Thorpy, MJ. Treatment of chronic insomnia by restriction of time in bed. Sleep, 1987;10(1):45–56

35. Smith, MT, Neubauer, DN. Cognitive behavior therapy for chronic insomnia. Clin Cornerstone, 2003;5(3):28–40

36. Edinger, JD, Wohlgemuth, WK, Radtke, RA, Marsh, GR, Quillian, RE. Cognitive behavioral therapy for treatment of chronic primary insomnia: a randomized controlled trial. JAMA, 2001;285(14):1856–64

37. Buysse, DJ, Reynolds, CF, III, Monk, TH, Berman, SR, Kupfer, DJ. The Pittsburgh Sleep Quality Index: a new instrument for psychiatric practice and research. Psychiatry Res, 1989;28(2):193–213

38. Bastien, CH, Vallieres, A, Morin, CM. Validation of the Insomnia Severity Index as an outcome measure for insomnia research. Sleep Med, 2001;2(4):297–307

39. Cronlein, T, Geisler, P, Zulley, J, Hajak, G. Periodic leg movements and sleep disturbances: the role of actigraphy in the diagnosis of insomnia. J Sleep Res, 2006; 15(s1):179

Chapter 66
Posttraumatic Tinnitus

Dirk De Ridder and Berthold Langguth

Keypoints

1. Posttraumatic tinnitus can be both non-pulsatile and pulsatile.
2. Posttraumatic non-pulsatile tinnitus can result from trauma to the ear or neck. Trauma to the ear includes temporal bone fracture, labyrinthine concussion, ossicular chain disruption, perilymphatic fistula, barotraumas, or noise trauma.
3. Posttraumatic pulsatile tinnitus is related to vascular lesions. Posttraumatic carotid dissection, AV fistula or caroticocavernous fistula, can cause pulsatile tinnitus.
4. Posttraumatic stress disorder can worsen the tinnitus percept and distress.
5. The cause of posttraumatic non-pulsatile and pulsatile tinnitus may be a sign of life-threatening diseases, some of which are treatable.

Keywords Pulsatile • Tinnitus • Trauma • Vascular

Abbreviations

AV	Arteriovenous
AVM	Arteriovenous malformation
CCF	Carotid-cavernous fistula
CD	Carotid dissection
CSF	Cerebrospinal fluid
MVC	Microvascular compression
OChD	Ossicular chain disruption
PTSD	Posttraumatic stress disorder
TBI	Traumatic brain injury

D. De Ridder (✉)
TRI Tinnitus Clinic Antwerp, BRAI²N & Department of Neurosurgery, University Hospital Antwerp, Wilrijkstraat 10, 2650 Edegem, Belgium
e-mail: dirk.de.ridder@uza.be

Introduction

Tinnitus often arises after, or is associated with, a trauma to the head – especially to the ear. Mechanical, pressure-related, noise-related, or stress-related trauma can cause tinnitus. Posttraumatic tinnitus can be either non-pulsatile or pulsatile.

Noise-related trauma is the most common cause of tinnitus and hearing loss. It is discussed in detail in Chap. 37.

Head [1] and neck injuries [2] are common causes of tinnitus [3, 4]. 53% of individuals suffering traumatic brain injuries (TBI) develop tinnitus; hyperacusis (intolerance to sudden or loud noise) develops in up to 87% of all TBI cases [4].

Non-pulsatile tinnitus in head injury can be due to injuries to the ear or brain. Injuries to the ear may consist of petrous bone fractures, ossicular chain disruption, and perilymphatic fistulas, as well as barotraumas and noise trauma. Posttraumatic damage to the auditory nerve and brain injuries can cause tinnitus as well. About 10–15% of whiplash injuries develop a whiplash syndrome consisting of persistent tinnitus combined with one or more of the following symptoms: headache, vertigo, instability, nausea, and hearing loss [5] (Table 66.1).

Pulsatile Tinnitus

Posttraumatic pulsatile tinnitus can be the result of a carotid dissection, AV fistula, or caroticocavernous fistula. Traumatic carotid dissections (CD) occur in approximately 1% of all individuals who have had blunt traumatic injury [6]. Pulsatile tinnitus is experienced in 16–27% of carotid dissections at the side of the dissection.

A.R. Møller et al. (eds.), *Textbook of Tinnitus*,
DOI 10.1007/978-1-60761-145-5_66, © Springer Science+Business Media, LLC 2011

Table 66.1 Causes of posttraumatic tinnitus

1. Non-pulsatile tinnitus
   (a) Ear
       i. Temporal bone fracture
       ii. Labyrinthine concussion
       iii. Ossicular chain disruption
       iv. Perilymphatic fistula
       v. Barotrauma
       vi. Noise trauma
   (b) Nervous System
   (c) Auditory nerve
   (d) Brain injury
   (e) Posttraumatic stress disorder
   (f) Neck
   (i) Neck trauma
2. Pulsatile tinnitus
   (a) Carotid dissection
   (b) AV fistula
   (c) Caroticocavernous fistula

CD is asymptomatic in less than 10%, whereas more than 90% of individuals with CD develop carotid territory ischemia and/or local signs and symptoms on the side of dissection. Signs and symptoms from the side of dissection include head (65–68%), facial (34–53%), or neck pain (9–26%), Horner syndrome[1] (28–41%), and cranial nerve palsy (8–16%) of the hypoglossal nerve in particular. The facial nerve may also be involved; dysgeusia[2] results mainly from involvement of the chorda tympani (0.5–7.0%) or the glossopharyngeal nerve. A metal-like taste is typical after chorda tympani lesions. Transient pareses of the ocular motor (III, IV, and VI) and the trigeminal nerve have been observed. In ¾ of carotid dissections, an ischemic event occurs, which includes ischemic stroke in 80–84%, transient ischemic attack in 15–16%, amaurosis fugax[3] in 3%, neuropathy in 4%, and retinal infarct in 1% [7].

Posttraumatic AV fistulas often result in an audible bruit, thus objective tinnitus or pulsatile tinnitus [8–10]. AV fistulas can develop after days, weeks, or even years [11].[4] The incidence at the middle meningeal artery in head injuries is 1.8% [9]. However, they can also occur along the superior sagittal sinus [10], the posterior auricular artery (internal jugular vein) [8], vertebral artery-vertebral plexus [11], sigmoid and transverse sinuses [11], or even the scalp [11]. The middle meningeal artery fistula to the sphenoparietal sinus is often the result of linear fractures and are most common in elderly people who have an adherent dura [9]. The sinus fistulas developing after trauma are often the result of a venous thrombosis and are similar to the non-traumatic variant of AV fistulas.

The most common posttraumatic fistula is the carotid-cavernous fistula (CCF). They are divided in the more common high- and rare low-flow fistulas. In 3.8% of traumatic skull base fractures, a traumatic carotid-cavernous fistula is seen, especially in middle fossa fractures, where up to 8.3% develop a CCF [12]. These are characterized by pulsatile tinnitus, pulsating exophthalmia, chemosis[5], and visual deficit of the afflicted side [11]. Endovascular treatment is the most commonly used treatment.

Non-pulsatile Posttraumatic Tinnitus

Ear

Temporal Bone Fracture

Tinnitus develops in nearly 50% of individuals with temporal bone fractures [13]. The common causes of temporal bone fractures are road accidents, falls, beatings, and gunshot wounds [14–16]. Forty-four percent of temporal bone fractures occur after a motor vehicle accident [15]. Head trauma occurs in 75% of traffic accidents; in 5% of these, petrous bone fracture is noted [17]. Of all head injuries requiring hospitalization,

---

[1] Horner syndrome: Ipsilateral myosis, ptosis, and facial anhydrosis; usually unilateral and due to an ipsilateral lesion of the cervical sympathetic chain or its central pathway; an ominous sign when it accompanies an ipsilateral traumatic brachial plexopathy because it usually indicates an avulsion of the C8 and T1 primary roots from the spinal cord. From Stedman's Electronic Medical Dictionary

[2] Dysgeusia: Distortion or perversion in the perception of a tastant. An unpleasant perception may occur when a normally pleasant taste is present, or the perception may occur when no tastant is present (gustatory hallucination). From Stedman's Electronic Medical Dictionary.

[3] Amaurosis fugax: A transient blindness that may result from a transient ischemia resulting from carotid artery insufficiency or retinal artery embolus, or to centrifugal force (visual blackout in flight). From Stedman's Electronic Medical Dictionary.

[4] Exophthalmos: Protrusion of one or both eyeballs; can be congenital and familial, or due to pathology, such as a retro-orbital tumor (usually unilateral) or thyroid disease (usually bilateral). From Stedman's Electronic Medical Dictionary.

[5] Chemosis: Edema of the bulbar conjunctiva, forming a swelling around the cornea. From Stedman's Electronic Medical Dictionary.

9% have a skull fracture and 2% of all these have temporal bone fractures [15]. Three kinds of fractures are noted after a substantial trauma to the temporal region: transverse, longitudinal, and mixed fractures. The most common fracture is the longitudinal fracture (82%) [14], characterized by visible laceration and fracture line of the external ear canal. Lateral impact to the head can cause tympanic membrane perforation or blood in the middle-ear cavity with an ossicular chain disruption in about half of the patients [14]. Facial paralysis occurs in 3% [13]. Hearing loss is predominately conductive but may have a sensorineural component as well. CSF leaks occur in 36% of patients with longitudinal temporal bone fractures [13].

Transverse fractures (11%) [14] resulting from antero-posterior impact have a higher rate of sensorineural hearing loss (53%) [18], vertigo [18], and facial paralysis (63%) [14]. Tinnitus develops in 41% of transverse fractures [18]. CSF leaks occur in 25% of patients with transverse fractures [13]. Mixed fractures occur in 7% [14] of the traumata. Some head injuries can severely damage the auditory nerve causing deafness and sometimes tinnitus.

Labyrinthine Concussion

Labyrinthine concussion may occur after less serious blows to the head [19], on the side of the trauma or, sometimes, on the opposite side [20]. Tinnitus, dizziness, vertigo, and high-frequency sensorineural hearing loss (4,000–8,000 Hz) are particularly common [21]. In some individuals, onset may be delayed for several days [19], and concomitant conductive hearing loss may occur from disruption of the ossicular chain or from bleeding into the middle-ear cavity [21]. A blow to the mastoid or occiput may damage labyrinth membranes [19] causing the symptoms, as has been suggested by animal experiments [22, 23].

Ossicular Chain Disruption

Ossicular chain disruption (OChD) may occur without rupture of the eardrum or temporal bone fracture and result in conductive hearing loss and tinnitus. Traffic accidents are the most common cause of OChD [24]. Twenty-two percent of the OChD are associated with a temporal bone fracture [24], and OChD occurs in 15% of such fractures [25]. There is often a long delay

between the injury and treatment (average of 5.7 years) [24]. The most common disruption is the incudostapedial joint followed by the incudomalleal joint [14]. The stapes is most commonly fractured followed by the malleus, with the incus almost never fractured [14]. There is no literature available on tinnitus in posttraumatic ossicular chain disruption specifically, but any hearing loss may cause tinnitus because it activates neural plasticity. Treatment consists of ossicular chain reconstruction if symptoms persist after 2–3 months of recovery or a disappearance of blood in the middle-ear cavity.

Perilymphatic Fistula

A perilymphatic fistula results from disruption of the membranes of the labyrinth, most often at the round or oval window [19]. In half of the patients, barotraumas such as blowing the nose, lifting heavy goods, and landing in an airplane are the cause [26]; in about 40% a trauma is the cause [27].

The most prominent symptoms are tinnitus (61–76%), sudden or fluctuating hearing loss (83–93%), vertigo and dizziness (77–91%), and aural fullness (31%) [26, 28]. Subjective positive signs (i.e., vertigo and nystagmus induced by pressure changes in the external ear canal or with coughing or straining [19]) of fistula are present in 71% of these patients [26].

Treatment consists of bed rest while elevating the head, preventing stressful physical activity, and packing both cochlear windows with soft tissue graft [19, 26–28]. If the symptoms persist, a ventriculoperitoneal shunt can be inserted [29, 30]. In general, vestibular symptoms respond to treatment better than auditory symptoms [19, 26–28].

Barotrauma

Barotrauma to the ear may occur during rapid change in pressure, such as descent from high altitudes or during underwater diving. It is usually associated with sudden severe ear pain [19]. The cause is that the Eustachian tube fails to equilibrate the pressure in the middle-ear cavity to that of the increasing atmospheric pressures [31]. It causes inward displacement of the tympanic membrane, increased blood flow, and swelling with fluid, sometimes, even blood [19], oozing into the middle-ear cavity, which may lead to hearing loss and tinnitus [32]. In severe situations, it can cause rupture of the eardrum and ossicular chain disruption and even rupture of the round window causing a perilymphatic fistula [31].

Blast injuries are special forms of combined baro- and noise trauma resulting in hearing loss (55–72%) and tinnitus (66–88%) in most individuals exposed to large explosions; both tinnitus and hearing loss occur in 41% [33–35]. Other symptoms include ear pain (41%) and distortion of sounds (28%) [34]. Two-thirds have a perforation of the eardrum, often on both sides (70%) [35]. In seventy-five percent of cases, the perforation heals spontaneously [35, 36].

Treatment of barotraumas is conservative, but when ossicular chain disruption has occurred and a perilymphatic fistula is present, the treatment may be surgical.

Noise Trauma

There is a significant correlation between a history of exposure to noise trauma and the presence of a high-pitched "whistling" tinnitus; the presence of such tinnitus is significantly correlated with high-frequency hearing loss [37] (see also Chap. 37). The most commonly observed frequency of tinnitus on pitch matching is the same as the worst frequency for hearing [38], most often at 4,000 Hz [39]. The effect of exposure to noise on hearing loss has been well studied (see Chap. 37), but the relationship between noise exposure and tinnitus has been researched to a lesser extent. One study shows that the prevalence of tinnitus in noise-exposed workers is 24% [40], significantly higher than in the general population [41]. It has also been shown that noise-induced hearing loss usually has a steep slope, which is a risk factor for tinnitus prevalence and intensity [42]. Furthermore, the more pronounced the hearing loss is the more discomfort the tinnitus generates [43] and the louder it is perceived [42]. The patients presenting with noise-induced tinnitus are mainly male and on average were 10 years younger than other tinnitus patients suffering from bilateral high-pitched "whistling" tinnitus in correlation with their high-frequency hearing loss [37]. Between 50 and 70% of young people who expose themselves to loud recreational noise have temporarily experienced tinnitus [44]. Disc jockeys develop hearing loss both at

high frequencies and at low frequencies and have tinnitus of the same sound spectra [45]. Up to 75% of DJs develop tinnitus [45].

Cervical

Whiplash-Associated Tinnitus

Ten to fifteen percent of individuals who have suffered a whiplash injury develop symptoms such as tinnitus, deafness, and vertigo [5, 46, 47]. It has been hypothesized that tinnitus might develop because of the somatosensory influences on the dorsal cochlear nucleus [48]. (For more information on somatosensory tinnitus, see Chap. 43.)

Neuropsychological

Posttraumatic Stress Disorder

Posttraumatic stress disorder (PTSD) is an anxiety disorder caused by exposure to terrifying events. It is often accompanied by tinnitus. The prevalence of tinnitus in individuals with PTSD is much higher than the prevalence in noise-exposed workers (24%) [40]. For example, 50% of Cambodian refugees suffer from tinnitus [49], and the prevalence of PTSD in these individuals is significantly higher than among individuals who do not have tinnitus. Of those patients who seek help for their tinnitus at a veterans tinnitus clinic, 34% have PTSD [50]. It is not known if it is the increased vigilance that causes the tinnitus.

Summary

Tinnitus can be both non-pulsatile and pulsatile after a trauma. Non-pulsatile tinnitus is a common symptom after head and neck injuries, after noise trauma, barotrauma, and in PTSD. Some of the causes involved (e.g., ossicular chain disruption, perilymphatic fistula) can be treated successfully. Posttraumatic pulsatile tinnitus can be a sign of life-threatening disorders such as carotid-cavernous fistulas, AVMs, and carotid dissections.

References

1. Sindhusake D, M Golding, D Wigney et al (2004) Factors predicting severity of tinnitus: a population-based assessment. J Am Acad Audiol 15:269–80.
2. Sindhusake D, P Mitchell, P Newall et al (2003) Prevalence and characteristics of tinnitus in older adults: the Blue Mountains Hearing Study. Int J Audiol 42:289–94.
3. Folmer RL and SE Griest (2003) Chronic tinnitus resulting from head or neck injuries. Laryngoscope 113:821–7.
4. Jury MA and MC Flynn (2001) Auditory and vestibular sequelae to traumatic brain injury: a pilot study. N Z Med J 114:286–8.
5. Claussen CF and E Claussen (1995) Neurootological contributions to the diagnostic follow-up after whiplash injuries. Acta Otolaryngol Suppl 520 Pt 1:53–6.
6. Redekop GJ (2008) Extracranial carotid and vertebral artery dissection: a review. Can J Neurol Sci 35:146–52.
7. Baumgartner RW and J Bogousslavsky (2005) Clinical manifestations of carotid dissection. Front Neurol Neurosci 20:70–6.
8. Chae SW, HJ Kang, HM Lee et al (2001) Tinnitus caused by traumatic posterior auricular artery–internal jugular vein fistula. J Laryngol Otol 115:313–5.
9. Freckmann N, K Sartor and HD Herrmann (1981) Traumatic arteriovenous fistulae of the middle meningeal artery and neighbouring veins or dural sinuses. Acta Neurochir (Wien) 55:273–81.
10. Fukai J, T Torada, T Kuwata et al (2001) Transarterial intravenous coil embolization of dural arteriovenous fistula involving the superior sagittal sinus. Surg Neurol 55:353–8.
11. D'Alise M, C Caetano and H Batjer (1997) Vascular complications of head injury, in Cerebrovascular disease, H Batjer, Editor. Lippincott-Raven: Philadelphia.
12. Liang W, Y Xiaofeng, L Weiguo et al (2007) Traumatic carotid cavernous fistula accompanying basilar skull fracture: a study on the incidence of traumatic carotid cavernous fistula in the patients with basilar skull fracture and the prognostic analysis about traumatic carotid cavernous fistula. J Trauma 63:1014-20; discussion 20.
13. Chen J, C Ji, C Yang et al (2001) Temporal bone fracture and its complications. Chin J Traumatol 4:106–9.
14. Wysocki J (2005) Cadaveric dissections based on observations of injuries to the temporal bone structures following head trauma. Skull Base 15:99–106; discussion -7.
15. Cannon CR and RA Jahrsdoerfer (1983) Temporal bone fractures. Review of 90 cases. Arch Otolaryngol 109:285–8.
16. Brodie HA and TC Thompson (1997) Management of complications from 820 temporal bone fractures. Am J Otol 18:188–97.
17. Granier M, L Renaud-Picard, JC Chobaut et al (2006) Mild head trauma: complications and acousticovestibular sequelae. Rev Stomatol Chir Maxillofac 107:253–63.
18. Heid L, CF Claussen, M Kersebaum et al (2004) Vertigo, dizziness, and tinnitus after otobasal fractures. Int Tinnitus J 10:94–100.
19. Baloh RW (1998) Dizziness, hearing loss and tinnitus. Vol. 29. F.A. Davis: Philadelphia. 250.
20. Ulug T and SA Ulubil (2006) Contralateral labyrinthine concussion in temporal bone fractures. J Otolaryngol 35:380–3.
21. Davies RA and LM Luxon (1995) Dizziness following head injury: a neuro-otological study. J Neurol 242:222–30.
22. Schuknecht HF (1951) Deafness following blows to the head: a clinical and experimental study. Trans Am Acad Ophthalmol Otolaryngol 55:407–17.
23. Schuknecht HF, WD Neff and HB Perlman (1951) An experimental study of auditory damage following blows to the head. Ann Otol Rhinol Laryngol 60:273–89.
24. Yetiser S, Y Hidir, H Birkent et al (2008) Traumatic ossicular dislocations: etiology and management. Am J Otolaryngol 29:31–6.
25. Wennmo C and O Spandow (1993) Fractures of the temporal bone-chain incongruencies. Am J Otolaryngol 14:38–42.
26. Goto F, K Ogawa, T Kunihiro et al (2001) Perilymph fistula – 45 case analysis. Auris Nasus Larynx 28:29–33.
27. Fitzgerald DC (1995) Persistent dizziness following head trauma and perilymphatic fistula. Arch Phys Med Rehabil 76:1017–20.
28. Glasscock ME, 3rd, MJ Hart, JD Rosdeutscher et al (1992) Traumatic perilymphatic fistula: how long can symptoms persist? A follow-up report. Am J Otol 13:333–8.
29. Lollis SS, DJ Weider, JM Phillips et al (2006) Ventriculoperitoneal shunt insertion for the treatment of refractory perilymphatic fistula. J Neurosurg 105:1–5.
30. Weider DJ, DW Roberts and J Phillips (2005) Ventriculoperitoneal shunt as treatment for perilymphatic fistula: a report of six cases. Int Tinnitus J 11:137–45.
31. Mirza S and H Richardson (2005) Otic barotrauma from air travel. J Laryngol Otol 119:366–70.
32. Becker GD and GJ Parell (2001) Barotrauma of the ears and sinuses after scuba diving. Eur Arch Otorhinolaryngol 258:159–63.
33. Persaud R, D Hajioff, M Wareing et al (2003) Otological trauma resulting from the Soho Nail Bomb in London, April 1999. Clin Otolaryngol Allied Sci 28:203–6.
34. Mrena R, R Paakkonen, L Back et al (2004) Otologic consequences of blast exposure: a Finnish case study of a shopping mall bomb explosion. Acta Otolaryngol 124:946–52.
35. Tungsinmunkong S, C Chongkolwatana, W Piyawongvisal et al (2007) Blast injury of the ears: the experience from Yala Hospital, Southern Thailand. J Med Assoc Thai 90:2662–8.
36. Kronenberg J, J Ben-Shoshan and M Wolf (1993) Perforated tympanic membrane after blast injury. Am J Otol 14:92–4.
37. Nicolas-Puel C, T Akbaraly, R Lloyd et al (2006) Characteristics of tinnitus in a population of 555 patients: specificities of tinnitus induced by noise trauma. Int Tinnitus J 12:64–70.
38. Axelsson A and D Prasher (2000) Tinnitus induced by occupational and leisure noise. Noise Health 2:47–54.
39. Cooper JC and JH Owen (1976) Audiologic profile of noise-induced hearing loss. Arch Otolaryngol 102:148–50.
40. Phoon W, H Lee and S Chia (1993) Tinnitus in noise-exposed workers. Occup Med (Lond). 43:35–8.

41. Axelsson A and A Ringdahl (1989) Tinnitus – a study of its prevalence and characteristics. Br J Audiol 23:53–62.
42. Demeester K, A van Wieringen, JJ Hendrickx et al (2007) Prevalence of tinnitus and audiometric shape. B-ENT Suppl 7:37–49.
43. Dias A and R Cordeiro (2008) Association between hearing loss level and degree of discomfort introduced by tinnitus in workers exposed to noise. Braz J Otorhinolaryngol 74:876–83.
44. Quintanilla-Dieck Mde L, M Artunduaga and R Eavey (2009) Intentional exposure to loud music: the second MTV.com survey reveals an opportunity to educate. J Pediatr. 55:550–5.
45. Potier M, C Hoquet, R Lloyd et al (2009) The risks of amplified music for disc-jockeys working in nightclubs. Ear Hear 30: 291–3.
46. Tranter RM and JR Graham (2009) A review of the otological aspects of whiplash injury. J Forensic Leg Med 16:53–5.
47. Claussen C and L Constantinescu (1995) Tinnitus in whiplash injury. Int Tinnitus J 1:105–14.
48. Levine RA (1999) Somatic (craniocervical) tinnitus and the dorsal cochlear nucleus hypothesis. Am J Otolaryngol 20:351–62.
49. Hinton DE, D Chhean, V Pich et al (2006) Tinnitus among Cambodian refugees: relationship to PTSD severity. J Trauma Stress 19:541–6.
50. Fagelson MA (2007) The association between tinnitus and posttraumatic stress disorder. Am J Audiol 16:107–17.

Chapter 67
Traumatic Brain Injury and Blast Exposures: Auditory and Vestibular Pathology

Michael E. Hoffer and Carey Balaban

Keywords Tinnitus • Traumatic brain injury • Tinnitus • Vestibular disorders • Hearing loss

Abbreviations

mTHB Mild traumatic brain injury
TBI   Traumatic brain injury

Introduction

Brain injury has been associated with a variety of neurologic sequelae including the auditory symptoms of hearing loss and tinnitus. Traditionally, we think of brain injury as being secondary to head impact and classify the resultant neurologic damage as mild, moderate, or severe [1]. This classification depends on a variety of factors including length of alteration of consciousness, force of the impact, associated injuries, and neuropathology (such as bleeding). This classification is important since it guides management of the injury and gives health care providers some information about the expected pathologies and best practices for management. There has been a great deal of work done over the years on blunt head injury; however, not all brain injury is secondary to blunt head impact.

The most common etiology of injuries in modern warfare is blast exposure. The use of explosives for terrorism has extended this threat to the civilian world. Such as blunt injury, blast exposure can produce traumatic brain injury. This chapter describes differences between blast injury and blunt head injury from a clinical perspective. We will then consider the audiologic sequelae of blast injury, including tinnitus.

Pathophysiological Features of Traumatic Brain Injury

A heuristic diagram for understanding the progression of signs and symptoms of traumatic brain injury is shown in Fig. 67.1.

1. The direct injury to the brain is presumed to be the "textbook" neuropathological hallmarks of concussive brain injury, which include subdural hematoma, cerebral contusion, and subarachnoid hematoma.
2. The subdural hematoma can be delayed, emerging later in subacute or chronic stages after injury [1]. Tissue injury responses include, at the cellular level, cellular repair and metabolic pathways and, at the tissue level, wound healing and vascular regulatory responses. Secondary damage includes ischemia and excitotoxic events that reflect imbalances in homeostatic control of both the intracellular and extracellular environments. Plasticity of intact neuronal pathways can also contribute to recovery. The outcomes (functional recovery and permanent functional loss) will obviously depend upon the severity (and location) of the primary trauma and the efficacy of the biological responses to the primary and secondary damage. The signs and symptoms of a patient at any given time will reflect the interplay

M.E. Hoffer (✉)
Spatial Orientation Center, Department of Otolaryngology,
Naval Medical Center San Diego, 34800 Bob Wilson Drive,
San Diego, CA 92134-2200, USA
e-mail: Michael.hoffer@med.navy.mil

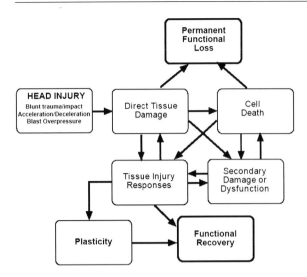

Fig. 67.1 Schematic representation of the development of neurological and otoneurological signs and symptoms after head injury from blunt and/or blast exposure. Direct damage to intracranial (brain, blood vessels, and meninges) and extracranial tissues triggers sequences of downstream injury and recovery processes that result in an evolving clinical presentation during the acute and subacute post-injury periods. These multiple processes can contribute to tinnitus

between these dynamic mechanisms. One example of this approach is the growing recognition that subarachnoid hemorrhage can contribute to both early and delayed mechanisms of secondary brain injury, including vasospasm, transient ischemia, oxidative stress, excitotoxicity, cortical spreading depression, microcirculatory dysfunction, and delayed thromboembolism [2–4].

An Introduction to Blast Injury

A shock wave, a blast wind, and an electromagnetic pulse are generated by detonations of explosives. Primary blast injury is defined as the effects of shock wave propagation through tissue. The blast front is a supersonic over-pressure wave, followed immediately by a negative pressure component termed "the under-pressure" [5]. The blast wave produces a positive–negative shift in intracranial pressure that mirrors the incident waveform [6–8]. Unlike primary blunt or acceleration–deceleration brain trauma, low-level blast exposure produces a global compression–decompression of the cranial contents rather than localized brain

contusions from impact with the skull. Secondary blast injury is produced by shrapnel or fragments. Tertiary blast injury can produce blunt trauma by impact with objects in the environment. Quaternary blast injury is produced by other detonation products such as heat, electromagnetic pulses, and detonation toxins.

Clinical Contrasts: Neurologic Aspects of Mild Blast Trauma Vs. Mild Blunt Head Trauma

A clinical picture is now emerging from a series of studies conducted with active duty military personnel who sustained a mild traumatic brain injury (mTBI) as a consequence of pure blunt head injury or pure blast head injury. These studies have been presented in detail in other publications, but will be summarized here [9, 10]. The mTBI was defined by the Department of Defense Policy for Mild Traumatic Brain Injury (October 2007) criteria as the presence of a documented head trauma or blast exposure event followed by a change in mental status, which could include nausea, dizziness/balance problems, temporary headache, sensitivity to noise or light, tinnitus, vomiting, fatigue, insomnia/sleep disturbances, drowsiness, blurred vision, memory problems, or poor concentration. One study examined males with purely blunt head injury during service in Iraq (34 individuals) or with purely blast injury during service in Iraq (21 individuals) within 9 months of injury. The clinical characteristics varied markedly between the blunt and blast-exposed patients. Specifically, the blast mTBI group had a much higher prevalence of clinically significant hearing loss (43% vs. 7% of the blunt head injury group) and cognitive impairment (90% vs. 17% of the blunt head injury group). Rotational chair balance test results also suggested a different pattern of functional impairment in the two groups with more unilateral, peripheral vestibular symptoms in the blunt group than the blast group [9, 10]. A second study used dynamic posturography to assess postural control after mTBI. The 33 blunt head injury patients and 39 blast injury patients in this study all received mTBI in Iraq and entered the study within 9 months after injury. There was a significant difference in the sensory organization test results of a portion of the blunt patients as compared to all the blast patients. The group mean scores of the motor control test of the patients with blast injuries were markedly worse than the group mean score of the patients who had suffered blunt injuries [9, 10]. In summary, our laboratory results demonstrate that the head injury and resultant sequelae seen after blast injuries are markedly different than those seen after blunt head injury. The implication of these findings is that we cannot utilize our decades of knowledge on blunt head injury to predict the pathologies or discern the best management practices in individuals with blast exposure.

Auditory Pathology after Blast Exposure

The rate of hearing loss, documented by pure-tone audiometry, increases slightly as a function of time from injury to presentation in individuals with blast exposure and resultant head trauma [9]. Tinnitus was noted initially by from 33% and in 43% of those seen later than 1 month after their most recent blast exposure. However, the occurrence of tinnitus is greater than the occurrence of hearing loss in both groups. Nearly 70% of individuals with documented mild traumatic brain injury report tinnitus in the first 72 h after the blast. This number decreases over time, but the rate of tinnitus exceeds the rate of hearing loss at all time points.

There are many factors that might account for the tinnitus seen after blast injury in our mild traumatic brain injury population. Of course, in many individuals, the tinnitus occurs along with the hearing loss, and the postulated etiology would be from primary damage to the ear. However, as stated earlier, tinnitus is more common than hearing loss, and many individuals who have been exposed to a blast wave have normal pure-tone hearing tests but show abnormalities in hearing noise and in central auditory processing. Most of these individuals complain of tinnitus despite their aforementioned normal audiograms. In this regard, it is critical to note that the subjective tinnitus can be produced by mechanisms that range from localized disturbances in the peripheral auditory system and central nervous system to systemic metabolic disturbances [11, 12]. Particularly, germane to blast TBI is the association of tinnitus with stroke and cerebral hemorrhage [11, 13–16]. Somatic tinnitus can accompany

acceleration–deceleration injuries, such as whiplash, in the absence of hearing loss [17]. Blast injury is also associated with a higher than expected rate of posttraumatic Ménière's disease. Thus, it is quite possible that the central and peripheral sequelae of blast injury produce tinnitus independent of direct ear damage. These factors may contribute to a higher than expected rate of tinnitus and suggest the need for more comprehensive diagnostic tests and a broader range of therapeutic approaches. At the same time, this may allow us to intervene specifically in the primary etiology of the tinnitus and/or more effectively manage the tinnitus after it develops.

Conclusions

Ultimately, the tinnitus seen after blast exposure and brain injury is likely multi-factorial and a product of end organ damage, brain injury, and/or a pathology that develops over time. Several factors remain unclear. We have very little data documenting the rate of tinnitus in those with blast exposure who do not have resultant mild traumatic brain injury. Given the rate of blast exposure in current operational settings, this is a very important piece of information. Also, while we have candidate pathologies to account for the tinnitus seen in blast-exposed individuals with mTBI, we still have a great deal of work to do in this area. More targeted and specific tinnitus tests need to be done on this population. We are obligated to better characterize the disorder, so that we can help develop diagnostic and management strategies to initially treat and, in the future, prevent tinnitus associated with blast exposure.

References

1. Greenfield JG. *Traumatic lesions of the central nervous system.* In: Greenfield JG, McMenemy WH, Meyer A and Norman RM (eds) Neuropathology. Edward Arnold Co., London, 1958:408–440
2. Cahill JJ, Calvert W, Zhang JH. *Mechanisms of early brain injury after subarachnoid hemorrhage.* J Cereb Blood Flow Metab 2006 **26**:1341–1353
3. Sehba FA, Bederson JB. *Mechanisms of acute brain injury after subarachnoid hemorrhage.* Neurol Res 2006 **28**: 381–398

4. Macdonald RL, Pluta MP, Zhang JH. Cerebral vasospasm after subarachnoid hemorrhage: the emerging revolution. Nat Clin Pract Neurol 2007 3:256–263

5. Stuhmiller JH, Phillips YY, Richmond DR. The physics and mechanisms of primary blast injury. In: Bellamy RF and Zajtchuk R (eds) Textbook of Military Medicine Conventional Warfare: Blast Ballistic and Burn Injuries. Department of the Army, Office of the Surgeon General, Borden Institute, Washington, DC, 1990:241–270

6. Chavko MW, Koller WA, Prusaczyk WK, McCarron RM. Measurement of blast wave by a miniature fiber optic pressure transducer in the rat brain. J Neurosci Meth 2007 159:277–281

7. Saljo A, Arrhenm F, Bolouri H, Mayorga M, Hamberger A. Neuropathology and pressure in the pig brain resulting from low-impulse noise exposure. J Neurotrauma 2008 25: 1397–1406

8. Moore DF, Jerusalem A, Nyein M, Noels L, Jaffee MS, Radovitzky RA. Computational biology – modeling of primary blast effects on the central nervous system. NeuroImage 2009 47:T10–T20

9. Hoffer ME, Balaban CD, Gottshall KR, Balough BJ. Blast Exposure: Vestibular consequences and associated characteristics. Otol Neurotol 2010 31:232–236

10. Hoffer ME, Donaldson C, Gottshall KR, Balaban C, Balough BJ. Blunt and blast head trauma: different entities. Int Tinnitus J 2009 15:115–118

11. Häusler RR, Levine R. Auditory dysfunction in stroke. Acta Otolaryngol 2000 120:689–703

12. Ahmad N, Seidman M. Tinnitus in the older adult: epidemiology, pathophysiology and treatment options. Drugs Aging 2004 21:297–305

13. Arnold M, Bousser M, Fahrni G, et al. Vertebral artery dissection: presenting findings and predictors of outcome. Stroke 2006 37:2499–2503

14. Matsuda Y, Inagawa T, Amano T. A case of tinnitus and hearing loss after cerebellar hemorrhage. Stroke 1993 24:906–908

15. Musiek F, Baran J. Audiological correlates to a rupture of a pontine arteriovenous malformation. J Am Acad Audiol 2004 15:161–171

16. Stimmer H, Borrmann A, Löer C, Arnold W, Rummeny EJ. Monaural tinnitus from a contralateral inferior colliculus hemorrhage. Audiol Neurootol 2009 14:35–38

17. Levine R. Somatic (craniocervical) tinnitus and the dorsal cochlear nucleus hypothesis. Am J Otolaryngol 1999 20:351–362

Part VI
Management of Tinnitus

Chapter 68
Introduction

Ron Goodey

Keypoints

1. Therapeutic tools include manipulating sensory inputs, modifying psychological influences and a variety of direct approaches to the central nervous system including drugs.
2. A combination of these therapeutic opportunity constitues a package of care.
3. In this section appropriate experts clarify almost every possible therapy.

Keywords Tinnitus therapy • Package of care

Introduction

For clinicians like me, the following section on management of tinnitus is the first section we look at and the one to which we shall refer most often. We want to know if we can improve the way we implement the therapeutic interventions we already use. We want to know if we should seek to adopt therapies which are already available but are ones we do not use. We want to know about new therapies which are being investigated and may, in the future, help our patients.

The editors are to be congratulated on bringing together such a comprehensive team of authors. Each is recognized as an authority on at least one aspect of tinnitus management. Collectively, they provide a detailed description, analysis, and instructions on almost every aspect of tinnitus management available to help us in the care of our patients.

Earlier sections of this book are also relevant to the management of tinnitus. However, as clinicians, we do not really manage tinnitus. We manage a patient who has tinnitus, and we help that patient to cope with this disorder. Our first contact with a patient, the obtaining of a history, items in a questionnaire, our clinical examination, and the tests performed are all part of our management of that patient. During a well-handled assessment process, anxiety may start to subside. Alternatively, new concerns may be raised. The first contact, even the making of a first appointment, may influence our patient's concerns and affect the therapeutic outcome. Every component of the assessment process is part of the therapeutic management of each patient troubled by tinnitus. However, this section is focussed on the various therapeutic tools we may utilize or recommend following assessment.

Tinnitus is most likely always multi-factorial. However, sometimes, one factor is dominant, and correcting that factor alone may be almost all that our patient requires, as far as their tinnitus management is concerned. Clearing the ear canals of wax or debris, surgical correction of hearing loss, the withdrawal of a drug, or facilitating the treatment of a psychiatric disturbance may stop tinnitus from being a problem. However, even in these "dominant factor" situations, other factors helped determine that awareness of tinnitus became a major feature and influence whether the tinnitus persists as a problem, even after the dominant factor has been treated.

In most of our patients, several factors are important in their awareness of tinnitus and the distress they experience. I find it helpful to group these factors into three broad categories.

R. Goodey (✉)
Department of Surgery, University of Auckland,
3 Wootton Road, Remuera, Auckland 1050, New Zealand
e-mail: rongoodey@xtra.co.nz

A.R. Møller et al. (eds.), *Textbook of Tinnitus*,
DOI 10.1007/978-1-60761-145-5_68, © Springer Science+Business Media, LLC 2011

- *Changes in sensory input.* These usually predisposed to the onset of tinnitus and help maintain it.
- *Psychological influences.* These include emotional state and emotional associations, lack of understanding and resultant anxiety, and unconscious conditioning ("neurophysiological model").
- *Changes in neural activity within the brain.* These have usually been triggered by the above factors, sometimes by direct injury, but then become self-perpetuating and are now regarded as the actual "generators" of tinnitus.

I then view the same three broad categories as distinguishing the avenues available for treating each patient who is troubled by tinnitus.

1. *Manipulating and where possible normalizing sensory inputs.* This applies most often to auditory input where hearing loss may be corrected or compensated, or therapeutic auditory stimulation applied. A lot of attention has recently been focused on somatosensory inputs, their ability to modulate and sometimes trigger tinnitus, and how these effects may be reduced. Visual, olfactory, vestibular, taste, and other sensory inputs may have influences on tinnitus, but have received little study in this context.
2. *Controlling emotional factors.* Successful management of tinnitus almost always requires reduction in concern about implications and often separation from anger about perceived causes. Disassociation of tinnitus from emotional factors, especially depression, anxiety, fear, and anger is essential. Explanation and understanding reduce anxiety and fear and the tendency for a patient to dwell upon their tinnitus. The most sophisticated and validated approach to achieving this "de-concerning" is cognitive behavioural therapy. At a less conscious level, de-conditioning techniques such as tinnitus-retraining therapy and desensitization with music are useful in reducing physiological changes associated with troublesome tinnitus.
3. *Direct approaches to the central nervous system.* Once tinnitus has become intrusive and distressing, then treatment through control of sensory input and psychological factors may be insufficient. Neuroplastic changes within the brain may need to be approached directly as well. The most readily available route is through the bloodstream, providing access for drugs and dietary factors. However, changes within the brain can also be approached directly by surgery, by direct electrical stimulation, and, especially in this context, by transcranial magnetic stimulation. Even if such direct approaches can reverse neuroplastic changes, they almost certainly need to be used in conjunction with the control of sensory input and psychological factors if relapse is to be prevented.

We are fortunate that the experts who have contributed to this section of the book have, between them, examined all avenues and clarified almost every possible therapy. Generally, they acknowledge, explicitly or implicitly, that each therapy described needs to be part of a package of care incorporating other approaches if it is to be of long-lasting benefit.

In managing sensory input, we find chapters on auditory training (Chap. 72), sound stimulation and hearing aids (Chap. 74), music treatment (Chap. 75), middle-ear implantable devices (Chap. 76), cochlear implants (Chap. 77), treatment directed to the ear (Chap. 83), and surgical treatments (Chap. 82), all of which may improve or manipulate auditory sensory input. Some pharmacological and nutritional therapies have their effect by improving inner ear function and auditory input (Chaps 78, 79 and 92). Chapters on temporomandibular joint dysfunction (Chap. 95), cutaneous stimulation (Chap. 91), focus on techniques which probably alter somatosensory influences on tinnitus, as may neuro-biofeedback (Chap. 87) and low-level laser therapy (and Chap. 93).

Psychological factors are addressed at a conscious level through chapters on counselling (Chap. 70) and cognitive behavioural treatment (Chap. 71) but may also be important components of sensory stimulation such as in music treatment (Chap. 75). De-conditioning at an unconscious level is inherent in tinnitus retaining therapy (Chap. 73) but may also be important in some forms of sound treatment. There are benefits in more holistic approaches (Chap. 92).

Most of the pharmacological treatments described act directly on the central nervous system (Chap. 78) as may some non-conventional therapies, nutritional factors, and vitamins (Chap. 92). Principals of neuro-modulation are discussed (Chap. 86) prior to descriptions of neuro-biofeedback (Chap. 87) and of direct stimulation both magnetically (Chap. 88) and electrically (Chaps. 89 and 90).

Some specific treatments for particular problems are also described, such as treatment of vestibular schwannoma (Chap. 85) and microvascular decompression (Chap. 84). Chapter 94 is devoted to the similarities between treatment of tinnitus and that of pain. The final chapter is devoted to the methodology of clinical trials for tinnitus. Treatment of disorders that are closely associated with tinnitus such as temporomandibular and masticatory disorders can often relieve tinnitus (Chaps. 95 and 96).

This section is an authoritative description and assessment of almost all the approaches to tinnitus therapy currently in use and others with potential for future benefit. Where a potential therapeutic approach has not been addressed, it is mostly because it has not been reliably reported. There is still room for more innovation.

Our improved understanding of the influences of sensory input and psychological factors and the neuroplastic changes, which result, has given us far greater sophistication in managing our patients who feel distressed by their tinnitus. For each patient, we have to identify the most helpful ways in which sensory inputs can be manipulated, how best to improve understanding and disassociate emotional factors, and whether there is a place for centrally acting agents and other direct approaches. The chapters in this section are a reference library of all the information available to help us make the most appropriate recommendations for each patient in the context of what is available for them.

Chapter 69
The Prevention of Tinnitus and Noise-Induced Hearing Loss

Larry E. Roberts, William Hal Martin, and Daniel J. Bosnyak

Keypoints

1. Although tinnitus is more common in older individuals, it can occur at any age. Because tinnitus in most individuals is associated with hearing impairment, prevalence may be increasing among youthful populations owing to exposure to environmental and recreational sound.

2. At present, there are no effective medical treatments for chronic tinnitus. Because hearing loss is a major risk factor, primary prevention is possible. Primary prevention is effective in other health domains, although it takes time for such programs to have impact.

3. Public education programs, role modeling by parents, cooperation from employers and industry, awareness campaigns, education of health professionals about avoidable risk factors, legislated standards for sound-emitting devices, and protection strategies that are acceptable to the young as well as adults, all have a role to play.

4. "Dangerous Decibels" is an example of a successful program aimed at reducing noise-induced hearing loss and tinnitus among school-aged children and young adults.

5. Epidemiological research tracking the prevalence of hearing loss and tinnitus at all ages, and research on intervention approaches, can provide essential information about effectiveness and long-term trends.

Keywords Tinnitus • Hearing loss • Prevention • Noise exposure • Epidemiology • Dangerous Decibels

Abbreviations

HL	Hearing level
TEN	Threshold equalizing noise test
DPOAE	Distortion product otoacoustic emissions
ABRs	Auditory brainstem responses
NIOSH	National Institute for Occupational Safety and Health
NIHL	Noise induced hearing loss
WHO	World Health Organization
OMSI	Oregon Museum of Science and Industry

Introduction

It is a common perception that tinnitus is an affliction of older individuals, which is to a significant extent true. Although reported prevalence varies widely among studies (see Chap. 5), it has been estimated that between 8 and 20% of individuals over the age of 60 report a persisting tinnitus, and among these individuals approximately 25% describe their tinnitus "moderate" and another 6.6% as "severe" [1] implying an adverse effect on quality of life in the latter group, which translates into millions of Americans and many more around the globe. However, it is well documented by national surveys [2] and confirmed by clinical experience that persisting tinnitus can occur at any age. Because in most individuals tinnitus is associated with hearing impairment, prevalence may be increasing among youthful populations owing to exposure to environmental and recreational sound in our electronic age.

L.E. Roberts (✉)
Department of Psychology, Neuroscience, and Behavior, McMaster University, 1280 Main Street West, Hamilton, Ontario, Canada L8S 4K1
e-mail: roberts@mcmaster.ca

A.R. Møller et al. (eds.), *Textbook of Tinnitus*,
DOI 10.1007/978-1-60761-145-5_69, © Springer Science+Business Media LLC, 2011

This state of affairs is by itself sufficient cause for concern among those who formulate public health policy. However, the problem is compounded by the fact that while treatments exist that often can reduce the impact of chronic tinnitus on individual lives, elimination of the disturbing tinnitus sensation itself remains largely beyond the reach of medicine (see Section V of this book). It is especially worrisome that although tinnitus experienced by younger individuals after noise exposure often subsides, tinnitus may return later in life as changes in brain function related to aging unmask a hidden vulnerability. The prospect of a growing cohort in future years calls not only for intensified research into the causes of tinnitus and its treatment but also for programs aimed at its prevention.

Programs and policies aimed at primary prevention have worked in other domains (see Fig. 69.1). In the three decades following publication of the US Surgeon General's Report on Smoking and Health in 1964, the incidence of smoking (a major preventable cause of respiratory and cardiovascular disease) in the United States declined from 42% of adults in 1964 to 26% in 1998, with this decline being particularly steep among men more of whom smoked (53%) than did women (33%) in 1964, compared to 28% and 23%, respectively, in 1998 [3]. Public education, anti-smoking campaigns, government restrictions on advertising and conditions of use, and litigation have undoubtedly contributed to this outcome, which (although it is not a simple matter to quantify health benefits) is an important medical success story. Use of seat belts in automobiles and helmets for cyclists have also doubtlessly reduced the risk of injury and subsequent social and health costs associated with driving and cycling. These well-known examples illustrate some of the key ingredients of successful prevention. Public awareness is essential, and cooperation from industry (sometimes resisted) is needed. When the need is urgent, government policies, law making, and legal action can mobilize interventions to reduce risk. The personal costs associated with prevention including convenience and expense must be acceptable. Persistence and patience over the long haul are required, and monitoring is needed to gauge effectiveness.

It must be acknowledged that prevention of tinnitus does not have the same urgency as that associated with tobacco use or passenger protection, which are examples that address risks affecting a substantial proportion of the population and if ignored can have catastrophic personal consequences. However, for millions of individuals severely affected, tinnitus is a debilitating and costly condition for which no effective medical treatments are currently available. Tinnitus also shares in common with these examples evidence of a role for a causal and tractable factor that makes prevention of new cases of tinnitus a practical goal. Epidemiological and neuroscience studies indicate that among the many benefits of preserving normal hearing is likely to be the prevention of tinnitus.

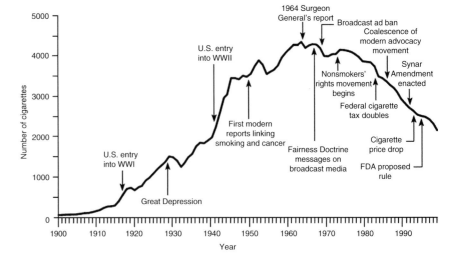

Fig. 69.1 Adult per capita cigarette consumption and major smoking and health events, United States 1900–1990. From the report of the US Surgeon General (2001) *Women and Smoking*

Tinnitus and Hearing Loss

One of the highest risk factors for tinnitus is noise exposure. Individuals who regularly worked in loud sound situations or were frequently exposed to impulse noise were nearly three times more likely to have tinnitus than those who did not have regular, loud sound exposures [4]. Henry et al. [5] noted that prolonged sound exposure and noise trauma represented the most commonly known factor associated with the onset of tinnitus. The Oregon Tinnitus Data Registry reported that sound exposures represented the most commonly reported onset factor in a tinnitus clinic population of 2,503 individuals [6]. Tinnitus has also been found to be an early indicator of permanent sensory neural hearing loss in work settings with prolonged loud sound exposure [7]. When measured within individuals, there is a close correspondence between the frequencies that are present in the tinnitus sensation and the sound frequencies at which hearing loss is present in the audiogram [8–11]. The nature of this relation is that ratings of sound frequencies for their similarity to tinnitus increase incrementally at the audiometric edge and continue to increase with the depth of threshold shift up to about 12 kHz [10, 11] (see Chap. 13). Konig et al. [12] reported that tinnitus is associated with steeper slopes of hearing loss, and also noted a strong relationship between the frequency with the steepest slope and the dominant tinnitus pitch

for tonal cases. Restoration of hearing is often associated with a decrease in tinnitus, provided that the tinnitus has not been present for too long. It is commonly reported in the clinic and confirmed by systematic study [13] that many individuals with tinnitus experience a reduction of their symptoms when fitted with a hearing aid (see Chap. 74).

However, many people have hearing loss without having tinnitus, and many people who have "normal" hearing according to their audiograms have tinnitus. For example, Barnea et al. [14] found that 8% of their patients suffering from tinnitus had normal hearing thresholds (<25 dB HL) up to 8 kHz, and Roberts et al. [15] reported that 8 of 32 individuals with tinnitus (25%) had normal hearing similarly defined. However, in the latter study, all 32 individuals with tinnitus had hearing thresholds exceeding 25 dB HL when measured above 8 kHz, underscoring the need for more thorough audiometric assessments. In a subsequent study, Roberts et al. [11] measured hearing thresholds up to 16 kHz in two groups of individuals with tinnitus: one consisting of individuals aged 50 years or older ($n=40$) and the other aged less than 50 years ($n=7$). As expected, the older group exhibited threshold elevations commencing above about 2 kHz, but the younger group had normal hearing thresholds up to 10 kHz (see Fig. 69.2). However, when the people in these tinnitus groups were compared to age-matched controls without tinnitus, both tinnitus groups had

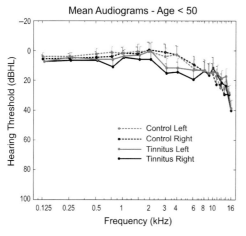
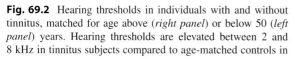
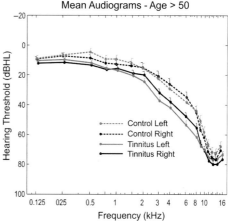

Fig. 69.2 Hearing thresholds in individuals with and without tinnitus, matched for age above (*right panel*) or below 50 (*left panel*) years. Hearing thresholds are elevated between 2 and 8 kHz in tinnitus subjects compared to age-matched controls in

both age groups, even though the audiograms for the younger tinnitus group were in the normal range up to 10 kHz. From Roberts et al. [11]

hearing thresholds that were elevated by approximately 11 dB compared to controls over the frequency regions corresponding to their tinnitus. These findings suggest that tinnitus and hearing impairment are related and that the degree of impairment needed to increase the risk for tinnitus is not large [16].

An alternative interpretation of the results of Fig. 69.2 is that the threshold elevations seen in the audiograms of individuals with tinnitus do not reflect reduced hearing, but confusion of the test sound with their tinnitus, which overlaps the same frequency range. Measures other than the conventional audiogram provide another approach. Tests for off-frequency listening can indicate the presence of cochlear dead regions that may lead to the development of tinnitus. Weisz et al. [17] administered the Threshold Equalizing Noise (TEN) test for off-frequency listening in individuals with tinnitus who were selected for study because their audiometric thresholds were within the normal range. Evidence was found for circumscribed cochlear damage in the frequency ranges that were rated as being similar to the tinnitus percept. Cochlear dead regions also appear to influence the shape of tinnitus spectra when band-limited noises differing in center frequency are used to measure these spectra, implying that individuals with tinnitus are listening off frequency to sounds in the stimulus where hearing thresholds are better preserved [11]. Measurement of distortion product otoacoustic emissions (DPOAEs) is another approach to detecting changes in hearing. Shiomi et al. [18] found significant decreases in DPOAE amplitudes over limited frequency ranges in 93% of ears in individuals with tinnitus and normal audiograms, in 96% of ears in patients with tinnitus and hearing impairment, and in only 15.4% of control ears. Similarly, Gouveris et al. [19] found decreased amplitudes in the 1,650–2,400 Hz range and increased amplitudes in the 4–6.3 kHz range in tinnitus patients. These studies point to some degree of impairment of outer hair cell function in tinnitus. Studies of auditory brain stem responses (ABRs) have provided more ambiguous results, with some authors reporting shortened wave V latency [20], others prolongations of waves I, III, and V [21, 22], and others no effects on the latency of waves I–V [14, 23].

If it is accepted that hearing loss is a substantial risk factor for tinnitus, how is tinnitus generated when hearing impairment occurs? Neuroscience studies have begun to answer this question (for a review see Chap. 13). Briefly, hearing loss induced by experimental noise trauma in animals leads to a reorganization of tonotopic maps in the primary auditory cortex, as thalamocortical input to the affected region is impaired [24–26]. This reorganization likely occurs because when thalamocortical input is reduced, neurons in the hearing loss region begin to express the frequency tuning of their unaffected neighbors via horizontal connections in the tonotopic map. It has also been found that the spontaneous firing rate of the affected neurons is increased and that there is an increase in neural synchrony (temporally coupled neural activity, sometimes called temporal coherence) in the region of hearing impairment [24]. Evidence from physiological, psychoacoustic, and human brain imaging studies suggests that increased neural synchrony in the hearing loss region may underlie the tinnitus sound [27].

Notwithstanding these lines of research pointing to a role for hearing loss in tinnitus, it is undeniable that there are individuals who have hearing loss but not tinnitus (see the older control group of Fig. 69.2). This is a puzzle to be explained. One factor that might distinguish between individuals with and without tinnitus despite the presence of hearing impairment is a difference in the prevalence of cochlear dead regions in the two groups. To date, this possibility has not been investigated. Age-related changes in intracortical inhibition [28, 29] may also play a role, with lags favoring normal tonotopic structure and conferring a benefit in preventing tinnitus. Some older individuals who have high-frequency hearing loss without tinnitus may eventually come to experience tinnitus, reducing the disparity between the two phenomena. Nevertheless, what protects many elderly individuals with hearing loss from tinnitus is presently unknown.

Hearing Loss in the Young

Noise exposure, which can lead to hearing loss, is an increasing problem among children. Blair et al. [30] reported that at some time during their young lives, 97% of 273 third graders surveyed had been exposed to sound levels that are regarded to be hazardous to their hearing. Another recent study indicated that 16% of 14- to 18-year-olds listen to their personal stereo systems at levels exceeding the recommendations of the National Institute for Occupational Safety and Health (NIOSH) on a daily basis [31]. Thirty percent of the students said they sometimes participated in other noisy activities (such as shooting firearms or attending auto races); however, only 5.5% of the students ever used hearing protection while engaged in these activities. Sources of excessive sound exposure for children include loud music [32, 33], real or toy firearms [34], power tools [35, 36], fireworks [37], loud toys [8, 38], and snowmobiles or other loud engines such as jet skis or motorcycles [39]. The World Health Organization reported that North American children "may receive more noise at school than workers from an 8-h work day at a factory"[40]. Surveys of junior high and high school students have identified large deficiencies in their knowledge about normal hearing as well as hearing loss, and that students know little about the damaging effects of noise exposure [41, 42]. Results from the third National Health and Nutrition Examination Survey indicated that 12.5% of 6- to 19-year-olds in the United States (5.2 million) have documented evidence of elevated hearing thresholds directly attributed to noise exposure [43]. Early exposure to noise causes cumulative damage that accelerates age-related changes and long-term consequences [44].

The good news is that nearly all noise-induced hearing loss (NIHL) and related tinnitus can be prevented. Educational interventions can increase knowledge about NIHL issues. One study that evaluated the effectiveness of hearing conservation education in high school students found an average increase of 16% correct responses after participation in an educational program [45]. A second study presented an educational program on hearing conservation to elementary school children and found that their knowledge regarding NIHL improved by an average of 23% [46]. Recent work using resources from the Dangerous Decibels program (see below) has shown that several interventions, including classroom programs, museum exhibits, and online interactives can improve knowledge, attitudes, and intended behaviors related to sound exposure and use of hearing protection strategies [47–49]. Knowledge of potentially dangerous sounds, their consequences, and simple ways to protect oneself are all significant factors in prevention of NIHL and tinnitus. Public education can promote hearing health and behavior to reduce noise-induced hearing loss, a fully preventable condition.

Dangerous Decibels

The health behavior literature has shown that attention to specific components of an intervention affects the success of that intervention. Strategies that tailor messages to the target group [50–53], use interactive not passive instruction [54], and incorporate teaching skills and self-efficacy [52, 53, 55, 56] have been most effective. *Dangerous Decibels*® is an exemplary program that has been built on health promotion theory applied to hearing loss and tinnitus prevention.

The Dangerous Decibels partnership began in 1999 and has been locally, regionally, nationally, and internationally active in hearing health promotion [48, 57]. The total number of individuals reached by Dangerous Decibels activities, including the museum exhibition at Oregon Museum of Science and Industry (OMSI), classroom education, web-based activities, OMSI Science Festivals at county fairs, and educator training workshops, approaches one million annually. It is the most extensively developed, disseminated, and evaluated hearing loss and tinnitus prevention program in the world with materials in 46 US States and 17 different countries. Between 2001 and 2006, 4,634 elementary and middle school students and adults participated in the formative and summative evaluation process for the Dangerous Decibels interventions. The results showed that the interventions were effective at changing knowledge, attitudes, and behaviors regarding exposure to loud sound and use of appropriate hearing protective strategies [47].

The Dangerous Decibels resources include the following components, some of which are illustrated in Fig. 69.3:

- A permanent Dangerous Decibels exhibition at the OMSI including 12 components covering over 2,000 ft^2 and providing information to approximately 670,000 visitors each year 70,000 of whom are K-12 students on school group field trips.
- A virtual Dangerous Decibels museum exhibition at the Dangerous Decibels website (www.dangerousdecibels.org).
- An interactive, inquiry-based classroom program targeting kindergarten through 12th grade students covering the physics of sound, normal hearing function, the pathophysiology and functional consequences of noise exposure, and tinnitus and hearing loss protective strategies.
- Educator training workshops that fully equip and certify individuals to present the classroom program in a manner proven to be effective, plus a Teachers Resource Guide with activities, images, and graphics intended to supplement the classroom program.

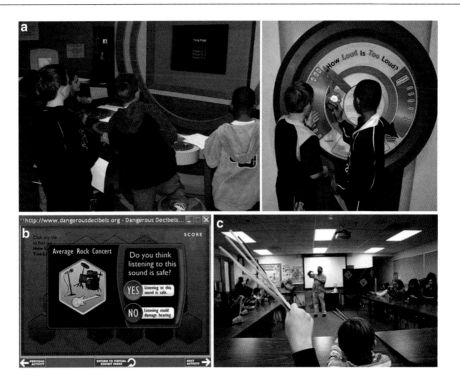

Fig. 69.3 Dangerous Decibels. (**a**) Fourth grade students playing "Whatta ya know?" (*left panel* and "How loud is too loud?" (*right panel*), two of the of the exhibit components at the Oregon Museum of Science and Industry. (**b**) Image from the Dangerous Decibels Virtual Exhibit game "How loud is too loud?" conducted over the Web. (**c**) Dangerous Decibels classroom program being delivered to fourth grade students (hair cell function is being illustrated here). (Photos by Genevieve Y. Martin)

- The "Jolene" system for measuring the sound pressure levels generated by personal music systems through headphones. The *Jolene Cookbook* [58] describes how students can make their own version of a Jolene.

These and other Dangerous Decibels activities are designed to communicate information about three questions important for the protection of hearing: (1) What are sources of dangerous sounds? (2) What are the consequences of being exposed to dangerous sounds? (3) How can I protect myself from dangerous sounds? Tinnitus is one of the potential consequences, and information about the role of hearing loss in tinnitus is essential to prevention.

Conclusion

Noise-induced hearing loss and tinnitus prevention activities have historically been emphasized in, or perhaps even limited to, occupational and military settings with the assumption that those settings provided the highest risks. However, recent epidemiologic evidence [59] indicates that cumulative hearing loss in the population has not declined over the past 30 years despite expected decreases in NIHL due to mandatory hearing conservation programs in occupational settings, suggesting that sound-related hearing loss may be resulting from exposures in non-occupational settings. Teaching individuals from an early age to cherish and protect the gift of hearing and equipping them to do so provides the highest likelihood of reducing the incidence of tinnitus.

Primary prevention takes time (Fig. 69.1), and education about noise exposure, while fundamental to success, is not the only factor that may bring benefits. Role modeling by parents, cooperation from employers and from industry, public awareness campaigns, education of health professionals about avoidable risk factors, legislated standards for sound-emitting devices, and protection strategies that are acceptable to the young as well as adults, are needed for a successful outcome. Epidemiological research into the prevalence of hearing loss and tinnitus at all ages, and research on the effectiveness of intervention approaches, can provide essential information about the magnitude of the problem and long-term trends. In addition to reducing the incidence of tinnitus, other benefits of hearing protection are reductions in health care costs and in disability claims as well as improved social and workplace communication. Primary prevention is especially important for tinnitus, because while some treatments exist that may reduce the impact of tinnitus on individual lives, elimination of the tinnitus sensation itself remains largely beyond the reach of medicine.

Acknowledgments Preparation of this chapter was assisted by grants from the Canadian Institutes for Health Research, the Natural Sciences and Engineering Research Council of Canada, the American Tinnitus Association, and the Tinnitus Research Initiative (LER); Oregon Health & Science University Tinnitus Clinic and the OHSU Center for Healthy Communities, and the Oregon Prevention Research Center (Centers for Disease Control and Prevention – CDC1 U43 DP00002401) (WHM).

References

1. Coles RRA, AC Davis and MP Haggard (1981) Medical Research Council's Institute of Hearing Research. Epidemiology of tinnitus. CIBA Found. Symp. 85:16–34.
2. Axelsson A and A Ringdahl (1989) Tinnitus--a study of its prevalence and characteristics. Br J Audiol 23:53–62.
3. Fishman YI, DH Reser , JC Arezzo et al. (2001) Neural correlates of auditory stream segregation in primary auditory cortex of the awake monkey. Hear Res 151:167–87.
4. Hoffman HJ, (2004) Epidemiology of tinnitus., in Tinnitus: theory and management., JB Snow, Jr., Editor, BC Decker: Lewiston, NY. 16–41.
5. Henry JA, KC Dennis and MA Schechter (2005) General review of tinnitus: prevalence, mechanisms, effects, and management. J Speech Lang Hear Res 48:1204–35.
6. Meikle MB, TA Creedon and SE Griest (2004) Tinnitus Archive, second edition (http://www.tinnitusArchive.org/). 2004.
7. Griest SE and PM Bishop (1998) Tinnitus as an early indicator of permanent hearing loss. A 15 year longitudinal study of noise exposed workers. AAOHN J 46:325–9.
8. Axelsson A and T Jerson (1985) Noisy toys: a possible source of sensorineural hearing loss. Pediatrics 76:574–8.
9. Henry JA, CL Flick, A Gilbert et al. (1999) Reliability of tinnitus loudness matches under procedural variation. J Am Acad Audiol 10:502–20.
10. Norena A, C Micheyl, S Chery-Croze et al. (2002) Psychoacoustic characterization of the tinnitus spectrum: implications for the underlying mechanisms of tinnitus. Audiol Neurootol 7:358–69.
11. Roberts LE, G Moffat, M Baumann et al. (2008) Residual inhibition functions overlap tinnitus spectra and the region of auditory threshold shift. J Assoc Res Otolaryngol 9:417–35.
12. Konig O, R Schaette, R Kempter et al. (2006) Course of hearing loss and occurrence of tinnitus. Hear Res 221:59–64.
13. Folmer RL and JR Carroll (2006) Long-term effectiveness of ear-level devices for tinnitus. Otolaryngol Head Neck Surg 134:132–7.
14. Barnea G, J Attias, S Gold et al. (1990) Tinnitus with normal hearing sensitivity: extended high-frequency audiometry and auditory-nerve brain-stem-evoked responses. Audiology 29:36–45.
15. Roberts LE, G Moffat and DJ Bosnyak (2006) Residual inhibition functions in relation to tinnitus spectra and auditory threshold shift. Acta Otolaryngol Suppl 556:27–33.
16. Wienbruch C, I Paul, N Weisz et al. (2006) Frequency organization of the 40-Hz auditory steady-state response in normal hearing and in tinnitus. Neuroimage 33:180–94.
17. Weisz N, T Hartmann, K Dohrmann et al. (2006) High-frequency tinnitus without hearing loss does not mean absence of deafferentation. Hear Res 222:108–14.
18. Shiomi Y, J Tsuji, Y Naito et al. (1997) Characteristics of DPOAE audiogram in tinnitus patients. Hear Res 108:83–8.
19. Gouveris H, J Maurer and W Mann (2005) DPOAE-grams in patients with acute tonal tinnitus. Otolaryngol Head Neck Surg 132:550–3.
20. Møller AR, MB Møller, PJ Jannetta et al. (1992) Compound action potentials recorded from the exposed eighth nerve in patients with intractable tinnitus. Laryngoscope 102: 187–97.
21. Ikner CL and AH Hassen (1990) The effect of tinnitus on ABR latencies. Ear Hear 11:16–20.
22. Rosenhall U and A Axelsson (1995) Auditory brainstem response latencies in patients with tinnitus. Scand Audiol 24:97–100.
23. Gerken GM, PS Hesse and JJ Wiorkowski (2001) Auditory evoked responses in control subjects and in patients with problem-tinnitus. Hear Res 157:52–64.
24. Norena AJ and JJ Eggermont (2003) Changes in spontaneous neural activity immediately after an acoustic trauma: implications for neural correlates of tinnitus. Hear Res 183:137–53.
25. Rajan R and DR Irvine (1998) Neuronal responses across cortical field A1 in plasticity induced by peripheral auditory organ damage. Audiol Neurootol 3:123–44.
26. Robertson D and DR Irvine (1989) Plasticity of frequency organization in auditory cortex of guinea pigs with partial unilateral deafness. J Comp Neurol 282:456–71.
27. Eggermont JJ and LE Roberts (2004) The neuroscience of tinnitus. Trends Neurosci 27:676–82.
28. Caspary DM, TA Schatteman and LF Hughes (2005) Age-related changes in the inhibitory response properties of dorsal cochlear nucleus output neurons: role of inhibitory inputs. J Neurosci 25:10952–9.
29. Ling LL, LF Hughes and DM Caspary (2005) Age-related loss of the GABA synthetic enzyme glutamic acid decarboxylase in rat primary auditory cortex. Neuroscience 132: 1103–13.
30. Blair JC, D Hardegree and PV Benson (1996) Necessity and effectiveness of a hearing conservation program for elementary students. J Edu Aud 4:12–6.

31. Martin WH. How loud is your music? Beliefs and practices regarding use of personal stereo systems. in Proceedings of the 9th International Congress on Noise as a Public Health Problem. 2008. Mystic, Connecticut.

32. Lipscomb DM (1972) The increase in prevalence of high frequency hearing impairment among college students. Audiology 11:231–7.

33. Meyer-Bisch C (1996) Epidemiological evaluation of hearing damage related to strongly amplified music (personal cassette players, discotheques, rock concerts)--high-definition audiometric survey on 1364 subjects. Audiology 35:121–42.

34. Lipscomb DM, (1974) Dangerous playthings., in Noise: the unwanted sounds., DM Lipscomb, Editor. 1974: Chicago.

35. Plakke BL (1985) Hearing conservation in secondary industrial arts classes: a challenge for school audiologists. Lang Speech Hear Ser Schools 16:75–9.

36. Roeser RJ (1980) Industrial hearing conservation programs in the high schools (Protect the Ear Before the 12th Year). Ear Hear 1:119–20.

37. Gupta D and SK Vishwakarma (1989) Toy weapons and firecrackers: a source of hearing loss. Laryngoscope 99:330–4.

38. Hellstrom PA, HA Dengerink and A Axelsson (1992) Noise levels from toys and recreational articles for children and teenagers. Br J Audiol 26:267–70.

39. Bess FH, J Dodd-Murphy and RA Parker (1998) Children with minimal sensorineural hearing loss: prevalence, educational performance, and functional status. Ear Hear 19:339–54.

40. Strategies for prevention of deafness and hearing impairment. Prevention of noise-induced hearing loss. 1997, WHO.

41. Lass NJ, CM Woodford, C Lundeen et al. (1987) A Survey of High School Students' Knowledge and Awareness of Hearing, Hearing Loss, and Hearing Health. Hearing J. 40:15–19.

42. Lass NJ, CM Woodford, C Lundeen et al. (1987) A Hearing-Conservation Program for a Junior High School. Hearing J. 40:32–40.

43. Niskar AS, SM Kieszak, AE Holmes et al. (2001) Estimated prevalence of noise-induced hearing threshold shifts among children 6 to 19 years of age: the Third National Health and Nutrition Examination Survey, 1988–1994, United States. Pediatrics 108:40–3.

44. Kujawa SG and MC Liberman (2006) Acceleration of age-related hearing loss by early noise exposure: evidence of a misspent youth. J Neurosci 26:2115–23.

45. Lass NJ, CM Woodford, C Lundeen et al. (1986) The prevention of noise-induced hearing loss in the school-aged population: a school educational hearing conservation program. J Aud Res 26:247–54.

46. Report on the Activities for the Year 1991 of the Select Committee on Children, Youth, and Families. 1991, 102d Congress, First Session: Washington, D.C.

47. Griest SE, RL Folmer and WH Martin (2007) Effectiveness of "Dangerous Decibels," a school-based hearing loss prevention program. Am J Audiol 16:S165–81.

48. Martin WH, SE Griest, C Spain et al. Effectiveness of web-based edutainment for hearing loss prevention in children. in Conference on Noise-induced Hearing Loss in Children at Work & Play. 2006. Cincinnati.

49. Martin WH, JL Sobel, SE Griest et al. (2006) Noise-induced hearing loss in children: preventing the silent epidemic. J. Otology 1:11–21.

50. Foshee VA, KE Bauman, XB Arriaga et al. (1998) An evaluation of Safe Dates, an adolescent dating violence prevention program. Am J Public Health 88:45–50.

51. MacDonald SA (1999) The cardiovascular health education program: assessing the impact on rural and urban adolescents' health knowledge. Appl Nurs Res 12:86–90.

52. Main DS, DC Iverson, J McGloin et al. (1994) Preventing HIV infection among adolescents: evaluation of a school-based education program. Prev Med 23:409–17.

53. Noland MP, RJ Kryscio, RS Riggs et al. (1998) The effectiveness of a tobacco prevention program with adolescents living in a tobacco-producing region. Am J Public Health 88:1862–5.

54. Black DR, NS Gobler and JP Sciacca (1998) Peer helping/ involvement: an efficacious way to meet the challenge of reducing alcohol, tobacco, and other drug use among youth. J Sch Health 68:87–93.

55. Price JH, P Beach, S Everett et al. (1998) Evaluation of a three-year urban elementary school tobacco prevention program. J Sch Health 68:26–31.

56. Reding DJ, V Fischer, P Gunderson et al. (1996) Teens teach skin cancer prevention. J Rural Health 12:265–72.

57. Martin WH (2008) Dangerous Decibels®: partnership for preventing noise-induced hearing loss and tinnitus in children. Seminars in Hearing 1:102–10.

58. Martin GY, and Martin, W.H (2007,2009) The Jolene Cookbook Instruction Guide. 2007,2009: Oregon Health & Science University.

59. Dobie RA. Age-related hearing loss in the USA since 1960. in Proceedings of the National Hearing Conservation Association annual meeting. 2009. Atlanta.

Chapter 70
Counseling and Psycho-Education for Tinnitus Management

Grant D. Searchfield, Jane Magnusson, Georgina Shakes, Eberhard Biesinger, and Orianna Kong

Keypoints

1. Tinnitus is a dysfunction of the auditory system that has proven to be highly resistant to a wide variety of treatments (Laryngoscope 109:1202–1211, 1999) making it a difficult condition to treat and to live with (*The psychological management of chronic tinnitus: a cognitive-behavioral approach.* Allyn & Bacon: Boston, 2001).

2. As there are no easy cures for tinnitus, the tinnitus patient has to adjust to not only the perception of internal noise but also to the often negative beliefs and consequences that accompany it (Psychological aspects of tinnitus, in *Contributions to medical psychology.* Pergamon: New York, 1984).

3. Some of the difficulties that tinnitus patients encounter include high levels of emotional distress, sleep difficulties, loss of concentration, attention problems, and disruption to their personal, occupational, and social lives (J Speech Hear Disord 48:150–154, 1983).

4. The need to address these "psychological" aspects of tinnitus has been known for many years (Lancet 36:828–829, 1841) but has only recently been given adequate consideration.

5. Fundamentally, the goal of tinnitus treatment is to reduce the negative impact this condition has on the patient's life. To facilitate this, counseling helps individuals understand their tinnitus, which can reduce the occurrence and level of distress.

6. Providing patients with education about what their tinnitus is, and what it is not, helps to demystify the condition, which can greatly change how they perceive and respond to their tinnitus.

7. This chapter focuses on one counseling approach and provides resource materials that will enable the practitioner to provide support for their patients' efforts to reduce tinnitus distress.

Keywords Tinnitus • Counseling • Treatment • Attention • Education • Habituation

Abbreviations

ASA	Auditory Scene Analysis
CBT	Cognitive Behavioral Therapy
CD	Compact (audio) Disc
COSI	Client Orientated Scale of Improvement
MP3 MPEG-1	(Moving Picture Experts Group) Audio Layer 3
OAEs	Otoacoustic Emissions
S.M.A.R.T	Specific Measurable, Attainable, Realistic, and Timely

Introduction

Men are disturbed not by things, but by the view which they take of them.

(Greek philosopher Epectuetus)

To help people cope with their tinnitus and its consequences, counseling is recognized as a vital component of virtually all tinnitus management options [6]. Yet despite the important role that counseling plays, it can be difficult to ensure that this aspect of tinnitus management is undertaken. Nonpsychologists often feel uncomfortable in their role as a patient's counselor, frequently feeling uncertain as to how far their counseling efforts should

G.D. Searchfield (✉)
Hearing and Tinnitus Clinic, Audiology Section, School of Population Health, The University of Auckland, Private Bag 92019, Auckland, New Zealand
e-mail: g.searchfield@auckland.ac.nz

go [7]. It is therefore the intent of this chapter to clarify the need to provide counseling for tinnitus patients, the role of counseling, and who should deliver this very important component of a tinnitus treatment program.

What is Counseling?

For the purpose of the chapter, we define counseling as the process of facilitating change by informing, advising, and empowering individuals who need support. To help patients understand tinnitus and facilitate their coping with the condition, clinical approaches to the management of tinnitus include the use of education, psychological interventions, and counseling approaches. As the term "counseling" has many connotations and is used by many professionals, it is important to be clear what "counseling" refers to, what role it has in the management of tinnitus, and who should be providing the counseling. Just as the term "counseling" can cover a variety of topics, those who undertake counseling can include a wide range of professionals including psychologists, audiologists, counselors, social workers, general physicians, nurses, and medical specialists. In this chapter, we refer to counseling in the broad psycho-educational context that can be provided by any number of health professions.

With regard to its role in tinnitus, it has been said that counseling is the single most important component in the management of tinnitus [6]. Virtually, all treatment strategies incorporate some form of counseling. These treatments include the use of hearing aids [8] tinnitus retraining therapy [9], tinnitus masking [10], and cognitive behavioral therapy [11]. The importance of counseling was emphasized by Tyler [12], who encouraged all sound-based therapies to go hand-in-hand with counseling. The rationale and the form of counseling may differ across treatments [13], but regardless of which strategy is employed, it is necessary to help the patient understand and learn to cope with their tinnitus [6].

Tinnitus is a Complex Condition: Why is Counseling Needed?

Tinnitus is the involuntary perception of sound originating in the head (or ears) [14]. Tinnitus is experienced as an occasional slight irritation by the majority of the population [8, 14]. Between 6 and 17% of the population have tinnitus to a significant degree, with 0.5–2% reporting tinnitus that produces sufficient annoyance to interfere with day-to-day activities and quality of life [15–17]. To date, there is no cure for tinnitus. However, there are ways of minimizing the effects of tinnitus on the patient's life [18]. While today it is accepted that tinnitus can impact the patient's life in many ways, awareness of the broad-ranging consequences and potential contributors to distress caused by tinnitus was facilitated by studies designed to assess how tinnitus patients experienced this condition. One of the early attempts to investigate the problems experienced by tinnitus patients was undertaken by Tyler and Baker [4], who asked tinnitus sufferers in a self-help group to list the difficulties they experienced as a consequence of their tinnitus. The primary problems reported included negative effects on lifestyle (93%), general health (55.6%), hearing (52.7%), and emotional problems (69.4%). Participants particularly noted difficulties with the persistence of tinnitus (48.6%), and sleep (56.9%) [4]. Further demonstrating the distress that tinnitus can cause the patient, 6.9% of the respondents in Tyler and Baker's [4] study had considered suicide. The findings of this study (i.e., the potentially negative impact that tinnitus can have on the patient's life) have been confirmed in other studies, which have reported that severe tinnitus is often associated with depression [19] and, rarely, suicide [20, 21]. Clearly, tinnitus has widespread effects on the lives of those with this condition, which would normally require a multidisciplinary approach to manage it. Consideration must therefore be given to both the physiological aspects of this condition and the psychological factors that can impact the experience of the disorder and, hence, the level of distress it creates for the patient.

When considering how people react to tinnitus, people with tinnitus generally fall within two distinct groups: those who have marked distress or handicap associated with their tinnitus and those who do not [22]. Why this difference occurs between patients is not always clear. For example, vulnerable people exposed to significant stressful events, such as war and accidents, may suffer tinnitus related to posttraumatic stress disorder [23]. Also, personality traits may play a significant role in tinnitus [24]. For those working with tinnitus, it is important to appreciate the influence of factors that can impact on the experience of tinnitus, as these factors can increase the level of distress caused by the tinnitus as well as the patient's ability to benefit from treatment (see Fig. 70.1).

Of those who experience distress and disability related to their tinnitus, there is considerable variability regarding the nature and extent of the psychological distress they experience [4, 25]. It is therefore essential that the difficulties experienced by those tinnitus, patients negatively affected by their tinnitus, be carefully assessed in order to determine the factors that may cause and/or maintain their difficulties [2]. When assessing the impact of tinnitus on the patient's life, it is important to realize that how, and why, a person experiences distress is variable and may not relate to the more "obvious" elements of their condition. For example, it may appear obvious that the loudness of the tinnitus is the factor most likely to influence the degree of distress experienced by a person with tinnitus [2], yet this is not always the case. Several studies have considered features of tinnitus such as loudness and unpleasantness and have found that the loudness of tinnitus (either self-rated or determined by loudness matching) was unrelated to complaint dimensions [26–28]. This highlights the importance of understanding that the perception of tinnitus is only one dimension of tinnitus and it is the psychological dimension that leads to the emergence of tinnitus-related distress [2].

Although tinnitus is a sensory experience, how individuals respond to their tinnitus tends to be more multidimensional, involving their perceptual, attentional, and emotional processes [29]. In describing the impact of psychological factors on tinnitus, Hallam and colleagues [3] proposed a psychological model based on the process of habituation. They suggested that the distress caused by tinnitus is due to an individual's inability to habituate to the signal, which should occur as it does to any other constant stimulus that does not present as something harmful to the individual [30]. The significance associated to the signal or any arousal-elevating condition can be influenced by the person's emotional state and/or personality, slowing the natural progression of habituation [3]. For example, if the person is someone who experiences negative thinking, this can overlay all processing of incoming sensations. Such persons may perceive the tinnitus as distressing, harmful, and something that they will be unable to cope with. The importance of understanding how people interpret their situation is eloquently summarized by the Greek philosopher Epectetus' quote at the beginning of this chapter. It is, after all, the person's perceived disability that is going to have the greatest impact on their life.

The treatment of tinnitus patients can be further complicated by a considerable delay in patients

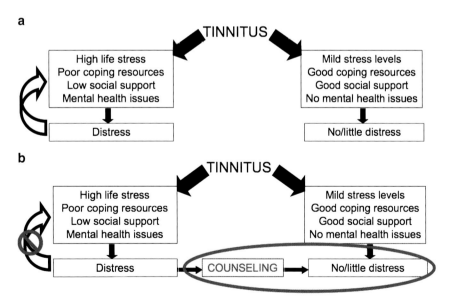

Fig. 70.1 The effect of counseling on tinnitus annoyance. (**a**) Distress caused by tinnitus is greatest when a person has high stress levels; mental health issues (anxiety, depression) poor coping strategies and little support. (**b**) Counseling can break a cycle of distress and provide the patient with the resources to accommodate the tinnitus

seeking medical attention from the onset of their tinnitus. It is not always clear why the person has not sought help for their tinnitus earlier and why their tinnitus has now become distressing [18]. The delay in seeking assistance may be due to people's developing strategies to distract themselves from their tinnitus to help them cope with the condition [18]. Alternatively it may be that their resources to endure and manage their tinnitus become weakened over time, and as the condition persists, they require assistance in adapting or strengthening their resources. Furthermore, patients often report difficulties in accessing appropriate information and referral to specialist services for tinnitus.

The negative consequences of tinnitus may include emotional states such as depression, anger, and anxiety, resulting in sleep disturbance, concentration difficulties, and interference with personal and social activities [4, 29, 30, 31]. Accordingly, psychological treatments aim to reduce the negative impact of tinnitus; often through the use of cognitive behavioral therapy (CBT see Chap. 21). CBT attempts to address the negative or unhelpful thought patterns and consequential behavioral problems accompanying tinnitus. The therapeutic approach of CBT has been shown to be effective in reducing the negative impact of tinnitus (i.e., distress and tinnitus annoyance) [32, 33] through cognitive restructuring and behavioral modification [34]. While CBT has been shown to be an effective treatment approach for tinnitus, some of the techniques are considered beyond the scope of practice for nonpsychologists; a more general approach is required for those who are working with tinnitus patients, but are not trained in CBT.

The Role of Counseling in Tinnitus Management

The goal of tinnitus management is the reduction of either the tinnitus itself or the patient's perception of the annoyance related to the tinnitus [7]. As reactions to tinnitus and the ability to cope with this condition vary from person to person, tinnitus is a complex condition to treat. Counseling should be the cornerstone of all tinnitus consultations. To facilitate the treatment of tinnitus, the practitioner must work toward establishing as in-depth an assessment of the individual's complaints

as possible, including a thorough tinnitus interview as well as assessment measures. The assessment allows better understanding of the person's experience of their tinnitus, the impact it has on their life, and their ability to cope [12]. Patient's perception of their tinnitus, their ability to cope with their tinnitus, their overall level of disability, and their ability to benefit from treatment interventions should be evaluated. As tinnitus can be associated with psychological distress from anxiety and/or depression, it is appropriate that an initial assessment determines their presence. The Beck Depression Inventory [35] and State-Trait Anxiety Inventory [36] have been used to assess baseline states of anxiety and depression. A useful alternative measure of the presence of psychological distress is the Hospital Anxiety and Depression Scale [37], which provides an easy to administer and well-validated measure of psychological distress in physical health conditions and is suggested as a crucial first step in identifying when to refer patients for psychological assessment [38].

The strong relationship between psychological symptoms (e.g., distress, depression, and anxiety) and tinnitus means that psychological approaches have been included in the treatment of tinnitus. There are many approaches to treating complex health conditions such as tinnitus [4]. Which psychological approaches are incorporated into the treatment of tinnitus will reflect a variety of factors, including the resources available to provide the patient and the training of the clinician. Common elements of a management approach include providing education and means to cope with the tinnitus and its effects. How these are provided to the patient varies considerably between programs and practices (again due to resources, practitioner experience, and practicality of program delivery). For those that do not have access to a multidimensional team approach, there is still a great deal that can be offered to the tinnitus patient in terms of tools to help them to understand and cope with their tinnitus.

Who Should Provide Tinnitus Counseling?

There is an opinion that interventions involving psychological therapy for tinnitus should include qualified psychologists [39]. It is also argued that an audiologist may be satisfactorily skilled to provide the CBT for patients with problematic tinnitus [34]. There are differences across country borders as to whom and how tinnitus management is provided. It is our opinion that provision of good counseling is important no matter the professional and that all clinicians should be aware of their own limitations and establish appropriate collegial networks. As the role of counseling and its definition will differ across professional groups, the varied background of participants in the counseling process will inevitably require that their expertise be used in different ways. Knowledge and training will determine to some extent the amount of, and style of, counseling. How the counseling is provided will also be determined by the environment (i.e., physical location, resources, type of patients, support networks, and referral options). For example, an otolaryngologist in a small rural center may be required to undertake greater counseling across a broader scope of practice than a clinician based in a large urban hospital working as part of a multidisciplinary team. While it is ideal for tinnitus patients to have access to a professional trained in the psychological management of this condition, it is not always possible or practical, as many practices do not have the resources or funding to provide such treatment. It is, however, possible to provide tinnitus patients with effective approaches to manage their condition, as audiologists or other tinnitus specialists can provide professional counseling [18] by familiarizing themselves with general counseling skills and principles (good basic texts exist for this purpose [7]).

Due to the chronic and distressing nature of the condition, tinnitus patients require engagement at a greater level than many other otologic or audiologic problems; as a consequence, clinicians should be prepared for an ongoing relationship with the patient. It is important that the professional be knowledgeable in their area of specialty, be sympathetic and caring for the patient, and demonstrate an understanding of the patient's problem [13]. The professional also needs to provide a clear therapy plan and express their belief in the chosen treatment [13]. Clear communication processes need to be established about when and how patients can contact the clinician (e.g., email, telephone, consultation). It is important not to foster dependence on the clinician but still maintain an easy means for the parties to communicate.

Counseling Approaches for the Management of Tinnitus

As a chronic condition, a primary focus in counseling and psychological approaches to the management of tinnitus is to reduce the distress caused by the tinnitus and the impact the condition has on the person's life. That is to say that tinnitus is a persistent condition with no easy cure and the focus of interventions therefore are to alter any negative thoughts the person has about the condition and its impact on their life, as this will decrease the role that tinnitus plays in their life.

Counseling interventions can range from simply providing information [29, 40] or educational sessions [41, 42] to psychologically influenced techniques such as relaxation training (e.g., [43]), attention control training (e.g., [44]), and sleep hygiene (e.g., [45]). Some counseling-based therapies include sound therapy as important elements. These approaches include masking and partial masking [2], tinnitus retraining therapy [46], tinnitus activities treatment [47], and audiological tinnitus management [48]. Counseling is the critical component in these therapies [49].

The Psycho-Educational Approach

Psycho-education is a patient-focused approach based on the premise that the more knowledgeable the patients are about their condition, the better the therapeutic outcome [50]. Readers are referred to Lukens and McFarlane [50] for a review of the effectiveness of psycho-education in health care. Providing information is considered by many to be a critical part of tinnitus management [29, 40, 51]. It has been suggested that an educational approach be the first step in tinnitus treatment before additional intervention is ventured into [39]. This helps with correcting the maladaptive thoughts and behaviors that can develop from false beliefs about tinnitus, which would be counterproductive to any accompanying management strategy [13]. Educating the patient about tinnitus and peoples' responses to this condition enables both the patient and the clinician to explore the problem and clarify the purpose and expected outcomes of subsequent interventions [41]. During the education sessions, it is important that there is opportunity for sufficient feedback and participation by the patient, as this will allow them to express any uncertainties and demonstrate any problematic patterns of thinking that could be a barrier to the success of any treatments offered (e.g., negative thinking about possible sinister causes of the tinnitus).

Counseling Content and Context

Tinnitus treatments use either group or individual sessions, but sometimes both have been applied. The integration of both contact styles has been effective in tinnitus management [52]. From a clinician's perspective, group therapy is a more cost- and time-effective method; it allows for the presentation of information to more patients in less time [52]. Individuals in a group may be role models to each other, which helps with the realization that there are others in similar situations [52, 53]. Another benefit of the group educational approach is its abilities to attract those who are not drawn to counseling, per se, due to the stigma and uncertainty attached to nonmedical or psychological approaches [54]. However, a disadvantage of the group session is the lack of an one-on-one relationship between the patient and the clinician [52]. Also, unless sessions are well managed, outgoing individuals may dominate discussions to the detriment of more reserved participants. Additionally, within the group format, the observation of another group member's success might evoke envy or confirm the uniqueness and difficulty of one's problem [55], making the person feel more distressed. In contrast to group therapy, individual sessions allow for specific issues pertaining to each individual patient to be addressed, which might be necessary for some. The decision to provide group or individual counseling depends on factors such as the availability of groups (this is not always feasible for some practices) and the patient's preference [56].

With regard to the content of the counseling, in an individual setting, it should be adjusted to suit each individual because a patient's lack of understanding will be a barrier, thereby defeating therapeutic interventions [8]. In a group setting, the content should be broadly based to encompass the essential elements applicable to most patients. It has been suggested that successful counseling programs include: the capability to change the way patients think about tinnitus; the ability to alter their behavioral or emotional reactions toward tinnitus; and an understanding of each patient's needs [8]. Shorter term counseling interventions have become increasingly favorable in a variety of clinical settings and are usually designed to be part of an overall management plan [42]. Topics usually covered include: the hearing system and hearing loss, the epidemiology and causes of tinnitus, perception (including habituation and attention), and treatment options [13]. In the following sections, we will briefly outline the main contents of one approach to counseling and the rationale for using them. Effective counseling on this basis requires that the clinician has good working knowledge of the physiology of the auditory system, as well as the mechanism and management of tinnitus and be able to convey this information in layman's terms to de-medicalize the condition.

Counseling Topics

Although for presentation purposes, the topics are presented here in a linear fashion (2 follows 1, etc.), the person providing counseling should be prepared to take a very nonlinear approach – the clinician should guide and react to patient responses, rather than follow a script. The elements that the authors believe are important to convey to the patient are:

1. Needs and goal setting
2. Anatomy/neurophysiology of the ear
3. Results of audiological assessment
4. Perception of sound and tinnitus
5. Habituation
6. Attention
7. Treatment approaches
8. Self-management/coping strategies
9. Referral
10. Relapse prevention
11. Hyperacusis
12. Homework

Needs and Goal Setting

A technique commonly used in counseling of chronic conditions such as tinnitus is goal setting, as it is an important skill to help patients work toward, achieve, and maintain treatment success [12]. Research has shown the importance of goals in improving self-efficacy and performance; it has been reported that the enthusiasm to match performance to goals derives from an anticipated increase in self-satisfaction [57]. Goal setting is said to positively impact an individual's performance through a self-regulatory process. These processes include enabling the individual to focus their attention, promote effort, and initiate task-related strategies [58]. While there are many ways to set goals, one of the most successful methods is setting S.M.A.R.T goals, which require the person to make their goals specific, measurable, achievable, realistic, and time bound [59]. The clinician's role is to help patients identify the areas they want to change and then guide them in ways to achieve these goals.

The purpose of using a goal setting technique is to help the patient focus on ways to move themselves forward, thereby reducing their focus on the negative and distressing aspects of their tinnitus. The use of the motivational effects of goal setting in the acquisition of new skills has been demonstrated in various fields (e.g., [58, 60]). It is necessary to ensure that the goals are adequately difficult to motivate, but not so difficult to discourage an individual from achieving them [61–63]. Several studies [57, 61] also emphasize the need to have explicit performance levels, including concrete and quantifiable outcomes. Regardless of the nature of an assignment, a person is usually advised to set short-term goals, as this increases their motivation and expectations toward the task at hand [64].

An important aspect of helping patients' progress through treatment is determining their needs (i.e., what they want/expect from treatment). Many audiologists will be familiar with the Client Orientated Scale of Improvement (COSI, [65]). This tool is used to determine specific hearing needs and the extent to which they are achieved following the fitting of hearing aids. A slight modification of this scale can also be applied to help determine needs and set goals for tinnitus management [8]. Using the Client Orientated Scale of Improvement in Tinnitus (COSIT), the clinician and patient identify specific situations in which tinnitus is bothersome (e.g., "Tinnitus affects my ability to concentrate at work") and discuss ways of reducing tinnitus in these situations (e.g., "Amplify sound to reduce tinnitus audibility"). At stages throughout the tinnitus rehabilitation process, the problems

identified using the COSIT are re-examined and in each situation, the degree of tinnitus improvement is determined. If improvement is not shown, appropriate steps (change in strategy, different techniques, or referral) are undertaken to address the problem until realistic goals are achieved.

Anatomy/Neurophysiology of the Ear

Counseling based on neurophysiology will commonly attempt to explain, in some detail, the normal and abnormal physiology of the auditory system and related neural networks. In so doing, the aims are to provide knowledge of the processes occurring in the generation of tinnitus and eliminate unfounded fears or presumptions as to the underlying causes [46]. It is also vital that misconceptions are corrected and patients are given sufficient reassurance that tinnitus is not a life-threatening injury or a psychiatric disease.

The elements of anatomy/physiology of the ear thought to be important for discussion (using diagrams and scripts similar to Appendix 1 as a starting point) are outlined below. It is important to pitch the amount of detail to the perceived level of the patient's understanding. Starting simple is best, but allow the patient to guide you as to the depth of their understanding through questions and answers. It is better that a patient leaves their consultation with a firm grasp of basic concepts, than a collection of confusing neuroanatomical nomenclature. Examples:

1. Outer and middle ear are responsible for conduction and amplification of sounds to the inner ear. The Eustachian tube as a source of repetitive sounds during swallowing.

We demonstrate and say to patients:

> Although swallowing is louder than your tinnitus, it is not perceived. The brain is able to filter sound, when it has no "importance."

2. Inner ear: hair cells, possible pathologies (e.g., noise trauma, ototoxicity) (Fig. 70.2).
3. Nerve ruling out possibility of acoustic neuroma (assuming investigation has been undertaken).
4. Brainstem: reaction to sound when detecting danger and provoking a strong and subconscious reaction. Tinnitus as a new signal to the brain creating arousal, fear, and threat-related reaction.

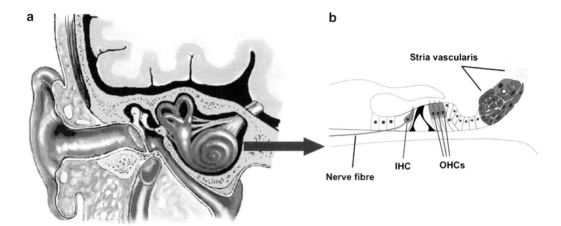

Fig. 70.2 For counseling about the anatomy and physiology of the ear. (**a**) Discuss role of outer, middle, and inner ear and transduction of sound from physical vibrations to electrical discharge of nerve. (**b**) Explain role of structures of the organ of Corti and relate patient's audiometric results to likely source of cochlear injury (e.g., outer hair cells). Discuss the stria vascularis as the battery of the inner ear, outer hair cells (OHCs) as amplifiers (relate to OAE results) inner hair cells (IHCs) as switches to send information via the auditory nerve

We explain to patients:

> Our reactions to tinnitus are a consequence of hearing a new and unknown annoying sound; they are not signs of mental illness.

5. Midbrain and cortex: addition of emotions and complex association of the sound to templates of normal sounds and depending on the subconscious evaluation we may focus even more on the tinnitus sound.

We say to patients:

> Tinnitus sound can be "stored" and become longer lasting the more you are focused on it.

and

> It is thought that tinnitus becomes magnified because of how the brain analyses tinnitus and how we think about it. Tinnitus happens because the brain misunderstands information from the inner ear. The inner ear sends nerves (think of these as wires in an electrical circuit) to information centers in the brain. When damage occurs to a specific region of the ear, there is less activity from the ear; the brain reacts to this over time creating new activity.

and

> People react to tinnitus in different ways. Tinnitus usually begins following ear injury, even small amounts of damage can start tinnitus (we relate the patient's tinnitus to audiometry and discuss different measures such as otoacoustic emissions (OAEs)). But the parts of the brain involved in hearing and emotion are also involved downstream from the ear. Most of the "wiring" of the auditory system is involved in the development and appearance of tinnitus itself (relate to Fig. 70.3 and describe the nonauditory centers, explaining that the limbic and autonomic nervous systems are primarily responsible to a large degree for tinnitus annoyance).

Results of Audiological Assessment

The first step in the evaluation of tinnitus, and then its management, is a comprehensive case history including questions of onset, description of the tinnitus "sound," location, possible cause (noise, medications, stress), and severity (Chaps. 46 and 47). If the tinnitus is objective, pulsatile, unilateral, or associated with a tempromandibular joint complaint, referral to an otolaryngologist or other specialist is recommended to the patient (Chaps. 48 and 50). We explain that the underlying cause in these cases may possibly be medically treatable, we are careful not to build expectations of a cure, nor are we pessimistic as to the potential for an effective intervention. We also explain that while there is currently no objective measure of tinnitus, psychoacoustical assessments of tinnitus qualities (pitch and loudness) (Chap. 49) and psychometric evaluations (Chap. 54) of tinnitus severity are often used by clinicians to characterize tinnitus.

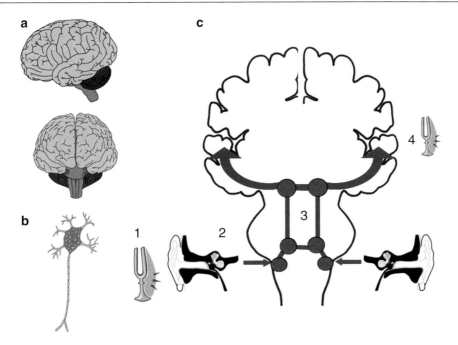

Fig. 70.3 For counseling of brain anatomy and physiology. Follow on from explanation of cochlear physiology. (**a**) Explain to patient the various sections and orientation of the brain. (**b**) Discuss neurons as the wiring of the brain relaying information (**c**). Sound (*1*) travels from the cochlea (*2*) (discuss

using analogy with light switch), auditory nerve (wiring) via auditory nuclei (*3*) (junction boxes) to auditory cortex (*4*) (light bulb – light goes on – we hear). Adjust detail according to patient knowledge. (**c**) Modeled on figure of the auditory pathway http://research.meei.harvard.edu/EPL/

Perception of Sound and Tinnitus

Tinnitus does not obey the normal rules which apply to sound perception [66]. For example, tinnitus intensity matches are out of step with its perceived loudness – tinnitus may subjectively match to a quiet external sound but be perceived by the sufferer as being extremely loud, e.g., "as loud as a train." Although tinnitus may have a low-intensity match, it can be difficult to mask – even when using high-intensity frequency-matched sounds (Chap. 49). Also, tinnitus does not have an external source or object to relate to. One reason for the annoyance and "strangeness" of tinnitus could be its conflict with normal Auditory Scene Analysis (ASA) [66, 67] (Fig. 70.4). Using Fig. 70.5a, we address the perception principle that describes the mind's tendency to seek figure and ground distinctions (e.g., Rubin's figure ground vase) and how the brain extracts important features. We also use visual analogs to explain phantom perceptions (such as lateral inhibition, Fig. 70.5b).

We say to patients:

> In our daily activities we are able to listen to one sound of interest, such as a friends voice buried in a background of competing noise. To do this we must categorize sound features occurring simultaneously (e.g., pitch and loudness) to the correct source. Tinnitus disobeys rules we would normally apply when listening to real sounds.

Feldmann [68] eloquently described that the natural reaction of people to tinnitus onset is to search for it and place it in context of a sound in the environment. With true sounds, we can localize them to something we can see, touch, and sometimes even smell. Multisensory recognition of objects is normal, tinnitus lacks this sense of reality, making it difficult to ignore.

We say to patients:

> One of the reasons tinnitus is so annoying is that we hear it, but can't see it or find where it is coming from. Imagine for a moment that tinnitus comes from this pen instead of your ears. If it was from the pen it would appear real, and be easier to ignore. It is natural for us to want to find and identify the source of sounds, when we can't it becomes frustrating (e.g., finding the source of a dripping sound in the house, is it a water leak?)

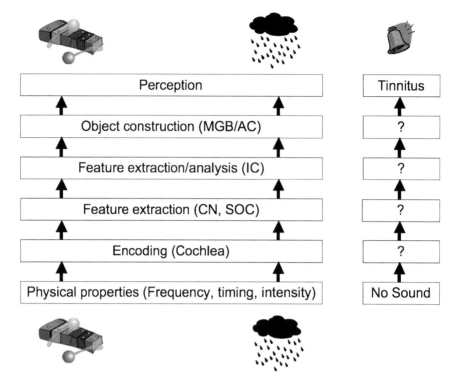

Fig. 70.4 For counseling about sound perception processes. Describe perception of sound as a process of sound (e.g., xylophone and rain) being broken into elements before being reassembled by the brain as an object. Relate to the anatomy in Fig. 70.3. Contrast this with tinnitus perception where no auditory object is present but a similar process of constructing the image of sound must occur. Use this to explain the unusual nature of tinnitus and how it differs from sound, with regard to tinnitus assessment and attempts to interfere with the tinnitus using sound. For a patient with a good understanding of physiology explanation of the various processes within the cochlear nucleus (CN) superior olivary complex (SOC), inferior colliculus (IC), medial geniculate body (MGB), and auditory cortex (AC) can be provided. Otherwise, these can be described as "Junction" or "decision" boxes

The above examples help to relate the sufferer's experiences within a simple philosophical framework that can be adjusted to suit the patient and the therapeutic approaches described in the following sections.

Habituation

A decline in behavioral responses to a sound signal due to repeated exposure is known as auditory habituation [69]. It appears that habituation is not caused just by the repetition of the sound but by the meaning or association the stimulus holds in the particular situation [69]. A lack of habituation was possibly first postulated by Hallam et al. [3] to play an important role in tinnitus persistence and annoyance. Habituation has become a common feature of most counseling and sound therapy practice [46, 47].

We say:

If a person moves from the country to the city often they become annoyed by the noise of city traffic. Sometimes the noise keeps them awake and is a great irritation. Usually this annoyance reduces and the person becomes less and less aware of the city noise with time. They – automatically – learn to ignore the noise, as it is not an important sound. The sound becomes classified as unimportant by the brain. It is as if the sound is no longer there. The same thing can happen with your tinnitus, we need to find ways to help your hearing system treat the tinnitus as an unimportant background "sound."

Attention

Attention may play a large role in tinnitus annoyance and should be addressed in counseling [12]. Tinnitus can often become the main focus in a person's life, consuming their attention resources and ability to

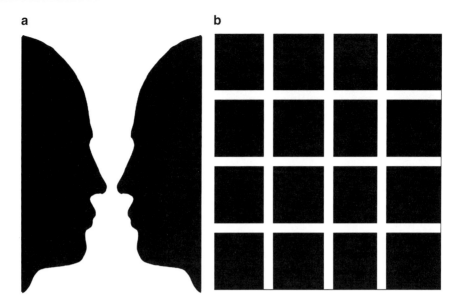

Fig. 70.5 For counseling about tinnitus perception – using visual analogs. (**a**) Rubin's vase can be used to demonstrate the concept of figure ground. Tinnitus can be viewed as an auditory object standing out from the background. By shifting attention from the faces to the vase, the patient can be informed about the use of attention strategies to focus less on tinnitus than background sound. (**b**) Visual analog of lateral inhibition. Have the patient stare at the center of the crosses, they should notice the emergence of gray spots at the intersections of the lines. Explain that the brain is tricked into seeing something that actually is not there. Relate this to tinnitus by explaining that the white lines depict activity – normal hearing, while the *black squares* depict absent activity – hearing loss. The area between the activity and nonactivity has created a phantom image. This diagram can be useful to explain how ear damage might result in activity in the CNS and how the fitting of hearing aids might "remove" areas of decreased acuity

concentrate in other tasks. Tinnitus can become the dominant element in a person's awareness. The acquisition of attention control skills, such as distraction, allows a person to shift their attention to and from tinnitus during stressful situations [13, 43]. These techniques may provide the individual with some sense of control over their tinnitus and the related distressing experiences [29, 44]. Apparently, it is the assumed uncontrollability of the tinnitus sensation which plays a key role in tinnitus being aversively interpreted [27, 68].

Attention control techniques aim to help listeners learn strategies to switch focus of attention from one thing to another, so that attention can be brought under voluntary control to direct thought to and from one's tinnitus. Henry and Wilson [2] suggest that by exerting control over attention, tinnitus-related distress will be reduced. Their technique can be used to alternate attention from tinnitus to others sounds and is consistent with the process of ASA discussed with patients:

We say:

We need to teach your hearing system to pay less attention to the unnatural sound of tinnitus and instead listen more to other "real" sounds. Use your ears like a search light – listen for sounds around you, what do you hear? Where is it coming from? Can you tell me more about the sound? When you were listening for the sound – were you aware of the tinnitus – possibly not as the other sound was competing for attention against the tinnitus, we can't hear everything around us all at once, we must pick and choose. Let's practice

and

Focus your awareness on the noises in your head – tune into the noises. What can you hear? Now quickly redirect your attention. Focus on external noises in the room and outside…notice you can only focus on one thing at a time.

(see Henry and Wilson page 106 [2] for complete dialog)

Treatment Approaches

The different treatment types (Chaps. 70–94 in this volume) can be discussed in layperson's terms to facilitate the patient's understanding of their tinnitus and the role that different treatment approaches can play in the management process. We provide the following simple information to patients about treatments.

Hearing Aids

It is likely that tinnitus is the response of the hearing system to altered output of the inner ear following hearing loss. One treatment approach is to identify any underlying reasons for the hearing system being overly active and to interfere with how the brain analyses the tinnitus. When hearing loss accompanies tinnitus, this would involve the fitting of hearing aids to the injured ears in an attempt to normalize activity. There are a number of ways the fitting of appropriate hearing aids can help in reducing tinnitus [8]:

- Psychological benefit from reducing hearing handicap
- By reducing the attention being paid to hearing and consequently tinnitus
- Modification of neural networks responsible for tinnitus
- Amplified sound can partially mask the tinnitus

Masking

Masking is the process of covering, usually partially, the tinnitus with an external sound. The sound used does not appear to be crucial, but should be less bothersome than the tinnitus. Masking often allows the tinnitus sufferer to gain control over their tinnitus by determining when they do not wish to hear it. Long-term use of partial masking, along with counseling, may lead to tinnitus habituation. Some idea of the potential benefit of masking can be assessed in the clinic by listening to an assortment of sounds over headphones.

Habituation Therapy

If the patient has no reason to attend to tinnitus, they should get used (habituate) to it. Even loud sounds can be habituated to if they are nonthreatening, for example, people living near railroad tracks seem unaware of the sound of trains passing. The difference between a person who experiences tinnitus and one who "suffers" from it may be the person's ability to habituate to the

tinnitus. Habituation therapies sometimes combine sound therapy with counseling. Hearing aids, broadband noise generators, and devices combining both amplification and generation of sound (combination aids) are used to reduce tinnitus audibility to facilitate the habituation of tinnitus. The sound therapy is thought to help by allowing the patient to become used to tinnitus as the sound fades into the background.

Cognitive Behavioral Therapy (CBT)

Psychologists often use CBT. They teach strategies and techniques to enable patients to cope with tinnitus. This therapy enables sufferers to change the way they think about their tinnitus. By minimizing the impact of unhelpful or negative thoughts about tinnitus, through challenging and changing responses, tinnitus annoyance can be reduced.

Self-Management/Coping Strategies

It has been shown that a person vulnerable to stress is more likely to experience tinnitus distress, whereas a more stress-tolerant or resilient person might be able to handle a greater degree of tinnitus before seeking help [70]. Although tinnitus and its associated symptoms can be a frequent source of stress and distress, stress in return can often exacerbate the existing effects of tinnitus. Therefore, managing stress and learning to relax helps reduce the effects of tinnitus and prevent further aggravation. As a stress-reduction technique, relaxation training enables an individual to become calmer and less reactive, hopefully reducing tinnitus perception [40]. As a first step, relaxation exercises such as progressive muscular relaxation and abdominal breathing [2] are potentially helpful. Patients can be informed about relaxation and be provided with resources for undertaking it (Appendix 1).

Improving Sleep

A very common complaint amongst tinnitus sufferers is difficulty in sleeping [4, 12, 15, 27]. Sleep problems may include regularly waking during the night and difficulty in falling asleep [72]. It is possible that tinnitus seems louder and more noticeable at bedtime due to the decrease in ambient noise at night [72]. Improving the quality and ability of individuals to sleep may reduce the adverse effects of tinnitus.

Sleep hygiene is a treatment tool for insomnia which involves behavioral practices that promote good sleep [45]. Patients should be asked about their bedtime routines and sleep patterns. There are different treatment versions of sleep hygiene [73, 74]. However, they all generally involve learning about sleep scheduling, attitudes and feelings that affect sleep, appropriate prebedtime activities, maintaining a good sleep environment, and the importance of daytime behavior [74]. Caffeine and nicotine both have stimulating effects, and intake should thus be regulated [53]. Regular exercise promotes sleep, but should not be carried out close to bedtime [53]. The use of sleep hygiene alone has produced variable success; however, when applied with other forms of intervention (for instance, relaxation exercises or cognitive behavioral treatment) greater improvement in tinnitus symptoms has been observed [75].

Music

One easily implemented self-help sound therapy measure is the use of low-level music played in the background in quiet situations to draw attention away from the tinnitus.

For best results, the following has been recommended to patients [76]:

- Listening to music or background sound that induces positive feelings.
- Music without vocals.
- Music without pronounced bass beat.
- Music should be pleasant but not too interesting.
- For short-term relief, when tinnitus is severe, attention capturing music can be beneficial.
- For long-term tinnitus, habituation music which induces relaxation while reducing tinnitus audibility.
- Music should be played at a low level, ideally where the music blends with the tinnitus.

Extra stimulation could be provided at night by a bedside sound generator or compact discs (CDs) designed to interfere with tinnitus detection [77]. This could involve the use of a pillow speaker in combination with a pre-existing CD or MP3 player. If these are not available,

purchase of a purpose-built bedside sound generator or tinnitus reduction CD could be considered (the clinic could have these available or a source for clients to obtain them).

Referring to Clinical Psychology

On the basis of cost-effectiveness, it is proposed that combining education and self-help advice should produce significant tinnitus reducing benefits when used as routine treatment. Those patients not profiting from the use of the minimal-contact approach could be offered CBT [78] or another psychological intervention. A common reason why tinnitus becomes stressful and disabling relates to the persons' perception of the auditory stimuli in terms of what could be causing the sensation and their ability to cope with it. Psychological therapy is therefore an appropriate treatment approach for tinnitus, as psychological techniques, including CBT, aim to change how a person thinks about something that will then impact how they react to that situation, stimulus, or event. Within a tinnitus management program, the intent is therefore to change how the person perceives and responds to their tinnitus, so that they are not as negatively impacted by the condition.

Relapse Prevention

Once made aware of potential triggers and means to manage them, the patient should be able to identify signs that a previously compensated tinnitus may re-emerge. New stressors, anxieties, and life events could retrigger tinnitus onset. Reassurance that the re-emerged tinnitus is likely a consequence of these events and that management of these issues should again reduce the salience of tinnitus is important. Changes in hearing could also trigger a resumption of tinnitus. As noise is the primary cause of tinnitus-related ear injury, it warrants attention. Hearing conservation should be addressed with caution. Care should be taken to distinguish damaging from helpful sound. An over emphasis on hearing protection may lead to an auditory deprivation effect – potentially reactive plasticity and tinnitus [79] and hyperacusis

(Chaps. 3 and 4). At the same time, patients should be made aware of dangerous sounds and how to avoid further injury [80]. One method to avoid resumption of annoying tinnitus is for the individual to be equipped to manage any re-emergence. Written materials to refer to can be useful, "The Consumer Handbook of Tinnitus" [81] and "Tinnitus. A Self-Management Guide for the Ringing in Your Ears" [82] being examples. Another way is to have access to homework tools that can be used independent of the clinician.

Hyperacusis

Although this chapter focuses on counseling for tinnitus, the underlying counseling principles can be applied to other symptoms of auditory injury such as hyperacusis. Care should be taken to explain the concept of hypersensitized auditory pathways, hearing protection vs. hearing isolation, and the importance of sound exposure to achieve some degree of normal tolerance to sound (Chap. 3).

Homework

Homework permits the practitioner to use the time between sessions effectively by engaging the patient in tasks aimed toward the therapy goals [83]. Although homework assignments are not commonly applied as part of a tinnitus intervention plan, research on home work in other disorders has demonstrated improved treatment outcomes [84]. One of the primary benefits of using homework is that the techniques learned during the intervention are practiced outside the session [83]. CBT [11, 29], cognitive therapies [85, 86], and rational-emotive therapy [87] have all incorporated homework as part of their therapy plans. Anxiety disorders [88] and certain phobias [89] are examples of clinical conditions that have been aided by homework activities. As part of a SMART approach, homework need not be complex or onerous, but it should encourage participation and ownership of the problem by the patient.

The benefits of the inclusion of homework assignments into therapies can be seen through such effects as significantly improving treatment outcomes [84]

and modifying behavior without supervision of a clinician [90]. It is important to note, however, that the benefits a person gains from the homework assigned depends on the clarity of its description and rationale, as well as the degree of patient involvement and level of compliance [84]. Kong [56] investigated the effectiveness of two CBT-based homework exercises alongside group-based information sessions to manage tinnitus. Simple, stand-alone take-home tasks were specifically designed, so that they could be provided to participants without needing to have a psychologist involved in their delivery. Two experimental groups, ACTIVE and PASSIVE, received identical educational sessions, once a week, for five consecutive weeks. All participants were given information sheets with general instructions to carry out the homework tasks that were meant to help in areas of difficulty caused by tinnitus. Additionally, the ACTIVE group participants received detailed and specific assignments to complete during the week. The majority of participants tended to benefit from the participant education sessions. A slightly greater reduction in tinnitus effect was recorded for the ACTIVE group participants at the end of this study when compared to the participants in the PASSIVE group. It was concluded that group-based information sessions including specific "active" homework assignments have the potential to be used alongside audiological management to reduce tinnitus impact [56]. The decision for the weekly topics was based on areas of difficulty frequently experienced by people with tinnitus, which were identified in previous research [4, 11, 30]. Kong [56] compiled the self-help strategies presented in Appendix 1 from various psychological management publications (e.g., [29, 91, 92]).

Resources

We the approach, we recommend that it is useful for the clinician to have charts of the ear and the central nervous system, and cartoons/schematic diagrams of perceptual principles available. In this chapter, we have provided some examples that we, as clinicians, have found useful. Pubmed is a great source for up-to-date information on tinnitus, while hearing aid manufacturers often have excellent anatomy charts. In addition, clinicians have offered helpful counseling tools in print [92] and on the internet (http://www.uihealthcare.com/depts/med/otolaryngology/clinics/tinnitus/activitytherapy.html). Patients should be guided in how to undertake internet searches for tinnitus information and informed of the frequency of poor quality information and misinformation on the World Wide Web.

Summary

Education alone can be a sufficient intervention for some patients [43, 78, 93]. Due to the complexity and multiple factors which impact upon the emotional well-being of an individual, a multidisciplinary team approach is best when treating a patient with complex tinnitus [52, 94]. However, circumstances will determine which professionals will be providing counseling within different settings. We have suggested a method that works in our clinic practices. We have found the education approach a very useful counseling method to empower patients to de-attend and habituate to tinnitus. Clinicians will have their own counseling "tricks" and methods, but the essence of approaches will likely be similar, to make the patient feel less fearful of their tinnitus and provide tools to minimize and, hopefully, eradicate any negative effects from the perception of tinnitus.

Acknowledgments Our thanks to Dr David Munoz who drew the image of the organ of Corti (Fig. 70.2b) and Kim Wise who used her clinical experience of counseling tinnitus to critique the text.

Appendix 1: Homework

The following homework exercises were compiled and trialed by Kong [56] on the basis of several previous studies [including: 2, 27, 92]. They are presented here in a format for clinicians to provide to patients.

Topics for Take-Home Tasks

1. Goal-setting
   S.M.A.R.T goal-setting strategy

2. Sleep hygiene
   Going to bed strategies
   Falling asleep strategies
   Sleeping environment
   Daytime habits
3. Relaxation techniques
   Progressive muscle relaxation
   Deep breathing exercises
4. Attention control
   Attention control techniques
   Distraction
5. Communication strategies (when tinnitus accompanies hearing loss)
   Communication tips

Task 1 Goal Setting

Background for Clinician

Tinnitus may result in a withdrawal from work and social activities that might normally provide a sense of achievement and enjoyment. The loss of these positive feelings, along with isolation, may lead to the person strongly attending to their tinnitus. Goal setting is about identifying and then overcoming barriers to participation and activity.

For Person with Tinnitus

Goal setting is the process of determining what your goals are, and making plans to achieve them. The goal-setting strategy explained here is known by the acronym S.M.A.R.T. This strategy has five components:

Goals need to be Specific, Measurable, Attainable, Realistic, and Timely.

Specific: Goals need to be specific in order to make reaching them easier. Specific goals have a much greater chance of being accomplished than do broad and general ones.

For example, a specific goal, "to be able to read without becoming annoyed by tinnitus," is easier to reach, make a plan for, measure progress, and to know when it is achieved than a general goal of, "I want the tinnitus to be gone."

Answering these questions can help to ensure a goal is a specific one:

Who is involved? What do I want to accomplish? Where am I going to do this? When will this occur? Why do I want to accomplish this goal?

Measurable: Goals need to be measurable. This way you will be able to see the progress you are making, will know when your goal is reached, and will know when it is time to celebrate! Celebrating your success is an important part of goal setting.

To determine if your goal is measurable, ask questions such as:

How much? How often? How will I know that I have reached my goal?

How will I know that I am making progress towards my goal?

For an example of a measurable goal, let us say your goal is to read in the evening without becoming annoyed by tinnitus. When you have achieved this, you will know that you have reached your goal. You can set mini-goals along the way of reading for 10 min at a time. Each time you reach one of these mini-goals you know that you are making good progress towards your overall goal. This allows you to monitor progress – and to have mini-celebrations along the way!

Attainable: The goals you set for yourself need to be achievable. The goals also need to be important for you so as to encourage you to make the commitment and put the effort in to reaching them. While goals should challenge you slightly, it is important to set goals which you are likely to achieve. This will set you up for success. Succeeding will encourage you, help to keep you motivated, and give you confidence to set and achieve further goals.

For example, setting a goal of reading an entire book without being annoyed by the tinnitus may not be feasible, whereas reading several chapters may be.

Realistic: Goals need to be realistic. Realistic does not mean easy, but it does mean do-able. The goals you set need to be reachable, relevant, and meaningful to you. You will need to devise a plan that makes reaching your goal a realistic proposition.

Timely: Put a timeframe on your goal. Setting an endpoint for your goal gives you a clear target to work towards and helps to encourage you to put in a consistent effort. Look for signposts along the way indicating progress towards your goal. Include these mini-goals in your time frame. Without a time frame in which to accomplish your goals, the commitment to achieving them becomes too vague.

TIPS:

Telling others about your goals may provide you with support and encouragement.

Take the time to look back, notice the progress you have made, and celebrate your successes!

Use these SMART strategies to get you where you want to be. Identify what you want to do. Set your goals and GO FOR IT!

Task 2 Sleep Hygiene

Background for Clinician

One of the most common tinnitus complaints is poor sleep. Good sleep practices along with relaxation exercises may improve the amount or quality of sleep.

For Person with Tinnitus

Using a number of strategies and forming new sleeping habits can improve quality of sleep. These strategies are commonly referred to as "sleep hygiene." Good sleep refers not only to quantity of sleep, but also quality of sleep. We want to make sure you get enough, and that what you get is refreshing. In practice, this means getting to sleep and not waking until fully rested!

People tend not to spend a lot of time thinking about their sleeping habits. You might have your dinner, do whatever it is that you normally do, and then just go to bed for the night. However, there are often things that we can do to make a good night's sleep more likely.

The quality and quantity of our sleep can be much improved by changing some of our habits!

Good sleep hygiene includes the following:

Going to Bed Strategies

Maintain a routine. Try to go to bed and wake up at the same time every day, even on the weekends. Keeping a regular schedule will help your body expect sleep at the same time each day.

Use bedtime rituals. Doing regular things before sleep tells your body that it's time to slow down and begin to prepare for sleep (e.g., a warm bath each night before bed).

Relax for a while before going to bed. Some quiet time can make falling asleep easier. Try relaxation techniques.

Write down all of your concerns and worries. Write down your worries and possible solutions before you go to bed so you don't need to dwell on them in the middle of the night. This allows you to put away your concerns until the next day.

Go to sleep when you are sleepy. When you feel tired at night, go to bed.

Don't nap through the day. If you find you have to, limit naps to 30 min, as daytime sleep can upset your body clock for sleeping at night.

Falling Asleep (or Getting Back to Sleep) Strategies

Practice your attention control techniques. This will help to keep your mind occupied, will increase your relaxation, and help you to fall back to sleep.

Get out of bed if unable to sleep. Don't lie in bed awake. Go into another room and do something relaxing until you feel sleepy. Worrying about falling asleep actually keeps many people awake.

Don't do anything stimulating. Don't read or watch a stimulating TV program (as the brain receives a mixed message of having to pay attention to something and yet wanting to go to sleep). Don't expose yourself to bright light. The light gives cues to your brain that it is time to wake up.

Drink some warm milk. Milk may help create feelings of sleepiness.

Consider changing your bedtime. If you are frequently experiencing sleeplessness, think about going to bed later so that the time you spend in bed is spent sleeping.

Sleeping Environment

Make sure your bed is large enough and comfortable.

Make your bedroom primarily a place for sleeping. Use your bed for sleeping or intimacy only. Help your body recognize that your bedroom is primarily a place for rest.

Keep your bedroom peaceful and comfortable. Make sure your room is well ventilated and the temperature is fairly constant. You could use a fan or a bedside sound conditioner to help reduce attention to tinnitus.

Hide your clock. A highly visible clock may cause you to focus on the time and make you feel stressed and anxious. Place your clock so you can't see the time when you are in bed.

Daytime Habits

Limit caffeine and alcohol. Avoid drinking caffeinated or alcoholic beverages for several hours before bedtime.

Expose yourself to bright light/sunlight soon after awakening. This will help to regulate your body's natural biological clock. Likewise, try to keep your bedroom dark while you are sleeping so that the light will not interfere with your rest.

Exercise early in the day. Twenty to thirty minutes of exercise every day can help you sleep, but be sure to exercise in the morning or afternoon, not evening. Exercise stimulates the body and aerobic activity before bedtime may make falling asleep more difficult.

Check your iron level. Iron deficient women tend to have more problems sleeping so if your blood is iron poor, a supplement might help your health and your ability to sleep. Check with your doctor as to whether this is a concern for you.

Establishing good sleeping habits will have many positive benefits for you. Remember to give yourself and your body time to adjust to your new sleeping routine. Some of the strategies will be of more use to you than others. The "going to bed" and "falling asleep" strategies may be the ones that create the biggest change in your quality of sleep, so focus on establishing these first.

Here's wishing you many nights of great sleep!

Task 3 Relaxation

Background for Clinician

Tinnitus can be increased with stress and tension. Relaxation is one strategy toward overcoming the negative consequences of stress and alleviating some tinnitus effects.

For Person with Tinnitus

By relaxing and becoming more calm, the stress driving your tinnitus, or resulting from tinnitus, may be reduced. This may have a positive effect on your mood and reduction in tinnitus annoyance.

Abbreviated Progressive Relaxation

After learning the skill of relaxation, this can be quickly tapped into at times of stress.

This exercise involves four muscle groups. You can modify this exercise if needed, simply be sure to include the areas listed below. Follow the principals of holding a muscle tense for 10–20 s and releasing, then relaxing for 15–20 s before moving on to tensing the next muscle.

1. Hands, forearms and biceps
2. Head, face, throat and shoulders, including concentration on forehead, cheeks nose, eyes, jaws, lips, tongue and neck
3. Chest, stomach and lower back
4. Thighs, buttocks, calves and feet

Find a quiet, comfortable place to sit where there are minimal distractions. Use a squeeze ball while doing these muscle-relaxing exercises, as it a useful aid to help a person to identify when a muscle is being tensed and when it is relaxed.

To begin:

1. Curl both fists
2. Tighten the upper arm and forearms as tight as possible
3. Hold them for 10–20 s and then relax them (this is the same for every part that follows)
4. Next wrinkle up the forehead. Simultaneously, press your head back as far as possible and roll it in a clockwise fashion. Then reverse the head roll
5. Now wrinkle up the muscles of your face like a walnut, and then relax them
6. Arch your back (but be careful if you have a bad back) and take a deep breath. Press out your stomach and relax.
7. Put both feet flat on the floor and now pull your toes back toward your face as far as possible. Tighten your shins; now your calves, thighs, and buttocks; now relax them.

Don't stand up in a hurry after finishing – take a few deep breaths and stand up slowly to give your body a chance to re-orientate itself.

Deep Breathing Exercises

Another form of relaxation is deep breathing. This is a simple exercise that does not take a lot of time. Slow deep abdominal breathing is a useful method of reducing anxiety and causing relaxation. Abdominal breathing expands the belly as it expands the lungs. Chest breathing is shallower and does not provide the relaxation that comes with abdominal breathing.

To begin:

- Close your eyes.
- Focus on your breathing.
- Place your hand flat on your stomach.
- Take slow deep breaths, breathing in through your nose to a count of 1-2-3-4.
- As you breathe in, feel your stomach rise under your hand. If you cannot feel your stomach rise under your hand keep practicing to learn the technique – you will know when it is right because you will feel your stomach rise under your hand. Sometimes it can feel awkward to have your stomach go out when you breathe in. To help learn this technique, imagine that when you take a breath in you are inflating a balloon in your stomach – deep breathing inflates the balloon and your stomach goes out and exhaling deflates the balloon and your stomach goes in.
- Pause.
- Exhale slowly through your nose (or mouth if you prefer) and count down 4-3-2-1.
- Repeat this breathing technique.
- After a few minutes of breathing like this, as you breathe in, think of the work "relax" and as you breathe out say the words "let go".

Task 4 Attention Control

Background for Clinician

People may experience tinnitus as intrusive, constantly on their mind and in their thoughts. It can become the unwanted over riding focus of their attention and make it difficult to think about anything else. This constant awareness can be overwhelming and the cause of much distress. Simple attention control exercises can be useful to shift attention from tinnitus to more useful perceptions. See also Henry and Wilson [2].

For Person with Tinnitus

How much of your *time and attention* does your tinnitus take from you? The answer is quite likely "Too much!" One of the most common complaints amongst those with bothersome tinnitus is that it is always on their mind. It takes up too much of their attention. *But – it doesn't need to be this way!* Although we are not always aware of it, we have some control over what we pay attention to – and we make these decisions many times a day. For example, we might be working on a crossword puzzle while others are watching TV. In that situation there are a number of things competing for our attention, but we are able to choose to pay more attention to one (e.g., doing our crossword puzzle) and less to the other (e.g., watching TV). *With practice, it is possible to take that same control over the attention that you give to your tinnitus.*

Learning this skill of attention control means you will be able to give less consideration to your tinnitus. It won't be constantly on your mind and in your thoughts. You will be able to better manage your tinnitus and to reduce the associated distress. You may even be able to do more of the things that you enjoy!

With tinnitus (or anything else really!) it is impossible to simply choose not to think about it anymore. But *we can* control where we focus our attention. We can redirect the focus of our attention from the tinnitus to something else; with practice this can become nearly second nature! There are a number of strategies that can help you learn how to direct the focus of your attention. These include attention control, imagery, and distraction. Without consciously thinking about it, you probably use some of these techniques already. You can use these very same techniques to manage your tinnitus. The aim of all of these techniques is to learn how to control the focus of your attention – to be able to direct your attention from one thing to another at will. The idea is that you will learn how to direct your attention, to and from, the tinnitus under your own control.

Attention Control Techniques

A characteristic of human behavior is that we can really only concentrate on one thing at a time. As we focus on a particular thing, other things become less of the focus of our attention and recede into the background of our mind. We can work this to your advantage, with tinnitus becoming less the center of attention and receding into the background of your awareness. The following are two examples of attention control techniques simplified from a self-help book "Tinnitus. A self-help management guide for the ringing in your ears" by Drs' Henry and Wilson (2002) which you might find useful. Modify them to suit you, and practice making up your own.

Example 1: Focus on your breathing. Breathe in and out. Think about breathing in through your nose and out through your mouth. Breathe slowly, deeply. Become aware of each breath. As you focus on your breathing, *notice that you have been less aware of other parts of your body.* Gently shift the focus of attention from your breathing to your feet. Without moving your feet become aware of any sensations they are feeling. Become aware of each toe. Picture them in your mind. How do they feel? Are they warm, cold? Can you feel your toes resting next to each other? As you focus your mind on your feet, notice that you have become less aware of your breathing. Gently shift the focus of your attention back to your breathing. As before, think about breathing in through your nose, out through your mouth. Become aware of each breath.

Practice switching your attention from your breathing to your hands. Focus on the details of each hand. Then practice directing your attention back to your breathing. Do this with different parts of your body, going back to your breathing in between. Notice how you can control where you focus your attention. *Notice that as you focus your attention on one thing, other things fade into the background.*

Example 2: Find a comfortable place to sit. Ask yourself "Where is my attention now?" Is it focused on a thought, a feeling, or a noise outside? Now change your focus to the physical sensations of your body. Does your skin feel cool or warm? Become aware of any other sensations in your body. Spend some time exploring these. Now refocus your attention to the noises around you. Try to identify what they are. Perhaps you can hear traffic outside, birds chirping, or people talking. Now refocus again, focusing your attention to your hands, picturing each one in your mind. Notice that you can become aware of where your attention is and that you can change the focus of your attention. *You are able to deliberately change your attention from one thing to another.*

Distraction

Distraction can be helpful in taking your mind off what is causing you distress or worry. You probably have some distraction techniques that you already use. These might include going for a walk, watching TV, or reading a book. Here are some others that you could try. Some will suit you more than others – try them all and see!

- Make a list of five things you enjoy doing most
- Listen to some nice music
- Take a walk
- Play a computer game
- In your mind, run through the alphabet backwards from Z to A
- Count backwards from 100 subtracting 6 at a time
- Search for a movie you would like to see
- Plan a shopping list
- Do something nice – for yourself or for somebody else!
- Make a list of other possible distraction techniques you could use

Task 5 Communication

Background for Clinician

Tinnitus and accompanying hearing loss can lead to communication difficulties. Communication is such an important activity we seldom think of the detrimental effects of being unable to effectively communicate. Reduced communication can lead to isolation and miscommunication can lead to negative consequences for relationships with family and friends.

For person with tinnitus and hearing loss

- Let other people know you have difficulties hearing. Tell them what they can do to help make things

easier. Be specific. Let them know that you need their help because you value what they have to say.
- Place your back to the main source of background noise and face the speaker.
- Ask people to get your attention before they start talking to you.
- Face the person you are talking to so their gestures and facial expressions will help you understand what they're saying.
- Try to choose a place that is well lit, so it is easy to see the target speaker.
- Try to keep calm and don't panic. If you become anxious or flustered, it might be harder for you to follow what's being said.
- Have patience, good humor, and be understanding with yourself.
- If your hearing is not the same in both ears, try turning your better side towards the person speaking to you.
- If you don't catch what someone says, don't be afraid to ask him or her to repeat it or say it in a different way.
- If necessary, ask people to slow down and speak more clearly.
- *Don't be too hard on yourself. No one hears correctly all the time!*

References

1. Dobie RA (1999) A review of randomized clinical trials in tinnitus. Laryngoscope 109:1202–11.
2. Henry J and P Wilson (2001) The psychological management of chronic tinnitus: a cognitive-behavioral approach. Allyn & Bacon: Boston.
3. Hallam R, S Rachman and R Hinchcliffe, (1984) Psychological aspects of tinnitus, in Contributions to medical psychology, S Rachman, Editor. 1984, Pergamon Press: New York. 31–53.
4. Tyler RS and LJ Baker (1983) Difficulties experienced by tinnitus sufferers. J Speech Hear Disord 48:150–4.
5. Curtis J (1841) Tinnitus aurium [letter to the editor]. Lancet 36:828–9.
6. Coles RR and RS Hallam (1987) Tinnitus and its management. Br Med Bull 43:983–98.
7. Clark J and K English (2004) Counseling in Audioloigic Practice: Helping Patients and Families Adjust to Hearing Loss. 2004, Pearson Education: New York.
8. Searchfield G (2006) Hearing aids and tinnitus, in Tinnitus treatment: Clinical protocols, R Tyler, Editor. 2006, Thieme: New York. 161–75.
9. Jastreboff PJ (2000) Tinnitus habituation therapy (THT) and tinnitus retraining therapy (TRT), in Tinnitus Handbook, R Tyler, Editor. 2000, Singular Publishing Group: San Diego. 357–76.

10. Henry JA, MA Schechter, SM Nagler et al (2002) Comparison of tinnitus masking and tinnitus retraining therapy. J Am Acad Audiol 13:559–81.

11. Andersson G (2002) Psychological aspects of tinnitus and the application of cognitive-behavioral therapy. Clin Psychol Rev 22:977–90.

12. Tyler RS, (2006) Neurophysiological models, psychological models, and treatments for tinnitus, in Tinnitus treatment: Clinical protocols., RS Tyler, Editor. 2006, Thieme Medical Publishers, Inc.: New York. 1–22.

13. Tyler R, W Noble, JP Preece et al (2004) Psychological treatments for tinnitus, in Tinnitus: theory and management, JB Snow, Editor. 2004, BC Decker: Ontario. 314–25.

14. McFadden D (1982) Tinnitus: Facts, theories, and treatments. 1982, Washington, D.C.: National Academy Press. 150.

15. Axelsson A and A Ringdahl (1989) Tinnitus: a study of its prevalence and characteristics. British Journal of Audiology 23:53-62.

16. Coles R (1984) Epidemiology of tinnitus (2). Demographic and clinical features. Journal of Laryngology and Otology Suppl 2:195-202.

17. Cooper JC (1994) Health and nutrition examination survey of 1971-75: Part II. Tinnitus, subjective hearing loss, and well being. J Am Acad Audiol 5:37–43.

18. Aazh H, B Moore and B Glasberg (2008) Simplified form of tinnitus retraining therapy in adults: a retrospective study. BMC Ear Nose Throat Disord 3:7.

19. Folmer RL, SE Griest, MB Meikle et al (1999) Tinnitus severity, loudness, and depression. Otolaryngol Head Neck Surg 121:48–51.

20. Lewis JE, GP Jacobson and DL McCaslin (2002) Tinnitus and suicide [letter to the editor]. J Am Acad Audiol 13:339; author reply 41.

21. Lewis JE, SD Stephens and L McKenna (1994) Tinnitus and suicide. Clin Otolaryngol Allied Sci 19:50–4.

22. Lindberg P and B Scott (1999) The use and predictive value of psychological profiles in helpseeking and nonhelpseeking tinnitus sufferers, in Proceedings of the Sixth International Tinnitus Seminar, Cambridge UK. September 5th-9th 1999, JW Hazell, Editor. 1999, The Tinnitus and Hyperacusis Centre: London. 114–7.

23. Fagelson MA (2007) The association between tinnitus and posttraumatic stress disorder. Am J Audiol 16:107–17.

24. Welch D and P Dawes (2008) Personality and perception of tinnitus. Ear Hear 29:684–92.

25. Holgers KM, S Erlandsson and M-L Barrenäs (1999) Early identification of therapy resistant tinnitus, in Proceedings of the Sixth International Tinnitus Seminar, Cambridge UK. September 5th-9th 1999, JW Hazell, Editor. 1999, The Tinnitus and Hyperacusis Centre: London. 268–70.

26. House JW (1981) Management of the tinnitus patient. Ann Otol Rhinol Laryngol 90:597–601.

27. Jakes S, R Hallam, C Chambers et al (1985) A factor analytical study of tinnitus complaint behaviour. Audiology. 24:195–206.

28. Reed G (1960) An audiometric study of two hundred cases of subjective tinnitus. Arch Otolaryngol. 71:84–94.

29. Henry J and PH Wilson (2001) The psychological management of chronic tinnitus: a cognitive-behavioural approach. 2001, Masachusetts: Allyn & Bacon.

30. Stephens D, SI Erlandsson, L Sanchez et al (1992) Some psychological aspects of tinnitus. in Fourth International Tinnitus Seminar. Amsterdam: Kugler.

31. Halford JB and SD Anderson (1991) Anxiety and depression in tinnitus sufferers. J Psychosom Res 35:383–90.

32. Andersson G (1995) A review of psychological treatment approaches for patients suffering from tinnitus. Soc Behav Med 17:357–66.

33. Andersson G and L Lyttkens (1999) A meta-analytic review of psychological treatments for tinnitus. Br J Audiol 33:201–10.

34. Sweetow R (2000) Cognitive-behavioural modification, in Handbook of tinnitus, R Tyler, Editor. 2000, Singular Publications: San Diego. 297–312.

35. Beck A, C Ward, M Mendelson et al (1961) An inventory for measuring depression. Arch Gen Psychiatry 4:561–71.

36. Spielberger CD (1983) Manual for the State-Trait Anxiety Inventory (STAI). 1983, PaloAlto, CA: Consulting Psychologists Press.

37. Zigmond A and R Snaith (1983) The hospital anxiety and depression scale. Acta Psychiatr Scand 67:361–70.

38. Andersson G, D Baguley, L McKenna et al (2005) Tinnitus: a multidisciplinary approach. London: Whurr Publishers.

39. Kroner-Herwig B, E Biesinger, F Gerhards et al (2000) Retraining therapy for chronic tinnitus. A critical analysis of its status. Scand Audiol 29:67–78.

40. Hallam RS (1993) Tinnitus: living with the ringing in your ears. London: Harper Collins Publishers.

41. Hallam RS and L McKenna, (2005) Tinnitus habituation therapy, in Tinnitus treatment: clinical protocols, R Tyler, Editor. 2005, Thieme: New York. 65–80.

42. Niemann SH (2002) Guidance/Psychoeducational groups, in Introduction to group counseling, D Capuzzi and DR Gross, Editors. 2002, Love: Denver. 265–90.

43. Henry J and PH Wilson (1996) The psychological management of tinnitus: comparison of a combined cognitive educational program, education alone and a waiting-list control. Int Tinnitus J 1:9–20.

44. Lindberg P, B Scott, L Melin et al (1989) The psychological treatment of tinnitus: an experimental evaluation. Behav Res Ther 27:593–603.

45. Jefferson CD, CL Drake, HM Scofield et al (2005) Sleep hygiene practices in a population-based sample of insomniacs. Sleep 28:611-5.

46. Jastreboff PJ and JWP Hazell (1993) A neurophysiological approach to tinnitus management. Br J Audiol 27:7–17.

47. Tyler RS, AK Gehringer, W Noble et al (2006) Tinnitus activities treatment, in Tinnitus treatment: Clinical protocols, RS Tyler, Editor. 2006. 116–31.

48. Henry JA, TL Zaugg and MA Schechter (2005) Clinical guide for audiologic tinnitus management II: Treatment. Am J Audiol 14:49–70.

49. McKenna L and R Irwin (2008) Sound therapy for tinnitus – Sacred cow or idol worship?: An investigation of the evidence. Audiol Med 6:16–24.

50. Lukens EP and W McFarlane (2004) Psychoeducation as evidence-based practice: considerations for practice, research, and policy. Brief Treat. Crisis Interv 4:205–25.

51. Stouffer JL and RS Tyler (1990) Characterization of tinnitus by tinnitus patients. J Speech Hear Disord 55:439–53.

52. Newman CW and SA Sandridge, (2005) Incorporating group and individual sessions into a tinnitus management

clinic, in Tinnitus treatment: clinical protocols, R Tyler, Editor. 2005, Thieme Medical Publishers, Inc.: New York. 187–97.

53. McKenna L and HC Daniel (2005) Tinnitus-related insomnia treatment, in Tinnitus treatment: clinical protocols, R Tyler, Editor. 2005, Thieme Medical Publishers, Inc.: New York. 81–95.

54. Niemann SH, (2002) Guidance/Psychoeducational groups, in Introduction to group counseling, D Capuzzi, Editor. 2002, Love: Denver.

55. Jakes SC, RS Hallam, L McKenna et al (1992) Group cognitive therapy for medical patients: an application to tinnitus. Cognit Ther Res 16:67–82.

56. Kong O, Group-Based Informational Counselling and Homework for Tinnitus Management. Unpublished Master of Audiology Dissertation. 2006, The University of Auckland: Auckland.

57. Locke EA (1968) Toward a theory of task motivation and incentives. Organ Behav Hum Perform 3(2):157–89.

58. Locke EA and GP Latham (1990) A theory of goal setting & task performance. Prentice Hall: Englewood Cliffs. 413.

59. Swinton L. Project YOU Part I: Goal setting guide. 2004 [cited 2005 November 13]; Available from: http://www.uncommon-knowledge.co.uk/goal_setting/Goal_Setting_Guide.pdf.

60. Schunk DH (1990) Goal setting and self-efficacy during self-regulated learning. Educ Psychol 25:71–86.

61. Lee TW, EA Locke and GP Latham (1989) Goal setting theory and job performance. 1989: Pervin LA (Ed). Goal concepts in personality and social psychology. Lawrence Erlbaum: Hillsdale.

62. Bandura A (1989) Self-regulation of motivation and action through internal standards and goal systems, in Goal concepts in personality and social psychology, LA Pervin, Editor. Lawrence Erlbaum: Hillsdale.

63. Locke EA (1968) Toward a Theory of task motivation and incentives. Organ Behav Hum Perform 3(2):157–189 http://www.elsevier.com/wps/find/journaldescription.cws_home/622929/description#description.

64. Manderlink G and JM Harackiewicz (1984) Proximal versus distal goal setting and intrinsic motivation. J Pers Soc Psychol 47:918–28.

65. Dillon H, A James and J Ginis (1997) Client Oriented Scale of Improvement (COSI) and its relationship to several other measures of benefit and satisfaction provided by hearing aids. J Am Acad Audiol 8:27–43.

66. Yost W (1991) Auditory image perception and analysis: the basis for hearing. Hear Res 56:8–18.

67. Bregman AS (1990) Auditory Scene Analysis: The Perceptual Organization of Sound. Cambridge: MIT Press.

68. Feldmann H (1992) Tinnitus – reality or phantom?, in Proceedings of the Fourth International Tinnitus Seminar, J Aran and R Dauman, Editors. Kugler: Amsterdam. 7–14.

69. Worden FG (1973) Auditory habituation, in Habituation: Physiological substrates, HVS Peeke and MJ Herz, Editors. Academic Press: New York. 109–33.

70. Andersson G and L McKenna (1998) Tinnitus masking and depression. Audiology 37:174–82.

71. Tyler R, (2000) Psychoacoustical measurement, in Handbook of tinnitus, R Tyler, Editor. Singular Publications: San Diego. 149–80.

72. Hallam RS (1996) Correlates of sleep disturbance in chronic distressing tinnitus. Scand Audiol 25:263–6.

73. Stepanski EJ and JK Wyatt (2003) Use of sleep hygiene in the treatment of insomnia. Sleep Med Rev 7:215–25.

74. Nau SD and JK Walsh (1983) Sleep hygiene of insomnia patients. Sleep Hygiene 12:268.

75. Harvey L, SJ Inglis and CA Espie (2002) Insomniacs' reported use of CBT components and relationship to long-term clinical outcome. Behav Res Ther 40:75–83.

76. Hann D, GD Searchfield, M Sanders et al (2008) Strategies for the selection of music in the short-term management of mild tinnitus. Aust N Z J Audiol 30:129–40.

77. Henry JA, B Rheinsburg and T Zaugg (2004) Comparison of custom sounds for achieving tinnitus relief. J Am Acad Audiol 15:585–98.

78. Kroner-Herwig B, A Frenzel, G Fritsche et al (2003) The management of chronic tinnitus: comparison of an outpatient cognitive-behavioral group training to minimal-contact interventions. J Psychosom Res 54:381–9.

79. Noreña AJ and S Chery-Croze (2007) Enriched acoustic environment rescales auditory sensitivity. NeuroReport 18:1251–5.

80. Martin WH (2008) Dangerous decibels: Partnership for preventing noise-induced hearing loss and tinnitus in children. Semin Hear 29:102–10.

81. Tyler R (2008) The Consumer Handbook on Tinnitus. Auricle Ink Publishers: Sedona.

82. Henry J and P Wilson (2002) Tinnitus. A self-help management guide for the ringing in your ears. Allyn and Bacon: Boston.

83. Kazantzis N and GK Lampropoulos (2002) The use of homework in psychotherapy: an introduction. J Clin Psychol 58:487–8.

84. Kazantzis N, FP Deane and KR Ronan (2000) Homework assignments in cognitive and behavioural therapy: a meta-analysis. Clin Psychol Sci Prac 7:189–202.

85. Beck AT, JA Rush, BF Shaw et al (1979) Cognitive therapy of depression. Guilford Press: New York.

86. Badgio PC, GS Halperin and JP Barber (1999) Acquisition of adaptive skills: psychotherapeutic change in cognitive and dynamic therapies. Clini Psychol Rev 19:721–37.

87. Dryden W (1994) Reason and emotion in psychotherapy: Thirty years on. J Ration Emot Cogn Behav Ther 12:83–99.

88. Barlow DH, JL Esler and AE Vitali (1998) Psychosocial treatments for panic disorders, phobias, and generalized anxiety disorder, in A guide to treatments that work, PE Nathan, Gorman JM, Editors. Oxford University Press: New York.

89. Wanderer Z and BL Ingram (1991) The therapeutic use of tape-recorded repetitions of flooding stimuli. J Behav Ther Exp Psychiatry 22:31–5.

90. Shelton JL and R Levy (1979) Home practice activities and compliance: Two sources of error variance in behavioral research. J Appl Behav Anal 12:324.

91. Jakes SC, RS Hallam, S Rachman et al (1986) The effects of reassurance, relaxation training and distraction on chronic tinnitus sufferers. Behav Res Ther 24:497-507.

92. Henry J and PH Wilson (1998) An evaluation of two types of cognitive intervention in the management of chronic tinnitus. Scand J Behav Ther 27:156–66.

96. Laurikainen E, R Johansson, E Akaan-Penttila et al (2000) Treatment of severe tinnitus. Acta Oto-Laryngol Suppl 543:77–8.

97. Andersson G, D Baguley, L McKenna et al (2005) Tinnitus: a multidisciplinary approach. Whurr : London. 205.

Chapter 71
Cognitive Behavioral Treatment (CBT)

Karoline V. Greimel and Birgit Kröner-Herwig

Keypoints

1. Cognitive behavioral interventions are the most widely used psychological strategies for coping with tinnitus.
2. The goal of the therapy is to alter maladaptive cognitive, emotional, and behavioral responses to tinnitus and not to abolish the sound itself.
3. There are two main components to this approach:

    (a) Cognitive restructuring and
    (b) Behavioral modification.

4. Treatment programs comprise of techniques like relaxation training, cognitive restructuring, attention control techniques, imagery training, and exposure to difficult situations.
5. The combined approach assists patients in identifying and modifying maladaptive behavior and promotes habituation to tinnitus.
6. The collaboration of patient and therapist is a prerequisite for a positive outcome of therapy.

Keywords Tinnitus • Cognitive behavioral therapy • Relaxation training • Cognitive restructuring • Attention control techniques • Imagery techniques • Behavioral techniques

Abbreviations

CBT   Cognitive behavioral therapy
PMR   Progressive muscle relaxation
RET   Rational-Emotive Therapy

K.V. Greimel (✉)
Salzburg University Hospital, Muellner Hauptstrasse 48,
5020 Salzburg, Austria, Germany
e-mail: k.greimel@salk.at

Introduction

In the history of tinnitus research and treatment, many attempts have been directed toward abolishing or minimizing tinnitus. Despite all these efforts, until now no treatment has been found to successfully eliminate tinnitus permanently. As a consequence, increasing efforts have been undertaken by behavioral scientists and psychologists to eliminate or at least ameliorate psychological symptoms associated with tinnitus. The aim of psychological interventions is not to "cure" or to eliminate the inner noise but to reduce tinnitus-related distress and increase quality of life. If patients are no longer bothered by their inner noises and the question of how tinnitus can be removed, they might become secondary. As long as tinnitus itself cannot be eliminated, the main intention of all therapeutic interventions is to alleviate suffering from tinnitus.

Cognitive Theories of Behavior Regulation

Most interventions in reducing tinnitus-related distress are predicated on cognitive theories of behavior regulation. One of the most influential theories was developed by Beck [1, 2]. Cognitive behavior therapy is based on the "rationale that an individual's affect and behavior are largely determined by the way in which he structures the world."

A general cognitive framework as shown in Fig. 71.1 asserts that the emotional and behavioral consequences of an event or situation experienced by a person are modified by the way a person thinks about it. In other words, emotions and behavioral reactions are the result of

Fig. 71.1 A-B-C model

Fig. 71.2 Association between tinnitus, specific beliefs, and emotional consequences

Activating Event (A)	Beliefs (B)	Emotional Consequences (C)
 *buzzing*	"I can not live with it" >>	desperate, hopeless
	"There is nothing I can do about it" >>	helpless, depressed
	"If I did not have to work in this noisy environment, I would not have gotten tinnitus" >>	anger, hostility

appraisals of an event and are not the result of the event itself. This model dates back to Ellis (1973) [3], who termed it the A-B-C model. A stands for activating events, B for beliefs, and C for consequences (see Fig. 71.1).

Patients have to be educated and instructed according to this model. It is made clear that mainly the thoughts, beliefs, and expectations about tinnitus are creating the problem. Tinnitus itself does not have the power to ruin one's life. This assumption can be illustrated by the fact that the majority of individuals permanently afflicted by tinnitus – even if they describe it as loud – do not feel distressed by it. Nevertheless, the therapist should make it explicitly clear that he or she knows that the tinnitus is real, not imagined, and that the patient's response to the abnormal tinnitus perception can be well understood.

In general, patients blame their tinnitus for their emotional impairment. They are convinced that the tinnitus is "making" them depressed, anxious, and worried and that their ways of dealing with tinnitus are of no account. Furthermore, if the patient thinks that there is nothing that can be done to alleviate the symptoms, he or she will likely become hopeless and depressed. Blaming a situation or person for the onset of tinnitus will create anger and hostility (see Fig. 71.2).

Cognitive responses to tinnitus can be very different. Regardless of the cause of tinnitus, "suffering" is a function of how the patient reacts to tinnitus – how he or she copes with it. Patients have to be made aware that their way of coping can be modified. The goal of the therapy is to alter maladaptive cognitive, emotional, and behavioral responses to tinnitus and not the sound itself.

A comprehensive model for the chronification of tinnitus, including various dysfunctional cognition and behavior, is described by Kroener-Herwig [4] based on the assumptions regarding tinnitus tolerance made by Hallam and Jakes [5] (see Fig. 71.3).

This model describes the vicious cycle of tinnitus distress and demonstrates how different cognitive, emotional, and behavioral factors interact and create positive feedback loops generating and maintaining tinnitus-related annoyance and discomfort. Attention plays a pivotal role. Focusing attention on tinnitus, accompanied by specific dysfunctional cognitive processes of appraisal like catastrophic thoughts and rumination, leads to negative emotional consequences. Furthermore, behavior resulting from illness often based on avoidance learning (e.g., exculpation from daily routine, justification for absence of work) can be reinforced by family or friends.

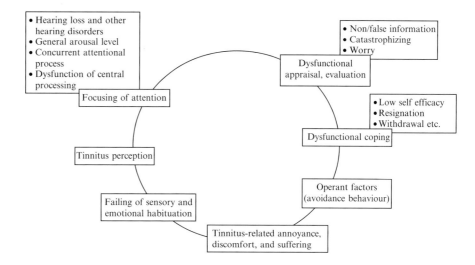

Fig. 71.3 A vicious circle model of tinnitus [17], after [16]

Cognitive Behavioral Therapy

The origin of cognitive behavioral therapy goes back to the 1950s and 1960s when Wolpe and Lazarus [6] developed new techniques for changing behavior – in particular in patients with anxiety disorders – based on experimental psychology. In the early phases, therapy (then called behavior therapy) was dominated by techniques like operant conditioning [7], systematic desensitization [8], or aversion therapy [9], which were directed at overt behavior change. In the 1970s, increasingly cognition-centered theories of behavior regulation were established and, consequently, cognitive interventions were implemented into therapy. Beck [2] has been most influential in introducing cognitive interventions into therapeutic strategies. In accordance with this trend, Ellis [10] introduced Rational-Emotive Therapy (RET) based on his A-B-C model. Meichenbaum [11] introduced the notion of the specific importance of self-talk and self-instructions for behavior regulation. Bandura [12] states in his social learning theory that self-efficacy beliefs play a most important role in guiding behavior.

Cognitive behavioral therapy was developed mainly as a treatment for affective disorders such as depression and anxiety. Subsequently, this therapy has been successfully utilized for patients with aversive medical conditions (e.g., chronic pain). A cognitive behavioral approach was first applied in the treatment of patients with tinnitus in the 1980s [13–16]. Nowadays,

it is one of the most widely used and accepted psychological strategies for coping with intractable disorders [17–19].

There are two main components to this approach:

– Cognitive restructuring
– Behavioral modification

The combined approach assists patients in identifying and modifying maladaptive behavior and promotes habituation to tinnitus. The collaboration of patient and therapist is a prerequisite for a positive outcome of therapy.

Treatment programs comprise of techniques like relaxation training, cognitive restructuring, attention control, imagery training, and exposure to difficult situations.

Relaxation Training

Relaxation methods were one of the earliest psychological treatments applied to patients with tinnitus [20]. There are several forms of relaxation training. The most common is progressive muscle relaxation (PMR). In this technique, a person is shown how to decrease muscular tension and to achieve states of relaxation in a very brief period of time after detecting tension. The therapist instructs patients how to sequentially tense and relax various muscle groups, moving from practice in comfortable settings to practice in real-life situations such as sitting at a desk, watching television, etc. Relaxation techniques may be helpful in assisting people in learning a way of coping with tension and anxiety related to tinnitus. Furthermore, it is commonly reported by patients that stress exacerbates tinnitus or causes a person to experience the tinnitus more intensely, and that a reduction in stress levels may reduce loudness and annoyance. Also, listening to one's tinnitus in a relaxed state can foster habituation and retain serenity in the presence of tinnitus.

Despite the popularity of relaxation training in clinical practice, research shows that relaxation seems to be of limited value for most tinnitus patients when used as the sole treatment [21]. To be successful, it has to be an integral part of a larger treatment program.

Cognitive Restructuring

In general, cognitive therapy involves the identification of dysfunctional beliefs and negative thoughts, which occur in response to life events or sources of distress. Patients are taught methods of challenging those thoughts and substituting their catastrophic, unrealistic thoughts with more constructive ones (cognitive restructuring). Cognitive restructuring helps patients think differently and adopt a different attitude about their problem. It is used as a method to guide patients recognize and subsequently abandon rigid, unhelpful thinking patterns and replace them with constructive cognitions and thoughts. This is different from simple "positive thinking" or from "directive counseling," a treatment component of tinnitus retraining therapy [22], because in cognitive restructuring the therapist and patient collaborate in identifying, testing, and challenging dysfunctional thoughts, beliefs, attitudes, or attributions [4, 23]. It is theorized that for patients with tinnitus, the source of distress is not the sound itself, but the way in which the person evaluates and interprets the sound. A person may have negative thoughts such as "The noise is driving me crazy" or "This is the worst thing that could ever happen." Alternatively, he or she could think: "The noise doesn't hurt me – it is bad, but it generally gets better by-and-by" or "Do something enjoyable, rather than being occupied with the noise in your head."

The therapist helps the clients to challenge and test the validity of their automatic thoughts and to learn ways to substitute them with more constructive ones.

Attention Control Techniques

Attention control interventions make patients aware that they indeed have control over their attentional focus, and that directing attention to other aspects of the external or internal environment can make the tinnitus "disappear." Instructing patients to switch attention to and from tinnitus illustrates that tinnitus can be "controlled." Patients are encouraged to augment their use of other sensory modalities (e.g., smelling coffee, tasting honey). Furthermore, strategies to specifically manipulate the acoustical environment are recommended.

Imagery Techniques

Imagery techniques are used to change the negative associations related to tinnitus either by "masking" the noises or by integrating them into positive scenes. In imagery exercises, a patient may be asked to imagine that the tinnitus is masked by the sound of a waterfall or the waves of the sea. No real sounds are used to mask tinnitus in this exercise. Masking is achieved by imagination. Tinnitus also may be incorporated into pleasant scenes. Patients might be instructed to imagine walking through a landscape by listening to the singing of birds or lying on a blooming field and hearing the noises of bumblebees, cicadas, and other insects. Alternatively, a patient may imagine a cold and snowy winter day, sitting comfortably in front of the fire place, hearing the sizzling of a teakettle, and looking forward to enjoying a cup of hot tea.

In clinical practice, these approaches are rarely used as sole therapeutic methods, but are incorporated into relaxation training or cognitive restructuring interventions.

Behavioral Techniques

Tinnitus patients may tend to avoid situations where they feel impaired or distressed by their tinnitus, i.e., conversations with more than one person, a concert, a stroll in the city. This may have developed into generalized avoidance behavior. Cognitive behavioral therapy (CBT) encourages patients to expose themselves to those situations in order to realize that they can cope without major negative consequences. These behavioral "experiments" must be well prepared and these new skills should be frequently practiced.

In some patients, "suffering" from tinnitus allows her/him to avoid situations, which were threatening, and anxiety inducing for non-tinnitus-related reasons, e.g., office work or participating in social events. Tinnitus for them is an acceptable solution or "a legitimate excuse" for avoiding these situations. Thus, tinnitus complaints are under operant control and are therefore maintained. In these cases, patients have to become aware of the underlying problem and are assisted in finding adaptive problem solutions.

Multimodal CBT has been evaluated in several studies. The meta-analysis of Anderson and Lytthens [21] showed that psychological treatments are very effective regarding the reduction of tinnitus-related distress. The average effect size of 0.86 reveals a high efficacy. Recently, Martinez Devesa et al. [24] prepared a meta-analysis of randomized controlled group trials on CBT for the Cochrane Collaboration and came to the conclusion that the CBT is effective for improving the quality of life based on the analysis of 24 trials.

References

1. Beck, AT (1976) *Cognitive therapy and the emotional disorders*. International University Press: New York
2. Beck, AT, Rush AJ, Shaw, B and Emery, G (1979) *Cognitive therapy of depression*. Guilford Press: New York
3. Ellis, A (1973) *Humanistic psychotherapy the rational-emotive approach*. McGraw-Hill: New York
4. Kroener-Herwig, B, Biesinger, E, Gerhards, F, Goebel, G, Greimel, KV and Hiller, W (2000) Retraining therapy for chronic tinnitus A critical analysis of its status. *Scand Audiol* **29**: 67–78
5. Hallam, RS and Jakes SC (1987) An evaluation of relaxation training in chronic tinnitus sufferers In: *Proceedings of the Third International Tinnitus Seminar*. pp 363–365 Ed H Feldmann Harsch Verlag: Karlsruhe
6. Wolpe, J and Lazarus, AA (1966) *Behavior therapy techniques: a guide to the treatment of neuroses*. Pergamon Press: Elmsford
7. Skinner, BF (1953) *Science and human behavior*. Macmillan: Oxford
8. Wolpe, J (1958) *Psychotherapy by reciprocal inhibition*. Stanford University Press: Oxford
9. Cautela, JR and Kearney AJ (1986) *The covert conditioning handbook*. Springer: New York
10. Ellis, A (1962) *Reason and emotion in psychotherapy*. Lyle Stuart: New York
11. Meichenbaum, D (1977) *Kognitive Verhaltensmodifikation*. Urban and Schwarzenberg: München
12. Bandura, A (1977) Self-efficacy: toward a unifying theory of behavioral change. *Psychol Rev* **84**, 191–215
13. Hallam, RS (1984) Psychological aspects of tinnitus In: *Contributions to medical psychology pp. 31–53 Ed* S Rachmann Pergamon Press: Oxford
14. Sweetow, RW (1984) Cognitive behavioral modification in tinnitus management *Hearing Instruments* **35**, 14–18
15. Sweetow, RW (1986) Cognitive aspects of tinnitus-patient management *Ear hear* **7**, 390–396
16. Hallam, RS (1987) Psychological approaches to the evaluation and management of tinnitus distress In: *Tinnitus* pp 156–175 Ed J Hazell Churchill Livingstone: Edinburgh
17. Kroener-Herwig, B (1997) *Psychologische behandlung des chronischen Tinnitus*. Beltz: Weinheim
18. Sweetow, RW (2000) Cognitive-behavior modification In: *Tinnitus handbook* pp 297–313 Ed RS Tyler, Singular Publishing Group: San Diego
19. Wilson, PH, Bowen, M and Farag, P (1992) Cognitive and relaxation techniques in the management of tinnitus In: *Proceedings of the Fourth International Tinnitus Conference* Bordeaux
20. Wilson, PH and JL Henry (2000) Psychological management of tinnitus In: *Tinnitus handbook* Ed RS Tyler Singular Publishing Group: San Diego
21. Andersson, G, and Lyttkens, L (1999) A meta-analytic review of psychological treatments for tinnitus. *Br J Audiol* **33**, 201–210
22. Jastreboff, PJ and Hazell J (1993) A neurophysiological approach tinnitus: clinical implication. *Br J Audiol* **27**, 7–17
23. Wilson, PH, Henry, JL, Anderson, G, Lindberg, P and Hallam RS (1998) A critical analysis of directive counselling as a component of tinnitus retraining therapy. *Br J Audiol* **32**, 273–86
24. Martinez Devesa, P, Waddell, A, Perera, R and Theodoulou M (2009) Cognitive behavioral therapy for tinnitus. Cochrane Database Syst Rev. 2010 Sep 8;9:CD005233

Chapter 72
Auditory Training in Tinnitus

Larry E. Roberts and Daniel J. Bosnyak

Keypoints

1. We reviewed sensory training studies from the point of view that tinnitus is caused by synchronous neural activity that develops in tonotopic regions of primary auditory cortex deafferented by hearing loss. Studies were classified according to whether training was conducted within the tinnitus frequency region or outside of it, and whether training was active (requiring behavioral responses) or passive (sounds were presented as background signals). Effects of training on the psychoacoustic properties of tinnitus were distinguished from those on the distress behavior that accompanies tinnitus.
2. Studies in all four categories have reported significant reductions compared to untreated controls in tinnitus distress, measured by standardized questionnaires and visual analogue scales at the first compared to untreated controls in-course assessment, with little further change thereafter. Because the particular details of sensory training do not appear to matter, these gains could reflect important nonspecific effects of the treatment procedures.
3. Psychoacoustic measures may more directly assess tinnitus sensations. Reductions in minimum masking level (MML) on the order of 5–10 dB have been reported by several studies, implying that tinnitus has become weaker. Improvements in loudness discomfort levels (LDL) have also been reported, as have changes in the frequency content of tinnitus. Improvements in MML and LDL

are more gradual than those on distress behavior assessed by questionnaires, suggesting that neural plasticity may be at work.
4. Several studies reporting improvements in psychoacoustic measures and questionnaire data used passive sound presentation procedures. Hence, active sensory training requiring discriminated behavioral responses is not needed for these changes.
5. Systematic manipulation of the frequency content of trained sounds has been attempted in only a few studies. This step is needed to determine whether sound training induces specific changes in tinnitus. Alternatively, sound therapy may amplify the nonspecific effect of elements common to all tinnitus therapies.
6. Future studies should continue the practice of specifying how many participants of the total recruited contributed to a data analysis, and why and when exclusions occurred. Substantial sample sizes will be needed to establish treatment effects. Neural correlates offer the advantage of comparative immunity to patient expectations and self-report bias. When sounds are used to evoke neural responses, changes in loudness recruitment consequent on rescaling of loudness growth functions by sound exposure are a potential contributing factor.

Keywords Tinnitus • Sensory training • Tinnitus distress • Minimum masking level • Loudness discomfort levels

Abbreviations

A1 Primary auditory cortex
A2 Secondary auditory cortex
ADT Auditory discrimination training
AOIL Auditory object identification and localization

L.E. Roberts (✉)
Department of Psychology, Neuroscience, and Behavior, McMaster University, 1280 Main Street West, Hamilton, ON, Canada L8S 4K1
e-mail: roberts@mcmaster.ca

A.R. Møller et al. (eds.), *Textbook of Tinnitus*, DOI 10.1007/978-1-60761-145-5_72, © Springer Science+Business Media, LLC 2011
563

ASSR   Auditory steady-state response
EAE   Enriched acoustic environment
LDL   Loudness discomfort level
LM   Loudness matching
MML   Minimum masking level
QE   Quiet environment
RI   Residual inhibition
THI   Tinnitus handicap inventory
THQ   Tinnitus handicap questionnaire
TRQ   Tinnitus reaction questionnaire
TRT   Tinnitus retraining therapy
TSI   Tinnitus severity index
VAS   Visual analog scales

Introduction

In 1995, Jastreboff [1] proposed a comprehensive model of tinnitus that addressed three clinically prominent features of this condition. These were (a) the tinnitus sensation itself, generated by pathology in the inner ear; (b) the ability of the tinnitus sensation to command attention; and (c) the patient's disturbing emotional reaction to the tinnitus percept. Jastreboff suggested that although elimination of the tinnitus sensation by treatment of cochlear pathology was in most cases not practical, the latter two features of tinnitus were likely modifiable and if treated would benefit the tinnitus patient. Tinnitus retraining therapy (TRT) was devised to foster extinction of attentional and emotional responses by presenting low-level tinnitus-like external sounds that could be filtered out along with the tinnitus by perceptual mechanisms (see Chap. 73). Studies of TRT and clinical experience have confirmed that emotional responses diminish with time for most tinnitus sufferers, as does the extent to which tinnitus sufferers attend to their tinnitus percept [2]. These are important and beneficial effects for tinnitus sufferers. Attempts to reduce or eliminate the tinnitus sensation itself, however, have met with less success.

One approach that has gained attention with respect to the latter goal in recent years is sensory training aimed at modifying the neural basis of tinnitus sounds. The inspiration for this approach was based in part on the discovery that hearing loss induced by noise exposure in animal models leads to a substantial reorganization of tonotopic maps in primary auditory cortex, such that frequencies near the edge of normal hearing come

to be overrepresented at the expense of frequencies in the hearing loss region [3–5]. Because hearing loss is a putative cause of tinnitus, it was suggested that this overrepresentation, or changes in the response properties of auditory neurons associated with it, may correspond to the tinnitus percept [6, 7]. A second foundation was laid by experiments conducted in the last 15 years that demonstrated that cortical representations for sound in the primary auditory cortex are not fixed after early development, as was once believed, but can be modified by auditory training well into adulthood [8, 9]. This phenomenon is called "neural plasticity" (see Chap. 12). These two lines of research have converged to ask whether sensory training procedures derived from animal research can be adapted to humans, with the goal of modifying neural representations that appear to underlie tinnitus.

A Framework for Sensory Training Studies

For this goal to be achieved, the neural modifications induced by sensory training must intersect with the neural mechanisms generating tinnitus. In Chap. 13, we reviewed evidence pointing to a role for *neural synchrony* (temporally coupled neural activity) in tinnitus. According to this viewpoint, tinnitus may be generated by synchronous neural activity that develops in reorganized tonotopic regions of primary auditory cortex that receive diminished input from the ear owing to hearing impairment caused by noise exposure, otological disease, or the aging process [7]. Changes in subcortical structures appear to contribute [10] and may account, as well, for some distinct properties of tinnitus including its modulation by somatosensory activity in many individuals [11, 12]. Although the thalamocortical input to the affected neurons in the primary auditory cortex (A1) is altered by hearing loss, their synchronous output remains intact and may be a driving force underlying tinnitus. This output may recruit other brain regions into a network identified by functional imaging studies [13], including frontal and limbic areas that subserve, respectively, the attentional and emotional aspects of tinnitus described by Jastreboff [1].

In this chapter, we use the neural synchrony model as a template for reviewing auditory training studies of tinnitus. This perspective suggests that it is necessary to reduce synchronous neural activity occurring in regions of A1 that have been affected by hearing loss, in order to reduce the loudness of tinnitus sounds. Training for sounds in the tinnitus frequency region, with the aim of segregating synchronous network activity in this region, would appear to be the most direct approach. Masking sounds presented to this frequency region induce optimal post-masking suppression of tinnitus [residual inhibition, (RI)], confirming that such sounds interact with the tinnitus generating mechanism [14]. Training in the tinnitus frequency region requires that significant residual hearing be present in this region, which is the case for many, but not all, tinnitus patients. Alternatively, training can be delivered outside of the tinnitus frequency region where hearing is generally better preserved. For example, training at or below the edge frequency region may alter neural representations in these regions, which send collateral inputs into the tinnitus region that may disrupt neural synchrony. Lateral inhibition arising from augmented representations below the tinnitus frequency range could also distribute into the tinnitus region and suppress tinnitus percepts. Inhibitory interactions have been demonstrated by human electrophysiological studies [15, 16] and are known to span several octaves in primate A1 [17], suggesting the feasibility of this approach. While the neural synchrony model focuses on A1 as a preferred site of action, several brain structures are active in tinnitus, including regions of the secondary auditory cortex (A2) that may distribute re-entrant feedback into the auditory core region and disrupt neural activity underlying tinnitus [18]. Remodeling of cortical representations in A2 by sensory training appears to proceed normally in the tinnitus brain (see Chap. 13) and may confer a benefit.

Several methodological limitations should be acknowledged in advance of this review. Auditory training procedures are aimed at modifying the neural processes that generate tinnitus sensations. In order to assess whether this goal has been achieved, it is desirable to employ psychoacoustic tools that more or less directly measure the sensory attributes of tinnitus, such as loudness matching (LM), in which the loudness of an external sound in the range of normal hearing is adjusted to equal the loudness of tinnitus, and minimum masking level (MML), the minimum loudness of a masking sound required to just cover tinnitus. Loudness discomfort level (LDL) is another useful psychoacoustic method, which measures loudness growth functions that are frequently elevated in individuals with tinnitus [19], as are their audiograms. Standardized procedures for measuring tinnitus spectra are also available [14, 20] and beneficial for characterizing tinnitus. However, only a minority of studies report such measures. More often, standardized questionnaires such as the tinnitus handicap questionnaire (THQ) [21], tinnitus severity index (TSI) [22], tinnitus handicap inventory (THI) [23], and tinnitus reaction questionnaire (TRQ) [24] are employed in which tinnitus patients rate on subjective scales the loudness and intrusiveness of their tinnitus and its effect on quality of life including mood and anxiety, interference with sleep, concentration, work productivity, and interpersonal relationships. While these questionnaires – often supplemented with tinnitus ratings on visual analog scales (VAS) – likely reflect to some degree the sensory properties of tinnitus, they tend to focus on the distressful consequences of having tinnitus emphasized by Jastreboff [1]. A further limitation is that few studies have controlled for the contribution of procedural elements that are likely common to all therapeutic approaches and may affect outcome regardless of any direct effect of auditory processing on the neural substrate of tinnitus. Examples of such elements include (a) beneficial effects of discussion with informed and sympathetic staff, (b) knowledge about tinnitus, (c) investment by patient and staff in a therapeutic process, and (d) the effect of these components on a hopeful attitude and expectations for success. In this chapter, we will refer to effects of these elements as "nonspecific effects", not to diminish their considerable importance for benefiting patients, but in order to distinguish them from effects attributable to the specific sounds incorporated into an auditory training procedure.

Notwithstanding these limitations, several approaches to auditory training have been tried or are currently under assessment. The results give a picture of the methods used, whether the goal of auditory training can be realized, and if not for all tinnitus patients, which variables may be important for treatment success. Because active training requiring explicit behavioral responses might confer a benefit in tinnitus, we categorize the studies into active procedures that require such responses and passive procedures that do not. We also categorize the studies according to whether sounds are presented to the tinnitus frequency (hearing loss) region or outside of this region. Animal studies are included where they are relevant. One novel approach is described that does not fit into these categories.

Active Training Within the Tinnitus Frequency Region

Several studies have assessed the effects of auditory training procedures at or near the tinnitus "pitch" (likely resembling the modal pitch in a tinnitus spectrum). Based on their results studying phantom limb pain where it had been shown that the amount of cortical reorganization was positively correlated with amount of pain [25] and that discrimination training in sensory areas adjacent to the deafferented region reduced phantom limb pain [26], Flor et al. [27] trained seven tinntius patients on a frequency discrimination task for tones matched to their tinnitus frequency (proximal frequency group), with an additional seven patients trained at a frequency distant from the tinnitus frequency (distal group). The participants in this study were asked to determine if two tones presented successively were either identical (50% of trials) or different in frequency and were given feedback for correctness. The difficulty of the task was increased with performance improvement across sessions. Training was to be carried out every day for 2 h over a 4-week period. Interestingly, two of the seven distant-frequency participants dropped from the study complaining of increases in tinnitus severity, suggesting an adverse effect of training below the tinnitus frequency region. At the end of training, the proximal and the remaining distal patients did not differ on any outcome measures, so they were combined for analysis. Given the unreliability of tinnitus pitch match procedures [28], some patients in the distal group may still have trained at frequencies within their tinnitus spectrum. No significant training effect on tinnitus severity was found, but not all patients complied with the training requirements. When the participants were separated post hoc into those who trained more ($n=7$) or less ($n=5$) over the 4-week period, the extensive training group showed significant reduction in self-reported tinnitus severity while the limited training group showed a significant increase in tinnitus severity. Cortical reorganization or changes in the psychoacoustic properties of the tinnitus

were not assessed. Given that the treatment effect was not limited to the group training on frequencies within the tinnitus frequency region, it appears that potentially nonspecific factors such as focusing attention away from tinnitus might have been responsible for the lessening in severity.

Herriaz et al. [29, 30] described the results of a number of similar procedures, which they collectively referred to as ADT (auditory discrimination training). In all patients, the stimuli to be discriminated fell within the region of hearing loss. However, the procedures differed from those used by Flor et al. in that the discrimination in most cases was relatively easy (for example, discrimination between a broadband noise and an 8 kHz pure tone) and task difficulty did not increase with training (non-adaptive procedure). Training sessions were relatively short in the largest test group ($n=29$), with the participants required to perform 10-min sessions twice daily for a 1-month period. These procedural changes allowed the patients to perform the task at home using an MP3 device. Significant improvements in self-reported tinnitus severity on a VAS scale of loudness and total score on the THI questionnaire were found compared to waitlist controls. However, because no assessments of the psychoacoustic properties of tinnitus (LM, MML, or tinnitus spectrum) were performed, it is difficult to attribute the tinnitus improvement to a reversal of the presumed cortical reorganization. In another study, participants in one group (SAME, $n=11$) trained at frequency discrimination at a pitch judged to be the same as the tinnitus pitch while the second group (NONSAME, $n=11$) trained at a frequency different from the tinnitus pitch but still within the region of hearing loss. The NONSAME group showed a larger reduction in THI score with the difference between the groups being significant. Like Flor et al. [27], these results suggest that training at the "tinnitus pitch" was not a requirement for reduction in tinnitus severity. However, because the trained pitch in the NONSAME group was in the region of hearing loss, some degree of overlap with the tinnitus spectrum was likely.

Norena et al. [20] trained a single individual on a frequency discrimination task for four frequencies within the participant's measured tinnitus spectrum, and also measured the frequency discrimination threshold during training using an adaptive forced-choice staircase procedure. Training occurred in seven sessions over 3 weeks and was performed monaurally although the participant had bilateral tinnitus. The tinnitus spectrum changed significantly post-training in the trained ear but not the untrained one, showing a marked reduction in likeness ratings at the highest frequencies. This individual reported informally that the tinnitus sensation shifted from the initially more salient trained ear toward the untrained ear. However, the changes in the tinnitus spectrum occurred at the highest measured frequencies rather than at the frequencies used in the training procedure. This raises the possibility that the changes observed in the tinnitus spectrum could be attributed to an improved ability of the participant to make better discriminations at higher frequencies, allowing more refined judgments of the tinnitus spectrum. The unilateral effect of the tinnitus spectrum change supports the idea that the discrimination training process induced changes in the frequency organization in the auditory cortex. Follow-up studies employing more participants are called for.

In a preliminary study of our own (see Chap. 13 and [31]), we departed from the frequency discrimination training paradigm to one requiring detection of targets of increased sound *intensity* that were embedded in a 40-Hz amplitude-modulated tone of 1-s duration (carrier frequency 5 kHz, in the tinnitus frequency region). This type of stimulus evokes the stimulus-driven 40-Hz "auditory steady-state response" (ASSR) that localizes tonotopically to the region of primary auditory cortex and gives a picture of events occurring in this region during auditory training. Previous research with frequency (not intensity) discrimination had shown that acoustic training advanced the phase of the ASSR (a shortened time delay between the 40-Hz stimulus and response waveforms), but the amplitude of the response (signaling a map expansion) did not change [32]. We therefore switched to the intensity discrimination procedure using a single carrier frequency, which reduced competitive interactions that may obstruct map expansions when several carrier frequencies are experienced [33]. If training at 5 kHz strengthened the thalamocortical tuning of the trained neurons, tinnitus might diminish at this frequency as the affected neurons were removed from synchronous network behavior underlying tinnitus. Measurement of the tinnitus spectrum before and after training showed little change at 5 kHz or any other tinnitus frequency after training. However, in individuals with tinnitus, auditory training did not change ASSR phase either ($n = 8$ participants, $p = 0.44$), although it did so in their age-matched controls ($n = 11$ participants, $p = 0.006$) suggesting impaired remodeling of primary auditory cortex in the tinnitus group. A different brain response that is known to be neuroplastic [32] and to localize to secondary auditory areas is the P2-evoked auditory potential (latency ~ 180 ms). P2 amplitude increased with training in both groups ([31]; see Chap. 13), suggesting normal remodeling of secondary areas in tinnitus. However, this remodeling had no effect on tinnitus. The results of this study could change as additional participants and groups are tested.

Active Training Outside the Tinnitus Frequency Region

Based on the proposal that the tinnitus percept elicits abnormal levels of attention, Searchfield et al. [34] trained 10 individuals with tinnitus on an auditory object identification and localization (AOIL) task designed to refocus the participants' attention on external stimuli. Training (approximately 30 min per day over 15 days) consisted of up to 20 listening tasks that required subjects to identify and locate in space (left, right, centre) a number of common sounds (e.g., spoken words, owl hooting, coughing, dog barking) against a variety of background noises. The frequency of the sounds and background noises were not explicitly designed to fall below the frequency region of hearing loss or tinnitus spectrum, although the dominant frequencies were likely in this region. Subjects showed a 6-dB reduction in tinnitus loudness assessed by LM, and a significant reduction in pitched matched MML (in eight of ten participants, up to 30 dB in one person). The experiment is noteworthy for its inclusion of psychoacoustic measures. This type of training explicitly targeting the attentional system (but not using sounds focused within the tinnitus region) produced changes similar to those seen in other training procedures that presented stimuli within the tinnitus spectrum.

Another approach similar to active training on sound discrimination is the restoration of behaviorally relevant input via prostheses. There are a number of studies that report cochlear implants having a suppressive effect on tinnitus (see Baguley and Atlas [35] for a review) (see Chap. 77), and hearing aids have also proven to be beneficial (see Chap. 74). Folmer et al. [36]

found that out of 50 patients purchasing and wearing a hearing aid, 46 reported at least "a little" improvement in their tinnitus, with 11 reporting "very much" after 6–48 months. The self-rated loudness of their tinnitus was significantly reduced from 7.5 to 6.3 out of 10 on a VAS. The matched pitch of their tinnitus was 4.3 kHz, which likely means that the aids (which typically have low-frequency amplification profiles) restored little input near their tinnitus frequency. However, Moffat et al. [37] fitted nine subjects with hearing aids with a high bandwidth amplification regime (20 dB threshold reductions at 6 and 8 kHz) and found no changes in the tinnitus spectrum or tinnitus loudness after 30 days. Interestingly, a second group fitted with a low-medium frequency amplification hearing aid showed a significant diminution of low-frequency components of the tinnitus spectrum, with no effect seen at middle or high frequencies. The authors suggested that the perceptual characteristics of tinnitus depend on a contrast between adjacent central auditory regions of more and less afferent activity, which was increased by the low frequency amplification profile. The limited malleability of the tinnitus percept in the high amplification group may be due to the extent of hearing loss in this region and the robustness of neuroplastic changes that give rise to tinnitus. Neither amplification group, however, reported a reduction in tinnitus when assessed by LM.

Passive Experience Within the Tinnitus Frequency Region

Restoration of input via prostheses restores auditory input in a behaviorally relevant manner, which supports classification of these procedures as active training. However, animal data (and training studies in normal hearing humans) suggest sound input need not be behaviorally relevant in order to effect changes. Norena and Eggermont [38] found that tonotopic map reorganization in cats exposed to traumatic noise can be prevented by subsequent immersion in an enriched acoustic environment (EAE) containing background sounds designed to compensate for the frequency-dependent decrease in sensory inputs from the hearing loss region. This procedure also led to a recovery from hearing loss between 16 and 32 kHz in the EAE cats, compared to cats exposed to an identical noise trauma but placed in a quiet environment (QE). The increased spontaneous

firing rates and increased neural synchrony, which underlies the neural synchrony model, were also absent in EAE cats [39]. Subsequent research showed that passive exposure to the EAE for 6 weeks can produce tonotopic reorganization in normal adult cats in the *absence* of any noise trauma, *suppressing* sound representations in the EAE frequency region, and without inducing any threshold changes [40]. These findings accord with other data indicating that passive exposure to environmental sounds can lead to neuroplastic changes in the absence of explicit training requirements [41–44].

Is restoring acoustic input in the tinnitus frequency region, even if this input is not behaviorally relevant, sufficient to normalize frequency representations and reduce the neural synchrony possibly underling tinnitus, in subjects for whom significant residual hearing is present in this frequency region? The most direct evidence comes from three studies initiated by Neuromonics (see Chap. 75), a private company (http://www.neuromonics.com) that markets a device that delivers spectrally manipulated music tailored to augment frequencies in the hearing loss region of the patient's audiological profile. Because the tinnitus spectrum typically tracks the hearing loss region [14], this sound (presented at levels covering fully or partially the tinnitus) would be expected to inject feed forward and surround inhibition into the relevant region, disrupting the tinnitus sound. Patients screened for residual hearing in the loss region were instructed to listen passively to the sound for at least 2 hours per day using a high fidelity sound player with ear phones over a treatment period of 12 months. In the initial months, patients were told to set the sound level so that their tinnitus was fully masked, and then in subsequent months to gradually reduce this level, so that tinnitus was intermittently heard. This sound therapy approach was combined with counseling following the method of systematic desensitization in which aversive stimuli (in this case, tinnitus) are experienced gradually and in a context conducive to relaxation. In three studies [45–47], Neuromonics treatment led to a substantial reduction in tinnitus distress measured by the TRQ at the first assessment taken 2 months into the study, with little further improvement and little remission in the 10 months of treatment following thereafter. VAS ratings assessing tinnitus severity, ability to relax, and loudness tolerance also improved, following a course similar to the TRQ data. Notably, psychoacoustic measurements of MML and LDL were also taken in each study. In each study, MML decreased progressively over the 12-month treatment interval, while LDL levels increased.

In order to assess whether sound therapy contributed to these beneficial results, Davis et al. [46] contrasted questionnaire and psychoacoustic data among groups that received Neuromonics treatment (Neuromonics sound therapy with counseling, $n = 21$ subjects), broadband noise masking with counseling ($n = 15$), or counseling alone ($n = 13$). After 12 months, subjects in the Neuromonics treatment group reported a 66% reduction in TRQ scores, compared to reductions of 22 and 15% reported by subjects in the masking and counseling alone groups, respectively (the differences between the Neuromonics group and other two groups were statistically significant). In agreement with these results, tinnitus severity assessed by VAS was reduced in the Neuromonics group, compared to the two control conditions. The Neuromonics group also reported a reduction of 11.3 dB in MML ($p < 0.001$) at 12 months, compared to non-significant reductions of 0.4 and 1.5 dB in the masking and counseling alone groups, suggesting a benefit of Neuromonics treatment on tinnitus loudness. However, an aspect of this study that should be noted is the high proportion of subjects who were either eliminated prior to treatment for failure to meet admission criteria ($n = 19/88$) or were excluded from the final analysis for other reasons ($n = 24/88$, overall exclusion rate 48.9%). Among the exclusions were subjects with entering TRQ scores lower than 14/100 who typically show little gain from treatment [2, 47]. It should also be noted that while improvements in the psychoacoustic measures in the Neuromonics group suggest that sound exposure mattered, the effect of spectrally enhancing sounds outside rather than inside the tinnitus frequency region has not been investigated. Evidence on this question is needed to determine whether the specific frequency of the sounds that subjects listen to is crucial for therapeutic gains, or whether the experience of sound (regardless of frequency) amplifies nonspecific contributions by increasing patient involvement and treatment plausibility.

Other evidence supports the contention that passive listening to sounds that cover tinnitus frequencies can reduce tinnitus. In a study cited previously, Folmer et al. [36] fitted 50 subjects with in the ear sound generators producing broadband (100–8,000 Hz) noise and found that self-rated tinnitus loudness significantly

reduced from 7.6 to 6.2 on a ten-point VAS scale. However, this improvement was about the same as a group fitted with hearing aids that likely did not restore much high-frequency input. TRT provides exposure to a broadband masking stimulus that resembles tinnitus but is presented at lower loudness levels (called the "mixing point") approximating the tinnitus loudness [1] (see Chap. 73). TRT has been found to lead to decreases in tinnitus distress (measured by the TSI, THI, and THQ) that are initially less than improvements produced by masker therapy [2]. However, after 12–18 months of treatment, improvements induced by TRT exceeded those of masker therapy [2], suggesting that the listening protocol may contribute a role.

Whether covering the tinnitus frequencies are crucial remains unclear, however. In a study modeled on animal data reported by Norena and Eggermont [38, 39], Norena and Chery-Croze [19] exposed individuals reporting abnormal loudness recruitment (hyperacusis) to a background sound containing high frequencies spectrally enhanced over the region of hearing impairment, in a manner similar to EAE-exposed cats. The participants in the study listened to the sound in the background for 3 h per day over 15 weeks. Passive listening rescaled loudness growth functions in the direction of normal hearing over this interval, with some regression over a period of 1 month after passive listening ceased. Effects on tinnitus were not assessed, although a majority of subjects with hyperacusis typically report tinnitus as well [48]. The specific frequency content of the sound was not manipulated in this study (all subjects received a high-frequency amplification profile). In a study of individuals with normal hearing, Formby et al. [49] found that loudness growth functions can be bi-directionally rescaled by enhancing or reducing background acoustic environments. These results, which appear to be mediated in part by subcortical mechanisms [50], show that passive exposure can selectively remodel auditory processing in humans. Whether concomitant effects are seen on tinnitus remains to be investigated.

Passive Experience Outside the Tinnitus Frequency Region

Except for the possibility (discussed above) that effects of hearing aid amplification on tinnitus may be attributable in part to passive exposure to sounds below the tinnitus frequency region, passive sound therapies restricted to this region have not been widely studied. However, a recent study by Okamoto et al. [51] can be discussed here.

These investigators reasoned that because hearing loss is often present in the tinnitus frequency region, auditory training may be more effective if delivered to frequency regions where hearing is better preserved. Their approach was based on an earlier series of studies by their group in normal hearing subjects [16], which showed that notched sound can suppress neural activations in the notched region by distributing lateral inhibition to these regions. Okamoto et al. [51] therefore gave chronic tonal tinnitus patients in a treatment group daily experience with their favorite music that had a one-octave notch around their dominant tinnitus frequency removed. A placebo group listened to similar musical stimuli, except that the notch shifted over the course of training but was never at the tinnitus frequency. Subjects in the treatment and placebo groups listened for about 12 hs/week over 12 months. A further control group (monitoring) received no treatment but participated in the study measurements. Tinnitus loudness measured by a VAS was significantly reduced from baseline in the treatment group, but changes in VAS ratings did not reach significance in the placebo or monitoring groups. A comparison of the VAS changes between the treatment and placebo group ratings was also significant (this comparison was not made for the monitoring group). Notably, the amplitude of the 40-Hz ASSR and the N1m response to tonal stimuli delivered at the tinnitus frequency were also reduced in the treatment group after their sound therapy, relative to these responses evoked by a control frequency (500 Hz). These brain measures did not change in either of the control groups (a comparison of the treatment and placebo groups was also significant in this measure). Hence, evidence for a brain correlate of tinnitus suppression was observed with the notching procedure. This study is notable for inclusion of control conditions designed to evaluate whether the specific frequency content of auditory training is crucial for tinnitus improvement and for carrying out brain imaging measures. A limitation, however, is that of 39 subjects that met the criteria for entry into the study, only 23 contributed data in the treatment ($n=8$), placebo ($n=8$), and monitoring ($n=7$) groups. Subjects were included in the final statistical analyses only if their subjective tinnitus pitch did not change over the study and if the median of repeated pitch matches fell within the notched region for subjects in the experimental group, which are reasonable criteria for a study of this design. Further research is called for to corroborate the findings and assess the limits and magnitude of possible treatment effects.

Other Approaches

Jepsen and her colleagues have proposed an alternative approach to the treatment of tinnitus based on the concept of category training [52]. This approach is modeled on studies by Guenther et al. [53] in normal hearing subjects, which found that training to classify non-speech stimuli within a particular frequency range as members of the same category (frequency categorization training) led to a decrease in discrimination ability for frequencies within the category. In subsequent research [54], frequency categorization training led to a relative decrease in neural activation measured by fMRI for the trained frequencies, whereas conventional training for discrimination among the same frequencies augmented neural activation for the trained stimuli.

Jepsen et al. [52] hypothesized that it would be advantageous to train subjects experiencing tinnitus to assign tinnitus frequencies to a common category, which might lead to a reduction in activation in this area of cortex and presumably a concomitant decrease in the tinnitus sensation. They trained 20 subjects for 30 min per day for 3 weeks, either to categorize tinnitus frequencies into a group or to discriminate among the frequencies, in each case using a take-home training device. The two groups did not differ markedly in their pre–post THI score changes, but did show differences in auditory-evoked potentials. The categorization group showed a reduction in P2-N1 amplitude post-training while the discrimination group showed an increase, which is in line with the observations of Guenther et al. [54]. However, this change was most evident for a control (untrained) frequency rather than the trained frequency, again indicating a more nonspecific effect of training rather than a reduction in cortical activation for the tinnitus region. Category training merits further investigation for its effects on discrimination ability, neural responses, and tinnitus.

Overview and Conclusion

Animal research in the last two decades has established that neural plasticity is a fundamental property of neurons in the auditory and other sensory systems. Evidence has also accumulated that hearing loss (a triggering factor in many if not most people with tinnitus) leads to changes in central auditory pathways, including tonotopic map reorganization and increased neuron firing rates that may be forged by neuroplastic mechanisms into abnormal network behavior generating tinnitus sounds. These findings have spawned renewed research into the question of whether tinnitus can be reduced or eliminated by auditory training specifically designed to normalize aberrant auditory neural representations that are believed to be responsible for tinnitus. For this goal to be achieved, it must be possible to modify auditory representations by acoustic training in individuals with tinnitus, and the neural modifications induced by training must intersect with the underlying tinnitus mechanisms.

In this chapter, we reviewed auditory training studies from the point of view that tinnitus is caused by synchronous neural activity that develops in tonotopic regions of primary auditory cortex that have been deafferented by hearing impairments. Studies were classified according to whether training was conducted within the tinnitus frequency region or outside of it, and whether the trained sounds served as cues for behavioral responses and were therefore processed actively in attention, or whether the sounds were presented passively as background signals. We also attempted to separate the effects of auditory training on two distinct aspects of tinnitus emphasized by Jastreboff [1], namely, effects on the tinnitus percept itself and effects on distress behavior that accompanies tinnitus. The following summary statements appear to be justified.

1. The number of auditory training studies is not large, and the studies do not evenly cover the four categories we used for classifying them.
2. Studies in all categories have reported significant reductions in tinnitus distress measured by standardized questionnaires (THQ, TRQ, TSI) and VAS ratings. These reductions typically achieved their maxima at the first in-course assessment, with relatively little if any gain thereafter. A noteworthy result is that two treatment procedures that manipulated

the frequency content of sounds in the tinnitus frequency region in opposite directions [46, 51] reported similar tinnitus reductions in VAS ratings. If the particular details of auditory training do not matter for these improvements, these gains would appear to be attributable to nonspecific effects of the treatment procedure.

3. Because these changes on questionnaires and VAS ratings are beneficial for patients, it is important to identify the factors responsible for them. Benefits may be greater when some form of sound therapy is employed, although further evidence on this point and particular sound therapy used is needed. Another factor relevant to a successful treatment outcome is opportunity for improvement. Several studies have reported that reductions in distress behavior are minimal when tinnitus distress is low at study commencement.
4. Changes in psychoacoustic measures have been reported that may more directly measure tinnitus sensations. Reductions in MML on the order of 5–10 dB have been reported by several studies [34, 45–47], implying that the tinnitus sensation has become weaker. MML may be a better measure of tinnitus loudness than adjusting external sounds to match tinnitus, which is known to be frequency dependent [14]. Improvements in loudness tolerance (LDL) have also been reported [45–47], as have changes in the frequency content of tinnitus [20, 37]. Improvements in MML and LDL are more gradual than those on distress behavior, suggesting that some form of neural plasticity may be at work.
5. Several of the studies reporting improvements in psychoacoustic measures used passive sound presentation procedures. Hence, active training requiring discriminated behavioral responses does not appear to be necessary for changes in psychoacoustic measures. This observation aligns with experiments in normal hearing animals and humans which found that passive exposure to sound can be sufficient to remodel auditory representations.
6. Animal data and the neural synchrony model of tinnitus imply that training for sounds that cover the tinnitus frequency region is likely to be most effective in modifying tinnitus, provided that residual hearing is present in this region. The results on this point are, however, conflicting. With a few exceptions [27, 37, 51], systematic manipulation of the

frequency content of the trained sounds has not been attempted in auditory training studies. Loudness growth curves are rescaled in normal hearing individuals by augmenting or reducing background sound [49], and rescaling occurs in hyperacusis patients exposed to high-frequency complex sounds [39], in both situations with broad frequency selectivity. However, applications of these procedures to tinnitus remain largely untested. Because the measurement of brain correlates often involves presenting sounds, effects of sound therapy on loudness recruitment are potential contributing factors to such measurements in tinnitus.

While these conclusions are less than satisfying, they do give guidance for continuing study. Future research should emphasize psychoacoustic measures, particularly MML and LDL, as well as standardized measures of tinnitus spectra [14, 20] which can obviate some of the unreliability of single-pitch matches, in addition to standardized questionnaires. Systematic variation of trained frequencies between groups or within individuals is highly desirable, including untreated control conditions. Such evidence is needed to determine whether auditory training induces specific changes in tinnitus, or whether it instead amplifies the nonspecific effect of procedures common to all tinnitus therapies. Neural correlates offer the advantage of comparative immunity to response bias. Finally, care should be taken to specify clearly how many participants of the total recruited contributed to a data analysis, and why and when exclusions occurred. Progress toward an optimal auditory training treatment will be limited until replications are reported involving substantial sample sizes.

We also suggest that applications of auditory training will be enriched when we know more about how neural plasticity works in normal hearing individuals and in individuals with tinnitus. Current findings showing that passive exposure to sound is sufficient to remodel auditory representations in people with normal hearing could be good news for tinnitus, since compliance with treatment procedures may improve when performance requirements are minimal. The results reflect the propensity of the human auditory system to extract and represent the features of salient environmental sounds, regardless of behavioral response requirements. However, that passive exposure is sufficient does not preclude the possibility that active processing may yield more long-lasting outcomes [51].

Acknowledgements Preparation of this chapter was assisted by grants from the Canadian Institutes for Health Research, the Natural Sciences and Engineering Research Council of Canada, the American Tinnitus Association, and the Tinnitus Research Initiative.

References

1. Jastreboff PJ (1995) Tinnitus as a phantom perception: Theories and clinical applications. In: Vernon J, Moeller AR, Editors. Mechanisms of Tinnitus. Boston, MA: Allyn and Bacon, pp. 73–94.
2. Henry JA, MA Schechter, TL Zaugg et al (2006) Outcomes of clinical trial: Tinnitus masking versus tinnitus retraining therapy. J. Am. Acad. Audiol. 17:104–132.
3. Robertson D, DRF Irvine (1989) Plasticity of frequency organization in auditory cortex of guinea pigs with partial unilateral deafness. J. Comp. Neurol. 282:456–461.
4. Rajan R, DRF Irvine (1998) Neuronal responses across cortical field A1 in plasticity induced by peripheral auditory organ damage. Audiol. Neurootol. 3:123–144.
5. Noreña AJ, M Tomita, JJ Eggermont (2003) Neural changes in cat auditory cortex after a transient pure-tone trauma. J. Neurophysiol. 90:2387–2401.
6. Rauschecker JP (1999) Auditory cortical plasticity: a comparison with other sensory systems. Trends Neurosci. 22:74–80.
7. Eggermont JJ, LE Roberts (2004) The neuroscience of tinnitus. Trends Neurosci. 27:676–682.
8. Fritz J, M Elhilali, S Shamma (2005) Active listening: task-dependent plasticity of spectrotemporal receptive fields in primary auditory cortex. Hear. Res. 206:159–176.
9. Weinberger NM (2007) Auditory associative memory and representational plasticity in the primary auditory cortex. Hear. Res. 229:54–68.
10. Finlayson PG, JA Kaltenbach (2009) Alterations in the spontaneous discharge patterns of single units in the dorsal cochlear nucleus following intense sound exposure. Hear. Res. doi:10.1016.
11. Cacace AT (2003) Expanding the biological basis of tinnitus: crossmodal origins and the role of neuroplasticity. Hear. Res. 175:112–132.
12. Shore SE, S Koehler, M Oldakowski, LF Hughes, S Syed (2008) Dorsal cochlear nucleus responses to somatosensory stimulation are enhanced after noise-induced hearing loss. Eur. J. Neurosci. 27:155–168.
13. Lanting CP, E de Kleine, P van Dijk (2009) Neural activity underlying tinnitus generation: Results from PET and fMRI. Hear. Res. 255:1–13.
14. Roberts LE, G Moffat, M Baumann et al (2008) Residual inhibition functions overlap tinnitus spectra and the region of auditory threshold shift. J. Assoc. Res. Otolaryngol. 9: 417–435.
15. Ross B, R Draganova, TW Picton, C Pantev (2003) Frequency specificity of 40-Hz auditory steady-state responses. Hear. Res. 186:57–68.
16. Pantev C, H Okamoto, B Ross, W Stoll, E Ciurlia-Guy, R Kakigi, T Kubo (2004) Lateral inhibition and habituation of the human auditory cortex. Eur. J. Neurosci. 19: 2337–2344.

17. Kadia SC, X Wang (2003) Spectral integration in A1 of awake primates: neurons with single and multipeaked tuning characteristics. J Neurophysiol. 89:1603–1622.

18. Plewnia C, M Reimold, A Najib, B Brehm, G Reischl, SK Plontke, C Gerloff (2007) Dose-dependent attenuation of auditory phantom perception (tinnitus) by PET-guided repetitive transcranial magnetic stimulation. Hum. Brain Mapp. 28:238–246.

19. Noreña AJ, S Chery-Croze (2007) Enriched acoustic environment rescales auditory sensitivity. NeuroReport 18:1251–1255

20. Noreña A, C Micheyl, S Chéry-Croze, L Collet (2002) Psychoacoustic characterization of the tinnitus spectrum: implications for the underlying mechanisms of tinnitus. Audiol. Neurootol. 7:358–369.

21. Kuk FK, RS Tyler, D Russell, H Jordan (1990) The psychometric properties of a tinnitus handicap questionnaire. Ear Hear. 11:434–445.

22. Meikle MB, SE Griest, BJ Stewart, LS Press (1995) Measuring the negative impact of tinnitus: A brief severity index. Abstr. Assoc. Res. Otolaryngol. p.167.

23. Newman CW, GP Jacobson, JB Spitzer (1996) Development of the tinnitus handicap inventory. Arch. Otolaryngol. Head Neck Surg. 122:143–148.

24. Wilson PH, J Henry, M Bowen, G Haralambous (1991) Tinnitus reaction questionnaire: psychometric properties of a measure of distress associated with tinnitus. J. Speech Hear. Res. 34:197–201.

25. Flor H, T Elbert, S Knecht, C Wienbruch, C Pantev, N Birbaumer et al (1995) Phantom limb pain as perceptual correlate of cortical reorganization. Nature 357:482–484.

26. Flor H, C Denke, M Schaefer, S Grusser (2001) Effect of sensory discrimination training on cortical reorganization and phantom limb pain. The Lancet 357:1763–1764.

27. Flor H, D Hoffmann, M Struve, E Diesch (2004) Auditory discrimination training for the treatment of tinnitus. Appl. Psychophysiol. Biofeedback 29(2):113–120.

28. Burns E (1984) A comparison of variability among measurements of subjective tinnitus and objective stimuli. Audiology 23:426–440.

29. Herriaz C, I Diges, P Cobo, G Plaza, J Aparicio (2006) Auditory discrimination therapy (ADT) for tinnitus management: preliminary results. Acta Oto-Laryngologica 126:8083.

30. Herriaz C, I Diges, P Cobo, J Aparicio (2009) Cortical reorganization and tinnitus: principles of auditory discrimination training for tinnitus management. Eur. Arch. Otorhinolaryngol. 266:9–16.

31. Roberts LE, DJ Bosnyak (2010) Neural synchrony and neural plasticity in tinnitus. In: Searchfield GD, Goodey R Editors. Proceedings of Tinnitus Discovery: Asia-Pacific Tinnitus Symposium. N. Z. Med. J. 123:39–50.

32. Bosnyak DJ, RA Eaton, LE Roberts (2004) Distributed auditory cortical representations are modified by training at pitch discrimination with 40-Hz amplitude modulated tones. Cereb. Cortex 14:1088–1099.

33. Kilgard MP, PK Pandya, J Vazquez, A Gehi, CE Schreiner, MM Merzenich (2001) Sensory input directs spatial and temporal plasticity in primary auditory cortex. J. Neurophysiol. 86:326–338.

34. Searchfield G, J Morrison-Low, K Wise (2007) Object identification and attention training for treating tinnitus. Prog. Brain Res. 166:369–75.

35. Baguley D, M Atlas (2007) Cochlear implants and tinnitus. Prog. Brain Res. 166:369–375.

36. Folmer R, J Carroll (2006) Long-term effectiveness of ear-level devices for tinnitus. Otolaryng. Head Neck Surg. 134:132–137.

37. Moffat G, K Adjout, S Gallego, H Thai-Van, L Collet, A Norena (2009) Effects of hearing aid fitting on the perceptual characteristics of tinnitus. Hear. Res. 254:82–91.

38. Noreña A, JJ Eggermont (2005) Enriched acoustic environment after noise trauma reduces hearing loss and prevents cortical map reorganization. J. Neurosci. 25(3):699–705.

39. Noreña A, JJ Eggermont (2006) Enriched acoustic environment after noise trauma abolishes neural signs of tinnitus. Neuroreport 17(6):559–563.

40. Pienkowski M, JJ Eggermont (2009) Long-term, partially-reversible reorganization of frequency tuning in mature cat primary auditory cortex can be induced by passive exposure to moderate-level sounds. Hear. Res. 257:24–40.

41. Gander PE, DJ Bosnyak, LE Roberts (2010) Acoustic experience but not attention modifies neural population phase expressed in human primary auditory cortex. Hear. Res. doi:10.1016 (on-line ahead of print).

42. Ross B, K Tremblay (2009) Stimulus experience modifies auditory neuromagnetic responses in young and older listeners. Hear. Res. 248:48–59.

43. Sheehan KA, GM McArthur, DV Bishop (2005) Is discrimination training necessary to cause changes in the P2 auditory event-related brain potential to speech sounds? Brain Res. Cogn. Brain Res. 25:547–553.

44. Stanton SG, RV Harrison (1996) Abnormal cochleotopic organization in the auditory cortex of cats reared in a frequency augmented environment. Aud. Neurosci. 2:97–107.

45. Davis PB, B Paki, PJ Hanley (2007) Neuromonics tinnitus treatment: third clinical trial. Ear Hear. 28(2):242–259.

46. Davis PB, RA Wilde, LG Steed, PJ Hanley (2008) Treatment of tinnitus with a customized acoustic neural stimulus: a controlled clinical study. Ear Nose Throat J. 87:330–339.

47. Hanley PJ, PB Davis, B Paki, SA Quinn, SR Bellekom (2008) Treatment of tinnitus with a customized, dynamic acoustic neural stimulus: Clinical outcomes in general private practice. Ann. Otol. Rhinol. Laryngol. 117:791–799.

48. Anari M, A Axelsson, A Eliasson, L Magnusson (1999) Hypersensitivity to sound – questionnaire data, audiometry and classification. Scand. Audiol. 28:219–230.

49. Formby C, LP Sherlock, SL Gold (2003) Adaptive plasticity of loudness induced by chronic attenuation and enhancement of the acoustic background. J. Acoust. Soc. Am. 114:55–58.

50. Munro KJ, J Blount (2009) Adaptive plasticity in brainstem of adult listeners following earplug-induced deprivation. J. Acoust. Soc. Am. 126:568–571.

51. Okamoto H, C Pantev, H Stracke, O Thiede (2009) Listening to tailor-made music reverses maladaptive auditory cortex reorganization and alleviates tinnitus. Proc. Natl. Acad. Sci. USA; doi:10.1073/pnas.0911268107.

52. Jepsen K, MP Sanders, GD Searchfield, K Kobayashi (2009) Perceptual training for tinnitus management. Tinnitus Discovery: Asia Pacific Tinnitus Symposium, Auckland, 11–12 September.

53. Guenther F, F Husain, M Cohen, B Shinn-Cunningham (1999) Effects of categorization and discrimination training on auditory perceptual space. JASA 106:2900–2912.

54. Guenther FH, A Nieto-Castanon, SS Ghosh, JA Tourville (2004) Representation of sound categories in auditory cortical maps. J. Speech Lang. Hear. Res. 47:46–57.

Chapter 73
Tinnitus Retraining Therapy

Pawel J. Jastreboff

Keypoints

1. Tinnitus Retraining Therapy (TRT) is strictly based on the neurophysiological model of tinnitus.
2. Tinnitus is a phantom auditory perception, i.e. perception of tinnitus is not linked to any vibratory activity within the cochlea.
3. The model postulates that it is necessary to include interconnections within a network of systems in the brain in the study and treatment of tinnitus.
4. The auditory system, while needed for perception of tinnitus, is secondary for clinically relevant tinnitus (i.e. tinnitus which is bothersome to the extent of requiring treatment).
5. The limbic and autonomic nervous systems are the main systems responsible for negative tinnitus-evoked reactions.
6. Tinnitus is frequently accompanied by a decreased sound tolerance, consisting of hyperacusis and misophonia.
7. Hyperacusis results from an increased gain within the auditory pathways and is determined solely by physical characteristics of sound (i.e. its intensity and spectrum).
8. Misophonia results from enhanced functional connections between the auditory and the limbic and autonomic nervous systems, and reactions occur to specific patterns of sound, with the total spectral energy being secondary or irrelevant.
9. In misophonia, the meaning of sound and an individual's past history of encountering it is crucial, with the auditory characteristics of the sound playing a secondary role.
10. There are two loops in network processing tinnitus signal:

    a. High loop, which involves cognitive processing of the signal and which is dominant at the initial stages of tinnitus.
    b. Low, subconscious loop, which appears to become dominant in chronic tinnitus.

    Connections within the neural networks that are involved in the adverse effects of tinnitus are governed by the principles of conditioned reflexes.

11. The primary goal of TRT is habituation of reactions evoked by tinnitus.
12. Habituation is initiated and further facilitated using the method of modified passive extinction of the conditioned reflexes and involves:

    a. Teaching/counseling aimed at reclassification of the tinnitus signal to the category of neutral stimuli.
    b. Sound therapy, which decreases the strength of the tinnitus signal by increasing the level of background neuronal activity in the auditory system achieved by providing an enhanced sound background.

13. Habituation of perception happens automatically once sufficient level of habituation of reactions is achieved.
14. Decreased sound tolerance must be treated concurrently with tinnitus.
15. Different protocols must be used for hyperacusis than for misophonia.

P.J. Jastreboff (✉)
Department of Otolaryngology, Emory University School of Medicine, 1365A Clifton Road, NE, 30322 Atlanta, GA, USA
e-mail: pjastre@emory.edu

A.R. Møller et al. (eds.), *Textbook of Tinnitus*,
DOI 10.1007/978-1-60761-145-5_73, © Springer Science+Business Media, LLC 2011

16. A specific variant of treatment, related to classifying a patient to one of 5 categories, is determined by the following factors:

    a. Impact of tinnitus on patients' lives and/or duration of clinically significant tinnitus.
    b. The presence of hyperacusis.
    c. The presence and significance of hearing loss.
    d. Prolonged exacerbation of tinnitus/hyperacusis by sound.

17. Misophonia is treated independently by specific protocols concurrently with tinnitus, hyperacusis, and hearing loss.
18. Results from many centers have confirmed the effectiveness of the tinnitus retraining therapy (TRT) for tinnitus, reporting a success rate of more than 80%.
19. Specific studies performed to assess the stability of improvement after 3 and 5 years revealed that improvement continues to be present with patients over time. These studies show a trend of continuing improvement, even after ending the treatment.
20. Prevention of clinically significant tinnitus or potential worsening of already existing tinnitus could be achieved by:

    a. Avoidance of silence and providing enriched sound environment.
    b. Avoidance of negative counseling and providing proper information in advance.

21. Certain populations are at high risk of developing clinically significant tinnitus, such as military personnel, police officers and firefighters, and patients who are going to have ear-related surgery. Providing them with a proper short informational session about tinnitus would significantly decrease the risk of developing bothersome tinnitus. People will still hear tinnitus, but it will not be a problem for them.

Keywords Tinnitus • Habituation of reaction • Habituation of perception • Conditioned reflexes • Phantom perception • Retraining • Neurophysiological model of tinnitus • Sound therapy • Counseling • Teaching

Abbreviations

TRT   Tinnitus retraining therapy
LDL   Loudness discomfort level
DDT   Discordant dysfunction theory
OHC   Outer hair cells
IHC   Inner hair cells
REM   Real ear measurements

Outline of the Concepts Presented in this Chapter

The theoretical ideas and the description of treatments presented in this chapter propose a different view on the phenomenon of tinnitus and its treatment than those found in the majority of other published hypotheses about tinnitus and descriptions of treatments. Therefore, definitions of tinnitus and decreased sound tolerance (hyperacusis and misophonia), as used in this chapter, will be provided first, followed by a brief outline of the main concepts of the neurophysiological model of tinnitus [1]. Tinnitus Retraining Therapy (TRT) is strictly based on this model and is one of several potential implementations of therapies aimed at habituation of tinnitus. Furthermore, as it is argued in this chapter, tinnitus should not be treated alone, but as one of the components of a more general dysfunction of the auditory system (including hearing loss and decreased sound tolerance), which needs concurrent treatment. Furthermore, the emphasis is on dynamic interaction of the auditory system with other systems in the brain, which is governed by principles of conditioned reflexes, and the role of subconscious pathways is stressed as well. The main goal of TRT is habituation of negative reactions evoked by tinnitus, with habituation of perception occurring as the subsequent, but inevitable, process.

Definitions of Tinnitus and Decreased Sound Tolerance

Tinnitus is defined as a phantom auditory perception, namely perception of sound without corresponding vibratory, mechanical activity in the cochlea [1, 2]. This perception is absolutely real and can be compared to phantom pain (see Chaps. 14 and 15) and the phantom limb phenomena. There is a tinnitus signal in the form of neural activity somewhere in the brain that is perceived as a sound, thus tinnitus. It is not known exactly where in the brain this occurs, but some studies indicate that the secondary auditory cortex plays an important role in this respect. Understanding the phantom aspect of tinnitus is fundamental for understanding the interaction of tinnitus with external sounds and thus is the basis for the different forms of sound therapies currently in use. Problems can arise from misunderstanding of the role of external sounds on tinnitus, such as when the suppression of tinnitus perception by external sound is called "masking" [3]. Masking represents interaction of two traveling waves at the basilar membrane of the cochlea and therefore exhibits a "V-shaped" masking curve and depends on the phenomenon of the critical band (i.e. it is impossible to mask one sound by a second if there is a sufficient frequency difference between the two sounds). None of these phenomena exists in connection with tinnitus, which can be equally easily suppressed by sounds from wide range of frequencies [4]. Obviously, it is possible to interact with the tinnitus signal, including suppression of the perception that it leads to, but the mechanism is one of interactions between sound-evoked neural activity and the tinnitus-related neuronal activity. Furthermore, it is possible to decrease the strength of the tinnitus signal by increasing the general level of sound-evoked neuronal activity, and thus by decreasing the difference between the tinnitus signal and the background neuronal activity.

Consequently, the author is against classification of tinnitus into "subjective" and "objective" tinnitus and instead supports using the term "somatosound" in place of "objective tinnitus" as well as reserving the term "tinnitus" for what other authors have referred to as "subjective tinnitus." This terminology is used in this chapter.

Tinnitus is frequently accompanied by decreased sound tolerance [5–7]. It is possible to identify two components of decreased sound tolerance, hyperacusis (see also Chap. 3) and misophonia (see also Chap. 4) [7–9]. Results from several centers show that about 25–30% of individuals with tinnitus also have hyperacusis. Our results from the Emory Tinnitus & Hyperacusis Center showed that out of 149 consecutive patients, 66% required treatment for decreased sound tolerance and 33% required treatment for hyperacusis while 57% required treatment for misophonia [8]. Most patients with decreased sound tolerance have both hyperacusis and misophonia, contributing to a decreased sound tolerance to different degrees. While these two components evoke a similar extent of behavioral reaction, there are significant differences in the categories of sound which trigger hyperacusis compared with misophonia, and the

physiological mechanisms and treatments of hyperacusis and misophonia are distinctively different. Treatments that are effective for hyperacusis are not effective for misophonia, and treatments for misophonia have only limited impact on hyperacusis.

It is characteristic for hyperacusis that the reaction depends exclusively on the physical characteristics of a bothersome sound, such as its energy and frequency spectrum. The meaning of a sound and an individual's past history are irrelevant. For example, a person may have a strong negative reaction to speech sounds. If this speech signal is recorded, the spectrum is determined, and then the sound is re-synthesized from individual frequencies with randomly assigned phases, this procedure will yield a sound with the identical energy spectrum as the original speech sound; however, this sound will be perceived as a noise without any meaning. A person with hyperacusis will react in the same manner to both such sounds; it is irrelevant whether this sound is familiar to the person or being encountered for the first time. The environment in which this sound is presented (e.g. doctor's office, home, part of a sound track of a favorite movie) will not affect how a person with hyperacusis reacts to the sound. People with hyperacusis have a tendency to react stronger (or have lower sound tolerance levels) to sound of higher frequencies (e.g. sound of a metal spoon hitting china, washing machines with clicking plates), reflecting the general tendency of high-frequency sound being more bothersome even for individuals who do not have hyperacusis.

It is proposed that the neural mechanisms of hyperacusis involve abnormally high amplification within the auditory system, with only secondary activation of other centers of the brain responsible for negative reactions (i.e. the limbic and autonomic nervous systems). In other words, the activity that occurs within the auditory pathways after stimulation by 80 dB HL sound in a person with hyperacusis would be similar to that occurring in an individual who does not have hyperacusis and is exposed to a much louder sound such as a sound of 120 dB HL. Studies in animals support proposed mechanism [10, 11]; however, lack of an animal model of hyperacusis hinders researchers from performing more specific studies.

It is characteristic for misophonia that the adverse reactions occur due to specific patterns of sound, with the sound's spectrum being secondary or irrelevant. The meaning of a sound and the past history of an individual encountering it is crucial. Sounds, which in the past have been associated with something negative (e.g. discomfort, pain, or other situations associated with strong negative emotions), will trigger misophonic negative reactions. Basically, the mechanism of misophonia involves the creation of a conditioned reflex linking specific patterns of a sound to negative reinforcement. Significant hyperacusis, even present for a short period of time, will automatically create misophonia, because exposure to the sound will create discomfort/pain and it will consequently provide the negative reinforcement associated with the sound. Once this reflex is created, it will persist, even when hyperacusis ceases to exist.

For example, in a situation such as the one described above, a person with misophonia may react very strongly to normal speech but show no reaction to re-synthesized speech sounds that seem like meaningless noise. People who have misophonia may exhibit strong reactions to soft sounds (e.g. sounds of eating or speech of certain people) while not having problems with even very loud sounds. Many individuals with misophonia react to sounds "louder than" a certain level, yielding Loudness Discomfort Levels (LDL) determined for pure tones following the shape of audiogram and being better for frequencies where hearing loss exists [8, 12] (see Chap. 4).

The auditory system is perfectly normal in persons with pure misophonia; however, selective connections from the auditory system to the limbic and autonomic nervous systems for specific patterns of sound are abnormally activated or enhanced. Functional properties of these connections are governed by principles of conditioned reflexes. Consequently, the strength of the reactions they cause depends on the strength of the reinforcement, and the sound level plays a secondary role.

Sounds-evoking misophonic reactions do not have to be unpleasant on their own, but it will be sufficient that the individual who has misophonia identify sounds, exposure to which enhances tinnitus for some time. These sounds will be associated with an increased emotionally negative status, caused by enhancement of tinnitus which will be sufficient to create a conditioned reflex arc evoking misophonic reaction to these sounds, even at lower levels than that needed to increase tinnitus loudness.

Physiological Basis for Tinnitus-Induced Negative Reactions

It is crucial to distinguish between mechanisms involved in the generation of tinnitus perception and mechanisms involved in tinnitus-evoked negative reactions. Most individuals who have tinnitus are just experiencing a sound sensation, without any problems related to it. Only about 20% of people with tinnitus have negative reactions evoked by tinnitus (see Chap. 5). It is interesting that the psychoacoustic characteristics of tinnitus in these two subpopulations are undistinguishable and not related to the severity of the tinnitus as it is experienced by the people who have the bothersome tinnitus.

These observations indicate that there are different mechanisms involved in the generation of the neural signal that causes tinnitus perception, and other mechanisms responsible for evoking negative reactions to this signal. Recognition of this distinction is important, and by aiming treatments at the mechanism of tinnitus-induced negative reactions, it should be possible to remove the problems of the tinnitus without trying to remove tinnitus perception. In the past, most research and treatment attempts were aimed at removing, or at least decreasing tinnitus perception. These approaches were not particularly successful and so far we do not have any reliable method that would make it possible to achieve this goal. Notably, decrease of tinnitus perception does not automatically translate into decrease of tinnitus severity, and actually there is no relation between tinnitus loudness match and the perceived severity of the tinnitus [13].

Analysis of the negative effects of tinnitus on individuals provides information about which system in the brain may be involved in this process. It is possible to distinguish between two main categories of negative effects: (1) physiological responses to tinnitus (e.g. anxiety, depression, sleep problems, increased stress level) and (2) behavioral responses and consequences (e.g. attention and concentration problems, decreased joy of life, and affected life activities such as social interactions, work impairment, family problems). Two major systems in the brain are involved in generating the negative effects of tinnitus, namely the limbic and autonomic nervous systems, which interact with many other systems such as the prefrontal cortex, thalamus, reticular formation, and cerebellum playing some role as well. It has been proposed that it is necessary to include these systems in the analysis of the generation of tinnitus and a person's reaction to the tinnitus (see Chaps. 20 and 21) and its treatment [1, 12].

The Neurophysiological Model of Tinnitus

The basic concept of the neurophysiological model of tinnitus is that it is necessary to include variety of systems in the brain in study and treatment of tinnitus [1, 12] (see also Chaps. 20 and 21). The auditory system, while needed for perception of tinnitus, plays a secondary role for clinically relevant tinnitus (i.e. tinnitus which is bothersome to the extent of requiring treatment). In the past, studies and treatments of tinnitus have tended to be cochleo-centric. The neurophysiological model of tinnitus proposed earlier [1] and outlined here shifts the attention away not only from the cochlea but also from the auditory nervous system. The main focus of the model can be envisioned in a form of a diagram, first published in late 1990s [14] (Fig. 73.1). This concept is currently generally accepted and it is believed that any valid neurophysiological model of tinnitus must include several different systems in the brain to represent mechanisms of tinnitus and to be useful in the treatment of tinnitus (see also Chaps. 20 and 21).

According to their model, the tinnitus signal – the generation of which is typically linked to the periphery of the auditory system – is detected and processed by subconscious centers of the auditory pathways and finally interpreted at the highest level of the auditory system (probably the secondary auditory cortices). If a person just perceives tinnitus without having a negative reaction induced by it, the tinnitus signal may be constrained within the auditory pathways. If, however, this activity spreads to the limbic and autonomic nervous systems by activation of specifically the sympathetic part of the autonomic system, it evokes several negative reactions such as annoyance, anxiety, and panic and triggers survival reflexes resulting in a decreased ability to enjoy life activities. This last mentioned effect has a profound impact on a person's life by depriving an individual of positive aspects of life which may push a person into depression [12] (and see Chaps. 62 and 63). The model shown in Fig. 73.1 has been described in detail already [15–23] and only the main aspects are outlined in this text.

Two Loops

All the systems in the brain are interconnected and work in the dynamic balance scenario, i.e. if a connection is frequently active it becomes stronger, if it is not activated it gradually becomes weaker (see also Chaps. 12, 13, and 20). This feature is reflected in the diagram of the model (Fig. 73.1), with the main systems mutually interconnected. It was postulated that tinnitus as a problem results mainly from over-activation of the

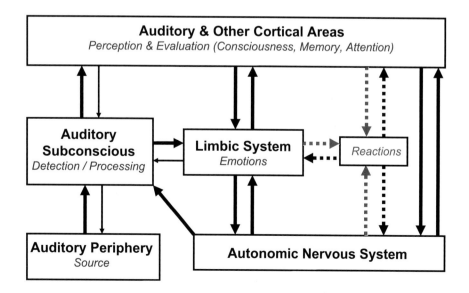

Fig. 73.1 The neurophysiological model of tinnitus

sympathetic part of the autonomic system [1, 19, 22]. It is, therefore, important to analyze pathways involved in tinnitus-related activation of these systems. Firstly, it should be noted that continuous activation of the connections illustrated in Fig. 73.1 causes their strengthening and yields stronger activation of the limbic and autonomic nervous systems by the same tinnitus signal according to the general rules of neural plasticity. Secondly, increased activation of the limbic and autonomic nervous systems occurs via reciprocal connections (feedback) and causes increased activity in the system from which the initial signal was coming. For example, autonomic system activation via a backward feedback can increase the activity in the limbic system, in cognitive brain areas, as well as auditory system. Therefore, the term "loop" is used instead of the term "connections" to emphasize the feedback aspects of the interaction between the different systems.

The tinnitus signal activates the limbic and autonomic nervous systems via two such loops. The upper one ("high loop") (named the "high route" by LeDoux [24], see Chap. 8) involves conscious areas of the cerebral cortex, involves perception, evaluation, verbalization, conscious associations, and fears. This loop is crucial in the initial stage of developing clinically significant tinnitus. The second, lower ("low loop", named the "low route" by LeDoux [24], (see Chap. 14)), involves subconscious centers in the brain. It branches from the auditory system at the level of extralemniscal subnuclei of the medial geniculate body, reaching the lateral nucleus of amygdala and, via other parts of the limbic system, reaches centers of the autonomic nervous system (see Chaps. 8, 12 and 21). Documented connections link the amygdala with the inferior colliculus, and therefore both connections (from auditory system to limbic system and back) are included in the diagram. The importance of these connections described in the model has been documented [25–27].

Both high and low loops contribute to the final activation of the autonomic nervous system and the negative reactions evoked by tinnitus. High loop is dominant in the acute stage of tinnitus development, but once tinnitus reaches a chronic stage, the subconscious becomes more important or even dominant (see Chap. 8). The analysis of results from over 300 patients with chronic tinnitus revealed that the proportion of time when patients are aware of tinnitus and subjectively ranked tinnitus loudness does not contribute significantly to tinnitus severity [28]. These results argue strongly against the dominant role of the conscious, high loop, because then tinnitus awareness and tinnitus loudness would be expected to be highly significant factors. These findings have a profound implication on tinnitus treatment.

Conditioned Reflexes

The connections between the brain systems involved in processing the tinnitus signal are governed by principles of conditioned reflexes. The tinnitus signal in the auditory pathways acts as a conditioning stimulus, which, via one or more reflex arc, activates the limbic and autonomic nervous systems and thereby evokes negative reactions. Several different scenarios may create these conditioned reflexes. The most common is the situation of "negative counseling," i.e. a person is told something which links tinnitus with a threatening, unpleasant, or dangerous situation such as "nothing can be done, you will have tinnitus up to the end of your life, you need to learn to cope with it, and we need to do a brain scan just to eliminate the possibility of a brain tumor." An extreme example of such negative counseling is when a patient is told that he/she has tinnitus because "he/she has a bad brain." The negative counseling provides a reinforcement which creates a conditioned reflex arc causing the tinnitus signal to subsequently evoke strong reactions of the limbic and autonomic nervous systems, causing physiological and behavioral reactions.

Another common scenario occurs when a person with tinnitus is under strong emotionally negative stress, such as during retirement, divorce, or from non-related health problems. Indeed, a study ranking ordered factors present when a person's tinnitus became a clinical problem revealed that there was no auditory-related factor in the top 10 most frequent situations [29]. While noise exposure is regarded a frequent cause of the appearance of tinnitus perception, it is not the case for emergence of tinnitus as a problem. Non-bothersome tinnitus may be present for years, and only when it becomes associated with something negative does it become a problem. It should be noted that no causal link is necessary for the creation of a conditioned reflex of any kind, but a close temporal association of a conditioning signal and reinforcement is sufficient to create the reflex.

The neurophysiological model described above and presented in simplified form in Fig. 73.1 predicts that a combination of rapid appearance of tinnitus together with high-level emotional stress is particularly effective in evoking clinically significant tinnitus. Indeed, bothersome tinnitus is evoked typically as a result of sudden hearing loss or when tinnitus starts at a specific time when a person is in the state of highly negative emotions due to sudden hearing loss. Consequently, clinically significant tinnitus can be expected to be more prevalent in professions where there is a combination of a high level of noise, particularly impulsive noise (e.g. gun fire) with a high level of negative emotional stress. Policeman, firefighters, and soldiers are typical examples of members of such professions.

This prediction has been confirmed by the fact that tinnitus occurs in a high rate (49%) of soldiers returning from Iraq and Afghanistan who were exposed to blast noise, the occurrence of which is even higher than the reported proportion of soldiers with blast-induced hearing loss (25%) (see Chap. 67). This unfortunate issue has significant financial connotations, as the American Veterans Administration spent $1.1 billion in 2009 (doubling from $540 million spent in 2006) on compensation for tinnitus alone, with the expected compensation for tinnitus reaching $2.3 billion by 2014 [30]. Since impulse noise can evoke hyperacusis and misophonia, in addition to tinnitus, adding significant problems for the Veterans health care system that must be taken care of in the near future and which will persist for many years to come (untreated clinically significant tinnitus tends to be stable for many years and untreated misophonia tends to worsen with time).

Once the reflex is established, a negative reaction can be evoked without a negative reinforcement, which means that while general health may improve and work problems may be resolved, a person's tinnitus will keep evoking negative reactions. One of the reasons is that a tinnitus-evoked negative reaction acts as the reinforcement to the reflex arc that has been created and which causes these negative reactions. This aspect of tinnitus explains the low rate of spontaneous recovery, since clinically significant tinnitus is constantly present and that it evokes constant negative reactions, passive extinction of this reflex will not occur and it may actually cause further reinforcement of the reflex arc that causes the negative reactions.

Tinnitus Treatments

There are different methods in use for treatment of tinnitus, and before discussing TRT, it may be useful to briefly discuss some of these other main treatments for tinnitus. Traditionally, the goal has been to eliminate the tinnitus source and tinnitus perception, thus, aiming at achieving a cure of the tinnitus. So far, however, this goal is rarely achieved. Many treatments, typically aimed at the cochlea by delivering drugs directly to the cochlea or through the middle ear, have been tried, and some studies of the outcome of such treatments are currently in progress. Another traditional approach for treatment of tinnitus has been aimed at eliminating tinnitus perception. Suppression of tinnitus perception by external sound, labeled "masking," has been widely promoted. This approach has not been as successful as hoped, with reported effectiveness from zero [31] to 60% [32]. Recently, "masking" has been re-defined as use of any sound which provides some immediate relief for tinnitus [33]. This approach has shown some effectiveness [34, 35], but it is not clear if it is better that any other type of sound therapy (see Chaps. 72, 74 and 75).

Different investigators have used the term "masking" in different ways to describe tinnitus suppression. Auditory masking results from interaction between two traveling waves on the basilar membrane of the cochlea, and as such exhibits phenomena of "critical band" and "V-shaped suppression curve." None of this is true for tinnitus, it is possible to suppress tinnitus perception equally easy by sound of any frequency, and there is lack of significant dependence on the intensity of the sounds needed to suppress tinnitus from a frequency of the tone [4]. These findings support the hypothesis that tinnitus is a phantom auditory perception without any correspondence to the vibratory activity within the cochlea.

Another approach to suppress tinnitus perception that has been described makes use of electrical stimulation of the cochlea/auditory nerve (see Chap. 77) or, recently, electrical stimulation of the auditory cortex [36–39] (see Chap. 90). In the case of the auditory cortex, in addition to direct electrical stimulation, Transcranial Magnetic Stimulation (TMS) has been used [40–42] (see Chap. 88). In TMS, impulses of a very strong magnetic field are applied locally to the skull and the induced electrical current stimulates the cerebral cortex. All these attempts to treat patients with tinnitus were partially successful, with an average rate of about 50%. These methods are now under further investigation.

Different classes of treatment have been aimed at decreasing tinnitus-evoked reactions by improving coping strategies, modifying an individual's thinking about tinnitus, or by using psychotropic drugs to attenuate activity of the limbic system [12, 43–46] (see Chaps. 78 and 79). Psychological approaches have shown effectiveness in the range of 50% (see Chaps. 71 and 72), while so far none of the drugs tested have shown significantly positive effects.

Last, but not least, a variety of sound therapies based on the concept of attenuating tinnitus or making it less noticeable have been described [33, 47–51] (see Chaps. 72, 74, and 75). These treatments have shown some effectiveness, but for most of these methods lack of systematic, independent studies have made it impossible to accurately assess their efficacy. Recently, the concept of using sounds where the energy at frequencies around the pitch of a person's tinnitus were eliminated has been re-introduced [52]. The use of such sounds is based on the hypothesis that utilizing the mechanism of lateral inhibition in the auditory cortex would suppress tinnitus. Lateral inhibition, which occurs commonly in the brain and reflects situation that stimulation of one neuron, is frequently accompanied by inhibition of nearby neurons [12, 53]. In the case of the auditory system, which exhibits tonotopic organization, stimulation with a given frequency can inhibit neurons that respond best to nearby frequencies. Specifically, in case of tinnitus, it has been postulated that by removing the music's frequencies around a person's tinnitus pitch, the neurons in this range will be inhibited due to activation of neurons which respond best to nearby frequencies (see Chap. 75).

Treatments Aimed at Habituation of Reactions to Tinnitus and Its Perception

Above Outlined treatments aim at removing or attenuating source of tinnitus signal, or at alleviation reactions evoked by tinnitus. The neurophysiological model of tinnitus suggests another possible direction for treatment, namely the possibility of blocking the spread of the tinnitus signal to other than auditory regions of the brain, particularly to the limbic and autonomic nervous systems. If such treatment is

successful, a person may still perceive their tinnitus, but tinnitus will not bother her/him. This process is called habituation of tinnitus-evoked reactions. Notably, once sufficient level of habituation of reactions is achieved, habituation of perception automatically follows and a person is aware of tinnitus for smaller and smaller proportions of time as the brain automatically habituates all stimuli that are not important [12] (see Chap. 20). As a result, an individual with tinnitus changes from being a sufferer to becoming a member of the population of people with tinnitus who experience it, but are not bothered by it. It is important to note that this treatment will not work when attempts have been made to first induce habituation of perception. Any method yielding habituation of tinnitus may be labeled Tinnitus Habituation Therapy [54].

According to the model outlined in Fig. 73.1, habituation of reactions will occur when all connections carrying the tinnitus signal to the limbic and autonomic nervous systems are attenuated and preferably blocked (Fig. 73.2). Proper counseling can relatively easily modify the functional connections from the cognitive areas down to the limbic and autonomic nervous systems. Retraining subconscious connections between the auditory system and the limbic and autonomic nervous systems, however, is more complex and difficult to accomplish. Counseling alone will not work, and it is necessary to utilize methods appropriate for retraining the conditioned reflexes.

From the time of Pavlov, it is well known that a conditioned reflex created by exposing a person many times to a sensory stimulus spontaneously undergoes extinction if reinforcement is not given (e.g. using the classical example of the Pavlovian dog, the bell keeps ringing but food is no longer given). This process is known as passive extinction of conditioned reflexes or habituation of reaction [12, 55, 56] (see also Chap. 87). While effective in many situations, this technique cannot be applied in its original form to tinnitus, because the tinnitus signal and its perception are constant and cannot be eliminated. Reinforcement is provided by reactions of the limbic and autonomic nervous systems and, consequently, is constant and cannot be blocked. To solve the problem, the author proposed a modified version of passive extinction of conditioned reflexes using a simultaneous decrease of the sensory signal and reinforcement with these changes maintained for some time (corresponding to the ringing of the Pavlov bell being softer and less food given). This process

Fig. 73.2 Habituation of reactions (HR) and habituation of perception (HP)

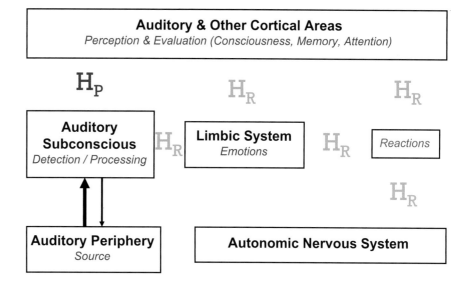

should be effective, but it requires more time than classical passive extinction. In the case of tinnitus, it requires that the strength of the tinnitus signal is decreased, with a decrease of the strength of negative reactions happening at the same time. These interventions must be carried on for some time to obtain good results.

Tinnitus Retraining Therapy and Its Clinical Goals

TRT is a specific implementation of general Tinnitus Habituation Therapy, which utilizes counseling to decrease tinnitus-evoked reactions and sound to decrease the strength of the tinnitus signal. The primary goal of TRT is to achieve habituation of tinnitus-evoked negative reactions and remove the effect of tinnitus on patients' lives. As pointed out above, once habituation of reactions has been at least partially achieved, habituation of perception automatically occurs without the need of any additional action. At the end of a successful treatment, people are not bothered by tinnitus (or bothered very little), even when perceiving it, and tinnitus has no impact on their lives. Additionally, their awareness of tinnitus typically drops to 5 or 10% of their waking time.

Counseling: Habituation cannot be achieved to stimuli indicating danger or are threatening and is achieved with difficulty to stimuli that evoke strong emotional reactions (negative or positive). Therefore, the primary role of counseling in TRT is to achieve reclassification of tinnitus to a category of neutral stimuli. This is achieved by intensive teaching about mechanisms of the tinnitus origin and its benign nature (as perception), which nevertheless may evoke strong negative reactions affecting patients' lives. Patients typically have many incorrect concepts about tinnitus and, at the same time, tinnitus remains a mystery for them. Therefore, demystification of tinnitus and providing patients with solid knowledge is important.

The modified method of passive extinction requires a decrease of the strengths of both the activation of the limbic and the autonomic nervous systems and the tinnitus signal. It is impossible to modify the activity of the subconscious low loop that connects information from the thalamus to the limbic system directly [12] (see Chap. 8), but it is possible to attenuate and finally remove the contribution of cognitive components (the high loop). As both the high and low loops contribute to the final activation of the limbic and autonomic nervous systems, it is possible to achieve a decrease of activation of the limbic system by removing or at least decreasing the transmission and processing of tinnitus signals in the high loop, thus removing its contribution.

By reclassifying tinnitus to the category of neutral stimuli, showing its benign character, providing explanation about its origin and mechanisms, pointing out that the patients have "a proper reaction but to an improper stimulus," and answering questions, etc., it is possible to eliminate transmission of the tinnitus signal in the high loop in a relatively short time.

Another, more general mechanism of attenuation of the effects of the high loop in tinnitus is based on the fact that people react stronger to unknown dangers than to even significant dangers which are known. Therefore, once patients are able to predict the behavior of their tinnitus (e.g. typical increase of the tinnitus when in quiet places or in a stressful situation) and their own reactions to it, they may still be annoyed and bothered by their tinnitus, but to a smaller extent.

Even complete abolishment of tinnitus signal processing and transmission in the high loop is not sufficient to remove negative reactions evoked by tinnitus because the low loop remains fully active and unchanged.

The negative reaction to a person's tinnitus will undergo gradual extinction as the result of this modified method of passive extinction, but the process will be slower than eliminating processing and transmission of tinnitus signals in the high loop. Nevertheless, on average, patients show clear improvement after just one month of TRT treatment. This observation has been recently collaborated by reports from other centers [57, 58].

The counseling/teaching session is crucial for achieving high effectiveness of the TRT treatment. Without it, sound therapy will have some positive effect, as well as using some general counseling, but the effectiveness of such treatments is clearly lower [34] because they will not eliminate processing and transmission of the tinnitus signal in the high loop, and patients will still have negative cognitive association with tinnitus.

Sound therapy: In principle, many different methods may be used to decrease the tinnitus signal (e.g. drugs, electrical stimulation, TMS), but in practice, the use of sound is simple and can be easily controlled and adapted to the needs of an individual patient (see Chap. 74). Sound therapy utilizes the principle that the strength of the neuronal signal within the brain is based on the contrast principle, thus the difference of the signal is from background sound or background neuronal activity. Therefore, the strength of the tinnitus signal can be deceased by systematically increasing the background neuronal activity within the auditory pathways. This can be achieved by enhancing background sound levels to which patients are exposed, thereby affecting the perception of the tinnitus.

Specifics regarding the implementation of sound therapy, including use of sound generators, combination instruments, and hearing aids, have been described in detail elsewhere [5, 8, 15, 59]. It is crucial to remember the basic rule for its successful implementation: "Never use sound as a part of sound therapy, which would create annoyance or discomfort for any reason." Use of a sound which would evoke any negative reactions would activate the limbic and autonomic nervous systems, worsening the situation and making habituation more difficult to achieve. Other recommendations, which are helpful while less critical, include the use of sound enrichment preferably all the time, 24/7, use more than one type of sound source (e.g. sound generators and tabletop sound machines) and preferentially use nature sounds in the background. Music is typically used in the basic protocol for misophonia [8, 12] (see also Chap. 75).

Decreased Sound Tolerance

Tinnitus is typically accompanied by decreased sound tolerance, both hyperacusis and misophonia (see also Chap. 3). Results from many centers indicate that hyperacusis coexists with tinnitus in 25–30% of people who seek help for their tinnitus. Our own data indicate that misophonia is present in about 60% of the patients we treat [8]. Proper diagnosis and treatment of decreased sound tolerance and its components is crucial for successful outcome of tinnitus treatment. Hyperacusis is relatively easy to treat with the desensitization protocol [12], and typically it can be attenuated or eliminated within a couple of months of treatment. Treatment of misophonia is much more complex and lengthy and requires specific protocols. This reflects the fact that the same neuronal networks are involved in tinnitus and misophonia, and consequently, treatment of misophonia takes a similar amount of time as treatment of tinnitus (see also Chap. 20). Methods used for successful treatment of hyperacusis are not effective for treatment of misophonia.

The situation is further worsened by the fact that the presence of tinnitus frequently induces or enhances misophonia, as patients dislike and start to avoid sounds in general, which makes their tinnitus worse (or patients think that this is happening). Last, but not least, misophonia tends to trigger the tensor tympani syndrome (fullness in the ears, pain, feeling of pulsation, vestibular problems, headaches, etc.) [60], which may become a significant, or even a dominant problem.

Severe decreased sound tolerance is more debilitating than severe or even catastrophic tinnitus and can totally disable people. Without adequate treatment of decreased sound tolerance, and particularly misophonia, the effectiveness of tinnitus treatment becomes substantially decreased.

On the positive side, TRT is very effective for treatment of both hyperacusis and misophonia, and it is possible to achieve a cure in most patients, which means total elimination of hyperacusis and misophonia. Another positive aspect is that after successful treatment of misophonia, the tensor tympani syndrome disappears as well, and that tinnitus, if still bothersome, typically also improves.

Outline of Treatment by TRT

Patient Evaluation

In evaluation of patients with tinnitus and decreased sound tolerance, the detailed initial interview is crucial for the diagnosis. We are using a structured interview for initial and follow-up visits conducted with help of specific forms [61, 62] (see Appendix A). While information provided by this interview gives good insight into many aspects of tinnitus including its severity, the Tinnitus Handicap Inventory (THI) is used as well to assess tinnitus severity in a more formal manner [63, 64].

An audiological evaluation includes a pure-tone audiogram (up to 12 kHz), determination of pure-tone Loudness Discomfort Levels (LDL) (measured for all frequencies evaluated in the audiogram), evaluation of speech discrimination, and high-frequency resolution Distortion Product Otoacoustic Emission (DPOAE) (10 points per octave, frequency range of f2 from 1 to 10 kHz), all are tests that are needed for evaluation of patients for treatment using TRT. Audiogram and speech discrimination scores show the patient's hearing ability. LDLs are crucial in assessing decreased sound

tolerance, and DPOAE is extremely helpful during counseling, particularly when Discordant Dysfunction Theory (DDT) is used [1, 12, 65]. This theory postulates that the tinnitus signal originates from the regions of the basilar membrane where there is decreased activity of Outer Hair Cells (OHC) while Inner Hair Cells (IHC) are functional. Measurements of tinnitus pitch and loudness match are performed as well, but these results have no impact on diagnosis or treatment. Determination of Minimal Masking Levels (MML) is done for research purposes.

The acoustic reflexes and reflex decay are not a part of routine evaluation. They are not necessary or sufficient to determine presence of vestibular schwannoma (if it is suspected). Since most patients with tinnitus have decreased sound tolerance, the exposure to loud sounds (which are necessary for testing the acoustic middle-ear reflexes) may cause worsening of the symptoms and make subsequent interaction with patients more difficult.

Diagnosis

The following information is used for diagnosis and categorizing the patients' category and variant of TRT treatment in TRT which should be used.

Impact of Tinnitus on Patients' Lives and/or the Duration of Clinically Significant Tinnitus

This information provides insight regarding the strength of neuronal connections in the network processing the tinnitus signal. If tinnitus has a low severity, the connections are likely to be weak because it has been shown that tinnitus severity does not depend on the loudness to which a patient matches his/her tinnitus, and it is as well established that the strength of reactions that occurs through activation of conditioned reflexes depends primarily on the strength of the reinforcement; the strength of the conditioned stimulus plays a limited role. Therefore, weak reactions indicate weak strength of the connections in the neural networks involved in causing the tinnitus-evoked reactions. If an individual's tinnitus is very recent (a few weeks), these connections have not had enough time to become permanent, which would make it easier to modify them (see chapter neural plasticity). In this connection, it should be noted that the duration of the symptoms regards clinically significant tinnitus and not the duration of the tinnitus perception as such. Tinnitus may be perceived for many years, without bothering a person, before suddenly becoming a problem.

Hyperacusis

Presence of hyperacusis imposes some constraints on the use of sound therapy, including the allowed category of protocols for misophonia. The differentiation between hyperacusis and misophonia is complex, but a detailed interview, together with a comparison of the shape of a person's audiogram and that of the LDLs, typically provides enough information to make this distinction [8]. A positive diagnosis of hyperacusis requires that the average LDL is less than about 90 dB. A low value of the LDL does not prove the presence of hyperacusis, however, because a low value of LDLs may be due to misophonia. The behavioral reactions evoked by hyperacusis and misophonia are identical, thus they cannot be used for differentiation either. Detailed interview with attention paid to sounds evoking negative reactions is necessary for differentiation of hyperacusis form misophonia and assign their relative contribution to decreased sound tolerance. If both hyperacusis and misophonia are present together and hyperacusis is treated successfully, but misophonia is not treated and disappears, misophonia typically may be enhanced, and at the behavioral level, no improvement in the patient's condition is achieved.

The Presence and Significance of Hearing Loss

Approximately 70–80% of individuals with tinnitus have some degree of hearing loss, which is typically less than 60 dB HL in the frequency range up to 8 kHz. It is important to consider whether such hearing loss has any impact on a person's everyday life (see Chap. 5). The same degree of hearing loss can be of large significance to one person (e.g. professions requiring communication in noise or musicians) while having no significance to another (e.g. farmers). A factor to consider when evaluating a person's hearing is whether the hearing loss is accompanied by a "strain to hear" in everyday life because this increases the severity of

tinnitus. Only after all these factors have been taken into consideration can a patient be classified as having hearing loss of significance for treatment of tinnitus. It should be noted that a patient's subjective awareness of her/his hearing loss has little relevance because patients often do not acknowledge mild or even significant hearing loss.

Prolonged Exacerbation of Tinnitus/Hyperacusis by Sound

Over 50% of patients report that their tinnitus becomes worse for some time after exposure to sound (loud, moderate, or even soft). This time is in the range of minutes to hours for most individuals with tinnitus and typically affects hyperacusis or misophonia more than tinnitus. Some patients report that the effect persists through the next day, even after a good night's sleep, or it may even last several days. This observation can be due to two scenarios and has profound impact on the diagnosis and treatment: (1) it may involve functional plastic changes in the nervous system that occurs as the "kindling" or "wind up" phenomenon (see also Chaps. 10 and 12) or (2) strong misophonia (see also Chap. 4). "Kindling" is a term from the field of epilepsy that describes the phenomenon that may occur when a weak stimulus that initially does not evoke a seizure evokes epileptic seizures after being presented repeatedly over several weeks.

The "Wind-up" phenomenon is a term from the field of chronic pain and describes the situation when the second presentation of a painful stimuli causes a stronger reaction than caused by the first presentation or when a stimulus presented for a limited time (e.g. a few minutes) is not inducing pain; when its duration is longer, it becomes painful (see also Chaps. 14 and 15). This is similar to what occurs when a sound, which initially is without any effect causes a worsening of tinnitus or hyperacusis after the sound has been presented for a longer period of time. These phenomena are particularly observed in people with certain medical problems, such as after head injury, brain surgery, Lyme disease, or symptoms associated with hormonal changes (for instance, during menopause).

In the past, it has not been appreciated that perception of prolonged sounds can often cause misophonia, causing elements of phonophobia to become worse. People with tinnitus may become afraid that exposure to sound may cause their hyperacusis or tinnitus to become permanently worse and by paying extra attention to such problems and avoiding sounds (using ear protection) can enhance tinnitus and hyperacusis/misophonia or cause prolongation of an initial worsening. The experience of treating patients with tinnitus has shown that most incidences of worsening were due to the development of misophonia; only a few people have had indications that the worsening had a medical basis. Nevertheless, when medical reasons are reported by a patient, it should be considered.

Categories of Tinnitus

Five categories of patients are proposed on the basis of the factors listed above [12, 22, 66], and specific variant of TRT treatment has been associated with each one of these categories. These categories, listed below, provide general directions, and the borders between them are not sharp. While the categorization forms a continuum that provides some general guidelines that can help in avoiding some mistakes in the treatment, there is a certain degree of overlap between neighboring categories. For example, patients can be categorized as C 2/3 or 3/2 in case of coexisting hearing loss (category 2) and hyperacusis (category 3), depending on which problem is dominant. If ear-level instrumentation is used, it should be aimed at preserving or restoring symmetrical stimulation of the auditory pathways. Consequently, most of those who use instruments use these bilaterally, with exception being for cases with no hearing in one ear.

Misophonia may be present or absent in all these categories since treatment of misophonia is different from treatment of hyperacusis and tinnitus and can be conducted simultaneously with treatments aimed at the patient's tinnitus and their hyperacusis. Consequently, misophonia is not included as a discriminating factor in the categorization. A detailed description of the categories and associated variants of treatments has been presented earlier [7, 19].

In the following, each one of the 5 categories is described as well as the methods in which patients with each category are treated using proper variant of TRT method.

Category 0

This category of patients is characterized by a low degree of severity (or hyperacusis) or a short duration of the problem. An abbreviated version of counseling is conducted providing basic information aimed at reclassification of tinnitus into a category of neutral stimuli, furthermore, following the principle that the problem should not be presented, so that it gives an impression that it could be worse than the patient reports (e.g. patients are not told that tinnitus or decreased sound tolerance can be debilitating and push them into depression or suicide!). All the remaining 4 categories have higher severity tinnitus and/or hyperacusis as well as potentially having tinnitus of a longer duration.

Treatment of patients with this category of tinnitus consists of providing basic information about sound therapy, with a short discussion about enrichment from environmental sounds by using sound machines producing nature sounds, or by using other sound sources. The benefit from the principle "Avoid Silence" during the treatment is pointed out. Ear-level instrumentations (e.g. sound generators) are typically not needed in this category, but such devices may anyhow be beneficial. However, as they are not essential for a successful outcome of the treatment and due to financial reasons, they are not recommended.

While an initial visit is typically sufficient to achieve noticeable improvement in this category of patients, a short follow-up visit or telephone call at 1, 3, and 6 months after treatment is worthwhile. Patients who are not improving should be reassessed and, if needed, have more extensive counseling, and recommendation of an ear-level instrumentation should be considered.

Category 1

Patients with this category of tinnitus have significant tinnitus, without hyperacusis, but misophonia may also be present. There is no significant hearing loss, and there is no sound-induced prolonged worsening of tinnitus (except when induced by misophonia). The treatment involves full counseling focused on the patient's tinnitus, with omitted elements related to hyperacusis.

Sound generators are recommended as part of the therapy, providing well-controlled sound delivery. The sound level is typically determined by the level that evokes annoyance, and only in some patients it is possible to reach the sound level where the patient can perceive their tinnitus and the external sounds as separate entities, but with both sounds start to mix or blend together (the "mixing point").

Formally, this is the level where partial suppression ("partial masking") starts to occur. Reaching the mixing point is not important for successful outcome of the treatment. In fact, pushing patients toward reaching the mixing point at the expense of going above the level evoking annoyance or discomfort is counterproductive and works against facilitation of habituation. Sound levels which are low should be avoided, however, because of the effect of stochastic resonance will enhance a person's tinnitus and work against its habituation [67, 68]. Real Ear Measurements (REM) are highly recommended as a part of fitting an in-the-ear device and are repeated at follow-up visits.

Category 2

The characteristic feature of this category of patients is the presence of significant hearing loss as defined above. Full counseling is performed with stressing matters that are related to hearing loss. Combination instruments (a combination of an independently controlled sound generator and hearing aid in one shell) are preferable for sound therapy to be used in conjunction with enrichment of environmental sounds, as recommended for other categories. If such devices cannot be used due to technical or financial issues, the focus should be on achieving sufficient enrichment of background sounds, typically including the use of tabletop sound machines, with increased stimulation of the auditory system further enhanced by hearing aids. Fitting and use of hearing aids is specific for individuals with tinnitus and different than for people without tinnitus [59, 69].

Sound generators alone are not used for this category of patients, as they would make the understanding of speech even more difficult. Such devices would make tinnitus worse due to an increase in the strain to hear and understand speech.

Category 3

The characteristic feature of this category of tinnitus is a presence of significant hyperacusis that must be treated first. Full counseling is performed, stressing

issues related to hyperacusis (e.g. both peripheral and central mechanisms controlling amplification within the auditory pathways are explained). Sound generators are always recommended for sound therapy in patients without hearing loss. Combination instruments are used in patients with hearing loss with stress in the initial stage on sound generators (and low amplification of hearing aid part) followed by second stage when amplification is increased. In both stages, sound generator and hearing aids parts are used concurrently. When combination instruments cannot be utilized, a two-stage procedure may be considered: the first stage with use of sound generators and in the second stage, they are replaced by hearing aids. In this scenario, patients need to be counseled properly to ensure that they expect and accept increased impairment of understanding of speech while using sound generators during the first stage of treatment. Patients should not use these devices when speech communication is essential. Another option is to make use of enrichment of sound background for treatment of hyperacusis before proceeding to the stage in the treatment where hearing aids are used. As hyperacusis is relatively easy to treat and the treatment is fast, this approach may be considered as well.

Combination instruments are the most versatile ear-level instruments for tinnitus treatment and, in theory, they can be used in about 80% of all patients. Technical limitations of currently available instruments as well as their high costs hinder their general use. Another significant aspect is that they require a specific fitting, and lack of proper theoretical and technical know-how by the people who do the fitting results in a high return rate of such instruments. In our experience, we have excellent results with the use of combination instruments and very few were returned.

It should be noted that the presence or absence of misophonia is irrelevant for treatment of patients with this category, which has hyperacusis present. If misophonia is present, it may be treated in the same way as described for the other categories of tinnitus, and for example patients with tinnitus and misophonia will be classified as category 1 with misophonia. Therefore, the presence of decreased sound tolerance is not sufficient to classify patient as belonging to category 3; presence of hyperacusis is required. If misophonia is present in this category, due to presence of hyperacusis, certain restrictions are imposed on the type of protocol that can be used for the treatment of misophonia. Note that the basic features of the protocol for misophonia can be used even for patients with severe hyperacusis [8, 19].

Category 4

The characteristic feature of the tinnitus in this category is a prolonged exacerbation of the patients' worst problem; typically, hyperacusis that may last at least after a good night's sleep and does not result from misophonia. If there are medical problems involved that cannot be treated medically, such as from the effect of brain injury after car accidents, blast injuries from military operations, or brain operations, the treatment is highly individualized and difficult. Checking for the presence of Lyme disease may be worthwhile, because it has been reported that hyperacusis is present in 48% of Lyme disease cases [70]. If Lyme disease is the base of the problem, treatment for Lyme disease with antibiotics could be helpful even regarding the tinnitus.

Results of TRT

TRT works independent of the cause of the tinnitus, and the habituation of the reaction to the tinnitus occurs outside the central auditory pathways. Therefore, the etiology of tinnitus is irrelevant, and TRT can be successfully used for any type of tinnitus, e.g. bilateral, unilateral, continuous, or intermittent, as well as for somatosounds. This prediction from the neurophysiological model of tinnitus has been confirmed by results of clinical studies. The results of our past studies showed significant improvement in over 80% of the patients with noteworthy improvement as observed after about 12 months after the beginning of the therapy disregarding the etiology of tinnitus [23, 71]. Recent results of studies of over 300 patients treated in the Emory Tinnitus & Hyperacusis Center showed statistically significant improvement after only 3 months of TRT treatment, with further improvement occurring when the treatment was continued [15, 72].

Results of open studies reported from various centers using TRT also consistently showed significant improvement in over 80% of the patients who were treated [57, 73–87].

The results of a 5-year follow-up study showed that TRT had a high degree of effectiveness in treatment of patients with tinnitus and hyperacusis and that the improvement is persistent [88]. A recently published study evaluated the effects of 18 months of TRT treatment (and the following 18 months without continuing the treatment) [89]. Results immediately following the treatment show a high level of statistically significant improvement which persisted for the 18 months after the study's treatment completion. Moreover, the proportion of patients reporting disappearance of their tinnitus-evoked difficulties while attempting to relax and concentrate and reporting problems with sleep, social interaction, and work increased continuously after treatment completion [89].

Of interest are also reports presenting results of a systematic randomized study, which showed that TRT is not only highly effective in general but is also effective for patients with severe symptoms typically reported to be particularly difficult to treat using other approaches [34, 35]. Interestingly, there was no indication of the results reaching a plateau after the 18 months the treatment, suggesting the possibility for achieving even better results with further continuation of the treatment.

Prevention and Early Treatment

Tinnitus and decreased sound tolerance present a big problem once they are established. Obviously, prevention of the occurrence of bothersome tinnitus, or treatment at the very early stage of tinnitus, would have a significant impact on the extent of problems created by tinnitus in the general population (see also Chap. 69). Unfortunately, tinnitus prevention is an area that has been largely ignored. The neurophysiological model as described earlier [1, 17, 19, 90–92] and outlined in this chapter provides guidelines for prevention of the appearance of clinically significant tinnitus and indicates how to achieve relief of problems related to tinnitus shortly after they appear [19].

Avoidance of Silence and Providing an Enriched Sound Environment

The vast majority of our patients at the Emory Tinnitus & Hyperacusis Center and at University of Maryland in Baltimore describe the initial appearance of their tinnitus occurred during a period where they were in a silent environment. Experiments have documented that it is possible to evoke tinnitus perception in most people after a few minutes in a quiet environment [93–95]. If a person is in a negative emotional state while perceiving tinnitus, it may lead to development of conditioned reflexes producing tinnitus-evoked negative reactions. Exposure to sound, particularly by being in an environment enriched by natural sounds or sounds generated by tabletop machines, music players, etc., decreases the probability of bothersome tinnitus materializing.

The neurophysiological model of tinnitus developed by the author and described earlier [1, 17, 19, 90–92] predicts that if a person is exposed to an enriched sound environment shortly after the occurrence of tinnitus perception due to any reason (e.g. explosion or exposure to another damaging sound), it will decrease the probability of development of clinically significant tinnitus or, if it does occur, exposure to sound will increase the likelihood of habituation of the tinnitus. Neuronal connections responsible for the tinnitus-evoked reactions will then not have enough time to become permanent, and it is easier to retrain them if tinnitus is treated early after its occurrence (see Hebb's principle in Chap. 12). This prediction has support from the results of both clinical studies and recent experiments on animals, showing that it is possible to prevent or reverse the reorganization of cortical maps that have been induced by sound overexposure by providing animals with an enriched sound environment [96, 97].

It is obvious that avoidance of excessive noise, which may cause damage to the cochlea or other changes in the auditory system (see Chap. 37), is recommended; however, recommendations given to patients with tinnitus frequently result in overprotection and have the opposite effect. The phenomenon of auditory toughening (i.e. increased resistance of the cochlea to damage and protection against loud, damaging sound offered by pre-exposure to moderate to loud sound) [98–100] (see Chap. 37), is not appreciated in general and even more in case of hyperacusis and tinnitus.

Sound exposure is necessary for keeping normal gain in the auditory nervous system; if it does not receive enough sound input, the gain increases and contributes to the development of tinnitus and/or hyperacusis. The experience from treating patients with tinnitus and animal experiments is that both

overexposure to sound and overprotection from sound can be harmful. This message needs to be strongly emphasized in both public and professional health education. Exposure to appropriate forms of sound should be promoted as an integral part of our life that is essential for personal well-being.

Avoidance of Negative Counseling and Providing Proper Information in Advance

Negative counseling frequently provided by health care professionals, patient support groups, and the Internet can trigger mechanism that can create clinically significant tinnitus and make existing tinnitus worse. Health professionals should be alerted to the danger of such negative counseling that is offered to people with tinnitus. Instead, the general population should be educated with correct and basic knowledge about tinnitus, pointing out that there is much that can be done to alleviate the harm from tinnitus and that there is a high likelihood of successful treatment and of decreased sound tolerance (hyperacusis and misophonia). The most frequent issues related to negative counseling (e.g. "nothing can be done, let's take a brain scan to exclude a brain tumor") should be properly presented, so that the effect of negative counseling a person may receive is eliminated or at least prevented from having any profound effect.

Such education is particularly important for individuals who have a high risk of acquiring tinnitus, such as soldiers. For example, a huge amount of suffering and money would be spared if all soldiers going into combat situations undergo just one thoughtfully prepared 1–2-h educational session. Identification of other high-risk populations (e.g. police officers, firefighters, construction workers, and patients before any type of ear operation) and providing them with proper education would be highly beneficial as well.

Conclusions

TRT is a specific implementation of the Tinnitus Habituation Therapy, which utilizes teaching/counseling to reclassify tinnitus into the category of neutral stimuli, and sound therapy to decrease the tinnitus-related neuronal activity (tinnitus signal) within the brain. As a result of TRT, habituation of both a person's reactions evoked by the tinnitus and its perception occurs. TRT is strictly based on the neurophysiological model of tinnitus developed by the author [1, 19, 22] (outlined in Fig. 73.1), which stresses the necessity of including a network of interaction between many different systems in the brain in models of tinnitus and hyperacusis. From the beginning, the model stressed that the auditory system plays a secondary role [19] (see also Chap. 20). Emphasis instead is placed on structures involved in evoking tinnitus-induced negative reactions, mainly but not exclusively, the limbic and autonomic nervous systems.

TRT has been used clinically for treatment of tinnitus and decreased sound tolerance since 1988. The method of TRT underwent many modifications since its first description, and the method does not have a stagnant protocol but continues to evolve on the basis of information gathered from both treatment of patients and animal research findings. While the main features and assumptions of TRT remained the same, imple-mentation of TRT has changed substantially regarding both the counseling part and sound therapy. In counseling, main changes included introduction of the concept of misophonia, the emphasis on conditional reflexes, subconscious processing of information, and on direct teaching about using a modified version of passive extinction of conditioned reflexes. The use of sound therapy has also undergone changes from the introduction of specific protocols for misophonia, changing the parameters for the sound stimulation from the use of levels, which could evoke annoyance or discomfort, to the use of lower levels. These modifications resulted in a significant reduction of the time needed to achieve improvement in the patients' problems, from 1 year to 1 month.

Results from many tinnitus treatment centers show that TRT causes noticeable improvements or cures in and above 80% of patients with any type of tinnitus. Notably, refined counseling and sound therapy increased the effectiveness of TRT in treatment of decreased sound tolerance, so that it now becomes possible to achieve complete elimination (cure) in most patients.

Appendix A: Forms for Structured Initial and Follow-up Interviews

Form 1: Tinnitus/Hyperacusis initial interview form

I	**TINNITUS / HYPERACUSIS INITIAL INTERVIEW FORM**	Clinic # :

T&HC#:

tel:
e-mail:

Clinic #   :
Name   :
DOB   :
SSN   :
Insurance :
Date   :

T I N N I T U S

RE / LE / Both / Head = >   Intermittent / Constant
                                           Fluctuations in volume Y / N
Description of T sound(s)

Onset: Gradual / Sudden   When
"Bad days" Y / N   Frequency

Activities prevented or affected:
◯Concentration ◯Sleep ◯QRA ◯Work
◯Restaurants ◯Sports ◯Social ◯Other

Effect of sound: None / Louder / Softer
           How long: min / hours / days

% of time when: Aware   Annoyed
Severity: 0 1 2 3 4 5 6 7 8 9 10
Annoyance: 0 1 2 3 4 5 6 7 8 9 10
Effect on Life: 0 1 2 3 4 5 6 7 8 9 10

Ear overprotection Y / N   % of time
                   in quiet Y / N
Any other T specific treatments

Why is T a problem

Comments:

S O U N D T O L E R A N C E

Oversensitivity: Y / N   Physical discomfort? Y / N
Description of troublesome sounds

"Bad days" Y / N   Frequency

Activities prevented or affected:
◯Concerts ◯Shopping ◯Movies ◯Work
◯Restaurants ◯Driving ◯Sports ◯Church
◯Housekeeping ◯Childcare ◯Social ◯Other

Effect of sound: None / Stronger / Weaker
           How long: min / hours / days

Severity: 0 1 2 3 4 5 6 7 8 9 10
Annoyance: 0 1 2 3 4 5 6 7 8 9 10
Effect on Life: 0 1 2 3 4 5 6 7 8 9 10

Ear overprotection Y / N   % of time
                   in quiet Y / N
Any other ST specific treatments

Why is ST a problem

Comments:

H L

Hearing problem   Y / N
Hearing Aid(s)   Y / N type:
Ever recommended Y / N

Category:
Recommendation:

Ranking problems: Tinnitus: 0 1 2 3 4 5 6 7 8 9 10
            Sound tolerance: 0 1 2 3 4 5 6 7 8 9 10
                    Hearing: 0 1 2 3 4 5 6 7 8 9 10

Ptn decision:
Next visit:

T - tinnitus   ST - sound tolerance (hyperacusis + phonophobia)
Is you T preventing or affecting any activities in your life.
QRA - quiet recreational activities: Is your T interfering with QRA such as reading or meditating.
% of time when: Aware - What % of time were you aware of your T over last month?
                    Annoyed - What % of the time over last months T bothered you?
Severity - How strong or loud was your T on average over last month? 0 - no T, 10 - as strong as you can imagine.
Annoyance - How much was T annoying you on average over last month 0 - not at all; 10 - as much as you can imagine.
Effect on life - How much was T affecting your life on average over last month. 0 - no effect; 10 - as much as you can imagine.
Any other T specific treatments - Are you using any other treatments for your T.
Sound tolerance - Is your tolerance to louder sounds the same as people around you?
Hearing - Do you think you have a hearing problem?
Ranking - rank importance of your problems with 0 - no problem, 10 - as large as you can imagine   MM & PJ Jastreboff, 1999

Form 2: Tinnitus/Hyperacusis follow-up interview form

FU	**TINNITUS / HYPERACUSIS** **FOLLOW-UP INTERVIEW FORM**	Clinic # : Name : DOB : SSN : Insurance : Date :

CATEGORY:
Date of init. couns.
T&HC#:   Date of instr. fitt.
                      SG:
tel: HA:
                      FUQ #:
                      Month #:
                      Type of visit:

TINNITUS

"Bad days" Y / N   Frequency
Are they: as frequent Y /N   as bad Y / N

Activities prevented or affected: Changes: Y / N
◯◯Concentration ◯◯Sleep   ◯◯QRA   ◯◯Work
◯◯Restaurants   ◯◯Sports   ◯◯Social ◯◯Other

Effect of sound: None / Louder / Softer
                    How long: min / hours / days

% of time when: Aware   (1ˢᵗ   ) Annoyed   (1ˢᵗ   )
Has it changed
Severity: 0 1 2 3 4 5 6 7 8 9 10
Annoyance: 0 1 2 3 4 5 6 7 8 9 10
Effect on Life: 0 1 2 3 4 5 6 7 8 9 10

Ear overprotection Y / N   % of time
                    in quiet Y / N
Any other T specific treatments

Comments:

SOUND TOLERANCE

"Bad days" Y / N   Frequency
Are they: as frequent Y /N   as bad Y / N

Description of troublesome sounds

Activities prevented or affected: Changes: Y / N
◯◯Concerts   ◯◯Shopping   ◯◯Movies ◯◯Work
◯◯Restaurants   ◯◯Driving   ◯◯Sports ◯◯Church
◯◯Housekeeping ◯◯Childcare   ◯◯Social ◯◯Other

Effect of sound: None / Stronger / Weaker
                    How long: min / hours / days

Severity: 0 1 2 3 4 5 6 7 8 9 10
Annoyance: 0 1 2 3 4 5 6 7 8 9 10
Effect on Life: 0 1 2 3 4 5 6 7 8 9 10

Ear overprotection Y / N   % of time
                    in quiet Y / N
Any other ST specific treatments

Comments:

HL

Hearing problem

Recommendation:

The problem in general: Same / Better / Worse
Ranking problems: Tinnitus: 0 1 2 3 4 5 6 7 8 9 10
                     Sound tolerance: 0 1 2 3 4 5 6 7 8 9 10
                     Hearing: 0 1 2 3 4 5 6 7 8 9 10

Next visit:

How would you feel if you had to give back your instruments
Are you glad you started this program? Y / N / NS
Main problems discussed:

T - tinnitus   **ST** - sound tolerance (hyperacusis + phonophobia)
Is you T preventing or affecting any activities in your life.
QRA - quiet recreational activities: Is your T interfering with QRA such as reading or meditating.
% of time when: Aware - What % of time were you aware of your T over last month?
                   Annoyed - What % of the time over last months T bothered you?
Severity - How strong or loud was your T on average over last month? 0 - no T, 10 - as strong as you can imagine.
Annoyance - How much was T annoying you on average over last month 0 - not at all; 10 - as much as you can imagine.
Effect on life - How much was T affecting your life on average over last month. 0 - no effect; 10 - as much as you can imagine.
Any other T specific treatments - Are you using any other treatments for your T.
Sound tolerance - Is your tolerance to louder sounds the same as people around you?
Hearing - Do you think you have a hearing problem?
Ranking - rank importance of your problems with 0 - no problem, 10 - as large as you can imagine

Type of visit: - phone, fax, e-mail, office visit
●◯ - an activity affected at first visit
◯● - an activity affected as for today

MM & PJ Jastreboff, 1999

References

1. Jastreboff PJ (1990) Phantom auditory perception (tinnitus): mechanisms of generation and perception. Neurosci Res 8:221–254

2. Jastreboff PJ (1995) Tinnitus as a phantom perception: theories and clinical implications. In: Mechanisms of Tinnitus. Vernon J, Møller AR, editors Boston, London: Allyn & Bacon, pp 73–94

3. Vernon J (1977) Attemps to relieve tinnitus. J Am Audiol Soc 2:124–131

4. Feldmann H (1971) Homolateral and contralateral masking of tinnitus by noise-bands and by pure tones. Audiology 10:138–144

5. Jastreboff PJ, Jastreboff MM (2007) Tinnitus and decreased sound tolerance: theory and treatment. In: Clinical otology. Huges G, Pensak M, editors, 3rd ed. New York: Thieme Medical Publishers, Inc.

6. Jastreboff PJ, Jastreboff MM (2004) Decreased sound tolerance. In: Tinnitus: theory and management. Snow JB, editor Hamilton, London: BC Decker, pp 8–15

7. Jastreboff PJ, Jastreboff MM (2003) Tinnitus and hyperacusis. In: Ballenger's otorhinolaryngology head and neck surgery. Snow JB, Jr., Ballenger JJ, editors16th ed. Hamilton, Ontario, Canada: BC Decker, pp 456–475

8. Jastreboff MM, Jastreboff PJ (2002) Decreased sound tolerance and tinnitus retraining therapy (TRT). Aust N Z J Audiol 21(2):74–81

9. Jastreboff MM, Jastreboff PJ (2001) Component of decreased sound tolerance: hyperacusis, misophonia, phonophobia. ITHS News Lett 2(Summer 2001):5–7

10. Boettcher FA, Salvi RJ (1993) Functional changes in the ventral cochlear nucleus following acute acoustic overstimulation. J Acoust Soc Am 94:2123–2134

11. Gerken GM (1993) Alteration of central auditory processing of brief stimuli: a review and a neural model. J Acoust Soc Am 93:2038–2049

12. Jastreboff PJ, Hazell JWP (2004) Tinnitus retraining therapy: implementing the neurophysiological model. Cambridge: Cambridge University Press

13. Monzani D, Genovese E, Marrara A et al (2008) Validity of the Italian adaptation of the Tinnitus Handicap Inventory; focus on quality of life and psychological distress in tinnitus-sufferers. Acta Otorhinolaryngol Ital 28(3): 126–134

14. Jastreboff PJ (1999) The neurophysiological model of tinnitus and hyperacusis. In: Proceedings of the sixth international tinnitus seminar, 1999, Cambridge, UK. Hazell JWP, editor London, UK: THC; pp 32–38

15. Jastreboff PJ (2007) Tinnitus retraining therapy. Prog Brain Res 166:415–423

16. Jastreboff PJ, Jastreboff MM (2006) Tinnitus retraining therapy: a different view on tinnitus. ORL J Otorhinolaryngol Relat Spec 68(1):23–29

17. Jastreboff PJ (2004) The neurophysiological model of tinnitus. In: Tinnitus: theory and management. Snow JB, editor Hamilton, London: BC Decker; pp 96–106

18. Jastreboff PJ (2004) Tinnitus retraining therapy. In: Tinnitus: theory and management. Snow JB, editor Hamilton, London: BC Decker; pp 295–309

19. Jastreboff PJ, Hazell JWP (2004) Tinnitus retraining therapy: implementing the neurophysiological model. Cambridge: Cambridge University Press

20. Jastreboff PJ, Jastreboff MM (2003) Tinnitus retraining therapy for patients with tinnitus and decreased sound tolerance. Otolaryngol Clin North Am 36(2):321–336

21. Jastreboff PJ, Jastreboff MM (2001) The neurophysiological model of tinnitus and its practical implementation: Current status. In: Advances in Otolaryngology-Head and Neck Surgery, vol 15. Myers EN, Bluestone CD, Brackman DE, Krause CJ, Tutchko MJ, editors St. Louis: Mosby, pp 135–147

22. Jastreboff PJ (2000) Tinnitus habituation therapy (THT) and tinnitus retraining therapy (TRT). In: Tinnitus handbook. Tyler R, editor San Diego: Singular, Thomson Learning; pp 357–376

23. Jastreboff PJ, Jastreboff MM (2000) Tinnitus retraining therapy (TRT) as a method for treatment of tinnitus and hyperacusis patients. J Am Acad Audiol 11(3):156–161

24. LeDoux JE (1992) Brain mechanisms of emotion and emotional learning. Curr Opin Neurobiol 2(2):191–197

25. Woodson W, Farb CR, LeDoux JE (2000) Afferents from the auditory thalamus synapse on inhibitory interneurons in the lateral nucleus of the amygdala. Synapse 38(2): 124–137

26. Farb CR, LeDoux JE (1997) NMDA and AMPA receptors in the lateral nucleus of the amygdala are postsynaptic to auditory thalamic afferents. Synapse 27(2):106–121

27. Marsh RA, Fuzessery ZM, Grose CD, Wenstrup JJ (2002) Projection to the inferior colliculus from the basal nucleus of the amygdala. J Neurosci 22(23):10449–10460

28. Jastreboff PJ (2008) The role of subconscious pathways in tinnitus and decreased sound tolerance. Nineth International Tinnitus Seminar, Goeteborg, Sweden

29. Hazell JWP, McKinney CJ (1996) Support for a neurophysiological model of tinnitus. In: Proceedings of the Fifth International Tinnitus Seminar, 1995, Portland, OR, U.S.A. Vernon JA, Reich G, editors Portland, OR: American Tinnitus Association; pp 51–57

30. (2010) http://www.ata.org/advocacy/tool-kit

31. Erlandsson S, Ringdahl A, Hutchins T, Carlsson SG (1987) Treatment of tinnitus: a controlled comparison of masking and placebo. Br J Audiol 21:37–44

32. Vernon JA, Meikle MB (2000) Tinnitus masking. In: Tinnitus Handbook. Tyler R, editor San Diego: Singular, Thomson Learning; pp 313–356

33. Henry JA, Schechter MA, Zaugg TL et al (2006) Outcomes of clinical trial: tinnitus masking vs. tinnitus retraining therapy. JAAA 17(2):104–132

34. Henry JA, Schechter MA, Zaugg TL et al (2006) Outcomes of clinical trial: tinnitus masking versus tinnitus retraining therapy. J Am Acad Audiol 17(2):104–132

35. Henry JA, Schechter MA, Zaugg TL et al (2006) Clinical trial to compare tinnitus masking and tinnitus retraining therapy. Acta Otolaryngol Suppl 556:64–69

36. De Ridder D, De MG, Verstraeten E et al (2006) Primary and secondary auditory cortex stimulation for intractable tinnitus. ORL J Otorhinolaryngol Relat Spec 68(1):48–54

37. Rubinstein JT, Tyler RS, Johnson A, Brown CJ (2003) Electrical suppression of tinnitus with high-rate pulse trains. Otol Neurotol 24(3):478–485

38. Dauman R (2000) Electrical stimulation for tinnitus supression. In: Tinnitus handbook. Tyler R, editor San Diego: Singular, Thomson Learning; pp 377–398

39. Dobie RA (1999) A review of randomized clinical trials in tinnitus. Laryngoscope 109(8):1202–1211

40. Rossi S, De CA, Ulivelli M et al (2007) Effects of repetitive transcranial magnetic stimulation on chronic tinnitus. A randomised, cross over, double blind, placebo-controlled study. J Neurol Neurosurg Psychiatry 78(8):857–863

41. Langguth B, Zowe M, Landgrebe M et al (2006) Transcranial magnetic stimulation for the treatment of tinnitus: a new coil positioning method and first results. Brain Topogr 18(4): 241–247

42. Langguth B, Hajak G, Kleinjung T, Pridmore S, Sand P, Eichhammer P (2006) Repetitive transcranial magnetic stimulation and chronic tinnitus. Acta Otolaryngol Suppl 556:102–104

43. Wilson PH (2006) Classical conditioning as the basis for the effective treatment of tinnitus-related distress. ORL J Otorhinolaryngol Relat Spec 68(1):6–11

44. Henry JL, Wilson PH (2001) Psychological management of chronic tinnitus: a cognitive-behavioral approach. Boston: Allyn & Bacon

45. Dobie RA (2004) Clinical trials and drug therapy for tinnitus. In: Snow JB (ed) Tinnitus: theory and management. BC Decker, Hamilton, London, pp 266–277

46. Dobie RA (1999) A review of randomized clinical trials in tinnitus. Laryngoscope 109(8):1202–1211

47. Jastreboff MM (2007) Sound therapies for tinnitus management. In: Tinnitus: pathophysiology and treatment. Langguth B, Hajak G, Kleinjung T, Cacace A, Møller A, editors Elsevier, Amsterdam, pp 449–454

48. Nickel AK, Hillecke T, Argstatter H, Bolay HV (2005) Outcome research in music therapy: a step on the long road to an evidence-based treatment. Ann N Y Acad Sci 1060: 283–293

49. Herraiz C, Diges I, Cobo P, Plaza G, Aparicio JM (2006) Auditory discrimination therapy (ADT) for tinnitus managment: preliminary results. Acta Otolaryngol Suppl 556:80–83

50. Davis P, Paki B, Hanley P (2007) Neuromonics tinnitus treatment: third clinical trail. Ear Hearing 28(2):242–259

51. Jastreboff PJ, Jastreboff MM (2009) The role of hearing aids in tinnitus management. In: Hearing aid book. Derebery J, Luxford W editors Plural Publishing, San Diego, CA, pp 119–131

52. Okamoto H, Stracke H, Stoll W, Pantev C (2010) Listening to tailor-made notched music reduces tinnitus loudness and tinnitus-related auditory cortex activity. Proc Natl Acad Sci U S A 107(3):1207–1210

53. Gerken GM (1996) Central tinnitus and lateral inhibition: an auditory brainstem model. Hearing Res 97:75–83

54. Jastreboff PJ (2000) Tinnitus Habituation Therapy (THT) and Tinnitus Retraining Therapy (TRT). In: Tinnitus Handbook. Tyler R, editor San Diego: Singular, Thomson Learning; pp 357–376

55. Tinnitus (2009) In: Encyclopedia of neuroscience. Squire LR, editor Oxford Academic Press, pp 1001–1008

56. Okamoto H, Stracke H, Stoll W, Pantev C (2010) Listening to tailor-made notched music reduces tinnitus loudness and tinnitus-related auditory cortex activity. Proc Natl Acad Sci U S A 107(3):1207–1210

57. Ito M, Soma K, Ando R (2009) Association between tinnitus retraining therapy and a tinnitus control instrument. Auris Nasus Larynx 36(5):536–540

58. Hatanaka A, Ariizumi Y, Kitamura K (2008) Pros and cons of tinnitus retraining therapy. Acta Otolaryngol 128(4): 365–368

59. Jastreboff PJ, Jastreboff MM (2009) The role of hearing aids in tinnitus management. In: Hearing aid book. Derebery J, Luxford W editors Plural Publishing, San Diego, CA, pp 119–131

60. Impedance fluctuation and a "Tensor Tympani Syndrome". 79 Sep 25; Lisbon: Universidad Nova de Lisboa Ed Penha & Pizarro; 1979, Ref ID: 8065

61. Henry JA, Jastreboff MM, Jastreboff PJ, Schechter MA, Fausti SA (2003) Guide to conducting tinnitus retraining therapy initial and follow-up interviews. J Rehabil Res Dev 40(2):157–177

62. Jastreboff MM, Jastreboff PJ (1999) Questionnaires for assessment of the patients and treatment outcome. In: Proceedings of the Sixth International Tinnitus Seminar, 1999, Cambridge, UK. Hazell JWP, editor London, UK: THC, pp 487–490

63. Newman CW, Sandridge SA, Jacobson GP (1998) Psychometric adequacy of the Tinnitus Handicap Inventory (THI) for evaluating treatment outcome. J Am Acad Audiol 9(2):153–160

64. Newman CW, Wharton JA, Jacobson GP (1995) Retest stability of the tinnitus handicap questionnaire. Ann Otol Rhinol Laryngol 104:718–723

65. Jastreboff PJ, Hazell JWP (1998) Treatment of tinnitus based on a neurophysiological model. In: Tinnitus: treatment and relief. Vernon J, editor Allyn & Bacon, pp 201–216

66. Jastreboff PJ (1999) Categories of the patients and the treatment outcome. In: Proceedings of the Sixth International Tinnitus Seminar, 1999, Cambridge, UK. Hazell JWP, editor London, UK: THC, pp 394–398

67. Jastreboff PJ, Jastreboff MM (2000) Potential impact of stochastic resonance on tinnitus and its treatment. Assoc Res Otolaryngol 23:5542

68. Jastreboff PJ, Jastreboff MM (2009) Tinnitus and decreased sound tolerance. In: Ballenger's Otorhinolaryngology Head and Neck Surgery. Ballenger JJ, Snow JB, Ashley WP, editors17 ed. San Diego: Singular Publishing, pp 351–362

69. Sheldrake JB, Jastreboff MM (2004) Role of hearing aids in management of tinnitus. In: Tinnitus: Theory and Management. Snow JB, editor Hamilton, London: BC Decker, pp 312–315

70. Nields JA, Fallon BA, Jastreboff PJ (1999) Carbamazepine in the treatment of Lyme disease-induced hyperacusi. J Neuropsychiatry Clin Neurosci 11(1):97–99

71. Jastreboff PJ, Gray WC, Gold SL (1996) Neurophysiological approach to tinnitus patients. Am J Otol 17:236–240

72. Jastreboff PJ, Jastreboff MM (2009) Tinnitus and decreased sound tolerance. In: Ballenger's Otorhinolaryngology Head and Neck Surgery. Ballenger JJ, Snow JB, Ashley WP, editors17 ed. San Diego: Singular Publishing, pp 351–362

73. McKinney CJ, Hazell JWP, Graham RL (1999) An evaluation of the TRT method. In: Proceedings of the Sixth International Tinnitus Seminar, 1999, Cambridge, UK. Hazell JWP, editor London, UK: THC, pp 99–105

74. Sheldrake JB, Hazell JWP, Graham RL (1999) Results of tinnitus retraining therapy. In: Proceedings of the Sixth International Tinnitus Seminar, 1999, Cambridge, UK. Hazell JWP, editor London, UK: THC, pp 292–296

75. Bartnik G, Fabijanska A, Rogowski M (2001) Effects of tinnitus retraining therapy (TRT) for patients with tinnitus and subjective hearing loss versus tinnitus only. Scand Audiol Suppl (52):206–208

76. Bartnik G, Fabijanska A, Rogowski M (1999) Our experience in treatment of patients with tinnitus and/or hyperacusis using the habituation method. In: Proceedings of the Sixth International Tinnitus Seminar, 1999, Cambridge, UK. Hazell JWP, editor London, UK: THC, pp 415–417

77. Heitzmann T, Rubio L, Cardenas MR, Zofio E (1999) The importance of continuity in TRT patients: Results at 18 months. In: Proceedings of the Sixth International Tinnitus Seminar, 1999, Cambridge, UK. Hazell JWP, editor London, UK: THC, pp 509–511

78. Mazurek B, Fischer F, Haupt H, Georgiewa P, Reisshauer A, Klapp BF (2006) A modified version of tinnitus retraining therapy: observing long-term outcome and predictors. Audiol Neurootol 11(5):276–286

79. Herraiz C, Larrea JL (2004) Implementation of habituation theory to pulsatile somato-sounds (tinnitus): the heart valve prosthesis sound model]. Acta Otorrinolaringol Esp 55(2):49–54

80. Mazurek B, Fischer F, Haupt H, Georgiewa P, Reisshauer A, Klapp BF (2006) A modified version of tinnitus retraining therapy: observing long-term outcome and predictors. Audiol Neurootol 11(5):276–286

81. Madeira G, Montmirail C, Decat M, Gersdorff M (2007) TRT: results after one year treatment. Rev Laryngol Otol Rhinol (Bord) 128(3):145–148

82. Hatanaka A, Ariizumi Y, Kitamura K (2008) Pros and cons of tinnitus retraining therapy. Acta Otolaryngol 128(4):365–368

83. Molini E, Faralli M, Calenti C, Ricci G, Longari F, Frenguelli A (2010) Personal experience with tinnitus retraining therapy. Eur Arch Otorhinolaryngol 267:51–56

84. Seydel C, Haupt H, Szczepek AJ, Klapp BF, Mazurek B (2010) Long-term improvement in tinnitus after modified tinnitus retraining therapy enhanced by a variety of psychological approaches. Audiol Neurootol 15(2):69–80

85. Herraiz C, Hernandez FJ, Plaza G, De los SG (2005) Long-term clinical trial of tinnitus retraining therapy. Otolaryngol Head Neck Surg 133(5):774–779

86. Proceedings of the Sixth International Tinnitus Seminar, 1999, Cambridge, UK. (1999) London, UK: THC

87. Baracca GN, Forti S, Crocetti A et al (2007) Results of TRT after eighteen months: our experience. Int J Audiol 46(5):217–222

88. Lux-Wellenhof G, Hellweg FC (2002) Longterm follow up study of TRT in Frankfurt. In: Proceedings of the Seventh International Tinnitus Seminar. Patuzzi R, editor Perth, Australia: The University of Western Australia, pp 277–279

89. Forti S, Costanzo S, Crocetti A, Pignataro L, Del BL, Ambrosetti U (2009) Are results of tinnitus retraining therapy maintained over time? 18-month follow-up after completion of therapy. Audiol Neurootol 14(5):286–289

90. Jastreboff PJ (1999) The neurophysiological model of tinnitus and hyperacusis. In: Proceedings of the Sixth International Tinnitus Seminar, 1999, Cambridge, UK. Hazell JWP, editor London, UK: THC, pp 32–38

91. Jastreboff PJ, Hazell JW, Graham RL (1994) Neurophysiological model of tinnitus: dependence of the minimal masking level on treatment outcome. Hear Res 80(2):216–232

92. Jastreboff PJ, Hazell JWP (1993) A neurophysiological approach to tinnitus: clinical implications. Br J Audiol 27:1–11

93. Heller MF, Bergman M (1953) Tinnitus in normally hearing persons. Ann Otol 62:73–93

94. Tucker DA, Phillips SL, Ruth RA, Clayton WA, Royster E, Todd AD (2005) The effect of silence on tinnitus perception. Otolaryngol Head Neck Surg 132(1):20–24

95. Del BL, Forti S, Ambrosetti U et al (2008) Tinnitus aurium in persons with normal hearing: 55 years later. Otolaryngol Head Neck Surg 139(3):391–394

96. Eggermont JJ (2006) Cortical tonotopic map reorganization and its implications for treatment of tinnitus. Acta Otolaryngol Suppl (556):9–12

97. Norena AJ, Eggermont JJ (2006) Enriched acoustic environment after noise trauma abolishes neural signs of tinnitus. Neuroreport 17(6):559–563

98. Hamernik RP, Qiu W, Davis B (2003) Cochlear toughening, protection, and potentiation of noise-induced trauma by non-Gaussian noise. J Acoust Soc Am 113(2):969–976

99. Niu X, Tahera Y, Canlon B (2004) Protection against acoustic trauma by forward and backward sound conditioning. Audiol Neurootol 9(5):265–273

100. Niu X, Canlon B (2002) Protective mechanisms of sound conditioning. Adv Otorhinolaryngol 59:96–105

Chapter 74
Sound Stimulation

Luca Del Bo, Giovanna Baracca, Stella Forti, and Arnaud Norena

Keypoints

1. There is considerable evidence that many forms of tinnitus are caused by central changes that may occur after peripheral lesions.
2. Auditory stimulation is one of the most employed therapeutic methods for tinnitus, and one of the most beneficial.
3. Sound generators that emulate environmental sounds are small devices that allow a person to select the favorite kind of sound at the most comfortable volume.
4. Custom sound generators, for normal hearing persons, are similar to hearing aids, very light, and to be worn behind the ear. They generate a wide-band sound that can be adjusted to the user's needs.
5. Hearing aids designed for people with tinnitus and hearing loss provide amplification that facilitates auditory stimulation to ameliorate tinnitus.
6. Implantable hearing aids are now used by many people, which made it possible to assess their efficacy in tinnitus treatment.
7. Other devices can be used for tinnitus management for immediate relief before a more complete sound therapy can be initiated.
8. Prosthesis and "open-ear" hearing aids are preferred for treatment of tinnitus. These devices provide amplification in narrow frequency bands which can be adjusted to coincide with the frequencies of the patient's hearing loss.
9. Sound stimulation has its beneficial effect on most forms of tinnitus by activating neural plasticity, which requires time to develop. The time it takes for sound stimulation to reduce an individual's tinnitus varies and may require a 6- to 8-month time frame.
10. The selection of hearing aids must be tailored to individual patients, based on the patient's clinical picture.
11. The specific guidelines on hearing aid device adaptation are crucial for an effective auditory stimulation of tinnitus-affected patients.

Keywords Tinnitus • Hearing aid • Sound enrichment • Hearing loss • Auditory stimulation

Abbreviations

Combi	Combination hearing aid
dB	Decibel
Hz	Hertz
SA	Spontaneous activity
TRT	Tinnitus retraining therapy

Introduction

Effective treatment of tinnitus depends on understanding the cause of tinnitus. Especially regarding treatment with sound, it is important to know if tinnitus is caused by pathology of the ear or the auditory nervous system.

The past years have witnessed a change in the understanding of the cause of tinnitus. Previously, tinnitus was believed to originate from the peripheral auditory

L.D. Bo (✉)
Audiology Unit, Fondazione IRCCS Ospedale Policlinico, Fondazione Ascolta e Vivi, Mangiagalli e Regina Elena, Milan, Milano, Italy
e-mail: delbo@sordita.it

system [1, 2]. There is now considerable evidence that most forms of tinnitus are caused by changes in the central nervous system after peripheral lesions [3, 4]. For treatment of tinnitus, it is important to distinguish between these two models, as they imply different therapeutic strategies. In fact, the peripheral model suggests that the aberrant neural activity is responsible for tinnitus perception. This hypothesis has been inspired by the results of an animal study [5], by showing an increase in the spontaneous activity (SA) in the cochlear nerve after the administration of a high dose of salicylate (400 mg/kg in cats) assumed to cause tinnitus. A recent study [6] has shown that salicylate-induced tinnitus may be caused by activation of NMDA receptors expressed in the synapses of cochlear hair cells and dendrites of spiral ganglion neurons. If tinnitus was normally caused by increased activation of NMDA receptors, a possible therapeutic approach that could suppress such "peripheral tinnitus" would be inactivating NMDA receptors [6, 7]. However, NMDA receptor blockage has not been shown as effective treatment of tinnitus.

High doses of salicylate are also known to cause nonspecific (toxic) effects, especially in cats, which lack the enzyme necessary to metabolize salicylate (glucuronyltransferase). Such nonspecific effects could account for the increase in SA in the cochlear nerve after the administration of high doses of salicylate (see above). More recent studies have shown that salicylate, at a dose of approximately 200 mg/kg, known to induce tinnitus in animals [8], does not increase SA in the cochlear nerve [9, 10], but increases neural activity in auditory centers [11–13]. These studies then question the peripheral origin of salicylate-induced tinnitus. It is also worth noting that recent studies suggest that salicylate has strong effects on the central auditory nervous system [14–17]. These findings indicate that salicylate may induce tinnitus through central mechanisms.

The most frequent causes of tinnitus seem to be cochlear damage, as almost all individuals with tinnitus have hearing loss. Importantly, cochlear damages – induced after noise trauma, for instance – cause a dramatic decrease of SA in the cochlear nerve [18, 19]. Damages to the inner hair cells (or their stereocils) have been shown to decrease the spontaneous release of glutamate from the inner hair cells (cochlear nerve synapses), thereby causing the decrease in SA. This strongly argues against a peripheral origin of tinnitus encountered in human subjects (related to peripheral damages). If the neural activity is decreased in the cochlear nerve, there should be a kind of compensatory mechanism, which could generate an aberrant neural activity in the auditory centers. In this context, it has been shown that cochlear damage decreases the inhibitory neurotransmission in the auditory centers [20–23]. This decrease in central inhibition is supposed to account for the changes in the evoked and SA after cochlear damage. First, hearing loss of a sufficient extent induces a reorganization of the tonotopic map, i.e., neurons with their characteristic frequency corresponding to the hearing loss region change their frequency tuning toward the cut-off frequency of hearing loss [24, 25]. In addition, a strong neural hyperactivity has been observed in the auditory cortex after a noise trauma [26]. This hyperactivity could be a neural correlate of hyperacusis, i.e., overestimation of loudness, sometimes reported by subjects presenting a hearing loss. Finally, changes in the pattern of spontaneous discharge (increase in firing rate and synchrony), consistent with the psychoacoustic properties of tinnitus [4], have been observed after acoustic trauma [3, 27]. These neural changes of the SA could then be neural correlates of tinnitus.

Rationale for Stimulating the Frequency Range of Hearing Loss: Reversing Central Changes Induced by a Decrease in Afferent Inputs

In summary, the decrease in afferent input caused by peripheral lesions could trigger dramatic central changes, such as a release from central inhibition. These central changes could ultimately result in the emergence of an aberrant neural activity that could induce tinnitus. In this context, we have suggested an approach consisting of preventing/compensating the decrease in afferent input related to hearing loss. This could reverse the central changes normally associated to it and, as a consequence, decrease/suppress tinnitus [3, 4, 28, 29]. The aim of this approach is to normalize the SA over frequency (in patients with high-frequency hearing loss, the approach consists of increasing sensory inputs in this frequency band) and/ or increase the overall level of sensory input (in patients with flat and severe hearing loss). Central inhibition could control a kind of central gain [28, 30], increasing central inhibition, by providing the auditory system with augmented input that is supposed to decrease neural hyperactivity induced after hearing loss. In animals, we have shown that an acoustic environment enriched in high frequencies could prevent the central changes normally induced after a noise-induced hearing loss [24, 31]. Moreover, we could induce a dramatic decrease of hypersensitivity in human subjects reporting hyperacusis, after these subjects were stimulated a few hours a day for several weeks with a customized stimulus (the long-term spectrum of the stimulus corresponded to the hearing loss of each subject [28]).

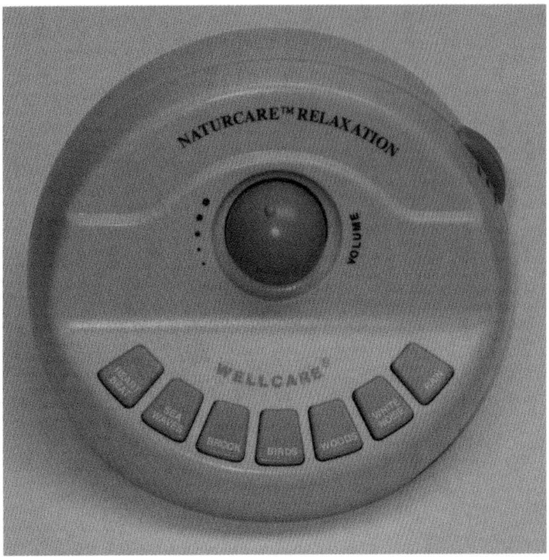

Fig. 74.1 Environmental sound generators used in sound therapy

Auditory Stimulation Delivery

Auditory stimulation is one of the most employed therapeutic methods and one of the most beneficial for patients suffering from tinnitus [32] (see also Chap. 75). Such therapy has no noticeable side effects and may be administered through simple devices [33]. Sounds used may resemble environment sounds, which enrich the atmosphere in the room they are used. In case sound enrichment should be required all day long (and tinnitus is not associated to hearing loss), "custom" ear level sound generators may be suitable. These are small electronic devices fitted to the ear. For individuals with hearing loss, open-ear hearing aids are suitable [34, 35], as well as tinnitus control combination instruments (Combi), which combine a prosthesis and a sound generator. These devices both amplify environmental sounds and generate sound enrichment.

Sound Environment Generators

Sound environment generators are contained in a small case, in which batteries and speakers are also housed. The volume can be regulated by means of a small roller on the side of the device. Different buttons may be pushed to select different sounds such as sea waves, creeks, waterfalls, rain, the woodlands, and white noise. For most users, these sounds are relaxing, as they are monotonous and repetitive without interruption. Once a given sound has been selected and the volume has been regulated, the user can use the environmental sound as background noise. For this reason, such sound generators are particularly useful during night rest (Fig. 74.1).

Custom Sound Generators

Custom sound generators look like regular hearing aids; they are light and designed to be worn behind the ear. A thin wire connects the generator to the speaker placed at the entrance of the ear canal.

Unlike the sound generated by environmental sound machines, the sound generated by custom sound generators can only be heard by the person wearing the device. These devices generate a wide band sound that can be adjusted by the audiologist to meet the final user's needs by means of high-pass or low-pass filters and may even be modulated in width.

The size of the mini speaker placed at the entrance of the auditory canal is such that it does not affect normal hearing. Custom sound generators are beneficial for individuals with normal hearing.

The small size of these sound generators makes them easy to wear during everyday activity. Once they have been worn and the volume regulated, the person may

Fig. 74.2 Real size of a custom sound generator or a combi hearing aid used in sound therapy

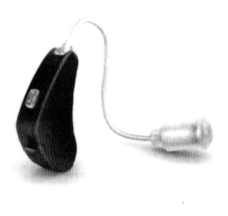
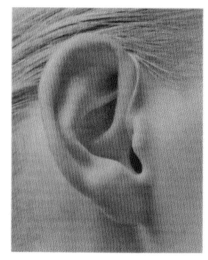

"forget" they are wearing them for the rest of the day. Their maintenance is limited to periodically replacing the battery which can be done by the user. Custom sound generators are both useful for total masking therapy [36] and for partial masking therapy, according to tinnitus retraining therapy (TRT) [37] (Fig. 74.2).

Hearing Aid Devices

The most suitable hearing aids for sound therapy are the open-ear hearing aids [38, 39], which have a mini speaker placed at the entrance of the ear canal. The size of the small case housing the battery resembles that of a bean. Like the custom sound generators, their ease is such that wearers often do not even feel them.

Hearing aids are designed to compensate for hearing loss and lack of auditory stimulation. Unfortunately, hearing aids currently available are not able to amplify sounds with a frequency above 6–7 kHz, a range of hearing that is often impaired in individuals with tinnitus; for this reason, ordinary hearing aids may be less efficient in compensating for lost auditory stimulation. Besides hearing aids, the new generation Combi (combination hearing aids) now available, combine common prostheses with the ability to generate an enrichment sound, similar to what custom sound generators provide. The Combi devices represent the most innovative and efficient therapeutic tools for tinnitus and hearing loss, because they can combine auditory stimulation in impaired hearing areas with either partial or total tinnitus masking [40, 41].

Implantable Hearing Aids

Traditional acoustic prostheses and Combi hearing aids are not generally recommended for patients with conductive hearing loss caused by external and middle-ear malformations or in patients with chronic middle-ear infection. Such individuals may benefit from the bone-anchored hearing aids, which transmit sound vibrations to the inner ear through a titanium rod implanted into the bone. The increase in use of implantable hearing aids during recent years has made it possible to assess their efficacy for treatment of tinnitus. Implantable middle-ear prostheses provide better sound therapy for some patients with tinnitus than traditional hearing aids [42], probably because they provide amplification in a wider frequency range and because of the "naturalness of the amplification". The cost, as well as the required surgery, limits the use of these devices. Cochlear implants can provide input to the auditory nervous system that can reduce tinnitus in many individuals, both in those with severe hearing loss and in individuals with good hearing on one ear who have severe tinnitus referred to that side [43] (see also Chaps. 76 and 77).

Other Sound Therapy Devices

Besides sound generators and acoustic prostheses, other devices that are not specifically designed for treatment of tinnitus can be used for tinnitus management. In fact, a simple fan or fish tank can be used as first-aid treatment of tinnitus. Music players, such as MP3 players with headphones, are often employed to reduce tinnitus. Recorded nature sounds played through home stereo systems are used for this purpose as well.

Can such devices replace custom sound generators or acoustic prostheses? We do not believe they can for the following reasons: MP3 players and headphones can hardly be worn by individuals carrying out nonsedentary activities; they partially occlude the ear; and they may become intrusive and cannot be worn (and forgotten) for 6–8 h a day. Conversely, these devices may be useful for immediate relief before a more complete sound therapy is started.

Auditory Stimulation from Theory to Practice

Clinical studies [29, 34, 35] have shown that not only do hearing aids improve hearing ability, but they can also reduce or suppress tinnitus.

For instance, in a study carried out in 1999 [44], 50% of hearing aid wearers experienced relief from tinnitus, with a median improvement of 10% after only 6 weeks from the first application. These results were confirmed by subsequent studies, which extended the investigation to individuals who had tinnitus and mild hearing loss [34, 45].

Prosthesis and open-ear hearing aids are important for proper treatment of tinnitus. Modern hearing aids can provide amplification at the frequencies where hearing loss occurs, without uncomfortable side effects, such as over amplification or rumbling, which were typical in the old generation devices.

Individuals with hearing loss that is limited to mild damage of hair cells not affecting the subjective hearing sensitivity benefit from custom sound generators or sound environment generators [46]. Our experience from daily clinical practice, as well as the experience of others reported in published studies [47], has shown that hearing aids and sound generators can achieve the following goals:

- Making patients with mild hearing loss less aware of tinnitus or masking it.
- Favoring the ability to listen to tinnitus according to Jastreboff's neurophysiologic hypothesis.

- Improving communication and reducing the discomfort often reported by patients as sounds and voices covered by tinnitus.
- Stimulating the auditory nervous system in a normal way and not only with tinnitus (phantom sounds).

The Approach to Sound Therapy

The role of the therapist should not be limited to the technical aspects of hearing aids and their application, but should aim at developing an empathic and confident relationship with the individual patient. Only a comprehensive evaluation may allow the therapist to have an accurate picture, in order to tailor the most appropriate and effective therapeutic plan. Hearing device application and control for adaptation may require a series of scheduled visits every 3–4 months, although in some cases a stricter follow-up schedule may be necessary. The results of long-term treatment may be assessed through visual analog questionnaires and the use of different kinds of scales [37] to allow tracking treatment progress. Audiometric test results do not usually reflect variations in tinnitus and thus, are not valid measures of relief [48]; tests, therefore, do not need to be periodically repeated. Cerebral plasticity requires some time to develop, and the needed duration of therapy may, therefore, vary from patient to patient [49]. Optimal relief from tinnitus may require a 6- to 8-month therapy using hearing aids and sound generators [50, 51].

Hearing Aid Selection

The selection of the most appropriate hearing aid device should be based on the individual patient's needs. For example, sound environment generators are mostly indicated during night rest in patients affected by mild tinnitus. However, patients with disturbing tinnitus and without subjective hearing impairments benefit from custom sound generators, which should be worn at least 8 h during the daytime, in combination with an environment generator during night rest. Combi-type devices are suitable for patients with mild hearing loss. These can also provide environmental sound enrichment during night rest.

Hearing Aid Device Adaptation

In order to achieve an optimal auditory stimulation, specific guidelines on hearing aid device adaptation should be followed, for custom sound generators, Combi devices, or prostheses [29, 34]. The parameters are crucial for auditory stimulation achieving maximal benefits on tinnitus.

The best results are achieved when the external auditory canal is left as accessible as possible. In fact, even partial occlusion of the auditory canal may cause unease of use and may even increase tinnitus perception. It may also affect the natural acoustic properties of the external ear, with further negative side effects causing a loss of the natural acoustic resonance, which is important for naturalness of hearing. Occlusion of the ear canal also causes over-emphasis of low frequencies with rumbling sensations resulting together with diminished perception of sound in the most important frequency range of hearing. It is also important not to underestimate the hearing of one's own voice which often causes difficulties in the understanding of speech, as well as being unpleasant for the individual and may cause a sensation of "closure" that can worsen tinnitus. The introduction of the so-called open-ear hearing aids helped overcome some of these problems, allowing application of hearing aids to individuals with mild hearing loss, such as many individuals with tinnitus have. Open-ear hearing aids also provide a stimulation mainly in the frequency region of the tinnitus pitch. The open-ear hearing aids, thus, provide important advantages, such as sound enrichment, that reduce tinnitus by activating the neural plasticity. Open-ear prostheses can also be employed in patients with severe hearing loss; acoustic feedback is reduced (or eliminated) by computer programs in modern digital hearing aids. Hearing naturalness and ease of use are important factors or advantages of digital hearing aids. In the selection of hearing aids, all elements that can cause a patient's discomfort and increase the perception of tinnitus must be taken into account, including cosmetic aspects. Hearing aids and sound generators should ideally be forgotten after they have been applied. In other words, people should become unaware of wearing a hearing aid device.

Hearing aid devices should simultaneously be worn in both ears, in order to favor a complete and simultaneous stimulation of the entire auditory nervous system. This is also important for unilateral tinnitus. Moreover, the frequency band of hearing aids should be adjusted to mostly amplifying the frequency range that is most important for hearing. Sound generators should be adjusted to the frequency of the tinnitus in order to activate the auditory nerve close to tinnitus frequency.

Our clinical experience supports the use of prescription formulas of gain/output suggested by device manufacturers, although major modifications are very often necessary. In fact, many tinnitus patients are sensitive to amplification, which sometimes requires less gain and maximum output than in patients who do not have tinnitus. Patients with moderate to severe hearing loss often benefit from amplifications that are 50–70% lower than traditional prescription formulas. The large variability of the requirements for tinnitus patients regarding amplification has prevented adaptation of an uniform formula that is suitable for all tinnitus patients. Individuals with tinnitus often benefit from having the option of noise reduction switched off or turned down.

Patients must be properly instructed in how to adjust the volume on their devices. Patients are generally able to fully understand the volume regulation procedure and to safely carry it out, but often more than one round of counseling is necessary and analog scales should be used to track the intensity of both tinnitus and therapeutic sound. During TRT therapy, the correct balance between sound stimulation and amplification can be determined with in situ instruments after some weeks of use [52]. The intensity of auditory stimulation should be 5–6 dB higher than the threshold level in order to prevent stochastic resonance phenomena [37].

Optimal results in management of tinnitus are not only obtained with the application of technologically advanced hearing aid devices but, most of all, with their adjustment to the individual person's needs and through patient counseling. Each single patient must be listened to, counseled, and informed throughout therapy planning and during follow-up. This enables therapists to fully understand their patient's problems and to solve them to the greatest extent through a proper selection of prosthetic devices and finding the optimal settings.

References

1. Tonndorf J (1987) The analogy between tinnitus and pain: a suggestion for a physiological basis of chronic tinnitus. Hear Res 28:271–5.
2. Jastreboff PJ (1990) Phantom auditory perception (tinnitus): mechanisms of generation and perception. Neurosci Res 8:221–54.

3. Norena AJ and JJ Eggermont (2003) Changes in spontaneous neural activity immediately after an acoustic trauma: implications for neural correlates of tinnitus. Hear Res 183:137–53.

4. Norena A, C Micheyl, S Chery-Croze et al (2002) Psychoacoustic characterization of the tinnitus spectrum: implications for the underlying mechanisms of tinnitus. Audiol Neurootol 7:358–69.

5. Evans EF and TA Borerwe (1982) Ototoxic effects of salicylates on the responses of single cochlear nerve fibres and on cochlear potentials. Br J Audiol 16:101–8.

6. Puel JL, J Ruel, M Guitton et al (2002) The inner hair cell synaptic complex: physiology, pharmacology and new therapeutic strategies. Audiol Neurootol 7:49–54.

7. Puel JL (2007) Cochlear NMDA receptor blockade prevents salicylate-induced tinnitus. B-Ent 3 Suppl 7:19–22.

8. Jastreboff PJ and CT Sasaki (1994) An animal model of tinnitus: a decade of development. Am J Otol 15:19–27.

9. Stypulkowski PH (1990) Mechanisms of salicylate ototoxicity. Hear Res 46:113–45.

10. Muller M, R Klinke, W Arnold et al (2003) Auditory nerve fibre responses to salicylate revisited. Hear Res 183:37–43.

11. Chen GD and PJ Jastreboff (1995) Salicylate-induced abnormal activity in the inferior colliculus of rats. Hear Res 82:158–78.

12. Ochi K and JJ Eggermont (1996) Effects of salicylate on neural activity in cat primary auditory cortex. Hear Res 95:63–76.

13. Jastreboff PJ and CT Sasaki (1986) Salicylate-induced changes in spontaneous activity of single units in the inferior colliculus of the guinea pig. J Acoust Soc Am 80:1384–91.

14. Bauer CA, TJ Brozoski, TM Holder et al (2000) Effects of chronic salicylate on GABAergic activity in rat inferior colliculus. Hear Res 147:175–82.

15. Wang HT, B Luo, KQ Zhou et al (2006) Sodium salicylate reduces inhibitory postsynaptic currents in neurons of rat auditory cortex. Hear Res 215:77–83.

16. Sun W, J Lu, D Stolzberg et al (2009) Salicylate increases the gain of the central auditory system. Neuroscience 159:325–34.

17. Su YY, B Luo, HT Wang et al (2009) Differential effects of sodium salicylate on current-evoked firing of pyramidal neurons and fast-spiking interneurons in slices of rat auditory cortex. Hear Res 253:60–6.

18. Liberman MC and LW Dodds (1984) Single-neuron labeling and chronic cochlear pathology. III. Stereocilia damage and alterations of threshold tuning curves. Hear Res 16:55-74.

19. Liberman MC and LW Dodds (1984) Single-neuron labeling and chronic cochlear pathology. II. Stereocilia damage and alterations of spontaneous discharge rates. Hear Res 16:43–53.

20. Milbrandt JC, TM Holder, MC Wilson et al (2000) GAD levels and muscimol binding in rat inferior colliculus following acoustic trauma. Hear Res 147:251–60.

21. Argence M, I Saez, R Sassu et al (2006) Modulation of inhibitory and excitatory synaptic transmission in rat inferior colliculus after unilateral cochleectomy: an in situ and immunofluorescence study. Neuroscience 141:1193–207.

22. Kotak VC, S Fujisawa, FA Lee et al (2005) Hearing loss raises excitability in the auditory cortex. J Neurosci 25: 3908–18.

23. Dong S, WH Mulders, J Rodger et al (2009) Changes in neuronal activity and gene expression in guinea-pig auditory brainstem after unilateral partial hearing loss. Neuroscience 159:1164–74.

24. Norena AJ and JJ Eggermont (2005) Enriched acoustic environment after noise trauma reduces hearing loss and prevents cortical map reorganization. J Neurosci 25:699–705.

25. Robertson D and DR Irvine (1989) Plasticity of frequency organization in auditory cortex of guinea pigs with partial unilateral deafness. J Comp Neurol 282:456–71.

26. Norena AJ, M Tomita and JJ Eggermont (2003) Neural changes in cat auditory cortex after a transient pure-tone trauma. J Neurophysiol 90:2387–401.

27. Mulders WH and D Robertson (2009) Hyperactivity in the auditory midbrain after acoustic trauma: dependence on cochlear activity. Neuroscience 164:733–46.

28. Norena AJ and S Chery-Croze (2007) Enriched acoustic environment rescales auditory sensitivity. Neuroreport 18:1251–5.

29. Moffat G, K Adjout, S Gallego et al (2009) Effects of hearing aid fitting on the perceptual characteristics of tinnitus. Hear Res 254:82–91.

30. Formby C, LP Sherlock and SL Gold, (2003) Adaptive recalibration of chronic auditory gain : interim findings, in Proceedings of the Seventh International Tinnitus Seminar, Perth, Australia : March 5th-9th, 2002, RB Patuzzi, Editor. 2003, Physiology Dept., University of Western Australia: Perth, Australia. 165–9.

31. Norena AJ and JJ Eggermont (2006) Enriched acoustic environment after noise trauma abolishes neural signs of tinnitus. Neuroreport 17:559–63.

32. Han BI, HW Lee, TY Kim et al (2009) Tinnitus: characteristics, causes, mechanisms, and treatments. J Clin Neurol 5:11–9.

33. Jastreboff PJ (2007) Tinnitus retraining therapy. Prog Brain Res 166:415–23.

34. Del Bo L and U Ambrosetti (2007) Hearing aids for the treatment of tinnitus. Prog Brain Res 166:341–5.

35. Trotter MI and I Donaldson (2008) Hearing aids and tinnitus therapy: a 25-year experience. J Laryngol Otol 122:1052–6.

36. Vernon JA and MB Meikle, (2000) Tinnitus masking, in Tinnitus handbook, RS Tyler, Editor. 2000, Singular Pub. Group: San Diego. 313–56.

37. Jastreboff PJ and JWP Hazell (2004) Tinnitus retraining therapy: implementing the neurophysiological model. Cambridge, U.K.: Cambridge University Press. 276.

38. Del Bo L, U Ambrosetti, M Bettinelli et al (2006) Using open-ear hearing aids in tinnitus therapy. Hear Rev 13:30–2.

39. Lantz J, OD Jensen, A Haastrup et al (2007) Real-ear measurement verification for open, non-occluding hearing instruments. Int J Audiol 46:11–6.

40. Carrabba L, G Coad, M Costantini et al. Combination open ear instrument for tinnitus sound treatment. in IXth International Tinnitus Seminars 2009. Sweden.

41. Van de Heyning P, K Vermeire, M Diebl et al (2008) Incapacitating unilateral tinnitus in single-sided deafness treated by cochlear implantation. Ann Otol Rhinol Laryngol 117:645–52.

42. Holgers KM and BE Hakansson (2002) Sound stimulation via bone conduction for tinnitus relief: a pilot study. Int J Audiol 41:293–300.

43. Baguley DM and MD Atlas (2007) Cochlear implants and tinnitus. Prog Brain Res 166:347–55.

44. Surr RK, JA Kolb, MT Cord et al (1999) Tinnitus Handicap Inventory (THI) as a hearing aid outcome measure. J Am Acad Audiol 10:489–95.

45. Folmer RL and JR Carroll (2006) Long-term effectiveness of ear-level devices for tinnitus. Otolaryngol Head Neck Surg 134:132–7.
46. Henry JA, TL Zaugg and MA Schechter (2005) Clinical guide for audiologic tinnitus management II: treatment. Am J Audiol 14:49–70.
47. Molini E, M Faralli, C Calenti et al (2009) Personal experience with tinnitus retraining therapy. Eur Arch Otorhinolaryngol. In press.
48. Forti S, S Costanzo, A Crocetti et al (2009) Are results of tinnitus retraining therapy maintained over time?. 18-month follow-up after completion of therapy. Audiol Neurootol 14:286–9.
49. Hatanaka A, Y Ariizumi and K Kitamura (2008) Pros and cons of tinnitus retraining therapy. Acta Otolaryngol 128: 365–8.
50. Baracca GN, S Forti, A Crocetti et al (2007) Results of TRT after eighteen months: Our experience. Int J Audiol 46: 217–22.
51. Sheldrake JB, JWP Hazell and RL Graham, (1999) Results of tinnitus retraining therapy, in Proceedings of the sixth International Tinnitus Seminar, Cambridge UK September 5th-9th 1999, J Hazell, Editor. 1999, Tinnitus and Hyperacusis Centre: London. 292–6.
52. Ito M, K Soma and R Ando (2009) Association between tinnitus retraining therapy and a tinnitus control instrument. Auris Nasus Larynx 36:536–40.

Chapter 75
Rehabilitation of Tinnitus Patients Using the Neuromonics Tinnitus Treatment

Dayse Távora-Vieira and Paul B. Davis

Keypoints

1. Tinnitus, a phantom perception of sound, is a frequent clinical condition that may cause significant debilitation.
2. Tinnitus treatments can focus on the condition itself or on patients' reaction to their tinnitus.
3. There is a growing acceptance that sound stimulation incites a neuroplastic change in the auditory pathways.
4. Neuromonics utilizes highly tailored music and broad frequency wave sounds, in the context of a structured counseling, support, and monitoring program, with the intention of reversing the neurological, psychological, and audiological processes that caused the disturbance.
5. Neuromonics also aims to facilitate a relaxation response and shift of attention, leading to a desensitization effect.
6. Clinical trial and private clinic outcomes show that the neuromonics tinnitus treatment can consistently provide clinically significant levels of desensitization to tinnitus perception over a relatively short period of time.

Keywords Neuromonics • Tinnitus • Hyperacusis • Desensitization • Acoustic stimulation

P.B. Davis (✉)
Department of Audiology, Nova Southeastern University,
Fort Lauderdale 33328-2709, FL, USA
and
Scientific Advisor to Neuromonics, Sydney, Australia
e-mail: pauldavi@nova.edu

Abbreviations

HL	Hearing level
LDL	Loudness discomfort levels
MML	Minimum masking levels
NTT	Neuromonics tinnitus treatment
RI	Residual inhibition
THQ	Tinnitus history questionnaire
TRQ	Tinnitus reaction questionnaire
TRT	Tinnitus retraining therapy

Introduction

Tyler [1] categorizes tinnitus treatment in two ways: one focused on tinnitus reduction or elimination (e.g., medications, electrical suppression) and the other focused on a patient's reaction to the condition. Current thinking on the underlying mechanism of tinnitus emphasizes changes in the auditory and neural systems that can be broadly related to the aspects of perception, attentional, and emotional reaction to tinnitus [1–4] (see Chap. 73). Recent animal studies have shown that tinnitus may be linked to cortical reorganization [5]. In addition, brain imaging studies have shown altered levels of activation in several areas of the brain in tinnitus sufferers. These areas include, for instance, the left temporal lobe (Brodman area 21 & 41), left hippocampus and posterior thalamic region [6], right middle frontal and right middle temporal gyri [7], amygdala, parahippocampal gyrus and hippocampus [8], inferior colliculus [9], subcallosal area [10], right inferior colliculus in the left hippocampus [11], and the Heschl's gyrus [12].

The neuromonics tinnitus treatment (NTT) is a structured tinnitus rehabilitation program consistent with these current models, incorporating structured

A.R. Møller et al. (eds.), *Textbook of Tinnitus*,
DOI 10.1007/978-1-60761-145-5_75, © Springer Science+Business Media, LLC 2011

counseling and individually customized broad frequency sounds including music for relaxation. The sounds are spectrally shaped to individually correct for each patient's hearing loss configuration and it aims to address the auditory deprivation element of tinnitus pathogenesis, providing most the broadest stimulation of the auditory pathways. The purpose is to decrease the limbic system/amygdala's involvement in the patient's perception and reaction to tinnitus, thus promoting relaxation and relief [13–16]. This chapter provides an overview of the underlying principles of NTT, describes the standard protocol, and outlines candidacy for NTT in the context of published clinical trial and private practice data. The importance of counseling and the main challenges faced by patients and clinicians will be discussed.

Theoretical Basis for Counseling and Sound Treatment

Most hypotheses about the pathology of tinnitus agree that the abnormal neural activity in the brain that is perceived as a sound is a result of neuroplastic processes (e.g., [17, 5]). There is a general agreement that the limbic system and autonomic nervous system are involved in generating the awareness and annoyance from tinnitus [1–3, 17, 18]. This can explain why an individual's reaction to tinnitus seems to be linked to the person's emotional state.

The cognitive and emotional reaction to tinnitus is the target for tinnitus treatment that uses counseling. Some commonly used forms of tinnitus treatment combine counseling with acoustic stimulation: tinnitus retraining therapy (Chap. 73) and a hearing aid program (Chap. 74) are among these approaches.

NTT is based on correcting the abnormal neural activity that causes tinnitus by inducing neural modification within areas of the brain related to audition, attention, and emotion [15]. NTT involves counseling and sound stimulation consisting of music and broad frequency sound (shower noise-like sound) [13–18].

A unique aspect of NTT is that the spectrum of the sound is individually modified to account for each patient's hearing loss; this enables the intensity to be set to a comfortably relaxing level. In a study of 35 patients, the average reduction in loudness of their tinnitus was 16.11 dB in a paired comparison between the

original source music and the corresponding customized music, which the patient had set to their minimum masking level (MML) [13]. The mean level of the source music was 72 dBA, which would make sleep onset and concentration difficult. The mean customized signal was 56 dB. This 16 dB difference is quite clinically significant when one recalls that 6 dB constitutes a perceptual halving of loudness. This ability to provide a high degree of relief at a comfortable level tends to greatly facilitate a sense of control over the tinnitus. As a result, it greatly reduces the significance of the tinnitus [15].

The purpose of the "shower noise", combined with music, is to restore normal activation of the auditory system that may have been deprived of stimulation due to hearing loss or other forms of auditory dysfunction. The rationale is this maximizes the efficiency of sound stimulation to induce a neuroplastic change in the auditory pathways [18]. This has been shown in numerous studies by the marked improvement over treatment in neuroplastic-mediated processes that are reflected by MML and loudness discomfort levels (LDL) [13, 14, 16].

Asymmetric hearing loss is compensated for to allow a balanced loudness perception. Consequently, a true stereo sound is afforded by the system's ability to phase-lock the left and right channels. Considerable peak compression is also applied to fit within the typically narrow dynamic ranges of those with disturbing tinnitus. Further details of the algorithms for the customization of the sound stimuli are described in Hanley and Davis [15].

If the tinnitus is considered to be important, it will become part of patients' consciousness and has been hypothesized to trigger a strong negative emotional reaction [19, 20]. In tinnitus retraining therapy (TRT), the use of noise was proposed because it may be considered "neutral" to the limbic system. Some patients may find noise to be unpleasant, thus possibly contributing to reasons why some patients have rejected the use of TRT [21, 22]. NTT uses relaxation music as the predominant signal in order to activate the limbic system with positive associations. The sound is presented within the context of a counseling program with a more collaborative, patient-centered orientation.

Music has long been recognized to provide a therapeutic effect and has been empirically used for facilitating a major relaxation response, a welcomed shift of attention [23]. Tyler [1] suggests the use of music

Fig. 75.1 Summary of how neuromonics tinnitus treatment addresses the various neurological aspects underlying the tinnitus, mechanism (reproduced from [15]). Reprinted by permission of SAGE Publications

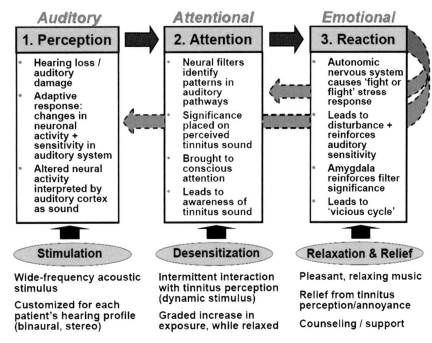

to provide distraction from tinnitus and notes that it has otherwise been highly underutilized. The use of music in NTT enables tinnitus sufferers to have a pleasant and relaxing sound to listen to while being treated. This approach facilitates patients' compliance to treatment and provides gradual desensitization to the tinnitus signal [13, 18].

In summary, NTT aims to facilitate the process of gradual desensitization of tinnitus disturbance. Together with a structured counseling program, NTT uses acoustic stimulation in a way that is effective, yet enjoyable (Fig. 75.1).

What follows is the standard NTT protocol aiming to assist clinicians in delivering the program to the most highly suitable "Tier 1" patients, who comprise around 43% of a typical tinnitus clinic population [16].

The NTT Protocol and Patient Selection

Based on clinical trials [13, 14] and outcomes of the treatment reported by private clinics [15], the most suitable candidates are as follows:

• Patients with four-frequency average hearing thresholds better than 50 dB in at least one ear
• Clinically significant tinnitus disturbance reported in the tinnitus reaction questionnaire with score of at least 17

• Normal or decreased sound tolerance
• Tinnitus is neither pulsatile nor multi-tone
• Tinnitus is not exacerbated by normal level of acoustic stimulation (i.e., not highly reactive)
• No active Ménière's disease or other causes of wide fluctuations in hearing levels
• Patient is well protected when exposed to a noisy environment.

Assessment

A comprehensive tinnitus history questionnaire (THQ) is mailed to the patient prior to his/her first visit to the clinic. The THQ involves data on the nature of the tinnitus, tinnitus history, general hearing difficulties, effect of tinnitus, and general patient's health. It helps the patient to recall all relevant factors and information relevant to the rehabilitation process. It also helps to determine the cause and influencing/exacerbating factors of the tinnitus and assess the patient's candidacy [18]. The patient also completes the tinnitus reaction questionnaire (TRQ). The score on the TRQ is used for counseling purposes, rehabilitation planning, and to monitor the patient's progress throughout treatment [13]. It has five response options that relate to the previous week of treatment, so it is more sensitive than most other tinnitus questionnaires [24].

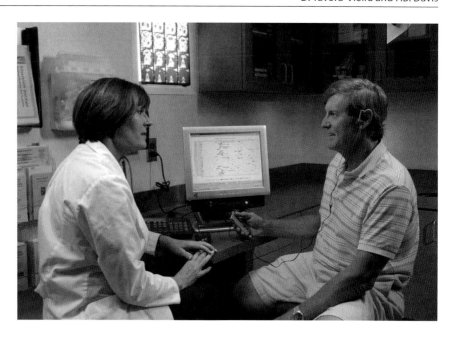

Fig. 75.2 Oasis neuromonics device

The following baseline audiological measures are obtained: tympanometry, but no acoustic reflexes in patients with decreased sound tolerance; pure-tone audiometry up to at least 12.5 kHz; tinnitus pitch match; tinnitus loudness balance; MML; LDL at 0.5, 1, and 4 kHz; and residual inhibition (RI) (Fig. 75.2).

Practical Use of NTT

Prior to commencing the treatment, patients are taught how to manage the device (Fig. 75.2), and discussion on the realistic outcomes during the first phase and neural changes related to the desensitization process over the second phase is considered of high priority for NTT. A good understanding of tinnitus and the proposed treatment are likely to make the patient more compliant and positive about the therapy [1]. Patients are provided with take-home reading material about their assessment results, how NTT works, what to expect at each phase of the treatment, advice on factors that can exacerbate tinnitus perception, and a list of suggested activities that can be done while using the device. The first stage of NTT lasts for approximately 2 months after the fitting date. Patients are instructed to initially use the device for at least 2–4 h a day, and especially during the times that his/her tinnitus is the most disturbing. Patients are also instructed to set the

volume at the beginning of each session to a comfortable level that provides a high level of interaction with his/her tinnitus. The high level of interaction aims to increase the amount of neurostimulation (representing the deprived sounds at the auditory cortex) and to provide maximal relief and relaxation for the tinnitus sufferers. This approach would facilitate the desensitization process of the tinnitus signal at a later stage by enabling them to relax despite their tinnitus and overcome prior problems like concentration disturbance and sleep onset/maintenance [15]. As observed by the authors and other clinicians in private clinics, the patients' monitoring of their tinnitus is contra-productive, potentially delaying, or even stopping the benefit of the treatment. Therefore, patients are encouraged to undertake another quiet activity while using the customized device to avoid monitoring the music and consequently risk monitoring the tinnitus. The second phase of the treatment aims to gradually promote desensitization to the tinnitus signal as a more permanent effect. Patients are re-instructed to set the volume to a level that only covers up their tinnitus around half of the time. Hence, the patient will experience an intermittent interaction with their tinnitus, which happens during the intensity troughs of the music. This fleeting exposure to the tinnitus whilst in a relaxed state is intended to help the brain develop a capability of placing the tinnitus in the background. This phase usually lasts for approximately 4 months, and the progress is reviewed at weeks 16 and 24. The MML and LDL are measured again at 2, 4, and 6 months after beginning the program to evaluate the patient's progress. The TRQ is also re-administered and the patient needs to estimate how often they have been aware of (and also how often they have been disturbed by) their tinnitus over the past week. The measures are used to determine the current progress and link back toward the stage-specific pretreatment goals. The patient's response to the second stage of treatment is checked at the tenth week, as there are a few cases where the patient feels too anxious about not having the extra "shower sound" to fill in the quieter parts of the dynamic signal, and they can worry that their tinnitus is increasing. Few patients may benefit from extra time on phase one. For instance, recent data from the authors suggest that patients with higher levels of hearing loss or protected exposure to noise may benefit from a few extra weeks of high level of interaction [25].

The clinical trials have shown that once the systematic desensitization starts to occur, patients typically report that their tinnitus annoyance gradually decreases, and often their current data suggest improvement from their TRQ, their audiometric MML, LDL, and even their estimates of the percentage of time they are aware of their tinnitus (e.g., [16]). Desensitization is deemed to have occurred when the patient reports that they do not need the device to distract them from the tinnitus. That represents the end of the second stage. A few patients will occasionally use the device in certain situations that trigger their tinnitus, for instance, high levels of stress, noise exposure, middle-ear pathology. [18].

Once tinnitus is no longer a problem, the third phase begins. The patients are encouraged to use the device at least once a week to maintain their improvement because complete withdrawal from treatment may cause re-emergence of tinnitus or decreased sound tolerance. This is consistent with the notion that the subsequent lack of stimulation had caused the auditory deprivation process to reappear. Rebound has not been found to be a factor when patients have kept using their devices, suggesting that the constant tonotopic representation of the hearing loss-frequencies at the cortex has been successful at maintaining their gains [18].

The first step for adequate counseling is the patient's understanding of hearing and tinnitus mechanisms [1]. Patient should be aware of the factors or illnesses that influence on the habituation process. They should also be advised about specific habits and behaviors that can interfere with the treatment, such as diet, alcohol, excess caffeine intake, insufficient exercise, noise exposure, stress levels.

Motivation and realistic expectations are very important matters for tinnitus treatment, particularly in private practice. Clinicians need to certify that the patient acknowledges the success of the treatment demands their active participation in the rehabilitation program. A number of patients continue to find it hard to understand the difference between tinnitus and tinnitus consequences, and that the NTT can only work on consequences such as the level of awareness and disturbance. If inadequately prepared, patients can display significant decreases on their TRQ score and percentage of disturbance, but show disappointment because they still have tinnitus and often may need revisiting if the patients begin to "move the goalposts".

Special Considerations

Based on clinical outcomes for the first 400 patients treated with NTT [16], patients are assigned to one of three categories: Tier 1 candidacy includes the most suitable patients for NTT; Tier 2 suitability includes patients with TRQ score of less than 17, high psychological disturbance, and four-frequency average hearing thresholds worse than 50 dB; and Tier 3 suitability includes patients with reactive, pulsatile or multi-tone tinnitus, ongoing noise exposure, Ménière's disease, or hearing loss greater than 50 dB in both ears. The standard (Tier 1) patient group represents the largest cohort in NTT populations found in regular private practice (48%); Tier 2 represents 37% and Tier 3 represents 15%. Whilst Tiers 2 and 3 can still be treated with NTT, they need to understand and acknowledge that their progress may be slower and more modest than usual [16].

Patients with very decreased sound tolerance (mean LDLs < 85 dBHL) are common, comprising 66% of participants in Trial 3 [13]. These patients were found to respond consistently well to NTT, with a > 5 dB improvement in LDLs found in 85% of those patients using the two-stage stimuli (mean change was 11 dB). A hyperacusis protocol has been subsequently formulated [26] (neuromonics, ND). This hyperacusis protocol constitutes a variation on the usual protocol. They are not encouraged to strive for a high level of interaction in the first phase, but instead just keep it as high as it can be whilst remaining comfortable. In case of history of even every day sounds making their tinnitus flare up, they should begin on the second phase of treatment immediately, again emphasizing comfort in setting the device intensity levels.

Patients with significant hearing loss across the speech range should be considered for hearing aid fitting in conjunction with NTT, but only if the patients have sufficient dynamic range to make the hearing aids tolerable (see Chap. 74). Many hearing impaired patients have tried or are wearing hearing aids, but report that tinnitus is most disturbing during quiet times, mainly when trying to sleep at night [26]. Some may find difficult to tolerate amplified sounds. These patients have found that NTT can improve their LDLs and reduce their reactivity, so that they become progressively better candidates for amplification [16].

Patients with high levels of hearing loss are likely to need to be kept in phase one of the treatment longer, as they can progress slower. They should be advised to wear the treatment for longer each day, and that the full program will also be extended for a longer period of time [25].

Patients with unilateral severe to profound hearing loss and those with asymmetric hearing loss (difference greater than 45 dB between the ears) are still considered candidates for NTT, applying a variation of the standard protocol with contra-lateral stimulation, which has been found to be effective in a cohort of 40 participants with severe unilateral hearing loss [27]. The thresholds of the better ear are used to customize the device, and the stimulation is provided only in that ear.

Patients with a level of tinnitus disturbance that is not having a significant effect on their quality of life (TRQ composite score less than 17) [24] have been found to be poor responders to NTT [16], perhaps because there is little central gain to reduce. These patients are more likely to benefit from counseling and an educational training. The clinician should provide information on the hearing and tinnitus mechanism and offer a follow-up appointment if the patient feels it is needed. Patients can still be good candidates for NTT when they have low TRQ, but a high level of specific distress (e.g., major concentration disturbance). As the TRQ is more relevant to tinnitus than hyperacusis, when the hyperacusis is the main problem, the TRQ can be low. However, these patients are in great need of treatment and are usually excellent NTT candidates.

Finally, patients pursuing compensation related to his/her tinnitus are encouraged to complete the case prior to treatment, given their responses have been found to be reduced and far less consistent [28]. The stress of the legal process and the continual reminders of the significance tends to be very counterproductive to a desensitization program such as neuromonics. However, if they are prepared to pay for the program themselves, it may be an indication that they may have enough intrinsic motivation to start sooner (see also Chap. 70).

Clinical Trials

NTT has been the subject of three major clinical trials. The first clinical trial strongly supported the idea that customization of music according to a patient's hearing profile is clinically more effective in tinnitus masking than customized noise [29]. The second clinical trial was a randomized controlled study of 50 tinnitus patients [14]. The exclusion criteria for this study were severe hearing loss in the better ear (four-frequency average hearing threshold greater than 70 dB), tinnitus-related compensation claim, ongoing noise exposure, major psychological disturbance (such as depression or psychosis), cognitive impairment, TRQ score of less than 17, and another simultaneous tinnitus treatment.

The second clinical trial compared clinical outcomes obtained with NTT, counseling alone, and counseling plus broadband noise set at the TRT mixing point. All groups had equal amounts of clinician time, and the in-depth counseling was reinforced by use of the self-help book, "Living with Tinnitus" [30]. Patients were evaluated at 3, 6, and 12 months after commencing treatment. They were asked to report their current tinnitus disturbance using TRQ. After 6 months of treatment, the results demonstrated that NTT was significantly more effective in improving tinnitus symptoms than the two reference groups. Patients receiving NTT presented a mean TRQ improvement of 66%, compared with mean of 22% for patients receiving noise plus counseling, and a mean of 15% for those receiving only counseling [14]. By 12 months, the mean gains of the neuromonics group had improved significantly more, but not for the other two groups. In terms of mechanisms, the study demonstrated that counseling was helpful (at a similar level to other studies), and the use of one-size-fits-all-type noise made a further improvement, but the highly tailored intermittent acoustic stimulation was far more effective. In terms of consistency of response, the proportion of patients who had a clinically significant improvement (TRQ improvement > 40%) was 86% of the neuromonics group, 47% of the noise and counseling group, and 23% of the counseling alone group.

The third clinical trial included 35 individuals with clinically significant tinnitus distress [13]. Participants were randomly allocated into two groups: the first group, called the one-stage group, received intermittent tinnitus interaction throughout the 6-months program, while the second group, or two-stage group, received high interaction for 2 months. Then it moved to intermittent interaction for the last 4 months. Both groups had the same structured support program and followed the suitability criteria discussed earlier in this chapter.

All the audiometric and psychometric measures were performed at pretreatment, 2, 4, and 6 months after commencing the program. The results suggested that patients from both groups improved significantly, both statistically and clinically. At the conclusion of the 6-month program, the TRQ scores showed that 91% of the participants displayed an improvement of their tinnitus disturbance greater than 40%, with a mean improvement of 65%. The two-stage group was found to have a faster response to treatment. In a questionnaire administered after 12 months of commencing the treatment, more than three-quarters of the patients reported that the treatment had provided relief and increased their general well-being by a moderate or large amount [13]. This Ear and Hearing article compared the neuromonics results to a similarly randomized and controlled trial of TRT and masking [31]. It found that at 6 months, the neuromonics group had a higher proportion of patients having a clinically significant response (91%) compared to the TRT group (29%); it took the TRT group 18 months to achieve a more comparable outcome of 74%. Similarly, the TRT group required 15 h of clinician time per patient, whilst the neuromonics group required less than half the total amount of clinician's time per patient.

A team of tinnitus specialists over eight centers across the US, led by the Cleveland clinic, has recently reported the 6-month post-therapy preliminary results of their study of the effectiveness of NTT [32]. Their dataset of 45 patients displayed clinically significant improvements of a very similar magnitude (88% of patients displayed this level of improvement of their tinnitus disturbance) to the prior Australian clinical trials and private practice results [16], and independently replicated those results. Another independent study reported on the long-term outcome of NTT [33]. The results of this report revealed that more than 85% of tinnitus patients treated with NTT sustained the full benefits of treatment 6–24 months after concluding the program.

Conclusion

Based on results from the clinical trials and outcomes showed by the private clinics, NTT can promote a major desensitization of tinnitus perception in a high proportion of patients. Among its advantages are that it is non-invasive, easy and pleasant to use, suitable for patients with a wide range of hearing and tinnitus characteristics, and it is not relatively time consuming for the clinician.

References

1. Tyler RS (2005) Neurophysiological models, psychological models, and treatment for tinnitus. In R Tyler (Ed), Tinnitus Treatments: Clinical Protocols. Thieme, New York: 1–22
2. Georgiewa P, Klapp BF, Fischer F (2006) An integrative model of developing tinnitus based on recent neurobiological findings. Medical Hypotheses; 66(3): 592–600
3. Kaltenbach JA (2006) The dorsal cochlear nucleus as a participant in the auditory, attentional and emotional components in tinnitus. Hearing Research; 216–217: 224–234
4. Møller A (2007) The role of neural plasticity in tinnitus. Progress in Brain Research; 166: 37–46
5. Eggermont JJ, Roberts LE (2004) The neuroscience of tinnitus. Trends in Neurosciences; 27: 676–682
6. Lockwood AH, Salvi RJ, Coad ML, Towsley ML, Wack DS, Murphy BW (1998) The functional neuroanatomy of tinnitus: Evidence for limbic system links and neural plasticity. Neurology 50(1): 114–120
7. Mirz F, Pedersen CB, Ishizu K, Johannsen P, Ovesen T, Stodkilde-Jorgensen H, Gjedde A (1999) Positron emission tomography of cortical centers of tinnitus. Hearing Research; 134: 133–144.
8. Mirz F, Gjedde A, Ishizu K, Brahe-Pedersen C (2000) Cortical networks subserving the perception of tinnitus – a PET study. Acta Otolaryngologica. Supplement 543: 241–243
9. Melcher JR, Sigalovsky IS, Guinan JJ, Levine RA (2000) Lateralized tinnitus studied with functional magnetic resonance imaging: Abnormal inferior colliculus activation. Journal of Neurophysiology 83(2): 1058–1072

10. Muhlau M, Rauschecker JP, Oestreicher E, Gaser C, Rottinger M, Wohlschlager AM, Simon F, Etgen T, Conrad B, Sander D (2006) Structural brain changes in tinnitus. Cerebral Cortex 16(9): 1283–1288

11. Landgrebe M, Langguth B, Rosengarth K, Braun S, Koch A, Kleinjung T, May A, de Ridder Dirk, Hajak G (2009) Structural brain changes in tinnitus: grey matter decrease in auditory and non-auditory brain areas. Neuroimage 46(1): 213–218

12. Schneider P, Andermann Ma, Wengenroth M, Goebel R, Flor H, Rupp A, Diesch E (2009) Reduced volume of Heschl's gyrus in tinnitus. Neuroimage 45(3): 927–939

13. Davis PB, Paki B, Hanley PJ (2007) The neuromonics tinnitus treatment: third clinical trial. Ear and Hearing; 28: 242–259

14. Davis PB, Wilde RA, Steed LG, Hanley PJ (2008) Treatment of tinnitus with a customized acoustic neural stimulus: A controlled clinical study. The ENT Journal; 87(6): 330–339

15. Hanley PJ, Davis PB (2008) Treatment of tinnitus with a customized, dynamic acoustic neural stimulus: underlying principles and clinical efficacy. Trends in Amplification; 12(3): 210–222

16. Hanley PJ, Davis PB, Paki B, Quinn SA, Bellekom SR (2008) Treatment of tinnitus with a customized, dynamic acoustic neural stimulus: clinical outcomes in general private practice annals of otology. Rhinology & Laryngology; 117(11): 791–799

17. Norena AJ, Eggernont J (2005) Enriched acoustic environment after noise trauma reduces hearing loss and prevents cortical map reorganization. The Journal of Neuroscience 25:699–705

18. Davis PB (2005) Music and the acoustic desensitization protocol for tinnitus. In R Tyler (Ed), Tinnitus Treatments. Thieme, New York: 146–160

19. Jastreboff PJ (2004) The neurophysiological model of tinnitus. In JB Snow (Ed), Tinnitus: Theory and Management. Decker, Ontario, BC: 96–107

20. Jastreboff PJ (1990) Phantom auditory perception (tinnitus): mechanisms of generation and perception. Neuroscience Research; 8: 221–254

21. Hiller W, Haerkötter C (2005) Does sound stimulation have additive effects on cognitive-behavioral treatment of chronic tinnitus? Behaviour Research and Therapy; 43: 595–612

22. Hatanaka A, Ariizumi Y, Kitamura, K (2008) Pros and cons of tinnitus retraining therapy. Acta Oto-Laryngologica; 128: 365–368

23. Yulis S, Brahm G, Jacard L, Picota E, Rutman F (1974) The extinction of phobic behaviour as a function of attention shifts. Behavior Research and Therapy; 13: 173–176

24. Wilson PH, Henry J, Bowen M, Haralambous G (1991) Tinnitus reaction questionnaire: Psychometric properties of a measure of distress associated with tinnitus. Journal of Speech and Hearing Research; 34: 197–201

25. Távora-Vieira D, Davis PB, Miller S (2009) Acoustic Stimulation in Tinnitus Treatment in Patients with Significant Levels of Hearing Loss Poster Presented at the Third Tinnitus Research Initiative Meeting, Stressa, Italy, June 23–26th 2009

26. Hallam RS, Jakes SC, Hinchcliffe R (1998) Cognitive variables in tinnitus annoyance. British Journal of Clinical Psychology; 27: 213–222

27. Davis PB (2009) Effects of Severe Unilateral Hearing Loss on Tinnitus Rehabilitation Poster Presented at the Third Tinnitus Research Initiative Meeting, Stressa, Italy, June 23–26th 2009

28. Davis PB, Wilde RA, Steed L (1999) Changes in tinnitus distress over a four month no-treatment period: Effects of audiological variables and litigation status. Proceedings of the Sixth International Tinnitus Seminar. The Tinnitus and Hyperacusis Centre, London: 384–390.

29. Davis PB, Wilde RA (1995) Clinical trial of a new tinnitus masking technique: In JA Vernon and G Reich (Eds), Tinnitus 95. ATA, Portland, Oregon: 305–309

30. Davis PB (1995) Living with Tinnitus Gore and Osment Publications. Health Book Series, Sydney

31. Henry JA, Schechter MA, Loovis C, Zaugg T, Kaelin C, Montero, M (2005) Clinical management of tinnitus using a "progressive intervention" approach. Journal of Rehabilitation Research and Development; 42: 95–116

32. Sandridge SA, Newman CW (2009) Long Term Benefits of Neuromonics Treatment: Preliminary Findings Research Poster Presented at the American Academy of Audiology, April 1–4th 2009, Dallas, TX

33. Távora-Vieira D, Miller S (2009) Long-Term Clinical Outcomes for Tinnitus Treatment Based on Acoustic Stimulation Poster Presented at the Ninth European Federation of Audiology Societies, Spain, June 21–24th 2009

Chapter 76
Middle Ear Implantable Devices in Tinnitus Treatment

Eberhard Biesinger and Manuela Mazzoli

Keypoints

1. Tinnitus is often associated with high-frequency hearing loss.
2. Rehabilitation with hearing aids has shown effectiveness in reducing tinnitus. However, in some individuals with severe high-frequency hearing loss, classical hearing aids are not always able to amplify the high frequencies sufficiently and provide enough power.
3. Active middle ear implants are an alternative to conventional hearing aids that allow more power delivered to the cochlea, especially at high frequencies, and can also be used when middle ear ossicles are damaged.
4. A study supported by the Tinnitus Research Initiative (TRI) and MED-EL of the effect of a middle ear implant showed that individuals with severe tinnitus and high-frequency hearing loss achieved relief of their tinnitus after implantation.
5. Some patients had complete relief of their tinnitus after activation of the middle ear implant. Similar effects cannot be achieved by conventional hearing aids.
6. Individuals who have significant residual inhibition of their tinnitus and high-frequency hearing loss seem to be the best candidates for implantations.

Keywords Tinnitus • Middle ear implants • High-frequency hearing loss

Abbreviations

CE	Conformity mark in the European economic market
DACS	Direct acoustical cochlear stimulation
FDA	Food and Drug Administration
FMT	Floating mass transducer
MET	Middle ear transducer
SR	Stochastic resonance
TBF	Tinnitus Beinträchtigungs Fragebogen (engl: tinnitus handicap inventory)
THI	Tinnitus handicap inventory
TRI	Tinnitus Research Initiative

Introduction

Individuals with tinnitus, who also suffer from hearing loss, often benefit from amplification. The use of hearing aids in tinnitus patients may make the patient less aware of the tinnitus as well as improve communication by reducing masking by the tinnitus. Hearing aids may also reduce the tinnitus, because they provide input to the nervous system that may reverse some of the plastic changes from deprivation of sound that has caused tinnitus and may counteract the deprivation of sound that causes some forms of tinnitus.

It has been reported that up to 67% of individuals who received unilateral hearing aids and 69% of individuals who received bilateral hearing aids report improvement in their tinnitus [1].

The quality of sound contributes many aspects. The effect of the pinna and the resonance in the external auditory canal contribute to optimize gain at higher frequencies [2].

E. Biesinger (✉)
Otolaryngology Department of Klinikum Traunstein,
Maxplatz 5, D-83278 Traumstein, Germany
e-mail: dr.eberhard.biesinger@t-online.de

A.R. Møller et al. (eds.), *Textbook of Tinnitus*,
DOI 10.1007/978-1-60761-145-5_76, © Springer Science+Business Media, LLC 2011

Hearing aids often increase the perceived quality (color, crispness, clarity, pureness) of sounds, which could be important in reducing tinnitus annoyance, but unfortunately is not measured in routine clinical practice and is difficult to define.

Today's digital hearing instruments are very advanced, offering maximum performance and reducing many of the difficulties encountered in earlier designs. In past years, improvements in hearing devices have substantially helped control feedback, widening the frequency range, and, to some degree, have improved sound quality. However, some individuals still experience the stigma and practical problems of using these devices.

Traditional hearing aids lack amplification of high frequencies (above 6,000 Hz) and fail to provide sufficient power. This is a problem in connection with suppression of tinnitus, which requires that high-frequency sounds are delivered to the ear at sufficient intensity.

Good reproduction of high-frequency sounds is also necessary for directional hearing and hearing when background noise is present.

Using a conventional "loudspeaker" at the end of the amplification chain seems to be the limiting factor for a sophisticated development of these devices.

Relocating the loudspeaker to the outer ear canal increased the performance of amplification in the high-frequency range.

Recognizing these problems and the fact that sound quality will always be an issue for those who use traditional hearing instruments and individuals with tinnitus, promoted the development of active middle ear implants. This has solved many of the problems of traditional hearing aids. It was therefore of great advantage in the treatment of some forms of tinnitus, occurring together with hearing loss, when devices that provide sound delivered directly to the middle ear bones or directly into the cochlea were developed. The amplification and the power that can be delivered to the cochlea using such devices exceed those of conventional hearing aids. Particularly, amplification is achieved in a larger frequency range than what is possible using traditional hearing aids.

With customized active middle ear implants, there is no need for a "loudspeaker" (receiver), thus reducing the distortion and reduction in the quality of sounds that occurs in traditional hearing aids. Furthermore, the ear canal is never occluded when implantable hearing aids are used.

History of Implantable Hearing Aids

Middle ear implants started in 1935 when Wilska [3] experimented with iron particles placed on the tympanic membrane. Wilska generated a magnetic field from an electromagnetic coil inside an earphone, which caused the iron filings to vibrate in synchrony with the magnetic field. This vibration in turn caused the eardrum to vibrate and allowed sound to be transduced to the cochlea in normal fashion. Later, Rutschmann (1959) [4] successfully stimulated the ossicles by gluing 10-mg magnets onto the umbo. An electromagnetic coil created a magnetic field that caused the ossicles to vibrate. Devices actually placed into the middle ear did not appear until 1970s [5].

Today, three general types of transducers are used in middle ear implants, each with advantages and disadvantages related to power, performance, frequency range, and reliability. The types of transducers used in middle ear implants consist of piezoelectric, electromagnetic, and electromechanical transducers.

Yanagihara and his colleagues [6] described an implantable piezoelectric device attached to the head of the stapes and performed the earliest human trials using these devices [7–12]. Their device was intended for patients with conductive and sensorineural loss.

A totally implantable piezoelectric device, known as the Esteem Hearing implant [13], was developed by St. Croix Medical, Inc. (now Envoy Medical Corporation) (Fig. 76.1).

Electromagnetic transduction devices consist of a magnet and an energizing coil. The magnet is attached to the ossicular chain, tympanic membrane, or the inner ear (round window or oval window). Specific experiences with regard to the influence on tinnitus have not been published.

Another implantable middle ear device known as Carina™ is shown in Fig. 76.2.

Figure 76.3: Otologics MET fully implantable middle ear device (Carina™, /Photo: Otologics). Reproduced with permission from OTOlogics GmbH, Heidelberg, Germany.

OLD Fig. 76.3: Otologics MET fully implantable middle ear device (Carina™, Photo: Otologics). Reproduced with permission fromMed-El, Innsbruck.

The Soundbridge

Soundbridge is the middle ear implant with the longest clinical experiences, 3,000 patients so far (2009). It was first marked by Symphonix Devices in San Jose, California, as the Vibrant Soundbridge. It has received both European CE-mark in March 1998 and FDA approval in the U.S. in August 2000 [14–16]. However, the company went out of business in 2002 only to return in March 2003 as the Med-EL Vibrant Soundbridge.

Fig. 76.1 Envoy piezoelectric device "esteem" (Photo: Envoy Medical Corporation, 5000 Township Parkway, Saint Paul, MN 55110, USA). Reproduced with permission from Envoy Medical

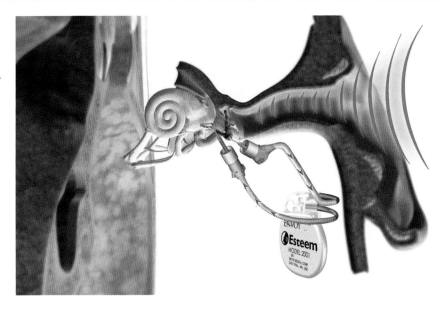

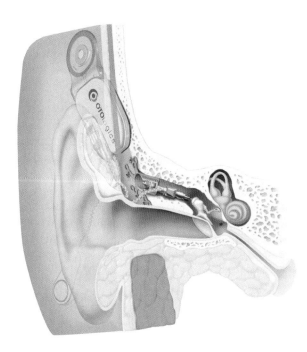

Fig. 76.2 Otologics MET fully implantable middle ear device ("Carina", Photo: Otologics, OTOlogics GmbH Im Neuenheimer Feld 581, 69120 Heidelberg, Germany). Reproduced with permission from Otologics

The semi-implantable device consists of an outward audio processor which is placed over the implanted coil and magnet. The coil is linked by a golden wire to the floating mass transducer (FMT) (Fig. 76.3). The frequency range is 1,000–8,000 Hz, but technically amplification up to 16,000 Hz is possible.

In the last 2 years, the Vibrant Soundbridge has assumed particular importance through the fact that the FMT can also be implanted in the round window [17] (Fig. 76.4). The indication here refers to a destroyed middle ear, such as after removal of the petrosal bone, malformations, cholesteatoma, sclerosis of the footplate, etc. The FMT provides a better way to induce sound energy into the cochlea than using the ossicular chain.

A special form of implanting the FMT was achieved by Hüttenbrink with "TORP-Y-Vibroplasty" [18].

Tinnitus-Related Clinical Observations and Studies

In the ENT Clinic in Traunstein, 52 patients have been equipped with the implant since 1998 (four of them bilaterally). All patients were provided with conventional hearing aids before and, for different reasons, were not content with these devices. All patients continue to use their middle ear implant as of August 2009 without any technical problems. It was surprising that most patients, who simultaneously suffered from tinnitus, reported that the middle ear implant largely reduced their tinnitus which could not have been achieved by traditional hearing aids.

In 2000, a patient implanted on both sides with middle ear implants reported that this tinnitus disappeared completely after activating the implant. Six years later, inspired by the results obtained by the middle ear implant in this person, the Tinnitus Research Initiative

Fig. 76.3 The "vibrant soundbridge" system. Photo: MED-EL, MED-EL, Fürstenweg 77a, A-6020 Innsbruck, Austria. Reproduced with permission from Med-El

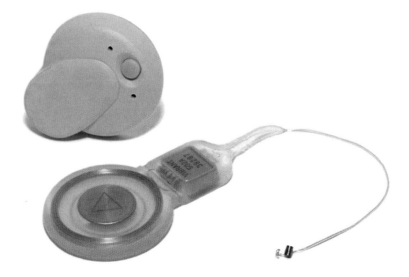

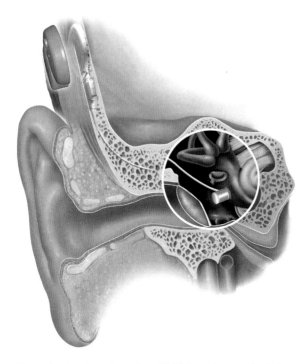

Fig. 76.4 Implantation of an FMT into the round window. Reproduced with permission from Med-El Innsbruck

(http://www.tinnitusresearch.org) offered a grant to study the effect of the middle ear implants on tinnitus. The participants had sensorineural hearing loss at high frequencies and tinnitus and had been given middle ear implants. All patients reveived the Vibrant soundbridge. They were studied for 1 year using a visual analogue scale (VAS), Goebel–Hiller score [19], and the Tinnitus Handicap Inventory (the German TBF-12 [20, 21]).

The first patient was implanted in January 2007 on the left side. His audiogram showed severe hearing loss on the left side and minor hearing loss on the right side (Fig. 76.5). The combination, with a good dynamic range assessed by the level of discomfort, gave a good indication for implantation.

After the operation, the audio processor was activated, and the reaction of his tinnitus was surprising: the tinnitus shifted from his left side to his right side.

Figure 76.6 shows the result: because of the remaining tinnitus, there was no improvement regarding annoyance after 2 months, and the person did not develop any habituation. Facing the fact that this individual now had tinnitus on the right side, we also implanted the right side with the Soundbridge 12 weeks after the original implantation. With the activation of both audio processors, the annoyance due to tinnitus diminished, and the quality of life improved.

Figure 76.7 shows the functional gain (green line) after the implantation of the Soundbridge in both ears. The patient describes that his tinnitus decreases already by switching on the device, although he is not able to hear the receiver noise. This indicates that in addition to a masking effect, there might be other effects from the implanted device.

At the 1-year follow-up exam (patient "M.A."), this patient is no longer annoyed by tinnitus when the audio processor is activated.

The first patient of a new study, sponsored by the company Med-El® with five participants with unilateral tinnitus and reproducible residual inhibition, received a Soundbridge implantation in June 2008. The device

Fig. 76.5 Audiogram participant "B.A." Reproduced with permission from the authors

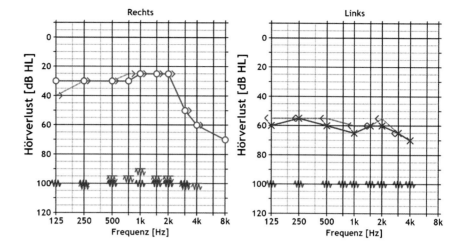

Fig. 76.6 One-year follow-up of participant "B.A." with tinnitus questionnaires and VAS shows his improvement with tinnitus after implantation on both ears. Reproduced with permission from the authors

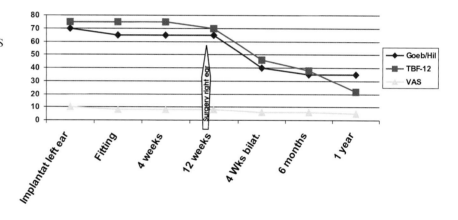

Fig. 76.7 Functional gains of both ears of participant "B.A." Reproduced with permission from the authors

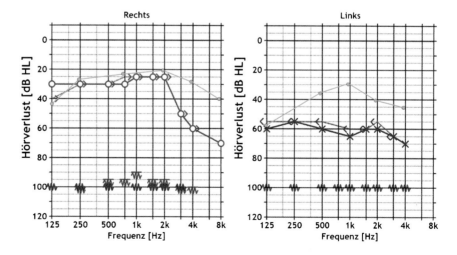

was activated and fitted in August 2008. Immediately after the fitting process, the patient's tinnitus disappeared completely after switching on the device. Although they were once greatly bothered and annoyed by the tinnitus, the activation of the device gave complete relief.

Three other participants in this study reported similar effects.

Conclusion

Implantable hearing aids have shown to be effective in reducing tinnitus in individuals with severe hearing loss and tinnitus, where the hearing loss was caused by middle ear or cochlear pathologies. The reason the middle ear implantable devices provide relief of tinnitus may be masking, but it seems more likely that the benefit is caused because these devices provide effective activation of the auditory nervous system, and thereby counteract the effect of deprivation of sound input that had activated neural plasticity causing the tinnitus. This means that the effect of the implanted hearing aids on tinnitus is similar to that of cochlear implants (see Chap. 77).

One reason for the success of implantation might be that it facilitates residual inhibition.

References

1. Trotter MI, Donaldson I (2008) Hearing aids and tinnitus therapy: a 25-year experience. J Laryngol Otol 22(10), 1052–6
2. Møller AR (2006) Hearing: Anatomy, Physiology, and Disorders of the Auditory System, 2nd Ed. Amsterdam: Academic Press
3. Wilska A (1935) Ein Methode zur Bestimmung der horsch wellenamplituden des Trommelfells bei verschieden Frequenzen. Skand Arch Physiol 72, 161–5
4. Rutschmann J (1959) Magnetic audition: Auditory stimulation by means of alternating magnetic fields acting on a permanent magnet fixed to the eardrum. IRE Trans Med Electron 6, 22–23
5. Goode RL (1988) Electromagnetic implantable hearing aids. In: Advances in Audiology. Ed. JI Suzuki. Karger: Basel, pp 31–44
6. Yanagihara N, Suzuki J, Gyo K, Syono H, Ikeda H (1984) Development of an implantable hearing aid using a piezoelectric vibrator of bimorph design: state of the art. Otolaryngol Head Neck Surg 92(6), 706–12
7. Yanagihara N, Aritomo H, Yamanaka E, Gyo K (1987) Implantable hearing aid: Report of the first human applications Arch. Otolaryngol Head Neck Surg 113(8), 869–72
8. Yanagihara N, Gyo K, Hinohira Y (1995) Partially implantable hearing aid using piezoelectric ceramic ossicular vibrator. Results of the implant operation and assessment of the hearing afforded by the device. Otolaryngol Clin North Am 28(1), 85–97
9. Yanagihara N, Sato H, Hinohira Y, Gyo K, Hori K (2001) Long-term results using a piezoelectric semi-implantable middle ear hearing device: The Rion device E-type. Otolaryngol Clin North Am 34(2), 389–400
10. Suzuki J-I, Yanagihara N, Kadera K (1987) The partially implantable middle ear implant, case reports. Ann Otol Rhinol Laryngol 37, 178–84
11. Suzuki J, Kodera K, Nagai K, Yabe T (1994) Long-term clinical results of the partially implantable piezoelectric middle ear implant. Ear Nose Throat J 73(2), 104–7
12. Gyo K, Yanagihara N, Saiki T, Hinohira Y (1990) Present status and outlook of the implantable hearing aid. Am J Otol 11(4), 250–3
13. Kroll K, Grant IL, Javel E (2002) The envoy totally implantable hearing system, St Croix Medical. Trends Amplif 6(2), 73–80
14. Snik AF, Cremers CW (2001) Vibrant semi-implantable hearing device with digital sound processing: effective gain and speech perception. Arch Otolaryngol Head Neck Surg 127, 1433–7
15. Snik FM, Cremers WRJ (1999) First audiometric results with the Vibrant Soundbridge, a semi-implantable hearing device for sensorineural hearing loss. Audiology 38, 335–8
16. Sterkers O, Boucarra D, Labassi S (2003) A middle ear implant, the Symphonix Vibrant Soundbridge. Retrospective study of the first 125 patients implanted in France. Otol Neurotol 24, 427–36
17. Colletti V, Carner M, Colletti L (2009) TORP vs round window implantat for hearing restoration of patients with extensive ossicular chain defect. Acta Otolaryngol 129(4):449–52.
18. Hüttenbrink K-B, Zahnert T, Bornitz M, Beutne D (2008) TORP Vibroplasty: a new alternative for the chronically disabled middle ear. Otol Neurotol 29(7), 965–71
19. Goebel G, Hiller W (1998) Tinnitus-Fragebogen (TF) Ein Instrument zur Erfassung von Belastung und Schweregrad bei Tinnitus. Göttingen, Bern, Toronto, Seattle: Hogrefe Verlag für Psychologie
20. Greimel KV, Leibetseder M, Unterrainer J, Albegger K (1999) Ist Tinnitus meßbar? Methoden zur Erfassung tinnitusspezifischer Beeinträchtigungen und Präsentation des Tinnitus-Beeinträchtigungs-Fragebogens (TBF-12). HNO 47, 196–201
21. Newman CW, Jacobson GP, Spitzer JB (1996) Development of the tinnitus handicap inventory. Arch Otolaryngol Head Neck Surg 122, 143–8

Chapter 77
Cochlear Implants and Tinnitus

Andrea Kleine Punte, Olivier Meeus, and Paul Van de Heyning

Keypoints

1. Many forms of tinnitus are caused by deprivation of sounds, and electrical stimulation has been applied to the promontory for treatment of tinnitus, providing significant relief from tinnitus by supplying input to the auditory nervous system.
2. Immediate relief of tinnitus has been reported in approximately 82% of the patients and longer term tinnitus suppression in 45% of such treatment.
3. Cochlear implants, therefore, may offer long-term tinnitus suppression in patients with severe sensorineural hearing loss by providing input to the auditory nervous system.
4. This chapter provides evidence of tinnitus relief in up to 90% of individuals with severe tinnitus following cochlear implantation.
5. An indication for the use of cochlear implants in individuals who are deaf in one ear while having incapacitating tinnitus on that side is provided in this chapter.
6. Research in the field of cochlear implants and tinnitus is discussed, and suggestions for future research are made.

Keywords Tinnitus • Cochlear implants • Promontory stimulation • Treatment

---

P. Van de Heyning (✉)
University Department of Otorhinolaryngology and Head and Neck Surgery, Antwerp University Hospital, Wilrijkstraat 10, Edegem 2650, Belgium
e-mail: paul.van.de.heyning@uza.be

Abbreviations

EPS   Electrical Promontory Stimulation
SNHL   Sensorineural Hearing Loss
SSD   Single-sided Deafness
VAS   Visual Analogue Scale

Introduction

Tinnitus is one of the most common otological complaints, affecting 10–15% of the adult population (see Chap. 5). Various treatments have been developed to suppress or reduce tinnitus (see chapters in Sect. 5). Many forms of tinnitus are now thought to be caused by auditory deprivation (see Chap. 11), and hearing aids can, therefore, provide relief from tinnitus in some individuals. Reduction of tinnitus following the use of a hearing aid was first reported in 1947 [1]. Later, several studies confirmed the beneficial effect of hearing aids for tinnitus relief. In 1981, a significant improvement of the value of binaural aids compared to monaural hearing aids in reduction of tinnitus and associated problems was reported. The improvement was present in almost half of the individuals surveyed [2]. Similar conclusions were drawn from another study by Surr et al. [3], in which approximately half of the respondents with tinnitus reported that their hearing aids provided either partial or total relief from tinnitus. Individuals rating their tinnitus as being severe reported partial relief of tinnitus rather than total relief, but other studies showed no effect of hearing aids on tinnitus [4].

A.R. Møller et al. (eds.), *Textbook of Tinnitus*,
DOI 10.1007/978-1-60761-145-5_77, © Springer Science+Business Media, LLC 2011

Hearing aids are not useful for treatment of individuals with severe sensorineural hearing loss (SNHL) and tinnitus, but if the auditory nerve is preserved, electrical stimulation of the inner ear can supply necessary auditory input in deaf individuals.

Electrical promontory stimulation (EPS) seems to be a promising tinnitus treatment, providing significant relief. Research on EPS shows at least temporary and partial tinnitus suppression. Immediate relief of tinnitus has been reported in approximately 82% of patients and longer term tinnitus suppression in 45% of these patients [5]. Rubinstein et al. [6] also described the effect of high-frequency EPS on tinnitus, and the authors advocated that the effect should be investigated with an implantable device. There are indications that cochlear implants may provide long-term tinnitus suppression in individuals with severe sensorineural hearing loss. Cochlear implants have been reported to provide tinnitus relief in up to 90% of patients. There is evidence that deafferentation of the auditory pathway plays an important role in causing tinnitus (see Chaps. 10 and 11), and that the effect can be reversed by electrical stimulation of the auditory system via EPS or through cochlear implants. A particularly new indication for cochlear implants is single-sided deafness (SSD) with concomitant incapacitating tinnitus [7]. In this chapter, results of studies of the use of cochlear implants for treatment of tinnitus are discussed and suggestions for future studies are made.

Electrical Promontory Stimulation and Tinnitus

Nearly 200 years ago, electrical stimulation was first described as possible tinnitus treatment. Only in the 1960s and 1970s, the potential beneficial effect of electrical stimulation on tinnitus was rediscovered. Feldmann [8] reported suppressed tinnitus by Volta's platinum–zinc cell. Since then, electrical stimulation as treatment for profound SNHL and tinnitus has been widely investigated. Originally, electrical stimulation of the cochlea was used to assess the integrity of the neural structure in the cochlear prior to cochlea implantation. A side effect of this test in some cases was a suppression of the accompanied tinnitus [9–13].

Electrical stimulation of the cochlea is possible with EPS or round window stimulation. In EPS, a needle electrode is placed on the promontory in order to stimulate the cochlea. This technique has been investigated thoroughly and is used pre-operatively to predict speech reception results with a cochlear implant (CI) [14–16]. An overview of the literature of tinnitus suppression with EPS [17–19] is given in Fig. 77.1.

Portmann et al. [20] suggested that the effectiveness of electrical stimulation depends on the electrode placement and electrical stimulation at the round window was better than promontory stimulation. Also, temporary tinnitus suppression was most effective

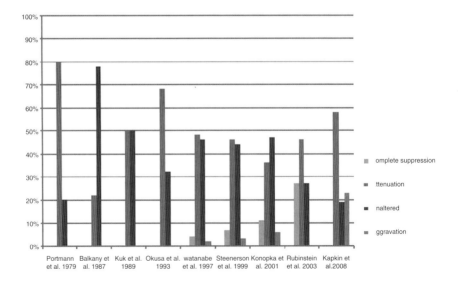

Fig. 77.1 Tinnitus modulation after electrical stimulation of the inner ear

when using positive electrical pulses. In the reported studies, the efficacy of EPS for suppressing tinnitus was done using stimulation for only a very short time in acute experimental set-ups. Repeatability of the tinnitus suppression remains unclear, and the long-term effects of EPS on the cochlea and acoustic thresholds have not been thoroughly investigated [6].

Cochlear Implant for Bilateral Profound Hearing Loss and Tinnitus

Many people who have bilateral profound sensorineural hearing loss have severe tinnitus. The first report showing that suppression of tinnitus could occur after cochlear implantation was published in 1976 by House [21]. Baguley [22] and Quaranta [23] reviewed the results of studies of suppression (or modulation) of tinnitus after cochlear implantation. Recent studies provided additional support of these findings [24, 25].

Figure 77.2 summarizes the results obtained concerning tinnitus modulation after cochlear implantation [24–32]. It is clear that tinnitus decreased after cochlear implantation in most of the people receiving these implants as treatment. For these individuals, the tinnitus was a secondary complaint to the main problem of deafness.

Cochlear Implant for Single-Sided Deafness and Incapacitating Tinnitus

A small group of people have suffered from SSD, and due to this deafness, incapacitating tinnitus developed. The tinnitus was referred to the deaf ear, with the other ear having normal hearing or showing only moderate hearing loss and no tinnitus. At the Antwerp University Hospital, such individuals received a cochlear implant in the deaf ear in order to reduce tinnitus and also to restore some hearing (Medel Combi 40+ with an M-electrode or Pulsar CI[100] with Flex*soft* electrode). We studied these individuals in a prospective clinical study to assess the long-term effects of cochlear implantation on tinnitus in people with SSD and ipsilateral incapacitating tinnitus [7]. Twenty-one individuals who received a cochlear implant and suffered from severe incapacitating tinnitus that was unresponsive to other treatments participated in this study. Tinnitus loudness was measured using a Visual Analogue Scale (VAS); loudness perception of tinnitus was recorded with the CI both activated and deactivated. Tinnitus distress was measured using the Tinnitus Questionnaire (TQ) pre- and post-operatively.

All 21 patients reported a subjective benefit when the cochlear implant was activated. Tinnitus loudness was reduced significantly after cochlear implantation.

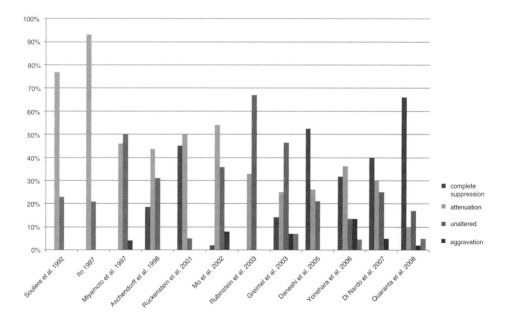

Fig. 77.2   Tinnitus modulation after cochlear implantation

At the 12-month follow-up exam, the loudness of their tinnitus had decreased from an average of 8.5 to 2.5 on the VAS (of 0–10). Also, the tinnitus questionnaire (TQ) total score decreased significantly. Figure 77.3 shows the average tinnitus loudness as a function of time.

Cochlear Implantation seems to be a successful treatment of severe tinnitus in patients with SSD. A significant suppression of tinnitus occurred already after 1 month of cochlear implantation. All patients but one had a tinnitus score lower than 5/10 on a VAS. The tinnitus largely recurred when their cochlear implant was deactivated.

The results of this study show that after a long period, tinnitus does not reoccur, and there is no adaptation of the tinnitus to the electrical stimulation presented by the cochlear implants. Long-term results up to 48 months after cochlear implantation also suggest cochlear implantation provides durable tinnitus relief in these individuals (Kleine Punte et al.) [33]. It must, however, be emphasized that other causes of tinnitus have to be excluded before cochlear implantation for tinnitus is recommended and severe depression is a contra-indication.

Experience from the use of cochlear implants to treat patients with tinnitus indicates that electrical stimulation of the auditory nerve can reverse the reorganization associated with peripheral deafferentation that causes tinnitus and thus, reverse plastic changes that may have caused the tinnitus (see Chap. 12). Also, the increase in activation of the auditory nerve may provide inhibitory influence on the cells in the auditory nervous system, which may play a role in its effect on tinnitus. Enhanced attentiveness to environmental sounds could contribute to the observed suppression of tinnitus. The results from this study suggest that inhibition of tinnitus by cochlear implants is stable, and tinnitus does not return over time. This long-term stability suggests that cochlear implants may permanently suppress tinnitus in these patients. Besides providing significant tinnitus relief, patients with SSD also experienced an improvement in their hearing capabilities after cochlear implantation [34].

It should be taken into account that other factors may also be responsible for the tinnitus relief obtained after cochlear implantation. Psychological factors may have an influence on tinnitus loudness and tinnitus annoyance: the long inclusion procedure before the implantation includes thorough psychological assistance, which may increase the well-being of the patient. However, in the months before cochlear implantation, no attenuation of tinnitus occurred in our study group, which is consistent with the Blue Mountain follow-up study [35]. Finally, an increased assurance after a recuperation of the auditory function may also have contributed to diminishing the tinnitus annoyance.

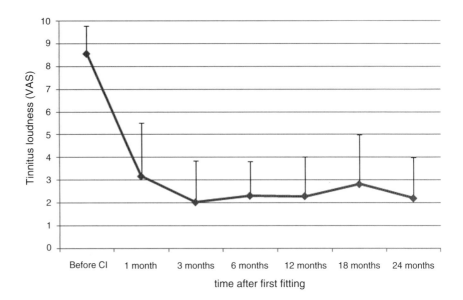

Fig. 77.3 Average tinnitus loudness and standard deviation with CI activated as function of time after first CI fitting

Development of Tinnitus After Cochlear Implantation

Although in the majority of cases, cochlear implantation results in an abolishment or suppression of tinnitus, a small percentage of individuals have been reported to develop tinnitus or experience an increase of their tinnitus after cochlear implantation. The reported incidence ranges from 0 to 9% [22, 30, 36–38]. Akdogan et al. [39] investigated the tinnitus properties due to cochlear implantation and found that 4 out of 17 patients (23.5%) developed tinnitus after cochlear implantation. The mean tinnitus loudness was 17.5 dB SL. Quaranta et al. [24] reported that 7 out of 41 individuals (17%) developed tinnitus immediately after the insertion of the electrode array for a cochlear implant. However, 1 month later, only two of these individuals still perceived the tinnitus they acquired at the time of the implantation and their tinnitus became mild. Although the risk of getting tinnitus from cochlear implantation is minimal, it is important to counsel candidates about the risk of cochlear implants.

Suppression of Bilateral Tinnitus After Unilateral Cochlear Implantation

A few reports about bilateral tinnitus suppression after unilateral cochlear implantation have been published. A study by Di Nardo et al. [25] reported complete tinnitus suppression bilaterally in 4 of 9 (44%) individuals who received a cochlear implant in one ear, while four others (44%) experienced bilateral attenuation of tinnitus. Another study performed in 14 individuals who had bilateral tinnitus before implantation reported bilateral suppression of their tinnitus or attenuation of the tinnitus in 12 (86%), while the tinnitus increased bilaterally in 2 (14%) of the participants in the study [32].

The effect of cochlear implantation on bilateral tinnitus was more extensively described in a study performed in 41 individuals with bilateral tinnitus [24]. When their cochlear implant was turned on, the tinnitus was abolished bilaterally in 23 participants of the study (56.1%). Tinnitus was completely suppressed in the implanted ear only in 4 (9.7%) individuals and contralaterally in 4 (9.7%) of the participants. That means tinnitus suppression occurred in 31 (76.5%) participants in this study.

Patients with bilateral tinnitus sometimes experience tinnitus suppression after sequential bilateral cochlear implantation [40]. Increase of tinnitus was also described after bilateral cochlear implantation, similar to tinnitus aggravation after unilateral cochlear implantation.

Future Research

Although many reports of tinnitus suppression after cochlear implantation have been published, more detailed studies are needed to assess the advantages of cochlear implants for treatment of tinnitus. Since double-blind studies are impossible in the field of cochlear implantation, the emphasis should lie on conducting randomized controlled studies on the effects of cochlear implantation on tinnitus. Also, the working mechanisms of tinnitus suppression after cochlear implantation are not totally understood and need to be further explored in studies of humans.

Conclusion

Tinnitus can be influenced by electrical stimulation of the inner ear, at least when the tinnitus occurs in connection with sensorineural hearing loss. Transtympanic electrical promontory stimulation or round window stimulation can provide temporary tinnitus relief. In individuals with profound hearing loss, cochlear implantation can provide more permanent tinnitus suppression.

Table 77.1 Inclusion and exclusion criteria of cochlear implantation as tinnitus treatment in patients with SSD

Inclusion criteria	Exclusion criteria
Severe tinnitus: tinnitus loudness 6–10 on VAS for >6 months	Major depression
Subjective tinnitus due to ipsilateral profound SNHL	Not willing to attend regular follow-up and rehabilitation
Tinnitus as primary complaint	Duration of tinnitus >10 years
Standard treatments of tinnitus have no effect	
Realistic expectations	
Normal hearing to moderate hearing loss contralaterally	
Patent Scala tympani	

References

1. Saltzman M, Ersner MS. A hearing aid for the relief of tinnitus aurium. Laryngoscope 1947;57(5):358–366
2. Brooks DN, Bulmer D. Survey of binaural hearing aid users. Ear Hear 1981;2:220–224
3. Surr RK, Montgomery AA, Mueller HG. Effect of amplification on tinnitus among new hearing aid users. Ear Hear 1985;6:71–75
4. Melin L, Scott B, Lindberg P, Lyttkens L. Hearing aids and tinnitus – an experimental group study. Br J Audiol 1987;21: 91–97
5. Di Nardo W, Cianfrone F, Scorpecci A, Cantore I, Giannantonio S, Paludetti G. Transtympanic electrical stimulation for immediate and long-term tinnitus suppression. Int Tinnitus J 2009;15(1):100–6
6. Rubinstein JT, Tyler RS, Johnson A, and Brown CJ. Electrical suppresion of tinnitus with high-rate pulse trains. Otol Neurotol 2003;24:478–485
7. Van de Heyning P, Vermeire K, Diebl M, Nopp P, Anderson I, De Ridder D. Incapacitating unilateral tinnitus in single-sided deafness treated by cochlear implantation. Ann Otol Rhinol Laryngol 2008;117(9):645–52
8. Feldmann, H. Suppression of tinnitus by electrical stimulation: a contribution to the history of medicine. J laryngol Otol Suppl 1986;9:123–124
9. Graham JM, Hazell JW. Electrical stimulation of the human cochlea using a transtympanic electrode. Br J Audiol 1977; 11(2):59–62
10. Cazals Y, Negrevergne M, and Aran JM. Electrical stimulation of the cochlea in Man: hearing introduction and tinnitus suppression. J Amer Audiol Soc 1978;3:209–213
11. Okusa M, Shiraishi T, Kubo T, Matsunaga T, Sugimoto K, Tamaki A. Suppression of tinnitus by electrical promontory stimulation. Audiol Jpn 1992;35:77–82
12. Kitahara M, Suzuki M, Kodama A. Electrical promontory stimulation. J Otolaryngol Head Neck Surg 1993; 9:83–86
13. Steerneson RL, Cronin GW. The treatment of tinnitus with electrical stimulation. Otolaryngol Head Neck Surg 1999; 121:511–513
14. Lee JC, Yoo MH, Ahn JH, Lee KS. Value of the promontory stimulation test in predicting speech perception after cochlear implantation. Laryngoscope 2007;117(11):1988–92
15. Kuo SC, Gibson WP The role of the promontory stimulation test in cochlear implantation. Cochlear Implants Int 2002; 3(1):19–28
16. Nikolopoulos T, Mason SM, Gibbin KP, O'Donoghue GM. The prognostic value of promontory electric auditory brain stem response in pediatric cochlear implantation. Ear Hear 2000;21(3):236–241
17. Okusa M, Shiraishi T, Kubo T, Matsunaga T Tinnitus suppression by electrical promontory stimulation in sensorineural deaf patients. Acta Otolaryngol Suppl 1993;501:54–8
18. Watanabe K, Okawara D, Baba S, Yagi T. Electrocochleographic analysis of tinnitus by electrical promontory stimulation. Audiology 1997;36:147–154
19. Konopka W, Zalewski P, Olszewski A, Olszewska-Ziaber A and Pietkiewics P. Tinnitus suppression by electrical promontory stimulation (EPS) in patients with sensorineural hearing loss. Auris Nasus Larynx 2001;28:35–40
20. Portmann M, Cazals Y, Negrevergne M, Aran JM. Temprary tinnitus suppression in man through electrical stimulation of the cochlea. Acta Oto Laryngologica. 1979;87:3,294–299
21. House WF. Cochlear implants. Ann Otol Rhinol Laryngol 1976;85 suppl 27:1–93
22. Baguley DM, Atlas MD. Cochlear implants and tinnitus. Prog Brain Res 2007;166:347–355
23. Quaranta N, Wagstaff S, Baguley DM. Tinnitus and cochlear implantation. Int J Audiol 2004;43:245–251
24. Quaranta N, Fernandez-Vega S, D'Elia C et al. The effect of unilateral multichannel cochlear implant on bilaterally perceived tinnitus. Acta Oto-Laryngologica 2008;128:159–163
25. Di Nardo W, Cantore I, Cianfrone F et al. Tinnitus modifications after cochlear implantation. Eur Arch Otorhinolaryngol 2007;264:1145–1149
26. Souliere CR Jr, Kileny PR, Zwolan TA, Kemink JL. Tinnitus suppression following cochlear implantation A multifactorial investigation. Arch Otolaryngol Head Neck Surg 1992;118:1291–7
27. Ito J, Sakakihara J. Tinnitus suppression by electrical stimulation of the cochlear wall and by cochlear implantation. Laryngoscope 1994; 104(6 Pt 1):752–4
28. Ruckenstein MJ, Hedgepeth C, Rafter KO, Montes ML, Bigelow DC. Tinnitus suppression in patients with cochlear implants. Otol Neurotol 2001;22:200–204
29. Greimel, KV, Meco, C, Mair, A, Kohlbock, G, Albegger, K. How is tinnitus influenced by cochlear implantation. HNO 2003;51:226–231
30. Mo B, Harris S, Lindbaek M. Tinnitus in cochlear implant patients–a comparison with other hearing-impaired patients. Int J Audiol 2002;41:527–534
31. Daneshi A, Mahmoudian S, Farhadi M et al. Auditory electrical tinnitus suppression in patients with and without implants. Int Tinnitus J 2005;11:85–91
32. Yonehara E, Mezzalira R, Porto PR, Bianchini WA, Calonga L, Curi SB, Stoler G. Can cochlear implants decrease tinnitus? Int Tinnitus J 2006;12:172–174
33. Kleine Punte A, Vermeire K, Hofkens A Van de Heyning P. Durable tinnitus reduction and bimodal hearing after cochlear implantation in single-sided deafness; results up to 48 months post-implantation 8th Wullstein Symposium, Treatment of Unilateral Deafness Wurzburg, 2009
34. Vermeire K, Van de Heyning P Binaural hearing after cochlear implantation in subjects with unilateral sensorineural deafness and tinnitus. Audiol Neurootol. 2009;14(3):163–71.
35. Gopinath B, McMahon CM, Rochtchina E, Karpa MJ, Mitchell P. Incidence, persistence, and progression of tinnitus symptoms in older adults: the blue mountains hearing study. Ear Hear 2010; Jan 29 [Epub ahead of print]
36. Tyler RS and Kelsay D. Advantages and disadvantages reported by some of the better cochlear-implant patients. Am J Otol 1990;11(4):282–9
37. Miyamoto RT, Wynne MK, McKnight C, Bichey B. Electrical Suppression of Tinnitus via Cochlear Implants. Int Tinnitus J 1997;3:35–38
38. McKerrow WS, Schreiner CE, Snyder RL, Merzenich MM, Toner JG. Tinnitus suppression by cochlear implants. Ann Otol Rhinol Laryngol 1991;100:552–88
39. Akdogan O, Ozcan I, Ozbek I, Huseyin D. Tinnitus after cochlear implantation. Auris Nasus Larynx 2009;36:2:210–212
40. Summerfield AQ, Barton GR, Toner J, McAnallen C, Proops D, Harries C, Cooper H, Court I, Gray R, Osborne J, Doran M, Ramsden R, Mawman D, O'Driscoll M, Graham J, Aleksy W, Meerton L, Verschure C, Ashcroft P, Pringle M. Self-reported benefits from successive bilateral cochlear implantation in post-lingually deafened adults: randomised controlled trial. Int J Audiol 2006;45(Suppl 1):S99-S107.

Chapter 78
Pharmacological Approaches to Tinnitus Treatment

Ana Belén Elgoyhen and Berthold Langguth

Keypoints

1. Available treatments for the management of tinnitus are diverse.
2. Although most patients benefit from treatment to some degree a large percentage of them are left untreated and in despair with the notion that "they have to learn to live with their tinnitus".
3. Currently there is no drug that is approved by the Food and Drug Administration (FDA) or the European Medicines Agency (EMEA) for the treatment of tinnitus. Thus, tinnitus is still a clinically unmet need, and most patients would welcome a drug that abolishes their phantom sound once and for all.
4. There are different forms of tinnitus which probably differ in their response to pharmacological treatment. Thus, even if a specific drug has failed to demonstrate efficacy in controlled clinical trials in a large sample, a beneficial effect in a subgroup of tinnitus patients should not be precluded. At present, most evidence-based pharmacological treatments treat specific comorbidities rather than the core of the disorder itself.
5. There is an urgent need for effective treatment approaches. Since in some individuals, tinnitus causes irritability agitation, stress, depression, insomnia, and interferes with normal life – leading to suicidal attempts in severe cases – even a drug

that produces a small but significant effect would have an enormous therapeutic impact. This review describes strategies currently available for tinnitus pharmacotherapy.

Keywords Tinnitus • Phantom sound • Lidocaine • Neramexane • Hearing • Noise trauma

Abbreviations

EMEA	European Medicines Agency
RNID	Royal National Institute for Deaf People (UK)
SSRI	Selective serotonin reuptake inhibitors
THQ	Tinnitus handicap questionnaire
SNRI	Serotonin-norepinephrine reuptake inhibitors
GABA	Gamma amino butyric acid
PDE5	Phosphodiesterase type 5
NMDA	N-methyl-D-aspartate

Introduction

Available treatments for the management of tinnitus are diverse. These include counseling and cognitive behavioral therapies; different forms of sound therapies; methods that attempt to increase input to the auditory system, such as hearing aids and cochlear implants (for use in patients whose tinnitus is caused by deprivation of signals to the auditory nervous system); neurobiofeedback; and various forms of electrical stimulation of brain structures, either through implanted electrodes or by inducing electrical current in the brain with transcranial magnetic stimulation and drug treatments [1–9]. Although most patients benefit to some degree from the above-mentioned therapies, a big fraction of them are

A.B. Elgoyhen (✉)
Instituto de Investigaciones en Ingeniería Genética y Biología Molecular, Consejo Nacional de Investigaciones Científicas y Técnicas, 1428, Buenos Aires, Argentina
and
Departamento de Farmacología, Facultad de Medicina, Universidad de Buenos Aires, Buenos Aires, Argentina
e-mail: elgoyhen@dna.uba.ar

A.R. Møller et al. (eds.), *Textbook of Tinnitus*,
DOI 10.1007/978-1-60761-145-5_78, © Springer Science+Business Media, LLC 2011

left untreated and in despair with the notion that "they have to learn to live with their tinnitus". Thus, tinnitus is still a clinically unmet need. Most patients would welcome a drug that abolishes their phantom sound once and for all.

The market for a drug specifically for tinnitus relief is huge. There have been numerous patents filed worldwide on drugs with the potential to offer relief. Furthermore, tinnitus can be found attached to many more patents filed on molecules aimed at a range of diverse therapeutic classes. The Royal National Institute for Deaf People (RNID) in the UK estimates that a novel tinnitus drug could have a product value of US \$689 million in its first year of launch [10]. However, we are still left without a single FDA-approved drug on the market targeting tinnitus relief. For the majority of tinnitus sufferers who seek medical advice, the treatment goals are aimed at symptomatic relief of their phantom sound and/or the management of the associated distress. This approach is usually justified, as serious underlying pathologies are rare. Over four million prescriptions are written each year for tinnitus relief in Europe and the US, but these are all off-label prescriptions from a wide variety of therapeutic drugs (Table 78.1) [10]. Most clinicians who treat tinnitus patients urge for an effective drug therapy targeted at tinnitus. Thus, there is a tremendous need both from patients and medical doctors to develop a drug targeting tinnitus relief. Since in some individuals, tinnitus causes irritability, agitation, stress, depression, insomnia, and interferes with normal life – leading to suicidal attempts in severe cases [11] – even a drug that produces a small but significant effect would have an enormous therapeutic impact. However, ideally a disappearance of tinnitus should be the ultimate goal of any research and development platform toward designing a tinnitus drug.

The lidocaine experience: tinnitus can be pharmacologically targeted.

Tinnitus is a symptom that is associated with virtually all diseases and disorders affecting the auditory system and can arise from a lesion in any part of the auditory pathway. Some causes that trigger tinnitus are well known. In particular, noise traumas, administration of ototoxic drugs, and head and neck injuries have been associated with the development of subjective tinnitus. Interestingly, while the initial lesion might affect the peripheral organ of the auditory system, the neural correlate of the sound perceived is most likely

Table 78.1 Number of prescriptions in 2001 in primary care for diagnosis of tinnitus in Western Europe (UK, France, Germany, Spain, Italy, Netherlands, Belgium, Denmark, Finland, Austria, Greece, Portugal, Republic of Ireland and Switzerland) (only substances with at least 10,000 prescriptions are included) Vio M. Tinnitus market situation analysis. London: RNID, 2003 • A market report for a virtual new tinnitus drug, provided by the Royal National Institute of Deafness (http://www.rnid.org.uk/marketreports).

Substance	Number of prescriptions in 2001 (in thousands)
Ginkgo biloba	782
Trimetazidine	650
Betahistine	314
Pentoxifylline	312
Piracetam	197
Naftidrofuryl	184
Buflomedil	144
Cinnarizine	141
Clonazepam	137
Nicergoline	119
Dihydroergocristine	91
Flunarizine	73
Nimodipine	56
Acetylsalicylic acid	53
Hetastarch	50
Ajmalicine	42
Moxaverine	32
Piribedil	31
Almitrine	21
Prednisolone	21
Amitriptyline	21
Dihydroergocryptine	18
Caffeine	16
Mesoglicane	14
Vitamin E	14
Dihydroergotixine	14
Retinol	13
Cyclandelate	12
Gold	10
Viscum album	10
Hypericum perforatum	10

in the central auditory circuitry [12, 13] and involves non-auditory brain areas [11, 14, 15]. A central origin of the tinnitus percept is demonstrated by the fact that the phantom sound sensation persists after deprivation of input from the periphery via sectioning of the auditory nerve [16]. Although the mechanisms of the production of tinnitus are far from being fully understood, there is growing evidence that changes in neuronal activity, neuronal synchrony, disruption of the balance between excitation and inhibition, and rearrangements of the tonotopic organization in different parts of the auditory pathway, including the dorsal cochlear nucleus, inferior colliculus, thalamus, and/or auditory cortex underlie tinnitus pathology [12, 15, 17–20]. Neuronal excitability can be modulated by different neurotransmitters, neuromodulators, and voltage-gated channel acting compounds [21–25]. Thus, there is no reason to believe that tinnitus cannot be pharmacologically approached. The fact that the voltage-gated sodium channel blocker lidocaine that is used as a local anesthetic and an antiarrythmic, given intravenously, leads to the temporary disappearance of tinnitus or a major change in the nature of the tinnitus in 70% of patients [26–28], indicates that activity-driven changes underlying tinnitus can be pharmacologically targeted.

Although intravenous lidocaine seems to be effective in a great number of tinnitus patients, the effect is short lasting and the route of administration is not a practical one in a clinical setting of a chronic condition. Moreover, side effects are considerable and include cardiac arrhythmia, drowsiness, dizziness, confusion, and restlessness [29]. Several other oral antiarrhythmic drugs like tocainide, flecainide, and mexiletine have been studied for tinnitus. None of these compounds have been demonstrated to be particularly useful. Almost all of them exhibit severe side effects and are now in disuse [6–8]. Given the positive results with lidocaine, the possibility of novel local anesthetics like tonicaine and sameridine with longer duration of action [30] has been suggested [31]. Tonicaine is a quaternary ammonium and most likely does not efficiently pass the blood–brain barrier. Thus, its use in tinnitus is probably limited. Sameridine has additional μ-opioid antagonist properties [30], a biological system that has not been targeted so far as a treatment for tinnitus, and a possible avenue to explore. Moreover, alternative delivery systems with prolonged duration of action, as has been suggested for the treatment of pain with a liposomal bupivacaine formulation and intradermal injection [32], could be tested. A preliminary report has shown some positive results in tinnitus patients with an intradermal lidocaine injection [33]. The pharmaceutical company Epicept (http://www.epicept.com) has a lidocaine patch formulation currently at Phase II for tinnitus. However, it has to be considered that the systemic concentrations that can be reached with the currently available lidocaine patches are probably much lower than the concentrations needed to suppress tinnitus.

Pharmacological Treatment of Tinnitus

The management of tinnitus sufferers is a pressing need faced by medical doctors in their daily practice. Drug therapy is one approach to the problem, and a large variety of different drugs are used (Table 78.1), even if supporting evidence is scarce. Since tinnitus is a symptom that might be the manifest of different underlying pathologies and has several etiologies and comorbidities – which can include various degrees of affective disorders – heterogeneity within tinnitus patients is expected [11, 34]. Thus, the pharmacological treatment of tinnitus faces the "one drug won't fit all" scenario. Once (and if) the different forms of tinnitus are established, different treatment approaches will be devised. Up front, there is a consensus among clinicians treating tinnitus that the pathophysiology underlying the onset of tinnitus may differ from that of chronic tinnitus. Therefore, treatment approaches will probably vary with the duration of the disease. Immediately after tinnitus onset, more casually oriented treatment approaches might be possible, and involvement of the cochlea might still be important. In case of abrupt onset tinnitus associated with sudden hearing loss or noise trauma, treatment strategies which restore hearing function are expected to have beneficial effects on tinnitus. There is no clear boarder between "acute" and "chronic" tinnitus. The currently used distinction is arbitrary and varies between 3 and 6 months. Furthermore, recent data suggest that the neural correlate of tinnitus might change even after a duration of several years [15].

"Acute State"

One form of acute tinnitus that deserves special attention is associated to sudden hearing loss. Sudden hearing loss is characterized by the abrupt loss of hearing, typically unilateral [35–37]. A proportion of patients also experience dizziness and tinnitus with the hearing loss. Most individuals are able to pinpoint the precise moment of hearing reduction, such as awakening with the symptom. No specific sound frequency region in the cochlea appears to be preferentially affected, and the severity of hearing loss ranges from mild to profound. The spontaneous recovery rate is high; up to

Table 78.2 Off-label drugs investigated for the treatment of tinnitus

• Antiarrythmics	• Antidepressants
Lidocaine	Amitriptyline
Tocainide	Trimipramine
Flecainide	Nortriptyline
Mexiletine	Paroxetine
• Anticonvulsants	Sertraline
Carbamazepine	Fluoxetine
Gabapentine	• Dopaminergic
Lamotrigine	Sulpiride
Valproic Acid	Piribedil
• Anxiolytics	• Others
Alprazolam	Atorvastatin
Clonazepam	Cyclandelate
Diazepam	Furosemide
• Glutamate receptor	Herbal products
antagonists	Misoprostol
Acamprosate	Melatonin
Caroverine	Nimodipine
Memantine	Vardenafil
	Zinc

65% of patients may experience recovery of pre-loss hearing. The high variability of the spontaneous course probably reflects the fact that there are different forms of sudden hearing loss with different etiologies. Among others, vascular, inflammatory, and infectious mechanisms are probably involved. However, in most cases, the exact etiology remains unknown. Many potential prognostic factors have been identified. Vertigo, persistent or profound hearing loss, and prolonged duration of hearing loss are negative prognostic factors. Subjects with good recovery usually experience that recovery within 2 weeks of the onset of hearing loss. Proposed treatments have included systemic or intratympanic steroids [36–38], vasodilators [39], antiviral agents [40, 41], and hyperbaric oxygen [42, 43]. Although some studies report positive results in subset of patients, none have proven effective in well-controlled studies [35, 41, 42].

Acute tinnitus associated to noise-induced hearing loss of abrupt onset such as that produced by exposure to a blast or after a rock concert also deserves special consideration. Noise is the greatest causative factor among the defined etiologies of tinnitus. Since the industrial revolution, an increasing number of people are being exposed to extreme levels of noise. Noise at levels of 85 dBA and higher can lead to both mechanical and metabolic damage of the cochlea [44]. Single, repeated, or continuous exposure to high levels of

noise can cause noise-induced hearing loss and tinnitus. In developed countries, the appetite for leisure noise among the young (like attending rock concerts or discos or the use of MP3 players) is expected to have a substantial, deleterious impact on hearing loss and tinnitus incidence in older generations in the near future [10, 45, 46]. In a retrospective study of 3,466 claimants who sought compensation for occupational noise-induced hearing loss, the prevalence of those reporting tinnitus as a function of hearing loss at 4 kHz, ranged from 41.7 to 56.5%, regardless of the amount of hearing loss sustained [47]. Excessive noise can cause structural damage to the hair cell bundles and can generate excitotoxic effects on the sensory nerve terminals [48]. Compared to the millions of photoreceptors in the eye or the number of olfactory neurons in the nose, the number of sensory hair cells in the cochlea is extremely modest (~15,000). Hair cells die by apoptosis and unlike supporting cells in non-mammalian epithelia, mammalian supporting cells in the organ of Corti do not proliferate to replace lost hair cells, and they do not naturally change their phenotype [49]. Loss of hair cells leads to loss of spiral ganglion neurons, which depend on hair cells for the production of survival factors such as the neurotrophin NT-3 and brain-derived neurotrophic factor. Accumulation of free radicals, excitotoxicity mediated by glutamate receptors, and activation of apoptosis, are predictable players in the loss of cells [46]. Animal experiments show that growth factors and drugs directed against apoptosis, excitotoxicity, and oxidative stress can provide valuable protection from hearing loss and tinnitus if applied during exposure [50] and also probably immediately after exposure.

Otoprotectants at clinical development to prevent noise-induced hearing loss and associated tinnitus are various. In a double-blind placebo-controlled study involving 300 young and healthy military recruits, those supplemented daily with 4 g of oral Mg granulate (6.7 mmol Mg aspartate) showed significantly less permanent threshold shift 1 week post noise than those in the placebo control group (11.2% vs. 21.5%) [51]. In a recent study, normal-hearing adults were dosed orally with placebo or 900 mg of the glutathione prodrug *N*-acetylcysteine 30 min before entering a nightclub where they were exposed to 2 h of loud music. Personal dosimeters recorded a mean noise level of 98.1 dB (A-weighted). An average of 14 dB themporal threshold shift at 4 kHz was reported in subjects immediately after exposure (within 15 min). No significant differences between groups were identified [52]. This observation might be related to the requirement of a high dose of *N*-acetylcysteine to effectively prevent noise-induced hearing loss in animal models, or possibly to the limited ability of the compound to prevent temporary threshold shifts. Several ongoing trials are being performed to test the efficacy of this compound [53]. Sound Pharmaceuticals is developing SPI-1005 (ebselen), an antioxidant. In Phase I studies, it has been shown to have a favorable toxicity and pharmacokinetic profile. The company is now testing the compound in Phase II trials with the Navy/Marine Corps. Auris Medical has a Phase II trial to test AM-101, an NMDA antagonist for the treatment of tinnitus derived from excitotoxicity in the cochlea due to noise trauma, and AM-111 (a JNK MAPK-mediated apoptosis blocker) at pre-clinical studies for the treatment of acute sensorineural hearing loss from acute acoustic trauma, sudden deafness, and inner-ear surgery.

Summarizing, there is consensus among clinicians that acute tinnitus deserves specific attention and that there might be a short therapeutic window for specific pharmacologic interventions. However, there are no treatments available, which have shown repeated efficacy in controlled trials. This might be due to etiologic heterogeneity of acute hearing loss and a high rate of spontaneous recovery. Probably, the most widely used treatment strategy is systemic and intratympanic steroid administration. Further clinical trials to validate treatments of acute tinnitus are urgently needed.

"Chronic Form"

Antidepressants

Antidepressants are commonly used in pharmacological protocols for the management of chronic tinnitus [6–8] (Table 78.2). The reason for such a large use of antidepressants can be found in the well-described comorbidity between depressive disorders and tinnitus. Among all antidepressants that have been investigated for tinnitus, a particular interest has been paid to tricyclic antidepressants, mainly because of their beneficial effects on chronic pain syndromes [54]. This

property of several tricyclic drugs is interesting in view of the proposed etiological similarities between tinnitus and neuropathic pain (see Chaps. 14, 15 and 94) [55]. Among the tricyclic antidepressants analyzed (amitriptyline, trimipramine, and nortriptyline), nortriptyline is worth mentioning. In a small-scale, single-blind placebo-washout study involving patients with severe tinnitus and major depression, nortriptyline significantly reduced depression and tinnitus loudness (10 dB reduction) [56]. In a follow-up double blind-placebo-controlled study involving subjects with severe tinnitus and severe depression or depressive symptoms, nortriptyline significantly reduced depression scores, tinnitus disability scores, and tinnitus loudness (6.4 dB reduction) relative to placebo [57]. There was a significant correlation between the reduction in tinnitus disability scores and depression scores, suggesting that nortriptyline is effective in reducing tinnitus loudness and severity in severely depressed tinnitus patients, but has less benefit in non-depressed individuals [58]. One study has compared amitriptyline with placebo and found after 6 weeks of 100 mg amitriptyline a significant reduction of tinnitus complaints and tinnitus loudness compared to the placebo group [59]. In another study, where amitriptyline was compared with biofeedback, 27.5% of patients reported improvement. However, this was less effective than biofeedback per se [60]. Trimipramine has been evaluated in a small double-blind placebo cross-over study, which did not demonstrate a difference between trimipramine and placebo treatment [61]. It should be noted that the induction of tinnitus with tricyclic antidepressants has been described [62–64].

Selective serotonin reuptake inhibitors (SSRI) such as paroxetine or sertraline have been tested. In a randomized double-blind placebo-controlled study of patients without severe hearing loss, but with depression, anxiety, and a high risk for developing severe tinnitus, sertraline was significantly more effective than placebo in reducing tinnitus loudness and tinnitus severity [65]. In a double-blind, placebo-controlled study involving chronic tinnitus patients, few of whom suffered from depression, the paroxetine group showed little difference from placebo on tinnitus loudness matching, tinnitus handicap questionnaire (THQ) scores, and other measures; however, the paroxetine group showed a significant improvement on tinnitus aggravation compared to the control group [66]. The combination of paroxetine with vestipitant and vestipitant alone is currently undergoing a phase II clinical trial for the treatment of tinnitus (http://clinicaltrials.gov/ct2/show/NCT00394056) by GlaxoSmith Kline. Vestipitant is a novel neurokinin-1 substance P receptor antagonist. Substance P receptor antagonists have been shown to be effective with pain [67]. Information on the clinical effectiveness of these drugs is currently unavailable. Very little has been reported for serotonin norepinephrine reuptake inhibitors (SNRI), such as duloxetine and venlafaxine, or for the dual acting drug mirtazapine. Since activity on norepinephrine reuptake is considered necessary for an antidepressant to be effective on neuropathic pain [54], it might be worthwhile to investigate this group of drugs for its use in tinnitus treatment.

It has to be considered that the scales used for the measurement of tinnitus correlate highly with depression scales. Thus, the observed reduction of tinnitus severity under antidepressant treatment might, at least to some extent, be a pure consequence of the antidepressant effect of the investigated drugs. Nevertheless, available data provide converging evidence that tinnitus patients with depression and anxiety may gain benefit from antidepressant treatment and clearly suggest that the use of an antidepressant in this patient group is highly indicated. However, available results do not allow for determining whether one specific compound is superior to others [66]. Therefore, in clinical practice, selection of the antidepressant drug should be guided by the patient's comorbidities and the side effect profile of the specific drug. For example, in tinnitus patients with insomnia, the use of a sedating antidepressant such as amitriptyline might be preferable. Available studies and clinical experience suggest that the dose of antidepressants for the treatment of tinnitus is in a similar range as that used in the treatment of depression. In general, a low starting dose and slow increase of the dosage reduce side effects. Since beneficial effects do not occur immediately, minimum treatment duration of 6–12 weeks at the effective dose is recommended. If treatment effects are unsatisfactory and the decision is made to discontinue or change treatment, dosage should be reduced slowly. If a patient experiences beneficial effects, treatment should be continued at a stable effective dose for about 6 months, then the dose can be reduced over the course of weeks to months. Should the tinnitus get worse during a reduction of the dose, it is recommended to keep the dosage at the minimum providing relief.

Benzodiazepines

Severe tinnitus can be an extremely stressful condition, heavily influencing every aspects of the patient's life. Since benzodiazepines are allosteric potentiators of the $GABA_A$ receptor [68] and tinnitus is thought to be the result of an imbalance between excitatory and inhibitory neurotransmission toward the former [12], benzodiazepines should have a positive effect on tinnitus by increasing inhibitory neurotransmission. Furthermore, due to their anxioloytic and sleep-inducing properties, benzodiazepines should have beneficial effects on comorbid anxiety and insomnia, and thus may help patients cope with their tinnitus.

In a prospective double-blind placebo-controlled study, 12 weeks of alprazolam administration at an individually adjusted dosage reduced tinnitus loudness in 76% of subjects – measured with a tinnitus synthesizer and a visual analog scale – whereas only 5% showed a reduction in tinnitus loudness in the control group [69]. Although the strong positive effects of alprazolam are encouraging, the study has been criticized because of the small sample size, drug dosing method, and failure to assess emotional effect [7]. On the other hand, diazepam, evaluated in a double-blind triple cross-over trial involving 21 tinnitus patients, had no effect on tinnitus loudness [70]. In a retrospective study of medical records from over 3,000 patients taking clonazepam (0.5–1 mg/day, 60–180 days) for vestibular or cochleovestibular disorders, 32% reported an improvement in their tinnitus [71]. However, the lack of a control group makes it difficult to evaluate the significance of these findings. In a prospective, randomized, single-blind clinical trial involving ten patients per group, clonazepam significantly reduced tinnitus loudness and annoyance (visual analog scale) relative to the control group [72]. Summarizing, available results seem to suggest a beneficial effect of benzodiazepines on tinnitus. However, additional studies are needed in order to evaluate the efficacy of benzodiazepines on tinnitus.

Due to their immediate effects, short-acting benzodiazepines such as lorazepam or alprazolam are widely used for acute treatment of anxiety, agitation, and insomnia – symptoms that frequently occur with tinnitus. The longer acting clonazepam provides some relief in a considerable subgroup of patients. The use of benzodiazepines should be restricted to short periods of time due to the risk of drug dependency. Moreover, caution is warranted since protracted tinnitus has been reported after discontinuation of benzodiazepines [73, 74].

Non-Benzodiazepine Anticonvulsants

Anticonvulsants are increasingly used in the treatment of several non-epileptic conditions, including various psychiatric disorders and pain syndromes [75]. Some of them have also been investigated for the treatment of tinnitus Table 78.2. Diverse pharmacological mechanisms of action are responsible for the therapeutic effects of antiepileptics; among them effects on voltage-gated sodium and calcium channels, and on synaptic transmission – mainly mediated by gamma amino butyric acid type A (GABA$_A$) receptors [76]. Since antiepileptics reduce neuronal excitability, in principle, they should be beneficial for the treatment of tinnitus.

The anticonvulsant carbamazepine, which binds to voltage-gated sodium channels and stabilizes the sodium inactivation state, thereby reducing neural firing [77, 78], has been investigated for tinnitus with mixed results. Based on the assumption that carbamazepine resembles lidocaine in its mechanism of action, three studies investigated the effect of carbamazepine in tinnitus patients who previously had responded to intravenous lidocaine [79–81]. About half of these patients had a positive response to carbamazepine (600–1,000 mg daily). However, controlled studies have not demonstrated benefits of the drug compared to placebo [82–84]. A significant benefit from carbamazepine has been reported for a rare group of patients who have intermittent tinnitus that sounds like a typewriter, popcorn, or ear clicking, and which is caused by a neurovascular conflict [85, 86].

The anticonvulsant gabapentin acts on voltage-gated calcium channels and is also used for the treatment of seizures, neuropathic pain, and migraine [87–89]. The results with gabapentin for the treatment of tinnitus are contradictory. One controlled trial has shown a significant improvement in tinnitus annoyance and loudness for a subgroup of participants with tinnitus related to acoustic trauma [90]. A second study did not detect any improvement in tinnitus handicap, but did report a significant improvement in tinnitus annoyance when compared to placebo [91]. However, further controlled trials did not report any benefit of the compound on tinnitus annoyance or loudness [92, 93].

Thus, although the effects of gabapentin are limited, it might benefit a subpopulation of patients in which tinnitus is associated with acoustic trauma [94].

Pregabalin, which resembles gabapentin in its mechanisms of action, is indicated not only for the treatment of partial seizures but also for neuropathic pain, fibromyalgia, and anxiety [95–97]. Beneficial effects on sleep have also been reported [98]. There are no data available for its use in tinnitus, but based on available data and clinical experience, pregabalin seems to be a promising option for the treatment of tinnitus-related anxiety and insomnia.

Lamotrigine, which stabilizes neuronal membranes by inhibiting voltage-sensitive sodium channels, has been investigated in a double-blind placebo-controlled cross-over clinical trial on 33 patients where it failed to demonstrate a beneficial effect [99]. Valproic acid, which is one of the most frequently prescribed antiepileptic drugs and which acts by multiple mechanisms has not been systematically investigated and only been reported in case reports as useful in tinnitus [100, 101].

Antiglutamatergic Compounds

Glutamate receptor antagonists have been tried in tinnitus sufferers. The rationale behind it is that imbalance between inhibitory vs. excitatory neurotransmission is observed in several regions of the auditory pathway in tinnitus [12, 13]. Moreover, blocking glutamatergic neurotransmission could also exert neuroprotectant effects, as it is known that noise overexposure is followed by an excitotoxic injury of the hair cells [102]. The putative non-selective NMDA receptor antagonist acomprosate has been tried in a double-blind study [103]. Patients received placebo or acamprosate (333 mg, three times per day) and rated the loudness and annoyance of their tinnitus before and at monthly intervals of treatment. Acamprosate had no beneficial effects after 30 days of treatment, a modest benefit at 60 days, and a significant effect at 90 days. Approximately 87% of the subjects in the acamprosate group showed some improvement, including three subjects in which tinnitus disappeared, compared to 44% in the placebo group. A larger clinical trial is currently underway to analyze the encouraging results from this preliminary study (http://clinicaltrials.gov/ct2/show/NCT00596531). Treatment with i.v. caroverine, an antagonist of non-NMDA and NMDA receptors, has been analyzed with contradictory results [104, 105]. In a prospective randomized double-blind cross-over study using the tinnitus handicap inventory to assess efficacy, 90-day treatment with the non-selective NMDA antagonist memantine was no more effective than placebo [106]. The memantine analogue ner-amexane, which blocks both NMDA [107] and α9α10 nicotinic cholinergic receptors [108] is at phase III of a clinical trial setting (http://clinicaltrials.gov/ct2/show/NCT00405886).

Dopaminergic–Antidopaminergic Drugs

Both dopaminergic and antidopaminergic drugs have been proposed for treating tinnitus. Dopaminergic pathways in limbic and prefrontal areas may be involved in mediating emotional aspects of tinnitus [109, 110]. In one double-blind placebo-controlled study, sulpiride significantly reduced subjective ratings of tinnitus and tinnitus visual analogue scores. Effects were more pronounced when sulpiride was combined with either hydroxyzine (an antihistamine and anxi-olytic) or melatonin [111, 112]. The dopamine agonist piribedil was investigated recently in a double-blind placebo-controlled cross-over study. In this study, piribedil was not superior to placebo; however, a post hoc analysis suggested that a subgroup of patients with specific findings in the electrocochleography may benefit from piribedil [113]. Although these results are preliminary and need further studies, they are encouraging and indicate that the dopaminergic pathway might be a promising target for tinnitus relief. A clinical trial is under way to assess the efficacy of flupen-thixol (a type of thioxanthene drug that acts by antagonism of D1 and D2 dopamine, and serotonin type 2A receptors [114]) plus clonazepam, compared to clonazepam alone (http://clinicaltrials.gov/ct2/show/NCT00841230).

Other

Some other miscellaneous drugs have been tested with limited efficacy or that require further controlled trials Table 78.2. These include the HMG-CoA reductase ator-vastatin, the vasodilator cyclandelate, the loop diuretic

furosemide, some herbal products like *Ginkgo biloba*, melatonin, the prostagaldin E1 analogue misoprostol, the L-type calcium blocker nimodipine, the phosphodi-esterase type 5 inhibitor vardenafil, and minerals includ-ing zinc.

Atorvastatin reduces the synthesis of cholesterol by inhibiting HMG-CoA reductase [115]. In a random-ized double-blind placebo-controlled study over 13 months involving elderly patients with elevated cholesterol, atorvastatin failed to slow the progression of age-related hearing loss and significantly reduce tinnitus [116].

Cyclandelate, a vasodilator used in the treatment of cerebrovascular and peripheral vascular disorders, that is believed to act by blocking calcium influx [117], has been investigated for the treatment of tinnitus based on the assumption that some forms of tinnitus may arise from cerebrovascular insufficiency. In an open multi-centric clinical trial of patients with tinnitus, vertigo, and visual disturbances, 90-day treatment with cyclan-delate reduced the severity and frequency of these symptoms with minimal side effects [118]. However, in a subsequent placebo-controlled double-blind study, cyclandelate did not significantly change audiometric measures of tinnitus loudness and pitch and caused side effects in many patients [119].

Furosemide is a loop inhibiting diuretic used to treat congestive heart failure and edema [120]. Furosemide has been proposed as a treatment for tinnitus of "cochlear" origin because it strongly suppresses the endolymphatic potential and other cochlear responses [121]. One initial study has shown that approximately 50% of patients exhibited a reduction of tinnitus symp-toms following intravenous furosemide treatment [122]. Moreover, furosemide has also been found to suppress tinnitus in approximately 40% of patients with Ménière's disease [123]. However, high doses of furosemide can also induce temporary hearing loss and tinnitus [124].

Ginkgo biloba has been proposed for the treatment of a wide range of disorders including tinnitus [125]. In western countries, *Ginkgo biloba* is commonly available in form of leaf extracts, which in Europe and in the United States are among the most widely used and appreciated herbal medications. *Ginkgo* extract contains two main pharmacologically active substances such as flavonoid glycosides and terpene lactones, responsible for many biological effects. Even if some studies have suggested beneficial effects of *Gingko* on tinnitus, particularly in patients with short duration symptoms [126, 127], there is a growing body of evidence from large, well-controlled double-blind placebo-controlled clinical studies clearly indicating that *Gingko* is no more effective in alleviating tinnitus symptoms than placebo [128, 129]. EGb-761 is a concentrated extract of *Ginkgo biloba* (enriched in flavonoids and terpenes) which has a broad spectrum of pharmacologic actions, including a free-radical scavenger effect, and which has shown efficacy for tinnitus in a phase I trial. Several other herbs have been proposed for tinnitus therapy, such as *Cimicifuga racemosa, Cornus officinalis, Verbascum densiflorum*, and *Yoku-kan-san*, but none of them *have* been tested in well-controlled trials [130].

Melatonin is a neurohormone that is primarily produced by the pineal gland. Since it can influence sleep and circadian rhythms, melatonin is nowadays widely used for treating sleep disturbances [131]. This effect of melatonin may have been the rationale for using this drug in the treatment of tinnitus. An open label study found statistically significant improvements on ratings of tinnitus severity and sleep quality scores [132], whereas a double-blind placebo-controlled cross-over study did not demonstrate superiority of melatonin over placebo [133]. A more recent randomized double-blind placebo-controlled study found that melatonin in combination with sulpiride reduced subjective rating of tinnitus and tinnitus loudness more than placebo [112].

Misoprostol is a synthetic prostaglandin E1 analogue which is primarily used to prevent gastric ulcers induced by non-steroidal anti-inflammatory drugs [134]. In a small, placebo-controlled cross-over study, tinnitus severity improved in 33% of subjects during misoprostol treatment (escalating to 800 mg/day), while none improved with placebo [135]. A subsequent double-blind placebo-controlled study has shown a significant reduction of tinnitus loudness with misoprostol treatment, but no differences in subjective measures of tinnitus severity [136]. A further study has shown efficacy of misoprostol in the treatment for chronic tinnitus in hypertensive and/or diabetic patients [137].

Nimodipine is a calcium antagonist, which crosses the blood–brain barrier and blocks L-type calcium channels [138]. Although a first open clinical trial suggested positive effects of nimodipine on tinnitus in some patients [139], these could not be confirmed in a second open clinical trial [140].

Vardenafil represents a potent and highly selective phosphodiesterase type 5 (PDE5) inhibitor that induces an increase of nitric oxide-mediated vasodilatation and which is marketed for treatment of erectile dysfunction and pulmonary hypertension. A prospective randomized double-blind placebo-controlled trial did not show any benefit of vardenafil over placebo [141].

Zinc is an essential catalytic or structural element of many proteins and a signaling messenger that is released by neural activity at many central excitatory synapses. Growing evidence suggests that zinc may also be a key mediator and modulator of the neuronal death associated with transient global ischemia and sustained seizures, as well as perhaps other neurological disease states [142]. While positive results have been reported in some tinnitus patients with hypozincemia, zinc therapy did not result in tinnitus improvement in patients with normal zinc levels in several double-blind placebo-controlled studies [143–148].

Conclusions

Despite the significant unmet clinical need for a safe and effective drug targeting tinnitus relief, there is currently not a single FDA-approved drug on the market. Although the available treatments for the management of the tinnitus patient are diverse, most patients and clinicians are waiting for a drug than can suppress or significantly reduce tinnitus. Thus, there is a pressing need to develop a drug targeting tinnitus relief. A wide variety of drugs with different therapeutic uses have been used off-label with some effect in a limited subset of patients. Tinnitus-related comorbidities such as depression or anxiety can especially be addressed successfully with pharmacological treatment. Since pharmaceutical companies are slowly entering the tinnitus field, this scenario most likely will change in the near future.

References

1. Langguth B, G Hajak, T Kleinjung et al (2006) Repetitive transcranial magnetic stimulation and chronic tinnitus. Acta Otolaryngol Suppl 556–5.

2. Van de Heyning P, K Vermeire, M Diebl et al (2008) Incapacitating unilateral tinnitus in single-sided deafness treated by cochlear implantation. Ann Otol Rhinol Laryngol 117:645–52.

3. Goodey R (2007) Tinnitus treatment: state of the art. Prog Brain Res 166:237–46.

4. Dohrmann K, N Weisz, W Schlee et al (2007) Neurofeedback for treating tinnitus. Prog Brain Res 166:473–85.

5. Jastreboff PJ and MM Jastreboff (2006) Tinnitus retraining therapy: a different view on tinnitus. ORL J Otorhinolaryngol Relat Spec 68:23–9; discussion 9–30.

6. Darlington CL and PF Smith (2007) Drug treatments for tinnitus. Prog Brain Res 166:249–62.

7. Dobie RA (1999) A review of randomized clinical trials in tinnitus. Laryngoscope 109:1202–11.

8. Patterson MB and BJ Balough (2006) Review of pharmacological therapy for tinnitus. Int Tinnitus J 12:149–59.

9. De Ridder D, G De Mulder, T Menovsky et al (2007) Electrical stimulation of auditory and somatosensory cortices for treatment of tinnitus and pain. Prog Brain Res 166:377–88.

10. Vio MM and RH Holme (2005) Hearing loss and tinnitus: 250 million people and a US$10 billion potential market. Drug Discov Today 10:1263–5.

11. Møller AR (2007) Tinnitus: presence and future. Prog Brain Res 166:3–16.

12. Eggermont JJ and LE Roberts (2004) The neuroscience of tinnitus. Trends Neurosci 27:676–82.

13. Eggermont JJ (2007) Pathophysiology of tinnitus. Prog Brain Res 166:19–35.

14. Jastreboff PJ (1990) Phantom auditory perception (tinnitus): mechanisms of generation and perception. Neurosci Res 8:221–54.

15. Schlee W, T Hartmann, B Langguth et al (2009) Abnormal resting-state cortical coupling in chronic tinnitus. BMC Neurosci 10:11.

16. House JW and DE Brackmann (1981) Tinnitus: surgical treatment. Ciba Found Symp 85:204–16.

17. Bauer CA, JG Turner, DM Caspary et al (2008) Tinnitus and inferior colliculus activity in chinchillas related to three distinct patterns of cochlear trauma. J Neurosci Res 86:2564–78.

18. Kaltenbach JA and DA Godfrey (2008) Dorsal cochlear nucleus hyperactivity and tinnitus: are they related? Am J Audiol 17:S148–61.

19. Melcher JR, IS Sigalovsky, JJ Guinan, Jr. et al (2000) Lateralized tinnitus studied with functional magnetic resonance imaging: abnormal inferior colliculus activation. J Neurophysiol 83:1058–72.

20. Weisz N, K Dohrmann and T Elbert (2007) The relevance of spontaneous activity for the coding of the tinnitus sensation. Prog Brain Res 166:61–70.

21. Lambert RC, T Bessaih and N Leresche (2006) Modulation of neuronal T-type calcium channels. CNS Neurol Disord Drug Targets 5:611–27.

22. Surmeier DJ, J Ding, M Day et al (2007) D1 and D2 dopamine-receptor modulation of striatal glutamatergic signaling in striatal medium spiny neurons. Trends Neurosci 30:228–35.

23. Wonnacott S, J Barik, J Dickinson et al (2006) Nicotinic receptors modulate transmitter cross talk in the CNS: nicotinic modulation of transmitters. J Mol Neurosci 30:137–40.

24. Slassi A, M Isaac, L Edwards et al (2005) Recent advances in non-competitive mGlu5 receptor antagonists and their potential therapeutic applications. Curr Top Med Chem 5:897–911.

25. Blank T, I Nijholt, MJ Kye et al (2004) Small conductance Ca2+-activated K+ channels as targets of CNS drug development. Curr Drug Targets CNS Neurol Disord 3:161–7.

26. Duckert LG and TS Rees (1983) Treatment of tinnitus with intravenous lidocaine: a double-blind randomized trial. Otolaryngol Head Neck Surg 91:550–5.

27. Israel JM, JS Connelly, ST McTigue et al (1982) Lidocaine in the treatment of tinnitus aurium. A double-blind study. Arch Otolaryngol 108:471–3.

28. Melding PS, RJ Goodey and PR Thorne (1978) The use of intravenous lignocaine in the diagnosis and treatment of tinnitus. J Laryngol Otol 92:115–21.

29. Gil-Gouveia R and PJ Goadsby (2009) Neuropsychiatric side-effects of lidocaine: examples from the treatment of headache and a review. Cephalalgia 29:496–508.

30. Hollmann MW, ME Durieux and BM Graf (2001) Novel local anaesthetics and novel indications for local anaesthetics. Curr Opin Anaesthesiol 14:741–9.

31. Trellakis S, J Lautermann and G Lehnerdt (2007) Lidocaine: neurobiological targets and effects on the auditory system. Prog Brain Res 166:303–22.

32. Grant GJ, Y Barenholz, EM Bolotin et al (2004) A novel liposomal bupivacaine formulation to produce ultralong-acting analgesia. Anesthesiology 101:133–7.

33. Savastano M (2004) Lidocaine intradermal injection – a new approach in tinnitus therapy: preliminary report. Adv Ther 21:13–20.

34. Tyler R, C Coelho, P Tao et al (2008) Identifying tinnitus subgroups with cluster analysis. Am J Audiol 17:S176–84.

35. Doyle KJ, C Bauch, R Battista et al (2004) Intratympanic steroid treatment: a review. Otol Neurotol 25:1034–9.

36. Slattery WH, LM Fisher, Z Iqbal et al (2005) Intratympanic steroid injection for treatment of idiopathic sudden hearing loss. Otolaryngol Head Neck Surg 133:251–9.

37. Slattery WH, LM Fisher, Z Iqbal et al (2005) Oral steroid regimens for idiopathic sudden sensorineural hearing loss. Otolaryngol Head Neck Surg 132:5–10.

38. Wilson WR, FM Byl and N Laird (1980) The efficacy of steroids in the treatment of idiopathic sudden hearing loss. A double-blind clinical study. Arch Otolaryngol 106:772–6.

39. Narozny W, J Kuczkowski, J Kot et al (2006) Prognostic factors in sudden sensorineural hearing loss: our experience and a review of the literature. Ann Otol Rhinol Laryngol 115:553–8.

40. Stokroos RJ, FW Albers and EM Tenvergert (1998) Antiviral treatment of idiopathic sudden sensorineural hearing loss: a prospective, randomized, double-blind clinical trial. Acta Otolaryngol 118:488–95.

41. Westerlaken BO, RJ Stokroos, IJ Dhooge et al (2003) Treatment of idiopathic sudden sensorineural hearing loss with antiviral therapy: a prospective, randomized, double-blind clinical trial. Ann Otol Rhinol Laryngol 112:993–1000.

42. Bennett MH, T Kertesz and P Yeung (2005) Hyperbaric oxygen for idiopathic sudden sensorineural hearing loss and tinnitus. Cochrane Database Syst Rev CD004739.

43. Lamm K, H Lamm and W Arnold (1998) Effect of hyperbaric oxygen therapy in comparison to conventional or placebo

therapy or no treatment in idiopathic sudden hearing loss, acoustic trauma, noise-induced hearing loss and tinnitus. A literature survey. Adv Otorhinolaryngol 54:86–99.

44. Lim DJ (1986) Effects of noise and ototoxic drugs at the cellular level in the cochlea: a review. Am J Otolaryngol 7:73–99.

45. Biassoni EC, MR Serra, U Richtert et al (2005) Recreational noise exposure and its effects on the hearing of adolescents. Part II: development of hearing disorders. Int J Audiol 44:74–85.

46. Holley MC (2005) Keynote review: The auditory system, hearing loss and potential targets for drug development. Drug Discov Today 10:1269–82.

47. McShane DP, ML Hyde and PW Alberti (1988) Tinnitus prevalence in industrial hearing loss compensation claimants. Clin Otolaryngol Allied Sci 13:323–30.

48. Puel JL, J Ruel, M Guitton et al (2002) The inner hair cell afferent/efferent synapses revisited: a basis for new therapeutic strategies. Adv Otorhinolaryngol 59:124–30.

49. Brigande JV and S Heller (2009) Quo vadis, hair cell regeneration? Nat Neurosci 12:679–85.

50. Lynch ED and J Kil (2005) Compounds for the prevention and treatment of noise-induced hearing loss. Drug Discov Today 10:1291–8.

51. Attias J, G Weisz, S Almog et al (1994) Oral magnesium intake reduces permanent hearing loss induced by noise exposure. Am J Otolaryngol 15:26–32.

52. Kramer S, L Dreisbach, J Lockwood et al (2006) Efficacy of the antioxidant N-acetylcysteine (NAC) in protecting ears exposed to loud music. J Am Acad Audiol 17:265–78.

53. Kopke RD, RL Jackson, JK Coleman et al (2007) NAC for noise: from the bench top to the clinic. Hear Res 226:114–25.

54. Mico JA, D Ardid, E Berrocoso et al (2006) Antidepressants and pain. Trends Pharmacol Sci 27:348–54.

55. Møller AR (2007) Tinnitus and pain. Prog Brain Res 166:47–53.

56. Sullivan MD, RA Dobie, CS Sakai et al (1989) Treatment of depressed tinnitus patients with nortriptyline. Ann Otol Rhinol Laryngol 98:867–72.

57. Sullivan M, W Katon, J Russo et al (1993) A randomized trial of nortriptyline for severe chronic tinnitus. Effects on depression, disability, and tinnitus symptoms. Arch Intern Med 153:2251–9.

58. Katon W, M Sullivan, J Russo et al (1993) Depressive symptoms and measures of disability: a prospective study. J Affect Disord 27:245–54.

59. Bayar N, B Boke, E Turan et al (2001) Efficacy of amitriptyline in the treatment of subjective tinnitus. J Otolaryngol 30:300–3.

60. Podoshin L, Y Ben-David, M Fradis et al (1995) Idiopathic subjective tinnitus treated by amitriptyline hydrochloride/biofeedback. Int Tinnitus J 1:54–60.

61. Mihail RC, JM Crowley, BE Walden et al (1988) The tricyclic trimipramine in the treatment of subjective tinnitus. Ann Otol Rhinol Laryngol 97:120–3.

62. Feder R (1990) Tinnitus associated with amitriptyline. J Clin Psychiatry 51:85–6.

63. Mendis D and M Johnston (2008) An unusual case of prolonged tinnitus following low-dose amitriptyline. J Psychopharmacol 22:574–5.

64. Tandon R, L Grunhaus and JF Greden (1987) Imipramine and tinnitus. J Clin Psychiatry 48:109–11.

65. Zoger S, J Svedlund and KM Holgers (2006) The effects of sertraline on severe tinnitus suffering--a randomized, double-blind, placebo-controlled study. J Clin Psychopharmacol 26:32–9.

66. Robinson S (2007) Antidepressants for treatment of tinnitus. Prog Brain Res 166:263–71.

67. Dionne RA, MB Max, SM Gordon et al (1998) The substance P receptor antagonist CP-99,994 reduces acute postoperative pain. Clin Pharmacol Ther 64:562–8.

68. Smith GB and RW Olsen (1995) Functional domains of GABAA receptors. Trends Pharmacol Sci 16:162–8.

69. Johnson RM, R Brummett and A Schleuning (1993) Use of alprazolam for relief of tinnitus. A double-blind study. Arch Otolaryngol Head Neck Surg 119:842–5.

70. Kay NJ (1981) Oral chemotherapy in tinnitus. Br J Audiol 15:123–4.

71. Gananca MM, HH Caovilla, FF Gananca et al (2002) Clonazepam in the pharmacological treatment of vertigo and tinnitus. Int Tinnitus J 8:50–3.

72. Bahmad FM Jr, AR Venosa and CA Oliveira (2006) Benzodiazepines and GABAergics in treating severe disabling tinnitus of predominantly cochlear origin. Int Tinnitus J 12:140–4.

73. Busto U, L Fornazzari and CA Naranjo (1988) Protracted tinnitus after discontinuation of long-term therapeutic use of benzodiazepines. J Clin Psychopharmacol 8:359–62.

74. Busto U, EM Sellers, CA Naranjo et al (1986) Withdrawal reaction after long-term therapeutic use of benzodiazepines. N Engl J Med 315:854–9.

75. Ettinger AB and CE Argoff (2007) Use of antiepileptic drugs for nonepileptic conditions: psychiatric disorders and chronic pain. Neurotherapeutics 4:75–83.

76. Neligan A and SD Shorvon (2009) The history of status epilepticus and its treatment. Epilepsia 50 Suppl 3:56–68.

77. Catterall WA (1999) Molecular properties of brain sodium channels: an important target for anticonvulsant drugs. Adv Neurol 79:441–56.

78. Willow M, T Gonoi and WA Catterall (1985) Voltage clamp analysis of the inhibitory actions of diphenylhydantoin and carbamazepine on voltage-sensitive sodium channels in neuroblastoma cells. Mol Pharmacol 27:549–58.

79. Melding PS and RJ Goodey (1979) The treatment of tinnitus with oral anticonvulsants. J Laryngol Otol 93:111–22.

80. Sanchez TG, AP Balbani, RS Bittar et al (1999) Lidocaine test in patients with tinnitus: rationale of accomplishment and relation to the treatment with carbamazepine. Auris Nasus Larynx 26:411–7.

81. Shea JJ and M Harell (1978) Management of tinnitus aurium with lidocaine and carbamazepine. Laryngoscope 88:1477–84.

82. Donaldson I (1981) Tegretol: a double blind trial in tinnitus. J Laryngol Otol 95:947–51.

83. Hulshof JH and P Vermeij (1985) The value of carbamazepine in the treatment of tinnitus. ORL J Otorhinolaryngol Relat Spec 47:262–6.

84. Marks NJ, C Onisiphorou and JR Trounce (1981) The effect of single doses of amylobarbitone sodium and carbamazepine in tinnitus. J Laryngol Otol 95:941–5.

85. Levine RA (2006) Typewriter tinnitus: a carbamazepine-responsive syndrome related to auditory nerve vascular compression. ORL J Otorhinolaryngol Relat Spec 68:43–6; discussion 6–7.

86. Mardini MK (1987) Ear-clicking "tinnitus" responding to carbamazepine. N Engl J Med 317:1542.

87. Sivenius J, R Kalviainen, A Ylinen et al (1991) Double-blind study of Gabapentin in the treatment of partial seizures. Epilepsia 32:539–42.

88. Levendoglu F, CO Ogun, O Ozerbil et al (2004) Gabapentin is a first line drug for the treatment of neuropathic pain in spinal cord injury. Spine 29:743–51.

89. Di Trapani G, D Mei, C Marra et al (2000) Gabapentin in the prophylaxis of migraine: a double-blind randomized placebo-controlled study. Clin Ter 151:145–8.

90. Bauer CA and TJ Brozoski (2006) Effect of gabapentin on the sensation and impact of tinnitus. Laryngoscope 116:675–81.

91. Witsell DL, MT Hannley, S Stinnet et al (2007) Treatment of tinnitus with gabapentin: a pilot study. Otol Neurotol 28:11–5.

92. Bakhshaee M, M Ghasemi, M Azarpazhooh et al (2008) Gabapentin effectiveness on the sensation of subjective idiopathic tinnitus: a pilot study. Eur Arch Otorhinolaryngol 265:525–30.

93. Piccirillo JF, J Finnell, A Vlahiotis et al (2007) Relief of idiopathic subjective tinnitus: is gabapentin effective? Arch Otolaryngol Head Neck Surg 133:390–7.

94. Bauer CA and TJ Brozoski (2007) Gabapentin. Prog Brain Res 166:287–301.

95. Hauser W, K Bernardy, N Uceyler et al (2009) Treatment of fibromyalgia syndrome with gabapentin and pregabalin – A meta-analysis of randomized controlled trials. Treatment of postherpetic neuralgia: focus on pregabalin. Pain 4:17–23.

96. Cappuzzo KA (2009) Treatment of postherpetic neuralgia: focus on pregabalin. Clin Interv Aging 4:17–23.

97. Montgomery SA, BK Herman, E Schweizer et al (2009) The efficacy of pregabalin and benzodiazepines in generalized anxiety disorder presenting with high levels of insomnia. Int Clin Psychopharmacol 24:214–22.

98. Russell IJ, LJ Crofford, T Leon et al (2009) The effects of pregabalin on sleep disturbance symptoms among individuals with fibromyalgia syndrome. Sleep Med 10:604–10.

99. Simpson JJ, AM Gilbert, GM Weiner et al (1999) The assessment of lamotrigine, an antiepileptic drug, in the treatment of tinnitus. Am J Otol 20:627–31.

100. Mansbach AL and P Freyens (1983) Tinnitus: current data and treatment with sodium valproate. Acta Otorhinolaryngol Belg 37:697–705.

101. Menkes DB and PM Larson (1998) Sodium valproate for tinnitus. J Neurol Neurosurg Psychiatry 65:803.

102. Guitton MJ, J Wang and JL Puel (2004) New pharmacological strategies to restore hearing and treat tinnitus. Acta Otolaryngol 124:411–5.

103. Azevedo AA and RR Figueiredo (2007) Treatment of tinnitus with acamprosate. Prog Brain Res 166:273–7.

104. Denk DM, H Heinzl, P Franz et al (1997) Caroverine in tinnitus treatment. A placebo-controlled blind study. Acta Otolaryngol 117:825–30.

105. Domeisen H, MA Hotz and R Hausler (1998) Caroverine in tinnitus treatment. Acta Otolaryngol 118:606–8.

106. Figueiredo RR, B Langguth, P Mello de Oliveira et al (2008) Tinnitus treatment with memantine. Otolaryngol Head Neck Surg 138:492–6.

107. Danysz W, CG Parsons, A Jirgensons et al (2002) Amino-alkyl-cyclohexanes as a novel class of uncompetitive NMDA receptor antagonists. Curr Pharm Des 8:835–43.

108. Plazas PV, J Savino, S Kracun et al (2007) Inhibition of the alpha9alpha10 nicotinic cholinergic receptor by neramexane, an open channel blocker of N-methyl-d-aspartate receptors. Eur J Pharmacol 566:11–9.

109. Lockwood AH, RJ Salvi, ML Coad et al (1998) The functional neuroanatomy of tinnitus: evidence for limbic system links and neural plasticity. Neurology 50:114–20.

110. Jastreboff PJ and JW Hazell (1993) A neurophysiological approach to tinnitus: clinical implications. Br J Audiol 27:7–17.

111. Lopez-Gonzalez MA, F Moliner-Peiro, J Alfaro-Garcia et al (2007) Sulpiride plus hydroxyzine decrease tinnitus perception. Auris Nasus Larynx 34:23–7.

112. Lopez-Gonzalez MA, AM Santiago and F Esteban-Ortega (2007) Sulpiride and melatonin decrease tinnitus perception modulating the auditolimbic dopaminergic pathway. J Otolaryngol 36:213–9.

113. Azevedo A, B Langguth, P de Oliveira et al (2009) Tinnitus treatment with piribedil guided by electrocochleography and acoustic otoemisions. Otology and Neurotology. 30:676–80.

114. Reimold M, C Solbach, S Noda et al (2007) Occupancy of dopamine D(1), D (2) and serotonin (2A) receptors in schizophrenic patients treated with flupentixol in comparison with risperidone and haloperidol. Psychopharmacology (Berl) 190:241–9.

115. Sniderman A (2009) Targets for LDL-lowering therapy. Curr Opin Lipidol. 20:282–7.

116. Olzowy B, M Canis, JM Hempel et al (2007) Effect of atorvastatin on progression of sensorineural hearing loss and tinnitus in the elderly: results of a prospective, randomized, double-blind clinical trial. Otol Neurotol 28:455–8.

117. Timmerman H (1987) Calcium modulation and clinical effect. Profile of cyclandelate. Drugs 33 Suppl 2:1–4.

118. Memin Y (1987) Perceived efficacy of cyclandelate in the treatment of cochleovestibular and retinal disturbances related to cerebrovascular insufficiency. A study in general practice comprising 2772 patients. Drugs 33 Suppl 2: 120–4.

119. Hester TO, G Theilman, W Green et al (1998) Cyclandelate in the management of tinnitus: a randomized, placebo-controlled study. Otolaryngol Head Neck Surg 118: 329–32.

120. Hutcheon D, ME Vincent and RS Sandhu (1981) Clinical use of diuretics in congestive heart failure. J Clin Pharmacol 21:668–72.

121. Rybak LP and T Morizono (1982) Effect of furosemide upon endolymph potassium concentration. Hear Res 7: 223–31.

122. Risey JA, PS Guth and RG Amedee (1995) Furosemide distinguishes central and peripheral tinnitus. Int Tinnitus J 1:99–103.

123. Futaki T, M Kitahara and M Morimoto (1977) A comparison of the furosemide and glycerol tests for Meniere's disease. With special reference to the bilateral lesion. Acta Otolaryngol 83:272–8.

124. Kuchar DL and MF O'Rourke (1985) High dose furosemide in refractory cardiac failure. Eur Heart J 6:954–8.

125. Mahadevan S and Y Park (2008) Multifaceted therapeutic benefits of Ginkgo biloba L.: chemistry, efficacy, safety, and uses. J Food Sci 73:R14–9.

126. Holstein N (2000) Ginkgo extract helps patients suffering from tinnitus. Review of the literature shows: tinnitus decreases. MMW Fortschr Med 142:46.

127. Morgenstern C and E Biermann (2002) The efficacy of Ginkgo special extract EGb 761 in patients with tinnitus. Int J Clin Pharmacol Ther 40:188–97.

128. Drew S and E Davies (2001) Effectiveness of Ginkgo biloba in treating tinnitus: double blind, placebo controlled trial. Br Med J 322:73.

129. Rejali D, A Sivakumar and N Balaji (2004) Ginkgo biloba does not benefit patients with tinnitus: a randomized placebo-controlled double-blind trial and meta-analysis of randomized trials. Clin Otolaryngol Allied Sci 29:226–31.

130. Enrico P, D Sirca and M Mereu (2007) Antioxidants, minerals, vitamins, and herbal remedies in tinnitus therapy. Prog Brain Res 166:323–30.

131. Srinivasan V, SR Pandi-Perumal, I Trahkt et al (2009) Melatonin and melatonergic drugs on sleep: possible mechanisms of action. Int J Neurosci 119:821–46.

132. Megwalu UC, JE Finnell and JF Piccirillo (2006) The effects of melatonin on tinnitus and sleep. Otolaryngol Head Neck Surg 134:210–3.

133. Rosenberg SI, H Silverstein, PT Rowan et al (1998) Effect of melatonin on tinnitus. Laryngoscope 108:305–10.

134. Lazzaroni M and GB Porro (2009) Management of NSAID-induced gastrointestinal toxicity: focus on proton pump inhibitors. Drugs 69:51–69.

135. Briner W, J House and M O'Leary (1993) Synthetic prostaglandin E1 misoprostol as a treatment for tinnitus. Arch Otolaryngol Head Neck Surg 119:652–4.

136. Yilmaz I, B Akkuzu, O Cakmak et al (2004) Misoprostol in the treatment of tinnitus: a double-blind study. Otolaryngol Head Neck Surg 130:604–10.

137. Akkuzu B, I Yilmaz, O Cakmak et al (2004) Efficacy of misoprostol in the treatment of tinnitus in patients with diabetes and/or hypertension. Auris Nasus Larynx 31: 226–32.

138. Scriabine A and W van den Kerckhoff (1988) Pharmacology of nimodipine. A review. Ann N Y Acad Sci 522: 698–706.

139. Theopold HM (1985) Nimodipine (Bay e 9736) a new therapy concept in diseases of the inner ear? Laryngol Rhinol Otol (Stuttg) 64:609–13.

140. Davies E, E Knox and I Donaldson (1994) The usefulness of nimodipine, an L-calcium channel antagonist, in the treatment of tinnitus. Br J Audiol 28:125–9.

141. Mazurek B, H Haupt, AJ Szczepek et al (2009) Evaluation of vardenafil for the treatment of subjective tinnitus: a controlled pilot study. J Negat Results Biomed 8:3.

142. Choi DW and JY Koh (1998) Zinc and brain injury. Annu Rev Neurosci 21:347–75.

143. Shambaugh GE, Jr. (1986) Zinc for tinnitus, imbalance, and hearing loss in the elderly. Am J Otol 7:476–7.

144. Coelho CB, R Tyler and M Hansen (2007) Zinc as a possible treatment for tinnitus. Prog Brain Res 166: 279–85.

145. Ochi K, H Kinoshita, M Kenmochi et al (2003) Zinc deficiency and tinnitus. Auris Nasus Larynx 30 Suppl: S25–8.

146. Yetiser S, F Tosun, B Satar et al (2002) The role of zinc in management of tinnitus. Auris Nasus Larynx 29:329–33.

147. Paaske PB, CB Pedersen, G Kjems et al (1991) Zinc in the management of tinnitus. Placebo-controlled trial. Ann Otol Rhinol Laryngol 100:647–9.

148. Arda HN, U Tuncel, O Akdogan et al (2003) The role of zinc in the treatment of tinnitus. Otol Neurotol 24:86–9.

Chapter 79
The Endocannabinoid System in the Cochlear Nucleus and Its Implications for Tinnitus Treatment

Paul F. Smith

Keypoints

1. One of the main theories of tinnitus is that it is a form of sensory epilepsy, sometimes arising from neuronal hyperactivity in the brainstem cochlear nucleus.
2. Antiepileptic drugs have therefore been explored as one potential treatment option.
3. Increasing evidence suggests that cannabinoid drugs can also have antiepileptic effects.
4. Recently, it has been reported that cannabinoid CB1 and CB2 receptors and the endogenous cannabinoid, 2-arachidonylglycerol (2-AG), are expressed in the cochlear nucleus.
5. CB1 receptors appear to negatively regulate the release of glutamate, and it is possible that their down-regulation during the development of tinnitus is responsible for the neuronal hyperactivity associated with the condition.
6. This chapter explores the possibility that cannabinoid drugs might be useful in the treatment of tinnitus.

Keywords Tinnitus • Cochlear nucleus • Cannabinoid receptors • Endocannabinoids

Abbreviations

2-AG	2-Arachidonylglycerol
ACPA	CB1 receptor agonist
CB	Cannabinoid
CN	Cochlear nucleus
Δ^9-THC	Δ^9-tetrahydrocannabinol
DAG	Diacylglycerol lipase
DCN	Dorsal cochlear nucleus
FAAH	Fatty acid amide hydrolase
GABA	Gamma-amino butyric acid
IPSC	Inhibitory post-synaptic currents
LTD	Long-term depression
LTP	Long-term potentiation
MAGL	Monoacylglycerol lipase
NAPE-PLD	N-arachidonoylphosphatidylethanolamine-phospholipase-D
PEA	*N*-palmitoylethanolamide
PSP	Post-synaptic potentials
SCE	Standard cannabis extracts
VCN	Ventral cochlear nucleus

Introduction

Subjective tinnitus is often caused by exposure to loud noise, and sometimes by head/neck injuries or exposure to ototoxic drugs (e.g., salicylate) [1]. Many theorists believe that the mechanisms for initiating tinnitus ('ignition' mechanisms) may be somewhat separate from those that maintain it [2, 3]. While cochlear hair cell dysfunction may trigger noise-induced tinnitus, there is evidence that the maintenance of tinnitus is associated with neuronal hyperactivity in the central auditory nervous system. Acoustic trauma has been correlated with increased spontaneous activity in the dorsal cochlear nucleus, (e.g., [4–9], but see [10, 11] for contradictory data), the inferior colliculus [12–14], and the primary (but not the secondary) auditory cortex [15, 16]. On the basis of such studies, it has been proposed that tinnitus is a form of sensory epilepsy

P.F. Smith (✉)
Department of Pharmacology and Toxicology, School
of Medical Sciences, University of Otago Medical School,
Dunedin, New Zealand
e-mail: paul.smith@stonebow.otago.ac.nz

A.R. Møller et al. (eds.), *Textbook of Tinnitus*,
DOI 10.1007/978-1-60761-145-5_79, © Springer Science+Business Media, LLC 2011

that might therefore be responsive to antiepileptic drugs [17, 18].

However, the evidence supporting the efficacy of antiepileptic drugs in the treatment of tinnitus is inconsistent [see 19 for a review]. Gananca et al. [20] performed a retrospective survey of 25 years of the use of clonazepam and concluded that it was at least partially effective in 32% of cases of tinnitus. Shulman et al. [21] suggested that for tinnitus of central origin, benzodiazepines provided long-term relief in 90% of cases. However, there are no systematic well-controlled clinical trials (i.e., double-blind, placebo-controlled) of the effects of benzodiazepines on tinnitus. Menkes and Larson [22] published a single case study reporting that sodium valproate was effective in suppressing tinnitus; however, there has never been a properly controlled clinical trial conducted to evaluate its efficacy. Carbamazepine has also been used, but other than case studies, e.g., [22, 23], only 3 clinical trials have been published. Melding and Goodey [24] reported that 56% of patients who had responded positively to lidocaine experienced relief from tinnitus following carbamazepine treatment. Sanchez et al. [25] also reported that carbamazepine was effective in reducing tinnitus in 58% of patients and abolished tinnitus in 18% of patients. However, Hulshof and Vermeij [26] reported that carbamazepine was less effective than a placebo in relieving tinnitus.

By far, the best studied antiepileptic drug in the context of tinnitus is gabapentin [27]. Following a positive case study [28], Bauer and Brozoski [29] conducted a prospective, placebo-controlled, single-blind trial of the effects of gabapentin on 39 patients with tinnitus. They found that the drug was effective in reducing tinnitus in some patients, especially those in whom the condition was related to acoustic trauma. However, Witsell et al. [30], in a more recent study using a randomized, placebo-controlled, double-blind trial reported that gabapentin had no significant effect on the severity of tinnitus. Piccirillo et al. [31] reported similar results from an 8-week double-blind, randomized trial.

Cannabinoids as Antiepileptic Drugs

In the late 1980s, Δ^9-tetrahydrocannabinol (Δ^9-THC), the principal psychoactive constituent of the *Cannabis sativa* plant, was demonstrated to act on a specific G-protein–coupled cannabinoid receptor (the "CB1 receptor") [see 32, 33 for reviews]. By 1993, an endogenous cannabinoid named 'anandamide' (arachidonylethanolamide) had been discovered in the porcine brain. A second cannabinoid receptor subtype, the "CB2 receptor", was identified in the peripheral nervous system and immune system [see 32, 33 for reviews]. During the 1990s, these findings were replicated and extended, and it became clear that the endogenous cannabinoid ("endocannabinoid") signaling system was central to many aspects of brain function. A second endocannabinoid, 2-arachidonylglycerol (2-AG), was discovered. It was shown that these arachidonic acid derivatives were synthesized by enzymes such as *N*-arachidonoylphosph atidylethanolamine-phospholipase-D (NAPE-PLD for anandamide) and diacylglycerol lipase (DAG for 2-AG) and metabolized by enzymes such as fatty acid amide hydrolase (FAAH for anandamide and 2-AG) and monoacylglycerol lipase (MAGL for 2-AG) [see 32, 34 for reviews]. As a consequence of these revolutionary developments in cannabinoid pharmacology, there has been intense interest in the development of both synthetic and natural cannabinoid compounds for the treatment of a wide range of disorders, including spasticity, pain, urinary dysfunction, and epilepsy [35].

Cannabinoids have been reported to have pro- or anticonvulsant effects under different circumstances [36, 37]. Epidemiological studies suggest that cannabis' use is common amongst people with epilepsy and that the drug is believed by users to have anticonvulsant actions [38]. Gordon and Devinsky [36] reviewed the literature on the effects of marijuana on epileptic symptoms and concluded that although cannabis' use can reduce seizure frequency in many cases and provoke seizure activity in some cases, it probably has no effect in most cases. Unfortunately, there have been a very few clinical studies of the effects of cannabinoids on seizure activity in humans, and no large, well-controlled, double-blind studies [36, 37]. Nonetheless, some recent reports of the anti-epileptic effects of the synthetic Δ^9-THC, dronabinol, have been published, e.g., [39].

CB1 receptors are thought to be localized mainly presynaptically and in many cases, through the inhibition of calcium influx at presynaptic terminals, inhibit the release of classical neurotransmitters, including glutamate [40, 41]. Wallace et al. [42] used the rat pilocarpine model of epilepsy to investigate the effects of cannabinoids on seizure activity. Δ^9-THC, as well as the synthetic cannabinoid receptor agonist $R(+)$

WIN55,212, completely blocked spontaneous seizure activity. The CB1 receptor antagonist SR141716A potentiated seizure duration and frequency, suggesting that endocannabinoids might have been suppressing seizure activity. Biochemical analyses of the hippocampus indicated that 2-AG was present in elevated concentrations during the seizure activity, which the authors hypothesized might play a role in termination of the seizures. Immunohistochemical and western blot analyses also showed that CB1 receptor expression was increased throughout the hippocampus during the seizure activity, again suggesting the possibility that the endocannabinoid system might serve some form of anti-epileptic function. Using the pentylenetetrazole model of epilepsy in mice, Shafaroodi et al. [43] demonstrated that the CB1 receptor agonist ACPA increased the seizure threshold, whereas the CB1 receptor antagonist AM251 blocked this anticonvulsant effect.

Not all studies have demonstrated an anti-epileptic action for CB1 receptor agonists, suggesting that where CB1 receptors are localized to GABAergic terminals, cannabinoids could potentiate epileptiform activity [44]. Nakatsuka et al. [45] used patch clamp recordings in granule cells of the human dentate gyrus to show that activation of CB1 receptors could suppress inhibitory synaptic activity. Bath application of WIN55212-2 suppressed the frequency of spontaneous inhibitory postsynaptic currents (IPSCs) as well as reducing their amplitude. The CB1 receptor antagonist AM251 completely blocked these effects, suggesting that they were mediated by CB1 receptors. It is likely that the activation of CB1 receptors on presynaptic GABAergic terminals results in decreased GABA release, which was responsible for the reduction in IPSC frequency and amplitude. These and similar previous results demonstrate that CB1 receptor agonists have the potential to induce as well as decrease epileptiform activity, depending on which presynaptic terminals the drugs affect.

Whalley et al. [46] have provided evidence that emphasizes the potential complexity of the effects of cannabis itself on epileptiform activity. Comparing standard cannabis extracts (SCEs) with and without Δ^9-THC, they found that while Δ^9-THC depressed depolarizing post-synaptic potentials (PSPs) in rat olfactory cortex neurons, SCEs with and without Δ^9-THC could potentiate PSPs. This effect could be blocked by the CB1 receptor antagonist SR141716A. One of the most surprising findings from this study was that the potentiation of PSPs was actually greater when a Δ^9-THC–free SCE was used. The authors suggested that a novel, unknown component in cannabis may override the decrease in excitatory synaptic transmission caused by Δ^9-THC and that this constituent may be partly responsible for the pro-convulsant effects of cannabis that have sometimes been reported. In a similar study, Wilkinson et al.[47], using seizure activity induced in rat piriform cortical brain slices by oxotremorine-M, found that an SCE had a more potent anticonvulsant action than Δ^9-THC alone, but that the Δ^9-THC–free extract also had anticonvulsant activity.

Marsicano et al. [48] bred mutant mice lacking CB1 receptors on principal forebrain neurons, but not on inhibitory interneurons, and found that kainic acid caused extreme seizure activity in vivo compared to wild-type littermates. In vitro, the threshold for neuronal excitation caused by kainic acid was reduced in the hippocampi of CB1 receptor–deficient mice. In wild-type mice, kainic acid administration resulted in increased concentrations of anandamide in the hippocampus. However, 2-AG or palmitoylethanolamide (PEA) levels were not affected and principal hippocampal neurons appeared to be protected. The anandamide uptake inhibitor UCM707 was also shown to protect against kainic acid–induced seizures. However, no protective effects occurred in the mutant mice, suggesting that CB1 receptors are necessary for the brain to protect against kainic acid–induced hyperexcitability. Mechoulam and Lichtman [49] have suggested that the endocannabinoid system may serve as a natural, endogenous anticonvulsant network. The fact that endocannabinoids such as anandamide and 2-AG are synthesized on demand and are rapidly metabolized adds validity to the concept that they may function as an "on-demand" defense system [37]. Recently, Ludanyi et al. [50] have reported that in hippocampi from humans with chronic epilepsy, CB1 receptor gene and protein expression, as well as DAG expression, were down-regulated in a way that correlated with the degree of sclerosis.

Wallace et al. [51] have also demonstrated that anandamide and its analogue, O-1812, have potent anticonvulsant effects in the maximal electroshock seizure model in mice. These effects could be blocked by the CB1 receptor antagonist SR141716A. Similar to the results of Wallace et al. [42], SR141716A significantly reduced the seizure threshold, consistent with the idea that activation of cannabinoid receptors by naturally occurring anandamide serves an anticonvulsant role. Anandamide and the synthetic CB1 receptor agonist WIN-55212-2 (but not the inactive isomer WIN 55212-3) have both been shown to reduce epileptiform activity in hippocampal slices. This effect can be blocked by SR141716A [52]. It is likely that these effects were mediated by anandamide and WIN-55212-2 acting on cannabinoid receptors on presynaptic glutamatergic terminals.

N-palmitoylethanolamide (PEA) is another member of the family of endogenous lipid amides and is a putative endocannabinoid. PEA has been reported to demonstrate anticonvulsant activity in the mouse maximal electroshock and chemically induced convulsion models (e.g., pentylentetrazol, bicuculline, strychnine) [53]. In the maximal electroshock model, the anticonvulsant effects of PEA were comparable to phenytoin [53]. PEA has also been shown to have an anticonvulsant action in the kindling model of epilepsy in rats [54].

All together, this evidence suggests that the endocannabinoid system serves a critical function in the control of hyperexcitability and that endocannabinoids and cannabinoid drugs may have antiepileptic effects that might be useful in the treatment of tinnitus.

Endocannabinoids and Cannabinoid Receptors in the Cochlear Nucleus

Until recently, there have been a few studies of cannabinoid receptors in the cochlear nucleus (CN). CB1 receptors were identified in the CN in early autoradiographic studies; however, Herkenham et al. [55] concluded that the CN had the lowest density of CB1 receptors of any brain region. This finding may have discouraged researchers from investigating CB1 receptors in the CN. However, the density of receptors is not the only indication of their likely significance. Receptor affinity and efficacy (i.e., the intracellular effect of receptor activation) are also important. In fact, Brievogel et al. [56] have reported that CB1 receptors in many brainstem regions have greater coupling to their G proteins (i.e., greater efficacy) than those in limbic and neocortical areas.

The first studies of CB1 receptors in the CN were published by Zheng et al. [57] and Tzounopoulos et al. [58]. Zheng et al. [57] used immunohistochemistry and stereological methods to quantify CB1 receptor expression in the dorsal and ventral cochlear nuclei (DCN and VCN, respectively). They found substantial CB1 receptor labeling on many different cell types, such as stellate cells, giant cells, fusiform cells, and corn cells in the DCN, as well as globular bushy cells, elongate cells, and octopus cells in the VNC (Figs. 79.1 and 79.2). Some of the labeling was cytoplasmic, which seemed inconsistent with the accepted presynaptic localization of CB1 receptors; however, it has been reported that the CB1 receptor undergoes extensive trafficking between the cytoplasm and the presynaptic terminals, especially in brain regions where it is very active. An earlier western blot study by Ashton et al. [59] had reported CB1 receptor levels in the CN that were similar to the cerebellar granule cell layer and cerebellar nuclei.

These results were confirmed and extended by Tzounopoulos et al. [58], who found CB1 receptors at

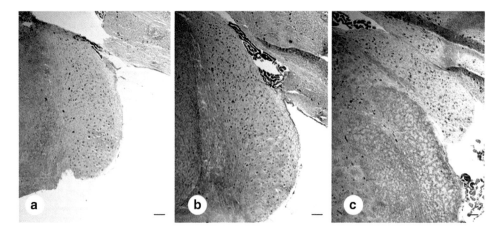

Fig. 79.1 CB1 receptor immunoreactivity in the rat cochlear nucleus. Reproduced from [57] with permission

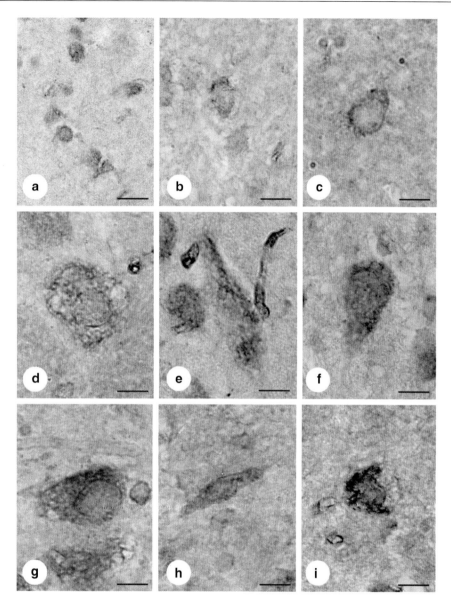

Fig. 79.2 High magnification view of CB1 receptor immunoreactivity in different cell types of the cochlear nucleus. (**a**): Granule cells in the molecular layer of the dorsal cochlear nucleus. (**b**): A stellate cell. (**c**): A cartwheel cell. (**d**): A giant cell. (**e**): A fusiform cell. (**f**): A corn cell. (**g**): A globular bushy cell. (**h**): An elongate cell. (**i**): An octopus cell. Reproduced from [57] with permission

the parallel fiber/cartwheel cell, parallel fiber/fusiform cell synapses, and on the dendritic spines of cartwheel cells using electron microscopy. In the same study, using patch clamp recording from cartwheel cells, they demonstrated that while the CB1 receptor antagonist AM-251 had no effect on basal synaptic transmission, it not only blocked the induction of long-term depression (LTD) but also induced long-term potentiation (LTP).

In a further study, Zhao et al. [60] showed that glutamate terminals in the DCN expressed more CB1 receptors than glycinergic terminals, and that both fusiform and cartwheel cells expressed DAG α and β, the two enzymes necessary for the production of 2-AG. Both forms of DAG were found in the dendritic spines of cartwheel but not fusiform cells, suggesting that the production of 2-AG is closer to parallel fiber synapses in cartwheel cells compared to fusiform cells. This was

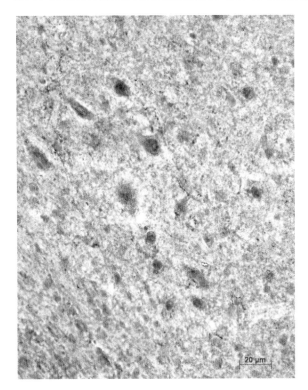

Fig. 79.3 CB2 receptor immunoreactivity in the rat cochlear nucleus (×63). Reproduced from [61] with permission

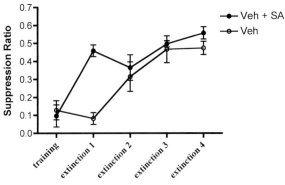

Fig. 79.4 Confirmation of tinnitus in rats used for the CB1 receptor study. Drinking suppression ratios for rats receiving vehicle + saline injections (*solid circles*, $n=6$) or a vehicle injection (*open circles*, $n=6$). Symbols represent means and bars 1 SD. Reproduced from [57] with permission

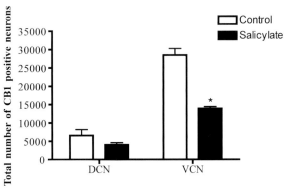

Fig. 79.5 Down-regulation of CB1 receptor-positive neurons in the dorsal and ventral cochlear nuclei (DCN and VCN) in control (*open bars*) and salicylate-treated (*filled bars*) rats. Data are expressed as means and bars as 1 SEM. *$P<0.01$ compared to the control group. Reproduced from [57] with permission

the first evidence for a complete endocannabinoid system in the DCN, involving, at the very least, 2-AG acting on CB1 receptors. Zhao et al. [60] concluded that the endocannabinoid system exerts a greater control over excitatory than inhibitory inputs in the DCN and that endocannabinoid signaling is a major factor affecting the balance of excitation and inhibition in this part of the central auditory system.

The expression of the second subtype of cannabinoid receptor in the brain, the CB2 receptor, is controversial. However, Baek et al. [61] found CB2 receptor labeling in the CN, which suggests the possibility that both cannabinoid receptor subtypes could be involved regulating the function of the CN (Fig. 79.3).

Cannabinoids, Cannabinoid Receptors, and Tinnitus

Only one study to date has investigated the relationship between CB1 receptors in the CN and the development of tinnitus. Zheng et al. [57] investigated the

expression of CB1 receptors in the DCN and VCN in rats in which tinnitus was induced with salicylate injections. They used a modification of the conditioned behavioral paradigm developed by Jastreboff et al. [62] in order to confirm that the animals were experiencing tinnitus (Fig. 79.4). In animals with tinnitus, they found a significant decrease in the number of neurons expressing CB1 receptors in the VCN compared to control animals. On the other hand, there was no significant difference in the DCN (Fig. 79.5). Zhao et al. [60] have suggested that if CB1 receptors were down-regulated on glutamatergic terminals synapsing on fusiform cells, this would increase the excitation of fusiform cells, possibly leading to hyperexcitability.

Unfortunately, there have been no systematic studies to date of the effects of cannabinoids on tinnitus, in either animals or humans. One case report has been published in which tinnitus was eliminated by administration of the synthetic Δ^9-THC, dronabinol [63]. However, the patient had intracranial hypertension with many other symptoms and had been previously using cannabis.

Given that agonists for the CB1 receptor have been shown to exert antiepileptic effects, that antiepileptic drugs do appear to alleviate tinnitus at least in some circumstances and that the endocannabinoid system is emerging as an important influence in the function of the CN; it seems worthwhile to pursue the possibility that cannabinoid drugs could be useful in the treatment of tinnitus. Since some of these drugs, including natural extracts (e.g., Sativex®), are already available in many countries for the treatment of nausea, wasting, chronic pain, and spasticity [see 64 for a review], it would not be difficult to test their effects in patients with tinnitus. Despite concerns about intoxication, most studies suggest that provided the levels of Δ^9-THC are low, few adverse side effects are experienced [65, 66].

Conclusions

This chapter has explored the possible significance of the endocannabinoid system for the cochlear nucleus and the treatment of tinnitus. There is substantial evidence to suggest that tinnitus is, in many cases at least, a form of sensory epilepsy [18]. Although the results of clinical trials of the effects of antiepileptic drugs on tinnitus are not consistent, these drugs have been shown to alleviate tinnitus in some cases. Therefore, since cannabinoids have been shown to exert antiepileptic effects in many parts of the brain, it is possible that they will exert similar effects in the central auditory system. In this respect, it is important to note that both an endocannabinoid (2-AG) and two cannabinoid receptor subtypes (CB1 and CB2) have been found in the CN [57, 58, 60, 61]; the CB1 receptors are functional, are preferentially localized to glutamatergic terminals, and indeed mediate synaptic plasticity in the CN [58, 61]; and CB1 receptors have been shown to down-regulate in the VCN in an animal model of tinnitus [57]. The functional significance of the endocannabinoid system for tinnitus, therefore, deserves urgent investigation.

Acknowledgements This research was generously supported by the Jean Cathie Estate.

References

1. Eggermont, JJ. Cortical tonotopic map reorganization and its implication for treatment of tinnitus. Acta Oto-laryngol (Stockh) 2006, 126:9–12
2. Eggermont, JJ and Roberts, LE. The neuroscience of tinnitus. Trends Neurosci 2004, 27(11):676–682
3. Baguley, DM. What progress have we made with tinnitus? Acta Otolaryngol (Stock) 2006, 126:4–8
4. Zhang, JS and Kaltenbach, JA. Increases in spontaneous activity in the dorsal cochlear nucleus of the rat following exposure to high intensity sound. Neurosci Lett 1998, 250:197–200
5. Kaltenbach, JA and Afman, CE. Hyperactivity in the dorsal cochlear nucleus after intense sound exposure and its resemblance to tone-evoked activity: a physiological model for tinnitus. Hear Res 2000, 140(1–2):165–172
6. Brozoski, TJ, Bauer, CA, and Caspary, DM. Elevated fusiform cell activity in the dorsal cochlear nucleus of chinchillas with psychophysical evidence of tinnitus. J Neurosci 2002, 22(6):2383–2390
7. Zacharek, MA, Kaltenbach, JA, Mathog, TA, and Zhang, J. Effects of cochlear ablation on noise induced hyperactivity in the hamster dorsal cochlear nucleus: implications for the origin of noise induced tinnitus. Hear Res 2002, 172(1–2):137–143
8. Kaltenbach, JA, Zacharek, MA, Zhang, J and Frederick, S. Activity in the dorsal cochlear nucleus of hamsters previously tested for tinnitus following intense tone exposure. Neurosci Lett 2004, 355(1–2):121–125
9. Kaltenbach, JA and Zhang, J. Intense sound-induced plasticity in the dorsal cochlear nucleus of rats: Evidence for cholinergic receptor upregulation. Hear Res 2007, 226(1–2):232–243
10. Chang, H, Chen, K, Kaltenbach, JA, Zhang, J and Godfrey, DA. Effects of acoustic trauma on dorsal cochlear nucleus neuron activity in slices. Hear Res 2002, 164:59–98
11. Ma, WLD and Young, ED. Dorsal cochlear response properties following acoustic trauma: response maps and spontaneous activity. Hear Res 2006, 216–217:176–188
12. Wang J, Ding D and Salvi RJ. Functional reorganization in chinchilla inferior colliculus associated with chronic and acute cochlear damage. Hear Res 2002, 168:238–249
13. Basta, D and Ernst, A. Noise-induced changes of neuronal spontaneous activity in mice inferior colliculus brain slices. Neurosci Lett 2004, 368:297–302
14. Basta, D and Ernst, A. Effects of salicylate on spontaneous activity in inferior colliculus brain slices. Neurosci Res 2004, 50:237–243
15. Norena, AJ and Eggermont, JJ. Changes in spontaneous neural activity immediately after an acoustic trauma: implications for neural correlates of tinnitus. Hear Res 2003, 183:137–153
16. Seki, S and Eggermont, JJ. Changes in spontaneous firing rate and neural synchrony in cat primary auditory cortex after tone-induced hearing loss. Hear Res 2003, 180:28–38
17. Møller, AR. Similarities between severe tinnitus and chronic pain. J Am Acad Audiol 2000, 11(3):115–124

18. Møller, AR. Pathophysiology of tinnitus. Otolaryngol Clin North Am 2003, 36:249–266

19. Simpson, JJ and Davies, WE. Recent advances in the pharmacological treatment of tinnitus. Trends Pharmacol Sci 1999, 20(1):12–18

20. Gananca, MM, Caovilla, HH, Gananca, FF, Gananca, CF, Munhoz, MS, da Silva, ML and Serafini, F. Clonazepam in the pharmacological treatment of vertigo and tinnitus. Int Tinnitus J 2002, 8:50–53

21. Shulman A, Strashun, AM and Goldstein, BA. GABA(A)-benzodiazepine-chloride receptor-targeted therapy for tinnitus control: preliminary report. Int Tinnitus J 2002, 8:30–36

22. Menkes, DB and Larson, PM. Sodium valproate for tinnitus. J Neurol Neurosurg Psychiatr 1998, 65:803

23. Levine, RA. Typewriter tinnitus: a carbamazepine-responsive syndrome related to auditory nerve vascular compression. J Otorhinolaryngol Relat Spec 2006, 68:43–46

24. Melding, PS and Goodey, RJ. The treatment of tinnitus with oral anticonvulsants. J Laryngol Otol 1979, 93(2):111–122

25. Sanchez, TG, Balbani, AP, Bittar, RS, Bento, RF and Camara, J. Lidocaine test in patients with tinnitus: rationale of accomplishment and relation to the treatment with carbamazepine Auris, Nasus. Larynx 1999, 26:411–417

26. Hulshof, JH and Vermeij. The value of carbamazepine in the treatment of tinnitus. J Otorhinolaryngol Related Spec 1985, 47:262–266

27. Bauer, CA and Brozoski, TJ. Gabapentin. Prog Brain Res 2007, 166:287–301

28. Zapp, JJ. Gabapentin for the treatment of tinnitus: a case report. Ear Nose Throat J 2001, 80:114–116

29. Bauer, CA and Brozoski, TJ. Effect of gabapentin on the sensation and impact of tinnitus. Laryngoscope 2006, 116:675–681

30. Witsell, DL, Hannley, MT, Stinnet, S and Tucci, DL. Treatment of tinnitus with gabapentin: a pilot study. Otol Neurol 2007, 28(1):11–15

31. Piccirillo, JF, Finnell, J, Vlahiotis, A, Chole RA and Spitznagel, E Jr. Relief of idiopathic subjective tinnitus: is gabapentin effective? Arch Otolaryngol Head Neck Surg 2007, 133:390–397

32. Iversen, L. Cannabis and the brain. Brain 2003, 126:1252–1270

33. Howlett, AC, Breivogel, CS and Childers, CR. Cannabinoid physiology and pharmacology: 30 years of progress. Neuropharmacology 2004, 47:345–358

34. De Petrocellis, L, Cascio, MG and Di Marzo, V. The endocannabinoid system: A general review and latest additions. Br J Pharmacol 2004, 141:765–774

35. Piomelli, D, Giuffrida, A, Calignano, A and Rodriguez de Fonseca, F. The endocannabinoid system as a target for therapeutic drugs. Trends Pharmacol Sci 2000, 21:218–224

36. Gordon, E and Devinsky, O. Alcohol and marijuana: Effects on epilepsy and use by patients with epilepsy. Epilepsia 2001, 42:1266–1272

37. Lutz, B. On-demand activation of the endocannabinoid system in the control of neuronal excitability and epileptiform seizures. Biochem Pharmacol 2004, 68:1691–1698

38. Zagnoni, PG and Albano, C. Psychostimulants and epilepsy. Epilepsia 2002, 43(Suppl 2):28–31

39. Lorenz, R. On the application of cannabis in paediatrics and epileptology. Neuro Endocrinol Lett 2004, 25:40–44

40. Alger, BE. Retrograde signalling in the regulation of synaptic transmission: focus on endocannabinoids. Prog Neurobiol 2002, 68:247–286

41. Kreitzer, AC and Regehr, WG. Retrograde signalling by endocannabinoids. Curr Opin Neurobiol 2002, 12:324–330

42. Wallace, MJ, Balir, RE, Falenski, KW, Martin, BR and Delorenzo, RJ. The endogenous cannabinoid system regulates seizure frequency and duration in a model of temporal lobe epilepsy. J Pharmacol Exp Ther 2003, 307:129–137

43. Shafaroodi, H, Samini, M, Moezi, L, Homayoun, H, Sadeghipour, H, Tavakoli, S, Hajrasouliha, AR and Dehpour, AR. The interaction of cannabinoids and opioids on pentylenetetrazole-induced seizure threshold in mice. Neuropharmacology 2004, 47:390–400

44. Hoffman, AF and Lupica, CR. Mechanisms of cannabinoid inhibition of GABA(A) synaptic transmission in the hippocampus. J Neurosci 2000, 20:2470–2479

45. Nakatsuka, T, Chen, H-X, Roper, SN and Gu, JG. Cannabinoid receptor-1 activation suppresses inhibitory synaptic activity in human dentate gyrus. Neuropharmacology 2003, 45:116–121

46. Whalley BJ, Wilkinson JD, Williamson, EM and Constanti, A. A novel component of cannabis extract potentiates excitatory synaptic transmission in rat olfactory cortex in vitro. Neurosci Lett 2004, 365:58–63

47. Wilkinson, JD, Whalley, BJ, Baker, D, Pryce, G, Constanti, A, Gibbons, S and Williamson, EM. Medicinal cannabis: Is delta-9-tetrahydrocannabinol necessary for all its effects? J Pharm Pharmacol 2003, 55:1687–1694

48. Marsicano, G, Goodenough, S, Monory, K, Hermann, H, Eder, M, Cannich, A, Azad, SC, Cascio, MG, Gutierrez, SO, van der Stelt, M, Lopez-Rodriguez, ML et al. CB1 cannabinoid receptors and on-demand defense against excitotoxicity. Science 2003, 302:84–88

49. Mechoulam, R and Lichtmanm AH. Stout guards of the central nervous system. Science 2003, 302:65–67

50. Ludanyi, A, Eross, L, Czirjak, S, Vajda, J, Halasz, P, Watanabe, M, Palkovits, M, Magloczky, Z, Freund, TF and Katona, I. Down regulation of the CB1 cannabinoid receptor and related molecular elements of the endocannabinoid system in epileptic human hippocampus. J Neurosci 2008, 28:2976–2990

51. Wallace, MJ, Martin, BR and Delorenzo, RJ. Evidence for a physiological role of endocannabinoids in the modulation of seizure threshold and severity. Eur J Pharmacol 2002, 452:295–301

52. Ameri, A, Wilhelm, A and Simmet, T. Effects of the endogenous cannabinoid, anandamide, on neuronal activity in rat hippocampal slices. Br J Pharmacol 1999, 126:1831–1839

53. Lambert, DM, Vandervoorde, S, Diependale, G, Govaerts, SJ and Robert, AR. Anticonvulsant activity of N-palmitoylethanolamide, a putative endocannabinoid, in mice. Epilepsia 2001, 42:321–327

54. Sheerin, AH, Zhang, X, Saucier, DM and Corcoran, ME. Selective antiepileptic effects of N-palmitoylethanolamide, a putative endocannabinoid. Epilepsia 2004, 45:1184–1188

55. Herkenkam, M, Lynn, AB, Johnson, MR, Melvin, LS, de Costa, BR and Rice, KC. Characterization and localization of cannabinoid receptors in rat brain: a quantitative in vitro autoradiographic study. J Neurosci 1991, 11:563–583

56. Brievogel, CS, Sim, LJ and Childers, SR. Regional differences in cannabinoid receptor/G protein coupling in rat brain. J Pharmacol Exp Ther 1997, 282:1632–1642

57. Zheng, Y, Baek, J-H, Smith, PF and Darlington, CL. Cannabinoid receptor down-regulation in the ventral cochlear nucleus in an animal model of tinnitus. Hear Res 2007, 228:105–111

58. Tzounopoulos, T, Rubio, ME, Keen, JE, and Trussell, LO. Coactivation of pre- and post-synaptic signaling mechanisms determines cell-specific spike-timing-dependent plasticity. Neuron 2007, 54:291–301

59. Ashton, JC, Zheng, Y, Liu, P, Darlington, CL and Smith, PF. Immunohistochemical characterization and localization of cannabinoid CB1 receptor protein in the rat vestibular nucleus complex and effects of unilateral vestibular deafferentation. Brain Res 2004, 1021:266–273

60. Zhao, Y, Rubio, ME and Tzounopoulos, T. Distinct functional and anatomical architecture of the endocannabinoid system in the auditory brainstem. J Neurophysiol 2009, 101:2434–2446

61. Baek, J-H, Zheng, Y, Darlington, CL and Smith, PF. Cannabinoid CB2 receptor expression in the vestibular and cochlear nuclei. Acta Otolaryngol (Stockh) 2008, 128(9): 961–967

62. Jastreboff, PJ, Brennan, JF, Coleman, JK, and Sasaki, CT. Phantom auditory sensation in rats: an animal model of tinnitus. Behav Neurosci 1988, 102(6):811–822

63. Raby, WN, Modica, PA, Wolintz, RJ, and Murtaugh, K. Dronabinol reduces signs and symptoms of idiopathic intracranial hypertension: a case report. J Ocul Pharmacol Ther 2006, 22(1):68–75

64. Smith, PF. Symptomatic treatment of multiple sclerosis using cannabinoids: Recent advances. Expert Rev Neurother 2007, 7(9):1157–1163

65. Wade, DT, Makela, PM, House, H, Bateman, C and Robson. Long-term use of a cannabis based medicine in the treatment of spasticity and other symptoms in multiple sclerosis. Multiple Sclerosis 2006, 12:639–645

66. Smith, F and Darlington, CL. Drug treatments for subjective tinnitus: serendipitous discovery versus rational drug design. Curr Opin Invest Drug 2005, 6(7):712–716

Chapter 80
Treatment of Somatosensory Tinnitus

Tanit Ganz Sanchez and Carina Bezerra Rocha

Keypoints

1. Treatment of somatosensory tinnitus often needs a multidisciplinary approach.
2. Treatment of patients who have signs of bone problems, muscular tension in the temporomandibular joint area or neck, should be directed to correct these problems as the first option.
3. If correction of bone or muscular disorders of temporomandibular joint and neck fails in relieving tinnitus, "symptomatic" treatment should be initiated.

Keywords Tinnitus • Somatic • Myofascial trigger point • Cervical spine • Temporomandibular joint • Treatment

Abbreviations

Bot-A	Botulinum toxin type A
CNS	Central nervous system
DCN	Dorsal cochlear nuclei
GET	Gaze-evoked tinnitus
MPS	Myofascial pain syndrome
MTP	Myofascial trigger point
TENS	Transdermelectrical nerve stimulation
THI	Tinnitus handicap inventory
TMD	Temporomandibular disorder
TMJ	Temporomandibular joint
VAS	Visual analogue scale

T.G. Sanchez (✉)
Department of Otolaryngology, University of São Paulo
Medical School São Paulo, Av. Padre Pereira de Andrade,
545/174-F, São Paulo, SP, Brazil 05469-000
e-mail: tanitsanchez@gmail.com

Introduction

As discussed in Chap. 43, tinnitus may have a somatosensory cause (primary origin in head and neck trauma, dental or cervical manipulation, or even in unknown chronic pain) or somatosensory modulation (auditory origin with temporary somatosensory influence in loudness, pitch or localization). Thus, it is logical to consider that these patients need evaluation of their temporomandibular joint (TMJ) and neck before deciding the best treatment option. However, otolaryngologists and neurologists are usually the first physicians to be sought by patients with tinnitus, and unfortunately little attention is often given to somatosensory influence on tinnitus [1]. Many patients with tinnitus would benefit from the opinion of a dentist or physiotherapist (according to customs and availability in each country). Whenever it is agreed that a patient with tinnitus has problems such as muscular tension in TMJ related to the TMJ or the neck, these problems should be addressed (see also Chaps. 95 and 96).

In this chapter, we will discuss different approaches for treating somatosensory tinnitus including certain methods that are generally used for patients with tinnitus but have been modified for somatosensory tinnitus.

Treatment Options to Somatosensory Tinnitus

Treatments for somatosensory tinnitus are now under development by several researchers, including a group associated with the Tinnitus Research Initiative, working to define the best options for patients with somatosensory tinnitus. This chapter will describe results from several such studies, some of which are under development.

A.R. Møller et al. (eds.), *Textbook of Tinnitus*,
DOI 10.1007/978-1-60761-145-5_80, © Springer Science+Business Media, LLC 2011

Relaxing Muscle Tension in Jaw and Neck

Considering that patients with temporomandibular disorders (TMD) often have muscular tension in both jaw and neck – as well as tinnitus, vertigo/dizziness, and aural fullness – the first aim of the treatment of somatosensory tinnitus should be to reduce such muscle tension [2].

Methods used for treatment of TMD by the dentist and the physiotherapist are described in Chaps. 95 and 96.

Many patients with such problems also benefit from performing regular stretching exercises of their suboccipital muscles at home, as well as rotation movements in the atlanto-occipital joint – especially to the restricted side – and relaxing exercises involving breathing with the diaphragm.

Such treatment of muscle tension in the jaw and neck can reduce tinnitus, as well as decrease other tension-related symptoms such as vertigo, aural fullness, and pain in the jaw, neck, or headache [2]. Björne showed that the intensity of all such symptoms was significantly reduced ($p < 0.001$) at a 3-year follow-up examination for patients who used this type of treatment.

Focal administration of lidocaine in jaw muscles (mainly the lateral pterygoid or masseter) or neck muscles (mainly trapezius and sternocleidomastoid) may temporarily reduce tension [3], and sometimes tinnitus decreases while the local anesthetic is active [2].

This means that relieving TMJ disorders and other forms of muscular tension may also relieve tinnitus. Felício et al. [4] observed that patients with TMD and auditory symptoms improved after using bite splints for 8 weeks. Wright and Bifano [5] reported 82.5% improvement of tinnitus in patients whose TMD improved with the association of cognitive therapy, bite splints, and home exercises.

Deactivating Myofascial Trigger Points (MTP)

The relationship between myofascial trigger point (MTP) deactivation and tinnitus relief was initially demonstrated by injecting a local anesthetic in these painful spots. In 1960, Travell [6] related a patient's tinnitus to a MTP located in the deep portion of masseter, because local injection of lidocaine on the ipsilateral masseter's myalgic spots relieved the patient's tinnitus. In this study, the injections were repeated eight times and the relief lasted from several days up to 4 weeks. Wyant [7] described two patients whose tinnitus was relieved after injections with steroid and lidocaine in MTPs in the cervical region. In this study, both tinnitus and pain relief occurred for 4 months.

In an unpublished study of 178 patients compared with a control group [3], tinnitus completely disappeared in 15% of the cases after cervical MTP injection. There were 178 people included in the treatment group. The control group consisted of 39 participants with tinnitus, who were not treated. In a 6-month follow-up after the last injection, tinnitus improved in more than 30%, as opposed to 15% of a control group.

Relief or reduction of tinnitus from injection of a local anesthetic (without corticosteroid or adrenalin) or dry needling depends on mechanical disruption of the myofascial trigger point and inactivation of the MTP. Inactivation of MTP can be done by injection of Botulinum toxin A because of its destruction of motor endplates. It is important for optimal effectiveness that the patients perform an active range of motion following the injection [8].

A 2005 study by Eriksson and co-workers [9] showed that some tinnitus patients benefited from stretching and massage. In a double-blind placebo-controlled randomized clinical trial, we have shown a significant decrease of tinnitus loudness ($p < 0.001$), decrease of pain intensity ($p < 0.001$), decrease of THI scores ($p = 0.01$), and decrease of the number of MTP ($p < 0.001$) from inactivation of MTPs.

The treatment was based on ten sessions of real and ten sessions of sham MTP deactivation in tinnitus patients. The real treatment used digital pressure in each MTP of eight possible muscles and some home orientations (muscle stretching, postural guidance, and hot pack). Seventeen patients from the experimental group and nine patients from the control group were analyzed by a blind researcher before treatment began and again after 10 weeks of the treatment. Moreover, two patients who had bilateral tinnitus now have complete relief, one who had bilateral tinnitus no longer has tinnitus in one ear, and another who had seven different kinds of tinnitus now only has three. Three patients with normal pure-tone audiograms, (i.e., tonal thresholds from 250 to 8,000 Hz better than 25 dBHL) were the ones with the best results after treatment, regardless of tinnitus being constant or intermittent, unilateral or bilateral.

Many techniques to relieve MTP have been published, but a few have been supported by scientific evidence.

The most commonly used treatment procedures for the myofascial pain syndrome (MPS) was reviewed by Vernon and co-workers [10] showing that these methods were supported by evidence from treatment. Laser therapy, transcutaneous electrical nerve stimulation, acupuncture, and magnet therapy for MTP and MPS are treatments, which are supported, in varying degrees, scientifically. The duration of relief fluctuates among therapies. Evidence is weak, however, for ultrasound therapy and is limited for electrical muscle stimulation, high-voltage galvanic stimulation, interferential current, and frequency-modulated neural stimulation.

We describe a patient below who was cured of her tinnitus through deactivation of MTPs in our institute:

> Case report: A 51-year-old female complained of bilateral tinnitus for the last 4 years (worse on the right), scoring 10 on the visual analog scale. She also had pain in her shoulders, cervical spine, and the left side of her face for 4 years (score of 9) together with other complaints such as dizziness, daily bruxism, subjective hearing loss, and depression. A physical ENT exam showed no pathologies, and she was referred to a physiotherapist because of her pain. During palpation of MTP of the left sternocleidomastoid, she noticed a complete disappearance of her tinnitus. Tinnitus returned when pressure was no longer applied. Palpation of MTP of the right trapezius caused a change in pitch of her tinnitus. Palpation of her left trapezius muscle caused temporary dizziness. Nine muscles of her head, neck, and shoulder girdle had myofascial trigger points. She was treated for her MPS by digital deactivation (pressure release, Fig. 80.1) of MTPs, together with exercise at home including muscle stretching, self-massage in the MTP, isometric strengthening,

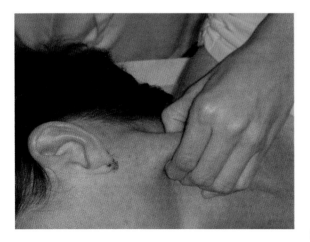

Fig. 80.1 Pressure release of the left sternocleidomastoid for deactivation of a myofascial trigger point in a patient with pain, tinnitus, and dizziness. This technique is used in the Tinnitus Research Group of the University of São Paulo School of Medicine

and postural guidance. During her weekly sessions in the clinic, she showed gradual and lasting improvement of her pain, tinnitus, and dizziness. After 6 months, she had total remission of these problems.

Manual Therapies: Cervical Manipulation

Chiropractic care is a popular and successful management option for reversible functional disorders of the cervical spine and other body structures. Some studies have demonstrated that such manipulation can relieve tinnitus [11–15].

> Thus, Alcantara and co-authors [13] described how chiropractic treatment of a patient with cervical subluxation and TMD could reduce the patient's tinnitus, vertigo, and hearing loss. The symptoms eventually ceased after 9 sessions. Kessinger and Boneva [11] documented clinical changes after some chiropractic sessions in a geriatric patient with tinnitus, vertigo, hearing loss, and cervical alterations from C_3 to C_7. Throughout the sessions, the patient's symptoms were alleviated, and structural/functional improvements were also evident through radiographic examination.
>
> Contrary to classical chiropractic treatment, Arlen's atlas therapy is performed without traction, rotation, or extension of the cervical spine. Kaute [16] considers that irritation and tension of posterior cervical muscle may precipitate a great afferent input to the vestibular nuclei in the brainstem, and this response seems to be one of the origins of idiopathic tinnitus. Diminishing the tension via atlas therapy seems to lower the proprioception and nociception output, leading to normalization of the flow of information to the brainstem and, as a consequence, the lessening of tinnitus.
>
> It seems that some somatosensory tinnitus could be alleviated by correcting the misalignment of the cervical spine through manual therapy (chiropractic or osteopathy), especially in the upper cervical. This readjustment may allow the entire spine to reposition itself and possibly readjust the input of the region through the somatosensory pathway on the auditory system.
> Nevertheless, as much as this topic has been receiving more attention in the current literature, it still needs further clarification.
>
> Transelectrical nerve stimulation (TENS): The use of electrical stimulation is used routinely in treatment of both pain and tinnitus. Its use in treatment of tinnitus is discussed in a separate chapter (Chap. 91).

Botulinum Toxin Type A

Botulinum toxin type A (Bot-A) is a neurotoxin that can inhibit the release of acetylcholine at the neuromuscular junction [17]. Due to its known paralytic effect, it is administered locally to control muscle hyperactivity in many different disorders, as well as in cosmetics.

Besides the paralytic effect, Bot-A might have a direct antinociceptive action through the blockage of the autonomic nervous system, in addition to the neuromuscular action [18–22]. Moreover, through a peripheral mechanism, it can inhibit the sensitization of central trigemino-vascular neurons [23]. Thus, Bot-A has more than one effect to control headache, migraine, and chronic neuropathic pain. Recently, Bot-A has been used for treatment of tinnitus [24, 25].

A crossover double-blind study of the effect of Bot-A on tinnitus showed that it had little effect on tinnitus [26]. One group was first injected with Bot-A and, 4 months later, with a saline injection into three sites around the ear: 1 cm above pinna, 1 cm behind – at 2 o'clock position – and 1 cm behind auricle – 5 o'clock position. The second group was first injected with placebo and, four months later, with BoNT-A injection. Seven participants reported a decrease in their tinnitus after the Bot-A injection and two improved after placebo.

When tinnitus was analyzed through global clinical impression by the patient ("better", "worse," or "the same") and through THI, the effects of Bot-A were significantly better than placebo ($p<0.05$), when comparing pre-treatment and 4 months after injection ($p=0.04$). Such results suggest that the Bot-A can play a role in tinnitus management by reducing the peripheral inputs from cervical, temporal, frontal, and periauricular muscles.

A similar study [24] showed that of 26 participants, 7 improved, 13 worsened, and 16 were unchanged. It should be considered when discussing treatment with botulinum toxin that it has potentially serious side effects, such as changing cardiac reflexes [26]. Eighty percent of people treated with botulinum toxin had abnormalities in their electrocardiogram. The fact that the treatment probably has to be repeated for long periods is a disadvantage that when used for treating other disorders such as hemifacial spasm has made many people discontinue treatment [27].

Training Exercises Repeating the Movements That Evoke Tinnitus Modulation

Exercise in general may be beneficial because it increases brain-derived neurotrophic factor (BDNF) [28]. Training by repetitive movements generates specific neurophysiological changes by activating neural plasticity. It has been demonstrated that activation of neural plasticity has a therapeutic effect on many disorders, such as vestibular diseases, where the repetition of specific maneuvers can decrease vestibular disturbances. Sanchez et al. [29] showed that muscle contractions may change the pattern of tinnitus, from temporary worsening to temporary improvement, with repetition of the maneuvers that modulate tinnitus. A similar strategy was able to cure one of our patients who had gaze-evoked tinnitus (GET) at the Tinnitus Research Group of the University of São Paulo School of Medicine by repeating all the eye maneuvers that evoked her tinnitus [1].

Case study: A 39-year-old woman with profound hearing loss in the right ear of unknown etiology since her teenage days developed a left vestibular schwannoma, which was subtotally removed. She received a right Nucleus 22 cochlear implant and 1 month after the surgery, at about the time the implant was activated, she developed a GET whenever her implant was on (without the implant, she had no tinnitus even with eye movements). A hissing occurred in the right ear with right- or down-gaze and in the left ear with left- or up-gaze; these symptoms had persisted for the last 4 years before the person decided to seek help. Motivated by the known benefit of vestibular rehabilitation for vestibular disorders, we recommended a habituation program to be done twice a day. The program consisted of gaze to the extreme right ten times and holding each position of gaze for 1 s before returning to the primary position of gaze. This exercise was then repeated to the left, up, and down directions of gaze. After 2 weeks, the tinnitus caused by vertical change of gaze from down stopped and the up-gaze tinnitus decreased after the 2-week period of exercise. The loudness of the tinnitus associated with vertical eye gaze decreased from 10 to 1 on the visual analog scale. However, her horizontal GET persisted and began to respond to treatment only when her gaze exercise program was modified by increasing the duration of each extreme of right and left gaze from 1 to 5 s. After 4 weeks, her right and left gaze-evoked tinnitus improved, and the loudness decreased from 10 to 6 and 10 to 2 on the visual analog scale, respectively. The increase of the duration of each gaze position from 5 to 30 s, for 3 more weeks, caused all GET to cease and not occur again out to an 18-month follow-up and at the end of all exercises. Her entire treatment program lasted 14 weeks.

The central element of vestibular rehabilitation is the repetition of a set of exercises, which compensates for the central nervous system abnormalities using eye movements, as well as cervical and body maneuvers. In the particular case discussed above, the habituation of GET occurred with the repetition of eye movements that used to trigger it. That the vertical component of patient's GET responded sooner to treatment than the horizontal component indicates that more than one neural network or process is involved in the habituation therapy.

Due to this surprising and long-term cure of tinnitus, we decided to use the modulation phenomenon as a basis for treating other patients through the repetition of the movements that modulate tinnitus. This treatment should be individually targeted to each patient, considering the particular movements that evoke tinnitus modulation, such as this example from work at the Tinnitus Research Group of the University of São Paulo School of Medicine.

Case Report: A 65-year-old woman with normal pure-tone thresholds complained about her constant bilateral (mostly left ear) "refrigerator's engine" tinnitus. The loudness of her tinnitus increased from bilateral compression of her temporal area. She was asked to perform a therapy involving repetitive pressure on temporal regions from where the tinnitus could be modulated making ten repetitions, three times a day. Her tinnitus began to decrease after 7 days of such training. After 2 months, her tinnitus could no longer be modulated by pressure on her temporal area for several days on the right side; after 4 months, her tinnitus could no longer be modulated, and the baseline tinnitus on the right side disappeared for several days. Tinnitus modulation and the perception of baseline tinnitus also decreased in the left ear, although this process took a longer time than for the right ear.

We are presently studying more details about the treatment of tinnitus through the repetition of maneuvers that modulate it.

In conclusion, individuals with somatosensory tinnitus or tinnitus that can be modulated may improve by coordinated exercise of the muscles that can modulate the tinnitus.

Acknowledgments The authors thank the Tinnitus Research Initiative for the creation and support of a workgroup of Somatosensory Tinnitus and Modulating Factors.

References

1. Sanchez, TG and Kii, MA (2008) Modulating tinnitus with visual, muscular and tactile stimulation. Seminars in Hearing, Tinnitus: Part II 29, 350–60
2. Björne, A (2007) Assessment of temporomandibular and cervical spine disorders in tinnitus patients. Prog Brain Res 166, 215–9
3. Estola-Partanen, M (2000) Muscular tension and tinnitus: an experimental trial of trigger point injections on tinnitus [dissertation]. Tampere: Faculty of Medicine, University of Tampere
4. Felício, CM, Melchior, MO, Ferreira, CL and Silva, MA (2008) Otologic symptoms of temporomandibular disorder and effect of orofacial myofunctional therapy. Cranio 26, 118–25
5. Wright, EF and Bifano, SL (1997) Tinnitus improvement through TMD therapy. J Am Dent Assoc 128, 1424–32
6. Travell, J (1960) Temporomandibular joint pain referred from muscle of the head and neck. J Prosthet Dent 10, 745–63
7. Wyant, GM (1979) Chronic pain syndrome and their treatment II: Trigger points. Canad Anaesth Soc J 26, 216–19
8. Travell, J and Simons, DG (1999) Myofascial pain and dysfunction: The trigger point manual, upper half of body. Baltimore: Williams & Wilkins
9. Eriksson, M, Gustafsson, S and Axelsson, A (1995) Tinnitus and trigger points: a randomized cross-over study. In: Proceedings of the Fifth International Tinnitus Seminar, Portland, OR, pp 81–3. Eds Reich, GE and Vernon, JA
10. Vernon, H and Schneider, M (2009) Chiropractic management of myofascial trigger points and myofascial pain syndrome: a systematic review of the literature. J Manipulative Physiol Ther 32, 14–24
11. Kessinger, RC and Boneva, DV (2000) Vertigo, tinnitus, and hearing loss in the geriatric patient. J Manipulative Physiol Ther 23, 352–62
12. Kessinger, RC and Boneva, DV (2000) Case study: acceleration/deceleration injury with angular kyphosis. J Manipulative Physiol Ther 23, 279–87
13. Alcantara, J, Plaugher, G, Klemp, DD and Salem, C (2002) Chiropractic care of a patient with temporomandibular disorder and atlas subluxation. J Manipulative Physiol Ther 25, 63–70
14. Leboeuf-Yde, C, Pedersen, EN, Bryner, P, Cosman, D, Hayek, R, Meeker, WC, Shaik, J, Terrazas, O, Tucker, J and Walsh, M (2005) Self-reported nonmusculoskeletal responses to chiropractic intervention: a multination survey. J Manipulative Physiol Ther 28, 294–302
15. DeVocht, JW, Schaeffer, W and Lawrence, DJ (2005) Chiropractic treatment of temporomandibular disorders using the activator adjusting instrument and protocol. Altern Ther Health Med 11, 70–3
16. Kaute, BB (1998) The influence of atlas therapy on tinnitus. Int Tinnitus J 4, 165–7
17. Simpson, LL (1986) Molecular pharmacology of botulinum toxin and tetanus toxin. Ann Rev Pharmacol Toxicol 26, 427–53
18. Blersch, W, Schulte-Mattler, WJ, Przywara, S, May, A, Bigalke, H and Wohlfarth, K (2002) Botulinum toxin A and the cutaneous nociception in humans: a prospective, double-blind, placebo-controlled, randomized study. J Neurol Sci 205, 59–63
19. Dolly, O (2003) Synaptic transmission: inhibition of neurotransmitter release by botulinum toxins. Headache 43(Suppl), 16–24
20. Aoki, KR (2005) Review of a proposed mechanism for the antinociceptive action of botulinum toxin type A. Neurotoxicology 26, 785–93
21. Cui, M, Khanijou, S, Rubino, J and Aoki, KR (2004) Subcutaneous administration of botulinum toxin A reduces formalin-induced pain. Pain 107, 125–33

22. Durham, PL and Cady, R (2004) Regulation of calcitonin gene-related peptide secretion from trigeminal nerve cells by botulinum toxin type A: implications for migraine therapy. Headache 44, 35–42

23. Oshinsky, M, Poso-Rosich, P, Luo, J, Hyman, S and Silberstein, SD (2004) Botulinum toxin A blocks sensitization of neurons in the trigeminal nucleus caudalis. Cephalalgia 24, 781

24. Stidham, KR, Solomon, PH and Roberson, JB (2005) Evaluation of botulinum toxin A in treatment of tinnitus. Otolaryngol Head Neck Surg 132, 883–89

25. Láinez, MJ and Piera, A (2007) Botulinum toxin for the treatment of somatic tinnitus. Prog Brain Res 166, 335–8

26. Girlanda, P, Vita, G, Nicolosi, C et al (1992) Botulinum toxin therapy: distant effects on neuromuscular transmission and autonomic nervous system. J Neurol Neurosurg Psychiatry 55, 844–5

27. Marion, M-H (1997) Hemifacial spasm: Treatment with botulinum toxin (long term results). In: Hemifacial Spasm. A Multidisiplinary Approach. Eds Sindou, M, Keravel, Y and Møller, AR. Wien: Springer, pp 141–4

28. Vaynman, S and Gomez-Pinilla, F (2005) License to run: exercise impacts functional plasticity in the intact and injured central nervous system by using neurotrophins. Neurorehabil Neural Repair 19, 283–95

29. Sanchez, TG, da Silva Lima, A, Brandão, AL, Lorenzi, MC and Bento RF (2007) Somatic modulation of tinnitus: test reliability and results after repetitive muscle contraction training. Ann Otol Rhinol Laryngol 116, 30–5

Chapter 81
Tinnitus Treatment: Botulinum Toxin

Miguel J.A. Láinez, Alejandro Ponz, and Anna Piera

Keypoints

1. Somatosensory tinnitus (objective or subjective) is tinnitus that can be modulated by stimulation of the somatosensory system.
2. Abnormal interactions between the auditory and the somatosensory nervous system that may occur at several levels of the central nervous system cause somatosensory tinnitus.
3. This chapter discusses how administration of a botulinum toxin can alleviate tinnitus and the mechanism of its action, and how that relates to its effects on chronic pain.
4. A proven benefit of botulinum toxin in patients with objective tinnitus is also discussed.

Keywords Somatosensory tinnitus • Botulinum toxin • Autonomic pathway • Headache • Dorsal cochlcar nucleus

Abbreviations

BoNT-A	Botulinum toxin type A
CGRP	Calcitonin gene related peptide
CNS	Central nervous system
DCN	Dorsal cochlear nucleus
HFS	Hemifacial spasm
MSN	Medullary-somatosensory nucleus
PAM	Posterior auricular muscle
PTA-2	Pure tone average 2

M.J.A. Láinez (✉)
Department of Neurology, Hospital Clínico Universitario,
University of Valencia, Avenida Blasco Ibáñez, 17,
46010 Valencia, Spain
e-mail: jlaineza@meditex.es

SDS	Speech discrimination scores
THI	Tinnitus handicap inventory
TMJ	Temporomandibular joint disorders

Introduction

While the pathophysiology of the different forms of tinnitus remains poorly understood, there is increasing evidence from electrophysiologic and functional neuroimaging studies that severe chronic tinnitus is caused by abnormal functioning of the central nervous system (CNS) [1] (see Chap. 10) brought about by activation of neural plasticity (see Chap. 12).

Somatosensory Tinnitus

The finding that people can develop tinnitus from forceful head and neck contractions [2] is an example of somatosensory tinnitus. Temporomandibular joint disorders (TMJ) are also often associated with tinnitus [3] (see Chap. 53), thus another example of somatosensory tinnitus. Effective treatment of the underlying disorder may resolve somatosensory tinnitus in some cases, but not in others [4]. The neural mechanisms of somatosensory tinnitus have been discussed elsewhere in this volume (see Chap. 9).

Reports have shown that somatic stimulation of the head or upper neck can suppress tinnitus through somatosensory pathways (see Chap. 80), supporting some forms of somatosensory tinnitus treatment such as administration of central muscle relaxants (benzodiazepines, etc.), acupuncture, biofeedback, and electrical stimulation for relaxing the muscles.

A.R. Møller et al. (eds.), *Textbook of Tinnitus*,
DOI 10.1007/978-1-60761-145-5_81, © Springer Science+Business Media, LLC 2011

Botulinum Toxin Type A

Botulinum toxin type A (BoNT-A) is a neurotoxin. Administered locally, it can inhibit the release of acetylcholine at the neuromuscular junction [5]. It is used therapeutically in disorders of muscle hyperactivity, including movement disorders, dystonia, spasticity, cerebral palsy, gastrointestinal disorders, and urological disorders. BoNT-A was first used to treat strabismus [6], and it is now widely used in cosmetics to diminish wrinkles and frown lines because of its paralytic effect [7]. It should be noted that botulinum toxin has system effects that include cardiovascular reflexes [8].

In vitro and in vivo studies [9] have demonstrated that BoNT-A inhibits the release of nociceptive mediators such as glutamate, substance P, and calcitonin gene-related peptide (CGRP) from nociceptive fibers [10], suggesting that BoNT-A may have a direct antinociceptive action through its effects on the autonomic nervous system in addition to its neuromuscular action [11–13]. Moreover, BoNT-A, through a peripheral mechanism, has also been shown to inhibit central sensitization of central trigeminovascular neurons [14], which takes an integral part in the development, progression, and maintenance of migraine headaches [14, 15]. Central sensitization is also considered to be a potential mechanism underlying the development of chronic daily headaches in patients with migraine (see Chap. 61) [16].

Clinical trials have suggested that BoNT-A may be an effective and safe prophylactic headache medication in the treatment of migraine and other headache disorders [17]. Thus, evidence has been presented that the blockage of the autonomic pathways, and not just its paralytic effect, contributes to the ability of BoNT-A to control headaches, chronic neuropathic pain, and migraines [10, 15, 18]. These similarities between tinnitus and pain were the reason that we investigated the effect of BoNT-A on tinnitus.

Botulinum Toxin in Tinnitus Treatment

In a prospective double-blind study of the effect of BoNT-A with 30 participants with tinnitus, 26 participants completed the two parts of the study, and the results were included in the analysis. Seven of the participants' tinnitus improved, in 3 it worsened, and in 16 it was unchanged; following placebo, the tinnitus of 2 participants improved, in 7 it worsened, and in 17 it was unchanged.

In this study, 30 patients with tinnitus were randomly placed into one of two treatment arms. Patients received either BoNT-A (20–50 units) or saline injection at the first treatment, and the opposite treatment 4 months later. Tinnitus and hearing were evaluated using questionnaires similar to the tinnitus handicap inventory (THI). Audiograms, pure-tone average-2 (PTA-2), and speech discrimination scores (SDS) were obtained prior to the first and second injection for all participants. BoNT-A or placebo were injected into three sites around the ear; 1 cm above the superior aspect of the auricle, 1 cm behind the auricle at the 2 o'clock position, and 1 cm behind the auricle at the 5 o'clock position [18].

When tinnitus was classified as "better", "worse," or "same" (global clinical impression estimated by patients), the treatment and placebo groups were statistically and significantly ($p<0.005$) different. Also, THI scores decreased significantly between pretreatment and 4 months after BoNT-A injection ($p=0.04$). The results of this study suggest that administration of BoNT-A may be useful in the management of tinnitus.

BoNT-A administered to the middle-ear cavity has been used to treat patients with tinnitus due to myoclonic tensor tympani contractions [19–21].

Animal studies of the possible adverse effects of administration of BoNT-A into the middle-ear cavity showed no negative effects [22].

In a study of patients with tinnitus from hemifacial spasm (HFS) in whom posterior auricular muscle is affected [23], BoNT-A was applied on the side to which the tinnitus was referred, obtaining a symptomatic improvement in 9 of 14 patients. Thus, patients who have spasm in their posterior auricular muscles (PAMs) may be candidates for treatment with botulinum toxin.

Conclusions

The effect of a local application of BoNT-A on tinnitus is assumed to be achieved through a reduction of inputs to the CNS from receptors in cervical, temporal, frontal, and periauricular muscles. This is assumed to produce a reduction of the activity in the medullary-somatosensory nucleus (MSN) (Nucleus Z), thereby reducing the input to the dorsal cochlear nucleus (DCN). This is assumed to be the basis for the use of BoNT-A in management of chronic headaches, and similar action may explain its effect on subjective tinnitus in patients with somatosensory tinnitus.

BoNT-A is proven to be effective for treatment of patients with objective tinnitus from palatal and middle-ear myoclonus when injected into the middle-ear cavity or injected in the palatal muscles with laryngoscopic guidance.

References

1. Møller AR (2003) Pathophysiology of tinnitus. Otolaryngol Clin North Am, 36: 249–266.
2. Levine RA, EC Nam, Y Oron et al, (2007) Evidence for a tinnitus subgroup responsive to somatosensory based treatment modalities, in Tinnitus: Pathophysiology and Treatment, Progress in Brain Research, B Langguth et al, Editors. Elsevier: Amsterdam. 195–207.
3. Morgan DH (1992) Tinnitus of TMJ origin. J Craniomandibul Pract, 10: 124–129.
4. Levine RA (2004) Somatic tinnitus, in Tinnitus: Theory and Management, JB Snow, Editor. Hamilton: Decker.
5. Simpson LL (1986) Molecular pharmacology of botulinum toxin and tetanus toxin. Ann Rev Pharmacol Toxicol, 26: 427–453.
6. Scott AB (1980) Botulinum toxin injections into extraocular muscles as an alternative to strabismus surgery. Ophthalmology, 87:1044–1049.
7. Klein A (2001) Introduction. Semin Cutan Med Surg, 20:69–70.
8. Girlanda P, G Vita, C Nicolosi, S Milone, and C Messina (1992) Botulinum toxin therapy: distant effects on neuromuscular transmission and autonomic nervous system. J Neurol Neurosurg Psychiatry, 55: 844–845.
9. Blersch W, W Schulte-Mattler, S Przywara, A May, H Bigalke, and K Wholfarth (2002) Botulinum toxina A and the cutaneous nociception in humans: a prospective double-blind, placebo-controlled, randomized study. J Neurol Sci, 205: 59–63.
10. Dolly O (2003) Synaptic transmission: inhibition of neurotransmitter release by botulinum toxins. Headache, 43 (Suppl 1): S16–S24.
11. Aoki KR (2003) Evidence for antinociceptive activity of botulinum toxin type A in pain management. Headache, 43 (Suppl 1): 9–15.
12. Cui M, S Kahanijou, J Rubino, and KR Aoki (2004) Subcutaneous administration of botulinum toxin A reduces formalin-induced pain. Pain, 107: 125–133.
13. Durham PL and R Cady (2004) Regulation of calcitonin gene-related peptide secretion from trigeminal nerve cells by botulinum toxin type A: implications for migraine therapy. Headache, 44: 35–42, Discussion 42–43.
14. Oshinsky ML, P Pozo-Rosich, J Luo, S Hyman, and S Silberstein (2004) Botulinum toxin type A blocks sensitization of neurons in the trigeminal nucleus caudalis. Cephalalgia, 24: 781.
15. Silberstein S, N Mathew, J Saper, and S Jenkins (2000) Group FtBMCR: botulinum toxin type A as a migraine preventive treatment. Headache, 40: 445–450.
16. Burstein R and M Jakubowsky (2004) Analgesic triptan action in an animal model of intracranial pain: a race against the development of central sensitization. Ann Neurol, 55: 27–36.
17. Dodick DW, A Mauskop, AH Elkind, et al, (2005) Botulinum toxin type A for the prophylaxia of chronic daily headache: subgroup analysis of patients not receiving other prophylactic medications: a randomized double-blind placebo-controlled study. Headache, 45: 315–324.
18. Barrientos N and P Chana (2003) Botulinum toxin type A in prophylactic treatment of migraine headaches: a preliminary study. J Headache Pain, 4: 146–151.
19. Stidham KR, PH Solomon, and JB Roberson (2005) Evaluation of botulinum toxin A in treatment of tinnitus. Otolaryngol Head Neck Surg, 132(6): 883–889.
20. Scolozzi P, E Carrera, B Jaques, and T Kuntzer (2005) Successful treatment of a postpolio tinnitus with type a botulinum toxin. Laryngoscope, 115(7): 1288–1290.
21. Bryce GE, and MD Morrison (1998) Botulinum toxin treatment of essential palatal myoclonus tinnitus. J Otolaryngol, 27(4): 213–216.
22. Zehlicke T, C Punke, D Dressler, and HW Pau (2008) Intratympanic application of botulinum toxin: experiments in guinea pigs for excluding ototoxic effects. Eur Arch Otorhinolaryngol, 265(2): 167–170.
23. Kiziltan M, R Sahin, N Uzun, and G Kiziltan (2006) Hemifacial spasm and posterior auricular muscle. Electromyogr Clin Neurophysiol, 46(5): 317–320.

Part VII
Surgical Treatments

Chapter 82
Surgical Treatments: Introduction

Tobias Kleinjung

Surgery has a definite role in the management of tinnitus associated with certain conditions as follows:

1. Surgery should be considered if hearing can be improved by surgery. Therefore, surgery plays a role in the management of tinnitus associated with conductive hearing loss. In patients with otosclerosis, tinnitus is most likely to disappear after stapes surgery (Chap. 83). Other options are tympanoplasty procedures in patients with tinnitus and chronic otitis media. Individuals with objective tinnitus due to middle-ear myoclonus will benefit from a surgical section of the tensor tympani or stapedial tendon.

   Conductive and cochlear hearing loss can also be improved by conventional hearing aids. In cases of failure, surgically implanted devices can be considered (Chap. 76). If tinnitus is associated with profound bilateral hearing loss or deafness, tinnitus suppression has been reported as a secondary benefit of cochlear implantation. Recently, cochlear implantation was discussed as a new treatment option irrespective of hearing restoration for patients with severe tinnitus due to unilateral deafness (see Chap. 77).

2. Some forms of tinnitus are associated with a clear structural cause that can be improved with surgery. Pulsatile tinnitus can occur due to vascular loops in the vicinity of the eighth nerve. Microvascular decompression procedures of these loops have shown some benefit in tinnitus suppression (Chap. 84).

Surgical treatment options for patients with pulsatile tinnitus of venous origin are ligation of the internal jugular vein, occlusion of the sigmoid sinus, or closure of a dural fistula. Tumors of the eighth nerve, like vestibular schwannoma, can cause tinnitus (Chap. 39). There are different surgical and non-surgical treatment options available to treat individuals with vestibular schwannoma. The surgical approaches differ in the conservation or destruction of the auditory part of the eighth nerve. The impact of surgical tumor removal on tinnitus suppression is discussed in Chap. 85. Sectioning of the eighth nerve (cochlear neurectomy) has also been tried for tinnitus suppression in individuals with tinnitus who do not have vestibular schwannoma. Improvement rates of less than 50% have to be considered in this destructive procedure as well as a chance of the condition worsening and development of complete hearing loss [1]. Therefore, candidates for this type of surgery should have no useful hearing on the affected side and should understand that effects of surgery are unpredictable.

3. Some individuals with Ménière's disease may have tinnitus reduction from surgical treatment options. The different techniques include transtympanic application of gentamycin, endolymphatic sac surgery, and destructive procedures like labyrinthectomy or vestibular neurectomy (Chap. 83).

4. Some people with temporomandibular joint (TMJ) disorder have severe tinnitus. In most cases, nonsurgical treatment options like physical therapy or local injections of anesthetics and corticoids can restore the joint function sufficiently. Some individuals with severe conditions may benefit from surgery. Surgical intervention can range from arthroscopy to a partial or total TMJ implant (Chap. 95).

5. Only a few incidences of tinnitus are direct consequences of pathologies of the ear or the auditory

T. Kleinjung (✉)
Department of Otorhinolaryngology, University Hospital
of Regensburg, Regensburg, Germany
e-mail: tobias.kleinjung@klinik.uni-regensburg.de

nerve. In most individuals with tinnitus, it is assumed that the tinnitus occurs as a series of reactions in the central nervous system due to deprivation of input to the central auditory pathway. Neuroimaging and neurophysiologic data suggest that chronic tinnitus is associated with focal brain activation of the auditory cortex or other parts of the auditory nervous system, such as the inferior colliculus (see Chap. 12). Therefore, targeted modulation of tinnitus-related neural hyperactivity has been considered as a new promising treatment strategy (Chap. 86). Besides the non-invasive neuromodulation techniques like repetitive transcranial magnetic stimulation (rTMS) and transcranial direct current stimulation (tDCS), an invasive direct electrical stimulation was suggested as a novel treatment option. If rTMS is capable of suppressing tinnitus transiently, the effect might be maintained by the surgical implantation of electrodes over the area of electrophysiological signal abnormality on the auditory cortex for direct electrical stimulation (Chap. 90).

Reference

1. House, J.W. and D.E. Brackmann, Tinnitus: surgical treatment. Ciba Found Symp, 1981. 85: p. 204–16.

Chapter 83
Surgical Treatment: The Ear

Tobias Kleinjung

Keypoints

1. Surgical restoration of hearing can improve tinnitus complaints in patients with tinnitus associated to conductive hearing loss.
2. Tinnitus is most likely to disappear after stapes surgery.
3. New-onset tinnitus or worsening of a pre-existing tinnitus can occur as an unwanted side effect of middle ear surgery.
4. Some patients with advanced Ménière's disease might benefit from a surgical approach to their tinnitus.

Keywords Tinnitus • Ear surgery • Tympanoplasty • Stapedotomy • Stapedectomy • Ménière's disease

Abbreviations

PORP   Partial ossicular replacement
TORP   Total ossicular replacement

Introduction

Any kind of conductive hearing loss may be accompanied by tinnitus, as outlined in detail in Chap. 34. Surgical efforts to improve hearing loss can, in some cases, also bring about the partial or complete remission of tinnitus. This chapter will discuss the possibility of reducing tinnitus through surgical operations in order to treat conductive hearing loss. The text will describe surgical procedures involving the middle ear that are indicated for treatment of different forms of objective tinnitus. Finally, it will also discuss otological surgery techniques used in the management of Ménière's disease. The topics of cochlear implant surgery (see Chap. 77) and surgery of the internal auditory canal (see Chap. 85) are dealt with in separate chapters. If the accompanying tinnitus is due to hearing loss, irrespective of its duration, then restoration of hearing can be beneficial to management of tinnitus, in addition to improving hearing (see Chap. 10).

Surgery of the External Auditory Canal

Space-occupying lesions that completely or partially obliterate the external auditory canal and lead to conductive hearing loss must be removed. This applies both to benign changes, such as auditory canal exostoses, and to malignant tumors. If normal hearing is restored after uncomplicated healing, any tinnitus that may have been present preoperatively can also be expected to resolve completely.

Middle Ear Surgery

Myringotomy with Tube Insertion

Myringotomy, followed by aspiration of fluid build-up in the middle ear and insertion of a small tube in the opening of the tympanic membrane, brings immediate relief of symptoms in cases of otitis media with

T. Kleinjung (✉)
Department of Otorhinolaryngology, University of Regensburg, Franz-Josef-Strauss-Allee 11, 93053 Regensburg, Germany
e-mail: tobias.kleinjung@klinik.uni-regensburg.de

A.R. Møller et al. (eds.), *Textbook of Tinnitus*,
DOI 10.1007/978-1-60761-145-5_83, © Springer Science+Business Media, LLC 2011

effusion. This procedure may also result in remission of tinnitus along with a reduction of aural fullness and conductive hearing loss. Myringotomy, with or without tube insertion, can also positively influence the course of acute otitis media that does not respond favorably to pharmacological therapy.

Tympanoplasty

"Tympanoplasty" is the term used to describe the surgical repair of the tympanic membrane after a perforation. This process includes inspection of the ossicular chain and, if necessary, its reconstruction by ossiculoplasty.

According to Wullstein, depending on the extent of reconstruction involved, there are five different types of tympanoplasty [1]. Tympanoplasty Type I merely involves the restoration of the perforated tympanic membrane by grafting. The ossicular chain is intact. In Type II and III procedures, ossiculoplasty is an integral part of tympanoplasty. Tympanoplasty Type II is a procedure in which the patient's own auditory ossicles (parts of the incus or the head of the malleus), i.e., organic material, are used for the reconstruction. In tympanoplasty Type III, alloplastic materials are used.

The defective ossicles are repaired using synthetic prostheses that replace the incus and are placed on the intact stapedial head (partial ossicular replacement prosthesis, PORP) or by prostheses that replace the incus and stapedial suprastructure and are placed directly on the intact stapes footplate (total ossicular replacement prosthesis, TORP). Tympanoplasty Types IV and V no longer play a role in middle ear surgery today.

The techniques of tympanoplasty have an application in the treatment of chronic otitis media. In chronic mesotympanic otitis media (chronic suppurative otitis media), reconstruction of the sound conduction mechanism is necessary in 20–25% of cases. In cholesteatoma, 80% of patients require tympanoplasty Type III [2]. Depending on the underlying pathology, the technique of tympanoplasty may be combined with procedures involving the external auditory canal (e.g., canaloplasty) and mastoid (e.g., mastoidectomy). The technique of tympanoplasty is used to correct malformations of the middle ear and following persistent traumatic eardrum perforation. Since the advent of microscopic middle ear surgery in the 1950s, many tympanoplasty techniques have been described. The techniques differ in terms of the approach, such as transcanal, endaural, retroauricular, graft material, used for tympanic membrane replacement (e.g., temporalis fascia, cartilage), and the design of the prosthesis and materials used (e.g., homologous incus, hydroxyapatite, gold, titanium) [2]. All metho ds aim at achieving complete eradication of infection, repairing the defective tympanic membrane, and improving hearing. These are the topics primarily addressed in the literature. Publication of results regarding relief of preoperative tinnitus has been few (summarized in Table 83.1). Nevertheless, results currently available show approximately 30% of patients who had tympanoplasty are no longer aware of tinnitus. In two of the three published studies, complete remission of tinnitus was achieved [3, 4] in about one-third of patients and more than 40% had partial remission and 4–8% became worse (Table 83.1). The assessment offered by Helms in an older study from 1981 [5] showed that one-third became worse. The improvement in tinnitus symptoms after surgery may be attributed primarily to closure of the air-bone gap. Accordingly, Lima Ada et al. [4] found a good correlation between postoperative hearing improvement and the reduction in tinnitus. In those patients who continue to suffer from tinnitus despite adequate hearing improvement, there must have been other causes for the reduced sound stimulation of tinnitus [4].

Stapes Surgery

Conductive hearing loss and tinnitus are the main symptoms of otosclerosis. With the development of microscopic middle ear surgery in the 1950s, surgical mobilization of the stapes in otosclerosis became the

Table 83.1 Effects of tympanoplasty on tinnitus

	n	Complete remission (%)	Partial remission (%)	No change (%)	Worse (%)
Baba et al. [3]	151	24.5	41.7	25.9	7.9
Helms [5]	59	33.3		33.3	33.3
Lima Ada et al. [4]	23	34.8	47.8	13	4.3

focal point of interest among middle ear surgeons. In 1958, Shea performed the first *stapedectomy*, where the stapes was replaced by prosthesis [6, 7]. In the following years, the technique of *stapedotomy* has evolved into a standard procedure, where only the suprastructure of the stapes is removed, a perforation of the footplate is made, and a piston prosthesis is attached to the long process of the incus extending into the perforation of the stapes footplate (for review, see [8]). The introduction of laser surgery permitted "no-touch" perforation of the stapes footplate [9]. The main objective of stapes surgery is to improve hearing. The most published studies regard hearing improvement achieved from different techniques. Hearing is improved in about 90% of patients [10] and approximately 60% of patients have an air-bone gap of between 0 and 10 dB [11]. No improvement in hearing occurs in approximately 8% of patients and a deterioration of hearing loss, including deafness, occurs in 2% of patients [10]. Few studies regarding the effect on tinnitus from stapes surgery have been published. Table 83.2 provides a summary of comparable studies conducted since 1990. On the average, complete remission of tinnitus was achieved in approximately half of patients from stapes surgery. Partial remission was achieved in 30% and approximately 80% of those who had stapes surgery benefited from the operation. Most of the remainder had no change, and fewer than 5% of patients reported worsening of their tinnitus.

Many studies showed improvement regarding tinnitus that was independent of the hearing improvement [12, 13], but one older study by Glasgold et al. [14] showed a correlation between hearing improvement and tinnitus improvement. Ayache et al. [15] found no difference in reduction of tinnitus between stapedotomy and stapedectomy. Sakai et al. [16] and Gersdorff et al. [12], on the other hand, noted better results after

stapedotomy than with stapedectomy. No significant correlation between gender, tinnitus frequency, tinnitus duration, or extent of hearing loss and the effect on the tinnitus from stapes surgery was reported [15]. These factors, therefore, do not have prognostic value for stapes operation. It is unclear whether the positive effect of the stapes surgery is due to the improvement of hearing or some other factors related to mobilization of the fixed footplate. The fact that many patients already experience an improvement in tinnitus immediately after surgery – i.e., in a state when the auditory canal is packed – favor the latter hypothesis.

Middle Ear Surgery for Objective Tinnitus

Objective tinnitus may be either vascular or muscular in nature. Objective tinnitus often accompanies disorders such as glomus tumors. When patients with glomus tumors are treated surgically, complete eradication of the pathological process is the main aim in the resection of such tumors. The patient's pulsatile tinnitus most often disappears, which is an additional benefit of the surgery. After embolizing the vessels feeding the tumor, resection of a glomus tumor located in the middle ear cavity is done using the same approaches as those for tympanoplasty. Reconstruction of the tympanic membrane and ossicular chain may be necessary. Surgery to excise glomus jugulare tumors is different and requires a wide approach via the lateral skull base [17].

Treatment of objective tinnitus, caused by contraction (repetitive myoclonus) of the middle ear muscles that results in rhythmic tinnitus, is to section the tendons of the stapedius or tensor tympani muscles [18, 19].

When the Eustachian tube fails to close normally, disabling breath-synchronous tinnitus may result.

Table 83.2 Effects of stapes surgery on tinnitus

	n	Complete remission (%)	Partial remission (%)	No change (%)	Worse (%)
Ayache et al. [15]	48	56.3	27.1	12.5	4.2
Da Silva Lima et al. [47]	23	39.1	56.5	4.4	0
Gersdorff et al. [12]	50	64	16	14	6
Oliveira [48]	19	52.6	37	10.4	0
Ramsay et al. [49]	268	48.2	33.2	7.8	10.8
Sakai et al. [16]	22	27	41	27	5
Sparano et al. [50]	40	52.5	32.5	12.5	2.5
Szymanski et al. [13]	149	73	17	10	0

The first remedy may be inserting a tympanostomy tube [20]. Other surgical procedures aim at narrowing or occluding the Eustachian tube from the middle ear or the nasopharynx. These methods are in a preliminary trial phase. Irreversible measures, such as the paratubular implantation of a Teflon graft [21], may lead to chronic otitis media due to Eustachian tube dysfunction if there is overcorrection. Endoscopic application of absorbable substances (hyaluronic acid, collagen) into the tubal elevation may bring transient symptom relief and is easy to regulate [22, 23].

Tinnitus as a Risk in Middle Ear Surgery

While middle ear surgery offers benefit regarding management of tinnitus, it can also, as a side effect, cause tinnitus or worsen existing tinnitus. Postoperative deafness is a serious complication of any middle ear surgery that can occur from intra-operative damage to cochlear structures. Together with deafness and vertigo, tinnitus may occur or pre-existing tinnitus may become worse [24]. The risk of serious postoperative inner ear damage in stapes surgery has been reported to be between 0.5 and 1% [2].

Operations for chronic otitis media extensive cholesteatoma resections, in particular, may have higher risks of postoperative tinnitus from damage to the inner ear from stapes luxation or development of a semicircular canal fistula [25]. In operations of large cholesteatoma involving the stapes, it is therefore recommended that some cholesteatoma be left behind. The remaining cholesteatoma then can be resected in a second operation after 6–9 months [26].

Surgical procedures directed at the middle ear or the external auditory canal involve extensive drilling which carries a risk of noise-induced hearing loss and increased risk of tinnitus. In addition, the effect of surgery and anesthesia on the central nervous system may explain postoperative increases in tinnitus.

Ear Surgery and Ménière's Disease

Two kinds of surgical treatment for advanced Ménière's disease are in use (see Chaps. 38 and 60). One is conservative and spares hearing while the other is a destructive

procedure. Conservative procedures compromising endolymphatic sac decompression, gentamycin infusion, are indicated when the symptoms are dominated by a frequent occurrence of severe attacks of vertigo with some residual hearing preserved. A third conservative procedure is an application of air puffs to the inner ear via a ventilation tube in the eardrum [27]. Surgery on the indication of tinnitus is rarely performed, and only in connection with deafness and reduced vertigo, when the tinnitus is highly distressing and resistive to other treatments.

Endolymphatic sac surgery is the most common surgical procedure for Ménière's disease. Its purpose is to treat the endolymphatic hydrops by inserting a permanent drain from the endolymphatic sac to the middle ear space. This is achieved by wide exposure of the endolymphatic sac following decompression of the sigmoid sinus in a mastoidectomy [28]. After saccotomy, silicone sheeting is inserted into the sac lumen to allow permanent drainage. The risk of suffering additional sensorineural hearing loss with this technique has been estimated at less than 2% [29]. Some debate surrounds the success rates obtained with this procedure in terms of the control of vertigo and tinnitus. Most of the reports published in the literature relate to vertigo, with successful vertigo control claimed to be achieved in 70–90% of cases [30, 31]. The success rate for tinnitus control with endolymphatic sac surgery is lower than that for vertigo control, with improvement or complete remission of tinnitus being reported in the 30–40% range [32, 33].

These reported success rates of endolymphatic sac decompression are being questioned after studies by Thomsen et al. [34] and Bretlau et al. [35], which showed similar effect of a placebo (sham) operation involving a classic mastoidectomy without decompression as was obtained in real endolymphatic sac decompression. Both real and placebo operations had success rates of 75%.

A similar placebo effect has also been attributed to insertion of a ventilating tube into the tympanic membrane with no additional measures [36], a technique that continues to find use in surgical practice [37]. Success rates for destructive procedures, such as labyrinthectomy, in improving tinnitus are not higher as compared with endolymphatic decompression. Labyrinthectomy is reported to improve tinnitus in 40% of the patients [38]. This rarely performed procedure may be considered for tinnitus and vertigo control in patients with Ménière's disease who have very poor hearing or are deaf. Higher success rates have been achieved when labyrinthectomy is combined with cochleovestibular neurectomy [39]. According to Jones et al. [40], good postoperative control of tinnitus can be expected with this technique in slightly less than 70% of cases. Effective control of vertigo symptoms can be achieved with this combination in nearly 100% of the patients [39].

Intratympanic gentamicin perfusion is designed to achieve chemical partial ablation of the vestibular system while still preserving cochlear function. For that, gentamicin is instilled into the middle ear cavity via a tube inserted in the ear drum or by direct puncture of the tympanic membrane. It diffuses across the round window membrane to reach the inner ear [41]. Several published studies have shown that good vertigo control can be achieved in 70–90% of the patients [28, 41, 42]. It is an advantage of this method that morbidity is low and the incidence of sensorineural hearing loss has been reduced to about 20% of all those treated [43]. This technique is currently regarded as the standard therapy for controlling vertigo attacks [42]. Little has been reported regarding the effect on tinnitus from gentamicin treatment. In one study, Lange et al. [44] reported improvement in tinnitus in 26 out of 56 patients treated (46%). Two small studies reported improvements in tinnitus in only 5 and 27% of patients, respectively [45, 46].

References

1. Tos, M, Manual of middle ear surgery, Volume 1 1993, Stuttgart: Georg Thieme
2. Hildmann, H, Sudhoff, H, Middle ear surgery 2006, Heidelberg: Springer
3. Baba, S, Yagi, T, and Fujikura, T, Subjective evaluation and overall satisfaction after tympanoplasty for chronic simple suppurative otitis media J Nippon Med Sch, 2004 71(1):17–24
4. Lima Ada, S, et al, The effect of timpanoplasty on tinnitus in patients with conductive hearing loss: a six month follow-up Braz J Otorhinolaryngol, 2007 73(3):384–9
5. Helms, J, Tympanoplasty and Tinnitus (author's transl) Laryngol Rhinol Otol (Stuttg), 1981 60(3):99–100
6. Shea, JJ, Jr, Fenestration of the oval window Ann Otol Rhinol Laryngol, 1958 67(4):932–51
7. Shea, JJ, Jr, A personal history of stapedectomy Am J Otol, 1998 19(5 Suppl):S2–12
8. Hausler, R, General history of stapedectomy Adv Otorhinolaryngol, 2007 65:1–5
9. Minovi, A, Probst, G, and Dazert, S, [Current concepts in the surgical management of otosclerosis] HNO, 2009 57(3):273–86
10. Shohet, JA, Middle ear, otosclerosis 2008 http://emedicine-medscapecom/article/859760-overview
11. Fisch, U, Tympanoplasty, mastoidectomy and stapes surgery 1994, Stuttgart: Georg Thieme
12. Gersdorff, M, Nouwen J, Gilain C, Decat M, and Betsch C, Tinnitus and otosclerosis Eur Arch Otorhinolaryngol, 2000 257(6):314–6
13. Szymanski, M, Golabek, W, and Mills, R, Effect of stapedectomy on subjective tinnitus J Laryngol Otol, 2003 117(4): 261–4
14. Glasgold, A and Altman, F, The effect of stapes surgery on tinnitus in otosclerosis Laryngoscope, 1966 76:1524–32
15. Ayache, D, Earally, F, and Elbaz, P, Characteristics and postoperative course of tinnitus in otosclerosis Otol Neurotol, 2003 24(1):48–51
16. Sakai, M, Sato M, Iida M, Ogata T, and Ishida K, The effect on tinnitus of stapes surgery for otosclerosis Rev Laryngol Otol Rhinol (Bord), 1995 116(1):27–30
17. Fisch, U and Mattox, D, Microsurgery of the skull base 1998, Stuttgart: Georg Thieme
18. Zipfel, TE, Kaza, SR, and Greene, JS, Middle ear myoclonus J Laryngol Otol, 2000 114(3):207–9
19. Golz, A, Fradis M, Martzu D, Netzer A, and Joachims HZ, Stapedius muscle myoclonus Ann Otol Rhinol Laryngol, 2003 112(6):522–4
20. Bluestone, CD, Eustachian tube Structure, function, role in otitis media 2005, Hamilton: BC Decker
21. Pulec, JL, Abnormally patent eustachian tubes: treatment with injection of polytetrafluoroethylene (Teflon) paste Laryngoscope, 1967 77(8):1543–54
22. Mees, K and Beimert, U, [Correction of the gaping eustachian tube osteum with injectable collagen] Laryngol Rhinol Otol (Stuttg), 1988 67(2):87
23. Grimmer, JF and Poe, DS, Update on eustachian tube dysfunction and the patulous eustachian tube Curr Opin Otolaryngol Head Neck Surg, 2005 13(5):277–82
24. Douek, E, Tinnitus following surgery, in Proceedings of the III International Tinnitus Seminar, H Feldmann, Editor 1987, Harsch: Karlsruhe 64–69
25. Weber, PC, Iatrogenic complications from chronic ear surgery Otolaryngol Clin North Am, 2005 38(4):711–22
26. Wiet, RJ, Harvet, SA, and Bauer, GP, Management of complications of chronic otitis media, in Otologic surgery, Shelton, C, Brackmann, E, and Bauer, GP, Editor 1994, Philadelphia:WB Saunders 257–76
27. Gates, GA, Green JD Jr, Tucci DL, and Telian SA The effects of transtympanic micropressure treatment in people with unilateral Meniere's disease Arch Otolaryngol Head Neck Surg, 2004 130(6):718–25
28. Sajjadi, H and Paparella, MM, Meniere's disease Lancet, 2008 372(9636):406–14
29. Paparella, MM and Fina, M, Endolymphatic sac enhancement: reversal of pathogenesis Otolaryngol Clin North Am, 2002 35(3):621–37
30. Ostrowski, VB and Kartush, JM, Endolymphatic sac-vein decompression for intractable Meniere's disease: long term treatment results Otolaryngol Head Neck Surg, 2003 128(4):550–9

31. Huang, TS, Endolymphatic sac surgery for Meniere's disease: experience with over 3000 cases Otolaryngol Clin North Am, 2002 35(3):591–606

32. Moffat, DA, Endolymphatic sac surgery: analysis of 100 operations Clin Otolaryngol Allied Sci, 1994 19(3):261–6

33. Quaranta, N, et al, [Long-term audition results in patients with chronic endolymphatic hydrops after selective vestibular neurotomy and endolymphatic sac surgery] Acta Otorhinolaryngol Ital, 2001 21(3):131–7

34. Thomsen, J, et al, Meniere's disease: endolymphatic sac decompression compared with sham (placebo) decompression Ann N Y Acad Sci, 1981 374:820–30

35. Bretlau, P, et al, Placebo effect in surgery for Meniere's disease: a three-year follow-up study of patients in a double blind placebo controlled study on endolymphatic sac shunt surgery Am J Otol, 1984 5(6):558–61

36. Thomsen, J, et al, The non-specific effect of endolymphatic sac surgery in treatment of Meniere's disease: a prospective, randomized controlled study comparing "classic" endolymphatic sac surgery with the insertion of a ventilating tube in the tympanic membrane Acta Otolaryngol, 1998 118(6): 769–73

37. Smith, WK, Sankar, V, and Pfleiderer, AG, A national survey amongst UK otolaryngologists regarding the treatment of Meniere's disease J Laryngol Otol, 2005 119(2):102–5

38. Pedersen, CB and Sorensen, H, Clinical effect of labyrinthectomy Arch Otolaryngol, 1970 92(4):307–10

39. Silverstein, H, Transmeatal labyrinthectomy with and without cochleovestibular neurectomy Laryngoscope, 1976 86(12):1777–91

40. Jones, R, Silverstein, H, and Smouha, E, Long-term results of transmeatal cochleovestibular neurectomy: an analysis of 100 cases Otolaryngol Head Neck Surg, 1989 100(1):22–9

41. Light, JP and Silverstein, H, Transtympanic perfusion: indications and limitations Curr Opin Otolaryngol Head Neck Surg, 2004 12(5):378–83

42. Minor, LB, Schessel, DA, and Carey, JP, Meniere's disease Curr Opin Neurol, 2004 17(1):9–16

43. Carey, J, Intratympanic gentamicin for the treatment of Meniere's disease and other forms of peripheral vertigo Otolaryngol Clin North Am, 2004 37(5):1075–90

44. Lange, G, Mann, W, and Maurer, J, [Intratympanic interval therapy of Meniere disease with gentamicin with preserving cochlear function] HNO, 2003 51(11):898–902

45. Smith, WK, Sandooram, D, and Prinsley, PR, Intratympanic gentamicin treatment in Meniere's disease: patients' experiences and outcomes J Laryngol Otol, 2006 120(9): 730–5

46. Suryanarayanan, R, Srinivasan, VR, and O'Sullivan, G, Transtympanic gentamicin treatment using Silverstein MicroWick in Meniere's disease patients: long term outcome J Laryngol Otol, 2009 123(1):45–9

47. Lima Ada, S, et al, The effect of stapedotomy on tinnitus in patients with otospongiosis Ear Nose Throat J, 2005 84(7):412–4

48. Oliveira, CA, How does stapes surgery influence severe disabling tinnitus in otosclerosis patients? Adv Otorhinolaryngol, 2007 65:343–7

49. Ramsay, H, Karkkainen, J, and Palva, T, Success in surgery for otosclerosis: hearing improvement and other indicators Am J Otolaryngol, 1997 18(1):23–8

50. Sparano, A, et al, Effects of stapedectomy on tinnitus in patients with otosclerosis Int Tinnitus J, 2004 10(1):73–7

Chapter 84
Long-Term Follow-Up of Microvascular Decompression for Tinnitus

Jacques Magnan, Benoit Lafont, and Charbel Rameh

Keypoints

1. The concept of cochlear nerve compression by an offending vessel as a cause for a small percentage of tinnitus cases is a controversial topic.
2. The diagnosis of tinnitus secondary to a neurovascular conflict requires a combination of the following:

    (a) Unilateral tinnitus
    (b) Radiographic presence of a vascular compression of the cochlear nerve
    (c) Prolonged latencies of waves I–III in ABR

3. Following these criteria, 43 patients between 1993 and 2006 underwent an endoscope-assisted microvascular decompression of the cochlear nerve via a minimally invasive retrosigmoid approach.
4. Our results were studied 1 week, 2 months, and 2 years postoperatively. On the long term, there was resolution of tinnitus in 9 cases (21%), a marked decrease of tinnitus in 13 cases (31%), and no change of tinnitus in 19 cases (44%).
5. A significant statistical correlation was found between the resolution of tinnitus and the improvement of hearing postoperatively.
6. The best results were in cases where the subarcuate artery was responsible for the conflict. The worse results were when the course of the offending vessel (AICA) was inside the internal auditory canal or between the facial and vestibulocochlear nerves.
7. Although the results of vascular decompression of the cochlear nerve involving select cases with incapacitating tinnitus are less rewarding than those

reached in hemifacial spasm or trigeminal neuralgia, they confirm the hypothesis of vascular compression syndrome of the auditory nerve and the need for better selection criteria.

Keywords Tinnitus • Endoscope assisted • Microvascular decompression • Results

Abbreviations

ABR	Auditory brainstem responses
AICA	Anterior inferior cerebellar artery
CCAP	Cochlear compound action potential
CISS	Constructive interference in steady state
CPA	Cerebella-pontine angle
CSF	Cerebrospinal fluid
FT	Fourier transform
IAC	Internal auditory meatus
MRI	Magnetic resonance imaging
MVD	Microvascular decompression
PICA	Posterior inferior cerebella artery
VNG	Vestibulonystagmography

Introduction

There are several etiologies for tinnitus. Among these, cochlear nerve compression by an arterial loop or a vein in the cerebellopontine angle (CPA) represents a very small percentage, which is difficult to quantify (see also Chaps. 10 and 40). Therefore, the vascular compression theory of the auditory cranial nerve is still questionable and has not yet gained the wide acceptance that trigeminal and facial nerve decompression for trigeminal neuralgia and hemifacial spasm has received.

J. Magnan (✉)
University Aix-Marseille II, Hopital Nord,
Marseille Cedex 20, 13915, France
e-mail: jmagnan@ap-hm.fr

A.R. Møller et al. (eds.), *Textbook of Tinnitus*,
DOI 10.1007/978-1-60761-145-5_84, © Springer Science+Business Media, LLC 2011

By presenting our results on endoscope-assisted microvascular decompression (MVD) of the auditory nerve, we will try to shed the light on this concept which was first suggested in 1934 by Dandy [1], popularized in 1975 by Jannetta [2], and utilized in 1993 by Møller and Jannetta [3] for the management of severe tinnitus.

Microsurgical Anatomy of the Cochlear Nerve

A prolonged contact or "conflict" between the cochlear nerve and an adjacent vascular structure will lead to an alteration in the myelin sheath. Studies have shown a better resistance of the peripheral myelin compared to the central myelin to such insults. Thus, the configuration of central myelin in the cochlear nerve has significant implications. The area of central myelin forming the root entry zone of the nerve is truly a cone shape and extends as far as the internal auditory canal. Therefore, a blood vessel can cause symptoms by compression not only at the junctional area close to the brainstem, as in the case of the motor facial nerve, but anywhere along the course of the nerve, whether cisternal or intracanalicular. The area of the nerve surrounded by central myelin, called the transitional glial zone or "Obersteiner-Redlich" zone, is fragile and very sensitive to external compressions. Its length is variable between the different cranial nerves. It is 1.2 mm for the glossopharyngeal nerve, 1.7 mm for the facial nerve, 2.6 mm for the trigeminal nerve, and 8.3 mm for the cochlear nerve [4].

The permanent and pulsatile contact of an artery with the transitional zone of the nerve will lead to histological and physiopathological changes in the root of the nerve [5].

1. Local demyelination (Fig. 84.1) will result in aberrant connections between the axons and ultimately to the phenomenon of localized hyper-excitability (Fig. 84.2).
2. Stimulation of neighboring axons and the orthodromic recruitment (ephapse phenomenon) [6].
3. Antidromic stimulation of neighboring neurons and the permanent nuclear hyperactivity (Kindling effect) [7, 8].
4. Endoneural fibrosis of the compressed zone: this leads to an alteration in nerve conduction and

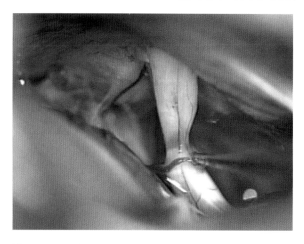

Fig. 84.1 Prolonged contact between the cochlear nerve and arterial branches from the AICA leads both to alteration of the myelin sheet and constriction of the nerve

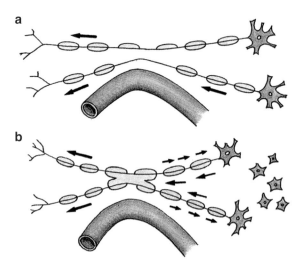

Fig. 84.2 (**a**): Ephapse effect by pulsatile stimulation of the cranial nerve. (**b**): Kindling effect by antidromic stimulation of the nucleus

a change in the auditory brainstem-evoked response (ABR) [5].

Patient Selection Criteria for Operative Treatment

The specification of tinnitus due to a neurovascular conflict is difficult. The decision to perform a microvascular decompression is not made unless a full workup has been done. Patients with tinnitus are quite demanding of a radical solution, and thus decision making should be very careful. The patients must have specific clinical evaluations and a battery of tests before being advised of surgery.

Most important is the unilaterality of tinnitus. In addition to the audiogram, we order a magnetic resonance imaging (MRI) to search for any associated pathology along the course of the auditory pathways, in particular at the level of the CPA.

Clinical Criteria

Tinnitus has to be unilateral, severe (following Reed's classification, significantly affecting the quality of life and considered as a handicap for the patient) [9], present over several months, and persistent despite therapy with the available medical treatments.

The pulsatile nature and the tonality of the tinnitus are not decision-influencing criteria. In addition, tinnitus associated with a low-frequency fluctuating hearing loss as in Ménière's disease or with progressive hearing loss was for us an exclusion criterion for MVD.

Radiological Criteria

MRI is able to reproduce the anatomy of the CPA and demonstrate the presence of a neurovascular conflict. It also eliminates other potential causes of unilateral tinnitus such as an acoustic neuroma. MRI in both T1 and T2 three-dimensional Fourier transfer (FT) is the most effective method of delineating both the acoustic facial nerve bundle and the surrounding vascular structures in the CPA and the IAC. T2 is carried out using constructive interference in steady-state (CISS) sequence (Fig. 84.3). Also, postcontrast reformatted turbo flash in the axial plane helps in delineating the conflict vessels [10]. The image assessment includes all the CPA with serial thin slices of 0.4 mm thickness.

To confirm the diagnosis, the single presence of a neurovascular contact is not sufficient. Other radiological criteria are required (Figs. 84.3, 84.4, 84.5):

1. Perpendicular contact between the vascular loop and the nerve along two different perpendicular planes.

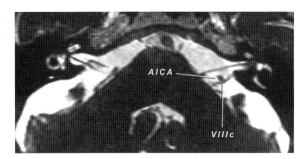

Fig. 84.3 Axial T2 CISS sequence MRI showing on the right side a normal vascular loop of the internal auditory canal and on the left side a vascular compression by the AICA on the cochlear nerve (VIIIc)

Fig. 84.4 Axial T2 CISS sequence MRI showing a typical neurovascular conflict with a perpendicular contact between the AICA and the cochlear nerve, the distortion of the nerve

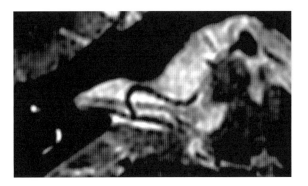

Fig. 84.5 An adjacent cut of the same MRI as in Fig. 84.4, with 0.4 mm thickness, showing clearly the imprint on the nerve by the vascular loop and the reduction of the diameter of the cochlear nerve

2. Displacement of the cochlear nerve, with a certain distance between the facial and cochlear nerves.
3. Imprint on the cochlear nerve and reduction in its diameter.

4. Brainstem distortion caused by the vascular structure at the level of the root entry zone of the cochlear nerve.

The presence of an arterial loop in the internal auditory canal (IAC) may be responsible for tinnitus but is not a sufficient criterion by itself.

Electrophysiological Criteria

1. Pure-tone audiometry: Pure-tone audiometry can identify an unilateral sensorineural hearing loss, on the same side as the tinnitus. In general, the hearing loss is of moderate severity over all the frequencies tested (250–8 KHz) but occurs predominantly at the higher frequencies. This hearing loss is of statistical significance when we compare it to the contralateral ear ($p < 0.05$) and is proof that the nerve is in a pathological state.

2. Auditory brainstem response (ABR): ABR, in the case of a retrocochlear lesion, will reveal a prolongation of the latencies or a desynchronization. We use Møller criteria to identify pathological ABRs with a prolonged interwave latency of peaks I–III of more than 0.2 ms (Fig. 84.6) [3].

3. Vestibulonystagmography (VNG): Vestibular tests allow a search for an ipsilateral vestibular deficit on the same side as the tinnitus, though it may be a subclinical deficit. The vascular compression might be responsible for a vestibular deficit following the same mechanism as that of tinnitus.

In summary, the diagnosis of a neurovascular conflict with the cochlear nerve requires the combination of a

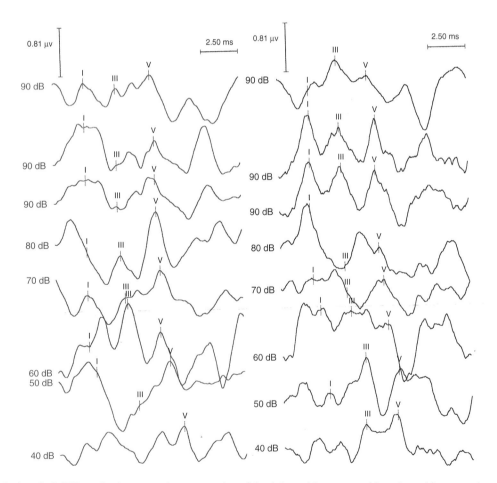

Fig. 84.6 A typical ABR confirming a vascular compression of the right cochlear nerve with prolonged interwave latencies I–III and I–V, and de-synchronisation of the wave

clinically incapacitating unilateral tinnitus, radiological presence of a vascular compression, and electrophysiological alteration of ABR with increased latencies or de-synchronization of waves.

These criteria should convince the surgeon of the involvement of the CPA vessel in the etiology of tinnitus and the possible benefit of the decompression. It was not uncommon that simply making the diagnosis of a vascular compression on the cochlear nerve as a cause of tinnitus reassured the patient, rendered the tinnitus more tolerable, and consequently did not require operative treatment.

Minimally Invasive Surgery of the Cerebellopontine Angle Using a Keyhole Retrosigmoid Approach

For this procedure, the patient is in a dorsal decubitus position, with the head flexed and turned to the contralateral side. General endotracheal anesthesia uses analgesics, hypnotics, or neuroleptics (Diprivan, Sulfentanyl). The patient is hyperventilated to obtain a hypocapnea (Pressure of CO_2 around 25 mmHg at the time of dural opening) to diminish the intracranial pressure and help spontaneous cerebellar retraction. Due to this process, lumbar puncture and mannitol solution are no longer used.

The electrodes monitoring the facial or cochlear nerve are put in place after the induction of anesthesia. With intraoperative ABR monitoring, we obtain the cochlear compound action potentials (CCAPs) from the entire surface of the cochlear nerve with a surface multipolar electrode. The return of the ABR to normal after the decompression is a sign of good prognosis, but unfortunately it is not constant.

A curvilinear retro-auricular skin incision is made, two finger widths behind the pinna. It is 6–8 cm long and passes over the posterior part of the anticipated craniotomy. The cutaneous flap is anteriorly based, while the underlying musculoperiosteal flap is fashioned to be posteriorly based. The mastoid emissary vein is identified. Drilling for the craniotomy is centered on the emissary vein and is done using a cutting then a diamond burr. Bone dust is collected to make a bone pâté that will be used in closure. The craniotomy is usually elliptical in shape, 20 mm × 10 mm in

dimensions. It must reach the posterior border of the sigmoid sinus without skeletonizing it. Any mastoid cells should be obliterated with bone wax to prevent cerebrospinal fluid (CSF) rhinorrhea.

Opening of the dura is done under the operating microscope. The dural flap is based and suspended anteriorly. The cerebellum is protected using a synthetic dura mater. The posterior cistern is opened inferiorly at the level of the lower cranial nerves. The arachnoid wrapping surrounding the acoustico-facial nerve bundle is dissected to expose the neurovascular conflict. The offending vessels characteristically induce pressure and distort the cochlear nerve at any place along its course. The compressive effect is most commonly due to sharp-angled loops at areas of vessel bifurcations. Two other typical aspects are when the loop pinches the nerve or when the subarcuate artery constricts the nerve.

Using the 4 mm 30° endoscope, a panoramic view of all the CPA structures is obtained. The tip of the endoscope is passed above and below the acoustico-facial bundle to identify the precise location and course of the offending vessels.

Whatever be the location of the neurovascular conflict, the purpose of the microvascular decompression procedure is to change the axis of the offending vascular loop and keep it away from the offended nerve. This surgical maneuver is done under the operating microscope. First, the offending vessel is carefully mobilized using microelevators and microhooks, respecting the labyrinthine and perforating arteries. Then, the MVD is performed using a small Teflon pad which is adjusted with a microhook to isolate the nerve from the artery. Teflon is an inert material very well tolerated in the CPA. The most common offending vessel, the AICA, has a course between the seventh and eighth nerve in 50% of cases, which prevents a fully efficient and complete microvascular decompression from being completed. An intracanalicular AICA loop requires a complementary drilling of the internal auditory canal.

CCAPs are monitored during decompression (Figs. 84.7 and 84.8) by placing the recording electrode beneath the flocculus or above the cochlear nerve depending on the course of the offending vessels.

The operation ends by another endoscopic control of the quality of the surgical act to confirm the good positioning of the Teflon pad.

At the end of the procedure, the dura mater is sutured meticulously using 5/0 silk sutures. Then, the craniotomy is filled with a mixture of bone pâté and fibrin glue.

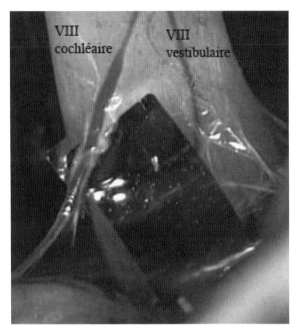

Fig. 84.7 Recording electrode on the medial part of the cochear nerve

The musculo-aponeurotic flap is sutured in place. The subcutaneous layer is sutured followed by skin closure.

The duration of the intervention is usually between 1.5 and 2 h.

The patient stays in the recovery room for 2 h and is then transferred to his/her room without the need for an intensive care unit (ICU), no matter what the patient's age is [11].

Results

Literature

The literature has sufficient data to prove that MVD can cure severe incapacitating tinnitus in carefully selected patients [3, 12–15]. However, the success rate of this procedure is inferior to that of MVD for hemifacial spasm or trigeminal neuralgia. This is mainly due to the anatomic difficulty in isolating the offending vessels as well as the multitude of other confounding etiologies for tinnitus. Following microvascular decompression for tinnitus, a result considered as "good" is a patient who had a total resolution or a significant decrease in tinnitus [3, 12, 13]. The frequency

of "good" results in the literature has ranged from 33 to 77% with more success in women than in men [3]. Some authors have performed revision surgeries before obtaining their final "good" results of 77% [12]. The only report that exceeded this range was by Okamura et al [16] who had 94% good results following the surgery. However, their selection criteria were much more flexible than the ones we used for our patients, and they included cases of low-frequency fluctuating hearing loss and intermittent tinnitus [16].

As for the offending vessels and their relation to the results of MVD, it seems that when the vertebral artery was the offender, decompression gave the best results, compared to AICA or PICA decompression [13].

Some authors have found a relation between the duration and character of the tinnitus and the postoperative results [3], while others found no such relation [13]. Several authors also report that ABR returns to normal in patients who had good results for the tinnitus [13], and that hearing loss is also improved [16].

Our Results

Between 1993 and 2006, 60 patients with tinnitus underwent endoscope-assisted microvascular decompression. Among them, 43 patients (22 women and 21 men) had a long-term follow-up. Their ages ranged from 37 to 71 years, and the average patient age was 57 years. The mean duration of tinnitus before surgery was 3.2 years (the range was between 1 and 8 years).

Tinnitus

In the immediate postoperative period (7 days following surgery), we have found the following results (Table 84.1):

1. Total relief in 16 patients (37%)
2. Marked improvement in 11 patients (26%)
3. No improvement in 16 patients (37%)

At 2 months postoperatively, the results are the following:

1. Total relief in 9 patients (21%)
2. Marked improvement in 14 patients (33%)
3. No improvement in 19 patients (44%)
4. Worsening in 1 patient (2%)

Fig. 84.8 Modification of CCAPS during the vascular decompression surgery

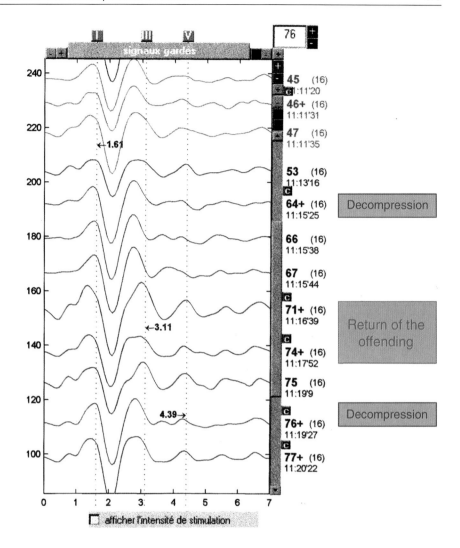

Table 84.1 Changes in tinnitus following miscrovascular decompression

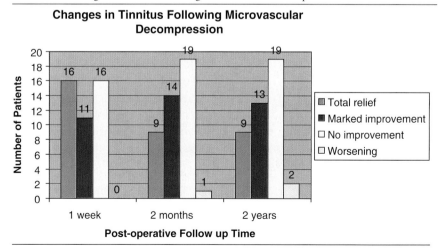

At 2 years postoperatively, the results are the following:

1. Total relief in 9 patients (21%)
2. Marked improvement in 13 patients (31%)
3. No improvement in 19 patients (44%)
4. Worsening in 2 patients (4%)

The characteristics of the tinnitus (pulsatility, pitch, persistence, or intermittency) are very labile parameters that were not quantified.

In our series, the results did not change significantly with time after 2 months postoperatively. This is not consistent with the data of other authors who mention some improvement until up to 1 year.

Postoperative Hearing

It is reasonable to believe that when pulsatile compression on the cochlear nerve is released, hearing loss due to such compression might be improved. We considered that there is an improvement in hearing if there is a gain superior or equal to 5 dB over a minimum of three standard frequencies of the audiogram. As such, we found that 12 patients had an improvement of hearing over three or more frequencies. On the preoperative audiograms, we notice that the high frequencies were mostly altered (4,000 and 8,000 Hz). We found an improvement by more than 5 dB over these two frequencies in 17 patients, but this improvement did not reach statistical significance ($p > 0.05$). Hearing remained unchanged in 20 subjects. On the other hand, eight patients presented a 5–10 dB worsening of their hearing, and one patient had a more significant loss of more than 30 dB. Two causes might explain this complication: the manipulation of the arteries, or the thermal effect from the light of the tip of the endoscope. In the year following the surgery, two other patients had a loss of hearing: one patient had a sudden hearing loss 11 weeks after the surgery, which never recovered, and another patient had a fluctuating hearing loss.

Correlation Between Tinnitus and Hearing

There exists a significant statistical correlation between the resolution of the tinnitus and the improvement in hearing. In fact, a 5 dB improvement over at least three frequencies of the audiogram is statistically associated with a resolution of the tinnitus (Fisher exact test) ($p = 0.034$ for an improvement over three frequencies, $p = 0.009$ over four frequencies, and $p = 0.050$ over five frequencies).

In addition, the sum of the auditory gains over the seven tested frequencies (250, 500, 1,000, 2,000, 4,000, 6,000, and 8,000 Hz) is statistically better in patients without any postoperative tinnitus compared to those who still have tinnitus. These former patients present an average sum auditory gain of 20 dB ($p = 0.039$).

Correlation Between Tinnitus and ABR

The ABR returned to normal (I–III < 0.2 ms relative to the non-operated side) in all patients who had successful results (total relief and marked improvement patients).

Correlation Between Tinnitus and VNG

Out of our 43 patients, only one had vestibular test normalization with relief of tinnitus.

Vascular Structures Responsible for the Conflict

We have grouped the causes of cochlear nerve compression into the following groups:

1. AICA only: 18/43 (39%) (Fig. 84.9)
2. AICA and PICA (pinching the nerve): 4/43 (9%) (Fig. 84.10)
3. PICA with or without vertebral artery: 12/43 (28%) (Fig. 84.11)
4. Subarcuate artery ("hugging" the cochlear nerve): 7/43 (19%) (Fig. 84.12)
5. Vein: 2/43 (5%) (when present, the cause effect is questionable).

Though it might be difficult to predict the clinical results in relation to the incriminated vessel, it seems that the seven patients whose conflicts were related to the subarcuate artery had the best results. Among the

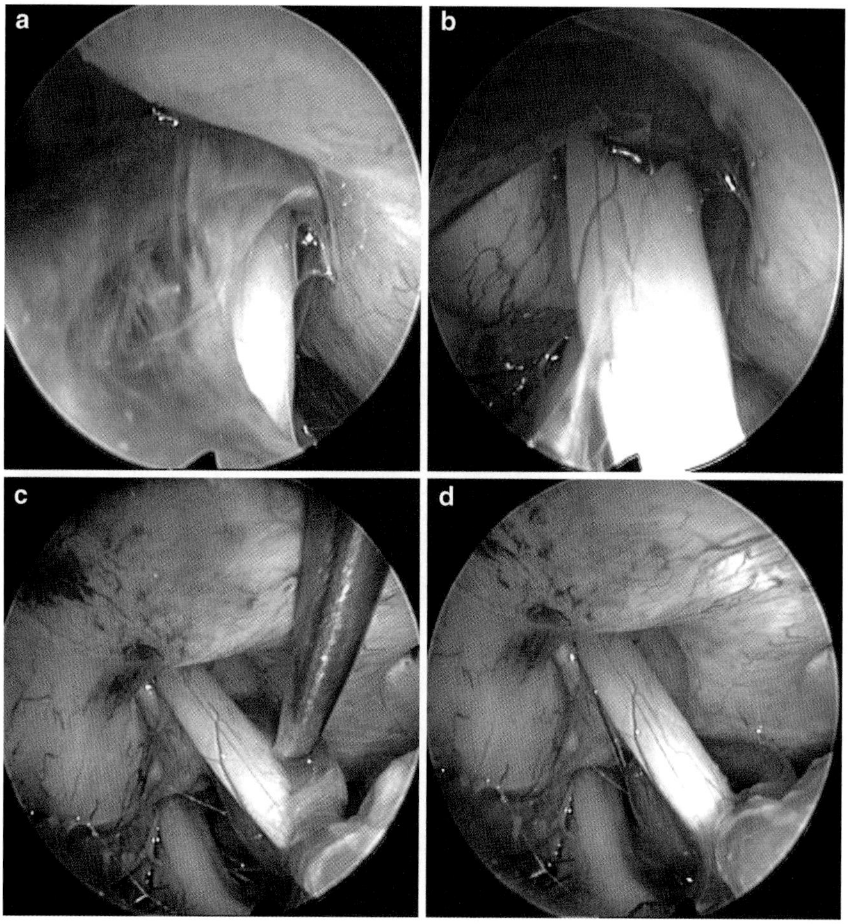

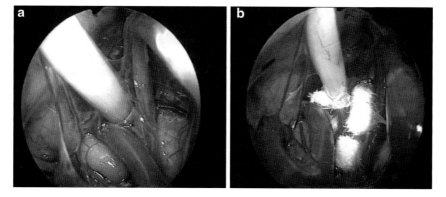

Fig. 84.9 AICA at the level of the porus compressing the cochlear nerve (tinnitus was reduced in this patient). (**a**): AICA and acoustico-facial nerve bundle within the arachnoid wrapping. (**b**): Closer view showing the offending contact between the vessel and the nerve at the entrance of the internal auditory canal. (**c**): Decompression of the vascular loop which is mobilised medially and inferiorly. (**d**): Vascular decompression done, not the labyrinthine artery emerging from the loop

Fig. 84.10 Different loops of the AICA pinching the cochlear nerve at its root entry zone (tinnitus was relieved in this patient). (**a**): Surgical aspect of the same vascular structure AICA looping around the cochlear nerve and compressing both sides of the nerve. (**b**): Vascular decompression using several small Teflon pads and isolating the cochlear nerve

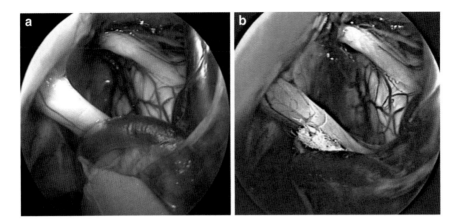

Fig. 84.11 (**a**) and (**b**): PICA deforming the course of the cochlear nerve (result: after an immediate good result, the tinnitus recurred on follow up)

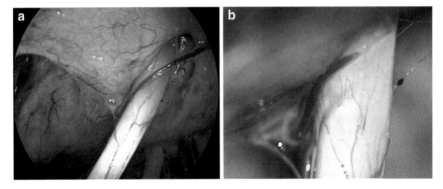

Fig. 84.12 Subarcuate artery crossing the cochlear nerve (result: relief of tinnitus). (**a**): The subarcuate artery distorting and constricting the cochlear nerve. (**b**): After coagulation of the subarcuate artery, the imprint made by the artery can be clearly seen on the nerve

seven operated cases, four had a total resolution of tinnitus, two had a decrease in tinnitus, and one had no change. On the other hand, in cases of an aberrant vein or a vascular loop inside the internal auditory canal, there was no improvement at all. For the other cases, no statistical correlation was found between the incriminated vessel and the postoperative result.

Morbidity

In our neuro-otological experience (1,117 retrosigmoid approach surgeries for functional indications), we have very little morbidity. This should be the rule in the functional surgical indications. In the surgeries of cochlear nerve decompression, no neurological sequalae were present postoperatively. There was no facial paralysis. There was one case of a profound hearing loss in the immediate postoperative period, probably related to a thermal heating effect from the tip of the endoscope. This happened in the earlier stages of our development of this technique. Two other hearing loss cases occurred in the first year after surgery. In one case, a sudden hearing loss appeared and did not recover despite adequate medical treatment. In the other case, a fluctuating hearing loss occurred, with vertigo, establishing the diagnosis of Ménière's disease that manifested itself 6 months postoperatively.

In total, based on our experience with the MVD surgery using the minimally invasive endoscope-assisted retrosigmoid approach, we can reduce the patient morbidity whatever the patient age is, but we did not succeed in increasing the rate of successful results above 50%. MVD of the auditory cranial nerve is less rewarding when compared to MVD of the trigeminal or the facial cranial nerves. This can be explained first by the difficulty in making a certain diagnosis, and second, by the complexity of the offending vascular loop anatomy which could limit the surgical maneuver.

Conclusion

When the neurovascular conflict is proven, decompression represents the only real treatment for these cases of tinnitus. This hypothesis is supported by the comparable management of hemifacial spasm and trigeminal neuralgia.

Our patient selection criteria are: unilateral tinnitus, positive offending vascular loop on MRI, and retrocochlear ABR abnormalities.

Out of 43 patients operated on by MVD of the cochlear nerve, the result was relief of tinnitus in 21% and decrease in its intensity in 31% of patients. There was a significant statistical correlation between the resolution of tinnitus and the postoperative hearing improvement confirming the concept of compression of the cochlear nerve. The failures of the eighth cranial nerve MVD must be analyzed with respect to the complex process of patient selection that is not yet definitively defined, the surgical findings, which can limit the efficacy of the surgical procedure, and the duration of the tinnitus with a central component.

References

1. Dandy W (1934) Concerning the cause of the trigeminal neuralgia, Am J Surg 24, 447–455
2. Jannetta PJ (1975) Neurovascular cross-compression in patients with hyperactive dysfunction symptoms of the eighth cranial nerve, Surg Forum 26, 467–469
3. Møller MB, Møller AR, Jannetta PJ, Jho HD (1993) Vascular decompression surgery for severe tinnitus: selection criteria and results, Laryngoscope 103(4), 421–427
4. De Ridder D, Møller A, Verlooy J, Cornelissen M, De Ridder L (2002) Is the root entry/exit zone important in microvascular compression syndromes? Neurosurgery 51(2), 427–434
5. Sekiya T, Møller AR (1987) Cochlear nerve injuries caused by cerebellopontine angle manipulations An electrophysiological and morphological study in dogs, J Neurosurg 67(2), 244–249
6. Arvanitaki A (1942) Effect evoked in an axon by the activity of a contiguous one, J Neurophysiol 5, 89–108
7. Møller AR, Jannetta PJ (1984) On the origin of synkinesis in hemifacial spasm: results of intracranial recordings, J Neurosurg 61(3), 569–576
8. Schwaber MK, Whetsell WO (1992) Cochleovestibular nerve compression syndrome II Vestibular nerve histopathology and theory of pathophysiology, Laryngoscope 102(9), 1030–1036
9. Reed GF (1960) An audiometric study of two hundred cases of subjective tinnitus, AMA Arch otolaryngol 71, 84–94
10. Girard N, Poncet M, Caces F, Tallon Y, Chays A, Martin-Bouyer P, Magnan J, Raybaud C (1997) Three-dimensional MRI of hemifacial spasm with surgical correlation, Neuroradiology 39(1), 46–51
11. Miyazaki H, Deveze A, Magnan J (2005) Neuro-otologic surgery through minimally invasive retrosigmoid approach: endoscope assisted microvascular decompression, vestibular neurotomy, and tumor removal, Laryngoscope 115(9), 1612–1617
12. Brookes GB (1996) Vascular decompression surgery for severe tinnitus, Am J Otol 17, 569–576
13. Guevara N, Deveze A, Buza V, Laffont B, Magnan J (2008) Microvascular decompression of cochlear nerve for tinnitus incapacity: pre-surgical data, surgical analyses and long-term follow-up of 15 patients, Eur Arch Otorhinolaryngol 265(4), 397–401
14. Ryu H, Yamamoto S, Sugiyama K, Nozue M (1998) Neurovascular compression syndrome of the eighth cranial nerve What are the most reliable diagnostic signs? Acta Neurochir (Wien) 140(12), 1279–1286
15. Vasama JP, Møller MB, Møller AR (1998) Microvascular decompression of the cochlear nerve in patients with severe tinnitus Preoperative findings and operative outcome in 22 patients. Neurol Res 20(3), 242–248
16. Okamura T, Kurokawa Y, Ikeda N, Abiko S, Ideguchi M, Watanabe K, Kido T (2000) Microvascular decompression for cochlear symptoms, J Neurosurg 93(3), 421–426

Chapter 85
Vestibular Schwannoma

Dirk De Ridder

Keypoints

1. Tinnitus is a common symptom in individuals with vestibular schwannoma (VS).
2. In 70–80% of cases, VS is ipsilateral to the tumor. It is the principal symptom in 10% and is moderate to severe in 14% of individuals.
3. Tinnitus in VS is typically associated with hearing loss (95%) and disorders of balance (50%).
4. Tinnitus in VS is mostly of high pitch.
5. Tinnitus is the predominant symptom in very small and very large tumors.
6. On the average tinnitus is not altered by gamma knife treatment, translabyrinth surgery, or retrosigmoid microneurosurgery, but the tinnitus of individual patients may improve or worsen after such treatments.
7. After retrosigmoid microneurosurgery tinnitus is often less troublesome than before the surgery.
8. Tinnitus might worsen after retrosigmoid tumor removal in operations in which attempts are made to spare hearing.

Keywords Tinnitus • Vestibular schwannoma • Acoustic neuroma • Gamma knife • Microsurgery • Natural history

Abbreviations

Gy   Gray
SRS   Stereotactic radiosurgery

THI   Tinnitus handicap inventory
VS   Vestibular schwannoma

Introduction

The name "acoustic neuroma" (correctly known as vestibular schwannoma) is a misnomer because histologically the benign lesions derive from the neurilemma sheath, most commonly of the superior vestibular nerve and not the auditory nerve [1]. These tumors occur in two forms: 95% are unilateral, mostly presenting after the age of 50; 5% occur bilaterally as a part of the signs of neurofibromatosis type 2, presenting at younger age (often before the age of 30) [2]. In neurofibromatosis type 1, unilateral VS are rare, with an incidence of about 2%. Bilateral VS are virtually non-existent in neurofibromatosis type 1 [2].

The incidence of VS is 1/100,000, 6% of intracranial tumors [2]. Postmortem studies indicate that the actual incidence is much higher (0.8%) [3] because many schwannoma remain asymptomatic.

Some epidemiological studies have found an association between the use of mobile phones and the incidence of VS [4–6], whereas other studies have not found such association [7]. Similarly, some epidemiological studies suggest an association between loud noise and VS [8].

The symptoms and signs of VS depend on the size of the lesion. When still intracanalicular, VS typically presents with a triad of symptoms: unilateral tinnitus (73%) [9], hearing loss (90–98%) [9–11], and balance problems (50%) [2]. The most common symptom is unilateral hearing loss [11], predominantly in high frequencies [2]. The hearing loss is progressive in most individuals with VS, but sudden deafness occurs in

D. De Ridder(✉)
TRI Tinnitus Clinic Antwerp, BRAIN and Department of Neurosurgery, University Hospital, Wilrijkstraat 10, 2650 Antwerp, Edegem, Belgium
e-mail: dirk.de.ridder@uza.be

A.R. Møller et al. (eds.), *Textbook of Tinnitus*,
DOI 10.1007/978-1-60761-145-5_85, © Springer Science+Business Media, LLC 2011

12% [12]. Low-frequency hearing loss occurs in individuals with large tumors [13]. Disequilibrium is more common than vertigo, and when disequilibrium is the first symptom, it seems to be correlated with rapidly growing tumors [14]. VS-related vertigo often occurs without nausea [10]. Tinnitus usually develops when the tumor is still intracanalicular [11] and is reported as the principal symptom in 1 of 10 patients who seek medical help [9]. Tinnitus is more common in small and large tumors than in medium-sized tumors [11].

When tumors extend into the cisternal space, hearing loss worsens and associated symptoms from compression of nearby cranial nerves may develop, such as facial numbness (in the midface area), facial palsy, otalgia, changes in taste, and, rarely, hoarseness or dysphagia. Compression of the brainstem and cerebellum can induce ataxia, diplopia, and other cerebellar signs. When a VS becomes very large, it obstructs the aqueduct causing collapse of the fourth ventricle leading to hydrocephalus and ultimately results in death if left untreated.

The rate of growth of a VS is unpredictable, but the average growth is 0.7 [15] to 1 mm/year [16], with 92% growing less than 2 mm/year [16]. In about 60% of patients, the annual tumor growth rate is <1 mm/year; in about 30%, 1–3 mm/year; and in about 10%, >3 mm/year [17]. Growth is manifest in 90% of tumors in the first 3 years after presentation [18], and if a VS growth is demonstrated by serial imaging, it usually continues to grow (63.9%). Only 30.6% arrest without treatment and 5.6% regress in size [19]. Intracanalicular tumors might grow slower than cisternal tumors [16], but this is not supported by all studies [17]. This might be related to the fact that growth rate is variable. In intracanalicular lesions, between 21.3 [20] and 70.6% [21] of patients demonstrate no tumor progression, but this variability signifies that potentially in as much as 76.6% of cases the tumor grows with resultant hearing loss [20].

Treatment for VS is still controversial. Treatment options consist of a wait and scan approach, stereotactic radiosurgery (SRS) (Gamma knife) and microsurgery [22]. A conservative approach can be elected in intracanalicular, asymptomatic, or elderly patients (>65 years) [14, 16, 17, 20, 21, 23, 24]. Furthermore, patients who fail conservative management have clinical outcomes that are not different from those who undergo primary treatment without a period of conservative management [16].

Microsurgery is elected for large and giant tumors, as large VS are more difficult to control with SRS and liable to produce ataxia due to transient expansion post-irradiation [25].

For small- and medium-sized VS, both microsurgery and SRS are valuable options. SRS, compared to surgical resection, seems to show superior outcomes for VS patients. A long-term tumor control rate of 94% after 5 years and 92.8% after 8 years [25] (transient facial palsy lower than 1%, and a probability of functional hearing preservation between 50 and 95%) can be achieved in experienced gamma knife centers treating large volumes of VS patients with state-of-the-art SRS [26]. Therefore, it has been suggested that unless a long-term follow-up examination indicates tumor progression at currently used radiation doses, SRS should be considered the best management strategy for the majority of VS patients [27, 28]. However, SRS does not arrest tumor growth in all patients: in 10% of patients who had SRS, tumor progression continues [29]. A second SRS treatment can often arrest further growth [29, 30], but if it does not, then radical surgery results in facial nerve worsening in half of the patients [31] due to severe adhesions or changes of the facial nerve [32]. Partial or subtotal resection can be proposed when SRS fails since the residual tumor does not seem to grow after subtotal resection [32]. A large study comparing 5,005 operations and 1,485 patients treated by SRS (gamma knife surgery) demonstrated that 96% of patients had total removal rates after microsurgical treatment, with a 1.8% recurrence rate, which compares favorably to recurrence rates after gamma knife surgery [33].

Based on these data, the following approach has been proposed: for lesions smaller than 2 cm, a conservative wait and scan approach; for growing lesions or lesions between 2 and 2.5 cm, either gamma knife or microsurgery; and for lesions bigger than 2.5 cm, microsurgery [22]. A combination of subtotal resection with adjunct SRS has been suggested as well to improve functional outcome in patients with VS that are larger than 4 cm [34, 35].

Tinnitus and Vestibular Schwannoma

Tinnitus is a very common symptom in VS: between 45 and 80% of VS patients have tinnitus [2, 9–11, 36–42]. It usually develops when the tumor is still intracanalicular [11] and is reported as the principal presenting symptom in 1 of 10 patients who seek medical help [9].

When tinnitus is the main presenting symptom, it seems to be perceived as severe [37]. The presence of tinnitus in VS is unrelated to patient age, gender, audiometric thresholds between 2,000 and 4,000 Hz, ipsilateral auditory brainstem response abnormalities, or caloric test abnormalities [37]. VS are most commonly associated with high-frequency hearing loss; the tinnitus is usually high pitched and localized to the tumor ear [2]. There is a correlation between the presence of tinnitus and the type of hearing loss with a tendency for patients without hearing loss to be less likely to experience tinnitus [37]. Greater age at the time of diagnosis seems to be associated with greater severity of the tinnitus. Abnormal caloric responses are also associated with a greater severity of tinnitus [37].

The presence of tinnitus is related to the tumor size [37]: it is more common when the tumor is small or when it is larger than 4.5 cm. This suggests that the tinnitus might be related to two different pathophysiological mechanisms, similarly to what has been described for microvascular compressions (see Chap. 40). The rate of tinnitus in VS is higher in individuals with functional hearing than in deaf individuals [43]. Deafness does not mean relief from tinnitus, and tinnitus persists in 46% of individuals who were deaf before the operation for VS [43]. This may suggest that the tinnitus is initially caused by aberrant signal transmission in the auditory nerve [37], whereas at a later stage, the tinnitus results from deafferentation, similarly to the tinnitus that occurs in connection with microvascular compressions (Fig. 85.1).

Treatment Options for Tinnitus in Patients with Vestibular Schwannoma

Conservative Treatment

It is uncertain if treating a small tumor leaves the patient with a better chance of obtaining relief from future tinnitus by observing it without treatment [22]. Between one third [33] and one half [44] of patients who are followed conservatively develop progressive hearing loss, which could result in more tinnitus. However, it is not known whether or not this is the case.

Microsurgery

After VS microneurosurgery, tinnitus disappears in 0–45%, becomes better in 16–17% of patients, while 30–60% do not experience any change, and 8–29% become worse [45, 46]. Neither tumor size nor age at the time of the operation has an impact on the tinnitus that occurs after surgery [45]. Therefore, these factors cannot be used as predictors for who will improve, remain unchanged, or worsen postoperatively. Furthermore, there is no association between changes in the tinnitus and changes in the quality of life following surgical treatment of VS, suggesting that tinnitus may be of relatively minor importance in the overall quality of life of patients following microneurosurgery for VS [45]. If no tinnitus is perceived before surgery, almost 40–50% develop it afterwards [39, 47].

Tinnitus and VS size

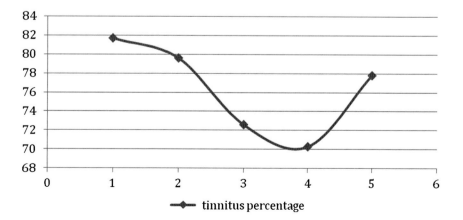

Fig. 85.1 Tinnitus percentage related to tumor size, based on [37]

Retrosigmoid (Suboccipital) Resection

Tinnitus disappears in 25.2%, improves in 33.3%, remains unchanged in 31.6%, and worsens in 9.9% after tumor removal using a retrosigmoid approach [48]. Although the proportion of patients complaining of frequent tinnitus increases postoperatively, the number of patients who find the tinnitus troublesome decreases markedly [49]. There is no difference in tinnitus incidence whether the auditory nerve is resected or not during surgery [48]. If no tinnitus is present before surgery, it develops postoperatively in 8.5%, again, whether the auditory nerve was resected or not [48]. Risk factors for developing tinnitus after microsurgery are sudden drops in perioperative blood pressure and hearing preservation surgery. A sudden drop in blood pressure during or after surgery is a negative prognostic factor not only for hearing preservation but also for ipsilateral tinnitus in patients undergoing vestibular schwannoma surgery [50]. When attempting to achieve hearing preservation during removal of a VS in patients without preoperatively tinnitus, 85% develop tinnitus postoperatively compared to 31% of patients in operations where hearing preservation is not attempted in the translabyrinth resection group [36]. However, a number of smaller studies seem to have opposite results: 50% of patients who had tinnitus preoperatively complained of it postoperatively, and only 8% developed tinnitus as a result of VS surgery which saved hearing [40].

Translabyrinthine Resection

The tinnitus in individuals with VS is usually not bothersome [2, 37, 41, 42]. Fourteen percent suffer from moderate to severe tinnitus according to a tinnitus handicap inventory (THI), and postoperatively the tinnitus handicap is neither alleviated nor exacerbated by translabyrinthine surgery as a group. On an individual basis, the tinnitus handicap was worse in 6.5%, unchanged in 87%, and better in 6.5% [42]. There is a 35% risk for developing tinnitus when no preoperative tinnitus is present and a 15% chance that tinnitus disappears when present preoperatively with translabyrinth surgery [41]. Patients who had a probable or definite nerve section had significantly lower postoperative tinnitus severity [51]. Based on these results, it may be suggested that patients with no tinnitus preoperatively

undergoing this form of surgery are unlikely to develop tinnitus after the operation, and if they do it will not be severe enough to significantly affect their quality of life [52]. When asked what affects the postoperative quality of life, less than 4% of the patients mentioned tinnitus [53].

Gamma Knife Surgery (SRS)

Tinnitus only changes or develops in a few patients (4%) after SRS for VS [28, 54, 55]. Preoperative tinnitus does not seem to exacerbate on a group level, thus similar to microsurgery [56]. Also in patients with small VS and no hearing, results from SRS and microsurgery are not significantly different with regard to tinnitus [57]. Some studies, however, do show less tinnitus in about 45% of patients who were treated with SRS [55, 58]. Whether hearing preservation in SRS is related to this is unknown. The functional hearing preservation at 3 years is 80% in patients with tinnitus as a first symptom [59]. Based on a systematic review of hearing results, on average 57% hearing preservation rate can be expected [60, 61]. The probability of preserving functional hearing is not only dependent of the presence of tinnitus as a first symptom. Hearing preservation is higher in patients who have an initial symptom other than hearing decrease (91.1%), in patients younger than 50 years (83.7%), and in those treated with a dose to the cochlea of less than 4 Gy (90.9%) [62]. Three years after GKS for VS, 71% of patients have unchanged hearing levels [63].

Conclusion

Tinnitus is a common symptom in VS, but rarely distressing. In only 10% of patients, harboring a VS tinnitus is the principal symptom and in only 14% of these, the tinnitus is perceived as moderately to severely distressing. Using gamma knife (SRS) or translabyrinthine surgical removal does not alter the tinnitus at a group level, even though some individual patients may experience less tinnitus after the treatment. Retrosigmoid surgery seems to have an impact on the tinnitus, decreasing its severity, except when associated with surgery which saves hearing. This should be remembered when treating patients with VS presenting with tinnitus.

References

1. Eldridge R and D Parry (1992) Vestibular schwannoma (acoustic neuroma). Consensus development conference. Neurosurgery 30:962–4.
2. Jackler R, (1994) Acoustic Neuroma (Vestibular Schwannoma), in Neurotology, R Jackler and D Brackmann, Editors. 1994, Mosby: St Louis. 729–85.
3. Leonard JR and ML Talbot (1970) Asymptomatic acoustic neurilemoma. Arch Otolaryngol 91:117–24.
4. Ahlbom A, M Feychting, A Green et al. (2009) Epidemiologic evidence on mobile phones and tumor risk: a review. Epidemiology 20:639–52.
5. Hardell L, M Carlberg, F Soderqvist et al. (2008) Meta-analysis of long-term mobile phone use and the association with brain tumours. Int J Oncol 32:1097–103.
6. Hardell L, K Hansson Mild, M Sandstrom et al. (2003) Vestibular schwannoma, tinnitus and cellular telephones. Neuroepidemiology 22:124–9.
7. Croft RJ, RJ McKenzie, I Inyang et al. (2008) Mobile phones and brain tumours: a review of epidemiological research. Australas Phys Eng Sci Med 31:255–67.
8. Hours M, M Bernard, M Arslan et al. (2009) Can loud noise cause acoustic neuroma? Analysis of the INTERPHONE study in France. Occup Environ Med 66:480–6.
9. Moffat DA, DM Baguley, GJ Beynon et al. (1998) Clinical acumen and vestibular schwannoma. Am J Otol 19:82–7.
10. Kentala E and I Pyykko (2001) Clinical picture of vestibular schwannoma. Auris Nasus Larynx 28:15–22.
11. Haapaniemi J, E Laurikainen, R Johansson et al. (2000) Cochleovestibular symptoms related to the site of vestibular schwannoma. Acta Otolaryngol Suppl 543:14–6.
12. Moffat DA, DM Baguley, H von Blumenthal et al. (1994) Sudden deafness in vestibular schwannoma. J Laryngol Otol 108:116–9.
13. Nadol JB, Jr., PF Diamond and AR Thornton (1996) Correlation of hearing loss and radiologic dimensions of vestibular schwannomas (acoustic Neuromas). Am J Otol 17:312–6.
14. Malhotra PS, P Sharma, MA Fishman et al. (2009) Clinical, radiographic, and audiometric predictors in conservative management of vestibular schwannoma. Otol Neurotol 30:507–14.
15. Battaglia A, B Mastrodimos and R Cueva (2006) Comparison of growth patterns of acoustic neuromas with and without radiosurgery. Otol Neurotol 27:705–12.
16. Hajioff D, VV Raut, RM Walsh et al. (2008) Conservative management of vestibular schwannomas: third review of a 10-year prospective study. Clin Otolaryngol 33:255–9.
17. Bakkouri WE, RE Kania, JP Guichard et al. (2009) Conservative management of 386 cases of unilateral vestibular schwannoma: tumor growth and consequences for treatment. J Neurosurg 110:662–9.
18. Martin TP, L Senthil, SV Chavda et al. (2009) A protocol for the conservative management of vestibular schwannomas. Otol Neurotol 30:381–5.
19. Mick P, BD Westerberg, R Ngo et al. (2009) Growing vestibular schwannomas: what happens next? Otol Neurotol 30:101–4.
20. Roche PH, O Soumare, JM Thomassin et al. (2008) The wait and see strategy for intracanalicular vestibular schwannomas. Prog Neurol Surg 21:83–8.
21. Solares CA and B Panizza (2008) Vestibular schwannoma: an understanding of growth should influence management decisions. Otol Neurotol 29:829–34.
22. Myrseth E, PH Pedersen, P Moller et al. (2007) Treatment of vestibular schwannomas. Why, when and how? Acta Neurochir (Wien) 149:647–60; discussion 60.
23. Ferri GG, GC Modugno, A Pirodda et al. (2008) Conservative management of vestibular schwannomas: an effective strategy. Laryngoscope 118:951–7.
24. Rosenberg SI (2000) Natural history of acoustic neuromas. Laryngoscope 110:497–508.
25. Fukuoka S, M Takanashi, A Hojyo et al. (2009) Gamma knife radiosurgery for vestibular schwannomas. Prog Neurol Surg 22:45–62.
26. Regis J, PH Roche, C Delsanti et al. (2007) Modern management of vestibular schwannomas. Prog Neurol Surg 20:129–41.
27. Pollock BE (2008) Vestibular schwannoma management: an evidence-based comparison of stereotactic radiosurgery and microsurgical resection. Prog Neurol Surg 21:222–7.
28. Myrseth E, P Moller, PH Pedersen et al. (2009) Vestibular schwannoma: surgery or gamma knife radiosurgery? A prospective, nonrandomized study. Neurosurgery 64:654–61; discussion 61–3.
29. Liscak R, V Vladyka, D Urgosik et al. (2009) Repeated treatment of vestibular schwannomas after gamma knife radiosurgery. Acta Neurochir (Wien) 151:317–24; discussion 24.
30. Yomo S, Y Arkha, C Delsanti et al. (2009) Repeat gamma knife surgery for regrowth of vestibular schwannomas. Neurosurgery 64:48–54; discussion 5.
31. Roche PH, M Khalil, JM Thomassin et al. (2008) Surgical removal of vestibular schwannoma after failed gamma knife radiosurgery. Prog Neurol Surg 21:152–7.
32. Shuto T, S Inomori, S Matsunaga et al. (2008) Microsurgery for vestibular schwannoma after gamma knife radiosurgery. Acta Neurochir (Wien) 150:229–34; discussion 34.
33. Yamakami I, Y Uchino, E Kobayashi et al. (2003) Conservative management, gamma-knife radiosurgery, and microsurgery for acoustic neurinomas: a systematic review of outcome and risk of three therapeutic options. Neurol Res 25:682–90.
34. Fuentes S, Y Arkha, G Pech-Gourg et al. (2008) Management of large vestibular schwannomas by combined surgical resection and gamma knife radiosurgery. Prog Neurol Surg 21:79–82.
35. Park CK, HW Jung, JE Kim et al. (2006) Therapeutic strategy for large vestibular schwannomas. J Neurooncol 77:167–71.
36. Kanzaki J, A Satoh and T Kunihiro (1999) Does hearing preservation surgery for acoustic neuromas affect tinnitus? Skull Base Surg 9:169–76.
37. Baguley DM, RL Humphriss, PR Axon et al. (2006) The clinical characteristics of tinnitus in patients with vestibular schwannoma. Skull Base 16:49–58.
38. Humphriss RL, DM Baguley, PR Axon et al. (2006) Preoperative audiovestibular handicap in patients with vestibular schwannoma. Skull Base 16:193–9.
39. Levo H, G Blomstedt and I Pyykko (2000) Tinnitus and vestibular schwannoma surgery. Acta Otolaryngol Suppl 543:28–9.
40. Catalano PJ and KD Post (1996) Elimination of tinnitus following hearing preservation surgery for acoustic neuromas. Am J Otol 17:443–5.

41. Andersson G, A Kinnefors, L Ekvall et al. (1997) Tinnitus and translabyrinthine acoustic neuroma surgery. Audiol Neurootol 2:403–9.

42. Baguley DM, RL Humphriss, PR Axon et al. (2005) Change in tinnitus handicap after translabyrinthine vestibular schwannoma excision. Otol Neurotol 26:1061–3.

43. Matthies C and M Samii (1997) Management of 1000 vestibular schwannomas (acoustic neuromas): clinical presentation. Neurosurgery 40:1–9; discussion 10.

44. Smouha EE, M Yoo, K Mohr et al. (2005) Conservative management of acoustic neuroma: a meta-analysis and proposed treatment algorithm. Laryngoscope 115:450–4.

45. Fahy C, TP Nikolopoulos and GM O'Donoghue (2002) Acoustic neuroma surgery and tinnitus. Eur Arch Otorhinolaryngol 259:299–301.

46. Henrich DE, BF McCabe and BJ Gantz (1995) Tinnitus and acoustic neuromas: analysis of the effect of surgical excision on postoperative tinnitus. Ear Nose Throat J 74:462–6.

47. Berliner KI, C Shelton, WE Hitselberger et al. (1992) Acoustic tumors: effect of surgical removal on tinnitus. Am J Otol 13:13–7.

48. Kameda K, T Shono, K Hashiguchi et al. (2009) Effect of tumor removal on tinnitus in patients with vestibular schwannoma. J Neurosurg 112(1):152–7.

49. Rigby PL, SB Shah, RK Jackler et al. (1997) Acoustic neuroma surgery: outcome analysis of patient-perceived disability. Am J Otol 18:427–35.

50. Schaller BJ, J Rasper, A Filis et al. (2008) Difference in functional outcome of ipsilateral tinnitus after intraoperative occurrence of the trigemino-cardiac reflex in surgery for vestibular schwannomas. Acta Neurochir (Wien) 150:157–60.

51. Harcourt J, J Thomsen and M Tos (1997) Translabyrinthine vestibular schwannoma surgery: postoperative tinnitus and cochlear nerve integrity. Auris Nasus Larynx 24:21–6.

52. Baguley DM, DA Moffat and DG Hardy (1992) What is the effect of translabyrinthine acoustic schwannoma removal upon tinnitus? J Laryngol Otol 106:329–31.

53. Bateman N, TP Nikolopoulos, K Robinson et al. (2000) Impairments, disabilities, and handicaps after acoustic neuroma surgery. Clin Otolaryngol Allied Sci 25:62–5.

54. Hempel JM, E Hempel, B Wowra et al. (2006) Functional outcome after gamma knife treatment in vestibular schwannoma. Eur Arch Otorhinolaryngol 263:714–8.

55. Bertalanffy A, W Dietrich, M Aichholzer et al. (2001) Gamma knife radiosurgery of acoustic neurinomas. Acta Neurochir (Wien) 143:689–95.

56. Karpinos M, BS Teh, O Zeck et al. (2002) Treatment of acoustic neuroma: stereotactic radiosurgery vs. microsurgery. Int J Radiat Oncol Biol Phys 54:1410–21.

57. Coelho DH, JT Roland, Jr., SA Rush et al. (2008) Small vestibular schwannomas with no hearing: comparison of functional outcomes in stereotactic radiosurgery and microsurgery. Laryngoscope 118:1909–16.

58. Niranjan A, LD Lunsford, JC Flickinger et al. (1999) Dose reduction improves hearing preservation rates after intracanalicular acoustic tumor radiosurgery. Neurosurgery 45:753–62; discussion 62–5.

59. Regis J, M Tamura, C Delsanti et al. (2008) Hearing preservation in patients with unilateral vestibular schwannoma after gamma knife surgery. Prog Neurol Surg 21:142–51.

60. Yang I, D Aranda, SJ Han et al. (2009) Hearing preservation after stereotactic radiosurgery for vestibular schwannoma: a systematic review. J Clin Neurosci 16:742–7.

61. Yang I, ME Sughrue, SJ Han et al. (2009) A comprehensive analysis of hearing preservation after radiosurgery for vestibular schwannoma. J Neurosurg 112(4):851–9

62. Tamura M, R Carron, S Yomo et al. (2009) Hearing preservation after gamma knife radiosurgery for vestibular schwannomas presenting with high-level hearing. Neurosurgery 64:289–96; discussion 96.

63. Chopra R, D Kondziolka, A Niranjan et al. (2007) Long-term follow-up of acoustic schwannoma radiosurgery with marginal tumor doses of 12 to 13 Gy. Int J Radiat Oncol Biol Phys 68:845–51.

Chapter 86
Neuromodulation: Introduction

Berthold Langguth and Dirk De Ridder

Keypoints

1. Tinnitus is related to altered activity in the central nervous system.
2. Tinnitus can be treated by interfering with this abnormal activity in the central nervous system.
3. Potential therapeutic approaches include sensory modulation, sensory stimulation, brain modulation, and brain stimulation.
4. Pilot studies have shown first promising results for somatosensory stimulation, neurobiofeedback, transcranial direct current stimulation, repetitive transcranial magnetic stimulation, and epidural electrical stimulation.
5. All therapeutic strategies presented are still at an early stage of development.
6. More research is needed to further improve the efficacy of the presented techniques.

Keywords Tinnitus • Brain stimulation • Nerve stimulation • Neural activity • Neural excitability • Neurobiofeedback • Transcranial magnetic stimulation • Electrical stimulation • Transcranial direct current stimulation • Nerve stimulation • Neuromodulation

Abbreviations

EEG   Electroencephalogram
fMRI   Functional magnetic resonance imaging
rTMS   Repetitive transcranial magnetic stimulation
tDCS   Transcranial direct current stimulation

As described in detail in Part I of this book, there is now compelling evidence that the phantom perception of sound is a consequence of altered activity in the central nervous system. An increasing number of animal studies and experimental neuroimaging studies in individuals with tinnitus together with experience from similar studies in patients who seek treatment for tinnitus have contributed to an increasingly detailed identification of the neural correlate of tinnitus. With the neural correlate of tinnitus, we mean the minimal neuronal mechanisms, which are jointly sufficient for the conscious percept [1] of tinnitus. In short, alterations of neural firing and oscillatory activity [2–4], alterations of neural synchrony and temporal coherence [5], and changes in the tonotopic maps of the auditory cortices [6] have been observed in connection with tinnitus and described in many studies (Chap. 10). Importantly, these changes are not restricted to one specific brain area. Rather, they can be conceived as alterations of a network involving auditory and non-auditory brain areas [7–9] (for more details see Chaps. 17, 20, and 21). These changes of neural activity seem to arise from dysfunctional activation of neural plasticity (Chap. 12) induced by altered sensory input, which is auditory deprivation in most cases (Chap. 11) [10, 11], but can also be altered somatosensory input (Chap. 9) [12]. Frontal and parietal brain areas seem to have an important modulatory role [7, 9, 13, 14].

Any causally oriented therapy should aim to normalize this disturbed neuronal network activity. In principle, there are two possibilities. The first approach consists of normalizing the disturbed auditory input to the auditory cortex, which can be done indirectly by hearing aids [15] or cochlear [16, 17], auditory

B. Langguth (✉)
Department of Psychiatry and Psychotherapy,
University of Regensburg, Universitätsstraße 84,
93053 Regensburg, Germany
and
Interdisciplinary Tinnitus Clinic, University of Regensburg,
Regensburg, Germany
e-mail: Berthold.Langguth@medbo.de

A.R. Møller et al. (eds.), *Textbook of Tinnitus*,
DOI 10.1007/978-1-60761-145-5_86, © Springer Science+Business Media, LLC 2011

nerve [18], and brainstem implants [19], which all were shown to improve tinnitus in selected patients. If this approach is not possible, there is still the option to use other sensory pathways for influencing the disturbed networks (e.g., somatosensory stimulation [20, 21]) or a combination of different sensory modalities (e.g., virtual reality) [22]. Whereas the efficacy of somatosensory stimulation has been demonstrated in several studies for a subgroup of patients (see Chap. 91), virtual reality treatment is currently under investigation [22].

Another option is to supply the missing information directly to the auditory cortex [23] or interfere with the distributed "tinnitus network" directly. This can be done at the auditory cortex by implanted electrodes [24–26] (Chap. 90), by transcranial direct current stimulation (tDCS) (Chap. 89), and by repetitive transcranial magnetic stimulation (rTMS) (Chap. 88) [27–30]. Another option is to target other hubs [8] of the distributed "tinnitus network" [7, 9], e.g. both auditory and non-auditory areas [31]. Neurobiofeedback can also be used to modulate the abnormal tinnitus-related activity or metabolism by operant conditioning of the reward system [32]. Neurobiofeedback can be performed to normalize pathological oscillatory activity directly [EEG based (Chap. 87)] [33] or indirectly (fMRI based) [34]. Whereas stimulation by implanted electrodes or pharmacotherapy can be performed permanently, rTMS, tDCS, or neurofeedback can only be applied for a limited amount of time. Nevertheless, these methods hold therapeutic potential since all of them can induce plastic changes, which outlast the treatment period. These long-lasting effects with limited treatment time can be explained by either learning-like effects (activation of neural plasticity) or the disruption of dysfunctional networks, which then allow the re-establishment of a more physiological state.

All techniques presented in Chaps. 87, 88, 89, 90 and 91 have been only recently introduced as treatment options for tinnitus. All these approaches have been based on new insights in brain-based pathophysiology of tinnitus and have shown promising results in pilot studies. However, none of them have supplied enough evidence for a general application in routine treatment. Being at an early stage of development, an increase in efficacy can be expected for all these methods in the next years, especially with increasing knowledge of both the pathophysiology of the different forms of tinnitus and the neurobiological mechanisms involved in the modulatory effects of the different interventions being used already.

References

1. Crick F and C Koch (1990) Toward a neurobiological theory of consciousness. Semin Neurosci 2:263–75
2. Llinas RR, U Ribary, D Jeanmonod et al (1999) Thalamo-cortical dysrhythmia: a neurological and neuropsychiatric syndrome characterized by magnetoencephalography. Proc Natl Acad Sci U S A 96:15222–7.
3. Weisz N, S Muller, W Schlee et al (2007) The neural code of auditory phantom perception. J Neurosci 27:1479–84.
4. van der Loo E, S Gais, M Congedo et al (2009) Tinnitus intensity dependent gamma oscillations of the contralateral auditory cortex. PLoS one 4:e7396.
5. Eggermont JJ (2003) Central tinnitus. Auris Nasus Larynx 30 Suppl:S7–12.
6. Muhlnickel W, T Elbert, E Taub et al (1998) Reorganization of auditory cortex in tinnitus. Proc Natl Acad Sci USA 95:10340–3.
7. Schlee W, T Hartmann, B Langguth et al (2009) Abnormal resting-state cortical coupling in chronic tinnitus. BMC Neurosci 10:11.
8. Schlee W, N Mueller, T Hartmann et al (2009) Mapping cortical hubs in tinnitus. BMC Biol 7:80.
9. Schlee W, N Weisz, O Bertrand et al (2008) Using auditory steady state responses to outline the functional connectivity in the tinnitus brain. PLoS one 3:e3720.
10. Norena A, C Micheyl, S Chery-Croze et al (2002) Psycho-acoustic characterization of the tinnitus spectrum: implications for the underlying mechanisms of tinnitus. Audiol Neurootol 7:358–69.
11. Norena AJ and JJ Eggermont (2005) Enriched acoustic environment after noise trauma reduces hearing loss and prevents cortical map reorganization. J Neurosci 25:699–705.
12. Shore SE and J Zhou (2006) Somatosensory influence on the cochlear nucleus and beyond. Hear Res 216–217:90–9.
13. Andersson G, L Lyttkens, C Hirvela et al (2000) Regional cerebral blood flow during tinnitus: a PET case study with lidocaine and auditory stimulation. Acta Otolaryngol 120:967–72.
14. Gardner A, M Pagani, H Jacobsson et al (2002) Differences in resting state regional cerebral blood flow assessed with 99mTc-HMPAO SPECT and brain atlas matching between depressed patients with and without tinnitus. Nucl Med Commun 23:429–39.
15. Moffat G, K Adjout, S Gallego et al (2009) Effects of hearing aid fitting on the perceptual characteristics of tinnitus. Hear Res 254:82–91.
16. Van de Heyning P, K Vermeire, M Diebl et al (2008) Incapacitating unilateral tinnitus in single-sided deafness treated by cochlear implantation. Ann Otol Rhinol Laryngol 117:645–52.
17. Brackmann DE (1981) Reduction of tinnitus in cochlear-implant patients. J Laryngol Otol Suppl 163–5.
18. Holm AF, MJ Staal, JJ Mooij et al (2005) Neurostimulation as a new treatment for severe tinnitus: a pilot study. Otol Neurotol 26:425–8; discussion 428.
19. Soussi T and SR Otto (1994) Effects of electrical brainstem stimulation on tinnitus. Acta Otolaryngol 114:135–40.
20. Møller AR, MB Møller and M Yokota (1992) Some forms of tinnitus may involve the extralemniscal auditory pathway. Laryngoscope 102:1165–71.

21. Herraiz C, A Toledano and I Diges (2007) Trans-electrical nerve stimulation (TENS) for somatic tinnitus. Prog Brain Res 166:389–94.
22. Londero A, I Viaud-Delmon, A Baskind et al (2010) Auditory and visual 3D virtual reality therapy for chronic subjective tinnitus: theoretical framework. Virtual Real 14:143–151.
23. De Ridder D and P Van de Heyning (2007) The Darwinian plasticity hypothesis for tinnitus and pain. Prog Brain Res 166:55–60.
24. De Ridder D, G De Mulder, E Verstraeten et al (2006) Primary and secondary auditory cortex stimulation for intractable tinnitus. ORL J Otorhinolaryngol Relat Spec 68:48–54; discussion 54–5.
25. Seidman MD, DD Ridder, K Elisevich et al (2008) Direct electrical stimulation of Heschl's gyrus for tinnitus treatment. Laryngoscope 118:491–500.
26. Friedland DR, W Gaggl, C Runge-Samuelson et al (2007) Feasibility of auditory cortical stimulation for the treatment of tinnitus. Otol Neurotol 28:1005–12.
27. De Ridder D, E Verstraeten, K Van der Kelen et al (2005) Transcranial magnetic stimulation for tinnitus: influence of tinnitus duration on stimulation parameter choice and maximal tinnitus suppression. Otol Neurotol 26:616–9.
28. Kleinjung T, T Steffens, A Londero et al (2007) Transcranial magnetic stimulation (TMS) for treatment of chronic tinnitus: clinical effects. Prog Brain Res 166:359–551.
29. Londero A, B Langguth, D De Ridder et al (2006) Repetitive transcranial magnetic stimulation (rTMS): a new therapeutic approach in subjective tinnitus? Neurophysiol Clin 36:145–55.
30. Khedr EM, H Kotb, NF Kamel et al (2005) Longlasting antalgic effects of daily sessions of repetitive transcranial magnetic stimulation in central and peripheral neuropathic pain. J Neurol Neurosurg Psychiatry 76:833–8.
31. Kleinjung T, P Eichhammer, M Landgrebe et al (2008) Combined temporal and prefrontal transcranial magnetic stimulation for tinnitus treatment: a pilot study. Otolaryngol Head Neck Surg 138:497–501.
32. Sterman MB and T Egner (2006) Foundation and practice of neurofeedback for the treatment of epilepsy. Appl Psychophysiol Biofeedback 31:21–35.
33. Dohrmann K, N Weisz, W Schlee et al (2007) Neurofeedback for treating tinnitus. Prog Brain Res 166:473–85.
34. Haller S, N Birbaumer and R Veit (2009) Real-time fMRI feedback training may improve chronic tinnitus. Eur Radiol 20:696–703.

Chapter 87
Neurobiofeedback

Thomas Hartmann, Isabel Lorenz, and Nathan Weisz

Keypoints

1. While neurofeedback has been used for the treatment of various diseases for about 40 years, research on using it as a treatment against tinnitus has begun only recently.
2. This is mainly due to the fact that the first studies concerning electrophysiological abnormalities in tinnitus patients were done in the early 2000s.
3. This chapter first outlines the history of neurofeedback as well as the theory behind it.
4. This is followed by a short description of the electrophysiological abnormalities in tinnitus patients applied in the studies provided at the end of the chapter.
5. These studies not only show effects on electrophysiological measurements but also demonstrate a great impact on tinnitus sensation and distress.

Keywords Chronic tinnitus • Neurofeedback • EEG

Abbreviations

ADHD	Attention deficit and hyperactivity disorder
dB	Decibel
EEG	Electroencephalography
fMRI	Functional magnetic resonance imaging
HL	Hearing level
MEG	Magnetoencephalography
QEEG	Quantitative electroencephalography
TQ	Tinnitus questionnaire

T. Hartmann (✉)
Department of Psychology, University of Konstanz,
P.O. Box D25, 78457 Constance, Germany
e-mail: thomas.hartmann@uni-konstanz.de

Theory and History

Bioneurofeedback (also known as neurofeedback, electroencephalography (EEG), biofeedback, or EEG operant conditioning) exploits a simple learning rule: the operant modification of signals acquired from the brain of a participant or patient. Although, advances in technology allow for more sophisticated forms of neurofeedback than was possible earlier, the basic principle has not changed over the past 40 years: A signal is acquired from the participant's brain in the form of a recorded EEG, relevant aspects of this signal are extracted (e.g., power in a distinct frequency band), and fed back to the participant in real time. As soon as the signal reaches a predefined target, the participant is rewarded. It is important to note that this principle is agnostic to both the signal and the reward used. Furthermore, there are no assumptions about the direct behavioral relevance of the signal for the patient, as, for instance, there is no direct link between a certain group of cortical oscillations and a particular disorder the patient might suffer from. Moreover, changes of the respective signals normally do not have an immediate relevance. Thus, it is vital for every successful neurofeedback training approach to increase the behavioral relevance of the signal for the patient (e.g., by choosing an appropriate reward). A further aspect to be emphasized is that the participant cannot be aware of the acquired signal without the help of a feedback, which leads to the ultimate goal of any neurofeedback approach: learning via operant modification to control a signal, putatively reflecting a distinct brain state, which is normally beyond the individual's awareness and thereby uncontrollable.

Following the seminal work of Miller [1], demonstrating that autonomic functions can be modified

A.R. Møller et al. (eds.), *Textbook of Tinnitus*,
DOI 10.1007/978-1-60761-145-5_87, © Springer Science+Business Media, LLC 2011

through operant conditioning, Sterman and Friar showed that not only it is possible to use operant conditioning to increase sensorimotor rhythms but also this modification leads to a decrease in the amount of seizures experienced by an epileptic patient [2]. Similar encouraging results were found 4 years later for attention-deficit hyperactive disorder (ADHD) [3], training enhancement in the alpha and reduction in the theta band. These patients successfully learned to control their EEG oscillations and modify them into the desired direction, and the ADHD symptoms improved on 13 behavioral categories like "Out-Of-Seat-Behavior" and "sustained attention". A worsening of the symptoms was reported when the contingency of the training was reversed, resulting in a reward for decreasing alpha and increasing theta oscillations.

These studies present important results, but they were based on single cases. Controlled studies involving groups of patients as well as control groups and/or treatments were needed to confirm these results. One of the first controlled studies concerning epilepsy and neurofeedback was conducted in 1993 [4]. Twenty-five patients suffering from epilepsy learned to control their "Slow Cortical Potentials" (SCP) an event-related component indexing neuronal excitability. One year after the training, 13 of 18 patients reported a significant decrease in seizure incidence. In this study, patients not only learned to reduce the SCPs, leading to lower excitability and thereby preventing seizures. The protocol involved training both directions, thus teaching the patients to actually control this aspect of their brain waves in a more complete manner. Trying to achieve a transfer from laboratory experience to real-life situations, transfer trials and distraction were introduced. Transfer trials are trials in the same neurofeedback setting as used during the 'real' training, but without any feedback provided for the patient. Hence, the participants should be enabled to incorporate the strategy learned during the training and transfer it into their everyday routine. Distraction is used to further enhance the transfer to everyday life, as the patient is required to apply the strategy in situations outside the laboratory with some kind of distraction, such as background noise. Transfer trials and distraction ought to be considered as an important aspect in modern neurofeedback therapy.

Several controlled studies have now demonstrated promising effects of neurofeedback on epilepsy, ADHD, and other disorders such as depression (for a review see [5]).

Independent of the type of disorder, neurofeedback training always involves prior identification of an abnormal recordable signal pattern differentiating patients from healthy controls (e.g., a significant increase or decrease of power in distinct frequency bands). A further challenge is the demand for almost instantaneous feedback, excluding several signal-processing algorithms such as averaging data from numerous trials. Identification of abnormal signals can be achieved by either controlled studies or using QEEG (Quantitative EEG). QEEG is a method comparing EEG signals acquired and processed with a standardized setting to a normative database of either healthy individuals or patients exhibiting abnormal oscillatory activity due to a certain defined condition. Thus, significant deviations from the standard EEG-recordings can be found and used for neurofeedback trainings [5].

The design of neurofeedback training may be regarded to be independent from the disease or the signal to be trained. It always involves the acquisition of the signal using appropriate devices which is then further processed using either proprietary software bound to the specific equipment or freely available software like ConSole [6]. Although EEG signals are usually utilized for neurofeedback, today other signal sources, such as fMRI, are used as well. The software then reduces the information of the signal to an essential minimum which is then made visible and/or audible to the patient. A common example of such a neurofeedback cue is an object moving from the left to the right side on a computer screen, whereas the information of the signal is represented by the height of the symbol on the screen. If the participant in the study is able to reach a pre-defined target (e.g., to "move the symbol" above a certain height), he/she receives a reward, which can be positive visual feedback (e.g., smiley face) appearing on the screen or, in some cases, monetary compensation as well.

Treatment of subjective tinnitus by means of neurofeedback is a relatively new application. In the next section, we will give a short review of the identified abnormal spontaneous EEG patterns, followed by an overview of current neurofeedback approaches pursued in our laboratory.

Electrophysiological Correlates of Tinnitus

Using neurofeedback as a treatment for tinnitus, it is important to identify abnormal aspects of brain activity, which are correlated with measures of subjective tinnitus, such as its intensity and/or distress. This is fundamental, both for the conceptualization of a neurofeedback strategy and for the assessment of the training success. If behavioral measurements such as questionnaires assessing core symptoms of tinnitus are associated with the amount of modification gained throughout the training process, the argument that the abnormal EEG pattern is a critical clinical marker is strengthened.

During the last few years, several studies were published on electrophysiological correlates of tinnitus [7–9], stimulating the emergence of innovative theories and models as well as treatment approaches [10–14].

Although not directly related to neurofeedback, it is of value to consider current electrophysiological findings regarding possible and actual applications of neurofeedback. (For a more extensive review see Chap. 20.)

Results of Central Mechanisms of Tinnitus

In their 2004 review, Eggermont and Roberts provide an extensive overview on central mechanisms underlying tinnitus derived largely from animal studies [7]. Unlike studies involving humans, animal studies can directly explore the instantaneous effects of certain tinnitus-inducing treatments, like noise trauma and high doses of salicylate, in central and peripheral structures using single- and multi-unit recordings. Besides proving that subjective tinnitus is a central phenomenon, the review concludes that changes in neural activation related to peripheral changes cannot be isolated from the rest of the brain, but are likely to lead to changes in the balance of intracortical inhibition/excitation. This can lead to drastic changes of spike rate and temporal aspects of spiking activity (synchrony) in several areas of the brain, most notably in the auditory

cortex. Particularly, changes in synchrony can be, if sufficiently large, captured using non-invasive techniques, such as EEG or MEG, and are reflected in alterations in *ongoing* oscillatory activity. In tinnitus, ongoing (spontaneous) synchronized activity probably engages the higher order brain regions that are responsible for conscious perception of tinnitus. Recently, this view has been further elaborated upon in a model framework by Weisz et al. [8] and extended by notions on inter-areal coupling of distant brain regions (see Chap. 20).

Basis for Neurofeedback Therapy of Tinnitus

Empirically, our neurofeedback tinnitus therapy was based on the identification of electrophysiological signals that differ markedly from people not experiencing chronic tinnitus. Our first paper on abnormal spontaneous brain activity was published in 2005 [9] not only demonstrating that tinnitus patients exhibit higher energy in the delta band and lower energy in the alpha band compared to healthy controls but also showing that a correlation exists between tinnitus distress and abnormal oscillatory activity patterns in right temporal and left frontal areas. These results were later supported and extended in a study revealing, furthermore, a marked increase of gamma band power in tinnitus patients [8]. Another paper shows a decrease in delta band power during residual inhibition [15].

The above-mentioned studies all point in the same direction: the resting state of brain oscillations is different in individuals with tinnitus and in individuals who do not have tinnitus in the delta, alpha, and gamma band (see Weisz et al. [8]). Thus, it seems reasonable to suggest that these EEG anomalies in individuals with tinnitus can be important for the therapy of tinnitus aimed at normalizing these oscillatory patterns. Cortical oscillations like respiratory rate or blood pressure are autonomous functions or a reflection of these. Therefore, operant modification of cortical oscillations should be possible by means of neurofeedback, as it has been demonstrated before regarding other aspects of electrophysiological signals.

Treating Tinnitus with Neurofeedback: An Overview Over Recent Studies

Studies exploring the effect of neurofeedback on subjective tinnitus are few. Two studies have supported the assumption that distress in general is associated with a reduction of power in the alpha band of EEG recorded from posterior sites and enhancement of power in the beta band [16, 17]. On the basis of these findings, it has been hypothesized that the vicious circle between strain, anxiety, and depression initiated in tinnitus can be interrupted through relaxation and by up-regulating the alpha activity (sign of increased relaxation) as well as down-regulating the beta activity (sign of decreased stress).

The approaches described in this chapter differ essentially from other studies in that the activity being modified is different in terms of assumed anatomical localization and generator types. While posterior recording sites have been the regions of interest in many studies, we focus on recordings from temporal and frontal regions, which we believe are mainly involved in the psychoacoustic and distress aspects of chronic tinnitus.

It is important that alpha oscillations in our approach are interpreted as an indicator of the excitatory–inhibitory balance in cortical neurons [8].

Here, we present the results of two recent studies by our workgroup in detail (Study 1 and 2) and pilot data from a new and innovative study (Study 3). Although all three studies differ in methodological details, the basic principles remain unchanged insofar as the objective of all training is to reestablish the excitatory–inhibitory imbalance putatively underlying tinnitus via a normalization of the ongoing spontaneous activity, particularly in the alpha band. The differences in the presented approaches lie mainly in which frequency bands are trained and how the feedback is presented to the patients.

Study 1

In the first study, 21 patients with chronic subjective tinnitus participated in a training aimed at controlling alpha power (5 patients), delta power (5 patients) or a ratio of alpha and delta power (11 patients). EEG was recorded at four fronto-central positions and the average power (in case of training a single frequency band) or ratio (in case of training alpha and delta simultaneously)

of the respective frequency bands was displayed as the height of a fish "swimming" across the screen. No instructions on how to solve the task were given, except the notice that the position of the fish represented the cortical oscillations which had to be modulated by mental activity. Additionally, the participants were asked not to engage in muscular activities and to avoid eye blinks throughout the training session. Training success was monitored by matching the participant's perception of their tinnitus to the intensity of their tinnitus to a 1-kHz test-tone using an audiometer and by measuring the power of the trained frequency bands during a 5-min resting condition before and after the training. The distress related to the tinnitus was surveyed once a week using a German adaptation of the Tinnitus Questionnaire [18]. Results showed a significant enhancement of the alpha–delta ratio within sessions and a significant linear trend between sessions. Thus, patients did not only learn to control their cortical EEG oscillations within a single session but also experienced an effect between sessions over the entire length of the training. Furthermore, a significant reduction of tinnitus intensity and tinnitus distress was revealed. The average tinnitus intensity was significantly reduced from 25 to 16 dB HL, and the average tinnitus distress measure decreased from 27 to 19 points at the end of the training. It is important to note that the amount of reduction of tinnitus intensity was strongly correlated with enhancements in the alpha/delta ratio, disregarding the exact training protocol. No significant differences were found between the different training groups (Alpha alone, Delta alone, Alpha/Delta ratio) or regarding tinnitus-related measures or ongoing oscillatory activity. This supports our notion that normalization of ongoing oscillatory activity might contribute to a reversal of the abnormal excitatory/inhibitory imbalance.

Although the study yielded promising results, it was not free of methodological problems. Thus, it is not clear and cannot be deducted post hoc what the patients actually trained as only the ratio of alpha/delta or one of the frequency bands was fed back. An increase of this ratio may have been an increase of alpha, a decrease of delta, or both, while a static ratio could have also been an increase in both bands or no change in these frequency bands at all. As the other two groups only trained one of the two frequency bands, no evidence about the effect of training both frequency bands could be concluded from the study. We thus developed a new training, providing two-dimensional feedback to the patients.

Study 2

Sixteen patients participated in the second study. EEG was recorded from 31 electrodes covering the whole scalp. The data were projected online on a source montage with eight sources covering major areas of the brain. Alpha and Delta power were computed for both temporal sources. During the training, patients saw a football (serving as the feedback cue) moving in the middle of the screen, which was supposed to be moved upwards, indicating increased alpha power, and sidewards (to the right-hand side), indicating decreasing delta power. A coordinate system was superimposed on the screen, dividing it into four quadrants, wherein the right upper quadrant was the patients' target to reach (i.e., increased alpha power and decreased delta power).

Training success was, again, monitored using electrophysiological measurements as well as the tinnitus intensity matched to a 1-kHz test-tone using an audiometer and by measuring the power of the trained frequency bands during a 5-min resting condition before and after the training [18].

Patients were able to normalize their alpha and delta power significantly, which means there was a significant enhancement of alpha power and a significant reduction of delta power after the training. Behavioral measures also demonstrated a certain relief from the tinnitus. Thus, there was a significant decrease of TQ values from an average of 22 points before the start of the training to an average of 17 points after the last training session. Tinnitus intensity was also significantly reduced from an average of 26 dB to an average of 23 dB HL.

Although this study exhibits an alleviation of tinnitus symptoms in some patients, it is also clear that many patients were not able to learn the task, mainly due to the abstract nature of the task and insufficient instructions.

Study 3

We offered the participants one possible strategy (out of numerous others) to be successful in the neurofeedback task as described below. In contrast to the previous studies, an amplitude-modulated sound with a frequency spectrum close to the individual's tinnitus was presented to both ears. Sound stimulation normally leads to desynchronization (decrease) of alpha oscillations recorded from auditory areas and is also modulated by top–down influence such as from attention [19]. By training a suppression of alpha desynchronization and thereby reducing cortical excitation, the aim was to aid patients in finding strategies of drawing away attention from their own internally generated sound.

Preliminary analyses of the results obtained from nine patients demonstrate highly significant effects regarding alpha normalization: Alpha power was increased by about 80% from the first to the last session. Behavioral measures point to an alleviation of tinnitus distress inasmuch as TQ values were significantly decreased from an average of 28 points to an average of 20 points.

Summary

Although neurofeedback has been available in clinical practice and research for 40 years, only recent advances in computer technology, amplifiers, and signal-processing routines made it possible to develop sophisticated techniques for biofeedback trainings. It is now possible to use knowledge about abnormal oscillatory patterns in the EEG that occurs in individuals with a disease to design a neurofeedback training program that is aimed at normalizing these patterns and thereby alleviating the disease condition.

Here, we have briefly reviewed the literature on abnormal cortical oscillations in individuals with tinnitus. Although such studies have been few and the results have not always been consistent, the central origin of tinnitus is now undisputed. Findings from our workgroup showed a decrease in alpha components of the EEG and an increase of delta and gamma activity in individuals who have tinnitus. On the basis of that, we designed and tested three kinds of neurofeedback trainings, which differed in methodological issues but shared the goal of normalizing these cortical oscillations.

In accordance with early neurofeedback studies, we showed that the participants were able to learn how to control the oscillations in their EEG. We could also show that this normalization had a positive impact on the perceived loudness of their tinnitus and/or the distress caused by their tinnitus.

Research on the cortical processes involved in the generation of tinnitus is new, and limited understanding of the phenomenon involved is an obstacle in achieving success in therapy using biofeedback. Models and theories incorporating recent knowledge of the brain's internal processes are evolving and will provide a better understanding of tinnitus as a central phenomenon. Together with new developments in techniques of signal processing and in neurofeedback, we may expect that innovative neurofeedback designs against tinnitus will be devised in the future. The recent findings suggest that training of coherences or connectivity between brain regions involved in the processing or generation of tinnitus will be promising areas in the future.

References

1. Miller NE. Learning of visceral and glandular responses. Science. 1969;163(3866):434–445.
2. Sterman M, Friar L. Suppression of seizures in an epileptic following sensorimotor EEG feedback training. Electroencephalogr Clin Neurophysiol. 1972 Jul;33(1):89–95.
3. Lubar JF, Shouse MN. EEG and behavioral changes in a hyperkinetic child concurrent with training of the sensorimotor rhythm (SMR). Appl Psychophysiol Biofeedback. 1976;1(3):293–306.
4. Rockstroh B, Elbert T, Birbaumer N, Wolf P, Düchting-Röth A, Reker M, et al. Cortical self-regulation in patients with epilepsies. Epilepsy Res. 1993 Jan;14(1):63–72.
5. Masterpasqua F, Healey K. Neurofeedback in psychological practice. Prof Psychol Res Pract. 2003;34(6):652–656.
6. Hartmann T. ConSole [Internet]. Available from: http://console-kn.sf.net
7. Eggermont JJ, Roberts LE. The neuroscience of tinnitus. Trends Neurosci. 2004 Nov;27(11):676–682.
8. Weisz N, Dohrmann K, Elbert T. The relevance of spontaneous activity for the coding of the tinnitus sensation. Prog Brain Res. 2007;166:61–70.
9. Weisz N, Moratti S, Meinzer M, Dohrmann K, Elbert T. Tinnitus perception and distress is related to abnormal spontaneous brain activity as measured by magnetoencephalography. PLOS Med. 2005 Jun;2(6):e153
10. Flor H, Hoffmann D, Struve M, Diesch E. Auditory discrimination training for the treatment of tinnitus. Appl Psychophysiol Biofeedback. 2004 Jun;29(2):113–120.
11. Norena AJ, Eggermont JJ. Enriched acoustic environment after noise trauma reduces hearing loss and prevents cortical map reorganization. J Neurosci. 2005 Jan;25(3): 699–705.
12. Noreña AJ, Eggermont JJ. Enriched acoustic environment after noise trauma abolishes neural signs of tinnitus. NeuroReport. 2006 Apr;17(6):559–563.
13. Ridder DD, Loo EVD, Kelen KVD, Menovsky T, Heyning PVD, Moller A. Theta, alpha and beta burst transcranial magnetic stimulation: brain modulation in tinnitus. Int J Med Sci. 2007;4(5):237–241.
14. Kleinjung T, Vielsmeier V, Landgrebe M, Hajak G, Langguth B. Transcranial magnetic stimulation: a new diagnostic and therapeutic tool for tinnitus patients. Int Tinnitus J. 2008; 14(2):112–118.
15. Kahlbrock N, Weisz N. Transient reduction of tinnitus intensity is marked by concomitant reductions of delta band power. BMC Biol. 2008;6(1):4.
16. Gosepath K, Nafe B, Ziegler E, Mann WJ. Neurofeedback in therapy of tinnitus. HNO. 2001 Jan;49(1):29–35.
17. Schenk S, Lamm K, Gündel H, Ladwig K. Neurofeedback-based EEG alpha and EEG beta training. Effectiveness in patients with chronically decompensated tinnitus. HNO. 2005 Jan;53(1):29–37.
18. Goebel G, Hiller W. The tinnitus questionnaire. A standard instrument for grading the degree of tinnitus. Results of a multicenter study with the tinnitus questionnaire. HNO. 1994 Mar;42(3):166–172.
19. Bastiaansen MC, Brunia CH. Anticipatory attention: an event-related desynchronization approach. Int J Psychophysiol. 2001 Dec;43(1):91–107.

Chapter 88
Transcranial Magnetic Stimulation

Tobias Kleinjung, Berthold Langguth, and Eman Khedr

Keypoints

1. Repetitive transcranial magnetic stimulation (rTMS) is a noninvasive method for applying electromagnetic fields to the brain.
2. rTMS can induce alterations of neuronal activity that outlast the stimulation period.
3. By modulating the excitability of the auditory cortex, rTMS can influence tinnitus perception.
4. Single sessions of rTMS over the temporal or temporoparietal cortex have been successful in transiently reducing tinnitus perception.
5. Repeated sessions of rTMS have resulted in tinnitus relief in a subgroup of patients lasting from several days to several months.
6. However, effect sizes of rTMS in the treatment of tinnitus are only moderate, and interindividual variability is high.
7. Further research is needed before this technique can be recommended for routine clinical use.

Keywords Tinnitus • Transcranial magnetic stimulation • Functional imaging • Cortical excitability • Neuromodulation

Abbreviations

DLFP   Dorsolateral prefrontal cortex
EEG   Electroencephalography
FDG   [^{18}F]deoxyglucose
MRI   Magnetic resonance imaging
MT   Motor threshold
PET   Positron emission tomography
rTMS   Repetitive transcranial magnetic stimulation
TMS   Transcranial magnetic stimulation

Transcranial Magnetic Stimulation

Transcranial magnetic stimulation (TMS) is an experimental tool for stimulating neurons via brief magnetic pulses delivered by a coil placed on the scalp [1]. In brief, the stimulator delivers a short-lasting, high-intensity current pulse through an insulated stimulating coil. This induces a magnetic field perpendicular to the coil which penetrates the scalp and brain with little attenuation (see Fig. 88.1). The magnetic field reaches a maximum of approximately 1.5–2 T (same size as that of an MRI scanner) in about 100 μs and then decays back to zero [2]. The magnetic coils that are used have different shapes. Round coils are relatively powerful. Figure eight-shaped coils are more focal with a maximal current delivered at the intersection of the two round components [3] (see Fig. 88.2).

Because the field changes rapidly with time, it induces an electrical current in the brain under the coil which is similar in duration and amplitude to a conventional electrical stimulator used to activate peripheral nerves. Due to the strong decline of the magnetic field with increasing distance from the coil, the direct stimulation is limited to superficial cortical areas, but the stimulation effects can be propagated transsynaptically to functionally connected remote areas and thus indirectly affect large areas of the brain.

T. Kleinjung (✉)
Department of Otorhinolaryngology, University of Regensburg, Franz-Josef-Strauss-Allee 11, 93053 Regensburg, Germany
e-mail: tobias.kleinjung@klinik.uni-regensburg.de

A.R. Møller et al. (eds.), *Textbook of Tinnitus*,
DOI 10.1007/978-1-60761-145-5_88, © Springer Science+Business Media, LLC 2011

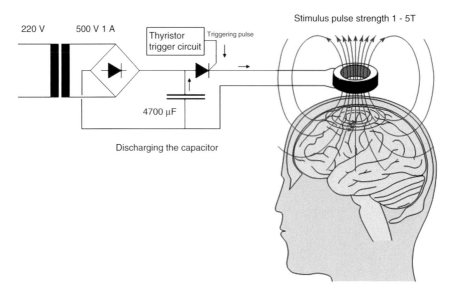

Fig. 88.1 Diagram of the underlying principle of TMS: The strong current in the coil produces a magnetic field perpendicular to the plane of the coil. The magnetic field passes unimpeded through the skull and induces oppositely directed electric current in the brain (adapted with permission from [66])

Whereas single magnetic pulses do not seem to have longer lasting effects on the brain, the application of multiple pulses, called repetitive TMS (rTMS), leads to effects on the brain that outlast the duration of the stimulation. These effects resemble those seen in animal experiments where repeated stimulation of many pathways has been shown to produce changes in the effectiveness of synapses in the same circuits [4]. Low-frequency (≤ 1 Hz) rTMS has been repeatedly shown to result in a decrease in cortical excitability [5], whereas high-frequency (5–20 Hz) rTMS results in an increase in excitability [6]. These changes include the phenomena of long-term potentiation (LTP) and long-term depression (LTD), which have been shown to be important in learning and memory [7]. Repetitive TMS can also be used to transiently disturb ongoing neural activity in the stimulated cortical area, thus creating a transient functional lesion. Such an approach can help to identify whether a given brain area is critically involved in a specific behavioral task.

Because of these unique and powerful features, rTMS has been widely used in various fields, including cognitive neuroscience and several clinical applications (for review see [8, 9]). However, despite its practical usefulness, the mechanisms of how rTMS stimulates neurons and interferes with neural functions are still incompletely understood.

Rationale for the Application of TMS in Tinnitus

Tinnitus is often associated with a lesion in the peripheral auditory system. It often occurs together with presbycusis, Ménière's disease, noise trauma, sudden deafness, or drug-related ototoxicity [10, 11]. However, these pathologies are not directly causing tinnitus. Rather, the neuroplastic changes which occur in the brain as reaction to sensory deafferentation represent the neural correlate of most forms of tinnitus [12] (see Chaps. 10 and 12). Thus, the mechanisms involved in tinnitus generation share similarities with those responsible for phantom pain after limb amputation [11]. Support for these hypotheses comes from functional imaging studies demonstrating that tinnitus is associated with neuroplastic alterations in the central auditory system and associated areas (see Chap. 18). In detail, positron emission tomography (PET) investigations revealed abnormal asymmetry in the auditory cortices of tinnitus patients with higher levels of spontaneous neuronal activity on the left side, irrespective of tinnitus laterality [13–15]. However, changes of neural activity are not limited to the central auditory pathways. Temporoparietal regions, as well as frontal and limbic areas, are also involved [16–18].

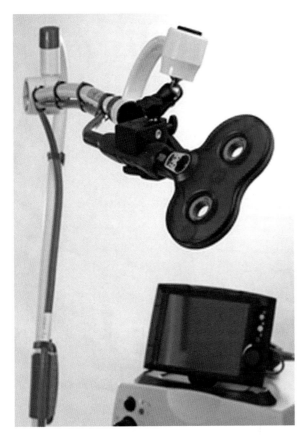

Fig. 88.2 The "figure of eight" coil consists of two overlapping loops of copper wire in a "figure of eight" arrangement. Current is induced under each of the two circular loops, but at the meeting point of the two loops the current sums up and is twice that beneath the edges of the two loops. Furthermore, this arrangement allows the stimulus to be more focal (1–2cm^2). Replicated by permission of The Magstim Company Ltd, Spring Gardens, Whitland, UK

Since rTMS has the ability to focally modulate cortical activity, it has been assumed that it can interfere with the abnormal neural activity in the auditory cortex associated with tinnitus and thereby influence the perception of tinnitus. If this is the case, repeated applications of rTMS might represent a potential treatment for some forms of tinnitus by producing longer lasting modulation of cortical activity. Additional support for this approach comes from clinical trials in which rTMS was used in an attempt to treat other pathological conditions with potential cortical hyperactivity, such as auditory hallucinations [19], writers' cramp [20], and obsessive compulsive disorders [21].

Studies Using Single Sessions of rTMS in Tinnitus

Within the last few years, results of several studies using single sessions of rTMS have been published (for references see Table 88.1). The goal of these studies was to transiently reduce tinnitus perception (see Table 88.1). In these kinds of studies, trains of high-frequency rTMS (10–20 Hz) were mainly administered. In a pilot study, stimulation of the left temporoparietal cortex with high-frequency rTMS (10 Hz) resulted in a transient reduction of tinnitus in 57% of the participants [22]. This result has been confirmed in a large series of 114 patients with unilateral tinnitus [23]. In this study, repetitive TMS at frequencies between 1 and 20 Hz was applied over the auditory cortex contralateral to the site of tinnitus perception. The best tinnitus suppression was achieved using higher stimulation frequencies, and patients who had their tinnitus for a shorter duration had the best results. These studies indicate that rTMS can be a valuable diagnostic tool for differentiating different forms of chronic tinnitus. This approach has been used for screening purposes to select patients for surgical implantation of cortical electrodes [24, 25] (see Chap. 90).

Two studies [26, 27] confirmed the result of transient tinnitus reduction after high-frequency stimulation of the left temporoparietal cortex, whereas one study [28] demonstrated reliable tinnitus suppression in only 1 out of 13 subjects after a single session of high-frequency rTMS. Additionally, one small study has shown [26] that the participants with significant tinnitus reduction after rTMS also had good response to anodal transcranial direct current stimulation (tDCS).

Different methods have been used to identify the target for stimulation. In one study, changes of cerebral blood flow were determined before and after lidocaine injection [17]. Single sessions of low-frequency (1 Hz) rTMS with the coil navigated to individually determined areas in the temporoparietal cortex resulted in tinnitus reduction in 6 out of 8 participants lasting up to 30 min.

Studies Using Repeated Sessions of rTMS in Tinnitus

The application of low-frequency rTMS in repeated sessions followed the hypothesis that longer lasting

Table 88.1 Effects of single sessions of rTMS on tinnitus

Authors	N	Stimulation site	Coil positioning	Frequency	Intensity	Pulses/session	Control condition	Results
Plewnia et al. [22]	14	Various scalp positions	10–20 EEG system	10 Hz	120% MT	30	Stimulation of nonauditory cortical areas	In 8 patients (58%) tinnitus suppression after left temporal/temporoparietal stimulation
De Ridder et al. [23]	114	Auditory cortex contralateral to tinnitus site	Anatomical landmarks	1, 5, 10, 20 Hz	90% MT	200	Coil angulation	In 60 patients (53 %) good or partial tinnitus suppression after active rTMS, in 33% suppression after sham rTMS
Fregni et al. [26]	7	Left temporoparietal areas	10–20 EEG system	10 Hz	120% MT	30	Sham coil and active stimulation of mesial parietal cortex	In 3 patients (42%) tinnitus suppression after left temporoparietal stimulation, no effect for both control rTMS conditions
Folmer et al. [27]	15	Left and right temporal cortex	10–20 EEG system	10 Hz	100% MT	150	Sham coil	In 6 patients (40%) tinnitus suppression after active rTMS, in four of the patients after contralateral rTMS in two patient after ipsilat. TMS; in 2 patients suppression after sham rTMS
Londero et al. [28]	13	Contralateral auditory cortex	fMRI guided neuronavigation	1, 10 Hz	120% MT	30	Stimulation over nonauditory cortical areas	Eight patients were stimulated over the auditory cortex with 1 Hz; in 5 of them (62.5%) tinnitus suppression; no suppression after 1 Hz rTMS of nonauditory targets; no suppression after 10 Hz, in 2 patients suppression after stimulation of a control position
Plewnia et al. [17]	8	Area of maximum tinnitus related PET activation (temporoparietal cortex)	Neuronavigational system, based on H_2O PET with and without Lidocaine	1 Hz	120% MT	300, 900, 1,800	Control position (occipital cortex)	In 6 patients (75%) tinnitus reduction after active rTMS, better suppression with more pulses

Study	N	Stimulation site	Localization	Stimulation pattern	Intensity	Number of stimuli	Placebo/control	Results
De Ridder et al. [47, 48]	46	Auditory cortex contralateral to tinnitus site	Anatomical landmarks	5, 10, 20 Hz tonic; 5, 10, 20 Hz burst	90%MT	200	Coil angulation	14 placebo-negative patients were analyzed: In those with narrow band/white noise tinnitus burst TMS was more effective in tinnitus suppression as compared to tonic TMS, whereas for pure tone tinnitus no difference was found between burst and tonic
Poreisz et al. [46]	20	Inferior temporal cortex	10–20 EEG electrode system, T3	Continuous theta burst, intermittent theta burst, immediate theta burst	80%MT	600	No placebo condition	Significant tinnitus reduction only for continuous theta burst immediately after stimulation
Meeus et al. [51]	50	Auditory cortex contralateral to tinnitus site	Anatomical landmarks	1,5, 10, 20 Hz tonic; 5, 10, 20 Hz burst	50% maximal stimulator output (independently of individual MT)	200	Coil angulation	No difference between tonic and burst rTMS in pure tone tinnitus (about 50% average suppression in unilateral and 30% in bilateral tinnitus). For bilateral narrow band tinnitus superiority of burst stimulation compared to tonic stimulation; better effects in patients with lower MT

MT motor threshold

improvement of tinnitus complaints can be achieved by reducing auditory cortex hyperactivity. An increasing number of studies using this approach as a treatment for tinnitus have been published recently (Table 88.2). Most rTMS treatment studies applied low-frequency rTMS in long trains of 1,200–2,000 pulses repeatedly over 5–10 days. In all controlled studies, a statistically significant improvement of tinnitus complaints has been documented. However, the degree of improvement and its duration varied across studies, probably due to differences in study design, stimulation parameters, and selection criteria of the participants.

Repetitive TMS has been applied over temporal or temporoparietal cortical areas. One placebo-controlled study with 14 participants used [^{18}F]deoxyglucose (FDG) PET and a neuronavigational system for the exact positioning of the TMS coil over the site of maximum activation in the auditory cortex [14] (see Fig. 88.3). After active treatment, the participants experienced a significant decrease in their tinnitus, as reflected by the score of the tinnitus questionnaire, whereas sham treatment showed no effect. Treatment effects were still detectable 6 months after treatment. Another study concerned the effects of 2 weeks of rTMS applied over the cortical area where lidocaine-induced activity change was largest as determined by [^{15}O]H$_2$O PET [29]. This approach also resulted in moderate, but significant effects after active stimulation. Placing the coil over the left temporal area according to the 10–20 EEG coordinate systems [30] resulted in a significant reduction of tinnitus severity after 10 sessions of 1 Hz rTMS. Beneficial effects of low-frequency rTMS have been confirmed by several further controlled studies [31–33].

While some studies demonstrated effects that outlasted the stimulation period for as much as 12 months [14, 34, 35], others were not able to achieve long-lasting effects [29, 32]. The number of daily sessions may be an important factor regarding long-term effects in tinnitus patients [36], thus similar to the experience from TMS applications for other disorders such as depression [37] and auditory hallucinations [38].

A recent case report showed that rTMS may be used as a maintenance treatment to manage chronic tinnitus [39]. In this patient, tinnitus could be reduced by rTMS each time it reoccurred using one to three sessions of rTMS; it finally remained stable on a low level after the third stimulation series. The positive effect of this maintenance stimulation could also be confirmed by reduced cerebral metabolism in PET imaging after treatment. The approach to use rTMS for maintenance treatment of tinnitus is further supported by the observation that those patients, who respond once to rTMS treatment, also experience further positive effects from a second series of rTMS [40].

Enhancement Strategies

In previous studies, when repeated sessions of rTMS were introduced as a therapeutic approach, stimulation has been performed at a frequency of 1 Hz [41]. This was motivated by the finding that 1 Hz rTMS reduces neuronal excitability over the motor cortex [5] and by the successful use of low-frequency rTMS in treatment of neuropsychiatric disorders, which are associated with focal hyperexcitability [42]. This concept has been challenged by a recent study with a relatively large sample size which compared effects of 1, 10, and 25 Hz rTMS [34]. Whereas sham rTMS treatment had no effect, active stimulation over the left temporoparietal cortex resulted in a reduction of tinnitus irrespective of the stimulation frequency. A follow-up assessment 1 year after treatment suggested a trend for higher efficiency of stimulation at 10 and 25 Hz, as compared to 1 Hz [35].

Experimental data from motor cortex stimulation in healthy subjects indicate that the effect of low-frequency rTMS can be enhanced by high-frequency priming stimulation [43]. However, in a clinical study, high-frequency priming stimulation failed to enhance the therapeutic efficacy of low-frequency rTMS for the treatment of tinnitus [44].

Repetitive TMS can be applied in a tonic and a burst mode. The burst stimulation technique has been proposed for enhancing rTMS effects. In detail, bursts of three stimuli at a frequency of 50 Hz (interval of 20 ms between each stimulus), applied every 200 ms (5 Hz, Theta burst), have been shown to induce more pronounced and longer lasting effects on human motor cortex than tonic stimulation [45]. Single sessions of continuous theta burst stimulation (3 pulses at 50 Hz, repeated at 200 ms intervals for up to 600 pulses for 40 s continuously) over the temporal cortex in tinnitus patients did only result in short-lasting reduction of tinnitus loudness, comparable to effects achieved with single sessions of tonic stimulation, whereas other

Table 88.2 Effects of repeated sessions of rTMS in tinnitus patients

Authors	N	Stimulation site	Coil positioning	Frequency (Hz)	Intensity	sessions	Pulses/session	Design	Control condition	Results
Kleinjung et al. [14]	14	Area of maximum PET activation in the temporal cortex, (12 left, 2 right)	Neuronavigational system, based on FDG-PET	1	110% MT	5	2,000	Sham-controlled, cross-over	Sham coil	Significant reduction of tinnitus after active rTMS as compared to sham rTMS; lasting tinnitus reduction (6 months)
Langguth et al. [30]	28	Left auditory cortex	10–20 EEG system	1	110% MT	10	2,000	Open	No control condition	Significant reduction of tinnitus until end of follow-up (3 months)
Plewnia et al. [29]	6	Area of maximum tinnitus related PET activation (temporoparietal cortex; 3 left, 3 right)	Neuronavigational system, based on H_2O PET with and without Lidocaine	1	120% MT	10	1,800	Sham-controlled, cross-over	Occipital cortex	Significant reduction of tinnitus after active rTMS, as compared to the control condition; no lasting effects
Kleinjung et al. [56]	45	Left auditory cortex	Neuronavigational system, based on structural MRI	1	110% MT	10	2,000	Open	No control condition	Significant tinnitus reduction after rTMS,lasting up furing follow-up period (3 months) responders were characterized by shorter tinnitus duration and less hearing impairment

(continued)

Table 88.2 (continued)

Authors	N	Stimulation site	Coil positioning	Frequency (Hz)	Intensity	sessions	Pulses/ session	Design	Control condition	Results
Rossi et al. [31]	16	Left secondary auditory cortex	Eight patients: neuronaviga-tional systemEight patients: according to 10–20 EEG system, halfway between T3 and C3/T5	1	120% MT	5	1,200	Sham-controlled, cross-over	Coil angulation + electrical stimula-tion of facial nerve	Significant reduction of tinnitus after active rTMS, as compared to the control condition, no lasting effects
Smith et al. [32]	4	Area of maximal PET activation in the temporal cortex, neuronaviga-tional system	Neuronavigational system, based on FDG-PET	1	110% MT	5	1,800	Sham-controlled, cross-over	Coil angulation	Modest response to active treatment in 3 patients (75%)
Khedr et al. [34, 35]	66	Left temporopa-rietal cortex	10–20 EEG system	1, 10, 25	100% MT	10	1,500	Sham-controlled, parallel group design	Occipital cortex	Significant reduction of tinnitus after all three active rTMS conditions, as compared to the control condition; tinnitus reduction lasting during follow-up period (4 months and 12 months)
Langguth et al. [44]	32	Left auditory cortex,	Neuronavigational system, based on structural MRI	1; 6 + 6	110% MT (90% MT for 6 Hz rTMS)	10	2,000	Randomization between two active treatment conditions, parallel group design	No sham control condition	Significant improvement for both stimulation conditions, no difference between conditions, no lasting effects

Study	N	Site	Localization	Frequency	Intensity	Sessions	Pulses	Design	Control	Results
Lee et al. [65]	8	Left temporoparietal cortex	??	0.5	100%MT	5	600	Open study	No control condition	No significant reduction of tinnitus
Kleinjung et al. [53]	32	Left auditory cortex; left dorsolateral prefrontal cortex	neuronavigational system, based on structural MRI	1, 20 (DLPFC) + 1	110%MT	10	2,000	Two active treatment conditions, parallel group design	No sham control condition	Directly after stimulation significant improvement for both stimulation conditions, at 3 month follow-up significantly better results for the combined frontal and temporal stimulation
Kleinjung et al. [55]	32	Left auditory cortex	Neuronavigational system, based on structural MRI	1; 1 + Levodopa	110% MT	10	2,000	Randomization between two active treatment conditions, parallel group design	No sham control condition	Significant improvement for both stimulation conditions, no difference between conditions, no lasting effects
Marcondes et al. [33]	19	Left temporoparietal cortex	10–20 EEG system	1	110% MT	5	1,020	Sham controlled, parallel group design	Sham coil	Significant improvement after active rTMS but not after sham rTMS, beneficial treatment effects still detectable at 6 months follow-up

MT motor threshold

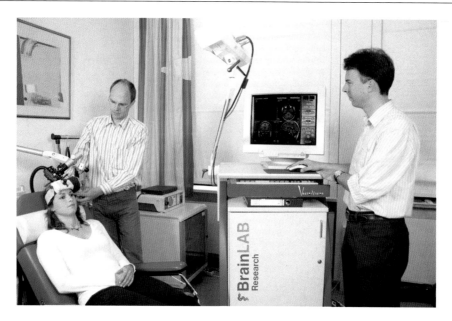

Fig. 88.3 Laboratory setting of a rTMS application to the left temporal cortex in a tinnitus patient. The coil is held by a mechanical arm which is fixed to the wall. The neuronavigational system allows the optimum position of the coil in relation to the target area as determined by functional and structural neuroimaging. Reproduced by permission from Hals-Nasen-Ohren-Klinik und Poliklinik Director: Professor Dr. med. Jurgen Strutz, Regensburg

theta burst protocols had no effect at all [46]. In two other studies, single sessions of burst stimulation were compared with tonic stimulation [47, 48]. Burst stimulation had similar effects as tonic stimulation in patients with pure-tone tinnitus but was superior in patients with noise-like tinnitus. A possible explanation for this finding is that pure-tone tinnitus may be due to increased neuronal activity in the classical (lemniscal) auditory pathways, which mainly fire tonically, whereas noise-like tinnitus may be the result of increased activity in the nonclassical (extralemniscal) pathways, characterized by burst firing [47, 49, 50]. A follow-up study of the same group could replicate this result for bilateral tinnitus, but not for unilateral tinnitus [51]. Furthermore, this study suggests that higher stimulation intensity may result in slightly better tinnitus suppression.

The neurobiology of chronic tinnitus suggests that neuronal changes are not limited to the auditory pathways [16]. Recent progress in neuroscientific research demonstrated that hyperactivity within primary sensory areas alone is not sufficient for conscious tinnitus perception. Rather, synchronized co-activation of frontal and parietal areas seems to be necessary [52]. In one pilot study, 32 patients received either low-frequency temporal rTMS or a combination of high-frequency prefrontal and low-frequency temporal rTMS [53]. Directly after therapy, there was an improvement of the tinnitus questionnaire score for both groups, but there were no differences between groups. Evaluation after 3 months revealed a remarkable advantage for combined prefrontal and temporal rTMS treatment. These data indicate that modulation of both frontal and temporal cortex activity might represent a promising enhancement strategy for improving TMS effects in tinnitus patients.

Combination of rTMS with pharmacologic intervention has been suggested for potentiating of rTMS effects. It is known from animal experiments that neuronal plasticity can be enhanced by dopaminergic receptor activation [54]. However, in a clinical pilot study, the administration of 100 mg of levodopa before rTMS was not successful in enhancing rTMS effects in tinnitus patients [55].

There is some evidence from several studies that the histories of patients who are treated may affect the therapeutic outcome of rTMS in tinnitus patients. Several studies reported that patients who have had their tinnitus for a short duration had better treatment outcomes [14, 23, 34, 56]. Normal hearing was also identified as a positive clinical predictor for good treatment response [33, 56]. Interestingly, short tinnitus duration and normal hearing have been demonstrated to be positive predictors in other treatment options for tinnitus as well [57, 58].

Methodological Considerations

Tinnitus is a phantom perception of sound and is susceptible for placebo effects. Evaluation of treatment efficacy requires adequate methodology for control of unspecific effects related or unrelated to the treatment (see Chap. 22). The majority of controlled studies, published so far, have compared the effect of the active treatment with placebo treatment in cross-over designs. Potential shortcomings of this approach include carry-over effects and missed long-term effects due to short observation periods. Also, different kinds of sham treatments have been reported so far. Besides the sham coil system [14, 59], which mimics the sound of the active coil without generating a magnetic field, an angulation of an active coil tilted 45° [32] or 90° [31] to the skull surface or a stimulation of nonauditory brain areas [29] have been described. Finding an optimal control condition for treatment studies is also difficult because of limitations in blinding of patients and operators to different stimulus conditions and due to the fact that TMS itself results in auditory and somatosensory stimulation in addition to the anticipated specific effect. One possible solution is a control condition which involves electrical stimulation of the facial nerve [31].

In most studies, validated tinnitus questionnaires and visual analog scales serve as primary outcome measurements due to the lack of objective signs of tinnitus. One pilot study demonstrated that an improvement in tinnitus rating after stimulation was also reflected by a reduction of activity in the PET scan after rTMS therapy, as compared to pretreatment values [32]. Therefore, functional imaging might be suggested as an important objective marker of treatment effects.

Safety Aspects

An extensive body of data has confirmed that rTMS is a safe and well-tolerated technique [60] when performed within a range of parameters defined according to a consensus on safety guidelines [60, 61]. Most available data regarding safety originate from rTMS studies in depressed subjects. A study showed that 2–4 weeks of daily prefrontal rTMS resulted in no sign of structural MRI changes [62], no significant changes in auditory thresholds, and no significant electroencephalogram abnormalities [63]. Adverse auditory effects such as hearing loss or auditory

hallucinations have not been reported after temporal rTMS. The risk of rTMS induced epileptic seizures, which had been reported in individual cases after high-intensity and high-frequency rTMS, has been largely reduced since the introduction of safety guidelines [61]. Mild adverse effects such as physical discomfort on the skull during stimulation or transient headache after stimulation are reported by about 10% of treated patients. It is essential that contraindications such as electronic implants (e.g., cardiac pace makers and cochlea implants), intracranial pieces of metal, or previous epileptic seizures are considered before treatment with rTMS.

Conclusion

In summary, the results from an increasing number of studies must be considered as preliminary due to small sample sizes, methodological heterogeneity, and high variability of results. However, the results of these studies are promising and show a similar percentage of beneficial effects. Data on the effect of the duration of treatment are still controversial. Effects outlasted the stimulation period up to 12 months in some studies; others could not demonstrate any after-effects. Replication in multicenter trials with many patients and long-term follow-up are needed before further conclusions can be drawn [64]. Further clinical research is also needed to get a clear definition of which subgroups of patients with tinnitus benefit most from rTMS and how their medical histories affect the outcome. Better understanding of the pathophysiology of the different forms of tinnitus and the neurobiological effects of rTMS will be critical for optimizing or even individualizing treatment protocols.

References

1. Barker AT, R Jalinous and IL Freeston (1985) Non-invasive magnetic stimulation of human motor cortex. Lancet 1:1106–7.
2. Ridding MC and JC Rothwell (2007) Is there a future for therapeutic use of transcranial magnetic stimulation? Nat Rev Neurosci 8:559–67.
3. Hallett M (2000) Transcranial magnetic stimulation and the human brain. Nature 406:147–50.
4. Post A and ME Keck (2001) Transcranial magnetic stimulation as a therapeutic tool in psychiatry: what do we know about the neurobiological mechanisms? J Psychiatr Res 35:193–215.

5. Chen R, J Classen, C Gerloff et al (1997) Depression of motor cortex excitability by low-frequency transcranial magnetic stimulation. Neurology 48:1398–403.

6. Pascual-Leone A, J Valls-Sole, EM Wassermann et al (1994) Responses to rapid-rate transcranial magnetic stimulation of the human motor cortex. Brain 117 (Pt 4):847–58.

7. Wang H, X Wang and H Scheich (1996) LTD and LTP induced by transcranial magnetic stimulation in auditory cortex. Neuroreport 7:521–5.

8. Walsh V and A Cowey (2000) Transcranial magnetic stimulation and cognitive neuroscience. Nat Rev Neurosci 1:73–9.

9. Simons W and M Dierick (2005) Transcranial magnetic stimulation as a therapeutic tool in psychiatry. World J Biol Psychiatry 6:6–25.

10. Møller AR, (2003) Pathophysiology of Tinnitus, in Otolaryngologic Clinics of North America, A Sismanis, Editor. 2003, W.B.Saunders: Amsterdam. 249–66.

11. Møller AR, (2007) Tinnitus and Pain, in Tinnitus: Pathophysiology and Treatment, Progress in Brain Research, B Langguth et al, Editors. 2007, Elsevier: Amsterdam. 47–53.

12. Møller AR (2007) The role of neural plasticity, in Tinnitus: Pathophysiology and Treatment, Progress in Brain Research, B Langguth et al, Editors. 2007, Elsevier: Amsterdam. 37–45.

13. Arnold W, P Bartenstein, E Oestreicher et al (1996) Focal metabolic activation in the predominant left auditory cortex in patients suffering from tinnitus: a PET study with [18F]deoxyglucose. ORL J Otorhinolaryngol Relat Spec 58:195–9.

14. Kleinjung T, P Eichhammer, B Langguth et al (2005) Long-term effects of repetitive transcranial magnetic stimulation (rTMS) in patients with chronic tinnitus. Otolaryngol Head Neck Surg 132:566–9.

15. Langguth B, P Eichhammer, A Kreutzer et al (2006) The impact of auditory cortex activity on characterizing and treating patients with chronic tinnitus–first results from a PET study. Acta Otolaryngol Suppl 84–8.

16. Lockwood A, R Salvi, M Coad et al (1998) The functional neuroanatomy of tinnitus. Evidence for limbic system links and neural plasticity. Neurology 50:114–20.

17. Plewnia C, M Reimold, A Najib et al (2007) Dose-dependent attenuation of auditory phantom perception (tinnitus) by PET-guided repetitive transcranial magnetic stimulation. Hum Brain Mapp 28:238–46.

18. Giraud AL, S Chery-Croze, G Fischer et al (1999) A selective imaging of tinnitus. Neuroreport 10:1–5.

19. Hoffman RE, KA Hawkins, R Gueorguieva et al (2003) Transcranial magnetic stimulation of left temporoparietal cortex and medication-resistant auditory hallucinations. Arch Gen Psychiatry 60:49–56.

20. Siebner HR, JM Tormos, AO Ceballos-Baumann et al (1999) Low-frequency repetitive transcranial magnetic stimulation of the motor cortex in writer's cramp. Neurology 52:529–37.

21. Mantovani A, SH Lisanby, F Pieraccini et al (2006) Repetitive transcranial magnetic stimulation (rTMS) in the treatment of obsessive-compulsive disorder (OCD) and Tourette's syndrome (TS). Int J Neuropsychopharmacol 9:95–100.

22. Plewnia C, M Bartels and C Gerloff (2003) Transient suppression of tinnitus by transcranial magnetic stimulation. Ann Neurol 53:263–6.

23. De Ridder D, E Verstraeten, K Van der Kelen et al (2005) Transcranial magnetic stimulation for tinnitus: influence of tinnitus duration on stimulation parameter choice and maximal tinnitus suppression. Otol Neurotol 26:616–9

24. De Ridder D, G De Mulder, V Walsh et al (2004) Magnetic and electrical stimulation of the auditory cortex for intractable tinnitus. J Neurosurg 100:560–4.

25. De Ridder D, G De Mulder, E Verstraeten et al (2006) Primary and secondary auditory cortex stimulation for intractable tinnitus. ORL J Otorhinolaryngol Relat Spec 68:48–54.

26. Fregni F, R Marcondes, PS Boggio et al (2006) Transient tinnitus suppression induced by repetitive transcranial magnetic stimulation and transcranial direct current stimulation. Eur J Neurol 13:996–1001.

27. Folmer RL, JR Carroll, A Rahim et al (2006) Effects of repetitive transcranial magnetic stimulation (rTMS) on chronic tinnitus. Acta Otolaryngol Suppl 96–101.

28. Londero A, JP Lefaucheur, D Malinvaud et al (2006) [Magnetic stimulation of the auditory cortex for disabling tinnitus: preliminary results]. Presse Med 35:200–6.

29. Plewnia C, M Reimold, A Najib et al (2007) Moderate therapeutic efficacy of positron emission tomography-navigated repetitive transcranial magnetic stimulation for chronic tinnitus: a randomised, controlled pilot study. J Neurol Neurosurg Psychiatry 78:152–6.

30. Langguth B, M Zowe, M Landgrebe et al (2006) Transcranial magnetic stimulation for the treatment of tinnitus: a new coil positioning method and first results. Brain Topogr 18:241–7.

31. Rossi S, A De Capua, M Ulivelli et al (2007) Effects of repetitive transcranial magnetic stimulation on chronic tinnitus: a randomised, crossover, double blind, placebo controlled study. J Neurol Neurosurg Psychiatry 78:857–63.

32. Smith JA, M Mennemeier, T Bartel et al (2007) Repetitive transcranial magnetic stimulation for tinnitus: a pilot study. Laryngoscope 117:529–34.

33. Marcondes RA, TG Sanchez, MA Kii et al (2009) Repetitive transcranial magnetic stimulation improve tinnitus in normal hearing patients: a double-blind controlled, clinical and neuroimaging outcome study. Eur J Neurol 17: 38–44.

34. Khedr EM, JC Rothwell, MA Ahmed et al (2008) Effect of daily repetitive transcranial magnetic stimulation for treatment of tinnitus: comparison of different stimulus frequencies. J Neurol Neurosurg Psychiatry 79:212–5.

35. Khedr EM, JC Rothwell and A El-Atar (2009) One-year follow up of patients with chronic tinnitus treated with left temporoparietal rTMS. Eur J Neurol 16:404–8.

36. Langguth B, P Eichhammer, R Wiegand et al (2003) Neuronavigated rTMS in a patient with chronic tinnitus. Effects of 4 weeks treatment. Neuroreport 14:977–80.

37. Gershon AA, PN Dannon and L Grunhaus (2003) Transcranial magnetic stimulation in the treatment of depression. Am J Psychiatry 160:835–45.

38. Hoffman RE, R Gueorguieva, KA Hawkins et al (2005) Temporoparietal transcranial magnetic stimulation for auditory hallucinations: Safety, efficacy and moderators in a fifty patient sample. Biol Psychiatry 58:97–104.

39. Mennemeier M, KC Chelette, J Myhill et al (2008) Maintenance repetitive transcranial magnetic stimulation can inhibit the return of tinnitus. Laryngoscope 118:1228–32.

40. Langguth B, M Landgrebe, G Hajak et al (2008) Re: Maintenance repetitive transcranial magnetic stimulation can inhibit the return of tinnitus. Laryngoscope 118:2264; author reply 5.

41. Kleinjung T, V Vielsmeier, M Landgrebe et al (2008) Transcranial magnetic stimulation: a new diagnostic and therapeutic tool for tinnitus patients. Int Tinnitus J 14:112–8.

42. Hoffman RE and I Cavus (2002) Slow transcranial magnetic stimulation, long-term depotentiation, and brain hyperexcitability disorders. Am J Psychiatry 159:1093–102.

43. Iyer MB, N Schleper and EM Wassermann (2003) Priming stimulation enhances the depressant effect of low-frequency repetitive transcranial magnetic stimulation. J Neurosci 23:10867–72.

44. Langguth B, T Kleinjung, E Frank et al (2008) High-frequency priming stimulation does not enhance the effect of low-frequency rTMS in the treatment of tinnitus. Exp Brain Res 184:587–91.

45. Huang YZ, MJ Edwards, E Rounis et al (2005) Theta burst stimulation of the human motor cortex. Neuron 45:201–6.

46. Poreisz C, W Paulus, T Moser et al (2009) Does a single session of theta-burst transcranial magnetic stimulation of inferior temporal cortex affect tinnitus perception? BMC Neurosci 10:54.

47. De Ridder D, E van der Loo, K Van der Kelen et al (2007) Do tonic and burst TMS modulate the lemniscal and extralemniscal system differentially? Int J Med Sci 4:242–6.

48. De Ridder D, E van der Loo, K Van der Kelen et al (2007) Theta, alpha and beta burst transcranial magnetic stimulation: brain modulation in tinnitus. Int J Med Sci 4:237–41.

49. Hu B, V Senatorov and D Mooney (1994) Lemniscal and non-lemniscal synaptic transmission in rat auditory thalamus. J Physiol 479 (Pt 2):217–31.

50. De Ridder D, S Vanneste, E van der Loo et al (2009) Burst stimulation of the auditory cortex: a new form of neurostimulation for noise-like tinnitus suppression. J Neurosurg 112:1289–94.

51. Meeus O, C Blaivie, J Ost et al (2009) Influence of tonic and burst transcranial magnetic stimulation characteristics on acute inhibition of subjective tinnitus. Otol Neurotol 30:697–703.

52. Boly M, ME Faymonville, P Peigneux et al (2004) Auditory processing in severely brain injured patients: differences between the minimally conscious state and the persistent vegetative state. Arch Neurol 61:233–8.

53. Kleinjung T, P Eichhammer, M Landgrebe et al (2008) Combined temporal and prefrontal transcranial magnetic stimulation for tinnitus treatment: a pilot study. Otolaryngol Head Neck Surg 138:497–501.

54. Otani S, O Blond, JM Desce et al (1998) Dopamine facilitates long-term depression of glutamatergic transmission in rat prefrontal cortex. Neuroscience 85:669–76.

55. Kleinjung T, T Steffens, M Landgrebe et al (2009) Levodopa does not enhance the effect of low-frequency repetitive transcranial magnetic stimulation in tinnitus treatment. Otolaryngol Head Neck Surg 140:92–5.

56. Kleinjung T, T Steffens, P Sand et al (2007) Which tinnitus patients benefit from transcranial magnetic stimulation? Otolaryngol Head Neck Surg 137:589–95.

57. Møller MB, AR Møller, PJ Jannetta et al (1993) Vascular decompression surgery for severe tinnitus: selection criteria and results. Laryngoscope 103:421–7.

58. Ryu H, S Yamamoto, K Sugiyama et al (1998) Neurovascular decompression of the eighth cranial nerve in patients with hemifacial spasm and incidental tinnitus: an alternative way to study tinnitus. J Neurosurg 88:232–6.

59. Eichhammer P, B Langguth, J Marienhagen et al (2003) Neuronavigated repetitive transcranial magnetic stimulation in patients with tinnitus: a short case series. Biol Psychiatry 54:862–5.

60. Rossi S, M Hallett, PM Rossini et al (2009) Safety, ethical considerations, and application guidelines for the use of transcranial magnetic stimulation in clinical practice and research. Clin Neurophysiol 120:2008–39.

61. Wassermann EM (1998) Risk and safety of repetitive transcranial magnetic stimulation: report and suggested guidelines from the international workshop on the safety of repetitive transcranial magnetic stimulation, June 5–7, 1996. Electroencephalogr Clin Neurophysiol 108:1–16.

62. Nahas Z, C DeBrux, V Chandler et al (2000) Lack of significant changes on magnetic resonance scans before and after 2 weeks of daily left prefrontal repetitive transcranial magnetic stimulation for depression. J ECT 16:380–90.

63. Loo C, P Sachdev, H Esayed et al (2001) Effects of a 2-to 4-week course of repetitive transcranial magnetic stimulation (rTMS) on neuropsychologic functioning, electroencephalogram, and auditory threshold in depressed patients. Biol Psychiatry 49:615–23.

64. Landgrebe M, H Binder, M Koller et al (2008) Design of a placebo-controlled, randomized study of the efficacy of repetitive transcranial magnetic stimulation for the treatment of chronic tinnitus. BMC Psychiatry 8:23.

65. Lee SL, M Abraham, AT Cacace et al (2008) Repetitive transcranial magnetic stimulation in veterans with debilitating tinnitus: A pilot study. Otolaryngol Head Neck Surg 138: 398–399.

66. Malmivuo J, R Plonsey (1995) Bioelectromagnetism – Principles and Application of Bioelectric and Biomagnetic Fields. Oxford University Press: New York.

Chapter 89
Transcranial Direct Current Stimulation (tDCS): A New Tool for the Treatment of Tinnitus?

Sven Vanneste and Dirk De Ridder

Keypoints

1. Transcranial direct current stimulation (tDCS) is a non-invasive technique of cortical stimulation encompassing a relatively weak constant current flow (between 0, 5 and 2 mA) through the cerebral cortex via scalp electrodes.
2. Several studies already revealed that tDCS can influence working memory, decision making, risk-taking behavior, impulsiveness, and emotions responsive to visual material in healthy humans.
3. Major depression and tinnitus have also shown promise in few pilot studies.
4. This chapter will review tDCS and its potential as treatment for tinnitus.

Keywords Tinnitus • Transcranial direct current stimulation • Transcranial magnetic stimulation • tDCS • TMS • Neuroplasticity

Transcranial Direct Current Stimulation

Transcranial Direct Current stimulation (tDCS) is a non-invasive procedure of cortical stimulation that was introduced in the 1960s. In these early studies, it was shown that subthreshold direct current stimulation increases spontaneous neuronal activity in the brain [1–3]. Apart from changes of spontaneous discharge rates, direct current stimulation of levels below behavioral threshold was shown to modulate the cortical response to thalamic stimulation in animals [3, 4]. It was further demonstrated that in addition to an acute effect of direct current stimulation, this technique can also induce a long-lasting after-effect on neuronal excitability and activity [1, 3, 5, 6]. Although these findings on direct current stimulation were obtained in animal studies, most of the results can probably be applied to humans. Nevertheless, it took almost 40 years before direct current stimulation gained attention as a possible tool for patient treatment and research in humans.

When tDCS is applied in humans, a relatively weak constant current (between 0, 5 and 2 mA) is passed through the cerebral cortex via scalp electrodes. Depending on the polarity of the stimulation, tDCS can increase or decrease cortical excitability in the brain regions to which it is applied [7]. Currently, tDCS is usually applied through two surface electrodes, one serving as the anode and the other as the cathode. Some of the applied current is shunted through scalp tissue and only a part of the applied current passes through the brain. Anodal tDCS typically has an excitatory effect on the local cerebral cortex by depolarizing neurons, while the opposite is the case under the cathode where hyperpolarization occurs. This effect of tDCS typically outlasts the stimulation by an hour or longer after a single treatment session of sufficiently long stimulation duration [8–11].

Blocking voltage-dependent ion channels pharmacologically abolishes any effect of depolarizing anodal tDCS on cortical excitability and does not influence the impact of hyperpolarizing cathodal tDCS. This means that the effect of tDCS on the cerebral cortex might be a subtreshold modulation of neuronal resting membrane potential [12], but this cannot explain the after-effects of tDCS. The NMDA receptor antagonist dextrometorphan blocks the after-effect of tDCS, whereas the NMDA receptor agonist D-cycloserine

S. Vanneste (✉)
BRAI²N TRI Tinnitus Clinic and Department of Neurosurgery University Hospital Antwerp, Wilrijkstraat 10, 2650, Edegem, Belgium
e-mail: sven.vanneste@ua.ac.be

A.R. Møller et al. (eds.), *Textbook of Tinnitus*,
DOI 10.1007/978-1-60761-145-5_89, © Springer Science+Business Media, LLC 2011

partially extends this effect [13–15]. This means that the after-effects of tDCS might depend on a modification of NMDA receptors efficacy. This tDCS polarity-dependent alteration of NMDA receptor function seems to be initiated by the respective membrane potential shift and probably by the accompanying cortical activity modification, because sodium channel blocker carbamazepine eliminates both the immediate and after-effect. Intraneuronal calcium concentration also contributes, since calcium channel antagonists eliminate the excitability-enhancing after-effect of anodal tDCS [12]. The mechanism of action of tDCS thus appears to depend on NMDA receptor activity [16] and involve a combination of hyper- and de-polarizing effect on neuronal axons.

Increasing the size of the reference electrode and reducing the size of the stimulation electrode allow for more focal treatment effects [17]. Moving the electrodes a few centimeters shifts the efficacy of tDCS dramatically [18]. Moreover, the electrical field strength is relatively homogeneous under the electrodes, but diminishes exponentially away from the electrode [7, 19]. In contrast to the relatively focal electrophysiological effect under the electrodes, widespread remote effects of tDCS on different cortical and subcortical areas were revealed in a PET study, suggesting that these effects might be caused by neural connection and not by direct electrical stimulation [20].

Safety of tDCS in Humans

To date, more than 2,000–3,000 individuals have participated in tDCS studies with no significant adverse effects reported using standard protocols consisting of 1–2 mA intensity, electrode size between 25 and 35 cm^2, and stimulation between 20 and 30°min per session. Slight tingling under the electrodes, headache, fatigue, and nausea might occur [21] and high current amplitudes (2 mA) can induce burns under the electrodes (Frank et al. 2010; Palm et al. 2008). tDCS does not elevate serum neuron-specific enolase levels (i.e. a sensitive marker of neuronal damage) [9]. No brain edema, no alternations of the blood–brain barrier, and no cerebral tissue damage were detectable by magnetic resonance imaging after tDCS [13]. Also, no worsening of cognitive function has been observed as a consequence of treatment [22]. However, for safety reasons, electrodes should not be positioned above cranial foraminae and

fissures because these could increase effective current density in neural tissue.

TMS vs. tDCS

As a method for neuromodulation, tDCS has been compared with repetitive transcranial magnetic stimulation (rTMS) [23, 24]. As in rTMS, the effect produced by tDCS depends on the stimulation duration, the stimulation intensity, and the location of stimulating electrodes. While both techniques allow focal neuromodulation, there are fundamental differences between these methods; whereas TMS is thought to exert its effects by inducing action potentials in cortical neurons, tDCS is believed to modulate neuronal excitability without inducing neuronal firing.

Moreover, the two methods differ in several practical aspects, and tDCS has several advantages over rTMS. Since tDCS produces less artifacts, such as acoustic noise and muscle twitching, it is more suitable for double-blind, sham-controlled studies and clinical applications of tinnitus research. The equipment for tDCS is compact and portable and less expensive. Seizure incidents have not been reported in tDCS studies, and the effects of tDCS seem to last longer than that of rTMS, which makes it more suitable as a treatment tool. The use of tDCS should therefore be considered as a complementary tool to rTMS.

Rationale for Using tDCS in the Treatment of Tinnitus

Considerable evidence that neural plasticity can cause tinnitus has been recently presented [25, 26]. Neural plasticity is a property of the nervous system to change its function and its organization [27], change synaptic efficacy, generate or reduce synapses, and produce new connections by developing and eliminating axons and dendrites (see Chap. 12). For tinnitus in particular, a reorganization of the auditory cortex consisting of a shift in tonotopic maps contralateral to the tinnitus side has been demonstrated [28]. Abnormal symmetry in the auditory cortex activity in tinnitus has been shown, indicating a higher level of spontaneous activity [29–32].

Other studies revealed changes in non-auditory brain areas, namely in frontal and limbic areas [33–36]. In the subcollosal anterior cingulate area, including the nucleus accumbens, a reduction of gray matter density has been shown in tinnitus as compared to controls [37]. MEG studies have found a reduction in alpha (8–12 Hz) and an increase in delta (1.5–4 Hz) in temporal regions, left frontal, and right parietal areas [38] as well as increased functional connectivity between the right frontal lobe and anterior cingulum [39].

Since tDCS has the ability to modulate cortical neural activity, it seems likely that application of tDCS to specific regions could alter tinnitus. Several studies already revealed that tDCS can have beneficial effects on disorders such as depression and pain. Preliminary results suggest that tDCS applied to the temperal lobe [24] and the dorsal lateral prefrontal cortex can supress tinnitus [58].

tDCS of the Temporal Lobe

Neuroimaging and electrophysiological studies have shown high spontaneous activity in the central auditory nervous system and changes in the tonotopic map of the auditory cortex in some individuals with tinnitus [33, 40–42]. Based on these findings, Fregni et al. initiated a tDCS study on a small sample ($N = 7$) with bilateral non-pulsatile tinnitus (tinnitus duration range: 1–17 years) in an attempt to modulate neural activity in the left temporoparietal cortex [24]. A single session of anodal tDCS applied over the left temporoparietal area and cathode placed contralateral over the supraorbital area resulted in a transient reduction of tinnitus, similar to what has been shown to occur after applying TMS at 10 Hz [24]. No effect was found from a single session of cathodal tDCS applied over the left temporoparietal area with the anode placed over the contralateral supraorbital area. This was surprising, since it was cathodal, tDCS has a general inhibitory effect. One possible reason might be that cathodal tDCS was too weak to disrupt ongoing activity. Anodal tDCS, however, had a transient suppressive effect on the tinnitus of the participants in this study. As large electrodes were used, it was assumed that anodal tDCS would additionally excite surrounding areas that might, by competition or inhibitory connections, decrease the pathologically increased activity of some areas related to tinnitus pathophysiology. Yet, an alternative explanation might be that anodal tDCS affects targeted not only the brain region but also distant cortical and subcortical structures because these regions are connected

to the areas that were stimulated. This would be in accordance with a recent PET study that demonstrated anodal tDCS of the motor cortex compared with cathodal tDCS induced a more widespread increase of regional cerebral blood flow [20].

The results from this study thus suggest that anodal stimulation of the temporoparietal area can produce an immediate reduction of tinnitus lasting a short time. Cathodal stimulation of the temporoparietal area may produce a similar effect, provided the duration of the stimulation is sufficiently long. This may be comparable with TMS, where short session of high-frequency TMS induces immediate change in tinnitus perception, while several sessions of low-frequency TMS induce prolonged decreases in tinnitus [43, 44].

tDCS of the Dorsolateral Prefrontal Cortex

New insights into the neurobiology of tinnitus suggest that neuronal changes are not limited to the classical auditory pathways [37, 38, 41, 45]. In particular, the dorsolateral prefrontal cortex (DLPFC) seems to play a specific role in auditory processing; the DLPC has a bilateral facilitatory effect on auditory memory storage [46] and contains auditory memory cells [47]. The DLPFC also exerts early inhibitory modulation of input to the primary auditory cortex in humans [48] and has been found to be associated with auditory attention [46, 49, 50] resulting in top–down modulation of auditory processing [51]. This was further confirmed by electrophysiological data indicating that tinnitus might occur as the result of a dysfunction in the top–down inhibitory processes [52].

Interestingly, several tDCS studies focused on DLPFC and found successful results for treating major depression [53] and mood changes in depression [54], as well as reducing impulsiveness [55] and pain threshold [56, 57]. As the DLPFC is involved in attention-mediated top–down control of auditory processing and tinnitus, and tDCS seems to be a promising tool for modulating the DLPFC, it is possible that bifrontal application of tDCS might be a useful technique for the suppressing tinnitus. The common rational is to modify activity in the prefrontal cortex and also to re-establish the balance of left and right prefrontal cortex activation.

In a preliminary study involving 418 individuals with non-pulsatile tinnitus, it was shown that tDCS, with the anode over the right DLPFC and the cathode over the left DLPFC, could cause tinnitus suppression in 29.9% of the participants [58]. In contrast, recent results of a study of 28 individuals with non-pulsatile tinnitus indicate that bilateral application of tDCS, with anode on the left and cathode on the right DLPFC, has no suppressive effect on tinnitus. Taken these results together, suppression of tinnitus by tDCS seems to be related by the ability to enhance excitability of the right prefrontal cortex and reducing the excitability of the left prefrontal cortex. A comparison between both groups did not show differences in tinnitus duration, tinnitus laterality, or tinnitus type and could therefore not explain the obtained results.

In conclusion, these studies indicate that anodal stimulation of the right DLPFC can produce an immediate reduction of tinnitus in some individuals. However, repeated sessions of tDCS might have better effects than single sessions as used in the present pilot study. Previous studies have already shown that anodal tDCS of the left DLPFC can affect depressive symptoms after one daily 20-min session of tDCS for a duration of 5 days [54]. Further studies are needed to explore the potential of frontal tDCS in reducing tinnitus-related distress.

Conclusion

Preliminary studies suggest that tDCS can modulate tinnitus in some individuals. However, further clinical and neurobiological research is needed before tDCS can be considered a practical treatment option for routine use. Therefore, multicenter placebo-controlled randomized trials with many patients and longer follow-up periods are required in order to estimate the efficacy of tDCS for the treatment of tinnitus. Further research is also needed to define selection criteria for patients for tDCS treatments. It may be possible to optimize and individualize stimulation protocols.

References

1. Bindman LJ, OC Lippold and JW Redfearn (1964) The action of brief polarizing currents on the cerebral cortex of the rat (1) during current flow and (2) in the production of long-Lasting after-effects. J Physiol 172:369–82

2. Creutzfeldt OD, GH Fromm and H Kapp (1962) Influence of transcortical d-c currents on cortical neuronal activity. Exp Neurol 5:436–52

3. Purpura DP and JG McMurtry (1965) Intracellular activities and evoked potential changes during polarization of motor cortex. J Neurophysiol 28:166–85

4. Landau WM, GH Bishop and MH Clare (1964) Analysis of the form and distribution of evoked cortical potentials under the influence of polarizing currents. J Neurophysiol 27: 788–813

5. Gartside IB (1968) Mechanisms of sustained increases of firing rate of neurons in the rat cerebral cortex after polarization: reverberating circuits or modification of synaptic conductance? Nature 220:382–3

6. Gartside IB (1968) Mechanisms of sustained increases of firing rate of neurones in the rat cerebral cortex after polarization: role of protein synthesis. Nature 220:383–4

7. Miranda PC, M Lomarev and M Hallett (2006) Modeling the current distribution during transcranial direct current stimulation. Clin Neurophysiol 117:1623–9

8. Nitsche MA and W Paulus (2000) Excitability changes induced in the human motor cortex by weak transcranial direct current stimulation. J Physiol 527 Pt 3:633–9

9. Nitsche MA and W Paulus (2001) Sustained excitability elevations induced by transcranial DC motor cortex stimulation in humans. Neurology 57:1899–901

10. Nitsche MA, MS Nitsche, CC Klein et al (2003) Level of action of cathodal DC polarisation induced inhibition of the human motor cortex. Clin Neurophysiol 114:600–4

11. Antal A, TZ Kincses, MA Nitsche et al (2004) Excitability changes induced in the human primary visual cortex by transcranial direct current stimulation: direct electrophysiological evidence. Invest Ophthalmol Vis Sci 45:702–7

12. Nitsche MA, K Fricke, U Henschke et al (2003) Pharmacological modulation of cortical excitability shifts induced by transcranial direct current stimulation in humans. J Physiol 553:293–301

13. Nitsche MA, L Niehaus, KT Hoffmann et al (2004) MRI study of human brain exposed to weak direct current stimulation of the frontal cortex. Clin Neurophysiol 115:2419–23

14. Nitsche MA, D Liebetanz, F Tergau et al (2002) Modulation of cortical excitability by transcranial direct current stimulation. Nervenarzt 73:332–5

15. Liebetanz D, MA Nitsche, F Tergau et al (2002) Pharmacological approach to the mechanisms of transcranial DC-stimulation-induced after-effects of human motor cortex excitability. Brain 125:2238–47

16. Paulus W (2004) Outlasting excitability shifts induced by direct current stimulation of the human brain. Suppl Clin Neurophysiol 57:708–14

17. Nitsche MA, S Doemkes, T Karakose et al (2007) Shaping the effects of transcranial direct current stimulation of the human motor cortex. J Neurophysiol 97:3109–17

18. Nitsche MA, A Schauenburg, N Lang et al (2003) Facilitation of implicit motor learning by weak transcranial direct current stimulation of the primary motor cortex in the human. J Cogn Neurosci 15:619–26

19. Rush S and DA Driscoll (1968) Current distribution in the brain from surface electrodes. Anesth Analg 47:717–23

20. Lang N, HR Siebner, NS Ward et al (2005) How does transcranial DC stimulation of the primary motor cortex alter regional neuronal activity in the human brain? Eur J Neurosci 22:495–504

21. Poreisz C, K Boros, A Antal et al (2007) Safety aspects of transcranial direct current stimulation concerning healthy subjects and patients. Brain Res Bull 72:208–14

22. Iyer MB, U Mattu, J Grafman et al (2005) Safety and cognitive effect of frontal DC brain polarization in healthy individuals. Neurology 64:872–5

23. Tanaka S and K Watanabe (2009) Transcranial direct current stimulation – a new tool for human cognitive neuroscience. Brain Nerve 61:53–64

24. Fregni F, R Marcondes, PS Boggio et al (2006) Transient tinnitus suppression induced by repetitive transcranial magnetic stimulation and transcranial direct current stimulation. Eur J Neurol 13:996–1001

25. Eggermont JJ and LE Roberts (2004) The neuroscience of tinnitus. Trends Neurosci 27:676–82

26. Møller A (2006) Neural plasticity and disorders of the nervous system. 2006, Cambridge: Cambridge University Press

27. Møller AR (2007) The role of neural plasticity in tinnitus. Prog Brain Res 166:37–45

28. Muhlnickel W, T Elbert, E Taub et al (1998) Reorganization of auditory cortex in tinnitus. Proc Natl Acad Sci USA 95:10340–3

29. Smits M, S Kovacs, D de Ridder et al (2007) Lateralization of functional magnetic resonance imaging (fMRI) activation in the auditory pathway of patients with lateralized tinnitus. Neuroradiology 49:669–79

30. Lockwood AH, RJ Salvi and RF Burkard (2002) Tinnitus. N Engl J Med 347:904–10

31. Weisz N, S Muller, W Schlee et al (2007) The neural code of auditory phantom perception. J Neurosci 27:1479–84

32. Arnold W, P Bartenstein, E Oestreicher et al (1996) Focal metabolic activation in the predominant left auditory cortex in patients suffering from tinnitus: a PET study with [18F]deoxyglucose. ORL J Otorhinolaryngol Relat Spec 58:195–9

33. Lockwood AH, RJ Salvi, ML Coad et al (1998) The functional neuroanatomy of tinnitus: evidence for limbic system links and neural plasticity. Neurology 50:114–20

34. Mirz F, A Gjedde, K Ishizu et al (2000) Cortical networks subserving the perception of tinnitus – a PET study. Acta Otolaryngol Suppl 543:241–3

35. Mirz F, B Pedersen, K Ishizu et al (1999) Positron emission tomography of cortical centers of tinnitus. Hear Res 134:133–44

36. Giraud AL, S Chery-Croze, G Fischer et al (1999) A selective imaging of tinnitus. Neuroreport 10:1–5

37. Muhlau M, JP Rauschecker, E Oestreicher et al (2006) Structural brain changes in tinnitus. Cereb Cortex 16: 1283–8

38. Weisz N, S Moratti, M Meinzer et al (2005) Tinnitus perception and distress is related to abnormal spontaneous brain activity as measured by magnetoencephalography. PLoS Med 2:e153

39. Schlee W, N Weisz, O Bertrand et al (2008) Using auditory steady state responses to outline the functional connectivity in the tinnitus brain. PLoS ONE 3:e3720

40. Salvi RJ, J Wang and D Ding (2000) Auditory plasticity and hyperactivity following cochlear damage. Hear Res 147:261–74

41. Schlee W, T Hartmann, B Langguth et al (2009) Abnormal resting-state cortical coupling in chronic tinnitus. BMC Neurosci 10:11

42. Smits M, S Kovacs, D de Ridder et al (2007) Lateralization of functional magnetic resonance imaging (fMRI) activation in the auditory pathway of patients with lateralized tinnitus. Neuroradiology 49:669–79

43. Eichhammer P, B Langguth, J Marienhagen et al (2003) Neuronavigated repetitive transcranial magnetic stimulation in patients with tinnitus: a short case series. Biol Psychiatry 54:862–5

44. Langguth B, P Eichhammer, R Wiegand et al (2003) Neuronavigated rTMS in a patient with chronic tinnitus. Effects of 4 weeks treatment. Neuroreport 14:977–80

45. Landgrebe M, B Langguth, K Rosengarth et al (2009) Structural brain changes in tinnitus: grey matter decrease in auditory and non-auditory brain areas. Neuroimage 46:213–8

46. Alain C, DL Woods and RT Knight (1998) A distributed cortical network for auditory sensory memory in humans. Brain Res 812:23–37

47. Bodner M, J Kroger and JM Fuster (1996) Auditory memory cells in dorsolateral prefrontal cortex. Neuroreport 7:1905–8

48. Knight RT, D Scabini and DL Woods (1989) Prefrontal cortex gating of auditory transmission in humans. Brain Res 504:338–42

49. Voisin J, A Bidet-Caulet, O Bertrand et al (2006) Listening in silence activates auditory areas: a functional magnetic resonance imaging study. J Neurosci 26:273–8

50. Lewis JW, MS Beauchamp and EA DeYoe (2000) A comparison of visual and auditory motion processing in human cerebral cortex. Cereb Cortex 10:873–88

51. Mitchell TV, RA Morey, S Inan et al (2005) Functional magnetic resonance imaging measure of automatic and controlled auditory processing. Neuroreport 16:457–61

52. Norena A, H Cransac and S Chery-Croze (1999) Towards an objectification by classification of tinnitus. Clin Neurophysiol 110:666–75

53. Fregni F, PS Boggio, MA Nitsche et al (2006) Cognitive effects of repeated sessions of transcranial direct current stimulation in patients with depression. Depress Anxiety 23:482–4

54. Fregni F, PS Boggio, MA Nitsche et al (2006) Treatment of major depression with transcranial direct current stimulation. Bipolar Disord 8:203–4

55. Beeli G, G Casutt, T Baumgartner et al (2008) Modulating presence and impulsiveness by external stimulation of the brain. Behav Brain Funct 4:33

56. Boggio PS, S Zaghi, M Lopes et al (2008) Modulatory effects of anodal transcranial direct current stimulation on perception and pain thresholds in healthy volunteers. Eur J Neurol 15:1124–30

57. Boggio PS, S Zaghi and F Fregni (2009) Modulation of emotions associated with images of human pain using anodal transcranial direct current stimulation (tDCS). Neuropsychologia 47:212–7

58. Vanneste, S., De Ridder, D., Plazier, M., Ost, J., van der Loo, E., and van Heyning, P (2009) Modulation of the bilateral dorsal lateral prefrontal cortex by transcranial direct current stimulation for tinnitus: a preliminary clinical study. Submitted for publication

59. Frank, E., Wilfurth, S., Landgrebe, M., Eichhammer, P., Hajak, G., Langguth, B (2010) Anodal skin lesions after treatment with transcranial direct current stimulation. Brain Stimul 3, 58–59.

60. Palm, U., Keeser, D., Schiller, C., Fintescu, Z., Reisinger, E., Nitsche, M., Padberg, F (2008) Skin lesions after treatment with transcranial direct current stimulation (tDCS). Brain Stimul 1, 386–387.

Chapter 90
Auditory Cortex Stimulation for Tinnitus

Dirk De Ridder and Sven Vanneste

Keypoints

1. The most frequent cause of tinnitus is hearing loss.
2. The auditory deprivation can lead to pathological theta–gamma coupling linked to a decrease of alpha oscillations also known as thalamocortical dysrhythmia.
3. Auditory deprivation also leads to auditory tract and auditory cortex tonotopic reorganization via activation of neural plasticity.
4. Presenting the missing information can reverse cortical reorganization.
5. Cortical stimulation can also reorganize tonotopic organization.
6. Auditory cortex stimulation can decrease tinnitus.
7. Auditory cortex stimulation interferes with ongoing oscillatory activity.
8. One in three patients responds to tonic stimulation and one in three to burst resulting in two out of three patients responding to auditory cortex stimulation.
9. Average improvement for auditory cortex stimulation is 50%.
10. Individuals with pure-tone tinnitus respond best to tonic stimulation of the cortex.
11. Individuals with noise-like tinnitus respond best to burst stimulation.
12. Tinnitus duration gender, or age is not predictive for successful stimulation.

Keywords Auditory cortex stimulation • Tinnitus • Deafferentation • fMRI • Gamma • Darwin • Plasticity • Reorganization

D. De Ridder (✉)
TRI Tinnitus Clinic Antwerp, BRAI²N and Department of Neurosurgery, University Hospital Antwerp, Wilrijkstraat 10, 2650 Edegem, Belgium
e-mail: dirk.de.ridder@uza.be

Abbreviations

BOLD	Blood oxygen level dependent
EEG	Electroencephalography
ERP	Event related potential
fMRI	Functional magnetic resonance imaging
Hz	Hertz
iEEG	Intracranial EEG
MEG	Magnetoencephalography
MSI	Magnetic source imaging
PET	Positron emission tomography
rTMS	Repetitive transcranial magnetic stimulation
TRI	Tinnitus research initiative

Introduction

Until recently, people suffering from tinnitus were told "to learn and live with it." This was largely due to the fact that there were no treatments available because of a lack of knowledge on how tinnitus is generated and the fact that tinnitus was considered solely an ear problem. In recent years, however, our understanding of the brain mechanisms involved in the generation of tinnitus has increased quite substantially [1, 2]. Even though for the majority of individuals with tinnitus, the original problem was located to the ear, and more specifically to hearing loss, most forms of tinnitus are caused by pathologic changes in the function of the brain.

Tinnitus Intensity

Tinnitus can be considered as a phantom phenomenon [3], similar to phantom pain [4–7]. People are well aware that when a hand or another part of the body is

A.R. Møller et al. (eds.), *Textbook of Tinnitus,*
DOI 10.1007/978-1-60761-145-5_90, © Springer Science+Business Media, LLC 2011

amputated, the missing part can generate phantom feelings [8]. This occurs in up to 85% of amputations, and in 15% the feeling is expressed as phantom pain [8]. Hearing loss, being considered analogous to amputation, can thus induce a phantom percept (such as phantom sound), better known as tinnitus. Much of the advancement in brain research on tinnitus is based on what is known from pain [5–7].

A heuristic model of tinnitus (see Chap. 21) is based on studies of consciousness suggesting that any conscious percept, including tinnitus, is related to gamma band activity (30–80 Hz) [9]. At rest, the auditory thalamocortical loop produces oscillations at alpha frequencies (8–12 Hz). When there is hearing loss, the cells that do not receive information from the cochlea will initially oscillate at lower frequencies (theta, 3–7 Hz) because there is less information to be processed [10]. In the brain high frequency activity (>10 Hz) in cells will suppress the activity in surrounding cells through lateral inhibition [11]. However, 10-Hz activity does not produce lateral inhibition [11], and lateral inhibition from activity at lower frequencies (<10 Hz) is decreased [12]. At low theta frequencies, lateral inhibition will decrease, inducing a halo of high-frequency gamma activity, also called the "edge effect." So when there is hearing loss, due to slower firing rate caused by the nerve fibers transmitting the missing frequencies, a decrease in lateral inhibition (i.e., less suppression of the surrounding activity arises) will result in an associated halo of faster gamma band activity (30–80 Hz) at the lesion edge. This is called thalamocortical dysrhythmia [13]. Magnetoencephalography (MEG) studies have indeed shown that in tinnitus patients, decreased alpha is linked to increased gamma [9, 14, 15] and theta coupled to gamma [12, 13], supportive of this idea.

The brain can be considered a Darwinian structure, analogous to nature [16]. An animal can be considered analogous to the synapse that connects nerve cells. Synapse formation is analogous to animal reproduction; competition for connections is analogous to competition for resources and survival of the fittest synapse analogous to survival of the fittest animal [17]. Therefore, the cortex cells that do not receive information, also known as deafferented cells, will look for information in order to survive and open connections to neighboring cells, processing the same incoming information as the neighboring cells but generating the perception of the frequency to which these cells are programmed to process. This hypothetical mechanism is called Darwinian plasticity [18] and is basically analogous to dendritic plasticity [19, 20]. Subsequently, the decreased oscillation rates of the deafferented cells will increase to the same rate as the halo as such abolish thalamocortical dysrhythmia. Due to increased lateral inhibition of the deafferented area and lesion edge, a new halo of low-frequency activity will develop around the lesion edge. This could be called reverse thalamo-cortical dysrhythmia (see Chap. 21). No consensus exists yet on the exact mechanism of how tinnitus is generated in the brain, but the hypothetical mechanism could explain that the tinnitus pitch matches the frequencies of the deafferented nerve cells.

Another explanation of how certain features of tinnitus may be related to plastic changes in the nervous system suggests that "re-routing" of activity through thalamic and cortico-cortical connections could transmit information from a lesion edge toward the deafferented area. This is parallel to axonal sprouting into a deafferented region. The main difference between these two models is that in Darwinian plasticity the auditory cortex cells that do not receive information any more will attract information, whereas in classical plasticity the auditory cortex cells that are adjacent to the cells that do not receive information invade the area of deprived cells [21]. Probably both dendritic and axonal sprouting occur simultaneously.

Irrespective of whether Darwinian plasticity or classical plasticity can explain generation of the neural activity that causes tinnitus, the end result is that the deafferented cells become hyperactive and cause a phantom sound.

Reafferenting the Auditory Cortex

The tinnitus treatment based on this model focuses on reafferenting the auditory cortex, which means that the missing information is supplied back to the auditory cortex and differs from the classical tinnitus treatments which predominantly target the ear. This does not mean that the ear is not important in tinnitus generation, as the changes in the brain are induced by a lack of information from the ear. Therefore, everybody suffering from tinnitus should undergo a complete tinnitus work-up by a specialized neuro-otologist (see Chap. 46).

Reafferenting the auditory cortex can happen in two ways: by compensating for the hearing loss to normalize the input to the cortex or by reafferenting the cerebral cortex. Reestablishing input to the cortex can be done by using hearing aids [22] (see Chap. 74) or cochlear implants in completely deaf people [23] (see Chap. 77), both of which are capable of reducing tinnitus. If this fails, the auditory cortex can be reafferented electrically by supplying the missing information directly or indirectly to the deafferented area of the auditory cortex. The electrical information can be supplied indirectly by electrical stimulation of the auditory nerve [24, 25], cochlear nuclei [26], inferior colliculus, or thalamus. The missing input to the cortex can be supplied directly to the deafferented area of the cortex by electrical stimulation [4, 27–30]. Electrical stimulation of the cortex may also result in suppressing the tinnitus by interfering with the neural network that functions abnormally instead of specifically reafferenting the cortex.

Electrical simulation through an electrode that is placed on the area of cortical hyperactivity can reestablish normal organization of the reorganized maps [31] through egocentric selection [32] of the entire tonotopic pathway all the way to the cochlea [33].

Another explanation for tinnitus relates the disorder to hypersynchronous gamma band activity [9, 13, 34]. The gamma band activity might code the tinnitus intensity [34], and the tinnitus percept per se could be the result of an emergent network property [15, 35, 36]. In a recent study using MEG during electrical stimulation of the auditory cortex, the stimulation increased spectral correlation across low and high gamma band activity; between alpha and beta activity, but delta/theta activity decreased, suggesting that auditory cortex stimulation does indeed affect thalamocortical dysrhythmia [37].

Electrical stimulation might, thus, do nothing more than disrupt the abnormal thalamocortical dysrhythmia embedded in a larger tinnitus network (see Chap. 21), and subsequently the emergent property of the network, the tinnitus, disappears.

Interfering with Tinnitus-Related Distress

Interfering with tinnitus-related distress requires an understanding of the pathophysiology of tinnitus distress.

The exact mechanisms are unknown, but based on the available literature and data from research on pain [38, 39], dyspnea [39], and post-traumatic stress syndrome (PTSD) [40], it seems likely that a "general distress network" exists, consisting of the amygdala, anterior cingulate, and anterior insula. Activity in this network might generate a feeling of distress, perceived as tinnitus distress if the activity in the "general distress network" is synchronized with the dysrhythmic activity in thalamocortical loop, i.e., with the (theta and/or) gamma activity in the auditory cortex [15] (see Chap. 21). This is consistent with the hypothesis that broad band [41] and gamma synchronization [42] is a potential binding mechanism to generate a unified percept of the simultaneously presenting stimuli.

Auditory Cortex Stimulation in Clinical Practice

Auditory cortex stimulation is based on a four-step rationale (Fig. 90.1):

1. Tinnitus is related to synchronized gamma band activity.
2. Synchronized gamma band activity correlates with the blood oxygen level-dependent (BOLD) imaging signal of functional MRI (fMRI).
3. fMRI-guided neuronavigated transcranial magnetic stimulation (TMS) can suppress gamma band-related tinnitus.
4. If TMS is successful in tinnitus suppression, fMRI-guided neuronavigated electrode implant can suppress tinnitus permanently.

For successful treatment of tinnitus, two problems must be addressed. First of all, the exact localization in the brain of the auditory cortical hyperactivity must be determined. This is done by means of magnetoencephalography (MEG) [30] or fMRI [29, 43, 44]. In fMRI, two MRI scans are combined: a morphological brain scan and a scan performed during auditory exposure. In the MRI machine, the tinnitus pitch is first determined by tinnitus matching. Subsequently, the tinnitus pitch the patient perceives is presented via ear phones, assuming that the generator of this frequency is the same as the tinnitus generator. Since both the activities seen on fMRI scan, i.e., the BOLD effect

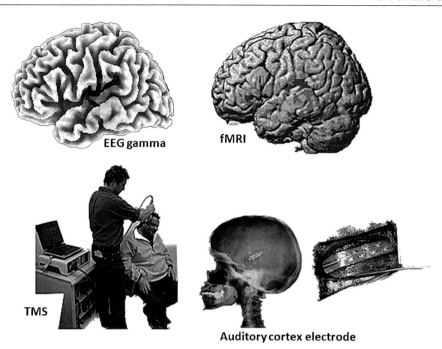

Fig. 90.1 Rationale for auditory cortex implants in the treatment for tinnitus. Tinnitus is related to gamma band activity (30–80 Hz) in the auditory cortex which can be demonstrated by EEG (*upper left*). This gamma band activity correlates with the BOLD effect on fMRI (*upper right*). This gamma band and BOLD activity can be used as a target for non-invasive TMS (*lower left*). If tinnitus can be successfully suppressed by TMS, an electrode can be implanted on the same target (*lower right*)

and the tinnitus [9], or tinnitus intensity [34], are related to gamma band synchronization [45], the activity seen on fMRI can be correlated to the anatomical location of the tinnitus generator. In a similar way, the MEG can be fused with an MRI scan to obtain a magnetic source imaging (MSI) in order to localize the area in the brain generating the neural activity that causes the perception of a phantom sound. These tinnitus-matched frequencies behave differently than the non-tinnitus-generating frequencies in the auditory cortex (Kovacs, unpublished data), suggesting that presenting the tinnitus-matched frequencies might indeed be capable of demonstrating a part of the auditory cortex that functions abnormally.

The second problem is localizing the zone of hyperactivity exactly from results of the scan of the patient's brain. The use of neuronavigation guided by the fMRI is helpful in this task.

Subsequently, a non-invasive stimulation can be performed targeting this area on the auditory cortex that shows abnormal activity. This is done by TMS.

If this non-invasive test shows that the abnormal neural activity assumed to cause tinnitus has been successfully suppressed, an electrode can subsequently be placed extradurally, overlying the secondary auditory cortical area of hyperactivity for permanent tinnitus suppression (on the exact same site as where the TMS was successful). The electrode is activated by an internal pulse generator, similar to a cardiac pacemaker, placed in the abdomen. The stimulation parameters (frequency, amplitude, and pulse width) can be changed postoperatively by remote control to find the best parameters for maximal tinnitus control.

In summary, the hypothesis behind auditory cortex stimulation for treatment of tinnitus is: (1) tinnitus is related to gamma band synchronization of the auditory cortical activity, (2) the anatomical location of the tinnitus generator can be determined by fMRI, (3) the activity of neurons in this location can be modulated by non-invasive TMS applied with the aid of neuronavigation, and (4) if TMS can suppress the tinnitus electrical stimulation through an electrode implanted on the same area, it can permanently provide the same tinnitus suppression by electrical stimulation as was achieved using TMS.

Implantations

Three different methods have been developed for auditory cortex stimulation via implanted electrodes:

1. Extradurally, on an area overlying the secondary auditory cortex [28, 29].
2. Intradurally, on the surface of the brain, placing the stimulating electrode in an existing groove or sulcus (intrasulcal grey matter) of the primary auditory cortex. Such placements of the stimulating electrode provide predominant stimulation of cell bodies and not so much of the incoming or leaving fibers [28, 46], and
3. Intradurally, inside the brain similar to deep brain stimulation. Such placement of the stimulating electrode will activate intraparenchymatous white matter, thus, nerve tracts of fibers coming into and leaving the primary auditory cortex [30].

The electrodes that are implanted can have 4–16 electrode contacts (Figs. 90.1 and 90.2).

The surgery for an extradural electrode placement has been described in some detail [29, 47] and has minimal risk of complications. An incision is made 5–6 cm above the external ear canal, based on the fMRI. The location of the auditory cortex varies among different individuals and between the left and right

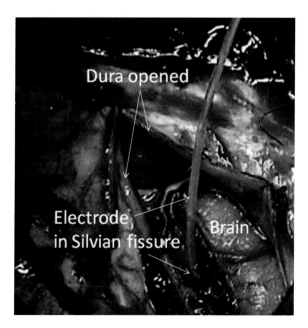

Fig. 90.2 Intraoperative picture showing the opened dura and electrode, inserted in the posterior part of the Silvian fissure

side. The location of the incision in the skin is therefore guided by the fMRI. The skin incision is about 5 cm long and followed by a split of the temporal muscle. A small 1 by 5 cm hole is made in the skull and the small sensory fibers that innervate the dura are coagulated. This is necessary because the electrical stimulation used for tinnitus suppression may also cause pain by activating these fibers. After that is completed, the stimulating electrode is placed on the exact spot with 1–2 mm accuracy based on the fMRI and sutured to the dura. The small skull defect is repositioned and fixated with small titanium screws and plates.

For intradural grey matter stimulation, the electrode is inserted in the posterior part of the Silvian fissure after opening the dura (Fig. 90.2). For intraparenchymal white matter stimulation, the stimulating electrode is inserted into the auditory cortex, parallel to the Sylvian fissure. In both intradural procedures, the dura is closed after the insertion of the electrode. After that, the lead to the stimulating electrode is tunneled to the chest where it is connected to an extension lead, and further tunneled to the abdomen where it is passed through the skin to the outside of the body.

The electrode leads that exit the abdomen are connected to a stimulator, usually after 3 days, as on the first day the tinnitus is often markedly decreased from the operation. During external trial stimulation, the different electrode contacts are activated, one by one, or more than one at a time, depending on what gives the best suppression. The trial sessions are limited to one hour because it is difficult for the patient to keep concentrating for longer times. Once a good suppressive effect is obtained, which can occur after one day (sometimes, it takes a week or even a month), a programmable internal pulse generator (IPG) is implanted in the abdomen and the electrode is connected with a new extension lead to the IPG.

Stimulation is not performed continuously because of the risk for eliciting an epileptic seizure. Usually, the stimulator is active for 5 s and switched off for 5 s. During these 5 s that the IPG is silent, the tinnitus remains suppressed because of residual inhibition. As the patient does not feel the electrical impulses, he or she does not know whether the stimulator is on or off. During the first period after the implantation, the tinnitus returns very quickly when the stimulator is turned off. After a couple of seconds, the sound starts to come back, thus the residual inhibition is not very long. However, after years of stimulation when the

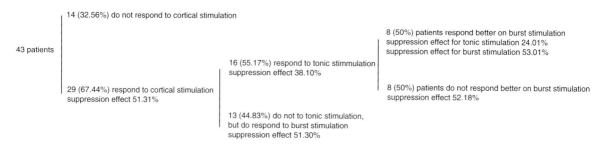

Fig. 90.3 Summary of the results obtained by electrical stimulation of auditory cortex for the treatment of tinnitus

stimulator is switched off or the battery has become drained, it may take weeks before the tinnitus returns full scale. It can only be hoped that after many years of stimulation, the tinnitus might stay away for longer and longer periods of residual inhibition and finally forever, even without further stimulation.

Results

In total, 43 patients with intractable grade 3 and 4 tinnitus, i.e., severe tinnitus according to the tinnitus questionnaire [48], were implanted with a cortical electrode overlying the secondary auditory cortex. Before implantation, all patients underwent tests in two TMS sessions on separate dates performed by a person not involved in the surgery. If TMS resulted in suppression of the tinnitus (>20% improvement on a visual analog scale (VAS)) on two separate occasions, the patients were regarded to be eligible for implantation.

Although all patients reacted to TMS, 1 out of 3 patients did not respond to the cortical stimulation after implantation. Two out of 3 patients responded to cortical stimulation with an average decrease in the perceived tinnitus loudness of 51.3%. A significant but weak positive correlation ($p<0.05$) between suppression effect from the test TMS and cortical stimulation after implantation was exists in responders to both TMS and electrical stimulation.

Of the patients who were implanted with a cortical electrode, the use of burst stimulation (5 stimuli of 1 ms pulse width, 1 ms interpulse interval, at 500 Hz delivered 40 times a second) improved the total results dramatically. When only tonic stimulation is used, only one in three patients obtained tinnitus suppression. However, using burst stimulation, half of the non-responding patients could benefit. In a similar way, half of the

patients who did respond to tonic stimulation had better suppression with burst stimulation. Earlier studies have shown that the suppression effect on TMS depends on how long the patient had tinnitus prior to TMS, indicating that the suppression effect on TMS decreases over time [15, 49, 50]. Similar results were obtained for the patients who were eligible for implantation. A negative correlation was found between tinnitus suppression from TMS and tinnitus duration $r=-0.37$, $p<0.05$. However, no correlation was found between the suppression effect based on electrical cortical stimulation and tinnitus duration. The latter result is quite interesting, as it suggests cortical stimulation is different from TMS and that it affects the neural activity that causes tinnitus in a different way than TMS since it seems to help in a way independent from tinnitus duration.

However, it was revealed that tinnitus type (pure tone, narrow band noise, or both) and laterality, whether unilateral or bilateral, whether unilateral or bilateral had a significant influence on the amount of suppression. Pure-tone tinnitus was suppressed more than narrow band noise or the combination of pure tone and narrow band noise and unilateral tinnitus was suppressed more than bilateral tinnitus.

Another study of eight patients using a similar technique but different hardware [27] showed only temporary tinnitus suppression in six of the patients studied. However, tinnitus distress decreased, even without suppression of tinnitus intensity. This is more similar to the effect of 1-Hz rTMS [51] than the results of our previous study [52]. Two explanations have been proposed for these differences [53], namely, a different stimulation device with different stimulus parameters and different electrodes. The stimulation parameters may be important for the ability to induce tinnitus suppression. Using an electrode with only two contacts limits the way the electrodes can be programmed. The tinnitus always reoccurs after auditory cortex stimulation using implanted electrodes and therefore requires the use of several different stimulation programs using multiple electrode contacts to run alternately to prevent tinnitus recurrence [29, 52].

The fact that tinnitus distress does decrease without tinnitus intensity reduction could possibly be explained by disruption of the phase synchronization between the "general distress network" and the thalamocortical dysrhythmia. Intracortical microstimulation in the auditory cortex of animals disrupts not only local ongoing activity but also long-range connections in a larger network [54], similarly to what has been described in humans using TMS of the auditory cortex [55].

Side Effects

Side effects are limited and do not occur at stimulation parameters required for tinnitus suppression. Side effects may occur when high-frequency, high-intensity stimulation is used. Different kinds of side effects have occurred when testing is performed to discover the limits of the applied stimulation design, so that permanent stimulation can be programmed without these side effects. A feeling of intoxication, altered spatial localization of external sounds, difficulty in finding appropriate words, dizziness, vertigo and hearing perception changes (hearing perceived as being clearer, related to even their own voice) [28], as well as out of body experiences [56] were noted. Some patients with tinnitus have an associated feeling of aural pressure, the feeling as if there is water inside the ear. In all patients with successful tinnitus suppression, these associated pressure feelings decreased, however. The stimulation designs that best suppressed tinnitus and best suppressed pressure feelings are not always identical.

Complications

Complications are limited but can be severe. Epileptic seizures occurred in 3 of the 43 patients studied. In these three patients, the epileptic seizures most likely occurred because of prolonged stimulation without interruption and also occurred while the patients still had an external stimulator which could not be programmed

by the investigator (it relies on patient cooperation). Therefore, patients with epilepsy are not candidates for this procedure. One patient developed an epileptic seizure during prolonged trial stimulation. Therefore, trial programs should probably best be limited to 1-h sessions.

The major complications occurred with intradural implants. One of the four patients implanted with the electrode directly on the surface of the primary auditory cortex developed a postoperative intracranial bleed in the superior temporal sulcus at a distance from the Sylvian fissure, where the electrode was inserted. Speech disturbances occurred as a result. However, a decrease in tinnitus also occurred as a result of the bleeding. One of the four patients developed an intracranial abscess that required surgical evacuation, with good outcome. Thus, this treatment should be preferentially performed extradurally. Extradural techniques in our last 30 patients experienced no serious complications.

Failures of Auditory Cortex Stimulation

Not all patients benefit from stimulation via implanted electrodes as detailed above.

Some of the conceivable reasons for failure are:

- Contralateral auditory cortex is not involved in all patients
- TMS is not a good predictor of subsequent implant success
- The stimulation design is not optimal for the individual patient
- The neural network that causes the tinnitus has become permanent
- The adjustments in the network that causes tinnitus also change over time

We have placed the stimulating electrode on the contralateral secondary auditory cortex for unilateral tinnitus and on the right secondary auditory cortex for bilateral tinnitus. It is possible that all electrodes should have been implanted at the left auditory cortex similarly to what has been done for rTMS [51]. This suggestion is supported by the finding that PET studies usually show increased metabolism on the left auditory cortex [57, 58] in individuals with tinnitus, irrespective of the side on which the tinnitus is perceived, and that TMS applied to the left side can suppress this metabolic activity [59]. On the other hand, fMRI [44, 58, 60, 61] and EEG [34] and MEG [9, 31] studies suggest that the neural generator of tinnitus is located contralaterally to the tinnitus side.

It is clear that TMS, even though performed twice and placebo controlled before every implant, is not a perfect predictor of success in subsequent implants. However, a correlation does exist between the amount of tinnitus suppression obtained by TMS and by stimulation via implanted electrodes.

Another reason for failure may be that the stimulus protocol used is not optimal for the individual patient. For example, noise-like tinnitus does not seem to respond to tonic stimulation, responding to burst stimulation instead [47]. If burst stimulation had not been used, the results obtained in the series of 43 patients discussed above would have been poor, with only 33% of patients showing benefit from the stimulation by implanted electrodes. In this study, 45% of patients only experienced benefit from burst stimulation.

Regarding the difference between the effect of TMS and stimulation with implanted electrodes, it is possible that TMS reaches more fibers or penetrates deeper into the auditory cortex than the implanted electrode. It is conceivable that TMS reaches auditory cortex fibers that go to the parahippocampus directly and therefore influences the parahippocampus where the implant does not. (The parahippocampal involvement in tinnitus is detailed in Chap. 21.)

Another explanation for the failure of cortex stimulation may be that the tinnitus network might have become too hard wired for stimulation to disrupt it. Even though this is conceptually possible, it is unlikely that this is the cause of the observed failures. While it is true that the results from TMS are affected by how long the patient has had the tinnitus [49, 55, 62–64], the results of our studies of patients with implanted electrodes indicate that the tinnitus duration does not seem to affect the outcome. Therefore, this argument is most likely not valid for explaining treatment failure. It, however, points to yet another interesting difference between TMS and stimulation from intracranial electrodes.

The tinnitus network might change in time. The recent development of network science [65–68] (see Chap. 21) with its application to tinnitus by the seminal work of Schlee et al. [15, 35, 36] has altered the way researchers think about the pathophysiology of tinnitus. Since tinnitus should be considered an emergent property of a large network, it is possible that the weight of the hubs and their individual' connectivity change in time [15]. Therefore, whether stimulation is beneficial or not could be dependent on the state of the network; the exact state cannot be derived from group data but should be analyzed on an individual level of the patients eligible for implant. Further studies exploring the differences of resting-state activity, as recorded by EEG or MEG, between responders and non-responders could help to elucidate these prognostic problems.

The Future of Neurostimulation for Tinnitus

Based on the new network science, it should be possible to retrieve good alternative targets to the auditory cortex for neuromodulation. This requires a thorough analysis of resting-state data of an individual patient, looking for the hubs in a scale-free network model (see Chap. 21) of tinnitus. Once these methods become easily accessible, results of the promising technique of neuromodulation should improve.

Conclusion

Brain stimulation is an option for patients with severe and intractable tinnitus. With proper selection of the patients, extradural stimulation is capable of suppressing tinnitus completely or partially in 67% of patients. Extradural stimulation is preferred because of less risk of complications than intradural placements of the stimulating electrodes. Using the results from TMS seems logical as a prognostic criterion. However, even with TMS as a preoperative test, 33% or more of patients will still fail to benefit from stimulation through implanted electrodes. Several reasons why not all patients benefit from auditory cortex stimulation may exist. Development of new stimulation designs as well as the application of network science might, in the near future, improve results of the techniques.

References

1. Eggermont JJ and LE Roberts (2004) The neuroscience of tinnitus. Trends Neurosci 27:676–82.
2. Lockwood AH, RJ Salvi and RF Burkard (2002) Tinnitus. N Engl J Med 347:904–10.
3. Jastreboff PJ (1990) Phantom auditory perception (tinnitus): mechanisms of generation and perception. Neurosci Res 8:221–54.
4. De Ridder D, G De Mulder, T Menovsky et al (2007) Electrical stimulation of auditory and somatosensory cortices for treatment of tinnitus and pain. Prog Brain Res 166:377–88.
5. Møller AR (2000) Similarities between severe tinnitus and chronic pain. J Am Acad Audiol 11:115–24.
6. Møller AR (1997) Similarities between chronic pain and tinnitus. Am J Otol 18:577–85.
7. Tonndorf J (1987) The analogy between tinnitus and pain: a suggestion for a physiological basis of chronic tinnitus. Hear Res 28:271–5.
8. Ramachandran VS and W Hirstein (1998) The perception of phantom limbs. The D. O. Hebb lecture. Brain 121 (Pt 9): 1603–30.
9. Weisz N, S Muller, W Schlee et al (2007) The neural code of auditory phantom perception. J Neurosci 27:1479–84.
10. Borst A and FE Theunissen (1999) Information theory and neural coding. Nat Neurosci 2:947–57.
11. Contreras D and R Llinas (2001) Voltage-sensitive dye imaging of neocortical spatiotemporal dynamics to afferent activation frequency. J Neurosci 21:9403–13.
12. Llinas R, FJ Urbano, E Leznik et al (2005) Rhythmic and dysrhythmic thalamocortical dynamics: GABA systems and the edge effect. Trends Neurosci 28:325–33.
13. Llinas RR, U Ribary, D Jeanmonod et al (1999) Thalamocortical dysrhythmia: A neurological and neuropsychiatric syndrome characterized by magnetoencephalography. Proc Natl Acad Sci USA 96:15222–7.
14. Lorenz I, N Muller, W Schlee et al (2009) Loss of alpha power is related to increased gamma synchronization-A marker of reduced inhibition in tinnitus? Neurosci Lett 453:225–8.
15. Schlee W, T Hartmann, B Langguth et al (2009) Abnormal resting-state cortical coupling in chronic tinnitus. BMC Neurosci 10:11.
16. Deacon T (1997) Evolution and Intelligence: Beyond the Argument from Design, in The Origin and Evolution of Intelligence, A Scheibel and J Schopf, Editors, Jones and Bartlett: Boston. 103–36.
17. Battelli L, A Pascual-Leone and P Cavanagh (2007) The 'when' pathway of the right parietal lobe. Trends Cogn Sci 11:204–10.
18. De Ridder D and P Van de Heyning (2007) The Darwinian plasticity hypothesis for tinnitus and pain. Prog Brain Res 166:55–60.
19. Holtmaat A and K Svoboda (2009) Experience-dependent structural synaptic plasticity in the mammalian brain. Nat Rev Neurosci 10:647–58.
20. Lendvai B, EA Stern, B Chen et al (2000) Experience-dependent plasticity of dendritic spines in the developing rat barrel cortex in vivo. Nature 404:876–81.
21. Kaas JH (1996) Plasticity of sensory representations in the auditory and other systems of adult mammals, in Auditory System Plasticity and Regeneration, RJ Salvi and D Henderson, Editors, Thieme Medical Publishers: New York. 213–23.
22. Moffat G, K Adjout, S Gallego et al (2009) Effects of hearing aid fitting on the perceptual characteristics of tinnitus. Hear Res 254:82–91.
23. Van de Heyning P, K Vermeire, M Diebl et al (2008) Incapacitating unilateral tinnitus in single-sided deafness treated by cochlear implantation. Ann Otol Rhinol Laryngol 117:645–52.
24. Bartels H, MJ Staal, AF Holm et al (2007) Long-term evaluation of treatment of chronic, therapeutically refractory tinnitus by neurostimulation. Stereotact Funct Neurosurg 85:150–7.
25. Holm AF, MJ Staal, JJ Mooij et al (2005) Neurostimulation as a new treatment for severe tinnitus: a pilot study. Otol Neurotol 26:425–8; discussion 8.
26. Soussi T and SR Otto (1994) Effects of electrical brainstem stimulation on tinnitus. Acta Otolaryngol 114:135–40.
27. Friedland DR, W Gaggl, C Runge-Samuelson et al (2007) Feasibility of auditory cortical stimulation for the treatment of tinnitus. Otol Neurotol 28:1005–12.
28. De Ridder D, G De Mulder, E Verstraeten et al (2006) Primary and secondary auditory cortex stimulation for intractable tinnitus. ORL J Otorhinolaryngol Relat Spec 68(1):48–54.
29. De Ridder D, G De Mulder, V Walsh et al (2004) Magnetic and electrical stimulation of the auditory cortex for intractable tinnitus. Case report. J Neurosurg 100:560–4.
30. Seidman MD, DD Ridder, K Elisevich et al (2008) Direct electrical stimulation of Heschl's gyrus for tinnitus treatment. Laryngoscope 118:491–500.
31. Muhlnickel W, T Elbert, E Taub et al (1998) Reorganization of auditory cortex in tinnitus. Proc Natl Acad Sci USA 95:10340–3.
32. Suga N, E Gao, Y Zhang et al (2000) The corticofugal system for hearing: recent progress. Proc Natl Acad Sci USA 97:11807–14.
33. Perrot X, P Ryvlin, J Isnard et al (2006) Evidence for corticofugal modulation of peripheral auditory activity in humans. Cereb Cortex 16:941–8.
34. van der Loo E, S Gais, M Congedo et al (2009) Tinnitus intensity dependent gamma oscillations of the contralateral auditory cortex. PLoS ONE 4:e7396.
35. Schlee W, N Mueller, T Hartmann et al (2009) Mapping cortical hubs in tinnitus. BMC Biol 7:80.
36. Schlee W, N Weisz, O Bertrand et al (2008) Using auditory steady state responses to outline the functional connectivity in the tinnitus brain. PLoS ONE 3:e3720.
37. Ramirez RR, BH Kopell, CR Butson et al (2009) Neuromagnetic source imaging of abnormal spontaneous activity in tinnitus patient modulated by electrical cortical stimulation. Conf Proc IEEE Eng Med Biol Soc 1:1940–4.
38. Kulkarni B, DE Bentley, R Elliott et al (2005) Attention to pain localization and unpleasantness discriminates the functions of the medial and lateral pain systems. Eur J Neurosci 21:3133–42.
39. von Leupoldt A, T Sommer, S Kegat et al (2009) Dyspnea and pain share emotion-related brain network. Neuroimage 48:200–6.
40. Etkin A and TD Wager (2007) Functional neuroimaging of anxiety: a meta-analysis of emotional processing in PTSD,

social anxiety disorder, and specific phobia. Am J Psychiatry 164:1476–88.

41. Bressler SL, R Coppola and R Nakamura (1993) Episodic multiregional cortical coherence at multiple frequencies during visual task performance. Nature 366:153–6.

42. Varela FJ (1995) Resonant cell assemblies: a new approach to cognitive functions and neuronal synchrony. Biol Res 28:81–95.

43. Kovacs S, R Peeters, M Smits et al (2005) Activation of cortical and subcortical auditory structures at 3T by means of a fMRI paradigm suitable for clinical use. . European Radiology (in press).

44. Smits M, S Kovacs, D de Ridder et al (2007) Lateralization of functional magnetic resonance imaging (fMRI) activation in the auditory pathway of patients with lateralized tinnitus. Neuroradiology.

45. Nir Y, L Fisch, R Mukamel et al (2007) Coupling between neuronal firing rate, gamma LFP, and BOLD fMRI is related to interneuronal correlations. Curr Biol 17:1275–85.

46. De Ridder D, G De Mulder, E Verstraeten et al (2007) Auditory cortex stimulation for tinnitus. Acta Neurochir Suppl 97:451–62.

47. De Ridder D, S Vanneste, E van der Loo et al (2009) Burst stimulation of the auditory cortex: a new form of neurostimulation for noise-like tinnitus suppression. J Neurosurg.

48. Goebel G and W Hiller (1994) [The tinnitus questionnaire. A standard instrument for grading the degree of tinnitus. Results of a multicenter study with the tinnitus questionnaire]. HNO 42:166–72.

49. Kleinjung T, T Steffens, P Sand et al (2007) Which tinnitus patients benefit from transcranial magnetic stimulation? Otolaryngol Head Neck Surg 137:589–95.

50. De Ridder D, E van der Loo, K Van der Kelen et al (2007) Theta, alpha and beta burst transcranial magnetic stimulation: brain modulation in tinnitus. Int J Med Sci 4:237–41.

51. Londero A, B Langguth, D De Ridder et al (2006) Repetitive transcranial magnetic stimulation (rTMS): a new therapeutic approach in subjective tinnitus? Neurophysiol Clin 36:145–55.

52. De Ridder D, G De Mulder, E Verstraeten et al (2006) Primary and secondary auditory cortex stimulation for intractable tinnitus. ORL J Otorhinolaryngol Relat Spec 68:48-54; discussion -5.

53. De Ridder D, T Menovsky and P van de Heyning (2008) Auditory cortex stimulation for tinnitus suppression. Otol Neurotol 29:574–5; author reply 5.

54. Deliano M, H Scheich and FW Ohl (2009) Auditory cortical activity after intracortical microstimulation and its role for sensory processing and learning. J Neurosci 29: 15898–909.

55. Plewnia C, M Reimold, A Najib et al (2006) Dose-dependent attenuation of auditory phantom perception (tinnitus) by PET-guided repetitive transcranial magnetic stimulation. Hum Brain Mapp 28(3):238–46.

56. De Ridder D, K Van Laere, P Dupont et al (2007) Visualizing out-of-body experience in the brain. N Engl J Med 357: 1829–33.

57. Langguth B, P Eichhammer, A Kreutzer et al (2006) The impact of auditory cortex activity on characterizing and treating patients with chronic tinnitus--first results from a PET study. Acta Otolaryngol Suppl 84–8.

58. Lanting CP, E de Kleine and P van Dijk (2009) Neural activity underlying tinnitus generation: results from PET and fMRI. Hear Res 255:1–13.

59. Marcondes RA, TG Sanchez, MA Kii et al (2009) Repetitive transcranial magnetic stimulation improve tinnitus in normal hearing patients: a double-blind controlled, clinical and neuroimaging outcome study. Eur J Neurol.

60. Kovacs S, R Peeters, M Smits et al (2006) Activation of cortical and subcortical auditory structures at 3 T by means of a functional magnetic resonance imaging paradigm suitable for clinical use. Invest Radiol 41:87–96.

61. Melcher JR, IS Sigalovsky, JJ Guinan, Jr. et al (2000) Lateralized tinnitus studied with functional magnetic resonance imaging: abnormal inferior colliculus activation. J Neurophysiol 83:1058–72.

62. De Ridder D, E Verstraeten, K Van der Kelen et al (2005) Transcranial magnetic stimulation for tinnitus: influence of tinnitus duration on stimulation parameter choice and maximal tinnitus suppression Otol Neurotol 26:616–9.

63. Khedr EM, JC Rothwell, MA Ahmed et al (2008) Effect of daily repetitive transcranial magnetic stimulation for treatment of tinnitus: comparison of different stimulus frequencies. J Neurol Neurosurg Psychiatry 79:212–5.

64. Khedr EM, JC Rothwell and A El-Atar (2009) One-year follow up of patients with chronic tinnitus treated with left temporoparietal rTMS. Eur J Neurol 16:404–8.

65. Barabasi AL (2009) Scale-free networks: a decade and beyond. Science 325:412–3.

66. Barabasi AL and R Albert (1999) Emergence of scaling in random networks. Science 286:509–12.

67. Bullmore E and O Sporns (2009) Complex brain networks: graph theoretical analysis of structural and functional systems. Nat Rev Neurosci 10:186–98.

68. Strogatz SH (2001) Exploring complex networks. Nature 410:268–76.

Chapter 91
Cutaneous Stimulation

Aage R. Møller

Keypoints

1. Electrical stimulation of the skin around the ears was one of the first described methods used clinically for treating tinnitus, but the results vary widely among authors.
2. Recordings from cells in the dorsal cochlear nucleus (DCN) show that stimulation of the skin around the ears can cause both increased and decreased excitation of neurons in the dorsal cochlear nucleus.
3. The skin around the ears is innervated by the upper spinal cord (C_2) and the caudal trigeminal nucleus, the neurons of which project to the DCN and the external nucleus (ICX) of the inferior colliculus. This is believed to be the basis for the observed effect on tinnitus from electrical stimulation of the skin.
4. Electrical stimulation of the middle ear mucosa (bony capsule of the cochlea) has also been used to treat tinnitus. The mucosa is innervated mainly by the trigeminal nerve.
5. A few studies have shown that cutaneous electrical stimulation in other places of the body can modulate tinnitus, indicating that the nonclassical auditory pathways are involved in such forms of tinnitus.

Keywords Cutaneous stimulation • Tinnitus • Trigeminal nucleus • Dorsal column nuclei

Abbreviations

C_{2-4} Upper cervical spine segment
DC Dorsal cortex (of IC)

DCN Dorsal cochlear nucleus
DR Dorsal raphe nucleus
IC Inferior colliculus
ICX External nucleus (of IC)
LC Locus coeruleus
Sp5 Spinal trigeminal nucleus
STT Spinothalamic tract
TENS Transderm electrical nerve stimulation
V1 Upper branch of the trigeminal nerve
VAS Visual analog scale

Introduction

Cutaneous electrical stimulation has been described as one of the earliest methods for managing tinnitus by means of electrical stimulation [1]. Most studies have used various forms of electrical stimulation through electrodes placed on the skin around the ears [2]. Results from stimulation of the skin at other places of the body or peripheral nerves, such as the median nerve at the wrist, [3] have also shown to be an influence on some individual's tinnitus. Electrical stimulation of the mucosa in the middle ear (bony capsule of the cochlea) has also been shown to modulate tinnitus in some individuals [4].

Electrical Stimulation of the Skin Around the Ears

One of the first to describe the results of cutaneous electrical stimulation around the ears was Shulman and Tonndorf [2, 5]. Different investigators have used different kinds of electrical stimulation, such as

A.R. Møller (✉)
The University of Texas at Dallas, School of Behavioral and Brain Sciences, GR 41, 800 West Campbell Road, Richardson, TX 75080, USA
e-mail: amoller@utdallas.edu

A.R. Møller et al. (eds.), *Textbook of Tinnitus*,
DOI 10.1007/978-1-60761-145-5_91, © Springer Science+Business Media, LLC 2011

impulses presented at different rates, high frequency electrical current, and direct current (DC). The beneficial effects reported by the different investigators vary greatly.

Some investigators [2] using a commercially available device reported beneficial effect of 82% in a study of 27 individuals. The effect lasted 3 months or more in 47% of the participants. However, when the effect of using the same device was tested in a single-blind crossover study by other investigators [6], the benefit was found to be minimal (only 7% of the participants reported improvement). More recent studies of transcutaneous electrical stimulation [7] found improvement in 42.8% from electrical stimulation of the skin in front of the ears and 28.5% had improvement from placebo (sham stimulation with electrodes placed on the skin, but no stimulation). The study had 42 patients, 31 received stimulation, and 11 had electrodes placed on the skin, but no stimulation.

In a recent study of the effect of electrical stimulation through electrodes placed on the right and left C_2 dermatome, Vanneste et al. found that such stimulation reduced the scores on a visual analog scale (VAS) of the strength of the tinnitus from a mean value of 6.16 (SD = 2.18) to 5.56 (SD = 2.42), thus 17.9% decrease [8]. Six participants had total disappearance of their tinnitus, and only 6% of the participants had a reduction in their tinnitus from the sham stimulation. The study had 240 participants with tinnitus (147 males and 93 females). Sixty-three of the participants had left-sided tinnitus, 44 had right-sided tinnitus, and 133 had bilateral tinnitus; 65 had pure tone tinnitus, 164 narrow band tinnitus, and 11 had both. The mean duration of their tinnitus was 6.19 years (SD = 7.92).

The stimulation lasted 10 min and consisted of constant current impulses at a rate of 6 per second, followed by 10 minutes stimulation at a rate of 40 impulses per second. The impulses (duration 250 µS (microseconds)) were presented at a subthreshold intensity. Sham stimulation was done with the same electrode placement and the stimulator turned on only for 30 seconds. The results were independent on the kind of tinnitus.

In a large study comprising 500 individuals with tinnitus, Steenerson and Cronin [9] found that 53% had improvement from electrical stimulation of the skin around the ears with at least two points on a subjective rating scale [10]. A month after the last treatment, 72% reported sustained benefit (when individuals with Ménière's disease were excluded, 94% had sustained effect).

In a prospective descriptive study of 26 individuals with tinnitus, Herraiz and coworkers [11] found that electrical stimulation of the skin around the ears improved the tinnitus in 46% of the participants (23% did not hear it anymore, and in another 23% its intensity was reduced). When using a VAS, scores improved from 6.5 to 6.0 after 2 weeks of treatment ($p < 0.01$). The participants used the electrical stimulation at home for 2 h, once per day for 2 weeks [alternating ramped burst, 150 pps, with pulse duration of 100 µS, the average intensity was 27 mA].

Intermittent "typewriter" type of tinnitus [described by Levine [12]] was the most responsive. The participants in the study were selected according to two criteria:

1. Their tinnitus was triggered by an acute somatic event.
2. The tinnitus could be modulated by orofacial movements or posture changes. Eight of the participants had "typewriter" tinnitus. This study shows the importance of selecting patients for treatment.

While these studies show that existing tinnitus can be modulated, tinnitus may also be elicited by the activation of the somatosensory system through touching the skin or through muscle contractions [13], change in gaze, etc. [14].

Mechanisms of Beneficial Effect from Stimulating the Skin Around the Ears

The investigators who placed stimulating electrodes on the skin behind the ears [2] were interested in stimulating the cochlea. However, electrical current from stimulation of the skin around the ears with tolerable intensities does not reach the cochlea with a strength that can possibly have any biological effect. Instead, such stimulation activates receptors or nerves in the skin. The skin behind the ears has dual innervations by spinal C_2 and the upper branch of the trigeminal nerve (V1). The effect on the auditory nervous system, and thereby modulating tinnitus, is most likely caused by activating neurons in the trigeminal nucleus and the dorsal column nuclei that project to the dorsal cochlear nucleus (DCN) [4, 15–18] (see Chap. 9). This means that the beneficial effect on tinnitus from electrical stimulation of the skin was achieved by the effect the stimulation had on the neurons in the DCN. Animal studies by other investigators have found it likely that the DCN is involved in tinnitus [19, 20].

Recordings from cells (multiunit recordings) in hamsters' DCN show sound stimulation after the animals had been exposed to high intensity sounds of the kind that normally cause tinnitus. These animal studies [21] have shown that electrical stimulation of the pinna, and in the spinal trigeminal nucleus (Sp5), dorsal raphe nucleus (DR), and locus coeruleus (LC) increase activity in neurons in the DCN (number of Fos-positive neurons increases). The sound stimulation caused hyperactivity that lasted several weeks after exposure [22].

Electrical stimulation of the skin behind the pinna caused several different kinds of changes in the recorded unit or multiunit activity. Suppression–suppression, excitation–suppression, suppression–excitation, and excitation–excitation were observed. The results were interpreted to show DCN hyperactivity is a direct neural correlate of tinnitus and somatosensory electrical stimulation can modulate DCN hyperactivity.

Results of tracing experiments indicate that the DCN received inputs from the Sp5, DR, and LC. The above results suggest that the modulation of DCN activity through somatosensory electrical stimulation may involve both direct pathways via the Sp5 and indirect pathways via the DR and LC. The relief of tinnitus caused by somatosensory electrical stimulation may involve manipulations of both auditory and nonauditory functions. For example, the stimulation of trigeminal fibers that innervate the cochlea may affect blood flow in the cochlea [23, 24].

The nerves that are activated by electrical stimulation of the skin behind the ears or in the middle ear cavity contain fibers of different diameters. These different fiber types innervate different populations of cells in the trigeminal nucleus and the dorsal horn of the spinal cord and project to different structures in the brain. It is not known which fibers are most effective in modulating tinnitus, but it seems likely fibers that belong to the pain system and those that mediate innocuous stimulation (touch and vibration) may have a different ability to cause tinnitus suppression. Electrical stimulation activates all these different types of fibers, but to different degrees depending on the stimulus parameters.

Receptors in the skin are innervated by three kinds of nerve fibers, large myelinated fibers (Aβ), small diameter myelinated fibers (Aδ), and unmyelinated small diameter fibers [25]. These fibers innervate different kinds of cells in the spinal cord (see Chap. 15) and the trigeminal nucleus. These cells project centrally in different pathways [26]. The Aβ fibers mediate touch and vibration. The fibers terminate on cells in the spinal cord located in the dorsal column nuclei from which fibers cross the midline and form the medial lemniscus – thus, the classical somatosensory pathway. Aδ fibers terminate on cells located in layer I of the dorsal horn of the spinal cord. C fibers terminate on cells in layer II, which make connections to cells in layer I. From these connections, fibers cross the midline at segmental levels and form the anterior spinothalamic tract that mainly mediates pain as well as hot and cold sensations. C-fibers mediate slow burning pain. These fibers terminate on other cells in the spinal cord, the projections of which also join the anterior lateral system. The Aβ fibers have inhibitory influence on the cells that receive pain signals through Aδ and C fibers. Trigeminal nerve fibers are similar, and all fibers have synaptic contact with cells in the trigeminal nucleus. It is not known which fiber groups of cutaneous nerves mediate the effect on tinnitus from cutaneous electrical stimulation.

Nerve cells innervated by cutaneous receptors can also be activated by mechanical and by chemical stimulation. These forms of stimulation do not seem to have been used for the management of tinnitus, but may offer advantages or electrical stimulation which is perceived by many individuals as being unpleasant.

Little attention seems to have been paid to the parameters of the electrical stimulation used for pain and tinnitus control. Electrical stimulation of nerve fibers can activate or inactivate the target cells depending on the frequency of the stimulation. Low frequency stimulation typically activates the target nerve cells while high frequency stimulation may constantly depolarize cells, and thereby inactivates them.

It would be interesting to compare specific stimulations of these receptors, such as using capsaicin that activates pain receptors compared with vibrations used for pain control [27]. Such stimulation activates receptors innervated by larger myelinated fibers (Aβ) [23].

Acupuncture, which may be regarded as a form of electrical stimulation of cutaneous nerve fibers, has been used for pain control [27] and tinnitus [28].

Stimulation of the Surface of the Cochlea

Placing electrodes on the bony capsule of the cochlea has been used to treat tinnitus. It has been assumed that the observed effect was caused by electrical current reaching the hair cells in the cochlea [29]. The mucosa of the middle ear, and also the surface of the cochlear capsule, is innervated by several somatosensory structures such as the dorsal root ganglia of C_{2-4}, and the trigeminal nucleus. The latter contributed the most [30]. Electrical stimulation applied to electrodes placed on the cochlear capsule may therefore activate the somatosensory system in a similar way as stimulating the skin around the ears. There are also autonomous fibers in the middle ear mucosa and in the skin, stimulation of which may change blood flow in the cochlea [23] which may affect tinnitus.

Subcutaneous Stimulation of the Skin at Other Places of the Body

Other investigators placed stimulating electrodes on places of the body other than the skin around the ears and found that stimulation could affect some individuals' tinnitus. Stimulation of the medial nerve at the wrist that innervates the skin of the hand can modulate tinnitus in some individuals [3].

Cacace and coauthors described [14] a form of tinnitus that could be evoked directly by cutaneous stimulation of the upper hand and fingertip regions in two adults after surgical removal of space-occupying lesions at the base of the skull and posterior fossa. Hearing and vestibular functions were lost in one ear and facial nerve paralysis was present after the operation. It was assumed that these abnormal sensations were caused by anatomical and physiological interactions between auditory and somatosensory structures in the brain.

Since somatic tinnitus can be elicited by muscle contraction, treatments that reduce contractions (botulinum toxin) have been tried as a treatment for some forms of tinnitus [31].

Anatomical Basis for Involvement of the Nonclassical Pathways in Modulation of Tinnitus by Cutaneous Stimulation

It was mentioned above that somatic input to the cochlear nuclei may be responsible for the effect on tinnitus from electrical stimulation of the skin around the ears. Increasing the somatic input to the nonclassical auditory pathways is another possible explanation for the beneficial effect of electrical stimulation of the skin around the ears. When the nonclassical auditory pathways are active, somatic stimulation may influence

(modulate) the activity in the nonclassical auditory pathways. It is generally assumed that the nonclassical auditory pathways are involved in the cross-modal sensory effects between somatic and auditory senses. Such cross-modal interaction has been studied in connection with tinnitus [3, 32, 33] and in connection with the perception of physical sounds [3, 34].

Zhou and Shore [35] have shown in anatomical studies that the external nucleus (ICX) of the IC receives projections from the Sp5 (in the guinea pig). The ICX is known to belong to the nonclassical ascending auditory pathways [36] and receives projections from mostly contralateral DCN [35]. The DC and ICX receive somatic input mainly originating in somatosensory innervation of the upper part of the body [36]. Electrical and other forms of stimulation of the skin, joints or muscles can thereby influence (modulate) the nonclassical auditory pathways.

Conclusions

Electrical stimulation of the skin can affect tinnitus; for some individuals, it can relieve tinnitus. The exact mechanisms for the effect are complex and incompletely understood, but it may have similarities with the techniques that have been in use for many years in the management of pain such as TENS. New discoveries regarding anatomical and functional connections between the somatosensory system and cochlear nuclei have provided new insights into the mechanisms of electrical skin stimulation.

References

1. Hatton DS, SD Erulkar and PE Rosenberg (1960) Some preliminary observations on the effect of galvanic current on tinnitus aurium. Laryngoscope 70:123–30.
2. Shulman A (1987) External electrical tinnitus suppression: a review. Am J Otol 8:479–84.
3. Møller AR, MB Møller and M Yokota (1992) Some forms of tinnitus may involve the extralemniscal auditory pathway. Laryngoscope 102:1165–71.
4. Itoh K, H Kamiya, A Mitani et al (1987) Direct projections from dorsal column nuclei and the spinal trigeminal nuclei to the cochlear nuclei in the cat. Brain Res. 400:145–50.
5. Shulman A, J Tonndorf and B Goldstein (1985) Electrical tinnitus control. Acta Otolaryngol 99:318–25.

6. Thedinger BS, E Karlsen and SH Schack (1987) Treatment of tinnitus with electrical stimulation: an evaluation of the Audimax Theraband. Laryngoscope 97:33–7.

7. Kapkin O, B Satar and S Yetiser (2008) Transcutaneous electrical stimulation of subjective tinnitus. A placebo-controlled, randomized and comparative analysis. ORL J Otorhinolaryngol Relat Spec 70:156–61.

8. Vanneste S, M Plazier, E van der Loo et al (2009) Transcutaneous electrical nerve stimulation (TENS) of upper cervical nerve (C2) for the treatment of somatic tinnitus. Exp Brain Res 204:283–7.

9. Steenerson RL and GW Cronin (2003) Tinnitus reduction using transcutaneous electrical stimulation. Otolaryngol Clin North Am 36:337–44.

10. Steenerson RL and GW Cronin (1999) The treatment of annoying tinnitus with electrical stimualtion. Int Tinnitus J 5:30–1.

11. Herraiz C, A Toledano and I Diges (2007) Trans-electrical nerve stimulation (TENS) for somatic tinnitus. Prog Brain Res 166:389–94.

12. Levine RA (2006) Typewriter tinnitus: a carbamazepine-responsive syndrome related to auditory nerve vascular compression. ORL J Otorhinolaryngol 68:43–6.

13. Levine RA, EC Nam, Y Oron et al. (2007) Evidence for a tinnitus subgroup responsive to somatosensory based treatment modalities. In Tinnitus: Pathophysiology and Treatment, Progress in Brain Research, B Langguth et al., Editors. Elsevier: Amsterdam. 195–207.

14. Cacace AT, JP Cousins, SM Parnes et al (1999) Cutaneous-evoked tinnitus. I: Phenomenology, psychophysics and functional imaging. Audiol Neurotol 4:247–57.

15. Shore SE (2005) Multisensory integration in the dorsal cochlear nucleus: unit responses to acoustic and trigeminal ganglion stimulation. Eur J Neurosci 21:3334–48.

16. Zhou J and S Shore (2004) Projections from the trigeminal nuclear complex to the cochlear nuclei: a retrograde and anterograde tracing study in the guinea pig. J Neurosci Res 78:901–7.

17. Shore SE, Z Vass, NL Wys et al (2000) Trigeminal ganglion innervates the auditory brainstem. J Comp Neurol 419:271–85.

18. Young ED, I Nelken, RA Conley (1995) Somatosensory effects on neurons in dorsal cochlear nucleus. J Neurophysiol 73:743–65.

19. Kaltenbach JA (2007) The dorsal cochlear nucleus as a contributor to tinnitus: mechanisms underlying the induction of hyperactivity. In Tinnitus: Pathophysiology and Treatment, Progress in Brain Research, B Langguth et al., Editors. Elevier: Amsterdam. 89–106.

20. Kaltenbach JA (2000) Neurophysiologic mechanisms of tinnitus. J Am Acad Audiol 11:125–37.

21. Zhang J, Z Guan (2007) Pathways involved in somatosensory electrical modulation of dorsal cochlear nucleus activity. Brain Res 1184:121–31.

22. Zhang J, Z Guan (2008) Modulatory effects of somatosensory electrical stimulation on neural activity of the dorsal cochlear nucleus of hamsters. J Neurosci Res 86:1178–87.

23. Vass Z, PS Steyger, AJ Hordichok et al (2001) Capsaicin stimulation of the cochlea and electric stimulation of the trigeminal ganglion mediate vascular permeability in cochlear and vertebro-basilar arteries: a potential cause of inner ear dysfunction in headache. Neuroscience 103:189–201.

24. Vass Z, SE Shore, AL Nuttall et al (1997) Trigeminal ganglion innervation of the cochlea–a retrograde transport study. Neuroscience 79:605–15.

25. Møller AR (2003) Sensory Systems: Anatomy and Physiology. Amsterdam: Academic.

26. Møller AR (2006) Neural Plasticity and Disorders of the Nervous System. Cambridge: Cambridge University Press.

27. Hansson P, T Lundeberg (1999) Transcutaneous electrical nerve stimulation, vibration and acupuncture as pain-relieving measures. In Textbook of Pain, PD Wall, R Melzack, Editors. Edinburgh: Churchill Livingstone. 1341–51.

28. Dobie RA (1999) A review of randomized clinical trials in tinnitus. Laryngoscope 109:1202–11.

29. Cazals Y, M Negrevergne, JM Aran (1978) Electrical stimulation of the cochlea in man: hearing induction and tinnitus suppression. J Am Audiol Soc 3:209–13.

30. Uddman R, T Grunditz, A Larsson et al (1988) Sensory innervation of the ear drum and middle-ear mucosa: retrograde tracing and immunocytochemistry. Cell Tissue Res 252:141–6.

31. Láinez MJ, A Piera (2007) Botulinum toxin for the treatment of somatic tinnitus. Prog Brain Res 166:335–8.

32. Cacace AT (2003) Expanding the biological basis of tinnitus: crossmodal origins and the role of neuroplasticity. Hear Res 175:112–32.

33. Cacace AT, TJ Lovely, DJ McFarland et al (1994) Anomalous cross-modal plasticity following posterior fossa surgery: Some speculations on gaze-evoked tinnitus. Hear Res 81:22–32.

34. Møller AR, P Rollins (2002) The non-classical auditory -system is active in children but not in adults. Neurosci Lett 319:41–4.

35. Zhou J, S Shore (2006) Convergence of spinal trigeminal and cochlear nucleus projections in the inferior colliculus of the guinea pig. J Comp Neurol 495:100–12.

36. Aitkin LM (1986) The auditory midbrain, structure and function in the central auditory pathway. Clifton: Humana.

Chapter 92
Complementary Tinnitus Therapies

Manuela Mazzoli

Keypoints

1. Several different complementary therapies have been attempted, but few studies have been published regarding the efficacy of complementary treatments for tinnitus.
2. Acupuncture seems to be mostly effective in acute and recent tinnitus as well as in somatic tinnitus. Other therapies that are in the area of musculoskeletal therapies, such as electrical stimulation applied to skin, the use of manipulations, or exercising, have been studied for somatic tinnitus.
3. There are strong indications that a metabolic component is involved in a subgroup of individuals with tinnitus, but only few studies have been performed of this aspect of tinnitus.
4. Training in mindfulness (including awareness), breathing techniques, meditation, and hypnosis are useful as complementary therapies for tinnitus that can reduce annoyance and fixation on the presence of tinnitus, improving sleep, anxiety, and the perceived quality of life.
5. Methodologies and study design for studies of efficacy of treatment are critical for the interpretation of the results. Difficulty to reach significance is not only an issue for complementary therapies, but also for drug trials or other kinds of therapies.

Keywords Tinnitus • Complementary • Acupuncture • TENS • Manipulations • Nutrition • Metabolic • Mindfulness

M. Mazzoli (✉)
ENT – Otosurgery Department, Azienda Ospedaliera di Padova, Via Giustiniani 2, 35128 Padova, Italy
e-mail: manuela.mazzoli@gmail.com

Abbreviations

CIC	Chloride ion channels
CoQ	Coenzyme Q
MBSR	Mindfulness-Based Stress Reduction
MEG	Magnetic Electroencephalography
MSG	Monosodium glutamate
NADPH	Nicotinamide adenine dinucleotide phosphate
NGF	Neural growth factor
NMDA	N-methyl-D-aspartate
NOX-3	NADPH oxidase
OAE	Otoacoustic emissions
ROS	Reactive oxygen species
TENS	Transcutaneous electrical neural stimulation
THI	Tinnitus handicap inventory
TCM	Traditional Chinese medicine
TOAE	Transiently evoked otoacoustic emissions
TQ	Tinnitus questionnaire
VAS	Visual analogic scale
VMA	Vanillic mandelic acid

Introduction

So far, no drug or medication has been found to be clearly useful in treating tinnitus. There is, therefore, reason to study other and different complementary therapies, such as acupuncture and herbal therapy, as well as methods that have been found useful in the treatment of other conditions. Physical therapy, osteopathy, nutrition, and hypnosis or mindfulness have been proposed or sought after by patients for the treatment of tinnitus.

This should not be surprising since tinnitus mechanisms are complex and often associated with other symptoms; it

A.R. Møller et al. (eds.), *Textbook of Tinnitus*,
DOI 10.1007/978-1-60761-145-5_92, © Springer Science+Business Media, LLC 2011

typically affects many aspects of a person's life, such as sleep, mood, lifestyle, stress, perceived quality of life, etc.

Before we judge these therapies as inadequate or unproven, we should consider that often in clinical practice there is wide use and acceptance of therapies that do not have any evidence-based efficacy from conventional surveys. For example, two surveys of the treatment used for Ménière's disease showed large differences in the treatment used routinely by different physicians. In one study, Smith and colleagues [1] reported that 52% of ENT physicians treated patients with Ménière's disease using many different medical and surgical therapies with little or no evidence of efficacy. The survey found that 94% of surgeons prescribed betahistine, 63% diuretics, and 71% advised salt restriction to their patients while 52% of surgeons continued to recommend endolyphatic sac decompression and 50% are still inserting a tympanostomy tube (PE tubes) in the eardrum despite suggestions these treatments have only a placebo effect [2].

Also the search for a treatment for tinnitus has been frustrating in all fields, including the more conventional pharmacology (see Chap. 42). This may be due to the lack of understanding of the pathology of tinnitus and of mechanisms underlying the different types of tinnitus in each patient. The fact that "annoyance" can be caused by symptoms such as fear, insomnia, etc., a nonhomogeneous design of the studies and the lack of more sensitive or objective measure for tinnitus and its annoyance are obstacles in the assessment of the efficacy of different treatments.

In this chapter, we review the most commonly used complementary therapies and different approaches aimed at reducing tinnitus annoyance. These are possibilities, at times promising, that should be explored in rigorous trials in order to understand if such treatments would benefit the tinnitus sufferers.

Physical Treatment

Acupuncture

Traditional Chinese medicine (TCM) is a complex and sophisticated diagnostic and therapeutic method used for the last 3,000–4,000 years, for which the Federal and Drug Administration (FDA) and the scientific community have approved the efficacy in the cure of

several conditions [3]. According to TCM, the body is an intercorrelated system, and a healthy condition is obtained when all physiological functions are in a dynamic balance within the body and between body and environment (climate, food, physical activity, etc.). This concept in modern terms is defined as homeostasis. TCM treatment, that can include acupuncture or herbal pharmacology, is personalized for the patient since the same symptoms can arise from different types of unbalances.

According to classical textbooks of TCM, for acute tinnitus a cure can be attempted, it is more difficult to reduce chronic tinnitus (symptom of a long lasting unbalance in the body), with either acupuncture or herbal therapy [4].

Several studies have been done using a scientific approach to verify the efficacy of acupuncture in tinnitus therapy. Park and colleagues [5] reviewed 33 papers on the treatment of tinnitus with acupuncture. Most of these studies [6] did not report clinical trial, of the remaining, five were not randomized and only six included a control group in the trial. The results of these latter studies seem to indicate that acupuncture may be effective in some patients, although conclusions on the efficacy of acupuncture for tinnitus treatment cannot be drawn. In fact, in these studies, the participants who reported an improvement after acupuncture ranged between 8–84% [7–10], but in some studies the results were not significantly different from a control group [11, 12].

An interesting study by Podoshin and colleagues [10] compared the effect of three different treatments for tinnitus: acupuncture, biofeedback, and cinnarizine. Patients with known pathologic conditions, such as Ménière's disease, vestibular schwannoma, or otosclerosis, were excluded. Sixty individuals with idiopathic subjective tinnitus were randomly divided into five groups to receive one of the three treatments mentioned above or placebo. Fifty-eight participants completed the study. Assessment was by subjective severity rating for tinnitus disturbance during activity and rest and by tinnitus matching. Although there was a nonsignificant trend toward the improvement in tinnitus disturbance in the acupuncture group, the percentage of participants who were improved with acupuncture (30%) was greater than the percentage of participants who were improved with cinnarizine (10%) or with either placebo biofeedback (0%) or placebo cinnarizine (10%), but less than with biofeedback (50%). Tinnitus matching showed no objective difference between either one of the three treatments and placebo.

In these studies, the design varied and methodologies of the treatments given to the participants were different (electrical, traditional, auricular acupuncture). In acupuncture, the treatment is often tailored to the participant's individual needs. The tinnitus of the participants in these studies varied; the participants were not divided into subgroups according to such factors as their hearing status or whether their tinnitus was acute or chronic, with or without somatic components, etc. The measures of tinnitus discomfort were highly subjective – only visual analog scales (VAS) were used. However, tinnitus questionnaires were not used, nor were anxiety questionnaires used in the evaluation. It is therefore difficult to draw definite conclusions on the efficacy of acupuncture treatment for tinnitus based on these earlier studies.

More recently, papers describing studies that were more rigorously designed, using a more conventional approach to tinnitus research, have been published.

Jackson et al. [13] described a rigorously designed study with a small series of six participants with chronic tinnitus (longer than 6 months) using an individualized treatment approach to obtain the best treatment according to TCM principles. This study found improvement in most of the parameters analyzed for most of the participants (loudness, pitch, THI, the number of waking hours affected by tinnitus, and the quality of sleep). The oldest person in the group (79 years) who had had tinnitus for 20 years did not improve, while the person who improved the most, was the youngest in the group with shortest duration of tinnitus. This is similar to what has been found in other studies analyzing other types of treatment, mainly that individuals who have had tinnitus for a long period have poor outcomes of treatment (see Chap. 10). The sample in this study was too small to draw definite conclusions.

In a study by Zhou and colleagues [14] similar conclusions were recorded on a greater sample (140 participants who had both hearing loss and tinnitus). In this study, neural growth factor (NGF) was injected into selected acupoints on channels that, according to TCM, connect to the ears. The control group received intramuscular injections of vitamin B1 and B12. The study found an overall improvement regarding both hearing and tinnitus in 78.6% of the treatment group and in 31.8% of the controls ($p < 0.05$). The effect of the treatment was especially good in patients with milder hearing impairment, those with recent onset of the symptoms and younger age, thus confirming other studies showing that tinnitus that has lasted a short time is more likely to get favorable results of treatment.

In a study by Okada et al. [15], acute tinnitus improved significantly more in the acupuncture treatment group compared to the sham acupuncture measured using a VAS scale. Average duration of symptom relief (90.24 ± 77.5 h) varied from 106.9 h in the study group to 72.3 h in controls. Eight participants (10.5%) reported improved quality of sleep – not only four in the study group, but also four among the controls – and the authors suggest the use of acupuncture for the relief of acute tinnitus.

Acupuncture indeed seems to have a direct effect on the function of the inner ear objectively measured with otoacoustic emissions (OAE). In a study by De Azevedo et al. [16], 38 patients with tinnitus were randomized between treatment and sham acupuncture. Transient otoacoustic emission (TOAE) were measured in the two groups before and after the treatment as well as contra lateral suppression. After the treatment with acupuncture, the amplitude of TOAEs increased significantly while in the sham group there was no significant increase. They also found higher suppression of the tinnitus after the acupuncture session compared with the sham group.

These later studies are promising and emphasize the importance of rigorous study design. The participants in the studies of treatment for tinnitus should be divided in appropriate subgroups to better identify the kinds of tinnitus that can respond best to acupuncture treatment. It is also worthy to consider that it has been widely demonstrated that many somatic complaints can be treated successfully with acupuncture [17–20]. Therefore, if there are somatic components to the onset or modulation of the tinnitus, such as neck or head trauma or whiplash, or if there are chronic inflammatory problems in the neck and upper back or head, acupuncture may be a treatment of choice.

Physical Therapies

Several studies have shown evidence that the somatosensory system of the upper cervical region and head is involved in some forms of tinnitus (see Chaps. 9 and 10). Studies have shown that tinnitus can arise directly from a disorder of the head and upper neck through the activation of the somatosensory system, which can trigger or modulate the tinnitus in 64–80%

of the participants [6, 21–28]. Other studies have shown that tinnitus can be evoked or modulated by pressure on painful trigger points in the upper back, neck, or shoulders [29].

Transcutaneous Electrical Nervous Stimulation

The transcutaneous electrical nervous stimulation (TENS) is a clinical form of electrical stimulation of the somatosensory system. It is the electrotherapy most commonly used in physiotherapy for pain, muscle contractions, and inflammation in several neural and osteo articular conditions as well as those affecting tendons and ligaments (see Chap. 15).

There are few reports on the application of somatosensory stimulation for treating tinnitus and the results of studies of the efficacy of this treatment are still controversial (see Chap. 14).

Kapkin et al. [30] reported a rate of tinnitus worsening after TENS therapy of 16.6% (7/42) with 42.8% (6/14) in the placebo, and the rate of improvement after therapy was 42.8% (18/42). However, an improvement was seen in 28.5% (4/14) of the controls. This is in agreement with other studies that showed electrical stimulation of the median nerve at the wrist could cause tinnitus to increase in some individuals and decrease in others [31].

Herraiz et al. [155] reports the improvement of tinnitus in 46% of their sample of 26 individuals with tinnitus receiving 2 h treatment daily (alternated stimuli, 150 pps, pulse duration of 10 µs, 0–60 mA amplitude, mean amplitude 27 mA) for 10 days. If tinnitus was intermittent and not associated with other symptoms, results were more consistent. In this study, participants were selected having some clinical clues to somatic influence on tinnitus, such as painful trigger points and modulation of tinnitus with head and neck or jaw movements.

In a study by Aydemir et al. [32], after TENS treatment the subjective improvement of tinnitus measured by VAS scale was only marginally significant ($p=0.059$). However, after electrical stimulation, there was statistically significant improvement regarding tinnitus severity scores, tinnitus handicap inventory scores, NHP fatigue, social isolation, and emotional problems scores. Many parameters were measured by the SF-36 ($p<0.05$), such as physical functioning, general health, vitality, social functioning, role limitations due to emotional problems and mental health.

Manipulations

Many of the manipulative treatments used for musculoskeletal disorders, such as chiropractic manipulations, osteopathy, and massages may be considered in tinnitus treatment not only in patients with somatic tinnitus, but also in some other patients because these therapies may elicit reflex effects on nonmusculoskeletal symptoms.

In published data, chiropractic manipulations are used mainly for musculoskeletal disorders, but the improvements of nonmusculoskeletal symptoms after chiropractic manipulations have been described to occur in 2–10% of all patients treated and by 3–27% of those who complained to have nonmusculoskeletal problems [33, 34]. The success of spinal manipulative therapy, particularly of the atlanto-occipital joint, can be up to 82% of patients with dizziness (46% total relief, 36% high improvement). In contrast, only 10% of patients with tinnitus showed an improvement according to one study ($p<0.001$) [35].

In some cases, cervical problems, such as cervical degeneration or cervical instability, can present with symptoms mimicking Ménière's disease: dizziness, fluctuating hearing loss, and tinnitus [36–38]. Cervical problems in the generation of tinnitus should be taken into account, especially in the elderly with a later onset of symptoms.

Osteopathy is a well-known system founded by Dr. A.T. Still (1828–1917), focusing on the diagnosis, treatment, prevention, and rehabilitation of musculoskeletal disorders and the effects of these conditions on a patient's general health. Osteopathy is based on the principle that the body has the ability to heal. Osteopathic care focuses on strengthening the musculoskeletal systems to treat existing conditions and prevent illness. This holistic approach ensures that all treatment is tailored to the individual patient. According to osteopathic textbooks, the therapy for tinnitus aims at the identification of structural problems to correct; the relaxation of muscles especially in the neck, upper back, and TMJ; and the improvement of lymphatic local circulation.

In a randomized study comparing osteopathic with electrical stimulation of the skin over the neck, shoulders, and upper back (dynamic TENS, InterX®) for tinnitus, we have found the treatments reduced tinnitus annoyance measured as THI scores and VAS (for perceived loudness, percentage of time of annoyance and perceived quality of life) in 60% of the participants who were treated with osteopathic manipulations and in 46% of those treated with electrical stimulation, with a longer duration of the effects in the osteopathic treated group (Mazzoli et al.: in preparation). The benefit from both the osteopathic treatment and the electrical stimulation was more evident in patients with associated postural or somatic problems. No benefit was seen in the participants with noise-induced tinnitus.

The use of osteopathy could be useful not only in somatic tinnitus, but also in individuals with tinnitus that mimics chronic pain since osteopathic treatment can interfere with the mechanisms of modulation of pain [39].

Many individuals with tinnitus can modulate or evoke their tinnitus by the manipulation of myofascial trigger points [40, 41]. Trigger points are small hypersensitive areas of skeletal muscles in which a tight muscular band is often present. These small areas can be painful either spontaneously or after mechanical stimulation and can raise local or referred pain [42]. In the presence of painful trigger points, tinnitus can be an isolated symptom or be part of the so called myofascial syndrome, usually affecting the upper back or neck, and accompanied by several physical symptoms and clinical findings, such as sleep disturbance, lacrimation, vertigo, and skin reddening which all greatly affect the quality of life [43]. Trigger points can also be found in individuals who report no modulation of their tinnitus with the manipulation of trigger points. The presence of chronic pain in the areas of trigger points should be regarded as a characteristic that seems to correlate with modulated tinnitus compared to nonmodulated tinnitus [28], pointing once more to common mechanisms of action between pain and tinnitus (see Chap. 14).

Voluntary Exercise

If there is clinical evidence for somatic modulation of tinnitus, especially in noncontinuous tinnitus triggered,

in particular, by some movements, exercising those movements can lead to habituation and a reduction of the tinnitus annoyance or to the disappearance of the symptom as described by Sanchez et al. [6]. In their study, they evaluated 38 individuals with tinnitus triggered or exacerbated by specific movements of the head and neck, as well as the shoulders or jaw. The participants were then instructed to exercise that movement for 10 min for 2 months and report the changes in their tinnitus and whether the exercise changed the pattern of tinnitus modulation. The participants were tested in different visits and the test retest was reliable for the modulation.

Influence on Tinnitus from Nutrition

Tinnitus can be triggered by drugs and is listed among the undesired effect of several medications (http://www.t-gone.com/tinnitus/drugs.asp) such as aspirin, diuretics, pain medications, etc. Despite this, there is little scientific evidence regarding metabolic or dietary treatments for tinnitus.

There are indications that the ear is particularly sensitive to nutritional and metabolic factors, specifically, several dietary changes are recommended for Ménière's disease, such as reducing salt intake or eliminating allergenic foods [44–46]. Some individuals with Ménière's disease may experience the increase of symptoms when drinking coffee or eating chocolate and other foods – similar to individuals with migraine [47] – and diet alone can work well in reducing the symptoms.

Even though up to now there are few scientific studies on metabolites or nutritional factors in tinnitus, we can try to analyze some substances that might be involved in triggering or modulating tinnitus.

Sodium Chloride

It is also known that salt intake may affect relapses in Ménière's disease [48]. Some individuals with tinnitus report that after excessive salt intake their tinnitus increases. Sodium chloride may influence the inner ear in several ways: through its action on the blood pressure, inducing vasoconstriction in the cochlea, increasing renal fluid retention, or acting on specific ion channels changing the composition of endolymph and therefore affecting the inner ear function. There is considerable relationship between impaired renal function and hearing loss [49]. Some inherited renal diseases are accompanied by hearing disorders, such as Alport syndrome and Bartter syndrome [50]. Also, the incidence of hearing loss is higher among patients with chronic renal failure than in the general population [51]. The renal adverse effects of some drugs (e.g., aminoglycosides and loop diuretics) may be accompanied by ototoxicity. Kidney and inner ear tissues are related immunologically, biochemically, and functionally. For example, the stria vascularis and the tubular epithelium in the kidney have similar ion transport processes [51] and the chloride ion channels of the ClC-K family are expressed exclusively in the kidneys and ears [52] and are involved in NaCl renal tubular reabsorption.

Monosodium Glutamate

Monosodium glutamate (MSG) is a sodium salt of the nonessential amino acid glutamic acid. It is used as a food additive and in its free form is commonly marketed as a flavor enhancer. It has the HS code 29224220 and E number E621. It is also included under the denomination "natural flavorings." It is thought to cause the "Chinese restaurant syndrome" the symptoms that may include headache, throbbing of the head and ears, dizziness, tinnitus, lightheadedness, a feeling of facial pressure, tightness of the jaw, burning or tingling sensations over parts of the body, chest pain, and back pain, although mechanisms are yet unclear and the reality of the syndrome is controversial. [53, 54].

Glutamate is an excitatory neurotransmitter and is released in high quantity when hair cells are damaged by noise, or when ototoxic medications or infections affect the inner ear. An excess amount of glutamate is released, which leads to cell and neuron death mediated by high Ca^{++} flux into cells [55, 56].

No studies have been published that evaluate the real effect of MSG taken orally on the inner ear or auditory pathways, but damages to other organs have been consistently described in animal models [57–59]. In particular, it can induce diabetes [60], which is associated with increased risk for inner ear disorders and tinnitus.

Glucose

Several studies report a higher incidence of tinnitus and hearing loss in up to 27–76% of individuals who have diabetes, subclinical diabetes, or abnormal glucose metabolism, such as hyperinsulinemia (insulin resistance) or hypoglycemia [61–65]. The improvement of tinnitus after a diabetic-like diet has been reported [63].

Glucose metabolism can influence the inner ear in several ways. The inner ear, like the brain, does not have energy reserves. Its metabolism depends directly on the supply of oxygen and nutrients, including glucose from the blood supply. Alterations in glucose metabolism, therefore, have the potential to disturb the workings of the inner ear. Altered glucose metabolism can cause damage to several systems leading to peripheral neuropathy or microvascular disease. Fukushima et al. [66] described histological findings of the cochlea in individuals with diabetes type 2 that showed the walls of the vessels of the basilar membrane and stria vascularis in all turns were significantly thicker in individuals treated with either insulin or oral hypoglycemic than those of controls. The stria vascularis was atrophied in most turns of the cochlea in the insulin group and in the lower and middle turn of the oral hypoglycemic group. The difference was significant compared to the controls. The loss of cochlear outer hair cells was significantly greater in the lower and upper basal turns in both diabetic groups while no significant difference was found in the number of spiral ganglion cells or inner hair cells between groups.

High levels of circulating glucose and hyperinsulinemia can also influence renal sodium reabsorption leading to salt sensitive hypertension [66–68], which could be mediated by oxidative stress factors [69, 70].

High levels of insulin are influenced by carbohydrate intake. It is therefore important to identify individuals at risk, that may include overweight patients with a craving for sugar or carbohydrates, who get lightheaded when fasting. Also blood testing could present hyperglycemia, although most frequently fasting glycemia can be normal while abnormal levels of glucose load curve response, hyperinsulinemia, hyperlipidemia, increased plasma aldosterone concentrations, or microalbuminuria, and sometimes chronic renal disease can be found.

Artificial Sweeteners

Discovered in 1965, aspartame is a low-calorie sweetener with a sugar-like taste but is approximately 200 times sweeter than sucrose. Aspartame is unique among low-calorie sweeteners in that it is completely broken down by the body to its components – the amino acids aspartic acid, phenylalanine, and a small amount of methanol. The safety of this aspartame is still controversial [71–74].

It has been reported that the consumption of aspartame could cause neurological and behavioral disturbances in certain individuals [73, 74]. Headaches, insomnia, and seizures are also some of the neurological effects that have been encountered, and these may be accredited to changes in regional brain concentrations of catecholamines (norepinephrine, epinephrine, and dopamine) [73, 74]. Consumption of large doses of aspartame in a single bolus dose will have an effect on some biochemical parameters, including plasma amino acid levels and brain neurotransmitter levels. The data from extensive investigations in humans into the possibility of neurotoxic effects of aspartame, in general, do not support the hypothesis that aspartame in the human diet will affect nervous system function, learning, or behavior [72].

Nevertheless, the use of aspartame or other sweeteners should be careful in specific patients, such as individuals with migraine, insomnia, dizziness, and possibly tinnitus. Even for diabetic patients, who seem to be the ideal consumers of the product, there are some concerns since aspartame intake has been associated to increase in baseline glucose and insulin levels in diabetes type 2 patients [71, 75].

Antioxidants

The suggestion that antioxidants should be used for the prevention or the repair of damage to the labyrinth comes from the studies on ototoxicity, although so far no clinical trials on patients with tinnitus have been published.

The most common ototoxic drugs in clinical use are aminoglycosides antibiotics, platinum-based chemotherapeutic agents (cisplatin and carboplatin), loop diuretics, macrolide antibiotics, and antimalarials. It is well established that oxidative reaction and free radicals in the cochlea are involved in causing damage to the cochlea from drugs and acoustic trauma [75–81].

Both aminoglycosides and cisplatin ototoxicity appear to involve the production of reactive oxygen species (ROS) in target tissues in the inner ear by activating the nicotinamide adenine dinucleotide phosphate (NADPH) oxidase, NOX-3, an enzyme unique to the cochlea. ROS can then deplete cochlear tissues of antioxidant protective molecules, for example, glutathione and antioxidant enzymes. This leads to a cascade resulting in oxidation of lipids, increased calcium influx, and apoptosis in cells of the cochlea [75, 78, 79]. The upregulation of endogenous protective mechanisms in the cochlea or the treatment with exogenous compounds reduces ototoxicity. Experimental studies in animals have shown that a variety of antioxidants, including aspirin, *Ginkgo biloba*, inhibitors of caspase-3, and caspase-9 can attenuate the ototoxicity of either aminoglycosides or cisplatin [79–82].

Similar mechanisms involving free radicals mediated damage can occur also in the nervous system at the level of the dorsal cochlear nucleus as well as inferior colliculus [83, 84]. Also, there is some evidence that psychological stress may cause oxidative damage in vivo, both in animal models and in humans [85–88].

A combination of antioxidant agents (vitamins A, C, and E) acts in synergy with magnesium to effectively prevent noise-induced trauma [87]. Neither the antioxidant agents nor magnesium used alone seems able to reduce noise-induced hearing loss or sensory cell death. In combination, however, they are highly effective in reducing both hearing loss and cell death, even with treatment initiated just 1 h prior to noise exposure [77, 89, 90]. These mechanisms could be involved also in aging and/or vascular problems associated with diabetes or inflammation generating tinnitus.

Preliminary results of a study by [91] on the effect of administration of Nanoquinone, a source of Coenzyme Q10 (CoQ10), on chronic tinnitus found no general improvement of tinnitus after increased CoQ10 levels. However, patients with a low CoQ10 level before treatment and with a significant increase in the CoQ10 level afterward showed a decrease of the total tinnitus score and of all its dimensions, except for emotional distress. CoQ10 is a 2, 3-dimethoxy, 5-methyl, 6-polyisoprene parabenzoquinone, and is located in all membranes throughout the cell. The highest concentrations are found in the heart, the liver, the kidneys, and the pancreas. It is an endogenously synthesized substance involved in a variety of essential processes, such as influence on the mitochondrial electron transport chain. However, it also appears to have membrane-stabilizing properties and to act as an antioxidant in conjunction with vitamin E [92].

Zinc

One of the few nutrients that have been studied in relation to tinnitus is zinc. Deficiency can be related to tinnitus, especially in the elderly [93]. Zinc deficiency affects many organ systems where it plays an essential role in numerous biochemical pathways, including the integumentary, gastrointestinal, central nervous system, immune, skeletal, and reproductive systems and is needed for maintaining DNA integrity [94, 95]).

The brain has the highest zinc content in the body [96] and is implicated in the function of glutaminergic neurons [97]. It has also been reported that hypozincemia activates the N-methyl-D-aspartate (NMDA) receptor, of the glutamate family, which may play an important role in the induction of epileptic discharge [97, 98]. Interestingly, it has been found that behavioral stress can modulate cellular influx of zinc changing the pattern of neural elements firing, especially in the hippocampus [96]. For these reasons, zinc has been proposed as a likely modulator of tinnitus.

Ochi and colleagues [99] have found that hypozincemia was related to the perceived loudness of tinnitus. However, in their study the average hearing sensitivities of patients with hypozincemia did not differ significantly from those of patients with normal serum zinc levels, suggesting zinc deficiency is likely related to tinnitus originating more centrally rather than hearing loss due to a peripheral disorder. On the other hand, the authors excluded people older than 59 from the study [99], and zinc deficiency increases over the age of 60 [93].

Most authors suggest administration of 50–66 mg of elemental zinc daily for individuals with hypozincemia [99–101]. The method by which zinc levels are measured can affect the definition of hypozincemia and may influence clinical decisions. Less than 2% of zinc in the organism is found free in plasma and most of the zinc in the body is located outside cells [93, 102]. Zinc level in the serum is therefore not a good measure for assessing zinc balance in the organism. In plasma, zinc is primarily bound to albumin and copper, and zinc is reciprocal in the serum. Because of this reverse and competitive correlation between zinc and copper, serum copper and albumin levels should also be assessed to prevent the risk that individuals given zinc supplementation develop hematologic abnormalities that occur in individuals with low copper levels [100].

Herbal Therapy

In TCM, there is a complex and sophisticated pharmacopeia where herbal remedies are knowledgeably mixed in combinations not only to obtain the desired synergic effect, but also to reduce side effects or correct the effect of specific ingredients. In TCM, the symptom is cured by reducing the functional unbalance that is assumed to cause the symptoms, and this can be different from patient to patient. A few randomized control studies on the treatment of tinnitus have been reported in the Chinese literature regarding the use of herbal drugs, claiming improvement in 40–55% of the participants, [103, 104]. Similar studies have been reported in behavioral animal models [105]. These studies have so far not been replicated at an international level.

Herbal medications should be considered as drugs since they contain pharmacological active substances in the form of phytocomplexes, some of which can be beneficial while others are toxic. Most modern medication derive from the isolation of the active substances (e.g., digitalis), and the herbal medications are often as effective as their synthetic counterpart [106, 107]. Nevertheless, investigations of the effects of herbal remedies on tinnitus, like other potential drug treatments, have often suffered from the lack of useful animal models and systematic clinical trials employing double-blind and placebo-controlled designs.

Ginkgo biloba

G. biloba leaves have been used therapeutically by the Chinese for centuries for the treatment of asthma and bronchitis and have also been used for tinnitus relief. The active ingredient has been isolated as EGb-761 containing 24% flavonoids, 7% proanthocyanidins, and 6% terpenoids. The flavonoids are mainly flavonol-glycosides with antioxidant properties, while the terpenoid fraction contains ginkgolides, sesquiterpene, and bilobalide. Ginkgolide B, in particular, has potent platelet-activating factor (PAF) receptor antagonist properties. Many of the CNS effects of EGb-761 have been attributed to the combination of its antioxidant and PAF receptor antagonist actions. It is also a vasodilator and along with its antioxidant properties these are the reasons for thinking that it would be useful in the management of tinnitus [108].

Despite the claims that *G. biloba* extracts have some efficacy in treating tinnitus [109–111], there is very little objective evidence to support this. Hilton and Stuart [112] reviewed the clinical evidence relating to the use of *G. biloba* by individuals with tinnitus and concluded that there were no reliable data on which to base a conclusion, due to the methodological shortcomings of the available studies. In particular, very few studies have employed double-blind, placebo-controlled designs, where possible experimenter bias and patient expectation can be controlled. Where these sorts of controls have been used, the results have usually been negative [113, 114].

The use of *G. biloba* extracts can lead to potential undesired effects. Due to the fact that these extracts have vasodilator effects, combined with drugs, such as aspirin, they could potentially increase bleeding [114].

Black Cohosh

Black Cohosh (*Cimicifuga racemosa*), a buttercup plant grown in North America, is a popular preparation for the treatment of menopausal and other symptoms, including fatigue, neuralgia, rheumatism, sore throat, asthma, bronchial spasms, bronchitis, and whooping cough [115]. Black Cohosh has been used for centuries by women to stimulate menstrual flow, ease the strains of childbirth, and confer relief from premenstrual syndrome and menopause. With its mildly sedative and relaxing effect, Black Cohosh has been used also as a tinnitus herb to treat anxiety, nervousness, and chronic tinnitus. Black Cohosh may indeed have a dopaminergic effects and serotonin-

binding properties in the brain. As a central nervous system depressant, Black Cohosh directly inhibits vasomotor centers involved with inner ear balance and hearing. As such, Black Cohosh has been used clinically for relief of tinnitus [116], although clinical trials on the therapeutic effect for tinnitus are missing.

There are few known health concerns regarding Black Cohosh, and consuming large amounts (over 5 g per day) is known to cause dizziness, vomiting, lowered blood pressure, limb pain, and can damage the liver [117].

Ligustrum

Ligustrum (*Ligustrum lucidum*) has been advocated by traditional herbalists for the management of tinnitus. It is considered, without scientific proof, to have a powerful liver and kidney protecting function; it supports adrenal function and has been found to have hypoglycemic, hypolipidemic, and antioxidant efficacy, and its use has been suggested for individuals with diabetes [118]. The recommended dosage for tinnitus is 400 mg three times per day. In this dosage, there are no known side effects from administration of this herb. No clinical trials have been published that have assessed its efficacy in tinnitus.

Other herbs have been suggested as possible remedies for tinnitus including: Mullein (*Verbascum densiflorum*); *Pulsatilla*; *Lycium* fruit (*Lycium barbarum* or *Lycium chinense*); *Cornus* (*Cornus officinalis*), only in association with Chinese fox glove root and Chinese yam; *Cuscuta chinensis* seeds are used alone and in combination with astragalus seeds (*Astragalus complanatus*), but no scientific studies of the effect on tinnitus of these herbs have been published for these herbs.

Unconventional Treatment

Mindfulness

Mindfulness involves bringing one's awareness to focus on experience within the mind at the present moment (from the past, the future, or the mechanical stream of consciousness). Mindfulness, such as meditation, yoga, Tai Chi, breathing techniques, etc., has been used in practice of spiritual healing in parts of the world for more than 5,000 years. During the last 40 years, the practice of meditation has become increasingly popular in Western countries as a complementary mind–body therapeutic strategy for a variety of health-related problems. By paying close attention to the present experience, practitioners begin to see both inner and outer aspects of reality as aspects of the mind in a nonjudgmental way, learning to observe without the continuous internal commentary or judgment. However, mindfulness does not have to be constrained to a formal meditation session. Mindfulness is an activity that can be done at any time and can be learned through several practical techniques that help reconnecting to the present moment each time the mechanical stream of thoughts drives us into our subjective mental "virtual reality."

Presumably, via activation of limbic system parasympathetic pathways [119], mindfulness techniques have been shown to shift the balance between sympathetic and parasympathetic activation toward the parasympathetic in activity as studied in short- and long-term practitioners compared to controls. This included a reduction in heart, respiratory and pulse rates; of systolic blood pressure and oxygen metabolism; of urinary vanillic mandelic acid (VMA); and increases of skin resistance because of reduced sympathetic activity [120–122]. These physiological alterations are indicators of increased parasympathetic and decreased sympathetic activation [123] and therefore physiological relaxation that has been related to stress relief and may have a role in the prevention of stress-related illness, such as respiratory illness and hypertensive cardiovascular disease [124].

Also, mindfulness training has been found to improve chronic pain and associated symptoms [125–130], and given the similarities between tinnitus and chronic pain (see Chap. 14) [131], a beneficial effect of mindfulness in tinnitus patients can be expected.

Furthermore, there is evidence that mindfulness-based stress reduction (MBSR) programs are useful not only in treating chronic depression and anxiety problems [132, 133], but also in reducing depression relapses [134–136] and improving the measures of sleep quality or duration [137, 138]. Affective symptoms may increase the level of tinnitus annoyance.

Also, there is evidence that the acceptance of the symptom obtained with mindfulness training has a therapeutic effect on tinnitus perceived annoyance [139, 140].

A marked reduction in alpha waves (8–12 Hz) at magnetic electro encephalography (MEG) recordings and an increase in delta waves (1.5–4 Hz) have been observed in individuals with tinnitus, especially when recorded from the temporal and left frontal areas. These anomalies have been associated with distress [141, 142, 156]. Meditation, on the other hand, causes increased theta coherence as well as increased alpha power [143]. The emergence of the slow (delta) waves in the attention-related frontal regions that occur during meditation provides strong support for the hypothesis that meditative states are not the same as relaxation states and that attentional processing is involved [144, 156]. This indicates that MBSR can be useful for the treatment of tinnitus since they have significantly higher everyday cognitive failures than nontinnitus patients, and this is related to the control of attentional processes [146]. Mindfulness training indeed improves attention skills possibly also reducing tinnitus-induced cognitive insufficiencies [147].

Hypnosis

Erickson's hypnosis [148, 149][1] includes relaxation and emotional management techniques. The hypnotic trance leads to a modified state of consciousness characterized by a shift of hemisphere dominance from the logic dominant to the analogical dominant. The purpose of hypnosis, according to Erickson, was that of having access to the subconscious potential and natural learning ability while avoiding limited conditioned schemes [150].

---

[1] Erickson's hypnosis: Hypnosis is a mental state (state theory) or set of attitudes (non-state theory), usually induced by a procedure known as a hypnotic induction, which is commonly composed of a series of preliminary instructions and suggestions.

Milton H. Erickson, M.D. (1901–1980) was one of the most influential post-war hypnotherapists. He wrote several books and journal articles on the subject. During the 1960s, Erickson was responsible for popularizing a new branch of hypnotherapy, which became known as "Ericksonian hypnotherapy" Ericksonian hypnotherapy, eventually characterized by, amongst other things, the absence of a formal hypnotic inductions, the use of indirect suggestion, a "metaphor" (actually they were analogies, rather than "metaphors"), confusion techniques, and double binds (Erickson, 1977; Barker, 1986).

A few studies have been published regarding the treatment of tinnitus with hypnosis and the results seem promising. Ross and colleagues [151] reported the results of a study with 392 participants who were treated for 28 days with hypnosis. The tinnitus questionnaire (TQ) scores decreased in 90.5% of the participants who had subacute tinnitus and in 88.3% of those with chronic tinnitus. The improvement of the TQ score at the end of therapy was 15.9/14.1 points, which was highly significant. Effect sizes in the treatment groups (0.94/0.80) were superior to those in the waiting-list controls (0.14/0.23). The TQ score remained stable in the 1-year follow-up controls. Significant improvement in the quality of life has been observed after the treatment but depends on initial level of tinnitus severity.

In another study of hypnosis treatment on tinnitus, Maudoux et al. [152] showed that the THI score improved from 60.23 before hypnosis therapy to 16.9 at the end of the treatment, which was highly significant ($p \leq 0.005$).

Other studies have shown that greater success of hypnotherapy was achieved in individuals who did not have hearing loss associated to their tinnitus [153]. This means that a subgroup of individuals would benefit more than others. The paper by Cope [154] provides a review of peer reviewed studies of the efficacy of hypnosis in the treatment of tinnitus.

Conclusions

Many of the complementary therapies described in the literature for treating tinnitus are promising, but the mechanisms of the beneficial effect are not known. Many of the studies that have been published indicate the importance of identifying subgroups of different types of tinnitus that would respond better to specific treatments. Methodology and study design are important to obtain clear indications of the efficacy of the therapies that are studied. Many of the tests that are used are not sensitive enough for tinnitus annoyance since THI questionnaires do not correspond to loudness or pitch of tinnitus, and are not sensitive enough. These issues contribute to the difficulty of defining "improvement" after tinnitus therapy and to compare the results between studies.

References

1. Smith, PF, Zheng, Y and Darlington, CL, Ginkgo biloba extracts for tinnitus: more hype than hope? J Ethnopharmacology, 2005 100:95–99
2. Kim, HH, Wiet, RJ and Battista, RA Trends in the diagnosis and the management of Meniere's disease: results of a survey Otolaryngol Head Neck Surg, 2005 132(5):722–726
3. Birch, S Hesselink, JK Jonkman, FAM, Hekker, TAM and Bos, A, Clinical research on acupuncture: part 1 what have reviews of the efficacy and safety of acupuncture told us so far? J Altern Complement Med, 2004 10(3):468–480
4. Maciocia, G, Acufeni In: La clinica in Medicina Cinese G Maciocia, Editor 1995 p307–316
5. Park, J, White, AR, Enst, E, Efficacy of acupuncure as a treatment for tinnitus: a systematic review Arch Otolaryngol Head Neck Surg, 2000 126:489–492
6. Sanchez, TG, Guerra, GC and Lorenzi, MC, The influence of voluntary muscle contractions upon the onset and modulation of tinnitus Audiol Neurootol, 2002 7:370–375
7. Marks, NJ, Emery and Onisiphorou, C, A controlled trial of acupuncture in tinnitus J Laryngol Otol, 1984 98: 1103–1109
8. Furugard, S, Hedin, PJ, Eggertz, A and Laurent, C, Acupuncture worth trying in severe tinnitus Lakartidningen, 1998 95:1922–1928
9. Axelsson, A and Ringdahl, A, Tinnitus: a study of its prevalence and characteristics Br J Audiol, 1989 23:53–62
10. Podoshin, L, Ben-David, Y, Fradis, M, Gerstel, R and Felner, H, Idiopathic subjective tinnitus treated by biofeedback, acupuncture and drug therapy Ear Nose Throat J, 1991 70:284–289
11. Hansen, PE, Hansen, JH and Bentzen, O, Acupuncture treatment of chronic unilateral tinnitus: a double-blind crossover trial Clin Otolaryngol, 1982 7:325–329
12. Vilholm, OJ, Møller, K and Jorgensen, K, Effect of traditional Chinese acupuncture on severe tinnitus: a double blind study, placebo-controlled clinical investigation with open therapeutic control Br J Audiol, 1998 32: 197–204
13. Jackson, A, MacPherson, H and Hahn, S, Acupuncure for tinnitus: A series of six n=1 controlled trials Compl Ther Med, 2006 14:39–46
14. Zhou, F, Wu, P, Wang, L, Wang, H, Zhangs, S, Lin, Y, Zhong, H and Chen, Y, The NGF Point-injection for treatment of the sound-perceiving nerve deafness and tinnitus in 68 cases J Tradit Chin Med, 2009 29(1):39–42
15. Okada, DM, Onishi, ET, Chami, FI, Borin, A, Cassola, N and Guerreiro, VM, Acupuncture for tinnitus immediate relief Rev Bras Otorrinolaringol, 2006 72(2):182–186
16. De Azevedo, RF, Chiari, BM, Okada, DM and Onishi, ET, Impact of acupuncture on otoacoustic emissions in patients with tinnitus Rev Bras Otorrinolaringol, 2007 73(5):599–607
17. Sator-Katzenschlager, SM, Szeles, JC, Scharbert, G, Michalek-Sauberer, A, Kober, A, Heinze, G and Kozek-Langenecker, SA, Electrical stimulation of auricular acupuncture points is more effective than conventional manual auricular acupuncture in chronic cervical pain: a pilot study Anesth Analg, 2003 97:1469–1473

18. Sator-Katzenschlager, SM, Scharbert, G, Kozek-Langenecker, SA, Szeles, JC, Finster, G, Schiesser, AW, Heinze, G and Kress, HG, The short and long term benefit in chronic low back pain through adjuvant electrical versus manual auricular acupuncture Anesth Analg, 2004 98:1359–1364

19. Witt, CM, Jena, S, Brinkhaus, B, Liecker, B, Wegscheider, K and Willich, SN, Acupuncture for patients with chronic neck pain Pain, 2006 125(1–2):98–106

20. Reinhold, T, Witt, CM, Jena, S, Brinkhaus, B and Willich, SN, Quality of life and cost-effectiveness of acupuncture treatment in patients with osteoarthritis pain Eur J Health Econ, 2008 9(3):209–219

21. Tjell, C, Tenenbaum, A and Rosenhall, U, Auditory function in whiplash-associated disorders Scand Audiol, 1999 28(4):203–209

22. Gelb, H, Gelb, ML and Wagner, ML, The relationship of tinnitus to craniocervical mandibular disorders Cranio, 1997 15(2):136–143

23. Herráiz, C, Hernández-Calvin, FJ, Plaza, G, Toledano, A and De Los Santos, G, Multi-sensory interactions in tinnitus: visual evoked potentials and somatosensory stimulation Acta Otorrinolaringol Esp, 2003 54(5):329–336

24. Levine, RA, Abel, M and Cheng, H, CNS somatosensory-auditory interactions elicit or modulate Exp Brain Res, 2003 153:643–648

25. Levine, RA, Somatic tinnitus In: Tinnitus theory and management JB Snow, Editor 2004 p108–204

26. Levine, RA, Nam, EC, Oron, Y and Melcher, JR, Evidence for a tinnitus subgroup responsive to somatosensory based treatment modalities Prog Brain Res, 2007 166:195–207

27. Rowlands, RG, Campbell, IK and Kenyon, GS, Otological and vestibular symptoms in patients with low grade (Quebec grades one and two) whiplash injury J Laryngol Otol, 2009 123(2):182–185

28. Rocha, CA, Sanchez, TG and De Siqueira, TJT, Myofacial trigger point: a possible way of modulating tinnitus Audiol Neurotool, 2008 13:153–160

29. Sanchez, TG, Da Silva-Lima, A, Brandão, AL, Lorenzi, MC and Bento, RF, Somatic modulation of tinnitus: test reliability and results after repetitive muscle contraction training Ann Otol Rhinol Laryngol, 2007 116(1):30–35

30. Kapkin, O, Satar, B and Yetiser, S, Transcutaneous electrical stimulation of subjective tinnitus. A placebo-controlled, randomized and comparative analysis ORL J Otorhinolaryngol Relat Spec, 2008 70(3):156–161

31. Møller, A R, Møller, M B and Yokota, M, Some forms of tinnitus may involve the extralemniscal auditory pathway Laryngoscope, 1992 102: 1165–1171

32. Aydemir, G, Tezer, MS, Borman, P, Bodur, H and Unal, A, Treatment of tinnitus with transcutaneous electrical nerve stimulation improves patients' quality of life J Laryngol Otol, 2006 120(6):442–445

33. Leboeuf-Yde, C, Pedersen, EN, Bryner, P, Cosman, D, Hayek, R, Meeker, WC, Shaik, J, Terrazas, O, Tucker, J and Walsh, M, Self-reported nonmusculoskeletal responses to chiropractic intervention: a multination survey J Manipulative Physiol Ther, 2005 28(5):294–302

34. Hawk, C, Khorsan, R, Lisi, AJ, Ferrance, RJ and Evans, MW, Chiropractic care for nonmusculoskeletal conditions: a systematic review with implications for whole systems research J Altern Complement Med, 2007 13(5):491–512

35. Hülse, M and Hölzl, M, The efficiency of spinal manipulation in otorhinolaryngology. A retrospective long-term study HNO, 2004 52(3):227–234

36. Decher, H, Morbus Meniere and cervical symptoms Arch Otorhinolaryngol, 1976 212:369–374

37. Biesinger, E, Diagnosis and therapy of vertebrogenic vertigo Laryngol Rhinol Otol (Stuttg), 1987 66(1):32–36

38. Kessinger, RC and Boneva, DV, Vertigo, tinnitus, and hearing loss in the geriatric patient J Manipul Physiol Ther, 2000 23(5):352–262

39. Kuchera, ML, Applying osteopathic principles to formulate treatment for patients with chronic pain J Am Osteopathic Assoc, 2007 107(Suppl 10):ES28–ES38

40. Eriksson, M, Gustafsson, S and Axelsson, A, Tinnitus and trigger points: a randomized cross over study In: Proceedings of the Fifth International Tinnitus Seminar, GE Rerich and JA Vernon, Editors 1995 81–83

41. Rocha, CA and Sanchez, TG, Myofascial trigger points: another way of modulating tinnitus Prog Brain Res, 2007 166:209–214

42. Alvarez, DJ and Rockwell, PG, Trigger points: diagnosis and management Am Fam Physician, 2002 65:653–660

43. Sahin, N, Karataş, O, Ozkaya, M, Cakmak, A and Berker, E, Demographics features, clinical findings and functional status in a group of subjects with cervical myofascial pain syndrome Agri, 2008 20(3):14–19

44. Shaver, EF Jr, Allergic management of Meniere disease Arch Otolaryngol, 1975 101(2):96–99

45. Derebery, MJ and Berliner, KI, Prevalence of allergy in Meniere's disease Otolaryngol Head Neck Surg, 2000 123(1):69–75

46. Derebery, MJ, Allergic management of Meniere's disease: an outcome study Otolaryngol Head Neck Surg, 2000 122(2):174–182

47. Folmer, RL, Matin, WH, Shi, Y and Edlefsen, LL, Lifestyle changes for tinnitus self-management In: Tinnitus treatment: clinical protocols RS Tyler, Editor 2006 51–64

48. Jackson, CG, Glasscock, ME, Hughes, GB and Sismanis, A, Medical-management of Menieres disease Ann Otol Rhinol Laryngol, 1981 90:142–147

49. Abbasi, AH, Ramadan, R, Hoffman, A and Abassi, Z, Kidney-ear axis Isr Med Assoc J, 2007 9(11):814–818

50. Izzedine, H, Tankere, F, Launay-Vacher, V and Deray, G, Ear and kidney syndromes: molecular versus clinical approach Kidney Int, 2004 65(2):369–385

51. Lang, F, Vallon, V, Knipper, M and Wangemann, P, Functional significance of channels and transporters expressed in the inner ear and kidney Am J Physiol Cell Physiol, 2007 293:C1187–C1208

52. Peters, TA, Monnens, LA, Cremers, CW and Curfs, JH, Genetic disorders of transporters/channels in the inner ear and their relation to the kidney Ped Nephrol, 2004 19:1194–1201

53. Geha, RS, Beiser, A, Ren, C, Patterson, R, Greenberger, PA, Grammer, LC, Ditto, AM, Harris, KE, Shaughnessy, MA, Yarnold, PR, Corren, J, Saxon, A, Review of alleged reaction to monosodium glutamate and outcome of a multicenter double-blind placebo-controlled study J Nutr, 2000 130(Suppl 4):1058S–1062S

54. Lawrence, DT, Dobmeier, SG, Bechtel, LK, Holstege, CP, Food poisoning Emerg Med Clin North Am, 2007 25(2):357–373

55. Puel, JL, Ruel, J, Guitton, M, Wang, J and Pujol, R, The inner hair cell synaptic complex: physiology, pharmacology and new therapeutic strategies Audiol Neurootol, 2002 7(1):49–54

56. Anne, S, Kisley, LB, Tajuddin, ST, Leahy, P, Alagramam, KN and Megerian CA, Molecular changes associated with the endolymphatic hydrops model Otol Neurotol, 2007 28(6):834–841

57. Dawson, R, Pelleymounter, MA and Millard, UJ, Attenuation of leptin-mediated effects by monosodium glutamate-induced arcade nucleus damages Am J Physiol, 1997 273:202–206

58. Bergen, HT, Mizuno, TM, Taylor, J and Mobbs, CV, Hyperphagia and weight gain after gold-thioglucose: relation to hypothalamic neuropeptide Y and proopiomelanocortin Endocrinology, 1998 139(11):4483–4488

59. Nakanishi, Y, Tsuneyama, K, Fujimoto, M, Salunga, TL, Nomoto, K, An, JL, Takano, Y, Iizuka, S, Nagata, M, Suzuki, W, Shimada, T, Aburada, M, Nakano, M, Selmi, C and Gershwin, ME, Monosodium glutamate (MSG): a villain and promoter of liver inflammation and dysplasia J Autoimmun, 2008 30(1–2):42–50

60. Nagata, M, Suzuki, W, Iizuka, S, Tabuchi, M, Maruyama, H, Takeda, S, Aburada, M, Miyamoto, K, Type 2 diabetes mellitus in obese mouse model induced by monosodium glutamate Exp Anim, 2006 55:109–115

61. Kraft, JR, Hyperinsulinemia: A merging history with idiopathic tinnitus, vertigo, and hearing loss Int Tinnitus J, 1998 4(2):127–130

62. Kaźmierczak, H and Doroszewska, G, Metabolic disorders in vertigo, tinnitus, and hearing loss Int Tinnitus J, 2001 7(1):54–58

63. Lavinsky, L, Oliveira, MW, Bassanesi, HJ, D'Avila, C and Lavinsky, M, Hyperinsulinemia and tinnitus: a historical cohort Int Tinnitus J 2004 10(1):24–30

64. Klagenberg, KF, Zeigelboim, BS, Jurkiewicz, AL and Martins-Bassetto J, Vestibulocochlear manifestations in patients with type I diabetes mellitus Rev Bras Otorrinolaringol, 2007 73(3):353–358

65. Pessin, AB, Martins, RH, Pimenta, WP, Simões, AC, Marsiglia, A and Amaral, AV, Auditory evaluation in patients with type 1 diabetes Ann Otol Rhinol Laryngol, 2008 117(5):366–370

66. Brands, MW and Hall, JE, Insulin resistance, hyperinsulinemia, and obesity-associated hypertension J Am Soc Nephrol, 1992 3(5):1064–1077

67. Fukushima, H, Cureoglu, S, Schachern, PA, Paparella, MM, Harada, T and Oktay, MF, Effects of type 2 diabetes mellitus on cochlear structure in humans Arch Otolaryngol Head Neck Surg, 2006 132:934–938

68. Brands, MW, Bell, TD, Rodriquez, NA, Polavarapu and Panteleyev, D, Chronic glucose infusion causes sustained increases in tubular sodium reabsorption and renal blood flow in dogs Am J Physiol Regul Integr ComPhysiol, 2009 296(2):R265–R271

69. Fujita, T, Aldosterone in salt-sensitive hypertension and metabolic syndrome J Mol Med, 2008 86(6):729–734

70. Sarafidis, PA and Grekas, DM, Insulin resistance and oxidant stress: an interrelation with deleterious renal consequences? J Cardiometab Syndr, 2007 2(2):139–142

71. Ferland, A, Brassard, P, Poirier, P, Is aspartame really safer in reducing the risk of hypoglycemia during exercise in patients with type 2 diabetes? Diabetes Care, 2007 30(7):e59

72. Magnuson, BA, Burdock, GA, Doull, J, Kroes, RM, Marsh, GM, Pariza, MW, Spencer, PS, Waddell, WJ, Walker, R and Williams, GM, Aspartame: a safety evaluation based on current use levels, regulations, and toxicological and epidemiological studies Crit Rev Toxicol, 2007 37(8):629–727

73. Humphries, P, Pretorius, E and Naudé, H, Direct and indirect cellular effects of aspartame on the brain Eur J Clin Nutr, 2008 62(4):451–462

74. Jacob, SE and Stechschulte, S, Formaldehyde, aspartame, and migraines: a possible connection Dermatitis, 2008 19(3):E10–E11

75. Clerici, WJ, DiMartino, DL and Prasad, MR, Direct effect of reactive oxygen species on cochlear outer hair cells Hear Res, 1995 84:30–40

76. Colagiuri, S, Miller, JJ and Edwards, RA, Metabolic effects of adding sucrose and aspartame to the diet of subjects with noninsulin-dependent diabetes mellitus Am J Clin Nutr, 1989 50:474–478

77. Fechter, LD, Oxidative stress: a potential basis for potentiation of noise-induced hearing loss Environ Toxicol Pharmacol, 2005 19:543–546

78. Lee, JE, Nakagawa, T, Kim, TS, Endo, T, Shiga, A, Iguchi, F, Lee, SH and Ito, J, Role of reactive radicals in degeneration of the auditory system of mice following cisplatin treatment Acta Otolaryngol, 2004 124:1131–1135

79. Huang T, Cheng AG, Stupak H, Liu W, Kim A, Staecker H, Lefebvre PP, Malgrange B, Kopke R, Moonen G, Van De Water TR Oxidative stress-induced apoptosis of cochlear sensory cells: otoprotective strategies Int J Dev Neurosci 2000 18:259–270

80. Rybak, LP, Whitworth, CA, Mukherjea, D and Ramkumar, V, Mechanisms of cisplatin induced totoxicity and prevention Hear Res, 2007 226:157–167

81. Yamasoba, T, Schachta, J, Shojia, F and Miller, JM, Attenuation of cochlear damage from noise trauma by an iron chelator, a free radical scavenger and glial cell line-derived neurotrophic factor in vivo Brain Res, 1999 815:317–325

82. Huang X, Whitworth CA, Rybak LP: Ginkgo biloba extract (EGb 761) protects against cisplatin-induced ototoxicity in rats Otol Neurotol 2007 28(6):828–833

83. Melamed, SB, Kaltenbach, JA, Church, MW, Burgio, DL and Afman, CE, Cisplatin-induced increases in spontaneous neural activity in the dorsal cochlear nucleus and associated outer hair cell loss Audiology, 2000 39(1):24–29

84. Rachel, JD, Kaltenbach, JA and Janisse, J, Increases in spontaneous neural activity in the hamster dorsal cochlear nucleus following cisplatin treatment: a possible basis for cisplatin-induced tinnitus Hear Res, 2002 164(1–2):206–214

85. Liu, J, Wang, X, Shigenaga, MK, Yeo, HC, Mori, A and Ames, BN, Immobilization stress causes oxidative damage to lipid, protein and DNA in the brain of rats FASEB J, 1996 10:1532–1538

86. Sivonova, M, Zitnanova, I, Hlincikova, L, Skodacek, I, Trebaticka, J and Durackova, Z, Oxidative stress in university students during examinations Stress, 2004 7:183–188

87. Mercanoglu, G, Safran, N, Uzun, H and Eroglu, L, Chronic emotional stress exposure increases infarct size in rats: the role of oxidative and nitrosative damage in response to sympathetic hyperactivity Methods Find Exp Clin Pharmacol, 2008 30(10):745–752

88. Inoue, A, Kawakami, N, Ishizaki, M, Tabata, M, Tsuchiya, M, Akiyama, M, Kitazume, A, Kuroda, M and Shimazu, A, Three job stress models/concepts and oxidative DNA damage in a sample of workers in Japan J Psychosom Res, 2009 66(4):329–334

89. Le Prell, CG, Hughes, LF and Miller, JM, Free radical scavengers, vitamins A, C, and E, plus magnesium reduces noise trauma Free Radic Biol Med, 2007 42(9):1454–1463

90. Henderson, D, McFadden, SL, Liu, CC, Hight, N and Zheng, XY, The role of antioxidants in protection from impulse noise Ann N Y Acad Sci, 1999 884:368–380

91. Khan, M, Gross, J, Haupt, H, Jainz, A, Niklowitz, P, Scherer, H, Schmidt, FP, Klapp, BF, Reisshauer, A and Mazurek, B, A pilot clinical trial of the effects of coenzyme Q10 on chronic tinnitus aurium Otolaryngol Head Neck Surg, 2007 136(1):72–77

92. Crane, FL, Biochemical functions of coenzyme Q10 J Am Coll Nutr, 2001 20:591–598

93. Shambaugh GE Jr, Zinc for tinnitus, imbalance and hearing loss in the elderly Am J Otol, 1986 7:476–477

94. Song, Y, Chung, CS, Bruno, RS, Traber, MG, Brown, KH, King, JC and Ho, E, Dietary zinc restriction and repletion affects DNA integrity in healthy men Am J Clin Nutr, 2009 90(2):321–328

95. Tuerk, MJ and Fazel, N, Zinc deficiency Curr Opin Gastroenterol, 2009 25(2):136–143

96. Takeda, A, Ando, M, Kanno, S and Oku, N Unique response of zinc in the hippocampus to behavioral stress and attenuation of subsequent mossy fiber long-term potentiation Neurotoxicol, 2009 30:712–717

97. Frederickson, CJ and Moncrieff, DW, Zinc-containing neurons Biol Signals, 1994 3:127–139

98. Izumi, Y, Ishii, K, Akiba, K and Hayashi, T, Hypozincemia during fever may trigger febrile convulsion Med Hypotheses, 1990 32:77–80

99. Ochi, K, Kinoshita, H, Kenmochi, M, Nishino, H and Ohashi, T, Zinc deficiency and tinnitus Auris Nasus Larynx, 2003 30:S25–S28

100. Yetiser, S, Tosun, F, Satar, B, Arslanhan, M, Akcam, T and Ozkaptan, Y, The role of zinc in management of tinnitus Auris, Nasus, Larynx, 2002 29:329–333

101. Arda, HN, Tuncel, U, Akdogan, O and Ozluoglu, LN, The role of zinc in the treatment of tinnitus Otol Neurotol, 2003 24(1):86–89

102. Shambaugh, GE Jr, Zinc and presbycusis Am J Otol, 1985 6(1):116–117

103. Yang, DJ, Tinnitus treated with combined traditional Chinese medicine and Western medicine Zhong Xi Yi Jie He Za Zhi, 1989 9(5):270–271

104. Tan, KQ, Zhang, C, Liu, MX and Qiu, L, Comparative study on therapeutic effects of acupuncture, Chinese herbs and Western medicine on nervous tinnitus Zhongguo Zhen Jiu, 2007 27(4):249–251

105. Wang, H, Jiang, S, Yang, W and Han, D, Evaluating effects of some medicine on tinnitus with animal behavioral model in rats Zhonghua Er Bi Yan Hou Ke Za Zhi, 2000 35(5):331–334

106. Szegedi, A, Kohnen, R, Dienel, A and Kieser, M, Acute treatment of moderate to severe depression with hypericum extract WS 5570 (St John's wort): randomised controlled double blind non-inferiority trial versus paroxetine BMJ, 2005 330(7490):503

107. Enrico, P, Sirca, D and Mereu, M, Antioxidants, minerals, vitamins, and herbal remedies in tinnitus therapy Prog Brain Res, 2007 166:323–330

108. Maclennan, K, Darlington, CL and Smith, PF, The CNS effects of Ginkgo biloba extracts and ginkgolide B Prog Neurobiol, 2002 67:236–258

109. Meyer, B, Etude multicentrique des acouphenes Ann Otolaryngol, 1986b 103:185–188

110. Meyer, B, Etude multicentrique randomisee a double insuface au placebo du traitement des acouphenes par l'extrait de Ginkgo biloba La Presse Medicale, 1986a 15:1562–1564

111. Morgenstern, C and Biermann, E, Ginkgo-Spezialextrakt Egb 761 in der Behandlung des Tinnitus aurium Fortschr der Medizin, 1997 115:7–11

112. Hilton, M and Stuart, E, Ginkgo biloba for tinnitus Cochrane Database Syst Rev, 2004 2:CD003852

113. Meehan, T, Eisenhut, M and Stephens, D, A review of alternative treatments for tinnitus Audiol Med, 2004 2:74–82

114. Smith, WK, Sankar, V and Pfleiderer, AG, A national survey amongst UK otolaryngologists regarding the treatment of Ménière's disease J Laryngol Otol, 2005 119(2):102–105

115. Newell, CA, Anderson, LA and Phillipson, JD, Herbal Medicines, a Guide for Health-Care Professionals, The Pharmaceutical Press, London, England,1996

116. Genazzani, E and Sorrentino, L, Black cohosh Nature, 1962 194:544–545

117. Anonymous. Cimicifuga racemosa Altern Med Rev, 2003 8:(2):186–189

118. Gao, D, Li, Q, Li, Y, Liu, Z, Fan, Y, Liu, Z, Zhao, H, Li, J and Han, Z, Antidiabetic and antioxidant effects of oleanolic acid from Ligustrum lucidum Ait in alloxan-induced diabetic rats Phytother Res, 2009 9 (Epub ahead of print)

119. Harrison, LJ, Manosh, R and Rubia, K, Sahaja yoga meditation as a family treatment program for attention deficit hyperactivity disorder children Clin Child Psychol Psychiatry, 2004 9(4):479–497

120. Rai, UC, Seti, S and Singh, SH, Some effects of Sahaja Yoga and its role in the prevention of stress disorders J Int Med Sci, 1988 19–23

121. Peng, CK, Henry, IC, Mietus, JE, Hausdorff, JM, Gurucharan, K, Benson, H and Goldberger, AL, Heart rate dynamics during three forms of meditation Int J Cardiology, 2004 95(1):19–27

122. Ditto, B, Eclache, M and Goldman, N, Short-term autonomic and cardiovascular effects of mindfulness body scan meditation Ann Behav Med, 2006 32(3):227–234

123. Wu, SD and Lo, PC Inward-attention meditation increases parasympathetic activity: a study based on heart rate variability Biomed Res, 2008 29(5):245–250

124. Cahn, BR and Polich, J, Meditation states and traits: EEG, ERP, and neuroimaging studies Psychological Bulletin, 2006 132 (2):180–211

125. Caudill, M, Schnable, R, Zuttermeister, P, Benson, H and Friedman, R, Decreased clinic utilization by chronic pain patients: response to behavioral medicine intervention Clin J Pain, 1991 7(4):305–310

126. Kabat-Zinn, J, Lipworth, L and Burney, R, The clinical use of mindfulness meditation for the self-regulation of chronic pain J Behav Med, 1985 8:163–190

127. Kabat-Zinn, J, Lipworth, L, Burney, R and Sellers, W, Four year follow-up of a meditation-based program for the self-regulation of chronic pain treatment outcomes and compliance Clin J Pain, 1986 2:159–173

128. Kaplan, KH, Goldenberg, DL and Galvin-Nadeau, M, The impact of a meditation-based stress reduction program on fibromyalgia Gen Hosp Psychiatry, 1993 15:284–289

129. Callahan, LF, Wiley-Exley, EK, Mielenz, TJ, Brady, TJ, Xiao, C, Currey, SS, Sleath, BL, Sloane, PD, DeVellis, RF and Sniezek, J, Use of complementary and alternative medicine among patients with arthritis Prev Chronic Dis, 2009 6(2):A44

130. Lush, E, Salmon, P, Floyd, A, Studts, JL, Weissbecker, I and Sephton, SE, Mindfulness meditation for symptom reduction in fibromyalgia: psychophysiological correlates J Clin Psychol Med Settings 2009 16(2):200–207

131. Møller, AR, Tinnitus and pain Prog Brain Res, 2007 166:47–53

132. Finucane, A and Mercer, SW, An exploratory mixed methods study of the acceptability and effectiveness of mindfulness-based cognitive therapy for patients with active depression and anxiety in primary care BMC Psychiatry, 2006 6:1–14

133. Evans, S, Ferrando, S, Findler, M, Stowell, C, Smart, C and Haglin, D, Mindfulness-based cognitive therapy for generalized anxiety disorder J Anxiety Disord, 2008 22(4):716–721

134. Teasdale, JD, Segal, ZV, Williams, JMG, Ridgeway, V, Soulsby, JM and Lau, M, Prevention of relapse/recurrence in major depression by mindfulness-based cognitive therapy J Consult Clin Psychol, 2000 68:615–623

135. Ma, SH and Teasdale, JD, Mindfulness-based cognitive therapy for depression: replication and exploration of differential relapse prevention effects J ConsultClin Psychology, 2004 72:31–40

136. Kuyken, W, Byford, S, Taylor, RS, Watkins, E, Holden, E, White, K, Barrett, B, Byng, R, Evans, A, Mullan, E and Teasdale, JD, Mindfulness-based cognitive therapy to prevent relapse in recurrent depression J Consult Clin Psychol, 2008 76(6):966–978

137. Winbush, NY, Gross, CR and Kreitzer, MJ, The effects of mindfulness-based stress reduction on sleep disturbance: a systematic review Explore (NY), 2007 3(6):585–591

138. Yook, K, Lee, SH, Ryu, M, Kim, KH, Choi, TK, Suh, SY, Kim, YW, Kim, B, Kim, MY and Kim, MJ, Usefulness of mindfulness-based cognitive therapy for treating insomnia in patients with anxiety disorders: a pilot study J Nerv Ment Dis, 2008 196(6):501–503

139. Sadlier, M, Stephens, SDG and Kennedy, V, Tinnitus rehabilitation: a mindfulness meditation cognitive behavioural therapy approach J Laryngol Otol, 2008 122(1):31–37

140. Hesser, H, Westin, V, Hayes, SC and Andersson, G, Clients' in-session acceptance and cognitive defusion behaviors in acceptance-based treatment of tinnitus distress Behav Res Ther, 2009 47(6):523–528

141. Weisz, N, Moratti, S, Meinzer, M, Dohrmann, K and Elbert, T, Tinnitus perception and distress is related to abnormal spontaneous brain activity as measured by magnetoencephalography PLoS Med (2005 2(6):e153

142. Weisz, N, Dohrmann, K and Elbert, T, The relevance of spontaneous activity for the coding of the tinnitus sensation Prog Brain Res, 2007 166:61–70

143. Lutz, A, Greischar, LL, Rawlings, NB, Ricard, M and Davidson, RJ, Long-term meditators self-induce high-amplitude gamma synchrony during mental practice Proc Natl Acad Sci USA, 2004 101:16369–16373

144. Khare, KC and Nigam, SK, A study of electroencephalogram in meditators Indian J Physiol Pharmacol, 2000 44(2):173–178

145. Baijal, S and Srinivasan, N, Theta activity and meditative states: spectral changes during concentrative meditation Cogn Process, 2009 22 [Epub ahead of print]

146. Hallam, RS, McKenna, L and Shurlock, L, Tinnitus impairs cognitive efficiency Int J Audiol, 2004 43(4):218–226

147. Tang, YY, Ma, Y, Wang, J, Fan, Y, Feng, S, Lu, Q, Yu, Q, Sui, D, Rothbart, MK, Fan, M and Posner, MI, Short-term meditation training improves attention and self-regulation Proc Natl Acad Sci USA, 2007 23 104(43):17152–17156

148. Erickson, MH, Control of physiological functions by hypnosis Am J Clin Hypn, 1977 20(1):8–19

149. Barker, P, Milton Erickson's contribution to psychiatry Br J Psychiatry, 1986 148:471–475

150. Flammer, E and Bongartz ,W, The efficacy of hypnosis: a meta-analytic study Contemp Hypn, 2003 20:179–197

151. Ross, UH, Lange, O, Unterrainer, J and Laszig, R, Ericksonian hypnosis in tinnitus therapy: effects of a 28-day inpatient multimodal treatment concept measured by Tinnitus Questionnaire and Health Survey SF-36 Eur Arch Otorhinolaryngol, 2007 264(5):483–488

152. Maudoux, A, Bonnet, S, Lhonneux-Ledoux, F and Lefebvre, P, Ericksonian hypnosis in tinnitus therapy B-ENT, 2007 7(Suppl 3):75–77

153. Mason, J and Rogerson, D, Client-centered hypnotherapy for tinnitus: who is likely to benefit? Am J Clin Hypn, 1995 37(4):294–299

154. Cope, TE, Clinical hypnosis for the alleviation of tinnitus Int Tinnitus J, 2008 14(2):135–138

155. Herráiz, C, Toledano, A and Diges, I, Trans-electrical nerve stimulation (TENS) for somatic tinnitus Prog Brain Res, 2007 166:389–394

156. Splevins, K, Smith, A and Simpson, J Do improvements in emotional distress correlate with becoming more mindful? A study of older adults Aging Ment Health, 2009 13(3):328–335

Chapter 93
Low-Level Laser Therapy

Tobias Kleinjung

Keypoints

1. Despite nearly 20 years of experience with low-level laser therapy (LLLT) for tinnitus concerns remain as to its effectiveness as a treatment modality for tinnitus.
2. Only a few reports show that LLLT is an effective treatment for tinnitus and other inner-ear conditions.
3. Many conflicting reports show no benefit whatsoever.
4. This chapter provides an outline of the biological basis for LLLT and reviews findings of controlled clinical studies of the use of LLLT in tinnitus treatment.

Keywords Tinnitus • Low level laser • Therapy • Biostimulation • Photostimulation

Abbreviation

LLLT   Low level laser therapy

Introduction

The last 30 years have seen an enormous increase of research work in the clinical application of laser technology in Otorhinolaryngology. Surgical removal of tumors of the larynx and pharynx was revolutionized by the many advantages offered by "hard" or "hot" surgical lasers (such as Carbon dioxide, Erbium yttrium aluminum garnet, and Neodymium yttrium aluminum garnet). The ability to remove soft-tissue lesions under microscopic control in combination with excellent control of bleeding, due to the coagulative capacity of these lasers, results in good functional outcome even after extensive surgery [1]. The perforation of the footplate in stapes surgery represents another use of these different types of lasers [2]. Some otologists prefer to use a laser for stapes surgery because they do not have to touch the footplate manually.

At the other end of the spectrum of available lasers are semiconductor diode lasers, or combined helium–neon and gallium–arsenide lasers, which are sometimes referred to as "cold" or "soft" lasers. These lasers have only about one hundredth of the power of a surgical laser. In clinical medicine, diode lasers have been predominantly used to accelerate the healing of injured peripheral nerves [3, 4] and soft-tissue injury [5], and to reduce inflammation [6] and pain [7]. The clinical effectiveness for these applications termed low-level laser therapy (LLLT) or low-intensity laser irradiation or "biostimulation" is still controversial.

Biological Effects of LLLT

Low-Level Laser Therapy

Low-level laser therapy (LLLT) uses a light source for treatment. This light source is usually red to near infrared (wavelengths in the range of 630–904 nm) and is obtained from diode lasers or a combination of helium–neon and gallium–arsenide lasers. LLLT produces no noticeable heat, sound, or vibration. Instead, LLLT may act via non-thermal or photochemical reactions in the cells that are also referred to as "photobiology" or

T. Kleinjung (✉)
Department of Otorhinolaryngology, University of Regensburg,
Franz-Josef-Strauss-Allee 11, 93053 Regensburg, Germany
e-mail: tobias.kleinjung@klinik.uni-regensburg.de

A.R. Møller et al. (eds.), *Textbook of Tinnitus*,
DOI 10.1007/978-1-60761-145-5_93, © Springer Science+Business Media, LLC 2011

"biostimulation." The red visible and near-infrared laser wavelength used may be mainly absorbed in proteins, but the identity of the photoreceptors responsible for the biological effects of LLLT is unknown [8]. The laser light may act on the mitochondrial cytochrome system, endogenous porphyrins in the cell, or the energy-absorbing chromophores in LLLT [9]. In vitro studies using cell cultures have demonstrated stimulatory effects of such laser radiation on fibroblasts, immune cells, epithelial cells, neurons, and the blood vascular system (for review see [8]).

Clinical Application

Clinical applications of LLLT show some potential effectiveness in treating soft-tissue injury [10], chronic pain [11], and wound healing [12]. Other studies have failed to demonstrate similar effectiveness [13, 14]. Optimal wavelength, dose, dose-rate effects, tissue penetration, the role of coherence and peak power, and repetition rates for the different applications are still unknown in clinical use of these lasers. Earlier studies have shown that LLLT can prevent neuronal degeneration, promote improved neuronal function and repair, and enhance neural growth [15]. Based on these studies, LLLT was proposed for treatment of tinnitus and sensorineural hearing loss more than one decade ago [16].

Use of LLLT to Treat Tinnitus

Low-level laser radiation has been tried for treatment of tinnitus [16–18]. For that purpose, the laser light is applied through the ear canal. It was assumed that low-intensity laser irradiation was capable of penetrating soft tissue to reach the cochlea, but it remains unclear if the intensity is adequate to affect cochlear hair cells when applied through the ear canal. Multiple scattering of the laser energy by erythrocytes and microvessels has to be taken into consideration [19]. Physical measurement performed on human petrous bones showed that only the transmeatal application provided sufficient light to reach all parts of the cochlea, whereas mastoidal application did not provide sufficient energy of light in the cochlea [20]. Several biological effects in the cochlea were assumed to occur: LLLT could

possibly increase cell proliferation, synthesis of ATP and collagen; affect the release of growth factors; promote the local blood flow in the inner ear; and activate repair mechanisms in the inner ear through photochemical and photophysical stimulation of the hair-cell mitochondria ("mitochondrial energy transfer") [18, 21]. There is some experimental support for this theory from basic science [22, 23]. However, experimental data from the ear are rare. One animal study showed suppression of the compound action potential of the eighth nerve from low-level laser irradiation [24].

Though the exact peripheral mechanism of tinnitus is still uncertain, it is generally accepted that the conscious perception of tinnitus must involve the cerebral cortex. Interestingly, a study of Siedentopf et al. [25] demonstrated functional activation after transmeatal LLLT of healthy human subjects in different auditory and non-auditory structures of the brain by means of fMRI, which indicates that LLLT may affect central mechanisms.

Clinical Studies of LLLT in Patients with Tinnitus

Few reports on laser therapy of tinnitus have been published [16–18, 26–32]. Both positive and negative effects have been reported. Different wavelengths, pulsing, dosage, target of irradiation, and treatment schedule have been used. The outcome criteria and placebo control vary among the published studies making it difficult to assess the efficacy of laser treatment for tinnitus.

Earlier studies have used a combination of intravenous application of Ginkgo biloba extracts with mastoidal laser irradiation [26–28]. The rationale for the combination was the assumption in synergistic effects, as anecdotal reports supposed that Gingko extracts should increase cerebral blood flow, accelerate oxygen supply, and therefore improve tinnitus complaints [33]. Later studies changed the target to the external auditory meatus und used the laser as a monotherapy [16, 17, 29–32]. Tinnitus improvement rates varied from 15 to 67% of patients [16]. Some studies summarized that LLLT showed no efficacy in tinnitus treatment [17, 26, 27, 30, 32]. Others found LLLT to be useful in tinnitus treatment and were encouraging for further investigations [16, 29, 31]. Clear positive results were demonstrated by Wilden and Dindinger

[18] in a treatment study without placebo control. However, a systematic review of randomized controlled clinical trials of LLLT treatment found no statistically significant difference between laser and placebo [34]. Only Wilden and Ellerbrock [35] described improvement of hearing thresholds after LLLT in more than 80% of treated subjects, whereas other studies did not observe any significant changes in hearing thresholds [16, 17, 26, 28, 32]. Nakashima et al. [30] reported on one patient who suffered from acute hearing detoriation after the third laser irradiation. All other studies could not observe any severe complications or side effects.

Conclusion

As the exact treatment mechanisms remain unclear and multiple placebo-controlled clinical studies failed to demonstrate significant efficacy, further studies are needed before this treatment modality can be recommended for routine clinical use.

References

1. Yao M, Epstein JB, Modi BJ, Pytynia KB, Mundt AJ, Feldman LE. Current surgical treatment of squamous cell carcinoma of the head and neck. Oral Oncol, 2007 43(3):213–23
2. Frenz M. Physical characteristics of various lasers used in stapes surgery. Adv Otorhinolaryngol, 2007 65:237–49
3. Rochkind S, Rousso M, Nissan M, Villarreal M, Barr-Nea L, Rees DG. Systemic effects of low-power laser irradiation on the peripheral and central nervous system, cutaneous wounds, and burns. Lasers Surg Med, 1989 9(2):174–82
4. Rochkind S, Nissan M, Alon M, Shamir M, Salame K. Effects of laser irradiation on the spinal cord for the regeneration of crushed peripheral nerve in rats. Lasers Surg Med, 2001 28(3):216–9
5. Nemeth AJ. Lasers and wound healing. Dermatol Clin, 1993 11(4):783–9
6. Harris DM. Laser biostimulation: review and hypothesis. Laser Topics, 1988 1:9–14
7. Walker J. Relief from chronic pain by low power laser irradiation. Neurosci Lett, 1983 43(2–3):339–44
8. Walsh LJ. The current status of low level laser therapy in dentistry. Part 1. Soft tissue applications. Aust Dent J, 1997 42(4):247–54
9. Lubart R, Wollman Y, Friedmann H, Rochkind S, Laulicht I. Effects of visible and near-infrared lasers on cell cultures. J Photochem Photobiol B, 1992 12(3):305–10
10. Vasseljen O Jr, Høeg N, Kjeldstad B, Johnsson A, Larsen S. Low level laser versus placebo in the treatment of tennis elbow. Scand J Rehabil Med, 1992 24(1):37–42
11. Walker JB, Akhanjee LK, Cooney MM, Goldstein J, Tamyoshi S, Sgal-Gidan F. Laser therapy for pain of rheumathoid arthritis. Clin J Pain, 1987 3(1):54–69
12. Sugrue ME, Carolan J, Leen EJ, Feeley TM, Moore DJ, Shanik GD. The use of infrared laser therapy in the treatment of venous ulceration. Ann Vasc Surg, 1990 4(2):179–81
13. Lowe AS, McDowell BC, Walsh DM, Baxter GD, Allen JM. Failure to demonstrate any hypoalgesic effect of low intensity laser irradiation (830 nm) of Erb's point upon experimental ischaemic pain in humans. Lasers Surg Med, 1997 20(1):69–76
14. Hall J, Clarke AK, Elvins DM, Ring EF. Low level laser therapy is ineffective in the management of rheumatoid arthritic finger joints. Br J Rheumatol, 1994 33(2):142–7
15. Belkin M, Schwartz M. Evidence for the existence of low-energy laser bioeffects on the nervous system. Neurosurg Rev, 1994 17(1):7–17
16. Tauber S, Schorn K, Beyer W, Baumgartner R. Transmeatal cochlear laser (TCL) treatment of cochlear dysfunction: a feasibility study for chronic tinnitus. Lasers Med Sci, 2003 18(3):154–61
17. Mirz F, Zachariae R, Andersen SE, Nielsen AG, Johansen LV, Bjerring P, Pedersen CB. The low-power laser in the treatment of tinnitus. Clin Otolaryngol Allied Sci, 1999 24(4):346–54
18. Wilden L, Dindinger D. Treatment of chronic disease of the inner ear with low-level laser therapy (LLLT): a pilot project. Laser Therapy, 1996 8:209–12
19. Gush RJ, King TA. Discrimination of capillary and arteriovenular blood flow in skin by laser Doppler flowmetry. Med Biol Eng Comput, 1991 29(4):387–92
20. Tauber S, Baumgartner R, Schorn K, Beyer W. Lightdosimetric quantitative analysis of the human petrous bone: experimental study for laser irradiation of the cochlea. Lasers Surg Med, 2001 28(1):18–26
21. Wilden L, Karthein R. Import of radiation phenomena of electrons and therapeutic low-level laser in regard to the mitochondrial energy transfer. J Clin Laser Med Surg, 1998 16(3):159–65
22. Karu TI. Mitochondrial signaling in mammalian cells activated by red and near-IR radiation. Photochem Photobiol, 2008 84(5):1091–9
23. Karu TI, Pyatibrat LV, Afanasyeva NI. A novel mitochondrial signaling pathway activated by visible-to-near infrared radiation. Photochem Photobiol, 2004 80(2):366–72
24. Shiomi Y, Tuji J, Naito Y. Effect of low power laser irradiation on inner ear. Pract Otol (Kyoto), 1994 87:1135–40
25. Siedentopf CM, Ischebeck A, Haala IA, Mottaghy FM, Schikora D, Verius M, Koppelstaetter F, Buchberger W, Schlager A, Felber SR, Golaszewski SM. Neural correlates of transmeatal cochlear laser (TCL) stimulation in healthy human subjects. Neurosci Lett, 2007 411(3):189–93
26. Partheniadis-Stumpf M, Maurer J, Mann W. [Soft laser therapy in combination with tebonin iv in tinnitus]. Laryngorhinootologie, 1993 72(1):28–31
27. Wedel H, Calero L, Walger M, Hoenen S, Rutwalt D. Soft laser/Gingko therapy in tinnitus A placebo-controlled study. Adv Otorhinolaryngol, 1995 49:105–8

28. Plath P, Olivier J. Results of combined low-power laser therapy and extracts of Gingko biloba in cases of sensorineural hearing loss and tinnitus. Adv Otorhinolaryngol, 1995 49:101–4

29. Shiomi Y, Takahashi H, Honjo I, Kojima H, Naito Y, Fujiki N. Efficacy of transmeatal low power laser irradiation on tinnitus: a preliminary report. Auris Nasus Larynx, 1997 24(1):39–42

30. Nakashima T, Ueda H, Misawa H, Suzuki T, Tominaga M, Ito A, Numata S, Kasai S, Asahi K, Vernon JA, Meikle MB. Transmeatal low-power laser irradiation for tinnitus. Otol Neurotol, 2002 23(3):296–300

31. Gungor A, Dogru S, Cincik H, Erkul E, Poyrazoglu E. Effectiveness of transmeatal low power laser irradiation for chronic tinnitus. J Laryngol Otol, 2008 122(5):447–51

32. Teggi R, Bellini C, Piccioni LO, Palonta F, Bussi M. Transmeatal low-level laser therapy for chronic tinnitus with cochlear dysfunction. Audiol Neurootol, 2009 14(2):115–20

33. Susan J. Gingko – fact or fiction? Tinnitus Today, 1993 18:10

34. Meehan T, Eisenhut M, Stephens D. A review of alternative treatments for tinnitus. Audiol Med, 2004 2:74–82

35. Wilden L, Ellerbrock D. Amelioration of the hearing capacity by low-level-laser-light (LLLL). Lasermedizin, 1999 14:129–38

Chapter 94
Similarities Between Treatments of Tinnitus and Central Pain

Dirk De Ridder and Aage R. Møller

Keypoints

1. Neurobiology, pathophysiology, neuroimaging, and clinical presentation share many common aspects between neuropathic pain and tinnitus.
2. Similar treatments for pain and tinnitus exist, but pharmacological methods are more successful for treatment of pain than for treatment of tinnitus.
3. Peripheral and intracranial ablative neurosurgical treatments yield common results and complications for pain and tinnitus.
4. The most promising analogous treatments for pain and tinnitus are non-invasive and invasive methods for neuromodulation, such as various forms of brain stimulation using transcranial magnetic stimulation (TMS) and transcranial direct current stimulation (tDCS).
5. TENS, for stimulation of peripheral nerves, and neurofeedback, have beneficial effects on both pain and tinnitus.
6. Invasive neuromodulatory treatments such as cochlear implants, dorsal column stimulation/auditory brainstem implant, subthalamic nucleus stimulation, and sensory cortex stimulation are beneficial for both tinnitus and pain.

Keywords Tinnitus • Central pain • Treatment • Cortical stimulation • Peripheral nerve stimulation • Transcranial magnetic stimulation • Transcranial direct current stimulation

D. De Ridder (✉)
TRI Tinnitus Clinic Antwerp, BRAI²N & Department of Neurosurgery, University Hospital Antwerp, Wilrijkstraat 10, Edegem 2650, Belgium
e-mail: dirk.de.ridder@uza.be

Abbreviations

ABI	Auditory brainstem implant
CI	Cochlear implant
DBS	Deep brain stimulation
DCN	Dorsal cochlear nucleus
DCSCS	Dorsal column spinal cord stimulation
DLPFC	Dorsolateral prefrontal cortex
EEG	Electroencephalography
fMRI	Functional MRI
MRI	Magnetic resonance imaging
MSI	Magnetic source imaging
MVD	Microvascular decompression
PET	Positron emission tomography
rTMS	Repetitive TMS
STN	Subthalamic nucleus
tDCS	Transcranial direct current stimulation
TENS	Transderm electric nerve stimulation
TMS	Transcranial magnetic stimulation
TMS	Trans cranial magnetic stimulation
VTA	Ventral tegmental area

Introduction

Similarities between pain and tinnitus were discussed in Chap. 14. Similarities Between Tinnitus and Pain. In this chapter, we will discuss similarities in treatment of neuropathic pain and some forms of tinnitus. Apart from the developmental and reorganizational analogy, a clear clinical analogy exists between phantom pain and tinnitus [1–4]. Both symptoms are wholly subjective sensations, events that may change in character and quality. Both can be masked and relieved by electrical stimulation with a residual inhibition. Transection

A.R. Møller et al. (eds.), *Textbook of Tinnitus*,
DOI 10.1007/978-1-60761-145-5_94, © Springer Science+Business Media, LLC 2011

of an afferent nerve usually does not help relieve tinnitus or chronic pain. In both systems, the ascending system is modified by a descending counterpart. This leads to similar characteristic symptoms in both tinnitus and phantom pain [2–4].

A normal stimulus to the skin in individuals with phantom pain can create a painful sensation (allodynia) in the same way tinnitus patients can perceive a sound as unpleasant or painful. A painful stimulus often generates an explosive and prolonged reaction to the stimulus (hyperpathia) in individuals with phantom pain similar to the hyperacusis seen in tinnitus patients [5]. The wind-up phenomenon, a worsening of pain sensation with repeated stimuli of the same intensity, is also present in some individuals with tinnitus, where it is described as an increasingly unpleasant sensation on repeating the same sound [2, 3]. Furthermore, a feeling of anxiety, nausea, and a clear stress response is often encountered both in individuals with phantom pain and tinnitus [2, 3] (see also Chap. 14).

There are at least two distinct forms of pain: normal physiological pain, by activation of nociceptors in a normally functioning somatosensory system, and neuropathic pain, which is the result of deafferentation and activation of a hereby pathologically functioning somatosensory system. There is no physiological tinnitus that is analogous to physiological pain, and therefore there are no similarities for the treatment of tinnitus to the common analgesics that are quite efficient for acute physiological body pain. Many different kinds of medications for physiological pain are readily available and have few side effects. There are also medications for neuropathic pain. Medications such as gabapentin and pregabalin are effective in treatment of central neuropathic pain. Similar medication that has a generally beneficial effect on central tinnitus does not exist either. Several other treatments are used for neuropathic pain with varying results including other pharmacological treatments [6], epidural treatments [7], regional nerve blocks [7], destructive lesions [8], treatment with calcitonin [7], transcutaneous electrical nerve stimulation [7], motor cortex stimulation (MCS) [9–11], and thalamic stimulation [12–14]. Existing treatments for various forms of pain are far more efficient than treatment of tinnitus. So even between the pathophysiology of neuropathic deafferentation pain and deafferentation tinnitus, there have to be some fundamental differences.

Medication

Some medications are used for both neuropathic pain and tinnitus, for example, clonazepam [15, 16] and gabapentin (and this only in acoustic trauma related tinnitus) [17]; however, most pain medication will not benefit tinnitus patients. For a detailed analysis of pharmacological approaches to tinnitus, the reader is referred to Chap. 78.

Destructive Procedures

Nerve Sections

The auditory information is brought to the brain via the auditory or cochlear nerve, and feedback from the cortex to the cochlea is mediated via the vestibular nerve [18, 19]. The inferior vestibular nerve connects to the auditory nerve via a small nerve fiber bundle [20]: Oort's bundle which contains about 360 myelinated and 1,000 unmyelinated axons [21]. As always, there is some variability, but vestibulocochlear anastomoses can be found in 80% of the population [22]. Based on this anatomical knowledge, both cochlear and vestibular nerve sections have been performed in an attempt to cure tinnitus.

In a recent review paper on vestibular nerve section performed for tinnitus [23], the proportion of patients in whom tinnitus was exacerbated postoperatively ranged from 0 to 60%, with a mean of 16.4% (standard deviation 14.0). The proportion of patients in whom tinnitus was unchanged was 17–72% (mean 38.5%, standard deviation 15.6), and in whom tinnitus was improved was 6–61% (mean 37.2%, standard deviation 15.2). In the majority of patients undergoing vestibular nerve section, ablation of auditory efferent input (and thus total efferent dysfunction) to the cochlea was not associated with an exacerbation of tinnitus [23]. Therefore, if a nerve section is elected, vestibular nerve section is to be preferred to cochlear nerve section in which the success rate in abolishing tinnitus is disappointing and the results generally unpredictable [24]; an important part of the patients (55%) report no effect or a worsening of their tinnitus [25]. Only one paper reports good results with cochlear nerve section for tinnitus [26]: two-thirds completely relieved, 28% improved, and only 5% non-responders, without a single patient worsening (see Chap. 39).

Section of the auditory nerve is controversial and now regarded contraindicated because it involves causing deprivation of signals to the auditory system, which is known to promote plastic changes. Despite a long history of ablative procedures in neurosurgery for pain control, the evidence supporting destructive procedures for benign pain conditions remains limited to class III evidence (retrospective studies) [8]. The fact that nerve lesioning is worse than non-destructive treatments [e.g., microvascular decompression (MVD)] in pain is demonstrated in trigeminal neuralgia where MVDs are better than destructive treatments such as rhizotomies or gamma knife surgery. MVD has the highest rate of long-term patient satisfaction with the lowest rate of pain recurrence [27, 28].

After surgical removal of vestibular schwannoma with resection of the auditory nerve, most patients have a small improvement of their tinnitus, but 50% of the people who do not present with tinnitus develop it after the surgery [29].

Frontal Lobotomies

Tinnitus and pain distress have both been linked to a neural network consisting of the anterior cingulate, frontal cortex, and insula [30–33]. These brain areas are also implicated in the distress perceived by people with posttraumatic stress disorder [34, 35], as well as asthma-related dyspnea [36], suggesting that these areas may constitute a "general distress network". In the 1930–1940s frontal lobotomies were performed both for pain [37, 38] and tinnitus [39, 40]. The net results of these treatments were the persistence of the perception of pain and tinnitus, but the affective component related to the pain and tinnitus disappeared. For treatment of pain, the frontal lobotomies have now been refined and restricted to anterior cingulotomies. Except for a decline in focused attention performance [41–43], other neurocognitive functions (including language, memory, motor, visual-constructional, and intellectual functions) remained unaffected after the anterior cingulotomies [43]. The decreased attention modulates (decreases) the emotional experience of pain that was related to self-perceived tension and which was expressed

by anger before the treatment, which also improved mood and decreased psychasthenia [44]. Cingulotomy also reduced behavioral spontaneity, expressed as a decrease in self-initiated action [42]. When performing cingulotomies for intractable pain, 72% of patients report improvements in their pain, 55% no longer take narcotics, 67% note improvement in their family life, and 72% note improvement in their social interactions. Fifty-six percent of patients report that the cingulotomy was beneficial and 28% return to their usual activities or work [45]. No reports have been published on the use of cingulotomy for treatment of tinnitus.

Thalamic Lesions

Thalamic lesioning has been used for both pain and tinnitus suppression based on the idea of thalamocortical dysrhythmia [46] as unifying pathophysiological mechanism of tinnitus and pain [47]. However, the experience is very limited up to now; so no definitive conclusions can be drawn of the value of this treatment for tinnitus suppression.

Lesioning of Autonomic Nervous System

It is well known that the sympathetic system influences both pain and tinnitus perception [2, 3]. Both pain and tinnitus tend to worsen under stressful situations. Therefore, interfering with the sympathetic system has been performed both in pain and tinnitus [48–51]. If tinnitus responds to a stellate block, a complete suppression of the tinnitus was possible in 31%, in 50% a partial response, and in 19% no response was obtained by surgical sympathectomy [51]. In Ménière's disease, the patients who did not improve their tinnitus intensity were no more distressed by their tinnitus [51]. The patient should be warned that 24 h after operation the deafness and tinnitus may be slightly worse, possibly as the result of irritation of the sympathetic nerve trunk; it may take a week or 10 days to settle down [51]. It can be expected, however, that cervical sympathectomies for tinnitus relief might only yield a temporary benefit, in a couple of months, similar to what is known for sympathectomies at C2 and C3 for occipital neuralgia [52].

Neuromodulation

Cortex Stimulation

The neurobiological, pathophysiological, and clinical analogies between deafferentation tinnitus and deafferentation pain [1–4, 53] suggest that the resulting phantom symptoms of central pain and central tinnitus are caused by cortical hyperactivity/reorganization. Therefore, it can be assumed that the same basic strategy for treating these two conditions can be applied.

The basic strategy can be summarized as follows:

1. The hyperactivity/reorganization that is associated with central pain and some forms of tinnitus can be demonstrated by functional neuroimaging techniques such as PET scan, fMRI, or MSI (magnetic source imaging).
2. The anatomical area of hyperactivity/reorganization can then be influenced by (neuronavigated) transcranial magnetic stimulation.
3. If successfully suppressed by TMS, an electrode can be permanently implanted extradurally over the anatomical area of cortical hyperactivity/reorganization.

The details of this approach are presented in the chapter on cortex stimulation for tinnitus (Chap. 90). In summary, a selection criterion of more than 50% transient tinnitus improvement, lasting only a few seconds, on two separated placebo-controlled TMS sessions was used for implanting cortical stimulation electrodes.

Deep Brain Stimulation (DBS)

Subthalamic nucleus (STN) stimulation is capable of both improving pain [54, 55] and tinnitus [56] in patients with Parkinson's disease, but the mechanism is unknown. STN stimulation also modulates olfactory [57] and visual [58] function suggesting that the STN has a general modulatory action on sensory processing. Stimulation of the auditory cortex, which does not send direct projections to the subthalamic nucleus, induces only late excitatory responses in the STN via the indirect cortico-striato-pallido-subthalamic pathway [59]. Many cells in the STN respond to both motor and auditory cortex stimulation as well as to frontal cortex

stimulation [59]. Therefore, it is possible that DBS of the STN improves tinnitus via its influence on the motor–auditory integration cells in the STN or indirectly via the frontal cortex. Another possibility is that it occurs via an indirect pathway involving the medial forebrain bundle. Activation of connections between the medial (limbic) STN and the medial forebrain bundle has been proposed as a mechanism for the emotional and motivational influences of STN stimulation [60]. The medial forebrain bundle connects the ventral tegmental area (VTA) to the nucleus accumbens, which has been implicated in tinnitus as well [61].

Transcutaneous Electrical Nerve Stimulation and Cochlear Implants

Neuropathic pain and tinnitus are both related to deprivation of sensory input to the brain (deafferentation symptoms). One way of compensating for the effect of deafferentation is by supplying the missing information through direct electrical activation of the peripheral receptors or the sensory nerves. Electrical stimulation of the peripheral somatosensory nerves, transcutaneous electrical nerve stimulation (TENS), and the auditory nerve [cochlear implants (CI)] has been used to suppress hyperactive clinical states of the respective system, which develop as a result of the deafferentation. Neuropathic pain can be modulated by TENS [62]. The effect on pain from such stimulation of the skin or peripheral nerves is mediated by the inhibitory influence from Aβ fibers on neurons in the spinal cord that receive nocuous input from C and Aδ fibers (see Chap. 14). TENS may also affect central pain, probably through activation of neural plasticity [1].

In the auditory system, peripheral nerve stimulation is performed by CI (see Chap. 77). The use of CI for tinnitus has shown promising results with regards to tinnitus suppression [63–68]. TENS is commonly used in the treatment of pain but has been used in tinnitus as well [69–75]. TENS modulates tinnitus most likely via somatosensory–auditory interactions at the level of the cochlear nuclei [76–78] or the inferior colliculus [79] (see Chap. 9). The DCN has been implicated in the pathophysiology of tinnitus [80, 81] (see Chaps. 9 and 31), and therefore modulating its activity could be useful in some forms of tinnitus (see Chap. 31). Using c-fos studies, it was recently shown that electrical stimulation of the skin around the ear modulates dorsal cochlear nucleus activity through both direct pathways via the trigeminal system and indirect pathways via the dorsal raphe and the locus coeruleus [82]. When auditory input to the DCN is diminished, an increase in somatosensory influence on auditory neurons occurs, which could be due to cross-modal reinnervation or increased synaptic strength [83]. This favors the use of TENS in auditory deafferentation tinnitus, even though clinical data not always support the use of TENS for tinnitus [84]. Selecting who benefits from TENS and who does not will be important for the future clinical application of this method.

Dorsal Column Stimulation and Auditory Brainstem Implants (ABI)

Electrical stimulation of the second neuron in the somatosensory system is known as dorsal column stimulation (DCS) and is used in the management of chronic, intractable neuropathic pain [85]. The method is based on the "gate–control" theory presented by Melzack and Wall [86], who postulated that activity in large diameter cutaneous fibers (type Aß) inhibits the transmission of noxious information to the brain. Electrical stimulation of these large afferents by an electrode placed dorsomedially in the epidural space elicits a tingling sensation (paresthesia) in the corresponding dermatomes. To obtain successful treatment of chronic, neuropathic pain by DCS, the stimulation-induced paresthesia has to cover the anatomical areas of pain completely [87, 88].

Electrical stimulation of the cochlear nucleus in the auditory brainstem yields suppressive effects on tinnitus in 80% of patients who use their auditory brainstem implants (ABI) daily [89]. This is supportive of the theory that the DCN is critically involved in tinnitus [80, 81] (see Chap. 9).

Transcranial Direct Current Stimulation

Transcranial direct current stimulation (tDCS) involves stimulation by a weak constant current (between 0.5 and 2 mA) flow through the cerebral cortex via scalp electrodes. Anodal tDCS typically has an excitatory effect on the local cerebral cortex by depolarizing neurons, while the opposite occurs under the cathode electrode through a process of hyperpolarization [90]. This effect of tDCS lasts for an hour or longer after a single 20–30 min treatment session [90–93].

With the anode electrode placed over the dorsolateral prefrontal cortex, tDCS can modulate both pain [94] and tinnitus (see Chap. 89), possibly via a similar mechanism, most likely a top-down modulation of auditory [95] and somatosensory [96] processing.

For pain, cathodal tDCS stimulation of the somatosensory cortex contralateral to the side to which the pain is referred [97] and left-sided anodal tDCS over the auditory cortex [98] can influence pain and tinnitus, respectively, via a more direct effect than tDCS applied through electrodes placed on the frontal part of the scalp (anode right side, cathode left side).

Transcranial Magnetic Stimulation

TMS is a non-invasive method of inducing electrical current in the brain [99]. It uses a coil placed on the scalp that generates magnetic pulses of very short duration (100–300 µs) at approximately 1.5–2.0 T in strength [100]. Because magnetic fields pass largely undistorted through the scalp and skull, TMS is powerful enough to cause neuronal depolarization in the cortex. TMS originally delivered single impulses. Further development of TMS equipment allowed repetitive magnetic impulses (rTMS) to be delivered, which are more effective than single impulses. The area of the brain that is stimulated and the intensity of the electromagnetic field depend on physical properties and rapidly decrease with the distance to the coil. It was estimated that a "figure of eight coil" stimulates an area of approximately 3×2 cm at cortical surface, but the induced current falls to near zero at a depth of 3 cm [101].

TMS has been used as a putative prognostic tool for cortex implants at the auditory cortex for treatment of tinnitus [102, 104] and for implants on the somatosensory cortex [103, 105] and motor cortex [106] for treatment of neuropathic pain. Details can be found in the chapter on cortex stimulation for tinnitus (Chap. 90).

Repetitive sessions of TMS (rTMS) have also been used as a treatment for pain [107, 108] and tinnitus [101, 109–112]. Details can be found in Chap. 88.

Neurobiofeedback

Tinnitus and pain are associated with abnormally coupled low and high frequency synchronous oscillatory activity in the brain [31, 46, 113–117]. If this abnormal oscillatory activity is related to the auditory and somatosensory phantom percept, a logical attempt to treat these symptoms is by normalizing this abnormal activity. Neurofeedback is a biofeedback technique using electroencephalographic (EEG) or fMRI signals for training individuals to alter their brain activity via operant conditioning. This has been used for both tinnitus [118–119] and fibromyalgia pain [120]. A detailed description of this technique is given in Chap. 87.

A better understanding of the spectral and connectivity changes, as well as alterations in independent components in tinnitus and pain, combined with new software development for source-analyzed neurofeedback training is expected to permit this technique to become a more powerful tool in treatment of both tinnitus and pain.

Conclusion

Tinnitus does not seem to respond to medication used for physiological or neuropathic pain. This means that pharmacological treatment does not seem to benefit from the neurobiological, pathophysiological, neuroimaging, and clinical analogy between tinnitus and pain, and pharmacological treatment [122], in general, has had little success in treatment of tinnitus.

Methods such as ablative neurosurgical approaches consisting of nerve sections or intracranial destructive lesions have found use in treatment of both tinnitus and pain.

Different kinds of invasive and non-invasive neuromodulation seem to be more promising analogous treatments. For invasive stimulation implanted electrodes on the auditory and somatosensory cortex, deep brain stimulation of the subthalamic nucleus and thalamus, TENS/cochlear implants, and dorsal column stimulation/auditory brainstem implants most likely use similar mechanisms to improve pain and tinnitus. Non-invasive neuromodulation techniques such as cortical transcranial magnetic stimulation, transcranial

direct current stimulation, transcutaneous electrical nerve stimulation, and neurofeedback appear to be analogous in their effect on pain and tinnitus as well.

References

1. Møller A (2006) Neural plasticity and disorders of the nervous system. Cambridge: Cambridge University Press.
2. Møller AR (2000) Similarities between severe tinnitus and chronic pain. J Am Acad Audiol 11:115–24.
3. Møller AR (1997) Similarities between chronic pain and tinnitus. Am J Otol 18:577–85.
4. Tonndorf J (1987) The analogy between tinnitus and pain: a suggestion for a physiological basis of chronic tinnitus. Hear Res 28:271–5.
5. Møller A (2006) Hearing: Its physiology and pathophysiology. Amsterdam: Elsevier Science.
6. Nikolajsen L and TS Jensen (2001) Phantom limb pain. Br J Anaesth 87:107–16.
7. Halbert J, M Crotty and ID Cameron (2002) Evidence for the optimal management of acute and chronic phantom pain: a systematic review. Clin J Pain 18:84–92.
8. Cetas JS, T Saedi and KJ Burchiel (2008) Destructive procedures for the treatment of nonmalignant pain: a structured literature review. J Neurosurg 109:389–404.
9. Brown JA and NM Barbaro (2003) Motor cortex stimulation for central and neuropathic pain: current status. Pain 104:431–5.
10. Tsubokawa T, Y Katayama, T Yamamoto et al (1991) Chronic motor cortex stimulation for the treatment of central pain. Acta Neurochir Suppl (Wien) 52:137–9.
11. Nguyen JP, JP Lefaucheur, P Decq et al (1999) Chronic motor cortex stimulation in the treatment of central and neuropathic pain. Correlations between clinical, electrophysiological and anatomical data. Pain 82:245–51.
12. Katayama Y, T Yamamoto, K Kobayashi et al (2001) Motor cortex stimulation for phantom limb pain: comprehensive therapy with spinal cord and thalamic stimulation. Stereotact Funct Neurosurg 77:159–62.
13. Kumar K, C Toth and RK Nath (1997) Deep brain stimulation for intractable pain: a 15-year experience. Neurosurgery 40:736–46; discussion 46–7.
14. Levy RM (2003) Deep brain stimulation for the treatment of intractable pain. Neurosurg Clin N Am 14:389–99, vi.
15. Gananca MM, HH Caovilla, FF Gananca et al (2002) Clonazepam in the pharmacological treatment of vertigo and tinnitus. Int Tinnitus J 8:50–3.
16. Murai K, RS Tyler, LA Harker et al (1992) Review of pharmacologic treatment of tinnitus. Am J Otol 13:454–64.
17. Bauer CA and TJ Brozoski (2006) Effect of gabapentin on the sensation and impact of tinnitus. Laryngoscope 116: 675–81.
18. Williams EA, GB Brookes and DK Prasher (1994) Effects of olivocochlear bundle section on otoacoustic emissions in humans: efferent effects in comparison with control subjects. Acta Otolaryngol 114:121–9.

19. Williams EA, GB Brookes and DK Prasher (1993) Effects of contralateral acoustic stimulation on otoacoustic emissions following vestibular neurectomy. Scand Audiol 22:197–203.

20. Ozdogmus O, O Sezen, U Kubilay et al (2004) Connections between the facial, vestibular and cochlear nerve bundles within the internal auditory canal. J Anat 205:65–75.

21. Arnesen AR (1984) Fibre population of the vestibulocochlear anastomosis in humans. Acta Otolaryngol 98:501–18.

22. Tian GY, DC Xu, DL Huang et al (2008) The topographical relationships and anastomosis of the nerves in the human internal auditory canal. Surg Radiol Anat 30:243–7.

23. Baguley DM, P Axon, IM Winter et al (2002) The effect of vestibular nerve section upon tinnitus. Clin Otolaryngol Allied Sci 27:219–26.

24. Jackson P (1985) A comparison of the effects of eighth nerve section with lidocaine on tinnitus. J Laryngol Otol 99:663–6.

25. House JW and DE Brackmann (1981) Tinnitus: surgical treatment. Ciba Found Symp 85:204–16.

26. Pulec JL (1995) Cochlear nerve section for intractable tinnitus. Ear Nose Throat J 74:468, 70–6.

27. Tatli M, O Satici, Y Kanpolat et al (2008) Various surgical modalities for trigeminal neuralgia: literature study of respective long-term outcomes. Acta Neurochir (Wien) 150:243–5.

28. Linskey ME, V Ratanatharathorn and J Penagaricano (2008) A prospective cohort study of microvascular decompression and Gamma Knife surgery in patients with trigeminal neuralgia. J Neurosurg 109 Suppl:160–72.

29. Berliner KI, C Shelton, WE Hitselberger et al (1992) Acoustic tumors: effect of surgical removal on tinnitus. Am J Otol 13:13–7.

30. Maihofner C, M Schmelz, C Forster et al (2004) Neural activation during experimental allodynia: a functional magnetic resonance imaging study. Eur J Neurosci 19:3211–8.

31. Stern J, D Jeanmonod and J Sarnthein (2006) Persistent EEG overactivation in the cortical pain matrix of neurogenic pain patients. Neuroimage 31:721–31.

32. Moisset X and D Bouhassira (2007) Brain imaging of neuropathic pain. Neuroimage 37 Suppl 1:S80–8.

33. Schlee W, N Weisz, O Bertrand et al (2008) Using auditory steady state responses to outline the functional connectivity in the tinnitus brain. PLoS ONE 3:e3720.

34. Etkin A and TD Wager (2007) Functional neuroimaging of anxiety: a meta-analysis of emotional processing in PTSD, social anxiety disorder, and specific phobia. Am J Psychiatry 164:1476–88.

35. Vermetten E, C Schmahl, SM Southwick et al (2007) Positron tomographic emission study of olfactory induced emotional recall in veterans with and without combat-related posttraumatic stress disorder. Psychopharmacol Bull 40:8–30.

36. von Leupoldt A, T Sommer, S Kegat et al (2009) Dyspnea and pain share emotion-related brain network. Neuroimage 48:200–6.

37. Freeman W and JW Watts (1948) Pain mechanisms and the frontal lobes; a study of prefrontal lobotomy for intractable pain. Ann Intern Med 28:747–54.

38. Freeman W and JW Watts (1950) Psychosurgery. Springfield, IL: Charles C Thomas.

39. Elithorn A (1953) Prefrontal leucotomy in the treatment of tinnitus. Proc R Soc Med 46:832–3.

40. Beard AW (1965) Results of leucotomy operations for tinnitus. J Psychosom Res 9:29–32.

41. Cohen RA, RF Kaplan, DJ Moser et al (1999) Impairments of attention after cingulotomy. Neurology 53:819–24.

42. Cohen RA, RF Kaplan, P Zuffante et al (1999) Alteration of intention and self-initiated action associated with bilateral anterior cingulotomy. J Neuropsychiatry Clin Neurosci 11:444–53.

43. Yen CP, CY Kuan, J Sheehan et al (2009) Impact of bilateral anterior cingulotomy on neurocognitive function in patients with intractable pain. J Clin Neurosci 16:214–9.

44. Cohen RA, R Paul, TM Zawacki et al (2001) Emotional and personality changes following cingulotomy. Emotion 1:38–50.

45. Wilkinson HA, KM Davidson and RI Davidson (1999) Bilateral anterior cingulotomy for chronic noncancer pain. Neurosurgery 45:1129–34; discussion 34–6.

46. Llinas RR, U Ribary, D Jeanmonod et al (1999) Thalamocortical dysrhythmia: A neurological and neuropsychiatric syndrome characterized by magnetoencephalography. Proc Natl Acad Sci U S A 96:15222–7.

47. Jeanmonod D, M Magnin and A Morel (1996) Low-threshold calcium spike bursts in the human thalamus. Common physiopathology for sensory, motor and limbic positive symptoms. Brain 119(Pt 2):363–75.

48. Adams DA and TJ Wilmot (1982) Meniere's disease: long-term results of sympathectomy. J Laryngol Otol 96:705–10.

49. Wilmot TJ (1969) Sympathectomy for Meniere's disease – a long-term reviews. J Laryngol Otol 83:323–31.

50. Wilmot TJ (1961) Sympathectomy for inner-ear vascular insufficiency. J Laryngol Otol 75:259–67.

51. Passe ER (1952) Sympathectomy in relation to Meniere's disease, nerve deafness and tinnitus; a report on 110 cases. Acta Otolaryngol 42:133–51.

52. Acar F, J Miller, KJ Golshani et al (2008) Pain relief after cervical ganglionectomy (C2 and C3) for the treatment of medically intractable occipital neuralgia. Stereotact Funct Neurosurg 86:106–12.

53. Jastreboff PJ (1990) Phantom auditory perception (tinnitus): mechanisms of generation and perception. Neurosci Res 8:221–54.

54. Kim HJ, SH Paek, JY Kim et al (2008) Chronic subthalamic deep brain stimulation improves pain in Parkinson disease. J Neurol 255:1889–94.

55. Samura K, Y Miyagi, T Morioka et al (2008) Intractable facial pain in advanced Parkinson's disease alleviated by subthalamic nucleus stimulation. J Neurol Neurosurg Psychiatry 79:1410–1.

56. Shi Y, KJ Burchiel, VC Anderson et al (2009) Deep brain stimulation effects in patients with tinnitus. Otolaryngol Head Neck Surg 141:285–7.

57. Guo X, G Gao, X Wang et al (2008) Effects of bilateral deep brain stimulation of the subthalamic nucleus on olfactory function in Parkinson's disease patients. Stereotact Funct Neurosurg 86:237–44.

58. Jech R, E Ruzicka, D Urgosik et al (2006) Deep brain stimulation of the subthalamic nucleus affects resting EEG and visual evoked potentials in Parkinson's disease. Clin Neurophysiol 117:1017–28.

59. Kolomiets BP, JM Deniau, P Mailly et al (2001) Segregation and convergence of information flow through the cortico-subthalamic pathways. J Neurosci 21:5764–72.

60. Coenen VA, CR Honey, T Hurwitz et al (2009) Medial forebrain bundle stimulation as a pathophysiological mechanism for hypomania in subthalamic nucleus deep brain stimulation for Parkinson's disease. Neurosurgery 64:1106–14; discussion 14–5.

61. Muhlau M, JP Rauschecker, E Oestreicher et al (2006) Structural brain changes in tinnitus. Cereb Cortex 16: 1283–8.

62. Cruccu G, TZ Aziz, L Garcia-Larrea et al (2007) EFNS guidelines on neurostimulation therapy for neuropathic pain. Eur J Neurol 14:952–70.

63. Van de Heyning P, K Vermeire, M Diebl et al (2008) Incapacitating unilateral tinnitus in single-sided deafness treated by cochlear implantation. Ann Otol Rhinol Laryngol 117:645–52.

64. Aschendorff A, G Pabst, T Klenzner et al (1998) Tinnitus in cochlear implant users: The Freiburg experience. Int Tinnitus J 4:162–4.

65. Brackmann DE (1981) Reduction of tinnitus in cochlear-implant patients. J Laryngol Otol Suppl. 4:163 5.

66. Di Nardo W, I Cantore, F Cianfrone et al (2007) Tinnitus modifications after cochlear implantation. Eur Arch Otorhinolaryngol 264:1145–9.

67. Ito J and J Sakakihara (1994) Tinnitus suppression by electrical stimulation of the cochlear wall and by cochlear implantation. Laryngoscope 104:752–4.

68. Miyamoto RT, MK Wynne, C McKnight et al (1997) Electrical suppression of tinnitus via cochlear implants. Int Tinnitus J 3:35–8.

69. Aydemir G, MS Tezer, P Borman et al (2006) Treatment of tinnitus with transcutaneous electrical nerve stimulation improves patients' quality of life. J Laryngol Otol 120: 442–5.

70. Cazals Y, M Bourdin, M Negrevergne et al (1986) [Transcutaneous electric stimulation in the treatment of tinnitus]. Rev Laryngol Otol Rhinol (Bord) 107:433–6.

71. Engelberg M and W Bauer (1985) Transcutaneous electrical stimulation for tinnitus. Laryngoscope 95:1167–73.

72. Herraiz C, A Toledano and I Diges (2007) Trans-electrical nerve stimulation (TENS) for somatic tinnitus. Prog Brain Res 166:389–94.

73. Kaada B, S Hognestad and J Havstad (1989) Transcutaneous nerve stimulation (TNS) in tinnitus. Scand Audiol 18: 211–7.

74. Vernon JA and JA Fenwick (1985) Attempts to suppress tinnitus with transcutaneous electrical stimulation. Otolaryngol Head Neck Surg 93:385–9.

75. Møller AR, MB Møller and M Yokota (1992) Some forms of tinnitus may involve the extralemniscal auditory pathway. Laryngoscope 102:1165–71.

76. Shore SE (2005) Multisensory integration in the dorsal cochlear nucleus: unit responses to acoustic and trigeminal ganglion stimulation. Eur J Neurosci 21:3334–48.

77. Shore SE, H El Kashlan and J Lu (2003) Effects of trigeminal ganglion stimulation on unit activity of ventral cochlear nucleus neurons. Neuroscience 119:1085–101.

78. Young ED, I Nelken and RA Conley (1995) Somatosensory effects on neurons in dorsal cochlear nucleus. J Neurophysiol 73:743–65.

79. Szczepaniak WS and AR Møller (1993) Interaction between auditory and somatosensory systems: a study of evoked potentials in the inferior colliculus. Electroencephalogr Clin Neurophysiol 88:508–15.

80. Kaltenbach JA (2000) Neurophysiologic mechanisms of tinnitus. J Am Acad Audiol 11:125–37.

81. Kaltenbach JA (2007) The dorsal cochlear nucleus as a contributor to tinnitus: mechanisms underlying the induction of hyperactivity. Prog Brain Res 166:89–106.

82. Zhang J and Z Guan (2007) Pathways involved in somatosensory electrical modulation of dorsal cochlear nucleus activity. Brain Res 1184:121–31.

83. Dehmel S, YL Cui and SE Shore (2008) Cross-modal interactions of auditory and somatic inputs in the brainstem and midbrain and their imbalance in tinnitus and deafness. Am J Audiol 17:S193–209.

84. Kapkin O, B Satar and S Yetiser (2008) Transcutaneous electrical stimulation of subjective tinnitus. A placebo-controlled, randomized and comparative analysis. ORL J Otorhinolaryngol Relat Spec 70:156–61.

85. Taylor RS (2006) Spinal cord stimulation in complex regional pain syndrome and refractory neuropathic back and leg pain/failed back surgery syndrome: results of a systematic review and meta-analysis. J Pain Symptom Manage 31:S13–9.

86. Melzack R and PD Wall (1965) Pain mechanisms: a new theory. Science 150:971–9.

87. North RB and GL Roark (1995) Spinal cord stimulation for chronic pain. Neurosurg Clin N Am 6:145–55.

88. Simpson BA (1997) Spinal cord stimulation. Br J Neurosurg 11:5–11.

89. Soussi T and SR Otto (1994) Effects of electrical brainstem stimulation on tinnitus. Acta Otolaryngol 114:135–40.

90. Nitsche MA and W Paulus (2001) Sustained excitability elevations induced by transcranial DC motor cortex stimulation in humans. Neurology 57:1899–901.

91. Nitsche MA and W Paulus (2000) Excitability changes induced in the human motor cortex by weak transcranial direct current stimulation. J Physiol 527 Pt 3:633–9.

92. Nitsche MA, MS Nitsche, CC Klein et al (2003) Level of action of cathodal DC polarisation induced inhibition of the human motor cortex. Clin Neurophysiol 114:600–4.

93. Antal A, TZ Kincses, MA Nitsche et al (2004) Excitability changes induced in the human primary visual cortex by transcranial direct current stimulation: direct electrophysiological evidence. Invest Ophthalmol Vis Sci 45:702–7.

94. Boggio PS, S Zaghi, M Lopes et al (2008) Modulatory effects of anodal transcranial direct current stimulation on perception and pain thresholds in healthy volunteers. Eur J Neurol 15:1124–30.

95. Mitchell TV, RA Morey, S Inan et al (2005) Functional magnetic resonance imaging measure of automatic and controlled auditory processing. Neuroreport 16:457–61.

96. Hannula H, T Neuvonen, P Savolainen et al (2010) Increasing top-down suppression from prefrontal cortex facilitates tactile working memory. Neuroimage 49:1091–8.

97. Antal A, N Brepohl, C Poreisz et al (2008) Transcranial direct current stimulation over somatosensory cortex decreases experimentally induced acute pain perception. Clin J Pain 24:56–63.

98. Fregni F, R Marcondes, PS Boggio et al (2006) Transient tinnitus suppression induced by repetitive transcranial magnetic stimulation and transcranial direct current stimulation. Eur J Neurol 13:996–1001.

99. Hallett M (2000) Transcranial magnetic stimulation and the human brain. Nature 406:147–50.

100. Walsh V and M Rushworth (1999) A primer of magnetic stimulation as a tool for neuropsychology. Neuropsychologia 37:125–35.

101. Londero A, B Langguth, D De Ridder et al (2006) Repetitive transcranial magnetic stimulation (rTMS): a new therapeutic approach in subjective tinnitus? Neurophysiol Clin 36: 145–55.

102. De Ridder D, G De Mulder, E Verstraeten et al (2007) Auditory cortex stimulation for tinnitus. Acta Neurochir Suppl 97:451–62.

103. De Ridder D, G De Mulder, E Verstraeten et al (2006) Primary and secondary auditory cortex stimulation for intractable tinnitus. ORL J Otorhinolaryngol Relat Spec 68:48–54; discussion 54–5.

104. De Ridder D, G De Mulder, V Walsh et al (2004) Magnetic and electrical stimulation of the auditory cortex for intractable tinnitus. Case report. J Neurosurg 100:560–4.

105. De Ridder D, G De Mulder, E Verstraeten et al (2007) Somatosensory cortex stimulation for deafferentation pain. Acta Neurochir Suppl 97:67–74.

106. Hosomi K, Y Saitoh, H Kishima et al (2008) Electrical stimulation of primary motor cortex within the central sulcus for intractable neuropathic pain. Clin Neurophysiol 119:993–1001.

107. Lefaucheur JP, X Drouot, I Menard-Lefaucheur et al (2008) Motor cortex rTMS in chronic neuropathic pain: pain relief is associated with thermal sensory perception improvement. J Neurol Neurosurg Psychiatry 79:1044–9.

108. Leung A, M Donohue, R Xu et al (2009) rTMS for suppressing neuropathic pain: a meta-analysis. J Pain 10:1205–16.

109. De Ridder D, E van der Loo, K Van der Kelen et al (2007) Theta, alpha and beta burst transcranial magnetic stimulation: brain modulation in tinnitus. Int J Med Sci 4:237–41.

110. Khedr EM, JC Rothwell, MA Ahmed et al (2008) Effect of daily repetitive transcranial magnetic stimulation for treatment of tinnitus: comparison of different stimulus frequencies. J Neurol Neurosurg Psychiatry 79:212–5.

111. Kleinjung T, P Eichhammer, B Langguth et al (2005) Long-term effects of repetitive transcranial magnetic stimulation (rTMS) in patients with chronic tinnitus. Otolaryngol Head Neck Surg 132:566–9.

112. Langguth B, P Eichhammer, A Kreutzer et al (2006) The impact of auditory cortex activity on characterizing and treating patients with chronic tinnitus – first results from a PET study. Acta Otolaryngol Suppl. 556:84–8.

113. Weisz N, S Moratti, M Meinzer et al (2005) Tinnitus perception and distress is related to abnormal spontaneous brain activity as measured by magnetoencephalography. PLoS Med 2:e153.

114. Weisz N, S Muller, W Schlee et al (2007) The neural code of auditory phantom perception. J Neurosci 27:1479–84.

115. Weisz N, C Wienbruch, K Dohrmann et al (2005) Neuromagnetic indicators of auditory cortical reorganization of tinnitus. Brain 128:2722–31.

116. De Pascalis V and I Cacace (2005) Pain perception, obstructive imagery and phase-ordered gamma oscillations. Int J Psychophysiol 56:157–69.

117. Sarnthein J and D Jeanmonod (2008) High thalamocortical theta coherence in patients with neurogenic pain. Neuroimage 39:1910–7.

118. Busse M, YF Low, FI Corona-Strauss et al (2008) Neurofeedback by neural correlates of auditory selective attention as possible application for tinnitus therapies. Conf Proc IEEE Eng Med Biol Soc 1:5136–9.

119. Dohrmann K, N Weisz, W Schlee et al (2007) Neurofeedback for treating tinnitus. Prog Brain Res 166:473–85.

120. Kayiran S, E Dursun, N Ermutlu et al (2007) Neurofeedback in fibromyalgia syndrome. Agri 19:47–53.

121. Dobie RA (1999) A review of randomized clinical trials in tinnitus. Laryngoscope 109:1202–11.

Chapter 95
Treatment Strategies of Temporomandibular Joint and Masticatory Muscle Disorders in Patients with Tinnitus

Ralf Bürgers, Michael Behr, and Martin Gosau

Keypoints

1. Temporomandibular joint disorders (TMD) are often accompanied by tinnitus.
2. Improvement or total remission of tinnitus from treatment of TMD is a secondary effect.
3. Treatment of TMD is suggested for patients with impaired range of jaw motion, painful jaw movements, pain in masticatory muscles or temporomandibular joint (TMJ), or oral parafunction and masticatory muscle hyperactivity.
4. Treatment of TMD includes:
   a. Intraocclusal stabilization appliances (occlusal splints);
   b. Selective adjustment of the occlusal surface of teeth and artificial dentition;
   c. Reassurance and counseling
   d. Medication, physical therapy or physiotherapy
   e. EMG biofeedback with progressive relaxation, hypnosis, and acupuncture;
   f. Joint injections (hydrocortisone), injection of local anesthetics intomuscle trigger points;
   g. TMJ surgery.

Keywords Temporomandibular disorders • Tinnitus • Treatment

Abbreviations

TMD   Temporomandibular disorder(s)
TMJ   Temporomandibular joint

Introduction

In dentistry, the most common approach to treating patients with symptoms of temporomandibular disorders (TMD) and concomitant tinnitus targets on the therapy of the TMD, more or less independent of the severity and quality of the tinnitus symptoms [1–3]. This approach is based on the assumption that appropriate TMD treatment will also eliminate or at least reduce tinnitus symptoms [1, 4–8]. This "dental approach" to the treatment of TMD with concomitant tinnitus may be adequate for patients who suffer from tinnitus as a secondary complaint due to a primary dysfunction of the temporomandibular system. In contrast, sole treatment of TMD is inadequate in patients who suffer from TMD as an implication of the tinnitus (as occurs in individuals who process their tinnitus symptoms through nightly grinding) or in whom both TMD and tinnitus symptoms may be caused by a third "collective trigger," such as mental pressure or a specific medication [9–11]. In such patients, sole treatment of tinnitus with an isolated TMD therapy is doomed to failure from the very start. This fact emphasizes the importance of interdisciplinary therapeutic concepts for the clinical treatment of individual patients with tinnitus.

This chapter will mainly consider such treatments of TMD that are beneficial on tinnitus when it accompanies temporomandibular problems. For general coverage of treatment of TMD, the reader is referred to the considerable literature covering this topic.

R. Bürgers (✉)
Department of Prosthetic Dentistry, University Medical Center Regensburg, 93042, Regensburg Germany
e-mail: ralf.buergers@klinik.uni-regensburg.de

A.R. Møller et al. (eds.), *Textbook of Tinnitus*,
DOI 10.1007/978-1-60761-145-5_95, © Springer Science+Business Media, LLC 2011

Treatment of TMD

Indication for TMD Therapy

Therapeutic intervention is beneficial to patients with TMD if one of the following symptoms is present:

1. Impaired range of jaw motion (limitation of mouth opening, deviation, or deflection)
2. Painful jaw movements
3. Pain in masticatory muscles, temporomandibular joint (TMJ), or trigger zones that occurs when palpated (myofascial pain or arthralgia[1])
4. Oral parafunction[2]) and masticatory muscle hyperactivities (bruxism[3]), clenching, and rocking of teeth

Usually, TMD treatment does not benefit patients with painless TMJ sounds or symptom-free occlusal interferences. Nevertheless, conservative (non-surgical) TMD therapy might alleviate patients with TMD who also have tinnitus if the tinnitus is related to TMD symptoms (e.g., ipsilateral occurrence of TMJ clicking and tinnitus).

TMD Therapy

Therapeutic interventions for TMD are complex because of the diversity of symptoms that may be caused by many different disorders of the TMJ (arthogenic), the masticatory muscles (myogenic) or both. TMD treatment options include intraocclusal stabilization appliances (occlusal splints), selective adjustment of the occlusal surface of teeth and artificial dentition, reassurance and counseling, medication, physical therapy or physiotherapy, EMG biofeedback with progressive relaxation, hypnosis, acupuncture, joint injections (hydrocortisone), injection of local anesthetics into muscle trigger points, and TMJ surgery. However, it would be negligent to give only one general recommendation or regime for the therapy of TMD or TMD-related tinnitus [12].

Approximately 30% of patients with TMD (with myogenic or arthogenic pain) report persisting pain after

TMD therapy [13]. In most patients, TMD will abate without active professional intervention [14]. Two kinds of therapy are available: conservative treatments, consisting of intraoral splints, counseling, physiotherapy, and medications; and invasive treatments (TMJ surgery), ranging from arthrocentesis and lavage to diskectomy. Most patients with TMD respond to conservative treatment and such reversible therapy does not change the structures of the masticatory system [14]. Invasive treatment is irreversible and can cause minor or more extensive structural changes. In this chapter, only the most important and generally approved treatment modalities will be presented, focusing on treatment modifications for patients with TMD and tinnitus.

It has been the main goal of TMD therapy to eliminate or at least reduce pain and discomfort and achieve normalization of the mandibular range of motion [12], but attention on tinnitus in patients with TMJ problems has been increased, and improvement or total remission of tinnitus has now become an important therapeutic goal of TMD therapy.

Counseling

Patients with TMD and TMD-related tinnitus benefit from receiving background information on their disorder and its implications [15–18]. Detailed explanation of the possible correlation between tinnitus and TMD, as well as the special features of a combined therapy, can have beneficial effects on both the pain and the tinnitus [14].

Medication

Some of the medications usually prescribed for TMJ pain have been reported to cause tinnitus and hearing loss [19, 20].

Treatment of TMD-Related Tinnitus

Improvement or relief of tinnitus has been reported after TMJ surgery [21–25].

In general, no difference exists between the dental therapy of TMD and the therapy of TMD-related tinnitus. In some patients with TMD, the intensity of the

---

[1]Arthralgia: Pain in a joint.
[2]Parafunction: Movements (e.g., bruxism, clenching, and rocking of teeth) that are considered outside or beyond function and that result in worn facets. Dictionary of Dental Term. Copyright© 1999, 2004 Rich Masel.
[3]Bruxism: clenching, and rocking of teeth.

tinnitus can be modulated by mandibular movements, pressure on the TMJ, or biting (mostly by enhancement) [12, 17, 26, 27]. If the quality and severity of tinnitus change during passive and active movement of the jaw, the chances for improvement by dental therapy might be higher [17, 26].

Many patients with tinnitus, who are referred to a dentist, have chronic tinnitus. The success of treatment of TMD-related tinnitus decreases with the duration of the tinnitus [28]. While therapy of acute TMD-related tinnitus may be aimed at total elimination, or significant reduction, of the tinnitus, the likelihood of complete remission of tinnitus is small in patients who have had their tinnitus for a long time [28]. Patients with objective tinnitus related to the TMJ or masticatory muscles (clicking and crepitation) are distinguished from those with subjective tinnitus. Treatment of objective tinnitus should focus on localizing and eliminating the source of the sound. Some investigators have questioned the significance of TMJ sounds and their clinical and pathological relevance [12].

Prognosis

Conflicting evidence of the effect of TMD therapy on TMD-related tinnitus exists. Various studies about the effect of different TMD treatment strategies on tinnitus have been ruled out, and an astonishing high percentage of improvement or elimination of tinnitus symptoms has been reported in some investigations (see Table 95.1) [3, 6, 20, 22, 26, 29, 30, 31]. No significant differences were found between various TMD therapies (splint vs. physical therapy vs. self-observation, etc.) [28].

Few prospective controlled randomized studies on the efficacy of TMD therapy for TMD-related tinnitus have been published, and many studies are only descriptive. Most studies that included a control group found that the placebo effect on tinnitus was considerable [26]. The great individual variation in the tinnitus of patients with TMD makes it difficult to compare the stated efficacy of treatments used in different studies [12, 28, 32].

Table 95.1 Effect of TMD therapy on tinnitus: literature overview

| Source | Total no. of patients | TMD therapy | Effect on tinnitus, no (%) of patients | | |
			Complete remission or improvement	Complete remission	Improvement
Bernstein et al. [33]	28	Adjusting deflective tooth contacts, counseling		21 (75%)	
Bürgers (unpublished)	25	Occlusal splints, physiotherapy	1 (44%)	2 (8%)	9 (36%)
Bush [6]	35	Oral splint, physiotherapy, surgery, medication	30 (86%)	11 (31%)	19 (55%)
Dolowitz [34]	43	Muscle exercises			40 (93%)
Gelb et al. [1]	26	Treatment "to establish maxillomandibular balance"	25 (96%)	17 (65%)	8 (31%)
Hankey [2]	6	Various stomathognathic treatment			3 (50%)
Ioannides et al. [35]	2	Counseling, physiotherapy, restoration of occlusion		1 (50%)	
Kelly et al. [5]	46	Occlusal splints (cast metal overlays)	37 (80%)	20 (43%)	17 (37%)
Koskinen et al.[7]	8	Selective grinding, occlusal splints, thermotherapy, muscle relaxants, muscle exercises	5 (63%)	2 (25%)	3 (38%)
Linsen et al. [8]	22	Distraction splints	17 (77%)	8 (36%)	9 (41%)
Rubinstein et al. [3]	57	Occlusal splints, occlusal adjustment, muscle exercises			26 (46%)
Tullberg et al. [36]	73	Counseling, jaw exercises, occlusal bite splints			31 (43%)
Wright et al. [29]	93	Splints, self care instructions, medication	80 (86%)	52 (65%)	28 (30%)

Summary and Conclusions

1. General TMD treatment recommendations are inadequate for patients with TMD-related tinnitus. There is no typical TMD patient and no typical TMD therapy, just as there is no typical tinnitus patient and no typical tinnitus therapy.
2. Different TMD treatment options are in use for TMD-related tinnitus, but no significant differences have been found between different TMD therapies regarding tinnitus.
3. Complete remission of tinnitus symptoms remains an unrealistic therapeutic goal. At best, the dental approach can provide an additional therapeutic option in individual patients with tinnitus. TMD treatment options contribute to inter- and multidisciplinary approaches to the clinical management of the symptoms of tinnitus.

References

1. Gelb, H, Calderone, JP, Gross, SM, Kantor, ME, The role of the dentist and the otolaryngologist in evaluating temporomandibular joint syndromes J Prosthet Dent 1967, 18:497–503
2. Hankey, GT, Painful disorders of the temporomandibular joint Proc R Soc Med 1962, 55:787–792
3. Rubinstein, B, Carlsson, GE, Effects of stomatognathic treatment on tinnitus: a retrospective study Cranio 1987, 5:254–259
4. Morgan, DH, Discussion: attributes of tinnitus that may predict TMJ syndromes Cranio 1992, 10:287–288
5. Kelly, HT, Goodfriend, DJ, Vertigo attrubutable to dental and temporomandibular joint causes J Prosthet Dent 1964, 14:159–173
6. Bush, FM, Tinnitus and otalgia in temporomandibular disorders J Prosthet Dent 1987, 58:495–498
7. Koskinen, J, Paavolainen, M, Raivio M, Roschier J, Otological manifestations in temporomandibular joint dysfunction J Oral Rehabil 1980, 7:249–254
8. Linsen, S, Schmidt-Beer, U, Koeck, B [Tinnitus-Verbesserung durch Kiefergelenk-Distraktions-Therapie] Dtsch Zahnärztl Z 2006, 61:27–31
9. Parker, WZ, Chole, RA, Tinnitus, vertigo, and temporomandibular disorders Am J Orthod Dentofacial Orthop 1995, 107:153–158
10. Brookes, GB, Maw, AR, Coleman, MJ, "Costen´s syndrome" – correlation or coincidence: a review of 45 patients with temporomandibular joint dysfunction, otalgia and other aural symptoms Clin Otolaryngol Allied Sci 1980, 5:23–36
11. Laskin, DM, Block, S, Diagnosis and treatment of myofascial pain-dysfunction (MPD) syndrome J Prosthet Dent 1986, 56:75–84
12. Turp, JC, Correlation between myoarthropathies of the masticatory system and ear symptoms (otalgia, tinnitus) HNO 1998, 46:303–310
13. Pedersen, A, Hansen, HJ, Long-term evaluation of 211 patients with internal derangement of the temporomandibular joint Community Dent Oral Epidemiol 1987, 15:344–347
14. Zarb, GA, Carlsson, GE, Sessle, BJ, Mohl, ND, Temporomandibular joint and masticatory muscle disorders 1994, Munksgaard: Copenhagen
15. Mejersjo, C, Long-term development after treatment of mandibular dysfunction and osteoarthrosis A clinical-radiographic follow-up and an animal experimental study Swed Dent J Suppl 1984, 22:1–58
16. Keersmaekers, K, De Boever, JA, Van Den, BL, Otalgia in patients with temporomandibular joint disorders J Prosthet Dent 1996, 75:72–76
17. Vernon, J, Griest, S, Press, L, Attributes of tinnitus that may predict temporomandibular joint dysfunction Cranio 1992, 10:282–287
18. Kopp, S, Short term evaluation of counselling and occlusal adjustment in patients with mandibular dysfunction involving the temporomandibular joint J Oral Rehabil 1979, 6:101–109
19. Seligmann, H, Podoshin, L, Ben-David, J, Fradis, M, Goldsher, M, Drug-induced tinnitus and other hearing disorders Drug Saf 1996, 14:198–212
20. Chan, SW, Reade, PC, Tinnitus and temporomandibular pain-dysfunction disorder Clin Otolaryngol Allied Sci 1994, 19:37–80
21. Morgan, DH, Surgical correction of temporomandibular joint arthritis J Oral Surg 1975, 33:766–773
22. House, LR, Morgan, DH, Hall, WP, Vamvas, SJ, Temporomandibular joint surgery: results of a 14-year joint implant study Laryngoscope 1984, 94:534–538
23. Bell, WH, Yamaguchi, Y, Poor, MR, Treatment of temporomandibular joint dysfunction by intraoral vertical ramus osteotomy Int J Adult Orthodon Orthognath Surg 1990, 5:9–27
24. Anderson, DM, Sinclair, PM, McBride, KM, A clinical evaluation of temporomandibular joint disk plication surgery Am J Orthod Dentofacial Orthop 1991, 100:156–62
25. Griffitts, TM, Collins, CP, Collins, PC, Beirne, OR, Walker repair of the temporomandibular joint: a retrospective evaluation of 117 patients J Oral Maxillofac Surg 2007, 65:1958–1962
26. Rubinstein, B, Tinnitus and craniomandibular disorders – is there a link? Swed Dent J Suppl 1993, 95:1–46
27. Peroz, I, Dysfunctions of the stomatognathic system in tinnitus patients compared to controls HNO 2003, 51:544–549
28. Bosel, C, Mazurek, B, Haupt, H, Peroz, I [Chronic tinnitus and craniomandibular disorders Effectiveness of functional therapy on perceived tinnitus distress] HNO 2008, 56:707–713
29. Wright, EF, Bifano, SL, The relationship between tinnitus and temporomandibular disorder (TMD) therapy Int Tinnitus J 1997, 3:55-61
30. Wright, EF, Syms, CA, Bifano, SL, Tinnitus, dizziness, and nonotologic otalgia improvement through temporomandibular disorder therapy Mil Med 2000, 165:733–736

31. Bjorne, A., Agerberg, G., Symptom relief after treatment of temporomandibular and cervical spine disorders in patients with Meniere's disease: a three-year follow-up Cranio 2003, 21:50–60

32. Chole, R.A., Parker, W.S. Tinnitus and vertigo in patients with temporomandibular disorder Arch Otolaryngol Head Neck Surg 1992, 118:817–821

33. Bernstein, J.M., Mohl, N.D., Spiller, H., Temporomandibular joint dysfunction masquerading as disease of ear, nose and throat Trans Am Acad Ophthalmol Otolaryngol 1969, 73:1208–1217

34. Dolowitz, D.A., Ward, J.W., Fingerle, C.O., Smith, C.C., The role of muscular incoordination in the pathogenesis of the temporomandibular joint syndrome Trans Am Laryngol Rhinol Otol Soc 1964, 44:253–255

35. Ionnides, C.A., Hoogland, G.A., The disco-malleolar ligament: a possible cause of subjective hearing loss in patients with temporomandibular joint dysfunction J Maxillofac Surg 1983, 11:227–231

36. Tullberg, M., ernberg, M., long-term effect on tinnitus by treatment of temporomandibular disorders: a two-year follow-up by questionnaire Acta Odontol Scan 2006, 64:89–96.

Author Index

A.R. Møller et al. (eds.), *Textbook of Tinnitus*,
DOI 10.1007/978-1-60761-145-5, © Springer Science+Business Media, LLC 2011

Subject Index

A.R. Møller et al. (eds.), *Textbook of Tinnitus*,
DOI 10.1007/978-1-60761-145-5, © Springer Science+Business Media, LLC 2011

Printed in the United States of America